W9-CGR-567

WEBSTER'S
New Spanish-English Dictionary

WEBSTER'S New Spanish-English Dictionary

Created in Cooperation with
the Editors of
Merriam-Webster

POPULAR PUBLISHING
New York

Copyright © by Merriam-Webster, Incorporated

All rights reserved. No part of this book covered by the copyrights hereon may be reproduced or copied in any form or by any means—graphic, electronic, or mechanical, including photocopying, taping, or information storage and retrieval systems—without written permission of the publisher.

This 2001 edition published by arrangement with Federal Street Press, a division of Merriam-Webster, Incorporated.

Popular Publishing Company, LLC
3 Park Avenue
New York, New York 10016

ISBN 1-59027-002-9

Printed in the United States of America
01 02 03 04 05 5 4 3 2 1

Contents		Índice

Preface

WEBSTER'S NEW SPANISH-ENGLISH DICTIONARY is a completely new dictionary designed to meet the needs of English and Spanish speakers in a time of ever-expanding communication among the countries of the Western Hemisphere. It is intended for language learners, teachers, office workers, tourists, business travelers—anyone who needs to communicate effectively in the Spanish and English languages as they are spoken and written in the Americas. This new dictionary provides accurate and up-to-date coverage of current vocabulary in both languages, as well as abundant examples of words used in context to illustrate idiomatic usage. The selection of Spanish words and idioms was based on evidence drawn from a wide variety of modern Latin-American sources and interpreted by trained Merriam-Webster bilingual lexicographers. The English entries were chosen by Merriam-Webster editors from the most recent Merriam-Webster dictionaries, and they represent the current basic vocabulary of American English.

All of this material is presented in a format that emphasizes convenience and ease of use, clarity and conciseness of the information presented, precise discrimination of senses, and frequent inclusion of example phrases showing words in actual use. Also included are pronunciations (in the International Phonetic Alphabet) for all English words, full coverage of irregular verbs in both languages, a section on basic Spanish grammar, a table of the most common Spanish abbreviations, and a detailed Explanatory Notes section that answers any questions the reader might have concerning the use of this book.

Eileen M. Haraty
Editor

Explanatory Notes

Entries

1. Main Entries

A boldface letter, word, or phrase appearing flush with the left-hand margin of each column of type is a main entry or entry word. The main entry may consist of letters set solid, of letters joined by a hyphen, or of letters separated by a space:

cafetalero[1], **-ra** *adj*. . .
eye–opener. . . *n*. . .
walk out *vi* . . .

The main entry, together with the material that follows it on the same line and succeeding indented lines, constitutes a dictionary entry.

2. Order of Main Entries

Alphabetical order throughout the book follows the order of the English alphabet, with one exception: words beginning with the Spanish letter *ñ* follow all entries for the letter *n*. The main entries follow one another alphabetically letter by letter without regard to intervening spaces or hyphens; for example, *shake-up* follows *shaker.*

Homographs (words with the same spelling) having different parts of speech are usually given separate dictionary entries. These entries are distinguished by superscript numerals following the entry word:

hail[1]. . . *vt*. . .

hail[2] *n*. . .

hail[3] *interj*. . .

madrileño[1], **-ña** *adj*. . .

madrileño[2], **-ña** *n*. . .

Numbered homograph entries are listed in the following order: verb, adverb, adjective, noun, conjunction, preposition, pronoun, interjection, article.

Homographs having the same part of speech are normally included at the same dictionary entry, without regard to their different semantic origins. On the English-to-Spanish side, however, separate entries are made if the homographs have distinct inflected forms or if they have distinct pronunciations.

3. Guide Words

A pair of guide words is printed at the top of each page, indicating the first and last main entries that appear on that page:

fregar • fuego

4. Variants

When a main entry is followed by the word *or* and another spelling, the two spellings are variants. Both are standard, and either one may be used according to personal inclination:

jailer *or* **jailor**. . . *n*. . .
quizá *or* **quizás** *adv*. . .

Occasionally, a variant spelling is used only for a particular sense of a word. In these cases, the variant spelling is listed after the sense number of the sense to which it pertains:

electric. . . *adj* **1** *or* **electrical**. . .

Sometimes the entry word is used interchangeably with a longer phrase containing the entry word. For the purposes of this dictionary, such phrases are considered variants of the headword:

bunk[2] *n* **1** *or* **bunk bed**. . .

angina *nf* **1** *or* **angina de pecho** : angina . . .

Variant wordings of boldface phrases may also be shown:

> **madera** *nf.* . . **3 madera dura** *or* **madera noble**. . .
>
> **atención**[1] *nf.* . . **2 poner atención** *or* **prestar atención**. . .

5. Run-On Entries

A main entry may be followed by one or more derivatives or by a homograph with a different functional label. These are run-on entries. Each is introduced by a boldface dash and each has a functional label. They are not defined, however, since their equivalents can be readily derived by adding the corresponding foreign-language suffix to the terms used to define the entry word or, in the case of homographs, simply substituting the appropriate part of speech:

> **illegal**. . . *adj* **:** ilegal **— illegally** *adv*
> (the Spanish adverb is *ilegalmente*)
>
> **transferir**. . . *vt* TRASLADAR **:** to transfer **— transferible** *adj*
> (the English adjective is **transferable**)
>
> **Bosnian** *n* **:** bosnio *m,* -nia *f* **— Bosnian** *adj*
> (the Spanish adjective is *bosnio, -nia*)

On the Spanish side of the book, reflexive verbs are sometimes run on undefined:

> **enrollar** *vt* **:** to roll up, to coil **— enrollarse** *vr*

The absence of a definition means that *enrollarse* has the simple reflexive meaning "to become rolled up or coiled," "to roll itself up."

6. Bold Notes

A main entry may be followed by one or more phrases containing the entry word or an inflected form of the entry word. These are bold notes. Each bold note is defined at its own numbered sense:

> **álamo** *nm* **1 :** poplar **2 álamo temblón :** aspen
>
> **hold**[1]. . . *vi*. . . **4 to hold to :**. . . **5 to hold with :**. . .

If the bold note consists only of the entry word and a single preposition, the entry word is represented by a boldface swung dash **~**.

> **pegar** . . . *vi* . . . **3 ~ con :** to match, to go with . . .

The same bold note phrase may appear at two or more senses if it has more than one distinct meaning:

> **wear**[1]. . . *vt*. . . **3 to wear out :** gastar <he wore out his shoes. . . > **4 to wear out** EXHAUST **:** agotar, fatigar <to wear oneself out . . .> . . .
>
> **estar** . . . *vi* . . . **15 ~ por :** to be in favor of **16 ~ por :** to be about to <está por cerrar . . .> . . .

If the use of the entry word is commonly restricted to one particular phrase, then a bold note may be given as the entry word's only sense:

> **ward**[1]. . . *vt* **to ward off :**. . .

Pronunciation

1. Pronunciation of English Entry Words

The matter between a pair of brackets [ ] following the entry word of an English-to-Spanish entry indicates the pronunciation. The symbols used are explained in the International Phonetic Alphabet chart on page 25a.

The presence of variant pronunciations indicates that not all educated speakers pronounce words the same way. A second-place variant is not to be regarded as less acceptable than the pronunciation that is given first. It may, in fact, be used by as many educated speakers as the first variant, but the requirements of the printed page are such that one must precede the other:

tomato [tə'meɪt̬o, -'mɑ-]. . .

When a compound word has less than a full pronunciation, the missing part is to be supplied from the pronunciation at the entry for the unpronounced element of the compound:

gamma ray ['gæmə]. . .

ray ['reɪ]. . .

smoke[1] ['smo:k]. . .

smoke detector [dɪ'tɛktər]. . .

In general, no pronunciation is given for open compounds consisting of two or more English words that are main entries at their own alphabetical place:

water lily *n* **:** nenúfar *m*

Only the first entry in a series of numbered homographs is given a pronunciation if their pronunciations are the same:

dab[1] ['dæb] *vt*. . .

dab[2] *n*. . .

No pronunciation is shown for principal parts of verbs that are formed by regular suffixation, nor for other derivative words formed by common suffixes.

2. Pronunciation of Spanish Entry Words

Spanish pronunciation is highly regular, so no pronunciations are given for most Spanish-to-English entries. Exceptions have been made for certain words (such as foreign borrowings) whose Spanish pronunciations are not evident from their spellings:

pizza ['pitsa, 'pisa] . . .

footing ['fu,tɪŋ]. . .

Functional Labels

An italic label indicating a part of speech or some other functional classification follows the pronunciation or, if no pronunciation is given, the main entry. The eight traditional parts of speech, adjective, adverb, conjunction, interjection, noun, preposition, pronoun, and verb, are indicated as follows:

daily[2] *adj*. . .

vagamente *adv*. . .

and. . . *conj*. . .

huy *interj*. . .

jackal. . . *n*. . .

para *prep*. . .

neither[3] *pron*. . .

leer. . . *v*. . .

Verbs that are intransitive are labeled *vi,* and verbs that are transitive are labeled *vt.* Entries for verbs that are both transitive and intransitive are labeled *v;* if such an entry includes irregular verb inflections, it is labeled *v* immediately after the main entry, with the labels *vi* and *vt* serving to introduce transitive and intransitive subdivisions when both are present:

deliberar *vi* : to deliberate

necessitate. . . *vt* **-tated; -tating :** necesitar, requerir

satisfy. . . *v* **-fied; -fying** *vt*. . . — *vi*. . .

Two other labels are used to indicate functional classifications of verbs: *v aux* (auxiliary verb) and *v impers* (impersonal verb).

may. . . *v aux, past* **might**. . .

haber[1]. . . *v aux* **1 :** have. . . — *v impers* **1 hay :** there is, there are. . .

Gender Labels

In Spanish-to-English noun entries, the gender of the entry word is indicated by an italic *m* (masculine), *f* (feminine), or *mf* (masculine or feminine), immediately following the functional label:

magnesio *nm. . .*

galaxia *nf. . .*

turista *nmf. . .*

If both the masculine and feminine forms are shown for a noun referring to a person, the label is simply *n:*

director, -tora *n. . .*

Spanish noun equivalents of English entry words are also labeled for gender:

amnesia. . . *n* **:** amnesia *f*

earache. . . *n* **:** dolor *m* de oído

gamekeeper. . . *n* **:** guardabosque *mf*

Inflected Forms

1. Nouns

The plurals of nouns are shown in this dictionary when they are irregular, when plural suffixation brings about a change in accentuation or in the spelling of the root word, when an English noun ends in a consonant plus *-o* or in *-ey,* when an English noun ends in *-oo,* when an English noun is a compound that pluralizes any element but the last, when a noun has variant plurals, or whenever the dictionary user might have reasonable doubts regarding the spelling of a plural:

> **tooth**. . . *n, pl* **teeth**. . .
>
> **garrafón** *nm, pl* **-fones**. . .
>
> **potato**. . . *n, pl* **-toes**. . .
>
> **abbey**. . . *n, pl* **-beys**. . .
>
> **cuckoo**[2] *n, pl* **-oos**. . .
>
> **brother–in–law**. . . *n, pl* **brothers–in–law** . . .
>
> **quail**[2] *n, pl* **quail** *or* **quails**. . .
>
> **hábitat** *nm, pl* **-tats**. . .
>
> **tahúr** *nm, pl* **tahúres**. . .

Cutback inflected forms are used for most nouns on the English-to-Spanish side, regardless of the number of syllables. On the Spanish-to-English side, cutback inflections are given for nouns that have three or more syllables; plurals for shorter words are written out in full:

> **shampoo**[2] *n, pl* **-poos**. . .
>
> **calamity** . . . *n, pl* **-ties**. . .
>
> **mouse** . . . *n, pl* **mice**. . .
>
> **sartén** *nmf, pl* **sartenes**. . .
>
> **hámster** *nm, pl* **hámsters**. . .
>
> **federación** *nf, pl* **-ciones**. . .

If only one gender form has a plural which is irregular, that plural form will be given with the appropriate label:

> **campeón, -ona** *n, mpl* **-ones** : champion

The plurals of nouns are usually not shown when the base word is unchanged by the addition of the regular plural suffix or when the noun is unlikely to occur in the plural:

apple. . . *n* : manzana *f*

inglés[3] *nm* : English (language)

Nouns that are plural in form and that regularly occur in plural constructions are labeled as *npl* (for English nouns), *nmpl* (for Spanish masculine nouns), or *nfpl* (for Spanish feminine nouns):

knickers. . . *npl*. . .

enseres *nmpl*. . .

mancuernas *nfpl*. . .

Entry words that are unchanged in the plural are labeled *ns & pl* (for English nouns), *nms & pl* (for Spanish masculine nouns), *nfs & pl* (for Spanish feminine nouns), and *nmfs & pl* (for Spanish gender-variable nouns):

deer. . . *ns & pl* . . .

lavaplatos *nms & pl*. . .

tesis *nfs & pl* . . .

rompehuelgas *nmfs & pl* . . .

2. Verbs

ENGLISH VERBS

The principal parts of verbs are shown in English-to-Spanish entries when they are irregular, when suffixation brings about a change in spelling of the root word, when the verb ends in *-ey,* when there are variant inflected forms, or whenever it is believed that the dictionary user might have reasonable doubts about the spelling of an inflected form:

break[1]. . . *v* **broke**. . . ; **broken**. . . ; **breaking**. . .

drag[1]. . . *v* **dragged; dragging**. . .

monkey[1]. . . *vi* **-keyed; -keying**. . .

label[1]. . . *vt* **-beled** *or* **-belled; -beling** *or* **-belling**. . .

imagine. . . *vt* **-ined; -ining**. . .

Cutback inflected forms are usually used when the verb has two or more syllables:

multiply. . . *v* **-plied; -plying**. . .

bevel[1]. . . *v* **-eled** *or* **-elled; -eling** *or* **-elling**. . .

forgo *or* **forego**. . . *vt* **-went; -gone; -going**. . .

commit . . . *vt* **-mitted; -mitting** . . .

The principal parts of an English verb are not shown when the base word is unchanged by suffixation:

delay[1]. . . *vt*

pitch[1]. . . *vt*

SPANISH VERBS

Entries for irregular Spanish verbs are cross-referenced by number to the model conjugations appearing in the Conjugation of Spanish Verbs section:

abnegarse {49} *vr*. . .

volver {89} *vi*. . .

Entries for Spanish verbs with regular conjugations are not cross-referenced; however, model conjugations for regular Spanish verbs are included in the Conjugation of Spanish Verbs section beginning on page 44a.

Adverbs and Adjectives

The comparative and superlative forms of English adjective and adverb main entries are shown when suffixation brings about a change in spelling of the root word, when the inflection is irregular, and when there are variant inflected forms:

wet[2] *adj* **wetter; wettest**. . .

good[2] *adj* **better**. . . ; **best**. . .

evil[1]. . . *adj* **eviler** *or* **eviller; evilest** *or* **evillest**. . .

The superlative forms of adjectives and adverbs of two or more syllables are usually cut back; the superlative is shown in full, however, when it is desirable to indicate the pronunciation of the inflected form:

early[1]. . . *adv* **earlier; -est**. . .

gaudy. . . *adj* **gaudier; -est**. . .

secure[2] *adj* **-curer; -est**. . .

but

young[1]. . . *adj* **younger** [ˈjʌŋgər]; **youngest** [-gəst]. . .

At a few entries only the superlative form is shown:

mere *adj, superlative* **merest**. . .

The absence of the comparative form indicates that there is no evidence of its use.

The comparative and superlative forms of adjectives and adverbs are usually not shown when the base word is unchanged by suffixation:

quiet[3] *adj* **1**. . .

Usage

1. Usage Labels

Two types of usage labels are used in this dictionary—regional and stylistic. Spanish words that are limited in use to a specific area or areas of Latin America, or to Spain, are given labels indicating the countries in which they are most commonly used:

> **guarachear** *vi Cuba, PRi fam. . .*
>
> **bucket**. . . *n* **:**. . . cubeta *f Mex*

The following regional labels are used in this book: *Arg* (Argentina), *Bol* (Bolivia), *CA* (Central America), *Car* (Caribbean), *Chile* (Chile), *Col* (Colombia), *CoRi* (Costa Rica), *Cuba* (Cuba), *DomRep* (Dominican Republic), *Ecua* (Ecuador), *Sal* (El Salvador), *Guat* (Guatemala), *Hond* (Honduras), *Mex* (Mexico), *Nic* (Nicaragua), *Pan* (Panama), *Par* (Paraguay), *Peru* (Peru), *PRi* (Puerto Rico), *Spain* (Spain), *Uru* (Uruguay), *Ven* (Venezuela).

Since this book focuses on the Spanish spoken in Latin America, only the most common regionalisms from Spain have been included in order to allow for more thorough coverage of Latin-American forms.

A number of Spanish words are given a *fam* (familiar) label as well, indicating that these words are suitable for informal contexts but would not normally be used in formal writing or speaking. The stylistic label *usu considered vulgar* is added for a word which is usually considered vulgar or offensive but whose widespread use justifies its inclusion in this book. The label is intended to warn the reader that the word in question may be inappropriate in polite conversation.

2. Usage Notes

Definitions are sometimes preceded by parenthetical usage notes that give supplementary semantic information:

> **not**. . . *adv* **1** (*used to form a negative*) **:** no. . .
>
> **within**[2] *prep* . . . **2** (*in expressions of distance*) **:**. . . **3** (*in expressions of time*) **:** . . .

e[2] *conj* (*used instead of* **y** *before words beginning with i or hi*) **:**. . .

poder[1]. . . *v aux*. . . **2** (*expressing possibility*) **:**. . . **3** (*expressing permission*) **:**. . .

Additional semantic orientation is also sometimes given in the form of parenthetical notes appearing within the definition:

calibrate. . . *vt*. . . **:** calibrar (armas), graduar (termómetros)

palco *nm* **:** box (in a theater or stadium)

Occasionally a usage note is used in place of a definition. This is usually done when the entry word has no single foreign-language equivalent. This type of usage note will be accompanied by examples of common use:

shall. . . *v aux*. . . **1** (*used to express a command*) <you shall do as I say **:** harás lo que te digo> . . .

3. Illustrations of Usage

Definitions are sometimes followed by verbal illustrations that show a typical use of the word in context or a common idiomatic usage. These verbal illustrations include a translation and are enclosed in angle brackets:

lejos *adv* **1 :** far away, distant <a lo lejos **:** in the distance, far off> . . .

make[1]. . . **9** . . .**:** ganar <to make a living **:** ganarse la vida> . . .

Sense Division

A boldface colon is used to introduce a definition:

fable. . . *n* **:** fábula *f*

Boldface Arabic numerals separate the senses of a word that has more than one sense:

laguna *nf* **1 :** lagoon **2 :** lacuna, gap

Whenever some information (such as a synonym, a boldface word or phrase, a usage note, a cross-reference, or a label) follows a sense number, it applies only to that specific numbered sense and not to any other boldface numbered senses:

abanico *nm.* . . **2** GAMA **:**. . .

tonic[2] *n.* . . **2** *or* **tonic water :**. . .

grillo *nm.* . . **2 grillos** *nmpl* **:**. . .

fairy. . . *n, pl* **fairies**. . . **2 fairy tale :**. . .

myself. . . *pron* **1** (*used reflexively*) **:**. . .

pike. . . *n.* . . **3 → turnpike**

atado[2] *nm.* . . **2** *Arg* **:**. . .

Cross-References

Three different kinds of cross-references are used in this dictionary: synonymous, cognate, and inflectional. In each instance the cross-reference is readily recognized by the boldface arrow following the entry word.

Synonymous and cognate cross-references indicate that a definition at the entry cross-referred to can be substituted for the entry word:

scapula. . . **→ shoulder blade**

amuck. . . **→ amok**

An inflectional cross-reference is used to identify the entry word as an inflected form of another word (as a noun or verb):

fue, etc. → ir, ser

mice → mouse

Synonyms

At many entries or senses in this book, a synonym in small capital letters is provided before the boldface colon and the following defining text. These synonyms are all main entries or bold notes elsewhere in the book. They serve as a helpful guide to the meaning of the entry or sense and also give the reader an additional term that might be substituted in a similar context. On the English-to-Spanish side synonyms are particularly abundant, since special care has been taken to guide the English speaker—by means of synonyms, verbal illustrations, or usage notes—to the meaning of the Spanish terms at each sense of a multisense entry.

Abbreviations in this Work

adj	adjective
adv	adverb
Arg	Argentina
Bol	Bolivia
Brit	British
CA	Central America
Car	Caribbean region
Col	Colombia
conj	conjuction
CoRi	Costa Rica
DomRep	Dominican Republic
Ecua	Ecuador
esp	especially
f	feminine
fam	familiar or colloquial
fpl	feminine plural
Guat	Guatemala
Hond	Honduras
interj	interjection
m	masculine
Mex	Mexico
mf	masculine or feminine
mpl	masculine plural
n	noun
nf	feminine noun
nfpl	feminine plural noun
nfs & pl	invariable singular or plural feminine noun
Nic	Nicaragua
nm	masculine noun
nmf	masculine or feminine noun
nmfpl	plural noun invariable for gender
nmfs & pl	noun invariable for both gender and number
nmpl	masculine plural noun
nms & pl	invariable singular or plural masculine noun
npl	plural noun
ns & pl	noun invariable for plural
Pan	Panama
Par	Paraguay
pl	plural
pp	past participle
prep	preposition
PRi	Puerto Rico
pron	pronoun
s	singular
Sal	El Salvador
Uru	Uruguay
usu	usually
v	verb (transitive and intransitive)
v aux	auxiliary verb
Ven	Venezuela
vi	intransitive verb
v impers	impersonal verb
vr	reflexive verb
vt	transitive verb

Pronunciation Symbols

VOWELS

- æ **a**sk, b**a**t, gl**a**d
- ɑ c**o**t, b**o**mb
- a *New England* **au**nt, *British* **a**sk, gl**a**ss, *Spanish* c**a**s**a**
- e *Spanish* p**e**so, j**e**f**e**
- ɛ **e**gg, b**e**t, f**e**d
- ə **a**bout, jav**e**lin, Al**a**bam**a**
- *ə* when italicized as in *ə*l, *ə*m, *ə*n, indicates a syllabic pronunciation of the consonant as in bott**le**, pris**m**, butt**on**
- i ver**y**, an**y**, thirt**y**, *Spanish* p**i**ña
- iː **ea**t, b**ea**d, b**ee**
- ɪ **i**d, b**i**d, p**i**t
- o **O**hio, yell**o**wer, potat**o**, *Spanish* **ó**valo
- oː **oa**ts, **ow**n, z**o**ne, bl**ow**
- ɔ **aw**l, m**au**l, c**au**ght, p**aw**
- ʊ s**u**re, sh**ou**ld, c**ou**ld
- u *Spanish* **u**va, c**u**lpa
- uː b**oo**t, f**ew**, c**oo**
- ʌ **u**nder, p**u**tt, b**u**d
- eɪ **ei**ght, w**a**de, b**ay**
- aɪ **i**ce, b**i**te, t**ie**
- aʊ **ou**t, g**ow**n, pl**ow**
- ɔɪ **oy**ster, c**oi**l, b**oy**
- ɒ *British* b**o**nd, g**o**d
- ø *French* d**eu**x, *German* H**öh**le
- œ *French* b**œu**f, *German* H**ö**lle
- y *French* l**u**ne, *German* f**üh**len
- ʏ *German* f**ü**llt
- ~ (tilde as in ã, ɔ̃, ɛ̃) *French* v**in**, b**on**, bi**en**
- ː indicates that the preceding vowel is long. Long vowels are almost always diphthongs in English, but not in Spanish.

STRESS MARKS

ˈ	high stress	**pen**manship
ˌ	low stress	penman**ship**

CONSONANTS

- b **b**a**b**y, la**b**or, ca**b**
- β *Spanish* ca**b**o, ó**v**alo
- d **d**ay, rea**d**y, ki**d**
- dʒ **j**ust, ba**dg**er, fu**dge**
- ð **th**en, ei**th**er, ba**the**
- f **f**oe, tou**gh**, bu**ff**
- g **g**o, bi**gg**er, ba**g**
- ɣ *Spanish* tra**g**ar, da**g**a
- h **h**ot, a**h**a
- j **y**es, vine**y**ard
- ʲ marks palatalization as in *French* digne [dinʲ]
- k **c**at, **k**eep, la**cqu**er, flo**ck**
- l **l**aw, ho**ll**ow, boi**l**
- m **m**at, he**m**p, ha**mm**er, ri**m**
- n **n**ew, te**n**t, te**n**or, ru**n**
- ŋ ru**ng**, ha**ng**, swi**ng**er
- ɲ *Spanish* caba**ñ**a, pi**ñ**a
- p **p**ay, la**p**se, to**p**
- r **r**ope, bu**r**n, ta**r**
- s **s**ad, mi**s**t, ki**ss**
- ʃ **sh**oe, mi**ss**ion, slu**sh**
- t **t**oe, bu**tt**on, ma**t**
- ṭ indicates that some speakers of English pronounce this as a voiced alveolar flap [ɾ], as in la**t**er, ca**tt**y, ba**tt**le
- tʃ **ch**oose, ba**tch**
- θ **th**in, e**th**er, ba**th**
- v **v**at, ne**v**er, ca**v**e
- w **w**et, soft**w**are
- x *German* Ba**ch**, *Scots* lo**ch**, *Spanish* **g**ente, **j**efe
- z **z**oo, ea**s**y, bu**zz**
- ʒ **j**aborandi, a**z**ure, bei**ge**
- ʔ indicates a glottal stop, the sound beginning the syllables in **uh-oh**
- *h, k, p, t* when italicized indicate sounds which are present in the pronunciation of some speakers of English but absent in that of others, so that *whence* [ˈ*h*wɛn*t*s] can be pronounced as [ˈwɛns], [ˈhwɛns], [ˈwɛnts], or [ˈhwɛnts]

Spanish Grammar

Accentuation

Spanish word stress is generally determined according to the following rules:

- Words ending in a vowel, or in *-n* or *-s,* are stressed on the penultimate syllable (*za**pa**to, **lla**man*).
- Words ending in a consonant other than *-n* or *-s* are stressed on the last syllable (*per**diz***, *curiosi**dad***).

Exceptions to these rules have a written accent mark over the stressed vowel (***fá**cil, habla**rá**, **úl**timo*). There are also a few words which take accent marks in order to distinguish them from homonyms (*si, sí; que, qué; el, él;* etc.).

Adverbs ending in *-mente* have two stressed syllables since they retain both the stress of the root word and of the *-mente* suffix (***len**ta**men**te, di**fí**cil**men**te*). Many compounds also have two stressed syllables (***lim**piapara**bri**sas*).

Punctuation and Capitalization

Questions and exclamations in Spanish are preceded by an inverted question mark ¿ and an inverted exclamation mark ¡, respectively:

¿Cuándo llamó Ana?
Y tú, ¿qué piensas?

¡No hagas eso!
Pero, ¡qué lástima!

In Spanish, unlike English, the following words are not capitalized:

- Names of days, months, and languages (*jueves, octubre, español*).
- Spanish adjectives or nouns derived from proper nouns (*los nicaragüenses, una teoría marxista*).

Articles

1. Definite Article

Spanish has five forms of the definite article: *el* (masculine singular), *la* (feminine singular), *los* (masculine plural), *las* (feminine plural), and *lo* (neuter). The first four agree in gender and number with the nouns they limit (*el carro,* the car; *las tijeras,* the scissors), although the form *el* is used with feminine singular nouns beginning with a stressed *a-* or *ha-* (*el águila, el hambre*).

The neuter article *lo* is used with the masculine singular form of an adjective to express an abstract concept (*lo mejor de este método,* the best thing about this method; *lo meticuloso de su trabajo,* the meticulousness of her work; *lo mismo para mí,* the same for me).

Whenever the masculine article *el* immediately follows the words *de* or *a,* it combines with them to form the contractions *del* and *al,* respectively (*viene* ***del*** *campo, vi* ***al*** *hermano de Roberto*).

The use of *el, la, los,* and *las* in Spanish corresponds largely to the use of *the* in English; some exceptions are noted below.

The definite article is used:

- When referring to something as a class (*los gatos son ágiles,* cats are agile; *me gusta el café,* I like coffee).
- In references to meals and in most expressions of time (*¿comiste el almuerzo?,* did you eat lunch?; *vino el año pasado,* he came last year; *son las dos,* it's two o'clock; *prefiero el verano,* I prefer summer; *la reunión es el lunes,*

the meeting is on Monday; but: *hoy es lunes,* today is Monday).

- Before titles (except *don, doña, san, santo, santa, fray,* and *sor*) in third-person references to people (*la señora Rivera llamó,* Mrs. Rivera called; but: *hola, señora Rivera,* hello, Mrs. Rivera).
- In references to body parts and personal possessions (*me duele la cabeza,* my head hurts; *dejó el sombrero,* he left his hat).
- To mean "the one" or "the ones" when the subject is already understood (*la de madera,* the wooden one; *los que vi ayer,* the ones I saw yesterday).

The definite article is omitted:

- Before a noun in apposition, if the noun is not modified (*Caracas, capital de Venezuela;* but: *Pico Bolívar, la montaña más alta de Venezuela*).
- Before a number in a royal title (*Carlos Quinto,* Charles the Fifth).

2. Indefinite Article

The forms of the indefinite article in Spanish are *un* (masculine singular), *una* (feminine singular), *unos* (masculine plural), and *unas* (feminine plural). They agree in number and gender with the nouns they limit (*una mesa,* a table; *unos platos,* some plates), although the form *un* is used with feminine singular nouns beginning with a stressed *a-* or *ha-* (*un ala, un hacha*).

The use of *un, una, unos,* and *unas* in Spanish corresponds largely to the use of *a, an,* and *some* in English, with some exceptions:

- Indefinite articles are generally omitted before nouns identifying someone or something as a member of a class or category (*Paco es profesor/católico,* Paco is a professor/Catholic; *se llama páncreas,* it's called a pancreas).

- They are also often omitted in instances where quantity is understood from context (*vine sin chaqueta,* I came without a jacket; *no tengo carro,* I don't have a car).

Nouns

1. Gender

Nouns in Spanish are either masculine or feminine. A noun's gender can often be determined according to the following guidelines:

- Nouns ending in *-aje, -o,* or *-or* are usually masculine (*el traje, el libro, el sabor*), with some exceptions (*la mano, la foto, la labor,* etc.).
- Nouns ending in *-a, -dad, -ión, -tud,* or *-umbre* are usually feminine (*la alfombra, la capacidad, la excepción, la juventud, la certidumbre*). Exceptions include: *el día, el mapa,* and many learned borrowings ending in *-ma* (*el idioma, el tema*).

Most nouns referring to people or animals agree in gender with the subject (*el hombre, la mujer; el hermano, la hermana; el perro, la perra*). However, some nouns referring to people, including those ending in *-ista,* use the same form for both sexes (*el artista, la artista; el modelo, la modelo;* etc.).

A few names of animals exist in only one gender form (*la jirafa, el sapo,* etc.). In these instances, the adjectives *macho* and *hembra* are sometimes used to distinguish males and females (*una jirafa macho,* a male giraffe).

2. Pluralization

Plurals of Spanish nouns are formed as follows:

- Nouns ending in an unstressed vowel or an accented *-é* are pluralized by adding *-s* (*la vaca, las vacas; el café, los cafés*).

- Nouns ending in a consonant other than *-s*, or in a stressed vowel other than *-é*, are generally pluralized by adding *-es* (*el papel, los papeles; el rubí, los rubíes*). Exceptions include *papá* (*papás*) and *mamá* (*mamás*).

- Nouns with an unstressed final syllable ending in *-s* usually have a zero plural (*la crisis, las crisis; el jueves, los jueves*). Other nouns ending in *-s* add *-es* to form the plural (*el mes, los meses; el país, los países*).

- Nouns ending in *-z* are pluralized by changing the *-z* to *-c* and adding *-es* (*el lápiz, los lápices; la vez, las veces*).

- Many compound nouns have a zero plural (*el paraguas, los paraguas; el aguafiestas, los aguafiestas*).

- The plurals of *cualquiera* and *quienquiera* are *cualesquiera* and *quienesquiera,* respectively.

Adjectives

1. Gender and Number

Most adjectives agree in gender and number with the nouns they modify (un chico *alto,* una chica *alta,* unos chicos *altos,* unas chicas *altas*). Some adjectives, including those ending in *-e* and *-ista* (*fuerte, altruista*) and comparative adjectives ending in *-or* (*mayor, mejor*), vary only for number.

Adjectives whose masculine singular forms end in *-o* generally change the *-o* to *-a* to form the feminine (*pequeño* → *pequeña*). Masculine adjectives ending in *-án, -ón,* or *-dor,* and masculine adjectives of nationality which end in a consonant, usually add *-a* to form the feminine (*holgazán* → *holgazana*; *llorón* → *llorona*; *trabajador* → *trabajadora*; *irlandés* → *irlandesa*).

Adjectives are pluralized in much the same manner as nouns:

- The plurals of adjectives ending in an unstressed vowel or an accented *-é* are formed by adding an *-s* (un postre *rico,* unos postres *ricos;* una camisa *café,* unas camisas *cafés*).

- Adjectives ending in a consonant, or in a stressed vowel other than *-é,* are generally pluralized by adding *-es* (un niño *cortés,* unos niños *corteses;* una persona *iraní,* unas personas *iraníes*).
- Adjectives ending in *-z* are pluralized by changing the *-z* to *-c* and adding *-es* (una respuesta *sagaz*, unas respuestas *sagaces*).

2. Shortening

- The following masculine singular adjectives drop their final *-o* when they occur before a masculine singular noun: *bueno* (*buen*), *malo* (*mal*), *uno* (*un*), *alguno* (*algún*), *ninguno* (*ningún*), *primero* (*primer*), *tercero* (*tercer*).
- *Grande* shortens to *gran* before any singular noun.
- *Ciento* shortens to *cien* before any noun.
- The title *Santo* shortens to *San* before all masculine names except those beginning with *To-* or *Do-* (*San Juan, Santo Tomás*).

3. Position

Descriptive adjectives generally follow the nouns they modify (*una cosa útil, un actor famoso*). However, adjectives that express an inherent quality often precede the noun (*la blanca nieve*).

Some adjectives change meaning depending on whether they occur before or after the noun: *un pobre niño,* a poor (pitiable) child; *un niño pobre,* a poor (not rich) child; *un gran hombre,* a great man; *un hombre grande,* a big man; *el único libro,* the only book; *el libro único,* the unique book, etc.

4. Comparative and Superlative Forms

The comparative of Spanish adjectives is generally rendered as *más . . . que* (more . . . than) or *menos . . . que* (less . . . than): *soy más alta que él,* I'm taller than he; *son menos inteligentes que tú,* they're less intelligent than you.

The superlative of Spanish adjectives usually follows the formula *definite article* + (*noun* +) *más/menos* + *adjective: ella es la estudiante más trabajadora,* she is the hardest-working student; *él es el menos conocido,* he's the least known.

A few Spanish adjectives have irregular comparative and superlative forms:

Adjective	Comparative/Superlative
bueno (good)	**mejor** (better, best)
malo (bad)	**peor** (worse, worst)
grande[1] (big, great), **viejo** (old)	**mayor** (greater, older; greatest, oldest)
pequeño[1] (little), **joven** (young)	**menor** (lesser, younger; least, youngest)
mucho (much), **muchos** (many)	**más** (more, most)
poco (little), **pocos** (few)	**menos** (less, least)

[1]These words have regular comparative and superlative forms when used in reference to physical size: *él es más grande que yo; nuestra casa es la más pequeña.*

ABSOLUTE SUPERLATIVE

The absolute superlative is formed by placing *muy* before the adjective, or by adding the suffix *-ísimo* (*ella es muy simpática* or *ella es simpatiquísima,* she is very nice). The absolute superlative using *-ísimo* is formed according to the following rules:

- Adjectives ending in a consonant other than *-z* simply add the *-ísimo* ending (*fácil* → *facilísimo*).
- Adjectives ending in *-z* change this consonant to *-c* and add *-ísimo* (*feliz* → *felicísimo*).
- Adjectives ending in a vowel or diphthong drop the vowel or diphthong and add *-ísimo* (*claro* → *clarísimo; amplio* → *amplísimo*).

- Adjectives ending in *-co* or *-go* change these endings to *qu* and *gu*, respectively, and add *-ísimo* (*rico* → *riquísimo; largo* → *larguísimo*).
- Adjectives ending in *-ble* change this ending to *-bil* and add *-ísimo* (*notable* → *notabilísimo*).
- Adjectives containing the stressed diphthong *ie* or *ue* will sometimes change these to *e* and *o*, respectively (*ferviente* → *fervientísimo* or *ferventísimo; bueno* → *buenísimo* or *bonísimo*).

Adverbs

Adverbs can be formed by adding the adverbial suffix *-mente* to virtually any adjective (*fácil* → *fácilmente*). If the adjective varies for gender, the feminine form is used as the basis for forming the adverb (*rápido* → *rápidamente*).

Pronouns

1. Personal Pronouns

The personal pronouns in Spanish are:

Person	Singular		Plural	
FIRST	**yo**	I	**nosotros, nosotras**	we
SECOND	**tú**	you (familiar)	**vosotros**[2], **vosotras**[2]	you, all of you
	vos[1]	you		
	usted	you (formal)	**ustedes**[3]	you, all of you
THIRD	**él**	he	**ellos, ellas**	they
	ella	she		
	ello	it (neuter)		

[1] Familiar form used in addition to *tú* in South and Central America.
[2] Familiar form used in Spain.
[3] Formal form used in Spain; familiar and formal form used in Latin America.

FAMILIAR VS. FORMAL

The second person personal pronouns exist in both familiar and formal forms. The familiar forms are generally used when addressing relatives, friends, and children, although usage varies considerably from region to region; the formal forms are used in other contexts to show courtesy, respect, or emotional distance.

In Spain and in the Caribbean, *tú* is used exclusively as the familiar singular "you." In South and Central America, however, *vos* either competes with *tú* to varying degrees or replaces it entirely. (For a more detailed explanation of *vos* and its corresponding verb forms, refer to the Conjugation of Spanish Verbs section.)

The plural familiar form *vosotros, -as* is used only in Spain, where *ustedes* is reserved for formal contexts. In Latin America, *vosotros, -as* is not used, and *ustedes* serves as the all-purpose plural "you."

It should be noted that while *usted* and *ustedes* are regarded as second person pronouns, they take the third person form of the verb.

USAGE

In Spanish, personal pronouns are generally omitted (*voy al cine,* I'm going to the movies; *¿llamaron?,* did they call?), although they are sometimes used for purposes of emphasis or clarity (*se lo diré yo,* I will tell them; *vino ella, pero él se quedó,* she came, but he stayed behind). The forms *usted* and *ustedes* are usually included out of courtesy (*¿cómo está usted?,* how are you?).

Personal pronouns are not generally used in reference to inanimate objects or living creatures other than humans; in these instances, the pronoun is most often omitted (*¿es nuevo? no, es viejo,* is it new? no, it's old).

The neuter third person pronoun *ello* is reserved for indefinite subjects (as abstract concepts): *todo ello implica . . . ,* all of this implies . . . ; *por si ello fuera poco . . . ,* as if that weren't enough . . . . It most commonly appears in formal writing and speech. In less formal contexts, *ello* is often either omitted or replaced with *esto, eso,* or *aquello.*

2. Prepositional Pronouns

Prepositional pronouns are used as the objects of prepositions (*¿es para mí?,* is it for me?; *se lo dio a ellos,* he gave it to them).

The prepositional pronouns in Spanish are:

Singular		Plural	
mí	me	**nosotros, nosotras**	us
ti	you	**vosotros[1], vosotras[1]**	you
usted	you (formal)	**ustedes**	you
él	him	**ellos, ellas**	them
ella	her		
ello	it (neuter)		
sí	yourself, himself, herself, itself, oneself	**sí**	yourselves, themselves

[1]Used primarily in Spain.

When the preposition *con* is followed by *mí, ti,* or *sí,* both words are replaced by *conmigo, contigo,* and *consigo,* respectively (*¿vienes conmigo?,* are you coming with me?; *habló contigo,* he spoke with you; *no lo trajo consigo,* she didn't bring it with her).

3. Object Pronouns

DIRECT OBJECT PRONOUNS

Direct object pronouns represent the primary goal or result of the action of a verb. The direct object pronouns in Spanish are:

Singular		Plural	
me	me	**nos**	us
te	you	**os[1]**	you
le[2]	you, him	**les[2]**	you, them
lo	you, him, it	**los**	you, them
la	you, her, it	**las**	you, them

[1]Used only in Spain.
[2]Used mainly in Spain.

Agreement

The third person forms agree in both gender and number with the nouns they replace or the people they refer to (*pintó las paredes,* she painted the walls → *las pintó,* she painted them; *visitaron al señor Juárez*, they visited Mr. Juárez → *lo visitaron*, they visited him). The remaining forms vary only for number.

Position

Direct object pronouns are normally affixed to the end of an affirmative command, a simple infinitive, or a present participle (*¡hazlo!,* do it!; *es difícil hacerlo,* it's difficult to do it; *haciéndolo, aprenderás,* you'll learn by doing it). With constructions involving an auxiliary verb and an infinitive or present participle, the pronoun may occur either immediately before the construction or suffixed to it (*lo voy a hacer* or *voy a hacerlo,* I'm going to do it; *estoy haciéndolo* or *lo estoy haciendo,* I'm doing it). In all other cases, the pronoun immediately precedes the conjugated verb (*no lo haré,* I won't do it).

Regional Variation

In Spain and in a few areas of Latin America, *le* and *les* are used in place of *lo* and *los* when referring to or addressing people (*le vieron,* they saw him; *les vistió,* she dressed them). In most parts of Latin America, however, *los* and *las* are used for the second person plural in both formal and familiar contexts.

The second person plural familiar form *os* is restricted to Spain.

INDIRECT OBJECT PRONOUNS

Indirect object pronouns represent the secondary goal of the action of a verb (*me dio el regalo,* he gave me the gift; *les dije que no,* I told them no). The indirect object pronouns in Spanish are:

Singular		Plural	
me	(to, for, from) me	**nos**	(to, for, from) us
te	(to, for, from) you	**os**[1]	(to, for, from) you
le	(to, for, from) you, him, her, it	**les**	(to, for, from) you, them
se[2]		**se**[2]	

[1]Used only in Spain.
[2]See explanation below.

Position

Indirect object pronouns follow the same rules as direct object pronouns with regard to their position in relation to verbs. When they occur with direct object pronouns, the indirect object pronoun always precedes (*nos lo dio,* she gave it to us; *estoy trayéndotela,* I'm bringing it to you).

Use of *Se*

When the indirect object pronouns *le* or *les* occur before any direct object pronoun beginning with an *l-,* the indirect object pronouns *le* and *les* convert to *se* (*les mandé la carta,* I sent them the letter → *se la mandé,* I sent it to them; *vamos a comprarle los aretes,* let's buy her the earrings → *vamos a comprárselos,* let's buy them for her).

4. Reflexive Pronouns

Reflexive pronouns are used to refer back to the subject of the verb (*me hice daño,* I hurt myself; *se vistieron,* they got dressed, they dressed themselves; *nos lo compramos,* we bought it for ourselves).

The reflexive pronouns in Spanish are:

Singular		Plural	
me	myself	**nos**	ourselves
te	yourself	**os**[1]	yourselves
se	yourself, himself, herself, itself	**se**	yourselves, themselves

[1]Used only in Spain.

Reflexive pronouns are also used:

- When the verb describes an action performed to one's own body, clothing, etc. (*me quité los zapatos,* I took off my shoes; *se arregló el pelo,* he fixed his hair).

- In the plural, to indicate reciprocal action (*se hablan con frecuencia,* they speak with each other frequently).
- In the third person singular and plural, as an indefinite subject reference (*se dice que es verdad,* they say it's true; *nunca se sabe,* one never knows; *se escribieron miles de páginas,* thousands of pages were written).

It should be noted that many verbs which take reflexive pronouns in Spanish have intransitive equivalents in English (*ducharse,* to shower; *quejarse,* to complain; etc.).

5. Relative Pronouns

Relative pronouns introduce subordinate clauses acting as nouns or modifiers (*el libro que escribió . . . ,* the book that he wrote . . . ; *las chicas a quienes conociste . . . ,* the girls whom you met . . .). In Spanish, the relative pronouns are:

que (that, which, who, whom)

quien, quienes (who, whom, that, whoever, whomever)

el cual, la cual, los cuales, las cuales (which, who)

el que, la que, los que, las que (which, who, whoever)

lo cual (which)

lo que (what, which, whatever)

cuanto, cuanta, cuantos, cuantas (all those that, all that, whatever, whoever, as much as, as many as)

Relative pronouns are not omitted in Spanish as they often are in English: *el carro que vi ayer,* the car (that) I saw yesterday. When relative pronouns are used with prepositions, the preposition precedes the clause (*la película sobre la cual le hablé,* the film I spoke to you about).

The relative pronoun *que* can be used in reference to both people and things. Unlike other relative pronouns, *que* does not take the personal *a* when used as a direct object referring to a person (*el hombre que llamé,* the man that I called; but: *el hombre a quien llamé,* the man whom I called).

Quien is used only in reference to people. It varies in number with the explicit or implied antecedent (*las mujeres con quienes charlamos . . .,* the women we chatted with; *quien lo hizo pagará,* whoever did it will pay).

El cual and *el que* vary for both number and gender, and are therefore often used in situations where *que* or *quien(es)* might create ambiguity: *nos contó algunas cosas sobre los libros, las cuales eran interesantes,* he told us some things about the books which (the things) were interesting.

Lo cual and *lo que* are used to refer back to a whole clause, or to something indefinite (*dijo que iría, lo cual me alegró,* he said he would go, which made me happy; *pide lo que quieras,* ask for whatever you want).

Cuanto varies for both number and gender with the implied antecedent: *conté a cuantas (personas) pude,* I counted as many (people) as I could. If an indefinite mass quantity is referred to, the masculine singular form is used (*anoté cuanto decía,* I jotted down whatever he said).

Possessives

1. Possessive Adjectives

UNSTRESSED FORMS

Singular		Plural	
mi(s)	my	**nuestro(s), nuestra(s)**	our
tu(s)	your	**vuestro(s)**[1], **vuestra(s)**[1]	your
su(s)	your, his, her, its	**su(s)**	your, their

[1]Used only in Spain.

STRESSED FORMS

Singular		Plural	
mío(s), mía(s)	my, mine, of mine	**nuestro(s), nuestra(s)**	our, ours, of ours
tuyo(s), tuya(s)	your, yours, of yours	**vuestro(s)**[1], **vuestra(s)**[1]	your, yours, of yours
suyo(s), suya(s)	your, yours, of yours; his, of his; her, hers, of hers; its, of its	**suyo(s), suya(s)**	your, yours, of yours; their, theirs, of theirs

[1]Used only in Spain.

The unstressed forms of possessive adjectives precede the nouns they modify (*mis zapatos,* my shoes; *nuestra escuela,* our school).

The stressed forms occur after the noun and are often used for purposes of emphasis (*el carro tuyo,* your car; *la pluma es mía,* the pen is mine; *unos amigos nuestros,* some friends of ours).

All possessive adjectives agree with the noun in number. The stressed forms, as well as the unstressed forms *nuestro* and *vuestro,* also vary for gender.

2. Possessive Pronouns

The possessive pronouns have the same forms as the stressed possessive adjectives (see table above). They are always preceded by the definite article, and they agree in number and gender with the nouns they replace (*las llaves mías,* my keys → *las mías,* mine; *los guantes nuestros,* our gloves → *los nuestros,* ours).

Demonstratives

1. Demonstrative Adjectives

The demonstrative adjectives in Spanish are:

Singular		Plural	
este, esta	this	**estos, estas**	these
ese, esa	that	**esos, esas**	those
aquel, aquella	that	**aquellos, aquellas**	those

Demonstrative adjectives agree with the nouns they modify in gender and number (*esta chica, aquellos árboles*). They normally precede the noun, but may occasionally occur after for purposes of emphasis or to express contempt: *en la época aquella de cambio,* in that era of change; *el perro ese ha ladrado toda la noche,* that (awful, annoying, etc.) dog barked all night long.

The forms *aquel, aquella, aquellos,* and *aquellas* are generally used in reference to people and things that are relatively distant from the speaker in space or time: *ese libro,* that book (a few feet away); *aquel libro,* that book (way over there).

2. Demonstrative Pronouns

The demonstrative pronouns in Spanish are orthographically identical to the demonstrative adjectives except that they take an accent mark over the stressed vowel (*éste, ése, aquél,* etc.). In addition, there are three neuter forms—*esto, eso,* and *aquello*—which are used when referring to abstract ideas or unidentified things (*¿te dijo eso?,* he said that to you?; *¿qué es esto?,* what is this?; *tráeme todo aquello,* bring me all that stuff).

Except for the neuter forms, demonstrative pronouns agree in gender and number with the nouns they replace (*esta silla,* this chair → *ésta,* this one; *aquellos vasos,* those glasses → *aquéllos,* those ones).

Spanish Numbers

Cardinal Numbers

1	uno	33	treinta y tres
2	dos	34	treinta y cuatro
3	tres	35	treinta y cinco
4	cuatro	36	treinta y seis
5	cinco	37	treinta y siete
6	seis	38	treinta y ocho
7	siete	39	treinta y nueve
8	ocho	40	cuarenta
9	nueve	41	cuarenta y uno
10	diez	50	cincuenta
11	once	60	sesenta
12	doce	70	setenta
13	trece	80	ochenta
14	catorce	90	noventa
15	quince	100	cien
16	dieciséis	101	ciento uno
17	diecisiete	102	ciento dos
18	dieciocho	200	doscientos
19	diecinueve	300	trescientos
20	veinte	400	cuatrocientos
21	veintiuno	500	quinientos
22	veintidós	600	seiscientos
23	veintitrés	700	setecientos
24	veinticuatro	800	ochocientos
25	veinticinco	900	novecientos
26	veintiséis	1,000	mil
27	veintisiete	1,001	mil uno
28	veintiocho	2,000	dos mil
29	veintinueve	100,000	cien mil
30	treinta	1,000,000	un millón
31	treinta y uno	1,000,000,000	mil millones
32	treinta y dos		

Ordinal Numbers

1st	primero, -ra	18th	decimoctavo, -va
2nd	segundo, -da	19th	decimonoveno, -na; *or* decimonono, -na
3rd	tercero, -ra	20th	vigésimo, -ma
4th	cuarto, -ta	21st	vigésimoprimero, vigésimaprimera
5th	quinto, -ta	22nd	vigésimosegundo, vigésimasegunda
6th	sexto, -ta	30th	trigésimo, -ma
7th	séptimo, -ma	40th	cuadragésimo, -ma
8th	octavo, -va	50th	quincuagésimo, -ma
9th	noveno, -na	60th	sexagésimo, -ma
10th	décimo, -ma	70th	septuagésimo, -ma
11th	undécimo, -ma	80th	octogésimo, -ma
12th	duodécimo, -ma	90th	nonagésimo, -ma
13th	decimotercero, -ra	100th	centésimo, -ma
14th	decimocuarto, -ta		
15th	decimoquinto, -ta		
16th	decimosexto, -ta		
17th	decimoséptimo, -ma		

Conjugation of Spanish Verbs

Simple Tenses

TENSE	REGULAR VERBS ENDING IN -AR	
	hablar	
PRESENT INDICATIVE	hablo	hablamos
	hablas	habláis
	habla	hablan
PRESENT SUBJUNCTIVE	hable	hablemos
	hables	habléis
	hable	hablen
PRETERIT INDICATIVE	hablé	hablamos
	hablaste	hablasteis
	habló	hablaron
IMPERFECT INDICATIVE	hablaba	hablábamos
	hablabas	hablabais
	hablaba	hablaban
IMPERFECT SUBJUNCTIVE	hablara	habláramos
	hablaras	hablarais
	hablara	hablaran
	or	
	hablase	hablásemos
	hablases	hablaseis
	hablase	hablasen
FUTURE INDICATIVE	hablaré	hablaremos
	hablarás	hablaréis
	hablará	hablarán
FUTURE SUBJUNCTIVE	hablare	habláremos
	hablares	hablareis
	hablare	hablaren
CONDITIONAL	hablaría	hablaríamos
	hablarías	hablaríais
	hablaría	hablarían
IMPERATIVE		hablemos
	habla	hablad
	hable	hablen
PRESENT PARTICIPLE (GERUND)	hablando	
PAST PARTICIPLE	hablado	

REGULAR VERBS ENDING IN -ER		REGULAR VERBS ENDING IN -IR	
	comer		vivir
como	comemos	vivo	vivimos
comes	coméis	vives	vivís
come	comen	vive	viven
coma	comamos	viva	vivamos
comas	comáis	vivas	viváis
coma	coman	viva	vivan
comí	comimos	viví	vivimos
comiste	comisteis	viviste	vivisteis
comió	comieron	vivió	vivieron
comía	comíamos	vivía	vivíamos
comías	comíais	vivías	vivíais
comía	comían	vivía	vivían
comiera	comiéramos	viviera	viviéramos
comieras	comierais	vivieras	vivierais
comiera	comieran	viviera	vivieran
or		*or*	
comiese	comiésemos	viviese	viviésemos
comieses	comieseis	vivieses	vivieseis
comiese	comiesen	viviese	viviesen
comeré	comeremos	viviré	viviremos
comerás	comeréis	vivirás	viviréis
comerá	comerán	vivirá	vivirán
comiere	comiéremos	viviere	viviéremos
comieres	comiereis	vivieres	viviereis
comiere	comieren	viviere	vivieren
comería	comeríamos	viviría	viviríamos
comerías	comeríais	vivirías	viviríais
comería	comerían	viviría	vivirían
	comamos		vivamos
come	comed	vive	vivid
coma	coman	viva	vivan
comiendo		viviendo	
comido		vivido	

Compound Tenses

1. Perfect Tenses

The perfect tenses are formed with *haber* and the past participle:

PRESENT PERFECT

he hablado, etc. (*indicative*);
haya hablado, etc. (*subjunctive*)

PAST PERFECT

había hablado, etc. (*indicative*);
hubiera hablado, etc. (*subjuntive*)
or
hubiese hablado, etc. (*subjunctive*)

PRETERIT PERFECT

hube hablado, etc. (*indicative*)

FUTURE PERFECT

habré hablado, etc. (*indicative*)

CONDITIONAL PERFECT

habría hablado, etc. (*indicative*)

2. Progressive Tenses

The progressive tenses are formed with *estar* and the present participle:

PRESENT PROGRESSIVE

estoy llamando, etc. (*indicative*);
esté llamando, etc. (*subjunctive*)

IMPERFECT PROGRESSIVE

estaba llamando, etc. (*indicative*);
estuviera llamando, etc. (*subjunctive*)
or
estuviese llamando, etc. (*subjunctive*)

PRETERIT PROGRESSIVE

estuve llamando, etc. (*indicative*)

FUTURE PROGRESSIVE

estaré llamando, etc. (*indicative*)

CONDITIONAL PROGRESSIVE

estaría llamando, etc. (*indicative*)

PRESENT PERFECT PROGRESSIVE

he estado llamando, etc. (*indicative*);
haya estado llamando, etc. (*subjunctive*)

PAST PERFECT PROGRESSIVE

había estado llamando, etc. (*indicative*);
hubiera estado llamando, etc. (*subjunctive*)
or
hubiese estado llamando, etc. (*subjunctive*)

Use of *Vos*

In parts of South and Central America, *vos* often replaces or competes with *tú* as the second person familiar personal pronoun. It is particularly well established in the Río de la Plata region and much of Central America.

The pronoun *vos* often takes a distinct set of verb forms, usually in the present tense and the imperative. These vary widely from region to region; examples of the most common forms are shown below.

INFINITIVE FORM	hablar	comer	vivir
PRESENT INDICATIVE	vos hablás	vos comés	vos vivís
PRESENT SUBJUNCTIVE	vos hablés	vos comás	vos vivás
IMPERATIVE	hablá	comé	viví

In some areas, *vos* may take the *tú* or *vosotros* forms of the verb, while in others (as Uruguay), *tú* is combined with the *vos* verb forms.

Irregular Verbs

The *imperfect subjunctive,* the *future subjunctive,* the *conditional*, and the remaining forms of the *imperative* are not included in the model conjugations list, but can be derived as follows:

The *imperfect subjunctive* and the *future subjunctive* are formed from the third person plural form of the preterit tense by removing the last syllable (*-ron*) and adding the appropriate suffix:

PRETERIT INDICATIVE, THIRD PERSON PLURAL (querer)	quisieron
IMPERFECT SUBJUNCTIVE (querer)	quisiera, quisieras, etc. *or* quisiese, quisieses, etc.
FUTURE SUBJUNCTIVE (querer)	quisiere, quisieres, etc.

The conditional uses the same stem as the future indicative:

FUTURE INDICATIVE (poner)	pondré, pondrás, etc.
CONDITIONAL (poner)	pondría, pondrías, etc.

The third person singular, first person plural, and third person plural forms of the *imperative* are the same as the corresponding forms of the present subjunctive.

The second person plural *(vosotros)* form of the *imperative* is formed by removing the final *-r* of the infinitive form and adding a *-d* (ex.: *oír* → *oíd).*

Model Conjugations of Irregular Verbs

The model conjugations below include the following simple tenses: the *present indicative* (*IND*), the *present subjunctive* (*SUBJ*), the *preterit indicative* (*PRET*), the *imperfect indicative* (*IMPF*), the *future indicative* (*FUT*), the second person singular form of the *imperative* (*IMPER*), the *present participle* or *gerund* (*PRP*), and the *past participle* (*PP*). Each set of conjugations is preceded by the corresponding infinitive form of the verb, shown in bold type. Only tenses containing irregularities are listed, and the irregular verb forms within each tense are displayed in bold type.

Conjugation of Spanish Verbs

Each irregular verb entry in the Spanish-English section of this dictionary is cross-referred by number to one of the following model conjugations. These cross-reference numbers are shown in curly braces { } immediately following the entry's functional label.

1 **abolir** *(defective verb)* **:** IND abolimos, abolís *(other forms not used);* SUBJ *(not used);* IMPER *(only second person plural is used)*

2 **abrir :** PP abierto

3 **actuar :** IND **actúo**, **actúas**, **actúa**, actuamos, actuáis, **actúan;** SUBJ **actúe, actúes, actúe,** actuemos, actuéis, **actúen;** IMPER **actúa**

4 **adquirir :** IND **adquiero, adquieres, adquiere,** adquirimos, adquirís, **adquieren;** SUBJ **adquiera, adquieras, adquiera,** adquiramos, adquiráis, **adquieran;** IMPER **adquiere**

5 **airar :** IND **aíro, aíras, aíra,** airamos, airáis, **aíran;** SUBJ **aíre, aíres, aíre,** airemos, airéis, **aíren;** IMPER **aíra**

6 **andar :** PRET **anduve, anduviste, anduvo, anduvimos, anduvisteis, anduvieron**

7 **asir :** IND **asgo,** ases, ase, asimos, asís, asen; SUBJ **asga, asgas, asga, asgamos, asgáis, asgan**

8 **aunar :** IND **aúno, aúnas, aúna,** aunamos, aunáis, **aúnan;** SUBJ **aúne, aúnes, aúne,** aunemos, aunéis, **aúnen;** IMPER **aúna**

9 **avergonzar :** IND **avergüenzo, avergüenzas, avergüenza,** avergonzamos, avergonzáis, **avergüenzan;** SUBJ **avergüence, avergüences, avergüence, avergoncemos, avergoncéis, avergüencen;** PRET **avergoncé;** IMPER **avergüenza**

10 **averiguar :** SUBJ **averigüe, averigües, averigüe, averigüemos, averigüéis, averigüen;** PRET **averigüé,** averiguaste, averiguó, averiguamos, averiguasteis, averiguaron

11 **bendecir :** IND **bendigo, bendices, bendice,** bendecimos, bendecís, **bendicen;** SUBJ **bendiga, bendigas, bendiga, bendigamos, bendigáis, bendigan;** PRET **bendije, bendijiste, bendijo, bendijimos, bendijisteis, bendijeron;** IMPER **bendice**

12 **caber :** IND **quepo,** cabes, cabe, cabemos, cabéis, caben; SUBJ **quepa, quepas, quepa, quepamos, quepáis, quepan;** PRET **cupe, cupiste, cupo, cupimos, cupisteis, cupieron;** FUT **cabré, cabrás, cabrá, cabremos, cabréis, cabrán**

13 **caer :** IND **caigo,** caes, cae, caemos, caéis, caen; SUBJ **caiga, caigas, caiga, caigamos, caigáis, caigan;** PRET caí, **caíste, cayó, caímos, caísteis, cayeron;** PRP **cayendo;** PP **caído**

14 **cocer :** IND **cuezo, cueces, cuece,** cocemos, cocéis, **cuecen;** SUBJ **cueza, cuezas, cueza, cozamos, cozáis, cuezan;** IMPER **cuece**

15 **coger :** IND **cojo,** coges, coge, cogemos, cogéis, cogen; SUBJ **coja, cojas, coja, cojamos, cojáis, cojan**

16 **colgar :** IND **cuelgo, cuelgas, cuelga,** colgamos, colgáis, **cuelgan;** SUBJ **cuelgue, cuelgues, cuelgue, colguemos, colguéis, cuelguen;** PRET **colgué,** colgaste, colgó, colgamos, colgasteis, colgaron; IMPER **cuelga**

17 **concernir** *(defective verb; used only in the third person singular and plural of the present indicative, present subjunctive, and imperfect subjunctive) see* 25 **discernir**

18 **conocer :** IND **conozco,** conoces, conoce, conocemos, conocéis, conocen; SUBJ **conozca, conozcas, conozca, conozcamos, conozcáis, conozcan**

19 **contar :** IND **cuento, cuentas, cuenta,** contamos, contáis, **cuentan;** SUBJ **cuente, cuentes, cuente,** contemos, contéis, **cuenten;** IMPER **cuenta**

20 **creer :** PRET creí, **creíste, creyó, creímos, creísteis, creyeron;** PRP **creyendo;** PP **creído**

21 **cruzar :** SUBJ **cruce, cruces, cruce, crucemos, crucéis, crucen;** PRET **crucé,** cruzaste, cruzó, cruzamos, cruzasteis, cruzaron

22 **dar :** IND **doy,** das, da, damos, **dais,** dan; SUBJ **dé,** des, **dé,** demos, **deis,** den; PRET **di, diste, dio, dimos, disteis, dieron**

23 **decir :** IND **digo, dices, dice,** decimos, decís, **dicen;** SUBJ **diga, digas, diga, digamos, digáis, digan;** PRET **dije, dijiste, dijo,**

dijimos, dijisteis, dijeron; *FUT* **diré, dirás, dirá, diremos, diréis, dirán;** *IMPER* **di;** *PRP* **diciendo;** *PP* **dicho**

24 **delinquir :** *IND* **delinco,** delinques, delinque, delinquimos, delinquís, delinquen; *SUBJ* **delinca, delincas, delinca, delincamos, delincáis, delincan**

25 **discernir :** *IND* **discierno, disciernes, discierne,** discernimos, discernís, **disciernen;** *SUBJ* **discierna, disciernas, discierna,** discernamos, discernáis, **disciernan;** *IMPER* **discierne**

26 **distinguir :** *IND* **distingo,** distingues, distingue, distinguimos, distinguís, distinguen; *SUBJ* **distinga, distingas, distinga, distingamos, distingáis, distingan**

27 **dormir :** *IND* **duermo, duermes, duerme,** dormimos, dormís, **duermen;** *SUBJ* **duerma, duermas, duerma, durmamos, durmáis, duerman;** *PRET* dormí, dormiste, **durmió,** dormimos, dormisteis, **durmieron;** *IMPER* **duerme;** *PRP* **durmiendo**

28 **elegir :** *IND* **elijo, eliges, elige,** elegimos, elegís, **eligen;** *SUBJ* **elija, elijas, elija, elijamos, elijáis, elijan;** *PRET* elegí, elegiste, **eligió,** elegimos, elegisteis, **eligieron;** *IMPER* **elige;** *PRP* **eligiendo**

29 **empezar :** *IND* **empiezo, empiezas, empieza,** empezamos, empezáis, **empiezan;** *SUBJ* **empiece, empieces, empiece, empecemos, empecéis, empiecen;** *PRET* **empecé,** empezaste, empezó, empezamos, empezasteis, empezaron; *IMPER* **empieza**

30 **enraizar :** *IND* **enraízo, enraízas, enraíza,** enraizamos, enraizáis, **enraízan;** *SUBJ* **enraíce, enraíces, enraíce, enraicemos, enraicéis, enraícen;** *PRET* **enraicé,** enraizaste, enraizó, enraizamos, enraizasteis, enraizaron; *IMPER* **enraíza**

31 **erguir :** *IND* **irgo** *or* **yergo, irgues** *or* **yergues, irgue** *or* **yergue,** erguimos, erguís, **irguen** *or* **yerguen;** *SUBJ* **irga** *or* **yerga, irgas** *or* **yergas, irga** *or* **yerga, irgamos, irgáis, irgan** *or* **yergan;** *PRET* erguí, erguiste, **irguió,** erguimos, erguisteis, **irguieron;** *IMPER* **irgue** *or* **yergue;** *PRP* **irguiendo**

32 **errar :** *IND* **yerro, yerras, yerra,** erramos, erráis, **yerran;** *SUBJ* **yerre, yerres, yerre,** erremos, erréis, **yerren;** *IMPER* **yerra**

33 **escribir** : *PP* **escrito**

34 **estar** : *IND* **estoy, estás, está,** estamos, estáis, **están;** *SUBJ* **esté, estés, esté,** estemos, estéis, **estén;** *PRET* **estuve, estuviste, estuvo, estuvimos, estuvisteis, estuvieron;** *IMPER* **está**

35 **exigir** : *IND* **exijo,** exiges, exige, exigimos, exigís, exigen; *SUBJ* **exija, exijas, exija, exijamos, exijáis, exijan**

36 **forzar** : *IND* **fuerzo, fuerzas, fuerza,** forzamos, forzáis, **fuerzan;** *SUBJ* **fuerce, fuerces, fuerce, forcemos, forcéis, fuercen;** *PRET* **forcé,** forzaste, forzó, forzamos, forzasteis, forzaron; *IMPER* **fuerza**

37 **freír** : *IND* **frío, fríes, fríe, freímos,** freís, **fríen;** *SUBJ* **fría, frías, fría, friamos, friáis, frían;** *PRET* freí, **freíste, frió, freímos, freísteis, frieron;** *IMPER* **fríe;** *PRP* **friendo;** *PP* **frito**

38 **gruñir** : *PRET* gruñí, gruñiste, **gruñó,** gruñimos, gruñisteis, **gruñeron;** *PRP* **gruñendo**

39 **haber** : *IND* **he, has, ha, hemos,** habéis, **han;** *SUBJ* **haya, hayas, haya, hayamos, hayáis, hayan;** *PRET* **hube, hubiste, hubo, hubimos, hubisteis, hubieron;** *FUT* **habré, habrás, habrá, habremos, habréis, habrán;** *IMPER* **he**

40 **hacer** : *IND* **hago,** haces, hace, hacemos, hacéis, hacen; *SUBJ* **haga, hagas, haga, hagamos, hagáis, hagan;** *PRET* **hice, hiciste, hizo, hicimos, hicisteis, hicieron;** *FUT* **haré, harás, hará, haremos, haréis, harán;** *IMPER* **haz;** *PP* **hecho**

41 **huir** : *IND* **huyo, huyes, huye,** huimos, huís, **huyen;** *SUBJ* **huya, huyas, huya, huyamos, huyáis, huyan;** *PRET* huí, huiste, **huyó,** huimos, huisteis, **huyeron;** *IMPER* **huye;** *PRP* **huyendo**

42 **imprimir** : *PP* **impreso**

43 **ir** : *IND* **voy, vas, va, vamos, vais, van;** *SUBJ* **vaya, vayas, vaya, vayamos, vayáis, vayan;** *PRET* **fui, fuiste, fue, fuimos, fuisteis, fueron;** *IMPF* **iba, ibas, iba, íbamos, ibais, iban;** *IMPER* **ve;** *PRP* **yendo;** *PP* **ido**

44 **jugar** : *IND* **juego, juegas, juega,** jugamos, jugáis, **juegan;** *SUBJ* **juegue, juegues, juegue, juguemos, juguéis, jueguen;** *PRET* **jugué,** jugaste, jugó, jugamos, jugasteis, jugaron; *IMPER* **juega**

45 **lucir :** IND **luzco,** luces, luce, lucimos, lucís, lucen; SUBJ **lucza, luzcas, luzca, luzcamos, luzcáis, luzcan**

46 **morir :** IND **muero, mueres, muere,** morimos, morís, **mueren;** SUBJ **muera, mueras, muera, muramos, muráis, mueran;** PRET morí, moriste, **murió,** morimos, moristeis, **murieron;** IMPER **muere;** PRP **muriendo;** PP **muerto**

47 **mover :** IND **muevo, mueves, mueve,** movemos, movéis, **mueven;** SUBJ **mueva, muevas, mueva,** movamos, mováis, **muevan;** IMPER **mueve**

48 **nacer :** IND **nazco,** naces, nace, nacemos, nacéis, nacen; SUBJ **nazca, nazcas, nazca, nazcamos, nazcáis, nazcan**

49 **negar :** IND **niego, niegas, niega,** negamos, negáis, **niegan;** SUBJ **niegue, niegues, niegue, neguemos, neguéis, nieguen;** PRET **negué,** negaste, negó, negamos, negasteis, negaron; IMPER **niega**

50 **oír :** IND **oigo, oyes, oye, oímos,** oís, **oyen;** SUBJ **oiga, oigas, oiga, oigamos, oigáis, oigan;** PRET oí, **oíste, oyó, oímos, oísteis, oyeron;** IMPER **oye;** PRP **oyendo;** PP **oído**

51 **oler :** IND **huelo, hueles, huele,** olemos, oléis, **huelen;** SUBJ **huela, huelas, huela,** olamos, oláis, **huelan;** IMPER **huele**

52 **pagar :** SUBJ **pague, pagues, pague, paguemos, paguéis, paguen;** PRET **pagué,** pagaste, pagó, pagamos, pagasteis, pagaron

53 **parecer :** IND **parezco,** pareces, parece, parecemos, parecéis, parecen; SUBJ **parezca, parezcas, parezca, parezcamos, parezcáis, parezcan**

54 **pedir :** IND **pido, pides, pide,** pedimos, pedís, **piden;** SUBJ **pida, pidas, pida, pidamos, pidáis, pidan;** PRET pedí, pediste, **pidió,** pedimos, pedisteis, **pidieron;** IMPER **pide;** PRP **pidiendo**

55 **pensar :** IND **pienso, piensas, piensa,** pensamos, pensáis, **piensan;** SUBJ **piense, pienses, piense,** pensemos, penséis, **piensen;** IMPER **piensa**

56 **perder :** IND **pierdo, pierdes, pierde,** perdemos, perdéis, **pierden;** SUBJ **pierda, pierdas, pierda,** perdamos, perdáis, **pierdan;** IMPER **pierde**

57 **placer** : *IND* **plazco,** places, place, placemos, placéis, placen; *SUBJ* **plazca, plazcas, plazca, plazcamos, plazcáis, plazcan;** *PRET* plací, placiste, plació *or* **plugo,** placimos, placisteis, placieron *or* **pluguieron**

58 **poder** : *IND* **puedo, puedes, puede,** podemos, podéis, **pueden;** *SUBJ* **pueda, puedas, pueda,** podamos, podáis, **puedan;** *PRET* **pude, pudiste, pudo, pudimos, pudisteis, pudieron;** *FUT* **podré, podrás, podrá, podremos, podréis, podrán;** *IMPER* **puede;** *PRP* **pudiendo**

59 **podrir** *or* **pudrir** : *PP* **podrido** *(all other forms based on* pudrir*)*

60 **poner** : *IND* **pongo,** pones, pone, ponemos, ponéis, ponen; *SUBJ* **ponga, pongas, ponga, pongamos, pongáis, pongan;** *PRET* **puse, pusiste, puso, pusimos, pusisteis, pusieron;** *FUT* **pondré, pondrás, pondrá, pondremos, pondréis, pondrán;** *IMPER* **pon;** *PP* **puesto**

61 **producir** : *IND* **produzco,** produces, produce, producimos, producís, producen; *SUBJ* **produzca, produzcas, produzca, produzcamos, produzcáis, produzcan;** *PRET* **produje, produjiste, produjo, produjimos, produjisteis, produjeron**

62 **prohibir** : *IND* **prohíbo, prohíbes, prohíbe,** prohibimos, prohibís, **prohíben;** *SUBJ* **prohíba, prohíbas, prohíba,** prohibamos, prohibáis, **prohíban;** *IMPER* **prohíbe**

63 **proveer** : *PRET* proveí, **proveíste, proveyó, proveímos, proveísteis, proveyeron;** *PRP* **proveyendo;** *PP* **provisto**

64 **querer** : *IND* **quiero, quieres, quiere,** queremos, queréis, **quieren;** *SUBJ* **quiera, quieras, quiera,** queramos, queráis, **quieran;** *PRET* **quise, quisiste, quiso, quisimos, quisisteis, quisieron;** *FUT* **querré, querrás, querrá, querremos, querréis, querrán;** *IMPER* **quiere**

65 **raer** : *IND* rao *or* **raigo** *or* **rayo,** raes, rae, raemos, raéis, raen; *SUBJ* **raiga** *or* **raya, raigas** *or* **rayas, raiga** *or* **raya, raigamos** *or* **rayamos, raigáis** *or* **rayáis, raigan** *or* **rayan;** *PRET* **raí, raíste, rayó, raímos, raísteis, rayeron;** *PRP* **rayendo;** *PP* **raído**

66 **reír** : *IND* **río, ríes, ríe, reímos,** reís, **ríen;** *SUBJ* **ría, rías, ría, riamos, riáis, rían;** *PRET* reí, **reíste, rió, reímos, reísteis, rieron;** *IMPER* **ríe;** *PRP* **riendo;** *PP* **reído**

67 **reñir :** IND **riño, riñes, riñe,** reñimos, reñís, **riñen;** SUBJ **riña, riñas, riña, riñamos, riñáis, riñan;** PRET reñí, reñiste, **riñó,** reñimos, reñisteis, **riñeron;** PRP **riñendo**

68 **reunir :** IND **reúno, reúnes, reúne,** reunimos, reunís, **reúnen;** SUBJ **reúna, reúnas, reúna,** reunamos, reunáis, **reúnan;** IMPER **reúne**

69 **roer :** IND roo *or* **roigo** *or* **royo,** roes, roe, roemos, roéis, roen; SUBJ roa *or* **roiga** *or* **roya,** roas *or* **roigas** *or* **royas,** roa *or* **roiga** *or* **roya,** roamos *or* **roigamos** *or* **royamos,** roáis *or* **roigáis** *or* **royáis,** roan *or* **roigan** *or* **royan;** PRET roí, **roíste, royó, roímos, roísteis, royeron;** PRP **royendo;** PP **roído**

70 **romper :** PP **roto**

71 **saber :** IND **sé,** sabes, sabe, sabemos, sabéis, saben; SUBJ **sepa, sepas, sepa, sepamos, sepáis, sepan;** PRET **supe, supiste, supo, supimos, supisteis, supieron;** FUT **sabré, sabrás, sabrá, sabremos, sabréis, sabrán**

72 **sacar :** SUBJ **saque, saques, saque, saquemos, saquéis, saquen;** PRET **saqué,** sacaste, sacó, sacamos, sacasteis, sacaron

73 **salir :** IND **salgo,** sales, sale, salimos, salís, salen; SUBJ **salga, salgas, salga, salgamos, salgáis, salgan;** FUT **saldré, saldrás, saldrá, saldremos, saldréis, saldrán;** IMPER **sal**

74 **satisfacer :** IND **satisfago,** satisfaces, satisface, satisfacemos, satisfacéis, satisfacen; SUBJ **satisfaga, satisfagas, satisfaga, satisfagamos, satisfagáis, satisfagan;** PRET **satisfice, satisficiste, satisfizo, satisficimos, satificisteis, satisficieron;** FUT **satisfaré, satisfarás, satisfará, satisfaremos, satisfaréis, satisfarán;** IMPER **satisfaz** *or* **satisface;** PP **satisfecho**

75 **seguir :** IND **sigo, sigues, sigue,** seguimos, seguís, **siguen;** SUBJ **siga, sigas, siga, sigamos, sigáis, sigan;** PRET seguí, seguiste, **siguió,** seguimos, seguisteis, **siguieron;** IMPER **sigue;** PRP **siguiendo**

76 **sentir :** IND **siento, sientes, siente,** sentimos, sentís, **sienten;** SUBJ **sienta, sientas, sienta, sintamos, sintáis, sientan;** PRET sentí, sentiste, **sintió,** sentimos, sentisteis, **sintieron;** IMPER **siente;** PRP **sintiendo**

77 **ser** : *IND* **soy, eres, es, somos, sois, son;** *SUBJ* **sea, seas, sea, seamos, seáis, sean;** *PRET* **fui, fuiste, fue, fuimos, fuisteis, fueron;** *IMPF* **era, eras, era, éramos, erais, eran;** *IMPER* **sé;** *PRP* **siendo;** *PP* **sido**

78 **soler** *(defective verb; used only in the present, preterit, and imperfect indicative, and the present and imperfect subjunctive) see* 47 **mover**

79 **tañer** : *PRET* tañí, tañiste, **tañó,** tañimos, tañisteis, **tañeron;** *PRP* **tañendo**

80 **tener** : *IND* **tengo, tienes, tiene,** tenemos, tenéis, **tienen;** *SUBJ* **tenga, tengas, tenga, tengamos, tengáis, tengan;** *PRET* **tuve, tuviste, tuvo, tuvimos, tuvisteis, tuvieron;** *FUT* **tendré, tendrás, tendrá, tendremos, tendréis, tendrán;** *IMPER* **ten**

81 **traer** : *IND* **traigo,** traes, trae, traemos, traéis, traen; *SUBJ* **traiga, traigas, traiga, traigamos, traigáis, traigan;** *PRET* **traje, trajiste, trajo, trajimos, trajisteis, trajeron;** *PRP* **trayendo;** *PP* **traído**

82 **trocar** : *IND* **trueco, truecas, trueca,** trocamos, trocáis, **truecan;** *SUBJ* **trueque, trueques, trueque, troquemos, troquéis, truequen;** *PRET* **troqué,** trocaste, trocó, trocamos, trocasteis, trocaron; *IMPER* **trueca**

83 **uncir** : *IND* **unzo,** unces, unce, uncimos, uncís, uncen; *SUBJ* **unza, unzas, unza, unzamos, unzáis, unzan**

84 **valer** : *IND* **valgo,** vales, vale, valemos, valéis, valen; *SUBJ* **valga, valgas, valga, valgamos, valgáis, valgan;** *FUT* **valdré, valdrás, valdrá, valdremos, valdréis, valdrán**

85 **variar** : *IND* **varío, varías, varía,** variamos, variáis, **varían;** *SUBJ* **varíe, varíes, varíe,** variemos, variéis, **varíen;** *IMPER* **varía**

86 **vencer** : *IND* **venzo,** vences, vence, vencemos, vencéis, vencen; *SUBJ* **venza, venzas, venza, venzamos, venzáis, venzan**

87 **venir** : *IND* **vengo, vienes, viene,** venimos, venís, **vienen;** *SUBJ* **venga, vengas, venga, vengamos, vengáis, vengan;** *PRET* **vine, viniste, vino, vinimos, vinisteis, vinieron;** *FUT* **vendré, vendrás, vendrá, vendremos, vendréis, vendrán;** *IMPER* **ven;** *PRP* **viniendo**

88 **ver :** *IND* veo, **ves, ve, vemos, veis, ven;** *PRET* **vi, viste, vio, vimos, visteis, vieron;** *IMPER* **ve;** *PRP* **viendo;** *PP* **visto**

89 **volver :** *IND* **vuelvo, vuelves, vuelve,** volvemos, volvéis, **vuelven;** *SUBJ* **vuelva, vuelvas, vuelva,** volvamos, volváis, **vuelvan;** *IMPER* **vuelve;** *PP* **vuelto**

90 **yacer :** *IND* **yazco** *or* **yazgo** *or* **yago,** yaces, yace, yacemos, yacéis, yacen; *SUBJ* **yazca** *or* **yazga** *or* **yaga, yazcas** *or* **yazgas** *or* **yagas, yazca** *or* **yazga** *or* **yaga, yazcamos** *or* **yazgamos** *or* **yagamos, yazcáis** *or* **yazgáis** *or* **yagáis, yazcan** *or* **yazgan** *or* **yagan;** *IMPER* yace *or* **yaz**

Spanish–English Dictionary

A

a[1] *nf* : first letter of the Spanish alphabet

a[2] *prep* **1 :** to <nos vamos a México : we're going to Mexico> **2** (*used before direct or indirect objects referring to persons*) <¿llamaste a tu papá? : did you call your dad?> <como a usted le guste : as you wish> **3 :** in the manner of <papas a la francesa : french fries> **4 :** on, by means of <a pie : on foot> **5 :** per, each <tres pastillas al día : three pills per day> **6** (*with infinitive*) <enséñales a leer : teach them to read> <problemas a resolver : problems to be solved>

ábaco *nm* : abacus

abad *nm* : abbot

abadesa *nf* : abbess

abadía *nf* : abbey

abajo *adv* **1 :** down <póngalo más abajo : put it further down> <arriba y abajo : up and down> **2 :** downstairs **3 :** under, beneath <el abajo firmante : the undersigned> **4 :** down with <¡abajo la inflación! : down with inflation!> **5 ~ de :** under, beneath **6 de ~ :** bottom <el cajón de abajo : the bottom drawer> **7 hacia ~** *or* **para ~ :** downwards **8 cuesta abajo :** downhill **9 río abajo :** downstream

abalanzarse {21} *vr* : to hurl oneself, to rush

abanderado, -da *n* : standard-bearer

abandonado, -da *adj* **1 :** abandoned, deserted **2 :** neglected **3 :** slovenly, unkempt

abandonar *vt* **1** DEJAR **:** to abandon, to leave **2 :** to give up, to quit <abandonaron la búsqueda : they gave up the search> — **abandonarse** *vr* **1 :** to neglect oneself **2 ~ a :** to succumb to, to give oneself over to

abandono *nm* **1 :** abandonment **2 :** neglect **3 :** withdrawal <ganar por abandono : to win by default>

abanicar {72} *vt* : to fan — **abanicarse** *vr*

abanico *nm* **1 :** fan **2** GAMA **:** range, gamut

abaratamiento *nm* : price reduction

abaratar *vt* : to lower the price of — **abaratarse** *vr* : to go down in price

abarcar {72} *vt* **1 :** to cover, to include, to embrace **2 :** to undertake **3 :** to monopolize

abaritonado, -da *adj* : baritone

abarrotado, -da *adj* : packed, crammed

abarrotar *vt* : to fill up, to pack

abarrotería *nf CA, Mex* : grocery store

abarrotero, -ra *n Col, Mex* : grocer

abarrotes *nmpl* **1 :** groceries, supplies **2 tienda de abarrotes :** general store, grocery store

abastecedor, -dora *n* : supplier

abastecer {53} *vt* : to supply, to stock — **abastecerse** *vr* : to stock up

abastecimiento → **abasto**

abasto *nm* : supply, supplying <no da abasto : there isn't enough for all>

abatido, -da *adj* : dejected, depressed

abatimiento *nm* **1 :** drop, reduction **2 :** dejection, depression

abatir *vt* **1** DERRIBAR **:** to demolish, to knock down **2 :** to shoot down **3** DEPRIMIR **:** to depress, to bring low — **abatirse** *vr* **1** DEPRIMIRSE **:** to get depressed **2 ~ sobre :** to swoop down on

abdicación *nf, pl* **-ciones** : abdication

abdicar {72} *vt* : to relinquish, to abdicate

abdomen *nm, pl* **-dómenes** : abdomen

abdominal *adj* : abdominal

abecé *nm* : ABC

abecedario *nm* ALFABETO : alphabet

abedul *nm* : birch (tree)

abeja *nf* : bee

abejorro *nm* : bumblebee

aberración *nf, pl* **-ciones** : aberration

aberrante *adj* : aberrant, perverse

abertura *nf* **1 :** aperture, opening **2** AGUJERO **:** hole **3 :** slit (in a skirt, etc.) **4** GRIETA **:** crack

abeto *nm* : fir (tree)

abierto[1] *pp* → **abrir**

abierto[2]**, -ta** *adj* **1 :** open **2 :** candid, frank **3 :** generous — **abiertamente** *adv*

abigarrado, -da *adj* : multicolored, variegated

abigeato *nm* : rustling (of livestock)

abismal *adj* : abysmal, vast

abismo *nm* : abyss, chasm <al borde del abismo : on the brink of ruin>

abjurar *vi* **~ de :** to abjure — **abjuración** *nf*

ablandamiento *nm* : softening, moderation

ablandar *vt* **1** SUAVIZAR **:** to soften **2** CALMAR **:** to soothe, to appease — *vi* **:** to moderate, to get milder — **ablandarse** *vr* **1 :** to become soft, to soften **2** CEDER **:** to yield, to relent

ablución *nf, pl* **-ciones** : ablution

abnegación *nf, pl* **-ciones** : abnegation, self-denial

abnegado, -da *adj* : self-sacrificing, selfless

abnegarse {49} *vr* : to deny oneself

abobado, -da *adj* **1 :** silly, stupid **2 :** bewildered

abocarse {72} *vr* **1** DIRIGIRSE **:** to head, to direct oneself **2** DEDICARSE **:** to dedicate oneself

abochornar *vt* AVERGONZAR : to embarrass, to shame — **abochornarse** *vr*

abofetear *vt* : to slap

abogacía *nf* : law, legal profession

abogado, -da *n* : lawyer, attorney

abogar {52} *vi* ~ **por** : to plead for, to defend, to advocate
abolengo *nm* LINAJE : lineage, ancestry
abolición *nf, pl* **-ciones** : abolition
abolir {1} *vt* DEROGAR : to abolish, to repeal
abolladura *nf* : dent
abollar *vt* : to dent
abombar *vt* : to warp, to cause to bulge — **abombarse** *vr* : to decompose, to go bad
abominable *adj* ABORRECIBLE : abominable
abominación *nf, pl* **-ciones** : abomination
abominar *vt* ABORRECER : to abominate, to abhor
abonado, -da *n* : subscriber
abonar *vt* **1** : to pay **2** FERTILIZAR : to fertilize — **abonarse** *vr* : to subscribe
abono *nm* **1** : payment, installment **2** FERTILIZANTE : fertilizer **3** : season ticket
abordaje *nm* : boarding
abordar *vt* **1** : to address, to broach **2** : to accost, to waylay **3** : to come on board
aborigen[1] *adj, pl* **-rígenes** : aboriginal, native
aborigen[2] *nmf, pl* **-rígenes** : aborigine, indigenous inhabitant
aborrecer {53} *vt* ABOMINAR, ODIAR : to abhor, to detest, to hate
aborrecible *adj* ABOMINABLE, ODIOSO : abominable, detestable
aborrecimiento *nm* : abhorrence, loathing
abortar *vi* : to have an abortion — *vt* **1** : to abort **2** : to quash, to suppress
abortista *nmf* : abortionist
abortivo, -va *adj* : abortive
aborto *nm* **1** : abortion **2** : miscarriage
abotonar *vt* : to button — **abotonarse** *vr* : to button up
abovedado, -da *adj* : vaulted
abrasador, -dora *adj* : burning, scorching
abrasar *vt* QUEMAR : to burn, to sear, to scorch
abrasivo[1], **-va** *adj* : abrasive
abrasivo[2] *nm* : abrasive
abrazadera *nf* : clamp, brace
abrazar {21} *vt* : to hug, to embrace — **abrazarse** *vr*
abrazo *nm* : hug, embrace
abrebotellas *nms & pl* : bottle opener
abrelatas *nms & pl* : can opener
abrevadero *nm* BEBEDERO : watering trough
abreviación *nf, pl* **-ciones** : abbreviation
abreviar *vt* **1** : to abbreviate **2** : to shorten, to cut short
abreviatura *nf* → **abreviación**
abridor *nm* : bottle opener, can opener
abrigadero *nm* : shelter, windbreak
abrigado, -da *adj* **1** : sheltered **2** : warm, wrapped up (with clothing)
abrigar {52} *vt* **1** : to shelter, to protect **2** : to keep warm, to dress warmly **3** : to cherish, to harbor <abrigar esperanzas : to cherish hopes> — **abrigarse** *vr* : to dress warmly
abrigo *nm* **1** : coat, overcoat **2** : shelter, refuge
abril *nm* : April
abrillantador *nm* : polish
abrillantar *vt* : to polish, to shine
abrir {2} *vt* **1** : to open **2** : to unlock, to undo **3** : to turn on (a tap or faucet) — *vi* : to open, to open up — **abrirse** *vr* **1** : to open up **2** : to clear (of the skies)
abrochar *vt* : to button, to fasten — **abrocharse** *vr* : to fasten, to hook up
abrogación *nf, pl* **-ciones** : abrogation, annulment, repeal
abrogar {52} *vt* : to abrogate, to annul, to repeal
abrojo *nm* : bur (of a plant)
abrumador, -dora *adj* : crushing, overwhelming
abrumar *vt* **1** AGOBIAR : to overwhelm **2** OPRIMIR : to oppress, to burden
abrupto, -ta *adj* **1** : abrupt **2** ESCARPADO : steep — **abruptamente** *adv*
absceso *nm* : abscess
absolución *nf, pl* **-ciones** **1** : absolution **2** : acquittal
absolutismo *nm* : absolutism
absoluto, -ta *adj* **1** : absolute, unconditional **2** **en** ~ : not at all <no me gustó en absoluto : I did not like it at all> — **absolutamente** *adv*
absolver {89} *vt* **1** : to absolve **2** : to acquit
absorbente *adj* **1** : absorbent **2** : absorbing, engrossing
absorber *vt* **1** : to absorb, to soak up **2** : to occupy, to take up, to engross
absorción *nf, pl* **-ciones** : absorption
absorto, -ta *adj* : absorbed, engrossed
abstemio[1], **-mia** *adj* : abstemious, teetotal
abstemio[2], **-mia** *n* : teetotaler
abstención *nf, pl* **-ciones** : abstention
abstenerse {80} *vr* : to abstain, to refrain
abstinencia *nf* : abstinence
abstracción *nf, pl* **-ciones** : abstraction
abstracto, -ta *adj* : abstract
abstraer {81} *vt* : to abstract — **abstraerse** *vr* : to lose oneself in thought
abstraído, -da *adj* : preoccupied, withdrawn
abstruso, -sa *adj* : abstruse
abstuvo, etc. → **abstenerse**
absuelto *pp* → **absolver**
absurdo[1], **-da** *adj* DISPARATADO, RIDÍCULO : absurd, ridiculous — **absurdamente** *adv*
absurdo[2] *nm* : absurdity
abuchear *vt* : to boo, to jeer
abucheo *nm* : booing, jeering
abuela *nf* **1** : grandmother **2** : old woman **3** **¡tu abuela!** *fam* : no way!, forget about it!

abuelo *nm* **1 :** grandfather **2 :** old man **3 abuelos** *nmpl* **:** grandparents, ancestors
abulia *nf* **:** apathy, lethargy
abúlico, -ca *adj* **:** lethargic, apathetic
abultado, -da *adj* **:** bulging, bulky
abultar *vi* **:** to bulge — *vt* **:** to enlarge, to expand
abundancia *nf* **:** abundance
abundante *adj* **:** abundant, plentiful — **abundantemente** *adv*
abundar *vi* **1 :** to abound, to be plentiful **2 ~ en :** to be in agreement with
aburrido, -da *adj* **1 :** bored, tired, fed up **2** TEDIOSO **:** boring, tedious
aburrimiento *nm* **:** boredom, weariness
aburrir *vt* **:** to bore, to tire — **aburrirse** *vr* **:** to get bored
abusado, -da *adj Mex fam* **:** sharp, on the ball
abusador, -dora *n* **:** abuser
abusar *vi* **1 :** to go too far, to do something to excess **2 ~ de :** to abuse (as drugs) **3 ~ de :** to take unfair advantage of
abusivo, -va *adj* **1 :** abusive **2 :** outrageous, excessive
abuso *nm* **1 :** abuse **2 :** injustice, outrage
abyecto, -ta *adj* **:** despicable, contemptible
acá *adv* AQUÍ **:** here, over here <¡ven acá! : come here!>
acabado¹, -da *adj* **1 :** finished, done, completed **2 :** old, worn-out
acabado² *nm* **:** finish <un acabado brillante : a glossy finish>
acabar *vi* **1** TERMINAR **:** to finish, to end **2 ~ de :** to have just (done something) <acabo de ver a tu hermano : I just saw your brother> **3 ~ con :** to put an end to, to stamp out — *vt* TERMINAR **:** to finish — **acabarse** *vr* TERMINARSE **:** to come to an end, to run out <se me acabó el dinero : I ran out of money>
academia *nf* **:** academy
académico¹, -ca *adj* **:** academic, scholastic — **académicamente** *adv*
académico², -ca *n* **:** academic, academician
acaecer {53} *vi* (*3rd person only*) **:** to happen, to take place
acalambrarse *vr* **:** to cramp up, to get a cramp
acallar *vt* **:** to quiet, to silence
acalorado, -da *adj* **:** emotional, heated
acaloramiento *nm* **1 :** heat **2 :** ardor, passion
acalorar *vt* **:** to heat up, to inflame — **acalorarse** *vr* **:** to get upset, to get worked up
acampada *nf* **:** camp, camping <ir de acampada : to go camping>
acampar *vi* **:** to camp
acanalar *vt* **1 :** to groove, to furrow **2 :** to corrugate
acantilado *nm* **:** cliff
acanto *nm* **:** acanthus
acantonar *vt* **:** to station, to quarter
acaparador, -dora *adj* **:** greedy, selfish
acaparar *vt* **1 :** to stockpile, to hoard **2 :** to monopolize
acápite *nm* **:** paragraph
acariciar *vt* **:** to caress, to stroke, to pet
ácaro *nm* **:** mite
acarrear *vt* **1 :** to haul, to carry **2 :** to bring, to give rise to <los problemas que acarrea : the problems that come along with it>
acarreo *nm* **:** transport, haulage
acartonarse *vr* **1 :** to stiffen **2 :** to become wizened
acaso *adv* **1 :** perhaps, by any chance **2 por si acaso :** just in case
acatamiento *nm* **:** compliance, observance
acatar *vt* **:** to comply with, to respect
acaudalado, -da *adj* RICO **:** wealthy, rich
acaudillar *vt* **:** to lead, to command
acceder *vi* **~ a 1 :** to accede to, to agree to **2 :** to assume (a position) **3 :** to gain access to
accesar *vt* **:** to access (on a computer)
accesibilidad *nf* **:** accessibility
accesible *adj* ASEQUIBLE **:** accessible, attainable
acceso *nm* **1 :** access **2 :** admittance, entrance
accesorio¹, -ria *adj* **1 :** accessory **2 :** incidental
accesorio² *nm* **1 :** accessory **2 :** prop (in the theater)
accidentado¹, -da *adj* **1 :** eventful, turbulent **2 :** rough, uneven **3 :** injured
accidentado², -da *n* **:** accident victim
accidental *adj* **:** accidental, unintentional — **accidentalmente** *adv*
accidentarse *vr* **:** to have an accident
accidente *nm* **1 :** accident **2 :** unevenness **3 accidente geográfico :** geographical feature
acción *nf, pl* **acciones 1 :** action **2** ACTO **:** act, deed **3 :** share, stock
accionamiento *nm* **:** activation
accionar *vt* **:** to put into motion, to activate — *vi* **:** to gesticulate
accionario, -ria *adj* **:** stock <mercado accionario : stock market>
accionista *nmf* **:** stockholder, shareholder
acebo *nm* **:** holly
acechar *vt* **1 :** to watch, to spy on **2 :** to stalk, to lie in wait for
acecho *nm* **al acecho :** lying in wait
acedera *nf* **:** sorrel (herb)
acéfalo, -la *adj* **:** leaderless
aceitar *vt* **:** to oil
aceite *nm* **1 :** oil **2 aceite de ricino :** castor oil **3 aceite de oliva :** olive oil
aceitera *nf* **1 :** cruet (for oil) **2 :** oilcan **3** *Mex* **:** oil refinery
aceitoso, -sa *adj* **:** oily
aceituna *nf* OLIVA **:** olive
aceituno *nm* OLIVO **:** olive tree

aceleración *nf, pl* **-ciones :** acceleration, speeding up
acelerado, -da *adj* **:** accelerated, speedy
acelerador *nm* **:** accelerator
aceleramiento *nm* → **aceleración**
acelerar *vt* **1 :** to accelerate, to speed up **2** AGILIZAR **:** to expedite — *vi* **:** to accelerate (of an automobile) — **acelerarse** *vr* **:** to hasten, to hurry up
acelga *nf* **:** chard, Swiss chard
acendrado, -da *adj* **:** pure, unblemished
acendrar *vt* **:** to purify, to refine
acento *nm* **1 :** accent **2 :** stress, emphasis
acentuación *nf, pl* **-ciones :** accentuation
acentuado, -da *adj* **:** marked, pronounced
acentuar {3} *vt* **1 :** to accent **2 :** to emphasize, to stress — **acentuarse** *vr* **:** to become more pronounced
acepción *nf, pl* **-ciones** SIGNIFICADO **:** sense, meaning
aceptabilidad *nf* **:** acceptability
aceptable *adj* **:** acceptable
aceptación *nf, pl* **-ciones 1 :** acceptance **2** APROBACIÓN **:** approval
aceptar *vt* **1 :** to accept **2 :** to approve
acequia *nf* **1 :** irrigation ditch **2** *Mex* **:** sewer
acera *nf* **:** sidewalk
acerado, -da *adj* **1 :** made of steel **2 :** steely, tough
acerbo, -ba *adj* **1 :** harsh, cutting <comentarios acerbos : cutting remarks> **2 :** bitter — **acerbamente** *adv*
acerca *prep* **~ de :** about, concerning
acercamiento *nm* **:** rapprochement, reconciliation
acercar {72} *vt* APROXIMAR, ARRIMAR **:** to bring near, to bring closer — **acercarse** *vr* APROXIMARSE, ARRIMARSE **:** to approach, to draw near
acería *nf* **:** steel mill
acerico *nm* **:** pincushion
acero *nm* **:** steel <acero inoxidable : stainless steel>
acérrimo, -ma *adj* **1 :** staunch, steadfast **2 :** bitter <un acérrimo enemigo : a bitter enemy>
acertado, -da *adj* CORRECTO **:** accurate, correct, on target — **acertadamente** *adv*
acertante[1] *adj* **:** winning
acertante[2] *nmf* **:** winner
acertar {55} *vt* **:** to guess correctly — *vi* ATINAR **:** to be accurate, to be on target
acertijo *nm* ADIVINANZA **:** riddle
acervo *nm* **1 :** pile, heap **2 :** wealth, heritage <el acervo artístico del instituto : the artistic treasures of the institute>
acetato *nm* **:** acetate
acético, -ca *adj* **:** acetic <ácido acético : acetic acid>
acetileno *nm* **:** acetylene
acetona *nf* **1 :** acetone **2 :** nail-polish remover
achacar {72} *vt* **:** to attribute, to impute <te achaca todos sus problemas : he blames all his problems on you>
achacoso, -sa *adj* **:** frail, sickly
achaparrado, -da *adj* **:** stunted, scrubby <árboles achaparrados : scrubby trees>
achaque *nm* DOLENCIA **:** ailment, malady, discomfort
achatar *vt* **:** to flatten
achicar {72} *vt* **1** REDUCIR **:** to make smaller, to reduce **2 :** to intimidate **3 :** to bail out (water) — **achicarse** *vr* **:** to become intimidated
achicharrar *vt* **:** to scorch, to burn to a crisp
achicoria *nf* **:** chicory
achispado, -da *adj fam* **:** tipsy
achote *or* **achiote** *nm* **:** annatto seed
achuchón *nm, pl* **-chones 1 :** push, shove **2** *fam* **:** squeeze, hug **3** *fam* **:** mild illness
aciago, -ga *adj* **:** fateful, unlucky
acicalar *vt* **1** PULIR **:** to polish **2 :** to dress up, to adorn — **acicalarse** *vr* **:** to get dressed up
acicate *nm* **1 :** spur **2** INCENTIVO **:** incentive, stimulus
acidez *nf, pl* **-deces 1 :** acidity **2 :** sourness **3 acidez estomacal :** heartburn
acidificar {72} *vt* **:** to acidify
ácido[1]**, -da** *adj* AGRIO **:** acid, sour
ácido[2] *nm* **:** acid
acierto *nm* **1 :** correct answer, right choice **2 :** accuracy, skill, deftness
acimut *nm* **:** azimuth
acitronar *vt Mex* **:** to fry until crisp
aclamación *nf, pl* **-ciones :** acclaim, acclamation
aclamar *vt* **:** to acclaim, to cheer, to applaud
aclaración *nf, pl* **-ciones** CLARIFICACIÓN **:** clarification, explanation
aclarar *vt* **1** CLARIFICAR **:** to clarify, to explain, to resolve **2 :** to lighten **3 aclarar la voz :** to clear one's throat — *vi* **1 :** to get light, to dawn **2 :** to clear up — **aclararse** *vr* **:** to become clear
aclaratorio, -ria *adj* **:** explanatory
aclimatar *vt* **:** to acclimatize — **aclimatarse** *vr* **~ a :** to get used to — **aclimatación** *nf*
acné *nm* **:** acne
acobardar *vt* INTIMIDAR **:** to frighten, to intimidate — **acobardarse** *vr* **:** to be frightened, to cower
acodarse *vr* **~ en :** to lean (one's elbows) on
acogedor, -dora *adj* **:** cozy, warm, friendly
acoger {15} *vt* **1** REFUGIAR **:** to take in, to shelter **2 :** to receive, to welcome — **acogerse** *vr* **1** REFUGIARSE **:** to take refuge **2 ~ a :** to resort to, to avail oneself of

acogida *nf* **1** AMPARO, REFUGIO **:** refuge, protection **2** RECIBIMIENTO **:** reception, welcome
acolchar *vt* **1 :** to pad (a wall, etc.) **2 :** to quilt
acólito *nm* **1** MONAGUILLO **:** altar boy **2 :** follower, helper, acolyte
acomedido, -da *adj* **:** helpful, obliging
acometer *vt* **1** ATACAR **:** to attack, to assail **2** EMPRENDER **:** to undertake, to begin — *vi* **~ contra :** to rush against
acometida *nf* ATAQUE **:** attack, assault
acomodado, -da *adj* **1 :** suitable, appropriate **2 :** well-to-do, prosperous
acomodador, -dora *n* **:** usher, usherette *f*
acomodar *vt* **1 :** to accommodate, to make room for **2 :** to adjust, to adapt — **acomodarse** *vr* **1 :** to settle in **2 ~ a :** to adapt to
acomodaticio, -cia *adj* **:** accommodating, obliging
acomodo *nm* **1 :** job, position **2 :** arrangement, placement **3 :** accommodation, lodging
acompañamiento *nm* **:** accompaniment
acompañante *nmf* **1** COMPAÑERO **:** companion **2 :** accompanist
acompañar *vt* **:** to accompany, to go with
acompasado, -da *adj* **:** rhythmic, regular, measured
acomplejado, -da *adj* **:** full of complexes, neurotic
acondicionado, -da *adj* **1 :** equipped, fitted-out **2 bien acondicionado :** in good shape, in a fit state
acondicionador *nm* **1 :** conditioner **2 acondicionador de aire :** air conditioner
acondicionar *vt* **1 :** to condition **2 :** to fit out, to furnish
acongojado, -da *adj* **:** distressed, upset
acongojarse *vr* **:** to grieve, to become distressed
aconsejable *adj* **:** advisable
aconsejar *vt* **:** to advise, to counsel
acontecer {53} *vi* (*3rd person only*) **:** to occur, to happen
acontecimiento *nm* SUCESO **:** event
acopiar *vt* **:** to gather, to collect, to stockpile
acopio *nm* **:** collection, stock
acoplamiento *nm* **:** connection, coupling
acoplar *vt* **:** to couple, to connect — **acoplarse** *vr* **:** to fit together
acoquinar *vt* **:** to intimidate
acorazado¹, -da *adj* BLINDADO **:** armored
acorazado² *nm* **:** battleship
acordado, -da *adj* **:** agreed upon
acordar {19} *vt* **1 :** to agree on **2** OTORGAR **:** to award, to bestow — **acordarse** *vr* RECORDAR **:** to remember, to recall
acorde¹ *adj* **1 :** in agreement, in accordance **2 ~ con :** in keeping with
acorde² *nm* **:** chord
acordeón *nm, pl* **-deones :** accordion — **acordeonista** *nmf*
acordonar *vt* **1 :** to cordon off **2 :** to lace up **3 :** to mill (coins)
acorralar *vt* ARRINCONAR **:** to corner, to hem in, to corral
acortar *vt* **:** to shorten, to cut short — **acortarse** *vr* **1 :** to become shorter **2 :** to end early
acosar *vt* PERSEGUIR **:** to pursue, to hound, to harass
acoso *nm* ASEDIO **:** harassment <acoso sexual : sexual harassment>
acostar {19} *vt* **1 :** to lay (something) down **2 :** to put to bed — **acostarse** *vr* **1 :** to lie down **2 :** to go to bed
acostumbrado, -da *adj* **1** HABITUADO **:** accustomed **2** HABITUAL **:** usual, customary
acostumbrar *vt* **:** to accustom — *vi* **:** to be accustomed, to be in the habit — **acostumbrarse** *vr*
acotación *nf, pl* **-ciones 1 :** marginal note **2 :** stage direction
acotado, -da *adj* **:** enclosed
acotamiento *nm Mex* **:** shoulder (of a road)
acotar *vt* **1** ANOTAR **:** to note, to annotate **2** DELIMITAR **:** to mark off (land), to demarcate
acre¹ *adj* **1 :** acrid, pungent **2** MORDAZ **:** caustic, biting
acre² *nm* **:** acre
acrecentamiento *nm* **:** growth, increase
acrecentar {55} *vt* AUMENTAR **:** to increase, to augment
acreditación *nf, pl* **-ciones :** accreditation
acreditado, -da *adj* **1 :** accredited, authorized **2 :** reputable
acreditar *vt* **1 :** to accredit, to authorize **2 :** to credit **3 :** to prove, to verify — **acreditarse** *vr* **:** to gain a reputation
acreedor¹, -dora *adj* **:** deserving, worthy
acreedor², -dora *n* **:** creditor
acribillar *vt* **1 :** to riddle, to pepper (with bullets, etc.) **2 :** to hound, to harass
acrílico *nm* **:** acrylic
acrimonia *nf* **1 :** pungency **2 :** acrimony
acrimonioso, -sa *adj* **:** acrimonious
acriollarse *vr* **:** to adopt local customs, to go native
acritud *nf* **1 :** pungency, bitterness **2 :** intensity, sharpness **3 :** harshness, asperity
acrobacia *nf* **:** acrobatics
acróbata *nmf* **:** acrobat
acrónimo *nm* **:** acronym
acta *nf* **1 :** document, certificate <acta de nacimiento : birth certificate> **2 actas** *nfpl* **:** minutes (of a meeting)
actitud *nf* **1 :** attitude **2 :** posture, position

activación *nf, pl* **-ciones 1 :** activation, stimulation **2** ACELERACIÓN **:** acceleration, speeding up
activar *vt* **1 :** to activate **2 :** to stimulate, to energize **3 :** to speed up
actividad *nf* **:** activity
activista *nmf* **:** activist
activo[1], -va *adj* **:** active **— activamente** *adv*
activo[2] *nm* **:** assets *pl* <activo y pasivo : assets and liabilities>
acto *nm* **1** ACCIÓN **:** act, deed **2 :** act (in a play) **3 el acto sexual :** sexual intercourse **4 en el acto :** right away, on the spot **5 acto seguido :** immediately after
actor *nm* ARTISTA **:** actor
actriz *nf, pl* **actrices** ARTISTA **:** actress
actuación *nf, pl* **-ciones 1 :** performance **2 actuaciones** *nfpl* DILIGENCIAS **:** proceedings
actual *adj* PRESENTE **:** present, current
actualidad *nf* **1 :** present time <en la actualidad : at present> **2 actualidades** *nfpl* **:** current affairs
actualización *nf, pl* **-ciones :** updating, modernization
actualizar {21} *vt* **:** to modernize, to bring up to date
actualmente *adv* **:** at present, nowadays
actuar {3} *vi* **:** to act, to perform
actuarial *adj* **:** actuarial
actuario, -ria *n* **:** actuary
acuarela *nf* **:** watercolor
acuario *nm* **:** aquarium
Acuario *nmf* **:** Aquarius, Aquarian
acuartelar *vt* **:** to quarter (troops)
acuático, -ca *adj* **:** aquatic, water
acuchillar *vt* APUÑALAR **:** to knife, to stab
acuciante *adj* **:** pressing, urgent
acucioso, -sa → acuciante
acudir *vi* **1 :** to go, to come (someplace for a specific purpose) <acudió a la puerta : he went to the door> <acudimos en su ayuda : we came to her aid> **2 :** to be present, to show up <acudí a la cita : I showed up for the appointment> **3 ~ a :** to turn to, to have recourse to <hay que acudir al médico : you must consult the doctor>
acueducto *nm* **:** aqueduct
acuerdo *nm* **1 :** agreement **2 estar de acuerdo :** to agree **3 de acuerdo con :** in accordance with **4 de ~ :** OK, all right
acuicultura *nf* **:** aquaculture
acullá *adv* **:** yonder, over there
acumulación *nf, pl* **-ciones :** accumulation
acumulador *nm* **:** storage battery
acumular *vt* **:** to accumulate, to amass **— acumularse** *vr* **:** to build up, to pile up
acumulativo, -va *adj* **:** cumulative **— acumulativamente** *adv*
acunar *vt* **:** to rock, to cradle
acuñar *vt* **:** to coin, to mint
acuoso, -sa *adj* **:** aqueous, watery
acupuntura *nf* **:** acupuncture
acurrucarse {72} *vr* **:** to cuddle, to nestle, to curl up
acusación *nf, pl* **-ciones 1 :** accusation, charge **2 la acusación :** the prosecution
acusado[1], -da *adj* **:** prominent, marked
acusado[2], -da *n* **:** defendant
acusador, -dora *n* **1 :** accuser **2** FISCAL **:** prosecutor
acusar *vt* **1 :** to accuse, to charge **2 :** to reveal, to betray <sus ojos acusaban la desconfianza : his eyes revealed distrust> **— acusarse** *vr* **:** to confess
acusatorio, -ria *adj* **:** accusatory
acuse *nm* **acuse de recibo :** acknowledgment of receipt
acústica *nf* **:** acoustics
acústico, -ca *adj* **:** acoustic
adagio *nm* **1** REFRÁN **:** adage, proverb **2 :** adagio
adalid *nm* **:** leader, champion
adaptable *adj* **:** adaptable **— adaptabilidad** *nf*
adaptación *nf, pl* **-ciones :** adaptation, adjustment
adaptado, -da *adj* **:** suited, adapted
adaptador *nm* **:** adapter (in electricity)
adaptar *vt* **1** MODIFICAR **:** to adapt **2 :** to adjust, to fit **— adaptarse** *vr* **:** to adapt oneself, to conform
adecentar *vt* **:** to tidy up
adecuación *nf, pl* **-ciones** ADAPTACIÓN **:** adaptation
adecuadamente *adv* **:** adequately
adecuado, -da *adj* **1** IDÓNEO **:** suitable, appropriate **2 :** adequate
adecuar {8} *vt* **:** to adapt, to make suitable **— adecuarse** *vr* **~ a :** to be appropriate for, to fit in with
adefesio *nm* **:** eyesore, monstrosity
adelantado, -da *adj* **1 :** advanced, ahead **2 :** fast (of a clock or watch) **3 por ~ :** in advance
adelantamiento *nm* **1 :** advancement **2 :** speeding up
adelantar *vt* **1 :** to advance, to move forward **2 :** to overtake, to pass **3 :** to reveal (information) in advance **4 :** to advance, to lend (money) **— adelantarse** *vr* **1 :** to advance, to get in front **2 ~ a :** to forestall, to preempt
adelante *adv* **1 :** ahead, in front, forward **2 más adelante :** further on, later on **3 ¡adelante! :** come in!
adelanto *nm* **1 :** advance, progress **2 :** advance payment **3 :** earliness <llevamos una hora de adelanto : we're running an hour ahead of time>
adelfa *nf* **:** oleander
adelgazar {21} *vt* **:** to thin, to reduce **—** *vi* **:** to lose weight
ademán *nm, pl* **-manes 1** GESTO **:** gesture **2 ademanes** *nmpl* **:** manners
además *adv* **1 :** besides, furthermore **2 ~ de :** in addition to, as well as

adenoides *nfpl* **:** adenoids
adentrarse *vr* **~ en :** to go into, to penetrate
adentro *adv* **:** inside, within
adentros *nmpl* **decirse para sus adentros :** to say to oneself <me dije para mis adentros que nunca regresaría : I told myself that I'd never go back>
adepto[1], **-ta** *adj* **:** supportive <ser adepto a : to be a follower of>
adepto[2], **-ta** *n* PARTIDARIO **:** follower, supporter
aderezar {21} *vt* **1** SAZONAR **:** to season, to dress (salad) **2 :** to embellish, to adorn
aderezo *nm* **1 :** dressing, seasoning **2 :** adornment, embellishment
adeudar *vt* **1 :** to debit **2** DEBER **:** to owe
adeudo *nm* **1** DÉBITO **:** debit **2** *Mex* **:** debt, indebtedness
adherencia *nf* **1 :** adherence, adhesiveness **2 :** appendage, accretion
adherente *adj* **:** adhesive, sticky
adherirse {76} *vr* **:** to adhere, to stick
adhesión *nf, pl* **-siones 1 :** adhesion **2 :** attachment, commitment (to a cause, etc.)
adhesivo[1], **-va** *adj* **:** adhesive
adhesivo[2] *nm* **:** adhesive
adicción *nf, pl* **-ciones :** addiction
adición *nf, pl* **-ciones :** addition
adicional *adj* **:** additional **— adicionalmente** *adv*
adicionar *vt* **:** to add
adicto[1], **-ta** *adj* **1 :** addicted **2 :** devoted, dedicated
adicto[2], **-ta** *n* **1 :** addict **2** PARTIDARIO **:** supporter, advocate
adiestrador, -dora *n* **:** trainer
adiestramiento *nm* **:** training
adiestrar *vt* **:** to train
adinerado, -da *adj* **:** moneyed, wealthy
adiós *nm, pl* **adioses 1** DESPEDIDA **:** farewell, good-bye **2 ¡adiós! :** good-bye!
aditamento *nm* **:** attachment, accessory
aditivo *nm* **:** additive
adivinación *nf, pl* **-ciones 1 :** guess **2 :** divination, prediction
adivinanza *nf* ACERTIJO **:** riddle
adivinar *vt* **1 :** to guess **2 :** to foretell, to predict
adivino, -na *n* **:** fortune-teller
adjetivo[1], **-va** *adj* **:** adjectival
adjetivo[2] *nm* **:** adjective
adjudicación *nf, pl* **-ciones 1 :** adjudication **2 :** allocation, awarding, granting
adjudicar {72} *vt* **1 :** to adjudge, to adjudicate **2 :** to assign, to allocate <adjudicar la culpa : to assign the blame> **3 :** to award, to grant
adjuntar *vt* **:** to enclose, to attach
adjunto[1], **-ta** *adj* **:** enclosed, attached
adjunto[2], **-ta** *n* **:** deputy, assistant
adjunto[3] *nm* **:** adjunct
administración *nf, pl* **-ciones 1 :** administration, management **2 administración de empresas :** business administration
administrador, -dora *n* **:** administrator, manager
administrar *vt* **:** to administer, to manage, to run
administrativo, -va *adj* **:** administrative
admirable *adj* **:** admirable, impressive **— admirablemente** *adv*
admiración *nf, pl* **-ciones :** admiration
admirador, -dora *n* **:** admirer
admirar *vt* **1 :** to admire **2 :** to amaze, to astonish **— admirarse** *vr* **:** to be amazed
admirativo, -va *adj* **:** admiring
admisibilidad *nf* **:** admissibility
admisible *adj* **:** admissible, allowable
admisión *nf, pl* **-siones :** admission, admittance
admitir *vt* **1 :** to admit, to let in **2 :** to acknowledge, to concede **3 :** to allow, to make room for <la ley no admite cambios : the law doesn't allow for changes>
admonición *nf, pl* **-ciones :** admonition, warning
admonitorio, -ria *adj* **:** admonitory
ADN *nm* **:** DNA
adobar *vt* **:** to marinate
adobe *nm* **:** adobe
adobo *nm* **1 :** marinade, seasoning **2** *Mex* **:** spicy marinade used for cooking pork
adoctrinamiento *nm* **:** indoctrination
adoctrinar *vt* **:** to indoctrinate
adolecer {53} *vi* PADECER **:** to suffer <adolece de timidez : he suffers from shyness>
adolescencia *nf* **:** adolescence
adolescente[1] *adj* **:** adolescent, teenage
adolescente[2] *nmf* **:** adolescent, teenager
adonde *conj* **:** where <el lugar adonde vamos es bello : the place where we're going is beautiful>
adónde *adv* **:** where <¿adónde vamos? : where are we going?>
adondequiera *adv* **:** wherever, anywhere <adondequiera que vayas : anywhere you go>
adopción *nf, pl* **-ciones :** adoption
adoptar *vt* **1 :** to adopt (a measure), to take (a decision) **2 :** to adopt (children)
adoptivo, -va *adj* **1 :** adopted (children, country) **2 :** adoptive (parents)
adoquín *nm, pl* **-quines :** paving stone, cobblestone
adorable *adj* **:** adorable, lovable
adoración *nf, pl* **-ciones :** adoration, worship
adorador[1], **-dora** *adj* **:** adoring, worshipping
adorador[2], **-dora** *n* **:** worshipper
adorar *vt* **:** to adore, to worship
adormecer {53} *vt* **1 :** to make sleepy, to lull to sleep **2 :** to numb **— ador-**

mecerse *vr* **1** : to doze off **2** : to go numb
adormecimiento *nm* **1** SUEÑO : drowsiness, sleepiness **2** INSENSIBILIDAD : numbness
adormilarse *vr* : to doze, to drowse
adornar *vt* DECORAR : to decorate, to adorn
adorno *nm* : ornament, decoration
adquirido, -da *adj* **1** : acquired **2 mal adquirido** : ill-gotten
adquirir {4} *vt* **1** : to acquire, to gain **2** COMPRAR : to purchase
adquisición *nf, pl* **-ciones** **1** : acquisition **2** COMPRA : purchase
adquisitivo, -va *adj* **poder adquisitivo** : purchasing power
adrede *adv* : intentionally, on purpose
adrenalina *nf* : adrenaline
adscribir {33} *vt* : to assign, to appoint — **adscribirse** *vr* **~ a** : to become a member of
adscripción *nf, pl* **-ciones** : assignment, appointment
adscrito *pp* → **adscribir**
aduana *nf* : customs, customs office
aduanero[1], -ra *adj* : customs
aduanero[2], -ra *n* : customs officer
aducir {61} *vt* : to adduce, to offer as proof
adueñarse *vr* **~ de** : to take possession of, to take over
adulación *nf, pl* **-ciones** : adulation, flattery
adulador[1], -dora *adj* : flattering
adulador[2], -dora *n* : flatterer, toady
adular *vt* LISONJEAR : to flatter
adulteración *nf, pl* **-ciones** : adulteration
adulterar *vt* : to adulterate
adulterio *nm* : adultery
adúltero[1], -ra *adj* : adulterous
adúltero[2], -ra *n* : adulterer
adultez *nf* : adulthood
adulto, -ta *adj & n* : adult
adusto, -ta *adj* : harsh, severe
advenedizo, -za *n* **1** : upstart, parvenu **2** : newcomer
advenimiento *nm* : advent
adventicio, -cia *adj* : adventitious
adverbio *nm* : adverb — **adverbial** *adj*
adversario[1], -ria *adj* : opposing, contrary
adversario[2], -ria *n* OPOSITOR : adversary, opponent
adversidad *nf* : adversity
adverso, -sa *adj* DESFAVORABLE : adverse, unfavorable — **adversamente** *adv*
advertencia *nf* AVISO : warning
advertir {76} *vt* **1** AVISAR : to warn **2** : to notice, to tell <no advertí que estuviera enojada : I couldn't tell she was angry>
adviento *nm* : Advent
adyacente *adj* : adjacent
aéreo, -rea *adj* **1** : aerial, air **2 correo aéreo** : airmail
aeróbic *nm* : aerobics
aeróbico, -ca *adj* : aerobic
aerobio, -bia *adj* : aerobic
aerodinámica *nf* : aerodynamics
aerodinámico, -ca *adj* : aerodynamic, streamlined
aeródromo *nm* : airfield
aeroespacial *adj* : aerospace
aerolínea *nf* : airline
aeromozo, -za *n* : flight attendant, steward *m,* stewardess *f*
aeronáutica *nf* : aeronautics
aeronáutico, -ca *adj* : aeronautical
aeronave *nf* : aircraft
aeropostal *adj* : airmail
aeropuerto *nm* : airport
aerosol *nm* : aerosol, aerosol spray
aeróstata *nmf* : baloonist
aerotransportado, -da *adj* : airborne
aerotransportar *vt* : to airlift
afabilidad *nf* : affability
afable *adj* : affable — **afablemente** *adv*
afamado, -da *adj* : well-known, famous
afán *nm, pl* **afanes** **1** ANHELO : eagerness, desire **2** EMPEÑO : effort, determination
afanador, -dora *n Mex* : cleaning person, cleaner
afanarse *vr* : to toil, to strive
afanosamente *adv* : zealously, industriously, busily
afanoso, -sa *adj* **1** : eager, industrious **2** : arduous, hard
afear *vt* : to make ugly, to disfigure
afección *nf, pl* **-ciones** **1** : fondness, affection **2** : illness, complaint
afectación *nf, pl* **-ciones** : affectation
afectado, -da *adj* **1** : affected, mannered **2** : influenced **3** : afflicted **4** : feigned
afectar *vt* **1** : to affect **2** : to upset **3** : to feign, to pretend
afectísimo, -ma *adj* **suyo afectísimo** : yours truly
afectivo, -va *adj* : emotional
afecto[1], -ta *adj* **1** : affected, afflicted **2** : fond, affectionate
afecto[2] *nm* CARIÑO : affection
afectuoso, -sa *adj* CARIÑOSO : affectionate, caring
afeitar *vt* RASURAR : to shave — **afeitarse** *vr*
afelpado, -da *adj* : plush
afeminado, -da *adj* : effeminate
aferrado, -da *adj* : obstinate, stubborn
aferrarse {55} *vr* : to cling, to hold on
AFI *nm* (*Alfabeto Fonético Internacional*) : IPA
affidávit *nm, pl* **-dávits** : affidavit
afgano, -na *adj & n* : Afghan
afianzar {21} *vt* **1** : to secure, to strengthen **2** : to guarantee, to vouch for — **afianzarse** *vr* ESTABLECERSE : to establish oneself
afiche *nm* : poster
afición *nf, pl* **-ciones** **1** : enthusiasm, penchant, fondness <afición al de-

porte : love of sports> **2** PASATIEMPO : hobby

aficionado[1], -da *adj* ENTUSIASTA : enthusiastic, keen

aficionado[2], -da *n* **1** ENTUSIASTA : enthusiast, fan **2** : amateur

áfido *nm* : aphid

afiebrado, -da *adj* : feverish

afilado, -da *adj* **1** : sharp **2** : long, pointed <una nariz afilada : a sharp nose>

afilador *nm* : sharpener

afilalápices *nms & pl* : pencil sharpener

afilar *vt* : to sharpen

afiliación *nf, pl* **-ciones** : affiliation

afiliado[1], -da *adj* : affiliated

afiliado[2], -da *n* : member

afiliarse *vr* : to become a member, to join, to affiliate

afín *adj, pl* **afines 1** PARECIDO : related, similar <la biología y disciplinas afines : biology and related disciplines> **2** PRÓXIMO : adjacent, nearby

afinación *nf, pl* **-ciones 1** : tune-up **2** : tuning (of an instrument)

afinador, -dora *n* : tuner (of musical instruments)

afinar *vt* **1** : to perfect, to refine **2** : to tune (an instrument) — *vi* : to sing or play in tune

afincarse {72} *vr* : to establish oneself, to settle in

afinidad *nf* : affinity, similarity

afirmación *nf, pl* **-ciones 1** : statement **2** : affirmation

afirmar *vt* **1** : to state, to affirm **2** REFORZAR : to make firm, to strengthen

afirmativo, -va *adj* : affirmative — **afirmativamente** *adj*

aflicción *nf, pl* **-ciones** DESCONSUELO, PESAR : grief, sorrow

afligido, -da *adj* : grief-stricken, sorrowful

afligir {35} *vt* **1** : to distress, to upset **2** : to afflict — **afligirse** *vr* : to grieve

aflojar *vt* **1** : to loosen, to slacken **2** *fam* : to pay up, to fork over — *vi* : to slacken, to ease up — **aflojarse** *vr* : to become loose, to slacken

afloramiento *nm* : outcropping, emergence

aflorar *vi* : to come to the surface, to emerge

afluencia *nf* **1** : flow, influx **2** : abundance, plenty

afluente *nm* : tributary

afluir {41} *vi* **1** : to flock <la gente afluía a la frontera : people were flocking to the border> **2** : to flow

aforismo *nm* : aphorism

aforo *nm* **1** : appraisal, assessment **2** : maximum capacity (of a theater, highway, etc.)

afortunado, -da *adj* : fortunate, lucky — **afortunadamente** *adv*

afrecho *nm* : bran, mash

afrenta *nf* : affront, insult

afrentar *vt* : to affront, to dishonor, to insult

africano, -na *adj & n* : African

afroamericano, -na *adj & n* : Afro-American

afrodisiaco *or* **afrodisíaco** *nm* : aphrodisiac

afrontamiento *nm* : confrontation

afrontar *vt* : to confront, to face up to

afrutado, -da *adj* : fruity

afuera *adv* **1** : out <¡afuera! : get out!> **2** : outside, outdoors

afueras *nfpl* ALEDAÑOS : outskirts

agachadiza *nf* : snipe (bird)

agachar *vt* : to lower (a part of the body) <agachar la cabeza : to bow one's head> — **agacharse** *vr* : to crouch, to stoop, to bend down

agalla *nf* **1** BRANQUIA : gill **2 tener agallas** *fam* : to have guts, to have courage

agarradera *nf* ASA, ASIDERO : handle, grip

agarrado, -da *adj fam* : cheap, stingy

agarrar *vt* **1** : to grab, to grasp **2** : to catch, to take — *vi* **agarrar y** *fam* : to do (something) abruptly <el día siguiente agarró y se fue : the next day he up and left> — **agarrarse** *vr* **1** : to hold on, to cling **2** *fam* : to get into a fight <se agarraron a golpes : they came to blows>

agarre *nm* : grip, grasp

agasajar *vt* : to fête, to wine and dine

agasajo *nm* : lavish attention

ágata *nf* : agate

agave *nm* : agave

agazaparse *vr* **1** AGACHARSE : to crouch **2** : to hide

agencia *nf* : agency, office

agenciar *vt* : to obtain, to procure — **agenciarse** *vr* : to manage, to get by

agenda *nf* **1** : agenda **2** : appointment book

agente *nmf* **1** : agent **2 agente de viajes** : travel agent **3 agente de bolsa** : stockbroker **4 agente de tráfico** : traffic officer

agigantado, -da *adj* GIGANTESCO : gigantic

agigantar *vt* **1** : to increase greatly, to enlarge **2** : to exaggerate

ágil *adj* **1** : agile, nimble **2** : sharp, lively (of a response, etc.) — **ágilmente** *adv*

agilidad *nf* : agility, nimbleness

agilizar {21} *vt* ACELERAR : to expedite, to speed up

agitación *nf, pl* **-ciones 1** : agitation **2** NERVIOSISMO : nervousness

agitado, -da *adj* **1** : agitated, excited **2** : choppy, rough, turbulent

agitador, -dora *n* PROVOCADOR : agitator

agitar *vt* **1** : to agitate, to shake **2** : to wave, to flap **3** : to stir up — **agitarse** *vr* **1** : to toss about, to flap around **2** : to get upset

aglomeración *nf, pl* **-ciones 1 :** conglomeration, mass **2** GENTÍO **:** crowd

aglomerar *vt* **:** to cluster, to amass — **aglomerarse** *vr* **:** to crowd together

aglutinar *vt* **:** to bring together, to bind

agnóstico, -ca *adj & n* **:** agnostic

agobiado, -da *adj* **:** weary, worn-out, weighted-down

agobiante *adj* **1 :** exhausting, overwhelming **2 :** stifling, oppressive

agobiar *vt* **1** OPRIMIR **:** to oppress, to burden **2** ABRUMAR **:** to overwhelm **3 :** to wear out, to exhaust

agonía *nf* **:** agony, death throes

agonizante *adj* **:** dying

agonizar {21} *vi* **1 :** to be dying **2 :** to be in agony **3 :** to dim, to fade

agorero, -ra *adj* **:** ominous

agostar *vt* **1 :** to parch **2 :** to wither — **agostarse** *vr*

agosto *nm* **1 :** August **2 hacer uno su agosto :** to make a fortune, to make a killing

agotado, -da *adj* **1 :** exhausted, used up **2 :** sold out **3** FATIGADO **:** worn-out, tired

agotador, -dora *adj* **:** exhausting

agotamiento *nm* FATIGA **:** exhaustion

agotar *vt* **1 :** to exhaust, to use up **2 :** to weary, to wear out — **agotarse** *vr*

agraciado[1], -da *adj* **1 :** attractive **2 :** fortunate

agraciado[2], -da *n* **:** winner

agradable *adj* GRATO, PLACENTERO **:** pleasant, agreeable — **agradablemente** *adv*

agradar *vi* **:** to be pleasing <nos agradó mucho el resultado : we were very pleased with the result>

agradecer {53} *vt* **1 :** to be grateful for **2 :** to thank

agradecido, -da *adj* **:** grateful, thankful

agradecimiento *nm* **:** gratitude, thankfulness

agrado *nm* **1** GUSTO **:** taste, liking <no es de su agrado : it's not to his liking> **2 :** graciousness, agreeableness **3 con ~ :** with pleasure, willingly <lo haré con agrado : I will be happy to do it>

agrandar *vt* **1 :** to exaggerate **2 :** to enlarge — **agrandarse** *vr*

agrario, -ria *adj* **:** agrarian, agricultural

agravación *nf, pl* **-ciones :** aggravation, worsening

agravante *adj* **:** aggravating

agravar *vt* **1 :** to increase (weight), to make heavier **2** EMPEORAR **:** to aggravate, to worsen — **agravarse** *vr*

agraviar *vt* INJURIAR, OFENDER **:** to offend, to insult

agravio *nm* INJURIA **:** affront, offense, insult

agredir {1} *vt* **:** to assail, to attack

agregado[1], -da *n* **1 :** attaché **2 :** assistant professor

agregado[2] *nm* **1 :** aggregate **2** AÑADIDURA **:** addition, something added

agregar {52} *vt* **1** AÑADIR **:** to add, to attach **2 :** to appoint — **agregarse** *vr* **:** to join

agresión *nf, pl* **-siones 1 :** aggression **2** ATAQUE **:** attack

agresividad *nf* **:** aggressiveness, aggression

agresivo, -va *adj* **:** aggressive — **agresivamente** *adv*

agresor[1], -sora *adj* **:** hostile, attacking

agresor[2], -sora *n* **1 :** aggressor **2 :** assailant, attacker

agreste *adj* **1** CAMPESTRE **:** rural **2 :** wild, untamed

agriar *vt* **1 :** to sour, to make sour **2 :** to embitter — **agriarse** *vr* **:** to turn sour

agrícola *adj* **:** agricultural

agricultor, -tora *n* **:** farmer, grower

agricultura *nf* **:** agriculture, farming

agridulce *adj* **1 :** bittersweet **2 :** sweet-and-sour

agrietar *vt* **:** to crack — **agrietarse** *vr* **1 :** to crack **2 :** to chap

agrimensor, -sora *n* **:** surveyor

agrimensura *nf* **:** surveying

agrio, agria *adj* **1** ÁCIDO **:** sour **2 :** caustic, acrimonious

agriparse *vr* **:** to catch the flu

agroindustria *nf* **:** agribusiness

agronomía *nf* **:** agronomy

agropecuario, -ria *adj* **:** pertaining to livestock and agriculture

agrupación *nf, pl* **-ciones** GRUPO **:** group, association

agrupamiento *nm* **:** grouping, concentration

agrupar *vt* **:** to group together

agua *nf* **1 :** water **2 agua oxigenada :** hydrogen peroxide **3 aguas negras** *or* **aguas residuales :** sewage **4 como agua para chocolate** *Mex fam* **:** furious **5 echar aguas** *Mex fam* **:** to keep an eye out, to be on the lookout

aguacate *nm* **:** avocado

aguacero *nm* **:** shower, downpour

aguado, -da *adj* **1** DILUIDO **:** watered-down, diluted **2** *CA, Col, Mex fam* **:** soft, flabby **3** *Mex, Peru fam* **:** dull, boring

aguafiestas *nmfs & pl* **:** killjoy, stick-in-the-mud, spoilsport

aguafuerte *nm* **:** etching

aguamanil *nm* **:** ewer, pitcher

aguanieve *nf* **:** sleet <caer aguanieve : to be sleeting>

aguantar *vt* **1** SOPORTAR **:** to bear, to tolerate, to withstand **2 :** to hold **3 aguantar las ganas :** to resist an urge <no pude aguantar las ganas de reír : I couldn't keep myself from laughing> — *vi* **:** to hold out, to last — **aguantarse** *vr* **1 :** to resign oneself **2 :** to restrain oneself

aguante *nm* **1** TOLERANCIA **:** tolerance, patience **2** RESISTENCIA **:** endurance, strength

aguar {10} *vt* **1 :** to water down, to dilute **2 aguar la fiesta** *fam* **:** to spoil the party

aguardar *vt* ESPERAR **:** to wait for, to await — *vi* **:** to be in store
aguardiente *nm* **:** clear brandy
aguarrás *nm* **:** turpentine
agudeza *nf* **1 :** keenness, sharpness **2 :** shrillness **3 :** witticism
agudizar {21} *vt* **:** to intensify, to heighten
agudo, -da *adj* **1 :** acute, sharp **2 :** shrill, high-pitched **3** PERSPICAZ **:** clever, shrewd
agüero *nm* AUGURIO, PRESAGIO **:** augury, omen
aguijón *nm, pl* **-jones 1 :** stinger (of a bee, etc.) **2 :** goad
aguijonear *vt* **:** to goad
águila *nf* **1 :** eagle **2 águila o sol** *Mex* **:** heads or tails
aguileño, -ña *adj* **:** aquiline
aguilera *nf* **:** aerie, eagle's nest
aguilón *nm, pl* **-lones :** gable
aguinaldo *nm* **1 :** Christmas bonus, year-end bonus **2** *PRi, Ven* **:** Christmas carol
agüitarse *vr Mex fam* **:** to have the blues, to feel discouraged
aguja *nf* **1 :** needle **2 :** steeple, spire
agujerear *vt* **:** to make a hole in, to pierce
agujero *nm* **1 :** hole **2 agujero negro :** black hole (in astronomy)
agujeta *nf* **1** *Mex* **:** shoelace **2 agujetas** *nfpl* **:** muscular soreness or stiffness
agusanado, -da *adj* **:** worm-eaten
aguzar {21} *vt* **1 :** to sharpen <aguzar el ingenio : to sharpen one's wits> **2 aguzar el oído :** to prick up one's ears
ahí *adv* **1 :** there <ahí está : there it is> **2 por ~ :** somewhere, thereabouts **3 de ahí que :** with the result that, so that
ahijado, -da *n* **:** godchild, godson *m*, goddaughter *f*
ahijar {5} *vt* **:** to adopt (a child)
ahínco *nm* **:** eagerness, zeal
ahogar {52} *vt* **1 :** to drown **2 :** to smother **3 :** to choke back, to stifle — **ahogarse** *vr*
ahogo *nm* **:** breathlessness, suffocation
ahondar *vt* **:** to deepen — *vi* **:** to elaborate, to go into detail
ahora *adv* **1 :** now **2 ahora mismo :** right now **3 hasta ~ :** so far **4 por ~ :** for the time being
ahorcar {72} *vt* **:** to hang, to kill by hanging — **ahorcarse** *vr*
ahorita *adv fam* **:** right now, right away
ahorquillado, -da *adj* **:** forked
ahorrador, -dora *adj* **:** thrifty
ahorrar *vt* **1 :** to save (money) **2 :** to spare, to conserve — *vi* **:** to save up — **ahorrarse** *vr* **:** to spare oneself
ahorrativo, -va *adj* **:** thrifty, frugal
ahorro *nm* **:** saving <cuenta de ahorros : savings account>
ahuecar {72} *vt* **1 :** to hollow out **2 :** to cup (one's hands) **3 :** to plump up, to fluff up
ahuizote *nm Mex fam* **:** annoying person, pain in the neck
ahumar {8} *vt* **:** to smoke, to cure
ahuyentar *vt* **1 :** to scare away, to chase away **2 :** to banish, to dispel <ahuyentar las dudas : to dispel doubts>
airado, -da *adj* FURIOSO **:** angry, irate
airar {5} *vt* **:** to make angry, to anger
aire *nm* **1 :** air **2 aire acondicionado :** air-conditioning **3 darse aires :** to give oneself airs
airear *vt* **:** to air, to air out — **airearse** *vr* **:** to get some fresh air
airoso, -sa *adj* **1 :** elegant, graceful **2 salir airoso :** to come out winning
aislacionismo *nm* **:** isolationism
aislacionista *adj & nmf* **:** isolationist
aislado, -da *adj* **:** isolated, alone
aislamiento *nm* **1 :** isolation **2 :** insulation
aislante *nm* **:** insulator, nonconductor
aislar {5} *vt* **1 :** to isolate **2 :** to insulate
ajado, -da *adj* **1 :** worn, shabby **2 :** wrinkled, crumpled
ajar *vt* **:** to wear out, to spoil
ajardinado, -da *adj* **:** landscaped
ajedrecista *nmf* **:** chess player
ajedrez *nm, pl* **-dreces 1 :** chess **2 :** chess set
ajeno, -na *adj* **1 :** alien **2 :** of another, of others <propiedad ajena : somebody else's property> **3 ~ a :** foreign to **4 ~ de :** devoid of, free from
ajetreado, -da *adj* **:** hectic, busy
ajetrearse *vr* **:** to bustle about, to rush around
ajetreo *nm* **:** hustle and bustle, fuss
ají *nm, pl* **ajíes :** chili pepper
ajo *nm* **:** garlic
ajonjolí *nm, pl* **-líes :** sesame
ajuar *nm* **:** trousseau
ajustable *adj* **:** adjustable
ajustado, -da *adj* **1** CEÑIDO **:** tight, tight-fitting **2 :** reasonable, fitting
ajustar *vt* **1 :** to adjust, to adapt **2 :** to take in (clothing) **3 :** to settle, to resolve — **ajustarse** *vr* **:** to fit, to conform
ajuste *nm* **1 :** adjustment **2 :** tightening
ajusticiar *vt* EJECUTAR **:** to execute, to put to death
al (*contraction of* **a** *and* **el**) → **a²**
ala *nf* **1 :** wing **2 :** brim (of a hat)
Alá *nm* **:** Allah
alabanza *nf* ELOGIO **:** praise
alabar *vt* **:** to praise — **alabarse** *vr* **:** to boast
alabastro *nm* **:** alabaster
alabear *vt* **:** to warp — **alabearse** *vr*
alabeo *nm* **:** warp, warping
alacena *nf* **:** cupboard, larder
alacrán *nm, pl* **-cranes** ESCORPIÓN **:** scorpion
alado, -da *adj* **:** winged
alambique *nm* **:** still (to distill alcohol)
alambre *nm* **1 :** wire **2 alambre de púas :** barbed wire

alameda *nf* **1** : poplar grove **2** : tree-lined avenue
álamo *nm* **1** : poplar **2 álamo temblón** : aspen
alar *nm* : eaves *pl*
alarde *nm* **1** : show, display **2 hacer alarde de** : to make show of, to boast about
alardear *vi* PRESUMIR : to boast, to brag
alargado, -da *adj* : elongated, slender
alargamiento *nm* : lengthening, extension, elongation
alargar {52} *vt* **1** : to extend, to lengthen **2** PROLONGAR : to prolong — **alargarse** *vr*
alarido *nm* : howl, shriek
alarma *nf* : alarm
alarmante *adj* : alarming — **alarmantemente** *adv*
alarmar *vt* : to alarm
alazán *nm, pl* **-zanes** : sorrel (color or animal)
alba *nf* AMANECER : dawn, daybreak
albacea *nmf* TESTAMENTARIO : executor, executrix *f*
albahaca *nf* : basil
albanés, -nesa *adj & n, mpl* **-neses** : Albanian
albañil *nmf* : bricklayer, mason
albañilería *nf* : bricklaying, masonry
albaricoque *nm* : apricot
albatros *nm* : albatross
albedrío *nm* : will <libre albedrío : free will>
alberca *nf* **1** : reservoir, tank **2** *Mex* : swimming pool
albergar {52} *vt* ALOJAR : to house, to lodge, to shelter
albergue *nm* **1** : shelter, refuge **2** : hostel
albino, -na *adj & n* : albino — **albinismo** *nm*
albóndiga *nf* : meatball
albor *nm* **1** : dawning, beginning **2** BLANCURA : whiteness
alborada *nf* : dawn
alborear *v impers* : to dawn
alborotado, -da *adj* **1** : excited, agitated **2** : rowdy, unruly
alborotador[1], -dora *adj* **1** : noisy, boisterous **2** : rowdy, unruly
alborotador[2], -dora *n* : agitator, troublemaker, rioter
alborotar *vt* **1** : to excite, to agitate **2** : to incite, to stir up — **alborotarse** *vr* : to riot
alboroto *nm* **1** : disturbance, ruckus **2** MOTÍN : riot
alborozado, -da *adj* : jubilant
alborozar {21} *vt* : to gladden, to cheer
alborozo *nm* : joy, elation
álbum *nm* : album <álbum de recortes : scrapbook>
albúmina *nf* : albumin
albur *nm* **1** : chance, risk **2** *Mex* : pun
alca *nf* : auk
alcachofa *nf* : artichoke
alcahuete, -ta *n* CHISMOSO : gossip
alcaide *nm* : warden (in a prison)
alcalde, -desa *n* : mayor
alcaldía *nf* **1** : mayoralty **2** AYUNTAMIENTO : city hall
álcali *nm* : alkali
alcalino, -na *adj* : alkaline — **alcalinidad** *nf*
alcance *nm* **1** : reach **2** : range, scope
alcancía *nf* **1** : piggy bank, money box **2** : collection box (for alms, etc.)
alcanfor *nm* : camphor
alcantarilla *nf* CLOACA : sewer, drain
alcanzar {21} *vt* **1** : to reach **2** : to catch up with **3** LOGRAR : to achieve, to attain — *vi* **1** DAR : to suffice, to be enough **2 ~ a** : to manage to
alcaparra *nf* : caper
alcapurria *nf PRi* : stuffed fritter made with taro and green banana
alcaravea *nf* : caraway
alcatraz *nm, pl* **-traces** : gannet
alcázar *nm* : fortress, castle
alce[1], **etc.** → **alzar**
alce[2] *nm* : moose, European elk
alcoba *nf* : bedroom
alcohol *nm* : alcohol
alcohólico, -ca *adj & n* : alcoholic
alcoholismo *nm* : alcoholism
alcoholizarse {21} *vr* : to become an alcoholic
alcornoque *nm* **1** : cork oak **2** *fam* : idiot, fool
alcurnia *nf* : ancestry, lineage
aldaba *nf* : door knocker
aldea *nf* : village
aldeano[1], -na *adj* : village, rustic
aldeano[2], -na *n* : villager
aleación *nf, pl* **-ciones** : alloy
alear *vt* : to alloy
aleatorio, -ria *adj* : random, fortuitous — **aleatoriamente** *adv*
alebrestar *vt* : to excite, to make nervous — **alebrestarse** *vr*
aledaño, -ña *adj* : bordering, neighboring
aledaños *nmpl* AFUERAS : outskirts, surrounding area
alegar {52} *vt* : to assert, to allege — *vi* DISCUTIR : to argue
alegato *nm* **1** : allegation, claim **2** *Mex* : argument, summation (in law) **3** : argument, dispute
alegoría *nf* : allegory
alegórico, -ca *adj* : allegorical
alegrar *vt* : to make happy, to cheer up — **alegrarse** *vr* : to be glad, to rejoice
alegre *adj* **1** : glad, cheerful **2** : colorful, bright **3** *fam* : tipsy
alegremente *adv* : happily, cheerfully
alegría *nf* : joy, cheer, happiness
alejado, -da *adj* : remote
alejamiento *nm* **1** : removal, separation **2** : estrangement
alejar *vt* **1** : to remove, to move away **2** : to estrange, to alienate — **alejarse** *vr* **1** : to move away, to stray **2** : to drift apart
alelado, -da *adj* **1** : bewildered, stupefied **2** : foolish, stupid
aleluya *interj* : hallelujah!, alleluia!

alemán[1], **-mana** *adj & n, mpl* **-manes** : German
alemán[2] *nm* : German (language)
alentador, -dora *adj* : encouraging
alentar {55} *vt* : to encourage, to inspire — *vi* : to breathe
alerce *nm* : larch
alérgeno *nm* : allergen
alergia *nf* : allergy
alérgico, -ca *adj* : allergic
alergista *nmf* : allergist
alero *nm* **1** : eaves *pl* **2** : forward (in basketball)
alerón *nm, pl* **-rones** : aileron
alerta[1] *adv* : on the alert
alerta[2] *nf* : alert, alarm
alertar *vt* : to alert
alerto, -ta *adj* : alert, watchful
aleta *nf* **1** : fin **2** : flipper **3** : small wing
aletargado, -da *adj* : lethargic, sluggish, torpid
aletargarse {52} *vr* : to feel drowsy, to become lethargic
aleteo *nm* : flapping, flutter
alevosía *nf* **1** : treachery **2** : premeditation
alevoso, -sa *adj* : treacherous
alfabético, -ca *adj* : alphabetical — **alfabéticamente** *adv*
alfabetismo *nm* : literacy
alfabetizado, -da *adj* : literate
alfabetizar {21} *vt* : to alphabetize
alfabeto *nm* : alphabet
alfalfa *nf* : alfalfa
alfanje *nm* : cutlass, scimitar
alfarería *nf* : pottery
alfarero, -ra *n* : potter
alféizar *nm* : sill, windowsill
alfeñique *nm fam* : wimp, weakling
alférez *nmf, pl* **-reces 1** : second lieutenant **2** : ensign
alfiler *nm* **1** : pin **2** BROCHE : brooch
alfiletero *nm* : pincushion
alfombra *nf* : carpet, rug
alfombrado *nm* : carpeting
alfombrar *vt* : to carpet
alfombrilla *nf* : small rug, mat
alforfón *nm, pl* **-fones** : buckwheat
alforja *nf* : saddlebag
alforza *nf* : pleat, tuck
alga *nf* **1** : aquatic plant, alga **2** : seaweed
algáceo, -cea *adj* : algal
algarabía *nf* **1** : gibberish, babble **2** : hubbub, uproar
álgebra *nf* : algebra
algebraico, -ca *adj* : algebraic
álgido, -da *adj* **1** : critical, decisive **2** : icy cold
algo[1] *adv* : somewhat, rather <es simpático, pero algo tacaño : he's nice but rather stingy>
algo[2] *pron* **1** : something **2 ~ de** : some, a little <tengo algo de dinero : I've got some money>
algodón *nm, pl* **-dones** : cotton
algoritmo *nm* : algorithm
alguacil *nm* : constable
alguien *pron* : somebody, someone
alguno[1], **-na** *adj* (**algún** *before masculine singular nouns*) **1** : some, any <algún día : someday, one day> **2** (*in negative constructions*) : not any, not at all <no tengo noticia alguna : I have no news at all> **3 algunas veces** : sometimes
alguno[2], **-na** *pron* **1** : one, someone, somebody <alguno de ellos : one of them> **2 algunos, -nas** *pron pl* : some, a few <algunos quieren trabajar : some want to work>
alhaja *nf* : jewel, gem
alhajar *vt* : to adorn with jewels
alharaca *nf* : fuss
alhelí *nm* : wallflower
aliado[1], **-da** *adj* : allied
aliado[2], **-da** *n* : ally
alianza *nf* : alliance
aliarse {85} *vr* : to form an alliance, to ally oneself
alias *adv & nm* : alias
alicaído, -da *adj* : depressed, discouraged
alicates *nmpl* PINZAS : pliers
aliciente *nm* **1** INCENTIVO : incentive **2** ATRACCIÓN : attraction
alienación *nf, pl* **-ciones** : alienation, derangement
alienar *vt* ENAJENAR : to alienate
aliento *nm* **1** : breath **2** : courage, strength **3 dar aliento a** : to encourage
aligerar *vt* **1** : to lighten **2** ACELERAR : to hasten, to quicken
alijo *nm* : cache, consignment (of contraband)
alimaña *nf* : pest, vermin
alimentación *nf, pl* **-ciones** NUTRICIÓN : nutrition, nourishment
alimentar *vt* **1** NUTRIR : to feed, to nourish **2** MANTENER : to support (a family) **3** FOMENTAR : to nurture, to foster — **alimentarse** *vr* **~ con** : to live on
alimentario, -ria → **alimenticio**
alimenticio, -cia *adj* **1** : nutritional, food, dietary **2** : nutritious, nourishing
alimento *nm* : food, nourishment
alineación *nf, pl* **-ciones 1** : alignment **2** : lineup (in sports)
alineamiento *nm* : alignment
alinear *vt* **1** : to align **2** : to line up — **alinearse** *vr* **1** : to fall in, to line up **2 ~ con** : to align oneself with
aliño *nm* : seasoning, dressing
alipús *nm, pl* **-puses** *Mex fam* : booze, drink
alisar *vt* : to smooth
aliso *nm* : alder
alistamiento *nm* : enlistment, recruitment
alistar *vt* **1** : to recruit **2** : to make ready — **alistarse** *vr* : to join up, to enlist
aliteración *nf, pl* **-ciones** : alliteration
aliterado, -da *adj* : alliterative

aliviar *vt* MITIGAR : to relieve, to alleviate, to soothe — **aliviarse** *vr* : to recover, to get better
alivio *nm* : relief
aljaba *nf* : quiver (for arrows)
aljibe *nm* : cistern, well
allá *adv* **1** : there, over there **2 más allá** : farther away **3 más allá de** : beyond **4 allá tú** : that's up to you
allanamiento *nm* **1** : (police) raid **2 allanamiento de morada** : breaking and entering
allanar *vt* **1** : to raid, to search **2** : to resolve, to solve **3** : to smooth, to level out
allegado[1], **-da** *adj* : close, intimate
allegado[2], **-da** *n* : close friend, relation <parientes y allegados : friends and relations>
allegar {52} *vt* : to gather, to collect
allende[1] *adv* : beyond, on the other side
allende[2] *prep* : beyond <allende las montañas : beyond the mountains>
allí *adv* : there, over there <allí mismo : right there> <hasta allí : up to that point>
alma *nf* **1** : soul **2** : person, human being **3 no tener alma** : to be pitiless **4 tener el alma en un hilo** : to have one's heart in one's mouth
almacén *nm, pl* **-cenes 1** BODEGA : warehouse, storehouse **2** TIENDA : shop, store **3 gran almacén** *Spain* : department store
almacenaje → **almacenamiento**
almacenamiento *nm* : storage <almacenamiento de datos : data storage>
almacenar *vt* : to store, to put in storage
almacenero, -ra *n* : shopkeeper
almacenista *nm* MAYORISTA : wholesaler
almádena *nf* : sledgehammer
almanaque *nm* : almanac
almeja *nf* : clam
almendra *nf* **1** : almond **2** : kernel
almendro *nm* : almond tree
almiar *nm* : haystack
almíbar *nm* : syrup
almidón *nm, pl* **-dones** : starch
almidonar *vt* : to starch
alminar *nm* MINARETE : minaret
almirante *nm* : admiral
almizcle *nm* : musk
almohada *nf* : pillow
almohadilla *nf* **1** : small pillow, cushion **2** : bag, base (in baseball)
almohadón *nm, pl* **-dones** : bolster, cushion
almohazar {21} *vt* : to curry (a horse)
almoneda *nf* SUBASTA : auction
almorranas *nfpl* HEMORROIDES : hemorrhoids, piles
almorzar {36} *vi* : to have lunch — *vt* : to have for lunch
almuerzo *nm* : lunch
alocado, -da *adj* **1** : crazy **2** : wild, reckless **3** : silly, scatterbrained
alocución *nf, pl* **-ciones** : speech, address
áloe *or* **aloe** *nm* : aloe
alojamiento *nm* : lodging, accommodations *pl*
alojar *vt* ALBERGAR : to house, to lodge — **alojarse** *vr* : to lodge, to room
alondra *nf* : lark, skylark
alpaca *nf* : alpaca
alpinismo *nm* : mountain climbing, mountaineering
alpinista *nmf* : mountain climber
alpino, -na *adj* : Alpine, alpine
alpiste *nm* : birdseed
alquilar *vt* ARRENDAR : to rent, to lease
alquiler *nm* ARRENDAMIENTO : rent, rental
alquimia *nf* : alchemy
alquimista *nmf* : alchemist
alquitrán *nm, pl* **-tranes** BREA : tar
alquitranar *vt* : to tar, to cover with tar
alrededor[1] *adv* **1** : around, about <todo temblaba alrededor : all around things were shaking> **2 ~ de** : around, approximately <alrededor de quince personas : around fifteen people>
alrededor[2] *prep* **~ de** : around, about <corrió alrededor de la casa : she ran around the house> <llegaré alrededor de diciembre : I will get there around December>
alrededores *nmpl* ALEDAÑOS : surroundings, outskirts
alta *nf* **1** : admission, entry, enrollment **2 dar de alta** : to release, to discharge (a patient)
altanería *nf* ALTIVEZ, ARROGANCIA : arrogance, haughtiness
altanero, -ra *adj* ALTIVO, ARROGANTE : arrogant, haughty — **altaneramente** *adv*
altar *nm* : altar
altavoz *nm, pl* **-voces** ALTOPARLANTE : loudspeaker
alteración *nf, pl* **-ciones 1** MODIFICACIÓN : alteration, modification **2** PERTURBACIÓN : disturbance, disruption
alterado, -da *adj* : upset
alterar *vt* **1** MODIFICAR : to alter, to modify **2** PERTURBAR : to disturb, to disrupt — **alterarse** *vr* : to get upset, to get worked up
altercado *nm* DISCUSIÓN, DISPUTA : altercation, argument, dispute
alternador *nm* : alternator
alternancia *nf* : alternation, rotation
alternar *vi* **1** : to alternate **2** : to mix, to socialize — *vt* : to alternate — **alternarse** *vr* : to take turns
alternativa *nf* OPCIÓN : alternative, option
alternativo, -va *adj* **1** : alternating **2** : alternative — **alternativamente** *adv*
alterno, -na *adj* : alternate <corriente alterna : alternating current>
alteza *nf* **1** : loftiness, lofty height **2 Alteza** : Highness

altibajos *nmpl* **1 :** unevenness (of terrain) **2 :** ups and downs
altímetro *nm* **:** altimeter
altiplano *nm* **:** high plateau
altisonante *adj* **1 :** pompous, affected (of language) **2** *Mex* **:** rude, obscene (of language)
altitud *nf* **:** altitude
altivez *nf, pl* **-veces** ALTANERÍA, ARROGANCIA **:** arrogance, haughtiness
altivo, -va *adj* ALTANERO, ARROGANTE **:** arrogant, haughty
alto[1] *adv* **1 :** high **2 :** loud, loudly
alto[2]**, -ta** *adj* **1 :** tall, high **2 :** loud <en voz alta : aloud, out loud>
alto[3] *nm* **1** ALTURA **:** height, elevation **2 :** stop, halt **3 altos** *nmpl* **:** upper floors
alto[4] *interj* **:** halt!, stop!
altoparlante *nm* ALTAVOZ **:** loudspeaker
altozano *nm* **:** hillock
altruismo *nm* **:** altruism
altruista[1] *adj* **:** altruistic
altruista[2] *nmf* **:** altruist
altura *nf* **1 :** height **2 :** altitude **3 :** loftiness, nobleness **4 a la altura de :** near, up by <en la avenida San Antonio a la altura de la Calle Tres : on San Antonio Avenue up near Third Street> **5 a estas alturas :** at this point, at this stage of the game
alubia *nf* **:** kidney bean
alucinación *nf, pl* **-ciones :** hallucination
alucinante *adj* **:** hallucinatory
alucinar *vi* **:** to hallucinate
alucinógeno[1]**, -na** *adj* **:** hallucinogenic
alucinógeno[2] *nm* **:** hallucinogen
alud *nm* AVALANCHA **:** avalanche, landslide
aludido, -da *n* **1 :** person in question <el aludido : the aforesaid> **2 darse por aludido :** to take personally
aludir *vi* **:** to allude, to refer
alumbrado *nm* ILUMINACIÓN **:** lighting
alumbramiento *nm* **1 :** lighting **2 :** childbirth
alumbrar *vt* **1** ILUMINAR **:** to light, to illuminate **2 :** to give birth to
alumbre *nm* **:** alum
aluminio *nm* **:** aluminum
alumnado *nm* **:** student body
alumno, -na *n* **1 :** pupil, student **2 ex–alumno, -na :** alumnus, alumna *f* **3 ex–alumnos, -nas** *npl* **:** alumni, alumnae *f*
alusión *nf, pl* **-siones :** allusion, reference
alusivo, -va *adj* **1 :** allusive **2 ~ a :** in reference to, regarding
aluvión *nm, pl* **-viones :** flood, barrage
alza *nf* SUBIDA **:** rise <precios en alza : rising prices>
alzamiento *nm* LEVANTAMIENTO **:** uprising, insurrection
alzar {21} *vt* **1** ELEVAR, LEVANTAR **:** to lift, to raise **2 :** to erect — **alzarse** *vr* LEVANTARSE **:** to rise up
ama *nf* → **amo**
amabilidad *nf* **:** kindness
amable *adj* **:** kind, nice — **amablemente** *adv*
amado[1]**, -da** *adj* **:** beloved, darling
amado[2]**, -da** *n* **:** sweetheart, loved one
amaestrar *vt* **:** to train (animals)
amafiarse *vr Mex fam* **:** to conspire, to be in cahoots
amagar {52} *vt* **1 :** to show signs of (an illness, etc.) **2 :** to threaten — *vi* **1 :** to be imminent, to threaten **2 :** to feint, to dissemble
amago *nm* **1** AMENAZA **:** threat **2 :** sign, hint
amainar *vi* **:** to abate, to ease up, to die down
amalgama *nf* **:** amalgam
amalgamar *vt* **:** to amalgamate, to unite
amamantar *v* **:** to breast-feed, to nurse, to suckle
amanecer[1] {53} *v impers* **1 :** to dawn **2 :** to begin to show, to appear **3 :** to wake up (in the morning)
amanecer[2] *nm* ALBA **:** dawn, daybreak
amanerado, -da *adj* **:** affected, mannered
amansar *vt* **1 :** to tame **2 :** to soothe, to calm down — **amansarse** *vr*
amante[1] *adj* **:** loving, fond
amante[2] *nmf* **:** lover
amañar *vt* **:** to rig, to fix, to tamper with — **amañarse** *vr* **amañárselas :** to manage
amaño *nm* **1 :** skill, dexterity **2 :** trick, ruse
amapola *nf* **:** poppy
amar *vt* **:** to love — **amarse** *vr*
amargado, -da *adj* **:** embittered, bitter
amargar {52} *vt* **:** to make bitter, to embitter — *vi* **:** to taste bitter
amargo[1]**, -ga** *adj* **:** bitter — **amargamente** *adv*
amargo[2] *nm* **:** bitterness, tartness
amargura *nf* **1 :** bitterness **2 :** grief, sorrow
amarilis *nf* **:** amaryllis
amarillear *vi* **:** to yellow, to turn yellow
amarillento, -ta *adj* **:** yellowish
amarillismo *nm* **:** yellow journalism, sensationalism
amarillo[1]**, -lla** *adj* **:** yellow
amarillo[2] *nm* **:** yellow
amarra *nf* **1 :** mooring, mooring line **2 soltar las amarras de :** to loosen one's grip on
amarrar *vt* **1 :** to moor (a boat) **2** ATAR **:** to fasten, to tie up, to tie down
amartillar *vt* **:** to cock (a gun)
amasar *vt* **1 :** to amass **2 :** to knead **3 :** to mix, to prepare
amasijo *nm* **:** jumble, hodgepodge
amasio, -sia *n* **:** lover, paramour
amateur *adj & nmf* **:** amateur — **amateurismo** *nm*
amatista *nf* **:** amethyst
amatorio, -ria *adj* **:** amatory, love

amazona *nf* **1 :** Amazon (in mythology) **2 :** horsewoman
amazónico, -ca *adj* **:** amazonian
ambages *mpl* **sin ~ :** without hesitation, straight to the point
ámbar *nm* **1 :** amber **2 ámbar gris :** ambergris
ambición *nf, pl* **-ciones :** ambition
ambicionar *vt* **:** to aspire to, to seek
ambicioso, -sa *adj* **:** ambitious — **ambiciosamente** *adv*
ambidextro, -tra *adj* **:** ambidextrous
ambientación *nf, pl* **-ciones :** setting, atmosphere
ambiental *adj* **:** environmental — **ambientalmente** *adv*
ambientalista *nmf* **:** environmentalist
ambientar *vt* **:** to give atmosphere to, to set (in literature and drama) — **ambientarse** *vr* **:** to adjust, to get one's bearings
ambiente *nm* **1 :** atmosphere **2 :** environment **3 :** surroundings *pl*
ambigüedad *nf* **:** ambiguity
ambiguo, -gua *adj* **:** ambiguous
ámbito *nm* **:** domain, field, area
ambivalencia *nf* **:** ambivalence
ambivalente *adj* **:** ambivalent
ambos, -bas *adj & pron* **:** both
ambulancia *nf* **:** ambulance
ambulante *adj* **1 :** traveling, itinerant **2 vendedor ambulante :** street vendor
ameba *nf* **:** amoeba
amedrentar *vt* **:** to frighten, to intimidate — **amedrentarse** *vr*
amén *nm* **1 :** amen **2 ~ de :** in addition to, besides **3 en un decir amén :** in an instant
amenaza *nf* **:** threat, menace
amenazador, -dora *adj* **:** threatening, menacing
amenazante → **amenazador**
amenazar {21} *v* **:** to threaten
amenguar {10} *vt* **1 :** to diminish **2 :** to belittle, to dishonor
amenidad *nf* **:** pleasantness, amenity
amenizar {21} *vt* **1 :** to make pleasant **2 :** to brighten up, to add life to
ameno, -na *adj* **:** agreeable, pleasant
amento *nm* **:** catkin
americano, -na *adj & n* **:** American
amerindio, -dia *adj & n* **:** Amerindian
ameritar *vt* MERECER **:** to deserve
ametralladora *nf* **:** machine gun
amianto *nm* **:** asbestos
amiba *nf* → **ameba**
amigable *adj* **:** friendly, amicable — **amigablemente** *adv*
amígdala *nf* **:** tonsil
amigdalitis *nf* **:** tonsilitis
amigo[1]**, -ga** *adj* **:** friendly, close
amigo[2]**, -ga** *n* **:** friend
amigote *nm* **:** crony, pal
amilanar *vt* **1 :** to frighten **2 :** to daunt, to discourage — **amilanarse** *vr* **:** to lose heart
aminoácido *nm* **:** amino acid
aminorar *vt* **:** to reduce, to lessen — *vi* **:** to diminish
amistad *nf* **:** friendship
amistoso, -sa *adj* **:** friendly — **amistosamente** *adv*
amnesia *nf* **:** amnesia
amnésico, -ca *adj & n* **:** amnesiac, amnesic
amnistía *nf* **:** amnesty
amnistiar {85} *vt* **:** to grant amnesty to
amo, ama *n* **1 :** master *m,* mistress *f* **2 :** owner, keeper (of an animal) **3 ama de casa :** housewife **4 ama de llaves :** housekeeper
amodorrado, -da *adj* **:** drowsy
amolar {19} *vt* **1 :** to grind, to sharpen **2 :** to pester, to annoy
amoldable *adj* **:** adaptable
amoldar *vt* **1 :** to mold **2 :** to adapt, to adjust — **amoldarse** *vr*
amonestación *nf, pl* **-ciones 1** APERCIBIMIENTO **:** admonition, warning **2** AMONESTACIONES *nfpl* **:** banns
amonestar *vt* APERCIBIR **:** to admonish, to warn
amoníaco *or* **amoniaco** *nm* **:** ammonia
amontonamiento *nm* **:** accumulation, piling up
amontonar *vt* **1** APILAR **:** to pile up, to heap up **2 :** to collect, to gather **3 :** to hoard — **amontonarse** *vr*
amor *nm* **1 :** love **2 :** loved one, beloved **3 amor propio :** self-esteem **4 hacer el amor :** to make love
amoral *adj* **:** amoral
amoratado, -da *adj* **:** black-and-blue, bruised, livid
amordazar {21} *vt* **1 :** to gag, to muzzle **2 :** to silence
amorfo, -fa *adj* **:** shapeless, amorphous
amorío *nm* **:** love affair, fling
amoroso, -sa *adj* **1 :** loving, affectionate **2 :** amorous <una mirada amorosa : an amorous glance> **3 :** charming, cute — **amorosamente** *adv*
amortiguación *nf* **:** cushioning, absorption
amortiguador *nm* **:** shock absorber
amortiguar {10} *vt* **:** to soften (an impact)
amortizar {21} *vt* **:** to amortize, to pay off — **amortización** *nf*
amotinado[1]**, -da** *adj* **:** rebellious, insurgent, mutinous
amotinado[2]**, -da** *n* **:** rebel, insurgent, mutineer
amotinamiento *nm* **:** uprising, rebellion
amotinar *vt* **:** to incite (to riot), to agitate — **amotinarse** *vr* **1 :** to riot, to rebel **2 :** to mutiny
amparar *vt* **:** to safeguard, to protect — **ampararse** *vr* **1 ~ de :** to take shelter from **2 ~ en :** to have recourse to
amparo *nm* ACOGIDA, REFUGIO **:** protection, refuge
amperímetro *nm* **:** ammeter

amperio *nm* : ampere

ampliable *adj* : expandable, enlargeable, extendible

ampliación *nf, pl* **-ciones** : expansion, extension

ampliar {85} *vt* **1** : to expand, to extend **2** : to widen **3** : to enlarge (photographs) **4** : to elaborate on, to develop (ideas)

amplificador *nm* : amplifier

amplificar {72} *vt* : to amplify — **amplificación** *nf*

amplio, -plia *adj* : broad, wide, ample — **ampliamente** *adj*

amplitud *nf* **1** : breadth, extent **2** : spaciousness

ampolla *nf* **1** : blister **2** : vial, ampoule

ampollar *vt* : to blister — **ampollarse** *vr*

ampolleta *nf* **1** : small vial **2** : hourglass **3** *Chile* : light bulb

ampulosidad *nf* : pompousness, bombast

ampuloso, -sa *adj* GRANDILOCUENTE : pompous, bombastic — **ampulosamente** *adv*

amputar *vt* : to amputate — **amputación** *nf*

amueblar *vt* : to furnish

amuleto *nm* TALISMÁN : amulet, charm

amurallar *vt* : to wall in, to fortify

anacardo *nm* : cashew nut

anaconda *nf* : anaconda

anacrónico, -ca *adj* : anachronistic

anacronismo *nm* : anachronism

ánade *nmf* **1** : duck **2 ánade real** : mallard

anagrama *nm* : anagram

anal *adj* : anal

anales *nmpl* : annals

analfabetismo *nm* : illiteracy

analfabeto, -ta *adj & n* : illiterate

analgésico[1], -ca *adj* : analgesic, painkilling

analgésico[2] *nm* : painkiller, analgesic

análisis *nm* : analysis

analista *nmf* **1** : analyst **2** : annalist

analítico, -ca *adj* : analytical, analytic — **analíticamente** *adv*

analizar {21} *vt* : to analyze

analogía *nf* : analogy

analógico, -ca *adj* **1** : analogical **2** : analog <computadora analógica : analog computer>

análogo, -ga *adj* : analogous, similar

ananá *or* **ananás** *nm, pl* **-nás** : pineapple

anaquel *nm* REPISA : shelf

anaranjado[1], -da *adj* NARANJA : orange-colored

anaranjado[2] *nm* NARANJA : orange (color)

anarquía *nf* : anarchy

anárquico, -ca *adj* : anarchic

anarquismo *nm* : anarchism

anarquista *adj & nmf* : anarchist

anatema *nm* : anathema

anatomía *nf* : anatomy — **anatomista** *nmf*

anatómico, -ca *adj* : anatomical — **anatómicamente** *adv*

anca *nm* **1** : haunch, hindquarter **2 ancas de rana** : frogs' legs

ancestral *adj* **1** : ancient, traditional **2** : ancestral

ancestro *nm* ASCENDIENTE : ancestor, forefather *m*

ancho[1], -cha *adj* **1** : wide, broad **2** : ample, loose-fitting

ancho[2] *nm* : width, breadth

anchoa *nf* : anchovy

anchura *nf* : width, breadth

ancianidad *nf* SENECTUD : old age

anciano[1], -na *adj* : aged, old, elderly

anciano[2], -na *n* : elderly person

ancla *nf* : anchor

ancladero *nm* → **anclaje**

anclaje *nm* : anchorage

anclar *v* FONDEAR : to anchor

andadas *nfpl* **1** : tracks **2 volver a las andadas** : to go back to one's old ways, to backslide

andador[1] *nm* **1** : walker, baby walker **2** *Mex* : walkway

andador[2], -dora *n* : walker, one who walks

andadura *nf* : course, journey <su agotadora andadura al campeonato : his exhausting journey to the championship>

andaluz, -luza *adj & n, mpl* **-luces** : Andalusian

andamiaje *nm* **1** : scaffolding **2** ESTRUCTURA : structure, framework

andamio *nm* : scaffold

andanada *nf* **1** : volley, broadside **2 soltar una andanada a** : to reprimand

andanzas *nfpl* : adventures

andar[1] {6} *vi* **1** CAMINAR : to walk **2** IR : to go, to travel **3** FUNCIONAR : to run, to function <el auto anda bien : the car runs well> **4** : to ride <andar a caballo : to ride on horseback> **5** : to be <anda sin dinero : he's broke> — *vt* : to walk, to travel

andar[2] *nm* : walk, gait

andas *nfpl* : stand (for a coffin), bier

andén *nm, pl* **andenes 1** : (train) platform **2** *CA, Col* : sidewalk

andino, -na *adj* : Andean

andorrano, -na *adj & n* : Andorran

andrajos *nmpl* : rags, tatters

andrajoso, -sa *adj* : ragged, tattered

andrógino, -na *adj* : androgynous

andurriales *nmpl* : remote place

anea *nf* : cattail

anduvo, etc. → **andar**

anécdota *nf* : anecdote

anecdótico, -ca *adj* : anecdotal

anegar {52} *vt* **1** INUNDAR : to flood **2** AHOGAR : to drown **3** : to overwhelm — **anegarse** *vr* : to be flooded

anejo *nm* → **anexo[2]**

anemia *nf* : anemia

anémico, -ca *adj* : anemic

anémona *nf* : anemone

anestesia *nf* : anesthesia

anestesiar *vt* : to anesthetize
anestésico[1], **-ca** *adj* : anesthetic
anestésico[2] *nm* : anesthetic
anestesista *nmf* : anesthetist
aneurisma *nmf* : aneurism
anexar *vt* : to annex, to attach
anexión *nf, pl* **-xiones** : annexation
anexo[1], **-xa** *adj* : attached, joined, annexed
anexo[2] *nm* **1** : annex **2** : supplement (to a book), appendix
anfetamina *nf* : amphetamine
anfibio[1], **-bia** *adj* : amphibious
anfibio[2] *nm* : amphibian
anfiteatro *nm* **1** : amphitheater **2** : lecture hall
anfitrión, -triona *n, mpl* **-triones** : host, hostess *f*
ánfora *nf* **1** : amphora **2** *Mex, Peru* : ballot box
ángel *nm* : angel
angelical *adj* : angelic, angelical
angina *nf* **1** *or* **angina de pecho** : angina **2** *Mex* : tonsil
anglicano, -na *adj & n* : Anglican
angloparlante[1] *adj* : English-speaking
angloparlante[2] *nmf* : English speaker
anglosajón, -jona *adj & n, mpl* **-jones** : Anglo-Saxon
angoleño, -ña *adj & n* : Angolan
angora *nf* : angora
angostar *vt* : to narrow — **angostarse** *vr*
angosto, -ta *adj* : narrow
angostura *nf* : narrowness
anguila *nf* : eel
angular *adj* : angular — **angularidad** *nf*
ángulo *nm* **1** : angle **2** : corner **3 ángulo muerto** : blind spot
anguloso, -sa *adj* : angular, sharp <una cara angulosa : an angular face> — **angulosidad** *nf*
angustia *nf* **1** CONGOJA : anguish, distress **2** : anxiety, worry
angustiar *vt* **1** : to anguish, to distress **2** : to worry — **angustiarse** *vr*
angustioso, -sa *adj* **1** : anguished, distressed **2** : distressing, worrisome
anhelante *adj* : yearning, longing
anhelar *vt* : to yearn for, to crave
anhelo *nm* : longing, yearning
anidar *vi* **1** : to nest **2** : to make one's home, to dwell — *vt* : to shelter
anillo *nm* SORTIJA : ring
ánima *n* ALMA : soul
animación *nf, pl* **-ciones** **1** : animation **2** VIVEZA : liveliness
animado, -da *adj* **1** : animated, lively **2** : cheerful — **animadamente** *adv*
animador, -dora *n* **1** : (television) host **2** : cheerleader
animadversión *nf, pl* **-siones** ANIMOSIDAD : animosity, antagonism
animal[1] *adj* **1** : animal **2** ESTÚPIDO : stupid, idiotic **3** : rough, brutish
animal[2] *nm* : animal
animal[3] *nmf* **1** IDIOTA : idiot, fool **2** : brute, beastly person
animar *vt* **1** ALENTAR : to encourage, to inspire **2** : to animate, to enliven **3** : to brighten up, to cheer up — **animarse** *vr*
anímico, -ca *adj* : mental <estado anímico : state of mind>
ánimo *nm* **1** ALMA : spirit, soul **2** : mood, spirits *pl* **3** : encouragement **4** PROPÓSITO : intention, purpose <sociedad sin ánimo de lucro : nonprofit organization> **5** : energy, vitality
animosidad *nf* ANIMADVERSIÓN : animosity, ill will
animoso, -sa *adj* : brave, spirited
aniñado, -da *adj* : childlike
aniquilación *nf* → **aniquilamiento**
aniquilamiento *nm* : annihilation, extermination
aniquilar *vt* **1** : to annihilate, to wipe out **2** : to overwhelm, to bring to one's knees — **aniquilarse** *vr*
anís *nm* **1** : anise **2 semilla de anís** : aniseed
aniversario *nm* : anniversary
ano *nm* : anus
anoche *adv* : last night
anochecer[1] {53} *v impers* : to get dark
anochecer[2] *nm* : dusk, nightfall
anodino, -na *adj* : insipid, dull
ánodo *nm* : anode
anomalía *nf* : anomaly
anómalo, -la *adj* : anomalous
anonadado, -da *adj* : dumbfounded, speechless
anonadar *vt* : to dumbfound, to stun
anonimato *nm* : anonymity
anónimo, -ma *adj* : anonymous — **anónimamente** *adv*
anorexia *nf* : anorexia
anoréxico, -ca *adj* : anorexic
anormal *adj* : abnormal — **anormalmente** *adv*
anormalidad *nf* : abnormality
anotación *nf, pl* **-ciones** **1** : annotation, note **2** : scoring (in sports) <lograron una anotación : they managed to score a goal>
anotar *vt* **1** : to annotate **2** APUNTAR, ESCRIBIR : to write down, to jot down **3** : to score (in sports) — *vi* : to score
anquilosado, -da *adj* **1** : stiff-jointed **2** : stagnated, stale
anquilosamiento *nm* **1** : stiffness (of joints) **2** : stagnation, paralysis
anquilosarse *vr* **1** : to stagnate **2** : to become stiff or paralyzed
anquilostoma *nm* : hookworm
ánsar *nm* : goose
ansarino *nm* : gosling
ansia *nf* **1** INQUIETUD : apprehensiveness, uneasiness **2** ANGUSTIA : anguish, distress **3** ANHELO : longing, yearning
ansiar {85} *vt* : to long for, to yearn for
ansiedad *nf* : anxiety
ansioso, -sa *adj* **1** : anxious, worried **2** : eager — **ansiosamente** *adv*
antagónico, -ca *adj* : conflicting, opposing
antagonismo *nm* : antagonism

antagonista[1] *adj* **:** antagonistic
antagonista[2] *nmf* **:** antagonist, opponent
antaño *adv* **:** yesteryear, long ago
antártico, -ca *adj* **1 :** antarctic **2 círculo antártico :** antarctic circle
ante[1] *nm* **1 :** elk, moose **2 :** suede
ante[2] *prep* **1 :** before, in front of **2 :** considering, in view of **3 ante todo :** first and foremost, above all
anteanoche *adv* **:** the night before last
anteayer *adv* **:** the day before yesterday
antebrazo *nm* **:** forearm
antecedente[1] *adj* **:** previous, prior
antecedente[2] *nm* **1 :** precedent **2 antecedentes** *nmpl* **:** record, background
anteceder *v* **:** to precede
antecesor, -sora *n* **1** ANTEPASADO **:** ancestor **2** PREDECESOR **:** predecessor
antedicho, -cha *adj* **:** aforesaid, above
antelación *nf, pl* **-ciones 1 :** advance notice **2 con ~ :** in advance, beforehand
antemano *adv* **de ~ :** in advance <se lo agradezco de antemano : I thank you in advance>
antena *nf* **:** antenna
antenoche → anteanoche
anteojera *nf* **1 :** eyeglass case **2 anteojeras** *nfpl* **:** blinders
anteojos *nmpl* GAFAS **:** glasses, eyeglasses
antepasado[1]**, -da** *adj* **:** before last <el domingo antepasado : the Sunday before last>
antepasado[2]**, -da** *n* ANTECESOR **:** ancestor
antepecho *nm* **1 :** guardrail **2 :** ledge, sill
antepenúltimo, -ma *adj* **:** third from last
anteponer {60} *vt* **1 :** to place before <anteponer al interés de la nación el interés de la comunidad : to place the interests of the community before national interest> **2 :** to prefer
anteproyecto *nm* **1 :** draft, proposal **2 anteproyecto de ley :** bill
antera *nf* **:** anther
anterior *adj* **1 :** previous **2 :** earlier <tiempos anteriores : earlier times> **3 :** anterior, forward, front
anterioridad *nf* **1 :** priority **2 con ~ :** beforehand, in advance
anteriormente *adv* **:** previously, beforehand
antes *adv* **1 :** before, earlier **2 :** formerly, previously **3 :** rather, sooner <antes prefiero morir : I'd rather die> **4 ~ de :** before, previous to <antes de hoy : before today> **5 antes que :** before <antes que llegue Luis : before Luis arrives> **6 cuanto antes :** as soon as possible **7 antes bien :** on the contrary
antesala *nf* **1 :** anteroom, waiting room, lobby **2 :** prelude, prologue
antiaborto, -ta *adj* **:** antiabortion
antiácido *nm* **:** antacid
antiadherente *adj* **:** nonstick
antiaéreo, -rea *adj* **:** antiaircraft
antiamericano, -na *adj* **:** anti-American
antibalas *adj* **:** bulletproof
antibiótico[1]**, -ca** *adj* **:** antibiotic
antibiótico[2] *nm* **:** antibiotic
antichoque *adj* **:** shockproof
anticipación *nf, pl* **-ciones 1 :** expectation, anticipation **2 con ~ :** in advance
anticipado, -da *adj* **1 :** advance, early **2 por ~ :** in advance
anticipar *vt* **1 :** to anticipate, to forestall, to deal with in advance **2 :** to pay in advance **— anticiparse** *vr* **1 :** to be early **2** ADELANTARSE **:** to get ahead
anticipo *nm* **1 :** advance (payment) **2 :** foretaste, preview
anticlerical *adj* **:** anticlerical
anticlimático, -ca : anticlimatic
anticlímax *nm* **:** anticlimax
anticomunismo *nm* **:** anticommunism
anticomunista *adj & nmf* **:** anticommunist
anticoncepción *nf, pl* **-ciones :** birth control, contraception
anticonceptivo *nm* **:** contraceptive
anticongelante *nm* **:** antifreeze
anticuado, -da *adj* **:** antiquated, outdated
anticuario[1]**, -ria** *adj* **:** antique, antiquarian
anticuario[2]**, -ria** *n* **:** antiquarian, antiquary
anticuario[3] *nm* **:** antique shop
anticuerpo *nm* **:** antibody
antidemocrático, -ca *adj* **:** antidemocratic
antideportivo, -va *adj* **:** unsportsmanlike
antidepresivo *nm* **:** antidepressant
antídoto *nm* **:** antidote
antidrogas *adj* **:** antidrug
antier → anteayer
antiestético, -ca *adj* **:** unsightly, unattractive
antifascista *adj & nmf* **:** antifascist
antifaz *nm, pl* **-faces :** mask
antifeminista *adj & nmf* **:** antifeminist
antífona *nf* **:** anthem
antígeno *nm* **:** antigen
antigualla *nf* **1 :** antique **2 :** relic, old thing
antiguamente *adv* **1 :** formerly, once **2 :** long ago
antigüedad *nf* **1 :** antiquity **2 :** seniority **3 :** age <con siglos de antigüedad : centuries-old> **4 antigüedades** *nfpl* **:** antiques
antiguo, -gua *adj* **1 :** ancient, old **2 :** former **3 :** old-fashioned <a la antigua : in the old-fashioned way>
antihigiénico, -ca *adj* INSALUBRE **:** unhygienic, unsanitary
antihistamínico *nm* **:** antihistamine
antiimperialismo *nm* **:** anti-imperialism

antiimperialista *adj & nmf* : anti-imperialist

antiinflacionario, -ria *adj* : anti-inflationary

antiinflamatorio, -ria *adj* : anti-inflammatory

antillano[1], -na *adj* CARIBEÑO : Caribbean, West Indian

antillano[2], -na *n* : West Indian

antílope *nm* : antelope

antimilitarismo *nm* : antimilitarism

antimilitarista *adj & nmf* : antimilitarist

antimonio *nm* : antimony

antimonopolista *adj* : antimonopoly, antitrust

antinatural *adj* : unnatural, perverse

antipatía *nf* : aversion, dislike

antipático, -ca *adj* : obnoxious, unpleasant

antipatriótico, -ca *adj* : unpatriotic

antirrábico, -ca *adj* : antirabies <vacuna antirrábica : rabies vaccine>

antirreglamentario, -ria *adj* **1** : unlawful, illegal **2** : foul (in sports)

antirrevolucionario, -ria *adj & n* : antirevolutionary

antirrobo, -ba *adj* : antitheft

antisemita *adj* : anti-Semitic

antisemitismo *nm* : anti-Semitism

antiséptico[1], -ca *adj* : antiseptic

antiséptico[2] *nm* : antiseptic

antisocial *adj* : antisocial

antitabaco *adj* : antismoking

antiterrorista *adj* : antiterrorist

antítesis *nf* : antithesis

antitoxina *nf* : antitoxin

antitranspirante *nm* : antiperspirant

antojadizo, -za *adj* CAPRICHOSO : capricious

antojarse *vr* **1** APETECER : to be appealing, to be desirable <se me antoja un helado : I feel like having ice cream> **2** : to seem, to appear <los árboles se antojaban fantasmas : the trees seemed like ghosts>

antojitos *nmpl Mex* : traditional Mexican snack foods

antojo *nm* **1** CAPRICHO : whim **2** : craving

antología *nf* **1** : anthology **2 de ~** *fam* : fantastic, incredible

antónimo *nm* : antonym

antonomasia *nf* **por ~** : par excellence

antorcha *nf* : torch

antracita *nf* : anthracite

antro *nm* **1** : cave, den **2** : dive, seedy nightclub

antropofagia *nf* CANIBALISMO : cannibalism

antropófago[1], -ga *adj* : cannibalistic

antropófago[2], -ga *n* CANÍBAL : cannibal

antropoide *adj & nmf* : anthropoid

antropología *nf* : anthropology

antropológico, -ca *adj* : anthropological

antropólogo, -ga *n* : anthropologist

anual *adj* : annual, yearly — **anualmente** *adv*

anualidad *nf* : annuity

anuario *nm* : yearbook, annual

anudar *vt* : to knot, to tie in a knot — **anudarse** *vr*

anuencia *nf* : consent

anulación *nf, pl* **-ciones** : annulment, nullification

anular *vt* : to annul, to cancel

anunciador, -dora *n* → **anunciante**

anunciante *nmf* : advertiser

anunciar *vt* **1** : to announce **2** : to advertise

anuncio *nm* **1** : announcement **2** : advertisement, commercial

anzuelo *nm* **1** : fishhook **2 morder el anzuelo** : to take the bait

añadido *nm* : addition

añadidura *nf* **1** : additive, addition **2 por ~** : in addition, furthermore

añadir *vt* **1** AGREGAR : to add **2** AUMENTAR : to increase

añejar *vt* : to age, to ripen

añejo, -ja *adj* **1** : aged, vintage **2** : age-old, musty, stale

añicos *nmpl* : smithereens, bits <hacer(se) añicos : to shatter>

añil *nm* **1** : indigo **2** : bluing

año *nm* **1** : year <en el año 1990 : in (the year) 1990> <tiene diez años : she is ten years old> **2** : grade <cuarto año : fourth grade> **3 año bisiesto** : leap year **4 año luz** : light-year **5 Año Nuevo** : New Year

añoranza *nf* : longing, yearning

añorar *vt* **1** DESEAR : to long for **2** : to grieve for, to miss — *vi* : to mourn, to grieve

añoso, -sa *adj* : aged, old

aorta *nf* : aorta

apabullante *adj* : overwhelming, crushing

apabullar *vt* : to overwhelm

apacentar {55} *vt* : to pasture, to put to pasture

apache *adj & nmf* : Apache

apachurrado, -da *adj fam* : depressed, down

apachurrar *vt* : to crush, to squash

apacible *adj* : gentle, mild, calm — **apaciblemente** *adv*

apaciguador, -dora *adj* : calming

apaciguamiento *nm* : appeasement

apaciguar {10} *vt* APLACAR : to appease, to pacify — **apaciguarse** *vr* : to calm down

apadrinar *vt* **1** : to be a godparent to **2** : to sponsor, to support

apagado, -da *adj* **1** : off, out <la luz está apagada : the light is off> **2** : dull, subdued

apagador *nm Mex* : switch

apagar {52} *vt* **1** : to turn off, to shut off **2** : to extinguish, to put out — **apagarse** *vr* **1** : to go out, to fade **2** : to wane, to die down

apagón *nm, pl* **-gones** : blackout (of power)

apalancamiento *nm* : leverage

apalancar {72} *vt* **1** : to jack up **2** : to pry open

apalear *vt* : to beat up, to thrash

apantallar *vt Mex* : to dazzle, to impress

apañar *vt* **1** : to seize, to grasp **2** : to repair, to mend — **apañarse** *vr* : to manage, to get along

apaño *nm fam* **1** : patch **2** HABILIDAD : skill, knack

apapachar *vt Mex fam* : to cuddle, to caress — **apapacharse** *vr*

aparador *nm* **1** : sideboard, cupboard **2** ESCAPARATE, VITRINA : shop window

aparato *nm* **1** : machine, appliance, apparatus <aparato auditivo : hearing aid> <aparato de televisión : television set> **2** : system <aparato digestivo : digestive system> **3** : display, ostentation <sin aparato : without ceremony> **4 aparatos** *nmpl* : braces (for the teeth)

aparatoso, -sa *adj* **1** : ostentatious **2** : spectacular

aparcamiento *nm Spain* **1** : parking **2** : parking lot

aparcar {72} *v Spain* : to park

aparcero, -ra *n* : sharecropper

aparear *vt* **1** : to mate (animals) **2** : to match up — **aparearse** *vr* : to mate

aparecer {53} *vi* **1** : to appear **2** PRESENTARSE : to show up **3** : to turn up, to be found — **aparecerse** *vr* : to appear

aparejado, -da *adj* **1 ir aparejado con** : to go hand in hand with **2 llevar aparejado** : to entail

aparejar *vt* **1** PREPARAR : to prepare, to make ready **2** : to harness (a horse) **3** : to fit out (a ship)

aparejo *nm* **1** : equipment, gear **2** : harness, saddle **3** : rig, rigging (of a ship)

aparentar *vt* **1** : to seem, to appear <no aparentas tu edad : you don't look your age> **2** FINGIR : to feign, to pretend

aparente *adj* **1** : apparent **2** : showy, striking — **aparentemente** *adv*

aparición *nf, pl* **-ciones 1** : appearance **2** PUBLICACIÓN : publication, release **3** FANTASMA : apparition, vision

apariencia *nf* **1** ASPECTO : appearance, look **2 en ~** : seemingly, apparently

apartado *nm* **1** : section, paragraph **2 apartado postal** : post office box

apartamento *nm* DEPARTAMENTO : apartment

apartar *vt* **1** ALEJAR : to move away, to put at a distance **2** : to put aside, to set aside, to separate — **apartarse** *vr* **1** : to step aside, to move away **2** DESVIARSE : to stray

aparte[1] *adv* **1** : apart, aside <modestia aparte : if I say so myself> **2** : separately **3 ~ de** : apart from, besides

aparte[2] *adj* : separate, special

aparte[3] *nm* : aside (in theater)

apartheid *nm* : apartheid

apasionado, -da *adj* : passionate, enthusiastic — **apasionadamente** *adv*

apasionante *adj* : fascinating, exciting

apasionar *vt* : to enthuse, to excite — **apasionarse** *vr*

apatía *nf* : apathy

apático, -ca *adj* : apathetic

apearse *vr* **1** DESMONTAR : to dismount **2** : to get out of or off (a vehicle)

apedrear *vt* : to stone, to throw stones at

apegado, -da *adj* : attached, close, devoted <es muy apegado a su familia : he is very devoted to his family>

apegarse {52} *vr* **~ a** : to become attached to, to grow fond of

apego *nm* AFICIÓN : attachment, fondness, inclination

apelación *nf, pl* **-ciones** : appeal (in court)

apelar *vi* **1** : to appeal **2 ~ a** : to resort to

apelativo *nm* APELLIDO : last name, surname

apellidarse *vr* : to have for a last name <¿cómo se apellida? : what is your last name?>

apellido *nm* : last name, surname

apelotonar *vt* : to roll into a ball, to bundle up

apenar *vt* : to aggrieve, to sadden — **apenarse** *vr* **1** : to be saddened **2** : to become embarrassed

apenas[1] *adv* : hardly, scarcely

apenas[2] *conj* : as soon as

apéndice *nm* **1** : appendix **2** : appendage

apendicectomía *nf* : appendectomy

apendicitis *nf* : appendicitis

apercibimiento *nm* **1** : preparation **2** AMONESTACIÓN : warning

apercibir *vt* **1** DISPONER : to prepare, to make ready **2** AMONESTAR : to warn **3** OBSERVAR : to observe, to perceive — **apercibirse** *vr* **1** : to get ready **2 ~ de** : to notice

aperitivo *nm* **1** : appetizer **2** : aperitif

apero *nm* : tool, implement

apertura *nf* **1** : opening, aperture **2** : commencement, beginning **3** : openness

apesadumbrar *vt* : to distress, to sadden — **apesadumbrarse** *vr* : to be weighed down

apestar *vt* **1** : to infect with the plague **2** : to corrupt — *vi* : to stink

apestoso, -sa *adj* : stinking, foul

apetecer {53} *vt* **1** : to crave, to long for <apeteció la fama : he longed for fame> **2** : to appeal to <me apetece un bistec : I feel like having a steak> <¿cuándo te apetece ir? : when do you want to go?> — *vi* : to be appealing

apetecible *adj* : appetizing, appealing

apetito *nm* : appetite

apetitoso, -sa *adj* : appetizing

apiario *nm* : apiary

ápice *nm* **1** : apex, summit **2** PIZCA : bit, smidgen

apicultor, -tora *n* : beekeeper

apicultura *nf* : beekeeping

apilar *vt* AMONTONAR : to heap up, to pile up — **apilarse** *vr*

apiñado, -da *adj* : jammed, crowded

apiñar *vt* : to pack, to cram — **apiñarse** *vr* : to crowd together, to huddle

apio *nm* : celery

apisonadora *nf* : steamroller

apisonar *vt* : to pack down, to tamp

aplacamiento *nm* : appeasement

aplacar {72} *vt* APACIGUAR : to appease, to placate — **aplacarse** *vr* : to calm down

aplanadora *nf* : steamroller

aplanar *vt* : to flatten, to level

aplastante *adj* : crushing, overwhelming

aplastar *vt* : to crush, to squash

aplaudir *v* : to applaud

aplauso *nm* **1** : applause, clapping **2** : praise, acclaim

aplazamiento *nm* : postponement

aplazar {21} *vt* : to postpone, to defer

aplicable *adj* : applicable — **aplicabilidad** *nf*

aplicación *nf, pl* **-ciones** **1** : application **2** : diligence, dedication

aplicado, -da *adj* : diligent, industrious

aplicador *nm* : applicator

aplicar {72} *vt* : to apply — **aplicarse** *vr* : to apply oneself

aplique *or* **apliqué** *nm* : appliqué

aplomar *vt* : to plumb, to make vertical

aplomo *nm* : aplomb, composure

apocado, -da *adj* : timid

apocalipsis *nms & pl* : apocalypse <el Libro del Apocalipsis : the Book of Revelation>

apocalíptico, -ca *adj* : apocalyptic

apocamiento *nm* : timidity

apocarse {72} *vr* **1** : to shy away, to be intimidated **2** : to humble oneself, to sell oneself short

apócrifo, -fa *adj* : apocryphal

apodar *vt* : to nickname, to call — **apodarse** *vr*

apoderado, -da *n* : proxy, agent

apoderar *vt* : to authorize, to empower — **apoderarse** *vr* **~ de** : to seize, to take over

apodo *nm* SOBRENOMBRE : nickname

apogeo *nm* : acme, peak, zenith

apología *nf* : defense, apology

apoplejía *nf* : apoplexy, stroke

apoplético, -ca *adj* : apoplectic

aporrear *vt* : to bang on, to beat, to bludgeon

aportación *nf, pl* **-ciones** : contribution

aportar *vt* CONTRIBUIR : to contribute, to provide

aporte *nm* → **aportación**

apostador, -dora *n* : bettor, better

apostar {19} *v* : to bet, to wager <I bet he's not coming : apuesto que no viene>

apostasía *nf* : apostasy

apóstata *nmf* : apostate

apostilla *nf* : note

apostillar *vt* : to annotate

apóstol *nm* : apostle

apostólico, -ca *adj* : apostolic

apóstrofe *nmf* : apostrophe

apostura *nf* : elegance, gracefulness

apoyacabezas *nms & pl* : headrest

apoyapiés *nms & pl* : footrest

apoyar *vt* **1** : to support, to back **2** : to lean, to rest — **apoyarse** *vr* **1 ~ en** : to lean on **2 ~ en** : to be based on, to rest on

apoyo *nm* : support, backing

apreciable *adj* : appreciable, substantial, considerable

apreciación *nf, pl* **-ciones** **1** : appreciation **2** : appraisal, evaluation

apreciar *vt* **1** ESTIMAR : to appreciate, to value **2** EVALUAR : to appraise, to assess — **apreciarse** *vr* : to appreciate, to increase in value

aprecio *nm* **1** ESTIMO : esteem, appreciation **2** EVALUACIÓN : appraisal, assessment

aprehender *vt* **1** : to apprehend, to capture **2** : to conceive of, to grasp

aprehensión *nf, pl* **-siones** : apprehension, capture, arrest

apremiante *adj* : pressing, urgent

apremiar *vt* INSTAR : to pressure, to urge — *vi* URGIR : to be urgent <el tiempo apremia : time is of the essence>

apremio *nm* : pressure, urgency

aprender *v* : to learn — **aprenderse** *vr*

aprendiz, -diza *n, mpl* **-dices** : apprentice, trainee

aprendizaje *nm* : apprenticeship

aprensión *nf, pl* **-siones** : apprehension, dread

aprensivo, -va *adj* : apprehensive, worried

apresamiento *nm* : seizure, capture

apresar *vt* : to capture, to seize

aprestar *vt* : to make ready, to prepare — **aprestarse** *vr* : to get ready

apresuradamente *adv* **1** : hurriedly **2** : hastily, too fast

apresurado, -da *adj* : hurried, in a rush

apresuramiento *nm* : hurry, haste

apresurar *vt* : to quicken, to speed up — **apresurarse** *vr* : to hurry up, to make haste

apretado, -da *adj* **1** : tight **2** *fam* : cheap, tightfisted — **apretadamente** *adv*

apretar {55} *vt* **1** : to press, to push (a button) **2** : to tighten **3** : to squeeze — *vi* **1** : to press, to push **2** : to fit tightly, to be too tight <los zapatos me aprietan : my shoes are tight>

apretón *nm, pl* **-tones** **1** : squeeze **2** **apretón de manos** : handshake

apretujar *vt* : to squash, to squeeze — **apretujarse** *vr*
aprieto *nm* APURO : predicament, difficulty <estar en un aprieto : to be in a fix>
aprisa *adv* : quickly, hurriedly
aprisionar *vt* **1** : to imprison **2** : to trap, to box in
aprobación *nf, pl* **-ciones** : approval, endorsement
aprobar {19} *vt* **1** : to approve of **2** : to pass (a law, an exam) — *vi* : to pass (in school)
aprobatorio, -ria *adj* : approving
apropiación *nf, pl* **-ciones** : appropriation
apropiado, -da *adj* : appropriate, proper, suitable — **apropiadamente** *adv*
apropiarse *vr* **~ de** : to take possession of, to appropriate
aprovechable *adj* : usable
aprovechado¹, -da *adj* **1** : diligent, hardworking **2** : pushy, opportunistic
aprovechado², -da *n* : pushy person, opportunist
aprovechamiento *nm* : use, exploitation
aprovechar *vt* : to take advantage of, to make good use of — *vi* **1** : to be of use **2** : to progress, to improve — **aprovecharse** *vr* **~ de** : to take advantage of, to exploit
aprovisionamiento *nm* : provisions *pl*, supplies *pl*
aprovisionar *vt* : to provide, to supply (with provisions)
aproximación *nf, pl* **-ciones** **1** : approximation, estimate **2** : rapprochement
aproximado, -da *adj* : approximate, estimated — **aproximadamente** *adv*
aproximar *vt* ACERCAR, ARRIMAR : to approximate, to bring closer — **aproximarse** *vr* ACERCARSE, ARRIMARSE : to approach, to move closer
aptitud *nf* : aptitude, capability
apto, -ta *adj* **1** : suitable, suited, fit **2** HÁBIL : capable, competent
apuesta *nf* : bet, wager
apuesto, -ta *adj* : elegant, good-looking
apuntador, -dora *n* : prompter
apuntalar *vt* : to prop up, to shore up
apuntar *vt* **1** : to aim, to point **2** ANOTAR : to write down, to jot down **3** INDICAR, SEÑALAR : to point to, to point out **4** : to prompt (in the theater) — *vi* **1** : to take aim **2** : to become evident — **apuntarse** *vr* **1** : to sign up, to enroll **2** : to score, to chalk up
apunte *nm* : note
apuñalar *vt* : to stab
apuradamente *adv* **1** : with difficulty **2** : hurriedly, hastily
apurado, -da *adj* **1** APRESURADO : rushed, pressured **2** : poor, needy **3** : difficult, awkward **4** : embarrassed
apurar *vt* **1** APRESURAR : to hurry, to rush **2** : to use up, to exhaust **3** : to trouble — **apurarse** *vr* **1** APRESURARSE : to hurry up **2** PREOCUPARSE : to worry
apuro *nm* **1** APRIETO : predicament, jam **2** : rush, hurry **3** : embarrassment
aquejar *vt* : to afflict
aquel, aquella *adj, mpl* **aquellos** : that, those
aquél, aquélla *pron, mpl* **aquéllos** **1** : that (one), those (ones) **2** : the former
aquello *pron* (*neuter*) : that, that matter, that business <aquello fue algo serio : that was something serious>
aquí *adv* **1** : here **2** : now <de aquí en adelante : from now on> **3 por ~** : around here, hereabouts
aquiescencia *nf* : acquiescence, approval
aquietar *vt* : to allay, to calm — **aquietarse** *vr* : to calm down
aquilatar *vt* **1** : to assay **2** : to assess, to size up
ara *nf* **1** : altar **2 en aras de** : in the interests of, for the sake of
árabe¹ *adj & nmf* : Arab, Arabian
árabe² *nm* : Arabic (language)
arabesco *nm* : arabesque — **arabesco, -ca** *adj*
arábigo, -ga *adj* **1** : Arabic, Arabian **2 número arábigo** : Arabic numeral
arable *adj* : arable
arado *nm* : plow
aragonés, -nesa *adj & n, mpl* **-neses** : Aragonese
arancel *nm* : tariff, duty
arándano *nm* : blueberry
arandela *nf* : washer (for a faucet, etc.)
araña *nf* **1** : spider **2** : chandelier
arañar *v* : to scratch, to claw
arañazo *nm* : scratch
arar *v* : to plow
arbitraje *nm* **1** : arbitration **2** : refereeing (in sports)
arbitrar *v* **1** : to arbitrate **2** : to referee, to umpire
arbitrariedad *nf* **1** : arbitrariness **2** INJUSTICIA : injustice, wrong
arbitrario, -ria *adj* **1** : arbitrary **2** : unfair, unjust — **arbitrariamente** *adv*
arbitrio *nm* **1** ALBEDRÍO : will **2** JUICIO : judgment
árbitro, -tra *n* **1** : arbitrator, arbiter **2** : referee, umpire
árbol *nm* **1** : tree **2 árbol genealógico** : family tree
arbolado¹, -da *adj* : wooded
arbolado² *nm* : woodland
arboleda *nf* : grove, wood
arbóreo, -rea *adj* : arboreal
arbusto *nm* : shrub, bush, hedge
arca *nf* **1** : ark **2** : coffer, chest
arcada *nf* **1** : arcade, series of arches **2 arcadas** *nfpl* : retching <hacer arcadas : to retch>
arcaico, -ca *adj* : archaic
arcángel *nm* : archangel
arcano, -na *adj* : arcane

arce *nm* **:** maple tree
arcén *nm, pl* **arcenes :** hard shoulder, berm
archidiócesis *nfs & pl* **:** archdiocese
archipiélago *nm* **:** archipelago
archivador *nm* **:** filing cabinet
archivar *vt* **1 :** to file **2 :** to archive
archivista *nmf* **:** archivist
archivo *nm* **1 :** file **2 :** archive, archives *pl*
arcilla *nf* **:** clay
arco *nm* **1 :** arch, archway **2 :** bow (in archery) **3 :** arc **4 :** wicket (in croquet) **5** PORTERÍA **:** goal, goalposts *pl* **6 arco iris :** rainbow
arder *vi* **1 :** to burn <el bosque está ardiendo : the forest is in flames> <arder de ira : to burn with anger, to be seething> **2 :** to smart, to sting, to burn <le ardía el estómago : he had heartburn>
ardid *nm* **:** scheme, ruse
ardiente *adj* **1 :** burning **2 :** ardent, passionate — **ardientemente** *adv*
ardilla *nf* **1 :** squirrel **2** *or* **ardilla listada :** chipmunk
ardor *nm* **1 :** heat **2 :** passion, ardor
ardoroso, -sa *adj* **:** heated, impassioned
arduo, -dua *adj* **:** arduous, grueling — **arduamente** *adv*
área *nf* **:** area
arena *nf* **1 :** sand <arena movediza : quicksand> **2 :** arena
arenga *nf* **:** harangue, lecture
arengar {52} *vt* **:** to harangue, to lecture
arenilla *nf* **1 :** fine sand **2 arenillas** *nfpl* **:** kidney stones
arenisca *nf* **:** sandstone
arenoso, -sa *adj* **:** sandy, gritty
arenque *nm* **:** herring
arepa *nf* **:** cornmeal bread
arete *nm* **:** earring
argamasa *nf* **:** mortar (cement)
argelino, -na *adj & n* **:** Algerian
argentino, -na *adj & n* **:** Argentinian, Argentine
argolla *nf* **:** hoop, ring
argón *nm* **:** argon
argot *nm* **:** slang
argucia *nf* **:** sophistry, subtlety
argüir {41} *vi* **:** to argue — *vt* **1** ARGUMENTAR **:** to contend, to argue **2** INFERIR **:** to deduce **3** PROBAR **:** to prove
argumentación *nf, pl* **-ciones :** line of reasoning, argument
argumentar *vt* **:** to argue, to contend
argumento *nm* **1 :** argument, reasoning **2 :** plot, story line
aria *nf* **:** aria
aridez *nf, pl* **-deces :** aridity, dryness
árido, -da *adj* **:** arid, dry
Aries *nmf* **:** Aries
ariete *nm* **:** battering ram
arisco, -ca *adj* **:** surly, sullen, unsociable
arista *nf* **1 :** ridge, edge **2 :** beard (of a plant) **3 aristas** *nfpl* **:** rough edges, complications, problems
aristocracia *nf* **:** aristocracy
aristócrata *nmf* **:** aristocrat
aristocrático, -ca *adj* **:** aristocratic
aritmética *nf* **:** arithmetic
aritmético, -ca *adj* **:** arithmetic, arithmetical — **aritméticamente** *adv*
arlequín *nm, pl* **-quines :** harlequin
arma *nf* **1 :** weapon **2 armas** *nfpl* **:** armed forces **3 arma de fuego :** firearm
armada *nf* **:** navy, fleet
armadillo *nm* **:** armadillo
armado, -da *adj* **1 :** armed **2 :** assembled, put together **3** *PRi* **:** obstinate, stubborn
armador, -dora *n* **:** shipowner
armadura *nf* **1 :** armor **2** ARMAZÓN **:** skeleton, framework
armamento *nm* **:** armament, arms *pl*, weaponry
armar *vt* **1 :** to assemble, to put together **2 :** to create, to cause <armar un escándalo : to cause a scene> **3 :** to arm — **armarse** *vr* **armarse de valor :** to steel oneself
armario *nm* **1** CLÓSET, ROPERO **:** closet **2** ALACENA **:** cupboard
armatoste *nm fam* **:** monstrosity, contraption
armazón *nmf, pl* **-zones 1** ESQUELETO **:** framework, skeleton <armazón de acero : steel framework> **2 :** frames *pl* (of eyeglasses)
armenio, -nia *adj & n* **:** Armenian
armería *nf* **1 :** armory **2 :** arms museum **3 :** gunsmith's shop **4 :** gunsmith's craft
armiño *nm* **:** ermine
armisticio *nm* **:** armistice
armonía *nf* **:** harmony
armónica *nf* **:** harmonica
armónico, -ca *adj* **1 :** harmonic **2 :** harmonious — **armónicamente** *adv*
armonioso, -sa *adj* **:** harmonious — **armoniosamente** *adv*
armonizar {21} *vt* **1 :** to harmonize **2 :** to reconcile — *vi* **:** to harmonize, to blend together
arnés *nm, pl* **arneses :** harness
aro *nm* **1 :** hoop **2 :** napkin ring **3** *Arg, Chile, Uru* **:** earring
aroma *nm* **:** aroma, scent
aromático, -ca *adj* **:** aromatic
arpa *nf* **:** harp
arpegio *nm* **:** arpeggio
arpía *nf* **:** shrew, harpy
arpista *nmf* **:** harpist
arpón *nm, pl* **arpones :** harpoon — **arponear** *vt*
arquear *vt* **:** to arch, to bend — **arquearse** *vr* **:** to bend, to bow
arqueología *nf* **:** archaeology
arqueológico, -ca *adj* **:** archaeological
arqueólogo, -ga *n* **:** archaeologist
arquero, -ra *n* **1 :** archer **2** PORTERO **:** goalkeeper, goalie

arquetípico, -ca *adj* : archetypal
arquetipo *nm* : archetype
arquitecto, -ta *n* : architect
arquitectónico, -ca *adj* : architectural — **aquitectónicamente** *adv*
arquitectura *nf* : architecture
arrabal *nm* **1** : slum **2 arrabales** *nmpl* : outskirts, outlying area
arracada *nf* : hoop earring
arracimarse *vr* : to cluster together
arraigado, -da *adj* : deep-seated, ingrained
arraigar {52} *vi* : to take root, to become established — **arraigarse** *vr*
arraigo *nm* : roots *pl* <con mucho arraigo : deep-rooted>
arrancar {72} *vt* **1** : to pull out, to tear out **2** : to pick, to pluck (a flower) **3** : to start (an engine) **4** : to boot (a computer) — *vi* **1** : to start an engine **2** : to get going — **arrancarse** *vr* : to pull out, to pull off
arrancón *nm, pl* **-cones** *Mex* **1** : sudden loud start (of a car) **2 carrera de arrancones** : drag race
arranque *nm* **1** : starter (of a car) **2** ARREBATO : outburst, fit **3 punto de arranque** : beginning, starting point
arrasar *vt* **1** : to level, to smooth **2** : to devastate, to destroy **3** : to fill to the brim
arrastrar *vt* **1** : to drag, to tow **2** : to draw, to attract — *vi* : to hang down, to trail — **arrastrarse** *vr* **1** : to crawl **2** : to grovel
arrastre *nm* **1** : dragging **2** : pull, attraction **3 red de arrastre** : dragnet, trawling net
arrayán *nm, pl* **-yanes 1** MIRTO : myrtle **2 arrayán brabántico** : bayberry, wax myrtle
arrear *vt* : to urge on, to drive — *vi* : to hurry along
arrebatado, -da *adj* **1** PRECIPITADO : impetuous, hotheaded, rash **2** : flushed, blushing
arrebatar *vt* **1** : to snatch, to seize **2** CAUTIVAR : to captivate — **arrebatarse** *vr* : to get carried away (with anger, etc.)
arrebato *nm* ARRANQUE : fit, outburst
arreciar *vi* : to intensify, to worsen
arrecife *nm* : reef
arreglado, -da *adj* **1** : fixed, repaired **2** : settled, sorted out **3** : neat, tidy **4** : smart, dressed-up
arreglar *vt* **1** COMPONER : to repair, to fix **2** : to tidy up <arregla tu cuarto : pick up your room> **3** : to solve, to work out <quiero arreglar este asunto : I want to settle this matter> — **arreglarse** *vr* **1** : to get dressed (up) <arreglarse el pelo : to get one's hair done> **2 arreglárselas** *fam* : to get by, to manage
arreglo *nm* **1** : repair **2** : arrangement **3** : agreement, understanding
arrellanarse *vr* : to settle (in a chair)
arremangarse {52} *vr* : to roll up one's sleeves
arremeter *vi* EMBESTIR : to attack, to charge
arremetida *nf* EMBESTIDA : attack, onslaught
arremolinarse *vr* **1** : to crowd around, to mill about **2** : to swirl (about)
arrendador, -dora *n* **1** : landlord, landlady *f* **2** : tenant, lessee
arrendajo *nm* : jay
arrendamiento *nm* **1** ALQUILER : rental, leasing **2 contrato de arrendamiento** : lease
arrendar {55} *vt* ALQUILAR : to rent, to lease
arrendatario, -ria *n* : tenant, lessee, renter
arreos *nmpl* GUARNICIONES : tack, harness, trappings
arrepentido, -da *adj* : repentant, remorseful
arrepentimiento *nm* : regret, remorse, repentance
arrepentirse {76} *vr* **1** : to regret, to be sorry **2** : to repent
arrestar *vt* DETENER : to arrest, to detain
arresto *nm* **1** DETENCIÓN : arrest **2 arrestos** *nmpl* : boldness, daring
arriate *nm Mex, Spain* : bed (for plants), border
arriba *adv* **1** : up, upwards **2** : above, overhead **3** : upstairs **4 ~ de** : more than **5 de arriba abajo** : from top to bottom, from head to foot
arribar *vi* **1** : to arrive **2** : to dock, to put into port
arribista *nmf* : parvenu, upstart
arribo *nm* : arrival
arriendo *nm* ARRENDAMIENTO : rent, rental
arriero, -ra *n* : mule driver, muleteer
arriesgado, -da *adj* **1** : risky **2** : bold, daring
arriesgar {52} *vt* : to risk, to venture — **arriesgarse** *vr* : to take a chance
arrimado, -da *n Mex fam* : sponger, freeloader
arrimar *vt* ACERCAR, APROXIMAR : to bring closer, to draw near — **arrimarse** *vr* ACERCARSE, APROXIMARSE : to approach, to get close
arrinconar *vt* **1** ACORRALAR : to corner, to box in **2** : to push aside, to abandon
arroba *nf* : arroba (Spanish unit of measurement)
arrobamiento *nm* : rapture, ecstasy
arrobar *vt* : to enrapture, to enchant — **arrobarse** *vr*
arrocero[1]**, -ra** *adj* : rice
arrocero[2]**, -ra** *n* : rice grower
arrodillarse *vr* : to kneel (down)
arrogancia *nf* ALTANERÍA, ALTIVEZ : arrogance, haughtiness
arrogante *adj* ALTANERO, ALTIVO : arrogant, haughty
arrogarse {52} *vr* : to usurp, to arrogate

arrojado, -da *adj* **:** daring, fearless
arrojar *vt* **1 :** to hurl, to cast, to throw **2 :** to give off, to spew out **3 :** to yield, to produce **4** *fam* **:** to vomit — **arrojarse** *vr* PRECIPITARSE **:** to throw oneself, to leap
arrojo *nm* **:** boldness, fearlessness
arrollador, -dora *adj* **:** sweeping, overwhelming
arrollar *vt* **1 :** to sweep away, to carry away **2 :** to crush, to overwhelm **3 :** to run over (with a vehicle)
arropar *vt* **:** to clothe, to cover (up) — **arroparse** *vr*
arrostrar *vt* **:** to confront, to face (up to)
arroyo *nm* **1** RIACHUELO **:** brook, creek, stream **2 :** gutter
arroz *nm, pl* **arroces :** rice
arrozal *nm* **:** rice field, rice paddy
arruga *nf* **:** wrinkle, fold, crease
arrugado, -da *adj* **:** wrinkled, creased, lined
arrugar {52} *vt* **:** to wrinkle, to crease, to pucker — **arrugarse** *vr*
arruinar *vt* **:** to ruin, to wreck — **arruinarse** *vr* **1 :** to be ruined **2 :** to fall into ruin, to go bankrupt
arrullar *vt* **:** to lull to sleep — *vi* **:** to coo
arrullo *nm* **1 :** lullaby **2 :** coo (of a dove)
arrumaco *nm fam* **:** kissing, cuddling
arrumbar *vt* **1 :** to lay aside, to put away **2 :** to floor, to leave speechless
arsenal *nm* **:** arsenal
arsénico *nm* **:** arsenic
arte *nmf* (*usually m in singular, f in plural*) **1 :** art <artes y oficios : arts and crafts> <bellas artes : fine arts> **2** HABILIDAD **:** skill **3 :** cunning, cleverness
artefacto *nm* **1 :** artifact **2** DISPOSITIVO **:** device
artemisa *nf* **:** sagebrush
arteria *nf* **:** artery — **arterial** *adj*
arteriosclerosis *nf* **:** arteriosclerosis, hardening of the arteries
artero, -ra *adj* **:** wily, crafty
artesanal *adj* **:** pertaining to crafts or craftsmanship, handmade
artesanía *nm* **1 :** craftsmanship **2 :** handicrafts *pl*
artesano, -na *n* **:** artisan, craftsman *m,* craftsperson
artesiano, -na *adj* **:** artesian <pozo artesiano : artesian well>
ártico, -ca *adj* **:** arctic
articulación *nf, pl* **-ciones 1 :** articulation, pronunciation **2** COYUNTURA **:** joint
articular *vt* **1 :** to articulate, to utter **2 :** to connect with a joint **3 :** to coordinate, to orchestrate
articulista *nmf* **:** columnist
artículo *nm* **1 :** article, thing **2 :** item, feature, report **3 artículo de comercio :** commodity **4 artículos de primera necesidad :** essentials **5 artículos de tocador :** toiletries
artífice *nmf* **1** ARTESANO **:** artisan **2 :** mastermind, architect
artificial *adj* **1 :** artificial, man-made **2 :** feigned, false — **artificialmente** *adv*
artificio *nm* **1** HABILIDAD **:** skill **2** APARATO **:** device, appliance **3** ARDID **:** artifice, ruse
artificioso, -sa *adj* **1 :** skillful **2 :** cunning, deceptive
artillería *nf* **:** artillery
artillero, -ra *n* **:** artilleryman *m,* gunner
artilugio *nm* **:** gadget, contraption
artimaña *nf* **:** ruse, trick
artista *nmf* **1 :** artist **2** ACTOR, ACTRIZ **:** actor, actress *f*
artístico, -ca *adj* **:** artistic — **artísticamente** *adv*
artrítico, -ca *adj* **:** arthritic
artritis *nms & pl* **:** arthritis
artrópodo *nm* **:** arthropod
arveja *nf* GUISANTE **:** pea
arzobispado *nm* **:** archbishopric
arzobispo *nm* **:** archbishop
as *nm* **:** ace
asa *nf* AGARRADERA, ASIDERO **:** handle, grip
asado¹, -da *adj* **:** roasted, grilled, broiled
asado² *nm* **1 :** roast **2 :** barbecued meat **3 :** barbecue, cookout
asador *nm* **:** spit, rotisserie
asaduras *nfpl* **:** entrails, offal
asalariado¹, -da *adj* **:** wage-earning, salaried
asalariado², -da *n* **:** wage earner
asaltante *nmf* **1 :** mugger, robber **2 :** assailant
asaltar *vt* **1 :** to assault **2 :** to mug, to rob **3 asaltar al poder :** to seize power
asalto *nm* **1 :** assault **2 :** mugging, robbery **3 :** round (in boxing) **4 asalto al poder :** coup d'etat
asamblea *nf* **:** assembly, meeting
asambleísta *nmf* **:** assemblyman *m,* assemblywoman *f*
asar *vt* **:** to roast, to grill — **asarse** *vr fam* **:** to roast, to be dying from heat
asbesto *nm* **:** asbestos
ascendencia *nf* **1 :** ancestry, descent **2 ~ sobre :** influence over
ascendente *adj* **:** ascending, upward <un curso ascendente : an upward trend>
ascender {56} *vi* **1 :** to ascend, to rise up **2 :** to be promoted <ascendió a gerente : she was promoted to manager> **3 ~ a :** to amount to, to reach <las deudas ascienden a 20 millones de pesos : the debt amounts to 20 million pesos> — *vt* **:** to promote
ascendiente¹ *nmf* ANCESTRO **:** ancestor
ascendiente² *nm* INFLUENCIA **:** influence, ascendancy

ascensión *nf, pl* **-siones 1 :** ascent, rise **2 Fiesta de la Ascensión :** Ascension Day

ascenso *nm* **1 :** ascent, rise **2 :** promotion

ascensor *nm* ELEVADOR **:** elevator

asceta *nmf* **:** ascetic

ascético, -ca *adj* **:** ascetic

ascetismo *nm* **:** asceticism

asco *nm* **1 :** disgust <¡qué asco! : that's disgusting!, how revolting!> **2 darle asco (a alguien) :** to sicken, to revolt **3 estar hecho un asco :** to be filthy **4 hacerle ascos a :** to turn up one's nose at

ascua *nf* **1** BRASA **:** ember **2 estar en ascuas** *fam* **:** to be on edge

asear *vt* **1 :** to wash, to clean **2 :** to tidy up — **asearse** *vr*

asechanza *nf* **:** snare, trap

asechar *vt* **:** to set a trap for

asediar *vt* **1** SITIAR **:** to besiege **2** ACOSAR **:** to harass

asedio *nm* **1 :** siege **2** ACOSO **:** harassment

asegurador[1], -dora *adj* **1 :** insuring, assuring **2 :** pertaining to insurance

asegurador[2], -dora *n* **:** insurer, underwriter

aseguradora *nf* **:** insurance company

asegurar *vt* **1 :** to assure **2 :** to secure **3 :** to insure — **asegurarse** *vr* **1** CERCIORARSE **:** to make sure **2 :** to take out insurance, to insure oneself

asemejar *vt* **1 :** to make similar <ese bigote te asemeja a tu abuelo : that mustache makes you look like your grandfather> **2** *Mex* **:** to be similar to, to resemble — **asemejarse** *vr* **~ a :** to be look like, to resemble

asentaderas *nfpl fam* **:** bottom, buttocks *pl*

asentado, -da *adj* **:** settled, established

asentamiento *nm* **:** settlement

asentar {55} *vt* **1 :** to lay down, to set down, to place **2 :** to settle, to establish **3** *Mex* **:** to state, to affirm — **asentarse** *vr* **1 :** to settle **2** ESTABLECERSE **:** to settle down, to establish oneself

asentimiento *nm* **:** assent, consent

asentir {76} *vi* **:** to consent, to agree

aseo *nm* **:** cleanliness

aséptico, -ca *adj* **:** aseptic, germ-free

asequible *adj* ACCESIBLE **:** accessible, attainable

aserción *nf* → **aserto**

aserradero *nm* **:** sawmill

aserrar {55} *vt* **:** to saw

aserrín *nm, pl* **-rrines :** sawdust

aserto *nm* **:** assertion, affirmation

asesinar *vt* **1 :** to murder **2 :** to assassinate

asesinato *nm* **1 :** murder **2 :** assassination

asesino[1], -na *adj* **:** murderous, homicidal

asesino[2], -na *n* **1 :** murderer, killer **2 :** assassin

asesor, -sora *n* **:** advisor, consultant

asesoramiento *nm* **:** advice, counsel

asesorar *vt* **:** to advise, to counsel — **asesorarse** *vr* **~ de :** to consult

asesoría *nf* **1 :** consulting, advising **2 :** consultant's office

asestar {55} *vt* **1 :** to aim, to point (a weapon) **2 :** to deliver, to deal (a blow)

aseveración *nf, pl* **-ciones :** assertion, statement

aseverar *vt* **:** to assert, to state

asexual *adj* **:** asexual — **asexualmente** *adv*

asfaltado[1], -da *adj* **:** asphalted, paved

asfaltado[2] *nm* PAVIMENTO **:** pavement, asphalt

asfaltar *vt* **:** to pave, to blacktop

asfalto *nm* **:** asphalt

asfixia *nf* **:** asphyxia, asphyxiation, suffocation

asfixiar *vt* **:** to asphyxiate, to suffocate, to smother — **asfixiarse** *vr*

asga, etc. → **asir**

así[1] *adv* **1 :** like this, like that **2 :** so, thus <así sea : so be it> **3 ~ de :** so, about so <una caja así de grande : a box about so big> **4 así que :** so, therefore **5 ~ como :** as well as **6 así así :** so-so, fair

así[2] *adj* **:** such, such a <un talento así es inestimable : a talent like that is priceless>

así[3] *conj* AUNQUE **:** even if, even though <no irá, así le paguen : he won't go, even if they pay him>

asiático[1], -ca *adj* **:** Asian, Asiatic

asiático[2], -ca *n* **:** Asian

asidero *nm* **1** AGARRADA, ASA **:** grip, handle **2** AGARRE **:** grip, hold

asiduamente *adv* **:** regularly, frequently

asiduidad *nf* **1 :** assiduousness **2 :** regularity, frequency

asiduo, -dua *adj* **1 :** assiduous **2 :** frequent, regular

asiento *nm* **1 :** seat, chair <asiento trasero : back seat> **2 :** location, site

asignación *nf, pl* **-ciones 1 :** allocation **2 :** appointment, designation **3 :** allowance, pay **4** *PRi* **:** homework, assignment

asignar *vt* **1 :** to assign, to allocate **2 :** to appoint

asignatura *nf* MATERIA **:** subject, course

asilado, -da *n* **:** exile, refugee

asilo *nm* **:** asylum, refuge, shelter

asimetría *nf* **:** asymmetry

asimétrico, -ca *adj* **:** asymmetrical, asymmetric

asimilación *nf, pl* **-ciones :** assimilation

asimilar *vt* **:** to assimilate — **asimilarse** *vr* **~ a :** to be similar to, to resemble

asimismo *adv* **1** IGUALMENTE **:** similarly, likewise **2** TAMBIÉN **:** as well, also

asir {7} *vt* : to seize, to grasp — **asirse** *vr* ~ **a** : to cling to

asistencia *nf* **1** : attendance **2** : assistance **3** : assist (in sports)

asistente[1] *adj* : attending, in attendance

asistente[2] *nmf* **1** : assistant **2 los asistentes** : those present, those in attendance

asistir *vi* : to attend, to be present <asistir a clase : to attend class> — *vt* : to aid, to assist

asma *nf* : asthma

asmático, -ca *adj* : asthmatic

asno *nm* BURRO : ass, donkey

asociación *nf, pl* **-ciones 1** : association, relationship **2** : society, group, association

asociado[1], **-da** *adj* : associate, associated

asociado[2], **-da** *n* : associate, partner

asociar *vt* **1** : to associate, to connect **2** : to pool (resources) **3** : to take into partnership — **asociarse** *vr* **1** : to become partners **2** ~ **a** : to join, to become a member of

asolar {19} *vt* : to devastate, to destroy

asoleado, -da *adj* : sunny

asolear *vt* : to put in the sun — **asolearse** *vr* : to sunbathe

asomar *vt* : to show, to stick out — *vi* : to appear, to become visible — **asomarse** *vr* **1** : to show, to appear **2** : to lean out, to look out <se asomó por la ventana : he leaned out the window>

asombrar *vt* MARAVILLAR : to amaze, to astonish — **asombrarse** *vr* : to marvel, to be amazed

asombro *nm* : amazement, astonishment

asombroso, -sa *adj* : amazing, astonishing — **asombrosamente** *adv*

asomo *nm* **1** : hint, trace **2 ni por asomo** : by no means

aspa *nf* : blade (of a fan or propeller)

aspaviento *nm* : exaggerated movement, fuss, flounce

aspecto *nm* **1** : aspect **2** APARIENCIA : appearance, look

aspereza *nf* RUDEZA : roughness, coarseness

áspero, -ra *adj* : rough, coarse, abrasive — **ásperamente** *adv*

aspersión *nf, pl* **-siones** : sprinkling

aspersor *nm* : sprinkler

aspiración *nf, pl* **-ciones 1** : inhalation, breathing in **2** ANHELO : aspiration, desire

aspiradora *nf* : vacuum cleaner

aspirante *nmf* : applicant, candidate

aspirar *vi* ~ **a** : to aspire to — *vt* : to inhale, to breathe in

aspirina *nf* : aspirin

asquear *vt* : to sicken, to disgust

asquerosidad *nf* : filth, foulness

asqueroso, -sa *adj* : disgusting, sickening, repulsive — **asquerosamente** *adv*

asta *nf* **1** : flagpole <a media asta : at half-mast> **2** : horn, antler **3** : shaft (of a weapon)

ástaco *nm* : crayfish

astado, -da *adj* : horned

áster *nm* : aster

asterisco *nm* : asterisk

asteroide *nm* : asteroid

astigmatismo *nm* : astigmatism

astil *nm* : shaft (of an arrow or feather)

astilla *nf* **1** : splinter, chip **2 de tal palo, tal astilla** : like father, like son

astillar *vt* : to splinter — **astillarse** *vr*

astillero *nm* : dry dock, shipyard

astral *adj* : astral

astringente *adj & nm* : astringent — **astringencia** *nf*

astro *nm* **1** : heavenly body **2** : star

astrología *nf* : astrology

astrológico, -ca *adj* : astrological

astrólogo, -ga *n* : astrologer

astronauta *nmf* : astronaut

astronáutica *nf* : astronautics

astronautico, -ca *adj* : astronautic, astronautical

astronave *nf* : spaceship

astronomía *nf* : astronomy

astronómico, -ca *adj* : astronomical — **astronómicamente** *adv*

astrónomo, -ma *n* : astronomer

astroso, -sa *adj* DESALIÑADO : slovenly, untidy

astucia *nf* **1** : astuteness, shrewdness **2** : cunning, guile

astuto, -ta *adj* **1** : astute, shrewd **2** : crafty, tricky — **astutamente** *adv*

asueto *nm* : time off, break

asumir *vt* **1** : to assume, to take on <asumir el cargo : to take office> **2** SUPONER : to assume, to suppose

asunción *nf, pl* **-ciones** : assumption

asunto *nm* **1** CUESTIÓN, TEMA : affair, matter, subject **2 asuntos** *nmpl* : affairs, business

asustadizo, -za *adj* : nervous, jumpy, skittish

asustado, -da *adj* : frightened, afraid

asustar *vt* ESPANTAR : to scare, to frighten — **asustarse** *vr*

atacante *nmf* : assailant, attacker

atacar {72} *v* : to attack

atado[1], **-da** *adj* : shy, inhibited

atado[2] *nm* **1** : bundle, bunch **2** *Arg* : pack (of cigarettes)

atadura *nf* LIGADURA : tie, bond

atajar *vt* **1** IMPEDIR : to block, to stop **2** INTERRUMPIR : to interrupt, to cut off **3** CONTENER : to hold back, to restrain — *vi* ~ **por** : to take a shortcut through

atajo *nm* : shortcut

atalaya *nf* **1** : watchtower **2** : vantage point

atañer {79} *vi* (*3rd person only*) : to concern, to have to do with <eso no me atañe : that does not concern me>

ataque *nm* **1** : attack, assault **2** : fit <ataque de risa : fit of laughter> **3 ataque de nervios** : nervous breakdown **4 ataque cardíaco** *or* **ataque al corazón :** heart attack

atar *vt* AMARRAR **:** to tie, to tie up, to tie down — **atarse** *vr*

atarantado, -da *adj fam* **1 :** restless **2 :** dazed, stunned

atarantar *vt fam* **:** to daze, to stun

atarazana *nf* **:** shipyard

atardecer[1] {53} *v impers* **:** to get dark

atardecer[2] *v impers* **:** late afternoon, dusk

atareado, -da *adj* **:** busy, overworked

atascar {72} *vt* **1** ATORAR **:** to block, to clog, to stop up **2 :** to hinder — **atascarse** *vr* **1 :** to become obstructed **2 :** to get bogged down **3** PARARSE **:** to stall

atasco *nm* **1 :** blockage **2** EMBOTELLAMIENTO **:** traffic jam

ataúd *nm* **:** coffin, casket

ataviar {85} *vt* **:** to dress, to clothe — **ataviarse** *vr* **:** to dress up

atavío *nm* ATUENDO **:** dress, attire

ateísmo *nm* **:** atheism

atemorizar {21} *vt* **:** to frighten, to intimidate — **atemorizarse** *vr*

atemperar *vt* **:** to temper, to moderate

atención[1] *nf, pl* **-ciones 1 :** attention **2 poner atención** *or* **prestar atención :** to pay attention **3 llamar la atención :** to attract attention **4 en atención a :** in view of

atención[2] *interj* **1 :** attention! **2 :** watch out!

atender {56 } *vt* **1 :** to help, to wait on **2 :** to look after, to take care of **3 :** to heed, to listen to — *vi* **:** to pay attention

atenerse {80} *vr* **:** to abide <tendrás que atenerte a las reglas : you will have to abide by the rules>

atentado *nm* **:** attack, assault

atentamente *adv* **1 :** attentively, carefully **2** (*used in correspondence*) **:** sincerely, sincerely yours

atentar {55} *vi* **~ contra :** to make an attempt on, to threaten <atentaron contra su vida : they made an attempt on his life>

atento, -ta *adj* **1 :** attentive, mindful **2** CORTÉS **:** courteous

atenuación *nf, pl* **-ciones 1 :** lessening **2 :** understatement

atenuante[1] *adj* **:** extenuating, mitigating

atenuante[2] *nmf* **:** extenuating circumstance, excuse

atenuar {3} *vt* **1** MITIGAR **:** to extenuate, to mitigate **2 :** to dim (light), to tone down (colors) **3 :** to minimize, to lessen

ateo[1], **atea** *adj* **:** atheistic

ateo[2], **atea** *n* **:** atheist

aterciopelado, -da *adj* **:** velvety, downy

aterido, -da *adj* **:** freezing, frozen

aterrador, -dora *adj* **:** terrifying

aterrar {55} *vt* **:** to terrify, to frighten

aterrizaje *nm* **:** landing (of a plane)

aterrizar {21} *vi* **:** to land, to touch down

aterrorizar {21} *vt* **1 :** to terrify **2 :** to terrorize — **aterrorizarse** *vr* **:** to be terrified

atesorar *vt* **:** to hoard, to amass

atestado, -da *adj* **:** crowded, packed

atestar {55} *vt* **1** ATIBORRAR **:** to crowd, to pack **2 :** to witness, to testify to — *vi* **:** to testify

atestiguar {10} *vt* **:** to testify to, to bear witness to — *vi* DECLARAR **:** to testify

atiborrar *vt* **:** to pack, to crowd — **atiborrarse** *vr* **:** to stuff oneself

ático *nm* **1 :** penthouse **2** BUHARDILLA, DESVÁN **:** attic

atigrado, -da *adj* **:** tabby (of cats), striped (of fur)

atildado, -da *adj* **:** smart, neat, dapper

atildar *vt* **1 :** to put a tilde over **2 :** to clean up, to smarten up — **atildarse** *vr* **:** to get spruced up

atinar *vi* ACERTAR **:** to be accurate, to be on target

atingencia *nf* **:** bearing, relevance

atípico, -ca *adj* **:** atypical

atiplado, -da *adj* **:** shrill, high-pitched

atirantar *vt* **:** to make taut, to tighten

atisbar *vt* **1 :** to spy on, to watch **2 :** to catch a glimpse of, to make out

atisbo *nm* **:** glimpse, sign, hint

atizador *nm* **:** poker (for a fire)

atizar {21} *vt* **1 :** to poke, to stir, to stoke (a fire) **2 :** to stir up, to rouse **3** *fam* **:** to give, to land (a blow)

atlántico, -ca *adj* **:** Atlantic

atlas *nm* **:** atlas

atleta *nmf* **:** athlete

atlético, -ca *adj* **:** athletic

atletismo *nm* **:** athletics

atmósfera *nf* **:** atmosphere

atmosférico, -ca *adj* **:** atmospheric

atole *nm Mex* **1 :** thick hot beverage prepared with corn flour **2 darle atole con el dedo (a alguien) :** to string (someone) along

atollarse *vr* **:** to get stuck, to get bogged down

atolón *nm, pl* **-lones :** atoll

atolondrado, -da *adj* **1** ATURDIDO **:** bewildered, dazed **2** DESPISTADO **:** scatterbrained, absentminded

atómico, -ca *adj* **:** atomic

atomizador *nm* **:** atomizer

atomizar {21} *vt* FRAGMENTAR **:** to fragment, to break into bits

átomo *nm* **:** atom

atónito, -ta *adj* **:** astonished, amazed

atontar *vt* **1 :** to stupefy **2 :** to bewilder, to confuse

atorar *vt* ATASCAR **:** to block, to clog — **atorarse** *vr* **1** ATASCARSE **:** to get stuck **2** ATRAGANTARSE **:** to choke

atormentador, -dora *n* **:** tormenter

atormentar *vt* **:** to torment, to torture — **atormentarse** *vr* **:** to torment oneself, to agonize

atornillar *vt* **:** to screw (in, on, down)

atorrante *nmf Arg* **:** bum, loafer
atosigar {52} *vt* **:** to harass, to annoy
atracadero *nm* **:** dock, pier
atracador, -dora *n* **:** robber, mugger
atracar {72} *vi* **:** to dock, to land — *vt* **:** to hold up, to rob, to mug — **atracarse** *vr fam* **~ de :** to gorge oneself with
atracción *nf, pl* **-ciones :** attraction
atraco *nm* **:** holdup, robbery
atractivo[1], -va *adj* **:** attractive
atractivo[2] *nm* **:** attraction, appeal, charm
atraer {81} *vt* **:** to attract — **atraerse** *vr* **1 :** to attract (each other) **2** GANARSE **:** to gain, to win
atragantarse *vr* **:** to choke (on food)
atrancar {72} *vt* **:** to block, to bar — **atrancarse** *vr*
atrapada *nf* **:** catch
atrapar *vt* **:** to trap, to capture
atrás *adv* **1** DETRÁS **:** back, behind <se quedó atrás : he stayed behind> **2** ANTES **:** ago <mucho tiempo atrás : long ago> **3 para ~** *or* **hacia ~ :** backwards, toward the rear **4 ~ de :** in back of, behind
atrasado, -da *adj* **1 :** late, overdue **2 :** backwards **3 :** old-fashioned **4 :** slow (of a clock or watch)
atrasar *vt* **:** to delay, to put off — *vi* **:** to lose time — **atrasarse** *vr* **:** to fall behind
atraso *nm* **1** RETRASO **:** lateness, delay <llegó con 20 minutos de atraso : he was 20 minutes late> **2 :** backwardness **3 atrasos** *nmpl* **:** arrears
atravesar {55} *vt* **1** CRUZAR **:** to cross, to go across **2 :** to pierce **3 :** to lay across **4 :** to go through (a situation or crisis) — **atravesarse** *vr* **1 :** to be in the way <se me atravesó : it blocked my path> **2 :** to interfere, to meddle
atrayente *adj* **:** attractive
atreverse *vr* **1 :** to dare **2 :** to be insolent
atrevido, -da *adj* **1 :** bold, daring **2 :** insolent
atrevimiento *nm* **1 :** daring, boldness **2 :** insolence
atribución *nf, pl* **-ciones :** attribution
atribuible *adj* IMPUTABLE **:** attributable, ascribable
atribuir {41} *vt* **1 :** to attribute, to ascribe **2 :** to grant, to confer — **atribuirse** *vr* **:** to take credit for
atribular *vt* **:** to afflict, to trouble — **atribularse** *vr*
atributo *nm* **:** attribute
atril *nm* **:** lectern, stand
atrincherar *vt* **:** to entrench — **atrincherarse** *vr* **1 :** to dig in, to entrench oneself **2 ~ en :** to hide behind
atrio *nm* **1 :** atrium **2 :** portico
atrocidad *nf* **:** atrocity
atrofia *nf* **:** atrophy
atrofiar *v* **:** to atrophy
atronador, -dora *adj* **:** thunderous, deafening
atropellado, -da *adj* **1 :** rash, hasty **2 :** brusque, abrupt
atropellamiento *nm* → **atropello**
atropellar *vt* **1 :** to knock down, to run over **2 :** to violate, to abuse — **atropellarse** *vr* **:** to rush through (a task), to trip over one's words
atropello *nm* **:** abuse, violation, outrage
atroz *adj, pl* **atroces :** atrocious, appalling — **atrozamente** *adv*
atuendo *nm* ATAVÍO **:** attire, costume
atufar *vt* **:** to vex, to irritate — **atufarse** *vr* **1 :** to get angry **2 :** to smell bad, to stink
atún *nm, pl* **atunes :** tuna fish, tuna
aturdimiento *nm* **:** bewilderment, confusion
aturdir *vt* **1 :** to stun, to shock **2 :** to bewilder, to confuse, to stupefy
atuvo, etc. → **atenerse**
audacia *nf* OSADÍA **:** boldness, audacity
audaz *adj, pl* **audaces :** bold, audacious, daring — **audazmente** *adv*
audible *adj* **:** audible
audición *nf, pl* **-ciones 1 :** hearing **2 :** audition
audiencia *nf* **:** audience
audífono *nm* **1 :** hearing aid **2 audífonos** *nmpl* **:** headphones, earphones
audio *nm* **:** audio
audiovisual *adj* **:** audiovisual
auditar *vt* **:** to audit
auditivo, -va *adj* **:** auditory, hearing, aural <aparato auditivo : hearing aid>
auditor, -tora *n* **:** auditor
auditoría *nf* **:** audit
auditorio *nm* **1 :** auditorium **2 :** audience
auge *nm* **1 :** peak, height **2 :** boom, upturn
augurar *vt* **:** to predict, to foretell
augurio *nm* AGÜERO, PRESAGIO **:** augury, omen
augusto, -ta *adj* **:** august
aula *nf* **:** classroom
aullar {8} *vi* **:** to howl, to wail
aullido *nm* **:** howl, wail
aumentar *vt* ACRECENTAR **:** to increase, to raise — *vi* **:** to rise, to increase, to grow
aumento *nm* INCREMENTO **:** increase, rise
aun *adv* **1 :** even <ni aun en coche llegaría a tiempo : I wouldn't arrive on time even if I drove> **2 aun así :** even so **3 aun más :** even more
aún *adv* **1** TODAVÍA **:** still, yet <¿aún no ha llegado el correo? : the mail still hasn't come?> **2 más aún :** furthermore
aunar {8} *vt* **:** to join, to combine — **aunarse** *vr* **:** to unite
aunque *conj* **1 :** though, although, even if, even though **2 aunque sea :** at least
aura *nf* **1 :** aura **2 :** turkey buzzard
áureo, -rea *adj* **:** golden

aureola *nf* 1 : halo 2 : aura (of power, fame, etc.)
aurícula *nf* : auricle
auricular *nm* : telephone receiver
aurora *nf* 1 : dawn 2 **aurora boreal** : aurora borealis
ausencia *nf* : absence
ausentarse *vr* 1 : to leave, to go away 2 ~ **de** : to stay away from
ausente[1] *adj* : absent, missing
ausente[2] *nmf* 1 : absentee 2 : missing person
auspiciar *vt* 1 PATROCINAR : to sponsor 2 FOMENTAR : to foster, to promote
auspicios *nmpl* : sponsorship, auspices
austeridad *nf* : austerity
austero, -ra *adj* : austere
austral[1] *adj* : southern
austral[2] *nm* : former monetary unit of Argentina
australiano, -na *adj & n* : Australian
austriaco *or* **austríaco, -ca** *adj & n* : Austrian
autenticar {72} *vt* : to authenticate — **autenticación** *nf*
autenticidad *nf* : authenticity
auténtico, -ca *adj* : authentic — **auténticamente** *adv*
autentificar {72} *vt* : to authenticate — **autentificación** *nf*
autismo *nm* : autism
autista *adj* : autistic
auto *nm* : auto, car
autoayuda *nf* : self-help
autobiografía *nf* : autobiography
autobiográfico, -ca *adj* : autobiographical
autobús *nm, pl* **-buses** : bus
autocompasión *nf* : self-pity
autocontrol *nm* : self-control
autocracia *nf* : autocracy
autócrata *nmf* : autocrat
autocrático, -ca *adj* : autocratic
autóctono, -na *adj* : indigenous, native <arte autóctono : indigenous art>
autodefensa *nf* : self-defense
autodestrucción *nf* : self-destruction — **autodestructivo, -va** *adj*
autodeterminación *nf* : self-determination
autodidacta *adj* : self-taught
autodisciplina *nf* : self-discipline
autoestima *nf* : self-esteem
autogobierno *nm* : self-government
autografiar *vt* : to autograph
autógrafo *nm* : autograph
autoinfligido, -da *adj* : self-inflicted
automación *nf* → **automatización**
autómata *nm* : automaton
automático, -ca *adj* : automatic — **automáticamente** *adv*
automatización *nf* : automation
automatizar {21} *vt* : to automate
automotor, -tora *adj* 1 : self-propelled 2 : automotive, car
automotriz[1] *adj, pl* **-trices** : automotive, car
automotriz[2] *nf, pl* **-trices** : car dealership
automóvil *nm* : automobile
automovilista *nmf* : motorist
automovilístico, -ca *adj* : automobile, car <accidente automovilístico : automobile accident>
autonombrado, -da *adj* : self-appointed
autonomía *nf* : autonomy
autónomo, -ma *adj* : autonomous — **autónomamente** *adv*
autopista *nf* : expressway, highway
autopropulsado, -da *adj* : self-propelled
autopsia *nf* : autopsy
autor, -tora *n* 1 : author 2 : perpetrator
autoría *nf* : authorship
autoridad *nf* : authority
autoritario, -ria *adj* : authoritarian
autorización *nf, pl* **-ciones** : authorization
autorizado, -da *adj* 1 : authorized 2 : authoritative
autorizar {21} *vt* : to authorize, to approve
autorretrato *nm* : self-portrait
autoservicio *nm* 1 : self-service restaurant 2 SUPERMERCADO : supermarket
autostop *nm* 1 : hitchhiking 2 **hacer autostop** : to hitchhike
autostopista *nmf* : hitchhiker
autosuficiencia *nf* : self-sufficiency — **autosuficiente** *adj*
auxiliar[1] *vt* : to aid, to assist
auxiliar[2] *adj* : assistant, auxiliary
auxiliar[3] *nmf* 1 : assistant, helper 2 **auxiliar de vuelo** : flight attendant
auxilio *nm* 1 : aid, assistance 2 **primeros auxilios** : first aid
aval *nm* : guarantee, endorsement
avalancha *nf* ALUD : avalanche
avalar *vt* : to guarantee, to endorse
avaluar {3} *vt* : to evaluate, to appraise
avalúo *nm* : appraisal, evaluation
avance *nm* ADELANTO : advance
avanzado, -da *adj* 1 : advanced 2 : progressive
avanzar {21} *v* : to advance, to move forward
avaricia *nf* CODICIA : greed, avarice
avaricioso, -sa *adj* : avaricious, greedy
avaro[1], **-ra** *adj* : miserly, greedy
avaro[2], **-ra** *n* : miser
avasallador, -dora *adj* : overwhelming
avasallamiento *nm* : subjugation, domination
avasallar *vt* : to overpower, to subjugate
ave *nf* 1 : bird 2 **aves de corral** : poultry 3 **ave rapaz** *or* **ave de presa** : bird of prey
avecinarse *vr* : to approach, to come near
avecindarse *vr* : to settle, to take up residence
avellana *nf* : hazelnut, filbert
avena *nf* 1 : oat, oats *pl* 2 : oatmeal

avenencia *nf* : agreement, pact
avenida *nf* : avenue
avenir {87} *vt* : to reconcile, to harmonize — **avenirse** *vr* **1** : to agree, to come to terms **2** : to get along
aventajado, -da *adj* : outstanding
aventajar *vt* **1** : to be ahead of, to lead **2** : to surpass, to outdo
aventar {55} *vt* **1** : to fan **2** : to winnow **3** *Col, Mex* : to throw, to toss — **aventarse** *vr* **1** *Col, Mex* : to hurl oneself **2** *Mex fam* : to dare, to take a chance
aventón *nm, pl* **-tones** *Col, Mex fam* : ride, lift
aventura *nf* **1** : adventure **2** RIESGO : venture, risk **3** : love affair
aventurado, -da *adj* : hazardous, risky
aventurar *vt* : to venture, to risk — **aventurarse** *vr* : to take a risk
aventurero[1], -ra *adj* : adventurous
aventurero[2], -ra *n* : adventurer
avergonzado, -da *adj* **1** : ashamed **2** : embarrassed
avergonzar {9} *vt* APENAR : to shame, to embarrass — **avergonzarse** *vr* APENARSE : to be ashamed, to be embarrassed
avería *nf* **1** : damage **2** : breakdown, malfunction
averiado, -da *adj* **1** : damaged, faulty **2** : broken down
averiar {85} *vt* : to damage — **averiarse** *vr* : to break down
averiguación *nf, pl* **-ciones** : investigation, inquiry
averiguar {10} *vt* **1** : to find out, to ascertain **2** : to investigate
aversión *nf, pl* **-siones** : aversion, dislike
avestruz *nm, pl* **-truces** : ostrich
avezado, -da *adj* : seasoned, experienced
aviación *nf, pl* **-ciones** : aviation
aviador, -dora *n* : aviator, flyer
aviar {85} *vt* **1** : to prepare, to make ready **2** : to tidy up **3** : to equip, to supply
avicultor, -tora *n* : poultry farmer
avicultura *nf* : poultry farming
avidez *nf, pl* **-deces** : eagerness
ávido, -da *adj* : eager, avid — **ávidamente** *adv*
avieso, -sa *adj* **1** : twisted, distorted **2** : wicked, depraved
avinagrado, -da *adj* : vinegary, sour
avío *nm* **1** : preparation, provision **2** : loan (for agriculture or mining) **3** **avíos** *nmpl* : gear, equipment
avión *nm, pl* **aviones** : airplane
avioneta *nf* : light airplane
avisar *vt* **1** : to notify, to inform **2** : to advise, to warn
aviso *nm* **1** : notice **2** : advertisement, ad **3** ADVERTENCIA : warning **4** **estar sobre aviso** : to be on the alert
avispa *nf* : wasp
avispado, -da *adj fam* : clever, sharp
avispero *nm* : wasps' nest
avispón *nm, pl* **-pones** : hornet
avistar *vt* : to sight, to catch sight of
avituallar *vt* : to suppy with food, to provision
avivar *vt* **1** : to enliven, to brighten **2** : to strengthen, to intensify
avizorar *vt* **1** ACECHAR : to spy on, to watch **2** : to observe, to perceive <se avizoran dificultades : difficulties are expected>
axila *nf* : underarm, armpit
axioma *nm* : axiom
axiomático, -ca *adj* : axiomatic
ay *interj* **1** : oh! **2** : ouch!, ow!
ayer[1] *adv* : yesterday
ayer[2] *nm* ANTAÑO : yesteryear, days gone by
ayote *nm CA, Mex* : squash, pumpkin
ayuda *nf* **1** : help, assistance **2** **ayuda de cámara** : valet
ayudante *nmf* : helper, assistant
ayudar *vt* : to help, to assist — **ayudarse** *vr* **~ de** : to make use of
ayunar *vi* : to fast
ayunas *nfpl* **en ~** : fasting <este medicamento ha de tomarse en ayunas : this medication should be taken on an empty stomach>
ayuno *nm* : fast
ayuntamiento *nm* **1** : town hall, city hall **2** : town or city council
azabache *nm* : jet <negro azabache : jet black>
azada *nf* : hoe
azafata *nf* **1** : stewardess *f* **2** : hostess *f* (on a TV show)
azafrán *nm, pl* **-franes** **1** : saffron **2** : crocus
azahar *nm* : orange blossom
azalea *nf* : azalea
azar *nm* **1** : chance <juegos de azar : games of chance> **2** : accident, misfortune **3** **al azar** : at random, randomly
azaroso, -sa *adj* **1** : perilous, hazardous **2** : turbulent, eventful
azimut *nm* : azimuth
azogue *nm* : mercury, quicksilver
azorar *vt* **1** : to alarm, to startle **2** : to fluster, to embarrass — **azorarse** *vr* : to get embarrassed
azotar *vt* **1** : to whip, to flog **2** : to lash, to batter **3** : to devastate, to afflict
azote *nm* **1** LÁTIGO : whip, lash **2** *fam* : spanking, licking **3** : calamity, scourge
azotea *nf* : flat roof, terraced roof
azteca *adj & nmf* : Aztec
azúcar *nmf* : sugar — **azucarar** *vt*
azucarado, -da *adj* : sweetened, sugary
azucarera *nf* : sugar bowl
azucarero, -ra *adj* : sugar <industria azucarera : sugar industry>
azucena *nf* : white lily
azuela *nf* : adz
azufre *nm* : sulphur — **azufroso, -sa** *adj*

azul *adj & nm* : blue

azulado, -da *adj* : bluish

azulejo *nm* : ceramic tile, floor tile

azulete *nm* : bluing

azuloso, -sa *adj* : bluish

azur[1] *adj* CELESTE : azure

azur[2] *n* CELESTE : azure, sky blue

azuzar {21} *vt* : to incite, to egg on

B

b *nf* : second letter of the Spanish alphabet

baba *nf* **1** : spittle, saliva **2** : dribble, drool (of a baby) **3** : slime, ooze

babear *vi* **1** : to drool, to slobber **2** : to ooze

babel *nf* : babel, chaos, bedlam

babero *nm* : bib

babor *nm* : port, port side

babosa *nf* : slug (mollusk)

babosada *nf CA, Mex* : silly act or remark

baboso, -sa *adj* **1** : drooling, slobbering **2** : slimy **3** *CA, Mex fam* : silly, dumb

babucha *nf* : slipper

babuino *nm* : baboon

bacalao *nm* : cod (fish)

bache *nm* **1** : pothole **2** *PRi* : deep puddle **3** : bad period, rough time <bache económico : economic slump>

bachiller *nmf* : high school graduate

bachillerato *nm* : high school diploma

bacilo *nm* : bacillus

backgammon *nm* : backgammon

bacon *nm Spain* : bacon

bacteria *nf* : bacterium

bacteriano, -na *adj* : bacterial

bacteriología *nf* : bacteriology

bacteriológico, -ca *adj* : bacteriologic, bacteriological

bacteriólogo, -ga *n* : bacteriologist

báculo *nm* **1** : staff, stick **2** : comfort, support

badajo *nm* : clapper (of a bell)

badén *nm, pl* **badenes 1** : (paved) ford, channel **2** : dip, ditch (in a road)

bádminton *nm* : badminton

bafle *or* **baffle** *nm* **1** : baffle **2** : speaker, loudspeaker

bagaje *nm* **1** EQUIPAJE : baggage, luggage **2** : background <bagaje cultural : cultural baggage>

bagatela *nf* : trifle, trinket

bagre *nm* : catfish

bahía *nf* : bay

bailar *vt* : to dance — *vi* **1** : to dance **2** : to spin **3** : to be loose, to be too big

bailarín[1], **-rina** *adj, mpl* **-rines 1** : dancing **2** : fond of dancing

bailarín[2], **-rina** *n, mpl* **-rines 1** : dancer **2** : ballet dancer, ballerina *f*

baile *nm* **1** : dance **2** : dance party, ball **3 llevarse al baile a** *Mex fam* : to take for a ride, to take advantage of

baja *nf* **1** DESCENSO : fall, drop **2** : slump, recession **3** : loss, casualty **4 dar de baja** : to discharge, to dismiss **5 darse de baja** : to withdraw, to drop out

bajada *nf* **1** : descent **2** : dip, slope **3** : decrease, drop

bajar *vt* **1** DESCENDER : to lower, to let down, to take down **2** REDUCIR : to reduce (prices) 3 INCLINAR : to lower, to bow (the head) **4** : to go down, to descend **5 bajar de categoría** : to downgrade — *vi* **1** : to drop, to fall **2** : to come down, to go down **3** : to ebb (of tides) — **bajarse** *vr* **~ de** : to get off, to get out of (a vehicle)

bajeza *nf* **1** : low or despicable act **2** : baseness

bajío *nm* **1** : lowland **2** : shoal, sandbank, shallows

bajista *nmf* : bass player, bassist

bajo[1] *adv* **1** : down, low **2** : softly, quietly <habla más bajo : speak more softly>

bajo[2], **-ja** *adj* **1** : low **2** : short (of stature) **3** : soft, faint, deep (of sounds) **4** : lower <el bajo Amazonas : the lower Amazon> **5** : lowered <con la mirada baja : with lowered eyes> **6** : base, vile **7 los bajos fondos** : the underworld

bajo[3] *nm* **1** : bass (musical instrument) **2** : first floor, ground floor **3** : hemline

bajo[4] *prep* : under, beneath, below

bajón *nm, pl* **bajones** : sharp drop, slump

bajorrelieve *m* : bas-relief

bala *nf* **1** : bullet **2** : bale

balacera *nf* TIROTEO : shoot-out, gunfight

balada *nf* : ballad

balance *nm* **1** : balance **2** : balance sheet

balancear *vt* **1** : to balance **2** : to swing (one's arms, etc.) **3** : to rock (a boat) — **balancearse** *vr* **1** OSCILAR : to swing, to sway, to rock **2** VACILAR : to hesitate, to vacillate

balanceo *nm* **1** : swaying, rocking **2** : vacillation

balancín *nm, pl* **-cines 1** : rocking chair **2** SUBIBAJA : seesaw

balandra *nf* : sloop

balanza *nf* BÁSCULA : scales *pl,* balance

balar *vi* : to bleat

balaustrada *nf* : balustrade

balaustre *nm* : baluster

balazo *nm* **1** TIRO : shot, gunshot **2** : bullet wound

balboa *nf* : balboa (monetary unit of Panama)

balbucear *vi* **1** : to mutter, to stammer **2** : to prattle, to babble <los niños están balbuceando : the children are prattling away>

balbuceo *nm* : mumbling, stammering

balbucir → **balbucear**

balcánico, -ca *adj* : Balkan

balcón *nm, pl* **balcones** : balcony

balde *nm* **1** CUBO : bucket, pail **2 en ~** : in vain, to no avail

baldío[1], -día *adj* **1** : fallow, uncultivated **2** : useless, vain

baldío[2] *nm* **1** : wasteland **2** *Mex* : vacant lot

baldosa *nf* LOSETA : floor tile

balear *vt* : to shoot, to shoot at

balero *nm* **1** *Mex* : ball bearing **2** *Mex, PRi* : cup-and-ball toy

balido *nm* : bleat

balín *nm, pl* **balines** : pellet

balística *nf* : ballistics

balístico, -ca *adj* : ballistic

baliza *nf* **1** : buoy **2** : beacon (for aircraft)

ballena *nf* : whale

ballenero[1], -ra *adj* : whaling

ballenero[2], -ra *n* : whaler

ballenero[3] *nm* : whaleboat, whaler

ballesta *nf* **1** : crossbow **2** : spring (of an automobile)

ballet *nm* : ballet

balneario *nm* : spa, bathing resort

balompié *nm* FUTBOL : soccer

balón *nm, pl* **balones** : ball

baloncesto *nm* BASQUETBOL : basketball

balsa *nf* **1** : raft **2** : balsa

balsámico, -ca *adj* : soothing

bálsamo *nm* : balsam, balm

báltico, -ca *adj* : Baltic

baluarte *nm* BASTIÓN : bulwark, bastion

bambolear *vi* **1** : to sway, to swing **2** : to wobble — **bambolearse** *vr*

bamboleo *nm* **1** : swaying, swinging **2** : wobbling

bambú *nm, pl* **bambúes** *or* **bambús** : bamboo

banal *adj* : banal, trivial

banalidad *nf* : banality

banana *nf* : banana

bananero[1], -ra *adj* : banana

bananero[2] *nm* : banana tree

banano *nm* **1** : banana tree **2** *CA,Col* : banana

banca *nf* **1** : banking **2** BANCO : bench

bancada *nf* **1** : group, faction **2** : workbench

bancal *nm* **1** : terrace (in agriculture) **2** : plot (of land)

bancario, -ria *adj* : bank, banking

bancarrota *nf* QUIEBRA : bankruptcy

banco *nm* **1** : bank <banco central : central bank> <banco de datos : data bank> <banco de arena : sandbank> <banco de sangre : blood bank> **2** BANCA : stool, bench **3** : pew **4** : school (of fish)

banda *nf* **1** : band, strip **2** *Mex* : belt <banda transportadora : conveyor belt> **3** : band (of musicians) **4** : gang (of persons), flock (of birds) **5 banda de rodadura** : tread (of a tire, etc.) **6 banda sonora** *or* **banda de sonido** : sound track

bandada *nf* : flock (of birds), school (of fish)

bandazo *nm* : swerving, lurch

bandearse *vr* : to look after oneself, to cope

bandeja *nf* : tray, platter

bandera *nf* : flag, banner

banderazo *nm* : starting signal (in sports)

banderilla *nf* : banderilla, dart (in bullfighting)

banderín *nm, pl* **-rines** : pennant, small flag

bandidaje *nm* : banditry

bandido, -da *n* BANDOLERO : bandit, outlaw

bando *nm* **1** FACCIÓN : faction, side **2** EDICTO : proclamation

bandolerismo *nm* : banditry

bandolero, -ra *n* BANDIDO : bandit, outlaw

banjo *nm* : banjo

banquero, -ra *n* : banker

banqueta *nf* **1** : footstool, stool, bench **2** *Mex* : sidewalk

banquete *nm* : banquet

banquetear *v* : to feast

banquillo *nm* **1** : bench (in sports) **2** : dock, defendant's seat

bañadera *nf* → **bañera**

bañar *vt* **1** : to bathe, to wash **2** : to immerse, to dip **3** : to coat, to cover <bañado en lágrimas : bathed in tears> — **bañarse** *vr* **1** : to take a bath, to bathe **2** : to go for a swim

bañera *nf* TINA : bathtub

bañista *nmf* : bather

baño *nm* **1** : bath **2** : swim, dip **3** : bathroom **4 baño María** : double-boiler

baqueta *nf* **1** : ramrod **2 baquetas** *nfpl* : drumsticks

bar *nm* : bar, tavern

baraja *nf* : deck of cards

barajar *vt* **1** : to shuffle (cards) **2** : to consider, to toy with

baranda *nf* : rail, railing

barandal *nm* **1** : rail, railing **2** : bannister, handrail

barandilla *nf Spain* : bannister, handrail, railing

barata *nf* **1** *Mex* : sale, bargain **2** *Chile* : cockroach

baratija *nf* : bauble, trinket

baratillo *nm* : rummage sale, flea market

barato[1] *adv* : cheap, cheaply <te lo vendo barato : I'll sell it to you cheap>

barato[2], -ta *adj* : cheap, inexpensive

baratura *nf* **1** : cheapness **2** : cheap thing

barba *nf* **1** : beard, stubble **2** : chin

barbacoa *nf* : barbecue

bárbaramente *adv* : barbarously
barbaridad *nf* **1** : barbarity, atrocity **2** **¡qué barbaridad!** : that's outrageous!
barbarie *nf* : barbarism, savagery
bárbaro[1] *adv fam* : wildly <anoche lo pasamos bárbaro : we had a wild time last night>
bárbaro[2], **-ra** *adj* **1** : barbarous, wild, uncivilized **2** *fam* : great, fantastic
bárbaro[3], **-ra** *n* : barbarian
barbecho *nm* : fallow land <dejar en barbecho : to leave fallow>
barbero, -ra *n* : barber
barbilla *nf* MENTÓN : chin
barbitúrico *nm* : barbiturate
barbudo[1], **-da** *adj* : bearded
barbudo[2] *nm* : bearded man
barca *nf* **1** : boat **2** **barca de pasaje** : ferryboat
barcaza *nf* : barge
barcia *nf* : chaff
barco *nm* **1** BARCA : boat **2** BUQUE, NAVE : ship
bardo *nm* : bard
bario *nm* : barium
barítono *nm* : baritone
barlovento *nm* : windward
barman *nm* : bartender
barniz *nm, pl* **barnices** **1** LACA : varnish, lacquer **2** : glaze (on ceramics, etc.)
barnizar {21} *vt* **1** : to varnish **2** : to glaze
barométrico, -ca *adj* : barometric
barómetro *nm* : barometer
barón *nm, pl* **barones** : baron
baronesa *nf* : baroness
baronet *nm* : baronet
barquero, -ra : boatman *m,* boatwoman *f*
barquillo *nm* : wafer, thin cookie or cracker
barra *nf* : bar
barraca *nf* **1** CABAÑA, CHOZA : hut, cabin **2** : booth, stall
barracuda *nf* : barracuda
barranca *nf* **1** : hillside, slope **2** → **barranco**
barranco *nm* : ravine, gorge
barredora *nf* : street sweeper (machine)
barrena *nf* **1** TALADRO : drill, auger, gimlet **2** : tailspin
barrenar *vt* **1** : to drill **2** : to undermine
barrendero, -ra *n* : sweeper, street cleaner
barrer *v* : to sweep — **barrerse** *vr* : to slide (in sports)
barrera *nf* OBSTÁCULO : barrier, obstacle <barrera de sonido : sound barrier>
barreta *nf* : crowbar
barriada *nf* **1** : district, quarter **2** : slums *pl*
barrica *nf* BARRIL, TONEL : barrel, cask, keg
barricada *nf* : barricade
barrida *nf* **1** : sweep **2** : slide (in sports)
barrido *nm* : sweeping
barriga *nf* PANZA : belly, paunch
barrigón, -gona *adj, mpl* **-gones** *fam* : potbellied, paunchy
barril *nm* **1** BARRICA : barrel, keg **2** **cerveza de barril** : draft beer
barrio *nm* **1** : neighborhood, district **2** **barrios bajos** : slums *pl*
barro *nm* **1** LODO : mud **2** ARCILLA : clay **3** ESPINILLA, GRANO : pimple, blackhead
barroco, -ca *adj* : baroque
barroso, -sa *adj* ENLODADO : muddy
barrote *nm* : bar (on a window)
barrunto *nm* **1** SOSPECHA : suspicion **2** INDICIO : sign, indication, hint
bártulos *nmpl* : things, belongings <liar los bártulos : to pack one's things>
barullo *nm* BULLA : racket, ruckus
basa *nf* : base, pedestal
basalto *nm* : basalt
basar *vt* FUNDAR : to base — **basarse** *vr* FUNDARSE **~ en** : to be based on
báscula *nf* BALANZA : balance, scales *pl*
base *nf* **1** : base, bottom **2** : base (in baseball) **3** FUNDAMENTO : basis, foundation **4** **base de datos** : database **5** **a base de** : based on, by means of **6** **en base a** : based on, on the basis of
básico, -ca *adj* FUNDAMENTAL : basic — **básicamente** *adv*
basílica *nf* : basilica
basquetbol *or* **básquetbol** *nm* BALONCESTO : basketball
basset *nm* : basset hound
bastante[1] *adv* **1** : enough, sufficiently <he trabajado bastante : I have worked enough> **2** : fairly, rather, quite <llegaron bastante temprano : they arrived quite early>
bastante[2] *adj* : enough, sufficient
bastante[3] *pron* : enough <hemos visto bastante : we have seen enough>
bastar *vi* : to be enough, to suffice
bastardilla *nf* CURSIVA : italic type, italics *pl*
bastardo, -da *adj & n* : bastard
bastidor *nm* **1** : framework, frame **2** : wing (in theater) <entre bastidores : backstage, behind the scenes>
bastilla *nf* : hem
bastión *nf, pl* **bastiones** BALUARTE : bastion, bulwark
basto, -ta *adj* : coarse, rough
bastón *nm, pl* **bastones** **1** : cane, walking stick **2** : baton **3** **bastón de mando** : staff (of authority)
basura *nf* DESECHOS : garbage, waste, refuse
basurero[1], **-ra** *n* : garbage collector
basurero[2] *nm Mex* : garbage can
bata *nf* **1** : bathrobe, housecoat **2** : smock, coverall, lab coat
batalla *nf* **1** : battle **2** : fight, struggle **3** **de ~** : ordinary, everyday <mis

zapatos de batalla : my everyday shoes>

batallar *vi* LIDIAR, LUCHAR : to battle, to fight

batallón *nm, pl* **-llones** : battalion

batata *nf* : yam, sweet potato

batazo *nm* HIT : hit (in baseball)

bate *nm* : baseball bat

batea *nf* **1** : tray, pan **2** : flat-bottomed boat, punt

bateador, -dora *n* : batter, hitter

batear *vi* : to bat — *vt* : to hit

batería *nf* **1** PILA : battery **2** : drum kit, drums *pl* **3** : artillery **4 batería de cocina** : kitchen utensils *pl*

baterista *nmf* : drummer

batido *nm* LICUADO : milk shake

batidor *nm* : eggbeater, whisk, mixer

batidora *nf* : (electric) mixer

batir *vt* **1** GOLPEAR : to beat, to hit **2** VENCER : to defeat **3** REVOLVER : to mix, to beat **4** : to break (a record) — **batirse** *vr* : to fight

batista *nf* : batiste, cambric

batuta *nf* **1** : baton **2 llevar la batuta** : to be the leader, to call the tune

baúl *nm* : trunk, chest

bautismal *adj* : baptismal

bautismo *nm* : baptism, christening

bautista *adj & nmf* : Baptist

bautizar {21} *vt* : to baptize, to christen

bautizo *nm* → **bautismo**

bávaro, -ra *adj & n* : Bavarian

baya *nf* **1** : berry **2 baya de saúco** : elderberry

bayeta *nf* : cleaning cloth

bayoneta *nf* : bayonet

baza *nf* **1** : trick (in card games) **2 meter baza en** : to butt in on

bazar *nm* : bazaar

bazo *nm* : spleen

bazofia *nf* **1** : table scraps *pl* **2** : slop, swill **3** : hogwash, rubbish

bazuca *nf* : bazooka

beagle *nm* : beagle

beatificar {72} *vt* : to beatify — **beatificación** *nf*

beatífico, -ca *adj* : beatific

beatitud *nf* : beatitude

beato, -ta *adj* **1** : blessed **2** : pious, devout **3** : sanctimonious, overly devout

bebé *nm* : baby

bebedero *nm* **1** ABREVADERO : watering trough **2** *Mex* : drinking fountain

bebedor, -dora *n* : drinker

beber *v* TOMAR : to drink

bebida *nf* : drink, beverage

beca *nf* : grant, scholarship

becado, -da *n* : scholar, scholarship holder

becerro, -rra *n* : calf

begonia *nf* : begonia

beige *adj & nm* : beige

beisbol *or* **béisbol** *nm* : baseball

beisbolista *nmf* : baseball player

beldad *nf* BELLEZA, HERMOSURA : beauty

belén *nf, pl* **belenes** NACIMIENTO : Nativity scene

belga *adj & nmf* : Belgian

beliceño, -ña *adj & n* : Belizean

belicista[1] *adj* : militaristic

belicista[2] *nmf* : warmonger

bélico, -ca *adj* GUERRERO : war, fighting <esfuerzos bélicos : war efforts>

belicosidad *nf* : bellicosity

belicoso, -sa *adj* **1** : warlike, martial **2** : aggressive, belligerent

beligerancia *nf* : belligerence

beligerante *adj & nmf* : belligerent

bellaco[1], **-ca** *adj* : sly, cunning

bellaco[2], **-ca** *n* : rogue, scoundrel

belleza *nf* BELDAD, HERMOSURA : beauty

bello, -lla *adj* **1** HERMOSO : beautiful **2 bellas artes** : fine arts

bellota *nf* : acorn

bemol *nm* : flat (in music) — **bemol** *adj*

benceno *nm* : benzene

bendecir {11} *vt* **1** CONSAGRAR : to bless, to consecrate **2** ALABAR : to praise, to extol **3 bendecir la mesa** : to say grace

bendición *nf, pl* **-ciones** : benediction, blessing

bendiga, bendijo, etc. → **bendecir**

bendito, -ta *adj* **1** : blessed, holy **2** : fortunate **3** : silly, simple-minded

benedictino, -na *adj & n* : Benedictine

benefactor[1], **-tora** *adj* : beneficent

benefactor[2], **-tora** *n* : benefactor, benefactress *f*

beneficencia *nf* : beneficence, charity

beneficiar *vt* : to benefit, to be of assistance to — **beneficiarse** *vr* : to benefit, to profit

beneficiario, -ria *n* : beneficiary

beneficio *nm* **1** GANANCIA, PROVECHO : gain, profit **2** : benefit

beneficioso, -sa *adj* PROVECHOSO : beneficial

benéfico, -ca *adj* : charitable, beneficent

benemérito, -ta *adj* : meritorious, worthy

beneplácito *nm* : approval, consent

benevolencia *nf* BONDAD : benevolence, kindness

benévolo, -la *adj* BONDADOSO : benevolent, kind, good

bengala *nf* **luz de bengala 1** : flare (signal) **2** : sparkler

bengalí[1] *adj & nmf* : Bengali

bengalí[2] *nm* : Bengali (language)

benignidad *nf* : mildness, kindness

benigno, -na *adj* : benign, mild

beninés, -nesa *adj & n* : Beninese

benjamín, -mina *n, mpl* **-mines** : youngest child

beodo[1], **-da** *adj* : drunk, inebriated

beodo[2], **-da** *n* : drunkard

berberecho *nm* : cockle

berbiquí *nm* : brace (in carpentry)

berenjena *nf* : eggplant

bergantín *nm, pl* **-tines** : brig (ship)

berilo *nm* : beryl

bermudas *nfpl* : Bermuda shorts
berrear *vi* **1** : to bellow, to low **2** : to bawl, to howl
berrido *nm* **1** : bellowing **2** : howl, scream
berrinche *nm fam* : tantrum, conniption
berro *nm* : watercress
berza *nf* : cabbage
besar *vt* : to kiss
beso *nm* : kiss
bestia[1] *adj* **1** : ignorant, stupid **2** : boorish, rude
bestia[2] *nf* : beast, animal
bestia[3] *nmf* **1** IGNORANTE : ignoramus **2** : brute
bestial *adj* **1** : bestial, beastly **2** *fam* : huge, enormous <hace un frío bestial : it's terribly cold> **3** *fam* : great, fantastic
besuquear *vt fam* : to cover with kisses — **besuquearse** *vr fam* : to neck, to smooch
betabel *nm Mex* : beet
betún *nm, pl* **betunes 1** : shoe polish **2** *Mex* : icing
bianual *adj* : biannual
biatlón *nm, pl* **-lones** : biathlon
biberón *nm, pl* **-rones** : baby's bottle
biblia *nf* **1** : bible **2 la Biblia** : the Bible
bíblico, -ca *adj* : biblical
bibliografía *nf* : bibliography
bibliográfico, -ca *adj* : bibliographic, bibliographical
bibliógrafo, -fa *n* : bibliographer
biblioteca *nf* : library
bibliotecario, -ria *n* : librarian
bicameral *adj* : bicameral
bicarbonato *nm* **1** : bicarbonate **2 bicarbonato de soda** : sodium bicarbonate, baking soda
bicentenario *nm* : bicentennial
bíceps *nms & pl* : biceps
bicho *nm* : small animal, bug, insect
bici *nf fam* : bike
bicicleta *nf* : bicycle
bicolor *adj* : two-tone
bicúspide *adj* : bicuspid
bidón *nm, pl* **bidones** : large can, (oil) drum
bien[1] *adv* **1** : well <¿dormiste bien? : did you sleep well?> **2** CORRECTAMENTE : correctly, properly, right <hay que hacerlo bien : it must be done correctly> **3** : very, quite <el libro era bien divertido : the book was very amusing> **4** : easily <bien puede acabarlo en un día : he can easily finish it in a day> **5** : willingly, readily <bien lo aceptaré : I'll gladly accept it> **6 bien que** : although **7 más bien** : rather
bien[2] *adj* **1** : well, OK, all right <¿te sientes bien? : are you feeling all right?> **2** : pleasant, agreeable <las flores huelen bien : the flowers smell very nice> **3** : satisfactory **4** : correct, right
bien[3] *nm* **1** : good <el bien y el mal : good and evil> **2 bienes** *nmpl* : property, goods, possessions
bienal *adj & nf* : biennial — **bienalmente** *adv*
bienaventurado, -da *adj* **1** : blessed **2** : fortunate, happy
bienaventuranzas *nfpl* : Beatitudes
bienestar *nm* **1** : welfare, well-being **2** CONFORT : comfort
bienhechor[1], **-chora** *adj* : beneficent, benevolent
bienhechor[2], **-chora** *n* : benefactor, benefactress *f*
bienintencionado, -da *adj* : well-meaning
bienvenida *nf* **1** : welcome **2 dar la bienvenida a** : to welcome
bienvenido, -da *adj* : welcome
bies *nm* : bias (in sewing)
bife *nm Arg, Chile, Uru* : steak
bífido, -da *adj* : forked
bifocal *adj* : bifocal
bifocales *nmpl* : bifocals
bifurcación *nf, pl* **-ciones** : fork (in a river or road)
bifurcarse {72} *vr* : to fork
bigamia *nf* : bigamy
bígamo, -ma *n* : bigamist
bigote *nm* **1** : mustache **2** : whisker (of an animal)
bigotudo, -da *adj* : mustached, having a big mustache
bikini *nm* : bikini
bilateral *adj* : bilateral — **bilateralmente** *adv*
bilingüe *adj* : bilingual
bilioso, -sa *adj* **1** : bilious **2** : irritable
bilis *nf* : bile
billar *nm* : pool, billiards
billete *nm* **1** : bill <un billete de cinco dólares : a five-dollar bill> **2** BOLETO : ticket <billete de ida y vuelta : round-trip ticket>
billetera *nf* : billfold, wallet
billón *nm, pl* **billones 1** : billion (Great Britain) **2** : trillion (U.S.A.)
bimestral *adj* : bimonthly — **bimestralmente** *adv*
bimotor *adj* : twin-engined
binacional *adj* : binational
binario, -ria *adj* : binary
binocular *adj* : binocular
binoculares *nmpl* : binoculars
binomio *nm* : binomial
biodegradable *adj* : biodegradable
biodegradarse *vr* : to biodegrade
biodiversidad *nf* : biodiversity
biofísica *nf* : biophysics
biofísico[1], **-ca** *adj* : biophysical
biofísico[2], **-ca** *n* : biophysicist
biografía *nf* : biography
biográfico, -ca *adj* : biographical
biógrafo, -fa *n* : biographer
biología *nf* : biology
biológico, -ca *adj* : biological, biologic — **biológicamente** *adv*
biólogo, -ga *n* : biologist

biombo *nm* MAMPARA : folding screen, room divider

biomecánica *nf* : biomechanics

biopsia *nf* : biopsy

bioquímica *nf* : biochemistry

bioquímico[1], -ca *adj* : biochemical

bioquímico[2], -ca *n* : biochemist

biosfera *or* **biósfera** *nf* : biosphere

biotecnología *nf* : biotechnology

biótico, -ca *adj* : biotic

bipartidismo *nm* : two-party system

bipartidista *adj* : bipartisan

bípedo *nm* : biped

birlar *vt fam* : to swipe, to pinch

birmano, -na *adj & n* : Burmese

bis[1] *adv* **1** : twice, again (in music) **2** : a, A <artículo 47 bis : Article 47A> <calle Bolívar, número 70 bis : Bolívar Street, number 70A>

bis[2] *nm* : encore

bisabuelo, -la *n* : great-grandfather *m,* great-grandmother *f,* great-grandparent

bisagra *nf* : hinge

bisbisar *vt fam* : to mutter, to mumble

bisecar {72} *vt* : bisect — **bisección** *nf*

bisel *nm* : bevel

biselar *vt* : to bevel

bisexual *adj* : bisexual

bisiesto *adj* **año bisiesto** : leap year

bismuto *nm* : bismuth

bisnieto, -ta *n* : great-grandson *m,* great-granddaughter *f,* great-grandchild

bisonte *nm* : bison, buffalo

bisoñé *nm* : hairpiece, toupee

bisoño[1], -ña *adj* : inexperienced, green

bisoño[2], -ña *n* : rookie, greenhorn

bistec *nm* : steak, beefsteak

bisturí *nm* ESCALPELO : scalpel

bisutería *nf* : costume jewelry

bit *nm* : bit (unit of information)

bituminoso, -sa *adj* : bituminous

bivalvo *nm* : bivalve

bizarría *nf* **1** : courage, gallantry **2** : generosity

bizarro, -rra *adj* **1** VALIENTE : courageous, valiant **2** GENEROSO : generous

bizco, -ca *adj* : cross-eyed

bizcocho *nm* **1** : sponge cake **2** : biscuit **3** *Mex* : breadstick

bizquera *nf* : crossed eyes, squint

blanco[1], -ca *adj* : white

blanco[2], -ca *n* : white person

blanco[3] *nm* **1** : white **2** : target, bull's-eye <dar en el blanco : to hit the target, to hit the nail on the head> **3** : blank space, blank <un cheque en blanco : a blank check>

blancura *nf* : whiteness

blancuzco, -ca *adj* **1** : whitish, off-white **2** PÁLIDO : pale

blandir {1} *vt* : to wave, to brandish

blando, -da *adj* **1** SUAVE : soft, tender **2** : weak (in character) **3** : lenient

blandura *nf* **1** : softness, tenderness **2** : leniency

blanqueador *nm* : bleach, whitener

blanquear *vt* **1** : to whiten, to bleach **2** : to shut out (in sports) **3** : to launder (money) — *vi* : to turn white

blanquillo *nm CA, Mex* : egg

blasfemar *vi* : to blaspheme

blasfemia *nf* : blasphemy

blasfemo, -ma *adj* : blasphemous

blazer *nm* : blazer

bledo *nm* **no me importa un bledo** *fam* : I couldn't care less, I don't give a damn

blindado, -da *adj* ACORAZADO : armored

blindaje *nm* **1** : armor, armor plating **2** : shield (for cables, machinery, etc.)

bloc *nm, pl* **blocs** : writing pad, pad of paper

blof *nm Col, Mex* : bluff

blofear *vi Col, Mex* : to bluff

blondo, -da *adj* : blond, flaxen

bloque *nm* **1** : block **2** GRUPO : bloc <el bloque comunista : the Communist bloc>

bloquear *vt* **1** OBSTRUIR : to block, to obstruct **2** : to blockade

bloqueo *nm* **1** OBSTRUCCIÓN : blockage, obstruction **2** : blockade

blusa *nf* : blouse

blusón *nm, pl* **blusones** : loose shirt, smock

boa *nf* : boa

boato *nm* : ostentation, show

bobada *nf* : folly, nonsense

bobalicón, -cona *adj, mpl* **-cones** *fam* : silly, stupid

bobina *nf* CARRETE : bobbin, reel

bobo[1], -ba *adj* : silly, stupid

bobo[2], -ba *n* : fool, simpleton

boca *nf* **1** : mouth **2** **boca arriba** : face up, on one's back **3** **boca abajo** : face down, prone **4** **boca de riego** : hydrant **5** **en boca de** : according to

bocacalle *nf* : entrance to a street <gire a la última bocacalle : take the last turning>

bocadillo *nm Spain* : sandwich

bocado *nm* **1** : bite, mouthful **2** FRENO : bit (of a bridle)

bocajarro *nm* **a ~** : point-blank, directly

bocallave *nf* : keyhole

bocanada *nf* **1** : swig, swallow **2** : puff, mouthful (of smoke) **3** : gust (of air) **4** : stream (of people)

boceto *nm* : sketch, outline

bochinche *nm fam* : ruckus, uproar

bochorno *nm* **1** VERGÜENZA : embarrassment **2** : hot and humid weather **3** : hot flash

bochornoso, -sa *adj* **1** EMBARAZOSO : embarrassing **2** : hot and muggy

bocina *nf* **1** : horn, trumpet **2** : automobile horn **3** : mouthpiece (of a telephone) **4** *Mex* : loudspeaker

bocinazo *nm* : honk (of a horn)

bocio *nm* : goiter

bocón, -cona *n, mpl* **bocones** *fam* : blabbermouth, loudmouth

boda *nf* : wedding

bodega *nf* **1 :** wine cellar **2** *Chile, Col, Mex* **:** storeroom, warehouse **3** (*in various countries*) **:** grocery store

bofetada *nf* CACHETADA **:** slap on the face

bofetear *vt* CACHETEAR **:** to slap

bofetón *nm* → **bofetada**

bofo, -fa *adj* **:** flabby

boga *nf* **:** fashion, vogue <estar en boga : to be in style>

bogotano[1], -na *adj* **:** of or from Bogotá

bogotano[2], -na *n* **:** person from Bogotá

bohemio, -mia *adj & n* **:** bohemian, Bohemian

boicot *nm, pl* **boicots :** boycott

boicotear *vt* **:** to boycott

boina *nf* **:** beret

boiserie *nf* **:** wood paneling, wainscoting

boj *nm, pl* **bojes :** box (plant), boxwood

bola *nf* **1 :** ball <bola de nieve : snowball> **2** *fam* **:** lie, fib **3** *Mex fam* **:** bunch, group <una bola de rateros : a bunch of thieves> **4** *Mex* **:** uproar, tumult

bolear *vt Mex* **:** to polish (shoes)

bolera *nf* **:** bowling alley

bolero *nm* **:** bolero

boleta *nf* **1 :** ballot **2 :** ticket **3 :** receipt

boletería *nf* TAQUILLA **:** box office, ticket office

boletín *nm, pl* **-tines 1 :** bulletin **2 :** journal, review **3 boletín de prensa :** press release

boleto *nm* BILLETE **:** ticket

boliche *nm* **1** BOLOS **:** bowling **2** *Arg* **:** bar, tavern

bolígrafo *nm* **:** ballpoint pen

bolillo *nm* **1 :** bobbin **2** *Mex* **:** roll, bun

bolívar *nm* **:** bolivar (monetary unit of Venezuela)

boliviano[1], -na *adj & n* **:** Bolivian

boliviano[2] *nm* **:** boliviano (monetary unit of Bolivia)

bollo *nm* **:** bun, sweet roll

bolo *nm* **:** bowling pin, tenpin

bolos *nmpl* BOLICHE **:** bowling

bolsa *nf* **1 :** bag, sack **2** *Mex* **:** pocketbook, purse **3** *Mex* **:** pocket **4 la Bolsa :** the stock market, the stock exchange **5 bolsa de trabajo :** employment agency

bolsear *vi Mex* **:** to pick pockets

bolsillo *nm* **1 :** pocket **2 dinero de bolsillo :** pocket change, loose change

bolso *nm* **:** pocketbook, handbag

bomba *nf* **1 :** bomb **2 :** bubble **3 :** pump <bomba de gasolina : gas pump>

bombachos *nmpl* **:** baggy pants, bloomers

bombardear *vt* **1 :** to bomb **2 :** to bombard

bombardeo *nm* **1 :** bombing, shelling **2 :** bombardment

bombardero *nm* **:** bomber (airplane)

bombástico, -ca *adj* **:** bombastic

bombear *vt* **:** to pump

bombero, -ra *n* **:** firefighter, fireman *m*

bombilla *nf* **:** lightbulb

bombillo *nm CA, Col, Ven* **:** lightbulb

bombo *nm* **1 :** bass drum **2** *fam* **:** exaggerated praise, hype <con bombos y platillos : with great fanfare>

bombón *nm, pl* **bombones 1 :** bonbon, chocolate **2** *Mex* **:** marshmallow

bonachón[1], -chona *adj, mpl* **-chones** *fam* **:** good-natured, kindhearted

bonachón[2], -chona *n, mpl* **-chones** *fam* BUENAZO **:** kindhearted person

bonaerense[1] *adj* **:** of or from Buenos Aires

bonaerense[2] *nmf* **:** person from Buenos Aires

bonanza *nf* **1** PROSPERIDAD **:** prosperity <bonanza económica : economic boom> **2 :** calm weather **3 :** rich ore deposit, bonanza

bondad *nf* BENEVOLENCIA **:** goodness, kindness <tener la bondad de hacer algo : to be kind enough to do something>

bondadoso, -sa *adj* BENÉVOLO **:** kind, kindly, good — **bondadosamente** *adv*

bonete *nm* **:** cap, mortarboard

boniato *nm* **:** sweet potato

bonificación *nf, pl* **-ciones 1 :** discount **2 :** bonus, extra

bonito[1] *adv* **:** nicely, well <¡qué bonito canta tu hermana! : your sister sings wonderfully!>

bonito[2], -ta *adj* LINDO **:** pretty, lovely <tiene un apartamento bonito : she has a nice apartment>

bonito[3] *nm* **:** bonito (tuna)

bono *nm* **1 :** bond <bono bancario : bank bond> **2 :** voucher

boqueada *nf* **:** gasp <to give one's last gasp : dar la última boqueada>

boquear *vi* **1 :** to gasp **2 :** to be dying

boquete *nm* **:** gap, opening, breach

boquiabierto, -ta *adj* **:** open-mouthed, speechless, agape

boquilla *nf* **:** mouthpiece (of a musical instrument)

borbollar *vi* **:** to bubble

borbotar *or* **borbotear** *vi* **:** to boil, to bubble, to gurgle

borboteo *nm* **:** bubbling, gurgling

borda *nf* **:** gunwale

bordado *nm* **:** embroidery, needlework

bordar *v* **:** to embroider

borde *nm* **1 :** border, edge **2 al borde de :** on the verge of <estoy al borde de la locura : I'm about to go crazy>

bordear *vt* **1 :** to border, to skirt <el Río Este bordea Manhattan : the East River borders Manhattan> **2 :** to border on <bordea la irrealidad : it borders on unreality> **3 :** to line <una calle bordeada de árboles : a street lined with trees>

bordillo *nm* **:** curb

bordo *nm* **a ~ :** aboard, on board

boreal *adj* **:** northern

borgoña *nf* **:** burgundy

bórico, -ca *adj* : boric <ácido bórico : boric acid>
boricua *adj & nmf fam* : Puerto Rican
borinqueño, -ña → **boricua**
borla *nf* **1** : pom-pom, tassel **2** : powder puff
boro *nm* : boron
borrachera *nf* : drunkenness <agarró una borrachera : he got drunk>
borrachín, -china *n, mpl* **-chines** *fam* : lush, drunk
borracho[1], -cha *adj* EBRIO : drunk, intoxicated
borracho[2], -cha *n* : drunk, drunkard
borrador *nm* **1** : rough copy, first draft <en borrador : in the rough> **2** : eraser
borrar *vt* : to erase, to blot out — **borrarse** *vr* **1** : to fade, to fade away **2** : to resign, to drop out **3** *Mex fam* : to split, to leave <me borro : I'm out of here>
borrascoso, -sa *adj* : gusty, blustery
borrego, -ga *n* **1** : lamb, sheep **2** : simpleton, fool
borrico *nm* → **burro**
borrón *nm, pl* **borrones** : smudge, blot <borrón y cuenta nueva : let's start on a clean slate, let's start over again>
borronear *vt* : to smudge, to blot
borroso, -sa *adj* **1** : blurry, smudgy **2** CONFUSO : unclear, confused
boscoso, -sa *adj* : wooded
bosnio, -nia *adj & n* : Bosnian
bosque *nm* : woods, forest
bosquecillo *nm* : grove, copse, thicket
bosquejar *vt* ESBOZAR : to outline, to sketch
bosquejo *nm* **1** TRAZADO : outline, sketch **2** : draft
bostezar {21} *vi* : to yawn
bostezo *nm* : yawn
bota *nf* **1** : boot **2** : wineskin
botana *nf Mex* : snack, appetizer
botanear *vi Mex* : to have a snack
botánica *nf* : botany
botánico[1], -ca *adj* : botanical
botánico[2], -ca *n* : botanist
botar *vt* **1** ARROJAR : to throw, to fling, to hurl **2** TIRAR : to throw out, to throw away **3** : to launch (a ship)
bote *nm* **1** : small boat <bote de remos : rowboat> **2** : can, jar **3** : jump, bounce **4** *Mex fam* : jail
botella *nf* : bottle
botica *nf* FARMACIA : drugstore, pharmacy
boticario, -ria *n* FARMACÉUTICO : pharmacist, druggist
botín *nm, pl* **botines 1** : baby's bootee **2** : ankle boot **3** : booty, plunder
botiquín *nm, pl* **-quines 1** : medicine cabinet **2** : first-aid kit
botón *nm, pl* **botones 1** : button **2** : bud **3** INSIGNIA : badge
botones *nmfs & pl* : bellhop
botulismo *nm* : botulism
boulevard [ˌbule'var] *nm* → **bulevar**
bouquet *nm* **1** : fragrance, bouquet (of wine) **2** RAMILLETE : bouquet (of flowers)
boutique *nf* : boutique
bóveda *nf* **1** : vault, dome **2** CRIPTA : crypt
bovino, -na *adj* : bovine
box *nm, pl* **boxes 1** : pit (in auto racing) **2** *Mex* : boxing
boxeador, -dora *n* : boxer
boxear *vi* : to box
boxeo *nm* : boxing
boya *nf* : buoy
boyante *adj* **1** : buoyant **2** : prosperous, thriving
bozal *nm* **1** : muzzle **2** : halter (for a horse)
bracear *vi* **1** : to wave one's arms **2** : to make strokes (in swimming)
bracero, -ra *n* : migrant worker, day laborer
braguero *nm* : truss (in medicine)
bragueta *nf* : fly, pants zipper
braille *adj & nm* : braille
bramante *nm* : twine, string
bramar *vi* **1** RUGIR : to roar, to bellow **2** : to howl (of the wind)
bramido *nm* : bellowing, roar
brandy *nm* : brandy
branquia *nf* AGALLA : gill
brasa *nf* ASCUA : ember, live coal
brasero *nm* : brazier
brasier *nm Col, Mex* : brassiere, bra
brasileño, -ña *adj & n* : Brazilian
bravata *nf* **1** JACTANCIA : boast, bravado **2** AMENAZA : threat
bravo, -va *adj* **1** FEROZ : ferocious, fierce <un perro bravo : a ferocious dog> **2** EXCELENTE : excellent, great <¡bravo! : bravo!, well done!> **3** : rough, rugged, wild **4** : annoyed, angry
bravucón, -cona *n, mpl* **-cones** : bully
bravuconadas *nfpl* : bravado
bravura *nf* **1** FEROCIDAD : fierceness, ferocity **2** VALENTÍA : bravery
braza *nf* **1** : breaststroke **2** : fathom (unit of length)
brazada *nf* : stroke (in swimming)
brazalete *nm* PULSERA : bracelet, bangle
brazo *nm* **1** : arm **2 brazo derecho** : right-hand man **3 brazos** *nmpl* : hands, laborers
brea *nf* ALQUITRÁN : tar, pitch
brebaje *nm* : potion, brew
brecha *nf* **1** : gap, breach <estar siempre en la brecha : to be always there when needed, to stay in the thick of things> **2** : gash
brécol *nm* : broccoli
brega *nf* **1** LUCHA : struggle, fight **2** : hard work
bregar {52} *vi* **1** LUCHAR : to struggle **2** : to toil, to work hard **3 ~ con** : to deal with
brete *nm* : jam, tight spot
breve *adj* **1** CORTO : brief, short **2 en ~** : shortly, in short — **brevemente** *adv*
brevedad *nf* : brevity, shortness
breviario *nm* : breviary

brezal *nm* : heath, moor
brezo *nm* : heather
bribón, -bona *n, mpl* **bribones** : rascal, scamp
bricolaje *or* **bricolage** *nm* : do-it-yourself
brida *nf* : bridle
brigada *nf* **1** : brigade **2** : gang, team, squad
brigadier *nm* : brigadier
brillante[1] *adj* : brilliant, bright — **brillantemente** *adv*
brillante[2] *nm* DIAMANTE : diamond
brillantez *nf* : brilliance, brightness
brillar *vi* : to shine, to sparkle
brillo *nm* **1** LUSTRE : luster, shine **2** : brilliance
brilloso, -sa *adj* LUSTROSO : lustrous, shiny
brincar {72} *vi* **1** SALTAR : to jump around, to leap about **2** : to frolic, to gambol
brinco *nm* **1** SALTO : jump, leap, skip **2 pegar un brinco** : to give a start, to jump
brindar *vi* : to drink a toast <brindó por los vencedores : he toasted the victors> — *vt* OFRECER, PROPORCIONAR : to offer, to provide — **brindarse** *vr* : to offer one's assistance, to volunteer
brindis *nm* : toast, drink <hacer un brindis : to drink a toast>
brinque, etc. → **brincar**
brío *nm* **1** : force, determination **2** : spirit, verve
brioso, -sa *adj* : spirited, lively
briqueta *nf* : briquette
brisa *nf* : breeze
británico[1], **-ca** *adj* : British
británico[2], **-ca** *n* **1** : British person **2 los británicos** : the British
brizna *nf* **1** : strand, thread **2** : blade (of grass)
brocado *nm* : brocade
brocha *nf* : paintbrush
broche *nm* **1** ALFILER : brooch **2** : fastener, clasp **3 broche de oro** : finishing touch
brocheta *nf* : skewer
brócoli *nm* : broccoli
broma *nf* **1** CHISTE : joke, prank **2** : fun, merriment **3 en ~** : in jest, jokingly
bromear *vi* : to joke, to fool around <sólo estaba bromeando : I was only kidding>
bromista[1] *adj* : fun-loving, joking
bromista[2] *nmf* : joker, prankster
bromo *nm* : bromine
bronca *nf fam* : fight, quarrel, fuss
bronce *nm* : bronze
bronceado[1], **-da** *adj* **1** : tanned, suntanned **2** : bronze
bronceado[2] *nm* **1** : suntan, tan **2** : bronzing
broncearse *vr* : to get a suntan
bronco, -ca *adj* **1** : harsh, rough **2** : untamed, wild
bronquial *adj* : bronchial
bronquio *nm* : bronchial tube, bronchus
bronquitis *nf* : bronchitis
broqueta *nf* : skewer
brotar *vi* **1** : to bud, to sprout **2** : to spring up, to stream, to gush forth **3** : to break out, to appear
brote *nm* **1** : outbreak **2** : sprout, bud, shoot
broza *nf* **1** : brushwood **2** MALEZA : scrub, undergrowth
brujería *nf* HECHICERÍA : witchcraft, sorcery
brujo[1], **-ja** *adj* : bewitching
brujo[2], **-ja** *n* : warlock *m*, witch *f*, sorcerer
brújula *nf* : compass
bruma *nf* : haze, mist
brumoso, -sa *adj* : hazy, misty
bruñir {38} *vt* : to burnish, to polish (metals)
brusco, -ca *adj* **1** SÚBITO : sudden, abrupt **2** : curt, brusque — **bruscamente** *adv*
brusquedad *nf* **1** : abruptness, suddenness **2** : brusqueness
brutal *adj* **1** : brutal **2** *fam* : incredible, terrific — **brutalmente** *adv*
brutalidad *nf* CRUELDAD : brutality
brutalizar {21} *vt* : to brutalize, to maltreat
bruto[1], **-ta** *adj* **1** : gross <peso bruto : gross weight> <ingresos brutos : gross income> **2** : unrefined <petróleo bruto : crude oil> **3** : brutish, stupid
bruto[2], **-ta** *n* **1** : brute **2** : dunce, blockhead
bucal *adj* : oral
bucanero *nm* : buccaneer, pirate
buccino *nm* : whelk
buceador, -dora *n* : diver, scuba diver
bucear *vi* **1** : to dive, to swim underwater **2** : to explore, to delve
buceo *nm* **1** : diving, scuba diving **2** : exploration, searching
buche *nm* **1** : crop (of a bird) **2** *fam* : belly, gut **3** : mouthful <hacer buches : to rinse one's mouth>
bucle *nm* **1** : curl, ringlet **2** : loop
bucólico, -ca *adj* : bucolic
budín *nm, pl* **budines** : pudding
budismo *nm* : Buddhism
budista *adj & nmf* : Buddhist
buen → **bueno**[1]
buenamente *adv* **1** : easily **2** : willingly
buenaventura *nf* **1** : good luck **2** : fortune, future <le dijo la buenaventura : she told his fortune>
buenazo, -za *n fam* BONACHÓN : kindhearted person
bueno[1], **-na** *adj* (**buen** *before masculine singular nouns*) **1** : good <una buena idea : a good idea> **2** BONDADOSO : nice, kind **3** APROPIADO : proper, appropriate **4** SANO : well, healthy **5** : considerable, goodly <una buena cantidad : a lot> **6 buenos días**

: hello, good day **7 buenas tardes** : good afternoon **8 buenas noches** : good evening, good night
bueno[2] *interj* **1** : OK!, all right! **2** *Mex* : hello! (on the telephone)
buey *nm* : ox, steer
búfalo *nm* **1** : buffalo **2 búfalo de agua** : water buffalo
bufanda *nf* : scarf, muffler
bufar *vi* : to snort
bufet *or* **bufé** *nm* : buffet-style meal
bufete *nm* **1** : law firm, law office **2** : writing desk
bufido *nm* : snort
bufo, -fa *adj* : comic
bufón, -fona *n, mpl* **bufones** : clown, buffoon, jester
bufonada *nf* **1** : jest, buffoonery **2** : sarcasm
buhardilla *nf* **1** ÁTICO, DESVÁN : attic **2** : dormer window
búho *nm* **1** : owl **2** *fam* : hermit, recluse
buhonero, -ra *n* MERCACHIFLE : peddler
buitre *nm* : vulture
bujía *nf* : spark plug
bulbo *nm* : bulb
bulboso, -sa *adj* : bulbous
bulevar *nm* : boulevard
búlgaro, -ra *adj & n* : Bulgarian
bulla *nf* BARULLO : racket, rowdiness
bullicio *nm* **1** : ruckus, uproar **2** : hustle and bustle
bullicioso, -sa *adj* : noisy, busy, turbulent
bullir {38} *vi* **1** HERVIR : to boil **2** MOVERSE : to stir, to bustle about
bulto *nm* **1** : package, bundle **2** : piece of luggage, bag **3** : size, bulk, volume **4** : form, shape **5** : lump (on the body), swelling, bulge
bumerán *nm, pl* **-ranes** : boomerang
búnker *nm, pl* **búnkers** : bunker
búnquer *nm* → **búnker**
buñuelo *nm* : fried pastry
buque *nm* BARCO : ship, vessel
burbuja *nf* : bubble, blister (on a surface)
burbujear *vi* **1** : to bubble **2** : to fizz
burbujeo *nm* : bubbling
burdel *nm* : brothel, whorehouse
burdo, -da *adj* **1** : coarse, rough **2** : crude, clumsy <una burda mentira : a clumsy lie> — **burdamente** *adj*
burgués, -guesa *adj & n, mpl* **burgueses** : bourgeois
burguesía *nf* : bourgeoisie, middle class
burla *nf* **1** : mockery, ridicule **2** : joke, trick **3 hacer burla de** : to make fun of, to mock
burlar *vt* ENGAÑAR : to trick, to deceive — **burlarse** *vr* **~ de** : to make fun of, to ridicule
burlesco, -ca *adj* : burlesque, comic
burlón[1], **-lona** *adj, mpl* **burlones** : joking, mocking
burlón[2], **-lona** *n, mpl* **burlones** : joker
burocracia *nf* : bureaucracy
burócrata *nmf* : bureaucrat
burocrático, -ca *adj* : bureaucratic
burrada *nf fam* : stupid act, nonsense
burrito *nm* : burrito
burro[1], **-rra** *adj fam* : dumb, stupid
burro[2], **-rra** *n* **1** ASNO : donkey, ass **2** *fam* : dunce, poor student
burro[3] *nm* **1** : sawhorse **2** *Mex* : ironing board **3** *Mex* : stepladder
bursátil *adj* : stock-market
burundés, -desa *adj & n* : Burundian
bus *nm* : bus
busca *nf* : search
buscador, -dora *n* : hunter (for treasure, etc.), prospector
buscapleitos *nmfs & pl* : troublemaker
buscar {72} *vt* **1** : to look for, to seek **2** : to pick up, to collect **3** : to provoke — *vi* : to look, to search <buscó en los bolsillos : he searched through his pockets>
buscavidas *nmfs & pl* **1** : busybody **2** : go-getter
busque, etc. → **buscar**
búsqueda *nf* : search
busto *nm* : bust
butaca *nf* **1** SILLÓN : armchair **2** : seat (in a theatre) **3** *Mex* : pupil's desk
butano *nm* : butane
buzo[1], **-za** *adj Mex fam* : smart, astute <¡ponte buzo! : get with it!, get on the ball!>
buzo[2] *nm* : diver, scuba diver
buzón *nm, pl* **buzones** : mailbox
byte *nm* : byte

C

c *nf* : third letter of the Spanish alphabet
cabal *adj* **1** : exact, correct **2** : complete **3** : upright, honest
cabales *nmpl* **no estar en sus cabales** : not to be in one's right mind
cabalgar {52} *vi* : to ride (on horseback)
cabalgata *nf* : cavalcade, procession
cabalidad *nf* **a ~** : thoroughly, conscientiously
caballa *nf* : mackerel
caballada *nf* **1** : herd of horses **2** *fam* : nonsense, stupidity, outrageousness
caballar *adj* EQUINO : horse, equine
caballeresco, -ca *adj* : gallant, chivalrous
caballería *nf* **1** : cavalry **2** : horse, mount **3** : knighthood, chivalry
caballeriza *nf* : stable
caballero[1] → **caballeroso**
caballero[2] *nm* **1** : gentleman **2** : knight

caballerosidad *nf* : chivalry, gallantry
caballeroso, -sa *adj* : gentlemanly, chivalrous
caballete *nm* **1** : ridge **2** : easel **3** : trestle (for a table, etc.) **4** : bridge (of the nose) **5** : sawhorse
caballista *nmf* : horseman *m,* horsewoman *f*
caballito *nm* **1** : rocking horse **2 caballito de mar** : seahorse **3 caballitos** *nmpl* : merry-go-round
caballo *nm* **1** : horse **2** : knight (in chess) **3 caballo de fuerza** *or* **caballo de vapor** : horsepower
cabalmente *adv* : fully, exactly
cabaña *nf* CHOZA : cabin, hut
cabaret *nm, pl* **-rets** : nightclub, cabaret
cabecear *vt* : to head (in soccer) — *vi* **1** : to nod one's head **2** : to lurch, to pitch
cabecera *nf* **1** : headboard **2** : head <cabecera de la mesa : head of the table> **3** : heading, headline **4** : headwaters *pl* **5 médico de cabecera** : family doctor **6 cabecera municipal** *CA, Mex* : downtown area
cabecilla *nmf* : ringleader, kingpin
cabellera *nf* : head of hair, mane
cabello *nm* : hair
cabelludo, -da *adj* **1** : hairy **2 cuero cabelludo** : scalp
caber {12} *vi* **1** : to fit, to go <no sé si cabremos todos en el coche : I don't know if we'll all fit in the car> **2** : to be possible <no cabe duda alguna : there's no doubt about it> <cabe que llegue mañana : he may come tomorrow>
cabestro *nm* : halter (for an animal)
cabeza *nf* **1** : head **2 cabeza hueca** : scatterbrain **3 de ~** : head first **4 dolor de cabeza** : headache
cabezada *nf* **1** : butt, blow with the head **2** : nod <echar una cabezada : to take a nap, to doze off>
cabezal *nm* : bolster
cabezazo *nm* : butt, blow with the head
cabezón, -zona *adj, mpl* **-zones** *fam* **1** : having a big head **2** : pigheaded, stubborn
cabida *nf* **1** : room, space, capacity **2 dar cabida a** : to accomodate, to hold
cabildear *vi* : to lobby
cabildeo *nm* : lobbying
cabildero, -ra *n* : lobbyist
cabildo *nm* AYUNTAMIENTO **1** : town or city hall **2** : town or city council
cabina *nf* **1** : cabin **2** : booth **3** : cab (of a truck), cockpit (of an airplane)
cabizbajo, -ja *adj* : dejected, downcast
cable *nm* : cable
cableado *nm* : wiring
cabo *nm* **1** : end <al cabo de dos semanas : at the end of two weeks> **2** : stub, end piece **3** : corporal **4** : cape, headland <el Cabo Cañaveral : Cape Canaveral> **5 al fin y al cabo** : after all, in the end **6 llevar a cabo** : to carry out, to do
caboverdiano, -na *adj & n* : Cape Verdean
cabrá, etc. → **caber**
cabra *nf* : goat
cabrestante *nm* : windlass
cabrío, -ría *adj* : goat, caprine
cabriola *nf* **1** : skip, jump **2 hacer cabriolas** : to prance
cabriolar *vi* : to prance
cabrito *nm* : kid, baby goat
cabús *nm, pl* **cabuses** *Mex* : caboose
cacahuate *or* **cacahuete** *nm* : peanut
cacalote *nm Mex* : crow
cacao *nm* : cacao, cocoa bean
cacarear *vi* : to crow, to cackle, to cluck — *vt fam* : to boast about, to crow about <cacarear un huevo : to brag about an accomplishment>
cacatúa *nf* : cockatoo
cace, etc. → **cazar**
cacería *nf* **1** CAZA : hunt, hunting **2** : hunting party
cacerola *nf* : pan, saucepan
cacha *nf* : butt (of a gun)
cachar *vt fam* : to catch
cacharro *nm* **1** *fam* : thing, piece of junk **2** *fam* : jalopy **3 cacharros** *nmpl* : pots and pans
cache *nm* : cache, cache memory
cachear *vt* : to search, to frisk
cachemir *nm* : cashmere
cachetada *nf* BOFETADA : slap on the face
cachete *nm* : cheek
cachetear *vt* BOFETEAR : to slap
cachiporra *nf* : bludgeon, club, blackjack
cachirul *nm Mex fam* : cheating <hacer cachirul : to cheat>
cachivache *nm fam* : thing <mete tus cachivaches en el maletero : put your stuff in the trunk>
cacho *nm fam* : piece, bit
cachorro, -rra *n* **1** : cub **2** PERRITO : puppy
cachucha *nf Mex* : cap, baseball cap
cacique *nm* **1** : chief (of a tribe) **2** : boss (in politics)
cacofonía *nf* : cacophony
cacofónico, -ca *adj* : cacophonous
cacto *nm* : cactus
cactus *nm* → **cacto**
cada *adj* **1** : each <cuestan diez pesos cada una : they cost ten pesos each> **2** : every <cada vez : every time> **3** : such, some <sales con cada historia : you come up with such crazy stories> **4 cada vez más** : more and more, increasingly **5 cada vez menos** : less and less
cadalso *nm* : scaffold, gallows
cadáver *nm* : corpse, cadaver
cadavérico, -ca *adj* **1** : cadaverous **2** PÁLIDO : deathly pale
caddie *or* **caddy** *nmf, pl* **caddies** : caddy

cadena *nf* **1 :** chain **2 :** network, channel **3 cadena de montaje :** assembly line **4 cadena perpetua :** life sentence

cadencia *nf* **:** cadence, rhythm

cadencioso, -sa *adj* **:** rhythmic, rhythmical

cadera *nf* **:** hip

cadete *nmf* **:** cadet

cadmio *nm* **:** cadmium

caducar {72} *vi* **:** to expire

caducidad *nf* **:** expiration

caduco, -ca *adj* **1 :** outdated, obsolete **2 :** deciduous

caer {13} *vi* **1 :** to fall, to drop **2 :** to collapse **3 :** to hang (down) **4 caer bien** *fam* **:** to be pleasant, to be likeable <me caes bien : I like you> **5 caer mal** *or* **caer gordo** *fam* **:** to be unpleasant, to be unlikeable — **caerse** *vr* **:** to fall down

café[1] *adj* **:** brown <ojos cafés : brown eyes>

café[2] *nm* **1 :** coffee **2 :** café

cafeína *nf* **:** caffeine

cafetal *nm* **:** coffee plantation

cafetalero[1], **-ra** *adj* **:** coffee <cosecha cafetalera : coffee harvest>

cafetalero[2], **-ra** *n* **:** coffee grower

cafetera *nf* **:** coffeepot, coffeemaker

cafetería *nf* **1 :** coffee shop, café **2 :** lunchroom, cafeteria

cafetero[1], **-ra** *adj* **:** coffee-producing

cafetero[2], **-ra** *n* **:** coffee grower

cafeticultura *nf Mex* **:** coffee industry

caguama *nf* **1 :** large Caribbean turtle **2** *Mex* **:** large bottle of beer

caída *nf* **1** BAJA, DESCENSO **:** fall, drop **2 :** collapse, downfall

caiga, etc. → **caer**

caimán *nm, pl* **caimanes :** alligator, caiman

caimito *nm* **:** star apple

caja *nf* **1 :** box, case **2 :** cash register, checkout counter **3 :** bed (of a truck) **4** *fam* **:** coffin **5 caja fuerte** *or* **caja de caudales :** safe **6 caja de seguridad :** safe-deposit box **7 caja torácica :** rib cage

cajero, -ra *n* **1 :** cashier **2 :** teller **3 cajero automático :** automated teller machine, ATM

cajeta *nf Mex* **:** a sweet carmel-flavored spread

cajetilla *nf* **:** pack (of cigarettes)

cajón *nm, pl* **cajones 1 :** drawer, till **2 :** crate, case **3 cajón de estacionamiento** *Mex* **:** parking space

cajuela *nf Mex* **:** trunk (of a car)

cal *nf* **:** lime, quicklime

cala *nf* **:** cove, inlet

calabacín *nm, pl* **-cines :** zucchini

calabacita *nf Mex* **:** zucchini

calabaza *nf* **1 :** pumpkin, squash **2 :** gourd **3 dar calabazas a :** to give the brush-off to, to jilt

calabozo *nm* **1 :** prison **2 :** jail cell

calado[1], **-da** *adj* **1 :** drenched **2 :** openworked

calado[2] *nm* **1 :** draft (of a ship) **2 :** openwork

calafatear *vt* **:** to caulk

calamar *nm* **1 :** squid **2 calamares** *nmpl* **:** calamari

calambre *nm* **1** ESPASMO **:** cramp **2 :** electric shock, jolt

calamidad *nf* DESASTRE **:** calamity, disaster

calamina *nf* **:** calamine

calamitoso, -sa *adj* **:** calamitous, disastrous

calaña *nf* **:** ilk, kind, sort <una persona de mala calaña : a bad sort>

calar *vt* **1 :** to soak through **2 :** to pierce, to penetrate — *vi* **:** to catch on — **calarse** *vr* **:** to get drenched

calavera[1] *nf* **1 :** skull **2** *Mex* **:** taillight

calavera[2] *nm* **:** rake, rogue

calcar {72} *vt* **1 :** to trace **2 :** to copy, to imitate

calce, etc. → **calzar**

calceta *nf* **:** knee-high stocking

calcetería *nf* **:** hosiery

calcetín *nm, pl* **-tines :** sock

calcificar {72} *v* **:** to calcify — **calcificarse** *vr*

calcinar *vt* **:** to char, to burn

calcio *nm* **:** calcium

calco *nm* **1 :** transfer, tracing **2 :** copy, image

calcomanía *nf* **:** decal, transfer

calculador, -dora *adj* **:** calculating

calculadora *nf* **:** calculator

calcular *vt* **1 :** to calculate, to estimate **2 :** to plan, to scheme

cálculo *nm* **1 :** calculation, estimation **2 :** calculus **3 :** plan, scheme **4 cálculo biliar :** gallstone **5 hoja de cálculo :** spreadsheet

caldas *nfpl* **:** hot springs

caldear *vt* **:** to heat, to warm — **caldearse** *vr* **1 :** to heat up **2 :** to become heated, to get tense

caldera *nf* **1 :** cauldron **2 :** boiler

caldo *nm* **1** CONSOMÉ **:** broth, stock **2 caldo de cultivo :** culture medium, breeding ground

caldoso, -sa *adj* **:** watery

calefacción *nf, pl* **-ciones :** heating, heat

calefactor *nm* **:** heater

caleidoscopio *nm* → **calidoscopio**

calendario *nm* **1 :** calendar **2 :** timetable, schedule

caléndula *nf* **:** marigold

calentador *nm* **:** heater

calentamiento *nm* **1 :** heating, warming **2 :** warm-up (in sports)

calentar {55} *vt* **1 :** to heat, to warm **2** *fam* **:** to annoy, to anger **3** *fam* **:** to excite, to turn on — **calentarse** *vr* **1 :** to get warm, to heat up **2 :** to warm up (in sports) **3** *fam* **:** to become sexually aroused **4** *fam* **:** to get mad

calentura *nf* **1** FIEBRE **:** temperature, fever **2 :** cold sore

calibrador *nm* **:** gauge, calipers *pl*

calibrar *vt* : to calibrate — **calibración** *nf*

calibre *nm* **1** : caliber, gauge **2** : importance, excellence **3** : kind, sort <un problema de grueso calibre : a serious problem>

calidad *nf* **1** : quality, grade **2** : position, status **3 en calidad de** : as, in the capacity of

cálido, -da *adj* **1** : hot <un clima cálido : a hot climate> **2** : warm <una cálida bienvenida : a warm welcome>

calidoscopio *nm* : kaleidoscope

caliente *adj* **1** : hot, warm <mantenerse caliente : to stay warm> **2** : heated, fiery <una disputa caliente : a heated argument> **3** *fam* : sexually excited, horny

califa *nm* : caliph

calificación *nf, pl* **-ciones 1** NOTA : grade (for a course) **2** : rating, score **3** CLASIFICACIÓN : qualification, qualifying <ronda de calificación : qualifying round>

calificar {72} *vt* **1** : to grade **2** : to describe, to rate <la calificaron de buena alumna : they described her as a good student> **3** : to qualify, to modify (in grammar)

calificativo[1], -va *adj* : qualifying

calificativo[2] *nm* : qualifier, epithet

caligrafía *nf* **1** ESCRITURA : handwriting **2** : calligraphy

calistenia *nf* : calisthenics

cáliz *nm, pl* **cálices 1** : chalice, goblet **2** : calyx

caliza *nf* : limestone

callado, -da *adj* : quiet, silent — **calladamente** *adv*

callar *vi* : to keep quiet, to be silent — *vt* **1** : to silence, to hush <¡calla a los niños! : keep the children quiet!> **2** : to keep secret — **callarse** *vr* : to remain silent <¡cállate! : be quiet!, shut up!>

calle *nf* : street, road

callejear *vi* : to wander about the streets, to hang out

callejero, -ra *adj* : street <perro callejero : stray dog>

callejón *nm, pl* **-jones 1** : alley **2 callejón sin salida** : dead-end street

callo *nm* : callus, corn

calloso, -sa *adj* : callous

calma *nf* : calm, quiet

calmante[1] *adj* : calming, soothing

calmante[2] *nm* : tranquilizer, sedative

calmar *vt* TRANQUILIZAR : to calm, to soothe — **calmarse** *vr* : to calm down

calmo, -ma *adj* TRANQUILO : calm, tranquil

calmoso, -sa *adj* **1** TRANQUILO : calm, quiet **2** LENTO : slow, sluggish

calor *nm* **1** : heat <hace calor : it's hot outside> <tener calor : to feel hot> **2** : warmth, affection **3** : ardor, passion

caloría *nf* : calorie

calórico, -ca *adj* : caloric

calque, etc. → **calcar**

calumnia *nf* : slander, libel — **calumnioso, -sa** *adj*

calumniar *vt* : to slander, to libel

caluroso, -sa *adj* **1** : hot **2** : warm, enthusiastic

calva *nf* : bald spot, bald head

calvario *nm* **1** : Calvary **2** : Stations of the Cross *pl* **3 vivir un calvario** : to suffer great adversity

calvicie *nf* : baldness

calvo[1], -va *adj* : bald

calvo[2], -va *n* : bald person

calza *nf* : block, wedge

calzada *nf* : roadway, avenue

calzado *nm* : footwear

calzador *nm* : shoehorn

calzar {21} *vt* **1** : to wear (shoes) <¿de cuál calza? : what is your shoe size?> <siempre calzaban tenis : they always wore sneakers> **2** : to provide with shoes

calzo *nm* : chock, wedge

calzoncillos *nmpl* : underpants, briefs

calzones *nmpl* : underpants, panties

cama *nf* **1** : bed **2 cama elástica** : trampoline

camada *nf* : litter, brood

camafeo *nm* : cameo

camaleón *nm, pl* **-leones** : chameleon

cámara *nf* **1** : camera **2** : chamber, room **3** : house (in government) **4** : inner tube

camarada *nmf* **1** : comrade, companion **2** : colleague

camaradería *nf* : camaraderie

camarero, -ra *n* **1** MESERO : waiter, waitress *f* **2** : bellboy *m*, chambermaid *f* (in a hotel) **3** : steward *m*, stewardess *f* (on a ship, etc.)

camarilla *nf* : political clique

camarógrafo, -fa *n* : cameraman *m*, camerawoman *f*

camarón *nm, pl* **-rones 1** : shrimp **2** : prawn

camarote *nm* : cabin, stateroom

camastro *nm* : small hard bed, pallet

cambalache *nm fam* : swap

cambiante *adj* **1** : changing **2** VARIABLE : changeable, variable

cambiar *vt* **1** ALTERAR, MODIFICAR : to change **2** : to exchange, to trade — *vi* **1** : to change **2 cambiar de velocidad** : to shift gears — **cambiarse** *vr* **1** : to change (clothing) **2** MUDARSE : to move (to a new address)

cambio *nm* **1** : change, alteration **2** : exchange **3** : change (money) **4 en cambio** : instead **5 en cambio** : however, on the other hand

cambista *nmf* : exchange broker

camboyano, -na *adj & n* : Cambodian

cambur *nm Ven* : banana

camelia *nf* : camellia

camello *nm* : camel

camellón *nm, pl* **-llones** *Mex* : traffic island

camerino *nm* : dressing room

camerunés, -nesa *adj, mpl* **-neses** : Cameroonian

camilla *nf* : stretcher
camillero, -ra *n* : orderly (in a hospital)
caminante *nmf* : wayfarer, walker
caminar *vi* ANDAR : to walk, to move — *vt* : to walk, to cover (a distance)
caminata *nf* : hike, long walk
camino *nm* **1** : path, road **2** : journey <ponerse en camino : to set off> **3** : way <a medio camino : halfway there>
camión *nm, pl* **camiones 1** : truck **2** *Mex* : bus
camionero, -ra *n* **1** : truck driver **2** *Mex* : bus driver
camioneta *nm* : light truck, van
camisa *nf* **1** : shirt **2 camisa de fuerza** : straitjacket
camiseta *nf* **1** : T-shirt **2** : undershirt
camisón *nm, pl* **-sones** : nightshirt, nightgown
camorra *nf fam* : fight, trouble <buscar camorra : to pick a fight>
camote *nm* **1** : root vegetable similar to the sweet potato **2 hacerse camote** *Mex fam* : to get mixed up
campal *adj* : pitched, fierce <batalla campal : pitched battle>
campamento *nm* : camp
campana *nf* : bell
campanada *nf* TAÑIDO : stroke (of a bell), peal
campanario *nm* : bell tower, belfry
campanilla *nf* **1** : small bell, handbell **2** : uvula
campante *adj* : nonchalant, smug <seguir tan campante : to go on as if nothing had happened>
campaña *nf* **1** CAMPO : countryside, country **2** : campaign **3 tienda de campaña** : tent
campañol *nm* : vole
campechana *nf Mex* : puff pastry
campechanía *nf* : geniality
campechano, -na *adj* : open, cordial, friendly
campeón, -peona *n, mpl* **-peones** : champion
campeonato *nm* : championship
cámper *nm* : camper (vehicle)
campero, -ra *adj* : country, rural
campesino, -na *n* : peasant, farm laborer
campestre *adj* : rural, rustic
camping *nm* **1** : camping **2** : campsite
campiña *nf* CAMPO : countryside, country
campista *nmf* : camper
campo *nm* **1** CAMPAÑA : countryside, country **2** : field <campo de aviación : airfield> <su campo de responsabilidad : her field of responsibility>
camposanto *nm* : graveyard, cemetery
campus *nms & pl* : campus
camuflaje *nm* : camouflage
camuflajear *vt* : to camouflage
camuflar → **camuflajear**
can *nm* : hound, dog
cana *nf* **1** : gray hair **2 salirle canas** : to go gray, to get gray hair **3 echar una cana al aire** : to let one's hair down
canadiense *adj & nmf* : Canadian
canal[1] *nm* **1** : canal **2** : channel
canal[2] *nmf* : gutter, groove
canalé *nm* : rib, ribbing (in fabric)
canaleta *nf* : gutter
canalete *nm* : paddle
canalizar {21} *vt* : to channel
canalla[1] *adj fam* : low, rotten
canalla[2] *nmf fam* : bastard, swine
canapé *nm* **1** : hors d'oeuvre, canapé **2** SOFÁ : couch, sofa
canario[1], **-ria** *adj* : of or from the Canary Islands
canario[2], **-ria** *n* : Canarian, Canary Islander
canario[3] *nm* : canary
canasta *nf* **1** : basket **2** : canasta (card game)
cancel *nm* **1** : sliding door **2** : partition
cancelación *nf, pl* **-ciones 1** : cancellation **2** : payment in full
cancelar *vt* **1** : to cancel **2** : to pay off, to settle
cáncer *nm* : cancer
Cáncer *nmf* : Cancer
cancerígeno[1], **-na** *adj* : carcinogenic
cancerígeno[2] *nm* : carcinogen
canceroso, -sa *adj* : cancerous
cancha *nf* : court, field (for sports)
canciller *nm* : chancellor
cancillería *nf* : chancellery, ministry
canción *nf, pl* **canciones 1** : song **2 canción de cuna** : lullaby
cancionero[1] *nm* : songbook
cancionero[2], **-ra** *n Mex* : songster, songstress *f*
candado *nm* : padlock
candela *nf* **1** : flame, fire **2** : candle
candelabro *nm* : candelabra
candelero *nm* **1** : candlestick **2 estar en el candelero** : to be the center of attention
candente *adj* : red-hot
candidato, -ta *n* : candidate, applicant
candidatura *nf* : candidacy
candidez *nf* **1** : simplicity **2** INGENUIDAD : naïveté, ingenuousness
cándido, -da *adj* **1** : simple, unassuming **2** INGENUO : naive, ingenuous
candil *nm* : oil lamp
candilejas *nfpl* : footlights
candor *nm* : naïveté, innocence
candoroso, -sa *adj* : naive, innocent
canela *nf* : cinnamon
canesú *nm* : yoke (of clothing)
cangrejo *nm* JAIBA : crab
canguro *nm* **1** : kangaroo **2 hacer de canguro** *Spain* : to baby-sit
caníbal[1] *adj* : cannibalistic
caníbal[2] *nmf* ANTROPÓFAGO : cannibal
canibalismo *nm* ANTROPOFAGIA : cannibalism
canibalizar {21} *vt* : to cannibalize
canica *nf* **1** : marble **2 canicas** *nfpl* : marbles (toys)
caniche *nm* : poodle

canijo, -ja *adj* **1** *fam* **:** puny, weak **2** *Mex fam* **:** tough, hard <un examen muy canijo : a very tough exam>
canilla *nf* **1 :** shin, shinbone **2** *Arg, Uru* **:** faucet
canino[1], -na *adj* **:** canine
canino[2] *nm* **1** COLMILLO **:** canine (tooth) **2 :** dog, canine
canje *nm* INTERCAMBIO **:** exchange, trade
canjear *vt* INTERCAMBIAR **:** to exchange, to trade
cannabis *nm* **:** cannabis
cano, -na *adj* **:** gray <un hombre de pelo cano : a gray-haired man>
canoa *nf* **:** canoe
canon *nm, pl* **cánones :** canon
canónico, -ca *adj* **1 :** canonical **2 derecho canónico :** canon law
canonizar {21} *vt* **:** to canonize — **canonización** *nf*
canoso, -sa → cano
cansado, -da *adj* **1 :** tired <estar cansado : to be tired> **2 :** tiresome, wearying <ser cansado : to be tiring>
cansancio *nm* FATIGA **:** fatigue, weariness
cansar *vt* FATIGAR **:** to wear out, to tire — *vi* **:** to be tiresome — **cansarse** *vr* **1 :** to wear oneself out **2 :** to get bored
cansino, -na *adj* **:** slow, weary, lethargic
cantaleta *nf fam* **:** nagging <la misma cantaleta : the same old story>
cantalupo *nm* **:** cantaloupe
cantante *nmf* **:** singer
cantar[1] *v* **:** to sing
cantar[2] *nm* **:** song, ballad
cántaro *nm* **1 :** pitcher, jug **2 llover a cántaros** *fam* **:** to rain cats and dogs
cantata *nf* **:** cantata
cantera *nf* **:** quarry <cantera de piedra : stone quarry>
cántico *nm* **:** canticle, chant
cantidad[1] *adv fam* **:** really <ese carro me costó cantidad : that car cost me plenty>
cantidad[2] *nf* **1 :** quantity **2 :** sum, amount (of money) **3** *fam* **:** a lot, a great many <había cantidad de niños en el parque : there were tons of kids in the park>
cantimplora *nf* **:** canteen, water bottle
cantina *nf* **1 :** tavern, bar **2 :** canteen, mess, dining quarters *pl*
cantinero, -ra *n* **:** bartender
canto *nm* **1 :** singing **2 :** chant <canto gregoriano : Gregorian chant> **3 :** song (of a bird) **4 :** edge, end <de canto : on end, sideways> **5 canto rodado :** boulder
cantón *nm, pl* **cantones 1 :** canton **2** *Mex fam* **:** place, home
cantor[1], -tora *adj* **1 :** singing **2 pájaro cantor :** songbird
cantor[2], -tora *n* **1 :** singer **2 :** cantor
caña *nf* **1 :** cane <caña de azúcar : sugarcane> **2 :** reed **3 caña de pescar :** fishing rod **4 caña del timón :** tiller (of a boat)
cañada *nf* **:** ravine, gully
cáñamo *nm* **:** hemp
cañaveral *nm* **:** sugarcane field
cañería *nf* TUBERÍA **:** pipes *pl*, piping
caño *nm* **1 :** pipe **2 :** spout **3 :** channel (for navigation)
cañón *nm, pl* **cañones 1 :** cannon **2 :** barrel (of a gun) **3 :** canyon
cañonear *vt* **:** to shell, to bombard
cañoneo *nm* **:** shelling, bombardment
cañonero *nm* **:** gunboat
caoba *nf* **:** mahogany
caos *nm* **:** chaos
caótico, -ca *adj* **:** chaotic
capa *nf* **1 :** cape, cloak **2 :** coating **3 :** layer, stratum **4 :** (social) class, stratum
capacidad *nf* **1 :** capacity **2 :** capability, ability
capacitación *nf, pl* **-ciones :** training
capacitar *vt* **:** to train, to qualify
caparazón *nm, pl* **-zones :** shell, carapace
capataz *nmf, pl* **-taces :** foreman *m*, forewoman *f*
capaz *adj, pl* **capaces 1** APTO **:** capable, able **2** COMPETENTE **:** competent **3 :** spacious <capaz para : with room for>
capcioso, -sa *adj* **:** cunning, deceptive <pregunta capciosa : trick question>
capea *nf* **:** amateur bullfight
capear *vt* **1 :** to make a pass with the cape (in bullfighting) **2 :** to dodge, to weather <capear el temporal : to ride out the storm>
capellán *nm, pl* **-llanes :** chaplain
capilar *nm* **:** capillary — **capilar** *adj*
capilla *nf* **:** chapel
capirotada *nf Mex* **:** traditional bread pudding
capirotazo *nm* **:** flip, flick
capital[1] *adj* **1 :** capital **2 :** chief, principal
capital[2] *nm* **:** capital <capital de riesgo : venture capital>
capital[3] *nf* **:** capital, capital city
capitalino[1], -na *adj* **:** of or from a capital city
capitalino[2], -na *n* **:** inhabitant of a capital city
capitalismo *nm* **:** capitalism
capitalista *adj & nmf* **:** capitalist
capitalizar {21} *vt* **:** to capitalize — **capitalización** *nf*
capitán, -tana *n, mpl* **-tanes :** captain
capitanear *vt* **:** to captain, to command
capitanía *nf* **:** captaincy
capitel *nm* **:** capital (of a column)
capitolio *nm* **:** capitol
capitulación *nf, pl* **-ciones :** capitulation
capitular *vi* **:** to capitulate, to surrender
capítulo *nm* **1 :** chapter, section **2 :** matter, subject
capó *nm* **:** hood (of a car)
capón *nm, pl* **capones :** capon

caporal *nm* **1 :** chief, leader **2 :** foreman (on a ranch)

capota *nf* **:** top (of a convertible)

capote *nm* **1 :** cloak, overcoat **2 :** bullfighter's cape **3** *Mex* COFRE **:** hood (of a car)

capricho *nm* ANTOJO **:** whim, caprice

caprichoso, -sa *adj* ANTOJADIZO **:** capricious, fickle

Capricornio *nmf* **:** Capricorn

cápsula *nf* **:** capsule

captar *vt* **1 :** to catch, to grasp **2 :** to gain, to attract **3 :** to harness, to collect (waters)

captor, -tora *n* **:** captor

captura *nf* **:** capture, seizure

capturar *vt* **:** to capture, to seize

capucha *nf* **:** hood, cowl

capuchina *nf* **:** nasturtium

capuchino *nm* **1 :** Capuchin (monk) **2 :** capuchin (monkey) **3 :** cappuccino

capullo *nm* **1 :** cocoon **2 :** bud (of a flower)

caqui *adj & nm* **:** khaki

cara *nf* **1 :** face **2** ASPECTO **:** look, appearance <¡qué buena cara tiene ese pastel! : that cake looks delicious!> **3** *fam* **:** nerve, gall **4 ~ a** *or* **de cara a :** facing **5 de cara a :** in view of, in the light of

carabina *nf* **:** carbine

caracol *nm* **1 :** snail **2** CONCHA **:** conch, seashell **3 :** cochlea **4 :** ringlet

caracola *nf* **:** conch

carácter *nm, pl* **caracteres 1** ÍNDOLE **:** character, kind, nature **2** TEMPERAMENTO **:** disposition, temperament **3 :** letter, symbol <caracteres chinos : Chinese characters>

característica *nf* RASGO **:** trait, feature, characteristic

característico, -ca *adj* **:** characteristic **— característicamente** *adv*

caracterizar {21} *vt* **:** to characterize **— caracterización** *nf*

caramba *interj* **:** darn!, heck!

carámbano *nm* **:** icicle

carambola *nf* **1 :** carom **2 :** ruse, trick <por carambola : by a lucky chance>

caramelo *nm* **1 :** caramel **2** DULCE **:** candy

caramillo *nm* **1 :** pipe, small flute **2 :** heap, pile

caraqueño[1], -ña *adj* **:** of or from Caracas

caraqueño[2], -ña *n* **:** person from Caracas

carátula *nf* **1 :** title page **2 :** cover, dust jacket **3** CARETA **:** mask **4** *Mex* **:** face, dial (of a clock or watch)

caravana *nf* **1 :** caravan **2 :** convoy, motorcade **3** REMOLQUE **:** trailer

caray → caramba

carbohidrato *nm* **:** carbohydrate

carbón *nm, pl* **carbones 1 :** coal **2 :** charcoal

carbonatado, -da *adj* **:** carbonated

carbonato *nm* **:** carbonate

carboncillo *nm* **:** charcoal

carbonera *nf* **:** coal cellar, coal bunker (on a ship)

carbonero, -ra *adj* **:** coal

carbonizar {21} *vt* **:** to carbonize, to char

carbono *nm* **:** carbon

carbunco *or* **carbunclo** *nm* **:** carbuncle

carburador *nm* **:** carburetor

carca *nmf fam* **:** old fogy

carcacha *nf fam* **:** jalopy, wreck

carcaj *nm* **:** quiver (for arrows)

carcajada *nf* **:** loud laugh, guffaw <reírse a carcajadas : to roar with laughter>

carcajearse *vr* **:** to roar with laughter, to be in stitches

cárcel *nf* PRISIÓN **:** jail, prison

carcelero, -ra *n* **:** jailer

carcinogénico, -ca *adj* **:** carcinogenic

carcinógeno *nm* CANCERÍGENO **:** carcinogen

carcinoma *nm* **:** carcinoma

carcomer *vt* **:** to eat away at, to consume

carcomido, -da *adj* **1 :** worm-eaten **2 :** decayed, rotten

cardán *nm, pl* **cardanes :** universal joint

cardar *vt* **:** to card, to comb

cardenal *nm* **1 :** cardinal (in religion) **2 :** bruise

cardíaco *or* **cardiaco, -ca** *adj* **:** cardiac, heart

cárdigan *nm, pl* **-gans :** cardigan

cardinal *adj* **:** cardinal

cardiología *nf* **:** cardiology

cardiólogo, -ga *n* **:** cardiologist

cardiovascular *adj* **:** cardiovascular

cardo *nm* **:** thistle

cardumen *nm* **:** school of fish

carear *vt* **:** to bring face-to-face

carecer {53} *vi* **~ de :** to lack <el cheque carecía de fondos : the check lacked funds>

carencia *nf* **1** FALTA **:** lack **2** ESCASEZ **:** shortage **3** DEFICIENCIA **:** deficiency

carente *adj* **~ de :** lacking (in)

carero, -ra *adj fam* **:** pricey

carestía *nf* **1 :** rise in cost <la carestía de la vida : the high cost of living> **2 :** dearth, scarcity

careta *nf* MÁSCARA **:** mask

carey *nm* **1 :** hawksbill turtle, sea turtle **2 :** tortoiseshell

carga *nf* **1 :** loading **2 :** freight, load, cargo **3 :** burden, responsibility **4 :** charge <carga eléctrica : electrical charge> **5 :** attack, charge

cargado, -da *adj* **1 :** loaded **2 :** bogged down, weighted down **3 :** close, stuffy **4 :** charged <cargado de tensión : charged with tension> **5** FUERTE **:** strong <café cargado : strong coffee> **6 cargado de hombros :** stoop-shouldered

cargador[1], -dora *n* **:** longshoreman *m*, longshorewoman *f*

cargador[2] *nm* **1 :** magazine (for a firearm) **2 :** charger (for batteries)
cargamento *nm* **:** cargo, load
cargar {52} *vt* **1 :** to carry **2 :** to load, to fill **3 :** to charge — *vi* **1 :** to load **2 :** to rest (in architecture) **3 ~ sobre :** to fall upon
cargo *nm* **1 :** burden, load **2 :** charge <a cargo de : in charge of> **3 :** position, office
cargue, etc. → **cargar**
carguero[1], **-ra** *adj* **:** freight, cargo <tren carguero : freight train>
carguero[2] *nm* **:** freighter, cargo ship
cariarse *vr* **:** to decay (of teeth)
caribe *adj* **:** Caribbean <el mar caribe : the Caribbean Sea>
caribeño, -ña *adj* **:** Caribbean
caribú *nm* **:** caribou
caricatura *nf* **1 :** caricature **2 :** cartoon
caricaturista *nmf* **:** caricaturist, cartoonist
caricaturizar {21} *vt* **:** to caricature
caricia *nf* **1 :** caress **2 hacer caricias :** to pet, to stroke
caridad *nf* **1 :** charity **2** LIMOSNA **:** alms *pl*
caries *nfs & pl* **:** cavity (in a tooth)
carillón *nm, pl* **-llones 1 :** carillon **2 :** glockenspiel
cariño *nm* AFECTO **:** affection, love
cariñoso, -sa *adj* AFECTUOSO **:** affectionate, loving — **cariñosamente** *adv*
carioca[1] *adj* **:** of or from Rio de Janeiro
carioca[2] *nmf* **:** person from Rio de Janeiro
carisma *nf* **:** charisma
carismático, -ca *adj* **:** charismatic
carita *adj Mex fam* **:** cute (said of a man) <tu primo se cree muy carita : your cousin thinks he's gorgeous>
caritativo, -va *adj* **:** charitable
cariz *nm, pl* **carices :** appearance, aspect
carmesí *adj & nm* **:** crimson
carmín *nm, pl* **carmines 1 :** carmine **2 carmín de labios :** lipstick
carnada *nf* CEBO **:** bait
carnal *adj* **1 :** carnal **2 primo carnal :** first cousin
carnaval *nm* **:** carnival
carnaza *nf* **:** bait
carne *nf* **1 :** meat <carne molida : ground beef> **2 :** flesh <carne de gallina : goose bumps>
carné *nm* → **carnet**
carnero *nm* **1 :** ram, sheep **2 :** mutton
carnet *nm* **1 :** identification card, ID **2 :** membership card **3 carnet de conducir** *Spain* **:** driver's license
carnicería *nf* **1 :** butcher shop **2** MATANZA **:** slaughter, carnage
carnicero, -ra *n* **:** butcher
carnívoro[1], **-ra** *adj* **:** carnivorous
carnívoro[2] *nm* **:** carnivore
carnoso, -sa *adj* **:** fleshy, meaty
caro[1] *adv* **:** dearly, a lot <pagué caro : I paid a high price>
caro[2], **-ra** *adj* **1 :** expensive, dear **2** QUERIDO **:** dear, beloved
carpa *nf* **1 :** carp **2 :** big top (of a circus) **3 :** tent
carpelo *nm* **:** carpel
carpeta *nf* **:** folder, binder, portfolio (of drawings, etc.)
carpetazo *nm* **dar carpetazo a :** to shelve, to defer
carpintería *nf* **1 :** carpentry **2 :** carpenter's workshop
carpintero, -ra *n* **:** carpenter
carraspear *vi* **:** to clear one's throat
carraspera *nf* **:** hoarseness <tener carraspera : to have a frog in one's throat>
carrera *nf* **1 :** run, running <a la carrera : at full speed> <de carrera : hastily> **2 :** race **3 :** course of study **4 :** career, profession **5 :** run (in baseball)
carreta *nf* **:** cart, wagon
carrete *nm* **1** BOBINA **:** reel, spool **2 :** roll of film
carretel *nm* → **carrete**
carretera *nf* **:** highway, road <carretera de peaje : turnpike>
carretero, -ra *adj* **:** highway <el sistema carretero nacional : the national highway system>
carretilla *nf* **1 :** wheelbarrow **2 carretilla elevadora :** forklift
carril *nm* **1 :** lane <carretera de doble carril : two-lane highway> **2 :** rail (on a railroad track)
carrillo *nm* **:** cheek, jowl
carrito *nm* **:** cart <carrito de compras : shopping cart>
carrizo *nm* JUNCO **:** reed
carro *nm* **1** COCHE **:** car **2 :** cart **3** *Chile, Mex* **:** coach (of a train) **4 carro alegórico :** float (in a parade)
carrocería *nf* **:** bodywork
carroña *nf* **:** carrion
carroñero, -ra *n* **:** scavenger (animal)
carroza *nf* **1 :** carriage **2 :** float (in a parade)
carruaje *nm* **:** carriage
carrusel *nm* **1 :** merry-go-round **2 :** carousel <carrusel de equipaje : luggage carousel>
carta *nf* **1 :** letter **2** NAIPE **:** playing card **3 :** charter, constitution **4** MENÚ **:** menu **5 :** map, chart **6 tomar cartas en :** to intervene in
cártamo *nm* **:** safflower
cartearse *vr* ESCRIBIRSE **:** to write to one another, to correspond
cartel *nm* **:** sign, poster
cártel *or* **cartel** *nm* **:** cartel
cartelera *nf* **1 :** billboard **2 :** marquee
cartera *nf* **1** BILLETERA **:** wallet, billfold **2** BOLSO **:** pocketbook, purse **3 :** portfolio <cartera de acciones : stock portfolio>
carterista *nmf* **:** pickpocket
cartero, -ra *n* **:** letter carrier, mailman *m*

cartilaginoso, -sa *adj* : cartilaginous, gristly

cartílago *nm* : cartilage

cartilla *nf* **1** : primer, reader **2** : booklet <cartilla de ahorros : bankbook>

cartografía *nf* : cartography

cartógrafo, -fa *n* : cartographer

cartón *nm, pl* **cartones 1** : cardboard <cartón madera : fiberboard> **2** : carton

cartucho *nm* : cartridge

cartulina *nf* : poster board, cardboard

carúncula *nf* : wattle (of a bird)

casa *nf* **1** : house, building **2** HOGAR : home **3** : household, family **4** : company, firm **5 echar la casa por la ventana** : to spare no expense

casaca *nf* : jacket

casado[1], -da *adj* : married

casado[2], -da *n* : married person

casamentero, -ra *n* : matchmaker

casamiento *nm* **1** : marriage **2** BODA : wedding

casar *vt* : to marry — *vi* : to go together, to match up — **casarse** *vr* **1** : to get married **2 ~ con** : to marry

casateniente *nmf Mex* : landlord, landlady *f*

cascabel[1] *nm* : small bell

cascabel[2] *nf* : rattlesnake

cascada *nf* CATARATA, SALTO : waterfall, cascade

cascajo *nm* **1** : pebble, rock fragment **2** *fam* : piece of junk

cascanueces *nms & pl* : nutcracker

cascar {72} *vt* : to crack (a shell) — **cascarse** *vr* : to crack, to chip

cáscara *nf* **1** : skin, peel, rind, husk **2** : shell (of a nut or egg)

cascarón *nm, pl* **-rones 1** : eggshell **2** *Mex* : shell filled with confetti

cascarrabias *nmfs & pl fam* : grouch, crab

casco *nm* **1** : helmet **2** : hull **3** : hoof **4** : fragment, shard **5** : center (of a town) **6** *Mex* : empty bottle **7 cascos** *nmpl* : headphones

caserío *nm* **1** : country house **2** : hamlet

casero[1], -ra *adj* **1** : domestic, household **2** : homemade

casero[2], -ra *n* DUEÑO : landlord *m,* landlady *f*

caseta *nf* : booth, stand, stall <caseta telefónica : telephone booth>

casete *nmf* → **cassette**

casi *adv* **1** : almost, nearly, virtually **2** (*in negative phrases*) : hardly <casi nunca : hardly ever>

casilla *nf* **1** : booth **2** : pigeonhole **3** : box (on a form)

casino *nm* **1** : casino **2** : (social) club

caso *nm* **1** : case **2 en caso de** : in case of, in the event of **3 hacer caso de** : to pay attention to, to notice **4 hacer caso omiso de** : to ignore, to take no notice of **5 no venir al caso** : to be beside the point

caspa *nf* : dandruff

casque, etc. → **cascar**

casquete *nm* **1** : skullcap **2 casquete glaciar** : ice cap **3 casquete corto** *Mex* : crew cut

cassette *nmf* : cassette

casta *nf* **1** : caste **2** : lineage, stock <de casta : thoroughbred, purebred> **3 sacar la casta** *Mex* : to come out ahead

castaña *nf* : chestnut

castañetear *vi* : to chatter (of teeth)

castaño[1], -ña *adj* : chestnut, brown

castaño[2], -ña *nm* **1** : chestnut tree **2** : chestnut, brown

castañuela *nf* : castanet

castellano[1], -na *adj & n* : Castilian

castellano[2] *nm* ESPAÑOL : Spanish, Castilian (language)

castidad *nf* : chastity

castigar {52} *vt* : to punish

castigo *nm* : punishment

castillo *nm* **1** : castle **2 castillo de proa** : forecastle

casto, -ta *adj* : chaste, pure — **castamente** *adv*

castor *nm* : beaver

castración *nf, pl* **-ciones** : castration

castrar *vt* **1** : to castrate, to spay, to neuter, to geld **2** DEBILITAR : to weaken, to debilitate

castrense *adj* : military

casual *adj* **1** FORTUITO : fortuitous, accidental **2** *Mex* : casual (of clothing)

casualidad *nf* **1** : chance **2 por ~** *or* **de ~** : by chance, by any chance

casualmente *adv* : accidentally, by chance

casucha *or* **casuca** *nf* : shanty, hovel

cataclismo *nm* : cataclysm

catacumbas *nfpl* : catacombs

catador, -dora *n* : wine taster

catalán[1], -lana *adj & n, mpl* **-lanes** : Catalan

catalán[2] *nm* : Catalan (language)

catálisis *nm* : catalysis

catalítico, -ca *adj* : catalytic

catalizador *nm* **1** : catalyst **2** : catalytic converter

catalogar {52} *vt* : to catalog, to classify

catálogo *nm* : catalog

catamarán *nm, pl* **-ranes** : catamaran

cataplasma *nf* : poultice

catapulta *nf* : catapult

catapultar *vt* : to catapult

catar *vt* **1** : to taste, to sample **2** : to look at, to examine

catarata *nf* **1** CASCADA, SALTO : waterfall **2** : cataract

catarro *nm* RESFRIADO : cold, catarrh

catarsis *nf* : catharsis

catártico, -ca *adj* : cathartic

catástrofe *nf* DESASTRE : catastrophe, disaster

catastrófico, -ca *adj* DESASTROSO : catastrophic, disastrous

catcher *nmf* : catcher (in baseball)

catecismo *nm* : catechism

cátedra *nf* **1** : chair, professorship **2** : subject, class **3 libertad de cátedra** : academic freedom

catedral *nf* : cathedral

catedrático, -ca *n* PROFESOR : professor

categoría *nf* **1** CLASE : category **2** RANGO : rank, standing **3 categoría gramatical** : part of speech **4 de ~** : first-rate, outstanding

categórico, -ca *adj* : categorical, unequivocal — **categóricamente** *adv*

catéter *nm* : catheter

cátodo *nm* : cathode

catolicismo *nm* : Catholicism

católico, -ca *adj & n* : Catholic

catorce *adj & nm* : fourteen

catorceavo *nm* : fourteenth

catre *nm* : cot

catsup *nm* : ketchup

caucásico, -ca *adj & n* : Caucasian

cauce *nm* **1** LECHO : riverbed **2** : means *pl,* channel

caucho *nm* **1** GOMA : rubber **2** : rubber tree **3** *Ven* : tire

caución *nf, pl* **cauciones** FIANZA : bail, security

caudal *nm* **1** : volume of water **2** RIQUEZA : capital, wealth **3** ABUNDANCIA : abundance

caudillaje *nm* : leadership

caudillo *nm* : leader, commander

causa *nf* **1** MOTIVO : cause, reason, motive <a causa de : because of> **2** IDEAL : cause <morir por una causa : to die for a cause> **3** : lawsuit

causal[1] *adj* : causal

causal[2] *nm* : cause, grounds *pl*

causalidad *nf* : causality

causante[1] *adj* **~ de** : causing, responsible for

causante[2] *nmf Mex* : taxpayer

causar *vt* **1** : to cause **2** : to provoke, to arouse <eso me causa gracia : that strikes me as being funny>

cáustico, -ca *adj* : caustic

cautela *nf* : caution, prudence

cautelar *adj* : precautionary, preventive

cauteloso, -sa *adj* : cautious, prudent — **cautelosamente** *adv*

cauterizar {21} *vt* : to cauterize

cautivador, -dora *adj* : captivating

cautivar *vt* HECHIZAR : to captivate, to charm

cautiverio *nm* : captivity

cautivo, -va *adj & n* : captive

cauto, -ta *adj* : cautious, careful

cavar *vt* : to dig — *vi* **~ en** : to delve into, to probe

caverna *nf* : cavern, cave

cavernoso, -sa *adj* **1** : cavernous **2** : deep, resounding

caviar *nm* : caviar

cavidad *nf* : cavity

cavilar *vi* : to ponder, to deliberate

cayado *nm* : crook, staff, crosier

cayena *nf* : cayenne pepper

cayó, etc. → **caer**

caza[1] *nf* **1** CACERÍA : hunt, hunting **2** : game

caza[2] *nm* : fighter plane

cazador, -dora *n* **1** : hunter **2 cazador furtivo** : poacher

cazar {21} *vt* **1** : to hunt **2** : to catch, to bag **3** *fam* : to land (a job, a spouse) — *vi* : to go hunting

cazatalentos *nmfs & pl* : talent scout

cazo *nm* **1** : saucepan, pot **2** CUCHARÓN : ladle

cazuela *nf* **1** : pan, saucepan **2** : casserole

cazurro, -ra *adj* : sullen, surly

CD *nm* : CD, compact disk

cebada *nf* : barley

cebar *vt* **1** : to bait **2** : to feed, to fatten **3** : to prime (a pump, etc.) — **cebarse** *vr* **~ en** : to take it out on

cebo *nm* **1** CARNADA : bait **2** : feed **3** : primer (for firearms)

cebolla *nf* : onion

cebolleta *nf* : scallion, green onion

cebollino *nm* **1** : chive **2** : scallion

cebra *nf* : zebra

cebú *nm, pl* **cebús** *or* **cebúes** : zebu (cattle)

cecear *vi* : to lisp

ceceo *nm* : lisp

cecina *nf* : dried beef, beef jerky

cedazo *nm* : sieve

ceder *vi* **1** : to yield, to give way **2** : to diminish, to abate **3** : to give in, to relent — *vt* : to cede, to hand over

cedro *nm* : cedar

cédula *nf* : document, certificate

céfiro *nm* : zephyr

cegador, -dora *adj* : blinding

cegar {49} *vt* **1** : to blind **2** : to block, to stop up — *vi* : to be blinded, to go blind

cegatón, -tona *adj, mpl* **-tones** *fam* : blind as a bat

ceguera *nf* : blindness

ceiba *nf* : ceiba, silk-cotton tree

ceja *nf* **1** : eyebrow <fruncir las cejas : to knit one's brows> **2** : flange, rim

cejar *vi* : to give in, to back down

celada *nf* : trap, ambush

celador, -dora *n* GUARDIA : guard, warden

celda *nf* : cell (of a jail)

celebración *nf, pl* **-ciones** : celebration

celebrado, -da *adj* CÉLEBRE, FAMOSO : famous, celebrated

celebrante *nmf* OFICIANTE : celebrant

celebrar *vt* **1** FESTEJAR : to celebrate **2** : to hold (a meeting) **3** : to say (Mass) **4** : to welcome, to be happy about — *vi* : to be glad — **celebrarse** *vr* **1** : to be celebrated, to fall **2** : to be held, to take place

célebre *adj* CELEBRADO, FAMOSO : celebrated, famous

celebridad *nf* **1** : celebrity **2** FAMA : fame, renown

celeridad *nf* : celerity, swiftness

celeste[1] *adj* **1** : celestial **2** : sky blue, azure

celeste[2] *nm* : sky blue
celestial *adj* : heavenly, celestial
celibato *nm* : celibacy
célibe *adj & nmf* : celibate
cello *nm* : cello
celo *nm* **1** : zeal, fervor **2** : heat (of females), rut (of males) **3 celos** *nmpl* : jealousy <tenerle celos a alguien : to be jealous of someone>
celofán *nm, pl* **-fanes** : cellophane
celosía *nf* **1** : lattice window **2** : latticework, trellis
celoso, -sa *adj* **1** : jealous **2** : zealous — **celosamente** *adv*
celta[1] *adj* : Celtic
celta[2] *nmf* : Celt
célula *nf* : cell
celular *adj* : cellular
celuloide *nm* **1** : celluloid **2** : film, cinema
celulosa *nf* : cellulose
cementar *vt* : to cement
cementerio *nm* : cemetery
cemento *nm* : cement
cena *nf* : supper, dinner
cenador *nm* : arbor
cenagal *nm* : bog, quagmire
cenagoso, -sa *adj* : swampy
cenar *vi* : to have dinner, to have supper — *vt* : to have for dinner or supper <anoche cenamos tamales : we had tamales for supper last night>
cencerro *nm* : cowbell
cenicero *nm* : ashtray
ceniciento, -ta *adj* : ashen
cenit *nm* : zenith, peak
ceniza *nf* **1** : ash **2 cenizas** *nfpl* : ashes (of a deceased person)
cenizo, -za *n* : jinx
cenote *nm Mex* : natural deposit of spring water
censar *vt* : to take a census of
censo *nm* : census
censor, -sora *n* : censor, critic
censura *nf* **1** : censorship **2** : censure, criticism
censurable *adj* : reprehensible, blameworthy
censurar *vt* **1** : to censor **2** : to censure, to criticize
centauro *nm* : centaur
centavo *nm* **1** : cent (in English-speaking countries) **2** : unit of currency in various Latin-American countries
centella *nf* **1** : lightning flash **2** : spark
centellear *vi* **1** : to twinkle **2** : to gleam, to sparkle
centelleo *nm* : twinkling, sparkle
centenar *nm* **1** : hundred **2 a centenares** : by the hundreds
centenario[1], **-ria** *adj & n* : centenarian
centenario[2] *nm* : centennial
centeno *nm* : rye
centésimo[1], **-ma** *adj* : hundredth
centésimo[2] *nm* : hundredth
centígrado *adj* : centigrade, Celsius
centigramo *nm* : centigram
centímetro *nm* : centimeter
centinela *nmf* : sentinel, sentry
central[1] *adj* **1** : central **2** PRINCIPAL : main, principal
central[2] *nf* **1** : main office, headquarters **2 central camionera** *Mex* : bus terminal
centralita *nf* : switchboard
centralizar {21} *vt* : to centralize — **centralización** *nf*
centrar *vt* **1** : to center **2** : to focus — **centrarse** *vr* **~ en** : to focus on, to concentrate on
céntrico, -ca *adj* : central
centrífugo, -ga *adj* : centrifugal
centrípeto, -ta *adj* : centripetal
centro[1] *nmf* : center (in sports)
centro[2] *nm* **1** MEDIO : center <centro de atención : center of attention> <centro de gravedad : center of gravity> **2** : downtown **3 centro de mesa** : centerpiece
centroamericano, -na *adj & n* : Central American
ceñido, -da *adj* AJUSTADO : tight, tight-fitting
ceñir {67} *vt* **1** : to encircle, to surround **2** : to hug, to cling to <me ciñe demasiado : it's too tight on me> — **ceñirse** *vr* **~ a** : to restrict oneself to, to stick to
ceño *nm* **1** : frown, scowl **2 fruncir el ceño** : to frown, to knit one's brows
cepa *nf* **1** : stump (of a tree) **2** : stock (of a vine) **3** LINAJE : ancestry, stock
cepillar *vt* **1** : to brush **2** : to plane (wood) — **cepillarse** *vr*
cepillo *nm* **1** : brush <cepillo de dientes : toothbrush> **2** : plane (for woodworking)
cepo *nm* : trap (for animals)
cera *nf* **1** : wax <cera de abejas : beeswax> **2** : polish
cerámica *nf* **1** : ceramics *pl* **2** : pottery
cerámico, -ca *adj* : ceramic
ceramista *nmf* ALFARERO : potter
cerca[1] *adv* **1** : close, near, nearby **2 ~ de** : nearly, almost
cerca[2] *nf* **1** : fence **2** : (stone) wall
cercado *nm* : enclosure
cercanía *nf* **1** PROXIMIDAD : proximity, closeness **2 cercanías** *nfpl* : outskirts, suburbs
cercano, -na *adj* : near, close
cercar {72} *vt* **1** : to fence in, to enclose **2** : to surround
cercenar *vt* **1** : to cut off, to amputate **2** : to diminish, to curtail
cerceta *nf* : teal (duck)
cerciorarse *vr* ASEGURARSE **~ de** : to make sure of, to verify
cerco *nm* **1** : siege **2** : cordon, circle **3** : fence
cerda *nf* **1** : bristle **2** : sow
cerdo *nm* **1** : pig, hog **2 carne de cerdo** : pork
cereal *nm* : cereal — **cereal** *adj*
cerebelo *nm* : cerebellum
cerebral *adj* : cerebral
cerebro *nm* : brain

ceremonia *nf* : ceremony — **ceremonial** *adj*
ceremonioso, -sa *adj* : ceremonious
cereza *nf* : cherry
cerezo *nm* : cherry tree
cerilla *nf* **1** : match **2** : earwax
cerillo *nm* (*in various countries*) : match
cerner {56} *vt* : to sift — **cernerse** *vr* **1** : to hover **2 ~ sobre** : to loom over, to threaten
cernidor *nm* : sieve
cernir → **cerner**
cero *nm* : zero
ceroso, -sa *adj* : waxy
cerque, etc. → **cercar**
cerquita *adv fam* : very close, very near
cerrado, -da *adj* **1** : closed, shut **2** : thick, broad <tiene un acento cerrado : she has a thick accent> **3** : cloudy, overcast **4** : quiet, reserved **5** : dense, stupid
cerradura *nf* : lock
cerrajería *nf* : locksmith's shop
cerrajero, -ra *n* : locksmith
cerrar {55} *vt* **1** : to close, to shut **2** : to turn off **3** : to bring to an end — *vi* **1** : to close up, to lock up **2** : to close down — **cerrarse** *vr* **1** : to close **2** : to fasten, to button up **3** : to conclude, to end
cerrazón *nf, pl* **-zones** : obstinacy, stubbornness
cerro *nm* COLINA, LOMA : hill
cerrojo *nm* PESTILLO : bolt, latch
certamen *nm, pl* **-támenes** : competition, contest
certero, -ra *adj* : accurate, precise — **certeramente** *adv*
certeza *nf* : certainty
certidumbre *nf* : certainty
certificable *adj* : certifiable
certificación *nf, pl* **-ciones** : certification
certificado¹, -da *adj* **1** : certified **2** : registered (of mail)
certificado² *nm* **1** : certificate **2** : registered letter
certificar {72} *vt* **1** : to certify **2** : to register (mail)
cervato *nm* : fawn
cervecería *nf* **1** : brewery **2** : beer hall, bar
cerveza *nf* : beer <cerveza de barril : draft beer>
cervical *adj* : cervical
cerviz *nf, pl* **cervices** : nape of the neck, cervix
cesación *nf, pl* **-ciones** : cessation, suspension
cesante *adj* : laid off, unemployed
cesantía *nf* : unemployment
cesar *vi* : to cease, to stop — *vt* : to dismiss, to lay off
cesárea *nf* : cesarean, C-section
cese *nm* **1** : cessation, stop <cese del fuego : cease-fire> **2** : dismissal
cesio *nm* : cesium
cesión *nf, pl* **cesiones** : transfer, assignment <cesión de bienes : transfer of property>
césped *nm* : lawn, grass
cesta *nf* **1** : basket **2** : jai alai racket
cesto *nm* **1** : hamper **2** : basket (in basketball) **3 cesto de (la) basura** : wastebasket
cetrería *nf* : falconry
cetrino, -na *adj* : sallow
cetro *nm* : scepter
chabacano¹, -na *adj* : tacky, tasteless
chabacano² *nm Mex* : apricot
chacal *nm* : jackal
cháchara *nf fam* **1** : small talk, chatter **2 cháchara**s *nfpl* : trinkets, junk
chacharear *vi fam* : to chatter, to gab
chacra *nf Arg, Chile, Peru* : small farm
chadiano, -na *adj & n* : Chadian
chal *nm* MANTÓN : shawl
chalado¹, -da *adj fam* : crazy, nuts
chalado², -da *n* : nut, crazy person
chalán *nm, pl* **chalanes** *Mex* : barge
chalé *nm* → **chalet**
chaleco *nm* : vest
chalet *nm Spain* : house
chalupa *nf* **1** : small boat **2** *Mex* : small stuffed tortilla
chamaco, -ca *n Mex fam* : kid, boy *m*, girl *f*
chamarra *nf* **1** : sheepskin jacket **2** : poncho, blanket
chamba *nf Mex, Peru fam* : job, work
chambear *vi Mex, Peru fam* : to work
chamo -ma *n Ven fam* **1** : kid, boy *m*, girl *f* **2** : buddy, pal
champaña *or* **champán** *nm* : champagne
champiñón *nm, pl* **-ñones** : mushroom
champú *nm, pl* **-pus** *or* **-púes** : shampoo
champurrado *nm Mex* : hot chocolate thickened with cornstarch
chamuco *nm Mex fam* : devil
chamuscar {72} *vt* : to singe, to scorch — **chamuscarse** *vr*
chamusquina *nf* : scorch
chance *nm* OPORTUNIDAD : chance, opportunity
chancho¹, -cha *adj fam* : dirty, filthy, gross
chancho², -cha *n* **1** : pig, hog **2** *fam* : slob
chanchullero, -ra *adj fam* : shady, crooked
chanchullo *nm fam* : shady deal, scam
chancla *nf* **1** : thong sandal, slipper **2** : old shoe
chancleta *nf* → **chancla**
chanclo *nm* **1** : clog **2 chanclos** *nmpl* : overshoes, galoshes, rubbers
chancro *nm* : chancre
changarro *nm Mex* : small shop, stall
chango, -ga *n Mex* : monkey
chantaje *nm* : blackmail
chantajear *vt* : to blackmail
chantajista *nmf* : blackmailer
chanza *nf* **1** : joke, jest **2** *Mex fam* : chance, opportunity

chapa *nf* **1** : sheet, panel, veneer **2** : lock **3** : badge
chapado, -da *adj* **1** : plated **2 chapado a la antigua** : old-fashioned
chapar *vt* **1** : to veneer **2** : to plate (metals)
chaparrón *nm, pl* **-rrones 1** : downpour **2** : great quantity, torrent
chapeado, -da *adj Col, Mex* : flushed
chapopote *nm Mex* : tar, blacktop
chapotear *vi* : to splash about
chapucero[1], -ra *adj* **1** : crude, shoddy **2** *Mex fam* : dishonest
chapucero[2], -ra *n* **1** : sloppy worker, bungler **2** *Mex fam* : cheat, swindler
chapulín *nm, pl* **-lines** *CA, Mex* : grasshopper, locust
chapuza *nf* **1** : botched job **2** *Mex fam* : fraud, trick <hacer chapuzas : to cheat>
chapuzón *nm, pl* **-zones** : dip, swim <darse un chapuzón : to go for a quick dip>
chaqueta *nf* : jacket
charada *nf* : charades (game)
charango *nm* : traditional Andean stringed instrument
charca *nf* : pond, pool
charco *nm* : puddle, pool
charcutería *nf* : delicatessen
charla *nf* : chat, talk
charlar *vi* : to chat, to talk
charlatán[1], -tana *adj* : talkative, chatty
charlatán[2], -tana *n, mpl* **-tanes 1** : chatterbox **2** FARSANTE : charlatan, phony
charlatanear *vi* : to chatter away
charol *nm* **1** : lacquer, varnish **2** : patent leather **3** : tray
charola *nf Bol, Mex, Peru* : tray
charreada *nf Mex* : charro show, rodeo
charretera *nf* : epaulet
charro[1], -rra *adj* **1** : gaudy, tacky **2** *Mex* : pertaining to charros
charro[2], -rra *n Mex* : charro (Mexican cowboy or cowgirl)
chascarrillo *nm fam* : joke, funny story
chasco *nm* **1** BROMA : trick, joke **2** DECEPCIÓN, DESILUSIÓN : disillusionment, disappointment
chasis *or* **chasís** *nm* : chassis
chasquear *vt* **1** : to click (the tongue, fingers, etc.) **2** : to snap (a whip)
chasquido *nm* **1** : click (of the tongue or fingers) **2** : snap, crack
chatarra *nf* : scrap metal
chato, -ta *adj* **1** : pug-nosed **2** : flat
chauvinismo *nm* : chauvinism
chauvinista[1] *adj* : chauvinistic
chauvinista[2] *nmf* : chauvinist
chaval, -vala *n fam* : kid, boy *m,* girl *f*
chavo[1], -va *adj Mex fam* : young
chavo[2], -va *n Mex fam* : kid, boy *m,* girl *f*
chavo[3] *nm fam* : cent, buck <no tengo un chavo : I'm broke>
chayote *nm* : chayote (plant, fruit)
checar {72} *vt Mex* : to check, to verify
checo[1], -ca *adj & n* : Czech
checo[2] *nm* : Czech (language)
checoslovaco, -ca *adj & n* : Czechoslovakian
chef *nm* : chef
chelín *nm, pl* **chelines** : shilling
cheque[1], etc. → **checar**
cheque[2] *nm* **1** : check **2 cheque de viajero** : traveler's check
chequear *vt* **1** : to check, to verify **2** : to check in (baggage)
chequeo *nm* **1** INSPECCIÓN : check, inspection **2** : checkup, examination
chequera *nf* : checkbook
chévere *adj fam* : great, fantastic
chic *adj & nm* : chic
chica → **chico**
chicano, -na *adj & n* : Chicano, Chicana *f*
chicha *nf* : fermented alcoholic beverage made from corn
chícharo *nm* : pea
chicharra *nf* **1** CIGARRA : cicada **2** : buzzer
chicharrón *nm, pl* **-rrones 1** : pork rind **2 darle chicharrón a** *Mex fam* : to get rid of
chichón *nm, pl* **chichones** : bump, swelling
chicle *nm* : chewing gum
chicloso *nm Mex* : taffy
chico[1], -ca *adj* **1** : little, small **2** : young
chico[2], -ca *n* **1** : child, boy *m,* girl *f* **2** : young man *m,* young woman *f*
chicote *nm* LÁTIGO : whip, lash
chiffon *nm* → **chifón**
chiflado[1], -da *adj fam* : nuts, crazy
chiflado[2], -da *n fam* : crazy person, lunatic
chiflar *vi* : to whistle — *vt* : to whistle at, to boo — **chiflarse** *vr fam* **~ por** : to be crazy about
chiflido *nm* : whistle, whistling
chiflón *nm, pl* **chiflones** : draft (of air)
chifón *nm, pl* **chifones** : chiffon
chilango[1], -ga *adj Mex fam* : of or from Mexico City
chilango[2], -ga *n Mex fam* : person from Mexico City
chilaquiles *nmpl Mex* : shredded tortillas in sauce
chile *nm* : chili pepper
chileno, -na *adj & n* : Chilean
chillar *vi* **1** : to squeal, to screech **2** : to scream, to yell **3** : to be gaudy, to clash
chillido *nm* **1** : scream, shout **2** : squeal, screech, cry (of an animal)
chillo *nm PRi* : red snapper
chillón, -llona *adj, mpl* **chillones 1** : piercing, shrill **2** : loud, gaudy
chilpayate *nmf Mex fam* : child, little kid
chimenea *nf* **1** : chimney **2** : fireplace
chimichurri *nm Arg* : traditional hot sauce

chimpancé *nm* : chimpanzee

china *nf* **1** : pebble, small stone **2** *PRi* : orange

chinchar *vt fam* : to annoy, to pester — **chincharse** *vr fam* : to put up with something, to grin and bear it

chinchayote *nm Mex* : chayote root

chinche[1] *nf* **1** : bedbug **2** *Ven* : ladybug **3** : thumbtack

chinche[2] *nmf fam* : nuisance, pain in the neck

chinchilla *nf* : chinchilla

chino[1], **-na** *adj* **1** : Chinese **2** *Mex* : curly, kinky

chino[2], **-na** *n* : Chinese person

chino[3] *nm* : Chinese (language)

chip *nm, pl* **chips** : chip <chip de memoria : memory chip>

chipote *nm Mex fam* : bump (on the head)

chipotle *nm Mex* : type of chili pepper

chipriota *adj & nmf* : Cypriot

chiquear *vt Mex* : to spoil, to indulge

chiquero *nm* POCILGA : pigpen, pigsty

chiquillada *nf* : childish prank

chiquillo[1], **-lla** *adj* : very young, little

chiquillo[2], **-lla** *n* : kid, youngster

chiquito[1], **-ta** *adj* : tiny

chiquito[2], **-ta** *n* : little one, baby

chiribita *nf* **1** : spark **2 chiribitas** *nfpl* : spots before the eyes

chiribitil *nm* **1** DESVÁN : attic, garret **2** : cubbyhole

chirigota *nf fam* : joke

chirimía *nf* : traditional reed pipe

chirimoya *nf* : cherimoya, custard apple

chiripa *nf* **1** : fluke **2 de ~** : by sheer luck

chirivía *nf* : parsnip

chirona *nf fam* : slammer, jail

chirriar {85} *vi* **1** : to squeak, to creak **2** : to screech — **chirriante** *adj*

chirrido *nm* **1** : squeak, squeaking **2** : screech, screeching

chirrión *nm, pl* **chirriones** *Mex* : whip, lash

chisme *nm* **1** : gossip, tale **2** *Spain fam* : gadget, thingamajig

chismear *vi* : to gossip

chismoso[1], **-sa** *adj* : gossipy, gossiping

chismoso[2], **-sa** *n* **1** : gossiper, gossip **2** *Mex fam* : tattletale

chispa[1] *adj* **1** *Mex fam* : lively, vivacious <un perrito chispa : a frisky puppy> **2** *Spain fam* : tipsy

chispa[2] *nf* **1** : spark **2 echar chispas** : to be furious

chispeante *adj* : sparkling, scintillating

chispear *vi* **1** : to give off sparks **2** : to sparkle

chisporrotear *vi* : to crackle, to sizzle

chiste *nm* **1** : joke, funny story **2 tener chiste** : to be funny **3 tener su chiste** *Mex* : to be tricky

chistoso[1], **-sa** *adj* **1** : funny, humorous **2** : witty

chistoso[2], **-sa** *n* : wit, joker

chivas *nfpl Mex fam* : stuff, odds and ends

chivo[1], **-va** *n* **1** : kid, young goat **2 chivo expiatorio** : scapegoat

chivo[2] *nm* **1** : billy goat **2** : fit of anger

chocante *adj* **1** : shocking **2** : unpleasant, rude

chocar {72} *vi* **1** : to crash, to collide **2** : to clash, to conflict **3** : to be shocking <le chocó : he was shocked> **4** *Mex, Ven fam* : to be unpleasant or obnoxious <me choca tu jefe : I can't stand your boss> — *vt* **1** : to shake (hands) **2** : to clink glasses

chochear *vi* **1** : to be senile **2 ~ por** : to dote on, to be soft on

chochín *nm, pl* **-chines** : wren

chocho, -cha *adj* **1** : senile **2** : doting

choclo *nm* **1** : ear of corn, corncob **2** : corn **3 meter el choclo** *Mex fam* : to make a mistake

chocolate *nm* **1** : chocolate **2** : hot chocolate, cocoa

chofer *or* **chófer** *nm* **1** : chauffeur **2** : driver

choke *nm* : choke (of an automobile)

chole *interj Mex fam* **¡ya chole!** : enough!, cut it out!

cholo, -la *adj & n* : mestizo

cholla *nf fam* : head

chollo *nm Spain fam* : bargain

chongo *nm Mex* **1** : bun (chignon) **2 chongos** *nmpl Mex* : dessert made with fried bread

choque[1], **etc.** → **chocar**

choque[2] *nm* **1** : crash, collision **2** : clash, conflict **3** : shock

chorizo *nm* : chorizo, sausage

chorrear *vi* **1** : to drip **2** : to pour out, to gush out

chorrito *nm* : squirt, splash

chorro *nm* **1** : flow, stream, jet **2** *Mex fam* : heap, ton

choteado, -da *adj Mex fam* : worn-out, stale <esa canción está bien choteada : that song's been played to death>

chotear *vt* : to make fun of

choteo *nm* : joking around, kidding

chovinismo, chovinista → **chauvinismo, chauvinista**

choza *nf* BARRACA, CABAÑA : hut, shack

chubasco *nm* : downpour, storm

chuchería *nf* : knickknack, trinket

chueco, -ca *adj* **1** : crooked, bent **2** *Chile, Mex fam* : dishonest, shady

chulada *nf Mex, Spain fam* : cute or pretty thing <¡qué chulada de vestido! : what a lovely dress!>

chulear *vt Mex fam* : to compliment

chuleta *nf* : cutlet, chop

chulo[1], **-la** *adj* **1** *fam* : cute, pretty **2** *Spain fam* : cocky, arrogant

chulo[2] *nm Spain* : pimp

chupada *nf* **1** : suck, sucking **2** : puff, drag (on a cigarette)

chupado, -da *adj fam* **1** : gaunt, skinny **2** : plastered, drunk

chupaflor *nm* COLIBRÍ : hummingbird

chupamirto *nm Mex* : hummingbird

chupar *vt* **1 :** to suck **2 :** to absorb **3 :** to puff on **4** *fam* **:** to drink, to guzzle — *vi* **:** to suckle — **chuparse** *vr* **1 :** to waste away **2** *fam* **:** to put up with **3 ¡chúpate esa!** *fam* **:** take that!

chupete *nm* **1 :** pacifier **2** *Chile, Peru* **:** lollipop

chupetear *vt* **:** to suck (at)

chupón *nm, pl* **chupones 1 :** sucker (of a plant) **2 :** baby bottle, pacifier

churrasco *nm* **1 :** steak **2 :** barbecued meat

churro *nm* **1 :** fried dough **2** *fam* **:** botch, mess **3** *fam* **:** attractive person, looker

chusco, -ca *adj* **:** funny, amusing

chusma *nf* GENTUZA **:** riffraff, rabble

chutar *vi* **:** to shoot (in soccer)

chute *nm* **:** shot (in soccer)

cianuro *nm* **:** cyanide

cibernética *nf* **:** cybernetics

cicatriz *nf, pl* **-trices :** scar

cicatrizarse {21} *vr* **:** to form a scar, to heal

cíclico, -ca *adj* **:** cyclical

ciclismo *nm* **:** bicycling

ciclista *nmf* **:** bicyclist

ciclo *nm* **:** cycle

ciclomotor *nm* **:** moped

ciclón *nm, pl* **ciclones :** cyclone

cicuta *nf* **:** hemlock

cidra *nf* **:** citron (fruit)

ciega, ciegue, etc. → **cegar**

ciego[1], -ga *adj* **1** INVIDENTE **:** blind **2 a ciegas :** blindly **3 quedarse ciego :** to go blind — **ciegamente** *adv*

ciego[2], -ga *n* INVIDENTE **:** blind person

cielo *nm* **1 :** sky **2 :** heaven **3 :** ceiling

ciempiés *nms & pl* **:** centipede

cien[1] *adj* **1 :** a hundred, hundred <las primeras cien páginas : the first hundred pages> **2 cien por cien** *or* **cien por ciento :** a hundred percent, through and through, wholeheartedly

cien[2] *nm* **:** one hundred

ciénaga *nf* **:** swamp, bog

ciencia *nf* **1 :** science **2 :** learning, knowledge **3 a ciencia cierta :** for a fact, for certain

cieno *nm* **:** mire, mud, silt

científico[1], -ca *adj* **:** scientific — **científicamente** *adv*

científico[2], -ca *n* **:** scientist

ciento[1] *adj* (*used in compound numbers*) **:** one hundred <ciento uno : one hundred and one>

ciento[2] *nm* **1 :** hundred, group of a hundred **2 por ~ :** percent

cierne, etc. → **cerner**

cierra, etc. → **cerrar**

cierre *nm* **1 :** closing, closure **2 :** fastener, clasp, zipper

cierto, -ta *adj* **1 :** true, certain, definite <lo cierto es que... : the fact is that...> **2 :** certain, one <cierto día de verano : one summer day> <bajo ciertas circunstancias : under certain circumstances> **3 por ~ :** in fact, as a matter of fact — **ciertamente** *adv*

ciervo, -va *n* **:** deer, stag *m,* hind *f*

cifra *nf* **1 :** figure, number **2 :** quantity, amount **3** CLAVE **:** code, cipher

cifrar *vt* **1 :** to write in code **2 :** to place, to pin <cifró su esperanza en la lotería : he pinned his hopes on the lottery> — **cifrarse** *vr* **:** to amount <la multa se cifra en millares : the fine amounts to thousands>

cigarra *nf* CHICHARRA **:** cicada

cigarrera *nf* **:** cigarette case

cigarrillo *nm* **:** cigarrette

cigarro *nm* **1 :** cigarette **2** PURO **:** cigar

cigoto *nm* **:** zygote

cigüeña *nf* **:** stork

cilantro *nm* **:** cilantro, coriander

cilíndrico, -ca *adj* **:** cylindrical

cilindro *nm* **:** cylinder

cima *nf* CUMBRE **:** peak, summit, top

cimarrón, -rrona *adj, mpl* **-rrones :** untamed, wild

címbalo *nm* **:** cymbal

cimbel *nm* **:** decoy

cimbrar *vt* **:** to shake, to rock — **cimbrarse** *vr* **:** to sway, to swing

cimentar {55} *vt* **1 :** to lay the foundation of, to establish **2 :** to strengthen, to cement

cimientos *nmpl* **:** base, foundation(s)

cinc *nm* **:** zinc

cincel *nm* **:** chisel

cincelar *vt* **1 :** to chisel **2 :** to engrave

cincha *nf* **:** cinch, girth

cinchar *vt* **:** to cinch (a horse)

cinco *adj & nm* **:** five

cincuenta *adj & nm* **:** fifty

cincuentavo[1], -va *adj* **:** fiftieth

cincuentavo[2] *nm* **:** fiftieth (fraction)

cine *nm* **1 :** cinema, movies *pl* **2 :** movie theater

cineasta *nmf* **:** filmmaker

cinematográfico, -ca *adj* **:** movie, film, cinematic <la industria cinematográfica : the film industry>

cingalés[1], -lesa *adj & n* **:** Sinhalese

cingalés[2] *nm* **:** Sinhalese (language)

cínico[1], -ca *adj* **1 :** cynical **2 :** shameless, brazen — **cínicamente** *adv*

cínico[2], -ca *n* **:** cynic

cinismo *nm* **:** cynicism

cinta *nf* **1 :** ribbon **2 :** tape <cinta métrica : tape measure> **3 :** strap, belt <cinta transportadora : conveyor belt>

cinto *nm* **:** strap, belt

cintura *nf* **1 :** waist, waistline **2 meter en cintura** *fam* **:** to bring into line, to discipline

cinturón *nm, pl* **-rones 1 :** belt **2 cinturón de seguridad :** seat belt

ciñe, etc. → **ceñir**

ciprés *nm, pl* **cipreses :** cypress

circo *nm* **:** circus

circón *nm, pl* **circones :** zircon

circonio *nm* **:** zirconium

circuitería *nf* **:** circuitry

circuito *nm* **:** circuit

circulación *nf, pl* **-ciones 1 :** circulation **2 :** movement **3 :** traffic

circular[1] *vi* **1 :** to circulate **2 :** to move along **3 :** to drive
circular[2] *adj* **:** circular
circular[3] *nf* **:** circular, flier
circulatorio, -ria *adj* **:** circulatory
círculo *nm* **1 :** circle **2 :** club, group
circuncidar *vt* **:** to circumcise
circuncisión *nf, pl* **-siones :** circumcision
circundar *vt* **:** to surround — **circundante** *adj*
circunferencia *nf* **:** circumference
circunflejo, -ja *adj* **acento circunflejo :** circumflex
circunlocución *nf, pl* **-ciones :** circumlocution
circunloquio *nm* → **circunlocución**
circunnavegar {52} *vt* **:** to circumnavigate — **circunnavegación** *nf*
circunscribir {33} *vt* **:** to circumscribe, to constrict, to limit — **circunscribirse** *vr*
circunscripción *nf, pl* **-ciones 1 :** limitation, restriction **2 :** constituency
circunscrito *pp* → **circunscribir**
circunspección *nf, pl* **-ciones :** circumspection, prudence
circunspecto, -ta *adj* **:** circumspect, prudent
circunstancia *nf* **:** circumstance
circunstancial *adj* **:** circumstantial, incidental
circunstante *nmf* **1 :** onlooker, bystander **2 los circunstantes :** those present
circunvalación *nf, pl* **-ciones :** surrounding, encircling <carretera de circunvalación : bypass, beltway>
circunvecino, -na *adj* **:** surrounding, neighboring
cirio *nm* **:** large candle
cirro *nm* **:** cirrus (cloud)
cirrosis *nf* **:** cirrhosis
ciruela *nf* **1 :** plum **2 ciruela pasa :** prune
cirugía *nf* **:** surgery
cirujano, -na *n* **:** surgeon
cisma *nm* **:** schism, rift
cisne *nm* **:** swan
cisterna *nf* **:** cistern, tank
cita *nf* **1 :** quote, quotation **2 :** appointment, date
citable *adj* **:** quotable
citación *nf, pl* **-ciones** EMPLAZAMIENTO **:** summons, subpoena
citadino[1], **-na** *adj* **:** of the city, urban
citadino[2], **-na** *n* **:** city dweller
citado, -da *adj* **:** said, aforementioned
citar *vt* **1 :** to quote, to cite **2 :** to make an appointment with **3 :** to summon (to court), to subpoena — **citarse** *vr* **~ con :** to arrange to meet (someone)
cítara *nf* **:** zither
citatorio *nm* **:** subpoena
citoplasma *nm* **:** cytoplasm
cítrico[1], **-ca** *adj* **:** citric
cítrico[2] *nm* **:** citrus fruit
ciudad *nf* **1 :** city, town **2 ciudad universitaria :** college or university campus **3 ciudad perdida** *Mex* **:** shantytown
ciudadanía *nf* **1 :** citizenship **2 :** citizenry, citizens *pl*
ciudadano[1], **-na** *adj* **:** civic, city
ciudadano[2], **-na** *n* **1** NACIONAL **:** citizen **2** HABITANTE **:** resident, city dweller
ciudadela *nf* **:** citadel, fortress
cívico, -ca *adj* **1 :** civic **2 :** public-spirited
civil[1] *adj* **1 :** civil **2 :** civilian
civil[2] *nmf* **:** civilian
civilidad *nf* **:** civility, courtesy
civilización *nf, pl* **-ciones :** civilization
civilizar {21} *vt* **:** to civilize
civismo *nm* **:** community spirit, civic-mindedness, civics
cizaña *nf* **:** discord, rift
clamar *vi* **:** to clamor, to raise a protest — *vt* **:** to cry out for
clamor *nm* **:** clamor, outcry
clamoroso, -sa *adj* **:** clamorous, resounding, thunderous
clan *nm* **:** clan
clandestinidad *nf* **:** secrecy <en la clandestinidad : underground>
clandestino, -na *adj* **:** clandestine, secret
clara *nf* **:** egg white
claraboya *nf* **:** skylight
claramente *adv* **:** clearly
clarear *v impers* **1 :** to clear, to clear up **2 :** to get light, to dawn — *vi* **:** to go gray, to turn white
claridad *nf* **1** NITIDEZ **:** clarity, clearness **2 :** brightness, light
clarificación *nf, pl* **-ciones** ACLARACIÓN **:** clarification, explanation
clarificar {72} *vt* ACLARAR **:** to clarify, to explain
clarín *nm, pl* **clarines :** bugle
clarinete *nm* **:** clarinet
clarividencia *nf* **1 :** clairvoyance **2 :** perspicacity, discernment
clarividente[1] *adj* **1 :** clairvoyant **2 :** perspicacious, discerning
clarividente[2] *nmf* **:** clairvoyant
claro[1] *adv* **1 :** clearly <habla más claro : speak more clearly> **2 :** of course, surely <¡claro!, ¡claro que sí! : absolutely!, of course!> <claro que entendió : of course she understood>
claro[2], **-ra** *adj* **1 :** bright, clear **2 :** pale, fair, light **3 :** clear, evident
claro[3] *nm* **1 :** clearing **2 claro de luna :** moonlight
clase *nf* **1 :** class **2** ÍNDOLE, TIPO **:** sort, kind, type
clasicismo *nm* **:** classicism
clásico[1], **-ca** *adj* **1 :** classic **2 :** classical
clásico[2] *nm* **:** classic
clasificación *nf, pl* **-ciones 1 :** classification, sorting out **2 :** rating **3** CALIFICACIÓN **:** qualification (in competitions)
clasificado, -da *adj* **:** classified <aviso clasificado : classified ad>
clasificar {72} *vt* **1 :** to classify, to sort out **2 :** to rate, to rank — *vi* CALIFICAR

: to qualify (in competitions) — **clasificarse** *vr*
claudicación *nf, pl* **-ciones** : surrender, abandonment of one's principles
claudicar {72} *vi* : to back down, to abandon one's principles
claustro *nm* : cloister
claustrofobia *nf* : claustrophobia
claustrofóbico, -ca *adj* : claustrophobic
cláusula *nf* : clause
clausura *nf* **1** : closure, closing **2** : closing ceremony **3** : cloister
clausurar *vt* **1** : to close, to bring to a close **2** : to close down
clavadista *nmf* : diver
clavado[1], -da *adj* **1** : nailed, fixed, stuck **2** *fam* : punctual, on the dot **3** *fam* : identical <es clavado a su padre : he's the image of his father>
clavado[2] *nm* : dive
clavar *vt* **1** : to nail, to hammer **2** HINCAR : to plunge, to stick **3** : to fix (one's eyes) on — **clavarse** *vr* : to stick oneself (with a sharp object)
clave[1] *adj* : key, essential
clave[2] *nf* **1** CIFRA : code **2** : key <la clave del misterio : the key to the mystery> **3** : clef **4** : keystone
clavel *nm* : carnation
clavelito *nm* : pink (flower)
clavicémbalo *nm* : harpsichord
clavícula *nf* : collarbone
clavija *nf* **1** : plug **2** : peg, pin
clavo *nm* **1** : nail <clavo grande : spike> **2** : clove **3 dar en el clavo** : to hit the nail on the head
claxon *nm, pl* **cláxones** : horn (of an automobile)
clemencia *nf* : clemency, mercy
clemente *adj* : merciful
cleptomanía *nf* : kleptomania
cleptómano, -na *n* : kleptomaniac
clerecía *nf* : ministry, ministers *pl*
clerical *adj* : clerical
clérigo, -ga *n* : cleric, member of the clergy
clero *nm* : clergy
cliché *nm* **1** : cliché **2** : stencil **3** : negative (of a photograph)
cliente, -ta *n* : customer, client
clientela *nf* : clientele, customers *pl*
clima *nm* **1** : climate **2** AMBIENTE : atmosphere, ambience
climático, -ca *adj* : climatic
climatización *nf, pl* **-ciones** : air-conditioning
climatizar {21} *vt* : to air-condition — **climatizado, -da** *adj*
clímax *nm* : climax
clínica *nf* : clinic
clínico, -ca *adj* : clinical — **clínicamente** *adv*
clip *nm* **1** : clip **2** : paper clip
clítoris *nms & pl* : clitoris
cloaca *nf* ALCANTARILLA : sewer
clocar {82} *vi* : to cluck
cloche *nm CA, Car, Col, Ven* : clutch (of an automobile)
clon *nm* : clone
cloqué, etc. → **clocar**
cloquear *vi* : to cluck
clorar *vt* : to chlorinate — **cloración** *nf*
cloro *nm* : chlorine
clorofila *nf* : chlorophyll
cloroformo *nm* : chloroform
cloruro *nm* : chloride
clóset *nm, pl* **clósets 1** : closet **2** : cupboard
club *nm* : club
clueca, clueque, etc. → **clocar**
coa *nf Mex* : hoe
coacción *nf, pl* **-ciones** : coercion, duress
coaccionar *vt* : to coerce
coactivo, -va *adj* : coercive
coagular *v* : to clot, to coagulate — **coagulación** *nf*
coágulo *nm* : clot
coalición *nf, pl* **-ciones** : coalition
coartada *nf* : alibi
coartar *vt* : to restrict, to limit
cobalto *nm* : cobalt
cobarde[1] *adj* : cowardly
cobarde[2] *nmf* : coward
cobardía *nf* : cowardice
cobaya *nf* : guinea pig
cobertizo *nm* : shed, shelter
cobertor *nm* COLCHA : bedspread, quilt
cobertura *nf* **1** : coverage **2** : cover, collateral
cobija *nf* FRAZADA, MANTA : blanket
cobijar *vt* : to shelter — **cobijarse** *vr* : to take shelter
cobra *nf* : cobra
cobrador, -dora *n* **1** : collector **2** : conductor (of a bus or train)
cobrar *vt* **1** : to charge **2** : to collect, to draw, to earn **3** : to acquire, to gain **4** : to recover, to retrieve **5** : to cash (a check) **6** : to claim, to take (a life) **7** : to shoot (game), to bag — *vi* **1** : to be paid **2 llamar por cobrar** *Mex* : to call collect
cobre *nm* : copper
cobro *nm* : collection (of money), cashing (of a check)
coca *nf* **1** : coca **2** *fam* : coke, cocaine
cocaína *nf* : cocaine
cocal *nm* : coca plantation
cocción *nf, pl* **cocciones** : cooking
cocear *vi* : to kick (of an animal)
cocer {14} *vt* **1** COCINAR : to cook **2** HERVIR : to boil
cochambre *nmf fam* : filth, grime
cochambroso, -sa *adj* : filthy, grimy
coche *nm* **1** : car, automobile **2** : coach, carriage **3 coche cama** : sleeping car **4 coche fúnebre** : hearse
cochecito *nm* : baby carriage, stroller
cochera *nf* : garage, carport
cochinada *nf fam* **1** : filthy language **2** : disgusting behavior **3** : dirty trick
cochinillo *nm* : suckling pig, piglet
cochino[1], -na *adj* **1** : dirty, filthy, disgusting **2** *fam* : rotten, lousy
cochino[2], -na *n* : pig, hog

cocido[1], -da *adj* **1** : boiled, cooked **2 bien cocido** : well-done

cocido[2] *nm* ESTOFADO, GUISADO : stew

cociente *nm* : quotient

cocimiento *nm* : cooking, baking

cocina *nf* **1** : kitchen **2** : stove **3** : cuisine, cooking

cocinar *v* : to cook

cocinero, -ra *n* : cook, chef

cocineta *nf Mex* : kitchenette

coco *nm* **1** : coconut **2** *fam* : head **3** *fam* : bogeyman

cocoa *nf* : cocoa, hot chocolate

cocodrilo *nm* : crocodile

cocotero *nm* : coconut palm

coctel *or* **cóctel** *nm* **1** : cocktail **2** : cocktail party

coctelera *nf* : cocktail shaker

codazo *nm* **1 darle un codazo a** : to elbow, to nudge **2 abrirse paso a codazos** : to elbow one's way through

codearse *vr* : to rub elbows, to hobnob

códice *nm* : codex, manuscript

codicia *nf* AVARICIA : avarice, covetousness

codiciar *vt* : to covet

codicilo *nm* : codicil

codicioso, -sa *adj* : avaricious, covetous

codificación *nf, pl* **-ciones 1** : codification **2** : coding, encoding

codificar {72} *vt* **1** : to codify **2** : to code, to encode

código *nm* **1** : code **2 código postal** : zip code **3 código morse** : Morse code

codo[1], -da *adj Mex* : cheap, stingy

codo[2], -da *n Mex* : tightwad, cheapskate

codo[3] *nm* : elbow

codorniz *nf, pl* **-nices** : quail

coeficiente *nm* **1** : coefficient **2 coeficiente intelectual** : IQ, intelligence quotient

coexistir *vi* : to coexist — **coexistencia** *nf*

cofa *nm* : crow's nest

cofre *nm* **1** BAÚL : trunk, chest **2** *Mex* CAPOTE : hood (of a car)

coger {15} *vt* **1** : to seize, to take hold of **2** : to catch **3** : to pick up **4** : to gather, to pick **5** : to gore — **cogerse** *vr* AGARRARSE : to hold on

cogida *nf* **1** : gathering, harvest **2** : goring

cognición *nf, pl* **-ciones** : cognition

cognitivo, -va *adj* : cognitive

cogollo *nm* **1** : heart (of a vegetable) **2** : bud, bulb **3** : core, crux <el cogollo de la cuestión : the heart of the matter>

cogote *nm* : scruff, nape

cohabitar *vi* : to cohabit — **cohabitación** *nf*

cohechar *vt* SOBORNAR : to bribe

cohecho *nm* SOBORNO : bribe, bribery

coherencia *nf* : coherence — **coherente** *adj*

cohesión *nf, pl* **-siones** : cohesion

cohesivo, -va *adj* : cohesive

cohete *nm* : rocket

cohibición *nf, pl* **-ciones 1** : (legal) restraint **2** INHIBICIÓN : inhibition

cohibido, -da *adj* : inhibited, shy

cohibir {62} *vt* : to inhibit, to make self-conscious — **cohibirse** *vr* : to feel shy or embarrassed

cohorte *nf* : cohort

coima *nf Arg, Chile, Peru* : bribe

coimear *vt Arg, Chile, Peru* : to bribe

coincidencia *nf* : coincidence

coincidir *vi* **1** : to coincide **2** : to agree

coito *nm* : sexual intercourse, coitus

coja, etc. → **coger**

cojear *vi* **1** : to limp **2** : to wobble, to rock **3 cojear del mismo pie** : to be two of a kind

cojera *nf* : limp

cojín *nm, pl* **cojines** : cushion, throw pillow

cojinete *nm* **1** : bearing, bushing **2 cojinete de bola** : ball bearing

cojo[1], -ja *adj* **1** : limping, lame **2** : wobbly **3** : weak, ineffectual

cojo[2], -ja *n* : lame person

cojones *nmpl usu considered vulgar* **1** : testicles *pl* **2** : guts *pl,* courage

col *nf* **1** REPOLLO : cabbage **2 col de Bruselas** : Brussels sprout **3 col rizada** : kale

cola *nf* **1** RABO : tail <cola de caballo : ponytail> **2** FILA : line (of people) <hacer cola : to wait in line> **3** : cola, drink **4** : train (of a dress) **5** : tails *pl* (of a tuxedo) **6** PEGAMENTO : glue **7** *fam* : buttocks *pl,* rear end

colaboracionista *nmf* : collaborator, traitor

colaborador, -dora *n* **1** : contributor (to a periodical) **2** : collaborator

colaborar *vi* : to collaborate — **colaboración** *nf*

colación *nf, pl* **-ciones 1** : light meal **2** : comparison, collation <sacar a colación : to bring up, to broach> **3** : conferral (of a degree)

colador *nm* **1** : colander, strainer **2** *PRi* : small coffeepot

colapso *nm* **1** : collapse **2** : standstill

colar {19} *vt* : to strain, to filter — **colarse** *vr* **1** : to sneak in, to cut in line, to gate-crash **2** : to slip up, to make a mistake

colateral[1] *adj* : collateral — **colateralmente** *adv*

colateral[2] *nm* : collateral

colcha *nf* COBERTOR : bedspread, quilt

colchón *nm, pl* **colchones 1** : mattress **2** : cushion, padding, buffer

colchoneta *nf* : mat (for gymnastic sports)

colear *vi* **1** : to wag its tail **2 vivito y coleando** *fam* : alive and kicking

colección *nf, pl* **-ciones** : collection

coleccionar *vt* : to collect, to keep a collection of

coleccionista *nmf* : collector

colecta *nf* : collection (of donations)

colectar *vt* : to collect
colectividad *nf* : community, group
colectivo[1], -va *adj* : collective — **colectivamente** *adv*
colectivo[2] *nm* **1** : collective **2** *Arg, Bol, Peru* : city bus
colector[1], -tora *n* : collector <colector de impuestos : tax collector>
colector[2] *nm* **1** : sewer **2** : manifold (of an engine)
colega *nmf* **1** : colleague **2** HOMÓLOGO : counterpart **3** *fam* : buddy
colegiado[1], -da *adj* : collegiate
colegiado[2], -da *n* **1** ÁRBITRO : referee **2** : member (of a professional association)
colegial[1], -giala *adj* **1** : school, collegiate **2** *Mex fam* : green, inexperienced
colegial[2], -giala *n* : schoolboy *m*, schoolgirl *f*
colegiatura *nf Mex* : tuition
colegio *nm* **1** : school **2** : college <colegio electoral : electoral college> **3** : professional association
colegir {28} *vt* **1** JUNTAR : to collect, to gather **2** INFERIR : to infer, to deduce
cólera[1] *nm* : cholera
cólera[2] *nf* FURIA, IRA : anger, rage
colérico, -ca *adj* **1** FURIOSO : angry **2** IRRITABLE : irritable
colesterol *nm* : cholesterol
coleta *nf* **1** : ponytail **2** : pigtail
coletazo *nm* : lash, flick (of a tail)
colgado, -da *adj* **1** : hanging, hanged **2** : pending **3 dejar colgado a** : to disappoint, to let down
colgante[1] *adj* : hanging, dangling
colgante[2] *nm* : pendant, charm (on a bracelet)
colgar {16} *vt* **1** : to hang (up), to put up **2** AHORCAR : to hang (someone) **3** : to hang up (a telephone) **4** *fam* : to fail (an exam) — **colgarse** *vr* **1** : to hang, to be suspended **2** AHORCARSE : to hang oneself **3** : to hang up a telephone
colibrí *nm* CHUPAFLOR : hummingbird
cólico *nm* : colic
coliflor *nf* : cauliflower
colilla *nf* : butt (of a cigarette)
colina *nf* CERRO, LOMA : hill
colindante *adj* CONTIGUO : adjacent, neighboring
colindar *vi* : to adjoin, to be adjacent
coliseo *nm* : coliseum
colisión *nf, pl* **-siones** : collision
colisionar *vi* : to collide
collage *nm* : collage
collar *nm* **1** : collar (for an animal) **2** : necklace <collar de perlas : string of pearls>
colmado, -da *adj* : heaping
colmar *vt* **1** : to fill to the brim **2** : to fulfill, to satisfy **3** : to heap, to shower <me colmaron de regalos : they showered me with gifts>
colmena *nf* : beehive
colmenar *nm* APIARIO : apiary
colmillo *nm* **1** CANINO : canine (tooth), fang **2** : tusk
colmilludo, -da *adj Mex, PRi* : astute, shrewd, crafty
colmo *nm* : height, extreme, limit <el colmo de la locura : the height of folly> <¡eso es el colmo! : that's the last straw!>
colocación *nf, pl* **-ciones 1** : placement, placing **2** : position, job **3** : investment
colocar {72} *vt* **1** PONER : to place, to put **2** : to find a job for **3** : to invest — **colocarse** *vr* **1** SITUARSE : to position oneself **2** : to get a job
colofón *nm, pl* **-fones 1** : ending, finale **2** : colophon
colofonia *nf* : rosin
colombiano, -na *adj & n* : Colombian
colon *nm* : (intestinal) colon
colón *nm, pl* **colones** : Costa Rican and Salvadoran unit of currency
colonia *nf* **1** : colony **2** : cologne **3** *Mex* : residential area, neighborhood
colonial *adj* : colonial
colonización *nf, pl* **-ciones** : colonization
colonizador[1], -dora *adj* : colonizing
colonizador[2], -dora *n* : colonizer, colonist
colonizar {21} *vt* : to colonize, to settle
colono, -na *n* **1** : settler, colonist **2** : tenant farmer
coloquial *adj* : colloquial
coloquio *nm* **1** : discussion, talk **2** : conference, symposium
color *nm* **1** : color **2** : paint, dye **3 colores** *nmpl* : colored pencils
coloración *nf, pl* **-ciones** : coloring, coloration
colorado[1], -da *adj* **1** ROJO : red **2 ponerse colorado** : to blush **3 chiste colorado** *Mex* : off-color joke
colorado[2] *nm* ROJO : red
colorante *nm* : coloring <colorante de alimentos : food coloring>
colorear *vt* : to color — *vi* **1** : to redden **2** : to ripen
colorete *nm* : rouge, blusher
colorido *nm* : color, coloring
colorín *nm, pl* **-rines 1** : bright color **2** : goldfinch
colosal *adj* : colossal
coloso *nm* : colossus
coludir *vi* : to be in collusion, to conspire
columna *nf* **1** : column **2 columna vertebral** : spine, backbone
columnata *nf* : colonnade
columnista *nmf* : columnist
columpiar *vt* : to push (on a swing) — **columpiarse** *vr* : to swing
columpio *nm* : swing
colusión *nf, pl* **-siones** : collusion
colza *nf* : rape (plant)
coma[1] *nm* : coma
coma[2] *nf* : comma
comadre *nf* **1** : godmother of one's child **2** : mother of one's godchild **3**

fam **:** neighbor, female friend **4** *fam* **:** gossip
comadrear *vi fam* **:** to gossip
comadreja *nf* **:** weasel
comadrona *nf* **:** midwife
comanche *nmf* **:** Comanche
comandancia *nf* **1 :** command headquarters **2 :** command
comandante *nmf* **1 :** commander, commanding officer **2 :** major
comandar *vt* **:** to command, to lead
comando *nm* **1 :** commando **2 :** command (for computers)
comarca *nf* REGIÓN **:** region
comarcal *adj* REGIONAL **:** regional, local
combar *vt* **:** to bend, to curve — **combarse** *vr* **1 :** to bend, to buckle **2 :** to warp, to bulge, to sag
combate *nm* **1 :** combat **2 :** fight, boxing match
combatiente *nmf* **:** combatant, fighter
combatir *vt* **:** to combat, to fight against — *vi* **:** to fight
combatividad *nf* **:** fighting spirit
combativo, -va *adj* **:** combative, spirited
combinación *nf, pl* **-ciones 1 :** combination **2 :** connection (in travel)
combinar *vt* **1** UNIR **:** to combine, to mix together **2 :** to match, to put together — **combinarse** *vr* **:** to get together, to conspire
combo *nm* **1 :** (musical) band **2** *Chile, Peru* **:** sledgehammer **3** *Chile, Peru* **:** punch
combustible[1] *adj* **:** combustible
combustible[2] *nm* **:** fuel
combustión *nf, pl* **-tiones :** combustion
comedero *nm* **:** trough, feeder
comedia *nf* **:** comedy
comediante *nmf* **:** actor, actress *f*
comedido, -da *adj* MESURADO **:** moderate, restrained
comediógrafo, -fa *n* **:** playwright
comedor *nm* **:** dining room
comején *nm, pl* **-jenes :** termite
comelón[1], **-lona** *adj, mpl* **-lones** *fam* **:** gluttonous
comelón[2] **-lona** *n, pl* **-lones** *fam* **:** big eater, glutton
comensal *nmf* **:** dinner guest
comentador, -dora *n* → **comentarista**
comentar *vt* **1 :** to comment on, to discuss **2 :** to mention, to remark
comentario *nm* **1 :** comment, remark <sin comentarios : no comment> **2 :** commentary
comentarista *nmf* **:** commentator
comenzar {29} *v* EMPEZAR **:** to begin, to start
comer[1] *vt* **1 :** to eat **2 :** to consume, to eat up, to eat into — *vi* **1 :** to eat **2** CENAR **:** to have a meal **3 dar de comer :** to feed — **comerse** *vr* **:** to eat up
comer[2] *nm* **:** eating, dining
comercial *adj & nm* **:** commercial — **comercialmente** *adv*
comercializar {21} *vt* **1 :** to commercialize **2 :** to market
comerciante *nmf* **:** merchant, dealer
comerciar *vi* **:** to do business, to trade
comercio *nm* **1 :** commerce, trade **2** NEGOCIO **:** business, place of business
comestible *adj* **:** edible
comestibles *nmpl* VÍVERES **:** groceries, food
cometa[1] *nm* **:** comet
cometa[2] *nf* **:** kite
cometer *vt* **1 :** to commit **2 cometer un error :** to make a mistake
cometido *nm* **:** assignment, task
comezón *nf, pl* **-zones** PICAZÓN **:** itchiness, itching
comible *adj fam* **:** eatable, edible
comic *or* **cómic** *nm* **:** comic strip, comic book
comicastro, -tra *n* **:** second-rate actor, ham
comicidad *nf* HUMOR **:** humor, wit
comicios *nmpl* **:** elections, voting
cómico[1], **-ca** *adj* **:** comic, comical
cómico[2], **-ca** *n* HUMORISTA **:** comic, comedian, comedienne *f*
comida *nf* **1 :** food **2 :** meal **3 :** dinner **4 comida basura :** junk food **5 comida rápida :** fast food
comidilla *nf* **:** talk, gossip
comienzo *nm* **1 :** start, beginning **2 al comienzo :** at first **3 dar comienzo :** to begin
comillas *nfpl* **:** quotation marks <entre comillas : in quotes>
comilón, -lona → **comelón, -lona**
comilona *nf fam* **:** feast
comino *nm* **1 :** cumin **2 me vale un comino** *fam* **:** not to matter to someone <no me importa un comino : I couldn't care less>
comisaría *nf* **:** police station
comisario, -ria *n* **:** commissioner
comisión *nf, pl* **-siones 1 :** commission, committing **2 :** committee **3 :** percentage, commission <comisión sobre las ventas : sales commission>
comisionado[1], **-da** *adj* **:** commissioned, entrusted
comisionado[2], **-da** *n* → **comisario**
comisionar *vt* **:** to commission
comité *nm* **:** committee
comitiva *nf* **:** retinue, entourage
como[1] *adv* **1 :** around, about <cuesta como 500 pesos : it costs around 500 pesos> **2 :** kind of, like <tengo como mareos : I'm kind of dizzy>
como[2] *conj* **1 :** how, as <hazlo como dijiste que lo harías : do it the way you said you would> **2 :** since, given that <como estaba lloviendo, no salí : since it was raining, I didn't go out> **3 :** if <como lo vuelva a hacer lo arrestarán : if he does that again he'll be arrested> **4 como quiera :** in any way

como[3] *prep* **1 :** like, as <ligero como una pluma : light as a feather> **2 así como :** as well as
cómo *adv* **:** how <¿cómo estás? : how are you?> <¿a cómo están las manzanas? : how much are the apples?> <¿cómo? : excuse me?, what was that?> <¿se puede? ¡cómo no! : may I? please do!>
cómoda *nf* **:** bureau, chest of drawers
comodidad *nf* **1 :** comfort **2 :** convenience
comodín *nm, pl* **-dines 1 :** joker, wild card **2 :** all-purpose word or thing **3 :** pretext, excuse
cómodo, -da *adj* **1** CONFORTABLE **:** comfortable **2 :** convenient — **cómodamente** *adv*
comodoro *nm* **:** commodore
comoquiera *adv* **1 :** in any way **2 comoquiera que :** in whatever way, however <comoquiera que sea eso : however that may be>
compa *nm fam* **:** buddy, pal
compactar *vt* **:** to compact, to compress
compacto, -ta *adj* **:** compact
compadecer {53} *vt* **:** to sympathize with, to feel sorry for — **compadecerse** *vr* **1 ~ de :** to take pity on, to commiserate with **2 ~ con :** to fit, to accord (with)
compadre *nm* **1 :** godfather of one's child **2 :** father of one's godchild **3** *fam* **:** buddy, pal
compaginar *vt* **1** COORDINAR **:** to combine, to coordinate **2 :** to collate
compañerismo *nm* **:** comradeship, camaraderie
compañero, -ñera *n* **:** companion, mate, partner
compañía *nf* **1 :** company <llegó en compañía de su madre : he arrived with his mother> **2** EMPRESA, FIRMA **:** firm, company
comparable *adj* **:** comparable
comparación *nf, pl* **-ciones :** comparison
comparado, -da *adj* **:** comparative <literatura comparada : comparative literature>
comparar *vt* **:** to compare
comparativo[1], **-va** *adj* **:** comparative, relative — **comparativamente** *adv*
comparativo[2] *nm* **:** comparative degree or form
comparecencia *nf* **1 :** appearance (in court) **2 orden de comparecencia :** subpoena, summons
comparecer {53} *vi* **:** to appear (in court)
compartimiento *or* **compartimento** *nm* **:** compartment
compartir *vt* **:** to share
compás *nm, pl* **-pases 1 :** beat, rhythm, time **2 :** compass
compasión *nf, pl* **-siones :** compassion, pity
compasivo, -va *adj* **:** compassionate, sympathetic
compatibilidad *nf* **:** compatibility
compatible *adj* **:** compatible
compatriota *nmf* PAISANO **:** compatriot, fellow countryman
compeler *vt* **:** to compel
compendiar *vt* **:** to summarize, to condense
compendio *nm* **:** summary
compenetración *nf, pl* **-ciones :** rapport, mutual understanding
compenetrarse *vr* **1 :** to understand each other **2 ~ con :** to identify oneself with
compensación *nf, pl* **-ciones :** compensation
compensar *vt* **:** to compensate for, to make up for — *vi* **:** to be worth one's while
compensatorio, -ria *adj* **:** compensatory
competencia *nf* **1 :** competition, rivalry **2 :** competence
competente *adj* **:** competent, able — **competentemente** *adv*
competición *nf, pl* **-ciones :** competition
competidor[1], **-dora** *adj* RIVAL **:** competing, rival
competidor[2], **-dora** *n* RIVAL **:** competitor, rival
competir {54} *vi* **:** to compete
competitividad *nf* **:** competitiveness
competitivo, -va *adj* **:** competitive — **competitivamente** *adv*
compilar *vt* **:** to compile — **compilación** *nf*
compinche *nmf fam* **1 :** buddy, pal **2 :** partner in crime, accomplice
complacencia *nf* **:** pleasure, satisfaction
complacer {57} *vt* **:** to please — **complacerse** *vr* **~ en :** to take pleasure in
complaciente *adj* **:** obliging, eager to please
complejidad *nf* **:** complexity
complejo[1], **-ja** *adj* **:** complex
complejo[2] *nm* **:** complex
complementar *vt* **:** to complement, to supplement — **complementarse** *vr*
complementario, -ria *adj* **:** complementary
complemento *nm* **1 :** complement, supplement **2 :** supplementary pay, allowance
completamente *adv* **:** completely, totally
completar *vt* TERMINAR **:** to complete, to finish
completo, -ta *adj* **1 :** complete **2 :** perfect, absolute **3 :** full, detailed — **completamente** *adv*
complexión *nf, pl* **-xiones :** (physical) constitution
complicación *nf, pl* **-ciones :** complication
complicado, -da *adj* **:** complicated

complicar {72} *vt* **1** : to complicate **2** : to involve — **complicarse** *vr*
cómplice *nmf* : accomplice
complicidad *nf* : complicity
complot *nm, pl* **complots** CONFABULACIÓN, CONSPIRACIÓN : conspiracy, plot
componenda *nf* : shady deal, scam
componente *adj & nm* : component, constituent
componer {60} *vt* **1** ARREGLAR : to fix, to repair **2** CONSTITUIR : to make up, to compose **3** : to compose, to write **4** : to set (a bone) — **componerse** *vr* **1** : to improve, to get better **2 ~ de** : to consist of
comportamiento *nm* CONDUCTA : behavior, conduct
comportarse *vr* : to behave, to conduct oneself
composición *nf, pl* **-ciones 1** OBRA : composition, work **2** : makeup, arrangement
compositor, -tora *n* : composer, songwriter
compostura *nf* **1** : composure **2** : mending, repair
compra *nf* **1** : purchase **2 ir de compras** : to go shopping **3 orden de compra** : purchase order
comprador, -dora *n* : buyer, shopper
comprar *vt* : to buy, to purchase
compraventa *nf* : buying and selling
comprender *vt* **1** ENTENDER : to comprehend, to understand **2** ABARCAR : to cover, to include — *vi* : to understand <¡ya comprendo! : now I understand!>
comprensible *adj* : understandable — **comprensiblemente** *adv*
comprensión *nf, pl* **-siones 1** : comprehension, understanding, grasp **2** : understanding, sympathy
comprensivo, -va *adj* : understanding
compresa *nf* **1** : compress **2** *or* **compresa higiénica** : sanitary napkin
compresión *nf, pl* **-siones** : compression
compresor *nm* : compressor
comprimido *nm* PÍLDORA, TABLETA : pill, tablet
comprimir *vt* : to compress
comprobable *adj* : verifiable, provable
comprobación *nf, pl* **-ciones** : verification, confirmation
comprobante *nm* **1** : proof <comprobante de identidad : proof of identity> **2** : voucher, receipt <comprobante de ventas : sales slip>
comprobar {19} *vt* **1** : to verify, to check **2** : to prove
comprometedor, -dora *adj* : compromising
comprometer *vt* **1** : to compromise **2** : to jeopardize **3** : to commit, to put under obligation — **comprometerse** *vr* **1** : to commit oneself **2 ~ con** : to get engaged to
comprometido, -da *adj* **1** : compromising, awkward **2** : committed, obliged **3** : engaged (to be married)
compromiso *nm* **1** : obligation, commitment **2** : engagement <anillo de compromiso : engagement ring> **3** : agreement **4** : awkward situation, fix
compuerta *nf* : floodgate
compuesto[1] *pp* → **componer**
compuesto[2], **-ta** *adj* **1** : fixed, repaired **2** : compound, composite **3** : decked out, spruced up **4 ~ de** : made up of, consisting of
compuesto[3] *nm* : compound
compulsión *nf, pl* **-siones** : compulsion
compulsivo, -va *adj* **1** : compelling, urgent **2** : compulsive — **compulsivamente** *adv*
compungido, -da *adj* : contrite, remorseful
compungirse {35} *vr* : to feel remorse
compuso, etc. → **componer**
computación *nf, pl* **-ciones** : computing, computers *pl*
computador *nm* → **computadora**
computadora *nf* **1** : computer **2 computadora portátil** : laptop computer
computar *vt* : to compute, tc calculate
computarizar {21} *vt* : to computerize
cómputo *nm* : computation, calculation
comulgar {52} *vi* : to receive Communion
común *adj, pl* **comunes 1** : common **2 común y corriente** : ordinary, regular **3 por lo común** : generally, as a rule
comuna *nf* : commune
comunal *adj* : communal
comunicación *nf, pl* **-ciones 1** : communication **2** : access, link **3** : message, report
comunicado *nm* **1** : communiqué **2 comunicado de prensa** : press release
comunicar {72} *vt* **1** : to communicate, to convey **2** : to notify — **comunicarse** *vr* **~ con 1** : to contact, to get in touch with **2** : to be connected to
comunicativo, -va *adj* : communicative, talkative
comunidad *nf* : community
comunión *nf, pl* **-niones 1** : communion, sharing **2** : Communion
comunismo *nm* : communism, Communism
comúnmente *adv* : commonly
con *prep* **1** : with <vengo con mi padre : I'm going with my father> <¿con quién hablas? : who are you speaking to?> **2** : in spite of <con todo : in spite of it all> **3** : to, towards <ella es amable con los niños : she is kind to the children> **4** : by <con llegar temprano : by arriving early> **5 con (tal) que** : as long as, so long as
conato *nm* : attempt, effort <conato de robo : attempted robbery>

cóncavo, -va *adj* : concave
concebible *adj* : conceivable
concebir {54} *vt* **1** : to conceive **2** : to conceive of, to imagine — *vi* : to conceive, to become pregnant
conceder *vt* **1** : to grant, to bestow **2** : to concede, to admit
concejal, -jala *n* : councilman *m,* councilwoman *f,* alderman *m,* alderwoman *f*
concejo *nm* : council <concejo municipal : town council>
concentración *nf, pl* **-ciones** : concentration
concentrado *nm* : concentrate
concentrar *vt* : to concentrate — **concentrarse** *vr*
concéntrico, -ca *adj* : concentric
concepción *nf, pl* **-ciones** : conception
concepto *nm* NOCIÓN : concept, idea, opinion
conceptuar {3} *vt* : to regard, to judge
concernir {17} *vi* : to be of concern
concertar {55} *vt* **1** : to arrange, to set up **2** : to agree on, to settle **3** : to harmonize — *vi* : to be in harmony
concesión *nf, pl* **-siones 1** : concession **2** : awarding, granting
concha *nf* : conch, seashell
conciencia *nf* **1** : conscience **2** : consciousness, awareness
concientizar {21} *vt* : to make aware — **concientizarse** *vr* **~ de** : to realize, to become aware of
concienzudo, -da *adj* : conscientious
concierto *nm* **1** : concert **2** : agreement **3** : concerto
conciliador[1]**, -dora** *adj* : conciliatory
conciliador[2]**, -dora** *n* : arbitrator, peacemaker
conciliar *vt* : to conciliate, to reconcile — **conciliación** *nf*
concilio *nm* : (church) council
conciso, -sa *adj* : concise — **concisión** *nf*
conciudadano, -na *n* : fellow citizen
cónclave *nm* : conclave, private meeting
concluir {41} *vt* **1** TERMINAR : to conclude, to finish **2** DEDUCIR : to deduce, to infer — *vi* : to end, to conclude
conclusión *nf, pl* **-siones** : conclusion
concluyente *adj* : conclusive
concomitante *adj* : concomitant
concordancia *nf* : agreement, accordance
concordar {19} *vi* : to agree, to coincide — *vt* : to reconcile
concordia *nf* : concord, harmony
concretar *vt* **1** : to pinpoint, to specify **2** : to fulfill, to realize — **concretarse** *vr* : to become real, to take shape
concretizar → **concretar**
concreto[1]**, -ta** *adj* **1** : concrete, actual **2** : definite, specific <en concreto : specifically> — **concretamente** *adv*
concreto[2] *nm* HORMIGÓN : concrete
concubina *nf* : concubine
concurrencia *nf* **1** : audience, turnout **2** : concurrence
concurrente *adj* : concurrent — **concurrentemente** *adv*
concurrido, -da *adj* : busy, crowded
concurrir *vi* **1** : to converge, to come together **2** : to concur, to agree **3** : to take part, to participate **4** : to attend, to be present <concurrir a una reunión : to attend a meeting> **5 ~ a** : to contribute to
concursante *nmf* : contestant, competitor
concursar *vt* : to compete in — *vi* : to compete, to participate
concurso *nm* **1** : contest, competition **2** : concurrance, coincidence **3** : crowd, gathering **4** : cooperation, assistance
condado *nm* **1** : county **2** : earldom
conde, -desa *n* : count *m,* earl *m,* countess *f*
condecoración *nf, pl* **-ciones** : decoration, medal
condecorar *vt* : to decorate, to award (a medal)
condena *nf* **1** REPROBACIÓN : disapproval, condemnation **2** SENTENCIA : sentence, conviction
condenación *nf, pl* **-ciones 1** : condemnation **2** : damnation
condenado[1]**, -da** *adj* **1** : fated, doomed **2** : convicted, sentenced **3** *fam* : darn, damned
condenado[2]**, -da** *n* : convict
condenar *vt* **1** : to condemn **2** : to sentence **3** : to board up, to wall up — **condenarse** *vr* : to be damned
condensación *nf, pl* **-ciones** : condensation
condensar *vt* : to condense
condesa *nf* → **conde**
condescendencia *nf* : condescension
condescender {56} *vi* **1** : to condescend **2** : to agree, to acquiesce
condición *nf, pl* **-ciones 1** : condition, state **2** : capacity, position **3 condiciones** *nfpl* : conditions, circumstances <condiciones de vida : living conditions>
condicional *adj* : conditional — **condicionalmente** *adv*
condicionamiento *nm* : conditioning
condicionar *vt* **1** : to condition, to determine **2 ~ a** : to be contingent on, to depend on
condimentar *vt* SAZONAR : to season, to spice
condimento *nm* : condiment, seasoning, spice
condolencia *nf* : condolence, sympathy
condolerse {47} *vr* : to sympathize
condominio *nm* : condominium, condo
condón *nm, pl* **condones** : condom
cóndor *nm* : condor
conducción *nf, pl* **-ciones 1** : conduction (of electricity, etc.) **2** DIRECCIÓN : management, direction

conducir {61} *vt* **1** DIRIGIR, GUIAR **:** to direct, to lead **2** MANEJAR **:** to drive (a vehicle) — *vi* **1 :** to drive a vehicle **2 ~ a :** to lead to — **conducirse** *vr* PORTARSE **:** to behave, to conduct oneself

conducta *nf* COMPORTAMIENTO **:** conduct, behavior

conducto *nm* **:** conduit, channel, duct

conductor[1], -tora *adj* **:** conducting, leading

conductor[2], -tora *n* **:** driver

conductor[3] *nm* **:** conductor (of electricity, etc.)

conectar *vt* **:** to connect — *vi* **~ con :** to link up with, to communicate with

conector *nm* **:** connector

conejera *nf* **:** rabbit hutch

conejillo *nm* **conejillo de Indias :** guinea pig

conejo, -ja *n* **:** rabbit

conexión *nf, pl* **-xiones :** connection

confabulación *nf, pl* **-ciones** COMPLOT, CONSPIRACIÓN **:** plot, conspiracy

confabularse *vr* **:** to plot, to conspire

confección *nf, pl* **-ciones 1 :** preparation **2 :** tailoring, dressmaking

confeccionar *vt* **:** to make, to produce, to prepare

confederación *nf, pl* **-ciones :** confederation

confederarse *vr* **:** to confederate, to form a confederation

conferencia *nf* **1** REUNIÓN **:** conference, meeting **2 :** lecture

conferenciante *nmf* **:** lecturer

conferencista *nmf* → **conferenciante**

conferir {76} *vt* **:** to confer, to bestow

confesar {55} *v* **:** to confess — **confesarse** *vr* **:** to go to confession

confesión *nf, pl* **-siones 1 :** confession **2 :** creed, denomination

confesionario *nm* **:** confessional

confesor *nm* **:** confessor

confeti *nm* **:** confetti

confiable *adj* **:** trustworthy, reliable

confiado, -da *adj* **1 :** confident, self-confident **2 :** trusting — **confiadamente** *adv*

confianza *nf* **1 :** trust <de poca confiaza : untrustworthy> **2 :** confidence, self-confidence

confianzudo, -da *adj* **:** forward, presumptuous

confiar {85} *vi* **:** to have trust, to be trusting — *vt* **1 :** to confide **2 :** to entrust — **confiarse** *vr* **1 :** to be overconfident **2 ~ a :** to confide in

confidencia *nf* **:** confidence, secret

confidencial *adj* **:** confidential — **confidencialmente** *adv*

confidencialidad *nf* **:** confidentiality

confidente *nmf* **1 :** confidant, confidante *f* **2 :** informer

configuración *nf, pl* **-ciones :** configuration, shape

configurar *vt* **:** to shape, to form

confín *nm, pl* **confines :** boundary, limit

confinamiento *nm* **:** confinement

confinar *vt* **1 :** to confine, to limit **2 :** to exile — *vi* **~ con :** to border on

confirmación *nf, pl* **-ciones :** confirmation

confirmar *vt* **:** to confirm, to substantiate

confiscar {72} *vt* DECOMISAR **:** to confiscate, to seize

confitado, -da *adj* **:** candied

confite *nm* **:** comfit, candy

confitería *nm* **1** DULCERÍA **:** candy store, confectionery **2 :** tearoom, café

confitero, -ra *n* **:** confectioner

confitura *nf* **:** preserves, jam

conflagración *nf, pl* **-ciones 1 :** conflagration, fire **2 :** war

conflictivo, -va *adj* **1 :** troubled **2 :** controversial

conflicto *nm* **:** conflict

confluencia *nf* **:** junction, confluence

confluir {41} *vi* **1 :** to converge, to join **2 :** to gather, to assemble

conformar *vt* **1 :** to form, to create **2 :** to constitute, to make up — **conformarse** *vr* **1** RESIGNARSE **:** to resign oneself **2 :** to comply, to conform **3 ~ con :** to content oneself with, to be satisfied with

conforme[1] *adj* **1 :** content, satisfied **2 ~ a :** in accordance with

conforme[2] *conj* **:** as <entreguen sus tareas conforme vayan saliendo : hand in your homework as you leave>

conformidad *nf* **1 :** agreement, consent **2 :** resignation

confort *nm* **:** comfort

confortable *adj* CÓMODO **:** comfortable

confortar *vt* CONSOLAR **:** to comfort, to console

confraternidad *nf* **:** brotherhood, fraternity

confrontación *nf, pl* **-ciones :** confrontation

confrontar *vt* **1** ENCARAR **:** to confront **2 :** to compare **3 :** to bring face-to-face — *vi* **:** to border — **confrontarse** *vr* **~ con :** to face up to

confundir *vt* **:** to confuse, to mix up — **confundirse** *vr* **:** to make a mistake, to be confused <confundirse de número : to get the wrong number>

confusión *nf, pl* **-siones :** confusion

confuso, -sa *adj* **1 :** confused, mixed-up **2 :** obscure, indistinct

congelación *nf, pl* **-ciones 1 :** freezing **2 :** frostbite

congelado, -da *adj* HELADO **:** frozen

congelador *nm* HELADORA **:** freezer

congelamiento *nm* → **congelación**

congelar *vt* **:** to freeze — **congelarse** *vr*

congeniar *vi* **:** to get along (with someone)

congénito, -ta *adj* **:** congenital

congestión *nf, pl* **-tiones :** congestion

congestionado, -da *adj* **:** congested

congestionamiento *nm* → **congestión**

congestionarse *vr* **1 :** to become flushed **2 :** to become congested
conglomerado[1], **-da** *adj* **:** conglomerate, mixed
conglomerado[2] *nm* **:** conglomerate, conglomeration
congoja *nf* ANGUSTIA **:** anguish, grief
congoleño, -ña *adj & n* **:** Congolese
congraciarse *vr* **:** to ingratiate oneself
congratular *vt* FELICITAR **:** to congratulate
congregación *nf, pl* **-ciones :** congregation, gathering
congregar {52} *vt* **:** to bring together — **congregarse** *vr* **:** to congregate, to assemble
congresista *nmf* **:** congressman *m*, congresswoman *f*
congreso *nm* **:** congress, conference
congruencia *nf* **1 :** congruence **2** COHERENCIA **:** coherence — **congruente** *adj*
cónico, -ca *adj* **:** conical, conic
conífera *nf* **:** conifer
conífero, -ra *adj* **:** coniferous
conjetura *nf* **:** conjecture, guess
conjeturar *vt* **:** to guess, to conjecture
conjugación *nf, pl* **-ciones :** conjugation
conjugar {52} *vt* **1 :** to conjugate **2 :** to combine
conjunción *nf, pl* **-ciones :** conjunction
conjuntivo, -va *adj* **:** connective <tejido conjuntivo : connective tissue>
conjunto[1], **-ta** *adj* **:** joint
conjunto[2] *nm* **1 :** collection, group **2 :** ensemble, outfit <conjunto musical : musical ensemble> **3 :** whole, entirety <en conjunto : as a whole, altogether>
conjurar *vt* **1 :** to exorcise **2 :** to avert, to ward off — *vi* CONSPIRAR **:** to conspire, to plot
conjuro *nm* **1 :** exorcism **2 :** spell
conllevar *vt* **1 :** to bear, to suffer **2** IMPLICAR **:** to entail, to involve
conmemorar *vt* **:** to commemorate — **conmemoración** *nf*
conmemorativo, -va *adj* **:** commemorative, memorial
conmigo *pron* **:** with me <habló conmigo : he talked with me>
conminar *vt* AMENAZAR **:** to threaten, to warn
conmiseración *nf, pl* **-ciones :** pity, conmiseration
conmoción *nf, pl* **-ciones 1 :** shock, upheaval **2** *or* **conmoción cerebral :** concussion
conmocionar *vt* **:** to shake, to shock
conmovedor, -dora *adj* EMOCIONANTE **:** moving, touching
conmover {47} *vt* **1** EMOCIONAR **:** to move, to touch **2 :** to shake up — **conmoverse** *vr*
conmutador *nm* **1 :** switch **2 :** switchboard
connivencia *nf* **:** connivance
connotación *nf, pl* **-ciones :** connotation
connotar *vt* **:** to connote, to imply
cono *nm* **:** cone
conocedor[1], **-dora** *adj* **:** knowledgeable
conocedor[2], **-dora** *n* **:** connoisseur, expert
conocer {18} *vt* **1 :** to know, to be acquainted with <ya la conocí : I've already met him> **2 :** to meet **3** RECONOCER **:** to recognize — **conocerse** *vr* **1 :** to know each other **2 :** to meet **3 :** to know oneself
conocido[1], **-da** *adj* **1 :** familiar **2 :** well-known, famous
conocido[2], **-da** *n* **:** acquaintance
conocimiento *nm* **1 :** knowledge **2** SENTIDO **:** consciousness
conque *conj* **:** so, so then, and so <¡ah, conque esas tenemos! : oh, so that's what's going on!>
conquista *nf* **:** conquest
conquistador[1], **-dora** *adj* **:** conquering
conquistador[2], **-dora** *n* **:** conqueror
conquistar *vt* **:** to conquer
consabido, -da *adj* **:** usual, typical
consagración *nf, pl* **-ciones :** consecration
consagrar *vt* **1 :** to consecrate **2** DEDICAR **:** to dedicate, to devote
consciencia *nf* → **conciencia**
consciente *adj* **:** conscious, aware — **conscientemente** *adv*
conscripción *nf, pl* **-ciones :** conscription, draft
conscripto, -ta *n* **:** conscript, inductee
consecución *nf, pl* **-ciones :** attainment
consecuencia *nf* **1 :** consequence, result <a consecuencia de : as a result of> **2 en ~ :** accordingly
consecuente *adj* **:** consistent — **consecuentemente** *adv*
consecutivo, -va *adj* **:** consecutive, successive — **consecutivamente** *adv*
conseguir {75} *vt* **1 :** to get, to obtain **2 :** to achieve, to attain **3 :** to manage to <consiguió acabar el trabajo : she managed to finish the job>
consejero, -ra *n* **:** adviser, counselor
consejo *nm* **1 :** advice, counsel **2 :** council <consejo de guerra : court-martial>
consenso *nm* **:** consensus
consentido, -da *adj* **:** spoiled, pampered
consentimiento *nm* **:** consent, permission
consentir {76} *vt* **1** PERMITIR **:** to consent to, to allow **2** MIMAR **:** to pamper, to spoil — *vi* **~ en :** to agree to, to approve of
conserje *nmf* **:** custodian, janitor, caretaker
conserva *nf* **1 :** preserve(s), jam **2 conservas** *nfpl* **:** canned goods
conservación *nf, pl* **-ciones :** conservation, preservation

conservacionista *nmf* : conservationist

conservador[1], **-dora** *adj & n* : conservative

conservador[2] *nm* : preservative

conservadurismo *nf* : conservatism

conservante *nm* : preservative

conservar *vt* **1** : to preserve **2** GUARDAR : to keep, to conserve

conservatorio *nm* : conservatory

considerable *adj* : considerable — **considerablemente** *adv*

consideración *nf, pl* **-ciones 1** : consideration **2** : respect **3 de ~** : considerable, important

considerado, -da *adj* **1** : considerate, thoughtful **2** : respected

considerar *vt* **1** : to consider, to think over **2** : to judge, to deem **3** : to treat with respect

consigna *nf* **1** ESLOGAN : slogan **2** : assignment, orders *pl* **3** : checkroom

consignar *vt* **1** : to consign **2** : to record, to write down **3** : to assign, to allocate

consigo *pron* : with her, with him, with you, with oneself <se llevó las llaves consigo : she took the keys with her>

consiguiente *adj* **1** : resulting, consequent **2 por ~** : consequently, as a result

consistencia *nf* : consistency

consistente *adj* **1** : firm, strong, sound **2** : consistent — **consistentemente** *adv*

consistir *vi* **1 ~ en** : to consist of **2 ~ en** : to lie in, to consist in

consola *nf* : console

consolación *nf, pl* **-ciones** : consolation <premio de consolación : consolation prize>

consolar {19} *vt* CONFORTAR : to console, to comfort

consolidar *vt* : to consolidate — **consolidación** *nf*

consomé *nm* CALDO : consommé, clear soup

consonancia *nf* **1** : consonance, harmony **2 en consonancia con** : in accordance with

consonante[1] *adj* : consonant, harmonious

consonante[2] *nf* : consonant

consorcio *nm* : consortium

consorte *nmf* : consort, spouse

conspicuo, -cua *adj* : eminent, famous

conspiración *nf, pl* **-ciones** COMPLOT, CONFABULACIÓN : conspiracy, plot

conspirador, -dora *n* : conspirator

conspirar *vi* CONJURAR : to conspire, to plot

constancia *nf* **1** PRUEBA : proof, certainty **2** : record, evidence <que quede constancia : for the record> **3** : perseverance, constancy

constante[1] *adj* : constant — **constantemente** *adv*

constante[2] *nm* : constant

constar *vi* **1** : to be evident, to be on record <que conste : believe me, have no doubt> **2 ~ de** : to consist of

constatación *nf, pl* **-ciones** : confirmation, proof

constatar *vt* **1** : to verify **2** : to state

constelación *nf, pl* **-ciones** : constellation

consternación *nf, pl* **-ciones** : consternation, dismay

consternar *vt* : to dismay, to appall

constipación *nf, pl* **-ciones** : constipation

constipado[1], **-da** *adj* **estar constipado** : to have a cold

constipado[2] *nm* RESFRIADO : cold

constiparse *vr* : to catch a cold

constitución *nf, pl* **-ciones** : constitution — **constitucional** *adj* — **constitucionalmente** *adv*

constitucionalidad *nf* : constitutionality

constituir {41} *vt* **1** FORMAR : to constitute, to make up, to form **2** FUNDAR : to establish, to set up — **constituirse** *vr* **~ en** : to set oneself up as, to become

constitutivo, -va *adj* : constituent, component

constituyente *adj & nmf* : constituent

constreñir {67} *vt* **1** FORZAR, OBLIGAR : to constrain, to oblige **2** LIMITAR : to restrict, to limit

construcción *nf, pl* **-ciones** : construction, building

constructivo, -va *adj* : constructive — **constructivamente** *adv*

constructor, -tora *n* : builder

constructora *nf* : construction company

construir {41} *vt* : to build, to construct

consuelo *nm* : consolation, comfort

consuetudinario, -ria *adj* **1** : customary, habitual **2 derecho consuetudinario** : common law

cónsul *nmf* : consul — **consular** *adj*

consulado *nm* : consulate

consulta *nf* **1** : consultation **2** : inquiry

consultar *vt* : to consult

consultor[1], **-tora** *adj* : consulting <firma consultora : consulting firm>

consultor[2], **-tora** *n* : consultant

consultorio *nm* : office (of a doctor or dentist)

consumación *nf, pl* **-ciones** : consummation

consumado, -da *adj* : consummate, perfect

consumar *vt* **1** : to consummate, to complete **2** : to commit, to carry out

consumible *adj* : consumable

consumición *nf, pl* **-ciones 1** : consumption **2** : drink (in a restaurant)

consumido, -da *adj* : thin, emaciated

consumidor, -dora *n* : consumer

consumir *vt* : to consume — **consumirse** *vr* : to waste away

consumo *nm* : consumption

contabilidad *nf* **1 :** accounting, bookkeeping **2 :** accountancy
contabilizar {21} *vt* **:** to enter, to record (in accounting)
contable[1] *adj* **:** countable
contable[2] *nmf Spain* **:** accountant, bookkeeper
contactar *vt* **:** to contact — *vi* **~ con :** to get in touch with, to contact
contacto *nm* **:** contact
contado[1], **-da** *adj* **1 :** counted <tenía los días contados : his days were numbered> **2 :** rare, scarce <en contadas ocasiones : on rare occasions>
contado[2] *nm* **al contado :** cash <pagar al contado : to pay in cash>
contador[1], **-dora** *n* **:** accountant
contador[2] *nm* **:** meter <contador de agua : water meter>
contaduría *nf* **1 :** accounting office **2** CONTABILIDAD **:** accountancy
contagiar *vt* **1 :** to infect **2 :** to transmit (a disease) — **contagiarse** *vr* **1 :** to be contagious **2 :** to become infected
contagio *nm* **:** contagion, infection
contagioso, -sa *adj* **:** contagious, catching
contaminación *nf, pl* **-ciones :** contamination, pollution
contaminante *nm* **:** pollutant, contaminant
contaminar *vt* **:** to contaminate, to pollute
contar {19} *vt* **1 :** to count **2 :** to tell **3 :** to include — *vi* **1 :** to count (up) **2 :** to matter, to be of concern <eso no cuenta : that doesn't matter> **3 ~ con :** to rely on, to count on — **contarse** *vr* **~ entre :** to be numbered among
contemplación *nf, pl* **-ciones :** contemplation — **contemplativo, -va** *adj*
contemplar *vt* **1 :** to contemplate, to ponder **2 :** to gaze at, to look at
contemporáneo, -nea *adj & n* **:** contemporary
contención *nf, pl* **-ciones :** containment, holding
contencioso, -sa *adj* **:** contentious
contender {56} *vi* **1 :** to contend, to compete **2 :** to fight
contendiente *nmf* **:** contender
contenedor *nm* **1 :** container, receptacle **2 :** Dumpster™
contener {80} *vt* **1 :** to contain, to hold **2** ATAJAR **:** to restrain, to hold back — **contenerse** *vr* **:** to restrain oneself
contenido[1], **-da** *adj* **:** restrained, reserved
contenido[2] *nm* **:** contents *pl*, content
contentar *vt* **:** to please, to make happy — **contentarse** *vr* **:** to be satisfied, to be pleased
contento[1], **-ta** *adj* **:** contented, glad, happy
contento[2] *nm* **:** joy, happiness
contestación *nf, pl* **-ciones 1 :** answer, reply **2 :** protest
contestar *vt* RESPONDER **:** to answer — *vi* **1** RESPONDER **:** to answer, to reply **2** REPLICAR **:** to answer back
contexto *nm* **:** context
contienda *nf* **1 :** dispute, conflict **2 :** contest, competition
contigo *pron* **:** with you <voy contigo : I'm going with you>
contiguo, -gua *adj* COLINDANTE **:** contiguous, adjacent
continencia *nf* **:** continence
continente *nm* **:** continent — **continental** *adj*
contingencia *nf* **:** contingency, eventuality
contingente *adj & nm* **:** contingent
continuación *nf, pl* **-ciones 1 :** continuation **2 a ~ :** next <lo demás sigue a continuación : the rest follows> **3 a continuación de :** after, following
continuar {3} *v* **:** to continue
continuidad *nf* **:** continuity
continuo, -nua *adj* **:** continuous, steady, constant — **continuamente** *adv*
contonearse *vr* **:** to sway one's hips
contoneo *nm* **:** swaying, wiggling (of the hips)
contorno *nm* **1 :** outline **2 contornos** *nmpl* **:** outskirts
contorsión *nf, pl* **-siones :** contortion
contra[1] *nf* **1** *fam* **:** difficulty, snag **2 llevar la contra a :** to oppose, to contradict
contra[2] *nm* **:** con <los pros y los contras : the pros and cons>
contra[3] *prep* **:** against
contraalmirante *nm* **:** rear admiral
contraatacar {72} *v* **:** to counterattack — **contraataque** *nm*
contrabajo *nm* **:** double bass
contrabalancear *vt* **:** to counterbalance — **contrabalanza** *nf*
contrabandear *v* **:** to smuggle
contrabandista *nmf* **:** smuggler, black marketeer
contrabando *nm* **1 :** smuggling **2 :** contraband
contracción *nf, pl* **-ciones :** contraction
contracepción *nf, pl* **-ciones :** contraception
contrachapado *nm* **:** plywood
contraconceptivo *nm* ANTICONCEPTIVO **:** contraceptive — **contracepción** *nf*
contracorriente *nf* **1 :** crosscurrent **2 ir a contracorriente :** to go against the tide
contractual *adj* **:** contractual
contradecir {11} *vt* DESMENTIR **:** to contradict — **contradecirse** *vr* DESDECIRSE **:** to contradict oneself
contradicción *nf, pl* **-ciones :** contradiction
contradictorio, -ria *adj* **:** contradictory
contraer {81} *vt* **1 :** to contract (a disease) **2 :** to establish by contract

<contraer matrimonio : to get married> **3** : to tighten, to contract — **contraerse** *vr* : to contract, to tighten up

contrafuerte *nm* : buttress

contragolpe *nm* **1** : counterblow **2** : backlash

contrahecho, -cha *adj* : deformed, hunchbacked

contraindicado, -da *adj* : contraindicated — **contraindicación** *nf*

contralor, -lora *n* : comptroller

contralto *nmf* : contralto

contramaestre *nm* **1** : boatswain **2** : foreman

contramandar *vt* : to countermand

contramano *nm* **a ~** : the wrong way (on a street)

contramedida *nf* : countermeasure

contraorden *nf* : countermand

contraparte *nf* **1** : counterpart **2 en ~** : on the other hand

contrapartida *nf* : compensation

contrapelo *nm* **a ~** : in the wrong direction, against the grain

contrapeso *nm* : counterbalance

contraponer {60} *vt* **1** : to counter, to oppose **2** : to contrast, to compare

contraposición *nf, pl* **-ciones** : comparison

contraproducente *adj* : counterproductive

contrapunto *nm* : counterpoint

contrariar {85} *vt* **1** : to contradict, to oppose **2** : to vex, to annoy

contrariedad *nf* **1** : setback, obstacle **2** : vexation, annoyance

contrario, -ria *adj* **1** : contrary, opposite <al contrario : on the contrary> **2** : conflicting, opposed

contrarrestar *vt* : to counteract

contrarrevolución *nf, pl* **-ciones** : counterrevolution — **contrarrevolucionario, -ria** *adj & n*

contrasentido *nm* : contradiction

contraseña *nf* : password

contrastante *adj* : contrasting

contrastar *vt* **1** : to resist **2** : to check, to confirm — *vi* : to contrast

contraste *nm* : contrast

contratar *vt* **1** : to contract for **2** : to hire, to engage

contratiempo *nm* **1** PERCANCE : mishap, accident **2** DIFICULTAD : setback, difficulty

contratista *nmf* : contractor

contrato *nm* : contract

contravenir {87} *vt* : to contravene, to infringe

contraventana *nf* : shutter

contribución *nf, pl* **-ciones** : contribution

contribuidor, -dora *n* : contributor

contribuir {41} *vt* **1** APORTAR : to contribute **2** : to pay (in taxes) — *vi* **1** : contribute, to help out **2** : to pay taxes

contribuyente[1] *adj* : contributing

contribuyente[2] *nmf* : taxpayer

contrición *nf, pl* **-ciones** : contrition

contrincante *nmf* : rival, opponent

contrito, -ta *adj* : contrite, repentant

control *nm* **1** : control **2** : inspection, check **3** : checkpoint, roadblock

controlador, -dora *n* : controller <controlador aéreo : air traffic controller>

controlar *vt* **1** : to control **2** : to monitor, to check

controversia *nf* : controversy

controversial → **controvertido**

controvertido, -da *adj* : controversial

controvertir {76} *vt* : to dispute, to argue about — *vi* : to argue, to debate

contubernio *nm* : conspiracy

contumacia *nf* : obstinacy, stubbornness

contumaz *adj, pl* **-maces** : obstinate, stubbornly disobedient

contundencia *nf* **1** : forcefulness, weight **2** : severity

contundente *adj* **1** : blunt <un objeto contundente : a blunt instrument> **2** : forceful, convincing — **contundentemente** *adv*

contusión *nf, pl* **-siones** : bruise, contusion

contuvo, etc. → **contener**

convalecencia *nf* : convalescence

convalecer {53} *vi* : to convalesce, to recover

convaleciente *adj & nmf* : convalescent

convección *nf, pl* **-ciones** : convection

convencer {86} *vt* : to convince, to persuade — **convencerse** *vr*

convencimiento *nm* : belief, conviction

convención *nf, pl* **-ciones** **1** : convention, conference **2** : pact, agreement **3** : convention, custom

convencional *adj* : conventional — **convencionalmente** *adv*

convencionalismo *nm* : conventionality

conveniencia *nf* **1** : convenience **2** : fitness, suitability, advisability

conveniente *adj* **1** : convenient **2** : suitable, advisable

convenio *nm* PACTO : agreement, pact

convenir {87} *vi* **1** : to be suitable, to be advisable **2** : to agree

convento *nm* **1** : convent **2** : monastery

convergencia *nf* : convergence

convergente *adj* : convergent, converging

converger {15} *vi* **1** : to converge **2 ~ en** : to concur on

conversación *nf, pl* **-ciones** : conversation

conversador, -dora *n* : conversationalist, talker

conversar *vi* : to converse, to talk

conversión *nf, pl* **-siones** : conversion

converso, -sa *n* : convert

convertible *adj & nm* : convertible

convertidor *nm* : converter

convertir {76} *vt* **1** : to convert **2** : to transform, to change **3** : to exchange (money) — **convertirse** *vr* ~ **en** : to turn into
convexo, -xa *adj* : convex
convicción *nf, pl* **-ciones** : conviction
convicto¹, -ta *adj* : convicted
convicto², -ta *n* : convict, prisoner
convidado, -da *n* : guest
convidar *vt* **1** INVITAR : to invite **2** : to offer
convincente *adj* : convincing — **convincentemente** *adv*
convivencia *nf* **1** : coexistence **2** : cohabitation
convivir *vi* **1** : to coexist **2** : to live together
convocación *nf, pl* **-ciones** : convocation
convocar {72} *vt* : to convoke, to call together
convocatoria *nf* : summons, call
convoy *nm* : convoy
convulsión *nf, pl* **-siones 1** : convulsion **2** : agitation, upheaval
convulsivo, -va *adj* : convulsive
conyugal *adj* : conjugal
cónyuge *nmf* : spouse, partner
coñac *nm* : cognac, brandy
cooperación *nf, pl* **-ciones** : cooperation
cooperador, -dora *adj* : cooperative
cooperar *vi* : to cooperate
cooperativa *nf* : cooperative, co-op
cooperativo, -va *adj* : cooperative
cooptar *vt* : to co-opt
coordenada *nf* : coordinate
coordinación *nf, pl* **-ciones** : coordination
coordinador, -dora *n* : coordinator
coordinar *vt* COMPAGINAR : to coordinate, to combine
copa *nf* **1** : wineglass, goblet **2** : drink <irse de copas : to go out drinking> **3** : cup, trophy
copar *vt* **1** : to take <ya está copado el puesto : the job is already taken> **2** : to fill, to crowd
copartícipe *nmf* : joint partner
copete *nm* **1** : tuft (of hair) **2 estar hasta el copete** : to be completely fed up
copia *nf* **1** : copy **2** : imitation, replica
copiadora *nf* : photocopier
copiar *vt* : to copy
copiloto *nmf* : copilot
copioso, -sa *adj* : copious, abundant
copla *nf* **1** : popular song or ballad **2** : couplet, stanza
copo *nm* **1** : snowflake **2 copos de avena** : rolled oats **3 copos de maíz** : cornflakes
copra *nf* : copra
cópula *nf* : copulation
copular *vi* : to copulate
coque *nm* : coke (fuel)
coqueta *nf* : dressing table
coquetear *vi* : to flirt
coqueteo *nm* : flirting, coquetry
coqueto¹, -ta *adj* : flirtatious, coquettish
coqueto², -ta *n* : flirt
coraje *nm* **1** VALOR : valor, courage **2** IRA : anger <darle coraje a alguien : to make someone angry>
coral¹ *nm* **1** : coral **2** : chorale
coral² *nf* : choir
Corán *nm* **el Corán** : the Koran
coraza *nf* **1** : armor, armor plating **2** : shell (of an animal)
corazón *nm, pl* **-zones 1** : heart <de todo corazón : wholeheartedly> <de buen corazón : kindhearted> **2** : core **3** : darling, sweetheart
corazonada *nf* : hunch, impulse
corbata *nf* : tie, necktie
corcel *nm* : steed, charger
corchete *nm* **1** : hook and eye, clasp **2** : square bracket
corcho *nm* : cork
corcholata *nf Mex* : cap, bottle top
corcovear *vi* : to buck
cordel *nm* : cord, string
cordero *nm* : lamb
cordial¹ *adj* : cordial, affable — **cordialmente** *adv*
cordial² *nm* : cordial (liqueur)
cordialidad *nf* : cordiality, warmth
cordillera *nf* : mountain range
córdoba *nf* : Nicaraguan unit of currency
cordón *nm, pl* **cordones 1** : cord <cordón umbilical : umbilical cord> **2** : cordon
cordura *nf* **1** : sanity **2** : prudence, good judgment
coreano¹, -na *adj & n* : Korean
coreano² *nm* : Korean (language)
corear *vt* : to chant, to chorus
coreografía *nf* : choreography
coreografiar {85} *vt* : to choreograph
coreográfico, -ca *adj* : choreographic
coreógrafo, -fa *n* : choreographer
cormorán *nm, pl* **-ranes** : cormorant
cornada *nf* : goring, butt (with the horns)
córnea *nf* : cornea
cornear *vt* : to gore
cornejo *nm* : dogwood (tree)
corneta *nf* : bugle, horn, cornet
cornisa *nf* : cornice
cornudo, -da *adj* : horned
coro *nm* **1** : choir **2** : chorus
corola *nf* : corolla
corolario *nm* : corollary
corona *nf* **1** : crown **2** : wreath, garland **3** : corona (in astronomy)
coronación *nf, pl* **-ciones** : coronation
coronar *vt* **1** : to crown **2** : to reach the top of, to culminate
coronel, -nela *n* : colonel
coronilla *nf* **1** : crown (of the head) **2 estar hasta la coronilla** : to be completely fed up
corpiño *nm* **1** : bodice **2** *Arg* : brassiere, bra
corporación *nf, pl* **-ciones** : corporation

corporal *adj* **:** corporal, bodily
corporativo, -va *adj* **:** corporate
corpóreo, -rea *adj* **:** corporeal, physical
corpulencia *nf* **:** corpulence, stoutness, sturdiness
corpulento, -ta *adj* ROBUSTO **:** robust, stout, sturdy
corpúsculo *nm* **:** corpuscle
corral *nm* **1 :** farmyard **2 :** corral, pen, stockyard **3** *or* **corralito :** playpen
correa *nf* **:** strap, belt
correcaminos *nms & pl* **:** roadrunner
corrección *nf, pl* **-ciones 1 :** correction **2 :** correctness, propriety **3 :** rebuke, reprimand **4 corrección de pruebas :** proofreading
correccional *nm* REFORMATORIO **:** reformatory
correctivo, -va *adj* **:** corrective <lentes correctivos : corrective lenses>
correcto, -ta *adj* **1 :** correct, right **2 :** courteous, polite — **correctamente** *adv*
corrector, -tora *n* **:** proofreader
corredizo, -za *adj* **:** sliding <puerta corrediza : sliding door>
corredor[1], -dora *n* **1 :** runner, racer **2 :** agent, broker <corredor de bolsa : stockbroker>
corredor[2] *nm* PASILLO **:** corridor, hallway
correduría *nf* → **corretaje**
corregir {28} *vt* **1** ENMENDAR **:** to correct, to emend **2 :** to reprimand **3 corregir pruebas :** to proofread — **corregirse** *vr* **:** to reform, to mend one's ways
correlación *nf, pl* **-ciones :** correlation
correo *nm* **1 :** mail <correo aéreo : airmail> **2 :** post office
correoso, -sa *adj* **:** leathery, rough
correr *vi* **1 :** to run, to race **2 :** to rush **3 :** to flow — *vt* **1 :** to travel over, to cover **2 :** to move, to slide, to roll, to draw (curtains) **3 correr un riesgo :** to run a risk — **correrse** *vr* **1 :** to move along **2 :** to run, to spill over
correspondencia *nf* **1 :** correspondence, mail **2 :** equivalence **3 :** connection, interchange
corresponder *vi* **1 :** to correspond **2 :** to pertain, to belong **3 :** to be appropriate, to fit **4 :** to reciprocate — **corresponderse** *vr* **:** to write to each other
correspondiente *adj* **:** corresponding, respective
corresponsal *nmf* **:** correspondent
corretaje *nm* **:** brokerage
corretear *vi* **1** VAGAR **:** to loiter, to wander about **2 :** to run around, to scamper about — *vt* **:** to pursue, to chase
corrida *nf* **1 :** run, dash **2 :** bullfight
corrido[1], -da *adj* **1 :** straight, continuous **2 :** wordly, experienced
corrido[2] *nm* **:** Mexican narrative folk song
corriente[1] *adj* **1 :** common, everyday **2 :** current, present **3** *Mex* **:** cheap, trashy **4 perro corriente** *Mex* **:** mutt
corriente[2] *nf* **1 :** current <corriente alterna : alternating current> <direct current : corriente continua> **2 :** draft **3** TENDENCIA **:** tendency, trend
corrillo *nm* **:** small group, clique
corro *nm* **:** ring, circle (of people)
corroborar *vt* **:** to corroborate
corroer {69} *vt* **1 :** to corrode **2 :** to erode, to wear away
corromper *vt* **1 :** to corrupt **2 :** to rot — **corromperse** *vr*
corrompido, -da *adj* CORRUPTO **:** corrupt, rotten
corrosión *nf, pl* **-siones :** corrosion
corrosivo, -va *adj* **:** corrosive
corrugar {52} *vt* **:** to corrugate — **corrugación** *nf*
corrupción *nf, pl* **-ciones 1 :** decay **2 :** corruption
corruptela *nf* **:** corruption, abuse of power
corrupto, -ta *adj* CORROMPIDO **:** corrupt
corsario *nm* **:** privateer
corsé *nm* **:** corset
cortada *nf* **:** cut, gash
cortador, -dora *n* **:** cutter
cortadora *nf* **:** cutter, slicer
cortadura *nm* **:** cut, slash
cortafuego *nm* **:** firebreak
cortante *adj* **:** cutting, sharp
cortar *vt* **1 :** to cut, to slice, to trim **2 :** to cut out, to omit **3 :** to cut off, to interrupt **4 :** to block, to close off **5 :** to curdle (milk) — *vi* **1 :** to cut **2 :** to break up **3 :** to hang up (the telephone) — **cortarse** *vr* **1 :** to cut oneself <cortarse el pelo : to cut one's hair> **2 :** to be cut off **3 :** to sour (of milk)
cortauñas *nms & pl* **:** nail clippers
corte[1] *nm* **1 :** cut, cutting <corte de pelo : haircut> **2 :** style, fit
corte[2] *nf* **1 :** court <corte suprema : supreme court> **2 hacer la corte a :** to court, to woo
cortejar *vt* GALANTEAR **:** to court, to woo
cortejo *nm* **1** GALANTEO **:** courtship **2 :** retinue, entourage
cortés *adj* **:** courteous, polite — **cortésmente** *adv*
cortesano[1], -na *adj* **:** courtly
cortesano[2], -na *n* **:** courtier
cortesía *nf* **1 :** courtesy, politeness **2 de ~ :** complimentary, free
corteza *nf* **1 :** bark **2 :** crust **3 :** peel, rind **4 :** cortex <corteza cerebral : cerebral cortex>
cortijo *nm* **:** farmhouse
cortina *nm* **:** curtain
cortisona *nf* **:** cortisone
corto, -ta *adj* **1 :** short (in length or duration) **2 :** scarce **3 :** timid, shy **4 corto de vista :** nearsighted
cortocircuito *nm* **:** short circuit
corvo, -va *adj* **:** curved, bent

cosa *nf* **1 :** thing, object **2 :** matter, affair **3 otra cosa :** anything else, something else

cosecha *nf* **:** harvest, crop

cosechador, -dora *n* **:** harvester, reaper

cosechadora *nf* **:** harvester (machine)

cosechar *vt* **1 :** to harvest, to reap **2 :** to win, to earn, to garner — *vi* **:** to harvest

coser *vt* **1 :** to sew **2 :** to stitch up — *vi* **:** to sew

cosmético[1], **-ca** *adj* **:** cosmetic

cosmético[2] *nm* **:** cosmetic

cósmico, -ca *adj* **:** cosmic

cosmonauta *nmf* **:** cosmonaut

cosmopolita *adj & nmf* **:** cosmopolitan

cosmos *nm* **:** cosmos

cosquillas *nfpl* **1 :** tickling **2 hacer cosquillas :** to tickle

cosquilleo *nm* **:** tickling sensation, tingle

cosquilloso, -sa *adj* **:** ticklish

costa *nf* **1 :** coast, shore **2 :** cost <a toda costa : at all costs>

costado *nm* **1 :** side **2 al costado :** alongside

costar {19} *v* **:** to cost <¿cuánto cuesta? : how much does it cost?>

costarricense *adj & nmf* **:** Costa Rican

costarriqueño, -ña → **costarricense**

coste *nm* → **costo**

costear *vt* **:** to pay for, to finance

costero, -ra *adj* **:** coastal, coast

costilla *nf* **1 :** rib **2 :** chop, cutlet **3** *fam* **:** better half, wife

costo *nm* **1 :** cost, price **2 costo de vida :** cost of living

costoso, -sa *adj* **:** costly, expensive

costra *nf* **1 :** crust **2** POSTILLA **:** scab

costumbre *nf* **1 :** custom **2** HÁBITO **:** habit

costura *nf* **1 :** seam **2 :** sewing, dressmaking **3 alta costura :** haute couture

costurera *nf* **:** seamstress *f*

cotejar *vt* **:** to compare, to collate

cotejo *nm* **:** comparison, collation

cotidiano, -na *adj* **:** daily, everyday <la vida cotidiana : daily life>

cotización *nf, pl* **-ciones 1 :** market price **2 :** quote, estimate

cotizado, -da *adj* **:** in demand, sought after

cotizar {21} *vt* **:** to quote, to value — **cotizarse** *vr* **:** to be worth

coto *nm* **1 :** enclosure, reserve **2 poner coto a :** to put a stop to

cotorra *nf* **1 :** small parrot **2** *fam* **:** chatterbox, windbag

cotorrear *vi fam* **:** to chatter, to gab, to blab

cotorreo *nm fam* **:** chatter, prattle

coyote *nm* **1 :** coyote **2** *Mex fam* **:** smuggler (of illegal immigrants)

coyuntura *nf* **1** ARTICULACIÓN **:** joint **2 :** occasion, moment

coz *nm, pl* **coces :** kick (of an animal)

crac *nm, pl* **cracs :** crash (of the stock market)

cozamos, etc. → **cocer**

craneal *adj* **:** cranial

cráneo *nf* **:** cranium, skull — **craneano, -na** *adj*

cráter *nm* **:** crater

creación *nf, pl* **-ciones :** creation

creador[1], **-dora** *adj* **:** creative, creating

creador[2], **-dora** *n* **:** creator

crear *vt* **1 :** to create, to cause **2 :** to originate

creatividad *nf* **:** creativity

creativo, -va *adj* **:** creative

crecer {53} *vi* **1 :** to grow **2 :** to increase

crecida *nf* **:** flooding, floodwater

crecido, -da *adj* **1 :** grown, grown-up **2 :** large (of numbers)

creciente *adj* **1 :** growing, increasing **2 luna creciente :** waxing moon

crecientemente *adv* **:** increasingly

crecimiento *nm* **1 :** growth **2 :** increase

credencial *adj* **cartas credenciales :** credentials

credenciales *nfpl* **:** documents, documentation, credentials

credibilidad *nf* **:** credibility

crédito *nm* **:** credit

credo *nm* **:** creed, credo

credulidad *nf* **:** credulity

crédulo, -la *adj* **:** credulous, gullible

creencia *nf* **:** belief

creer {20} *v* **1 :** to believe **2 :** to suppose, to think <creo que sí : I think so> — **creerse** *vr* **1 :** to believe, to think **2 :** to regard oneself as <se cree guapísimo : he thinks he's so handsome>

creíble *adj* **:** believable, credible

creído, -da *adj* **1** *fam* **:** conceited **2 :** confident, sure

crema *nf* **1 :** cream **2 la crema y nata :** the pick of the crop

cremación *nf, pl* **-ciones :** cremation

cremallera *nf* **:** zipper

cremar *vt* **:** to cremate

cremoso, -sa *adj* **:** creamy

crepa *nf Mex* **:** crepe (pancake)

crepe *or* **crep** *nmf* **:** crepe (pancake)

crepé *nm* **1** → **crespón 2 papel crepé :** crepe paper

crepitar *vi* **:** to crackle

crepúsculo *nm* **:** twilight

crescendo *nm* **:** crescendo

crespo, -pa *adj* **:** curly, frizzy

crespón *nm, pl* **crespones :** crepe (fabric)

cresta *nf* **1 :** crest **2 :** comb (of a rooster)

creta *nf* **:** chalk (mineral)

cretino, -na *n* **:** cretin

creyente *nmf* **:** believer

creyó, etc. → **creer**

crezca, etc. → **crecer**

cría *nf* **1 :** breeding, rearing **2 :** young **3 :** litter

criadero *nm* **:** hatchery

criado[1], **-da** *adj* **1 :** raised, brought up **2 bien criado :** well-bred

criado[2], **-da** *n* **:** servant, maid *f*

criador, -dora *n* **:** breeder

crianza *nf* : upbringing, rearing
criar {85} *vt* **1** : to breed **2** : to bring up, to raise
criatura *nf* **1** : baby, child **2** : creature
criba *nf* : sieve, screen
cribar *vt* : to sift
cric *nm, pl* **crics** : jack
crimen *nm, pl* **crímenes** : crime
criminal *adj & nmf* : criminal
crin *nf* **1** : mane **2** : horsehair
criollo[1], **-lla** *adj* **1** : Creole **2** : native, national <comida criolla : native cuisine>
criollo[2], **-lla** *n* : Creole
criollo[3] *nm* : Creole (language)
cripta *nf* : crypt
críptico, -ca *adj* **1** : cryptic, coded **2** : enigmatic, cryptic
criptón *nm* : krypton
críquet *nm* : cricket (game)
crisálida *nf* : chrysalis, pupa
crisantemo *nm* : chrysanthemum
crisis *nf* **1** : crisis **2** **crisis nerviosa** : nervous breakdown
crisma *nf fam* : head <romperle la crisma a alguien : to knock someone's block off>
crisol *nm* **1** : crucible **2** : melting pot
crispar *vt* **1** : to cause to contract **2** : to irritate, to set on edge <eso me crispa : that gets on my nerves> — **crisparse** *vr* : to tense up
cristal *nm* **1** VIDRIO : glass, piece of glass **2** : crystal
cristalería *nf* **1** : glassware shop <como chivo en cristalería : like a bull in a china shop> **2** : glassware, crystal
cristalino[1], **-na** *adj* : crystalline, clear
cristalino[2] *nm* : lens (of the eye)
cristalizar {21} *vi* : to crystallize — **cristalización** *nf*
cristianismo *nm* : Christianity
cristiano, -na *adj & n* : Christian
criterio *nm* **1** : criterion **2** : judgment, sense
crítica *nf* **1** : criticism **2** : review, critique
criticar {72} *vt* : to criticize
crítico[1], **-ca** *adj* : critical — **críticamente** *adv*
crítico[2], **-ca** *n* : critic
criticón[1], **-cona** *adj, mpl* **-cones** *fam* : hypercritical, captious
criticón[2], **-cona** *n, mpl* **-cones** *fam* : faultfinder, critic
croar *vi* : to croak
croata *adj & nmf* : Croatian
crocante *adj* : crunchy
croché *or* **crochet** *nm* : crochet
cromático, -ca *adj* : chromatic
cromo *nm* **1** : chromium, chrome **2** : picture card, sports card
cromosoma *nm* : chromosome
crónica *nf* **1** : news report **2** : chronicle, history
crónico, -ca *adj* : chronic
cronista *nmf* **1** : reporter, newscaster **2** HISTORIADOR : chronicler, historian
cronología *nf* : chronology
cronológico, -ca *adj* : chronological — **cronológicamente** *adv*
cronometrador, -dora *n* : timekeeper
cronometrar *vt* : to time, to clock
cronómetro *nm* : chronometer
croquet *nm* : croquet
croqueta *nf* : croquette
croquis *nm* : rough sketch
cruce[1], etc. → **cruzar**
cruce[2] *nm* **1** : crossing, cross **2** : crossroads, intersection <cruce peatonal : crosswalk>
crucero *nm* **1** : cruise **2** : cruiser, warship **3** *Mex* : intersection
crucial *adj* : crucial — **crucialmente** *adv*
crucificar {72} *vt* : to crucify
crucifijo *nm* : crucifix
crucifixión *nf, pl* **-xiones** : crucifixion
crucigrama *nm* : crossword puzzle
crudo[1], **-da** *adj* **1** : raw **2** : crude, harsh
crudo[2] *nm* : crude oil
cruel *adj* : cruel — **cruelmente** *adv*
crueldad *nf* : cruelty
cruento, -ta *adj* : bloody
crujido *nm* **1** : rustling **2** : creaking **3** : crackling (of a fire) **4** : crunching
crujiente *adj* : crunchy, crisp
crujir *vi* **1** : to rustle **2** : to creak, to crack **3** : to crunch
crup *nm* : croup
crustáceo *nm* : crustacean
crutón *nm, pl* **crutones** : crouton
cruz *nf, pl* **cruces** : cross
cruza *nf* : cross (hybrid)
cruzada *nf* : crusade
cruzado[1], **-da** *adj* : crossed <espadas cruzadas : crossed swords>
cruzado[2] *nm* **1** : crusader **2** : Brazilian unit of currency
cruzar {21} *vt* **1** : to cross **2** : to exchange (words, greetings) **3** : to cross, to interbreed — **cruzarse** *vr* **1** : to intersect **2** : to meet, to pass each other
cuaderno *nm* LIBRETA : notebook
cuadra *nf* **1** : city block **2** : stable
cuadrado[1], **-da** *adj* : square
cuadrado[2] *nm* : square <elevar al cuadrado : to square (a number)>
cuadragésimo[1] *adj* : fortieth, forty-
cuadragésimo[2], **-ma** *n* : fortieth, forty- (in a series)
cuadrante *nm* **1** : quadrant **2** : dial
cuadrar *vi* : to conform, to agree — *vt* : to square — **cuadrarse** *vr* : to stand at attention
cuadriculado *nm* : grid (on a map, etc.)
cuadrilátero *nm* **1** : quadrilateral **2** : ring (in sports)
cuadrilla *nf* : gang, team, group
cuadro *nm* **1** : square <una blusa a cuadros : a checkered blouse> **2** : painting, picture **3** : baseball diamond, infield **4** : panel, board, cadre
cuadrúpedo *nm* : quadruped
cuadruple *adj* : quadruple

cuadruplicar {72} *vt* : to quadruple — **cuadruplicarse** *vr*

cuajada *nf* : curd

cuajar *vi* **1** : to curdle **2** COAGULAR : to clot, to coagulate **3** : to set, to jell **4** : to be accepted <su idea no cuajó : his idea didn't catch on> — *vt* **1** : to curdle **2** : to adorn

cual[1] *prep* : like, as

cual[2] *pron* **1 el cual, la cual, los cuales, las cuales** : who, whom, which <la razón por la cual lo dije : the reason I said it> **2 lo cual** : which <se rió, lo cual me dio rabia : he laughed, which made me mad> **3 cada cual** : everyone, everybody

cuál[1] *adj* : which, what <¿cuáles libros? : which books?>

cuál[2] *pron* **1** (*in questions*) : which (one), what (one) <¿cuál es el mejor? : which one is the best?> <¿cuál es tu apellido? : what is your last name?> **2 cuál más, cuál menos** : some more, some less

cualidad *nf* : quality, trait

cualitativo, -va *adj* : qualitative — **cualitativamente** *adv*

cualquier → **cualquiera**[1]

cualquiera[1] (**cualquier** *before nouns*) *adj, pl* **cualesquiera 1** : any, whichever <cualquier persona : any person> **2** : everyday, ordinary <un hombre cualquiera : an ordinary man>

cualquiera[2] *pron, pl* **cualesquiera 1** : anyone, anybody, whoever **2** : whatever, whichever

cuán *adv* : how <¡cuán risible fue todo eso! : how funny it all was!>

cuando[1] *conj* **1** : when <cuando llegó : when he arrived> **2** : since, if <cuando lo dices : if you say so> **3 cuando más** : at the most **4 de vez en cuando** : from time to time

cuando[2] *prep* : during, at the time of <cuando la guerra : during the war>

cuándo *adv & conj* **1** : when <¿cuándo llegará? : when will she arrive?> <no sabemos cuándo será : we don't know when it will be> **2 ¿de cuándo acá?** : since when?, how come?

cuantía *nf* **1** : quantity, extent **2** : significance, import

cuántico, -ca *adj* : quantum <teoría cuántica : quantum theory>

cuantioso, -sa *adj* **1** : abundant, considerable **2** : heavy, grave <cuantiosos daños : heavy damage>

cuantitativo, -va *adj* : quantitative — **cuantitativamente** *adv*

cuanto[1] *adv* **1** : as much as <come cuanto puedas : eat as much as you can> **2 cuanto antes** : as soon as possible **3 en ~** : as soon as **4 en cuanto a** : as for, as regards

cuanto[2], **-ta** *adj* : as many, whatever <llévate cuantas flores quieras : take as many flowers as you wish>

cuanto[3], **-ta** *pron* **1** : as much as, all that, everything <tengo cuanto deseo : I have all that I want> **2 unos cuantos, unas cuantas** : a few

cuánto[1] *adv* : how much, how many <¿a cuánto están las manzanas? : how much are the apples?> <no sé cuánto desean : I don't know how much they want>

cuánto[2], **-ta** *adj* : how much, how many <¿cuántos niños tiene? : how many children do you have?>

cuánto[3] *pron* : how much, how many <¿cuántos quieren participar? : how many want to take part?> <¿cuánto cuesta? : how much does it cost?>

cuarenta *adj & nm* : forty

cuarentavo[1] *adj* : fortieth

cuarentavo[2] *nm* : fortieth (fraction)

cuarentena *nf* **1** : group of forty **2** : quarantine

Cuaresma *nf* : Lent

cuartear *vt* **1** : to quarter **2** : to divide up — **cuartearse** *vr* AGRIETARSE : to crack, to split

cuartel *nm* **1** : barracks, headquarters **2** : mercy <una guerra sin cuartel : a merciless war>

cuartelazo *nm* : coup d'état

cuarteto *nm* : quartet

cuartilla *nf* : sheet (of paper)

cuarto[1], **-ta** *adj* : fourth

cuarto[2], **-ta** *n* : fourth (in a series)

cuarto[3] *nm* **1** : quarter, fourth <cuarto de galón : quart> **2** HABITACIÓN : room

cuarzo *nm* : quartz

cuate, -ta *n Mex* **1** : twin **2** *fam* : buddy, pal

cuatrero, -ra *n* : rustler

cuatrillizo, -za *n* : quadruplet

cuatro *adj & nm* : four

cuatrocientos[1], **-tas** *adj* : four hundred

cuatrocientos[2] *nms & pl* : four hundred

cuba *nf* BARRÍL : cask, barrel

cubano, -na *adj & n* : Cuban

cubertería *nf* : flatware, silverware

cubeta *nf* **1** : keg, cask **2** : bulb (of a thermometer) **3** *Mex* : bucket, pail

cúbico, -ca *adj* : cubic, cubed

cubículo *nm* : cubicle

cubierta *nf* **1** : covering **2** FORRO : cover, jacket (of a book) **3** : deck

cubierto[1] *pp* → **cubrir**

cubierto[2] *nm* **1** : cover, shelter <bajo cubierto : under cover> **2** : table setting **3** : utensil, piece of silverware

cubil *nm* : den, lair

cúbito *nm* : ulna

cubo *nm* **1** : cube **2** BALDE : pail, bucket, can <cubo de basura : garbage can> **3** : hub (of a wheel)

cubrecama *nm* COLCHA : bedspread

cubrir {2} *vt* : to cover — **cubrirse** *vr*

cucaracha *nf* : cockroach, roach

cuchara *nf* : spoon

cucharada *nf* : spoonful

cucharilla *or* **cucharita** *nf* : teaspoon

cucharón *nf, pl* **-rones** : ladle

cuchichear *vi* : to whisper

cuchicheo *nm* : whisper

cuchilla *nf* **1 :** kitchen knife, cleaver **2 :** blade <cuchilla de afeitar : razor blade> **3 :** crest, ridge
cuchillada *nf* **:** stab, knife wound
cuchillo *nm* **:** knife
cuclillas *nfpl* **en ~ :** squatting, crouching
cuco¹, -ca *adj fam* **:** pretty, cute
cuco² *nm* **:** cuckoo
cuece, cueza, etc. → cocer
cuela, etc. → colar
cuelga, cuelgue, etc. → colgar
cuello *nm* **1 :** neck **2 :** collar (of a shirt) **3 cuello del útero :** cervix
cuenca *nf* **1 :** river basin **2 :** eye socket
cuenco *nm* **:** bowl, basin
cuenta¹, etc. → contar
cuenta² *nf* **1 :** calculation, count **2 :** account **3 :** check, bill **4 darse cuenta :** to realize **5 tener en cuenta :** to bear in mind
cuentagotas *nfs & pl* **1 :** dropper **2 con ~ :** little by little
cuentista *nmf* **1 :** short story writer **2** *fam* **:** liar, fibber
cuento *nm* **1 :** story, tale **2 cuento de hadas :** fairy tale **3 sin ~ :** countless
cuerda *nf* **1 :** cord, rope, string **2 cuerdas vocales :** vocal cords **3 darle cuerda a :** to wind up (a clock, a toy, etc.)
cuerdo, -da *adj* **:** sane, sensible
cuerno *nm* **1 :** horn, antler **2 :** cusp (of the moon) **3 :** horn (musical instrument)
cuero *nm* **1 :** leather, hide **2 cuero cabelludo :** scalp
cuerpo *nm* **1 :** body **2 :** corps
cuervo *nm* **:** crow, raven
cuesta¹, etc. → costar
cuesta² *nf* **1 :** slope <cuesta arriba : uphill> **2 a cuestas :** on one's back
cuestión *nf, pl* **-tiones** ASUNTO, TEMA **:** matter, affair
cuestionable *adj* **:** questionable, dubious
cuestionar *vt* **:** to question
cuestionario *nm* **1 :** questionnaire **2 :** quiz
cueva *nf* **:** cave
cuidado *nm* **1 :** care **2 :** worry, concern **3 tener cuidado :** to be careful **4 ¡cuidado! :** watch out!, be careful!
cuidadoso, -sa *adj* **:** careful, attentive — **cuidadosamente** *adv*
cuidar *vt* **1 :** to take care of, to look after **2 :** to pay attention to — *vi* **1 ~ de :** to look after **2 cuidar de que :** to make sure that — **cuidarse** *vr* **:** to take care of oneself
culata *nf* **:** butt (of a gun)
culatazo *nf* **:** kick, recoil
culebra *nf* SERPIENTE **:** snake
culi *nmf* **:** coolie
culinario, -ria *adj* **:** culinary
culminante *adj* **punto culminante :** peak, high point, climax
culminar *vi* **:** to culminate — **culminación** *nf*
culo *nm* **1** *fam* **:** backside, behind **2 :** bottom (of a glass)
culpa *nf* **1 :** fault, blame <echarle la culpa a alguien : to blame someone> **2 :** sin
culpabilidad *nf* **:** guilt
culpable¹ *adj* **:** guilty
culpable² *nmf* **:** culprit, guilty party
culpar *vt* **:** to blame
cultivado, -da *adj* **1 :** cultivated, farmed **2 :** cultured
cultivador, -dora *n* **:** cultivator
cultivar *vt* **1 :** to cultivate **2 :** to foster
cultivo *nm* **1 :** cultivation, farming **2 :** crop
culto¹, -ta *adj* **:** cultured, educated
culto² *nm* **1 :** worship **2 :** cult
cultura *nf* **:** culture
cultural *adj* **:** cultural — **culturalmente** *adv*
cumbre *nf* CIMA **:** top, peak, summit
cumpleaños *nms & pl* **:** birthday
cumplido¹, -da *adj* **1 :** complete, full **2 :** courteous, correct
cumplido² *nm* **:** compliment, courtesy <por cumplido : out of courtesy> <andarse con cumplidos : to stand on ceremony, to be formal>
cumplimentar *vt* **1 :** to congratulate **2 :** to carry out, to perform
cumplimiento *nm* **1 :** completion, fulfillment **2 :** performance
cumplir *vt* **1 :** to accomplish, to carry out **2 :** to comply with, to fulfill **3 :** to attain, to reach <su hermana cumple los 21 el viernes : her sister will be 21 on Friday> — *vi* **1 :** to expire, to fall due **2 :** to fulfill one's obligations <cumplir con el deber : to do one's duty> <cumplir con la palabra : to keep one's word> — **cumplirse** *vr* **1 :** to come true, to be fulfilled <se cumplieron sus sueños : her dreams came true> **2 :** to run out, to expire
cúmulo *nm* **1** MONTÓN **:** heap, pile **2 :** cumulus
cuna *nf* **1 :** cradle **2 :** birthplace <Puerto Rico es la cuna de la música salsa : Puerto Rico is the birthplace of salsa music>
cundir *vi* **1 :** to propagate, to spread <cundió el pánico en el vecindario : panic spread throughout the neighborhood> **2 :** to progress, to make headway
cuneta *nf* **:** ditch (in a road), gutter
cuña *nf* **:** wedge
cuñado, -da *n* **:** brother-in-law *m*, sister-in-law *f*
cuño *nm* **:** die (for stamping)
cuota *nf* **1 :** fee, dues **2 :** quota, share **3 :** installment, payment
cupé *nm* **:** coupe
cupo¹, etc. → caber
cupo² *nm* **1 :** quota, share **2 :** capacity, room
cupón *nm, pl* **cupones 1 :** coupon, voucher **2 cupón federal :** food stamp
cúpula *nf* **:** dome, cupola

cura[1] *nm* : priest

cura[2] *nf* **1** CURACIÓN, TRATAMIENTO : cure, treatment **2** : dressing, bandage

curación *nf, pl* **-ciones** CURA, TRATAMIENTO : cure, treatment

curandero, -ra *nm* **1** : witch doctor **2** : quack, charlatan

curar *vt* **1** : to cure, to heal **2** : to treat, to dress **3** CURTIR : to tan **4** : to cure (meat) — *vi* : to get well, to recover — **curarse** *vr*

curativo, -va *adj* : curative, healing

curiosear *vi* **1** : to snoop, to pry **2** : to browse — *vt* : to look over, to check

curiosidad *nf* **1** : curiosity **2** : curio

curioso, -sa *adj* **1** : curious, inquisitive **2** : strange, unusual, odd — **curiosamente** *adv*

currículo *nm* → **currículum**

currículum *nm, pl* **-lums** **1** : résumé, curriculum vitae **2** : curriculum, course of study

curry ['kurri] *nm, pl* **-rries** **1** : curry powder **2** : curry (dish)

cursar *vt* **1** : to attend (school), to take (a course) **2** : to dispatch, to pass on

cursi *adj fam* : affected, pretentious

cursilería *nf* **1** : vulgarity, poor taste **2** : pretentiousness

cursiva *nf* BASTARDILLA : italic type, italics *pl*

curso *nm* **1** : course, direction **2** : school year **3** : course, subject (in school)

cursor *nm* : cursor

curtido, -da *adj* : weather-beaten, leathery (of skin)

curtidor, -dora *n* : tanner

curtiduría *nf* : tannery

curtir *vt* **1** : to tan **2** : to harden, to weather — **curtirse** *vr*

curva *nf* : curve, bend

curvar *vt* : to bend

curvatura *nf* : curvature

curvilíneo, -nea *adj* : curvaceous, shapely

curvo, -va *adj* : curved, bent

cúspide *nf* : zenith, apex, peak

custodia *nf* : custody

custodiar *vt* : to guard, to look after

custodio, -dia *n* : keeper, guardian

cúter *nm* : cutter (boat)

cutícula *nf* : cuticle

cutis *nms & pl* : skin, complexion

cuyo, -ya *adj* **1** : whose, of whom, of which **2** **en cuyo caso** : in which case

D

d *nf* : fourth letter of the Spanish alphabet

dable *adj* : feasible, possible

dactilar *adj* **huellas dactilares** : fingerprints

dádiva *nf* : gift, handout

dadivoso, -sa *adj* : generous

dado, -da *adj* **1** : given **2** **dado que** : given that, since

dador, -dora *n* : giver, donor

dados *nmpl* : dice

daga *nf* : dagger

dalia *nf* : dahlia

dálmata *nm* : dalmatian

daltónico, -ca *adj* : color-blind

daltonismo *nm* : color blindness

dama *nf* **1** : lady **2** **damas** *nfpl* : checkers

damasco *nm* : damask

damisela *nf* : damsel

damnificado, -da *n* : victim (of a disaster)

damnificar {72} *vt* : to damage, to injure

dance, etc. → **danzar**

dandi *nm* : dandy, fop

danés[1], **-nesa** *adj* : Danish

danés[2], **-nesa** *n, mpl* **daneses** : Dane, Danish person

danza *nf* : dance, dancing <danza folklórica : folk dance>

danzante, -ta *n* BAILARÍN : dancer

danzar {21} *v* BAILAR : to dance

dañar *vt* **1** : to damage, to spoil **2** : to harm, to hurt — **dañarse** *vr*

dañino, -na *adj* : harmful

daño *nm* **1** : damage **2** : harm, injury **3** **hacer daño a** : to harm, to damage **4** **daños y perjuicios** : damages

dar {22} *vt* **1** : to give **2** ENTREGAR : to deliver, to hand over **3** : to hit, to strike **4** : to yield, to produce **5** : to perform **6** : to give off, to emit **7** **~ como** *or* **~ por** : to regard as, to consider — *vi* **1** ALCANZAR : to suffice, to be enough <no me da para dos pasajes : I don't have enough for two fares> **2** **~ a** *or* **~ sobre** : to overlook, to look out on **3** **~ con** : to run into **4** **~ con** : to hit upon (an idea) **5** **dar de sí** : to give, to stretch — **darse** *vr* **1** : to give in, to surrender **2** : to occur, to arise **3** : to grow, to come up **4** **~ con** *or* **~ contra** : to hit oneself against **5** **dárselas de** : to boast about <se las da de muy listo : he thinks he's very smart>

dardo *nm* : dart

datar *vt* : to date — *vi* **~ de** : to date from, to date back to

dátil *nm* : date (fruit)

dato *nm* **1** : fact, piece of information **2** **datos** *nmpl* : data, information

dé → **dar**

de *prep* **1** : of <la casa de Pepe : Pepe's house> <un niño de tres años : a three-year-old boy> **2** : from <es de Managua : she's from Managua> <salió del edificio : he left the building> **3** : in, at <a las tres de la mañana

: at three in the morning> <salen de noche : they go out at night> **4** : than <más de tres : more than three>

deambular *vi* : to wander, to roam

debajo *adv* **1** : underneath, below, on the bottom **2** ~ **de** : under, underneath **3 por** ~ : below, beneath

debate *nm* : debate

debatir *vt* : to debate, to discuss — **debatirse** *vr* : to struggle

debe *nm* : debit column, debit

deber[1] *vt* : to owe — *v aux* **1** : must, have to <debo ir a la oficina : I must go to the office> **2** : should, ought to <deberías buscar trabajo : you ought to look for work> **3** (*expressing probability*) : must <debe ser mexicano : he must be Mexican> — **deberse** *vr* ~ **a** : to be due to

deber[2] *nm* **1** OBLIGACIÓN : duty, obligation **2 deberes** *nmpl Spain* : homework

debidamente *adv* : properly, duly

debido, -da *adj* **1** : right, proper, due **2** ~ **a** : due to, owing to

débil *adj* : weak, feeble — **débilmente** *adv*

debilidad *nf* : weakness, debility, feebleness

debilitamiento *nm* : debilitation, weakening

debilitar *vt* : to debilitate, to weaken — **debilitarse** *vr*

debilucho[1], **-cha** *adj* : weak, frail

debilucho[2], **-cha** *n* : weakling

debitar *vt* : to debit

débito *nm* **1** DEUDA : debt **2** : debit

debut [deˈbut] *nm, pl* **debuts** : debut

debutante[1] *nmf* : beginner, newcomer

debutante[2] *nf* : debutante *f*

debutar *vi* : to debut, to make a debut

década *nf* DECENIO : decade

decadencia *nf* **1** : decadence **2** : decline

decadente *adj* **1** : decadent **2** : declining

decaer {13} *vi* **1** : to decline, to decay, to deteriorate **2** FLAQUEAR : to weaken, to flag

decaiga, etc. → **decaer**

decano, -na *n* **1** : dean **2** : senior member

decantar *vt* : to decant

decapitar *vt* : to decapitate, to behead

decayó, etc. → **decaer**

decena *nf* : group of ten

decencia *nf* : decency

decenio *nm* DÉCADA : decade

decente *adj* : decent — **decentemente** *adv*

decepción *nf, pl* **-ciones** : disappointment, letdown

decepcionante *adj* : disappointing

decepcionar *vt* : to disappoint, to let down — **decepcionarse** *vr*

deceso *nm* DEFUNCIÓN : death, passing

dechado *nm* **1** : sampler (of embroidery) **2** : model, paragon

decibelio *or* **decibel** *nm* : decibel

decidido, -da *adj* : decisive, determined, resolute — **decididamente** *adv*

decidir *vt* **1** : to decide, to determine <no he decidido nada : I haven't made a decision> **2** : to persuade, to decide <su padre lo decidió a estudiar : his father persuaded him to study> — *vi* : to decide — **decidirse** *vr* : to make up one's mind

decimal *adj* : decimal

décimo, -ma *adj* : tenth — **décimo, -ma** *n*

decimoctavo[1], **-va** *adj* : eighteenth

decimoctavo[2], **-va** *nm* : eighteenth (in a series)

decimocuarto[1], **-ta** *adj* : fourteenth

decimocuarto[2], **-ta** *nm* : fourteenth (in a series)

decimonoveno[1], **-na** *or* **decimonono, -na** *adj* : nineteenth

decimonoveno[2], **-na** *or* **decimonono, -na** *nm* : nineteenth (in a series)

decimoquinto[1], **-ta** *adj* : fifteenth

decimoquinto[2], **-ta** *nm* : fifteenth (in a series)

decimoséptimo[1], **-ma** *adj* : seventeenth

decimoséptimo[2], **-ma** *nm* : seventeenth (in a series)

decimosexto[1], **-ta** *adj* : sixteenth

decimosexto[2], **-ta** *nm* : sixteenth (in a series)

decimotercero[1], **-ra** *adj* : thirteenth

decimotercero[2], **-ra** *nm* : thirteenth (in a series)

decir[1] {23} *vt* **1** : to say <dice que no quiere ir : she says she doesn't want to go> **2** : to tell <dime lo que estás pensando : tell me what you're thinking> **3** : to speak, to talk <no digas tonterías : don't talk nonsense> **4** : to call <me dicen Rosy : they call me Rosy> **5 es decir** : that is to say **6 querer decir** : to mean — **decirse** *vr* **1** : to say to oneself **2** : to be said <¿cómo se dice "lápiz" en francés? : how do you say "pencil" in French?>

decir[2] *nm* DICHO : saying, expression

decisión *nf, pl* **-siones** : decision, choice

decisivo, -va *adj* : decisive, conclusive — **decisivamente** *adv*

declamar *vi* : to declaim — *vt* : to recite

declaración *nf, pl* **-ciones 1** : declaration, statement **2** TESTIMONIO : deposition, testimony **3 declaración de derechos** : bill of rights **4 declaración jurada** : affidavit

declarado, -da *adj* : professed, open — **declaradamente** *adv*

declarar *vt* : to declare, to state — *vi* ATESTIGUAR : to testify — **declararse** *vr* **1** : to declare oneself, to make a statement **2** : to confess one's love **3**

: to plead (in court) <declararse inocente : to plead not guilty>
declinación *nf, pl* **-ciones 1** : drop, downward trend **2** : declination **3** : declension (in grammar)
declinar *vt* : to decline, to turn down — *vi* **1** : to draw to a close **2** : to diminish, to decline
declive *nm* **1** DECADENCIA : decline **2** : slope, incline
decodificador *nm* : decoder
decolar *vi Chile, Col, Ecua* : to take off (of an airplane)
decolorar *vt* : to bleach — **decolorarse** *vr* : to fade
decomisar *vt* CONFISCAR : to seize, to confiscate
decomiso *nm* : seizure, confiscation
decoración *nf, pl* **-ciones 1** : decoration **2** : decor **3** : stage set, scenery
decorado *nm* : stage set, scenery
decorador, -dora *n* : decorator
decorar *vt* ADORNAR : to decorate, to adorn
decorativo, -va *adj* : decorative, ornamental
decoro *nm* : decorum, propriety
decoroso, -sa *adj* : decent, proper, respectable
decrecer {53} *vi* : to decrease, to wane, to diminish — **decreciente** *adj*
decrecimiento *nm* : decrease, decline
decrépito, -ta *adj* : decrepit
decretar *vt* : to decree, to order
decreto *nm* : decree
decúbito *nm* : horizontal position <en decúbito prono : prone> <en decúbito supino : supine>
dedal *nm* : thimble
dedalera *nf* DIGITAL : foxglove
dedicación *nf, pl* **-ciones** : dedication, devotion
dedicar {72} *vt* CONSAGRAR : to dedicate, to devote — **dedicarse** *vr* **~ a** : to devote oneself to, to engage in
dedicatoria *nf* : dedication (of a book, song, etc.)
dedo *nm* **1** : finger <dedo meñique : little finger> **2 dedo del pie** : toe
deducción *nf, pl* **-ciones** : deduction
deducible *adj* **1** : deducible, inferable **2** : deductible
deducir {61} *vt* **1** INFERIR : to deduce **2** DESCONTAR : to deduct
defecar {72} *vi* : to defecate — **defecación** *nf*
defecto *nm* **1** : defect, flaw, shortcoming **2 en su defecto** : lacking that, in the absence of that
defectuoso, -sa *adj* : defective, faulty
defender {56} *vt* : to defend, to protect — **defenderse** *vr* **1** : to defend oneself **2** : to get by, to know the basics <su inglés no es perfecto pero se defiende : his English isn't perfect but he gets by>
defendible *adj* : defensible, tenable
defensa[1] *nf* : defense
defensa[2] *nmf* : defender, back (in sports)
defensiva *nf* : defensive, defense
defensivo, -va *adj* : defensive — **defensivamente** *adv*
defensor[1], **-sora** *adj* : defending, defense
defensor[2], **-sora** *n* **1** : defender, advocate **2** : defense counsel
defeño, -ña *n* : person from the Federal District (Mexico City)
deficiencia *nf* : deficiency, flaw
deficiente *adj* : deficient
déficit *nm, pl* **-cits 1** : deficit **2** : shortage, lack
definición *nf, pl* **-ciones** : definition
definido, -da *adj* : definite, well-defined
definir *vt* **1** : to define **2** : to determine
definitivamente *adv* **1** : finally **2** : permanently, for good **3** : definitely, absolutely
definitivo, -va *adj* **1** : definitive, conclusive **2 en definitiva** : all in all, on the whole **3 en definitiva** *Mex* : permanently, for good
deflación *nf, pl* **-ciones** : deflation
deforestación *nf, pl* **-ciones** : deforestation
deformación *nf, pl* **-ciones 1** : deformation **2** : distortion
deformar *vt* **1** : to deform, to disfigure **2** : to distort — **deformarse** *vr*
deforme *adj* : deformed, misshapen
deformidad *nf* : deformity
defraudación *nf, pl* **-ciones** : fraud
defraudar *vt* **1** ESTAFAR : to defraud, to cheat **2** : to disappoint
defunción *nf, pl* **-ciones** DECESO : death, passing
degeneración *nf, pl* **-ciones 1** : degeneration **2** : degeneracy, depravity
degenerado, -da *adj* DEPRAVADO : degenerate
degenerar *vi* : to degenerate
degenerativo, -va *adj* : degenerative
degollar {19} *vt* **1** : to slit the throat of, to slaughter **2** DECAPITAR : to behead **3** : to ruin, to destroy
degradación *nf, pl* **-ciones 1** : degradation **2** : demotion
degradar *vt* **1** : to degrade, to debase **2** : to demote
degustación *nf, pl* **-ciones** : tasting, sampling
degustar *vt* : to taste
deidad *nf* : deity
deificar {72} *vt* : to idolize, to deify
dejado, -da *adj* **1** : slovenly **2** : careless, lazy
dejar *vt* **1** : to leave **2** ABANDONAR : to abandon, to forsake **3** : to let be, to let go **4** PERMITIR : to allow, to permit — *vi* **~ de** : to stop, to quit <dejar de fumar : to quit smoking> — **dejarse** *vr* **1** : to let oneself be <se deja insultar : he lets himself be insulted> **2** : to forget, to leave <me dejé las llaves en el carro : I left the keys in

the car> **3 :** to neglect oneself, to let oneself go **4 :** to grow <nos estamos dejando el pelo largo : we're growing our hair long>

dejo *nm* **1 :** aftertaste **2 :** touch, hint **3 :** (regional) accent

delación *nf, pl* **-ciones :** denunciation, betrayal

delantal *nm* **1 :** apron **2 :** pinafore

delante *adv* **1** ENFRENTE **:** ahead, in front **2 ~ de :** before, in front of

delantera *nf* **1 :** front, front part, front row <tomar la delantera : to take the lead> **2 :** forward line (in sports)

delantero[1]**, -ra** *adj* **1 :** front, forward **2 tracción delantera :** front-wheel drive

delantero[2]**, -ra** *n* **:** forward (in sports)

delatar *vt* **1 :** to betray, to reveal **2 :** to denounce, to inform against

delegación *nf, pl* **-ciones :** delegation

delegado, -da *n* **:** delegate, representative

delegar {52} *vt* **:** to delegate

deleitar *vt* **:** to delight, to please — **deleitarse** *vr*

deleite *nm* **:** delight, pleasure

deletrear *vi* **:** to spell <¿como se deletrea? : how do you spell it?>

deleznable *adj* **1 :** brittle, crumbly **2 :** slippery **3 :** weak, fragile <una excusa deleznable : a weak excuse>

delfín *nm, pl* **delfines 1 :** dolphin **2 :** dauphin, heir apparent

delgadez *nf* **:** thinness, skinniness

delgado, -da *adj* **1** FLACO **:** thin, skinny **2** ESBELTO **:** slender, slim **3** DELICADO **:** delicate, fine **4** AGUDO **:** sharp, clever

deliberación *nf, pl* **-ciones :** deliberation

deliberado, -da *adj* **:** deliberate, intentional — **deliberadamente** *adv*

deliberar *vi* **:** to deliberate

deliberativo, -va *adj* **:** deliberative

delicadeza *nf* **1 :** delicacy, fineness **2 :** gentleness, softness **3 :** tact, discretion, consideration

delicado, -da *adj* **1 :** delicate, fine **2 :** sensitive, frail **3 :** difficult, tricky **4 :** fussy, hard to please **5 :** tactful, considerate

delicia *nf* **:** delight

delicioso, -sa *adj* **1** RICO **:** delicious **2 :** delightful

delictivo, -va *adj* **:** criminal

delictuoso, -sa → **delictivo**

delimitación *nf, pl* **-ciones 1 :** demarcation **2 :** defining, specifying

delimitar *vt* **1 :** to demarcate **2 :** to define, to specify

delincuencia *nf* **:** delinquency, crime

delincuente[1] *adj* **:** delinquent

delincuente[2] *nmf* CRIMINAL **:** delinquent, criminal

delinear *vt* **1 :** to delineate, to outline **2 :** to draft, to draw up

delinquir {24} *vi* **:** to break the law

delirante *adj* **:** delirious

delirar *vi* DESVARIAR **1 :** to be delirious **2 :** to rave, to talk nonsense

delirio *nm* **1** DESVARÍO **:** delirium **2** DISPARATE **:** nonsense, ravings *pl* <delirios de grandeza : delusions of grandeur> **3** FRENESÍ **:** mania, frenzy <¡fue el delirio! : it was wild!>

delito *nm* **:** crime, offense

delta *nm* **:** delta

demacrado, -da *adj* **:** emaciated, gaunt

demagogia *nf* **:** demagogy

demagógico, -ca *adj* **:** demagogic, demagogical

demagogo, -ga *n* **:** demagogue

demanda *nf* **1 :** demand <la oferta y la demanda : supply and demand> **2 :** petition, request **3 :** lawsuit

demandado, -da *n* **:** defendant

demandante *nmf* **:** plaintiff

demandar *vt* **1 :** to demand **2** REQUERIR **:** to call for, to require **3 :** to sue, to file a lawsuit against

demarcar {72} *vt* **:** to demarcate — **demarcación** *nf*

demás[1] *adj* **:** remaining <acabó las demás tareas : she finished the rest of the chores>

demás[2] *pron* **1 lo (la, los, las) demás :** the rest, everyone else, everything else <Pepe, Rosa, y los demás : Pepe, Rosa, and everybody else> **2 estar por demás :** to be of no use, to be pointless <no estaría por demás : it couldn't hurt, it's worth a try> **3 por demás :** extremely **4 por lo demás :** otherwise **5 y demás :** and so on, et cetera

demasía *nf* **en ~ :** excessively, in excess

demasiado[1] *adv* **1 :** too <vas demasiado aprisa : you're going too fast> **2 :** too much <estoy comiendo demasiado : I'm eating too much>

demasiado[2]**, -da** *adj* **:** too much, too many, excessive

demencia *nf* **1 :** dementia **2** LOCURA **:** madness, insanity

demente[1] *adj* **:** insane, mad

demente[2] *nmf* **:** insane person

demeritar *vt* **1 :** to detract from **2 :** to discredit

demérito *nm* **1 :** fault **2 :** discredit, disrepute

democracia *nf* **:** democracy

demócrata[1] *adj* **:** democratic

demócrata[2] *nmf* **:** democrat

democrático, -ca *adj* **:** democratic — **democráticamente** *adv*

democratizar {21} *vt* **:** to democratize, to make democratic

demografía *nf* **:** demography

demográfico, -ca *adj* **:** demographic

demoledor, -dora *adj* **:** devastating

demoler {47} *vt* DERRIBAR, DERRUMBAR **:** to demolish, to destroy

demolición *nf, pl* **-ciones :** demolition

demonio *nm* DIABLO **:** devil, demon

demora *nf* **:** delay

demorar *vt* **1** RETRASAR **:** to delay **2** TARDAR **:** to take, to last <la reparación demorará varios días : the repair will take several days> — *vi* **:** to delay, to linger — **demorarse** *vr* **1 :** to be slow, to take a long time **2 :** to take too long
demostración *nf, pl* **-ciones :** demonstration
demostrar {19} *vt* **:** to demonstrate, to show
demostrativo, -va *adj* **:** demonstrative
demudar *vt* **:** to change, to alter — **demudarse** *vr* **:** to change one's expression
denegación *nf, pl* **-ciones :** denial, refusal
denegar {49} *vt* **:** to deny, to turn down
denigrante *adj* **:** degrading, humiliating
denigrar *vt* **1** DIFAMAR **:** to denigrate, to disparage **2 :** to degrade, to humiliate
denodado, -da *adj* **:** bold, dauntless
denominación *nf, pl* **-ciones 1 :** name, designation **2 :** denomination (of money)
denominador *nm* **:** denominator
denominar *vt* **:** to designate, to name
denostar {19} *vt* **:** to revile
denotar *vt* **:** to denote, to show
densidad *nf* **:** density, thickness
denso, -sa *adj* **:** dense, thick — **densamente** *adv*
dentado, -da *adj* SERRADO **:** serrated, jagged
dentadura *nf* **1 :** teeth *pl* **2 dentadura postiza :** dentures *pl*
dental *adj* **:** dental
dentellada *nf* **1 :** bite **2 :** tooth mark
dentera *nf* **1 :** envy, jealousy **2 dar dentera :** to set one's teeth on edge
dentición *nf, pl* **-ciones 1 :** teething **2 :** dentition, set of teeth
dentífrico *nm* **:** toothpaste
dentista *nmf* **:** dentist
dentro *adv* **1 :** in, inside **2 :** indoors **3 ~ de :** within, inside, in **4 dentro de poco :** soon, shortly **5 dentro de todo :** all in all, all things considered **6 por ~ :** inwardly, inside
denuedo *nm* **:** valor, courage
denuesto *nm* **:** insult
denuncia *nf* **1 :** denunciation, condemnation **2 :** police report
denunciante *nmf* **:** accuser (of a crime)
denunciar *vt* **1 :** to denounce, to condemn **2 :** to report (to the authorities)
deparar *vt* **:** to have in store for, to provide with <no sabemos lo que nos depara el destino : we don't know what fate has in store for us>
departamental *adj* **1 :** departmental **2 tienda departamental** *Mex* **:** department store
departamento *nm* **1 :** department **2** APARTAMENTO **:** apartment
departir *vi* **:** to converse
dependencia *nf* **1 :** dependence, dependency <dependencia emocional : emotional dependence> <dependencia del alcohol : dependence on alcohol> **2 :** agency, branch office
depender *vi* **1 :** to depend **2 ~ de :** to depend on **3 ~ de :** to be subordinate to
dependiente¹ *adj* **:** dependent
dependiente², -ta *n* **:** clerk, salesperson
deplorable *adj* **:** deplorable
deplorar *vt* **1 :** to deplore **2** LAMENTAR **:** to regret
deponer {60} *vt* **1 :** to depose, to overthrow **2 :** to abandon (an attitude or stance) **3 deponer las armas :** to lay down one's arms — *vi* **1** TESTIFICAR **:** to testify, to make a statement **2** EVACUAR **:** to defecate
deportación *nf, pl* **-ciones :** deportation
deportar *vt* **:** to deport
deporte *nm* **:** sport, sports *pl* <hacer deporte : to engage in sports>
deportista¹ *adj* **1 :** fond of sports **2 :** sporty
deportista² *nmf* **1 :** sports fan **2 :** athlete, sportsman *m,* sportswoman *f*
deportividad *nf Spain* **:** sportsmanship
deportivo, -va *adj* **1 :** sports, sporting <artículos deportivos : sporting goods> **2 :** sporty
deposición *nf, pl* **-ciones 1 :** statement, testimony **2 :** removal from office
depositante *nmf* **:** depositor
depositar *vt* **1 :** to deposit, to place **2 :** to store — **depositarse** *vr* **:** to settle
depósito *nm* **1 :** deposit **2 :** warehouse, storehouse
depravado, -da *adj* DEGENERADO **:** depraved, degenerate
depravar *vt* **:** to deprave, to corrupt
depreciación *nf, pl* **-ciones :** depreciation
depreciar *vt* **:** to depreciate, to reduce the value of — **depreciarse** *vr* **:** to lose value
depredación *nf* SAQUEO **:** depredation, plunder
depredador¹, -dora *adj* **:** predatory
depredador² *nm* **1 :** predator **2** SAQUEADOR **:** plunderer
depresión *nf, pl* **-siones 1 :** depression **2 :** hollow, recess **3 :** drop, fall **4 :** slump, recession
depresivo¹, -va *adj* **1 :** depressive **2 :** depressant
depresivo² *nm* **:** depressant
deprimente *adj* **:** depressing
deprimir *vt* **1 :** to depress **2 :** to lower — **deprimirse** *vr* ABATIRSE **:** to get depressed
depuesto *pp* → **deponer**
depuración *nf, pl* **-ciones 1** PURIFICACIÓN **:** purification **2** PURGA **:** purge **3 :** refinement, polish
depurar *vt* **1** PURIFICAR **:** to purify **2** PURGAR **:** to purge
depuso, etc. → **deponer**
derecha *nf* **1 :** right **2 :** right hand, right side **3 :** right wing, right (in politics)

derechazo *nm* **1 :** pass with the cape on the right hand (in bullfighting) **2 :** right (in boxing) **3 :** forehand (in tennis)

derechista[1] *adj* **:** rightist, right-wing

derechista[2] *nmf* **:** right-winger

derecho[1] *adv* **1 :** straight **2 :** upright **3 :** directly

derecho[2]**, -cha** *adj* **1 :** right **2 :** right-hand **3 :** RECTO **:** straight, upright, erect

derecho[3] *nm* **1 :** right <derechos humanos : human rights> **2 :** law <derecho civil : civil law> **3 :** right side (of cloth or clothing)

deriva *nf* **1 :** drift **2 a la deriva :** adrift

derivación *nf, pl* **-ciones :** derivation

derivar *vi* **1 :** to drift **2 ~ de :** to come from, to derive from **3 ~ en :** to result in — *vt* **:** to steer, to direct <derivó la discusión hacia la política : he steered the discussion over to politics> — **derivarse** *vr* **:** to be derived from, to arise from

dermatología *nf* **:** dermatology

dermatológico, -ca *adj* **:** dermatological

dermatólogo, -ga *n* **:** dermatologist

derogación *nf, pl* **-ciones :** abolition, repeal

derogar {52} *vt* ABOLIR **:** to abolish, to repeal

derramamiento *nm* **1 :** spilling, overflowing **2 derramamiento de sangre :** bloodshed

derramar *vt* **1 :** to spill **2 :** to shed (tears, blood) — **derramarse** *vr* **1 :** to spill over **2 :** to scatter

derrame *nm* **1 :** spilling, shedding **2 :** leakage, overflow **3 :** discharge, hemorrhage

derrapar *vi* **:** to skid

derrape *nm* **:** skid

derredor *nm* **al derredor** *or* **en derredor :** around, round about

derrengado, -da *adj* **1 :** bent, twisted **2 :** exhausted

derretir {54} *vt* **:** to melt, to thaw — **derretirse** *vr* **1 :** to melt, to thaw **2 ~ por** *fam* **:** to be crazy about

derribar *vt* **1** DEMOLER, DERRUMBAR **:** to demolish, to knock down **2 :** to shoot down, to bring down (an airplane) **3** DERROCAR **:** to overthrow

derribo *nm* **1 :** demolition, razing **2 :** shooting down **3 :** overthrow

derrocamiento *nm* **:** overthrow

derrocar {72} *vt* DERRIBAR **:** to overthrow, to topple

derrochador[1]**, -dora** *adj* **:** extravagant, wasteful

derrochador[2]**, -dora** *n* **:** spendthrift

derrochar *vt* **:** to waste, to squander

derroche *nm* **:** extravagance, waste

derrota *nf* **1 :** defeat, rout **2 :** course (at sea)

derrotar *vt* **:** to defeat

derrotero *nm* RUTA **:** course

derrotista *adj & nmf* **:** defeatist

derruir {41} *vt* **:** to demolish, to tear down

derrumbamiento *nm* **:** collapse

derrumbar *vt* **1** DEMOLER, DERRIBAR **:** to demolish, to knock down **2** DESPEÑAR **:** to cast down, to topple — **derrumbarse** *vr* DESPLOMARSE **:** to collapse, to break down

derrumbe *nm* **1** DESPLOME **:** collapse, fall <el derrumbe del comunismo : the fall of Communism> **2 :** landslide

desabastecimiento *nm* **:** shortage, scarcity

desabasto *nm Mex* **:** shortage, scarcity

desabrido, -da *adj* **:** tasteless, bland

desabrigar {52} *vt* **1 :** to undress **2 :** to uncover **3 :** to deprive of shelter

desabrochar *vt* **:** to unbutton, to undo — **desabrocharse** *vr* **:** to come undone

desacato *nm* **1 :** disrespect **2 :** contempt (of court)

desacelerar *vi* **:** to decelerate, to slow down

desacertado, -da *adj* **1 :** mistaken **2 :** unwise

desacertar {55} *vi* ERRAR **:** to err, to be mistaken

desacierto *nm* ERROR **:** error, mistake

desaconsejado, -da *adj* **:** ill-advised, unwise

desacorde *adj* **1 :** conflicting **2 :** discordant

desacostumbrado, -da *adj* **:** unaccustomed, unusual

desacreditar *vt* DESPRESTIGIAR **:** to discredit, to disgrace

desactivar *vt* **:** to deactivate, to defuse

desacuerdo *nm* **:** disagreement

desafiante *adj* **:** defiant

desafiar {85} *vt* RETAR **:** to defy, to challenge

desafilado, -da *adj* **:** blunt

desafinado, -da *adj* **:** out-of-tune, offkey

desafinarse *vr* **:** to go out of tune

desafío *nm* **1** RETO **:** challenge **2** RESISTENCIA **:** defiance

desafortunado, -da *adj* **:** unfortunate, unlucky — **desafortunadamente** *adv*

desafuero *nm* ABUSO **:** injustice, outrage

desagradable *adj* **:** unpleasant, disagreeable — **desagradablemente** *adv*

desagradar *vi* **:** to be unpleasant, to be disagreeable

desagradecido, -da *adj* **:** ungrateful

desagrado *nm* **1 :** displeasure **2 con ~ :** reluctantly

desagravio *nm* **1 :** apology **2 :** amends, reparation

desagregarse {52} *vr* **:** to break up, to disintegrate

desaguar {10} *vi* **:** to drain, to empty

desagüe *nm* **1 :** drain **2 :** drainage

desahogado, -da *adj* **1 :** well-off, comfortable **2 :** spacious, roomy

desahogar {52} *vt* **1** : to relieve, to ease **2** : to give vent to — **desahogarse** *vr* **1** : to recover, to feel better **2** : to unburden oneself, to let off steam
desahogo *nm* **1** : relief, outlet **2 con ~** : comfortably
desahuciar *vt* **1** : to deprive of hope **2** : to evict — **desahuciarse** *vr* : to lose all hope
desahucio *nm* : eviction
desairar {5} *vt* : to snub, to rebuff
desaire *nm* : rebuff, snub, slight
desajustar *vt* **1** : to disarrange, to put out of order **2** : to upset (plans)
desajuste *nm* **1** : maladjustment **2** : imbalance **3** : upset, disruption
desalentar {55} *vt* DESANIMAR : to discourage, to dishearten — **desalentarse** *vr*
desaliento *nm* : discouragement
desaliñado, -da *adj* : slovenly, untidy
desalmado, -da *adj* : heartless, callous
desalojar *vt* **1** : to remove, to clear **2** EVACUAR : to evacuate, to vacate **3** : to evict
desalojo *nm* **1** : removal, expulsion **2** : evacuation **3** : eviction
desamor *nm* **1** FRIALDAD : indifference **2** ENEMISTAD : dislike, enmity
desamparado, -da *adj* DESVALIDO : helpless, destitute
desamparar *vt* : to abandon, to forsake
desamparo *nm* **1** : abandonment, neglect **2** : helplessness
desamueblado, -da *adj* : unfurnished
desandar {6} *vt* : to go back, to return to the starting point
desangelado, -da *adj* : dull, lifeless
desangrar *vt* : to bleed, to bleed dry — **desangrarse** *vr* **1** : to be bleeding **2** : to bleed to death
desanimar *vt* DESALENTAR : to discourage, to dishearten — **desanimarse** *vr*
desánimo *nm* DESALIENTO : discouragement, dejection
desanudar *vt* : to untie, to disentangle
desapacible *adj* : unpleasant, disagreeable
desaparecer {53} *vt* : to cause to disappear — *vi* : to disappear, to vanish
desaparecido[1], **-da** *adj* **1** : late, deceased **2** : missing
desaparecido[2], **-da** *n* : missing person
desaparición *nf, pl* **-ciones** : disappearance
desapasionado, -da *adj* : dispassionate, impartial — **desapasionadamente** *adv*
desapego *nm* : coolness, indifference
desapercibido, -da *adj* **1** : unnoticed **2** DESPREVENIDO : unprepared, off guard
desaprobación *nf, pl* **-ciones** : disapproval
desaprobar {19} *vt* REPROBAR : to disapprove of
desaprovechar *vt* MALGASTAR : to waste, to misuse — *vi* : to lose ground, to slip back
desarmador *nm Mex* : screwdriver
desarmar *vt* **1** : to disarm **2** DESMONTAR : to disassemble, to take apart
desarme *nm* : disarmament
desarraigado, -da *adj* : rootless
desarraigar {52} *vt* : to uproot, to root out
desarreglado, -da *adj* : untidy, disorganized
desarreglar *vt* **1** : to mess up **2** : to upset, to disrupt
desarreglo *nm* **1** : untidiness **2** : disorder, confusion
desarrollar *vt* : to develop — **desarrollarse** *vr* : to take place
desarrollo *nm* : development
desarticulación *nf, pl* **-ciones** **1** : dislocation **2** : breaking up, dismantling
desarticular *vt* **1** DISLOCAR : to dislocate **2** : to break up, to dismantle
desaseado, -da *adj* **1** : dirty **2** : messy, untidy
desastre *nm* CATÁSTROFE : disaster
desastroso, -sa *adj* : disastrous, catastrophic
desatar *vt* **1** : to undo, to untie **2** : to unleash **3** : to trigger, to precipitate — **desatarse** *vr* : to break out, to erupt
desatascar {72} *vt* : to unblock, to clear
desatención *nf, pl* **-ciones** **1** : absentmindedness, distraction **2** : discourtesy
desatender {56} *vt* **1** : to disregard **2** : to neglect
desatento, -ta *adj* **1** DISTRAÍDO : absentminded **2** GROSERO : discourteous, rude
desatinado, -da *adj* : foolish, silly
desatino *nm* : folly, mistake
desautorizar {21} *vt* : to deprive of authority, to discredit
desavenencia *nf* DISCORDANCIA : disagreement, dispute
desayunar *vi* : to have breakfast — *vt* : to have for breakfast
desayuno *nm* : breakfast
desazón *nf, pl* **-zones** INQUIETUD : uneasiness, anxiety
desbalance *nm* : imbalance
desbancar {72} *vt* : to displace, to oust
desbandada *nf* : scattering, dispersal
desbarajuste *nm* DESORDEN : disarray, disorder, mess
desbaratar *vt* **1** ARRUINAR : to destroy, to ruin **2** DESCOMPONER : to break, to break down — **desbaratarse** *vr* : to fall apart
desbloquear *vt* **1** : to open up, to clear, to break through **2** : to free, to release
desbocado, -da *adj* : unbridled, rampant
desbocarse {72} *vr* : to run away, to bolt
desbordamiento *nm* : overflowing
desbordante *adj* : overflowing, bursting <desbordante de energía : bursting with energy>
desbordar *vt* **1** : to overflow, to spill over **2** : to surpass, to exceed **3** : to

burst with, to brim with — **desbordarse** *vr*

descabellado, -da *adj* : outlandish, ridiculous

descafeinado, -da *adj* : decaffeinated

descalabrar *vt* : to hit on the head — **descalabrarse** *vr*

descalabro *nm* : setback, misfortune, loss

descalificar {72} *vt* : to disqualify — **descalificarse** *vr*

descalzarse {21} *vr* : take off one's shoes

descalzo, -za *adj* : barefoot

descansado, -da *adj* **1** : rested, refreshed **2** : restful, peaceful

descansar *vi* : to rest, to relax — *vt* : to rest <descansar la vista : to rest one's eyes>

descansillo *nm* : landing (of a staircase)

descanso *nm* **1** : rest, relaxation **2** : break **3** : landing (of a staircase) **4** : intermission

descapotable *adj & nm* : convertible

descarado, -da *adj* : brazen, impudent — **descaradamente** *adv*

descarga *nf* **1** : discharge **2** : unloading

descargar {52} *vt* **1** : to discharge **2** : to unload **3** : to release, to free **4** : to take out, to vent (anger, etc.) — **descargarse** *vr* **1** : to unburden oneself **2** : to quit **3** : to lose power

descargo *nm* **1** : unloading **2** : defense <testigo de descargo : witness for the defense>

descarnado, -da *adj* : scrawny, gaunt

descaro *nm* : audacity, nerve

descarriado, -da *adj* : lost, gone astray

descarrilar *vi* : to derail — **descarrilarse** *vr*

descartar *vt* : to rule out, to reject — **descartarse** *vr* : to discard

descascarar *vt* : to peel, to shell, to husk — **descascararse** *vr* : to peel off, to chip

descendencia *nf* **1** : descendants *pl* **2** LINAJE : descent, lineage

descendente *adj* : downward, descending

descender {56} *vt* **1** : to descend, to go down **2** BAJAR : to lower, to take down, to let down — *vi* **1** : to descend, to come down **2** : to drop, to fall **3** ~ **de** : to be a descendant of

descendiente *adj & nm* : descendant

descenso *nm* **1** : descent **2** BAJA, CAÍDA : drop, fall

descentralizar {21} *vt* : to decentralize — **descentralizarse** *vr* — **descentralización** *nf*

descifrable *adj* : decipherable

descifrar *vt* : to decipher, to decode

descolgar {16} *vt* **1** : to take down, to let down **2** : to pick up, to answer (the telephone)

descollar {19} *vi* SOBRESALIR : to stand out, to be outstanding, to excel

descolorarse *vr* : to fade

descolorido, -da *adj* : discolored, faded

descomponer {60} *vt* **1** : to rot, to decompose **2** DESBARATAR : to break, to break down — **descomponerse** *vr* **1** : to break down **2** : to decompose

descomposición *nf, pl* **-ciones** **1** : breakdown, decomposition **2** : decay

descompresión *nf* : decompression

descompuesto[1] *pp* → **descomponer**

descompuesto[2], **-ta** *adj* **1** : broken down, out of order **2** : rotten, decomposed

descomunal *adj* **1** ENORME : enormous, huge **2** EXTRAORDINARIO : extraordinary

desconcertante *adj* : disconcerting

desconcertar {55} *vt* : to disconcert — **desconcertarse** *vr*

desconchar *vt* : to chip — **desconcharse** *vr* : to chip off, to peel

desconcierto *nm* : uncertainty, confusion

desconectar *vt* **1** : to disconnect, to switch off **2** : to unplug

desconfiado, -da *adj* : distrustful, suspicious

desconfianza *nf* RECELO : distrust, suspicion

desconfiar {85} *vi* ~ **de** : to distrust, to be suspicious of

descongelar *vt* **1** : to thaw **2** : to defrost **3** : to unfreeze (assets) — **descongelarse** *vr*

descongestionante *adj & nm* : decongestant

desconocer {18} *vt* **1** IGNORAR : to be unaware of **2** : to fail to recognize

desconocido[1], **-da** *adj* : unknown, unfamiliar

desconocido[2], **-da** *n* EXTRAÑO : stranger

desconocimiento *nm* : ignorance

desconsiderado, -da *adj* : inconsiderate, thoughtless — **desconsideradamente** *adj*

desconsolado, -da *adj* : disconsolate, heartbroken

desconsuelo *nm* AFLICCIÓN : grief, distress, despair

descontaminar *vt* : to decontaminate — **descontaminación** *nf*

descontar {19} *vt* **1** : to discount, to deduct **2** EXCEPTUAR : to except, to exclude

descontento[1], **-ta** *adj* : discontented, dissatisfied

descontento[2] *nm* : discontent, dissatisfaction

descontrol *nm* : lack of control, disorder, chaos

descontrolarse *vr* : to get out of control, to be out of hand

descorazonado, -da *adj* : disheartened, discouraged

descorrer *vt* : to draw back

descortés *adj, pl* **-teses** : discourteous, rude

descortesía *nf* : discourtesy, rudeness

descrédito *nm* DESPRESTIGIO **:** discredit
descremado, -da *adj* **:** nonfat, skim
describir {33} *vt* **:** to describe
descripción *nf, pl* **-ciones :** description
descriptivo, -va *adj* **:** descriptive
descrito *pp* → **describir**
descuartizar {21} *vt* **1 :** to cut up, to quarter **2 :** to tear to pieces
descubierto[1] *pp* → **descubrir**
descubierto[2], **-ta** *adj* **1 :** exposed, revealed **2 al descubierto :** out in the open
descubridor, -dora *n* **:** discoverer, explorer
descubrimiento *nm* **:** discovery
descubrir {2} *vt* **1** HALLAR **:** to discover, to find out **2** REVELAR **:** to uncover, to reveal — **descubrirse** *vr*
descuento *nm* REBAJA **:** discount
descuidado, -da *adj* **1 :** neglectful, careless **2 :** neglected, unkempt
descuidar *vt* **:** to neglect, to overlook — *vi* **:** to be careless — **descuidarse** *vr* **1 :** to be careless, to drop one's guard **2 :** to let oneself go
descuido *nm* **1 :** carelessness, negligence **2 :** slip, oversight
desde *prep* **1 :** from **2 :** since **3 desde ahora :** from now on **4 desde entonces :** since then **5 desde hace :** for, since (a time) <ha estado nevando desde hace dos días : it's been snowing for two days> **6 desde luego :** of course **7 desde que :** since, ever since **8 desde ya :** right now, immediately
desdecir {11} *vi* **~ de 1 :** to be unworthy of **2 :** to clash with — **desdecirse** *vr* **1** CONTRADECIRSE **:** to contradict oneself **2** RETRACTARSE **:** to go back on one's word
desdén *nm, pl* **desdenes** DESPRECIO **:** disdain, scorn
desdentado, -da *adj* **:** toothless
desdeñar *vt* DESPRECIAR **:** to disdain, to scorn, to despise
desdeñoso, -sa *adj* **:** disdainful, scornful — **desdeñosamente** *adv*
desdibujar *vt* **:** to blur — **desdibujarse** *vr*
desdicha *nf* **1 :** misery **2 :** misfortune
desdichado[1], **-da** *adj* **1 :** unfortunate **2 :** miserable, unhappy
desdichado[2], **-da** *n* **:** wretch
desdicho *pp* → **desdecir**
desdiga, desdijo, etc. → **desdecir**
desdoblar *vt* DESPLEGAR **:** to unfold
deseable *adj* **:** desirable
desear *vt* **1 :** to wish <te deseo buena suerte : I wish you good luck> **2** QUERER **:** to want, to desire
desechable *adj* **:** disposable
desechar *vt* **1 :** to discard, to throw away **2** RECHAZAR **:** to reject
desecho *nm* **1 :** reject **2 desechos** *nmpl* RESIDUOS **:** rubbish, waste
desembarazarse {21} *vr* **~ de :** to get rid of
desembarcadero *nm* **:** jetty, landing pier
desembarcar {72} *vi* **:** to disembark — *vt* **:** to unload
desembarco *nm* **1 :** landing, arrival **2 :** unloading
desembarque *nm* → **desembarco**
desembocadura *nf* **1 :** mouth (of a river) **2 :** opening, end (of a street)
desembocar {72} *vi* **~ en** *or* **~ a 1 :** to flow into, to join **2 :** to lead to, to result in
desembolsar *vt* PAGAR **:** to disburse, to pay out
desembolso *nm* PAGO **:** disbursement, payment
desempacar {72} *v* **:** to unpack
desempate *nm* **:** tiebreaker, play-off
desempeñar *vt* **1 :** to play (a role) **2 :** to fulfill, to carry out **3 :** to redeem (from a pawnshop) — **desempeñarse** *vr* **:** to function, to act
desempeño *nm* **1 :** fulfillment, carrying out **2 :** performance
desempleado[1], **-da** *adj* **:** unemployed
desempleado[2], **-da** *n* **:** unemployed person
desempleo *nm* **:** unemployment
desempolvar *vt* **1 :** to dust off **2 :** to resurrect, to revive
desencadenar *vt* **1 :** to unchain **2 :** to trigger, to unleash — **desencadenarse** *vr*
desencajar *vt* **1 :** to dislocate **2 :** to disconnect, to disengage
desencantar *vt* **:** to disenchant, to disillusion — **desencantarse** *vr*
desencanto *nm* **:** disenchantment, disillusionment
desenchufar *vt* **:** to disconnect, to unplug
desenfadado, -da *adj* **1 :** uninhibited, carefree **2 :** confident, self-assured
desenfado *nm* **1** DESENVOLTURA **:** self-assurance, confidence **2 :** naturalness, ease
desenfrenadamente *adv* **:** wildly, with abandon
desenfrenado, -da *adj* **:** unbridled, unrestrained
desenfreno *nm* **:** abandon, unrestraint
desenganchar *vt* **:** to unhitch, to uncouple
desengañar *vt* **:** to disillusion, to disenchant — **desengañarse** *vr*
desengaño *nm* **:** disenchantment, disillusionment
desenlace *nm* **:** ending, outcome
desenlazar {21} *vt* **1 :** to untie **2 :** to clear up, to resolve
desenmarañar *vt* **:** to disentangle, to unravel
desenmascarar *vt* **:** to unmask, to expose
desenredar *vt* **:** to untangle, to disentangle
desenrollar *vt* **:** to unroll, to unwind
desentenderse {56} *vr* **~ de 1 :** to want nothing to do with, to be uninterested in **2 :** to pretend ignorance of

desenterrar {55} *vt* **1** EXHUMAR **:** to exhume **2 :** to unearth, to dig up
desentonar *vi* **1 :** to clash, to conflict **2 :** to be out of tune, to sing off-key
desentrañar *vt* **:** to get to the bottom of, to unravel
desenvainar *vt* **:** to draw, to unsheathe (a sword)
desenvoltura *nf* **1** DESENFADO **:** confidence, self-assurance **2** ELOCUENCIA **:** eloquence, fluency
desenvolver {89} *vt* **:** to unwrap, to open — **desenvolverse** *vr* **1 :** to unfold, to develop **2 :** to manage, to cope
desenvuelto[1] *pp* → **desenvolver**
desenvuelto[2], **-ta** *adj* **:** confident, relaxed, self-assured
deseo *nm* **:** wish, desire
deseoso, -sa *adj* **:** eager, anxious
desequilibrar *vt* **:** to unbalance, to throw off balance — **desequilibrarse** *vr*
desequilibrio *nm* **:** imbalance
deserción *nf, pl* **-ciones :** desertion, defection
desertar *vi* **1 :** to desert, to defect **2 ~ de :** to abandon, to neglect
desertor, -tora *n* **:** deserter, defector
desesperación *nf, pl* **-ciones :** desperation, despair
desesperado, -da *adj* **:** desperate, despairing, hopeless — **desesperadamente** *adv*
desesperanza *nf* **:** despair, hopelessness
desesperar *vt* **:** to exasperate — *vi* **:** to despair, to lose hope — **desesperarse** *vr* **:** to become exasperated
desestimar *vt* **1 :** to reject, to disallow **2 :** to have a low opinion of
desfachatez *nf, pl* **-teces :** audacity, nerve, cheek
desfalcador, -dora *n* **:** embezzler
desfalcar {72} *vt* **:** to embezzle
desfalco *nm* **:** embezzlement
desfallecer {53} *vi* **1 :** to weaken **2 :** to faint
desfallecimiento *nm* **1 :** weakness **2 :** fainting
desfasado, -da *adj* **1 :** out of sync **2 :** out of step, behind the times
desfase *nm* **:** gap, lag <desfase horario : jet lag>
desfavorable *adj* **:** unfavorable, adverse — **desfavorablemente** *adv*
desfavorecido, -da *adj* **:** underprivileged
desfigurar *vt* **1 :** to disfigure, to mar **2 :** to distort, to misrepresent
desfiladero *nm* **:** narrow gorge, defile
desfilar *vi* **:** to parade, to march
desfile *nm* **:** parade, procession
desfogar {52} *vt* **1 :** to vent **2** *Mex* **:** to unclog, to unblock — **desfogarse** *vr* **:** to vent one's feelings, to let off steam
desforestación *nf, pl* **-ciones :** deforestation
desgajar *vt* **1 :** to tear off **2 :** to break apart — **desgajarse** *vr* **:** to come apart
desgana *nf* **1** INAPETENCIA **:** lack of appetite **2** APATÍA **:** apathy, unwillingness, reluctance
desgano *nm* → **desgana**
desgarbado, -da *adj* **:** ungainly
desgarrador, -dora *adj* **:** heartrending, heartbreaking
desgarradura *nf* **:** tear, rip
desgarrar *vt* **1 :** to tear, to rip **2 :** to break (one's heart) — **desgarrarse** *vr*
desgarre *nm* → **desgarro**
desgarro *nm* **:** tear
desgarrón *nm, pl* **-rrones :** rip, tear
desgastar *vt* **1 :** to use up **2 :** to wear away, to wear down
desgaste *nm* **:** deterioration, wear and tear
desglosar *vt* **:** to break down, to itemize
desglose *nm* **:** breakdown, itemization
desgobierno *nm* **:** anarchy, disorder
desgracia *nf* **1 :** misfortune **2 :** disgrace **3 por ~ :** unfortunately
desgraciadamente *adv* **:** unfortunately
desgraciado[1], **-da** *adj* **1 :** unfortunate, unlucky **2 :** vile, wretched
desgraciado[2], **-da** *n* **:** unfortunate person, wretch
desgranar *vt* **:** to shuck, to shell
deshabitado, -da *adj* **:** unoccupied, uninhabited
deshacer {40} *vt* **1 :** to destroy, to ruin **2** DESATAR **:** to undo, to untie **3 :** to break apart, to crumble **4 :** to dissolve, to melt **5 :** to break, to cancel — **deshacerse** *vr* **1 :** to fall apart, to come undone **2 ~ de :** to get rid of
deshecho[1] *pp* → **deshacer**
deshecho[2], **-cha** *adj* **1 :** destroyed, ruined **2 :** devastated, shattered **3 :** undone, untied
desherbar {55} *vt* **:** to weed
desheredado, -da *adj* MARGINADO **:** dispossessed, destitute
desheredar *vt* **:** to disinherit
deshicieron, etc. → **deshacer**
deshidratar *vt* **:** to dehydrate — **deshidratación** *nf*
deshielo *nm* **:** thaw, thawing
deshilachar *vt* **:** to fray — **deshilacharse** *vr*
deshizo → **deshacer**
deshonestidad *nf* **:** dishonesty
deshonesto, -ta *adj* **:** dishonest
deshonra *nf* **:** dishonor, disgrace
deshonrar *vt* **:** to dishonor, to disgrace
deshonroso, -sa *adj* **:** dishonorable, disgraceful
deshuesar *vt* **1 :** to pit (a fruit, etc.) **2 :** to bone, to debone
deshumanizar {21} *vt* **:** to dehumanize — **deshumanización** *nf*
desidia *nf* **1** APATÍA **:** apathy, indolence **2** NEGLIGENCIA **:** negligence, sloppiness
desierto[1], **-ta** *adj* **:** deserted, uninhabited

desierto² *nm* : desert
designación *nf, pl* **-ciones** NOMBRAMIENTO : appointment, naming (to an office, etc.)
designar *vt* NOMBRAR : to designate, to appoint, to name
designio *nm* : plan
desigual *adj* **1** : unequal **2** DISPAREJO : uneven
desigualdad *nf* **1** : inequality **2** : unevenness
desilusión *nf, pl* **-siones** DESENCANTO, DESENGAÑO : disillusionment, disenchantment
desilusionar *vt* DESENCANTAR, DESENGAÑAR : to disillusion, to disenchant — **desilusionarse** *vr*
desinfectante *adj & nm* : disinfectant
desinfectar *vt* : to disinfect — **desinfección** *nf*
desinflar *vt* : to deflate — **desinflarse** *vr*
desinhibido, -da *adj* : unihibited, unrestrained
desintegración *nf, pl* **-ciones** : disintegration
desintegrar *vt* : to disintegrate, to break up — **desintegrarse** *vr*
desinterés *nm* **1** : lack of interest, indifference **2** : unselfishness
desinteresado, -da *adj* GENEROSO : unselfish
desintoxicar {72} *vt* : to detoxify, to detox
desistir *vi* **1** : to desist, to stop **2 ~ de** : to give up, to relinquish
deslave *nm Mex* : landslide
desleal *adj* INFIEL : disloyal — **deslealmente** *adv*
deslealtad *nf* : disloyalty
desleír {66} *vt* : to dilute, to dissolve
desligar {52} *vt* **1** : to separate, to undo **2** : to free (from an obligation) — **desligarse** *vr* **~ de** : to extricate oneself from
deslindar *vt* **1** : to mark the limits of, to demarcate **2** : to define, to clarify
deslinde *nm* : demarcation
desliz *nm, pl* **deslices** : error, mistake, slip <desliz de la lengua : slip of the tongue>
deslizar {21} *vt* **1** : to slide, to slip **2** : to slip in — **deslizarse** *vr* **1** : to slide, to glide **2** : to slip away
deslucido, -da *adj* **1** : unimpressive, dull **2** : faded, dingy, tarnished
deslucir {45} *vt* **1** : to spoil **2** : to fade, to dull, to tarnish **3** : to discredit
deslumbrar *vt* : to dazzle — **deslumbrante** *adj*
deslustrado, -da *adj* : dull, lusterless
deslustrar *vt* : to tarnish, to dull
deslustre *nm* : tarnish
desmán *nm, pl* **desmanes** **1** : outrage, abuse **2** : misfortune
desmandarse *vr* : to behave badly, to get out of hand
desmantelar *vt* DESMONTAR : to dismantle
desmañado, -da *adj* : clumsy, awkward
desmayado, -da *adj* **1** : fainting, weak **2** : dull, pale
desmayar *vi* : to lose heart, to falter — **desmayarse** *vr* DESVANECERSE : to faint, to swoon
desmayo *nm* **1** : faint, fainting **2 sufrir un desmayo** : to faint
desmedido, -da *adj* DESMESURADO : excessive, undue
desmejorar *vt* : to weaken, to make worse — *vi* : to decline (in health), to get worse
desmembramiento *nm* : dismemberment
desmembrar {55} *vt* **1** : to dismember **2** : to break up
desmemoriado, -da *adj* : absent-minded, forgetful
desmentido *nm* : denial
desmentir {76} *vt* **1** NEGAR : to deny, to refute **2** CONTRADECIR : to contradict
desmenuzar {21} *vt* **1** : to break down, to scrutinize **2** : to crumble, to shred — **desmenuzarse** *vr*
desmerecer {53} *vt* : to be unworthy of — *vi* **1** : to decline in value **2 ~ de** : to compare unfavorably with
desmesurado, -da *adj* DESMEDIDO : excessive, inordinate — **desmesuradamente** *adv*
desmigajar *vt* : to crumble — **desmigajarse** *vr*
desmilitarizado, -da *adj* : demilitarized
desmontar *vt* **1** : to clear, to level off **2** DESMANTELAR : to dismantle, to take apart — *vi* : to dismount
desmonte *nm* : clearing, leveling
desmoralizador, -dora *adj* : demoralizing
desmoralizar {21} *vt* DESALENTAR : to demoralize, to discourage
desmoronamiento *nm* : crumbling, falling apart
desmoronar *vt* : to wear away, to erode — **desmoronarse** *vr* : to crumble, to deteriorate, to fall apart
desmotadora *nf* : gin, cotton gin
desmovilizar {21} *vt* : to demobilize — **desmovilización** *nf*
desnaturalizar {21} *vt* **1** : to denature **2** : to distort, to alter
desnivel *nm* **1** : disparity, difference **2** : unevenness (of a surface) **3 paso a desnivel** *Mex* : underpass
desnivelado, -da *adj* **1** : uneven **2** : unbalanced
desnudar *vt* **1** : to undress **2** : to strip, to lay bare — **desnudarse** *vr* : to undress, to strip off one's clothing
desnudez *nf, pl* **-deces** : nudity, nakedness
desnudismo *nm* → **nudismo**
desnudista → **nudista**
desnudo¹, -da *adj* : nude, naked, bare
desnudo² *nm* : nude

desnutrición *nf, pl* **-ciones** : MALNUTRICIÓN : malnutrition, undernourishment

desnutrido, -da *adj* MALNUTRIDO : malnourished, undernourished

desobedecer {53} *v* : to disobey

desobediencia *nf* : disobedience — **desobediente** *adj*

desocupación *nf, pl* **-ciones** : unemployment

desocupado, -da *adj* **1** : vacant, empty **2** : free, unoccupied **3** : unemployed

desocupar *vt* **1** : to empty **2** : to vacate, to move out of — **desocuparse** *vr* : to leave, to quit (a job)

desodorante *adj & nm* : deodorant

desolación *nf, pl* **-ciones** : desolation

desolado, -da *adj* **1** : desolate **2** : devastated, distressed

desolador, -dora *adj* **1** : devastating **2** : bleak, desolate

desollar *vt* : to skin, to flay

desorbitado, -da *adj* **1** : excessive, exorbitant **2 con los ojos desorbitados** : with eyes popping out of one's head

desorden *nm, pl* **desórdenes** **1** DESBARAJUSTE : disorder, mess **2** : disorder, disturbance, upset

desordenado, -da *adj* **1** : untidy, messy **2** : disorderly, unruly

desorganización *nf, pl* **-ciones** : disorganization

desorganizar {21} *vt* : to disrupt, to disorganize

desorientación *nf, pl* **-ciones** : disorientation, confusion

desorientar *vt* : to disorient, to mislead, to confuse — **desorientarse** *vr* : to become disoriented, to lose one's way

desovar *vi* : to spawn

despachar *vt* **1** : to complete, to conclude **2** : to deal with, to take care of, to handle **3** : to dispatch, to send off **4** *fam* : to finish off, to kill — **despacharse** *vr fam* : to gulp down, to polish off

despacho *nm* **1** : dispatch, shipment **2** OFICINA : office, study

despacio *adv* LENTAMENTE, LENTO : slowly, slow <¡despacio! : take it easy!, easy does it!>

desparasitar *vt* : to worm (an animal), to delouse

desparpajo *nm* **1** *fam* : self-confidence, nerve **2** *CA fam* : confusion, muddle

desparramar *vt* **1** : to spill, to splatter **2** : to spread, to scatter

despatarrarse *vr* : to sprawl (out)

despavorido, -da *adj* : terrified, horrified

despecho *nm* **1** : spite **2 a despecho de** : despite, in spite of

despectivo, -va *adj* **1** : contemptuous, disparaging **2** : derogatory, pejorative

despedazar {21} *vt* : to cut to pieces, to tear apart

despedida *nf* **1** : farewell, good-bye **2 despedida de soltera** : bridal shower

despedir {54} *vt* **1** : to see off, to show out **2** : to dismiss, to fire **3** EMITIR : to give off, to emit <despedir un olor : to give off an odor> — **despedirse** *vr* : to take one's leave, to say good-bye

despegado, -da *adj* **1** : separated, detached **2** : cold, distant

despegar {52} *vt* : to remove, to detach — *vi* : to take off, to lift off, to blast off

despegue *nm* : takeoff, liftoff

despeinado, -da *adj* : disheveled, tousled <estoy despeinada : my hair's a mess>

despejado, -da *adj* **1** : clear, fair **2** : alert, clear-headed **3** : uncluttered, unobstructed

despejar *vt* **1** : to clear, to free **2** : to clarify — *vi* **1** : to clear up **2** : to punt (in sports)

despeje *nm* **1** : clearing **2** : punt (in sports)

despellejar *vt* : to skin (an animal)

despenalizar {21} *vt* : to legalize — **despenalización** *nf*

despensa *nf* **1** : pantry, larder **2** PROVISIONES : provisions *pl,* supplies *pl*

despeñar *vt* : to hurl down

despepitar *vt* : to seed, to remove the seeds from

desperdiciar *vt* **1** DESAPROVECHAR, MALGASTAR : to waste **2** : to miss, to miss out on

desperdicio *nm* **1** : waste **2 desperdicios** *nmpl* RESIDUOS : refuse, scraps, rubbish

desperdigar {52} *vt* DISPERSAR : to disperse, to scatter

desperfecto *nm* **1** DEFECTO : flaw, defect **2** : damage

despertador *nm* : alarm clock

despertar {55} *vi* : to awaken, to wake up — *vt* **1** : to arouse, to wake **2** EVOCAR : to elicit, to evoke — **despertarse** *vr* : to wake (oneself) up

despiadado, -da *adj* CRUEL : cruel, merciless, pitiless — **despiadadamente** *adv*

despido *nm* : dismissal, layoff

despierto, -ta *adj* **1** : awake, alert **2** LISTO : clever, sharp <con la mente despierta : with a sharp mind>

despilfarrador[1], -dora *adj* : extravagant, wasteful

despilfarrador[2], -dora *n* : spendthrift, prodigal

despilfarrar *vt* MALGASTAR : to squander, to waste

despilfarro *nm* : extravagance, wastefulness

despintar *vt* : to strip the paint from — **despintarse** *vr* : to fade, to wash off, to peel off

despistado[1], -da *adj* **1** DISTRAÍDO : absentminded, forgetful **2** CONFUSO : confused, bewildered

despistado[2], -da *n* : scatterbrain, absentminded person

despistar *vt* : to throw off the track, to confuse — **despistarse** *vr*

despiste *nm* **1** : absentmindedness **2** : mistake, slip

desplantador *nm* : garden trowel

desplante *nm* : insolence, rudeness

desplazamiento *nm* **1** : movement, displacement **2** : journey

desplazar {21} *vt* **1** : to replace, to displace **2** TRASLADAR : to move, to shift

desplegar {49} *vt* **1** : to display, to show, to manifest **2** DESDOBLAR : to unfold, to unfurl **3** : to spread (out) **4** : to deploy

despliegue *nm* **1** : display **2** : deployment

desplomarse *vr* **1** : to plummet, to fall **2** DERRUMBARSE : to collapse, to break down

desplome *nm* **1** : fall, drop **2** : collapse

desplumar *vt* : to pluck (a chicken, etc.)

despoblado[1], -da *adj* : uninhabited, deserted

despoblado[2] *nm* : open country, deserted area

despoblar {19} *vt* : to depopulate

despojar *vt* **1** : to strip, to clear **2** : to divest, to deprive — **despojarse** *vr* **1** **~ de** : to remove (clothing) **2** **~ de** : to relinquish, to renounce

despojos *nmpl* **1** : remains, scraps **2** : plunder, spoils

desportilladura *nf* : chip, nick

desportillar *vt* : to chip — **desportillarse** *vr*

desposeer {20} *vt* : to dispossess

déspota *nmf* : despot, tyrant

despotismo *nm* : despotism — **despótico, -ca** *adj*

despotricar {72} *vi* : to rant and rave, to complain excessively

despreciable *adj* **1** : despicable, contemptible **2** : negligible <nada despreciable : not inconsiderable, significant>

despreciar *vt* DESDEÑAR, MENOSPRECIAR : to despise, to scorn, to disdain

despreciativo, -va *adj* : scornful, disdainful

desprecio *nm* DESDÉN, MENOSPRECIO : disdain, contempt, scorn

desprender *vt* **1** SOLTAR : to detach, to loosen, to unfasten **2** EMITIR : to emit, to give off — **desprenderse** *vr* **1** : to come off, to come undone **2** : to be inferred, to follow **3** **~ de** : to part with, to get rid of

desprendido, -da *adj* : generous, unselfish, disinterested

desprendimiento *nm* **1** : detachment **2** GENEROSIDAD : generosity **3 desprendimiento de tierras** : landslide

despreocupación *nf, pl* **-ciones** : indifference, lack of concern

despreocupado, -da *adj* : carefree, easygoing, unconcerned

desprestigiar *vt* DESACREDITAR : to discredit, to disgrace — **desprestigiarse** *vr* : to lose prestige

desprestigio *nm* DESCRÉDITO : discredit, disrepute

desprevenido, -da *adj* DESAPERCIBIDO : unprepared, off guard, unsuspecting

desproporción *nf, pl* **-ciones** : disproportion, disparity

desproporcionado, -da : out of proportion

despropósito *nm* : piece of nonsense, absurdity

desprotegido, -da *adj* : unprotected, vulnerable

desprovisto, -ta *adj* **~ de** : devoid of, lacking in

después *adv* **1** : afterward, later **2** : then, next **3** **~ de** : after, next after <después de comer : after eating> **4** **después (de) que** : after <después que lo acabé : after I finished it> **5** **después de todo** : after all **6** **poco después** : shortly after, soon thereafter

despuntado, -da *adj* : blunt, dull

despuntar *vt* : to blunt — *vi* **1** : to dawn **2** : to sprout **3** : to excel, to stand out

desquiciar *vt* **1** : to unhinge (a door) **2** : to drive crazy — **desquiciarse** *vr* : to go crazy

desquitarse *vr* **1** : to get even, to retaliate **2** **~ con** : to take it out on

desquite *nm* : revenge

desregulación *nf, pl* **-ciones** : deregulation

desregular *vt* : to deregulate

destacadamente *adv* : outstandingly, prominently

destacado, -da *adj* **1** : outstanding, prominent **2** : stationed, posted

destacar {72} *vt* **1** ENFATIZAR, SUBRAYAR : to emphasize, to highlight, to stress **2** : to station, to post — *vi* : to stand out

destajo *nm* **1** : piecework **2** **a ~** : by the item, by the job

destapador *nm* : bottle opener

destapar *vt* **1** : to open, to take the top off **2** DESCUBRIR : to reveal, to uncover **3** : to unblock, to unclog

destape *nm* : uncovering, revealing

destartalado, -da *adj* : dilapidated, tumbledown

destellar *vi* **1** : to sparkle, to flash, to glint **2** : to twinkle

destello *nm* **1** : flash, sparkle, twinkle **2** : glimmer, hint

destemplado, -da *adj* **1** : out of tune **2** : irritable, out of sorts **3** : unpleasant (of weather)

desteñir {67} *vi* : to run, to fade — **desteñirse** DESCOLORARSE : to fade

desterrado[1], -da *adj* : banished, exiled

desterrado[2], -da *n* : exile

desterrar {55} *vt* **1** EXILIAR **:** to banish, to exile **2** ERRADICAR **:** to eradicate, to do away with
destetar *vt* **:** to wean
destiempo *adv* **a ~ :** at the wrong time
destierro *nm* EXILIO **:** exile
destilación *nf, pl* **-ciones :** distillation
destilador, -dora *n* **:** distiller
destilar *vt* **1 :** to exude **2 :** to distill
destilería *nf* **:** distillery
destinación *nf, pl* **-ciones** DESTINO **:** destination
destinado, -da *adj* **:** destined, bound
destinar *vt* **1 :** to appoint, to assign **2** ASIGNAR **:** to earmark, to allot
destinatario, -ria *n* **1 :** addressee **2 :** payee
destino *nm* **1 :** destiny, fate **2** DESTINACIÓN **:** destination **3 :** use **4 :** assignment, post
destitución *nf, pl* **-ciones :** dismissal, removal from office
destituir {41} *vt* **:** to dismiss, to remove from office
destorcer {14} *vt* **:** to untwist
destornillador *nm* **:** screwdriver
destornillar *vt* **:** to unscrew
destrabar *vt* **1 :** to untie, to undo, to ease up **2 :** to separate
destreza *nf* HABILIDAD **:** dexterity, skill
destronar *vt* **:** to depose, to dethrone
destrozado, -da *adj* **1 :** ruined, destroyed **2 :** devastated, brokenhearted
destrozar {21} *vt* **1 :** to smash, to shatter **2 :** to destroy, to wreck — **destrozarse** *vr*
destrozo *nm* **1** DAÑO **:** damage **2 :** havoc, destruction
destrucción *nf, pl* **-ciones :** destruction
destructivo, -va *adj* **:** destructive
destructor[1]**, -tora** *adj* **:** destructive
destructor[2] *nm* **:** destroyer (ship)
destruir {41} *vt* **:** to destroy — **destruirse** *vr*
desubicado, -da *adj* **1 :** out of place **2 :** confused, disoriented
desunión *nf, pl* **-niones :** disunity
desunir *vt* **:** to split, to divide
desusado, -da *adj* **1** INSÓLITO **:** unusual **2** OBSOLETO **:** obsolete, disused, antiquated
desuso *nm* **:** disuse, obsolescence <caer en desuso : to fall into disuse>
desvaído, -da *adj* **1 :** pale, washed-out **2 :** vague, blurred
desvainar *vt* **:** to shell
desvalido, -da *adj* DESAMPARADO **:** destitute, helpless
desvalijar *vt* **1 :** to ransack **2 :** to rob
desvalorización *nf, pl* **-ciones 1** DEVALUACIÓN **:** devaluation **2 :** depreciation
desvalorizar {21} *vt* **:** to devalue
desván *nm, pl* **desvanes** ÁTICO, BUHARDILLA **:** attic
desvanecer {53} *vt* **1** DISIPAR **:** to make disappear, to dispel **2 :** to fade, to blur — **desvanecerse** *vr* **1 :** to vanish, to disappear **2 :** to fade **3** DESMAYARSE **:** to faint, to swoon
desvanecimiento *nm* **1 :** disappearance **2** DESMAYO **:** faint **3 :** fading
desvariar {85} *vi* **1** DELIRAR **:** to be delirious **2 :** to rave, to talk nonsense
desvarío *nm* DELIRIO **:** delirium
desvelado, -da *adj* **:** sleepless
desvelar *vt* **1 :** to keep awake **2** REVELAR **:** to reveal, to disclose — **desvelarse** *vr* **1 :** to stay awake **2 :** to do one's utmost
desvelo *nm* **1 :** sleeplessness **2 desvelos** *nmpl* **:** efforts, pains
desvencijado, -da *adj* **:** dilapidated, rickety
desventaja *nf* **:** disadvantage, drawback
desventajoso, -sa *adj* **:** disadvantageous, unfavorable
desventura *nf* INFORTUNIO **:** misfortune
desventurado, -da *adj* **:** unfortunate, ill-fated
desvergonzado, -da *adj* **:** shameless, impudent
desvergüenza *nf* **:** shamelessness, impudence
desvestir {54} *vt* **:** to undress — **desvestirse** *vr* **:** to get undressed
desviación *nf, pl* **-ciones 1 :** deviation, departure **2 :** detour, diversion
desviar {85} *vt* **1 :** to change the course of, to divert **2 :** to turn away, to deflect — **desviarse** *vr* **1 :** to branch off **2** APARTARSE **:** to stray
desvinculación *nf, pl* **-ciones :** dissociation
desvincular *vt* **~ de :** to separate from, to dissociate from — **desvincularse** *vr*
desvío *nm* **1 :** diversion, detour **2 :** deviation
desvirtuar {3} *vt* **1 :** to impair, to spoil **2 :** to detract from **3 :** to distort, to misrepresent
detalladamente *adv* **:** in detail, at great length
detallar *vt* **:** to detail
detalle *nm* **1 :** detail **2 al detalle :** retail
detallista[1] *adj* **1 :** meticulous **2 :** retail
detallista[2] *nmf* **1 :** perfectionist **2 :** retailer
detección *nf, pl* **-ciones :** detection
detectar *vt* **:** to detect — **detectable** *adj*
detective *nmf* **:** detective
detector *nm* **:** detector <detector de mentiras : lie detector>
detención *nf, pl* **-ciones 1** ARRESTO **:** detention, arrest **2 :** stop, halt **3 :** delay, holdup
detener {80} *vt* **1** ARRESTAR **:** to arrest, to detain **2** PARAR **:** to stop, to halt **3 :** to keep, to hold back — **detenerse** *vr* **1 :** to stop **2 :** to delay, to linger
detenidamente *adv* **:** thoroughly, at length
detenimiento *nm* **con ~ :** carefully, in detail

detentar *vt* : to hold, to retain
detergente *nm* : detergent
deteriorado, -da *adj* : damaged, worn
deteriorar *vt* ESTROPEAR : to damage, to spoil — **deteriorarse** *vr* **1** : to get damaged, to wear out **2** : to deteriorate, to worsen
deterioro *nm* **1** : deterioration, wear **2** : worsening, decline
determinación *nf, pl* **-ciones 1** : determination, resolve **2 tomar una determinación** : to make a decision
determinado, -da *adj* **1** : certain, particular **2** : determined, resolute
determinante[1] *adj* : determining, deciding
determinante[2] *nm* : determinant
determinar *vt* **1** : to determine **2** : to cause, to bring about — **determinarse** *vr* : to make up one's mind, to decide
detestar *vt* : to detest — **detestable** *adj*
detonación *nf, pl* **-ciones** : detonation
detonador *nm* : detonator
detonante[1] *adj* : detonating, explosive
detonante[2] *nm* **1** → **detonador 2** : catalyst, cause
detonar *vi* : to detonate, to explode
detractor, -tora *n* : detractor, critic
detrás *adv* **1** : behind **2 ~ de** : in back of **3 por ~** : from behind
detuvo, etc. → **detener**
deuda *nf* **1** DÉBITO : debt **2 en deuda con** : indebted to
deudo, -da *n* : relative
deudor[1], **-dora** *adj* : indebted
deudor[2], **-dora** *n* : debtor
devaluación *nf, pl* **-ciones** DESVALORIZACIÓN : devaluation
devaluar {3} *vt* : to devalue — **devaluarse** *vr* : to depreciate
devanarse *vr* **devanarse los sesos** : to rack one's brains
devaneo *nm* **1** : flirtation, fling **2** : idle pursuit
devastador, -dora *adj* : devastating
devastar *vt* : to devastate — **devastación** *nf*
devenir {87} *vi* **1** : to come about **2 ~ en** : to become, to turn into
devoción *nf, pl* **-ciones** : devotion
devolución *nf, pl* **-ciones** REEMBOLSO : return, refund
devolver {89} *vt* **1** : to return, to give back **2** REEMBOLSAR : to refund, to pay back **3** : to vomit, to bring up — *vi* : to vomit, to throw up — **devolverse** *vr* : to return, to come back, to go back
devorar *vt* **1** : to devour **2** : to consume
devoto[1], **-ta** *adj* : devout — **devotamente** *adv*
devoto[2], **-ta** *n* : devotee, admirer
di → **dar, decir**
día *nm* **1** : day <todos los días : every day> **2** : daytime, daylight <de día : by day, in the daytime> <en pleno día : in broad daylight> **3 al día** : up-to-date **4 en su día** : in due time
diabetes *nf* : diabetes
diabético, -ca *adj & n* : diabetic
diablillo *nm* : little devil, imp
diablo *nm* DEMONIO : devil
diablura *nf* **1** : prank **2 diabluras** *nfpl* : mischief
diabólico, -ca *adj* : diabolical, diabolic, devilish
diaconisa *nf* : deaconess
diácono *nm* : deacon
diadema *nf* : diadem, crown
diáfano, -na *adj* : diaphanous
diafragma *nm* : diaphragm
diagnosticar {72} *vt* : to diagnose
diagnóstico[1], **-ca** *adj* : diagnostic
diagnóstico[2] *nm* : diagnosis
diagonal *adj & nf* : diagonal — **diagonalmente** *adv*
diagrama *nm* **1** : diagram **2 diagrama de flujo** ORGANIGRAMA : flowchart
dialecto *nm* : dialect
dialogar {52} *vi* : to have a talk, to converse
diálogo *nm* : dialogue
diamante *nm* : diamond
diametral *adj* : diametric, diametrical — **diametralmente** *adv*
diámetro *nm* : diameter
diana *nf* **1** : target, bull's-eye **2** *or* **toque de diana** : reveille
diapositiva *nf* : slide, transparency
diario[1] *adv Mex* : every day, daily
diario[2], **-ria** *adj* : daily, everyday — **diariamente** *adv*
diario[3] *nm* **1** : diary **2** PERIÓDICO : newspaper
diarrea *nf* : diarrhea
diatriba *nf* : diatribe, tirade
dibujante *nmf* **1** : draftsman *m*, draftswoman *f* **2** CARICATURISTA : cartoonist
dibujar *vt* **1** : to draw, to sketch **2** : to portray, to depict
dibujo *nm* **1** : drawing **2** : design, pattern **3 dibujos animados** : (animated) cartoons
dicción *nf, pl* **-ciones** : diction
diccionario *nm* : dictionary
dícese → **decir**
dicha *nf* **1** SUERTE : good luck **2** FELICIDAD : happiness, joy
dicho[1] *pp* → **decir**
dicho[2], **-cha** *adj* : said, aforementioned
dicho[3] *nm* DECIR : saying, proverb
dichoso, -sa *adj* **1** : blessed **2** FELIZ : happy **3** AFORTUNADO : fortunate, lucky
diciembre *nm* : December
diciendo → **decir**
dictado *nm* : dictation
dictador, -dora *n* : dictator
dictadura *nf* : dictatorship
dictamen *nm, pl* **dictámenes 1** : report **2** : judgment, opinion
dictaminar *vt* : to report — *vi* : to give an opinion, to pass judgment
dictar *vt* **1** : to dictate **2** : to pronounce (a judgment) **3** : to give, to deliver <dictar una conferencia : to give a lecture>
dictatorial *adj* : dictatorial

didáctico, -ca *adj* : didactic

diecinueve *adj & nm* : nineteen

diecinueveavo[1], **-va** *adj* : nineteenth

diecinueveavo[2] *nm* : nineteenth (fraction)

dieciocho *adj & nm* : eighteen

dieciochoavo[1], **-va** *or* **dieciochavo, -va** *adj* : eighteenth

dieciochoavo[2] *or* **dieciochavo** *nm* : eighteenth (fraction)

dieciséis *adj & nm* : sixteen

dieciseisavo[1], **-va** *adj* : sixteenth

dieciseisavo[2] *nm* : sixteenth (fraction)

diecisietaeavo[1], **-va** *adj* : seventeenth

diecisietaeavo[2] *nm* : seventeenth (fraction)

diecisiete *adj & nm* : seventeen

diecisieteavo[1], **-va** *adj* : seventeenth

diecisieteavo[2] *nm* : seventeenth

diente *nm* **1** : tooth <diente canino : eyetooth, canine tooth> **2** : tusk, fang **3** : prong, tine **4 diente de león** : dandelion

dieron, etc. → **dar**

diesel [ˈdisɛl] *nm* : diesel

diestra *nf* : right hand

diestramente *adv* : skillfully, adroitly

diestro[1], **-tra** *adj* **1** : right **2** : skillful, accomplished

diestro[2] *nm* : bullfighter, matador

dieta *nf* : diet

dietética *nf* : dietetics

dietético, -ca *adj* : dietetic

dietista *nmf* : dietitian

diez *adj & nm, pl* **dieces** : ten

difamación *nf, pl* **-ciones** : defamation, slander

difamar *vt* : to defame, to slander

difamatorio, -ria *adj* : slanderous, defamatory, libelous

diferencia *nf* **1** : difference **2 a diferencia de** : unlike, in contrast to

diferenciación *nf, pl* **-ciones** : differentiation

diferenciar *vt* : to differentiate between, to distinguish — **diferenciarse** *vr* : to differ

diferendo *nm* : dispute, conflict

diferente *adj* DISTINTO : different — **diferentemente** *adv*

diferir {76} *vt* DILATAR, POSPONER : to postpone, to put off — *vi* : to differ

difícil *adj* : difficult, hard

difícilmente *adv* **1** : with difficulty **2** : hardly

dificultad *nf* : difficulty

dificultar *vt* : to make difficult, to obstruct

dificultoso, -sa *adj* : difficult, hard

difteria *nf* : diphtheria

difundir *vt* **1** : to diffuse, to spread out **2** : to broadcast, to spread

difunto, -ta *adj & n* FALLECIDO : deceased

difusión *nf, pl* **-siones 1** : spreading **2** : diffusion (of heat, etc.) **3** : broadcast, broadcasting <los medios de difusión : the media>

difuso, -sa *adj* : diffuse, widespread

diga, etc. → **decir**

digerir {76} *vt* : to digest — **digerible** *adj*

digestión *nf, pl* **-tiones** : digestion

digestivo, -va *adj* : digestive

digital[1] *adj* : digital — **digitalmente** *adv*

digital[2] *nm* **1** DEDALERA : foxglove **2** : digitalis

dígito *nm* : digit

dignarse *vr* : to deign, to condescend <no se dignó contestar : he didn't deign to answer>

dignatario, -ria *n* : dignitary

dignidad *nf* **1** : dignity **2** : dignitary

dignificar {72} *vt* : to dignify

digno, -na *adj* **1** HONORABLE : honorable **2** : worthy — **dignamente** *adv*

digresión *nf, pl* **-ciones** : digression

dije *nm* : charm (on a bracelet)

dijo, etc. → **decir**

dilación *nf, pl* **-ciones** : delay

dilapidar *vt* : to waste, to squander

dilatar *vt* **1** : to dilate, to widen, to expand **2** DIFERIR, POSPONER : to put off, to postpone — **dilatarse** *vr* **1** : to expand (of gases, metals, etc.) **2** *Mex* : to take long, to be long

dilatorio, -ria *adj* : dilatory, delaying

dilema *nm* : dilemma

diligencia *nf* **1** : diligence, care **2** : promptness, speed **3** : action, step **4** : task, errand **5** : stagecoach **6 diligencias** *nfpl* : judicial procedures, formalities

diligente *adj* : diligent — **diligentemente** *adv*

dilucidar *vt* : to elucidate, to clarify

diluir {41} *vt* : to dilute

diluviar *v impers* : to pour (with rain), to pour down

diluvio *nm* **1** : flood **2** : downpour

dimensión *nf, pl* **-siones** : dimension — **dimensional** *adj*

dimensionar *vt* : to measure, to gauge

diminuto, -ta *adj* : minute, tiny

dimisión *nf, pl* **-siones** : resignation

dimitir *vi* : to resign, to step down

dimos → **dar**

dinámica *nf* : dynamics

dinámico, -ca *adj* : dynamic — **dinámicamente** *adv*

dinamita *nf* : dynamite

dinamitar *vt* : to dynamite

dínamo *or* **dinamo** *nm* : dynamo

dinastía *nf* : dynasty

dineral *nm* : fortune, large sum of money

dinero *nm* : money

dinosaurio *nm* : dinosaur

dintel *nm* : lintel

dio, etc. → **dar**

diocesano, -na *adj* : diocesan

diócesis *nfs & pl* : diocese

dios, diosa *n* : god, goddess *f*

Dios *nm* : God

diploma *nm* : diploma

diplomacia *nf* : diplomacy

diplomado[1], **-da** *adj* : qualified, trained
diplomado[2] *nm Mex* : seminar
diplomático[1], **-ca** *adj* : diplomatic — **diplomáticamente** *adv*
diplomático[2], **-ca** *n* : diplomat
diputación *nf, pl* **-ciones** : deputation, delegation
diputado, -da *n* : delegate, representative
dique *nm* : dike
dirá, etc. → **decir**
dirección *nf, pl* **-ciones 1** : address **2** : direction **3** : management, leadership **4** : steering (of an automobile)
direccional[1] *adj* : directional
direccional[2] *nf* : directional, turn signal
directa *nf* : high gear
directamente *adv* : straight, directly
directiva *nf* **1** ORDEN : directive **2** DIRECTORIO, JUNTA : board of directors
directivo[1], **-va** *adj* : executive, managerial
directivo[2], **-va** *n* : executive, director
directo, -ta *adj* **1** : direct, straight, immediate **2 en ~** : live (in broadcasting)
director, -tora *n* **1** : director, manager, head **2** : conductor (of an orchestra)
directorial *adj* : managing, executive
directorio *nm* **1** : directory **2** DIRECTIVA, JUNTA : board of directors
directriz *nf, pl* **-trices** : guideline
dirigencia *nf* : leaders *pl*, leadership
dirigente[1] *adj* : directing, leading
dirigente[2] *nmf* : director, leader
dirigible *nm* : dirigible, blimp
dirigir {35} *vt* **1** : to direct, to lead **2** : to address **3** : to aim, to point **4** : to conduct (music) — **dirigirse** *vr* **~ a 1** : to go towards **2** : to speak to, to address
dirimir *vt* **1** : to resolve, to settle **2** : to annul, to dissolve (a marriage)
discapacidad *nf* MINUSVALÍA : disability, handicap
discapacitado[1], **-da** *adj* : disabled, handicapped
discapacitado[2], **-da** *n* : disabled person, handicapped person
discernimiento *nm* : discernment
discernir {25} *v* : to discern, to distinguish
disciplina *nf* : discipline
disciplinar *vt* : to discipline — **disciplinario, -ria** *adj*
discípulo, -la *n* : disciple, follower
disc jockey [ˌdiskˈjoke, -ˈdʒo-] *nmf* : disc jockey
disco *nm* **1** : phonograph record **2** : disc, disk <disco compacto : compact disc> **3** : discus
díscolo, -la *adj* : unruly, disobedient
disconforme *adj* : in disagreement
discontinuidad *nf* : discontinuity
discontinuo, -nua *adj* : discontinuous
discordancia *nf* DESAVENENCIA : conflict, disagreement
discordante *adj* **1** : discordant **2** : conflicting
discordia *nf* : discord
discoteca *nf* **1** : disco, discotheque **2** *CA, Mex* : record store
discreción *nf, pl* **-ciones** : discretion
discrecional *adj* : discretionary
discrepancia *nf* : discrepancy
discrepar *vi* **1** : to disagree **2** : to differ
discreto, -ta *adj* : discreet — **discretamente** *adv*
discriminación *nf, pl* **-ciones** : discrimination
discriminar *vt* **1** : to discriminate against **2** : to distinguish, to differentiate
discriminatorio, -ria *adj* : discriminatory
disculpa *nf* **1** : apology **2** : excuse
disculpable *adj* : excusable
disculpar *vt* : to excuse, to pardon — **disculparse** *vr* : to apologize
discurrir *vi* **1** : to flow **2** : to pass, to go by **3** : to ponder, to reflect
discurso *nm* **1** ORACIÓN : speech, address **2** : discourse, treatise
discusión *nf, pl* **-siones 1** : discussion **2** ALTERCADO, DISPUTA : argument
discutible *adj* : arguable, debatable
discutidor, -dora *adj* : argumentative
discutir *vt* **1** : to discuss **2** : to dispute — *vi* ALTERCAR : to argue, to quarrel
disecar {72} *vt* **1** : to dissect **2** : to stuff (for preservation)
disección *nf, pl* **-ciones** : dissection
diseminación *nf, pl* **-ciones** : dissemination, spreading
diseminar *vt* : to disseminate, to spread
disensión *nf, pl* **-siones** : dissension, disagreement
disentería *nf* : dysentery
disentir {76} *vi* : to dissent, to disagree
diseñador, -dora *n* : designer
diseñar *vt* **1** : to design, to plan **2** : to lay out, to outline
diseño *nm* : design
disertación *nf, pl* **-ciones 1** : lecture, talk **2** : dissertation
disertar *vi* : to lecture, to give a talk
disfraz *nm, pl* **disfraces 1** : disguise **2** : costume **3** : front, pretense
disfrazar {21} *vt* **1** : to disguise **2** : to mask, to conceal — **disfrazarse** *vr* : to wear a costume, to be in disguise
disfrutar *vt* : to enjoy — *vi* : to enjoy oneself, to have a good time
disfrute *nm* : enjoyment
disfunción *nf, pl* **-ciones** : dysfunction — **disfuncional** *adj*
disgresión *nf* → **digresión**
disgustar *vt* : to upset, to displease, to make angry — **disgustarse** *vr*
disgusto *nm* **1** : annoyance, displeasure **2** : argument, quarrel **3** : trouble, misfortune
disidencia *nf* : dissidence, dissent
disidente *adj & nmf* : dissident
disímbolo, -la *adj Mex* : dissimilar

disímil *adj* : dissimilar

disimulado, -da *adj* **1** : concealed, disguised **2** : furtive, sly

disimular *vi* : to dissemble, to pretend — *vt* : to conceal, to hide

disimulo *nm* **1** : dissembling, pretense **2** : slyness, furtiveness **3** : tolerance

disipar *vt* **1** : to dissipate **2** : to dispel — **disiparse** *vr*

diskette [di'skɛt] *nm* : floppy disk, diskette

dislocar {72} *vt* : to dislocate — **dislocación** *nf*

disminución *nf, pl* **-ciones** : decrease, drop, fall

disminuir {41} *vt* REDUCIR : to reduce, to decrease, to lower — *vi* **1** : to lower **2** : to drop, to fall

disociación *nf, pl* **-ciones** : dissociation

disociar *vt* : to dissociate, to separate

disolución *nf, pl* **-ciones** **1** : dissolution, dissolving **2** : breaking up **3** : dissipation

disoluto, -ta *adj* : dissolute, dissipated

disolver {89} *vt* **1** : to dissolve **2** : to break up — **disolverse** *vr*

disonancia *nf* : dissonance — **disonante** *adj*

disparado, -da *adj* **salir disparado** *fam* : to take off in a hurry, to rush away

disparar *vi* **1** : to fire (a gun) **2** *Mex fam* : to pay — *vt* **1** : to shoot **2** : to rush off **3** *Mex fam* : to treat to, to buy — **dispararse** *vr* : to shoot up, to skyrocket

disparatado, -da *adj* ABSURDO, RIDÍCULO : absurd, ridiculous, crazy

disparate *nm* : silliness, stupidity <decir disparates : to talk nonsense>

disparejo, -ja *adj* DESIGUAL : uneven

disparidad *nf* : disparity

disparo *nm* TIRO : shot

dispendio *nm* : wastefulness, extravagance

dispendioso, -sa *adj* : wasteful, extravagant

dispensa *nf* : dispensation

dispensable *adj* **1** : dispensable **2** : excusable

dispensar *vt* **1** : to dispense, to give, to grant **2** EXCUSAR : to excuse, to forgive **3** EXIMIR : to exempt

dispensario *nm* **1** : dispensary, clinic **2** *Mex* : dispenser

dispersar *vt* DESPERDIGAR : to disperse, to scatter

dispersión *nf, pl* **-siones** : dispersion

disperso, -sa *adj* : dispersed, scattered

displicencia *nf* : indifference, coldness, disdain

displicente *adj* : indifferent, cold, disdainful

disponer {60} *vt* **1** : to arrange, to lay out **2** : to stipulate, to order **3** : to prepare — *vi* **~ de** : to have at one's disposal — **disponerse** *vr* **~ a** : to prepare to, to be about to

disponibilidad *nf* : availability

disponible *adj* : available

disposición *nf, pl* **-ciones** **1** : disposition **2** : aptitude, talent **3** : order, arrangement **4** : willingness, readiness **5 última disposición** : last will and testament

dispositivo *nm* **1** APARATO, MECANISMO : device, mechanism **2** : force, detachment

dispuesto[1] *pp* → **disponer**

dispuesto[2], **-ta** *adj* PREPARADO : ready, prepared, disposed

dispuso, etc. → **disponer**

disputa *nf* ALTERCADO, DISCUSIÓN : dispute, argument

disputar *vi* : to argue, to contend, to vie — *vt* : to dispute, to question — **disputarse** *vr* : to be in competition for <se disputan la corona : they're fighting for the crown>

disquera *nf* : record label, recording company

disquete *nm* → **diskette**

disquisición *nf, pl* **-ciones** **1** : formal discourse **2 disquisiciones** *nfpl* : digressions

distancia *nf* : distance

distanciamiento *nm* **1** : distancing **2** : rift, estrangement

distanciar *vt* **1** : to space out **2** : to draw apart — **distanciarse** *vr* : to grow apart, to become estranged

distante *adj* **1** : distant, far-off **2** : aloof

distar *vi* **~ de** : to be far from <dista de ser perfecto : he is far from perfect>

diste → **dar**

distender {56} *vt* : to distend, to stretch

distensión *nf, pl* **-siones** : distension

distinción *nf, pl* **-ciones** : distinction

distinguido, -da *adj* : distinguished, refined

distinguir {26} *vt* **1** : to distinguish **2** : to honor — **distinguirse** *vr*

distintivo, -va *adj* : distinctive, distinguishing

distinto, -ta *adj* **1** DIFERENTE : different **2** CLARO : distinct, clear, evident

distorsión *nf, pl* **-siones** : distortion

distorsionar *vt* : to distort

distracción *nf, pl* **-ciones** **1** : distraction, amusement **2** : forgetfulness **3** : oversight

distraer {81} *vt* **1** : to distract **2** ENTRETENER : to entertain, to amuse — **distraerse** *vr* **1** : to get distracted **2** : to amuse oneself

distraídamente *adv* : absentmindedly

distraído[1] *pp* → **distraer**

distraído[2], **-da** *adj* **1** : distracted, preoccupied **2** DESPISTADO : absentminded

distribución *nf, pl* **-ciones** : distribution

distribuidor, -dora *n* : distributor

distribuir {41} *vt* : to distribute

distrital *adj* : district, of the district

distrito *nm* : district
distrofia *nf* : dystrophy <distrofia muscular : muscular dystrophy>
disturbio *nm* : disturbance
disuadir *vt* : to dissuade, to discourage
disuasión *nf, pl* **-siones** : dissuasion
disuasorio, -ria *adj* : discouraging
disuelto *pp* → **disolver**
disyuntiva *nf* : dilemma
diurético[1], -ca *adj* : diuretic
diurético[2] *nm* : diuretic
diurno, -na *adj* : day, daytime
diva *nf* → **divo**
divagar {52} *vi* : to digress
diván *nm, pl* **divanes** : divan
divergencia *nf* : divergence, difference
divergente *adj* : divergent, differing
divergir {35} *vi* **1** : to diverge **2** : to differ, to disagree
diversidad *nf* : diversity, variety
diversificación *nf, pl* **-ciones** : diversification
diversificar {72} *vt* : to diversify
diversión *nf, pl* **-siones** ENTRETENIMIENTO : fun, amusement, diversion
diverso, -sa *adj* : diverse, various
divertido, -da *adj* **1** : amusing, funny **2** : entertaining, enjoyable
divertir {76} *vt* ENTRETENER : to amuse, to entertain — **divertirse** *vr* : to have fun, to have a good time
dividendo *nm* : dividend
dividir *vt* **1** : to divide, to split **2** : to distribute, to share out — **dividirse** *vr*
divieso *nm* : boil
divinidad *nf* : divinity
divino, -na *adj* : divine
divisa *nf* **1** : currency **2** LEMA : motto **3** : emblem, insignia
divisar *vt* : to discern, to make out
divisible *adj* : divisible
división *nf, pl* **-siones** : division
divisionismo *nm* : factionalism
divisivo, -va *adj* : divisive
divisor *nm* : denominator
divisorio, -ria *adj* : dividing
divo, -va *n* **1** : prima donna **2** : celebrity, star
divorciado[1], -da *adj* **1** : divorced **2** : split, divided
divorciado[2], -da *n* : divorcé *m*, divorcée *f*
divorciar *vt* : to divorce — **divorciarse** *vr* : to get a divorce
divorcio *nm* : divorce
divulgación *nf, pl* **-ciones** **1** : spreading, dissemination **2** : popularization
divulgar {52} *vt* **1** : to spread, to circulate **2** REVELAR : to divulge, to reveal **3** : to popularize — **divulgarse** *vr*
dizque *adv* : supposedly, apparently
dobladillar *vt* : to hem
dobladillo *nm* : hem
doblar *vt* **1** : to double **2** PLEGAR : to fold, to bend **3** : to turn <doblar la esquina : to turn the corner> **4** : to dub — *vi* **1** : to turn **2** : to toll, to ring — **doblarse** *vr* **1** : to fold up, to double over **2** : to give in, to yield
doble[1] *adj* : double — **doblemente** *adv*
doble[2] *nm* **1** : double **2** : toll (of a bell), knell
doble[3] *nmf* : stand-in, double
doblegar {52} *vt* **1** : to fold, to crease **2** : to force to yield — **doblegarse** *vr* : to yield, to bow
doblez[1] *nm, pl* **dobleces** : fold, crease
doblez[2] *nmf* : duplicity, deceitfulness
doce *adj & nm* : twelve
doceavo[1], -va *adj* : twelfth
doceavo[2] *nm* : twelfth (fraction)
docena *nf* **1** : dozen **2 docena de fraile** : baker's dozen
docencia *nf* : teaching
docente[1] *adj* : educational, teaching
docente[2] *n* : teacher, lecturer
dócil *adj* : docile — **dócilmente** *adv*
docilidad *nf* : docility
docto, -ta *adj* : learned, erudite
doctor, -tora *n* : doctor
doctorado *nm* : doctorate
doctrina *nf* : doctrine — **doctrinal** *adj*
documentación *nf, pl* **-ciones** : documentation
documental *adj & nm* : documentary
documentar *vt* : to document
documento *nm* : document
dogma *nm* : dogma
dogmático, -ca *adj* : dogmatic
dogmatismo *nm* : dogmatism
dólar *nm* : dollar
dolencia *nf* : ailment, malaise
doler {47} *vi* **1** : to hurt, to ache **2** : to grieve — **dolerse** *vr* **1** : to be distressed **2** : to complain
doliente *nmf* : mourner, bereaved
dolor *nm* **1** : pain, ache <dolor de cabeza : headache> **2** PENA, TRISTEZA : grief, sorrow
dolorido, -da *adj* **1** : sore, aching **2** : hurt, upset
doloroso, -sa *adj* **1** : painful **2** : distressing — **dolorosamente** *adv*
doloso, -sa *adj* : fraudulent — **dolosamente** *adv*
domador, -dora *n* : tamer
domar *vt* : to tame, to break in
domesticado, -da *adj* : domesticated, tame
domesticar {72} *vt* : to domesticate, to tame
doméstico, -ca *adj* : domestic, household
domiciliado, -da *adj* : residing
domiciliario, -ria *adj* **1** : home **2 arresto domiciliario** : house arrest
domiciliarse *vr* RESIDIR : to reside
domicilio *nm* : home, residence <cambio de domicilio : change of address>
dominación *nf, pl* **-ciones** : domination
dominancia *nf* : dominance
dominante *adj* **1** : dominant **2** : domineering

dominar *vt* **1 :** to dominate **2 :** to master, to be proficient at — *vi* **:** to predominate, to prevail — **dominarse** *vr* **:** to control oneself

domingo *nm* **:** Sunday

dominical *adj* **:** Sunday <periódico dominical : Sunday newspaper>

dominicano, -na *adj & n* **:** Dominican

dominio *nm* **1 :** dominion, power **2 :** mastery **3 :** domain, field

dominó *nm, pl* **-nós 1 :** domino (tile) **2 :** dominoes *pl* (game)

domo *nm* **:** dome

don[1] *nm* **1 :** gift, present **2 :** talent

don[2] *nm* **1 :** title of courtesy preceding a man's first name **2 don nadie :** nobody, insignificant person

dona *nf Mex* **:** doughnut, donut

donación *nf, pl* **-ciones :** donation

donador, -dora *n* **:** donor

donaire *nm* **1** GARBO **:** grace, poise **2 :** witticism

donante *nf* → **donador**

donar *vt* **:** to donate

donativo *nm* **:** donation

doncella *nf* **:** maiden, damsel

doncellez *nf* **:** maidenhood

donde[1] *conj* **:** where, in which <el pueblo donde vivo : the town where I live>

donde[2] *prep* **:** over by <lo encontré donde la silla : I found it over by the chair>

dónde *adv* **:** where <¿dónde está su casa? : where is your house?>

dondequiera *adv* **1 :** anywhere, no matter where **2 dondequiera que :** wherever, everywhere

doña *nf* **:** title of courtesy preceding a woman's first name

doquier *adv* **por ~ :** everywhere, all over

dorado[1], **-da** *adj* **:** gold, golden

dorado[2], **-da** *nm* **:** gilt

dorar *vt* **1 :** to gild **2 :** to brown

dormido, -da *adj* **1 :** asleep **2 :** numb <tiene el pie dormido : her foot's numb, her foot's gone to sleep>

dormilón, -lona *n* **:** sleepyhead, late riser

dormir {27} *vt* **:** to put to sleep — *vi* **:** to sleep — **dormirse** *vr* **:** to fall asleep

dormitar *vi* **:** to snooze, to doze

dormitorio *nm* **1 :** bedroom **2 :** dormitory

dorsal[1] *adj* **:** dorsal

dorsal[2] *nm* **:** number (worn in sports)

dorso *nm* **1 :** back <el dorso de la mano : the back of the hand> **2** *Mex* **:** backstroke

dos *adj & nm* **:** two

doscientos[1], **-tas** *adj* **:** two hundred

doscientos[2] *nms & pl* **:** two hundred

dosel *nm* **:** canopy

dosificación *nf, pl* **-ciones :** dosage

dosis *nfs & pl* **1 :** dose **2 :** amount, quantity

dotación *nf, pl* **-ciones 1 :** endowment, funding **2 :** staff, personnel

dotado, -da *adj* **1 :** gifted **2 ~ de :** endowed with, equipped with

dotar *vt* **1 :** to provide, to equip **2 :** to endow

dote *nf* **1 :** dowry **2 dotes** *nfpl* **:** talent, gift

doy → **dar**

draga *nf* **:** dredge

dragado *nm* **:** dredging

dragar {52} *vt* **:** to dredge

dragón *nm, pl* **dragones 1 :** dragon **2 :** snapdragon

drague, etc. → **dragar**

drama *nm* **:** drama

dramático, -ca *adj* **:** dramatic — **dramáticamente** *adv*

dramatizar {21} *vt* **:** to dramatize — **dramatización** *nf*

dramaturgo, -ga *n* **:** dramatist, playwright

drástico, -ca *adj* **:** drastic — **drásticamente** *adv*

drenaje *nm* **:** drainage

drenar *vt* **:** to drain

drene *nm Mex* **:** drain

driblar *vi* **:** to dribble (in basketball)

drible *nm* **:** dribble (in basketball)

droga *nf* **:** drug

drogadicción *nf, pl* **-ciones :** drug addiction

drogadicto, -ta *n* **:** drug addict

drogar {52} *vt* **:** to drug — **drogarse** *vr* **:** to take drugs

drogue, etc. → **drogar**

droguería *nf* FARMACIA **:** drugstore

dual *adj* **:** dual

dualidad *nf* **:** duality

dualismo *nm* **:** dualism

ducha *nf* **:** shower <darse una ducha : to take a shower>

ducharse *vr* **:** to take a shower

ducho, -cha *adj* **:** experienced, skilled, expert

ducto *nm* **1 :** duct, shaft **2 :** pipeline

duda *nf* **:** doubt <no cabe duda : there's no doubt about it>

dudar *vt* **:** to doubt — *vi* **~ en :** to hesitate to <no dudes en pedirme ayuda : don't hesitate to ask me for help>

dudoso, -sa *adj* **1 :** doubtful **2 :** dubious, questionable — **dudosamente** *adv*

duele, etc. → **doler**

duelo *nm* **1 :** duel **2** LUTO **:** mourning

duende *nm* **1 :** elf, goblin **2** ENCANTO **:** magic, charm <una bailarina que tiene duende : a dancer with a certain magic>

dueño, -na *nmf* **1 :** owner, proprietor, proprietress *f* **2 :** landlord, landlady *f*

duerme, etc. → **dormir**

dueto *nm* **:** duet

dulce[1] *adv* **:** sweetly, softly

dulce[2] *adj* **1 :** sweet **2 :** mild, gentle, mellow — **dulcemente** *adv*

dulce[3] *nm* **:** candy, sweet

dulcería *nf* : candy store

dulcificante *nm* : sweetener

dulzura *nf* **1** : sweetness **2** : gentleness, mellowness

duna *nf* : dune

dúo *nm* : duo, duet

duodécimo[1], **-ma** *adj* : twelfth

duodécimo[2], **-ma** *nm* : twelfth (in a series)

dúplex *nms & pl* : duplex apartment

duplicación *nf, pl* **-ciones** : duplication, copying

duplicado *nm* : duplicate, copy

duplicar {72} *vt* **1** : to double **2** : to duplicate, to copy

duplicidad *nf* : duplicity

duque *nm* : duke

duquesa *nf* : duchess

durabilidad *nf* : durability

durable → **duradero**

duración *nf, pl* **-ciones** : duration, length

duradero, -ra *adj* : durable, lasting

duramente *adv* **1** : harshly, severely **2** : hard

durante *prep* : during <durante todo el día : all day long> <trabajó durante tres horas : he worked for three hours>

durar *vi* : to last, to endure

durazno *nm* **1** : peach **2** : peach tree

dureza *nf* **1** : hardness, toughness **2** : severity, harshness

durmiente[1] *adj* : sleeping

durmiente[2] *nmf* : sleeper

durmió, etc. → **dormir**

duro[1] *adv* : hard <trabajé tan duro : I worked so hard>

duro[2], -ra *adj* **1** : hard, tough **2** : harsh, severe

E

e[1] *nf* : fifth letter of the Spanish alphabet

e[2] *conj* (*used instead of* **y** *before words beginning with i or hi*) : and

ebanista *nmf* : cabinetmaker

ebanistería *nf* : cabinetmaking

ébano *nm* : ebony

ebriedad *nf* EMBRIAGUEZ : inebriation, drunkenness

ebrio, -bria *adj* EMBRIAGADO : inebriated, drunk

ebullición *nf, pl* **-ciones** : boiling

eccéntrico → **excéntrico**

echar *vt* **1** LANZAR : to throw, to cast, to hurl **2** EXPULSAR : to throw out, to expel **3** EMITIR : to emit, give off **4** BROTAR : to sprout, to put forth **5** DESPEDIR : to fire, to dismiss **6** : to put in, to add **7 echar a perder** : to spoil, to ruin **8 echar de menos** : to miss <echan de menos a su madre : they miss their mother> — *vi* **1** : to start off **2 ~ a** : to begin to — **echarse** *vr* **1** : to throw oneself **2** : to lie down **3** : to put on **4 ~ a** : to start to **5 echarse a perder** : to go bad, to spoil **6 echárselas de** : to pose as

ecléctico, -ca *adj* : eclectic

eclesiástico[1], **-ca** *adj* : ecclesiastical, ecclesiastic

eclesiástico[2] *nm* CLÉRIGO : cleric, clergyman

eclipsar *vt* **1** : to eclipse **2** : to outshine, to surpass

eclipse *nm* : eclipse

eco *nm* : echo

ecografía *nf* : ultrasound scanning

ecología *nf* : ecology

ecológico, -ca *adj* : ecological — **ecológicamente** *adv*

ecologista *nmf* : ecologist, environmentalist

ecólogo, -ga *n* : ecologist

economía *nf* **1** : economy **2** : economics

económicamente *adv* : financially

económico, -ca *adj* : economic, economical

economista *nmf* : economist

economizar {21} *vt* : to save, to economize on — *vi* : to save up, to be frugal

ecosistema *nm* : ecosystem

ecuación *nf, pl* **-ciones** : equation

ecuador *nm* : equator

ecuánime *adj* **1** : even-tempered **2** : impartial

ecuanimidad *nf* **1** : equanimity **2** : impartiality

ecuatorial *adj* : equatorial

ecuatoriano, -na *adj & n* : Ecuadorian

ecuestre *adj* : equestrian

ecuménico, -ca *adj* : ecumenical

eczema *nm* : eczema

edad *nf* **1** : age <¿qué edad tiene? : how old is she?> **2** ÉPOCA, ERA : epoch, era

edema *nm* : edema

Edén *nm, pl* **Edenes** : Eden, paradise

edición *nf, pl* **-ciones** **1** : edition **2** : publication, publishing

edicto *nm* : edict, proclamation

edificación *nf, pl* **-ciones** **1** : edification **2** : construction, building

edificante *adj* : edifying

edificar {72} *vt* **1** : to edify **2** CONSTRUIR : to build, to construct

edificio *nm* : building, edifice

editar *vt* **1** : to edit **2** PUBLICAR : to publish

editor[1], **-tora** *adj* : publishing <casa editora : publishing house>

editor[2], **-tora** *n* **1** : editor **2** : publisher

editora *nf* : publisher, publishing company

editorial[1] *adj* **1** : publishing **2** : editorial

editorial[2] *nm* : editorial

editorial[3] *nf* : publishing house

editorializar {21} *vi* : to editorialize
edredón *nm, pl* **-dones** COBERTOR, COLCHA : comforter, eiderdown, quilt
educable *adj* : educable, teachable
educación *nf, pl* **-ciones 1** ENSEÑANZA : education **2** : manners *pl* — **educacional** *adj*
educado, -da *adj* : polite, well-mannered
educador, -dora *n* : educator
educando, -da *n* ALUMNO, PUPILO : pupil, student
educar {72} *vt* **1** : to educate **2** CRIAR : to bring up, to raise **3** : to train — **educarse** *vr* : to be educated
educativo, -va *adj* : educational
efectista *adj* : dramatic, sensational
efectivamente *adv* : really, actually
efectividad *nf* : effectiveness
efectivo[1], **-va** *adj* **1** : effective **2** : real, actual **3** : permanent, regular (of employment)
efectivo[2] *nm* : cash
efecto *nm* **1** : effect **2 en ~** : actually, in fact **3 efectos** *nmpl* : goods, property <efectos personales : personal effects>
efectuar {3} *vt* : to carry out, to bring about
efervescencia *nf* **1** : effervescence **2** : vivacity, high spirits *pl*
efervescente *adj* **1** : effervescent **2** : vivacious
eficacia *nf* **1** : effectiveness, efficacy **2** : efficiency
eficaz *adj, pl* **-caces 1** : effective **2** EFICIENTE : efficient — **eficazmente** *adv*
eficiencia *nf* : efficiency
eficiente *adj* EFICAZ : efficient — **eficientemente** *adv*
eficientizar {21} *vt Mex* : to streamline, to make more efficient
efigie *nf* : effigy
efímera *nf* : mayfly
efímero, -ra *adj* : ephemeral
efusión *nf, pl* **-siones 1** : effusion **2** : warmth, effusiveness **3 con ~** : effusively
efusivo, -va *adj* : effusive — **efusivamente** *adv*
egipcio, -cia *adj & n* : Egyptian
eglefino *nm* : haddock
ego *nm* : ego
egocéntrico, -ca *adj* : egocentric, self-centered
egoísmo *nm* : selfishness, egoism
egoísta[1] *adj* : selfish, egoistic
egoísta[2] *nmf* : egoist, selfish person
egotismo *nm* : egotism, conceit
egotista[1] *adj* : egotistic, egotistical, conceited
egotista[2] *nmf* : egotist, conceited person
egresado, -da *n* : graduate
egresar *vi* : to graduate
egreso *nm* **1** : graduation **2 ingresos y egresos** : income and expenditure
eje *nm* **1** : axle **2** : axis
ejecución *nf, pl* **-ciones** : execution
ejecutante *nmf* : performer
ejecutar *vt* **1** : to execute, to put to death **2** : to carry out, to perform
ejecutivo, -va *adj & n* : executive
ejecutor, -tora *n* : executor
ejemplar[1] *adj* : exemplary, model
ejemplar[2] *nm* **1** : copy (of a book, magazine, etc.) **2** : specimen, example
ejemplificar {72} *vt* : to exemplify, to illustrate
ejemplo *nm* **1** : example **2 por ~** : for example **3 dar ejemplo** : to set an example
ejercer {86} *vi* **~ de** : to practice as, to work as — *vt* **1** : to practice **2** : exercise (a right) **3** : to exert
ejercicio *nm* **1** : exercise **2** : practice
ejercitar *vt* **1** : to exercise **2** ADIESTRAR : to drill, to train
ejército *nm* : army
ejidal *adj Mex* : cooperative
ejido *nm* **1** : common land **2** *Mex* : cooperative
ejote *nm Mex* : green bean
el[1] *pron* (*referring to masculine nouns*) **1** : the one <tengo mi libro y el tuyo : I have my book and yours> <de los cantantes me gusta el de México : I prefer the singer from México> **2 el que** : he who, whoever, the one that <el que vino ayer : the one who came yesterday> <el que trabaja duro estará contento : he who works hard will be happy>
el[2], **la** *art, pl* **los, las** : the <los niños están en la casa : the boys are in the house> <me duele el pie : my foot hurts>
él *pron* : he, him <él es mi amigo : he's my friend> <hablaremos con él : we will speak with him>
elaboración *nf, pl* **-ciones 1** PRODUCCIÓN : production, making **2** : preparation, devising
elaborado, -da *adj* : elaborate
elaborar *vt* **1** : to make, to produce **2** : to devise, to draw up
elasticidad *nf* : elasticity
elástico[1], **-ca** *adj* **1** FLEXIBLE : flexible **2** : elastic
elástico[2] *nm* **1** : elastic (material) **2** : rubber band
elección *nf, pl* **-ciones 1** SELECCIÓN : choice, selection **2** : election
electivo, -va *adj* : elective
electo, -ta *adj* : elect <el presidente electo : the president-elect>
elector, -tora *n* : elector, voter
electorado *nm* : electorate
electoral *adj* : electoral, election
electricidad *nf* : electricity
electricista *nmf* : electrician
eléctrico, -ca *adj* : electric, electrical
electrificar {72} *vt* : to electrify — **electrificación** *nf*
electrizar {21} *vt* : to electrify, to thrill — **electrizante** *adj*

electrocardiógrafo *nm* : electrocardiograph
electrocardiograma *nm* : electrocardiogram
electrocutar *vt* : to electrocute — **electrocución** *nf*
electrodo *nm* : electrode
electrodoméstico *nm* : electric appliance
electroimán *nm, pl* **-manes** : electromagnet
electrólisis *nfs & pl* : electrolysis
electrolito *nm* : electrolyte
electromagnético, -ca *adj* : electromagnetic
electromagnetismo *nm* : electromagnetism
electrón *nm, pl* **-trones** : electron
electrónica *nf* : electronics
electrónico, -ca *adj* : electronic — **electrónicamente** *adv*
elefante, -ta *n* : elephant
elegancia *nf* : elegance
elegante *adj* : elegant, smart — **elegantemente** *adv*
elegía *nf* : elegy
elegíaco, -ca *adj* : elegiac
elegibilidad *nf* : eligibility
elegible *adj* : eligible
elegido, -da *adj* **1** : chosen, selected **2** : elected
elegir {28} *vt* **1** ESCOGER, SELECCIONAR : to choose, to select **2** : to elect
elemental *adj* **1** : elementary, basic **2** : fundamental, essential
elemento *nm* : element
elenco *nm* : cast (of actors)
elepé *nm* : long-playing record
elevación *nf, pl* **-ciones** : elevation, height
elevado, -da *adj* **1** : elevated, lofty **2** : high
elevador *nm* ASCENSOR : elevator
elevar *vt* **1** ALZAR : to raise, to lift **2** AUMENTAR : to raise, to increase **3** : to elevate (in a hierarchy), to promote **4** : to present, to submit — **elevarse** *vr* : to rise
elfo *nm* : elf
eliminación *nf, pl* **-ciones** : elimination, removal
eliminar *vt* **1** : to eliminate, to remove **2** : to do in, to kill
elipse *nf* : ellipse
elipsis *nf* : ellipsis
elíptico, -ca *adj* : elliptical, elliptic
elite *or* **élite** *nf* : elite
elixir *or* **elíxir** *nm* : elixir
ella *pron* : she, her <ella es mi amiga : she is my friend> <nos fuimos con ella : we left with her>
ello *pron* : it <es por ello que me voy : that's why I'm going>
ellos, ellas *pron pl* **1** : they, them **2 de ellos, de ellas** : theirs
elocución *nf, pl* **-ciones** : elocution
elocuencia *nf* : eloquence
elocuente *adj* : eloquent — **elocuentemente** *adv*
elogiar *vt* ENCOMIAR : to praise
elogio *nm* : praise
elote *nm* **1** *Mex* : corn, maize **2** *CA, Mex* : corncob
elucidación *nf, pl* **-ciones** ESCLARECIMIENTO : elucidation
elucidar *vt* ESCLARECER : to elucidate
eludir *vt* EVADIR : to evade, to avoid, to elude
emanación *nf, pl* **-ciones** : emanation
emanar *vi* **~ de** : to emanate from — *vt* : to exude
emancipar *vt* : to emancipate — **emancipación** *nf*
embadurnar *vt* EMBARRAR : to smear, to daub
embajada *nf* : embassy
embajador, -dora *n* : ambassador
embalaje *nm* : packing, packaging
embalar *vt* EMPAQUETAR : to pack
embaldosar *vt* : to tile, to pave with tiles
embalsamar *vt* : to embalm
embalsar *vt* : to dam, to dam up
embalse *nm* : dam, reservoir
embarazada *adj* ENCINTA, PREÑADA : pregnant, expecting
embarazar {21} *vt* **1** : to obstruct, to hamper **2** PREÑAR : to make pregnant
embarazo *nm* : pregnancy
embarazoso, -sa *adj* : embarrassing, awkward
embarcación *nf, pl* **-ciones** : boat, craft
embarcadero *nm* : wharf, pier, jetty
embarcar {72} *vi* : to embark, to board — *vt* : to load
embarco *nm* : embarkation
embargar {52} *vt* **1** : to seize, to impound **2** : to overwhelm
embargo *nm* **1** : seizure **2** : embargo **3 sin ~** : however, nevertheless
embarque *nm* **1** : embarkation **2** : shipment
embarrancar {72} *vi* **1** : to run aground **2** : to get bogged down
embarrar *vt* **1** : to cover with mud **2** EMBADURNAR : to smear
embarullar *vt fam* : to muddle, to confuse — **embarullarse** *vr fam* : to get mixed up
embate *nm* **1** : onslaught **2** : battering (of waves or wind)
embaucador, -dora *n* : swindler, deceiver
embaucar {72} *vt* : to trick, to swindle
embeber *vt* : to absorb, to soak up — *vi* : to shrink
embelesado, -da *adj* : spellbound
embelesar *vt* : to enchant, to captivate
embellecer {53} *vt* : to embellish, to beautify
embellecimiento *nm* : beautification, embellishment
embestida *nf* **1** : charge (of a bull) **2** ARREMETIDA : attack, onslaught
embestir {54} *vt* : to hit, to run into, to charge at — *vi* ARREMETER : to charge, to attack

emblanquecer {53} *vt* BLANQUEAR **:** to bleach, to whiten — **emblanquecerse** *vr* **:** to turn white

emblema *nm* **:** emblem

emblemático, -ca *adj* **:** emblematic

embolia *nf* **:** embolism

émbolo *nm* **:** piston

embolsarse *vr* **1 :** to pocket (money) **2 :** to collect (payment)

emborracharse *vr* EMBRIAGARSE **:** to get drunk

emborronar *vt* **1 :** to blot, to smudge **2** GARABATEAR **:** to scribble

emboscada *nf* **:** ambush

emboscar {72} *vt* **:** to ambush — **emboscarse** *vr* **:** to lie in ambush

embotadura *nf* **:** bluntness, dullness

embotar *vt* **1 :** to dull, to blunt **2 :** to weaken, to enervate

embotellamiento *nm* ATASCO **:** traffic jam

embotellar *vt* ENVASAR **:** to bottle

embragar {52} *vi* **:** to engage the clutch

embrague *nm* **:** clutch

embravecerse {53} *vr* **1 :** to get furious **2 :** to get rough <el mar se embraveció : the sea became tempestuous>

embriagado, -da *adj* **:** inebriated, drunk

embriagador, -dora *adj* **:** intoxicating

embriagarse {52} *vr* EMBORRACHARSE **:** to get drunk

embriaguez *nf* EBRIEDAD **:** drunkenness, inebriation

embrión *nm, pl* **embriones :** embryo

embrionario, -ria *adj* **:** embryonic

embrollo *nm* ENREDO **:** imbroglio, confusion

embrujar *vt* HECHIZAR **:** to bewitch

embrujo *nm* **:** spell, curse

embudo *nm* **:** funnel

embuste *nm* **1** MENTIRA **:** lie, fib **2** ENGAÑO **:** trick, hoax

embustero[1], -ra *adj* **:** lying, deceitful

embustero[2], -ra *n* **:** liar, cheat

embutido *nm* **1 :** sausage **2 :** inlaid work

embutir *vt* **1 :** to cram, to stuff, to jam **2 :** to inlay

emergencia *nf* **1 :** emergency **2 :** emergence

emergente *adj* **1 :** emergent **2 :** consequent, resultant

emerger {15} *vi* **:** to emerge, to surface

emético[1], -ca *adj* **:** emetic

emético[2] *nm* **:** emetic

emigración *nf, pl* **-ciones 1 :** emigration **2 :** migration

emigrante *adj & nmf* **:** emigrant

emigrar *vi* **1 :** to emigrate **2 :** to migrate

eminencia *nf* **:** eminence

eminente *adj* **:** eminent, distinguished

eminentemente *adv* **:** basically, essentially

emisario[1], -ria *n* **:** emissary

emisario[2] *nm* **:** outlet (of a body of water)

emisión *nf, pl* **-siones 1 :** emission **2 :** broadcast **3 :** issue <emisión de acciones : stock issue>

emisor *nm* TRANSMISOR **:** television or radio transmitter

emisora *nf* **:** radio station

emitir *vt* **1 :** to emit, to give off **2 :** to broadcast **3 :** to issue **4 :** to cast (a vote)

emoción *nf, pl* **-ciones :** emotion — **emocional** *adj* — **emocionalmente** *adv*

emocionado, -da *adj* **1 :** moved, affected by emotion **2** ENTUSIASMADO **:** excited

emocionante *adj* **1** CONMOVEDOR **:** moving, touching **2** EXCITANTE **:** exciting, thrilling

emocionar *vt* **1** CONMOVER **:** to move, to touch **2 :** to excite, to thrill — **emocionarse** *vr*

emotivo, -va *adj* **:** emotional, moving

empacador, -dora *n* **:** packer

empacar {72} *vt* **1** EMPAQUETAR **:** to pack **2 :** to bale — *vi* **:** to pack — **empacarse** *vr* **1 :** to balk, to refuse to budge **2** *Col, Mex fam* **:** to eat ravenously, to devour

empachar *vt* **1** ESTORBAR **:** to obstruct **2 :** to give indigestion to **3** DISFRAZAR **:** to disguise, to mask — **empacharse** *vr* **1** INDIGESTARSE **:** to get indigestion **2** AVERGONZARSE **:** to be embarrassed

empacho *nm* **1** INDIGESTIÓN **:** indigestion **2** VERGÜENZA **:** embarrassment **3 no tener empacho en :** to have no qualms about

empadronarse *vr* **:** to register to vote

empalagar {52} *vt* **1 :** to cloy, to surfeit **2** FASTIDIAR **:** to annoy, to bother

empalagoso, -sa *adj* MELOSO **:** cloying, excessively sweet

empalar *vt* **:** to impale

empalizada *nf* **:** palisade (fence)

empalmar *vt* **1 :** to splice, to link **2 :** to combine — *vi* **:** to meet, to converge

empalme *nm* **1** CONEXIÓN **:** connection, link **2 :** junction

empanada *nf* **:** pie, turnover

empanadilla *nf* **:** meat or seafood pie

empanar *vt* **:** to bread

empantanado, -da *adj* **:** bogged down, delayed

empañar *vt* **1 :** to steam up **2 :** to tarnish, to sully

empapado, -da *adj* **:** soggy, sodden

empapar *vt* MOJAR **:** to soak, to drench — **empaparse** *vr* **1 :** to get soaking wet **2 ~ de :** to absorb, to be imbued with

empapelar *vt* **:** to wallpaper

empaque *nm fam* **1 :** presence, bearing **2 :** pomposity **3** DESCARO **:** impudence, nerve

empaquetar *vt* EMBALAR **:** to pack, to package — **empaquetarse** *vr fam* **:** to dress up

emparedado *nm* : sandwich
emparedar *vt* : to wall in, to confine
emparejar *vt* **1** : to pair, to match up **2** : to make even — *vi* : to catch up — **emparejarse** *vr* : to pair up
emparentado, -da *adj* : related
emparentar {55} *vi* : to become related by marriage
emparrillado *nm Mex* : gridiron (in football)
empastar *vt* **1** : to fill (a tooth) **2** : to bind (a book)
empaste *nm* : filling (of a tooth)
empatar *vt* : to tie, to connect — *vi* : to result in a draw, to be tied — **empatarse** *vr Ven* : to hook up, to link together
empate *nm* : draw, tie
empatía *nf* : empathy
empecinado, -da *adj* TERCO : stubborn
empecinarse *vr* OBSTINARSE : to be stubborn, to persist
empedernido, -da *adj* INCORREGIBLE : hardened, inveterate
empedrado *nm* : paving, pavement
empedrar {55} *vt* : to pave (with stones)
empeine *nm* : instep
empellón *nm, pl* **-llones** : shove, push
empelotado, -da *adj* **1** *Mex fam* : madly in love **2** *fam* : stark naked
empeñado, -da *adj* : determined, committed
empeñar *vt* **1** : to pawn **2** : to pledge, to give (one's word) — **empeñarse** *vr* **1** : to insist stubbornly **2** : to make an effort
empeño *nm* **1** : pledge, commitment **2** : insistence **3** ESFUERZO : effort, determination **4** : pawning <casa de empeños : pawnshop>
empeoramiento *nm* : worsening, deterioration
empeorar *vi* : to deteriorate, to get worse — *vt* : to make worse
empequeñecer {53} *vi* : to diminish, to become smaller — *vt* : to minimize, to make smaller
emperador *nm* : emperor
emperatriz *nf, pl* **-trices** : empress
empero *conj* : however, nevertheless
empezar {29} *v* COMENZAR : to start, to begin
empinado, -da *adj* : steep
empinar *vt* ELEVAR : to lift, to raise — **empinarse** *vr* : to stand on tiptoe
empírico, -ca *adj* : empirical — **empíricamente** *adv*
emplasto *nm* : poultice, dressing
emplazamiento *nm* **1** : location, site **2** CITACIÓN : summons, subpoena
emplazar {21} *vt* **1** CONVOCAR : to convene, to summon **2** : to subpoena **3** UBICAR : to place, to position
empleado, -da *n* : employee
empleador, -dora *n* PATRÓN : employer
emplear *vt* **1** : to employ **2** USAR : to use — **emplearse** *vr* **1** : to get a job **2** : to occupy oneself
empleo *nm* **1** OCUPACIÓN : employment, occupation, job **2** : use, usage
empobrecer {53} *vt* : to impoverish — *vi* : to become poor — **empobrecerse** *vr*
empobrecimiento *nm* : impoverishment
empollar *vi* : to brood eggs — *vt* : to incubate
empolvado, -da *adj* **1** : dusty **2** : powdered, powdery
empolvar *vt* **1** : to cover with dust **2** : to powder — **empolvarse** *vr* **1** : to gather dust **2** : to powder one's face
emporio *nm* **1** : center, capital, empire <un emporio cultural : a cultural center> <un emporio financiero : a financial empire> **2** : department store
empotrado, -da *adj* : built-in <armarios empotrados : built-in cabinets>
empotrar *vt* : to build into, to embed
emprendedor, -dora *adj* : enterprising
emprender *vt* : to undertake, to begin
empresa *nf* **1** COMPAÑÍA, FIRMA : company, corporation, firm **2** : undertaking, venture
empresariado *nm* **1** : business world **2** : management, managers *pl*
empresarial *adj* : business, managerial, corporate
empresario, -ria *n* **1** : manager **2** : businessman *m*, businesswoman *f* **3** : impresario
empujar *vi* : to push, to shove — *vt* **1** : to push **2** PRESIONAR : to spur on, to press
empuje *nm* : impetus, drive
empujón *nm, pl* **-jones** : push, shove
empuñadura *nf* MANGO : hilt, handle
empuñar *vt* **1** ASIR : to grasp **2 empuñar las armas** : to take up arms
emú *nm* : emu
emular *vt* IMITAR : to emulate — **emulación** *nf*
emulsión *nf, pl* **-siones** : emulsion
emulsionante *nm* : emulsifier
emulsionar *vt* : to emulsify
en *prep* **1** : in <en el bolsillo : in one's pocket> <en una semana : in a week> **2** : on <en la mesa : on the table> **3** : at <en casa : at home> <en el trabajo : at work> <en ese momento : at that moment>
enagua *nf* : petticoat, slip
enajenación *nf, pl* **-ciones** **1** : transfer (of property) **2** : alienation **3** : absentmindedness
enajenado, -da *adj* : out of one's mind
enajenar *vt* **1** : to transfer (property) **2** : to alienate **3** : to enrapture — **enajenarse** *vr* **1** : to become estranged **2** : to go mad
enaltecer {53} *vt* : to praise, to extol
enamorado[1], -da *adj* : in love
enamorado[2], -da *n* : lover, sweetheart
enamoramiento *nm* : infatuation, crush

enamorar *vt* : to enamor, to win the love of — **enamorarse** *vr* : to fall in love
enamoriscarse {72} *vr fam* : to have a crush, to be infatuated
enamorizado, -da *adj* : amorous, passionate
enano[1], **-na** *adj* : tiny, minute
enano[2], **-na** *n* : dwarf, midget
enarbolar *vt* **1** : to hoist, to raise **2** : to brandish
enarcar {72} *vt* : to arch, to raise
enardecer {53} *vt* **1** : to arouse (anger, passions) **2** : to stir up, to excite — **enardecerse** *vr*
encabezado *nm Mex* : headline
encabezamiento *nm* **1** : heading **2** : salutation, opening
encabezar {21} *vt* **1** : to head, to lead **2** : to put a heading on
encabritarse *vr* **1** : to rear up **2** *fam* : to get angry
encadenar *vt* **1** : to chain **2** : to connect, to link **3** INMOVILIZAR : to immobilize
encajar *vi* : to fit, to fit together, to fit in — *vt* **1** : to insert, to stick **2** : to take, to cope with <encajó el golpe : he withstood the blow>
encaje *nm* **1** : lace **2** : financial reserve
encajonar *vt* **1** : to box, to crate **2** : to cram in
encalar *vt* : to whitewash
encallar *vi* **1** : to run aground **2** : to get stuck
encallecido, -da *adj* : callused
encamar *vt* : to confine to a bed
encaminado, -da *adj* **1** : on the right track **2** ~ **a** : aimed at, designed to
encaminar *vt* **1** : to direct, to channel **2** : to head in the right direction — **encaminarse** *vr* ~ **a** : to head for, to aim at
encandilar *vt* : to dazzle
encanecer {53} *vi* : to gray, to go gray
encantado, -da *adj* **1** : charmed, bewitched **2** : delighted
encantador[1], **-dora** *adj* : charming, delightful
encantador[2], **-dora** *n* : magician
encantamiento *nm* : enchantment, spell
encantar *vt* **1** : to enchant, to bewitch **2** : to charm, to delight <me encanta esta canción : I love this song>
encanto *nm* **1** : charm, fascination **2** HECHIZO : spell **3** : delightful person or thing
encañonar *vt* : to point (a gun) at, to hold up
encapotado, -da *adj* : cloudy, overcast
encapotarse *vr* : to cloud over, to become overcast
encaprichado, -da *adj* : infatuated
encaprichamiento *nm* : infatuation
encapuchado, -da *adj* : hooded
encarado, -da *adj* **estar mal encarado** *fam* : to be ugly-looking, to look mean
encaramar *vt* : to raise, to lift up — **encaramarse** *vr* : to perch
encarar *vt* CONFRONTAR : to face, to confront
encarcelación *nf* → **encarcelamiento**
encarcelamiento *nm* : incarceration, imprisonment
encarcelar *vt* : to incarcerate, to imprison
encarecer {53} *vt* **1** : to increase, to raise (price, value) **2** : to beseech, to entreat — **encarecerse** *vr* : to become more expensive
encarecidamente *adv* : insistently, urgently
encarecimiento *nm* : increase, rise (in price)
encargado[1], **-da** *adj* : in charge
encargado[2], **-da** *n* : manager, person in charge
encargar {52} *vt* **1** : to put in charge of **2** : to recommend, to advise **3** : to order, to request — **encargarse** *vr* ~ **de** : to take charge of
encargo *nm* **1** : errand **2** : job assignment **3** : order <hecho de encargo : custom-made, made to order>
encariñarse *vr* ~ **con** : to become fond of, to grow attached to
encarnación *nf, pl* **-ciones** : incarnation, embodiment
encarnado[1], **-da** *adj* **1** : incarnate **2** : flesh-colored **3** : red **4** : ingrown
encarnado[2] *nm* : red
encarnar *vt* : to incarnate, to embody — **encarnarse** *vr* **encarnarse una uña** : to have an ingrown nail
encarnizado, -da *adj* **1** : bloodshot, inflamed **2** : fierce, bloody
encarnizar {21} *vt* : to enrage, to infuriate — **encarnizarse** *vr* : to be brutal, to attack viciously
encarrilar *vt* : to guide, to put on the right track
encasillar *vt* CLASIFICAR : to classify, to pigeonhole, to categorize
encausar *vt* : to prosecute, to charge
encauzar {21} *vt* : to channel, to guide — **encauzarse** *vr*
encebollado, -da *adj* : cooked with onions
encefalitis *nms & pl* : encephalitis
encendedor *nm* : lighter
encender {56} *vi* : to light — *vt* **1** : to light, to set fire to **2** PRENDER : to switch on **3** : to start (a motor) **4** : to arouse, to kindle — **encenderse** *vr* **1** : to get excited **2** : to blush
encendido[1], **-da** *adj* **1** : burning **2** : flushed **3** : fiery, passionate
encendido[2] *nm* : ignition
encerado *nm* **1** : waxing, polishing **2** : blackboard
encerar *vt* : to wax, to polish
encerrar {55} *vt* **1** : to lock up, to shut away **2** : to contain, to include **3** : to involve, to entail
encerrona *nf* **1** TRAMPA : trap, setup **2** **prepararle una encerrona a alguien**

: to set a trap for someone, to set someone up

encestar *vi* : to make a basket (in basketball)

enchapado *nm* : plating, coating (of metal)

encharcamiento *nm* : flood, flooding

encharcar {72} *vt* : to flood, to swamp — **encharcarse** *vr*

enchilada *nf* : enchilada

enchilar *vt Mex* : to season with chili

enchuecar {72} *vt Chile, Mex fam* : to make crooked, to twist

enchufar *vt* **1** : to plug in **2** : to connect, to fit together

enchufe *nm* **1** : connection **2** : plug, socket

encía *nf* : gum (tissue)

encíclica *nf* : encyclical

enciclopedia *nf* : encyclopedia

enciclopédico, -ca *adj* : encyclopedic

encierro *nm* **1** : confinement **2** : enclosure

encima *adv* **1** : on top, above **2** ADEMÁS : as well, besides **3 ~ de** : on, on top of, over **4 por encima de** : above, beyond <por encima de la ley : above the law> **5 echarse encima** : to take upon oneself **6 estar encima de** *fam* : to nag, to criticize **7 quitarse de encima** : to get rid of

encina *nf* : evergreen oak

encinta *adj* EMBARAZADA, PREÑADA : pregnant, expecting

enclaustrado, -da *adj* : cloistered, shut away

enclavado, -da *adj* : buried

enclenque *adj* : weak, sickly

encoger {15} *vt* **1** : to shrink, to make smaller **2** : to intimidate — *vi* : to shrink, to contract — **encogerse** *vr* **1** : to shrink **2** : to be intimidated, to cower, to cringe **3 encogerse de hombros** : to shrug <one's shoulders>

encogido, -da *adj* **1** : shriveled, shrunken **2** TÍMIDO : shy, inhibited

encogimiento *nm* **1** : shrinking, shrinkage **2** : shrug **3** TIMIDEZ : shyness

encolar *vt* : to paste, to glue

encolerizar {21} *vt* ENFURECER : to enrage, to infuriate — **encolerizarse** *vr*

encomendar {55} *vt* CONFIAR : to entrust, to commend — **encomendarse** *vr*

encomiable *adj* : commendable, praiseworthy

encomiar *vt* ELOGIAR : to praise, to pay tribute to

encomienda *nf* **1** : charge, mission **2** : royal land grant **3** : parcel

encomio *nm* : praise, eulogy

encomioso, -sa *adj* : eulogistic, laudatory

enconar *vt* **1** : to irritate, to anger **2** : to inflame — **enconarse** *vr* **1** : to become heated **2** : to fester

encono *nm* **1** RENCOR : animosity, rancor **2** : inflamation, infection

encontrado, -da *adj* : contrary, opposing

encontrar {19} *vt* **1** HALLAR : to find **2** : to encounter, to meet — **encontrarse** *vr* **1** REUNIRSE : to meet **2** : to clash, to conflict **3** : to be <su abuelo se encuentra mejor : her grandfather is doing better>

encorvar *vt* : to bend, to curve — **encorvarse** *vr* : to hunch over, to stoop

encrespar *vt* **1** : to curl, to ruffle, to ripple **2** : to annoy, to irritate — **encresparse** *vr* **1** : to curl one's hair **2** : to become choppy **3** : to get annoyed

encrucijada *nf* : crossroads

encuadernación *nf, pl* **-ciones** : bookbinding

encuadernar *vt* EMPASTAR : to bind (a book)

encuadrar *vt* **1** ENMARCAR : to frame **2** ENCAJAR : to fit, to insert **3** COMPRENDER : to contain, to include

encubierto *pp* → **encubrir**

encubrimiento *nm* : cover-up

encubrir {2} *vt* : to cover up, to conceal

encuentro *nm* **1** : meeting, encounter **2** : conference, congress

encuerado, -da *adj fam* : naked

encuerar *vt fam* : to undress

encuesta *nf* **1** INVESTIGACIÓN, PESQUISA : inquiry, investigation **2** SONDEO : survey

encuestador, -dora *n* : pollster

encuestar *vt* : to poll, to take a survey of

encumbrado, -da *adj* **1** : lofty, high **2** : eminent, distinguished

encumbrar *vt* **1** : to exalt, to elevate **2** : to extol — **encumbrarse** *vr* : to reach the top

encurtir *vt* ESCABECHAR : to pickle

ende *adv* **por ~** : therefore, consequently

endeble *adj* : feeble, weak

endeblez *nf* : weakness, frailty

endémico, -ca *adj* : endemic

endemoniado, -da *adj* : fiendish, diabolical

endentecer {53} *vi* : to teethe

enderezar {21} *vt* **1** : to straighten (out) **2** : to stand on end, to put upright

endeudado, -da *adj* : in debt, indebted

endeudamiento *nm* : indebtedness

endeudarse *vr* **1** : to go into debt **2** : to feel obliged

endiabladamente *adv* : extremely, diabolically

endiablado, -da *adj* **1** : devilish, diabolical **2** : complicated, difficult

endibia *or* **endivia** *nm* : endive

endilgar {52} *vt fam* : to spring, to foist <me endilgó la responsabilidad : he saddled me with the responsibility>

endocrino, -na *adj* : endocrine

endogamia *nf* : inbreeding

endosar *vt* : to endorse
endoso *nm* : endorsement
endulzante *nm* : sweetener
endulzar {21} *vt* **1** : to sweeten **2** : to soften, to mellow — **endulzarse** *vr*
endurecer {53} *vt* : to harden, to toughen — **endurecerse** *vr*
enebro *nm* : juniper
eneldo *nm* : dill
enema *nm* : enema
enemigo, -ga *adj & n* : enemy
enemistad *nf* : enmity, hostility
enemistar *vt* : to make enemies of — **enemistarse** *vr* **~ con** : to fall out with
energía *nf* : energy
enérgico, -ca *adj* **1** : energetic, vigorous **2** : forceful, emphatic — **enérgicamente** *adv*
energúmeno, -na *n fam* : lunatic, crazy person
enero *nm* : January
enervar *vt* **1** : to enervate **2** *fam* : to annoy, to get on one's nerves — **enervante** *adj*
enésimo, -ma *adj* : umpteenth, nth
enfadar *vt* **1** : to annoy, to make angry **2** *Mex fam* : to bore — **enfadarse** *vr* : to get angry, to get annoyed
enfado *nm* : anger, annoyance
enfadoso, -sa *adj* : irritating, annoying
enfardar *vt* : to bale
énfasis *nms & pl* : emphasis
enfático, -ca *adj* : emphatic — **enfáticamente** *adv*
enfatizar {21} *vt* DESTACAR, SUBRAYAR : to emphasize
enfermar *vt* : to make sick — *vi* : to fall ill, to get sick — **enfermarse** *vr*
enfermedad *nf* **1** INDISPOSICIÓN : sickness, illness **2** : disease
enfermería *nf* : infirmary
enfermero, -ra *n* : nurse
enfermizo, -za *adj* : sickly
enfermo[1], **-ma** *adj* : sick, ill
enfermo[2], **-ma** *n* **1** : sick person, invalid **2** PACIENTE : patient
enfilar *vt* **1** : to take, to go along <enfiló la carretera de Montevideo : she went up the road to Montevideo> **2** : to line up, to put in a row **3** : to string, to thread **4** : to aim, to direct — *vi* : to make one's way
enflaquecer {53} *vi* : to lose weight, to become thin — *vt* : to emaciate
enfocar {72} *vt* **1** : to focus (on) **2** : to consider, to look at
enfoque *nm* : focus
enfrascamiento *nm* : immersion, absorption
enfrascarse {72} *vr* **~ en** : to immerse oneself in, to get caught up in
enfrentamiento *nm* : clash, confrontation
enfrentar *vt* : to confront, to face — **enfrentarse** *vr* **1 ~ con** : to clash with **2 ~ a** : to face up to
enfrente *adv* **1** DELANTE : in front **2** : opposite
enfriamiento *nm* **1** CATARRO : chill, cold **2** : cooling off, damper
enfriar {85} *vt* **1** : to chill, to cool **2** : to cool down, to dampen — *vi* : to get cold — **enfriarse** *vr* : to get chilled, to catch a cold
enfundar *vt* : to sheathe, to encase
enfurecer {53} *vt* ENCOLERIZAR : to infuriate — **enfurecerse** *vr* : to fly into a rage
enfurecido, -da *adj* : furious, raging
enfurruñarse *vr fam* : to sulk
engalanar *vt* : to decorate, to deck out — **engalanarse** *vr* : to dress up
enganchar *vt* **1** : to hook, to snag **2** : to attach, to hitch up — **engancharse** *vr* **1** : to get snagged, to get hooked **2** : to enlist
enganche *nm* **1** : hook **2** : coupling, hitch **3** *Mex* : down payment
engañar *vt* **1** EMBAUCAR : to trick, to deceive, to mislead **2** : to cheat on, to be unfaithful to — **engañarse** *vr* **1** : to be mistaken **2** : to deceive oneself
engaño *nm* **1** : deception, trick **2** : fake, feint (in sports)
engañoso, -sa *adj* **1** : deceitful **2** : misleading, deceptive
engarrotarse *vr* : to stiffen up, to go numb
engatusamiento *nm* : cajolery
engatusar *vt* : to coax, to cajole
engendrar *vt* **1** : to beget, to father **2** : to give rise to, to engender
engentarse *vr Mex* : to be in a daze
englobar *vt* : to include, to embrace
engomar *vt* : to glue
engordar *vt* : to fatten, to fatten up — *vi* : to gain weight
engorro *nm* : nuisance, bother
engorroso, -sa *adj* : bothersome
engranaje *nm* : gears *pl,* cogs *pl*
engranar *vt* : to mesh, to engage — *vi* : to mesh gears
engrandecer {53} *vt* **1** : to enlarge **2** : to exaggerate **3** : to exalt
engrandecimiento *nm* **1** : enlargement **2** : exaggeration **3** : exaltation
engrane *nm Mex* : cogwheel
engrapadora *nf* : stapler
engrapar *vt* : to staple
engrasar *vt* : to grease, to lubricate
engrase *nm* : greasing, lubrication
engreído, -da *adj* PRESUMIDO, VANIDOSO : vain, conceited, stuck-up
engreimiento *nm* ARROGANCIA : arrogance, conceit
engreír {66} *vt* ENVANECER : to make vain — **engreírse** *vr* : to become conceited
engrosar {19} *vt* : to enlarge, to increase, to swell — *vi* ENGORDAR : to gain weight
engrudo *nm* : paste
engullir {38} *vt* : to gulp down, to gobble up — **engullirse** *vr*
enharinar *vt* : to flour
enhebrar *vt* ENSARTAR : to string, to thread

enhiesto, -ta *adj* **1 :** erect, upright **2 :** lofty, towering
enhilar *vt* **:** to thread (a needle, etc.)
enhorabuena *nf* FELICIDADES **:** congratulations *pl*
enigma *nm* **:** enigma, mystery
enigmático, -ca *adj* **:** enigmatic — **enigmáticamente** *adv*
enjabonar *vt* **:** to soap up, to lather — **enjabonarse** *vr*
enjaezar {21} *vt* **:** to harness
enjalbegar {52} *vt* **:** to whitewash
enjambrar *vi* **:** to swarm
enjambre *nm* **1 :** swarm **2** MUCHEDUMBRE **:** crowd, mob
enjaular *vt* **1 :** to cage **2** *fam* **:** to jail, to lock up
enjuagar {52} *vt* **:** to rinse — **enjuagarse** *vr* **:** to rinse out
enjuague *nm* **1 :** rinse **2 enjuague bucal :** mouthwash
enjugar {52} *vt* **:** to wipe away (tears)
enjuiciar *vt* **1 :** to indict, to prosecute **2** JUZGAR **:** to try
enjundioso, -sa *adj* **:** substantial, weighty
enjuto, -ta *adj* **:** lean, gaunt
enlace *nm* **1 :** bond, link, connection **2 :** liaison
enladrillado *nm* **:** brick paving
enladrillar *vt* **:** to pave with bricks
enlatar *vt* ENVASAR **:** to can
enlazar {21} *v* **:** to join, to link, to fit together
enlistar *vt* **:** to list — **enlistarse** *vr* **:** to enlist
enlodado, -da *adj* BARROSO **:** muddy
enlodar *vt* **1 :** to cover with mud **2 :** to stain, to sully — **enlodarse** *vr*
enlodazar → **enlodar**
enloquecedor, -dora *adj* **:** maddening
enloquecer {53} *vt* ALOCAR **:** to drive crazy — **enloquecerse** *vr* **:** to go crazy
enlosado *nm* **:** flagstone pavement
enlosar *vt* **:** to pave with flagstone
enlutarse *vr* **:** to go into mourning
enmaderado *nm* **1 :** wood paneling **2 :** hardwood floor
enmarañar *vt* **1 :** to tangle **2 :** to complicate **3 :** to confuse, to mix up — **enmarañarse** *vr*
enmarcar {72} *vt* **1** ENCUADRAR **:** to frame **2 :** to provide the setting for
enmascarar *vt* **:** to mask, to disguise
enmasillar *vt* **:** to putty, to caulk
enmendar {55} *vt* **1 :** to amend **2** CORREGIR **:** to emend, to correct **3** COMPENSAR **:** to compensate for — **enmendarse** *vr* **:** to mend one's ways
enmienda *nf* **1 :** amendment **2 :** correction, emendation
enmohecerse {53} *vr* **1 :** to become moldy **2** OXIDARSE **:** to rust, to become rusty
enmudecer {53} *vt* **:** to mute, to silence — *vi* **:** to fall silent
enmugrar *vt* **:** to soil, to make dirty — **enmugrarse** *vr* **:** to get dirty
ennegrecer {53} *vt* **:** to blacken, to darken — **ennegrecerse** *vr*
ennoblecer {53} *vt* **1 :** to ennoble **2 :** to embellish
enojadizo, -za *adj* IRRITABLE **:** irritable, cranky
enojado, -da *adj* **1 :** annoyed **2 :** angry, mad
enojar *vt* **1 :** to anger **2 :** to annoy, to upset — **enojarse** *vr*
enojo *nm* **1** CÓLERA **:** anger **2 :** annoyance
enojón, -jona *adj, pl* **-jones** *Chile, Mex fam* **:** irritable, cranky
enojoso, -sa *adj* FASTIDIOSO, MOLESTOSO **:** annoying, irritating
enorgullecer {53} *vt* **:** to make proud — **enorgullecerse** *vr* **:** to pride oneself
enorme *adj* INMENSO **:** enormous, huge — **enormemente** *adv*
enormidad *nf* **1 :** enormity, seriousness **2 :** immensity, hugeness
enraizado, -da *adj* **:** deep-seated, deeply rooted
enraizar {30} *vi* **:** to take root
enramada *nf* **:** arbor, bower
enramar *vt* **:** to cover with branches
enrarecer {53} *vt* **:** to rarefy — **enrarecerse** *vr*
enredadera *nf* **:** climbing plant, vine
enredar *vt* **1 :** to tangle up, to entangle **2 :** to confuse, to complicate **3 :** to involve, to implicate — **enredarse** *vr*
enredo *nm* **1** EMBROLLO **:** muddle, confusion **2** MARAÑA **:** tangle
enredoso, -sa *adj* **:** complicated, tricky
enrejado *nm* **1 :** railing **2 :** grating, grille **3 :** trellis, lattice
enrevesado, -da *adj* **:** complicated, involved
enriquecer {53} *vt* **:** to enrich — **enriquecerse** *vr* **:** to get rich
enriquecido, -da *adj* **:** enriched
enriquecimiento *nm* **:** enrichment
enrojecer {53} *vt* **:** to make red, to redden — **enrojecerse** *vr* **:** to blush
enrolar *vt* RECLUTAR **:** to recruit — **enrolarse** *vr* INSCRIBIRSE **:** to enlist, to sign up
enrollar *vt* **:** to roll up, to coil — **enrollarse** *vr*
enronquecerse {53} *vr* **:** to become hoarse
enroscar {72} *vt* TORCER **:** to twist — **enroscarse** *vr* **:** to coil, to twine
ensacar {72} *vt* **:** to bag (up)
ensalada *nf* **:** salad
ensaladera *nf* **:** salad bowl
ensalmo *nm* **:** incantation, spell
ensalzar {21} *vt* **1 :** to praise, to extol **2** EXALTAR **:** to exalt
ensamblaje *nm* **:** assembly
ensamblar *vt* **1 :** to assemble **2 :** to join, to fit together
ensanchar *vt* **1 :** to widen **2 :** to expand, to extend — **ensancharse** *vr*
ensanche *nm* **1 :** widening **2 :** expansion, development

ensangrentado, -da *adj* **:** bloody, bloodstained
ensañarse *vr* **:** to act cruelly, to be merciless
ensartar *vt* **1** ENHEBRAR **:** to string, to thread **2 :** to skewer, to pierce
ensayar *vi* **:** to rehearse — *vt* **1 :** to try out, to test **2 :** to assay
ensayista *nmf* **:** essayist
ensayo *nm* **1 :** essay **2 :** trial, test **3 :** rehearsal **4 :** assay (of metals)
enseguida *adv* INMEDIATAMENTE **:** right away, immediately, at once
ensenada *nf* **:** cove, inlet
enseña *nf* **1** INSIGNIA **:** emblem, insignia **2 :** standard, banner
enseñanza *nf* **1** EDUCACIÓN **:** education **2 :** teaching
enseñar *vt* **1 :** to teach **2** MOSTRAR **:** to show, to display — **enseñarse** *vr* **~ a :** to learn to, to get used to
enseres *nmpl* **:** equipment, furnishings *pl* <enseres domésticos : household goods>
ensillar *vt* **:** to saddle (up)
ensimismado, -da *adj* **:** absorbed, engrossed
ensimismarse *vr* **:** to lose oneself in thought
ensoberbecerse {53} *vr* **:** to become haughty
ensombrecer {53} *vt* **:** to cast a shadow over, to darken — **ensombrecerse** *vr*
ensoñación *nf, pl* **-ciones :** fantasy
ensopar *vt* **1 :** to drench **2 :** to dunk, to dip
ensordecedor, -dora *adj* **:** deafening, thunderous
ensordecer {53} *vt* **:** to deafen — *vi* **:** to go deaf
ensuciar *vt* **:** to soil, to dirty — **ensuciarse** *vr*
ensueño *nm* **1 :** daydream, revery **2** FANTASÍA **:** illusion, fantasy
entablar *vt* **1 :** to cover with boards **2 :** to initiate, to enter into, to start
entallar *vt* AJUSTAR **:** to tailor, to fit, to take in — *vi* QUEDAR **:** to fit
ente *nm* **1 :** being, entity **2 :** body, organization <ente rector : ruling body> **3** *fam* **:** eccentric, crackpot
enteco, -ca *adj* **:** gaunt, frail
entenado, -da *n Mex* **:** stepchild, stepson *m,* stepdaughter *f*
entender[1] {56} *vt* **1** COMPRENDER **:** to understand **2** OPINAR **:** to think, to believe **3** QUERER **:** to mean, to intend **4** DEDUCIR **:** to infer, to deduce — *vi* **1 :** to understand <¡ya entiendo! : now I understand!> **2 ~ de :** to know about, to be good at **3 ~ en :** to be in charge of — **entenderse** *vr* **1 :** to be understood **2 :** to get along well, to understand each other **3 ~ con :** to deal with
entender[2] *nm* **a mi entender :** in my opinion
entendible *adj* **:** understandable
entendido[1], **-da** *adj* **1 :** skilled, expert **2 tener entendido :** to understand, to be under the impression <teníamos entendido que vendrías : we were under the impression you would come> **3 darse por entendido :** to go without saying
entendido[2] *nm* **:** expert, authority, connoisseur
entendimiento *nm* **1 :** intellect, mind **2 :** understanding, agreement
enterado, -da *adj* **:** aware, well-informed <estar enterado de : to be privy to>
enteramente *adv* **:** entirely, completely
enterar *vt* INFORMAR **:** to inform — **enterarse** *vr* INFORMARSE **:** to find out, to learn
entereza *nf* **1** INTEGRIDAD **:** integrity **2** FORTALEZA **:** fortitude **3** FIRMEZA **:** resolve
enternecedor, -dora *adj* CONMOVEDOR **:** touching, moving
enternecer {53} *vt* CONMOVER **:** to move, to touch
entero[1], **-ra** *adj* **1 :** entire, whole **2 :** complete, absolute **3 :** intact — **enteramente** *adv*
entero[2] *nm* **1 :** integer, whole number **2 :** point (in finance)
enterramiento *nm* **:** burial
enterrar {55} *vt* **:** to bury
entibiar *vt* **:** to cool (down) — **entibiarse** *vr* **:** to become lukewarm
entidad *nf* **1** ENTE **:** entity **2 :** body, organization **3 :** firm, company **4 :** importance, significance
entierro *nm* **1 :** burial **2 :** funeral
entintar *vt* **:** to ink
entoldado *nm* **:** awning
entomología *nf* **:** entomology
entomólogo, -ga *n* **:** entomologist
entonación *nf, pl* **-ciones :** intonation
entonar *vi* **:** to be in tune — *vt* **1 :** to intone **2 :** to tone up
entonces *adv* **1 :** then **2 desde ~ :** since then **3 en aquel entonces :** in those days
entornado, -da *adj* ENTREABIERTO **:** half-closed, ajar
entornar *vt* ENTREABRIR **:** to leave ajar
entorno *nm* **:** surroundings *pl,* environment
entorpecer {53} *vt* **1 :** to hinder, to obstruct **2 :** to dull — **entorpecerse** *vr* **:** to dull the senses
entrada *nf* **1 :** entrance, entry **2 :** ticket, admission **3 :** beginning, onset **4 :** entrée **5 :** cue (in music) **6 entradas** *nfpl* **:** income <entradas y salidas : income and expenditures> **7 tener entradas :** to have a receding hairline
entrado, -da *adj* **entrado en años :** elderly
entramado *nm* **:** framework
entrampar *vt* **1** ATRAPAR **:** to entrap, to ensnare **2** ENGAÑAR **:** to deceive, to trick

entrante *adj* **1** : next, upcoming <el año entrante : next year> **2** : incoming, new <el presidente entrante : the president elect>
entraña *nf* **1** MEOLLO : core, heart, crux **2 entrañas** *nfpl* VÍSCERAS : entrails
entrañable *adj* : close, intimate
entrañar *vt* : to entail, to involve
entrar *vi* **1** : to enter, to go in, to come in **2** : to begin — *vt* **1** : to bring in, to introduce **2** : to access
entre *prep* **1** : between **2** : among
entreabierto[1] *pp* → **entreabrir**
entreabierto[2], **-ta** *adj* ENTORNADO : half-open, ajar
entreabrir {2} *vt* ENTORNAR : to leave ajar
entreacto *nm* : intermission, interval
entrecano, -na *adj* : grayish, graying
entrecejo *nm* **fruncir el entrecejo** : to knit one's brows
entrecomillar *vt* : to place in quotation marks
entrecortado, -da *adj* **1** : labored, difficult <respiración entrecortada : shortness of breath> **2** : faltering, hesitant <con la voz entrecortada : with a catch in his voice>
entrecruzar {21} *vt* ENTRELAZAR : to interweave, to intertwine — **entrecruzarse** *vr*
entredicho *nm* **1** DUDA : doubt, question **2** : prohibition
entrega *nf* **1** : delivery **2** : handing over, surrender **3** : installment <entrega inicial : down payment>
entregar {52} *vt* **1** : to deliver **2** DAR : to give, to present **3** : to hand in, to hand over — **entregarse** *vr* **1** : to surrender, to give in **2** : to devote oneself
entrelazar {21} *vt* ENTRECRUZAR : to interweave, to intertwine
entremedias *adv* **1** : in between, halfway **2** : in the meantime
entremés *nm, pl* **-meses 1** APERITIVO : appetizer, hors d'oeuvre **2** : interlude, short play
entremeterse → **entrometerse**
entremetido *nm* → **entrometido**
entremezclar *vt* : to intermingle
entrenador, -dora *n* : trainer, coach
entrenamiento *nm* : training, drill, practice
entrenar *vt* : to train, to drill, to practice — **entrenarse** *vr* : to train, to spar (in boxing)
entreoír {50} *vt* : to hear indistinctly
entrepierna *nf* **1** : inner thigh **2** : crotch **3** : inseam
entrepiso *nm* ENTRESUELO : mezzanine
entresacar {72} *vt* **1** SELECCIONAR : to pick out, to select **2** : to thin out
entresuelo *nm* ENTREPISO : mezzanine
entretanto[1] *adv* : meanwhile
entretanto[2] *nm* **en el entretanto** : in the meantime
entretejer *vt* : to interweave
entretela *nf* : facing (of a garment)
entretener {80} *vt* **1** DIVERTIR : to entertain, to amuse **2** DISTRAER : to distract **3** DEMORAR : to delay, to hold up — **entretenerse** *vr* **1** : to amuse oneself **2** : to dally
entretenido, -da *adj* DIVERTIDO : entertaining, amusing
entretenimiento *nm* **1** : entertainment, pastime **2** DIVERSIÓN : fun, amusement
entrever {88} *vt* **1** : to catch a glimpse of **2** : to make out, to see indistinctly
entreverar *vt* : to mix, to intermingle
entrevero *nm* : confusion, disorder
entrevista *nf* : interview
entrevistador, -dora *n* : interviewer
entrevistar *vt* : to interview — **entrevistarse** *vr* REUNIRSE **~ con** : to meet with
entristecer {53} *vt* : to sadden
entrometerse *vr* : to interfere, to meddle
entrometido, -da *n* : meddler, busybody
entroncar {72} *vt* RELACIONAR : to establish a relationship between, to connect — *vi* **1** : to be related **2** : to link up, to be connected
entronque *nm* **1** : kinship **2** VÍNCULO : link, connection
entuerto *nm* : wrong, injustice
entumecer {53} *vt* : to make numb, to be numb — **entumecerse** *vr* : to go numb, to fall asleep
entumecido, -da *adj* **1** : numb **2** : stiff (of muscles, joints, etc.)
entumecimiento *nm* : numbness
enturbiar *vt* **1** : to cloud **2** : to confuse — **enturbiarse** *vr*
entusiasmar *vt* : to excite, to fill with enthusiasm — **entusiasmarse** *vr* : to get excited
entusiasmo *nm* : enthusiasm
entusiasta[1] *adj* : enthusiastic
entusiasta[2] *nmf* AFICIONADO : enthusiast
enumerar *vt* : to enumerate — **enumeración** *nf*
enunciación *nf, pl* **-ciones** : enunciation, statement
enunciar *vt* : to enunciate, to state
envainar *vt* : to sheathe
envalentonar *vt* : to make bold, to encourage — **envalentonarse** *vr*
envanecer {53} *vt* ENGREÍR : to make vain — **envanecerse** *vr*
envasar *vt* **1** EMBOTELLAR : to bottle **2** ENLATAR : to can **3** : to pack in a container
envase *nm* **1** : packaging, packing **2** : container **3** LATA : can **4** : empty bottle
envejecer {53} *vt* : to age, to make look old — *vi* : to age, to grow old
envejecido, -da *adj* : aged, old-looking
envejecimiento *nm* : aging
envenenamiento *nm* : poisoning
envenenar *vt* **1** : to poison **2** : to embitter

envergadura *nf* **1** : span, breadth, spread **2** : importance, scope
envés *nm, pl* **enveses** : reverse, opposite side
enviado, -da *n* : envoy, correspondent
enviar {85} *vt* **1** : to send **2** : to ship
envidia *nf* : envy, jealousy
envidiar *vt* : to envy — **envidiable** *adj*
envidioso, -sa *adj* : envious, jealous
envilecer {53} *vt* : to degrade, to debase
envilecimiento *nm* : degradation, debasement
envío *nm* **1** : shipment **2** : remittance
enviudar *vi* : to be widowed, to become a widower
envoltorio *nm* **1** : bundle, package **2** : wrapping, wrapper
envoltura *nf* : wrapper, wrapping
envolver {89} *vt* **1** : to wrap **2** : to envelop, to surround **3** : to entangle, to involve — **envolverse** *vr* **1** : to become involved **2** : to wrap oneself (up)
envuelto *pp* → **envolver**
enyerbar *vt Mex* : to bewitch
enyesar *vt* **1** : to plaster **2** ESCAYOLAR : to put in a plaster cast
enzima *nf* : enzyme
éon *nm, pl* **eones** : aeon
eperlano *nm* : smelt (fish)
épico, -ca *adj* : epic
epicúreo[1], -rea *adj* : epicurean
epicúreo[2], -rea *n* : epicure
epidemia *nf* : epidemic
epidémico, -ca *adj* : epidemic
epidermis *nf* : epidermis
epifanía *nf* : feast of the Epiphany (January 6th)
epigrama *nm* : epigram
epilepsia *nf* : epilepsy
epiléptico, -ca *adj & n* : epileptic
epílogo *nm* : epilogue
episcopal *adj* : episcopal
episcopalista *adj & nmf* : Episcopalian
episódico, -ca *adj* : episodic
episodio *nm* : episode
epístola *nf* : epistle
epitafio *nm* : epitaph
epíteto *nm* : epithet, name
epítome *nm* : summary, abstract
época *nf* **1** EDAD, ERA, PERÍODO : epoch, age, period **2** : time of year, season **3** **de ~** : vintage, antique
epopeya *nf* : epic poem
equidad *nf* JUSTICIA : equity, justice, fairness
equilátero, -ra *adj* : equilateral
equilibrado, -da *adj* : well-balanced
equilibrar *vt* : to balance — **equilibrarse** *vr*
equilibrio *nm* **1** : balance, equilibrium <perder el equilibrio : to lose one's balance> <equilibrio político : balance of power> **2** : poise, aplomb
equilibrista *nmf* ACRÓBATA, FUNÁMBULO : acrobat, tightrope walker
equino, -na *adj* : equine
equinoccio *nm* : equinox
equipaje *nm* BAGAJE : baggage, luggage
equipamiento *nm* : equipping, equipment
equipar *vt* : to equip — **equiparse** *vr*
equiparable *adj* : comparable
equiparar *vt* **1** IGUALAR : to put on a same level, to make equal **2** COMPARAR : to compare
equipo *nm* **1** : team, crew **2** : gear, equipment
equitación *nf, pl* **-ciones** : horseback riding, horsemanship
equitativo, -va *adj* JUSTO : equitable, fair, just — **equitativamente** *adv*
equivalencia *nf* : equivalence
equivalente *adj & nm* : equivalent
equivaler {84} *vi* : to be equivalent
equivocación *nf, pl* **-ciones** ERROR : error, mistake
equivocado, -da *adj* : mistaken, wrong — **equivocadamente** *adv*
equivocar {72} *vt* : to mistake, to confuse — **equivocarse** *vr* : to make a mistake, to be wrong
equívoco[1], -ca *adj* AMBIGUO : ambiguous, equivocal
equívoco[2] *nm* : misunderstanding
era[1], etc. → **ser**
era[2] *nf* EDAD, ÉPOCA : era, age
erario *nm* : public treasury
erección *nf, pl* **-ciones** : erection, raising
eremita *nmf* ERMITAÑO : hermit
ergonomía *nf* : ergonomic
erguido, -da *adj* : erect, upright
erguir {31} *vt* : to raise, to lift up — **erguirse** *vr* : to straighten up
erial *nm* : uncultivated land
erigir {35} *vt* : to build, to erect — **erigirse** *vr* **~ en** : to set oneself up as
erizado, -da : bristly
erizarse {21} *vr* : to bristle, to stand on end
erizo *nm* **1** : hedgehog **2** **erizo de mar** : sea urchin
ermitaño[1], -ña *n* EREMITA : hermit, recluse
ermitaño[2] *nm* : hermit crab
erogación *nf, pl* **-ciones** : expenditure
erogar {52} *vt* **1** : to pay out **2** : to distribute
erosión *nf, pl* **-siones** : erosion
erosionar *vt* : to erode
erótico, -ca *adj* : erotic
erotismo *nm* : eroticism
errabundo, -da *adj* ERRANTE, VAGABUNDO : wandering
erradicar {72} *vt* : to eradicate — **erradicación** *nf*
errado, -da *adj* : wrong, mistaken
errante *adj* ERRABUNDO, VAGABUNDO : errant, wandering
errar {32} *vt* FALLAR : to miss — *vi* **1** DESACERTAR : to be wrong, to be mistaken **2** VAGAR : to wander
errata *nf* : misprint, error

errático, -ca *adj* : erratic — **erráticamente** *adv*
erróneo, -nea *adj* EQUIVOCADO : erroneous, wrong — **erróneamente** *adv*
error *nm* EQUIVOCACIÓN : error, mistake
eructar *vi* : to belch, to burp
eructo *nm* : belch, burp
erudición *nf, pl* **-ciones** : erudition, learning
erudito[1], **-ta** *adj* LETRADO : erudite, learned
erudito[2], **-ta** *n* : scholar
erupción *nf, pl* **-ciones 1** : eruption **2** SARPULLIDO : rash
eruptivo, -va *adj* : eruptive
es → **ser**
esbelto, -ta *adj* DELGADO : slender, slim
esbirro *nm* : henchman
esbozar {21} *vt* BOSQUEJAR : to sketch, to outline
esbozo *nm* **1** : sketch **2** : rough draft
escabechar *vt* **1** ENCURTIR : to pickle **2** *fam* : to kill, to rub out
escabeche *nm* : brine (for pickling)
escabechina *nf* MASACRE : massacre, bloodbath
escabel *nm* : footstool
escabroso, -sa *adj* **1** : rugged, rough **2** : difficult, tough **3** : risqué
escabullirse {38} *vr* : to slip away, to escape
escala *nf* **1** : scale **2** ESCALERA : ladder **3** : stopover
escalada *nf* : ascent, climb
escalador, -dora *n* ALPINISTA : mountain climber
escalafón *nm, pl* **-fones 1** : list of personnel **2** : salary scale, rank
escalar *vt* : to climb, to scale — *vi* **1** : to go climbing **2** : to escalate
escaldar *vt* : to scald
escalera *nf* **1** : ladder <escalera de tijera : stepladder> **2** : stairs *pl*, staircase **3 escalera mecánica** : escalator
escalfador *nm* : chafing dish
escalfar *vt* : to poach (eggs)
escalinata *nf* : flight of stairs
escalofriante *adj* : horrifying, bloodcurdling
escalofrío *nm* : shiver, chill, shudder
escalón *nm, pl* **-lones 1** : echelon **2** : step, rung
escalonado, -da *adj* GRADUAL : gradual, staggered
escalonar *vt* **1** : to terrace **2** : to stagger, to alternate
escalpelo *nm* BISTURÍ : scalpel
escama *nf* **1** : scale (of fish or reptiles) **2** : flake (of skin)
escamar *vt* **1** : to scale (fish) **2** : to make suspicious
escamocha *nf Mex* : fruit salad
escamoso, -sa *adj* : scaly
escamotear *vt* **1** : to palm, to conceal **2** *fam* : to lift, to swipe **3** : to hide, to cover up
escandalizar {21} *vt* : to shock, to scandalize — *vi* : to make a fuss — **escandalizarse** *vr* : to be shocked
escándalo *nm* **1** : scandal **2** : scene, commotion
escandaloso, -sa *adj* **1** : shocking, scandalous **2** RUIDOSO : noisy, rowdy **3** : flagrant, outrageous — **escandalosamente** *adv*
escandinavo, -va *adj & n* : Scandinavian
escandir *vt* : to scan (poetry)
escáner *nm* : scanner, scan
escaño *nm* **1** : seat (in a legislative body) **2** BANCO : bench
escapada *nf* HUIDA : flight, escape
escapar *vi* HUIR : to escape, to flee, to run away — **escaparse** *vr* : to escape notice, to leak out
escaparate *nm* **1** : shop window **2** : showcase
escapatoria *nf* **1** : loophole, excuse, pretext <no tener escapatoria : to have no way out> **2** ESCAPADA : escape, flight
escape *nm* **1** FUGA : escape **2** : exhaust (from a vehicle)
escapismo *nm* : escapism
escápula *nm* OMÓPLATO : scapula, shoulder blade
escapulario *nm* : scapular
escarabajo *nm* : beetle
escaramuza *nf* **1** : skirmish **2** : scrimmage
escaramuzar {21} *vi* : to skirmish
escarapela *nf* : rosette (ornament)
escarbar *vt* **1** : to dig, to scratch up **2** : to poke, to pick **3 ~ en** : to investigate, to pry into
escarcha *nf* **1** : frost **2** *Mex, PRi* : glitter
escarchar *vt* **1** : to frost (a cake) **2** : to candy (fruit)
escardar *vt* **1** : to weed, to hoe **2** : to weed out
escariar *vt* : to ream
escarlata *adj & nf* : scarlet
escarlatina *nf* : scarlet fever
escarmentar {55} *vt* : to punish, to teach a lesson to — *vi* : to learn one's lesson
escarmiento *nm* **1** : lesson, warning **2** CASTIGO : punishment
escarnecer {53} *vt* RIDICULIZAR : to ridicule, to mock
escarnio *nm* : ridicule, mockery
escarola *nf* : escarole
escarpa *nf* : escarpment, steep slope
escarpado, -da *adj* : steep, sheer
escarpia *nf* : hook, spike
escasamente *adv* : scarcely, barely
escasear *vi* : to be scarce, to run short
escasez *nf, pl* **-seces** : shortage, scarcity
escaso, -sa *adj* **1** : scarce, scant **2 ~ de** : short of
escatimar *vt* : to skimp on, to be sparing with <no escatimar esfuerzos : to spare no effort>
escayola *nf* **1** : plaster (for casts) **2** : plaster cast
escayolar *vt* : to put in a plaster cast

escena *nf* **1** : scene **2** : stage
escenario *nm* **1** ESCENA : stage **2** : setting, scene <el escenario del crimen : the scene of the crime>
escénico, -ca *adj* **1** : scenic **2** : stage
escenificar {72} *vt* : to stage, to dramatize
escepticismo *nm* : skepticism
escéptico¹, -ca *adj* : skeptical
escéptico², -ca *n* : skeptic
escindirse *vr* **1** : to split **2** : to break away
escisión *nf, pl* **-siones 1** : split, division **2** : excision
esclarecer {53} *vt* **1** ELUCIDAR : to elucidate, to clarify **2** ILUMINAR : to illuminate, to light up
esclarecimiento *nm* ELUCIDACIÓN : elucidation, clarification
esclavitud *nf* : slavery
esclavización *nf, pl* **-ciones** : enslavement
esclavizar {21} *vt* : to enslave
esclavo, -va *n* : slave
esclerosis *nf* **esclerosis múltiple** : multiple sclerosis
esclusa *nf* : floodgate, lock (of a canal)
escoba *nf* : broom
escobilla *nf* : small broom, brush, whisk broom
escobillón *nm, pl* **-llones** : swab
escocer {14} *vi* ARDER : to smart, to sting — **escocerse** *vr* : to be sore
escocés¹, -cesa *adj, mpl* **-ceses 1** : Scottish **2** : tartan, plaid
escocés², -cesa *n, mpl* **-ceses** : Scottish person, Scot
escocés³ *nm* **1** : Scots (language) **2** *pl* **-ceses** : Scotch (whiskey)
escofina *nf* : file, rasp
escoger {15} *vt* ELEGIR, SELECCIONAR : to choose, to select
escogido, -da *adj* : choice, select
escolar¹ *adj* : school
escolar² *nmf* : student, pupil
escolaridad *nf* : schooling <escolaridad obligatoria : compulsory education>
escolarización *nf, pl* **-ciones** : education, schooling
escollo *nm* **1** : reef **2** OBSTÁCULO : obstacle
escolta *nmf* : escort
escoltar *vt* : to escort, to accompany
escombro *nm* **1** : debris, rubbish **2 escombros** *nmpl* : ruins, rubble
esconder *vt* OCULTAR : to hide, to conceal
escondidas *nfpl* **1** : hide-and-seek **2 a ~** : secretly, in secret
escondimiento *nm* : concealment
escondite *nm* **1** ENCONDRIJO : hiding place **2** ESCONDIDAS : hide-and-seek
escondrijo *nm* ESCONDITE : hiding place
escopeta *nf* : shotgun
escoplear *vt* : to chisel (out)
escoplo *nm* : chisel
escora *nf* : list, heeling
escorar *vi* : to list, to heel (of a boat)
escorbuto *nm* : scurvy
escoria *nf* **1** : slag, dross **2** HEZ : dregs *pl,* scum <la escoria de la sociedad : the dregs of society>
Escorpio *or* **Escorpión** *nmf* : Scorpio
escorpión *nm, pl* **-piones** ALACRÁN : scorpion
escote *nm* **1** : low neckline **2 pagar a escote** : to go dutch
escotilla *nf* : hatch, hatchway
escotillón *nf, pl* **-llones** : trapdoor
escozor *nm* : smarting, stinging
escriba *nm* : scribe
escribano, -na *n* **1** : court clerk **2** NOTARIO : notary public
escribir {33} *v* **1** : to write **2** : to spell — **escribirse** *vr* CARTEARSE : to write to one another, to correspond
escrito¹ *pp* → **escribir**
escrito², -ta *adj* : written
escrito³ *nm* **1** : written document **2 escritos** *nmpl* : writings, works
escritor, -tora *n* : writer
escritorio *nm* : desk
escritorzuelo, -la *n* : hack (writer)
escritura *nf* **1** : writing, handwriting **2** : deed
escroto *nm* : scrotum
escrúpulo *nm* : scruple
escrupuloso, -sa *adj* **1** : scrupulous **2** METICULOSO : exact, meticulous — **escrupulosamente** *adv*
escrutador, -dora *adj* : penetrating, searching
escrutar *vt* ESCUDRIÑAR : to scrutinize, to examine closely
escrutinio *nm* : scrutiny
escuadra *nf* **1** : square (instrument) **2** : fleet, squadron
escuadrilla *nf* : squadron, formation, flight
escuadrón *nm, pl* **-drones** : squadron
escuálido, -da *adj* **1** : skinny, scrawny **2** INMUNDO : filthy, squalid
escuchar *vt* **1** : to listen to **2** : to hear — *vi* : to listen — **escucharse** *vr*
escudar *vt* : to shield — **escudarse** *vr* **~ en** : to hide behind
escudero *nm* : squire
escudo *nm* **1** : shield **2 escudo de armas** : coat of arms
escudriñar *vt* **1** ESCRUTAR : to scrutinize **2** : to inquire into, to investigate
escuela *nf* : school
escueto, -ta *adj* **1** : plain, simple **2** : succinct, concise — **escuetamente** *adv*
escuincle, -cla *n Mex fam* : child, kid
esculcar {72} *vt* : to search
esculpir *vt* **1** : to sculpt **2** : to carve, to engrave — *vi* : to sculpt
escultor, -tora *n* : sculptor
escultórico, -ca *adj* : sculptural
escultura *nf* : sculpture
escultural *adj* : statuesque
escupidera *nf* : spittoon, cuspidor
escupir *v* : to spit
escupitajo *nm* : spit
escurridizo, -za *adj* : slippery, elusive

escurridor *nm* **1 :** dish rack **2 :** colander
escurrir *vt* **1 :** to wring out **2 :** to drain — *vi* **1 :** to drain **2 :** to drip, to drip-dry — **escurrirse** *vr* **:** to slip away
ese, esa *adj, mpl* **esos :** that, those
ése, ésa *pron, mpl* **ésos :** that one, those ones *pl*
esencia *nf* **:** essence
esencial *adj* **:** essential — **esencialmente** *adv*
esfera *nf* **1 :** sphere **2 :** face, dial (of a watch)
esférico[1]**, -ca** *adj* **:** spherical
esférico[2] *nm* **:** ball (in sports)
esfinge *nf* **:** sphinx
esforzado, -da *adj* **1 :** energetic, vigorous **2** VALIENTE **:** courageous, brave
esforzar {36} *vt* **:** to strain — **esforzarse** *vr* **:** to make an effort
esfuerzo *nm* **1 :** effort **2** ÁNIMO, VIGOR **:** spirit, vigor **3 sin ~ :** effortlessly
esfumar *vt* **:** to tone down, to soften — **esfumarse** *vr* **1 :** to fade away, to vanish **2** *fam* **:** to take off, to leave
esgrima *nf* **:** fencing (sport)
esgrimidor, -dora *n* **:** fencer
esgrimir *vt* **1 :** to brandish, to wield **2 :** to use, to resort to — *vi* **:** to fence
esguince *nm* **:** sprain, strain (of a muscle)
eslabón *nm, pl* **-bones :** link
eslabonar *vt* **:** to link, to connect, to join
eslavo[1]**, -va** *adj* **:** Slavic
eslavo[2]**, -va** *n* **:** Slav
eslogan *nm, pl* **-lóganes :** slogan
eslovaco, -ca *adj & n* **:** Slovakian, Slovak
esloveno, -na *adj & nm* **:** Slovene, Slovenian
esmaltar *vt* **:** to enamel
esmalte *nm* **1 :** enamel **2 esmalte de uñas :** nail polish
esmerado, -da *adj* **:** careful, painstaking
esmeralda *nf* **:** emerald
esmerarse *vr* **:** to take great pains, to do one's utmost
esmeril *nm* **:** emery
esmero *nm* **:** meticulousness, great care
esmoquin *nm, pl* **-quins :** tuxedo
esnob[1] *adj, pl* **esnobs :** snobbish
esnob[2] *nmf, pl* **esnobs :** snob
esnobismo *nm* **:** snobbery, snobbishness
eso *pron* (*neuter*) **1 :** that <eso no me gusta : I don't like that> **2 ¡eso es! :** that's it!, that's right! **3 a eso de :** around <a eso de las tres : around three o'clock> **4 en ~ :** at that point, just then
esófago *nm* **:** esophagus
esos → **ese**
ésos → **ése**
esotérico, -ca *adj* **:** esoteric — **esotéricamente** *adv*
espabilado, -da *adj* **:** bright, smart
espabilarse *vr* **1 :** to awaken **2 :** to get a move on **3 :** to get smart, to wise up
espacial *adj* **1 :** space **2 :** spatial
espaciar *vt* DISTANCIAR **:** to space out, to spread out
espacio *nm* **1 :** space, room **2 :** period, length (of time) **3 espacio exterior :** outer space
espacioso, -sa *adj* **:** spacious, roomy
espada[1] *nf* **1 :** sword **2 espadas** *nfpl* **:** spades (in playing cards)
espada[2] *nm* MATADOR, TORERO **:** bullfighter, matador
espadaña *nf* **1 :** belfry **2 :** cattail
espadilla *nf* **:** scull, oar
espagueti *nm or* **espaguetis** *nmpl* **:** spaghetti
espalda *nf* **1 :** back **2 espaldas** *nfpl* **:** shoulders, back **3 por la espalda :** from behind
espaldarazo *nm* **1 :** recognition, support **2 :** slap on the back
espaldera *nf* **:** trellis
espantajo *nm* **:** scarecrow
espantapájaros *nms & pl* **:** scarecrow
espantar *vt* ASUSTAR **:** to scare, to frighten — **espantarse** *vr*
espanto *nm* **:** fright, fear, horror
espantoso, -sa *adj* **1 :** frightening, terrifying **2 :** frightful, dreadful
español[1]**, -ñola** *adj* **:** Spanish
español[2]**, -ñola** *n* **:** Spaniard
español[3] *nm* CASTELLANO **:** Spanish (language)
esparadrapo *nm* **:** adhesive bandage, Band-Aid™
esparcimiento *nm* **1** DIVERSIÓN, RECREO **:** entertainment, recreation **2** DESCANSO **:** relaxation **3** DISEMINACIÓN **:** dissemination, spreading
esparcir {83} *vt* DISPERSAR **:** to scatter, to spread — **esparcirse** *vr* **1 :** to spread out **2** DESCANSARSE **:** to take it easy **3** DIVERTIRSE **:** to amuse oneself
espárrago *nm* **:** asparagus
espartano, -na *adj* **:** severe, austere
espasmo *nm* **:** spasm
espasmódico, -ca *adj* **:** spasmodic
espástico, -ca *adj* **:** spastic
espátula *nf* **:** spatula
especia *nf* **:** spice
especial *adj & nm* **:** special
especialidad *nf* **:** specialty
especialista *nmf* **:** specialist, expert
especializarse {21} *vr* **:** to specialize
especialmente *adv* **:** especially, particularly
especie *nf* **1 :** species **2** CLASE, TIPO **:** type, kind, sort
especificación *nf, pl* **-ciones :** specification
especificar {72} *vt* **:** to specify
específico, -ca *adj* **:** specific — **específicamente** *adv*
espécimen *nm, pl* **especímenes :** specimen
especioso, -sa *adj* **:** specious
espectacular *adj* **:** spectacular — **espectacularmente** *adv*

espectáculo *nm* **1** : spectacle, sight **2** : show, performance

espectador, -dora *n* : spectator, onlooker

espectro *nm* **1** : ghost, specter **2** : spectrum

especulación *nf, pl* **-ciones** : speculation

especulador, -dora *n* : speculator

especular *vi* : to speculate

especulativo, -va *adj* : speculative

espejismo *nm* **1** : mirage **2** : illusion

espejo *nm* : mirror

espejuelos *nmpl* ANTEOJOS : spectacles, glasses

espeluznante *adj* : hair-raising, terrifying

espera *nf* : wait

esperanza *nf* : hope, expectation

esperanzado, -da *adj* : hopeful

esperanzador, -dora *adj* : encouraging, promising

esperanzar {21} *vt* : to give hope to

esperar *vt* **1** AGUARDAR : to wait for, to await **2** : to expect **3** : to hope <espero poder trabajar : I hope to be able to work> <espero que sí : I hope so> — *vi* : to wait — **esperarse** *vr* **1** : to expect, to be hoped <como podría esperarse : as would be expected> **2** : to hold on, to hang on <espérate un momento : hold on a minute>

esperma *nmf* : sperm

esperpéntico, -ca *adj* GROTESCO : grotesque

esperpento *nm fam* MAMARRACHO : sight, fright <voy hecha un esperpento : I really look a sight>

espesante *nm* : thickener

espesar *vt* : to thicken — **espesarse** *vr*

espeso, -sa *adj* : thick, heavy, dense

espesor *nm* : thickness, density

espesura *nf* **1** : thickness **2** : thicket

espetar *vt* **1** : to blurt out **2** : to skewer

espía *nmf* : spy

espiar {85} *vt* : to spy on, to observe — *vi* : to spy

espiga *nf* **1** : ear (of wheat) **2** : spike (of flowers)

espigado, -da *adj* : willowy, slender

espigar {52} *vt* : to glean, to gather — **espigarse** *vr* : to grow quickly, to shoot up

espigón *nm, pl* **-gones** : breakwater

espina *nf* **1** : thorn **2** : spine <espina dorsal : spinal column> **3** : fish bone

espinaca *nf* **1** : spinach (plant) **2 espinacas** *nfpl* : spinach (food)

espinal *adj* : spinal

espinazo *nm* : backbone

espineta *nf* : spinet

espinilla *nf* **1** BARRO, GRANO : pimple **2** : shin

espino *nm* : hawthorn

espinoso, -sa *adj* **1** : thorny, prickly **2** : bony (of fish) **3** : knotty, difficult

espionaje *nm* : espionage

espiración *nf, pl* **-ciones** : exhalation

espiral *adj & nf* : spiral

espirar *vt* EXHALAR : to breathe out, to give off — *vi* : to exhale

espiritismo *nm* : spiritualism

espiritista *nmf* : spiritualist

espíritu *nm* **1** : spirit **2** ÁNIMO : state of mind, spirits *pl* **3 el Espíritu Santo** : the Holy Ghost

espiritual *adj* : spiritual — **espiritualmente** *adv*

espiritualidad *nf* : spirituality

espita *nf* : spigot, tap

esplendidez *nf, pl* **-deces** ESPLENDOR : magnificence, splendor

espléndido, -da *adj* **1** : splendid, magnificent **2** : generous, lavish — **espléndidamente** *adv*

esplendor *nm* ESPLENDIDEZ : splendor

esplendoroso, -sa *adj* MAGNÍFICO : magnificent, grand

espliego *nm* LAVANDA : lavender

espolear *vt* : to spur on

espoleta *nf* **1** DETONADOR : detonator, fuse **2** : wishbone

espolón *nm, pl* **-lones** : spur (of poultry), fetlock (of a horse)

espolvorear *vt* : to sprinkle, to dust

esponja *nf* **1** : sponge **2 tirar la esponja** : to throw in the towel

esponjado, -da *adj* : spongy

esponjoso, -sa *adj* **1** : spongy **2** : soft, fluffy

esponsales *nmpl* : betrothal, engagement

espontaneidad *nf* : spontaneity

espontáneo, -nea *adj* : spontaneous — **espontáneamente** *adv*

espora *nf* : spore

esporádico, -ca *adj* : sporadic — **esporádicamente** *adv*

esposar *vt* : to handcuff

esposas *nfpl* : handcuffs

esposo, -sa *n* : spouse, wife *f*, husband *m*

esprint *nm* : sprint

esprintar *vi* : to sprint

esprinter *nmf* : sprinter

espuela *nf* : spur

espuerta *nf* : two-handled basket

espulgar {52} *vt* **1** : to delouse **2** : to scrutinize

espuma *nf* **1** : foam **2** : lather **3** : froth, head (on beer)

espumar *vi* : to foam, to froth — *vt* : to skim off

espumoso, -sa *adj* : foamy, frothy

espurio, -ria *adj* : spurious

esputar *v* : to expectorate, to spit

esputo *nm* : spit, sputum

esqueje *nm* : cutting (from a plant)

esquela *nf* **1** : note **2** : notice, announcement

esquelético, -ca *adj* : emaciated, skeletal

esqueleto *nm* **1** : skeleton **2** ARMAZÓN : framework

esquema *nf* BOSQUEJO : outline, sketch, plan

esquemático, -ca *adj* : schematic

esquí *nm* **1** : ski **2 esquí acuático** : water ski, waterskiing

esquiador, -dora *n* : skier

esquiar {85} *vi* : to ski

esquife *nm* : skiff

esquila *nf* **1** CENCERRO : cowbell **2** : shearing

esquilar *vt* TRASQUILAR : to shear

esquimal *adj & nmf* : Eskimo

esquina *nf* : corner

esquinazo *nm* **1** : corner **2 dar esquinazo a** *fam* : to stand up, to give the slip to

esquirla *nf* : splinter (of bone, glass, etc.)

esquirol *nm* ROMPEHUELGAS : strikebreaker, scab

esquisto *nm* : shale

esquivar *vt* **1** EVADIR : to dodge, to evade **2** EVITAR : to avoid

esquivez *nf, pl* **-veces 1** : aloofness **2** TIMIDEZ : shyness

esquivo, -va *adj* **1** HURAÑO : aloof, unsociable **2** : shy **3** : elusive, evasive

esquizofrenia *nf* : schizophrenia

esquizofrénico, -ca *adj & n* : schizophrenic

esta → **este**[1]

ésta → **éste**

estabilidad *nf* : stability

estabilización *nf, pl* **-ciones** : stabilization

estabilizador *nm* : stabilizer

estabilizar {21} *vt* : to stabilize — **estabilizarse** *vr*

estable *adj* : stable, steady

establecer {53} *vt* FUNDAR, INSTITUIR : to establish, to found, to set up — **establecerse** *vr* INSTALARSE : to settle, to establish oneself

establecimiento *nm* **1** : establishing **2** : establishment, institution, office

establo *nm* : stable

estaca *nf* : stake, picket, post

estacada *nf* **1** : picket fence **2** : stockade

estacar {72} *vt* **1** : to stake out **2** : to fasten down with stakes — **estacarse** *vr* : to remain rigid

estación *nf, pl* **-ciones 1** : station <estación de servicio : service station, gas station> **2** : season

estacional *adj* : seasonal

estacionamiento *nm* **1** : parking **2** : parking lot

estacionar *vt* **1** : to place, to station **2** : to park — **estacionarse** *vr* **1** : to park **2** : to remain stationary

estacionario, -ria *adj* **1** : stationary **2** : stable

estada *nf* : stay

estadía *nf* ESTANCIA : stay, sojourn

estadio *nm* **1** : stadium **2** : phase, stage

estadista *nmf* : statesman

estadística *nf* **1** : statistic, figure **2** : statistics

estadístico[1], **-ca** *adj* : statistical — **estadísticamente** *adv*

estadístico[2], **-ca** *n* : statistician

estado *nm* **1** : state **2** : status <estado civil : marital status> **3** CONDICIÓN : condition

estadounidense *adj & nmf* AMERICANO, NORTEAMERICANO : American

estafa *nf* : swindle, fraud

estafador, -dora *n* : cheat, swindler

estafar *vt* DEFRAUDAR : to swindle, to defraud

estalactita *nf* : stalactite

estalagmita *nf* : stalagmite

estallar *vi* **1** REVENTAR : to burst, to explode, to erupt **2** : to break out

estallido *nm* **1** EXPLOSIÓN : explosion **2** : report (of a gun) **3** : outbreak, outburst

estambre *nm* **1** : worsted (fabric) **2** : stamen

estampa *nf* **1** ILUSTRACIÓN, IMAGEN : printed image, illustration **2** ASPECTO : appearance, demeanor

estampado[1], **-da** *adj* : patterned, printed

estampado[2] *nm* : print, pattern

estampar *vt* : to stamp, to print, to engrave

estampida *nf* : stampede

estampilla *nf* **1** : rubber stamp **2** SELLO, TIMBRE : postage stamp

estancado, -da *adj* : stagnant

estancamiento *nm* : stagnation

estancar {72} *vt* **1** : to dam up, to hold back **2** : to bring to a halt, to deadlock — **estancarse** *vr* **1** : to stagnate **2** : to be brought to a standstill, to be deadlocked

estancia *nf* **1** ESTADÍA : stay, sojourn **2** : ranch, farm

estanciero, -ra *n* : rancher, farmer

estanco, -ca *adj* : watertight

estándar *adj & nm* : standard

estandarización *nf, pl* **-ciones** : standardization

estandarizar {21} *vt* : to standardize

estandarte *nm* : standard, banner

estanque *nm* **1** : pool, pond **2** : tank, reservoir

estante *nm* REPISA : shelf

estantería *nf* : shelves *pl,* bookcase

estaño *nm* : tin

estaquilla *nf* **1** : peg **2** ESPIGA : spike

estar {34} *v aux* : to be <estoy aprendiendo inglés : I'm learning English> <está terminado : it's finished> — *vi* **1** (*indicating a state or condition*) : to be <está muy alto : he's so tall, he's gotten very tall><¿ya estás mejor? : are you feeling better now?> <estoy casado : I'm married> **2** (*indicating location*) : to be <están en la mesa : they're on the table> <estamos en la página 2 : we're on page 2> **3** : to be at home <¿está María? : is Maria in?> **4** : to remain <estaré aquí 5 días : I'll be here for 5 days> **5** : to be ready, to be done <estará para las diez : it will be ready by ten o'clock> **6** : to agree <¿estamos? : are we in agreement?> <estoy contigo : I'm with you> **7**

¿cómo estás? : how are you? **8 ¡está bien! :** all right!, that's fine! **9 ~ a :** to cost **10 ~ a :** to be <¿a qué dia estamos? : what's today's date?> **11 ~ con** to have <está con fiebre : she has a fever> **12 ~ de :** to be <estoy de vacaciones : I'm on vacation> <está de director hoy : he's acting as director today> **13 estar bien (mal) :** to be well (sick) **14 ~ para :** to be in the mood for **15 ~ por :** to be in favor of **16 ~ por :** to be about to <está por cerrar : it's on the verge of closing> **17 estar de más :** to be unnecessary **18 estar que :** to be (in a state or condition) <está que echa chispas : he's hopping mad> — **estarse** *vr* QUEDARSE **:** to stay, to remain <¡estáte quieto! : be still!>
estarcir {83} *vt* **:** to stencil
estatal *adj* **:** state, national
estática *nf* **:** static
estático, -ca *adj* **:** static
estatizar {21} *vt* **:** to nationalize — **estatización** *nf*
estatua *nf* **:** statue
estatuilla *nf* **:** statuette, figurine
estatura *nf* **:** height, stature <de mediana estatura : of medium height>
estatus *nm* **:** status, prestige
estatutario, -ria *adj* **:** statutory
estatuto *nm* **:** statute
este[1], esta *adj, mpl* **estos :** this, these
este[2] *adj* **:** eastern, east
este[3] *nm* **1** ORIENTE **:** east **2 :** east wind **3 el Este :** the East, the Orient
éste, ésta *pron, mpl* **éstos 1 :** this one, these ones *pl* **2 :** the latter
estela *nf* **1 :** wake (of a ship) **2** RASTRO **:** trail (of dust, smoke, etc.)
estelar *adj* **:** stellar
estelarizar {21} *vt Mex* **:** to star in, to be the star of
esténcil *nm* **:** stencil
estentóreo, -rea *adj* **:** loud, thundering
estepa *nf* **:** steppe
éster *nf* **:** ester
estera *nf* **:** mat
estercolero *nm* **:** dunghill
estéreo *adj & nm* **:** stereo
estereofónico, -ca *adj* **:** stereophonic
estereotipado, -da *adj* **:** stereotyped
estereotipar *vt* **:** to stereotype
estereotipo *nm* **:** stereotype
estéril *adj* **1 :** sterile, germ-free **2 :** infertile, barren **3 :** futile, vain
esterilidad *nf* **1 :** sterility **2 :** infertility
esterilizar {21} *vt* **1 :** to sterilize, to disinfect **2 :** to sterilize (a person), to spay (an animal) — **esterilización** *nf*
esterlina *adj* **:** sterling
esternón *nm, pl* **-nones :** sternum
estero *nm* **:** estuary
estertor *nm* **:** death rattle
estética *nf* **:** aesthetics
estético, -ca *adj* **:** aesthetic — **estéticamente** *adv*
estetoscopio *nm* **:** stethoscope
estibador, -dora *n* **:** longshoreman, stevedore
estibar *vt* **:** to load (freight)
estiércol *nm* **:** dung, manure
estigma *nm* **:** stigma
estigmatizar {21} *vt* **:** to stigmatize, to brand
estilarse *vr* **:** to be in fashion
estilete *nm* **:** stiletto
estilista *nmf* **:** stylist
estilizar {21} *vt* **:** to stylize
estilo *nm* **1 :** style **2 :** fashion, manner **3 :** stylus
estima *nf* ESTIMACIÓN **:** esteem, regard
estimable *adj* **1 :** considerable **2 :** estimable, esteemed
estimación *nf, pl* **-ciones 1** ESTIMA **:** esteem, regard **2 :** estimate
estimado, -da *adj* **:** esteemed, dear <Estimado señor Ortiz : Dear Mr. Ortiz>
estimar *vt* **1** APRECIAR **:** to esteem, to respect **2** EVALUAR **:** to estimate, to appraise **3** OPINAR **:** to consider, to deem
estimulación *nf, pl* **-ciones :** stimulation
estimulante[1] *adj* **:** stimulating
estimulante[2] *nm* **:** stimulant
estimular *vt* **1 :** to stimulate **2 :** to encourage
estímulo *nm* **1 :** stimulus **2** INCENTIVO **:** incentive, encouragement
estío *nm* **:** summertime
estipendio *nm* **1 :** salary **2 :** stipend, remuneration
estipular *vt* **:** to stipulate — **estipulación** *nf*
estirado, -da *adj* **1 :** stretched, extended **2** PRESUMIDO **:** stuck-up, conceited
estiramiento *nm* **1 :** stretching **2 estiramiento facial :** face-lift
estirar *vt* **:** to stretch (out), to extend — **estirarse** *vr*
estirón *nm, pl* **-rones 1 :** pull, tug **2 dar un estirón :** to grow quickly, to shoot up
estirpe *nf* LINAJE **:** lineage, stock
estival *adj* VERANIEGO **:** summer
esto *pron (neuter)* **1 :** this <¿qué es esto? : what is this?> **2 en ~ :** at this point **3 por ~ :** for this reason
estocada *nf* **1 :** final thrust (in bullfighting) **2 :** thrust, lunge (in fencing)
estofa *nf* CLASE **:** class, quality <de baja estofa : low-class, poor-quality>
estofado *nm* COCIDO, GUISADO **:** stew
estofar *vt* GUISAR **:** to stew
estoicismo *nm* **:** stoicism
estoico[1], -ca *adj* **:** stoic, stoical
estoico[2], -ca *n* **:** stoic
estola *nf* **:** stole
estomacal *adj* GÁSTRICO **:** stomach, gastric
estómago *nm* **:** stomach
estoniano, -na *adj & n* **:** Estonian
estopa *nf* **1 :** tow (yarn or cloth) **2 :** burlap

estopilla *nf* : cheesecloth
estoque *nm* : rapier, sword
estorbar *vt* OBSTRUIR : to obstruct, to hinder — *vi* : to get in the way
estorbo *nm* **1** : obstacle, hindrance **2** : nuisance
estornino *nm* : starling
estornudar *vi* : to sneeze
estornudo *nm* : sneeze
estos → **este**[1]
éstos → **éste**
estoy → **estar**
estrabismo *nm* : squint
estrado *nm* **1** : dais, platform, bench (of a judge) **2** ESTRADOS *nmpl* : courts of law
estrafalario, -ria *adj* ESTRAMBÓTICO, EXCÉNTRICO : eccentric, bizarre
estragar {52} *vt* DEVASTAR : to ruin, to devastate
estragón *nm* : tarragon
estragos *nmpl* **1** : ravages, destruction, devastation <los estragos de la guerra : the ravages of war> **2 hacer estragos en** *or* **causar estragos entre** : to play havoc with
estrambótico, -ca *adj* ESTRAFALARIO, EXCÉNTRICO : eccentric, bizarre
estrangulamiento *nm* : strangling, strangulation
estrangular *vt* AHOGAR : to strangle — **estrangulación** *nf*
estratagema *nf* ARTIMAÑA : stratagem, ruse
estratega *nmf* : strategist
estrategia *nf* : strategy
estratégico, -ca *adj* : strategic, tactical — **estratégicamente** *adv*
estratificación *nf, pl* **-ciones** : stratification
estratificado, -da *adj* : stratified
estrato *nm* : stratum, layer
estratosfera *nf* : stratosphere
estratosférico, -ca *adj* **1** : stratospheric **2** : astronomical, exorbitant
estrechamiento *nm* **1** : narrowing **2** : narrow point **3** : tightening, strengthening (of relations)
estrechar *vt* **1** : to narrow **2** : to tighten, to strengthen (a bond) **3** : to hug, to embrace **4 estrechar la mano de** : to shake hands with — **estrecharse** *vr*
estrechez *nf, pl* **-checes 1** : tightness, narrowness **2 estrecheces** *nfpl* : financial problems
estrecho[1], **-cha** *adj* **1** : tight, narrow **2** ÍNTIMO : close — **estrechamente** *adv*
estrecho[2] *nm* : strait, narrows
estrella *nf* **1** ASTRO : star <estrella fugaz : shooting star> **2** : destiny <tener buena estrella : to be born lucky> **3** : movie star **4 estrella de mar** : starfish
estrellado, -da *adj* **1** : starry **2** : star-shaped **3 huevos estrellados** : fried eggs
estrellamiento *nm* : crash, collision
estrellar *vt* : to smash, to crash — **estrellarse** *vr* : to crash, to collide
estrellato *nm* : stardom
estremecedor, -dora *adj* : horrifying
estremecer {53} *vt* : to cause to shake — *vi* : to tremble, to shake — **estremecerse** *vr* : to shudder, to shiver (with emotion)
estremecimiento *nm* : trembling, shaking, shivering
estrenar *vt* **1** : to use for the first time **2** : to premiere, to open — **estrenarse** *vr* : to make one's debut
estreno *nm* DEBUT : debut, premiere
estreñimiento *nm* : constipation
estreñirse {67} *vr* : to be constipated
estrépito *nm* ESTRUENDO : clamor, din
estrepitoso, -sa *adj* : clamorous, noisy — **estrepitosamente** *adv*
estrés *nm, pl* **estreses** : stress
estresante *adj* : stressful
estresar *vt* : to stress, to stress out
estría *nf* : fluting, groove
estribación *nf, pl* **-ciones 1** : spur, ridge **2 estribaciones** *nfpl* : foothills
estribar *vi* FUNDARSE **~ en** : to be due to, to stem from
estribillo *nm* : refrain, chorus
estribo *nm* **1** : stirrup **2** : abutment, buttress **3 perder los estribos** : to lose one's temper
estribor *nm* : starboard
estricnina *nf* : strychnine
estricto, -ta *adj* SEVERO : strict, severe — **estrictamente** *adv*
estridente *adj* : strident, shrill, loud — **estridentemente** *adv*
estrofa *nf* : stanza, verse
estrógeno *nm* : estrogen
estropajo *nm* : scouring pad
estropear *vt* **1** ARRUINAR : to ruin, to spoil **2** : to break, to damage — **estropearse** *vr* **1** : to spoil, to go bad **2** : to break down
estropicio *nm* DAÑO : damage, breakage
estructura *nf* : structure, framework
estructuración *nf, pl* **-ciones** : structuring, structure
estructural *adj* : structural — **estructuralmente** *adv*
estructurar *vt* : to structure, to organize
estruendo *nm* ESTRÉPITO : racket, din, roar
estruendoso, -sa *adj* : resounding, thunderous
estrujar *vt* APRETAR : to press, to squeeze
estuario *nm* : estuary
estuche *nm* : kit, case
estuco *nm* : stucco
estudiado, -da *adj* : affected, mannered
estudiantado *nm* : student body, students *pl*
estudiante *nmf* : student
estudiantil *adj* : student <la vida estudiantil : student life>

estudiar *v* : to study
estudio *nm* **1** : study **2** : studio **3 estudios** *nmpl* : studies, education
estudioso, -sa *adj* : studious
estufa *nf* **1** : stove, heater **2** *Col, Mex* : cooking stove, range
estupefacción *nf, pl* **-ciones** : stupefaction, astonishment
estupefaciente[1] *adj* : narcotic
estupefaciente[2] *nm* DROGA, NARCÓTICO : drug, narcotic
estupefacto, -ta *adj* : astonished, stunned
estupendo, -da *adj* MARAVILLOSO : stupendous, marvelous — **estupendamente** *adv*
estupidez *nf, pl* **-deces 1** : stupidity **2** : nonsense
estúpido[1], **-da** *adj* : stupid — **estúpidamente** *adj*
estúpido[2], **-da** *n* IDIOTA : idiot, fool
estupor *nm* **1** : stupor **2** : amazement
esturión *nm, pl* **-riones** : sturgeon
estuvo, etc. → **estar**
etano *nm* : ethane
etanol *nm* : ethanol
etapa *nf* FASE : stage, phase
etcétera[1] : et cetera, and so on
etcétera[2] *nmf* : etcetera
éter *nm* : ether
etéreo, -rea *adj* : ethereal, heavenly
eternidad *nf* : eternity
eternizar {21} *vt* PERPETUAR : to make eternal, to perpetuate — **eternizarse** *vr fam* : to take forever
eterno, -na *adj* : eternal, endless — **eternamente** *adv*
ética *nf* : ethics
ético, -ca *adj* : ethical — **éticamente** *adv*
etimología *nf* : etymology
etimológico, -ca *adj* : etymological
etimólogo, -ga *n* : etymologist
etíope *adj & nmf* : Ethiopian
etiqueta *nf* **1** : etiquette **2** : tag, label **3 de ~** : formal, dressy
etiquetar *vt* : to label
étnico, -ca *adj* : ethnic
etnología *nf* : ethnology
etnólogo, -ga *n* : ethnologist
eucalipto *nm* : eucalyptus
Eucaristía *nf* : Eucharist, communion
eucarístico, -ca *adj* : eucharistic
eufemismo *nm* : euphemism
eufemístico, -ca *adj* : euphemistic
eufonía *nf* : euphony
eufónico, -ca *adj* : euphonious
euforia *nf* : euphoria, joyousness
eufórico, -ca *adj* : euphoric, exuberant, joyous — **eufóricamente** *adv*
eunuco *nm* : eunuch
europeo, -pea *adj & n* : European
euskera *nm* : Basque (language)
eutanasia *nf* : euthanasia
evacuación *nf, pl* **-ciones** : evacuation
evacuar *vt* **1** : to evacuate, to vacate **2** : to carry out — *vi* : to have a bowel movement
evadir *vt* ELUDIR : to evade, to avoid — **evadirse** *vr* : to escape, to slip away
evaluación *nf, pl* **-ciones** : assessment, evaluation
evaluar {3} *vt* : to evaluate, to assess, to appraise
evangélico, -ca *adj* : evangelical — **evangélicamente** *adv*
evangelio *nm* : gospel
evangelismo *nm* : evangelism
evangelista *nm* : evangelist
evangelizador, -dora *n* : evangelist, missionary
evaporación *nf, pl* **-ciones** : evaporation
evaporar *vt* : to evaporate — **evaporarse** *vr* ESFUMARSE : to disappear, to vanish
evasión *nf, pl* **-siones 1** : escape, flight **2** : evasion, dodge
evasiva *nf* : excuse, pretext
evasivo, -va *adj* : evasive
evento *nm* : event
eventual *adj* **1** : possible **2** : temporary <trabajadores eventuales : temporary workers> — **eventualmente** *adv*
eventualidad *nf* : possibility, eventuality
evidencia *nf* **1** : evidence, proof **2 poner en evidencia** : to demonstrate, to make clear
evidenciar *vt* : to demonstrate, to show — **evidenciarse** *vr* : to be evident
evidente *adj* : evident, obvious, clear — **evidentemente** *adv*
eviscerar *vt* : to eviscerate
evitable *adj* : avoidable, preventable
evitar *vt* **1** : to avoid **2** PREVENIR : to prevent **3** ELUDIR : to escape, to elude
evocación *nf, pl* **-ciones** : evocation
evocador, -dora *adj* : evocative
evocar {72} *vt* **1** : to evoke **2** RECORDAR : to recall
evolución *nf, pl* **-ciones 1** : evolution **2** : development, progress
evolucionar *vi* **1** : to evolve **2** : to change, to develop
evolutivo, -va *adj* : evolutionary
exabrupto *nm* : pointed remark
exacción *nf, pl* **-ciones** : levying, exaction
exacerbar *vt* **1** : to exacerbate, to aggravate **2** : to irritate, to exasperate
exactamente *adv* : exactly
exactitud *nf* PRECISIÓN : accuracy, precision, exactitude
exacto, -ta *adj* PRECISO : accurate, precise, exact
exageración *nf, pl* **-ciones** : exaggeration
exagerado, -da *adj* **1** : exaggerated **2** : excessive — **exageradamente** *adv*
exagerar *v* : to exaggerate
exaltación *nf, pl* **-ciones 1** : exaltation **2** : excitement, agitation
exaltado[1], **-da** *adj* : excitable, hotheaded
exaltado[2], **-da** *n* : hothead

exaltar *vt* **1** ENSALZAR **:** to exalt, to extol **2 :** to excite, to agitate — **exaltarse** *vr* ACALORARSE **:** to get overexcited

ex–alumno → **alumno**

examen *nm, pl* **exámenes 1 :** examination, test **2 :** consideration, investigation

examinar *vt* **1 :** to examine **2** INSPECCIONAR **:** to inspect — **examinarse** *vr* **:** to take an exam

exánime *adj* **1 :** lifeless **2 :** exhausted

exasperar *vt* IRRITAR **:** to exasperate, to irritate — **exasperación** *nf*

excavación *nf, pl* **-ciones :** excavation

excavadora *nf* **:** excavator

excavar *v* **:** to excavate, to dig

excedente[1] *adj* **1 :** excessive **2 :** excess, surplus

excedente[2] *nm* **:** surplus, excess

exceder *vt* **:** to exceed, to surpass — **excederse** *vr* **:** to go too far

excelencia *nf* **1 :** excellence **2 :** excellency <Su Excelencia : His Excellency>

excelente *adj* **:** excellent — **excelentemente** *adv*

excelso, -sa *adj* **:** lofty, sublime

excentricidad *nf* **:** eccentricity

excéntrico, -ca *adj & n* **:** eccentric

excepción *nf, pl* **-ciones :** exception

excepcional *adj* EXTRAORDINARIO **:** exceptional, extraordinary, rare

excepto *prep* SALVO **:** except

exceptuar {3} *vt* EXCLUIR **:** to except, to exclude

excesivo, -va *adj* **:** excessive — **excesivamente** *adv*

exceso *nm* **1 :** excess **2 excesos** *nmpl* **:** excesses, abuses **3 exceso de velocidad :** speeding

excitabilidad *nf* **:** excitability

excitación *nf, pl* **-ciones :** excitement

excitante *adj* **:** exciting

excitar *vt* **:** to excite, to arouse — **excitarse** *vr*

exclamación *nf, pl* **-ciones :** exclamation

exclamar *v* **:** to exclaim

excluir {41} *vt* EXCEPTUAR **:** to exclude, to leave out

exclusión *nf, pl* **-siones :** exclusion

exclusividad *nf* **1 :** exclusiveness **2 :** exclusive rights *pl*

exclusivo, -va *adj* **:** exclusive — **exclusivamente** *adv*

excomulgar {52} *vt* **:** to excommunicate

excomunión *nf, pl* **-niones :** excommunication

excreción *nf, pl* **-ciones :** excretion

excremento *nm* **:** excrement

excretar *vt* **:** to excrete

exculpar *vt* **:** to exonerate, to exculpate — **exculpación** *nf*

excursión *nf, pl* **-siones :** excursion, outing

excursionista *nmf* **1 :** sightseer, tourist **2 :** hiker

excusa *nf* **1** PRETEXTO **:** excuse **2** DISCULPA **:** apology

excusar *vt* **1 :** to excuse **2 :** to exempt — **excusarse** *vr* **:** to apologize, to send one's regrets

execrable *adj* **:** detestable, abominable

exención *nf, pl* **-ciones :** exemption

exento, -ta *adj* **1 :** exempt, free **2 exento de impuestos :** tax-exempt

exequias *nfpl* FUNERALES **:** funeral rites

exhalar *vt* ESPIRAR **:** to exhale, to give off

exhaustivo, -va *adj* **:** exhaustive — **exhaustivamente** *adv*

exhausto, -ta *adj* AGOTADO **:** exhausted, worn-out

exhibición *nf, pl* **-ciones 1 :** exhibition, show **2 :** showing

exhibir *vt* **:** to exhibit, to show, to display — **exhibirse** *vr*

exhortación *nf, pl* **-ciones :** exhortation

exhortar *vt* **:** to exhort

exhumar *vt* DESENTERRAR **:** to exhume — **exhumación** *nf*

exigencia *nf* **:** demand, requirement

exigente *adj* **:** demanding, exacting

exigir {35} *vt* **1 :** to demand, to require **2 :** to exact, to levy

exiguo, -gua *adj* **:** meager

exiliado[1]**, -da** *adj* **:** exiled, in exile

exiliado[2]**, -da** *n* **:** exile

exiliar *vt* DESTERRAR **:** to exile, to banish — **exiliarse** *vr* **:** to go into exile

exilio *nm* DESTIERRO **:** exile

eximio, -mia *adj* **:** distinguished, eminent

eximir *vt* EXONERAR **:** to exempt

existencia *nf* **1 :** existence **2 existencias** *nfpl* MERCANCÍA **:** goods, stock

existente *adj* **1 :** existing, in existence **2 :** in stock

existir *vi* **:** to exist

éxito *nm* **1** TRIUNFO **:** success, hit **2 tener éxito :** to be successful

exitoso, -sa *adj* **:** successful — **exitosamente** *adv*

éxodo *nm* **:** exodus

exoneración *nf, pl* **-ciones** EXENCIÓN **:** exoneration, exemption

exonerar *vt* **1** EXIMIR **:** to exempt, to exonerate **2** DESPEDIR **:** to dismiss

exorbitante *adj* **:** exorbitant

exorcismo *nm* **:** exorcism — **exorcista** *nmf*

exorcizar {21} *vt* **:** to exorcize

exótico, -ca *adj* **:** exotic

expandir *vt* EXPANSIONAR **:** to expand — **expandirse** *vr* **:** to spread

expansión *nf, pl* **-siones 1 :** expansion, spread **2** DIVERSIÓN **:** recreation, relaxation

expansionar *vt* EXPANDIR **:** to expand — **expansionarse** *vr* **1 :** to expand **2** DIVERTIRSE **:** to amuse oneself, to relax

expansivo, -va *adj* **:** expansive

expatriado, -da *adj & n* **:** expatriate

expatriarse {85} *vr* **1** EMIGRAR **:** to emigrate **2 :** to go into exile

expectación *nf, pl* **-ciones** : expectation, anticipation

expectante *adj* : expectant

expectativa *nf* **1** : expectation, hope **2 expectativas** *nfpl* : prospects

expedición *nf, pl* **-ciones** : expedition

expediente *nm* **1** : expedient, means **2** ARCHIVO : file, dossier, record

expedir {54} *vt* **1** EMITIR : to issue **2** DESPACHAR : to dispatch, to send

expedito, -ta *adj* **1** : free, clear **2** : quick, easy

expeler *vt* : to expel, to eject

expendedor, -dora *n* : dealer, seller

expendio *nm* TIENDA : store, shop

expensas *nfpl* **1** : expenses, costs **2 a expensas de** : at the expense of

experiencia *nf* **1** : experience **2** EXPERIMENTO : experiment

experimentación *nf, pl* **-ciones** : experimentation

experimental *adj* : experimental

experimentar *vi* : to experiment — *vt* **1** : to experiment with, to test out **2** : to experience

experimento *nm* EXPERIENCIA : experiment

experto, -ta *adj & n* : expert

expiación *nf, pl* **-ciones** : expiation, atonement

expiar {85} *vt* : to expiate, to atone for

expiración *nf, pl* **-ciones** VENCIMIENTO : expiration

expirar *vi* **1** FALLECER, MORIR : to pass away, to die **2** : to expire

explanada *nf* : esplanade, promenade

explayar *vt* : to extend — **explayarse** *vr* : to expound, to speak at length

explicable *adj* : explicable, explainable

explicación *nf, pl* **-ciones** : explanation

explicar {72} *vt* : to explain — **explicarse** *vr* : to understand

explicativo, -va *adj* : explanatory

explicitar *vt* : to state explicitly, to specify

explícito, -ta *adj* : explicit — **explícitamente** *adv*

exploración *nf, pl* **-ciones** : exploration

explorador, -dora *n* : explorer, scout

explorar *vt* : to explore — **exploratorio, -ria** *adj*

explosión *nf, pl* **-siones 1** ESTALLIDO : explosion **2** : outburst <una explosión de ira : an outburst of anger>

explosivo, -va *adj* : explosive

explotación *nf, pl* **-ciones 1** : exploitation **2** : operation, running

explotar *vt* **1** : to exploit **2** : to operate, to run — *vi* ESTALLAR, REVENTAR : to explode

exponente *nm* : exponent

exponential *adj* : exponential — **exponentialmente** *adv*

exponer {60} *vt* **1** : to exhibit, to show, to display **2** : to explain, to present, to set forth **3** : to expose, to risk — *vi* : to exhibit

exportación *nf, pl* **-ciones 1** : exportation **2 exportaciones** *nfpl* : exports

exportador, -dora *n* : exporter

exportar *vt* : to export — **exportable** *adj*

exposición *nf, pl* **-ciones 1** EXHIBICIÓN : exposition, exhibition **2** : exposure **3** : presentation, statement

expositor, -tora *n* **1** : exhibitor **2** : exponent

exprés *nms & pl* **1** : express, express train **2** : espresso

expresamente *adv* : expressly, on purpose

expresar *vt* : to express — **expresarse** *vr*

expresión *nf, pl* **-siones** : expression

expresivo, -va *adj* **1** : expressive **2** CARIÑOSO : affectionate — **expresivamente** *adv*

expreso[1]**, -sa** *adj* : express, specific

expreso[2] *nm* : express train, express

exprimidor *nm* : squeezer, juicer

exprimir *vt* **1** : to squeeze **2** : to exploit

expropiar *vt* : to expropriate, to commandeer — **expropiación** *nf*

expuesto[1] *pp* → **exponer**

expuesto[2]**, -ta** *adj* **1** : exposed **2** : hazardous, risky

expulsar *vt* : to expel, to eject

expulsión *nf, pl* **-siones** : expulsion

expurgar {52} *vt* : to expurgate

expuso, etc. → **exponer**

exquisitez *nf, pl* **-teces 1** : exquisiteness, refinement **2** : delicacy, special dish

exquisito, -ta *adj* **1** : exquisite **2** : delicious

extasiarse {85} *vr* : to be in ecstasy, to be enraptured

éxtasis *nms & pl* : ecstasy, rapture

extático, -ta *adj* : ecstatic

extemporáneo, -nea *adj* **1** : unseasonable **2** : untimely

extender {56} *vt* **1** : to spread out, to stretch out **2** : to broaden, to expand <extender la influencia : to broaden one's influence> **3** : to draw up (a document), to write out (a check) — **extenderse** *vr* **1** : to spread **2** : to last

extendido, -da *adj* **1** : outstretched **2** : widespread

extensamente *adv* : extensively, at length

extensible *adj* : extensible, extendable

extensión *nf, pl* **-siones 1** : extension, stretching **2** : expanse, spread **3** : extent, range **4** : length, duration

extenso, -sa *adj* **1** : extensive, detailed **2** : spacious, vast

extenuar {3} *vt* : to exhaust, to tire out — **extenuarse** *vr* — **extenuante** *adj*

exterior[1] *adj* **1** : exterior, external **2** : foreign <asuntos exteriores : foreign affairs>

exterior[2] *nm* **1** : outside **2** : abroad

exteriorizar {21} *vt* : to express, to reveal

exteriormente *adv* : outwardly

exterminar *vt* : to exterminate — **exterminación** *nf*
exterminio *nm* : extermination
externar *vt Mex* : to express, to display
externo, -na *adj* : external, outward
extinción *nf, pl* **-ciones** : extinction
extinguidor *nm* : fire extinguisher
extinguir {26} *vt* **1** APAGAR : to extinguish, to put out **2** : to wipe out — **extinguirse** *vr* **1** APAGARSE : to go out, to fade out **2** : to die out, to become extinct
extinto, -ta *adj* : extinct
extintor *nm* : extinguisher
extirpación *n, pl* **-ciones** : removal, excision
extirpar *vt* : to eradicate, to remove, to excise — **extirparse** *vr*
extorsión *nf, pl* **-siones** **1** : extortion **2** : harm, trouble
extorsionar *vt* : to extort
extra[1] *adv* : extra
extra[2] *adj* **1** : additional, extra **2** : superior, top-quality
extra[3] *nmf* : extra (in movies)
extra[4] *nm* : extra expense <paga extra : bonus>
extracción *nf, pl* **-ciones** : extraction
extracto *nm* **1** : extract <extracto de vainilla : vanilla extract> **2** : abstract, summary
extradición *nf, pl* **-ciones** : extradition
extraditar *vt* : to extradite
extraer {81} *vt* : to extract
extraído *pp* → **extraer**
extrajudicial *adj* : out-of-court
extramatrimonial *adj* : extramarital
extranjerizante *adj* : foreign-sounding, foreign-looking
extranjero[1], **-ra** *adj* : foreign
extranjero[2], **-ra** *n* : foreigner
extranjero[3] *nm* : foreign countries *pl* <viajó al extranjero : he traveled abroad> <trabajan en el extranjero : they work overseas>
extrañamente *adv* : strangely, oddly
extrañamiento *nm* ASOMBRO : amazement, surprise, wonder
extrañar *vt* : to miss (someone) — **extrañarse** *vr* : to be surprised
extrañeza *nf* **1** : strangeness, oddness **2** : surprise
extraño[1], **-ña** *adj* **1** RARO : strange, odd **2** EXTRANJERO : foreign
extraño[2], **-ña** *n* DESCONOCIDO : stranger
extraoficial *adj* OFICIOSO : unofficial — **extraoficialmente** *adv*
extraordinario, -ria *adj* EXCEPCIONAL : extraordinary — **extraordinariamente** *adv*
extrasensorial *adj* : extrasensory <percepción extrasensorial : extrasensory perception>
extraterrestre *adj & nmf* : extraterrestrial, alien
extravagancia *nf* : extravagance, outlandishness, flamboyance
extravagante *adj* : extravagant, outrageous, flamboyant
extraviar {85} *vt* **1** : to mislead, to lead astray **2** : to misplace, to lose — **extraviarse** *vr* : to get lost, to go astray
extravío *nm* **1** PÉRDIDA : loss, misplacement **2** : misconduct
extremado, -da *adj* : extreme — **extremadamente** *adv*
extremar *vt* : to carry to extremes — **extremarse** *vr* : to do one's utmost
extremidad *nf* **1** : extremity, tip, edge **2 extremidades** *nfpl* : extremities
extremista *adj & nmf* : extremist
extremo[1], **-ma** *adj* **1** : extreme, utmost **2** EXCESIVO : excessive **3 en caso extremo** : as a last resort
extremo[2] *nm* **1** : extreme, end **2 al extremo de** : to the point of **3 en ~** : in the extreme
extrovertido[1] **-da** *adj* : extroverted, outgoing
extrovertido[2], **-da** *n* : extrovert
extrudir *vt* : to extrude
exuberancia *nf* **1** : exuberance **2** : luxuriance, lushness
exuberante *adj* : exuberant, luxuriant — **exuberantemente** *adv*
exudar *vt* : to exude
exultación *nf, pl* **-ciones** : exultation, elation
exultante *adj* : exultant, elated — **exultantemente** *adv*
exultar *vi* : to exult, to rejoice
eyacular *vi* : to ejaculate — **eyaculación** *nf*
eyección *nf, pl* **-ciones** : ejection, expulsion
eyectar *vt* : to eject, to expel — **eyectarse** *vr*

F

f *nf* : sixth letter of the Spanish alphabet
fábrica *nf* FACTORÍA : factory
fabricación *nf, pl* **-ciones** : manufacture
fabricante *nmf* : manufacturer
fabricar {72} *vt* MANUFACTURAR : to manufacture, to make
fabril *adj* INDUSTRIAL : industrial, manufacturing
fábula *nf* **1** : fable **2** : fabrication, fib
fabuloso, -sa *adj* **1** : fabulous, fantastic **2** : mythical, fabled
facción *nf, pl* **facciones** **1** : faction **2 facciones** *nfpl* RASGOS : features
faccioso, -sa *adj* : factious
faceta *nf* : facet
facha *nf* : appearance, look <estar hecho una facha : to look a sight>
fachada *nf* : facade

facial *adj* : facial
fácil *adj* **1** : easy **2** : likely, probable <es fácil que no pase : it probably won't happen>
facilidad *nf* **1** : facility, ease **2 facilidades** *nfpl* : facilities, services **3 facilidades** *nfpl* : opportunities
facilitar *vt* **1** : to facilitate **2** : to provide, to supply
fácilmente *adv* : easily, readily
facsímil *or* **facsímile** *nm* **1** : facsimile, copy **2** : fax
facsimilar *adj* : facsimile
factibilidad *nf* : feasibility
factible *adj* : feasible, practicable
facticio, -cia *adj* : artificial, factitious
factor[1], **-tora** *n* **1** : agent, factor **2** : baggage clerk
factor[2] *nm* ELEMENTO : factor, element
factoría *nf* FÁBRICA : factory
factótum *nm* : factotum
factura *nf* **1** : making, manufacturing **2** : bill, invoice
facturación *nf, pl* **-ciones 1** : invoicing, billing **2** : check-in
facturar *vt* **1** : to bill, to invoice **2** : to register, to check in
facultad *nf* **1** : faculty, ability <facultades mentales : mental faculties> **2** : authority, power **3** : school (of a university) <facultad de derecho : law school>
facultar *vt* : to authorize, to empower
facultativo, -va *adj* **1** OPTATIVO : voluntary, optional **2** : medical <informe facultativo : medical report>
faena *nf* : task, job, work <faenas domésticas : housework>
faenar *vi* **1** : to work, to labor **2** PESCAR : to fish
fagot *nm* : bassoon
faisán *nm, pl* **faisanes** : pheasant
faja *nf* **1** : sash, belt **2** : girdle **3** : strip (of land)
fajar *vt* **1** : to wrap (a sash or girdle) around **2** : to hit, to thrash — **fajarse** *vr* **1** : to put on a sash or girdle **2** : to come to blows
fajo *nm* : bundle, sheaf <un fajo de billetes : a wad of cash>
falacia *nf* : fallacy
falaz, -laza *adj, mpl* **falaces** FALSO : fallacious, false
falda *nf* **1** : skirt <falda escocesa : kilt> **2** REGAZO : lap (of the body) **3** VERTIENTE : side, slope
falible *adj* : fallible
fálico, -ca *adj* : phallic
falla *nf* **1** : flaw, defect **2** : (geological) fault **3** : fault, failing
fallar *vi* **1** FRACASAR : to fail, to go wrong **2** : to rule (in a court of law) — *vt* **1** ERRAR : to miss (a target) **2** : to pronounce judgment on
fallecer {53} *vi* MORIR : to pass away, to die
fallecido, -da *adj & n* DIFUNTO : deceased
fallecimiento *nm* : demise, death
fallido, -da *adj* : failed, unsuccessful
fallo *nm* **1** SENTENCIA : sentence, judgment, verdict **2** : error, fault
falo *nm* : phallus, penis
falsamente *adv* : falsely
falsear *vt* **1** : to falsify, to fake **2** : to distort — *vi* **1** CEDER : to give way **2** : to be out of tune
falsedad *nf* **1** : falseness, hypocrisy **2** MENTIRA : falsehood, lie
falsete *nm* : falsetto
falsificación *nf, pl* **-ciones 1** : counterfeit, forgery **2** : falsification
falsificador, -dora *n* : counterfeiter, forger
falsificar {72} *vt* **1** : to counterfeit, to forge **2** : to falsify
falso, -sa *adj* **1** FALAZ : false, untrue **2** : counterfeit, forged
falta *nf* **1** CARENCIA : lack <hacer falta : to be lacking, to be needed> **2** DEFECTO : defect, fault, error **3** : offense, misdemeanor **4** : foul (in basketball), fault (in tennis)
faltar *vi* **1** : to be lacking, to be needed <me falta ayuda : I need help> **2** : to be absent, to be missing **3** QUEDAR : to remain, to be left <faltan pocos días para la fiesta : the party is just a few days away> **4 ¡no faltaba más!** : don't mention it!, you're welcome!
falto, -ta *adj* **~ de** : lacking (in), short of
fama *nf* **1** : fame **2** REPUTACIÓN : reputation **3 de mala fama** : disreputable
famélico, -ca *adj* HAMBRIENTO : starving, famished
familia *nf* **1** : family **2 familia política** : in-laws
familiar[1] *adj* **1** CONOCIDO : familiar **2** : familial, family **3** INFORMAL : informal
familiar[2] *nmf* PARIENTE : relation, relative
familiaridad *nf* **1** : familiarity **2** : informality
familiarizarse {21} *vr* **~ con** : to familiarize oneself with
famoso[1], **-sa** *adj* CÉLEBRE : famous
famoso[2], **-sa** *n* : celebrity
fanal *nm* **1** : beacon, signal light **2** *Mex* : headlight
fanático, -ca *adj & n* : fanatic
fanatismo *nm* : fanaticism
fandango *nm* : fandango
fanfarria *nf* **1** : (musical) fanfare **2** : pomp, ceremony
fanfarrón[1], **-rrona** *adj, mpl* **-rrones** *fam* : bragging, boastful
fanfarrón[2], **-rrona** *n, mpl* **-rrones** *fam* : braggart
fanfarronada *nf* : boast, bluster
fanfarronear *vi* : to brag, to boast
fango *nm* LODO : mud, mire
fangosidad *nf* : muddiness
fangoso, -sa *adj* LODOSO : muddy
fantasear *vi* : to fantasize, to daydream
fantasía *nf* **1** : fantasy **2** : imagination

fantasma *nm* : ghost, phantom
fantasmal *adj* : ghostly
fantástico, -ca *adj* **1** : fantastic, imaginary, unreal **2** *fam* : great, fantastic
faquir *nm* : fakir
farándula *nf* : show business, theater
faraón *nm, pl* **faraones** : pharaoh
fardo *nm* **1** : bale **2** : bundle
farfulla *nf* : jabbering
farfullar *v* : to jabber, to gabble
faringe *nf* : pharynx
faríngeo, -gea *adj* : pharyngeal
fariña *nf* : coarse manioc flour
farmacéutico[1]**, -ca** *adj* : pharmaceutical
farmacéutico[2]**, -ca** *n* : pharmacist
farmacia *nf* : drugstore, pharmacy
fármaco *nm* : medicine, drug
farmacodependencia *nf* : drug addiction
farmacología *nf* : pharmacology
faro *nm* **1** : lighthouse **2** : headlight
farol *nm* **1** : streetlight **2** : lantern, lamp **3** *fam* : bluff **4** *Mex* : headlight
farola *nf* **1** : lamppost **2** : streetlight
farolero, -ra *n fam* : bluffer
farra *nf* : spree, revelry
fárrago *nm* REVOLTIJO : hodgepodge, jumble
farsa *nf* **1** : farce **2** : fake, sham
farsante *nmf* CHARLATÁN : charlatan, fraud, phony
fascículo *nm* : fascicle, part (of a publication)
fascinación *nf, pl* **-ciones** : fascination
fascinante *adj* : fascinating
fascinar *vt* **1** : to fascinate **2** : to charm, to captivate
fascismo *nm* : fascism
fascista *adj & nmf* : fascist
fase *nf* : phase, stage
fastidiar *vt* **1** MOLESTAR : to annoy, to bother, to hassle **2** ABURRIR : to bore — *vi* : to be annoying or bothersome
fastidio *nm* **1** MOLESTIA : annoyance, nuisance, hassle **2** ABURRIMIENTO : boredom
fastidioso, -sa *adj* **1** MOLESTO : annoying, bothersome **2** ABURRIDO : boring
fatal *adj* **1** MORTAL : fatal **2** *fam* : awful, terrible **3** : fateful, unavoidable
fatalidad *nf* **1** : fatality **2** DESGRACIA : misfortune, bad luck
fatalismo *nm* : fatalism
fatalista[1] *adj* : fatalistic
fatalista[2] *nmf* : fatalist
fatalmente *adv* **1** : unavoidably **2** : unfortunately
fatídico, -ca *adj* : fateful, momentous
fatiga *nf* CANSANCIO : fatigue
fatigado, -da *adj* AGOTADO : weary, tired
fatigar {52} *vt* CANSAR : to fatigue, to tire — **fatigarse** *vr* : to wear oneself out
fatigoso, -sa *adj* : fatiguing, tiring
fatuidad *nf* **1** : fatuousness **2** VANIDAD : vanity, conceit
fatuo, -tua *adj* **1** : fatuous **2** PRESUMIDO : vain
fauces *nfpl* : jaws *pl,* maw
faul *nm, pl* **fauls** : foul, foul ball
fauna *nf* : fauna
fausto *nm* : splendor, magnificence
favor *nm* **1** : favor **2 a favor de** : in favor of **3 por ~** : please
favorable *adj* : favorable — **favorablemente** *adv*
favorecedor, -dora *adj* : becoming, flattering
favorecer {53} *vt* **1** : to favor **2** : to look well on, to suit
favorecido, -da *adj* **1** : flattering **2** : fortunate
favoritismo *nm* : favoritism
favorito, -ta *adj & n* : favorite
fax *nm* : fax, facsimile
fayuca *nf Mex* **1** : contraband **2** : black market
fayuquero *nm Mex* : smuggler, black marketeer
faz *nf* **1** : face, countenance <la faz de la tierra : the face of the earth> **2** : side (of coins, fabric, etc.)
fe *nf* **1** : faith **2** : assurance, testimony <dar fe de : to bear witness to> **3** : intention, will <de buena fe : bona fide, in good faith>
fealdad *nf* : ugliness
febrero *nm* : February
febril *adj* : feverish — **febrilmente** *adv*
fecal *adj* : fecal
fecha *nf* **1** : date **2 fecha de caducidad** *or* **fecha de vencimiento** : expiration date **3 fecha límite** : deadline
fechar *vt* : to date, to put a date on
fechoría *nf* : misdeed
fécula *nf* : starch
fecundar *vt* : to fertilize (an egg) — **fecundación** *nf*
fecundidad *nf* **1** : fecundity, fertility **2** : productiveness
fecundo, -da *adj* FÉRTIL : fertile, fecund
federación *nf, pl* **-ciones** : federation
federal *adj* : federal
federalismo *nm* : federalism
federalista *adj & nmf* : federalist
federar *vt* : to federate
fehaciente *adj* : reliable, irrefutable — **fehacientemente** *adv*
feldespato *nm* : feldspar
felicidad *nf* **1** : happiness **2 ¡felicidades!** : best wishes!, congratulations!, happy birthday!
felicitación *nf, pl* **-ciones** **1** : congratulation <¡felicitaciones! : congratulations!> **2** : greeting card
felicitar *vt* CONGRATULAR : to congratulate — **felicitarse** *vr* : to be glad about
feligrés, -gresa *n, mpl* **-greses** : parishioner
feligresía *nf* : parish
felino, -na *adj & n* : feline
feliz *adj, pl* **felices** **1** : happy **2 Feliz Navidad** : Merry Christmas

felizmente *adv* **1 :** happily **2 :** fortunately, luckily
felonía *nf* **:** felony
felpa *nf* **1 :** terry cloth **2 :** plush
felpudo *nm* **:** doormat
femenil *adj* **:** women's, girls' <futbol femenil : women's soccer>
femenino, -na *adj* **1 :** feminine **2 :** women's <derechos femeninos : women's rights> **3 :** female
femineidad *nf* **:** femininity
feminidad *nf* **:** femininity
feminismo *nm* **:** feminism
feminista *adj & nmf* **:** feminist
femoral *adj* **:** femoral
fémur *nm* **:** femur, thighbone
fenecer {53} *vi* **1 :** to die, to pass away **2 :** to come to an end, to cease
fénix *nm* **:** phoenix
fenomenal *adj* **1 :** phenomenal **2** *fam* **:** fantastic, terrific — **fenomenalmente** *adv*
fenómeno *nm* **1 :** phenomenon **2 :** prodigy, genius
feo[1] *adv* **:** badly, bad
feo[2], fea *adj* **1 :** ugly **2 :** unpleasant, nasty
féretro *nm* ATAÚD **:** coffin, casket
feria *nf* **1 :** fair, market **2 :** festival, holiday **3** *Mex* **:** change (money)
feriado, -da *adj* **día feriado :** public holiday
ferial *nm* **:** fairground
fermentar *v* **:** to ferment — **fermentación** *nf*
fermento *nm* **:** ferment
ferocidad *nf* **:** ferocity, fierceness
feroz *adj, pl* **feroces** FIERO **:** ferocious, fierce — **ferozmente** *adv*
férreo, -rrea *adj* **1 :** iron **2 :** strong, steely <una voluntad férrea : an iron will> **3 :** strict, severe **4 vía férrea :** railroad track
ferretería *nf* **1 :** hardware store **2 :** hardware **3 :** foundry, ironworks
férrico, -ca *adj* **:** ferric
ferrocarril *nm* **:** railroad, railway
ferrocarrilero → **ferroviario**
ferroso, -sa *adj* **:** ferrous
ferroviario, -ria *adj* **:** rail, railroad
ferry *nm, pl* **ferrys :** ferry
fértil *adj* FECUNDO **:** fertile, fruitful
fertilidad *nf* **:** fertility
fertilizante[1] *adj* **:** fertilizing <droga fertilizante : fertility drug>
fertilizante[2] *nm* ABONO **:** fertilizer
fertilizar *vt* ABONAR **:** to fertilize — **fertilización** *nf*
ferviente *adj* FERVOROSO **:** fervent
fervor *nm* **:** fervor, zeal
fervoroso, -sa *adj* FERVIENTE **:** fervent, zealous
festejar *vt* **1** CELEBRAR **:** to celebrate **2** AGASAJAR **:** to entertain, to wine and dine **3** *Mex fam* **:** to thrash, to beat
festejo *nm* **:** celebration, festivity
festín *nm, pl* **festines :** banquet, feast
festinar *vt* **:** to hasten, to hurry up
festival *nm* **:** festival
festividad *nf* **1 :** festivity **2 :** (religious) feast, holiday
festivo, -va *adj* **1 :** festive **2 día festivo :** holiday — **festivamente** *adv*
fetal *adj* **:** fetal
fetiche *nm* **:** fetish
fétido, -da *adj* **:** fetid, foul
feto *nm* **:** fetus
feudal *adj* **:** feudal — **feudalismo** *nm*
feudo *nm* **1 :** fief **2 :** domain, territory
fiabilidad *nf* **:** reliability, trustworthiness
fiable *adj* **:** trustworthy, reliable
fiado, -da *adj* **:** on credit
fiador, -dora *n* **:** bondsman, guarantor
fiambrería *nf* **:** delicatessen
fiambres *nfpl* **:** cold cuts
fianza *nf* **1** CAUCIÓN **:** bail, bond **2 :** surety, deposit
fiar {85} *vt* **1 :** to sell on credit **2 :** to guarantee — **fiarse** *vr* **~ de :** to place trust in
fiasco *nm* FRACASO **:** fiasco, failure
fibra *nf* **1 :** fiber **2 fibra de vidrio :** fiberglass
fibrilar *vi* **:** to fibrillate — **fibrilación** *nf*
fibroso, -sa *adj* **:** fibrous
ficción *nf, pl* **ficciones 1 :** fiction **2 :** fabrication, lie
ficha *nf* **1 :** index card **2 :** file, record **3 :** token **4 :** domino, checker, counter, poker chip
fichar *vt* **1 :** to open a file on **2 :** to sign up — *vi* **:** to punch in, to punch out
fichero *nm* **1 :** card file **2 :** filing cabinet
ficticio, -cia *adj* **:** fictitious
fidedigno, -na *adj* FIABLE **:** reliable, trustworthy
fideicomisario, -ria *n* **:** trustee
fideicomiso *nm* **:** trusteeship, trust <guardar en fideicomiso : to hold in trust>
fidelidad *nf* **:** fidelity, faithfulness
fideo *nm* **:** noodle
fiduciario[1], -ria *adj* **:** fiduciary
fiduciario[2], -ria *n* **:** trustee
fiebre *nf* **1** CALENTURA **:** fever, temperature <fiebre amarilla : yellow fever> <fiebre palúdica : malaria> **2 :** fever, excitement
fiel[1] *adj* **1 :** faithful, loyal **2 :** accurate — **fielmente** *adv*
fiel[2] *nm* **1 :** pointer (of a scale) **2 los fieles :** the faithful
fieltro *nm* **:** felt
fiera *nf* **1 :** wild animal, beast **2 :** fiend, demon <una fiera para el trabajo : a demon for work>
fiero, -ra *adj* FEROZ **:** fierce, ferocious
fierro *nm* HIERRO **:** iron
fiesta *nf* **1 :** party, fiesta **2 :** holiday, feast day
figura *nf* **1 :** figure **2 :** shape, form **3 figura retórica :** figure of speech
figurado, -da *adj* **:** figurative — **figuradamente** *adv*

figurar *vi* **1 :** to figure, to be included <Rivera figura entre los más grandes pintores de México : Rivera is among Mexico's greatest painters> **2 :** to be prominent, to stand out — *vt* **:** to represent <esta línea figura el horizonte : this line represents the horizon> — **figurarse** *vr* **:** to imagine, to think <¡figúrate el lío en que se metió! : imagine the mess she got into!>
fijación *nf, pl* **-ciones 1 :** fixation, obsession **2 :** fixing, establishing **3 :** fastening, securing
fijador *nm* **1 :** fixative **2 :** hair spray
fijamente *adv* **:** fixedly
fijar *vt* **1 :** to fasten, to affix **2** ESTABLECER **:** to establish, to set up **3** CONCRETAR **:** to set, to fix <fijar la fecha : to set the date> — **fijarse** *vr* **1 :** to settle, to become fixed **2 ~ en :** to notice, to pay attention to
fijeza *nf* **1 :** firmness (of convictions) **2 :** persistence, constancy <mirar con fijeza a : to stare at>
fijiano, -na *adj & n* **:** Fijian
fijo, -ja *adj* **1 :** fixed, firm, steady **2** PERMANENTE **:** permanent
fila *nf* **1** HILERA **:** line, file <ponerse en fila : to get in line> **2 :** rank, row **3 filas** *nfpl* **:** ranks <cerrar filas : to close ranks>
filamento *nm* **:** filament
filantropía *nf* **:** philanthropy
filantrópico, -ca *adj* **:** philanthropic
filántropo, -pa *n* **:** philanthropist
filatelia *nf* **:** philately, stamp collecting
filatelista *nmf* **:** stamp collector, philatelist
filete *nm* **1 :** fillet **2** SOLOMILLO **:** sirloin **3 :** thread (of a screw)
filiación *nf, pl* **-ciones 1 :** affiliation, connection **2 :** particulars *pl,* (police) description
filial[1] *adj* **:** filial
filial[2] *nf* **:** affiliate, subsidiary
filibustero *nm* **:** freebooter, pirate
filigrana *nf* **1 :** filigree **2 :** watermark (on paper)
filipino, -na *adj & n* **:** Filipino
filmación *nf, pl* **-ciones :** filming, shooting
filmar *vt* **:** to film, to shoot
filme *or* **film** *nm* PELÍCULA **:** film, movie
filmina *nf* **:** slide, transparency
filo *nm* **1 :** cutting edge, blade **2 :** edge <al filo del escritorio : at the edge of the desk> <al filo de la medianoche : at the stroke of midnight>
filología *nf* **:** philology
filólogo, -ga *n* **:** philologist
filón *nm, pl* **filones 1 :** seam, vein (of minerals) **2** *fam* **:** successful business, gold mine
filoso, -sa *adj* **:** sharp
filosofar *vi* **:** to philosophize
filosofía *nf* **:** philosophy
filosófico, -ca *adj* **:** philosophic, philosophical — **filosóficamente** *adv*
filósofo, -fa *n* **:** philosopher
filtración *nf* **:** seepage, leaking
filtrar *v* **:** to filter — **filtrarse** *vr* **:** to seep through, to leak
filtro *nm* **:** filter
filudo, -da *adj* **:** sharp
fin *nm* **1 :** end **2 :** purpose, aim, objective **3 en ~ :** in short **4 fin de semana :** weekend **5 por ~ :** finally, at last
finado, -da *adj & n* DIFUNTO **:** deceased
final[1] *adj* **:** final, ultimate — **finalmente** *adv*
final[2] *nm* **1 :** end, conclusion, finale **2 finales** *nmpl* **:** play-offs
finalidad *nf* **1 :** purpose, aim **2 :** finality
finalista *nmf* **:** finalist
finalización *nf* **:** completion, end
finalizar {21} *v* **:** to finish, to end
financiación *nf, pl* **-ciones :** financing, funding
financiamiento *nm* → **financiación**
financiar *vt* **:** to finance, to fund
financiero[1]**, -ra** *adj* **:** financial
financiero[2]**, -ra** *n* **:** financier
financista *nmf* **:** financier
finanzas *nfpl* **:** finances, finance <altas finanzas : high finance>
finca *nf* **1 :** farm, ranch **2 :** country house
fineza *nf* FINURA, REFINAMIENTO **:** refinement
fingido, -da *adj* **:** false, feigned
fingimiento *nm* **:** pretense
fingir {35} *v* **:** to feign, to pretend
finiquitar *vt* **1 :** to settle (an account) **2 :** to conclude, to bring to an end
finiquito *nm* **:** settlement (of an account)
finito, -ta *adj* **:** finite
finja, etc. → **fingir**
finlandés, -desa *adj & n* **:** Finnish
fino, -na *adj* **1 :** fine, excellent **2 :** delicate, slender **3** REFINADO **:** refined **4 :** sharp, acute <olfato fino : keen sense of smell> **5 :** subtle
finta *nf* **:** feint
fintar *or* **fintear** *vi* **:** to feint
finura *nf* **1 :** fineness, high quality **2** FINEZA, REFINAMIENTO **:** refinement
fiordo *nm* **:** fjord
fique *nm* **:** sisal
firma *nf* **1 :** signature **2 :** signing **3** EMPRESA **:** firm, company
firmamento *nm* **:** firmament, sky
firmante *nmf* **:** signer, signatory
firmar *v* **:** to sign
firme *adj* **1 :** firm, resolute **2 :** steady, stable
firmemente *adv* **:** firmly
firmeza *nf* **1 :** firmness, stability **2 :** strength, resolve
firuletes *nmpl* **:** frills, adornments
fiscal[1] *adj* **:** fiscal — **fiscalmente** *adv*
fiscal[2] *nmf* **:** district attorney, prosecutor
fiscalizar {21} *vt* **1 :** to audit, to inspect **2 :** to oversee **3 :** to criticize
fisco *nm* **:** national treasury, exchequer

fisgar {52} *vt* HUSMEAR : to pry into, to snoop on
fisgón, -gona *n, mpl* **fisgones** : snoop, busybody
fisgonear *vi* : to snoop, to pry
fisgue, etc. → **fisgar**
física *nf* : physics
físico[1], **-ca** *adj* : physical — **físicamente** *adv*
físico[2], **-ca** *n* : physicist
físico[3] *nm* : physique, figure
fisiología *nf* : physiology
fisiológico, -ca *adj* : physiological, physiologic
fisiólogo, -ga *n* : physiologist
fisión *nf, pl* **fisiones** : fission — **fisionable** *adj*
fisionomía *nf* → **fisonomía**
fisioterapeuta *nmf* : physical therapist
fisioterapia *nf* : physical therapy
fisonomía *nf* : physiognomy, features *pl*
fistol *nm Mex* : tie clip
fisura *nf* : fissure, crevasse
fláccido, -da *or* **flácido, -da** *adj* : flaccid, flabby
flaco, -ca *adj* **1** DELGADO : thin, skinny **2** : feeble, weak <una excusa flaca : a feeble excuse>
flagelar *vt* : to flagellate — **flagelación** *nf*
flagelo *nm* **1** : scourge, whip **2** : calamity
flagrante *adj* : flagrant, glaring, blatant — **flagrantemente** *adv*
flama *nf* LLAMA : flame
flamante *adj* **1** : bright, brilliant **2** : brand-new
flamear *vi* **1** LLAMEAR : to flame, to blaze **2** ONDEAR : to flap, to flutter
flamenco[1], **-ca** *adj* **1** : flamenco **2** : Flemish
flamenco[2], **-ca** *n* : Fleming, Flemish person
flamenco[3] *nm* **1** : Flemish (language) **2** : flamingo **3** : flamenco (music or dance)
flanco *nm* : flank, side
flanquear *vt* : to flank
flaquear *vi* DECAER : to flag, to weaken
flaqueza *nf* **1** DEBILIDAD : frailty, feebleness **2** : thinness **3** : weakness, failing
flato *nm* : gloom, melancholy
flatulento, -ta *adj* : flatulent — **flatulencia** *nf*
flauta *nf* **1** : flute **2** **flauta dulce** : recorder
flautín *nm, pl* **flautines** : piccolo
flautista *nmf* : flute player, flutist
flebitis *nf* : phlebitis
flecha *nf* : arrow
fleco *nm* **1** : bangs *pl* **2** : fringe
flema *nf* : phlegm
flemático, -ca *adj* : phlegmatic, stolid, impassive
flequillo *nm* : bangs *pl*
fletar *vt* **1** : to charter, to hire **2** : to load (freight)
flete *nm* **1** : charter fee **2** : shipping cost **3** : freight, cargo
fletero *nm* : shipper, carrier
flexibilidad *nf* : flexibility
flexibilizar {21} *vt* : to make more flexible
flexible[1] *adj* : flexible
flexible[2] *nm* **1** : flexible electrical cord **2** : soft hat
flirtear *vi* : to flirt
flojear *vi* **1** DEBILITARSE : to weaken, to flag **2** : to idle, to loaf around
flojedad *nf* : weakness
flojera *nf fam* **1** : lethargy, feeling of weakness **2** : laziness
flojo, -ja *adj* **1** SUELTO : loose, slack **2** : weak, poor <está flojo en las ciencias : he's weak in science> **3** PEREZOSO : lazy
flor *nf* **1** : flower **2** **flor de Pascua** : poinsettia
flora *nf* : flora
floración *nf* : flowering <en plena floración : in full bloom>
floral *adj* : floral
floreado, -da *adj* : flowered, flowery
florear *vi* FLORECER : to flower, to bloom — *vt* **1** : to adorn with flowers **2** *Mex* : to flatter, to compliment
florecer {53} *vi* **1** : to bloom, to blossom **2** : to flourish, to thrive
floreciente *adj* **1** : flowering **2** PROSPERO : flourishing, thriving
florecimiento *nm* : flowering
floreo *nm* : flourish
florería *nf* : flower shop, florist's
florero[1], **-ra** *n* : florist
florero[2] *nm* JARRÓN : vase
floresta *nf* **1** : glade, grove **2** BOSQUE : woods
florido, -da *adj* **1** : full of flowers **2** : florid, flowery <escritos floridos : flowery prose>
florista *nmf* : florist
floritura *nf* : frill, embellishment
flota *nf* : fleet
flotabilidad *nf* : buoyancy
flotación *nf, pl* **-ciones** : flotation
flotador *nm* **1** : float **2** : life preserver
flotante *adj* : floating, buoyant
flotar *vi* : to float
flote *nm* **a ~** : afloat
flotilla *nf* : flotilla, fleet
fluctuar {3} *vi* **1** : to fluctuate **2** VACILAR : to vacillate — **fluctuación** *nf* — **fluctuante** *adj*
fluidez *nf* **1** : fluency **2** : fluidity
fluido[1], **-da** *adj* **1** : flowing **2** : fluent **3** : fluid
fluido[2] *nm* : fluid
fluir {41} *vi* : to flow
flujo *nm* **1** : flow **2** : discharge
flúor *nm* : fluorine
fluoración *nf, pl* **-ciones** : fluoridation
fluorescencia *nf* : fluorescence — **fluorescente** *adj*
fluorizar {21} *vt* : to fluoridate
fluoruro *nm* : fluoride
fluvial *adj* : fluvial, river

fluye, etc. → **fluir**
fobia *nf* : phobia
foca *nf* : seal (animal)
focal *adj* : focal
focha *nf* : coot
foco *nm* **1** : focus **2** : center, pocket **3** : lightbulb **4** : spotlight **5** : headlight
fofo, -fa *adj* **1** ESPONJOSO : soft, spongy **2** : flabby
fogaje *nm* **1** FUEGO : skin eruption, cold sore **2** BOCHORNO : hot and humid weather
fogata *nf* : bonfire
fogón *nm, pl* **fogones** : bonfire
fogonazo *nm* : flash, explosion
fogonero, -ra *n* : stoker (of a furnace), fireman
fogoso, -sa *adj* ARDIENTE : ardent
foguear *vt* : to inure, to accustom
foja *nf* : sheet (of paper)
folículo *nm* : follicle
folio *nm* : folio, leaf
folklore *nm* : folklore
folklórico, -ca *adj* : folk, traditional
follaje *nm* : foliage
folleto *nm* : pamphlet, leaflet, circular
fomentar *vt* **1** : to foment, to stir up **2** PROMOVER : to promote, to foster
fomento *nm* : promotion, encouragement
fonda *nf* **1** POSADA : inn **2** : small restaurant
fondeado, -da *adj fam* : rich, in the money
fondear *vt* **1** : to sound **2** : to sound out, to examine **3** *Mex* : to fund, to finance — *vi* ANCLAR : to anchor — **fondearse** *vr fam* : to get rich
fondeo *nm* **1** : anchoring **2** *Mex* : funding, financing
fondillos *mpl* : seat, bottom (of clothing)
fondo *nm* **1** : bottom **2** : rear, back, end **3** : depth **4** : background **5** : sea bed **6** : fund <fondo de inversiones : investment fund> **7** *Mex* : slip, petticoat **8** **fondos** *nmpl* : funds, resources <cheque sin fondos : bounced check> **9 a ~** : thoroughly, in depth **10 en ~** : abreast
fonema *nm* : phoneme
fonética *nf* : phonetics
fonético, -ca *adj* : phonetic
fontanería *nf* PLOMERÍA : plumbing
fontanero, -ra *n* PLOMERO : plumber
footing [ˈfuˌtɪŋ] *nm* : jogging <hacer footing : to jog>
foque *nm* : jib
forajido, -da *n* : bandit, fugitive, outlaw
foráneo, -nea *adj* : foreign, strange
forastero, -ra *n* : stranger, outsider
forcejear *vi* : to struggle
forcejeo *nm* : struggle
fórceps *nms & pl* : forceps *pl*
forense *adj* : forensic, legal
forestal *adj* : forest
forja *nf* FRAGUA : forge
forjar *vt* **1** : to forge **2** : to shape, to create <forjar un compromiso : to hammer out a compromise> **3** : to invent, to concoct
forma *nf* **1** : form, shape **2** MANERA, MODO : manner, way **3** : fitness <estar en forma : to be fit, to be in shape> **4** **formas** *nfpl* : appearances, conventions
formación *nf, pl* **-ciones** **1** : formation **2** : training <formación profesional : vocational training>
formal *adj* **1** : formal **2** : serious, dignified **3** : dependable, reliable
formaldehído *nm* : formaldehyde
formalidad *nf* **1** : formality **2** : seriousness, dignity **3** : dependability, reliability
formalizar {21} *vt* : to formalize, to make official
formalmente *adv* : formally
formar *vt* **1** : to form, to make **2** CONSTITUIR : to constitute, to make up **3** : to train, to educate — **formarse** *vr* **1** DESARROLLARSE : to develop, to take shape **2** EDUCARSE : to be educated
formatear *vt* : to format
formativo, -va *adj* : formative
formato *nm* : format
formidable *adj* **1** : formidable, tremendous **2** *fam* : fantastic, terrific
formón *nm, pl* **formones** : chisel
fórmula *nf* : formula
formulación *nf, pl* **-ciones** : formulation
formular *vt* **1** : to formulate, to draw up **2** : to make, to lodge (a protest or complaint)
formulario *nm* : form <rellenar un formulario : to fill out a form>
fornicar {72} *vi* : to fornicate — **fornicación** *nf*
fornido, -da *adj* : well-built, burly, hefty
foro *nm* **1** : forum **2** : public assembly, open discussion
forraje *nm* **1** : forage, fodder **2** : foraging **3** *fam* : hodgepodge
forrajear *vi* : to forage
forrar *vt* **1** : to line (a garment) **2** : to cover (a book)
forro *nm* **1** : lining **2** CUBIERTA : book cover
forsitia *nf* : forsythia
fortachón, -chona *adj, pl* **-chones** *fam* : brawny, strong, tough
fortalecer {53} *vt* : to strengthen, to fortify — **fortalecerse** *vr*
fortalecimiento *nm* **1** : strengthening, fortifying **2** : fortifications
fortaleza *nf* **1** : fortress **2** FUERZA : strength **3** : resolution, fortitude
fortificación *nf, pl* **-ciones** : fortification
fortificar {72} *vt* **1** : to fortify **2** : to strengthen
fortín *nm, pl* **fortines** : small fort
fortuito, -ta *adj* : fortuitous

fortuna *nf* **1** SUERTE : fortune, luck **2** RIQUEZA : wealth, fortune

forzar {36} *vt* **1** OBLIGAR : to force, to compel **2** : to force open **3** : to strain <forzar los ojos : to strain one's eyes>

forzosamente *adv* **1** : forcibly, by force **2** : necessarily, inevitably <forzosamente tendrán que pagar : they'll have no choice but to pay>

forzoso, -sa *adj* **1** : forced, compulsory **2** : necessary, inevitable

fosa *nf* **1** : ditch, pit <fosa séptica : septic tank> **2** TUMBA : grave **3** : cavity <fosas nasales : nasal cavities, nostrils>

fosfato *nm* : phosphate

fosforescencia *nf* : phosphorescence — **fosforescente** *adj*

fósforo *nm* **1** CERILLA : match **2** : phosphorus

fósil[1] *adj* : fossilized, fossil

fósil[2] *nm* : fossil

fosilizarse {21} *vr* : to fossilize, to become fossilized

foso *nm* **1** FOSA, ZANJA : ditch **2** : pit (of a theater) **3** : moat

foto *nf* : photo, picture

fotocopia *nf* : photocopy — **fotocopiar** *vt*

fotocopiadora *nf* COPIADORA : photocopier

fotoeléctrico, -ca *adj* : photoelectric

fotogénico, -ca *adj* : photogenic

fotografía *nf* **1** : photograph **2** : photography

fotografiar {85} *vt* : to photograph

fotográfico, -ca *adj* : photographic — **fotográficamente** *adv*

fotógrafo, -fa *n* : photographer

fotosíntesis *nf* : photosynthesis

fotosintético, -ca *adj* : photosynthetic

fracasado[1], **-da** *adj* : unsuccessful, failed

fracasado[2], **-da** *n* : failure

fracasar *vi* **1** FALLAR : to fail **2** : to fall through

fracaso *nm* FIASCO : failure

fracción *nf, pl* **fracciones 1** : fraction **2** : part, fragment **3** : faction, splinter group

fraccionamiento *nm* **1** : division, breaking up **2** *Mex* : residential area, housing development

fraccionar *vt* : to divide, to break up

fractura *nf* **1** : fracture **2 fractura complicada** : compound fracture

fracturarse *vr* QUEBRARSE, ROMPERSE : to fracture, to break <fracturarse el brazo : to break one's arm>

fragancia *nf* : fragrance, scent

fragante *adj* : fragrant

fragata *nf* : frigate

frágil *adj* **1** : fragile **2** : frail, delicate

fragilidad *nf* **1** : fragility **2** : frailty, delicacy

fragmentar *vt* : to fragment — **fragmentación** *nf*

fragmentario, -ria *adj* : fragmentary, sketchy

fragmento *nm* **1** : fragment, shard **2** : bit, snippet **3** : excerpt, passage

fragor *nm* : clamor, din, roar

fragoroso, -sa *adj* : thunderous, deafening

fragoso, -sa *adj* **1** : rough, uneven **2** : thick, dense

fragua *nf* FORJA : forge

fraguar {10} *vt* **1** : to forge **2** : to conceive, to concoct, to hatch — *vi* : to set, to solidify

fraile *nm* : friar, monk

frambuesa *nf* : raspberry

francamente *adv* **1** : frankly, candidly **2** REALMENTE : really <es francamente admirable : it's really impressive>

francés[1], **-cesa** *adj, mpl* **franceses** : French

francés[2], **-cesa** *n, mpl* **franceses** : French person, Frenchman *m*, Frenchwoman *f*

francés[3] *nm* : French (language)

franciscano, -na *adj & n* : Franciscan

francmasón, -sona *n, mpl* **-sones** : Freemason — **francmasonería** *nf*

franco[1], **-ca** *adj* **1** CÁNDIDO : frank, candid **2** PATENTE : clear, obvious **3** : free <franco a bordo : free on board>

franco[2] *nm* : franc

francotirador, -dora *n* : sniper

franela *nf* : flannel

franja *nf* **1** : stripe, band **2** : border, fringe

franquear *vt* **1** : to clear **2** ATRAVESAR : to cross, to go through **3** : to pay the postage on

franqueo *nm* : postage

franqueza *nf* : frankness

franquicia *nf* **1** EXENCIÓN : exemption **2** : franchise

frasco *nm* : small bottle, flask, vial

frase *nf* **1** : phrase **2** ORACIÓN : sentence

frasear *vt* : to phrase

fraternal *adj* : fraternal, brotherly

fraternidad *nf* **1** : brotherhood **2** : fraternity

fraternizar {21} *vi* : to fraternize — **fraternización** *nf*

fraterno, -na *adj* : fraternal, brotherly

fratricida *adj* : fratricidal

fratricidio *nm* : fratricide

fraude *nm* : fraud

fraudulento, -ta *adj* : fraudulent — **fraudulentamente** *adv*

fray *nm* : brother (title of a friar) <Fray Bartolomé : Brother Bartholomew>

frazada *nf* COBIJA, MANTA : blanket

frecuencia *nf* : frequency

frecuentar *vt* : to frequent, to haunt

frecuente *adj* : frequent — **frecuentemente** *adv*

fregadera *nf fam* : hassle, pain in the neck

fregadero *nm* : kitchen sink

fregado[1], **-da** *adj fam* : annoying, bothersome

fregado[2] *nm* **1** : scrubbing, scouring **2** *fam* : mess, muddle

fregar {49} *vt* **1 :** to scrub, to scour, to wash <fregar los trastes : to do the dishes> <fregar el suelo : to scrub the floor> **2** *fam* **:** to annoy — *vi* **1 :** to wash the dishes **2 :** to clean, to scrub **3** *fam* **:** to be annoying

freidera *nf Mex* **:** frying pan

freír {37} *vt* **:** to fry — **freírse** *vr*

frenar *vt* **1 :** to brake **2** DETENER **:** to curb, to check — *vi* **:** to apply the brakes — **frenarse** *vr* **:** to restrain oneself

frenesí *nm* **:** frenzy

frenético, -ca *adj* **:** frantic, frenzied — **frenéticamente** *adv*

freno *nm* **1 :** brake **2 :** bit (of a bridle) **3 :** check, restraint **4 frenos** *nmpl Mex* **:** braces (for teeth)

frente[1] *nm* **1 :** front <al frente de : at the head of> <en frente : in front, opposite> **2 :** facade **3 :** front line, sphere of activity **4 :** front (in meteorology) <frente frío : cold front> **5 hacer frente a :** to face up to, to brave

frente[2] *nf* **1 :** forehead, brow **2 frente a frente :** face to face

fresa *nf* **1 :** strawberry **2 :** drill (in dentistry)

fresco[1]**, -ca** *adj* **1 :** fresh **2 :** cool **3** *fam* **:** insolent, nervy

fresco[2] *nm* **1 :** coolness **2 :** fresh air <al fresco : in the open air, outdoors> **3 :** fresco

frescor *nm* **:** cool air <el frescor de la noche : the cool of the evening>

frescura *nf* **1 :** freshness **2 :** coolness **3 :** calmness **4** DESCARO **:** nerve, audacity

fresno *nm* **:** ash (tree)

freza *nf* **:** spawn, roe

frezar {21} *vi* DESOVAR **:** to spawn

friable *adj* **:** friable

frialdad *nf* **1 :** coldness **2** INDIFERENCIA **:** indifference, unconcern

fríamente *adv* **:** coldly, indifferently

fricasé *nm* **:** fricassee

fricción *nf, pl* **fricciones 1 :** friction **2 :** rubbing, massage **3 :** discord, disagreement <fricción entre los hermanos : friction between the brothers>

friccionar *vt* **1** FROTAR **:** to rub **2 :** to massage

friega[1]**, friegue, etc. → fregar**

friega[2] *nf* **1** FRICCIÓN **:** rubdown, massage **2 :** annoyance, bother

frigidez *nf* **:** (sexual) frigidity

frigorífico *nm Spain* **:** refrigerator

frijol *nm* **:** bean <frijoles refritos : refried beans>

frío[1]**, fría** *adj* **1 :** cold **2** INDIFERENTE **:** cool, indifferent

frío[2] *nm* **1 :** cold <hace mucho frío esta noche : it's very cold tonight> **2** INDIFERENCIA **:** coldness, indifference **3 tener frío :** to feel cold <tengo frío : I'm cold> **4 tomar frío** RESFRIARSE **:** to catch a cold

friolento, -ta *adj* **:** sensitive to cold

friolera *nf* (*used ironically or humorously*) **:** trifling amount <una friolera de mil dólares : a mere thousand dollars>

friso *nm* **:** frieze

fritar *vt* **:** to fry

frito[1] *pp* **→ freír**

frito[2]**, -ta** *adj* **1 :** fried **2** *fam* **:** worn-out, fed up <tener frito a alguien : to get on someone's nerves> **3** *fam* **:** fast asleep <se quedó frito en el sofá : she fell asleep on the couch>

fritura *nf* **1 :** frying **2 :** fried food

frivolidad *nf* **:** frivolity

frívolo, -la *adj* **:** frivolous — **frívolamente** *adv*

fronda *nf* **1 :** frond **2 frondas** *nfpl* **:** foliage

frondoso, -sa *adj* **:** leafy, luxuriant

frontal *adj* **:** frontal, head-on <un choque frontal : a head-on collision>

frontalmente *adv* **:** head-on

frontera *nf* **:** border, frontier

fronterizo, -za *adj* **:** border, on the border <estados fronterizos : neighboring states>

frotar *vt* **1 :** to rub **2 :** to strike (a match) — **frotarse** *vr* **:** to rub (together)

frote *nm* **:** rubbing, rub

fructífero, -ra *adj* **:** fruitful, productive

fructificar {72} *vi* **1 :** to bear or produce fruit **2 :** to be productive

fructuoso, -sa *adj* **:** fruitful

frugal *adj* **:** frugal, thrifty — **frugalmente** *adv*

frugalidad *adj* **:** frugality

frunce *nm* **:** gather (in cloth), pucker

fruncido *nm* **:** gathering, shirring

fruncir {83} *vt* **1 :** to gather, to shirr **2 fruncir el ceño :** to knit one's brow, to frown **3 fruncir la boca :** to pucker up, to purse one's lips

frunza, etc. → fruncir

frustración *nf, pl* **-ciones :** frustration

frustrado, -da *adj* **1 :** frustrated **2 :** failed, unsuccessful

frustrante *adj* **:** frustrating

frustrar *vt* **:** to frustrate, to thwart — **frustrarse** *vr* FRACASAR **:** to fail, to come to nothing <se frustraron sus esperanzas : his hopes were dashed>

fruta *nf* **:** fruit

frutal[1] *adj* **:** fruit, fruit-bearing

frutal[2] *nm* **:** fruit tree

frutilla *nf* **:** South American strawberry

fruto *nm* **1 :** fruit, agricultural product <los frutos de la tierra : the fruits of the earth> **2 :** result, consequence <los frutos de su trabajo : the fruits of his labor>

fucsia *adj & nm* **:** fuchsia

fue, etc. → ir, ser

fuego *nm* **1 :** fire **2 :** light <¿tienes fuego? : have you got a light?> **3 :** flame, burner (on a stove) **4 :** ardor, passion **5** FOGAJE **:** skin eruption, cold sore 6 **fuegos artificiales** *nmpl* : fireworks

fuelle *nm* : bellows

fuente *nf* 1 MANANTIAL : spring 2 : fountain 3 ORIGEN : source <fuentes informativas : sources of information> 4 : platter, serving dish

fuera *adv* 1 : outside, out 2 : abroad, away 3 **~ de** : outside of, out of, beyond 4 **~ de** : besides, in addition to <fuera de eso : aside from that> 5 **fuera de lugar** : out of place, amiss

fuerce, fuerza, etc. → **forzar**

fuero *nm* 1 JURISDICCIÓN : jurisdiction 2 : privilege, exemption 3 **fuero interno** : conscience, heart of hearts

fuerte[1] *adv* 1 : strongly, tightly, hard 2 : loudly 3 : abundantly

fuerte[2] *adj* 1 : strong 2 : intense <un fuerte dolor : an intense pain> 3 : loud 4 : extreme, excessive

fuerte[3] *nm* 1 : fort, stronghold 2 : forte, strong point

fuerza *nf* 1 : strength, vigor <fuerza de voluntad : willpower> 2 : force <fuerza bruta : brute force> 3 : power, might <fuerza de brazos : manpower> 4 **fuerzas** *nfpl* : forces <fuerzas armadas : armed forces> 5 **a fuerza de** : by, by dint of

fuetazo *nm* : lash

fuga *nf* 1 HUIDA : flight, escape 2 : fugue 3 : leak <fuga de gas : gas leak>

fugarse {52} *vr* 1 : to escape 2 HUIR : to flee, to run away 3 : to elope

fugaz *adj, pl* **fugaces** : brief, fleeting

fugitivo, -va *adj & n* : fugitive

fulana *nf* : hooker, slut

fulano, -na *n* : so-and-so, what's-his-name, what's-her-name <fulano, mengano, y zutano : Tom, Dick, and Harry> <señora fulana de tal : Mrs. so-and-so>

fulcro *nm* : fulcrum

fulgor *nm* : brilliance, splendor

fulgurar *vi* : to shine brightly, to gleam, to glow

fulminante *adj* 1 : fulminating, explosive 2 : devastating, terrible <una mirada fulminante : a withering look>

fulminar *vt* 1 : to strike with lightning 2 : to strike down <fulminar a alguien con la mirada : to look daggers at someone>

fumador, -dora *n* : smoker

fumar *v* : to smoke

fumble *nm* : fumble (in football)

fumblear *vt* : to fumble (in football)

fumigante *nm* : fumigant

fumigar {52} *vt* : to fumigate — **fumigación** *nf*

funámbulo, -la *n* EQUILIBRISTA : tightrope walker

función *nf, pl* **funciones** 1 : function 2 : duty 3 : performance, show

funcional *adj* : functional — **funcionalmente** *adv*

funcionamiento *nm* 1 : functioning 2 **en ~** : in operation

funcionar *vi* 1 : to function 2 : to run, to work

funcionario, -ria *n* : civil servant, official

funda *nf* 1 : case, cover, sheath 2 : pillowcase

fundación *nf, pl* **-ciones** : foundation, establishment

fundado, -da *adj* : well-founded, justified

fundador, -dora *n* : founder

fundamental *adj* BÁSICO : fundamental, basic — **fundamentalmente** *adv*

fundamentar *vt* 1 : to lay the foundations for 2 : to support, to back up 3 : to base, to found

fundamento *nm* : basis, foundation, groundwork

fundar *vt* 1 ESTABLECER, INSTITUIR : to found, to establish 2 BASAR : to base — **fundarse** *vr* **~ en** : to be based on, to stem from

fundición *nf, pl* **-ciones** 1 : founding, smelting 2 : foundry

fundir *vt* 1 : to melt down, to smelt 2 : to fuse, to merge 3 : to burn out (a lightbulb) — **fundirse** *vr* 1 : to fuse together, to blend, to merge 2 : to melt, to thaw 3 : to fade (in television or movies)

fúnebre *adj* 1 : funeral, funereal 2 LÚGUBRE : gloomy, mournful

funeral[1] *adj* : funeral, funerary

funeral[2] *nm* 1 : funeral 2 **funerales** *nmpl* EXEQUIAS : funeral rites

funeraria *nf* 1 : funeral home, funeral parlor 2 **director de funeraria** : funeral director, undertaker

funerario, -ria *adj* : funeral

funesto, -ta *adj* : terrible, disastrous <consecuencias funestas : disastrous consequences>

fungicida[1] *adj* : fungicidal

fungicida[2] *nm* : fungicide

fungir {35} *vi* : to act, to function <fungir de asesor : to act as a consultant>

fungoso, -sa *adj* : fungous

funja, etc. → **fungir**

furgón *nm, pl* **furgones** 1 : van, truck 2 : freight car, boxcar 3 **furgón de cola** : caboose

furgoneta *nf* : van

furia *nf* 1 CÓLERA, IRA : fury, rage 2 : violence, fury <la furia de la tormenta : the fury of the storm>

furibundo, -da *adj* : furious

furiosamente *adv* : furiously, frantically

furioso, -sa *adj* 1 AIRADO : furious, irate 2 : intense, violent

furor *nm* 1 : fury, rage 2 : violence (of the elements) 3 : passion, frenzy 4 : enthusiasm <hacer furor : to be all the rage>

furtivo, -va *adj* : furtive — **furtivamente** *adv*

furúnculo *nm* DIVIESO **:** boil
fuselaje *nm* **:** fuselage
fusible *nm* **:** (electrical) fuse
fusil *nm* **:** rifle
fusilar *vt* **1 :** to shoot, to execute (by firing squad) **2** *fam* **:** to plagiarize, to pirate
fusilería *nf* **1 :** rifles *pl,* rifle fire **2 descarga de fusilería :** fusillade
fusión *nf, pl* **fusiones 1 :** fusion **2 :** union, merger
fusionar *vt* **1 :** to fuse **2 :** to merge, to amalgamate — **fusionarse** *vr*
fusta *nf* **:** riding crop
fustigar {52} *vt* **1** AZOTAR **:** to whip, to lash **2 :** to upbraid, to berate
futbol *or* **fútbol** *nm* **1 :** soccer **2 futbol americano :** football
futbolista *nmf* **:** soccer player
futesa *nf* **1 :** small thing, trifle **2 futesas** *nfpl* **:** small talk
fútil *adj* **:** trifling, trivial
futurista *adj* **:** futuristic
futuro[1], -ra *adj* **:** future
futuro[2] *nm* PORVENIR **:** future

G

g *nf* **:** seventh letter of the Spanish alphabet
gabán *nm, pl* **gabanes :** topcoat, overcoat
gabardina *nf* **1 :** gabardine **2 :** trench coat, raincoat
gabarra *nf* **:** barge
gabinete *nm* **1 :** cabinet (in government) **2 :** study, office (in the home) **3 :** (professional) office
gablete *nm* **:** gable
gabonés, -nesa *adj & n, mpl* **-neses :** Gabonese
gacela *nf* **:** gazelle
gaceta *nf* **:** gazette, newspaper
gachas *nfpl* **:** porridge
gacho, -cha *adj* **1 :** drooping, turned downward **2** *Mex fam* **:** nasty, awful **3 ir a gachas** *fam* **:** to go on all fours
gaélico[1], -ca *adj* **:** Gaelic
gaélico[2] *nm* **:** Gaelic (language)
gafas *nfpl* ANTEOJOS **:** eyeglasses, glasses
gaita *nf* **:** bagpipes *pl*
gajes *nmpl* **gajes del oficio :** occupational hazards
gajo *nm* **1 :** broken branch (of a tree) **2 :** cluster, bunch (of fruit) **3 :** segment (of citrus fruit)
gala *nf* **1 :** gala <vestido de gala : formal dress> <tener algo a gala : to be proud of something> **2 galas** *nfpl* **:** finery, attire
galáctico, -ca *adj* **:** galactic
galán *nm, pl* **galanes 1 :** ladies' man, gallant **2 :** leading man, hero **3 :** boyfriend, suitor
galano, -na *adj* **1 :** elegant **2** *Mex* **:** mottled
galante *adj* **:** gallant, attentive — **galantemente** *adv*
galantear *vt* **1** CORTEJAR **:** to court, to woo **2 :** to flirt with
galanteo *nm* **1** CORTEJO **:** courtship **2 :** flirtation, flirting
galantería *nf* **1 :** gallantry, attentiveness **2 :** compliment
galápago *nm* **:** aquatic turtle
galardón *nm, pl* **-dones :** award, prize
galardonado, -da *adj* **:** prize-winning
galardonar *vt* **:** to give an award to
galaxia *nf* **:** galaxy
galeno *nm fam* **:** physician, doctor
galeón *nm, pl* **galeones :** galleon
galera *nf* **:** galley
galería *nf* **1 :** gallery, balcony (in a theater) <galería comercial : shopping mall> **2 :** corridor, passage
galerón *nm, pl* **-rones** *Mex* **:** large hall
galés[1], -lesa *adj* **:** Welsh
galés[2], -lesa *n, mpl* **galeses 1 :** Welshman *m,* Welshwoman *f* **2 los galeses :** the Welsh
galés[3] *nm* **:** Welsh (language)
galgo *nm* **:** greyhound
galimatías *nms & pl* **:** gibberish, nonsense
galio *nm* **:** gallium
gallardete *nm* **:** pennant, streamer
gallardía *nf* **1** VALENTÍA **:** bravery **2** APOSTURA **:** elegance, gracefulness
gallardo, -da *adj* **1** VALIENTE **:** brave **2** APUESTO **:** elegant, graceful
gallear *vi* **:** to show off, to strut around
gallego[1], -ga *adj* **1 :** Galician **2** *fam* **:** Spanish
gallego[2], -ga *n* **1 :** Galician **2** *fam* **:** Spaniard
galleta *nf* **1 :** cookie **2 :** cracker
gallina *nf* **1 :** hen **2 gallina de Guinea :** guinea fowl
gallinazo *nm* **:** vulture, buzzard
gallinero *nm* **:** chicken coop, henhouse
gallito, -ta *adj fam* **:** cocky, belligerent
gallo *nm* **1 :** rooster, cock **2** *fam* **:** squeak or crack in the voice **3** *Mex* **:** serenade **4 gallo de pelea :** gamecock
galo[1], -la *adj* **1 :** Gaulish **2 :** French
galo[2], -la *n* **:** Frenchman *m,* Frenchwoman *f*
galocha *nf* **:** galosh
galón *nm, pl* **galones 1 :** gallon **2 :** stripe (military insignia)
galopada *nf* **:** gallop
galopante *adj* **:** galloping <inflación galopante : galloping inflation>
galopar *vi* **:** to gallop
galope *nm* **:** gallop

galpón *nm, pl* **galpones** : shed, storehouse

galvanizar {21} *vt* : to galvanize — **galvanización** *nf*

gama *nf* **1** : range, spectrum, gamut **2** → **gamo**

gamba *nf* : large shrimp, prawn

gameto *nm* : gamete

gamo, -ma *n* : fallow deer

gamuza *nf* **1** : suede **2** : chamois

gana *nf* **1** : desire, inclination **2 de buena gana** : willingly, readily, gladly **3 de mala gana** : reluctantly, half-heartedly **4 tener ganas de** : to feel like, to be in the mood for <tengo ganas de bailar : I feel like dancing> **5 ponerle ganas a algo** : to put effort into something

ganadería *nf* **1** : cattle raising, stockbreeding **2** : cattle ranch **3** GANADO : cattle *pl,* livestock

ganadero[1], **-ra** *adj* : cattle, ranching

ganadero[2], **-ra** *n* : rancher, stockbreeder

ganado *nm* **1** : cattle *pl,* livestock **2 ganado ovino** : sheep *pl* **3 ganado porcino** : swine *pl*

ganador[1], **-dora** *adj* : winning

ganador[2], **-dora** *n* : winner

ganancia *nf* **1** : profit **2 ganancias** *nfpl* : winnings, gains

ganancioso, -sa *adj* : profitable

ganar *vt* **1** : to win **2** : to gain <ganar tiempo : to buy time> **3** : to earn <ganar dinero : to make money> **4** : to acquire, to obtain — *vi* **1** : to win **2** : to profit <salir ganando : to come out ahead> — **ganarse** *vr* **1** : to gain, to win <ganarse a alguien : to win someone over> **2** : to earn <ganarse la vida : to make a living> **3** : to deserve

gancho *nm* **1** : hook **2** : clothes hanger **3** : hairpin, bobby pin **4** *Col* : safety pin

gandul[1] *nm CA, Car, Col* : pigeon pea

gandul[2], **-dula** *n fam* : idler, lazybones

gandulear *vi* : to idle, to loaf, to lounge about

ganga *nf* : bargain

ganglio *nm* **1** : ganglion **2** : gland

gangrena *nf* : gangrene — **gangrenoso, -sa** *adj*

gángster *nmf, pl* **gángsters** : gangster

gansada *nf* : silly thing, nonsense

ganso, -sa *n* **1** : goose, gander *m* **2** : idiot, fool

gañido *nm* : yelp (of a dog)

gañir {38} *vi* : to yelp

garabatear *v* : to scribble, to scrawl, to doodle

garabato *nm* **1** : doodle **2 garabatos** *nmpl* : scribble, scrawl

garaje *nm* : garage

garante *nmf* : guarantor

garantía *nf* **1** : guarantee, warranty **2** : security <garantía de trabajo : job security>

garantizar {21} *vt* : to guarantee

garapiña *nf* : pineapple drink

garapiñar *vt* : to candy

garbanzo *nm* : chickpea, garbanzo

garbo *nm* **1** DONAIRE : grace, poise **2** : jauntiness

garboso, -sa *adj* **1** : graceful **2** : elegant, stylish

garceta *nf* : egret

gardenia *nf* : gardenia

garfio *nm* : hook, gaff, grapnel

gargajo *nm* : phlegm

garganta *nf* **1** : throat **2** : neck (of a person or a bottle) **3** : ravine, narrow pass

gargantilla *nf* : choker, necklace

gárgara *nf* **1** : gargle, gargling **2 hacer gárgaras** : to gargle

gargarizar *vi* : to gargle

gárgola *nf* : gargoyle

garita *nf* **1** : cabin, hut **2** : sentry box, lookout post

garoso, -sa *adj Col, Ven* : gluttonous, greedy

garra *nf* **1** : claw **2** : hand, paw **3 garras** *nfpl* : claws, clutches <caer en las garras de alguien : to fall into someone's clutches>

garrafa *nf* : decanter, carafe

garrafal *adj* : terrible, monstrous

garrafón *nm, pl* **-fones** : large decanter, large bottle

garrapata *nf* : tick

garrobo *nm CA* : large lizard, iguana

garrocha *nf* **1** PICA : lance, pike **2** : pole <salto con garrocha : pole vault>

garrotazo *nm* : blow (with a club)

garrote *nm* **1** : club, stick **2** *Mex* : brake

garúa *nf* : drizzle

garuar {3} *v impers* LLOVIZNAR : to drizzle

garza *nf* : heron

gas *nm* : gas, vapor, fumes *pl* <gas lagrimógeno : tear gas>

gasa *nf* : gauze

gasear *vt* **1** : to gas **2** : to aerate (a liquid)

gaseosa *nf* REFRESCO : soda, soft drink

gaseoso, -sa *adj* **1** : gaseous **2** : carbonated, fizzy

gasoducto *nm* : gas pipeline

gasolina *nf* : gasoline, gas

gasolinera *nf* : gas station, service station

gastado, -da *adj* **1** : spent **2** : worn, worn-out

gastador[1], **-dora** *adj* : extravagant, spendthrift

gastador[2], **-dora** *n* : spendthrift

gastar *vt* **1** : to spend **2** CONSUMIR : to consume, to use up **3** : to squander, to waste **4** : to wear <gasta un bigote : he sports a mustache> — **gastarse** *vr* **1** : to spend, to expend **2** : to run down, to wear out

gasto *nm* **1** : expense, expenditure **2** DETERIORO : wear **3 gastos generales** *or* **gastos indirectos** : overhead

gástrico, -ca *adj* : gastric

gastritis *nf* : gastritis

gastronomía *nf* : gastronomy
gastronómico, -ca *adj* : gastronomic
gastrónomo, -ma *n* : gourmet
gatas *adv* **andar a gatas** : to crawl, to go on all fours
gatear *vi* **1** : to crawl **2** : to climb, to clamber (up)
gatillero *nm Mex* : gunman
gatillo *nm* : trigger
gatito, -ta *n* : kitten
gato[1], -ta *n* : cat
gato[2] *nm* : jack (for an automobile)
gauchada *nf Arg, Uru* : favor, kindness
gaucho *nm* : gaucho
gaveta *nf* **1** CAJÓN : drawer **2** : till
gavilla *nf* **1** : gang, band **2** : sheaf
gaviota *nf* : gull, seagull
gay ['ge, 'gai] *adj* : gay (homosexual)
gaza *nf* : loop
gazapo *nm* **1** : young rabbit **2** : misprint, error
gazmoñería *nf* MOJIGATERÍA : prudery, primness
gazmoño[1], -ña *adj* : prudish, prim
gazmoño[2], -ña *n* MOJIGATO : prude, prig
gaznate *nm* : throat, gullet
gazpacho *nm* : gazpacho
géiser *or* **géyser** *nm* : geyser
gel *nm* : gel
gelatina *nf* : gelatin
gélido, -da *adj* : icy, freezing cold
gelificarse *vr* : to jell
gema *nf* : gem
gemelo[1], -la *adj & n* MELLIZO : twin
gemelo[2] *nm* **1** : cuff link **2 gemelos** *nmpl* BINOCULARES : binoculars
gemido *nm* : moan, groan, wail
Géminis *nmf* : Gemini
gemir {54} *vi* : to moan, to groan, to wail
gen *or* **gene** *nm* : gene
gendarme *nmf* POLICÍA : police officer, policeman *m,* policewoman *f*
gendarmería *nf* : police
genealogía *nf* : genealogy
genealógico, -ca *adj* : genealogical
generación *nf, pl* **-ciones 1** : generation <tercera generación : third generation> **2** : generating, creating **3** : class <la generación del '97 : the class of '97>
generacional *adj* : generation, generational
generador *nm* : generator
general[1] *adj* **1** : general **2 en ~** *or* **por lo general** : in general, generally
general[2] *nmf* **1** : general **2 general de división** : major general
generalidad *nf* **1** : generality, generalization **2** : majority
generalización *nf, pl* **-ciones 1** : generalization **2** : escalation, spread
generalizado, -da *adj* : generalized, widespread
generalizar {21} *vi* : to generalize — *vt* : to spread, to spread out — **generalizarse** *vr* : to become widespread
generalmente *adv* : usually, generally
generar *vt* : to generate — **generarse** *vr*
genérico, -ca *adj* : generic
género *nm* **1** : genre, class, kind <el género humano : the human race, mankind> **2** : gender (in grammar) **3 géneros** *nmpl* : goods, commodities
generosidad *nf* : generosity
generoso, -sa *adj* **1** : generous, unselfish **2** : ample — **generosamente** *adv*
genética *nf* : genetics
genético, -ca *adj* : genetic — **genéticamente** *adv*
genetista *nmf* : geneticist
genial *adj* **1** AGRADABLE : genial, pleasant **2** : brilliant <una obra genial : a work of genius> **3** *fam* FORMIDABLE : fantastic, terrific
genialidad *nf* **1** : genius **2** : stroke of genius **3** : eccentricity
genio *nm* **1** : genius **2** : temper, disposition <de mal genio : bad-tempered> **3** : genie
genital *adj* : genital
genitales *nmpl* : genitals, genitalia
genocidio *nm* : genocide
genotipo *nm* : genotype
gente *nf* **1** : people **2** : relatives *pl,* folks *pl* **3 gente menuda** *fam* : children, kids *pl* **4 ser buena gente** : to be nice, to be kind
gentil[1] *adj* **1** AMABLE : kind **2** : gentile
gentil[2] *nmf* : gentile
gentileza *nf* **1** AMABILIDAD : kindness **2** CORTESÍA : courtesy
gentilicio, -cia *adj* **1** : national, tribal **2** : family
gentío *nm* MUCHEDUMBRE, MULTITUD : crowd, mob
gentuza *nf* CHUSMA : riffraff, rabble
genuflexión *nf, pl* **-xiones 1** : genuflection **2 hacer una genuflexión** : to genuflect
genuino, -na *adj* : genuine — **genuinamente** *adv*
geofísica *nf* : geophysics
geofísico, -ca *adj* : geophysical
geografía *nf* : geography
geográfico, -ca *adj* : geographic, geographical — **geográficamente** *adv*
geógrafo, -fa *n* : geographer
geología *nf* : geology
geológico, -ca *adj* : geologic, geological — **geológicamente** *adv*
geólogo, -ga *n* : geologist
geometría *nf* : geometry
geométrico, -ca *adj* : geometric, geometrical — **geométricamente** *adv*
geopolítica *nf* : geopolitics
geopolítico, -ca *adj* : geopolitical
georgiano, -na *adj & n* : Georgian
geranio *nm* : geranium
gerbo *nm* : gerbil
gerencia *nf* : management, administration
gerencial *adj* : managerial
gerente *nmf* : manager, director
geriatría *nf* : geriatrics

geriátrico, -ca *adj* : geriatric
germanio *nm* : germanium
germano, -na *adj* : Germanic, German
germen *nm, pl* **gérmenes** : germ
germicida *nf* : germicide
germinación *nf, pl* **-ciones** : germination
germinar *vi* : to germinate, to sprout
gerontología *nf* : gerontology
gerundio *nm* : gerund
gesta *nf* : deed, exploit
gestación *nf, pl* **-ciones** : gestation
gesticulación *nf, pl* **-ciones** : gesturing, gesticulation
gesticular *vi* : to gesticulate, to gesture
gestión *nf, pl* **gestiones 1** TRÁMITE : procedure, step **2** ADMINISTRACIÓN : management **3 gestiones** *nfpl* : negotiations
gestionar *vt* **1** : to negotiate, to work towards **2** ADMINISTRAR : to manage, to handle
gesto *nm* **1** ADEMÁN : gesture **2** : facial expression **3** MUECA : grimace
gestor[1], -tora *adj* : facilitating, negotiating, managing
gestor[2], -tora *n* : facilitator, manager
géyser *nm* → **géiser**
ghanés, -nesa *adj & n, mpl* **ghaneses** : Ghanaian
ghetto → **gueto**
giba *nf* **1** : hump (of an animal) **2** : hunchback (of a person)
gibón *nm, pl* **gibones** : gibbon
giboso[1], -sa *adj* : hunchbacked, humpbacked
giboso[2], -sa *n* : hunchback, humpback
gigante[1] *adj* : giant, gigantic
gigante[2], -ta *n* : giant
gigantesco, -ca *adj* : gigantic, huge
gime, etc. → **gemir**
gimnasia *nf* : gymnastics
gimnasio *nm* : gymnasium, gym
gimnasta *nmf* : gymnast
gimnástico, -ca *adj* : gymnastic
gimotear *vi* LLORIQUEAR : to whine, to whimper
gimoteo *nm* : whimpering
ginebra *nf* : gin
ginecología *nf* : gynecology
ginecológico, -ca *adj* : gynecologic, gynecological
ginecólogo, -ga *n* : gynecologist
gira *nf* : tour
giralda *nf* : weather vane
girar *vi* **1** : to turn around, to revolve **2** : to swing around, to swivel — *vt* **1** : to turn, to twist, to rotate **2** : to draft (checks) **3** : to transfer (funds)
girasol *nm* MIRASOL : sunflower
giratorio, -ria *adj* : revolving
giro *nm* **1** VUELTA : turn, rotation **2** : change of direction <giro de 180 grados : U-turn, about-face> **3 giro bancario** : bank draft **4 giro postal** : money order
giroscopio *or* **giróscopo** *nm* : gyroscope
gis *nm Mex* : chalk
gitano, -na *adj & n* : Gypsy
glacial *adj* : glacial, icy — **glacialmente** *adv*
glaciar *nm* : glacier
gladiador *nm* : gladiator
gladiolo *or* **gladíolo** *nm* : gladiolus
glándula *nf* : gland — **glandular** *adj*
glaseado *nm* : glaze, icing
glasear *vt* : to glaze
glaucoma *nm* : glaucoma
glicerina *nf* : glycerin, glycerol
glicinia *nf* : wisteria
global *adj* **1** : global, worldwide **2** : full, comprehensive **3** : total, overall
globalizar {21} *vt* **1** ABARCAR : to include, to encompass **2** : to extend worldwide
globalmente *adv* : globally, as a whole
globo *nm* **1** : globe, sphere **2** : balloon **3 globo ocular** : eyeball
glóbulo *nm* **1** : globule **2** : blood cell, corpuscle
gloria *nf* **1** : glory **2** : fame, renown **3** : delight, enjoyment **4** : star, legend <las glorias del cine : the great names in motion pictures>
glorieta *nf* **1** : rotary, traffic circle **2** : bower, arbor
glorificar {72} *vt* ALABAR : to glorify — **glorificación** *nf*
glorioso, -sa *adj* : glorious — **gloriosamente** *adv*
glosa *nf* **1** : gloss **2** : annotation, commentary
glosar *vt* **1** : to gloss **2** : to annotate, to comment on (a text)
glosario *nm* : glossary
glotis *nf* : glottis
glotón[1], -tona *adj, mpl* **glotones** : gluttonous
glotón[2], -tona *n, mpl* **glotones** : glutton
glotón[3] *nm, pl* **glotones** : wolverine
glotonería *nf* GULA : gluttony
glucosa *nf* : glucose
glutinoso, -sa *adj* : glutinous
gnomo *nm* : gnome
gobernación *nf, pl* **-ciones** : governing, government
gobernador, -dora *n* : governor
gobernante[1] *adj* : ruling, governing
gobernante[2] *nmf* : ruler, leader, governor
gobernar {55} *vt* **1** : to govern, to rule **2** : to steer, to sail (a ship) — *vi* **1** : to govern **2** : to steer
gobierno *nm* : government
goce[1], etc. → **gozar**
goce[2] *nm* **1** PLACER : enjoyment, pleasure **2** : use, possession
gol *nm* : goal (in soccer)
golear *vt* : to rout, to score many goals against (in soccer)
goleta *nf* : schooner
golf *nm* : golf
golfista *nmf* : golfer
golfo *nm* : gulf, bay
golondrina *nf* **1** : swallow (bird) **2 golondrina de mar** : tern

golosina *nf* : sweet, snack

goloso, -sa *adj* : fond of sweets <ser goloso : to have a sweet tooth>

golpazo *nm* : heavy blow, bang, thump

golpe *nm* **1** : blow <caerle a golpes a alguien : to give someone a beating> **2** : knock **3 de ~** : suddenly **4 de un golpe** : all at once, in one fell swoop **5 golpe de estado** : coup, coup d'etat **6 golpe de suerte** : stroke of luck

golpeado, -da *adj* **1** : beaten, hit **2** : bruised (of fruit) **3** : dented

golpear *vt* **1** : to beat (up), to hit **2** : to slam, to bang, to strike — *vi* **1** : to knock (at a door) **2** : to beat <la lluvia golpeaba contra el tejado : the rain beat against the roof> — **golpearse** *vr*

golpetear *v* : to knock, to rattle, to tap

golpeteo *nm* : banging, knocking, tapping

goma *nf* **1** : gum <goma de mascar : chewing gum> **2** CAUCHO : rubber <goma espuma : foam rubber> **3** PEGAMENTO : glue **4** : rubber band **5** *Arg* : tire **6** *or* **goma de borrar** : eraser

gomita *nf* : rubber band

gomoso, -sa *adj* : gummy, sticky

góndola *nf* : gondola

gong *nm* : gong

gonorrea *nf* : gonorrhea

gorda *nf Mex* : thick corn tortilla

gordinflón[1], -flona *adj, mpl* **-flones** *fam* : chubby, pudgy

gordinflón[2], -flona *n, mpl* **-flones** *fam* : chubby person

gordo[1], -da *adj* **1** : fat **2** : thick **3** : fatty, greasy, oily **4** : unpleasant <me cae gorda tu tía : I can't stand your aunt>

gordo[2], -da *n* : fat person

gordo[3] *nm* **1** GRASA : fat **2** : jackpot

gordura *nf* : fatness, flab

gorgojo *nm* : weevil

gorgotear *vi* : to gurgle, to bubble

gorgoteo *nm* : gurgle

gorila *nm* : gorilla

gorjear *vi* **1** : to chirp, to tweet, to warble **2** : to gurgle

gorjeo *nm* **1** : chirping, warbling **2** : gurgling

gorra *nf* **1** : bonnet **2** : cap **3 de ~** *fam* : for free, at someone else's expense <vivir de gorra : to sponge, to freeload>

gorrear *vt fam* : to bum, to scrounge — *vi fam* : to freeload

gorrero, -ra *n fam* : freeloader, sponger

gorrión *nm, pl* **gorriones** : sparrow

gorro *nm* **1** : cap **2 estar hasta el gorro** : to be fed up

gorrón, -rrona *n fam, mpl* **gorrones** : freeloader, scrounger

gorronear *vt fam* : to bum, to scrounge — *vi fam* : to freeload

gota *nf* **1** : drop <una gota de sudor : a bead of sweat> <como dos gotas de agua : like two peas in a pod> <sudar la gota gorda : to sweat buckets, to work very hard> **2** : gout

gotear *v* **1** : to drip **2** : to leak — *v impers* LLOVIZNAR : to drizzle

goteo *nm* : drip, dripping

gotera *nf* **1** : leak **2** : stain (from dripping water)

gotero *nm* : (medicine) dropper

gótico, -ca *adj* : Gothic

gourmet *nmf* : gourmet

gozar {21} *vi* **1** : to enjoy oneself, to have a good time **2 ~ de** : to enjoy, to have, to possess <gozar de buena salud : to enjoy good health> **3 ~ con** : to take delight in

gozne *nm* BISAGRA : hinge

gozo *nm* **1** : joy **2** PLACER : enjoyment, pleasure

gozoso, -sa *adj* : joyful

grabación *nf, pl* **-ciones** : recording

grabado *nm* **1** : engraving **2 grabado al aguafuerte** : etching

grabador, -dora *n* : engraver

grabadora *nf* : tape recorder

grabar *vt* **1** : to engrave **2** : to record, to tape — *vi* **grabar al aguafuerte** : to etch — **grabarse** *vr* **grabársele a alguien en la memoria** : to become engraved on someone's mind

gracia *nf* **1** : grace **2** : favor, kindness **3** : humor, wit <su comentario no me hizo gracia : I wasn't amused by his remark> **4 gracias** *nfpl* : thanks <¡gracias! : thank you!> <dar gracias : to give thanks>

grácil *adj* **1** : graceful **2** : delicate, slender, fine

gracilidad *nm* : gracefulness

gracioso, -sa *adj* **1** CHISTOSO : funny, amusing **2** : cute, attractive

grada *nf* **1** : harrow **2** PELDAÑO : step, stair **3 gradas** *nfpl* : bleachers, grandstand

gradación *nf, pl* **-ciones** : gradation, scale

gradar *vt* : to harrow, to hoe

gradería *nf* : tiers *pl,* stands *pl,* rows *pl* (in a theater)

gradiente *nf* : gradient, slope

grado *nm* **1** : degree (in meteorology and mathematics) <grado centígrado : degree centigrade> **2** : extent, level, degree <en grado sumo : greatly, to the highest degree> **3** RANGO : rank **4** : year, class (in education) **5 de buen grado** : willingly, readily

graduable *adj* : adjustable

graduación *nf, pl* **-ciones** **1** : graduation (from a school) **2** GRADO : rank **3** : alcohol content, proof

graduado[1], -da *adj* **1** : graduated **2 lentes graduados** : prescription lenses

graduado[2], -da *n* : graduate

gradual *adj* : gradual — **gradualmente** *adv*

graduar {3} *v* **1** : to regulate, to adjust **2** CALIBRAR : to calibrate, to gauge —

graduarse *vr* : to graduate (from a school)
gráfica *nf* → **gráfico**[2]
gráfico[1], **-ca** *adj* : graphic — **gráficamente** *adv*
gráfico[2] *nm* **1** : graph, chart **2** : graphic (for a computer, etc.) **3 gráfico de barras** : bar graph
grafismo *nm* : graphics *pl*
grafito *nm* : graphite
gragea *nf* **1** : coated pill or tablet **2 grageas** *nfpl* : sprinkles, jimmies
grajo *nm* : rook (bird)
grama *nf* : grass
gramática *nf* : grammar
gramatical *adj* : grammatical — **gramaticalmente** *adv*
gramo *nm* : gram
gran → **grande**
grana *nf* : scarlet, deep red
granada *nf* **1** : pomegranate **2** : grenade <granada de mano : hand grenade>
granadero *nm* **1** : grenadier **2 granaderos** *nmpl Mex* : riot squad
granadino, -na *adj & n* : Grenadian
granado, -da *adj* **1** DISTINGUIDO : distinguished **2** : choice, select
granate *nm* **1** : garnet **2** : deep red, maroon
grande *adj* (**gran** *before singular nouns*) **1** : large, big <un libro grande : a big book> **2** ALTO : tall **3** NOTABLE : great <un gran autor : a great writer> **4** (*indicating intensity*) : great <con gran placer : with great pleasure> **5** : old, grown-up <hijos grandes : grown children>
grandeza *nf* **1** MAGNITUD : greatness, size **2** : nobility **3** : generosity, graciousness **4** : grandeur, magnificence
grandilocuencia *nf* : grandiloquence — **grandilocuente** *adj*
grandiosidad *nf* : grandeur
grandioso, -sa *adj* **1** MAGNÍFICO : grand, magnificent **2** : grandiose
granel *adv* **1 a ~** : galore, in great quantities **2 a ~** : in bulk <vender a granel : to sell in bulk>
granero *nm* : barn, granary
granito *nm* : granite
granizada *nf* : hailstorm
granizar {21} *v impers* : to hail
granizo *nm* : hail
granja *nf* : farm
granjear *vt* : to earn, to win — **granjearse** *vr* : to gain, to earn
granjero, -ra *n* : farmer
grano *nm* **1** PARTÍCULA : grain, particle <un grano de arena : a grain of sand> **2** : grain (of rice, etc.), bean (of coffee), seed **3** : grain (of wood or rock) **4** BARRO, ESPINILLA : pimple **5 ir al grano** : to get to the point
granuja *nmf* PILLUELO : rascal, urchin
granular[1] *vt* : to granulate — **granularse** *vr* : to break out in spots
granular[2] *adj* : granular, grainy
granza *nf* : chaff
grapa *nf* **1** : staple **2** : clamp
grapadora *nf* ENGRAPADORA : stapler
grapar *vt* ENGRAPAR : to staple
grasa *nf* **1** : grease **2** : fat **3** *Mex* : shoe polish
grasiento, -ta *adj* : greasy, oily
graso, -sa *adj* **1** : fatty **2** : greasy, oily
grasoso, -sa *adj* GRASIENTO : greasy, oily
gratificación *nf, pl* **-ciones 1** SATISFACCIÓN : gratification **2** : bonus **3** RECOMPENSA : recompense, reward
gratificar {72} *vt* **1** SATISFACER : to satisfy, to gratify **2** RECOMPENSAR : to reward **3** : to give a bonus to
gratinado, -da *adj* : au gratin
gratis[1] *adv* GRATUITAMENTE : free, for free, gratis
gratis[2] *adj* GRATUITO : free, gratis
gratitud *nf* : gratitude
grato, -ta *adj* AGRADABLE, PLACENTERO : pleasant, agreeable — **gratamente** *adv*
gratuitamente *adv* **1** : gratuitously **2** GRATIS : free, for free, gratis
gratuito, -ta *adj* **1** : gratuitous, unwarranted **2** GRATIS : free, gratis
grava *nf* : gravel
gravamen *nm, pl* **-vámenes 1** : burden, obligation **2** : (property) tax
gravar *vt* **1** : to burden, to encumber **2** : to levy (a tax)
grave *adj* **1** : grave, important **2** : serious, somber **3** : serious (of an illness)
gravedad *nf* **1** : gravity <centro de gravedad : center of gravity> **2** : seriousness, severity
gravemente *adv* : gravely, seriously
gravilla *nf* : (fine) gravel
gravitación *nf, pl* **-ciones** : gravitation
gravitar *vi* **1** : to gravitate **2 ~ sobre** : to rest on **3 ~ sobre** : to loom over
gravoso, -sa *adj* **1** ONEROSO : burdensome, onerous **2** : costly
graznar *vi* : to caw, to honk, to quack, to squawk
graznido *nm* : cawing, honking, quacking, squawking
gregario, -ria *adj* : gregarious
gregoriano, -na *adj* : Gregorian
gremial *adj* SINDICAL : union, labor
gremio *nm* SINDICATO : union, guild
greña *nf* **1** : mat, tangle **2 greñas** *nfpl* MELENAS : shaggy hair, mop
greñudo, -da *n* HIPPIE, MELENUDO : longhair, hippie
grey *nf* : congregation, flock
griego[1], **-ga** *adj & n* : Greek
griego[2] *nm* : Greek (language)
grieta *nf* : crack, crevice
grifo *nm* **1** : faucet <agua del grifo : tap water> **2** : griffin
grillete *nm* : shackle
grillo *nm* **1** : cricket **2 grillos** *nmpl* : fetters, shackles
grima *nf* **1** : disgust, uneasiness **2 darle grima a alguien** : to get on someone's nerves

gringo, -ga *adj & n* YANQUI : Yankee, gringo
gripa *nf Col, Mex* : flu
gripe *nf* : flu
gris *adj* **1** : gray **2** : overcast, cloudy
grisáceo, -cea *adj* : grayish
gritar *v* : to shout, to scream, to cry
gritería *nf* : shouting, clamor
grito *nm* : shout, scream, cry <a grito pelado : at the top of one's voice>
groenlandés, -desa *adj & n* : Greenlander
grogui *adj fam* : dazed, groggy
grosella *nf* **1** : currant **2 grosella espinosa** : gooseberry
grosería *nf* **1** : insult, coarse language **2** : rudeness, discourtesy
grosero[1], -ra *adj* **1** : rude, fresh **2** : coarse, vulgar
grosero[2], -ra *n* : rude person
grosor *nm* : thickness
grosso *adj* **a grosso modo** : roughly, broadly, approximately
grotesco, -ca *adj* : grotesque, hideous
grúa *nf* **1** : crane (machine) **2** : tow truck
gruesa *nf* : gross
grueso[1], -sa *adj* **1** : thick, bulky **2** : heavy, big **3** : heavyset, stout
grueso[2] *nm* **1** : thickness **2** : main body, mass **3 en ~** : in bulk
grulla *nf* : crane (bird)
grumo *nm* : lump, glob
gruñido *nm* : growl, grunt
gruñir {38} *vi* **1** : to growl, to grunt **2** : to grumble
gruñón[1], -ñona *adj, mpl* **gruñones** *fam* : grumpy, crabby
gruñón[2], -ñona *n, mpl* **gruñones** *fam* : grumpy person, nag
grupa *nf* : rump, hindquarters *pl*
grupo *nm* : group
gruta *nf* : grotto, cave
guacal *nm Col, Mex, Ven* : crate
guacamayo *nm* : macaw
guacamole *or* **guacamol** *nm* : guacamole
guacamote *nm Mex* : yuca, cassava
guachinango → **huachinango**
guacho, -cha *adj* **1** *Arg, Col, Chile, Peru* : orphaned **2** *Chile, Peru* : odd, unmatched
guadaña *nf* : scythe
guagua *nf* **1** *Arg, Col, Chile, Peru* : baby **2** *Cuba, PRi* : bus
guaira *nf* **1** *CA* : traditional flute **2** *Peru* : smelting furnace
guajiro, -ra *n Cuba* : peasant
guajolote *nm Mex* : turkey
guanábana *nf* : guanabana, soursop (fruit)
guanaco *nm* : guanaco
guandú *nm CA, Car, Col* : pigeon pea
guango, -ga *adj Mex* **1** : loose-fitting, baggy **2** : slack, loose
guano *nm* : guano
guante *nm* **1** : glove <guante de boxeo : boxing glove> **2 arrojarle el guante (a alguien)** : to throw down the gauntlet (to someone)
guantelete *nm* : gauntlet
guapo, -pa *adj* **1** : handsome, good-looking, attractive **2** : elegant, smart **3** *fam* : bold, dashing
guapura *nf fam* : handsomeness, attractiveness, good looks *pl* <¡qué guapura! : what a vision!>
guarache → **huarache**
guarachear *vi Cuba, PRi fam* : to go on a spree, to go out on the town
guaraní[1] *adj & nmf* : Guarani
guaraní[2] *nm* : Guarani (language of Paraguay)
guarda *nmf* **1** GUARDIÁN : security guard **2** : keeper, custodian
guardabarros *nms & pl* : fender, mudguard
guardabosque *nmfs & pl* : forest ranger, gamekeeper
guardacostas[1] *nmfs & pl* : coastguardsman
guardacostas[2] *nms & pl* : coast guard vessel
guardaespaldas *nmfs & pl* : bodyguard
guardafangos *nms & pl* : fender, mudguard
guardameta *nmf* ARQUERO, PORTERO : goalkeeper, goalie
guardapelo *nm* : locket
guardapolvo *nm* **1** : dustcover **2** : duster, housecoat
guardar *vt* **1** : to guard **2** : to maintain, to preserve **3** CONSERVAR : to put away **4** RESERVAR : to save **5** : to keep (a secret or promise) — **guardarse** *vr* **1 ~ de** : to refrain from **2 ~ de** : to guard against, to be careful not to
guardarropa *nm* **1** : cloakroom, checkroom **2** ARMARIO : closet, wardrobe
guardería *nf* : nursery, day-care center
guardia[1] *nf* **1** : guard, defense **2** : guard duty, watch **3 en ~** : on guard
guardia[2] *nmf* **1** : sentry, guardsman, guard **2** : police officer, policeman *m*, policewoman *f*
guardián, -diana *n, mpl* **guardianes** **1** GUARDA : security guard, watchman **2** : guardian, keeper **3 perro guardián** : watchdog
guarecer {53} *vt* : to shelter, to protect — **guarecerse** *vr* : to take shelter
guarida *nf* **1** : den, lair **2** : hideout
guarismo *nm* : figure, numeral
guarnecer {53} *vt* **1** : to adorn **2** : to garnish **3** : to garrison
guarnición *nf, pl* **-ciones** **1** : garnish **2** : garrison **3** : decoration, trimming, setting (of a jewel)
guaro *nm CA* : liquor distilled from sugarcane
guasa *nf fam* **1** : joking, fooling around **2 de ~** : in jest, as a joke
guasón[1], -sona *adj, mpl* **guasones** *fam* : funny, witty

guasón[2], -sona *n, mpl* **guasones** *fam* : joker, clown
guatemalteco, -ca *adj & n* : Guatemalan
guau *interj* : wow!
guayaba *nf* : guava (fruit)
gubernamental *adj* : governmental
gubernativo, -va → **gubernamental**
gubernatura *nf Mex* : governing body
guepardo *nm* : cheetah
güero, -ra *adj Mex* : blond, fair
guerra *nf* **1** : war <declarar la guerra : to declare war> <guerra sin cuartel : all-out war> **2** : warfare **3** LUCHA : conflict, struggle
guerrear *vi* : to wage war
guerrero[1], -ra *adj* **1** : war, fighting **2** : warlike
guerrero[2], -ra *n* : warrior
guerrilla *nf* : guerrilla warfare
guerrillero, -ra *adj & n* : guerrilla
gueto *nm* : ghetto
guía[1] *nf* **1** : directory, guidebook **2** ORIENTACIÓN : guidance, direction <la conciencia me sirve como guía : conscience is my guide>
guía[2] *nmf* : guide, leader <guía de turismo : tour guide>
guiar {85} *vt* **1** : to guide, to lead **2** CONDUCIR : to manage — **guiarse** *vr* : to be guided by, to go by
guija *nf* : pebble
guijarro *nm* : pebble
guillotina *nf* : guillotine — **guillotinar** *vt*
guinda[1] *adj & nm Mex* : burgundy (color)
guinda[2] *nf* : morello (cherry)
guineo *nm Car* : banana
guinga *nf* : gingham
guiñada → **guiño**
guiñar *vi* : to wink
guiño *nm* : wink
guión *nm, pl* **guiones** **1** : script, screenplay **2** : hyphen, dash **3** ESTANDARTE : standard, banner
guirnalda *nf* : garland
guisa *nf* **1** : manner, fashion **2 a guisa de** : like, by way of **3 de tal guisa** : in such a way
guisado ESTOFADO *nm* : stew
guisante *nm* : pea
guisar *vt* **1** ESTOFAR : to stew **2** *Spain* : to cook
guiso *nm* **1** : stew **2** : casserole
güisqui → **whisky**
guita *nf* : string, twine
guitarra *nf* : guitar
guitarrista *nmf* : guitarist
gula *nf* GLOTONERÍA : gluttony, greed
gusano *nm* **1** LOMBRIZ : worm, earthworm <gusano de seda : silkworm> **2** : caterpillar, maggot, grub
gustar *vt* **1** : to taste **2** : to like <¿gustan pasar? : would you like to come in?> — *vi* **1** : to be pleasing <me gustan los dulces : I like sweets> <a María le gusta Carlos : Maria is attracted to Carlos> <no me gusta que me griten : I don't like to be yelled at> **2 ~ de** : to like, to enjoy <no gusta de chismes : she doesn't like gossip> **3 como guste** : as you wish, as you like
gustativo, -va *adj* : taste <papilas gustativas : taste buds>
gusto *nm* **1** : flavor, taste **2** : taste, style **3** : pleasure, liking **4** : whim, fancy <a gusto : at will> **5 a ~** : comfortable, at ease **6 al gusto** : to taste, as one likes **7 mucho gusto** : pleased to meet you
gustosamente *adv* : gladly
gustoso, -sa *adj* **1** : willing, glad <nuestra empresa participará gustosa : our company will be pleased to participate> **2** : zesty, tasty
gutural *adj* : guttural

H

h *nf* : eighth letter of the Spanish alphabet
ha → **haber**
haba *nf* : broad bean
habanero[1], -ra *adj* : of or from Havana
habanero[2], -ra *n* : native or resident of Havana
haber[1] {39} *v aux* **1** : have, has <no ha llegado el envío : the shipment hasn't arrived> **2 ~ de** : must <ha de ser tarde : it must be late> — *v impers* **1 hay** : there is, there are <hay dos mensajes : there are two messages> <¿qué hay de nuevo? : what's new?> **2 hay que** : it is necessary <hay que trabajar más rápido : you have to work faster>
haber[2] *nm* **1** : assets *pl* **2** : credit, credit side **3 haberes** *nmpl* : salary, income, remuneration
habichuela *nf* **1** : bean, kidney bean **2** : green bean
hábil *adj* **1** : able, skillful **2** : working <días hábiles : working days>
habilidad *nf* CAPACIDAD : ability, skill
habilidoso, -sa *adj* : skillful, clever
habilitación *nf, pl* **-ciones** **1** : authorization **2** : furnishing, equipping
habilitar *vt* **1** : to enable, to authorize, to empower **2** : to equip, to furnish
hábilmente *adv* : skillfully, expertly
habitable *adj* : habitable, inhabitable
habitación *nf, pl* **-ciones** **1** CUARTO : room **2** DORMITORIO : bedroom **3** : habitation, occupancy

habitante *nmf* **:** inhabitant, resident
habitar *vt* **:** to inhabit — *vi* **:** to reside, to dwell
hábitat *nm, pl* **-tats :** habitat
hábito *nm* **1 :** habit, custom **2 :** habit (of a monk or nun)
habitual *adj* **:** habitual, customary — **habitualmente** *adv*
habituar {3} *vt* **:** to accustom, to habituate — **habituarse** *vr* **~ a :** to get used to, to grow accustomed to
habla *nf* **1 :** speech **2 :** language, dialect **3 de ~ :** speaking <de habla inglesa : English-speaking>
hablado, -da *adj* **1 :** spoken **2 mal hablado :** foulmouthed
hablador[1], -dora *adj* **:** talkative
hablador[2], -dora *n* **:** chatterbox
habladuría *nf* **1 :** rumor **2 habladurías** *nfpl* **:** gossip, scandal
hablante *nmf* **:** speaker
hablar *vi* **1 :** to speak, to talk <hablar en broma : to be joking> **2 ~ de :** to mention, to talk about **3 dar que hablar :** to make people talk — *vt* **1 :** to speak (a language) **2 :** to talk about, to discuss <háblalo con tu jefe : discuss it with your boss> — **hablarse** *vr* **1 :** to speak to each other, to be on speaking terms **2 se habla inglés (etc.) :** English (etc.) spoken
habrá, etc. → **haber**
hacedor, -dora *n* **:** creator, maker, doer
hacendado, -da *n* **:** landowner
hacer {40} *vt* **1 :** to make **2 :** to do, to perform **3 :** to force, to oblige <los hice esperar : I made them wait> — *vi* **:** to act <haces bien : you're doing the right thing> — *v impers* **1** (*referring to weather*) <hacer frío : to be cold> <hace viento : it's windy> **2 hace :** ago <hace mucho tiempo : a long time ago, for a long time> **3 no le hace :** it doesn't matter, it makes no difference **4 hacer falta :** to be necessary, to be needed — **hacerse** *vr* **1 :** to become **2 :** to pretend, to act, to play <hacerse el tonto : to play dumb> **3 :** to seem <el examen se me hizo difícil : the exam seemed difficult to me> **4 :** to get, to grow <se hace tarde : it's growing late>
hacha *nf* **:** hatchet, ax
hachazo *nm* **:** blow, chop (with an ax)
hachís *nm* **:** hashish
hacia *prep* **1 :** toward, towards <hacia abajo : downward> <hacia adelante : forward> **2 :** near, around, about <hacia las seis : about six o'clock>
hacienda *nf* **1 :** estate, ranch, farm **2 :** property **3 :** livestock **4 la Hacienda :** department of revenue, tax office
hacinar *vt* **1 :** to pile up, to stack **2 :** to overcrowd — **hacinarse** *vr* **:** to crowd together
hada *nf* **:** fairy
hado *nm* **:** destiny, fate
haga, etc. → **hacer**
haitiano, -na *adj & n* **:** Haitian
halagador[1], -dora *adj* **:** flattering
halagador[2], -dora *n* **:** flatterer
halagar {52} *vt* **:** to flatter, to compliment
halago *nm* **:** flattery, praise
halagüeño, -ña *adj* **1 :** flattering **2 :** encouraging, promising
halcón *nm, pl* **halcones :** hawk, falcon
halibut *nm, pl* **-buts :** halibut
hálito *nm* **1 :** breath **2 :** gentle breeze
hallar *vt* **1** ENCONTRAR **:** to find **2** DESCUBRIR **:** to discover, to find out — **hallarse** *vr* **1 :** to be situated, to find oneself **2 :** to feel <no se halla bien : he doesn't feel comfortable, he feels out of place>
hallazgo *nm* **1 :** discovery **2 :** find <¡es un verdadero hallazgo! : it's a real find!>
halo *nm* **1 :** halo **2 :** aura
halógeno *nm* **:** halogen
hamaca *nf* **:** hammock
hambre *nf* **1 :** hunger **2 :** starvation **3 tener hambre :** to be hungry **4 dar hambre :** to make hungry
hambriento, -ta *adj* **:** hungry, starving
hambruna *nf* **:** famine
hamburguesa *nf* **:** hamburger
hampa *nf* **:** criminal underworld
hampón, -pona *n, mpl* **hampones :** criminal, thug
hámster *nm, pl* **hámsters :** hamster
han → **haber**
handicap *or* **hándicap** [ˈhandiˌkap] *nm, pl* **-caps :** handicap (in sports)
hangar *nm* **:** hangar
hará, etc. → **hacer**
haragán[1], -gana *adj, mpl* **-ganes :** lazy, idle
haragán[2], -gana *n, mpl* **-ganes** HOLGAZÁN **:** slacker, good-for-nothing
haraganear *vi* **:** to be lazy, to waste one's time
haraganería *nf* **:** laziness
harapiento, -ta *adj* **:** ragged, tattered
harapos *nmpl* ANDRAJOS **:** rags, tatters
hardware [ˈhardˌwɛr] *nm* **:** computer hardware
harén *nm, pl* **harenes :** harem
harina *nf* **1 :** flour **2 harina de maíz :** cornmeal
hartar *vt* **1 :** to glut, to satiate **2** FASTIDIAR **:** to tire, to irritate, to annoy — **hartarse** *vr* **:** to be weary, to get fed up
harto[1] *adv* **:** most, extremely, very
harto[2], -ta *adj* **1 :** full, satiated **2 :** fed up
hartura *nf* **1 :** surfeit **2 :** abundance, plenty
has → **haber**
hasta[1] *adv* **:** even
hasta[2] *prep* **1 :** until, up until <hasta entonces : until then> <¡hasta luego! : see you later!> **2 :** as far as <nos fuimos hasta Managua : we went all the way to Managua> **3 :** up to <hasta cierto punto : up to a certain point> **4 hasta que :** until

hastiar {85} *vt* **1 :** to make weary, to bore **2 :** to disgust, to sicken — **hastiarse** *vr* **~ de :** to get tired of
hastío *nm* **1** TEDIO **:** tedium **2** REPUGNANCIA **:** disgust
hato *nm* **1 :** flock, herd **2 :** bundle (of possessions)
hawaiano, -na *adj & n* **:** Hawaiian
hay → **haber**
haya[1], **etc.** → **haber**
haya[2] *nf* **:** beech (tree and wood)
hayuco *nm* **:** beechnut
haz[1] → **hacer**
haz[2] *nm, pl* **haces 1** FARDO **:** bundle **2 :** beam (of light)
haz[3] *nf, pl* **haces 1 :** face **2 haz de la tierra :** surface of the earth
hazaña *nf* PROEZA **:** feat, exploit
hazmerreír *nm fam* **:** laughingstock
he[1] {39} → **haber**
he[2] *v impers* **he aquí :** here is, here are, behold
hebilla *nf* **:** buckle, clasp
hebra *nf* **:** strand, thread
hebreo[1], **-brea** *adj & n* **:** Hebrew
hebreo[2] *nm* **:** Hebrew (language)
hecatombe *nm* **1** MATANZA **:** massacre **2 :** disaster
heces → **hez**
hechicería *nf* **1** BRUJERÍA **:** sorcery, witchcraft **2 :** curse, spell
hechicero[1], **-ra** *adj* **:** bewitching, enchanting
hechicero[2], **-ra** *n* **:** sorcerer, sorceress *f*
hechizar {21} *vt* **1** EMBRUJAR **:** to bewitch **2** CAUTIVAR **:** to charm
hechizo *nm* **1** SORTILEGIO **:** spell, enchantment **2** ENCANTO **:** charm, fascination
hecho[1] *pp* → **hacer**
hecho[2], **-cha** *adj* **1 :** made, done **2 :** ready-to-wear **3 :** complete, finished <hecho y derecho : full-fledged>
hecho[3] *nm* **1 :** fact **2 :** event <hechos históricos : historic events> **3 :** act, action **4 de ~ :** in fact, in reality
hechura *nf* **1 :** style **2 :** craftsmanship, workmanship **3 :** product, creation
hectárea *nf* **:** hectare
heder {56} *vi* **:** to stink, to reek
hediondez *nf* **:** stink, stench
hediondo, -da *adj* MALOLIENTE **:** foul-smelling, stinking
hedor *nm* **:** stench, stink
hegemonía *nf* **1 :** dominance **2 :** hegemony (in politics)
helada *nf* **:** frost (in meteorology)
heladería *nf* **:** ice-cream parlor, ice-cream stand
helado[1], **-da** *adj* **1** GÉLIDO **:** icy, freezing cold **2** CONGELADO **:** frozen
helado[2] *nm* **:** ice cream
heladora *nf* CONGELADOR **:** freezer
helar {55} *v* CONGELAR **:** to freeze — *v impers* **:** to produce frost <anoche heló : there was frost last night> — **helarse** *vr*
helecho *nm* **:** fern, bracken
hélice *nf* **1 :** spiral, helix **2 :** propeller
helicóptero *nm* **:** helicopter
helio *nm* **:** helium
helipuerto *nm* **:** heliport
hembra *adj & nf* **:** female
hemisférico, -ca *adj* **:** hemispheric, hemispherical
hemisferio *nm* **:** hemisphere
hemofilia *nf* **:** hemophilia
hemofílico, -ca *adj & n* **:** hemophiliac
hemoglobina *nf* **:** hemoglobin
hemorragia *nf* **1 :** hemorrhage **2 hemorragia nasal :** nosebleed
hemorroides *nfpl* ALMORRANAS **:** hemorrhoids, piles
hemos → **haber**
henchido, -da *adj* **:** swollen, bloated
henchir {54} *vt* **1 :** to stuff, to fill **2 :** to swell, to swell up — **henchirse** *vr* **:** to stuff oneself **2** LLENARSE **:** to fill up, to be full
hender {56} *vt* **:** to cleave, to split
hendidura *nf* **:** crack, crevice, fissure
henequén *nm, pl* **-quenes :** sisal hemp
heno *nm* **:** hay
hepatitis *nf* **:** hepatitis
heráldica *nf* **:** heraldry
heráldico, -ca *adj* **:** heraldic
heraldo *nm* **:** herald
herbario, -ria *adj* **:** herbal
herbicida *nm* **:** herbicide, weed killer
herbívoro[1], **-ra** *adj* **:** herbivorous
herbívoro[2] *nm* **:** herbivore
herbolario, -ria *n* **:** herbalist
hercúleo, -lea *adj* **:** herculean
heredar *vt* **:** to inherit
heredero, -ra *n* **:** heir, heiress *f*
hereditario, -ria *adj* **:** hereditary
hereje *nmf* **:** heretic
herejía *nf* **:** heresy
herencia *nf* **1 :** inheritance **2 :** heritage **3 :** heredity
herético, -ca *adj* **:** heretical
herida *nf* **:** injury, wound
herido[1], **-da** *adj* **1 :** injured, wounded **2 :** hurt, offended
herido[2], **-da** *n* **:** injured person, casualty
herir {76} *vt* **1 :** to injure, to wound **2 :** to hurt, to offend
hermafrodita *nmf* **:** hermaphrodite
hermanar *vt* **1 :** to unite, to bring together **2 :** to match up, to twin (cities)
hermanastro, -tra *n* **:** half brother *m*, half sister *f*
hermandad *nf* **1** FRATERNIDAD **:** brotherhood <hermandad de mujeres : sisterhood, sorority> **2 :** association
hermano, -na *n* **:** sibling, brother *m*, sister *f*
hermético, -ca *adj* **:** hermetic, watertight — **herméticamente** *adv*
hermoso, -sa *adj* BELLO **:** beautiful, lovely — **hermosamente** *adv*
hermosura *nf* BELLEZA **:** beauty, loveliness
hernia *nf* **:** hernia
héroe *nm* **:** hero
heroicidad *nf* **:** heroism, heroic deed

heroico, -ca *adj* : heroic — **heroicamente** *adv*

heroína *nf* **1** : heroine **2** : heroin

heroísmo *nm* : heroism

herpes *nms & pl* **1** : herpes **2** : shingles

herradura *nf* : horseshoe

herraje *nm* : ironwork

herramienta *nf* : tool

herrar {55} *vt* : to shoe (a horse)

herrería *nf* : blacksmith's shop

herrero, -ra *n* : blacksmith

herrumbre *nf* ORÍN : rust

herrumbroso, -sa *adj* OXIDADO : rusty

hertzio *nm* : hertz

hervidero *nm* **1** : mass, swarm **2** : hotbed (of crime, etc.)

hervidor *nm* : kettle

hervir {76} *vi* **1** BULLIR : to boil, to bubble **2 ~ de** : to teem with, to be swarming with — *vt* : to boil

hervor *nm* **1** : boiling **2** : fervor, ardor

heterogeneidad *nf* : heterogeneity

heterogéneo, -nea *adj* : heterogeneous

heterosexual *adj & nmf* : heterosexual

heterosexualidad *nf* : heterosexuality

hexágono *nm* : hexagon — **hexagonal** *adj*

hez *nf, pl* **heces 1** ESCORIA : scum, dregs *pl* **2** : sediment, lees *pl* **3 heces** *nfpl* : feces, excrement

hiato *nm* : hiatus

hibernar *vi* : to hibernate — **hibernación** *nf*

híbrido[1], **-da** *adj* : hybrid

híbrido[2] *nm* : hybrid

hicieron, etc. → **hacer**

hidalgo, -ga *n* : nobleman *m,* noblewoman *f*

hidrante *nm CA, Col* : hydrant

hidratar *vt* : to moisturize — **hidratante** *adj*

hidrato *nm* **1** : hydrate **2 hidrato de carbono** : carbohydrate

hidráulico, -ca *adj* : hydraulic

hidroavión *nm, pl* **-viones** : seaplane

hidrocarburo *nm* : hydrocarbon

hidroeléctrico, -ca *adj* : hydroelectric

hidrofobia *nf* RABIA : hydrophobia, rabies

hidrófugo, -ga *adj* : water-repellent

hidrógeno *nm* : hydrogen

hidroplano *nm* : hydroplane

hiede, etc. → **heder**

hiedra *nf* **1** : ivy **2 hiedra venenosa** : poison ivy

hiel *nf* **1** BILIS : bile **2** : bitterness

hiela, etc. → **helar**

hielo *nm* **1** : ice **2** : coldness, reserve <romper el hielo : to break the ice>

hiena *nf* : hyena

hiende, etc. → **hender**

hierba *nf* **1** : herb **2** : grass **3 mala hierba** : weed

hierbabuena *nf* : mint, spearmint

hiere, etc. → **herir**

hierra, etc. → **herrar**

hierro *nm* **1** : iron <hierro fundido : cast iron> **2** : branding iron

hierve, etc. → **hervir**

hígado *nm* : liver

higiene *nf* : hygiene

higiénico, -ca *adj* : hygienic — **higiénicamente** *adv*

higienista *nmf* : hygienist

higo *nm* **1** : fig **2 higo chumbo** : prickly pear (fruit)

higrómetro *nm* : hygrometer

higuera *nf* : fig tree

hijastro, -tra *n* : stepson *m,* stepdaughter *f*

hijo, -ja *n* **1** : son *m,* daughter *f* **2 hijos** *nmpl* : children, offspring

híjole *interj Mex* : wow!, good grief!

hilacha *nf* **1** : ravel, loose thread **2 mostrar la hilacha** : to show one's true colors

hilado *nm* **1** : spinning **2** HILO : yarn, thread

hilar *vt* **1** : to spin (thread) **2** : to consider, to string together (ideas) — *vi* **1** : to spin **2 hilar delgado** : to split hairs

hilarante *adj* **1** : humorous, hilarious **2 gas hilarante** : laughing gas

hilaridad *nf* : hilarity

hilera *nf* FILA : file, row, line

hilo *nm* **1** : thread <colgar de un hilo : to hang by a thread> <hilo dental : dental floss> **2** LINO : linen **3** : (electric) wire **4** : theme, thread (of a discourse) **5** : trickle (of water, etc.)

hilvanar *vt* **1** : to baste, to tack **2** : to piece together

himnario *nm* : hymnal

himno *nm* **1** : hymn **2 himno nacional** : national anthem

hincapié *nm* **hacer hincapié en** : to emphasize, to stress

hincar {72} *vt* CLAVAR : to stick, to plunge — **hincarse** *vr* **hincarse de rodillas** : to kneel down, to fall to one's knees

hinchado, -da *adj* **1** : swollen, inflated **2** : pompous, overblown

hinchar *vt* **1** INFLAR : to inflate **2** : to exaggerate — **hincharse** *vr* **1** : to swell up **2** : to become conceited, to swell with pride

hinchazón *nf, pl* **-zones** : swelling

hinche, etc. → **henchir**

hindú *adj & nmf* : Hindu

hinduismo *nm* : Hinduism

hiniesta *nf* : broom (plant)

hinojo *nm* **1** : fennel **2 de hinojos** : on bended knee

hinque, etc. → **hincar**

hipar *vi* : to hiccup

hiperactividad *nf* : hyperactivity

hiperactivo, -va *adj* : hyperactive, overactive

hipérbole *nf* : hyperbole

hiperbólico, -ca *adj* : hyperbolic, exaggerated

hipercrítico, -ca *adj* : hypercritical

hipermetropía *nf* : farsightedness

hipersensibilidad *nf* : hypersensitivity

hipersensible *adj* : hypersensitive

hipertensión *nf, pl* **-siones** : hypertension, high blood pressure
hípico, -ca *adj* : equestrian <concurso hípico : horse show>
hipil *nm* → **huipil**
hipnosis *nfs & pl* : hypnosis
hipnótico, -ca *adj* : hypnotic
hipnotismo *nm* : hypnotism
hipnotizador[1], -dora *adj* **1** : hypnotic **2** : spellbinding, mesmerizing
hipnotizador[2], -dora *n* : hypnotist
hipnotizar {21} *vt* : to hypnotize
hipo *nm* : hiccup, hiccups *pl*
hipocampo *nm* : sea horse
hipocondría *nf* : hypochondria
hipocondríaco, -ca *adj & n* : hypochondriac
hipocresía *nf* : hypocrisy
hipócrita[1] *adj* : hypocritical — **hipócritamente** *adv*
hipócrita[2] *nmf* : hypocrite
hipodérmico, -ca *adj* **aguja hipodérmica** : hypodermic needle
hipódromo *nm* : racetrack
hipopótamo *nm* : hippopotamus
hipoteca *nf* : mortgage
hipotecar {72} *vt* **1** : to mortgage **2** : to compromise, to jeopardize
hipotecario, -ria *adj* : mortgage
hipotensión *nf* : low blood pressure
hipotenusa *nf* : hypotenuse
hipótesis *nfs & pl* : hypothesis
hipotético, -ca *adj* : hypothetical — **hipotéticamente** *adv*
hippie *or* **hippy** ['hipi] *nmf, pl* **hippies** [-pis] : hippie
hiriente *adj* : hurtful, offensive
hirió, etc. → **herir**
hirsuto, -ta *adj* **1** : hirsute, hairy **2** : bristly, wiry
hirviente *adj* : boiling
hirvió, etc. → **hervir**
hisopo *nm* **1** : hyssop **2** : cotton swab
hispánico, -ca *adj & n* : Hispanic
hispano[1], -na *adj* : Hispanic <de habla hispana : Spanish-speaking>
hispano[2], -na *n* : Hispanic (person)
hispanoamericano[1], -na *adj* LATINOAMERICANO : Latin-American
hispanoamericano[2], -na *n* LATINOAMERICANO : Latin American
hispanohablante[1] *adj* : Spanish-speaking
hispanohablante[2] *nmf* : Spanish speaker
histerectomía *nf* : hysterectomy
histeria *nf* **1** : hysteria **2** : hysterics
histérico, -ca *adj* : hysterical — **histéricamente** *adv*
histerismo *nm* **1** : hysteria **2** : hysterics
historia *nf* **1** : history **2** NARRACIÓN, RELATO : story
historiador, -dora *n* : historian
historial *nm* **1** : record, document **2** CURRÍCULUM : résumé, curriculum vitae
histórico, -ca *adj* **1** : historical **2** : historic, important — **históricamente** *adv*
historieta *nf* : comic strip
histrionismo *nm* : histrionics, acting
hit ['hit] *nm, pl* **hits** **1** ÉXITO : hit, popular song **2** : hit (in baseball)
hito *nm* : milestone, landmark
hizo → **hacer**
hobby ['hɔbi] *nm, pl* **hobbies** [-bis] : hobby
hocico *nm* : snout, muzzle
hockey ['hɔke, -ki] *nm* : hockey
hogar *nm* **1** : home **2** : hearth, fireplace
hogareño, -ña *adj* **1** : home-loving **2** : domestic, homelike
hogaza *nf* : large loaf (of bread)
hoguera *nf* **1** FOGATA : bonfire **2** **morir en la hoguera** : to burn at the stake
hoja *nf* **1** : leaf, petal, blade (of grass) **2** : sheet (of paper), page (of a book) <hoja de cálculo : spreadsheet> **3** FORMULARIO : form <hoja de pedido : order form> **4** : blade (of a knife) <hoja de afeitar : razor blade>
hojalata *nf* : tinplate
hojaldra *or* **hojaldre** *nm* : puff pastry
hojarasca *nf* : fallen leaves *pl*
hojear *vt* : to leaf through (a book or magazine)
hojuela *nf* **1** : leaflet, young leaf **2** : flake
hola *interj* : hello!, hi!
holandés[1], -desa *adj, mpl* **-deses** : Dutch
holandés[2], -desa *n, mpl* **-deses** : Dutch person, Dutchman *m*, Dutchwoman *f* <los holandeses : the Dutch>
holandés[3] *nm* : Dutch (language)
holgadamente *adv* : comfortably, easily <vivir holgadamente : to be well-off>
holgado, -da *adj* **1** : loose, baggy **2** : at ease, comfortable
holganza *nf* : leisure, idleness
holgazán[1], -zana *adj, mpl* **-zanes** : lazy
holgazán[2], -zana *n, mpl* **-zanes** HARAGÁN : slacker, idler
holgazanear *vi* HARAGANEAR : to laze around, to loaf
holgazanería *nf* PEREZA : idleness, laziness
holgura *nf* **1** : looseness **2** COMODIDAD : comfort, ease
holístico, -ca *adj* : holistic
hollar {19} *vt* : to tread on, to trample
hollín *nm, pl* **hollines** TIZNE : soot
holocausto *nm* : holocaust
holograma *nm* : hologram
hombre *nm* **1** : man <el hombre : man, mankind> **2** **hombre de estado** : statesman **3** **hombre de negocios** : businessman **4** **hombre lobo** : werewolf
hombrera *nf* **1** : shoulder pad **2** : epaulet
hombría *nf* : manliness
hombro *nm* : shoulder <encogerse de hombros : to shrug one's shoulders>
hombruno, -na *adj* : mannish

homenaje *nm* : homage, tribute <rendir homenaje a : to pay tribute to>

homenajear *vt* : to pay homage to, to honor

homeopatía *nf* : homeopathy

homicida[1] *adj* : homicidal, murderous

homicida[2] *nmf* ASESINO : murderer

homicidio *nm* ASESINATO : homicide, murder

homilía *nf* : homily, sermon

homófono *nm* : homophone

homogeneidad *nf* : homogeneity

homogeneización *nf* : homogenization

homogeneizar {21} *vt* : to homogenize

homogéneo, -nea *adj* : homogeneous

homógrafo *nm* : homograph

homologación *nf, pl* **-ciones 1** : sanctioning, approval **2** : parity

homologar {52} *vt* **1** : to sanction **2** : to bring into line

homólogo[1], **-ga** *adj* : homologous, equivalent

homólogo[2], **-ga** *n* : counterpart

homónimo[1], **-ma** *n* TOCAYO : namesake

homónimo[2] *nm* : homonym

homosexual *adj & nmf* : homosexual

homosexualidad *nf* : homosexuality

honda *nf* : sling

hondo[1] *adv* : deeply

hondo[2], **-da** *adj* PROFUNDO : deep <en lo más hondo de : in the depths of> — **hondamente** *adv*

hondonada *nf* **1** : hollow, depression **2** : ravine, gorge

hondura *nf* : depth

hondureño, -ña *adj & n* : Honduran

honestidad *nf* **1** : decency, modesty **2** : honesty, uprightness

honesto, -ta *adj* **1** : decent, virtuous **2** : honest, honorable — **honestamente** *adv*

hongo *nm* **1** : fungus **2** : mushroom

honor *nm* **1** : honor <en honor a la verdad : to be quite honest> **2 honores** *nmpl* : honors <hacer los honores : to do the honors>

honorable *adj* HONROSO : honorable — **honorablemente** *adv*

honorario, -ria *adj* : honorary

honorarios *nmpl* : payment, fees (for professional services)

honorífico, -ca *adj* : honorary <mención honorífica : honorable mention>

honra *nf* **1** : dignity, self-respect <tener a mucha honra : to take great pride in> **2** : good name, reputation

honradamente *adv* : honestly, decently

honradez *nf, pl* **-deces** : honesty, integrity, probity

honrado, -da *adj* **1** HONESTO : honest, upright **2** : honored

honrar *vt* **1** : to honor **2** : to be a credit to <su generosidad lo honra : his generosity does him credit>

honroso, -sa *adj* HONORABLE : honorable — **honrosamente** *adv*

hora *nf* **1** : hour <media hora : half an hour> <a la última hora : at the last minute> <a la hora en punto : on the dot> <horas de oficina : office hours> **2** : time <¿qué hora es? : what time is it?> **3** CITA : appointment

horario *nm* : schedule, timetable, hours *pl* <horario de visita : visiting hours>

horca *nf* **1** : gallows *pl* **2** : pitchfork

horcajadas *nfpl* **a ~** : astride, astraddle

horcón *nm, pl* **horcones** : wooden post, prop

horda *nf* : horde

horizontal *adj* : horizontal — **horizontalmente** *adv*

horizonte *nm* : horizon, skyline

horma *nf* **1** : shoe tree **2** : shoemaker's last

hormiga *nf* : ant

hormigón *nm, pl* **-gones** CONCRETO : concrete

hormigonera *nf* : cement mixer

hormigueo *nm* **1** : tingling, pins and needles *pl* **2** : uneasiness

hormiguero *nm* **1** : anthill **2** : swarm (of people)

hormona *nf* : hormone — **hormonal** *adj*

hornacina *nf* : niche, recess

hornada *nf* : batch

hornear *vt* : to bake

hornilla *nf* : burner (of a stove)

horno *nm* **1** : oven <horno crematorio : crematorium> <horno de microondas : microwave oven> **2** : kiln

horóscopo *nm* : horoscope

horqueta *nf* **1** : fork (in a river or road) **2** : crotch (in a tree) **3** : small pitchfork

horquilla *nf* **1** : hairpin, bobby pin **2** : pitchfork

horrendo, -da *adj* : horrendous, horrible

horrible *adj* : horrible, dreadful — **horriblemente** *adv*

horripilante *adj* : horrifying, hair-raising

horripilar *vt* : to horrify, to terrify

horror *nm* : horror, dread

horrorizado, -da *adj* : terrified

horrorizar {21} *vt* : to horrify, to terrify — **horrorizarse** *vr*

horroroso, -sa *adj* **1** : horrifying, terrifying **2** : dreadful, bad

hortaliza *nf* **1** : vegetable **2 hortalizas** *nfpl* : garden produce

hortera *adj Spain fam* : tacky, gaudy

hortícola *adj* : horticultural

horticultor, -ra *n* : horticulturist

horticultura *nf* : horticulture

hosco, -ca *adj* : sullen, gloomy

hospedaje *nm* : lodging, accomodations *pl*

hospedar *vt* : to provide with lodging, to put up — **hospedarse** *vr* : to stay, to lodge

hospicio *nm* : orphanage

hospital *nm* : hospital

hospitalario, -ria *adj* : hospitable

hospitalidad *nf* : hospitality

hospitalización *nf, pl* **-ciones** : hospitalization

hospitalizar {21} *vt* : to hospitalize — **hospitalizarse** *vr*

hostería *nf* POSADA : inn

hostia *nf* : host, Eucharist

hostigamiento *nm* : harassment

hostigar {52} *vt* ACOSAR, ASEDIAR : to harass, to pester

hostil *adj* : hostile

hostilidad *nf* **1** : hostility, antagonism **2 hostilidades** *nfpl* : (military) hostilities

hostilizar {21} *vt* : to harass

hotel *nm* : hotel

hotelero[1], **-ra** *adj* : hotel <la industria hotelera : the hotel business>

hotelero[2], **-ra** *n* : hotel manager, hotelier

hoy *adv* **1** : today <hoy mismo : right now, this very day> **2** : now, nowadays <de hoy en adelante : from now on>

hoyo *nm* AGUJERO : hole

hoyuelo *nm* : dimple

hoz *nf, pl* **hoces** : sickle

hozar {21} *vi* : to root (of a pig)

huachinango *nm Mex* : red snapper

huarache *nm* : huarache sandal

hubo, etc. → **haber**

hueco[1], **-ca** *adj* **1** : hollow, empty **2** : soft, spongy **3** : hollow-sounding, resonant **4** : proud, conceited **5** : superficial

hueco[2] *nm* **1** : hole, hollow, cavity **2** : gap, space **3** : recess, alcove

huele, etc. → **oler**

huelga *nf* **1** PARO : strike **2 hacer huelga** : to strike, to go on strike

huelguista *nmf* : striker

huella[1], **etc.** → **hollar**

huella[2] *nf* **1** : footprint <seguir las huellas de alguien : to follow in someone's footsteps> **2** : mark, impact <dejar huella : to leave one's mark> <sin dejar huella : without a trace> **3 huella digital** *or* **huella dactilar** : fingerprint

huérfano[1], **-na** *adj* **1** : orphan, orphaned **2** : defenseless **3 ~ de** : lacking, devoid of

huérfano[2], **-na** *n* : orphan

huerta *nf* **1** : large vegetable garden, truck farm **2** : orchard **3** : irrigated land

huerto *nm* **1** : vegetable garden **2** : orchard

hueso *nm* **1** : bone **2** : pit, stone (of a fruit)

huésped[1], **-peda** *n* INVITADO : guest

huésped[2] *nm* : host <organismo huésped : host organism>

huestes *nfpl* **1** : followers **2** : troops, army

huesudo, -da *adj* : bony

hueva *nf* : roe, spawn

huevo *nm* : egg <huevos revueltos : scrambled eggs>

huida *nf* : flight, escape

huidizo, -za *adj* **1** ESCURRIDIZO : elusive, slippery **2** : shy, evasive

huipil *nm CA, Mex* : traditional sleeveless blouse or dress

huir {41} *vi* **1** ESCAPAR : to escape, to flee **2 ~ de** : to avoid

huiro *nm Chile, Peru* : seaweed

huizache *nm* : huisache, acacia

hule *nm* **1** : oilcloth, oilskin **2** *Mex* : rubber **3 hule espuma** *Mex* : foam rubber

humanidad *nf* **1** : humanity, mankind **2** : humaneness **3 humanidades** *nfpl* : humanities *pl*

humanismo *nm* : humanism

humanista *nmf* : humanist

humanístico, -ca *adj* : humanistic

humanitario, -ria *adj & n* : humanitarian

humano[1], **-na** *adj* **1** : human **2** BENÉVOLO : humane , benevolent — **humanamente** *adv*

humano[2] *nm* : human being, human

humareda *nf* : cloud of smoke

humeante *adj* **1** : smoky **2** : smoking, steaming

humear *vi* **1** : to smoke **2** : to steam

humectante[1] *adj* : moisturizing

humectante[2] *nm* : moisturizer

humedad *nf* **1** : humidity **2** : dampness, moistness

humedecer {53} *vt* **1** : to humidify **2** : to moisten, to dampen

húmedo, -da *adj* **1** : humid **2** : moist, damp

humidificador *nm* : humidifier

humidificar {72} *vt* : to humidify

humildad *nf* **1** : humility **2** : lowliness

humilde *adj* **1** : humble **2** : lowly <gente humilde : poor people>

humildemente *adv* : meekly, humbly

humillación *nf, pl* **-ciones** : humiliation

humillante *adj* : humiliating

humillar *vt* : to humiliate — **humillarse** *vr* : to humble oneself <humillarse a hacer algo : to stoop to doing something>

humo *nm* **1** : smoke, steam, fumes **2 humos** *nmpl* : airs *pl,* conceit

humor *nm* **1** : humor **2** : mood, temper <está de buen humor : she's in a good mood>

humorada *nf* **1** BROMA : joke, witticism **2** : whim, caprice

humorismo *nm* : humor, wit

humorista *nmf* : humorist, comedian, comedienne *f*

humorístico, -ca *adj* : humorous — **humorísticamente** *adv*

humoso, -sa *adj* : smoky, steamy

humus *nm* : humus

hundido, -da *adj* **1** : sunken **2** : depressed

hundimiento *nm* **1 :** sinking **2 :** collapse, ruin

hundir *vt* **1 :** to sink **2 :** to destroy, to ruin — **hundirse** *vr* **1 :** to sink down **2 :** to cave in **3 :** to break down, to go to pieces

húngaro[1], -ra *adj & n* **:** Hungarian

húngaro[2] *nm* **:** Hungarian (language)

huracán *nm, pl* **-canes :** hurricane

huraño, -ña *adj* **1 :** unsociable, aloof **2 :** timid, skittish (of an animal)

hurgar {52} *vt* **:** to poke, to jab, to rake (a fire) — *vi* **~ en :** to rummage in, to poke through

hurgue, etc. → **hurgar**

hurón *nm, pl* **hurones :** ferret

huronear *vi* **:** to pry, to snoop

hurra *interj* **:** hurrah!, hooray!

hurtadillas *nfpl* **a ~ :** stealthily, on the sly

hurtar *vt* ROBAR **:** to steal

hurto *nm* **1 :** theft, robbery **2 :** stolen property, loot

husmear *vt* **1 :** to follow the scent of, to track **2 :** to sniff out, to pry into — *vi* **1 :** to pry, to snoop **2 :** to sniff around (of an animal)

huso *nm* **1 :** spindle **2 huso horario :** time zone

huy *interj* **:** ow!, ouch!

huye, etc. → **huir**

I

i *nf* **:** ninth letter of the Spanish alphabet

iba, etc. → **ir**

ibérico, -ca *adj* **:** Iberian

ibero, -ra *or* **íbero, -ra** *adj & n* **:** Iberian

iberoamericano, -na *adj* HISPANOAMERICANO, LATINOAMERICANO **:** Latin-American

ibis *nfs & pl* **:** ibis

ice, etc. → **izar**

iceberg *nm, pl* **icebergs :** iceberg

icono *nm* **:** icon

iconoclasia *nf* **:** iconoclasm

iconoclasta *nmf* **:** iconoclast

ictericia *nf* **:** jaundice

ida *nf* **1 :** going, departure **2 ida y vuelta :** round-trip **3 idas y venidas :** comings and goings

idea *nf* **1 :** idea, notion **2 :** opinion, belief **3** PROPÓSITO **:** intention

ideal *adj & nm* **:** ideal — **idealmente** *adv*

idealismo *nm* **:** idealism

idealista[1] *adj* **:** idealistic

idealista[2] *nmf* **:** idealist

idealizar {21} *vt* **:** to idealize — **idealización** *nf*

idear *vt* **:** to devise, to think up

ideario *nm* **:** ideology

ídem *nm* **:** idem, the same, ditto

idéntico, -ca *adj* **:** identical, alike — **idénticamente** *adv*

identidad *nf* **:** identity

identificable *adj* **:** identifiable

identificación *nf, pl* **-ciones 1 :** identification, identifying **2 :** identification document, ID

identificar {72} *vt* **:** to identify — **identificarse** *vr* **1 :** to identify oneself **2 ~ con :** to identify with

ideología *nf* **:** ideology — **ideológicamente** *adv*

ideológico, -ca *adj* **:** ideological

idílico, -ca *adj* **:** idyllic

idilio *nm* **:** idyll

idioma *nm* **:** language <el idioma inglés : the English language>

idiomático, -ca *adj* **:** idiomatic — **idiomáticamente** *adv*

idiosincrasia *nf* **:** idiosyncrasy

idiosincrásico, -ca *adj* **:** idiosyncratic

idiota[1] *adj* **:** idiotic, stupid, foolish

idiota[2] *nmf* **:** idiot, foolish person

idiotez *nf, pl* **-teces 1 :** idiocy **2 :** idiotic act or remark <¡no digas idioteces! : don't talk nonsense!>

ido *pp* → **ir**

idólatra[1] *adj* **:** idolatrous

idólatra[2] *nmf* **:** idolater

idolatrar *vt* **:** to idolize

idolatría *nf* **:** idolatry

ídolo *nm* **:** idol

idoneidad *nf* **:** suitability

idóneo, -nea *adj* ADECUADO **:** suitable, fitting

iglesia *nf* **:** church

iglú *nm* **:** igloo

ignición *nf, pl* **-ciones :** ignition

ignífugo, -ga *adj* **:** fire-resistant, fireproof

ignominia *nf* **:** ignominy, disgrace

ignominioso, -sa *adj* **:** ignominious, shameful

ignorancia *nf* **:** ignorance

ignorante[1] *adj* **:** ignorant

ignorante[2] *nmf* **:** ignorant person, ignoramus

ignorar *vt* **1 :** to ignore **2** DESCONOCER **:** to be unaware of <lo ignoramos por absoluto : we have no idea>

ignoto, -ta *adj* **:** unknown

igual[1] *adv* **1 :** in the same way **2 por ~ :** equally

igual[2] *adj* **1 :** equal **2** IDÉNTICO **:** the same, alike **3 :** even, smooth **4** SEMEJANTE **:** similar **5** CONSTANTE **:** constant

igual[3] *nmf* **:** equal, peer

igualación *nf* **1 :** equalization **2 :** leveling, smoothing **3 :** equating (in mathematics)

igualado, -da *adj* **1 :** even (of a score) **2 :** level **3** *Mex* **:** disrespectful

igualar *vt* **1 :** to equalize **2 :** to tie <igualar el marcador : to even the score>

igualdad *nf* **1 :** equality **2** UNIFORMIDAD **:** evenness, uniformity

igualmente *adv* **1 :** equally **2** ASIMISMO **:** likewise

iguana *nf* **:** iguana

ijada *nf* **:** flank, loin, side

ijar *nm* → **ijada**

ilegal[1] *adj* **:** illegal, unlawful — **ilegalmente** *adv*

ilegal[2] *nmf CA, Mex* **:** illegal alien

ilegalidad *nf* **:** illegality, unlawfulness

ilegibilidad *nf* **:** illegibility

ilegible *adj* **:** illegible — **ilegiblemente** *adv*

ilegitimidad *nf* **:** illegitimacy

ilegítimo, -ma *adj* **:** illegitimate, unlawful

ileso, -sa *adj* **:** uninjured, unharmed

ilícito, -ta *adj* **:** illicit — **ilícitamente** *adv*

ilimitado, -da *adj* **:** unlimited

ilógico, -ca *adj* **:** illogical — **ilógicamente** *adv*

iluminación *nf, pl* **-ciones 1 :** illumination **2** ALUMBRADO **:** lighting

iluminado, -da *adj* **:** illuminated, lighted

iluminar *vt* **1 :** to illuminate, to light (up) **2 :** to enlighten

ilusión *nf, pl* **-siones 1 :** illusion, delusion **2** ESPERANZA **:** hope <hacerse ilusiones : to get one's hopes up>

ilusionado, -da *adj* ESPERANZADO **:** hopeful, eager

ilusionar *vt* **:** to build up hope, to excite — **ilusionarse** *vr* **:** to get one's hopes up

iluso[1]**, -sa** *adj* **:** naive, gullible

iluso[2]**, -sa** *n* SOÑADOR **:** dreamer, visionary

ilusorio, -ria *adj* ENGAÑOSO **:** illusory, misleading

ilustración *nf, pl* **-ciones 1 :** illustration **2 :** erudition, learning <la Ilustración : the Enlightenment>

ilustrado, -da *adj* **1 :** illustrated **2** DOCTO **:** learned, erudite

ilustrador, -dora *n* **:** illustrator

ilustrar *vt* **1 :** to illustrate **2** ACLARAR, CLARIFICAR **:** to explain

ilustrativo, -va *adj* **:** illustrative

ilustre *adj* **:** illustrious, eminent

imagen *nf, pl* **imágenes :** image, picture

imaginable *adj* **:** imaginable, conceivable

imaginación *nf, pl* **-ciones :** imagination

imaginar *vt* **:** to imagine — **imaginarse** *vr* **1 :** to suppose, to imagine **2 :** to picture

imaginario, -ria *adj* **:** imaginary

imaginativo, -va *adj* **:** imaginative — **imaginativamente** *adv*

imán *nm, pl* **imanes :** magnet

imantar *vt* **:** to magnetize

imbatible *adj* **:** unbeatable

imbécil[1] *adj* **:** stupid, idiotic

imbécil[2] *nmf* **1 :** imbecile **2** *fam* **:** idiot, dope

imborrable *adj* **:** indelible

imbuir {41} *vt* **:** to imbue — **imbuirse** *vr*

imitación *nf, pl* **-ciones 1 :** imitation **2 :** mimicry, impersonation

imitador[1]**, -dora** *adj* **:** imitative

imitador[2]**, -dora** *n* **1 :** imitator **2 :** mimic

imitar *vt* **1 :** to imitate, to copy **2 :** to mimic, to impersonate

impaciencia *nf* **:** impatience

impacientar *vt* **:** to make impatient, to exasperate — **impacientarse** *vr*

impaciente *adj* **:** impatient — **impacientemente** *adv*

impactado, -da *adj* **:** shocked, stunned

impactante *adj* **1 :** shocking **2 :** impressive, powerful

impactar *vt* **1** GOLPEAR **:** to hit **2** IMPRESIONAR **:** to impact, to affect — **impactarse** *vr*

impacto *nm* **1 :** impact, effect **2 :** shock, collision

impagable *adj* **1 :** unpayable **2 :** priceless

impago *nm* **:** nonpayment

impalpable *adj* INTANGIBLE **:** impalpable, intangible

impar[1] *adj* **:** odd <números impares : odd numbers>

impar[2] *nm* **:** odd number

imparable *adj* **:** unstoppable

imparcial *adj* **:** impartial — **imparcialmente** *adv*

imparcialidad *nf* **:** impartiality

impartir *vt* **:** to impart, to give

impasible *adj* **:** impassive, unmoved — **impasiblemente** *adv*

impasse *nm* **:** impasse

impávido, -da *adj* **:** undaunted, unperturbed

impecable *adj* INTACHABLE **:** impeccable, faultless — **impecablemente** *adv*

impedido, -da *adj* **:** disabled, crippled

impedimento *nm* **1 :** impediment, obstacle **2 :** disability

impedir {54} *vt* **1 :** to prevent, to block **2 :** to impede, to hinder

impeler *vt* **1 :** to drive, to propel **2 :** to impel

impenetrable *adj* **:** impenetrable — **impenetrabilidad** *nf*

impenitente *adj* **:** unrepentant, impenitent

impensable *adj* **:** unthinkable

impensado, -da *adj* **:** unforeseen, unexpected

imperante *adj* **:** prevailing

imperar *vi* **1 :** to reign, to rule **2** PREDOMINAR **:** to prevail

imperativo[1]**, -va** *adj* **:** imperative

imperativo[2] *nm* **:** imperative

imperceptible *adj* **:** imperceptible — **imperceptiblemente** *adv*

imperdible *Spain nm* **:** safety pin

imperdonable *adj* : unpardonable, unforgivable
imperecedero, -ra *adj* **1** : imperishable **2** INMORTAL : immortal, everlasting
imperfección *nf, pl* **-ciones 1** : imperfection **2** DEFECTO : defect, flaw
imperfecto[1], **-ta** *adj* : imperfect, flawed
imperfecto[2] *nm* : imperfect tense
imperial *adj* : imperial
imperialismo *nm* : imperialism
imperialista *adj & nmf* : imperialist
impericia *nf* : lack of skill, incompetence
imperio *nm* : empire
imperioso, -sa *adj* **1** : imperious **2** : pressing, urgent — **imperiosamente** *adv*
impermeabilizante *adj* : water-repellent
impermeabilizar {21} *vt* : to waterproof
impermeable[1] *adj* **1** : impervious **2** : impermeable, waterproof
impermeable[2] *nm* : raincoat
impersonal *adj* : impersonal — **impersonalmente** *adv*
impertinencia *nf* INSOLENCIA : impertinence, insolence
impertinente *adj* **1** INSOLENTE : impertinent, insolent **2** INOPORTUNO : inappropriate, uncalled-for **3** IRRELEVANTE : irrelevant
imperturbable *adj* : imperturbable, impassive, stolid
ímpetu *nm* **1** : impetus, momentum **2** : vigor, energy **3** : force, violence
impetuoso, -sa *adj* : impetuous, impulsive — **impetuosamente** *adv*
impiedad *nf* : impiety
impío, -pía *adj* : impious, ungodly
implacable *adj* : implacable, relentless — **implacablemente** *adv*
implantación *nf, pl* **-ciones 1** : implantation **2** ESTABLECIMIENTO : establishment, introduction
implantado, -da *adj* : well-established
implantar *vt* **1** : to implant **2** ESTABLECER : to establish, to introduce — **implantarse** *vr*
implante *nm* : implant
implementar *vt* : to implement — **implementarse** *vr* — **implementación** *nf*
implemento *nm* : implement, tool
implicación *nf, pl* **-ciones** : implication
implicar {72} *vt* **1** ENREDAR, ENVOLVER : to involve, to implicate **2** : to imply
implícito, -ta *adj* : implied, implicit — **implícitamente** *adv*
implorar *vt* : to implore
implosión *nf, pl* **-siones** : implosion — **implosivo, -va** *adj*
implosionar *vi* : to implode
imponderable *adj & nm* : imponderable
imponente *adj* : imposing, impressive
imponer {60} *vt* **1** : to impose **2** : to confer — *vi* : to be impressive, to command respect — **imponerse** *vr* **1** : to take on (a duty) **2** : to assert oneself **3** : to prevail
imponible *adj* : taxable
impopular *adj* : unpopular — **impopularidad** *nf*
importación *nf, pl* **-ciones 1** : importation **2 importaciones** *nfpl* : imports
importado, -da *adj* : imported
importador[1], **-dora** *adj* : importing
importador[2], **-dora** *n* : importer
importancia *nf* : importance
importante *adj* : important — **importantemente** *adv*
importar *vi* : to matter, to be important <no le importa lo que piensen : she doesn't care what they think> — *vt* : to import
importe *nm* **1** : price, cost **2** : sum, amount
importunar *vt* : to bother, to inconvenience — *vi* : to be inconvenient
importuno, -na *adj* **1** : inopportune, inconvenient **2** : bothersome, annoying
imposibilidad *nf* : impossibility
imposibilitado, -da *adj* **1** : disabled, crippled **2 verse imposibilitado** : to be unable (to do something)
imposibilitar *vt* **1** : to make impossible **2** : to disable, to incapacitate — **imposibilitarse** *vr* : to become disabled
imposible *adj* : impossible
imposición *nf, pl* **-ciones 1** : imposition **2** EXIGENCIA : demand, requirement **3** : tax **4** : deposit
impositivo, -va *adj* : tax <tasa impositiva : tax rate>
impostor, -tora *n* : impostor
impotencia *nf* **1** : impotence, powerlessness **2** : impotence (in medicine)
impotente *adj* **1** : powerless **2** : impotent
impracticable *adj* : impracticable
imprecisión *nf, pl* **-siones 1** : imprecision, vagueness **2** : inaccuracy
impreciso, -sa *adj* **1** : imprecise, vague **2** : inaccurate
impredecible *adj* : unpredictable
impregnar *vt* : to impregnate
imprenta *nf* **1** : printing **2** : printing shop, press
imprescindible *adj* : essential, indispensable
impresentable *adj* : unpresentable, unfit
impresión *nf, pl* **-siones 1** : print, printing **2** : impression, feeling
impresionable *adj* : impressionable
impresionante *adj* : impressive, incredible, amazing — **impresionantemente** *adv*
impresionar *vt* **1** : to impress, to strike **2** : to affect, to move — *vi* : to make an impression — **impresionarse** *vr* : to be affected, to be removed
impresionismo *nm* : impressionism

impresionista[1] *adj* : impressionist, impressionistic
impresionista[2] *nmf* : impressionist
impreso[1] *pp* → **imprimir**
impreso[2], **-sa** *adj* : printed
impreso[3] *nm* PUBLICACIÓN : printed matter, publication
impresor, -sora *n* : printer
impresora *nf* : (computer) printer
imprevisible *adj* : unforeseeable
imprevisión *nf, pl* **-siones** : lack of foresight, thoughtlessness
imprevisto[1], **-ta** *adj* : unexpected, unforeseen
imprevisto[2] *nm* : unexpected occurrence, contingency
imprimir {42} *vt* **1** : to print **2** : to imprint, to stamp, to impress
improbabilidad *nf* : improbability
improbable *adj* : improbable, unlikely
improcedente *adj* **1** : inadmissible **2** : inappropriate, improper
improductivo, -va *adj* : unproductive
improperio *nm* : affront, insult
impropio, -pia *adj* **1** : improper, incorrect **2** INADECUADO : unsuitable, inappropriate
improvisación *nf, pl* **-ciones** : improvisation, ad-lib
improvisado, -da *adj* : improvised, ad-lib
improvisar *v* : to improvise, to ad-lib
improviso *adj* **de ~** : all of a sudden, unexpectedly
imprudencia *nf* INDISCRECIÓN : imprudence, indiscretion
imprudente *adj* INDISCRETO : imprudent, indiscreet — **imprudentemente** *adv*
impúdico, -ca *adj* : shameless, indecent
impuesto[1] *pp* → **imponer**
impuesto[2] *nm* : tax
impugnar *vt* : to challenge, to contest
impulsar *vt* : to propel, to drive
impulsividad *nf* : impulsiveness
impulsivo, -va *adj* : impulsive — **impulsivamente** *adv*
impulso *nm* **1** : drive, thrust **2** : impulse, urge
impune *adj* : unpunished
impunemente *adv* : with impunity
impunidad *nf* : impunity
impureza *nf* : impurity
impuro, -ra *adj* : impure
impuso, etc. → **imponer**
imputable *adj* ATRIBUIBLE : attributable
imputación *nf, pl* **-ciones** **1** : attribution, imputation **2** : accusation
imputar *vt* ATRIBUIR : to impute, to attribute
inacabable *adj* : endless
inacabado, -da *adj* INCONCLUSO : unfinished
inaccesibilidad *nf* : inaccessibility
inaccesible *adj* **1** : inaccessible **2** : unattainable
inacción *nf, pl* **-ciones** : inactivity, inaction
inaceptable *adj* : unacceptable
inactividad *nf* : inactivity, idleness
inactivo, -va *adj* : inactive, idle
inadaptado[1], **-da** *adj* : maladjusted
inadaptado[2], **-da** *n* : misfit
inadecuación *nf, pl* **-ciones** : inadequacy
inadecuado, -da *adj* **1** : inadequate **2** IMPROPIO : inappropriate — **inadecuadamente** *adv*
inadmisible *adj* **1** : inadmissible **2** : unacceptable
inadvertencia *nf* : oversight
inadvertidamente *adv* : inadvertently
inadvertido, -da *adj* **1** : unnoticed <pasar inadvertido : to go unnoticed> **2** DESPISTADO, DISTRAÍDO : inattentive, distracted
inagotable *adj* : inexhaustible
inaguantable *adj* INSOPORTABLE : insufferable, unbearable
inalámbrico, -ca *adj* : wireless, cordless
inalcanzable *adj* : unreachable, unattainable
inalienable *adj* : inalienable
inalterable *adj* **1** : unalterable, unchangeable **2** : impassive **3** : colorfast
inamovible *adj* : immovable, fixed
inanición *nf, pl* **-ciones** : starvation
inanimado, -da *adj* : inanimate
inapelable *adj* : indisputable
inapetencia *nf* : lack of appetite
inaplicable *adj* : inapplicable
inapreciable *adj* **1** : imperceptible, negligible **2** : invaluable
inapropiado, -da *adj* : inappropriate, unsuitable
inarticulado, -da *adj* : inarticulate, unintelligible — **inarticuladamente** *adv*
inasequible *adj* : unattainable, inaccessible
inasistencia *nf* AUSENCIA : absence
inatacable *adj* : unassailable, indisputable
inaudible *adj* : inaudible
inaudito, -ta *adj* : unheard-of, unprecedented
inauguración *nf, pl* **-ciones** : inauguration
inaugural *adj* : inaugural, opening
inaugurar *vt* **1** : to inaugurate **2** : to open
inca *adj & nmf* : Inca
incalculable *adj* : incalculable
incalificable *adj* : indescribable
incandescencia *nf* : incandescence — **incandescente** *adj*
incansable *adj* INFATIGABLE : tireless — **incansablemente** *adv*
incapacidad *nf* **1** : inability, incapacity **2** : disability, handicap
incapacitado, -da *adj* **1** : disqualified **2** : disabled, handicapped
incapacitar *vt* **1** : to incapacitate, to disable **2** : to disqualify
incapaz *adj, pl* **-paces** **1** : incapable, unable **2** : incompetent, inept

incautación *nf, pl* **-ciones** : seizure, confiscation

incautar *vt* CONFISCAR : to confiscate, to seize — **incautarse** *vr*

incauto, -ta *adj* : unwary, unsuspecting

incendiar *vt* : to set fire to, to burn (down) — **incendiarse** *vr* : to catch fire

incendiario[1], **-ria** *adj* : incendiary, inflammatory

incendiario[2], **-ria** *n* : arsonist

incendio *nm* **1** : fire **2 incendio premeditado** : arson

incentivar *vt* : to encourage, to stimulate

incentivo *nm* : incentive

incertidumbre *nf* : uncertainty, suspense

incesante *adj* : incessant — **incesantemente** *adv*

incesto *nm* : incest

incidencia *nf* **1** : incident **2** : effect, impact **3 por ~** : by chance, accidentally

incidental *adj* : incidental

incidentalmente *adv* : by chance

incidente *nm* : incident, occurrence

incidir *vi* **1 ~ en** : to fall into, to enter into <incidimos en el mismo error : we fell into the same mistake> **2 ~ en** : to affect, to influence, to have a bearing on

incienso *nm* : incense

incierto, -ta *adj* **1** : uncertain **2** : untrue **3** : unsteady, insecure

incineración *nf, pl* **-ciones 1** : incineration **2** : cremation

incinerador *nm* : incinerator

incinerar *vt* **1** : to incinerate **2** : to cremate

incipiente *adj* : incipient

incisión *nf, pl* **-siones** : incision

incisivo[1], **-va** *adj* : incisive

incisivo[2] *nm* : incisor

inciso *nm* : digression, aside

incitación *nf, pl* **-ciones** : incitement

incitante *adj* : provocative

incitar *vt* : to incite, to rouse

incivilizado, -da *adj* : uncivilized

inclemencia *nf* : inclemency, severity

inclemente *adj* : inclement

inclinación *nf, pl* **-ciones 1** PROPENSIÓN : inclination, tendency **2** : incline, slope

inclinado, -da *adj* **1** : sloping **2** : inclined, apt

inclinar *vt* : to tilt, to lean, to incline <inclinar la cabeza : to bow one's head> — **inclinarse** *vr* **1** : to lean, to lean over **2 ~ a** : to be inclined to

incluir {41} *vt* : to include

inclusión *nf, pl* **-siones** : inclusion

inclusive *adv* : inclusively, up to and including

inclusivo, -va *adj* : inclusive

incluso *adv* **1** AUN : even, in fact <es importante e incluso crucial : it is important and even crucial> **2** : inclusively

incógnita *nf* **1** : unknown quantity (in mathematics) **2** : mystery

incógnito, -ta *adj* **1** : unknown **2 de incógnito** : incognito

incoherencia *nf* : incoherence

incoherente *adj* : incoherent — **incoherentemente** *adv*

incoloro, -ra *adj* : colorless

incombustible *adj* : fireproof

incomible *adj* : inedible

incomodar *vt* **1** : to make uncomfortable **2** : to inconvenience — **incomodarse** *vr* : to put oneself out, to take the trouble

incomodidad *nf* **1** : discomfort, awkwardness **2** MOLESTIA : inconvenience, bother

incómodo, -da *adj* **1** : uncomfortable, awkward **2** INCONVENIENTE : inconvenient

incomparable *adj* : incomparable

incompatibilidad *nf* : incompatibility

incompatible *adj* : incompatible, uncongenial

incompetencia *nf* : incompetence

incompetente *adj & nmf* : incompetent

incompleto, -ta *adj* : incomplete

incomprendido, -da *adj* : misunderstood

incomprensible *adj* : incomprehensible

incomprensión *nf, pl* **-siones** : lack of understanding, incomprehension

incomunicación *nf, pl* **-ciones** : lack of communication

incomunicado, -da *adj* **1** : cut off, isolated **2** : in solitary confinement

inconcebible *adj* : inconceivable, unthinkable — **inconcebiblemente** *adv*

inconcluso, -sa *adj* INACABADO : unfinished

incondicional *adj* : unconditional — **incondicionalmente** *adv*

inconexo, -xa *adj* : unconnected, disconnected

inconfesable *adj* : unspeakable, shameful

inconforme *adj & nmf* : nonconformist

inconformidad *nf* : nonconformity

inconformista *adj & nmf* : nonconformist

inconfundible *adj* : unmistakable, obvious — **inconfundiblemente** *adv*

incongruencia *nf* : incongruity

incongruente *adj* : incongruous

inconmensurable *adj* : vast, immeasurable

inconquistable *adj* : unyielding

inconsciencia *nf* **1** : unconsciousness, unawareness **2** : irresponsibility

inconsciente[1] *adj* **1** : unconscious, unaware **2** : reckless, needless — **inconscientemente** *adv*

inconsciente[2] *n* **el inconsciente** : the unconscious

inconsecuente *adj* : inconsistent — **inconsecuencia** *nf*

inconsiderado, -da *adj* : inconsiderate, thoughtless

inconsistencia *nf* : inconsistency

inconsistente *adj* **1** : weak, flimsy **2** : watery, runny (of a sauce, etc.) **3** : inconsistent, weak (of an argument)

inconsolable *adj* : inconsolable — **inconsolablemente** *adv*

inconstancia *nf* : inconstancy

inconstante *adj* : inconstant, fickle, changeable

inconstitucional *adj* : unconstitutional

inconstitucionalidad *nf* : unconstitutionality

incontable *adj* INNUMERABLE : countless, innumerable

incontenible *adj* : uncontrollable, unstoppable

incontestable *adj* INCUESTIONABLE, INDISCUTIBLE : irrefutable, indisputable

incontinencia *nf* : incontinence — **incontinente** *adj*

incontrolable *adj* : uncontrollable

incontrolado, -da *adj* : uncontrolled, out of control

incontrovertible *adj* : indisputable

inconveniencia *nf* **1** : inconvenience, trouble **2** : unsuitability, inappropriateness **3** : tactless remark

inconveniente[1] *adj* **1** INCÓMODO : inconvenient **2** INAPROPIADO : improper, unsuitable

inconveniente[2] *nm* : obstacle, problem, snag <no tengo inconveniente en hacerlo : I don't mind doing it>

incorporación *nf, pl* **-ciones** : incorporation

incorporar *vt* **1** : to incorporate **2** : to add, to include — **incorporarse** *vr* **1** : to sit up **2** ~ **a** : to join

incorpóreo, -rea *adj* : incorporeal, bodiless

incorrección *n, pl* **-ciones** : impropriety, improper word or action

incorrecto, -ta *adj* : incorrect — **incorrectamente** *adv*

incorregible *adj* : incorrigible — **incorregibilidad** *nf*

incorruptible *adj* : incorruptible

incredulidad *nf* : incredulity, skepticism

incrédulo[1], **-la** *adj* : incredulous, skeptical

incrédulo[2], **-la** *n* : skeptic

increíble *adj* : incredible, unbelievable — **increíblemente** *adv*

incrementar *vt* : to increase — **incrementarse** *vr*

incremento *nm* AUMENTO : increase

incriminar *vt* : to incriminate — **incriminación** *nf*

incruento, -ta *adj* : bloodless

incrustación *nf, pl* **-ciones** : inlay

incrustar *vt* **1** : to embed **2** : to inlay — **incrustarse** *vr* : to become embedded

incubación *nf, pl* **-ciones** : incubation

incubadora *nf* : incubator

incubar *v* : to incubate

incuestionable *adj* INCONTESTABLE, INDISCUTIBLE : unquestionable, indisputable — **incuestionablemente** *adv*

inculcar {72} *vt* : to inculcate, to instill

inculpar *vt* ACUSAR : to accuse, to charge

inculto, -ta *adj* **1** : uncultured, ignorant **2** : uncultivated, fallow

incumbencia *nf* : obligation, responsibility

incumbir *vi* (*3rd person only*) ~ **a** : to be incumbent upon, to be of concern to <a mí no me incumbe : it's not my concern>

incumplido, -da *adj* : irresponsible, unreliable

incumplimiento *nm* **1** : nonfulfillment, neglect **2 incumplimiento de contrato** : breach of contract

incumplir *vt* : to fail to carry out, to break (a promise, a contract)

incurable *adj* : incurable

incurrir *vi* **1** ~ **en** : to incur <incurrir en gastos : to incur expenses> **2** ~ **en** : to fall into, to commit <incurrió en un error : he made a mistake>

incursión *nf, pl* **-siones** : incursion, raid

incursionar *vi* **1** : to raid **2** ~ **en** : to go into, to enter <el actor incursionó en el baile : the actor worked in dance for a while>

indagación *nf, pl* **-ciones** : investigation, inquiry

indagar {52} *vt* : to inquire into, to investigate

indebido, -da *adj* : improper, undue — **indebidamente** *adv*

indecencia *nf* : indecency, obscenity

indecente *adj* : indecent, obscene

indecible *adj* : indescribable, inexpressible

indecisión *nf, pl* **-siones** : indecision

indeciso, -sa *adj* **1** IRRESOLUTO : indecisive **2** : undecided

indeclinable *adj* : unavoidable

indecoro *nm* : impropriety, indecorousness

indecoroso, -sa *adj* : indecorous, unseemly

indefectible *adj* : unfailing, sure

indefendible *adj* : indefensible

indefenso, -sa *adj* : defenseless, helpless

indefinido, -da *adj* **1** : undefined, vague **2** INDETERMINADO : indefinite — **indefinidamente** *adv*

indeleble *adj* : indelible — **indeleblemente** *adv*

indelicado, -da *adj* : indelicate, tactless

indemnización *nf, pl* **-ciones** **1** : indemnity **2 indemnización por despido** : severance pay

indemnizar {21} *vt* : to indemnify, to compensate

independencia *nf* : independence

independiente *adj* : independent — **independientemente** *adv*

independizarse {21} *vr* : to become independent, to gain independence

indescifrable *adj* : indecipherable

indescriptible *adj* : indescribable — **indescriptiblemente** *adv*

indeseable *adj & nmf* : undesirable

indestructible *adj* : indestructible

indeterminación *nf, pl* **-ciones** : indeterminacy

indeterminado, -da *adj* **1** INDEFINIDO : indefinite **2** : indeterminate

indexar *vt* INDICIAR : to index (wages, prices, etc.)

indicación *nf, pl* **-ciones 1** : sign, signal **2** : direction, instruction **3** : suggestion, hint

indicado, -da *adj* **1** APROPIADO : appropriate, suitable **2** : specified, indicated <al día indicado : on the specified day>

indicador *nm* **1** : gauge, dial, meter **2** : indicator <indicadores económicos : economic indicators>

indicar {72} *vt* **1** SEÑALAR : to indicate **2** ENSEÑAR, MOSTRAR : to show

indicativo[1], **-va** *adj* : indicative

indicativo[2] *nm* : indicative (mood)

índice *nm* **1** : index **2** : index finger, forefinger **3** INDICIO : indication

indiciar *vt* : to index (prices, wages, etc.)

indicio *nm* : indication, sign

indiferencia *nf* : indifference

indiferente *adj* **1** : indifferent, unconcerned **2 ser indiferente** : to be of no concern <me es indiferente : it doesn't matter to me>

indígena[1] *adj* : indigenous, native

indígena[2] *nmf* : native

indigencia *nf* MISERIA : poverty, destitution

indigente *adj & nmf* : indigent

indigestarse *vr* **1** EMPACHARSE : to have indigestion **2** *fam* : to nauseate, to disgust <ese tipo se me indigesta : that guy makes me sick>

indigestión *nf, pl* **-tiones** EMPACHO : indigestion

indigesto, -ta *adj* : indigestible, difficult to digest

indignación *nf, pl* **-ciones** : indignation

indignado, -da *adj* : indignant

indignante *adj* : outrageous, infuriating

indignar *vt* : to outrage, to infuriate — **indignarse** *vr*

indignidad *nf* : indignity

indigno, -na *adj* : unworthy

indio[1], **-dia** *adj* **1** : American Indian, Indian, Amerindian **2** : Indian (from India)

indio[2], **-dia** *n* **1** : American Indian **2** : Indian (from India)

indirecta *nf* **1** : hint, innuendo **2 echar indirectas** *or* **lanzar indirectas** : to drop a hint, to insinuate

indirecto, -ta *adj* : indirect — **indirectamente** *adv*

indisciplina *nf* : indiscipline, unruliness

indisciplinado, -da *adj* : undisciplined, unruly

indiscreción *nf, pl* **-ciones 1** IMPRUDENCIA : indiscretion **2** : tactless remark

indiscreto, -ta *adj* IMPRUDENTE : indiscreet, imprudent — **indiscretamente** *adv*

indiscriminado, -da *adj* : indiscriminate — **indiscriminadamente** *adv*

indiscutible *adj* INCONTESTABLE, INCUESTIONABLE : indisputable, unquestionable — **indiscutiblemente** *adv*

indispensable *adj* : indispensable — **indispensablemente** *adv*

indisponer {60} *vt* **1** : to spoil, to upset **2** : to make ill — **indisponerse** *vr* **1** : to become ill **2 ~ con** : to fall out with

indisposición *nf, pl* **-ciones** : indisposition, illness

indispuesto, -ta *adj* : unwell, indisposed

indistinguible *adj* : indistinguishable

indistintamente *adv* **1** : indistinctly **2** : indiscriminately

indistinto, -ta *adj* : indistinct, vague, faint

individual *adj* : individual — **individualmente** *adv*

individualidad *nf* : individuality

individualismo *nm* : individualism

individualista[1] *adj* : individualistic

individualista[2] *nmf* : individualist

individualizar {21} *vt* : to individualize

individuo *nm* : individual, person

indivisible *adj* : indivisible — **indivisibilidad** *nf*

indocumentado, -da *n* : illegal immigrant

índole *nf* **1** : nature, character **2** CLASE, TIPO : sort, kind

indolencia *nf* : indolence, laziness

indolente *adj* : indolent, lazy

indoloro, -ra *adj* : painless

indomable *adj* **1** : indomitable **2** : unruly, unmanageable

indómito, -ta *adj* : indomitable

indonesio, -sia *adj & n* : Indonesian

inducción *nf, pl* **-ciones** : induction

inducir {61} *vt* **1** : to induce, to cause **2** : to infer, to deduce

inductivo, -va *adj* : inductive

indudable *adj* : unquestionable, beyond doubt

indudablemente *adv* : undoubtedly, unquestionably

indulgencia *nf* **1** : indulgence, leniency **2** : indulgence (in religion)

indulgente *adj* : indulgent, lenient

indultar *vt* : to pardon, to reprieve

indulto *nm* : pardon, reprieve

indumentaria *nf* : clothing, attire

industria *nf* : industry

industrial[1] *adj* : industrial

industrial[2] *nmf* : industrialist, manufacturer
industrialización *nf, pl* **-ciones** : industrialization
industrializar {21} *vt* : to industrialize
industrioso, -sa *adj* : industrious
inédito, -ta *adj* **1** : unpublished **2** : unprecedented
inefable *adj* : ineffable
ineficacia *nf* **1** : inefficiency **2** : ineffectiveness
ineficaz *adj, pl* **-caces 1** : inefficient **2** : ineffective — **ineficazmente** *adv*
ineficiencia *nf* : inefficiency
ineficiente *adj* : inefficient — **ineficientemente** *adv*
inelegancia *nf* : inelegance — **inelegante** *adj*
inelegible *adj* : ineligible — **inelegibilidad** *nf*
ineludible *adj* : inescapable, unavoidable — **ineludiblemente** *adv*
ineptitud *nf* : ineptitude, incompetence
inepto, -ta *adj* : inept, incompetent
inequidad *nf* : inequity
inequitativo, -va *adj* : inequitable
inequívoco, -ca *adj* : unequivocal, unmistakable — **inequívocamente** *adv*
inercia *nf* **1** : inertia **2** : apathy, passivity **3 por ~** : out of habit
inerme *adj* : unarmed, defenseless
inerte *adj* : inert
inescrupuloso, -sa *adj* : unscrupulous
inescrutable *adj* : inscrutable
inesperado, -da *adj* : unexpected — **inesperadamente** *adv*
inestabilidad *nf* : instability, unsteadiness
inestable *adj* : unstable, unsteady
inestimable *adj* : inestimable, invaluable
inevitabilidad *nf* : inevitability
inevitable *adj* : inevitable, unavoidable — **inevitablemente** *adv*
inexactitud *nf* : inaccuracy
inexacto, -ta *adj* : inexact, inaccurate
inexcusable *adj* : inexcusable, unforgivable
inexistencia *nf* : lack, nonexistence
inexistente *adj* : nonexistent
inexorable *adj* : inexorable — **inexorablemente** *adv*
inexperiencia *nf* : inexperience
inexperto, -ta *adj* : inexperienced, unskilled
inexplicable *adj* : inexplicable — **inexplicablemente** *adv*
inexplorado, -da *adj* : unexplored
inexpresable *adj* : inexpressible
inexpresivo, -va *adj* : inexpressive, expressionless
inextinguible *adj* **1** : inextinguishable **2** : unquenchable
inextricable *adj* : inextricable — **inextricablemente** *adv*
infalible *adj* : infallible — **infaliblemente** *adv*
infame *adj* **1** : infamous **2** : loathsome, vile <tiempo infame : terrible weather>
infamia *nf* : infamy, disgrace
infancia *nf* **1** NIÑEZ : infancy, childhood **2** : children *pl* **3** : beginnings *pl*
infante *nm* **1** : infante, prince **2** : infantryman
infantería *nf* : infantry
infantil *adj* **1** : childish, infantile **2** : child's, children's
infarto *nm* : heart attack
infatigable *adj* : indefatigable, tireless — **infatigablemente** *adv*
infección *nf, pl* **-ciones** : infection
infeccioso, -sa *adj* : infectious
infectar *vt* : to infect — **infectarse** *vr*
infecto, -ta *adj* **1** : infected **2** : repulsive, sickening
infecundidad *nf* : infertility
infecundo, -da *adj* : infertile, barren
infelicidad *nf* : unhappiness
infeliz[1] *adj, pl* **-lices 1** : unhappy **2** : hapless, unfortunate, wretched
infeliz[2] *nmf, pl* **-lices** : wretch
inferior[1] *adj* : inferior, lower
inferior[2] *nmf* : inferior, underling
inferioridad *nf* : inferiority
inferir {76} *vt* **1** DEDUCIR : to infer, to deduce **2** : to cause (harm or injury), to inflict
infernal *adj* : infernal, hellish
infestación *n, pl* **-ciones** : infestation
infestar *vt* **1** : to infest **2** : to overrun, to invade
infición *nf, pl* **-ciones** *Mex* : pollution
infidelidad *nf* : unfaithfulness, infidelity
infiel[1] *adj* : unfaithful, disloyal
infiel[2] *nmf* : infidel, heathen
infierno *nm* **1** : hell **2 el quinto infierno** : the middle of nowhere
infiltrar *vt* : to infiltrate — **infiltrarse** *vr* — **infiltración** *nf*
infinidad *nf* **1** : infinity **2** SINFÍN : great number, huge quantity <una infinidad de veces : countless times>
infinitesimal *adj* : infinitesimal
infinitivo *nm* : infinitive
infinito[1] *adv* : infinitely, vastly
infinito[2], **-ta** *adj* **1** : infinite **2** : limitless, endless **3 hasta lo infinito** : ad infinitum — **infinitamente** *adv*
infinito[3] *nm* : infinity
inflable *adj* : inflatable
inflación *nf, pl* **-ciones** : inflation
inflacionario, -ria *adj* : inflationary
inflamable *adj* : flammable
inflamación *nf, pl* **-ciones** : inflammation
inflamar *vt* : to inflame
inflamatorio, -ria *adj* : inflammatory
inflar *vt* HINCHAR : to inflate — **inflarse** *vr* **1** : to swell **2** : to become conceited
inflexibilidad *nf* : inflexibility
inflexible *adj* : inflexible, unyielding
inflexión *nf, pl* **-xiones** : inflection
infligir {35} *vt* : to inflict
influencia *nf* INFLUJO : influence

influenciable *adj* : easily influenced, suggestible
influenciar *vt* : to influence
influenza *nf* : influenza
influir {41} *vt* : to influence — *vi* ~ **en** *or* ~ **sobre** : to have an influence on, to affect
influjo *nm* INFLUENCIA : influence
influyente *adj* : influential
información *nf, pl* **-ciones** 1 : information 2 INFORME : report, inquiry 3 NOTICIAS : news
informado, -da *adj* : informed <bien informado : well-informed>
informador, -dora *n* : informer, informant
informal *adj* 1 : unreliable (of persons) 2 : informal, casual — **informalmente** *adv*
informalidad *nf* : informality
informante *nmf* : informant
informar *vt* ENTERAR : to inform — *vi* : to report — **informarse** *vr* ENTERARSE : to get information, to find out
informática *nf* : computer science, computing
informativo[1], **-va** *adj* : informative
informativo[2] *nm* : news program, news
informatización *nf, pl* **-ciones** : computerization
informatizar {21} *vt* : to computerize
informe[1] *adj* AMORFO : shapeless, formless
informe[2] *nm* 1 : report 2 : reference (for employment) 3 INFORMES *nmpl* : information, data
infortunado, -da *adj* : unfortunate, unlucky
infortunio *nm* 1 DESGRACIA : misfortune 2 CONTRATIEMPO : mishap
infracción *nf, pl* **-ciones** : violation, offense, infraction
infractor, -tora *n* : offender
infraestructura *nf* : infrastructure
infrahumano, -na *adj* : subhuman
infranqueable *adj* 1 : impassable 2 : insurmountable
infrarrojo, -ja *adj* : infrared
infrecuente *adj* : infrequent
infringir {35} *vt* : to infringe, to breach
infructuoso, -sa *adj* : fruitless — **infructuosamente** *adv*
ínfulas *nfpl* 1 : conceit 2 **darse ínfulas** : to put on airs
infundado, -da *adj* : unfounded, baseless
infundio *nm* : false story, lie, tall tale <todo eso son infundios : that's a pack of lies>
infundir *vt* 1 : to instill 2 **infundir ánimo a** : to encourage 3 **infundir miedo a** : to intimidate
infusión *nf, pl* **-siones** : infusion
ingeniar *vt* : to devise, to think up — **ingeniarse** *vr* : to manage, to find a way
ingeniería *nf* : engineering
ingeniero, -ra *n* : engineer
ingenio *nm* 1 : ingenuity 2 CHISPA : wit, wits 3 : device, apparatus 4 **ingenio azucarero** : sugar refinery
ingenioso, -sa *adj* 1 : ingenious 2 : clever, witty — **ingeniosamente** *adv*
ingente *adj* : huge, enormous
ingenuidad *nf* : naïveté, ingenuousness
ingenuo[1], **-nua** *adj* CÁNDIDO : naive — **ingenuamente** *adv*
ingenuo[2], **-nua** *n* : naive person
ingerencia → **injerencia**
ingerir {76} *vt* : to ingest, to consume
ingestión *nf, pl* **-tiones** : ingestion
ingle *nf* : groin
inglés[1], **-glesa** *adj, mpl* **ingleses** : English
inglés[2], **-glesa** *n, mpl* **ingleses** : Englishman *m,* Englishwoman *f*
inglés[3] *nm* : English (language)
inglete *nm* : miter joint
ingobernable *adj* : ungovernable, lawless
ingratitud *nf* : ingratitude
ingrato[1], **-ta** *adj* 1 : ungrateful 2 : thankless
ingrato[2], **-ta** *n* : ingrate
ingrediente *nm* : ingredient
ingresar *vt* 1 : to admit <ingresaron a Luis al hospital : Luis was admitted into the hospital> 2 : to deposit — *vi* 1 : to enter, to go in 2 ~ **en** : to join, to enroll in
ingreso *nm* 1 : entrance, entry 2 : admission 3 **ingresos** *nmpl* : income, earnings *pl*
íngrimo, -ma *adj* : all alone, all by oneself
inhábil *adj* : unskillful, clumsy
inhabilidad *nf* 1 : unskillfulness 2 : unfitness
inhabilitar *vt* 1 : to disqualify, to bar 2 : to disable
inhabitable *adj* : uninhabitable
inhabituado, -da *adj* ~ **a** : unaccustomed to
inhalante *nm* : inhalant
inhalar *vt* : to inhale — **inhalación** *nf*
inherente *adj* : inherent
inhibición *nf, pl* **-ciones** COHIBICIÓN : inhibition
inhibir *vt* : to inhibit — **inhibirse** *vr*
inhóspito, -ta *adj* : inhospitable
inhumación *nf, pl* **-ciones** : interment, burial
inhumanidad *nf* : inhumanity
inhumano, -na *adj* : inhuman, cruel, inhumane
inhumar *vt* : to inter, to bury
iniciación *nf, pl* **-ciones** 1 : initiation 2 : introduction
iniciado, -da *n* : initiate
iniciador[1], **-dora** *adj* : initiatory
iniciador[2], **-dora** *n* : initiator, originator
inicial[1] *adj* : initial, original — **inicialmente** *adv*
inicial[2] *nf* : initial (letter)

iniciar *vt* COMENZAR : to initiate, to begin — **iniciarse** *vr*

iniciativa *nf* : initiative

inicio *nm* COMIENZO : beginning

inicuo, -cua *adj* : iniquitous, wicked

inigualado, -da *adj* : unequaled

inimaginable *adj* : unimaginable

inimitable *adj* : inimitable

ininteligible *adj* : unintelligible

ininterrumpido, -da *adj* : uninterrupted, continuous — **ininterrumpidamente** *adv*

iniquidad *nf* : iniquity, wickedness

injerencia *nf* : interference

injerirse {76} *vr* ENTROMETERSE, INMISCUIRSE : to meddle, to interfere

injertar *vt* : to graft

injerto *nm* : graft <injerto de piel : skin graft>

injuria *nf* AGRAVIO : affront, insult

injuriar *vt* INSULTAR : to insult, to revile

injurioso, -sa *adj* : insulting, abusive

injusticia *nf* : injustice, unfairness

injustificable *adj* : unjustifiable

injustificadamente *adv* : unjustifiably, unfairly

injustificado, -da *adj* : unjustified, unwarranted

injusto, -ta *adj* : unfair, unjust — **injustamente** *adv*

inmaculado, -da *adj* : immaculate, spotless

inmadurez *nf, pl* **-reces** : immaturity

inmaduro, -ra *adj* **1** : immature **2** : unripe

inmediaciones *nfpl* : environs, surrounding area

inmediatamente *adv* ENSEGUIDA : immediately

inmediatez *nf, pl* **-teces** : immediacy

inmediato, -ta *adj* **1** : immediate **2** CONTIGUO : adjoining **3 de ~** : immediately, right away **4 ~ a** : next to, close to

inmejorable *adj* : excellent, unbeatable

inmensidad *nf* : immensity, vastness

inmenso, -sa *adj* ENORME : immense, huge, vast — **inmensamente** *adv*

inmensurable *adj* : boundless, immeasurable

inmerecido, -da *adj* : undeserved — **inmerecidamente** *adv*

inmersión *nf, pl* **-siones** : immersion

inmerso, -sa *adj* **1** : immersed **2** : involved, absorbed

inmigración *nf, pl* **-ciones** : immigration

inmigrado, -da *adj & n* : immigrant

inmigrante *adj & nmf* : immigrant

inmigrar *vi* : to immigrate

inminencia *nf* : imminence

inminente *adj* : imminent — **inminentemente** *adv*

inmiscuirse {41} *vr* ENTROMETERSE, INJERIRSE : to meddle, to interfere

inmobiliario, -ria *adj* : real estate, property

inmoderación *n, pl* **-ciones** : immoderation, intemperance

inmoderado, -da *adj* : immoderate, excessive — **inmoderamente** *adv*

inmodestia *nf* : immodesty — **inmodesto, -ta** *adj*

inmolar *vt* : to immolate — **inmolación** *nf*

inmoral *adj* : immoral

inmoralidad *nf* : immorality

inmortal *adj & nmf* : immortal

inmortalidad *nf* : immortality

inmortalizar {21} *vt* : to immortalize

inmotivado, -da *adj* **1** : unmotivated **2** : groundless

inmovible *adj* : immovable, fixed

inmóvil *adj* **1** : still, motionless **2** : steadfast

inmovilidad *nf* : immobility

inmovilizar {21} *vt* : to immobilize

inmueble *nm* : building, property

inmundicia *nf* : dirt, filth, trash

inmundo, -da *adj* : dirty, filthy, nasty

inmune *adj* : immune

inmunidad *nf* : immunity

inmunizar {21} *vt* : to immunize — **inmunización** *nf*

inmunología *nf* : immunology

inmunológico, -ca *adj* : immune <sistema inmunológico : immune system>

inmutabilidad *nf* : immutability

inmutable *adj* : immutable, unchangeable

innato, -ta *adj* : innate, inborn

innecesario, -ria *adj* : unnecessary — **innecesariamente** *adv*

innegable *adj* : undeniable

innoble *adj* : ignoble — **innoblemente** *adv*

innovación *nf, pl* **-ciones** : innovation

innovador, -dora *adj* : innovative

innovar *vt* : to introduce — *vi* : to innovate

innumerable *adj* INCONTABLE : innumerable, countless

inobjetable *adj* : indisputable, unobjectionable

inocencia *nf* : innocence

inocente[1] *adj* **1** : innocent **2** INGENUO : naive — **inocentemente** *adv*

inocente[2] *nmf* : innocent person

inocentón[1], -tona *adj, mpl* **-tones** : naive, gullible

inocentón[2], -tona *n, mpl* **-tones** : simpleton, dupe

inocuidad *nf* : harmlessness

inocular *vt* : to inoculate, to vaccinate — **inoculación** *nf*

inocuo, -cua *adj* : innocuous, harmless

inodoro[1], -ra *adj* : odorless

inodoro[2] *nm* : toilet

inofensivo, -va *adj* : inoffensive, harmless

inolvidable *adj* : unforgettable

inoperable *adj* : inoperable

inoperante *adj* : ineffective, inoperative

inopinado, -da *adj* : unexpected — **inopinadamente** *adv*
inoportuno, -na *adj* : untimely, inopportune, inappropriate
inorgánico, -ca *adj* : inorganic
inoxidable *adj* **1** : rustproof **2 acero inoxidable** : stainless steel
inquebrantable *adj* : unshakable, unwavering
inquietante *adj* : disturbing, worrisome
inquietar *vt* PREOCUPAR : to disturb, to upset, to worry — **inquietarse** *vr*
inquieto, -ta *adj* **1** : anxious, uneasy, worried **2** : restless
inquietud *nf* **1** : anxiety, uneasiness, worry **2** AGITACIÓN : restlessness
inquilinato *nm* : tenancy
inquilino, -na *n* : tenant, occupant
inquina *nf* **1** : aversion, dislike **2** : ill will <tener inquina a alguien : to have a grudge against someone>
inquirir {4} *vi* : to make inquiries — *vt* : to investigate
inquisición *nf, pl* **-ciones** : investigation, inquiry
inquisidor, -dora *adj* : inquisitive
inquisitivo, -va *adj* : inquisitive, curious — **inquisitivamente** *adv*
insaciable *adj* : insatiable
insalubre *adj* **1** : unhealthy **2** ANTIHIGIÉNICO : unsanitary
insalubridad *nf* : unhealthiness
insalvable *adj* : insuperable, insurmountable
insano, -na *adj* **1** LOCO : insane, mad **2** INSALUBRE : unhealthy
insatisfacción *nf, pl* **-ciones** : dissatisfaction
insatisfactorio *nm* : unsatisfactory
insatisfecho, -cha *adj* **1** : dissatisfied **2** : unsatisfied
inscribir {33} *vt* **1** MATRICULAR : to enroll, to register **2** GRABAR : to engrave — **inscribirse** *vr* : to register, to sign up
inscripción *nf, pl* **-ciones 1** MATRÍCULA : enrollment, registration **2** : inscription
inscrito *pp* → **inscribir**
insecticida[1] *adj* : insecticidal
insecticida[2] *nm* : insecticide
insecto *nm* : insect
inseguridad *nf* **1** : insecurity **2** : lack of safety **3** : uncertainty
inseguro, -ra *adj* **1** : insecure **2** : unsafe **3** : uncertain
inseminar *vt* : to inseminate — **inseminación** *nf*
insensatez *nf, pl* **-teces** : foolishness, stupidity
insensato[1]**, -ta** *adj* : foolish, senseless
insensato[2]**, -ta** *n* : fool
insensibilidad *nf* : insensitivity
insensible *adj* : insensitive, unfeeling
inseparable *adj* : inseparable — **inseparablemente** *adv*
inserción *nf, pl* **-ciones** : insertion
insertar *vt* : to insert
inservible *adj* INÚTIL : useless, unusable
insidia *nf* **1** : snare, trap **2** : malice
insidioso, -sa *adj* : insidious
insigne *adj* : noted, famous
insignia *nf* ENSEÑA : insignia, emblem, badge
insignificancia *nf* **1** : insignificance **2** NIMIEDAD : trifle, triviality
insignificante *adj* : insignificant
insincero, -ra *adj* : insincere — **insinceridad** *nf*
insinuación *nf, pl* **-ciones** : insinuation, hint
insinuante *adj* : suggestive
insinuar {3} *vt* : to insinuate, to hint at — **insinuarse** *vr* **1 ~ a** : to make advances to **2 ~ en** : to worm one's way into
insipidez *nf, pl* **-deces** : insipidness, blandness
insípido, -da *adj* : insipid, bland
insistencia *nf* : insistence
insistente *adj* : insistent — **insistentemente** *adv*
insistir *v* : to insist
insociable *adj* : unsociable
insolación *nf, pl* **-ciones** : sunstroke
insolencia *nf* IMPERTINENCIA : insolence
insolente *adj* IMPERTINENTE : insolent
insólito, -ta *adj* : rare, unusual
insoluble *adj* : insoluble — **insolubilidad** *nf*
insolvencia *nf* : insolvency, bankruptcy
insolvente *adj* : insolvent, bankrupt
insomne *adj & nmf* : insomniac
insomnio *nm* : insomnia
insondable *adj* : fathomless, deep
insonorizado, -da *adj* : soundproof
insoportable *adj* INAGUANTABLE : unbearable, intolerable
insoslayable *adj* : unavoidable, inescapable
insospechado, -da *adj* : unexpected, unforeseen
insostenible *adj* : untenable
inspección *nf, pl* **-ciones** : inspection
inspeccionar *vt* : to inspect
inspector, -tora *n* : inspector
inspiración *nf, pl* **-ciones 1** : inspiration **2** INHALACIÓN : inhalation
inspirador, -dora *adj* : inspiring
inspirar *vt* : to inspire — *vi* INHALAR : to inhale
instalación *nf, pl* **-ciones** : installation
instalar *vt* **1** : to install **2** : to instate — **instalarse** *vr* ESTABLECERSE : to settle, to establish oneself
instancia *nf* **1** : petition, request **2 en última instancia** : as a last resort
instantánea *nf* : snapshot
instantáneo, -nea *adj* : instantaneous — **instantáneamente** *adv*
instante *nm* **1** : instant, moment **2 al instante** : immediately **3 a cada instante** : frequently, all the time **4 por instantes** : constantly, incessantly

instar *vt* APREMIAR : to urge, to press — *vi* URGIR : to be urgent or pressing <insta que vayamos pronto : it is imperative that we leave soon>

instauración *nf, pl* **-ciones** : establishment

instaurar *vt* : to establish

instigador, -dora *n* : instigator

instigar {52} *vt* : to instigate, to incite

instintivo, -va *adj* : instinctive — **instintivamente** *adv*

instinto *nm* : instinct

institución *nf, pl* **-ciones** : institution

institucional *adj* : institutional — **institucionalmente** *adv*

institucionalización *nf, pl* **-ciones** : institutionalization

institucionalizar {21} *vt* : to institutionalize

instituir {41} *vt* ESTABLECER, FUNDAR : to institute, to establish, to found

instituto *nm* : institute

institutriz *nf, pl* **-trices** : governess *f*

instrucción *nf, pl* **-ciones 1** EDUCACIÓN : education **2 instrucciones** *nfpl* : instructions, directions

instructivo, -va *adj* : instructive, educational

instructor, -tora *n* : instructor

instruir {41} *vt* **1** ADIESTRAR : to instruct, to train **2** ENSEÑAR : to educate, to teach

instrumentación *nf, pl* **-ciones** : orchestration

instrumental *adj* : instrumental

instrumentar *vt* : to orchestrate

instrumentista *nmf* : instrumentalist

instrumento *nm* : instrument

insubordinado, -da *adj* : insubordinate — **insubordinación** *nf*

insubordinarse *vr* : to rebel

insuficiencia *nf* **1** : insufficiency, inadequacy **2 insuficiencia cardíaca** : heart failure

insuficiente *adj* : insufficient, inadequate — **insuficientemente** *adv*

insufrible *adj* : insufferable

insular *adj* : insular

insulina *nf* : insulin

insulso, -sa *adj* **1** INSÍPIDO : insipid, bland **2** : dull

insultante *adj* : insulting

insultar *vt* : to insult

insulto *nm* : insult

insumos *nmpl* : supplies <insumos agrícolas : agricultural supplies>

insuperable *adj* : insuperable, insurmountable

insurgente *adj & nmf* : insurgent — **insurgencia** *nf*

insurrección *nf, pl* **-ciones** : insurrection, uprising

insustancial *adj* : insubstantial, flimsy

insustituible *adj* : irreplaceable

intachable *adj* : irreproachable, faultless

intacto, -ta *adj* : intact

intangible *adj* IMPALPABLE : intangible, impalpable

integración *nf, pl* **-ciones** : integration

integral *adj* **1** : integral, essential **2 pan integral** : whole grain bread

integrante[1] *adj* : integrating, integral

integrante[2] *nmf* : member

integrar *vt* : to make up, to compose — **integrarse** *vr* : to integrate, to fit in

integridad *nf* **1** RECTITUD : integrity, honesty **2** : wholeness, completeness

integrismo *nm* : fundamentalism

integrista *adj & nmf* : fundamentalist

íntegro, -gra *adj* **1** : honest, upright **2** ENTERO : whole, complete **3** : unabridged

intelecto *nm* : intellect

intelectual *adj & nmf* : intellectual — **intelectualmente** *adv*

intelectualidad *nf* : intelligentsia

inteligencia *nf* : intelligence

inteligente *adj* : intelligent — **inteligentemente** *adv*

inteligible *adj* : intelligible — **inteligibilidad** *nf*

intemperancia *adj* : intemperance, excess

intemperie *nf* **1** : bad weather, elements *pl* **2 a la intemperie** : in the open air, outside

intempestivo, -va *adj* : inopportune, untimely — **intempestivamente** *adv*

intención *nf, pl* **-ciones** : intention, plan

intencional *adj* : intentional — **intencionalmente** *adv*

intendencia *nf* : management, administration

intendente *nmf* : quartermaster

intensidad *nf* : intensity

intensificar {72} *vt* : to intensify — **intensificarse** *vr*

intensivo, -va *adj* : intensive — **intensivamente** *adv*

intenso, -sa *adj* : intense — **intensamente** *adv*

intentar *vt* : to attempt, to try

intento *nm* **1** PROPÓSITO : intent, intention **2** TENTATIVA : attempt, try

interacción *nf, pl* **-ciones** : interaction

interactivo, -va *adj* : interactive

interactuar {3} *vi* : to interact

intercalar *vt* : to intersperse, to insert

intercambiable *adj* : interchangeable

intercambiar *vt* CANJEAR : to exchange, to trade

intercambio *nm* CANJE : exchange, trade

interceder *vi* : to intercede

intercepción *nf, pl* **-ciones** : interception

interceptar *vt* **1** : to intercept, to block **2 interceptar las líneas** : to wiretap

intercesión *nf, pl* **-siones** : intercession

intercomunicación *nf, pl* **-ciones** : intercommunication

interconexión *nf, pl* **-xiones** : interconnection

interconfesional *adj* : interdenominational

interdependencia *nf* : interdependence — **interdependiente** *adj*
interdicción *nf, pl* **-ciones** : interdiction, prohibition
interés *nm, pl* **-reses** : interest
interesado, -da *adj* **1** : interested **2** : selfish, self-seeking
interesante *adj* : interesting
interesar *vt* : to interest — *vi* : to be of interest, to be interesting — **interesarse** *vr*
interestatal *adj* : interstate <autopista interestatal : interstate highway>
interestelar *adj* : interstellar
interfaz *nf, pl* **-faces** : interface
interferencia *nf* : interference, static
interferir {76} *vi* : to interfere, to meddle — *vt* : to interfere with, to obstruct
interín[1] *or* **ínterin** *adv* : meanwhile
interín[2] *or* **ínterin** *nm, pl* **-rines** : meantime, interim <en el interín : in the meantime>
interinamente *adv* : temporarily
interino, -na *adj* : acting, temporary, interim
interior[1] *adj* : interior, inner
interior[2] *nm* **1** : interior, inside **2** : inland region
interiormente *adv* : inwardly
interjección *nf, pl* **-ciones** : interjection
interlocutor, -tora *n* : interlocutor, speaker
intermediario, -ria *adj & n* : intermediary, go-between
intermedio[1], **-dia** *adj* : intermediate
intermedio[2] *nm* **1** : intermission **2 por intermedio de** : by means of
interminable *adj* : interminable, endless — **interminablemente** *adv*
intermisión *nf, pl* **-siones** : intermission, pause
intermitente[1] *adj* **1** : intermittent **2 luz intermitente** : strobe light — **intermitentemente** *adv*
intermitente[2] *nm* : blinker, turn signal
internacional *adj* : international — **internacionalmente** *adv*
internacionalismo *nm* : internationalism
internacionalizar {21} *vt* : to internationalize
internado *nm* : boarding school
internar *vt* : to commit, to confine — **internarse** *vr* **1** : to penetrate, to advance into **2 ~ en** : to go into, to enter
internista *nmf* : internist
interno[1], **-na** *adj* : internal — **internamente** *adv*
interno[2], **-na** *n* **1** : intern **2** : inmate, internee
interpelación *nf, pl* **-ciones** : appeal, plea
interpelar *vt* : to question (formally)
interpolar *vt* : to insert, to interpolate
interponer {60} *vt* : to interpose — **interponerse** *vr* : to intervene
interpretación *nf, pl* **-ciones** : interpretation
interpretar *vt* **1** : to interpret **2** : to play, to perform
interpretativo, -va *adj* : interpretive
intérprete *nmf* **1** TRADUCTOR : interpreter **2** : performer
interpuesto *pp* → **interponer**
interracial *adj* : interracial
interrelación *nf, pl* **-ciones** : interrelationship
interrelacionar *vi* : to interrelate
interrogación *nf, pl* **-ciones 1** : interrogation, questioning **2 signo de interrogación** : question mark
interrogador, -dora *n* : interrogator, questioner
interrogante[1] *adj* : questioning
interrogante[2] *nm* **1** : question mark **2** : query
interrogar {52} *vt* : to interrogate, to question
interrogativo, -va *adj* : interrogative
interrogatorio *nm* : interrogation, questioning
interrumpir *v* : to interrupt
interrupción *nf, pl* **-ciones** : interruption
interruptor *nm* **1** : (electrical) switch **2** : circuit breaker
intersección *nf, pl* **-ciones** : intersection
intersticio *nm* : interstice — **intersticial** *adj*
intervalo *nm* : interval
intervención *nf, pl* **-ciones 1** : intervention **2** : audit **3 intervención quirúrgica** : operation
intervencionista *adj & nmf* : interventionist
intervenir {87} *vi* **1** : to take part **2** INTERCEDER : to intervene, to intercede — *vt* **1** : to control, to supervise **2** : to audit **3** : to operate on **4** : to tap (a telephone)
interventor, -tora *n* **1** : inspector **2** : auditor, comptroller
intestado, -da *adj* : intestate
intestinal *adj* : intestinal
intestino *nm* : intestine
intimar *vi* **~ con** : to become friendly with — *vt* : to require, to call on
intimidación *nf, pl* **-ciones** : intimidation
intimidad *nf* **1** : intimacy **2** : privacy, private life
intimidar *vt* ACOBARDAR : to intimidate
íntimo, -ma *adj* **1** : intimate, close **2** PRIVADO : private — **íntimamente** *adv*
intitular *vt* : to entitle, to title
intocable *adj* : untouchable
intolerable *adj* : intolerable, unbearable
intolerancia *nf* : intolerance
intolerante[1] *adj* : intolerant
intolerante[2] *nmf* : intolerant person, bigot
intoxicación *nf, pl* **-ciones** : poisoning
intoxicante *nm* : poison

intoxicar {72} *vt* : to poison
intranquilidad *nf* PREOCUPACIÓN : worry, anxiety
intranquilizar {21} *vt* : to upset, to make uneasy — **intranquilizarse** *vr* : to get worried, to be anxious
intranquilo, -la *adj* PREOCUPADO : uneasy, worried
intransigencia *nf* : intransigence
intransigente *adj* : intransigent, unyielding
intransitable *adj* : impassable
intransitivo, -va *adj* : intransitive
intrascendente *adj* : unimportant, insignificant
intratable *adj* **1** : intractable **2** : awkward **3** : unsociable
intravenoso, -sa *adj* : intravenous
intrepidez *nf* : fearlessness
intrépido, -da *adj* : intrepid, fearless
intriga *nf* : intrigue
intrigante *nmf* : schemer
intrigar {52} *v* : to intrigue — **intrigante** *adj*
intrincado, -da *adj* : intricate, involved
intrínseco, -ca *adj* : intrinsic — **intrínsecamente** *adv*
introducción *nf, pl* **-ciones** : introduction
introducir {61} *vt* **1** : to introduce **2** : to bring in **3** : to insert **4** : to input, to enter — **introducirse** *vr* : to penetrate, to get into
introductorio, -ria *adj* : introductory
intromisión *nf, pl* **-siones** : interference, meddling
introspección *nf, pl* **-ciones** : introspection
introspectivo, -va *adj* : introspective
introvertido[1], -da *adj* : introverted
introvertido[2], -da *n* : introvert
intrusión *nf, pl* **-siones** : intrusion
intruso[1], -sa *adj* : intrusive
intruso[2], -sa *n* : intruder
intuición *nf, pl* **-ciones** : intuition
intuir {41} *vt* : to intuit, to sense
intuitivo, -va *adj* : intuitive — **intuitivamente** *adv*
inundación *nf, pl* **-ciones** : flood, inundation
inundar *vt* : to flood, to inundate
inusitado, -da *adj* : unusual, uncommon — **inusitadamente** *adv*
inusual *adj* : unusual, uncommon — **inusualmente** *adv*
inútil[1] *adj* INSERVIBLE : useless — **inútilmente** *adv*
inútil[2] *nmf* : good-for-nothing
inutilidad *nf* : uselessness
inutilizar {21} *vt* **1** : to make useless **2** INCAPACITAR : to disable, to put out of commission
invadir *vt* : to invade
invalidar *vt* : to nullify, to invalidate
invalidez *nf, pl* **-deces 1** : invalidity **2** : disablement
inválido, -da *adj & n* : invalid
invariable *adj* : invariable — **invariablemente** *adv*
invasión *nf, pl* **-siones** : invasion
invasivo, -va *adj* : invasive
invasor[1], -sora *adj* : invading
invasor[2], -sora *n* : invader
invectiva *nf* : invective, abuse
invencible *adj* **1** : invincible **2** : insurmountable
invención *nf, pl* **-ciones 1** INVENTO : invention **2** MENTIRA : fabrication, lie
inventar *vt* **1** : to invent **2** : to fabricate, to make up
inventariar {85} *vt* : to inventory
inventario *nm* : inventory
inventiva *nf* : ingenuity, inventiveness
inventivo, -va *adj* : inventive
invento *nm* INVENCIÓN : invention
inventor, -tora *n* : inventor
invernadero *nm* : greenhouse, hothouse
invernal *adj* : winter, wintry
invernar {55} *vi* **1** : to spend the winter **2** HIBERNAR : to hibernate
inverosímil *adj* : unlikely, farfetched
inversión *nf, pl* **-siones 1** : inversion **2** : investment
inversionista *nmf* : investor
inverso[1], -sa *adj* **1** : inverse, inverted **2** CONTRARIO : opposite **3 a la inversa** : on the contrary, vice versa **4 en orden inverso** : in reverse order — **inversamente** *adv*
inverso[2] *n* : inverse
inversor, -sora *n* : investor
invertebrado[1], -da *adj* : invertebrate
invertebrado[2] *nm* : invertebrate
invertir {76} *vt* **1** : to invert, to reverse **2** : to invest — *vi* : to make an investment — **invertirse** *vr* : to be reversed
investidura *nf* : investiture, inauguration
investigación *nf, pl* **-ciones 1** ENCUESTA, INDAGACIÓN : investigation, inquiry **2** : research
investigador[1], -dora *adj* : investigative
investigador[2], -dora *n* **1** : investigator **2** : researcher
investigar {52} *vt* **1** INDAGAR : to investigate **2** : to research — *vi* **~ sobre** : to do research into
investir {54} *vt* **1** : to empower **2** : to swear in, to inaugurate
inveterado, -da *adj* : inveterate, deep-seated
invicto, -ta *adj* : undefeated
invidente[1] *adj* CIEGO : blind, sightless
invidente[2] *nmf* CIEGO : blind person
invierno *nm* : winter, wintertime
inviolable *adj* : inviolable — **inviolabilidad** *nf*
inviolado, -da *adj* : inviolate, pure
invisibilidad *nf* : invisibility
invisible *adj* : invisible — **invisiblemente** *adv*
invitación *nf, pl* **-ciones** : invitation
invitado, -da *n* : guest

invitar *vt* : to invite

invocación *nf, pl* **-ciones** : invocation

invocar {72} *vt* : to invoke, to call on

involucramiento *nm* : involvement

involucrar *vt* : to implicate, to involve — **involucrarse** *vr* : to get involved

involuntario, -ria *adj* : involuntary — **involuntariamente** *adv*

invulnerable *adj* : invulnerable

inyección *nf, pl* **-ciones** : injection, shot

inyectado, -da *adj* **ojos inyectados** : bloodshot eyes

inyectar *vt* : to inject

ion *nm* : ion

ionizar {21} *vt* : to ionize — **ionización** *nf*

ionosfera *nf* : ionosphere

ir {43} *vi* **1** : to go <ir a pie : to go on foot, to walk> <ir a caballo : to ride horseback> <ir a casa : to go home> **2** : to lead, to extend, to stretch <el camino va de Cali a Bogotá : the road goes from Cali to Bogotá> **3** FUNCIONAR : to work, to function <esta computadora ya no va : this computer doesn't work anymore> **4** : to get on, to get along <¿cómo te va? : how are you?, how's it going?> <el negocio no va bien : the business isn't doing well> **5** : to suit <ese vestido te va bien : that dress really suits you> **6** ~ **con** : to be <ir con prisa : to be in a hurry> **7** ~ **por** : to follow, to go along <fueron por la costa : they followed the shoreline> **8 dejarse ir** : to let oneself go **9 ir a parar** : to end up **10 vamos a ver** : let's see — *v aux* **1** (*with present participle*) <ir caminando : to walk> <¡voy corriendo! : I'll be right there!> **2** ~ **a** : to be going to <voy a hacerlo : I'm going to do it> <el avión va a despegar : the plane is about to take off> — **irse** *vr* **1** : to leave, to go <¡vámonos! : let's go!> <todo el mundo se fue : everyone left> **2** ESCAPARSE : to leak **3** GASTARSE : to be used up, to be gone

ira *nf* CÓLERA, FURIA : wrath, anger

iracundo, -da *adj* : irate, angry

iraní *adj & nmf* : Iranian

iraquí *adj & nmf* : Iraqi

irascible *adj* : irascible, irritable — **irascibilidad** *nf*

irga, irgue, etc. → **erguir**

iridio *nm* : iridium

iridiscencia *nf* : iridescence — **iridiscente** *adj*

iris *nms & pl* **1** : iris **2 arco iris** : rainbow

irlandés[1], **-desa** *adj, mpl* **-deses** : Irish

irlandés[2], **-desa** *n, pl* **-deses** : Irish person, Irishman *m,* Irishwoman *f*

irlandés[3] *nm* : Irish (language)

ironía *nf* : irony

irónico, -ca *adj* : ironic, ironical — **irónicamente** *adv*

irracional *adj* : irrational — **irracionalmente** *adv*

irracionalidad *nf* : irrationality

irradiar *vt* : to radiate, to irradiate

irrazonable *adj* : unreasonable

irreal *adj* : unreal

irrebatible *adj* : unanswerable, irrefutable

irreconciliable *adj* : irreconcilable

irreconocible *adj* : unrecognizable

irrecuperable *adj* : irrecoverable, irretrievable

irredimible *adj* : irredeemable

irreductible *adj* : unyielding

irreemplazable *adj* : irreplaceable

irreflexión *nf, pl* **-xiones** : thoughtlessness, impetuosity

irreflexivo, -va *adj* : rash, unthinking — **irreflexivamente** *adv*

irrefrenable *adj* : uncontrollable, unstoppable <un impulso irrefrenable : an irresistable urge>

irrefutable *adj* : irrefutable

irregular *adj* : irregular — **irregularmente** *adv*

irregularidad *nf* : irregularity

irrelevante *adj* : irrelevant — **irrelevancia** *nf*

irreligioso, -sa *adj* : irreligious

irremediable *adj* : incurable — **irremediablemente** *adv*

irreparable *adj* : irreparable

irreprimible *adj* : irrepressible

irreprochable *adj* : irreproachable

irresistible adj : irresistible — **irresistiblemente** adv

irresolución *nf, pl* **-ciones** : indecision, hesitation

irresoluto, -ta *adj* INDECISO : undecided

irrespeto *nm* : disrespect

irrespetuoso, -sa *adj* : disrespectful — **irrespetuosamente** *adv*

irresponsabilidad *nf* : irresponsibility

irresponsable *adj* : irresponsible — **irresponsablemente** *adv*

irrestricto, -ta *adj* : unrestricted, unconditional <apoyo irrestricto : unconditional support>

irreverencia *nf* : disrespect

irreverente *adj* : disrespectful

irreversible *adj* : irreversible

irrevocable *adj* : irrevocable — **irrevocablemente** *adv*

irrigar {52} *vt* : to irrigate — **irrigación** *nf*

irrisible *adj* : laughable

irrisión *nf, pl* **-siones** : derision, ridicule

irrisorio, -ria *adj* RISIBLE : ridiculous, ludicrous

irritabilidad *nf* : irritability

irritable *adj* : irritable

irritación *nf, pl* **-ciones** : irritation

irritante *adj* : irritating

irritar *vt* : to irritate — **irritación** *nf*

irrompible *adj* : unbreakable

irrumpir *vi* ~ **en** : to burst into

irrupción *nf, pl* **-ciones 1** : irruption **2** : invasion

isla *nf* : island

islámico, -ca *adj* **:** Islamic, Muslim
islandés[1]**, -desa** *adj, mpl* **-deses :** Icelandic
islandés[2]**, -desa** *n, mpl* **-deses :** Icelander
islandés[3] *nm* **:** Icelandic (language)
isleño, -ña *n* **:** islander
islote *nm* **:** islet
isometría *nfs & pl* **:** isometrics
isométrico, -ca *adj* **:** isometric
isósceles *adj* **:** isosceles <triángulo isósceles : isosceles triangle>
isótopo *nm* **:** isotope
israelí *adj & nmf* **:** Israeli
istmo *nm* **:** isthmus
itacate *nm Mex* **:** pack, provisions *pl*
italiano[1]**, -na** *adj & n* **:** Italian
italiano[2] *nm* **:** Italian (language)
iterbio *nm* **:** ytterbium
itinerante *adj* AMBULANTE **:** traveling, itinerant
itinerario *nm* **:** itinerary, route
itrio *nm* **:** yttrium
izar {21} *vt* **:** to hoist, to raise <izar la bandera : to raise the flag>
izquierda *nf* **:** left
izquierdista *adj & nmf* **:** leftist
izquierdo, -da *adj* **:** left

J

j *nf* **:** tenth letter of the Spanish alphabet
jabalí *nm* **:** wild boar
jabalina *nf* **:** javelin
jabón *nm, pl* **jabones :** soap
jabonar *vt* ENJABONAR **:** to soap up, to lather — **jabonarse** *vr*
jabonera *nf* **:** soap dish
jabonoso, -sa *adj* **:** soapy
jaca *nf* **1 :** pony **2** YEGUA **:** mare
jacal *nm Mex* **:** shack, hut
jacinto *nm* **:** hyacinth
jactancia *nf* **1 :** boastfulness **2 :** boasting, bragging
jactancioso[1]**, -sa** *adj* **:** boastful
jactancioso[2]**, -sa** *n* **:** boaster, braggart
jactarse *vr* **:** to boast, to brag
jade *nm* **:** jade
jadear *vi* **:** to pant, to gasp, to puff — **jadeante** *adj*
jadeo *nm* **:** panting, gasping, puffing
jaez *nm, pl* **jaeces 1 :** harness **2 :** kind, sort, ilk **3 jaeces** *nmpl* **:** trappings
jaguar *nm* **:** jaguar
jai alai *nm* **:** jai alai
jaiba *nf* CANGREJO **:** crab
jalapeño *nm Mex* **:** jalapeño pepper
jalar *vt* **1 :** to pull, to tug **2** *fam* **:** to attract, to draw in <las ideas nuevas lo jalan : new ideas appeal to him> — *vi* **1 :** to pull, to pull together **2** *fam* **:** to hurry up, to get going **3** *Mex fam* **:** to be in working order <esta máquina no jala : this machine doesn't work>
jalbegue *nm* **:** whitewash
jalea *nf* **:** jelly
jalear *vt* **:** to encourage, to urge on
jaleo *nm fam* **1 :** uproar, ruckus, racket **2** *fam* **:** confusion, hassle **3 :** cheering and clapping (for a dance)
jalón *nm, pl* **jalones 1 :** milestone, landmark **2** TIRÓN **:** pull, tug
jalonar *vt* **:** to mark, to stake out
jalonear *vt Mex, Peru fam* **:** to tug at — *vi* **1** *fam* **:** to pull, to tug **2** *CA fam* **:** to haggle
jamaica *nf* **:** hibiscus
jamaicano, -na → **jamaiquino**
jamaiquino, -na *adj & n* **:** Jamaican
jamás *adv* **1** NUNCA **:** never **2 nunca jamás** *or* **jamás de los jamases :** never ever **3 para siempre jamás :** for ever and ever
jamba *nf* **:** jamb
jamelgo *nm* **:** nag (horse)
jamón *nm, pl* **jamones :** ham
Janucá *nmf* **:** Hanukkah
japonés, -nesa *adj & n, mpl* **-neses :** Japanese
jaque *nm* **1 :** check (in chess) <jaque mate : checkmate> **2 tener en jaque :** to intimidate, to bully
jaqueca *nf* **:** headache, migraine
jarabe *nm* **1 :** syrup **2 :** Mexican folk dance
jarana *nf* **1** *fam* **:** revelry, partying, spree **2** *fam* **:** joking, fooling around **3 :** small guitar
jaranear *vi fam* **:** to go on a spree, to party
jarcia *nf* **1 :** rigging **2 :** fishing tackle
jardín *nm, pl* **jardines 1 :** garden **2 jardín de niños :** kindergarten **3 los jardines** *nmpl* **:** the outfield
jardinería *nf* **:** gardening
jardinero, -ra *n* **1 :** gardener **2 :** outfielder (in baseball)
jarra *nf* **1 :** pitcher, jug **2 :** stein, mug **3 de jarras** *or* **en jarras :** akimbo
jarrete *nm* **1 :** back of the knee **2 :** hock (of an animal)
jarro *nm* **1 :** pitcher, jug **2 :** mug
jarrón *nm, pl* **jarrones** FLORERO **:** vase
jaspe *nm* **:** jasper
jaspeado, -da *adj* **1** VETEADO **:** streaked, veined **2 :** speckled, mottled
jaula *nf* **:** cage
jauría *nf* **:** pack of hounds
javanés, -nesa *adj & n* **:** Javanese
jazmín *nm, pl* **jazmines :** jasmine
jazz ['jas, 'dʒas] *nm* **:** jazz
jeans ['jins, 'dʒins] *nmpl* **:** jeans
jeep ['jip, 'dʒip] *nm, pl* **jeeps :** jeep
jefatura *nf* **1 :** leadership **2 :** headquarters <jefatura de policía : police headquarters>
jefe, -fa *n* **1 :** chief, head, leader <jefe de bomberos : fire chief> **2 :** boss
Jehová *nm* **:** Jehovah

jején *nm, pl* **jejenes** : gnat, small mosquito
jengibre *nm* : ginger
jeque *nm* : sheikh, sheik
jerarca *nmf* : leader, chief
jerarquía *nf* **1** : hierarchy **2** RANGO : rank
jerárquico, -ca *adj* : hierarchical
jerbo *nm* : gerbil
jerez *nm, pl* **jereces** : sherry
jerga *nf* **1** : jargon, slang **2** : coarse cloth
jerigonza *nf* GALIMATÍAS : mumbo jumbo, gibberish
jeringa *nf* : syringe
jeringar {52} *vt* **1** : to inject **2** *fam* JOROBAR : to annoy, to pester — *vi fam* JOROBAR : to be annoying, to be a nuisance
jeringuear → **jeringar**
jeringuilla *nf* → **jeringa**
jeroglífico *nm* : hieroglyphic
jersey *nm, pl* **jerseys 1** : jersey (fabric) **2** *Spain* : sweater
jesuita *adj & nm* : Jesuit
Jesús *nm* : Jesus
jeta *nf* **1** : snout **2** *fam* : face, mug
jíbaro, -ra *adj* **1** : Jivaro **2** : rustic, rural
jibia *nf* : cuttlefish
jícama *nf* : jicama
jícara *nf Mex* : calabash
jilguero *nm* : European goldfinch
jinete *nmf* : horseman, horsewoman *f,* rider
jinetear *vt* **1** : to ride, to perform (on horseback) **2** DOMAR : to break in (a horse) — *vi* CABALGAR : to ride horseback
jingoísmo [ˌjɪŋgoˈizmo, ˌdʒɪŋ-] *nm* : jingoism
jingoísta *adj* : jingoist, jingoistic
jiote *nm Mex* : rash
jira *nf* : outing, picnic
jirafa *nf* **1** : giraffe **2** : boom microphone
jirón *nm, pl* **jirones** : shred, rag <hecho jirones : in tatters>
jitomate *nm Mex* : tomato
jockey [ˈjɔki, ˈdʒɔ-] *nmf, pl* **jockeys** [-kis] : jockey
jocosidad *nf* : humor, jocularity
jocoso, -sa *adj* : playful, jocular — **jocosamente** *adv*
jofaina *nf* : washbowl
jogging [ˈjɔgɪŋ, ˈdʒɔ-] *nm* : jogging
jolgorio *nm* : merrymaking, fun
jonrón *nm, pl* **jonrones** : home run
jordano, -na *adj & n* : Jordanian
jornada *nf* **1** : expedition, day's journey **2 jornada de trabajo** : working day **3 jornadas** *nfpl* : conference, congress
jornal *nm* **1** : day's pay **2 a ~** : by the day
jornalero, -ra *n* : day laborer
joroba *nf* **1** GIBA : hump **2** *fam* : nuisance, pain in the neck
jorobado[1], -da *adj* GIBOSO : hunchbacked, humpbacked
jorobado[2], -da *n* GIBOSO : hunchback, humpback
jorobar *vt fam* JERINGAR : to bother, to annoy — *vi fam* JERINGAR : to be annoying, to be a nuisance
jorongo *nm Mex* : full-length poncho
jota *nf* **1** : jot, bit <no entiendo ni jota : I don't understand a word of it> <no se ve ni jota : you can't see a thing> **2** : jack (in playing cards)
joven[1] *adj, pl* **jóvenes 1** : young **2** : youthful
joven[2] *nmf, pl* **jóvenes** : young man *m,* young woman *f,* young person
jovial *adj* : jovial, cheerful — **jovialmente** *adv*
jovialidad *nf* : joviality, cheerfulness
joya *nf* **1** : jewel, piece of jewelry **2** : treasure, gem <la nueva empleada es una joya : the new employee is a real gem>
joyería *nf* **1** : jewelry store **2** : jewelry **3 joyería de fantasía** : costume jewelry
joyero, -ra *n* : jeweler
juanete *nm* : bunion
jubilación *nf, pl* **-ciones 1** : retirement **2** PENSIÓN : pension
jubilado[1], -da *adj* : retired, in retirement
jubilado[2], -da *nmf* : retired person, retiree
jubilar *vt* **1** : to retire, to pension off **2** *fam* : to get rid of, to discard — **jubilarse** *vr* : to retire
jubileo *nm* : jubilee
júbilo *nm* : jubilation, joy
jubiloso, -sa *adj* : jubilant, joyous
judaico, -ca *adj* : Judaic, Jewish
judaísmo *nm* : Judaism
judía *nf* **1** : bean **2** *or* **judía verde** : green bean, string bean
judicatura *nf* **1** : judiciary, judges *pl* **2** : office of judge
judicial *adj* : judicial — **judicialmente** *adv*
judío[1], -día *adj* : Jewish
judío[2], -día *n* : Jewish person, Jew
judo [ˈjuðo, ˈdʒu-] *nm* : judo
juega, juegue, etc. → **jugar**
juego *nm* **1** : play, playing <poner en juego : to bring into play> **2** : game, sport <juego de cartas : card game> <Juegos Olímpicos : Olympic Games> **3** : gaming, gambling <estar en juego : to be at stake> **4** : set <un juego de llaves : a set of keys> **5 hacer juego** : to go together, to match **6 juego de manos** : conjuring trick, sleight of hand
juerga *nf* : partying, binge <irse de juerga : to go on a spree>
juerguista *nmf* : reveler, carouser
jueves *nms & pl* : Thursday
juez *nmf, pl* **jueces 1** : judge **2** ÁRBITRO : umpire, referee

jugada *nf* **1 :** play, move **2 :** trick <hacer una mala jugada : to play a dirty trick>
jugador, -dora *n* **1 :** player **2 :** gambler
jugar {44} *vi* **1 :** to play <jugar a la pelota : to play ball> **2** APOSTAR **:** to gamble, to bet **3 :** to joke, to kid — *vt* **1 :** to play <jugar un papel : to play a role> <jugar una carta : to play a card> **2 :** to bet — **jugarse** *vr* **1 :** to risk, to gamble away <jugarse la vida : to risk one's life> **2 jugarse el todo por el todo :** to risk everything
jugarreta *nf fam* **:** prank, dirty trick
juglar *nm* **:** minstrel
jugo *nm* **1 :** juice **2 :** substance, essence <sacarle el jugo a algo : to get the most out of something>
jugosidad *nf* **:** juiciness, succulence
jugoso, -sa *adj* **:** juicy
juguete *nm* **:** toy
juguetear *vi* **1 :** to play, to cavort, to frolic **2 :** to toy, to fiddle
juguetería *nf* **:** toy store
juguetón, -tona *adj, mpl* **-tones :** playful — **juguetonamente** *adv*
juicio *nm* **1 :** good judgment, reason, sense **2 :** opinion <a mi juicio : in my opinion> **3 :** trial <llevar a juicio : to take to court>
juicioso, -sa *adj* **:** judicious, wise — **juiciosamente** *adv*
julio *nm* **:** July
juncia *nf* **:** sedge
junco *nm* **1 :** reed, rush **2 :** junk (boat)
jungla *nf* **:** jungle
junio *nm* **:** June
junquillo *nm* **:** jonquil
junta *nf* **1 :** board, committee <junta directiva : board of directors> **2** REUNIÓN **:** meeting, session **3 :** junta **4 :** joint, gasket
juntamente *adv* **1 :** jointly, together <juntamente con : together with> **2 :** at the same time
juntar *vt* **1** UNIR **:** to unite, to combine, to put together **2** REUNIR **:** to collect, to gather together, to assemble **3 :** to close partway <juntar la puerta : to leave the door ajar> — **juntarse** *vr* **1 :** to join together **2 :** to socialize, to get together
junto, -ta *adj* **1** UNIDO **:** joined, united **2 :** close, adjacent <colgaron los dos retratos juntos : they hung the two paintings side by side> **3** (*used adverbially*) **:** together <llegamos juntos : we arrived together> **4 ~ a :** next to, alongside of **5 ~ con :** together with, along with
juntura *nf* **:** joint, coupling
Júpiter *nm* **:** Jupiter
jura *nf* **:** oath, pledge <jura de bandera : pledge of allegiance>
jurado[1] *nm* **:** jury
jurado[2]**, -da** *n* **:** juror
juramento *nm* **1 :** oath <juramento hipocrático : Hippocratic oath> **2 :** swearword, oath
jurar *vt* **1 :** to swear <jurar lealtad : to swear loyalty> **2 :** to take an oath <el alcalde juró su cargo : the mayor took the oath of office> — *vi* **:** to curse, to swear
jurídico, -ca *adj* **:** legal
jurisdicción *nf, pl* **-ciones :** jurisdiction
jurisdiccional *adj* **:** jurisdictional, territorial
jurisprudencia *nf* **:** jurisprudence, law
justa *nf* **1 :** joust **2** TORNEO **:** tournament, competition
justamente *adv* **1** PRECISAMENTE **:** precisely, exactly **2 :** justly, fairly
justar *vi* **:** to joust
justicia *nf* **1 :** justice, fairness <hacerle justicia a : to do justice to> <ser de justicia : to be only fair> **2 la justicia :** the law <tomarse la justicia por su mano : to take the law into one's own hands>
justiciero, -ra *adj* **:** righteous, avenging
justificable *adj* **:** justifiable
justificación *nf, pl* **-ciones :** justification
justificante *nm* **1 :** justification **2 :** proof, voucher
justificar {72} *vt* **1 :** to justify **2 :** to excuse, to vindicate
justo[1] *adv* **1 :** justly **2 :** right, exactly <justo a tiempo : just in time> **3 :** tightly
justo[2]**, -ta** *adj* **1 :** just, fair **2 :** right, exact **3 :** tight <estos zapatos me quedan muy justos : these shoes are too tight>
justo[3]**, -ta** *n* **:** just person <los justos : the just>
juvenil *adj* **1 :** juvenile, young, youthful **2** ADOLESCENTE **:** teenage
juventud *nf* **1 :** youth **2 :** young people
juzgado *nm* TRIBUNAL **:** court, tribunal
juzgar {52} *vt* **1 :** to try, to judge (a case in court) **2 :** to pass judgment on **3** CONSIDERAR **:** to consider, to deem
juzgue, etc. → **juzgar**

K

k *nf* **:** eleventh letter of the Spanish alphabet
kaki *adj & nm* → **caqui**
kaleidoscopio *nm* → **caleidoscopio**
kamikaze *adj & nm* **:** kamikaze
kampucheano, -na *adj & n* **:** Kampuchean
kan *nm* **:** khan
karaoke *nm* **:** karaoke
karate *or* **kárate** *nm* **:** karate

kayac *or* **kayak** *nm, pl* **kayacs** *or* **kayaks** : kayak
keniano, -na *adj & n* : Kenyan
kepí *nm* : kepi
kermesse *or* **kermés** [kɛr'mɛs] *nf, pl* **kermesses** *or* **kermeses** [-'mɛsɛs] : charity fair, bazaar
kerosene *or* **kerosén** *or* **keroseno** *nm* : kerosene, paraffin
kilo *nm* **1** : kilo, kilogram **2** *fam* : large amount
kilobyte [,kilo'bait] *nm* : kilobyte
kilociclo *nm* : kilocycle
kilogramo *nm* : kilogram
kilohertzio *nm* : kilohertz
kilometraje *nm* : distance in kilometers, mileage
kilométrico, -ca *adj fam* : endless, very long
kilómetro *nm* : kilometer
kilovatio *nm* : kilowatt
kimono *nm* : kimono
kinder ['kɪndɛr] *nm* → **kindergarten**
kindergarten [,kɪndɛr'gartɛn] *nm, pl* **kindergartens** [-tɛns] : kindergarten, nursery school
kinesiología *nf* : physical therapy
kinesiólogo, -ga *n* : physical therapist
kiosco *nm* → **quiosco**
kit *nm, pl* **kits** : kit
kiwi ['kiwi] *nm* **1** : kiwi (bird) **2** : kiwifruit
klaxon *nm* → **claxon**
knockout [nɔ'kaut] *nm* → **nocaut**
koala *nm* : koala bear
kriptón *nm* : krypton
kurdo[1], -da *adj* : Kurdish
kurdo[2], -da *n* : Kurd
kuwaití [ku,wai'ti] *adj & nmf* : Kuwaiti

L

l *nf* : twelfth letter of the Spanish alphabet
la[1] *pron* **1** : her, it <llámala hoy : call her today> <sacó la botella y la abrió : he took out the bottle and opened it> **2** (*formal*) : you <no la vi a usted, Señora Díaz : I didn't see you, Mrs. Díaz> **3** : the one <mi casa y la de la puerta roja : my house and the one with the red door> **4 la que** : the one who
la[2] *art* → **el[2]**
laberíntico, -ca *adj* : labyrinthine
laberinto *nm* : labyrinth, maze
labia *nf fam* : gift of gab <tu amigo tiene labia : your friend has a way with words>
labial *adj* : labial, lip <lápiz labial : lipstick>
labio *nm* **1** : lip **2 labio leporino** : harelip
labor *nf* : work, labor
laborable *adj* **1** : arable **2 día laborable** : workday, business day
laboral *adj* **1** : work, labor <costos laborales : labor costs> **2 estancia laboral** : workstation
laborar *vi* : to work
laboratorio *nm* : laboratory, lab
laboriosidad *nf* : industriousness, diligence
laborioso, -sa *adj* **1** : laborious, hard **2** : industrious, hard-working
labrado[1], -da *adj* **1** : cultivated, tilled **2** : carved, wrought
labrado[2] *nm* : cultivated field
labrador, -dora *n* : farmer
labranza *nf* : farming
labrar *vt* **1** : to carve, to work (metal) **2** : to cultivate, to till **3** : to cause, to bring about
laca *nf* **1** : lacquer, shellac **2** : hair spray **3 laca de uñas** : nail polish
lacayo *nm* : lackey
lace, etc. → **lazar**
lacear *vt* : to lasso
laceración *nf, pl* **-ciones** : laceration
lacerante *adj* : hurtful, wounding
lacerar *vt* **1** : to lacerate, to cut **2** : to hurt, to wound (one's feelings)
lacio, -cia *adj* **1** : limp, lank **2 pelo lacio** : straight hair
lacónico, -ca *adj* : laconic — **lacónicamente** *adv*
lacra *nf* **1** : scar, mark (on the skin) **2** : stigma, blemish
lacrar *vt* : to seal (with wax)
lacrimógeno, -na *adj* **gas lacrimógeno** : tear gas
lacrimoso, -sa *adj* : tearful, moving
lactancia *nf* **1** : lactation **2** : breastfeeding
lactante *nmf* : nursing infant, suckling
lactar *v* : to breast-feed
lácteo, -tea *adj* **1** : dairy **2 Vía Láctea** : Milky Way
láctico, -ca *adj* : lactic
lactosa *nf* : lactose
ladeado, -da *adj* : crooked, tilted, lopsided
ladear *vt* : to tilt, to tip — **ladearse** *vr* : to bend (over)
ladera *nf* : slope, hillside
ladino[1], -na *adj* **1** : cunning, shrewd **2** *CA, Mex* : mestizo
ladino[2], -na *n* **1** : trickster **2** *CA, Mex* : Spanish-speaking Indian **3** *CA, Mex* : mestizo
lado *nm* **1** : side **2** PARTE : place <miró por todos lados : he looked everywhere> **3 al lado de** : next to, beside **4 de ~** : tilted, sideways <está de lado : it's lying on its side> **5 hacerse a un lado** : to step aside **6 lado a lado** : side by side **7 por otro lado** : on the other hand
ladrar *vi* : to bark
ladrido *nm* : bark (of a dog), barking

ladrillo *nm* : brick
ladrón, -drona *n, mpl* **ladrones** : robber, thief, burglar
lagartija *nf* : small lizard
lagarto *nm* **1** : lizard **2 lagarto de Indias** : alligator
lago *nm* : lake
lágrima *nf* : tear, teardrop
lagrimear *vi* **1** : to water (of eyes) **2** : to weep easily
laguna *nf* **1** : lagoon **2** : lacuna, gap
laicado *nm* : laity
laico[1], -ca *adj* : lay, secular
laico[2], -ca *n* : layman *m,* laywoman *f*
laja *nf* : slab
lama[1] *nf* : slime, ooze
lama[2] *nm* : lama
lamber *vt* : to lick
lamentable *adj* **1** : unfortunate, lamentable **2** : pitiful, sad
lamentablemente *adv* : unfortunately, regrettably
lamentación *nf, pl* **-ciones** : lamentation, groaning, moaning
lamentar *vt* **1** : to lament **2** : to regret <lo lamento : I'm sorry> — **lamentarse** *vr* : to grumble, to complain
lamento *nm* : lament, groan, cry
lamer *vt* **1** : to lick **2** : to lap against
lamida *nf* : lick
lámina *nf* **1** PLANCHA : sheet, plate **2** : plate, illustration
laminado[1], -da *adj* : laminated
laminado[2] *nm* : laminate
laminar *vt* : to laminate — **laminación** *nf*
lámpara *nf* : lamp
lampiño, -ña *adj* : hairless
lamprea *nf* : lamprey
lana *nf* **1** : wool <lana de acero : steel wool> **2** *Mex fam* : money, dough
lance[1], etc. → **lanzar**
lance[2] *nm* **1** INCIDENTE : event, incident **2** RIÑA : quarrel **3** : throw, cast (of a net, etc.) **4** : move, play (in a game), throw (of dice)
lancear *vt* : to spear
lanceta *nf* : lancet
lancha *nf* **1** : small boat, launch **2 lancha motora** : motorboat, speedboat
langosta *nf* **1** : lobster **2** : locust
langostino *nm* : prawn, crayfish
languidecer {53} *vi* : to languish
languidez *nf, pl* **-deces** : languor, listlessness
lánguido, -da *adj* : languid, listless — **lánguidamente** *adv*
lanolina *nf* : lanolin
lanudo, -da *adj* : woolly
lanza *nf* : spear, lance
lanzadera *nf* **1** : shuttle (for weaving) **2 lanzadera espacial** : space shuttle
lanzado, -da *adj* **1** : impulsive, brazen **2** : forward, determined <ir lanzado : to hurtle along>
lanzador, -dora *n* : thrower, pitcher
lanzallamas *nms & pl* : flamethrower
lanzamiento *nm* **1** : throw **2** : pitch (in baseball) **3** : launching, launch
lanzar {21} *vt* **1** : to throw, to hurl **2** : to pitch **3** : to launch — **lanzarse** *vr* **1** : to throw oneself (at, into) **2** ~ **a** : to embark upon, to undertake
laosiano, -na *adj & n* : Laotian
lapicero *nm* **1** : mechanical pencil **2** *CA, Peru* : ballpoint pen
lápida *nf* : marker, tombstone
lapidar *vt* APEDREAR : to stone
lapidario, -ria *adj & n* : lapidary
lápiz *nm, pl* **lápices 1** : pencil **2 lápiz de labios** *or* **lápiz labial** : lipstick
lapón, -pona *adj & n, mpl* **lapones** : Lapp
lapso *nm* : lapse, space (of time)
lapsus *nms & pl* : error, slip
laquear *vt* : to lacquer, to varnish, to shellac
largamente *adv* **1** : at length, extensively **2** : easily, comfortably **3** : generously
largar {52} *vt* **1** SOLTAR : to let loose, to release **2** AFLOJAR : to loosen, to slacken **3** *fam* : to give, to hand over **4** *fam* : to hurl, to let fly (insults, etc.) — **largarse** *vr fam* : to scram, to beat it
largo[1], -ga *adj* **1** : long **2 a lo largo** : lengthwise **3 a lo largo de** : along **4 a la larga** : in the long run
largo[2] *nm* : length <tres metros de largo : three meters long>
largometraje *nm* : feature film
largue, etc. → **largar**
larguero *nm* : crossbeam
largueza *nf* : generosity, largesse
larguirucho, -cha *adj fam* : lanky
largura *nf* : length
laringe *nf* : larynx
laringitis *nfs & pl* : laryngitis
larva *nf* : larva — **larval** *adj*
las → **el[2], los[1]**
lasaña *nf* : lasagna
lasca *nf* : chip, chipping
lascivia *nf* : lasciviousness, lewdness
lascivo, -va *adj* : lascivious, lewd — **lascivamente** *adv*
láser *nm* : laser
lasitud *nf* : lassitude, weariness
laso, -sa *adj* : languid, weary
lástima *nf* **1** : compassion, pity **2** PENA : shame, pity <¡qué lástima! : what a shame!>
lastimadura *nf* : injury, wound
lastimar *vt* **1** DAÑAR, HERIR : to hurt, to injure **2** AGRAVIAR : to offend — **lastimarse** *vr* : to hurt oneself
lastimero, -ra *adj* : pitiful, wretched
lastimoso, -sa *adj* **1** : shameful **2** : pitiful, terrible
lastrar *vt* **1** : to ballast **2** : to burden, to encumber
lastre *nm* **1** : burden **2** : ballast
lata *nf* **1** : tinplate **2** : tin can **3** *fam* : pest, bother, nuisance **4 dar lata** *fam* : to bother, to annoy
latencia *nf* : latency
latente *adj* : latent

lateral[1] *adj* **1 :** lateral, side **2 :** indirect — **lateralmente** *adv*

lateral[2] *nm* **:** end piece, side

látex *nms & pl* **:** latex

latido *nm* **:** beat, throb <latido del corazón : heartbeat>

latifundio *nm* **:** large estate

latigazo *nm* **:** lash (with a whip)

látigo *nm* AZOTE **:** whip

latín *nm* **:** Latin (language)

latino[1], **-na** *adj* **1 :** Latin **2** *fam* **:** Latin-American

latino[2], **-na** *n fam* **:** Latin American

latinoamericano[1], **-na** *adj* HISPANOAMERICANO **:** Latin American

latinoamericano, -na *n* **:** Latin American

latir *vi* **1 :** to beat, to throb **2 latirle a uno** *Mex fam* **:** to have a hunch <me late que no va a venir : I have a feeling he's not going to come>

latitud *nf* **1 :** latitude **2 :** breadth

lato, -ta *adj* **1 :** extended, lengthy **2 :** broad (in meaning)

latón *nm, pl* **latones :** brass

latoso[1], **-sa** *adj fam* **:** annoying, bothersome

latoso[2], **-sa** *n fam* **:** pest, nuisance

latrocinio *nm* **:** larceny

laúd *nm* **:** lute

laudable *adj* **:** laudable, praiseworthy

laudo *nm* **:** findings, decision

laureado, -da *adj & n* **:** laureate

laurear *vt* **:** to award, to honor

laurel *nm* **1 :** laurel **2 :** bay leaf **3 dormirse en sus laureles :** to rest on one's laurels

lava *nf* **:** lava

lavable *adj* **:** washable

lavabo *nm* **1** LAVAMANOS **:** sink, washbowl **2 :** lavatory, toilet

lavadero *nm* **:** laundry room

lavado *nm* **1 :** laundry, wash **2 :** laundering <lavado de dinero : money laundering>

lavadora *nf* **:** washing machine

lavamanos *nms & pl* LAVABO **:** sink, washbowl

lavanda *nf* ESPLIEGO **:** lavender

lavandería *nf* **:** laundry (service)

lavandero, -ra *n* **:** launderer, laundress *f*

lavaplatos *nms & pl* **1 :** dishwasher **2** *Chile, Col, Mex* **:** kitchen sink

lavar *vt* **1 :** to wash, to clean **2 :** to launder (money) **3 lavar en seco :** to dry-clean — **lavarse** *vr* **1 :** to wash oneself **2 lavarse las manos de :** to wash one's hands of

lavativa *nf* **:** enema

lavatorio *nm* **:** lavatory, washroom

lavavajillas *nms & pl* **:** dishwasher

laxante *adj & nm* **:** laxative

laxitud *nf* **:** laxity, slackness

laxo, -xa *adj* **:** lax, slack

lazada *nf* **:** bow, loop

lazar {21} *vt* **:** to rope, to lasso

lazo *nm* **1** VÍNCULO **:** link, bond **2 :** bow, ribbon **3 :** lasso, lariat

le *pron* **1 :** to her, to him, to it <¿qué le dijiste? : what did you tell him?> **2 :** from her, from him, from it <el ladrón le robó la cartera : the thief stole his wallet> **3 :** for her, for him, for it <cómprale flores a tu mamá : buy your mom some flowers> **4** (*formal*) **:** to you, for you <le traje un regalo : I brought you a gift>

leal *adj* **:** loyal, faithful — **lealmente** *adv*

lealtad *nf* **:** loyalty, allegiance

lebrel *nm* **:** hound

lección *nf, pl* **lecciones :** lesson

lechada *nf* **1 :** whitewash **2 :** grout

lechal *adj* **:** suckling, unweaned <cordero lechal : suckling lamb>

leche *nf* **1 :** milk <leche en polvo : powdered milk> <leche de magnesia : milk of magnesia> **2 :** milky sap

lechera *nf* **1 :** milk jug **2 :** dairymaid *f*

lechería *nf* **:** dairy store

lechero[1], **-ra** *adj* **:** dairy

lechero[2], **-ra** *n* **:** milkman *m,* milk dealer

lecho *nm* **1 :** bed <un lecho de rosas : a bed of roses> <lecho de muerte : deathbed> **2 :** riverbed **3 :** layer, stratum (in geology)

lechón, -chona *n, mpl* **lechones :** suckling pig

lechoso, -sa *adj* **:** milky

lechuga *nf* **:** lettuce

lechuza *nf* BÚHO **:** owl, barn owl

lectivo, -va *adj* **:** school <año lectivo : school year>

lector[1], **-tora** *adj* **:** reading <nivel lector : reading level>

lector[2], **-tora** *n* **:** reader

lector[3] *nm* **:** scanner, reader <lector óptico : optical scanner>

lectura *nf* **1 :** reading **2 :** reading matter

leer {20} *v* **:** to read

legación *nf, pl* **-ciones :** legation

legado *nm* **1 :** legacy, bequest **2 :** legate, emissary

legajo *nm* **:** dossier, file

legal *adj* **:** legal, lawful — **legalmente** *adv*

legalidad *nf* **:** legality, lawfulness

legalizar {21} *vt* **:** to legalize — **legalización** *nf*

legar {52} *vt* **1 :** to bequeath, to hand down **2** DELEGAR **:** to delegate

legendario, -ria *adj* **:** legendary

legible *adj* **:** legible

legión *nf, pl* **legiones :** legion

legionario, -ria *n* **:** legionnaire

legislación *nf* **1 :** legislation, lawmaking **2 :** laws *pl*, legislation

legislador[1], **-dora** *adj* **:** legislative

legislador[2], **-dora** *n* **:** legislator

legislar *vi* **:** to legislate

legislativo, -va *adj* **:** legislative

legislatura *nf* **1 :** legislature **2 :** term of office

legitimar *vt* **1 :** to legitimize **2 :** to authenticate — **legitimación** *nf*

legitimidad *nf* : legitimacy

legítimo, -ma *adj* **1** : legitimate **2** : genuine, authentic — **legítimamente** *adv*

lego[1], -ga *adj* **1** : secular, lay **2** : uniformed, ignorant

lego[2], -ga *n* : layperson, layman *m*, laywoman *f*

legua *nf* **1** : league **2 notarse a leguas** : to be very obvious <se notaba a leguas : you could tell from a mile away>

legue, etc. → **legar**

legumbre *nf* **1** HORTALIZA : vegetable **2** : legume

leíble *adj* : readable

leída *nf* : reading, read <de una leída : in one reading, at one go>

leído[1] *pp* → **leer**

leído[2], -da *adj* : well-read

lejanía *nf* : remoteness, distance

lejano, -na *adj* : remote, distant, far away

lejía *nf* **1** : lye **2** : bleach

lejos *adv* **1** : far away, distant <a lo lejos : in the distance, far off> <desde lejos : from a distance> **2** : long ago, a long way off <está lejos de los 50 años : he's a long way from 50 years old> **3 de ~** : by far <esta decisión fue de lejos la más fácil : this decision was by far the easiest> **4 ~ de** : far from <lejos de ser reprobado, recibió una nota de B : far from failing, he got a B>

lelo, -la *adj* : silly, stupid

lema *nm* : motto, slogan

lencería *nf* : lingerie

lengua *nf* **1** : tongue <morderse la lengua : to bite one's tongue> **2** IDIOMA : language <lengua materna : mother tongue, native language> <lengua muerta : dead language>

lenguado *nm* : sole, flounder

lenguaje *nm* **1** : language, speech **2 lenguaje gestual** *or* **lenguaje de gestos** : sign language **3 lenguaje de programación** : programming language

lengüeta *nf* **1** : tongue (of a shoe), tab, flap **2** : reed (of a musical instrument) **3** : barb, point

lengüetada *nf* **beber a lengüetadas** : to lap (up)

lenidad *nf* : leniency

lenitivo, -va *adj* : soothing

lente *nmf* **1** : lens <lentes de contacto : contact lenses> **2 lentes** *nmpl* ANTEOJOS : eyeglasses <lentes de sol : sunglasses>

lenteja *nf* : lentil

lentejuela *nf* : sequin, spangle

lentitud *nf* : slowness

lento[1] *adv* DESPACIO : slowly

lento[2], -ta *adj* **1** : slow **2** : slow-witted, dull — **lentamente** *adv*

leña *nf* : wood, firewood

leñador, -dora *n* : lumberjack, woodcutter

leñera *nf* : woodshed

leño *nm* : log

leñoso, -sa *adj* : woody

Leo *nmf* : Leo

león, -ona *n, mpl* **leones 1** : lion, lioness *f* **2** (*in various countries*) : puma, cougar

leonado, -da *adj* : tawny

leonino, -na *adj* **1** : leonine **2** : one-sided, unfair

leopardo *nm* : leopard

leotardo *nm* MALLA : leotard, tights *pl*

leperada *nf Mex* : obscenity

lépero, -ra *adj Mex* : vulgar, coarse

lepra *nf* : leprosy

leproso[1], -sa *adj* : leprous

leproso[2], -sa *n* : leper

lerdo, -da *adj* **1** : clumsy **2** : dull, oafish, slow-witted

les *pron* **1** : to them <dales una propina : give them a tip> **2** : from them <se les privó de su herencia : they were deprived of their inheritance> **3** : for them <les hice sus tareas : I did their homework for them> **4** : to you *pl*, for you *pl* <les compré un regalo : I bought you all a present>

lesbiana *nf* : lesbian — **lesbiano, -na** *adj*

lesbianismo *nm* : lesbianism

lesión *nf, pl* **lesiones** HERIDA : lesion, wound, injury <una lesión grave : a serious injury>

lesionado, -da *adj* HERIDO : injured, wounded

lesionar *vt* : to injure, to wound — **lesionarse** *vr* : to hurt oneself

lesivo, -va *adj* : harmful, damaging

letal *adj* MORTÍFERO : deadly, lethal — **letalmente** *adv*

letanía *nf* **1** : litany **2** *fam* : spiel, song and dance

letárgico, -ca *adj* : lethargic

letargo *nm* : lethargy, torpor

letón[1], -tona *adj & n, mpl* **letones** : Latvian

letón[2] *nm* : Latvian (language)

letra *nf* **1** : letter **2** CALIGRAFÍA : handwriting, lettering **3** : lyrics *pl* **4 al pie de la letra** : word for word, by the book **5 letras** *nfpl* : arts (in education)

letrado[1], -da *adj* ERUDITO : learned, erudite

letrado[2], -da *n* : attorney-at-law, lawyer

letrero *nm* RÓTULO : sign, notice

letrina *nf* : latrine

letrista *nmf* : lyricist, songwriter

leucemia *nf* : leukemia

levadizo, -za *adj* **1** : liftable **2 puente levadizo** : drawbridge

levadura *nf* **1** : yeast, leavening **2 levadura en polvo** : baking powder

levantamiento *nm* **1** ALZAMIENTO : uprising **2** : raising, lifting <levantamiento de pesas : weight lifting>

levantar *vt* **1** ALZAR : to lift, to raise **2** : to put up, to erect **3** : to call off, to adjourn **4** : to give rise to, to arouse

<levantar sospechas : to arouse suspicion> — **levantarse** *vr* **1 :** to rise, to stand up **2 :** to get out of bed

levar *vt* **levar anclas :** to weigh anchor

leve *adj* **1 :** light, slight **2 :** trivial, unimportant — **levemente** *adv*

levedad *nf* **:** lightness

levemente *adv* LIGERAMENTE **:** lightly, softly

léxico[1], -ca *adj* **:** lexical

léxico[2] *nm* **:** lexicon, glossary

lexicografía *nf* **:** lexicography

lexicográfico, -ca *adj* **:** lexicographical, lexicographic

lexicógrafo, -fa *n* **:** lexicographer

ley *nf* **1 :** law <fuera de la ley : outside the law> <la ley de gravedad : the law of gravity> **2 :** purity (of metals) <oro de ley : pure gold>

leyenda *nf* **1 :** legend **2 :** caption, inscription

leyó, etc. → **leer**

liar {85} *vt* **1** ATAR **:** to bind, to tie (up) **2 :** to roll (a cigarette) **3 :** to confuse — **liarse** *vr* **:** to get mixed up

libanés, -nesa *adj & n, mpl* **-neses :** Lebanese

libar *vt* **1 :** to suck (nectar) **2 :** to sip, to swig (liquor, etc.)

libelo *nm* **1 :** libel, lampoon **2 :** petition (in court)

libélula *nf* **:** dragonfly

liberación *nf, pl* **-ciones :** liberation, deliverance <liberación de la mujer : women's liberation>

liberado, -da *adj* **1 :** liberated <una mujer liberada : a liberated woman> **2 :** freed, delivered

liberal *adj & nmf* **:** liberal

liberalidad *nf* **:** generosity, liberality

liberalismo *nm* **:** liberalism

liberalizar {21} *vt* **:** to liberalize — **liberalización** *nf*

liberar *vt* **:** to liberate, to free — **liberarse** *vr* **:** to get free of

liberiano, -na *adj & n* **:** Liberian

libertad *nf* **1 :** freedom, liberty <tomarse la libertad de : to take the liberty of> **2 libertad bajo fianza :** bail **3 libertad condicional :** parole

libertador[1], -dora *adj* **:** liberating

libertador[2], -dora *n* **:** liberator

libertar *vt* LIBRAR **:** to set free

libertario, -ria *adj & n* **:** libertarian

libertinaje *nm* **:** licentiousness, dissipation

libertino[1], -na *adj* **:** licentious, dissolute

libertino[2], -na *n* **:** libertine

libidinoso, -sa *adj* **:** lustful, lewd

libido *nf* **:** libido

libio, -bia *adj & n* **:** Libyan

libra *nf* **1 :** pound **2 libra esterlina :** pound sterling

Libra *nmf* **:** Libra

libramiento *nm* **1 :** liberating, freeing **2** LIBRANZA **:** order of payment **3** *Mex* **:** beltway

libranza *nf* **:** order of payment

librar *vt* **1** LIBERTAR **:** to deliver, to set free **2 :** to wage <librar batalla : to do battle> **3 :** to issue <librar una orden : to issue an order> — **librarse** *vr* **~ de :** to free oneself from, to get out of

libre *adj* **1 :** free <un país libre : a free country> <libre de : free from, exempt from> <libre albedrío : free will> **2** DESOCUPADO **:** vacant **3 día libre :** day off

librea *nf* **:** livery

librecambio *nm* **:** free trade

libremente *adv* **:** freely

librería *nf* **:** bookstore

librero[1], -ra *n* **:** bookseller

librero[2] *nm Mex* **:** bookcase

libresco, -ca *adj* **:** bookish

libreta *nf* CUADERNO **:** notebook

libreto *nm* **:** libretto, script

libro *nm* **1 :** book <libro de texto : textbook> **2 libros** *nmpl* **:** books (in bookkeeping), accounts <llevar los libros : to keep the books>

licencia *nf* **1 :** permission **2 :** leave, leave of absence **3 :** permit, license <licencia de conducir : driver's license>

licenciado, -da *n* **1 :** university graduate **2** ABOGADO **:** lawyer

licenciar *vt* **1 :** to license, to permit, to allow **2 :** to discharge **3 :** to grant a university degree to — **licenciarse** *vr* **:** to graduate

licenciatura *nf* **1 :** college degree **2 :** course of study (at a college or university)

licencioso, -sa *adj* **:** licentious, lewd

liceo *nm* **:** secondary school, high school

licitación *nf, pl* **-ciones :** bid, bidding

licitar *vt* **:** to bid on

lícito, -ta *adj* **1 :** lawful, licit **2** JUSTO **:** just, fair

licor *nm* **1 :** liquor **2 :** liqueur

licorera *nf* **:** decanter

licuado *nm* BATIDO **:** milk shake

licuadora *nf* **:** blender

licuar {3} *vt* **:** to liquefy — **licuarse** *vr*

lid *nf* **1 :** fight, combat **2 :** argument, dispute **3 lides** *nfpl* **:** matters, affairs **4 en buena lid :** fair and square

líder[1] *adj* **:** leading, foremost

líder[2] *nmf* **:** leader

liderar *vt* DIRIGIR **:** to lead, to head

liderato *nm* **:** leadership, leading

liderazgo *nm* → **liderato**

lidiar *vt* **:** to fight — *vi* BATALLAR, LUCHAR **:** to struggle, to battle, to wrestle

liebre *nf* **:** hare

liendre *nf* **:** nit

lienzo *nm* **1 :** linen **2 :** canvas, painting **3 :** stretch of wall or fencing

liga *nf* **1** ASOCIACIÓN **:** league **2** GOMITA **:** rubber band **3 :** garter

ligado, -da *adj* **:** linked, connected

ligadura *nf* **1** ATADURA **:** tie, bond **2 :** ligature

ligamento *nm* **:** ligament

ligar {52} *vt* **:** to bind, to tie (up)

ligeramente *adv* **1** : slightly **2** LEVEMENTE : lightly, gently **3** : casually, flippantly
ligereza *nf* **1** : lightness **2** : flippancy **3** : agility
ligero, -ra *adj* **1** : light, lightweight **2** : slight, minor **3** : agile, quick **4** : lighthearted, superficial
ligue, etc. → **ligar**
lija *nf or* **papel de lija** : sandpaper
lijar *vt* : to sand
lila[1] *adj* : lilac, light purple
lila[2] *nf* : lilac
lima *nf* **1** : lime (fruit) **2** : file <lima de uñas : nail file>
limadora *nf* : polisher
limar *vt* **1** : to file **2** : to polish, to put the final touch on **3** : to smooth over <limar las diferencias : to iron out differences>
limbo *nm* **1** : limbo **2** : limb (in botany and astronomy)
limeño[1], **-ña** *adj* : of or from Lima, Peru
limeño[2], **-ña** *n* : person from Lima, Peru
limero *nm* : lime tree
limitación *nf, pl* **-ciones** **1** : limitation **2** : limit, restriction <sin limitación : unlimited>
limitado, -da *adj* **1** RESTRINGIDO : limited **2** : dull, slow-witted
limitar *vt* RESTRINGIR : to limit, to restrict — *vi* **~ con** : to border on — **limitarse** *vr* **~ a** : to limit oneself to
límite *nm* **1** : boundary, border **2** : limit <el límite de mi paciencia : the limit of my patience> <límite de velocidad : speed limit> **3 fecha límite** : deadline
limítrofe *adj* LINDANTE, LINDERO : bordering, adjoining
limo *nm* : slime, mud
limón *nm, pl* **limones** **1** : lemon **2** : lemon tree **3 limón verde** *Mex* : lime
limonada *nf* : lemonade
limosna *nf* : alms, charity
limosnear *vi* : to beg (for alms)
limosnero, -ra *n* MENDIGO : beggar
limoso, -sa *adj* : slimy
limpiabotas *nmfs & pl* : bootblack
limpiador[1], **-dora** *adj* : cleaning
limpiador[2], **-dora** *n* : cleaning person, cleaner
limpiamente *adv* : cleanly, honestly, fairly
limpiaparabrisas *nms & pl* : windshield wiper
limpiar *vt* **1** : to clean, to cleanse **2** : to clean up, to remove defects **3** *fam* : to clean out (in a game) **4** *fam* : to swipe, to pinch — *vi* : to clean — **limpiarse** *vr*
limpiavidrios *nmfs & pl Mex* : windshield wiper
límpido, -da *adj* : limpid
limpieza *nf* **1** : cleanliness, tidiness **2** : cleaning **3** HONRADEZ : integrity, honesty **4** DESTREZA : skill, dexterity
limpio[1] *adv* : fairly
limpio[2], **-pia** *adj* **1** : clean, neat **2** : honest <un juego limpio : a fair game> **3** : free <limpio de impurezas : pure, free from impurities> **4** : clear, net <ganancia limpia : clear profit>
limusina *nf* : limousine
linaje *nm* ABOLENGO : lineage, ancestry
linaza *nf* : linseed
lince *nm* : lynx
linchamiento *nm* : lynching
linchar *vt* : to lynch
lindante *adj* LIMÍTROFE, LINDERO : bordering, adjoining
lindar *vi* **1 ~ con** : to border, to skirt **2 ~ con** BORDEAR : to border on, to verge on
linde *nmf* : boundary, limit
lindero[1], **-ra** *adj* LIMÍTROFE, LINDANTE : bordering, adjoining
lindero[2] *nm* : boundary, limit
lindeza *nf* **1** : prettiness **2** : clever remark **3 lindezas** *nfpl* (*used ironically*) : insults
lindo[1] *adv* **1** : beautifully, wonderfully <canta lindo tu mujer : your wife sings beautifully> **2 de lo lindo** : a lot, a great deal <los zancudos nos picaban de lo lindo : the mosquitoes were biting away at us>
lindo[2], **-da** *adj* **1** BONITO : pretty, lovely **2** MONO : cute
línea *nf* **1** : line <línea divisoria : dividing line> <línea de banda : sideline> **2** : line, course, position <línea de conducta : course of action> <en líneas generales : in general terms, along general lines> **3** : line, service <línea aérea : airline> <línea telefónica : telephone line>
lineal *adj* : linear
linfa *nf* : lymph
linfático, -ca *adj* : lymphatic
lingote *nm* : ingot
lingüista *nmf* : linguist
lingüística *nf* : linguistics
lingüístico, -ca *adj* : linguistic
linimento *nm* : liniment
lino *nm* **1** : linen **2** : flax
linóleo *nm* : linoleum
linterna *nf* **1** : lantern **2** : flashlight
lío *nm fam* **1** : confusion, mess **2** : hassle, trouble, jam <meterse en un lío : to get into a jam> **3** : affair, liason
liofilizar {21} *vt* : to freeze-dry
lioso, -sa *adj fam* **1** : confusing, muddled **2** : troublemaking
liquen *nm* : lichen
liquidación *nf, pl* **-ciones** **1** : liquidation **2** : clearance sale **3** : settlement, payment
liquidar *vt* **1** : to liquefy **2** : to liquidate **3** : to settle, to pay off **4** *fam* : to rub out, to kill
liquidez *nf, pl* **-deces** : liquidity

líquido[1], **-da** *adj* **1** : liquid, fluid **2** : net <ingresos líquidos : net income>
líquido[2] *nm* **1** : liquid, fluid <líquido de frenos : brake fluid> **2** : ready cash, liquid assets
lira *nf* : lyre
lírica *nf* : lyric poetry
lírico, -ca *adj* : lyric, lyrical
lirio *nm* **1** : iris **2 lirio de los valles** MUGUETE : lily of the valley
lirismo *nm* : lyricism
lirón *nm, pl* **lirones** : dormouse
lisiado[1], **-da** *adj* : disabled, crippled
lisiado[2], **-da** *n* : disabled person, cripple
lisiar *vt* : to cripple, to disable — **lisiarse** *vr*
liso, -sa *adj* **1** : smooth **2** : flat **3** : straight <pelo liso : straight hair> **4** : plain, unadorned <liso y llano : plain and simple>
lisonja *nf* : flattery
lisonjear *vt* ADULAR : to flatter
lista *nf* **1** : list **2** : roster, roll <pasar lista : to take attendance> **3** : stripe, strip **4** : menu
listado[1], **-da** *adj* : striped
listado[2] *nm* : listing
listar *vt* : to list
listeza *nf* : smartness, alertness
listo, -ta *adj* **1** DISPUESTO, PREPARADO : ready <¿estás listo? : are you ready?> **2** : clever, smart
listón *nm, pl* **listones 1** : ribbon **2** : strip (of wood), lath **3** : high bar (in sports)
lisura *nf* : smoothness
litera *nf* : bunk bed, berth
literal *adj* : literal — **literalmente** *adv*
literario, -ria *adj* : literary
literato, -ta *n* : writer, author
literatura *nf* : literature
litigante *adj & nmf* : litigant
litigar {52} *vi* : to litigate, to be in litigation
litigio *nm* **1** : litigation, lawsuit **2 en ~** : in dispute
litigioso, -sa *adj* : litigious
litio *nm* : lithium
litografía *nf* **1** : lithography **2** : lithograph
litógrafo, -fa *n* : lithographer
litoral[1] *adj* : coastal
litoral[2] *nm* : shore, seaboard
litosfera *nf* : lithosphere
litro *nm* : liter
lituano[1], **-na** *adj & n* : Lithuanian
lituano[2] *nm* : Lithuanian (language)
liturgia *nf* : liturgy
litúrgico, -ca *adj* : liturgical — **litúrgicamente** *adv*
liviandad *nf* LIGEREZA : lightness
liviano, -na *adj* **1** : light, slight **2** INCONSTANTE : fickle
lividez *nf* PALIDEZ : pallor
lívido, -da *adj* **1** AMORATADO : livid **2** PÁLIDO : pallid, extremely pale
living *nm* : living room
llaga *nf* : sore, wound
llama *nf* **1** : flame **2** : llama
llamada *nf* : call <llamada a larga distancia : long-distance call> <llamada al orden : call to order>
llamado[1], **-da** *adj* : named, called <una mujer llamada Rosa : a woman called Rosa>
llamado[2] → **llamamiento**
llamador *nm* : door knocker
llamamiento *nm* : call, appeal
llamar *vt* **1** : to name, to call **2** : to call, to summon **3** : to phone, to call up — **llamarse** *vr* : to be called, to be named <¿cómo te llamas? : what's your name?>
llamarada *nf* **1** : flare-up, sudden blaze **2** : flushing (of the face)
llamativo, -va *adj* : flashy, showy, striking
llameante *adj* : flaming, blazing
llamear *vi* : to flame, to blaze
llana *nf* **1** : trowel **2** → **llano**[2]
llanamente *adv* : simply, plainly, straightforwardly
llaneza *nf* : simplicity, naturalness
llano[1], **-na** *adj* **1** : even, flat **2** : frank, open **3** LISO : plain, simple
llano[2] *nm* : plain
llanta *nf* **1** NEUMÁTICO : tire **2** : rim
llantén *nm, pl* **llantenes** : plantain (weed)
llanto *nm* : crying, weeping
llanura *nf* : plain, prairie
llave *nf* **1** : key **2** : faucet **3** INTERRUPTOR : switch **4** : brace (punctuation mark) **5 llave inglesa** : monkey wrench
llavero *nm* : key chain, key ring
llegada *nf* : arrival
llegar {52} *vi* **1** : to arrive, to come **2 ~ a** : to arrive at, to reach, to amount to **3 ~ a** : to manage to <llegó a terminar la novela : she managed to finish the novel> **4 llegar a ser** : to become <llegó a ser un miembro permanente : he became a permanent member>
llegue, etc. → **llegar**
llenar *vt* **1** : to fill, to fill up, to fill in **2** : to meet, to fulfill <los regalos no llenaron sus expectativas : the gifts did not meet her expectations> — **llenarse** *vr* : to fill up, to become full
llenito, -ta *adj fam* REGORDETE : chubby, plump
lleno[1], **-na** *adj* **1** : full, filled **2 de ~** : completely, fully **3 estar lleno de sí mismo** : to be full of oneself
lleno[2] *nm* **1** *fam* : plenty, abundance **2** : full house, sellout
llevadero, -ra *adj* : bearable
llevar *vt* **1** : to take away, to carry <me gusta, me lo llevo : I like it, I'll take it> **2** : to wear **3** : to take, to lead <llevamos a Pedro al cine : we took Pedro to the movies> **4 llevar a cabo** : to carry out **5 llevar adelante** : to carry on, to keep going — *vi* : to lead <un problema lleva al otro : one problem leads to another> — *v aux* : to

have <llevo mucho tiempo buscándolo : I've been looking for it for a long time> <lleva leído medio libro : he's halfway through the book> — **llevarse** *vr* **1** : to take away, to carry off **2** : to get along <siempre nos llevábamos bien : we always got along well>

llorar *vi* : to cry, to weep — *vt* : to mourn, to bewail

lloriquear *vi* : to whimper, to whine

lloriqueo *nm* : whimpering, whining

llorón, -rona *n, mpl* **llorones** : crybaby, whiner

lloroso, -sa *adj* : tearful, sad

llovedizo, -za *adj* : rain <agua llovediza : rainwater>

llover {47} *v impers* : to rain <está lloviendo : it's raining> <llover a cántaros : to rain cats and dogs> — *vi* : to rain down, to shower <le llovieron regalos : he was showered with gifts>

llovizna *nf* : drizzle, sprinkle

lloviznar *v impers* : to drizzle, to sprinkle

llueve, etc. → **llover**

lluvia *nf* **1** : rain, rainfall **2** : barrage, shower

lluvioso, -sa *adj* : rainy

lo[1] *pron* **1** : him, it <lo vi ayer : I saw him yesterday> <lo entiendo : I understand it> <no lo creo : I don't believe so> **2** (*formal, masculine*) : you <disculpe, señor, no lo oí : excuse me sir, I didn't hear you> **3 lo que** : what, that which <eso es lo que más le gusta : that's what he likes the most>

lo[2] *art* **1** : the <lo mejor : the best, the best thing> **2** : how <sé lo bueno que eres : I know how good you are>

loa *nf* : praise

loable *adj* : laudable, praiseworthy — **loablemente** *adv*

loar *vt* : to praise, to laud

lobato, -ta *n* : wolf cub

lobby *nm* : lobby, pressure group

lobo, -ba *n* : wolf

lóbrego, -ga *adj* SOMBRÍO : gloomy, dark

lobulado, -da *adj* : lobed

lóbulo *nm* : lobe <lóbulo de la oreja : earlobe>

locación *nf, pl* **-ciones 1** : location (in moviemaking) **2** *Mex* : place

local[1] *adj* : local — **localmente** *adv*

local[2] *nm* : premises *pl*

localidad *nf* : town, locality

localización *nf, pl* **-ciones 1** : locating, localization **2** : location

localizar {21} *vt* **1** UBICAR : to locate, to find **2** : to localize — **localizarse** *vr* UBICARSE : to be located <se localiza en el séptimo piso : it is located on the seventh floor>

locatario, -ria *n* : tenant

loción *nf, pl* **lociones** : lotion

lócker *nm, pl* **lóckers** : locker

loco[1], **-ca** *adj* **1** DEMENTE : crazy, insane, mad **2 a lo loco** : wildly, recklessly **3 volverse loco** : to go mad

loco[2], **-ca** *n* **1** : crazy person, lunatic **2 hacerse el loco** : to act the fool

locomoción *nf, pl* **-ciones** : locomotion

locomotor, -tora *adj* : locomotive

locomotora *nf* **1** : locomotive **2** : driving force

locuacidad *nf* : loquacity, talkativeness

locuaz *adj, pl* **locuaces** : loquacious, talkative

locución *nf, pl* **-ciones** : locution, phrase <locución adverbial : adverbial phrase>

locura *nf* **1** : insanity, madness **2** : crazy thing, folly

locutor, -tora *n* : announcer

lodazal *nm* : bog, quagmire

lodo *nm* BARRO : mud, mire

lodoso, -sa *adj* : muddy

logaritmo *nm* : logarithm

logia *nf* : lodge <logia masónica : Masonic lodge>

lógica *nf* : logic

lógico, -ca *adj* : logical — **lógicamente** *adv*

logística *nf* : logistics *pl*

logístico, -ca *adj* : logistic, logistical

logo *nm* → **logotipo**

logotipo *nm* : logo

logrado, -da *adj* : successful, well done

lograr *vt* **1** : to get, to obtain **2** : to achieve, to attain — **lograrse** *vr* : to be successful

logro *nm* : achievement, attainment

loma *nf* : hill, hillock

lombriz *nf, pl* **lombrices** : worm <lombriz de tierra : earthworm, night crawler> <lombriz solitaria : tapeworm> <tener lombrices : to have worms>

lomo *nm* **1** : back (of an animal) **2** : loin <lomo de cerdo : pork loin> **3** : spine (of a book) **4** : blunt edge (of a knife)

lona *nf* : canvas

loncha *nf* LONJA, REBANADA : slice

lonche *nm* **1** ALMUERZO : lunch **2** *Mex* : submarine sandwich

lonchería *nf Mex* : luncheonette

londinense[1] *adj* : of or from London

londinense[2] *nmf* : Londoner

longaniza *nf* : spicy pork sausage

longevidad *nf* : longevity

longevo, -va *adj* : long-lived

longitud *nf* **1** LARGO : length <longitud de onda : wavelength> **2** : longitude

longitudinal *adj* : longitudinal

lonja *nf* LONCHA, REBANADA : slice

lontananza *nf* : background <en lontananza : in the distance, far away>

lord *nm, pl* **lores** (*title in England*) : lord

loro *nm* : parrot

los[1], **las** *pron* **1** : them <hice galletas y se las di a los nuevos vecinos : I made cookies and gave them to the

new neighbors> **2** : you <voy a llevarlos a los dos : I am going to take both of you> **3 los que, las que** : those, who, the ones <los que van a cantar deben venir temprano : those who are singing must come early> **4** (*used with* **haber**) <los hay en varios colores : they come in various colors>

los[2] → **el**[2]

losa *nf* : flagstone, paving stone

loseta *nf* BALDOSA : floor tile

lote *nm* **1** : part, share **2** : batch, lot **3** : plot of land, lot

lotería *nf* : lottery

loto *nm* : lotus

loza *nf* **1** : crockery, earthenware **2** : china

lozanía *nf* **1** : healthiness, robustness **2** : luxuriance, lushness

lozano, -na *adj* **1** : robust, healthy-looking <un rostro lozano : a smooth, fresh face> **2** : lush, luxuriant

lubricante[1] *adj* : lubricating

lubricante[2] *nm* : lubricant

lubricar {72} *vt* : to lubricate, to oil — **lubricación** *nf*

lucero *nm* : bright star <lucero del alba : morning star>

lucha *nf* **1** : struggle, fight **2** : wrestling

luchador, -dora *n* **1** : fighter **2** : wrestler

luchar *vi* **1** : to fight, to struggle **2** : to wrestle

luchón, -chona *adj, mpl* **luchones** *Mex* : industrious, hardworking

lucidez *nf, pl* **-deces** : lucidity, clarity

lucido, -da *adj* MAGNÍFICO : magnificent, splendid

lúcido, -da *adj* : lucid

luciérnaga *nf* : firefly, glowworm

lucimiento *nm* **1** : brilliance, splendor, sparkle **2** : triumph, success <salir con lucimiento : to succeed with flying colors>

lucio *nm* : pike (fish)

lucir {45} *vi* **1** : to shine **2** : to look good, to stand out **3** : to seem, to appear <ahora luce contento : he looks happy now> — *vt* **1** : to wear, to sport **2** : to flaunt, to show off — **lucirse** *vr* **1** : to distinguish oneself, to excel **2** : to show off

lucrarse *vr* : to make a profit

lucrativo, -va *adj* : lucrative, profitable — **lucrativamente** *adv*

lucro *nm* GANANCIA : profit, gain

luctuoso, -sa *adj* : mournful, tragic

luego[1] *adv* **1** DESPUÉS : then, afterwards **2** : later (on) **3 desde ~** : of course **4 ¡hasta luego!** : see you later! **5 luego que** : as soon as **6 luego luego** *Mex fam* : right away, immediately

luego[2] *conj* : therefore <pienso, luego existo : I think, therefore I am>

lugar *nm* **1** : place, position <se llevó el primer lugar en su división : she took first place in her division> **2** ESPACIO : space, room **3 dar lugar a** : to give rise to, to lead to **4 en lugar de** : instead of **5 lugar común** : cliché, platitude **6 tener lugar** : to take place

lugareño[1], **-ña** *adj* : village, rural

lugareño[2], **-ña** *n* : villager

lugarteniente *nmf* : lieutenant, deputy

lúgubre *adj* : gloomy, lugubrious

lujo *nm* **1** : luxury **2 de ~** : deluxe

lujoso, -sa *adj* : luxurious

lujuria *nf* : lust, lechery

lujurioso, -sa *adj* : lustful, lecherous

lumbar *adj* : lumbar

lumbre *nf* **1** FUEGO : fire **2** : brilliance, splendor **3 poner en la lumbre** : to put on the stove, to warm up

lumbrera *nf* **1** : skylight **2** : vent, port **3** : brilliant person, luminary

luminaria *nf* **1** : altar lamp **2** LUMBRERA : luminary, celebrity

luminiscencia *nf* : luminescence — **luminiscente** *adj*

luminosidad *nf* : luminosity, brightness

luminoso, -sa *adj* : shining, luminous

luna *nf* **1** : moon **2 luna de miel** : honeymoon

lunar[1] *adj* : lunar

lunar[2] *nm* **1** : mole, beauty spot **2** : defect, blemish **3** : polka dot

lunático, -ca *adj & n* : lunatic

lunes *nms & pl* : Monday

luneta *nf* **1** : lens (of eyeglasses) **2** : windshield (of an automobile) **3** : crescent

lupa *nf* : magnifying glass

lúpulo *nm* : hops (plant)

lustrar *vt* : to shine, to polish

lustre *nm* **1** BRILLO : luster, shine **2** : glory, distinction

lustroso, -sa *adj* BRILLOSO : lustrous, shiny

luto *nm* : mourning <estar de luto : to be in mourning>

luz *nf, pl* **luces** **1** : light **2** : lighting **3** *fam* : electricity **4** : window, opening **5** : light, lamp **6** : span, spread (between supports) **7 a la luz de** : in light of **8 dar a luz** : to give birth **9 traje de luces** : matador's costume

luzca, etc. → **lucir**

M

m *nf* : thirteenth letter of the Spanish alphabet

macabro, -bra *adj* : macabre

macaco[1], **-ca** *adj* : ugly, misshapen

macaco[2], **-ca** *n* : macaque

macadán *nm, pl* **-danes** : macadam

macana *nf* **1** : club, cudgel **2** *fam* : nonsense, silliness **3** *fam* : lie, fib

macanudo, -da *adj fam* : great, fantastic

macarrón *nm, pl* **-rrones 1 :** macaroon **2 macarrones** *nmpl* **:** macaroni
maceta *nf* **1 :** flowerpot **2 :** mallet **3** *Mex fam* **:** head
machacar {72} *vt* **1 :** to crush, to grind **2 :** to beat, to pound — *vi* **:** to insist, to go on (about)
machacón, -cona *adj, mpl* **-cones :** insistent, tiresome
machete *nm* **:** machete
machetear *vt* **:** to hack with a machete — *vi Mex fam* **:** to plod, to work tirelessly
machismo *nm* **1 :** machismo **2 :** male chauvinism
machista *nm* **:** male chauvinist
macho[1] *adj* **1 :** male **2 :** macho, virile, tough
macho[2] *nm* **1 :** male **2 :** he-man
machote *nm* **1** *fam* **:** tough guy, he-man **2** *CA, Mex* **:** rough draft, model **3** *Mex* **:** blank form
machucar {72} *vt* **1 :** to pound, to beat, to crush **2 :** to bruise
machucón *nm, pl* **-cones 1** MORETÓN **:** bruise **2 :** smashing, pounding
macilento, -ta *adj* **:** gaunt, wan
macis *nm* **:** mace (spice)
macizo, -za *adj* **1 :** solid <oro macizo : solid gold> **2 :** strong, strapping **3 :** massive
macrocosmo *nm* **:** macrocosm
mácula *nf* **:** blemish, stain
madeja *nf* **1 :** skein, hank **2 :** tangle (of hair)
madera *nf* **1 :** wood **2 :** lumber, timber **3 madera dura** *or* **madera noble :** hardwood
maderero, -ra *adj* **:** timber, lumber
madero *nm* **:** piece of lumber, plank
madrastra *nf* **:** stepmother
madrazo *nm Mex fam* **:** punch, blow <se agarraron a madrazos : they beat each other up>
madre *nf* **1 :** mother **2 madre política :** mother-in-law **3 la Madre Patria :** the mother country (said of Spain)
madrear *vt Mex fam* **:** to beat up
madreperla *nf* NÁCAR **:** mother-of-pearl
madreselva *nf* **:** honeysuckle
madriguera *nf* **:** burrow, den, lair
madrileño[1], **-ña** *adj* **:** of or from Madrid
madrileño[2], **-ña** *n* **:** person from Madrid
madrina *nf* **1 :** godmother **2 :** bridesmaid **3 :** sponsor
madrugada *nf* **1 :** early morning, wee hours **2** ALBA **:** dawn, daybreak
madrugador, -dora *n* **:** early riser
madrugar {52} *vi* **1 :** to get up early **2 :** to get a head start
madurar *v* **1 :** to ripen **2 :** to mature
madurez *nf, pl* **-reces 1 :** maturity **2 :** ripeness
maduro, -ra *adj* **1 :** mature **2 :** ripe
maestría *nf* **1 :** mastery, skill **2 :** master's degree
maestro[1], **-tra** *adj* **1 :** masterly, skilled **2 :** chief, main **3 :** trained <un elefante maestro : a trained elephant>
maestro[2], **-tra** *n* **1 :** teacher (in grammar school) **2 :** expert, master **3 :** maestro
Mafia *nf* **:** Mafia
mafioso, -sa *n* **:** mafioso, gangster
magdalena *nf* **:** bun, muffin
magenta *adj & n* **:** magenta
magia *nf* **:** magic
mágico, -ca *adj* **:** magic, magical — **mágicamente** *adv*
magisterio *nm* **1 :** teaching **2 :** teachers *pl,* teaching profession
magistrado, -da *n* **:** magistrate, judge
magistral *adj* **1 :** masterful, skillful **2 :** magisterial
magistralmente *adv* **:** masterfully, brilliantly
magistratura *nf* **:** judgeship, magistracy
magma *nm* **:** magma
magnanimidad *nf* **:** magnanimity
magnánimo, -ma *adj* GENEROSO **:** magnanimous — **magnánimamente** *adv*
magnate *nmf* **:** magnate, tycoon
magnesia *nf* **:** magnesia
magnesio *nm* **:** magnesium
magnético, -ca *adj* **:** magnetic
magnetismo *nm* **:** magnetism
magnetizar {21} *vt* **:** to magnetize
magnetófono *nm* **:** tape recorder
magnetofónico, -ca *adj* **cinta magnetofónica :** magnetic tape
magnificar {72} *vt* **1 :** to magnify **2** EXAGERAR **:** to exaggerate **3** ENSALZAR **:** to exalt, to extol, to praise highly
magnificencia *nf* **:** magnificence, splendor
magnífico, -ca *adj* ESPLENDOROSO **:** magnificent, splendid — **magníficamente** *adv*
magnitud *nf* **:** magnitude
magnolia *nf* **:** magnolia (flower)
magnolio *nm* **:** magnolia (tree)
mago, -ga *n* **1 :** magician **2 :** wizard (in folk tales, etc.) **3 los Reyes Magos :** the Magi
magro, -gra *adj* **1 :** lean (of meat) **2 :** meager
maguey *nm* **:** maguey
magulladura *nf* MORETÓN **:** bruise
magullar *vt* **:** to bruise — **magullarse** *vr*
mahometano[1], **-na** *adj* ISLÁMICO **:** Islamic, Muslim
mahometano[2], **-na** *n* **:** Muslim
mahonesa *nf* → **mayonesa**
maicena *nf* **:** cornstarch
maíz *nm* **:** corn, maize
maizal *nm* **:** cornfield
maja *nf* **:** pestle
majadería *nf* **1** TONTERÍA **:** stupidity, foolishness **2** *Mex* LEPERADA **:** insult, obscenity
majadero[1], **-ra** *adj* **1 :** foolish, silly **2** *Mex* LÉPERO **:** crude, vulgar

majadero[2], **-ra** *n* **1** TONTO : fool **2** *Mex* : rude person, boor

majar *vt* : to crush, to mash

majestad *nf* : majesty <Su Majestad : Your Majesty>

majestuosamente *adv* : majestically

majestuosidad *nf* : majesty, grandeur

majestuoso, -sa *adj* : majestic, stately

majo, -ja *adj Spain* **1** : nice, likeable **2** GUAPO : attractive, good-looking

mal[1] *adv* **1** : badly, poorly <baila muy mal : he dances very badly> **2** : wrong, incorrectly <me entendió mal : she misunderstood me> **3** : with difficulty, hardly <mal puedo oírte : I can hardly hear you> **4 de mal en peor** : from bad to worse **5 menos mal** : it could have been worse

mal[2] *adj* → **malo**

mal[3] *nm* **1** : evil, wrong **2** DAÑO : harm, damage **3** DESGRACIA : misfortune **4** ENFERMEDAD : illness, sickness

malabar *adj* **juegos malabares** : juggling

malabarista *nmf* : juggler

malaconsejado, -da *adj* : ill-advised

malacostumbrado, -da *adj* CONSENTIDO : spoiled, pampered

malacostumbrar *vt* : to spoil

malagradecido, -da *adj* INGRATO : ungrateful

malaisio → **malasio**

malaquita *nf* : malachite

malaria *nf* PALUDISMO : malaria

malasio, -sia *adj & n* : Malaysian

malaventura *nf* : misadventure, misfortune

malaventurado, -da *adj* MALHADADO : ill-fated, unfortunate

malayo, -ya *adj & n* : Malay, Malayan

malbaratar *vt* **1** MALGASTAR : to squander **2** : to undersell

malcriado[1], **-da** *adj* **1** : ill-bred, bad-mannered **2** : spoiled, pampered

malcriado[2], **-da** *n* : spoiled brat

maldad *nf* **1** : evil, wickedness **2** : evil deed

maldecir {11} *vt* : to curse, to damn — *vi* **1** : to curse, to swear **2 ~ de** : to speak ill of, to slander, to defame

maldición *nf, pl* **-ciones** : curse

maldiga, maldijo, etc. → **maldecir**

maldito, -ta *adj* **1** : cursed, damned <¡maldita sea! : damn it all!> **2** : wicked

maldoso, -sa *adj Mex* : mischievous

maleable *adj* : malleable

maleante *nmf* : crook, thug

malecón *nm, pl* **-cones** : jetty, breakwater

maleducado, -da *adj* : ill-mannered, rude

maleficio *nm* : curse, hex

maléfico, -ca *adj* : evil, harmful

malentender {56} *vt* : to misunderstand

malentendido *nm* : misunderstanding

malestar *nm* **1** : discomfort **2** IRRITACIÓN : annoyance **3** INQUIETUD : uneasiness, unrest

maleta *nf* : suitcase, bag <haz tus maletas : pack your bags>

maletero[1], **-ra** *n* : porter

maletero[2] *nm* : trunk (of an automobile)

maletín *nm, pl* **-tines 1** PORTAFOLIO : briefcase **2** : overnight bag, satchel

malevolencia *nf* : malevolence, wickedness

malévolo, -la *adj* : malevolent, wicked

maleza *nf* **1** : thicket, underbrush **2** : weeds *pl*

malformación *nf, pl* **-ciones** : malformation

malgache *adj & nmf* : Madagascan

malgastar *vt* : to squander (resources), to waste (time, effort)

malhablado, -da *adj* : foul-mouthed

malhadado, -da *adj* MALAVENTURADO : ill-fated

malhechor, -chora *n* : criminal, delinquent, wrongdoer

malherir {76} *vt* : to injure seriously

malhumor *nm* : bad mood, sullenness

malhumorado, -da *adj* : bad-tempered, cross

malicia *nf* **1** : wickedness, malice **2** : mischief, naughtiness **3** : cunning, craftiness

malicioso, -sa *adj* **1** : malicious **2** PÍCARO : mischievous

malignidad *nf* **1** : malignancy **2** MALDAD : evil

maligno, -na *adj* **1** : malignant <un tumor maligno : a malignant tumor> **2** : evil, harmful, malign

malinchismo *nm Mex* : preference for foreign goods or people — **malinchista** *adj*

malintencionado, -da *adj* : malicious, spiteful

malinterpretar *vt* : to misinterpret

malla *nf* **1** : mesh **2** LEOTARDO : leotard, tights *pl* **3 malla de baño** : bathing suit

mallorquín, -quina *adj & n* : Majorcan

malnutrición *nf, pl* **-ciones** DESNUTRICIÓN : malnutrition

malnutrido, -da *adj* DESNUTRIDO : malnourished, undernourished

malo[1], **-la** *adj* (**mal** *before masculine singular nouns*) **1** : bad <mala suerte : bad luck> **2** : wicked, naughty **3** : cheap, poor (quality) **4** : harmful <malo para la salud : bad for one's health> **5** (*using the form* **mal**) : unwell <estar mal del corazón : to have heart trouble> **6 estar de malas** : to be in a bad mood

malo[2], **-la** *n* : villain, bad guy (in novels, movies, etc.)

malogrado, -da *adj* : failed, unsuccessful

malograr *vt* **1** : to spoil, to ruin **2** : to waste (an opportunity, time) — **mal-**

ograrse *vr* **1** FRACASAR **:** to fail **2 :** to die young

malogro *nm* **1 :** untimely death **2** FRACASO **:** failure

maloliente *adj* HEDIONDO **:** foul-smelling, smelly

malparado, -da *adj* **salir malparado** *or* **quedar malparado :** to come out of (something) badly, to end up in a bad state

malpensado, -da *adj* **:** distrustful, suspicious, nasty-minded

malquerencia *nf* AVERSIÓN **:** ill will, dislike

malquerer {64} *vt* **:** to dislike

malquiso, etc. → malquerer

malsano, -na *adj* **:** unhealthy

malsonante *adj* **:** rude, offensive <palabras malsonantes : foul language>

malta *nf* **:** malt

malteada *nf* **:** malted milk <malteada de chocolate : chocolate malt>

maltés, -tesa *adj & n, mpl* **malteses :** Maltese

maltratar *vt* **1 :** to mistreat, to abuse **2 :** to damage, to spoil

maltrato *nm* **:** mistreatment, abuse

maltrecho, -cha *adj* **:** battered, damaged

malucho, -cha *adj fam* **:** sick, under the weather

malva *adj & nm* **:** mauve

malvado[1], -da *adj* **:** evil, wicked

malvado[2], -da *n* **:** evildoer, wicked person

malvavisco *nm* **:** marshmallow

malvender *vt* **:** to sell at a loss

malversación *nf, pl* **-ciones :** misappropriation (of funds), embezzlement

malversador, -dora *n* **:** embezzler

malversar *vt* **:** to embezzle

malvivir *vi* **:** to live badly, to just scrape by

mamá *nf fam* **:** mom, mama

mamar *vi* **1 :** to suckle **2 darle de mamar a :** to breast-feed — *vt* **1 :** to suckle, to nurse **2 :** to learn from childhood, to grow up with — **mamarse** *vr fam* **:** to get drunk

mamario, -ria *adj* **:** mammary

mamarracho *nm fam* **1** ESPERPENTO **:** mess, sight **2 :** laughingstock, fool **3 :** rubbish, junk

mambo *nm* **:** mambo

mami *nf fam* **:** mommy

mamífero[1], -ra *adj* **:** mammalian

mamífero[2] *nm* **:** mammal

mamila *nf* **1 :** nipple **2** *Mex* **:** baby bottle, pacifier

mamografía *nf* **:** mammogram

mamola *nf* **:** pat, chuck under the chin

mamotreto *nm fam* **1 :** huge book, tome **2** ARMATOSTE **:** hulk, monstrosity

mampara *nf* BIOMBO **:** screen, room divider

mamparo *nm* **:** bulkhead

mampostería *nf* **:** masonry, stonemasonery

mampostero *nm* **:** mason, stonemason

mamut *nm, pl* **mamuts :** mammoth

maná *nm* **:** manna

manada *nf* **1 :** flock, herd, pack **2** *fam* **:** horde, mob <llegaron en manada : they came in droves>

manantial *nm* **1** FUENTE **:** spring **2 :** source

manar *vi* **1 :** to flow **2 :** to abound

manatí *nm* **:** manatee

mancha *nf* **1 :** stain, spot, mark <mancha de sangre : bloodstain> **2 :** blemish, blot <una mancha en su reputación : a blemish on his reputation> **3 :** patch

manchado, -da *adj* **:** stained

manchar *vt* **1** ENSUCIAR **:** to stain, to soil **2** DESHONRAR **:** to sully, to tarnish — **mancharse** *vr* **:** to get dirty

mancillar vt **:** to sully, to besmirch

manco, -ca *adj* **:** one-armed, one-handed

mancomunar *vt* **:** to combine, to pool — **mancomunarse** *vr* **:** to unite, to join together

mancomunidad *nf* **1 :** commonwealth **2 :** association, confederation

mancuernas *nfpl* **:** cuff links

mancuernillas *nf Mex* **:** cuff links

mandadero, -ra *n* **:** errand boy *m,* errand girl *f,* messenger

mandado *nm* **1 :** order, command **2 :** errand <hacer los mandados : to run errands, to go shopping>

mandamás *nmf, pl* **-mases** *fam* **:** boss, bigwig, honcho

mandamiento *nm* **1 :** commandment **2 :** command, order, warrant <mandamiento judicial : warrant, court order>

mandar *vt* **1** ORDENAR **:** to command, to order **2** ENVIAR **:** to send <te manda saludos : he sends you his regards> **3** ECHAR **:** to hurl, to throw **4 ¿mande?** *Mex* **:** yes?, pardon? — *vi* **:** to be the boss, to be in charge — **mandarse** *vr Mex* **:** to take liberties, to take advantage

mandarina *nf* **:** mandarin orange, tangerine

mandatario, -ria *n* **1 :** leader (in politics) <primer mandatario : head of state> **2 :** agent (in law)

mandato *nm* **1 :** term of office **2 :** mandate

mandíbula *nf* **1 :** jaw **2 :** mandible

mandil *nm* **1** DELANTAL **:** apron **2 :** horse blanket

mandilón *nm, pl* **-lones** *fam* **:** wimp, coward

mandioca *nf* **1 :** manioc, cassava **2 :** tapioca

mando *nm* **1 :** command, leadership **2 :** control (for a device) <mando a distancia : remote control> **3 al mando de :** in charge of **4 al mando de :** under the command of

mandolina *nf* **:** mandolin

mandón, -dona *adj, mpl* **mandones :** bossy, domineering

mandonear *vt fam* MANGONEAR : to boss around

mandrágora *nf* : mandrake

manecilla *nf* : hand (of a clock), pointer

manejable *adj* **1** : manageable **2** : docile, easily led

manejar *vt* **1** CONDUCIR : to drive (a car) **2** OPERAR : to handle, to operate **3** : to manage **4** : to manipulate (a person) — *vi* : to drive — **manejarse** *vr* **1** COMPORTARSE : to behave **2** : to get along, to manage

manejo *nm* **1** : handling, operation **2** : management

manera *nf* **1** MODO : way, manner, fashion **2 de cualquier manera** *or* **de todas maneras** : anyway, anyhow **3 de manera que** : so, in order that **4 de ninguna manera** : by no means, absolutely not **5 manera de ser** : personality, demeanor

manga *nf* **1** : sleeve **2** MANGUERA : hose

manganeso *nm* : manganese

mangle *nm* : mangrove

mango *nm* **1** : hilt, handle **2** : mango

mangonear *vt fam* : to boss around, to bully — *vi* **1** : to be bossy **2** : to loaf, to fool around

mangosta *nf* : mongoose

manguera *nf* : hose

maní *nm, pl* **maníes** : peanut

manía *nf* **1** OBSESIÓN : mania, obsession **2** : craze, fad **3** : odd habit, peculiarity **4** : dislike, aversion

maníaco[1], **-ca** *adj* : maniacal

maníaco[2], **-ca** *n* : maniac

maniatar *vt* : to tie the hands of, to manacle

maniático[1], **-ca** *adj* **1** MANÍACO : maniacal **2** : obsessive **3** : fussy, finicky

maniático[2], **-ca** *n* **1** MANÍACO : maniac, lunatic **2** : obsessive person, fanatic **3** : eccentric, crank

manicomio *nm* : insane asylum, madhouse

manicura *nf* : manicure

manicuro, -ra *n* : manicurist

manido, -da *adj* : hackneyed, stale, trite

manifestación *nf, pl* **-ciones 1** : manifestation, sign **2** : demonstration, rally

manifestante *nmf* : demonstrator

manifestar {55} *vt* **1** : to demonstrate, to show **2** : to declare — **manifestarse** *vr* **1** : to be or become evident **2** : to state one's position <se han manifestado a favor del acuerdo : they have declared their support for the agreement> **3** : to demonstrate, to rally

manifiesto[1], **-ta** *adj* : manifest, evident, clear — **manifiestamente** *adv*

manifiesto[2] *nm* : manifesto

manija *nf* MANGO : handle

manilla *nf* → **manecilla**

manillar *nm* : handlebars *pl*

maniobra *nf* : maneuver, stratagem

maniobrar *v* : to maneuver

manipulación *nf, pl* **-ciones** : manipulation

manipulador[1], **-dora** *adj* : manipulating, manipulative

manipulador[2], **-dora** *n* : manipulator

manipular *vt* **1** : to manipulate **2** MANEJAR : to handle

maniquí[1] *nmf, pl* **-quíes** : mannequin, model

maniquí[2] *nm, pl* **-quíes** : mannequin, dummy

manirroto[1], **-ta** *adj* : extravagant

manirroto[2], **-ta** *n* : spendthrift

manivela *nf* : crank

manjar *nm* : delicacy, special dish

mano[1] *nf* **1** : hand **2** : coat (of paint or varnish) **3 a ~** : by hand **4 a ~** *or* **a la mano** : handy, at hand, nearby **5 darse la mano** : to shake hands **6 de la mano** : hand in hand <la política y la economía van de la mano : politics and economics go hand in hand> **7 de primera mano** : firsthand, at firsthand **8 de segunda mano** : secondhand <ropa de segunda mano : secondhand clothing> **9 mano a mano** : one-on-one **10 mano de obra** : labor, manpower **11 mano de mortero** : pestle **12 echar una mano** : to lend a hand **13** *Mex fam* **mano negra** : shady dealings *pl*

mano[2], **-na** *n Mex fam* : buddy, pal <¡oye, mano! : hey man!>

manojo *nm* PUÑADO : handful, bunch

manopla *nf* **1** : mitten, mitt **2** : brass knuckles *pl*

manosear *vt* **1** : to handle or touch excessively **2** ACARICIAR : to fondle, to caress

manotazo *nm* : slap, smack, swipe

manotear *vi* : to wave one's hands, to gesticulate

mansalva *adv* **a ~** : at close range

mansarda *nf* BUHARDILLA : attic

mansedumbre *nf* **1** : gentleness, meekness **2** : tameness

mansión *nf, pl* **-siones** : mansion

manso, -sa *adj* **1** : gentle, meek **2** : tame — **mansamente** *adv*

manta *nf* **1** COBIJA, FRAZADA : blanket **2** : poncho **3** *Mex* : coarse cotton fabric

manteca *nf* **1** GRASA : lard, fat **2** : butter

mantecoso, -sa *adj* : buttery

mantel *nm* **1** : tablecloth **2** : altar cloth

mantelería *nf* : table linen

mantener {80} *vt* **1** SUSTENTAR : to support, to feed <mantener uno su familia : to support one's family> **2** CONSERVAR : to keep, to preserve **3** CONTINUAR : to keep up, to sustain <mantener una correspondencia : to keep up a correspondence> **4** AFIRMAR : to maintain, to affirm — **mantenerse** *vr* **1** : to support oneself, to subsist **2 mantenerse firme** : to hold one's ground

mantenimiento *nm* **1** : maintenance, upkeep **2** : sustenance, food **3** : preservation

mantequera *nf* **1** : churn **2** : butter dish

mantequería *nf* **1** : creamery, dairy **2** : grocery store

mantequilla *nf* : butter

mantilla *nf* : mantilla

manto *nm* **1** : cloak **2** : mantle (in geology)

mantón *nm, pl* **-tones** CHAL : shawl

mantuvo, etc. → **mantener**

manual[1] *adj* **1** : manual <trabajo manual : manual labor> **2** : handy, manageable — **manualmente** *adv*

manual[2] *nm* : manual, handbook

manualidades *nfpl* : handicrafts (in schools)

manubrio *nm* **1** : handle, crank **2** : handlebars *pl*

manufactura *nf* **1** FABRICACIÓN : manufacture **2** : manufactured item, product **3** FÁBRICA : factory

manufacturar *vt* FABRICAR : to manufacture

manufacturero[1], **-ra** *adj* : manufacturing

manufacturero[2], **-ra** *n* FABRICANTE : manufacturer

manuscrito[1], **-ta** *adj* : handwritten

manuscrito[2] *nm* : manuscript

manutención *nf, pl* **-ciones** : maintenance, support

manzana *nf* **1** : apple **2** CUADRA : block (enclosed by streets or buildings) **3** *or* **manzana de Adán** : Adam's apple

manzanal *nm* **1** : apple orchard **2** MANZANO : apple tree

manzanar *nm* : apple orchard

manzanilla *nf* **1** : chamomile **2** : chamomile tea

manzano *nm* : apple tree

maña *nf* **1** : dexterity, skill **2** : cunning, guile **3 mañas** *or* **malas mañas** *nfpl* : bad habits, vices

mañana *nf* **1** : morning **2** : tomorrow

mañanero, -ra *adj* MATUTINO : morning <rocío mañanero : morning dew>

mañanitas *nfpl Mex* : birthday serenade

mañoso, -sa *adj* **1** HÁBIL : skillful **2** ASTUTO : cunning, crafty **3** : fussy, finicky

mapa *nm* CARTA : map

mapache *nm* : raccoon

mapamundi *nm* : map of the world

maqueta *nf* : model, mock-up

maquillador, -dora *n* : makeup artist

maquillaje *nm* : makeup

maquillarse *vr* : to put on makeup, to make oneself up

máquina *nf* **1** : machine <máquina de coser : sewing machine> <máquina de escribir : typewriter> **2** LOCOMOTORA : engine, locomotive **3** : machine (in politics) **4 a toda máquina** : at full speed

maquinación *nf, pl* **-ciones** : machination, scheme, plot

maquinal *adj* : mechanical, automatic — **maquinalmente** *adv*

maquinar *vt* : to plot, to scheme

maquinaria *nf* **1** : machinery **2** : mechanism, works *pl*

maquinilla *nf* **1** : small machine or device **2** *CA, Car* : typewriter

maquinista *nmf* **1** : machinist **2** : railroad engineer

mar *nmf* **1** : sea <un mar agitado : a rough sea> <hacerse a la mar : to set sail> **2 alta mar** : high seas

maraca *nf* : maraca

maraña *nf* **1** : thicket **2** ENREDO : tangle, mess

marasmo *nm* : paralysis, stagnation

maratón *nm, pl* **-tones** : marathon

maravilla *nf* **1** : wonder, marvel <a las mil maravillas : wonderfully, marvelously> <hacer maravillas : to work wonders> **2** : marigold

maravillar *vt* ASOMBRAR : to astonish, to amaze — **maravillarse** *vr* : to be amazed, to marvel

maravilloso, -sa *adj* ESTUPENDO : wonderful, marvelous — **maravillosamente** *adv*

marbete *nm* **1** ETIQUETA : label, tag **2** *PRi* : registration sticker (of a car)

marca *nf* **1** : mark **2** : brand, make **3** : trademark <marca registrada : registered trademark> **4** : record (in sports) <batir la marca : to beat the record>

marcado, -da *adj* : marked <un marcado contraste : a marked contrast>

marcador *nm* **1** TANTEADOR : scoreboard **2** : marker, felt-tipped pen **3 marcador de libros** : bookmark

marcaje *nm* **1** : scoring (in sports) **2** : guarding (in sports)

marcapasos *nms & pl* : pacemaker

marcar {72} *vt* **1** : to mark **2** : to brand (livestock) **3** : to indicate, to show **4** RESALTAR : to emphasize **5** : to dial (a telephone) **6** : to guard (an opponent) **7** ANOTAR : to score (a goal, a point) — *vi* **1** ANOTAR : to score **2** : to dial

marcha *nf* **1** : march **2** : hike, walk <ir de marcha : to go hiking> **3** : pace, speed <a toda marcha : at top speed> **4** : gear (of an automobile) <marcha atrás : reverse, reverse gear> **5 en ~** : in motion, in gear, under way

marchar *vi* **1** IR : to go, to travel **2** ANDAR : to walk **3** FUNCIONAR : to work, to go **4** : to march — **marcharse** *vr* : to leave

marchitar *vi* : to make wither, to wilt — **marchitarse** *vr* **1** : to wither, to shrivel up, to wilt **2** : to languish, to fade away

marchito, -ta *adj* : withered, faded

marcial *adj* : martial, military

marco *nm* **1** : frame, framework **2** : goalposts *pl* **3** AMBIENTE : setting, atmosphere **4** : mark (unit of currency)

marea *nf* : tide

mareado, -da *adj* **1** : dizzy, lightheaded **2** : queasy, nauseous **3** : seasick

marear *vt* **1 :** to make sick <los gases me marearon : the fumes made me sick> **2 :** to bother, to annoy — **marearse** *vr* **1 :** to get sick, to become nauseated **2 :** to feel dizzy **3 :** to get tipsy

marejada *nf* **1 :** surge, swell (of the sea) **2 :** undercurrent, ferment, unrest

maremoto *nm* **:** tidal wave

mareo *nm* **1 :** dizzy spell **2 :** nausea **3 :** seasickness, motion sickness **4 :** annoyance, vexation

marfil *nm* **:** ivory

margarina *nf* **:** margarine

margarita *nf* **1 :** daisy **2 :** margarita (cocktail)

margen[1] *nf, pl* **márgenes :** bank (of a river), side (of a street)

margen[2] *nm, pl* **márgenes 1 :** edge, border **2 :** margin <margen de ganancia : profit margin>

marginación *nf, pl* **-ciones :** marginalization, exclusion

marginado[1], **-da** *adj* **1** DESHEREDADO **:** outcast, alienated, dispossessed **2 clases marginadas :** underclass

marginado[2], **-da** *n* **:** outcast, misfit

marginal *adj* **:** marginal, fringe

marginalidad *nf* **:** marginality

marginar *vt* **:** to ostracize, to exclude

mariachi *nm* **:** mariachi musician or band

maridaje *nm* **:** marriage, union

maridar *vt* UNIR **:** to marry, to unite

marido *nm* ESPOSO **:** husband

marihuana *or* **mariguana** *or* **marijuana** *nf* **:** marihuana

marimacho *nmf fam* **1 :** mannish woman **2 :** tomboy

marimba *nf* **:** marimba

marina *nf* **1 :** coast, coastal area **2 :** navy, fleet <marina mercante : merchant marine>

marinada *nf* **:** marinade

marinar *vt* **:** to marinate

marinero[1], **-ra** *adj* **1 :** seaworthy **2 :** sea, marine

marinero[2] *nm* **:** sailor

marino[1], **-na** *adj* **:** marine, sea

marino[2] *nm* **:** sailor, seaman

marioneta *nf* TÍTERE **:** puppet, marionette

mariposa *nf* **1 :** butterfly **2 mariposa nocturna :** moth

mariquita[1] *nf* **:** ladybug

mariquita[2] *nm fam* **:** sissy, wimp

mariscal *nm* **1 :** marshal **2 mariscal de campo :** field marshal (in the military), quarterback (in football)

marisco *nm* **1 :** shellfish **2 mariscos** *nmpl* **:** seafood

marisma *nf* **:** marsh, salt marsh

marital *adj* **:** marital, married <la vida marital : married life>

marítimo, -ma *adj* **:** maritime, shipping <la industria marítima : the shipping industry>

marmita *nf* **:** (cooking) pot

mármol *nm* **:** marble

marmóreo, -rea *adj* **:** marble, marmoreal

marmota *nf* **1 :** marmot **2 marmota de América :** woodchuck, groundhog

maroma *nf* **1 :** rope **2 :** acrobatic stunt **3** *Mex* **:** somersault

marque, etc. → **marcar**

marqués, -quesa *n, mpl* **marqueses :** marquis *m*, marquess *m*, marquise *f*, marchioness *f*

marquesina *nf* **:** marquee, canopy

marqueta *nf Mex* **:** block (of chocolate), lump (of sugar or salt)

marranada *nf* **1 :** disgusting thing **2 :** dirty trick

marrano[1], **-na** *adj* **:** filthy, disgusting

marrano[2], **-na** *n* **1** CERDO **:** pig, hog **2 :** dirty pig, slob

marrar *vt* **:** to miss (a target) — *vi* **:** to fail, to go wrong

marras *adv* **1 :** long ago **2 de ~ :** said, aforementioned <el individuo de marras : the individual in question>

marrasquino *nm* **:** maraschino

marrón *adj & nm, pl* **marrones** CASTAÑO **:** brown

marroquí *adj & nmf, pl* **-quíes :** Moroccan

marsopa *nf* **:** porpoise

marsupial *nm* **:** marsupial

marta *nf* **1 :** marten **2 marta cebellina :** sable (animal)

Marte *nm* **:** Mars

martes *nms & pl* **:** Tuesday

martillar *v* **:** to hammer

martillazo *nm* **:** blow with a hammer

martillo *nm* **1 :** hammer **2 martillo neumático :** jackhammer

martinete *nm* **1 :** heron **2 :** pile driver

mártir *nmf* **:** martyr

martirio *nm* **1 :** martyrdom **2 :** ordeal, torment

martirizar {21} *vt* **1 :** to martyr **2** ATORMENTAR **:** to torment

marxismo *nm* **:** Marxism

marxista *adj & nmf* **:** Marxist

marzo *nm* **:** March

mas *conj* PERO **:** but

más[1] *adv* **1 :** more <¿hay algo más grande? : is there anything bigger?> **2 :** most <Luis es el más alto : Luis is the tallest> **3 :** longer <el sabor dura más : the flavor lasts longer> **4 :** rather <más querría andar : I would rather walk> **5 a ~ :** besides, in addition **6 más allá :** further **7 qué . . . más . . . :** what . . ., what a . . . <¡qué día más bonito! : what a beautiful day!>

más[2] *adj* **1 :** more <dáme dos kilos más : give me two more kilos> **2 :** most <la que ganó más dinero : the one who earned the most money> **3 :** else <¿quién más quiere vino? : who else wants wine?>

más[3] *n* **:** plus sign

más[4] *prep* **:** plus <tres más dos es igual a cinco : three plus two equals five>

más[5] *pron* **1 :** more <¿tienes más? : do you have more?> **2 a lo más :** at most **3 de ~ :** extra, excess **4 más o menos :** more or less, approximately **5 por más que :** no matter how much <por más que corras no llegarás a tiempo : no matter how fast you run you won't arrive on time>
masa *nf* **1 :** mass, volume <masa atómica : atomic mass> <producción en masa : mass production> **2 :** dough, batter **3 masas** *nfpl* **:** people, masses <las masas populares : the common people> **4 masa harina** *Mex* **:** corn flour (for tortillas, etc.)
masacrar *vt* **:** to massacre
masacre *nf* **:** massacre
masaje *nm* **:** massage
masajear *vt* **:** to massage
masajista *nmf* **:** masseur *m,* masseuse *f*
mascar {72} *v* MASTICAR **:** to chew
máscara *nf* **1** CARETA **:** mask **2 :** appearance, pretense
mascarada *nf* **:** masquerade
mascarilla *nf* **1 :** mask (in medicine) <mascarilla de oxígeno : oxygen mask> **2 :** facial mask (in cosmetology)
mascota *nf* **:** mascot
masculinidad *nf* **:** masculinity
masculino, -na *adj* **1 :** masculine, male **2 :** manly **3 :** masculine (in grammar)
mascullar *v* **:** to mumble, to mutter
masificado, -da *adj* **:** overcrowded
masilla *nf* **:** putty
masivamente *adv* **:** en masse
masivo, -va *adj* **:** mass <comunicación masiva : mass communication>
masón *nm, pl* **masones** FRANCMASÓN **:** Mason, Freemason
masonería *nf* FRANCMASONERÍA **:** Masonry, Freemasonry
masónico, -ca *adj* **:** Masonic
masoquismo *nm* **:** masochism
masoquista[1] *adj* **:** masochistic
masoquista[2] *nmf* **:** masochist
masque, etc. → mascar
masticar {72} *v* MASCAR **:** to chew, to masticate
mástil *nm* **1 :** mast **2** ASTA **:** flagpole **3 :** neck (of a stringed instrument)
mastín *nm, pl* **mastines :** mastiff
mástique *nm* **:** putty, filler
mastodonte *nm* **:** mastodon
masturbación *nf, pl* **-ciones :** masturbation
masturbarse *vr* **:** to masturbate
mata *nf* **1** ARBUSTO **:** bush, shrub **2 :** plant <mata de tomate : tomato plant> **3 :** sprig, tuft **4 mata de pelo :** mop of hair
matadero *nm* **:** slaughterhouse, abattoir
matado, -da *adj Mex* **:** strenuous, exhausting
matador *nm* TORERO **:** matador, bullfighter
matamoscas *nms & pl* **:** flyswatter
matanza *nf* MASACRE **:** slaughter, butchering
matar *vt* **1 :** to kill **2 :** to slaughter, to butcher **3** APAGAR **:** to extinguish, to put out (fire, light) **4 :** to tone down (colors) **5 :** to pass, to waste (time) **6 :** to trump (in card games) — *vi* **:** to kill — **matarse** *vr* **1 :** to be killed **2** SUICIDARSE **:** to commit suicide **3** *fam* **:** to exhaust oneself <se mató tratando de terminarlo : he knocked himself out trying to finish it>
matasanos *nms & pl fam* **:** quack
matasellar *vt* **:** to cancel (a stamp), to postmark
matasellos *nms & pl* **:** postmark
matatena *nf Mex* **:** jacks
mate[1] *adj* **:** matte, dull
mate[2] *nm* **1 :** maté **2 jaque mate :** checkmate <darle mate a *or* darle jaque mate a : to checkmate>
matemática → matemáticas
matemáticas *nfpl* **:** mathematics, math
matemático[1], **-ca** *adj* **:** mathematical — **matemáticamente** *adv*
matemático[2], **-ca** *n* **:** mathematician
materia *nf* **1 :** matter <materia gris : gray matter> **2 :** material <materia prima : raw material> **3 :** (academic) subject **4 en materia de :** on the subject of, concerning
material[1] *adj* **1 :** material, physical, real **2 daños materiales :** property damage
material[2] *nm* **1 :** material <material de construcción : building material> **2** EQUIPO **:** equipment, gear
materialismo *nm* **:** materialism
materialista[1] *adj* **:** materialistic
materialista[2] *nmf* **1 :** materialist **2** *Mex* **:** truck driver
materializar {21} *vt* **:** to bring to fruition, to realize — **materializarse** *vr* **:** to materialize, to come into being
materialmente *adv* **1 :** materially, physically <materialmente imposible : physically impossible> **2 :** really, absolutely
maternal *adj* **:** maternal, motherly
maternidad *nf* **1 :** maternity, motherhood **2 :** maternity hospital, maternity ward
materno, -na *adj* **:** maternal
matinal *adj* MATUTINO **:** morning <la pálida luz matinal : the pale morning light>
matinée *or* **matiné** *nf* **:** matinee
matiz *nm, pl* **matices 1 :** hue, shade **2 :** nuance
matización *nf, pl* **-ciones 1 :** tinting, toning, shading **2 :** clarification (of a statement)
matizar {21} *vt* **1 :** to tinge, to tint (colors) **2 :** to vary, to modulate (sounds) **3 :** to qualify (statements)
matón *nm, pl* **matones :** thug, bully
matorral *nm* **1 :** thicket **2 :** scrub, scrubland

matraca *nf* **1 :** rattle, noisemaker **2 dar la matraca a :** to pester, to nag

matriarca *nf* **:** matriarch

matriarcado *nm* **:** matriarchy

matrícula *nf* **1 :** list, roll, register **2** INSCRIPCIÓN **:** registration, enrollment **3 :** license plate, registration number

matriculación *nf, pl* **-ciones :** matriculation, registration

matricular *vt* **1** INSCRIBIR **:** to enroll, to register (a person) **2 :** to register (a vehicle) — **matricularse** *vr* **:** to matriculate

matrimonial *adj* **:** marital, matrimonial <la vida matrimonial : married life>

matrimonio *nm* **1 :** marriage, matrimony **2 :** married couple

matriz *nf, pl* **matrices 1 :** uterus, womb **2 :** original, master copy **3 :** main office, headquarters **4 :** stub (of a check) **5 :** matrix <matriz de puntos : dot matrix>

matrona *nf* **:** matron

matronal *adj* **:** matronly

matutino[1], -na *adj* **:** morning <la edición matutina : the morning edition>

matutino[2] *nm* **:** morning paper

maullar {8} *vi* **:** to meow

maullido *nm* **:** meow

mauritano, -na *adj & n* **:** Mauritanian

mausoleo *nm* **:** mausoleum

maxilar *nm* **:** jaw, jawbone

máxima *nf* **:** maxim

máxime *adv* ESPECIALMENTE **:** especially, principally

maximizar {21} *vt* **:** to maximize

máximo[1], -ma *adj* **:** maximum, greatest, highest

máximo[2] *nm* **1 :** maximum **2 al máximo :** to the utmost **3 como ~ :** at the most, at the latest

maya[1] *adj & nmf* **:** Mayan

maya[2] *nmf* **:** Maya, Mayan

mayo *nm* **:** May

mayonesa *nf* **:** mayonnaise

mayor[1] *adj* **1** (*comparative of* **grande**) **:** bigger, larger, greater, elder, older **2** (*superlative of* **grande**) **:** biggest, largest, greatest, eldest, oldest **3 :** grown-up, mature **4 :** main, major **5 mayor de edad :** of (legal) age **6 al por mayor** *or* **por ~ :** wholesale

mayor[2] *nmf* **1 :** major (in the military) **2 :** adult

mayoral *nm* CAPATAZ **:** foreman, overseer

mayordomo *nm* **:** butler, majordomo

mayoreo *nm* **:** wholesale

mayores *nmpl* **:** grown-ups, elders

mayoría *nf* **1 :** majority **2 en su mayoría :** on the whole

mayorista[1] *adj* ALMACENISTA **:** wholesale

mayorista[2] *nmf* **:** wholesaler

mayoritariamente *adv* **:** primarily, chiefly

mayoritario, -ria *adj & n* **:** majority <un consenso mayoritario : a majority consensus>

mayormente *adv* **:** primarily, chiefly

mayúscula *nf* **:** capital letter

mayúsculo, -la *adj* **1 :** capital, uppercase **2 :** huge, terrible <un problema mayúsculo : a huge problem>

maza *nf* **1 :** mace (weapon) **2 :** drumstick **3** *fam* **:** bore, pest

mazacote *nm* **1 :** concrete **2 :** lumpy mess (of food) **3 :** eyesore, crude work of art

mazapán *nm, pl* **-panes :** marzipan

mazmorra *nf* CALABOZO **:** dungeon

mazo *nm* **1 :** mallet **2 :** pestle **3** MANOJO **:** handful, bunch

mazorca *nf* **1** CHOCLO **:** cob, ear of corn **2 pelar la mazorca** *Mex fam* **:** to smile from ear to ear

me *pron* **1 :** me <me vieron : they saw me> **2 :** to me, for me, from me <dame el libro : give me the book> <me lo compró : he bought it for me> <me robaron la cartera : they stole my pocketbook> **3 :** myself, to myself, for myself, from myself <me preparé una buena comida : I cooked myself a good dinner> <me equivoqué : I made a mistake>

mecánica *nf* **:** mechanics

mecánico[1], -ca *adj* **:** mechanical — **mecánicamente** *adv*

mecánico[2], -ca *n* **1 :** mechanic **2 :** technician <mecánico dental : dental technician>

mecanismo *nm* **:** mechanism

mecanización *nf, pl* **-ciones :** mechanization

mecanizar {21} *vt* **:** to mechanize

mecanografía *nf* **:** typing

mecanografiar {85} *vt* **:** to type

mecanógrafo, -fa *n* **:** typist

mecate *nm CA, Mex, Ven* **:** rope, twine, cord

mecedor *nm* **:** glider (seat)

mecedora *nf* **:** rocking chair

mecenas *nmfs & pl* **:** patron (of the arts), sponsor

mecenazgo *nm* PATROCINIO **:** sponsorship, patronage

mecer {86} *vt* **1 :** to rock **2** COLUMPIAR **:** to push (on a swing) — **mecerse** *vr* **:** to rock, to swing, to sway

mecha *nf* **1 :** fuse **2 :** wick **3 mechas** *nfpl* **:** highlights (in hair)

mechero *nm* **1 :** burner **2** *Spain* **:** lighter

mechón *nm, pl* **mechones :** lock (of hair)

medalla *nf* **:** medal, medallion

medallista *nmf* **:** medalist

medallón *nm, pl* **-llones 1 :** medallion **2 :** locket

media *nf* **1** CALCETÍN **:** sock **2 :** average, mean **3 medias** *nfpl* **:** stockings, hose, tights **4 a medias :** by halves, half and half, halfway <ir a medias : to go

halves> <verdad a medias : half-truth>

mediación *nf, pl* **-ciones :** mediation

mediado, -da *adj* **1 :** half full, half empty, half over **2 :** halfway through <mediada la tarea : halfway through the job>

mediador, -dora *n* **:** mediator

mediados *nmpl* **a mediados de :** halfway through, in the middle of <a mediados del mes : towards the middle of the month, mid-month>

medialuna *nf* **1 :** crescent **2 :** croissant, crescent roll

medianamente *adv* **:** fairly, moderately

medianero, -ra *adj* **1 :** dividing **2 :** mediating

medianía *nf* **1 :** middle position **2 :** mediocre person, mediocrity

mediano, -na *adj* **1 :** medium, average <la mediana edad : middle age> **2 :** mediocre

medianoche *nf* **:** midnight

mediante *prep* **:** through, by means of <Dios mediante : God willing>

mediar *vi* **1 :** to mediate **2 :** to be in the middle, to be halfway through **3 :** to elapse, to pass <mediaron cinco años entre el inicio de la guerra y el armisticio : five years passed between the start of the war and the armistice> **4 :** to be a consideration <media el hecho de que cuesta mucho : one must take into account that it is costly> **5 :** to come up, to happen <medió algo urgente : something pressing came up>

mediatizar {21} *vt* **:** to influence, to interfere with

medicación *nf, pl* **-ciones :** medication, treatment

medicamento *nm* **:** medication, medicine, drug

medicar {72} *vt* **:** to medicate — **medicarse** *vr* **:** to take medicine

medicina *nf* **:** medicine

medicinal *adj* **1 :** medicinal **2 :** medicated

medicinar *vt* **:** to give medication to, to dose

medición *nf, pl* **-ciones :** measuring, measurement

médico[1], -ca *adj* **:** medical <una receta médica : a doctor's prescription>

médico[2], -ca *n* DOCTOR **:** doctor, physician

medida *nf* **1 :** measurement, measure <hecho a medida : custom-made> **2 :** measure, step <tomar medidas : to take steps> **3 :** moderation, prudence <sin medida : immoderately> **4 :** extent, degree <en gran medida : to a great extent>

medidor *nm* **:** meter, gauge

medieval *adj* **:** medieval — **medievalista** *nmf*

medievo *nm* → **medioevo**

medio[1] *adv* **1 :** half <está medio dormida : she's half asleep> **2 :** rather, kind of <está medio aburrida esta fiesta : this party is rather boring>

medio[2], -dia *adj* **1 :** half <una media hora : half an hour> <medio hermano : half brother> <a media luz : in the half-light> <son las tres y media : it's half past three, it's three-thirty> **2 :** midway, halfway <a medio camino : halfway there> **3 :** middle <la clase media : the middle class> **4 :** average <la temperatura media : the average temperature>

medio[3] *nm* **1** CENTRO **:** middle, center <en medio de : in the middle of, amid> **2** AMBIENTE **:** milieu, environment **3 :** medium, spiritualist **4 :** means *pl,* way <por medio de : by means of> <los medios de comunicación : the media> **5 medios** *nmpl* **:** means, resources

mediocre *adj* **:** mediocre, average

mediocridad *nf* **:** mediocrity

mediodía *nm* **:** noon, midday

medioevo *nm* **:** Middle Ages

medir {54} *vt* **1 :** to measure **2 :** to weigh, to consider <medir los riesgos : to weigh the risks> — *vi* **:** to measure — **medirse** *vr* **:** to be moderate, to exercise restraint

meditabundo, -da *adj* PENSATIVO **:** pensive, thoughtful

meditación *nf, pl* **-ciones :** meditation, thought

meditar *vi* **:** to meditate, to think <meditar sobre la vida : to contemplate life> — *vt* **1 :** to think over, to consider **2 :** to plan, to work out

meditativo, -va *adj* **:** pensive

mediterráneo, -nea *adj* **:** Mediterranean

medrar *vi* **1** PROSPERAR **:** to prosper, to thrive **2** AUMENTAR **:** to increase, to grow

medro *nm* PROSPERIDAD **:** prosperity, growth

medroso, -sa *adj* **:** fainthearted, fearful

médula *nf* **1 :** marrow, pith **2 médula espinal :** spinal cord

medular *adj* **:** fundamental, core <el punto medular : the crux of the matter>

medusa *nf* **:** jellyfish, medusa

megabyte *nm* **:** megabyte

megáfono *nm* **:** megaphone

megahertzio *nm* **:** megahertz

megatón *nm, pl* **-tones :** megaton

megavatio *nm* **:** megawatt

mejicano → **mexicano**

mejilla *nf* **:** cheek

mejillón *nm, pl* **-llones :** mussel

mejor[1] *adv* **1 :** better <Carla cocina mejor que Ana : Carla cooks better than Ana> **2 :** best <ella es la que lo hace mejor : she's the one who does it best> **3 :** rather <mejor morir que rendirme : I'd rather die than give up> **4 :** it's better that . . . <mejor te

vas : you'd better go> **5 a lo mejor** : maybe, perhaps

mejor[2] *adj* **1** (*comparative of* **bueno**) : better <a falta de algo mejor : for lack of something better> **2** (*comparative of* **bien**) : better <está mucho mejor : he's much better> **3** (*superlative of* **bueno**) : best, the better <mi mejor amigo : my best friend> **4** (*superlative of* **bien**) : best, the better <duermo mejor en un clima seco : I sleep best in a dry climate> **5** PREFERIBLE : preferable, better **6 lo mejor** : the best thing, the best part

mejor[3] *nmf* (*with definite article*) : the better (one), the best (one)

mejora *nf* : improvement

mejoramiento *nm* : improvement

mejorana *nf* : marjoram

mejorar *vt* : to improve, to make better — *vi* : to improve, to get better — **mejorarse** *vr*

mejoría *nf* : improvement, betterment

mejunje *nm* : concoction, brew

melancolía *nf* : melancholy, sadness

melancólico, -ca *adj* : melancholy, sad

melanoma *nm* : melanoma

melaza *nf* : molasses

maleficio *nm* : curse, spell

melena *nf* **1** : mane **2** : long hair **3 melenas** *nfpl* GREÑAS : shaggy hair, mop

melenudo[1], **-da** *adj fam* : longhaired

melenudo[2], **-da** *n* GREÑUDO : longhair, hippie

melindres *nmpl* **1** : affectation, airs *pl* **2** : finickiness

melindroso[1], **-sa** *adj* **1** : affected **2** : fussy, finicky

melindroso[2], **-sa** *n* : finicky person, fussbudget

melisa *nf* : lemon balm

mella *nf* **1** : dent, nick **2 hacer mella en** : to have an effect on, to make an impression on

mellado, -da *adj* **1** : chipped, dented **2** : gap-toothed

mellar *vt* : to dent, to nick

mellizo, -za *adj & n* GEMELO : twin

melocotón *nm, pl* **-tones** : peach

melodía *nf* : melody, tune

melódico, -ca *adj* : melodic

melodioso, -sa *adj* : melodious

melodrama *nm* : melodrama

melodramático, -ca *adj* : melodramatic

melón *nm, pl* **melones** : melon, cantaloupe

meloso, -sa *adj* **1** : honeyed, sweet **2** EMPALAGOSO : cloying, saccharine

membrana *nf* **1** : membrane **2 membrana interdigital** : web, webbing (of a bird's foot) — **membranoso, -sa** *adj*

membresía *nf* : membership, members *pl*

membrete *nm* : letterhead, heading

membrillo *nm* : quince

membrudo, -da *adj* FORNIDO : muscular, well-built

memez *nf, pl* **memeces** : stupid thing

memo, -ma *adj* : silly, stupid

memorabilia *nf* : memorabilia

memorable *adj* : memorable

memorándum *or* **memorando** *nm, pl* **-dums** *or* **-dos 1** : memorandum, memo **2** : memo book, appointment book

memoria *nf* **1** : memory <de memoria : by heart> <hacer memoria : to try to remember> <traer a la memoria : to call to mind> **2** RECUERDO : remembrance, memory <su memoria perdurará para siempre : his memory will live forever> **3** : report <memoria anual : annual report> **4 memorias** *nfpl* : memoirs

memorizar {21} *vt* : to memorize — **memorización** *nf*

mena *nf* : ore

menaje *nm* : household goods *pl*, furnishings *pl*

mención *nf, pl* **-ciones** : mention

mencionar *vt* : to mention, to refer to

mendaz *adj, pl* **mendaces** : mendacious, lying

mendicidad *nf* : begging

mendigar {52} *vi* : to beg — *vt* : to beg for

mendigo, -ga *n* LIMOSNERO : beggar

mendrugo *nm* : crust (of bread)

menear *vt* **1** : to shake (one's head) **2** : to sway, to wiggle (one's hips) **3** : to wag (a tail) **4** : to stir (a liquid) — **menearse** *vr* **1** : to wiggle one's hips **2** : to fidget

meneo *nm* **1** : movement **2** : shake, toss **3** : swaying, wagging, wiggling **4** : stir, stirring

menester *nm* **1** : activity, occupation, duties *pl* **2 ser menester** : to be necessary <es menester que vengas : you must come>

mengano, -na *n* → **fulano**

mengua *nf* **1** : decrease, decline **2** : lack, want **3** : discredit, dishonor

menguar *vt* : to diminish, to lessen — *vi* **1** : to decline, to decrease **2** : to wane — **menguante** *adj*

meningitis *nf* : meningitis

menisco *nm* : meniscus, cartilage

menjurje *nm* → **mejunje**

menopausia *nf* : menopause

menor[1] *adj* **1** (*comparative of* **pequeño**) : smaller, lesser, younger **2** (*superlative of* **pequeño**) : smallest, least, youngest **3** : minor **4 al por menor** : retail **5 ser menor de edad** : to be a minor, to be underage

menor[2] *nmf* : minor, juvenile

menos[1] *adv* **1** : less <llueve menos en agosto : it rains less in August> **2** : least <el coche menos caro : the least expensive car> **3 ~ de** : less than, fewer than

menos[2] *adj* **1** : less, fewer <tengo más trabajo y menos tiempo : I have more

work and less time> **2 :** least, fewest <la clase que tiene menos estudiantes : the class that has the fewest students>

menos[3] *prep* **1** SALVO, EXCEPTO **:** except **2 :** minus <quince menos cuatro son once : fifteen minus four is eleven>

menos[4] *pron* **1 :** less, fewer <no deberías aceptar menos : you shouldn't accept less> **2 al menos** *or* **por lo menos :** at least **3 a menos que :** unless

menoscabar *vt* **1 :** to lessen, to diminish **2 :** to disgrace, to discredit **3** PERJUDICAR **:** to harm, to damage

menoscabo *nm* **1 :** lessening, diminishing **2 :** disgrace, discredit **3 :** harm, damage

menospreciar *vt* **1** DESPRECIAR **:** to scorn, to look down on **2 :** to underestimate, to undervalue

menosprecio *nm* DESPRECIO **:** contempt, scorn

mensaje *nm* **:** message

mensajero, -ra *n* **:** messenger

menso, -sa *adj Mex fam* **:** foolish, stupid

menstrual *adj* **:** menstrual

menstruar {3} *vi* **:** to menstruate — **menstruación** *nf*

mensual *adj* **:** monthly

mensualidad *nf* **1 :** monthly payment, installment **2 :** monthly salary

mensualmente *adv* **:** every month, monthly

mensurable *adj* **:** measurable

menta *nf* **1 :** mint, peppermint **2 menta verde :** spearmint

mentado, -da *adj* **1 :** aforementioned **2** FAMOSO **:** renowned, famous

mental *adj* **:** mental, intellectual — **mentalmente** *adv*

mentalidad *nf* **:** mentality

mentar {55} *vt* **1 :** to mention, to name **2 mentar la madre a** *fam* **:** to insult, to swear at

mente *nf* **:** mind <tener en mente : to have in mind>

mentecato[1], **-ta** *adj* **:** foolish, simple

mentecato[2], **-ta** *n* **:** fool, idiot

mentir {76} *vi* **:** to lie

mentira *nf* **:** lie

mentiroso[1], **-sa** *adj* EMBUSTERO **:** lying, untruthful

mentiroso[2], **-sa** *n* EMBUSTERO **:** liar

mentís *nm, pl* **mentises :** denial, repudiation <dar el mentís a : to deny, to refute>

mentol *nm* **:** menthol

mentón *nm, pl* **mentones** BARBILLA **:** chin

mentor *nm* **:** mentor, counselor

menú *nm, pl* **menús :** menu

menudear *vi* **:** to occur frequently — *vt* **:** to do repeatedly

menudencia *nf* **1 :** trifle **2 menudencias** *nfpl* **:** giblets

menudeo *nm* **:** retail, retailing

menudillos *nmpl* **:** giblets

menudo[1], **-da** *adj* **1 :** minute, small **2 a ~** FRECUENTEMENTE **:** often, frequently

menudo[2] *nm* **1** *Mex* **:** tripe stew **2 menudos** *nmpl* **:** giblets

meñique *nm or* **dedo meñique :** little finger, pinkie

meollo *nm* **1** MÉDULA **:** marrow **2** SESO **:** brains *pl* **3** ENTRAÑA **:** essence, core <el meollo del asunto : the heart of the matter>

mequetrefe *nm fam* **:** good-for-nothing

mercachifle *nm* **:** peddler, hawker

mercadeo *nm* **:** marketing

mercadería *nf* **:** merchandise, goods *pl*

mercado *nm* **:** market <mercado de trabajo *or* mercado laboral : labor market> <mercado de valores *or* mercado bursátil : stock market>

mercadotecnia *nf* **:** marketing

mercancía *nf* **:** merchandise, goods *pl*

mercante *nmf* **:** merchant, dealer

mercantil *adj* COMERCIAL **:** commercial, mercantile

merced *nf* **1 :** favor **2 ~ a :** thanks to, due to **3 a merced de :** at the mercy of

mercenario, -ria *adj & n* **:** mercenary

mercería *nf* **:** notions store

mercurio *nm* **:** mercury

Mercurio *nm* **:** Mercury (planet)

merecedor, -dora *adj* **:** deserving, worthy

merecer {53} *vt* **:** to deserve, to merit — *vi* **:** to be worthy

merecidamente *adv* **:** rightfully, deservedly

merecido *nm* **:** something merited, due <recibieron su merecido : they got their just deserts>

merecimiento *nm* **:** merit, worth

merendar {55} *vi* **:** to have an afternoon snack — *vt* **:** to have as an afternoon snack

merendero *nm* **1 :** lunchroom, snack bar **2 :** picnic area

merengue *nm* **1 :** meringue **2 :** merengue (dance)

meridiano[1], **-na** *adj* **1 :** midday **2 :** crystal clear

meridiano[2] *nm* **:** meridian

meridional *adj* SUREÑO **:** southern

merienda *nf* **:** afternoon snack, tea

mérito *nm* **:** merit

meritorio[1], **-ria** *adj* **:** deserving, meritorious

meritorio[2], **-ria** *n* **:** intern, trainee

merluza *nf* **:** hake

merma *nf* **1 :** decrease, cut **2 :** waste, loss

mermar *vi* **:** to decrease, to diminish — *vt* **:** to reduce, to cut down

mermelada *nf* **:** marmalade, jam

mero[1], **-ra** *adv Mex fam* **1 :** nearly, almost <ya mero me caí : I almost fell> **2 :** just, exactly <aquí mero : right here>

mero[2], **-ra** *adj* **1 :** mere, simple **2** *Mex fam* (*used as an intensifier*) **:** very <en el mero centro : in the very center of town>
mero[3] *nm* **:** grouper
merodeador, -dora *n* **1 :** marauder **2 :** prowler
merodear *vi* **1 :** to maraud, to pillage **2 :** to prowl around, to skulk
mes *nm* **:** month
mesa *nf* **1 :** table **2 :** committee, board
mesada *nf* **:** allowance, pocket money
mesarse *vr* **:** to pull at <mesarse los cabellos : to tear one's hair>
mesero, -ra *n* CAMARERO **:** waiter, waitress *f*
meseta *nf* **:** plateau, tableland
Mesías *nm* **:** Messiah
mesón *nm, pl* **mesones :** inn
mesonero, -ra *nm* **:** innkeeper
mestizo[1], **-za** *adj* **1 :** of mixed ancestry **2** HÍBRIDO **:** hybrid
mestizo[2], **-za** *n* **:** person of mixed ancestry
mesura *nf* **1** MODERACIÓN **:** moderation, discretion **2** CORTESÍA **:** courtesy **3** GRAVEDAD **:** seriousness, dignity
mesurado, -da *adj* COMEDIDO **:** moderate, restrained
mesurar *vt* **:** to moderate, to restrain, to temper — **mesurarse** *vr* **:** to restrain oneself
meta *nf* **:** goal, objective
metabólico, -ca *adj* **:** metabolic
metabolismo *nm* **:** metabolism
metabolizar {21} *vt* **:** to metabolize
metafísica *nf* **:** metaphysics
metafísico, -ca *adj* **:** metaphysical
metáfora *nf* **:** metaphor
metafórico, -ca *adj* **:** metaphoric, metaphorical
metal *nm* **1 :** metal **2 :** brass section (in an orchestra)
metálico, -ca *adj* **:** metallic, metal
metalistería *nf* **:** metalworking
metalurgia *nf* **:** metallurgy
metalúrgico[1], **-ca** *adj* **:** metallurgical
metalúrgico[2], **-ca** *n* **:** metallurgist
metamorfosis *nfs & pl* **:** metamorphosis
metano *nm* **:** methane
meteórico, -ca *adj* **:** meteoric
meteorito *nm* **:** meteorite
meteoro *nm* **:** meteor
meteorología *nf* **:** meteorology
meteorológico, -ca *adj* **:** meteorologic, meteorological
meteorólogo, -ga *n* **:** meteorologist
meter *vt* **1 :** to put (in) <metieron su dinero en el banco : they put their money in the bank> **2 :** to fit, to squeeze <puedes meter dos líneas más en esa página : you can fit two more lines on that page> **3 :** to place (in a job) <lo metieron de barrendero : they got him a job as a street sweeper> **4 :** to involve <lo metió en un buen lío : she got him in an awful mess> **5 :** to make, to cause <meten demasiado ruido : they make too much noise> **6 :** to spread (a rumor) **7 :** to strike (a blow) **8 :** to take up, to take in (clothing) **9 a todo meter :** at top speed — **meterse** *vr* **1 :** to get into, to enter **2** *fam* **:** to meddle <no te metas en lo que no te importa : mind your own business> **3 ~ con** *fam* **:** to pick a fight with, to provoke <no te metas conmigo : don't mess with me>
metiche[1] *adj Mex fam* **:** nosy
metiche[2] *nmf Mex fam* **:** busybody
meticulosidad *nf* **:** thoroughness, meticulousness
meticuloso, -sa *adj* **:** meticulous, thorough — **meticulosamente** *adv*
metida *nf* **metida de pata** *fam* **:** blunder, gaffe, blooper
metódico, -ca *adj* **:** methodical — **metódicamente** *adv*
metodista *adj & nmf* **:** Methodist
método *nm* **:** method
metodología *nf* **:** methodology
metomentodo *nmf fam* **:** busybody
metralla *nf* **:** shrapnel
metralleta *nf* **:** submachine gun
métrico, -ca *adj* **1 :** metric **2 cinta métrica :** tape measure
metro *nm* **1 :** meter **2 :** subway
metrónomo *nm* **:** metronome
metrópoli *nf or* **metrópolis** *nfs & pl* **:** metropolis
metropolitano, -na *adj* **:** metropolitan
mexicanismo *nm* **:** Mexican word or expression
mexicano, -na *adj & n* **:** Mexican
mexicoamericano, -na *adj & n* **:** Mexican-American
meza, etc. → **mecer**
mezcla *nf* **1 :** mixing **2 :** mixture, blend **3 :** mortar (masonry material)
mezclar *vt* **1 :** to mix, to blend **2 :** to mix up, to muddle **3** INVOLUCRAR **:** to involve — **mezclarse** *vr* **1 :** to get mixed up (in) **2 :** to mix, to mingle (socially)
mezclilla *nf Chile, Mex* **:** denim <pantalones de mezclilla : jeans>
mezcolanza *nf* **:** jumble, hodgepodge
mezquindad *nf* **1 :** meanness, stinginess **2 :** petty deed, mean action
mezquino[1], **-na** *adj* **1 :** mean, petty **2 :** stingy **3 :** paltry
mezquino[2] *nm Mex* **:** wart
mezquita *nf* **:** mosque
mezquite *nm* **:** mesquite
mi *adj* **:** my
mí *pron* **1 :** me <es para mí : it's for me> <a mí no me importa : it doesn't matter to me> **2 mí mismo, mí misma :** myself
miasma *nm* **:** miasma
miau *nm* **:** meow
mica *nf* **:** mica
mico *nm* **:** monkey, long-tailed monkey
micra *nf* **:** micron
microbio *nm* **:** microbe, germ
microbiología *nf* **:** microbiology

microbiólogico, -ca *adj* : microbiological
microbús *nm, pl* **-buses** : minibus
microcomputadora *nf* : microcomputer
microcosmos *nms & pl* : microcosm
microficha *nf* : microfiche
microfilm *nm, pl* **-films** : microfilm
micrófono *nm* : microphone
micrómetro *nm* : micrometer
microonda *nf* : microwave
microondas *nms & pl* : microwave, microwave oven
microordenador *nm Spain* : microcomputer
microorganismo *nm* : microorganism
microprocesador *nm* : microprocessor
microscópico, -ca *adj* : microscopic
microscopio *nm* : microscope
mide, etc. → **medir**
miedo *nm* **1** TEMOR : fear <le tiene miedo al perro : he's scared of the dog> <tenían miedo de hablar : they were afraid to speak> **2 dar miedo** : to frighten
miedoso, -sa *adj* TEMEROSO : fearful
miel *nf* : honey
miembro *nm* **1** : member **2** EXTREMIDAD : limb, extremity
mienta, etc. → **mentar**
miente, etc. → **mentir**
mientras[1] *adv* **1** *or* **mientras tanto** : meanwhile, in the meantime **2 mientras más** : the more <mientras más como, más quiero : the more I eat, the more I want>
mientras[2] *conj* **1** : while, as <roncaba mientras dormía : he snored while he was sleeping> **2** : as long as <luchará mientras pueda : he will fight as long as he is able> **3 mientras que** : while, whereas <él es alto mientras que ella es muy baja : he is tall, whereas she is very short>
miércoles *nms & pl* : Wednesday
miga *nf* **1** : crumb **2 hacer buenas (malas) migas con** : to get along well (poorly) with
migaja *nf* **1** : crumb **2 migajas** *nfpl* SOBRAS : leftovers, scraps
migración *nf, pl* **-ciones** : migration
migrante *nmf* : migrant
migraña *nf* : migraine
migratorio, -ria *adj* : migratory
mijo *nm* : millet
mil[1] *adj* : thousand
mil[2] *nm* : one thousand, a thousand
milagro *nm* : miracle <de milagro : miraculously>
milagroso, -sa *adj* : miraculous, marvelous — **milagrosamente** *adv*
milenio *nm* : millennium
milésimo, -ma *adj* : thousandth — **milésimo** *n*
milicia *nf* **1** : militia **2** : military service
miligramo *nm* : milligram
mililitro *nm* : milliliter
milímetro *nm* : millimeter
militancia *nf* : militancy
militante[1] *adj* : militant
militante[2] *nmf* : militant, activist
militar[1] *vi* **1** : to serve (in the military) **2** : to be active (in politics)
militar[2] *adj* : military
militar[3] *nmf* SOLDADO : soldier
militarizar {21} *vt* : to militarize
milla *nf* : mile
millar *nm* : thousand
millón *nm, pl* **millones** : million
millonario, -ria *n* : millionaire
millonésimo[1], **-ma** *adj* : millionth
millonésimo[2] *nm* : millionth
mil millones *nms & pl* : billion
milpa *nf CA, Mex* : cornfield
milpiés *nms & pl* : millipede
mimar *vt* CONSENTIR : to pamper, to spoil
mimbre *nm* : wicker
mimeógrafo *nm* : mimeograph
mímica *nf* **1** : mime, sign language **2** IMITACIÓN : mimicry
mimo *nm* **1** : pampering, indulgence <hacerle mimos a alguien : to pamper someone> **2** : mime
mimoso, -sa *adj* **1** : fussy, finicky **2** : affectionate, clinging
mina *nf* **1** : mine **2** : lead (for pencils)
minar *vt* **1** : to mine **2** DEBILITAR : to undermine
minarete *nm* ALMINAR : minaret
mineral *adj & nm* : mineral
minería *nf* : mining
minero[1], **-ra** *adj* : mining
minero[2], **-ra** *n* : miner, mine worker
miniatura *nf* : miniature
minicomputadora *nf* : minicomputer
minifalda *nf* : miniskirt
minifundio *nm* : small farm
minimizar {21} *vt* : to minimize
mínimo[1], **-ma** *adj* **1** : minimum <salario mínimo : minimum wage> **2** : least, smallest **3** : very small, minute
mínimo[2] *nm* **1** : minimum, least amount **2** : modicum, small amount **3 como ~** : at least
minino, -na *n fam* : pussy, pussycat
miniserie *nf* : miniseries
ministerial *adj* : ministerial
ministerio *nm* : ministry, department
ministro, -tra *n* : minister, secretary <primer ministro : prime minister> <Ministro de Defensa : Secretary of Defense>
minivan [ˌminiˈban, -ˈvan] *nf, pl* **-vanes** : minivan
minoría *nf* : minority
minorista[1] *adj* : retail
minorista[2] *nmf* : retailer
minoritario, -ria *adj* : minority
mintió, etc. → **mentir**
minuciosamente *adv* **1** : minutely **2** : in great detail **3** : thoroughly, meticulously
minucioso, -sa *adj* **1** : minute **2** DETALLADO : detailed **3** : thorough, meticulous
minué *nm* : minuet

minúsculo, -la *adj* DIMINUTO : tiny, miniscule

minusvalía *nf* : disability, handicap

minusválido[1], -da *adj* : handicapped, disabled

minusválido[2], -da *n* : handicapped person

minuta *nf* **1** BORRADOR : rough draft **2** : bill, fee

minutero *nm* : minute hand

minuto *nm* : minute

mío[1], mía *adj* **1** : my, of mine <¡Dios mío! : my God!, good heavens!> <una amiga mía : a friend of mine> **2** : mine <es mío : it's mine>

mío[2], mía *pron* (*with definite article*) : mine, my own <tus zapatos son iguales a los míos : your shoes are just like mine>

miope *adj* : nearsighted, myopic

miopía *nf* : myopia, nearsightedness

mira *nf* **1** : sight (of a firearm or instrument) **2** : aim, objective <con miras a : with the intention of, with a view to> <de amplias miras : broadminded> <poner la mira en : to aim at, to aspire to>

mirada *nf* **1** : look, glance, gaze **2** EXPRESIÓN : look, expression <una mirada de sorpresa : a look of surprise>

mirado, -da *adj* **1** : cautious, careful **2** : considerate **3 bien mirado** : well thought of **4 mal mirado** : disliked, disapproved of

mirador *nm* : balcony, lookout, vantage point

miramiento *nm* **1** CONSIDERACIÓN : consideration, respect **2 sin miramientos** : without due consideration, carelessly

mirar *vt* **1** : to look at **2** OBSERVAR : to watch **3** REFLEXIONAR : to consider, to think over — *vi* **1** : to look **2** : to face, to overlook **3 ~ por** : to look after, to look out for — **mirarse** *vr* **1** : to look at oneself **2** : to look at each other

mirasol *nm* GIRASOL : sunflower

miríada *nf* : myriad

mirlo *nm* : blackbird

mirra *nf* : myrrh

mirto *nm* ARRAYÁN : myrtle

misa *nf* : Mass

misantropía *nf* : misanthropy

misantrópico, -ca *adj* : misanthropic

misántropo, -pa *n* : misanthrope

miscelánea *nf* : miscellany

misceláneo, -nea *adj* : miscellaneous

miserable *adj* **1** LASTIMOSO : miserable, wretched **2** : paltry, meager **3** MEZQUINO : stingy, miserly **4** : despicable, vile

miseria *nf* **1** POBREZA : poverty **2** : misery, suffering **3** : pittance, meager amount

misericordia *nf* COMPASIÓN : mercy, compassion

misericordioso, -sa *adj* : merciful

mísero, -ra *adj* **1** : wretched, miserable **2** : stingy **3** : paltry, meager

misil *nm* : missile

misión *nf, pl* **misiones** : mission

misionero, -ra *adj & n* : missionary

misiva *nf* : missive, letter

mismísimo, -ma *adj* (*used as an intensifier*) : very, selfsame <el mismísimo día : that very same day>

mismo[1] *adv* (*used as an intensifier*) : right, exactly <hazlo ahora mismo : do it right now> <te llamará hoy mismo : he'll definitely call you today>

mismo[2], -ma *adj* **1** : same **2** (*used as an intensifier*) : very <en ese mismo momento : at that very moment> **3** : oneself <lo hizo ella misma : she made it herself> **4 por lo mismo** : for that reason

misoginia *nf* : misogyny

misógino *nm* : misogynist

misterio *nm* : mystery

misterioso, -sa *adj* : mysterious — **misteriosamente** *adv*

misticismo *nm* : mysticism

místico[1], -ca *adj* : mystic, mystical

místico[2], -ca *n* : mystic

mitad *nf* **1** : half <mitad y mitad : half and half> **2** MEDIO : middle <a mitad de : halfway through> <por la mitad : in half>

mítico, -ca *adj* : mythical, mythic

mitigar {52} *vt* ALIVIAR : to mitigate, to alleviate — **mitigación** *nf*

mitin *nm, pl* **mítines** : (political) meeting, rally

mito *nm* LEYENDA : myth, legend

mitología *nm* : mythology

mitológico, -ca *adj* : mythological

mitosis *nfs & pl* : mitosis

mitra *nf* : miter (bishop's hat)

mixto, -ta *adj* **1** : mixed, joint **2** : coeducational

mixtura *nf* : mixture, blend

mnemónico, -ca *adj* : mnemonic

mobiliario *nm* : furniture

mocasín *nm, pl* **-sines** : moccasin

mocedad *nf* **1** JUVENTUD : youth **2** : youthful prank

mochila *nf* MORRAL : backpack, knapsack

moción *nf, pl* **-ciones 1** MOVIMIENTO : motion, movement **2** : motion (to a court or assembly)

moco *nm* **1** : mucus **2** *fam* : snot <limpiarse los mocos : to wipe one's (runny) nose>

mocoso, -sa *n* : kid, brat

moda *nf* **1** : fashion, style **2 a la moda** *or* **de ~** : in style, fashionable **3 moda pasajera** : fad

modales *nmpl* : manners

modalidad *nf* **1** CLASE : kind, type **2** MANERA : way, manner

modelar *vt* : to model, to mold — **modelarse** *vr* : to model oneself after, to emulate

modelo[1] *adj* : model <una casa modelo : a model home>
modelo[2] *nm* : model, example, pattern
modelo[3] *nmf* : model, mannequin
módem *or* **modem** ['moðɛm] *nm* : modem
moderación *nf, pl* **-ciones** MESURA : moderation
moderado, -da *adj & n* : moderate — **moderadamente** *adv*
moderador, -dora *n* : moderator, chair
moderar *vt* **1** TEMPERAR : to temper, to moderate **2** : to curb, to reduce <moderar gastos : to curb spending> **3** PRESIDIR : to chair (a meeting) — **moderarse** *vr* **1** : to restrain oneself **2** : to diminish, to calm down
modernidad *nf* **1** : modernity, modernness **2** : modern age
modernismo *nm* : modernism
modernista[1] *adj* : modernist, modernistic
modernista[2] *nmf* : modernist
modernizar {21} *vt* : to modernize — **modernización** *nf*
moderno, -na *adj* : modern, up-to-date
modestia *nf* : modesty
modesto, -ta *adj* : modest — **modestamente** *adv*
modificación *nf, pl* **-ciones** : alteration
modificante *nm* : modifier
modificar {72} *vt* ALTERAR : to modify, to alter, to adapt
modismo *nm* : idiom
modista *nmf* **1** : dressmaker **2** : fashion designer
modo *nm* **1** MANERA : way, manner, mode <de un modo u otro : one way or another> <a mi modo de ver : to my way of thinking> **2** : mood (in grammar) **3** : mode (in music) **4 a modo de** : by way of, in the manner of, like <a modo de ejemplo : by way of example> **5 de cualquier modo** : in any case, anyway **6 de modo que** : so, in such a way that **7 de todos modos** : in any case, anyway **8 en cierto modo** : in a way, to a certain extent
modorra *nf* : drowsiness, lethargy
modular[1] *v* : to modulate — **modulación** *nf*
modular[2] *adj* : modular
módulo *nm* : module, unit
mofa *nf* **1** : mockery, ridicule **2 hacer mofa de** : to make fun of, to ridicule
mofarse *vr* **~ de** : to scoff at, to make fun of
mofeta *nf* ZORRILLO : skunk
mofle *nm CA, Mex* : muffler (of a car)
moflete *nm fam* : fat cheek
mofletudo, -da *adj fam* : fat-cheeked, chubby
mohín *nm, pl* **mohines** : grimace, face
mohino, -na *adj* : gloomy, melancholy
moho *nm* **1** : mold, mildew **2** : rust
mohoso, -sa *adj* **1** : moldy **2** : rusty
moisés *nm, pl* **moiseses** : bassinet, cradle
mojado[1], **-da** *adj* : wet
mojado[2], **-da** *n Mex fam* : illegal immigrant
mojar *vt* **1** : to wet, to moisten **2** : to dunk — **mojarse** *vr* : to get wet
mojigatería *nf* **1** : hypocrisy **2** GAZMOÑERÍA : primness, prudery
mojigato[1], **-ta** *adj* : prudish, prim — **mojigatamente** *adv*
mojigato[2], **-ta** *n* : prude, prig
mojón *nm, pl* **mojones** : boundary stone, marker
molar *nm* MUELA : molar
molcajete *nm Mex* : mortar
molde *nm* **1** : mold, form **2 letras de molde** : printing, block lettering
moldear *vt* **1** FORMAR : to mold, to shape **2** : to cast
moldura *nf* : molding
mole[1] *nm Mex* **1** : spicy sauce made with chilies and usually chocolate **2** : meat served with mole sauce
mole[2] *nf* : mass, bulk
molécula *nf* : molecule — **molecular** *adj*
moler {47} *vt* **1** : to grind, to crush **2** CANSAR : to exhaust, to wear out
molestar *vt* **1** FASTIDIAR : to annoy, to bother **2** : to disturb, to disrupt — *vi* : to be a nuisance — **molestarse** *vr* **~ en** : to take the trouble to
molestia *nf* **1** FASTIDIO : annoyance, bother, nuisance **2** : trouble <se tomó la molestia de investigar : she took the trouble to investigate> **3** MALESTAR : discomfort
molesto, -ta *adj* **1** ENOJADO : bothered, annoyed **2** FASTIDIOSO : bothersome, annoying
molestoso, -sa *adj* : bothersome, annoying
molido, -da *adj* **1** MACHACADO : ground, crushed **2 estar molido** : to be exhausted
molinero, -ra *n* : miller
molinillo *nm* : grinder, mill <molinillo de café : coffee grinder>
molino *nm* **1** : mill **2 molino de viento** : windmill
molla *nf* : soft fleshy part, flesh (of fruit), lean part (of meat)
molleja *nf* : gizzard
molusco *nm* : mollusk
momentáneamente *adv* : momentarily
momentáneo, -nea *adj* **1** : momentary **2** TEMPORARIO : temporary
momento *nm* **1** : moment, instant <espera un momentito : wait just a moment> **2** : time, period of time <momentos difíciles : hard times> **3** : present, moment <los atletas del momento : the athletes of the moment, today's popular athletes> **4** : momentum **5 al momento** : right away, at once **6 de ~** : at the moment, for the moment **7 de un momento a otro** : any time now **8 por momentos** : at times

momia *nf* : mummy
monaguillo *nm* ACÓLITO : altar boy
monarca *nmf* : monarch
monarquía *nf* : monarchy
monárquico, -ca *n* : monarchist
monasterio *nm* : monastery
monástico, -ca *adj* : monastic
mondadientes *nms & pl* PALILLO : toothpick
mondar *vt* : to peel
mondongo *nm* ENTRAÑAS : innards *pl,* insides *pl,* guts *pl*
moneda *nf* **1** : coin **2** : money, currency
monedero *nm* : change purse
monetario, -ria *adj* : monetary, financial
mongol, -gola *adj & n* : Mongol, Mongolian
monitor[1], **-tora** *n* : instructor (in sports)
monitor[2] *nm* : monitor <monitor de televisión : television monitor>
monitorear *vt* : to monitor
monja *nf* : nun
monje *nm* : monk
mono[1], **-na** *adj fam* : lovely, pretty, cute, darling
mono[2], **-na** *n* : monkey
monóculo *nm* : monocle
monogamia *nf* : monogamy
monógamo -ma *adj* : monogamous
monografía *nf* : monograph
monograma *nm* : monogram
monolingüe *adj* : monolingual
monolítico, -ca *adj* : monolithic
monolito *nm* : monolith
monólogo *nm* : monologue
monomanía *nf* : obsession
monopatín *nm, pl* **-tines** : scooter
monopolio *nm* : monopoly
monopolizar {21} *vt* : to monopolize — **monopolización** *nf*
monosilábico, -ca *adj* : monosyllabic
monosílabo *nm* : monosyllable
monoteísmo *nm* : monotheism
monoteísta[1] *adj* : monotheistic
monoteísta[2] *nmf* : monotheist
monotonía *nf* **1** : monotony **2** : monotone
monótono, -na *adj* : monotonous — **monótonamente** *adv*
monóxido *nm* : monoxide <monóxido de carbono : carbon monoxide>
monserga *nf* : gibberish, drivel
monstruo *nm* : monster
monstruosidad *nf* : monstrosity
monstruoso, -sa *adj* : monstrous — **monstruosamente** *adv*
monta *nf* **1** : sum, total **2** : importance, value <de poca monta : unimportant, insignificant>
montaje *nm* **1** : assembling, assembly **2** : montage
montante *nm* : transom, fanlight
montaña *nf* **1** MONTE : mountain **2** **montaña rusa** : roller coaster
montañero, -ra *n* : mountaineer, mountain climber
montañoso, -sa *adj* : mountainous
montar *vt* **1** : to mount **2** ESTABLECER : to set up, to establish **3** ARMAR : to assemble, to put together **4** : to edit (a film) **5** : to stage, to put on (a show) **6** : to cock (a gun) **7** **montar en bicicleta** : to get on a bicycle **8** **montar a caballo** CABALGAR : to ride horseback
monte *nm* **1** MONTAÑA : mountain, mount **2** : woodland, scrubland <monte bajo : underbrush> **3** : outskirts (of a town), surrounding country **4** **monte de piedad** : pawnshop
montés *adj, pl* **monteses** : wild (of animals or plants)
montículo *nm* **1** : mound, heap **2** : hillock, knoll
monto *nm* : amount, total
montón *nm, pl* **-tones** **1** : heap, pile **2** *fam* : ton, load <un montón de preguntas : a ton of questions> <montones de gente : loads of people>
montura *nf* **1** : mount (horse) **2** : saddle, tack **3** : setting, mounting (of jewelry) **4** : frame (of glasses)
monumental *adj fam* **1** : tremendous, terrific **2** : massive, huge
monumento *nm* : monument
monzón *nm, pl* **monzones** : monsoon
moño *nm* **1** : bun (chignon) **2** LAZO : bow, knot <corbata de moño : bow tie>
moquear *vi* : to snivel
moquillo *nm* : distemper
mora *nf* **1** : blackberry **2** : mulberry
morada *nf* RESIDENCIA : dwelling, abode
morado[1], **-da** *adj* : purple
morado[2] *nm* : purple
morador, -dora *n* : dweller, inhabitant
moral[1] *adj* : moral — **moralmente** *adv*
moral[2] *nf* **1** MORALIDAD : ethics, morality, morals *pl* **2** ÁNIMO : morale, spirits *pl*
moraleja *nf* : moral (of a story)
moralidad *nf* : morality
moralista[1] *adj* : moralistic
moralista[2] *nmf* : moralist
morar *vi* : to dwell, to reside
moratoria *nf* : moratorium
morboso, -sa *adj* : morbid — **morbosidad** *nf*
morcilla *nf* : blood sausage, blood pudding
mordacidad *nf* : bite, sharpness
mordaz *adj* : caustic, scathing
mordaza *nf* **1** : gag **2** : clamp
mordedura *nf* : bite (of an animal)
morder {47} *v* : to bite
mordida *nf* **1** : bite **2** *CA, Mex* : bribe, payoff
mordisco *nm* : bite, nibble
mordisquear *vt* : to nibble (on), to bite
morena *nf* **1** : moraine **2** : moray (eel)
moreno[1], **-na** *adj* **1** : brunette **2** : dark, dark-skinned
moreno[2], **-na** *n* **1** : brunette **2** : dark-skinned person

moretón *nm, pl* **-tones :** bruise
morfina *nf* **:** morphine
morfología *nf* **:** morphology
morgue *nf* **:** morgue
moribundo[1], **-da** *adj* **:** dying, moribund
moribundo[2], **-da** *n* **:** dying person
morillo *nm* **:** andiron
morir {46} *vi* **1** FALLECER **:** to die **2** APAGARSE **:** to die out, to go out
mormón, -mona *adj & n, pl* **mormones :** Mormon
moro[1], **-ra** *adj* **:** Moorish
moro[2], **-ra** *n* **1 :** Moor **2 :** Muslim
morosidad *nf* **1 :** delinquency (in payment) **2 :** slowness
moroso, -sa *adj* **1 :** delinquent, in arrears <cuentas morosas : delinquent accounts> **2 :** slow, sluggish
morral *nm* MOCHILA **:** backpack, knapsack
morralla *nf* **1 :** small fish **2 :** trash, riffraff **3** *Mex* **:** small change
morriña *nf* **:** homesickness
morro *nm* HOCICO **:** snout
morsa *nf* **:** walrus
morse *nm* **:** Morse code
mortaja *nf* SUDARIO **:** shroud
mortal[1] *adj* **1 :** mortal **2** FATAL **:** fatal, deadly — **mortalmente** *adv*
mortal[2] *nmf* **:** mortal
mortalidad *nf* **:** mortality
mortandad *nf* **1 :** loss of life, death toll **2 :** carnage, slaughter
mortero *nm* **:** mortar (bowl, cannon, or building material)
mortífero, -ra *adj* LETAL **:** deadly, fatal
mortificación *nf, pl* **-ciones 1 :** mortification **2** TORMENTO **:** anguish, torment
mortificar {72} *vt* **1 :** to mortify **2** TORTURAR **:** to trouble, to torment — **mortificarse** *vr* **:** to be mortified, to feel embarrassed
mosaico *nm* **:** mosaic
mosca *nf* **1 :** fly **2 mosca común :** housefly
moscada *adj* **nuez moscada :** nutmeg
moscovita *adj & nmf* **:** Muscovite
mosquearse *vr* **1 :** to become suspicious **2 :** to take offense
mosquete *nm* **:** musket
mosquetero *nm* **:** musketeer
mosquitero *nm* **:** mosquito net
mosquito *nm* ZANCUDO **:** mosquito
mostachón *nm, pl* **-chones :** macaroon
mostaza *nf* **:** mustard
mostrador *nm* **:** counter (in a store)
mostrar {19} *vt* **1 :** to show **2** EXHIBIR **:** to exhibit, to display — **mostrarse** *vr* **:** to show oneself, to appear
mota *nf* **1 :** fleck, speck **2 :** defect, blemish
mote *nm* SOBRENOMBRE **:** nickname
moteado, -da *adj* **:** dotted, spotted, dappled
motel *nm* **:** motel
motín *nm, pl* **motines 1 :** riot **2 :** rebellion, mutiny
motivación *nf, pl* **-ciones :** motivation — **motivacional** *adj*
motivar *vt* **1** CAUSAR **:** to cause **2** IMPULSAR **:** to motivate
motivo *nm* **1** MÓVIL **:** motive **2** CAUSA **:** cause, reason **3** TEMA **:** theme, motif
moto *nf* **:** motorcycle, motorbike
motocicleta *nf* **:** motorcycle
motociclismo *nm* **:** motorcycling
motociclista *nmf* **:** motorcyclist
motor[1], **-ra** *adj* MOTRIZ **:** motor
motor[2] *nm* **1 :** motor, engine **2 :** driving force, cause
motorista *nmf* **:** motorist
motriz *adj, pl* **motrices :** driving
motu proprio *adv* **de motu proprio** [de'motu'proprio] **:** voluntarily, of one's own accord
mousse ['mus] *nm* **:** mousse
mover {47} *vt* **1** TRASLADAR **:** to move, to shift **2** AGITAR **:** to shake, to nod (the head) **3** ACCIONAR **:** to power, to drive **4** INDUCIR **:** to provoke, to cause **5 :** to excite, to stir — **moverse** *vr* **1 :** to move, to move over **2 :** to hurry, to get a move on **3 :** to get moving, to make an effort
movible *adj* **:** movable
movida *nf* **:** move (in a game)
móvil[1] *adj* **:** mobile
móvil[2] *nm* **1** MOTIVO **:** motive **2 :** mobile
movilidad *nf* **:** mobility
movilizar {21} *vt* **:** to mobilize — **movilización** *nf*
movimiento *nm* **:** movement, motion <movimiento del cuerpo : bodily movement> <movimiento sindicalista : labor movement>
mozo[1], **-za** *adj* **:** young, youthful
mozo[2], **-za** *n* **1** JOVEN **:** young man *m,* young woman *f,* youth **2 :** helper, servant
mucamo, -ma *n* **:** servant, maid *f*
muchacha *nf* **:** maid
muchacho, -cha *n* **1 :** kid, boy *m,* girl *f* **2** JOVEN **:** young man *m,* young woman *f*
muchedumbre *nf* MULTITUD **:** crowd, multitude
mucho[1] *adv* **1 :** much, a lot <mucho más : much more> <le gusta mucho : he likes it a lot> **2 :** long, a long time <tardó mucho en venir : he was a long time getting here> **3 por mucho que :** no matter how much
mucho[2], **-cha** *adj* **1 :** a lot of, many, much <mucha gente : a lot of people> <hace mucho tiempo que no lo veo : I haven't seen him in ages> **2 muchas veces :** often
mucho[3], **-cha** *pron* **1 :** a lot, many, much <hay mucho que hacer : there is a lot to do> <muchas no vinieron : many didn't come> **2 cuando ~** *or* **como ~ :** at most **3 con ~ :** by far **4 ni mucho menos :** not at all, far from it
mucílago *nm* **:** mucilage
mucosidad *nf* **:** mucus

mucoso, -sa *adj* : mucous, slimy
muda *nf* **1** : change <muda de ropa : change of clothes> **2** : molt, molting
mudanza *nf* **1** CAMBIO : change **2** TRASLADO : move, moving
mudar *v* **1** CAMBIAR : to change **2** : to molt, to shed — **mudarse** *vr* **1** TRASLADARSE : to move (one's residence) **2** : to change (clothes)
mudo[1], **-da** *adj* **1** SILENCIOSO : silent <el cine mudo : silent films> **2** : mute, dumb
mudo[2], **-da** *n* : mute
mueble *nm* **1** : piece of furniture **2** **muebles** *nmpl* : furniture, furnishings
mueblería *nf* : furniture store
mueca *nf* : grimace, face
muela *nf* **1** : tooth, molar <dolor de muelas : toothache> <muela de juicio : wisdom tooth> **2** : millstone **3** : whetstone
muele, etc. → **moler**
muelle[1] *adj* : soft, comfortable, easy
muelle[2] *nm* **1** : wharf, dock **2** RESORTE : spring
muérdago *nm* : mistletoe
muerde, etc. → **morder**
muere, etc. → **morir**
muerte *nf* : death
muerto[1] *pp* → **morir**
muerto[2], **-ta** *adj* **1** : dead **2** : lifeless, flat, dull **3** ~ **de** : dying of <estoy muerto de hambre : I'm dying of hunger>
muerto[3], **-ta** *nm* DIFUNTO : dead person, deceased
muesca *nf* : nick, notch
muestra[1], **etc.** → **mostrar**
muestra[2] *nf* **1** : sample **2** SEÑAL : sign, show <una muestra de respeto : a show of respect> **3** EXPOSICIÓN : exhibition, exposition **4** : pattern, model
mueve, etc. → **mover**
mugido *nm* : moo, lowing, bellow
mugir {35} *vi* : to moo, to low, to bellow
mugre *nf* SUCIEDAD : grime, filth
mugriento, -ta *adj* : filthy
muguete *nm* : lily of the valley
muja, etc. → **mugir**
mujer *nf* **1** : woman **2** ESPOSA : wife
mulato, -ta *adj* & *n* : mulatto
muleta *nf* : crutch
mullido, -da *adj* **1** : soft, fluffy **2** : spongy, springy
mulo, -la *n* : mule
multa *nf* : fine
multicolor *adj* : multicolored
multicultural *adj* : multicultural
multidisciplinario, -ria *adj* : multidisciplinary
multifacético, -ca *adj* : multifaceted
multifamiliar *adj* : multifamily
multilateral *adj* : multilateral
multimedia *nf* : multimedia
multimillonario, -ria *n* : multimillionaire
multinacional *adj* : multinational
múltiple *adj* : multiple
multiplicación *nf, pl* **-ciones** : multiplication
multiplicar {72} *v* **1** : to multiply **2** : to increase — **multiplicarse** *vr* : to multiply, to reproduce
multiplicidad *nf* : multiplicity
múltiplo *nm* : multiple
multitud *nf* MUCHEDUMBRE : crowd, multitude
multiuso, -sa *adj* : multipurpose
multivitamínico, -ca *adj* : multivitamin
mundano, -na *adj* : worldly, earthly
mundial *adj* : world, worldwide
mundialmente *adv* : worldwide, all over the world
mundo *nm* **1** : world **2** **todo el mundo** : everyone, everybody
municiones *nfpl* : ammunition, munitions
municipal *adj* : municipal
municipio *nm* **1** : municipality **2** AYUNTAMIENTO : town council
muñeca *nf* **1** : doll **2** MANIQUÍ : mannequin **3** : wrist
muñeco *nm* **1** : doll, boy doll **2** MARIONETA : puppet
muñon *nm, pl* **muñones** : stump (of an arm or leg)
mural *adj* & *nm* : mural
muralista *nmf* : muralist
muralla *nf* : rampart, wall
murciélago *nm* : bat (animal)
murga *nf* : band of street musicians
murió, etc. → **morir**
murmullo *nm* **1** : murmur, murmuring **2** : rustling, rustle <el murmullo de las hojas : the rustling of the leaves>
murmurar *vt* **1** : to murmur, to mutter **2** : to whisper (gossip) — *vi* **1** : to murmur **2** CHISMEAR : to gossip
muro *nm* : wall
musa *nf* : muse
musaraña *nf* : shrew
muscular *adj* : muscular
musculatura *nf* : muscles *pl,* musculature
músculo *nm* : muscle
musculoso, -sa *adj* : muscular, brawny
muselina *nf* : muslin
museo *nm* : museum
musgo *nm* : moss
musgoso, -sa *adj* : mossy
música *nf* : music
musical *adj* : musical — **musicalmente** *adv*
músico[1], **-ca** *adj* : musical
músico[2], **-ca** *n* : musician
musitar *vt* : to mumble, to murmur
muslo *nm* : thigh
musulmán, -mana *adj* & *n, mpl* **-manes** : Muslim
mutación *nf, pl* **-ciones** : mutation
mutante *adj* & *nm* : mutant
mutar *v* : to mutate
mutilar *vt* : to mutilate — **mutilación** *nf*
mutis *nm* **1** : exit (in theater) **2** : silence
mutual *adj* : mutual

mutuo, -tua *adj* **:** mutual, reciprocal — **mutuamente** *adv*

muy *adv* **1 :** very, quite <es muy inteligente : she's very intelligent> <muy bien : very well, fine> <eso es muy americano : that's typically American> **2 :** too <es muy grande para él : it's too big for him>

N

n *nf* **:** fourteenth letter of the Spanish alphabet

nabo *nm* **:** turnip

nácar *nm* MADREPERLA **:** nacre, mother-of-pearl

nacarado, -da *adj* **:** pearly

nacer {48} *vi* **1 :** to be born <nací en Guatemala : I was born in Guatemala> <no nació ayer : he wasn't born yesterday> **2 :** to hatch **3 :** to bud, to sprout **4 :** to rise, to originate **5 nacer para algo :** to be born to be something **6 volver a nacer :** to have a lucky escape

nacido[1], -da *adj* **1 :** born **2 recién nacido :** newborn

nacido[2], -da *n* **1 los nacidos :** those born (at a particular time) **2 recién nacido :** newborn baby

naciente *adj* **1 :** newfound, growing **2 :** rising <el sol naciente : the rising sun>

nacimiento *nm* **1 :** birth **2 :** source (of a river) **3 :** beginning, origin **4** BELÉN **:** Nativity scene, crèche

nación *nf, pl* **naciones :** nation, country, people (of a country)

nacional[1] *adj* **:** national

nacional[2] *nmf* CIUDADANO **:** national, citizen

nacionalidad *nf* **:** nationality

nacionalismo *nm* **:** nationalism

nacionalista[1] *adj* **:** nationalist, nationalistic

nacionalista[2] *nmf* **:** nationalist

nacionalización *nf, pl* **-ciones 1 :** nationalization **2 :** naturalization

nacionalizar {21} *vt* **1 :** to nationalize **2 :** to naturalize (as a citizen) — **nacionalizarse** *vr*

naco, -ca *adj Mex* **:** trashy, vulgar, common

nada[1] *adv* **:** not at all, not in the least <no estamos nada cansados : we are not at all tired>

nada[2] *nf* **1 :** nothingness **2 :** smidgen, bit <una nada le disgusta : the slightest thing upsets him>

nada[3] *pron* **1 :** nothing <no estoy haciendo nada : I'm not doing anything> **2 casi nada :** next to nothing **3 de ~ :** you're welcome **4 dentro de nada :** very soon, in no time **5 nada más :** nothing else, nothing more

nadador, -dora *n* **:** swimmer

nadar *vi* **1 :** to swim **2 ~ en :** to be swimming in, to be rolling in — *vt* **:** to swim

nadería *nf* **:** small thing, trifle

nadie *pron* **:** nobody, no one <no vi a nadie : I didn't see anyone>

nadir *nm* **:** nadir

nado *nm* **1** *Mex* **:** swimming **2 a ~ :** swimming <cruzó el río a nado : he swam across the river>

nafta *nf* **1 :** naphtha **2** (*in various countries*) **:** gasoline

naftalina *nf* **:** naphthalene, mothballs *pl*

náhuatl[1] *adj & nmf, pl* **nahuas :** Nahuatl

náhuatl[2] *nm* **:** Nahuatl (language)

nailon → nilón

naipe *nm* **:** playing card

nalga *nf* **1 :** buttock **2 nalgas** *nfpl* **:** buttocks, bottom

nalgada *nf* **:** smack on the bottom, spanking

namibio, -bia *adj & n* **:** Namibian

nana *nf* **1 :** lullaby **2** *fam* **:** grandma **3** *CA, Col, Mex, Ven* **:** nanny

nanay *interj fam* **:** no way!, not likely!

naranja[1] *adj & nm* **:** orange (color)

naranja[2] *nf* **:** orange (fruit)

naranjal *nm* **:** orange grove

naranjo *nm* **:** orange tree

narcisismo *nm* **:** narcissism

narcisista[1] *adj* **:** narcissistic

narcisista[2] *nmf* **:** narcissist

narciso *nm* **:** narcissus, daffodil

narcótico[1], -ca *adj* **:** narcotic

narcótico[2] *nm* **:** narcotic

narcotizar {21} *vt* **:** to drug, to dope

narcotraficante *nmf* **:** drug trafficker

narcotráfico *nm* **:** drug trafficking

narigón, -gona *adj, mpl* **-gones :** big-nosed

narigudo → narigón

nariz *nf, pl* **narices 1 :** nose <sonar(se) la nariz : to blow one's nose> **2 :** sense of smell

narración *nf, pl* **-ciones :** narration, account

narrador, -dora *n* **:** narrator

narrar *vt* **:** to narrate, to tell

narrativa *nf* **:** narrative, story

narrativo, -va *adj* **:** narrative

narval *nm* **:** narwhal

nasa *nf* **:** creel

nasal *adj* **:** nasal

nata *nf* **1 :** cream <nata batida : whipped cream> **2 :** skin (on boiled milk)

natación *nf, pl* **-ciones :** swimming

natal *adj* **:** native, natal

natalicio *nm* **:** birthday <el natalicio de George Washington : George Washington's birthday>

natalidad *nf* **:** birthrate

natillas *nfpl* : custard
natividad *nf* : birth, nativity
nativo, -va *adj & n* : native
natural[1] *adj* **1** : natural **2** : normal <como es natural : naturally, as expected> **3 ~ de** : native of, from **4 de tamaño natural** : life-size
natural[2] *nm* **1** CARÁCTER : disposition, temperament **2** : native <un natural de Venezuela : a native of Venezuela>
naturaleza *nf* **1** : nature <la madre naturaleza : mother nature> **2** ÍNDOLE : nature, disposition, constitution <la naturaleza humana : human nature> **3 naturaleza muerta** : still life
naturalidad *nf* : simplicity, naturalness
naturalismo *nm* : naturalism
naturalista[1] *adj* : naturalistic
naturalista[2] *nmf* : naturalist
naturalización *nf, pl* **-ciones** : naturalization
naturalizar {21} *vt* : to naturalize — **naturalizarse** *vr* NACIONALIZARSE : to become naturalized
naturalmente *adv* **1** : naturally, inherently **2** : of course
naufragar {52} *vi* **1** : to be shipwrecked **2** FRACASAR : to fail, to collapse
naufragio *nm* **1** : shipwreck **2** FRACASO : failure, collapse
náufrago[1], **-ga** *adj* : shipwrecked, castaway
náufrago[2], **-ga** *n* : shipwrecked person, castaway
náusea *nf* **1** : nausea **2 dar náuseas** : to nauseate, to disgust **3 náuseas matutinas** : morning sickness
nauseabundo, -da *adj* : nauseating, sickening
náutica *nf* : navigation
náutico, -ca *adj* : nautical
nautilo *nm* : nautilus
navaja *nf* **1** : pocketknife, penknife <navaja de muelle : switchblade> **2 navaja de afeitar** : straight razor, razor blade
navajo, -ja *adj & n* : Navajo
naval *adj* : naval
nave *nf* **1** : ship <nave capitana : flagship> <nave espacial : spaceship> **2** : nave <nave lateral : aisle> **3 quemar uno sus naves** : to burn one's bridges
navegabilidad *nf* : navigability
navegable *adj* : navigable
navegación *nf, pl* **-ciones** : navigation
navegante[1] *adj* : sailing, seafaring
navegante[2] *nmf* : navigator
navegar {52} *v* : to navigate, to sail
Navidad *nf* : Christmas, Christmastime <Feliz Navidad : Merry Christmas>
navideño, -ña *adj* : Christmas
naviero, -ra *adj* : shipping
náyade *nf* : naiad
nazca, etc. → **nacer**
nazi *adj & nmf* : Nazi
nazismo *nm* : Nazism
nébeda *nf* : catnip
neblina *nf* : light fog, mist
neblinoso, -sa *adj* : misty, foggy
nebulosa *nf* : nebula
nebulosidad *nf* : mistiness, haziness
nebuloso, -sa *adj* **1** : hazy, misty **2** : nebulous, vague
necedad *nf* : stupidity, foolishness <decir necedades : to talk nonsense>
necesariamente *adv* : necessarily
necesario, -ria *adj* **1** : necessary **2 si es necesario** : if need be **3 hacerse necesario** : to be required
neceser *nm* : toilet kit, vanity case
necesidad *nf* **1** : need, necessity **2** : poverty, want **3 necesidades** *nfpl* : hardships **4 hacer sus necesidades** : to relieve oneself
necesitado, -da *adj* : needy
necesitar *vt* **1** : to need **2** : to necessitate, to require — *vi* **~ de** : to have need of
necio[1], **-cia** *adj* **1** : foolish, silly, dumb **2** *fam* : naughty
necio[2], **-cia** *n* ESTÚPIDO : fool, idiot
necrología *nf* : obituary
necrópolis *nfs & pl* : cemetery
néctar *nm* : nectar
nectarina *nf* : nectarine
neerlandés[1], **-desa** *adj, mpl* **-deses** HOLANDÉS : Dutch
neerlandés[2], **-desa** *n, mpl* **-deses** HOLANDÉS : Dutch person, Dutchman *m*
nefando, -da *adj* : unspeakable, heinous
nefario, -ria *adj* : nefarious
nefasto, -ta *adj* **1** : ill-fated, unlucky **2** : disastrous, terrible
negación *nf, pl* **-ciones** **1** : negation, denial **2** : negative (in grammar)
negar {49} *vt* **1** : to deny **2** REHUSAR : to refuse **3** : to disown — **negarse** *vr* **1** : to refuse **2** : to deny oneself
negativa *nf* **1** : denial **2** : refusal
negativo[1], **-va** *adj* : negative
negativo[2] *nm* : negative (of a photograph)
negligé *nm* : negligee
negligencia *nf* : negligence
negligente *adj* : neglectful, negligent — **negligentemente** *adv*
negociable *adj* : negotiable
negociación *nf, pl* **-ciones** **1** : negotiation **2 negociación colectiva** : collective bargaining
negociador, -dora *n* : negotiator
negociante *nmf* : businessman *m*, businesswoman *f*
negociar *vt* : to negotiate — *vi* : to deal, to do business
negocio *nm* **1** : business, place of business **2** : deal, transaction **3 negocios** *nmpl* : commerce, trade, business
negrero, -ra *n* **1** : slave trader **2** *fam* : slave driver, brutal boss
negrita *nf* : boldface (type)

negro[1], **-gra** *adj* **1** : black, dark **2** BRONCEADO : suntanned **3** : gloomy, awful, desperate <la cosa se está poniendo negra : things are looking bad> **4 mercado negro** : black market
negro[2], **-gra** *n* **1** : dark-skinned person, black person **2** *fam* : darling, dear
negro[3] *nm* : black (color)
negrura *nf* : blackness
negruzco, -ca *adj* : blackish
nene, -na *n* : baby, small child
nenúfar *nm* : water lily
neocelandés → **neozelandés**
neoclasicismo *nm* : neoclassicism
neoclásico, -ca *adj* : neoclassical
neófito, -ta *n* : neophyte, novice
neologismo *nm* : neologism
neón *nm, pl* **neones** : neon
neoyorquino[1], **-na** *adj* : of or from New York
neoyorquino[2], **-na** *n* : New Yorker
neozelandés[1], **-desa** *adj, mpl* **-deses** : of or from New Zealand
neozelandés[2], **-desa** *n, mpl* **-deses** : New Zealander
nepalés, -lesa *adj & n, mpl* **-leses** : Nepali
nepotismo *nm* : nepotism
neptunio *nm* : neptunium
Neptuno *nm* : Neptune
nervio *nm* **1** : nerve **2** : tendon, sinew, gristle (in meat) **3** : energy, drive **4** : rib (of a vault) **5 nervios** *nmpl* : nerves <estar mal de los nervios : to be a bundle of nerves> <ataque de nervios : nervous breakdown>
nerviosamente *adv* : nervously
nerviosidad *nf* → **nerviosismo**
nerviosismo *nf* : nervousness, anxiety
nervioso, -sa *adj* **1** : nervous, nerve <sistema nervioso : nervous system> **2** : high-strung, restless, anxious <ponerse nervioso : to get nervous> **3** : vigorous, energetic
nervudo, -da *adj* : sinewy, wiry
neta *nf Mex fam* : truth <la neta es que me cae mal : the truth is, I don't like her>
netamente *adv* : clearly, obviously
neto, -ta *adj* **1** : net <peso neto : net weight> **2** : clear, distinct
neumático[1], **-ca** *adj* : pneumatic
neumático[2] *nm* LLANTA : tire
neumonía *nf* PULMONÍA : pneumonia
neural *adj* : neural
neuralgia *nf* : neuralgia
neuritis *nf* : neuritis
neurología *nf* : neurology
neurológico, -ca *adj* : neurological, neurologic
neurólogo, -ga *n* : neurologist
neurosis *nfs & pl* : neurosis
neurótico, -ca *adj & n* : neurotic
neutral *adj* : neutral
neutralidad *nf* : neutrality
neutralizar {21} *vt* : to neutralize — **neutralización** *nf*
neutro, -tra *adj* **1** : neutral **2** : neuter
neutrón *nm, pl* **neutrones** : neutron
nevada *nf* : snowfall
nevado, -da *adj* **1** : snowcapped **2** : snow-white
nevar {55} *v impers* : to snow
nevasca *nf* : snowstorm, blizzard
nevera *nf* REFRIGERADOR : refrigerator
nevería *nf Mex* : ice cream parlor
nevisca *nf* : light snowfall, flurry
nevoso, -sa *adj* : snowy
nexo *nm* VÍNCULO : link, connection, nexus
ni *conj* **1** : neither, nor <afuera no hace ni frío ni calor : it's neither cold nor hot outside> **2 ni que** : not even if, not as if <ni que me pagaran : not even if they paid me> <ni que fuera (yo) su madre : it's not as if I were his mother> **3 ni siquiera** : not even <ni siquiera nos llamaron : they didn't even call us>
nicaragüense *adj & nmf* : Nicaraguan
nicho *nm* : niche
nicotina *nf* : nicotine
nido *nm* **1** : nest **2** : hiding place, den
niebla *nf* : fog, mist
niega, niegue, etc. → **negar**
nieto, -ta *n* **1** : grandson *m,* granddaughter *f* **2 nietos** *nmpl* : grandchildren
nieva, etc. → **nevar**
nieve *nf* **1** : snow **2** *Cuba, Mex, PRi* : sherbet
nigeriano, -na *adj & n* : Nigerian
nigua *nf* : sand flea, chigger
nihilismo *nm* : nihilism
nilón *or* **nilon** *nm, pl* **nilones** : nylon
nimbo *nm* **1** : halo **2** : nimbus
nimiedad *nf* INSIGNIFICANCIA : trifle, triviality
nimio, -mia *adj* INSIGNIFICANTE : insignificant, trivial
ninfa *nf* : nymph
ningunear *vt Mex fam* : to disrespect
ninguno[1], **-na** (**ningún** *before masculine singular nouns*) *adj, mpl* **ningunos** : no, none <no es ninguna tonta : she's no fool> <no debe hacerse en ningún momento : that should never be done>
ninguno[2], **-na** *pron* **1** : neither, none <ninguno de los dos ha vuelto aún : neither one has returned yet> **2** : no one, no other <te quiero más que a ninguna : I love you more than any other>
niña *nf* **1** PUPILA : pupil (of the eye) **2 la niña de los ojos** : the apple of one's eye
niñada *nf* **1** : childishness **2** : trifle, silly thing
niñería *nf* → **niñada**
niñero, -ra *n* : baby-sitter, nanny
niñez *nf, pl* **niñeces** INFANCIA : childhood
niño, -ña *n* : child, boy *m,* girl *f*
niobio *nm* : niobium
nipón, -pona *adj & n, mpl* **nipones** JAPONÉS : Japanese
níquel *nm* : nickel

nitidez *nf, pl* **-deces** CLARIDAD : clarity, vividness, sharpness

nítido, -da *adj* CLARO : clear, vivid, sharp

nitrato *nm* : nitrate

nítrico, -ca *adj* **ácido nítrico** : nitric acid

nitrito *nm* : nitrite

nitrógeno *nm* : nitrogen

nitroglicerina *nf* : nitroglycerin

nivel *nm* **1** : level, height <nivel del mar : sea level> **2** : level, standard <nivel de vida : standard of living>

nivelar *vt* : to level (out)

nixtamal *nm Mex* : limed corn used for tortillas

no *adv* **1** : no <¿quieres ir al mercado? no, voy más tarde : do you want to go shopping? no, I'm going later> **2** : not <¡no hagas eso! : don't do that!> <creo que no : I don't think so> **3** : non- <no fumador : non-smoker> **4** **¡como no!** : of course! **5** **no bien** : as soon as, no sooner

nobelio *nm* : nobelium

noble[1] *adj* : noble — **noblemente** *adv*

noble[2] *nmf* : nobleman *m,* noblewoman *f*

nobleza *nf* **1** : nobility **2** HONRADEZ : honesty, integrity

nocaut *nm* : knockout, KO

noche *nf* **1** : night, nighttime, evening **2** **buenas noches** : good evening, good night **3** **de noche** *or* **por la noche** : at night **4** **hacerse de noche** : to get dark

Nochebuena *nf* : Christmas Eve

nochecita *nf* : dusk

Nochevieja *nf* : New Year's Eve

noción *nf, pl* **nociones** **1** CONCEPTO : notion, concept **2** **nociones** *nfpl* : smattering, rudiments *pl*

nocivo, -va *adj* DAÑINO : harmful, noxious

noctámbulo, -la *n* **1** : sleepwalker **2** : night owl

nocturno[1], **-na** *adj* : night, nocturnal

nocturno[2] *nm* : nocturne

nodriza *nf* : wet nurse

nódulo *nm* : nodule

nogal *nm* **1** : walnut tree **2** *Mex* : pecan tree **3** **nogal americano** : hickory

nómada[1] *adj* : nomadic

nómada[2] *nmf* : nomad

nomás *adv* : only, just <lo hice nomás porque sí : I did it just because> <nomás de recordarlo me enojo : I get angry just remembering it> <nomás faltan dos semanas para Navidad : there are only two weeks left till Christmas>

nombradía *nf* RENOMBRE : fame, renown

nombrado, -da *adj* : famous, well-known

nombramiento *nm* : appointment, nomination

nombrar *vt* **1** : to appoint **2** : to mention, to name

nombre *nm* **1** : name <nombre de pluma : pseudonym, pen name> <en nombre : on behalf of> <sin nombre : nameless> **2** : noun <nombre propio : proper noun> **3** : fame, renown

nomenclatura *nf* : nomenclature

nomeolvides *nmfs & pl* : forget-me-not

nómina *nf* : payroll

nominación *nf, pl* **-ciones** : nomination

nominal *adj* : nominal — **nominalmente** *adv*

nominar *vt* : to nominate

nominativo[1], **-va** *adj* : nominative

nominativo[2] *nm* : nominative (case)

nomo *nm* : gnome

non[1] *adj* IMPAR : odd, not even

non[2] *nm* : odd number

nonagésimo[1], **-ma** *adj* : ninetieth, ninety-

nonagésimo[2], **-ma** *n* : ninetieth, ninety- (in a series)

nono, -na *adj* : ninth — **nono** *nm*

nopal *nm* : nopal, cactus

nopalitos *nmpl Mex* : pickled cactus leaves

noquear *vt* : to knock out, to KO

norcoreano, -na *adj & n* : North Korean

nordeste[1] *or* **noreste** *adj* **1** : northeastern **2** : northeasterly

nordeste[2] *or* **noreste** *nm* : northeast

nórdico, -ca *adj & n* ESCANDINAVO : Scandinavian

noreste → **nordeste**

noria *nf* **1** : waterwheel **2** : Ferris wheel

norirlandés[1], **-desa** *adj, mpl* **-deses** : Northern Irish

norirlandés[2], **-desa** *n, mpl* **-deses** : person from Northern Ireland

norma *nf* **1** : rule, regulation **2** : norm, standard

normal *adj* **1** : normal, usual **2** : standard **3** **escuela normal** : teacher-training college

normalidad *nf* : normality, normalcy

normalización *nf, pl* **-ciones** *nf* **1** REGULARIZACIÓN : normalization **2** ESTANDARIZACIÓN : standardization

normalizar {21} *vt* **1** REGULARIZAR : to normalize **2** ESTANDARIZAR : to standardize — **normalizarse** *vr* : to return to normal

normalmente *adv* GENERALMENTE : ordinarily, generally

noroeste[1] *adj* **1** : northwestern **2** : northwesterly

noroeste[2] *nm* : northwest

norte[1] *adj* : north, northern

norte[2] *nm* **1** : north **2** : north wind **3** META : aim, objective

norteamericano, -na *adj & n* **1** : North American **2** AMERICANO, ESTADOUNIDENSE : American, native or inhabitant of the United States

norteño[1], **-ña** *adj* : northern

norteño[2], **-ña** *n* : Northerner

noruego[1], **-ga** *adj & n* : Norwegian
noruego[2] *nm* : Norwegian (language)
nos *pron* **1** : us <nos enviaron a la frontera : they sent us to the border> **2** : ourselves <nos divertimos muchísimo : we enjoyed ourselves a great deal> **3** : each other, one another <nos vimos desde lejos : we saw each other from far away> **4** : to us, for us, from us <nos lo dio : he gave it to us> <nos lo compraron : they bought it from us>
nosotros, -tras *pron* **1** : we <nosotros llegamos ayer : we arrived yesterday> **2** : us <ven con nosotros : come with us> **3 nosotros mismos** : ourselves <lo arreglamos nosotros mismos : we fixed it ourselves>
nostalgia *nf* **1** : nostalgia, longing **2** : homesickness
nostálgico, -ca *adj* **1** : nostalgic **2** : homesick
nota *nf* **1** : note, message **2** : announcement <nota de prensa : press release> **3** : grade, mark (in school) **4** : characteristic, feature, touch **5** : note (in music) **6** : bill, check (in a restaraunt)
notable *adj* **1** : notable, noteworthy **2** : outstanding
notar *vt* **1** : to notice <hacer notar algo : to point out something> **2** : to tell <la diferencia se nota inmediatamente : you can tell the difference right away> — **notarse** *vr* **1** : to be evident, to show **2** : to feel, to seem
notario, -ria *n* : notary, notary public
noticia *nf* **1** : news item, piece of news **2 noticias** *nfpl* : news
noticiero *nm* : news program, newscast
noticioso, -sa *adj* : news <agencia noticiosa : news agency>
notificación *nf, pl* **-ciones** : notification
notificar {72} *vt* : to notify, to inform
notoriedad *nf* **1** : knowledge, obviousness **2** : fame, notoriety
notorio, -ria *adj* **1** OBVIO : obvious, evident **2** CONOCIDO : well-known
novato[1], **-ta** *adj* : inexperienced, new
novato[2], **-ta** *n* : beginner, novice
novecientos[1], **-tas** *adj* : nine hundred
novecientos[2] *nms & pl* : nine hundred
novedad *nf* **1** : newness, novelty **2** : innovation
novedoso, -sa *adj* : original, novel
novel *adj* NOVATO : inexperienced, new
novela *nf* **1** : novel **2** : soap opera
novelar *vt* : to fictionalize, to make a novel out of
novelesco, -ca *adj* **1** : fictional **2** : fantastic, fabulous
novelista *nmf* : novelist
novena *nf* : novena
noveno, -na *adj* : ninth — **noveno, -na** *n*
noventa *adj & nm* : ninety
noventavo[1], **-va** *adj* : ninetieth
noventavo[2] *nm* : ninetieth (fraction)
noviazgo *nm* **1** : courtship, relationship **2** : engagement, betrothal
novicio, -cia *n* **1** : novice (in religion) **2** PRINCIPIANTE : novice, beginner
noviembre *nm* : November
novilla *nf* : heifer
novillada *nf* : bullfight featuring young bulls
novillero, -ra *n* : apprentice bullfighter
novillo *nm* : young bull
novio, -via *n* **1** : boyfriend *m,* girlfriend *f* **2** PROMETIDO : fiancé *m,* fiancée *f* **3** : bridegroom *m,* bride *f*
novocaína *nf* : novocaine
nubarrón *nm, pl* **-rrones** : storm cloud
nube *nf* **1** : cloud <andar en las nubes : to have one's head in the clouds> <por las nubes : sky-high> **2** : cloud (of dust), swarm (of insects, etc.)
nublado[1], **-da** *adj* **1** NUBOSO : cloudy, overcast **2** : clouded, dim
nublado[2] *nm* **1** : storm cloud **2** AMENAZA : menace, threat
nublar *vt* **1** : to cloud **2** OSCURECER : to obscure — **nublarse** *vr* : to get cloudy
nubosidad *nf* : cloudiness
nuboso, -sa *adj* NUBLADO : cloudy
nuca *nf* : nape, back of the neck
nuclear *adj* : nuclear
núcleo *nm* **1** : nucleus **2** : center, heart, core
nudillo *nm* : knuckle
nudismo *nm* : nudism
nudista *adj & nmf* : nudist
nudo *nm* **1** : knot <square knot : nudo de rizo> <un nudo en la garganta : a lump in one's throat> **2** : node **3** : junction, hub <nudo de comunicaciones : communication center> **4** : crux, heart (of a problem, etc.)
nudoso, -sa *adj* : knotty, gnarled
nuera *nf* : daughter-in-law
nuestro[1], **-tra** *adj* : our
nuestro[2], **-tra** *pron* (*with definite article*) : ours, our own <el nuestro es más grande : ours is bigger> <es de los nuestros : it's one of ours>
nuevamente *adv* : again, anew
nuevas *nfpl* : tidings *pl*
nueve *adj & nm* : nine
nuevecito, -ta *adj* : brand-new
nuevo, -va *adj* **1** : new <una casa nueva : a new house> <¿qué hay de nuevo? : what's new?> **2 de ~** : again, once more
nuez *nf, pl* **nueces 1** : nut **2** : walnut **3** *Mex* : pecan **4 nuez de Adán** : Adam's apple **5 nuez moscada** : nutmeg
nulidad *nf* **1** : nullity **2** : incompetent person <¡es una nulidad! : he's hopeless!>
nulo, -la *adj* **1** : null, null and void **2** INEPTO : useless, inept <es nula para la cocina : she's hopeless at cooking>
numen *nm* : poetic muse, inspiration
numerable *adj* : countable

numeración *nf, pl* **-ciones 1 :** numbering **2 :** numbers *pl,* numerals *pl* <numeración romana : Roman numerals>
numerador *nm* **:** numerator
numeral *adj* **:** numeral
numerar *vt* **:** to number
numerario, -ria *adj* **:** long-standing, permanent <profesor numerario : tenured professor>
numérico, -ca *adj* **:** numerical **— numéricamente** *adv*
número *nm* **1 :** number <número impar : odd number> <número ordinal : ordinal number> <número arábico : Arabic numeral> <número quebrado : fraction> **2 :** issue (of a publication) **3 sin ~ :** countless
numeroso, -sa *adj* **:** numerous
numismática *nf* **:** numismatics
nunca *adv* **1 :** never, ever <nunca es tarde : it's never too late> <no trabaja casi nunca : he hardly ever works> **2 nunca más :** never again **3 nunca jamás :** never ever
nuncio *nm* **:** harbinger, herald
nupcial *adj* **:** nuptial, wedding
nupcias *nfpl* **:** nuptials *pl,* wedding
nutria *nf* **1 :** otter **2 :** nutria
nutrición *nf, pl* **-ciones :** nutrition, nourishment
nutrido, -da *adj* **1 :** nourished <mal nutrido : undernourished, malnourished> **2 :** considerable, abundant <de nutrido : full of, abounding in>
nutriente *nm* **:** nutrient
nutrimento *nm* **:** nutriment
nutrir *vt* **1** ALIMENTAR **:** to feed, to nourish **2 :** to foster, to provide
nutritivo, -va *adj* **:** nourishing, nutritious
nylon *nm* **→ nilón**

Ñ

ñ *nf* **:** fifteenth letter of the Spanish alphabet
ñame *nm* **:** yam
ñandú *nm* **:** rhea
ñapa *nf* **:** extra amount <de ñapa : for good measure>
ñoñear *vi fam* **:** to whine
ñoño, -ña *adj fam* **:** whiny, fussy <no seas tan ñoño : don't be such a wimp>
ñoquis *nmpl* **:** gnocchi *pl*
ñu *nm* **:** gnu, wildebeest

O

o[1] *nf* **:** sixteenth letter of the Spanish alphabet
o[2] *conj* (**u** *before words beginning with o- or ho-*) **1 :** or <¿vienes con nosotros o te quedas? : are you coming with us or staying?> **2 :** either <o vienes con nosotros o te quedas : either you come with us or you stay> **3 o sea :** that is to say, in other words
oasis *nms & pl* **:** oasis
obcecado, -da *adj* **1 :** blinded <obcecado por la ira : blinded by rage> **2 :** stubborn, obstinate
obcecar {72} *vt* **:** to blind (by emotions) **— obcecarse** *vr* **:** to become stubborn
obedecer {53} *vt* **:** to obey <obedecer órdenes : to obey orders> <obedece a tus padres : obey your parents> **—** *vi* **1 :** to obey **2 ~ a :** to respond to **3 ~ a :** to be due to, to result from
obediencia *nf* **:** obedience
obediente *adj* **:** obedient **— obedientemente** *adv*
obelisco *nm* **:** obelisk
obertura *nf* **:** overture
obesidad *nf* **:** obesity
obeso, -sa *adj* **:** obese
óbice *nm* **:** obstacle, impediment
obispado *nm* DIÓCESIS **:** bishopric, diocese
obispo *nm* **:** bishop
obituario *nm* **:** obituary
objeción *nf, pl* **-ciones :** objection <ponerle objeciones a algo : to object to something>
objetar *v* **:** to object <no tengo nada que objetar : I have no objections>
objetividad *nf* **:** objectivity
objetivo[1], **-va** *adj* **:** objective **— objetivamente** *adv*
objetivo[2] *nm* **1** META **:** objective, goal, target **2 :** lens
objeto *nm* **1** COSA **:** object, thing **2** OBJETIVO **:** objective, purpose <con objeto de : in order to, with the aim of> **3 objeto volador no identificado :** unidentified flying object
objetor, -tora *n* **:** objector <objetor de conciencia : conscientious objector>
oblea *nf* **1 :** wafer **2 hecho una oblea** *fam* **:** skinny as a rail
oblicuo, -cua *adj* **:** oblique **— oblicuamente** *adv*
obligación *nf, pl* **-ciones 1** DEBER **:** obligation, duty **2 :** bond, debenture
obligado, -da *adj* **1 :** obliged **2 :** obligatory, compulsory **3 :** customary
obligar {52} *vt* **:** to force, to require, to oblige **— obligarse** *vr* **:** to commit

oneself, to undertake (to do something)

obligatorio, -ria *adj* **:** mandatory, required, compulsory

obliterar *vt* **:** to obliterate, to destroy — **obliteración** *nf*

oblongo, -ga *adj* **:** oblong

obnubilación *nf, pl* **-ciones :** bewilderment, confusion

obnubilar *vt* **:** to daze, to bewilder

oboe[1] *nm* **:** oboe

oboe[2] *nmf* **:** oboist

obra *nf* **1 :** work <obra de arte : work of art> <obra de teatro : play> <obra de consulta : reference work> **2 :** deed <una buena obra : a good deed> **3 :** construction work **4 obra maestra :** masterpiece **5 obras públicas :** public works **6 por obra de :** thanks to, because of

obrar *vt* **:** to work, to produce <obrar milagros : to work miracles> — *vi* **1 :** to act, to behave <obrar con cautela : to act with caution> **2 obrar en poder de :** to be in possession of

obrero[1], -ra *adj* **:** working <la clase obrera : the working class>

obrero[2], -ra *n* **:** worker, laborer

obscenidad *nf* **:** obscenity

obsceno, -na *adj* **:** obscene

obscurecer, obscuridad, obscuro → **oscurecer, oscuridad, oscuro**

obsequiar *vt* REGALAR **:** to give, to present <lo obsequiaron con una placa : they presented him with a plaque>

obsequio *nm* REGALO **:** gift, present

obsequiosidad *nf* **:** attentiveness, deference

obsequioso, -sa *adj* **:** obliging, attentive

observación *nf, pl* **-ciones 1 :** observation, watching **2 :** remark, comment

observador[1], -dora *adj* **:** observant

observador[2], -dora *n* **:** observer, watcher

observancia *nf* **:** observance

observar *vt* **1 :** to observe, to watch <estábamos observando a los niños : we were watching the children> **2** NOTAR **:** to notice **3** ACATAR **:** to obey, to abide by **4** COMENTAR **:** to remark, to comment

observatorio *nm* **:** observatory

obsesión *nf, pl* **-siones :** obsession

obsesionar *vt* **:** to obsess, to preoccupy excessively — **obsesionarse** *vr*

obsesivo, -va *adj* **:** obsessive

obseso, -sa *adj* **:** obsessed

obsolescencia *nf* DESUSO **:** obsolescence — **obsolescente** *adj*

obsoleto, -ta *adj* DESUSADO **:** obsolete

obstaculizar {21} *vt* IMPEDIR **:** to obstruct, to hinder

obstáculo *nm* IMPEDIMENTO **:** obstacle

obstante[1] *conj* **no obstante :** nevertheless, however

obstante[2] *prep* **no obstante :** in spite of, despite <mantuvo su inocencia no obstante la evidencia : he maintained his innocence in spite of the evidence>

obstar *v impers* **~ a** *or* **~ para :** to hinder, to prevent <eso no obsta para que me vaya : that doesn't prevent me from leaving>

obstetra *nmf* TOCÓLOGO **:** obstetrician

obstetricia *nf* **:** obstetrics

obstétrico, -ca *adj* **:** obstetric, obstetrical

obstinación *nf, pl* **-ciones 1** TERQUEDAD **:** obstinacy, stubbornness **2 :** perseverance, tenacity

obstinado, -da *adj* **1** TERCO **:** obstinate, stubborn **2 :** persistent — **obstinadamente** *adv*

obstinarse *vr* EMPECINARSE **:** to be obstinate, to be stubborn

obstrucción *nf, pl* **-ciones :** obstruction, blockage

obstruccionismo *nm* **:** obstructionism, filibustering

obstructor, -tora *adj* **:** obstructive

obstruir {41} *vt* BLOQUEAR **:** to obstruct, to block, to clog — **obstruirse** *vr*

obtención *nf* **:** obtaining, procurement

obtener {80} *vt* **:** to obtain, to secure, to get — **obtenible** *adj*

obturador *nm* **:** shutter (of a camera)

obtuso, -sa *adj* **:** obtuse

obtuvo, etc. → **obtener**

obviar *vt* **:** to get around (a difficulty), to avoid

obvio, -via *adj* **:** obvious — **obviamente** *adv*

oca *nf* **:** goose

ocasión *nf, pl* **-siones 1 :** occasion, time **2 :** opportunity, chance **3 :** bargain **4 de ~ :** secondhand **5 aviso de ocasión** *Mex* **:** classified ad

ocasional *adj* **1 :** occasional **2 :** chance, fortuitous

ocasionalmente *adv* **1 :** occasionally **2 :** by chance

ocasionar *vt* CAUSAR **:** to cause, to occasion

ocaso *nm* **1** ANOCHECER **:** sunset, sundown **2** DECADENCIA **:** decline, fall

occidental *adj* **:** western, occidental

occidente *nm* **1** OESTE, PONIENTE **:** west **2 el Occidente :** the West

oceánico, -ca *adj* **:** oceanic

océano *nm* **:** ocean

oceanografía *nf* **:** oceanography

oceanográfico, -ca *adj* **:** oceanographic

ocelote *nm* **:** ocelot

ochenta *adj & nm* **:** eighty

ochentavo[1], -va *adj* **:** eightieth

ochentavo[2] *nm* **:** eightieth (fraction)

ocho *adj & nm* **:** eight

ochocientos[1], -tas *adj* **:** eight hundred

ochocientos[2] *nms & pl* **:** eight hundred

ocio *nm* **1 :** free time, leisure **2 :** idleness

ociosidad *nf* **:** idleness, inactivity

ocioso, -sa *adj* **1** INACTIVO : idle, inactive **2** INÚTIL : pointless, useless

ocre *nm* : ocher

octágono *nm* : octagon — **octagonal** *adj*

octava *nf* : octave

octavo, -va *adj* : eighth — **octavo, -va** *n*

octeto *nm* **1** : octet **2** : byte

octogésimo[1], **-ma** *adj* : eightieth, eighty-

octogésimo[2], **-ma** *n* : eightieth, eighty- (in a series)

octubre *nm* : October

ocular *adj* **1** : ocular, eye <músculos oculares : eye muscles> **2 testigo ocular** : eyewitness

oculista *nmf* : oculist, opthalmologist

ocultación *nf, pl* **-ciones** : concealment

ocultar *vt* ESCONDER : to conceal, to hide — **ocultarse** *vr*

oculto, -ta *adj* **1** ESCONDIDO : hidden, concealed **2** : occult

ocupación *nf, pl* **-ciones 1** : occupation, activity **2** : occupancy **3** EMPLEO : employment, job

ocupacional *adj* : occupational, job-related

ocupado, -da *adj* **1** : busy **2** : taken <este asiento está ocupado : this seat is taken> **3** : occupied <territorios ocupados : occupied territories> **4 señal de ocupado** : busy signal

ocupante *nmf* : occupant

ocupar *vt* **1** : to occupy, to take possession of **2** : to hold (a position) **3** : to employ, to keep busy **4** : to fill (space, time) **5** : to inhabit (a dwelling) **6** : to bother, to concern — **ocuparse** *vr* **~ de 1** : to be concerned with **2** : to take care of

ocurrencia *nf* **1** : occurrence, event **2** : witticism **3** : bright idea

ocurrente *adj* **1** : witty **2** : clever, sharp

ocurrir *vi* : to occur, to happen — **ocurrirse** *vr* **~ a** : to occur to, to strike <se me ocurrió una mejor idea : a better idea occurred to me>

oda *nf* : ode

odiar *vt* ABOMINAR, ABORRECER : to hate

odio *nm* : hate, hatred

odioso, -sa *adj* ABOMINABLE, ABORRECIBLE : hateful, detestable

odisea *nf* : odyssey

odontología *nf* : dentistry, dental surgery

odontólogo, -ga *n* : dentist, dental surgeon

oeste[1] *adj* **1** : west, western <la región oeste : the western region> **2** : westerly

oeste[2] *nm* **1** : west, West **2** : west wind

ofender *vt* AGRAVIAR : to offend, to insult — *vi* : to offend, to be insulting — **ofenderse** *vr* : to take offense

ofensa *nf* : offense, insult

ofensiva *nf* : offensive <pasar a la ofensiva : to go on the offensive>

ofensivo, -va *adj* : offensive, insulting

ofensor, -sora *n* : offender

oferente *nmf* **1** : supplier **2** FUENTE : source <un oferente no identificado : an unidentified source>

oferta *nf* **1** : offer **2** : sale, bargain <las camisas están en oferta : the shirts are on sale> **3 oferta y demanda** : supply and demand

ofertar *vt* OFRECER : to offer

oficial[1] *adj* : official — **oficialmente** *adv*

oficial[2] *nmf* **1** : officer, police officer, commissioned officer (in the military) **2** : skilled worker

oficializar {21} *vt* : to make official

oficiante *nmf* : celebrant

oficiar *vt* **1** : to inform officially **2** : to officiate at, to celebrate (Mass) — *vi* **~ de** : to act as

oficina *nf* : office

oficinista *nmf* : office worker

oficio *nm* **1** : trade, profession <es electricista de oficio : he's an electrician by trade> **2** : function, role **3** : official communication **4** : experience <tener oficio : to be experienced> **5** : religious ceremony

oficioso, -sa *adj* **1** EXTRAOFICIAL : unofficial **2** : officious — **oficiosamente** *adv*

ofrecer {53} *vt* **1** : to offer **2** : to provide, to give **3** : to present (an appearance, etc.) — **ofrecerse** *vr* **1** : to offer oneself, to volunteer **2** : to open up, to present itself

ofrecimiento *nm* : offer, offering

ofrenda *nf* : offering

oftalmología *nf* : ophthalmology

oftalmólogo, -ga *n* : ophthalmologist

ofuscación *nf, pl* **-ciones** : blindness, confusion

ofuscar {72} *vt* **1** : to blind, to dazzle **2** CONFUNDIR : to bewilder, to confuse — **ofuscarse** *vr* **~ con** : to be blinded by

ogro *nm* : ogre

ohm *nm, pl* **ohms** : ohm

ohmio *nm* → **ohm**

oídas *nfpl* **de ~** : by hearsay

oído *nm* **1** : ear <oído interno : inner ear> **2** : hearing <duro de oído : hard of hearing> **3 tocar de oído** : to play by ear

oiga, etc. → **oír**

oír {50} *vi* : to hear — *vt* **1** : to hear **2** ESCUCHAR : to listen to **3** : to pay attention to, to heed **4 ¡oye!** *or* **¡oiga!** : listen!, excuse me!, look here!

ojal *nm* : buttonhole

ojalá *interj* **1** : I hope so!, if only!, God willing! **2** : I hope, I wish, hopefully <¡ojalá que le vaya bien! : I hope things go well for her!> <¡ojalá no llueva! : hopefully it won't rain!>

ojeada *nf* : glimpse, glance <echar una ojeada : to have a quick look>

ojear *vt* : to eye, to have a look at

ojete *nm* : eyelet

ojiva *nf* : warhead
ojo *nm* **1** : eye **2** : judgment, sharpness <tener buen ojo para : to be a good judge of, to have a good eye for> **3** : hole (in cheese), eye (in a needle), center (of a storm) **4** : span (of a bridge) **5 a ojos vistas** : openly, publicly **6 andar con ojo** : to be careful **7 ojo de agua** *Mex* : spring, source **8 ¡ojo!** : look out!, pay attention!
ola *nf* **1** : wave **2 ola de calor** : heat wave
oleada *nf* : swell, wave <una oleada de protestas : a wave of protests>
oleaje *nm* : waves *pl*, surf
óleo *nm* **1** : oil **2** : oil painting
oleoducto *nm* : oil pipeline
oleoso, -sa *adj* : oily
oler {51} *vt* **1** : to smell **2** INQUIRIR : to pry into, to investigate **3** AVERIGUAR : to smell out, to uncover — *vi* **1** : to smell <huele mal : it smells bad> **2 ~ a** : to smell like, to smell of <huele a pino : it smells like pine> — **olerse** *vr* : to have a hunch, to suspect
olfatear *vt* **1** : to sniff **2** : to sense, to sniff out
olfativo, -va *adj* : olfactory
olfato *nm* **1** : sense of smell **2** : nose, instinct
oligarquía *nf* : oligarchy
olimpiada *or* **olimpíada** *nf* : Olympics *pl*, Olympic Games *pl*
olímpico, -ca *adj* : Olympic
olisquear *vt* : to sniff at
oliva *nf* ACEITUNA : olive <aceite de oliva : olive oil>
olivo *nm* : olive tree
olla *nf* **1** : pot <olla de presión : pressure cooker> **2 olla podrida** : Spanish stew
olmeca *adj & nmf* : Olmec
olmo *nm* : elm
olor *nm* : smell, odor
oloroso, -sa *adj* : scented, fragrant
olote *nm Mex* : cob, corncob
olvidadizo, -za *adj* : forgetful, absent-minded
olvidar *vt* **1** : to forget, to forget about <olvida lo que pasó : forget about what happened> **2** : to leave behind <olvidé mi chequera en la casa : I left my checkbook at home> — **olvidarse** *vr* : to forget <se me olvidó mi cuaderno : I forgot my notebook> <se le olvidó llamarme : he forgot to call me>
olvido *nm* **1** : forgetfulness **2** : oblivion **3** DESCUIDO : oversight
omaní *adj & nmf* : Omani
ombligo *nm* : navel, belly button
ombudsman *nmfs & pl* : ombudsman
omelette *nmf* : omelet
ominoso, -sa *adj* : ominous — **ominosamente** *adv*
omisión *nf, pl* **-siones** : omission, neglect
omiso, -sa *adj* **1** NEGLIGENTE : neglectful **2 hacer caso omiso de** : to ignore
omitir *vt* **1** : to omit, to leave out **2** : to fail to <omitió dar su nombre : he failed to give his name>
ómnibus *n, pl* **-bus** *or* **-buses** : bus, coach
omnipotencia *nf* : omnipotence
omnipotente *adj* TODOPODEROSO : omnipotent, almighty
omnipresencia *nf* : ubiquity, omnipresence
omnipresente *adj* : ubiquitous, omnipresent
omnisciente *adj* : omniscient — **omnisciencia** *nf*
omnívoro, -ra *adj* : omnivorous
omóplato *or* **omoplato** *nm* : shoulder blade
once *adj & nm* : eleven
onceavo[1]**, -va** *adj* : eleventh
onceavo[2] *nm* : eleventh (fraction)
onda *nf* **1** : wave, ripple, undulation <onda sonora : sound wave> **2** : wave (in hair) **3** : scallop (on clothing) **4** *fam* : wavelength, understanding <agarrar la onda : to get the point> <en la onda : on the ball, with it> **5 ¿qué onda?** *fam* : what's happening?, what's up?
ondear *vi* : to ripple, to undulate, to flutter
ondulación *nf, pl* **-ciones** : undulation
ondulado, -da *adj* **1** : wavy <pelo ondulado : wavy hair> **2** : undulating
ondular *vt* : to wave (hair) — *vi* : to undulate, to ripple
oneroso, -sa *adj* GRAVOSO : onerous, burdensome
ónix *nm* : onyx
onza *nf* : ounce
opacar {72} *vt* **1** : to make opaque or dull **2** : to outshine, to overshadow
opacidad *nf* **1** : opacity **2** : dullness
opaco, -ca *adj* **1** : opaque **2** : dull
ópalo *nm* : opal
opción *nf, pl* **opciones 1** ALTERNATIVA : option, choice **2** : right, chance <tener opción a : to be eligible for>
opcional *adj* : optional — **opcionalmente** *adv*
ópera *nf* : opera
operación *nf, pl* **-ciones 1** : operation **2** : transaction, deal
operacional *adj* : operational
operador, -dora *n* **1** : operator **2** : cameraman, projectionist
operante *adj* : operating, working
operar *vt* **1** : to produce, to bring about **2** INTERVENIR : to operate on **3** *Mex* : to operate, to run (a machine) — *vi* **1** : to operate, to function **2** : to deal, to do business — **operarse** *vr* **1** : to come about, to take place **2** : to have an operation
operario, -ria *n* : laborer, worker
operático, -ca → **operístico**
operativo[1]**, -va** *adj* **1** : operating <capacidad operativa : operating capacity> **2** : operative

operativo[2] *nm* : operation <operativo militar : military operation>
opereta *nf* : operetta
operístico, -ca *adj* : operatic
opiato *nm* : opiate
opinable *adj* : arguable
opinar *vi* **1 :** to think, to have an opinion **2 :** to express an opinion **3 opinar bien de :** to think highly of — *vt* : to think <opinamos lo mismo : we're of the same opinion, we're in agreement>
opinión *nf, pl* **-niones :** opinion, belief
opio *nm* : opium
oponente *nmf* : opponent
oponer {60} *vt* **1** CONTRAPONER : to oppose, to place against **2 oponer resistencia :** to resist, to put up a fight — **oponerse** *vr* **~ a :** to object to, to be against
oporto *nm* : port (wine)
oportunamente *adv* **1 :** at the right time, opportunely **2 :** appropriately
oportunidad *nf* : opportunity, chance
oportunismo *nm* : opportunism
oportunista[1] *adj* : opportunistic
oportunista[2] *nmf* : opportunist
oportuno, -na *adj* **1 :** opportune, timely **2 :** suitable, appropriate
oposición *nf, pl* **-ciones :** opposition
opositor, -tora *n* ADVERSARIO : opponent
oposum *nm* ZARIGÜEYA : opossum
opresión *nf, pl* **-siones 1 :** oppression **2 opresión de pecho :** tightness in the chest
opresivo, -va *adj* : oppressive
opresor[1]**, -sora** *adj* : oppressive
opresor[2]**, -sora** *n* : oppressor
oprimir *vt* **1 :** to oppress **2 :** to press, to squeeze <oprima el botón : push the button>
oprobio *nm* : opprobrium, shame
optar *vi* **1 ~ por :** to opt for, to choose **2 ~ a :** to aspire to, to apply for <dos candidatos optan a la presidencia : two candidates are running for president>
optativo, -va *adj* FACULTATIVO : optional
óptica *nf* **1 :** optics **2 :** optician's shop **3 :** viewpoint
óptico[1]**, -ca** *adj* : optical, optic
óptico[2]**, -ca** *n* : optician
optimismo *nm* : optimism
optimista[1] *adj* : optimistic
optimista[2] *nmf* : optimist
óptimo, -ma *adj* : optimum, optimal
optometría *nf* : optometry — **optometrista** *nmf*
opuesto[1] *pp* → **oponer**
opuesto[2] *adj* **1 :** opposite, contrary **2 :** opposed
opulencia *nf* : opulence — **opulento, -ta** *adj*
opus *nm* : opus
opuso, etc. → **oponer**
ora *conj* : now <los matices eran variados, ora verdes, ora ocres : the hues were varied, now green, now ocher>
oración *nf, pl* **-ciones 1** DISCURSO : oration, speech **2** PLEGARIA : prayer **3** FRASE : sentence, clause
oráculo *nm* : oracle
orador, -dora *n* : speaker, orator
oral *adj* : oral — **oralmente** *adv*
órale *interj Mex fam* **1 :** sure!, OK! <¿los dos por cinco pesos? ¡órale! : both for five pesos? you've got a deal!> **2 :** come on! <¡órale, vámonos! : come on, let's go!>
orangután *nm, pl* **-tanes :** orangutan
orar *vi* REZAR : to pray
oratoria *nf* : oratory
oratorio *nm* **1** CAPILLA : oratory, chapel **2 :** oratorio
orbe *nm* **1 :** orb, sphere **2** GLOBO : globe, world
órbita *nf* **1 :** orbit **2 :** eye socket **3** ÁMBITO : sphere, field
orbitador *nm* : space shuttle, orbiter
orbital *adj* : orbital
orden[1] *nm, pl* **órdenes 1 :** order <todo está en orden : everything's in order> <por orden cronológico : in chronological order> **2 orden del día :** agenda (at a meeting) **3 orden público :** law and order
orden[2] *nf, pl* **órdenes 1 :** order <una orden religiosa : a religious order> <una orden de tacos : an order of tacos> **2 orden de compra :** purchase order **3 estar a la orden del día :** to be the order of the day, to be prevalent
ordenación *nf, pl* **-ciones 1 :** ordination **2 :** ordering, organizing
ordenadamente *adv* : in an orderly fashion, neatly
ordenado, -da *adj* : orderly, neat
ordenador *nm Spain* : computer
ordenamiento *nm* **1 :** ordering, organizing **2 :** code (of laws)
ordenanza[1] *nf* REGLAMENTO : ordinance, regulation
ordenanza[2] *nm* : orderly (in the armed forces)
ordenar *vt* **1** MANDAR : to order, to command **2** ARREGLAR : to put in order, to arrange **3 :** to ordain (a priest)
ordeñar *vt* : to milk
ordeño *nm* : milking
ordinal *nm* : ordinal (number)
ordinariamente *adv* **1 :** usually **2 :** coarsely
ordinariez *nf* : coarseness, vulgarity
ordinario, -ria *adj* **1 :** ordinary **2 :** coarse, common, vulgar **3 de ~ :** usually
orear *vt* : to air
orégano *nm* : oregano
oreja *nf* : ear
orfanato *nm* : orphanage
orfanatorio *nm Mex* : orphanage
orfebre *nmf* : goldsmith, silversmith
orfebrería *nf* : articles of gold or silver

orfelinato *nm* : orphanage
orgánico, -ca *adj* : organic — **orgánicamente** *adv*
organigrama *nm* : organization chart, flowchart
organismo *nm* **1** : organism **2** : agency, organization
organista *nmf* : organist
organización *nf, pl* **-ciones** : organization
organizador[1], **-dora** *adj* : organizing
organizador[2], **-dora** *n* : organizer
organizar {21} *vt* : to organize, to arrange — **organizarse** *vr* : to get organized
organizativo, -va *adj* : organizational
órgano *nm* : organ
orgasmo *nm* : orgasm
orgía *nf* : orgy
orgullo *nm* : pride
orgulloso, -sa *adj* : proud — **orgullosamente** *adv*
orientación *nf, pl* **-ciones 1** : orientation **2** DIRECCIÓN : direction, course **3** GUÍA : guidance, direction
oriental[1] *adj* **1** : eastern **2** : oriental **3** *Arg, Uru* : Uruguayan
oriental[2] *nmf* **1** : Easterner **2** : Oriental **3** *Arg, Uru* : Uruguayan
orientar *vt* **1** : to orient, to position **2** : to guide, to direct — **orientarse** *vr* **1** : to orient oneself, to get one's bearings **2** ~ **hacia** : to turn towards, to lean towards
oriente *nm* **1** : east, East **2 el Oriente** : the Orient
orífice *nmf* : goldsmith
orificio *nm* : orifice, opening
origen *nm, pl* **orígenes 1** : origin **2** : lineage, birth **3 dar origen a** : to give rise to **4 en su origen** : originally
original *adj & nm* : original — **originalmente** *adv*
originalidad *nf* : originality
originar *vt* : to originate, to give rise to — **originarse** *vr* : to originate, to begin
originario, -ria *adj* ~ **de** : native of
originariamente *adv* : originally
orilla *nf* **1** BORDE : border, edge **2** : bank (of a river) **3** : shore
orillar *vt* **1** : to skirt, to go around **2** : to trim, to edge (cloth) **3** : to settle, to wind up **4** *Mex* : to pull over (a vehicle)
orín *nm* **1** HERRUMBRE : rust **2 orines** *nmpl* : urine
orina *nf* : urine
orinación *nf* : urination
orinal *nm* : urinal (vessel)
orinar *vi* : to urinate — **orinarse** *vr* : to wet oneself
oriol *nm* OROPÉNDOLA : oriole
oriundo, -da *adj* ~ **de** : native of
orla *nf* : border, edging
orlar *vt* : to edge, to trim
ornamentación *nf, pl* **-ciones** : ornamentation
ornamental *adj* : ornamental
ornamentar *vt* ADORNAR : to ornament, to adorn
ornamento *nm* : ornament, adornment
ornar *vt* : to adorn, to decorate
ornitología *nf* : ornithology
ornitólogo, -ga *n* : ornithologist
ornitorrinco *nm* : platypus
oro *nm* : gold
orondo, -da *adj* **1** : rounded, potbellied (of a container) **2** *fam* : smug, self-satisfied
oropel *nm* : glitz, glitter, tinsel
oropéndola *nf* : oriole
orquesta *nf* : orchestra — **orquestal** *adj*
orquestar *vt* : to orchestrate — **orquestación** *nf*
orquídea *nf* : orchid
ortiga *nf* : nettle
ortodoncia *nf* : orthodontics
ortodoncista *nmf* : orthodontist
ortodoxia *nf* : orthodoxy
ortodoxo, -xa *adj* : orthodox
ortografía *nf* : orthography, spelling
ortográfico, -ca *adj* : orthographic, spelling
ortopedia *nf* : orthopedics
ortopedista *nmf* : orthopedist
oruga *nf* **1** : caterpillar **2** : track (of a tank, etc.)
orzuelo *nm* : sty, stye (in the eye)
os *pron pl* (*objective form of* **vosotros**) *Spain* **1** : you, to you **2** : yourselves, to yourselves **3** : each other, to each other
osa *nf* → **oso**
osadía *nf* **1** VALOR : boldness, daring **2** AUDACIA : audacity, nerve
osado, -da *adj* **1** : bold, daring **2** : audacious, impudent — **osadamente** *adv*
osamenta *nf* : skeletal remains *pl*, bones *pl*
osar *vi* : to dare
oscilación *nf, pl* **-ciones 1** : oscillation **2** : fluctuation **3** : vacillation, wavering
oscilar *vi* **1** BALANCEARSE : to swing, to sway, to oscillate **2** FLUCTUAR : to fluctuate **3** : to vacillate, to waver
oscuramente *adv* : obscurely
oscurecer {53} *vt* **1** : to darken **2** : to obscure, to confuse, to cloud **3 al oscurecer** : at dusk, at nightfall — *v impers* : to grow dark, to get dark — **oscurecerse** *vr* : to darken, to dim
oscuridad *nf* **1** : darkness **2** : obscurity
oscuro, -ra *adj* **1** : dark **2** : obscure **3 a oscuras** : in the dark, in darkness
óseo, ósea *adj* : skeletal, bony
ósmosis *or* **osmosis** *nf* : osmosis
oso, osa *n* **1** : bear **2 Osa Mayor** : Big Dipper **3 Osa Menor** : Little Dipper **4 oso blanco** : polar bear **5 oso hormiguero** : anteater **6 oso de peluche** : teddy bear
ostensible *adj* : ostensible, apparent — **ostensiblemente** *adv*
ostentación *nf, pl* **-ciones** : ostentation, display

ostentar *vt* **1** : to display, to flaunt **2** POSEER : to have, to hold <ostenta el récord mundial : he holds the world record>
ostentoso, -sa *adj* : ostentatious, showy — **ostentosamente** *adv*
osteópata *nmf* : osteopath
osteopatía *n* : osteopathy
osteoporosis *nf* : osteoporosis
ostión *nm, pl* **ostiones 1** *Mex* : oyster **2** *Chile* : scallop
ostra *nf* : oyster
ostracismo *nm* : ostracism
otear *vt* : to scan, to survey, to look over
otero *nm* : knoll, hillock
otomana *nf* : ottoman
otoñal *adj* : autumn, autumnal
otoño *nm* : autumn, fall
otorgamiento *nm* : granting, awarding
otorgar {52} *vt* **1** : to grant, to award **2** : to draw up, to frame (a legal document)
otro[1], otra *adj* **1** : other **2** : another <en otro juego, ellos ganaron : in another game, they won> **3 otra vez** : again **4 de otra manera** : otherwise **5 otra parte** : elsewhere **6 en otro tiempo** : once, formerly
otro[2], otra *pron* **1** : another one <dame otro : give me another> **2** : other one <el uno o el otro : one or the other> **3 los otros, las otras** : the others, the rest <me dio una y se quedó con las otras : he gave me one and kept the rest>
ovación *nf, pl* **-ciones** : ovation
ovacionar *vt* : to cheer, to applaud
oval → **ovalado**
ovalado, -da *adj* : oval
óvalo *nm* : oval
ovárico, -ca *adj* : ovarian
ovario *nm* : ovary
oveja *nf* **1** : sheep, ewe **2 oveja negra** : black sheep
overol *nm* : overalls *pl*
ovillar *vt* : to roll into a ball
ovillo *nm* **1** : ball (of yarn) **2** : tangle
ovni *or* **OVNI** *nm* (*objeto volador no identificado*) : UFO
ovoide *adj* : ovoid, ovoidal
ovulación *nf, pl* **-ciones** : ovulation
ovular *vi* : to ovulate
óvulo *nm* : ovum
oxidación *nf, pl* **-ciones 1** : oxidation **2** : rusting
oxidado, -da *adj* : rusty
oxidar *vt* **1** : to cause to rust **2** : to oxidize — **oxidarse** *vr* : to rust, to become rusty
óxido *nm* **1** HERRUMBRE, ORÍN : rust **2** : oxide
oxigenar *vt* **1** : to oxygenate **2** : to bleach (hair)
oxígeno *nm* : oxygen
oxiuro *nm* : pinworm
oye, etc. → **oír**
oyente *nmf* **1** : listener **2** : auditor, auditing student
ozono *nm* : ozone

P

p *nf* : seventeenth letter of the Spanish alphabet
pabellón *nm, pl* **-llones 1** : pavilion **2** : summerhouse, lodge **3** : flag (of a vessel)
pabilo *nm* MECHA : wick
paca *nf* FARDO : bale
pacana *nf* : pecan
pacer {48} *v* : to graze, to pasture
paces → **paz**
pachanga *nf fam* : party, bash
paciencia *nf* : patience
paciente *adj & nmf* : patient — **pacientemente** *adv*
pacificación *nf, pl* **-ciones** : pacification
pacíficamente *adv* : peacefully, peaceably
pacificar {72} *vt* : to pacify, to calm — **pacificarse** *vr* : to calm down, to abate
pacífico, -ca *adj* : peaceful, pacific
pacifismo *nm* : pacifism
pacifista *adj & nmf* : pacifist
pacotilla *nf* **de ~** : shoddy, trashy
pactar *vt* : to agree on — *vi* : to come to an agreement
pacto *nm* CONVENIO : pact, agreement
padecer {53} *vt* : to suffer, to endure — *vi* ADOLECER **~ de** : to suffer from
padecimiento *nm* **1** : suffering **2** : ailment, condition
padrastro *nm* **1** : stepfather **2** : hangnail
padre[1] *adj Mex fam* : fantastic, great
padre[2] *nm* **1** : father **2 padres** *nmpl* : parents
padrenuestro *nm* : Lord's Prayer, paternoster
padrino *nm* **1** : godfather **2** : best man **3** : sponsor, patron
padrón *nm, pl* **padrones** : register, roll <padrón municipal : city register>
paella *nf* : paella
paga *nf* **1** : payment **2** : pay, wages *pl*
pagadero, -ra *adj* : payable
pagado, -da *adj* **1** : paid **2 pagado de sí mismo** : self-satisfied, smug
pagador, -dora *n* : payer
paganismo *nm* : paganism
pagano, -na *adj & n* : pagan
pagar {52} *vt* : to pay, to pay for, to repay — *vi* : to pay
pagaré *nm* VALE : promissory note, IOU
página *nf* : page

pago *nm* **1** : payment **2 en pago de** : in return for

pagoda *nf* : pagoda

pague, etc. → **pagar**

país *nm* **1** NACIÓN : country, nation **2** REGIÓN : region, territory

paisaje *nm* : scenery, landscape

paisano, -na *n* COMPATRIOTA : compatriot, fellow countryman

paja *nf* **1** : straw **2** *fam* : trash, tripe

pajar *nm* : hayloft, haystack

pajarera *nf* : aviary

pájaro *nm* : bird <pájaro cantor : songbird> <pájaro bobo : penguin> <pájaro carpintero : woodpecker>

pajita *nf* : (drinking) straw

pajote *nm* : straw, mulch

pala *nf* **1** : shovel, spade **2** : blade (of an oar or a rotor) **3** : paddle, racket

palabra *nf* **1** VOCABLO : word **2** PROMESA : word, promise <un hombre de palabra : a man of his word> **3** HABLA : speech **4** : right to speak <tener la palabra : to have the floor>

palabrería *nf* : empty talk

palabrota *nf* : swearword

palacio *nm* **1** : palace, mansion **2 palacio de justicia** : courthouse

paladar *nm* **1** : palate **2** GUSTO : taste

paladear *vt* SABOREAR : to savor

paladín *nm, pl* **-dines** : champion, defender

palanca *nf* **1** : lever, crowbar **2** *fam* : leverage, influence **3 palanca de cambio** *or* **palanca de velocidad** : gearshift

palangana *nf* : washbowl

palanqueta *nf* : jimmy, small crowbar

palco *nm* : box (in a theater or stadium)

palear *vt* **1** : to shovel **2** : to paddle

palenque *nm* **1** ESTACADA : stockade, palisade **2** : arena, ring

paleontología *nf* : paleontology

paleontólogo, -ga *n* : paleontologist

palestino, -na *adj & n* : Palestinian

palestra *nf* : arena <salir a la palestra : to join the fray>

paleta *nf* **1** : palette **2** : trowel **3** : spatula **4** : blade, vane **5** : paddle **6** *CA, Mex* : lollipop, Popsicle—

paletilla *nf* : shoulder blade

paliar *vt* MITIGAR : to alleviate, to palliate

paliativo[1], -va *adj* : palliative

paliativo[2] *nm* : palliative

palidecer {53} *vi* : to turn pale

palidez *nf, pl* **-deces** : paleness, pallor

pálido, -da *adj* : pale

palillo *nm* **1** MONDADIENTES : toothpick **2 palillos** *nmpl* : chopsticks **3 palillo de tambor** : drumstick

paliza *nf* : beating, pummeling <darle una paliza a : to beat, to thrash>

palma *nf* **1** : palm (of the hand) **2** : palm (tree or leaf) **3 batir palmas** : to clap, to applaud **4 llevarse la palma** *fam* : to take the cake

palmada *nf* **1** : pat **2** : slap **3** : clap

palmarés *nm* : record (of achievements)

palmario, -ria *adj* MANIFIESTO : clear, manifest

palmeado, -da *adj* : webbed

palmear *vt* : to slap on the back — *vi* : to clap, to applaud

palmera *nf* : palm tree

palmo *nm* **1** : span, small amount **2 palmo a palmo** : bit by bit, inch by inch **3 dejar con un palmo de narices** : to disappoint

palmotear *vi* : to applaud

palmoteo *nm* : clapping, applause

palo *nm* **1** : stick, pole, post **2** : shaft, handle <palo de escoba : broomstick> **3** : mast, spar **4** : wood **5** : blow (with a stick) **6** : suit (of cards)

paloma *nf* **1** : pigeon, dove **2 paloma mensajera** : carrier pigeon

palomilla *nf* : moth

palomitas *nfpl* : popcorn

palpable *adj* : palpable, tangible

palpar *vt* : to feel, to touch

palpitación *nf, pl* **-ciones** : palpitation

palpitar *vi* : to palpitate, to throb — **palpitante** *adj*

palta *nf* : avocado

paludismo *nm* MALARIA : malaria

palurdo, -da *n* : boor, yokel, bumpkin

pampa *nf* : pampa

pampeano, -na *adj* : pampean, pampas

pampero → **pampeano**

pan *nm* **1** : bread **2** : loaf of bread **3** : cake, bar <pan de jabón : bar of soap> **4 pan dulce** *CA, Mex* : traditional pastry **5 pan tostado** : toast **6 ser pan comido** *fam* : to be a piece of cake, to be a cinch

pana *nf* : corduroy

panacea *nf* : panacea

panadería *nf* : bakery, bread shop

panadero, -ra *n* : baker

panal *nm* : honeycomb

panameño, -ña *adj & n* : Panamanian

pancarta *nf* : placard, sign

pancita *nf Mex* : tripe

páncreas *nms & pl* : pancreas

panda *nmf* : panda

pandeado, -da *adj* : warped

pandearse *vr* **1** : to warp **2** : to bulge, to sag

pandemonio *or* **pandemónium** *nm* : pandemonium

pandereta *nf* : tambourine

pandero *nm* : tambourine

pandilla *nf* **1** : group, clique **2** : gang

panecito *nm* : roll, bread roll

panegírico[1], -ca *adj* : eulogistic, panegyrical

panegírico[2] *nm* : eulogy, panegyric

panel *nm* : panel — **panelista** *nmf*

panera *nf* : bread box

panfleto *nm* : pamphlet

pánico *nm* : panic

panorama *nm* **1** VISTA : panorama, view **2** : scene, situation <el pa-

norama nacional : the national scene> 3 PERSPECTIVA : outlook
panorámico, -ca *adj* : panoramic
panqueque *nm* : pancake
pantaletas *nfpl* : panties
pantalla *nf* **1** : screen, monitor **2** : lampshade **3** : fan
pantalón *nm, pl* **-lones 1** : pants *pl,* trousers *pl* **2 pantalones vaqueros** : jeans **3 pantalones de mezclilla** *Chile, Mex* : jeans **4 pantalones de montar** : jodhpurs
pantano *nm* **1** : swamp, marsh, bayou **2** : reservoir **3** : obstacle, difficulty
pantanoso, -sa *adj* **1** : marshy, swampy **2** : difficult, thorny
panteón *nm, pl* **-teones 1** CEMENTERIO : cemetery **2** : pantheon, mausoleum
pantera *nf* : panther
pantimedias *nfpl Mex* : panty hose
pantomima *nf* : pantomime
pantorrilla *nf* : calf (of the leg)
pantufla *nf* ZAPATILLA : slipper
panza *nf* BARRIGA : belly, paunch
panzón, -zona *adj, mpl* **panzones** : potbellied, paunchy
pañal *nm* : diaper
pañería *nf* **1** : cloth, material **2** : fabric store
pañito *nm* : doily
paño *nm* **1** : cloth **2** : rag, dust cloth **3 paño de cocina** : dishcloth **4 paño higiénico** : sanitary napkin
pañuelo *nm* **1** : handkerchief **2** : scarf
papa[1] *nm* : pope
papa[2] *nf* **1** : potato **2 papa dulce** : sweet potato **3 papas fritas** : potato chips, french fries **4 papas a la francesa** *Mex* : french fries
papá *nm fam* **1** : dad, pop **2 papás** *nmpl* : parents, folks
papada *nf* **1** : double chin, jowl **2** : dewlap
papagayo *nm* LORO : parrot
papal *adj* : papal
papalote *nm Mex* : kite
papaya *nf* : papaya
papel *nm* **1** : paper, piece of paper **2** : role, part **3 papel de estaño** : tinfoil **4 papel de empapelar** *or* **papel pintado** : wallpaper **5 papel higiénico** : toilet paper **6 papel de lija** : sandpaper
papeleo *nm* : paperwork, red tape
papelera *nf* : wastebasket
papelería *nf* : stationery store
papelero, -ra *adj* : paper
papeleta *nf* **1** : ballot **2** : ticket, slip
paperas *nfpl* : mumps
papi *nm fam* : daddy, papa
papilla *nf* **1** : pap, mash **2 hacer papilla** : to beat to a pulp
papiro *nm* : papyrus
paquete *nm* BULTO : package, parcel
paquistaní *adj & nmf* : Pakistani
par[1] *adj* : even (in number)
par[2] *nm* **1** : pair, couple **2** : equal, peer <sin par : matchless, peerless> **3** : par (in golf) **4** : rafter **5 de par en par** : wide open
par[3] *nf* **1** : par <por encima de la par : above par> **2 a la par que** : at the same time as, as well as <interesante a la par que instructivo : both interesting and informative>
para *prep* **1** : for <para ti : for you> <alta para su edad : tall for her age> <una cita para el lunes : an appointment for Monday> **2** : to, towards <para la derecha : to the right> <van para el río : they're heading towards the river> **3** : to, in order to <lo hace para molestarte : he does it to annoy you> **4** : around, by (a time) <para mañana estarán listos : they'll be ready by tomorrow> **5 para adelante** : forwards **6 para atrás** : backwards **7 para que** : so, so that, in order that <te lo digo para que sepas : I'm telling you so you'll know>
parabién *nm, pl* **-bienes** : congratulations *pl*
parábola *nf* **1** : parable **2** : parabola
parabrisas *nms & pl* : windshield
paracaídas *nms & pl* : parachute
paracaidista *nmf* **1** : parachutist **2** : paratrooper
parachoques *nms & pl* : bumper
parada *nf* **1** : stop <parada de autobús : bus stop> **2** : catch, save, parry (in sports) **3** DESFILE : parade
paradero *nm* : whereabouts
paradigma *nm* : paradigm
parado, -da *adj* **1** : motionless, idle, stopped **2** : standing (up) **3** : confused, bewildered **4 bien (mal) parado** : in good (bad) shape <salió bien parado : it turned out well for him>
paradoja *nf* : paradox
paradójico, -ca *adj* : paradoxical
parafernalia *nf* : paraphernalia
parafina *nf* : paraffin
parafrasear *vt* : to paraphrase
paráfrasis *nfs & pl* : paraphrase
paraguas *nms & pl* : umbrella
paraguayo, -ya *adj & n* : Paraguayan
paraíso *nm* **1** : paradise, heaven **2 paraíso fiscal** : tax shelter
paraje *nm* : spot, place
paralelismo *nm* : parallelism, similarity
paralelo[1], -la *adj* : parallel
paralelo[2] *nm* : parallel
paralelogramo *nm* : parallelogram
parálisis *nfs & pl* **1** : paralysis **2** : standstill **3 parálisis cerebral** : cerebral palsy
paralítico, -ca *adj & n* : paralytic
paralizar {21} *vt* **1** : to paralyze **2** : to bring to a standstill — **paralizarse** *vr*
parámetro *nm* : parameter
páramo *nm* : barren plateau, moor
parangón *nm, pl* **-gones 1** : comparison **2 sin ~** : incomparable
paraninfo *nm* : auditorium, assembly hall

paranoia *nf* : paranoia
paranoico, -ca *adj & n* : paranoid
parapeto *nm* : parapet, rampart
parapléjico, -ca *adj & n* : paraplegic
parar *vt* **1** DETENER : to stop **2** : to stand, to prop — *vi* **1** CESAR : to stop **2** : to stay, to put up **3 ir a parar** : to end up, to wind up — **pararse** *vr* **1** : to stop **2** ATASCARSE : to stall (out) **3** : to stand up, to get up
pararrayos *nms & pl* : lightning rod
parasitario, -ria *adj* : parasitic
parasitismo *nm* : parasitism
parásito *nm* : parasite
parasol *nm* SOMBRILLA : parasol
parcela *nf* : parcel, tract of land
parcelar *vt* : to parcel (land)
parchar *vt* : to patch, to patch up
parche *nm* : patch
parcial *adj* : partial — **parcialmente** *adv*
parcialidad *nf* : partiality, bias
parco, -ca *adj* **1** : sparing, frugal **2** : moderate, temperate
pardo, -da *adj* : brownish grey
pardusco → **pardo**
parecer[1] {53} *vi* **1** : to seem, to look, to appear to be <parece bien fácil : it looks very easy> <así parece : so it seems> <pareces una princesa : you look like a princess> **2** : to think, to have an opinion <me parece que sí : I think so> **3** : to like, to be in agreement <si te parece : if you like, if it's all right with you> — **parecerse** *vr* **~ a** : to resemble
parecer[2] *nm* **1** OPINIÓN : opinion **2** ASPECTO : appearance <al parecer : apparently>
parecido[1], **-da** *adj* **1** : similar, alike **2 bien parecido** : good-looking
parecido[2] *nm* : resemblance, similarity
pared *nf* : wall
pareja *nf* **1** : couple, pair **2** : partner, mate
parejo, -ja *adj* **1** : even, smooth, level **2** : equal, similar
parentela *nf* : relations *pl*, kinfolk
parentesco *nm* : relationship, kinship
paréntesis *nms & pl* **1** : parenthesis **2** : digression
parentético, -ca *adj* : parenthetic, parenthetical
paria *nmf* : pariah, outcast
paridad *nf* : parity, equality
pariente *nmf* : relative, relation
parir *vi* : to give birth — *vt* : to give birth to, to bear
parking *nm* : parking lot
parlamentar *vi* : to talk, to parley
parlamentario[1], **-ria** *adj* : parliamentary
parlamentario[2], **-ria** *n* : member of parliament
parlamento *nm* **1** : parliament **2** : negotiations *pl*, talks *pl*
parlanchín[1], **-china** *adj, mpl* **-chines** : chatty, talkative
parlanchín[2], **-china** *n, mpl* **-chines** : chatterbox
parlante *nm* ALTOPARLANTE : loudspeaker
parlotear *vi fam* : to gab, to chat, to prattle
parloteo *nm fam* : prattle, chatter
paro *nm* **1** HUELGA : strike **2** : stoppage, stopping **3 paro forzoso** : layoff
parodia *nf* : parody
parodiar *vt* : to parody
parpadear *vi* **1** : to blink **2** : to flicker
parpadeo *nm* **1** : blink, blinking **2** : flickering
párpado *nm* : eyelid
parque *nm* **1** : park **2 parque de atracciones** : amusement park
parquear *vt* : to park — **parquearse** *vr*
parqueo *nm* : parking
parquet *or* **parqué** *nm* : parquet
parquímetro *nm* : parking meter
parra *nf* : vine, grapevine
párrafo *nm* : paragraph
parranda *nf fam* : party, spree
parrilla *nf* **1** : broiler, grill **2** : grate
parrillada *nf* BARBACOA : barbecue
párroco *nm* : parish priest
parroquia *nf* **1** : parish **2** : parish church **3** : customers *pl*, clientele
parroquial *adj* : parochial
parroquiano, -na *nm* **1** : parishioner **2** : customer, patron
parsimonia *nf* **1** : calm **2** : parsimony, thrift
parsimonioso, -sa *adj* **1** : calm, unhurried **2** : parsimonious, thrifty
parte[1] *nm* : report, dispatch
parte[2] *nf* **1** : part, share **2** : part, place <en alguna parte : somewhere> <por todas partes : everywhere> **3** : party (in negotiations, etc.) **4 de parte de** : on behalf of **5 ¿de parte de quién?** : may I ask who's calling? **6 tomar parte** : to take part
partero, -ra *n* : midwife
partición *nf, pl* **-ciones** : division, sharing
participación *nf, pl* **-ciones 1** : participation **2** : share, interest **3** : announcement, notice
participante *nmf* **1** : participant **2** : competitor, entrant
participar *vi* **1** : to participate, to take part **2 ~ en** : to have a share in — *vt* : to announce, to notify
partícipe *nmf* : participant
participio *nm* : participle
partícula *nf* : particle
particular[1] *adj* **1** : particular, specific **2** : private, personal **3** : special, unique
particular[2] *nm* **1** : matter, detail **2** : individual
particularidad *nf* : characteristic, peculiarity
particularizar {21} *vt* **1** : to distinguish, to characterize **2** : to specify

partida *nf* **1 :** departure **2 :** item, entry **3 :** certificate <partida de nacimiento : birth certificate> **4 :** game, match, hand **5 :** party, group
partidario, -ria *n* **:** follower, supporter
partido *nm* **1 :** (political) party **2 :** game, match <partido de futbol : soccer game> **3** APOYO **:** support, following **4** PROVECHO **:** profit, advantage <sacar partido de : to profit from>
partir *vt* **1 :** to cut, to split **2 :** to break, to crack **3 :** to share (out), to divide — *vi* **1 :** to leave, to depart **2 ~ de :** to start from **3 a partir de :** as of, from <a partir de hoy : as of today> — **partirse** *vr* **1 :** to smash, to split open **2 :** to chap
partisano, -na *adj & n* **:** partisan
partitura *nf* **:** (musical) score
parto *nm* **1 :** childbirth, delivery, labor <estar de parto : to be in labor> **2 :** product, creation, brainchild
parvulario *nm* **:** nursery school
párvulo, -la *n* **:** toddler, preschooler
pasa *nf* **1 :** raisin **2 pasa de Corinto :** currant
pasable *adj* **:** passable, tolerable — **pasablemente** *adv*
pasada *nf* **1 :** passage, passing **2 :** pass, wipe, coat (of paint) **3 de ~ :** in passing **4 mala pasada :** dirty trick
pasadizo *nm* **:** passageway, corridor
pasado¹, -da *adj* **1 :** past <el año pasado : last year> <pasado mañana : the day after tomorrow> <pasadas las siete : after seven o'clock> **2 :** stale, bad, overripe **3 :** old-fashioned, out-of-date **4 :** overripe, slightly spoiled
pasado² *nm* **:** past
pasador *nm* **1 :** bolt, latch **2 :** barrette **3** *Mex* **:** bobby pin
pasaje *nm* **1 :** ticket (for travel) **2** TARIFA **:** fare **3 :** passageway **4 :** passengers *pl*
pasajero¹, -ra *adj* **:** passing, fleeting
pasajero², -ra *n* **:** passenger
pasamanos *nms & pl* **1 :** handrail **2 :** banister
pasante *nmf* **:** assistant
pasaporte *nm* **:** passport
pasar *vi* **1 :** to pass, to go by, to come by **2 :** to come in, to enter <¿se puede pasar? : may we come in?> **3 :** to happen <¿qué pasa? : what's happening?, what's going on?> **4 :** to manage, to get by **5 :** to be over, to end **6 ~ de :** to exceed, to go beyond **7 ~ por :** to pretend to be — *vt* **1 :** to pass, to give <¿me pasas la sal? : would you pass me the salt?> **2 :** to pass (a test) **3 :** to go over, to cross **4 :** to spend (time) **5 :** to tolerate **6 :** to go through, to suffer **7 :** to show (a movie, etc.) **8 :** to overtake, to pass, to surpass **9 :** to pass over, to wipe up **10 pasarlo bien** *or* **pasarla bien :** to have a good time **11 pasarlo mal** *or* **pasarla mal :** to have a bad time, to have a hard time **12 pasar por alto :** to overlook, to omit — **pasarse** *vr* **1 :** to move, to pass, to go away **2 :** to slip one's mind, to forget **3 :** to go too far
pasarela *nf* **1 :** gangplank **2 :** footbridge **3 :** runway, catwalk
pasatiempo *nm* **:** pastime, hobby
Pascua *nf* **1 :** Easter **2 :** Passover **3 :** Christmas **4 Pascuas** *nfpl* **:** Christmas season
pase *nm* **1** PERMISO **:** pass, permit **2 pase de abordar** *Mex* **:** boarding pass
pasear *vi* **:** to take a walk, to go for a ride — *vt* **1 :** to take for a walk **2 :** to parade around, to show off — **pasearse** *vr* **:** to walk around
paseo *nm* **1 :** walk, stroll **2 :** ride **3** EXCURSIÓN **:** outing, trip
pasiflora *nf* **:** passionflower
pasillo *nm* CORREDOR **:** hallway, corridor, aisle
pasión *nf, pl* **pasiones :** passion
pasional *adj* **:** passionate <crimen pasional : crime of passion>
pasionaria *nf* → **pasiflora**
pasivo¹, -va *adj* **:** passive — **pasivamente** *adv*
pasivo² *nm* **1 :** liability <activos y pasivos : assets and liabilities> **2 :** debit side (of an account)
pasmado, -da *adj* **:** stunned, flabbergasted
pasmar *vt* **:** to amaze, to stun — **pasmarse** *vr*
pasmo *nm* **1 :** shock, astonishment **2 :** wonder, marvel
pasmoso, -sa *adj* **:** incredible, amazing — **pasmosamente** *adv*
paso¹, -sa *adj* **:** dried <ciruela pasa : prune>
paso² *nm* **1 :** passage, passing <de paso : in passing, on the way> **2 :** way, path <abrirse paso : to make one's way> **3 :** crossing <paso de peatones : crosswalk> <paso a desnivel : underpass> <paso elevado : overpass> **4 :** step <paso a paso : step by step> **5 :** pace, gait <a buen paso : quickly, at a good rate>
pasta *nf* **1 :** paste <pasta de dientes *or* pasta dental : toothpaste> **2 :** pasta **3 :** pastry dough **4 libro en pasta dura :** hardcover book **5 tener pasta de :** to have the makings of
pastar *vi* **:** to graze — *vt* **:** to put to pasture
pastel¹ *adj* **:** pastel
pastel² *nm* **1 :** cake <pastel de cumpleaños : birthday cake> **2 :** pie, turnover **3 :** pastel
pastelería *nf* **:** pastry shop
pasteurización *nf, pl* **-ciones :** pasteurization
pasteurizar {21} *vt* **:** to pasteurize
pastilla *nf* **1** COMPRIMIDO, PÍLDORA **:** pill, tablet **2 :** lozenge <pastilla para la tos

: cough drop> 3 : cake (of soap), bar (of chocolate)

pastizal *nm* : pasture, grazing land

pasto *nm* 1 : pasture 2 HIERBA : grass, lawn

pastor, -tora *n* 1 : shepherd, shepherdess *f* 2 : minister, pastor

pastoral *adj & nf* : pastoral

pastorear *vt* : to shepherd, to tend

pastorela *nf* 1 : pastoral, pastourelle 2 *Mex* : a traditional Christmas play

pastoso, -sa *adj* 1 : pasty, doughy 2 : smooth, mellow (of sounds)

pata *nf* 1 : paw, leg (of an animal) 2 : foot, leg (of furniture) 3 **patas de gallo** : crow's-feet 4 **meter la pata** *fam* : to put one's foot in it, to make a blunder

patada *nf* 1 PUNTAPIÉ : kick 2 : stamp (of the foot)

patalear *vi* 1 : to kick 2 : to stamp one's feet

pataleta *nf fam* : tantrum

patán[1] *adj, pl* **patanes** : boorish, crude

patán[2] *nm, pl* **patanes** : boor, lout

patata *nf Spain* : potato

patear *vt* : to kick — *vi* : to stamp one's foot

patentar *vt* : to patent

patente[1] *adj* EVIDENTE : obvious, patent — **patentemente** *adv*

patente[2] *nf* : patent

paternal *adj* : fatherly, paternal

paternidad *nf* 1 : fatherhood, paternity 2 : parenthood 3 : authorship

paterno, -na *adj* : paternal <abuela paterna : paternal grandmother>

patético, -ca *adj* : pathetic, moving

patetismo *nm* : pathos

patíbulo *nm* : gallows, scaffold

patillas *nfpl* : sideburns

patín *nm, pl* **patines** : skate <patín de ruedas : roller skate>

patinador, -dora *n* : skater

patinaje *nm* : skating

patinar *vi* 1 : to skate 2 : to skid, to slip 3 *fam* : to slip up, to blunder

patinazo *nm* 1 : skid 2 *fam* : blunder, slipup

patineta *nf* 1 : scooter 2 : skateboard

patinete *nm* : scooter

patio *nm* 1 : courtyard, patio 2 **patio de recreo** : playground

patito, -ta *n* : duckling

pato, -ta *n* 1 : duck 2 **pato real** : mallard 3 **pagar el pato** *fam* : to take the blame

patología *nf* : pathology

patológico, -ca *adj* : pathological

patólogo, -ga *n* : pathologist

patraña *nf* : tall tale, humbug, nonsense

patria *nf* : native land

patriarca *nm* : patriarch — **patriarcal** *adj*

patriarcado *nm* : patriarchy

patrimonio *nm* : patrimony, legacy

patrio, -tria *adj* 1 : native, home <suelo patrio : native soil> 2 : paternal

patriota[1] *adj* : patriotic

patriota[2] *nmf* : patriot

patriotería *nf* : jingoism, chauvinism

patriotero[1], **-ra** *adj* : jingoistic, chauvinistic

patriotero[2], **-ra** *n* : jingoist, chauvinist

patriótico, -ca *adj* : patriotic

patriotismo *nm* : patriotism

patrocinador, -dora *n* : sponsor, patron

patrocinar *vt* : to sponsor

patrocinio *nm* : sponsorship, patronage

patrón[1], **-trona** *n, mpl* **patrones** 1 JEFE : boss 2 : patron saint

patrón[2] *nm, pl* **patrones** 1 : standard 2 : pattern (in sewing)

patronal *adj* 1 : management, employers' <sindicato patronal : employers' association> 2 : pertaining to a patron saint <fiesta patronal : patron saint's day>

patronato *nm* 1 : board, council 2 : foundation, trust

patrono, -na *n* 1 : employer 2 : patron saint

patrulla *nf* 1 : patrol 2 : police car, cruiser

patrullar *v* : to patrol

patrullero *nm* 1 : police car 2 : patrol boat

paulatino, -na *adj* : gradual

paupérrimo, -ma *adj* : destitute, poverty-stricken

pausa *nf* : pause, break

pausado[1] *adv* : slowly, deliberately <habla más pausado : speak more slowly>

pausado[2], **-da** *adj* : slow, deliberate — **pausadamente** *adv*

pauta *nf* 1 : rule, guideline 2 : lines *pl* (on paper)

pava *nf Arg, Bol, Chile* : kettle

pavimentar *vt* : pave

pavimento *nm* : pavement

pavo, -va *n* 1 : turkey 2 **pavo real** : peacock 3 **comer pavo** : to be a wallflower

pavón *nm, pl* **pavones** : peacock

pavonearse *vr* : to strut, to swagger

pavoneo *nm* : strut, swagger

pavor *nm* TERROR : dread, terror

pavoroso, -sa *adj* ATERRADOR : dreadful, terrifying

payasada *nf* BUFONADA : antic, buffoonery

payasear *vi* : to clown around

payaso, -sa *n* : clown

paz *nf, pl* **paces** 1 : peace 2 **dejar en paz** : to leave alone 3 **hacer las paces** : to make up, to reconcile

pazca, etc. → **pacer**

PC *nmf* : PC, personal computer

peaje *nm* : toll

peatón *nm, pl* **-tones** : pedestrian

peca *nf* : freckle

pecado *nm* : sin
pecador[1], -dora *adj* : sinful, sinning
pecador[2], -dora *n* : sinner
pecaminoso, -sa *adj* : sinful
pecar {72} *vi* **1** : to sin **2 ~ de** : to be too much (something) <no pecan de amabilidad : they're not overly friendly>
pécari *or* **pecarí** *nm* : peccary
pececillo *nm* : small fish
pecera *nf* : fishbowl, fish tank
pecho *nm* **1** : chest **2** SENO : breast, bosom **3** : heart, courage **4 dar el pecho** : to breast-feed **5 tomar a pecho** : to take to heart
pechuga *nf* : breast (of fowl)
pecoso, -sa *adj* : freckled
pectoral *adj* : pectoral
peculado *nm* : embezzlement
peculiar *adj* **1** CARACTERÍSTICO : particular, characteristic **2** RARO : peculiar, uncommon
peculiaridad *nf* : peculiarity
pecuniario, -ria *adj* : pecuniary
pedagogía *nf* : pedagogy
pedagógico, -ca *adj* : pedagogic, pedagogical
pedagogo, -ga *n* : educator, pedagogue
pedal *nm* : pedal
pedalear *vi* : to pedal
pedante[1] *adj* : pedantic
pedante[2] *nmf* : pedant
pedantería *nf* : pedantry
pedazo *nm* TROZO : piece, bit, chunk <caerse a pedazos : to fall to pieces> <hacer pedazos : to tear into shreds, to smash to pieces>
pedernal *nm* : flint
pedestal *nm* : pedestal
pedestre *adj* : commonplace, pedestrian
pediatra *nmf* : pediatrician
pediatría *nf* : pediatrics
pediátrico, -ca *adj* : pediatric
pedido *nm* **1** : order (of merchandise) **2** : request
pedigrí *nm* : pedigree
pedir {54} *vt* **1** : to ask for, to request <le pedí un préstamo a Claudia : I asked Claudia for a loan> **2** : to order (food, merchandise) **3 pedir disculpas** *or* **pedir perdón** : to apologize — *vi* **1** : to order **2** : to beg
pedrada *nf* **1** : blow (with a rock or stone) <la ventana se quebró de una pedrada : the window was broken by a rock> **2** *fam* : cutting remark, dig
pedregal *nm* : rocky ground
pedregoso, -sa *adj* : rocky, stony
pedrera *nf* CANTERA : quarry
pedrería *nf* : precious stones *pl*, gems *pl*
pegado, -da *adj* **1** : glued, stuck, stuck together **2 ~ a** : right next to
pegajoso, -sa *adj* **1** : sticky, gluey **2** : catchy <una tonada pegajosa : a catchy tune>
pegamento *nm* : adhesive, glue
pegar {52} *vt* **1** : to glue, to stick, to paste **2** : to attach, to sew on **3** : to infect with, to give <me pegó el resfriado : he gave me his cold> **4** GOLPEAR : to hit, to deal, to strike <me pegaron un puntapié : they gave me a kick> **5** : to give (out with) <pegó un grito : she let out a yell> — *vi* **1** : to adhere, to stick **2 ~ en** : to hit, to strike (against) **3 ~ con** : to match, to go with — **pegarse** *vr* **1** GOLPEARSE : to hit oneself, to hit each other **2** : to stick, to take hold **3** : to be contagious **4** *fam* : to tag along, to stick around
pegote *nm* **1** : sticky mess **2** *Mex* : sticker, adhesive label
pegue, etc. → **pegar**
peinado *nm* : hairstyle, hairdo
peinador, -dora *n* : hairdresser
peinar *vt* : to comb — **peinarse** *vr*
peine *nm* : comb
peineta *nf* : ornamental comb
peladez *nf, pl* **-deces** *Mex fam* : obscenity, bad language
pelado, -da *adj* **1** : bald, hairless **2** : peeled **3** : bare, barren **4** : broke, penniless **5** *Mex fam* : coarse, crude
pelador *nm* : peeler
pelagra *nf* : pellagra
pelaje *nm* : coat (of an animal), fur
pelar *vt* **1** : to peel, to shell **2** : to skin **3** : to pluck **4** : to remove hair from **5** *fam* : to clean out (of money) — **pelarse** *vr* **1** : to peel **2** *fam* : to get a haircut **3** *Mex fam* : to split, to leave
peldaño *nm* **1** : step, stair **2** : rung
pelea *nf* **1** LUCHA : fight **2** : quarrel
pelear *vi* **1** LUCHAR : to fight **2** DISPUTAR : to quarrel — **pelearse** *vr*
peleón, -ona *adj, mpl* **-ones** *Spain* : quarrelsome, argumentative
peleonero, -ra *adj Mex* : quarrelsome
peletería *nf* **1** : fur shop **2** : fur trade
peletero, -ra *n* : furrier
peliagudo, -da *adj* : tricky, difficult, ticklish
pelícano *nm* : pelican
película *nf* **1** : movie, film **2** : (photographic) film **3** : thin covering, layer
peligrar *vi* : to be in danger
peligro *nm* **1** : danger, peril **2** : risk <correr peligro de : to run the risk of>
peligroso, -sa *adj* : dangerous, hazardous
pelirrojo[1], -ja *adj* : red-haired, redheaded
pelirrojo[2], -ja *n* : redhead
pellejo *nm* **1** : hide, skin **2 salvar el pellejo** : to save one's neck
pellizcar {72} *vt* **1** : to pinch **2** : to nibble on
pellizco *nm* : pinch
pelo *nm* **1** : hair **2** : fur **3** : pile, nap **4 a pelo** : bareback **5 con pelos y señales** : in great detail **6 no tener pelos en la lengua** : to not mince words, to be blunt **7 tomarle el pelo a alguien** : to tease someone, to pull someone's leg

pelón, -lona *adj, mpl* **pelones 1 :** bald **2** *fam* **:** broke **3** *Mex fam* **:** tough, difficult

pelota *nf* **1 :** ball **2** *fam* **:** head **3 en pelotas** *fam* **:** naked **4 pelota vasca :** jai alai **5 pasar la pelota** *fam* **:** to pass the buck

pelotón *nm, pl* **-tones :** squad, detachment

peltre *nm* **:** pewter

peluca *nf* **:** wig

peluche *nm* **:** plush (fabric)

peludo, -da *adj* **:** hairy, shaggy, bushy

peluquería *nf* **1 :** hairdresser's, barber shop **2 :** hairdressing

peluquero, -ra *n* **:** barber, hairdresser

peluquín *nm, pl* **-quines** TUPÉ **:** hairpiece, toupee

pelusa *nf* **:** lint, fuzz

pélvico, -ca *adj* **:** pelvic

pelvis *nfs & pl* **:** pelvis

pena *nf* **1** CASTIGO **:** punishment, penalty <pena de muerte : death penalty> **2** AFLICCIÓN **:** sorrow, grief <morir de pena : to die of a broken heart> <¡que pena! : what a shame!, how sad!> **3** DOLOR **:** pain, suffering **4** DIFICULTAD **:** difficulty, trouble <a duras penas : with great difficulty> **5** VERGÜENZA **:** shame, embarrassment **6 valer la pena :** to be worthwhile

penacho *nm* **1 :** crest, tuft **2 :** plume (of feathers)

penal[1] *adj* **:** penal

penal[2] *nm* CÁRCEL **:** prison, penitentiary

penalidad *nf* **1 :** hardship **2 :** penalty, punishment

penalizar {21} *vt* **:** to penalize

penalty *nm* **:** penalty (in sports)

penar *vt* **:** to punish, to penalize — *vi* **:** to suffer, to grieve

pendenciero, -ra *adj* **:** argumentative, quarrelsome

pender *vi* **1 :** to hang **2 :** to be pending

pendiente[1] *adj* **1 :** pending **2 estar pendiente de :** to be watchful of, to be on the lookout for

pendiente[2] *nm Spain* **:** earring

pendiente[3] *nf* **:** slope, incline

pendón *nm, pl* **pendones :** banner

péndulo *nm* **:** pendulum

pene *nm* **:** penis

penetración *nf, pl* **-ciones 1 :** penetration **2 :** insight

penetrante *adj* **1 :** penetrating, piercing **2 :** sharp, acute **3 :** deep (of a wound)

penetrar *vi* **1 :** to penetrate, to sink in **2 ~ por** *or* **~ en :** to pierce, to go in, to enter into <el frío penetra por la ventana : the cold comes right in through the window> — *vt* **1 :** to penetrate, to permeate **2 :** to pierce <el dolor penetró su corazón : sorrow pierced her heart> **3 :** to fathom, to understand

penicilina *nf* **:** penicillin

península *nf* **:** peninsula — **peninsular** *adj*

penitencia *nf* **:** penance, penitence

penitenciaría *nf* **:** penitentiary

penitente *adj & nmf* **:** penitent

penol *nm* **:** yardarm

penoso, -sa *adj* **1 :** painful, distressing **2 :** difficult, arduous **3 :** shy, bashful

pensado, -da *adj* **1 bien pensado :** well thought-out **2 en el momento menos pensado :** when least expected **3 poco pensado :** badly thought-out **4 mal pensado :** evil-minded

pensador, -dora *n* **:** thinker

pensamiento *nm* **1 :** thought **2 :** thinking **3 :** pansy

pensar {55} *vi* **1 :** to think **2 ~ en :** to think about — *vt* **1 :** to think **2 :** to think about **3 :** to intend, to plan on — **pensarse** *vr* **:** to think over

pensativo, -va *adj* **:** pensive, thoughtful

pensión *nf, pl* **pensiones 1** JUBILACIÓN **:** pension **2 :** boarding house **3 pensión alimenticia :** alimony

pensionado, -da *n* → **pensionista**

pensionista *nmf* **1** JUBILADO **:** pensioner, retiree **2 :** boarder, lodger

pentágono *nm* **:** pentagon — **pentagonal** *adj*

pentagrama *nm* **:** staff (in music)

penúltimo, -ma *adj* **:** next to last, penultimate

penumbra *nf* **:** semidarkness

penuria *nf* **1** ESCASEZ **:** shortage, scarcity **2 :** poverty

peña *nf* **:** rock, crag

peñasco *nm* **:** crag, large rock

peñón *nm* → **peñasco**

peón *nm, pl* **peones 1 :** laborer, peon **2 :** pawn (in chess)

peonía *nf* **:** peony

peor[1] *adv* **1** (*comparative of* **mal**) **:** worse <se llevan peor que antes : they get along worse than before> **2** (*superlative of* **mal**) **:** worst <me fue peor que a nadie : I did the worst of all>

peor[2] *adj* **1** (*comparative of* **malo**) **:** worse <es peor que el original : it's worse than the original> **2** (*superlative of* **malo**) **:** worst <el peor de todos : the worst of all>

pepa *nf* **:** seed, pit (of a fruit)

pepenador, -dora *n CA, Mex* **:** scavenger

pepenar *vt CA, Mex* **:** to scavenge, to scrounge

pepinillo *nm* **:** pickle, gherkin

pepino *nm* **:** cucumber

pepita *nf* **1 :** seed, pip **2 :** nugget **3** *Mex* **:** dried pumpkin seed

peque, etc. → **pecar**

pequeñez *nf, pl* **-ñeces 1 :** smallness **2 :** trifle, triviality **3 pequeñez de espíritu :** pettiness

pequeño[1]**, -ña** *adj* **1 :** small, little <un libro pequeño : a small book> **2 :** young **3** BAJO **:** short

pequeño[2]**, -ña** *n* **:** child, little one

pera *nf* : pear
peraltar *vt* : to bank (a road)
perca *nf* : perch (fish)
percal *nm* : percale
percance *nm* : mishap, misfortune
percatarse *vr* **~ de** : to notice, to become aware of
percebe *nm* : barnacle
percepción *nf, pl* **-ciones 1** : perception **2** : idea, notion **3** COBRO : receipt (of payment), collection
perceptible *adj* : perceptible, noticeable — **perceptiblemente** *adv*
percha *nf* **1** : perch **2** : coat hanger **3** : coatrack, coat hook
perchero *nm* : coatrack
percibir *vt* **1** : to perceive, to notice, to sense **2** : to earn, to draw (a salary)
percudido, -da *adj* : grimy
percudir *vt* : to make grimy — **percudirse** *vr*
percusión *nf, pl* **-siones** : percussion
percusor *or* **percutor** *nm* : hammer (of a firearm)
perdedor[1], -dora *adj* : losing
perdedor[2], -dora *n* : loser
perder {56} *vt* **1** : to lose **2** : to miss <perdimos la oportunidad : we missed the opportunity> **3** : to waste (time) — *vi* : to lose — **perderse** *vr* EXTRAVIARSE : to get lost, to stray
perdición *nf, pl* **-ciones** : perdition, damnation
pérdida *nf* **1** : loss **2 pérdida de tiempo** : waste of time
perdidamente *adv* : hopelessly
perdido, -da *adj* **1** : lost **2** : inveterate, incorrigible <es un caso perdido : he's a hopeless case> **3** : in trouble, done for **4 de ~** *Mex fam* : at least
perdigón *nm, pl* **-gones** : shot, pellet
perdiz *nf, pl* **perdices** : partridge
perdón[1] *nm, pl* **perdones** : forgiveness, pardon
perdón[2] *interj* : excuse me!, sorry!
perdonable *adj* : forgivable
perdonar *vt* **1** DISCULPAR : to forgive, to pardon **2** : to exempt, to excuse
perdurable *adj* : lasting
perdurar *vi* : to last, to endure, to survive
perecedero, -ra *adj* : perishable
perecer {53} *vi* : to perish, to die
peregrinación *nf, pl* **-ciones** : pilgrimage
peregrinaje *nm* → **peregrinación**
peregrino[1], -na *adj* **1** : unusual, odd **2** MIGRATORIO : migratory
peregrino[2], -na *n* : pilgrim
perejil *nm* : parsley
perenne *adj* : perennial
pereza *nf* FLOJERA, HOLGAZANERÍA : laziness, idleness
perezoso[1], -sa *adj* FLOJO, HOLGAZÁN : lazy
perezoso[2] *nm* : sloth (animal)
perfección *nf, pl* **-ciones** : perfection
perfeccionamiento *nm* : perfecting, refinement
perfeccionar *vt* : to perfect, to refine
perfeccionismo *nm* : perfectionism
perfeccionista *nmf* : perfectionist
perfecto, -ta *adj* : perfect — **perfectamente** *adv*
perfidia *nf* : perfidy, treachery
pérfido, -da *adj* : perfidious
perfil *nm* **1** : profile **2 de ~** : sideways, from the side **3 perfiles** *nmpl* RASGOS : features, characteristics
perfilar *vt* : to outline, to define — **perfilarse** *vr* **1** : to be outlined, to be silhouetted **2** : to take shape
perforación *nf, pl* **-ciones 1** : perforation **2** : drilling
perforar *vt* **1** : to perforate, to pierce **2** : to drill, to bore
perfumar *vt* : to perfume, to scent — **perfumarse** *vr*
perfume *nm* : perfume, scent
pergamino *nm* : parchment
pérgola *nf* : pergola, arbor
pericia *nf* : skill, expertise
pericial *adj* : expert <testigo pericial : expert witness>
perico *nm* COTORRA : small parrot
periferia *nf* : periphery
periférico[1], -ca *adj* : peripheral
periférico[2] *nm* **1** *CA, Mex* : beltway **2** : peripheral
perilla *nf* **1** : goatee **2** : pommel (on a saddle) **3** *Col, Mex* : knob, handle **4 perilla de la oreja** : earlobe **5 de perillas** *fam* : handy, just right
perímetro *nm* : perimeter
periódico[1], -ca *adj* : periodic — **periódicamente** *adv*
periódico[2] *nm* DIARIO : newspaper
periodismo *nm* : journalism
periodista *nmf* : journalist
periodístico, -ca *adj* : journalistic, news
período *or* **periodo** *nm* : period
peripecia *nf* VICISITUD : vicissitude, reversal <las peripecias de su carrera : the ups and downs of her career>
periquito *nm* **1** : parakeet **2 periquito australiano** : budgerigar
periscopio *nm* : periscope
perito, -ta *adj & n* : expert
perjudicar {72} *vt* : to harm, to be detrimental to
perjudicial *adj* : harmful, detrimental
perjuicio *nm* **1** : harm, damage **2 en perjuicio de** : to the detriment of
perjurar *vi* : to perjure oneself
perjurio *nm* : perjury
perjuro, -ra *n* : perjurer
perla *nf* **1** : pearl **2 de perlas** *fam* : wonderfully <me viene de perlas : it suits me just fine>
permanecer {53} *vi* **1** QUEDARSE : to remain, to stay **2** SEGUIR : to remain, to continue to be
permanencia *nf* **1** : permanence, continuance **2** ESTANCIA : stay
permanente[1] *adj* **1** : permanent **2** : constant — **permanentemente** *adv*
permanente[2] *nf* : permanent (wave)

permeabilidad *nf* : permeability

permeable *adj* : permeable

permisible *adj* : permissible, allowable

permisividad *nf* : permissiveness

permisivo, -va *adv* : permissive

permiso *nm* **1** : permission **2** : permit, license **3** : leave, furlough **4 con ~** : excuse me, pardon me

permitir *vt* : to permit, to allow — **permitirse** *vr*

permuta *nf* : exchange

permutar *vt* INTERCAMBIAR : to exchange

pernicioso, -sa *adj* : pernicious, destructive

pernil *nm* **1** : haunch (of an animal) **2** : leg (of meat), ham **3** : trouser leg

perno *nm* : bolt, pin

pernoctar *vi* : to stay overnight, to spend the night

pero[1] *nm* **1** : fault, defect <ponerle peros a : to find fault with> **2** : objection

pero[2] *conj* : but

perogrullada *nf* : truism, platitude, cliché

peroné *nm* : fibula

perorar *vi* : to deliver a speech

perorata *nf* : oration, long-winded speech

peróxido *nm* : peroxide

perpendicular *adj & nf* : perpendicular

perpetrar *vt* : to perpetrate

perpetuar {3} *vt* ETERNIZAR : to perpetuate

perpetuidad *nf* : perpetuity

perpetuo, -tua *adj* : perpetual — **perpetuamente** *adv*

perplejidad *nf* : perplexity

perplejo, -ja *adj* : perplexed, puzzled

perrada *nf fam* : dirty trick

perrera *nf* : kennel, dog pound

perrero, -ra *n* : dogcatcher

perrito, -ta *n* CACHORRO : puppy, small dog

perro, -rra *n* **1** : dog, bitch *f* **2 perro caliente** : hot dog **3 perro salchicha** : dachsund **4 perro faldero** : lapdog **5 perro cobrador** : retriever

persa *adj & nmf* : Persian

persecución *nf, pl* **-ciones 1** : pursuit, chase **2** : persecution

perseguidor, -dora *n* **1** : pursuer **2** : persecutor

perseguir {75} *vt* **1** : to pursue, to chase **2** : to persecute **3** : to pester, to annoy

perseverancia *nf* : perseverance

perseverar *vi* : to persevere

persiana *nf* : blind, venetian blind

persignarse *vr* SANTIGUARSE : to cross oneself, to make the sign of the cross

persistir *vi* : to persist — **persistencia** *nf* — **persistente** *adj*

persona *nf* : person

personaje *nm* **1** : character (in drama or literature) **2** : personage, celebrity

personal[1] *adj* : personal — **personalmente** *adv*

personal[2] *nm* : personnel, staff

personalidad *nf* : personality

personalizar {21} *vt* : to personalize

personificar {72} *vi* : to personify — **personificación** *nf*

perspectiva *nf* **1** : perspective, view **2** : prospect, outlook

perspicacia *nf* : shrewdness, perspicacity, insight

perspicaz *adj, pl* **-caces** : shrewd, perspicacious

persuadir *vt* : to persuade — **persuadirse** *vr* : to become convinced

persuasión *nf, pl* **-siones** : persuasion

persuasivo, -va *adj* : persuasive

pertenecer {53} *vi* : to belong

perteneciente *adj* **~ a** : belonging to

pertenencia *nf* **1** : membership **2** : ownership **3 pertenencias** *nfpl* : belongings, possessions

pértiga *nf* GARROCHA : pole <salto de pértiga : pole vault>

pertinaz *adj, pl* **-naces 1** OBSTINADO : obstinate **2** PERSISTENTE : persistent

pertinencia *nf* : pertinence, relevance — **pertinente** *adj*

pertrechos *nmpl* : equipment, gear

perturbación *nf, pl* **-ciones** : disturbance, disruption

perturbador, -dora *adj* **1** INQUIETANTE : disturbing, troubling **2** : disruptive

perturbar *vt* **1** : to disturb, to trouble **2** : to disrupt

peruano, -na *adj & n* : Peruvian

perversidad *nf* : perversity, depravity

perversión *nf, pl* **-siones** : perversion

perverso, -sa *adj* : wicked, depraved

pervertido[1], **-da** *adj* DEPRAVADO : perverted, depraved

pervertido[2], **-da** *n* : pervert

pervertir {76} *vt* : to pervert, to corrupt

pesa *nf* **1** : weight **2 levantamiento de pesas** : weightlifting

pesadamente *adv* **1** : heavily **2** : slowly, clumsily

pesadez *nf, pl* **-deces 1** : heaviness **2** : slowness **3** : tediousness

pesadilla *nf* : nightmare

pesado[1], **-da** *adj* **1** : heavy **2** : slow **3** : irritating, annoying **4** : tedious, boring **5** : tough, difficult

pesado[2], **-da** *n fam* : bore, pest

pesadumbre *nf* AFLICCIÓN : grief, sorrow, sadness

pésame *nm* : condolences *pl* <mi más sentido pésame : my heartfelt condolences>

pesar[1] *vt* **1** : to weigh **2** EXAMINAR : to consider, to think over — *vi* **1** : to weigh <¿cuánto pesa? : how much does it weigh?> **2** : to be heavy **3** : to weigh heavily, to be a burden <no le pesa : it's not a burden on him> <pesa sobre mi corazón : it weighs upon my heart> **4** INFLUIR : to carry weight, to have bearing **5** (*with personal pro-*

nouns) **:** to grieve, to sadden <me pesa mucho : I'm very sorry> **6 pese a :** in spite of, despite

pesar[2] *nm* **1** AFLICCIÓN, PENA **:** sorrow, grief **2** REMORDIMIENTO **:** remorse **3 a pesar de :** in spite of, despite

pesaroso, -sa *adj* **1 :** sad, mournful **2** ARREPENTIDO **:** sorry, regretful

pesca *nf* **:** fishing

pescadería *nf* **:** fish market

pescado *nm* **:** fish (as food)

pescador, -dora *n* **:** fisherman *m,* fisherwoman *f*

pescar {72} *vt* **1 :** to fish for **2 :** to catch **3** *fam* **:** to get a hold of, to land — *vi* **:** to fish, to go fishing

pescuezo *nm* **:** neck

pesebre *nm* **:** manger

pesera *nf Mex* **:** minibus

peseta *nf* **:** peseta (Spanish unit of currency)

pesimismo *nm* **:** pessimism

pesimista[1] *adj* **:** pessimistic

pesimista[2] *nmf* **:** pessimist

pésimo, -ma *adj* **:** dreadful, abominable

peso *nm* **1 :** weight, heaviness **2 :** burden, responsibility **3 :** weight (in sports) **4** BÁSCULA **:** scales *pl* **5 :** peso

pesque, etc. → **pescar**

pesquería *nf* **:** fishery

pesquero[1], **-ra** *adj* **:** fishing <pueblo pesquero : fishing village>

pesquero[2] *nm* **:** fishing boat

pesquisa *nf* INVESTIGACIÓN **:** inquiry, investigation

pestaña *nf* **1 :** eyelash **2 :** flange, rim

pestañear *vi* **:** to blink

pestañeo *nm* **:** blink

peste *nf* **1 :** plague, pestilence **2 :** stench, stink **3 :** nuisance, pest

pesticida *nm* **:** pesticide

pestilencia *nf* **1 :** stench, foul odor **2 :** pestilence

pestilente *adj* **1 :** foul, smelly **2 :** pestilent

pestillo *nm* CERROJO **:** bolt, latch

petaca *nf* **1** *Mex* **:** suitcase **2 petacas** *nfpl Mex fam* **:** bottom, behind

pétalo *nm* **:** petal

petardear *vi* **:** to backfire

petardeo *nm* **:** backfiring

petardo *nm* **:** firecracker

petate *nm Mex* **:** mat

petición *nf, pl* **-ciones :** petition, request

peticionar *vt* **:** to petition

peticionario, -ria *n* **:** petitioner

petirrojo *nm* **:** robin

peto *nm* **:** bib (of clothing)

pétreo, -trea *adj* **:** stone, stony

petrificar {72} *vt* **:** to petrify

petróleo *nm* **:** oil, petroleum

petrolero[1], **-ra** *adj* **:** oil <industria petrolera : oil industry>

petrolero[2] *nm* **:** oil tanker

petulancia *nf* INSOLENCIA **:** insolence, petulance

petulante *adj* INSOLENTE **:** insolent, petulant — **petulantemente** *adv*

petunia *nf* **:** petunia

peyorativo, -va *adj* **:** pejorative

pez[1] *nm, pl* **peces 1 :** fish **2 pez de colores :** goldfish **3 pez espada :** swordfish **4 pez gordo :** big shot

pez[2] *nf, pl* **peces :** pitch, tar

pezón *nm, pl* **pezones :** nipple

pezuña *nf* **:** hoof <pezuña hendida : cloven hoof>

pi *nf* **:** pi

piadoso, -sa *adj* **1 :** compassionate, merciful **2** DEVOTO **:** pious, devout

pianista *nmf* **:** pianist, piano player

piano *nm* **:** piano

piar {85} *vi* **:** to chirp, to cheep, to tweet

pibe, -ba *n Arg, Uru fam* **:** kid, child

pica *nf* **1 :** pike, lance **2 :** goad (in bullfighting) **3 :** spade (in playing cards)

picada *nf* **1 :** bite, sting (of an insect) **2 :** sharp descent

picadillo *nm* **1 :** minced meat, hash **2 hacer picadillo a :** to beat to a pulp

picado, -da *adj* **1 :** perforated **2 :** minced, chopped **3 :** decayed (of teeth) **4 :** choppy, rough **5** *fam* **:** annoyed, miffed

picador *nm* **:** picador

picadura *nf* **1 :** sting, bite **2 :** prick, puncture **3 :** decay, cavity

picaflor *nm* COLIBRÍ **:** hummingbird

picana *nf* **:** goad, prod

picante[1] *adj* **1 :** hot, spicy **2 :** sharp, cutting **3 :** racy, risqué

picante[2] *nm* **1 :** spiciness **2 :** hot spices *pl,* hot sauce

picaporte *nm* **1 :** latch **2 :** door handle **3** ALDABA **:** door knocker

picar {72} *vt* **1 :** to sting, to bite **2 :** to peck at **3 :** to nibble on **4 :** to prick, to puncture, to punch (a ticket) **5 :** to grind, to chop **6 :** to goad, to incite **7 :** to pique, to provoke — *vi* **1 :** to itch **2 :** to sting **3 :** to be spicy **4 :** to nibble **5 :** to take the bait **6 ~ en :** to dabble in **7 picar muy alto :** to aim too high — **picarse** *vr* **1 :** to get a cavity, to decay **2 :** to get annoyed, to take offense

picardía *nf* **1 :** cunning, craftiness **2 :** prank, dirty trick

picaresco, -ca *adj* **1 :** picaresque **2 :** rascally, roguish

pícaro[1], **-ra** *adj* **1 :** mischievous **2 :** cunning, sly **3 :** off-color, risqué

pícaro[2], **-ra** *n* **1 :** rogue, scoundrel **2 :** rascal

picazón *nf, pl* **-zones** COMEZÓN **:** itch

picea *nf* **:** spruce (tree)

pichel *nm* **:** pitcher, jug

pichón, -chona *n, mpl* **pichones 1 :** young pigeon, squab **2** *Mex fam* **:** novice, greenhorn

picnic *nm* **:** picnic

pico *nm* **1 :** peak **2 :** point, spike **3 :** beak, bill **4 :** pick, pickax **5 y pico**

: and a little, and a bit <las siete y pico : a little after seven> <dos metros y pico : a bit over two meters>

picor *nm* : itch, irritation

picoso, -sa *adj Mex* : very hot, spicy

picota *nf* **1** : pillory, stock **2 poner a alguien en la picota** : to put someone on the spot

picotada *nf* → **picotazo**

picotazo *nm* : peck (of a bird)

picotear *vt* : to peck — *vi* : to nibble, to pick

pictórico, -ca *adj* : pictorial

picudo, -da *adj* **1** : pointy, sharp **2 ~ para** *Mex fam* : clever at, good at

pide, etc. → **pedir**

pie *nm* **1** : foot <a pie : on foot> <de pie : on one's feet, standing> **2** : base, bottom, stem, foot <pie de la cama : foot of the bed> <pie de una lámpera : base of a lamp> <pie de la escalera : bottom of the stairs> <pie de una copa : stem of a glass> **3** : foot (in measurement) <pie cuadrado : square foot> **4** : cue (in theater) **5 dar pie a** : to give cause for, to give rise to **6 en pie de igualidad** : on equal footing

piedad *nf* **1** COMPASIÓN : mercy, pity **2** DEVOCIÓN : piety, devotion

piedra *nf* **1** : stone **2** : flint (of a lighter) **3** : hailstone **4 piedra de afilar** : whetstone, grindstone **5 piedra angular** : cornerstone **6 piedra arenisca** : sandstone **7 piedra caliza** : limestone **8 piedra imán** : lodestone **9 piedra de molino** : millstone **10 piedra de toque** : touchstone

piel *nf* **1** : skin **2** CUERO : leather, hide <piel de venado : deerskin> **3** : fur, pelt **4** CÁSCARA : peel, skin **5 piel de gallina** : goose bumps *pl* <me pone la piel de gallina : it gives me goose bumps>

piélago *nm* **el piélago** : the deep, the ocean

piensa, etc. → **pensar**

pienso *nm* : feed, fodder

pierde, etc. → **perder**

pierna *nf* : leg

pieza *nf* **1** ELEMENTO : piece, part, component <vestido de dos piezas : two-piece dress> <pieza de recambio : spare part> <pieza clave : key element> **2** : piece (in chess) **3** OBRA : piece, work <pieza de teatro : play> **4** : room, bedroom

pifia *nf fam* : goof, blunder

pigargo *nm* : osprey

pigmentación *nf, pl* **-ciones** : pigmentation

pigmento *nm* : pigment

pigmeo, -mea *adj & n* : pygmy, Pygmy

pijama *nm* : pajamas *pl*

pila *nf* **1** BATERÍA : battery <pila de linterna : flashlight battery> **2** MONTÓN : pile, heap **3** : sink, basin, font <pila bautismal : baptismal font> <pila para pájaros : birdbath>

pilar *nm* **1** : pillar, column **2** : support, mainstay

píldora *nf* PASTILLA : pill

pillaje *nm* : pillage, plunder

pillar *vt fam* **1** : to catch <¡cuidado! ¡nos pillarán! : watch out! they'll catch us!> **2** : to grasp, to catch on <¿no lo pillas? : don't you get it?>

pillo[1], -lla *adj* : cunning, crafty

pillo[2], -lla *n* **1** : rascal, brat **2** : rogue, scoundrel

pilluelo, -la *n* : urchin

pilotar *vt* : to pilot, to drive

pilote *nm* : pile (stake)

pilotear → **pilotar**

piloto *nm* **1** : pilot, driver **2** : pilot light

piltrafa *nf* **1** : poor quality meat **2** : wretch **3 piltrafas** *nfpl* : food scraps

pimentero *nm* : pepper shaker

pimentón *nm, pl* **-tones 1** : paprika **2** : cayenne pepper

pimienta *nf* **1** : pepper (condiment) **2 pimienta de Jamaica** : allspice

pimiento *nm* : pepper (fruit) <pimiento verde : green pepper>

pináculo *nm* **1** : pinnacle (of a building) **2** : peak, acme

pincel *nm* : paintbrush

pincelada *nf* **1** : brushstroke **2 últimas pinceladas** : final touches

pinchar *vt* **1** PICAR : to puncture (a tire) **2** : to prick, to stick **3** : to goad, to tease, to needle — *vi* **1** : to be prickly **2** : to get a flat tire **3** *fam* : to get beaten, to lose out — **pincharse** *vr* : to give oneself an injection

pinchazo *nm* **1** : prick, jab **2** : puncture, flat tire

pingüe *adj* **1** : rich, huge (of profits) **2** : lucrative

pingüino *nm* : penguin

pininos *or* **pinitos** *nmpl* : first steps <hacer pininos : to take one's first steps, to toddle>

pino *nm* : pine, pine tree

pinta *nf* **1** : dot, spot **2** : pint **3** *fam* : aspect, appearance <las peras tienen buena pinta : the pears look good> **4 pintas** *nfpl Mex* : graffiti

pintadas *nfpl* : graffiti

pintar *vt* **1** : to paint **2** : to draw, to mark **3** : to describe, to depict — *vi* **1** : to paint, to draw **2** : to look <no pinta bien : it doesn't look good> **3** *fam* : to count <aquí no pinta nada : he has no say here> — **pintarse** *vr* **1** MAQUILLARSE : to put on makeup **2 pintárselas solo** *fam* : to manage by oneself, to know it all

pintarrajear *vt* : to daub (with paint)

pinto, -ta *adj* : speckled, spotted

pintor, -tora *n* **1** : painter **2 pintor de brocha gorda** : housepainter, dauber

pintoresco, -ca *adj* : picturesque, quaint

pintura *nf* **1** : paint **2** : painting (art, work of art)

pinza *nf* **1** : clothespin **2** : claw, pincer **3** : pleat, dart **4 pinzas** *nfpl* : tweezers **5 pinzas** *nfpl* ALICATES : pliers, pincers

pinzón *nm, pl* **pinzones** : finch

piña *nf* **1** : pineapple **2** : pine cone

piñata *nf* : piñata

piñón *nm, pl* **piñones 1** : pine nut **2** : pinion

pío[1], **pía** *adj* **1** DEVOTO : pious, devout **2** : piebald, pied, dappled

pío[2] *nm* : peep, tweet, cheep

piocha *nf* **1** : pickax **2** *Mex* : goatee

piojo *nm* : louse

piojoso, -sa *adj* **1** : lousy **2** : filthy

pionero[1], **-ra** *adj* : pioneering

pionero[2], **-ra** *n* : pioneer

pipa *nf* : pipe (for smoking)

pipián *nm, pl* **pipianes** *Mex* : a spicy sauce or stew

pipiolo, -la *n fam* **1** : greenhorn, novice **2** : kid, youngster

pique[1], **etc.** → **picar**

pique[2] *nm* **1** : pique, resentment **2** : rivalry, competition **3 a pique de** : about to, on the verge of **4 irse a pique** : to sink, to founder

piqueta *nf* : pickax

piquete *nm* **1** : picketers *pl*, picket line **2** : squad, detachment **3** *Mex* : prick, jab

piquetear *vt* **1** : to picket **2** *Mex* : to prick, to jab

pira *nf* : pyre

piragua *nf* : canoe — **piragüista** *nmf*

pirámide *nf* : pyramid

piraña *nf* : piranha

pirata[1] *adj* : bootleg, pirated

pirata[2] *nmf* **1** : pirate **2** : bootlegger **3 pirata aéreo** : hijacker

piratear *vt* **1** : to hijack, to commandeer **2** : to bootleg, to pirate

piratería *nf* : piracy, bootlegging

piromanía *nf* : pyromania

pirómano, -na *n* : pyromaniac

piropo *nm* : flirtatious compliment

pirotecnia *nf* : fireworks *pl*, pyrotechnics *pl*

pirotécnico, -ca *adj* : fireworks, pyrotechnic

pírrico, -ca *adj* : Pyrrhic

pirueta *nf* : pirouette

pirulí *nm* : cone-shaped lollipop

pisada *nf* **1** : footstep **2** HUELLA : footprint

pisapapeles *nms & pl* : paperweight

pisar *vt* **1** : to step on, to set foot in **2** : to walk all over, to mistreat — *vi* : to step, to walk, to tread

piscina *nf* **1** : swimming pool **2** : fish pond

Piscis *nmf* : Pisces

piso *nm* **1** PLANTA : floor, story **2** SUELO : floor **3** *Spain* : apartment

pisotear *vt* **1** : to stamp on, to trample **2** PISAR : to walk all over **3** : to flout, to disregard

pisotón *nm, pl* **-tones** : stamp, step <sufrieron empujones y pisotones : they were pushed and stepped on>

pista *nf* **1** RASTRO : trail, track <siguen la pista de los sospechosos : they're on the trail of the suspects> **2** : clue **3** CAMINO : road, trail **4** : track, racetrack **5** : ring, arena, rink **6 pista de aterrizaje** : runway, airstrip **7 pista de baile** : dance floor

pistacho *nm* : pistachio

pistilo *nm* : pistil

pistola *nf* **1** : pistol, handgun **2** : spray gun

pistolera *nf* : holster

pistolero *nm* : gunman

pistón *nm, pl* **pistones** : piston

pita *nf* **1** : agave **2** : pita fiber **3** : twine

pitar *vi* **1** : to blow a whistle **2** : to whistle, to boo **3** : to beep, to honk, to toot — *vt* : to whistle at, to boo

pitido *nm* **1** : whistle, whistling **2** : beep, honk, toot

pito *nm* **1** SILBATO : whistle **2 no me importa un pito** *fam* : I don't give a damn

pitón *nm, pl* **pitones** *nm* **1** : python **2** : point of a bull's horn

pituitario, -ria *adj* : pituitary

pívot *nmf, pl* **pívots** : center (in basketball)

pivote *nm* : pivot

piyama *nmf* : pajamas *pl*

pizarra *nf* **1** : slate **2** : blackboard **3** : scoreboard

pizarrón *nm, pl* **-rrones** : blackboard, chalkboard

pizca *nf* **1** : pinch <una pizca de canela : a pinch of cinnamon> **2** : speck, trace <ni pizca : not a bit> **3** *Mex* : harvest

pizcar {72} *vt Mex* : to harvest

pizque, etc. → **pizcar**

pizza ['pitsa, 'pisa] *nf* : pizza

pizzería *nf* : pizzeria, pizza parlor

placa *nf* **1** : sheet, plate **2** : plaque, nameplate **3** : plate (in photography) **4** : badge, insignia **5 placa de matrícula** : license plate, tag **6 placa dental** : plaque, tartar

placebo *nm* : placebo

placenta *nf* : placenta, afterbirth

placentero, -ra *adj* AGRADABLE, GRATO : pleasant, agreeable

placer[1] {57} *vi* GUSTAR : to be pleasing <hazlo como te plazca : do it however you please>

placer[2] *nm* **1** : pleasure, enjoyment **2 a ~** : as much as one wants

plácido, -da *adj* TRANQUILO : placid, calm

plaga *nf* **1** : plague, infestation, blight **2** CALAMIDAD : disaster, scourge

plagado, -da *adj* **~ de** : filled with, covered with

plagar {52} *vt* : to plague

plagiar *vt* **1** : to plagiarize **2** SECUESTRAR : to kidnap, to abduct

plagiario, -ria *n* **1 :** plagiarist **2** SECUESTRADOR **:** kidnapper, abductor
plagio *nm* **1 :** plagiarism **2** SECUESTRO **:** kidnapping, abduction
plague, etc. → **plagar**
plan *nm* **1 :** plan, strategy, program <plan de inversiones : investment plan> <plan de estudios : curriculum> **2** PLANO **:** plan, diagram **3 :** attitude, intent, purpose <ponte en plan serio : be serious> <estamos en plan de divertirnos : we're looking to have some fun>
plana *nf* **1 :** page <noticias en primera plana : front-page news> **2 plana mayor :** staff (in the military)
plancha *nf* **1 :** iron, ironing **2 :** grill, griddle <a la plancha : grilled> **3 :** sheet, plate <plancha para hornear : baking sheet> **4** *fam* **:** blunder, blooper
planchada *nf* **:** ironing, pressing
planchado *nm* → **planchada**
planchar *v* **:** to iron
planchazo *nm fam* **:** goof, blunder
plancton *nm* **:** plankton
planeación *nf* → **planeamiento**
planeador *nm* **:** glider (aircraft)
planeamiento *nm* **:** plan, planning
planear *vt* **:** to plan — *vi* **:** to glide (in the air)
planeo *nm* **:** gliding, soaring
planeta *nm* **:** planet
planetario[1], -ria *adj* **1 :** planetary **2 :** global, worldwide
planetario[2] *nm* **:** planetarium
planicie *nf* **:** plain
planificación *nf* **:** planning <planificación familiar : family planning>
planificar {72} *vt* **:** to plan
planilla *nf* **1** LISTA **:** list **2** NÓMINA **:** payroll **3** TABLA **:** chart, table **4** *Mex* **:** slate, ticket (of candidates) **5 planilla de cálculo** *Arg, Chile* **:** spreadsheet
plano[1], -na *adj* **:** flat, level, plane
plano[2] *nm* **1** PLAN **:** map, plan **2 :** plane (surface) **3** NIVEL **:** level <en un plano personal : on a personal level> **4 :** shot (in photography) **5 de ~ :** flatly, outright, directly <se negó de plano : he flatly refused>
planta *nf* **1 :** plant <planta de interior : houseplant> **2** FÁBRICA **:** plant, factory **3** PISO **:** floor, story **4 :** staff, employees *pl* **5 :** sole (of the foot)
plantación *nf, pl* **-ciones 1 :** plantation **2 :** planting
plantar *vt* **1 :** to plant, to sow **2 :** to put in, to place **3** *fam* **:** to plant, to land <plantar un beso : to plant a kiss> **4** *fam* **:** to leave, to jilt — **plantarse** *vr* **1 :** to stand firm **2** *fam* **:** to arrive, to show up **3** *fam* **:** to balk
planteamiento *nm* **1 :** approach, position <el planteamiento feminista : the feminist viewpoint> **2 :** explanation, exposition **3 :** proposal, suggestion, plan
plantear *vt* **1 :** to set forth, to bring up, to suggest **2 :** to establish, to set up **3 :** to create, to pose (a problem) — **plantearse** *vr* **1 :** to think about **2 :** to arise
plantel *nm* **1 :** educational institution **2 :** staff, team
planteo *nm* → **planteamiento**
plantilla *nf* **1 :** insole **2 :** pattern, template, stencil **3** *Mex, Spain* **:** staff, roster of employees
plantío *nm* **:** field (planted with a crop)
plantón *nm, pl* **plantones 1 :** seedling **2 :** long wait <darle a alguien un plantón : to stand someone up>
plañidero[1], -ra *adj* **:** mournful
plañidero[2], -ra *nf* **:** hired mourner
plañir {38} *v* **:** to mourn, to lament
plasma *nm* **:** plasma
plasmar *vt* **:** to express, to give form to — **plasmarse** *vr*
plasta *nf* **:** soft mass, lump
plástica *nf* **:** modeling, sculpture
plasticidad *nf* **:** plasticity
plástico[1], -ca *adj* **:** plastic
plástico[2] *nm* **:** plastic
plastificar {72} *vt* **:** to laminate
plata *nf* **1 :** silver **2 :** money
plataforma *nf* **1** ESTRADO, TARIMA **:** platform, dais **2 :** platform (in politics) **3 :** springboard, stepping stone **4 plataforma continental :** continental shelf **5 plataforma de lanzamiento :** launchpad **6 plataforma petrolífera :** oil rig (at sea)
platal *nm* **:** large sum of money, fortune
platanal *nm* **:** banana plantation
platanero[1], -ra *adj* **:** banana, banana-producing
platanero[2], -ra *n* **:** banana grower
plátano *nm* **1 :** banana **2 :** plantain **3 plátano macho** *Mex* **:** plantain
platea *nf* **:** orchestra, pit (in a theater)
plateado, -da *adj* **1 :** silver, silvery **2 :** silver-plated
plática *nf* **1 :** talk, lecture **2 :** chat, conversation
platicar {72} *vi* **:** to talk, to chat — *vt Mex* **:** to tell, to say
platija *nf* **:** flatfish, flounder
platillo *nm* **1 :** saucer <platillo volador : flying saucer> **2 :** cymbal **3** *Mex* **:** dish <platillos típicos : local dishes>
platino *nm* **:** platinum
plato *nm* **1 :** plate, dish <lavar los platos : to do the dishes> **2 :** serving, helping **3 :** course (of a meal) **4 :** dish <plato típico : typical dish> **5 :** home plate (in baseball) **6 plato hondo :** soup bowl
plató *nm* **:** set (in the movies)
platónico, -ca *adj* **:** platonic
playa *nf* **:** beach, seashore
playera *nf* **1 :** canvas sneaker **2** *CA, Mex* **:** T-shirt
plaza *nf* **1 :** square, plaza **2 :** marketplace **3 :** room, space, seat (in a vehicle) **4 :** post, position **5 plaza fuerte**

: stronghold, fortified city **6 plaza de toros** : bullring
plazca, etc. → **placer**
plazo *nm* **1** : period, term <un plazo de cinco días : a period of five days> <a largo plazo : long-term> **2** ABONO : installment <pagar a plazos : to pay in installments>
pleamar *nf* : high tide
plebe *nf* : common people, masses *pl*
plebeyo[1], -ya *adj* : plebeian
plebeyo[2], -ya *n* : plebeian, commoner
plegable *adj* : folding, collapsible
plegadizo → **plegable**
plegar {49} *vt* DOBLAR : to fold, to bend — **plegarse** *vr* : to give in, to yield
plegaria *nf* ORACIÓN : prayer
pleito *nm* **1** : lawsuit **2** : fight, argument, dispute
plenamente *adv* COMPLETAMENTE : fully, completely
plenario, -ria *adj* : plenary, full
plenilunio *nm* : full moon
plenipotenciario, -ria *n* : plenipotentiary
plenitud *nf* : fullness, abundance
pleno, -na *adj* COMPLETO (*often used as an intensifier*) : full, complete <en pleno uso de sus facultades : in full command of his faculties> <en plena noche : in the middle of the night> <en pleno corazón de la ciudad : right in the heart of the city>
plétora *nf* : plethora
pleuresía *nf* : pleurisy
pliega, pliegue, etc. → **plegar**
pliego *nm* **1** HOJA : sheet of paper **2** : sealed document
pliegue *nm* **1** DOBLEZ : crease, fold **2** : pleat
plisar *vt* : to pleat
plomada *nf* **1** : plumb line **2** : sinker
plomería *nf* FONTANERÍA : plumbing
plomero, -ra *n* FONTANERO : plumber
plomizo, -za *adj* : leaden
plomo *nm* **1** : lead **2** : plumb line **3** : fuse **4** *fam* : bore, drag **5 a ~** : plumb, straight
plugo, etc. → **placer**
pluma *nf* **1** : feather **2** : pen **3 pluma fuente** : fountain pen
plumaje *nm* : plumage
plumero *nm* : feather duster
plumilla *nf* : nib
plumón *nm, pl* **plumones** : down
plumoso, -sa *adj* : feathery, downy
plural *adj & nm* : plural
pluralidad *nf* : plurality
pluralizar {21} *vt* : to pluralize
pluriempleado, -da *adj* : holding more than one job
pluriempleo *nm* : moonlighting
plus *nm* : bonus
plusvalía *nf* : appreciation, capital gain
Plutón *nm* : Pluto
plutocracia *nf* : plutocracy
plutonio *nm* : plutonium
población *nf, pl* **-ciones 1** : population **2** : city, town, village
poblado[1], -da *adj* **1** : inhabited, populated **2** : full, thick <cejas pobladas : bushy eyebrows>
poblado[2] *nm* : village, settlement
poblador, -dora *n* : settler
poblar {19} *vt* **1** : to populate, to inhabit **2** : to settle, to colonize **3 ~ de** : to stock with, to plant with — **poblarse** *vr* : to fill up, to become crowded
pobre[1] *adj* **1** : poor, impoverished **2** : unfortunate <¡pobre de mí! : poor me!> **3** : weak, deficient <una dieta pobre : a poor diet>
pobre[2] *nmf* : poor person <los pobres : the poor> <¡pobre! : poor thing!>
pobremente *adv* : poorly
pobreza *nf* : poverty
pocilga *nf* CHIQUERO : pigsty, pigpen
pocillo *nm* : small coffee cup, demitasse
poción *nf, pl* **pociones** : potion
poco[1] *adv* **1** : little, not much <poco probable : not very likely> <come poco : he doesn't eat much> **2** : a short time, a while <tardaremos poco : we won't be very long> **3 poco antes** : shortly before **4 poco después** : shortly after
poco[2], -ca *adj* **1** : little, not much, (a) few <tengo poco dinero : I don't have much money> <en no pocas ocasiones : on more than a few occasions> <poca gente : few people> **2 pocas veces** : rarely
poco[3], -ca *pron* **1** : little, few <le falta poco para terminar : he's almost finished> <uno de los pocos que quedan : one of the remaining few> **2 un poco** : a little, a bit <un poco de vino : a little wine> <un poco extraño : a bit strange> **3 a ~** *Mex* (*used to express disbelief*) <¿a poco no se te hizo difícil? : you mean you didn't find it difficult?> **4 de a poco** : little by little **5 hace poco** : not long ago **6 poco a poco** : little by little **7 dentro de poco** : shortly, in a little while **8 por ~** : nearly, almost
podar *vt* : to prune, to trim
poder[1] {58} *v aux* **1** : to be able to, can <no puede hablar : he can't speak> **2** (*expressing possibility*) : might, may <puede llover : it may rain at any moment> <¿cómo puede ser? : how can that be?> **3** (*expressing permission*) : can, may <¿puedo ir a la fiesta? : can I go to the party?> <¿se puede? : may I come in?> — *vi* **1** : to beat, to defeat <cree que le puede a cualquiera : he thinks he can beat anyone> **2** : to be possible <¿crees que vendrán? — puede (que sí) : do you think they'll come? — maybe> **3 ~ con** : to cope with, to manage <¡no puedo con estos niños! : I can't handle these children!> **4 no poder más** : to have had enough <no puede más : she can't take anymore> **5 no poder menos**

que : to not be able to help <no pudo menos que asombrarse : she couldn't help but be amazed>

poder[2] *nm* **1** : control, power <poder adquisitivo : purchasing power> **2** : authority <el poder legislativo : the legislature> **3** : possession <está en mi poder : it's in my hands> **4** : strength, force <poder militar : military might>

poderío *nm* **1** : power **2** : wealth, influence

poderoso, -sa *adj* **1** : powerful **2** : wealthy, influential **3** : effective

podiatría *nf* : podiatry

podio *nm* : podium

pódium *nm* → **podio**

podología *nf* : podiatry, chiropody

podólogo, -ga *n* : podiatrist, chiropodist

podrá, etc. → **poder**

podredumbre *nf* **1** : decay, rottenness **2** : corruption

podrido, -da *adj* **1** : rotten, decayed **2** : corrupt

podrir → **pudrir**

poema *nm* : poem

poesía *nf* **1** : poetry **2** POEMA : poem

poeta *nmf* : poet

poético, -ca *adj* : poetic, poetical

pogrom *nm* : pogrom

póker *or* **poker** *nm* : poker (card game)

polaco[1], -ca *adj* : Polish

polaco[2], -ca *n* : Pole, Polish person

polaco[3] *nm* : Polish (language)

polar *adj* : polar

polarizar {21} *vt* : to polarize — **polarizarse** *vr* — **polarización** *nf*

polea *nf* : pulley

polémica *nf* CONTROVERSIA : controversy, polemics

polémico, -ca *adj* CONTROVERTIDO : controversial, polemical

polen *nm, pl* **pólenes** : pollen

policía[1] *nf* : police

policía[2] *nmf* : police officer, policeman *m,* policewoman *f*

policíaco, -ca *or* **policiaco, -ca** *adj* : police <novela policíaca : detective story>

policial *adj* : police

poliéster *nm* : polyester

poligamia *nf* : polygamy

polígamo[1], -ma *adj* : polygamous

polígamo[2], -ma *n* : polygamist

polígono *nm* : polygon — **polígonal** *adj*

poliinsaturado, -da *adj* : polyunsaturated

polilla *nf* : moth

polimerizar {21} *vt* : to polymerize

polímero *nm* : polymer

polinesio, -sia *adj & n* : Polynesian

polinizar {21} *vt* : to pollinate — **polinización** *nf*

polio *nf* : polio

poliomielitis *nf* : poliomyelitis, polio

polisón *nm, pl* **-sones** : bustle (on clothing)

politécnico, -ca *adj* : polytechnic

politeísmo *nm* : polytheism — **politeísta** *adj & nmf*

política *nf* **1** : politics **2** : policy

políticamente *adv* : politically

político[1], -ca *adj* **1** : political **2** : tactful, politic **3** : by marriage <padre político : father-in-law>

político[2], -ca *n* : politician

póliza *nf* : policy <póliza de seguros : insurance policy>

polizón *nm, pl* **-zones** : stowaway <viajar de polizón : to stow away>

polla *nf* APUESTA : bet

pollera *nf* **1** : chicken coop **2** : skirt

pollero, -ra *n* **1** : poulterer **2** : poultry farm **3** *Mex fam* COYOTE : smuggler of illegal immigrants

pollito, -ta *n* : chick, young bird, fledgling

pollo, -lla *n* **1** : chicken **2** POLLITO : chick **3** JOVEN : young man *m,* young lady *f*

polluelo *nm* → **pollito**

polo *nm* **1** : pole <el Polo Norte : the North Pole> <polo negativo : negative pole> **2** : polo (sport) **3** : polo shirt **4** : focal point, center **5 polo opuesto** : exact opposite

polución *nf, pl* **-ciones** CONTAMINACIÓN : pollution

polvareda *nf* **1** : cloud of dust **2** : uproar, fuss

polvera *nf* : compact (for face powder)

polvo *nm* **1** : dust **2** : powder **3 polvos** *nmpl* : face powder **4 polvos de hornear** : baking powder **5 hacer polvo** *fam* : to crush, to shatter <vas a hacer polvo el reloj : you're going to destroy your watch>

pólvora *nf* **1** : gunpowder **2** : fireworks *pl*

polvoriento, -ta *adj* : dusty, powdery

polvorín *nm, pl* **-rines** : magazine, storehouse (for explosives)

pomada *nf* : ointment, cream

pomelo *nm* : grapefruit

pómez *nm or* **piedra pómez** : pumice

pomo *nm* **1** : pommel (on a sword) **2** : knob, handle **3** : perfume bottle

pompa *nf* **1** : bubble **2** : pomp, splendor **3 pompas fúnebres** : funeral

pompón *nm, pl* **pompones** BORLA : pom-pom

pomposidad *nf* **1** : pomp, splendor **2** : pomposity, ostentation

pomposo, -sa *adj* : pompous — **pomposamente** *adv*

pómulo *nm* : cheekbone

pon → **poner**

ponchadura *nf Mex* : puncture, flat (tire)

ponchar *vt* **1** : to strike out (in baseball) **2** *Mex* : to puncture — **poncharse** *vr* **1** *Col, Ven* : to strike out (in baseball) **2** *Mex* : to blow out (of a tire)

ponche *nm* **1** : punch (drink) **2 ponche de huevo** : eggnog

poncho *nm* : poncho

ponderación *nf, pl* **-ciones 1** : consideration, deliberation **2** : high praise

ponderar *vt* **1** : to weigh, to consider **2** : to speak highly of

pondrá, etc. → **poner**

ponencia *nf* **1** DISCURSO : paper, presentation, address **2** INFORME : report

ponente *nmf* : speaker, presenter

poner {60} *vt* **1** COLOCAR : to put, to place <pon el libro en la mesa : put the book on the table> **2** AGREGAR, AÑADIR : to put in, to add **3** : to put on (clothes) **4** CONTRIBUIR : to contribute **5** ESCRIBIR : to put in writing <no le puso su nombre : he didn't put his name on it> **6** IMPONER : to set, to impose **7** EXPONER : to put, to expose <lo puso en peligro : she put him in danger> **8** : to prepare, to arrange <poner la mesa : to set the table> **9** : to name <le pusimos Ana : we called her Ana> **10** ESTABLECER : to set up, to establish <puso un restaurante : he opened up a restaurant> **11** INSTALAR : to install, to put in **12** (*with an adjective or adverb*) : to make <siempre lo pones de mal humor : you always put him in a bad mood> **13** : to turn on, to switch on **14** SUPONER : to suppose <pongamos que no viene : supposing he doesn't come> **15** : to lay (eggs) **16 ~ a** : to start (someone doing something) <lo puse a trabajar : I put him to work> **17 ~ de** : to place as <la pusieron de directora : they made her director> **18 ~ en** : to put in (a state or condition) <poner en duda : to call into question — *vi* **1** : to contribute **2** : to lay eggs — **ponerse** *vr* **1** : to move (into a position) <ponerse de pie : to stand up> **2** : to put on, to wear **3** : to become, to turn <se puso colorado : he turned red> **4** : to set (of the sun or moon)

poni *or* **poney** *nm* : pony

ponga, etc. → **poner**

poniente *nm* **1** OCCIDENTE : west **2** : west wind

ponqué *nm Col, Ven* : cake

pontifical *adj* : pontifical

pontificar {72} *vi* : to pontificate

pontífice *nm* : pontiff, pope

pontón *nm, pl* **pontones** : pontoon

ponzoña *nf* VENENO : poison — **ponzoñoso, -sa** *adj*

popa *nf* **1** : stern **2 a ~** : astern, abaft, aft

popelín *nm, pl* **-lines** : poplin

popelina *nf* : poplin

popote *nm Mex* : (drinking) straw

populachero, -ra *adj* : common, popular, vulgar

populacho *nm* : rabble, masses *pl*

popular *adj* **1** : popular **2** : traditional **3** : colloquial

popularidad *nf* : popularity

popularizar {21} *vt* : to popularize — **popularizarse** *vr*

populista *adj & nmf* : populist — **populismo** *nm*

populoso, -sa *adj* : populous

popurrí *nm* : potpourri

por *prep* **1** : for, during <se quedaron allí por la semana : they stayed there during the week> <por el momento : for now, at the moment> **2** : around, during <por noviembre empieza a nevar : around November it starts to snow> <por la mañana : in the morning> **3** : around (a place) <debe estar por allí : it must be over there> <por todas partes : everywhere> **4** : by, through, along <por la puerta : through the door> <pasé por tu casa : I stopped by your house> <por la costa : along the coast> **5** : for, for the sake of <lo hizo por su madre : he did it for his mother> <¡por Dios! : for heaven's sake!> **6** : because of, on account of <llegué tarde por el tráfico : I arrived late because of the traffic> <dejar por imposible : to give up as impossible> **7** : per <60 millas por hora : 60 miles per hour> <por docena : by the dozen> **8** : for, in exchange for, instead of <su hermana habló por él : his sister spoke on his behalf> **9** : by means of <hablar por teléfono : to talk on the phone> <por escrito : in writing> **10** : as for <por mí : as far as I'm concerned> **11** : times <tres por dos son seis : three times two is six> **12** SEGÚN : from, according to <por lo que dices : judging from what you're telling me> **13** : as, for <por ejemplo : for example> **14** : by <hecho por mi abuela : made by my grandmother> <por correo : by mail> **15** : for, in order to <lucha por ganar su respeto : he struggles to win her respect> **16 estar por** : to be about to **17 por ciento** : percent **18 por favor** : please **19 por lo tanto** : therefore, consequently **20 ¿por qué?** : why? **21 por que** → **porque 22 por . . . que** : no matter how <por mucho que intente : no matter how hard I try> **23 por si** *or* **por si acaso** : just in case

porcelana *nf* : china, porcelain

porcentaje *nm* : percentage

porche *nm* : porch

porción *nf, pl* **porciones 1** : portion **2** PARTE : part, share **3** RACIÓN : serving, helping

pordiosear *vi* MENDIGAR : beg

pordiosero, -ra *n* MENDIGO : beggar

porfiado, -da *adj* OBSTINADO, TERCO : obstinate, stubborn — : **porfiadamente** *adv*

porfiar {85} *vi* : to insist, to persist

pormenor *nm* DETALLE : detail

pormenorizar {21} *vi* : to go into detail — *vt* : to tell in detail

pornografía *nf* : pornography

pornográfico, -ca *adj* : pornographic

poro *nm* : pore

poroso, -sa *adj* : porous — **porosidad** *nf*

poroto *nm Arg, Chile, Uru* : bean

porque *conj* **1** : because **2** *or* **por que** : in order that

porqué *nm* : reason, cause

porquería *nf* **1** SUCIEDAD : dirt, filth **2** : nastiness, vulgarity **3** : worthless thing, trifle **4** : junk food

porra *nf* **1** : nightstick, club **2** *Mex* : cheer, yell <los aficionados le echaban porras : the fans cheered him on>

porrazo *nm* **1** : blow, whack **2 de golpe y porrazo** : suddenly

porrista *nmf* **1** : cheerleader **2** : fan, supporter

portaaviones *nms & pl* : aircraft carrier

portada *nf* **1** : title page **2** : cover **3** : facade, front

portador, -dora *n* : carrier, bearer

portafolio *or* **portafolios** *nm, pl* **-lios 1** MALETÍN : briefcase **2** : portfolio (of investments)

portal *nm* **1** : portal, doorway **2** VESTÍBULO : vestibule, hall

portar *vt* **1** : to carry, to bear **2** : to wear — **portarse** *vr* CONDUCIRSE : to behave <pórtate bien : behave yourself>

portátil *adj* : portable

portaviandas *nms & pl* : lunch box

portaviones *nm* → **portaaviones**

portavoz *nmf, pl* **-voces** : spokesperson, spokesman *m*, spokeswoman *f*

portazo *nm* : slam (of a door)

porte *nm* **1** ASPECTO : bearing, demeanor **2** TRANSPORTE : transport, carrying <porte pagado : postage paid>

portento *nm* MARAVILLA : marvel, wonder

portentoso, -sa *adj* MARAVILLOSO : marvelous, wonderful

porteño, -ña *adj* : of or from Buenos Aires

portería *nf* **1** ARCO : goal, goalposts *pl* **2** : superintendent's office

portero, -ra *n* **1** ARQUERO : goalkeeper, goalie **2** : doorman *m* **3** : janitor, superintendent

pórtico *nm* : portico

portilla *nf* : porthole

portón *nm, pl* **portones 1** : main door **2** : gate

portugués[1], -guesa *adj & n, mpl* **-gueses** : Portuguese

portugués[2] *nm* : Portuguese (language)

porvenir *nm* FUTURO : future

pos *adv* **en pos de** : in pursuit of

posada *nf* **1** : inn **2** *Mex* : Advent celebration

posadero, -ra *n* : innkeeper

posar *vi* : to pose — *vt* : to place, to lay — **posarse** *vr* **1** : to land, to light, to perch **2** : to settle, to rest

posavasos *nms & pl* : coaster (for drinks)

posdata *nf* → **postdata**

pose *nf* : pose

poseedor, -dora *n* : possessor, holder

poseer {20} *vt* : to possess, to hold, to have

poseído, -da *adj* : possessed

posesión *nf, pl* **-siones** : possession

posesionarse *vr* **~ de** : to take possession of, to take over

posesivo[1], -va *adj* : possessive

posesivo[2] *nm* : possessive case

posguerra *nf* : postwar period

posibilidad *nf* **1** : possibility **2 posibilidades** *nfpl* : means, income

posibilitar *vt* : to make possible, to permit

posible *adj* : possible — **posiblemente** *adv*

posición *nf, pl* **-ciones 1** : position, place **2** : status, standing **3** : attitude, stance

posicionar *vt* **1** : to position, to place **2** : to establish — **posicionarse** *vr*

positivo[1], -va *adj* : positive

positivo[2] *nm* : print (in photography)

poso *nm* **1** : sediment, dregs *pl* **2** : grounds *pl* (of coffee)

posoperatorio, -ria *adj* : postoperative

posponer {60} *vt* **1** : to postpone **2** : to put behind, to subordinate

pospuso, etc. → **posponer**

posta *nf* : relay race

postal[1] *adj* : postal

postal[2] *nm* : postcard

postdata *nf* : postscript

poste *nm* : post, pole <poste de teléfonos : telephone pole>

póster *or* **poster** *nm, pl* **pósters** *or* **posters** : poster, placard

postergación *nf, pl* **-ciones** : postponement, deferring

postergar {52} *vt* **1** : to delay, to postpone **2** : to pass over (an employee)

posteridad *nf* : posterity

posterior *adj* **1** ULTERIOR : later, subsequent **2** TRASERO : back, rear

postgrado *nm* : graduate course

postgraduado, -da *n* : graduate student, postgraduate

postigo *nm* **1** CONTRAVENTANA : shutter **2** : small door, wicket gate

postilla *nf* : scab

postizo, -za *adj* : artificial, false <dentadura postiza : dentures>

postnatal *adj* : postnatal

postor, -tora *n* : bidder <mejor postor : highest bidder>

postración *nf, pl* **-ciones 1** : prostration **2** ABATIMIENTO : depression

postrado, -da *adj* **1** : prostrate **2 postrado en cama** : bedridden

postrar *vt* DEBILITAR : to debilitate, to weaken — **postrarse** *vr* : to prostrate oneself

postre *nm* : dessert

postrero, -ra *adj* (**postrer** *before masculine singular nouns*) ÚLTIMO : last

postulación *nf, pl* **-ciones 1** : collection **2** : nomination (of a candidate)

postulado *nm* : postulate, assumption

postulante, -ta *n* **1** : postulant **2** : candidate, applicant

postular *vt* **1** : to postulate **2** : to nominate **3** : to propose — **postularse** *vr* : to run, to be a candidate

póstumo, -ma *adj* : posthumous — **póstumamente** *adv*

postura *nf* **1** : posture, position (of the body) **2** ACTITUD, POSICIÓN : position, stance

potable *adj* : drinkable, potable

potaje *nm* : thick vegetable soup, pottage

potasa *nf* : potash

potasio *nm* : potassium

pote *nm* **1** OLLA : pot **2** : jar, container

potencia *nf* **1** : power <potencias extranjeras : foreign powers> <elevado a la tercera potencia : raised to the third power> **2** : capacity, potency

potencial *adj & nm* : potential

potenciar *vt* : to promote, to foster

potenciómetro *nm* : dimmer, dimmer switch

potentado, -da *n* **1** SOBERANO : potentate, sovereign **2** MAGNATE : tycoon, magnate

potente *adj* **1** : powerful, strong **2** : potent, virile

potestad *nf* **1** AUTORIDAD : authority, jurisdiction **2 patria potestad** : custody, guardianship

potrero *nm* **1** : field, pasture **2** : cattle ranch

potro[1], -tra *n* : colt *m,* filly *f*

potro[2] *nm* **1** : rack (for torture) **2** : horse (in gymnastics)

pozo *nm* **1** : well <pozo de petróleo : oil well> **2** : deep pool (in a river) **3** : mine shaft **4** *Arg, Par, Uru* : pothole **5 pozo séptico** : cesspool

pozole *nm Mex* : spicy stew made with pork and hominy

práctica *nf* **1** : practice, experience **2** EJERCICIO : exercising <la práctica de la medicina : the practice of medicine> **3** APLICACIÓN : application, practice <poner en práctica : to put into practice> **4 prácticas** *nfpl* : training

practicable *adj* : practicable, feasible

prácticamente *adv* : practically

practicante[1] *adj* : practicing <católicos practicantes : practicing Catholics>

practicante[2] *nmf* : practicer, practitioner

practicar {72} *vt* **1** : to practice **2** : to perform, to carry out **3** : to exercise (a profession) — *vi* : to practice

práctico, -ca *adj* : practical, useful

pradera *nf* : grassland, prairie

prado *nm* **1** CAMPO : field, meadow **2** : park

pragmático, -ca *adj* : pragmatic — **pragmáticamente** *adv*

pragmatismo *nm* : pragmatism

preámbulo *nm* **1** INTRODUCCIÓN : preamble, introduction **2** RODEO : evasion <gastar preámbulos : to beat around the bush>

prebélico, -ca *adj* : antebellum

prebenda *nf* : privilege, perquisite

precalentar {55} *vt* : to preheat

precariedad *nf* : precariousness

precario, -ria *adj* : precarious — **precariamente** *adv*

precaución *nf, pl* **-ciones 1** : precaution <medidas de precaución : precautionary measures> **2** PRUDENCIA : caution, care <con precaución : cautiously>

precautorio, -ria *adj* : precautionary

precaver *vt* PREVENIR : to prevent, to guard against — **precaverse** *vr* PREVENIRSE : to take precautions, to be on guard

precavido, -da *adj* CAUTELOSO : cautious, prudent

precedencia *nf* : precedence, priority

precedente[1] *adj* : preceding, previous

precedente[2] *nm* : precedent

preceder *v* : to precede

precepto *nm* : rule, precept

preciado, -da *adj* : esteemed, prized, valuable

preciarse *vr* **1** JACTARSE : to boast, to brag **2 ~ de** : to pride oneself on

precinto *nm* : seal

precio *nm* **1** : price **2** : cost, sacrifice <a cualquier precio : whatever the cost>

preciosidad *nf* : beautiful thing <este vestido es una preciosidad : this dress is lovely>

precioso, -sa *adj* **1** HERMOSO : beautiful, exquisite **2** VALIOSO : precious, valuable

precipicio *nm* **1** : precipice **2** RUINA : ruin

precipitación *nf, pl* **-ciones 1** PRISA : haste, hurry, rush **2** : precipitation, rain, snow

precipitado, -da *adj* **1** : hasty, sudden **2** : rash — **precipitadamente** *adv*

precipitar *vt* **1** APRESURAR : to hasten, to speed up **2** ARROJAR : to hurl, to throw — **precipitarse** *vr* **1** APRESURARSE : to rush **2** : to act rashly **3** ARROJARSE : to throw oneself

precisamente *adv* JUSTAMENTE : precisely, exactly

precisar *vt* **1** : to specify, to determine exactly **2** NECESITAR : to need, to require — *vi* : to be necessary

precisión *nf, pl* **-siones 1** EXACTITUD : precision, accuracy **2** CLARIDAD : clarity (of style, etc.) **3** NECESIDAD : necessity <tener precisión de : to have need of>

preciso, -sa *adj* **1** EXACTO : precise **2** : very, exact <en ese preciso instante : at that very instant> **3** NECESARIO : necessary

precocidad *nf* **:** precocity
precocinar *vt* **:** to precook
preconcebir {54} *vt* **:** to preconceive
precondición *nf, pl* **-ciones :** precondition
preconizar {21} *vt* **1 :** to recommend, to advocate **2 :** to extol
precoz *adj, pl* **precoces 1 :** precocious **2 :** early, premature — **precozmente** *adv*
precursor, -sora *n* **:** forerunner, precursor
predecesor, -sora *n* ANTECESOR **:** predecessor
predecir {11} *vt* **:** to foretell, to predict
predestinado, -da *adj* **:** predestined, fated
predestinar *vt* **:** to predestine — **predestinación** *nf*
predeterminar *vt* **:** to predetermine
prédica *nf* SERMÓN **:** sermon
predicado *nm* **:** predicate
predicador, -dora *n* **:** preacher
predicar {72} *v* **:** to preach
predicción *nf, pl* **-ciones 1 :** prediction **2** PRONÓSTICO **:** forecast <predicción del tiempo : weather forecast>
prediga, predijo, etc. → **predecir**
predilección *nf, pl* **-ciones :** predilection, preference
predilecto, -ta *adj* **:** favorite
predio *nm* **:** property, piece of land
predisponer {60} *vt* **1 :** to predispose, to incline **2 :** to prejudice, to bias
predisposición *nf, pl* **-ciones 1 :** predisposition, tendency **2 :** prejudice, bias
predominante *adj* **:** predominant — **predominantemente** *adv*
predominar *vi* PREVALECER **:** to predominate, to prevail
predominio *nm* **:** predominance, prevalence
preeminente *adj* **:** preeminent — **preeminencia** *nf*
preescolar *adj & nm* **:** preschool
preestreno *nm* **:** preview
prefabricado, -da *adj* **:** prefabricated
prefacio *nm* **:** preface
prefecto *nm* **:** prefect
preferencia *nf* **1 :** preference **2** PRIORIDAD **:** priority **3 de ~ :** preferably
preferencial *adj* **:** preferential
preferente *adj* **:** preferential, special <trato preferente : special treatment>
preferentemente *adv* **:** preferably
preferible *adj* **:** preferable
preferido, -da *adj & n* **:** favorite
preferir {76} *vt* **:** to prefer
prefijo *nm* **:** prefix
pregonar *vt* **1 :** to proclaim, to announce **2 :** to hawk (merchandise) **3 :** to extol **4 :** to reveal, to disclose
pregunta *nf* **1 :** question **2 hacer una pregunta :** to ask a question
preguntar *vt* **:** to ask, to question — *vi* **:** to ask, to inquire — **preguntarse** *vr* **:** to wonder
preguntón, -tona *adj, mpl* **-tones :** inquisitive
prehistórico, -ca *adj* **:** prehistoric
prejuicio *nm* **:** prejudice
prejuzgar {52} *vt* **:** to prejudge
prelado *nm* **:** prelate
preliminar *adj & nm* **:** preliminary
preludio *nm* **:** prelude
prematrimonial *adj* **:** premarital
prematuro, -ra *adj* **:** premature
premeditación *nf, pl* **-ciones :** premeditation
premeditar *vt* **:** to premeditate, to plan
premenstrual *adj* **:** premenstrual
premiado, -da *adj* **:** winning, prizewinning
premiar *vt* **1 :** to award a prize to **2 :** to reward
premier *nmf* **:** premier, prime minister
premio *nm* **1 :** prize <premio gordo : grand prize, jackpot> **2 :** reward **3 :** premium
premisa *nf* **:** premise, basis
premolar *nm* **:** bicuspid (tooth)
premonición *nf, pl* **-ciones :** premonition
premura *nf* **:** haste, urgency
prenatal *adj* **:** prenatal
prenda *nf* **1 :** piece of clothing **2 :** security, pledge
prendar *vt* **1 :** to charm, to captivate **2 :** to pawn, to pledge — **prendarse** *vr* **~ de :** to fall in love with
prendedor *nm* **:** brooch, pin
prender *vt* **1** SUJETAR **:** to pin, to fasten **2** APRESAR **:** to catch, to apprehend **3 :** to light (a cigarette, a match) **4 :** to turn on <prende la luz : turn on the light> **5 prender fuego a :** to set fire to — *vi* **1 :** to take root **2 :** to catch fire **3 :** to catch on
prensa *nf* **1 :** printing press **2 :** press <conferencia de prensa : press conference>
prensar *vt* **:** to press
prensil *adj* **:** prehensile
preñado, -da *adj* **1 :** pregnant **2 ~ de :** filled with
preñar *vt* EMBARAZAR **:** to make pregnant
preñez *nf, pl* **preñeces :** pregnancy
preocupación *nf, pl* **-ciones** INQUIETUD **:** worry, concern
preocupante *adj* **:** worrisome
preocupar *vt* INQUIETAR **:** to worry, to concern — **preocuparse** *vr* APURARSE **:** to worry, to be concerned
preparación *nf, pl* **-ciones 1 :** preparation, readiness **2 :** education, training **3 :** (medicinal) preparation
preparado[1], -da *adj* **1 :** ready, prepared **2 :** trained
preparado[2] *nm* **:** preparation, mixture
preparar *vt* **1 :** to prepare, to make ready **2 :** to teach, to train, to coach — **prepararse** *vr*
preparativos *nmpl* **:** preparations
preparatoria *nf Mex* **:** high school
preparatorio, -ria *adj* **:** preparatory

preponderante *adj* : preponderant, predominant — **preponderancia** *nf* — **preponderantemente** *adv*

preposición *nf, pl* **-ciones** : preposition — **preposicional** *adj*

prepotente *adj* : arrogant, domineering, overbearing — **prepotencia** *nf*

prerrogativa *nf* : prerogative, privilege

presa *nf* **1** : capture, seizure <hacer presa de : to seize> **2** : catch, prey <presa de : prey to, seized with> **3** : claw, fang **4** DIQUE : dam **5** : morsel, piece (of food)

presagiar *vt* : to presage, to portend

presagio *nm* : omen, portent

presbiterio *nm* : presbytery, sanctuary (of a church)

presbítero *nm* : presbyter

presciencia *nf* : prescience

prescindir *vi* ~ **de 1** : to do without, to dispense with **2** DESATENDER : to ignore, to disregard **3** OMITIR : to omit, to skip

prescribir {33} *vt* : to prescribe

prescripción *nf, pl* **-ciones** : prescription

prescrito *pp* → **prescribir**

presencia *nf* **1** : presence **2** ASPECTO : appearance

presenciar *vt* : to be present at, to witness

presentación *nf, pl* **-ciones 1** : presentation **2** : introduction **3** : appearance

presentador, -dora *n* : newscaster, anchorman *m,* anchorwoman *f*

presentar *vt* **1** : to present, to show **2** : to offer, to give **3** : to submit (a document), to launch (a product) **4** : to introduce (a person) — **presentarse** *vr* **1** : to show up, to appear **2** : to arise, to come up **3** : to introduce oneself

presente[1] *adj* **1** : present, in attendance **2** : present, current **3 tener presente** : to keep in mind

presente[2] *nm* **1** : present (time, tense) **2** : one present <entre los presentes se encontraban . . . : those present included . . .>

presentimiento *nm* : premonition, hunch, feeling

presentir {76} *vt* : to sense, to intuit <presentía lo que iba a pasar : he sensed what was going to happen>

preservación *nf, pl* **-ciones** : preservation

preservar *vt* **1** : to preserve **2** : to protect

preservativo *nm* CONDÓN : condom

presidencia *nf* **1** : presidency **2** : chairmanship

presidencial *adj* : presidential

presidente, -ta *n* **1** : president **2** : chair, chairperson **3** : presiding judge

presidiario, -ria *n* : convict, prisoner

presidio *nm* : prison, penitentiary

presidir *vt* **1** MODERAR : to preside over, to chair **2** : to dominate, to rule over

presilla *nf* : eye, loop, fastener

presión *nf, pl* **presiones 1** : pressure **2 presión arterial** : blood pressure

presionar *vt* **1** : to pressure **2** : to press, to push — *vi* : to put on the pressure

preso[1], -sa *adj* : imprisoned

preso[2], -sa *n* : prisoner

prestado, -da *adj* **1** : borrowed, on loan **2 pedir prestado** : to borrow

prestamista *nmf* : moneylender, pawnbroker

préstamo *nm* : loan

prestar *vt* **1** : to lend, to loan **2** : to render (a service), to give (aid) **3 prestar atención** : to pay attention **4 prestar juramento** : to take an oath — **prestarse** *vr* : to lend oneself <se presta a confusiones : it lends itself to confusion>

prestatario, -ria *n* : borrower

presteza *nf* : promptness, speed

prestidigitación *nf, pl* **-ciones** : sleight of hand, prestidigitation

prestidigitador, -dora *n* : conjurer, magician

prestigio *nm* : prestige — **prestigioso, -sa** *adj*

presto[1] *adv* : promptly, at once

presto[2], -ta *adj* **1** : quick, prompt **2** DISPUESTO, PREPARADO : ready

presumido, -da *adj* VANIDOSO : conceited, vain

presumir *vt* SUPONER : to presume, to suppose — *vi* **1** ALARDEAR : to boast, to show off **2** ~ **de** : to consider oneself <presume de inteligente : he thinks he's intelligent>

presunción *nf, pl* **-ciones 1** SUPOSICIÓN : presumption, supposition **2** VANIDAD : conceit, vanity

presunto, -ta *adj* : presumed, supposed, alleged — **presuntamente** *adv*

presuntuoso, -sa *adj* : conceited

presuponer {60} *vt* : to presuppose

presupuestal *adj* : budget, budgetary

presupuestar *vi* : to budget — *vt* : to budget for

presupuestario, -ria *adj* : budget, budgetary

presupuesto *nm* **1** : budget, estimate **2** : assumption, supposition

presurizar {21} *vt* : to pressurize

presuroso, -sa *adj* : hasty, quick

pretencioso, -sa *adj* : pretentious

pretender *vt* **1** INTENTAR : to attempt, to try <pretendo estudiar : I'm trying to study> **2** AFIRMAR : to claim <pretende ser pobre : he claims he's poor> **3** : to seek, to aspire to <¿qué pretendes tú? : what are you after?> **4** CORTEJAR : to court **5 pretender que** : to expect <¿pretendes que lo crea? : do you expect me to believe you?>

pretendiente[1] *nmf* **1** : candidate, applicant **2** : pretender, claimant (to a throne, etc.)

pretendiente[2] *nm* : suitor

pretensión *nf, pl* **-siones 1 :** intention, hope, plan **2 :** pretension <sin pretensiones : unpretentious>

pretexto *nm* EXCUSA **:** pretext, excuse

pretil *nm* **:** parapet, railing

prevalecer {53} *vi* **:** to prevail, to triumph

prevaleciente *adj* **:** prevailing, prevalent

prevalerse {84} *vr* **~ de :** to avail oneself of, to take advantage of

prevención *nf, pl* **-ciones 1 :** prevention **2 :** preparation, readiness **3 :** precautionary measure **4 :** prejudice, bias

prevenido, -da *adj* **1** PREPARADO **:** prepared, ready **2** ADVERTIDO **:** forewarned **3** CAUTELOSO **:** cautious

prevenir {87} *vt* **1 :** to prevent **2 :** to warn — **prevenirse** *vr* **~ contra** *or* **~ de :** to take precautions against

preventivo, -va *adj* **:** preventive, precautionary

prever {88} *vt* ANTICIPAR **:** to foresee, to anticipate

previo, -via *adj* **1 :** previous, prior **2 :** after, upon <previo pago : after paying, upon payment>

previsible *adj* **:** foreseeable

previsión *nf, pl* **-siones 1 :** foresight **2 :** prediction, forecast **3 :** precaution

previsor, -sora *adj* **:** farsighted, prudent

prieto, -ta *adj* **1 :** blackish, dark **2 :** dark-skinned, swarthy **3 :** tight, compressed

prima *nf* **1 :** premium **2 :** bonus **3 → primo**

primacía *nf* **1 :** precedence, priority **2 :** superiority, supremacy

primado *nm* **:** primate (bishop)

primario, -ria *adj* **:** primary

primate *nm* **:** primate

primavera *nf* **1 :** spring (season) **2** PRÍMULA **:** primrose

primaveral *adj* **:** spring, springlike

primero[1] *adv* **1 :** first **2 :** rather, sooner

primero[2]**, -ra** *adj* (**primer** *before masculine singular nouns*) **1 :** first **2 :** top, leading **3 :** fundamental, basic **4 de primera :** first-rate

primero[3]**, -ra** *n* **:** first

primicia *nf* **1 :** first fruits **2 :** scoop, exclusive

primigenio, -nia *adj* **:** original, primary

primitivo, -va *adj* **1 :** primitive **2** ORIGINAL **:** original

primo, -ma *n* **:** cousin

primogénito, -ta *adj & n* **:** firstborn

primor *nm* **1 :** skill, care **2 :** beauty, elegance

primordial *adj* **1 :** primordial **2 :** basic, fundamental

primoroso, -sa *adj* **1 :** exquisite, fine, delicate **2 :** skillful

prímula *nf* **:** primrose

princesa *nf* **:** princess

principado *nm* **:** principality

principal[1] *adj* **1 :** main, principal **2 :** foremost, leading

principal[2] *nm* **:** capital, principal

príncipe *nm* **:** prince

prinipesco, -ca *adj* **:** princely

principiante[1] *adj* **:** beginning

principiante[2] *nmf* **:** beginner, novice

principiar *vt* EMPEZAR **:** to begin

principio *nm* **1** COMIENZO **:** beginning **2 :** principle **3 al principio :** at first **4 a principios de :** at the beginning of <a principios de agosto : at the beginning of August> **5 en ~ :** in principle

pringar {52} *vt* **1 :** to dip (in grease) **2 :** to soil, to spatter (with grease) — **pringarse** *vr*

pringoso, -sa *adj* **:** greasy

pringue[1]**, etc. → pringar**

pringue[2] *nm* **:** grease, drippings *pl*

prior, priora *n* **:** prior *m,* prioress *f*

priorato *nm* **:** priory

prioridad *nf* **:** priority, precedence

prisa *nf* **1 :** hurry, rush **2 a ~** *or* **de ~ :** quickly, fast **3 a toda prisa :** as fast as possible **4 darse prisa :** to hurry **5 tener prisa :** to be in a hurry

prisión *nf, pl* **prisiones 1** CÁRCEL **:** prison, jail **2** ENCARCELAMIENTO **:** imprisonment

prisionero, -ra *n* **:** prisoner

prisma *nf* **:** prism

prismáticos *nmpl* **:** binoculars

prístino, -na *adj* **:** pristine

privacidad *nf* **:** privacy

privación *nf, pl* **-ciones 1 :** deprivation **2 :** privation, want

privado, -da *adj* **:** private — **privadamente** *adv*

privar *vt* **1** DESPOJAR **:** to deprive **2 :** to stun, to knock out — **privarse** *vr* **:** to deprive oneself

privativo, -va *adj* **:** exclusive, particular

privilegiado, -da *adj* **:** privileged

privilegiar *vt* **:** to grant a privilege to, to favor

privilegio *nm* **:** privilege

pro[1] *nm* **1 :** pro, advantage <los pros y contras : the pros and cons> **2 en pro de :** for, in favor of

pro[2] *prep* **:** for, in favor of <grupos pro derechos humanos : groups supporting human rights>

proa *nf* **:** bow, prow

probabilidad *nf* **:** probability

probable *adj* **:** probable, likely

probablemente *adv* **:** probably

probar {19} *vt* **1 :** to demonstrate, to prove **2 :** to test, to try out **3 :** to try on (clothing) **4 :** to taste, to sample — *vi* **:** to try — **probarse** *vr* **:** to try on (clothing)

probeta *nf* **:** test tube

probidad *nf* **:** probity

problema *nm* **:** problem

problemática *nf* **:** set of problems <la problemática que debemos enfrentar : the problems we must face>

probóscide *nf* **:** proboscis

problemático, -ca *adj* : problematic
procaz *adj, pl* **procaces 1** : insolent, impudent **2** : indecent
procedencia *nf* : origin, source
procedente *adj* **1** : proper, fitting **2 ~ de** : coming from
proceder *vi* **1** AVANZAR : to proceed **2** : to act, to behave **3** : to be appropriate, to be fitting **4 ~ de** : to originate from, to come from
procedimiento *nm* : procedure, process
prócer *nmf* : eminent person, leader
procesado, -da *n* : accused, defendant
procesador *nm* : processor <procesador de textos : word processor>
procesamiento *nm* : processing <procesamiento de datos : data processing>
procesar *vt* **1** : to prosecute, to try **2** : to process
procesión *nf, pl* **-siones** : procession
proceso *nm* **1** : process **2** : trial, proceedings *pl*
proclama *nf* : proclamation
proclamación *nf, pl* **-ciones** : proclamation
proclamar *vt* : to proclaim — **proclamarse** *vr*
proclive *adj* **~ a** : inclined to, prone to
proclividad *nf* : proclivity, inclination
procrear *vi* : to procreate — **procreación** *nf*
procurador, -dora *n* ABOGADO : attorney
procurar *vt* **1** INTENTAR : to try, to endeavor **2** CONSEGUIR : to obtain, to procure **3 procurar hacer** : to manage to do
prodigar {52} *vt* : to lavish, to be generous with
prodigio *nm* : wonder, marvel
prodigioso, -sa *adj* : prodigious, marvelous
pródigo[1], -ga *adj* **1** : generous, lavish **2** : wasteful, prodigal
pródigo[2], -ga *n* : spendthrift, prodigal
producción *nf, pl* **-ciones 1** : production **2 producción en serie** : mass production
producir {61} *vt* **1** : to produce, to make, to manufacture **2** : to cause, to bring about **3** : to bear (interest) — **producirse** *vr* : to take place, to occur
productividad *nf* : productivity
productivo, -va *adj* **1** : productive **2** LUCRATIVO : profitable
producto *nm* **1** : product **2** : proceeds *pl*, yield
productor, -tora *n* : producer
proeza *nf* HAZAÑA : feat, exploit
profanar *vt* : to profane, to desecrate — **profanación** *nf*
profano[1], -na *adj* **1** : profane **2** : worldly, secular
profano[2], -na *n* : nonspecialist
profecía *nf* : prophecy
proferir {76} *vt* **1** : to utter **2** : to hurl (insults)
profesar *vt* **1** : to profess, to declare **2** : to practice, to exercise
profesión *nf, pl* **-siones** : profession
profesional *adj & nmf* : professional — **profesionalmente** *adv*
profesionalismo *nm* : professionalism
profesionalizar {21} *vt* : to professionalize
profesionista *nmf Mex* : professional
profesor, -sora *n* **1** MAESTRO : teacher **2** : professor
profesorado *nm* **1** : faculty **2** : teaching profession
profeta *nm* : prophet
profético, -ca *adj* : prophetic
profetisa *nf* : prophetess, prophet
profetizar {21} *vt* : to prophesy
prófugo, -ga *adj & n* : fugitive
profundidad *nf* : depth, profundity
profundizar {21} *vt* **1** : to deepen **2** : to study in depth — *vi* **~ en** : to go deeply into, to study in depth
profundo, -da *adj* **1** HONDO : deep **2** : profound — **profundamente** *adv*
profusión *nf, pl* **-siones** : abundance, profusion
profuso, -sa *adj* : profuse, abundant, extensive
progenie *nf* : progeny, offspring
progenitor, -tora *n* ANTEPASADO : ancestor, progenitor
prognóstico *nm* : prognosis
programa *nm* **1** : program **2** : plan **3 programa de estudios** : curriculum
programable *adj* : programmable
programación *nf, pl* **-ciones 1** : programming **2** : planning
programador, -dora *n* : programmer
programar *vt* **1** : to schedule, to plan **2** : to program (a computer, etc.)
progresar *vi* : to progress, to make progress
progresista *adj & nmf* : progressive
progresivo, -va *adj* : progressive, gradual
progreso *nm* : progress
prohibición *nf, pl* **-ciones** : ban, prohibition
prohibir {62} *vt* : to prohibit, to ban, to forbid
prohibitivo, -va *adj* : prohibitive
prohijar {5} *vt* ADOPTAR : to adopt
prójimo *nm* : neighbor, fellow man
prole *nf* : offspring, progeny
proletariado *nm* : proletariat, working class
proletario, -ria *adj & n* : proletarian
proliferar *vi* : to proliferate — **proliferación** *nf*
prolífico, -ca *adj* : prolific
prolijo, -ja *adj* : wordy, long-winded
prólogo *nm* : prologue, preface, foreword
prolongación *nf, pl* **-ciones** : extension, lengthening

prolongar {52} *vt* **1 :** to prolong **2 :** to extend, to lengthen — **prolongarse** *vr* CONTINUAR **:** to last, to continue

promediar *vt* **1 :** to average **2 :** to divide in half — *vi* **:** to be half over

promedio *nm* **1 :** average **2 :** middle, mid-point

promesa *nf* **:** promise

prometedor, -dora *adj* **:** promising, hopeful

prometer *vt* **:** to promise — *vi* **:** to show promise — **prometerse** *vr* COMPROMETERSE **:** to get engaged

prometido[1], **-da** *adj* **:** engaged

prometido[2], **-da** *n* NOVIO **:** fiancé *m,* fiancée *f*

prominente *adj* **:** prominent — **prominencia** *nf*

promiscuo, -cua *adj* **:** promiscuous — **promiscuidad** *nf*

promisorio, -ria *adj* **1 :** promising **2 :** promissory

promoción *nf, pl* **-ciones 1 :** promotion **2 :** class, year **3 :** play-off (in soccer)

promocionar *vt* **:** to promote — **promocional** *adj*

promontorio *nm* **:** promontory, headland

promotor, -tora *n* **:** promoter

promover {47} *vt* **1 :** to promote, to advance **2** FOMENTAR **:** to foster, to encourage **3** PROVOCAR **:** to provoke, to cause

promulgación *nf, pl* **-ciones 1 :** enactment **2 :** proclamation, enactment

promulgar {52} *vt* **1 :** to promulgate, to proclaim **2 :** to enact (a law or decree)

prono, -na *adj* **:** prone

pronombre *nm* **:** pronoun

pronosticar {72} *vt* **:** to predict, to forecast

pronóstico *nm* **1** PREDICCIÓN **:** forecast, prediction **2 :** prognosis

prontitud *nf* **1** PRESTEZA **:** promptness, speed **2 con ~ :** promptly, quickly

pronto[1] *adv* **1 :** quickly, promptly **2 :** soon **3 de ~ :** suddenly **4 lo más pronto posible :** as soon as possible **5 tan pronto como :** as soon as

pronto[2], **-ta** *adj* **1** RÁPIDO **:** quick, speedy, prompt **2** PREPARADO **:** ready

pronunciación *nf, pl* **-ciones :** pronunciation

pronunciado, -da *adj* **1 :** pronounced, sharp, steep **2 :** marked, noticeable

pronunciar *vt* **1 :** to pronounce, to say **2 :** to give, to deliver (a speech) **3 pronunciar un fallo :** to pronounce sentence — **pronunciarse** *vr* **:** to declare oneself

propagación *nf, pl* **-ciones :** propagation, spreading

propaganda *nf* **1 :** propaganda **2** PUBLICIDAD **:** advertising

propagar {52} *vt* **1 :** to propagate **2 :** to spread, to disseminate — **propagarse** *vr*

propalar *vt* **1 :** to divulge **2 :** to spread

propano *nm* **:** propane

propasarse *vr* **:** to go too far, to overstep one's bounds

propensión *nf, pl* **-siones** INCLINACIÓN **:** inclination, propensity

propenso, -sa *adj* **:** prone, susceptible

propiamente *adv* **1 :** properly, correctly **2 :** exactly, precisely <propiamente dicho : strictly speaking>

propiciar *vt* **1 :** to propitiate **2 :** to favor, to foster

propicio, -cia *adj* **:** favorable, propitious

propiedad *nf* **1 :** property <propiedad privada : private property> **2 :** ownership **3** CUALIDAD **:** property, quality **4 :** suitability, appropriateness

propietario[1], **-ria** *adj* **:** proprietary

propietario[2], **-ria** *n* DUEÑO **:** owner, proprietor

propina *nf* **:** tip, gratuity

propinar *vt* **:** to give, to strike <propinar una paliza : to give a beating>

propio, -pia *adj* **1 :** own <su propia casa : his own house> <sus recursos propios : their own resources> **2** APROPIADO **:** appropriate, suitable **3** CARACTERÍSTICO **:** characteristic, typical **4** MISMO **:** oneself <el propio director : the director himself>

proponer {60} *vt* **1 :** to propose, to suggest **2 :** to nominate — **proponerse** *vr* **:** to intend, to plan, to set out <lo que se propone lo cumple : he does what he sets out to do>

proporción *nf, pl* **-ciones 1 :** proportion **2 :** ratio (in mathematics) **3 proporciones** *nfpl* **:** proportions, size <de grandes proporciones : very large>

proporcionado, -da *adj* **1 :** proportionate **2 :** proportioned <bien proporcionado : well-proportioned> — **proporcionadamente** *adv*

proporcional *adj* **:** proportional — **proporcionalmente** *adv*

proporcionar *vt* **1 :** to provide, to give **2 :** to proportion, to adapt

proposición *nf, pl* **-ciones :** proposal, proposition

propósito *nm* **1** INTENCIÓN **:** purpose, intention **2 a ~ :** by the way **3 a ~ :** on purpose, intentionally

propuesta *nf* PROPOSICIÓN **:** proposal

propulsar *vt* **1** IMPULSAR **:** to propel, to drive **2** PROMOVER **:** to promote, to encourage

propulsión *nf, pl* **-siones :** propulsion

propulsor *nm* **:** propellant

propuso, etc. → **proponer**

prorrata *nf* **1 :** share, quota **2 a ~ :** pro rata, proportionately

prórroga *nf* **1 :** extension, deferment **2 :** overtime (in sports)

prorrogar {52} *vt* **1 :** to extend (a deadline) **2 :** to postpone

prorrumpir *vi* **:** to burst forth, to break out <prorrumpí en lágrimas : I burst into tears>

prosa *nf* **:** prose

prosaico, -ca *adj* **:** prosaic, mundane
proscribir {33} *v* **1** PROHIBIR **:** to prohibit, to ban, to proscribe **2** DESTERRAR **:** to banish, to exile
proscripción *nf, pl* **-ciones 1** PROHIBICIÓN **:** ban, proscription **2** DESTIERRO **:** banishment
proscrito[1] *pp* → **proscribir**
proscrito[2], **-ta** *n* **1** DESTERRADO **:** exile **2 :** outlaw
prosecución *nf, pl* **-ciones 1 :** continuation **2 :** pursuit
proseguir {75} *vt* **1** CONTINUAR **:** to continue **2 :** to pursue (studies, goals) — *vi* **:** to continue, to go on
prosélito, -ta *n* **:** proselyte
prospección *nf, pl* **-ciones :** prospecting, exploration
prospectar *vi* **:** to prospect
prospecto *nm* **:** prospectus, leaflet, brochure
prosperar *vi* **:** to prosper, to thrive
prosperidad *nf* **:** prosperity
próspero, -ra *adj* **:** prosperous, flourishing
próstata *nf* **:** prostate
prostitución *nf, pl* **-ciones :** prostitution
prostituir {41} *vt* **:** to prostitute — **prostituirse** *vr* **:** to prostitute oneself
prostituto, -ta *n* **:** prostitute
protagonista *nmf* **1 :** protagonist, main character **2 :** leader
protagonizar {21} *vt* **:** to star in
protección *nf, pl* **-ciones :** protection
protector[1], **-tora** *adj* **:** protective
protector[2], **-tora** *n* **1 :** protector, guardian **2 :** patron
protector[3] *nm* **:** protector, guard <chaleco protector : chest protector>
protectorado *nm* **:** protectorate
proteger {15} *vt* **:** to protect, to defend — **protegerse** *vr*
protegido, -da *n* **:** protégé
proteína *nf* **:** protein
prótesis *nfs & pl* **:** prosthesis
protesta *nf* **1 :** protest **2** *Mex* **:** promise, oath
protestante *adj & nmf* **:** Protestant
protestantismo *nm* **:** Protestantism
protestar *vi* **:** to protest, to object — *vt* **1 :** to protest, to object to **2 :** to declare, to profess
protocolo *nm* **:** protocol
protón *nm, pl* **protones :** proton
protoplasma *nm* **:** protoplasm
prototipo *nm* **:** prototype
protozoario *or* **protozoo** *nm* **:** protozoan
protuberancia *nf* **:** protuberance — **protuberante** *adj*
provecho *nm* **:** benefit, advantage
provechoso, -sa *adj* BENEFICIOSO **:** beneficial, profitable, useful — **provechosamente** *adv*
proveedor, -dora *n* **:** provider, supplier
proveer {63} *vt* **:** to provide, to supply — **proveerse** *vr* **~ de :** to obtain, to supply oneself with
provenir {87} *vi* **~ de :** to come from
provenzal[1] *adj* **:** Provençal
provenzal[2] *nmf* **:** Provençal
provenzal[3] *nm* **:** Provençal (language)
proverbio *nm* REFRÁN **:** proverb — **proverbial** *adj*
providencia *nf* **1 :** providence, foresight **2 :** Providence, God **3 providencias** *nfpl* **:** steps, measures
providencial *adj* **:** providential
provincia *nf* **:** province — **provincial** *adj*
provinciano, -na *adj* **:** provincial, unsophisticated
provisión *nf, pl* **-siones :** provision
provisional *adj* **:** provisional, temporary
provisionalmente *adv* **:** provisionally, tentatively
provisorio, -ria *adj* **:** provisional, temporary
provisto *pp* → **proveer**
provocación *nf, pl* **-ciones :** provocation
provocador[1], **-dora** *adj* **:** provocative, provoking
provocador[2], **-dora** *n* AGITADOR **:** agitator
provocar {72} *vt* **1** CAUSAR **:** to provoke, to cause **2** IRRITAR **:** to provoke, to pique
provocativo, -va *adj* **:** provocative
proxeneta *nmf* **:** pimp *m*
próximamente *adv* **:** shortly, soon
proximidad *nf* **1 :** nearness, proximity **2 proximidades** *nfpl* **:** vicinity
próximo, -ma *adj* **1 :** near, close <la Navidad está próxima : Christmas is almost here> **2** SIGUIENTE **:** next, following <la próxima semana : the following week>
proyección *nf, pl* **-ciones 1 :** projection **2 :** showing, screening (of a film) **3 :** range, influence, diffusion
proyectar *vt* **1 :** to plan **2** LANZAR **:** to throw, to hurl **3 :** to project, to cast (light or shadow) **4 :** to show, to screen (a film)
proyectil *nm* **:** projectile, missile
proyecto *nm* **1 :** plan, project **2 proyecto de ley :** bill
proyector *nm* **1 :** projector **2 :** spotlight
prudencia *nf* **:** prudence, care, discretion
prudente *adj* **:** prudent, sensible, reasonable
prueba[1], **etc.** → **probar**
prueba[2] *nf* **1 :** proof, evidence **2 :** trial, test **3 :** proof (in printing or photography) **4 :** event, qualifying round (in sports) **5 a prueba de agua :** waterproof **6 prueba de fuego :** acid test **7 poner a prueba :** to put to the test
prurito *nm* **1 :** itching **2 :** desire, urge
psicoanálisis *nm* **:** psychoanalysis — **psicoanalista** *nmf*

psicoanalítico, -ca *adj* : psychoanalytic
psicoanalizar {21} *vt* : to psychoanalyze
psicología *nf* : psychology
psicológico, -ca *adj* : psychological — **psicológicamente** *adv*
psicólogo, -ga *n* : psychologist
psicópata *nmf* : psychopath
psicopático, -ca *adj* : psycopathic
psicosis *nfs & pl* : psychosis
psicosomático, -ca *adj* : psychosomatic
psicoterapeuta *nmf* : psychotherapist
psicoterapia *nf* : psychotherapy
psicótico, -ca *adj & n* : psychotic
psique *nf* : psyche
psiquiatra *nmf* : psychiatrist
psiquiatría *nf* : psychiatry
psiquiátrico[1], -ca *adj* : psychiatric
psiquiátrico[2] *nm* : mental hospital
psíquico, -ca *adj* : psychic
psiquis *nfs & pl* : psyche
psoriasis *nf* : psoriasis
ptomaína *nf* : ptomaine
púa *nf* **1** : barb <alambre de púas : barbed wire> **2** : tooth (of a comb) **3** : quill, spine
pubertad *nf* : puberty
pubiano → **púbico**
púbico, -ca *adj* : pubic
publicación *nf, pl* **-ciones** : publication
publicar {72} *vt* **1** : to publish **2** DIVULGAR : to divulge, to disclose
publicidad *nf* **1** : publicity **2** : advertising
publicista *nmf* : publicist
publicitar *vt* **1** : to publicize **2** : to advertise
publicitario, -ria *adj* : advertising, publicity <agencia publicitaria : advertising agency>
público[1], -ca *adj* : public — **públicamente** *adv*
público[2] *nm* **1** : public **2** : audience, spectators *pl*
puchero *nm* **1** : pot **2** : stew **3** : pout <hacer pucheros : to pout>
pucho *nm* **1** : waste, residue **2** : cigarette butt **3 a puchos** : little by little, bit by bit
púdico, -ca *adj* : chaste, modest
pudiente *adj* **1** : powerful **2** : rich, wealthy
pudín *nm, pl* **pudines** BUDÍN : pudding
pudo, etc. → **poder**
pudor *nm* : modesty, reserve
pudoroso, -sa *adj* : modest, reserved, shy
pudrir {59} *vt* **1** : to rot **2** *fam* : to annoy, to upset — **pudrirse** *vr* **1** : to rot **2** : to languish
pueblerino, -na *adj* : provincial, countrified
puebla, etc. → **poblar**
pueblo *nm* **1** NACIÓN : people **2** : common people **3** ALDEA, POBLADO : town, village
puede, etc. → **poder**
puente *nm* **1** : bridge <puente levadizo : drawbridge> **2** : denture, bridge **3 puente aéreo** : airlift
puerco[1], -ca *adj* : dirty, filthy
puerco[2], -ca *n* **1** CERDO, MARRANO : pig, hog **2** : pig, dirty or greedy person **3 puerco espín** : porcupine
pueril *adj* : childish, puerile
puerro *nm* : leek
puerta *nf* **1** : door, entrance, gate **2 a puerta cerrada** : behind closed doors
puerto *nm* **1** : port, harbor **2** : mountain pass **3 puerto marítimo** : seaport
puertorriqueño, -ña *adj & n* : Puerto Rican
pues *conj* **1** : since, because, for <no puedo ir, pues no tengo plata : I can't go, since I don't have any money> <lo hace, pues a él le gusta : he does it because he likes to> **2** (*used interjectionally*) : well, then <¡pues claro que sí! : well, of course!> <¡pues no voy! : well then, I'm not going!>
puesta *nf* **1** : setting <puesta del sol : sunset> **2** : laying (of eggs) **3 puesta a punto** : tune-up **4 puesta en marcha** : start, starting up
puestero, -ra *n* : seller, vendor
puesto[1] *pp* → **poner**
puesto[2], -ta *adj* : dressed <bien puesto : well-dressed>
puesto[3] *nm* **1** LUGAR, SITIO : place, position **2** : position, job **3** : kiosk, stand, stall **4 puesto que** : since, given that
pugilato *nm* BOXEO : boxing, pugilism
pugilista *nm* BOXEADOR : boxer, pugilist
pugna *nf* **1** CONFLICTO, LUCHA : conflict, struggle **2 en ~** : at odds, in conflict
pugnar *vi* LUCHAR : to fight, to strive, to struggle
pugnaz *adj* : pugnacious
pujante *adj* : mighty, powerful
pujanza *nf* : strength, vigor <pujanza económica : economic strength>
pulcritud *nf* **1** : neatness, tidiness **2** ESMERO : meticulousness
pulcro, -cra *adj* **1** : clean, neat **2** : exquisite, delicate, refined
pulga *nf* **1** : flea **2 tener malas pulgas** : to be bad-tempered
pulgada *nf* : inch
pulgar *nm* **1** : thumb **2** : big toe
pulir *vt* **1** : to polish, to shine **2** REFINAR : to refine, to perfect
pulla *nf* **1** : cutting remark, dig, gibe **2** : obscenity
pulmón *nm, pl* **pulmones** : lung
pulmonar *adj* : pulmonary
pulmonía *nf* NEUMONÍA : pneumonia
pulpa *nf* : pulp, flesh
pulpería *nf* : small grocery store
púlpito *nm* : pulpit
pulpo *nm* : octopus
pulsación *nf, pl* **-ciones** **1** : beat, pulsation, throb **2** : keystroke
pulsar *vt* **1** APRETAR : to press, to push **2** : to strike (a key) **3** : to assess — *vi* : to beat, to throb

pulsera *nf* **:** bracelet

pulso *nm* **1 :** pulse <tomarle el pulso a alguien : to take someone's pulse> <tomarle el pulso a la opinión : to sound out opinion> **2 :** steadiness (of hand) <dibujo a pulso : freehand sketch>

pulular *vi* ABUNDAR **:** to abound, to swarm <en el río pululan los peces : the river is teeming with fish>

pulverizador *nm* **1 :** atomizer, spray **2 :** spray gun

pulverizar {21} *vt* **1 :** to pulverize, to crush **2 :** to spray

puma *nf* **:** cougar, puma

puna *nf* **:** bleak Andean tableland

punción *nf, pl* **punciones :** puncture

punible *adj* **:** punishable

punitivo, -va *adj* **:** punitive

punce, etc. → **punzar**

punta *nf* **1 :** tip, end <punta del dedo : fingertip> <en la punta de la lengua : at the tip of one's tongue> **2 :** point (of a weapon or pencil) <punta de lanza : spearhead> **3 :** point, headland **4 :** bunch, lot <una punta de ladrones : a bunch of thieves> **5 a punta de :** by, by dint of

puntada *nf* **1 :** stitch (in sewing) **2** PUNZADA **:** sharp pain, stitch, twinge **3** *Mex* **:** witticism, quip

puntal *nm* **1 :** prop, support **2 :** stanchion

puntapié *nm* PATADA **:** kick

puntazo *nm* CORNADA **:** wound (from a goring)

puntear *vt* **1 :** to pluck (a guitar) **2 :** to lead (in sports)

puntería *nf* **:** aim, marksmanship

puntero *nm* **1 :** pointer **2 :** leader

puntiagudo, -da *adj* **:** sharp, pointed

puntilla *nf* **1 :** lace edging **2 :** dagger (in bullfighting) **3 de puntillas :** on tiptoe

puntilloso, -sa *adj* **:** punctilious

punto *nm* **1 :** dot, point **2 :** period (in punctuation) **3 :** item, question **4 :** spot, place **5 :** moment, stage, degree **6 :** point (in a score) **7 :** stitch **8 en ~ :** on the dot, sharp <a las dos en punto : at two o'clock sharp> **9 al punto :** at once **10 a punto fijo :** exactly, certainly **11 dos puntos :** colon **12 hasta cierto punto :** up to a point **13 punto decimal :** decimal point **14 punto de vista :** point of view **15 punto y coma :** semicolon **16 y punto :** period <es el mejor que hay y punto : it's the best there is, period> **17 puntos cardinales :** points of the compass

puntuación *nf, pl* **-ciones 1 :** punctuation **2 :** scoring, score, grade

puntual *adj* **1 :** prompt, punctual **2 :** exact, accurate — **puntualmente** *adv*

puntualidad *nf* **1 :** promptness, punctuality **2 :** exactness, accuracy

puntualizar {21} *vt* **1 :** to specify, to state **2 :** to point out

puntuar {3} *vt* **:** to punctuate — *vi* **:** to score points

punzada *nf* **:** sharp pain, twinge, stitch

punzante *adj* **1 :** sharp **2** CÁUSTICO **:** biting, caustic

punzar {21} *vt* **:** to pierce, to puncture

punzón *nm, pl* **punzones 1 :** awl **2 :** hole punch

puñado *nm* **1 :** handful **2 a puñados :** lots of, by the handful

puñal *nm* DAGA **:** dagger

puñalada *nf* **:** stab, stab wound

puñetazo *nm* **:** punch (with the fist)

puño *nm* **1 :** fist **2 :** handful, fistful **3 :** cuff (of a shirt) **4 :** handle, hilt

pupila *nf* **:** pupil (of the eye)

pupilo, -la *n* **1 :** pupil, student **2 :** ward, charge

pupitre *nm* **:** writing desk

puré *nm* **:** purée <puré de papas : mashed potatoes>

pureza *nf* **:** purity

purga *nf* **1 :** laxative **2 :** purge

purgante *adj & nm* **:** laxative, purgative

purgar {52} *vt* **1 :** to purge, to cleanse **2 :** to liquidate (in politics) **3 :** to give a laxative to — **purgarse** *vr* **1 :** to take a laxative **2 ~ de :** to purge oneself of

purgatorio *nm* **:** purgatory

purgue, etc. → **purgar**

purificador *nm* **:** purifier

purificar {72} *vt* **:** to purify — **purificación** *nf*

puritano[1], -na *adj* **:** puritanical, puritan

puritano[2], -na *n* **1 :** Puritan **2 :** puritan

puro[1] *adv* **:** sheer, much <de puro terco : out of sheer stubbornness>

puro[2], -ra *adj* **1 :** pure <aire puro : fresh air> **2 :** plain, simple, sheer <por pura curiosidad : from sheer curiosity> **3 :** only, just <emplean puras mujeres : they only employ women> **4 pura sangre :** Thoroughbred horse

puro[3] *nm* **:** cigar

púrpura *nf* **:** purple

purpúreo, -rea *adj* **:** purple

purpurina *nf* **:** glitter (for decoration)

pus *nm* **:** pus

pusilánime *adj* COBARDE **:** pusillanimous, cowardly

puso, etc. → **poner**

pústula *nf* **:** pustule, pimple

puta *nf* **:** whore, slut

putrefacción *nf, pl* **-ciones :** putrefaction

putrefacto, -ta *adj* **1** PODRIDO **:** putrid, rotten **2 :** decayed

pútrido, -da *adj* **:** putrid, rotten

puya *nf* **1 :** point (of a lance) **2 lanzar una puya :** to gibe, to taunt

Q

q *nf* **:** eighteenth letter of the Spanish alphabet

que[1] *conj* **1 :** that <dice que está listo : he says that he's ready> <espero que lo haga : I hope that he does it> **2 :** than <más que nada : more than anything> **3** (*implying permission or desire*) <¡que entre! : send him in!> <¡que te vaya bien! : I wish you well!> **4** (*indicating a reason or cause*) <¡cuidado, que te caes! : be careful, you're about to fall!> <no provoques al perro, que te va a morder : don't provoke the dog or (else) he'll bite> **5 es que :** the thing is that, I'm afraid that **6 yo que tú :** if I were you

que[2] *pron* **1 :** who, that <la niña que viene : the girl who is coming> **2 :** whom, that <los alumnos que enseñé : the students that I taught> **3 :** that, which <el carro que me gusta : the car that I like> **4 el** (**la, lo, las, los**) **que** → **el**[1], **la**[1], **lo**[1], **los**[1]

qué[1] *adv* **:** how, what <¡qué bonito! : how pretty!>

qué[2] *adj* **:** what, which <¿qué hora es? : what time is it?>

qué[3] *pron* **:** what <¿qué quieres? : what do you want?>

quebracho *nm* **:** quebracho (tree)

quebrada *nf* DESFILADERO **:** ravine, gorge

quebradizo, -za *adj* FRÁGIL **:** breakable, delicate, fragile

quebrado[1], **-da** *adj* **1 :** bankrupt **2 :** rough, uneven **3** ROTO **:** broken

quebrado[2] *nm* **:** fraction

quebrantamiento *nm* **1 :** breaking **2 :** deterioration, weakening

quebrantar *vt* **1 :** to break, to split, to crack **2 :** to weaken **3 :** to violate (a law or contract)

quebranto *nm* **1 :** break, breaking **2** AFLICCIÓN **:** affliction, grief **3** PÉRDIDA **:** loss

quebrar {55} *vt* **1** ROMPER **:** to break **2** DOBLAR **:** to bend, to twist — *vi* **1 :** to go bankrupt **2 :** to fall out, to break up — **quebrarse** *vr*

queda *nf* **:** curfew

quedar *vi* **1** PERMANECER **:** to remain, to stay **2 :** to be <quedamos contentos con las mejoras : we were pleased with the improvements> **3 :** to be situated <queda muy lejos : it's very far, it's too far away> **4 :** to be left <quedan sólo dos alternativas : there are only two options left> **5 :** to fit, to suit <estos zapatos no me quedan : these shoes don't fit> **6 quedar bien (mal) :** to turn out well (badly) **7 ~ en :** to agree, to arrange <¿en qué quedamos? : what's the arrangement, then?> — **quedarse** *vr* **1 :** to stay <se quedó en casa : she stayed at home> **2 :** to keep on <se quedó esperando : he kept on waiting> **3 quedarse atrás :** to stay behind <no quedarse atrás : to be no slouch> **4 ~ con :** to remain <me quedé con hambre después de comer : I was still hungry after I ate>

quedo[1] *adv* **:** softly, quietly

quedo[2], **-da** *adj* **:** quiet, still

quehacer *nm* **1 :** work **2 quehaceres** *nmpl* **:** chores

queja *nf* **:** complaint

quejarse *vr* **1 :** to complain **2 :** to groan, to moan

quejido *nm* **1 :** groan, moan **2 :** whine, whimper

quejoso, -sa *adj* **:** complaining, whining

quejumbroso, -sa *adj* **:** querulous, whining

quema *nf* **1** FUEGO **:** fire **2 :** burning

quemado, -da *adj* **1 :** burned, burnt **2 :** annoyed **3 :** burned-out

quemador *nm* **:** burner

quemadura *nf* **:** burn

quemar *vt* **:** to burn, to set fire to — *vi* **:** to be burning hot — **quemarse** *vr*

quemarropa *nf* **a ~ :** point-blank

quemazón *nf, pl* **-zones 1 :** burning **2 :** intense heat **3 :** itch **4 :** cutting remark

quena *nf* **:** Peruvian reed flute

quepa, etc. → **caber**

querella *nf* **1 :** complaint **2 :** lawsuit

querellante *nmf* **:** plaintiff

querellarse *vr* **~ contra :** to bring suit against, to sue

querer[1] {64} *vt* **1** DESEAR **:** to want, to desire <quiere ser profesor : he wants to be a teacher> <¿cuánto quieres por esta computadora? : how much do you want for this computer?> **2 :** to love, to like, to be fond of <te quiero : I love you> **3** (*indicating a request*) <¿quieres pasarme la leche? : please pass the milk> **4 querer decir :** to mean **5 sin ~ :** unintentionally — *vi* **:** like, want <si quieras : if you like>

querer[2] *nm* **:** love, affection

querido[1], **-da** *adj* **:** dear, beloved

querido[2], **-da** *n* **:** dear, sweetheart

queroseno *nm* **:** kerosene

querúbico, -ca *adj* **:** cherubic

querrá, etc. → **querer**

querubín *nm, pl* **-bines :** cherub

quesadilla *nf* **:** quesadilla

quesería *nf* **:** cheese shop

queso *nm* **:** cheese

quetzal *nm* **1 :** quetzal (bird) **2 :** monetary unit of Guatemala

quicio *nm* **1 estar fuera de quicio :** to be beside oneself **2 sacar de quicio :** to exasperate, to drive crazy

quid *nm* **:** crux, gist <el quid de la cuestión : the crux of the matter>

quiebra[1], **etc.** → **quebrar**

quiebra[2] *nf* **1** : break, crack **2** BANCARROTA : failure, bankruptcy

quien *pron, pl* **quienes 1** : who, whom <no sé quien ganará : I don't know who will win> <las personas con quienes trabajo : the people with whom I work> **2** : whoever, whomever <quien quiere salir que salga : whoever wants to can leave> **3** : anyone, some people <hay quienes no están de acuerdo : some people don't agree>

quién *pron, pl* **quiénes 1** : who, whom <¿quién sabe? : who knows?> <¿con quién hablo? : with whom am I speaking?> **2 de ~** : whose <¿de quién es este libro? : whose book is this?>

quienquiera *pron, pl* **quienesquiera** : whoever, whomever

quiere, etc. → **querer**

quieto, -ta *adj* **1** : calm, quiet **2** INMÓVIL : still

quietud *nf* **1** : calm, tranquility **2** INMOVILIDAD : stillness

quijada *nf* : jaw, jawbone

quijotesco, -ca *adj* : quixotic

quilate *nm* : karat

quilla *nf* : keel

quimera *nf* : chimera, illusion

quimérico, -ca *adj* : chimeric, fanciful

química *nf* : chemistry

químico[1], **-ca** *adj* : chemical

químico[2], **-ca** *n* : chemist

quimioterapia *nf* : chemotherapy

quimono *nm* : kimono

quince *adj & nm* : fifteen

quinceañero, -ra *n* : fifteen-year-old, teenager

quinceavo[1], **-va** *adj* : fifteenth

quinceavo[2] *nm* : fifteenth (fraction)

quincena *nf* : two week period, fortnight

quincenal *adj* : bimonthly, twice a month

quingombó *nm* : okra

quincuagésimo[1], **-ma** *adj* : fiftieth, fifty-

quincuagésimo[2], **-ma** *n* : fiftieth, fifty- (in a series)

quiniela *nf* : sports lottery

quinientos[1], **-tas** *adj* : five hundred

quinientos[2] *nms & pl* : five hundred

quinina *nf* : quinine

quino *nm* : cinchona

quinqué *nm* : oil lamp

quinquenal *adj* : five-year <un plan quinquenal : a five-year plan>

quinta *nf* : country house, villa

quintaesencia *nf* : quintessence — **quintaesencial** *adj*

quintal *nm* : hundredweight

quinteto *nm* : quintet

quintillizo, -za *n* : quintuplet

quinto, -ta *adj* : fifth — **quinto, -ta** *n*

quíntuplo, -la *adj* : quintuple, fivefold

quiosco *nm* **1** : kiosk **2** : newsstand **3 quiosco de música** : bandstand

quirófano *nm* : operating room

quiromancia *nf* : palmistry

quiropráctica *nf* : chiropractic

quiropráctico, -ca *n* : chiropractor

quirúrgico, -ca *adj* : surgical — **quirúrgicamente** *adv*

quiso, etc. → **querer**

quisquilloso[1], **-sa** *adj* : fastidious, fussy

quisquilloso[2], **-sa** *n* : fussy person, fussbudget

quiste *nm* : cyst

quitaesmalte *nm* : nail polish remover

quitamanchas *nms & pl* : stain remover

quitanieves *nms & pl* : snowplow

quitar *vt* **1** : to remove, to take away **2** : to take off (clothes) **3** : to get rid of, to relieve — **quitarse** *vr* **1** : to withdraw, to leave **2** : to take off (one's clothes) **3 ~ de** : to give up (a habit) **4 quitar de encima** : to get rid of

quitasol *nm* : parasol

quiteño[1], **-ña** *adj* : of or from Quito

quiteño[2], **-ña** *n* : person from Quito

quizá *or* **quizás** *adv* : maybe, perhaps

quórum *nm, pl* **quórums** : quorum

R

r *nf* : nineteenth letter of the Spanish alphabet

rábano *nm* **1** : radish **2 rábano picante** : horseradish

rabí *nmf, pl* **rabíes** : rabbi

rabia *nf* **1** HIDROFOBIA : rabies, hydrophobia **2** : rage, anger

rabiar *vi* **1** : to rage, to be furious **2** : to be in great pain **3 a ~** *fam* : like crazy, like mad

rabieta *nf* BERRINCHE : tantrum

rabino, -na *n* : rabbi

rabioso, -sa *adj* **1** : enraged, furious **2** : rabid

rabo *nm* **1** COLA : tail **2 el rabo del ojo** : the corner of one's eye

racha *nf* **1** : gust of wind **2** : run, series, string <racha perdedora : losing streak>

racheado, -da *adj* : gusty, windy

racial *adj* : racial

racimo *nm* : bunch, cluster <un racimo de uvas : a bunch of grapes>

raciocinio *nm* : reason, reasoning

ración *nf, pl* **raciones 1** : share, ration **2** PORCIÓN : portion, helping

racional *adj* : rational, reasonable — **racionalmente** *adv*

racionalidad *nf* : rationality

racionalización *nf, pl* **-ciones** : rationalization
racionalizar {21} *vt* **1** : to rationalize **2** : to streamline
racionamiento *nm* : rationing
racionar *vt* : to ration
racismo *nm* : racism
racista *adj & nmf* : racist
radar *nm* : radar
radiación *nf, pl* **-ciones** : radiation, irradiation
radiactividad *nf* : radioactivity
radiactivo, -va *adj* : radioactive
radiador *nm* : radiator
radial *adj* **1** : radial **2** : radio, broadcasting <emisora radial : radio transmitter>
radiante *adj* : radiant
radiar *vt* **1** : to radiate **2** : to irradiate **3** : to broadcast (on the radio)
radical[1] *adj* : radical, extreme — **radicalmente** *adv*
radical[2] *nmf* : radical
radicalismo *nm* : radicalism
radicar {72} *vi* **1** : to be found, to lie **2** ARRAIGAR : to take root — **radicarse** *vr* : to settle, to establish oneself
radio[1] *nm* **1** : radius **2** : radium
radio[2] *nmf* : radio
radioactividad *nf* : radioactivity
radioactivo, -va *adj* : radioactive
radioaficionado, -da *n* : ham radio operator
radiodifusión *nf, pl* **-siones** : radio broadcasting
radiodifusora *nf* : radio station
radioemisora *nf* : radio station
radiofaro *nm* : radio beacon
radiofónico, -ca *adj* : radio <estación radiofónica pública : public radio station>
radiofrecuencia *nf* : radio frequency
radiografía *nf* : X ray (photograph)
radiografiar {85} *vt* : to x-ray
radiología *nf* : radiology
radiólogo, -ga *n* : radiologist
radón *nm* : radon
raer {65} *vt* RASPAR : to scrape, to scrape off
ráfaga *nf* **1** : gust (of wind) **2** : flash, burst <una ráfaga de luz : a flash of light>
raid *nm CA, Mex fam* : lift, ride
raído, -da *adj* : worn, shabby
raiga, etc. → **raer**
raíz *nf, pl* **raíces** **1** : root **2** : origin, source **3** **a raíz de** : following, as a result of **4** **echar raíces** : to take root
raja *nf* **1** : crack, slit **2** : slice, wedge
rajá *nm* : raja
rajadura *nf* : crack, split
rajar *vt* HENDER : to crack, to split — *vi* **1** *fam* : to chatter **2** *fam* : to boast, to brag — **rajarse** *vr* **1** : to crack, to split open **2** *fam* : to back out
rajatabla *adv* **a ~** : strictly, to the letter
ralea *nf* : kind, sort, ilk <son de la misma valea : they're two of a kind>
ralentí *nm* **dejar al ralentí** : to leave (a motor) idling
rallado, -da *adj* **1** : grated **2** **pan rallado** : bread crumbs *pl*
rallador *nm* : grater
rallar *vt* : to grate
ralo, -la *adj* : sparse, thin
rama *nf* : branch
ramaje *nm* : branches *pl*
ramal *nm* **1** : branchline **2** : halter, strap
ramera *nf* : harlot, prostitute
ramificación *nf, pl* **-ciones** : ramification
ramificarse {72} *vr* : to branch out, to divide into branches
ramillete *nm* **1** RAMO : bouquet **2** : select group, cluster
ramo *nm* **1** : branch **2** RAMILLETE : bouquet **3** : division (of science or industry) **4** **Domingo de Ramos** : Palm Sunday
rampa *nf* : ramp, incline
rana *nf* **1** : frog **2** **rana toro** : bullfrog
ranchera *nf Mex* : traditional folk song
ranchería *nf* : settlement
ranchero, -ra *n* : rancher, farmer
rancho *nm* **1** : ranch, farm **2** : hut **3** : settlement, camp **4** : food, mess (for soldiers, etc.)
rancio, -cia *adj* **1** : aged, mellow (of wine) **2** : ancient, old **3** : rancid
rango *nm* **1** : rank, status **2** : high social standing **3** : pomp, splendor
ranúnculo *nm* : buttercup
ranura *nf* : groove, slot
rapacidad *nf* : rapacity
rapar *vt* **1** : to crop **2** : to shave
rapaz[1] *adj, pl* **rapaces** : rapacious, predatory
rapaz[2], **-paza** *n, mpl* **rapaces** : youngster, child
rape *nm* : close haircut
rapé *nm* : snuff
rapidez *nf* : rapidity, speed
rápido[1] *adv* : quickly, fast <¡manejas tan rápido! : you drive so fast!>
rápido[2], **-da** *adj* : rapid, quick — **rápidamente** *adv*
rápido[3] *nm* **1** : express train **2** **rápidos** *nmpl* : rapids
rapiña *nf* **1** : plunder, pillage **2** **ave de rapiña** : bird of prey
raposa *nf* : vixen (fox)
rapsodia *nf* : rhapsody
raptar *vt* SEQUESTRAR : to abduct, to kidnap
rapto *nm* **1** SECUESTRO : kidnapping, abduction **2** ARREBATO : fit, outburst
raptor, -tora *n* SECUESTRADOR : kidnapper
raque *nm* : beachcombing
raquero, -ra *n* : beachcomber
raqueta *nf* **1** : racket (in sports) **2** : snowshoe
raquítico, -ca *adj* **1** : scrawny, weak **2** : measly, skimpy
raquitismo *nm* : rickets
raramente *adv* : seldom, rarely

rareza *nf* **1** : rarity **2** : peculiarity, oddity
raro, -ra *adj* **1** EXTRAÑO : odd, strange, peculiar **2** : unusual, rare **3** : exceptional **4 rara vez** : seldom, rarely
ras *nm* **a ras de** : level with
rasar *vt* **1** : to skim, to graze **2** : to level
rascacielos *nms & pl* : skyscraper
rascar {72} *vt* **1** : to scratch **2** : to scrape — **rascarse** *vr* : to scratch an itch
rasgadura *nf* : tear, rip
rasgar {52} *vt* : to rip, to tear — **rasgarse** *vr*
rasgo *nm* **1** : stroke (of a pen) <a grandes rasgos : in broad outlines> **2** CARACTERÍSTICA : trait, characteristic **3** : gesture, deed **4 rasgos** *nmpl* FACCIONES : features
rasgón *nm, pl* **rasgones** : rip, tear
rasgue, etc. → **rasgar**
rasguear *vt* : to strum
rasguñar *vt* **1** : to scratch **2** : to sketch, to outline
rasguño *nm* **1** : scratch **2** : sketch
raso[1], -sa *adj* **1** : level, flat **2 soldado raso** : private (in the army) <los soldados rasos : the ranks>
raso[2] *nm* : satin
raspadura *nf* **1** : scratching, scraping **2 raspaduras** *nfpl* : scrapings
raspar *vt* **1** : to scrape **2** : to file down, to smooth — *vi* : to be rough
rasque, etc. → **rascar**
rastra *nf* **1** : harrow **2 a rastras** : by dragging, unwillingly
rastrear *vt* **1** : to track, to trace **2** : to comb, to search **3** : to trawl
rastrero, -ra *adj* **1** : creeping, crawling **2** : vile, despicable
rastrillar *vt* : to rake, to harrow
rastrillo *nm* **1** : rake **2** *Mex* : razor
rastro *nm* **1** PISTA : trail, track **2** VESTIGIO : trace, sign
rastrojo *nm* : stubble (of plants)
rasurar *vt* AFEITAR : to shave — **rasurarse** *vr*
rata[1] *nm fam* : pickpocket, thief
rata[2] *nf* **1** : rat **2** *Col, Pan, Peru* : rate, percentage
ratear *vt* : to pilfer, to steal
ratero, -ra *n* : petty thief
ratificación *nf, pl* **-ciones** : ratification
ratificar {72} *vt* **1** : to ratify **2** : to confirm
rato *nm* **1** : while **2 pasar el rato** : to pass the time **3 a cada rato** : all the time, constantly <les sacaba dinero a cada rato : he was always taking money from them> **4 al poco rato** : later, shortly after
ratón[1], -tona *n, mpl* **ratones 1** : mouse **2 ratón de biblioteca** *fam* : bookworm
ratón[2] *nm, pl* **ratones 1** : (computer) mouse **2** *CoRi* : biceps
ratonera *nf* : mousetrap
raudal *nm* **1** : torrent **2 a raudales** : in abundance
raya[1], etc. → **raer**
raya[2] *nf* **1** : line **2** : stripe **3** : skate, ray **4** : part (in the hair) **5** : crease (in clothing)
rayar *vt* **1** ARAÑAR : to scratch **2** : to scrawl on, to mark up <rayaron las paredes : they covered the walls with graffiti> — *vi* **1** : to scratch **2** AMANECER : to dawn, to break <al rayar el alba : at break of day> **3 ~ con** : to be adjacent to, to be next to **4 ~ en** : to border on, to verge on <su respuesta raya en lo ridículo : his answer borders on the ridiculous> — **rayarse** *vr*
rayo *nm* **1** : ray, beam <rayo láser : laser beam> <rayo de gamma : gamma ray> <rayo de sol : sunbeam> **2** RELÁMPAGO : lightning bolt **3 rayo X** : X ray
rayón *nm, pl* **rayones** : rayon
raza *nf* **1** : race <raza humana : human race> **2** : breed, strain **3 de ~** : thoroughbred, pedigreed
razón *nf, pl* **razones 1** MOTIVO : reason, motive <en razón de : by reason of, because of> **2** JUSTICIA : rightness, justice <tener razón : to be right> **3** : reasoning, sense <perder la razón : to lose one's mind> **4** : ratio, proportion
razonable *adj* : reasonable — **razonablemente** *adv*
razonado, -da *adj* : itemized, detailed
razonamiento *nm* : reasoning
razonar *v* : to reason, to think
reabastecimiento *nm* : replenishment
reabierto *pp* → **reabrir**
reabrir {2} *vt* : to reopen — **reabrirse** *vr*
reacción *nf, pl* **-ciones 1** : reaction **2 motor a reacción** : jet engine
reaccionar *vi* : to react, to respond
reaccionario, -ria *adj & n* : reactionary
reacio, -cia *adj* : resistant, opposed
reacondicionar *vt* : to recondition
reactor *nm* **1** : reactor <reactor nuclear : nuclear reactor> **2** : jet engine **3** : jet airplane, jet
reafirmar *vt* : to reaffirm, to assert, to strengthen
reajustar *vt* : to readjust, to adjust
reajuste *nm* : readjustment <reajuste de precios : price increase>
real *adj* **1** : real, true **2** : royal
realce *nm* **1** : embossing, relief **2 dar realce** : to highlight, to bring out
realeza *nf* : royalty
realidad *nf* **1** : reality **2 en ~** : in truth, actually
realinear *vt* : to realign
realismo *nm* **1** : realism **2** : royalism
realista[1] *adj* **1** : realistic **2** : realist **3** : royalist
realista[2] *nmf* **1** : realist **2** : royalist
realización *nf, pl* **-ciones** : execution, realization
realizar {21} *vt* **1** : to carry out, to execute **2** : to produce, to direct (a

film or play) **3 :** to fulfill, to achieve **4 :** to realize (a profit) — **realizarse** *vr* **1 :** to come true **2 :** to fulfill oneself

realmente *adv* **:** really, in reality

realzar {21} *vt* **1 :** to heighten, to raise **2 :** to highlight, to enhance

reanimación *nf, pl* **-ciones :** revival, resuscitation

reanimar *vt* **1 :** to revive, to restore **2 :** to resuscitate — **reanimarse** *vr* **:** to come around, to recover

reanudar *vt* **:** to resume, to renew — **reanadarse** *vr* **:** to resume, to continue

reaparecer {53} *vi* **1 :** to reappear **2 :** to make a comeback

reaparición *nf, pl* **-ciones :** reappearance

reapertura *nf* **:** reopening

reata *nf* **1 :** rope **2** *Mex* **:** lasso, lariat **3 de ~ :** single file

reavivar *vt* **:** to revive, to reawaken

rebaja *nf* **1 :** reduction **2** DESCUENTO **:** discount **3 rebajas** *nfpl* **:** sale

rebajar *vt* **1 :** to reduce, to lower **2 :** to lessen, to diminish **3 :** to humiliate — **rebajarse** *vr* **: 1 :** to humble oneself **2 rebajarse a :** to stoop to

rebanada *nf* **:** slice

rebañar *vt* **:** to mop up, to sop up

rebaño *nm* **1 :** flock **2 :** herd

rebasar *vt* **1 :** to surpass, to exceed **2** *Mex* **:** to pass, to overtake

rebatiña *nf* **:** scramble, fight (over something)

rebatir *vt* REFUTAR **:** to refute

rebato *nm* **1 :** surprise attack **2 tocar a rebato :** to sound the alarm

rebelarse *vr* **:** to rebel

rebelde[1] *adj* **:** rebellious, unruly

rebelde[2] *nmf* **1 :** rebel **2 :** defaulter

rebeldía *nf* **1 :** rebelliousness **2 en ~ :** in default

rebelión *nf, pl* **-liones :** rebellion

rebobinar *vt* **:** to rewind

reborde *nm* **:** border, flange, rim

rebosante *adj* **:** brimming, overflowing <rebosante de salud : brimming with health>

rebosar *vi* **1 :** to overflow **2 ~ de :** to abound in, to be bursting with — *vt* **:** to radiate

rebotar *vi* **1 :** to bounce **2 :** to ricochet, to rebound

rebote *nm* **1 :** bounce **2 :** rebound, ricochet

rebozar {21} *vt* **:** to coat in batter

rebozo *nm* **1 :** shawl, wrap **2 sin ~ :** frankly, openly

rebullir {38} *v* **:** to move, to stir — **rebullirse** *vr*

rebuscado, -da *adj* **:** affected, pretentious

rebuscar {72} *vi* **:** to search thoroughly

rebuznar *vi* **:** to bray

rebuzno *nm* **:** bray, braying

recabar *vt* **1 :** to gather, to obtain, to collect **2 recabar fondos :** to raise money

recado *nm* **1 :** message <mandar recado : to send word> **2** *Spain* **:** errand

recaer {13} *vi* **1 :** to relapse **2 ~ en** *or* **~ sobre :** to fall on, to fall to

recaída *nf* **:** relapse

recaiga, etc. → **recaer**

recalar *vi* **:** to arrive

recalcar {72} *vt* **:** to emphasize, to stress

recalcitrante *adj* **:** recalcitrant

recalentar {55} *vt* **1 :** to reheat, to warm up **2 :** to overheat

recámara *nf* **1** *Col, Mex, Pan* **:** bedroom **2 :** chamber (of a firearm)

recamarera *nf Mex* **:** chambermaid

recambio *nm* **1 :** spare part **2 :** refill (for a pen, etc.)

recapacitar *vi* **1 :** to reconsider **2 ~ en :** to reflect on, to weigh

recapitular *v* **:** to recapitulate — **recapitulación** *nf*

recargable *adj* **:** rechargeable

recargado, -da *adj* **:** overly elaborate or ornate

recargar {52} *vt* **1 :** to recharge **2 :** to overload

recargo *nm* **:** surcharge

recatado, -da *adj* MODESTO **:** modest, demure

recato *nm* PUDOR **:** modesty

recaudación *nf, pl* **-ciones 1 :** collection **2 :** earnings *pl*, takings *pl*

recaudador, -dora *n* **recaudador de impuestos :** tax collector

recaudar *vt* **:** to collect

recaudo *nm* **:** safe place <a (buen) recaudo : in safe keeping>

recayó, etc. → **recaer**

rece, etc. → **rezar**

recelo *nm* **:** distrust, suspicion

receloso, -sa *adj* **:** distrustful, suspicious

recepción *nf, pl* **-ciones :** reception

recepcionista *nmf* **:** receptionist

receptáculo *nm* **:** receptacle

receptividad *nf* **:** receptivity, receptiveness

receptivo, -va *adj* **:** receptive

receptor[1], **-tora** *adj* **:** receiving

receptor[2], **-tora** *n* **1 :** recipient **2 :** catcher (in baseball), receiver (in football)

receptor[3] *nm* **:** receiver <receptor de televisión : television set>

recesión *nf, pl* **-siones :** recession

recesivo, -va *adj* **:** recessive

receso *nm* **:** recess, adjournment

receta *nf* **1 :** recipe **2 :** prescription

recetar *vt* **:** to prescribe (medications)

rechazar {21} *vt* **1 :** to reject **2 :** to turn down, to refuse

rechazo *nm* **:** rejection, refusal

rechifla *nf* **:** booing, jeering

rechinar *vi* **1 :** to squeak **2 :** to grind, to gnash <hacer rechinar los dientes : to grind one's teeth>
rechoncho, -cha *adj fam* **:** chubby, squat
recibidor *nm* **:** vestibule, entrance hall
recibimiento *nm* **:** reception, welcome
recibir *vt* **1 :** to receive, to get **2 :** to welcome — *vi* **:** to receive visitors — **recibirse** *vr* **~ de :** to qualify as
recibo *nm* **:** receipt
reciclable *adj* **:** recyclable
reciclado *nm* → **reciclaje**
reciclaje *nm* **1 :** recycling **2 :** retraining
reciclar *vt* **1 :** to recycle **2 :** to retrain
recién *adv* **1 :** newly, recently <recién nacido : newborn> <recién casados : newlyweds> <recién llegado : newcomer> **2 :** just, only just <recién ahora me acordé : I just now remembered>
reciente *adj* **:** recent — **recientemente** *adv*
recinto *nm* **1 :** enclosure **2 :** site, premises *pl*
recio[1] *adv* **1 :** strongly, hard **2 :** loudly, loud
recio[2]**, -cia** *adj* **1 :** severe, harsh **2 :** tough, strong
recipiente[1] *nm* **:** container, receptacle
recipiente[2] *nmf* **:** recipient
reciprocar {72} *vi* **:** to reciprocate
reciprocidad *nf* **:** reciprocity
recíproco, -ca *adj* **:** reciprocal, mutual
recitación *nf, pl* **-ciones :** recitation, recital
recital *nm* **:** recital
recitar *vt* **:** to recite
reclamación *nf, pl* **-ciones 1 :** claim, demand **2** QUEJA **:** complaint
reclamar *vt* **1** EXIGIR **:** to demand, to require **2 :** to claim — *vi* **:** to complain
reclamo *nm* **1 :** bird call, lure **2 :** lure, decoy **3 :** inducement, attraction **4 :** advertisement **5 :** complaint
reclinar *vt* **:** to rest, to lean — **reclinarse** *vr* **:** to recline, to lean back
recluir {41} *vt* **:** to confine, to lock up — **recluirse** *vr* **:** to shut oneself up, to withdraw
reclusión *nf, pl* **-siones :** imprisonment
recluso, -sa *n* **1 :** inmate, prisoner **2** SOLITARIO **:** recluse
recluta *nmf* **:** recruit, draftee
reclutamiento *nm* **:** recruitment, recruiting
reclutar *vt* ENROLAR **:** to recruit, to enlist
recobrar *vt* **:** to recover, to regain — **recobrarse** *vr* **:** to recover, to recuperate
recocer {14} *vt* **:** to overcook, to cook again
recodo *nm* **:** bend
recogedor *nm* **:** dustpan
recoger {15} *vt* **1 :** to collect, to gather **2 :** to get, to retrieve, to pick up **3 :** to clean up, to tidy (up)
recogido, -da *adj* **:** quiet, secluded
recogimiento *nm* **1 :** collecting, gathering **2 :** withdrawal **3 :** absorption, concentration
recolección *nf, pl* **-ciones 1 :** collection <recolección de basura : trash pickup> **2 :** harvest
recolectar *vt* **1 :** to gather, to collect **2 :** to harvest, to pick
recomendable *adj* **:** advisable, recommended
recomendación *nf, pl* **-ciones :** recommendation
recomendar {55} *vt* **1 :** to recommend **2** ACONSEJAR **:** to advise
recompensa *nf* **:** reward, recompense
recompensar *vt* **1** PREMIAR **:** to reward **2 :** to compensate
reconciliación *nf, pl* **-ciones :** reconciliation
reconciliar *vt* **:** to reconcile — **reconciliarse** *vr*
recóndito, -ta *adj* **1 :** remote, isolated **2 :** hidden, recondite **3 en lo más recóndito de :** in the depths of
reconfortar *vt* **:** to comfort — **reconfortante** *adj*
reconocer {18} *vt* **1 :** to recognize **2 :** to admit **3 :** to examine
reconocible *adj* **:** recognizable
reconocido, -da *adj* **1 :** recognized, accepted **2 :** grateful
reconocimiento *nm* **1 :** acknowledgment, recognition, avowal **2 :** (medical) examination **3 :** reconnaissance
reconsiderar *vt* **:** to reconsider — **reconsideración** *nf*
reconstrucción *nf, pl* **-ciones :** reconstruction
reconstruir {41} *vt* **:** to rebuild, to reconstruct
reconversión *nf, pl* **-siones :** restructuring
reconvertir {76} *vt* **1 :** to restructure **2 :** to retrain
recopilación *nf, pl* **-ciones 1 :** summary **2 :** collection, compilation
recopilar *vt* **:** to compile, to collect
récord *or* **record** [ˈrɛkɔr] *nm, pl* **récords** *or* **records** [-kɔrs] **:** record <record mundial : world record> — **récord** *or* **record** *adj*
recordar {19} *vt* **1 :** to recall, to remember **2 :** to remind — *vi* **1** ACORDARSE **:** to remember **2** DESPERTAR **:** to wake up
recordatorio[1]**, -ria** *adj* **:** commemorative
recordatorio[2] *nm* **:** reminder
recorrer *vt* **1 :** to travel through, to tour **2 :** to cover (a distance) **3 :** to go over, to look over
recorrido *nm* **1 :** journey, trip **2 :** path, route, course **3 :** round (in golf)
recortar *vt* **1 :** to cut, to reduce **2 :** to cut out **3 :** to trim, to cut off **4 :** to outline — **recortarse** *vr* **:** to stand out <los árboles se recortaban en el horizonte : the trees were silhouetted against the horizon>

recorte *nm* **1 :** cut, reduction **2 :** clipping <recortes de periódicos : newspaper clippings>

recostar {19} *vt* **:** to lean, to rest — **recostarse** *vr* **:** to lie down, recline

recoveco *nm* **1** VUELTA **:** bend, turn **2 :** nook, corner **3 recovecos** *nmpl* **:** intricacies, ins and outs

recreación *nf, pl* **-ciones 1 :** re-creation **2** DIVERSIÓN **:** recreation, entertainment

recrear *vt* **1 :** to re-create **2 :** to entertain, to amuse — **recrearse** *vr* **:** to enjoy oneself

recreativo, -va *adj* **:** recreational

recreo *nm* **1** DIVERSIÓN **:** entertainment, amusement **2 :** recess, break

recriminación *nf, pl* **-ciones :** reproach, recrimination

recriminar *vt* **:** to reproach — *vi* **:** to recriminate — **recriminarse** *vr*

recrudecer {53} *v* **:** to intensify, to worsen — **recrudecerse** *vr*

rectal *adj* **:** rectal

rectangular *adj* **:** rectangular

rectángulo *nm* **:** rectangle

rectificación *nf, pl* **-ciones :** rectification, correction

rectificar {72} *vt* **1 :** to rectify, to correct **2 :** to straighten (out)

rectitud *nf* **1 :** straightness **2 :** honesty, rectitude

recto[1] *adv* **:** straight

recto[2]**, -ta** *adj* **1 :** straight **2 :** upright, honorable **3 :** sound

recto[3] *nm* **:** rectum

rector[1]**, -tora** *adj* **:** governing, managing

rector[2]**, -tora** *n* **:** rector

rectoría *nf* **:** rectory

recubierto *pp* → **recubrir**

recubrir {2} *vt* **:** to cover, to coat

recuento *nm* **:** recount, count <un recuento de los votos : a recount of the votes>

recuerdo *nm* **1 :** memory **2 :** souvenir, memento **3 recuerdos** *nmpl* **:** regards

recuperación *nf, pl* **-ciones 1 :** recovery, recuperation **2 recuperación de datos :** data retrieval

recuperar *vt* **1 :** to recover, to get back, to retrieve **2 :** to recuperate **3 :** to make up for <recuperar el tiempo perdido : to make up for lost time> — **recuperarse** *vr* **~ de :** to recover from, to get over

recurrente *adj* **:** recurrent, recurring

recurrir *vi* **1 ~ a :** to turn to, to appeal to **2 ~ a :** to resort to **3 :** to appeal (in law)

recurso *nm* **1 :** recourse <el último recurso : the last resort> **2 :** appeal (in law) **3 recursos** *nmpl* **:** resources, means <recursos naturales : natural resources>

red *nf* **1 :** net, mesh **2 :** network, system, chain **3 :** trap, snare

redacción *nf, pl* **-ciones 1 :** writing, composition **2 :** editing

redactar *vt* **1 :** to write, to draft **2 :** to edit

redactor, -tora *n* **:** editor

redada *nf* **1 :** raid **2 :** catch, haul

redefinir *vt* **:** to redefine — **redefinición** *nf*

redención *nf, pl* **-ciones :** redemption

redentor[1]**, -tora** *adj* **:** redeeming

redentor[2]**, -tora** *n* **:** redeemer

redescubierto *pp* → **redescubrir**

redescubrir {2} *vt* **:** to rediscover

redicho, -cha *adj fam* **:** affected, pretentious

redil *nm* **1 :** sheepfold **2 volver al redil :** to return to the fold

redimir *vt* **:** to redeem, to deliver (from sin)

rediseñar *vt* **:** to redesign

redistribuir {41} *vt* **:** to redistribute — **redistribución** *nf*

rédito *nm* **:** return, yield

redituar {3} *vt* **:** to produce, to yield

redoblar *vt* **:** to redouble, to strengthen — **redoblado, -da** *adj*

redomado, -da *adj* **1 :** sly, crafty **2 :** utter, out-and-out

redonda *nf* **1 :** region, surrounding area **2 a la redonda** ALREDEDOR **:** around <de diez millas a la redonda : for ten miles around>

redondear *vt* **:** to round off, to round out

redondel *nm* **1 :** ring, circle **2 :** bullring, arena

redondez *nf* **:** roundness

redondo, -da *adj* **1 :** round <mesa redonda : round table> **2 :** great, perfect <un negocio redondo : an excellent deal> **3 :** straightforward, flat <un rechazo redondo : a flat refusal> **4** *Mex* **:** round-trip **5 en ~ :** around

reducción *nf, pl* **-ciones :** reduction, decrease

reducido, -da *adj* **1 :** reduced, limited **2 :** small

reducir {61} *vt* **1** DISMINUIR **:** to reduce, to decrease, to cut **2 :** to subdue **3 :** to boil down — **reducirse** *vr* **~ a :** to come down to, to be nothing more than

redundancia *nf* **:** reduncancy

redundante *adj* **:** redundant

reedición *nf, pl* **-ciones :** reprint

reelegir {28} *vt* **:** to reelect — **reelección** *nf*

reembolsable *adj* **:** refundable

reembolsar *vt* **1 :** to refund, to reimburse **2 :** to repay

reembolso *nm* **:** refund, reimbursement

reemplazable *adj* **:** replaceable

reemplazar {21} *vt* **:** to replace, to substitute

reemplazo *nm* **:** replacement, substitution

reencarnación *nf, pl* **-ciones :** reincarnation

reencuentro *nm* **:** reunion

reestablecer {53} *vt* **:** to reestablish

reestructurar *vt* **:** to restructure
reexaminar *vt* **:** to reexamine
refaccionar *vt* **:** to repair, to renovate
refacciones *nfpl* **:** repairs, renovations
referencia *nf* **1 :** reference **2 hacer referencia a :** to refer to
referendo *nm* → **referéndum**
referéndum *nm, pl* **-dums :** referendum
referente *adj* **~ a :** concerning
réferi *or* **referi** ['rɛfɛri] *nmf* **:** referee
referir {76} *vt* **1 :** to relate, to tell **2 :** to refer <nos refirió al diccionario : she referred us to the dictionary> — **referirse** *vr* **1 ~ a :** to refer to **2 ~ a :** to be concerned, to be in reference to <en lo que se refiere a la educación : as far as education is concerned>
refinado¹, -da *adj* **:** refined
refinado² *nm* **:** refining
refinamiento *nm* **1 :** refining **2** FINURA **:** refinement
refinanciar *vt* **:** to refinance
refinar *vt* **:** to refine
refinería *nf* **:** refinery
reflectante *adj* **:** reflective, reflecting
reflector¹, -tora *adj* **:** reflecting
reflector² *nm* **1 :** spotlight, searchlight **2 :** reflector
reflejar *vt* **:** to reflect — **reflejarse** *vr* **:** to be reflected <la decepción se refleja en su rostro : the disappointment shows on her face>
reflejo *nm* **1 :** reflection **2 :** reflex **3 reflejos** *nmpl* **:** highlights, streaks (in hair)
reflexión *nf, pl* **-xiones :** reflection, thought
reflexionar *vi* **:** to reflect, to think
reflexivo, -va *adj* **1 :** reflective, thoughtful **2 :** reflexive
reflujo *nm* **:** ebb, ebb tide
reforma *nf* **1 :** reform **2 :** alteration, renovation
reformador, -dora *n* **:** reformer
reformar *vt* **1 :** to reform **2 :** to change, to alter **3 :** to renovate, to repair — **reformarse** *vr* **:** to mend one's ways
reformatorio *nm* **:** reformatory
reformular *vt* **:** to reformulate — **reformulación** *nf*
reforzar {36} *vt* **1 :** to reinforce, to strengthen **2 :** to encourage, to support
refracción *nf, pl* **-ciones :** refraction
refractar *vt* **:** to refract — **refractarse** *vr*
refractario, -ria *adj* **:** refractory, obstinate
refrán *nm, pl* **refranes** ADAGIO **:** proverb, saying
refregar {49} *vt* **:** to scrub
refrenar *vt* **1 :** to rein in (a horse) **2 :** to restrain, to check — **refrenarse** *vr* **:** to restrain oneself
refrendar *vt* **1 :** to countersign, to endorse **2 :** to stamp (a passport)
refrescante *adj* **:** refreshing
refrescar {72} *vt* **1 :** to refresh, to cool **2 :** to brush up (on) **3 refrescar la memoria :** to refresh one's memory — *vi* **:** to turn cooler
refresco *nm* **:** refreshment, soft drink
refriega *nf* **:** skirmish, scuffle
refrigeración *nf, pl* **-ciones 1 :** refrigeration **2 :** air-conditioning
refrigerador *nmf* NEVERA **:** refrigerator
refrigeradora *nf Col, Peru* **:** refrigerator
refrigerante *nm* **:** coolant
refrigerar *vt* **1 :** to refrigerate **2 :** to air-condition
refrigerio *nm* **:** snack, refreshments *pl*
refrito¹, -ta *adj* **:** refried
refrito² *nm* **:** rehash
refuerzo *nm* **:** reinforcement, support
refugiado, -da *n* **:** refugee
refugiar *vt* **:** to shelter — **refugiarse** *vr* ACOGERSE **:** to take refuge
refugio *nm* **:** refuge, shelter
refulgencia *nf* **:** brilliance, splendor
refulgir {35} *vi* **:** to shine brightly
refundir *vt* **1 :** to recast (metals) **2 :** to revise, to rewrite
refunfuñar *vi* **:** to grumble, to groan
refutar *vt* **:** to refute — **refutación** *nf*
regadera *nf* **1 :** watering can **2 :** shower head, shower **3 :** sprinkler
regaderazo *nm Mex* **:** shower
regalar *vt* **1** OBSEQUIAR **:** to present (as a gift), to give away **2 :** to regale, to entertain **3 :** to flatter, to make a fuss over — **regalarse** *vr* **:** to pamper oneself
regalía *nf* **:** royalty, payment
regaliz *nm, pl* **-lices :** licorice
regalo *nm* **1** OBSEQUIO **:** gift, present **2 :** pleasure, comfort **3 :** treat
regañadientes *mpl* **a ~ :** reluctantly, unwillingly
regañar *vt* **:** to scold, to give a talking to — *vi* **1** QUEJARSE **:** to grumble, to complain **2** REÑIR **:** to quarrel, to argue
regaño *nm fam* **:** scolding
regañon, -ñona *adj, mpl* **-ñones** *fam* **:** grumpy, irritable
regar {49} *vt* **1 :** to irrigate **2 :** to water **3 :** to wash, to hose down **4 :** to spill, to scatter
regata *nf* **:** regatta, yacht race
regate *nm* **:** dodge, feint
regatear *vt* **1 :** to haggle over **2** ESCATIMAR **:** to skimp on, to be sparing with — *vi* **:** to bargain, to haggle
regateo *nm* **:** bargaining, haggling
regatón *nm, pl* **-tones :** ferrule, tip
regazo *nm* **:** lap (of a person)
regencia *nf* **:** regency
regenerar *vt* **:** to regenerate — **regenerarse** *vr* — **regeneración** *nf*
regentar *vt* **:** to run, to manage
regente *nmf* **:** regent
regidor, -dora *n* **:** town councillor
régimen *nm, pl* **regímenes 1 :** regime **2 :** diet **3 :** regimen, rules *pl* <régimen de vida : lifestyle>
regimiento *nm* **:** regiment

regio, -gia *adj* **1 :** great, magnificent **2 :** regal, royal
región *nf, pl* **regiones :** region, area
regional *adj* **:** regional — **regionalmente** *adv*
regir {28} *vt* **1 :** to rule **2 :** to manage, to run **3 :** to control, to govern <las costumbres que rigen la conducta : the customs which govern behavior> — *vi* **:** to apply, to be in force <las leyes rigen en los tres países : the laws apply in all three countries> — **regirse** *vr* **~ por :** to go by, to be guided by
registrador[1], -dora *adj* **caja registradora :** cash register
registrador[2], -dora *n* **:** registrar, recorder
registrar *vt* **1 :** to register, to record **2** GRABAR **:** to record, to tape **3 :** to search, to examine — **registrarse** *vr* **1** INSCRIBIRSE **:** to register **2** OCURRIR **:** to happen, to occur
registro *nm* **1 :** register **2 :** registration **3 :** registry, record office **4 :** range (of a voice or musical instrument) **5 :** search
regla *nf* **1** NORMA **:** rule, regulation **2 :** ruler <regla de cálculo : slide rule> **3** MENSTRUACIÓN **:** period, menstruation
reglamentación *nf, pl* **-ciones 1 :** regulation **2 :** rules *pl*
reglamentar *vt* **:** to regulate, to set rules for
reglamentario, -ria *adj* **:** regulation, official <equipo reglamentario : standard equipment>
reglamento *nm* **:** regulations *pl*, rules *pl* <reglamento de tráfico : traffic regulations>
regocijar *vt* **:** to gladden, to delight — **regocijarse** *vr* **:** to rejoice
regocijo *nm* **:** delight, rejoicing
regordete *adj fam* LLENITO **:** chubby
regresar *vt* DEVOLVER **:** to give back — *vi* **:** to return, to come back, to go back
regresión *nf, pl* **-siones :** regression, return
regresivo, -va *adj* **:** regressive
regreso *nm* **1 :** return **2 estar de regreso :** to be back, to be home
reguero *nm* **1 :** irrigation ditch **2 :** trail, trace **3 propagarse como reguero de pólvora :** to spread like wildfire
regulable *adj* **:** adjustable
regulación *nf, pl* **-ciones :** regulation, control
regulador[1], -dora *adj* **:** regulating, regulatory
regulador[2] *nm* **1 :** regulator, governor **2 regulador de tiro :** damper (in a chimney)
regular[1] *vt* **:** to regulate, to control
regular[2] *adj* **1 :** regular **2 :** fair, OK, so-so **3 :** medium, average **4 por lo regular :** in general, generally
regularidad *nf* **:** regularity
regularización *nf, pl* **-ciones** NORMALIZACIÓN **:** normalization
regularizar {21} *vt* NORMALIZAR **:** to normalize, to make regular
regularmente *adv* **:** regularly
rehabilitar *vt* **1 :** to rehabilitate **2 :** to reinstate **3 :** renovate, to restore — **rehabilitación** *nf*
rehacer {40} *vt* **1 :** to redo **2 :** to remake, to repair, to renew — **rehacerse** *vr* **1 :** to recover **2 ~ de :** to get over
rehecho *pp* → **rehacer**
rehén *nm, pl* **rehenes :** hostage
rehicieron, etc. → **rehacer**
rehizo → **rehacer**
rehuir {41} *vt* **:** to avoid, to shun
rehusar {8} *v* **:** to refuse
reimprimir *vt* **:** to reprint
reina *nf* **:** queen
reinado *nm* **:** reign
reinante *adj* **1 :** reigning **2 :** prevailing, current
reinar *vi* **1 :** to reign **2 :** to prevail
reincidencia *nf* **:** recidivism, relapse
reincidente *nmf* **:** backslider, recidivist
reincidir *vi* **:** to backslide, to retrogress
reincorporar *vt* **:** to reinstate — **reincorporarse** *vr* **~ a :** to return to, to rejoin
reino *nm* **:** kingdom, realm <reino animal : animal kingdom>
reinstalar *vt* **1 :** to reinstall **2 :** to reinstate
reintegrar *vt* **1 :** to reintegrate, reinstate **2 :** to refund, to reimburse — **reintegrarse** *vr* **~ a :** to return to, to rejoin
reír {66} *vi* **:** to laugh — *vt* **:** to laugh at — **reírse** *vr*
reiteración *nf, pl* **-ciones :** reiteration, repetition
reiterado, -da *adj* **:** repeated <lo explicó en reiteradas ocasiones : he explained it repeatedly> — **reiteradamente** *adv*
reiterar *vt* **:** to reiterate, to repeat
reiterativo, -va *adj* **:** repetitive, repetitious
reivindicación *nf, pl* **-ciones 1 :** demand, claim **2 :** vindication
reivindicar {72} *vt* **1 :** to vindicate **2 :** to demand, to claim **3 :** to restore
reja *nf* **1 :** grill, grating <entre rejas : behind bars> **2 :** plowshare
rejilla *nf* **:** grille, grate, screen
rejuvenecer {53} *vt* **:** to rejuvenate — *vi* **:** to be rejuvenated — **rejuvenecerse** *vr*
rejuvencimiento *m* **:** rejuvenation
relación *nf, pl* **-ciones 1 :** relation, connection, relevance **2 :** relationship **3** RELATO **:** account **4** LISTA **:** list **5 con relación a** *or* **en relación con :** in relation to, concerning **6 relaciones públicas :** public relations
relacionar *vt* **:** to relate, to connect — **relacionarse** *vr* **~ con :** to be connected to, to be linked with

relajación *nf, pl* **-ciones** : relaxation

relajado, -da *adj* **1** : relaxed, loose **2** : dissolute, depraved

relajar *vt* : to relax, to slacken — *vi* : to be relaxing — **relajarse** *vr*

relajo *nm* **1** : commotion, ruckus **2** : joke, laugh <lo hizo de relajo : he did it for a laugh>

relamerse *vr* : to smack one's lips, to lick one's chops

relámpago *nm* : flash of lightning

relampaguear *vi* : to flash

relanzar {21} *vt* : to relaunch

relatar *vt* : to relate, to tell

relativo, -va *adj* **1** : relative **2** **en lo relativo a** : with regard to, concerning — **relativamente** *adv*

relato *nm* **1** : story, tale **2** : account

releer {20} *vt* : to reread

relegar {52} *vt* **1** : to relegate **2** **relegar al olvido** : to consign to oblivion

relevante *adj* : outstanding, important

relevar *vt* **1** : to relieve, to take over from **2** **~ de** : to exempt from — **relevarse** *vr* : to take turns

relevo *nm* **1** : relief, replacement **2** : relay <carrera de relevos : relay race>

relicario *nm* **1** : reliquary **2** : locket

relieve *nm* **1** : relief, projection <mapa en relieve : relief map> <letras en relieve : embossed letters> **2** : prominence, importance **3** **poner en relieve** : to highlight, to emphasize

religión *nf, pl* **-giones** : religion

religiosamente *adv* : religiously, faithfully

religioso[1], **-sa** *adj* : religious

religioso[2], **-sa** *n* : monk *m,* nun *f*

relinchar *vi* : to neigh, to whinny

relincho *nm* : neigh, whinny

reliquia *nf* **1** : relic **2** **reliquia de familia** : family heirloom

rellenar *vt* **1** : to refill **2** : to stuff, to fill **3** : to fill out

relleno[1], **-na** *adj* : stuffed, filled

relleno[2] *nm* : stuffing, filling

reloj *nm* **1** : clock **2** : watch **3** **reloj de arena** : hourglass **4** **reloj de pulsera** : wristwatch **5** **como un reloj** : like clockwork

relojería *nf* **1** : watchmaker's shop **2** : watchmaking, clockmaking

reluciente *adj* : brilliant, shining

relucir {45} *vi* **1** : to glitter, to shine **2** **salir a relucir** : to come to the surface **3** **sacar a relucir** : to bring up, to mention

relumbrante *adj* : dazzling

relumbrar *vi* : to shine brightly

relumbrón *nm, pl* **-brones** **1** : flash, glare **2** **de ~** : flashy, showy

remachar *vt* **1** : to rivet **2** : to clinch (a nail) **3** : to stress, to drive home — *vi* : to smash, to spike (a ball)

remache *nm* **1** : rivet **2** : smash, spike (in sports)

remanente *nm* **1** : remainder, balance **2** : surplus

remanso *nm* : pool

remar *vi* **1** : to row, to paddle **2** : to struggle, to toil

remarcar {72} *vt* : to emphasize, to stress

rematado, -da *adj* : utter, complete

rematador, -dora *n* : auctioneer

rematar *vt* **1** : to finish off **2** : to auction — *vi* **1** : to shoot **2** : to end

remate *nm* **1** : shot (in sports) **2** : auction **3** : end, conclusion **4** **como ~** : to top it off **5** **de ~** : completely, utterly

remecer {86} *vt* : to sway, to swing

remedar *vt* **1** IMITAR : to imitate, to copy **2** : to mimic, to ape

remediar *vt* **1** : to remedy, to repair **2** : to help out, to assist **3** EVITAR : to prevent, to avoid

remedio *nm* **1** : remedy, cure **2** : solution **3** : option <no me quedó más remedio : I had no other choice> <no hay remedio : it can't be helped> **4** **poner remedio a** : to put a stop to **5** **sin ~** : unavoidable, inevitable

remedo *nm* : imitation

rememorar *vi* : to recall <rememorar los viejos tiempos : to reminisce>

remendar {55} *vt* **1** : to mend, to patch, to darn **2** : to correct

remero, -ra *n* : rower

remesa *nf* **1** : remittance **2** : shipment

remezón *nm, pl* **-zones** : mild earthquake, tremor

remiendo *nm* **1** : patch **2** : correction

remilgado, -da *adj* **1** : prim, prudish **2** : affected

remilgo *nm* : primness, affectation

reminiscencia *nf* : reminiscence

remisión *nf, pl* **-siones** **1** ENVÍO : sending, delivery **2** : remission **3** : reference, cross-reference

remiso, -sa *adj* **1** : lax, remiss **2** : reluctant

remitente[1] *nm* : return address

remitente[2] *nmf* : sender (of a letter, etc.)

remitir *vt* **1** : to send, to remit **2** **~ a** : to refer to, to direct to <nos remitió al diccionario : he referred us to the dictionary> — *vi* : to subside, to let up

remo *nm* **1** : paddle, oar **2** : rowing (sport)

remoción *nf, pl* **-ciones** **1** : removal **2** : dismissal

remodelación *nf, pl* **-ciones** **1** : remodeling **2** : reorganization, restructuring

remodelar *vt* **1** : to remodel **2** : to restructure

remojar *vt* **1** : to soak, to steep **2** : to dip, to dunk **3** : to celebrate with a drink

remojo *nm* **1** : soaking, steeping **2** **poner en remojo** : to soak, to leave soaking

remolacha *nf* : beet

remolcador *nm* : tugboat

remolcar {72} *vt* : to tow, to haul

remolino *nm* **1 :** whirlwind **2 :** eddy, whirlpool **3 :** crowd, throng **4 :** cowlick

remolque *nm* **1 :** towing, tow **2 :** trailer **3 a ~ :** in tow

remontar *vt* **1 :** to overcome **2** SUBIR **:** to go up — **remontarse** *vr* **1 :** to soar **2 ~ a :** to date from, to go back to

rémora *nf* **:** obstacle, hindrance

remorder {47} *vt* INQUIETAR **:** to trouble, to distress

remordimiento *nm* **:** remorse

remotamente *adv* **:** remotely, vaguely

remoto, -ta *adj* **1 :** remote, unlikely <hay una posibilidad remota : there is a slim possibility> **2 :** distant, far-off

remover {47} *vt* **1 :** to stir **2 :** to move around, to turn over **3 :** to stir up **4 :** to remove **5 :** to dismiss

remozamiento *nm* **:** renovation

remozar {21} *vt* **1 :** to renew, to brighten up **2 :** to redo, to renovate

remuneración *nf, pl* **-ciones :** remuneration, pay

remunerar *vt* **:** to pay, to remunerate

remunerativo, -va *adj* **:** remunerative

renacer {48} *vi* **:** to be reborn, to revive

renacimiento *nm* **1 :** rebirth, revival **2 el Renacimiento :** the Renaissance

renacuajo *nm* **:** tadpole, pollywog

renal *adj* **:** renal, kidney

rencilla *nf* **:** quarrel

renco, -ca *adj* **:** lame

rencor *nm* **1 :** rancor, enmity, hostility **2 guardar rencor :** to hold a grudge

rencoroso, -sa *adj* **:** resentful, rancorous

rendición *nf, pl* **-ciones 1 :** surrender, submission **2 :** yield, return

rendido, -da *adj* **1 :** submissive **2 :** worn-out, exhausted **3 :** devoted

rendija *nf* GRIETA **:** crack, split

rendimiento *nm* **1 :** performance **2 :** yield

rendir {54} *vt* **1 :** to render, to give <rendir las gracias : to give thanks> <rendir homenaje a : to pay homage to> **2 :** to yield **3** CANSAR **:** to exhaust — *vi* **1** CUNDIR **:** to progress, to make headway **2 :** to last, to go a long way — **rendirse** *vr* **:** to surrender, to give up

renegado, -da *n* **:** renegade

renegar {49} *vi* **1 ~ de :** to renounce, to disown, to give up **2 ~ de :** to complain about — *vt* **1 :** to deny vigorously **2 :** to abhor, to hate

renegociar *vt* **:** to renegotiate — **renegociación** *nf*

renglón *nm, pl* **renglones 1 :** line (of writing) **2 :** merchandise, line (of products)

rengo, -ga *adj* **:** lame

renguear *vi* **:** to limp

reno *nm* **:** reindeer

renombrado, -da *adj* **:** renowned, famous

renombre *nm* NOMBRADÍA **:** renown, fame

renovable *adj* **:** renewable

renovación *nf, pl* **-ciones 1 :** renewal <renovación de un contrato : renewal of a contract> **2 :** change, renovation

renovar {19} *vt* **1 :** to renew, to restore **2 :** to renovate

renquear *vi* **:** to limp, to hobble

renquera *nf* COJERA **:** limp, lameness

renta *nf* **1 :** income **2 :** rent **3 impuesto sobre la renta :** income tax

rentable *adj* **:** profitable

rentar *vt* **1 :** to produce, to yield **2** ALQUILAR **:** to rent

renuencia *nf* **:** reluctance, unwillingness

renuente *adj* **:** reluctant, unwilling

renuncia *nf* **1 :** resignation **2 :** renunciation **3 :** waiver

renunciar *vi* **1 :** to resign **2 ~ a :** to renounce, to relinquish <renunció al título : he relinquished the title>

reñido, -da *adj* **1 :** tough, hard-fought **2 :** at odds, on bad terms

reñir {67} *vi* **1 :** to argue **2 ~ con :** to fall out with, to go up against — *vt* **:** to scold, to reprimand

reo, rea *n* **1 :** accused, defendant **2 :** offender, culprit

reojo *nm* **de ~ :** out of the corner of one's eye <una mirada de reojo : a sidelong glance>

reorganizar {21} *vt* **:** to reorganize — **reorganización** *nf*

repantigarse {52} *vr* **:** to slouch, to loll about

reparación *nf, pl* **-ciones 1 :** reparation, amends **2 :** repair

reparar *vt* **1 :** to repair, to fix, to mend **2 :** to make amends for **3 :** to correct **4 :** to restore, to refresh — *vi* **1 ~ en :** to observe, to take notice of **2 ~ en :** to consider, to think about

reparo *nm* **1 :** repair, restoration **2 :** reservation, qualm <no tuvieron reparos en decírmelo : they didn't hesitate to tell me> **3 poner reparos a :** to find fault with, to object to

repartición *nf, pl* **-ciones 1 :** distribution **2 :** department, division

repartidor[1], -dora *adj* **:** delivery <camión repartidor : delivery truck>

repartidor[2], -dora *n* **:** delivery person, distributor

repartimiento *nm* → **repartición**

repartir *vt* **1 :** to allocate **2** DISTRIBUIR **:** to distribute, to hand out **3 :** to spread

reparto *nm* **1 :** allocation **2 :** distribution **3 :** cast (of characters)

repasar *vt* **1 :** to pass by again **2 :** to review, to go over **3 :** to mend

repaso *nm* **1 :** review **2 :** mending **3 :** checkup, overhaul

repatriar {85} *vt* **:** to repatriate — **repatriación** *nf*

repavimentar *vt* **:** to resurface

repelente[1] *adj* **:** repellent, repulsive

repelente[2] *nm* **:** repellent <repelente de insectos : insect repellent>

repeler *vt* **1 :** to repel, to resist, to repulse **2 :** to reject **3 :** to disgust <el sabor me repele : I find the taste repulsive>

repensar {55} *v* **:** to rethink, to reconsider

repente *nm* **1 :** sudden movement, start <de repente : suddenly> **2 :** fit, outburst <un repente de ira : a fit of anger>

repentino, -na *adj* **:** sudden — **repentinamente** *adv*

repercusión *nf, pl* **-siones :** repercussion

repercutir *vi* **1 :** to reverberate, to echo **2 ~ en :** to have effects on, to have repercussions on

repertorio *nm* **:** repertoire

repetición *nf, pl* **-ciones 1 :** repetition **2 :** rerun, repeat

repetidamente *adv* **:** repeatedly

repetido, -da *adj* **1 :** repeated, numerous **2 repetidas veces :** repeatedly, time and again

repetir {54} *vt* **1 :** to repeat **2 :** to have a second helping of — **repetirse** *vr* **1 :** to repeat oneself **2 :** to recur

repetitivo, -va *adj* **:** repetitive, repetitious

repicar {72} *vt* **:** to ring — *vi* **:** to ring out, to peal

repique *nm* **:** ringing, pealing

repisa *nf* **:** shelf, ledge <repisa de chimenea : mantelpiece> <repisa de ventana : windowsill>

replantear *vt* **:** to redefine, to restate — **replantearse** *vr* **:** to reconsider

replegar {49} *vt* **:** to fold — **replegarse** *vr* RETIRARSE **:** to retreat, to withdraw

repleto, -ta *adj* **1 :** replete, full **2 ~ de :** packed with, crammed with

réplica *nf* **1 :** reply **2 :** replica, reproduction **3** *Chile, Mex* **:** aftershock

replicación *nf, pl* **-ciones :** replication

replicar {72} *vi* **1 :** to reply, to retort **2 :** to argue, to answer back

repliegue *nm* **1 :** fold **2 :** retreat, withdrawal

repollo *nm* COL **:** cabbage

reponer {60} *vt* **1 :** to replace, to put back **2 :** to reinstate **3 :** to reply — **reponerse** *vr* **:** to recover

reportaje *nm* **:** article, story, report

reportar *vt* **1 :** to check, to restrain **2 :** to bring, to carry, to yield <me reportó numerosos beneficios : it brought me many benefits> **3 :** to report — **reportarse** *vr* **1** CONTENERSE **:** to control oneself **2** PRESENTARSE **:** to report, to show up

reporte *nm* **:** report

reportear *vt* **:** to report on, to cover

reportero, -ra *n* **1 :** reporter **2 reportero gráfico :** photojournalist

reposado, -da *adj* **:** calm

reposar *vi* **1 :** to rest, to repose **2 :** to stand, to settle <deje reposar la masa media hora : let the dough stand for half an hour> **3 :** to lie, to be buried — **reposarse** *vr* **:** to settle

reposición *nf, pl* **-ciones 1 :** replacement **2 :** reinstatement **3 :** revival

repositorio *nm* **:** repository

reposo *nm* **:** repose, rest

repostar *vi* **1 :** to stock up **2 :** to refuel

repostería *nf* **1 :** confectioner's shop **2 :** pastry-making

repostero, -ra *n* **:** confectioner

repreguntar *vt* **:** to cross-examine

repreguntas *nfpl* **:** cross-examination

reprender *vt* **:** to reprimand, to scold

reprensible *adj* **:** reprehensible

represa *nf* **:** dam

represalia *nf* **1 :** reprisal, retaliation **2 tomar represalias :** to retaliate

represar *vt* **:** to dam

representación *nf, pl* **-ciones 1 :** representation **2 :** performance **3 en representación de :** on behalf of

representante *nmf* **1 :** representative **2 :** performer

representar *vt* **1 :** to represent, to act for **2 :** to perform **3 :** to look, to appear as **4 :** to symbolize, to stand for **5 :** to signify, to mean — **representarse** *vr* **:** to imagine, to picture

representativo, -va *adj* **:** representative

represión *nf, pl* **-siones :** repression

represivo, -va *adj* **:** repressive

reprimenda *nf* **:** reprimand

reprimir *vt* **1 :** to repress **2 :** to suppress, to stifle

reprobable *adj* **:** reprehensible, culpable

reprobación *nf* **:** disapproval

reprobar {19} *vt* **1** DESAPROBAR **:** to condemn, to disapprove of **2 :** to fail (a course)

reprobatorio, -ria *adj* **:** disapproving, admonitory

reprochar *vt* **:** to reproach — **reprocharse** *vr*

reproche *nm* **:** reproach

reproducción *nf, pl* **-ciones :** reproduction

reproducir {61} *vt* **:** to reproduce — **reproducirse** *vr* **1 :** to breed, to reproduce **2 :** to recur

reproductor, -tora *adj* **:** reproductive

reptar *vi* **:** to crawl, to slither

reptil[1] *adj* **:** reptilian

reptil[2] *nm* **:** reptile

república *nf* **:** republic

republicanismo *nm* **:** republicanism

republicano, -na *adj & n* **:** republican

repudiar *vt* **:** to repudiate — **repudiación** *nf*

repudio *nm* **:** repudiation

repuesto[1] *pp* → **reponer**

repuesto[2] *nm* **1 :** spare part **2 de ~ :** spare <rueda de repuesto : spare wheel>

repugnancia *nf* **:** repugnance

repugnante *adj* **:** repulsive, repugnant, revolting

repugnar *vt* **:** to cause repugnance, to disgust — **repugnarse** *vr*

repujar *vt* **:** to emboss

repulsivo, -va *adj* **:** repulsive

repuntar *vt Arg, Chile* **:** to round up (cattle) — *vi* **:** to begin to appear — **repuntarse** *vr* **:** to fall out, to quarrel

repuso, etc. → **reponer**

reputación *nf, pl* **-ciones :** reputation

reputar *vt* **:** to consider, to deem

requerir {76} *vt* **1 :** to require, to call for **2 :** to summon, to send for

requesón *nm, pl* **-sones :** curd cheese, cottage cheese

réquiem *nm* **:** requiem

requisa *nf* **1 :** requisition **2 :** seizure **3 :** inspection

requisar *vt* **1 :** to requisition **2 :** to seize **3** INSPECCIONAR **:** to inspect

requisito *nm* **1 :** requirement **2 requisito previo :** prerequisite

res *nf* **1 :** beast, animal **2** *CA, Mex* **:** beef **3 reses** *nfpl* **:** cattle <60 reses : 60 head of cattle>

resabio *nm* **1** VICIO **:** bad habit, vice **2** DEJO **:** aftertaste

resaca *nf* **1 :** undertow **2 :** hangover

resaltar *vi* **1** SOBRESALIR **:** to stand out **2 hacer resaltar :** to bring out, to highlight — *vt* **:** to stress, to emphasize

resarcimiento *nm* **1 :** compensation **2 :** reimbursement

resarcir {83} *vt* **:** to compensate, to indemnify — **resarcirse** *vr* **~ de :** to make up for

resbaladizo, -za *adj* **1** RESBALOSO **:** slippery **2 :** tricky, ticklish, delicate

resbalar *vi* **1 :** to slip, to slide **2 :** to slip up, to make a mistake **3 :** to skid — **resbalarse** *vr*

resbalón *nm, pl* **-lones :** slip

resbaloso, -sa *adj* **:** slippery

rescatar *vt* **1 :** to rescue, to save **2 :** to recover, to get back

rescate *nm* **1 :** rescue **2 :** recovery **3 :** ransom

rescindir *vt* **:** to rescind, to annul, to cancel

rescisión *nf, pl* **-siones :** annulment, cancelation

rescoldo *nm* **:** embers *pl*

resecar {72} *vt* **:** to make dry, to dry up — **resecarse** *vr* **:** to dry up

reseco, -ca *adj* **:** dry, dried-up

resentido, -da *adj* **:** resentful

resentimiento *nm* **:** resentment

resentirse {76} *vr* **1 :** to suffer, to be weakened **2** OFENDERSE **:** to be upset <se resintió porque la insultaron : she got upset when they insulted her, she resented being insulted> **3 ~ de :** to feel the effects of

reseña *nf* **1 :** report, summary, review **2 :** description

reseñar *vt* **1 :** to review **2** DESCRIBIR **:** to describe

reserva *nf* **1 :** reservation **2 :** reserve **3 :** confidence, privacy <con la mayor reserva : in strictest confidence> **4 de ~ :** spare, in reserve **5 reservas** *nfpl* **:** reservations, doubts

reservación *nf, pl* **-ciones :** reservation

reservado, -da *adj* **1 :** reserved, reticent **2 :** confidential

reservar *vt* **:** to reserve — **reservarse** *vr* **1 :** to save oneself **2 :** to conceal, to keep to oneself

reservorio *nm* **:** reservoir, reserve

resfriado *nm* CATARRO **:** cold

resfriar {85} *vt* **:** to cool — **resfriarse** *vr* **1 :** to cool off **2 :** to catch a cold

resfrío *nm* **:** cold

resguardar *vt* **:** to safeguard, to protect — **resguardarse** *vr*

resguardo *nm* **1 :** safeguard, protection **2 :** receipt, voucher **3 :** border guard, coast guard

residencia *nf* **1 :** residence **2 :** boarding house

residencial *adj* **:** residential

residente *adj & nmf* **:** resident

residir *vi* **1** VIVIR **:** to reside, to dwell **2 ~ en :** to lie in, to consist of

residual *adj* **:** residual

residuo *nm* **1 :** residue **2 :** remainder **3 residuos** *nmpl* **:** waste <residuos nucleares : nuclear waste>

resignación *nf, pl* **-ciones :** resignation

resignar *vt* **:** to resign — **resignarse** *vr* **~ a :** to resign oneself to

resina *nf* **1 :** resin **2 resina epoxídica :** epoxy

resistencia *nf* **1 :** resistance **2** AGUANTE **:** endurance, strength, stamina

resistente *adj* **1 :** resistant **2 :** strong, tough

resistir *vt* **1 :** to stand, to bear, to tolerate **2 :** to withstand — *vi* **:** to resist <resistió hasta el último minuto : he held out until the last minute> — **resistirse** *vr* **~ a :** to be resistent to, to be reluctant

resollar {19} *vi* **:** to breathe heavily, to wheeze

resolución *nf, pl* **-ciones 1 :** resolution, settlement **2 :** decision **3 :** determination, resolve

resolver {89} *vt* **1 :** to resolve, to settle **2 :** to decide — **resolverse** *vr* **:** to make up one's mind

resonancia *nf* **1 :** resonance **2 :** impact, repercussions *pl*

resonante *adj* **1 :** resonant **2 :** tremendous, resounding <un éxito resonante : a resounding success>

resonar {19} *vi* **:** to resound, to ring

resoplar *vi* **1 :** to puff, to pant **2 :** to snort

resoplo *nm* **1 :** puffing, panting **2 :** snort

resorte *nm* **1** MUELLE **:** spring **2 :** elasticity **3 :** influence, means *pl* <tocar resortes : to pull strings>

resortera *nf Mex* **:** slingshot

respaldar *vt* **:** to back, to support, to endorse — **respaldarse** *vr* **:** to lean back

respaldo *nm* **1 :** back (of an object) **2 :** support, backing

respectar *vt* **:** to concern, to relate to <por lo que a mí respecta : as far as I'm concerned>

respectivo, -va *adj* **:** respective — **respectivamente** *adv*

respecto *nm* **1 ~ a :** in regard to, concerning **2 al respecto :** on this matter, in this respect

respetable *adj* **:** respectable — **respetabilidad** *nf*

respetar *vt* **:** to respect

respeto *nm* **1 :** respect, consideration **2 respetos** *nmpl* **:** respects <presentar sus respetos : to pay one's respects>

respetuosidad *nf* **:** respectfulness

respetuoso, -sa *adj* **:** respectful — **respetuosamente** *adv*

respingo *nm* **:** start, jump

respiración *nf, pl* **-ciones :** respiration, breathing

respiradero *nm* **:** vent, ventilation shaft

respirador *nm* **:** respirator

respirar *v* **:** to breathe

respiratorio, -ria *adj* **:** respiratory

respiro *nm* **1 :** breath **2 :** respite, break

resplandecer {53} *vi* **1 :** to shine **2 :** to stand out

resplandeciente *adj* **1 :** resplendent, shining **2 :** radiant

resplandor *nm* **1 :** brightness, brilliance, radiance **2 :** flash

responder *vt* **:** to answer — *vi* **1 :** to answer, to reply, to respond **2 ~ a :** to respond to <responder al tratamiento : to respond to treatment> **3 ~ de :** to answer for, to vouch for (something) **4 ~ por :** to vouch for (someone)

responsabilidad *nf* **:** responsibility

responsable *adj* **:** responsible — **responsablemente** *adv*

respuesta *nf* **:** answer, response

resquebrajar *vt* **:** to split, to crack — **resquebrajarse** *vr*

resquemor *nm* **:** resentment, bitterness

resquicio *nm* **1 :** crack **2 :** opportunity, chance **3 :** trace <sin un resquicio de remordimiento : without a trace of remorse> **4 resquicio legal :** loophole

resta *nf* SUSTRACCIÓN **:** subtraction

restablecer {53} *vt* **:** to reestablish, to restore — **restablecerse** *vr* **:** to recover

restablecimiento *nm* **1 :** reestablishment, restoration **2 :** recovery

restallar *vi* **:** to crack, to crackle, to click

restallido *nm* **:** crack, crackle

restante *adj* **1 :** remaining **2 lo restante, los restantes :** the rest

restañar *vt* **:** to stanch

restar *vt* **1 :** to deduct, to subtract <restar un punto : to deduct a point> **2 :** to minimize, to play down — *vi* **:** to remain, to be left

restauración *nf, pl* **-ciones 1 :** restoration **2 :** catering, food service

restaurante *nm* **:** restaurant

restaurar *vt* **:** to restore

restitución *nf, pl* **-ciones :** restitution, return

restituir {41} *vt* **:** to return, to restore, to reinstate

resto *nm* **1 :** rest, remainder **2 restos** *nmpl* **:** remains <restos de comida : leftovers> <restos arqueológicos : archeological ruins> **3 restos mortales :** mortal remains

restorán *nm, pl* **-ranes :** restaurant

restregadura *nf* **:** scrub, scrubbing

restregar {49} *vt* **1 :** to rub **2 :** to scrub — **restregarse** *vr*

restricción *nf, pl* **-ciones :** restriction, limitation

restrictivo, -va *adj* **:** restrictive

restringido, -da *adj* LIMITADO **:** limited, restricted

restringir {35} *vt* LIMITAR **:** to restrict, to limit

restructuración *nf* **:** restructuring

restructurar *vt* **:** to restructure

resucitación *nf* **:** resuscitation <resucitación cardiopulmonar : CPR, cardiopulmonary resuscitation>

resucitar *vt* **1 :** to resuscitate, to revive, to resurrect **2 :** to revitalize

resuello *nm* **1 :** puffing, heavy breathing, wheezing **2 :** break, breather

resuelto[1] *pp* → **resolver**

resuelto[2]**, -ta** *adj* **:** determined, resolved, resolute

resulta *nf* **1 :** consequence, result **2 a resultas de** *or* **de resultas de :** as a result of

resultado *nm* **:** result, outcome

resultante *adj & nf* **:** resultant

resultar *vi* **1 :** to work, to work out <mi idea no resultó : my idea didn't work out> **2 :** to prove, to turn out to be <resultó bien simpático : he turned out to be very nice> **3 ~ en :** to lead to, to result in **4 ~ de :** to be the result of

resumen *nm, pl* **-súmenes 1 :** summary, summation **2 en ~ :** in summary, in short

resumidero *nm* **:** drain

resumir *v* **:** to summarize, to sum up

resurgimiento *nm* **:** resurgence

resurgir {35} *vi* **:** to reappear, to revive

resurrección *nf, pl* **-ciones :** resurrection

retablo *nm* **1 :** tableau **2 :** altarpiece

retador, -dora *n* **:** challenger (in sports)

retaguardia *nf* **:** rear guard

retahíla *nf* **:** string, series <una retahíla de insultos : a volley of insults>

retaliación *nf, pl* **-ciones :** retaliation

retama *nf* **:** broom (plant)

retar *vt* DESAFIAR **:** to challenge, to defy

retardante *adj* **:** retardant

retardar *vt* **1** RETRASAR **:** to delay, to retard **2 :** to postpone

retazo *nm* **1 :** remnant, scrap **2 :** fragment, piece <retazos de su obra : bits and pieces from his writings>

retención *nf, pl* **-ciones 1 :** retention **2 :** deduction, withholding

retener {80} *vt* **1 :** to retain, to keep **2 :** to withhold **3 :** to detain

retentivo, -va *adj* **:** retentive

reticencia *nf* **1 :** reluctance, reticence **2 :** insinuation

reticente *adj* **1 :** reluctant, reticent **2 :** insinuating, misleading

retina *nf* **:** retina

retintín *nm, pl* **-tines 1 :** jingle, jangle **2 con ~ :** sarcastically

retirada *nf* **1 :** retreat <batirse en retirada : to withdraw, to beat a retreat> **2 :** withdrawl (of funds) **3 :** retirement **4 :** refuge, haven

retirado, -da *adj* **1 :** remote, distant, far off **2 :** secluded, quiet

retirar *vt* **1 :** to remove, to take away, to recall **2 :** to withdraw, to take out — **retirarse** *vr* **1** REPLEGARSE **:** to retreat, to withdraw **2** JUBILARSE **:** to retire

retiro *nm* **1** JUBILACIÓN **:** retirement **2 :** withdrawal, retreat **3 :** seclusion

reto *nm* DESAFÍO **:** challenge, dare

retocar {72} *vt* **:** to touch up

retoñar *vi* **:** to sprout

retoño *nm* **:** sprout, shoot

retoque *nm* **:** retouching

retorcer {14} *vt* **1 :** to twist **2 :** to wring — **retorcerse** *vr* **1 :** to get twisted, to get tangled up **2 :** to squirm, to writhe, to wiggle about

retorcijón *nm, pl* **-jones :** cramp, sharp pain

retorcimiento *nm* **1 :** twisting, wringing **2 :** deviousness

retórica *nf* **:** rhetoric

retórico, -ca *adj* **:** rhetorical — **retóricamente** *adv*

retornar *v* **:** to return

retorno *nm* **:** return

retozar {21} *vi* **:** to frolic, to romp

retozo *nm* **:** frolicking

retozón, -zona *adj, mpl* **-zones :** playful

retracción *nf, pl* **-ciones :** retraction, withdrawal

retractable *adj* **:** retractable

retractación *nf, pl* **-ciones :** retraction (of a statement, etc.)

retractarse *vr* **1 :** to withdraw, to back down **2 ~ de :** to take back, to retract

retraer {81} *vt* **1 :** to bring back **2 :** to dissuade — **retraerse** *vr* **1** RETIRARSE **:** to withdraw, to retire **2** REFUGIARSE **:** to take refuge

retraído, -da *adj* **:** withdrawn, retiring, shy

retraimiento *nm* **1 :** shyness, timidity **2 :** withdrawal

retrasado, -da *adj* **1 :** retarded, mentally slow **2 :** behind, in arrears **3 :** backward (of a country) **4 :** slow (of a watch)

retrasar *vt* **1** DEMORAR, RETARDAR **:** to delay, to hold up **2 :** to put off, to postpone — **retrasarse** *vr* **1 :** to be late **2 :** to fall behind

retraso *nm* **1** ATRASO **:** delay, lateness **2 retraso mental :** mental retardation

retratar *vt* **1 :** to portray, to depict **2 :** to photograph **3 :** to paint a portrait of

retrato *nm* **1 :** depiction, portrayal **2 :** portrait, photograph

retrete *nm* **:** restroom, toilet

retribución *nf, pl* **-ciones 1 :** pay, payment **2 :** reward

retribuir {41} *vt* **1 :** to pay **2 :** to reward

retroactivo, -va *adj* **:** retroactive — **retroactivamente** *adv*

retroalimentación *nf, pl* **-ciones :** feedback

retroceder *vi* **1 :** to move back, to turn back **2 :** to back off, to back down **3 :** to recoil (of a firearm)

retroceso *nm* **1 :** backward movement **2 :** backing down **3 :** setback, relapse **4 :** recoil

retrógrado, -da *adj* **1 :** reactionary **2 :** retrograde

retropropulsión *nf* **:** jet propulsion

retrospectiva *nf* **:** retrospective, hindsight

retrospectivo, -va *adj* **1 :** retrospective **2 mirada retrospectiva :** backward glance

retrovisor *nm* **:** rearview mirror

retruécano *nm* **:** pun, play on words

retumbar *vi* **1 :** to boom, to thunder **2 :** to resound, to reverberate

retumbo *nm* **:** booming, thundering, roll

retuvo, etc. → **retener**

reubicar {72} *vt* **:** to relocate — **reubicación** *nf*

reuma *or* **reúma** *nmf* → **reumatismo**

reumático, -ca *adj* **:** rheumatic

reumatismo *nm* **:** rheumatism

reunión *nf, pl* **-niones 1 :** meeting **2 :** gathering, reunion

reunir {68} *vt* **1 :** to unite, to join, to bring together **2 :** to have, to possess <reunieron los requisitos necesarios : they fulfilled the necessary requirements> **3 :** to gather, to collect, to raise (funds) — **reunirse** *vr* **:** to meet

reutilizable *adj* **:** reusable

reutilizar {21} *vt* **:** to recycle, to reuse

revalidar *vt* **1 :** to confirm, to ratify **2 :** to defend (a title)

revaluar {3} *vt* **:** to reevaluate — **revaluación** *n*

revancha *nf* **1** DESQUITE **:** revenge, requital **2 :** rematch

revelación *nf, pl* **-ciones :** revelation

revelado *nm* **:** developing (of film)

revelador[1], -dora *adj* **:** revealing

revelador[2] *nm* **:** developer

revelar *vt* **1 :** to reveal, to disclose **2 :** to develop (film)

revendedor, -dora *n* **1 :** scalper **2** DETALLISTA **:** retailer

revender *vt* **1 :** to resell **2 :** to scalp

reventa *nf* **1 :** resale **2 :** scalping

reventar {55} *vi* **1** ESTALLAR, EXPLOTAR **:** to burst, to blow up **2 ~ de :** to be bursting with — *vt* **1 :** to burst **2** *fam* **:** to annoy, to rile

reventón *nm, pl* **-tones 1 :** burst, bursting **2 :** blowout, flat tire **3** *Mex fam* **:** bash, party

reverberar *vi* **:** to reverberate — **reverberación** *nf*

reverdecer {53} *vi* **1 :** to grow green again **2 :** to revive

reverencia *nf* **1 :** reverence **2 :** bow, curtsy

reverenciar *vt* **:** to revere, to venerate

reverendo[1], -da *adj* **1 :** reverend **2** *fam* **:** total, absolute <es un reverendo imbécil : he is a complete idiot>

reverendo[2], -da *n* **:** reverend

reverente *adj* **:** reverent

reversa *nf Col, Mex* **:** reverse (gear)

reversible *adj* **:** reversible

reversión *nf, pl* **-siones :** reversion

reverso *nm* **1 :** back, other side **2 el reverso de la medalla :** the complete opposite

revertir {76} *vi* **1 :** to revert, to go back **2 ~ en :** to result in, to end up as

revés *nm, pl* **reveses 1 :** back, wrong side **2 :** setback, reversal **3 :** backhand (in sports) **4 al revés :** the other way around, upside down, inside out **5 al revés de :** contrary to

revestimiento *nm* **:** covering, facing (of a building)

revestir {54} *vt* **1 :** to coat, to cover, to surface **2 :** to conceal, to disguise **3 :** to take on, to assume <la reunión revistió gravedad : the meeting took on a serious note>

revisar *vt* **1 :** to examine, to inspect, to check **2 :** to check over, to overhaul (machinery) **3 :** to revise

revisión *nf, pl* **-siones 1 :** revision **2 :** inspection, check

revisor, -sora *n* **1 :** inspector **2 :** conductor (on a train)

revista *nf* **1 :** magazine, journal **2 :** revue **3 pasar revista :** to review, to inspect

revistar *vt* **:** to review, to inspect

revitalizar {21} *vt* **:** to revitalize — **revitalización** *nf*

revivir *vi* **:** to revive, to come alive again — *vt* **:** to relive

revocación *nf, pl* **-ciones :** revocation, repeal

revocar {72} *vt* **1 :** to revoke, to repeal **2 :** to plaster (a wall)

revolcar {82} *vt* **:** to knock over, to knock down — **revolcarse** *vr* **:** to roll around, to wallow

revolcón *nm, pl* **-cones** *fam* **:** tumble, fall

revolotear *vi* **:** to flutter around, to flit

revoloteo *nm* **:** fluttering, flitting

revoltijo *nm* **1** FÁRRAGO **:** mess, jumble **2** *Mex* **:** traditional seafood dish

revoltoso, -sa *adj* **:** unruly, rebellious

revolución *nf, pl* **-ciones :** revolution

revolucionar *vt* **:** to revolutionize

revolucionario, -ria *adj & n* **:** revolutionary

revolver {89} *vt* **1 :** to move about, to mix, to shake, to stir **2 :** to upset (one's stomach) **3 :** to mess up, to rummage through <revolver la casa : to turn the house upside down> — **revolverse** *vr* **1 :** to toss and turn **2** VOLVERSE **:** to turn around

revólver *nm* **:** revolver

revoque *nm* **:** plaster

revuelo *nm* **1 :** fluttering **2 :** commotion, stir

revuelta *nf* **:** uprising, revolt

revuelto[1] *pp* → **revolver**

revuelto[2], -ta *adj* **1 :** choppy, rough <mar revuelto : rough sea> **2 :** untidy **3 huevos revueltos :** scrambled eggs

rey *nm* **:** king

reyerta *nf* **:** brawl, fight

rezagado, -da *n* **:** straggler, latecomer

rezagar {52} *vt* **1 :** to leave behind **2 :** to postpone — **rezagarse** *vr* **:** to fall behind, to lag

rezar {21} *vi* **1 :** to pray **2 :** to say <como reza el refrán : as the saying goes> **3 ~ con :** to concern, to have to do with — *vt* **:** to say, to recite <rezar un Ave María : to say a Hail Mary>

rezo *nm* **:** prayer, praying

rezongar {52} *vi* **:** to gripe, to grumble

rezumar *v* **:** to ooze, to leak

ría[1], etc. → **reír**

ría[2] *nf* **:** estuary

riachuelo *nm* ARROYO **:** brook, stream

riada *nf* **:** flood

ribera *nf* **:** bank, shore

ribete *nm* **1 :** border, trim **2 :** frill, adornment **3 ribetes** *nmpl* **:** hint, touch <tiene sus ribetes de genio : there's a touch of genius in him>

ribetear *vt* **:** to border, to edge, to trim

ricamente *adv* **:** richly, splendidly

rice, etc. → **rizar**

rico[1], -ca *adj* **1 :** rich, wealthy **2 :** fertile **3 :** luxurious, valuable **4 :** delicious **5 :** adorable, lovely **6 :** great, wonderful

rico[2], -ca *n* **:** rich person

ridiculez *nf, pl* **-leces :** ridiculousness, absurdity

ridiculizar {21} *vt* **:** to ridicule

ridículo[1], -la *adj* ABSURDO, DISPARATADO **:** ridiculous, ludicrous — **ridículamente** *adv*

ridículo[2], -la *n* **1 hacer el ridículo :** to make a fool of oneself **2 poner en ridículo :** to ridicule

ríe, etc. → **reír**

riega, riegue, etc. → **regar**

riego *nm* **:** irrigation

riel *nm* **:** rail, track

rienda *nf* **1 :** rein **2 dar rienda suelta a :** to give free rein to **3 llevar las riendas :** to be in charge **4 tomar las riendas :** to take control

riesgo *nm* **:** risk

riesgoso, -sa *adj* **:** risky

rifa *nf* **:** raffle

rifar *vt* **:** to raffle — *vi* **:** to quarrel, to fight

rifle *nm* **:** rifle

rige, rija, etc. → **regir**

rigidez *nf, pl* **-deces 1 :** rigidity, stiffness <rigidez cadavérica : rigor mortis> **2 :** inflexibility

rígido, -da *adj* **1 :** rigid, stiff **2 :** strict — **rígidamente** *adv*

rigor *nm* **1 :** rigor, harshness **2 :** precision, meticulousness **3 de ~ :** usual <la respuesta de rigor : the standard reply> **4 de ~ :** essential, obligatory **5 en ~ :** strictly speaking, in reality

riguroso, -sa *adj* **:** rigorous — **rigurosamente** *adv*

rima *nf* **1 :** rhyme **2 rimas** *nfpl* **:** verse, poetry

rimar *vi* **:** to rhyme

rimbombante *adj* **1 :** grandiose, showy **2 :** bombastic, pompous

rímel *or* **rimel** *nm* **:** mascara

rin *nm Col, Mex* **:** wheel, rim (of a tire)

rincón *nm, pl* **rincones :** corner, nook

rinde, etc. → **rendir**

rinoceronte *nm* **:** rhinoceros

riña *nf* **1 :** fight, brawl **2 :** dispute, quarrel

riñe, etc. → **reñir**

riñón *nm, pl* **riñones :** kidney

río[1] → **reír**

río[2] *nm* **1 :** river **2 :** torrent, stream <un río de lágrimas : a flood of tears>

ripio *nm* **1 :** debris, rubble **2 :** gravel

riqueza *nf* **1 :** wealth, riches *pl* **2 :** richness **3 riquezas naturales :** natural resources

risa *nf* **1 :** laughter, laugh **2 dar risa :** to make laugh <me dio mucha risa : I found it very funny> **3** *fam* **morirse de la risa :** to die laughing, to crack up

risco *nm* **:** crag, cliff

risible *adj* IRRISORIO **:** ludicrous, laughable

risita *nf* **:** giggle, titter, snicker

risotada *nf* **:** guffaw

ristra *nf* **:** string, series *pl*

risueño, -ña *adj* **1 :** cheerful, pleasant **2 :** promising

rítmico, -ca *adj* **:** rhythmical, rhythmic — **rítmicamente** *adv*

ritmo *nm* **1 :** rhythm **2 :** pace, tempo <trabajó a ritmo lento : she worked at a slow pace>

rito *nm* **:** rite, ritual

ritual *adj & nm* **:** ritual — **ritualmente** *adv*

rival *adj & nmf* COMPETIDOR **:** rival

rivalidad *nf* **:** rivalry, competition

rivalizar {21} *vi* **~ con :** to rival, to compete with

rizado, -da *adj* **1 :** curly **2 :** ridged **3 :** ripply, undulating

rizar {21} *vt* **1 :** to curl **2 :** to ripple, to ruffle (a surface) **3 :** to crumple, to fold — **rizarse** *vr* **1 :** to frizz **2 :** to ripple

rizo *nm* **1 :** curl **2 :** loop (in aviation)

robalo *or* **róbalo** *nm* **:** sea bass

robar *vt* **1 :** to steal **2 :** to rob, to burglarize **3** SECUESTRAR **:** to abduct, to kidnap **4 :** to captivate — *vi* **~ en :** to break into

roble *nm* **:** oak

robo *nm* **:** robbery, theft

robot *nm, pl* **robots :** robot

robótica *nf* **:** robotics

robustecer {53} *vt* **:** to grow stronger, to strengthen

robustez *nf* **:** sturdiness, robustness

robusto, -ta *adj* **:** robust, sturdy

roca *nf* **:** rock, boulder

roce[1], **etc.** → **rozar**

roce[2] *nm* **1 :** rubbing, chafing **2 :** brush, graze, touch **3 :** close contact, familiarity **4 :** friction, disagreement

rociador *nm* **:** sprinkler

rociar {85} *vt* **:** to spray, to sprinkle

rocío *nm* **1 :** dew **2 :** shower, light rain

rocola *nf* **:** jukebox

rocoso, -sa *adj* **:** rocky

rodada *nf* **:** track (of a tire), rut

rodado, -da *adj* **1 :** wheeled **2 :** dappled (of a horse)

rodaja *nf* **:** round, slice

rodaje *nm* **1 :** filming, shooting **2 :** breaking in (of a vehicle)

rodamiento *nm* **1 :** bearing <rodamiento de bolas : ball bearings> **2 :** rolling

rodar {19} *vi* **1 :** to roll, to roll down, to roll along <rodé por la escalera : I tumbled down the stairs> <todo rodaba bien : everthing was going along well> **2** GIRAR **:** to turn, to go around **3 :** to move about, to travel <andábamos rodando por todas partes : we drifted along from place to place> — *vt* **1 :** to film, to shoot **2 :** to break in (a new vehicle)

rodear *vt* **1 :** to surround **2 :** to round up (cattle) — *vi* **1 :** to go around **2 :** to beat around the bush — **rodearse** *vr* **~ de :** to surround oneself with

rodeo *nm* **1 :** rodeo, roundup **2** DESVÍO **:** detour **3 :** evasion <andar con rodeos : to beat around the bush> <sin rodeos : without reservations>

rodilla *nf* **:** knee

rodillo *nm* **1 :** roller **2 :** rolling pin

rododendro *nm* **:** rhododendron

roedor[1], **-dora** *adj* **:** gnawing

roedor[2] *nm* **:** rodent

roer {69} *vt* **1 :** to gnaw **2 :** to eat away at, to torment

rogar {16} *vt* **:** to beg, to request — *vi* **1 :** to beg, to plead **2 :** to pray

rojez *nf* **:** redness

roiga, etc. → **roer**
rojizo, -za *adj* : reddish
rojo[1], **-ja** *adj* **1** : red **2 ponerse rojo** : to blush
rojo[2] *nm* : red
rol *nm* **1** : role **2** : list, roll
rollo *nm* **1** : roll, coil <un rollo de cinta : a roll of tape> <en rollo : rolled up> **2** *fam* : roll of fat **3** *fam* : boring speech, lecture
romance *nm* **1** : Romance language **2** : ballad **3** : romance **4 en buen romance** : simply stated, simply put
romano, -na *adj & n* : Roman
romanticismo *nm* : romanticism
romántico, -ca *adj* : romantic — **románticamente** *adv*
rombo *nm* : rhombus
romería *nf* **1** : pilgrimage, procession **2** : crowd, gathering
romero[1], **-ra** *n* PEREGRINO : pilgrim
romero[2] *nm* : rosemary
romo, -ma *adj* : blunt, dull
rompecabezas *nms & pl* : puzzle, riddle
rompehielos *nms & pl* : icebreaker (ship)
rompehuelgas *nmfs & pl* ESQUIROL : strikebreaker, scab
rompenueces *nms & pl* : nutcracker
rompeolas *ns & pl* : breakwater, jetty
romper {70} *vt* **1** : to break, to smash **2** : to rip, to tear **3** : to break off (relations), to break (a contract) **4** : to break through, to break down **5** GASTAR : to wear out — *vi* **1** : to break <al romper del día : at the break of day> **2 ~ a** : to begin to, to burst out with <romper a llorar : to burst into tears> **3 ~ con** : to break off with
rompope *nm CA, Mex* : drink similar to eggnog
ron *nm* : rum
roncar {72} *vi* **1** : to snore **2** : to roar
ronco, -ca *adj* **1** : hoarse **2** : husky (of the voice) — **roncamente** *adv*
ronda *nf* **1** : beat, patrol **2** : round (of drinks, of negotiations, of a game)
rondar *vt* **1** : to patrol **2** : to hang around <siempre está rondando la calle : he's always hanging around the street> **3** : to be approximately <debe rondar los cincuenta : he must be about 50> — *vi* **1** : to be on patrol **2** : to prowl around, to roam about
ronque, etc. → **roncar**
ronquera *nf* : hoarseness
ronquido *nm* **1** : snore **2** : roar
ronronear *vi* : to purr
ronroneo *nm* : purr, purring
ronzal *nm* : halter (for an animal)
ronzar {21} *v* : to munch, to crunch
roña *nf* **1** : mange **2** : dirt, filth **3** *fam* : stinginess
roñoso, -sa *adj* **1** : mangy **2** : dirty **3** *fam* : stingy
ropa *nf* **1** : clothes *pl,* clothing **2 ropa interior** : underwear
ropaje *nm* : apparel, garments *pl,* regalia
ropero *nm* ARMARIO, CLÓSET : wardrobe, closet
rosa[1] *adj* : rose-colored, pink
rosa[2] *nm* : rose, pink (color)
rosa[3] *nf* : rose (flower)
rosáceo, -cea *adj* : pinkish
rosado[1], **-da** *adj* **1** : pink **2 vino rosado** : rosé
rosado[2] *nm* : pink (color)
rosal *nm* : rosebush
rosario *nm* **1** : rosary **2** : series <un rosario de islas : a string of islands>
rosbif *nm* : roast beef
rosca *nf* **1** : thread (of a screw) <una tapa a rosca : a screw top> **2** : ring, coil
roseta *nf* : rosette
rosquilla *nf* : ring-shaped pastry, doughnut
rostro *nm* : face, countenance
rotación *nf, pl* **-ciones** : rotation
rotar *vt* : to rotate, to turn — *vi* : to turn, to spin
rotativo[1], **-va** *adj* : rotary
rotativo[2] *nm* : newspaper
rotatorio, -ria → **rotativo**[1]
roto[1] *pp* → **romper**
roto[2], **-ta** *adj* **1** : broken **2** : ripped, torn
rotonda *nf* **1** : traffic circle, rotary **2** : rotunda
rotor *nm* : rotor
rótula *nf* : kneecap
rotular *vt* **1** : to head, to entitle **2** : to label
rótulo *nm* **1** : heading, title **2** : label, sign
rotundo, -da *adj* **1** REDONDO : round **2** : categorical, absolute <un éxito rotundo : a resounding success> — **rotundamente** *adv*
rotura *nf* : break, tear, fracture
roya *nf* : plant rust
roya, etc. → **roer**
rozado, -da *adj* GASTADO : worn
rozadura *nf* **1** : scratch, abrasion **2** : rubbed spot, sore
rozar {21} *vt* **1** : to chafe, to rub against **2** : to border on, to touch on **3** : to graze, to touch lightly — **rozarse** *vr* **~ con** *fam* : to rub shoulders with
ruandés, -desa *adj & n* : Rwandan
ruano, -na *adj* : roan
rubí *nm, pl* **rubíes** : ruby
rubio, -bia *adj & n* : blond
rublo *nm* : ruble
rubor *nm* **1** : flush, blush **2** : rouge, blusher
ruborizarse {21} *vr* : to blush
rubrica *nf* : title, heading
rubricar {72} *vt* **1** : sign with a flourish <firmado y rubricado : signed and sealed> **2** : to endorse, to sanction
rubro *nm* **1** : heading, title **2** : line, area (in business)
rudeza *nf* ASPEREZA : roughness, coarseness

rudimentario, -ria *adj* : rudimentary — **rudimentariamente** *adv*

rudimento *nm* : rudiment, basics *pl*

rudo, -da *adj* **1** : rough, harsh **2** : coarse, unpolished — **rudamente** *adv*

rueda[1], etc. → **rodar**

rueda[2] *nf* **1** : wheel **2** RODAJA : round slice **3** : circle, ring **4 rueda de andar** : treadmill **5 rueda de prensa** : press conference **6 ir sobre ruedas** : to go smoothly

ruedita *nf* : caster (on furniture)

ruedo *nm* **1** : bullring, arena **2** : rotation, turn **3** : hem

ruega, ruegue, etc. → **rogar**

ruego *nm* : request, appeal, plea

rugido *nm* : roar

rugir {35} *vi* : to roar

ruibarbo *nm* : rhubarb

ruido *nm* : noise, sound

ruidoso, -sa *adj* : loud, noisy — **ruidosamente** *adv*

ruin *adj* **1** : base, despicable **2** : mean, stingy

ruina *nf* **1** : ruin, destruction **2** : downfall, collapse **3 ruinas** *nfpl* : ruins, remains

ruinoso, -sa *adj* **1** : run-down, dilapidated **2** : ruinous, disasterous

ruiseñor *nm* : nightingale

ruja, etc. → **rugir**

ruleta *nf* : roulette

rulo *nm* : curler, roller

rumano, -na *n* : Romanian, Rumanian

rumbo *nm* **1** : direction, course <con rumbo a : bound for, heading for> <perder el rumbo : to go off course, to lose one's bearings> <sin rumbo : aimless, aimlessly> **2** : ostentation, pomp **3** : lavishness, generosity

rumiante *adj & nm* : ruminant

rumiar *vt* : to ponder, to mull over — *vi* **1** : to chew the cud **2** : to ruminate, to ponder

rumor *nm* **1** : rumor **2** : murmur

rumorearse *or* **rumorarse** *vr* : to be rumored <se rumorea que se va : rumor has it that she's leaving>

rumoroso, -sa *adj* : murmuring, babbling <un arroyo rumoroso : a babbling brook>

rupia *nf* : rupee

ruptura *nf* **1** : break **2** : breaking, breach (of a contract) **3** : breaking off, breakup

rural *adj* : rural

ruso[1], -sa *adj & n* : Russian

ruso[2] *nm* : Russian (language)

rústico[1], -ca *adj* : rural, rustic

rústico[2], -ca *n* : rustic, country dweller

ruta *nf* : route

rutina *nf* : routine, habit

rutinario, -ria *adj* : routine, ordinary <visita rutinaria : routine visit> — **rutinariamente** *adv*

S

s *nf* : twentieth letter of the Spanish alphabet

sábado *nm* **1** : Saturday **2** : Sabbath

sábalo *nm* : shad

sabana *nf* : savanna

sábana *nf* : sheet, bedsheet

sabandija *nf* BICHO : bug, small reptile, pesky creature

sabático, -ca *adj* : sabbatical

sabedor, -dora *adj* : aware, informed

sabelotodo *nmf fam* : know-it-all

saber[1] {71} *vt* **1** : to know **2** : to know how to, to be able to <sabe tocar el violín : she can play the violin> **3** : to learn, to find out **4 a ~** : to wit, namely — *vi* **1** : to know, to suppose **2** : to be informed <supimos del desastre : we heard about the disaster> **3** : to taste <esto no sabe bien : this doesn't taste right> **4 ~ a** : to taste like <sabe a naranja : it tastes like orange> — **saberse** *vr* : to know <ese chiste no me lo sé : I don't know that joke>

saber[2] *nm* : knowledge, learning

sabiamente *adv* : wisely

sabido, -da *adj* : well-known

sabiduría *nf* **1** : wisdom **2** : learning, knowledge

sabiendas *adv* **1 a ~** : knowingly **2 a sabiendas de que** : knowing full well that

sabio[1], -bia *adj* **1** PRUDENTE : wise, sensible **2** DOCTO : learned

sabio[2], -bia *n* **1** : wise person **2** : savant, learned person

sable *nm* : saber, cutlass

sablear *vt fam* : to scrounge, to cadge

sabor *nm* **1** : flavor, taste **2 sin ~** : flavorless

saborear *vt* **1** : to taste, to savor **2** : to enjoy, to relish

sabotaje *nm* : sabotage

saboteador, -dora *n* : saboteur

sabotear *vt* : to sabotage

sabrá, etc. → **saber**

sabroso, -sa *adj* **1** RICO : delicious, tasty **2** AGRADABLE : pleasant, nice, lovely

sabueso *nm* **1** : bloodhound **2** *fam* : detective, sleuth

sacacorchos *nms & pl* : corkscrew

sacapuntas *nms & pl* : pencil sharpener

sacar {72} *vt* **1** : to pull out, to take out <saca el pollo del congelador : take the chicken out of the freezer> **2** : to get, to obtain <saqué un 100 en el examen : I got 100 on the exam> **3** : to get out, to extract <le saqué la infor-

mación : I got the information from him> **4** : to stick out <sacar la lengua : to stick out one's tongue> **5** : to bring out, to introduce <sacar un libro : to publish a book> <sacaron una moda nueva : they introduced a new style> **6** : to take (photos) **7** : to make (copies) — *vi* **1** : to kick off (in soccer or football) **2** : to serve (in sports)

sacarina *nf* : saccharin

sacarosa *nf* : sucrose

sacerdocio *nm* : priesthood

sacerdotal *adj* : priestly

sacerdote, -tisa *n* : priest *m*, priestess *f*

saciar *vt* **1** HARTAR : to sate, to satiate **2** SATISFACER : to satisfy

saciedad *nf* : satiety

saco *nm* **1** : bag, sack **2** : sac **3** : jacket, sport coat

sacramento *nm* : sacrament — **sacramental** *adj*

sacrificar {72} *vt* : to sacrifice — **sacrificarse** *vr* : to sacrifice oneself, to make sacrifices

sacrificio *nm* : sacrifice

sacrilegio *nm* : sacrilege

sacrílego, -ga *adj* : sacrilegious

sacristán *nm, pl* **-tanes** : sexton, sacristan

sacristía *nf* : sacristy, vestry

sacro, -cra *adj* SAGRADO : sacred <arte sacro : sacred art>

sacrosanto, -ta *adj* : sacrosanct

sacudida *nf* **1** : shaking **2** : jerk, jolt, shock **3** : shake-up, upheaval

sacudir *vt* **1** : to shake, to beat **2** : to jerk, to jolt **3** : to dust off **4** CONMOVER : to shake up, to shock — **sacudirse** *vr* : to shake off

sacudón *nm, pl* **-dones** : intense jolt or shake-up

sádico[1], -ca *adj* : sadistic

sádico[2], -ca *n* : sadist

sadismo *nm* : sadism

safari *nm* : safari

saga *nf* : saga

sagacidad *nf* : sagacity, shrewdness

sagaz *adj, pl* **sagaces** PERSPICAZ : shrewd, discerning, sagacious

Sagitario *nmf* : Sagittarius, Sagittarian

sagrado, -da *adj* : sacred, holy

sainete *nm* : comedy sketch, one-act farce <este proceso es un sainete : these proceedings are a farce>

sajar *vt* : to lance, to cut open

sal[1] → **salir**

sal[2] *nf* **1** : salt **2** *CA, Mex* : misfortune, bad luck

sala *nf* **1** : living room **2** : room, hall <sala de conferencias : lecture hall> <sala de urgencias : emergency room> <sala de baile : ballroom>

salado, -da *adj* **1** : salty **2 agua salada** : salt water

salamandra *nf* : salamander

salami *nm* : salami

salar *vt* **1** : to salt **2** : to spoil, to ruin **3** *CoRi, Mex* : to jinx, to bring bad luck

salarial *adj* : salary, salary-related

salario *nm* **1** : salary **2 salario mínimo** : minimum wage

salaz *adj, pl* **salaces** : salacious, lecherous

salchicha *nf* **1** : sausage **2** : frankfurter, wiener

salchichón *nf, pl* **-chones** : a type of deli meat

salchichonería *nf Mex* **1** : delicatessen **2** : cold cuts *pl*

saldar *vt* : to settle, to pay off <saldar una cuenta : to settle an account>

saldo *nm* **1** : settlement, payment **2** : balance <saldo de cuenta : account balance> **3** : remainder, leftover merchandise

saldrá, etc. → **salir**

salero *nm* **1** : saltshaker **2** : wit, charm

salga, etc. → **salir**

salida *nf* **1** : exit <salida de emergencia : emergency exit> **2** : leaving, departure **3** SOLUCIÓN : way out, solution **4** : start (of a race) **5** OCURRENCIA : wisecrack, joke **6 salida del sol** : sunrise

saliente[1] *adj* **1** : departing, outgoing **2** : projecting **3** DESTACADO : salient, prominent

saliente[2] *nm* **1** : projection, protrusion **2 ventana en saliente** : bay window

salinidad *nf* : salinity, saltiness

salino, -na *adj* : saline <solución salina : saline solution>

salir {73} *vi* **1** : to go out, to come out, to get out <salimos todas las noches : we go out every night> <su libro acaba de salir : her book just came out> **2** PARTIR : to leave, to depart **3** APARECER : to appear <salió en todos los diarios : it came out in all the papers> **4** : to project, to stick out **5** : to cost, to come to **6** RESULTAR : to turn out, to prove **7** : to come up, to occur <salga lo que salga : whatever happens> <salió una oportunidad : an opportunity came up> **8 ~ a** : to take after, to look like, to resemble **9 ~ con** : to go out with, to date — **salirse** *vr* **1** : to escape, to get out, to leak out **2** : to come loose, to come off **3 salirse con la suya** : to get one's own way

saliva *nf* : saliva

salivar *vi* : to salivate

salmo *nm* : psalm

salmón[1] *adj* : salmon-colored

salmón[2] *nm, pl* **salmones** : salmon

salmuera *nf* : brine

salobre *adj* : brackish, briny

salón *nm, pl* **salones 1** : hall, large room <salón de clase : classroom> <salón de baile : ballroom> **2** : salon <salón de belleza : beauty salon> **3** : parlor, sitting room

salpicadera *nf Mex* : fender

salpicadura *nf* : spatter, splash

salpicar {72} *vt* **1 :** to spatter, to splash **2 :** to sprinkle, to scatter about

salpimentar {55} *vt* **1 :** to season (with salt and pepper) **2 :** to spice up

salsa *nf* **1 :** sauce <salsa picante : hot sauce> <salsa inglesa : Worcestershire sauce> <salsa tártara : tartar sauce> **2 :** gravy **3 :** salsa (music) **4 salsa mexicana :** salsa (sauce)

salsero, -ra *n* **:** salsa musician

saltador, -dora *n* **:** jumper

saltamontes *nms & pl* **:** grasshopper

saltar *vi* **1** BRINCAR **:** to jump, to leap **2 :** to bounce **3 :** to come off, to pop out **4 :** to shatter, to break **5 :** to explode, to blow up — *vt* **1 :** to jump, to jump over **2 :** to skip, to miss — **saltarse** *vr* OMITIR **:** to skip, to omit <me salté ese capítulo : I skipped that chapter>

saltarín, -rina *adj, mpl* **-rines :** leaping, hopping <frijol saltarín : jumping bean>

salteado, -da *adj* **1 :** sautéed **2 :** jumbled up <los episodios se transmitieron salteados : the episodes were broadcast in random order>

salteador *nm* **:** highwayman

saltear *vt* **1** SOFREÍR **:** to sauté **2 :** to skip around, to skip over

saltimbanqui *nmf* **:** acrobat

salto *nm* **1** BRINCO **:** jump, leap, skip **2 :** jump, dive (in sports) **3 :** gap, omission **4 dar saltos :** to jump up and down **5** *or* **salto de agua** CATARATA **:** waterfall

saltón, -tona *adj, mpl* **saltones :** bulging, protruding

salubre *adj* **:** healthful, salubrious

salubridad *nf* **:** healthfulness, health

salud *nf* **1 :** health <buena salud : good health> **2 ¡salud! :** bless you! (when someone sneezes) **3 ¡salud! :** cheers!, to your health!

saludable *adj* **1** SALUBRE **:** healthful **2** SANO **:** healthy, well

saludar *vt* **1 :** to greet, to say hello to **2 :** to salute — **saludarse** *vr*

saludo *nm* **1 :** greeting, regards *pl* **2 :** salute

salutación *nf, pl* **-ciones :** salutation

salva *nf* **1 :** salvo, volley **2 salva de aplausos :** round of applause

salvación *nf, pl* **-ciones 1 :** salvation **2** RESCATE **:** rescue

salvado *nm* **:** bran

salvador, -dora *n* **1 :** savior, rescuer **2 el Salvador :** the Savior

salvadoreño, -ña *adj & n* **:** Salvadoran, El Salvadoran

salvaguardar *vt* **:** to safeguard

salvaguardia *or* **salvaguarda** *nf* **:** safeguard, defense

salvajada *nf* ATROCIDAD **:** atrocity, act of savagery

salvaje[1] *adj* **1 :** wild <animales salvajes : wild animals> **2 :** savage, cruel **3 :** primitive, uncivilized

salvaje[2] *nmf* **:** savage

salvajismo *nm* **:** savagery

salvamento *nm* **1 :** rescuing, lifesaving **2 :** salvation **3 :** refuge

salvar *vt* **1 :** to save, to rescue **2 :** to cover (a distance) **3 :** to get around (an obstacle), to overcome (a difficulty) **4 :** to cross, to jump across **5 salvando :** except for, excluding — **salvarse** *vr* **1 :** to survive, to escape **2 :** to save one's soul

salvavidas[1] *nms & pl* **1 :** life preserver **2 bote salvavidas :** lifeboat

salvavidas[2] *nmf* **:** lifeguard

salvedad *nf* **1** EXCEPCIÓN **:** exception **2 :** proviso, stipulation

salvia *nf* **:** sage (plant)

salvo[1], **-va** *adj* **1 :** unharmed, sound <sano y salvo : safe and sound> **2 a ~ :** safe from danger

salvo[2] *prep* **1** EXCEPTO **:** except (for), save <todos asistirán salvo Jaime : all will attend except for Jaime> **2 salvo que :** unless <salvo que llueva : unless it rains>

salvoconducto *nm* **:** safe-conduct

samba *nf* **:** samba

San → **santo**[1]

sanar *vt* **:** to heal, to cure — *vi* **:** to get well, to recover

sanatorio *nm* **1 :** sanatorium **2 :** clinic, private hospital

sanción *nf, pl* **sanciones :** sanction

sancionar *vt* **1 :** to penalize, to impose a sanction on **2 :** to sanction, to approve

sancochar *vt* **:** to parboil

sandalia *nf* **:** sandal

sándalo *nm* **:** sandalwood

sandez *nf, pl* **sandeces** ESTUPIDEZ **:** nonsense, silly thing to say

sandía *nf* **:** watermelon

sandwich [ˈsandwitʃ, ˈsaŋgwitʃ] *nm, pl* **sandwiches** [-dwitʃɛs, -gwi-] EMPAREDADO **:** sandwich

saneamiento *nm* **1 :** cleaning up, sanitation **2 :** reorganizing, streamlining

sanear *vt* **1 :** to clean up, to sanitize **2 :** to reorganize, to streamline

sangrante *adj* **1 :** bleeding **2 :** flagrant, blatant

sangrar *vi* **:** to bleed — *vt* **:** to indent (a paragraph, etc.)

sangre *nf* **1 :** blood **2 a sangre fría :** in cold blood **3 a sangre y fuego :** by violent force **4 pura sangre :** thoroughbred

sangría *nf* **1 :** bloodletting **2 :** sangria (wine punch) **3 :** drain, draining <una sangría fiscal : a financial drain> **4 :** indentation, indenting

sangriento, -ta *adj* **1 :** bloody **2 :** cruel

sanguijuela *nf* **1 :** leech, bloodsucker **2 :** sponger, leech

sanguinario, -ria *adj* **:** bloodthirsty

sanguíneo, -nea *adj* **1 :** blood <vaso sanguíneo : blood vessel> **2 :** sanguine, ruddy

sanidad *nf* **1 :** health **2 :** public health, sanitation

sanitario[1], **-ria** *adj* **1** : sanitary **2** : health <centro sanitario : health center>

sanitario[2], **-ria** *n* : sanitation worker

sanitario[3] *nm Col, Mex, Ven* : toilet <los sanitarios : the toilets, the restroom>

sano, -na *adj* **1** SALUDABLE : healthy **2** : wholesome **3** : whole, intact

santiaguino, -na *adj* : of or from Santiago, Chile

santiamén *nm* **en un santiamén** : in no time at all

santidad *nf* : holiness, sanctity

santificar {72} *vt* : to sanctify, to consecrate, to hallow

santiguarse {10} *vr* PERSIGNARSE : to cross oneself

santo[1], **-ta** *adj* **1** : holy, saintly <el Santo Padre : the Holy Father> <una vida santa : a saintly life> **2 Santo, Santa** (**San** *before names of masculine saints except those beginning with D or T*) : Saint <Santa Clara : Saint Claire> <Santo Tomás : Saint Thomas> <San Francisco : Saint Francis>

santo[2], **-ta** *n* : saint

santo[3] *nm* **1** : saint's day **2** CUMPLEAÑOS : birthday

santuario *nm* : sanctuary

santurrón, -rrona *adj, mpl* **-rrones** : overly pious, sanctimonious — **santurronamente** *adv*

saña *nf* **1** : fury, rage **2** : viciousness <con saña : viciously>

sapo *nm* : toad

saque[1], **etc.** → **sacar**

saque[2] *nm* **1** : kick-off (in soccer or football) **2** : serve, service (in sports)

saqueador, -dora *n* DEPREDADOR : plunderer, looter

saquear *vt* : to sack, to plunder, to loot

saqueo *nm* DEPREDACIÓN : sacking, plunder, looting

sarampión *nm* : measles *pl*

sarape *nm CA, Mex* : serape, blanket

sarcasmo *nm* : sarcasm

sarcástico, -ca *adj* : sarcastic

sarcófago *nm* : sarcophagus

sardina *nf* : sardine

sardónico, -ca *adj* : sardonic

sarga *nf* : serge

sargento *nmf* : sergeant

sarna *nf* : mange

sarnoso, -sa *adj* : mangy

sarpullido *nm* ERUPCIÓN : rash

sarro *nm* **1** : deposit, coating **2** : tartar, plaque

sartén *nmf, pl* **sartenes 1** : frying pan **2 tener la sartén por el mango** : to call the shots, to be in control

sasafrás *nm* : sassafras

sastre, -tra *n* : tailor

sastrería *nf* **1** : tailoring **2** : tailor's shop

Satanás *or* **Satán** *nm* : Satan, the devil

satánico, -ca *adj* : satanic

satélite *nm* : satellite

satín *or* **satén** *nm, pl* **satines** *or* **satenes** : satin

satinado, -da *adj* : satiny, glossy

sátira *nf* : satire

satírico, -ca *adj* : satirical, satiric

satirizar {21} *vt* : to satirize

sátiro *nm* : satyr

satisfacción *nf, pl* **-ciones** : satisfaction

satisfacer {74} *vt* **1** : to satisfy **2** : to fulfill, to meet **3** : to pay, to settle — **satisfacerse** *vr* **1** : to be satisfied **2** : to take revenge

satisfactorio, -ria *adj* : satisfactory — **satisfactoriamente** *adv*

satisfecho, -cha *adj* : satisfied, content, pleased

saturación *nf, pl* **-ciones** : saturation

saturar *vt* **1** : to saturate, to fill up **2** : to satiate, to surfeit

saturnismo *nm* : lead poisoning

Saturno *nm* : Saturn

sauce *nm* : willow

saúco *nm* : elder (tree)

saudí *or* **saudita** *adj & nmf* : Saudi, Saudi Arabian

sauna *nmf* : sauna

savia *nf* : sap

saxofón *nm, pl* **-fones** : saxophone

sazón[1] *nf, pl* **sazones 1** : flavor, seasoning **2** : ripeness, maturity <en sazón : in season, ripe> **3 a la sazón** : at that time, then

sazón[2] *nmf, pl* **sazones** *Mex* : flavor, seasoning

sazonar *vt* CONDIMENTAR : to season, to spice

sé → **saber, ser**

se *pron* **1** : to him, to her, to you, to them <se los daré a ella : I'll give them to her> **2** : each other, one another <se abrazaron : they hugged each other> **3** : himself, herself, itself, yourself, yourselves, themselves <se afeitó antes de salir : he shaved before leaving> **4** (*used in passive constructions*) <se dice que es hermosa : they say she's beautiful> <se habla inglés : English spoken>

sea, etc. → **ser**

sebo *nm* **1** : grease, fat **2** : tallow **3** : suet

secado *nm* : drying

secador *nm* : hair dryer

secadora *nf* **1** : dryer, clothes dryer **2** *Mex* : hair dryer

secante *nm* : blotting paper, blotter

secar {72} *v* : to dry — **secarse** *vr* **1** : to get dry **2** : to dry up

sección *nf, pl* **secciones 1** : section <sección transversal : cross section> **2** : department, division

seco, -ca *adj* **1** : dry **2** DISECADO : dried <fruta seca : dried fruit> **3** : thin, lean **4** : curt, brusque **5** : sharp <un golpe seco : a sharp blow> **6 a secas** : simply, just <se llama Chico, a secas : he's just called Chico> **7 en ~**

: abruptly, suddenly <frenar en seco : to make a sudden stop>

secoya *nf* : sequoia, redwood

secreción *nf, pl* **-ciones** : secretion

secretar *vt* : to secrete

secretaría *nf* **1** : secretariat, administrative department **2** *Mex* : ministry, cabinet office

secretariado *nm* **1** : secretariat **2** : secretarial profession

secretario, -ria *n* : secretary — **secretarial** *adj*

secreto[1], -ta *adj* **1** : secret **2** : secretive — **secretamente** *adv*

secreto[2] *nm* **1** : secret **2** : secrecy

secta *nf* : sect

sectario, -ria *adj & n* : sectarian

sector *nm* : sector

secuaz *nmf, pl* **secuaces** : follower, henchman, underling

secuela *nf* : consequence, sequel <las secuelas de la guerra : the aftermath of the war>

secuencia *nf* : sequence

secuestrador, -dora *n* **1** : kidnapper, abductor **2** : hijacker

secuestrar *vt* **1** RAPTAR : to kidnap, to abduct **2** : to hijack, to commandeer **3** CONFISCAR : to confiscate, to seize

secuestro *nm* **1** RAPTO : kidnapping, abduction **2** : hijacking **3** : seizure, confiscation

secular *adj* : secular — **secularismo** *nm* — **secularización** *nf*

secundar *vt* : to support, to second

secundaria *nf* **1** : secondary education, high school **2** *Mex* : junior high school, middle school

secundario, -ria *adj* : secondary

secuoya *nf* : sequoia

sed *nf* **1** : thirst <tener sed : to be thirsty> **2 tener sed de** : to hunger for, to thirst for

seda *nf* : silk

sedación *nf, pl* **-ciones** : sedation

sedal *nm* : fishing line

sedán *nm, pl* **sedanes** : sedan

sedante *adj & nm* CALMANTE : sedative

sedar *vt* : to sedate

sede *nf* **1** : seat, headquarters **2** : venue, site **3 la Santa Sede** : the Holy See

sedentario, -ria *adj* : sedentary

sedición *nf, pl* **-ciones** : sedition — **sedicioso, -sa** *adj*

sediento, -ta *adj* : thirsty, thirsting

sedimentación *nf, pl* **-ciones** : sedimentation

sedimentario, -ria *adj* : sedimentary

sedimento *nm* : sediment

sedoso, -sa *adj* : silky, silken

seducción *nf, pl* **-ciones** : seduction

seducir {61} *vt* **1** : to seduce **2** : to captivate, to charm

seductivo, -va *adj* : seductive

seductor[1], -tora *adj* **1** SEDUCTIVO : seductive **2** ENCANTADOR : charming, alluring

seductor[2], -tora *n* : seducer

segar {49} *vt* **1** : to reap, to harvest, to cut **2** : to sever abruptly <una vida segada por la enfermedad : a life cut short by illness>

seglar[1] *adj* LAICO : lay, secular

seglar[2] *nm* LAICO : layperson, layman *m,* laywoman *f*

segmentación *nm, pl* **-ciones** : segmentation

segmentado, -da *adj* : segmented

segmento *nm* : segment

segregar {52} *vt* **1** : to segregate **2** SECRETAR : to secrete

seguida *nf* **en ~** : right away, immediately <vuelvo en seguida : I'll be right back>

seguidamente *adv* **1** : next, immediately after **2** : without a break, continuously

seguido[1] *adv* **1** RECTO : straight, straight ahead **2** : often, frequently

seguido[2], -da *adj* **1** CONSECUTIVO : consecutive, successive <tres días seguidos : three days in a row> **2** : straight, unbroken **3 ~ por** *or* **~ de** : followed by

seguidor, -dora *n* : follower, supporter

seguimiento *nm* **1** : following, pursuit **2** : continuation **3** : tracking, monitoring

seguir {75} *vt* **1** : to follow <el sol sigue la lluvia : sunshine follows the rain> <seguiré tu consejo : I'll follow your advice> <me siguieron con la mirada : they followed me with their eyes> **2** : to go along, to keep on <seguimos toda la carretera panamericana : we continued along the Pan-American Highway> <siguió hablando : he kept on talking> <seguir el curso : to stay on course> **3** : to take (a course, a treatment) — *vi* **1** : to go on, to keep going <sigue adelante : keep going, carry on> **2** : to remain, to continue to be <¿todavía sigues aquí? : you're still here?> <sigue con vida : she's still alive> **3** : to follow, to come after <la frase que sigue : the following sentence>

según[1] *adv* : it depends <según y como : it all depends on>

según[2] *conj* **1** COMO, CONFORME : as, just as <según lo dejé : just as I left it> **2** : depending on how <según se vea : depending on how one sees it>

según[3] *prep* **1** : according to <según los rumores : according to the rumors> **2** : depending on <según los resultados : depending on the results>

segundo[1], -da *adj* : second <el segundo lugar : second place>

segundo[2], -da *n* **1** : second (in a series) **2** : second (person), second-in-command

segundo[3] *nm* : second <sesenta segundos : sixty seconds>

seguramente *adv* **1** : for sure, surely **2** : probably

seguridad *nf* **1** : safety, security **2** : (financial) security <seguridad social : Social Security> **3** CERTEZA : certainty, assurance <con toda seguridad : with complete certainty> **4** : confidence, self-confidence

seguro[1] *adv* : certainly, definitely <va a llover, seguro : it's going to rain for sure> <¡seguro que sí! : of course!>

seguro[2], **-ra** *adj* **1** : safe, secure **2** : sure, certain <estoy segura que es él : I'm sure that's him> **3** : reliable, trustworthy **4** : self-assured

seguro[3] *nm* **1** : insurance <seguro de vida : life insurance> **2** : fastener, clasp **3** *Mex* : safety pin

seis *adj & nm* : six

seiscientos[1], **-tas** *adj* : six hundred

seiscientos[2] *nms & pl* : six hundred

selección *nf, pl* **-ciones 1** ELECCIÓN : selection, choice **2 selección natural** : natural selection

seleccionar *vt* ELEGIR : to select, to choose

selectivo, -va *adj* : selective — **selectivamente** *adv*

selecto, -ta *adj* **1** : choice, select **2** EXCLUSIVO : exclusive

selenio *nm* : selenium

sellar *vt* **1** : to seal **2** : to stamp

sello *nm* **1** : seal **2** ESTAMPILLA, TIMBRE : postage stamp **3** : hallmark, characteristic

selva *nf* **1** BOSQUE : woods *pl*, forest <selva húmeda : rain forest> **2** JUNGLA : jungle

selvático, -ca *adj* **1** : forest, jungle <sendero selvático : jungle path> **2** : wild

semáforo *nm* **1** : traffic light **2** : stop signal

semana *nf* : week

semanal *adj* : weekly — **semanalmente** *adv*

semanario *nm* : weekly (publication)

semántica *nf* : semantics

semántico, -ca *adj* : semantic

semblante *nm* **1** : countenance, face **2** : appearance, look

semblanza *nf* : biographical sketch, profile

sembrado *nm* : cultivated field

sembrador, -dora *n* : planter, sower

sembradora *nf* : seeder (machine)

sembrar {55} *vt* **1** : to plant, to sow **2** : to scatter, to strew <sembrar el pánico : to spread panic>

semejante[1] *adj* **1** PARECIDO : similar, alike **2** TAL : such <nunca he visto cosa semejante : I have never seen such a thing>

semejante[2] *nm* PRÓJIMO : fellowman

semejanza *nf* PARECIDO : similarity, resemblance

semejar *vi* : to resemble, to look like — **semejarse** *vr* : to be similar, to look alike

semen *nm* : semen

semental *nm* : stud (animal) <caballo semental : stallion>

semestre *nm* : semester

semicírculo *nm* : semicircle, half circle

semiconductor *nm* : semiconductor

semidiós *nm, pl* **-dioses** : demigod *m*

semifinal *nf* : semifinal

semifinalista[1] *adj* : semifinal

semifinalista[2] *nmf* : semifinalist

semiformal *adj* : semiformal

semilla *nf* : seed

semillero *nm* **1** : seedbed **2** : hotbed, breeding ground

seminario *nm* **1** : seminary **2** : seminar, graduate course

seminarista *nm* : seminarian

semiprecioso, -sa *adj* : semiprecious

semita[1] *adj* : Semitic

semita[2] *nmf* : Semite

sémola *nf* : semolina

sempiterno, -na *adj* ETERNO : eternal, everlasting

senado *nm* : senate

senador, -dora *n* : senator

sencillamente *adv* : simply, plainly

sencillez *nf* : simplicity

sencillo[1], **-lla** *adj* **1** : simple, easy **2** : plain, unaffected **3** : single

sencillo[2] *nm* **1** : single (recording) **2** : small change (coins) **3** : one-way ticket

senda *nf* CAMINO, SENDERO : path, way

sendero *nm* CAMINO, SENDA : path, way

sendos, -das *adj pl* : each, both <llevaban sendos vestidos nuevos : they were each wearing a new dress>

senectud *nf* ANCIANIDAD : old age

senegalés, -lesa *adj & n, mpl* **-leses** : Senegalese

senil *adj* : senile — **senilidad** *nf*

seno *nm* **1** : breast, bosom <los senos : the breasts> <el seno de la familia : the bosom of the family> **2** : sinus **3 seno materno** : womb

sensación *nf, pl* **-ciones 1** IMPRESIÓN : feeling <tener la sensación : to have a feeling> **2** : sensation <causar sensación : to cause a sensation>

sensacional *adj* : sensational

sensacionalista *adj* : sensationalistic, lurid

sensatez *nf* **1** : good sense **2 con ~** : sensibly

sensato, -ta *n* : sensible, sound — **sensatamente** *adv*

sensibilidad *nf* **1** : sensitivity, sensibility **2** SENSACIÓN : feeling

sensibilizar {21} *vt* : to sensitize

sensible *adj* **1** : sensitive **2** APRECIABLE : considerable, significant

sensiblemente *adv* : considerably, significantly

sensiblería *nf* : sentimentality, mush

sensiblero, -ra *adj* : mawkish, sentimental, mushy

sensitivo, -va *adj* **1** : sense <órganos sensitivos : sense organs> **2** : sentient, capable of feeling

sensor *nm* : sensor

sensorial *adj* **:** sensory

sensual *adj* **:** sensual, sensuous — **sensualmente** *adv*

sensualidad *nf* **:** sensuality

sentado, -da *adj* **1 :** sitting, seated **2 :** established, settled <dar por sentado : to take for granted> <dejar sentado : to make clear> **3 :** sensible, steady, judicious

sentar {55} *vt* **1 :** to seat, to sit **2 :** to establish, to set — *vi* **1 :** to suit <ese color te sienta : that color suits you> **2 :** to agree with (of food or drink) <las cebollas no me sientan : onions don't agree with me> **3 :** to please <le sentó mal el paseo : she didn't enjoy the trip> — **sentarse** *vr* **:** to sit, to sit down <siéntese, por favor : please have a seat>

sentencia *nf* **1 :** sentence, judgment **2 :** maxim, saying

sentenciar *vt* **:** to sentence

sentido[1], -da *adj* **1 :** heartfelt, sincere <mi más sentido pésame : my sincerest condolences> **2 :** touchy, sensitive **3 :** offended, hurt

sentido[2] *nm* **1 :** sense <sentido común : common sense> <los cinco sentidos : the five senses> <sin sentido : senseless> **2** CONOCIMIENTO **:** consciousness **3** SIGNIFICADO **:** meaning, sense <doble sentido : double entendre> **4 :** direction <calle de sentido único : one-way street>

sentimental[1] *adj* **1 :** sentimental **2 :** love, romantic <vida sentimental : love life>

sentimental[2] *nmf* **:** sentimentalist

sentimentalismo *nm* **:** sentimentality, sentimentalism

sentimiento *nm* **1 :** feeling, emotion **2** PESAR **:** regret, sorrow

sentir {76} *vt* **1 :** to feel, to experience <no siento nada de dolor : I don't feel any pain> <sentía sed : he was feeling thirsty> <sentir amor : to feel love> **2** PERCIBIR **:** to perceive, to sense <sentir un ruido : to hear a noise> **3** LAMENTAR **:** to regret, to feel sorry for <lo siento mucho : I'm very sorry> — *vi* **1 :** to have feeling, to feel **2 sin ~ :** without noticing, inadvertently — **sentirse** *vr* **1 :** to feel <¿te sientes mejor? : are you feeling better?> **2** *Chile, Mex* **:** to take offense

seña *nf* **1 :** sign, signal **2 dar señas de :** to show signs of

señal *nf* **1 :** signal **2 :** sign <señal de tráfico : traffic sign> **3** INDICIO **:** indication <en señal de : as a token of> **4** VESTIGIO **:** trace, vestige **5 :** scar, mark **6 :** deposit, down payment

señalado, -da *adj* **:** distinguished, notable

señalador *nm* **:** marker <señalador de libros : bookmark>

señalar *vt* **1** INDICAR **:** to indicate, to show **2 :** to mark **3 :** to point out, to stress **4 :** to fix, to set — **señalarse** *vr* **:** to distinguish oneself

señor, -ñora *n* **1 :** gentleman *m,* man *m,* lady *f,* woman *f,* wife *f* **2 :** Sir *m,* Madam *f* <estimados señores : Dear Sirs> **3 :** Mr. *m,* Mrs. *f* **4 :** lord *m,* lady *f* <el Señor : the Lord>

señoría *nf* **1 :** lordship **2 Su Señoría :** Your Honor

señorial *adj* **:** stately, regal

señorío *nm* **1 :** manor, estate **2 :** dominion, power **3 :** elegance, class

señorita *nf* **1 :** young lady, young woman **2 :** Miss

señuelo *nm* **1 :** decoy **2 :** bait

sépalo *nm* **:** sepal

sepa, etc. → **saber**

separación *nf, pl* **-ciones 1 :** separation, division **2 :** gap, space

separadamente *adv* **:** separately, apart

separado, -da *adj* **1 :** separated **2 :** separate <vidas separadas : separate lives> **3 por ~ :** separately

separar *vt* **1 :** to separate, to divide **2 :** to split up, to pull apart — **separarse** *vr*

sepelio *nm* **:** interment, burial

sepia[1] *adj & nm* **:** sepia

sepia[2] *nf* **:** cuttlefish

septentrional *adj* **:** northern

séptico, -ca *adj* **:** septic

septiembre *nm* **:** September

séptimo[1], -ma *adj* **:** seventh

séptimo[2] *nm* **:** seventh

septuagésimo[1], -ma *adj* **:** seventieth

septuagésimo[2] *nm* **:** seventieth

sepulcral *adj* **1 :** sepulcral **2 :** dismal, gloomy

sepulcro *nm* TUMBA **:** tomb, sepulchre

sepultar *vt* ENTERRAR **:** to bury

sepultura *nf* **1 :** burial **2** TUMBA **:** grave, tomb

seque, etc. → **secar**

sequedad *nf* **1 :** dryness **2 :** brusqueness, curtness

sequía *nf* **:** drought

séquito *nm* **:** retinue, entourage

ser[1] {77} *vi* **1 :** to be <él es mi hermano : he is my brother> <Camila es linda : Camila is pretty> **2 :** to exist, to live <ser, o no ser : to be or not to be> **3 :** to take place, to occur <el concierto es el domingo : the concert is on Sunday> **4** (*used with expressions of time, date, season*) <son las diez : it's ten o'clock> <hoy es el 9 : today's the 9th> **5 :** to cost, to come to <¿cuánto es? : how much is it?> **6** (*with the future tense*) **:** to be able to be <¿será posible? : can it be possible?> **7 ~ de :** to come from <somos de Managua : we're from Managua> **8 ~ de :** to belong to <ese lápiz es de Juan : that's Juan's pencil> **9 es que :** the thing is that <es que no lo conozco : it's just that I don't know him> **10 ¡sea! :** agreed!, all right! **11 sea . . . sea :** either . . . or — *v aux* (*used in passive constructions*) **:** to be <la cuenta

ha sido pagada : the bill has been paid> <él fue asesinado : he was murdered>

ser[2] *nm* : being <ser humano : human being>

seráfico, -ca *adj* : angelic, seraphic

serbio[1]**, -bia** *adj & n* : Serb, Serbian

serbio[2] *nm* : Serbian (language)

serbocroata[1] *adj* : Serbo-Croatian

serbocroata[2] *nm* : Serbo-Croatian (language)

serenar *vt* : to calm, to soothe — **serenarse** *vr* CALMARSE : to calm down

serenata *nf* : serenade

serendipia *nf* : serendipity

serenidad *nf* : serenity, calmness

sereno[1]**, -na** *adj* **1** SOSEGADO : serene, calm, composed **2** : fair, clear (of weather) **3** : calm, still (of the sea) — **serenamente** *adv*

sereno[2] *nm* : night watchman

seriado, -da *adj* : serial

serial *nm* : serial (on radio or television)

seriamente *adv* : seriously

serie *nf* **1** : series **2** SERIAL : serial **3 fabricación en serie** : mass production **4 fuera de serie** : extraordinary, amazing

seriedad *nf* **1** : seriousness, earnestness **2** : gravity, importance

serio, -ria *adj* **1** : serious, earnest **2** : reliable, responsible **3** : important **4 en ~** : seriously, in earnest — **seriamente** *adv*

sermón *nm, pl* **sermones 1** : sermon **2** *fam* : harangue, lecture

sermonear *vt fam* : to harangue, to lecture

serpentear *vi* : to twist, to wind — **serpenteante** *adj*

serpentina *nf* : paper streamer

serpiente *nf* : serpent, snake

serrado, -da *adj* DENTADO : serrated

serranía *nf* : mountainous area

serrano, -na *adj* : from the mountains

serrar {55} *vt* : to saw

serrín *nm, pl* **serrines** : sawdust

serruchar *vt* : to saw up

serrucho *nm* : saw, handsaw

servicentro *nm Peru* : gas station

servicial *adj* : obliging, helpful

servicio *nm* **1** : service **2** SAQUE : serve (in sports) **3 servicios** *nmpl* : restroom

servidor, -dora *n* **1** : servant **2 su seguro servidor** : yours truly (in correspondence)

servidumbre *nf* **1** : servitude **2** : help, servants *pl*

servil *adj* **1** : servile, subservient **2** : menial

servilismo *nm* : servility, subservience

servilleta *nf* : napkin

servir {54} *vt* **1** : to serve, to be of use to **2** : to serve, to wait **3** SURTIR : to fill (an order) — *vi* **1** : to work <mi radio no sirve : my radio isn't working> **2** : to be of use, to be helpful <esa computadora no sirve para nada : that computer's perfectly useless> — **servirse** *vr* **1** : to help oneself to **2** : to be kind enough <sírvase enviarnos un catálogo : please send us a catalog>

sésamo *nm* AJONJOLÍ : sesame, sesame seeds *pl*

sesenta *adj & nm* : sixty

sesentavo[1]**, -va** *adj* : sixtieth

sesentavo[2] *n* : sixtieth (fraction)

sesgado, -da *adj* **1** : inclined, tilted **2** : slanted, biased

sesgar {52} *vt* **1** : to cut on the bias **2** : to tilt **3** : to bias, to slant

sesgo *nm* : bias

sesgue, etc. → **sesgar**

sesión *nf, pl* **sesiones 1** : session **2** : showing, performance

sesionar *vi* REUNIRSE : to meet, to be in session

seso *nm* **1** : brains, intelligence **2 sesos** *nmpl* : brains (as food)

sesudo, -da *adj* **1** : prudent, sensible **2** : brainy

set *nm, pl* **sets** : set (in tennis)

seta *nf* : mushroom

setecientos[1]**, -tas** *adj* : seven hundred

setecientos[2] *nms & pl* : seven hundred

setenta *adj & nm* : seventy

setentavo[1]**, -va** *adj* : seventieth

setentavo[2] *nm* : seventieth

setiembre *nm* → **septiembre**

seto *nm* **1** : fence, enclosure **2 seto vivo** : hedge

seudónimo *nm* : pseudonym

severidad *nf* **1** : harshness, severity **2** : strictness

severo, -ra *adj* **1** : harsh, severe **2** ESTRICTO : strict — **severamente** *adv*

sexagésimo[1]**, -ma** *adj* : sixtieth, sixty-

sexagésimo[2]**, -ma** *n* : sixtieth, sixty- (in a series)

sexismo *nm* : sexism — **sexista** *adj & nmf*

sexo *nm* : sex

sextante *nm* : sextant

sexteto *nm* : sextet

sexto, -ta *adj* : sixth — **sexto, -ta** *n*

sexual *adj* : sexual, sex <educación sexual : sex education> — **sexualmente** *adv*

sexualidad *nf* : sexuality

sexy *adj, pl* **sexy** *or* **sexys** : sexy

shock [ˈʃɔk, ˈtʃɔk] *nm* : shock <estado de shock : state of shock>

short *nm, pl* **shorts** : shorts *pl*

show *nm, pl* **shows** : show

si *conj* **1** : if <lo haré si me pagan : I'll do it if they pay me> <si lo supiera te lo diría : if I knew it I would tell you> **2** : whether, if <no importa si funciona o no : it doesn't matter whether it works (or not)> **3** (*expressing desire, protest, or surprise*) <si supiera la verdad : if only I knew the truth> <¡si no quiero! : but I don't want to!> **4 si bien** : although <si bien se ha progresado : although progress has been made> **5 si no** : otherwise, or else <si no, no voy : otherwise I won't go>

sí[1] *adv* **1** : yes <sí, gracias : yes, please> <creo que sí : I think so> **2 sí que** : indeed, absolutely <esta vez sí que ganaré : this time I'm sure to win> **3 porque sí** *fam* : because, just because <lo hizo porque sí : she did it just because>

sí[2] *nm* : yes <dar el sí : to say yes, to express consent>

sí[3] *pron* **1 de por sí** *or* **en sí** : by itself, in itself, per se **2 fuera de sí** : beside oneself **3 para sí (mismo)** : to himself, to herself, for himself, for herself **4 entre ~** : among themselves

siamés, -mesa *adj & n, mpl* **siameses** : Siamese

sibilante *adj & nf* : sibilant

siciliano, -na *adj & n* : Sicilian

sico- → **psico-**

sicomoro *or* **sicómoro** *nm* : sycamore

SIDA *or* **sida** *nm* : AIDS

siderurgia *nf* : iron and steel industry

siderúrgico, -ca *adj* : steel, iron <the steel industry : la industria siderúrgica>

sidra *nf* : hard cider

siega[1], **siegue, etc.** → **segar**

siega[2] *nf* **1** : harvesting **2** : harvest time **3** : harvested crop

siembra[1], **etc.** → **sembrar**

siembra[2] *nf* **1** : sowing **2** : sowing season **3** SEMBRADO : cultivated field

siempre *adv* **1** : always <siempre tienes hambre : you're always hungry> **2** : still <¿siempre te vas? : are you still going?> **3** *Mex* : after all <siempre no fui : I didn't go after all> **4 siempre que** : whenever, every time <siempre que pasa : every time he walks by> **5 para ~** : forever, for good **6 siempre y cuando** : provided that

sien *nf* : temple (on the forehead)

sienta, etc. → **sentar**

siente, etc. → **sentir**

sierpe *nf* : serpent, snake

sierra[1], **etc.** → **serrar**

sierra[2] *nf* **1** : saw <sierra de vaivén : jigsaw> **2** CORDILLERA : mountain range **3** : mountains *pl* <viven en la sierra : they live in the mountains>

siervo, -va *n* **1** : slave **2** : serf

siesta *nf* : nap, siesta

siete *adj & nm* : seven

sífilis *nf* : syphilis

sifón *nm, pl* **sifones** : siphon

siga, sigue, etc. → **seguir**

sigilo *nm* : secrecy, stealth

sigiloso, -sa *adj* FURTIVO : furtive, stealthy — **sigilosamente** *adv*

sigla *nf* : acronym, abbreviation

siglo *nm* **1** : century **2** : age <el Siglo de Oro : the Golden Age> <hace siglos que no te veo : I haven't seen you in ages> **3** : world, secular life

signar *vt* : to sign (a treaty or agreement)

signatario, -ria *n* : signatory

significación *nf, pl* **-ciones 1** : significance, importance **2** : signification, meaning

significado *nm* **1** : sense, meaning **2** : significance

significante *adj* : significant

significar {72} *vt* **1** : to mean, to signify **2** : to express, to make known — **significarse** *vr* **1** : to draw attention, to become known **2** : to take a stance

significativo, -va *adj* **1** : significant, important **2** : meaningful — **significativamente** *adv*

signo *nm* **1** : sign <signo de igual : equal sign> <un signo de alegría : a sign of happiness> **2** : (punctuation) mark <signo de interrogación : question mark> <signo de admiración : exclamation point> <signo de intercalación : caret>

siguiente *adj* : next, following

sílaba *nf* : syllable

silábico, -ca *adj* : syllabic

silbar *v* : to whistle

silbato *nm* PITO : whistle

silbido *nm* : whistle, whistling

silenciador *nm* **1** : muffler (of an automobile) **2** : silencer

silenciar *vt* **1** : to silence **2** : to muffle

silencio *nm* **1** : silence, quiet <¡silencio! : be quiet!> **2** : rest (in music)

silencioso, -sa *adj* : silent, quiet — **silenciosamente** *adv*

sílice *nf* : silica

silicio *nm* : silicon

silla *nf* **1** : chair **2 silla de ruedas** : wheelchair

sillón *nm, pl* **sillones** : armchair, easy chair

silo *nm* : silo

silueta *nf* **1** : silhouette **2** : figure, shape

silvestre *adj* : wild <flor silvestre : wildflower>

silvicultor, -tora *n* : forester

silvicultura *nf* : forestry

sima *nf* ABISMO : chasm, abyss

simbólico, -ca *adj* : symbolic — **simbólicamente** *adj*

simbolismo *nm* : symbolism

simbolizar {21} *vt* : to symbolize

símbolo *nm* : symbol

simetría *nf* : symmetry

simétrico, -ca *adj* : symmetrical, symmetric

simiente *nf* : seed

símil *nm* **1** : simile **2** : analogy, comparison

similar *adj* SEMEJANTE : similar, alike

similitud *nf* : similarity, resemblance

simio *nm* : ape

simpatía *nf* **1** : liking, affection <tomarle simpatía a : to take a liking to> **2** : warmth, friendliness **3** : support, solidarity

simpático, -ca *adj* : nice, friendly, likeable

simpatizante *nf* : sympathizer, supporter

simpatizar {21} *vi* **1** : to get along, to hit it off <simpaticé mucho con él : I really liked him> **2 ~ con** : to sympathize with, to support
simple¹ *adj* **1** SENCILLO : plain, simple, easy **2** : pure, mere <por simple vanidad : out of pure vanity> **3** : simpleminded, foolish
simple² *n* : fool, simpleton
simplemente *adv* : simply, merely, just
simpleza *nf* **1** : foolishness, simpleness **2** NECEDAD : nonsense
simplicidad *nf* : simplicity
simplificar {72} *vt* : to simplify — **simplificación** *nf*
simposio *or* **simposium** *nm* : symposium
simulación *nf, pl* **-ciones** : simulation
simulacro *nm* : imitation, sham <simulacro de juicio : mock trial>
simular *vt* **1** : to simulate **2** : to feign, to pretend
simultáneo, -nea *adj* : simultaneous — **simultáneamente** *adv*
sin *prep* **1** : without <sin querer : unintentionally> <sin refinar : unrefined> **2 sin que** : without <lo hicimos sin que él se diera cuenta : we did it without him noticing>
sinagoga *nf* : synagogue
sinceridad *nf* : sincerity
sincero, -ra *adj* : sincere, honest, true — **sinceramente** *adv*
síncopa *nf* : syncopation
sincopar *vt* : to syncopate
sincronizar {21} *vt* : to synchronize — **sincronización** *nf*
sindical *adj* GREMIAL : union, labor <representante sindical : union representative>
sindicalización *nf, pl* **-ciones** : unionizing, unionization
sindicalizar {21} *vt* : to unionize — **sindicalizarse** *vr* **1** : to form a union **2** : to join a union
sindicar → **sindicalizar**
sindicato *nm* GREMIO : union, guild
síndrome *nm* : syndrome
sinecura *nf* : sinecure
sinfín *nm* : endless number <un sinfín de problemas : no end of problems>
sinfonía *nf* : symphony
sinfónica *nf* : symphony orchestra
sinfónico, -ca *adj* : symphonic, symphony
singular¹ *adj* **1** : singular, unique **2** PARTICULAR : peculiar, odd **3** : singular (in grammar) — **singularmente** *adv*
singular² *nm* : singular
singularidad *nf* : uniqueness, singularity
singularizar {21} *vt* : to make unique or distinct — **singularizarse** *vr* : to stand out, to distinguish oneself
siniestrado, -da *adj* : damaged, wrecked <zona siniestrada : disaster zone>
siniestro¹, -tra *adj* **1** IZQUIERDO : left, left-hand **2** MALVADO : sinister, evil
siniestro² *nm* : accident, disaster
sinnúmero → **sinfín**
sino *conj* **1** : but, rather <no será hoy, sino mañana : it won't be today, but tomorrow> **2** EXCEPTO : but, except <no hace sino despertar suspicacias : it does nothing but arouse suspicion>
sinónimo¹, -ma *adj* : synonymous
sinónimo² *nm* : synonym
sinopsis *nfs & pl* RESUMEN : synopsis, summary
sinrazón *nf, pl* **-zones** : wrong, injustice
sinsabores *nmpl* : woes, troubles
sinsonte *nm* : mockingbird
sintáctico, -ca *adj* : syntactic, syntactical
sintaxis *nfs & pl* : syntax
síntesis *nfs & pl* **1** : synthesis, fusion **2** SINOPSIS : synopsis, summary
sintético, -ca *adj* : synthetic — **sintéticamente** *adv*
sintetizar {21} *vt* **1** : to synthesize **2** RESUMIR : to summarize
sintió, etc. → **sentir**
síntoma *nm* : symptom
sintomático, -ca *adj* : symptomatic
sintonía *nf* **1** : tuning in (of a radio) **2 en sintonía con** : in tune with, attuned to
sintonizador *nm* : tuner, knob for tuning (of a radio, etc.)
sintonizar {21} *vt* : to tune (in) to — *vi* **1** : to tune in **2 ~ con** : to be in tune with, to empathize with
sinuosidad *nf* : sinuosity
sinuoso, -sa *adj* **1** : winding, sinuous **2** : devious
sinvergüenza¹ *adj* **1** DESCARADO : shameless, brazen, impudent **2** TRAVIESO : naughty
sinvergüenza² *nmf* **1** : rogue, scoundrel **2** : brat, rascal
sionista *adj & nmf* : Zionist — **sionismo** *nm*
siqui- → **psiqui-**
siquiera *adv* **1** : at least <dame siquiera un poquito : at least give me a little bit> **2** (*in negative constructions*) : not even <ni siquiera nos saludaron : they didn't even say hello to us>
sirena *nf* **1** : mermaid **2** : siren <sirena de niebla : foghorn>
sirio, -ria *adj & n* : Syrian
sirope *nm* : syrup
sirve, etc. → **servir**
sirviente, -ta *n* : servant, maid *f*
sisal *nm* : sisal
sisear *vi* : to hiss
siseo *nm* : hiss
sísmico, -ca *adj* : seismic
sismo *nm* **1** TERREMOTO : earthquake **2** TEMBLOR : tremor
sismógrafo *nm* : seismograph
sistema *nm* : system

sistemático, -ca *adj* **:** systematic — **sistemáticamente** *adv*
sistematizar {21} *vt* **:** to systematize
sistémico, -ca *adj* **:** systemic
sitiar *vt* ASEDIAR **:** to besiege
sitio *nm* **1** LUGAR **:** place, site <vámonos a otro sitio **:** let's go somewhere else> **2** ESPACIO **:** room, space <hacer sitio a **:** to make room for> **3 :** siege <estado de sitio **:** state of siege> **4** *Mex* **:** taxi stand
situación *nf, pl* **-ciones :** situation
situado, -da *adj* **:** situated, placed
situar {3} *vt* UBICAR **:** to situate, to place, to locate — **situarse** *vr* **1 :** to be placed, to be located **2 :** to make a place for oneself, to do well
sketch *nm* **:** sketch, skit
slip *nm* **:** briefs *pl*, underpants *pl*
smog *nm* **:** smog
smoking *nm* ESMOQUIN **:** tuxedo
snob → **esnob**
so *prep* **:** under <so pena de **:** under penalty of>
sobaco *nm* **:** armpit
sobado, -da *adj* **1 :** worn, shabby **2 :** well-worn, hackneyed
sobar *vt* **1 :** to finger, to handle **2 :** to knead **3 :** to rub, to massage **4** *fam* **:** to beat, to pummel
soberanía *nf* **:** sovereignty
soberano, -na *adj & n* **:** sovereign
soberbia *nf* **1** ORGULLO **:** pride, arrogance **2** MAGNIFICENCIA **:** magnificence
soberbio, -bia *adj* **1 :** proud, arrogant **2 :** grand, magnificent
sobornable *adv* **:** venal, bribable
sobornar *vt* **:** to bribe
soborno *nm* **1 :** bribery **2 :** bribe
sobra *nf* **1 :** excess, surplus **2 de ~ :** extra, to spare **3 sobras** *nfpl* **:** leftovers, scraps
sobrado, -da *adj* **:** abundant, excessive, more than enough
sobrante[1] *adj* **:** remaining, superfluous
sobrante[2] *nm* **:** remainder, surplus
sobrar *vi* **:** to be in excess, to be superfluous <más vale que sobre a que falte **:** it's better to have too much than not enough>
sobre[1] *nm* **1 :** envelope **2 :** packet <un sobre de sazón **:** a packet of seasoning>
sobre[2] *prep* **1 :** on, on top of <sobre la mesa **:** on the table> **2 :** over, above **3 :** about <¿tiene libros sobre Bolivia? **:** do you have books on Bolivia?> **4 sobre todo :** especially, above all
sobrealimentar *vt* **:** to overfeed
sobrecalentar {55} *vt* **:** to overheat — **sobrecalentarse** *vr*
sobrecama *nmf* **:** bedspread
sobrecargar {52} *vt* **:** to overload, to overburden, to weigh down
sobrecoger {15} *vt* **1 :** to surprise, to startle **2 :** to scare — **sobrecogerse** *vr*
sobrecubierta *nf* **:** dust jacket
sobredosis *nfs & pl* **:** overdose
sobreentender {56} *vt* **:** to infer, to understand
sobreestimar *vt* **:** to overestimate, to overrate
sobreexitado, -da *adj* **:** overexcited
sobreexponer {60} *vt* **:** to overexpose
sobregirar *vt* **:** to overdraw
sobregiro *nm* **:** overdraft
sobrehumano, -na *adj* **:** superhuman
sobrellevar *vt* **:** to endure, to bear
sobremanera *adv* **:** exceedingly
sobremesa *nf* **:** after-dinner conversation
sobrenatural *adj* **:** supernatural
sobrenombre *nm* APODO **:** nickname
sobrentender → **sobreentender**
sobrepasar *vt* **:** to exceed, to surpass — **sobrepasarse** *vr* PASARSE **:** to go too far
sobrepelliz *nf, pl* **-pellices :** surplice
sobrepeso *nm* **1 :** excess weight **2 :** overweight, obesity
sobrepoblación, sobrepoblado → **superpoblación, superpoblado**
sobreponer {60} *vt* **1** SUPERPONER **:** to superimpose **2** ANTEPONER **:** to put first, to give priority to — **sobreponerse** *vr* **1 :** to pull oneself together **2 ~ a :** to overcome
sobreprecio *nm* **:** surcharge
sobreproducción *nf, pl* **-ciones :** overproduction
sobreproducir {61} *vt* **:** to overproduce
sobreprotector, -tora *adj* **:** overprotective
sobreproteger {15} *vt* **:** to overprotect
sobresaliente[1] *adj* **1 :** protruding, projecting **2 :** outstanding, noteworthy **3 :** significant, salient
sobresaliente[2] *nmf* **:** understudy
sobresalir {73} *vi* **1 :** to protrude, to jut out, to project **2 :** to stand out, to excel
sobresaltar *vt* **:** to startle, to frighten — **sobresaltarse** *vr*
sobresalto *nm* **:** start, fright
sobresueldo *nm* **:** bonus, additional pay
sobretasa *nf* **:** surcharge <sobretasa a la gasolina **:** gas tax>
sobretodo *nm* **:** overcoat
sobrevalorar *or* **sobrevaluar** {3} *vt* **:** to overvalue, to overrate
sobrevender *vt* **:** to oversell
sobrevenir {87} *vi* ACAECER **:** to take place, to come about <podrían sobrevenir complicaciones **:** complications could occur>
sobrevivencia *nf* → **supervivencia**
sobreviviente → **superviviente**
sobrevivir *vi* **:** to survive — *vt* **:** to outlive, to outlast
sobrevolar {19} *vt* **:** to fly over, to overfly
sobriedad *nf* **:** sobriety, moderation
sobrino, -na *n* **:** nephew *m,* niece *f*
sobrio, -bria *adj* **:** sober — **sobriamente** *adv*

socarrón, -rrona *adj, mpl* **-rrones 1** : sly, cunning **2** : sarcastic
socavar *vt* : to undermine
sociabilidad *nf* : sociability
sociable *adj* : sociable
social *adj* : social — **socialmente** *adv*
socialista *adj & nmf* : socialist — **socialismo** *nm*
sociedad *nf* **1** : society **2** : company, enterprise **3 sociedad anónima** : incorporated company
socio, -cia *n* **1** : member **2** : partner
socioeconómico, -ca *adj* : socioeconomic
sociología *nf* : sociology
sociológico, -ca *adj* : sociological — **sociológicamente** *adv*
sociólogo, -ga *n* : sociologist
socorrer *vt* : to assist, to come to the aid of
socorrido, -da *adj* ÚTIL : handy, practical
socorrista *nmf* **1** : rescue worker **2** : lifeguard
socorro *nm* AUXILIO **1** : aid, help <equipo de socorro : rescue team> **2 ¡socorro!** : help!
soda *nf* : soda, soda water
sodio *nf* : sodium
soez *adj, pl* **soeces** GROSERO : rude, vulgar — **soezmente** *adv*
sofá *nm* : couch, sofa
sofistería *nf* : sophistry — **sofista** *nmf*
sofisticación *nf, pl* **-ciones** : sophistication
sofisticado, -da *adj* : sophisticated
sofocante *adj* : suffocating, stifling
sofocar {72} *vt* **1** AHOGAR : to suffocate, to smother **2** EXTINGUIR : to extinguish, to put out (a fire) **3** APLASTAR : to crush, to put down <sofocar una rebelión : to crush a rebellion> — **sofocarse** *vr* **1** : to suffocate **2** *fam* : to get upset, to get mad
sofreír {66} *vt* : to sauté
sofrito[1], -ta *adj* : sautéed
sofrito[2] *nm* : seasoning sauce
softbol *nm* : softball
software *nm* : software
soga *nf* : rope
soja *nf* → **soya**
sojuzgar *vt* : to subdue, to conquer, to subjugate
sol *nm* **1** : sun **2** : Peruvian unit of currency
solamente *adv* SÓLO : only, just
solapa *nf* **1** : lapel (of a jacket) **2** : flap (of an envelope)
solapado, -da *adj* : secret, underhanded
solapar *vt* : to cover up, to keep secret — **solaparse** *vr* : to overlap
solar[1] {19} *vt* : to floor, to tile
solar[2] *adj* : solar, sun
solar[3] *nm* **1** TERRENO : lot, piece of land, site **2** *Cuba, Peru* : tenement building
solariego, -ga *adj* : ancestral
solaz *nm, pl* **solaces 1** CONSUELO : solace, comfort **2** DESCANSO : relaxation, recreation
solazarse {21} *vr* : to relax, to enjoy oneself
soldado *nm* **1** : soldier **2 soldado raso** : private, enlisted man
soldador[1], -dora *n* : welder
soldador[2] *nm* : soldering iron
soldadura *nf* **1** : welding **2** : soldering, solder
soldar {19} *vt* **1** : to weld **2** : to solder
soleado, -da *adj* : sunny
soledad *nf* : loneliness, solitude
solemne *adj* : solemn — **solemnemente** *adv*
solemnidad *nf* : solemnity
soler {78} *vi* : to be in the habit of, to tend to <solía tomar café por la tarde : she usually drank coffee in the afternoon> <eso suele ocurrir : that frequently happens>
solera *nf* **1** : prop, support **2** : tradition
solicitante *nmf* : applicant
solicitar *vt* **1** : to request, to solicit **2** : to apply for <solicitar empleo : to apply for employment>
solícito, -ta *adj* : solicitous, attentive, obliging
solicitud *nf* **1** : solicitude, concern **2** : request **3** : application
solidaridad *nf* : solidarity
solidario, -ria *adj* : supportive, united in support <se declararon solidarios con la nueva ley : they declared their support for the new law> <espíritu solidario : spirit of solidarity>
solidarizar {21} *vi* : to be in solidarity <solidarizamos con la huelga : we support the strike>
solidez *nf* **1** : solidity, firmness **2** : soundness (of an argument, etc.)
solidificar {72} *vt* : to solidify, to make solid — **solidificarse** *vr* — **solidificación** *nf*
sólido[1], -da *adj* **1** : solid, firm **2** : sturdy, well-made **3** : sound, well-founded — **sólidamente** *adv*
sólido[2] *nm* : solid
soliloquio *nm* : soliloquy
solista *nmf* : soloist
solitaria *nf* TENIA : tapeworm
solitario[1], -ria *adj* **1** : lonely **2** : lone, solitary **3** DESIERTO : deserted, lonely <una calle solitaria : a deserted street>
solitario[2], -ria *n* : recluse, loner
solitario[3] *nm* : solitaire
sollozar {21} *vi* : to sob
sollozo *nm* : sob
solo[1], -la *adj* **1** : alone, by oneself **2** : lonely **3** ÚNICO : only, sole, unique <hay un solo problema : there's only one problem> **4 a solas** : alone
solo[2] *nm* : solo
sólo *adv* SOLAMENTE : just, only <sólo quieren comer : they just want to eat>
solomillo *nm* : sirloin, loin
solsticio *nm* : solstice

soltar {19} *vt* **1 :** to let go of, to drop **2 :** to release, to set free **3** AFLOJAR **:** to loosen, to slacken

soltería *nf* **:** bachelorhood, spinsterhood

soltero[1], -ra *adj* **:** single, unmarried

soltero[2], -ra *n* **1 :** bachelor *m,* single man *m,* single woman *f* **2 apellido de soltera :** maiden name

soltura *nf* **1 :** looseness, slackness **2 :** fluency (of language) **3 :** agility, ease of movement

soluble *adj* **:** soluble — **solubilidad** *nf*

solución *nf, pl* **-ciones 1 :** solution (in a liquid) **2 :** answer, solution

solucionar *vt* RESOLVER **:** to solve, to resolve — **solucionarse** *vr*

solvencia *nf* **1 :** solvency **2 :** settling, payment (of debts) **3 :** reliability <solvencia moral : trustworthiness>

solvente[1] *adj* **1 :** solvent **2 :** reliable, trustworthy

solvente[2] *nm* **:** solvent

somalí *adj & nmf* **:** Somalian

sombra *nf* **1 :** shadow **2 :** shade **3 sombras** *nfpl* **:** darkness, shadows *pl* **4 sin sombra de duda :** without a shadow of a doubt

sombreado, -da *adj* **1 :** shady **2 :** shaded, darkened

sombrear *vt* **:** to shade

sombrerero, -ra *n* **:** milliner, hatter

sombrero *nm* **1 :** hat **2 sin ~ :** bareheaded **3 sombrero hongo :** derby

sombrilla *nf* **:** parasol, umbrella

sombrío, -bría *adj* LÓBREGO **:** dark, somber, gloomy — **sombríamente** *adv*

someramente *adv* **:** cursorily, summarily

somero, -ra *adj* **:** superficial, cursory, shallow

someter *vt* **1 :** to subjugate, to conquer **2 :** to subordinate **3 :** to subject (to treatment or testing) **4 :** to submit, to present — **someterse** *vr* **1 :** to submit, to yield **2 :** to undergo

sometimiento *nm* **1 :** submission, subjection **2 :** presentation

somnífero[1], -ra *adj* **:** soporific

somnífero[2] *nm* **:** sleeping pill

somnolencia *nf* **:** drowsiness, sleepiness

somnoliento, -ta *adj* **:** drowsy, sleepy

somorgujo *or* **somormujo** *nm* **:** loon, grebe

somos → **ser**

son[1] → **ser**

son[2] *nm* **1 :** sound <al son de la trompeta : at the sound of the trumpet> **2 :** news, rumor **3 en son de :** as, in the manner of, by way of <en son de broma : as a joke> <en son de paz : in peace>

sonado, -da *adj* **:** celebrated, famous, much-discussed

sonaja *nf* **:** rattle

sonajero *nm* **:** rattle (toy)

sonámbulo, -la *n* **:** sleepwalker

sonar[1] {19} *vi* **1 :** to sound <suena bien : it sounds good> **2 :** to ring (bells) **3 :** to look or sound familiar <me suena ese nombre : that name rings a bell> **4 ~ a :** to sound like — *vt* **1 :** to ring **2 :** to blow (a trumpet, a nose) — **sonarse** *vr* **:** to blow one's nose

sonar[2] *nm* **:** sonar

sonata *nf* **:** sonata

sonda *nf* **1 :** sounding line **2 :** probe **3** CATÉTER **:** catheter

sondar *vt* **1 :** to sound, to probe (in medicine, drilling, etc.) **2 :** to probe, to explore (outer space)

sondear *vt* **1 :** to sound **2 :** to probe **3 :** to sound out, to test (opinions, markets)

sondeo *nm* **1 :** sounding, probing **2 :** drilling **3** ENCUESTA **:** survey, poll

soneto *nm* **:** sonnet

sónico, -ca *adj* **:** sonic

sonido *nm* **:** sound

sonoridad *nf* **:** sonority, resonance

sonoro, -ra *adj* **1 :** resonant, sonorous, voiced (in linguistics) **2 :** resounding, loud **3 banda sonora :** soundtrack

sonreír {66} *vi* **:** to smile

sonriente *adj* **:** smiling

sonrisa *nf* **:** smile

sonrojar *vt* **:** to cause to blush — **sonrojarse** *vr* **:** to blush

sonrojo *nm* RUBOR **:** blush

sonrosado, -da *adj* **:** rosy, pink

sonsacar {72} *vt* **:** to wheedle, to extract

sonsonete *nm* **1 :** tapping **2 :** drone **3 :** mocking tone

soñador[1], -dora *adj* **:** dreamy

soñador[2], -dora *n* **:** dreamer

soñar {19} *v* **1 :** to dream **2 ~ con :** to dream about **3 soñar despierto :** to daydream

soñoliento, -ta *adj* **:** sleepy, drowsy

sopa *nf* **1 :** soup **2 estar hecho una sopa :** to be soaked to the bone

sopera *nf* **:** soup tureen

sopesar *vt* **:** to weigh, to evaluate

soplar *vi* **:** to blow — *vt* **:** to blow on, to blow out, to blow off

soplete *nm* **:** blowtorch

soplido *nm* **:** puff

soplo *nm* **:** puff, gust

soplón, -plona *n, mpl* **soplones** *fam* **:** tattletale, sneak

sopor *nm* SOMNOLENCIA **:** drowsiness, sleepiness

soporífero, -ra *adj* **:** soporific

soportable *adj* **:** bearable, tolerable

soportar *vt* **1** SOSTENER **:** to support, to hold up **2** RESISTIR **:** to withstand, to resist **3** AGUANTAR **:** to bear, to tolerate

soporte *nm* **:** base, stand, support

soprano *nmf* **:** soprano

sor *nf* **:** Sister (religious title)

sorber *vt* **1 :** to sip, to suck in **2 :** to absorb, to soak up

sorbete *nm* **:** sherbet

sorbo *nm* **1 :** sip, gulp, swallow **2 beber a sorbos :** to sip

sordera *nf* : deafness

sordidez *nf, pl* **-deces** : sordidness, squalor

sórdido, -da *adj* : sordid, dirty, squalid

sordina *nf* : mute (for a musical instrument)

sordo, -da *adj* **1** : deaf **2** : muted, muffled

sordomudo, -da *n* : deaf-mute

sorgo *nm* : sorghum

soriasis *nfs & pl* : psoriasis

sorna *nf* : sarcasm, mocking tone

sorprendente *adj* : surprising — **sorprendentemente** *adv*

sorprender *vt* : to surprise — **sorprenderse** *vr*

sorpresa *nf* : surprise

sorpresivo, -va *adj* **1** : surprising, surprise **2** IMPREVISTO : sudden, unexpected

sortear *vt* **1** RIFAR : to raffle, to draw lots for **2** : to dodge, to avoid

sorteo *nm* : drawing, raffle

sortija *nf* **1** ANILLO : ring **2** : curl, ringlet

sortilegio *nm* **1** HECHIZO : spell, charm **2** HECHICERÍA : sorcery

SOS *nm* : SOS

sosegado, -da *adj* SERENO : calm, tranquil, serene

sosegar {49} *vt* : to calm, to pacify — **sosegarse** *vr*

sosiego *nm* : tranquillity, serenity, calm

soslayar *vt* ESQUIVAR : to dodge, to evade

soslayo *nm* **de ~** : obliquely, sideways <mirar de soslayo : to look askance>

soso, -sa *adj* **1** INSÍPIDO : bland, flavorless **2** ABURRIDO : dull, boring

sospecha *nf* : suspicion

sospechar *vt* : to suspect — *vi* : to be suspicious

sospechosamente *adv* : suspiciously

sospechoso[1], -sa *adj* : suspicious, suspect

sospechoso[2], -sa *n* : suspect

sostén *nm, pl* **sostenes** **1** APOYO : support **2** : sustenance **3** : brassiere, bra

sostener {80} *vt* **1** : to support, to hold up **2** : to hold <sostenme la puerta : hold the door for me> <sostener una conversación : to hold a conversation> **3** : to sustain, to maintain — **sostenerse** *vr* **1** : to stand, to hold oneself up **2** : to continue, to remain

sostenible *adj* : sustainable, tenable

sostenido[1], -da *adj* **1** : sustained, prolonged **2** : sharp (in music)

sostenido[2] *nm* : sharp (in music)

sostuvo, etc. → **sostener**

sotana *nf* : cassock

sótano *nm* : basement

sotavento *nm* : lee <a sotavento : leeward>

soterrar {55} *vt* **1** : to bury **2** : to conceal, to hide away

soto *nm* : grove, copse

souvenir *nm, pl* **-nirs** RECUERDO : souvenir, memento

soviético, -ca *adj* : Soviet

soy → **ser**

soya *nf* : soy, soybean

spaghetti *nm* → **espagueti**

sport [ɛ'spor] *adj* : sport, casual

sprint [ɛ'sprin, -'sprint] *nm* : sprint — **sprinter** *nmf*

squash [ɛ'skwaʃ, -'skwatʃ] *nm* : squash (sport)

Sr. *nm* : Mr.

Sra. *nf* : Mrs., Ms.

Srta. *or* **Srita.** *nf* : Miss, Ms.

standard → **estándar**

stress *nm* → **estrés**

su *adj* **1** : his, her, its, their, one's <su libro : her book> <sus consecuencias : its consequences> **2** (*formal*) : your <tómese su medicina, señor : take your medicine, sir>

suave *adj* **1** BLANDO : soft **2** LISO : smooth **3** : gentle, mild **4** *Mex fam* : great, fantastic

suavemente *adj* : smoothly, gently, softly

suavidad *nf* : softness, smoothness, mellowness

suavizante *nm* : softener, fabric softener

suavizar {21} *vt* **1** : to soften, to smooth out **2** : to tone down — **suavizarse** *vr*

subacuático, -ca *adj* : underwater

subalterno[1], -na *adj* **1** SUBORDINADO : subordinate **2** SECUNDARIO : secondary

subalterno[2], -na *n* SUBORDINADO : subordinate

subarrendar {55} *vt* : to sublet

subasta *nf* : auction

subastador, -dora *n* : auctioneer

subastar *vt* : to auction, to auction off

subcampeón, -peona *n, mpl* **-peones** : runner-up

subcomité *nm* : subcommittee

subconsciente *adj & nm* : subconscious — **subconscientemente** *adv*

subcontratar *vt* : to subcontract

subcontratista *nmf* : subcontractor

subcultura *nf* : subculture

subdesarrollado, -da *adj* : underdeveloped

subdirector, -tora *n* : assistant manager

súbdito, -ta *n* : subject (of a monarch)

subdividir *vt* : to subdivide

subdivisión *nf, pl* **-siones** : subdivision

subestimar *vt* : to underestimate, to undervalue

subexponer {60} *vt* : to underexpose

subexposición *nf, pl* **-ciones** : underexposure

subgrupo *nm* : subgroup

subibaja *nm* : seesaw

subida *nf* **1** : ascent, climb **2** : rise, increase **3** : slope, hill <ir de subida : to go uphill>

subido, -da *adj* **1 :** intense, strong <amarillo subido : bright yellow> **2 subido de tono :** risqué

subir *vt* **1 :** to bring up, to take up **2 :** to climb, to go up **3 :** to raise — *vi* **1 :** to go up, to come up **2 :** to rise, to increase **3 :** to be promoted **4 ~ a :** to get on, to mount <subir a un tren : to get on a train> — **subirse** *vr* **1 :** to climb (up) **2 :** to pull up (clothing) **3 subirse a la cabeza :** to go to one's head

súbito, -ta *adj* **1** REPENTINO **:** sudden **2 de ~ :** all of a sudden, suddenly — **súbitamente** *adv*

subjetivo, -va *adj* **:** subjective — **subjetivamente** *adv* — **subjetividad** *nf*

subjuntivo[1], -va *adj* **:** subjunctive

subjuntivo[2] *nm* **:** subjunctive

sublevación *nf, pl* **-ciones** ALZAMIENTO **:** uprising, rebellion

sublevar *vt* **:** to incite to rebellion — **sublevarse** *vr* **:** to rebel, to rise up

sublimar *vt* **:** to sublimate — **sublimación** *nf*

sublime *adj* **:** sublime

submarinismo *nm* **:** scuba diving

submarinista *nmf* **:** scuba diver

submarino[1], -na *adj* **:** submarine, undersea

submarino[2] *nm* **:** submarine

suboficial *nmf* **:** noncommissioned officer, petty officer

subordinado, -da *adj & n* **:** subordinate

subordinar *vt* **:** to subordinate — **subordinarse** *vr* — **subordinación** *nf*

subproducto *nm* **:** by-product

subrayar *vt* **1 :** to underline, to underscore **2** ENFATIZAR **:** to highlight, to emphasize

subrepticio, -cia *adj* **:** surreptitious — **subrepticiamente** *adv*

subsahariano, -na *adj* **:** sub-Saharan

subsanar *vt* **1** RECTIFICAR **:** to rectify, to correct **2 :** to overlook, to excuse **3 :** to make up for

subscribir → **suscribir**

subsecretario, -ria *n* **:** undersecretary

subsecuente *adj* **:** subsequent — **subsecuentemente** *adv*

subsidiar *vt* **:** to subsidize

subsidiaria *nf* **:** subsidiary

subsidio *nm* **:** subsidy

subsiguiente *adj* **:** subsequent

subsistencia *nf* **1 :** subsistence **2 :** sustenance

subsistir *vi* **1 :** to subsist, to live **2 :** to endure, to survive

substancia *nf* → **sustancia**

subteniente *nmf* **:** second lieutenant

subterfugio *nm* **:** subterfuge

subterráneo[1], -nea *adj* **:** underground, subterranean

subterráneo[2] *nm* **1 :** underground passage, tunnel **2** *Arg, Uru* **:** subway

subtítulo *nm* **:** subtitle, subheading

subtotal *nm* **:** subtotal

suburbano, -na *adj* **:** suburban

suburbio *nm* **1 :** suburb **2 :** slum (outside a city)

subvención *nf, pl* **-ciones :** subsidy, grant

subvencionar *vt* **:** to subsidize

subversivo, -va *adj & n* **:** subversive — **subversión** *nf*

subvertir {76} *vt* **:** to subvert

subyacente *adj* **:** underlying

subyugar {52} *vt* **:** to subjugate — **subyugación** *nf*

succión *nf, pl* **succiones :** suction

succionar *vt* **:** to suck up, to draw in

sucedáneo *nm* **:** substitute <sucedáneo de azucar : sugar substitute>

suceder *vi* **1** OCURRIR **:** to happen, to occur <¿qué sucede? : what's going on?> <suceda lo que suceda : come what may> **2 ~ a :** to follow, to succeed <suceder al trono : to succeed to the throne> <a la primavera sucede el verano : summer follows sping>

sucesión *nf, pl* **-siones 1 :** succession **2 :** sequence, series **3 :** issue, heirs *pl*

sucesivamente *adv* **:** successively, consecutively <y así sucesivamente : and so on>

sucesivo, -va *adj* **:** successive <en los días sucesivos : in the days that followed>

suceso *nm* **1 :** event, happening, occurrence **2 :** incident, crime

sucesor, -sora *n* **:** successor

suciedad *nf* **1 :** dirtiness, filthiness **2** MUGRE **:** dirt, filth

sucinto, -ta *adj* CONCISO **:** succinct, concise — **sucintamente** *adv*

sucio, -cia *adj* **:** dirty, filthy

sucre *nm* **:** Ecuadoran unit of currency

suculento, -ta *adj* **:** succulent

sucumbir *vi* **:** to succumb

sucursal *nf* **:** branch (of a business)

sudadera *nf* **:** sweatshirt

sudado, -da → **sudoroso**

sudafricano, -na *adj & n* **:** South African

sudamericano, -na *adj & n* **:** South American

sudanés, -nesa *adj & n, mpl* **-neses :** Sudanese

sudar *vi* TRANSPIRAR **:** to sweat, to perspire

sudario *nm* **:** shroud

sudeste → **sureste**

sudoeste → **suroeste**

sudor *nm* TRANSPIRACIÓN **:** sweat, perspiration

sudoroso, -sa *adj* **:** sweaty

sueco[1], -ca *adj* **:** Swedish

sueco[2], -ca *n* **:** Swede

sueco[3] *nm* **:** Swedish (language)

suegro, -gra *n* **1 :** father-in-law *m*, mother-in-law *f* **2 suegros** *nmpl* **:** in-laws

suela *nf* **:** sole (of a shoe)

suelda, etc. → **soldar**

sueldo *nm* **:** salary, wage

suele, etc. → **soler**

suelo *nm* **1 :** ground <caerse al suelo : to fall down, to hit the ground> **2 :** floor, flooring **3** TIERRA **:** soil, land

suelta, etc. → **soltar**

suelto[1], -ta *adj* **:** loose, free, unattached

suelto[2] *nm* **:** loose change

suena, etc. → **sonar**

sueña, etc. → **soñar**

sueño *nm* **1 :** dream **2 :** sleep <perder el sueño : to lose sleep> **3 :** sleepiness <tener sueño : to be sleepy>

suero *nm* **1 :** serum **2 :** whey

suerte *nf* **1** FORTUNA **:** luck, fortune <tener suerte : to be lucky> <por suerte : luckily> **2** DESTINO **:** fate, destiny, lot **3** CLASE, GÉNERO **:** sort, kind <toda suerte de cosas : all kinds of things>

suertudo, -da *adj fam* **:** lucky

suéter *nm* **:** sweater

suficiencia *nf* **1 :** adequacy, sufficiency **2 :** competence, fitness **3 :** smugness, self-satisfaction

suficiente *adj* **1** BASTANTE **:** enough, sufficient <tener suficiente : to have enough> **2 :** suitable, fit **3 :** smug, complacent

suficientemente *adv* **:** sufficiently, enough

sufijo *nm* **:** suffix

suflé *nm* **:** soufflé

sufragar {52} *vt* **1** AYUDAR **:** to help out, to support **2 :** to defray (costs) — *vi* **:** to vote

sufragio *nm* **:** suffrage, vote

sufrido, -da *adj* **1 :** long-suffering, patient **2 :** sturdy, serviceable (of clothing)

sufrimiento *nm* **:** suffering

sufrir *vt* **1 :** to suffer <sufrir una pérdida : to suffer a loss> **2 :** to tolerate, to put up with <ella no lo puede sufrir : she can't stand him> — *vi* **:** to suffer

sugerencia *nf* **:** suggestion

sugerir {76} *vt* **1** PROPONER, RECOMENDAR **:** to suggest, to recommend, to propose **2 :** to suggest, to bring to mind

sugestión *nf, pl* **-tiones :** suggestion, prompting <poder de sugestión : power of suggestion>

sugestionable *adj* **:** suggestible, impressionable

sugestionar *vt* **:** to influence, to sway — **sugestionarse** *vr* **~ con :** to talk oneself into, to become convinced of

sugestivo, -va *adj* **1 :** suggestive **2 :** interesting, stimulating

suicida[1] *adj* **:** suicidal

suicida[2] *nmf* **:** suicide victim, suicide

suicidarse *vr* **:** to commit suicide

suicidio *nm* **:** suicide

suite *nf* **:** suite

suizo, -za *adj & n* **:** Swiss

sujeción *nf, pl* **-ciones 1 :** holding, fastening **2 :** subjection

sujetador *nm* **1 :** fastener **2 :** holder <sujetador de tazas : cup holder>

sujetalibros *nms & pl* **:** bookend

sujetapapeles *nms & pl* CLIP **:** paper clip

sujetar *vt* **1 :** to hold on to, to steady, to hold down **2** FIJAR **:** to fasten, to attach **3** DOMINAR **:** to subdue, to conquer — **sujetarse** *vr* **1 :** to hold on, to hang on **2 ~ a :** to abide by

sujeto[1], -ta *adj* **1 :** secure, fastened **2 ~ a :** subject to

sujeto[2] *nm* **1** INDIVIDUO **:** individual, character **2 :** subject (in grammar)

sulfúrico, -ca *adj* **:** sulfuric

sulfuro *nm* **:** sulfur

sultán *nm, pl* **sultanes :** sultan

suma *nf* **1** CANTIDAD **:** sum, quantity **2 :** addition

sumamente *adv* **:** extremely, exceedingly

sumar *vt* **1 :** to add, to add up **2 :** to add up to, to total — *vi* **:** to add up — **sumarse** *vr* **~ a :** to join

sumario[1], -ria *adj* SUCINTO **:** succinct, summary — **sumariamente** *adv*

sumario[2] *nm* **:** summary

sumergir {35} *vt* **:** to submerge, to immerse, to plunge — **sumergirse** *vr*

sumersión *nf, pl* **-siones :** submersion, immersion

sumidero *nm* **:** drain, sewer

suministrar *vt* **:** to supply, to provide

suministro *nm* **:** supply, provision

sumir *vt* SUMERGIR **:** to plunge, to immerse, to sink — **sumirse** *vr*

sumisión *nf, pl* **-siones 1 :** submission **2 :** submissiveness

sumiso, -sa *adj* **:** submissive, acquiescent, docile

sumo, -ma *adj* **1 :** extreme, great, high <la suma autoridad : the highest authority> **2 a lo sumo :** at the most — **sumamente** *adv*

suntuoso, -sa *adj* **:** sumptuous, lavish — **suntuosamente** *adv*

supeditar *vt* SUBORDINAR **:** to subordinate — **supeditación** *nf*

super[1] *or* **súper** *adj fam* **:** super, great

super[2] *nm* SUPERMERCADO **:** market, supermarket

superable *adj* **:** surmountable

superabundancia *nf* **:** overabundance, superabundance — **superabundante** *adj*

superar *vt* **1 :** to surpass, to exceed **2 :** to overcome, to surmount — **superarse** *vr* **:** to improve oneself

superávit *nm, pl* **-vit** *or* **-vits :** surplus

superchería *nf* **:** trickery, fraud

superestructura *nf* **:** superstructure

superficial *adj* **:** superficial — **superficialmente** *adv*

superficialidad *nf* **:** superficiality

superficie *nf* **1 :** surface **2 :** area <el superficie de un triángulo : the area of a triangle>

superfluidad *nf* **:** superfluity

superfluo, -flua *adj* **:** superfluous

superintendente *nmf* **:** supervisor, superintendent

superior[1] *adj* **1 :** superior **2 :** upper <nivel superior : upper level> **3 :** higher <educación superior : higher education> **4 ~ a :** above, higher than, in excess of
superior[2] *nm* **:** superior
superioridad *nf* **:** superiority
superlativo[1], **-va** *adj* **:** superlative
superlativo[2] *nm* **:** superlative
supermercado *nm* **:** supermarket
superpoblación *nf, pl* **-ciones :** overpopulation
superpoblado, -da *adj* **:** overpopulated
superponer {60} *vt* **:** to superimpose
superpotencia *nf* **:** superpower
superproducción *nf* → **sobreproducción**
supersónico, -ca *adj* **:** supersonic
superstición *nf, pl* **-ciones :** superstition
supersticioso, -sa *adj* **:** superstitious
supervisar *vt* **:** to supervise, to oversee
supervisión *nf, pl* **-siones :** supervision
supervisor, -sora *n* **:** supervisor, overseer
supervivencia *nf* **:** survival
superviviente *nmf* **:** survivor
supino, -na *adj* **:** supine
suplantar *vt* **:** to supplant, to replace
suplemental → **suplementario**
suplementario, -ria *adj* **:** supplementary, additional, extra
suplemento *nm* **:** supplement
suplencia *nf* **:** substitution, replacement
suplente *adj & nmf* **:** substitute <equipo suplente : replacement team>
supletorio, -ria *adj* **:** extra, additional <teléfono supletorio : extension phone> <cama supletoria : spare bed>
súplica *nf* **:** plea, entreaty
suplicar {72} *vt* IMPLORAR, ROGAR **:** to entreat, to implore, to supplicate
suplicio *nm* TORMENTO **:** ordeal, torture
suplir *vt* **1** COMPENSAR **:** to make up for, to compensate for **2** REEMPLAZAR **:** to replace, to substitute
supo, etc. → **saber**
suponer {60} *vt* **1** PRESUMIR **:** to suppose, to assume <supongo que sí : I guess so, I suppose so> <se supone que van a llegar mañana : they're supposed to arrive tomorrow> **2 :** to imply, to suggest **3 :** to involve, to entail <el éxito supone mucho trabajo : success involves a lot of work>
suposición *nf, pl* **-ciones** PRESUNCIÓN **:** supposition, assumption
supositorio *nm* **:** suppository
supremacía *nf* **:** supremacy
supremo, -ma *adj* **:** supreme
supresión *nf, pl* **-siones 1 :** suppression, elimination **2 :** deletion
suprimir *vt* **1 :** to suppress, to eliminate **2 :** to delete
supuestamente *adv* **:** supposedly, allegedly
supuesto, -ta *adj* **1 :** supposed, alleged **2 por ~ :** of course, absolutely
supurar *vi* **:** to ooze, to discharge
supuso, etc. → **suponer**
sur[1] *adj* **:** southern, southerly, south
sur[2] *nm* **1 :** south, South **2 :** south wind
surafricano, -na → **sudafricano**
suramericano, -na → **sudamericano**
surcar {72} *vt* **1 :** to plow (through) **2 :** to groove, to score, to furrow
surco *nm* **:** groove, furrow, rut
sureño[1], **-ña** *adj* **:** southern, Southern
sureño[2], **-ña** *n* **:** Southerner
sureste[1] *adj* **1 :** southeast, southeastern **2 :** southeasterly
sureste[2] *nm* **:** southeast, Southeast
surf *nm* **:** surfing
surfear *vi* **:** to surf
surfing *nm* → **surf**
surfista *nmf* **:** surfer
surgimiento *nm* **:** rise, emergence
surgir {35} *vi* **:** to rise, to arise, to emerge
suroeste[1] *adj* **1 :** southwest, southwestern **2 :** southwesterly
suroeste[2] *nm* **:** southwest, Southwest
surtido[1], **-da** *adj* **1 :** assorted, varied **2 :** stocked, provisioned
surtido[2] *nm* **:** assortment, selection
surtidor *nm* **1 :** jet, spout **2** *Arg, Chile, Spain* **:** gas pump
surtir *vt* **1 :** to supply, to provide <surtir un pedido : to fill an order> **2 surtir efecto :** to have an effect — *vi* **:** to spout, to spurt up — **surtirse** vr **:** to stock up
susceptible *adj* **:** susceptible, sensitive — **susceptibilidad** *nf*
suscitar *vt* **:** to provoke, to give rise to
suscribir {33} *vt* **1 :** to sign (a formal document) **2 :** to endorse, to sanction — **suscribirse** *vr* **~ a :** to subscribe to
suscripción *nf, pl* **-ciones 1 :** subscription **2 :** endorsement, sanction **3 :** signing
suscriptor, -tora *n* **:** subscriber
susodicho, -cha *adj* **:** aforementioned, aforesaid
suspender *vt* **1** COLGAR **:** to suspend, to hang **2 :** to suspend, to discontinue **3 :** to suspend, to dismiss
suspensión *nf, pl* **-siones :** suspension
suspenso *nm* **:** suspense
suspicacia *nf* **:** suspicion, mistrust
suspicaz *adj, pl* **-caces** DESCONFIADO **:** suspicious, wary
suspirar *vi* **:** to sigh
suspiro *nm* **:** sigh
surque, etc. → **surcar**
suscrito *pp* → **suscribir**
sustancia *nf* **1 :** substance **2 sin ~ :** shallow, lacking substance
sustancial *adj* **1 :** substantial **2** ESENCIAL, FUNDAMENTAL **:** essential, fundamental — **sustancialmente** *adv*

sustancioso, -sa *adj* **1** NUTRITIVO **:** hearty, nutritious **2 :** substantial, solid
sustantivo *nm* **:** noun
sustentación *nf, pl* **-ciones** SOSTÉN **:** support
sustentar *vt* **1 :** to support, to hold up **2 :** to sustain, to nourish **3 :** to maintain, to hold (an opinion) — **sustentarse** *vr* **:** to support oneself
sustento *nm* **1 :** means of support, livelihood **2 :** sustenance, food
sustitución *nf, pl* **-ciones :** replacement, substitution
sustituir {41} *vt* **1 :** to replace, to substitute for **2 :** to stand in for
sustituto, -ta *n* **:** substitute, stand-in
susto *nm* **:** fright, scare
sustracción *nf, pl* **-ciones 1** RESTA **:** subtraction **2 :** theft
sustraer {81} *vt* **1 :** to remove, to take away **2** RESTAR **:** to subtract **3 :** to steal — **sustraerse** *vr* **~ a :** to avoid, to evade
susurrar *vi* **1 :** to whisper **2 :** to murmur **3 :** to rustle (leaves, etc.) — *vt* **:** to whisper
susurro *nm* **1 :** whisper **2 :** murmur **3 :** rustle, rustling
sutil *adj* **1 :** delicate, thin, fine **2 :** subtle
sutileza *nf* **1 :** delicacy **2 :** subtlety
sutura *nf* **:** suture
suturar *vt* **:** to suture
suyo[1], -ya *adj* **1 :** his, her, its, theirs <los libros suyos : his books> <un amigo suyo : a friend of hers> <esta casa es suya : this house is theirs> **2** (*formal*) **:** yours <¿este abrigo es suyo, señor? : is this your coat, sir?>
suyo[2], -ya *pron* **1 :** his, hers, theirs <mi guitarra y la suya : my guitar and hers> <ellos trajeron las suyas : they brought theirs, they brought their own> **2** (*formal*) **:** yours <usted olvidó la suya : you forgot yours>
switch *nm* **:** switch

T

t *nf* **:** twenty-first letter of the Spanish alphabet
taba *nf* **:** anklebone
tabacalero[1], -ra *adj* **:** tobacco <industria tabacalera : tobacco industry>
tabacalero[2], -ra *n* **:** tobacco grower
tabaco *nm* **:** tobacco
tábano *nm* **:** horsefly
taberna *nf* **:** tavern, bar
tabernáculo *nm* **:** tabernacle
tabicar {72} *vt* **:** to wall up
tabique *nm* **:** thin wall, partition
tabla *nf* **1 :** table, list <tabla de multiplicar : multiplication table> **2 :** board, plank, slab <tabla de planchar : ironing board> **3 :** plot, strip (of land) **4 tablas** *nfpl* **:** stage, boards *pl*
tablado *nm* **1 :** flooring, floorboards **2 :** platform, scaffold **3 :** stage
tablero *nm* **1 :** bulletin board **2 :** board (in games) <tablero de ajedrez : chessboard> <tablero de damas : checkerboard> **3** PIZARRA **:** blackboard **4 :** switchboard **5 tablero de instrumentos :** dashboard, instrument panel
tableta *nf* **1** COMPRIMIDO, PÍLDORA **:** tablet, pill **2 :** bar (of chocolate)
tabletear *vi* **:** to rattle, to clack
tableteo *nm* **:** clack, rattling
tablilla *nf* **1 :** small board or tablet **2 :** bulletin board **3 :** splint
tabloide *nm* **:** tabloid
tablón *nm, pl* **tablones 1 :** plank, beam **2 tablón de anuncios :** bulletin board
tabú[1] *adj* **:** taboo
tabú[2] *nm, pl* **tabúes** or **tabús :** taboo
tabulador *nm* **:** tabulator
tabular[1] *vt* **:** to tabulate
tabular[2] *adj* **:** tabular
taburete *nm* **:** footstool, stool
tacañería *nf* **:** miserliness, stinginess
tacaño[1], -na *adj* MEZQUINO **:** stingy, miserly
tacaño[2], -ña *n* **:** miser, tightwad
tacha *nf* **1 :** flaw, blemish, defect **2 poner tacha a :** to find fault with **3 sin ~ :** flawless
tachadura *nf* **:** erasure, correction
tachar *vt* **1 :** to cross out, to delete **2 ~ de :** to accuse of, to label as <lo tacharon de mentiroso : they accused him of being a liar>
tachón *nm, pl* **tachones :** stud, hobnail
tachonar *vt* **:** to stud
tachuela *nf* **:** tack, hobnail, stud
tácito, -ta *adj* **:** tacit, implicit — **tácitamente** *adv*
taciturno, -na *adj* **1 :** taciturn **2 :** sullen, gloomy
tacle *nm* **:** tackle
taclear *vt* **:** to tackle (in football)
taco *nm* **1 :** wad, stopper, plug **2 :** pad (of paper) **3 :** cleat **4 :** heel (of a shoe) **5 :** cue (in billiards) **6 :** light snack, bite **7 :** taco
tacón *nm, pl* **tacones :** heel (of a shoe) <de tacón alto : high-heeled>
táctica *nf* **:** tactic, tactics *pl*
táctico[1], -ca *adj* **:** tactical
táctico[2], -ca *n* **:** tactician
táctil *adj* **:** tactile
tacto *nm* **1 :** touch, touching, feel **2** DELICADEZA **:** tact
tafetán *nm, pl* **-tanes :** taffeta
tahúr *nm, pl* **tahúres :** gambler
tailandés[1], -desa *adj & n, pl* **-deses :** Thai
tailandés[2] *nm* **:** Thai (language)

taimado, -da *adj* **1 :** crafty, sly **2** *Chile* **:** sullen, sulky

tajada *nf* **1 :** slice **2 sacar tajada** *fam* **:** to get one's share

tajante *adj* **1 :** cutting, sharp **2 :** decisive, categorical

tajantemente *adj* **:** emphatically, categorically

tajar *vt* **:** to cut, to slice

tajo *nm* **1 :** cut, slash, gash **2** ESCARPA **:** steep cliff

tal[1] *adv* **1 :** so, in such a way **2 tal como :** just as <tal como lo hice : just the way I did it> **3 con tal que :** provided that, as long as **4 ¿qué tal? :** how are you?, how's it going?

tal[2] *adj* **1 :** such, such a **2 tal vez :** maybe, perhaps

tal[3] *pron* **1 :** such a one, someone **2 :** such a thing, something **3 tal para cual :** two of a kind

tala *nf* **:** felling (of trees)

taladrar *vt* **:** to drill

taladro *nm* **:** drill, auger <taladro eléctrico : power drill>

talante *nm* **1** HUMOR **:** mood, disposition **2** VOLUNTAD **:** will, willingness

talar *vt* **1 :** to cut down, to fell **2** DEVASTAR **:** to devastate, to destroy

talco *nm* **1 :** talc **2 :** talcum powder

talego *nm* **:** sack

talento *nm* **:** talent, ability

talentoso, -sa *adj* **:** talented, gifted

talismán *nm, pl* **-manes** AMULETO **:** talisman, charm

talla *nf* **1** ESTATURA **:** height **2 :** size (in clothing) **3 :** stature, status **4 :** sculpture, carving

tallar *vt* **1 :** to sculpt, to carve **2 :** to measure (someone's height) **3 :** to deal (cards)

tallarín *nf, pl* **-rines :** noodle

talle *nm* **1 :** size **2 :** waist, waistline **3 :** figure, shape

taller *nm* **1 :** shop, workshop **2 :** studio (of an artist)

tallo *nm* **:** stalk, stem <tallo de maíz : cornstalk>

talón *nm, pl* **talones 1 :** heel (of the foot) **2 :** stub (of a check) **3 talón de Aquiles :** Achilles' heel

talud *nm* **:** slope, incline

tamal *nm* **:** tamale

tamaño[1], **-ña** *adj* **:** such a big <¿crees tamaña mentira? : do you believe such a lie?>

tamaño[2] *nm* **1 :** size **2 de tamaño natural :** life-size

tamarindo *nm* **:** tamarind

tambalearse *vr* **1 :** to teeter **2 :** to totter, to stagger, to sway — **tambaleante** *adj*

tambaleo *nm* **:** staggering, lurching, swaying

también *adv* **:** too, as well, also

tambor *nm* **:** drum

tamborilear *vi* **:** to drum, to tap

tamborileo *nm* **:** tapping, drumming

tamiz *nm* **:** sieve

tamizar {21} *vt* **:** to sift

tampoco *adv* **:** neither, not either <ni yo tampoco : me neither>

tampón *nm, pl* **tampones 1 :** ink pad **2 :** tampon

tam–tam *nm* **:** tom-tom

tan *adv* **1 :** so, so very <no es tan difícil : it is not that difficult> **2 :** as <tan pronto como : as soon as> **3 tan siquiera :** at least, at the least **4 tan sólo :** only, merely

tanda *nf* **1 :** turn, shift **2 :** batch, lot, series

tándem *nm* **1 :** tandem (bicycle) **2 :** duo, pair

tangente *adj & nf* **:** tangent — **tangencial** *adj*

tangible *adj* **:** tangible

tango *nm* **:** tango

tanino *nm* **:** tannin

tanque *nm* **1 :** tank, reservoir **2 :** tanker, tank (vehicle)

tanteador *nm* MARCADOR **:** scoreboard

tantear *vt* **1 :** to feel, to grope **2 :** to size up, to weigh — *vi* **1 :** to keep score **2 :** to feel one's way

tanteo *nm* **1 :** estimate, rough calculation **2 :** testing, sizing up **3 :** scoring

tanto[1] *adv* **1 :** so much <tanto mejor : so much the better> **2 :** so long <¿por qué te tardaste tanto? : why did you take so long?>

tanto[2], **-ta** *adj* **1 :** so much, so many, such <no hagas tantas preguntas : don't ask so many questions> <tiene tanto encanto : he has such charm, he's so charming> **2 :** as much, as many <come tantos dulces como yo : she eats as many sweets as I do> **3 :** odd, however many <cuarenta y tantos años : forty-odd years>

tanto[3] *nm* **1 :** certain amount **2 :** goal, point (in sports) **3 al tanto :** abreast, in the picture **4 un tanto :** somewhat, rather <un tanto cansado : rather tired>

tanto[4], **-ta** *pron* **1 :** so much, so many <tiene tanto que hacer : she has so much to do> <¡no me des tantos! : don't give me so many!> **2 entre ~ :** meanwhile **3 por lo tanto :** therefore

tañer {79} *vt* **1 :** to ring (a bell) **2 :** to play (a musical instrument)

tañido *nm* **1** CAMPANADA **:** ring, peal, toll **2 :** sound (of an instrument)

tapa *nf* **1 :** cover, top, lid **2** *Spain* **:** bar snack

tapacubos *nms & pl* **:** hubcap

tapadera *nf* **1 :** cover, lid **2 :** front, cover (for an organization or person)

tapar *vt* **1** CUBRIR **:** to cover, to cover up **2** OBSTRUIR **:** to block, to obstruct — **taparse** *vr*

tapete *nm* **1 :** small rug, mat **2 :** table cover **3 poner sobre el tapete :** to bring up for discussion

tapia *nf* **:** (adobe) wall, garden wall

tapiar *vt* **1 :** to wall in **2 :** to enclose, to block off

tapicería *nf* **1 :** upholstery **2** TAPIZ **:** tapestry
tapicero, -ra *n* **:** upholsterer
tapioca *nf* **:** tapioca
tapir *nm* **:** tapir
tapiz *nm, pl* **tapices :** tapestry
tapizar {21} *vt* **1 :** to upholster **2 :** to cover, to carpet
tapón *nm, pl* **tapones 1 :** cork **2 :** bottle cap **3 :** plug, stopper
tapujo *nm* **1 :** deceit, pretension **2 sin tapujos :** openly, frankly
taquigrafía *nf* **:** stenography, shorthand
taquigráfico, -ca *adj* **:** stenographic
taquígrafo, -fa *n* **:** stenographer
taquilla *nf* **1 :** box office, ticket office **2 :** earnings *pl*, take
taquillero, -ra *adj* **:** box-office, popular <un éxito taquillero : a box-office success>
tarántula *nf* **:** tarantula
tararear *vt* **:** to hum
tardanza *nf* **:** lateness, delay
tardar *vi* **1 :** to delay, to take a long time **2 :** to be late **3 a más tardar :** at the latest — *vt* DEMORAR **:** to take (time) <tarda una hora : it takes an hour>
tarde[1] *adv* **1 :** late **2 tarde o temprano :** sooner or later
tarde[2] *nf* **1 :** afternoon, evening **2 ¡buenas tardes! :** good afternoon!, good evening! **3 en la tarde** *or* **por la tarde :** in the afternoon, in the evening
tardío, -día *adj* **:** late, tardy
tardo, -da *adj* **:** slow
tarea *nf* **1 :** task, job **2 :** homework
tarifa *nf* **1 :** rate <tarifas postales : postal rates> **2 :** fare (for transportation) **3 :** price list **4** ARANCEL **:** duty
tarima *nf* PLATAFORMA **:** dais, platform, stage
tarjeta *nf* **:** card <tarjeta de crédito : credit card> <tarjeta postal : postcard>
tarro *nm* **1 :** jar, pot **2** *Arg, Chile* **:** can, tin
tarta *nf* **1 :** tart **2 :** cake
tartaleta *nf* **:** tart
tartamudear *vi* **:** to stammer, to stutter
tartamudeo *nm* **:** stutter, stammer
tartán *nm, pl* **tartanes :** tartan, plaid
tártaro *nm* **:** tartar <cream of tartar : crémor, tártaro>
tasa *nf* **1 :** rate <tasa de desempleo : unemployment rate> **2 :** tax, fee **3 :** appraisal, valuation
tasación *nf, pl* **-ciones :** appraisal, assessment
tasador, -dora *n* **:** assessor, appraiser
tasar *vt* **1** VALORAR **:** to appraise, to value **2 :** to set the price of **3 :** to ration, to limit
tasca *nf* **:** cheap bar, dive
tatuaje *nm* **:** tattoo, tattooing
tatuar {3} *vt* **:** to tattoo
taurino, -na *adj* **:** bull, bullfighting
Tauro *nmf* **:** Taurus
tauromaquia *nf* **:** (art of) bullfighting
taxi *nm, pl* **taxis :** taxi, taxicab
taxidermia *nf* **:** taxidermy
taxidermista *nmf* **:** taxidermist
taxímetro *nm* **:** taximeter
taxista *nmf* **:** taxi driver
taza *nf* **1 :** cup **2 :** cupful **3 :** (toilet) bowl **4 :** basin (of a fountain)
tazón *nm, pl* **tazones 1 :** bowl **2 :** large cup, mug
te *pron* **1 :** you <te quiero : I love you> **2 :** for you, to you, from you <me gustaría dártelo : I would like to give it to you> **3 :** yourself, for yourself, to yourself, from yourself <¡cálmate! : calm yourself!> <¿te guardaste uno? : did you keep one for yourself?> **4 :** thee
té *nm* **1 :** tea **2 :** tea party
tea *nf* **:** torch
teatral *adj* **:** theatrical — **teatralmente** *adv*
teatro *nm* **1 :** theater **2 hacer teatro :** to put on an act, to exaggerate
teca *nf* **:** teak
techado *nm* **1 :** roof **2 bajo techado :** under cover, indoors
techar *vt* **:** to roof, to shingle
techo *nm* **1** TEJADO **:** roof **2 :** ceiling **3 :** upper limit, ceiling
techumbre *nf* **:** roofing
tecla *nf* **1 :** key (of a musical instrument or a machine) **2 dar en la tecla :** to hit the nail on the head
teclado *nm* **:** keyboard
teclear *vt* **:** to type in, to enter
técnica *nf* **1 :** technique, skill **2 :** technology
técnico[1], **-ca** *adj* **:** technical — **técnicamente** *adv*
técnico[2], **-ca** *n* **:** technician, expert, engineer
tecnología *nf* **:** technology
tecnológico, -ca *adj* **:** technological — **tecnológicamente** *adv*
tecolote *nm Mex* **:** owl
tedio *nm* **:** tedium, boredom
tedioso, -sa *adj* **:** tedious, boring — **tediosamente** *adv*
teja *nf* **:** tile
tejado *nm* TECHO **:** roof
tejedor, -dora *n* **:** weaver
tejer *vt* **1 :** to knit, to crochet **2 :** to weave **3** FABRICAR **:** to concoct, to make up, to fabricate
tejido *nm* **1** TELA **:** fabric, cloth **2 :** weave, texture **3 :** tissue <tejido muscular : muscle tissue>
tejo *nm* **:** yew
tejón *nm, pl* **tejones :** badger
tela *nf* **1 :** fabric, cloth, material **2 tela de araña :** spiderweb **3 poner en tela de juicio :** to call into question, to doubt
telar *nm* **:** loom
telaraña *nf* **:** spiderweb, cobweb
tele *nf fam* **:** TV, television
telecomunicación *nf, pl* **-ciones :** telecommunication

teleconferencia *nf* : teleconference
teledifusión *nf, pl* **-siones** : television broadcasting
teledirigido, -da *adj* : remote-controlled
telefonear *v* : to telephone, to call
telefónico, -ca *adj* : phone, telephone <llamada telefónica : phone call>
telefonista *nmf* : telephone operator
teléfono *nm* **1** : telephone **2 llamar por teléfono** : to telephone, to make a phone call
telegrafiar {85} *v* : to telegraph
telegráfico, -ca *adj* : telegraphic
telégrafo *nm* : telegaph
telegrama *nm* : telegram
telenovela *nf* : soap opera
telepatía *nf* : telepathy
telepático, -ca *adj* : telepathic — **telepáticamente** *adv*
telescópico, -ca *adj* : telescopic
telescopio *nm* : telescope
telespectador, -dora *n* : television viewer
telesquí *nm, pl* **-squís** : ski lift
televidente *nmf* : television viewer
televisar *vt* : to televise
televisión *nf, pl* **-siones** : television, TV
televisivo, -va *adj* : television <serie televisiva : television series>
televisor *nm* : television set
telón *nm, pl* **telones 1** : curtain (in theater) **2 telón de fondo** : backdrop, background
tema *nm* **1** ASUNTO : theme, topic, subject **2** MOTIVO : motif, central theme
temario *nm* **1** : set of topics (for study) **2** : agenda
temática *nf* : subject matter
temático, -ca *adj* : thematic
temblar {55} *vi* **1** : to tremble, to shake, to shiver <le temblaban las rodillas : his knees were shaking> **2** : to shudder, to be afraid <tiemblo con sólo pensarlo : I shudder to think of it>
temblor *nm* **1** : shaking, trembling **2** : tremor, earthquake
tembloroso, -sa *adj* : tremulous, trembling, shaking <con la voz temblorosa : with a shaky voice>
temer *vt* : to fear, to dread — *vi* : to be afraid
temerario, -ria *adj* : reckless, rash — **temerariamente** *adv*
temeridad *nf* **1** : temerity, recklessness, rashness **2** : rash act
temeroso, -sa *adj* MIEDOSO : fearful, frightened
temible *adj* : fearsome, dreadful
temor *nm* MIEDO : fear, dread
témpano *nm* : ice floe
temperamento *nm* : temperament — **temperamental** *adj*
temperancia *nf* : temperance
temperar *vt* MODERAR : to temper, to moderate — *vi* : to have a change of air
temperatura *nf* : temperature
tempestad *nf* **1** : storm, tempest **2 tempestad de arena** : sandstorm
tempestuoso, -sa *adj* : tempestuous, stormy
templado, -da *adj* **1** : temperate, mild **2** : moderate, restrained **3** : warm, lukewarm **4** VALIENTE : courageous, bold
templanza *nf* **1** : temperance, moderation **2** : mildness (of weather)
templar *vt* **1** : to temper (steel) **2** : to restrain, to moderate **3** : to tune (a musical instrument) **4** : to warm up, to cool down — **templarse** *vr* **1** : to be moderate **2** : to warm up, to cool down
temple *nm* **1** : temper (of steel, etc.) **2** HUMOR : mood <de buen temple : in a good mood> **3** : tuning **4** VALOR : courage
templo *nm* **1** : temple **2** : church, chapel
tempo *nm* : tempo (in music)
temporada *nf* **1** : season, time <temporada de béisbol : baseball season> **2** : period, spell <por temporadas : on and off>
temporal[1] *adj* **1** : temporal **2** : temporary
temporal[2] *nm* **1** : storm **2 capear el temporal** : to weather the storm
temporalmente *adv* : temporarily
temporario, -ria *adj* : temporary — **temporariamente** *adv*
temporero[1], **-ra** *adj* : temporary, seasonal
temporero[2], **-ra** *n* : temporary or seasonal worker
temporizador *nm* : timer
tempranero, -ra *adj* **1** : early **2** : early-rising
temprano[1] *adv* : early <lo más temprano posible : as soon as possible>
temprano[2], **-na** *adj* : early <la parte temprana del siglo : the early part of the century>
ten → **tener**
tenacidad *nf* : tenacity, perseverance
tenaz *adj, pl* **tenaces 1** : tenacious, persistent **2** : strong, tough
tenaza *nf or* **tenazas** *nfpl* **1** : pliers, pincers **2** : tongs **3** : claw (of a crustacean)
tenazmente *adv* : tenaciously
tendedero *nm* : clothesline
tendencia *nf* **1** PROPENSIÓN : tendency, inclination **2** : trend
tendencioso, -sa *adj* : tendencious, biased
tendente → **tendiente**
tender {56} *vt* **1** EXTENDER : to spread out, to lay out **2** : to hang out (clothes) **3** : to lay (cables, etc.) **4** : to set (a trap) — *vi* **~ a** : to tend to, to have a tendency towards — **tenderse** *vr* : to stretch out, to lie down
tendero, -ra *n* : shopkeeper, storekeeper

tendido *nm* **1 :** laying (of cables, etc.) **2 :** seats *pl,* section (at a bullfight)

tendiente *adj* **~ a :** aimed at, designed to

tendón *nm, pl* **tendones :** tendon

tenebrosidad *nf* **:** darkness, gloom

tendrá, etc. → **tener**

tenebroso, -sa *adj* **1** OSCURO **:** gloomy, dark **2** SINIESTRO **:** sinister

tenedor[1], -dora *n* **1 :** holder **2 tenedor de libros, tenedora de libros :** bookkeeper

tenedor[2] *nm* **:** table fork

tenencia *nf* **1 :** possession, holding **2 :** tenancy **3 :** tenure

tener {80} *vt* **1 :** to have <tiene ojos verdes : she has green eyes> <tengo mucho que hacer : I have a lot to do> <tiene veinte años : he's twenty years old> <tiene un metro de largo : it's one meter long> **2 :** to hold <ten esto un momento : hold this for a moment> **3 :** to feel, to make <tengo frío : I'm cold> <eso nos tiene contentos : that makes us happy> **4 ~ por :** to think, to consider <me tienes por loco : you think I'm crazy> — *v aux* **1 tener que :** to have to <tengo que salir : I have to leave> <tiene que estar aquí : it has to be here, it must be here> **2** (*with past participle*) <tenía pensado escribirte : I've been thinking of writing to you> — **tenerse** *vr* **1 :** to stand up **2 ~ por :** to consider oneself <me tengo por afortunado : I consider myself lucky>

tenería *nf* CURTIDURÍA **:** tannery

tenga, etc. → **tener**

tenia *nf* SOLITARIA **:** tapeworm

teniente *nmf* **1 :** lieutenant **2 teniente coronel :** lieutenant colonel

tenis *nms & pl* **1 :** tennis **2 tenis** *nmpl* **:** sneakers *pl*

tenista *nmf* **:** tennis player

tenor *nm* **1 :** tenor **2 :** tone, sense

tensar *vt* **1 :** to tense, to make taut **2 :** to draw (a bow) — **tensarse** *vr* **:** to become tense

tensión *nf, pl* **tensiones 1 :** tension, tautness **2 :** stress, strain **3 tensión arterial :** blood pressure

tenso, -sa *adj* **:** tense

tentación *nf, pl* **-ciones :** temptation

tentáculo *nm* **:** tentacle, feeler

tentador[1], -dora *adj* **:** tempting

tentador[2], -dora *n* **:** tempter, temptress *f*

tentar {55} *vt* **1** TOCAR **:** to feel, to touch **2** PROBAR **:** to test, to try **3** ATRAER **:** to tempt, to entice

tentativa *nf* **:** attempt, try

tentempié *nm fam* **:** snack, bite

tenue *adj* **1 :** tenuous **2 :** faint, weak, dim **3 :** light, fine **4 :** thin, slender

teñir {67} *vt* **1 :** to dye **2 :** to stain

teodolito *nm* **:** theodolite, transit (for surveying)

teología *nf* **:** theology

teológico, -ca *adj* **:** theological

teólogo, -ga *n* **:** theologian

teorema *nm* **:** theorem

teoría *nf* **:** theory

teórico[1], -ca *adj* **:** theoretical — **teóricamente** *adv*

teórico[2], -ca *n* **:** theorist

teorizar {21} *vi* **:** to theorize

tepe *nm* **:** sod, turf

teponaztle *nm Mex* **:** traditional drum

tequila *nm* **:** tequila

terapeuta *nmf* **:** therapist

terapéutica *nf* **:** therapeutics

terapéutico, -ca *adj* **:** therapeutic

terapia *nf* **1 :** therapy **2 terapia intensiva :** intensive care

tercer → **tercero**

tercermundista *adj* **:** third-world

tercero[1], -ra *adj* (**tercer** *before masculine singular nouns*) **1 :** third **2 el Tercer Mundo :** the Third World

tercero[2], -ra *n* **:** third (in a series)

terciar *vt* **1 :** to place diagonally **2 :** to divide into three parts — *vi* **1 :** to mediate **2 ~ en :** to take part in

terciario, -ria *adj* **:** tertiary

tercio[1], -cia → **tercero**

tercio[2] *nm* **:** third <dos tercios : two thirds>

terciopelo *nm* **:** velvet

terco, -ca *adj* OBSTINADO **:** obstinate, stubborn

tergiversación *nf, pl* **-ciones :** distortion

tergiversar *vt* **:** to distort, to twist

termal *adj* **:** thermal, hot

termas *nfpl* **:** hot springs

térmico, -ca *adj* **:** thermal, heat <energía térmica : thermal energy>

terminación *nf, pl* **-ciones :** termination, conclusion

terminal[1] *adj* **:** terminal — **terminalmente** *adv*

terminal[2] *nm* (*in some regions f*) **:** (electric or electronic) terminal

terminal[3] *nf* (*in some regions m*) **:** terminal, station

terminante *adj* **:** final, definitive, categorical — **terminantemente** *adv*

terminar *vt* **1** CONCLUIR **:** to end, to conclude **2** ACABAR **:** to complete, to finish off — *vi* **1 :** to finish **2 :** to stop, to end — **terminarse** *vr* **1 :** to run out **2 :** to come to an end

término *nm* **1** CONCLUSIÓN **:** end, conclusion **2 :** term, expression **3 :** period, term of office **4 término medio :** happy medium **5 términos** *nmpl* **:** terms, specifications <los términos del acuerdo : the terms of the agreement>

terminología *nf* **:** terminology

termita *nf* **:** termite

termo *nm* **:** thermos

termodinámica *nf* **:** thermodynamics

termómetro *nm* **:** thermometer

termóstato *nm* **:** thermostat

ternera *nf* **:** veal

ternero, -ra *n* **:** calf

terno *nm* **1 :** set of three **2 :** three-piece suit

ternura *nf* **:** tenderness

terquedad *nf* OBSTINACIÓN **:** obstinacy, stubbornness

terracota *nf* **:** terra-cotta

terraplén *nm, pl* **-plenes :** terrace, embankment

terráqueo, -quea *adj* **1 :** earth **2 globo terráqueo :** the earth, globe (of the earth)

terrateniente *nmf* **:** landowner

terraza *nf* **1 :** terrace, veranda **2 :** balcony (in a theater) **3 :** terrace (in agriculture)

terremoto *nm* **:** earthquake

terrenal *adj* **:** worldly, earthly

terreno *nm* **1 :** terrain **2** SUELO **:** earth, ground **3 :** plot, tract of land **4 perder terreno :** to lose ground **5 preparar el terreno :** to pave the way

terrestre *adj* **:** terrestrial

terrible *adj* **:** terrible, horrible **— terriblemente** *adv*

terrier *nmf* **:** terrier

territorial *adj* **:** territorial

territorio *nm* **:** territory

terrón *nm, pl* **terrones 1 :** clod (of earth) **2 terrón de azúcar :** lump of sugar

terror *nm* **:** terror

terrorífico, -ca *adj* **:** horrific, terrifying

terrorismo *nm* **:** terrorism

terrorista *adj & nmf* **:** terrorist

terroso, -sa *adj* **:** earthy <colores terrosos : earthy colors>

terruño *nm* **:** native land, homeland

terso, -sa *adj* **1 :** smooth **2 :** glossy, shiny **3 :** polished, flowing (of a style)

tersura *nf* **1 :** smoothness **2 :** shine

tertulia *nf* **:** gathering, group <tertulia literaria : literary circle>

tesauro *nm* **:** thesaurus

tesis *nfs & pl* **:** thesis

tesón *nm* **:** persistence, tenacity

tesonero, -ra *adj* **:** persistent, tenacious

tesorería *nf* **:** treasurer's office

tesorero, -ra *n* **:** treasurer

tesoro *nm* **1 :** treasure **2 :** thesaurus

testaferro *nm* **:** figurehead

testamentario[1], -ria *adj* **:** testamentary

testamentario[2], -ria *n* ALBACEA **:** executor, executrix *f*

testamento *nm* **:** testament, will

testar *vi* **:** to draw up a will

testarudo, -da *adj* **:** stubborn, pigheaded

testículo *nm* **:** testicle

testificar {72} *v* **:** to testify

testigo *nmf* **:** witness

testimonial *adj* **1 :** testimonial **2 :** token

testimoniar *vi* **:** to testify

testimonio *nm* **:** testimony, statement

teta *nf* **:** teat

tétano *or* **tétanos** *nm* **:** tetanus, lockjaw

tetera *nf* **1 :** teapot **2 :** teakettle

tetilla *nf* **1 :** teat **2 :** nipple

tetina *nf* **:** nipple (on a bottle)

tétrico, -ca *adj* **:** somber, gloomy

textil *adj & nm* **:** textile

texto *nm* **:** text

textual *adj* **:** literal, exact **— textualmente** *adv*

textura *nf* **:** texture

tez *nf, pl* **teces :** complexion, coloring

ti *pron* **1 :** you <es para ti : it's for you> **2 ti mismo, ti misma :** yourself **3 :** thee

tía → tío

tiamina *nf* **:** thiamine

tianguis *nm Mex* **:** open-air market

tibetano, -na *adj & n* **:** Tibetan

tibia *nf* **:** tibia

tibieza *nf* **1 :** tepidness **2 :** halfheartedness

tibio, -bia *adj* **1 :** lukewarm, tepid **2 :** cool, unenthusiastic

tiburón *nm, pl* **-rones 1 :** shark **2 :** raider (in finance)

tic *nm* **1 :** click, tick **2 tic nervioso :** tic

tico, -ca *adj & n fam* **:** Costa Rican

tiembla, etc. → temblar

tiempo *nm* **1 :** time <justo a tiempo : just in time> <perder tiempo : to waste time> <tiempo libre : spare time> **2 :** period, age <en los tiempos que corren : nowadays> **3 :** season, moment <antes de tiempo : prematurely> **4 :** weather <hace buen tiempo : the weather is fine, it's nice outside> **5 :** tempo (in music) **6 :** half (in sports) **7 :** tense (in grammar)

tienda *nf* **1 :** store, shop **2** *or* **tienda de campaña :** tent

tiende, etc. → tender

tiene, etc. → tener

tienta[1], etc. → tentar

tienta[2] *nf* **andar a tientas :** to feel one's way, to grope around

tiernamente *adv* **:** tenderly

tierno, -na *adj* **1 :** affectionate, tender **2 :** tender, young

tierra *nf* **1 :** land **2** SUELO **:** ground, earth **3 :** country, homeland, soil **4 tierra natal :** native land **5 la Tierra :** the Earth

tieso, -sa *adj* **1 :** stiff, rigid **2 :** upright, erect

tiesto *nm* **1 :** potsherd **2** MACETA **:** flowerpot

tiesura *nf* **:** stiffness, rigidity

tifoidea *nf* **:** typhoid

tifoideo, -dea *adj* **:** typhoid <fiebre tifoidea : typhoid fever>

tifón *nm, pl* **tifones :** typhoon

tifus *nm* **:** typhus

tigre, -gresa *n* **1 :** tiger, tigress *f* **2 :** jaguar

tijera *nf* **1** *or* **tijeras** *nfpl* **:** scissors **2 de ~ :** folding <escalera de tijera : stepladder>

tijereta *nf* **:** earwig

tijeretada *nf or* **tijeretazo** *nm* **:** cut, snip

tildar *vt* ~ **de** : to brand as, to call <lo tildaron de traidor : they branded him as a traitor>

tilde *nf* **1** : accent mark **2** : tilde (accent over *ñ*)

tilo *nm* : linden (tree)

timador, -dora *n* : swindler

timar *vt* : to swindle, to cheat

timbal *nm* **1** : kettledrum **2 timbales** *nmpl* : timpani

timbre *nm* **1** : bell <tocar el timbre : to ring the doorbell> **2** : tone, timbre **3** SELLO : seal, stamp **4** *CA, Mex* : postage stamp

timidez *nf* : timidity, shyness

tímido, -da *adj* : timid, shy — **tímidamente** *adv*

timo *nm fam* : swindle, trick, hoax

timón *nm, pl* **timones** : rudder <estar al timón : to beat the helm>

timonel *nm* : helmsman, coxwain

timorato, -ta *adj* **1** : timorous **2** : sanctimonious

tímpano *nm* **1** : eardrum **2 tímpanos** *nmpl* : timpani, kettledrums

tina *nf* **1** BAÑERA : tub, bathtub **2** : vat

tinaco *nm Mex* : water tank

tinieblas *nfpl* **1** OSCURIDAD : darkness **2** : ignorance

tino *nm* **1** : good judgment, sense **2** : tact, sensitivity, insight

tinta *nf* : ink

tinte *nm* **1** : dye, coloring **2** : overtone <tintes raciales : racial overtones>

tintero *nm* **1** : inkwell **2 quedarse en el tintero** : to remain unsaid

tintinear *vt* : to jingle, to clink, to tinkle

tintineo *nm* : clink, jingle, tinkle

tinto, -ta *adj* **1** : dyed, stained <tinto en sangre : bloodstained> **2** : red (of wine)

tintorería *nf* : dry cleaner (service)

tintura *nf* **1** : dye, tint **2** : tincture <tintura de yodo : tincture of iodine>

tiña *nf* : ringworm

tiñe, etc. → **teñir**

tío, tía *n* : uncle *m,* aunt *f*

tiovivo *nm* : merry-go-round

tipi *nm* : tepee

típico, -ca *adj* : typical — **típicamente** *adv*

tipificar {72} *vt* **1** : to classify, to categorize **2** : to typify

tiple *nm* : soprano

tipo[1] *nm* **1** CLASE : type, kind, sort **2** : figure, build, appearance **3** : rate <tipo de interés : interest rate> **4** : (printing) type, typeface **5** : style, model <un vestido tipo 60's : a 60's-style dress>

tipo[2], **-pa** *n fam* : guy *m,* gal *f,* character

tipografía *nf* : typography, printing

tipográfico, -ca *adj* : typographic, typographical

tipográfo, -fa *n* : printer, typographer

tique *or* **tiquet** *nm* **1** : ticket **2** : receipt

tira *nf* **1** : strip, strap **2 tira cómica** : comic, comic strip

tirabuzón *nf, pl* **-zones** : corkscrew

tirada *nf* **1** : throw **2** : distance, stretch **3** IMPRESIÓN : printing, issue

tiradero *nm Mex* **1** : dump **2** : mess, clutter

tirador[1] *nm* : handle, knob

tirador[2], **-dora** *n* : marksman *m,* markswoman *f*

tiragomas *nms & pl* : slingshot

tiranía *nf* : tyranny

tiránico, -ca *adj* : tyrannical

tiranizar {21} *vt* : to tyrannize

tirano[1], **-na** *adj* : tyrannical, despotic

tirano[2], **-na** *n* : tyrant

tirante[1] *adj* **1** : tense, strained **2** : taut

tirante[2] *nm* **1** : shoulder strap **2 tirantes** *nmpl* : suspenders

tirantez *nf* **1** : tautness **2** : tension, friction, strain

tirar *vt* **1** : to throw, to hurl, to toss **2** BOTAR : to throw away, to throw out, to waste **3** DERRIBAR : to knock down **4** : to shoot, to fire, to launch **5** : to take (a photo) **6** : to print, to run off — *vi* **1** : to pull, to draw **2** : to shoot **3** : to attract **4** : to get by, to manage <va tirando : he's getting along, he's managing> **5** ~ **a** : to tend towards, to be rather <tira a picante : it's a bit spicy> — **tirarse** *vr* **1** : to throw oneself **2** *fam* : to spend (time)

tiritar *vi* : to shiver, to tremble

tiro *nm* **1** BALAZO, DISPARO : shot, gunshot **2** : shot, kick (in sports) **3** : flue **4** : team (of horses, etc.) **5 a** ~ : within range **6 al tiro** : right away **7 tiro de gracia** : coup de grace, death blow

tiroideo, -dea *adj* : thyroid

tiroides *nmf* : thyroid, thyroid gland — **tiroides** *adj*

tirolés, -lesa *adj* : Tyrolean

tirón *nm, pl* **tirones 1** : pull, tug, yank **2 de un tirón** : all at once, in one go

tiroteo *nm* **1** : shooting **2** : gunfight, shoot-out

tirria *nf fam* **tener tirria a** : to have a grudge against

titánico, -ca *adj* : titanic, huge

titanio *nm* : titanium

títere *nm* : puppet

tití *nm* : marmoset

titilar *vi* : to twinkle, to flicker

titileo *nm* : twinkle, flickering

titiritero, -ra *n* **1** : puppeteer **2** : acrobat

titubear *vi* **1** : to hesitate **2** : to stutter, to stammer — **titubeante** *adj*

titubeo *nm* **1** : hesitation **2** : stammering

titulado, -da *adj* **1** : titled, entitled **2** : qualified

titular[1] *vt* : to title, to entitle — **titularse** *vr* **1** : to be called, to be entitled **2** : to receive a degree

titular[2] *adj* : titular, official

titular[3] *nm* : headline

titular[4] *nmf* **1** : owner, holder **2** : officeholder, incumbent

título *nm* **1** : title **2** : degree, qualification **3** : security, bond **4 a título de** : by way of, in the capacity of

tiza *nf* : chalk

tiznar *vt* : to blacken (with soot, etc.)

tizne *nm* HOLLÍN : soot

tiznón *nm, pl* **tiznones** : stain, smudge

tlapalería *nf Mex* : hardware store

TNT *nm* : TNT

toalla *nf* : towel

toallita *nf* : washcloth

tobillo *nm* : ankle

tobogán *nm, pl* **-ganes 1** : toboggan, sled **2** : slide, chute

tocadiscos *nms & pl* : record player, phonograph

tocado[1], **-da** *adj* **1** : bad, bruised (of fruit) **2** *fam* : touched, not all there

tocado[2] *nm* : headdress

tocador[1] *nm* **1** : dressing table, vanity table **2 artículos de tocador** : toiletries

tocador[2], **-dora** *n* : player (of music)

tocante *adj* **~ a** : with regard to, regarding

tocar {72} *vt* **1** : to touch, to feel, to handle **2** : to touch on, to refer to **3** : to concern, to affect **4** : to play (a musical instrument) — *vi* **1** : to knock, to ring <tocar a la puerta : to rap on the door> **2 ~ en** : to touch on, to border on <eso toca en lo ridículo : that's almost ludicrous> **3 tocarle a** : to fall to, to be up to, to be one's turn <¿a quién le toca manejar? : whose turn is it to drive?>

tocayo, -ya *n* : namesake

tocineta *nf Col, Ven* : bacon

tocino *nm* **1** : bacon **2** : salt pork

tocología *nf* OBSTETRICIA : obstetrics

tocólogo, -ga *n* OBSTETRA : obstetrician

tocón *nm, pl* **tocones** CEPA : stump (of a tree)

todavía *adv* **1** AÚN : still, yet <todavía puedes verlo : you can still see it> **2** : even <todavía más rápido : even faster> **3 todavía no** : not yet

todo[1], **-da** *adj* **1** : all, whole, entire <con toda sinceridad : with all sincerity> <toda la comunidad : the whole community> **2** : every, each <a todo nivel : at every level> **3** : maximum <a toda velocidad : at top speed> **4 todo el mundo** : everyone, everybody

todo[2] *nm* : whole

todo[3], **-da** *pron* **1** : everything, all, every bit <lo sabe todo : he knows it all> <es todo un soldado : he's every inch a soldier> **2 todos, -das** *pl* : everybody, everyone, all

todopoderoso, -sa *adj* OMNIPOTENTE : almighty, all-powerful

toga *nf* **1** : toga **2** : gown, robe (for magistrates, etc.)

toldo *nm* : awning, canopy

tolerable *adj* : tolerable — **tolerablemente** *adv*

tolerancia *nf* : tolerance, toleration

tolerante *adj* : tolerant — **tolerantemente** *adv*

tolerar *vt* : to tolerate

tolete *nm* : oarlock

tolva *nf* : hopper (container)

toma *nf* **1** : taking, seizure, capture **2** DOSIS : dose **3** : take, shot **4 toma de corriente** : wall socket, outlet **5 toma y daca** : give-and-take

tomar *vt* **1** : to take <tomé el libro : I took the book> <tomar un taxi : to take a taxi> <tomar una foto : to take a photo> <toma dos años : it takes two years> <tomaron medidas drásticas : they took drastic measures> **2** BEBER : to drink **3** CAPTURAR : to capture, to seize **4 tomar el sol** : to sunbathe **5 tomar tierra** : to land — *vi* : to drink (alcohol) — **tomarse** *vr* **1** : to take <tomarse la molestia de : to take the trouble to> **2** : to drink, to eat, to have

tomate *nm* : tomato

tomillo *nm* : thyme

tomo *nm* : volume, tome

ton *nm* **sin ton ni son** : without rhyme or reason

tonada *nf* **1** : tune, song **2** : accent

tonalidad *nf* : tonality

tonel *nm* BARRICA : barrel, cask

tonelada *nf* : ton

tonelaje *nm* : tonnage

tónica *nf* **1** : tonic (water) **2** : tonic (in music) **3** : trend, tone <dar la tónica : to set the tone>

tónico[1], **-ca** *adj* : tonic

tónico[2] *nm* : tonic <tónico capilar : hair tonic>

tono *nm* **1** : tone <tono muscular : muscle tone> **2** : shade (of colors) **3** : key (in music)

tontamente *adv* : foolishly, stupidly

tontear *vi* **1** : to fool around, to play the fool **2** : to flirt

tontería *nf* **1** : foolishness **2** : stupid remark or action **3 decir tonterías** : to talk nonsense

tonto[1], **-ta** *adj* **1** : dumb, stupid **2** : silly **3 a tontas y a locas** : without thinking, haphazardly

tonto[2], **-ta** *n* : fool, idiot

topacio *nm* : topaz

toparse *vr* **~ con** : to bump into, to run into, to come across <me topé con algunas dificultades : I ran into some problems>

tope *nm* **1** : limit, end <hasta el tope : to the limit, to the brim> **2** : stop, check, buffer <tope de puerta : doorstop> **3** : bump, collision **4** *Mex* : speed bump

tópico[1], **-ca** *adj* **1** : topical, external **2** : trite, commonplace

tópico[2] *nm* **1** : topic, subject **2** : cliché, trite expression

topo *nm* **1 :** mole (animal) **2** *fam* **:** clumsy person, blunderer
topografía *nf* **:** topography
topográfico, -ca *adj* **:** topographic, topographical
topógrafo, -fa *n* **:** topographer
toque[1], etc. → tocar
toque[2] *nm* **1 :** touch <el último toque : the finishing touch> <un toque de color : a touch of color> **2 :** ringing, peal, chime **3** *Mex* **:** shock, jolt **4 toque de queda :** curfew **5 toque de diana :** reveille
toquetear *vt* **:** to touch, to handle, to finger
tórax *nm* **:** thorax
torbellino *nm* **:** whirlwind
torcedura *nf* **1 :** twisting, buckling **2 :** sprain
torcer {14} *vt* **1 :** to bend, to twist **2 :** to sprain **3 :** to turn (a corner) **4 :** to wring, to wring out **5 :** to distort — *vi* **:** to turn — **torcerse** *vr*
torcido, -da *adj* **1 :** twisted, crooked **2 :** devious
tordo *nm* ZORZAL **:** thrush
torear *vt* **1 :** to fight (bulls) **2 :** to dodge, to sidestep
toreo *nm* **:** bullfighting
torero, -ra *n* MATADOR **:** bullfighter, matador
tormenta *nf* **1 :** storm <tormenta de nieve : snowstorm> **2 :** turmoil, frenzy
tormento *nm* **1 :** torment, anguish **2 :** torture
tormentoso, -sa *adj* **:** stormy, turbulent
tornado *nm* **:** tornado
tornamesa *nmf* **:** turntable
tornar *vt* **1 :** to return, to give back **2 :** to make, to render — *vi* **:** to go back — **tornarse** *vr* **:** to become, to turn into
tornasol *nm* **1 :** reflected light **2 :** sunflower **3 :** litmus
tornear *vt* **:** to turn (in carpentry)
torneo *nm* **:** tournament
tornillo *nm* **1 :** screw **2 tornillo de banco :** vise
torniquete *nm* **1 :** tourniquet **2 :** turnstile
torno *nm* **1 :** lathe **2 :** winch **3 torno de banco :** vise **4 en torno a :** around, about <en torno a este asunto : about this issue> <en torno suyo : around him>
toro *nm* **:** bull
toronja *nf* **:** grapefruit
toronjil *nm* **:** balm, lemon balm
torpe *adj* **1** DESMAÑADO **:** clumsy, awkward **2 :** stupid, dull — **torpemente** *adv*
torpedear *vt* **:** to torpedo
torpedo *nm* **:** torpedo
torpeza *nf* **1 :** clumsiness, awkwardness **2 :** stupidity **3 :** blunder
torre *nf* **1 :** tower <torre de perforación : oil rig> **2 :** turret **3 :** rook, castle (in chess)
torrencial *adj* **:** torrential — **torrencialmente** *adv*
torrente *nm* **1 :** torrent **2 torrente sanguíneo :** bloodstream
torreón *nm, pl* **-rreones :** tower (of a castle)
torreta *nf* **:** turret (of a tank, ship, etc.)
tórrido, -da *adj* **:** torrid
torsión *nf, pl* **torsiones :** torsion — **torsional** *adj*
torso *nm* **:** torso, trunk
torta *nf* **1 :** torte, cake **2** *Mex* **:** sandwich
tortazo *nm fam* **:** blow, wallop
tortilla *nf* **1 :** tortilla **2** *or* **tortilla de huevo :** omelet
tórtola *nf* **:** turtledove
tortuga *nf* **1 :** turtle, tortoise **2 tortuga de agua dulce :** terrapin **3 tortuga boba :** loggerhead
tortuoso, -sa *adj* **:** tortuous, winding
tortura *nf* **:** torture
torturador, -dora *n* **:** torturer
torturar *vt* **:** to torture, to torment
torvo, -va *adj* **:** grim, stern, baleful
torzamos, etc. → torcer
tos *nf* **1 :** cough **2 tos ferina :** whooping cough
tosco, -ca *adj* **:** rough, coarse
toser *vi* **:** to cough
tosquedad *nf* **:** crudeness, coarseness, roughness
tostada *nf* **1 :** piece of toast **2 :** tostada
tostador *nm* **1 :** toaster **2 :** roaster (for coffee)
tostar {19} *vt* **1 :** to toast **2 :** to roast (coffee) **3 :** to tan — **tostarse** *vr* **:** to get a tan
tostón *nm, pl* **tostones** *Car* **:** fried plantain chip
total[1] *adv* **:** in the end, so <total, que no fui : in short, I didn't go>
total[2] *adj & nm* **:** total — **totalmente** *adv*
totalidad *nf* **:** totality, whole
totalitario, -ria *adj & n* **:** totalitarian
totalitarismo *nm* **:** totalitarianism
totalizar {21} *vt* **:** total, to add up to
tótem *nm, pl* **tótems :** totem
totopo *nm CA, Mex* **:** tortilla chip
totuma *nf* **:** calabash
tour ['tur] *nm, pl* **tours :** tour, excursion
toxicidad *nf* **:** toxicity
tóxico[1], -ca *adj* **:** toxic, poisonous
tóxico[2] *nm* **:** poison
toxicomanía *nf* **:** drug addiction
toxicómano, -na *n* **:** drug addict
toxina *nf* **:** toxin
tozudez *nf* **:** stubbornness, obstinancy
tozudo, -da *adj* **:** stubborn, obstinate — **tozudamente** *adv*
traba *nf* **1 :** tie, bond **2 :** obstacle, hinderance
trabajador[1], -dora *adj* **:** hard-working
trabajador[2], -dora *n* **:** worker

trabajar *vi* **1 :** to work <trabaja mucho : he works hard> <trabajo de secretaria : I work as a secretary> **2 :** to strive <trabajan por mejores oportunidades : they're striving for better opportunities> **3 :** to act, to perform <trabajar en una película : to be in a movie> — *vt* **1 :** to work (metal) **2 :** to knead **3 :** to till **4 :** to work on <tienes que trabajar el español : you need to work on your Spanish>

trabajo *nm* **1 :** work, job **2** LABOR **:** labor, work <tengo mucho trabajo : I have a lot of work to do> **3** TAREA **:** task **4** ESFUERZA **:** effort **5 costar trabajo :** to be difficult **6 tomarse el trabajo :** to take the trouble **7 trabajo en equipo :** teamwork **8 trabajos** *nmpl* **:** hardships, difficulties

trabajoso, -sa *adj* LABORIOSO **:** laborious — **trabajosamente** *adv*

trabalenguas *nms & pl* **:** tongue twister

trabar *vt* **1 :** to join, to connect **2 :** to impede, to hold back **3 :** to strike up (a conversation), to form (a friendship) **4 :** to thicken (sauces) — **trabarse** *vr* **1 :** to jam **2 :** to become entangled **3 :** to be tongue-tied, to stammer

trabucar {72} *vt* **:** to confuse, to mix up

trabuco *nm* **:** blunderbuss

tracalero, -ra *adj Mex* **:** dishonest, tricky

tracción *nf* **:** traction

trace, etc. → **trazar**

tracto *nm* **:** tract

tractor *nm* **:** tractor

tradición *nf, pl* **-ciones :** tradition

tradicional *adj* **:** traditional — **tradicionalmente** *adv*

traducción *nf, pl* **-ciones :** translation

traducible *adj* **:** translatable

traducir {61} *vt* **1 :** to translate **2 :** to convey, to express — **traducirse** *vr* **~ en :** to result in

traductor, -dora *n* **:** translator

traer {81} *vt* **1 :** to bring <trae una ensalada : bring a salad> **2** CAUSAR **:** to cause, to bring about <el problema puede traer graves consecuencias : the problem could have serious consequences> **3 :** to carry, to have <todos los periódicos traían las mismas noticias : all of the newspapers carried the same news> **4** LLEVAR **:** to wear — **traerse** *vr* **1 :** to bring along **2 traérselas :** to be difficult

traficante *nmf* **:** dealer, trafficker

traficar {72} *vi* **1 :** to trade, to deal **2 ~ en :** to traffic in

tráfico *nm* **1 :** trade **2 :** traffic

tragaluz *nf, pl* **-luces :** skylight, fanlight

tragar {52} *v* **:** to swallow — **tragarse**

tragedia *nf* **:** tragedy

trágico, -ca *adj* **:** tragic — **trágicamente** *adv*

trago *nm* **1 :** swallow, swig **2 :** drink, liquor **3 trago amargo :** hard time

trague, etc. → **tragar**

traición *nf, pl* **traiciones 1 :** treason **2 :** betrayal, treachery

traicionar *vt* **:** to betray

traicionero, -ra → **traidor**

traidor[1], -dora *adj* **:** traitorous, treasonous

traidor[2], -dora *n* **:** traitor

traiga, etc. → **traer**

tráiler *or* **trailer** *nm* **:** trailer

traílla *nf* **1 :** leash **2 :** harrow

traje *nm* **1 :** suit **2 :** dress **3 :** costume **4 traje de baño :** bathing suit

trajín *nm, pl* **trajines 1 :** transport 2 *fam* **:** hustle and bustle

trajinar *vt* **:** to transport, to carry — *vi* **:** to rush around

trajo, etc. → **traer**

trama *nf* **1 :** plot **2 :** weave, weft (fabric)

tramar *vt* **1 :** to plot, to plan **2 :** to weave

tramitar *vt* **:** to transact, to negotiate, to handle

trámite *nm* **:** procedure, step

tramo *nm* **1 :** stretch, section **2 :** flight (of stairs)

trampa *nf* **1 :** trap **2 hacer trampas :** to cheat

trampear *vt* **:** to cheat

trampero, -ra *n* **:** trapper

trampilla *nf* **:** trapdoor

trampolín *nm, pl* **-lines 1 :** diving board **2 :** trampoline **3 :** springboard <un trampolín al éxito : a springboard to success>

tramposo[1], -sa *adj* **:** crooked, cheating

tramposo[2], -sa *n* **:** cheat, swindler

tranca *nf* **1 :** stick, club **2 :** bar, crossbar

trancar {72} *vt* **:** to bar (a door or window)

trancazo *nm* GOLPE **:** blow, hit

trance *nm* **1 :** critical juncture, tough time **2 :** trance **3 en trance de :** in the process of <en trance de extinción : on the verge of extinction>

tranco *nm* **1 :** stride **2** UMBRAL **:** threshold

tranque, etc. → **trancar**

tranquilidad *nf* **:** tranquility, peace

tranquilizador, -dora *adj* **1 :** soothing **2 :** reassuring

tranquilizante[1] *adj* **1 :** reassuring **2 :** tranquilizing

tranquilizante[2] *nm* **:** tranquilizer

tranquilizar {21} *vt* CALMAR **:** to calm down, to soothe <tranquilizar la conciencia : to ease the conscience> — **tranquilizarse** *vr*

tranquilo, -la *adj* CALMO **:** calm, tranquil <una vida tranquila : a quiet life> — **tranquilamente** *adv*

transacción *nf, pl* **-ciones :** transaction

transar *vi* TRANSIGIR **:** to give way, to compromise — *vt* **:** to buy and sell

transatlántico[1], -ca *adj* **:** transatlantic

transatlántico[2] *nm* : ocean liner

transbordador *nm* **1** : ferry **2 transbordador espacial** : space shuttle

transbordar *v* : to transfer

transbordo *nm* : transfer

transcendencia *nf* → **trascendencia**

transcender → **trascender**

transcribir {33} *vt* : to transcribe

transcrito *pp* → **transcribir**

transcripción *nf, pl* **-ciones** : transcription

transcurrir *vi* : to elapse, to pass

transcurso *nm* : course, progression <en el transcurso de cien años : over the course of a hundred years>

transeúnte *nmf* **1** : passerby **2** : transient

transferencia *nf* : transfer, transference

transferir {76} *vt* TRASLADAR : to transfer — **transferible** *adj*

transfigurar *vt* : to transfigure, to transform — **transfiguración** *nf*

transformación *nf, pl* **-ciones** : transformation, conversion

transformador *nm* : transformer

transformar *vt* **1** CONVERTIR : to convert **2** : to transform, to change, to alter — **transformarse** *vr*

transfusión *nf, pl* **-siones** : transfusion

transgredir {1} *vt* : to transgress — **transgresión** *nf*

transgresor, -sora *n* : transgressor

transición *nf, pl* **-ciones** : transition <período de transición : transition period>

transido, -da *adj* : overcome, beset <transido de dolor : racked with pain>

transigir {35} *vi* **1** : to give in, to compromise **2 ~ con** : to tolerate, to put up with

transistor *nm* : transistor

transitable *adj* : passable

transitar *vi* : to go, to pass, to travel <transitar por la ciudad : to travel through the city>

transitivo, -va *adj* : transitive

tránsito *nm* **1** TRÁFICO : traffic <hora de máximo tránsito : rush hour> **2** : transit, passage, movement **3** : death, passing

transitorio, -ria *adj* **1** : transitory **2** : provisional, temporary — **transitoriamente** *adv*

translúcido, -da *adj* : translucent

translucir → **traslucir**

transmisión *nf, pl* **-siones 1** : transmission, broadcast **2** : transfer **3** : transmission (of an automobile)

transmisor *nm* : transmitter

transmitir *vt* **1** : to transmit, to broadcast **2** : to pass on, to transfer — *vi* : to transmit, to broadcast

transparencia *nf* : transparency

transparentar *vt* : to reveal, to betray — **transparentarse** *vr* **1** : to be transparent **2** : to show through

transparente[1] *adj* : transparent — **transparentemente** *adv*

transparente[2] *nm* : shade, blind

transpiración *nf, pl* **-ciones** SUDOR : perspiration, sweat

transpirado, -da *adj* : sweaty

transpirar *vi* **1** SUDAR : to perspire, to sweat **2** : to transpire

transplantar, transplante → **trasplantar, trasplante**

transponer {60} *vt* **1** : to transpose, to move about **2** TRASPLANTAR : to transplant — **transponerse** *vr* **1** OCULTARSE : to hide **2** PONERSE : to set, to go down (of the sun or moon) **3** DORMITAR : to doze off

transportación *nf, pl* **-ciones** : transportation

transportador *nm* **1** : protractor **2** : conveyor

transportar *vt* **1** : to transport, to carry **2** : to transmit **3** : to transpose (music) — **transportarse** *vr* : to get carried away

transporte *nm* : transport, transportation

transportista *nmf* : hauler, carrier, trucker

transpuso, etc. → **transponer**

transversal *adj* : transverse, cross <corte transversal : cross section>

transversalmente *adv* : obliquely

transverso, -sa *adj* : transverse

tranvía *nm* : streetcar, trolley

trapeador *nm* : mop

trapear *vt* : to mop

trapecio *nm* **1** : trapezoid **2** : trapeze

trapezoide *nm* : trapezoid

trapo *nm* **1** : cloth, rag <trapo de polvo : dust cloth> **2 soltar el trapo** : to burst into tears **3 trapos** *nmpl fam* : clothes

tráquea *nf* : trachea, windpipe

traquetear *vi* : to clatter, to jolt

traqueteo *nm* **1** : jolting **2** : clattering, clatter

tras *prep* **1** : after <día tras día : day after day> <uno tras otro : one after another> **2** : behind <tras la puerta : behind the door>

trasbordar, trasbordo → **transbordar, transbordo**

trascendencia *nf* **1** : importance, significance **2** : transcendence

trascendental *adj* **1** : transcendental **2** : important, momentous

trascendente *adj* **1** : important, significant **2** : transcendent

trascender {56} *vi* **1** : to leak out, to become known **2** : to spread, to have a wide effect **3 ~ a** : to smell of <la casa trascendía a flores : the house smelled of flowers> **4 ~ de** : to transcend, to go beyond — *vt* : to transcend

trasero[1], **-sa** *adj* POSTERIOR : rear, back

trasero[2] *nm* : buttocks

trasfondo *nm* **1** : background, backdrop **2** : undertone, undercurrent

trasformación *nf* → **transformación**

trasgo *nm* : goblin, imp

trasgredir → **transgredir**
trasladar *vt* **1** TRANSFERIR : to transfer, to move **2** POSPONER : to postpone **3** TRADUCIR : to translate **4** COPIAR : to copy, to transcribe — **trasladarse** *vr* MUDARSE : to move, to relocate
traslado *nm* **1** : transfer, move **2** : copy
traslapar *vt* : to overlap — **traslaparse** *vr*
traslapo *nm* : overlap
traslúcido, -da → **translúcido**
traslucir {45} *vi* : to reveal, to show — **traslucirse** *vr* : to show through
trasmano *nm* **a ~** : out of the way, out of reach
trasmisión, trasmitir → **transmisión, transmitir**
trasnochar *vi* : to stay up all night
trasparencia *nf,* **trasparente** → **transparencia, transparente**
traspasar *vt* **1** PERFORAR : to pierce, to go through **2** : to go beyond <traspasar los límites : to overstep the limits> **3** ATRAVESAR : to cross, to go across **4** : to sell, to transfer
traspaso *nm* : transfer, sale
traspié *nm* **1** : stumble **2** : blunder
traspiración *nf* → **transpiración**
trasplantar *vt* : to transplant
trasplante *nm* : transplant
trasponer → **transponer**
trasportar → **transportar**
trasquilar *vt* ESQUILAR : to shear
traste *nm* **1** : fret (on a guitar) **2** *CA, Mex, PRi* : kitchen utensil <lavar los trastes : to do the dishes> **3 dar al traste con** : to ruin, to destroy **4 irse al traste** : to fall through
trastornar *vt* : to disturb, to upset, to disrupt — **trastornarse** *vr*
trastorno *nm* **1** : disorder <trastorno mental : mental disorder> **2** : disturbance, upset
trastos *nmpl* **1** : implements, utensils **2** *fam* : pieces of junk, stuff
trasunto *nm* : image, likeness
tratable *adj* **1** : friendly, sociable **2** : treatable
tratado *nm* **1** : treatise **2** : treaty
tratamiento *nm* : treatment
tratante *nmf* : dealer, trader
tratar *vi* **1 ~ con** : to deal with, to have contact with <no trato mucho con los clientes : I don't have much contact with customers> **2 ~ de** : to try to <estoy tratando de comer : I am trying to eat> **3 ~ de** *or* **~ sobre** : to be about, to concern <el libro trata de las plantas : the book is about plants> **4 ~ en** : to deal in <trata en herramientas : he deals in tools> — *vt* **1** : to treat <tratan bien a sus empleados : they treat their employees well> **2** : to handle <trató el tema con delicadeza : he handled the subject tactfully> — **tratarse** *vr* **~ de** : to be about, to concern
trato *nm* **1** : deal, agreement **2** : relationship, dealings *pl* **3** : treatment <malos tratos : ill-treatment>
trauma *nm* : trauma
traumático, -ca *adj* : traumatic — **traumáticamente** *adv*
traumatismo *nm* : injury <traumatismo cervical : whiplash>
través *nm* **1 a través de** : across, through **2 al través** : crosswise, across **3 de través** : sideways
travesaño *nm* **1** : crossbar **2** : crossbeam, crosspiece, transom (of a window)
travesía *nf* : voyage, crossing (of the sea)
travesura *nf* **1** : prank, mischievous act **2 travesuras** *nfpl* : mischief
travieso, -sa *adj* : mischievous, naughty — **traviesamente** *adv*
trayecto *nm* **1** : journey **2** : route **3** : trajectory, path
trayectoria *nf* : course, path, trajectory
trayendo → **traer**
traza *nf* **1** DISEÑO : design, plan **2** : appearance
trazado *nm* **1** BOSQUEJO : outline, sketch **2** PLAN : plan, layout
trazar {21} *vt* **1** : to trace **2** : to draw up, to devise **3** : to outline, to sketch
trazo *nm* **1** : stroke, line **2** : sketch, outline
trébol *nm* **1** : clover, shamrock **2** : club (playing card)
trece *adj & nm* : thirteen
treceavo[1], -va *adj* : thirteenth
treceavo[2] *nm* : thirteenth (fraction)
trecho *nm* **1** : stretch, period <de trecho en trecho : at intervals> **2** : distance, space
tregua *nf* **1** : truce **2** : lull, respite **3 sin ~** : relentless, unrelenting
treinta *adj & nm* : thirty
treintavo[1], -va *adj* : thirtieth
treintavo[2] *nm* : thirtieth (fraction)
tremendo, -da *adj* **1** : tremendous, enormous **2** : terrible, dreadful **3** *fam* : great, super
trementina *nf* AGUARRÁS : turpentine
trémulo, -la *adj* **1** : trembling, shaky **2** : flickering
tren *nm* **1** : train **2** : set, assembly <tren de aterrizaje : landing gear> **3** : speed, pace <a todo tren : at top speed>
trence, etc. → **trenzar**
trenza *nf* : braid, pigtail
trenzar {21} *vt* : to braid — **trenzarse** *vr* : to get involved
trepador, -dora *adj* : climbing <rosal trepador : rambling rose>
trepadora *nf* **1** : climbing plant, climber **2** : nuthatch
trepar *vi* **1** : to climb <trepar a un árbol : to climb up a tree> **2** : to creep, to spread (of a plant)
trepidación *nf, pl* **-ciones** : vibration
trepidante *adj* **1** : vibrating **2** : fast, frantic

trepidar *vi* **1 :** to shake, to vibrate **2 :** to hesitate, to waver

tres *adj & nm* **:** three

trescientos[1], -tas *adj* **:** two hundred

trescientos[2] *nms & pl* **:** three hundred

treta *nf* **:** trick, ruse

tríada *nf* **:** triad

triángulo *nm* **:** triangle — **triangular** *adj*

tribal *adj* **:** tribal

tribu *nf* **:** tribe

tribulación *nf, pl* **-ciones :** tribulation

tribuna *nf* **1 :** dais, platform **2 :** stands *pl,* bleachers *pl,* grandstand

tribunal *nm* **:** court, tribunal

tributar *vt* **:** to pay, to render — *vi* **:** to pay taxes

tributario[1], -ria *adj* **:** tax <evasión tributaria : tax evasion>

tributario[2] *nm* **:** tributary

tributo *nm* **1 :** tax **2 :** tribute

triciclo *nm* **:** tricycle

tricolor *adj* **:** tricolor, tricolored

tridente *nm* **:** trident

tridimensional *adj* **:** three-dimensional, 3-D

trienal *adj* **:** triennial

trifulca *nf fam* **:** row, ruckus

trigésimo[1], -ma *adj* **:** thirtieth, thirty-

trigésimo[2], -ma *n* **:** thirtieth, thirty- (in a series)

trigo *nm* **1 :** wheat **2 trigo rubión :** buckwheat

trigonometría *nf* **:** trigonometry

trigueño, -ña *adj* **1 :** light brown (of hair) **2** MORENO **:** dark, olive-skinned

trillado, -da *adj* **:** trite, hackneyed

trilladora *nf* **:** thresher, threshing machine

trillar *vt* **:** to thresh

trillizo, -za *n* **:** triplet

trilogía *nf* **:** trilogy

trimestral *adj* **:** quarterly — **trimestralmente** *adv*

trinar *vi* **1 :** to thrill **2 :** to warble

trinchar *vt* **:** to carve, to cut up

trinchera *nf* **1 :** trench, ditch **2 :** trench coat

tridente *nm* **:** trident

trineo *nm* **:** sled, sleigh

trinidad *nf* **la Trinidad :** the Trinity

trino *nm* **:** trill, warble

trinquete *nm* **:** ratchet

trío *nm* **:** trio

tripa *nf* **1** INTESTINO **:** gut, intestine **2 tripas** *nfpl fam* **:** belly, tummy, insides *pl* <dolerle a uno las tripas : to have a stomach ache>

tripartito, -ta *adj* **:** tripartite

triple *adj & nm* **:** triple

triplicado *nm* **:** triplicate

triplicar {72} *vt* **:** to triple, to treble

trípode *nm* **:** tripod

tripulación *nf, pl* **-ciones :** crew

tripulante *nmf* **:** crew member

tripular *vt* **:** to man

tris *nm* **estar en un tris de :** to be within an inch of, to be very close to

triste *adj* **1 :** sad, gloomy <ponerse triste : to become sad> **2 :** desolate, dismal <una perspectiva triste : a dismal outlook> **3 :** sorry, sorry-looking <la triste verdad : the sorry truth>

tristeza *nf* DOLOR **:** sadness, grief

tristón, -tona *adj, mpl* **-tones :** melancholy, downhearted

tritón *nm, pl* **tritones :** newt

triturar *vt* **:** to crush, to grind

triunfal *adj* **:** triumphal, triumphant — **triunfalmente** *adv*

triunfante *adj* **:** triumphant, victorious

triunfar *vi* **:** to triumph, to win

triunfo *nm* **1 :** triumph, victory **2** ÉXITO **:** success **3 :** trump (in card games)

triunvirato *nm* **:** triumvirate

trivial *adj* **1 :** trivial **2 :** trite, commonplace

trivialidad *nf* **:** triviality

triza *nf* **1 :** shred, bit **2 hacer trizas :** to tear into shreds, to smash to pieces

trocar {82} *vt* **1** CAMBIAR **:** to exchange, to trade **2** CAMBIAR **:** to change, to alter, to transform **3** CONFUNDIR **:** to confuse, to mix up

trocha *nf* **:** path, trail

troce, etc. → **trozar**

trofeo *nm* **:** trophy

tromba *nf* **1 :** whirlwind **2 tromba de agua :** downpour, cloudburst

trombón *nm, pl* **trombones 1 :** trombone **2 :** trombonist — **trombonista** *nmf*

trombosis *nf* **:** thrombosis

trompa *nf* **1 :** trunk (of an elephant), proboscis (of an insect) **2 :** horn <trompa de caza : hunting horn> **3 :** tube, duct (in the body)

trompada *nf fam* **1 :** punch, blow **2 :** bump, collision (of persons)

trompeta *nf* **:** trumpet

trompetista *nmf* **:** trumpet player, trumpeter

trompo *nm* **:** spinning top

tronada *nf* **:** thunderstorm

tronar {19} *vi* **1 :** to thunder, to roar **2 :** to be furious, to rage **3** *CA, Mex fam* **:** to shoot — *v impers* **:** to thunder <está tronando : it's thundering>

tronchar *vt* **1 :** to snap, to break off **2 :** to cut off (relations)

tronco *nm* **1 :** trunk (of a tree) **2 :** log **3 :** torso

trono *nm* **1 :** throne **2** *fam* **:** toilet

tropa *nf* **1 :** troop, soldiers *pl* **2 :** crowd, mob **3 :** herd (of livestock)

tropel *nm* **:** mob, swarm

tropezar {29} *vi* **1 :** to trip, to stumble **2 :** to slip up, to blunder **3 ~ con :** to run into, to bump into **4 ~ con :** to come up against (a problem)

tropezón *nm, pl* **-zones 1 :** stumble **2 :** mistake, slip

tropical *adj* **:** tropical

trópico *nm* **1 :** tropic <trópico de Cáncer : tropic of Cancer> **2 el trópico :** the tropics

tropiezo *nm* **1** CONTRATIEMPO **:** snag, setback **2** EQUIVOCACIÓN **:** mistake, slip

troqué, etc. → **trocar**

troquel *nm* **:** die (for stamping)

trotamundos *nmf* **:** globe-trotter

trotar *vi* **1 :** to trot **2 :** to jog **3** *fam* **:** to rush about

trote *nm* **1 :** trot **2** *fam* **:** rush, bustle **3 de ~ :** durable, for everyday use

trovador, -dora *n* **:** troubadour

trozar {21} *vt* **:** to cut up, to dice

trozo *nm* **1** PEDAZO **:** piece, bit, chunk **2 :** passage, extract

trucha *nf* **:** trout

truco *nm* **1 :** trick **2 :** knack

truculento, -ta *adj* **:** horrifying, gruesome

trueca, trueque, etc. → **trocar**

truena, etc. → **tronar**

trueno *nm* **:** thunder

trueque *nm* **:** barter, exchange

trufa *nf* **:** truffle

truncar {72} *vt* **1 :** to truncate, to cut short **2 :** to thwart, to frustrate <truncó sus esperanzas : she shattered their hopes>

trunco, -ca *adj* **1 :** truncated **2 :** unfinished, incomplete

trunque, etc. → **truncar**

tu *adj* **1 :** your <tu vestido : your dress> <toma tus vitaminas : take your vitamins> **2 :** thy

tú *pron* **1 :** you <tú eres mi hijo : you are my son> **2 :** thou

tuba *nf* **:** tuba

tubérculo *nm* **:** tuber

tuberculosis *nf* **:** tuberculosis

tuberculoso, -sa *adj* **:** tuberculous, tubercular

tubería *nf* **:** pipes *pl*, tubing

tuberoso, -sa *adj* **:** tuberous

tubo *nm* **1 :** tube <tubo de ensayo : test tube> **2 :** pipe <tubo de desagüe : drainpipe> **3 tubo digestivo :** alimentary canal

tubular *adj* **:** tubular

tuerca *nf* **:** nut <tuercas y tornillos : nuts and bolts>

tuerce, etc. → **torcer**

tuerto, -ta *adj* **:** one-eyed, blind in one eye

tuerza, etc. → **torcer**

tuesta, etc. → **tostar**

tuétano *nm* **:** marrow

tufo *nm* **1 :** fume, vapor **2** *fam* **:** stench, stink

tugurio *nm* **:** hovel

tulipán *nm, pl* **-panes :** tulip

tumba *nf* **1** SEPULCRO **:** tomb **2** FOSA **:** grave **3 :** felling of trees

tumbar *vt* **1 :** to knock down **2 :** to fell, to cut down — *vi* **:** to fall down — **tumbarse** *vr* ACOSTARSE **:** to lie down

tumbo *nm* **1 :** tumble, fall **2 dar tumbos :** to jolt, to bump around

tumor *nm* **:** tumor

túmulo *nm* **:** burial mound

tumulto *nm* **1** ALBOROTO **:** commotion, tumult **2** MOTÍN **:** riot **3** MULTITUD **:** crowd

tumultuoso, -sa *adj* **:** tumultuous

tuna *nf* **:** prickly pear (fruit)

tundra *nf* **:** tundra

tunecino, -na *adj & n* **:** Tunisian

túnel *nm* **:** tunnel

tungsteno *nm* **:** tungsten

túnica *nf* **:** tunic

tupé *nm* PELUQUÍN **:** toupee

tupido, -da *adj* **1** DENSO **:** dense, thick **2** OBSTRUIDO **:** obstructed, blocked up

turba *nf* **1 :** peat **2 :** mob, throng

turbación *nf, pl* **-ciones 1 :** disturbance **2 :** alarm, concern **3 :** confusion

turbante *nm* **:** turban

turbar *vt* **1 :** to disturb, to disrupt **2 :** to worry, to upset **3 :** to confuse

turbina *nf* **:** turbine

turbio, -bia *adj* **1 :** cloudy, murky, turbid **2 :** dim, blurred **3 :** shady, crooked

turbopropulsor *nm* **:** turboprop

turborreactor *nm* **:** turbojet

turbulencia *nf* **:** turbulence

turbulento, -ta *adj* **:** turbulent

turco[1], -ca *adj* **:** Turkish

turco[2], -ca *n* **:** Turk

turgente *adj* **:** turgid, swollen

turismo *nm* **:** tourism, tourist industry

turista *nmf* **:** tourist, vacationer

turístico, -ca *adj* **:** tourist, travel

turnar *vi* **:** to take turns, to alternate

turno *nm* **1 :** turn <ya te tocará tu turno : you'll get your turn> **2 :** shift, duty <turno de noche : night shift> **3 por turno :** alternately

turón *nm, pl* **turones :** polecat

turquesa *nf* **:** turquoise

turrón *nm, pl* **turrones :** nougat

tusa *nf* **:** corn husk

tutear *vt* **:** to address as *tú*

tutela *nf* **1 :** guardianship **2 :** tutelage, protection

tuteo *nm* **:** addressing as *tú*

tutor, -tora *n* **1 :** tutor **2 :** guardian

tuvo, etc. → **tener**

tuyo[1], -ya *adj* **:** yours, of yours <un amigo tuyo : a friend of yours> <¿es tuya esta casa? : is this house yours?>

tuyo[2], -ya *pron* **1 :** yours <ése es el tuyo : that one is yours> <trae la tuya : bring your own> **2 los tuyos :** your relations, your friends <¿vendrán los tuyos? : are your folks coming?>

tweed ['twið] *nm* **:** tweed

U

u[1] *nf* : twenty-second letter of the Spanish alphabet
u[2] *conj* (*used instead of* **o** *before words beginning with o- or ho-*) : or
ualabí *nm* : wallaby
uapití *nm* : American elk, wapiti
ubicación *nf, pl* **-ciones** : location, position
ubicar {72} *vt* **1** SITUAR : to place, to put, to position **2** LOCALIZAR : to locate, to find — **ubicarse** *vr* **1** LOCALIZARSE : to be placed, to be located **2** SITUARSE : to position oneself
ubicuidad *nf* OMNIPRESENCIA : ubiquity
ubicuo, -cua *adj* OMNIPRESENTE : ubiquitous
ubre *nf* : udder
ucraniano, -na *adj & n* : Ukranian
Ud., Uds. → **usted**
ufanarse *vr* **~ de** : to boast about, to pride oneself on
ufano, -na *adj* **1** ORGULLOSO : proud **2** : self-satisfied, smug
ugandés, -desa *adj & n, mpl* **-deses** : Ugandan
ukelele *nm* : ukulele
úlcera *nf* : ulcer — **ulceroso, -sa** *adj*
ulcerar *vt* : to ulcerate — **ulcerarse** *vr* — **ulceración** *nf*
ulceroso, -sa *adj* : ulcerous
ulterior *adj* : later, subsequent — **ulteriormente** *adv*
últimamente *adv* : lately, recently
ultimar *vt* **1** CONCLUIR : to complete, to finish, to finalize **2** MATAR : to kill
ultimátum *nm, pl* **-tums** : ultimatum
último, -ma *adj* **1** : last, final <la última galleta : the last cookie> <en último caso : as a last resort> **2** : last, latest, most recent <su último viaje a España : her last trip to Spain> <en los últimos años : in recent years> **3 por ~** : finally
ultrajar *vt* INSULTAR : to offend, to outrage, to insult
ultraje *nm* INSULTO : outrage, insult
ultramar *nm* **de ~** *or* **en ~** : overseas, abroad
ultranza *nf* **a ~ 1** : to the extreme <lo defendió a ultranza : she defended him fiercely> **2** : extreme, out-and-out <perfeccionismo a ultranza : rabid perfectionism>
ultrarrojo, -ja *adj* : infrared
ultravioleta *adj* : ultraviolet
ulular *vi* **1** : to hoot **2** : to howl, to wail
ululato *nm* : hoot (of an owl), wail (of a person)
umbilical *adj* : umbilical <cordón umbilical : umbilical cord>
umbral *nm* : threshold, doorstep
un[1] → **uno**[1]
un[2], **una** *art, mpl* **unos 1** : a, an **2 unos** *or* **unas** *pl* : some, a few <hace unas semanas : a few weeks ago> **3 unos** *or* **unas** *pl* : about, approximately <unos veinte años antes : about twenty years before>
unánime *adj* : unanimous — **unánimemente** *adv*
unanimidad *nf* **1** : unanimity **2 por ~** : unanimously
unción *nf, pl* **-ciones** : unction
uncir {83} *vt* : to yoke
undécimo[1], **-ma** *adj* : eleventh
undécimo[2], **-ma** *n* : eleventh (in a series)
ungir {35} *vt* : to anoint
ungüento *nm* : ointment, salve
únicamente *adv* : only, solely
unicelular *adj* : unicellular
único[1], **-ca** *adj* **1** : only, sole **2** : unique, extraordinary
único[2], **-ca** *n* : only one <los únicos que vinieron : the only ones who showed up>
unicornio *nm* : unicorn
unidad *nf* **1** : unity **2** : unit
unidireccional *adj* : unidirectional
unido, -da *adj* **1** : joined, united **2** : close <unos amigos muy unidos : very close friends>
unificar {72} *vt* : to unify — **unificación** *nf*
uniformado, -da *adj* : uniformed
uniformar *vt* ESTANDARIZAR : to standardize, to make uniform
uniforme[1] *adj* : uniform — **uniformemente** *adv*
uniforme[2] *nm* : uniform
uniformidad *nf* : uniformity
unilateral *adj* : unilateral — **unilateralmente** *adv*
unión *nf, pl* **uniones 1** : union **2** JUNTURA : joint, coupling
unir *vt* **1** JUNTAR : to unite, to join, to link **2** COMBINAR : to combine, to blend — **unirse** *vr* **1** : to join together **2** : to combine, to mix together **3 ~ a** : to join <se unieron al grupo : they joined the group>
unísono *nm* : unison <al unísono : in unison>
unitario, -ria *adj* : unitary, unit <precio unitario : unit price>
universal *adj* : universal — **universalmente** *adv*
universidad *nf* : university
universitario[1], **-ria** *adj* : university, college
universitario[2], **-ria** *n* : university student, college student
universo *nm* : universe
unja, etc. → **ungir**
uno[1], **una** *adj* (**un** *before masculine singular nouns*) : one <una silla : one chair> <tiene treinta y un años : he's thirty-one years old> <el tomo uno : volume one>
uno[2] *nm* : one, number one
uno[3], **una** *pron* **1** : one (number) <uno por uno : one by one> <es la una : it's

one o'clock> **2 :** one (person or thing) <una es mejor que las otras : one (of them) is better than the others> <hacerlo uno mismo : to do it oneself> **3 unos, unas** *pl* **:** some (ones), some people **4 uno y otro :** both **5 unos y otros :** all of them **6 el uno al otro :** one another, each other <se enseñaron los unos a los otros : they taught each other>
untar *vt* **1 :** to anoint **2 :** to smear, to grease **3 :** to bribe
unza, etc. → **uncir**
uña *nf* **1 :** fingernail, toenail **2 :** claw, hoof, stinger
uranio *nm* **:** uranium
Urano *nm* **:** Uranus
urbanidad *nf* **:** urbanity, courtesy
urbanización *nf, pl* **-ciones :** housing development, residential area
urbano, -na *adj* **1 :** urban **2** CORTÉS **:** urbane, polite
urbe *nf* **:** large city, metropolis
urdimbre *nf* **:** warp (in a loom)
uretra *nf* **:** urethra
urgencia *nf* **1 :** urgency **2** EMERGENCIA **:** emergency
urgente *adj* **:** urgent — **urgentemente** *adv*
urgir {35} *v impers* **:** to be urgent, to be pressing <me urge localizarlo : I urgently need to find him> <el tiempo urge : time is running out>
urinario[1], -ria *adj* **:** urinary
urinario[2] *nm* **:** urinal (place)
urja, etc. → **urgir**
urna *nf* **1 :** urn **2 :** ballot box <acudir a las urnas : to go to the polls>
urogallo *nm* **:** grouse (bird)
urraca *nf* **1 :** magpie **2 urraca de América :** blue jay
urticaria *nf* **:** hives
uruguayo, -ya *adj & n* **:** Uruguayan
usado, -da *adj* **1 :** used, secondhand **2 :** worn, worn-out
usanza *nf* **:** custom, usage
usar *vt* **1** EMPLEAR, UTILIZAR **:** to use, to make use of **2** CONSUMIR **:** to consume, to use (up) **3** LLEVAR **:** to wear **4 de usar y tirar :** disposable — **usarse 1 :** to be used **2 :** to be in fashion
uso *nm* **1** EMPLEO, UTILIZACIÓN **:** use <de uso personal : for personal use> <hacer uso de : to make use of> **2 :** wear <uso y desgaste : wear and tear> **3** USANZA **:** custom, usage, habit <al uso de : in the manner of, in the style of>
usted *pron* **1** (*formal form of address in most countries; often written as* **Ud.** *or* **Vd.**) **:** you **2 ustedes** *pl* (*often written as* **Uds.** *or* **Vds.**) **:** you, all of you
usual *adj* **:** usual, common, normal <poco usual : not very common> — **usualmente** *adv*
usuario, -ria *n* **:** user
usura *nf* **:** usury — **usurario, -ria** *adj*
usurero, -ra *n* **:** usurer
usurpador, -dora *n* **:** usurper
usurpar *vt* **:** to usurp — **usurpación** *nf*
utensilio *nm* **:** utensil, tool
uterino, -na *adj* **:** uterine
útero *nm* **:** uterus, womb
útil *adj* **:** useful, handy, helpful
útiles *nmpl* **:** implements, tools
utilidad *nf* **1 :** utility, usefulness **2 utilidades** *nfpl* **:** profits
utilitario, -ria *adj* **:** utilitarian
utilizable *adj* **:** usable, fit for use
utilización *nf, pl* **-ciones :** utilization, use
utilizar {21} *vt* **:** to use, to utilize
útilmente *adv* **:** usefully
utopía *nf* **:** utopia
utópico, -ca *adj* **:** utopian
uva *nf* **:** grape
uvular *adj* **:** uvular

V

v *nf* **:** twenty-third letter of the Spanish alphabet
va → **ir**
vaca *nf* **:** cow
vacación *nf, pl* **-ciones 1 :** vacation <dos semanas de vacaciones : two weeks of vacation> **2 estar de vacaciones :** to be on vacation **3 irse de vacaciones :** to go on vacation
vacacionar *vi Mex* **:** to vacation
vacacionista *nmf CA, Mex* **:** vacationer
vacante[1] *adj* **:** vacant, empty
vacante[2] *nf* **:** vacancy (for a job)
vaciado *nm* **:** cast, casting <vaciado de yeso : plaster cast>
vaciar {85} *vt* **1 :** to empty, to empty out, to drain **2** AHUECAR **:** to hollow out **3 :** to cast (in a mold) — *vi* **~ en :** to flow into, to empty into
vacilación *nf, pl* **-ciones :** hesitation, vacillation
vacilante *adj* **1 :** hesitant, unsure **2 :** shaky, unsteady **3 :** flickering
vacilar *vi* **1 :** to hesitate, to vacillate, to waver **2 :** to be unsteady, to wobble **3 :** to flicker **4** *fam* **:** to joke, to fool around
vacío[1], -cía *adj* **1 :** vacant **2 :** empty **3 :** meaningless
vacío[2] *nm* **1 :** emptiness, void **2 :** space, gap **3 :** vacuum **4 hacerle el vacío a alguien :** to ostracize someone, to give someone the cold shoulder
vacuidad *nf* **:** vacuity, vacuousness
vacuna *nf* **:** vaccine
vacunación *nf, pl* **-ciones** INOCULACIÓN **:** vaccination, inoculation

vacunar *vt* INOCULAR : to vaccinate, to inoculate
vacuno¹, -na *adj* : bovine <ganado vacuno : beef cattle>
vacuno² *nm* : bovine
vacuo, -cua *adj* : empty, shallow, inane
vadear *vt* : to ford, to wade across
vado *nm* : ford
vagabundear *vi* : to wander, to roam about
vagabundo¹, -da *adj* **1** ERRANTE : wandering **2** : stray
vagabundo², -da *n* : vagrant, bum, vagabond
vagamente *adv* : vaguely
vagancia *nf* **1** : vagrancy **2** PEREZA : laziness, idleness
vagar {52} *vi* ERRAR : to roam, to wander
vagina *nf* : vagina — **vaginal** *adj*
vago¹, -ga *adj* **1** : vague **2** PEREZOSO : lazy, idle
vago², -ga *n* **1** : idler, loafer **2** VAGABUNDO : vagrant, bum
vagón *nm, pl* **vagones** : car (of a train)
vague, etc. → **vagar**
vaguear *vi* **1** : to loaf, to lounge around **2** VAGAR : to wander
vaguedad *nf* : vagueness
vahído *nm* : dizzy spell
vaho *nm* **1** : breath **2** : vapor, steam (on glass, etc.)
vaina *nf* **1** : sheath, scabbard **2** : pod (of a pea or bean) **3** *fam* : nuisance, bother
vainilla *nf* : vanilla
vaivén *nm, pl* **vaivenes 1** : swinging, swaying, rocking **2** : change, fluctuation <los vaivenes de la vida : life's ups and downs>
vajilla *nf* : dishes *pl*, set of dishes
valdrá, etc. → **valer**
vale *nm* **1** : voucher **2** PAGARÉ : promissary note, IOU
valedero, -ra *adj* : valid
valentía *nf* : courage, valor
valer {84} *vt* **1** : to be worth <valen una fortuna : they're worth a fortune> <no vale protestar : there's no point in protesting> <valer la pena : to be worth the trouble> **2** : to cost <¿cuánto vale? : how much does it cost?> **3** : to earn, to gain <le valió una reprimenda : it earned him a reprimand> **4** : to protect, to aid <¡válgame Dios! : God help me!> **5** : to be equal to — *vi* **1** : to have value <sus consejos no valen para nada : his advice is worthless> **2** : to be valid, to count <¡eso no vale! : that doesn't count!> **3 hacerse valer** : to assert oneself **4 más vale** : it's better <más vale que te vayas : you'd better go> — **valerse** *vr* **1 ~ de** : to take advantage of **2 valerse solo** *or* **valerse por sí mismo** : to look after oneself **3** *Mex* : to be fair <no se vale : it's not fair>
valeroso, -sa *adj* : brave, valiant
valet [ˈbalɛt, -ˈle] *nm* : jack (in playing cards)
valga, etc. → **valer**
valía *nf* : value, worth
validar *vt* : to validate — **validación** *nf*
validez *nf* : validity
válido, -da *adj* : valid
valiente *adj* **1** : brave, valiant **2** (*used ironically*) : fine, great <¡valiente amiga! : what a fine friend!> — **valientemente** *adv*
valija *nf* : suitcase, valise
valioso, -sa *adj* PRECIOSO : valuable, precious
valla *nf* **1** : fence, barricade **2** : hurdle (in sports) **3** : obstacle, hindrance
vallar *vt* : to fence, to put a fence around
valle *nm* : valley, vale
valor *nm* **1** : value, worth, importance **2** CORAJE : courage, valor **3 valores** *nmpl* : values, principles **4 valores** *nmpl* : securities, bonds **5 sin ~** : worthless
valoración *nf, pl* **-ciones 1** EVALUACIÓN : valuation, appraisal, assessment **2** APRECIACIÓN : appreciation
valorar *vt* **1** EVALUAR : to evaluate, to appraise, to assess **2** APRECIAR : to value, to appreciate
valorizarse {21} *vr* : to appreciate, to increase in value — **valorización** *nf*
vals *nm* : waltz
valsar *vi* : to waltz
valuación *nf, pl* **-ciones** : valuation, appraisal
valuar {3} *vt* : to value, to appraise, to assess
válvula *nf* **1** : valve **2 válvula reguladora** : throttle
vamos → **ir**
vampiro *nm* : vampire
van → **ir**
vanadio *nm* : vanadium
vanagloriarse *vr* : to boast, to brag
vanamente *adv* : vainly, in vain
vandalismo : vandalism
vándalo *nm* : vandal — **vandalismo** *nm*
vanguardia *nf* **1** : vanguard **2** : avantegarde **3 a la vanguardia** : at the forefront
vanidad *nf* : vanity
vanidoso, -sa *adj* PRESUMIDO : vain, conceited
vano, -na *adj* **1** INÚTIL : vain, useless **2** : vain, worthless <vanas promesas : empty promises> **3 en ~** : in vain, of no avail
vapor *nm* **1** : vapor, steam **2** : steamer, steamship **3 al vapor** : steamed
vaporizador *nm* : vaporizer
vaporizar {21} *vt* : to vaporize — **vaporizarse** *vr* — **vaporización** *nf*
vaporoso, -sa *adj* **1** : vaporous **2** : sheer, airy
vapulear *vt* : to beat, to thrash

vaquero[1], **-ra** *adj* : cowboy <pantalón vaquero : jeans>
vaquero[2], **-ra** *n* : cowboy *m,* cowgirl *f*
vaqueros *nmpl* JEANS : jeans
vaquilla *nf* : heifer
vara *nf* **1** : pole, stick, rod **2** : staff (of office) **3** : lance, pike (in bullfighting) **4** : yardstick **5 vara de oro** : goldenrod
varado, -da *adj* **1** : beached, aground **2** : stranded
varar *vt* : to beach (a ship), to strand — *vi* : to run aground
variable *adj & nf* : variable — **variabilidad** *nf*
variación *nf, pl* **-ciones** : variation
variado, -da *adj* : varied, diverse
variante *adj & nf* : variant
varianza *nf* : variance
variar {85} *vt* **1** : to change, to alter **2** : to diversify — *vi* **1** : to vary, to change **2 variar de opinión** : to change one's mind
varicela *nf* : chicken pox
varices *or* **várices** *nfpl* : varicose veins
varicoso, -sa *adj* : varicose
variedad *nf* DIVERSIDAD : variety, diversity
varilla *nf* **1** : rod, bar **2** : spoke (of a wheel) **3** : rib (of an umbrella)
vario, -ria *adj* **1** : varied, diverse **2** : variegated, motley **3** : changeable **4 varios, varias** *pl* : various, several
variopinto, -ta *adj* : diverse, assorted, motley
varita *nf* : wand <varita mágica : magic wand>
varón *nm, pl* **varones 1** HOMBRE : man, male **2** NIÑO : boy
varonil *adj* **1** : masculine, manly **2** : mannish
vas → **ir**
vasallo *nm* : vassal — **vasallaje** *nm*
vasco[1], **-ca** *adj & n* : Basque
vasco[2] *nm* : Basque (language)
vascular *adj* : vascular
vasija *nf* : container, vessel
vaso *nm* **1** : glass, tumbler **2** : glassful **3** : vessel <vaso sanguíneo : blood vessel>
vástago *nm* **1** : offspring, descendent **2** : shoot (of a plant)
vastedad *nf* : vastness, immensity
vasto, -ta *adj* : vast, immense
vataje *nm* : wattage
vaticinar *vt* : to predict, to foretell
vaticinio *nm* : prediction, prophecy
vatio *nm* : watt
vaya, etc. → **ir**
Vd., Vds. → **usted**
ve, etc. → **ir, ver**
vea, etc. → **ver**
vecinal *adj* : local
vecindad *nf* **1** : neighborhood, vicinity **2 casa de vecindad** : tenement
vecindario *nm* **1** : neighborhood, area **2** : residents *pl*
vecino, -na *n* **1** : neighbor **2** : resident, inhabitant
veda *nf* **1** PROHIBICIÓN : prohibition **2** : closed season (for hunting or fishing)
vedar *vt* **1** : to prohibit, to ban **2** IMPEDIR : to impede, to prevent
vega *nf* : fertile lowland
vegetación *nf, pl* **-ciones 1** : vegetation **2 vegetaciones** *nfpl* : adenoids
vegetal *adj & nm* : vegetable, plant
vegetar *vi* : to vegetate
vegetarianismo *nm* : vegetarianism
vegetariano, -na *adj & n* : vegetarian
vegetativo, -va *adj* : vegetative
vehemente *adj* : vehement — **vehemencia** *nf*
vehículo *nm* : vehicle — **vehicular** *adj*
veía, etc. → **ver**
veinte *adj & nm* : twenty
veinteavo[1], **-va** *adj* : twentieth
veinteavo[2] *nm* : twentieth (fraction)
veintena *nf* : group of twenty, score <una veintena de participantes : about twenty participants>
vejación *nf, pl* **-ciones** : ill-treatment, humiliation
vejar *vt* : to mistreat, to ridicule, to harass
vejete *nm* : old fellow, codger
vejez *nf* : old age
vejiga *nf* **1** : bladder **2** AMPOLLA : blister
vela *nf* **1** VIGILIA : wakefulness <pasé la noche en vela : I stayed awake all night> **2** : watch, vigil, wake **3** : candle **4** : sail
velada *nf* : evening party, soirée
velado, -da *adj* **1** : veiled, hidden **2** : blurred **3** : muffled
velador[1], **-dora** *n* : guard, night watchman
velador[2] *nm* **1** : candlestick **2** : night table
velar *vt* **1** : to hold a wake over **2** : to watch over, to sit up with **3** : to blur, to expose (a photo) **4** : to veil, to conceal — *vi* **1** : to stay awake **2 ~ por** : to watch over, to look after
velatorio *nm* VELORIO : wake (for the dead)
veleidad *nf* **1** : fickleness **2** : whim, caprice
veleidoso, -sa : fickle, capricious
velero *nm* **1** : sailing ship **2** : sailboat
veleta *nf* : weather vane
vello *nm* **1** : body hair **2** : down, fuzz
vellocino *nm* : fleece
vellón *nm, pl* **vellones 1** : fleece, sheepskin **2** *PRi* : nickel (coin)
vellosidad *nf* : downiness, hairiness
velloso, -sa *adj* : downy, fluffy, hairy
velo *nm* : veil
velocidad *nf* **1** : speed, velocity <velocidad máxima : speed limit> **2** MARCHA : gear (of an automobile)
velocímetro *nm* : speedometer
velocista *nmf* : sprinter
velorio *nm* VELATORIO : wake (for the dead)
velour *nm* : velour, velours

veloz *adj, pl* **veloces :** fast, quick, swift — **velozmente** *adv*

ven → **venir**

vena *nf* **1 :** vein <vena yugular : jugular vein> **2 :** vein, seam, lode **3 :** grain (of wood) **4 :** style <en vena lírica : in a lyrical vein> **5 :** strain, touch <una vena de humor : a touch of humor> **6 :** mood

venado *nm* **1 :** deer **2 :** venison

venal *adj* **:** venal — **venalidad** *nf*

vencedor, -dora *n* **:** winner, victor

vencejo *nm* **:** swift (bird)

vencer {86} *vt* **1** DERROTAR **:** to vanquish, to defeat **2** SUPERAR **:** to overcome, to surmount — *vi* **1** GANAR **:** to win, to triumph **2** CADUCAR **:** to expire <el plazo vence el jueves : the deadline is Thursday> **3 :** to fall due, to mature — **vencerse** *vr* **1** DOMINARSE **:** to control oneself **2 :** to break, to collapse

vencido, -da *adj* **1 :** defeated **2 :** expired **3 :** due, payable **4 darse por vencido :** to give up

vencimiento *nm* **1 :** defeat **2 :** expiration **3 :** maturity (of a loan)

venda *nf* **:** bandage

vendaje *nm* **:** bandage, dressing

vendar *vt* **1 :** to bandage **2 vendar los ojos :** to blindfold

vendaval *nm* **:** gale, strong wind

vendedor, -dora *n* **:** salesperson, salesman *m,* saleswoman *f*

vender *vt* **1 :** to sell **2 :** to sell out, to betray — **venderse 1 :** to be sold <se vende : for sale> **2 :** to sell out

vendetta *nf* **:** vendetta

vendible *adj* **:** salable, marketable

vendimia *nf* **:** grape harvest

vendrá, etc. → **venir**

veneno *nm* **1 :** poison **2 :** venom

venenoso, -sa *adj* **:** poisonous, venomous

venerable *adj* **:** venerable

veneración *nf, pl* **-ciones :** veneration, reverence

venerar *vt* **:** to venerate, to revere

venéreo, -rea *adj* **:** venereal

venero *nm* **1** VENA **:** seam, lode, vein **2** MANANTIAL **:** spring **3** FUENTE **:** origin, source

venezolano, -na *adj & n* **:** Venezuelan

venga, etc. → **venir**

vengador, -dora *n* **:** avenger

venganza *nf* **:** vengeance, revenge

vengar {52} *vt* **:** to avenge — **vengarse** *vr* **:** to get even, to revenge oneself

vengativo, -va *adj* **:** vindictive, vengeful

vengue, etc. → **vengar**

venia *nf* **1** PERMISO **:** permission, leave **2** PERDÓN **:** pardon **3 :** bow (of the head)

venial *adj* **:** venial

venida *nf* **1** LLEGADA **:** arrival, coming **2** REGRESO **:** return **3 idas y venidas :** comings and goings

venidero, -ra *adj* **:** coming, future

venir {87} *vi* **1 :** to come <lo vi venir : I saw him coming> <¡venga! : come on!> **2 :** to arrive <vinieron en coche : they came by car> **3 :** to come, to originate <sus zapatos vienen de Italia : her shoes are from Italy> **4 :** to come, to be available <viene envuelto en plástico : it comes wrapped in plastic> **5 :** to come back, to return **6 :** to affect, to overcome <me vino un vahído : a dizzy spell came over me> **7 :** to fit <te viene un poco grande : it's a little big for you> **8** (*with the present participle*) **:** to have been <viene entrenando diariamente : he's been training daily> **9 ~ a** (*with the infinitive*) **:** to end up, to turn out <viene a ser lo mismo : it comes out the same> **10 que viene :** coming, next <el año que viene : next year> **11 venir bien :** to be suitable, to be just right — **venirse** *vr* **1 :** to come, to arrive **2 :** to come back **3 venirse abajo :** to fall apart, to collapse

venta *nf* **1 :** sale **2 venta al por menor** *or* **venta al detalle :** retail sales

ventaja *nf* **1 :** advantage **2 :** lead, head start **3 ventajas** *nfpl* **:** perks, extras

ventajoso, -sa *adj* **1 :** advantageous **2 :** profitable — **ventajosamente** *adv*

ventana *nf* **1 :** window (of a building) **2 ventana de la nariz :** nostril

ventanal *nm* **:** large window

ventanilla *nf* **1 :** window (of a vehicle or airplane) **2 :** ticket window, box office

ventero, -ra *n* **:** innkeeper

ventilación *nf, pl* **-ciones :** ventilation

ventilador *nm* **1 :** ventilator **2 :** fan

ventilar *vt* **1 :** to ventilate, to air out **2 :** to air, to discuss **3 :** to make public, to reveal — **ventilarse** *vr* **:** to get some air

ventisca *nf* **:** snowstorm, blizzard

ventisquero *nm* **:** snowdrift

ventosear *vi* **:** to break wind

ventosidad *nf* **:** wind, flatulence

ventoso, -sa *adj* **:** windy

ventrículo *nm* **:** ventricle

ventrílocuo, -cua *n* **:** ventriloquist

ventriloquia *nf* **:** ventriloquism

ventura *nf* **1 :** fortune, luck, chance **2 :** happiness **3 a la ventura :** at random, as it comes

venturoso, -sa *adj* **1** AFORTUNADO **:** fortunate, lucky **2 :** successful

Venus *nm* **:** Venus

venza, etc. → **vencer**

ver[1] {88} *vt* **1 :** to see <vimos la película : we saw the movie> **2** ENTENDER **:** to understand <ya lo veo : now I get it> **3** EXAMINAR **:** to examine, to look into <lo veré : I'll take a look at it> **4** JUZGAR **:** to see, to judge <a mi manera de ver : to my way of thinking> **5** VISITAR **:** to meet with, to visit **6** AVERIGUAR **:** to find out **7 a ver** *or* **vamos a ver :** let's see — *vi* **1 :** to see **2** ENTERARSE **:** to learn, to find out **3**

ENTENDER : to understand — **verse** *vr* **1** HALLARSE : to find oneself **2** PARECER : to look, to appear **3** ENCONTRARSE : to see each other, to meet

ver[2] *nm* **1** : looks *pl*, appearance **2** : opinion <a mi ver : in my view>

vera *nf* : side <a la vera del camino : alongside the road>

veracidad *nf* : truthfulness, veracity

veranda *nf* : veranda

veraneante *nmf* : summer vacationer

veranear *vi* : to spend the summer

veraniego, -ga *adj* **1** ESTIVAL : summer <el sol veraniego : the summer sun> **2** : summery

verano *nm* : summer

veras *nfpl* **de ~** : really, truly

veraz *adj, pl* **veraces** : truthful, veracious

verbal *adj* : verbal — **verbalmente** *adv*

verbalizar {21} *vt* : to verbalize, to express

verbena *nf* **1** FIESTA : festival, fair **2** : verbena, vervain

verbigracia *adv* : for example

verbo *nm* : verb

verborrea *nf* : verbiage

verbosidad *nf* : verbosity, wordiness

verboso, -sa *adj* : verbose, wordy

verdad *nf* **1** : truth **2 de ~** : really, truly **3 ¿verdad?** : right?, isn't that so?

verdaderamente *adv* : really, truly

verdadero, -dera *adj* **1** REAL, VERÍDICO : true, real **2** AUTÉNTICO : genuine

verde[1] *adj* **1** : green (in color) **2** : green, unripe **3** : inexperienced, green **4** : dirty, risqué

verde[2] *nm* : green

verdear *vi* : to turn green, to become verdant

verdín *nm, pl* **verdines** : slime, scum

verdor *nm* **1** : greenness **2** : verdure

verdoso, -sa *adj* : greenish

verdugo *nm* **1** : executioner, hangman **2** : tyrant

verdugón *nm, pl* **-gones** : welt, wheal

verdura *nf* : vegetable(s), green(s)

vereda *nf* **1** SENDA : path, trail **2** : sidewalk, pavement

veredicto *nm* : verdict

verga *nf* : spar, yard (of a ship)

vergonzoso, -sa *adj* **1** : disgraceful, shameful **2** : bashful, shy — **vergonzosamente** *adv*

vergüenza *nf* **1** : disgrace, shame **2** : embarrassment **3** : bashfulness, shyness

vericueto *nm* : rough terrain

verídico, -ca *adj* **1** REAL, VERDADERO : true, real **2** VERAZ : truthful

verificación *nf, pl* **-ciones 1** : verification **2** : testing, checking

verificador, -dora *n* : inspector, tester

verificar {72} *vt* **1** : to verify, to confirm **2** : to test, to check **3** : to carry out, to conduct — **verificarse** *vr* **1** : to take place, to occur **2** : to come true

verja *nf* **1** : rails *pl* (of a fence) **2** : grating, grille **3** : gate

vermut *nm, pl* **vermuts** : vermouth

vernáculo, -la *adj* : vernacular

vernal *adj* : vernal, spring

verosímil *adj* **1** : probable, likely **2** : credible, realistic

verosimilitud *nf* **1** : probability, likeliness **2** : verisimilitude

verraco *nm* : boar

verruga *nf* : wart

versado, -da *adj* **~ en** : versed in, knowledgeable about

versar *vi* **~ sobre** : to deal with, to be about

versátil *adj* **1** : versatile **2** : fickle

versatilidad *nf* **1** : versatility **2** : fickleness

versículo *nm* : verse (in the Bible)

versión *nf, pl* **versiones 1** : version **2** : translation

verso *nm* : verse

versus *prep* : versus, against

vértebra *nf* : vertebra — **vertebral** *adj*

vertebrado[1], -da *adj* : vertebrate

vertebrado[2] *nm* : vertebrate

vertedero *nm* **1** : garbage dump **2** DESAGÜE : drain, outlet

verter {56} *vt* **1** : to pour **2** : to spill, to shed **3** : to empty out **4** : to express, to voice **5** : to translate, to render — *vi* : to flow

vertical *adj & nf* : vertical — **verticalmente** *adv*

vértice *nm* : vertex, apex

vertido *nm* : spilling, spill

vertiente *nf* **1** : slope **2** : aspect, side, element

vertiginoso, -sa *adj* : vertiginous — **vertiginosamente** *adv*

vértigo *nm* : vertigo, dizziness

vesícula *nf* **1** : vesicle **2 vesícula biliar** : gallbladder

vesicular *adj* : vesicular

vestíbulo *nm* : vestibule, hall, lobby, foyer

vestido *nm* **1** : dress, costume, clothes *pl* **2** : dress (garment)

vestidor *nm* : dressing room

vestiduras *nfpl* **1** : clothing, raiment, regalia **2** *or* **vestiduras sacerdotales** : vestments

vestigio *nm* : vestige, sign, trace

vestimenta *nf* ROPA : clothing, clothes *pl*

vestir {54} *vt* **1** : to dress, to clothe **2** LLEVAR : to wear **3** ADORNAR : to decorate, to dress up — *vi* **1** : to dress <vestir bien : to dress well> **2** : to look good, to suit the occasion — **vestirse** *vr* **1** : to get dressed **2 ~ de** : to dress up as <se vistieron de soldados : they dressed up as soldiers> **3 ~ de** : to wear, to dress in

vestuario *nm* **1** : wardrobe **2** : dressing room, locker room

veta *nf* **1** : grain (in wood) **2** : vein, seam, lode **3** : trace, streak <una veta de terco : a stubborn streak>

vetar *vt* : to veto

veteado, -da *adj* : streaked, veined

veterano, -na *adj & n* : veteran

veterinaria *nf* : veterinary medicine

veterinario[1], -ria *adj* : veterinary

veterinario[2], -ria *n* : veterinarian

veto *nm* : veto

vetusto, -ta *adj* ANTIGUO : ancient, very old

vez *nf, pl* **veces 1** : time, occasion <a la vez : at the same time> <a veces : at times, occasionally> <de vez en cuando : from time to time> **2** (*with numbers*) : time <una vez : once> <de una vez : all at once> <de una vez para siempre : once and for all> <dos veces : twice> **3** : turn <a su vez : in turn> <en vez de : instead of> <hacer las veces de : to act as, to stand in for>

vía[1] *nf* **1** RUTA, CAMINO : road, route, way <Vía Láctea : Milky Way> **2** MEDIO : means, way <por vía oficial : through official channels> **3** : track, line (of a railroad) **4** : tract, passage <por vía oral : orally> **5 en vías de** : in the process of <en vías de solución : on the road to a solution> **6 por ~** : by (in transportation) <por vía aérea : by air, airmail>

vía[2] *prep* : via

viable *adj* : viable, feasible — **viabilidad** *nf*

viaducto *nm* : viaduct

viajante *mf* : traveling salesman, traveling saleswoman

viajar *vi* : to travel, to journey

viaje *nm* : trip, journey <viaje de negocios : business trip>

viajero[1], -ra *adj* : traveling

viajero[2], -ra *n* **1** : traveler **2** PASAJERO : passenger

vial *adj* : road, traffic

viático *nm* : travel allowance, travel expenses *pl*

víbora *nf* : viper

vibración *nf, pl* **-ciones** : vibration

vibrador *nm* : vibrator

vibrante *adj* **1** : vibrant **2** : vibrating

vibrar *vi* : to vibrate

vibratorio, -ria *adj* : vibratory

vicario, -ria *n* : vicar

vicealmirante *nmf* : vice admiral

vicepresidente, -ta *n* : vice president — **vicepresidencia** *nf*

viceversa *adv* : vice versa, conversely

viciado, -da *adj* : stuffy, close

viciar *vt* **1** : to corrupt **2** : to invalidate **3** FALSEAR : to distort **4** : to pollute, to adulterate

vicio *nm* **1** : vice, depravity **2** : bad habit **3** : defect, blemish

vicioso, -sa *adj* : depraved, corrupt

vicisitud *nf* : vicissitude

víctima *nf* : victim

victimario, -ria *n* ASESINO : killer, murderer

victimizar {21} *vt Arg, Mex* : to victimize

victoria *nf* : victory — **victorioso, -sa** *adj* — **victoriosamente** *adv*

victoriano, -na *adj* : Victorian

vid *nf* : vine, grapevine

vida *nf* **1** : life <la vida cotidiana : everyday life> **2** : life span, lifetime **3** BIOGRAFÍA : biography, life **4** : way of life, lifestyle **5** : livelihood <ganarse la vida : to earn one's living> **6** VIVEZA : liveliness **7 media vida** : half-life

vidente *nmf* **1** : psychic, clairvoyant **2** : sighted person

video *or* **vídeo** *nm* : video

videocasete *or* **videocasette** *nm* : videocassette

videocasetera *or* **videocasettera** *nf* : videocassette recorder, VCR

videocinta *nf* : videotape

videograbar *vt* : to videotape

vidriado *nm* : glaze

vidriar *vt* : to glaze (pottery, tile, etc.)

vidriera *nf* **1** : stained-glass window **2** : glass door or window **3** : store window

vidriero, -ra *n* : glazier

vidrio *nm* **1** : glass, piece of glass **2** : windowpane

vidrioso, -sa *adj* **1** : brittle, fragile **2** : slippery **3** : glassy, glazed (of eyes) **4** : touchy, delicate

vieira *nf* **1** : scallop **2** : scallop shell

viejo[1], -ja *adj* **1** ANCIANO : old, elderly **2** ANTIGUO : former, longstanding <viejas tradiciones : old traditions> <viejos amigos : old friends> **3** GASTADO : old, worn, worn-out

viejo[2], -ja *n* ANCIANO : old man *m*, old woman *f*

viene, etc. → **venir**

viento *nm* **1** : wind **2 hacer viento** : to be windy **3 contra viento y marea** : against all odds **4 viento en popa** : splendidly, successfully

vientre *nm* **1** : abdomen, belly **2** : womb **3** : bowels *pl*

viernes *nms & pl* : Friday

vierte, etc. → **verter**

vietnamita *adj & nmf* : Vietnamese

viga *nf* **1** : beam, rafter, girder **2 viga voladiza** : cantilever

vigencia *nf* **1** : validity **2** : force, effect <entrar en vigencia : to go into effect>

vigente *adj* : valid, in force

vigésimo[1], -ma *adj* : twentieth, twenty- <la vigésima segunda edición : the twenty-second edition>

vigésimo[2], -ma *n* : twentieth, twenty- (in a series)

vigía *nmf* : lookout

vigilancia *nf* : vigilance, watchfulness <bajo vigilancia : under surveillance>

vigilante[1] *adj* : vigilant, watchful

vigilante[2] *nmf* : watchman, guard

vigilar *vt* **1** CUIDAR : to look after, to keep an eye on **2** GUARDAR : to watch over, to guard — *vi* **1** : to be watchful **2** : to keep watch

vigilia *nf* **1** VELA **:** wakefulness **2 :** night work **3 :** vigil (in religion)

vigor *nm* **1 :** vigor, energy, strength **2** VIGENCIA **:** force, effect

vigorizante *adj* **:** envigorating

vigorizar {21} *vt* **:** to strengthen, to invigorate

vigoroso, -sa *adj* **:** vigorous — **vigorosamente** *adv*

VIH *nm* **:** HIV

vil *adj* **:** vile, dispicable

vileza *nf* **1 :** vileness **2 :** despicable action, villainy

vilipendiar *vt* **:** to vilify, to revile

villa *nf* **1 :** town, village **2 :** villa

villancico *nm* **:** carol, Christmas carol

villano, -na *n* **1 :** villain **2 :** peasant

vilo *nm* **en ~ 1 :** in the air **2 :** uncertain, in suspense

vinagre *nm* **:** vinegar

vinagrera *nf* **:** cruet (for vinegar)

vinatería *nf* **:** wine shop

vinculación *nf, pl* **-ciones 1 :** linking **2** RELACIÓN **:** bond, link, connection

vincular *vt* CONECTAR, RELACIONAR **:** to tie, to link, to connect

vínculo *nm* LAZO **:** tie, link, bond

vindicación *nf, pl* **-ciones :** vindication

vindicar *vt* **1 :** to vindicate **2 :** to avenge

vinilo *nm* **:** vinyl

vino[1], etc. → venir

vino[2] *nm* **:** wine

viña *nf* **:** vineyard

viñedo *nm* **:** vineyard

vio, etc. → ver

viola *nf* **:** viola

violación *nf, pl* **-ciones 1 :** violation, offense **2 :** rape

violador[1], -dora *n* **:** violator, offender

violador[2] *nm* **:** rapist

violar *vt* **1 :** to rape **2 :** to violate (a law or right) **3** PROFANAR **:** to desecrate

violencia *nf* **:** violence

violentamente *adv* **:** by force, violently

violentar *vt* **1** FORZAR **:** to break open, to force **2 :** to distort (words or ideas) — **violentarse** *vr* **:** to force oneself

violento, -ta *adj* **1 :** violent **2** EMBARAZOSO, INCÓMODO **:** awkward, embarassing

violeta[1] *adj & nm* **:** violet (color)

violeta[2] *nf* **:** violet (flower)

violín *nm, pl* **-lines :** violin

violinista *nmf* **:** violinist

violonchelista *nmf* **:** cellist

violonchelo *nm* **:** cello, violoncello

VIP *nmf, pl* **VIPs :** VIP

vira *nf* **:** welt (of a shoe)

virago *nf* **:** virago, shrew

viraje *nm* **1 :** turn, swerve **2 :** change

viral *adj* **:** viral

virar *vi* **:** to tack, to turn, to veer

virgen[1] *adj* **:** virgin <lana virgen : virgin wool>

virgen[2] *nmf, pl* **vírgenes :** virgin <la Santísima Virgen : the Blessed Virgin>

virginal *adj* **:** virginal, chaste

virginidad *nf* **:** virginity

Virgo *nmf* **:** Virgo

vírico, -ca *adj* **:** viral

viril *adj* **:** virile — **virilidad** *nf*

virrey, -rreina *n* **:** viceroy *m,* vicereine *f*

virtual *adj* **:** virtual — **virtualmente** *adv*

virtud *nf* **1 :** virtue **2 en virtud de :** by virtue of

virtuosismo *nm* **:** virtuosity

virtuoso[1], -sa *adj* **:** virtuous — **virtuosamente** *adv*

virtuoso[2], -sa *n* **:** virtuoso

viruela *nf* **1 :** smallpox **2 :** pockmark

virulencia *nf* **:** virulence

virulento, -ta *adj* **:** virulent

virus *nm* **:** virus

viruta *nf* **:** shaving

visa *nf* **:** visa

visado *nm Spain* **:** visa

visaje *nm* **:** face, grimace <hacer visajes : to make faces>

visceral *adj* **:** visceral

vísceras *nfpl* **:** viscera, entrails

visconde, -desa *n* **:** viscount *m,* viscountess *f*

viscosidad *nf* **:** viscosity

viscoso, -sa *adj* **:** viscous

visera *nf* **:** visor

visibilidad *nf* **:** visibility

visible *adj* **:** visible — **visiblemente** *adv*

visión *nf, pl* **visiones 1 :** vision, eyesight **2 :** view, perspective **3 :** vision, illusion <ver visiones : to be seeing things>

visionario, -ria *adj & n* **:** visionary

visita *nf* **1 :** visit, call **2 :** visitor **3 ir de visita :** to go visiting

visitador, -dora *n* **:** visitor, frequent caller

visitante[1] *adj* **:** visiting

visitante[2] *nmf* **:** visitor

visitar *vt* **:** to visit

vislumbrar *vt* **1 :** to discern, to make out **2 :** to begin to see, to have an inkling of

vislumbre *nf* **:** glimmer, gleam

viso *nm* **1** APARIENCIA **:** appearance <tener visos de : to seem, to show signs of> **2** DESTELLO **:** glint, gleam **3 :** sheen, iridescence

visón *nm, pl* **visones :** mink

víspera *nf* **1 :** eve, day before **2 vísperas** *nfpl* **:** vespers

vista *nf* **1** VISIÓN **:** vision, eyesight **2** MIRADA **:** look, gaze, glance **3** PANORAMA **:** view, vista, panorama **4 :** hearing (in court) **5 a primera vista :** at first sight **6 en vista de :** in view of **7 hacer la vista gorda :** to turn a blind eye **8 ¡hasta la vista! :** so long!, see you! **9 perder de vista :** to lose sight of **10 punto de vista :** point of view

vistazo *nm* **:** glance, look

viste, etc. → ver, vestir

visto[1] *pp* → **ver**

visto[2], **-ta** *adj* **1** : obvious, clear **2** : in view of, considering **3 estar bien visto** : to be approved of **4 estar mal visto** : to be frowned upon **5 por lo visto** : apparently **6 nunca visto** : unheard-of **7 visto que** : since, given that

visto[3] *nm* **visto bueno** : approval

vistoso, -sa *adj* : colorful, bright

visual *adj* : visual — **visualmente** *adv*

visualización *nf, pl* **-ciones** : visualization

visualizar {21} *vt* **1** : to visualize **2** : to display (on a screen)

vital *adj* **1** : vital **2** : lively, dynamic

vitalicio, -cia *adj* : life, lifetime

vitalidad *nf* : vitality

vitamina *nf* : vitamin

vitamínico, -ca *adj* : vitamin <complejos vitamínicos : vitamin compounds>

vitorear *vt* : to cheer, to acclaim

vitral *nm* : stained-glass window

vítreo, -rea *adj* : vitreous, glassy

vitrina *nf* **1** : showcase, display case **2** : store window

vitriolo *nm* : vitriol

vituperar *vt* : to condemn, to vituperate against

vituperio *nm* : vituperation, censure

viudez *nf* : widowerhood, widowhood

viudo, -da *n* : widower *m,* widow *f*

vivacidad *nf* VIVEZA : vivacity, liveliness

vivamente *adv* **1** : in a lively manner **2** : vividly **3** : strongly, acutely <lo recomendamos vivamente : we strongly recommend it>

vivaque *nm* : bivouac

vivaquear *vi* : to bivouac

vivar *vi* : to cheer

vivaz *adj, pl* **vivaces 1** : lively, vivacious **2** : clever, sharp **3** : perennial

víveres *nmpl* : provisions, supplies, food

vivero *nm* **1** : nursery (for plants) **2** : hatchery, fish farm

viveza *nf* **1** VIVACIDAD : liveliness **2** BRILLO : vividness, brightness **3** ASTUCIA : cleverness, sharpness

vívido, -da *adj* : vivid, lively

vividor, -dora *n* : sponger, parasite

vivienda *nf* **1** : housing **2** MORADA : dwelling, home

viviente *adj* : living

vivificar {72} *vt* : to vivify, to give life to

vivir[1] *vi* **1** : to live, to be alive **2** SUBSISTIR : to subsist, to make a living **3** RESIDIR : to reside **4** : to spend one's life <vive para trabajar : she lives to work> **5 ~ de** : to live on — *vt* **1** : to live <vivir su vida : to live one's life> **2** EXPERIMENTAR : to go through, to experience

vivir[2] *nm* **1** : life, lifestyle **2 de mal vivir** : disreputable

vivisección *nf, pl* **-ciones** : vivisection

vivo, -va *adj* **1** : alive **2** INTENSO : vivid, bright, intense **3** ANIMADO : lively, vivacious **4** ASTUTO : sharp, clever **5 en ~** : live <transmisión en vivo : live broadcast> **6 al rojo vivo** : red-hot

vizconde, -desa *n* : viscount *m,* viscountess *f*

vocablo *nm* PALABRA : word

vocabulario *nm* : vocabulary

vocación *nf, pl* **-ciones** : vocation

vocacional *adj* : vocational

vocal[1] *adj* : vocal

vocal[2] *nmf* : member (of a committee, board, etc.)

vocal[3] *nf* : vowel

vocalista *nmf* CANTANTE : singer, vocalist

vocalizar {21} *vi* : to vocalize

vocear *v* : to shout

vocerío *nm* : clamor, shouting

vocero, -ra *n* PORTAVOZ : spokesperson, spokesman *m,* spokeswoman *f*

vociferante *adj* : vociferous

vociferar *vi* GRITAR : to shout, to yell

vodevil *nm* : vaudeville

vodka *nm* : vodka

voladizo[1], **-za** *adj* : projecting

voladizo[2] *nm* : projection

volador, -dora *adj* : flying

volando *adv* : quickly, in a hurry

volante[1] *adj* : flying

volante[2] *nm* **1** : steering wheel **2** FOLLETO : flier, circular **3** : shuttlecock **4** : flywheel **5** : balance wheel (of a watch) **6** : ruffle, flounce

volar {19} *vi* **1** : to fly **2** CORRER : to hurry, to rush <el tiempo vuela : time flies> <pasar volando : to fly past> **3** DIVULGARSE : to spread <unos rumores volaban : rumors were spreading around> **4** DESAPARECER : to disappear <el dinero ya voló : the money's already gone> — *vt* **1** : to blow up, to demolish **2** : to irritate

volátil *adj* : volatile — **volatilidad** *nf*

volatilizar {21} *vt* : to volatize — **volatilizarse** *vr*

volcán *nm, pl* **volcanes** : volcano

volcánico, -ca *adj* : volcanic

volcar {82} *vt, pl* **volcanes 1** : to upset, to knock over, to turn over **2** : to empty out **3** : to make dizzy **4** : to cause a change of mind in **5** : to irritate — *vi* **1** : to overturn, to tip over **2** : to capsize — **volcarse** *vr* **1** : to overturn **2** : to do one's utmost

volea *nf* : volley (in sports)

volear *vi* : to volley (in sports)

voleibol *nm* : volleyball

voleo *nm* **al voleo** : haphazardly, at random

volframio *nm* : wolfram, tungsten

volición *nf, pl* **-ciones** : volition

volqué, etc. → **volcar**

voltaje *nm* : voltage

voltear *vt* **1** : to turn over, to turn upside down **2** : to reverse, to turn inside out **3** : to turn <voltear la cara : to turn one's head> **4** : to knock down — *vi* **1 :** to roll over, to do somersaults **2 :** to turn <volteó a la izquierda : he turned left> — **voltearse** *vr* **1 :** to turn around **2 :** to change one's allegiance

voltereta *nf* **:** somersault, tumble

voltio *nm* **:** volt

volubilidad *nf* **:** fickleness, changeableness

voluble *adj* **:** fickle, changeable

volumen *nm, pl* **-lúmenes 1** TOMO **:** volume, book **2 :** capacity, size, bulk **3** CANTIDAD **:** amount <el volumen de ventas : the volume of sales> **4 :** volume, loudness

voluminoso, -sa *adj* **:** voluminous, massive, bulky

voluntad *nf* **1 :** will, volition **2** DESEO **:** desire, wish **3** INTENCIÓN **:** intention **4 a voluntad :** at will **5 buena voluntad :** good will **6 mala voluntad :** ill will **7 fuerza de voluntad :** willpower

voluntario[1], -ria *adj* **:** voluntary — **voluntariamente** *adv*

voluntario[2], -ria *n* **:** volunteer

voluntarioso, -sa *adj* **1 :** stubborn **2 :** willing, eager

voluptuosidad *nf* **:** voluptuousness

voluptuoso, -sa *adj* **:** voluptuous — **voluptuosamente** *adv*

voluta *nf* **:** spiral, column (of smoke)

volver {89} *vi* **1 :** to return, to come or go back <volver a casa : to return home> **2 :** to revert <volver al tema : to get back to the subject> **3 ~ a :** to do again <volvieron a llamar : they called again> **4 volver en sí :** to come to, to regain consciousness — *vt* **1 :** to turn, to turn over, to turn inside out **2 :** to return, to repay, to restore **3 :** to cause, to make <la volvía loca : it was driving her crazy> — **volverse** *vr* **1 :** to become <se volvió deprimido : he became depressed> **2 :** to turn around

vomitar *vi* **:** to vomit — *vt* **1 :** to vomit **2 :** to spew out (lava, etc.)

vómito *nm* **1 :** vomiting **2 :** vomit

voracidad *nf* **:** voracity

vorágine *nf* **:** whirlpool, maelstrom

voraz *adj, pl* **voraces :** voracious — **vorazmente** *adv*

vórtice *nm* **1 :** whirlpool, vortex **2** TORBELLINO **:** whirlwind

vos *pron* (*in some regions of Latin America*) **:** you

vosear *vt* **:** to address as *vos*

vosotros, -tras *pron pl Spain* **1 :** you, yourselves **2 :** ye

votación *nf, pl* **-ciones :** vote, voting

votante *nmf* **:** voter

votar *vi* **:** to vote — *vt* **:** to vote for

votivo, -va *adj* **:** votive

voto *nm* **1 :** vote **2 :** vow (in religion) **3 votos** *nmpl* **:** good wishes

voy → ir

voz *nf, pl* **voces 1 :** voice **2 :** opinion, say **3** GRITO **:** shout, yell **4 :** sound **5** VOCABLO **:** word, term **6 :** rumor **7 a voz en cuello :** at the top of one's lungs **8 dar voces :** to shout **9 en voz alta :** aloud, in a loud voice **10 en voz baja :** softly, in a low voice

vudú *nm* **:** voodoo

vuelco *nm* **:** upset, overturning <me dio un vuelco el corazón : my heart skipped a beat>

vuela, etc. → volar

vuelca, vuelque, etc. → volcar

vuelo *nm* **1 :** flight, flying <alzar el vuelo : to take flight> **2 :** flight (of an aircraft) <vuelo espacial : space flight> **3 :** flare, fullness (of clothing) **4 al vuelo :** on the wing

vuelta *nf* **1** GIRO **:** turn <se dio la vuelta : he turned around> **2** REVOLUCIÓN **:** circle, revolution <dio la vuelta al mundo : she went around the world> <las ruedas daban vueltas : the wheels were spinning> **3 :** flip, turn <le dio la vuelta : she flipped it over> **4 :** bend, curve <a la vuelta de la esquina : around the corner> **5** REGRESO **:** return <de ida y vuelta : round trip> <a vuelta de correo : return mail> **6 :** round, lap (in sports or games) **7** PASEO **:** walk, drive, ride <dio una vuelta : he went for a walk> **8** DORSO, REVÉS **:** back, other side <a la vuelta : on the back> **9 :** cuff (of pants) **10 darle vueltas :** to think over **11 estar de vuelta :** to be back

vuelto *pp* **→ volver**

vuelve, etc. → volver

vuestro[1], -stra *adj Spain* **:** your, of yours <vuestros coches : your cars> <una amiga vuestra : a friend of yours>

vuestro[2], -stra *pron Spain* (*with definite article*) **:** yours <la vuestra es más grande : yours is bigger> <esos son los vuestros : those are yours>

vulcanizar {21} *vt* **:** to vulcanize

vulgar *adj* **1 :** common **2 :** vulgar

vulgaridad *nf* **:** vulgarity

vulgarismo *nm* **:** vulgarism

vulgarizar {21} *vt* **:** to vulgarize, to popularize

vulgarmente *adv* **:** vulgarly, popularly

vulgo *nm* **el vulgo :** the masses, common people

vulnerable *adj* **:** vulnerable — **vulnerabilidad** *nf*

vulnerar *vt* **1 :** to injure, to damage (one's reputation or honor) **2 :** to violate, to break (a law or contract)

W

w *nf* **:** twenty-fourth letter of the Spanish alphabet
wafle *nm* **:** waffle
waflera *nf* **:** waffle iron
wapití *nm* **:** wapiti, elk
whisky *nm, pl* **whiskys** *or* **whiskies** **:** whiskey
wigwam *nm* **:** wigwam

X

x *nf* **:** twenty-fifth letter of the Spanish alphabet
xenofobia *nf* **:** xenophobia
xenófobo[1], -ba *adj* **:** xenophobic
xenófobo[2], -ba *n* **:** xenophobe
xenón *nm* **:** xenon
xerocopiar *vt* **:** to photocopy, to xerox
xilófono *nm* **:** xylophone

Y

y[1] *nf* **:** twenty-sixth letter of the Spanish alphabet
y[2] *conj* **1 :** and <mi hermano y yo : my brother and I> <¿y los demás? : and (what about) the others?> **2** (*used in numbers*) <cincuenta y cinco : fifty-five> **3** *fam* **:** well <y por supuesto : well, of course>
ya[1] *adv* **1 :** already <ya terminó : she's finished already> **2 :** now, right now <¡hazlo ya! : do it now!> <ya mismo : right away> **3 :** later, soon <ya iremos : we'll go later on> **4 :** no longer, anymore <ya no fuma : he no longer smokes> **5** (*used for emphasis*) **:** <¡ya lo sé! : I know!> <ya lo creo : of course> **6 no ya :** not only <no ya lloran sino gritan : they're not only crying but screaming> **7 ya que :** now that, since <ya que sabe la verdad : now that she knows the truth>
ya[2] *conj* **ya . . . ya :** whether . . . or, first . . . then <ya le gusta, ya no : first he likes it, then he doesn't>
yac *nm* **:** yak
yacer {90} *vi* **:** to lie <en esta tumba yacen sus abuelos : his grandparents lie in this grave>
yacimiento *nm* **:** bed, deposit <yacimiento petrolífero : oil field>
yaga, etc. → **yacer**
yanqui *adj & nmf* **:** Yankee
yarda *nf* **:** yard
yate *nm* **:** yacht
yaz, yazca, yazga, etc. → **yacer**
yedra *nf* **:** ivy
yegua *nf* **:** mare
yelmo *nm* **:** helmet
yema *nf* **1 :** bud, shoot **2 :** yolk (of an egg) **3 yema del dedo :** fingertip
yemenita *adj & nmf* **:** Yemenite
yendo → **ir**
yerba *nf* **1** *or* **yerba mate :** maté **2** → **hierba**
yerga, yergue, etc. → **erguir**
yermo[1], -ma *adj* **:** barren, deserted
yermo[2] *nm* **:** wasteland
yerno *nm* **:** son-in-law
yerra, etc. → **errar**
yerro *nm* **:** blunder, mistake
yerto, -ta *adj* **:** rigid, stiff
yesca *nf* **:** tinder
yeso *nm* **1 :** plaster **2 :** gypsum
yo[1] *nm* **:** ego, self
yo[2] *pron* **1 :** I **2 :** me <todos menos yo : everyone except me> <tan bajo como yo : as short as me> **3 soy yo :** it is I, it's me
yodado, -da *adj* **:** iodized
yodo *nm* **:** iodine
yoduro *nm* **:** iodide
yoga *nm* **:** yoga
yogui *nm* **:** yogi
yogurt *or* **yogur** *nm* **:** yogurt
yola *nf* **:** yawl
yoyo *or* **yoyó** *nm* **:** yo-yo
yuca *nf* **1 :** yucca (plant) **2 :** cassava, manioc
yucateco[1], -ca *adj* **:** of or from the Yucatán
yucateco[2], -ca *n* **:** person from the Yucatán
yudo → **judo**
yugo *nm* **:** yoke
yugoslavo, -va *adj & n* **:** Yugoslavian
yugular *adj* **:** jugular <vena yugular : jugular vein>
yungas *nfpl Bol, Chile, Peru* **:** warm tropical valleys
yunque *nm* **:** anvil
yunta *nf* **:** yoke, team (of oxen)
yute *nm* **:** jute
yuxtaponer {60} *vt* **:** to juxtapose — **yuxtaposición** *nf*

Z

z *nf* : twenty-seventh letter of the Spanish alphabet
zacate *nm CA, Mex* **1** : grass, forage **2** : hay
zafacón *nm, pl* **-cones** : wastebasket
zafar *vt* : to loosen, to untie — **zafarse** *vr* **1** : to loosen up, to come undone **2** : to get free of
zafio, -fia *adj* : coarse, crude
zafiro *nm* : sapphire
zaga *nf* **1** : defense (in sports) **2 a la zaga** *or* **en ~** : behind, in the rear
zagual *nm* : paddle (of a canoe)
zaguán *nm, pl* **zaguanes** : front hall, vestibule
zaherir {76} *vt* **1** : to criticize sharply **2** : to wound, to mortify
zahones *nmpl* : chaps
zaino, -na *adj* : chestnut (color)
zalamería *nf* : flattery, sweet talk
zalamero[1], -ra *adj* : flattering, fawning
zalamero[2], -ra *n* : flatterer
zambiano, -na *adj & nmf* : Zambian
zambullida *nf* : dive, plunge
zambullirse {38} *vr* : to dive, to plunge
zanahoria *nf* : carrot
zancada *nf* : stride, step
zancadilla *nf* **1** : trip, stumble **2** *fam* : trick, ruse
zancos *nmpl* : stilts
zancuda *nf* : wading bird
zancudo *nm* MOSQUITO : mosquito
zángano *nm* : drone, male bee
zanja *nf* : ditch, trench
zanjar *vt* ACLARAR : to settle, to clear up, to resolve
zapallo *nm Arg, Chile, Peru, Uru* : pumpkin
zapapico *nm* : pickax
zapata *nf* : brake shoe
zapatería *nf* **1** : shoemaker's, shoe factory **2** : shoe store
zapatero[1], -ra *adj* : dry, tough, poorly cooked
zapatero[2], -ra *n* : shoemaker, cobbler
zapatilla *nf* **1** PANTUFLA : slipper **2** *or* **zapatilla de deporte** : sneaker
zapato *nm* : shoe
zar, zarina *n* : czar *m*, czarina *f*
zarandear *vt* **1** : to sift, to sieve **2** : to shake, to jostle, to jiggle
zarapito *nm* : curlew
zarcillo *nm* **1** : earring **2** : tendril (of a plant)
zarigüeya *nf* : opossum
zarista *adj & nmf* : czarist
zarpa *nf* : paw
zarpar *vi* : to set sail, to raise anchor
zarza *nf* : bramble, blackberry bush
zarzamora *nf* **1** : blackberry **2** : bramble, blackberry bush
zarzaparrilla *nf* : sarsaparilla
zepelín *nm, pl* **-lines** : zeppelin
zigoto *nm* : zygote
zigzag *nm, pl* **zigzags** *or* **zigzagues** : zigzag
zigzaguear *vi* : to zigzag
zimbabuense *adj & nmf* : Zimbabwean
zinc *nm* : zinc
zinnia *nf* : zinnia
zíper *nm CA, Mex* : zipper
zircón *nm, pl* **zircones** : zircon
zócalo *nm Mex* : main square
zodíaco *nm* : zodiac — **zodíacal** *adj*
zombi *or* **zombie** *nmf* : zombie
zona *nf* : zone, district, area
zonzo[1], -za *adj* : stupid, silly
zonzo[2], -za *n* : idiot, nitwit
zoo *nm* : zoo
zoología *nf* : zoology
zoológico[1], -ca *adj* : zoological
zoológico[2] *nm* : zoo
zoólogo, -ga *n* : zoologist
zoom *nm* : zoom lens
zopilote *nm CA, Mex* : buzzard
zoquete *nmf fam* : oaf, blockhead
zorrillo *nm* MOFETA : skunk
zorro[1], -rra *adj* : sly, crafty
zorro[2], -rra *n* **1** : fox, vixen **2** : sly crafty person
zorzal *nm* : thrush
zozobra *nf* : anxiety, worry
zozobrar *vi* : to capsize
zueco *nm* : clog (shoe)
zulú[1] *adj & nmf* : Zulu
zulú[2] *nm* : Zulu (language)
zumaque *nm* : sumac
zumbar *vi* : to buzz, to hum — *vt fam* **1** : to hit, to thrash **2** : to make fun of
zumbido *nm* : buzzing, humming
zumo *nf* JUGO : juice
zurcir {83} *vt* : to darn, to mend
zurdo[1], -da *adj* : left-handed
zurdo[2], -da *n* : left-handed person
zurza, etc. → **zurcir**
zutano, -na → **fulano**

English–Spanish Dictionary

A

a[1] [ˈeɪ] *n, pl* **a's** *or* **as** [ˈeɪz] **:** primera letra del alfabeto inglés

a[2] [ə, ˈeɪ] *art* (**an** [ən, ˈæn] *before vowel or silent h*) **1 :** un *m,* una *f* <a house : una casa> <half an hour : media hora> <what a surprise! : ¡qué sorpresa!> **2** PER **:** por, a la, al <30 kilometers an hour : 30 kilómetros por hora> <twice a month : dos veces al mes>

aardvark [ˈɑrdˌvɑrk] *n* **:** oso *m* hormiguero

aback [əˈbæk] *adv* **1 :** por sorpresa **2 to be taken aback :** quedarse desconcertado

abacus [ˈæbəkəs] *n, pl* **abaci** [ˈæbəˌsaɪ, -ˌkiː] *or* **abacuses :** ábaco *m*

abaft [əˈbæft] *adv* **:** a popa

abalone [ˌæbəˈloːni] *n* **:** abulón *m,* oreja *f* marina

abandon[1] [əˈbændən] *vt* **1** DESERT, FORSAKE **:** abandonar, desamparar (a alguien), desertar de (algo) **2** GIVE UP, SUSPEND **:** renunciar a, suspender <he abandoned the search : suspendió la búsqueda> **3** EVACUATE, LEAVE **:** abandonar, evacuar, dejar <to abandon ship : abandonar el buque> **4 to abandon oneself :** entregarse, abandonarse

abandon[2] *n* **:** desenfreno *m* <with wild abandon : desenfrenadamente>

abandoned [əˈbændənd] *adj* **1** DESERTED **:** abandonado **2** UNRESTRAINED **:** desenfrenado, desinhibido

abandonment [əˈbændənmənt] *n* **:** abandono *m,* desamparo *m*

abase [əˈbeɪs] *vt* **abased; abasing :** degradar, humillar, rebajar

abash [əˈbæʃ] *vt* **:** avergonzar, abochornar

abashed [əˈbæʃt] *adj* **:** avergonzado

abate [əˈbeɪt] *vi* **abated; abating :** amainar, menguar, disminuir

abattoir [ˈæbəˌtwɑr] *n* **:** matadero *m*

abbess [ˈæbɪs, -ˌbɛs, -bəs] *n* **:** abadesa *f*

abbey [ˈæbi] *n, pl* **-beys :** abadía *f*

abbot [ˈæbət] *n* **:** abad *m*

abbreviate [əˈbriːviˌeɪt] *vt* **-ated; -ating :** abreviar

abbreviation [əˌbriːviˈeɪʃən] *n* **:** abreviación *f,* abreviatura *f*

abdicate [ˈæbdɪˌkeɪt] *v* **-cated; -cating :** abdicar

abdication [ˌæbdɪˈkeɪʃən] *n* **:** abdicación *f*

abdomen [ˈæbdəmən, æbˈdoːmən] *n* **:** abdomen *m,* vientre *m*

abdominal [æbˈdɑmənəl] *adj* **:** abdominal — **abdominally** *adv*

abduct [æbˈdʌkt] *vt* **:** raptar, secuestrar

abduction [æbˈdʌkʃən] *n* **:** rapto *m,* secuestro *m*

abductor [æbˈdʌktər] *n* **:** raptor *m,* -tora *f;* secuestrador *m,* -dora *f*

abed [əˈbɛd] *adv & adj* **:** en cama

aberrant [æˈbɛrənt, ˈæbərənt] *adj* **1** ABNORMAL **:** anormal, aberrante **2** ATYPICAL **:** anómalo, atípico

aberration [ˌæbəˈreɪʃən] *n* **1 :** aberración *f* **2** DERANGEMENT **:** perturbación *f* mental

abet [əˈbɛt] *vt* **abetted; abetting** ASSIST **:** ayudar <to aid and abet : ser cómplice de>

abeyance [əˈbeɪənts] *n* **:** desuso *m,* suspensión *f*

abhor [əbˈhɔr, æb-] *vt* **-horred; -horring :** abominar, aborrecer

abhorrence [əbˈhɔrənts, æb-] *n* **:** aborrecimiento *m,* odio *m*

abhorrent [əbˈhɔrənt, æb-] *adj* **:** abominable, aborrecible, odioso

abide [əˈbaɪd] *v* **abode** [əˈboːd] *or* **abided; abiding** *vt* STAND **:** soportar, tolerar <I can't abide them : no los puedo ver> — *vi* **1** ENDURE **:** quedar, permanecer **2** DWELL **:** morar, residir **3 to abide by :** atenerse a

ability [əˈbɪləti] *n, pl* **-ties 1** CAPABILITY **:** aptitud *f,* capacidad *f,* facultad *f* **2** COMPETENCE **:** competencia *f* **3** TALENT **:** talento *m,* don *m,* habilidad *f*

abject [ˈæbˌdʒɛkt, æbˈ-] *adj* **1** WRETCHED **:** miserable, desdichado **2** HOPELESS **:** abatido, desesperado **3** SERVILE **:** servil <abject flattery : halagos serviles> — **abjectly** *adv*

ablaze [əˈbleɪz] *adj* **1** BURNING **:** ardiendo, en llamas **2** RADIANT **:** resplandeciente, radiante

able [ˈeɪbəl] *adj* **abler; ablest 1** CAPABLE **:** capaz, hábil **2** COMPETENT **:** competente

ablution [əˈbluːʃən] *n* **:** ablución *f* <to perform one's ablutions : lavarse>

ably [ˈeɪbəli] *adv* **:** hábilmente, eficientemente

abnormal [æbˈnɔrməl] *adj* **:** anormal — **abnormally** *adv*

abnormality [ˌæbnərˈmæləti, -nɔr-] *n, pl* **-ties :** anormalidad *f*

aboard[1] [əˈbord] *adv* **:** a bordo

aboard[2] *prep* **:** a bordo de

abode[1] → **abide**

abode[2] [əˈboːd] *n* **:** morada *f,* residencia *f,* vivienda *f*

abolish [əˈbɑlɪʃ] *vt* **:** abolir, suprimir

abolition [ˌæbəˈlɪʃən] *n* **:** abolición *f,* supresión *f*

abominable [əˈbɑmənəbəl] *adj* DETESTABLE **:** abominable, aborrecible, espantoso

abominate [əˈbɑməˌneɪt] *vt* **-nated; -nating :** abominar, aborrecer

abomination [əˌbɑməˈneɪʃən] *n* **:** abominación *f*

aboriginal [ˌæbəˈrɪdʒənəl] *adj* **:** aborigen, indígena

aborigine [ˌæbəˈrɪdʒəni] *n* NATIVE : aborigen *mf,* indígena *mf*

abort [əˈbɔrt] *vt* **1** : abortar (en medicina) **2** CALL OFF : suspender, abandonar — *vi* : abortar, hacerse un aborto

abortion [əˈbɔrʃən] *n* : aborto *m*

abortive [əˈbɔrtɪv] *adj* UNSUCCESSFUL : fracasado, frustrado, malogrado

abound [əˈbaʊnd] *vi* **to abound in** : abundar en, estar lleno de

about[1] [əˈbaʊt] *adv* **1** APPROXIMATELY : aproximadamente, casi, más o menos **2** AROUND : por todas partes, alrededor <the children are running about : los niños están corriendo por todas partes> **3 to be about to** : estar a punto de **4 to be up and about** : estar levantado

about[2] *prep* **1** AROUND : alrededor de **2** CONCERNING : de, acerca de, sobre <he always talks about politics : siempre habla de política>

above[1] [əˈbʌv] *adv* **1** OVERHEAD : por encima, arriba **2** : más arriba <as stated above : como se indica más arriba>

above[2] *adj* : anterior, antedicho <for the above reasons : por las razones antedichas>

above[3] *prep* **1** OVER : encima de, arriba de, sobre **2** : superior a, por encima de <he's above those things : él está por encima de esas cosas> **3** : más de, superior a <he earns above $50,000 : gana más de $50,000> <a number above 10 : un número superior a 10> **4 above all** : sobre todo

aboveboard[1] [əˈbʌvˈbord, -ˌbord] *adv* **open and aboveboard** : sin tapujos

aboveboard[2] *adj* : legítimo, sincero

abrade [əˈbreɪd] *vt* **abraded; abrading 1** ERODE : erosionar, corroer **2** SCRAPE : escoriar, raspar

abrasion [əˈbreɪʒən] *n* **1** SCRAPE, SCRATCH : raspadura *f,* rasguño *m* **2** EROSION : erosión *f*

abrasive[1] [əˈbreɪsɪv] *adj* **1** ROUGH : abrasivo, áspero **2** BRUSQUE, IRRITATING : brusco, irritante

abrasive[2] *n* : abrasivo *m*

abreast [əˈbrɛst] *adv* **1** : en fondo, al lado <to march three abreast : marchar de tres en fondo> **2 to keep abreast** : mantenerse al día

abridge [əˈbrɪdʒ] *vt* **abridged; abridging** : compendiar, resumir

abridgment *or* **abridgement** [əˈbrɪdʒmənt] *n* : compendio *m,* resumen *m*

abroad [əˈbrɔd] *adv* **1** ABOUT, WIDELY : por todas partes, en todas direcciones <the news spread abroad : la noticia corrió por todas partes> **2** OVERSEAS : en el extranjero, en el exterior

abrupt [əˈbrʌpt] *adj* **1** SUDDEN : abrupto, repentino, súbito **2** BRUSQUE, CURT : brusco, cortante — **abruptly** *adv*

abscess [ˈæbˌsɛs] *n* : absceso *m*

abscond [æbˈskɑnd] *vi* : huir, fugarse

absence [ˈæbsənts] *n* **1** : ausencia *f* (de una persona) **2** LACK : falta *f,* carencia *f*

absent[1] [æbˈsɛnt] *vt* **to absent oneself** : ausentarse

absent[2] [ˈæbsənt] *adj* : ausente

absentee [ˌæbsənˈtiː] *n* : ausente *mf*

absentminded [ˌæbsəntˈmaɪndəd] *adj* : distraído, despistado

absentmindedly [ˌæbsəntˈmaɪndədli] *adv* : distraídamente

absentmindedness [ˌæbsəntˈmaɪndədnəs] *n* : distracción *f,* despiste *m*

absolute [ˈæbsəˌluːt, ˌæbsəˈluːt] *adj* **1** COMPLETE, PERFECT : completo, pleno, perfecto **2** UNCONDITIONAL : absoluto, incondicional **3** DEFINITE : categórico, definitivo

absolutely [ˈæbsəˌluːtli, ˌæbsəˈluːtli] *adv* **1** COMPLETELY : completamente, absolutamente **2** CERTAINLY : desde luego <do you agree? absolutely! : ¿estás de acuerdo? ¡desde luego!>

absolution [ˌæbsəˈluːʃən] *n* : absolución *f*

absolve [əbˈzɑlv, æb-, -ˈsɑlv] *vt* **-solved; -solving** : absolver, perdonar

absorb [əbˈzɔrb, æb-, -ˈsɔrb] *vt* **1** : absorber, embeber (un líquido), amortiguar (un golpe, la luz) **2** ENGROSS : absorber **3** ASSIMILATE : asimilar

absorbed [əbˈzɔrbd, æb-, -ˈsɔrbd] *adj* ENGROSSED : absorto, ensimismado

absorbency [əbˈzɔrbəntsi, æb-, -ˈsɔr-] *n* : absorbencia *f*

absorbent [əbˈzɔrbənt, æb-, -ˈsɔr-] *adj* : absorbente

absorbing [əbˈzɔrbɪŋ, æb-, -ˈsɔr-] *adj* : absorbente, fascinante

absorption [əbˈzɔrpʃən, æb-, -ˈsɔrp-] *n* **1** : absorción *f* **2** CONCENTRATION : concentración *f*

abstain [əbˈsteɪn, æb-] *vi* : abstenerse

abstainer [əbˈsteɪnər, æb-] *n* : abstemio *m,* -mia *f*

abstemious [æbˈstiːmiəs] *adj* : abstemio, sobrio — **abstemiously** *adv*

abstention [əbˈstɛntʃən, æb-] *n* : abstención *f*

abstinence [ˈæbstənənts] *n* : abstinencia *f*

abstract[1] [æbˈstrækt, ˈæbˌ-] *vt* **1** EXTRACT : abstraer, extraer **2** SUMMARIZE : compendiar, resumir

abstract[2] *adj* : abstracto — **abstractly** [æbˈstræktli, ˈæbˌ-] *adv*

abstract[3] [ˈæbˌstrækt] *n* : resumen *m,* compendio *m,* sumario *m*

abstraction [æbˈstrækʃən] *n* **1** : abstracción *f,* idea *f* abstracta **2** ABSENTMINDEDNESS : distracción *f*

abstruse [əbˈstruːs, æb-] *adj* : abstruso, recóndito — **abstrusely** *adv*

absurd [əbˈsərd, -ˈzərd] *adj* : absurdo, ridículo, disparatado — **absurdly** *adv*

absurdity [əbˈsərdəti, -ˈzər-] *n, pl* **-ties 1** : absurdo *m* **2** NONSENSE : disparate *m,* despropósito *m*

abundance [ə'bʌndənts] *n* : abundancia *f*
abundant [ə'bʌndənt] *adj* : abundante, cuantioso, copioso
abundantly [ə'bʌndəntli] *adv* : abundantemente, en abundancia
abuse[1] [ə'bju:z] *vt* **abused; abusing 1** MISUSE : abusar de **2** MISTREAT : maltratar **3** REVILE : insultar, injuriar, denostar
abuse[2] [ə'bju:s] *n* **1** MISUSE : abuso *m* **2** MISTREATMENT : abuso *m,* maltrato *m* **3** INSULTS : insultos *mpl,* improperios *mpl* <a string of abuse : una serie de improperios>
abuser [ə'bju:zər] *n* : abusador *m,* -dora *f*
abusive [ə'bju:sɪv] *adj* **1** ABUSING : abusivo **2** INSULTING : ofensivo, injurioso, insultante — **abusively** *adv*
abut [ə'bʌt] *v* **abutted; abutting** *vt* : bordear — *vi* **to abut on** : colindar con
abutment [ə'bʌtmənt] *n* **1** BUTTRESS : contrafuerte *m,* estribo *m* **2** CLOSENESS : contigüidad *f*
abysmal [ə'bɪzməl] *adj* **1** DEEP : abismal, insondable **2** TERRIBLE : atroz, desastroso
abysmally [ə'bɪzməli] *adv* : desastrosamente, terriblemente
abyss [ə'bɪs, 'æbɪs] *n* : abismo *m,* sima *f*
acacia [ə'keɪʃə] *n* : acacia *f*
academic[1] [,ækə'dɛmɪk] *adj* **1** : académico **2** THEORETICAL : teórico — **academically** [-mɪkli] *adv*
academic[2] *n* : académico *m,* -ca *f*
academy [ə'kædəmi] *n, pl* **-mies** : academia *f*
accede [æk'si:d] *vi* **-ceded; -ceding 1** AGREE : acceder, consentir **2** ASCEND : subir, acceder <he acceded to the throne : subió al trono>
accelerate [ɪk'sɛlə,reɪt, æk-] *v* **-ated; -ating** *vt* : acelerar, apresurar — *vi* : acelerar (dícese de un carro)
acceleration [ɪk,sɛlə'reɪʃən, æk-] *n* : aceleración *f*
accelerator [ɪk'sɛlə,reɪt̬ər, æk-] *n* : acelerador *m*
accent[1] ['æk,sɛnt, æk'sɛnt] *vt* : acentuar
accent[2] ['æk,sɛnt, -sənt] *n* **1** : acento *m* **2** EMPHASIS, STRESS : énfasis *m,* acento *m*
accentuate [ɪk'sɛntʃʊ,eɪt, æk-] *vt* **-ated; -ating** : acentuar, poner énfasis en
accept [ɪk'sɛpt, æk-] *vt* **1** : aceptar **2** ACKNOWLEDGE : admitir, reconocer
acceptability [ɪk,sɛptə'bɪlət̬i, æk-] *n* : aceptabilidad *f*
acceptable [ɪk'sɛptəbəl, æk-] *adj* : aceptable, admisible — **acceptably** [-bli] *adv*
acceptance [ɪk'sɛptənts, æk-] *n* : aceptación *f,* aprobación *f*
access[1] ['æk,sɛs] *vt* : obtener acceso a, entrar a
access[2] *n* : acceso *m*
accessible [ɪk'sɛsəbəl, æk-] *adj* : accesible, asequible
accession [ɪk'sɛʃən, æk-] *n* **1** : ascenso *f,* subida *f* (al trono, etc.) **2** ACQUISITION : adquisición *f*
accessory[1] [ɪk'sɛsəri, æk-] *adj* : auxiliar
accessory[2] *n, pl* **-ries 1** : accesorio *m,* complemento *m* **2** ACCOMPLICE : cómplice *mf*
accident ['æksədənt] *n* **1** MISHAP : accidente *m* **2** CHANCE : casualidad *f*
accidental [,æksə'dɛntəl] *adj* : accidental, casual, imprevisto, fortuito
accidentally [,æksə'dɛntəli, -'dɛntli] *adv* **1** BY CHANCE : por casualidad **2** UNINTENTIONALLY : sin querer, involuntariamente
acclaim[1] [ə'kleɪm] *vt* : aclamar, elogiar
acclaim[2] *n* : aclamación *f,* elogio *m*
acclamation [,æklə'meɪʃən] *n* : aclamación *f*
acclimate ['æklə,meɪt, ə'klaɪmət] → **acclimatize**
acclimatize [ə'klaɪmə,taɪz] *v* **-tized; -tizing** *vt* **1** : aclimatar **2 to acclimatize oneself** : aclimatarse
accolade ['ækə,leɪd, -,lɑd] *n* **1** PRAISE : elogio *m* **2** AWARD : galardón *m*
accommodate [ə'kɑmə,deɪt] *vt* **-dated; -dating 1** ADAPT : acomodar, adaptar **2** SATISFY : tener en cuenta, satisfacer **3** HOLD : dar cabida a, tener cabida para
accommodation [ə,kɑmə'deɪʃən] *n* **1** : adaptación *f,* adecuación *f* **2 accommodations** *npl* LODGING : alojamiento *m,* hospedaje *m*
accompaniment [ə'kʌmpənəmənt, -'kɑm-] *n* : acompañamiento *m*
accompanist [ə'kʌmpənɪst, -'kɑm-] *n* : acompañante *mf*
accompany [ə'kʌmpəni, -'kɑm-] *vt* **-nied; -nying** : acompañar
accomplice [ə'kɑmpləs, -'kʌm-] *n* : cómplice *mf*
accomplish [ə'kɑmplɪʃ, -'kʌm-] *vt* : efectuar, realizar, lograr, llevar a cabo
accomplished [ə'kɑmplɪʃt, -'kʌm-] *adj* : consumado, logrado
accomplishment [ə'kɑmplɪʃmənt, -'kʌm-] *n* **1** ACHIEVEMENT : logro *m,* éxito *m* **2** SKILL : destreza *f,* habilidad *f*
accord[1] [ə'kɔrd] *vt* GRANT : conceder, otorgar — *vi* **to accord with** : concordar con, conformarse con
accord[2] *n* **1** AGREEMENT : acuerdo *m,* convenio *m* **2** VOLITION : voluntad *f* <on one's own accord : voluntariamente, de motu proprio>
accordance [ə'kɔrdənts] *n* **1** ACCORD : acuerdo *m,* conformidad *f* **2 in ac-**

cordance with : conforme a, según, de acuerdo con
accordingly [ə'kɔrdɪŋli] *adv* **1** CORRESPONDINGLY : en consecuencia **2** CONSEQUENTLY : por consiguiente, por lo tanto
according to [ə'kɔrdɪŋ] *prep* : según, de acuerdo con, conforme a
accordion [ə'kɔrdiən] *n* : acordeón *m*
accordionist [ə'kɔrdiənɪst] *n* : acordeonista *mf*
accost [ə'kɔst] *vt* : abordar, dirigirse a
account[1] [ə'kaʊnt] *vt* : considerar, estimar <he accounts himself lucky : se considera afortunado> — *vi* **to account for** : dar cuenta de, explicar
account[2] *n* **1** : cuenta *f* <savings account : cuenta de ahorros> **2** EXPLANATION : versión *f,* explicación *f* **3** REPORT : relato *m,* informe *m* **4** IMPORTANCE : importancia *f* <to be of no account : no tener importancia> **5 on account of** BECAUSE OF : a causa de, debido a, por **6 on no account** : de ninguna manera
accountability [ə,kaʊntə'bɪləṱi] *n* : responsabilidad *f*
accountable [ə'kaʊntəbəl] *adj* : responsable
accountant [ə'kaʊntənt] *n* : contador *m,* -dora *f;* contable *mf Spain*
accounting [ə'kaʊntɪŋ] *n* : contabilidad *f*
accoutrements *or* **accouterments** [ə'kuːtrəmənts, -'kuːṱər-] *npl* **1** EQUIPMENT : equipo *m,* avíos *mpl* **2** ACCESSORIES : accesorios *mpl* **3** TRAPPINGS : símbolos *mpl* <the accoutrements of power : los símbolos del poder>
accredit [ə'krɛdət] *vt* : acreditar, autorizar
accreditation [ə,krɛdə'teɪʃən] *n* : acreditación *f,* homologación *f*
accrual [ə'kruːəl] *n* : incremento *m,* acumulación *f*
accrue [ə'kruː] *vi* **-crued; -cruing** : acumularse, aumentarse
accumulate [ə'kjuːmjə,leɪt] *v* **-lated; -lating** *vt* : acumular, amontonar — *vi* : acumularse, amontonarse
accumulation [ə,kjuːmjə'leɪʃən] *n* : acumulación *f,* amontonamiento *m*
accuracy ['ækjərəsi] *n* : exactitud *f,* precisión *f*
accurate ['ækjərət] *adj* : exacto, correcto, fiel, preciso — **accurately** *adv*
accusation [,ækjə'zeɪʃən] *n* : acusación *f*
accuse [ə'kjuːz] *vt* **-cused; -cusing** : acusar, delatar, denunciar
accused [ə'kjuːzd] *ns & pl* DEFENDANT : acusado *m,* -da *f*
accuser [ə'kjuːzər] *n* : acusador *m,* -dora *f*
accustom [ə'kʌstəm] *vt* : acostumbrar, habituar
ace ['eɪs] *n* : as *m*
acerbic [ə'sərbɪk, æ-] *adj* : acerbo, mordaz
acetate ['æsə,teɪt] *n* : acetato *m*
acetylene [ə'sɛṱələn, -ṱə,liːn] *n* : acetileno *m*
ache[1] ['eɪk] *vi* **ached; aching 1** : doler **2 to ache for** : anhelar, ansiar
ache[2] *n* : dolor *m*
achieve [ə'tʃiːv] *vt* **achieved; achieving** : lograr, alcanzar, conseguir, realizar
achievement [ə'tʃiːvmənt] *n* : logro *m,* éxito *m,* realización *f*
acid[1] ['æsəd] *adj* **1** SOUR : ácido, agrio **2** CAUSTIC, SHARP : acerbo, mordaz — **acidly** *adv*
acid[2] *n* : ácido *m*
acidic [ə'sɪdɪk, æ-] *adj* : ácido
acidity [ə'sɪdəṱi, æ-] *n, pl* **-ties** : acidez *f*
acknowledge [ɪk'nɑlɪdʒ, æk-] *vt* **-edged; -edging 1** ADMIT : reconocer, admitir **2** RECOGNIZE : reconocer **3 to acknowledge receipt of** : acusar recibo de
acknowledgment [ɪk'nɑlɪdʒmənt, æk-] *n* **1** RECOGNITION : reconocimiento *m* **2** THANKS : agradecimiento *m*
acme ['ækmi] *n* : colmo *m,* apogeo *m,* cúspide *f*
acne ['ækni] *n* : acné *m*
acorn ['eɪ,kɔrn, -kərn] *n* : bellota *f*
acoustic [ə'kuːstɪk] *or* **acoustical** [-stɪkəl] *adj* : acústico — **acoustically** *adv*
acoustics [ə'kuːstɪks] *ns & pl* : acústica *f*
acquaint [ə'kweɪnt] *vt* **1** INFORM : enterar, informar **2** FAMILIARIZE : familiarizar **3 to be acquainted with** : conocer a (una persona), estar al tanto de (un hecho)
acquaintance [ə'kweɪntənts] *n* **1** KNOWLEDGE : conocimiento *m* **2** : conocido *m,* -da *f* <friends and acquaintances : amigos y conocidos>
acquiesce [,ækwi'ɛs] *vi* **-esced; -escing** : consentir, conformarse
acquiescence [,ækwi'ɛsənts] *n* : consentimiento *m,* aquiescencia *f*
acquire [ə'kwaɪr] *vt* **-quired; -quiring** : adquirir, obtener
acquisition [,ækwə'zɪʃən] *n* : adquisición *f*
acquisitive [ə'kwɪzəṱɪv] *adj* : adquisitivo, codicioso
acquit [ə'kwɪt] *vt* **-quitted; -quitting 1** : absolver, exculpar **2 to acquit oneself** : comportarse, defenderse
acquittal [ə'kwɪṱəl] *n* : absolución *f,* exculpación *f*
acre ['eɪkər] *n* : acre *m*
acreage ['eɪkərɪdʒ] *n* : superficie *f* en acres
acrid ['ækrəd] *adj* **1** BITTER : acre **2** CAUSTIC : acre, mordaz — **acridly** *adv*
acrimonious [,ækrə'moːniəs] *adj* : áspero, cáustico, sarcástico
acrimony ['ækrə,moːni] *n, pl* **-nies** : acrimonia *f*

acrobat [ˈækrəˌbæt] *n* : acróbata *mf,* satimbanqui *mf*
acrobatic [ˌækrəˈbæt̬ɪk] *adj* : acrobático
acronym [ˈækrəˌnɪm] *n* : acrónimo *m*
across[1] [əˈkrɔs] *adv* **1** CROSSWISE : al través **2** : a través, del otro lado <he's already across : ya está del otro lado> **3** : de ancho <40 feet across : 40 pies de ancho>
across[2] *prep* **1** : al otro lado de <across the street : al otro lado de la calle> **2** : a través de <a log across the road : un tronco a través del camino>
acrylic [əˈkrɪlɪk] *n* : acrílico *m*
act[1] [ˈækt] *vi* **1** PERFORM : actuar, interpretar **2** FEIGN, PRETEND : fingir, simular **3** BEHAVE : comportarse **4** FUNCTION : actuar, servir, funcionar **5** : tomar medidas <he acted to save the business : tomó medidas para salvar el negocio> **6 to act as** : servir de, hacer de
act[2] *n* **1** DEED : acto *m,* hecho *m,* acción *f* **2** DECREE : ley *f,* decreto *m* **3** : acto *m* (en una obra de teatro), número *m* (en un espectáculo) **4** PRETENSE : fingimiento *m*
action [ˈækʃən] *n* **1** DEED : acción *f,* acto *m,* hecho *m* **2** BEHAVIOR : actuación *f,* comportamiento *m* **3** LAWSUIT : demanda *f* **4** MOVEMENT : movimiento *m* **5** COMBAT : combate *m* **6** PLOT : acción *f,* trama *f* **7** MECHANISM : mecanismo *m*
activate [ˈæktəˌveɪt] *vt* **-vated; -vating** : activar
active [ˈæktɪv] *adj* **1** MOVING : activo, en movimiento **2** LIVELY : vigoroso, enérgico **3** : en actividad <an active volcano : un volcán en actividad> **4** OPERATIVE : vigente
actively [ˈæktɪvli] *adv* : activamente, enérgicamente
activity [ækˈtɪvət̬i] *n, pl* **-ties 1** MOVEMENT : actividad *f,* movimiento *m* **2** VIGOR : vigor *m,* energía *f* **3** OCCUPATION : actividad *f,* ocupación *f*
actor [ˈæktər] *n* : actor *m,* artista *mf*
actress [ˈæktrəs] *n* : actriz *f*
actual [ˈæktʃʊəl] *adj* : real, verdadero
actuality [ˌæktʃʊˈælət̬i] *n, pl* **-ties** : realidad *f*
actually [ˈæktʃʊəli, -ʃəli] *adv* : realmente, en realidad
actuary [ˈæktʃʊˌɛri] *n, pl* **-aries** : actuario *m,* -ria *f* de seguros
acumen [əˈkjuːmən] *n* : perspicacia *f*
acupuncture [ˈækjʊˌpʌŋktʃər] *n* : acupuntura *f*
acute [əˈkjuːt] *adj* **acuter; acutest 1** SHARP : agudo **2** PERCEPTIVE : perspicaz, sagaz **3** KEEN : fino, muy desarrollado, agudo <an acute sense of smell : un fino olfato> **4** SEVERE : grave **5 acute angle** : ángulo *m* agudo
acutely [əˈkjuːtli] *adv* : intensamente <to be acutely aware : estar perfectamente consciente>
acuteness [əˈkjuːtnəs] *n* : agudeza *f*
ad [ˈæd] → **advertisement**
adage [ˈædɪdʒ] *n* : adagio *m,* refrán *m,* dicho *m*
adamant [ˈædəmənt, -ˌmænt] *adj* : firme, categórico, inflexible — **adamantly** *adv*
Adam's apple [ˈædəmz] *n* : nuez *f* de Adán
adapt [əˈdæpt] *vt* : adaptar, ajustar — *vi* : adaptarse
adaptability [əˌdæptəˈbɪlət̬i] *n* : adaptabilidad *f,* flexibilidad *f*
adaptable [əˈdæptəbəl] *adj* : adaptable, amoldable
adaptation [ˌæˌdæpˈteɪʃən, -dəp-] *n* **1** : adaptación *f,* modificación *f* **2** VERSION : versión *f*
adapter [əˈdæptər] *n* : adaptador *m*
add [ˈæd] *vt* **1** : añadir, agregar <to add a comment : añadir una observación> **2** : sumar <add these numbers : suma estos números> — *vi* : sumar (en total)
adder [ˈædər] *n* : víbora *f*
addict[1] [əˈdɪkt] *vt* : causar adicción en
addict[2] [ˈædɪkt] *n* **1** : adicto *m,* -ta *f* **2 drug addict** : drogadicto *m,* -ta *f;* toxicómano *m,* -na *f*
addiction [əˈdɪkʃən] *n* **1** : adicción *f,* dependencia *f* **2 drug addiction** : drogadicción *f*
addictive [əˈdɪktɪv] *adj* : adictivo
addition [əˈdɪʃən] *n* **1** : adición *f,* añadidura *f* **2 in ~** : además, también
additional [əˈdɪʃənəl] *adj* : extra, adicional, de más
additionally [əˈdɪʃənəli] *adv* : además, adicionalmente
additive [ˈædət̬ɪv] *n* : aditivo *m*
addle [ˈædəl] *vt* **-dled; -dling** : confundir, enturbiar
address[1] [əˈdrɛs] *vt* **1** : dirigirse a, pronunciar un discurso ante <to address a jury : dirigirse a un jurado> **2** : dirigir, ponerle la dirección a <to address a letter : dirigir una carta>
address[2] [əˈdrɛs, ˈæˌdrɛs] *n* **1** SPEECH : discurso *m,* alocución *f* **2** : dirección *f* (de una residencia, etc.)
adenoids [ˈædˌnɔɪd, -dənˌɔɪd] *npl* : adenoides *fpl*
adept [əˈdɛpt] *adj* : experto, hábil — **adeptly** *adv*
adequacy [ˈædɪkwəsi] *n, pl* **-cies** : cantidad *f* suficiente
adequate [ˈædɪkwət] *adj* **1** SUFFICIENT : adecuado, suficiente **2** ACCEPTABLE, PASSABLE : adecuado, aceptable
adequately [ˈædɪkwətli] *adv* : suficientemente, apropiadamente
adhere [ædˈhɪr, əd-] *vi* **-hered; -hering 1** STICK : pegarse, adherirse **2 to adhere to** : adherirse a (una política, etc.), cumplir con (una promesa)

adherence [æd'hɪrənts, əd-] *n* : adhesión *f,* adherencia *f,* observancia *f* (de una ley, etc.)

adherent[1] [æd'hɪrənt, əd-] *adj* : adherente, adhesivo, pegajoso

adherent[2] *n* : adepto *m,* -ta *f;* partidario *m,* -ria *f*

adhesive[1] [æd'hi:sɪv, əd-, -zɪv] *adj* : adhesivo

adhesive[2] *n* : adhesivo *m,* pegamento *m*

adjacent [ə'dʒeɪsənt] *adj* : adyacente, colindante, contiguo

adjective ['ædʒɪktɪv] *n* : adjetivo *m* — **adjectival** [ˌædʒɪk'taɪvəl] *adj*

adjoin [ə'dʒɔɪn] *vt* : lindar con, colindar con

adjoining [ə'dʒɔɪnɪŋ] *adj* : contiguo, colindante

adjourn [ə'dʒərn] *vt* : levantar, suspender <the meeting is adjourned : se levanta la sesión> — *vi* : aplazarse

adjournment [ə'dʒərnmənt] *n* : suspensión *f,* aplazamiento *m*

adjudicate [ə'dʒu:dɪˌkeɪt] *vt* **-cated; -cating** : juzgar, arbitrar

adjunct ['æˌdʒʌŋkt] *n* : adjunto *m,* complemento *m*

adjust [ə'dʒʌst] *vt* : ajustar, arreglar, regular — *vi* **to adjust to** : adaptarse a

adjustable [ə'dʒʌstəbəl] *adj* : ajustable, regulable, graduable

adjustment [ə'dʒʌstmənt] *n* : ajuste *m,* modificación *f*

ad–lib[1] ['æd'lɪb] *v* **-libbed; -libbing** : improvisar

ad–lib[2] *adj* : improvisado

administer [æd'mɪnəstər, əd-] *vt* : administrar

administration [ædˌmɪnə'streɪʃən, əd-] *n* **1** MANAGING : administración *f,* dirección *f* **2** GOVERNMENT, MANAGEMENT : administración *f,* gobierno *m*

administrative [æd'mɪnəˌstreɪt̬ɪv, əd-] *adj* : administrativo — **administratively** *adv*

administrator [æd'mɪnəˌstreɪt̬ər, əd-] *n* : administrador *m,* -dora *f*

admirable ['ædmərəbəl] *adj* : admirable, loable — **admirably** *adv*

admiral ['ædmərəl] *n* : almirante *mf*

admiration [ˌædmə'reɪʃən] *n* : admiración *f*

admire [æd'maɪr] *vt* **-mired; -miring** : admirar

admirer [æd'maɪrər] *n* : admirador *m,* -dora *f*

admiring [æd'maɪrɪŋ] *adj* : admirativo, de admiración

admiringly [æd'maɪrɪŋli] *adv* : con admiración

admissible [æd'mɪsəbəl] *adj* : admisible, aceptable

admission [æd'mɪʃən] *n* **1** ADMITTANCE : entrada *f,* admisión *f* **2** ACKNOWLEDGMENT : reconocimiento *m,* admisión *f*

admit [æd'mɪt, əd-] *vt* **-mitted; -mitting 1** : admitir, dejar entrar <the museum admits children : el museo deja entrar a los niños> **2** ACKNOWLEDGE : reconocer, admitir

admittance [æd'mɪtənts, əd-] *n* : admisión *f,* entrada *f,* acceso *m*

admittedly [æd'mɪt̬ədli, əd-] *adv* : la verdad es que, lo cierto es que <admittedly we went too fast : la verdad es que fuimos demasiado de prisa>

admonish [æd'mɑnɪʃ, əd-] *vt* : amonestar, reprender

admonition [ˌædmə'nɪʃən] *n* : admonición *f*

ado [ə'du:] *n* **1** FUSS : ruido *m,* alboroto *m* **2** TROUBLE : dificultad *f,* lío *m* **3 without further ado** : sin más preámbulos

adobe [ə'do:bi] *n* : adobe *m*

adolescence [ˌædəl'ɛsənts] *n* : adolescencia *f*

adolescent[1] [ˌædəl'ɛsənt] *adj* : adolescente, de adolescencia

adolescent[2] *n* : adolescente *mf*

adopt [ə'dɑpt] *vt* : adoptar

adoption [ə'dɑpʃən] *n* : adopción *f*

adorable [ə'dorəbəl] *adj* : adorable, encantador

adorably [ə'dorəbli] *adv* : de manera adorable

adoration [ˌædə'reɪʃən] *n* : adoración *f*

adore [ə'dor] *vt* **adored; adoring 1** WORSHIP : adorar **2** LOVE : querer, adorar **3** LIKE : encantarle (algo a uno), gustarle mucho (algo a uno) <I adore your new dress : me encanta tu vestido nuevo>

adorn [ə'dɔrn] *vt* : adornar, ornar, engalanar

adornment [ə'dɔrnmənt] *n* : adorno *m,* decoración *f*

adrift [ə'drɪft] *adj & adv* : a la deriva

adroit [ə'drɔɪt] *adj* : diestro, hábil — **adroitly** *adv*

adroitness [ə'drɔɪtnəs] *n* : destreza *f,* habilidad *f*

adult[1] [ə'dʌlt, 'æˌdʌlt] *adj* : adulto

adult[2] *n* : adulto *m,* -ta *f*

adulterate [ə'dʌltəˌreɪt] *vt* **-ated; -ating** : adulterar

adulterous [ə'dʌltərəs] *adj* : adúltero

adultery [ə'dʌltəri] *n, pl* **-teries** : adulterio *m*

adulthood [ə'dʌltˌhʊd] *n* : adultez *f,* edad *f* adulta

advance[1] [æd'vænts, əd-] *v* **-vanced; -vancing** *vt* **1** : avanzar, adelantar <to advance troops : avanzar las tropas> **2** PROMOTE : ascender, promover **3** PROPOSE : proponer, presentar **4** : adelantar, anticipar <they advanced me next month's salary : me adelantaron el sueldo del próximo mes> — *vi* **1** PROCEED : avanzar, adelantarse **2** PROGRESS : progresar

advance[2] *adj* : anticipado <advance notice : previo aviso>

advance[3] *n* **1** PROGRESSION : avance *m* **2** PROGRESS : adelanto *m,* mejora *f,* pro-

greso *m* 3 RISE : aumento *m,* alza *f* 4 LOAN : anticipo *m,* préstamo *m* 5 in ~ : por adelantado
advanced [æd'vænʦt, əd-] *adj* 1 DEVELOPED : avanzado, desarrollado 2 PRECOCIOUS : adelantado, precoz 3 HIGHER : superior
advancement [æd'vænʦmənt, əd-] *n* 1 FURTHERANCE : fomento *m,* adelantamiento *m,* progreso *m* 2 PROMOTION : ascenso *m*
advantage [əd'væntɪdʒ, æd-] *n* 1 SUPERIORITY : ventaja *f,* superioridad *f* 2 GAIN : provecho *m,* partido *m* 3 **to take advantage of** : aprovecharse de
advantageous [ˌædˌvæn'teɪdʒəs, -vən-] *adj* : ventajoso, provechoso — **advantageously** *adv*
advent ['ædˌvɛnt] *n* 1 **Advent** : Adviento *m* 2 ARRIVAL : advenimiento *m,* venida *f*
adventure [æd'vɛntʃər, əd-] *n* : aventura *f*
adventurer [æd'vɛntʃərər, əd-] *n* : aventurero *m,* -ra *f*
adventurous [æd'vɛntʃərəs, əd-] *adj* 1 : intrépido, aventurero <an adventurous traveler : un viajero intrépido> 2 RISKY : arriesgado, aventurado
adverb ['ædˌvərb] *n* : adverbio *m* — **adverbial** [æd'vərbiəl] *adj*
adversary ['ædvərˌsɛri] *n, pl* **-saries** : adversario *m,* -ria *f*
adverse [æd'vərs, 'æd-ˌ] *adj* 1 OPPOSING : opuesto, contrario 2 UNFAVORABLE : adverso, desfavorable — **adversely** *adv*
adversity [æd'vərsəṭi, əd-] *n, pl* **-ties** : adversidad *f*
advertise ['ædvərˌtaɪz] *v* **-tised; -tising** *vt* : anunciar, hacerle publicidad a — *vi* : hacer publicidad, hacer propaganda
advertisement ['ædvərˌtaɪzmənt; æd'vərṭəzmənt] *n* : anuncio *m*
advertiser ['ædvərˌtaɪzər] *n* : anunciante *mf*
advertising ['ædvərˌtaɪzɪŋ] *n* : publicidad *f,* propaganda *f*
advice [æd'vaɪs] *n* : consejo *m,* recomendación *f* <take my advice : sigue mis consejos>
advisability [ædˌvaɪzə'bɪləṭi, əd-] *n* : conveniencia *f*
advisable [æd'vaɪzəbəl, əd-] *adj* : aconsejable, recomendable, conveniente
advise [æd'vaɪz, əd-] *v* **-vised; -vising** *vt* 1 COUNSEL : aconsejar, asesorar 2 RECOMMEND : recomendar 3 INFORM : informar, notificar — *vi* : dar consejo
adviser *or* **advisor** [æd'vaɪzər, əd-] *n* : consejero *m,* -ra *f;* asesor *m,* -sora *f*
advisory [æd'vaɪzəri, əd-] *adj* 1 : consultivo 2 **in an advisory capacity** : como asesor
advocacy ['ædvəkəsi] *n* : promoción *f,* apoyo *m*
advocate[1] ['ædvəˌkeɪt] *vt* **-cated; -cating** : recomendar, abogar por, ser partidario de
advocate[2] ['ædvəkət] *n* : defensor *m,* -sora *f;* partidario *m,* -ria *f*
adze ['ædz] *n* : azuela *f*
aeon ['iːən, 'iːˌɑn] *n* : eón *m,* siglo *m,* eternidad *f*
aerate ['ærˌeɪt] *vt* **-ated; -ating** : gasear (un líquido), oxigenar (la sangre)
aerial[1] ['æriəl] *adj* : aéreo
aerial[2] *n* : antena *f*
aerie ['æri, 'ɪri, 'eɪəri] *n* : aguilera *f*
aerobic [ˌær'oːbɪk] *adj* : aerobio, aeróbico <aerobic exercises : ejercicios aeróbicos>
aerobics [ˌær'oːbɪks] *ns & pl* : aeróbic *m*
aerodynamic [ˌæroːdaɪ'næmɪk] *adj* : aerodinámico — **aerodynamically** [-mikli] *adv*
aerodynamics [ˌæroːdaɪ'næmɪks] *n* : aerodinámica *f*
aeronautical [ˌærə'nɔṭɪkəl] *adj* : aeronáutico
aeronautics [ˌærə'nɔṭɪks] *n* : aeronáutica *f*
aerosol ['ærəˌsɔl] *n* : aerosol *m*
aerospace[1] ['æroˌspeɪs] *adj* : aeroespacial
aerospace[2] *n* : espacio *m*
aesthetic [ɛs'θɛṭɪk] *adj* : estético — **aesthetically** [-ṭɪkli] *adv*
aesthetics [ɛs'θɛṭɪks] *n* : estética *f*
afar [ə'fɑr] *adv* : lejos, a lo lejos
affability [ˌæfə'bɪləṭi] *n* : afabilidad *f*
affable ['æfəbəl] *adj* : afable — **affably** *adv*
affair [ə'fær] *n* 1 MATTER : asunto *m,* cuestión *f,* caso *m* 2 EVENT : ocasión *f,* acontecimiento *m* 3 LIAISON : amorío *m,* aventura *f* 4 **business affairs** : negocios *mpl* 5 **current affairs** : actualidades *fpl*
affect [ə'fɛkt, æ-] *vt* 1 INFLUENCE, TOUCH : afectar, tocar 2 FEIGN : fingir
affectation [ˌæˌfɛk'teɪʃən] *n* : afectación *f*
affected [ə'fɛktəd, æ-] *adj* 1 FEIGNED : afectado, fingido 2 MOVED : conmovido
affecting [ə'fɛktɪŋ, æ-] *adj* : conmovedor
affection [ə'fɛkʃən] *n* : afecto *m,* cariño *m*
affectionate [ə'fɛkʃənət] *adj* : afectuoso, cariñoso — **affectionately** *adv*
affidavit [ˌæfə'deɪvət, 'æfəˌ-] *n* : declaración *f* jurada, affidávit *m*
affiliate[1] [ə'fɪliˌeɪt] *v* **-ated; -ating** *vt* : afiliar, asociar <to be affiliated with : estar afiliado a>
affiliate[2] [ə'fɪliət] *n* : afiliado *m,* -da *f* (persona), filial *f* (organización)
affiliation [əˌfɪli'eɪʃən] *n* : afiliación *f,* filiación *f*
affinity [ə'fɪnəṭi] *n, pl* **-ties** : afinidad *f*

affirm [ə'fərm] *vt* : afirmar, aseverar, declarar

affirmation [ˌæfər'meɪʃən] *n* : afirmación *f,* aserto *m,* declaración *f*

affirmative[1] [ə'fərmət̬ɪv] *adj* : afirmativo <affirmative action : acción afirmativa>

affirmative[2] *n* **1** : afirmativa *f* **2 to answer in the affirmative** : responder afirmativamente, dar una respuesta afirmativa

affix [ə'fɪks] *vt* : fijar, poner, pegar

afflict [ə'flɪkt] *vt* **1** : afligir, aquejar **2 to be afflicted with** : padecer de, sufrir de

affliction [ə'flɪkʃən] *n* **1** TRIBULATION : aflicción *f,* tribulación *f* **2** AILMENT : enfermedad *f,* padecimiento *m*

affluence ['æˌflu:ən*t*s; æ'flu:-, ə-] *n* : afluencia *f,* abundancia *f,* prosperidad *f*

affluent ['æˌflu:ənt; æ'flu:-, ə-] *adj* : próspero, adinerado

afford [ə'ford] *vt* **1** : tener los recursos para, permitirse el lujo de <I can afford it : puedo permitírmelo, tengo con que comprarlo> **2** PROVIDE : ofrecer, proporcionar, dar

affront[1] [ə'frʌnt] *vt* : afrentar, insultar, ofender

affront[2] *n* : afrenta *f,* insulto *m,* ofensa *f*

Afghan ['æfˌgæn, -gən] *n* : afgano *m,* -na *f* — **Afghan** *adj*

afire [ə'faɪr] *adj* : ardiendo, en llamas

aflame [ə'fleɪm] *adj* : llameante, en llamas

afloat [ə'flo:t] *adv & adj* : a flote

afoot [ə'fʊt] *adj* **1** WALKING : a pie, andando **2** UNDER WAY : en marcha <something suspicious is afoot : algo sospechoso se está tramando>

aforesaid [ə'forˌsɛd] *adj* : antes mencionado, antedicho

afraid [ə'freɪd] *adj* **1 to be afraid** : tener miedo **2 to be afraid that** : temerse que <I'm afraid not : me temo que no>

afresh [ə'frɛʃ] *adv* **1** : de nuevo, otra vez **2 to start afresh** : volver a empezar

African ['æfrɪkən] *n* : africano *m,* -na *f* — **African** *adj*

Afro–American[1] [ˌæfroə'mɛrɪkən] *adj* : afroamericano *m,* -na *f*

Afro–American[2] *n* : afroamericano

aft ['æft] *adv* : a popa

after[1] ['æftər] *adv* **1** AFTERWARD : después **2** BEHIND : detrás, atrás

after[2] *adj* : posterior, siguiente <in after years : en los años posteriores>

after[3] *conj* : después de, después de que <after we ate : después de que comimos, después de comer>

after[4] *prep* **1** FOLLOWING : después de, tras <after Saturday : después del sábado> <day after day : día tras día> **2** BEHIND : tras de, después de <I ran after the dog : corrí tras del perro> **3** CONCERNING : por <they asked after you : preguntaron por ti> **4 after all** : después de todo

aftereffect ['æftərɪˌfɛkt] *n* : efecto *m* secundario

afterlife ['æftərˌlaɪf] *n* : vida *f* venidera, vida *f* después de la muerte

aftermath ['æftərˌmæθ] *n* : consecuencias *fpl,* resultados *mpl*

afternoon [ˌæftər'nu:n] *n* : tarde *f*

afterthought ['æftərˌθɔt] *n* : ocurrencia *f* tardía, idea *f* tardía

afterward ['æftərwərd] *or* **afterwards** [-wərdz] *adv* : después, luego <soon afterward : poco después>

again [ə'gɛn, -'gɪn] *adv* **1** ANEW, OVER : de nuevo, otra vez **2** BESIDES : además **3 then again** : por otra parte <I may stay, then again I may not : puede ser que me quede, por otra parte, puede que no>

against [ə'gɛn*t*st, -'gɪn*t*st] *prep* **1** TOUCHING : contra <against the wall : contra la pared> **2** OPPOSING : contra, en contra de <I will vote against the proposal : votaré en contra de la propuesta> <against the grain : a contrapelo>

agape [ə'geɪp] *adj* : boquiabierto

agate ['ægət] *n* : ágata *f*

age[1] ['eɪdʒ] *vi* **aged; aging** : envejecer, madurar

age[2] *n* **1** : edad *f* <ten years of age : diez años de edad> <to be of age : ser mayor de edad> **2** PERIOD : era *f,* siglo *m,* época *f* **3 old age** : vejez *f* **4 ages** *npl* : siglos *mpl,* eternidad *f*

aged *adj* **1** ['eɪdʒəd, 'eɪdʒd] OLD : anciano, viejo, vetusto **2** ['eɪdʒd] (*indicating a specified age*) <a girl aged 10 : una niña de 10 años de edad>

ageless ['eɪdʒləs] *adj* **1** YOUTHFUL : eternamente joven **2** TIMELESS : eterno, perenne

agency ['eɪdʒən*t*si] *n, pl* **-cies 1** : agencia *f,* oficina *f* <travel agency : agencia de viajes> **2 through the agency of** : a través de, por medio de

agenda [ə'dʒɛndə] *n* : agenda *f,* orden *m* del día

agent ['eɪdʒənt] *n* **1** MEANS : agente *m,* medio *m,* instrumento *m* **2** REPRESENTATIVE : agente *mf,* representante *mf*

aggravate ['ægrəˌveɪt] *vt* **-vated; -vating 1** WORSEN : agravar, empeorar **2** ANNOY : irritar, exasperar

aggravation [ˌægrə'veɪʃən] *n* **1** WORSENING : empeoramiento *m* **2** ANNOYANCE : molestia *f,* irritación *f,* exasperación *f*

aggregate[1] ['ægrɪˌgeɪt] *vt* **-gated; -gating** : juntar, sumar

aggregate[2] ['ægrɪgət] *adj* : total, global, conjunto

aggregate[3] ['ægrɪgət] *n* **1** CONGLOMERATE : agregado *m,* conglomerado *m* **2** WHOLE : total *m,* conjunto *m*

aggression [əˈgrɛʃən] *n* **1** ATTACK : agresión *f* **2** AGGRESSIVENESS : agresividad *f*

aggressive [əˈgrɛsɪv] *adj* : agresivo — **aggressively** *adv*

aggressiveness [əˈgrɛsɪvnəs] *n* : agresividad *f*

aggressor [əˈgrɛsər] *n* : agresor *m*, -sora *f*

aggrieved [əˈgriːvd] *adj* : ofendido, herido

aghast [əˈgæst] *adj* : espantado, aterrado, horrorizado

agile [ˈædʒəl] *adj* : ágil

agility [əˈdʒɪləṭi] *n, pl* **-ties** : agilidad *f*

agitate [ˈædʒəˌteɪt] *v* **-tated; -tating** *vt* **1** SHAKE : agitar **2** UPSET : inquietar, perturbar — *vi* **to agitate against** : hacer campaña en contra de

agitation [ˌædʒəˈteɪʃən] *n* : agitación *f*, inquietud *f*

agitator [ˈædʒəˌteɪṭər] *n* : agitador *m*, -dora *f*

agnostic [ægˈnɑstɪk] *n* : agnóstico *m*, -ca *f*

ago [əˈgoː] *adv* : hace <two years ago : hace dos años> <long ago : hace tiempo, hace mucho tiempo>

agog [əˈgɑg] *adj* : ansioso, curioso

agonize [ˈægəˌnaɪz] *vi* **-nized; -nizing** : tormentarse, angustiarse

agonizing [ˈægəˌnaɪzɪŋ] *adj* : angustioso, terrible — **agonizingly** [-zɪŋli] *adv*

agony [ˈægəni] *n, pl* **-nies 1** PAIN : dolor *m* **2** ANGUISH : angustia *f*

agrarian [əˈgrɛriən] *adj* : agrario

agree [əˈgriː] *v* **agreed; agreeing** *vt* ACKNOWLEDGE : estar de acuerdo <he agreed that I was right : estuvo de acuerdo en que tenía razón> — *vi* **1** CONCUR : estar de acuerdo **2** CONSENT : ponerse de acuerdo **3** TALLY : concordar **4 to agree with** : sentarle bien (a alguien) <this climate agrees with me : este clima me sienta bien>

agreeable [əˈgriːəbəl] *adj* **1** PLEASING : agradable, simpático **2** WILLING : dispuesto **3** AGREEING : de acuerdo, conforme

agreeably [əˈgriːəbli] *adv* : agradablemente

agreement [əˈgriːmənt] *n* **1** : acuerdo *m*, conformidad *f* <in agreement with : de acuerdo con> **2** CONTRACT, PACT : acuerdo *m*, pacto *m*, convenio *m* **3** CONCORD, HARMONY : concordia *f*

agriculture [ˈægrɪˌkʌltʃər] *n* : agricultura *f* — **agricultural** [ˌægrɪˈkʌltʃərəl] *adj*

aground [əˈgraʊnd] *adj* : encallado, varado

ahead [əˈhɛd] *adv* **1** : al frente, delante, adelante <he walked ahead : caminó delante> **2** BEFOREHAND : por adelantado, con antelación **3** LEADING : a la delantera **4 to get ahead** : adelantar, progresar

ahead of *prep* **1** : al frente de, delante de, antes de **2 to get ahead of** : adelantarse a

ahoy [əˈhɔɪ] *interj* **ship ahoy!** : ¡barco a la vista!

aid[1] [ˈeɪd] *vt* : ayudar, auxiliar

aid[2] *n* **1** HELP : ayuda *f*, asistencia *f* **2** ASSISTANT : asistente *mf*

aide [ˈeɪd] *n* : ayudante *mf*

AIDS [ˈeɪdz] *n* : SIDA *m*, sida *m*

ail [ˈeɪl] *vt* : molestar, afligir — *vi* : sufrir, estar enfermo

aileron [ˈeɪləˌrɑn] *n* : alerón *m*

ailment [ˈeɪlmənt] *n* : enfermedad *f*, dolencia *f*, achaque *m*

aim[1] [ˈeɪm] *vt* **1** : apuntar (un arma), dirigir (una observación) **2** INTEND : proponerse, querer <he aims to do it tonight : se propone hacerlo esta noche> — *vi* **1** POINT : apuntar **2 to aim at** : aspirar a

aim[2] *n* **1** MARKSMANSHIP : puntería *f* **2** GOAL : propósito *m*, objetivo *m*, fin *m*

aimless [ˈeɪmləs] *adj* : sin rumbo, sin objeto

aimlessly [ˈeɪmləsli] *adv* : sin rumbo, sin objeto

air[1] [ˈær] *vt* **1** : airear, ventilar <to air out a mattress : airear un colchón> **2** EXPRESS : airear, manifestar, comunicar **3** BROADCAST : transmitir, emitir

air[2] *n* **1** : aire *m* **2** MELODY : aire *m* **3** APPEARANCE : aire *m*, aspecto *m* **4 airs** *npl* : aires *mpl*, afectación *f* **5 by ~** : por avión (dícese de una carta), en avión (dícese de una persona) **6 to be on the air** : estar en el aire, estar emitiendo

airborne [ˈærˌborn] *adj* **1** : aerotransportado <airborne troops : tropas aerotransportadas> **2** FLYING : volando, en el aire

air–condition [ˌærkənˈdɪʃən] *vt* : climatizar, condicionar con el aire

air conditioner [ˌærkənˈdɪʃənər] *n* : acondicionador *m* de aire

air–conditioning [ˌærkənˈdɪʃənɪŋ] *n* : aire *m* acondicionado

aircraft [ˈærˌkræft] *ns & pl* **1** : avión *m*, aeronave *f* **2 aircraft carrier** : portaaviones *m*

airfield [ˈærˌfiːld] *n* : aeródromo *m*, campo *m* de aviación

air force *n* : fuerza *f* aérea

airlift [ˈærˌlɪft] *n* : puente *m* aéreo, transporte *m* aéreo

airline [ˈærˌlaɪn] *n* : aerolínea *f*, línea *f* aérea

airliner [ˈærˌlaɪnər] *n* : avión *m* de pasajeros

airmail[1] [ˈærˌmeɪl] *vt* : enviar por vía aérea

airmail[2] *n* : correo *m* aéreo

airman [ˈærmən] *n, pl* **-men** [-mən, -ˌmɛn] **1** AVIATOR : aviador *m*, -dora *f* **2** : soldado *m* de la fuerza aérea

airplane [ˈærˌpleɪn] *n* : avión *m*

airport [ˈærˌport] *n* : aeropuerto *m*

airship [ˈær,ʃɪp] *n* : dirigible *m*, zepelín *m*
airstrip [ˈær,strɪp] *n* : pista *f* de aterrizaje
airtight [ˈærˈtaɪt] *adj* : hermético, herméticamente cerrado
airwaves [ˈær,weɪvz] *npl* : radio *m*, televisión *f*
airy [ˈæri] *adj* **airier** [-iər]; **-est 1** DELICATE, LIGHT : delicado, ligero **2** BREEZY : aireado, bien ventilado
aisle [ˈaɪl] *n* : pasillo *m*, nave *f* lateral (de una iglesia)
ajar [əˈdʒɑr] *adj* : entreabierto, entornado
akimbo [əˈkɪmbo] *adj & adv* : en jarras
akin [əˈkɪn] *adj* **1** RELATED : emparentado **2** SIMILAR : semejante, parecido
alabaster [ˈælə,bæstər] *n* : alabastro *m*
alacrity [əˈlækrət̬i] *n* : presteza *f*, prontitud *f*
alarm[1] [əˈlɑrm] *vt* **1** WARN : alarmar, alertar **2** FRIGHTEN : asustar
alarm[2] *n* **1** WARNING : alarma *f*, alerta *f* **2** APPREHENSION, FEAR : aprensión *f*, inquietud *f*, temor *m* **3 alarm clock** : despertador *m*
alas [əˈlæs] *interj* : ¡ay!
Albanian [ælˈbeɪniən] *n* : albanés *m*, -nesa *f* — **Albanian** *adj*
albatross [ˈælbə,trɔs] *n, pl* **-tross** *or* **-trosses** : albatros *m*
albeit [ɔlˈbiːət, æl-] *conj* : aunque
albino [ælˈbaɪno] *n, pl* **-nos** : albino *m*, -na *f*
album [ˈælbəm] *n* : álbum *m*
albumen [ælˈbjuːmən] *n* **1** : clara *f* de huevo **2** → **albumin**
albumin [ælˈbjuːmən] *n* : albúmina *f*
alcohol [ˈælkə,hɔl] *n* **1** ETHANOL : alcohol *m*, etanol *m* **2** LIQUOR : alcohol *m*, bebidas *fpl* alcohólicas
alcoholic[1] [,ælkəˈhɔlɪk] *adj* : alcohólico
alcoholic[2] *n* : alcohólico *m*, -ca *f*
alcoholism [ˈælkəhɔ,lɪzəm] *n* : alcoholismo *m*
alcove [ˈæl,koːv] *n* : nicho *m*, hueco *m*
alderman [ˈɔldərmən] *n, pl* **-men** [-mən, -,mɛn] : concejal *mf*
ale [ˈeɪl] *n* : cerveza *f*
alert[1] [əˈlərt] *vt* : alertar, poner sobre aviso
alert[2] *adj* **1** WATCHFUL : alerta, vigilante **2** QUICK : listo, vivo
alert[3] *n* : alerta *f*, alarma *f*
alertly [əˈlərtli] *adv* : con listeza
alertness [əˈlərtnəs] *n* **1** WATCHFULNESS : vigilancia *f* **2** ASTUTENESS : listeza *f*, viveza *f*
alfalfa [ælˈfælfə] *n* : alfalfa *f*
alga [ˈælgə] *n, pl* **-gae** [ˈæl,dʒiː] : alga *f*
algebra [ˈældʒəbrə] *n* : álgebra *m*
algebraic [,ældʒəˈbreɪɪk] *adj* : algebraico — **algebraically** [-ɪkli] *adv*
Algerian [ælˈdʒɪriən] *n* : argelino *m*, -na *f* — **Algerian** *adj*
alias[1] [ˈeɪliəs] *adv* : alias
alias[2] *n* : alias *m*
alibi[1] [ˈælə,baɪ] *vi* : ofrecer una coartada
alibi[2] *n* **1** : coartada *f* **2** EXCUSE : pretexto *m*, excusa *f*
alien[1] [ˈeɪliən] *adj* **1** STRANGE : ajeno, extraño **2** FOREIGN : extranjero, foráneo **3** EXTRATERRESTRIAL : extraterrestre
alien[2] *n* **1** FOREIGNER : extranjero *m*, -ra *f*; forastero *m*, -ra *f* **2** EXTRATERRESTRIAL : extraterrestre *mf*
alienate [ˈeɪliə,neɪt] *vt* **-ated; -ating 1** ESTRANGE : alienar, enajenar **2 to alienate oneself** : alejarse, distanciarse
alienation [,eɪliəˈneɪʃən] *n* : alienación *f*, enajenación *f*
alight [əˈlaɪt] *vi* **1** DISMOUNT : bajarse, apearse **2** LAND : posarse, aterrizar
align [əˈlaɪn] *vt* : alinear
alignment [əˈlaɪnmənt] *n* : alineación *f*, alineamiento *m*
alike[1] [əˈlaɪk] *adv* : igual, del mismo modo
alike[2] *adj* : igual, semejante, parecido
alimentary [,æləˈmɛntəri] *adj* **1** : alimenticio **2 alimentary canal** : tubo *m* digestivo
alimony [ˈælə,moːni] *n, pl* **-nies** : pensión *f* alimenticia
alive [əˈlaɪv] *adj* **1** LIVING : vivo, viviente **2** LIVELY : animado, activo **3** ACTIVE : vigente, en uso **4** AWARE : consciente <alive to the danger : consciente del peligro>
alkali [ˈælkə,laɪ] *n, pl* **-lies** [-,laɪz] *or* **-lis** [-,laɪz] : álcali *m*
alkaline [ˈælkələn, -,laɪn] *adj* : alcalino
all[1] [ˈɔl] *adv* **1** COMPLETELY : todo, completamente **2** : igual <the score is 14 all : es 14 iguales, están empatados a 14> **3 all the better** : tanto mejor **4 all the more** : aún más, todavía más
all[2] *adj* : todo <all the children : todos los niños> <in all likelihood : con toda probabilidad, con la mayor probabilidad>
all[3] *pron* **1** : todo, -da <they ate it all : lo comieron todo> <that's all : eso es todo> <enough for all : suficiente para todos> **2 all in all** : en general **3 not at all** (*in negative constructions*) : en absoluto, para nada
Allah [ˈɑlɑ, ɑˈlɑ] *n* : Alá *m*
all–around [,ɔləˈraʊnd] *adj* : completo, amplio
allay [əˈleɪ] *vt* **1** ALLEVIATE : aliviar, mitigar **2** CALM : aquietar, calmar
allegation [,ælɪˈgeɪʃən] *n* : alegato *m*, acusación *f*
allege [əˈlɛdʒ] *vt* **-leged; -leging 1** : alegar, afirmar **2 to be alleged** : decirse, pretenderse <she is alleged

to be wealthy : se dice que es adinerada>
alleged [ə'lɛdʒd, ə'lɛdʒəd] *adj* : presunto, supuesto
allegedly [ə'lɛdʒədli] : *adv* : supuestamente, según se alega
allegiance [ə'li:dʒən*t*s] *n* : lealtad *f,* fidelidad *f*
allegorical [ˌælə'gɔrɪkəl] *adj* : alegórico
allegory ['ælə͵gori] *n, pl* **-ries** : alegoría *f*
alleluia [ˌɑlə'lu:jə, ˌæ-] → **hallelujah**
allergic [ə'lərdʒɪk] *adj* : alérgico
allergy ['ælərdʒi] *n, pl* **-gies** : alergia *f*
alleviate [ə'li:vi͵eɪt] *vt* **-ated; -ating** : aliviar, mitigar, paliar
alleviation [ə͵li:vi'eɪʃən] *n* : alivio *m*
alley ['æli] *n, pl* **-leys 1** : callejón *m* **2 bowling alley** : bolera *f*
alliance [ə'laɪən*t*s] *n* : alianza *f,* coalición *f*
alligator ['ælə͵geɪtər] *n* : caimán *m*
alliteration [ə͵lɪtə'reɪʃən] *n* : aliteración *f*
allocate ['ælə͵keɪt] *vt* **-cated; -cating** : asignar, adjudicar
allocation [ˌælə'keɪʃən] *n* : asignación *f,* reparto *m,* distribución *f*
allot [ə'lɑt] *vt* **-lotted; -lotting** : repartir, distribuir, asignar
allotment [ə'lɑtmənt] *n* : reparto *m,* asignación *f,* distribución *f*
allow [ə'laʊ] *vt* **1** PERMIT : permitir, dejar **2** ALLOT : conceder, dar **3** ADMIT, CONCEDE : admitir, conceder — *vi* **to allow for** : tener en cuenta
allowable [ə'laʊəbəl] *adj* **1** PERMISSIBLE : permisible, lícito **2** : deducible <allowable expenditure : gasto deducible>
allowance [ə'laʊən*t*s] *n* **1** : complemento *m* (para gastos, etc.), mesada *f* (para niños) **2 to make allowance(s)** : tener en cuenta, disculpar
alloy ['æ͵lɔɪ] *n* : aleación *f*
all right[1] *adv* **1** YES : sí, por supuesto **2** WELL : bien <I did all right : me fue bien> **3** DEFINITELY : bien, ciertamente, sin duda <he's sick all right : está bien enfermo>
all right[2] *adj* **1** OK : bien <are you all right? : ¿estás bien?> **2** SATISFACTORY : bien, bueno <your work is all right : tu trabajo es bueno>
all–round [ˌɔl'raʊnd] → **all–around**
allspice ['ɔlspaɪs] *n* : pimienta *f* de Jamaica
allude [ə'lu:d] *vi* **-luded; -luding** : aludir, referirse
allure[1] [ə'lʊr] *vt* **-lured; -luring** : cautivar, atraer
allure[2] *n* : atractivo *m,* encanto *m*
allusion [ə'lu:ʒən] *n* : alusión *f*
ally[1] [ə'laɪ, 'æ͵laɪ] *vi* **-lied; -lying** : aliarse
ally[2] ['æ͵laɪ, ə'laɪ] *n* : aliado *m,* -da *f*
almanac ['ɔlmə͵næk, 'æl-] *n* : almanaque *m*
almighty [ɔl'maɪti] *adj* : omnipotente, todopoderoso
almond ['ɑmənd, 'ɑl-, 'æ-, 'æl-] *n* : almendra *f*
almost ['ɔl͵mo:st, ɔl'mo:st] *adv* : casi, prácticamente
alms ['ɑmz, 'ɑlmz, 'ælmz] *ns & pl* : limosna *f,* caridad *f*
aloft [ə'lɔft] *adv* : en alto, en el aire
alone[1] [ə'lo:n] *adv* : sólo, solamente, únicamente
alone[2] *adj* : solo <they're alone in the house : están solos en la casa>
along[1] [ə'lɔŋ] *adv* **1** FORWARD : adelante <farther along : más adelante> <move along! : ¡circulen, por favor!> **2 to bring along** : traer **3 ~ with** : con, junto con **4 all along** : desde el principio
along[2] *prep* **1** : por, a lo largo de <along the coast : a lo largo de la costa> **2** : en, en el curso de, por <along the way : en el curso del viaje>
alongside[1] [ə͵lɔŋ'saɪd] *adv* : al costado, al lado
alongside[2] *or* **alongside of** *prep* : junto a, al lado de
aloof [ə'lu:f] *adj* : distante, reservado
aloofness [ə'lu:fnəs] *n* : reserva *f,* actitud *f* distante
aloud [ə'laʊd] *adv* : en voz alta
alpaca [æl'pækə] *n* : alpaca *f*
alphabet ['ælfə͵bɛt] *n* : alfabeto *m*
alphabetical [ˌælfə'bɛtɪkəl] *or* **alphabetic** [-'bɛtɪk] *adj* : alfabético — **alphabetically** [-tɪkli] *adv*
alphabetize ['ælfəbə͵taɪz] *vt* **-ized; -izing** : alfabetizar, poner en orden alfabético
already [ɔl'rɛdi] *adv* : ya
also ['ɔl͵so:] *adv* : también, además
altar ['ɔltər] *n* : altar *m*
alter ['ɔltər] *vt* : alterar, cambiar, modificar
alteration [ˌɔltə'reɪʃən] *n* : alteración *f,* cambio *m,* modificación *f*
altercation [ˌɔltər'keɪʃən] *n* : altercado *m,* disputa *f*
alternate[1] ['ɔltər͵neɪt] *v* **-nated; -nating** : alternar
alternate[2] ['ɔltərnət] *adj* **1** : alterno <alternate cycles of inflation and depression : ciclos alternos de inflación y depresión> **2** : uno sí y uno no <he cooks on alternate days : cocina un día sí y otro no>
alternate[3] ['ɔltərnət] *n* : suplente *mf;* sustituto *m,* -ta *f*
alternately ['ɔltərnətli] *adv* : alternativamente, por turno
alternating current ['ɔltər͵neɪtɪŋ] *n* : corriente *f* alterna
alternation [ˌɔltər'neɪʃən] *n* : alternancia *f,* rotación *f*
alternative[1] [ɔl'tərnətɪv] *adj* : alternativo

alternative[2] *n* : alternativa *f*
alternator ['ɔltər,neɪt̬ər] *n* : alternador *m*
although [ɔl'ðoː] *conj* : aunque, a pesar de que
altitude ['æltə,tuːd, -,tjuːd] *n* : altitud *f,* altura *f*
alto ['æl,toː] *n, pl* **-tos** : alto *mf,* contralto *mf*
altogether [,ɔltə'gɛðər] *adv* **1** COMPLETELY : completamente, totalmente, del todo **2** ON THE WHOLE : en suma, en general
altruism ['æltrʊ,ɪzəm] *n* : altruismo *m*
altruistic [,æltrʊ'ɪstɪk] *adj* : altruista — **altruistically** [-tɪkli] *adv*
alum ['æləm] *n* : alumbre *m*
aluminum [ə'luːmənəm] *n* : aluminio *m*
alumna [ə'lʌmnə] *n, pl* **-nae** [-,niː] : ex-alumna *f*
alumnus [ə'lʌmnəs] *n, pl* **-ni** [-,naɪ] : ex-alumno *m*
always ['ɔlwiz, -,weɪz] *adv* **1** INVARIABLY : siempre, invariablemente **2** FOREVER : para siempre
am → **be**
amalgam [ə'mælgəm] *n* : amalgama *f*
amalgamate [ə'mælgə,meɪt] *vt* **-ated; -ating** : amalgamar, unir, fusionar
amalgamation [ə,mælgə'meɪʃən] *n* : fusión *f,* unión *f*
amaryllis [,æmə'rɪləs] *n* : amarilis *f*
amass [ə'mæs] *vt* : amasar, acumular
amateur ['æmətʃər, -tər, -,tʊr, -,tjʊr] *n* **1** : amateur *mf* **2** BEGINNER : principiante *mf;* aficionado *m,* -da *f*
amateurish ['æmə,tʃərɪʃ, -,tər-, -,tʊr-, -,tjʊr-] *adj* : amateur, inexperto
amaze [ə'meɪz] *vt* **amazed; amazing** : asombrar, maravillar, pasmar
amazement [ə'meɪzmənt] *n* : asombro *m,* sorpresa *f*
amazing [ə'meɪzɪŋ] *adj* : asombroso, sorprendente — **amazingly** [-zɪŋli] *adv*
ambassador [æm'bæsədər] *n* : embajador *m,* -dora *f*
amber ['æmbər] *n* : ámbar *m*
ambergris ['æmbər,grɪs, -,griːs] *n* : ámbar *m* gris
ambidextrous [,æmbɪ'dɛkstrəs] *adj* : ambidextro — **ambidextrously** *adv*
ambience *or* **ambiance** ['æmbiənts, 'ɑmbi,ɑnts] *n* : ambiente *m,* atmósfera *f*
ambiguity [,æmbə'gjuːət̬i] *n, pl* **-ties** : ambigüedad *f*
ambiguous [æm'bɪgjʊəs] *adj* : ambiguo
ambition [æm'bɪʃən] *n* : ambición *f*
ambitious [æm'bɪʃəs] *adj* : ambicioso — **ambitiously** *adv*
ambivalence [æm'bɪvələnts] *n* : ambivalencia *f*
ambivalent [æm'bɪvələnt] *adj* : ambivalente
amble[1] ['æmbəl] *vi* **-bled; -bling** : ir tranquilamente, pasearse despreocupadamente
amble[2] *n* : paseo *m* tranquilo
ambulance ['æmbjələnts] *n* : ambulancia *f*
ambush[1] ['æm,bʊʃ] *vt* : emboscar
ambush[2] *n* : emboscada *f,* celada *f*
ameliorate [ə'miːljə,reɪt] *v* **-rated; -rating** IMPROVE : mejorar
amelioration [ə,miːljə'reɪʃən] *n* : mejora *f*
amen ['eɪ'mɛn, 'ɑ-] *interj* : amén
amenable [ə'miːnəbəl, -'mɛ-] *adj* RESPONSIVE : susceptible, receptivo, sensible
amend [ə'mɛnd] *vt* **1** IMPROVE : mejorar, enmendar **2** CORRECT : enmendar, corregir
amendment [ə'mɛndmənt] *n* : enmienda *f*
amends [ə'mɛndz] *ns & pl* : compensación *f,* reparación *f,* desagravio *m*
amenity [ə'mɛnət̬i, -'miː-] *n, pl* **-ties** **1** PLEASANTNESS : lo agradable, amenidad *f* **2** **amenities** *npl* : servicios *mpl,* comodidades *fpl*
American [ə'mɛrɪkən] *n* : americano *m,* -na *f* — **American** *adj*
American Indian *n* : indio *m* (americano), india *f* (americana)
amethyst ['æməθəst] *n* : amatista *f*
amiability [,eɪmiːə'bɪlət̬i] *n* : amabilidad *f,* afabilidad *f*
amiable ['eɪmiːəbəl] *adj* : amable, afable — **amiably** [-bli] *adv*
amicable ['æmɪkəbəl] *adj* : amigable, amistoso, cordial — **amicably** [-bli] *adv*
amid [ə'mɪd] *or* **amidst** [ə'mɪdst] *prep* : en medio de, entre
amino acid [ə'miːno] *n* : aminoácido *m*
amiss[1] [ə'mɪs] *adv* : mal, fuera de lugar <to take amiss : tomar a mal, llevar a mal>
amiss[2] *adj* **1** WRONG : malo, inoportuno **2** **there's something amiss** : pasa algo, algo anda mal
ammeter ['æ,miːt̬ər] *n* : amperímetro *m*
ammonia [ə'moːnjə] *n* : amoníaco *m*
ammunition [,æmjə'nɪʃən] *n* **1** : municiones *fpl* **2** ARGUMENTS : argumentos *mpl*
amnesia [æm'niːʒə] *n* : amnesia *f*
amnesty ['æmnəsti] *n, pl* **-ties** : amnistía *f*
amoeba [ə'miːbə] *n, pl* **-bas** *or* **-bae** [-,biː] : ameba *f*
amoebic [ə'miːbɪk] *adj* : amébico
amok [ə'mʌk, -'mɑk] *adv* **to run amok** : correr a ciegas, enloquecerse, desbocarse (dícese de la economía, etc.)
among [ə'mʌŋ] *prep* : entre
amorous ['æmərəs] *adj* **1** PASSIONATE : enamoradizo, apasionado **2** ENAM-

ORED : enamorado **3** LOVING : amoroso, cariñoso
amorously ['æmərəsli] *adv* : con cariño
amorphous [ə'mɔrfəs] *adj* : amorfo, informe
amortize ['æmər,taɪz, ə'mɔr-] *vt* **-tized; -tizing** : amortizar
amount[1] [ə'maʊnt] *vi* **to amount to 1** : equivaler a, significar <that amounts to treason : eso equivale a la traición> **2** : ascender (a) <my debts amount to $2000 : mis deudas ascienden a $2000>
amount[2] *n* : cantidad *f,* suma *f*
ampere ['æm,pɪr] *n* : amperio *m*
ampersand ['æmpər,sænd] *n* : el signo *&*
amphibian [æm'fɪbiən] *n* : anfibio *m*
amphibious [æm'fɪbiəs] *adj* : anfibio
amphitheater ['æmfə,θiːəṱər] *n* : anfiteatro *m*
ample ['æmpəl] *adj* **-pler; -plest 1** LARGE, SPACIOUS : amplio, extenso, grande **2** ABUNDANT : abundante, generoso
amplifier ['æmplə,faɪər] *n* : amplificador *m*
amplify ['æmplə,faɪ] *vt* **-fied; -fying** : amplificar
amply ['æmpli] *adv* : ampliamente, abundantemente, suficientemente
amputate ['æmpjə,teɪt] *vt* **-tated; -tating** : amputar
amputation [,æmpjə'teɪʃən] *n* : amputación *f*
amuck [ə'mʌk] → **amok**
amulet ['æmjələt] *n* : amuleto *m,* talismán *m*
amuse [ə'mjuːz] *vt* **amused; amusing 1** ENTERTAIN : entretener, distraer **2** : hacer reír, divertir <the joke amused us : la broma nos hizo reír>
amusement [ə'mjuːzmənt] *n* **1** ENTERTAINMENT : diversión *f,* entretenimiento *m,* pasatiempo *m* **2** LAUGHTER : risa *f*
an → **a**[2]
anachronism [ə'nækrə,nɪzəm] *n* : anacronismo *m*
anachronistic [ə,nækrə'nɪstɪk] *adj* : anacrónico
anaconda [,ænə'kɑndə] *n* : anaconda *f*
anagram ['ænə,græm] *n* : anagrama *m*
anal ['eɪnəl] *adj* : anal
analgesic [,ænəl'dʒiːzɪk, -sɪk] *n* : analgésico *m*
analogical [,ænə'lɑdʒɪkəl] *adj* : analógico — **analogically** [-kli] *adv*
analogous [ə'næləgəs] *adj* : análogo
analogy [ə'nælədʒi] *n, pl* **-gies** : analogía *f*
analysis [ə'næləsəs] *n, pl* **-yses** [-,siːz] **1** : análisis *m* **2** PSYCHOANALYSIS : psicoanálisis *m*
analyst ['ænəlɪst] *n* **1** : analista *mf* **2** PSYCHOANALYST : psicoanalista *mf*
analytic [,ænə'lɪtɪk] *or* **analytical** [-tɪkəl] *adj* : analítico — **analytically** [-ṱikli] *adv*
analyze ['ænə,laɪz] *vt* **-lyzed; -lyzing** : analizar
anarchic [æ'nɑrkɪk] *adj* : anárquico — **anarchically** [-kɪkli] *adv*
anarchism ['ænər,kɪzəm, -nɑr-] *n* : anarquismo *m*
anarchist ['ænərkɪst, -nɑr-] *n* : anarquista *mf*
anarchy ['ænərki, -nɑr-] *n* : anarquía *f*
anathema [ə'næθəmə] *n* : anatema *m*
anatomic [,ænə'tɑmɪk] *or* **anatomical** [-mɪkəl] *adj* : anatómico — **anatomically** [-mɪkli] *adv*
anatomy [ə'næṱəmi] *n, pl* **-mies** : anatomía *f*
ancestor ['æn,sɛstər] *n* : antepasado *m,* -da *f;* antecesor *m,* -sora *f*
ancestral [æn'sɛstrəl] *adj* : ancestral, de los antepasados
ancestry ['æn,sɛstri] *n* **1** DESCENT : ascendencia *f,* linaje *m,* abolengo *m* **2** ANCESTORS : antepasados *mpl,* -das *fpl*
anchor[1] ['æŋkər] *vt* **1** MOOR : anclar, fondear **2** FASTEN : sujetar, asegurar, fijar
anchor[2] *n* **1** : ancla *f* **2** : presentador *m,* -dora *f* (en televisión)
anchorage ['æŋkərɪdʒ] *n* : anclaje *m*
anchovy ['æn,tʃoːvi, æn'tʃoː-] *n, pl* **-vies** *or* **-vy** : anchoa *f*
ancient ['eɪntʃənt] *adj* **1** : antiguo <ancient history : historia antigua> **2** OLD : viejo
ancients ['eɪntʃənts] *npl* : los antiguos *mpl*
and ['ænd] *conj* **1** : y (e *before words beginning with i- or hi-*) **2** : con <ham and eggs : huevos con jamón> **3** : a <go and see : ve a ver> **4** : de <try and finish it soon : trata de terminarlo pronto>
andiron ['æn,daɪərn] *n* : morillo *m*
Andorran [æn'dɔrən] *n* : andorrano *m,* -na *f* — **Andorran** *adj*
androgynous [æn'drɑdʒənəs] *adj* : andrógino
anecdotal [,ænɪk'doːṱəl] *adj* : anecdótico
anecdote ['ænɪk,doːt] *n* : anécdota *f*
anemia [ə'niːmiə] *n* : anemia *f*
anemic [ə'niːmɪk] *adj* : anémico
anemone [ə'nɛməni] *n* : anémona *f*
anesthesia [,ænəs'θiːʒə] *n* : anestesia *f*
anesthetic[1] [,ænəs'θɛṱɪk] *adj* : anestésico
anesthetic[2] *n* : anestésico *m*
anesthetist [ə'nɛsθətɪst] *n* : anestesista *mf*
anesthetize [ə'nɛsθə,taɪz] *vt* **-tize; -tized** : anestesiar
anew [ə'nuː, -'njuː] *adv* : de nuevo, otra vez, nuevamente
angel ['eɪndʒəl] *n* : ángel *m*

angelic [æn'dʒɛlɪk] *or* **angelical** [-lɪkəl] *adj* : angélico — **angelically** [-lɪkli] *adv*

anger[1] ['æŋgər] *vt* : enojar, enfadar

anger[2] *n* : enojo *m,* enfado *m,* ira *f,* cólera *f,* rabia *f*

angina [æn'dʒaɪnə] *n* : angina *f*

angle[1] ['æŋgəl] *v* **angled; angling** *vt* DIRECT, SLANT : orientar, dirigir — *vi* FISH : pescar (con caña)

angle[2] *n* **1** : ángulo *m* **2** POINT OF VIEW : perspectiva *f,* punto *m* de vista

angler ['æŋglər] *n* : pescador *m,* -dora *f*

Anglo–Saxon[1] [ˌæŋglo'sæksən] *adj* : anglosajón

Anglo–Saxon[2] *n* : anglosajón *m,* -jona *f*

Angolan [æŋ'go:lən, æn-] *n* : angoleño *m,* -ña *f* — **Angolan** *adj*

angora [æŋ'gorə, æn-] *n* : angora *f*

angrily ['æŋgrəli] *adv* : furiosamente, con ira

angry ['æŋgri] *adj* **-grier; -est** : enojado, enfadado, furioso

anguish ['æŋgwɪʃ] *n* : angustia *f,* congoja *f*

anguished ['æŋgwɪʃt] *adj* : angustiado, acongojado

angular ['æŋgjələr] *adj* : angular (dícese de las formas), anguloso (dícese de las caras)

animal ['ænəməl] *n* **1** : animal *m* **2** BRUTE : bruto *m,* -ta *f*

animate[1] ['ænəˌmeɪt] *vt* **-mated; -mating** : animar

animate[2] ['ænəmət] *adj* : animado

animated ['ænəˌmeɪt̬əd] *adj* **1** LIVELY : animado, vivo, vivaz **2 animated cartoon** : dibujos *mpl* animados

animation [ˌænə'meɪʃən] *n* : animación *f*

animosity [ˌænə'mɑsət̬i] *n, pl* **-ties** : animosidad *f,* animadversión *f*

anise ['ænəs] *n* : anís *m*

aniseed ['ænəsˌsi:d] *n* : anís *m,* semilla *f* de anís

ankle ['æŋkəl] *n* : tobillo *m*

anklebone ['æŋkəlˌbo:n] *n* : taba *f*

annals ['ænəlz] *npl* : anales *mpl,* crónica *f*

anneal [ə'ni:l] *vt* **1** TEMPER : templar **2** STRENGTHEN : fortalecer

annex[1] [ə'nɛks, 'æˌnɛks] *vt* : anexar

annex[2] ['æˌnɛks, -nɪks] *n* : anexo *m,* anejo *m*

annexation [ˌæˌnɛk'seɪʃən] *n* : anexión *f*

annihilate [ə'naɪəˌleɪt] *vt* **-lated; -lating** : aniquilar

annihilation [əˌnaɪə'leɪʃən] *n* : aniquilación *f,* aniquilamiento *m*

anniversary [ˌænə'vərsəri] *n, pl* **-ries** : aniversario *m*

annotate ['ænəˌteɪt] *vt* **-tated; -tating** : anotar

annotation [ˌænə'teɪʃən] *n* : anotación *f*

announce [ə'naʊnts] *vt* **-nounced; -nouncing** : anunciar

announcement [ə'naʊntsmənt] *n* : anuncio *m*

announcer [ə'naʊntsər] *n* : anunciador *m,* -dora *f;* comentarista *mf;* locutor *m,* -tora *f*

annoy [ə'nɔɪ] *vt* : molestar, fastidiar, irritar

annoyance [ə'nɔɪənts] *n* **1** IRRITATION : irritación *f,* fastidio *m* **2** NUISANCE : molestia *f,* fastidio *m*

annoying [ə'nɔɪɪŋ] *adj* : molesto, fastidioso, engorroso — **annoyingly** [-ɪŋli] *adv*

annual[1] ['ænjʊəl] *adj* : anual — **annually** *adv*

annual[2] *n* **1** : planta *f* anual **2** YEARBOOK : anuario *m*

annuity [ə'nu:ət̬i] *n, pl* **-ties** : anualidad *f*

annul [ə'nʌl] *vt* **anulled; anulling** : anular, invalidar

annulment [ə'nʌlmənt] *n* : anulación *f*

anode ['æˌno:d] *n* : ánodo

anoint [ə'nɔɪnt] *vt* : ungir

anomalous [ə'nɑmələs] *adj* : anómalo

anomaly [ə'nɑməli] *n, pl* **-lies** : anomalía *f*

anonymity [ˌænə'nɪmət̬i] *n* : anonimato *m*

anonymous [ə'nɑnəməs] *adj* : anónimo — **anonymously** *adv*

another[1] [ə'nʌðər] *adj* : otro

another[2] *pron* : otro, otra

answer[1] ['æntsər] *vt* **1** : contestar (a), responder (a) <to answer the telephone : contestar el teléfono> **2** FULFILL : satisfacer **3 to answer for** : ser responsable de, pagar por <she'll answer for that mistake : pagará por ese error> — *vi* : contestar, responder

answer[2] *n* **1** REPLY : respuesta *f,* contestación *f* **2** SOLUTION : solución *f*

answerable ['æntsərəbəl] *adj* : responsable

ant ['ænt] *n* : hormiga *f*

antagonism [æn'tægəˌnɪzəm] *n* : antagonismo *m,* hostilidad *f*

antagonist [æn'tægənɪst] *n* : antagonista *mf*

antagonistic [ænˌtægə'nɪstɪk] *adj* : antagonista, hostil

antagonize [æn'tægəˌnaɪz] *vt* **-nized; -nizing** : antagonizar

antarctic [ænt'ɑrktɪk, -'ɑrt̬ɪk] *adj* : antártico

antarctic circle *n* : círculo *m* antártico

antebellum [ˌæntɪ'bɛləm] *adj* : prebélico

antecedent[1] [ˌæntə'si:dənt] *adj* : antecedente, precedente

antecedent[2] *n* : antecedente *mf;* precursor *m,* -sora *f*

antelope ['æntəlˌo:p] *n, pl* **-lope** *or* **-lopes** : antílope *m*

antenna [æn'tɛnə] *n, pl* **-nae** [-ˌni:, -ˌnaɪ] *or* **-nas** : antena *f*

anterior [æn'tɪriər] *adj* : anterior

anthem ['ænθəm] *n* : himno *m* <national anthem : himno nacional>

anther ['ænθər] *n* : antera *f*
anthill ['ænt,hɪl] *n* : hormiguero *m*
anthology [æn'θɑləʤi] *n, pl* **-gies** : antología *f*
anthracite ['ænθrə,saɪt] *n* : antracita *f*
anthropoid[1] ['ænθrə,pɔɪd] *adj* : antropoide
anthropoid[2] *n* : antropoide *mf*
anthropological [,ænθrəpə'lɑʤɪkəl] *adj* : antropológico
anthropologist [,ænθrə'pɑləʤɪst] *n* : antropólogo *m*, -ga *f*
anthropology [,ænθrə'pɑləʤi] *n* : antropología *f*
antiabortion [,æntiə'bɔrʃən, ,æntaɪ-] *adj* : antiaborto
antiaircraft [,ænti'ær,kræft, ,æntaɪ-] *adj* : antiaéreo
anti–American [,æntiə'mɛrɪkən, ,æntaɪ-] *adj* : antiamericano
antibiotic[1] [,æntibaɪ'ɑṭɪk, ,æntaɪ-, -bi-] *adj* : antibiótico
antibiotic[2] *n* : antibiótico *m*
antibody ['ænti,bɑdi] *n, pl* **-bodies** : anticuerpo *m*
antic[1] ['æntɪk] *adj* : extravagante, juguetón
antic[2] *n* : payasada *f*, travesura *f*
anticipate [æn'tɪsə,peɪt] *vt* **-pated; -pating 1** FORESEE : anticipar, prever **2** EXPECT : esperar, contar con
anticipation [æn,tɪsə'peɪʃən] *n* **1** FORESIGHT : previsión *f* **2** EXPECTATION : anticipación *f*, expectación *f*, esperanza *f*
anticipatory [æn'tɪsəpə,tori] *adj* : en anticipación, en previsión
anticlimactic [,æntiklaɪ'mæktɪk] *adj* : anticlimático, decepcionante
anticlimax [,ænti'klaɪ,mæks] *n* : anticlímax *m*
anticommunism [,ænti'kɑmjə,nɪzəm, ,æntaɪ-] *n* : anticomunismo *m*
anticommunist[1] [,ænti'kɑmjənɪst, ,æntaɪ-] *adj* : anticomunista
anticommunist[2] *n* : anticomunista *mf*
antidemocratic [,ænti,dɛmə'kræṭɪk, ,æntaɪ-] *adj* : antidemocrático
antidote ['æntɪ,do:t] *n* : antídoto *m*
antidrug [,ænti'drʌg, ,æntaɪ-; 'ænti-,drʌg, 'æntaɪ-] *adj* : antidrogas
antifascist [,ænti'fæʃɪst, ,æntaɪ-] *adj* : antifascista
antifeminist [,ænti'fɛmənɪst, ,æntaɪ-] *adj* : antifeminista
antifreeze ['ænti,fri:z] *n* : anticongelante *m*
anti–imperialism [,æntiɪm'pɪriə,lɪzəm, ,æntaɪ-] *n* : antiimperialismo *m*
anti–imperialist [,æntiɪm'pɪriəlɪst, ,æntaɪ-] *adj* : antiimperialista
anti–inflationary [,æntiɪn'fleɪʃə,nɛri, ,æntaɪ-] *adj* : antiinflacionario
antimony ['æntə,mo:ni] *n* : antimonio *m*
antipathy [æn'tɪpəθi] *n, pl* **-thies** : antipatía *f*, aversión *f*
antiperspirant [,ænti'pərspərənt, ,æntaɪ-] *n* : antitranspirante *m*
antiquarian[1] [,æntə'kwɛriən] *adj* : antiguo, anticuario <an antiquarian book : un libro antiguo>
antiquarian[2] *n* : anticuario *m*, -ria *f*
antiquary ['æntə,kwɛri] → **antiquarian[2]**
antiquated ['æntə,kweɪṭəd] *adj* : anticuado, pasado de moda
antique[1] [æn'ti:k] *adj* **1** OLD : antiguo, de época <an antique mirror : un espejo antiguo> **2** OLD-FASHIONED : anticuado, pasado de moda
antique[2] *n* : antigüedad *f*
antiquity [æn'tɪkwəṭi] *n, pl* **-ties** : antigüedad
antirevolutionary [,ænti,rɛvə'lu:ʃə,nɛri, ,æntaɪ-] *adj* : antirrevolucionario
anti–Semitic [,æntisə'mɪṭɪk, ,æntaɪ-] *adj* : antisemita
anti–Semitism [,ænti'sɛmə,tɪzəm, ,æntaɪ-] *n* : antisemitismo *m*
antiseptic[1] [,æntə'sɛptɪk] *adj* : antiséptico — **antiseptically** [-tɪkli] *adv*
antiseptic[2] *n* : antiséptico *m*
antismoking [,ænti'smo:kɪŋ, ,æntaɪ-] *adj* : antitabaco
antisocial [,ænti'so:ʃəl, ,æntaɪ-] *adj* **1** : antisocial **2** UNSOCIABLE : poco sociable
antitheft [,ænti'θɛft, ,æntaɪ-] *adj* : antirrobo
antithesis [æn'tɪθəsɪs] *n, pl* **-eses** [-,si:z] : antítesis *f*
antitoxin [,ænti'tɑksən, ,æntaɪ-] *n* : antitoxina *f*
antitrust [,ænti'trʌst, ,æntaɪ-] *adj* : antimonopolista
antler ['æntlər] *n* : asta *f*, cuerno *m*
antonym ['æntə,nɪm] *n* : antónimo *m*
anus ['eɪnəs] *n* : ano *m*
anvil ['ænvəl, -vɪl] *n* : yunque *m*
anxiety [æŋ*k*'zaɪəṭi] *n, pl* **-eties 1** UNEASINESS : inquietud *f*, preocupación *f*, ansiedad *f* **2** APPREHENSION : ansiedad *f*, angustia *f*
anxious ['æŋ*k*ʃəs] *adj* **1** WORRIED : inquieto, preocupado, ansioso **2** WORRISOME : preocupante, inquietante **3** EAGER : ansioso, deseoso
anxiously ['æŋ*k*ʃəsli] *adv* : con inquietud, con ansiedad
any[1] ['ɛni] *adv* **1** : algo <is it any better? : ¿está (algo) mejor?> **2** : para nada <it is not any good : no sirve para nada>
any[2] *adj* **1** : alguno <is there any doubt? : ¿hay alguna duda?> <call me if you have any questions : llámeme si tiene alguna pregunta> **2** : cualquier <I can answer any question : puedo responder a cualquier pregunta> **3** : todo <in any case : en todo caso> **4** : ningún <he would not accept it under any circumstances : no lo aceptaría bajo ninguna circunstancia>
any[3] *pron* **1** : alguno *m*, -na *f* <are there any left? : ¿queda alguno?> **2** : nin-

guno *m,* -na *f* <I don't want any : no quiero ninguno>
anybody ['ɛni,bʌdi, -,bɑ-] → **anyone**
anyhow ['ɛni,haʊ] *adv* **1** HAPHAZARDLY : de cualquier manera **2** IN ANY CASE : de todos modos, en todo caso
anymore [,ɛni'mor] *adv* **1 :** ya, ya más <he doesn't dance anymore : ya no baila más> **2 :** todavía <do they sing anymore? : ¿cantan todavía?>
anyone ['ɛni,wʌn] *pron* **1 :** alguien <is anyone here? : ¿hay alguien aquí?> <if anyone wants to come : si alguno quiere venir> **2 :** cualquiera <anyone can play : cualquiera puede jugar> **3 :** nadie <I don't want anyone here : no quiero a nadie aquí>
anyplace ['ɛni,pleɪs] → **anywhere**
anything ['ɛni,θɪŋ] *pron* **1 :** algo, alguna cosa <do you want anything? : ¿quieres algo?, ¿quieres alguna cosa?> **2 :** nada <hardly anything : casi nada> **3 :** cualquier cosa <I eat anything : como de todo>
anytime ['ɛni,taɪm] *adv* **:** en cualquier momento, a cualquier hora, cuando sea
anyway ['ɛni,weɪ] → **anyhow**
anywhere ['ɛni,*h*wɛr] *adv* **1 :** en algún sitio, en alguna parte <do you see it anywhere? : ¿lo ves en alguna parte?> **2 :** en ningún sitio, por ninguna parte <I can't find it anywhere : no puedo encontrarlo por ninguna parte> **3 :** en cualquier parte, dondequiera, donde sea <put it anywhere : ponlo dondequiera>
aorta [eɪ'ɔrt̬ə] *n, pl* **-tas** *or* **-tae** [-t̬i, -taɪ] **:** aorta *f*
apart [ə'pɑrt] *adv* **1** SEPARATELY : aparte, separadamente **2** ASIDE : aparte, a un lado **3 to fall apart** : deshacerse, hacerse pedazos **4 to take apart :** desmontar, desmantelar
apartheid [ə'pɑr,teɪt, -,taɪt] *n* **:** apartheid *m*
apartment [ə'pɑrtmənt] *n* **:** apartamento *m,* departamento *m,* piso *m Spain*
apathetic [,æpə'θɛt̬ɪk] *adj* **:** apático, indiferente — **apathetically** [-tɪkli] *adv*
apathy ['æpəθi] *n* **:** apatía *f,* indiferencia *f*
ape[1] ['eɪp] *vt* **aped; aping :** imitar, remedar
ape[2] *n* **:** simio *m;* mono *m,* -na *f*
aperture ['æpərtʃər, -,tʃʊr] *n* **:** abertura *f,* rendija *f,* apertura *f* (en fotografía)
apex ['eɪ,pɛks] *n, pl* **apexes** *or* **apices** ['eɪpə,si:z, 'æ-] **:** ápice *m,* cúspide *f,* cima *f*
aphid ['eɪfɪd, 'æ-] *n* **:** áfido *m*
aphorism ['æfə,rɪzəm] *n* **:** aforismo *m*
aphoristic [,æfə'rɪstɪk] *adj* **:** aforístico
aphrodisiac [,æfrə'di:zi,æk, -'dɪ-] *n* **:** afrodisíaco *m*
apiary ['eɪpi,ɛri] *n, pl* **-aries :** apiario *m,* colmenar *m*
apiece [ə'pi:s] *adv* **:** cada uno
aplenty [ə'plɛnti] *adj* **:** en abundancia
aplomb [ə'plɑm, -'plʌm] *n* **:** aplomo *m*
apocalypse [ə'pɑkə,lɪps] *n* **:** apocalipsis *m*
apocalyptic [ə,pɑkə'lɪptɪk] *adj* **:** apocalíptico
apocrypha [ə'pɑkrəfə] *n* **:** textos *mpl* apócrifos
apocryphal [ə'pɑkrəfəl] *adj* **:** apócrifo
apologetic [ə,pɑlə'dʒɛt̬ɪk] *adj* **:** lleno de disculpas
apologetically [ə,pɑlə'dʒɛt̬ɪkli] *adv* **:** disculpándose, con aire de disculpas
apologize [ə'pɑlə,dʒaɪz] *vi* **-gized; -gizing :** disculparse, pedir perdón
apology [ə'pɑlədʒi] *n, pl* **-gies :** disculpa *f,* excusa *f*
apoplectic [,æpə'plɛktɪk] *adj* **:** apopléctico
apoplexy ['æpə,plɛksi] *n* **:** apoplejía *f*
apostasy [ə'pɑstəsi] *n, pl* **-sies :** apostasía *f*
apostate [ə'pɑs,teɪt] *n* **:** apóstata *mf*
apostle [ə'pɑsəl] *n* **:** apóstol *m*
apostleship [ə'pɑsəlʃɪp] *n* **:** apostolado *m*
apostolic [,æpə'stɑlɪk] *adj* **:** apostólico
apostrophe [ə'pɑstrə,fi:] *n* **:** apóstrofo *m*
apothecary [ə'pɑθə,kɛri] *n, pl* **-caries :** boticario *m,* -ria *f*
appall [ə'pɔl] *vt* **:** consternar, horrorizar
apparatus [,æpə'ræt̬əs, -'reɪ-] *n, pl* **-tuses** *or* **-tus :** aparato *m,* equipo *m*
apparel [ə'pærəl] *n* **:** atavío *m,* ropa *f*
apparent [ə'pærənt] *adj* **1** VISIBLE **:** visible **2** OBVIOUS **:** claro, evidente, manifiesto **3** SEEMING **:** aparente, ostensible
apparently [ə'pærəntli] *adv* **:** aparentemente, al parecer
apparition [,æpə'rɪʃən] *n* **:** aparición *f,* visión *f*
appeal[1] [ə'pi:l] *vt* **1 :** apelar <to appeal a decision : apelar contra una decisión> — *vi* **1 to appeal for :** pedir, solicitar **2 to appeal to :** atraer a <that doesn't appeal to me : eso no me atrae>
appeal[2] *n* **1 :** apelación *f* (en derecho) **2** PLEA **:** ruego *m,* súplica *f* **3** ATTRACTION **:** atracción *f,* atractivo *m,* interés *m*
appear [ə'pɪr] *vi* **1 :** aparecer, aparecerse, presentarse <he suddenly appeared : apareció de repente> **2** COME OUT **:** aparecer, salir, publicarse **3 :** comparecer (ante el tribunal), actuar (en el teatro) **4** SEEM **:** parecer
appearance [ə'pɪrən*t*s] *n* **1** APPEARING **:** aparición *f,* presentación *f,* comparecencia *f* (ante un tribunal), publicación *f* (de un libro) **2** LOOK **:** apariencia *f,* aspecto *m*

appease [ə'pi:z] *vt* **-peased; -peasing** 1 CALM, PACIFY : aplacar, apaciguar, sosegar 2 SATISFY : satisfacer, mitigar

appeasement [ə'pi:zmənt] *n* : aplacamiento *m,* apaciguamiento *m*

append [ə'pɛnd] *vt* : agregar, añadir, adjuntar

appendage [ə'pɛndɪdʒ] *n* 1 ADDITION : apéndice *m,* añadidura *f* 2 LIMB : miembro *m,* extremidad *f*

appendectomy [ˌæpən'dɛktəmi] *n, pl* **-mies** : apendicectomía *f*

appendicitis [əˌpɛndə'saɪtəs] *n* : apendicitis *f*

appendix [ə'pɛndɪks] *n, pl* **-dixes** *or* **-dices** [-dəˌsi:z] : apéndice *m*

appetite ['æpəˌtaɪt] *n* 1 CRAVING : apetito *m,* deseo *m,* ganas *fpl* 2 PREFERENCE : gusto *m,* preferencia *f* <the cultural appetites of today : los gustos culturales de hoy>

appetizer ['æpəˌtaɪzər] *n* : aperitivo *m,* entremés *m,* botana *f Mex,* tapa *f Spain*

appetizing ['æpəˌtaɪzɪŋ] *adj* : apetecible, apetitoso — **appetizingly** [-zɪŋli] *adv*

applaud [ə'plɔd] *v* : aplaudir

applause [ə'plɔz] *n* : aplauso *m*

apple ['æpəl] *n* : manzana *f*

appliance [ə'plaɪənts] *n* 1 : aparato *m* 2 **household appliance** : electrodoméstico *m,* aparato *m* electrodoméstico

applicability [ˌæplɪkə'bɪləti, əˌplɪkə-] *n* : aplicabilidad *f*

applicable ['æplɪkəbəl, ə'plɪkə-] *adj* : aplicable, pertinente

applicant ['æplɪkənt] *n* : solicitante *mf,* aspirante *mf,* postulante *mf;* candidato *m,* -ta *f*

application [ˌæplə'keɪʃən] *n* 1 USE : aplicación *f,* empleo *m,* uso *m* 2 DILIGENCE : aplicación *f,* diligencia *f,* dedicación *f* 3 REQUEST : solicitud *f,* petición *f,* demanda *f*

applicator ['æpləˌkeɪtər] *n* : aplicador *m*

appliqué[1] [ˌæplə'keɪ] *vt* : decorar con apliques

appliqué[2] *n* : aplique *m*

apply [ə'plaɪ] *v* **-plied; -plying** *vt* 1 : aplicar (una sustancia, los frenos, el conocimiento) 2 **to apply oneself** : dedicarse, aplicarse — *vi* 1 : aplicarse, referirse <the rules apply to everyone : las reglas se aplican a todos> 2 **to apply for** : solicitar, pedir

appoint [ə'pɔɪnt] *vt* 1 NAME : nombrar, designar 2 FIX, SET : fijar, señalar, designar <to appoint a date : fijar una fecha> 3 EQUIP : equipar <a well-appointed office : una oficina bien equipada>

appointee [əˌpɔɪn'ti:, ˌæ-] *n* : persona *f* designada

appointment [ə'pɔɪntmənt] *n* 1 APPOINTING : nombramiento *m,* designación *f* 2 ENGAGEMENT : cita *f,* hora *f* 3 POST : puesto *m*

apportion [ə'porʃən] *vt* : distribuir, repartir

apportionment [ə'porʃənmənt] *n* : distribución *f,* repartición *f,* reparto *m*

apposite ['æpəzət] *adj* : apropiado, oportuno, pertinente — **appositely** *adv*

appraisal [ə'preɪzəl] *n* : evaluación *f,* valoración *f,* tasación *f,* apreciación *f*

appraise [ə'preɪz] *vt* **-praised; -praising** : evaluar, valorar, tasar, apreciar

appraiser [ə'preɪzər] *n* : tasador *m,* -dora *f*

appreciable [ə'pri:ʃəbəl, -'prɪʃiə-] *adj* : apreciable, sensible, considerable — **appreciably** [-bli] *adv*

appreciate [ə'pri:ʃiˌeɪt, -'prɪ-] *v* **-ated; -ating** *vt* 1 VALUE : apreciar, valorar 2 : agradecer <we appreciate his frankness : agradecemos su franqueza> 3 UNDERSTAND : darse cuenta de, entender — *vi* : apreciarse, valorizarse

appreciation [əˌpri:ʃi'eɪʃən, -ˌprɪ-] *n* 1 GRATITUDE : agradecimiento *m,* reconocimiento *m* 2 VALUING : apreciación *f,* valoración *f,* estimación *f* <art appreciation : apreciación artística> 3 UNDERSTANDING : comprensión *f,* entendimiento *m*

appreciative [ə'pri:ʃətɪv, -'prɪ-; ə'pri:ʃiˌeɪ-] *adj* 1 : apreciativo <an appreciative audience : un público apreciativo> 2 GRATEFUL : agradecido 3 ADMIRING : de admiración

apprehend [ˌæprɪ'hɛnd] *vt* 1 ARREST : aprehender, detener, arrestar 2 DREAD : temer 3 COMPREHEND : comprender, entender

apprehension [ˌæprɪ'hɛntʃən] *n* 1 ARREST : arresto *m,* detención *f,* aprehensión *f* 2 ANXIETY : aprensión *f,* ansiedad *f,* temor *m* 3 UNDERSTANDING : comprensión *f,* percepción *f*

apprehensive [ˌæprɪ'hɛntsɪv] *adj* : aprensivo, inquieto — **apprehensively** *adv*

apprentice[1] [ə'prɛntɪs] *vt* **-ticed; -ticing** : colocar de aprendiz

apprentice[2] *n* : aprendiz *m,* -diza *f*

apprenticeship [ə'prɛntɪsˌʃɪp] *n* : aprendizaje *f*

apprise [ə'praɪz] *vt* **-prised; -prising** : informar, avisar

approach[1] [ə'pro:tʃ] *vt* 1 NEAR : acercarse a 2 APPROXIMATE : aproximarse a 3 : abordar, dirigirse a <I approached my boss with the proposal : me dirigí a mi jefe con la propuesta> 4 TACKLE : abordar, enfocar, considerar — *vi* : acercarse, aproximarse

approach[2] *n* 1 NEARING : acercamiento *m,* aproximación *f* 2 POSITION : enfoque *m,* planteamiento *m* 3 OFFER : propuesta *f,* oferta *f* 4 ACCESS : acceso *m,* vía *f* de acceso

approachable [ə'pro:tʃəbəl] *adj* : accesible, asequible

approbation [ˌæprəˈbeɪʃən] *n* : aprobación *f*
appropriate[1] [əˈproːpriˌeɪt] *vt* **-ated; -ating 1** SEIZE : apropiarse de **2** ALLOCATE : destinar, asignar
appropriate[2] [əˈproːpriət] *adj* : apropiado, adecuado, idóneo — **appropriately** *adv*
appropriateness [əˈproːpriətnəs] *n* : idoneidad *f,* propiedad *f*
appropriation [əˌproːpriˈeɪʃən] *n* **1** SEIZURE : apropiación *f* **2** ALLOCATION : asignación *f*
approval [əˈpruːvəl] *n* **1** : aprobación *f,* visto *m* bueno **2 on approval** : a prueba
approve [əˈpruːv] *vt* **-proved; -proving 1** : aprobar, sancionar, darle el visto bueno a **2 to approve of** : consentir en, aprobar <he doesn't approve of smoking : está en contra del tabaco>
approximate[1] [əˈprɑksəˌmeɪt] *vt* **-mated; -mating** : aproximarse a, acercarse a
approximate[2] [əˈprɑksəmət] *adj* : aproximado
approximately [əˈprɑksəmətli] *adv* : aproximadamente, más o menos
approximation [əˌprɑksəˈmeɪʃən] *n* : aproximación *f*
appurtenance [əˈpərtənənts] *n* : accesorio *m*
apricot [ˈæprəˌkɑt, ˈeɪ-] *n* : albaricoque *m,* chabacano *m Mex*
April [ˈeɪprəl] *n* : abril *m*
apron [ˈeɪprən] *n* : delantal *m,* mandil *m*
apropos[1] [ˌæprəˈpoː, ˈæprəˌpoː] *adv* : a propósito
apropos[2] *adj* : pertinente, oportuno, acertado
apropos of *prep* : a propósito de
apt [ˈæpt] *adj* **1** FITTING : apto, apropiado, acertado, oportuno **2** LIABLE : propenso, inclinado **3** CLEVER, QUICK : listo, despierto
aptitude [ˈæptəˌtuːd, -ˌtjuːd] *n* **1** : aptitud *f,* capacidad *f* <aptitude test : prueba de aptitud> **2** TALENT : talento *m,* facilidad *f*
aptly [ˈæptli] *adv* : acertadamente
aqua [ˈækwə, ˈɑ-] *n* : color *m* aguamarina
aquarium [əˈkwæriəm] *n, pl* **-iums** *or* **-ia** [-iə] : acuario *m*
Aquarius [əˈkwæriəs] *n* : Acuario *mf*
aquatic [əˈkwɑt̬ɪk, -ˈkwæ-] *adj* : acuático
aqueduct [ˈækwəˌdʌkt] *n* : acueducto *m*
aquiline [ˈækwəˌlaɪn, -lən] *adj* : aguileño
Arab[1] [ˈærəb] *adj* : árabe
Arab[2] *n* : árabe *mf*
arabesque [ˌærəˈbɛsk] *n* : arabesco *m*
Arabian[1] [əˈreɪbiən] *adj* : árabe
Arabian[2] *n* → **Arab[2]**
Arabic[1] [ˈærəbɪk] *adj* : árabe
Arabic[2] *n* : árabe *m* (idioma)
arable [ˈærəbəl] *adj* : arable, cultivable
arbiter [ˈɑrbət̬ər] *n* : árbitro *m,* -tra *f*
arbitrary [ˈɑrbəˌtrɛri] *adj* : arbitrario — **arbitrarily** [ˌɑrbəˈtrɛrəli] *adv*
arbitrate [ˈɑrbəˌtreɪt] *v* **-trated; -trating** : arbitrar
arbitration [ˌɑrbəˈtreɪʃən] *n* : arbitraje *m*
arbitrator [ˈɑrbəˌtreɪt̬ər] *n* : árbitro *m,* -tra *f*
arbor [ˈɑrbər] *n* : cenador *m,* pérgola *f*
arboreal [ɑrˈboriəl] *adj* : arbóreo
arc[1] [ˈɑrk] *vi* **arced; arcing** : formar un arco
arc[2] *n* : arco *m*
arcade [ɑrˈkeɪd] *n* **1** ARCHES : arcada *f* **2** MALL : galería *f* comercial
arcane [ɑrˈkeɪn] *adj* : arcano, secreto, misterioso
arch[1] [ˈɑrtʃ] *vt* : arquear, enarcar — *vi* : formar un arco, arquearse
arch[2] *adj* **1** CHIEF : principal **2** MISCHIEVOUS : malicioso, pícaro
arch[3] *n* : arco *m*
archaeological [ˌɑrkiəˈlɑdʒɪkəl] *adj* : arqueológico
archaeologist [ˌɑrkiˈɑlədʒɪst] *n* : arqueólogo *m,* -ga *f*
archaeology *or* **archeology** [ˌɑrkiˈɑlədʒi] *n* : arqueología *f*
archaic [ɑrˈkeɪɪk] *adj* : arcaico — **archaically** [-ɪkli] *adv*
archangel [ˈɑrkˌeɪndʒəl] *n* : arcángel *m*
archbishop [ɑrtʃˈbɪʃəp] *n* : arzobispo *m*
archdiocese [ɑrtʃˈdaɪəsəs, -ˌsiːz, -ˌsiːs] *n* : archidiócesis *f*
archer [ˈɑrtʃər] *n* : arquero *m,* -ra *f*
archery [ˈɑrtʃəri] *n* : tiro *m* al arco
archetype [ˈɑrkɪˌtaɪp] *n* : arquetipo *m*
archipelago [ˌɑrkəˈpɛləˌgoː, ˌɑrtʃə-] *n, pl* **-goes** *or* **-gos** [-goːz] : archipiélago *m*
architect [ˈɑrkəˌtɛkt] *n* : arquitecto *m,* -ta *f*
architectural [ˌɑrkəˈtɛktʃərəl] *adj* : arquitectónico — **architecturally** *adv*
architecture [ˈɑrkəˌtɛktʃər] *n* : arquitectura *f*
archives [ˈɑrˌkaɪvz] *npl* : archivo *m*
archivist [ˈɑrkəvɪst, -ˌkaɪ-] *n* : archivero *m,* -ra *f;* archivista *mf*
archway [ˈɑrtʃˌweɪ] *n* : arco *m,* pasadizo *m* abovedado
arctic [ˈɑrktɪk, ˈɑrt̬-] *adj* **1** : ártico <arctic regions : zonas árticas> **2** FRIGID : glacial
arctic circle *n* : círculo *m* ártico
ardent [ˈɑrdənt] *adj* **1** PASSIONATE : ardiente, fogoso, apasionado **2** FERVENT : ferviente, fervoroso — **ardently** *adv*
ardor [ˈɑrdər] *n* : ardor *m,* pasión *f,* fervor *m*
arduous [ˈɑrdʒʊəs] *adj* : arduo, duro, riguroso — **arduously** *adv*

arduousness [ˈɑrdʒʊəsnəs] *n* **:** dureza *f,* rigor *m*

are → **be**

area [ˈæriə] *n* **1** SURFACE **:** área *f,* superficie *f* **2** REGION **:** área *f,* región *f,* zona *f* **3** FIELD **:** área *f,* terreno *m,* campo *m* (de conocimiento)

area code *n* **:** código *m* de la zona, prefijo *m Spain*

arena [əˈriːnə] *n* **1 :** arena *f,* estadio *m* <sports arena : estadio deportivo> **2 :** arena *f,* ruedo *m* <the political arena : el ruedo político>

Argentine [ˈɑrdʒənˌtaɪn, -ˌtiːn] *or* **Argentinean** *or* **Argentinian** [ˌɑrdʒənˈtɪniən] *n* **:** argentino *m,* -na *f* — **Argentine** *or* **Argentinean** *or* **Argentinian** *adj*

argon [ˈɑrˌgɑn] *n* **:** argón *m*

argot [ˈɑrgət, -ˌgoː] *n* **:** argot *m*

arguable [ˈɑrgjʊəbəl] *adj* **:** discutible

argue [ˈɑrˌgjuː] *v* **-gued; -guing** *vi* **1** REASON **:** argüir, argumentar, razonar **2** DISPUTE **:** discutir, pelear(se), alegar — *vt* **1** SUGGEST **:** sugerir **2** MAINTAIN **:** alegar, argüir, sostener **3** DISCUSS **:** discutir, debatir

argument [ˈɑrgjəmənt] *n* **1** REASONING **:** argumento *m,* razonamiento *m* **2** DISCUSSION **:** discusión *f,* debate *m* **3** QUARREL **:** pelea *f,* riña *f,* disputa *f*

argumentative [ˌɑrgjəˈmɛntət̬ɪv] *adj* **:** discutidor

argyle [ˈɑrˌgaɪl] *n* **:** diseño *m* de rombos

aria [ˈɑriə] *n* **:** aria *f*

arid [ˈærəd] *adj* **:** árido

aridity [əˈrɪdət̬i, æ-] *n* **:** aridez *f*

Aries [ˈɛriːz, -iˌiːz] *n* **:** Aries *mf*

arise [əˈraɪz] *vi* **arose** [əˈroːz]; **arisen** [əˈrɪzən]; **arising 1** ASCEND **:** ascender, subir, elevarse **2** ORIGINATE **:** originarse, surgir, presentarse **3** GET UP **:** levantarse

aristocracy [ˌærəˈstɑkrəsi] *n, pl* **-cies :** aristocracia *f*

aristocrat [əˈrɪstəˌkræt] *n* **:** aristócrata *mf*

aristocratic [əˌrɪstəˈkræt̬ɪk] *adj* **:** aristocrático, noble

arithmetic[1] [ˌærɪθˈmɛt̬ɪk] *or* **arithmetical** [-t̬ɪkəl] *adj* **:** aritmético

arithmetic[2] [əˈrɪθməˌtɪk] *n* **:** aritmética

ark [ˈɑrk] *n* **:** arca *f*

arm[1] [ˈɑrm] *vt* **:** armar — *vi* **:** armarse

arm[2] *n* **1 :** brazo *m* (del cuerpo o de un sillón), manga *f* (de una prenda) **2** BRANCH **:** rama *f,* sección *f* **3** WEAPON **:** arma *f* <to take up arms : tomar las armas> **4 coat of arms :** escudo *m* de armas

armada [ɑrˈmɑdə, -ˈmeɪ-] *n* **:** armada *f,* flota *f*

armadillo [ˌɑrməˈdɪlo] *n, pl* **-los :** armadillo *m*

armament [ˈɑrməmənt] *n* **:** armamento *m*

armed [ˈɑrmd] *adj* **1 :** armado <armed robbery : robo a mano armada> **2 armed forces :** fuerzas *fpl* armadas

Armenian [ɑrˈmiːniən] *n* **:** armenio *m,* -nia *f* — **Armenian** *adj*

armistice [ˈɑrməstɪs] *n* **:** armisticio *m*

armor [ˈɑrmər] *n* **:** armadura *f,* coraza *f*

armored [ˈɑrmərd] *adj* **:** blindado, acorazado

armory [ˈɑrməri] *n, pl* **-mories :** arsenal *m* (almacén), armería *f* (museo), fábrica *f* de armas

armpit [ˈɑrmˌpɪt] *n* **:** axila *f,* sobaco *m*

army [ˈɑrmi] *n, pl* **-mies 1 :** ejército *m* (militar) **2** MULTITUDE **:** legión *f,* multitud *f,* ejército *m*

aroma [əˈroːmə] *n* **:** aroma *f*

aromatic [ˌærəˈmæt̬ɪk] *adj* **:** aromático

around[1] [əˈraʊnd] *adv* **1 :** de circunferencia <a tree three feet around : un árbol de tres pies de circunferencia> **2 :** alrededor, a la redonda <for miles around : por millas a la redonda> <all around : por todos lados, todo alrededor> **3 :** por ahí <they're somewhere around : deben estar por ahí> **4** APPROXIMATELY **:** más o menos, aproximadamente <around 5 o'clock : a eso de las 5> **5 to turn around :** darse la vuelta, voltearse

around[2] *prep* **1** SURROUNDING **:** alrededor de, en torno a **2** THROUGH **:** por, en <he traveled around Mexico : viajó por México> <around the house : en casa> **3 :** a la vuelta de <around the corner : a la vuelta de la esquina> **4** NEAR **:** alrededor de, cerca de

arousal [əˈraʊzəl] *n* **:** excitación *f*

arouse [əˈraʊz] *vt* **aroused; arousing 1** AWAKE **:** despertar **2** EXCITE **:** despertar, suscitar, excitar

arraign [əˈreɪn] *vt* **:** hacer comparecer (ante un tribunal)

arraignment [əˈreɪnmənt] *n* **:** orden *m* de comparecencia, acusación *f*

arrange [əˈreɪndʒ] *vt* **-ranged; -ranging 1** ORDER **:** arreglar, poner en orden, disponer **2** SETTLE **:** arreglar, fijar, concertar **3** ADAPT **:** arreglar, adaptar

arrangement [əˈreɪndʒmənt] *n* **1** ORDER **:** arreglo *m,* orden *m* **2** ARRANGING **:** disposición *f* <floral arrangement : arreglo floral> **3** AGREEMENT **:** arreglo *m,* acuerdo *m,* convenio *m* **4 arrangements** *npl* **:** preparativos *mpl,* planes *mpl*

array[1] [əˈreɪ] *vt* **1** ORDER **:** poner en orden, presentar, formar **2** GARB **:** vestir, ataviar, engalanar

array[2] *n* **1** ORDER **:** orden *m,* formación *f* **2** ATTIRE **:** atavío *m,* galas *mpl* **3** RANGE, SELECTION **:** selección *f,* serie *f,* gama *f* <an array of problems : una serie de problemas>

arrears [əˈrɪrz] *npl* **:** atrasos *mpl* <to be in arrears : estar atrasado en los pagos>

arrest[1] [ə'rɛst] *vt* **1** APPREHEND **:** arrestar, detener **2** CHECK, STOP **:** detener, parar

arrest[2] *n* **1** APPREHENSION **:** arresto *m,* detención *f* <under arrest : detenido> **2** STOPPING **:** paro *m*

arrival [ə'raɪvəl] *n* **:** llegada *f,* venida *f,* arribo *m*

arrive [ə'raɪv] *vi* **-rived; -riving 1** COME **:** llegar, arribar **2** SUCCEED **:** triunfar, tener éxito

arrogance ['ærəgənts] *n* **:** arrogancia *f,* soberbia *f,* altanería *f,* altivez *f*

arrogant ['ærəgənt] *adj* **:** arrogante, soberbio, altanero, altivo — **arrogantly** *adv*

arrogate ['ærəˌgeɪt] *vt* **-gated; -gating to arrogate to oneself :** arrogarse

arrow ['æro] *n* **:** flecha *f*

arrowhead ['æroˌhɛd] *n* **:** punta *f* de flecha

arroyo [ə'rɔɪo] *n* **:** arroyo *m*

arsenal ['ɑrsənəl] *n* **:** arsenal *m*

arsenic ['ɑrsənɪk] *n* **:** arsénico *m*

arson ['ɑrsən] *n* **:** incendio *m* premeditado

arsonist *n* ['ɑrsənɪst] **:** incendiario *m,* -ria *f;* pirómano *m,* -na *f*

art ['ɑrt] *n* **1 :** arte *m* **2** SKILL **:** destreza *f,* habilidad *f,* maña *f* **3 arts** *npl* **:** letras *fpl* (en la educación) **4 fine arts :** bellas artes *fpl*

arterial [ɑr'tɪriəl] *adj* **:** arterial

arteriosclerosis [ɑrˌtɪriosklə'roːsɪs] *n* **:** arteriosclerosis *f*

artery ['ɑrt̬əri] *n, pl* **-teries 1 :** arteria *f* **2** THOROUGHFARE **:** carretera *f* principal, arteria *f*

artesian well [ɑr'tiːʒən] *n* **:** pozo *m* artesiano

artful ['ɑrtfəl] *adj* **1** INGENIOUS **:** ingenioso, diestro **2** CRAFTY **:** astuto, taimado, ladino, artero — **artfully** *adv*

arthritic [ɑr'θrɪt̬ɪk] *adj* **:** artrítico

arthritis [ɑr'θraɪt̬əs] *n, pl* **-tides** [ɑr'θrɪt̬əˌdiːz] **:** artritis *f*

arthropod ['ɑrθrəˌpɑd] *n* **:** artrópodo *m*

artichoke ['ɑrt̬əˌtʃoːk] *n* **:** alcachofa *f*

article ['ɑrtɪkəl] *n* **1** ITEM **:** artículo *m,* objeto *m* **2** ESSAY **:** artículo *m* **3** CLAUSE **:** artículo *m,* cláusula *f* **4 :** artículo *m* <definite article : artículo determinado>

articulate[1] [ɑr'tɪkjəˌleɪt] *vt* **-lated; -lating 1** UTTER **:** articular, enunciar, expresar **2** CONNECT **:** articular (en anatomía)

articulate[2] [ɑr'tɪkjələt] *adj* **to be articulate :** poder articular palabras, expresarse bien

articulately [ɑr'tɪkjələtli] *adv* **:** elocuentemente, con fluidez

articulateness [ɑr'tɪkjələtnəs] *n* **:** elocuencia *f,* fluidez *f*

articulation [ɑrˌtɪkjə'leɪʃən] *n* **1** JOINT **:** articulación *f* **2** UTTERANCE **:** articulación *f,* declaración *f* **3** ENUNCIATION **:** articulación *f,* pronunciación *f*

artifact ['ɑrt̬əˌfækt] *n* **:** artefacto *m*

artifice ['ɑrt̬əfəs] *n* **:** artificio *m*

artificial [ˌɑrt̬ə'fɪʃəl] *adj* **1** SYNTHETIC **:** artificial, sintético **2** FEIGNED **:** artificial, falso, afectado

artificially [ˌɑrt̬ə'fɪʃəli] *adv* **:** artificialmente, con afectación

artillery [ɑr'tɪləri] *n, pl* **-leries :** artillería *f*

artisan ['ɑrt̬əzən, -sən] *n* **:** artesano *m,* -na *f*

artist ['ɑrtɪst] *n* **:** artista *mf*

artistic [ɑr'tɪstɪk] *adj* **:** artístico — **artistically** [-tɪkli] *adv*

artistry ['ɑrtəstri] *n* **:** maestría *f,* arte *m*

artless ['ɑrtləs] *adj* **:** sencillo, natural, ingenuo, cándido — **artlessly** *adv*

artlessness ['ɑrtləsnəs] *n* **:** ingenuidad *f,* candidez *f*

arty ['ɑrt̬i] *adj* **artier; -est :** pretenciosamente artístico

as[1] ['æz] *adv* **1 :** tan, tanto <this one's not as difficult : éste no es tan difícil> **2 :** como <some trees, as oak and pine : algunos árboles, como el roble y el pino>

as[2] *conj* **1** LIKE **:** como, igual que **2** WHEN, WHILE **:** cuando, mientras, a la vez que **3** BECAUSE **:** porque **4** THOUGH **:** aunque, por más que <strange as it may appear : por extraño que parezca> **5 as is :** tal como está

as[3] *prep* **1 :** de <I met her as a child : la conocí de pequeña> **2** LIKE **:** como <behave as a man : compórtate como un hombre>

as[4] *pron* **:** que <in the same building as my brother : en el mismo edificio que mi hermano>

asbestos [æz'bɛstəs, æs-] *n* **:** asbesto *m,* amianto *m*

ascend [ə'sɛnd] *vi* **:** ascender, subir — *vt* **:** subir, subir a, escalar

ascendancy [ə'sɛndəntsi] *n* **:** ascendiente *m,* predominio *m*

ascendant[1] [ə'sɛndənt] *adj* **1** RISING **:** ascendente **2** DOMINANT **:** superior, dominante

ascendant[2] *n* **to be in the ascendant :** estar en alza, ir ganando predominio

ascension [ə'sɛntʃən] *n* **:** ascensión *f*

ascent [ə'sɛnt] *n* **1** RISE **:** ascensión, *f,* subida *f,* ascenso *m* **2** SLOPE **:** cuesta *f,* pendiente *f*

ascertain [ˌæsər'teɪn] *vt* **:** determinar, establecer, averiguar

ascertainable [ˌæsər'teɪnəbəl] *adj* **:** determinable, averiguable

ascetic[1] [ə'sɛt̬ɪk] *adj* **:** ascético

ascetic[2] *n* **:** asceta *mf*

asceticism [ə'sɛt̬əˌsɪzəm] *n* **:** ascetismo *m*

ascribable [ə'skraɪbəbəl] *adj* **:** atribuible, imputable

ascribe [ə'skraɪb] *vt* **-cribed; -cribing :** atribuir, imputar

aseptic [eɪ'sɛptɪk] *adj* **:** aséptico

as for *prep* CONCERNING **:** en cuanto a, respecto a, para

ash ['æʃ] *n* **1 :** ceniza *f* <to reduce to ashes : reducir a cenizas> **2 :** fresno *m* (árbol)
ashamed [ə'ʃeɪmd] *adj* **:** avergonzado, abochornado, apenado — **ashamedly** [ə'ʃeɪmədli] *adv*
ashen ['æʃən] *adj* **:** lívido, ceniciento, pálido
ashore [ə'ʃor] *adv* **1 :** en tierra **2 to go ashore :** desembarcar
ashtray ['æʃ,treɪ] *n* **:** cenicero *m*
Asian[1] ['eɪʒən, -ʃən] *adj* **:** asiático
Asian[2] *n* **:** asiático *m*, -ca *f*
aside [ə'saɪd] *adv* **1 :** a un lado <to step aside : hacerse a un lado> **2 :** de lado, aparte <jesting aside : bromas aparte> **3 to set aside :** guardar, apartar, reservar
aside from *prep* **1** BESIDES **:** además de **2** EXCEPT **:** aparte de, menos
as if *conj* **:** como si
asinine ['æsən,aɪn] *adj* **:** necio, estúpido
ask ['æsk] *vt* **1 :** preguntar <ask him if he's coming : pregúntale si viene> **2** REQUEST **:** pedir, solicitar <to ask a favor : pedir un favor> **3** INVITE **:** invitar — *vi* **1** INQUIRE **:** preguntar <I asked about her children : pregunté por sus niños> **2** REQUEST **:** pedir <we asked for help : pedimos ayuda>
askance [ə'skænts] *adv* **1** SIDELONG **:** de reojo, de soslayo **2** SUSPICIOUSLY **:** con recelo, con desconfianza
askew [ə'skju:] *adj* **:** torcido, ladeado
asleep [ə'sli:p] *adj* **1 :** dormido, durmiendo **2 to fall asleep :** quedarse dormido
as of *prep* **:** desde, a partir de
asparagus [ə'spærəgəs] *n* **:** espárrago *m*
aspect ['æ,spɛkt] *n* **:** aspecto *m*
aspen ['æspən] *n* **:** álamo *m* temblón
asperity [æ'spɛrəṭi, ə-] *n, pl* **-ties :** aspereza *f*
aspersion [ə'spərʒən] *n* **:** difamación *f*, calumnia *f*
asphalt ['æs,fɔlt] *n* **:** asfalto *m*
asphyxia [æ'sfɪksiə, ə-] *n* **:** asfixia *f*
asphyxiate [æ'sfɪksi,eɪt] *v* **-ated; -ating** *vt* **:** asfixiar — *vi* **:** asfixiarse
asphyxiation [æ,sfɪksi'eɪʃən] *n* **:** asfixia *f*
aspirant ['æspərənt, ə'spaɪrənt] *n* **:** aspirante *mf*, pretendiente *mf*
aspiration [,æspə'reɪʃən] *n* **1** DESIRE **:** aspiración *f*, anhelo *m*, ambición *f* **2** BREATHING **:** aspiración *f*
aspire [ə'spaɪr] *vi* **-pired; -piring :** aspirar
aspirin ['æsprən, 'æspə-] *n, pl* **aspirin** *or* **aspirins :** aspirina *f*
ass ['æs] *n* **1 :** asno *m* **2** IDIOT **:** imbécil *mf*, idiota *mf*
assail [ə'seɪl] *vt* **:** atacar, asaltar
assailant [ə'seɪlənt] *n* **:** asaltante *mf*, atacante *mf*
assassin [ə'sæsən] *n* **:** asesino *m*, -na *f*
assassinate [ə'sæsən,eɪt] *vt* **-nated; -nating :** asesinar
assassination [ə,sæsən'eɪʃən] *n* **:** asesinato *m*
assault[1] [ə'sɔlt] *vt* **:** atacar, asaltar, agredir
assault[2] *n* **:** ataque *m*, asalto *m*, agresión *f*
assay[1] [æ'seɪ, 'æ,seɪ] *vt* **:** ensayar
assay[2] ['æ,seɪ, æ'seɪ] *n* **:** ensayo *m*
assemble [ə'sɛmbəl] *v* **-bled; -bling** *vt* **1** GATHER **:** reunir, recoger, juntar **2** CONSTRUCT **:** ensamblar, montar, construir — *vi* **:** reunirse, congregarse
assembly [ə'sɛmbli] *n, pl* **-blies 1** MEETING **:** reunión *f* **2** CONSTRUCTING **:** ensamblaje *m*, montaje *m*
assemblyman [ə'sɛmblimən] *n, pl* **-men** [-mən, -,mɛn] **:** asambleísta *m*
assemblywoman [ə'sɛmbli,wʊmən] *n, pl* **-women** [-,wɪmən] **:** asambleísta *f*
assent[1] [ə'sɛnt] *vi* **:** asentir, consentir
assent[2] *n* **:** asentimiento *m*, aprobación *f*
assert [ə'sərt] *vt* **1** AFFIRM **:** afirmar, aseverar, mantener **2 to assert oneself :** imponerse, hacerse valer
assertion [ə'sərʃən] *n* **:** afirmación *f*, aseveración *f*, aserto *m*
assertive [ə'sərṭɪv] *adj* **:** firme, enérgico
assertiveness [ə'sərṭɪvnəs] *n* **:** seguridad *f* en sí mismo
assess [ə'sɛs] *vt* **1** IMPOSE **:** gravar (un impuesto), imponer **2** EVALUATE **:** evaluar, valorar, aquilatar
assessment [ə'sɛsmənt] *n* **:** evaluación *f*, valoración *f*
assessor [ə'sɛsər] *n* **:** evaluador *m*, -dora *f*; tasador *m*, -dora *f*
asset ['æ,sɛt] *n* **1 :** ventaja *f*, recurso *m* **2 assets** *npl* **:** bienes *mpl*, activo *m* <assets and liabilities : activo y pasivo>
assiduous [ə'sɪdʒuəs] *adj* **:** diligente, aplicado, asiduo — **assiduously** *adv*
assign [ə'saɪn] *vt* **1** APPOINT **:** designar, nombrar **2** ALLOT **:** asignar, señalar **3** ATTRIBUTE **:** atribuir, dar, conceder
assignment [ə'saɪnmənt] *n* **1** TASK **:** función *f*, tarea *f*, misión *f* **2** HOMEWORK **:** tarea *f*, asignación *f PRi*, deberes *mpl Spain* **3** APPOINTMENT **:** nombramiento *m* **4** ALLOCATION **:** asignación *f*
assimilate [ə'sɪmə,leɪt] *v* **-lated; -lating** *vt* **:** asimilar — *vi* **:** adaptarse, integrarse
assimilation [ə,sɪmə'leɪʃən] *n* **:** asimilación *f*
assist[1] [ə'sɪst] *vt* **:** asistir, ayudar
assist[2] *n* **:** asistencia *f*, contribución *f*
assistance [ə'sɪstənts] *n* **:** asistencia *f*, ayuda *f*, auxilio *m*
assistant [ə'sɪstənt] *n* **:** ayudante *mf*, asistente *mf*
associate[1] [ə'so:ʃi,eɪt, -si-] *v* **-ated; -ating** *vt* **1** CONNECT, RELATE **:** asociar, relacionar **2 to be associated with**

: estar relacionado con, estar vinculado a — *vi* **to associate with** : relacionarse con, frecuentar
associate² [ə'soːʃiət, -siət] *n* : asociado *m*, -da *f*; colega *mf*; socio *m*, -cia *f*
association [əˌsoːʃi'eɪʃən, -si-] *n* **1** ORGANIZATION : asociación *f*, sociedad *f* **2** RELATIONSHIP : asociación *f*, relación *f*
as soon as *conj* : en cuanto, tan pronto como
assorted [ə'sɔrṭəd] *adj* : surtido
assortment [ə'sɔrtmənt] *n* : surtido *m*, variedad *f*, colección *f*
assuage [ə'sweɪdʒ] *vt* **-suaged; -suaging 1** EASE : aliviar, mitigar **2** CALM : calmar, aplacar **3** SATISFY : saciar, satisfacer
assume [ə'suːm] *vt* **-sumed; -suming 1** SUPPOSE : suponer, asumir **2** UNDERTAKE : asumir, encargarse de **3** TAKE ON : adquirir, adoptar, tomar <to assume importance : tomar importancia> **4** FEIGN : adoptar, afectar, simular
assumption [ə'sʌmpʃən] *n* : asunción *f*, presunción *f*
assurance [ə'ʃʊrən*t*s] *n* **1** CERTAINTY : certidumbre *f*, certeza *f* **2** CONFIDENCE : confianza *f*, aplomo *m*, seguridad *f*
assure [ə'ʃʊr] *vt* **-sured; -suring** : asegurar, garantizar <I assure you that I'll do it : te aseguro que lo haré>
assured [ə'ʃʊrd] *adj* **1** CERTAIN : seguro, asegurado **2** CONFIDENT : confiado, seguro de sí mismo
aster ['æstər] *n* : áster *m*
asterisk ['æstəˌrɪsk] *n* : asterisco *m*
astern [ə'stərn] *adv* **1** BEHIND : detrás, a popa **2** BACKWARDS : hacia atrás
asteroid ['æstəˌrɔɪd] *n* : asteroide *m*
asthma ['æzmə] *n* : asma *m*
asthmatic [æz'mæṭɪk] *adj* : asmático
as though → **as if**
astigmatism [ə'stɪgməˌtɪzəm] *n* : astigmatismo *m*
as to *prep* **1** ABOUT : sobre, acerca de **2** → **according to**
astonish [ə'stɑnɪʃ] *vt* : asombrar, sorprender, pasmar
astonishing [ə'stɑnɪʃɪŋ] *adj* : asombroso, sorprendente, increíble — **astonishingly** *adv*
astonishment [ə'stɑnɪʃmənt] *n* : asombro *m*, estupefacción *f*, sorpresa *f*
astound [ə'staʊnd] *vt* : asombrar, pasmar, dejar estupefacto
astounding [ə'staʊndɪŋ] *adj* : asombroso, pasmoso — **astoundingly** *adv*
astraddle [ə'strædəl] *adv* : a horcajadas
astral ['æstrəl] *adj* : astral
astray [ə'streɪ] *adv & adj* : perdido, extraviado, descarriado
astride [ə'straɪd] *adv* : a horcajadas
astringency [ə'strɪndʒən*t*si] *n* : astringencia *f*
astringent¹ [ə'strɪndʒənt] *adj* : astringente
astringent² *n* : astringente *m*
astrologer [ə'strɑlədʒər] *n* : astrólogo *m*, -ga *f*
astrological [ˌæstrə'lɑdʒɪkəl] *adj* : astrológico
astrology [ə'strɑlədʒi] *n* : astrología *f*
astronaut ['æstrəˌnɔt] *n* : astronauta *mf*
astronautic [ˌæstrə'nɔṭɪk] *or* **astronautical** [-ṭɪkəl] *adj* : astronáutico
astronautics [ˌæstrə'nɔṭɪks] *ns & pl* : astronáutica *f*
astronomer [ə'strɑnəmər] *n* : astrónomo *m*, -ma *f*
astronomical [ˌæstrə'nɑmɪkəl] *adj* **1** : astronómico **2** ENORMOUS : astronómico, enorme, gigantesco
astronomy [ə'strɑnəmi] *n, pl* **-mies** : astronomía *f*
astute [ə'stuːt, -'stjuːt] *adj* : astuto, sagaz, perspicaz — **astutely** *adv*
astuteness [ə'stuːtnəs, -'stjuːt-] *n* : astucia *f*, sagacidad *f*, perspicacia *f*
asunder [ə'sʌndər] *adv* : en dos, en pedazos <to tear asunder : hacer pedazos>
as well as¹ *conj* : tanto como
as well as² *prep* BESIDES : además de, aparte de
as yet *adv* : aún, todavía
asylum [ə'saɪləm] *n* **1** REFUGE : refugio *m*, santuario *m*, asilo *m* **2 insane asylum** : manicomio *m*
asymmetrical [ˌeɪsə'mɛtrɪkəl] *or* **asymmetric** [-'mɛtrɪk] *adj* : asimétrico
asymmetry [ˌeɪ'sɪmətri] *n* : asimetría *f*
at ['æt] *prep* **1** : en <at the top : en lo alto> <at peace : en paz> <at Ana's house : en casa de Ana> **2** : a <at the rear : al fondo> <at 10 o'clock : a las diez> **3** : por <at last : por fin> <to be surprised at something : sorprenderse por algo> **4** : de <he's laughing at you : está riéndose de ti> **5** : para <you're good at this : eres bueno para esto>
at all *adv* : en absoluto, para nada
ate → **eat**
atheism *n* ['eɪθiˌɪzəm] : ateísmo *m*
atheist ['eɪθiɪst] *n* : ateo *m*, atea *f*
atheistic [ˌeɪθi'ɪstɪk] *adj* : ateo
athlete ['æθˌliːt] *n* : atleta *mf*
athletic [æθ'lɛṭɪk] *adj* : atlético
athletics [æθ'lɛṭɪks] *ns & pl* : atletismo *m*
atlas ['ætləs] *n* : atlas *m*
atmosphere ['ætməˌsfɪr] *n* **1** AIR : atmósfera *f*, aire *m* **2** AMBIENCE : ambiente *m*, atmósfera *f*, clima *m*
atmospheric [ˌætmə'sfɪrɪk, -'sfɛr-] *adj* : atmosférico — **atmospherically** [-ɪkli] *adv*
atoll ['æˌtɔl, 'eɪ-, -ˌtɑl] *n* : atolón *m*
atom ['æṭəm] *n* **1** : átomo *m* **2** SPECK : ápice *m*, pizca *f*
atomic [ə'tɑmɪk] *adj* : atómico

atomic bomb *n* : bomba *f* atómica

atomizer [ˈæt̬əˌmaɪzər] *n* : atomizador *m,* pulverizador *m*

atone [əˈtoːn] *vt* **atoned; atoning to atone for** : expiar

atonement [əˈtoːnmənt] *n* : expiación *f,* desagravio *m*

atop[1] [əˈtɑp] *adj* : encima

atop[2] *prep* : encima de, sobre

atrium [ˈeɪtriəm] *n, pl* **atria** [-triə] *or* **atriums 1** : atrio *m* **2** : aurícula *f* (del corazón)

atrocious [əˈtroːʃəs] *adj* : atroz — **atrociously** *adv*

atrocity [əˈtrɑsət̬i] *n, pl* **-ties** : atrocidad *f*

atrophy[1] [ˈætrəfi] *vt* **-phied; -phying** : atrofiar

atrophy[2] *n, pl* **-phies** : atrofia *f*

atropine [ˈætrəˌpiːn] *n* : atropina *f*

attach [əˈtætʃ] *vt* **1** FASTEN : sujetar, atar, amarrar, pegar **2** JOIN : juntar, adjuntar **3** ATTRIBUTE : dar, atribuir <I attached little importance to it : le di poca importancia> **4** SEIZE : embargar **5 to become attached to someone** : encariñarse con alguien

attaché [ˌæt̬əˈʃeɪ, ˌæˌtæ-, əˌtæ-] *n* : agregado *m,* -da *f*

attachment [əˈtætʃmənt] *n* **1** ACCESSORY : accesorio *m* **2** CONNECTION : conexión *f,* acoplamiento *m* **3** FONDNESS : apego *m,* cariño *m,* afición *f*

attack[1] [əˈtæk] *vt* **1** ASSAULT : atacar, asaltar, agredir **2** TACKLE : acometer, combatir, enfrentarse con

attack[2] *n* **1** : ataque *m,* asalto *m,* acometida *f* <to launch an attack : lanzar un ataque> **2** : ataque *m,* crisis *f* <heart attack : ataque cardíaco, infarto> <attack of nerves : crisis nerviosa>

attacker [əˈtækər] *n* : asaltante *mf*

attain [əˈteɪn] *vt* **1** ACHIEVE : lograr, conseguir, alcanzar, realizar **2** REACH : alcanzar, llegar a

attainable [əˈteɪnəbəl] *adj* : alcanzable, realizable, asequible

attainment [əˈteɪnmənt] *n* : logro *m,* consecución *f,* realización *f*

attempt[1] [əˈtɛmpt] *vt* : intentar, tratar de

attempt[2] *n* : intento *m,* tentativa *f*

attend [əˈtɛnd] *vt* **1** : asistir a <to attend a meeting : asistir a una reunión> **2** : atender, ocuparse de, cuidar <to attend a patient : atender a un paciente> **3** HEED : atender a, hacer caso de **4** ACCOMPANY : acompañar

attendance [əˈtɛndən*t*s] *n* **1** ATTENDING : asistencia *f* **2** TURNOUT : concurrencia *f*

attendant[1] [əˈtɛndənt] *adj* : concomitante, inherente

attendant[2] *n* : asistente *mf,* acompañante *mf,* guarda *mf*

attention [əˈtɛntʃən] *n* **1** : atención *f* **2 to pay attention** : prestar atención, hacer caso **3 to stand at attention** : estar firme

attentive [əˈtɛntɪv] *adj* : atento — **attentively** *adv*

attentiveness [əˈtɛntɪvnəs] *n* **1** THOUGHTFULNESS : cortesía *f,* consideración *f* **2** CONCENTRATION : atención *f,* concentración *f*

attest [əˈtɛst] *vt* : atestiguar, dar fe de

attestation [ˌæˌtɛsˈteɪʃən] *n* : testimonio *m*

attic [ˈætɪk] *n* : ático *m,* desván *m,* buhardilla *f*

attire[1] [əˈtaɪr] *vt* **-tired; -tiring** : ataviar

attire[2] *n* : atuendo *m,* atavío *m*

attitude [ˈæt̬əˌtuːd, -ˌtjuːd] *n* **1** FEELING : actitud *f* **2** POSTURE : postura *f*

attorney [əˈtərni] *n, pl* **-neys** : abogado *m,* -da *f*

attract [əˈtrækt] *vt* **1** : atraer **2 to attract attention** : llamar la atención

attraction [əˈtrækʃən] *n* : atracción *f,* atractivo *m*

attractive [əˈtræktɪv] *adj* : atractivo, atrayente

attractively [əˈtræktɪvli] *adv* : de manera atractiva, de buen gusto, hermosamente

attractiveness [əˈtræktɪvnəs] *n* : atractivo *m*

attributable [əˈtrɪbjʊt̬əbəl] *adj* : atribuible, imputable

attribute[1] [əˈtrɪˌbjuːt] *vt* **-tributed; -tributing** : atribuir

attribute[2] [ˈætrəˌbjuːt] *n* : atributo *m,* cualidad *f*

attribution [ˌætrəˈbjuːʃən] *n* : atribución *f*

attune [əˈtuːn, -ˈtjuːn] *vt* **-tuned; -tuning 1** ADAPT : adaptar, adecuar **2 to be attuned to** : estar en armonía con

auburn [ˈɔbərn] *adj* : castaño rojizo

auction[1] [ˈɔkʃən] *vt* : subastar, rematar

auction[2] *n* : subasta *f,* remate *m*

auctioneer [ˌɔkʃəˈnɪr] *n* : subastador *m,* -dora *f;* rematador *m,* -dora *f*

audacious [ɔˈdeɪʃəs] *adj* : audaz, atrevido

audacity [ɔˈdæsət̬i] *n, pl* **-ties** : audacia *f,* atrevimiento *m,* descaro *m*

audible [ˈɔdəbəl] *adj* : audible — **audibly** [-bli] *adv*

audience [ˈɔdiən*t*s] *n* **1** INTERVIEW : audiencia *f* **2** PUBLIC : audiencia *f,* público *m,* auditorio *m,* espectadores *mpl*

audio[1] [ˈɔdiˌoː] *adj* : de sonido, de audio

audio[2] *n* : audio *m*

audiovisual [ˌɔdioˈvɪʒʊəl] *adj* : audiovisual

audit[1] [ˈɔdət] *vt* **1** : auditar (finanzas) **2** : asistir como oyente a (una clase o un curso)

audit[2] *n* : auditoría *f*

audition[1] [ɔˈdɪʃən] *vi* : hacer una audición

audition[2] *n* : audición *f*

auditor [ˈɔdət̬ər] *n* **1** : auditor *m,* -tora *f* (de finanzas) **2** STUDENT : oyente *mf*
auditorium [ˌɔdəˈtoriəm] *n, pl* **-riums** *or* **-ria** [-riə] : auditorio *m,* sala *f*
auditory [ˈɔdəˌtori] *adj* : auditivo
auger [ˈɔgər] *n* : taladro *m,* barrena *f*
augment [ɔgˈmɛnt] *vt* : aumentar, incrementar
augmentation [ˌɔgmənˈteɪʃən] *n* : aumento *m,* incremento *m*
augur¹ [ˈɔgər] *vt* : augurar, presagiar — *vi* **to augur well** : ser de buen agüero
augur² *n* : augur *m*
augury [ˈɔgjʊri, -gər-] *n, pl* **-ries** : augurio *m,* presagio *m,* agüero *m*
august [ɔˈgʌst] *adj* : augusto
August [ˈɔgəst] *n* : agosto *m*
auk [ˈɔk] *n* : alca *f*
aunt [ˈænt, ˈant] *n* : tía *f*
aura [ˈɔrə] *n* : aura *f*
aural [ˈɔrəl] *adj* : auditivo
auricle [ˈɔrɪkəl] *n* : aurícula *f*
aurora borealis [əˈrorəˌboriˈæləs] *n* : aurora *f* boreal
auspices [ˈɔspəsəz, -ˌsiːz] *npl* : auspicios *mpl*
auspicious [ɔˈspɪʃəs] *adj* : prometedor, propicio, de buen augurio
austere [ɔˈstɪr] *adj* : austero, severo, adusto — **austerely** *adv*
austerity [ɔˈstɛrət̬i] *n, pl* **-ties** : austeridad *f*
Australian [ɔˈstreɪljən] *n* : australiano *m,* -na *f* — **Australian** *adj*
Austrian [ˈɔstriən] *n* : austriaco *m,* -ca *f* — **Austrian** *adj*
authentic [əˈθɛntɪk, ɔ-] *adj* : auténtico, genuino — **authentically** [-tɪkli] *adv*
authenticate [əˈθɛntɪˌkeɪt, ɔ-] *vt* **-cated; -cating** : autenticar, autentificar
authenticity [ɔˌθɛnˈtɪsət̬i] *n* : autenticidad *f*
author [ˈɔθər] *n* **1** WRITER : escritor *m,* -tora *f;* autor *m,* -tora *f* **2** CREATOR : autor *m,* -tora *f;* creador *m,* -dora *f;* artífice *mf*
authoritarian [ɔˌθɔrəˈtɛriən, ə-] *adj* : autoritario
authoritative [əˈθɔrəˌteɪt̬ɪv, ɔ-] *adj* **1** RELIABLE : fidedigno, autorizado **2** DICTATORIAL : autoritario, dictatorial, imperioso
authoritatively [əˈθɔrəˌteɪt̬ɪvli, ɔ-] *adv* **1** RELIABLY : con autoridad **2** DICTATORIALLY : de manera autoritaria
authority [əˈθɔrət̬i, ɔ-] *n, pl* **-ties 1** EXPERT : autoridad *f;* experto *m,* -ta *f* **2** POWER : autoridad *f,* poder *m* **3** AUTHORIZATION : autorización *f,* licencia *f* **4 the authorities** : las autoridades *fpl* **5 on good authority** : de buena fuente
authorization [ˌɔθərəˈzeɪʃən] *n* : autorización *f*
authorize [ˈɔθəˌraɪz] *vt* **-rized; -rizing** : autorizar, facultar
authorship [ˈɔθərˌʃɪp] *n* : autoría *f*
auto [ˈɔt̬o] → **automobile**
autobiographical [ˌɔt̬oˌbaɪəˈgræfɪkəl] *adj* : autobiográfico
autobiography [ˌɔt̬obaɪˈɑgrəfi] *n, pl* **-phies** : autobiografía *f*
autocracy [ɔˈtɑkrəsi] *n, pl* **-cies** : autocracia *f*
autocrat [ˈɔt̬əˌkræt] *n* : autócrata *mf*
autocratic [ˌɔt̬əˈkræt̬ɪk] *adj* : autocrático — **autocratically** [-t̬ɪkli] *adv*
autograph¹ [ˈɔt̬əˌgræf] *vt* : autografiar
autograph² *n* : autógrafo *m*
automate [ˈɔt̬əˌmeɪt] *vt* **-mated; -mating** : automatizar
automatic [ˌɔt̬əˈmæt̬ɪk] *adj* : automático — **automatically** [-t̬ɪkli] *adv*
automation [ˌɔt̬əˈmeɪʃən] *n* : automatización *f*
automaton [ɔˈtɑməˌtɑn] *n, pl* **-atons** *or* **-ata** [-t̬ə, -ˌtɑ] : autómata *m*
automobile [ˌɔt̬əmoˈbiːl, -ˈmoːˌbiːl] *n* : automóvil *m,* auto *m,* carro *m,* coche *m*
automotive [ˌɔt̬əˈmoːt̬ɪv] *adj* : automotor
autonomous [ɔˈtɑnəməs] *adj* : autónomo — **autonomously** *adv*
autonomy [ɔˈtɑnəmi] *n, pl* **-mies** : autonomía *f*
autopsy [ˈɔˌtɑpsi, -təp-] *n, pl* **-sies** : autopsia *f*
autumn [ˈɔt̬əm] *n* : otoño *m*
autumnal [ɔˈtʌmnəl] *adj* : otoñal
auxiliary¹ [ɔgˈzɪljəri, -ˈzɪləri] *adj* : auxiliar
auxiliary² *n, pl* **-ries** : auxiliar *mf,* ayudante *mf*
avail¹ [əˈveɪl] *vt* **to avail oneself** : aprovecharse, valerse
avail² *n* **1** : provecho *m,* utilidad *f* **2 to no avail** : en vano **3 to be of no avail** : no servir de nada, ser inútil
availability [əˌveɪləˈbɪlət̬i] *n, pl* **-ties** : disponibilidad *f*
available [əˈveɪləbəl] *adj* : disponible
avalanche [ˈævəˌlæntʃ] *n* : avalancha *f,* alud *m*
avarice [ˈævərəs] *n* : avaricia *f,* codicia *f*
avaricious [ˌævəˈrɪʃəs] *adj* : avaricioso, codicioso
avenge [əˈvɛndʒ] *vt* **avenged; avenging** : vengar
avenger [əˈvɛndʒər] *n* : vengador *m,* -dora *f*
avenue [ˈævəˌnuː, -ˌnjuː] *n* **1** : avenida *f* **2** MEANS : vía *f,* camino *m*
average¹ [ˈævrɪdʒ, ˈævə-] *vt* **-aged; -aging 1** : hacer un promedio de <he averages 8 hours a day : hace un promedio de 8 horas diarias> **2** : calcular el promedio de, promediar (en matemáticas)
average² *adj* **1** MEAN : medio <the average temperature : la temperatura media> **2** ORDINARY : común, ordinario <the average man : el hombre común>

average[3] *n* : promedio *m*

averse [ə'vərs] *adj* : reacio, opuesto

aversion [ə'vərʒən] *n* : aversión *f*

avert [ə'vərt] *vt* **1** : apartar, desviar <he averted his eyes from the scene : apartó los ojos de la escena> **2** AVOID, PREVENT : evitar, prevenir

aviary ['eɪvi,ɛri] *n, pl* **-aries** : pajarera *f*

aviation [,eɪvi'eɪʃən] *n* : aviación *f*

aviator ['eɪvi,eɪt̬ər] *n* : aviador *m*, -dora *f*

avid ['ævɪd] *adj* **1** GREEDY : ávido, codicioso **2** ENTHUSIASTIC : ávido, entusiasta, ferviente — **avidly** *adv*

avocado [,ævə'kɑdo, ,ɑvə-] *n, pl* **-dos** : aguacate *m*, palta *f*

avocation [,ævə'keɪʃən] *n* : pasatiempo *m*, afición *f*

avoid [ə'vɔɪd] *vt* **1** SHUN : evitar, eludir **2** FORGO : evitar, abstenerse de <I always avoided gossip : siempre evitaba los chismes> **3** EVADE : evitar <if I can avoid it : si puedo evitarlo>

avoidable [ə'vɔɪdəbəl] *adj* : evitable

avoidance [ə'vɔɪdənts] *n* : el evitar

avoirdupois [,ævərdə'pɔɪz] *n* : sistema *m* inglés de pesos y medidas

avow [ə'vaʊ] *vt* : reconocer, confesar

avowal [ə'vaʊəl] *n* : reconocimiento *m*, confesión *f*

await [ə'weɪt] *vt* : esperar

awake[1] [ə'weɪk] *v* **awoke** [ə'wo:k]; **awoken** [ə'wo:kən] *or* **awaked; awaking** : despertar

awake[2] *adj* : despierto

awaken [ə'weɪkən] → **awake**[1]

award[1] [ə'wɔrd] *vt* : otorgar, conceder, conferir

award[2] *n* **1** PRIZE : premio *m*, galardón *m* **2** MEDAL : condecoración *f*

aware [ə'wær] *adj* : consciente <to be aware of : darse cuenta de, estar consciente de>

awareness [ə'wærnəs] *n* : conciencia *f*, conocimiento *m*

awash [ə'wɔʃ] *adj* : inundado

away[1] [ə'weɪ] *adv* **1** : de aquí <go away! : ¡fuera de aquí!, ¡vete!> **2** : de distancia <10 miles away : 10 millas de distancia, queda a 10 millas> **3 far away** : lejos, a lo lejos **4 right away** : en seguida, ahora mismo **5 to be away** : estar ausente, estar de viaje **6 to give away** : regalar (una posesión), revelar (un secreto) **7 to go away** : irse, largarse **8 to put away** : guardar **9 to turn away** : volver la cara

away[2] *adj* **1** ABSENT : ausente <away for the week : ausente por la semana> **2 away game** : partido *m* que se juega fuera

awe[1] ['ɔ] *vt* **awed; awing** : abrumar, asombrar, impresionar

awe[2] *n* : asombro *m*

awesome ['ɔsəm] *adj* **1** IMPOSING : imponente, formidable **2** AMAZING : asombroso

awestruck ['ɔ,strʌk] *adj* : asombrado

awful ['ɔfəl] *adj* **1** AWESOME : asombroso **2** DREADFUL : horrible, terrible, atroz **3** ENORMOUS : enorme, tremendo <an awful lot of people : muchísima gente, la mar de gente>

awfully ['ɔfəli] *adv* **1** EXTREMELY : terriblemente, extremadamente **2** BADLY : muy mal, espantosamente

awhile [ə'hwaɪl] *adv* : un rato, algún tiempo

awkward ['ɔkwərd] *adj* **1** CLUMSY : torpe, desmañado **2** EMBARRASSING : embarazoso, delicado — **awkwardly** *adv*

awkwardness ['ɔkwərdnəs] *n* **1** CLUMSINESS : torpeza *f* **2** INCONVENIENCE : incomodidad *f*

awl ['ɔl] *n* : punzón *m*

awning ['ɔnɪŋ] *n* : toldo *m*

awry [ə'raɪ] *adj* 1 ASKEW : torcido **2 to go awry** : salir mal, fracasar

ax *or* **axe** ['æks] *n* : hacha *m*

axiom ['æksiəm] *n* : axioma *m*

axiomatic [,æksiə'mæt̬ɪk] *adj* : axiomático

axis ['æksɪs] *n, pl* **axes** [-,si:z] : eje *m*

axle ['æksəl] *n* : eje *m*

aye[1] ['aɪ] *adv* : sí

aye[2] *n* : sí *m*

azalea [ə'zeɪljə] *n* : azalea *f*

azimuth ['æzəməθ] *n* : azimut *m*, acimut *m*

azure[1] ['æʒər] *adj* : azur, celeste

azure[2] *n* : azur *m*

B

b ['bi:] *n, pl* **b's** *or* **bs** ['bi:z] : segunda letra del alfabeto inglés

babble[1] ['bæbəl] *vi* **-bled; -bling 1** PRATTLE : balbucear **2** CHATTER : charlatanear, parlotear *fam* **3** MURMUR : murmurar

babble[2] *n* : balbuceo *m* (de bebé), parloteo *m* (de adultos), murmullo *m* (de voces, de un arroyo)

babe ['beɪb] → **baby**[3]

babel ['beɪbəl, 'bæ-] *n* : babel *f*, caos *m*

baboon [bæ'bu:n] *n* : babuino *m*

baby[1] ['beɪbi] *vt* **-bied; -bying** : mimar, consentir

baby[2] *adj* **1** : de niño <a baby carriage : un cochecito> <baby talk : habla infantil> **2** TINY : pequeño, minúsculo

baby[3] *n, pl* **-bies** : bebé *m*; niño *m*, -ña *f*

babyhood ['beɪbi,hʊd] *n* : niñez *f*, primera infancia *f*

babyish ['beɪbiɪʃ] *adj* : infantil, pueril

baby–sit ['beɪbi,sɪt] *vi* **-sat** [-,sæt]; **-sitting** : cuidar niños, hacer de canguro *Spain*

baby–sitter ['beɪbi,sɪṭər] *n* : niñero *m*, -ra *f*; canguro *mf Spain*

baccalaureate [,bækə'lɔriət] *n* : licenciatura *f*

bachelor ['bætʃələr] *n* **1** : soltero *m* **2** : licenciado *m*, -da *f* <bachelor of arts degree : licenciatura en filosofía y letras>

bacillus [bə'sɪləs] *n*, *pl* **-li** [-,laɪ] : bacilo *m*

back[1] ['bæk] *vt* **1** *or* **to back up** SUPPORT : apoyar, respaldar **2** *or* **to back up** REVERSE : darle marcha atrás a (un vehículo) **3** : estar detrás de, formar el fondo de <trees back the garden : unos árboles están detrás del jardín> — *vi* **1** *or* **to back up** : retroceder **2** **to back away** : echarse atrás **3** **to back down** *or* **to back out** : volverse atrás, echarse para atrás

back[2] *adv* **1** : atrás, hacia atrás, detrás <to move back : moverse atrás> <back and forth : de acá para allá> **2** AGO : atrás, antes, ya <some years back : unos años atrás, ya unos años> <10 months back : hace diez meses> **3** : de vuelta, de regreso <we're back : estamos de vuelta> <she ran back : volvió corriendo> <to call back : llamar de nuevo>

back[3] *adj* **1** REAR : de atrás, posterior, trasero **2** OVERDUE : atrasado **3** **back pay** : atrasos *mpl*

back[4] *n* **1** : espalda *f* (de un ser humano), lomo *m* (de un animal) **2** : respaldo *m* (de una silla), espalda *f* (de ropa) **3** REVERSE : reverso *m*, dorso *m*, revés *m* **4** REAR : fondo *m*, parte *f* de atrás **5** : defensa *mf* (en deportes)

backache ['bæk,eɪk] *n* : dolor *m* de espalda

backbite ['bæk,baɪt] *v* **-bit** [-,bɪt]; **-bitten** [-,bɪtən]; **-biting** *vt* : calumniar, hablar mal de — *vi* : murmurar

backbiter ['bæk,baɪṭər] *n* : calumniador *m*, -dora *f*

backbone ['bæk,bo:n] *n* **1** : columna *f* vertebral **2** FIRMNESS : firmeza *f*, carácter *m*

backdrop ['bæk,drɑp] *n* : telón *m* de fondo

backer ['bækər] *n* **1** SUPPORTER : partidario *m*, -ria *f* **2** SPONSOR : patrocinador *m*, -dora *f*

backfire[1] ['bæk,faɪr] *vi* **-fired; -firing** **1** : petardear (dícese de un automóvil) **2** FAIL : fallar, salir el tiro por la culata

backfire[2] *n* : petardeo *m*, explosión *f*

background ['bæk,graʊnd] *n* **1** : fondo *m* (de un cuadro, etc.), antecedentes *mpl* (de una situación) **2** EXPERIENCE, TRAINING : experiencia *f* profesional, formación *f*

backhand[1] ['bæk,hænd] *adv* : de revés, con el revés

backhand[2] *n* : revés *m*

backhanded ['bæk,hændəd] *adj* **1** : dado con el revés, de revés **2** INDIRECT : indirecto, ambiguo

backing ['bækɪŋ] *n* **1** SUPPORT : apoyo *m*, respaldo *m* **2** REINFORCEMENT : refuerzo *m* **3** SUPPORTERS : partidarios *mpl*, -rias *fpl*

backlash ['bæk,læʃ] *n* : reacción *f* violenta

backlog ['bæk,lɔg] *n* : atraso *m*, trabajo *m* acumulado

backpack[1] ['bæk,pæk] *vi* : viajar con mochila

backpack[2] *n* : mochila *f*

backrest ['bæk,rɛst] *n* : respaldo *m*

backslide ['bæk,slaɪd] *vi* **-slid** [-,slɪd]; **-slid** *or* **-slidden** [-,slɪdən]; **-sliding** : recaer, reincidir

backstage [,bæk'steɪdʒ, 'bæk,-] *adv & adj* : entre bastidores

backtrack ['bæk,træk] *vi* : dar marcha atrás, volverse atrás

backup ['bæk,ʌp] *n* **1** SUPPORT : respaldo *m*, apoyo *m* **2** : copia *f* de seguridad (para computadoras)

backward[1] ['bækwərd] *or* **backwards** [-wərdz] *adv* **1** : hacia atrás **2** : de espaldas <he fell backwards : se cayó de espaldas> **3** : al revés <you're doing it backwards : lo estás haciendo al revés> **4** **to bend over backwards** : hacer todo lo posible

backward[2] *adj* **1** : hacia atrás <a backward glance : una mirada hacia atrás> **2** RETARDED : retrasado **3** SHY : tímido **4** UNDERDEVELOPED : atrasado

backwardness ['bækwərdnəs] *n* : atraso *m* (dícese de una región), retraso *m* (dícese de una persona)

backwoods [,bæk'wʊdz] *npl* : monte *m*, región *f* alejada

bacon ['beɪkən] *n* : tocino *m*, tocineta *f Col, Ven*, bacon *m Spain*

bacterial [bæk'tɪriəl] *adj* : bacteriano

bacteriologist [bæk,tɪri'ɑlədʒɪst] *n* : bacteriólogo *m*, -ga *f*

bacteriology [bæk,tɪri'ɑlədʒi] *n* : bacteriología *f*

bacterium [bæk'tɪriəm] *n*, *pl* **-ria** [-iə] : bacteria *f*

bad[1] ['bæd] *adv* → **badly**

bad[2] *adj* **1** : malo **2** ROTTEN : podrido **3** SERIOUS, SEVERE : grave **4** DEFECTIVE : defectuoso <a bad check : un cheque sin fondos> **5** HARMFUL : perjudicial **6** CORRUPT, EVIL : malo, corrompido **7** NAUGHTY : travieso **8** **from bad to worse** : de mal en peor **9** **too bad!** : ¡qué lástima!

bad[3] *n* : lo malo <the good and the bad : lo bueno y lo malo>

bade → **bid**

badge ['bædʒ] *n* : insignia *f*, botón *m*, chapa *f*

badger[1] ['bædʒər] *vt* : fastidiar, acosar, importunar

badger[2] *n* : tejón *m*

badly [ˈbædli] *adv* **1** : mal **2** URGENTLY : mucho, con urgencia **3** SEVERELY : gravemente
badminton [ˈbæd,mɪntən, -,mɪt-] *n* : bádminton *m*
badness [ˈbædnəs] *n* : maldad *f*
baffle[1] [ˈbæfəl] *vi* **-fled; -fling 1** PERPLEX : desconcertar, confundir **2** FRUSTRATE : frustrar
baffle[2] *n* : deflector *m,* bafle *m* (acústico)
bafflement [ˈbæfəlmənt] *n* : desconcierto *m,* confusión *f*
bag[1] [ˈbæg] *v* **bagged; bagging** *vi* SAG : formar bolsas — *vt* **1** : ensacar, poner en una bolsa **2** : cobrar (en la caza), cazar
bag[2] *n* **1** : bolsa *f,* saco *m* **2** HANDBAG : cartera *f,* bolso *m,* bolsa *f Mex* **3** SUITCASE : maleta *f,* valija *f*
bagatelle [,bægəˈtɛl] *n* : bagatela *f*
bagel [ˈbeɪgəl] *n* : rosquilla *f* de pan
baggage [ˈbægɪdʒ] *n* : equipaje *m*
baggy [ˈbægi] *adj* **-gier; -est** : holgado, ancho
bagpipe [ˈbæg,paɪp] *n* : gaita *f*
bail[1] [ˈbeɪl] *vt* **1** : achicar (agua de un bote) **2 to bail out** : poner en libertad (de una cárcel) bajo fianza **3 to bail out** EXTRICATE : sacar de apuros
bail[2] *n* : fianza *f,* caución *f*
bailiff [ˈbeɪləf] *n* : aguacil *mf*
bailiwick [ˈbeɪli,wɪk] *n* : dominio *m*
bailout [ˈbeɪl,aʊt] *n* : rescate *m* (financial)
bait[1] [ˈbeɪt] *vt* **1** : cebar (un anzuelo o cepo) **2** HARASS : acosar
bait[2] *n* : cebo *m,* carnada *f*
bake[1] [ˈbeɪk] *vt* **baked; baking** : hornear, hacer al horno
bake[2] *n* : fiesta con platos hechos al horno
baker [ˈbeɪkər] *n* : panadero *m,* -ra *f*
baker's dozen *n* : docena *f* de fraile
bakery [ˈbeɪkəri] *n, pl* **-ries** : panadería *f*
bakeshop [ˈbeɪk,ʃɑp] *n* : pastelería *f,* panadería *f*
baking powder *n* : levadura *f* en polvo
baking soda → **sodium bicarbonate**
balance[1] [ˈbælənts] *v* **-anced; -ancing** *vt* **1** : hacer el balance de (una cuenta) <to balance the books : cuadrar las cuentas> **2** EQUALIZE : balancear, equilibrar **3** HARMONIZE : armonizar — *vi* : balancearse
balance[2] *n* **1** SCALES : balanza *f,* báscula *f* **2** COUNTERBALANCE : contrapeso *m* **3** EQUILIBRIUM : equilibrio *m* **4** REMAINDER : balance *m,* resto *m*
balanced [ˈbælənst] *adj* : equilibrado, balanceado
balcony [ˈbælkəni] *n, pl* **-nies 1** : balcón *m,* terraza *f* (de un edificio) **2** : galería *f* (de un teatro)
bald [ˈbɔld] *adj* **1** : calvo, pelado, pelón **2** PLAIN : simple, puro <the bald truth : la pura verdad>
balding [ˈbɔldɪŋ] *adj* : quedándose calvo
baldly [ˈbɔldli] *adv* : sin reparos, sin rodeos, francamente
baldness [ˈbɔldnəs] *n* : calvicie *f*
bale[1] [ˈbeɪl] *vt* **baled; baling** : empacar, hacer balas de
bale[2] *n* : bala *f,* fardo *m,* paca *f*
baleful [ˈbeɪlfəl] *adj* **1** DEADLY : mortífero **2** SINISTER : siniestro, funesto, torvo <a baleful glance : una mirada torva>
balk[1] [ˈbɔk] *vt* : obstaculizar, impedir — *vi* **1** : plantarse *fam* (dícese de un caballo, etc.) **2 to balk at** : resistarse a, mostrarse reacio a
balk[2] *n* : obstáculo *m*
Balkan [ˈbɔlkən] *adj* : balcánico
balky [ˈbɔki] *adj* **balkier; -est** : reacio, obstinado, terco
ball[1] [ˈbɔl] *vt* : apelotonar, ovillar
ball[2] *n* **1** : pelota *f,* bola *f,* balón *m,* ovillo *m* (de lana) **2** : juego *m* con pelota o bola **3** DANCE : baile *m,* baile *m* de etiqueta
ballad [ˈbæləd] *n* : romance *m,* balada *f*
balladeer [,bæləˈdɪr] *n* : cantante *mf* de baladas
ballast[1] [ˈbæləst] *vt* : lastrear
ballast[2] *n* : lastre *m*
ball bearing *n* : cojinete *m* de bola
ballerina [,bæləˈriːnə] *n* : bailarina *f*
ballet [bæˈleɪ, ˈbæ,leɪ] *n* : ballet *m*
ballistic [bəˈlɪstɪk] *adj* : balístico
ballistics [bəˈlɪstɪks] *ns & pl* : balística *f*
balloon[1] [bəˈluːn] *vi* **1** : viajar en globo **2** SWELL : hincharse, inflarse
balloon[2] *n* : globo *m*
balloonist [bəˈluːnɪst] *n* : aeróstata *mf*
ballot[1] [ˈbælət] *vi* : votar
ballot[2] *n* **1** : papeleta *f* (de voto) **2** BALLOTING : votación *f* **3** VOTE : voto *m*
ballpoint pen [ˈbɔl,pɔɪnt] *n* : bolígrafo *m*
ballroom [ˈbɔl,ruːm, -,rʊm] *n* : sala *f* de baile
ballyhoo [ˈbæli,huː] *n* : propaganda *f,* publicidad *f,* bombo *m fam*
balm [ˈbɑm, ˈbɑlm] *n* : bálsamo *m,* ungüento *m*
balmy [ˈbɑmi, ˈbɑl-] *adj* **balmier; -est 1** MILD : templado, agradable **2** SOOTHING : balsámico **3** CRAZY : chiflado *fam,* chalado *fam*
baloney [bəˈloːni] *n* NONSENSE : tonterías *fpl,* estupideces *fpl*
balsa [ˈbɔlsə] *n* : balsa *f*
balsam [ˈbɔlsəm] *n* **1** : bálsamo *m* **2** *or* **balsam fir** : abeto *m* balsámico
baluster [ˈbæləstər] *n* : balaustre *m*
balustrade [ˈbælə,streɪd] *n* : balaustrada *f*
bamboo [bæmˈbuː] *n* : bambú *m*
bamboozle [bæmˈbuːzəl] *vt* **-zled; -zling** : engañar, embaucar
ban[1] [ˈbæn] *vt* **banned; banning** : prohibir, proscribir

ban[2] *n* : prohibición *f,* proscripción *f*
banal [bəˈnɑl, bəˈnæl, ˈbeɪnəl] *adj* : banal, trivial
banality [bəˈnæləti] *n, pl* **-ties** : banalidad *f,* trivialidad *f*
banana [bəˈnænə] *n* : banano *m,* plátano *m,* banana *f,* cambur *m Ven,* guineo *m Car*
band[1] [ˈbænd] *vt* **1** BIND : fajar, atar **2 to band together** : unirse, juntarse
band[2] *n* **1** STRIP : banda *f,* cinta *f* (de un sombrero, etc.) **2** STRIPE : franja *f* **3** : banda *f* (de radiofrecuencia) **4** RING : anillo *m* **5** GROUP : banda *f,* grupo *m,* conjunto *m* <jazz band : conjunto de jazz>
bandage[1] [ˈbændɪdʒ] *vt* **-daged; -daging** : vendar
bandage[2] *n* : vendaje *m,* venda *f*
bandanna *or* **bandana** [bænˈdænə] *n* : pañuelo *m* (de colores)
bandit [ˈbændət] *n* : bandido *m,* -da *f;* bandolero *m,* -ra *f*
banditry [ˈbændətri] *n* : bandolerismo *m,* bandidaje *m*
bandstand [ˈbændˌstænd] *n* : quiosco *m* de música
bandwagon [ˈbændˌwægən] *n* **1** : carroza *f* de músicos **2 to jump on the bandwagon** : subirse al carro, seguir la moda
bandy[1] [ˈbændi] *vt* **-died; -dying 1** EXCHANGE : intercambiar **2 to bandy about** : circular, propagar
bandy[2] *adj* : arqueado, torcido <bandy-legged : de piernas arqueadas>
bane [ˈbeɪn] *n* **1** POISON : veneno *m* **2** RUIN : ruina *f,* pesadilla *f*
baneful [ˈbeɪnfəl] *adj* : nefasto, funesto
bang[1] [ˈbæŋ] *vt* **1** STRIKE : golpear, darse <he banged his elbow against the door : se dio con el codo en la puerta> **2** SLAM : cerrar (la puerta) con un portazo — *vi* **1** SLAM : cerrarse de un golpe **2 to bang on** : aporrear, golpear <she was banging on the table : aporreaba la mesa>
bang[2] *adv* : directamente, exactamente
bang[3] *n* **1** BLOW : golpe *m,* porrazo *m,* trancazo *m* **2** EXPLOSION : explosión *f,* estallido *m* **3** SLAM : portazo *m* **4 bangs** *npl* : flequilla *f,* fleco *m*
Bangladeshi [ˌbɑŋgləˈdɛʃi, ˌbæŋ-, ˌbʌŋ-, -ˈdeɪ-] *n* : bangladesí *mf* — **Bangladeshi** *adj*
bangle [ˈbæŋgəl] *n* : brazalete *m,* pulsera *f*
banish [ˈbænɪʃ] *vt* **1** EXILE : desterrar, exiliar **2** EXPEL : expulsar
banishment [ˈbænɪʃmənt] *n* **1** EXILE : destierro *m,* exilio *m* **2** EXPULSION : expulsión *f*
banister [ˈbænəstər] *n* **1** BALUSTER : balaustre *m* **2** HANDRAIL : pasamanos *m,* barandilla *f,* barandal *m*
banjo [ˈbænˌdʒoː] *n, pl* **-jos** : banjo *m*
bank[1] [ˈbæŋk] *vt* **1** TILT : peraltar (una carretera), ladear (un avión) **2** HEAP : amontonar **3** : cubrir (un fuego) **4** : depositar (dinero en un banco) — *vi* **1** : ladearse (dícese de un avión) **2** : tener una cuenta (en un banco) **3 to bank on** : contar con
bank[2] *n* **1** MASS : montón *m,* montículo *m,* masa *f* **2** : orilla *f,* ribera *f* (de un río) **3** : peralte *m* (de una carretera) **4** : banco *m* <World Bank : Banco Mundial> <banco de sangre : blood bank>
bankbook [ˈbæŋkˌbʊk] *n* : libreta *f* bancaria, libreta *f* de ahorros
banker [ˈbæŋkər] *n* : banquero *m,* -ra *f*
bankrupt[1] [ˈbæŋˌkrʌpt] *vt* : hacer quebrar, llevar a la quiebra, arruinar
bankrupt[2] *adj* **1** : en bancarrota, en quiebra **2 ~ of** LACKING : carente de, falto de
bankrupt[3] *n* : fallido *m,* -da *f;* quebrado *m,* -da *f*
bankruptcy [ˈbæŋˌkrʌp*t*si] *n, pl* **-cies** : ruina *f,* quiebra *f,* bancarrota *f*
banner[1] [ˈbænər] *adj* : excelente
banner[2] *n* : estandarte *m,* bandera *f*
banns [ˈbænz] *npl* : amonestaciones *fpl*
banquet[1] [ˈbæŋkwət] *vi* : celebrar un banquete
banquet[2] *n* : banquete *m*
banter[1] [ˈbæntər] *vi* : bromear, hacer bromas
banter[2] *n* : bromas *fpl*
baptism [ˈbæpˌtɪzəm] *n* : bautismo *m*
baptismal [bæpˈtɪzməl] *adj* : bautismal
baptize [bæpˈtaɪz, ˈbæpˌtaɪz] *vt* **-tized; -tizing** : bautizar
bar[1] [ˈbɑr] *vt* **barred; barring 1** OBSTRUCT : obstruir, bloquear **2** EXCLUDE : excluir **3** PROHIBIT : prohibir **4** SECURE : atrancar, asegurar <bar the door! : ¡atranca la puerta!>
bar[2] *n* **1** : barra *f,* barrote *m* (de una ventana), tranca *f* (de una puerta) **2** BARRIER : barrera *f,* obstáculo *m* **3** LAW : abogacía *f* **4** STRIPE : franja *f* **5** COUNTER : mostrador *m,* barra *f* **6** TAVERN : bar *m,* taberna *f*
bar[3] *prep* **1** : excepto, con excepción de **2 bar none** : sin excepción
barb [ˈbɑrb] *n* **1** POINT : púa *f,* lengüeta *f* **2** GIBE : pulla *f*
barbarian[1] [bɑrˈbæriən] *adj* **1** : bárbaro **2** CRUDE : tosco, bruto
barbarian[2] *n* : bárbaro *m,* -ra *f*
barbaric [bɑrˈbærɪk] *adj* **1** PRIMITIVE : primitivo **2** CRUEL : brutal, cruel
barbarity [bɑrˈbærəti] *n, pl* **-ties** : barbaridad *f*
barbarous [ˈbɑrbərəs] *adj* **1** UNCIVILIZED : bárbaro **2** MERCILESS : despiadado, cruel
barbarously [ˈbɑrbərəsli] *adv* : bárbaramente

barbecue[1] [ˈbɑrbɪˌkjuː] *vt* **-cued; -cuing :** asar a la parrilla
barbecue[2] *n* **:** barbacoa *f,* parrillada *f*
barber [ˈbɑrbər] *n* **:** barbero *m,* -ra *f*
barbiturate [bɑrˈbɪtʃərət] *n* **:** barbitúrico *m*
bard [ˈbɑrd] *n* **:** bardo *m*
bare[1] [ˈbær] *vt* **bared; baring :** desnudar
bare[2] *adj* **1** NAKED **:** desnudo **2** EXPOSED **:** descubierto, sin protección **3** EMPTY **:** desprovisto, vacío **4** MINIMUM **:** mero, mínimo <the bare necessities : las necesidades mínimas> **5** PLAIN **:** puro, sencillo
bareback [ˈbærˌbæk] *or* **barebacked** [-ˌbækt] *adv & adj* **:** a pelo
barefaced [ˈbærˌfeɪst] *adj* **:** descarado
barefoot [ˈbærˌfʊt] *or* **barefooted** [-ˌfʊtəd] *adv & adj* **:** descalzo
bareheaded [ˈbærˈhɛdəd] *adv & adj* **:** sin sombrero, con la cabeza descubierta
barely [ˈbærli] *adv* **:** apenas, por poco
bareness [ˈbærnəs] *n* **:** desnudez *f*
bargain[1] [ˈbɑrgən] *vi* HAGGLE **:** regatear, negociar — *vt* BARTER **:** trocar, cambiar
bargain[2] *n* **1** AGREEMENT **:** acuerdo *m,* convenio *m* <to strike a bargain : cerrar un trato> **2 :** ganga *f* <bargain price : precio de ganga>
barge[1] [ˈbɑrdʒ] *vi* **barged; barging 1 :** mover con torpeza **2 to barge in :** entrometerse, interrumpir
barge[2] *n* **:** barcaza *f,* gabarra *f*
bar graph *n* **:** gráfico *m* de barras
baritone [ˈbærəˌtoːn] *n* **:** barítono *m*
barium [ˈbæriəm] *n* **:** bario *m*
bark[1] [ˈbɑrk] *vi* **:** ladrar — *vt or* **to bark out :** gritar <to bark out an order : dar una orden a gritos>
bark[2] *n* **1 :** ladrido *m* (de un perro) **2 :** corteza *f* (de un árbol) **3** *or* **barque :** tipo de embarcación con velas de proa y popa
barley [ˈbɑrli] *n* **:** cebada *f*
barn [ˈbɑrn] *n* **:** granero *m* (para cosechas), establo *m* (para ganado)
barnacle [ˈbɑrnɪkəl] *n* **:** percebe *m*
barnyard [ˈbɑrnˌjɑrd] *n* **:** corral *m*
barometer [bəˈrɑmət̬ər] *n* **:** barómetro *m*
barometric [ˌbærəˈmɛtrɪk] *adj* **:** barométrico
baron [ˈbærən] *n* **1 :** barón *m* **2** TYCOON **:** magnate *mf*
baroness [ˈbærənɪs, -nəs, -ˌnɛs] *n* **:** baronesa *f*
baronet [ˌbærəˈnɛt, ˈbærənət] *n* **:** baronet *m*
baronial [bəˈroːniəl] *adj* **1 :** de barón **2** STATELY **:** señorial, majestuoso
baroque [bəˈroːk, -ˈrɑk] *adj* **:** barroco
barracks [ˈbærəks] *ns & pl* **:** cuartel *m*
barracuda [ˌbærəˈkuːdə] *n, pl* **-da** *or* **-das :** barracuda *f*
barrage [bəˈrɑʒ, -ˈrɑdʒ] *n* **1 :** descarga *f* (de artillería) **2** DELUGE **:** aluvión *m* <a barrage of questions : un aluvión de preguntas>
barred [ˈbɑrd] *adj* **:** excluido, prohibido
barrel[1] [ˈbærəl] *v* **-reled** *or* **-relled; -reling** *or* **-relling** *vt* **:** embarrilar — *vi* **:** ir disparado
barrel[2] *n* **1 :** barril *m,* tonel *m* **2 :** cañón *m* (de un arma de fuego), cilindro *m* (de una cerradura)
barren [ˈbærən] *adj* **1** STERILE **:** estéril (dícese de las plantas o la mujer), árido (dícese del suelo) **2** DESERTED **:** yermo, desierto
barrette [bɑˈrɛt, bə-] *n* **:** pasador *m,* broche *m* para el cabello
barricade[1] [ˈbærəˌkeɪd, ˌbærəˈ-] *vt* **-caded; -cading :** cerrar con barricadas
barricade[2] *n* **:** barricada *f*
barrier [ˈbæriər] *n* **1 :** barrera *f* **2** OBSTACLE **:** obstáculo *m,* impedimento *m*
barring [ˈbɑrɪŋ] *prep* **:** excepto, salvo, a excepción de
barrio [ˈbɑrio, ˈbær-] *n* **:** barrio *m*
barroom [ˈbɑrˌruːm, -ˌrʊm] *n* **:** bar *m*
barrow [ˈbærˌoː] → **wheelbarrow**
bartender [ˈbɑrˌtɛndər] *n* **:** camarero *m,* -ra *f;* barman *m*
barter[1] [ˈbɑrt̬ər] *vt* **:** cambiar, trocar
barter[2] *n* **:** trueque *m,* permuta *f*
basalt [bəˈsɔlt, ˈbeɪˌ-] *n* **:** basalto *m*
base[1] [ˈbeɪs] *vt* **based; basing :** basar, fundamentar, establecer
base[2] *adj* **baser; basest 1 :** de baja ley (dícese de un metal) **2** CONTEMPTIBLE **:** vil, despreciable
base[3] *n, pl* **bases :** base *f*
baseball [ˈbeɪsˌbɔl] *n* **:** beisbol *m,* béisbol *m*
baseless [ˈbeɪsləs] *adj* **:** infundado
basely [ˈbeɪsli] *adv* **:** vilmente
basement [ˈbeɪsmənt] *n* **:** sótano *m*
baseness [ˈbeɪsnəs] *n* **:** vileza *f,* bajeza *f*
bash[1] [ˈbæʃ] *vt* **:** golpear violentamente
bash[2] *n* **1** BLOW **:** golpe *m,* porrazo *m,* madrazo *m Mex fam* **2** PARTY**:** fiesta *f,* juerga *f fam*
bashful [ˈbæʃfəl] *adj* **:** tímido, vergonzoso, penoso
bashfulness [ˈbæʃfəlnəs] *n* **:** timidez *f*
basic [ˈbeɪsɪk] *adj* **1** FUNDAMENTAL **:** básico, fundamental **2** RUDIMENTARY **:** básico, elemental **3 :** básico (en química)
basically [ˈbeɪsɪkli] *adv* **:** fundamentalmente
basil [ˈbeɪzəl, ˈbæzəl] *n* **:** albahaca *f*
basilica [bəˈsɪlɪkə] *n* **:** basílica *f*
basin [ˈbeɪsən] *n* **1** WASHBOWL **:** palangana *f,* lavamanos *m,* lavabo *m* **2 :** cuenca *f* (de un río)
basis [ˈbeɪsəs] *n, pl* **bases** [-ˌsiːz] **1** BASE **:** base *f,* pilar *m* **2** FOUNDATION **:** fundamento *m,* base *f* **3 on a weekly basis :** semanalmente

bask [ˈbæsk] *vi* : disfrutar, deleitarse <to bask in the sun : disfrutar del sol>

basket [ˈbæskət] *n* : cesta *f,* cesto *m,* canasta *f*

basketball [ˈbæskət͵bɔl] *n* : baloncesto *m,* basquetbol *m*

bas–relief [͵bɑrɪˈliːf] *n* : bajorrelieve *m*

bass[1] [ˈbæs] *n, pl* **bass** *or* **basses** : róbalo *m* (pesca)

bass[2] [ˈbeɪs] *n* : bajo *m* (tono, voz, cantante)

bass drum *n* : bombo *m*

basset hound [ˈbæsət͵haʊnd] *n* : basset *m*

bassinet [͵bæsəˈnɛt] *n* : moisés *m,* cuna *f*

bassoon [bəˈsuːn, bæ-] *n* : fagot *m*

bass viol [ˈbeɪsˈvaɪəl, -͵oːl] → **double bass**

bastard[1] [ˈbæstərd] *adj* : bastardo

bastard[2] *n* : bastardo *m,* -da *f*

bastardize [ˈbæstər͵daɪz] *vt* **-ized; -izing** DEBASE : degradar, envilecer

baste [ˈbeɪst] *vt* **basted; basting 1** STITCH : hilvanar **2** : bañar (con su jugo durante la cocción)

bastion [ˈbæstʃən] *n* : bastión *m,* baluarte *m*

bat[1] [ˈbæt] *vt* **batted; batting 1** HIT : batear **2 without batting an eye** : sin pestañear

bat[2] *n* **1** : murciélago *m* (animal) **2** : bate *m* <baseball bat : bate de beisbol>

batch [ˈbætʃ] *n* : hornada *f,* tanda *f,* grupo *m,* cantidad *f*

bate [ˈbeɪt] *vt* **bated; bating 1** : aminorar, reducir **2 with bated breath** : con ansiedad, aguantando la respiración

bath [ˈbæθ, ˈbaθ] *n, pl* **baths** [ˈbæðz, ˈbæθs, ˈbaðz, ˈbaθs] **1** BATHING : baño *m* <to take a bath : bañarse> **2** : baño *m* (en fotografía, etc.) **3** BATHROOM : baño *m,* cuarto *m* de baño **4** SPA : balneario *m* **5** LOSS : pérdida *f*

bathe [ˈbeɪð] *v* **bathed; bathing** *vt* **1** WASH : bañar, lavar **2** SOAK : poner en remojo **3** FLOOD : inundar <to bathe with light : inundar de luz> — *vi* : bañarse, ducharse

bather [ˈbeɪðər] *n* : bañista *mf*

bathrobe [ˈbæθ͵roːb] *n* : bata *f* (de baño)

bathroom [ˈbæθ͵ruːm, -͵rʊm] *n* : baño *m,* cuarto *m* de baño

bathtub [ˈbæθ͵tʌb] *n* : bañera *f,* tina *f* (de baño)

batiste [bəˈtiːst] *n* : batista *f*

baton [bəˈtɑn] *n* : batuta *f,* bastón *m*

battalion [bəˈtæljən] *n* : batallón *m*

batten [ˈbætən] *vt* **to batten down the hatches** : cerrar las escotillas

batter[1] [ˈbæt̬ər] *vt* **1** BEAT : aporrear, golpear **2** MISTREAT : maltratar

batter[2] *n* **1** : masa *f* para rebozar **2** HITTER : bateador *m,* -dora *f*

battering ram *n* : ariete *m*

battery [ˈbæt̬əri] *n, pl* **-teries 1** : lesiones *fpl* <assault and battery : agresión con lesiones> **2** ARTILLERY : batería *f* **3** : batería *f,* pila *f* (de electricidad) **4** SERIES : serie *f*

batting [ˈbætɪŋ] *n* **1** *or* **cotton batting** : algodón *m* en láminas **2** : bateo *m* (en beisbol)

battle[1] [ˈbæt̬əl] *vi* **-tled; -tling** : luchar, pelear

battle[2] *n* : batalla *f,* lucha *f,* pelea *f*

battle–ax [ˈbæt̬əl͵æks] *n* : hacha *f* de guerra

battlefield [ˈbæt̬əl͵fɪːld] *n* : campo *m* de batalla

battlements [ˈbæt̬əlmənts] *npl* : almenas *fpl*

battleship [ˈbæt̬əl͵ʃɪp] *n* : acorazado *m*

batty [ˈbæti] *adj* **-tier; -est** : chiflado *fam,* chalado *fam*

bauble [ˈbɔbəl] *n* : chuchería *f,* baratija *f*

bawdiness [ˈbɔdinəs] *n* : picardía *f*

bawdy [ˈbɔdi] *adj* **bawdier; -est** : subido de tono, verde, colorado *Mex*

bawl[1] [ˈbɔl] *vi* : llorar a gritos

bawl[2] *n* : grito *m,* alarido *m*

bawl out *vt* SCOLD : regañar

bay[1] [ˈbeɪ] *vi* HOWL : aullar

bay[2] *adj* : castaño, zaino (dícese de los caballos)

bay[3] *n* **1** : bahía *f* <Bay of Campeche : Bahía de Campeche> **2** *or* **bay horse** : caballo *m* castaño **3** LAUREL : laurel *m* **4** HOWL : aullido *m* **5** : saliente *m* <bay window : ventana en saliente> **6** COMPARTMENT : área *f,* compartimento *m* **7 at ~** : acorralado

bayberry [ˈbeɪ͵bɛri] *n, pl* **-ries** : arrayán *m* brabántico

bayonet[1] [͵beɪəˈnɛt, ˈbeɪə͵nɛt] *vt* **-neted; -neting** : herir (*o* matar) con bayoneta

bayonet[2] *n* : bayoneta *f*

bayou [ˈbaɪ͵uː, -͵oː] *n* : pantano *m*

bazaar [bəˈzɑr] *n* **1** : bazar *m* **2** SALE : venta *f* benéfica

bazooka [bəˈzuːkə] *n* : bazuca *f*

BB [ˈbiːbi] *n* : balín *m*

be [ˈbiː] *v* **was** [ˈwəz, ˈwɑz], **were** [ˈwər]; **been** [ˈbɪn]; **being; am** [ˈæm], **is** [ˈɪz], **are** [ˈɑr] *vi* **1** (*expressing equality*) : ser <José is a doctor : José es doctor> <I'm Ana's sister : soy la hermana de Ana> **2** (*expressing quality*) : ser <the tree is tall : el árbol es alto> <you're silly! : ¡eres tonto!> **3** (*expressing origin or possession*) : ser <she's from Managua : es de Managua> <it's mine : es mío> **4** (*expressing location*) : estar <my mother is at home : mi madre está en casa> <the cups are on the table : las tazas están en la mesa> **5** (*expressing existence*) : ser, existir <to be or not to be : ser, o no ser> <I think, therefore I am : pienso, luego existo> **6** (*expressing a state of being*)

: estar, tener <how are you? : ¿cómo estás?> <I'm cold : tengo frío> <she's 10 years old : tiene 10 años> <they're both sick : están enfermos los dos> — *v impers* **1** (*indicating time*) : ser <it's eight o'clock : son las ocho> <it's Friday : hoy es viernes> **2** (*indicating a condition*) : hacer, estar <it's sunny : hace sol> <it's very dark outside : está bien oscuro afuera> — *v aux* **1** (*expressing progression*) : estar <what are you doing? —I'm working : ¿qué haces? —estoy trabajando> **2** (*expressing occurrence*) : ser <it was finished yesterday : fue acabado ayer, se acabó ayer> <it was cooked in the oven : se cocinó en el horno> **3** (*expressing possibility*) : poderse <can she be trusted? : ¿se puede confiar en ella?> **4** (*expressing obligation*) : deber <you are to stay here : debes quedarte aquí> <he was to come yesterday : se esperaba que viniese ayer>

beach[1] [ˈbiːtʃ] *vt* : hacer embarrancar, hacer varar, hacer encallar

beach[2] *n* : playa *f*

beachcomber [ˈbiːtʃˌkoːmər] *n* : raquero *m*, -ra *f*

beachhead [ˈbiːtʃˌhɛd] *n* : cabeza *f* de playa

beacon [ˈbiːkən] *n* : faro *m*

bead[1] [ˈbiːd] *vi* : formarse en gotas

bead[2] *n* **1** : cuenta *f* **2** DROP : gota *f* **3 beads** *npl* NECKLACE : collar *m*

beady [ˈbiːdi] *adj* **beadier; -est 1** : de forma de cuenta **2 beady eyes** : ojos *mpl* pequeños y brillantes

beagle [ˈbiːgəl] *n* : beagle *m*

beak [ˈbiːk] *n* : pico *m*

beaker [ˈbiːkər] *n* **1** CUP : taza *f* alta **2** : vaso *m* de precipitados (en un laboratorio)

beam[1] [ˈbiːm] *vi* **1** SHINE : brillar **2** SMILE : sonreír radiantemente — *vt* BROADCAST : transmitir, emitir

beam[2] *n* **1** : viga *f*, barra *f* **2** RAY : rayo *m*, haz *m* de luz **3** : haz *m* de radiofaro (para guiar pilotos, etc.)

bean [ˈbiːn] *n* **1** : habichuela *f*, frijol *m* **2 broad bean** : haba *f* **3 string bean** : judía *f*

bear[1] [ˈbær] *v* **bore** [ˈbor]; **borne** [ˈbɔrn]; **bearing** *vt* **1** CARRY : llevar, portar **2** : dar a luz a (un niño) **3** PRODUCE : dar (frutas, cosechas) **4** ENDURE, SUPPORT : soportar, resistir, aguantar — *vi* **1** TURN : doblar, dar la vuelta <bear right : doble a la derecha> **2 to bear up** : resistir

bear[2] *n, pl* **bears** *or* **bear** : oso *m*, osa *f*

bearable [ˈbærəbəl] *adj* : soportable

beard [ˈbɪrd] *n* **1** : barba *f* **2** : arista *f* (de plantas)

bearded [ˈbɪrdəd] *adj* : barbudo, de barba

bearer [ˈbærər] *n* : portador *m*, -dora *f*

bearing [ˈbærɪŋ] *n* **1** CONDUCT, MANNERS : comportamiento *m*, modales *mpl* **2** SUPPORT : soporte *f* **3** SIGNIFICANCE : relacíon *f*, importancia *f* <to have no bearing on : no tener nada que ver con> **4** : cojinete *m*, rodamiento *m* (de una máquina) **5** COURSE, DIRECTION : dirección *f*, rumbo *m* <to get one's bearings : orientarse>

beast [ˈbiːst] *n* **1** : bestia *f*, fiera *f* <beast of burden : animal de carga> **2** BRUTE : bruto *m*, -ta *f*; bestia *mf*

beastly [ˈbiːstli] *adj* : detestable, repugnante

beat[1] [ˈbiːt] *v* **beat; beaten** [ˈbiːtən] *or* **beat; beating** *vt* **1** STRIKE : golpear, pegar, darle una paliza (a alguien) **2** DEFEAT : vencer, derrotar **3** AVOID : anticiparse a, evitar <to beat the crowd : evitar el gentío> **4** MASH, WHIP : batir — *vi* THROB : palpitar, latir

beat[2] *adj* EXHAUSTED : derrengado, muy cansado <I'm beat! : ¡estoy molido!>

beat[3] *n* **1** : golpe *m*, redoble *m* (de un tambor), latido *m* (del corazón) **2** RHYTHM : ritmo *m*, tiempo *m*

beater [ˈbiːtər] *n* **1** : batidor *m*, -dora *f* **2** EGGBEATER : batidor *m*

beatific [ˌbiːəˈtɪfɪk] *adj* : beatífico

beatitude [biˈætəˌtuːd] *n* **1** : beatitud *f* **2 the Beatitudes** : las bienaventuranzas

beau [ˈboː] *n, pl* **beaux** *or* **beaus** : pretendiente *m*, galán *m*

beautification [ˌbjuːtəfəˈkeɪʃən] *n* : embellecimiento *m*

beautiful [ˈbjuːtɪfəl] *adj* : hermoso, bello, lindo, precioso

beautifully [ˈbjuːtɪfəli] *adv* **1** ATTRACTIVELY : hermosamente **2** EXCELLENTLY : maravillosamente, excelentemente

beauty [ˈbjuːti] *n, pl* **-ties** : belleza *f*, hermosura *f*, beldad *f*

beauty shop *or* **beauty salon** *n* : salón *m* de belleza

beaver [ˈbiːvər] *n* : castor *m*

because [bɪˈkʌz, -ˈkɔz] *conj* : porque

because of *prep* : por, a causa de, debido a

beck [ˈbɛk] *n* **to be at the beck and call of** : estar a la entera disposición de, estar sometido a la voluntad de

beckon [ˈbɛkən] *vi* **to beckon to someone** : hacerle señas a alguien

become [bɪˈkʌm] *v* **-came** [-ˈkeɪm]; **-come; -coming** *vi* : hacerse, volverse, ponerse <he became famous : se hizo famoso> <to become sad : ponerse triste> <to become accustomed to : acostumbrarse a> — *vt* **1** BEFIT : ser apropiado para **2** SUIT : favorecer, quedarle bien (a alguien) <that dress becomes you : ese vestido te favorece>

becoming [bɪˈkʌmɪŋ] *adj* **1** SUITABLE : apropiado **2** FLATTERING : favorecedor

bed[1] [ˈbɛd] *v* **bedded; bedding** *vt* : acostar — *vi* : acostarse

bed[2] *n* **1** : cama *f*, lecho *m* **2** : cauce *m* (de un río), fondo *m* (del mar) **3**

: arriate *m* (para plantas) **4** LAYER, STRATUM : estrato *m,* capa *f*
bedbug [ˈbɛd,bʌg] *n* : chinche *f*
bedclothes [ˈbɛd,klo:ðz, -,klo:z] *npl* : ropa *f* de cama, sábanas *fpl*
bedding [ˈbɛdɪŋ] *n* **1** → **bedclothes 2** : cama *f* (para animales)
bedeck [bɪˈdɛk] *vt* : adornar, engalanar
bedevil [bɪˈdɛvəl] *vt* **-iled** *or* **-illed; -iling** *or* **-illing** : acosar, plagar
bedlam [ˈbɛdləm] *n* : locura *f,* caos *m,* alboroto *m*
bedraggled [bɪˈdrægəld] *adj* : desaliñado, despeinado
bedridden [ˈbɛd,rɪdən] *adj* : postrado en cama
bedrock [ˈbɛd,rɑk] *n* : lecho *m* de roca
bedroom [ˈbɛd,ru:m, -,rʊm] *n* : dormitorio *m,* habitación *f,* pieza *f,* recámara *f Col, Mex, Pan*
bedspread [ˈbɛd,sprɛd] *n* : cubrecama *m,* colcha *f,* cobertor *m*
bee [ˈbi:] *n* **1** : abeja *f* (insecto) **2** GATHERING : círculo *m,* reunión *f*
beech [ˈbi:tʃ] *n, pl* **beeches** *or* **beech** : haya *f*
beechnut [ˈbi:tʃ,nʌt] *n* : hayuco *m*
beef[1] [ˈbi:f] *vt* **to beef up** : fortalecer, reforzar — *vi* COMPLAIN : quejarse
beef[2] *n, pl* **beefs** [ˈbi:fs] *or* **beeves** [ˈbi:vz] : carne *f* de vaca, carne *f* de res *CA, Mex*
beefsteak [ˈbi:f,steɪk] *n* : filete *m,* bistec *m*
beehive [ˈbi:,haɪv] *n* : colmena *f*
beekeeper [ˈbi:,ki:pər] *n* : apicultor *m,* -tora *f*
beeline [ˈbi:,laɪn] *n* **to make a beeline for** : ir derecho a, ir directo hacia
been → **be**
beep[1] [ˈbi:p] *v* : pitar
beep[2] *n* : pitido *m*
beeper [ˈbi:pər] *n* : busca *m,* buscapersonas *m*
beer [ˈbɪr] *n* : cerveza *f*
beeswax [ˈbi:z,wæks] *n* : cera *f* de abejas
beet [ˈbi:t] *n* : remolacha *f,* betabel *m Mex*
beetle [ˈbi:təl] *n* : escarabajo *m*
befall [bɪˈfɔl] *v* **-fell** [-ˈfɛl]; **-fallen** [-ˈfɔlən] *vt* : sucederle a, acontecerle a — *vi* : acontecer
befit [bɪˈfɪt] *vt* **-fitted; -fitting** : convenir a, ser apropiado para
before[1] [bɪˈfor] *adv* **1** : antes <before and after : antes y después> **2** : anterior <the month before : el mes anterior>
before[2] *conj* : antes que <he would die before surrendering : moriría antes que rendirse>
before[3] *prep* **1** : antes de <before eating : antes de comer> **2** : delante de, ante <I stood before the house : estaba parada delante de la casa> <before the judge : ante el juez>
beforehand [bɪˈfor,hænd] *adv* : antes, por adelantado, de antemano, con anticipación
befriend [bɪˈfrɛnd] *vt* : hacerse amigo de
befuddle [bɪˈfʌdəl] *vt* **-dled; -dling** : aturdir, ofuscar, confundir
beg [ˈbɛg] *v* **begged; begging** *vt* : pedir, mendigar, suplicar <I begged him to go : le supliqué que fuera> — *vi* : mendigar, pedir limosna
beget [bɪˈgɛt] *vt* **-got** [-ˈgɑt]; **-gotten** [-ˈgɑtən] *or* **-got; -getting** : engendrar
beggar [ˈbɛgər] *n* : mendigo *m,* -ga *f;* pordiosero *m,* -ra *f*
begin [bɪˈgɪn] *v* **-gan** [-ˈgæn]; **-gun** [-ˈgʌn]; **-ginning** *vt* : empezar, comenzar, iniciar — *vi* **1** START : empezar, comenzar, iniciarse **2** ORIGINATE : nacer, originarse **3 to begin with** : en primer lugar, para empezar
beginner [bɪˈgɪnər] *n* : principiante *mf*
beginning [bɪˈgɪnɪŋ] *n* : principio *m,* comienzo *m*
begone [biˈgɔn] *interj* : ¡fuera de aquí!
begonia [bɪˈgo:njə] *n* : begonia *f*
begrudge [bɪˈgrʌdʒ] *vt* **-grudged; -grudging 1** : dar de mala gana **2** ENVY : envidiar, resentir
beguile [bɪˈgaɪl] *vt* **-guiled; -guiling 1** DECEIVE : engañar **2** AMUSE : divertir, entretener
behalf [bɪˈhæf, -ˈhaf] *n* **1** : favor *m,* beneficio *m,* parte *f* **2 on behalf of** *or* **in behalf of** : de parte de, en nombre de
behave [bɪˈheɪv] *vi* **-haved; -having** : comportarse, portarse
behavior [bɪˈheɪvjər] *n* : comportamiento *m,* conducta *f*
behead [bɪˈhɛd] *vt* : decapitar
behest [bɪˈhɛst] *n* **1** : mandato *m,* orden *f* **2 at the behest of** : a instancia de
behind[1] [bɪˈhaɪnd] *adv* : atrás, detrás <to fall behind : quedarse atrás>
behind[2] *prep* **1** : atrás de, detrás de, tras <behind the house : detrás de la casa> <one behind another : uno tras otro> **2** : atrasado con, después de <behind schedule : atrasado con el trabajo> <I arrived behind the others : llegué después de los otros> **3** SUPPORTING : en apoyo de, detrás
behold [bɪˈho:ld] *vt* **-held; -holding** : contemplar
beholder [bɪˈho:ldər] *n* : observador *m,* -dora *f*
behoove [bɪˈhu:v] *vt* **-hooved; -hooving** : convenirle a, corresponderle a <it behooves us to help him : nos conviene ayudarlo>
beige[1] [ˈbeɪʒ] *adj* : beige
beige[2] *n* : beige *m*
being [ˈbi:ɪŋ] *n* **1** EXISTENCE : ser *m,* existencia *f* **2** CREATURE : ser *m,* ente *m*
belabor [bɪˈleɪbər] *vt* **to belabor the point** : extenderse sobre el tema

belated [bɪˈleɪt̬əd] *adj* : tardío, retrasado

belch[1] [ˈbɛltʃ] *vi* **1** BURP : eructar **2** EXPEL : expulsar, arrojar

belch[2] *n* : eructo *m*

beleaguer [bɪˈliːgər] *vt* **1** BESIEGE : asediar, sitiar **2** HARASS : fastidiar, molestar

belfry [ˈbɛlfri] *n, pl* **-fries** : campanario *m*

Belgian [ˈbɛldʒən] *n* : belga *mf* — **Belgian** *adj*

belie [bɪˈlaɪ] *vt* **-lied; -lying 1** MISREPRESENT : falsear, ocultar **2** CONTRADICT : contradecir, desmentir

belief [bəˈliːf] *n* **1** TRUST : confianza *f* **2** CONVICTION : creencia *f,* convicción *f* **3** FAITH : fe *f*

believable [bəˈliːvəbəl] *adj* : verosímil, creíble

believe [bəˈliːv] *v* **-lieved; -lieving** : creer

believer [bəˈliːvər] *n* **1** : creyente *mf* **2** : partidario *m,* -ria *f;* entusiasta *mf* <she's a great believer in vitamins : ella es una gran partidaria de las vitaminas>

belittle [bɪˈlɪt̬əl] *vt* **-littled; -littling 1** DISPARAGE : menospreciar, denigrar, rebajar **2** MINIMIZE : minimizar, quitar importancia a

Belizean [bəˈliːziən] *n* : beliceño *m,* -ña *f* — **Belizean** *adj*

bell[1] [ˈbɛl] *vt* : ponerle un cascabel a

bell[2] *n* : campana *f,* cencerro *m* (para una vaca o cabra), cascabel *m* (para un gato), timbre *m* (de teléfono, de la puerta)

belladonna [ˌbɛləˈdɑnə] *n* : belladona *f*

belle [ˈbɛl] *n* : belleza *f,* beldad *f*

bellhop [ˈbɛlˌhɑp] *n* : botones *m*

bellicose [ˈbɛlɪˌkoːs] *adj* : belicoso *m* — **bellicosity** [ˌbɛlɪˈkɑsət̬i] *n*

belligerence [bəˈlɪdʒərən*t*s] *n* : agresividad *f,* beligerancia *f*

belligerent[1] [bəˈlɪdʒərənt] *adj* : agresivo, beligerante

belligerent[2] *n* : beligerante *mf*

bellow[1] [ˈbɛˌloː] *vi* : bramar, mugir — *vt* : gritar

bellow[2] *n* : bramido *m,* grito *m*

bellows [ˈbɛˌloːz] *ns & pl* : fuelle *m*

bellwether [ˈbɛlˌwɛðər] *n* : líder *mf*

belly[1] [ˈbɛli] *vi* **-lied; -lying** SWELL : hincharse, inflarse

belly[2] *n, pl* **-lies** : abdomen *m,* vientre *m,* barriga *f,* panza *f*

belong [bɪˈlɔŋ] *vi* **1** : pertenecer (a), ser propiedad (de) <it belongs to her : pertenece a ella, es suyo, es de ella> **2** : ser parte (de), ser miembro (de) <he belongs to the club : es miembro del club> **3** : deber estar, ir <your coat belongs in the closet : tu abrigo va en el ropero>

belongings [bɪˈlɔŋɪŋz] *npl* : pertenencias *fpl,* efectos *mpl* personales

beloved[1] [bɪˈlʌvəd, -ˈlʌvd] *adj* : querido, amado

beloved[2] *n* : amado *m,* -da *f;* enamorado *m,* -da *f;* amor *m*

below[1] [bɪˈloː] *adv* : abajo

below[2] *prep* **1** : abajo de, debajo de <below the window : debajo de la ventana> **2** : por debajo de, bajo <below average : por debajo del promedio> <5 degrees below zero : 5 grados bajo cero>

belt[1] [ˈbɛlt] *vt* **1** : ceñir con un cinturón, ponerle un cinturón a **2** THRASH : darle una paliza a, darle un trancazo a

belt[2] *n* **1** : cinturón *m,* cinto *m* (para el talle) **2** BAND, STRAP : cinta *f,* correa *f,* banda *f Mex* **3** AREA : frente *m,* zona *f*

bemoan [bɪˈmoːn] *vt* : lamentarse de

bemuse [bɪˈmjuːz] *vt* **-mused; -musing 1** BEWILDER : confundir, desconcertar **2** ENGROSS : absorber

bench [ˈbɛntʃ] *n* **1** SEAT : banco *m,* escaño *m,* banca *f* **2** : estrado *m* (de un juez) **3** COURT : tribunal *m*

bend[1] [ˈbɛnd] *v* **bent** [ˈbɛnt]; **bending** *vt* : torcer, doblar, curvar, flexionar — *vi* **1** : torcerse, agacharse <to bend over : inclinarse> **2** TURN : torcer, hacer una curva

bend[2] *n* **1** TURN : vuelta *f,* recodo *m* **2** CURVE : curva *f,* ángulo *m,* codo *m*

beneath[1] [bɪˈniːθ] *adv* : bajo, abajo, debajo

beneath[2] *prep* : bajo de, abajo de, por debajo de

benediction [ˌbɛnəˈdɪkʃən] *n* : bendición *f*

benefactor [ˈbɛnəˌfæktər] *n* : benefactor *m,* -tora *f*

beneficence [bəˈnɛfəsən*t*s] *n* : beneficencia *f*

beneficent [bəˈnɛfəsənt] *adj* : benéfico, caritativo

beneficial [ˌbɛnəˈfɪʃəl] *adj* : beneficioso, provechoso — **beneficially** *adv*

beneficiary [ˌbɛnəˈfɪʃiˌɛri, -ˈfɪʃəri] *n, pl* **-ries** : beneficiario *m,* -ria *f*

benefit[1] [ˈbɛnəfɪt] *vt* : beneficiar — *vi* : beneficiarse

benefit[2] *n* **1** ADVANTAGE : beneficio *m,* ventaja *f,* provecho *m* **2** AID : asistencia *f,* beneficio *m* **3** : función *f* benéfica (para recaudar fondos)

benevolence [bəˈnɛvələn*t*s] *n* : bondad *f,* benevolencia *f*

benevolent [bəˈnɛvələnt] *adj* : benévolo, bondadoso — **benevolently** *adv*

Bengali [bɛnˈgɔli, bɛŋ-] *n* **1** : bengalí *mf* **2** : bengalí *m* (idioma) — **Bengali** *adj*

benign [bɪˈnaɪn] *adj* **1** GENTLE, KIND : benévolo, amable **2** FAVORABLE : propicio, favorable **3** MILD : benigno <a benign tumor : un tumor benigno>

Beninese [bəˌnɪˈniːz, -ˌniː-, -ˈniːs; ˌbɛnɪˈ-] *n* : beninés *m*, -nesa *f* — **Beninese** *adj*
bent [ˈbɛnt] *n* : aptitud *f*, inclinación *f*
benumb [bɪˈnʌm] *vt* : entumecer
benzene [ˈbɛnˌziːn] *n* : benceno *m*
bequeath [bɪˈkwiːθ, -ˈkwiːð] *vt* : legar, dejar en testamento
bequest [bɪˈkwɛst] *n* : legado *m*
berate [bɪˈreɪt] *vt* **-rated; -rating** : reprender, regañar
bereaved[1] [bɪˈriːvd] *adj* : que está de luto, afligido (por la muerte de alguien)
bereaved[2] *n* **the bereaved** : los deudos del difunto (o de la difunta)
bereavement [bɪˈriːvmənt] *n* **1** SORROW : dolor *m*, pesar *m* **2** LOSS : pérdida *f*
bereft [bɪˈrɛft] *adj* : privado, desprovisto
beret [bəˈreɪ] *n* : boina *f*
beriberi [ˌbɛriˈbɛri] *n* : beriberi *m*
berm [ˈbərm] *n* : arcén *m*
berry [ˈbɛri] *n, pl* **-ries** : baya *f*
berserk [bərˈsərk, -ˈzərk] *adj* **1** : enloquecido **2 to go beserk** : volverse loco
berth[1] [ˈbərθ] *vi* : atracar
berth[2] *n* **1** DOCK : atracadero *m* **2** ACCOMMODATION : litera *f*, camarote *m* **3** POSITION : trabajo *m*, puesto *m*
beryl [ˈbɛrəl] *n* : berilo *m*
beseech [bɪˈsiːtʃ] *vt* **-sought** [-ˈsɔt] *or* **-seeched; -seeching** : suplicar, implorar, rogar
beset [bɪˈsɛt] *vt* **-set; -setting 1** HARASS : acosar **2** SURROUND : rodear
beside [bɪˈsaɪd] *prep* : al lado de, junto a
besides[1] [bɪˈsaɪdz] *adv* **1** ALSO : además, también, aparte **2** MOREOVER : además, por otra parte
besides[2] *prep* **1** : además de, aparte de <six others besides you : seis otros además de ti> **2** EXCEPT : excepto, fuera de, aparte de
besiege [bɪˈsiːdʒ] *vt* **-sieged; -sieging** : asediar, sitiar, cercar
besmirch [bɪˈsmərtʃ] *vt* : ensuciar, mancillar
best[1] [ˈbɛst] *vt* : superar, ganar a
best[2] *adv* (*superlative of* **well**) : mejor <as best I can : lo mejor que puedo>
best[3] *adj* (*superlative of* **good**) : mejor <my best friend : mi mejor amigo>
best[4] *n* **1 the best** : lo mejor, el mejor, la mejor, los mejores, las mejores **2 at ∼** : a lo más **3 to do one's best** : hacer todo lo posible
bestial [ˈbɛstʃəl, ˈbiːs-] *adj* **1** : bestial **2** BRUTISH : brutal, salvaje
best man *n* : padrino *m*
bestow [bɪˈstoː] *vt* : conferir, otorgar, conceder
bestowal [bɪˈstoːəl] *n* : concesión *f*, otorgamiento *m*
bet[1] [ˈbɛt] *v* **bet; betting** *vt* : apostar — *vi* **to bet on** : apostarle a
bet[2] *n* : apuesta *f*
betoken [bɪˈtoːkən] *vt* : denotar, ser indicio de
betray [bɪˈtreɪ] *vt* **1** : traicionar <to betray one's country : traicionar uno a su patria> **2** DIVULGE, REVEAL : delatar, revelar <to betray a secret : revelar un secreto>
betrayal [bɪˈtreɪəl] *n* : traición *f*, delación *f*, revelación *f* <betrayal of trust : abuso de confianza>
betrothal [bɪˈtroːðəl, -ˈtrɔ-] *n* : esponsales *mpl*, compromiso *m*
betrothed [bɪˈtroːðd, -ˈtrɔθt] *n* FIANCÉ : prometido *m*, -da *f*
better[1] [ˈbɛt̬ər] *vt* **1** IMPROVE : mejorar **2** SURPASS : superar
better[2] *adv* (*comparative of* **well**) **1** : mejor **2** MORE : más <better than 50 miles : más de 50 millas>
better[3] *adj* (*comparative of* **good**) **1** : mejor <the weather is better today : hace mejor tiempo hoy> <I was sick, but now I'm better : estuve enfermo, pero ahora estoy mejor> **2** : mayor <the better part of a month : la mayor parte de un mes>
better[4] *n* **1** : el mejor, la mejor <the better of the two : el mejor de los dos> **2 to get the better of** : vencer a, quedar por encima de, superar
betterment [ˈbɛt̬ərmənt] *n* : mejoramiento *m*, mejora *f*
bettor *or* **better** [ˈbɛt̬ər] *n* : apostador *m*, -dora *f*
between[1] [bɪˈtwiːn] *adv* **1** : en medio, por lo medio **2 in ∼** : intermedio
between[2] *prep* : entre
bevel[1] [ˈbɛvəl] *v* **-eled** *or* **-elled; -eling** *or* **-elling** *vt* : biselar — *vi* INCLINE : inclinarse
bevel[2] *n* : bisel *m*
beverage [ˈbɛvrɪdʒ, ˈbɛvə-] *n* : bebida *f*
bevy [ˈbɛvi] *n, pl* **bevies** : grupo *m* (de personas), bandada *f* (de pájaros)
bewail [bɪˈweɪl] *vt* : lamentarse de, llorar
beware [bɪˈwær] *vi* **to beware of** : tener cuidado con <beware of the dog! : ¡cuidado con el perro!> — *vt* : guardarse de, cuidarse de
bewilder [bɪˈwɪldər] *vt* : desconcertar, dejar perplejo
bewilderment [bɪˈwɪldərmənt] *n* : desconcierto *m*, perplejidad *f*
bewitch [bɪˈwɪtʃ] *vt* **1** : hechizar, embrujar **2** CHARM : cautivar, encantar
bewitchment [bɪˈwɪtʃmənt] *n* : hechizo *m*
beyond[1] [biˈjɑnd] *adv* **1** FARTHER, LATER : más allá, más lejos (en el espacio), más adelante (en el tiempo) **2** MORE : más <$50 and beyond : $50 o más>
beyond[2] *n* **the beyond** : el más allá, lo desconocido
beyond[3] *prep* **1** : más allá de <beyond the frontier : más allá de la frontera>

2 : fuera de <beyond one's reach : fuera de su alcance> 3 BESIDES : además de

biannual [ˌbaɪ'ænjʊəl] *adj* : bianual — **biannually** *adv*

bias[1] ['baɪəs] *vt* **-ased** *or* **-assed; -asing** *or* **-assing 1** : predisponer, sesgar, influir en, afectar **2 to be biased against** : tener prejuicio contra

bias[2] *n* **1** : sesgo *m,* bies *m* (en la costura) **2** PREJUDICE : prejuicio *m* **3** TENDENCY : inclinación *f,* tendencia *f*

biased ['baɪəst] *adj* : tendencioso, parcial

bib ['bɪb] *n* **1** : peto *m* **2** : babero *m* (para niños)

Bible ['baɪbəl] *n* : Biblia *f*

biblical ['bɪblɪkəl] *adj* : bíblico

bibliographer [ˌbɪbli'ɑgrəfər] *n* : bibliógrafo *m,* -fa *f*

bibliographic [ˌbɪbliə'græfɪk] *adj* : bibliográfico

bibliography [ˌbɪbli'ɑgrəfi] *n, pl* **-phies** : bibliografía *f*

bicameral [ˌbaɪ'kæmərəl] *adj* : bicameral

bicarbonate [ˌbaɪ'kɑrbənət, -ˌneɪt] *n* : bicarbonato *m*

bicentennial [ˌbaɪsɛn'tɛniəl] *n* : bicentenario *m*

biceps ['baɪˌsɛps] *ns & pl* : bíceps *m*

bicker[1] ['bɪkər] *vi* : pelear, discutir, reñir

bicker[2] *n* : pelea *f,* riña *f,* discusión *f*

bicuspid [baɪ'kʌspɪd] *n* : premolar *m,* diente *m* bicúspide

bicycle[1] ['baɪsɪkəl, -ˌsɪ-] *vi* **-cled; -cling** : ir en bicicleta

bicycle[2] *n* : bicicleta *f*

bicycling ['baɪsɪkəlɪŋ] *n* : ciclismo *m*

bicyclist ['baɪsɪkəlɪst] *n* : ciclista *mf*

bid[1] ['bɪd] *vt* **bade** ['bæd, 'beɪd] *or* **bid; bidden** ['bɪdən] *or* **bid; bidding 1** ORDER : pedir, mandar **2** INVITE : invitar **3** SAY : dar, decir <to bid good evening : dar las buenas noches> <to bid farewell to : decir adiós a> **4** : ofrecer (en una subasta), declarar (en juegos de cartas)

bid[2] *n* **1** OFFER : oferta *f* (en una subasta), declaración *f* (en juegos de cartas) **2** INVITATION : invitación *f* **3** ATTEMPT : intento *m,* tentativa *f*

bidder ['bɪdər] *n* : postor *m,* -tora *f*

bide ['baɪd] *v* **bode** ['bo:d] *or* **bided; bided; biding** *vt* : esperar, aguardar <to bide one's time : esperar el momento oportuno> — *vi* DWELL : morar, vivir

biennial [baɪ'ɛniəl] *adj* : bienal — **biennially** *adv*

bier ['bɪr] *n* **1** STAND : andas *fpl* **2** COFFIN : ataúd *m,* féretro *m*

bifocals ['baɪˌfo:kəlz] *npl* : lentes *mpl* bifocales, bifocales *mpl*

big ['bɪg] *adj* **bigger; biggest 1** LARGE : grande **2** PREGNANT : embarazada **3** IMPORTANT, MAJOR : importante, grande <a big decision : una gran decisión> **4** POPULAR : popular, famoso, conocido

bigamist ['bɪgəmɪst] *n* : bígamo *m,* -ma *f*

bigamous ['bɪgəməs] *adj* : bígamo

bigamy ['bɪgəmi] *n* : bigamia *f*

Big Dipper → **dipper**

bighorn ['bɪgˌhɔrn] *n, pl* **-horn** *or* **-horns** *or* **bighorn sheep** : oveja *f* salvaje de las montañas

bight ['baɪt] *n* : bahía *f,* ensenada *f,* golfo *m*

bigot ['bɪgət] *n* : intolerante *mf*

bigoted ['bɪgət̬əd] *adj* : intolerante, prejuiciado, fanático

bigotry ['bɪgətri] *n, pl* **-tries** : intolerancia *f,* fanaticismo *m*

big shot *n* : pez *m* gordo *fam,* mandamás *mf*

bigwig ['bɪgˌwɪg] → **big shot**

bike ['baɪk] *n* **1** : bicicleta *f,* bici *f fam* **2** : motocicleta *f,* moto *f*

bikini [bə'ki:ni] *n* : bikini *m*

bilateral [baɪ'læt̬ərəl] *adj* : bilateral — **bilaterally** *adv*

bile ['baɪl] *n* **1** : bilis *f* **2** IRRITABILITY : mal genio *m*

bilingual [baɪ'lɪŋgwəl] *adj* : bilingüe

bilious ['bɪliəs] *adj* **1** : bilioso **2** IRRITABLE : bilioso, colérico

bilk ['bɪlk] *vt* : burlar, estafar, defraudar

bill[1] ['bɪl] *vt* : pasarle la cuenta a — *vi* : acariciar <to bill and coo : acariciarse>

bill[2] *n* **1** LAW : proyecto *m* de ley, ley *f* **2** INVOICE : cuenta *f,* factura *f* **3** POSTER : cartel *m* **4** PROGRAM : programa *m* (del teatro) **5** : billete *m* <a five-dollar bill : un billete de cinco dólares> **6** BEAK : pico *m*

billboard ['bɪlˌbɔrd] *n* : cartelera *f*

billet[1] ['bɪlət] *vt* : acuartelar, alojar

billet[2] *n* : alojamiento *m*

billfold ['bɪlˌfo:ld] *n* : billetera *f,* cartera *f*

billiards ['bɪljərdz] *n* : billar *m*

billion ['bɪljən] *n, pl* **billions** *or* **billion** : mil millones *mpl*

billow[1] ['bɪlo] *vi* : hincharse, inflarse

billow[2] *n* **1** WAVE : ola *f* **2** CLOUD : nube *f* <a billow of smoke : un nube de humo>

billowy ['bɪlowi] *adj* : ondulante

billy goat ['bɪliˌgo:t] *n* : macho *m* cabrío

bin ['bɪn] *n* : cubo *m,* cajón *m*

binary ['baɪnəri, -ˌnɛri] *adj* : binario *m*

bind ['baɪnd] *vt* **bound** ['baʊnd]; **binding 1** TIE : atar, amarrar **2** OBLIGATE : obligar **3** UNITE : aglutinar, ligar, unir **4** BANDAGE : vendar **5** : encuadernar (un libro)

binder ['baɪndər] *n* **1** FOLDER : carpeta *f* **2** : encuadernador *m,* -dora *f* (de libros)

binding ['baɪndɪŋ] *n* **1** : encuadernación *f* (de libros) **2** COVER : cubierta *f,* forro *m*

binge [ˈbɪndʒ] *n* : juerga *f,* parranda *f fam*
bingo [ˈbɪŋˌgoː] *n, pl* **-gos** : bingo *m*
binocular [baɪˈnɑkjələr, bə-] *adj* : binocular
binoculars [bəˈnɑkjələrz, baɪ-] *npl* : binoculares *mpl*
biochemical[1] [ˌbaɪoˈkɛmɪkəl] *adj* : bioquímico
biochemical[2] *n* : bioquímico *m*
biochemist [ˌbaɪoˈkɛmɪst] *n* : bioquímico *m,* -ca *f*
biochemistry [ˌbaɪoˈkɛməstri] *n* : bioquímica *f*
biodegradable [ˌbaɪodɪˈgreɪdəbəl] *adj* : biodegradable
biodegradation [ˌbaɪodɛgrəˈdeɪʃən] *n* : biodegradación *f*
biodegrade [ˌbaɪodɪˈgreɪd] *vi* **-graded; -grading** : biodegradarse
biographer [baɪˈɑgrəfər] *n* : biógrafo *m,* -fa *f*
biographical [ˌbaɪəˈgræfɪkəl] *adj* : biográfico
biography [baɪˈɑgrəfi, biː-] *n, pl* **-phies** : biografía *f*
biologic [ˌbaɪəˈlɑdʒɪk] *or* **biological** [-dʒɪkəl] *adj* : biológico
biologist [baɪˈɑlədʒɪst] *n* : biólogo *m,* -ga *f*
biology [baɪˈɑlədʒi] *n* : biología *f*
biophysical [ˌbaɪoˈfɪzɪkəl] *adj* : biofísico
biophysicist [ˌbaɪoˈfɪzəsɪst] *n* : biofísico *m,* -ca *f*
biophysics [ˌbaɪoˈfɪzɪks] *ns & pl* : biofísica *f*
biopsy [ˈbaɪˌɑpsi] *n, pl* **-sies** : biopsia *f*
biotechnology [ˌbaɪotɛkˈnɑlədʒi] *n* : biotecnología *f*
biotic [baɪˈɑtɪk] *adj* : biótico
bipartisan [baɪˈpɑrtəzən, -sən] *adj* : bipartidista, de dos partidas
biped [ˈbaɪˌpɛd] *n* : bípedo *m*
birch [ˈbərtʃ] *n* : abedul *m*
bird [ˈbərd] *n* : pájaro *m* (pequeño), ave *f* (grande)
birdbath [ˈbərdˌbæθ, -ˌbaθ] *n* : pila *f* para pájaros
bird dog *n* : perro *m,* -rra *f* de caza
bird of prey *n* : ave *f* rapaz, ave *f* de presa
birdseed [ˈbərdˌsiːd] *n* : alpiste *m*
bird's–eye [ˈbərdzˌaɪ] *adj* **1** : visto desde arriba <bird's-eye view : vista aérea> **2** CURSORY : rápido, somero
birth [ˈbərθ] *n* **1** : nacimiento *m,* parto *m* **2** ORIGIN : origen *m,* nacimiento *m*
birthday [ˈbərθˌdeɪ] *n* : cumpleaños *m,* aniversario *m*
birthmark [ˈbərθˌmɑrk] *n* : mancha *f* de nacimiento
birthplace [ˈbərθˌpleɪs] *n* : lugar *m* de nacimiento
birthrate [ˈbərθˌreɪt] *n* : índice *m* de natalidad
birthright [ˈbərθˌraɪt] *n* : derecho *m* de nacimiento
biscuit [ˈbɪskət] *n* : bizcocho *m*
bisect [ˈbaɪˌsɛkt, ˌbaɪˈ-] *vt* : bisecar
bisector [ˈbaɪˌsɛktər, ˌbaɪˈ-] *n* : bisectriz *f*
bishop [ˈbɪʃəp] *n* : obispo *m*
bismuth [ˈbɪzməθ] *n* : bismuto *m*
bison [ˈbaɪzən, -sən] *ns & pl* : bisonte *m*
bistro [ˈbiːstro, ˈbɪs-] *n, pl* **-tros** : bar *m,* restaurante *m* pequeño
bit [ˈbɪt] *n* **1** FRAGMENT, PIECE : pedazo *m,* trozo *m* <a bit of luck : un poco de suerte> **2** : freno *m,* bocado *m* (de una brida) **3** : broca *f* (de un taladro) **4** : bit *m* (de información)
bitch[1] [ˈbɪtʃ] *vi* COMPLAIN : quejarse, reclamar
bitch[2] *n* : perra *f*
bite[1] [ˈbaɪt] *v* **bit** [ˈbɪt]; **bitten** [ˈbɪtən]; **biting** *vt* **1** : morder **2** STING : picar **3** PUNCTURE : punzar, pinchar **4** GRIP : agarrar — *vi* **1** : morder <that dog bites : ese perro muerde> **2** STING : picar (dícese de un insecto), cortar (dícese del viento) **3** : picar <the fish are biting now : ya están picando los peces> **4** GRAB : agarrarse
bite[2] *n* **1** BITING : mordisco *m,* dentellada *f* **2** SNACK : bocado *m* <a bite to eat : algo de comer> **3** : picadura *f* (de un insecto), mordedura *f* (de un animal) **4** SHARPNESS : mordacidad *f,* penetración *f*
biting *adj* **1** PENETRATING : cortante, penetrante **2** CAUSTIC : mordaz, sarcástico
bitter [ˈbɪtər] *adj* **1** ACRID : amargo, acre **2** PENETRATING : cortante, penetrante <bitter cold : frío glacial> **3** HARSH : duro, amargo <to the bitter end : hasta el final> **4** INTENSE, RELENTLESS : intenso, extremo, implacable <bitter hatred : odio implacable>
bitterly [ˈbɪtərli] *adv* : amargamente
bittern [ˈbɪtərn] *n* : avetoro *m* común
bitterness [ˈbɪtərnəs] *n* : amargura *f*
bituminous coal [bəˈtuːmənəs, -ˈtjuː-] *n* : carbón *m* bituminoso
bivalve [ˈbaɪˌvælv] *n* : bivalvo *m* — **bivalve** *adj*
bivouac[1] [ˈbɪvəˌwæk, ˈbɪvˌwæk] *vi* **-ouacked; -ouacking** : acampar, vivaquear
bivouac[2] *n* : vivaque *m*
bizarre [bəˈzɑr] *adj* : extraño, singular, estrafalario, estrambótico — **bizarrely** *adv*
blab [ˈblæb] *vi* **blabbed; blabbing** : parlotear *fam,* cotorrear *fam*
black[1] [ˈblæk] *vt* : ennegrecer
black[2] *adj* **1** : negro (color, raza) **2** SOILED : sucio **3** DARK : oscuro, negro **4** WICKED : malvado, perverso, malo **5** GLOOMY : negro, sombrío, deprimente
black[3] *n* **1** : negro *m* (color) **2** : negro *m,* -gra *f* (persona)
black–and–blue [ˌblækənˈbluː] *adj* : amoratado

blackball [ˈblæk,bɔl] *vt* **1** OSTRACIZE : hacerle el vacío a, aislar **2** BOYCOTT : boicotear
blackberry [ˈblæk,bɛri] *n, pl* **-ries** : mora *f*
blackbird [ˈblæk,bərd] *n* : mirlo *m*
blackboard [ˈblæk,bɔrd] *n* : pizarra *f,* pizarrón *m*
blacken [ˈblækən] *vt* **1** BLACK : ennegrecer **2** DEFAME : deshonrar, difamar, manchar
blackhead [ˈblæk,hɛd] *n* : espinilla *f,* punto *m* negro
black hole *n* : agujero *m* negro
blackjack [ˈblæk,ʤæk] *n* **1** : cachiporra *f* (arma) **2** : veintiuna *f* (juego de cartas)
blacklist[1] [ˈblæk,lɪst] *vt* : poner en la lista negra
blacklist[2] *n* : lista *f* negra
blackmail[1] [ˈblæk,meɪl] *vt* : chantajear, hacer chantaje a
blackmail[2] *n* : chantaje *m*
blackmailer [ˈblæk,meɪlər] *n* : chantajista *mf*
blackout [ˈblæk,aʊt] *n* **1** : apagón *m* (de poder eléctrico) **2** FAINT : desmayo *m,* desvanecimiento *m*
black out *vt* : dejar sin luz — *vi* FAINT : perder el conocimiento, desmayarse
blacksmith [ˈblæk,smɪθ] *n* : herrero *m*
blacktop [ˈblæk,tɑp] *n* : asfalto *m*
bladder [ˈblædər] *n* : vejiga *f*
blade [ˈbleɪd] *n* : hoja *f* (de un cuchillo), cuchilla *f* (de un patín), pala *f* (de un remo o una hélice), brizna *f* (de hierba)
blamable [ˈbleɪməbəl] *adj* : culpable
blame[1] [ˈbleɪm] *vt* **blamed; blaming** : culpar, echar la culpa a
blame[2] *n* : culpa *f*
blameless [ˈbleɪmləs] *adj* : intachable, sin culpa, inocente — **blamelessly** *adv*
blameworthiness [ˈbleɪm,wərðinəs] *n* : culpa *f,* culpabilidad *f*
blameworthy [ˈbleɪm,wərði] *adj* : culpable, reprochable, censurable
blanch [ˈblænʧ] *vt* WHITEN : blanquear — *vi* PALE : palidecer
bland [ˈblænd] *adj* : soso, insulso, desabrido <a bland smile : una sonrisa insulsa> <a bland diet : una dieta fácil de digerir>
blandishments [ˈblændɪʃmənts] *npl* : lisonjas *fpl,* halagos *mpl*
blandly [ˈblændli] *adv* : de manera insulsa
blandness [ˈblændnəs] *n* : lo insulso, lo desabrido
blank[1] [ˈblæŋk] *vt* OBLITERATE : borrar
blank[2] *adj* **1** DAZED : perplejo, desconcertado **2** EXPRESSIONLESS : sin expresión, inexpresivo **3** : en blanco (dícese de un papel), liso (dícese de una pared) **4** EMPTY : vacío, en blanco <a blank stare : una mirada vacía> <his mind went blank : se quedó en blanco>
blank[3] *n* **1** SPACE : espacio *m* en blanco **2** FORM : formulario *m* **3** CARTRIDGE : cartucho *m* de fogueo **4** *or* **blank key** : llave *f* ciega
blanket[1] [blæŋkət] *vt* : cubrir
blanket[2] *adj* : global
blanket[3] *n* : manta *f,* cobija *f,* frazada *f*
blankly [ˈblænkli] *adv* : sin comprender
blankness [ˈblænknəs] *n* **1** PERPLEXITY : desconcierto *m,* perplejidad *f* **2** EMPTINESS : vacío *m,* vacuidad *f*
blare[1] [ˈblær] *vi* **blared; blaring** : resonar
blare[2] *n* : estruendo *m*
blarney [ˈblɑrni] *n* : labia *f fam*
blasé [blɑˈzeɪ] *adj* : displicente, indiferente
blaspheme [blæsˈfiːm, ˈblæs,-] *vi* **-phemed; -pheming** : blasfemar
blasphemer [blæsˈfiːmər, ˈblæs,-] *n* : blasfemo *m,* -ma *f*
blasphemous [ˈblæsfəməs] *adj* : blasfemo
blasphemy [ˈblæsfəmi] *n, pl* **-mies** : blasfemia *f*
blast[1] [ˈblæst] *vt* **1** BLOW UP : volar, hacer volar **2** ATTACK : atacar, arremeter contra
blast[2] *n* **1** GUST : ráfaga *f* **2** EXPLOSION : explosión *f*
blast-off [ˈblæst,ɔf] *n* : despegue *m*
blast off *vi* : despegar
blatant [ˈbleɪtənt] *adj* : descarado — **blatantly** [ˈbleɪtəntli] *adv*
blaze[1] [ˈbleɪz] *v* **blazed; blazing** *vi* SHINE : arder, brillar, resplandecer — *vt* MARK : marcar, señalar <to blaze a trail : abrir un camino>
blaze[2] *n* **1** FIRE : fuego *m* **2** BRIGHTNESS : resplandor *m,* brillantez *f* **3** OUTBURST : arranque *m* <a blaze of anger : un arranque de cólera> **4** DISPLAY : alarde *m,* llamarada *f* <a blaze of color : un derroche de color>
blazer [ˈbleɪzər] *n* : chaqueta *f* deportiva, blazer *m*
bleach[1] [ˈbliːʧ] *vt* : blanquear, decolorar
bleach[2] *n* : lejía *f,* blanqueador *m*
bleachers [ˈbliːʧərz] *ns & pl* : gradas *fpl,* tribuna *f* descubierta
bleak [ˈbliːk] *adj* **1** DESOLATE : inhóspito, sombrío, desolado **2** DEPRESSING : deprimente, triste, sombrío
bleakly [ˈbliːkli] *adv* : sombríamente
bleakness [ˈbliːknəs] *n* : lo inhóspito, lo sombrío
blear [ˈblɪr] *adj* : empañado, nublado
bleary [ˈblɪri] *adj* **1** : adormilado, fatigado **2** **bleary–eyed** : con los ojos nublados
bleat[1] [ˈbliːt] *vi* : balar
bleat[2] *n* : balido *m*
bleed [ˈbliːd] *v* **bled** [ˈblɛd]; **bleeding** *vi* **1** : sangrar **2** GRIEVE : sufrir, afligirse **3** EXUDE : exudar (dícese de una planta), correrse (dícese de los colo-

res) — *vt* **1** : sangrar (a una persona), purgar (frenos) **2 to bleed someone dry** : sacarle todo el dinero a alguien
blemish[1] [ˈblɛmɪʃ] *vt* : manchar, marcar
blemish[2] *n* : imperfección *f,* mancha *f,* marca *f*
blend[1] [ˈblɛnd] *vt* **1** MIX : mezclar **2** COMBINE : combinar, aunar
blend[2] *n* : mezcla *f,* combinación *f*
blender [ˈblɛndər] *n* : licuadora *f*
bless [ˈblɛs] *vt* **blessed** [ˈblɛst]; **blessing 1** CONSECRATE : bendecir, consagrar **2** : bendecir <may God bless you! : ¡que Dios te bendiga!> **3 to bless with** : dotar de **4 to bless oneself** : santiguarse
blessed [ˈblɛsəd] *or* **blest** [ˈblɛst] *adj* : bienaventurado, bendito, dichoso
blessedly [ˈblɛsədli] *adv* : felizmente, alegremente, afortunadamente
blessing [ˈblɛsɪŋ] *n* **1** : bendición *f* **2** APPROVAL : aprobación *f,* consentimiento *m*
blew → **blow**
blight[1] [ˈblaɪt] *vt* : arruinar, infestar
blight[2] *n* **1** : añublo *m* **2** PLAGUE : peste *f,* plaga *f* **3** DECAY : deterioro *m,* ruina *f*
blimp [ˈblɪmp] *n* : dirigible *m*
blind[1] [ˈblaɪnd] *vt* **1** : cegar, dejar ciego **2** DAZZLE : deslumbrar
blind[2] *adj* **1** SIGHTLESS : ciego **2** INSENSITIVE : ciego, insensible, sin razón **3** CLOSED : sin salida <blind alley : callejón sin salida>
blind[3] *n* **1** : persiana *f* (para una ventana) **2** COVER : escondite *m,* escondrijo *m*
blindfold[1] [ˈblaɪndˌfoːld] *vt* : vendar los ojos
blindfold[2] *n* : venda *f* (para los ojos)
blindly [ˈblaɪndli] *adv* : a ciegas, ciegamente
blindness [ˈblaɪndnəs] *n* : ceguera *f*
blink[1] [ˈblɪŋk] *vi* **1** WINK : pestañear, parpadear **2** : brillar intermitentemente
blink[2] *n* : pestañeo *m,* parpadeo *m*
blinker [ˈblɪŋkər] *n* : intermitente *m,* direccional *f*
bliss [ˈblɪs] *n* **1** HAPPINESS : dicha *f,* felicidad *f* absoluta **2** PARADISE : paraíso *m*
blissful [ˈblɪsfəl] *adj* : dichoso, feliz — **blissfully** *adv*
blister[1] [ˈblɪstər] *vi* : ampollarse
blister[2] *n* : ampolla *f* (en la piel o una superficie), burbuja *f* (en una superficie)
blithe [ˈblaɪθ, ˈblaɪð] *adj* **blither; blithest 1** CAREFREE : despreocupado **2** CHEERFUL : alegre, risueño — **blithely** *adv*
blitz[1] [ˈblɪts] *vt* **1** BOMBARD : bombardear **2** : atacar con rapidez
blitz[2] *n* **1** : bombardeo *m* aéreo **2** CAMPAIGN : ataque *m,* acometida *f*
blizzard [ˈblɪzərd] *n* : tormenta *f* de nieve, ventisca *f*
bloat [ˈbloːt] *vi* : hincharse, inflarse
blob [ˈblɑb] *n* : gota *f,* mancha *f,* borrón *m*
bloc [ˈblɑk] *n* : bloque *m*
block[1] [ˈblɑk] *vt* **1** OBSTRUCT : obstruir, bloquear **2** CLOG : atascar, atorar
block[2] *n* **1** PIECE : bloque *m* <building blocks : cubos de construcción> <auction block : plataforma de subastas> <starting block : taco de salida> **2** OBSTRUCTION : obstrucción *f,* bloqueo *m* **3** : cuadra *f,* manzana *f* (de edificios) <to go around the block : dar la vuelta a la cuadra> **4** BUILDING : edificio *m* (de apartamentos, oficinas, etc.) **5** GROUP, SERIES : serie *f,* grupo *m* <a block of tickets : una serie de entradas> **6 block and tackle** : aparejo *m* de poleas
blockade[1] [blɑˈkeɪd] *vt* **-aded; -ading** : bloquear
blockade[2] *n* : bloqueo *m*
blockage [ˈblɑkɪdʒ] *n* : bloqueo *m,* obstrucción *f*
blockhead [ˈblɑkˌhɛd] *n* : bruto *m,* -ta *f;* estúpido *m,* -da *f*
blond[1] *or* **blonde** [ˈblɑnd] *adj* : rubio, güero *Mex,* claro (dícese de la madera)
blond[2] *or* **blonde** *n* : rubio *m,* -bia *f;* güero *m,* -ra *f Mex*
blood [ˈblʌd] *n* **1** : sangre *f* **2** LIFEBLOOD : vida *f,* alma *f* **3** LINEAGE : linaje *m,* sangre *f*
blood bank *n* : banco *m* de sangre
bloodcurdling [ˈblʌdˌkərdəlɪŋ] *adj* : espeluznante, aterrador
blooded [ˈblʌdəd] *adj* : de sangre <cold-blooded animal : animal de sangre fría>
bloodhound [ˈblʌdˌhaʊnd] *n* : sabueso *m*
bloodless [ˈblʌdləs] *adj* **1** : incruento, sin derramamiento de sangre **2** LIFELESS : desanimado, insípido, sin vida
bloodmobile [ˈblʌdmoˌbiːl] *n* : unidad *f* móvil para donantes de sangre
blood pressure *n* : tensión *f,* presión *f* (arterial)
bloodshed [ˈblʌdˌʃɛd] *n* : derramamiento *m* de sangre
bloodshot [ˈblʌdˌʃɑt] *adj* : inyectado de sangre
bloodstain [ˈblʌdˌsteɪn] *n* : mancha *f* de sangre
bloodstained [ˈblʌdˌsteɪnd] *adj* : manchado de sangre
bloodstream [ˈblʌdˌstriːm] *n* : torrente *m* sanguíneo, corriente *f* sanguínea
bloodsucker [ˈblʌdˌsʌkər] *n* : sanguijuela *f*
bloodthirsty [ˈblʌdˌθərsti] *adj* : sanguinario
blood vessel *n* : vaso *m* sanguíneo
bloody [ˈblʌdi] *adj* **bloodier; -est** : ensangrentado, sangriento

bloom[1] [ˈbluːm] *vi* **1** FLOWER : florecer **2** MATURE : madurar

bloom[2] *n* **1** FLOWER : flor *f* <to be in bloom : estar en flor> **2** FLOWERING : floración *f* <in full bloom : en plena floración> **3** : rubor *m* (de la tez) <in the bloom of youth : en plena juventud, en la flor de la vida>

bloomers [ˈbluːmərz] *npl* : bombachos *mpl*

blooper [ˈbluːpər] *n* : metedura *f* de pata *fam*

blossom[1] [ˈblɑsəm] *vi* : florecer, dar flor

blossom[2] *n* : flor *f*

blot[1] [ˈblɑt] *vt* **blotted; blotting 1** SPOT : emborronar, borronear **2** DRY : secar

blot[2] *n* **1** STAIN : mancha *f,* borrón *m* **2** BLEMISH : mancha *f,* tacha *f*

blotch[1] [ˈblɑtʃ] *vt* : emborronar, borronear

blotch[2] *n* : mancha *f,* borrón *m*

blotchy [ˈblɑtʃi] *adj* **blotchier; -est** : lleno de manchas

blotter [ˈblɑt̬ər] *n* : hoja *f* de papel secante, secante *m*

blouse [ˈblaʊs, ˈblaʊz] *n* : blusa *f*

blow[1] [ˈbloː] *v* **blew** [ˈbluː]; **blown** [ˈbloːn]; **blowing** *vi* **1** : soplar, volar <the wind is blowing hard : el viento está soplando con fuerza> <it blew out the door : voló por la puerta> <the window blew shut : se cerró la ventana> **2** SOUND : sonar <the whistle blew : sonó el silbato> **3 to blow out** : fundirse (dícese de un fusible eléctrico), reventarse (dícese de una llanta) — *vt* **1** : soplar, echar <to blow smoke : echar humo> **2** SOUND : tocar, sonar **3** SHAPE : soplar, dar forma a <to blow glass : soplar vidrio> **4** BUNGLE : echar a perder

blow[2] *n* **1** PUFF : soplo *m,* soplido *m* **2** GALE : vendaval *f* **3** HIT, STROKE : golpe *m* **4** CALAMITY : golpe *m,* desastre *m* **5 to come to blows** : llegar a las manos

blower [ˈbloːər] *n* FAN : ventilador *m*

blowout [ˈbloːˌaʊt] *n* : reventón *m*

blowtorch [ˈbloːˌtɔrtʃ] *n* : soplete *m*

blow up *vi* EXPLODE : estallar, hacer explosión — *vt* BLAST : volar, hacer volar

blubber[1] [ˈblʌbər] *vi* : lloriquear

blubber[2] *n* : esperma *f* de ballena

bludgeon [ˈblʌdʒən] *vt* : aporrear

blue[1] [ˈbluː] *adj* **bluer; bluest 1** : azul **2** MELANCHOLY : melancólico, triste

blue[2] *n* : azul *m*

blueberry [ˈbluːˌbɛri] *n, pl* **-ries** : arándano *m*

bluebird [ˈbluːˌbərd] *n* : azulejo *m*

blue cheese *n* : queso *m* azul

blueprint [ˈbluːˌprɪnt] *n* **1** : plano *m,* proyecto *m,* cianotipo *m* **2** PLAN : anteproyecto *m,* programa *m*

blues [ˈbluːz] *npl* **1** DEPRESSION : depresión *f,* melancolía *f* **2** : blues *m* <to sing the blues : cantar blues>

bluff[1] [ˈblʌf] *vi* : hacer un farol, blofear *Col, Mex*

bluff[2] *adj* **1** STEEP : escarpado **2** FRANK : campechano, franco, directo

bluff[3] *n* **1** : farol *m,* blof *m Col, Mex* **2** CLIFF : acantilado *m,* risco *m*

bluffer [ˈblʌfər] *n* : farolero *m,* -ra *f fam;* blofeador *m,* -dora *f Col, Mex*

bluing *or* **blueing** [ˈbluːɪŋ] *n* : añil *m,* azulete *m*

bluish [ˈbluːɪʃ] *adj* : azulado

blunder[1] [ˈblʌndər] *vi* **1** STUMBLE : tropezar, dar traspiés **2** ERR : cometer un error, tropezar, meter la pata *fam*

blunder[2] *n* : error *m,* fallo *m* garrafal, metedura *f* de pata *fam*

blunderbuss [ˈblʌndərˌbʌs] *n* : trabuco *m*

blunt[1] [ˈblʌnt] *vt* : despuntar (aguja o lápiz), desafilar (cuchillo o tijeras), suavizar (crítica)

blunt[2] *adj* **1** DULL : desafilado, despuntado **2** DIRECT : directo, franco, categórico

bluntly [ˈblʌntli] *adv* : sin rodeos, francamente, bruscamente

bluntness [ˈblʌntnəs] *n* **1** DULLNESS : falta *f* de filo, embotadura *f* **2** FRANKNESS : franqueza *f*

blur[1] [ˈblər] *vt* **blurred; blurring** : desdibujar, hacer borroso

blur[2] *n* **1** SMEAR : mancha *f,* borrón *m* **2** : aspecto *m* borroso <everything was just a blur : todo se volvió borroso>

blurb [ˈblərb] *n* : propaganda *f,* nota *f* publicitaria

blurt [ˈblərt] *vt* : espetar, decir impulsivamente

blush[1] [ˈblʌʃ] *vi* : ruborizarse, sonrojarse, hacerse colorado

blush[2] *n* : rubor *m,* sonrojo *m*

bluster[1] [ˈblʌstər] *vi* **1** BLOW : soplar con fuerza **2** BOAST : fanfarronear, echar bravatas

bluster[2] *n* : fanfarronada *f,* bravata *f*

blustery [ˈblʌstəri] *adj* : borrascoso, tempestuoso

boa [ˈboːə] *n* : boa *f*

boar [ˈbor] *n* : cerdo *m* macho, verraco *m*

board[1] [ˈbord] *vt* **1** : embarcarse en, subir a bordo de (una nave o un avión), subir a (un tren o carro) **2** LODGE : hospedar, dar hospedaje con comidas a **3 to board up** : cerrar con tablas

board[2] *n* **1** PLANK : tabla *f,* tablón *m* **2** : tablero *m* <chessboard : tablero de ajedrez> **3** MEALS : comida *f* <board and lodging : comida y alojamiento> **4** COMMITTEE, COUNCIL : junta *f,* consejo *m*

boarder [ˈbordər] *n* LODGER : huésped *m,* -peda *f*

boardinghouse [ˈbordɪŋˌhaʊs] *n* : casa *f* de huéspedes

boarding school *n* : internado *m*

boardwalk [ˈbord͵wɔk] *n* : paseo *m* marítimo entablado
boast[1] [ˈboːst] *vi* : alardear, presumir, jactarse
boast[2] *n* : jactancia *f,* alarde *m*
boaster [ˈboːstər] *n* : presumido *m,* -da *f;* fanfarrón *m,* -rrona *f fam*
boastful [ˈboːstfəl] *adj* : jactancioso, fanfarrón *fam*
boastfully [ˈboːstfəli] *adv* : de manera jactanciosa
boat[1] [ˈboːt] *vt* : transportar en barco, poner a bordo
boat[2] *n* : barco *m,* embarcación *f,* bote *m,* barca *f*
boatman [ˈboːtmən] *n, pl* **-men** [-mən, -͵mɛn] : barquero *m*
boatswain [ˈboːsən] *n* : contramaestre *m*
bob[1] [ˈbɑb] *v* **bobbed; bobbing** *vi* **1** : balancearse, mecerse <to bob up and down : subir y bajar> **2** *or* **to bob up** APPEAR : presentarse, surgir — *vt* **1** : inclinar (la cabeza o el cuerpo) **2** CUT : cortar, recortar <she bobbed her hair : se cortó el pelo>
bob[2] *n* **1** : inclinación *f* (de la cabeza, del cuerpo), sacudida *f* **2** FLOAT : flotador *m,* corcho *m* (de pesca) **3** : pelo *m* corto
bobbin [ˈbɑbən] *n* : bobina *f,* carrete *m*
bobby pin [ˈbɑbi͵pɪn] *n* : horquilla *f*
bobcat [ˈbɑb͵kæt] *n* : lince *m* rojo
bobolink [ˈbɑbə͵lɪŋk] *n* : tordo *m* arrocero
bobsled [ˈbɑb͵slɛd] *n* : bobsleigh *m*
bobwhite [ˈbɑbˈhwaɪt] *n* : codorniz *m* (del Nuevo Mundo)
bode[1] [ˈboːd] *v* **boded; boding** *vt* : presagiar, augurar — *vi* **to bode well** : ser de buen agüero
bode[2] → **bide**
bodice [ˈbɑdəs] *n* : corpiño *m*
bodied [ˈbɑdid] *adj* : de cuerpo <lean-bodied : de cuerpo delgado> <able-bodied : no discapacitado>
bodiless [ˈbɑdiləs, ˈbɑdələs] *adj* : incorpóreo
bodily[1] [ˈbɑdəli] *adv* : en peso <to lift someone bodily : levantar a alguien en peso>
bodily[2] *adj* : corporal, del cuerpo <bodily harm : daños corporales>
body [ˈbɑdi] *n, pl* **bodies 1** : cuerpo *m,* organismo *m* **2** CORPSE : cadáver *m* **3** PERSON : persona *f,* ser *m* humano **4** : nave *f* (de una iglesia), carrocería (de un automóvil), fuselaje *m* (de un avión), casco *m* (de una nave) **5** COLLECTION, MASS : conjunto *m,* grupo *m,* masa *f* <in a body : todos juntos, en masa> **6** ORGANIZATION : organismo *m,* organización *f*
bodyguard [ˈbɑdi͵gɑrd] *n* : guardaespaldas *mf*
bog[1] [ˈbɑg, ˈbɔg] *vt* **bogged; bogging** : empantanar, inundar <to get bogged down : empantanarse>
bog[2] *n* : lodazal *m,* ciénaga *f,* cenagal *m*
bogey [ˈbʊgi, ˈboː-] *n, pl* **-geys** : terror *m,* coco *m fam*
boggle [ˈbɑgəl] *vi* **-gled; -gling** : quedarse atónito, quedarse pasmado <the mind boggles! : ¡es increíble!>
boggy [ˈbɑgi, ˈbɔ-] *adj* **boggier; -est** : cenagoso
bogus [ˈboːgəs] *adj* : falso, fingido, falaz
bohemian [boːˈhiːmiən] *n* : bohemio *m,* -mia *f* — **bohemian** *adj*
boil[1] [ˈbɔɪl] *vi* **1** : hervir **2 to make one's blood boil** : hervirle la sangre a uno — *vt* **1** : hervir, hacer hervir <to boil water : hervir agua> **2** : cocer, hervir <to boil potatoes : cocer papas>
boil[2] *n* **1** BOILING : hervor *m* **2** : furúnculo *m,* divieso *m* (in medicine)
boiler [ˈbɔɪlər] *n* : caldera *f*
boisterous [ˈbɔɪstərəs] *adj* : bullicioso, escandaloso — **boisterously** *adv*
bold [ˈboːld] *adj* **1** COURAGEOUS : valiente **2** INSOLENT : insolente, descarado **3** DARING : atrevido, audaz — **boldly** *adv*
boldface [ˈboːld͵feɪs] *n or* **boldface type** : negrita *f*
boldness [ˈboːldnəs] *n* **1** COURAGE : valor *m,* coraje *m* **2** INSOLENCE : atrevimiento *m,* insolencia *f,* descaro *m* **3** DARING : audacia *f*
bolero [bəˈlɛro] *n, pl* **-ros** : bolero *m*
Bolivian [bəˈlɪviən] *n* : boliviano *m,* -na *f* — **Bolivian** *adj*
boll [ˈboːl] *n* : cápsula *f* (del algodón)
boll weevil *n* : gorgojo *m* del algodón
bologna [bəˈloːni] *n* : salchicha *f* ahumada
bolster[1] [ˈboːlstər] *vt* **-stered; -stering** : reforzar, reafirmar <to bolster morale : levantar la moral>
bolster[2] *n* : cabezal *m,* almohadón *m*
bolt[1] [ˈboːlt] *vt* **1** atornillar, sujetar con pernos <bolted to the floor : sujetado con pernos al suelo> **2** : cerrar con pestillo, echar el cerrojo a <to bolt the door : echar el cerrojo a la puerta> **3 to bolt down** : engullir <she bolted down her dinner : engulló su comida> — *vi* : echar a correr, salir corriendo <he bolted from the room : salió corriendo de la sala>
bolt[2] *n* **1** LATCH : pestillo *m,* cerrojo *m* **2** : tornillo *m,* perno *m* <nuts and bolts : tuercas y tornillos> **3** : rollo *m* <a bolt of cloth : un rollo de tela> **4 lightning bolt** : relámpago *m,* rayo *m*
bomb[1] [ˈbɑm] *vt* : bombardear
bomb[2] *n* : bomba *f*
bombard [bɑmˈbɑrd, bəm-] *vt* : bombardear
bombardier [͵bɑmbəˈdɪr] *n* : bombardero *m,* -ra *f*
bombardment [bɑmˈbɑrdmənt] *n* : bombardeo *m*

bombast [ˈbɑmˌbæst] *n* : grandilocuencia *f,* ampulosidad *f*
bombastic [bɑmˈbæstɪk] *adj* : grandilocuente, ampuloso, bombástico
bomber [ˈbɑmər] *n* : bombardero *m*
bombproof [ˈbɑmˌpruːf] *adj* : a prueba de bombas
bombshell [ˈbɑmˌʃɛl] *n* : bomba *f* <a political bombshell : una bomba política>
bona fide [ˈboːnəˌfaɪd, ˈbɑ-; ˌboːnəˈfaɪdi] *adj* **1** : de buena fe <a bona fide offer : una oferta de buena fe> **2** GENUINE : genuino, auténtico
bonanza [bəˈnænzə] *n* : bonanza *f*
bonbon [ˈbɑnˌbɑn] *n* : bombón *m*
bond[1] [ˈbɑnd] *vt* **1** INSURE : dar fianza a, asegurar **2** STICK : adherir, pegar — *vi* : adherirse, pegarse
bond[2] *n* **1** LINK, TIE : vínculo *m,* lazo *m* **2** BAIL : fianza *f,* caución *f* **3** : bono *m* <stocks and bonds : acciones y bonos> **4 bonds** *npl* FETTERS : cadenas *fpl*
bondage [ˈbɑndɪdʒ] *n* : esclavitud *f*
bondholder [ˈbɑndˌhoːldər] *n* : tenedor *m,* -dora *f* de bonos
bondsman [ˈbɑndzmən] *n, pl* **-men** [-mən, -ˌmɛn] **1** SLAVE : esclavo *m* **2** SURETY : fiador *m,* -dora *f*
bone[1] [ˈboːn] *vt* **boned; boning** : deshuesar
bone[2] *n* : hueso *m*
boneless [ˈboːnləs] *adj* : sin huesos, sin espinas
boner [ˈboːnər] *n* : metedura *f* de pata, metida *f* de pata
bonfire [ˈbɑnˌfaɪr] *n* : hoguera *f,* fogata *f,* fogón *m*
bonito [bəˈniːt̬o] *n, pl* **-tos** *or* **-to** : bonito *m*
bonnet [ˈbɑnət] *n* : sombrero *m* (de mujer), gorra *f* (de niño)
bonus [ˈboːnəs] *n* **1** : prima *f,* bonificación *f* (pagado al empleado) **2** ADVANTAGE, BENEFIT : beneficio *m,* provecho *m*
bony [ˈboːni] *adj* **bonier; -est** : huesudo, osudo
boo[1] [ˈbuː] *vt* : abuchear
boo[2] *n, pl* **boos** : abucheo *m*
booby [ˈbuːbi] *n, pl* **-bies** : bobo *m,* -ba *f;* tonto *m,* -ta *f*
book[1] [ˈbʊk] *vt* : reservar <to book a flight : reservar un vuelo>
book[2] *n* **1** : libro *m* **2 the Book** : la Biblia **3 by the book** : según las reglas
bookcase [ˈbʊkˌkeɪs] *n* : estantería *f,* librero *m Mex*
bookend [ˈbʊkˌɛnd] *n* : sujetalibros *m*
bookie [ˈbʊki] → **bookmaker**
bookish [ˈbʊkɪʃ] *adj* : libresco
bookkeeper [ˈbʊkˌkiːpər] *n* : tenedor *m,* -dora *f* de libros; contable *mf Spain*
bookkeeping [ˈbʊkˌkiːpɪŋ] *n* : contabilidad *f,* teneduría *f* de libros
booklet [ˈbʊklət] *n* : folleto *m*
bookmaker [ˈbʊkˌmeɪkər] *n* : corredor *m,* -dora *f* de apuestas
bookmark [ˈbʊkˌmɑrk] *n* : señalador *m* de libros, marcador *m* de libros
bookseller [ˈbʊkˌsɛlər] *n* : librero *m,* -ra *f*
bookshelf [ˈbʊkˌʃɛlf] *n, pl* **-shelves 1** : estante *m* **2 bookshelves** *npl* : estantería *f*
bookstore [ˈbʊkˌstor] *n* : librería *f*
bookworm [ˈbʊkˌwərm] *n* : ratón *m* de biblioteca *fam*
boom[1] [ˈbuːm] *vi* **1** THUNDER : tronar, resonar **2** FLOURISH, PROSPER : estar en auge, prosperar
boom[2] *n* **1** BOOMING : bramido *m,* estruendo *m* **2** FLOURISHING : auge *m* <population boom : auge de población>
boomerang [ˈbuːməˌræŋ] *n* : bumerán *m*
boon[1] [ˈbuːn] *adj* **boon companion** : amigo *m,* -ga *f* del alma
boon[2] *n* : ayuda *f,* beneficio *m,* adelanto *m*
boondocks [ˈbuːnˌdɑks] *npl* : area *f* rural remota, región *f* alejada
boor [ˈbʊr] *n* : grosero *m,* -ra *f*
boorish [ˈbʊrɪʃ] *adj* : grosero
boost[1] [ˈbuːst] *vt* **1** LIFT : levantar, alzar **2** INCREASE : aumentar, incrementar **3** PROMOTE : promover, fomentar, hacer publicidad por
boost[2] *n* **1** THRUST : impulso *m,* empujón *m* **2** ENCOURAGEMENT : estímulo *m,* aliento *m* **3** INCREASE : aumento *m,* incremento *m*
booster [ˈbuːstər] *n* **1** SUPPORTER : partidario *m,* -ria *f* **2 booster rocket** : cohete *m* propulsor **3 booster shot** : vacuna *f* de refuerzo
boot[1] [ˈbuːt] *vt* KICK : dar una patada a, patear
boot[2] *n* **1** : bota *f,* botín *m* **2** KICK : puntapié *m,* patada *f*
bootee *or* **bootie** [ˈbuːt̬i] *n* : botita *f,* botín *m*
booth [ˈbuːθ] *n, pl* **booths** [ˈbuːðz, ˈbuːθs] : cabina *f* (de teléfono, de votar), caseta *f* (de información), barraca *f* (a una feria)
bootlegger [ˈbuːtˌlɛgər] *n* : contrabandista *mf* del alcohol
booty [ˈbuːt̬i] *n, pl* **-ties** : botín *m*
booze [ˈbuːz] *n* : trago *m,* bebida *f* (alcohólica)
borax [ˈbɔrˌæks] *n* : bórax *m*
border[1] [ˈbɔrdər] *vt* **1** EDGE : ribetear, bordear **2** BOUND : limitar con, lindar con — *vi* VERGE : rayar, lindar <that borders on absurdity : eso raya en el absurdo>
border[2] *n* **1** EDGE : borde *m,* orilla *f* **2** TRIM : ribete *m* **3** FRONTIER : frontera *f*
bore[1] [ˈbor] *vt* **bored; boring 1** PIERCE : taladrar, perforar <to bore metals : taladrar metales> **2** OPEN : hacer, abrir <to bore a tunnel : abrir un túnel> **3** WEARY : aburrir

bore[2] → **bear**[1]
bore[3] *n* **1** : pesado *m,* -da *f* (persona aburrida) **2** TEDIOUSNESS : pesadez *f,* lo aburrido **3** DIAMETER : calibre *m*
boredom [ˈbordəm] *n* : aburrimiento *m*
boring [ˈborɪŋ] *adj* : aburrido, pesado
born [ˈbɔrn] *adj* **1** : nacido **2** : nato <she's a born singer : es una cantante nata> <he's a born leader : nació para mandar>
borne → **bear**[1]
boron [ˈborˌɑn] *n* : boro *m*
borough [ˈbəro] *n* : distrito *m* municipal
borrow [ˈbɑro] *vt* **1** : pedir prestado, tomar prestado **2** APPROPRIATE : apropiarse de, adoptar
Bosnian [ˈbɑzniən, ˈbɔz-] *n* : bosnio *m,* -nia *f* — **Bosnian** *adj*
bosom[1] [ˈbʊzəm, ˈbuː-] *adj* : íntimo
bosom[2] *n* **1** CHEST : pecho *m* **2** BREAST : pecho *m,* seno *m* **3** CLOSENESS : seno *m* <in the bosom of her family : en el seno de su familia>
bosomed [ˈbʊzəmd, ˈbuː-] *adj* : con busto <big-bosomed : con mucho busto>
boss[1] [ˈbɔs] *vt* **1** SUPERVISE : dirigir, supervisar **2 to boss around** : mandonear *fam,* mangonear *fam*
boss[2] *n* : jefe *m,* -fa *f;* patrón *m,* -trona *f*
bossy [ˈbɔsi] *adj* **bossier; -est** : mandón *fam,* autoritario, dominante
botanist [ˈbɑtənɪst] *n* : botánico *m,* -ca *f*
botany [ˈbɑtəni] *n* : botánica *f* — **botanical** [bəˈtænɪkəl] *adj*
botch[1] [ˈbɑtʃ] *vt* : hacer una chapuza de, estropear
botch[2] *n* : chapuza *f*
both[1] [ˈboːθ] *adj* : ambos, los dos, las dos <both books : ambos libros, los dos libros>
both[2] *conj* : tanto como <both Ana and her mother are tall : tanto Ana como su madre son altas>
both[3] *pron* : ambos *m,* -bas *f;* los dos, las dos
bother[1] [ˈbɑðər] *vt* **1** IRK : preocupar <nothing's bothering me : nada me preocupa> <what's bothering him? : ¿qué le pasa?> **2** PESTER : molestar, fastidiar — *vi* **to bother to** : molestarse en, tomar la molestia de
bother[2] *n* **1** TROUBLE : molestia *f,* problemas *mpl* **2** ANNOYANCE : molestia *f,* fastidio *m*
bothersome [ˈbɑðərsəm] *adj* : molesto, fastidioso
bottle[1] [ˈbɑtəl] *vt* **bottled; bottling** : embotellar, envasar
bottle[2] *n* : botella *f,* frasco *m*
bottleneck [ˈbɑtəlˌnɛk] *n* **1** : cuello *m* de botello (en un camino) **2** : embotellamiento *m,* atasco *m* (de tráfico) **3** OBSTACLE : obstáculo *m*
bottom[1] [ˈbɑt̬əm] *adj* : más bajo, inferior, de abajo
bottom[2] *n* **1** : fondo *m* (de una caja, de una taza, del mar), pie *m* (de una escalera, una página, una montaña), asiento *m* (de una silla), parte *f* de abajo (de una pila) **2** CAUSE : origen *m,* causa *f* <to get to the bottom of : llegar al fondo de> **3** BUTTOCKS : trasero *m,* nalgas *fpl*
bottomless [ˈbɑt̬əmləs] *adj* : sin fondo, sin límites
botulism [ˈbɑtʃəˌlɪzəm] *n* : botulismo *m*
boudoir [bəˈdwɑr, bʊ-; ˈbuːˌ-, ˈbʊ-] *n* : tocador *m*
bough [ˈbaʊ] *n* : rama *f*
bought → **buy**[1]
bouillon [ˈbuːˌjɑn; ˈbʊlˌjɑn, -jən] *n* : caldo *m*
boulder [ˈboːldər] *n* : canto *m* rodado, roca *f* grande
boulevard [ˈbʊləˌvɑrd, ˈbuː-] *n* : bulevar *m,* boulevard *m*
bounce[1] [ˈbaʊnts] *v* **bounced; bouncing** *vt* : hacer rebotar — *vi* : rebotar
bounce[2] *n* : rebote *m*
bouncy [ˈbaʊntsi] *adj* **bouncier; -est 1** LIVELY : vivo, exuberante, animado **2** RESILIENT : elástico, flexible **3** : que rebota (dícese de una pelota)
bound[1] [ˈbaʊnd] *vt* : delimitar, rodear — *vi* LEAP : saltar, dar brincos
bound[2] *adj* **1** OBLIGED : obligado **2** : encuadernado, empastado <a book bound in leather : un libro encuadernado en cuero> **3** DETERMINED : decidido, empeñado **4 to be bound to** : ser seguro que, tener que, no caber duda que <it was bound to happen : tenía que suceder> **5 bound for** : con rumbo a <bound for Chicago : con rumbo a Chicago> <to be homeward bound : ir camino a casa>
bound[3] *n* **1** LIMIT : límite *m* **2** LEAP : salto *m,* brinco *m*
boundary [ˈbaʊndri, -dəri] *n, pl* **-aries** : límite *m,* línea *f* divisoria, linde *mf*
boundless [ˈbaʊndləs] *adj* : sin límites, infinito
bounteous [ˈbaʊntiəs] *adj* **1** GENEROUS : generoso **2** ABUNDANT : copioso, abundante — **bounteously** *adv*
bountiful [ˈbaʊntɪfəl] *adj* **1** GENEROUS, LIBERAL : munificente, pródigo, generoso **2** ABUNDANT : copioso, abundante
bounty [ˈbaʊnti] *n, pl* **-ties 1** GENEROSITY : generosidad *f,* munificiencia *f* **2** REWARD : recompensa *f*
bouquet [boːˈkeɪ, buː-] *n* **1** : ramo *m,* ramillete *m* **2** FRAGRANCE : bouquet *m,* aroma *m*
bourbon [ˈbərbən, ˈbʊr-] *n* : bourbon *m,* whiskey *m* americano
bourgeois[1] [ˈbʊrʒˌwɑ, bʊrʒˈwɑ] *adj* : burgués
bourgeois[2] *n* : burgués *m,* -guesa *f*
bourgeoisie [ˌbʊrʒˌwɑˈzi] *n* : burguesía *f*

bout [ˈbaʊt] *n* **1 :** encuentro *m,* combate *m* (en deportes) **2** ATTACK **:** ataque *m* (de una enfermedad) **3** PERIOD, SPELL **:** período *m* (de actividad)

boutique [buːˈtiːk] *n* **:** boutique *f*

bovine[1] [ˈboːˌvaɪn, -ˌviːn] *adj* **:** bovino, vacuno

bovine[2] *n* **:** bovino *m*

bow[1] [ˈbaʊ] *vi* **1 :** hacer una reverencia, inclinarse **2** SUBMIT **:** ceder, resignarse, someterse — *vt* **1** LOWER **:** inclinar, bajar **2** BEND **:** doblar

bow[2] [ˈbaʊː] *n* **1** BOWING **:** reverencia *f,* inclinación *f* **2 :** proa *f* (de un barco)

bow[3] [ˈboː] *vi* CURVE **:** arquearse, doblarse

bow[4] [ˈboː] *n* **1** ARCH, CURVE **:** arco *m,* curva *f* **2 :** arco *m* (arma o vara para tocar varios instrumentos de música) **3 :** lazo *m,* moño *m* <to tie a bow : hacer un moño>

bowels [ˈbaʊəls] *npl* **1** INTESTINES **:** intestinos *mpl* **2 :** entrañas *fpl* <in the bowels of the earth : en las entrañas de la tierra>

bower [ˈbaʊər] *n* **:** enramada *f*

bowl[1] [ˈboːl] *vi* **:** jugar a los bolos

bowl[2] *n* **:** tazón *m,* cuenco *m*

bowler [ˈboːlər] *n* **:** jugador *m,* -dora *f* de bolos

bowling [ˈboːlɪŋ] *n* **:** bolos *mpl*

box[1] [ˈbɑks] *vt* **1** PACK **:** empaquetar, embalar, encajonar **2** SLAP **:** bofetear, cachetear — *vi* **:** boxear

box[2] *n* **1** CONTAINER **:** caja *f,* cajón *m* **2** COMPARTMENT **:** compartimento *m,* palco *m* (en el teatro) **3** SLAP **:** bofetada *f,* cachetada *f* **4 :** boj *m* (planta)

boxcar [ˈbɑksˌkɑr] *n* **:** vagón *m* de carga, furgón *m*

boxer [ˈbɑksər] *n* **:** boxeador *m,* -dora *f*

boxing [ˈbɑksɪŋ] *n* **:** boxeo *m*

box office *n* **:** taquilla *f,* boletería *f*

boxwood [ˈbɑksˌwʊd] *n* **:** boj *m*

boy [ˈbɔɪ] *n* **:** niño *m,* chico *m*

boycott[1] [ˈbɔɪˌkɑt] *vt* **:** boicotear

boycott[2] *n* **:** boicot *m*

boyfriend [ˈbɔɪˌfrɛnd] *n* **1** FRIEND **:** amigo *m* **2** SWEETHEART **:** novio *m*

boyhood [ˈbɔɪˌhʊd] *n* **:** niñez *f*

boyish [ˈbɔɪɪʃ] *adj* **:** de niño, juvenil

bra [ˈbrɑ] → **brassiere**

brace[1] [ˈbreɪs] *v* **braced; bracing** *vt* **1** PROP UP, SUPPORT **:** apuntalar, apoyar, sostener **2** INVIGORATE **:** vigorizar **3** REINFORCE **:** reforzar — *vi* **to brace oneself** PREPARE **:** prepararse

brace[2] *n* **1 :** berbiquí *m* <brace and bit : berbiquí y barrena> **2** CLAMP, REINFORCEMENT **:** abrazadera *f,* refuerzo *m* **3 :** llave *f* (signo de puntuación) **4 braces** *npl* **:** aparatos *mpl* (de ortodoncia), frenos *mpl Mex*

bracelet [ˈbreɪslət] *n* **:** brazalete *m,* pulsera *f*

bracken [ˈbrækən] *n* **:** helecho *m*

bracket[1] [ˈbrækət] *vt* **1** SUPPORT **:** asegurar, apuntalar **2 :** poner entre corchetes **3** CATEGORIZE, GROUP **:** catalogar, agrupar

bracket[2] *n* **1** SUPPORT **:** soporte *m* **2 :** corchete *m* (marca de puntuación) **3** CATEGORY, CLASS **:** clase *f,* categoría *f*

brackish [ˈbrækɪʃ] *adj* **:** salobre

brad [ˈbræd] *n* **:** clavo *m* con cabeza pequeña, clavito *m*

brag[1] [ˈbræg] *vi* **bragged; bragging :** alardear, fanfarronear, jactarse

brag[2] *n* **:** alarde *m,* jactancia *f,* fanfarronada *f*

braggart [ˈbrægərt] *n* **:** fanfarrón *m,* -rrona *f fam;* jactancioso *m,* -sa *f*

braid[1] [ˈbreɪd] *vt* **:** trenzar

braid[2] *n* **:** trenza *f*

braille [ˈbreɪl] *n* **:** braille *m*

brain[1] [ˈbreɪn] *vt* **:** romper la crisma a, aplastar el cráneo a

brain[2] *n* **1 :** cerebro *m* **2 brains** *npl* INTELLECT **:** inteligencia *f,* sesos *mpl*

brainless [ˈbreɪnləs] *adj* **:** estúpido, tonto

brainstorm [ˈbreɪnˌstɔrm] *n* **:** idea *f* brillante, idea *f* genial

brainy [ˈbreɪni] *adj* **brainier; -est :** inteligente, listo

braise [ˈbreɪz] *vt* **braised; braising :** cocer a fuego lento, estofar

brake[1] [ˈbreɪk] *v* **braked; braking :** frenar

brake[2] *n* **:** freno *m*

bramble [ˈbræmbəl] *n* **:** zarza *f,* zarzamora *f*

bran [ˈbræn] *n* **:** salvado *m*

branch[1] [ˈbræntʃ] *vi* **1 :** echar ramas (dícese de una planta) **2** DIVERGE **:** ramificarse, separarse

branch[2] *n* **1 :** rama *f* (de una planta) **2** EXTENSION **:** ramal *m* (de un camino, un ferrocarril, un río), rama *f* (de una familia o un campo de estudiar), sucursal *f* (de una empresa), agencia *f* (del gobierno)

brand[1] [ˈbrænd] *vt* **1 :** marcar (ganado) **2** LABEL **:** tachar, tildar <they branded him as a liar : lo tacharon de mentiroso>

brand[2] *n* **1 :** marca *f* (de ganado) **2** STIGMA **:** estigma *m* **3** MAKE **:** marca *f* <brand name : marca de fábrica>

brandish [ˈbrændɪʃ] *vt* **:** blandir

brand–new [ˈbrændˈnuː, -ˈnjuː] *adj* **:** nuevo, flamante

brandy [ˈbrændi] *n, pl* **-dies :** brandy *m*

brash [ˈbræʃ] *adj* **1** IMPULSIVE **:** impulsivo, impetuoso **2** BRAZEN **:** excesivamente desenvuelto, descarado

brass [ˈbræs] *n* **1 :** latón *m* **2** GALL, NERVE **:** descaro *m,* cara *f fam* **3** OFFICERS **:** mandamases *mpl fam*

brassiere [brəˈzɪr, brɑ-] *n* **:** sostén *m,* brasier *m Col, Mex*

brassy [ˈbræsi] *adj* **brassier; -est :** dorado

brat [ˈbræt] *n* **:** mocoso *m,* -sa *f;* niño *m* mimado, niña *f* mimada

bravado [brəˈvɑdo] *n, pl* **-does** *or* **-dos** : bravuconadas *fpl*, bravatas *fpl*

brave[1] [ˈbreɪv] *vt* **braved; braving** : afrontar, hacer frente a

brave[2] *adj* **braver; bravest** : valiente, valeroso — **bravely** *adv*

brave[3] *n* : guerrero *m* indio

bravery [ˈbreɪvəri] *n* : valor *m*, valentía *f*

bravo [ˈbrɑˌvoː] *n, pl* **-vos** : bravo *m*

brawl[1] [ˈbrɔl] *vi* : pelearse, pegarse

brawl[2] *n* : pelea *f*, reyerta *f*

brawn [ˈbrɔn] *n* : fuerza *f* muscular

brawny [ˈbrɔni] *adj* **brawnier; -est** : musculoso

bray[1] [ˈbreɪ] *vi* : rebuznar

bray[2] *n* : rebuzno *m*

brazen [ˈbreɪzən] *adj* **1** : de latón **2** BOLD : descarado, directo

brazenly [ˈbreɪzənli] *adv* : descaradamente, insolentemente

brazenness [ˈbreɪzənnəs] *n* : descaro *m*, atrevimiento *m*

brazier [ˈbreɪʒər] *n* : brasero *m*

Brazilian [brəˈzɪljən] *n* : brasileño *m*, -ña *f* — **Brazilian** *adj*

Brazil nut [brəˈzɪlˌnʌt] *n* : nuez *f* de Brasil

breach[1] [ˈbriːtʃ] *vt* **1** PENETRATE : abrir una brecha en, penetrar **2** VIOLATE : infringir, violar

breach[2] *n* **1** VIOLATION : infracción *f*, violación *f* <breach of trust : abuso de confianza> **2** GAP, OPENING : brecha *f*

bread[1] [ˈbrɛd] *vt* : empanar

bread[2] *n* : pan *m*

breadth [ˈbrɛtθ] *n* : ancho *m*, anchura *f*

breadwinner [ˈbrɛdˌwɪnər] *n* : sostén *m* de la familia

break[1] [ˈbreɪk] *v* **broke** [ˈbroːk]; **broken** [ˈbroːkən]; **breaking** *vt* **1** SMASH : romper, quebrar **2** VIOLATE : infringir, violar, romper **3** SURPASS : batir, superar **4** CRUSH, RUIN : arruinar, deshacer, destrozar <to break one's spirit : quebrantar su espíritu> **5** : dar, comunicar <to break the news : dar las noticias> **6** INTERRUPT : cortar, interrumpir — *vi* **1** : romperse, quebrarse <my calculator broke : se me rompió la calculadora> **2** DISPERSE : dispersarse, despejarse **3** : estallar (dícese de una tormenta), romper (dícese del día) **4** CHANGE : cambiar (dícese del tiempo o de la voz) **5** DECREASE : bajar <my fever broke : me bajó la fiebre> **6** : divulgarse, revelarse <the news broke : la noticia se divulgó> **7 to break into** : forzar, abrir **8 to break out of** : escaparse de **9 to break through** : penetrar

break[2] *n* **1** : ruptura *f*, rotura *f*, fractura *f* (de un hueso), claro *m* (entre las nubes), cambio *m* (del tiempo) **2** CHANCE : oportunidad *f* <a lucky break : un golpe de suerte> **3** REST : descanso *m* <to take a break : tomar(se) un descanso>

breakable [ˈbreɪkəbəl] *adj* : quebradizo, frágil

breakage [ˈbreɪkɪdʒ] *n* **1** BREAKING : rotura *f* **2** DAMAGE : destrozos *mpl*, daños *mpl*

breakdown [ˈbreɪkˌdaʊn] *n* **1** : avería *f* (de máquinas), interrupción *f* (de comunicaciones), fracaso *m* (de negociaciones) **2** ANALYSIS : análisis *m*, desglose *m* **3** *or* **nervous breakdown** : crisis *f* nerviosa

break down *vi* **1** : estropearse, descomponerse <the machine broke down : la máquina se descompuso> **2** FAIL : fracasar **3** CRY : echarse a llorar — *vt* **1** DESTROY : derribar, echar abajo **2** OVERCOME : vencer (la resistencia), disipar (sospechas) **3** ANALYZE : analizar, descomponer

breaker [ˈbreɪkər] *n* **1** WAVE : ola *f* grande **2** : interruptor *m* automático (de electricidad)

breakfast[1] [ˈbrɛkfəst] *vi* : desayunar

breakfast[2] *n* : desayuno *m*

breakneck [ˈbreɪkˌnɛk] *adj* **at breakneck speed** : a una velocidad vertiginosa

break out *vi* **1** : salirse <she broke out in spots : le salieron granos> **2** ERUPT : estallar (dícese de una guerra, la violencia, etc.) **3** ESCAPE : fugarse, escaparse

break up *vt* **1** DIVIDE : dividir **2** : disolver (una muchedumbre, una pelea, etc.) — *vi* **1** BREAK : romperse **2** SEPARATE : deshacerse, separarse <I broke up with him : terminé con él>

breast [ˈbrɛst] *n* **1** : pecho *m*, seno *m* (de una mujer) **2** CHEST : pecho *m*

breastbone [ˈbrɛstˌboːn] *n* : esternón *m*

breast–feed [ˈbrɛstˌfiːd] *vt* **-fed** [-ˌfɛd]; **-feeding** : amamantar, darle de mamar (a un niño)

breath [ˈbrɛθ] *n* **1** BREATHING : aliento *m* <to hold one's breath : aguantar la respiración>**2** BREEZE : soplo *m* <a breath of fresh air : un soplo de aire freso>

breathe [ˈbriːð] *v* **breathed; breathing** *vi* **1** : respirar **2** LIVE : vivir, respirar — *vt* **1** : respirar, aspirar <to breathe fresh air : respirar el aire fresco> **2** UTTER : decir <I won't breathe a word of this : no diré nada de esto>

breathless [ˈbrɛθləs] *adj* : sin aliento, jadeante

breathlessly [ˈbrɛθləsli] *adv* : entrecortadamente, jadeando

breathlessness [ˈbrɛθləsnəs] *n* : dificultad *f* al respirar

breathtaking [ˈbrɛθˌteɪkɪŋ] *adj* IMPRESSIVE : impresionante, imponente

breeches [ˈbrɪtʃəz, ˈbriː-] *npl* : pantalones *mpl*, calzones *mpl*, bombachos *mpl*

breed[1] [ˈbriːd] *v* **bred** [ˈbrɛd]; **breeding** *vt* **1** : criar (animales) **2** ENGENDER

: engendrar, producir <familiarity breeds contempt : la confianza hace perder el respeto> **3** RAISE, REAR : criar, educar — *vi* REPRODUCE : reproducirse

breed[2] *n* **1** : variedad *f* (de plantas), raza *f* (de animales) **2** CLASS : clase *f,* tipo *m*

breeder ['bri:dər] *n* : criador *m,* -dora *f* (de animales); cultivador *m,* -dora *f* (de plantas)

breeze[1] ['bri:z] *vi* **breezed; breezing** : pasar con ligereza <to breeze in : entrar como si nada>

breeze[2] *n* : brisa *f,* soplo *m* (de aire)

breezy ['bri:zi] *adj* **breezier; -est 1** AIRY, WINDY : aireado, ventoso **2** LIVELY : animado, alegre **3** NONCHALANT : despreocupado

brethren → **brother**

brevity ['brɛvəti] *n, pl* **-ties** : brevedad *f,* concisión *f*

brew[1] ['bru:] *vt* **1** : fabricar, elaborar (cerveza) **2** FOMENT : tramar, maquinar, fomentar — *vi* **1** : fabricar cerveza **2** : amenazar <a storm is brewing : una tormenta amenaza>

brew[2] *n* **1** BEER : cerveza *f* **2** POTION : brebaje *m*

brewer ['bru:ər] *n* : cervecero *m,* -ra *f*

brewery ['bru:əri, 'brʊri] *n, pl* **-eries** : cervecería *f*

briar ['braɪər] → **brier**

bribe[1] ['braɪb] *vt* **bribed; bribing** : sobornar, cohechar, coimear *Arg, Chile, Peru*

bribe[2] *n* : soborno *m,* cohecho *m,* coima *f Arg, Chile, Peru,* mordida *f CA, Mex*

bribery ['braɪbəri] *n, pl* **-eries** : soborno *m,* cohecho *m,* coima *f,* mordida *f CA, Mex*

bric–a–brac ['brɪkə,bræk] *npl* : baratijas *fpl,* chucherías *fpl*

brick[1] ['brɪk] *vt* **to brick up** : tabicar, tapiar

brick[2] *n* : ladrillo *m*

bricklayer ['brɪk,leɪər] *n* : albañil *mf*

bricklaying ['brɪk,leɪɪŋ] *n* : albañilería *f*

bridal ['braɪdəl] *adj* : nupcial, de novia

bride ['braɪd] *n* : novia *f*

bridegroom ['braɪd,gru:m] *n* : novio *m*

bridesmaid ['braɪdz,meɪd] *n* : dama *f* de honor

bridge[1] ['brɪdʒ] *vt* **bridged; bridging 1** : tender un puente sobre **2 to bridge the gap** : salvar las diferencias

bridge[2] *n* **1** : puente *m* **2** : caballete *m* (de la nariz) **3** : puente *m* de mando (de un barco) **4** DENTURE : puente *m* (dental) **5** : bridge *m* (juego de naipes)

bridle[1] ['braɪdəl] *v* **-dled; -dling** *vt* **1** : embridar (un caballo) **2** RESTRAIN : refrenar, dominar, contener — *vi* **to bridle at** : molestarse por, picarse por

bridle[2] *n* : brida *f*

brief[1] ['bri:f] *vt* : dar órdenes a, instruir

brief[2] *adj* : breve, sucinto, conciso

brief[3] *n* : resumen *m,* sumario *m*

briefcase ['bri:f,keɪs] *n* : portafolio *m,* maletín *m*

briefly ['bri:fli] *adv* : brevemente, por poco tiempo <to speak briefly : discursar en pocas palabras>

brier ['braɪər] *n* **1** BRAMBLE : zarza *f,* rosal *m* silvestre **2** HEATH : brezo *m* veteado

brig ['brɪg] *n* **1** : bergantín *m* (barco) **2** : calabozo *m* (en un barco)

brigade [brɪ'geɪd] *n* : brigada *f*

brigadier general [,brɪgə'dɪr] *n* : general *m* de brigada

brigand ['brɪgənd] *n* : bandolero *m,* -ra *f;* forajido *m,* -da *f*

bright ['braɪt] *adj* **1** : brillante (dícese del sol, de los ojos), vivo (dícese de un color), claro, fuerte **2** CHEERFUL : alegre, animado <bright and early : muy temprano> **3** INTELLIGENT : listo, inteligente <a bright idea : una idea luminosa>

brighten ['braɪtən] *vt* **1** ILLUMINATE : iluminar **2** ENLIVEN : alegrar, animar — *vi* **1** : hacerse más brillante **2 to brighten up** : animarse, alegrarse, mejorar

brightly ['braɪtli] *adv* : vivamente, intensamente, alegremente

brightness ['braɪtnəs] *n* **1** LUMINOSITY : luminosidad *f,* brillantez *f,* resplandor *m,* brillo *m* **2** CHEERFULNESS : alegría *f,* ánimo *m*

brilliance ['brɪljən*t*s] *n* **1** BRIGHTNESS : resplandor *m,* fulgor *m,* brillo *m,* brillantez *f* **2** INTELLIGENCE : inteligencia *f,* brillantez *f*

brilliancy ['brɪljən*t*si] → **brilliance**

brilliant ['brɪljənt] *adj* : brillante

brilliantly ['brɪljəntli] *adv* : brillantemente, con brillantez

brim[1] ['brɪm] *vi* **brimmed; brimming 1** *or* **to brim over** : desbordarse, rebosar **2 to brim with tears** : llenarse de lágrimas

brim[2] *n* **1** : ala *f* (de un sombrero) **2** : borde *m* (de una taza o un vaso)

brimful ['brɪm'fʊl] *adj* : lleno hasta el borde, repleto, rebosante

brimless ['brɪmləs] *adj* : sin ala

brimstone ['brɪm,sto:n] *n* : azufre *m*

brindled ['brɪndəld] *adj* : manchado, pinto

brine ['braɪn] *n* **1** : salmuera *f,* escabeche *m* (para encurtir) **2** OCEAN : océano *m,* mar *m*

bring ['brɪŋ] *vt* **brought** ['brɔt]; **bringing 1** CARRY : traer <bring me some coffee : tráigame un café> **2** PRODUCE : traer, producir, conseguir <his efforts will bring him success : sus esfuerzos le conseguirán el éxito> **3** PERSUADE : convencer, persuadir **4** YIELD : rendir, alcanzar, venderse por <to bring a good price : alcanzar un

precio alto> **5 to bring to an end** : terminar (con) **6 to bring to light** : sacar a la luz

bring about *vt* : ocasionar, provocar, determinar

bring forth *vt* PRODUCE : producir

bring out *vt* : sacar, publicar (un libro, etc.)

bring to *vt* REVIVE : resucitar

bring up *vt* **1** REAR : criar **2** MENTION : sacar, mencionar

brininess [ˈbraɪninəs] *n* : salinidad *f*

brink [ˈbrɪŋk] *n* : borde *m*

briny [ˈbraɪni] *adj* **brinier; -est** : salobre

briquette *or* **briquet** [brɪˈkɛt] *n* : briqueta *f*

brisk [ˈbrɪsk] *adj* **1** LIVELY : rápido, enérgico, brioso **2** INVIGORATING : fresco, estimulante

brisket [ˈbrɪskət] *n* : falda *f*

briskly [ˈbrɪskli] *adv* : rápidamente, enérgicamente, con brío

briskness [ˈbrɪsknəs] *n* : brío *m,* rapidez *f*

bristle[1] [ˈbrɪsəl] *vi* **-tled; -tling 1** : erizarse, ponerse de punta **2** : enfurecerse, enojarse <she bristled at the suggestion : se enfureció ante tal sugerencia> **3** : estar plagado, estar repleto <a city bristling with tourists : una ciudad repleta de turistas>

bristle[2] *n* : cerda *f* (de un animal), pelo *m* (de una planta)

bristly [ˈbrɪsəli] *adj* **bristlier; -est** : erizado, cerdoso, hirsuto

British[1] [ˈbrɪt̬ɪʃ] *adj* : británico

British[2] *n* **the British** *npl* : los británicos

brittle [ˈbrɪt̬əl] *adj* **-tler; -tlest** : frágil, quebradizo

brittleness [ˈbrɪt̬əlnəs] *n* : fragilidad *f*

broach [ˈbroːtʃ] *vt* BRING UP : mencionar, abordar, sacar

broad [ˈbrɔd] *adj* **1** WIDE : ancho **2** SPACIOUS : amplio, extenso **3** FULL : pleno <in broad daylight : en pleno día> **4** OBVIOUS : claro, evidente **5** TOLERANT : tolerante, liberal **6** GENERAL : general **7** ESSENTIAL : principal, esencial <the broad outline : los rasgos esenciales>

broadcast[1] [ˈbrɔdˌkæst] *vt* **-cast; -casting 1** SCATTER : esparcir, diseminar **2** CIRCULATE, SPREAD : divulgar, difundir, propagar **3** TRANSMIT : transmitir, emitir

broadcast[2] *n* **1** TRANSMISSION : transmisión *f,* emisión *f* **2** PROGRAM : programa *m,* emisión *f*

broadcaster [ˈbrɔdˌkæstər] *n* : presentador *m,* -dora *f;* locutor *m,* -tora *f*

broadcloth [ˈbrɔdˌklɔθ] *n* : paño *m* fino

broaden [ˈbrɔdən] *vt* : ampliar, ensanchar — *vi* : ampliarse, ensancharse

broadloom [ˈbrɔdˌluːm] *adj* : tejido en telar ancho

broadly [ˈbrɔdli] *adv* **1** GENERALLY : en general, aproximadamente **2** WIDELY : extensivamente

broad–minded [ˈbrɔdˈmaɪndəd] *adj* : tolerante, de amplias miras

broad–mindedness [brɔdˈmaɪndədnəs] *n* : tolerancia *f*

broadside [ˈbrɔdˌsaɪd] *n* **1** VOLLEY : andanada *f* **2** ATTACK : ataque *m,* invectiva *f,* andanada *f*

brocade [broˈkeɪd] *n* : brocado *m*

broccoli [ˈbrɑkəli] *n* : brócoli *m,* brécol *m*

brochure [broˈʃʊr] *n* : folleto *m*

brogue [ˈbroːg] *n* : acento *m* irlandés

broil[1] [ˈbrɔɪl] *vt* : asar a la parrilla

broil[2] *n* : asado *m*

broiler [ˈbrɔɪlər] *n* **1** GRILL : parrilla *f* **2** : pollo *m* para asar

broke[1] [ˈbroːk] → **break**[1]

broke[2] *adj* : pelado, arruinado <to go broke : arruinarse, quebrar>

broken [ˈbroːkən] *adj* **1** DAMAGED, SHATTERED : roto, quebrado, fracturado **2** IRREGULAR, UNEVEN : accidentado, irregular, recortado **3** VIOLATED : roto, quebrantado **4** INTERRUPTED : interrumpido, descontinuo **5** CRUSHED : abatido, quebrantado <a broken man : un hombre destrozado> **6** IMPERFECT : mal <to speak broken English : hablar el inglés con dificultad>

brokenhearted [ˌbroːkənˈhɑrt̬əd] *adj* : descorazonado, desconsolado

broker[1] [ˈbroːkər] *vt* : hacer corretaje de

broker[2] *n* **1** : agente *mf;* corredor *m,* -dora *f* **2** → **stockbroker**

brokerage [ˈbroːkərɪdʒ] *n* : corretage *m,* agencia *f* de corredores

bromine [ˈbroːˌmiːn] *n* : bromo *m*

bronchitis [brɑnˈkaɪt̬əs, brɑŋ-] *n* : bronquitis *f*

bronze[1] [ˈbrɑnz] *vt* **bronzed; bronzing** : broncear

bronze[2] *n* : bronce *m*

brooch [ˈbroːtʃ, ˈbruːtʃ] *n* : broche *m,* prendedor *m*

brood[1] [ˈbruːd] *vt* **1** INCUBATE : empollar, incubar **2** PONDER : sopesar, considerar — *vi* **1** INCUBATE : empollar **2** REFLECT : rumiar, reflexionar **3** WORRY : ponerse melancólico, inquietarse

brood[2] *adj* : de cría

brood[3] *n* : nidada *f* (de pájaros), camada *f* (de mamíferos)

brooder [ˈbruːdər] *n* **1** THINKER : pensador *m,* -dora *f* **2** INCUBATOR : incubadora *f*

brook[1] [ˈbrʊk] *vt* TOLERATE : tolerar, admitir

brook[2] *n* : arroyo *m*

broom [ˈbruːm, ˈbrʊm] *n* **1** : retama *f,* hiniesta *f* **2** : escoba *f* (para barrer)

broomstick [ˈbruːmˌstɪk, ˈbrʊm-] *n* : palo *m* de escoba

broth [ˈbrɔθ] *n, pl* **broths** [ˈbrɔθs, ˈbrɔðz] : caldo *m*

brothel [ˈbrɑθəl, ˈbrɔ-] *n* : burdel *m*

brother [ˈbrʌðər] *n, pl* **brothers** *also* **brethren** [ˈbrɛðrən, -ðərn] **1** : hermano *m* **2** KINSMAN : pariente *m*, familiar *m*

brotherhood [ˈbrʌðərˌhʊd] *n* **1** FELLOWSHIP : fraternidad *f* **2** ASSOCIATION : hermandad *f*

brother–in–law [ˈbrʌðərɪnˌlɔ] *n, pl* **brothers–in–law:** cuñado *m*

brotherly [ˈbrʌðərli] *adj* : fraternal

brought → **bring**

brow [ˈbraʊ] *n* **1** EYEBROW : ceja *f* **2** FOREHEAD : frente *f* **3** : cima *f* <the brow of a hill : la cima de una colina>

browbeat [ˈbraʊˌbiːt] *vt* **-beat; -beaten** [-ˌbiːtən] *or* **-beat; -beating** : intimidar

brown[1] [ˈbraʊn] *vt* **1** : dorar (en cocinar) **2** TAN : broncear — *vi* **1** : dorarse (en cocinar) **2** TAN : broncearse

brown[2] *adj* : marrón, café, castaño (dícese del pelo), moreno (dícese de la piel)

brown[3] *n* : marrón *m*, café *m*

brownish [ˈbraʊnɪʃ] *adj* : pardo

browse [ˈbraʊz] *vi* **browsed; browsing** **1** GRAZE : pacer **2** LOOK : mirar, echar un vistazo

bruin [ˈbruːɪn] *n* BEAR : oso *m*

bruise[1] [ˈbruːz] *vt* **bruised; bruising** **1** : contusionar, machucar, magullar (a una persona) **2** DAMAGE : magullar, dañar (frutas) **3** CRUSH : majar **4** HURT : herir (los sentimientos)

bruise[2] *n* : moretón *m*, cardenal *m*, magulladura *f* (dícese de frutas)

brunch [ˈbrʌntʃ] *n* : combinación *f* de desayuno y almuerzo

brunet[1] *or* **brunette** [bruːˈnɛt] *adj* : moreno

brunet[2] *or* **brunette** *n* : moreno *m*, -na *f*

brunt [ˈbrʌnt] *n* **to bear the brunt of** : llevar el peso de, aguantar el mayor impacto de

brush[1] [ˈbrʌʃ] *vt* **1** : cepillar <to brush one's teeth : cepillarse uno los dientes> **2** SWEEP : barrer, quitar con un cepillo **3** GRAZE : rozar **4** **to brush off** DISREGARD : hacer caso omiso de, ignorar — *vi* **to brush up on** : repasar, refrescar, dar un repaso a

brush[2] *n* **1** *or* **brushwood** [ˈbrʌʃˌwʊd] : broza *f* **2** SCRUB, UNDERBRUSH : maleza *f* **3** : cepillo *m*, pincel *m* (de artista), brocha *f* (de pintor) **4** TOUCH : roce *m* **5** SKIRMISH : escaramuza *f*

brush–off [ˈbrʌʃˌɔf] *n* **to give the brush–off to** : dar calabazas a

brusque [ˈbrʌsk] *adj* : brusco — **brusquely** *adv*

brussels sprout [ˈbrʌsəlzˌspraʊt] *n* : col *f* de Bruselas

brutal [ˈbruːtəl] *adj* : brutal, cruel, salvaje — **brutally** *adv*

brutality [bruːˈtæləti] *n, pl* **-ties** : brutalidad *f*

brutalize [ˈbruːtəlˌaɪz] *vt* **-ized; -izing** : brutalizar, maltratar

brute[1] [ˈbruːt] *adj* : bruto <brute force : fuerza bruta>

brute[2] *n* **1** BEAST : bestia *f*, animal *m* **2** : bruto *m*, -ta *f*; bestia *mf* (persona)

brutish [ˈbruːtɪʃ] *adj* **1** : de animal **2** CRUEL : brutal, salvaje **3** STUPID : bruto, estúpido

bubble[1] [ˈbʌbəl] *vi* **-bled; -bling** : burbujear <to bubble over with joy : rebosar de alegría>

bubble[2] *n* : burbuja *f*

bubbly [ˈbʌbəli] *adj* **bubblier; -est** **1** BUBBLING : burbujeante **2** LIVELY : vivaz, lleno de vida

bubonic plague [buːˈbɑnɪk, ˈbjuː-] *n* : peste *f* bubónica

buccaneer [ˌbʌkəˈnɪr] *n* : bucanero *m*

buck[1] [ˈbʌk] *vi* **1** : corcovear (dícese de un caballo o un burro) **2** JOLT : dar sacudidas **3** **to buck against** : resistirse a, rebelarse contra **4** **to buck up** : animarse, levantar el ánimo — *vt* OPPOSE : oponerse a, ir en contra de

buck[2] *n, pl* **buck** *or* **bucks** **1** : animal *m* macho, ciervo *m* (macho) **2** DOLLAR : dólar *m* **3** **to pass the buck** *fam* : pasar la pelota *fam*

bucket [ˈbʌkət] *n* : balde *m*, cubo *m*, cubeta *f Mex*

bucketful [ˈbʌkətˌfʊl] *n* : balde *m* lleno

buckle[1] [ˈbʌkəl] *v* **-led; -ling** *vt* **1** FASTEN : abrochar **2** BEND, TWIST : combar, torcer — *vi* **1** BEND, TWIST : combarse, torcerse, doblarse (dícese de las rodillas) **2** **to buckle down** : ponerse a trabajar con esmero **3** **to buckle up** : abrocharse

buckle[2] *n* **1** : hebilla *f* **2** TWISTING : torcedura *f*

buckshot [ˈbʌkˌʃɑt] *n* : perdigón *m*

buckskin [ˈbʌkˌskɪn] *n* : gamuza *f*

bucktooth [ˈbʌkˌtuːθ] *n* : diente *m* saliente, diente *m* salido

buckwheat [ˈbʌkˌhwiːt] *n* : trigo *m* rubión, alforfón *m*

bucolic [bjuːˈkɑlɪk] *adj* : bucólico

bud[1] [ˈbʌd] *v* **budded; budding** *vt* GRAFT : injertar — *vi* : brotar, hacer brotes

bud[2] *n* : brote *m*, yema *f*, capullo *m* (de una flor)

Buddhism [ˈbuːˌdɪzəm, ˈbʊ-] *n* : Budismo *m*

Buddhist [ˈbuːdɪst, ˈbʊ-] *n* : budista *mf* — **Buddhist** *adj*

buddy [ˈbʌdi] *n, pl* **-dies** : amigo *m*, -ga *f*; compinche *mf fam*; cuate *m*, -ta *f Mex fam*

budge [ˈbʌdʒ] *vi* **budged; budging** **1** MOVE : moverse, desplazarse **2** YIELD : ceder

budget[1] [ˈbʌdʒət] *vt* : presupuestar (gastos), asignar (dinero) — *vi* : presupuestar, planear el presupuesto

budget[2] *n* : presupuesto

budgetary [ˈbʌdʒəˌtɛri] *adj* : presupuestario
buff¹ [ˈbʌf] *vt* POLISH : pulir, sacar brillo a, lustrar
buff² *adj* : beige, amarillento
buff³ *n* **1** : beige *m*, amarillento *m* **2** ENTHUSIAST : aficionado *m*, -da *f*; entusiasta *mf*
buffalo [ˈbʌfəˌloː] *n, pl* **-lo** *or* **-loes 1** : búfalo *m* **2** BISON : bisonte *m*
buffer [ˈbʌfər] *n* **1** BARRIER : barrera *f* <buffer state : estado tapón> **2** SHOCK ABSORBER : amortiguador *m*
buffet¹ [ˈbʌfət] *vt* : golpear, zarandear, sacudir
buffet² *n* BLOW : golpe *m*
buffet³ [ˌbʌˈfeɪ, ˌbuː-] *n* **1** : bufete *m*, bufé *m* (comida) **2** SIDEBOARD : aparador *m*
buffoon [ˌbʌˈfuːn] *n* : bufón *m*, -fona *f*; payaso *m*, -sa *f*
buffoonery [ˌbʌˈfuːnəri] *n, pl* **-eries** : bufonada *f*, payasada *f*
bug¹ [ˈbʌg] *vt* **bugged; bugging 1** PESTER : fastidiar, molestar **2** : ocultar micrófonos en
bug² *n* **1** INSECT : bicho *m*, insecto *m* **2** DEFECT : defecto *m*, falla *f*, problema *m* **3** GERM : microbio *m*, virus *m* **4** MICROPHONE : micrófono *m*
bugaboo [ˈbʌgəˌbuː] → **bogey**
bugbear [ˈbʌgˌbær] *n* : pesadilla *f*, coco *m*
buggy [ˈbʌgi] *n, pl* **-gies** : calesa *f* (tirada por caballos), cochecito *m* (para niños)
bugle [ˈbjuːgəl] *n* : clarín *m*, corneta *f*
bugler [ˈbjuːgələr] *n* : corneta *mf*
build¹ [ˈbɪld] *v* **built** [ˈbɪlt]; **building** *vt* **1** CONSTRUCT : construir, edificar, ensamblar, levantar **2** DEVELOP : desarrollar, elaborar, forjar **3** INCREASE : incrementar, aumentar — *vi* **to build up** : aumentar, intensificar
build² *n* PHYSIQUE : físico *m*, complexión *f*
builder [ˈbɪldər] *n* : constructor *m*, -tora *f*; contratista *mf*
building [ˈbɪldɪŋ] *n* **1** EDIFICE : edificio *m* **2** CONSTRUCTION : construcción *f*
built-in [ˈbɪltˈɪn] *adj* **1** : empotrado <built-in cabinets : armarios empotrados> **2** INHERENT : incorporado, intrínseco
bulb [ˈbʌlb] *n* **1** : bulbo *m* (de una planta), cabeza *f* (de ajo), cubeta *f* (de un termómetro) **2** LIGHTBULB : bombilla *f*, foco *m*, bombillo *m* *CA, Col, Ven*
bulbous [ˈbʌlbəs] *adj* : bulboso
Bulgarian [bʌlˈgæriən, bʊl-] *n* **1** : búlgaro *m*, -ra *f* **2** : búlgaro *m* (idioma) — **Bulgarian**
bulge¹ [ˈbʌldʒ] *vi* **bulged; bulging** : abultar, sobresalir
bulge² *n* : bulto *m*, protuberancia *f*
bulk¹ [ˈbʌlk] *vt* : hinchar — *vi* EXPAND, SWELL : ampliarse, hincharse
bulk² *n* **1** SIZE, VOLUME : volumen *m*, tamaño *m* **2** FIBER : fibra *f* **3** MASS : mole *f* **4 the bulk of** : la mayor parte de **5 in ~** : en grandes cantidades
bulkhead [ˈbʌlkˌhɛd] *n* : mamparo *m*
bulky [ˈbʌlki] *adj* **bulkier; -est** : voluminoso, grande
bull¹ [ˈbʊl] *adj* : macho
bull² *n* **1** : toro *m*, macho *m* (de ciertas especies) **2** : bula *f* (papal) **3** DECREE : decreto *m*, edicto *m*
bulldog [ˈbʊlˌdɔg] *n* : buldog *m*
bulldoze [ˈbʊlˌdoːz] *vt* **-dozed; -dozing 1** LEVEL : nivelar (el terreno), derribar (un edificio) **2** FORCE : forzar <he bulldozed his way through : se abrió paso a codazos>
bulldozer [ˈbʊlˌdoːzər] *n* : bulldozer *m*
bullet [ˈbʊlət] *n* : bala *f*
bulletin [ˈbʊlətən, -lətən] *n* **1** NOTICE : comunicado *m*, anuncio *m*, boletín *m* **2** NEWSLETTER : boletín *m* (informativo)
bulletin board *n* : tablón *m* de anuncios
bulletproof [ˈbʊlətˌpruːf] *adj* : antibalas, a prueba de balas
bullfight [ˈbʊlˌfaɪt] *n* : corrida *f* (de toros)
bullfighter [ˈbʊlˌfaɪtər] *n* : torero *m*, -ra *f*; matador *m*
bullfrog [ˈbʊlˌfrɔg] *n* : rana *f* toro
bullheaded [ˈbʊlˈhɛdəd] *adj* : testarudo
bullion [ˈbʊljən] *n* : oro *m* en lingotes, plata *f* en lingotes
bullock [ˈbʊlək] *n* **1** STEER : buey *m*, toro *m* castrado **2** : toro *m* joven, novillo *m*
bull's–eye [ˈbʊlzˌaɪ] *n, pl* **bull's–eyes** : diana *f*, blanco *m*
bully¹ [ˈbʊli] *vt* **-lied; -lying** : intimidar, amendrentar, mangonear
bully² *n, pl* **-lies** : matón *m*; bravucón *m*, -cona *f*
bulrush [ˈbʊlˌrʌʃ] *n* : especie *f* de junco
bulwark [ˈbʊlˌwərk, -ˌwɔrk; ˈbʌlˌwərk] *n* : baluarte *m*, bastión *f*
bum¹ [ˈbʌm] *v* **bummed; bumming** *vi* **to bum around** : vagabundear, vagar — *vt* : gorronear *fam*, sablear *fam*
bum² *adj* : inútil, malo <a bum rap : una acusación falsa>
bum³ *n* **1** LOAFER : vago *m*, -ga *f* **2** HOBO, TRAMP : vagabundo *m*, -da *f*
bumblebee [ˈbʌmbəlˌbiː] *n* : abejorro *m*
bump¹ [ˈbʌmp] *vt* : chocar contra, golpear contra, dar <to bump one's head : darse (un golpe) en la cabeza> — *vi* **to bump into** MEET : encontrarse con, tropezarse con
bump² *n* **1** BULGE : bulto *m*, protuberancia *f* **2** IMPACT : golpe *m*, choque *m* **3** JOLT : sacudida *f*
bumper¹ [ˈbʌmpər] *adj* : extraordinario, récord <a bumper crop : una cosecha abundante>

bumper[2] *n* : parachoques *mpl*

bumpkin [ˈbʌmpkən] *n* : palurdo *m*, -da *f*

bumpy [ˈbʌmpi] *adj* **bumpier; -est** : desigual, lleno de baches (dícese de un camino), agitado (dícese de un vuelo en avión)

bun [ˈbʌn] *n* : bollo *m*

bunch[1] [ˈbʌntʃ] *vt* : agrupar, amontonar — *vi* **to bunch up** : amontarse, agruparse, fruncirse (dícese de una tela)

bunch[2] *n* : grupo *m*, montón *m*, ramo *m* (de flores)

bundle[1] [ˈbʌndəl] *vt* **-dled; -dling** : liar, atar

bundle[2] *n* **1** : fardo *m*, atado *m*, bulto *m*, haz *m* (de palos) **2** PARCEL : paquete *m* **3** LOAD : montón *m* <a bundle of money : un montón de dinero>

bungalow [ˈbʌŋɡəˌloː] *n* : tipo de casa de un solo piso

bungle[1] [ˈbʌŋɡəl] *vt* **-gled; -gling** : echar a perder, malograr

bungle[2] *n* : chapuza *f*, desatino *m*

bungler [ˈbʌŋɡələr] *n* : chapucero *m*, -ra *f*; inepto *m*, -ta *f*

bunion [ˈbʌnjən] *n* : juanete *m*

bunk[1] [ˈbʌŋk] *vi* : dormir (en una litera)

bunk[2] *n* **1** *or* **bunk bed** : litera *f* **2** NONSENSE : tonterías *fpl*, bobadas *fpl*

bunker [ˈbʌŋkər] *n* **1** : carbonera *f* (en un barco) **2** SHELTER : búnker *m*

bunny [ˈbʌni] *n, pl* **-nies** : conejo *m*, -ja *f*

buoy[1] [ˈbuːi, ˈbɔɪ] *vt* **to buoy up 1** : mantener a flote **2** CHEER, HEARTEN : animar, levantar el ánimo a

buoy[2] *n* : boya *f*

buoyancy [ˈbɔɪən*t*si, ˈbuːjən-] *n* **1** : flotabilidad *f* **2** OPTIMISM : confianza *f*, optimismo *m*

buoyant [ˈbɔɪənt, ˈbuːjənt] *adj* : boyante, flotante

bur *or* **burr** [ˈbər] *n* : abrojo *m* (de una planta)

burden[1] [ˈbərdən] *vt* : cargar, oprimir

burden[2] *n* : carga *f*, peso *m*

burdensome [ˈbərdənsəm] *adj* : oneroso

burdock [ˈbərˌdɑk] *n* : bardana *f*

bureau [ˈbjʊro] *n* **1** CHEST OF DRAWERS : cómoda *f* **2** DEPARTMENT : departamento *m* (del gobierno) **3** AGENCY : agencia *f* <travel bureau : agencia de viajes>

bureaucracy [bjʊˈrɑkrəsi] *n, pl* **-cies** : burocracia *f*

bureaucrat [ˈbjʊrəˌkræt] *n* : burócrata *mf*

bureaucratic [ˌbjʊrəˈkræt̬ɪk] *adj* : burocrático

burgeon [ˈbərdʒən] *vi* : florecer, retoñar, crecer

burglar [ˈbərglər] *n* : ladrón *m*, -drona *f*

burglarize [ˈbərgləˌraɪz] *vt* **-ized; -izing** : robar

burglary [ˈbərgləri] *n, pl* **-glaries** : robo *m*

burgle [ˈbərgəl] *vt* **-gled; -gling** : robar

burgundy [ˈbərgəndi] *n, pl* **-dies** : borgoña *m*, vino *m* de Borgoña

burial [ˈbɛriəl] *n* : entierro *m*, sepelio *m*

burlap [ˈbərˌlæp] *n* : arpillera *f*

burlesque[1] [bərˈlɛsk] *vt* **-lesqued; -lesquing** : parodiar

burlesque[2] *n* **1** PARODY : parodia *f* **2** REVUE : revista *f* (musical)

burly [ˈbərli] *adj* **-lier; -liest** : fornido, corpulento, musculoso

burn[1] [ˈbərn] *v* **burned** [ˈbərnd, ˈbərnt] *or* **burnt** [ˈbərnt]; **burning** *vt* **1** : quemar, incendiar <to burn a building : incendiar un edificio> <I burned my hand : me quemé la mano> **2** CONSUME : usar, gastar, consumir — *vi* **1** : arder (dícese de un fuego o un edificio), quemarse (dícese de la comida, etc.) **2** : estar prendido, estar encendido <we left the lights burning : dejamos las luces encendidas> **3 to burn out** : consumirse, apagarse **4 to burn with** : arder de <he was burning with jealousy : ardía de celos>

burn[2] *n* : quemadura *f*

burner [ˈbərnər] *n* : quemador *m*

burnish [ˈbərnɪʃ] *vt* : bruñir

burp[1] [ˈbərp] *vi* : eructar — *vt* : hacer eructar

burp[2] *n* : eructo *m*

burr → **bur**

burro [ˈbəro, ˈbʊr-] *n, pl* **-os** : burro *m*

burrow[1] [ˈbəro] *vi* **1** : cavar, hacer una madriguera **2 to burrow into** : hurgar en — *vt* : cavar, excavar

burrow[2] *n* : madriguera *f*, conejera *f* (de un conejo)

bursar [ˈbərsər] *n* : administrador *m*, -dora *f*

bursitis [bərˈsaɪt̬əs] *n* : bursitis *f*

burst[1] [ˈbərst] *v* **burst** *or* **bursted; bursting** *vi* **1** : reventarse (dícese de una llanta o un globo), estallar (dícese de obuses o fuegos artificiales), romperse (dícese de un dique) **2 to burst in** : irrumpir en **3 to burst into** : empezar a, echar a <to burst into tears : echarse a llorar> — *vt* : reventar

burst[2] *n* **1** EXPLOSION : estallido *m*, explosión *f*, reventón *m* (de una llanta) **2** OUTBURST : arranque *m* (de actividad, de velocidad), arrebato *m* (de ira), salva *f* (de aplausos)

Burundian [bʊˈruːndiən, -ˈrʊn-] *n* : burundés *m*, -desa *f* — **Burundian** *adj*

bury [ˈbɛri] *vt* **buried; burying 1** INTER : enterrar, sepultar **2** HIDE : esconder, ocultar **3 to bury oneself in** : enfrascarse en

bus[1] [ˈbʌs] *v* **bused** *or* **bussed** [ˈbʌst]; **busing** *or* **bussing** [ˈbʌsɪŋ] *vt* : transportar en autobús — *vi* : viajar en autobús

bus[2] *n* : autobús *m,* bus *m,* camión *m Mex,* colectivo *m Arg, Bol, Peru*

busboy [ˈbʌsˌbɔɪ] *n* : ayudante *mf* de camarero

bush [ˈbʊʃ] *n* **1** SHRUB : arbusto *m,* mata *f* **2** THICKET : maleza *f,* matorral *m*

bushel [ˈbʊʃəl] *n* : medida de áridos igual a 35.24 litros

bushing [ˈbʊʃɪŋ] *n* : cojinete *m*

bushy [ˈbʊʃi] *adj* **bushier; -est** : espeso, poblado <bushy eyebrows : cejas pobladas>

busily [ˈbɪzəli] *adv* : afanosamente, diligentemente

business [ˈbɪznəs, -nəz] *n* **1** OCCUPATION : ocupación *f,* oficio *m* **2** DUTY, MISSION : misión *f,* deber *m,* responsabilidad *f* **3** ESTABLISHMENT, FIRM : empresa *f,* firma *f,* negocio *m,* comercio *m* **4** COMMERCE : negocios *mpl,* comercio *m* **5** AFFAIR, MATTER : asunto *m,* cuestión *f,* cosa *f* <it's none of your business : no es asunto tuyo>

businessman [ˈbɪznəsˌmæn, -nəz-] *n, pl* **-men** [-mən, -ˌmɛn] : empresario *m,* hombre *m* de negocios

businesswoman [ˈbɪznəsˌwʊmən, -nəz-] *n, pl* **-women** [-ˌwɪmən] : empresaria *f,* mujer *f* de negocios

bust[1] [ˈbʌst] *vt* **1** BREAK, SMASH : romper, estropear, destrozar **2** TAME : domar, amansar (un caballo) — *vi* : romperse, estropearse

bust[2] *n* **1** : busto *m* (en la escultura) **2** BREASTS : pecho *m,* senos *mpl,* busto *m*

bustle[1] [ˈbʌsəl] *vi* **-tled; -tling to bustle about** : ir y venir, trajinar, ajetrearse

bustle[2] *n* **1** *or* **hustle and bustle** : bullicio *m,* ajetreo *m* **2** : polisón *m* (en la ropa feminina)

busy[1] [ˈbɪzi] *vt* **busied; busying to busy oneself with** : ocuparse con, ponerse a, entretenerse con

busy[2] *adj* **busier; -est 1** OCCUPIED : ocupado, atareado <he's busy working : está ocupado en su trabajo> <the telephone was busy : el teléfono estaba ocupado> **2** BUSTLING : concurrido, animado <a busy street : una calle concurrida, una calle con mucho tránsito>

busybody [ˈbɪziˌbɑdi] *n, pl* **-bodies** : entrometido *m,* -da *f;* metiche *mf fam;* metomentodo *mf*

but[1] [ˈbʌt] *conj* **1** THAT : que <there is no doubt but he is lazy : no cabe duda que sea perezoso> **2** WITHOUT : sin que **3** NEVERTHELESS : pero, no obstante, sin embargo <I called her but she didn't answer : la llamé pero no contestó> **4** YET : pero <he was poor but proud : era pobre pero orgulloso>

but[2] *prep* EXCEPT : excepto, menos <everyone but Carlos : todos menos Carlos> <the last but one : el penúltimo>

butcher[1] [ˈbʊtʃər] *vt* **1** SLAUGHTER : matar (animales) **2** KILL : matar, asesinar, masacrar **3** BOTCH : estropear, hacer una chapuza

butcher[2] *n* **1** : carnicero *m,* -ra *f* **2** KILLER : asesino *m,* -na *f* **3** BUNGLER : chapucero *m,* -ra *f*

butler [ˈbʌtlər] *n* : mayordomo *m*

butt[1] [ˈbʌt] *vt* **1** : embestir (con los cuernos), darle un cabezazo a **2** ABUT : colindar con, bordear — *vi* **to butt in 1** INTERRUPT : interrumpir **2** MEDDLE : entrometerse, meterse

butt[2] *n* **1** BUTTING : embestida *f* (de cuernos), cabezazo *m* **2** TARGET : blanco *m* <the butt of their jokes : el blanco de sus bromas> **3** BOTTOM, END : extremo *m,* culata *f* (de un rifle), colilla *f* (de un cigarillo)

butte [ˈbjuːt] *n* : colina *f* empinada y aislada

butter[1] [ˈbʌt̬ər] *vt* **1** : untar con mantequilla **2 to butter up** : halagar

butter[2] *n* : mantequilla *f*

buttercup [ˈbʌt̬ərˌkʌp] *n* : ranúnculo *m*

butterfat [ˈbʌt̬ərˌfæt] *n* : grasa *f* de la leche

butterfly [ˈbʌt̬ərˌflaɪ] *n, pl* **-flies** : mariposa *f*

buttermilk [ˈbʌt̬ərˌmɪlk] *n* : suero *m* de la leche

butternut [ˈbʌtərˌnʌt] *n* : nogal *m* ceniciento (árbol)

butterscotch [ˈbʌt̬ərˌskɑtʃ] *n* : caramelo *m* duro hecho con mantequilla

buttery [ˈbʌt̬əri] *adj* : mantecoso

buttocks [ˈbʌt̬əks, -ˌtɑks] *npl* : nalgas *fpl,* trasero *m*

button[1] [ˈbʌtən] *vt* : abrochar, abotonar — *vi* : abrocharse, abotonarse

button[2] *n* : botón *m*

buttonhole[1] [ˈbʌtənˌhoːl] *vt* **-holed; -holing** : acorralar

buttonhole [2] *n* : ojal *m*

buttress[1] [ˈbʌtrəs] *vt* : apoyar, reforzar

buttress[2] *n* **1** : contrafuerte *m* (en la arquitectura) **2** SUPPORT : apoyo *m,* sostén *m*

buxom [ˈbʌksəm] *adj* : con mucho busto, con mucho pecho

buy[1] [ˈbaɪ] *vt* **bought** [ˈbɔt]; **buying** : comprar

buy[2] *n* BARGAIN : compra *f,* ganga *f*

buyer [ˈbaɪər] *n* : comprador *m,* -dora *f*

buzz[1] [ˈbʌz] *vi* : zumbar (dícese de un insecto), sonar (dícese de un teléfono o un despertador)

buzz[2] *n* **1** : zumbido *m* (de insectos) **2** : murmullo *m,* rumor *m* (de voces)

buzzard [ˈbʌzərd] *n* VULTURE : buitre *m,* zopilote *m CA, Mex*

buzzer [ˈbʌzər] *n* : timbre *m,* chicharra *f*

buzzword [ˈbʌzˌwərd] *n* : palabra *f* de moda

by[1] [ˈbaɪ] *adv* **1** NEAR : cerca <he lives close by : vive muy cerca> **2 to stop**

by : pasar por casa, hacer una visita **3 to go by** : pasar <they rushed by : pasaron corriendo> **4 to put by** : reservar, poner a un lado **5 by and by** : poco después, dentro de poco **6 by and large** : en general

by[2] *prep* **1** NEAR : cerca de, al lado de, junto a **2** VIA : por <she left by the door : salió por la puerta> **3** PAST : por, por delante de <they walked by him : pasaron por delante de él> **4** DURING : de, durante <by night : de noche> **5** (*in expressions of time*) : para <we'll be there by ten : estaremos allí para las diez> <by then : para entonces> **6** (*indicating cause or agent*) : por, de, a <built by the Romans : construido por los romanos> <a book by Borges : un libro de Borges> <made by hand : hecho a mano>

by and by *adv* : dentro de poco

bygone[1] [ˈbaɪˌgɔn] *adj* : pasado

bygone[2] *n* **let bygones be bygones** : lo pasado, pasado está

bylaw *or* **byelaw** [ˈbaɪˌlɔ] *n* : norma *f*, reglamento *m*

by–line [ˈbaɪˌlaɪn] *n* : data *f*

bypass[1] [ˈbaɪˌpæs] *vt* : evitar

bypass[2] *n* : carretera *f* de circunvalación, desvío *m*

by–product [ˈbaɪˌprɑdəkt] *n* : subproducto *m*, producto *m* derivado

bystander [ˈbaɪˌstændər] *n* : espectador *m*, -dora *f*

byway [ˈbaɪˌweɪ] *n* : camino *m* (apartado), carretera *f* secundaria

byword [ˈbaɪˌwərd] *n* **1** PROVERB : proverbio *m*, refrán *m* **2 to be a byword for** : estar sinónimo de

C

c [ˈsiː] *n*, *pl* **c's** *or* **cs** : tercera letra del alfabeto inglés

cab [ˈkæb] *n* **1** TAXI : taxi *m* **2** : cabina *f* (de un camión o una locomotora) **3** CARRIAGE : coche *m* de caballos

cabal [kəˈbɑl, -ˈbæl] *n* **1** INTRIGUE, PLOT : conspiración *f*, complot *m*, intriga *f* **2** : grupo *m* de conspiradores

cabaret [ˌkæbəˈreɪ] *n* : cabaret *m*

cabbage [ˈkæbɪdʒ] *n* : col *f*, repollo *m*

cabbie *or* **cabby** [ˈkæbi] *n* : taxista *mf*

cabin [ˈkæbən] *n* **1** HUT : cabaña *f*, choza *f*, barraca *f* **2** STATEROOM : camarote *m* **3** : cabina *f* (de un automóvil o avión)

cabinet [ˈkæbnət] *n* **1** CUPBOARD : armario *m* **2** : gabinete *m*, consejo *m* de ministros **3 medicine cabinet** : botiquín *m*

cabinetmaker [ˈkæbnətˌmeɪkər] *n* : ebanista *mf*

cabinetmaking [ˈkæbnətˌmeɪkɪŋ] *n* : ebanistería *f*

cable[1] [ˈkeɪbəl] *vt* **-bled; -bling** : enviar un cable, telegrafiar

cable[2] *n* **1** : cable *m* (para colgar o sostener algo) **2** : cable *m* eléctrico **3** → **cablegram**

cablegram [ˈkeɪbəlˌgræm] *n* : telegrama *m*, cable *m*

caboose [kəˈbuːs] *n* : furgón *m* de cola, cabús *m Mex*

cabstand [ˈkæbˌstænd] *n* : parada *f* de taxis

cacao [kəˈkaʊ, -ˈkeɪo] *n*, *pl* **cacaos** : cacao *m*

cache[1] [ˈkæʃ] *vt* **cached; caching** : esconder, guardar en un escondrijo

cache[2] *n* **1** : escondite *m*, escondrijo *m* <cache of weapons : escondite de armas> **2** : cache *m* <cache memory : memoria cache>

cachet [kæˈʃeɪ] *n* : caché *m*, prestigio *m*

cackle[1] [ˈkækəl] *vi* **-led; -ling 1** CLUCK : cacarear **2** : reírse o carcajearse estridentemente <he was cackling with delight : estaba carcajeándose de gusto>

cackle[2] *n* **1** : cacareo *m* (de una polla) **2** LAUGH : risa *f* estridente

cacophony [kæˈkɑfəni, -ˈkɔ-] *n*, *pl* **-cies** : cacofonía *f*

cactus [ˈkæktəs] *n*, *pl* **cacti** [-ˌtaɪ] *or* **-tuses** : cacto *m*, cactus *m*

cadaver [kəˈdævər] *n* : cadáver *m*

cadaverous [kəˈdævərəs] *adj* : cadavérico

caddie[1] *or* **caddy** [ˈkædi] *vi* **caddied; caddying** : trabajar de caddie, hacer de caddie

caddie[2] *or* **caddy** *n*, *pl* **-dies** : caddie *mf*

caddy [ˈkædi] *n*, *pl* **-dies** : cajita *f* para té

cadence [ˈkeɪdənts] *n* : cadencia *f*, ritmo *m*

cadenced [ˈkeɪdəntst] *adj* : cadencioso, rítmico

cadet [kəˈdɛt] *n* : cadete *mf*

cadmium [ˈkædmiəm] *n* : cadmio *m*

cadre [ˈkæˌdreɪ, ˈkɑ-, -ˌdriː] *n* : cuadro *m* (de expertos)

café [kæˈfeɪ, kə-] *n* : café *m*, cafetería *f*

cafeteria [ˌkæfəˈtɪriə] *n* : cafetería *f*, restaurante *m* de autoservicio

caffeine [kæˈfiːn] *n* : cafeína *f*

cage[1] [ˈkeɪdʒ] *vt* **caged; caging** : enjaular

cage[2] *n* : jaula *f*

cagey [ˈkeɪdʒi] *adj* **-gier; -est 1** CAUTIOUS : cauteloso, reservado **2** SHREWD : astuto, vivo — **cagily** [-dʒəli] *adv*

caisson ['keɪˌsɑn, -sən] *n* **1 :** cajón *m* de municiones **2 :** cajón *m* hidráulico
cajole [kə'ʤoːl] *vt* **-joled; -joling :** engatusar
cajolery [kə'ʤoːləri] *n* **:** engatusamiento *m*
cake[1] ['keɪk] *v* **caked; caking** *vt* **:** cubrir <caked with mud : cubierto de barro> — *vi* **:** endurecerse
cake[2] *n* **1 :** torta *f*, bizcocho *m*, pastel *m* **2 :** pastilla *f* (de jabón) **3 to take the cake :** llevarse la palma, ser el colmo
calabash ['kæləˌbæʃ] *n* **:** calabaza *f*
calamine ['kæləˌmaɪn] *n* **:** calamina *f* <calamine lotion : loción de calamina>
calamitous [kə'læmət̬əs] *adj* **:** desastroso, catastrófico, calamitoso — **calamitously** *adv*
calamity [kə'læmət̬i] *n, pl* **-ties :** desastre *m*, desgracia *f*, calamidad *f*
calcium ['kælsiəm] *n* **:** calcio *m*
calcium carbonate ['kɑrbəˌneɪt, -nət] *n* **:** carbonato *m* de calcio
calculable ['kælkjələbəl] *adj* **:** calculable, computable
calculate ['kælkjəˌleɪt] *v* **-lated; -lating** *vt* **1** COMPUTE **:** calcular, computar **2** ESTIMATE **:** calcular, creer **3** INTEND **:** planear, tener la intención de <I calculated on spending $100 : planeaba gastar $100> — *vi* **:** calcular, hacer cálculos
calculated ['kælkjəˌleɪt̬əd] *adj* **1** ESTIMATED **:** calculado **2** DELIBERATE **:** intencional, premeditado, deliberado
calculating ['kælkjəˌleɪt̬ɪŋ] *adj* SHREWD **:** calculador, astuto
calculation [ˌkælkjə'leɪʃən] *n* **:** cálculo *m*
calculator ['kælkjəˌleɪt̬ər] *n* **:** calculadora *f*
calculus ['kælkjələs] *n, pl* **-li** [-ˌlaɪ] **1 :** cálculo *m* <differential calculus : cálculo diferencial> **2** TARTAR **:** sarro *m* (dental)
caldron ['kɔldrən] → **cauldron**
calendar ['kæləndər] *n* **1 :** calendario *m* **2** SCHEDULE **:** calendario *m*, programa *m*, agenda *f*
calf ['kæf, 'kɑf] *n, pl* **calves** ['kævz, 'kɑvz] **1 :** becerro *m*, -rra *f*; ternero *m*, -ra *f* (de vacunos) **2 :** cría *f* (de otros mamíferos) **3 :** pantorrilla *f* (de la pierna)
calfskin ['kæfˌskɪn] *n* **:** piel *f* de becerro
caliber *or* **calibre** ['kæləbər] *n* **1 :** calibre *m* <a .38 caliber gun : una pistola de calibre .38> **2** ABILITY **:** calibre *m*, valor *m*, capacidad *f*
calibrate ['kæləˌbreɪt] *vt* **-brated; -brating :** calibrar (armas), graduar (termómetros)
calibration [ˌkælə'breɪʃən] *n* **:** calibrado *m*, calibración *f*
calico ['kælɪˌkoː] *n, pl* **-coes** *or* **-cos 1 :** calicó *m*, percal *m* **2** *or* **calico cat :** gato *m* manchado
calipers ['kæləpərz] *npl* **:** calibrador *m*
caliph *or* **calif** ['keɪləf, 'kæ-] *n* **:** califa *m*
calisthenics [ˌkæləs'θɛnɪks] *ns & pl* **:** calistenia *f*
calk ['kɔk] → **caulk**
call[1] ['kɔl] *vi* **1** CRY, SHOUT **:** gritar, vociferar **2** VISIT **:** hacer (una) visita, visitar **3 to call for :** exigir, requerir, necesitar <it calls for patience : requiere mucha paciencia> — *vt* **1** SUMMON **:** llamar, convocar **2** TELEPHONE **:** llamar por teléfono, telefonear **3** NAME **:** llamar, apodar
call[2] *n* **1** SHOUT **:** grito *m*, llamada *f* **2 :** grito *m* (de un animal), reclamo *m* (de un pájaro) **3** SUMMONS **:** llamada *f* **4** DEMAND **:** llamado *m*, petición *f* **5** VISIT **:** visita *f* **6** DECISION **:** decisión *f* (en deportes) **7** *or* **telephone call :** llamada *f* (telefónica)
call down *vt* REPRIMAND **:** reprender, reñir
caller ['kɔlər] *n* **1** VISITOR **:** visita *f* **2 :** persona *f* que llama (por teléfono)
calling ['kɔlɪŋ] *n* **:** vocación *f*, profesión *f*
calliope [kə'laɪəˌpiː, 'kæliˌoːp] *n* **:** órgano *m* de vapor
call off *vt* CANCEL **:** cancelar, suspender
callous[1] ['kæləs] *vt* **:** encallecer
callous[2] *adj* **1** CALLUSED **:** calloso, encallecido **2** UNFEELING **:** insensible, desalmado, cruel
callously ['kæləsli] *adv* **:** cruelmente, insensiblemente
callousness ['kæləsnəs] *n* **:** insensibilidad *f*, crueldad *f*
callow ['kælo] *adj* **:** inexperto, inmaduro
callus ['kæləs] *n* **:** callo m
callused ['kæləst] *adj* **:** encallecido, calloso
calm[1] ['kɑm, 'kɑlm] *vt* **:** tranquilizar, calmar, sosegar — *vi* **:** tranquilizarse, calmarse <calm down! : ¡tranquilízate!>
calm[2] *adj* **1** TRANQUIL **:** calmo, tranquilo, sereno, ecuánime **2** STILL **:** en calma (dícese del mar), sin viento (dícese del aire)
calm[3] *n* **:** tranquilidad *f*, calma *f*
calmly ['kɑmli, 'kɑlm-] *adv* **:** con calma, tranquilamente
calmness ['kɑmnəs, 'kɑlm-] *n* **:** calma *f*, tranquilidad *f*
caloric [kə'lɔrɪk] *adj* **:** calórico (dícese de los alimentos), calorífico (dícese de la energía)
calorie ['kæləri] *n* **:** caloría *f*
calumniate [kə'lʌmniˌeɪt] *vt* **-ated; -ating :** calumniar, difamar
calumny ['kæləmni] *n, pl* **-nies :** calumnia *f*, difamación *f*
calve ['kæv, 'kɑv] *vi* **calved; calving :** parir (dícese de los mamíferos)
calves → **calf**
calypso [kə'lɪpˌsoː] *n, pl* **-sos :** calipso *m*

calyx [ˈkeɪlɪks, ˈkæ-] *n, pl* **-lyxes** *or* **-lyces** [-ləˌsiːz] : cáliz *m*
cam [ˈkæm] *n* : leva *f*
camaraderie [ˌkɑmˈrɑdəri, ˌkæm-; ˌkɑməˈrɑ-] *n* : compañerismo *m,* camaradería *f*
Cambodian [kæmˈboːdiən] *n* : camboyano *m,* -na *f* — **Cambodian** *adj*
came → **come**
camel [ˈkæməl] *n* : camello *m*
camellia [kəˈmiːljə] *n* : camelia *f*
cameo [ˈkæmiˌoː] *n, pl* **-eos 1** : camafeo *m* **2** *or* **cameo performance** : actuación *f* especial
camera [ˈkæmrə, ˈkæmərə] *n* : cámara *f,* máquina *f* fotográfica
Cameroonian [ˌkæməˈruːniən] *n* : camerunés *m,* -nesa *f*
camouflage[1] [ˈkæməˌflɑʒ, -ˌflɑdʒ] *vt* **-flaged; -flaging** : camuflajear, camuflar
camouflage[2] *n* : camuflaje *m*
camp[1] [ˈkæmp] *vi* : acampar, ir de camping
camp[2] *n* **1** : campamento *m* **2** FACTION : campo *m,* bando *m* <in the same camp : del mismo bando> **3 to pitch camp** : acampar, poner el campamento **4 to break camp** : levantar el campamento
campaign[1] [kæmˈpeɪn] *vi* : hacer (una) campaña
campaign[2] *n* : campaña *f*
campanile [ˌkæmpəˈniːˌliː, -ˈniːl] *n, pl* **-niles** *or* **-nili** [-ˈniːˌliː] : campanario *m*
camper [ˈkæmpər] *n* **1** : campista *mf* (persona) **2** : cámper *m* (vehículo)
campground [ˈkæmpˌgraʊnd] *n* : campamento *m,* camping *m*
camphor [ˈkæmpfər] *n* : alcanfor *m*
campsite [ˈkæmpˌsaɪt] *n* : campamento *m,* camping *m*
campus [ˈkæmpəs] *n* : campus *m,* recinto *m* universitario
can[1] [ˈkæn] *v aux, past* **could** [ˈkʊd]; *present s & pl* **can 1** : poder <could you help me? : ¿podría ayudarme?> **2** : saber <she can't drive yet : todavía no sabe manejar> **3** MAY : poder, tener permiso para <can I sit down? : ¿puedo sentarme?> **4** : poder <it can't be! : ¡no puede ser!> <where can they be? : ¿dónde estarán?>
can[2] [ˈkæn] *vt* **canned; canning 1** : enlatar, envasar <to can tomatoes : enlatar tomates> **2** DISMISS, FIRE : despedir, echar
can[3] *n* : lata *f,* envase *m,* cubo *m* <a can of beer : una lata de cerveza> <garbage can : cubo de basura>
Canadian [kəˈneɪdiən] *n* : canadiense *mf* — **Canadian** *adj*
canal [kəˈnæl] *n* **1** : canal *m,* tubo *m* <alimentary canal : tubo digestivo> **2** : canal *m* <Panama Canal : Canal de Panamá>
canapé [ˈkænəpi, -ˌpeɪ] *n* : canapé *m*
canary [kəˈnɛri] *n, pl* **-naries** : canario *m*
cancel [ˈkæntsəl] *vt* **-celed** *or* **-celled; -celing** *or* **-celling** : cancelar
cancellation [ˌkæntsəˈleɪʃən] *n* : cancelación *f*
cancer [ˈkæntsər] *n* : cáncer *m*
Cancer *n* : Cáncer *mf*
cancerous [ˈkæntsərəs] *adj* : canceroso
candelabrum [ˌkændəˈlɑbrəm, -ˈlæ-] *or* **candelabra** [-brə] *n, pl* **-bra** *or* **-bras** : candelabro *m*
candid [ˈkændɪd] *adj* **1** FRANK : franco, sincero, abierto **2** : natural, espontáneo (en la fotografía)
candidacy [ˈkændədəsi] *n, pl* **-cies** : candidatura *f*
candidate [ˈkændəˌdeɪt, -dət] *n* : candidato *m,* -ta *f*
candidly [ˈkændɪdli] *adv* : con franqueza
candied [ˈkændid] *adj* : confitado
candle [ˈkændəl] *n* : vela *f,* candela *f,* cirio *m* (ceremonial)
candlestick [ˈkændəlˌstɪk] *n* : candelero *m*
candor [ˈkændər] *n* : franqueza *f*
candy [ˈkændi] *n, pl* **-dies** : dulce *m,* caramelo *m*
cane[1] [ˈkeɪn] *vt* **caned; caning 1** : tapizar (muebles) con mimbre **2** FLOG : azotar con una vara
cane[2] *n* **1** : bastón *m* (para andar), vara *f* (para castigar) **2** REED : caña *f,* mimbre *m* (para muebles)
canine[1] [ˈkeɪˌnaɪn] *adj* : canino
canine[2] *n* **1** DOG : canino *m;* perro *m,* -rra *f* **2** *or* **canine tooth** : colmillo *m,* diente *m* canino
canister [ˈkænəstər] *n* : lata *f,* bote *m*
canker [ˈkæŋkər] *n* : úlcera *f* bucal
cannery [ˈkænəri] *n, pl* **-ries** : fábrica *f* de conservas
cannibal [ˈkænəbəl] *n* : caníbal *mf;* antropófago *m,* -ga *f*
cannibalism [ˈkænəbəˌlɪzəm] *n* : canibalismo *m,* antropofagia *f*
cannily [ˈkænəbəˌlaɪz] *adv* : astutamente, sagazmente
cannon [ˈkænən] *n, pl* **-nons** *or* **-non** : cañón *m*
cannot (can not) [ˈkænˌɑt, kəˈnɑt] → **can**[1]
canny [ˈkæni] *adj* **-nier; -est** SHREWD : astuto, sagaz
canoe[1] [kəˈnuː] *vt* **-noed; -noeing** : ir en canoa
canoe[2] *n* : canoa *f,* piragua *f*
canon [ˈkænən] *n* **1** : canon *m* <canon law : derecho canónico> **2** WORKS : canon *m* <the canon of American literature : el canon de la literatura americana> **3** : canónigo *m* (de una catedral) **4** STANDARD : canon *m,* norma *f*
canonize [ˈkænəˌnaɪz] *vt* **-ized; -izing** : canonizar

canopy [ˈkænəpi] *n, pl* **-pies** : dosel *m,* toldo *m*

cant[1] [ˈkænt] *vt* TILT : ladear, inclinar — *vi* **1** SLANT : ladearse, inclinarse, escorar (dícese de un barco) **2** : hablar insinceramente

cant[2] *n* **1** SLANT : plano *m* inclinado **2** JARGON : jerga *f* **3** : palabras *fpl* insinceras

can't [ˈkænt, ˈkant] (*contraction of* **can not**) → **can**[1]

cantaloupe [ˈkæntəl,oːp] *n* : melón *m,* cantalupo *m*

cantankerous [kænˈtæŋkərəs] *adj* : irritable, irascible — **cantankerously** *adv*

cantankerousness [kænˈtæŋkərəsnəs] *n* : irritabilidad *f,* irascibilidad *f*

cantata [kənˈtɑt̬ə] *n* : cantata *f*

canteen [kænˈtiːn] *n* **1** FLASK : cantimplora *f* **2** CAFETERIA : cantina *f,* comedor *m* **3** : club *m* para actividades sociales y recreativas

canter[1] [ˈkæntər] *vi* : ir a medio galope

canter[2] *n* : medio galope *m*

cantilever [ˈkæntə,liːvər, -,lɛvər] *n* **1** : viga *f* voladiza **2** **cantilever bridge** : puente *m* voladizo

canto [ˈkæn,toː] *n, pl* **-tos** : canto *m*

cantor [ˈkæntər] *n* : solista *mf*

canvas [ˈkænvəs] *n* **1** : lona *f* **2** SAILS : velas *fpl* (de un barco) **3** : lienzo *m,* tela *f* (de pintar) **4** PAINTING : pintura *f,* óleo *m,* cuadro *m*

canvass[1] [ˈkænvəs] *vt* **1** SOLICIT : solicitar votos o pedidos de, hacer campaña entre **2** SOUND OUT : sondear (opiniones, etc.)

canvass[2] *n* SURVEY : sondeo *m,* encuesta *f*

canyon [ˈkænjən] *n* : cañón *m*

cap[1] [ˈkæp] *vt* **capped; capping** **1** COVER : tapar (un recipiente), enfundar (un diente), cubrir (una montaña) **2** CLIMAX : coronar, ser el punto culminante de <to cap it all off : para colmo> **3** LIMIT : limitar, poner un tope a

cap[2] *n* **1** : gorra *f,* gorro *m,* cachucha *f Mex* <baseball cap : gorra de béisbol> **2** COVER, TOP : tapa *f,* tapón *m* (de botellas), corcholata *f Mex* **3** LIMIT : tope *m,* límite *m*

capability [,keɪpəˈbɪlət̬i] *n, pl* **-ties** : capacidad *f,* habilidad *f,* competencia *f*

capable [ˈkeɪpəbəl] *adj* : competente, capaz, hábil — **capably** [-bli] *adv*

capacious [kəˈpeɪʃəs] *adj* : amplio, espacioso, de gran capacidad *f*

capacity[1] [kəˈpæsət̬i] *adj* : completo, total <a capacity crowd : un lleno completo>

capacity[2] *n, pl* **-ties** **1** ROOM, SPACE : capacidad *f,* cabida *f,* espacio *m* **2** CAPABILITY : habilidad *f,* competencia *f* **3** FUNCTION, ROLE : calidad *f,* función *f* <in his capacity as ambassador : en su calidad de embajador>

cape [ˈkeɪp] *n* **1** : capa *f* **2** : cabo *m* <Cape Horn : el Cabo de Hornos>

caper[1] [ˈkeɪpər] *vi* : dar saltos, correr y brincar

caper[2] *n* **1** : alcaparra *f* <olives and capers : aceitunas y alcaparras> **2** ANTIC, PRANK : broma *f,* travesura *f* **3** LEAP : brinco *m,* salto *m*

Cape Verdean [ˈkeɪpˈvərdiən] *n* : caboverdiano *m,* -na *f* — **Cape Verdean** *adj*

capful [ˈkæp,fʊl] *n* : tapa *f,* tapita *f*

capillary[1] [ˈkæpə,lɛri] *adj* : capilar

capillary[2] *n, pl* **-ries** : capilar *m*

capital[1] [ˈkæpət̬əl] *adj* **1** : capital <capital punishment : pena capital> **2** : mayúsculo (dícese de las letras) **3** : de capital <capital assets : activo fijo> <capital gain : ganancia de capital, plusvalía> **4** EXCELLENT : excelente, estupendo

capital[2] *n* **1** *or* **capital city** : capital *f,* sede *f* del gobierno **2** WEALTH : capital *m* **3** *or* **capital letter** : mayúscula *f* **4** : capitel *m* (de una columna)

capitalism [ˈkæpət̬əl,ɪzəm] *n* : capitalismo *m*

capitalist[1] [ˈkæpət̬əlɪst] *or* **capitalistic** [,kæpət̬əlˈɪstɪk] *adj* : capitalista

capitalist[2] *n* : capitalista *mf*

capitalization [,kæpət̬ələˈzeɪʃən] *n* : capitalización *f*

capitalize [ˈkæpət̬əl,aɪz] *v* **-ized; -izing** *vt* **1** FINANCE : capitalizar, financiar **2** : escribir con mayúscula — *vi* **to capitalize on** : sacar partido de, aprovechar

capitol [ˈkæpət̬əl] *n* : capitolio *m*

capitulate [kəˈpɪtʃə,leɪt] *vi* **-lated; -lating** : capitular

capitulation [kə,pɪtʃəˈleɪʃən] *n* : capitulación *f*

capon [ˈkeɪ,pɑn, -pən] *n* : capón *m*

caprice [kəˈpriːs] *n* : capricho *m,* antojo *m*

capricious [kəˈprɪʃəs, -ˈpriː-] *adj* : caprichoso — **capriciously** *adv*

Capricorn [ˈkæprɪ,kɔrn] *n* : Capricornio *mf*

capsize [ˈkæp,saɪz, kæpˈsaɪz] *v* **-sized; -sizing** *vi* : volcar, volcarse — *vt* : hacer volcar

capstan [ˈkæpstən, -,stæn] *n* : cabrestante *m*

capsule [ˈkæpsəl, -,suːl] *n* **1** : cápsula *f* (en la farmacéutica y botánica) **2** **space capsule** : cápsula *f* espacial

captain[1] [ˈkæptən] *vt* : capitanear

captain[2] *n* **1** : capitán *m,* -tana *f* **2** HEADWAITER : jefe *m,* -fa *f* de comedor **3** **captain of industry** : magnate *mf*

caption[1] [ˈkæpʃən] *vt* : ponerle una leyenda a (una ilustración), titular (un artículo), subtitular (una película)

caption[2] *n* **1** HEADING : titular *m,* encabezamiento *m* **2** : leyenda *f* (al pie de una ilustración) **3** SUBTITLE : subtítulo *m*

captivate [ˈkæptə,veɪt] *vt* **-vated; -vating** CHARM : cautivar, hechizar, encantar
captivating [ˈkæptə,veɪt̬ɪŋ] *adj* : cautivador, hechicero, encantador
captive[1] [ˈkæptɪv] *adj* : cautivo
captive[2] *n* : cautivo *m,* -va *f*
captivity [kæpˈtɪvət̬i] *n* : cautiverio *m*
captor [ˈkæptər] *n* : captor *m,* -tora *f*
capture[1] [ˈkæpʃər] *vt* **-tured; -turing** **1** SEIZE : capturar, apresar **2** CATCH : captar <to capture one's interest : captar el interés de uno>
capture[2] *n* : captura *f,* apresamiento *m*
car [ˈkɑr] *n* **1** AUTOMOBILE : automóvil *m,* coche *m,* carro *m* **2** : vagón *m,* coche *m* (de un tren) **3** : cabina *f* (de un ascensor)
carafe [kəˈræf, -ˈrɑf] *n* : garrafa *f*
caramel [ˈkɑrməl; ˈkærəməl, -,mɛl] *n* **1** : caramelo *m,* azúcar *f* quemada **2** *or* **caramel candy** : caramelo *m,* dulce *m* de leche
carat [ˈkærət] *n* : quilate *m*
caravan [ˈkærə,væn] *n* : caravana *f*
caraway [ˈkærə,weɪ] *n* : alcaravea *f*
carbine [ˈkɑr,baɪn, -,bi:n] *n* : carabina *f*
carbohydrate [,kɑrboˈhaɪ,dreɪt, -drət] *n* : carbohidrato *m,* hidrato *m* de carbono
carbon [ˈkɑrbən] *n* **1** : carbono *m* **2** → **carbon paper** **3** → **carbon copy**
carbonated [ˈkɑrbə,neɪt̬əd] *adj* : carbonatado (dícese del agua), gaseoso (dícese de las bebidas)
carbon copy *n* **1** : copia *f* al carbón **2** DUPLICATE : duplicado *m,* copia *f* exacta
carbon paper *n* : papel *m* carbón
carbuncle [ˈkɑr,bʌŋkəl] *n* : carbunco *m*
carburetor [ˈkɑrbə,reɪt̬ər, -bjə-] *n* : carburador *m*
carcass [ˈkɑrkəs] *n* : cuerpo *m* (de un animal muerto)
carcinogen [kɑrˈsɪnədʒən, ˈkɑrsənə,dʒɛn] *n* : carcinógeno *m,* cancerígeno *m*
carcinogenic [,kɑrsənoˈdʒɛnɪk] *adj* : carcinogénico
card[1] [ˈkɑrd] *vt* : cardar (fibras)
card[2] *n* **1** : carta *f,* naipe *m* <to play cards : jugar a las cartas> <a deck of cards : una baraja> **2** : tarjeta *f* <birthday card : tarjeta de cumpleaños> <business card : tarjeta (de visita)> **3** : carda *f* (para cardar fibras)
cardboard [ˈkɑrd,bord] *n* : cartón *m,* cartulina *f*
cardiac [ˈkɑrdi,æk] *adj* : cardíaco, cardiaco
cardigan [ˈkɑrdɪgən] *n* : cárdigan *m,* chaqueta *f* de punto
cardinal[1] [ˈkɑrdənəl] *adj* FUNDAMENTAL : cardinal, fundamental
cardinal[2] *n* : cardenal *m*
cardinal number *n* : número *m* cardinal
cardinal point *n* : punto *m* cardinal
cardiologist [,kɑrdiˈɑlədʒɪst] *n* : cardiólogo *m,* -ga *f*
cardiology [,kɑrdiˈɑlədʒi] *n* : cardiología *f*
cardiovascular [,kɑrdioˈvæskjələr] *adj* : cardiovascular
care[1] [ˈkær] *v* **cared; caring** *vi* **1** : importarle a uno <they don't care : no les importa> **2** : preocuparse, inquietarse <she cares about the poor : se preocupa por los pobres> **3 to care for** TEND : cuidar (de), atender, encargarse de **4 to care for** CHERISH : querer, sentir cariño por **5 to care for** LIKE : gustarle (algo a uno) <I don't care for your attitude : tu actitud no me agrada> — *vt* WISH : desear, querer <if you care to go : si deseas ir>
care[2] *n* **1** ANXIETY : inquietud *f,* preocupación *f* **2** CAREFULNESS : cuidado *m,* atención *f* <handle with care : manejar con cuidado> **3** CHARGE : cargo *m,* cuidado *m* **4 to take care of** : cuidar (de), atender, encargarse de
careen [kəˈri:n] *vi* **1** SWAY : oscilar, balancearse **2** CAREER : ir a toda velocidad
career[1] [kəˈrɪr] *vi* : ir a toda velocidad
career[2] *n* VOCATION : vocación *f,* profesión *f,* carrera *f*
carefree [ˈkær,fri:, ,kærˈ-] *adj* : despreocupado
careful [ˈkærfəl] *adj* **1** CAUTIOUS : cuidadoso, cauteloso **2** PAINSTAKING : cuidadoso, esmerado, meticuloso
carefully [ˈkærfəli] *adv* : con cuidado, cuidadosamente
carefulness [ˈkærfəlnəs] *n* **1** CAUTION : cuidado *m,* cautela *f* **2** METICULOUSNESS : esmero *m,* meticulosidad *f*
caregiver [ˈkær,gɪvər] *n* : persona *f* que cuida a niños o enfermos
careless [ˈkærləs] *adj* : descuidado, negligente — **carelessly** *adv*
carelessness [ˈkærləsnəs] *n* : descuido *m,* negligencia *f*
caress[1] [kəˈrɛs] *vt* : acariciar
caress[2] *n* : caricia *f*
caret [ˈkærət] *n* : signo *m* de intercalación
caretaker [ˈkɛr,teɪkər] *n* : conserje *mf;* velador *m,* -dora *f*
cargo [ˈkɑr,go:] *n, pl* **-goes** *or* **-gos** : cargamento *m,* carga *f*
caribou [ˈkærə,bu:] *n, pl* **-bou** *or* **-bous** : caribú *m*
caricature[1] [ˈkærɪkə,tʃʊr] *vt* **-tured; -turing** : caricaturizar
caricature[2] *n* : caricatura *f*
caricaturist [ˈkærɪkə,tʃʊrɪst] *n* : caricaturista *mf*
caries [ˈkær,i:z] *n, pl* **caries** : caries *f*
carillon [ˈkærə,lɑn] *n* : carillón *m*
carmine [ˈkɑrmən, -,maɪn] *n* : carmín *m*
carnage [ˈkɑrnɪdʒ] *n* : matanza *f,* carnicería *f*

carnal [ˈkɑrnəl] *adj* : carnal
carnation [kɑrˈneɪʃən] *n* : clavel *m*
carnival [ˈkɑrnəvəl] *n* : carnaval *m*, feria *f*
carnivore [ˈkɑrnəˌvor] *n* : carnívoro *m*
carnivorous [kɑrˈnɪvərəs] *adj* : carnívoro
carol[1] [ˈkærəl] *vi* **-oled** *or* **-olled; -oling** *or* **-olling** : cantar villancicos
carol[2] *n* : villancico *m*
caroler *or* **caroller** [ˈkærələr] *n* : persona *f* que canta villancicos
carom[1] [ˈkærəm] *vi* **1** REBOUND : rebotar <the bullet caromed off the wall : la bala rebotó contra el muro> **2** : hacer carambola (en billar)
carom[2] *n* : carambola *f*
carouse [kəˈraʊz] *vt* **-roused; -rousing** : irse de parranda, irse de juerga
carousel *or* **carrousel** [ˌkærəˈsɛl, ˈkærəˌ-] *n* : carrusel *m*, tiovivo *m*
carouser [kəˈraʊzər] *n* : juerguista *mf*
carp[1] [ˈkɑrp] *vi* **1** COMPLAIN : quejarse **2 to carp at** : criticar
carp[2] *n, pl* **carp** *or* **carps** : carpa *f*
carpel [ˈkɑrpəl] *n* : carpelo *m*
carpenter [ˈkɑrpəntər] *n* : carpintero *m*, -ra *f*
carpentry [ˈkɑrpəntri] *n* : carpintería *f*
carpet[1] [ˈkɑrpət] *vt* : alfombrar
carpet[2] *n* : alfombra *f*
carpeting [ˈkɑrpət̬ɪŋ] *n* : alfombrado *m*
carport [ˈkɑrˌpɔrt] *n* : cochera *f*, garaje *m* abierto
carriage [ˈkærɪdʒ] *n* **1** TRANSPORT : transporte *m* **2** POSTURE : porte *m*, postura *f* **3 horse–drawn carriage** : carruaje *m*, coche *m* **4 baby carriage** : cochecito *m*
carrier [ˈkæriər] *n* **1** : transportista *mf*, empresa *f* de transportes **2** : portador *m*, -dora *f* (de una enfermedad) **3 aircraft carrier** : portaaviones *m*
carrier pigeon : paloma *f* mensajera
carrion [ˈkæriən] *n* : carroña *f*
carrot [ˈkærət] *n* : zanahoria *f*
carry [ˈkæri] *v* **-ried; -rying** *vt* **1** TRANSPORT : llevar, cargar, transportar (cargamento), conducir (electricidad), portar (un virus) <to carry a bag : cargar una bolsa> <to carry money : llevar dinero encima, traer dinero consigo> **2** BEAR : soportar, aguantar, resistir (peso) **3** STOCK : vender, tener en abasto **4** ENTAIL : llevar, implicar, acarrear **5** WIN : ganar (una elección o competición), aprobar (una moción) **6 to carry oneself** : portarse, comportarse <he carried himself honorably : se comportó dignamente> — *vi* : oírse, proyectarse <her voice carries well : su voz se puede oír desde lejos>
carryall [ˈkæriˌɔl] *n* : bolsa *f* de viaje
carry away *vt* **to get carried away** : exaltarse, entusiasmarse
carry on *vt* CONDUCT : realizar, ejercer, mantener <to carry on research : realizar investigaciones> <to carry on a correspondence : mantener una correspondencia> — *vi* **1** : portarse de manera escandalosa o inapropiada <it's embarrassing how he carries on : su manera de comportarse da vergüenza> **2** CONTINUE : seguir, continuar
carry out *vt* **1** PERFORM : llevar a cabo, realizar **2** FULFILL : cumplir
cart[1] [ˈkɑrt] *vt* : acarrear, llevar
cart[2] *n* : carreta *f*, carro *m*
cartel [kɑrˈtɛl] *n* : cártel *m*
cartilage [ˈkɑrt̬əlɪdʒ] *n* : cartílago *m*
cartilaginous [ˌkɑrt̬əlˈædʒənəs] *adj* : cartilaginoso
cartographer [kɑrˈtɑgrəfər] *n* : cartógrafo *m*, -fa *f*
cartography [kɑrˈtɑgrəfi] *n* : cartografía *f*
carton [ˈkɑrtən] *n* : caja *f* de cartón
cartoon [kɑrˈtuːn] *n* **1** : chiste *m* (gráfico), caricatura *f* <a political cartoon : un chiste político> **2** COMIC STRIP : tira *f* cómica, historieta *f* **3** *or* **animated cartoon** : dibujo *m* animado
cartoonist [kɑrˈtuːnɪst] *n* : caricaturista *mf*, dibujante *mf* (de chistes)
cartridge [ˈkɑrtrɪdʒ] *n* : cartucho *m*
carve [ˈkɑrv] *vt* **carved; carving 1** : tallar (madera), esculpir (piedra), grabar <he carved his name in the bark : grabó su nombre en la corteza> **2** SLICE : cortar, trinchar (carne)
cascade[1] [kæsˈkeɪd] *vi* **-caded; -cading** : caer en cascada
cascade[2] *n* : cascada *f*, salto *m* de agua
case[1] [ˈkeɪs] *vt* **cased; casing 1** BOX, PACK : embalar, encajonar **2** INSPECT : observar, inspeccionar (antes de cometer un delito)
case[2] *n* **1** : caso *m* <an unusual case : un caso insólito> <ablative case : caso ablativo> <a case of the flu : un caso de gripe> **2** BOX : caja *f* **3** CONTAINER : funda *f*, estuche *m* **4 in any case** : de todos modos, en cualquier caso **5 in case** : como precaución <just in case : por si acaso> **6 in case of** : en caso de
casement [ˈkeɪsmənt] *n* : ventana *f* con bisagras
cash[1] [ˈkæʃ] *vt* : convertir en efectivo, cobrar, cambiar (un cheque)
cash[2] *n* : efectivo *m*, dinero *m* en efectivo
cashew [ˈkæˌʃuː, kəˈʃuː] *n* : anacardo *m*
cashier[1] [kæˈʃɪr] *vt* : destituir, despedir
cashier[2] *n* : cajero *m*, -ra *f*
cashmere [ˈkæʒˌmɪr, ˈkæʃ-] *n* : cachemir *m*
casino [kəˈsiːˌnoː] *n, pl* **-nos** : casino *m*
cask [ˈkæsk] *n* : tonel *m*, barrica *f*, barril *m*
casket [ˈkæskət] *n* COFFIN : ataúd *m*, féretro *m*

casserole [ˈkæsəˌroːl] *n* **1 :** cazuela *f* **2 :** guiso *m,* guisado *m* <tuna casserole : guiso de atún>
cassette [kəˈsɛt, kæ-] *n* **:** cassette *mf*
cassock [ˈkæsək] *n* **:** sotana *f*
cast[1] [ˈkæst] *vt* **cast; casting 1** THROW **:** tirar, echar, arrojar <the die is cast : la suerte está echada> **2 :** depositar (un voto) **3 :** asignar (papeles en una obra de teatro) **4** MOLD **:** moldear, fundir, vaciar **5 to cast off** ABANDON **:** desamparar, abandonar
cast[2] *n* **1** THROW **:** lance *m,* lanzamiento *m* **2** APPEARANCE **:** aspecto *m,* forma *f* **3 :** elenco *m,* reparto *m* (de una obra de teatro) **4 plaster cast :** molde *m* de yeso, escayola *f*
castanets [ˌkæstəˈnɛts] *npl* **:** castañuelas *fpl*
castaway[1] [ˈkæstəˌweɪ] *adj* **:** náufrago
castaway[2] *n* **:** náufrago *m,* -ga *f*
caste [ˈkæst] *n* **:** casta *f*
caster [ˈkæstər] *n* **:** ruedita *f* (de un mueble)
castigate [ˈkæstəˌgeɪt] *vt* **-gated; -gating :** castigar severamente, censurar, reprobar
cast iron *n* **:** hierro *m* fundido
castle [ˈkæsəl] *n* **1 :** castillo *m* **2 :** torre *f* (en ajedrez)
cast–off [ˈkæstˌɔf] *adj* **:** desechado
castoff [ˈkæstˌɔf] *n* **:** desecho *m*
castrate [ˈkæsˌtreɪt] *vt* **-trated; -trating :** castrar
castration [kæˈstreɪʃən] *n* **:** castración *f*
casual [ˈkæʒʊəl] *adj* **1** FORTUITOUS **:** casual, fortuito **2** INDIFFERENT **:** indiferente, despreocupado **3** INFORMAL **:** informal — **casually** [ˈkæʒʊəli, ˈkæʒəli] *adv*
casualness [ˈkæʒʊəlnəs] *n* **1** FORTUITOUSNESS **:** casualidad *f* **2** INDIFFERENCE **:** indiferencia *f,* despreocupación *f* **3** INFORMALITY **:** informalidad *f*
casualty [ˈkæʒʊəlti, ˈkæʒəl-] *n, pl* **-ties 1** ACCIDENT **:** accidente *m* serio, desastre *m* **2** VICTIM **:** víctima *f;* baja *f;* herido *m,* -da *f*
cat [ˈkæt] *n* **:** gato *m,* -ta *f*
cataclysm [ˈkæt̬əˌklɪzəm] *n* **:** cataclismo *m*
cataclysmal [ˌkæt̬əˈklɪzməl] *or* **cataclysmic** [ˌkæt̬əˈklɪzmɪk] *adj* **:** catastrófico
catacombs [ˈkæt̬əˌkoːmz] *npl* **:** catacumbas *fpl*
catalog[1] *or* **catalogue** [ˈkæt̬əˌlɔg] *vt* **-loged** *or* **-logued; -loging** *or* **-loguing :** catalogar
catalog[2] *n* **:** catálogo *m*
catalpa [kəˈtælpə, -ˈtɔl-] *n* **:** catalpa *f*
catalyst [ˈkæt̬ələst] *n* **:** catalizador *m*
catalytic [ˌkæt̬əlˈɪtɪk] *adj* **:** catalítico
catamaran [ˌkæt̬əməˈræn, ˈkæt̬əməˌræn] *n* **:** catamarán *m*
catapult[1] [ˈkæt̬əˌpʌlt, -ˌpʊlt] *vt* **:** catapultar
catapult[2] *n* **:** catapulta *f*
cataract [ˈkæt̬əˌrækt] *n* **:** catarata *f*
catarrh [kəˈtɑr] *n* **:** catarro *m*
catastrophe [kəˈtæstrəˌfiː] *n* **:** catástrofe *f*
catastrophic [ˌkæt̬əˈstrɑfɪk] *adj* **:** catastrófico — **catastrophically** [-fɪkli] *adv*
catcall [ˈkætˌkɔl] *n* **:** rechifla *f,* abucheo *m*
catch[1] [ˈkætʃ, ˈkɛtʃ] *v* **caught** [ˈkɔt]; **catching** *vt* **1** CAPTURE, TRAP **:** capturar, agarrar, atrapar, coger **2 :** agarrar, pillar *fam,* tomar de sorpresa <they caught him red-handed : lo pillaron con las manos en la masa> **3** GRASP **:** agarrar, captar **4** ENTANGLE **:** enganchar, enredar **5 :** tomar (un tren, etc.) **6 :** contagiarse de <to catch a cold : contagiarse de un resfriado, resfriarse> — *vi* **1** GRASP **:** agarrar **2** HOOK **:** engancharse **3** IGNITE **:** prender, agarrar
catch[2] *n* **1** CATCHING **:** captura *f,* atrapada *f,* parada *f* (de una pelota) **2 :** redada *f* (de pescado), presa *f* (de caza) <he's a good catch : es un buen partido> **3** LATCH **:** pestillo *m,* pasador *m* **4** DIFFICULTY, TRICK **:** problema *m,* trampa *f,* truco *m*
catcher [ˈkætʃər, ˈkɛ-] *n* **:** catcher *mf;* receptor *m* , -tora *f* (en béisbol)
catching [ˈkætʃɪŋ, ˈkɛ-] *adj* **:** contagioso
catchup [ˈkætʃəp, ˈkɛ-] → **ketchup**
catchword [ˈkætʃˌwərd, ˈkɛtʃ-] *n* **:** eslogan *m,* lema *m*
catchy [ˈkætʃi, ˈkɛ-] *adj* **catchier; -est :** pegajoso <a catchy song : una canción pegajosa>
catechism [ˈkæt̬əˌkɪzəm] *n* **:** catecismo *m*
categorical [ˌkæt̬əˈgɔrɪkəl] *adj* **:** categórico, absoluto, rotundo — **categorically** [-kli] *adv*
categorize [ˈkæt̬ɪgəˌraɪz] *vt* **-rized; -rizing :** clasificar, catalogar
category [ˈkæt̬əˌgori] *n, pl* **-ries :** categoría *f,* género *m,* clase *f*
cater [ˈkeɪt̬ər] *vi* **1 :** proveer alimentos (para fiestas, bodas, etc.) **2 to cater to :** atender a <to cater to all tastes : atender a todos los gustos>
catercorner[1] [ˈkæt̬iˌkɔrnər, ˈkæt̬ə-, ˈkɪti-] *or* **cater–cornered** [-ˌkɔrnərd] *adv* **:** diagonalmente, en diagonal
catercorner[2] *or* **cater–cornered** *adj* **:** diagonal
caterer [ˈkeɪt̬ərər] *n* **:** proveedor *m,* -dora *f* de comida
caterpillar [ˈkæt̬ərˌpɪlər] *n* **:** oruga *f*
catfish [ˈkætˌfɪʃ] *n* **:** bagre *m*
catgut [ˈkætˌgʌt] *n* **:** cuerda *f* de tripa
catharsis [kəˈθɑrsɪs] *n, pl* **catharses** [-ˌsiːz] **:** catarsis *f*
cathartic[1] [kəˈθɑrt̬ɪk] *adj* **:** catártico
cathartic[2] *n* **:** purgante *m*
cathedral [kəˈθiːdrəl] *n* **:** catedral *f*
catheter [ˈkæθət̬ər] *n* **:** catéter *m,* sonda *f*

cathode ['kæ,θo:d] *n* : cátodo *m*
catholic ['kæθəlɪk] *adj* **1** BROAD, UNIVERSAL : liberal, universal **2 Catholic** : católico
Catholic *n* : católico *m*, -ca *f*
Catholicism [kə'θɑlə,sɪzəm] *n* : catolicismo *m*
catkin ['kætkɪn] *n* : amento *m*, candelilla *f*
catlike ['kæt,laɪk] *adj* : gatuno, felino
catnap[1] ['kæt,næp] *vi* **-napped; -napping** : tomarse una siestecita
catnap[2] *n* : siesta *f* breve, siestecita *f*
catnip ['kæt,nɪp] *n* : nébeda *f*
catsup ['kɛtʃəp, 'kætsəp] → **ketchup**
cattail ['kæt,teɪl] *n* : espadaña *f*, anea *f*
cattiness ['kætinəs] *n* : malicia *f*
cattle ['kætəl] *npl* : ganado *m*, reses *mpl*
cattleman ['kætəlmən, -,mæn] *n, pl* **-men** [-mən, -,mɛn] : ganadero *m*
catty ['kæti] *adj* **-tier; -est** : malicioso, malintencionado
catwalk ['kæt,wɔk] *n* : pasarela *f*
Caucasian[1] [kɔ'keɪʒən] *adj* : caucásico
Caucasian[2] *n* : caucásico *m*, -ca *f*
caucus ['kɔkəs] *n* : junta *f* de políticos
caught → **catch**
cauldron ['kɔldrən] *n* : caldera *f*
cauliflower ['kɑlɪ,flaʊər, 'kɔ-] *n* : coliflor *f*
caulk[1] ['kɔk] *vt* : calafatear (un barco), enmasillar (una grieta)
caulk[2] *n* : masilla *f*
causal ['kɔzəl] *adj* : causal
cause[1] ['kɔz] *vt* **caused; causing** : causar, provocar, ocasionar
cause[2] *n* **1** ORIGIN : causa *f*, origen *m* **2** REASON : causa *f*, razón *f*, motivo *m* **3** LAWSUIT : litigio *m*, pleito *m* **4** MOVEMENT : causa *f*, movimiento *m*
causeless ['kɔzləs] *adj* : sin causa
causeway ['kɔz,weɪ] *n* : camino *m* elevado
caustic ['kɔstɪk] *adj* **1** CORROSIVE : cáustico, corrosivo **2** BITING : mordaz, sarcástico
cauterize ['kɔtə,raɪz] *vt* **-ized; -izing** : cauterizar
caution[1] ['kɔʃən] *vt* : advertir
caution[2] *n* **1** WARNING : advertencia *f*, aviso *m* **2** CARE, PRUDENCE : precaución *f*, cuidado *m*, cautela *f*
cautionary ['kɔʃə,nɛri] *adv* : admonitorio <cautionary tale : cuento moral>
cautious ['kɔʃəs] *adj* : cauteloso, cuidadoso, precavido
cautiously ['kɔʃəsli] *adv* : cautelosamente, con precaución
cautiousness ['kɔʃəsnəs] *n* : cautela *f*, precaución *f*
cavalcade [,kævəl'keɪd, 'kævəl,-] *n* **1** : cabalgata *f* **2** SERIES : serie *f*
cavalier[1] [,kævə'lɪr] *adj* : altivo, desdeñoso — **cavalierly** *adv*
cavalier[2] *n* : caballero *m*
cavalry ['kævəlri] *n, pl* **-ries** : caballería *f*
cave[1] ['keɪv] *vi* **caved; caving** *or* **to cave in** : derrumbarse
cave[2] *n* : cueva *f*
cavern ['kævərn] *n* : caverna *f*
cavernous ['kævərnəs] *adj* : cavernoso — **cavernously** *adv*
caviar *or* **caviare** ['kævi,ɑr, 'kɑ-] *n* : caviar *m*
cavity ['kævəti] *n, pl* **-ties 1** HOLE : cavidad *f*, hueco *m* **2** CARIES : caries *f*
cavort [kə'vɔrt] *vi* : brincar, hacer cabriolas
caw[1] ['kɔ] *vi* : graznar
caw[2] *n* : graznido *m*
cayenne pepper [,kaɪ'ɛn, ,keɪ-] *n* : pimienta *f* cayena, pimentón *m*
CD [,si:'di:] *n* : CD *m*, disco *m* compacto
cease ['si:s] *v* **ceased; ceasing** *vt* : dejar de <they ceased bickering : dejaron de discutir> — *vi* : cesar, pasarse
ceaseless ['si:sləs] *adj* : incesante, continuo
cedar ['si:dər] *n* : cedro *m*
cede ['si:d] *vt* **ceded; ceding** : ceder, conceder
ceiling ['si:lɪŋ] *n* **1** : techo *m*, cielo *m* **2** LIMIT : límite *m*, tope *m*
celebrant ['sɛləbrənt] *n* : celebrante *mf*, oficiante *mf*
celebrate ['sɛlə,breɪt] *v* **-brated; -brating** *vt* **1** : celebrar, oficiar <to celebrate Mass : celebrar la misa> **2** : celebrar, festejar <we're celebrating our anniversary : estamos celebrando nuestro aniversario> **3** EXTOL : alabar, ensalzar, exaltar — *vi* : estar de fiesta, divertirse
celebrated ['sɛlə,breɪtəd] *adj* : célebre, famoso, renombrado
celebration [,sɛlə'breɪʃən] *n* : celebración *f*, festejos *mpl*
celebrity [sə'lɛbrəti] *n, pl* **-ties 1** RENOWN : fama *f*, renombre *m*, celebridad *f* **2** PERSONALITY : celebridad *f*, personaje *m*
celery ['sɛləri] *n, pl* **-eries** : apio *m*
celestial [sə'lɛstʃəl, -'lɛstiəl] *adj* **1** : celeste **2** HEAVENLY : celestial, paradisiaco
celibacy ['sɛləbəsi] *n* : celibato *m*
celibate[1] ['sɛləbət] *adj* : célibe
celibate[2] *n* : célibe *mf*
cell ['sɛl] *n* **1** : célula *f* (de un organismo) **2** : celda *f* (en una cárcel, etc.) **3** : elemento *m* (de una pila)
cellar ['sɛlər] *n* **1** BASEMENT : sótano *m* **2** : bodega *f* (de vinos)
cellist ['tʃɛlɪst] *n* : violonchelista *mf*
cello ['tʃɛ,lo:] *n, pl* **-los** : violonchelo *m*
cellophane ['sɛlə,feɪn] *n* : celofán *m*
cellular ['sɛljələr] *adj* : celular
cellulose ['sɛljə,lo:s] *n* : celulosa *f*

Celsius ['sɛlsiəs] *adj* : centígrado <100 degrees Celsius : 100 grados centígrados>
Celt ['kɛlt, 'sɛlt] *n* : celta *mf*
Celtic[1] ['kɛltɪk, 'sɛl-] *adj* : celta
Celtic[2] *n* : celta *m* (idioma)
cement[1] [sɪ'mɛnt] *vi* : unir o cubrir algo con cemento, cementar
cement[2] *n* **1** : cemento *m* **2** GLUE : pegamento *m*
cemetery ['sɛmə,tɛri] *n, pl* **-teries** : cementerio *m,* panteón *m*
censer ['sɛntsər] *n* : incensario *m*
censor[1] ['sɛntsər] *vt* : censurar
censor[2] *n* : censor *m,* -sora *f*
censorious [sɛn'soriəs] *adj* : de censura, crítico
censorship ['sɛntsər,ʃɪp] *n* : censura *f*
censure[1] ['sɛntʃər] *vt* **-sured; -suring** : censurar, criticar, reprobar — **censurable** [-tʃərəbəl] *adj*
censure[2] *n* : censura *f,* reproche *f* oficial
census ['sɛntsəs] *n* : censo *m*
cent ['sɛnt] *n* : centavo *m*
centaur ['sɛn,tɔr] *n* : centauro *m*
centennial[1] [sɛn'tɛniəl] *adj* : del centenario
centennial[2] *n* : centenario *m*
center[1] ['sɛntər] *vt* **1** : centrar **2** CONCENTRATE : concentrar, fijar, enfocar — *vi* : centrarse, enfocarse
center[2] *n* **1** : centro *m* <center of gravity : centro de gravedad> **2** : centro *mf* (en futbol americano), pívot *mf* (en basquetbol)
centerpiece ['sɛntər,pi:s] *n* : centro *m* de mesa
centigrade ['sɛntə,greɪd, 'sɑn-] *adj* : centígrado
centigram ['sɛntə,græm, 'sɑn-] *n* : centigramo *m*
centimeter ['sɛntə,mi:tər, 'sɑn-] *n* : centímetro *m*
centipede ['sɛntə,pi:d] *n* : ciempiés *m*
central ['sɛntrəl] *adj* **1** : céntrico, central <in a central location : en un lugar céntrico> **2** MAIN, PRINCIPAL : central, fundamental, principal
Central American[1] *adj* : centroamericano
Central American[2] *n* : centroamericano *m,* -na *f*
centralization [,sɛntrələ'zeɪʃən] *n* : centralización *f*
centralize ['sɛntrə,laɪz] *vt* **-ized; -izing** : centralizar
centrally ['sɛntrəli] *adv* **1 centrally heated** : con calefacción central **2 centrally located** : céntrico, en un lugar céntrico
centre ['sɛntər] → **center**
centrifugal force [sɛn'trɪfjəgəl, -'trɪfɪgəl] *n* : fuerza *f* centrífuga
century ['sɛntʃəri] *n, pl* **-ries** : siglo *m*
ceramic[1] [sə'ræmɪk] *adj* : de cerámica
ceramic[2] *n* **1** : objeto *m* de cerámica, cerámica *f* **2 ceramics** *npl* : cerámica *f*
cereal[1] ['sɪriəl] *adj* : cereal
cereal[2] *n* : cereal *m*
cerebellum [,sɛrə'bɛləm] *n, pl* **-bellums** *or* **-bella** [-'bɛlə] : cerebelo *m*
cerebral [sə'ri:brəl, 'sɛrə-] *adj* : cerebral
cerebral palsy *n* : parálisis *f* cerebral
cerebrum [sə'ri:brəm, 'sɛrə-] *n, pl* **-brums** *or* **-bra** [-brə] : cerebro *m*
ceremonial[1] [,sɛrə'mo:niəl] *adj* : ceremonial
ceremonial[2] *n* : ceremonial *m*
ceremonious [,sɛrə'mo:niəs] *adj* **1** FORMAL : ceremonioso, formal **2** CEREMONIAL : ceremonial
ceremony ['sɛrə,mo:ni] *n, pl* **-nies** : ceremonia *f*
cerise [sə'ri:s] *n* : rojo *m* cereza
certain[1] ['sərtən] *adj* **1** DEFINITE : cierto, determinado <a certain percentage : un porcentaje determinado> **2** TRUE : cierto, con certeza <I don't know for certain : no sé exactamente> **3** : cierto, alguno <it has a certain charm : tiene cierta gracia> **4** INEVITABLE : seguro, inevitable **5** ASSURED : seguro, asegurado <she's certain to do well : seguro que le irá bien>
certain[2] *pron* : ciertos *pl,* algunos *pl* <certain of my friends : algunos de mis amigos>
certainly ['sərtənli] *adv* **1** DEFINITELY : ciertamente, seguramente **2** OF COURSE : por supuesto
certainty ['sərtənti] *n, pl* **-ties** : certeza *f,* certidumbre *f,* seguridad *f*
certifiable [,sərtə'faɪəbəl] *adj* : certificable
certificate [sər'tɪfɪkət] *n* : certificado *m,* acta *f* <birth certificate : acta de nacimiento>
certification [,sərtəfə'keɪʃən] *n* : certificación *f*
certify ['sərtə,faɪ] *vt* **-fied; -fying 1** VERIFY : certificar, verificar, confirmar **2** ENDORSE : endosar, aprobar oficialmente
certitude ['sərtə,tu:d, -,tju:d] *n* : certeza *f,* certidumbre *f*
cervical ['sərvɪkəl] *adj* **1** : cervical (dícese del cuello) **2** : del cuello del útero
cervix ['sərvɪks] *n, pl* **-vices** [-və-,si:z] *or* **-vixes 1** NECK : cerviz *f* **2** *or* **uterine cervix** : cuello *m* del útero
cesarean[1] [sɪ'zæriən] *adj* : cesáreo
cesarean[2] *n* : cesárea *f*
cesium ['si:ziəm] *n* : cesio *m*
cessation [sɛ'seɪʃən] *n* : cesación *f,* cese *m*
cesspool ['sɛs,pu:l] *n* : pozo *m* séptico
Chadian ['tʃædiən] *n* : chadiano *m,* -na *f* — **Chadian** *adj*
chafe ['tʃeɪf] *v* **chafed; chafing** *vi* : enojarse, irritarse — *vt* : rozar
chaff ['tʃæf] *n* **1** : barcia *f,* granzas *fpl* **2 to separate the wheat from the chaff** : separar el grano de la paja

chafing dish [ˈtʃeɪfɪŋˌdɪʃ] *n* : escalfador *m*

chagrin[1] [ʃəˈgrɪn] *vt* : desilusionar, avergonzar

chagrin[2] *n* : desilusión *f,* disgusto *m*

chain[1] [ˈtʃeɪn] *vt* : encadenar

chain[2] *n* **1** : cadena *f* <steel chain : cadena de acero> <restaurant chain : cadena de restaurantes> **2** SERIES : serie *f* <chain of events : serie de eventos> **3 chains** *npl* FETTERS : grillos *mpl*

chair[1] [ˈtʃɛr] *vt* : presidir, moderar

chair[2] *n* **1** : silla *f* **2** CHAIRMANSHIP : presidencia *f* **3** → **chairman, chairwoman**

chairman [ˈtʃɛrmən] *n, pl* **-men** [-mən, -ˌmɛn] : presidente *m*

chairmanship [ˈtʃɛrmənˌʃɪp] *n* : presidencia *f*

chairwoman [ˈtʃɛrˌwʊmən] *n, pl* **-women** [-ˌwɪmən] : presidenta *f*

chaise longue [ˈʃeɪzˈlɔŋ] *n, pl* **chaise longues** [-lɔŋ, -ˈlɔŋz] : chaise longue *f*

chalet [ʃæˈleɪ] *n* : chalet *m,* chalé *m*

chalice [ˈtʃælɪs] *n* : cáliz *m*

chalk[1] [ˈtʃɔk] *vt* : escribir con tiza

chalk[2] *n* **1** LIMESTONE : creta *f,* caliza *f* **2** : tiza *f,* gis *m Mex* (para escribir)

chalkboard [ˈtʃɔkˌbord] → **blackboard**

chalk up *vt* **1** ASCRIBE : atribuir, adscribir **2** SCORE : apuntarse, anotarse (una victoria, etc.)

chalky [ˈtʃɔki] *adj* **chalkier; -est** : calcáreo

challenge[1] [ˈtʃælɪndʒ] *vt* **-lenged; -lenging 1** DISPUTE : disputar, cuestionar, poner en duda **2** DARE : desafiar, retar **3** STIMULATE : estimular, incentivar

challenge[2] *n* : reto *m,* desafío *m*

challenger [ˈtʃælɪndʒər] *n* : retador *m,* -dora *f;* contendiente *mf*

chamber [ˈtʃeɪmbər] *n* **1** ROOM : cámara *f,* sala *f* <the senate chamber : la cámara del senado> **2** : recámara *f* (de un arma de fuego), cámara *f* (de combustión) **3** : cámara *f* <chamber of commerce : cámara de comercio> **4 chambers** *npl or* **judge's chambers** : despacho *m* del juez

chambermaid [ˈtʃeɪmbərˌmeɪd] *n* : camarera *f*

chamber music *n* : música *f* de cámara

chameleon [kəˈmiːljən, -liən] *n* : camaleón *m*

chamois [ˈʃæmi] *n, pl* **chamois** [-mi, -miz] : gamuza *f*

champ[1] [ˈtʃæmp, ˈtʃɑmp] *vi* **1** : masticar ruidosamente **2 to champ at the bit** : impacientarse, comerle a uno la impaciencia

champ[2] [ˈtʃæmp] *n* : campeón *m,* -peona *f*

champagne [ʃæmˈpeɪn] *n* : champaña *m,* champán *m*

champion[1] [ˈtʃæmpiən] *vt* : defender, luchar por (una causa)

champion[2] *n* **1** ADVOCATE, DEFENDER : paladín *m;* campeón *m,* -peona *f;* defensor *m,* -sora *f* **2** WINNER : campeón *m,* -peona *f* <world champion : campeón mundial>

championship [ˈtʃæmpiənˌʃɪp] *n* : campeonato *m*

chance[1] [ˈtʃænts] *v* **chanced; chancing** *vi* **1** HAPPEN : ocurrir por casualidad **2 to chance upon** : encontrar por casualidad — *vt* RISK : arriesgar

chance[2] *adj* : fortuito, casual <a chance encounter : un encuentro casual>

chance[3] *n* **1** FATE, LUCK : azar *m,* suerte *f,* fortuna *f* **2** OPPORTUNITY : oportunidad *f,* ocasión *f* **3** PROBABILITY : probabilidad *f,* posibilidad *f* **4** RISK : riesgo *m* **5** : boleto *m* (de una rifa o lotería) **6 by chance** : por casualidad

chancellor [ˈtʃæntsələr] *n* **1** : canciller *m* **2** : rector *m,* -tora *f* (de una universidad)

chancre [ˈʃæŋkər] *n* : chancro *m*

chancy [ˈtʃæntsi] *adj* **chancier; -est** : riesgoso, arriesgado

chandelier [ˌʃændəˈlɪr] *n* : araña *f* de luces

change[1] [ˈtʃeɪndʒ] *v* **changed; changing** *vt* **1** ALTER : cambiar, alterar, modificar **2** EXCHANGE : cambiar de, intercambiar <to change places : cambiar de sitio> — *vi* **1** VARY : cambiar, variar, transformarse <you haven't changed : no has cambiado> **2** *or* **to change clothes** : cambiarse (de ropa)

change[2] *n* **1** ALTERATION : cambio *m* **2** : cambio *m,* vuelto *m* <two dollars change : dos dólares de vuelto> **3** COINS : cambio *m,* monedas *fpl*

changeable [ˈtʃeɪndʒəbəl] *adj* : cambiante, variable

changeless [ˈtʃeɪndʒləs] *adj* : invariable, constante

changer [ˈtʃeɪndʒər] *n* **1** : cambiador *m* <record changer : cambiador de discos> **2** *or* **money changer** : cambista *mf* (de dinero)

channel[1] [ˈtʃænəl] *vt* **-neled** *or* **-nelled; -neling** *or* **-nelling** : encauzar, canalizar

channel[2] *n* **1** RIVERBED : cauce *m* **2** STRAIT : canal *m,* estrecho *m* <English Channel : Canal de la Mancha> **3** COURSE, MEANS : vía *f,* conducto *m* <the usual channels : las vías normales> **4** : canal *m* (de televisión)

chant[1] [ˈtʃænt] *v* : salmodiar, cantar

chant[2] *n* : **1** : salmodia *f* **2 Gregorian chant** : canto *m* gregoriano

Chanukah [ˈxɑnəkə, ˈhɑ-] → **Hanukkah**

chaos [ˈkeɪˌɑs] *n* : caos *m*

chaotic [keɪˈɑtɪk] *adj* : caótico — **chaotically** [-tɪkli] *adv*

chap[1] [ˈtʃæp] *vi* **chapped; chapping** : partirse, agrietarse

chap[2] *n* FELLOW : tipo *m,* hombre *m*

chapel [ˈtʃæpəl] *n* : capilla *f*

chaperon[1] *or* **chaperone** [ˈʃæpəˌroːn] *vt* **-oned; -oning :** ir de chaperón, acompañar

chaperon[2] *or* **chaperone** *n* **:** chaperón *m*, -rona *f;* acompañante *mf*

chaplain [ˈtʃæplɪn] *n* **:** capellán *m*

chapter [ˈtʃæptər] *n* **1 :** capítulo *m* (de un libro) **2** BRANCH **:** sección *f,* división *f* (de una organización)

char [ˈtʃɑr] *vt* **charred; charring 1** BURN **:** carbonizar **2** SCORCH **:** chamuscar

character [ˈkærɪktər] *n* **1** LETTER, SYMBOL **:** carácter *m* <Chinese characters : caracteres chinos> **2** DISPOSITION **:** carácter *m,* personalidad *f* <of good character : de buena reputación> **3 :** tipo *m,* personaje *m* peculiar <he's quite a character! : ¡él es algo serio!> **4 :** personaje *m* (ficticio)

characteristic[1] [ˌkærɪktəˈrɪstɪk] *adj* **:** característico, típico — **characteristically** [-tɪkli] *adv*

characteristic[2] *n* **:** característica *f*

characterization [ˌkærɪktərəˈzeɪʃən] *n* **:** caracterización *f*

characterize [ˈkærɪktəˌraɪz] *vt* **-ized; -izing :** caracterizar

charades [ʃəˈreɪdz] *ns & pl* **:** charada *f*

charcoal [ˈtʃɑrˌkoːl] *n* **:** carbón *m*

chard [ˈtʃɑrd] → **Swiss chard**

charge[1] [ˈtʃɑrdʒ] *v* **charged; charging** *vt* **1 :** cargar <to charge the batteries : cargar las pilas> **2** ENTRUST **:** encomendar, encargar **3** COMMAND **:** ordenar, mandar **4** ACCUSE **:** acusar <charged with robbery : acusado de robo> **5 :** cargar a una cuenta, comprar a crédito — *vi* **1 :** cargar (contra el enemigo) <charge! : ¡a la carga!> **2 :** cobrar <they charge too much : cobran demasiado>

charge[2] *n* **1 :** carga *f* (eléctrica) **2** BURDEN **:** carga *f,* peso *m* **3** RESPONSIBILITY **:** cargo *m,* responsabilidad *f* <to take charge of : hacerse cargo de> **4** ACCUSATION **:** cargo *m,* acusación *f* **5** COST **:** costo *m,* cargo *m,* precio *m* **6** ATTACK **:** carga *f,* ataque *m*

charge card → **credit card**

chargeable [ˈtʃɑrdʒəbəl] *adj* **1 :** acusable, perseguible (dícese de un delito) **2 ~ to :** a cargo de (una cuenta)

charger [ˈtʃɑrdʒər] *n* **:** corcel *m,* caballo *m* (de guerra)

chariot [ˈtʃæriət] *n* **:** carro *m* (de guerra)

charisma [kəˈrɪzmə] *n* **:** carisma *m*

charismatic [ˌkærəzˈmætɪk] *adj* **:** carismático

charitable [ˈtʃærət̬əbəl] *adj* **1** GENEROUS **:** caritativo <a charitable organization : una organización benéfica> **2** KIND, UNDERSTANDING **:** generoso, benévolo, comprensivo — **charitably** [-bli] *adv*

charitableness [ˈtʃærət̬əbəlnəs] *n* **:** caridad *f*

charity [ˈtʃærət̬i] *n, pl* **-ties 1** GENEROSITY **:** caridad *f* **2** ALMS **:** caridad *f,* limosna *f* **3 :** organización *f* benéfica, obra *f* de beneficencia

charlatan [ˈʃɑrlətən] *n* **:** charlatán *m,* -tana *f;* farsante *mf*

charley horse [ˈtʃɑrliˌhɔrs] *n* **:** calambre *m*

charm[1] [ˈtʃɑrm] *vt* **:** encantar, cautivar, fascinar

charm[2] *n* **1** AMULET **:** amuleto *m,* talismán *m* **2** ATTRACTION **:** encanto *m,* atractivo *m* <it has a certain charm : tiene cierto atractivo> **3 :** dije *m,* colgante *m* <charm bracelet : pulsera de dijes>

charmer [ˈtʃɑrmər] *n* **:** persona *f* encantadora

charming [ˈtʃɑrmɪŋ] *adj* **:** encantador, fascinante

chart[1] [ˈtʃɑrt] *vt* **1 :** trazar un mapa de, hacer un gráfico de **2** PLAN **:** trazar, planear <to chart a course : trazar un derrotero>

chart[2] *n* **1** MAP **:** carta *f,* mapa *m* **2** DIAGRAM **:** gráfico *m,* cuadro *m,* tabla *f*

charter[1] [ˈtʃɑrt̬ər] *vt* **1 :** establecer los estatutos de (una organización) **2** RENT **:** alquilar, fletar

charter[2] *n* **1** STATUTES **:** estatutos *mpl* **2** CONSTITUTION **:** carta *f,* constitución *f*

chartreuse [ʃɑrˈtruːz, -ˈtruːs] *n* **:** color *m* verde-amarillo intenso

chary [ˈtʃæri] *adj* **charier; -est 1** WARY **:** cauteloso, precavido **2** SPARING **:** parco

chase[1] [ˈtʃeɪs] *vt* **chased; chasing 1** PURSUE **:** perseguir, ir a la caza de **2** DRIVE **:** ahuyentar, echar <he chased the dog from the garden : ahuyentó al perro del jardín> **3 :** grabar (metales)

chase[2] *n* **1** PURSUIT **:** persecución *f,* caza *f* **2 the chase** HUNTING **:** caza *f*

chaser [ˈtʃeɪsər] *n* **1** PURSUER **:** perseguidor *m,* -dora *f* **2 :** bebida *f* que se toma después de un trago de licor

chasm [ˈkæzəm] *n* **:** abismo *m,* sima *f*

chassis [ˈtʃæsi, ˈʃæsi] *n, pl* **chassis** [-siz] **:** chasis *m,* armazón *m*

chaste [ˈtʃeɪst] *adj* **chaster; -est 1 :** casto **2** MODEST **:** modesto, puro **3** AUSTERE **:** austero, sobrio

chastely [ˈtʃeɪstli] *adv* **:** castamente

chasten [ˈtʃeɪsən] *vt* **:** castigar, sancionar

chasteness [ˈtʃeɪstnəs] *n* **1** MODESTY **:** modestia *f,* castidad *f* **2** AUSTERITY **:** sobriedad *f,* austeridad *f*

chastise [ˈtʃæsˌtaɪz, tʃæsˈ-] *vt* **-tised; -tising 1** REPRIMAND **:** reprender, corregir, reprobar **2** PUNISH **:** castigar

chastisement [ˈtʃæsˌtaɪzmənt, tʃæsˈtaɪz-, ˈtʃæstəz-] *n* **:** castigo *m,* corrección *f*

chastity [ˈtʃæstət̬i] *n* **:** castidad *f,* decencia *f,* modestia *f*

chat[1] [ˈtʃæt] *vi* **chatted; chatting :** charlar, platicar

chat[2] *n* : charla *f,* plática *f*
château [ʃæˈtoː] *n, pl* **-teaus** [-ˈtoː, -ˈtoːz] *or* **-teaux** [-ˈtoːz] : mansión *f* campestre
chattel [ˈtʃætəl] *n* : bienes *fpl* muebles, enseres *mpl*
chatter[1] [ˈtʃætər] *vi* **1** : castañetear (dícese de los dientes) **2** GAB : parlotear *fam,* cotorrear *fam*
chatter[2] *n* **1** CHATTERING : castañeteo *m* (de dientes) **2** GABBING : parloteo *m fam,* cotorreo *m fam,* cháchara *f fam*
chatterbox [ˈtʃætərˌbɑks] *n* : parlanchín *m,* -china *f;* charlatán *m,* -tana *f;* hablador *m,* -dora *f*
chatty [ˈtʃæti] *adj* **chattier; chattiest** **1** TALKATIVE : parlanchín, charlatán **2** CONVERSATIONAL : familiar, conversador <a chatty letter : una carta llena de noticias>
chauffeur[1] [ˈʃoːfər, ʃoˈfər] *vi* : trabajar de chofer privado — *vt* : hacer de chofer para
chauffeur[2] *n* : chofer *m* privado
chauvinism [ˈʃoːvəˌnɪzəm] *n* : chauvinismo *m,* patriotería *f*
chauvinist [ˈʃoːvənɪst] *n* : chauvinista *mf;* patriotero *m,* -ta *f*
chauvinistic [ˌʃoːvəˈnɪstɪk] *adj* : chauvinista, patriotero
cheap[1] [ˈtʃiːp] *adv* : barato <to sell cheap : vender barato>
cheap[2] *adj* **1** INEXPENSIVE : barato, económico **2** SHODDY : barato, mal hecho **3** STINGY : tacaño, agarrado *fam,* codo *Mex*
cheapen [ˈtʃiːpən] *vt* : degradar, rebajar
cheaply [ˈtʃiːpli] *adv* : barato, a precio bajo
cheapness [ˈtʃiːpnəs] *n* **1** : baratura *f,* precio *m* bajo **2** STINGINESS : tacañería *f*
cheapskate [ˈtʃiːpˌskeɪt] *n* : tacaño *m,* -ña *f;* codo *m,* -da *f Mex*
cheat[1] [ˈtʃiːt] *vt* : defraudar, estafar, engañar — *vi* : hacer trampa
cheat[2] *n* **1** CHEATING : engaño *m,* fraude *m,* trampa *f* **2** → **cheater**
cheater [ˈtʃiːtər] *n* : estafador *m,* -dora *f;* tramposo *m,* -sa *f*
check[1] [ˈtʃɛk] *vt* **1** HALT : frenar, parar, detener **2** RESTRAIN : refrenar, contener, reprimir **3** VERIFY : verificar, comprobar **4** INSPECT : revisar, chequear, inspeccionar **5** MARK : marcar, señalar **6** : chequear, facturar (maletas, equipaje) **7** CHECKER : marcar con cuadros **8** **to check in** : registrarse en un hotel **9** **to check out** : irse de un hotel
check[2] *n* **1** HALT : detención *f* súbita, parada *f* **2** RESTRAINT : control *m,* freno *m* **3** INSPECTION : inspección *f,* verificación *f,* chequeo *m* **4** : cheque *m* <to pay by check : pagar con cheque> **5** VOUCHER : resguardo *m,* comprobante *m* **6** BILL : cuenta *f* (en un restaurante) **7** SQUARE : cuadro *m* **8** MARK : marca *f* **9** : jaque *m* (en ajedrez)
checker[1] [ˈtʃɛkər] *vt* : marcar con cuadros
checker[2] *n* **1** : pieza *f* (en el juego de damas) **2** : verificador *m,* -dora *f;* revisador *m,* -dora *f*
checkerboard [ˈtʃɛkərˌbord] *n* : tablero *m* de damas
checkers [ˈtʃɛkərz] *n* : damas *fpl*
checkmate[1] [ˈtʃɛkˌmeɪt] *vt* **-mated; -mating** **1** : dar jaque mate a (en ajedrez) **2** THWART : frustrar, arruinar
checkmate[2] *n* : jaque mate *m*
checkpoint [ˈtʃɛkˌpɔɪnt] *n* : puesto *m* de control
checkup [ˈtʃɛkˌʌp] *n* : examen *m* médico, chequeo *m*
cheddar [ˈtʃɛdər] *n* : queso *m* Cheddar
cheek [ˈtʃiːk] *n* **1** : mejilla *f,* cachete *m* **2** IMPUDENCE : insolencia *f,* descaro *m*
cheeky [ˈtʃiːki] *adj* **cheekier; -est** : descarado, insolente, atrevido
cheep[1] [ˈtʃiːp] *vi* : piar
cheep[2] *n* : pío *m*
cheer[1] [ˈtʃɪr] *vt* **1** ENCOURAGE : alentar, animar **2** GLADDEN : alegrar, levantar el ánimo a **3** ACCLAIM : aclamar, vitorear, echar porras a
cheer[2] *n* **1** CHEERFULNESS : alegría *f,* buen humor *m,* jovialidad *f* **2** APPLAUSE : aclamación *f,* ovación *f,* aplausos *mpl* <three cheers for the chief! : ¡viva el jefe!> **3** **cheers!** : ¡salud!
cheerful [ˈtʃɪrfəl] *adj* : alegre, de buen humor
cheerfully [ˈtʃɪrfəli] *adv* : alegremente, jovialmente
cheerfulness [ˈtʃɪrfəlnəs] *n* : buen humor *m,* alegría *f*
cheerily [ˈtʃɪrəli] *adv* : alegremente
cheeriness [ˈtʃɪrinəs] *n* : buen humor *m,* alegría *f*
cheerleader [ˈtʃɪrˌliːdər] *n* : porrista *mf*
cheerless [ˈtʃɪrləs] *adj* BLEAK : triste, sombrío
cheerlessly [ˈtʃɪrləsli] *adv* : desanimadamente
cheery [ˈtʃɪri] *adj* **cheerier; -est** : alegre, de buen humor
cheese [ˈtʃiːz] *n* : queso *m*
cheesecloth [ˈtʃiːzˌklɔθ] *n* : estopilla *f*
cheesy [ˈtʃiːzi] *adj* **cheesier; -est** **1** : a queso **2** : que contiene queso **3** CHEAP : barato, de mala calidad
cheetah [ˈtʃiːtə] *n* : guepardo *m*
chef [ˈʃɛf] *n* : chef *m*
chemical[1] [ˈkɛmɪkəl] *adj* : químico — **chemically** [-mɪkli] *adv*
chemical[2] *n* : sustancia *f* química
chemise [ʃəˈmiːz] *n* **1** : camiseta *f,* prenda *f* interior de una pieza **2** : vestido *m* holgado
chemist [ˈkɛmɪst] *n* : químico *m,* -ca *f*
chemistry [ˈkɛmɪstri] *n, pl* **-tries** : química *f*
chemotherapy [ˌkiːmoˈθɛrəpi, ˌkɛmo-] *n, pl* **-pies** : quimioterapia *f*

chenille [ʃə'niːl] *n* : felpilla *f*

cherish ['tʃɛrɪʃ] *vt* **1** VALUE : apreciar, valorar **2** HARBOR : abrigar, albergar

cherry ['tʃɛri] *n, pl* **-ries 1** : cereza *f* (fruta) **2** : cerezo *m* (árbol)

cherub ['tʃɛrəb] *n* **1** *pl* **-ubim** ['tʃɛrə,bɪm, 'tʃɛrjə-] ANGEL : ángel *m,* querubín *m* **2** *pl* **-ubs** : niño *m* regordete, niña *f* regordeta

cherubic [tʃə'ruːbɪk] *adj* : querúbico, angelical

chess ['tʃɛs] *n* : ajedrez *m*

chessboard ['tʃɛs,bord] *n* : tablero *m* de ajedrez

chessman ['tʃɛsmən, -,mæn] *n, pl* **-men** [-mən, -,mɛn] : pieza *f* de ajedrez

chest ['tʃɛst] *n* **1** : cofre *m,* baúl *m* **2** : pecho *m* <chest pains : dolores de pecho>

chestnut ['tʃɛst,nʌt] *n* **1** : castaña *f* (fruto) **2** : castaño *m* (árbol)

chest of drawers *n* : cómoda *f*

chevron ['ʃɛvrən] *n* : galón *m* (de un oficial militar)

chew[1] ['tʃuː] *vt* : masticar, mascar

chew[2] *n* : algo que se masca (como tabaco)

chewable ['tʃuːəbəl] *adj* : masticable

chewing gum *n* : goma *f* de mascar, chicle *m*

chewy ['tʃuːi] *adj* **chewier; -est 1** : fibroso (dícese de las carnes o los vegetales) **2** : pegajoso, chicloso (dícese de los los dulces)

chic[1] ['ʃiːk] *adj* : chic, elegante, de moda

chic[2] *n* : chic *m,* elegancia *f*

Chicano [tʃɪ'kɑno] *n* : chicano *m,* -na *f* — **Chicano** *adj*

chick ['tʃɪk] *n* : pollito *m,* -ta *f;* polluelo *m,* -la *f*

chicken ['tʃɪkən] *n* **1** FOWL : pollo *m* **2** COWARD : cobarde *mf*

chickenhearted ['tʃɪkən,hɑrṯəd] *n* : miedoso, cobarde

chicken pox *n* : varicela *f*

chicle ['tʃɪkəl] *n* : chicle *m* (resina)

chicory ['tʃɪkəri] *n, pl* **-ries 1** : endibia *f* (para ensaladas) **2** : achicoria *f* (aditivo de café)

chide ['tʃaɪd] *vt* **chid** ['tʃɪd] *or* **chided; chid** *or* **chidden** ['tʃɪdən] *or* **chided; chiding** ['tʃaɪdɪŋ] : regañar, reprender

chief[1] ['tʃiːf] *adj* : principal, capital <chief negotiator : negociador en jefe> — **chiefly** *adv*

chief[2] *n* : jefe *m,* -fa *f*

chieftain ['tʃiːftən] *n* : jefe *m,* -fa *f* (de una tribu)

chiffon [ʃɪ'fɑn, 'ʃɪ,-] *n* : chifón *m*

chigger ['tʃɪgər] *n* : nigua *f*

chignon ['ʃiːn,jɑn, -,jɔn] *n* : moño *m,* chongo *m Mex*

chilblain ['tʃɪl,bleɪn] *n* : sabañón *m*

child ['tʃaɪld] *n, pl* **children** ['tʃɪldrən] **1** BABY, YOUNGSTER : niño *m,* -ña *f;* criatura *f* **2** OFFSPRING : hijo *m,* -ja *f;* progenie *f*

childbearing[1] ['tʃaɪlbɛrɪŋ] *adj* : relativo al parto <of childbearing age : en edad fértil>

childbearing[2] → **childbirth**

childbirth ['tʃaɪld,bərθ] *n* : parto *m*

childhood ['tʃaɪld,hʊd] *n* : infancia *f,* niñez *f*

childish ['tʃaɪldɪʃ] *adj* : infantil, inmaduro — **childishly** *adv*

childishness ['tʃaɪldɪʃnəs] *n* : infantilismo *m,* inmadurez *f*

childless ['tʃaɪldləs] *adj* : sin hijos

childlike ['tʃaɪld,laɪk] *adj* : infantil, inocente <a childlike imagination : una imaginación infantil>

childproof ['tʃaɪld,pruːf] *adj* : a prueba de niños

Chilean ['tʃɪliən, tʃɪ'leɪən] : chileno *m,* -na *f* — **Chilean** *adj*

chili *or* **chile** *or* **chilli** ['tʃɪli] *n, pl* **chilies** *or* **chiles** *or* **chillies 1** *or* **chili pepper** : chile *m,* ají *m* **2** : chile *m* con carne

chill[1] ['tʃɪl] *v* : enfriar

chill[2] *adj* : frío, gélido <a chill wind : un viento frío>

chill[3] *n* **1** CHILLINESS : fresco *m,* frío *m* **2** SHIVER : escalofrío *m* **3** DAMPER : enfriamiento *m,* frío *m* <to cast a chill over : enfriar>

chilliness ['tʃɪlinəs] *n* : frío *m,* fresco *m*

chilly ['tʃɪli] *adj* **chillier; -est** : frío <it's chilly tonight : hace frío esta noche>

chime[1] ['tʃaɪm] *v* **chimed; chiming** *vt* : hacer sonar (una campana) — *vi* : sonar una campana, dar campanadas

chime[2] *n* **1** BELLS : juego *m* de campanitas sintonizadas, carillón *m* **2** PEAL : tañido *m,* campanada *f*

chime in *vi* : meterse en una conversación

chimera *or* **chimaera** [kaɪ'mɪrə, kə-] *n* : quimera *f*

chimney ['tʃɪmni] *n, pl* **-neys** : chimenea *f*

chimney sweep *n* : deshollinador *m,* -dora *f*

chimp ['tʃɪmp, 'ʃɪmp] → **chimpanzee**

chimpanzee [,tʃɪm,pæn'ziː, ,ʃɪm-; tʃɪm'pænzi, ʃɪm-] *n* : chimpancé *m*

chin ['tʃɪn] *n* : barbilla *f,* mentón *m,* barba *f*

china ['tʃaɪnə] *n* **1** PORCELAIN : porcelana *f,* loza *f* **2** CROCKERY, TABLEWARE : loza *f,* vajilla *f*

chinchilla [tʃɪn'tʃɪlə] *n* : chinchilla *f*

Chinese [tʃaɪ'niːz, -'niːs] *n* **1** : chino *m,* -na *f* **2** : chino *m* (idioma) — **Chinese** *adj*

chink ['tʃɪŋk] *n* : grieta *f,* abertura *f*

chintz ['tʃɪnts] *n* : chintz *m,* chinz *m*

chip[1] ['tʃɪp] *v* **chipped; chipping** *vt* : desportillar, desconchar, astillar (madera) — *vi* : desportillarse, desconcharse, descascararse (dícese de la pintura, etc.)

chip[2] *n* **1** : astilla *f* (de madera o vidrio), lasca *f* (de piedra) <he's a chip

off the old block : de tal palo, tal astilla> **2** : bocado *m* pequeño (en rodajas o rebanadas) <tortilla chips : totopos, tortillitas tostadas> **3** : ficha *f* (de póker, etc.) **4** NICK : desportilladura *f,* mella *f* **5** : chip *m* <memory chip : chip de memoria>

chip in *v* CONTRIBUTE : contribuir

chipmunk [ˈtʃɪpˌmʌŋk] *n* : ardilla *f* listada

chipper [ˈtʃɪpər] *adj* : alegre y vivaz

chiropodist [kəˈrɑpədɪst, ʃə-] *n* : podólogo *m,* -ga *f*

chiropody [kəˈrɑpədi, ʃə-] *n* : podología *f*

chiropractic [ˈkaɪrəˌpræktɪk] *n* : quiropráctica *f*

chiropractor [ˈkaɪrəˌpræktər] *n* : quiropráctico *m,* -ca *f*

chirp[1] [ˈtʃərp] *vi* : gorjear (dícese de los pájaros), chirriar (dícese de los grillos)

chirp[2] *n* : gorjeo *m* (de un pájaro), chirrido *m* (de un grillo)

chisel[1] [ˈtʃɪzəl] *vt* **-eled** *or* **-elled; -eling** *or* **-elling 1** : cincelar, tallar, labrar **2** CHEAT : estafar, defraudar

chisel[2] *n* : cincel *m* (para piedras y metales), escoplo *m* (para madera), formón *m*

chiseler [ˈtʃɪzələr] *n* SWINDLER : estafador *m,* -dora *f;* fraude *mf*

chit [ˈtʃɪt] *n* : resguardo *m,* recibo *m*

chitchat [ˈtʃɪtˌtʃæt] *n* : cotorreo *m,* charla *f*

chivalric [ʃəˈvælrɪk] → **chivalrous**

chivalrous [ˈʃɪvəlrəs] *adj* **1** KNIGHTLY : caballeresco, relativo a la caballería **2** GENTLEMANLY : caballeroso, honesto, cortés

chivalrousness [ˈʃɪvəlrəsnəs] *n* : caballerosidad *f,* cortesía *f*

chivalry [ˈʃɪvəlri] *n, pl* **-ries 1** KNIGHTHOOD : caballería *f* **2** CHIVALROUSNESS : caballerosidad *f,* nobleza *f,* cortesía *f*

chive [ˈtʃaɪv] *n* : cebollino *m*

chloride [ˈklorˌaɪd] *n* : cloruro *m*

chlorinate [ˈklorəˌneɪt] *vt* **-nated; -nating** : clorar

chlorination [ˌklorəˈneɪʃən] *n* : cloración *f*

chlorine [ˈklorˌiːn] *n* : cloro *m*

chloroform[1] [ˈklorəˌfɔrm] *vt* : cloroformizar

chloroform[2] *n* : cloroformo *m*

chlorophyll [ˈklorəˌfɪl] *n* : clorofila *f*

chock–full [ˈtʃɑkˈfʊl, ˈtʃʌk-] *adj* : colmado, repleto

chocolate [ˈtʃɑkələt, ˈtʃɔk-] *n* **1** : chocolate *m* **2** BONBON : bombón *m* **3** : color *m* chocolate, marrón *m*

choice[1] [ˈtʃɔɪs] *adj* **choicer; -est** : selecto, escogido, de primera calidad

choice[2] *n* **1** CHOOSING : elección *f,* selección *f* **2** OPTION : elección *f,* opción *f* <I have no choice : no tengo alternativa> **3** PREFERENCE : preferencia *f,* elección *f* **4** VARIETY : surtido *m,* selección *f* <a wide choice : un gran surtido>

choir [ˈkwaɪr] *n* : coro *m*

choirboy [ˈkwaɪrˌbɔɪ] *n* : niño *m* de coro

choke[1] [ˈtʃoːk] *v* **choked; choking** *vt* **1** ASPHYXIATE, STRANGLE : sofocar, asfixiar, ahogar, estrangular **2** BLOCK : tapar, obstruir — *vi* **1** SUFFOCATE : asfixiarse, sofocarse, ahogarse, atragantarse (con comida) **2** CLOG : taparse, obstruirse

choke[2] *n* **1** CHOKING : estrangulación *f* **2** : choke *m* (de un motor)

choker [ˈtʃoːkər] *n* : gargantilla *f*

cholera [ˈkɑlərə] *n* : cólera *m*

cholesterol [kəˈlɛstəˌrɔl] *n* : colesterol *m*

choose [ˈtʃuːz] *v* **chose** [ˈtʃoːz]; **chosen** [ˈtʃoːzən]; **choosing** *vt* **1** SELECT : escoger, elegir <choose only one : escoja sólo uno> **2** DECIDE : decidir <he chose to leave : decidió irse> **3** PREFER : preferir <which one do you choose? : ¿cuál prefiere?> — *vi* : escoger <much to choose from : mucho de donde escoger>

choosy *or* **choosey** [ˈtʃuːzi] *adj* **choosier; -est** : exigente, remilgado

chop[1] [ˈtʃɑp] *vt* **chopped; chopping 1** MINCE : picar, cortar, moler (carne) **2 to chop down** : cortar, talar (un árbol)

chop[2] *n* **1** CUT : hachazo *m* (con una hacha), tajo *m* (con una cuchilla) **2** BLOW : golpe *m* (penetrante) <karate chop : golpe de karate> **3** : chuleta *f* <pork chops : chuletas de cerdo>

chopper [ˈtʃɑpər] → **helicopter**

choppy [ˈtʃɑpi] *adj* **choppier; -est 1** : agitado, picado (dícese del mar) **2** DISCONNECTED : incoherente, inconexo

chops [ˈtʃɑps] *npl* **1** : quijada *f,* mandíbula *f,* boca *f* (de una persona) **2 to lick one's chops** : relamerse

chopsticks [ˈtʃɑpˌstɪks] *npl* : palillos *mpl*

choral [ˈkorəl] *adj* : coral

chorale [kəˈræl, -ˈrɑl] *n* **1** : coral *f* (composición musical vocal) **2** CHOIR, CHORUS : coral *f,* coro *m*

chord [ˈkɔrd] *n* **1** : acorde *m* (en música) **2** : cuerda *f* (en anatomía o geometría)

chore [ˈtʃor] *n* **1** TASK : tarea *f* rutinaria **2** BOTHER, NUISANCE : lata *f fam,* fastidio *m* **3 chores** *npl* WORK : quehaceres *mpl,* faenas *fpl*

choreograph [ˈkoriəˌgræf] *vt* : coreografiar

choreographer [ˌkoriˈɑgrəfər] *n* : coreógrafo *m,* -fa *f*

choreographic [ˌkoriəˈgræfɪk] *adj* : coreográfico

choreography [ˌkoriˈɑgrəfi] *n, pl* **-phies** : coreografía *f*

chorister [ˈkorəstər] *n* : corista *mf*

chortle[1] [ˈtʃɔrtəl] *vi* **-tled; -tling** : reírse (con satisfacción o júbilo)

chortle[2] *n* **:** risa *f* (de satisfacción o júbilo)
chorus[1] [ˈkorəs] *vt* **:** corear
chorus[2] *n* **1 :** coro *m* (grupo o composición musical) **2** REFRAIN **:** coro *m,* estribillo *m*
chose *pp* → **choose**
chosen [ˈtʃoːzən] *adj* **:** elegido, selecto
chow [ˈtʃaʊ] *n* **1** FOOD **:** comida *f* **2 :** chow-chow *m* (perro)
chowder [ˈtʃaʊdər] *n* **:** sopa *f* de pescado
christen [ˈkrɪsən] *vt* **1** BAPTIZE **:** bautizar **2** NAME **:** bautizar con el nombre de
Christendom [ˈkrɪsəndəm] *n* **:** cristiandad *f*
christening [ˈkrɪsənɪŋ] *n* **:** bautismo *m,* bautizo *m*
Christian[1] [ˈkrɪstʃən] *adj* **:** cristiano
Christian[2] *n* **:** cristiano *m,* -na *f*
Christianity [ˌkrɪstʃiˈænət̬i, ˌkrɪsˈtʃæ-] *n* **:** cristianismo *m*
Christian name *n* **:** nombre *m* de pila
Christmas [ˈkrɪsməs] *n* **:** Navidad *f* <Christmas season : las Navidades>
chromatic [kroːˈmæt̬ɪk] *adj* **:** cromático <chromatic scale : escala cromática>
chrome [ˈkroːm] *n* **:** cromo *m* (metal)
chromium [ˈkroːmiəm] *n* **:** cromo *m* (elemento)
chromosome [ˈkroːməˌsoːm, -ˌzoːm] *n* **:** cromosoma *m*
chronic [ˈkrɑnɪk] *adj* **:** crónico — **chronically** [-nɪkli] *adv*
chronicle[1] [ˈkrɑnɪkəl] *vt* **-cled; -cling :** escribir (una crónica o historia)
chronicle[2] *n* **:** crónica *f,* historia *f*
chronicler [ˈkrɑnɪklər] *n* **:** historiador *m,* -dora *f;* cronista *mf*
chronological [ˌkrɑnəlˈɑdʒɪkəl] *adj* **:** cronológico — **chronologically** [-kli] *adv*
chronology [krəˈnɑlədʒi] *n, pl* **-gies :** cronología *f*
chronometer [krəˈnɑmət̬ər] *n* **:** cronómetro *m*
chrysalis [ˈkrɪsələs] *n, pl* **chrysalides** [krɪˈsæləˌdiːz] *or* **chrysalises :** crisálida *f*
chrysanthemum [krɪˈsæntθəməm] *n* **:** crisantemo *m*
chubbiness [ˈtʃʌbinəs] *n* **:** gordura *f*
chubby [ˈtʃʌbi] *adj* **-bier; -est :** gordito, regordete, rechoncho
chuck[1] [ˈtʃʌk] *vt* **1** TOSS **:** tirar, lanzar, aventar *Col, Mex* **2 to chuck under the chin :** hacer la mamola
chuck[2] *n* **1** PAT **:** mamola *f,* palmada *f* **2** TOSS **:** lanzamiento *m* **3** *or* **chuck steak :** corte *m* de carne de res
chuckle[1] [ˈtʃʌkəl] *vi* **-led; -ling :** reírse entre dientes
chuckle[2] *n* **:** risita *f,* risa *f* ahogada
chug[1] [ˈtʃʌg] *vi* **chugged; chugging :** resoplar, traquetear
chug[2] *n* **:** resoplido *m,* traqueteo *m*
chum[1] [ˈtʃʌm] *vi* **chummed; chumming :** ser camaradas, ser cuates *Mex fam*
chum[2] *n* **:** amigo *m,* -ga *f;* camarada *mf;* compinche *mf fam*
chummy [ˈtʃʌmi] *adj* **-mier; -est :** amistoso <they're very chummy : son muy amigos>
chump [ˈtʃʌmp] *n* **:** tonto *m,* -ta *f;* idiota *mf*
chunk [ˈtʃʌnk] *n* **1** PIECE **:** cacho *m,* pedazo *m,* trozo *m* **2 :** cantidad *f* grande <a chunk of money : mucho dinero>
chunky [ˈtʃʌnki] *adj* **chunkier; -est 1** STOCKY **:** fornido, robusto **2 :** que contiene pedazos
church [ˈtʃərtʃ] *n* **1 :** iglesia *f* <to go to church : ir a la iglesia> **2** CHRISTIANS **:** iglesia *f,* conjunto *m* de fieles cristianos **3** DENOMINATION **:** confesión *f,* secta *f* **4** CONGREGATION **:** feligreses *mpl,* fieles *mpl*
churchgoer [ˈtʃərtʃˌgoːər] *n* **:** practicante *mf*
churchyard [ˈtʃərtʃˌjɑrd] *n* **:** cementerio *m* (junto a una iglesia)
churn[1] [ˈtʃərn] *vt* **1 :** batir (crema), hacer (mantequilla) **2 :** agitar con fuerza, revolver — *vi* **:** agitarse, arremolinarse
churn[2] *n* **:** mantequera *f*
chute [ˈʃuːt] *n* **:** conducto *m* inclinado, vertedero *m* (para basuras)
chutney [ˈtʃʌtni] *n, pl* **-neys :** chutney *m*
chutzpah [ˈhʊtspə, ˈxʊt-, -ˌspɑ] *n* **:** descaro *m,* frescura *f,* cara *f fam*
cicada [səˈkeɪdə, -ˈkɑ-] *n* **:** cigarra *f,* chicharra *f*
cider [ˈsaɪdər] *n* **1 :** jugo *m* (de manzana, etc.) **2 hard cider :** sidra *f*
cigar [sɪˈgɑr] *n* **:** puro *m,* cigarro *m*
cigarette [ˌsɪgəˈrɛt, ˈsɪgəˌrɛt] *n* **:** cigarrillo *m,* cigarro *m*
cinch[1] [ˈsɪntʃ] *vt* **1 :** cinchar (un caballo) **2** ASSURE **:** asegurar
cinch[2] *n* **1 :** cincha *f* (para caballos) **2 :** algo fácil o seguro <it's a cinch : es bien fácil, es pan comido>
cinchona [sɪŋˈkoːnə] *n* **:** quino *m*
cinder [ˈsɪndər] *n* **1** EMBER **:** brasa *f,* ascua *f* **2 cinders** *npl* ASHES **:** cenizas *fpl*
cinema [ˈsɪnəmə] *n* **:** cine *m*
cinematic [ˌsɪnəˈmæt̬ɪk] *adj* **:** cinematográfico
cinnamon [ˈsɪnəmən] *n* **:** canela *f*
cipher [ˈsaɪfər] *n* **1** ZERO **:** cero *m* **2** CODE **:** cifra *f,* clave *f*
circa [ˈsərkə] *prep* **:** alrededor de, hacia <circa 1800 : hacia el año 1800>
circle[1] [ˈsərkəl] *v* **-cled; -cling** *vt* **1 :** encerrar en un círculo, poner un círculo alrededor de **2 :** girar alrededor de, dar vueltas a <we circled the building twice : le dimos vueltas al edificio dos veces> — *vi* **:** dar vueltas

circle[2] *n* **1** : círculo *m* **2** CYCLE : ciclo *m* <to come full circle : volver al punto de partida> **3** GROUP : círculo *m*, grupo *m* (social)

circuit ['sərkət] *n* **1** BOUNDARY : circuito *m*, perímetro *m* (de una zona o un territorio) **2** TOUR : circuito *m*, recorrido *m*, tour *m* **3** : circuito *m* (eléctrico) <a short circuit : un cortocircuito>

circuitous [ˌsər'kju:ət̬əs] *adj* : sinuoso, tortuoso

circuitry ['sərkətri] *n, pl* **-ries** : sistema *m* de circuitos

circular[1] ['sərkjələr] *adj* ROUND : circular, redondo

circular[2] *n* : circular *f*

circulate ['sərkjəˌleɪt] *v* **-lated; -lating** *vi* : circular — *vt* **1** : circular (noticias, etc.) **2** DISSEMINATE : hacer circular, divulgar

circulation [ˌsərkjə'leɪʃən] *n* : circulación *f*

circulatory ['sərkjələˌtori] *adj* : circulatorio

circumcise ['sərkəmˌsaɪz] *vt* **-cised; -cising** : circuncidar

circumcision [ˌsərkəm'sɪʒən, 'sərkəmˌ-] *n* : circuncisión *f*

circumference [sər'kʌmpfrənts] *n* : circunferencia *f*

circumflex ['sərkəmˌflɛks] *n* : acento *m* circunflejo

circumlocution [ˌsərkəmlo'kju:ʃən] *n* : circunlocución *f*

circumnavigate [ˌsərkəm'nævəˌgeɪt] *vt* **-gated; -gating** : circunnavegar

circumscribe ['sərkəmˌskraɪb] *vt* **-scribed; -scribing 1** : circunscribir, trazar una figura alrededor de **2** LIMIT : circunscribir, limitar

circumspect ['sərkəmˌspɛkt] *adj* : circunspecto, prudente, cauto

circumspection [ˌsərkəm'spɛkʃən] *n* : circunspección *f*, cautela *f*

circumstance ['sərkəmˌstænts] *n* **1** EVENT : circunstancia *f*, acontecimiento *m* **2 circumstances** *npl* SITUATION : circunstancias *fpl*, situación *f* <under the circumstances : dadas las circunstancias> <under no circumstances : de ninguna manera, bajo ningún concepto> **3 circumstances** *npl* : situación *f* económica

circumstantial [ˌsərkəm'stæntʃəl] *adj* : circunstancial

circumvent [ˌsərkəm'vɛnt] *vt* : evadir, burlar (una ley o regla), sortear (una responsabilidad o dificultad)

circumvention [ˌsərkəm'vɛntʃən] *n* : evasión *f*

circus ['sərkəs] *n* : circo *m*

cirrhosis [sə'ro:sɪs] *n* : cirrosis *f*

cirrus ['sɪrəs] *n, pl* **-ri** ['sɪrˌaɪ] : cirro *m*

cistern ['sɪstərn] *n* : cisterna *f*, aljibe *m*

citadel ['sɪt̬ədəl, -ˌdɛl] *n* FORTRESS : ciudadela *f*, fortaleza *f*

citation [saɪ'teɪʃən] *n* **1** SUMMONS : emplazamiento *m*, citación *f*, convocatoria *f* (judicial) **2** QUOTATION : cita *f* **3** COMMENDATION : elogio *m*, mención *f* (de honor)

cite ['saɪt] *vt* **cited; citing 1** ARRAIGN, SUBPOENA : emplazar, citar, hacer comparecer (ante un tribunal) **2** QUOTE : citar **3** COMMEND : elogiar, honrar (oficialmente)

citizen ['sɪt̬əzən] *n* : ciudadano *m*, -na *f*

citizenry ['sɪt̬əzənri] *n, pl* **-ries** : ciudadanía *f*, conjunto *m* de ciudadanos

citizenship ['sɪt̬əzənˌʃɪp] *n* : ciudadanía *f* <Nicaraguan citizenship : ciudadanía nicaragüense>

citron ['sɪtrən] *n* : cidra *f*

citrus ['sɪtrəs] *n, pl* **-rus** *or* **-ruses** : cítrico *m*

city ['sɪti] *n, pl* **cities** : ciudad *f*

civic ['sɪvɪk] *adj* : cívico

civics ['sɪvɪks] *ns & pl* : civismo *m*

civil ['sɪvəl] *adj* **1** : civil <civil law : derecho civil> **2** POLITE : civil, cortés

civilian [sə'vɪljən] *n* : civil *mf* <soldiers and civilians : soldados y civiles>

civility [sə'vɪlət̬i] *n, pl* **-ties** : cortesía *f*, educación *f*

civilization [ˌsɪvələ'zeɪʃən] *n* : civilización *f*

civilize ['sɪvəˌlaɪz] *vt* **-lized; -lizing** : civilizar — **civilized** *adj*

civil liberties *npl* : derechos *mpl* civiles

civilly ['sɪvəli] *adv* : cortésmente

civil rights *npl* : derechos *mpl* civiles

civil service *n* : administración *f* pública

civil war *n* : guerra *f* civil

clack[1] ['klæk] *vi* : tabletear

clack[2] *n* : tableteo *m*

clad ['klæd] *adj* **1** CLOTHED : vestido **2** COVERED : cubierto

claim[1] ['kleɪm] *vt* **1** DEMAND : reclamar, reivindicar <she claimed her rights : reclamó sus derechos> **2** MAINTAIN : afirmar, sostener <they claim it's theirs : sostienen que es suyo>

claim[2] *n* **1** DEMAND : demanda *f*, reclamación *f* **2** DECLARATION : declaración *f*, afirmación *f* **3 to stake a claim** : reclamar, reivindicar

claimant ['kleɪmənt] *n* : demandante *mf* (ante un juez), pretendiente *mf* (al trono, etc.)

clairvoyance [klær'vɔɪənts] *n* : clarividencia *f*

clairvoyant[1] [klær'vɔɪənt] *adj* : clarividente

clairvoyant[2] *n* : clarividente *mf*

clam ['klæm] *n* : almeja *f*

clamber ['klæmbər] *vi* : treparse o subirse torpemente

clammy ['klæmi] *adj* **-mier; -est** : húmedo y algo frío

clamor[1] ['klæmər] *vi* : gritar, clamar

clamor[2] *n* : clamor *m*
clamorous [ˈklæmərəs] *adj* : clamoroso, ruidoso, estrepitoso
clamp[1] [ˈklæmp] *vt* : sujetar con abrazaderas
clamp[2] *n* : abrazadera *f*
clan [ˈklæn] *n* : clan *m*
clandestine [klænˈdɛstɪn] *adj* : clandestino, secreto
clang[1] [ˈklæŋ] *vi* : hacer resonar (dícese de un objeto metálico)
clang[2] *n* : ruido *m* metálico fuerte
clangor [ˈklæŋər, -gər] *n* : estruendo *m* metálico
clank[1] [ˈklæŋk] *vi* : producir un ruido metálico seco
clank[2] *n* : ruido *m* metálico seco
clannish [ˈklænɪʃ] *adj* : exclusivista
clap[1] [ˈklæp] *v* **clapped; clapping** *vt* **1** SLAP, STRIKE : golpear ruidosamente, dar una palmada <to clap one's hands : batir palmas, dar palmadas> **2** APPLAUD : aplaudir — *vi* APPLAUD : aplaudir
clap[2] *n* **1** SLAP : palmada *f*, golpecito *m* **2** NOISE : ruido *m* seco <a clap of thunder : un trueno>
clapboard [ˈklæbərd, ˈklæp,bord] *n* : tabla *f* de madera (para revestir muros)
clapper [ˈklæpər] *n* : badajo *m* (de una campana)
clarification [,klærəfəˈkeɪʃən] *n* : clarificación *f*
clarify [ˈklærə,faɪ] *vt* **-fied; -fying 1** EXPLAIN : aclarar **2** : clarificar (un líquido)
clarinet [,klærəˈnɛt] *n* : clarinete *m*
clarinetist *or* **clarinettist** [,klærəˈnɛṭɪst] *n* : clarinetista *mf*
clarion [ˈklæriən] *adj* : claro y sonoro
clarity [ˈklærəṭi] *n* : claridad *f*, nitidez *f*
clash[1] [ˈklæʃ] *vi* **1** : sonar, chocarse <the cymbals clashed : los platillos sonaron> **2** : chocar, enfrentarse <the students clashed with the police : los estudiantes se enfrentaron con la policía> **3** CONFLICT : estar en conflicto, oponerse **4** : desentonar (dícese de los colores), coincidir (dícese de los datos)
clash[2] *n* **1** : ruido *m* (producido por un choque) **2** CONFLICT, CONFRONTATION : enfrentamiento *m*, conflicto *m*, choque *m* **3** : desentono *m* (de colores), coincidencia *f* (de datos)
clasp[1] [ˈklæsp] *vt* **1** FASTEN : sujetar, abrochar **2** EMBRACE, GRASP : agarrar, sujetar, abrazar
clasp[2] *n* **1** FASTENING : broche *m*, cierre *m* **2** EMBRACE, SQUEEZE : apretón *m*, abrazo *m*
class[1] [ˈklæs] *vt* : clasificar, catalogar
class[2] *n* **1** KIND, TYPE : clase *f*, tipo *m*, especie *f* **2** : clase *f*, rango *m* social <the working class : la clase obrera> **3** LESSON : clase *f*, curso *m* <English class : clase de inglés> **4** : conjunto *m* de estudiantes, clase *f* <the class of '97 : la promoción del 97>
classic[1] [ˈklæsɪk] *adj* : clásico
classic[2] *n* : clásico *m*, obra *f* clásica
classical [ˈklæsɪkəl] *adj* : clásico — **classically** [-kli] *adv*
classicism [ˈklæsə,sɪzəm] *n* : clasicismo *m*
classification [,klæsəfəˈkeɪʃən] *n* : clasificación *f*
classified [ˈklæsə,faɪd] *adj* **1** : clasificado <classified ads : avisos clasificados> **2** RESTRICTED : confidencial, secreto <classified documents : documentos secretos>
classify [ˈklæsə,faɪ] *vt* **-fied; -fying** : clasificar, catalogar
classless [ˈklæsləs] *adj* : sin clases
classmate [ˈklæs,meɪt] *n* : compañero *m*, -ra *f* de clase
classroom [ˈklæs,ruːm] *n* : aula *f*, salón *m* de clase
clatter[1] [ˈklæṭər] *vi* : traquetear, hacer ruido
clatter[2] *n* : traqueteo *m*, ruido *m*, estrépito *m*
clause [ˈklɔz] *n* : cláusula *f*
claustrophobia [,klɔstrəˈfoːbiə] *n* : claustrofobia *f*
clavicle [ˈklævɪkəl] *n* : clavícula *f*
claw[1] [ˈklɔ] *v* : arañar
claw[2] *n* : garra *f*, uña *f* (de un gato), pinza *f* (de un crustáceo)
clay [ˈkleɪ] *n* : arcilla *f*, barro *m*
clayey [ˈkleɪi] *adj* : arcilloso
clean[1] [ˈkliːn] *vt* : limpiar, lavar, asear
clean[2] *adv* : limpio, limpiamente <to play clean : jugar limpio>
clean[3] *adj* **1** : limpio **2** UNADULTERATED : puro **3** IRREPROACHABLE : intachable, sin mancha <to have a clean record : no tener antecedentes penales> **4** DECENT : decente **5** COMPLETE : completo, absoluto <a clean break with the past : un corte radical con el pasado>
cleaner [ˈkliːnər] *n* **1** : limpiador *m*, -dora *f* **2** : producto *m* de limpieza **3** DRY CLEANER : tintorería *f* (servicio)
cleanliness [ˈklɛnlinəs] *n* : limpieza *f*, aseo *m*
cleanly[1] [ˈkliːnli] *adv* : limpiamente, con limpieza
cleanly[2] [ˈklɛnli] *adj* **-lier; -est** : limpio, pulcro
cleanness [ˈkliːnnəs] *n* : limpieza *f*
cleanse [ˈklɛnz] *vt* **cleansed; cleansing** : limpiar, purificar
cleanser [ˈklɛnzər] *n* : limpiador *m*, purificador *m*
clear[1] [ˈklɪr] *vt* **1** CLARIFY : aclarar, clarificar (un líquido) **2** : despejar (una superficie), desatascar (un tubo), desmontar (una selva) <to clear the table : levantar la mesa> <to clear one's throat : carraspear, aclararse la voz> **3** EXONERATE : absolver, limpiar el nombre de **4** EARN : ganar, sacar (una ganancia de) **5** : pasar sin tocar

<he cleared the hurdle : saltó por encima de la valla> **6 to clear up** RESOLVE : aclarar, resolver, esclarecer — *vi* **1** DISPERSE : irse, despejarse, disiparse **2** : ser compensado (dícese de un cheque) **3 to clear up** : despejar (dícese del tiempo), mejorarse (dícese de una enfermedad)
clear[2] *adv* : claro, claramente
clear[3] *adj* **1** BRIGHT : claro, lúcido **2** FAIR : claro, despejado **3** TRANSPARENT : transparente, translúcido **4** EVIDENT, UNMISTAKABLE : evidente, claro, obvio **5** CERTAIN : seguro **6** UNOBSTRUCTED : despejado, libre
clear[4] *n* **1 in the clear** : inocente, libre de toda sospecha **2 in the clear** SAFE : fuera de peligro
clearance [ˈklɪrən*t*s] *n* **1** CLEARING : despeje *m* **2** SPACE : espacio *m* (libre), margen *m* **3** AUTHORIZATION : autorización *f*, despacho *m* (de la aduana)
clearing [ˈklɪrɪŋ] *n* : claro *m* (de un bosque)
clearly [ˈklɪrli] *adv* **1** DISTINCTLY : claramente, directamente **2** OBVIOUSLY : obviamente, evidentemente
cleat [ˈkliːt] *n* **1** : taco *m* **2 cleats** *npl* : zapatos *mpl* deportivos (con tacos)
cleavage [ˈkliːvɪdʒ] *n* **1** CLEFT : hendidura *f*, raja *f* **2** : escote *m* (del busto)
cleave[1] [ˈkliːv] *vi* **cleaved** [ˈkliːvd] *or* **clove** [ˈkloːv]; **cleaving** ADHERE : adherirse, unirse
cleave[2] *vt* **cleaved; cleaving** SPLIT : hender, dividir, partir
cleaver [ˈkliːvər] *n* : cuchilla *f* de carnicero
clef [ˈklɛf] *n* : clave *f*
cleft [ˈklɛft] *n* : hendidura *f*, raja *f*, grieta *f*
clemency [ˈklɛmən*t*si] *n* : clemencia *f*
clement [ˈklɛmənt] *adj* **1** MERCIFUL : clemente, piadoso **2** MILD : clemente, apacible
clench [ˈklɛntʃ] *vt* **1** CLUTCH : agarrar **2** TIGHTEN : apretar (el puño, los dientes)
clergy [ˈklərdʒi] *n, pl* **-gies** : clero *m*
clergyman [ˈklərdʒimən] *n, pl* **-men** [-mən, -ˌmɛn] : clérigo *m*
cleric [ˈklɛrɪk] *n* : clérigo *m*, -ga *f*
clerical [ˈklɛrɪkəl] *adj* **1** : clerical <a clerical collar : un alzacuello> **2** : de oficina <clerical staff : personal de oficina>
clerk[1] [ˈklərk, *Brit* ˈklɑrk] *vi* : trabajar de oficinista, trabajar de dependiente
clerk[2] *n* **1** : funcionario *m*, -ria *f* (de una oficina gubernamental) **2** : oficinista *mf*, empleado *m*, -da *f* de oficina **3** SALESPERSON : dependiente *m*, -ta *f*
clever [ˈklɛvər] *adj* **1** SKILLFUL : ingenioso, hábil **2** SMART : listo, inteligente, astuto
cleverly [ˈklɛvərli] *adv* **1** SKILLFULLY : ingeniosamente, hábilmente **2** INTELLIGENTLY : inteligentemente
cleverness [ˈklɛvərnəs] *n* **1** SKILL : ingenio *m*, habilidad *f* **2** INTELLIGENCE : inteligencia *f*
clew [ˈkluː] → **clue**
cliché [kliˈʃeɪ] *n* : cliché *m*, tópico *m*
click[1] [ˈklɪk] *vt* : chasquear (la lengua, los dedos) — *vi* **1** : chasquear **2** SUCCEED : tener éxito **3** GET ALONG : congeniar, llevarse bien
click[2] *n* : chasquido *m*
client [ˈklaɪənt] *n* : cliente *m*, -ta *f*
clientele [ˌklaɪənˈtɛl, ˌkliː-] *n* : clientela *f*
cliff [ˈklɪf] *n* : acantilado *m*, precipicio *m*, risco *m*
climate [ˈklaɪmət] *n* : clima *m*
climax[1] [ˈklaɪˌmæks] *vi* : llegar al punto culminante, culminar — *vt* : ser el punto culminante de
climax[2] *n* : clímax *m*, punto *m* culminante
climb[1] [ˈklaɪm] *vt* : escalar, trepar a, subir a <to climb a mountain : escalar una montaña> — *vi* **1** RISE : subir, ascender <prices are climbing : los precios están subiendo> **2** subirse, treparse <to climb up a tree : treparse a un árbol>
climb[2] *n* : ascenso *m*, subida *f*
climber [ˈklaɪmər] *n* **1** : escalador *m*, -dora *f* <a mountain climber : un alpinista> **2** : trepadora *f* (planta)
clinch[1] [ˈklɪntʃ] *vt* **1** FASTEN, SECURE : remachar (un clavo), afianzar, abrochar **2** SETTLE : decidir, cerrar <to clinch the title : ganar el título>
clinch[2] *n* : abrazo *m*, clinch *m* (en el boxeo)
clincher [ˈklɪntʃər] *n* : argumento *m* decisivo
cling [ˈklɪŋ] *vi* **clung** [ˈklʌŋ]; **clinging** **1** STICK : adherirse, pegarse **2** : aferrarse, agarrarse <he clung to the railing : se aferró a la barandilla>
clinic [ˈklɪnɪk] *n* : clínica *f*
clinical [ˈklɪnɪkəl] *adj* : clínico — **clinically** [-kli] *adv*
clink[1] [ˈklɪŋk] *vi* : tintinear
clink[2] *n* : tintineo *m*
clip[1] [ˈklɪp] *vt* **clipped; clipping** **1** CUT : cortar, recortar **2** HIT : golpear, dar un puñetazo a **3** FASTEN : sujetar (con un clip)
clip[2] *n* **1** → **clippers** **2** BLOW : golpe *m*, puñetazo *m* **3** PACE : paso *m* rápido **4** FASTENER : clip *m* <a paper clip : un sujetapapeles>
clipper [ˈklɪpər] *n* **1** : clíper *m* (buque de vela) **2 clippers** *npl* : tijeras *fpl* <nail clippers : cortaúñas>
clique [ˈkliːk, ˈklɪk] *n* : grupo *m* exclusivo, camarilla *f* (de políticos)
clitoris [ˈklɪtərəs, klɪˈtɔrəs] *n, pl* **clitorides** [-ˈtɔrəˌdiːz] : clítoris *m*
cloak[1] [ˈkloːk] *vt* : encubrir, envolver (en un manto de)
cloak[2] *n* : capa *f*, capote *m*, manto *m* <under the cloak of darkness : al amparo de la oscuridad>

clobber ['klɑbər] *vt* : dar una paliza a
clock[1] ['klɑk] *vt* : cronometrar
clock[2] *n* **1** : reloj *m* (de pared), cronómetro *m* (en deportes o competencias) **2 around the clock** : las veinticuatro horas
clockwise ['klɑk,waɪz] *adv & adj* : en la dirección de las manecillas del reloj
clockwork ['klɑk,wərk] *n* : mecanismo *m* de relojería
clod ['klɑd] *n* **1** : terrón *m* **2** OAF : zoquete *mf*
clog[1] ['klɑg] *v* **clogged; clogging** *vt* **1** HINDER : estorbar, impedir **2** BLOCK : atascar, tapar — *vi* : atascarse, taparse
clog[2] *n* **1** OBSTACLE : traba *f*, impedimento *m*, estorbo *m* **2** : zueco *m* (zapato)
cloister[1] ['klɔɪstər] *vt* : enclaustrar
cloister[2] *n* : claustro *m*
clone ['klo:n] *n* **1** : clon *m* (de un organismo) **2** COPY : copia *f*, reproducción *f*
close[1] ['klo:z] *v* **closed; closing** *vt* : cerrar — *vi* **1** : cerrarse, cerrar **2** TERMINATE : concluirse, terminar **3 to close in** APPROACH : acercarse, aproximarse
close[2] ['klo:s] *adv* : cerca, de cerca
close[3] *adj* **closer; closest 1** CONFINING : restrictivo, estrecho **2** SECRETIVE : reservado **3** STRICT : estricto, detallado **4** STUFFY : cargado, bochornoso (dícese del tiempo) **5** TIGHT : apretado, entallado, ceñido <it's a close fit : es muy apretado> **6** NEAR : cercano, próximo **7** INTIMATE : íntimo <close friends : amigos íntimos> **8** ACCURATE : fiel, exacto **9** : reñido <a close election : una elección muy reñida>
close[4] ['klo:z] *n* : fin *m*, final *m*, conclusión *f*
closely ['klo:sli] *adv* : cerca, de cerca
closeness ['klo:snəs] *n* **1** NEARNESS : cercanía *f*, proximidad *f* **2** INTIMACY : intimidad *f*
closet[1] ['klɑzət] *vt* **to be closeted with** : estar encerrado con
closet[2] *n* : armario *m*, guardarropa *f*, clóset *m*
closure ['klo:ʒər] *n* **1** CLOSING, END : cierre *m*, clausura *f*, fin *m* **2** FASTENER : cierre *m*
clot[1] ['klɑt] *v* **clotted; clotting** *vt* : coagular, cuajar — *vi* : cuajarse, coagularse
clot[2] *n* : coágulo *m*
cloth ['klɔθ] *n, pl* **cloths** ['klɔðz, 'klɔθs] **1** FABRIC : tela *f* **2** RAG : trapo *m* **3** TABLECLOTH : mantel *m*
clothe ['klo:ð] *vt* **clothed** *or* **clad** ['klæd]; **clothing** DRESS : vestir, arropar, ataviar
clothes ['klo:z, 'klo:ðz] *npl* **1** CLOTHING : ropa *f* **2** BEDCLOTHES : ropa *f* de cama
clothespin ['klo:z,pɪn] *n* : pinza *f* (para la ropa)
clothing ['klo:ðɪŋ] *n* : ropa *f*, indumentaria *f*
cloud[1] ['klaʊd] *vt* : nublar, oscurecer — *vi* **to cloud over** : nublarse
cloud[2] *n* : nube *f*
cloudburst ['klaʊd,bərst] *n* : chaparrón *m*, aguacero *m*
cloudless ['klaʊdləs] *adj* : despejado, claro
cloudy ['klaʊdi] *adj* **cloudier; -est** : nublado, nuboso
clout[1] ['klaʊt] *vt* : bofetear, dar un tortazo a
clout[2] *n* **1** BLOW : golpe *m*, tortazo *m* *fam* **2** INFLUENCE : influencia *f*, palanca *f fam*
clove[1] ['klo:v] *n* **1** : diente *m* (de ajo) **2** : clavo *m* (especia)
clove[2] → **cleave**
cloven hoof ['klo:vən] : pezuña *f* hendida
clover ['klo:vər] *n* : trébol *m*
cloverleaf ['klo:vər,li:f] *n, pl* **-leafs** *or* **-leaves** [-,li:vz] : intersección *f* en trébol
clown[1] ['klaʊn] *vi* : payasear, bromear <stop clowning around : déjate de payasadas>
clown[2] *n* : payaso *m*, -sa *f*
clownish ['klaʊnɪʃ] *adj* **1** : de payaso **2** BOORISH : grosero — **clownishly** *adv*
cloying ['klɔɪɪŋ] *adj* : empalagoso, meloso
club[1] ['klʌb] *vt* **clubbed; clubbing** : aporrear, dar garrotazos a
club[2] *n* **1** CUDGEL : garrote *m*, porra *f* **2** : palo *m* <golf club : palo de golf> **3** : trébol *m* (naipe) **4** ASSOCIATION : club *m*
clubfoot ['klʌb,fʊt] *n, pl* **-feet** : pie *m* deforme
clubhouse ['klʌb,haʊs] *n* : sede *f* de un club
cluck[1] ['klʌk] *vi* : cloquear, cacarear
cluck[2] *n* : cloqueo *m*, cacareo *m*
clue[1] ['klu:] *vt* **clued; clueing** *or* **cluing** *or* **to clue in** : dar una pista a, informar
clue[2] *n* : pista *f*, indicio *m*
clump[1] ['klʌmp] *vi* **1** : caminar con pisadas fuertes **2** LUMP : agruparse, aglutinarse — *vt* : amontonar
clump[2] *n* **1** : grupo *m* (de arbustos o árboles), terrón *m* (de tierra) **2** : pisada *f* fuerte
clumsily ['klʌmzəli] *adv* : torpemente, sin gracia
clumsiness ['klʌmzinəs] *n* : torpeza *f*
clumsy ['klʌmzi] *adj* **-sier; -est 1** AWKWARD : torpe, desmañado **2** TACTLESS : carente de tacto, poco delicado
clung → **cling**
cluster[1] ['klʌstər] *vt* : agrupar, juntar — *vi* : agruparse, apiñarse, arracimarse
cluster[2] *n* : grupo *m*, conjunto *m*, racimo *m* (de uvas)
clutch[1] ['klʌtʃ] *vt* : agarrar, asir — *vi* **to clutch at** : tratar de agarrar

clutch[2] *n* **1** GRASP, GRIP : agarre *m,* apretón *m* **2** : embrague *m,* clutch *m* (de una máquina) **3 clutches** *npl* : garras *fpl* <he fell into their clutches : cayó en sus garras>
clutter[1] [ˈklʌtər] *vt* : atiborrar o atestar de cosas, llenar desordenadamente
clutter[2] *n* : desorden *m,* revoltijo *m*
coach[1] [ˈkoːtʃ] *vt* : entrenar (atletas, artistas), preparar (alumnos)
coach[2] *n* **1** CARRIAGE : coche *m,* carruaje *m,* carroza *f* **2** : vagón *m* de pasajeros (de un tren) **3** BUS : autobús *m,* ómnibus *m* **4** : pasaje *m* aéreo de segunda clase **5** TRAINER : entrenador *m,* -dora *f*
coagulate [koˈægjəˌleɪt] *v* **-lated; -lating** *vt* : coagular, cuajar — *vi* : coagularse, cuajarse
coal [ˈkoːl] *n* **1** EMBER : ascua *f,* brasa *f* **2** : carbón *m* <a coal mine : una mina de carbón>
coalesce [ˌkoːəˈlɛs] *vi* **-alesced; -alescing** : unirse
coalition [ˌkoːəˈlɪʃən] *n* : coalición *f*
coarse [ˈkors] *adj* **coarser; -est 1** : grueso (dícese de la arena o la sal), basto (dícese de las telas), áspero (dícese de la piel) **2** CRUDE, ROUGH : basto, tosco, ordinario **3** VULGAR : grosero — **coarsely** *adv*
coarsen [ˈkorsən] *vt* : hacer áspero o basto — *vi* : volverse áspero o basto
coarseness [ˈkorsnəs] *n* : aspereza *f,* tosquedad *f*
coast[1] [ˈkoːst] *vi* : deslizarse, rodar sin impulso
coast[2] *n* : costa *f,* litoral *m*
coastal [ˈkoːstəl] *adj* : costero
coaster [ˈkoːstər] *n* : posavasos *m*
coast guard *n* : guardia *f* costera, guardacostas *mpl*
coastline [ˈkoːstˌlaɪn] *n* : costa *f*
coat[1] [ˈkoːt] *vt* : cubrir, revestir, bañar (en un líquido)
coat[2] *n* **1** : abrigo *m* <a sport coat : una chaqueta, un saco> **2** : pelaje *m* (de animales) **3** LAYER : capa *f,* mano *f* (de pintura)
coating [ˈkoːtɪŋ] *n* : capa *f*
coat of arms *n* : escudo *m* de armas
coax [ˈkoːks] *vt* : engatusar, persuadir
cob [ˈkɑb] → **corncob**
cobalt [ˈkoːˌbɔlt] *n* : cobalto *m*
cobble [ˈkɑbəl] *vt* **cobbled; cobbling 1** : fabricar o remendar (zapatos) **2 to cobble together** : improvisar, hacer apresuradamente
cobbler [ˈkɑblər] *n* **1** SHOEMAKER : zapatero *m,* -ra *f* **2 fruit cobbler** : tarta *f* de fruta
cobblestone [ˈkɑbəlˌstoːn] *n* : adoquín *m*
cobra [ˈkoːbrə] *n* : cobra *f*
cobweb [ˈkɑbˌwɛb] *n* : telaraña *f*
cocaine [koːˈkeɪn, ˈkoːˌkeɪn] *n* : cocaína *f*
cock[1] [ˈkɑk] *vt* **1** : ladear <to cock one's head : ladear la cabeza> **2** : montar, amartillar (un arma de fuego)
cock[2] *n* **1** ROOSTER : gallo *m* **2** FAUCET : grifo *m,* llave *f* **3** : martillo *m* (de un arma de fuego)
cockatoo [ˈkɑkəˌtuː] *n, pl* **-toos** : cacatúa *f*
cockeyed [ˈkɑkˌaɪd] *adj* **1** ASKEW : ladeado, torcido, chueco **2** ABSURD : disparatado, absurdo
cockfight [ˈkɑkˌfaɪt] *n* : pelea *f* de gallos
cockiness [ˈkɑkinəs] *n* : arrogancia *f*
cockle [ˈkɑkəl] *n* : berberecho *m*
cockpit [ˈkɑkˌpɪt] *n* : cabina *f*
cockroach [ˈkɑkˌroːtʃ] *n* : cucaracha *f*
cocktail [ˈkɑkˌteɪl] *n* **1** : coctel *m,* cóctel *m* **2** APPETIZER : aperitivo *m*
cocky [ˈkɑki] *adj* **cockier; -est** : creído, engreído
cocoa [ˈkoːˌkoː] *n* **1** CACAO : cacao *m* **2** : cocoa *f,* chocolate *m* (bebida)
coconut [ˈkoːkəˌnʌt] *n* : coco *m*
cocoon [kəˈkuːn] *n* : capullo *m*
cod [ˈkɑd] *n, pl* **cod** : bacalao *m*
coddle [ˈkɑdəl] *vt* **-dled; -dling** : mimar, consentir
code [ˈkoːd] *n* **1** : código *m* <civil code : código civil> **2** : código *m,* clave *f* <secret code : clave secreta>
codeine [ˈkoːˌdiːn] *n* : codeína *f*
codger [ˈkɑdʒər] *n* : viejo *m,* vejete *m*
codify [ˈkɑdəˌfaɪ, ˈkoː-] *vt* **-fied; -fying** : codificar
coeducation [ˌkoːˌɛdʒəˈkeɪʃən] *n* : coeducación *f,* enseñanza *f* mixta
coeducational [ˌkoːˌɛdʒəˈkeɪʃənəl] *adj* : mixto
coefficient [ˌkoːəˈfɪʃənt] *n* : coeficiente *m*
coerce [koˈərs] *vt* **-erced; -ercing** : coaccionar, forzar, obligar
coercion [koˈərʒən, -ʃən] *n* : coacción *f*
coercive [koˈərsɪv] *adj* : coactivo
coexist [ˌkoːɪgˈzɪst] *vi* : coexistir
coexistence [ˌkoːɪgˈzɪstənts] *n* : coexistencia *f*
coffee [ˈkɔfi] *n* : café *m*
coffeepot [ˈkɔfiˌpɑt] *n* : cafetera *f*
coffer [ˈkɔfər] *n* : cofre *m*
coffin [ˈkɔfən] *n* : ataúd *m,* féretro *m*
cog [ˈkɑg] *n* : diente *m* (de una rueda dentada)
cogent [ˈkoːdʒənt] *adj* : convincente, persuasivo
cogitate [ˈkɑdʒəˌteɪt] *vi* **-tated; -tating** : reflexionar, meditar, discurrir
cogitation [ˌkɑdʒəˈteɪʃən] *n* : reflexión *f,* meditación *f*
cognac [ˈkoːnˌjæk] *n* : coñac *m*
cognate [ˈkɑgˌneɪt] *adj* : relacionado, afín
cogwheel [ˈkɑgˌhwiːl] *n* : rueda *f* dentada
cohabit [ˌkoːˈhæbət] *vi* : cohabitar
cohere [koˈhɪr] *vi* **-hered; -hering 1** ADHERE : adherirse, pegarse **2** : ser coherente o congruente

coherence [koˈhɪrənts] *n* : coherencia *f*, congruencia *f*

coherent [koˈhɪrənt] *adj* : coherente, congruente — **coherently** *adv*

cohesion [koˈhiːʒən] *n* : cohesión *f*

cohort [ˈkoːˌhɔrt] *n* **1** : cohorte *f* (de soldados) **2** COMPANION : compañero *m*, -ra *f*; colega *mf*

coiffure [kwɑˈfjʊr] *n* : peinado *m*

coil[1] [ˈkɔɪl] *vt* : enrollar — *vi* : enrollarse, enroscarse

coil[2] *n* : rollo *m* (de cuerda, etc.), espiral *f* (de humo)

coin[1] [ˈkɔɪn] *vt* **1** MINT : acuñar (moneda) **2** INVENT : acuñar, crear, inventar <to coin a phrase : como se suele decir>

coin[2] *n* : moneda *f*

coincide [ˌkoːɪnˈsaɪd, ˈkoːɪnˌsaɪd] *vi* **-cided; -ciding** : coincidir

coincidence [koˈɪntsədənts] *n* : coincidencia *f*, casualidad *f* <what a coincidence! : ¡qué casualidad!>

coincident [koˈɪntsədənt] *adj* : coincidente, concurrente

coincidental [koˌɪntsəˈdɛntəl] *adj* : casual, accidental, fortuito

coitus [ˈkoːətəs] *n* : coito *m*

coke [ˈkoːk] *n* : coque *m*

colander [ˈkɑləndər, ˈkʌ-] *n* : colador *m*

cold[1] [ˈkoːld] *adj* : frío <it's cold out : hace frío> <a cold reception : una fría recepción> <in cold blood : a sangre fría>

cold[2] *n* **1** : frío *m* <to feel the cold : sentir frío> **2** : resfriado *m*, catarro *m* <to catch a cold : resfriarse>

cold–blooded [ˈkoːldˈblʌdəd] *adj* **1** CRUEL : cruel, despiadado **2** : de sangre fría (dícese de los reptiles, etc.)

coldly [ˈkoːldli] *adv* : fríamente, con frialdad

coldness [ˈkoːldnəs] *n* : frialdad *f* (de una persona o una actitud), frío *m* (de la temperatura)

coleslaw [ˈkoːlˌslɔ] *n* : ensalada *f* de col

colic [ˈkɑlɪk] *n* : cólico *m*

coliseum [ˌkɑləˈsiːəm] *n* : coliseo *m*, arena *f*

collaborate [kəˈlæbəˌreɪt] *vi* **-rated; -rating** : colaborar

collaboration [kəˌlæbəˈreɪʃən] *n* : colaboración *f*

collaborator [kəˈlæbəˌreɪtər] *n* **1** COLLEAGUE : colaborador *m*, -dora *f* **2** TRAITOR : colaboracionista *mf*

collapse[1] [kəˈlæps] *vi* **-lapsed; -lapsing 1** : derrumbarse, desplomarse, hundirse <the building collapsed : el edificio se derrumbó> **2** FALL : desplomarse, caerse <he collapsed on the bed : se desplomó en la cama> <to collapse with laughter : morirse de risa> **3** FAIL : fracasar, quebrar, arruinarse **4** FOLD : plegarse

collapse[2] *n* **1** FALL : derrumbe *m*, desplome *m* **2** BREAKDOWN, FAILURE : fracaso *m*, colapso *m* (físico), quiebra *f* (económica)

collapsible [kəˈlæpsəbəl] *adj* : plegable

collar[1] [ˈkɑlər] *vt* : agarrar, atrapar

collar[2] *n* : cuello *m*

collarbone [ˈkɑlərˌboːn] *n* : clavícula *f*

collate [kəˈleɪt; ˈkɑˌleɪt, ˈkoː-] *vt* **-lated; -lating 1** COMPARE : cotejar, comparar **2** : ordenar, recopilar (páginas)

collateral[1] [kəˈlætərəl] *adj* : colateral

collateral[2] *n* : garantía *f*, fianza *f*, prenda *f*

colleague [ˈkɑˌliːg] *n* : colega *mf*; compañero *m*, -ra *f*

collect[1] [kəˈlɛkt] *vt* **1** GATHER : recopilar, reunir, recoger <she collected her thoughts : puso en orden sus ideas> **2** : coleccionar, juntar <to collect stamps : coleccionar timbres> **3** : cobrar (una deuda), recaudar (un impuesto) **4** DRAW : cobrar, percibir (un sueldo, etc.) — *vi* **1** ACCUMULATE : acumularse, juntarse **2** CONGREGATE : congregarse, reunirse

collect[2] *adv & adj* : por cobrar, a cobro revertido

collectible *or* **collectable** [kəˈlɛktəbəl] *adj* : coleccionable

collection [kəˈlɛkʃən] *n* **1** COLLECTING : colecta *f* (de contribuciones), cobro *m* (de deudas), recaudación *f* (de impuestos) **2** GROUP : colección *f* (de objetos), grupo *m* (de personas)

collective[1] [kəˈlɛktɪv] *adj* : colectivo — **collectively** *adv*

collective[2] *n* : colectivo *m*

collector [kəˈlɛktər] *n* **1** : coleccionista *mf* (de objetos) **2** : cobrador *m*, -dora *f* (de deudas)

college [ˈkɑlɪdʒ] *n* **1** : universidad *f* **2** : colegio *m* (de electores o profesionales)

collegiate [kəˈliːdʒət] *adj* : universitario

collide [kəˈlaɪd] *vi* **-lided; -liding** : chocar, colisionar, estrellarse

collie [ˈkɑli] *n* : collie *mf*

collision [kəˈlɪʒən] *n* : choque *m*, colisión *f*

colloquial [kəˈloːkwiəl] *adj* : coloquial

colloquialism [kəˈloːkwiəˌlɪzəm] *n* : expresión *f* coloquial

collusion [kəˈluːʒən] *n* : colusión *f*

cologne [kəˈloːn] *n* : colonia *f*

Colombian [kəˈlʌmbiən] *n* : colombiano *m*, -na *f* — **Colombian** *adj*

colon[1] [ˈkoːlən] *n, pl* **colons** *or* **cola** [-lə] : colon *m* (de los intestinos)

colon[2] *n, pl* **colons** : dos puntos *mpl* (signo ortográfico)

colonel [ˈkərnəl] *n* : coronel *m*

colonial[1] [kəˈloːniəl] *adj* : colonial

colonial[2] *n* : colono *m*, -na *f*

colonist [ˈkɑlənɪst] *n* : colono *m*, -na *f*; colonizador *m*, -dora *f*

colonization [ˌkɑlənəˈzeɪʃən] *n* : colonización *f*
colonize [ˈkɑləˌnaɪz] *vt* **-nized; -nizing** **1** : establecer una colonia en **2** SETTLE : colonizar
colonnade [ˌkɑləˈneɪd] *n* : columnata *f*
colony [ˈkɑləni] *n, pl* **-nies** : colonia *f*
color[1] [ˈkʌlər] *vt* **1** : colorear, pintar **2** INFLUENCE : influir en, influenciar — *vi* BLUSH : sonrojarse, ruborizarse
color[2] *n* **1** : color *m* <primary colors : colores primarios> **2** INTEREST, VIVIDNESS : color *m,* colorido *m* <local color : color local>
color–blind [ˈkʌlərˌblaɪnd] *adj* : daltónico
color blindness *n* : daltonismo *m*
colored [ˈkʌlərd] *adj* **1** : de color (dícese de los objetos) **2** : de color, negro (dícese de las personas)
colorfast [ˈkʌlərˌfæst] *adj* : que no se destiñe
colorful [ˈkʌlərfəl] *adj* **1** : lleno de colorido, de colores vivos **2** PICTURESQUE, STRIKING : pintoresco, llamativo
colorless [ˈkʌlərləs] *adj* **1** : incoloro, sin color **2** DULL : soso, aburrido
colossal [kəˈlɑsəl] *adj* : colosal
colossus [kəˈlɑsəs] *n, pl* **-si** [-ˌsaɪ] : coloso *m*
colt [ˈkoːlt] *n* : potro *m*
column [ˈkɑləm] *n* : columna *f*
columnist [ˈkɑləmnɪst, -ləmɪst] *n* : columnista *mf*
coma [ˈkoːmə] *n* : coma *m,* estado *m* de coma
comatose [ˈkoːməˌtoːs, ˈkɑ-] *adj* : comatoso, en estado de coma
comb[1] [ˈkoːm] *vt* **1** : peinar (el pelo) **2** SEARCH : peinar, rastrear, registrar a fondo
comb[2] *n* **1** : peine *m* **2** : cresta *f* (de un gallo)
combat[1] [kəmˈbæt, ˈkɑmˌbæt] *vt* **-bated** *or* **-batted; -bating** *or* **-batting** : combatir, luchar contra
combat[2] [ˈkɑmˌbæt] *n* : combate *m,* lucha *f*
combatant [kəmˈbætənt] *n* : combatiente *mf*
combative [kəmˈbæt̬ɪv] *adj* : combativo
combination [ˌkɑmbəˈneɪʃən] *n* : combinación *f*
combine[1] [kəmˈbaɪn] *v* **-bined; -bining** *vt* : combinar, aunar — *vi* : combinarse, mezclarse
combine[2] [ˈkɑmˌbaɪn] *n* **1** ALLIANCE : alianza *f* comercial o política **2** HARVESTER : cosechadora *f*
combustible [kəmˈbʌstəbəl] *adj* : inflamable, combustible
combustion [kəmˈbʌstʃən] *n* : combustión *f*
come [ˈkʌm] *vi* **came** [ˈkeɪm]; **come; coming** **1** APPROACH : venir, aproximarse <here they come : acá vienen> **2** ARRIVE : venir, llegar, alcanzar <they came yesterday : vinieron ayer> **3** ORIGINATE : venir, provenir <this wine comes from France : este vino viene de Francia> **4** AMOUNT : llegar, ascender <the investment came to two million : la inversión llegó a dos millones> **5 to come clean** : confesar, desahogar la conciencia **6 to come into** ACQUIRE : adquirir <to come into a fortune : heredar una fortuna> **7 to come off** SUCCEED : tener éxito, ser un éxito **8 to come out** : salir, aparecer, publicarse **9 to come to** REVIVE : recobrar el conocimiento, volver en sí **10 to come to pass** HAPPEN : acontecer **11 to come to terms** : llegar a un acuerdo
comeback [ˈkʌmˌbæk] *n* **1** RETORT : réplica *f,* respuesta *f* **2** RETURN : retorno *m,* regreso *m* <the champion announced his comeback : el campeón anunció su regreso>
come back *vi* **1** RETORT : replicar, contestar **2** RETURN : volver <come back here! : ¡vuelve acá!> <that style's coming back : ese estilo está volviendo>
comedian [kəˈmiːdiən] *n* : cómico *m,* -ca *f;* humorista *mf*
comedienne [kəˌmiːdiˈɛn] *n* : cómica *f,* humorista *f*
comedy [ˈkɑmədi] *n, pl* **-dies** : comedia *f*
comely [ˈkʌmli] *adj* **-lier; -est** : bello, bonito
comet [ˈkɑmət] *n* : cometa *m*
comfort[1] [ˈkʌmpfərt] *vt* **1** CHEER : confortar, alentar **2** CONSOLE : consolar
comfort[2] *n* **1** CONSOLATION : consuelo *m* **2** WELL-BEING : confort *m,* bienestar *m* **3** CONVENIENCE : comodidad *f* <the comforts of home : las comodidades del hogar>
comfortable [ˈkʌmpfərt̬əbəl, ˈkʌmpftə-] *adj* : cómodo, confortable — **comfortably** [ˈkʌmpfərt̬əbli, ˈkʌmpftə-] *adv*
comforter [ˈkʌmpfərt̬ər] *n* **1** : confortador *m,* -dora *f* **2** QUILT : edredón *m,* cobertor *m*
comic[1] [ˈkɑmɪk] *adj* : cómico, humorístico
comic[2] *n* **1** COMEDIAN : cómico *m,* -ca *f;* humorista *mf* **2** *or* **comic book** : historieta *f,* cómic *m*
comical [ˈkɑmɪkəl] *adj* : cómico, gracioso, chistoso
comic strip *n* : tira *f* cómica, historieta *f*
coming [ˈkʌmɪŋ] *adj* : siguiente, próximo, que viene
comma [ˈkɑmə] *n* : coma *f*
command[1] [kəˈmænd] *vt* **1** ORDER : ordenar, mandar **2** CONTROL, DIRECT : comandar, tener el mando de — *vi* **1** : dar órdenes **2** GOVERN : estar al mando *m,* gobernar

command[2] *n* **1** CONTROL, LEADERSHIP : mando *m,* control *m,* dirección *f* **2** ORDER : orden *f,* mandato *m* **3** MASTERY : maestría *f,* destreza *f,* dominio *m* **4** : tropa *f* asignada a un comandante

commandant [ˈkɑmən͵dɑnt, -͵dænt] *n* : comandante *mf*

commandeer [͵kɑmənˈdɪr] *vt* : piratear, secuestrar (un vehículo, etc.)

commander [kəˈmændər] *n* : comandante *mf*

commandment [kəˈmændmənt] *n* : mandamiento *m,* orden *f* <the Ten Commandments : los diez mandamientos>

commemorate [kəˈmɛmə͵reɪt] *vt* **-rated; -rating** : conmemorar

commemoration [kə͵mɛməˈreɪʃən] *n* : conmemoración *f*

commemorative [kəˈmɛmrəṭiv, -ˈmɛmə͵reɪṭiv] *adj* : conmemorativo

commence [kəˈmɛnts] *v* **-menced; -mencing** *vt* : iniciar, comenzar — *vi* : iniciarse, comenzar

commencement [kəˈmɛntsmənt] *n* **1** BEGINNING : inicio *m,* comienzo *m* **2** : ceremonia *f* de graduación

commend [kəˈmɛnd] *vt* **1** ENTRUST : encomendar **2** RECOMMEND : recomendar **3** PRAISE : elogiar, alabar

commendable [kəˈmɛndəbəl] *adj* : loable, meritorio, encomiable

commendation [͵kɑmənˈdeɪʃən, -͵mɛn-] *n* : elogio *m,* encomio *m*

commensurate [kəˈmɛntsərət, -ˈmɛntʃʊrət] *adj* : proporcionado <commensurate with : en proporción a>

comment[1] [ˈkɑ͵mɛnt] *vi* **1** : hacer comentarios **2 to comment on** : comentar, hacer observaciones sobre

comment[2] *n* : comentario *m,* observación *f*

commentary [ˈkɑmən͵tɛri] *n, pl* **-taries** : comentario *m,* crónica *f* (deportiva)

commentator [ˈkɑmən͵teɪṭər] *n* : comentarista *mf,* cronista *mf* (de deportes)

commerce [ˈkɑmərs] *n* : comercio *m*

commercial[1] [kəˈmərʃəl] *adj* : comercial — **commercially** *adv*

commercial[2] *n* : comercial *m*

commercialize [kəˈmərʃə͵laɪz] *vt* **-ized; -izing** : comercializar

commiserate [kəˈmɪzə͵reɪt] *vi* **-ated; -ating** : compadecerse, consolarse

commiseration [kə͵mɪzəˈreɪʃən] *n* : conmiseración *f*

commission[1] [kəˈmɪʃən] *vt* **1** : nombrar (un oficial) **2** : comisionar, encargar <to commission a painting : encargar una pintura>

commission[2] *n* **1** : nombramiento *m* (al grado de oficial) **2** COMMITTEE : comisión *f,* comité *m* **3** COMMITTING : comisión *f,* realización *f* (de un acto) **4** PERCENTAGE : comisión *f* <sales commissions : comisiones de venta>

commissioned officer *n* : oficial *mf*

commissioner [kəˈmɪʃənər] *n* **1** : comisionado *m,* -da *f;* miembro *m* de una comisión **2** : comisario *m,* -ria *f* (de policía, etc.)

commit [kəˈmɪt] *vt* **-mitted; -mitting** **1** ENTRUST : encomendar, confiar **2** CONFINE : internar (en un hospital), encarcelar (en una prisión) **3** PERPETRATE : cometer <to commit a crime : cometer un crimen> **4 to commit oneself** : comprometerse

commitment [kəˈmɪtmənt] *n* **1** RESPONSIBILITY : compromiso *m,* responsabilidad *f* **2** DEDICATION : dedicación *f,* devoción *f* <commitment to the cause : devoción a la causa>

committee [kəˈmɪṭi] *n* : comité *m*

commodious [kəˈmo:diəs] *adj* SPACIOUS : amplio, espacioso

commodity [kəˈmɑdəṭi] *n, pl* **-ties** : artículo *m* de comercio, mercancía *f,* mercadería *f*

commodore [ˈkɑmə͵dor] *n* : comodoro *m*

common[1] [ˈkɑmən] *adj* **1** PUBLIC : común, público <the common good : el bien común> **2** SHARED : común <a common interest : un interés común> **3** GENERAL : común, general <it's common knowledge : todo el mundo lo sabe> **4** ORDINARY : ordinario, común y corriente <the common man : el hombre medio, el hombre de la calle>

common[2] *n* **1** : tierra *f* comunal **2 in ~** : en común

common cold *n* : resfriado *m* común

common denominator *n* : denominador *m* común

commoner [ˈkɑmənər] *n* : plebeyo *m,* -ya *f*

commonly [ˈkɑmənli] *adv* **1** FREQUENTLY : comúnmente, frecuentemente **2** USUALLY : normalmente

common noun *n* : nombre *m* común

commonplace[1] [ˈkɑmən͵pleɪs] *adj* : común, ordinario

commonplace[2] *n* : cliché *m,* tópico *m*

common sense *n* : sentido *m* común

commonwealth [ˈkɑmən͵wɛlθ] *n* : entidad *f* política <the British Commonwealth : la Mancomunidad Británica>

commotion [kəˈmo:ʃən] *n* **1** RUCKUS : alboroto *m,* jaleo *m,* escándalo *m* **2** STIR, UPSET : revuelo *m,* conmoción *f*

communal [kəˈmju:nəl] *adj* : communal

commune[1] [kəˈmju:n] *vi* **-muned; -muning** : estar en comunión *f*

commune[2] [ˈkɑ͵mju:n, kəˈmju:n] *n* : comuna *f*

communicable [kəˈmju:nɪkəbəl] *adj* CONTAGIOUS : transmisible, contagioso

communicate [kəˈmju:nə͵keɪt] *v* **-cated; -cating** *vt* **1** CONVEY : comunicar, expresar, hacer saber **2** TRANSMIT : transmitir (una enfermedad), contagiar — *vi* : comunicarse, expresarse

communication [kə,mju:nə'keɪʃən] *n* : comunicación *f*

communicative [kə'mju:nɪ,keɪt̬ɪv, -kət̬ɪv] *adj* : comunicativo

communion [kə'mju:njən] *n* **1** SHARING : comunión *f* **2 Communion** : comunión *f,* eucaristía *f*

communiqué [kə'mju:nə,keɪ, -,mju:nə'keɪ] *n* : comunicado *m*

communism *or* **Communism** ['kɑmjə,nɪzəm] *n* : comunismo *m*

communist[1] *or* **Communist** ['kɑmjə,nɪst] *adj* : comunista <the Communist Party : el Partido Comunista>

communist[2] *or* **Communist** *n* : comunista *mf*

communistic *or* **Communistic** [,kɑmjə'nɪstɪk] *adj* : comunista

community [kə'mju:nət̬i] *n, pl* **-ties** : comunidad *f*

commute [kə'mju:t] *v* **-muted; -muting** *vt* REDUCE : conmutar, reducir (una sentencia) — *vi* : viajar de la residencia al trabajo

commuter [kə'mju:t̬ər] *n* : persona *f* que viaja diariamente al trabajo

compact[1] [kəm'pækt, 'kɑm,pækt] *vt* : compactar, consolidar, comprimir

compact[2] [kəm'pækt, 'kɑm,pækt] *adj* **1** DENSE, SOLID : compacto, macizo, denso **2** CONCISE : breve, conciso

compact[3] ['kɑm,pækt] *n* **1** AGREEMENT : acuerdo *m,* pacto *m* **2** : polvera *f,* estuche *m* de maquillaje **3** *or* **compact car** : auto *m* compacto

compact disc ['kɑm,pækt'dɪsk] *n* : disco *m* compacto, compact disc *m*

compactly [kəm'pæktli, 'kɑm,pækt-] *adv* **1** DENSELY : densamente, macizamente **2** CONCISELY : concisamente, brevemente

companion [kəm'pænjən] *n* **1** COMRADE : compañero *m,* -ra *f;* acompañante *mf* **2** MATE : pareja *f* (de un zapato, etc.)

companionable [kəm'pænjənəbəl] *adj* : sociable, amigable

companionship [kəm'pænjən,ʃɪp] *n* : compañerismo *m,* camaradería *f*

company ['kʌmpəni] *n, pl* **-nies 1** FIRM : compañía *f,* empresa *f* **2** GROUP : compañía *f* (de actores o soldados) **3** GUESTS : visita *f* <we have company : tenemos visita>

comparable ['kɑmpərəbəl] *adj* : comparable, parecido

comparative[1] [kəm'pærət̬ɪv] *adj* RELATIVE : comparativo, relativo — **comparatively** *adv*

comparative[2] *n* : comparativo *m*

compare[1] [kəm'pær] *v* **-pared; -paring** *vt* : comparar — *vi* **to compare with** : poder comparar con, tener comparación con

compare[2] *n* : comparación *f* <beyond compare : sin igual, sin par>

comparison [kəm'pærəsən] *n* : comparación *f*

compartment [kəm'pɑrtmənt] *n* : compartimento *m,* compartimiento *m*

compass ['kʌmpəs, 'kɑm-] *n* **1** RANGE, SCOPE : alcance *m,* extensión *f,* límites *mpl* **2** : compás *m* (para trazar circunferencias) **3** : compás *m,* brújula *f* <the points of the compass : los puntos cardinales>

compassion [kəm'pæʃən] *n* : compasión *f,* piedad *f,* misericordia *f*

compassionate [kəm'pæʃənət] *adj* : compasivo

compatibility [kəm,pæt̬ə'bɪlət̬i] *n* : compatibilidad *f*

compatible [kəm'pæt̬əbəl] *adj* : compatible, afín

compatriot [kəm'peɪtriət, -'pæ-] *n* : compatriota *mf;* paisano *m,* -na *f*

compel [kəm'pɛl] *vt* **-pelled; -pelling** : obligar, compeler

compendium [kəm'pɛndiəm] *n, pl* **-diums** *or* **-dia** [-diə] : compendio *m*

compensate ['kɑmpən,seɪt] *v* **-sated; -sating** *vi* **to compensate for** : compensar — *vt* : indemnizar, compensar

compensation [,kɑmpən'seɪʃən] *n* : compensación *f,* indemnización *f*

compensatory [kəm'pɛntsə,tori] *adj* : compensatorio

compete [kəm'pi:t] *vi* **-peted; -peting** : competir, contender, rivalizar

competence ['kɑmpətənts] *n* : competencia *f,* aptitud *f*

competency ['kɑmpətəntsi] → **competence**

competent ['kɑmpətənt] *adj* : competente, capaz

competition [,kɑmpə'tɪʃən] *n* : competencia *f,* concurso *m*

competitive [kəm'pɛt̬ət̬ɪv] *adj* : competitivo

competitor [kəm'pɛt̬ət̬ər] *n* : competidor *m,* -dora *f*

compile [kəm'paɪl] *vt* **-piled; -piling** : compilar, recopilar

complacency [kəm'pleɪsəntsi] *n* : satisfacción *f* consigo mismo, suficiencia *f*

complacent [kəm'pleɪsənt] *adj* : satisfecho de sí mismo, suficiente

complain [kəm'pleɪn] *vi* **1** GRIPE : quejarse, regañar, rezongar **2** PROTEST : reclamar, protestar

complaint [kəm'pleɪnt] *n* **1** GRIPE : queja *f* **2** AILMENT : afección *f,* dolencia *f* **3** ACCUSATION : reclamo *m,* acusación *f*

complement[1] ['kɑmplə,mɛnt] *vt* : complementar

complement[2] ['kɑmpləmənt] *n* : complemento *m*

complementary [,kɑmplə'mɛntəri] *adj* : complementario

complete[1] [kəm'pli:t] *vt* **-pleted; -pleting 1** : completar, hacer entero <this piece completes the collection : esta pieza completa la colección> **2** FINISH : completar, acabar, terminar

<she completed her studies : completó sus estudios>
complete[2] *adj* **-pleter; -est** **1** WHOLE : completo, entero, íntegro **2** FINISHED : terminado, acabado **3** TOTAL : completo, total, absoluto
completely [kəm'pliːtli] *adv* : completamente, totalmente
completion [kəm'pliːʃən] *n* : finalización *f,* cumplimiento *m*
complex[1] [kɑm'plɛks, kəm-; 'kɑm-ˌplɛks] *adj* : complejo, complicado
complex[2] ['kɑmˌplɛks] *n* : complejo *m*
complexion [kəm'plɛkʃən] *n* : cutis *m,* tez *f* <of dark complexion : de tez morena>
complexity [kəm'plɛksət̬i, kɑm-] *n, pl* **-ties** : complejidad *f*
compliance [kəm'plaɪənts] *n* : conformidad *f* <in compliance with the law : conforme a la ley>
compliant [kəm'plaɪənt] *adj* : dócil, sumiso
complicate ['kɑmpləˌkeɪt] *vt* **-cated; -cating** : complicar
complicated ['kɑmpləˌkeɪt̬əd] *adj* : complicado
complication [ˌkɑmplə'keɪʃən] *n* : complicación *f*
complicity [kəm'plɪsət̬i] *n, pl* **-ties** : complicidad *f*
compliment[1] ['kɑmpləˌmɛnt] *vt* : halagar, florear *Mex*
compliment[2] ['kɑmpləmənt] *n* **1** : halago *m,* cumplido *m* **2** **compliments** *npl* : saludos *mpl* <give them my compliments : déles saludos de mi parte>
complimentary [ˌkɑmplə'mɛntəri] *adj* **1** FLATTERING : halagador, halagüeño **2** FREE : de cortesía, gratis
comply [kəm'plaɪ] *vi* **-plied; -plying** : cumplir, acceder, obedecer
component[1] [kəm'poːnənt, 'kɑm-ˌpoː-] *adj* : componente
component[2] *n* : componente *m,* elemento *m,* pieza *f*
compose [kəm'poːz] *vt* **-posed; -posing** **1** : componer, crear <to compose a melody : componer una melodía > **2** CALM : calmar, serenar <to compose oneself : serenarse> **3** CONSTITUTE : constar, componer <to be composed of : constar de> **4** : componer (un texto a imprimirse)
composer [kəm'poːzər] *n* : compositor *m,* -tora *f*
composite[1] [kɑm'pɑzət, kəm-; 'kɑmpəzət] *adj* : compuesto (de varias partes)
composite[2] *n* : compuesto *m,* mezcla *f*
composition [ˌkɑmpə'zɪʃən] *n* **1** MAKEUP : composición *f* **2** ESSAY : ensayo *m,* trabajo *m*
compost ['kɑmˌpoːst] *n* : abono *m* vegetal
composure [kəm'poːʒər] *n* : compostura *f,* serenidad *f*
compound[1] [kɑm'paʊnd, kəm-; 'kɑmˌpaʊnd] *vt* **1** COMBINE, COMPOSE : combinar, componer **2** AUGMENT : agravar, aumentar <to compound a problem : agravar un problema>
compound[2] ['kɑmˌpaʊnd; kɑm-'paʊnd, kəm-] *adj* : compuesto <compound interest : interés compuesto>
compound[3] ['kɑmˌpaʊnd] *n* **1** MIXTURE : compuesto *m,* mezcla *f* **2** ENCLOSURE : recinto *m* (de residencias, etc.)
compound fracture *n* : fractura *f* complicada
comprehend [ˌkɑmprɪ'hɛnd] *vt* **1** UNDERSTAND : comprender, entender **2** INCLUDE : comprender, incluir, abarcar
comprehensible [ˌkɑmprɪ'hɛntsəbəl] *adj* : comprensible
comprehension [ˌkɑmprɪ'hɛntʃən] *n* : comprensión *f*
comprehensive [ˌkɑmprɪ'hɛntsɪv] *adj* **1** INCLUSIVE : inclusivo, exhaustivo **2** BROAD : extenso, amplio
compress[1] [kəm'prɛs] *vt* : comprimir
compress[2] ['kɑmˌprɛs] *n* : compresa *f*
compression [kəm'prɛʃən] *n* : compresión *f*
comprise [kəm'praɪz] *vt* **-prised; -prising** **1** INCLUDE : comprender, incluir **2** : componerse de, constar de <the installation comprises several buildings : la instalación está compuesta de varios edificios>
compromise[1] ['kɑmprəˌmaɪz] *v* **-mised; -mising** *vi* : transigir, avenirse — *vt* JEOPARDIZE : comprometer, poner en peligro
compromise[2] *n* : acuerdo *m* mutuo, compromiso *m*
comptroller [kən'troːlər, 'kɑmp-ˌtroː-] *n* : contralor *m,* -lora *f;* interventor *m,* -tora *f*
compulsion [kəm'pʌlʃən] *n* **1** COERCION : coacción *f* **2** URGE : compulsión *f,* impulso *m*
compulsive [kəm'pʌlsɪv] *adj* : compulsivo
compulsory [kəm'pʌlsəri] *adj* : obligatorio
compunction [kəm'pʌŋkʃən] *n* **1** QUALM : reparo *m,* escrúpulo *m* **2** REMORSE : remordimiento *m*
computation [ˌkɑmpjʊ'teɪʃən] *n* : cálculo *m,* cómputo *m*
compute [kəm'pjuːt] *vt* **-puted; -puting** : computar, calcular
computer [kəm'pjuːt̬ər] *n* : computadora *f,* computador *m,* ordenador *m* *Spain*
computerize [kəm'pjuːt̬əˌraɪz] *vt* **-ized; -izing** : computarizar, informatizar
comrade ['kɑmˌræd] *n* : camarada *mf;* compañero *m,* -ra *f*
con[1] ['kɑn] *vt* **conned; conning** SWINDLE : estafar, timar
con[2] *adv* : contra

con[3] *n* : contra *m* <the pros and cons : los pros y los contras>
concave [kɑn'keɪv, 'kɑn,keɪv] *adj* : cóncavo
conceal [kən'siːl] *vt* : esconder, ocultar, disimular
concealment [kən'siːlmənt] *n* : escondimiento *m,* ocultación *f*
concede [kən'siːd] *vt* **-ceded; -ceding** **1** ALLOW, GRANT : conceder **2** ADMIT : conceder, reconocer <to concede defeat : reconocer la derrota>
conceit [kən'siːt] *n* : engreimiento *m,* presunción *f*
conceited [kən'siːtəd] *adj* : presumido, engreído, presuntuoso
conceivable [kən'siːvəbəl] *adj* : concebible, imaginable
conceivably [kən'siːvəbli] *adv* : posiblemente, de manera concebible
conceive [kən'siːv] *v* **-ceived; -ceiving** *vi* : concebir, embarazarse — *vt* IMAGINE : concebir, imaginar
concentrate[1] ['kɑntsən,treɪt] *v* **-trated; -trating** *vt* : concentrar — *vi* : concentrarse
concentrate[2] *n* : concentrado *m*
concentration [,kɑntsən'treɪʃən] *n* : concentración *f*
concentric [kən'sɛntrɪk] *adj* : concéntrico
concept ['kɑn,sɛpt] *n* : concepto *m,* idea *f*
conception [kən'sɛpʃən] *n* **1** : concepción *f* (de un bebé) **2** IDEA : concepto *m,* idea *f*
concern[1] [kən'sərn] *vt* **1** : tratarse de, tener que ver con <the novel concerns a sailor : la novela se trata de un marinero> **2** INVOLVE : concernir, incumbir a, afectar <that does not concern me : eso no me incumbe>
concern[2] *n* **1** AFFAIR : asunto *m* **2** WORRY : inquietud *f,* preocupación *f* **3** BUSINESS : negocio *m*
concerned [kən'sərnd] *adj* **1** ANXIOUS : preocupado, ansioso **2** INTERESTED, INVOLVED : interesado, afectado
concerning [kən'sərnɪŋ] *prep* REGARDING : con respecto a, acerca de, sobre
concert ['kɑn,sərt] *n* **1** AGREEMENT : concierto *m,* acuerdo *m* **2** : concierto *m* (musical)
concerted [kən'sərtəd] *adj* : concertado, coordinado <to make a concerted effort : coordinar los esfuerzos>
concertina [,kɑntsər'tiːnə] *n* : concertina *f*
concerto [kən'tʃɛrtoː] *n, pl* **-ti** [-ti, -,tiː] *or* **-tos** : concierto *m* <violin concerto : concierto para violín>
concession [kən'sɛʃən] *n* : concesión *f*
conch ['kɑŋk, 'kɑntʃ] *n, pl* **conchs** ['kɑŋks] *or* **conches** ['kɑntʃəz] : caracol *m* (animal), caracola *f* (concha)
conciliatory [kən'sɪliə,tori] *adj* : conciliador, conciliatorio
concise [kən'saɪs] *adj* : conciso, breve — **concisely** *adv*
conclave ['kɑn,kleɪv] *n* : cónclave *m*
conclude [kən'kluːd] *v* **-cluded; -cluding** *vt* **1** END : concluir, finalizar <to conclude a meeting : concluir una reunión> **2** DECIDE : concluir, llegar a la conclusión de — *vi* END : concluir, terminar
conclusion [kən'kluːʒən] *n* **1** INFERENCE : conclusión *f* **2** END : fin *m,* final *m*
conclusive [kən'kluːsɪv] *adj* : concluyente, decisivo — **conclusively** *adv*
concoct [kən'kɑkt, kɑn-] *vt* **1** PREPARE : preparar, confeccionar **2** DEVISE : inventar, tramar
concoction [kən'kɑkʃən] *n* : invención *f,* mejunje *m,* brebaje *m*
concord ['kɑn,kɔrd, 'kɑŋ-] *n* **1** HARMONY : concordia *f,* armonía *f* **2** AGREEMENT : acuerdo *m*
concordance [kən'kɔrdənts] *n* : concordancia *f*
concourse ['kɑn,kors] *n* : explanada *f,* salón *m* (para pasajeros)
concrete[1] [kɑn'kriːt, 'kɑn,kriːt] *adj* **1** REAL : concreto <concrete objects : objetos concretos> **2** SPECIFIC : determinado, específico **3** : de concreto, de hormigón <concrete walls : paredes de concreto>
concrete[2] ['kɑn,kriːt, kɑn'kriːt] *n* : concreto *m,* hormigón *m*
concur [kən'kər] *vi* **concurred; concurring** **1** COINCIDE : concurrir, coincidir **2** AGREE : concurrir, estar de acuerdo
concurrent [kən'kərənt] *adj* : concurrente, simultáneo
concussion [kən'kʌʃən] *n* : conmoción *f* cerebral
condemn [kən'dɛm] *vt* **1** CENSURE : condenar, reprobar, censurar **2** : declarar insalubre (alimentos), declarar ruinoso (un edificio) **3** SENTENCE : condenar <condemned to death : condenado a muerte>
condemnation [,kɑn,dɛm'neɪʃən] *n* : condena *f,* reprobación *f*
condensation [,kɑn,dɛn'seɪʃən, -dən-] *n* : condensación *f*
condense [kən'dɛnts] *v* **-densed; -densing** *vt* **1** ABRIDGE : condensar, resumir **2** : condensar (vapor, etc.) — *vi* : condensarse
condescend [,kɑndɪ'sɛnd] *vi* **1** DEIGN : condescender, dignarse **2 to condescend to someone** : tratar a alguien con condescendencia
condescension [,kɑndɪ'sɛntʃən] *n* : condescendencia *f*
condiment ['kɑndəmənt] *n* : condimento *m*
condition[1] [kən'dɪʃən] *vt* **1** DETERMINE : condicionar, determinar **2** : acondicionar (el pelo o el aire), poner en forma (el cuerpo)

condition[2] *n* **1** STIPULATION : condición *f,* estipulación *f* <on the condition that : a condición de que> **2** STATE : condición *f,* estado *m* <in poor condition : en malas condiciones> **3 conditions** *npl* : condiciones *fpl,* situación *f* <working conditions : condiciones del trabajo>

conditional [kən'dɪʃənəl] *adj* : condicional — **conditionally** *adv*

condolence [kən'doːlənts] *n* **1** SYMPATHY : condolencia *f* **2 condolences** *npl* : pésame *m*

condominium [ˌkandə'mɪniəm] *n, pl* **-ums** : condominio *m*

condone [kən'doːn] *vt* **-doned; -doning** : aprobar, perdonar, tolerar

condor ['kandər, -ˌdɔr] *n* : cóndor *m*

conducive [kən'duːsɪv, -'djuː-] *adj* : propicio, favorable

conduct[1] [kən'dʌkt] *vt* **1** GUIDE : guiar, conducir <to conduct a tour : guiar una visita> **2** DIRECT : conducir, dirigir <to conduct an orchestra : dirigir una orquesta> **3** CARRY OUT : realizar, llevar a cabo <to conduct an investigation : llevar a cabo una investigación> **4** TRANSMIT : conducir, transmitir (calor, electricidad, etc.) **5 to conduct oneself** BEHAVE : conducirse, comportarse

conduct[2] ['kanˌdʌkt] *n* **1** MANAGEMENT : conducción *f,* dirección *f,* manejo *m* <the conduct of foreign affairs : la conducción de asuntos exteriores> **2** BEHAVIOR : conducta *f,* comportamiento *m*

conduction [kən'dʌkʃən] *n* : conducción *f*

conductivity [ˌkanˌdʌk'tɪvət̬i] *n, pl* **-ties** : conductividad *f*

conductor [kən'dʌktər] *n* **1** : conductor *m,* -tora *f;* revisor *m,* -sora *f* (en un tren); cobrador *m,* -dora *f* (en un bus); director *m,* -tora *f* (de una orquesta) **2** : conductor *m* (de electricidad, etc.)

conduit ['kanˌduːət, -ˌdjuː-] *n* : conducto *m,* canal *m,* vía *f*

cone ['koːn] *n* **1** : piña *f* (fruto de las coníferas) **2** : cono *m* (en geometría) **3 ice–cream cone** : cono *m,* barquillo *m,* cucurucho *m*

confection [kən'fɛkʃən] *n* : dulce *m*

confectioner [kən'fɛkʃənər] *n* : confitero *m,* -ra *f*

confederacy [kən'fɛdərəsi] *n, pl* **-cies** : confederación *f*

confederate[1] [kən'fɛdəˌreɪt] *v* **-ated; -ating** *vt* : unir, confederar — *vi* : confederarse, aliarse

confederate[2] [kən'fɛdərət] *adj* : confederado

confederate[3] *n* : cómplice *mf;* aliado *m,* -da *f*

confederation [kənˌfɛdə'reɪʃən] *n* : confederación *f,* alianza *f*

confer [kən'fər] *v* **-ferred; -ferring** *vt* : conferir, otorgar — *vi* **to confer with** : consultar

conference ['kanfrənts, -fərənts] *n* : conferencia *f* <press conference : conferencia de prensa>

confess [kən'fɛs] *vt* : confesar — *vi* **1** : confesar <the prisoner confessed : el detenido confesó> **2** : confesarse (en religión)

confession [kən'fɛʃən] *n* : confesión *f*

confessional [kən'fɛʃənəl] *n* : confesionario *m*

confetti [kən'fɛt̬i] *n* : confeti *m*

confidant ['kanfəˌdant, -ˌdænt] *n* : confidente *mf*

confide [kən'faɪd] *v* **-fided; -fiding** : confiar

confidence ['kanfədənts] *n* **1** TRUST : confianza *f* **2** SELF-ASSURANCE : confianza *f* en sí mismo, seguridad *f* en sí mismo **3** SECRET : confidencia *f,* secreto *m*

confident ['kanfədənt] *adj* **1** SURE : seguro **2** SELF-ASSURED : confiado, seguro de sí mismo

confidential [ˌkanfə'dɛntʃəl] *adj* : confidencial — **confidentially** [ˌkanfə'dɛntʃəli] *adv*

confidently ['kanfədəntli] *adv* : con seguridad, con confianza

configuration [kənˌfɪgjə'reɪʃən] *n* : configuración *f*

confine [kən'faɪn] *vt* **-fined; -fining 1** LIMIT : confinar, restringir, limitar **2** IMPRISON : recluir, encarcelar, encerrar

confinement [kən'faɪnmənt] *n* : confinamiento *m,* reclusión *f,* encierro *m*

confines ['kanˌfaɪnz] *npl* : límites *mpl,* confines *mpl*

confirm [kən'fərm] *vt* **1** RATIFY : ratificar **2** VERIFY : confirmar, verificar **3** : confirmar (en religión)

confirmation [ˌkanfər'meɪʃən] *n* : confirmación *f*

confiscate ['kanfəˌskeɪt] *vt* **-cated; -cating** : confiscar, incautar, decomisar

confiscation [ˌkanfə'skeɪʃən] *n* : confiscación *f,* incautación *f,* decomiso *m*

conflagration [ˌkanflə'greɪʃən] *n* : conflagración *f*

conflict[1] [kən'flɪkt] *vi* : estar en conflicto, oponerse

conflict[2] ['kanˌflɪkt] *n* : conflicto *m* <to be in conflict : estar en desacuerdo>

conform [kən'fɔrm] *vi* **1** ACCORD, COMPLY : ajustarse, adaptarse, conformarse <it conforms with our standards : se ajusta a nuestras normas> **2** CORRESPOND : corresponder, encajar <to conform to the truth : corresponder a la verdad>

conformity [kən'fɔrmət̬i] *n, pl* **-ties** : conformidad *f*

confound [kən'faʊnd, kan-] *vt* : confundir, desconcertar

confront [kən'frʌnt] *vt* : afrontar, enfrentarse a, encarar

confrontation [ˌkanfrən'teɪʃən] *n* : enfrentamiento *m,* confrontación *f*

confuse [kən'fjuːz] *vt* **-fused; -fusing 1** PUZZLE : confundir, enturbiar **2** COMPLICATE : confundir, enredar, complicar <to confuse the issue : complicar las cosas>
confusion [kən'fjuːʒən] *n* **1** PERPLEXITY : confusión *f* **2** MESS, TURMOIL : confusión *f,* embrollo *m,* lío *m fam*
congeal [kən'dʒiːl] *vi* **1** FREEZE : congelarse **2** COAGULATE, CURDLE : coagularse, cuajarse
congenial [kən'dʒiːniəl] *adj* : agradable, simpático
congenital [kən'dʒɛnət̬əl] *adj* : congénito
congest [kən'dʒɛst] *vt* **1** : congestionar (en la medicina) **2** OVERCROWD : abarrotar, atestar, congestionar (el tráfico) — *vi* : congestionarse
congestion [kən'dʒɛstʃən] *n* : congestión *f*
conglomerate[1] [kən'glɑmərət] *adj* : conglomerado
conglomerate[2] [kən'glɑmərət] *n* : conglomerado *m*
conglomeration [kən,glɑmə'reɪʃən] *n* : conglomerado *m,* acumulación *f*
Congolese [,kɑŋgə'liːz, -'liːs] *n* : congoleño *m,* -ña *f* — **Congolese** *adj*
congratulate [kən'grædʒə,leɪt, -'grætʃə-] *vt* **-lated; -lating** : felicitar
congratulation [kən,grædʒə'leɪʃən, -,grætʃə-] *n* : felicitación *f* <congratulations! : ¡felicidades!, ¡enhorabuena!>
congregate ['kɑŋgrɪ,geɪt] *v* **-gated; -gating** *vt* : congregar, reunir — *vi* : congregarse, reunirse
congregation [,kɑŋgrɪ'geɪʃən] *n* **1** GATHERING : congregación *f,* fieles *mpl* (a un servicio religioso) **2** PARISHIONERS : feligreses *mpl*
congress ['kɑŋgrəs] *n* : congreso *m*
congressional [kən'grɛʃənəl, kɑn-] *adj* : del congreso
congressman ['kɑŋgrəsmən] *n, pl* **-men** [-mən, -,mɛn] : congresista *m,* diputado *m*
congresswoman ['kɑŋgrəs,wʊmən] *n, pl* **-women** [-,wɪmən] : congresista *f,* diputada *f*
congruence [kən'gruːən*t*s, 'kɑŋgrʊən*t*s] *n* : congruencia *f*
congruent [kən'gruːənt, 'kɑŋgrʊənt] *adj* : congruente
conic ['kɑnɪk] → **conical**
conical ['kɑnɪkəl] *adj* : cónico
conifer ['kɑnəfər, 'koː-] *n* : conífera *f*
coniferous [koː'nɪfərəs, kə-] *adj* : conífero
conjecture[1] [kən'dʒɛktʃər] *v* **-tured; -turing** : conjeturar
conjecture[2] *n* : conjetura *f,* presunción *f*
conjugal ['kɑndʒɪgəl, kən'dʒuː-] *adj* : conyugal
conjugate ['kɑndʒə,geɪt] *vt* **-gated; -gating** : conjugar
conjugation [,kɑndʒə'geɪʃən] *n* : conjugación *f*
conjunction [kən'dʒʌŋkʃən] *n* : conjunción *f* <in conjunction with : en combinación con>
conjure ['kɑndʒər, 'kʌn-] *v* **-jured; -juring** *vt* **1** ENTREAT : rogar, suplicar **2 to conjure up** : hacer aparecer (apariciones), evocar (memorias, etc.) — *vi* : practicar la magia
conjurer *or* **conjuror** ['kɑndʒərər, 'kʌn-] *n* : mago *m,* -ga *f;* prestidigitador *m,* -dora *f*
connect [kə'nɛkt] *vi* : conectar, enlazar, empalmar, comunicarse — *vt* **1** JOIN, LINK : conectar, unir, juntar, vincular **2** RELATE : relacionar, asociar (ideas)
connection [kə'nɛkʃən] *n* : conexión *f,* enlace *m* <professional connections : relaciones profesionales>
connective [kə'nɛktɪv] *adj* : conectivo, conjuntivo <connective tissue : tejido conjuntivo>
connector [kə'nɛktər] *n* : conector *m*
connivance [kə'naɪvən*t*s] *n* : connivencia *f,* complicidad *f*
connive [kə'naɪv] *vi* **-nived; -niving** CONSPIRE, PLOT : actuar en connivencia, confabularse, conspirar
connoisseur [,kɑnə'sər, -'sʊr] *n* : conocedor *m,* -dora *f;* entendido *m,* -da *f*
connotation [,kɑnə'teɪʃən] *n* : connotación *f*
connote [kə'noːt] *vt* **-noted; -noting** : connotar
conquer ['kɑŋkər] *vt* : conquistar, vencer
conqueror ['kɑŋkərər] *n* : conquistador *m,* -dora *f*
conquest ['kɑn,kwɛst, 'kɑŋ-] *n* : conquista *f*
conscience ['kɑntʃən*t*s] *n* : conciencia *f,* consciencia *f* <to have a clear conscience : tener la conciencia limpia>
conscientious [,kɑntʃi'ɛntʃəs] *adj* : concienzudo — **conscientiously** *adv*
conscious ['kɑntʃəs] *adj* **1** AWARE : consciente <to become conscious of : darse cuenta de> **2** ALERT, AWAKE : consciente **3** INTENTIONAL : intencional, deliberado
consciously ['kɑntʃəsli] *adv* INTENTIONALLY : intencionalmente, deliberadamente, a propósito
consciousness ['kɑntʃəsnəs] *n* **1** AWARENESS : conciencia *f,* consciencia *f* **2** conocimiento *m* <to lose consciousness : perder el conocimiento>
conscript[1] [kən'skrɪpt] *vt* : reclutar, alistar, enrolar
conscript[2] ['kɑn,skrɪpt] *n* : conscripto *m,* -ta *f;* recluta *mf*
consecrate ['kɑn*t*sə,kreɪt] *vt* **-crated; -crating** : consagrar
consecration [,kɑn*t*sə'kreɪʃən] *n* : consagración *f,* dedicación *f*

consecutive [kən'sɛkjət̬iv] *adj* : consecutivo, seguido <on five consecutive days : cinco días seguidos>
consecutively [kən'sɛkjət̬ivli] *adv* : consecutivamente
consensus [kən'sɛntsəs] *n* : consenso *m*
consent[1] [kən'sɛnt] *vi* **1** AGREE : acceder, ponerse de acuerdo **2 to consent to do something** : consentir en hacer algo
consent[2] *n* : consentimiento *m*, permiso *m* <by common consent : de común acuerdo>
consequence ['kɑntsə,kwɛnts, -kwənts] *n* **1** RESULT : consecuencia *f*, secuela *f* **2** IMPORTANCE : importancia *f*, trascendencia *f*
consequent ['kɑntsəkwənt, -,kwɛnt] *adj* : consiguiente
consequential [,kɑntsə'kwɛntʃəl] *adj* **1** CONSEQUENT : consiguiente **2** IMPORTANT : importante, trascendente, trascendental
consequently ['kɑntsəkwəntli, -,kwɛnt-] *adv* : por consiguiente, por ende, por lo tanto
conservation [,kɑntsər'veɪʃən] *n* : conservación *f*, protección *f*
conservationist [,kɑntsər'veɪʃənɪst] *n* : conservacionista *mf*
conservatism [kən'sərvə,tɪzəm] *n* : conservadurismo *m*
conservative[1] [kən'sərvət̬iv] *adj* **1** : conservador **2** CAUTIOUS : moderado, cauteloso <a conservative estimate : un cálculo moderado>
conservative[2] *n* : conservador *m*, -dora *f*
conservatory [kən'sərvə,tori] *n*, *pl* **-ries** : conservatorio *m*
conserve[1] [kən'sərv] *vt* **-served; -serving** : conservar, preservar
conserve[2] ['kɑn,sərv] *n* PRESERVES : confitura *f*
consider [kən'sɪdər] *vt* **1** CONTEMPLATE : considerar, pensar en <we'd considered attending : habíamos pensado en asistir> **2** : considerar, tener en cuenta <consider the consequences : considera las consecuencias> **3** JUDGE, REGARD : considerar, estimar
considerable [kən'sɪdərəbəl] *adj* : considerable — **considerably** [-bli] *adv*
considerate [kən'sɪdərət] *adj* : considerado, atento
consideration [kən,sɪdə'reɪʃən] *n* : consideración *f* <to take into consideration : tener en cuenta>
considering [kən'sɪdərɪŋ] *prep* : teniendo en cuenta, visto
consign [kən'saɪn] *vt* **1** COMMIT, ENTRUST : confiar, encomendar **2** TRANSFER : consignar, transferir **3** SEND : consignar, enviar (mercancía)
consignment [kən'saɪnmənt] *n* **1** : envío *m*, remesa *f* **2 on ~** : en consignación
consist [kən'sɪst] *vi* **1** LIE : consistir <success consists in hard work : el éxito consiste en trabajar duro> **2** : constar, componerse <the set consists of 5 pieces : el juego se compone de 5 piezas>
consistency [kən'sɪstəntsi] *n*, *pl* **-cies 1** : consistencia *f* (de una mezcla o sustancia) **2** COHERENCE : coherencia *f* **3** UNIFORMITY : regularidad *f*, uniformidad *f*
consistent [kən'sɪstənt] *adj* **1** COMPATIBLE : compatible, coincidente <consistent with policy : coincidente con la política> **2** UNIFORM : uniforme, constante, regular — **consistently** [kən'sɪstəntli] *adv*
consolation [,kɑntsə'leɪʃən] *n* **1** : consuelo *m* **2 consolation prize** : premio *m* de consolación
console[1] [kən'so:l] *vt* **-soled; -soling** : consolar
console[2] ['kɑn,so:l] *n* : consola *f*
consolidate [kən'sɑlə,deɪt] *vt* **-dated; -dating** : consolidar, unir
consolidation [kən,sɑlə'deɪʃən] *n* : consolidación *f*
consommé [,kɑntsə'meɪ] *n* : consomé *m*
consonant ['kɑntsənənt] *n* : consonante *m*
consort[1] [kən'sɔrt] *vi* : asociarse, relacionarse, tener trato <to consort with criminals : tener trato con criminales>
consort[2] ['kɑn,sɔrt] *n* : consorte *mf*
conspicuous [kən'spɪkjʊəs] *adj* **1** OBVIOUS : visible, evidente **2** STRIKING : llamativo
conspicuously [kən'spɪkjʊəsli] *adv* : de manera llamativa
conspiracy [kən'spɪrəsi] *n*, *pl* **-cies** : conspiración *f*, complot *m*, confabulación *f*
conspirator [kən'spɪrət̬ər] *n* : conspirador *m*, -dora *f*
conspire [kən'spaɪr] *vi* **-spired; -spiring** : conspirar, confabularse
constable ['kɑntstəbəl, 'kʌntstə-] *n* : agente *mf* de policía (en un pueblo)
constancy ['kɑntstəntsi] *n*, *pl* **-cies** : constancia *f*
constant[1] ['kɑntstənt] *adj* **1** FAITHFUL : leal, fiel **2** INVARIABLE : constante, invariable **3** CONTINUAL : constante, continuo
constant[2] *n* : constante *f*
constantly ['kɑntstəntli] *adv* : constantemente, continuamente
constellation [,kɑntstə'leɪʃən] *n* : constelación *f*
consternation [,kɑntstər'neɪʃən] *n* : consternación *f*
constipate ['kɑntstə,peɪt] *vt* **-pated; -pating** : estreñir
constipation ['kɑntstə'peɪʃən] *n* : estreñimiento *m*, constipación *f* (de vientre)

constituency [kən'stɪtʃʊəntsi] *n, pl* **-cies 1 :** distrito *m* electoral **2 :** residentes *mpl* de un distrito electoral

constituent[1] [kən'stɪtʃʊənt] *adj* **1** COMPONENT **:** constituyente, componente **2 :** constituyente, constitutivo <a constituent assembly : una asamblea constituyente>

constituent[2] *n* **1** COMPONENT **:** componente *m* **2** ELECTOR, VOTER **:** elector *m*, -tora *f;* votante *mf*

constitute ['kɑntstə,tu:t, -,tju:t] *vt* **-tuted; -tuting 1** ESTABLISH **:** constituir, establecer **2** COMPOSE, FORM **:** constituir, componer

constitution [,kɑntstə'tu:ʃən, -'tju:-] *n* **:** constitución *f*

constitutional [,kɑntstə'tu:ʃənəl, -'tju:-] *adj* **:** constitucional

constitutionality [,kɑntstə,tu:ʃə'nælət̬i, -,tju:-] *n* **:** constitucionalidad *f*

constrain [kən'streɪn] *vt* **1** COMPEL **:** constreñir, obligar **2** CONFINE **:** constreñir, limitar, restringir **3** RESTRAIN **:** contener, refrenar

constraint [kən'streɪnt] *n* **:** restricción *f*, limitación *f*

constrict [kən'strɪkt] *vt* **:** estrechar, apretar, comprimir

constriction [kən'strɪkʃən] *n* **:** estrechamiento *m*, compresión *f*

construct [kən'strʌkt] *vt* **:** construir

construction [kən'strʌkʃən] *n* **:** construcción *f*

constructive [kən'strʌktɪv] *adj* **:** constructivo

construe [kən'stru:] *vt* **-strued; -struing :** interpretar

consul ['kɑntsəl] *n* **:** cónsul *mf*

consular ['kɑntsələr] *adj* **:** consular

consulate ['kɑntsələt] *n* **:** consulado *m*

consult [kən'sʌlt] *vt* **:** consultar — *vi* **to consult with :** consultar con, solicitar la opinión de

consultant [kən'sʌltənt] *n* **:** consultor *m*, -tora *f;* asesor *m*, -sora *f*

consultation [,kɑntsəl'teɪʃən] *n* **:** consulta *f*

consumable [kən'su:məbəl] *adj* **:** consumible

consume [kən'su:m] *vt* **-sumed; -suming :** consumir, usar, gastar

consumer [kən'su:mər] *n* **:** consumidor *m*, -dora *f*

consummate[1] ['kɑntsə,meɪt] *vt* **-mated; -mating :** consumar

consummate[2] [kən'sʌmət, 'kɑntsəmət] *adj* **:** consumado, perfecto

consummation [,kɑntsə'meɪʃən] *n* **:** consumación *f*

consumption [kən'sʌmpʃən] *n* **1** USE **:** consumo *m*, uso *m* <consumption of electricity : consumo de electricidad> **2** TUBERCULOSIS **:** tisis *f*, consunción *f*

contact[1] ['kɑn,tækt, kən'-] *vt* **:** ponerse en contacto con, contactar (con)

contact[2] ['kɑn,tækt] *n* **1** TOUCHING **:** contacto *m*, tocamiento *m* <to come into contact with : entrar en contacto con> **2** TOUCH **:** contacto *m*, comunicación *f* <to lose contact with : perder contacto con> **3** CONNECTION **:** contacto *m* (en negocios) **4** → **contact lens**

contact lens ['kɑn,tækt'lɛnz] *n* **:** lente *mf* de contacto, pupilente *m Mex*

contagion [kən'teɪdʒən] *n* **:** contagio *m*

contagious [kən'teɪdʒəs] *adj* **:** contagioso

contain [kən'teɪn] *vt* **1 :** contener **2 to contain oneself :** contenerse

container [kən'teɪnər] *n* **:** recipiente *m*, envase *m*

contaminate [kən'tæmə,neɪt] *vt* **-nated; -nating :** contaminar

contamination [kən,tæmə'neɪʃən] *n* **:** contaminación *f*

contemplate ['kɑntəm,pleɪt] *v* **-plated; -plating** *vt* **1** VIEW **:** contemplar **2** PONDER **:** contemplar, considerar **3** CONSIDER, PROPOSE **:** proponerse, proyectar, pensar en <to contemplate a trip : pensar en viajar> — *vi* MEDITATE **:** meditar

contemplation [,kɑntəm'pleɪʃən] *n* **:** contemplación *f*

contemplative [kən'tɛmplət̬ɪv, 'kɑntəm,pleɪt̬ɪv] *adj* **:** contemplativo

contemporaneous [kən,tɛmpə'reɪniəs] → **contemporary[1]**

contemporary[1] [kən'tɛmpə,rɛri] *adj* **:** contemporáneo

contemporary[2] *n, pl* **-raries :** contemporáneo *m*, -nea *f*

contempt [kən'tɛmpt] *n* **1** DISDAIN **:** desprecio *m*, desdén *m* <to hold in contempt : despreciar> **2 :** desacato *m* (ante un tribunal)

contemptible [kən'tɛmptəbəl] *adj* **:** despreciable, vil

contemptuous [kən'tɛmptʃʊəs] *adj* **:** despectivo, despreciativo, desdeñoso

contemptuously [kən'tɛmptʃʊəsli] *adv* **:** despectivamente, con desprecio

contend [kən'tɛnd] *vi* **1** STRUGGLE **:** luchar, lidiar, contender <to contend with a problem : lidiar con un problema> **2** COMPETE **:** competir <to contend for a position : competir por un puesto> — *vt* **1** ARGUE, MAINTAIN **:** argüir, sostener, afirmar <he contended that he was right : afirmó que tenía razón> **2** CONTEST **:** protestar contra (una decisión, etc.), disputar

contender [kən'tɛndər] *n* **:** contendiente *mf;* aspirante *mf;* competidor *m*, -dora *f*

content[1] [kən'tɛnt] *vt* SATISFY **:** contentar, satisfacer

content[2] *adj* **:** conforme, contento, satisfecho

content[3] *n* CONTENTMENT **:** contento *m*, satisfacción *f* <to one's heart's content : hasta quedar satisfecho, a más no poder>

content[4] [ˈkɑnˌtɛnt] *n* **1** MEANING : contenido *m,* significado *m* **2** PROPORTION : contenido *m,* proporción *f* <fat content : contenido de grasa> **3 contents** *npl* : contenido *m,* sumario *m* (de un libro) <table of contents : índice de materias>

contented [kənˈtɛntəd] *adj* : conforme, satisfecho <a contented smile : una sonrisa de satisfacción>

contentedly [kənˈtɛntədli] *adv* : con satisfacción

contention [kənˈtɛntʃən] *n* **1** DISPUTE : disputa *f,* discusión *f* **2** COMPETITION : competencia *f,* contienda *f* **3** OPINION : argumento *m,* opinión *f*

contentious [kənˈtɛntʃəs] *adj* : disputador, pugnaz, combativo

contentment [kənˈtɛntmənt] *n* : satisfacción *f,* contento *m*

contest[1] [kənˈtɛst] *vt* : disputar, cuestionar, impugnar <to contest a will : impugnar un testamento>

contest[2] [ˈkɑnˌtɛst] *n* **1** STRUGGLE : lucha *f,* contienda *f* **2** GAME : concurso *m,* competencia *f*

contestable [kənˈtɛstəbəl] *adj* : discutible, cuestionable

contestant [kənˈtɛstənt] *n* : concursante *mf;* competidor *m,* -dora *f*

context [ˈkɑnˌtɛkst] *n* : contexto *m*

contiguous [kənˈtɪgjʊəs] *adj* : contiguo

continence [ˈkɑntənənts] *n* : continencia *f*

continent[1] [ˈkɑntənənt] *adj* : continente

continent[2] *n* : continente *m* — **continental** [ˌkɑntənˈɛntəl] *adj*

contingency [kənˈtɪndʒəntsi] *n, pl* **-cies** : contingencia *f,* eventualidad *f*

contingent[1] [kənˈtɪndʒənt] *adj* **1** POSSIBLE : contingente, eventual **2** ACCIDENTAL : fortuito, accidental **3 to be contingent on** : depender de, estar sujeto a

contingent[2] *n* : contingente *m*

continual [kənˈtɪnjʊəl] *adj* : continuo, constante — **continually** [kənˈtɪnjʊəli, -ˈtɪnjəli] *adv*

continuance [kənˈtɪnjʊənts] *n* **1** CONTINUATION : continuación *f* **2** DURATION : duración *f* **3** : aplazamiento *m* (de un proceso)

continuation [kənˌtɪnjʊˈeɪʃən] *n* : continuación *f,* prolongación *f*

continue [kənˈtɪnjuː] *v* **-tinued; -tinuing** *vi* **1** CARRY ON : continuar, seguir, proseguir <please continue : continúe, por favor> **2** ENDURE, LAST : continuar, prolongarse, durar **3** RESUME : continuar, reanudarse — *vt* **1** : continuar, seguir <she continued writing : continuó escribiendo> **2** RESUME : continuar, reanudar **3** EXTEND, PROLONG : continuar, prolongar

continuity [ˌkɑntənˈuːəṭi, -ˈjuː-] *n, pl* **-ties** : continuidad *f*

continuous [kənˈtɪnjʊəs] *adj* : continuo — **continuously** *adv*

contort [kənˈtɔrt] *vt* : torcer, retorcer, contraer (el rostro) — *vi* : contraerse, demudarse

contortion [kənˈtɔrʃən] *n* : contorsión *f*

contour [ˈkɑnˌtʊr] *n* **1** OUTLINE : contorno *m* **2 contours** *npl* SHAPE : forma *f,* curvas *fpl* **3 contour map** : mapa *m* topográfico

contraband [ˈkɑntrəˌbænd] *n* : contrabando *m*

contraception [ˌkɑntrəˈsɛpʃən] *n* : anticoncepción *f,* contracepción *f*

contraceptive[1] [ˌkɑntrəˈsɛptɪv] *adj* : anticonceptivo, contraceptivo

contraceptive[2] *n* : anticonceptivo *m,* contraceptivo *m*

contract[1] [kənˈtrækt, 1 *usu* ˈkɑnˌtrækt] *vt* **1** : contratar (servicios profesionales) **2** : contraer (una enfermedad, una deuda) **3** TIGHTEN : contraer (un músculo) **4** SHORTEN : contraer (una palabra) — *vi* : contraerse, reducirse

contract[2] [ˈkɑnˌtrækt] *n* : contrato *m*

contraction [kənˈtrækʃən] *n* : contracción *f*

contractor [ˈkɑnˌtræktər, kənˈtræk-] *n* : contratista *mf*

contractual [kənˈtræktʃʊəl] *adj* : contractual — **contractually** *adv*

contradict [ˌkɑntrəˈdɪkt] *vt* : contradecir, desmentir

contradiction [ˌkɑntrəˈdɪkʃən] *n* : contradicción *f*

contradictory [ˌkɑntrəˈdɪktəri] *adj* : contradictorio

contralto [kənˈtrælˌtoː] *n, pl* **-tos** : contralto *m* (voz), contralto *mf* (vocalista)

contraption [kənˈtræpʃən] *n* DEVICE : aparato *m,* artefacto *m*

contrary[1] [ˈkɑnˌtrɛri, 2 *often* kənˈtrɛri] *adj* **1** OPPOSITE : contrario, opuesto **2** BALKY, STUBBORN : terco, testarudo **3 contrary to** : al contrario de, en contra de <contrary to the facts : en contra de los hechos>

contrary[2] [ˈkɑnˌtrɛri] *n, pl* **-traries 1** OPPOSITE : lo contrario, lo opuesto **2 on the contrary** : al contrario, todo lo contrario

contrast[1] [kənˈtræst] *vi* DIFFER : contrastar, diferir — *vt* COMPARE : contrastar, comparar

contrast[2] [ˈkɑnˌtræst] *n* : contraste *m*

contravene [ˌkɑntrəˈviːn] *vt* **-vened; -vening** : contravenir, infringir

contribute [kənˈtrɪbjət] *v* **-uted; -uting** *vt* : contribuir, aportar (dinero, bienes, etc.) — *vi* : contribuir

contribution [ˌkɑntrəˈbjuːʃən] *n* : contribución *f*

contributor [kənˈtrɪbjəṭər] *n* : contribuidor *m,* -dora *f;* colaborador *m,* -dora *f* (en periodismo)

contrite ['kɑn,traɪt, kən'traɪt] *adj* REPENTANT : contrito, arrepentido

contrition [kən'trɪʃən] *n* : contrición *f,* arrepentimiento *m*

contrivance [kən'traɪvənts] *n* **1** DEVICE : aparato *m,* artefacto *m* **2** SCHEME : artimaña *f,* treta *f,* ardid *m*

contrive [kən'traɪv] *vt* **-trived; -triving 1** DEVISE : idear, ingeniar, maquinar **2** MANAGE : lograr, ingeniárselas para <she contrived a way out of the mess : se las ingenió para salir del enredo>

control[1] [kən'troːl] *vt* **-trolled; -trolling** : controlar, dominar

control[2] *n* **1** : control *m,* dominio *m,* mando *m* <to be under control : estar bajo control> **2** RESTRAINT : control *m,* limitación *f* <birth control : control natal> **3** : control *m,* dispositivo *m* de mando <remote control : control remoto>

controllable [kən'troːləbəl] *adj* : controlable

controller [kən'troːlər, 'kɑn,-] *n* **1** → **comptroller 2** : controlador *m,* -dora *f* <air traffic controller : controlador aéreo>

controversial [,kɑntrə'vərʃəl, -siəl] *adj* : controvertido <a controversial decision : una decisión controvertida>

controversy ['kɑntrə,vərsi] *n, pl* **-sies** : controversia *f*

controvert ['kɑntrə,vərt, ,kɑntrə'-] *vt* : controvertir, contradecir

contusion [kən'tuːʒən, -tjuː-] *n* BRUISE : contusión *f,* moretón *m*

conundrum [kə'nʌndrəm] *n* RIDDLE : acertijo *m,* adivinanza *f*

convalesce [,kɑnvə'lɛs] *vi* **-lesced; -lescing** : convalecer

convalescence [,kɑnvə'lɛsənts] *n* : convalecencia *f*

convalescent[1] [,kɑnvə'lɛsənt] *adj* : convaleciente

convalescent[2] *n* : convaleciente *mf*

convection [kən'vɛkʃən] *n* : convección *f*

convene [kən'viːn] *v* **-vened; -vening** *vt* : convocar — *vi* : reunirse

convenience [kən'viːnjənts] *n* **1** : conveniencia *f* <at your convenience : cuando le resulte conveniente> **2** AMENITY : comodidad *f* <modern conveniences : comodidades modernas>

convenient [kən'viːnjənt] *adj* : conveniente, cómodo — **conveniently** *adv*

convent ['kɑnvənt, -,vɛnt] *n* : convento *m*

convention [kən'vɛntʃən] *n* **1** PACT : convención *f,* convenio *m,* pacto *m* <the Geneva Convention : la Convención de Ginebra> **2** MEETING : convención *f,* congreso *m* **3** CUSTOM : convención *f,* convencionalismo *m*

conventional [kən'vɛntʃənəl] *adj* : convencional — **conventionally** *adv*

converge [kən'vərdʒ] *vi* **-verged; -verging** : converger, convergir

conversant [kən'vərsənt] *adj* **conversant with** : versado con, experto en

conversation [,kɑnvər'seɪʃən] *n* : conversación *f*

conversational [,kɑnvər'seɪʃənəl] *adj* : familiar <a conversational style : un estilo familiar>

converse[1] [kən'vərs] *vi* **-versed; -versing** : conversar

converse[2] [kən'vərs, 'kɑn,vɛrs] *adj* : contrario, opuesto, inverso

conversely [kən'vərsli, 'kɑn,vɛrs-] *adv* : a la inversa

conversion [kən'vərʒən] *n* **1** CHANGE : conversión *f,* transformación *f,* cambio *m* **2** : conversión *f* (a una religión)

convert[1] [kən'vərt] *vt* **1** : convertir (a una religión o un partido) **2** CHANGE : convertir, cambiar — *vi* : convertirse

convert[2] ['kɑn,vərt] *n* : converso *m,* -sa *f*

converter *or* **convertor** [kən'vərt̬ər] *n* : convertidor *m*

convertible[1] [kən'vərt̬əbəl] *adj* : convertible

convertible[2] *n* : convertible *m,* descapotable *m*

convex [kɑn'vɛks, 'kɑn,-, kən'-] *adj* : convexo

convey [kən'veɪ] *vt* **1** TRANSPORT : transportar, conducir **2** TRANSMIT : transmitir, comunicar, expresar (noticias, ideas, etc.)

conveyance [kən'veɪənts] *n* **1** TRANSPORT : transporte *m,* transportación *f* **2** COMMUNICATION : transmisión *f,* comunicación *f* **3** TRANSFER : transferencia *f,* traspaso *m* (de una propiedad)

conveyor [kən'veɪər] *n* : transportador *m,* -dora *f* <conveyor belt : cinta transportadora>

convict[1] [kən'vɪkt] *vt* : declarar culpable

convict[2] ['kɑn,vɪkt] *n* : preso *m,* -sa *f;* presidiario *m,* -ria *f;* recluso *m,* -sa *f*

conviction [kən'vɪkʃən] *n* **1** : condena *f* (de un acusado) **2** BELIEF : convicción *f,* creencia *f*

convince [kən'vɪnts] *vt* **-vinced; -vincing** : convencer

convincing [kən'vɪntsɪŋ] *adj* : convincente, persuasivo

convincingly [kən'vɪntsɪŋli] *adv* : de forma convincente

convivial [kən'vɪvjəl, -'vɪviəl] *adj* : jovial, festivo, alegre

conviviality [kən,vɪvi'ælət̬i] *n, pl* **-ties** : jovialidad *f*

convoke [kən'voːk] *vt* **-voked; -voking** : convocar

convoluted ['kɑnvə,luːt̬əd] *adj* : intrincado, complicado

convoy ['kɑn,vɔɪ] *n* : convoy *m*

convulse [kən'vʌls] *v* **-vulsed; -vulsing** *vt* : convulsionar <convulsed with laughter : muerto de risa> — *vi* : sufrir convulsiones

convulsion [kən'vʌlʃən] *n* : convulsión *f*
convulsive [kən'vʌlsɪv] *adj* : convulsivo — **convulsively** *adv*
coo[1] ['ku:] *vi* : arrullar
coo[2] *n* : arrullo *m* (de una paloma)
cook[1] ['kʊk] *vi* : cocinar — *vt* **1** : preparar (comida) **2 to cook up** CONCOCT : inventar, tramar
cook[2] *n* : cocinero *m*, -ra *f*
cookbook ['kʊk,bʊk] *n* : libro *m* de cocina
cookery ['kʊkəri] *n, pl* **-eries** : cocina *f*
cookie *or* **cooky** ['kʊki] *n, pl* **-ies** : galleta *f* (dulce)
cookout ['kʊk,aʊt] *n* : comida *f* al aire libre
cool[1] ['ku:l] *vt* : refrescar, enfriar — *vi* **1** : refrescarse, enfriarse <the pie is cooling : el pastel se está enfriando> **2** : calmarse, tranquilizarse <his anger cooled : su ira se calmó>
cool[2] *adj* **1** : fresco, frío <cool weather : tiempo fresco> **2** CALM : tranquilo, sereno **3** ALOOF : frío, distante
cool[3] *n* **1** : fresco *m* <the cool of the evening : el fresco de la tarde> **2** COMPOSURE : calma *f*, serenidad *f*
coolant ['ku:lənt] *n* : refrigerante *m*
cooler ['ku:lər] *n* : nevera *f* portátil
coolie ['ku:li] *n* : culi *m*
coolly ['ku:lli] *adv* **1** CALMLY : con calma, tranquilamente **2** COLDLY : fríamente, con frialdad
coolness ['ku:lnəs] *n* **1** : frescura *f*, frescor *m* <the coolness of the evening : el frescor de la noche> **2** CALMNESS : tranquilidad *f*, serenidad *f* **3** COLDNESS, INDIFFERENCE : frialdad *f*, indiferencia
coop[1] ['ku:p, 'kʊp] *vt or* **to coop up** : encerrar <cooped up in the house : encerrado en la casa>
coop[2] *n* : gallinero *m*
co–op ['ko:,ɑp] → **cooperative**[2]
cooperate [ko'ɑpə,reɪt] *vi* **-ated; -ating** : cooperar, colaborar
cooperation [ko,ɑpə'reɪʃən] *n* : cooperación *f*, colaboración *f*
cooperative[1] [ko'ɑpərət̬iv, -'ɑpə,reɪt̬iv] *adj* : cooperativo
cooperative[2] [ko'ɑpərət̬iv] *n* : cooperativa *f*
co–opt [ko'ɑpt] *vt* **1** : nombrar como miembro, cooptar **2** APPROPRIATE : apropiarse de
coordinate[1] [ko'ɔrdən,eɪt] *v* **-nated; -nating** *vt* : coordinar — *vi* : coordinarse, combinar, acordar
coordinate[2] [ko'ɔrdənət] *adj* **1** COORDINATED : coordinado **2** EQUAL : igual, semejante
coordinate[3] [ko'ɔrdənət] *n* : coordenada *f*
coordination [ko,ɔrdən'eɪʃən] *n* : coordinación *f*
coordinator [ko'ɔrdən,eɪt̬ər] *n* : coordinador *m*, -dora *f*
cop ['kɑp] → **police officer**
cope ['ko:p] *vi* **coped; coping 1** : arreglárselas **2 to cope with** : hacer frente a, poder con <I can't cope with all this! : ¡no puedo con todo esto!>
copier ['kɑpiər] *n* : copiadora *f*, fotocopiadora *f*
copilot ['ko:,paɪlət] *n* : copiloto *m*
copious ['ko:piəs] *adj* : copioso, abundante — **copiously** *adv*
copiousness ['ko:piəsnəs] *n* : abundancia *f*
copper ['kɑpər] *n* : cobre *m*
coppery ['kɑpəri] *adj* : cobrizo
copra ['ko:prə, 'kɑ-] *n* : copra *f*
copse ['kɑps] *n* THICKET : soto *m*, matorral *m*
copulate ['kɑpjə,leɪt] *vi* **-lated; -lating** : copular
copulation [,kɑpjə'leɪʃən] *n* : cópula *f*, relaciones *fpl* sexuales
copy[1] ['kɑpi] *vt* **copied; copying 1** DUPLICATE : hacer una copia de, duplicar, reproducir **2** IMITATE : copiar, imitar
copy[2] *n, pl* **copies 1** : copia *f*, duplicado *m* (de un documento), reproducción *f* (de una obra de arte) **2** : ejemplar *m* (de un libro), número *m* (de una revista) **3** TEXT : manuscrito *m*, texto *m*
copyright[1] ['kɑpi,raɪt] *vt* : registrar los derechos de
copyright[2] *n* : derechos *mpl* de autor
coral[1] ['kɔrəl] *adj* : de coral <a coral reef : un arrecife de coral>
coral[2] *n* : coral *m*
coral snake *n* : serpiente *f* de coral
cord ['kɔrd] *n* **1** ROPE, STRING : cuerda *f*, cordón *m*, cordel *m* **2** : cuerda *f*, cordón *m*, médula *f* (en la anatomía) <vocal cords : cuerdas vocales> **3** : cuerda *f* <a cord of firewood : una cuerda de leña> **4** *or* **electric cord** : cable *m* eléctrico
cordial[1] ['kɔrdʒəl] *adj* : cordial — **cordially** *adv*
cordial[2] *n* : cordial *m*
cordiality [,kɔrdʒi'ælət̬i] *n* : cordialidad *f*
cordon[1] ['kɔrdən] *vt* **to cordon off** : acordonar
cordon[2] *n* : cordón *m*
corduroy ['kɔrdə,rɔɪ] *n* **1** : pana *f* **2 corduroys** *npl* : pantalones *mpl* de pana
core[1] ['kor] *vt* **cored; coring** : quitar el corazón a (una fruta)
core[2] *n* **1** : corazón *m*, centro *m* (de algunas frutas) **2** CENTER : núcleo *m*, centro *m* **3** ESSENCE : núcleo *m*, meollo *m* <to the core : hasta la médula>
cork[1] ['kɔrk] *vt* : ponerle un corcho a
cork[2] *n* : corcho *m*
corkscrew ['kɔrk,skru:] *n* : tirabuzón *m*, sacacorchos *m*
cormorant ['kɔrmərənt, -,rænt] *n* : cormorán *m*
corn[1] ['kɔrn] *vt* : conservar en salmuera <corned beef : carne en conserva>

corn[2] *n* 1 GRAIN : grano *m* 2 : maíz *m,* elote *m Mex* <corn tortillas : tortillas de maíz> 3 : callo *m* <corn plaster : emplasto para callos>

corncob ['kɔrn,kɑb] *n* : mazorca *f* (de maíz), choclo *m,* elote *m CA, Mex*

cornea ['kɔrniə] *n* : córnea *f*

corner[1] ['kɔrnər] *vt* 1 TRAP : acorralar, arrinconar 2 MONOPOLIZE : monopolizar, acaparar (un mercado) — *vi* : tomar una curva, doblar una esquina (en un automóvil)

corner[2] *n* 1 ANGLE : rincón *m,* esquina *f,* ángulo *m* <the corner of a room : el rincón de una sala> <all corners of the world : todos los rincones del mundo> <to cut corners : atajar, economizar esfuerzos> 2 INTERSECTION : esquina *f* 3 IMPASSE, PREDICAMENT : aprieto *m,* impasse *m* <to be backed into a corner : estar acorralado>

cornerstone ['kɔrnər,sto:n] *n* : piedra *f* angular

cornet [kɔr'nɛt] *n* : corneta *f*

cornice ['kɔrnɪs] *n* : cornisa *f*

cornmeal ['kɔrn,mi:l] *n* : harina *f* de maíz

cornstalk ['kɔrn,stɔk] *n* : tallo *m* del maíz

cornstarch ['kɔrn,stɑrtʃ] *n* : maicena *f,* almidón *m* de maíz

cornucopia [,kɔrnə'ko:piə, -njə-] *n* : cornucopia *f*

corolla [kə'rɑlə] *n* : corola *f*

corollary ['kɔrə,lɛri] *n, pl* **-laries** : corolario *m*

corona [kə'ro:nə] *n* : corona *f* (del sol)

coronary[1] ['kɔrə,nɛri] *adj* : coronario

coronary[2] *n, pl* **-naries** 1 : trombosis *f* coronaria 2 HEART ATTACK : infarto *m,* ataque *m* al corazón

coronation [,kɔrə'neɪʃən] *n* : coronación *f*

coroner ['kɔrənər] *n* : médico *m* forense

corporal[1] ['kɔrpərəl] *adj* : corporal <corporal punishment : castigos corporales>

corporal[2] *n* : cabo *m*

corporate ['kɔrpərət] *adj* : corporativo, empresarial

corporation [,kɔrpə'reɪʃən] *n* : sociedad *f* anónima, corporación *f,* empresa *f*

corporeal [kɔr'poriəl] *adj* 1 PHYSICAL : corpóreo 2 MATERIAL : material, tangible — **corporeally** *adv*

corps ['kor] *n, pl* **corps** ['korz] : cuerpo *m* <medical corps : cuerpo médico> <diplomatic corps : cuerpo diplomático>

corpse ['kɔrps] *n* : cadáver *m*

corpulence ['kɔrpjələn*t*s] *n* : obesidad *f,* gordura *f*

corpulent ['kɔrpjələnt] *adj* : obeso, gordo

corpuscle ['kɔr,pʌsəl] *n* : corpúsculo *m,* glóbulo *m* (sanguíneo)

corral[1] [kə'ræl] *vt* **-ralled; -ralling** : acorralar, encorralar (ganado)

corral[2] *n* : corral *m*

correct[1] [kə'rɛkt] *vt* 1 RECTIFY : corregir, rectificar 2 REPRIMAND : corregir, reprender

correct[2] *adj* 1 ACCURATE, RIGHT : correcto, exacto <to be correct : estar en lo cierto> 2 PROPER : correcto, apropiado

correction [kə'rɛkʃən] *n* : corrección *f*

corrective [kə'rɛktɪv] *adj* : correctivo

correctly [kə'rɛktli] *adv* : correctamente

correlate ['kɔrə,leɪt] *vt* **-lated; -lating** : relacionar, poner en correlación

correlation [,kɔrə'leɪʃən] *n* : correlación *f*

correspond [,kɔrə'spɑnd] *vi* 1 MATCH : corresponder, concordar, coincidir 2 WRITE : corresponderse, escribirse

correspondence [,kɔrə'spɑndən*t*s] *n* : correspondencia *f*

correspondent [,kɔrə'spɑndənt] *n* : corresponsal *mf*

correspondingly [,kɔrə'spɑndɪŋli] *adv* : en consecuencia, de la misma manera

corridor ['kɔrədər, -,dɔr] *n* : corredor *m,* pasillo *m*

corroborate [kə'rɑbə,reɪt] *vt* **-rated; -rating** : corroborar

corroboration [kə,rɑbə'reɪʃən] *n* : corroboración *f*

corrode [kə'ro:d] *v* **-roded; -roding** *vt* : corroer — *vi* : corroerse

corrosion [kə'ro:ʒən] *n* : corrosión *f*

corrosive [kə'ro:sɪv] *adj* : corrosivo

corrugate ['kɔrə,geɪt] *vt* **-gated; -gating** : ondular, acanalar, corrugar

corrugated ['kɔrə,geɪṱəd] *adj* : ondulado, acanalado <corrugated cardboard : cartón ondulado>

corrupt[1] [kə'rʌpt] *vt* 1 PERVERT : corromper, pervertir, degradar (información) 2 BRIBE : sobornar

corrupt[2] *adj* : corrupto, corrompido

corruptible [kə'rʌptəbəl] *adj* : corruptible

corruption [kə'rʌpʃən] *n* : corrupción *f*

corsage [kɔr'sɑʒ, -'sɑdʒ] *n* : ramillete *m* que se lleva como adorno

corset ['kɔrsət] *n* : corsé *m*

cortex ['kɔr,tɛks] *n, pl* **-tices** ['kɔrṱə,si:z] *or* **-texes** : corteza *f* <cerebral cortex : corteza cerebral>

cortisone ['kɔrṱə,so:n, -zo:n] *n* : cortisona *f*

cosmetic[1] [kɑz'mɛṱɪk] *adj* : cosmético

cosmetic[2] *n* : cosmético *m*

cosmic ['kɑzmɪk] *adj* 1 : cósmico <cosmic ray : rayo cósmico> 2 VAST : grandioso, inmenso, vasto

cosmonaut ['kɑzmə,nɔt] *n* : cosmonauta *mf*

cosmopolitan[1] [,kɑzmə'pɑlətən] *adj* : cosmopolita

cosmopolitan[2] *n* : cosmopolita *mf*

cosmos [ˈkɑzməs, -ˌmoːs, -ˌmɑs] *n* : cosmos *m,* universo *m*

cost[1] [ˈkɔst] *v* **cost; costing** *vt* : costar <how much does it cost? : ¿cuánto cuesta?, ¿cuánto vale?> — *vi* : costar <these cost more : éstos cuestan más>

cost[2] *n* : costo *m,* precio *m,* coste *m* <cost of living : costo de vida> <victory at all costs : victoria a toda costa>

Costa Rican[1] [ˌkɔstəˈriːkən] *adj* : costarricense

Costa Rican[2] *n* : costarricense *mf*

costly [ˈkɔstli] *adj* : costoso, caro

costume [ˈkɑsˌtuːm, -ˌtjuːm] *n* **1** : traje *m* <national costume : traje típico> **2** : disfraz *m* <costume party : fiesta de disfraces> **3** OUTFIT : vestimenta *f,* traje *m,* conjunto *m*

cosy [ˈkoːzi] → **cozy**

cot [ˈkɑt] *n* : catre *m*

coterie [ˈkoːt̬əˌri, ˌkoːt̬əˈ-] *n* : tertulia *f,* círculo *m* (social)

cottage [ˈkɑt̬ɪʤ] *n* : casita *f* (de campo)

cottage cheese *n* : requesón *m*

cotton [ˈkɑtən] *n* : algodón *m*

cottonmouth [ˈkɑtənˌmaʊθ] → **moccasin**

cottonseed [ˈkɑtənˌsiːd] *n* : semilla *f* de algodón

cotton swab → **swab**

cottontail [ˈkɑtənˌteɪl] *n* : conejo *m* de cola blanca

couch[1] [ˈkaʊʧ] *vt* : expresar, formular <couched in strong language : expresado en lenguaje enérgico>

couch[2] *n* SOFA : sofá *m*

cougar [ˈkuːgər] *n* : puma *m*

cough[1] [ˈkɔf] *vi* : toser

cough[2] *n* : tos *f*

could [ˈkʊd] → **can**

council [ˈkaʊntsəl] *n* **1** : concejo *m* <city council : concejo municipal, ayuntamiento> **2** MEETING : concejo *m,* junta *f* **3** BOARD : consejo *m* **4** : concilio *m* (eclesiástico)

councillor *or* **councilor** [ˈkaʊntsələr] *n* : concejal *m,* -jala *f*

councilman [ˈkaʊntsəlmən] *n, pl* **-men** [-mən, -ˌmɛn] : concejal *m*

councilwoman [ˈkaʊntsəlˌwʊmən] *n, pl* **-women** [-ˌwɪmən] : concejala *f*

counsel[1] [ˈkaʊntsəl] *v* **-seled** *or* **-selled; -seling** *or* **-selling** *vt* ADVISE : aconsejar, asesorar, recomendar — *vi* CONSULT : consultar

counsel[2] *n* **1** ADVICE : consejo *m,* recomendación *f* **2** CONSULTATION : consulta *f* **3 counsel** *ns & pl* LAWYER : abogado *m,* -da *f*

counselor *or* **counsellor** [ˈkaʊntsələr] *n* : consejero *m,* -ra *f;* consultor *m,* -tora *f;* asesor *m,* -sora *f*

count[1] [ˈkaʊnt] *vt* : contar, enumerar — *vi* **1** : contar <to count out loud : contar en voz alta> **2** MATTER : contar, valer, importar <that's what counts : eso es lo que cuenta> **3 to count on** : contar con

count[2] *n* **1** COMPUTATION : cómputo *m,* recuento *m,* cuenta *f* <to lose count : perder la cuenta> **2** CHARGE : cargo *m* <two counts of robbery : dos cargos de robo> **3** : conde *m* (noble)

countable [ˈkaʊntəbəl] *adj* : numerable

countdown [ˈkaʊntˌdaʊn] *n* : cuenta *f* atrás

countenance[1] [ˈkaʊntənənts] *vt* **-nanced; -nancing** : permitir, tolerar

countenance[2] *n* FACE : semblante *m,* rostro *m*

counter[1] [ˈkaʊntər] *vt* **1** → **counteract** **2** OPPOSE : oponerse a, resistir — *vi* RETALIATE : responder, contraatacar

counter[2] *adv* **counter to** : contrario a, en contra de

counter[3] *adj* : contrario, opuesto

counter[4] *n* **1** PIECE : ficha *f* (de un juego) **2** : mostrador *m* (de un negocio), ventanilla *f* (en un banco) **3** : contador *m* (aparato) **4** COUNTERBALANCE : fuerza *f* opuesta, contrapeso *m*

counteract [ˌkaʊntərˈækt] *vt* : contrarrestar

counterattack [ˈkaʊntərəˌtæk] *n* : contraataque *m*

counterbalance[1] [ˌkaʊntərˈbælənts] *vt* **-anced; -ancing** : contrapesar

counterbalance[2] [ˈkaʊntərˌbælənts] *n* : contrapeso *m*

counterclockwise [ˌkaʊntərˈklɑkˌwaɪz] *adv & adj* : en el sentido opuesto al de las manecillas del reloj

counterfeit[1] [ˈkaʊntərˌfɪt] *vt* **1** : falsificar (dinero) **2** PRETEND : fingir, aparentar

counterfeit[2] *adj* : falso, inauténtico

counterfeit[3] *n* : falsificación *f*

counterfeiter [ˈkaʊntərˌfɪt̬ər] *n* : falsificador *m,* -dora *f*

countermand [ˈkaʊntərˌmænd, ˌkaʊntərˈ-] *vt* : contramandar

countermeasure [ˈkaʊntərˌmɛʒər] *n* : contramedida *f*

counterpart [ˈkaʊntərˌpɑrt] *n* : homólogo *m,* contraparte *f Mex*

counterpoint [ˈkaʊntərˌpɔɪnt] *n* : contrapunto *m*

counterproductive [ˌkaʊntərprəˈdʌktɪv] *adj* : contraproducente

counterrevolution [ˌkaʊntərˌrɛvəˈluːʃən] *n* : contrarrevolución *f*

counterrevolutionary[1] [ˌkaʊntərˌrɛvəˈluːʃənˌɛri] *adj* : contrarrevolucionario

counterrevolutionary[2] *n, pl* **-ries** : contrarrevolucionario *m,* -ria *f*

countersign [ˈkaʊntərˌsaɪn] *n* : contraseña *f*

countess [ˈkaʊntɪs] *n* : condesa *f*

countless [ˈkaʊntləs] *adj* : incontable, innumerable

country[1] [ˈkʌntri] *adj* : campestre, rural

country[2] *n, pl* **-tries** **1** NATION : país *m,* nación *f,* patria *f* <country of origin : país de origen> <love of one's country : amor a la patria> **2** : campo *m*

<they left the city for the country : se fueron de la ciudad al campo>
countryman [ˈkʌntrimən] *n, pl* **-men** [-mən, -ˌmɛn] : compatriota *mf;* paisano *m,* -na *f*
countryside [ˈkʌntriˌsaɪd] *n* : campo *m,* campiña *f*
county [ˈkaʊnti] *n, pl* **-ties** : condado *m*
coup [ˈkuː] *n, pl* **coups** [ˈkuːz] **1** : golpe *m* maestro **2** *or* **coup d'etat** : golpe *m* (de estado), cuartelazo *m*
coupe [ˈkuːp] *n* : cupé *m*
couple[1] [ˈkʌpəl] *vt* **-pled; -pling** : acoplar, enganchar, conectar
couple[2] *n* **1** PAIR : par *m* <a couple of hours : un par de horas, unas dos horas> **2** : pareja *f* <a young couple : una pareja joven>
coupling [ˈkʌplɪŋ] *n* : acoplamiento *m*
coupon [ˈkuːˌpɑn, ˈkjuː-] *n* : cupón *m*
courage [ˈkərɪdʒ] *n* : valor *m,* valentía *f,* coraje *m*
courageous [kəˈreɪdʒəs] *adj* : valiente, valeroso
courier [ˈkʊriər, ˈkəriər] *n* : mensajero *m,* -ra *f*
course[1] [ˈkors] *vi* **coursed; coursing** : correr (a toda velocidad)
course[2] *n* **1** PROGRESS : curso *m,* transcurso *m* <to run its course : seguir su curso> **2** DIRECTION : rumbo *m* (de un avión), derrota *f,* derrotero *m* (de un barco) **3** PATH, WAY : camino *m,* vía *f* <course of action : línea de conducta> **4** : plato *m* (de una cena) <the main course : el plato principal> **5** : curso *m* (académico) **6 of course** : desde luego, por supuesto <yes, of course! : ¡claro que sí!>
court[1] [ˈkort] *vt* WOO : cortejar, galantear
court[2] *n* **1** PALACE : palacio *m* **2** RETINUE : corte *f,* séquito *m* **3** COURTYARD : patio *m* **4** : cancha *f* (de tenis, baloncesto, etc.) **5** TRIBUNAL : corte *f,* tribunal *m* <the Supreme Court : la Corte Suprema>
courteous [ˈkərt̬iəs] *adj* : cortés, atento, educado — **courteously** *adv*
courtesan [ˈkort̬əzən, ˈkər-] *n* : cortesana *f*
courtesy [ˈkərt̬əsi] *n, pl* **-sies** : cortesía *f*
courthouse [ˈkortˌhaʊs] *n* : palacio *m* de justicia, juzgado *m*
courtier [ˈkortiər, ˈkortjər] *n* : cortesano *m,* -na *f*
courtly [ˈkortli] *adj* **-lier; -est** : distinguido, elegante, cortés
court–martial[1] [ˈkortˌmɑrʃəl] *vt* : someter a consejo de guerra
court–martial[2] *n, pl* **courts–martial** [ˈkortsˌmɑrʃəl] : consejo *m* de guerra
court order *n* : mandamiento *m* judicial
courtroom [ˈkortˌruːm] *n* : tribunal *m,* corte *f*
courtship [ˈkortˌʃɪp] *n* : cortejo *m,* noviazgo *m*
courtyard [ˈkortˌjɑrd] *n* : patio *m*
cousin [ˈkʌzən] *n* : primo *m,* -ma *f*
cove [ˈkoːv] *n* : ensenada *f,* cala *f*
covenant [ˈkʌvənənt] *n* : pacto *m,* contrato *m*
cover[1] [ˈkʌvər] *vt* **1** : cubrir, tapar <cover your head : tápate la cabeza> <covered with mud : cubierto de lodo> **2** HIDE, PROTECT : encubrir, proteger **3** TREAT : tratar **4** INSURE : asegurar, cubrir
cover[2] *n* **1** SHELTER : cubierta *f,* abrigo *m,* refugio *m* <to take cover : ponerse a cubierto> <under cover of darkness : al amparo de la oscuridad> **2** LID, TOP : cubierta *f,* tapa *f* **3** : cubierta *f* (de un libro), portada *f* (de una revista) **4 covers** *npl* BEDCLOTHES : ropa *f* de cama, cobijas *fpl,* mantas *fpl*
coverage [ˈkʌvərɪdʒ] *n* : cobertura *f*
coverlet [ˈkʌvərlət] *n* : cobertor *m*
covert[1] [ˈkoːˌvərt, ˈkʌvərt] *adj* : encubierto, secreto <covert operations : operaciones encubiertas>
covert[2] [ˈkʌvərt, ˈkoː-] *n* THICKET : espesura *f,* maleza *f*
cover–up [ˈkʌvərˌʌp] *n* : encubrimiento
covet [ˈkʌvət] *vt* : codiciar
covetous [ˈkʌvət̬əs] *adj* : codicioso
covey [ˈkʌvi] *n, pl* **-eys 1** : bandada *f* pequeña (de codornices, etc.) **2** GROUP : grupo *m*
cow[1] [ˈkaʊ] *vt* : intimidar, acobardar
cow[2] *n* : vaca *f,* hembra *f* (de ciertas especies)
coward [ˈkaʊərd] *n* : cobarde *mf*
cowardice [ˈkaʊərdɪs] *n* : cobardía *f*
cowardly [ˈkaʊərdli] *adj* : cobarde
cowboy [ˈkaʊˌbɔɪ] *n* : vaquero *m,* cowboy *m*
cower [ˈkaʊər] *vi* : encogerse (de miedo), acobardarse
cowgirl [ˈkaʊˌgərl] *n* : vaquera *f*
cowherd [ˈkaʊˌhərd] *n* : vaquero *m,* -ra *f*
cowhide [ˈkaʊˌhaɪd] *n* : cuero *m,* piel *f* de vaca
cowl [ˈkaʊl] *n* : capucha *f* (de un monje)
cowlick [ˈkaʊˌlɪk] *n* : remolino *m*
cowpuncher [ˈkaʊˌpʌntʃər] → **cowboy**
cowslip [ˈkaʊˌslɪp] *n* : prímula *f,* primavera *f*
coxswain [ˈkɑksən, -ˌsweɪn] *n* : timonel *m*
coy [ˈkɔɪ] *adj* **1** SHY : tímido, cohibido **2** COQUETTISH : coqueto
coyote [kaɪˈoːt̬i, ˈkaɪˌoːt] *n, pl* **coyotes** *or* **coyote** : coyote *m*
cozy [ˈkoːzi] *adj* **-zier; -est** : acogedor, cómodo
crab [ˈkræb] *n* : cangrejo *m,* jaiba *f*
crabby [ˈkræbi] *adj* **-bier; -est** : gruñón, malhumorado
crabgrass [ˈkræbˌgræs] *n* : garranchuelo *m*

crack[1] ['kræk] *vi* **1 :** chasquear, restallar <the whip cracked : el látigo restalló> **2** SPLIT **:** rajarse, resquebrajarse, agrietarse **3 :** quebrarse (dícese de la voz) — *vt* **1 :** restallar, chasquear (un látigo, etc.) **2** SPLIT **:** rajar, agrietar, resquebrajar **3** BREAK **:** romper (un huevo), cascar (nueces), forzar (una caja fuerte) **4** SOLVE **:** resolver, descifrar (un código)

crack[2] *adj* FIRST-RATE **:** buenísimo, de primera

crack[3] *n* **1 :** chasquido *m,* restallido *m,* estallido *m* (de un arma de fuego), crujido *m* (de huesos) <a crack of thunder : un trueno> **2** WISECRACK **:** chiste *m,* ocurrencia *f,* salida *f* **3** CREVICE **:** raja *f,* grieta *f,* fisura *f* **4** BLOW **:** golpe *m* **5** ATTEMPT **:** intento *m*

crackdown ['kræk,daʊn] *n* **:** medidas *fpl* enérgicas

crack down *vt* **:** tomar medidas enérgicas

cracker ['krækər] *n* **:** galleta *f* (de soda, etc.)

crackle[1] ['krækəl] *vi* **-led; -ling :** crepitar, chisporrotear

crackle[2] *n* **:** crujido *m,* chisporroteo *m*

crackpot ['kræk,pɑt] *n* **:** excéntrico *m,* -ca *f;* chiflado *m,* -da *f*

crack–up ['kræk,ʌp] *n* **1** CRASH **:** choque *m,* estrellamiento *m* **2** BREAKDOWN **:** crisis *f* nerviosa

crack up *vt* WRECK **:** estrellar (un vehículo) — *vi* **:** sufrir una crisis nerviosa

cradle[1] ['kreɪdəl] *vt* **-dled; -dling :** acunar, mecer (a un niño)

cradle[2] *n* **:** cuna *f*

craft ['kræft] *n* **1** TRADE **:** oficio *m* <the craft of carpentry : el oficio de carpintero> **2** CRAFTSMANSHIP, SKILL **:** arte *m,* artesanía *f,* destreza *f* **3** CRAFTINESS **:** astucia *f,* maña *f* **4** *pl usually* **craft** BOAT **:** barco *m,* embarcación *f* **5** *pl usually* **craft** AIRCRAFT **:** avión *m,* aeronave *f*

craftiness ['kræftinəs] *n* **:** astucia *f,* maña *f*

craftsman ['kræftsmən] *n, pl* **-men** [-mən, -,mɛn] **:** artesano *m,* -na *f*

craftsmanship ['kræftsmən,ʃɪp] *n* **:** artesanía *f,* destreza *f*

crafty ['kræfti] *adj* **craftier; -est :** astuto, taimado

crag ['kræg] *n* **:** peñasco *m*

craggy ['krægi] *adj* **-gier; -est :** peñascoso

cram ['kræm] *v* **crammed; cramming** *vt* **1** JAM **:** embutir, meter **2** STUFF **:** atiborrar, abarrotar <crammed with people : atiborrado de gente> — *vi* **:** estudiar a última hora, memorizar (para un examen)

cramp[1] ['kræmp] *vt* **1 :** dar calambre en **2** RESTRICT **:** limitar, restringir, entorpecer <to cramp someone's style : cortarle el vuelo a alguien> — *vi or* **to cramp up :** acalambrarse

cramp[2] *n* **1** SPASM **:** calambre *m,* espasmo *m* (de los músculos) **2 cramps** *npl* **:** retorcijones *mpl* <stomach cramps : retorcijones de estómago>

cranberry ['kræn,bɛri] *n, pl* **-berries :** arándano *m* (rojo y agrio)

crane[1] ['kreɪn] *vi* **craned; craning :** estirar <to crane one's neck : estirar el cuello>

crane[2] *n* **1 :** grulla *f* (ave) **2 :** grúa *f* (máquina)

cranial ['kreɪniəl] *adj* **:** craneal, craneano

cranium ['kreɪniəm] *n, pl* **-niums** *or* **-nia** [-niə]**:** cráneo *m*

crank[1] ['kræŋk] *vt or* **to crank up :** arrancar (con una manivela)

crank[2] *n* **1 :** manivela *f,* manubrio *m* **2** ECCENTRIC **:** excéntrico *m,* -ca *f*

cranky ['kræŋki] *adj* **crankier; -est :** irritable, malhumorado, enojadizo

cranny ['kræni] *n, pl* **-nies :** grieta *f* <every nook and cranny : todos los rincones>

crash[1] ['kræʃ] *vi* **1** SMASH **:** caerse con estrépito, estrellarse **2** COLLIDE **:** estrellarse, chocar **3** BOOM, RESOUND **:** retumbar, resonar — *vt* **1** SMASH **:** estrellar **2 to crash one's car :** tener un accidente

crash[2] *n* **1** DIN **:** estrépito *m* **2** COLLISION **:** choque *m,* colisión *f* <car crash : accidente automovilístico> **3** FAILURE **:** quiebra *f* (de un negocio), crac *m* (de la bolsa)

crass ['kræs] *adj* **:** grosero, de mal gusto

crate[1] ['kreɪt] *vt* **crated; crating :** empacar en un cajón

crate[2] *n* **:** cajón *m* (de madera)

crater ['kreɪt̬ər] *n* **:** cráter *m*

cravat [krə'væt] *n* **:** corbata *f*

crave ['kreɪv] *vt* **craved; craving :** ansiar, apetecer, tener muchas ganas de

craven ['kreɪvən] *adj* **:** cobarde, pusilánime

craving ['kreɪvɪŋ] *n* **:** ansia *f,* antojo *m,* deseo *m*

crawfish ['krɔ,fɪʃ] → **crayfish**

crawl[1] ['krɔl] *vi* **1** CREEP **:** arrastrarse, gatear (dícese de un bebé) **2** TEEM **:** estar plagado

crawl[2] *n* **:** paso *m* lento

crayfish ['kreɪ,fɪʃ] *n* **1 :** ástaco *m* (de agua dulce) **2 :** langostino *m* (de mar)

crayon ['kreɪ,ɑn, -ən] *n* **:** crayón *m*

craze ['kreɪz] *n* **:** moda *f* pasajera, manía *f*

crazed ['kreɪzd] *adj* **:** enloquecido

crazily ['kreɪzəli] *adv* **:** locamente, erráticamente, insensatamente

craziness ['kreɪzinəs] *n* **:** locura *f,* demencia *f*

crazy ['kreɪzi] *adj* **-zier; -est 1** INSANE **:** loco, demente <to go crazy : volverse loco> **2** ABSURD, FOOLISH **:** loco, insensato, absurdo **3 to be crazy about :** estar loco por

creak[1] [ˈkriːk] *vi* : chirriar, rechinar, crujir
creak[2] *n* : chirrido *m,* crujido *m*
creaky [ˈkriːki] *adj* **creakier; -est** : chirriante, que cruje
cream[1] [ˈkriːm] *vt* **1** BEAT, MIX : batir, mezclar (azúcar y mantequilla, etc.) **2** : preparar (alimentos) con crema
cream[2] *n* **1** : crema *f* (de leche) **2** LOTION : crema *f,* loción *f* **3** ELITE : crema *f,* elite *f* <the cream of the crop : la crema y nata, lo mejor>
creamery [ˈkriːməri] *n, pl* **-eries** : fábrica *f* de productos lácteos
creamy [ˈkriːmi] *adj* **creamier; -est** : cremoso
crease[1] [ˈkriːs] *vt* **creased; creasing 1** : plegar, poner una raya en (pantalones) **2** WRINKLE : arrugar
crease[2] *n* : pliegue *m,* doblez *m,* raya *f* (de pantalones)
create [kriˈeɪt] *vt* **-ated; -ating** : crear, hacer
creation [kriˈeɪʃən] *n* : creación *f*
creative [kriˈeɪt̬ɪv] *adj* : creativo, original <creative people : personas creativas> <a creative work : un obra original>
creatively [kriˈeɪt̬ɪvli] *adv* : creativamente, con originalidad
creativity [ˌkriːeɪˈtɪvət̬i] *n* : creatividad *f*
creator [kriˈeɪt̬ər] *n* : creador *m,* -dora *f*
creature [ˈkriːtʃər] *n* : ser *m* viviente, criatura *f,* animal *m*
credence [ˈkriːdənts] *n* : crédito *m*
credentials [krɪˈdɛntʃəlz] *npl* : referencias *fpl* oficiales, cartas *fpl* credenciales
credibility [ˌkrɛdəˈbɪlət̬i] *n* : credibilidad *f*
credible [ˈkrɛdəbəl] *adj* : creíble
credit[1] [ˈkrɛdɪt] *vt* **1** BELIEVE : creer, dar crédito a **2** : ingresar, abonar <to credit $100 to an account : ingresar $100 en (una) cuenta> **3** ATTRIBUTE : atribuir <they credit the invention to him : a él se le atribuye el invento>
credit[2] *n* **1** : saldo *m* positivo, saldo *m* a favor (de una cuenta) **2** : crédito *m* <to buy on credit : comprar a crédito> <credit card : tarjeta de crédito> **3** CREDENCE : crédito *m* <I gave credit to everything he said : di crédito a todo lo que dijo> **4** RECOGNITION : reconocimiento *m* **5** : orgullo *m,* honor *m* <she's a credit to the school : ella es el orgullo de la escuela>
creditable [ˈkrɛdɪt̬əbəl] *adj* : encomiable, loable — **creditably** [-bli] *adv*
credit card *n* : tarjeta de crédito
creditor [ˈkrɛdɪt̬ər] *n* : acreedor *m,* -dora *f*
credulity [krɪˈduːlət̬i, -ˈdjuː-] *n* : credulidad *f*
credulous [ˈkrɛdʒələs] *adj* : crédulo
creed [ˈkriːd] *n* : credo *m*
creek [ˈkriːk, ˈkrɪk] *n* : arroyo *m,* riachuelo *m*
creel [ˈkriːl] *n* : nasa *f,* cesta *f* (de pescador)
creep[1] [ˈkriːp] *vi* **crept** [ˈkrɛpt]; **creeping 1** CRAWL : arrastrarse, gatear **2** : moverse lentamente o sigilosamente <he crept out of the house : salió sigilosamente de la casa> **3** SPREAD : trepar (dícese de una planta)
creep[2] *n* **1** CRAWL : paso *m* lento **2** **creeps** *npl* : escalofríos *mpl* <that gives me the creeps : eso me da escalofríos>
creeper [ˈkriːpər] *n* : planta *f* trepadora, trepadora *f*
cremate [ˈkriːˌmeɪt] *vt* **-mated; -mating** : cremar
cremation [krɪˈmeɪʃən] *n* : cremación *f*
creosote [ˈkriːəˌsoːt] *n* : creosota *f*
crepe *or* **crêpe** [ˈkreɪp] *n* **1** : crespón *m* (tela) **2** PANCAKE : crepe *mf,* crepa *f Mex*
crescendo [krɪˈʃɛnˌdoː] *n, pl* **-dos** *or* **-does** : crescendo *m*
crescent [ˈkrɛsənt] *n* : creciente *m*
crest [ˈkrɛst] *n* **1** : cresta *f,* penacho *m* (de un ave) **2** PEAK, TOP : cresta *f* (de una ola), cima *f* (de una colina) **3** : emblema *m* (sobre un escudo de armas)
crestfallen [ˈkrɛstˌfɔlən] *adj* : alicaído, abatido
cretin [ˈkriːtən] *n* : cretino *m,* -na *f*
crevasse [krɪˈvæs] *n* : grieta *f,* fisura *f*
crevice [ˈkrɛvɪs] *n* : grieta *f,* hendidura *f*
crew [ˈkruː] *n* **1** : tripulación *f* (de una nave) **2** TEAM : equipo *m* (de trabajadores o atletas)
crib [ˈkrɪb] *n* **1** MANGER : pesebre *m* **2** GRANARY : granero *m* **3** : cuna *f* (de un bebé)
crick [ˈkrɪk] *n* : calambre *m,* espasmo *m* muscular
cricket [ˈkrɪkət] *n* **1** : grillo *m* (insecto) **2** : críquet *m* (juego)
crime [ˈkraɪm] *n* **1** : crimen *m,* delito *m* <to commit a crime : cometer un delito> **2** : crimen *m,* delincuencia *f* <organized crime : crimen organizado>
criminal[1] [ˈkrɪmənəl] *adj* : criminal
criminal[2] *n* : criminal *mf,* delincuente *mf*
crimp [ˈkrɪmp] *vt* : ondular, rizar (el pelo), arrugar (una tela, etc.)
crimson [ˈkrɪmzən] *n* : carmesí *m*
cringe [ˈkrɪndʒ] *vi* **cringed; cringing** : encogerse
crinkle[1] [ˈkrɪŋkəl] *v* **-kled; -kling** *vt* : arrugar — *vi* : arrugarse
crinkle[2] *n* : arruga *f*
crinkly [ˈkrɪŋkəli] *adj* : arrugado
cripple[1] [ˈkrɪpəl] *vt* **-pled; -pling 1** DISABLE : lisiar, dejar inválido **2** INCAPACITATE : inutilizar, incapacitar
cripple[2] *n* : lisiado *m,* -da *f*

crisis ['kraɪsɪs] *n, pl* **crises** [-ˌsiːz] **:** crisis *f*
crisp[1] ['krɪsp] *vt* **:** tostar, hacer crujiente
crisp[2] *adj* **1** CRUNCHY **:** crujiente, crocante **2** FIRM, FRESH **:** firme, fresco <crisp lettuce : lechuga fresca> **3** LIVELY **:** vivaz, alegre <a crisp tempo : un ritmo alegre> **4** INVIGORATING **:** fresco, vigorizante <the crisp autumn air : el fresco aire otoñal> — **crisply** *adv*
crispy ['krɪspi] *adj* **crispier; -est** **:** crujiente <crispy potato chips : papitas crujientes>
crisscross ['krɪsˌkrɔs] *vt* **:** entrecruzar
criterion [kraɪ'tɪriən] *n, pl* **-ria** [-iə] **:** criterio *m*
critic ['krɪt̬ɪk] *n* **1 :** crítico *m,* -ca *f* (de las artes) **2** FAULTFINDER **:** detractor *m,* -tora *f;* criticón *m,* -cona *f*
critical ['krɪt̬ɪkəl] *adj* **:** crítico
critically ['krɪt̬ɪkli] *adv* **:** críticamente <critically ill : gravemente enfermo>
criticism ['krɪt̬əˌsɪzəm] *n* **:** crítica *f*
criticize ['krɪt̬əˌsaɪz] *vt* **-cized; -cizing** **1** EVALUATE, JUDGE **:** criticar, analizar, evaluar **2** CENSURE **:** criticar, reprobar
critique [krɪ'tiːk] *n* **:** crítica *f,* evaluación *f*
croak[1] ['kroːk] *vi* **:** croar
croak[2] *n* **:** croar *m,* canto *m* (de la rana)
Croatian [kro'eɪʃən] *n* **:** croata *mf* — **Croatian** *adj*
crochet[1] [kroː'ʃeɪ] *v* **:** tejer al croché
crochet[2] *n* **:** croché *m,* crochet *m*
crock ['krɑk] *n* **:** vasija *f* de barro
crockery ['krɑkəri] *n* **:** vajilla *f* (de barro)
crocodile ['krɑkəˌdaɪl] *n* **:** cocodrilo *m*
crocus ['kroːkəs] *n, pl* **-cuses** **:** azafrán *m*
crone ['kroːn] *n* **:** vieja *f* arpía, vieja *f* bruja
crony ['kroːni] *n, pl* **-nies** **:** amigote *m fam;* compinche *mf fam*
crook[1] ['krʊk] *vt* **:** doblar (el brazo o el dedo)
crook[2] *n* **1** STAFF **:** cayado *m* (de pastor), báculo *m* (de obispo) **2** THIEF **:** ratero *m,* -ra *f;* ladrón *m,* -drona *f*
crooked ['krʊkəd] *adj* **1** BENT **:** chueco, torcido **2** DISHONEST **:** deshonesto
crookedness ['krʊkədnəs] *n* **1 :** lo torcido, lo chueco **2** DISHONESTY **:** falta *f* de honradez
croon ['kruːn] *v* **:** cantar suavemente
crop[1] ['krɑp] *v* **cropped; cropping** *vt* TRIM **:** recortar, cortar — *vi* **to crop up** **:** aparecer, surgir <these problems keep cropping up : estos problemas no cesan de surgir>
crop[2] *n* **1 :** buche *m* (de un ave o insecto) **2** WHIP **:** fusta *f* (de jinete) **3** HARVEST **:** cosecha *f,* cultivo *m*
croquet [ˌkroː'keɪ] *n* **:** croquet *m*
croquette [ˌkroː'kɛt] *n* **:** croqueta *f*
cross[1] ['krɔs] *vt* **1 :** cruzar, atravesar <to cross the street : cruzar la calle> <several canals cross the city : varios canales atraviesan la ciudad> **2** CANCEL **:** tachar, cancelar <he crossed his name off the list : tachó su nombre de la planilla> **3** INTERBREED **:** cruzar (en genética)
cross[2] *adj* **1 :** que atraviesa <cross ventilation : ventilación que atraviesa un cuarto> **2** CONTRARY **:** contrario, opuesto <cross purposes : objetivos opuestos> **3** ANGRY **:** enojado, de mal humor
cross[3] *n* **1 :** cruz *f* <the sign of the cross : la señal de la cruz> **2 :** cruza *f* (en biología)
crossbones ['krɔsˌboːnz] *npl* **1 :** huesos *mpl* cruzados **2** → **skull**
crossbow ['krɔsˌboː] *n* **:** ballesta *f*
crossbreed ['krɔsˌbriːd] *vt* **-bred** [-+bred]; **-breeding** **:** cruzar
cross–examination [ˌkrɔsɪgˌzæmə'neɪʃən] *n* **:** repreguntas *fpl,* interrogatorio *m*
cross–examine [ˌkrɔsɪg'zæmən] *vt* **-ined; -ining** **:** repreguntar
cross–eyed ['krɔsˌaɪd] *adj* **:** bizco
crossing ['krɔsɪŋ] *n* **1** INTERSECTION **:** cruce *m,* paso *m* <pedestrian crossing : paso de peatones> **2** VOYAGE **:** travesía *f* (del mar)
crossly ['krɔsli] *adv* **:** con enojo, con enfado
cross–reference [ˌkrɔs'rɛfrənts, -'rɛfərənts] *n* **:** referencia *f,* remisión *f*
crossroads ['krɔsˌroːdz] *n* **:** cruce *m,* encrucijada *f,* crucero *m Mex*
cross section *n* **1** SECTION **:** corte *m* transversal **2** SAMPLE **:** muestra *f* representativa <a cross section of the population : una muestra representativa de la población>
crosswalk ['krɔsˌwɔk] *n* **:** cruce *m* peatonal, paso *m* de peatones
crossways ['krɔsˌweɪz] → **crosswise**
crosswise[1] ['krɔsˌwaɪz] *adv* **:** transversalmente, diagonalmente
crosswise[2] *adj* **:** transversal, diagonal
crossword puzzle ['krɔsˌwərd] *n* **:** crucigrama *m*
crotch ['krɑtʃ] *n* **:** entrepierna *f*
crotchety ['krɑtʃət̬i] *adj* CRANKY **:** malhumorado, irritable, enojadizo
crouch ['kraʊtʃ] *vi* **:** agacharse, ponerse de cuclillas
croup ['kruːp] *n* **:** crup *m*
crouton ['kruːˌtɑn] *n* **:** crutón *m*
crow[1] ['kroː] *vi* **1 :** cacarear, cantar (como un cuervo) **2** BRAG **:** alardear, presumir
crow[2] *n* **1 :** cuervo *m* (ave) **2 :** cantar *m* (del gallo)
crowbar ['kroːˌbɑr] *n* **:** palanca *f*
crowd[1] ['kraʊd] *vi* **:** aglomerarse, amontonarse — *vt* **:** atestar, atiborrar, llenar
crowd[2] *n* **:** multitud *f,* muchedumbre *f,* gentío *m*
crown[1] ['kraʊn] *vt* **:** coronar
crown[2] *n* **:** corona *f*

crow's nest *n* : cofa *f*
crucial [ˈkruːʃəl] *adj* : crucial, decisivo
crucible [ˈkruːsəbəl] *n* : crisol *m*
crucifix [ˈkruːsəˌfɪks] *n* : crucifijo *m*
crucifixion [ˌkruːsəˈfɪkʃən] *n* : crucifixión *f*
crucify [ˈkruːsəˌfaɪ] *vt* **-fied; -fying** : crucificar
crude [ˈkruːd] *adj* **cruder; -est 1** RAW, UNREFINED : crudo, sin refinar <crude oil : petróleo crudo> **2** VULGAR : grosero, de mal gusto **3** ROUGH : tosco, burdo, rudo
crudely [ˈkruːdli] *adv* **1** VULGARLY : groseramente **2** ROUGHLY : burdamente, de manera rudimentaria
crudity [ˈkruːdət̬i] *n, pl* **-ties 1** VULGARITY : grosería *f* **2** COARSENESS, ROUGHNESS : tosquedad *f,* rudeza *f*
cruel [ˈkruːəl] *adj* **-eler** *or* **-eller; -elest** *or* **-ellest** : cruel
cruelly [ˈkruːəli] *adv* : cruelmente
cruelty [ˈkruːəlti] *n, pl* **-ties** : crueldad *f*
cruet [ˈkruːɪt] *n* : vinagrera *f,* aceitera *f*
cruise[1] [ˈkruːz] *vi* **cruised; cruising 1** : hacer un crucero **2** : navegar o conducir a una velocidad constante <cruising speed : velocidad de crucero>
cruise[2] *n* : crucero *m*
cruiser [ˈkruːzər] *n* **1** WARSHIP : crucero *m,* buque *m* de guerra **2** : patrulla *f* (de policía)
crumb [ˈkrʌm] *n* : miga *f,* migaja *f*
crumble [ˈkrʌmbəl] *v* **-bled; -bling** *vt* : desmigajar, desmenuzar — *vi* : desmigajarse, desmoronarse, desmenuzarse
crumbly [ˈkrʌmbli] *adj* : que se desmenuza fácilmente, friable
crumple [ˈkrʌmpəl] *v* **-pled; -pling** *vt* RUMPLE : arrugar — *vi* **1** WRINKLE : arrugarse **2** COLLAPSE : desplomarse
crunch[1] [ˈkrʌntʃ] *vt* **1** : ronzar (con los dientes) **2** : hacer crujir (con los pies, etc.) — *vi* : crujir
crunch[2] *n* : crujido *m*
crunchy [ˈkrʌntʃi] *adj* **crunchier; -est** : crujiente
crusade[1] [kruːˈseɪd] *vi* **-saded; -sading** : hacer una campaña (a favor de o contra algo)
crusade[2] *n* **1** : campaña *f* (de reforma, etc.) **2 Crusade** : cruzada *f*
crusader [kruːˈseɪdər] *n* **1** : cruzado *m* (en la Edad Media) **2** : campeón *m,* -peona *f* (de una causa)
crush[1] [ˈkrʌʃ] *vt* **1** SQUASH : aplastar, apachurrar **2** GRIND, PULVERIZE : triturar, machacar **3** SUPPRESS : aplastar, suprimir
crush[2] *n* **1** CROWD, MOB : gentío *m,* multitud *f,* aglomeración *f* **2** INFATUATION : enamoramiento *m*
crushing [ˈkrʌʃɪŋ] *adj* : aplastante, abrumador
crust [ˈkrʌst] *n* **1** : corteza *f,* costra *f* (de pan) **2** : tapa *f* de masa, pasta *f* (de un pastel) **3** LAYER : capa *f,* corteza *f* <the earth's crust : la corteza terrestre>
crustacean [ˌkrʌsˈteɪʃən] *n* : crustáceo *m*
crusty [ˈkrʌsti] *adj* **crustier; -est 1** : de corteza dura **2** CROSS, GRUMPY : enojado, malhumorado
crutch [ˈkrʌtʃ] *n* : muleta *f*
crux [ˈkrʌks, ˈkrʊks] *n, pl* **cruxes** : quid *m,* esencia *f,* meollo *m* <the crux of the problem : el quid del problema>
cry[1] [ˈkraɪ] *vi* **cried; crying 1** SHOUT : gritar <they cried for more : a gritos pidieron más> **2** WEEP : llorar
cry[2] *n, pl* **cries 1** SHOUT : grito *m* **2** WEEPING : llanto *m* **3** : chillido *m* (de un animal)
crybaby [ˈkraɪˌbeɪbi] *n, pl* **-bies** : llorón *m,* -rona *f*
crypt [ˈkrɪpt] *n* : cripta *f*
cryptic [ˈkrɪptɪk] *adj* : enigmático, críptico
crystal [ˈkrɪstəl] *n* : cristal *m*
crystalline [ˈkrɪstəlɪn] *adj* : cristalino
crystallize [ˈkrɪstəˌlaɪz] *v* **-lized; -lizing** *vt* : cristalizar, materializar <to crystallize one's thoughts : cristalizar uno sus pensamientos> — *vi* : cristalizarse
cub [ˈkʌb] *n* : cachorro *m*
Cuban [ˈkjuːbən] *n* : cubano *m,* -na *f* — **Cuban** *adj*
cubbyhole [ˈkʌbiˌhoːl] *n* : chiribitil *m*
cube[1] [ˈkjuːb] *vt* **cubed; cubing 1** : elevar (un número) al cubo **2** : cortar en cubos
cube[2] *n* **1** : cubo *m* **2 ice cube** : cubito *m* de hielo **3 sugar cube** : terrón *m* de azúcar
cubic [ˈkjuːbɪk] *adj* : cúbico
cubicle [ˈkjuːbɪkəl] *n* : cubículo *m*
cuckoo[1] [ˈkuːˌkuː, ˈkʊ-] *adj* : loco, chiflado
cuckoo[2] *n, pl* **-oos** : cuco *m,* cuclillo *m*
cucumber [ˈkjuːˌkʌmbər] *n* : pepino *m*
cud [ˈkʌd] *n* **to chew the cud** : rumiar
cuddle [ˈkʌdəl] *v* **-dled; -dling** *vi* : abrazarse tiernamente, acurrucarse — *vt* : abrazar
cudgel[1] [ˈkʌdʒəl] *vt* **-geled** *or* **-gelled; -geling** *or* **-gelling** : apalear, aporrear
cudgel[2] *n* : garrote *m,* porra *f*
cue[1] [ˈkjuː] *vt* **cued; cuing** *or* **cueing** : darle el pie a, darle la señal a
cue[2] *n* **1** SIGNAL : señal *f,* pie *m* (en teatro), entrada *f* (en música) **2** : taco *m* (de billar)
cuff[1] [ˈkʌf] *vt* : bofetear, cachetear
cuff[2] *n* **1** : puño *m* (de una camisa), vuelta *f* (de pantalones) **2** SLAP : bofetada *f,* cachetada *f* **3 cuffs** *npl* HANDCUFFS : esposas *fpl*
cuisine [kwɪˈziːn] *n* : cocina *f* <Mexican cuisine : la cocina mexicana>

culinary [ˈkʌləˌnɛri, ˈkjuːlə-] *adj* : culinario
cull [ˈkʌl] *vt* : seleccionar, entresacar
culminate [ˈkʌlməˌneɪt] *vi* **-nated; -nating** : culminar
culmination [ˌkʌlməˈneɪʃən] *n* : culminación *f,* punto *m* culminante
culpable [ˈkʌlpəbəl] *adj* : culpable
culprit [ˈkʌlprɪt] *n* : culpable *mf*
cult [ˈkʌlt] *n* : culto *m*
cultivate [ˈkʌltəˌveɪt] *vt* **-vated; -vating 1** TILL : cultivar, labrar **2** FOSTER : cultivar, fomentar **3** REFINE : cultivar, refinar <to cultivate the mind : cultivar la mente>
cultivation [ˌkʌltəˈveɪʃən] *n* **1** : cultivo *m* <under cultivation : en cultivo> **2** CULTURE, REFINEMENT : cultura *f,* refinamiento *m*
cultural [ˈkʌltʃərəl] *adj* : cultural — **culturally** *adv*
culture [ˈkʌltʃər] *n* **1** CULTIVATION : cultivo *m* **2** REFINEMENT : cultura *f,* educación *f,* refinamiento *m* **3** CIVILIZATION : cultura *f,* civilización *f* <the Incan culture : la cultura inca>
cultured [ˈkʌltʃərd] *adj* **1** EDUCATED, REFINED : culto, educado, refinado **2** : de cultivo, cultivado <cultured pearls : perlas de cultivo>
culvert [ˈkʌlvərt] *n* : alcantarilla *f*
cumbersome [ˈkʌmbərsəm] *adj* : torpe y pesado, difícil de manejar
cumulative [ˈkjuːmjələt̬ɪv, -ˌleɪt̬ɪv] *adj* : acumulativo
cumulus [ˈkjuːmjələs] *n, pl* **-li** [-ˌlaɪ, -ˌliː] : cúmulo *n*
cunning[1] [ˈkʌnɪŋ] *adj* **1** CRAFTY : astuto, taimado **2** CLEVER : ingenioso, hábil **3** CUTE : mono, gracioso, lindo
cunning[2] *n* **1** SKILL : habilidad *f* **2** CRAFTINESS : astucia *f,* maña *f*
cup[1] [ˈkʌp] *vt* **cupped; cupping** : ahuecar (las manos)
cup[2] *n* **1** : taza *f* <a cup of coffee : una taza de café> **2** CUPFUL : taza *f* **3** : media pinta *f* (unidad de medida) **4** GOBLET : copa *f* **5** TROPHY : copa *f,* trofeo *m*
cupboard [ˈkʌbərd] *n* : alacena *f,* armario *m*
cupcake [ˈkʌpˌkeɪk] *n* : pastelito *m*
cupful [ˈkʌpˌfʊl] *n* : taza *f*
cupola [ˈkjuːpələ, -ˌloː] *n* : cúpula *f*
cur [ˈkər] *n* : perro *m* callejero, perro *m* corriente *Mex*
curate [ˈkjʊrət] *n* : cura *m,* párroco *m*
curator [ˈkjʊrˌeɪt̬ər, kjʊˈreɪt̬ər] *n* : conservador *m,* -dora *f* (de un museo); director *m,* -tora *f* (de un zoológico)
curb[1] [ˈkərb] *vt* : refrenar, restringir, controlar
curb[2] *n* **1** RESTRAINT : freno *m,* control *m* **2** : borde *m* de la acera
curd [ˈkərd] *n* : cuajada *f*
curdle [ˈkərdəl] *v* **-dled; -dling** *vi* : cuajarse — *vt* : cuajar <to curdle one's blood : helarle la sangre a uno>
cure[1] [ˈkjʊr] *vt* **cured; curing 1** HEAL : curar, sanar **2** REMEDY : remediar **3** PROCESS : curar (alimentos, etc.)
cure[2] *n* **1** RECOVERY : curación *f,* recuperación *f* **2** REMEDY : cura *f,* remedio *m*
curfew [ˈkərˌfjuː] *n* : toque *m* de queda
curio [ˈkjʊriˌoː] *n, pl* **-rios** : curiosidad *f,* objeto *m* curioso
curiosity [ˌkjʊriˈɑsət̬i] *n, pl* **-ties** : curiosidad *f*
curious [ˈkjʊriəs] *adj* **1** INQUISITIVE : curioso **2** STRANGE : curioso, raro
curl[1] [ˈkərl] *vt* **1** : rizar, ondular (el pelo) **2** COIL : enrollar **3** TWIST : torcer <to curl one's lip : hacer una mueca> — *vi* **1** : rizarse, ondularse **2 to curl up** : acurrucarse (con un libro, etc.)
curl[2] *n* **1** RINGLET : rizo *m* **2** COIL : espiral *f,* rosca *f*
curler [ˈkərlər] *n* : rulo *m*
curlew [ˈkərˌluː, ˈkərlˌjuː] *n, pl* **-lews** *or* **-lew** : zarapito *m*
curly [ˈkərli] *adj* **curlier; -est** : rizado, crespo
currant [ˈkərənt] *n* **1** : grosella *f* (fruta) **2** RAISIN : pasa *f* de Corinto
currency [ˈkərəntsi] *n, pl* **-cies 1** PREVALENCE, USE : uso *m,* aceptación *f,* difusión *f* <to be in currency : estar en uso> **2** MONEY : moneda *f,* dinero *m*
current[1] [ˈkərənt] *adj* **1** PRESENT : actual <current events : actualidades> **2** PREVALENT : corriente, común — **currently** *adv*
current[2] *n* : corriente *f*
curriculum [kəˈrɪkjələm] *n, pl* **-la** [-lə] : currículum *m,* currículo *m,* programa *m* de estudio
curriculum vitae [ˈviːˌtaɪ, ˈvaɪt̬i] *n, pl* **curricula vitae** : currículum *m,* currículo *m*
curry[1] [ˈkəri] *vt* **-ried; -rying 1** GROOM : almohazar (un caballo) **2** : condimentar con curry **3 to curry favor** : congraciarse (con alguien)
curry[2] *n, pl* **-ries** : curry *m*
curse[1] [ˈkərs] *v* **cursed; cursing** *vt* **1** DAMN : maldecir **2** INSULT : injuriar, insultar, decir malas palabras a **3** AFFLICT : afligir — *vi* : maldecir, decir malas palabras
curse[2] *n* **1** : maldición *f* <to put a curse on someone : echarle una maldición a alguien> **2** AFFLICTION : maldición *f,* aflicción *f,* cruz *f*
cursor [ˈkərsər] *n* : cursor *m*
cursory [ˈkərsəri] *adj* : rápido, superficial, somero
curt [ˈkərt] *adj* : cortante, brusco, seco — **curtly** *adv*
curtail [kərˈteɪl] *vt* : acortar, limitar, restringir
curtailment [kərˈteɪlmənt] *n* : restricción *f,* limitación *f*
curtain [ˈkərtən] *n* : cortina *f* (de una ventana), telón *m* (en un teatro)
curtness [ˈkərtnəs] *n* : brusquedad *f,* sequedad *f*

curtsy[1] *or* **curtsey** [ˈkərtsi] *vt* **-sied** *or* **-seyed; -sying** *or* **-seying :** hacer una reverencia

curtsy[2] *or* **curtsey** *n, pl* **-sies** *or* **-seys :** reverencia *f*

curvature [ˈkərvəˌtʃʊr] *n* **:** curvatura *f*

curve[1] [ˈkərv] *v* **curved; curving** *vi* **:** torcerse, describir una curva — *vt* **:** encorvar

curve[2] *n* **:** curva *f*

cushion[1] [ˈkʊʃən] *vt* **1 :** poner cojines o almohadones a **2** SOFTEN **:** amortiguar, mitigar, suavizar <to cushion a blow : amortiguar un golpe>

cushion[2] *n* **1 :** cojín *m,* almohadón *m* **2** PROTECTION **:** colchón *m,* protección *f*

cusp [ˈkʌsp] *n* **:** cúspide *f* (de un diente), cuerno *m* (de la luna)

cuspid [ˈkʌspɪd] *n* **:** diente *m* canino, colmillo *m*

custard [ˈkʌstərd] *n* **:** natillas *fpl*

custodian [ˌkʌˈstoːdiən] *n* **:** custodio *m,* -dia *f;* guardián, -diana *f*

custody [ˈkʌstədi] *n, pl* **-dies :** custodia *f,* cuidado *m* <to be in custody : estar detenido>

custom[1] [ˈkʌstəm] *adj* **:** a la medida, a la orden

custom[2] *n* **1 :** costumbre *f,* tradición *f* **2 customs** *npl* **:** aduana *f*

customarily [ˌkʌstəˈmɛrəli] *adv* **:** habitualmente, normalmente, de costumbre

customary [ˈkʌstəˌmɛri] *adj* **1** TRADITIONAL **:** tradicional **2** USUAL **:** habitual, de costumbre

customer [ˈkʌstəmər] *n* **:** cliente *m,* -ta *f*

custom–made [ˈkʌstəmˈmeɪd] *adj* **:** hecho a la medida

cut[1] [ˈkʌt] *v* **cut; cutting** *vt* **1 :** cortar <to cut paper : cortar papel> **2 :** cortarse <to cut one's finger : cortarse uno el dedo> **3** TRIM **:** cortar, recortar <to have one's hair cut : cortarse el pelo> **4** INTERSECT **:** cruzar, atravesar **5** SHORTEN **:** acortar, abreviar **6** REDUCE **:** reducir, rebajar <to cut prices : rebajar los precios> **7 to cut one's teeth :** salirle los dientes a uno — *vi* **1 :** cortar, cortarse **2 to cut in :** entrometerse

cut[2] *n* **1 :** corte *m* <a cut of meat : un corte de carne> **2** SLASH **:** tajo *m,* corte *m,* cortadura *f* **3** REDUCTION **:** rebaja *f,* reducción *f* <a cut in the rates : una rebaja en las tarifas>

cute [ˈkjuːt] *adj* **cuter; -est :** mono *fam,* lindo

cuticle [ˈkjuːtɪkəl] *n* **:** cutícula *f*

cutlass [ˈkʌtləs] *n* **:** alfanje *m*

cutlery [ˈkʌtləri] *n* **:** cubiertos *mpl*

cutlet [ˈkʌtlət] *n* **:** chuleta *f*

cutter [ˈkʌtər] *n* **1 :** cortadora *f* (implemento) **2 :** cortador *m,* -dora *f* (persona) **3 :** cúter *m* (embarcación)

cutthroat [ˈkʌtˌθroːt] *adj* **:** despiadado, desalmado <cutthroat competition : competencia feroz>

cutting[1] [ˈkʌtɪŋ] *adj* **1 :** cortante <a cutting wind : un viento cortante> **2** CAUSTIC **:** mordaz

cutting[2] *n* **:** esqueje *m* (de una planta)

cuttlefish [ˈkʌtəlˌfɪʃ] *n, pl* **-fish** *or* **-fishes :** jibia *f,* sepia *f*

cyanide [ˈsaɪəˌnaɪd, -nɪd] *n* **:** cianuro *m*

cycle[1] [ˈsaɪkəl] *vi* **-cled; -cling :** andar en bicicleta, ir en bicicleta

cycle[2] *n* **1 :** ciclo *m* <life cycle : ciclo de vida, ciclo vital> **2** BICYCLE **:** bicicleta *f* **3** MOTORCYCLE **:** motocicleta *f*

cyclic [ˈsaɪklɪk, ˈsɪ-] *or* **cyclical** [-klɪkəl] *adj* **:** cíclico

cyclist [ˈsaɪklɪst] *n* **:** ciclista *mf*

cyclone [ˈsaɪˌkloːn] *n* **1 :** ciclón *m* **2** TORNADO **:** tornado *m*

cyclopedia *or* **cyclopaedia** [ˌsaɪkləˈpiːdiə] → **encyclopedia**

cylinder [ˈsɪləndər] *n* **:** cilindro *m*

cylindrical [səˈlɪndrɪkəl] *adj* **:** cilíndrico

cymbal [ˈsɪmbəl] *n* **:** platillo *m,* címbalo *m*

cynic [ˈsɪnɪk] *n* **:** cínico *m,* -ca *f*

cynical [ˈsɪnɪkəl] *adj* **:** cínico

cynicism [ˈsɪnəˌsɪzəm] *n* **:** cinismo *m*

cypress [ˈsaɪprəs] *n* **:** ciprés *m*

Cypriot [ˈsɪpriət, -ˌɑt] *n* **:** chipriota *mf* — **Cypriot** *adj*

cyst [ˈsɪst] *n* **:** quiste *m*

cytoplasm [ˈsaɪt̬oˌplæzəm] *n* **:** citoplasma *m*

czar [ˈzɑr, ˈsɑr] *n* **:** zar *m*

czarina [zɑˈriːnə, sɑ-] *n* **:** zarina *f*

Czech [ˈtʃɛk] *n* **1 :** checo *m,* -ca *f* **2 :** checo *m* (idioma) — **Czech** *adj*

Czechoslovak [ˌtʃɛkoˈsloːˌvɑk, -ˌvæk] *or* **Czechoslovakian** [-sloˈvɑkiən, -ˈvæ-] *n* **:** checoslovaco *m,* -ca *f* — **Czechoslovak** *or* **Czechoslovakian** *adj*

D

d [ˈdiː] *n, pl* **d's** *or* **ds** [ˈdiːz] **:** cuarta letra del alfabeto inglés

dab[1] [ˈdæb] *vt* **dabbed; dabbing :** darle toques ligeros a, aplicar suavemente

dab[2] *n* **1** BIT **:** toque *m,* pizca *f,* poco *m* <a dab of ointment : un toque de ungüento> **2** PAT **:** toque *m* ligero, golpecito *m*

dabble [ˈdæbəl] *v* **-bled; -bling** *vt* SPATTER **:** salpicar — *vi* **1** SPLASH **:** chapotear **2** TRIFLE **:** jugar, interesarse superficialmente

dabbler ['dæbələr] *n* : diletante *mf*
dachshund ['dɑks,hʊnt, -,hʊnd; 'dɑksənt, -sənd] *n* : perro *m* salchicha
dad ['dæd] *n* : papá *m fam*
daddy ['dædi] *n, pl* **-dies** : papi *m fam*
daffodil ['dæfə,dɪl] *n* : narciso *m*
daft ['dæft] *adj* : tonto, bobo
dagger ['dægər] *n* : daga *f,* puñal *m*
dahlia ['dæljə, 'dɑl-, 'deɪl-] *n* : dalia *f*
daily[1] ['deɪli] *adv* : a diario, diariamente
daily[2] *adj* : diario, cotidiano
daily[3] *n, pl* **-lies** : diario *m,* periódico *m*
daintily ['deɪntəli] *adv* : delicadamente, con delicadeza
daintiness ['deɪntinəs] *n* : delicadeza *f,* finura *f*
dainty[1] ['deɪnti] *adj* **-tier; -est 1** DELICATE : delicado **2** FASTIDIOUS : remilgado, melindroso **3** DELICIOUS : exquisito, sabroso
dainty[2] *n, pl* **-ties** DELICACY : exquisitez *f,* manjar *m*
dairy ['dæri] *n, pl* **-ies 1** *or* **dairy store** : lechería *f* **2** *or* **dairy farm** : granja *f* lechera
dairymaid ['dæri,meɪd] *n* : lechera *f*
dairyman ['dærimən, -,mæn] *n, pl* **-men** [-mən, -,mɛn] : lechero *m*
dais ['deɪəs] *n* : tarima *f,* estrado *m*
daisy ['deɪzi] *n, pl* **-sies** : margarita *f*
dale ['deɪl] *n* : valle *m*
dally ['dæli] *vi* **-lied; -lying 1** TRIFLE : juguetear **2** DAWDLE : entretenerse, perder tiempo
dalmatian [dæl'meɪʃən, dɔl-] *n* : dálmata *m*
dam[1] ['dæm] *vt* **dammed; damming** : represar, embalsar
dam[2] *n* **1** : represa *f,* dique *m* **2** : madre *f* (de animales domésticos)
damage[1] ['dæmɪdʒ] *vt* **-aged; -aging** : dañar (un objeto o una máquina), perjudicar (la salud o una reputación)
damage[2] *n* **1** : daño *m,* perjuicio *m* **2** **damages** *npl* : daños y perjuicios *mpl*
damask ['dæməsk] *n* : damasco *m*
dame ['deɪm] *n* LADY : dama *f,* señora *f*
damn[1] ['dæm] *vt* **1** CONDEMN : condenar **2** CURSE : maldecir
damn[2] *or* **damned** ['dæmd] *adj* : condenado *fam,* maldito *fam*
damn[3] *n* : pito *m,* bledo *m,* comino *m* <it's not worth a damn : no vale un pito> <I don't give a damn : me importa un comino>
damnable ['dæmnəbəl] *adj* : condenable, detestable
damnation [dæm'neɪʃən] *n* : condenación *f*
damned[1] ['dæmd] *adv* VERY : muy
damned[2] *adj* **1** → **damnable 2** REMARKABLE : extraordinario
damp[1] ['dæmp] *vt* → **dampen**
damp[2] *adj* : húmedo
damp[3] *n* MOISTURE : humedad *f*
dampen ['dæmpən] *vt* **1** MOISTEN : humedecer **2** DISCOURAGE : desalentar, desanimar
damper ['dæmpər] *n* **1** : regulador *m* de tiro (de una chimenea) **2** : sordina *f* (de un piano) **3 to put a damper on** : desanimar, apagar (el entusiasmo), enfriar
dampness ['dæmpnəs] *n* : humedad *f*
damsel ['dæmzəl] *n* : damisela *f*
dance[1] ['dænts] *v* **danced; dancing** : bailar
dance[2] *n* : baile *m*
dancer ['dæntsər] *n* : bailarín *m,* -rina *f*
dandelion ['dændəl,aɪən] *n* : diente *m* de león
dandruff ['dændrəf] *n* : caspa *f*
dandy[1] ['dændi] *adj* **-dier; -est** : excelente, magnífico, macanudo *fam*
dandy[2] *n, pl* **-dies 1** FOP : dandi *m* **2** : algo *m* excelente <this new program is a dandy : este programa nuevo es algo excelente>
Dane ['deɪn] *n* : danés *m,* -nesa *f*
Danish[1] ['deɪnɪʃ] *adj* : danés
Danish[2] *n* : danés *m* (idioma)
danger ['deɪndʒər] *n* : peligro *m*
dangerous ['deɪndʒərəs] *adj* : peligroso
dangle ['dæŋgəl] *v* **-gled; -gling** *vi* HANG : colgar, pender — *vt* **1** SWING : hacer oscilar **2** PROFFER : ofrecer (como incentivo) **3 to keep someone dangling** : dejar a alguien en suspenso
dank ['dæŋk] *adj* : frío y húmedo
dapper ['dæpər] *adj* : pulcro, atildado
dappled ['dæpəld] *adj* : moteado <a dappled horse : un caballo rodado>
dare[1] ['dær] *v* **dared; daring** *vi* : osar, atreverse <how dare you! : ¡cómo te atreves!> — *vt* **1** CHALLENGE : desafiar, retar **2 to dare to do something** : atreverse a hacer algo, osar hacer algo
dare[2] *n* : desafío *m,* reto *m*
daredevil ['dær,dɛvəl] *n* : persona *f* temeraria
daring[1] ['dærɪŋ] *adj* : osado, atrevido, audaz
daring[2] *n* : arrojo *m,* coraje *m,* audacia *f*
dark ['dɑrk] *adj* **1** : oscuro (dícese del ambiente o de los colores), moreno (dícese del pelo o de la piel) **2** SOMBER : sombrío, triste
darken ['dɑrkən] *vt* **1** DIM : oscurecer **2** SADDEN : entristecer — *vi* : ensombrecerse, nublarse
darkly ['dɑrkli] *adv* **1** DIMLY : oscuramente **2** GLOOMILY : tristemente **3** MYSTERIOUSLY : misteriosamente, enigmáticamente
darkness ['dɑrknəs] *n* : oscuridad *f,* tinieblas *f*
darling[1] ['dɑrlɪŋ] *adj* **1** BELOVED : querido, amado **2** CHARMING : encantador, mono *fam*

darling[2] *n* **1** BELOVED : querido *m,* -da *f;* amado *m,* -da *f;* cariño *m,* -ña *f* **2** FAVORITE : preferido *m,* -da *f;* favorito *m,* -ta *f*
darn[1] ['dɑrn] *vt* : zurcir
darn[2] *n* **1** : zurcido *m* **2** → **damn**[3]
dart[1] ['dɑrt] *vt* THROW : lanzar, tirar — *vi* DASH : lanzarse, precipitarse
dart[2] *n* **1** : dardo *m* **2 darts** *npl* : juego *m* de dardos
dash[1] ['dæʃ] *vt* **1** SMASH : romper, estrellar **2** HURL : arrojar, lanzar **3** SPLASH : salpicar **4** FRUSTRATE : frustrar **5 to dash off** : hacer (algo) rápidamente — *vi* **1** SMASH : romperse, estrellarse **2** DART : lanzarse, irse apresuradamente
dash[2] *n* **1** BURST, SPLASH : arranque *m,* salpicadura *f* (de aguas) **2** : guión *m* largo (signo de puntuación) **3** DROP : gota *f,* pizca *f* **4** VERVE : brío *m* **5** RACE : carrera *f* <a 100-meter dash : una carrera de 100 metros> **6 to make a dash for it** : precipitarse (hacia), echarse a correr **7** → **dashboard**
dashboard ['dæʃˌbord] *n* : tablero *m* de instrumentos
dashing ['dæʃɪŋ] *adj* : gallardo, apuesto
data ['deɪt̬ə, 'dæ-, 'dɑ-] *ns & pl* : datos *mpl,* información *f*
database ['deɪt̬əˌbeɪs, 'dæ-, 'dɑ-] *n* : base *f* de datos
date[1] ['deɪt] *v* **dated; dating** *vt* **1** : fechar (una carta, etc.), datar (un objeto) <it was dated June 9 : estaba fechada el 9 de junio> **2** : salir con <she's dating my brother : sale con mi hermano> — *vi* : datar
date[2] *n* **1** : fecha *f* <to date : hasta la fecha> **2** EPOCH, PERIOD : época *f,* período *m* **3** APPOINTMENT : cita *f* **4** COMPANION : acompañante *mf* **5** : dátil *m* (fruta)
dated ['deɪt̬əd] *adj* OUT-OF-DATE : anticuado, pasado de moda
datum ['deɪt̬əm, 'dæ-, 'dɑ-] *n, pl* **-ta** [-t̬ə] *or* **-tums** : dato *m*
daub[1] ['dɔb] *vt* : embadurnar
daub[2] *n* : mancha *f*
daughter ['dɔt̬ər] *n* : hija *f*
daughter–in–law ['dɔt̬ərɪnˌlɔ] *n, pl* **daughters–in–law** : nuera *f,* hija *f* política
daunt ['dɔnt] *vt* : amilanar, acobardar, intimidar
dauntless ['dɔntləs] *adj* : intrépido, impávido
davenport ['dævənˌport] *n* : sofá *m*
dawdle ['dɔdəl] *vi* **-dled; -dling 1** DALLY : demorarse, entretenerse, perder tiempo **2** LOITER : vagar, holgazanear, haraganear
dawn[1] ['dɔn] *vi* **1** : amanecer, alborear, despuntar <Saturday dawned clear and bright : el sábado amaneció claro y luminoso> **2 to dawn on** : hacerse obvio <it dawned on me that she was right : me di cuenta de que tenía razón>
dawn[2] *n* **1** DAYBREAK : amanecer *m,* alba *f* **2** BEGINNING : albor *m,* comienzo *m* <the dawn of history : los albores de la historia> **3 from dawn to dusk** : de sol a sol
day ['deɪ] *n* **1** : día *m* **2** DATE : fecha *f* **3** TIME : día *m,* tiempo *m* <in olden days : antaño> **4** WORKDAY : jornada *f* laboral
daybreak ['deɪˌbreɪk] *n* : alba *f,* amanecer *m*
day care *n* : servicio *m* de guardería infantil
daydream[1] ['deɪˌdriːm] *vi* : soñar despierto, fantasear
daydream[2] *n* : ensueño *m,* ensoñación *f,* fantasía *f*
daylight ['deɪˌlaɪt] *n* **1** : luz *f* del día <in broad daylight : a plena luz del día> **2** → **daybreak 3** → **daytime**
daylight saving time *n* : hora *f* de verano
daytime ['deɪˌtaɪm] *n* : horas *fpl* diurnas, día *m*
daze[1] ['deɪz] *vt* **dazed; dazing 1** STUN : aturdir **2** DAZZLE : deslumbrar, ofuscar
daze[2] *n* **1** : aturdimiento *m* **2 in a daze** : aturdido, atonado
dazzle[1] ['dæzəl] *vt* **-zled; -zling** : deslumbrar, ofuscar
dazzle[2] *n* : resplandor *m,* brillo *m*
DDT [ˌdiːˌdiː'tiː] *n* : DDT *m*
deacon ['diːkən] *n* : diácono *m*
dead[1] ['dɛd] *adv* **1** ABRUPTLY : repentinamente, súbitamente <to stop dead : parar en seco> **2** ABSOLUTELY : absolutamente <I'm dead certain : estoy absolutamente seguro> **3** DIRECTLY : justo <dead ahead : justo adelante>
dead[2] *adj* **1** LIFELESS : muerto **2** NUMB : entumecido **3** INDIFFERENT : indiferente, frío **4** INACTIVE : inactivo <a dead volcano : un volcán inactivo> **5** : desconectado (dícese del teléfono), descargado (dícese de una batería) **6** EXHAUSTED : agotado, derrengado, muerto **7** OBSOLETE : obsoleto, muerto <a dead language : una lengua muerta> **8** EXACT : exacto <in the dead center : justo en el blanco>
dead[3] *n* **1 the dead** : los muertos **2 in the dead of night** : a las altas horas de la noche **3 in the dead of winter** : en pleno invierno
deadbeat ['dɛdˌbiːt] *n* **1** LOAFER : vago *m,* -ga *f;* holgazán *m,* -zana *f* **2** FREELOADER : gorrón *m,* -rrona *f fam;* gorrero *m,* -ra *f fam*
deaden ['dɛdən] *vt* **1** : atenuar (un dolor), entorpecer (sensaciones) **2** DULL : deslustrar **3** DISPIRIT : desanimar **4** MUFFLE : amortiguar, reducir (sonidos)
dead–end ['dɛd'ɛnd] *adj* **1** : sin salida <dead-end street : calle sin salida> **2** : sin futuro <a dead-end job : un trabajo sin porvenir>
dead end *n* : callejón *m* sin salida

dead heat *n* : empate *m*

deadline [ˈdɛdˌlaɪn] *n* : fecha *f* límite, fecha *f* tope, plazo *m* (determinado)

deadlock[1] [ˈdɛdˌlɑk] *vt* : estancar — *vi* : estancarse, llegar a punto muerto

deadlock[2] *n* : punto *m* muerto, impasse *m*

deadly[1] [ˈdɛdli] *adv* : extremadamente, sumamente <deadly serious : muy en serio>

deadly[2] *adj* **-lier; -est 1** LETHAL : mortal, letal, mortífero **2** ACCURATE : certero, preciso <a deadly aim : una puntería infalible> **3** CAPITAL : capital <the seven deadly sins : los siete pecados capitales> **4** DULL : funesto, aburrido **5** EXTREME : extremo, absoluto <a deadly calm : una calma absoluta>

deadpan[1] [ˈdɛdˌpæn] *adv* : de manera inexpresiva, sin expresión

deadpan[2] *adj* : inexpresivo, impasible

deaf [ˈdɛf] *adj* : sordo

deafen [ˈdɛfən] *vt* **-ened; -ening** : ensordecer

deaf–mute [ˈdɛfˈmjuːt] *n* : sordomudo *m,* -da *f*

deafness [ˈdɛfnəs] *n* : sordera *f*

deal[1] [ˈdiːl] *v* **dealt; dealing** *vt* **1** APPORTION : repartir <to deal justice : repartir la justicia> **2** DISTRIBUTE : repartir, dar (naipes) **3** DELIVER : asestar, propinar <to deal a blow : asestar un golpe> — *vi* **1** : dar, repartir (en juegos de naipes) **2 to deal in** : comerciar en, traficar con (drogas) **3 to deal with** CONCERN : tratar de, tener que ver con <the book deals with poverty : el libro trata de la pobreza> **4 to deal with** HANDLE : tratar (con), encargarse de **5 to deal with** TREAT : tratar <the judge dealt with him severely : el juez lo trató con severidad> **6 to deal with** ACCEPT : aceptar (una situación o desgracia)

deal[2] *n* **1** : reparto *m* (de naipes) **2** AGREEMENT, TRANSACTION : trato *m,* acuerdo *m,* transacción *f* **3** TREATMENT : trato *m* <he got a raw deal : le hicieron una injusticia> **4** BARGAIN : ganga *f,* oferta *f* **5 a good deal** *or* **a great deal** : mucho, una gran cantidad

dealer [ˈdiːlər] *n* : comerciante *mf,* traficante *mf*

dealings [ˈdiːlɪŋz] *npl* **1** : relaciones *fpl* (personales) **2** TRANSACTIONS : negocios *mpl,* transacciones *fpl*

dean [ˈdiːn] *n* **1** : deán *m* (del clero) **2** : decano *m,* -na *f* (de una facultad o profesión)

dear[1] [ˈdɪr] *adj* **1** ESTEEMED, LOVED : querido, estimado <a dear friend : un amigo querido> <Dear Sir : Estimado Señor> **2** COSTLY : caro, costoso

dear[2] *n* : querido *m,* -da *f;* amado *m,* -da *f*

dearly [ˈdɪrli] *adv* **1** : mucho <I love them dearly : los quiero mucho> **2** : caro <to pay dearly : pagar caro>

dearth [ˈdərθ] *n* : escasez *f,* carestía *f*

death [ˈdɛθ] *n* **1** : muerte *f,* fallecimiento *m* <to be the death of : matar> **2** FATALITY : víctima *f* (mortal); muerto *m,* -ta *f* **3** END : fin *m* <the death of civilization : el fin de la civilización>

deathbed [ˈdɛθˌbɛd] *n* : lecho *m* de muerte

deathblow [ˈdɛθˌbloː] *n* : golpe *m* mortal

deathless [ˈdɛθləs] *adj* : eterno, inmortal

deathly [ˈdɛθli] *adj* : de muerte, sepulcral (dícese del silencio), cadavérico (dícese de la palidez)

debacle [dɪˈbɑkəl, -ˈbæ-] *n* : desastre *m,* debacle *m,* fiasco *m*

debar [diˈbɑr] *vt* **-barred; -barring** : excluir, prohibir

debase [diˈbeɪs] *vt* **-based; -basing** : degradar, envilecer

debasement [diˈbeɪsmənt] *n* : degradación *f,* envilecimiento *m*

debatable [diˈbeɪtəbəl] *adj* : discutible

debate[1] [diˈbeɪt] *vt* **-bated; -bating** : debatir, discutir

debate[2] *n* : debate *m,* discusión *f*

debauch [diˈbɔtʃ] *vt* : pervertir, corromper

debauchery [diˈbɔtʃəri] *n, pl* **-eries** : libertinaje *m,* disipación *f,* intemperancia *f*

debilitate [diˈbɪləˌteɪt] *vt* **-tated; -tating** : debilitar

debility [diˈbɪləṱi] *n, pl* **-ties** : debilidad *f*

debit[1] [ˈdɛbɪt] *vt* : adeudar, cargar, debitar

debit[2] *n* : débito *m,* cargo *m,* debe *m*

debonair [ˌdɛbəˈnær] *adj* : elegante y desenvuelto, apuesto

debris [dəˈbriː, deɪ-; ˈdeɪˌbriː] *n, pl* **-bris** [-ˈbriːz, -ˌbriːz] **1** RUBBLE, RUINS : escombros *mpl,* ruinas *fpl,* restos *mpl* **2** RUBBISH : basura *f,* deshechos *mpl*

debt [ˈdɛt] *n* **1** : deuda *f* <to pay a debt : saldar una deuda> **2** INDEBTEDNESS : endeudamiento *m*

debtor [ˈdɛṱər] *n* : deudor *m,* -dora *f*

debunk [diˈbʌŋk] *vt* DISCREDIT : desacreditar, desprestigiar

debut[1] [deɪˈbjuː, ˈdeɪˌbjuː] *vi* : debutar

debut[2] *n* **1** : debut *m* (de un actor), estreno *m* (de una obra) **2** : debut *m,* presentación *f* (en sociedad)

debutante [ˈdɛbjʊˌtɑnt] *n* : debutante *f*

decade [ˈdɛˌkeɪd, dɛˈkeɪd] *n* : década *f*

decadence [ˈdɛkədənts] *n* : decadencia *f*

decadent [ˈdɛkədənt] *adj* : decadente

decal [ˈdiːˌkæl, diˈkæl] *n* : calcomanía *f*

decamp [di'kæmp] *vi* : irse, largarse *fam*

decant [di'kænt] *vt* : decantar

decanter [di'kæntər] *n* : licorera *f,* garrafa *f*

decapitate [di'kæpə,teɪt] *vt* **-tated; -tating** : decapitar

decay[1] [di'keɪ] *vi* **1** DECOMPOSE : descomponerse, pudrirse **2** DETERIORATE : deteriorarse **3** : cariarse (dícese de los dientes)

decay[2] *n* **1** DECOMPOSITION : descomposición *f* **2** DECLINE, DETERIORATION : decadencia *f,* deterioro *m* **3** : caries *f* (de los dientes)

decease[1] [di'si:s] *vi* **-ceased; -ceasing** : morir, fallecer

decease[2] *n* : fallecimiento *m,* defunción *f,* deceso *m*

deceit [di'si:t] *n* **1** DECEPTION : engaño *m* **2** DISHONESTY : deshonestidad *f*

deceitful [di'si:tfəl] *adj* : falso, embustero, engañoso, mentiroso

deceitfully [di'si:tfəli] *adv* : con engaño, con falsedad

deceitfulness [di'si:tfəlnəs] *n* : falsedad *f,* engaño *m*

deceive [di'si:v] *vt* **-ceived; -ceiving** : engañar, burlar

deceiver [di'si:vər] *n* : impostor *m,* -tora *f*

decelerate [di'sɛlə,reɪt] *vi* **-ated; -ating** : reducir la velocidad, desacelerar

December [di'sɛmbər] *n* : diciembre *m*

decency ['disəntsi] *n, pl* **-cies** : decencia *f,* decoro *m*

decent ['di:sənt] *adj* **1** CORRECT, PROPER : decente, decoroso, correcto **2** CLOTHED : vestido, presentable **3** MODEST : púdico, modesto **4** ADEQUATE : decente, adecuado <decent wages : paga adecuada>

decently ['di:səntli] *adv* : decentemente

deception [di'sɛpʃən] *n* : engaño *m*

deceptive [di'sɛptɪv] *adj* : engañoso, falaz — **deceptively** *adv*

decibel ['dɛsəbəl, -,bɛl] *n* : decibelio *m*

decide [di'saɪd] *v* **-cided; -ciding** *vt* **1** CONCLUDE : decidir, llegar a la conclusión de <he decided what to do : decidió qué iba a hacer> **2** DETERMINE : decidir, determinar <one blow decided the fight : un solo golpe determinó la pelea> **3** CONVINCE : decidir <her pleas decided me to help : sus súplicas me decidieron a ayudarla> **4** RESOLVE : resolver — *vi* : decidirse

decided [di'saɪdəd] *adj* **1** UNQUESTIONABLE : indudable **2** RESOLUTE : decidido, resuelto — **decidedly** *adv*

deciduous [di'sɪdʒʊəs] *adj* : caduco, de hoja caduca

decimal[1] ['dɛsəməl] *adj* : decimal

decimal[2] *n* : número *m* decimal

decipher [di'saɪfər] *vt* : descifrar — **decipherable** [-əbəl] *adj*

decision [dɪ'sɪʒən] *n* : decisión *f,* determinación *f* <to make a decision : tomar una decisión>

decisive [dɪ'saɪsɪv] *adj* **1** DECIDING : decisivo <the decisive vote : el voto decisivo> **2** CONCLUSIVE : decisivo, concluyente, contundente <a decisive victory : una victoria contundente> **3** RESOLUTE : decidido, resuelto, firme

decisively [dɪ'saɪsɪvli] *adv* : con decisión, de manera decisiva

decisiveness [dɪ'saɪsɪvnəs] *n* **1** FORCEFULNESS : contundencia *f* **2** RESOLUTION : firmeza *f,* decisión *f,* determinación *f*

deck[1] ['dɛk] *vt* **1** FLOOR : tumbar, derribar <she decked him with one blow : lo tumbó de un solo golpe> **2 to deck out** : adornar, engalanar

deck[2] *n* **1** : cubierta *f* (de un barco) **2** *or* **deck of cards** : baraja *f* (de naipes)

declaim [di'kleɪm] *v* : declamar

declaration [,dɛklə'reɪʃən] *n* : declaración *f,* pronunciamiento *m* (oficial)

declare [di'klær] *vt* **-clared; -claring** : declarar, manifestar <to declare war : declarar la guerra> <they declared their support : manifestaron su apoyo>

decline[1] [di'klaɪn] *v* **-clined; -clining** *vi* **1** DESCEND : descender **2** DETERIORATE : deteriorarse, decaer <her health is declining : su salud se está deteriorando> **3** DECREASE : disminuir, decrecer, decaer **4** REFUSE : rehusar — *vt* **1** INFLECT : declinar **2** REFUSE, TURN DOWN : declinar, rehusar

decline[2] *n* **1** DETERIORATION : decadencia *f,* deterioro *m* **2** DECREASE : disminución *f,* descenso *m* **3** SLOPE : declive *m,* pendiente *f*

decode [di'ko:d] *vt* **-coded; -coding** : descifrar (un mensaje), descodificar (una señal)

decompose [,di:kəm'po:z] *v* **-posed; -posing** *vt* **1** BREAK DOWN : descomponer **2** ROT : descomponer, pudrir — *vi* : descomponerse, pudrirse

decomposition [,di:,kɑmpə'zɪʃən] *n* : descomposición *f*

decongestant [,di:kən'dʒɛstənt] *n* : descongestionante *m*

decor *or* **décor** [deɪ'kɔr, 'deɪ,kɔr] *n* : decoración *f*

decorate ['dɛkə,reɪt] *vt* **-rated; -rating 1** ADORN : decorar, adornar **2** : condecorar <he was decorated for bravery : lo condecoraron por valor>

decoration [,dɛkə'reɪʃən] *n* **1** ADORNMENT : decoración *f,* adorno *m* **2** : condecoración *f* (de honor)

decorative ['dɛkərət̬ɪv, -,reɪ-] *adj* : decorativo, ornamental, de adorno

decorator ['dɛkə,reɪt̬ər] *n* : decorador *m,* -dora *f*

decorum [di'korəm] *n* : decoro *m*

decoy[1] [ˈdiːˌkɔɪ, diˈ-] *vt* : atraer (con señuelo)
decoy[2] *n* : señuelo *m,* reclamo *m,* cimbel *m*
decrease[1] [diˈkriːs] *v* **-creased; -creasing** *vi* : decrecer, disminuir, bajar — *vt* : reducir, disminuir
decrease[2] [ˈdiːˌkriːs] *n* : disminución *f,* descenso *m,* bajada *f*
decree[1] [diˈkriː] *vt* **-creed; -creeing** : decretar
decree[2] *n* : decreto *m*
decrepit [diˈkrɛpɪt] *adj* **1** FEEBLE : decrépito, débil **2** DILAPIDATED : deteriorado, ruinoso
decry [diˈkraɪ] *vt* **-cried; -crying** : censurar, criticar
dedicate [ˈdɛdɪˌkeɪt] *vt* **-cated; -cating** **1** : dedicar <she dedicated the book to Carlos : le dedicó el libro a Carlos> **2** : consagrar, dedicar <to dedicate one's life : consagrar uno su vida>
dedication [ˌdɛdɪˈkeɪʃən] *n* **1** DEVOTION : dedicación *f,* devoción *f* **2** : dedicatoria *f* (de un libro, una canción, etc.) **3** CONSECRATION : dedicación *f*
deduce [diˈduːs, -ˈdjuːs] *vt* **-duced; -ducing** : deducir, inferir
deduct [diˈdʌkt] *vt* : deducir, descontar, restar
deductible [diˈdʌktəbəl] *adj* : deducible
deduction [diˈdʌkʃən] *n* : deducción *f*
deed[1] [ˈdiːd] *vt* : ceder, transferir
deed[2] *n* **1** ACT : acto *m,* acción *f,* hecho *m* <a good deed : una buena acción> **2** FEAT : hazaña *f,* proeza *f* **3** TITLE : escritura *f,* título *m*
deem [ˈdiːm] *vt* : considerar, juzgar
deep[1] [ˈdiːp] *adv* : hondo, profundamente <to dig deep : cavar hondo>
deep[2] *adj* **1** : hondo, profundo <the deep end : la parte honda> <a deep wound : una herida profunda> **2** WIDE : ancho **3** INTENSE : profundo, intenso **4** DARK : intenso, subido <deep red : rojo subido> **5** LOW : profundo <a deep tone : un tono profundo> **6** ABSORBED : absorto <deep in thought : absorto en la meditación>
deep[3] *n* **1 the deep** : lo profundo, el piélago **2 the deep of night** : lo más profundo de la noche
deepen [ˈdiːpən] *vt* **1** : ahondar, profundizar **2** INTENSIFY : intensificar — *vi* **1** : hacerse más profundo **2** INTENSIFY : intensificarse
deeply [ˈdiːpli] *adv* : hondo, profundamente <I'm deeply sorry : lo siento sinceramente>
deep–seated [ˈdiːpˈsiːtəd] *adj* : profundamente arraigado, enraizado
deer [ˈdɪr] *ns & pl* : ciervo *m,* venado *m*
deerskin [ˈdɪrˌskɪn] *n* : piel *f* de venado
deface [diˈfeɪs] *vt* **-faced; -facing** MAR : desfigurar
defacement [diˈfeɪsmənt] *n* : desfiguración *f*
defamation [ˌdɛfəˈmeɪʃən] *n* : difamación *f*
defamatory [diˈfæməˌtori] *adj* : difamatorio
defame [diˈfeɪm] *vt* **-famed; -faming** : difamar, calumniar
default[1] [diˈfɔlt, ˈdiːˌfɔlt] *vi* **1** : no cumplir (con una obligación), no pagar **2** : no presentarse (en un tribunal)
default[2] *n* **1** NEGLECT : omisión *f,* negligencia *f* **2** NONPAYMENT : impago *m,* falta *f* de pago **3 to win by default** : ganar por abandono
defaulter [diˈfɔltər] *n* : moroso *m,* -sa *f;* rebelde *mf* (en un tribunal)
defeat[1] [diˈfiːt] *vt* **1** FRUSTRATE : frustrar **2** BEAT : vencer, derrotar
defeat[2] *n* : derrota *f,* rechazo *m* (de legislación), fracaso *m* (de planes, etc.)
defecate [ˈdɛfɪˌkeɪt] *vi* **-cated; -cating** : defecar
defect[1] [diˈfɛkt] *vi* : desertar
defect[2] [ˈdiːˌfɛkt, diˈfɛkt] *n* : defecto *m*
defection [diˈfɛkʃən] *n* : deserción *f,* defección *f*
defective [diˈfɛktɪv] *adj* **1** FAULTY : defectuoso **2** DEFICIENT : deficiente
defector [diˈfɛktər] *n* : desertor *m,* -tora *f*
defend [diˈfɛnd] *vt* : defender
defendant [diˈfɛndənt] *n* : acusado *m,* -da *f;* demandado *m,* -da *f*
defender [diˈfɛndər] *n* **1** ADVOCATE : defensor *m,* -sora *f* **2** : defensa *mf* (en deportes)
defense [diˈfɛnts, ˈdiːˌfɛnts] *n* : defensa *f*
defenseless [diˈfɛntsləs] *adj* : indefenso
defensive[1] [diˈfɛntsɪv] *adj* : defensivo
defensive[2] *n* **on the defensive** : a la defensiva
defer [diˈfər] *v* **-ferred; -ferring** *vt* POSTPONE : diferir, aplazar, posponer — *vi* **to defer to** : deferir a
deference [ˈdɛfərənts] *n* : deferencia *f*
deferential [ˌdɛfəˈrɛntʃəl] *adj* : respetuoso
deferment [diˈfərmənt] *n* : aplazamiento *m*
defiance [diˈfaɪənts] *n* : desafío *m*
defiant [diˈfaɪənt] *adj* : desafiante, insolente
deficiency [diˈfɪʃəntsi] *n, pl* **-cies** : deficiencia *f,* carencia *f*
deficient [diˈfɪʃənt] *adj* : deficiente, carente
deficit [ˈdɛfəsɪt] *n* : déficit *m*
defile [diˈfaɪl] *vt* **-filed; -filing** **1** DIRTY : ensuciar, manchar **2** CORRUPT : corromper **3** DESECRATE, PROFANE : profanar **4** DISHONOR : deshonrar
defilement [diˈfaɪlmənt] *n* **1** DESECRATION : profanación *f* **2** CORRUPTION

: corrupción *f* **3** CONTAMINATION : contaminación *f*
define [di'faɪn] *vt* **-fined; -fining 1** BOUND : delimitar, demarcar **2** CLARIFY : aclarar, definir **3** : definir <to define a word : definir una palabra>
definite ['dɛfənɪt] *adj* **1** CERTAIN : definido, determinado **2** CLEAR : claro, explícito **3** UNQUESTIONABLE : seguro, incuestionable
definite article *n* : artículo *m* definido
definitely ['dɛfənɪtli] *adv* **1** DOUBTLESSLY : indudablemente, sin duda **2** DEFINITIVELY : definitivamente, seguramente
definition [ˌdɛfə'nɪʃən] *n* : definición *f*
definitive [di'fɪnət̬ɪv] *adj* **1** CONCLUSIVE : definitivo, decisivo **2** AUTHORITATIVE : de autoridad, autorizado
deflate [di'fleɪt] *v* **-flated; -flating** *vt* **1** : desinflar (una llanta, etc.) **2** REDUCE : rebajar <to deflate one's ego : bajarle los humos a uno> — *vi* : desinflarse
deflect [di'flɛkt] *vt* : desviar — *vi* : desviarse
defoliant [di'foːliənt] *n* : defoliante *m*
deform [di'fɔrm] *vt* : deformar
deformed [di'fɔrmd] *adj* : deforme
deformity [di'fɔrmət̬i] *n, pl* **-ties** : deformidad *f*
defraud [di'frɔd] *vt* : estafar, defraudar
defray [di'freɪ] *vt* : sufragar, costear
defrost [di'frɔst] *vt* : descongelar, deshelar — *vi* : descongelarse, deshelarse
deft ['dɛft] *adj* : hábil, diestro — **deftly** *adv*
defunct [di'fʌŋkt] *adj* **1** DECEASED : difunto, fallecido **2** EXTINCT : extinto, fenecido
defy [di'faɪ] *vt* **-fied; -fying 1** CHALLENGE : desafiar, retar **2** DISOBEY : desobedecer **3** RESIST : resistir, hacer imposible, hacer inútil
degenerate[1] [di'dʒɛnəˌreɪt] *vi* **-ated; -ating** : degenerar
degenerate[2] [di'dʒɛnərət] *adj* : degenerado
degeneration [diˌdʒɛnə'reɪʃən] *n* : degeneración *f*
degradation [ˌdɛgrə'deɪʃən] *n* : degradación *f*
degrade [di'greɪd] *vt* **-graded; -grading 1** : degradar, envilecer **2 to degrade oneself** : rebajarse
degree [di'griː] *n* **1** EXTENT : grado *m* <a third degree burn : una quemadura de tercer grado> **2** : título *m* (de enseñanza superior) **3** : grado *m* (de un círculo, de la temperatura) **4 by degrees** : gradualmente, poco a poco
dehydrate [di'haɪˌdreɪt] *v* **-drated; -drating** *vt* : deshidratar — *vi* : deshidratarse
dehydration [ˌdiːhaɪ'dreɪʃən] *n* : deshidratación *f*
deice [ˌdiː'aɪs] *vt* **-iced; -icing** : deshelar, descongelar
deify ['diːəˌfaɪ, 'deɪ-] *vt* **-fied; -fying** : deificar
deign ['deɪn] *vi* : dignarse, condescender
deity ['diːət̬i, 'deɪ-] *n, pl* **-ties 1 the Deity** : Dios *m* **2** GOD, GODDESS : deidad *f;* dios *m,* diosa *f*
dejected [di'dʒɛktəd] *adj* : abatido, desalentado, desanimado
dejection [di'dʒɛkʃən] *n* : abatimiento *m,* desaliento *m,* desánimo *m*
delay[1] [di'leɪ] *vt* **1** POSTPONE : posponer, postergar **2** HOLD UP : retrasar, demorar — *vi* : tardar, demorar
delay[2] *n* **1** LATENESS : tardanza *f* **2** HOLDUP : demora *f,* retraso *m*
delectable [di'lɛktəbəl] *adj* **1** DELICIOUS : delicioso, exquisito **2** DELIGHTFUL : encantador
delegate[1] ['dɛlɪˌgeɪt] *v* **-gated; -gating** : delegar
delegate[2] ['dɛlɪgət, -ˌgeɪt] *n* : delegado *m,* -da *f*
delegation [ˌdɛlɪ'geɪʃən] *n* : delegación *f*
delete [di'liːt] *vt* **-leted; -leting** : suprimir, tachar, eliminar
deletion [di'liːʃən] *n* : supresión *f,* tachadura *f,* eliminación *f*
deliberate[1] [dɪ'lɪbəˌreɪt] *v* **-ated; -ating** *vt* : deliberar sobre, reflexionar sobre, considerar — *vi* : deliberar
deliberate[2] [dɪ'lɪbərət] *adj* **1** CONSIDERED : reflexionado, premeditado **2** INTENTIONAL : deliberado, intencional **3** SLOW : lento, pausado
deliberately [dɪ'lɪbərətli] *adv* **1** INTENTIONALLY : adrede, a propósito **2** SLOWLY : pausadamente, lentamente
deliberation [dɪˌlɪbə'reɪʃən] *n* **1** CONSIDERATION : deliberación *f,* consideración *f* **2** SLOWNESS : lentitud *f*
delicacy ['dɛlɪkəsi] *n, pl* **-cies 1** : manjar *m,* exquisitez *f* <caviar is a real delicacy : el caviar es un verdadero manjar> **2** FINENESS : delicadeza *f* **3** FRAGILITY : fragilidad *f*
delicate ['dɛlɪkət] *adj* **1** SUBTLE : delicado <a delicate fragrance : una fragancia delicada> **2** DAINTY : delicado, primoroso, fino **3** FRAGILE : frágil **4** SENSITIVE : delicado <a delicate matter : un asunto delicado>
delicately ['dɛlɪkətli] *adv* : delicadamente, con delicadeza
delicatessen [ˌdɛlɪkə'tɛsən] *n* : charcutería *f,* fiambrería *f,* salchichonería *f Mex*
delicious [di'lɪʃəs] *adj* : delicioso, exquisito, rico — **deliciously** *adv*
delight[1] [dɪ'laɪt] *vt* : deleitar, encantar — *vi* **to delight in** : deleitarse con, complacerse en
delight[2] *n* **1** JOY : placer *m,* deleite *m,* gozo *m* **2** : encanto *m* <your garden is a delight : su jardín es un encanto>

delightful [dɪˈlaɪtfəl] *adj* : delicioso, encantador

delightfully [dɪˈlaɪtfəli] *adv* : de manera encantadora, de maravilla

delineate [diˈlɪni,eɪt] *vt* **-eated; -eating** : delinear, trazar, bosquejar

delinquency [diˈlɪŋkwən*t*si] *n, pl* **-cies** : delincuencia *f*

delinquent[1] [diˈlɪŋkwənt] *adj* **1** : delincuente **2** OVERDUE : vencido y sin pagar, moroso

delinquent[2] *n* : delincuente *mf* <juvenile delinquent : delincuente juvenil>

delirious [diˈlɪriəs] *adj* : delirante <delirious with joy : loco de alegría>

delirium [diˈlɪriəm] *n* : delirio *m,* desvarío *m*

deliver [diˈlɪvər] *vt* **1** FREE : liberar, librar **2** DISTRIBUTE, HAND : entregar, repartir **3** : asistir en el parto de (un niño) **4** : pronunciar <to deliver a speech : pronunciar un discurso> **5** PROJECT : despachar, lanzar <he delivered a fast ball : lanzó un pelota rápida> **6** DEAL : propinar, asestar <to deliver a blow : asestar un golpe>

deliverance [diˈlɪvərən*t*s] *n* : liberación *f,* rescate *m,* salvación *f*

deliverer [diˈlɪvərər] *n* RESCUER : libertador *m,* -dora *f;* salvador *m,* -dora *f*

delivery [diˈlɪvəri] *n, pl* **-eries 1** LIBERATION : liberación *f* **2** : entrega *f,* reparto *m* <cash on delivery : entrega contra reembolso> <home delivery : servicio a domicilio> **3** CHILDBIRTH : parto *m,* alumbramiento *m* **4** SPEECH : expresión *f* oral, modo *m* de hablar **5** THROW : lanzamiento *m*

dell [ˈdɛl] *n* : hondonada *f,* valle *m* pequeño

delta [ˈdɛltə] *n* : delta *m*

delude [diˈluːd] *vt* **-luded; -luding 1** : engañar **2 to delude oneself** : engañarse

deluge[1] [ˈdɛl,juːdʒ, -,juːʒ] *vt* **-uged; -uging 1** FLOOD : inundar **2** OVERWHELM : abrumar <deluged with requests : abrumado de pedidos>

deluge[2] *n* **1** FLOOD : inundación *f* **2** DOWNPOUR : aguacero *m* **3** BARRAGE : aluvión *m*

delusion [diˈluːʒən] *n* **1** : ilusión *f* (falsa) **2 delusions of grandeur** : delirios *mpl* de grandeza

deluxe [diˈlʌks, -ˈlʊks] *adj* : de lujo

delve [ˈdɛlv] *vi* **delved; delving 1** DIG : escarbar **2 to delve into** PROBE : cavar en, ahondar en

demand[1] [diˈmænd] *vt* : demandar, exigir, reclamar

demand[2] *n* **1** REQUEST : petición *f,* pedido *m,* demanda *f* <by popular demand : a petición del público> **2** CLAIM : reclamación *f,* exigencia *f* **3** MARKET : demanda *f* <supply and demand : la oferta y la demanda>

demarcation [,diː,mɑrˈkeɪʃən] *n* : demarcación *f,* deslinde *m*

demean [diˈmiːn] *vt* : degradar, rebajar

demeanor [diˈmiːnər] *n* : comportamiento *m,* conducta *f*

demented [diˈmɛntəd] *adj* : demente, loco

demerit [diˈmɛrət] *n* : demérito *m*

demigod [ˈdɛmi,gɑd, -,gɔd] *n* : semidiós *m*

demise [dɪˈmaɪz] *n* **1** DEATH : fallecimiento *m,* deceso *m* **2** END : hundimiento *m,* desaparición *f* (de una institución, etc.)

demitasse [ˈdɛmi,tæs, -,tɑs] *n* : taza *f* pequeña (de café)

demobilization [di,moːbələˈzeɪʃən] *n* : desmovilización *f*

demobilize [diˈmoːbə,laɪz] *vt* **-lized; -lizing** : desmovilizar

democracy [diˈmɑkrəsi] *n, pl* **-cies** : democracia *f*

democrat [ˈdɛmə,kræt] *n* : demócrata *mf*

democratic [,dɛməˈkræt̬ɪk] *adj* : democrático — **democratically** [-t̬ɪkli] *adv*

demolish [diˈmɑlɪʃ] *vt* **1** RAZE : demoler, derribar, arrasar **2** DESTROY : destruir, destrozar

demolition [,dɛməˈlɪʃən, ,diː-] *n* : demolición *f,* derribo *m*

demon [ˈdiːmən] *n* : demonio *m,* diablo *m*

demonstrably [diˈmɑn*t*strəbli] *adv* : manifiestamente, claramente

demonstrate [ˈdɛmən,streɪt] *vt* **-strated; -strating 1** SHOW : demostrar **2** PROVE : probar, demostrar **3** EXPLAIN : explicar, ilustrar

demonstration [,dɛmənˈstreɪʃən] *n* **1** SHOW : muestra *f,* demostración *f* **2** RALLY : manifestación *f*

demonstrative [diˈmɑn*t*strət̬ɪv] *adj* **1** EFFUSIVE : efusivo, expresivo, demostrativo **2** : demostrativo (en lingüística) <demonstrative pronoun : pronombre demostrativo>

demonstrator [ˈdɛmən,streɪt̬ər] *n* **1** : demostrador *m,* -dora *f* (de productos) **2** PROTESTER : manifestante *mf*

demoralize [diˈmɔrə,laɪz] *vt* **-ized; -izing** : desmoralizar

demote [diˈmoːt] *vt* **-moted; -moting** : degradar, bajar de categoría

demotion [diˈmoːʃən] *n* : degradación *f,* descenso *m* de categoría

demur [diˈmər] *vi* **-murred; -murring 1** OBJECT : oponerse **2 to demur at** : ponerle objeciones a (algo)

demure [diˈmjʊr] *adj* : recatado, modesto — **demurely** *adv*

den [ˈdɛn] *n* **1** LAIR : cubil *m,* madriguera *f* **2** HIDEOUT : guarida *f* **3** STUDY : estudio *m,* gabinete *m*

denature [diˈneɪtʃər] *vt* **-tured; -turing** : desnaturalizar

denial [diˈnaɪəl] *n* **1** REFUSAL : rechazo *m,* denegación *f,* negativa *f* **2** REPUDIATION : negación *f* (de una creencia, etc.), rechazo *m*

denim [ˈdɛnəm] *n* **1 :** tela *f* vaquera, mezclilla *f Chile, Mex* **2 denims** *npl* → **jeans**
denizen [ˈdɛnəzən] *n* **:** habitante *mf;* morador *m,* -dora *f*
denomination [dɪˌnɑməˈneɪʃən] *n* **1** FAITH **:** confesión *f,* fe *f* **2** VALUE **:** denominación *f,* valor *m* (de una moneda)
denominator [dɪˈnɑməˌneɪt̬ər] *n* **:** denominador *m*
denote [diˈnoːt] *vt* **-noted; -noting 1** INDICATE, MARK **:** indicar, denotar, señalar **2** MEAN **:** significar
denouement [ˌdeɪˌnuːˈmɑ] *n* **:** desenlace *m*
denounce [diˈnaʊnts] *vt* **-nounced; -nouncing 1** CENSURE **:** denunciar, censurar **2** ACCUSE **:** denunciar, acusar, delatar
dense [ˈdɛnts] *adj* **denser; -est 1** THICK **:** espeso, denso <dense vegetation : vegetación densa> <a dense fog : una niebla espesa> **2** STUPID **:** estúpido, burro *fam*
densely [ˈdɛntsli] *adv* **1** THICKLY **:** densamente **2** STUPIDLY **:** torpemente
denseness [ˈdɛntsnəs] *n* **1** → **density 2** STUPIDITY **:** estupidez *f*
density [ˈdɛntsət̬i] *n, pl* **-ties :** densidad *f*
dent[1] [ˈdɛnt] *vt* **:** abollar, mellar
dent[2] *n* **:** abolladura *f,* mella *f*
dental [ˈdɛntəl] *adj* **:** dental
dental floss *n* **:** hilo *m* dental
dentifrice [ˈdɛntəfrɪs] *n* **:** dentífrico *m,* pasta *f* de dientes
dentist [ˈdɛntɪst] *n* **:** dentista *mf*
dentistry [ˈdɛntɪstri] *n* **:** odontología *f*
dentures [ˈdɛntʃərz] *npl* **:** dentadura *f* postiza
denude [diˈnuːd, -ˈnjuːd] *vt* **-nuded; -nuding** STRIP **:** desnudar, despojar
denunciation [diˌnʌntsiˈeɪʃən] *n* **:** denuncia *f,* acusación *f*
deny [diˈnaɪ] *vt* **-nied; -nying 1** REFUTE **:** desmentir, negar **2** DISOWN, REPUDIATE **:** negar, renegar de **3** REFUSE **:** denegar **4 to deny oneself :** privarse, sacrificarse
deodorant [diˈoːdərənt] *n* **:** desodorante *m*
deodorize [diˈoːdəˌraɪz] *vt* **-ized; -izing :** desodorizar
depart [diˈpɑrt] *vt* **:** salirse de — *vi* **1** LEAVE **:** salir, partir, irse **2** DIE **:** morir
department [diˈpɑrtmənt] *n* **1** DIVISION **:** sección *f* (de una tienda, una organización, etc.), departamento *m* (de una empresa, una universidad, etc.), ministerio *m* (del gobierno) **2** PROVINCE, SPHERE **:** esfera *f,* campo *m,* competencia *f*
departmental [diˌpɑrtˈmɛntəl, ˌdiː-] *adj* **:** departamental
department store *n* **:** grandes almacenes *mpl*
departure [diˈpɑrtʃər] *n* **1** LEAVING **:** salida *f,* partida *f* **2** DEVIATION **:** desviación *f*
depend [diˈpɛnd] *vi* **1** RELY **:** contar (con), confiar (en) <depend on me! : ¡cuenta conmigo!> **2 to depend on :** depender de <success depends on hard work : el éxito depende de trabajar duro> **3 that depends :** según, eso depende
dependable [diˈpɛndəbəl] *adj* **:** responsable, digno de confianza, fiable
dependence [diˈpɛndənts] *n* **:** dependencia *f*
dependency [diˈpɛndəntsi] *n, pl* **-cies 1** → **dependence 2 :** posesión *f* (de una unidad política)
dependent[1] [diˈpɛndənt] *adj* **:** dependiente
dependent[2] *n* **:** persona *f* a cargo de alguien
depict [diˈpɪkt] *vt* **1** PORTRAY **:** representar **2** DESCRIBE **:** describir
depiction [diˈpɪkʃən] *n* **:** representación *f,* descripción *f*
deplete [diˈpliːt] *vt* **-pleted; -pleting 1** EXHAUST **:** agotar **2** REDUCE **:** reducir
depletion [diˈpliːʃən] *n* **1** EXHAUSTION **:** agotamiento *m* **2** REDUCTION **:** reducción *f,* disminución *f*
deplorable [diˈplorəbəl] *adj* **1** CONTEMPTIBLE **:** deplorable, despreciable **2** LAMENTABLE **:** lamentable
deplore [diˈplor] *vt* **-plored; -ploring 1** REGRET **:** deplorar, lamentar **2** CONDEMN **:** condenar, deplorar
deploy [diˈplɔɪ] *vt* **:** desplegar
deployment [diˈplɔɪmənt] *n* **:** despliegue *m*
deport [diˈport] *vt* **1** EXPEL **:** deportar, expulsar (de un país) **2 to deport oneself** BEHAVE **:** comportarse
deportment [diˈportmənt] *n* **:** conducta *f,* comportamiento *f*
depose [diˈpoːz] *v* **-posed; -posing** *vt* **:** deponer
deposit[1] [diˈpɑzət] *vt* **-ited; -iting :** depositar
deposit[2] *n* **1 :** depósito *m* (en el banco) **2** DOWN PAYMENT **:** entrega *f* inicial **3 :** depósito *m,* yacimiento *m* (en geología)
depositor [diˈpɑzət̬ər] *n* **:** depositante *mf*
depository [diˈpɑzəˌtori] *n, pl* **-ries :** almacén *m,* depósito *m*
depot [*in sense 1 usu* ˈdɛˌpoː, *2 usu* ˈdiː-] *n* **1** STOREHOUSE **:** almacén *m,* depósito *m* **2** STATION, TERMINAL **:** terminal *mf,* estación *f* (de autobuses, ferrocarriles, etc.)
deprave [diˈpreɪv] *vt* **-praved; -praving :** depravar, pervertir
depraved [diˈpreɪvd] *adj* **:** depravado, degenerado
depravity [diˈprævət̬i] *n, pl* **-ties :** depravación *f*
depreciate [diˈpriːʃiˌeɪt] *v* **-ated; -ating** *vt* **1** DEVALUE **:** depreciar, de-

valuar 2 DISPARAGE : menospreciar, despreciar — *vi* : depreciarse, devaluarse
depreciation [di,pri:ʃi'eɪʃən] *n* : depreciación *f,* devaluación *f*
depress [di'prɛs] *vt* **1** PRESS, PUSH : apretar, presionar, pulsar **2** REDUCE : reducir, hacer bajar (precios, ventas, etc.) **3** SADDEN : deprimir, abatir, entristecer **4** DEVALUE : depreciar
depressant[1] [di'prɛsənt] *adj* : depresivo
depressant[2] *n* : depresivo *m*
depressed [di'prɛst] *adj* **1** DEJECTED : deprimido, abatido **2** : deprimido, en crisis (dícese de la economía)
depressing [di'prɛsɪŋ] *adj* : deprimente, triste
depression [di'prɛʃən] *n* **1** DESPONDENCY : depresión *f,* abatimiento *m* **2** : depresión (en una superficie) **3** RECESSION : depresión *f* económica, crisis *f*
deprivation [,dɛprə'veɪʃən] *n* : privación *f*
deprive [di'praɪv] *vt* **-prived; -priving** : privar
depth ['dɛpθ] *n, pl* **depths** ['dɛpθs, 'dɛps] : profundidad *f,* fondo *m* <to study in depth : estudiar a fondo> <in the depths of winter : en pleno invierno>
deputize ['dɛpjʊ,taɪz] *vt* **-tized; -tizing** : nombrar como segundo
deputy ['dɛpjʊṭi] *n, pl* **-ties** : suplente *mf;* sustituto *m,* -ta *f*
derail [di'reɪl] *v* : descarrilar
derailment [di'reɪlmənt] *n* : descarrilamiento *m*
derange [di'reɪndʒ] *vt* **-ranged; -ranging 1** DISARRANGE : desarreglar, desordenar **2** DISTURB, UPSET : trastornar, perturbar **3** MADDEN : enloquecer, volver loco
derangement [di'reɪndʒmənt] *n* **1** DISTURBANCE, UPSET : trastorno *m* **2** INSANITY : locura *f,* perturbación *f* mental
derby ['dərbi] *n, pl* **-bies 1** : derby *m* <the Kentucky Derby : el Derby de Kentucky> **2** : sombrero *m* hongo
deregulate [di'rɛgjʊ,leɪt] *vt* **-lated; -lating** : desregular
deregulation [di,rɛgjʊ'leɪʃən] *n* : desregularización *f*
derelict[1] ['dɛrə,lɪkt] *adj* **1** ABANDONED : abandonado, en ruinas **2** REMISS : negligente, remiso
derelict[2] *n* **1** : propiedad *f* abandonada **2** VAGRANT : vagabundo *m,* -da *f*
deride [di'raɪd] *vt* **-rided; -riding** : ridiculizar, burlarse de
derision [di'rɪʒən] *n* : escarnio *m,* irrisión *f,* mofa *f*
derisive [di'raɪsɪv] *adj* : burlón
derivative[1] [di'rɪvəṭɪv] *adj* **1** DERIVED : derivado **2** BANAL : carente de originalidad, banal
derivative[2] *n* : derivado *m*
derive [di'raɪv] *v* **-rived; -riving** *vt* **1** OBTAIN : obtener, sacar **2** DEDUCE : deducir, inferir — *vi* : provenir, derivar, proceder
dermatologist [,dərmə'tɑlədʒɪst] *n* : dermatólogo *m,* -ga *f*
dermatology [,dərmə'tɑlədʒi] *n* : dermatología *f*
derogatory [di'rɑgə,tori] *adj* : despectivo, despreciativo
derrick ['dɛrɪk] *n* **1** CRANE : grúa *f* **2** : torre *f* de perforación (sobre un pozo de petróleo)
descend [di'sɛnd] *vt* : descender, bajar — *vi* **1** : descender, bajar <he descended from the platform : descendió del estrado> **2** DERIVE : descender, provenir **3** STOOP : rebajarse <I descended to his level : me rebajé a su nivel> **4 to descend upon** : caer sobre, invadir
descendant[1] [di'sɛndənt] *adj* : descendente
descendant[2] *n* : descendiente *mf*
descent [di'sɛnt] *n* **1** : bajada *f,* descenso *m* <the descent from the mountain : el descenso de la montaña> **2** ANCESTRY : ascendencia *f,* linaje *f* **3** SLOPE : pendiente *f,* cuesta *f* **4** FALL : caída *f* **5** ATTACK : incursión *f,* ataque *m*
describe [di'skraɪb] *vt* **-scribed; -scribing** : describir
description [di'skrɪpʃən] *n* : descripción *f*
descriptive [di'skrɪptɪv] *adj* : descriptivo <descriptive adjective : adjetivo calificativo>
desecrate ['dɛsɪ,kreɪt] *vt* **-crated; -crating** : profanar
desecration [,dɛsɪ'kreɪʃən] *n* : profanación *f*
desegregate [di'sɛgrə,geɪt] *vt* **-gated; -gating** : eliminar la segregación racial de
desegregation [di,sɛgrə'geɪʃən] *n* : eliminación *f* de la segregación racial
desert[1] [di'zərt] *vt* : abandonar (una persona o un lugar), desertar de (una causa, etc.) — *vi* : desertar
desert[2] ['dɛzərt] *adj* : desierto <a desert island : una isla desierta>
desert[3] *n* **1** ['dɛzərt] : desierto *m* (en geografía) **2** [di'zərt] → **deserts**
deserter [di'zərṭər] *n* : desertor *m,* -tora *f*
desertion [di'zərʃən] *n* : abandono *m,* deserción *f* (militar)
deserts [di'zərts] *npl* : merecido *m* <to get one's just deserts : llevarse uno su merecido>
deserve [di'zərv] *vt* **-served; -serving** : merecer, ser digno de
desiccate ['dɛsɪ,keɪt] *vt* **-cated; -cating** : desecar, deshidratar
design[1] [di'zaɪn] *vt* **1** DEVISE : diseñar, concebir, idear **2** PLAN : proyectar **3** SKETCH : trazar, bosquejar

design[2] *n* **1** PLAN, SCHEME : plan *m,* proyecto *m* <by design : a propósito, intencionalmente> **2** SKETCH : diseño *m,* bosquejo *m* **3** PATTERN, STYLE : diseño *m,* estilo *m* **4 designs** *npl* INTENTIONS : propósitos *mpl,* designios *mpl*

designate [ˈdɛzɪgˌneɪt] *vt* **-nated; -nating 1** INDICATE, SPECIFY : indicar, especificar **2** APPOINT : nombrar, designar

designation [ˌdɛzɪgˈneɪʃən] *n* **1** NAMING : designación *f* **2** NAME : denominación *f,* nombre *m* **3** APPOINTMENT : designación *f,* nombramiento *m*

designer [diˈzaɪnər] *n* : diseñador *m,* -dora *f*

desirability [diˌzaɪrəˈbɪlət̬i] *n, pl* **-ties 1** ADVISABILITY : conveniencia *f* **2** ATTRACTIVENESS : atractivo *m*

desirable [diˈzaɪrəbəl] *adj* **1** ADVISABLE : conveniente, aconsejable **2** ATTRACTIVE : deseable, atractivo

desire[1] [diˈzaɪr] *vt* **-sired; -siring 1** WANT : desear **2** REQUEST : rogar, solicitar

desire[2] *n* : deseo *m,* anhelo *m,* ansia *m*

desist [diˈsɪst, -ˈzɪst] *vi* **to desist from** : desistir de, abstenerse de

desk [ˈdɛsk] *n* : escritorio *m,* pupitre *m* (en la escuela)

desolate[1] [ˈdɛsəˌleɪt, -zə-] *vt* **-lated; -lating** : devastar, desolar

desolate[2] [ˈdɛsələt, -zə-] *adj* **1** BARREN : desolado, desierto, yermo **2** DISCONSOLATE : desconsolado, desolado

desolation [ˌdɛsəˈleɪʃən, -zə-] *n* : desolación *f*

despair[1] [diˈspær] *vi* : desesperar, perder las esperanzas

despair[2] *n* : desesperación *f,* desesperanza *f*

desperate [ˈdɛspərət] *adj* **1** HOPELESS : desesperado, sin esperanzas **2** RASH : desesperado, precipitado **3** SERIOUS, URGENT : grave, urgente, apremiante <a desperate need : una necesidad apremiante>

desperately [ˈdɛspərətli] *adv* : desesperadamente, urgentemente

desperation [ˌdɛspəˈreɪʃən] *n* : desesperación *f*

despicable [diˈspɪkəbəl, ˈdɛspɪ-] *adj* : vil, despreciable, infame

despise [diˈspaɪz] *vt* **-spised; -spising** : despreciar

despite [dəˈspaɪt] *prep* : a pesar de, aún con

despoil [diˈspɔɪl] *vt* : saquear

despondency [diˈspɑndəntsi] *n* : desaliento *m,* desánimo *m,* depresión *f*

despondent [diˈspɑndənt] *adj* : desalentado, desanimado

despot [ˈdɛspət, -ˌpɑt] *n* : déspota *mf;* tirano *m,* -na *f*

despotic [dɛsˈpɑt̬ɪk] *adj* : despótico

despotism [ˈdɛspəˌtɪzəm] *n* : despotismo *m*

dessert [diˈzərt] *n* : postre *m*

destination [ˌdɛstəˈneɪʃən] *n* : destino *m,* destinación *f*

destined [ˈdɛstənd] *adj* **1** FATED : predestinado **2** BOUND : destinado, con destino (a), con rumbo (a)

destiny [ˈdɛstəni] *n, pl* **-nies** : destino *m*

destitute [ˈdɛstəˌtuːt, -ˌtjuːt] *adj* **1** LACKING : carente, desprovisto **2** POOR : indigente, en miseria

destitution [ˌdɛstəˈtuːʃən, -ˈtjuː-] *n* : indigencia *f,* miseria *f*

destroy [diˈstrɔɪ] *vt* **1** KILL : matar **2** DEMOLISH : destruir, destrozar

destroyer [diˈstrɔɪər] *n* : destructor *m* (buque)

destructible [diˈstrʌktəbəl] *adj* : destructible

destruction [diˈstrʌkʃən] *n* : destrucción *f,* ruina *f*

destructive [diˈstrʌktɪv] *adj* : destructor, destructivo

desultory [ˈdɛsəlˌtori] *adj* **1** AIMLESS : sin rumbo, sin objeto **2** DISCONNECTED : inconexo

detach [diˈtætʃ] *vt* : separar, quitar, desprender

detached [diˈtætʃt] *adj* **1** SEPARATE : separado, suelto **2** ALOOF : distante, indiferente **3** IMPARTIAL : imparcial, objetivo

detachment [diˈtætʃmənt] *n* **1** SEPARATION : separación *f* **2** DETAIL : destacamento *m* (de tropas) **3** ALOOFNESS : reserva *f,* indiferencia *f* **4** IMPARTIALITY : imparcialidad *f*

detail[1] [diˈteɪl, ˈdiːˌteɪl] *vt* : detallar, exponer en detalle

detail[2] *n* **1** : detalle *m,* pormenor *m* **2** : destacamento *m* (de tropas)

detailed [diˈteɪld, ˈdiːˌteɪld] *adj* : detallado, minucioso

detain [diˈteɪn] *vt* **1** HOLD : detener **2** DELAY : entretener, demorar, retrasar

detect [diˈtɛkt] *vt* : detectar, descubrir

detection [diˈtɛkʃən] *n* : descubrimiento *m*

detective [diˈtɛktɪv] *n* : detective *mf* <private detective : detective privado>

detention [diˈtɛntʃən] *n* : detención *m*

deter [diˈtər] *vt* **-terred; -terring** : disuadir, impedir

detergent [diˈtərdʒənt] *n* : detergente *m*

deteriorate [diˈtɪriəˌreɪt] *vi* **-rated; -rating** : deteriorarse, empeorar

deterioration [diˌtɪriəˈreɪʃən] *n* : deterioro *m,* empeoramiento *m*

determination [dɪˌtərməˈneɪʃən] *n* **1** DECISION : determinación *f,* decisión *f* **2** RESOLUTION : resolución *f,* determinación *f* <with grim determination : con una firme resolución>

determine [diˈtərmən] *vt* **-mined; -mining 1** ESTABLISH : determinar, establecer **2** SETTLE : decidir **3** FIND OUT : averiguar **4** BRING ABOUT : determinar

determined [di'tərmənd] *adj* RESOLUTE : decidido, resuelto
deterrent [di'tərənt] *n* : medida *f* disuasiva
detest [di'tɛst] *vt* : detestar, odiar, aborrecer
detestable [di'tɛstəbəl] *adj* : detestable, odioso, aborrecible
dethrone [di'θro:n] *vt* **-throned; -throning** : destronar
detonate ['dɛtən,eɪt] *v* **-nated; -nating** *vt* : hacer detonar — *vi* : detonar, estallar
detonator ['dɛtən,eɪt̬ər] *n* : detonador *m*
detour[1] ['di:,tʊr, di'tʊr] *vi* : desviarse
detour[2] *n* : desvío *m*, rodeo *m*
detract [di'trækt] *vi* **to detract from** : restarle valor a, quitarle méritos a
detriment ['dɛtrəmənt] *n* : detrimento *m*, perjuicio *m*
detrimental [,dɛtrə'mɛntəl] *adj* : perjudicial — **detrimentally** *adv*
devaluation [di,vælju'eɪʃən] *n* : devaluación *f*
devalue [di'væl,ju:] *vt* **-ued; -uing** : devaluar, depreciar
devastate ['dɛvə,steɪt] *vt* **-tated; -tating** : devastar, arrasar, asolar
devastation [,dɛvə'steɪʃən] *n* : devastación *f*, estragos *mpl*
develop [di'vɛləp] *vt* **1** FORM, MAKE : desarrollar, elaborar, formar **2** : revelar (en fotografía) **3** FOSTER : desarrollar, fomentar **4** EXPLOIT : explotar (recursos), urbanizar (un área) **5** ACQUIRE : adquirir <to develop an interest : adquirir un interés> **6** CONTRACT : contraer (una enfermedad) — *vi* **1** GROW : desarrollarse **2** ARISE : aparecer, surgir
developed [di'vɛləpt] *adj* : avanzado, desarrollado
development [di'vɛləpmənt] *n* **1** : desarrollo *m* <physical development : desarrollo físico> **2** : urbanización *f* (de un área), explotación *f* (de recursos), creación *f* (de inventos) **3** EVENT : acontecimiento *m*, suceso *m* <to await developments : esperar acontecimientos>
deviant ['di:viənt] *adj* : desviado, anormal
deviate ['di:vi,eɪt] *v* **-ated; -ating** *vi* : desviarse, apartarse — *vt* : desviar
deviation [,di:vi'eɪʃən] *n* : desviación *f*
device [di'vaɪs] *n* **1** MECHANISM : dispositivo *m*, aparato *m*, mecanismo *m* **2** EMBLEM : emblema *m*
devil[1] ['dɛvəl] *vt* **-iled** *or* **-illed; -iling** *or* **-illing 1** : sazonar con picante y especias **2** PESTER : molestar
devil[2] *n* **1** SATAN : el diablo, Satanás *m* **2** DEMON : diablo *m*, demonio *m* **3** FIEND : persona *f* diabólica; malvado *m*, -da *f*
devilish ['dɛvəlɪʃ] *adj* : diabólico
devilry ['dɛvəlri] *n, pl* **-ries** : diabluras *fpl*, travesuras *fpl*
devious ['di:viəs] *adj* **1** CRAFTY : taimado, artero **2** WINDING : tortuoso, sinuoso
devise [di'vaɪz] *vt* **-vised; -vising 1** INVENT : idear, concebir, inventar **2** PLOT : tramar
devoid [di'vɔɪd] *adj* **~ of** : carente de, desprovisto de
devote [di'vo:t] *vt* **-voted; -voting 1** DEDICATE : consagrar, dedicar <to devote one's life : dedicar uno su vida> **2 to devote oneself** : dedicarse
devoted [di'vo:t̬əd] *adj* **1** FAITHFUL : leal, fiel **2 to be devoted to someone** : tenerle mucho cariño a alguien
devotee [,dɛvə'ti:, -'teɪ] *n* : devoto *m*, -ta *f*
devotion [di'vo:ʃən] *n* **1** DEDICATION : dedicación *f*, devoción *f* **2 devotions** PRAYERS : oraciones *fpl*, devociones *fpl*
devour [di'vaʊər] *vt* : devorar
devout [di'vaʊt] *adj* **1** PIOUS : devoto, piadoso **2** EARNEST, SINCERE : sincero, ferviente — **devoutly** *adv*
devoutness [di'vaʊtnəs] *n* : devoción *f*, piedad *f*
dew ['du:, 'dju:] *n* : rocío *m*
dewlap ['du,læp, 'dju-] *n* : papada *f*
dew point *n* : punto *m* de condensación
dewy ['du:i, 'dju:i] *adj* **dewier; -est** : cubierto de rocío
dexterity [dɛk'stɛrət̬i] *n, pl* **-ties** : destreza *f*, habilidad *f*
dexterous ['dɛkstrəs] *adj* : diestro, hábil
dexterously ['dɛkstrəsli] *adv* : con destreza, con habilidad, hábilmente
dextrose ['dɛk,stro:s] *n* : dextrosa *f*
diabetes [,daɪə'bi:tiz] *n* : diabetes *f*
diabetic[1] [,daɪə'bɛt̬ɪk] *adj* : diabético
diabetic[2] *n* : diabético *m*, -ca *f*
diabolic [,daɪə'bɑlɪk] *or* **diabolical** [-lɪkəl] *adj* : diabólico, satánico
diacritical mark [,daɪə'krɪt̬ɪkəl] *n* : signo *m* diacrítico
diadem ['daɪə,dɛm, -dəm] *n* : diadema *f*
diagnose ['daɪɪg,no:s, ,daɪɪg'no:s] *vt* **-nosed; -nosing** : diagnosticar
diagnosis [,daɪɪg'no:sɪs] *n, pl* **-noses** [-'no:,si:z] : diagnóstico *m*
diagnostic [,daɪɪg'nɑstɪk] *adj* : diagnóstico
diagonal[1] [daɪ'ægənəl] *adj* : diagonal, en diagonal
diagonal[2] *n* : diagonal *f*
diagonally [daɪ'ægənəli] *adv* : diagonalmente, en diagonal
diagram[1] ['daɪə,græm] *vt* **-gramed** *or* **-grammed; -graming** *or* **-gramming** : hacer un diagrama de
diagram[2] *n* : diagrama *m*, gráfico *m*, esquema *m*
dial[1] ['daɪl] *v* **dialed** *or* **dialled; dialing** *or* **dialling** : marcar, discar

dial[2] *n* **:** esfera *f* (de un reloj), dial *m* (de un radio), disco *m* (de un teléfono)
dialect [ˈdaɪəˌlɛkt] *n* **:** dialecto *m*
dialogue [ˈdaɪəˌlɔg] *n* **:** diálogo *m*
diameter [daɪˈæmət̬ər] *n* **:** diámetro *m*
diamond [ˈdaɪmənd, ˈdaɪə-] *n* **1 :** diamante *m,* brillante *m* <a diamond necklace : un collar de brillantes> **2 :** rombo *m,* forma *f* de rombo **3 :** diamante *m* (en naipes) **4** INFIELD **:** cuadro *m,* diamante *m* (en béisbol)
diaper [ˈdaɪpər, ˈdaɪə-] *n* **:** pañal *m*
diaphragm [ˈdaɪəˌfræm] *n* **:** diafragma *m*
diarrhea [ˌdaɪəˈriːə] *n* **:** diarrea *f*
diary [ˈdaɪəri] *n, pl* **-ries:** diario *m*
diatribe [ˈdaɪəˌtraɪb] *n* **:** diatriba *f*
dice[1] [ˈdaɪs] *vt* **diced; dicing :** cortar en cubos
dice[2] *ns & pl* **1 → die**[2] **2 :** dados *mpl* (juego)
dicker [ˈdɪkər] *vt* **:** regatear
dictate[1] [ˈdɪkˌteɪt, dɪkˈteɪt] *v* **-tated; -tating** *vt* **1 :** dictar <to dictate a letter : dictar una carta> **2** ORDER **:** mandar, ordenar — *vi* **:** dar órdenes
dictate[2] [ˈdɪkˌteɪt] *n* **1 :** mandato *m,* orden *f* **2 dictates** *npl* **:** dictados *mpl* <the dictates of conscience : los dictados de la conciencia>
dictation [dɪkˈteɪʃən] *n* **:** dictado *m*
dictator [ˈdɪkˌteɪt̬ər] *n* **:** dictador *m,* -dora *f*
dictatorial [ˌdɪktəˈtoriəl] *adj* **:** dictatorial — **dictatorially** *adv*
dictatorship [dɪkˈteɪt̬ərˌʃɪp, ˈdɪkˌ-] *n* **:** dictadura *f*
diction [ˈdɪkʃən] *n* **1 :** lenguaje *m,* estilo *m* **2** ENUNCIATION **:** dicción *f,* articulación *f*
dictionary [ˈdɪkʃəˌnɛri] *n, pl* **-naries :** diccionario *m*
did → do
didactic [daɪˈdæktɪk] *adj* **:** didáctico
die[1] [ˈdaɪ] *vi* **died** [ˈdaɪd]; **dying** [ˈdaɪɪŋ] **1 :** morir **2** CEASE **:** morir, morirse <a dying civilization : una civilización moribunda> **3** STOP **:** apagarse, dejar de funcionar <the motor died : el motor se apagó> **4 to die down** SUBSIDE **:** amainar, disminuir **5 to die out :** extinguirse **6 to be dying for** *or* **to be dying to :** morirse por <I'm dying to leave : me muero por irme>
die[2] [ˈdaɪ] *n, pl* **dice** [ˈdaɪs] **:** dado *m*
die[3] *n, pl* **dies** [ˈdaɪz] **1** STAMP **:** troquel *m,* cuño *m* **2** MOLD **:** matriz *f,* molde *m*
diesel [ˈdiːzəl, -səl] *n* **:** diesel *m*
diet[1] [ˈdaɪət] *vi* **:** ponerse a régimen, hacer dieta
diet[2] *n* **:** régimen *m,* dieta *f*
dietary [ˈdaɪəˌtɛri] *adj* **:** alimenticio, dietético
dietitian *or* **dietician** [ˌdaɪəˈtɪʃən] *n* **:** dietista *mf*
differ [ˈdɪfər] *vi* **-ferred; -ferring 1 :** diferir, diferenciarse **2** VARY **:** variar **3** DISAGREE **:** discrepar, diferir, no estar de acuerdo
difference [ˈdɪfrənts, ˈdɪfərənts] *n* **:** diferencia *f*
different [ˈdɪfrənt, ˈdɪfərənt] *adj* **:** distinto, diferente
differentiate [ˌdɪfəˈrɛntʃiˌeɪt] *v* **-ated; -ating** *vt* **1 :** hacer diferente **2** DISTINGUISH **:** distinguir, diferenciar — *vi* **:** distinguir
differentiation [ˌdɪfəˌrɛntʃiˈeɪʃən] *n* **:** diferenciación *f*
differently [ˈdɪfrəntli, ˈdɪfərənt-] *adv* **:** de otra manera, de otro modo, distintamente
difficult [ˈdɪfɪˌkʌlt] *adj* **:** difícil
difficulty [ˈdɪfɪˌkʌlti] *n, pl* **-ties 1 :** dificultad *f* **2** PROBLEM **:** problema *f,* dificultad *f*
diffidence [ˈdɪfədənts] *n* **1** SHYNESS **:** retraimiento *m,* timidez *f,* apocamiento *m* **2** RETICENCE **:** reticencia *f*
diffident [ˈdɪfədənt] *adj* **1** SHY **:** tímido, apocado, inseguro **2** RESERVED **:** reservado
diffuse[1] [dɪˈfjuːz] *v* **-fused; -fusing** *vt* **:** difundir, esparcir — *vi* **:** difundirse, esparcirse
diffuse[2] [dɪˈfjuːs] *adj* **1** WORDY **:** prolijo, verboso **2** WIDESPREAD **:** difuso
diffusion [dɪˈjuːʒən] *n* **:** difusión *f*
dig[1] [ˈdɪg] *v* **dug** [ˈdʌg]; **digging** *vt* **1 :** cavar, excavar <to dig a hole : cavar un hoyo> **2** EXTRACT **:** sacar <to dig up potatoes : sacar papas del suelo> **3** POKE, THRUST **:** clavar, hincar <he dug me in the ribs : me dio un codazo en las costillas> **4 to dig up** DISCOVER **:** descubrir, sacar a luz — *vi* **:** cavar, excavar
dig[2] *n* **1** POKE **:** codazo *m* **2** GIBE **:** pulla *f* **3** EXCAVATION **:** excavación *f*
digest[1] [daɪˈdʒɛst, dɪ-] *vt* **1** ASSIMILATE **:** digerir, asimilar **2 :** digerir (comida) **3** SUMMARIZE **:** compendiar, resumir
digest[2] [ˈdaɪˌdʒɛst] *n* **:** compendio *m,* resumen *m*
digestible [daɪˈdʒɛstəbəl, dɪ-] *adj* **:** digerible
digestion [daɪˈdʒɛstʃən, dɪ-] *n* **:** digestión *f*
digestive [daɪˈdʒɛstɪv, dɪ-] *adj* **:** digestivo <the digestive system : el sistema digestivo>
digit [ˈdɪdʒət] *n* **1** NUMERAL **:** dígito *m,* número *m* **2** FINGER, TOE **:** dedo *m*
digital [ˈdɪdʒət̬əl] *adj* **:** digital — **digitally** *adv*
dignified [ˈdɪgnəˌfaɪd] *adj* **:** digno, decoroso
dignify [ˈdɪgnəˌfaɪ] *vt* **-fied; -fying :** dignificar, honrar
dignitary [ˈdɪgnəˌtɛri] *n, pl* **-taries :** dignatario *m,* -ria *f*
dignity [ˈdɪgnət̬i] *n, pl* **-ties :** dignidad *f*
digress [daɪˈgrɛs, də-] *vi* **:** desviarse del tema, divagar

digression [daɪˈgrɛʃən, də-] *n* : digresión *f*
dike *or* **dyke** [ˈdaɪk] *n* : dique *m*
dilapidated [dəˈlæpəˌdeɪt̬əd] *adj* : ruinoso, desvencijado, destartalado
dilapidation [dəˌlæpəˈdeɪʃən] *n* : deterioro *m,* estado *m* ruinoso
dilate [daɪˈleɪt, ˈdaɪˌleɪt] *v* **-lated; -lating** *vt* : dilatar — *vi* : dilatarse
dilemma [dɪˈlɛmə] *n* : dilema *m*
dilettante [ˈdɪləˌtɑnt, -ˌtænt] *n, pl* **-tantes** [-ˌtɑnts, -ˌtænts] *or* **-tanti** [ˌdɪləˈtɑnti, -ˈtæn-] : diletante *mf*
diligence [ˈdɪlədʒənts] *n* : diligencia *f,* aplicación *f*
diligent [ˈdɪlədʒənt] *adj* : diligente <a diligent search : una búsqueda minuciosa> — **diligently** *adv*
dill [ˈdɪl] *n* : eneldo *m*
dillydally [ˈdɪliˌdæli] *vi* **-lied; lying** : demorarse, perder tiempo
dilute [daɪˈluːt, də-] *vt* **-luted; -luting** : diluir, aguar
dilution [daɪˈluːʃən, də-] *n* : dilución *f*
dim[1] [ˈdɪm] *v* **dimmed; dimming** *vt* : atenuar (la luz), nublar (la vista), borrar (la memoria), opacar (una superficie) — *vi* : oscurecerse, apagarse
dim[2] *adj* **dimmer; dimmest 1** FAINT : oscuro, tenue (dícese de la luz), nublado (dícese de la vista), borrado (dícese de la memoria) **2** DULL : deslustrado **3** STUPID : tonto, torpe
dime [ˈdaɪm] *n* : moneda *f* de diez centavos
dimension [dəˈmɛntʃən, daɪ-] *n* **1** : dimensión *f* **2 dimensions** *npl* EXTENT, SCOPE : dimensiones *fpl,* extensión *f,* medida *f*
diminish [dəˈmɪnɪʃ] *vt* LESSEN : disminuir, reducir, amainar — *vi* DWINDLE, WANE : menguar, reducirse
diminutive [dəˈmɪnjʊt̬ɪv] *adj* : diminutivo, minúsculo
dimly [ˈdɪmli] *adv* : indistintamente, débilmente
dimmer [ˈdɪmər] *n* : potenciómetro *m,* conmutador *m* de luces (en automóviles)
dimness [ˈdɪmnəs] *n* : oscuridad *f,* debilidad *f* (de la vista), imprecisión *f* (de la memoria)
dimple [ˈdɪmpəl] *n* : hoyuelo *m*
din [ˈdɪn] *n* : estrépito *m,* estruendo *m*
dine [ˈdaɪn] *vi* **dined; dining** : cenar
diner [ˈdaɪnər] *n* **1** : comensal *mf* (persona) **2** : vagón *m* restaurante (en un tren) **3** : cafetería *f,* restaurante *m* barato
dinghy [ˈdɪŋi, ˈdɪŋgi, ˈdɪŋki] *n, pl* **-ghies** : bote *m*
dinginess [ˈdɪndʒinəs] *n* **1** DIRTINESS : suciedad *f* **2** SHABBINESS : lo gastado, lo deslucido
dingy [ˈdɪndʒi] *adj* **-gier; -est 1** DIRTY : sucio **2** SHABBY : gastado, deslucido
dinner [ˈdɪnər] *n* : cena *f,* comida *f*
dinosaur [ˈdaɪnəˌsɔr] *n* : dinosaurio *m*
dint [ˈdɪnt] *n* **by dint of** : a fuerza de
diocese [ˈdaɪəsəs, -ˌsiːz, -ˌsiːs] *n, pl* **-ceses** [ˈdaɪəsəsəz] : diócesis *f*
dip[1] [ˈdɪp] *v* **dipped; dipping** *vt* **1** DUNK, PLUNGE : sumergir, mojar, meter **2** LADLE : servir con cucharón **3** LOWER : bajar, arriar (una bandera) — *vi* **1** DESCEND, DROP : bajar en picada, descender **2** SLOPE : bajar, inclinarse
dip[2] *n* **1** SWIM : chapuzón *m* **2** DROP : descenso *m,* caída *f* **3** SLOPE : cuesta *f,* declive *m* **4** SAUCE : salsa *f*
diphtheria [dɪfˈθɪriə] *n* : difteria *f*
diphthong [ˈdɪfˌθɔŋ] *n* : diptongo *m*
diploma [dəˈploːmə] *n, pl* **-mas** : diploma *m*
diplomacy [dəˈploːməsi] *n* **1** : diplomacia *f* **2** TACT : tacto *m,* discreción *f*
diplomat [ˈdɪpləˌmæt] *n* **1** : diplomático *m,* -ca *f* (en relaciones internacionales) **2** : persona *f* diplomática
diplomatic [ˌdɪpləˈmæt̬ɪk] *adj* : diplomático <diplomatic immunity : inmunidad diplomática>
dipper [ˈdɪpər] *n* **1** LADLE : cucharón *m,* cazo *m* **2 Big Dipper** : Osa *f* Mayor **3 Little Dipper** : Osa *f* Menor
dire [ˈdaɪr] *adj* **direr; direst 1** HORRIBLE : espantoso, terrible, horrendo **2** EXTREME : extremo <dire poverty : pobreza extrema>
direct[1] [dəˈrɛkt, daɪ-] *vt* **1** ADDRESS : dirigir, mandar **2** AIM, POINT : dirigir **3** GUIDE : indicarle el camino (a alguien), orientar **4** MANAGE : dirigir <to direct a film : dirigir una película> **5** COMMAND : ordenar, mandar
direct[2] *adv* : directamente
direct[3] *adj* **1** STRAIGHT : directo **2** FRANK : franco
direct current *n* : corriente *f* continua
direction [dəˈrɛkʃən, daɪ-] *n* **1** SUPERVISION : dirección *f* **2** INSTRUCTION, ORDER : instrucción *f,* orden *f* **3** COURSE : dirección *f,* rumbo *m* <to change direction : cambiar de dirección> **4 to ask directions** : pedir indicaciones
directly [dəˈrɛktli, daɪ-] *adv* **1** STRAIGHT : directamente <directly north : directamente al norte> **2** FRANKLY : francamente **3** EXACTLY : exactamente, justo <directly opposite : justo enfrente> **4** IMMEDIATELY : en seguida, inmediatamente
directness [dəˈrɛktnəs, daɪ-] *n* : franqueza *f*
director [dəˈrɛktər, daɪ-] *n* **1** : director *m,* -tora *f* **2 board of directors** : junta *f* directiva, directorio *m*
directory [dəˈrɛktəri, daɪ-] *n, pl* **-ries** : guía *f,* directorio *m* <telephone directory : directorio telefónico>
dirge [ˈdərdʒ] *n* : canto *m* fúnebre
dirigible [ˈdɪrədʒəbəl, dəˈrɪdʒə-] *n* : dirigible *m,* zepelín *m*
dirt [ˈdərt] *n* **1** FILTH : suciedad *f,* mugre *f,* porquería *f* **2** SOIL : tierra *f*
dirtiness [ˈdərtinəs] *n* : suciedad *f*
dirty[1] [ˈdərt̬i] *vt* **dirtied; dirtying** : ensuciar, manchar

dirty[2] *adj* **dirtier; -est 1** SOILED, STAINED : sucio, manchado **2** DISHONEST : sucio, deshonesto <a dirty player : un jugador tramposo> <a dirty trick : una mala pasada> **3** INDECENT : indecente, cochino <a dirty joke : un chiste verde>

disability [ˌdɪsəˈbɪləti] *n, pl* **-ties** : minusvalía *f,* discapacidad *f,* invalidez *f*

disable [dɪsˈeɪbəl] *vt* **-abled; -abling** : dejar inválido, inutilizar, incapacitar

disabled [dɪsˈeɪbəld] *adj* : minusválido, discapacitado

disabuse [ˌdɪsəˈbjuːz] *vt* **-bused; -busing** : desengañar, sacar del error

disadvantage [ˌdɪsədˈvæntɪdʒ] *n* : desventaja *f*

disadvantageous [ˌdɪsˌædˌvænˈteɪdʒəs] *adj* : desventajoso, desfavorable

disagree [ˌdɪsəˈgriː] *vi* **1** DIFFER : discrepar, no coincidir **2** DISSENT : disentir, discrepar, no estar de acuerdo

disagreeable [ˌdɪsəˈgriːəbəl] *adj* : desagradable

disagreement [ˌdɪsəˈgriːmənt] *n* **1** : desacuerdo *m* **2** DISCREPANCY : discrepancia *f* **3** ARGUMENT : discusión *f,* altercado *m,* disputa *f*

disappear [ˌdɪsəˈpɪr] *vi* : desaparecer, desvanecerse <to disappear from view : perderse de vista>

disappearance [ˌdɪsəˈpɪrən*t*s] *n* : desaparición *f*

disappoint [ˌdɪsəˈpɔɪnt] *vt* : decepcionar, defraudar, fallar

disappointment [ˌdɪsəˈpɔɪntmənt] *n* : decepción *f,* desilusión *f,* chasco *m*

disapproval [ˌdɪsəˈpruːvəl] *n* : desaprobación *f*

disapprove [ˌdɪsəˈpruːv] *vi* **-proved; -proving** : desaprobar, estar en contra

disapprovingly [ˌdɪsəˈpruːvɪŋli] *adv* : con desaprobación

disarm [dɪsˈɑrm] *vt* : desarmar

disarmament [dɪsˈɑrməmənt] *n* : desarme *m* <nuclear disarmament : desarme nuclear>

disarrange [ˌdɪsəˈreɪndʒ] *vt* **-ranged; -ranging** : desarreglar, desordenar

disarray [ˌdɪsəˈreɪ] *n* : desorden *m,* confusión *f,* desorganización *f*

disaster [dɪˈzæstər] *n* : desastre *m,* catástrofe *f*

disastrous [dɪˈzæstrəs] *adj* : desastroso

disband [dɪsˈbænd] *vt* : disolver — *vi* : disolverse, dispersarse

disbar [dɪsˈbɑr] *vt* **-barred; -barring** : prohibir de ejercer la abogacía

disbelief [ˌdɪsbɪˈliːf] *n* : incredulidad *f*

disbelieve [ˌdɪsbɪˈliːv] *v* **-lieved; -lieving** : no creer, dudar

disburse [dɪsˈbərs] *vt* **-bursed; -bursing** : desembolsar

disbursement [dɪsˈbərsmənt] *n* : desembolso *m*

disc → **disk**

discard [dɪsˈkɑrd, ˈdɪsˌkɑrd] *vt* : desechar, deshacerse de, botar — *vi* : descartarse (en juegos de naipes)

discern [dɪˈsərn, -ˈzərn] *vt* : discernir, distinguir, percibir

discernible [dɪˈsərnəbəl, -ˈzər-] *adj* : perceptible, visible

discernment [dɪˈsərnmənt, -ˈzərn-] *n* : discernimiento *m,* criterio *m*

discharge[1] [dɪsˈtʃɑrdʒ, ˈdɪsˌ-] *v* **-charged; -charging 1** UNLOAD : descargar (carga), desembarcar (pasajeros) **2** SHOOT : descargar, disparar **3** FREE : liberar, poner en libertad **4** DISMISS : despedir **5** EMIT : despedir (humo, etc.), descargar (electricidad) **6** : cumplir con (una obligación), saldar (una deuda) — *vi* **1** : descargarse (dícese de una batería) **2** OOZE : supurar

discharge[2] [ˈdɪsˌtʃɑrdʒ, dɪsˈ-] *n* **1** EMISSION : descarga *f* (de electricidad), emisión *f* (de gases) **2** DISMISSAL : despido *m* (del empleo), baja *f* (del ejército) **3** SECRETION : secreción *f*

disciple [dɪˈsaɪpəl] *n* : discípulo *m,* -la *f*

discipline[1] [ˈdɪsəplən] *vt* **-plined; -plining 1** PUNISH : castigar, sancionar (a los empleados) **2** CONTROL : disciplinar **3 to discipline oneself** : disciplinarse

discipline[2] *n* **1** FIELD : disciplina *f,* campo *m* **2** TRAINING : disciplina *f* **3** PUNISHMENT : castigo *m* **4** SELF-CONTROL : dominio *m* de sí mismo

disc jockey *n* : disc jockey *mf*

disclaim [dɪsˈkleɪm] *vt* DENY : negar

disclose [dɪsˈkloːz] *vt* **-closed; -closing** : revelar, poner en evidencia

disclosure [dɪsˈkloːʒər] *n* : revelación *f*

discolor [dɪsˈkʌlər] *vt* **1** BLEACH : decolorar **2** FADE : desteñir **3** STAIN : manchar — *vi* : decolorarse, desteñirse

discoloration [dɪsˌkʌləˈreɪʃən] *n* **1** FADING : decoloración *f* **2** STAIN : mancha *f*

discomfort [dɪsˈkʌmfərt] *n* **1** PAIN : molestia *f,* malestar *m* **2** UNEASINESS : inquietud *f*

disconcert [ˌdɪskənˈsərt] *vt* : desconcertar

disconnect [ˌdɪskəˈnɛkt] *vt* : desconectar

disconnected [ˌdɪskəˈnɛktəd] *adj* : inconexo

disconsolate [dɪsˈkɑn*t*sələt] *adj* : desconsolado

discontent [ˌdɪskənˈtɛnt] *n* : descontento *m*

discontented [ˌdɪskənˈtɛntəd] *adj* : descontento

discontinue [ˌdɪskənˈtɪnˌjuː] *vt* **-ued; -uing** : suspender, descontinuar

discord [ˈdɪsˌkɔrd] *n* **1** STRIFE : discordia *f,* discordancia *f* **2** : disonancia *f* (en música)

discordant [dɪsˈkɔrdənt] *adj* **:** discordante, discorde — **discordantly** *adv*

discount¹ [ˈdɪsˌkaʊnt, dɪsˈ-] *vt* **1** REDUCE **:** descontar, rebajar (precios) **2** DISREGARD **:** descartar, ignorar

discount² [ˈdɪsˌkaʊnt] *n* **:** descuento *m,* rebaja *f*

discourage [dɪsˈkərɪdʒ] *vt* **-aged; -aging 1** DISHEARTEN **:** desalentar, desanimar **2** DISSUADE **:** disuadir

discouragement [dɪsˈkərɪdʒmənt] *n* **:** desánimo *m,* desaliento *m*

discourse¹ [dɪsˈkors] *vi* **-coursed; -coursing :** disertar, conversar

discourse² [ˈdɪsˌkors] *n* **1** TALK **:** conversación *f* **2** SPEECH, TREATISE **:** discurso *m,* tratado *m*

discourteous [dɪsˈkərt̬iəs] *adj* **:** descortés — **discourteously** *adv*

discourtesy [dɪsˈkərt̬əsi] *n, pl* **-sies :** descortesía *f*

discover [dɪsˈkʌvər] *vt* **:** descubrir

discoverer [dɪsˈkʌvərər] *n* **:** descubridor *m,* -dora *f*

discovery [dɪsˈkʌvəri] *n, pl* **-ries :** descubrimiento *m*

discredit¹ [dɪsˈkrɛdət] *vt* **1** DISBELIEVE **:** no creer, dudar **2 :** desacreditar, desprestigiar, poner en duda <they discredited his research : desacreditaron sus investigaciones>

discredit² *n* **1** DISREPUTE **:** descrédito *m,* desprestigio *m* **2** DOUBT **:** duda *f*

discreet [dɪsˈkriːt] *adj* **:** discreto — **discreetly** *adv*

discrepancy [dɪsˈkrɛpəntsi] *n, pl* **-cies :** discrepancia *f*

discretion [dɪsˈkrɛʃən] *n* **1** CIRCUMSPECTION **:** discreción *f,* circunspección *f* **2** JUDGMENT **:** discernimiento *m,* criterio *m*

discriminate [dɪsˈkrɪməˌneɪt] *v* **-nated; -nating** *vt* DISTINGUISH **:** distinguir, discriminar, diferenciar — *vi* **:** discriminar <to discriminate against women : discriminar a las mujeres>

discrimination [dɪsˌkrɪməˈneɪʃən] *n* **1** PREJUDICE **:** discriminación *f* **2** DISCERNMENT **:** discernimiento *m*

discriminatory [dɪsˈkrɪmənəˌtori] *adj* **:** discriminatorio

discus [ˈdɪskəs] *n, pl* **-cuses** [-kəsəz] **:** disco *m*

discuss [dɪsˈkʌs] *vt* **:** hablar de, discutir, tratar (de)

discussion [dɪsˈkʌʃən] *n* **:** discusión *f,* debate *m,* conversación *f*

disdain¹ [dɪsˈdeɪn] *vt* **:** desdeñar, despreciar <they disdained to reply : no se dignaron a responder>

disdain² *n* **:** desdén *m*

disdainful [dɪsˈdeɪnfəl] *adj* **:** desdeñoso — **disdainfully** *adv*

disease [dɪˈziːz] *n* **:** enfermedad *f,* mal *m,* dolencia *f*

diseased [dɪˈziːzd] *adj* **:** enfermo

disembark [ˌdɪsɪmˈbɑrk] *v* **:** desembarcar

disembarkation [dɪsˌɛmˌbɑrˈkeɪʃən] *n* **:** desembarco *m,* desembarque *m*

disembodied [ˌdɪsɪmˈbɑdid] *adj* **:** incorpóreo

disenchant [ˌdɪsɪnˈtʃænt] *vt* **:** desilusionar, desencantar, desengañar

disenchantment [ˌdɪsɪnˈtʃæntmənt] *n* **:** desencanto *m,* desilusión *f*

disengage [ˌdɪsɪnˈgeɪdʒ] *vt* **-gaged; -gaging 1 :** soltar, desconectar (un mecanismo) **2 to disengage the clutch :** desembragar

disentangle [ˌdɪsɪnˈtæŋgəl] *vt* **-gled; -gling** UNTANGLE **:** desenredar, desenmarañar

disfavor [dɪsˈfeɪvər] *n* **:** desaprobación *f*

disfigure [dɪsˈfɪgjər] *vt* **-ured; -uring :** desfigurar (a una persona), afear (un edificio, un área)

disfigurement [dɪsˈfɪgjərmənt] *n* **:** desfiguración *f,* afeamiento *m*

disfranchise [dɪsˈfrænˌtʃaɪz] *vt* **-chised; -chising :** privar del derecho a votar

disgrace¹ [dɪˈskreɪs] *vt* **-graced; -gracing :** deshonrar

disgrace² *n* **1** DISHONOR **:** desgracia *f,* deshonra *f* **2** SHAME **:** vergüenza *f* <he's a disgrace to his family : es una vergüenza para su familia>

disgraceful [dɪˈskreɪsfəl] *adj* **:** vergonzoso, deshonroso, ignominioso

disgracefully [dɪˈskreɪsfəli] *adv* **:** vergonzosamente

disgruntle [dɪsˈgrʌntəl] *vt* **-tled; -tling :** enfadar, contrariar

disguise¹ [dɪˈskaɪz] *vt* **-guised; -guising 1 :** disfrazar, enmascarar (el aspecto) **2** CONCEAL **:** encubrir, disimular

disguise² *n* **:** disfraz *m*

disgust¹ [dɪˈskʌst] *vt* **:** darle asco (a alguien), asquear, repugnar <eso me da asco : that disgusts me>

disgust² *n* **:** asco *m,* repugnancia *f*

disgusting [dɪˈskʌstɪŋ] *adj* **:** asqueroso, repugnante — **disgustingly** *adv*

dish¹ [ˈdɪʃ] *vt* SERVE **:** servir

dish² *n* **1 :** plato *m* <the national dish : el plato nacional> **2** PLATE **:** plato *m* <to wash the dishes : lavar los platos> **3 serving dish :** fuente *f*

dishcloth [ˈdɪʃˌklɔth] *n* **:** paño *m* de cocina (para secar), trapo *m* de fregar (para lavar)

dishearten [dɪsˈhɑrtən] *vt* **:** desanimar, desalentar

dishevel [dɪˈʃɛvəl] *vt* **-eled** *or* **-elled; -eling** *or* **-elling :** desarreglar, despeinar (el pelo)

disheveled *or* **dishevelled** [dɪˈʃɛvəld] *adj* **:** despeinado (dícese del pelo), desarreglado, desaliñado

dishonest [dɪˈsɑnəst] *adj* **:** deshonesto, fraudulento — **dishonestly** *adv*

dishonesty [dɪˈsɑnəsti] *n, pl* **-ties :** deshonestidad *f,* falta *f* de honradez

dishonor¹ [dɪˈsɑnər] *vt* **:** deshonrar

dishonor[2] *n* : deshonra *f*
dishonorable [dɪˈsɑnərəbəl] *adj* : deshonroso — **dishonorably** [-bli] *adv*
dishrag [ˈdɪʃˌræg] → **dishcloth**
dishwasher [ˈdɪʃˌwɔʃər] *n* : lavaplatos *m*, lavavajillas *m*
disillusion [ˌdɪsəˈluːʒən] *vt* : desilusionar, desencantar, desengañar
disillusionment [ˌdɪsəˈluːʒənmənt] *n* : desilusión *f*, desencanto *m*
disinclination [dɪsˌɪnkləˈneɪʃən, -ˌɪŋ-] *n* : aversión *f*
disinclined [ˌdɪsɪnˈklaɪnd] *adv* : poco dispuesto
disinfect [ˌdɪsɪnˈfɛkt] *vt* : desinfectar
disinfectant[1] [ˌdɪsɪnˈfɛktənt] *adj* : desinfectante
disinfectant[2] *n* : desinfectante *m*
disinherit [ˌdɪsɪnˈhɛrət] *vt* : desheredar
disintegrate [dɪsˈɪntəˌgreɪt] *v* **-grated; -grating** *vt* : desintegrar, deshacer — *vi* : desintegrarse, deshacerse
disintegration [dɪsˌɪntəˈgreɪʃən] *n* : desintegración *f*
disinterested [dɪsˈɪntərəstəd, -ˌrɛs-] *adj* **1** INDIFFERENT : indiferente **2** IMPARTIAL : imparcial, desinteresado
disinterestedness [dɪsˈɪntərəstədnəs, -ˌrɛs-] *n* : desinterés *m*
disjointed [dɪsˈdʒɔɪntəd] *adj* : inconexo, incoherente
disk *or* **disc** [ˈdɪsk] *n* : disco *m*
dislike[1] [dɪsˈlaɪk] *vt* **-liked; -liking** : tenerle aversión a (algo), tenerle antipatía (a alguien), no gustarle (algo a uno)
dislike[2] *n* : aversión *f*, antipatía *f*
dislocate [ˈdɪsloˌkeɪt, dɪsˈloː-] *vt* **-cated; -cating** : dislocar
dislocation [ˌdɪsloˈkeɪʃən] *n* : dislocación *f*
dislodge [dɪsˈlɑdʒ] *vt* **-lodged; -lodging** : sacar, desalojar, desplazar
disloyal [dɪsˈlɔɪəl] *adj* : desleal
disloyalty [dɪsˈlɔɪəlti] *n, pl* **-ties** : deslealtad *f*
dismal [ˈdɪzməl] *adj* **1** GLOOMY : sombrío, lúgubre, tétrico **2** DEPRESSING : deprimente, triste
dismantle [dɪsˈmæntəl] *vt* **-tled; -tling** : desmantelar, desmontar, desarmar
dismay[1] [dɪsˈmeɪ] *vt* : consternar
dismay[2] *n* : consternación *f*
dismember [dɪsˈmɛmbər] *vt* : desmembrar
dismiss [dɪsˈmɪs] *vt* **1** : dejar salir, darle permiso (a alguien) para retirarse **2** DISCHARGE : despedir, destituir **3** REJECT : descartar, desechar, rechazar
dismissal [dɪsˈmɪsəl] *n* **1** : permiso *m* para retirarse **2** DISCHARGE : despido *m* (de un empleado), destitución *f* (de un funcionario) **3** REJECTION : rechazo *m*
dismount [dɪsˈmaʊnt] *vi* : desmontar, bajarse, apearse
disobedience [ˌdɪsəˈbiːdiənts] *n* : desobediencia *f* — **disobedient** [-ənt] *adj*
disobey [ˌdɪsəˈbeɪ] *v* : desobedecer
disorder[1] [dɪsˈɔrdər] *vt* : desordenar, desarreglar
disorder[2] *n* **1** DISARRAY : desorden *m* **2** UNREST : disturbios *mpl*, desórdenes *mpl* **3** AILMENT : afección *f*, indisposición *f*, dolencia *f*
disorderly [dɪsˈɔrdərli] *adj* **1** UNTIDY : desordenado, desarreglado **2** UNRULY : indisciplinado, alborotado **3 disorderly conduct** : conducta *f* escandalosa
disorganization [dɪsˌɔrgənəˈzeɪʃən] *n* : desorganización *f*
disorganize [dɪsˈɔrgəˌnaɪz] *vt* **-nized; -nizing** : desorganizar
disown [dɪsˈoːn] *vt* : renegar de, repudiar
disparage [dɪsˈpærɪdʒ] *vt* **-aged; -aging** : menospreciar, denigrar
disparagement [dɪsˈpærɪdʒmənt] *n* : menosprecio *m*
disparate [ˈdɪspərət, dɪsˈpærət] *adj* : dispar, diferente
disparity [dɪsˈpærət̬i] *n, pl* **-ties** : disparidad *f*
dispassionate [dɪsˈpæʃənət] *adj* : desapasionado, imparcial — **dispassionately** *adv*
dispatch[1] [dɪsˈpætʃ] *vt* **1** SEND : despachar, enviar **2** KILL : despachar, matar **3** HANDLE : despachar
dispatch[2] *n* **1** SENDING : envío *m*, despacho *m* **2** MESSAGE : despacho *m*, reportaje *m* (de un periodista), parte *m* (en el ejército) **3** PROMPTNESS : prontitud *f*, rapidez *f*
dispel [dɪsˈpɛl] *vt* **-pelled; -pelling** : disipar, desvanecer
dispensation [ˌdɪspɛnˈseɪʃən] *n* EXEMPTION : exención *m*, dispensa *f*
dispense [dɪsˈpɛnts] *v* **-pensed; -pensing** *vt* **1** DISTRIBUTE : repartir, distribuir, dar **2** ADMINISTER, BESTOW : administrar (justicia), conceder (favores, etc.) **3** : preparar y despachar (medicamentos) — *vi* **to dispense with** : prescindir de
dispenser [dɪsˈpɛntsər] *n* : dispensador *m*, distibuidor *m* automático
dispersal [dɪsˈpərsəl] *n* : dispersión *f*
disperse [dɪsˈpərs] *v* **-persed; -persing** *vt* : dispersar, diseminar — *vi* : dispersarse
dispirit [dɪˈspɪrət] *vt* : desalentar, desanimar
displace [dɪsˈpleɪs] *vt* **-placed; -placing** **1** : desplazar (un líquido, etc.) **2** REPLACE : reemplazar
displacement [dɪsˈpleɪsmənt] *n* **1** : desplazamiento *m* (de personas) **2** REPLACEMENT : sustitución *f*, reemplazo *m*
display[1] [dɪsˈpleɪ] *vt* : exponer, exhibir, mostrar
display[2] *n* : muestra *f*, exposición *m*, alarde *m*

displease [dɪs'pliːz] *vt* **-pleased; -pleasing** : desagradar a, disgustar, contrariar

displeasure [dɪs'plɛʒər] *n* : desagrado *m*

disposable [dɪs'poːzəbəl] *adj* **1** : desechable <disposable diapers : pañales desechables> **2** AVAILABLE : disponible

disposal [dɪs'poːzəl] *n* **1** PLACEMENT : disposición *f,* colocación *f* **2** REMOVAL : eliminación *f* **3 to have at one's disposal** : disponer de, tener a su disposición

dispose [dɪs'poːz] *v* **-posed; -posing** *vt* **1** ARRANGE : disponer, colocar **2** INCLINE : predisponer — *vi* **1 to dispose of** DISCARD : desechar, deshacerse de **2 to dispose of** HANDLE : despachar

disposition [ˌdɪspə'zɪʃən] *n* **1** ARRANGEMENT : disposición *f* **2** TENDENCY : predisposición *f,* inclinación *f* **3** TEMPERAMENT : temperamento *m,* carácter *m*

disproportion [ˌdɪsprə'porʃən] *n* : desproporción *f*

disproportionate [ˌdɪsprə'porʃənət] *adj* : desproporcionado — **disproportionately** *adv*

disprove [dɪs'pruːv] *vt* **-proved; -proving** : rebatir, refutar

disputable [dɪs'pjuːtəbəl, 'dɪspjʊtəbəl] *adj* : disputable, discutible

dispute[1] [dɪs'pjuːt] *v* **-puted; -puting** *vt* **1** QUESTION : discutir, cuestionar **2** OPPOSE : combatir, resistir — *vi* ARGUE, DEBATE : discutir

dispute[2] *n* **1** DEBATE : debate *m,* discusión *f* **2** QUARREL : disputa *f,* discusión *f*

disqualification [dɪsˌkwɑləfə'keɪʃən] *n* : descalificación *f*

disqualify [dɪs'kwɑləˌfaɪ] *vt* **-fied; -fying** : descalificar, inhabilitar

disquiet[1] *vt* [dɪs'kwaɪət] : inquietar

disquiet[2] *n* : ansiedad *f,* inquietud *f*

disregard[1] [ˌdɪsrɪ'gɑrd] *vt* : ignorar, no prestar atención a

disregard[2] *n* : indiferencia *f*

disrepair [ˌdɪsrɪ'pær] *n* : mal estado *m*

disreputable [dɪs'rɛpjʊtəbəl] *adj* : de mala fama (dícese de una persona o un lugar), vergonzoso (dícese de la conducta)

disreputably [dɪs'rɛpjʊtəbli] *adv* : vergonzosamente

disrepute [ˌdɪsrɪ'pjuːt] *n* : descrédito *m,* mala fama *f,* deshonra *f*

disrespect [ˌdɪsrɪ'spɛkt] *n* : falta *f* de respeto

disrespectful [ˌdɪsrɪ'spɛktfəl] *adj* : irrespetuoso — **disrespectfully** *adv*

disrobe [dɪs'roːb] *v* **-robed; -robing** *vt* : desvestir, desnudar — *vi* : desvestirse, desnudarse

disrupt [dɪs'rʌpt] *vt* : trastornar, perturbar

disruption [dɪs'rʌpʃən] *n* : trastorno *m*

disruptive [dɪs'rʌptɪv] *adj* : perjudicial, perturbador — **disruptively** *adv*

dissatisfaction [dɪsˌsætəs'fækʃən] *n* : descontento *m,* insatisfacción *f*

dissatisfied [dɪs'sætəsˌfaɪd] *adj* : descontento, insatisfecho

dissatisfy [dɪs'sætəsˌfaɪ] *vt* **-fied; -fying** : no contentar, no satisfacer

dissect [dɪ'sɛkt] *vt* : disecar

dissemble [dɪ'sɛmbəl] *v* **-bled; -bling** *vt* HIDE : ocultar, disimular — *vi* PRETEND : fingir, disimular

disseminate [dɪ'sɛməˌneɪt] *vt* **-nated; -nating** : diseminar, difundir, divulgar

dissemination [dɪˌsɛmə'neɪʃən] *n* : diseminación *f,* difusión *f*

dissension [dɪ'sɛntʃən] *n* : disensión *f,* desacuerdo *m*

dissent[1] [dɪ'sɛnt] *vi* : disentir

dissent[2] *n* : disentimiento *m,* disensión *f*

dissertation [ˌdɪsər'teɪʃən] *n* **1** DISCOURSE : disertación *f,* discurso *m* **2** THESIS : tesis *f*

disservice [dɪs'sərvɪs] *n* : perjuicio *m*

dissident[1] ['dɪsədənt] *adj* : disidente

dissident[2] *n* : disidente *mf*

dissimilar [dɪ'sɪmələr] *adj* : distinto, diferente, disímil

dissipate ['dɪsəˌpeɪt] *vt* **-pated; -pating 1** DISPERSE : disipar, dispersar **2** SQUANDER : malgastar, desperdiciar, derrochar, disipar

dissipation [ˌdɪsə'peɪʃən] *n* : disipación *f,* libertinaje *m*

dissolute ['dɪsəˌluːt] *adj* : disoluto

dissolution [ˌdɪsə'luːʃən] *n* : disolución *f*

dissolve [dɪ'zɑlv] *v* **-solved; -solving** *vt* : disolver — *vi* : disolverse

dissonance ['dɪsənənts] *n* : disonancia *f*

dissuade [dɪ'sweɪd] *vt* **-suaded; -suading** : disuadir

distance ['dɪstənts] *n* **1** : distancia *f* <the distance between two points : la distancia entre dos puntos> <in the distance : a lo lejos> **2** RESERVE : actitud *f* distante, reserva *f* <to keep one's distance : guardar las distancias>

distant ['dɪstənt] *adj* **1** FAR : distante, lejano **2** REMOTE : distante, lejano, remoto **3** ALOOF : distante, frío

distantly ['dɪstəntli] *adv* **1** LOOSELY : aproximadamente, vagamente **2** COLDLY : fríamente, con frialdad

distaste [dɪs'teɪst] *n* : desagrado *m,* aversión *f*

distasteful [dɪs'teɪstfəl] *adj* : desagradable, de mal gusto

distemper [dɪs'tɛmpər] *n* : moquillo *m*

distend [dɪs'tɛnd] *vt* : dilatar, hinchar — *vi* : dilatarse, hincharse

distill [dɪ'stɪl] *vt* : destilar

distillation [ˌdɪstə'leɪʃən] *n* : destilación *f*

distiller [dɪˈstɪlər] *n* : destilador *m,* -dora *f*

distinct [dɪˈstɪŋkt] *adj* **1** DIFFERENT : distinto, diferente **2** CLEAR, UNMISTAKABLE : marcado, claro, evidente <a distinct possibility : una clara posibilidad>

distinction [dɪˈstɪŋkʃən] *n* **1** DIFFERENTIATION : distinción *f* **2** DIFFERENCE : diferencia *f* **3** EXCELLENCE : distinción *f,* excelencia *f* <a writer of distinction : un escritor destacado>

distinctive [dɪˈstɪŋktɪv] *adj* : distintivo, característico — **distinctively** *adv*

distinctiveness [dɪˈstɪŋktɪvnəs] *n* : peculiaridad *f*

distinctly [dɪˈstɪŋktli] *adv* : claramente, con claridad

distinguish [dɪsˈtɪŋgwɪʃ] *vt* **1** DIFFERENTIATE : distinguir, diferenciar **2** DISCERN : distinguir <he distinguished the sound of the piano : distinguió el sonido del piano> **3 to distinguish oneself** : señalarse, distinguirse — *vi* DISCRIMINATE : distinguir

distinguishable [dɪsˈtɪŋgwɪʃəbəl] *adj* : distinguible

distinguished [dɪsˈtɪŋgwɪʃt] *adj* : distinguido

distort [dɪˈstɔrt] *vt* **1** MISREPRESENT : distorsionar, tergiversar **2** DEFORM : distorsionar, deformar

distortion [dɪˈstɔrʃən] *n* : distorsión *f,* deformación *f,* tergiversación *f*

distract [dɪˈstrækt] *vt* : distraer, entretener

distracted [dɪˈstræktəd] *adj* : distraído

distraction [dɪˈstrækʃən] *n* **1** INTERRUPTION : distracción *f,* interrupción *f* **2** CONFUSION : confusión *f* **3** AMUSEMENT : diversión *f,* entretenimiento *m,* distracción *f*

distraught [dɪˈstrɔt] *adj* : afligido, turbado

distress[1] [dɪˈstrɛs] *vt* : afligir, darle pena (a alguien), hacer sufrir

distress[2] *n* **1** SORROW : dolor *m,* angustia *f,* aflicción *f* **2** PAIN : dolor *m* **3 in ~** : en peligro

distressful [dɪˈstrɛsfəl] *adj* : doloroso, penoso

distribute [dɪˈstrɪˌbjuːt, -bjʊt] *vt* **-uted; -uting** : distribuir, repartir

distribution [ˌdɪstrəˈbjuːʃən] *n* : distribución *f,* reparto *m*

distributive [dɪˈstrɪbjʊt̬ɪv] *adj* : distributivo

distributor [dɪˈstrɪbjʊt̬ər] *n* : distribuidor *m,* -dora *f*

district [ˈdɪsˌtrɪkt] *n* **1** REGION : región *f,* zona *f,* barrio *m* (de una ciudad) **2** : distrito *m* (zona política)

distrust[1] [dɪsˈtrʌst] *vt* : desconfiar de

distrust[2] *n* : desconfianza *f,* recelo *m*

distrustful [dɪsˈtrʌstfəl] *adj* : desconfiado, receloso, suspicaz

disturb [dɪˈstərb] *vt* **1** BOTHER : molestar, perturbar <sorry to disturb you : perdone la molestia> **2** DISARRANGE : desordenar **3** WORRY : inquietar, preocupar **4 to disturb the peace** : alterar el orden público

disturbance [dɪˈstərbənts] *n* **1** COMMOTION : alboroto *m,* disturbio *m* **2** INTERRUPTION : interrupción *f*

disuse [dɪsˈjuːs] *n* : desuso *m*

ditch[1] [ˈdɪtʃ] *vt* **1** : cavar zanjas en **2** DISCARD : deshacerse de, botar

ditch[2] *n* : zanja *f,* fosa *f,* cuneta *f* (en una carretera)

dither [ˈdɪðər] *n* **to be in a dither** : estar nervioso, ponerse como loco

ditto [ˈdɪtoː] *n, pl* **-tos 1** : lo mismo, ídem *m* **2 ditto marks** : comillas *fpl*

ditty [ˈdɪt̬i] *n, pl* **-ties** : canción *f* corta y simple

diurnal [daɪˈərnəl] *adj* **1** DAILY : diario, cotidiano **2** : diurno <a diurnal animal : un animal diurno>

divan [ˈdaɪˌvæn, dɪˈ-] *n* : diván *m*

dive[1] [ˈdaɪv] *vi* **dived** *or* **dove** [ˈdoːv]; **dived; diving 1** PLUNGE : tirarse al agua, zambullirse, dar un clavado **2** SUBMERGE : sumergirse **3** DROP : bajar en picada (dícese de un avión), caer en picada

dive[2] *n* **1** PLUNGE : zambullida *f,* clavado *m* (en el agua) **2** DESCENT : descenso *m* en picada **3** BAR, JOINT : antro *m*

diver [ˈdaɪvər] *n* : saltador *m,* -dora *f;* clavadista *mf*

diverge [dəˈvərdʒ, daɪ-] *vi* **-verged; -verging 1** SEPARATE : divergir, separarse **2** DIFFER : divergir, discrepar

divergence [dəˈvərdʒənts, daɪ-] *n* : divergencia *f* — **divergent** [-ənt] *adj*

diverse [daɪˈvərs, də-, ˈdaɪˌvərs] *adj* : diverso, variado

diversify [daɪˈvərsəˌfaɪ, də-] *vt* **-fied; -fying** : diversificar, variar

diversion [daɪˈvərʒən, də-] *n* **1** DEVIATION : desviación *f* **2** AMUSEMENT, DISTRACTION : diversión *f,* distracción *f,* entretenimiento *m*

diversity [daɪˈvərsət̬i, də-] *n, pl* **-ties** : diversidad *f*

divert [dəˈvərt, daɪ-] *vt* **1** DEVIATE : desviar **2** DISTRACT : distraer **3** AMUSE : divertir, entretener

divest [daɪˈvɛst, də-] *vt* **1** UNDRESS : desnudar, desvestir **2 to divest of** : despojar de

divide [dəˈvaɪd] *v* **-vided; -viding** *vt* **1** HALVE : dividir, partir por la mitad **2** SHARE : repartir, dividir **3** : dividir (números) — *vi* : dividirse, dividir (en matemáticas)

dividend [ˈdɪvəˌdɛnd, -dənd] *n* **1** : dividendo *m* (en finanzas) **2** BONUS : benefício *m,* provecho *m* **3** : dividendo *m* (en matemáticas)

divider [dɪˈvaɪdər] *n* **1** : separador *m* (para ficheros, etc.) **2** *or* **room divider** : mampara *f,* biombo *m*

divine[1] [dəˈvaɪn] *adj* **-viner; -est 1** : divino **2** SUPERB : divino, espléndido — **divinely** *adv*

divine[2] *n* : clérigo *m,* eclesiástico *m*

divinity [dəˈvɪnət̬i] *n, pl* **-ties** : divinidad *f*

divisible [dɪˈvɪzəbəl] *adj* : divisible

division [dɪˈvɪʒən] *n* **1** DISTRIBUTION : división *f,* reparto *m* <division of labor : distribución del trabajo> **2** PART : división *f,* sección *f* **3** : división *f* (en matemáticas)

divisor [dɪˈvaɪzər] *n* : divisor *m*

divorce[1] [dəˈvors] *v* **-vorced; -vorcing** *vt* : divorciar — *vi* : divorciarse

divorce[2] *n* : divorcio *m*

divorcé [dɪˌvorˈseɪ, -ˈsiː; -ˈvorˌ-] *n* : divorciado *m*

divorcée [dɪˌvorˈseɪ, -ˈsiː; -ˈvorˌ-] *n* : divorciada *f*

divulge [dəˈvʌldʒ, daɪ-] *vt* **-vulged; -vulging** : revelar, divulgar

dizzily [ˈdɪzəli] *adv* : vertiginosamente

dizziness [ˈdɪzinəs] *n* : mareo *m,* vahído *m,* vértigo *m*

dizzy [ˈdɪzi] *adj* **dizzier; -est 1** : mareado <I feel dizzy : estoy mareado> **2** : vertiginoso <a dizzy speed : una velocidad vertiginosa>

DNA [ˌdiːˌɛnˈeɪ] *n* : AND *m*

do [ˈduː] *v* **did** [ˈdɪd]; **done** [ˈdʌn]; **doing; does** [ˈdʌz] *vt* **1** CARRY OUT, PERFORM : hacer, realizar, llevar a cabo <she did her best : hizo todo lo posible> **2** PREPARE : preparar, hacer <do your homework : haz tu tarea> **3** ARRANGE : arreglar, peinar (el pelo) **4 to do in** RUIN : estropear, arruinar **5 to do in** KILL : matar, liquidar *fam* — *vi* **1** : hacer <you did well : hiciste bien> **2** FARE : estar, ir, andar <how are you doing? : ¿cómo estás?, ¿cómo te va?> **3** FINISH : terminar <now I'm done : ya terminé> **4** SERVE : servir, ser suficiente, alcanzar <this will do for now : esto servirá por el momento> **5 to do away with** ABOLISH : abolir, suprimir **6 to do away with** KILL : eliminar, matar **7 to do by** TREAT : tratar <he does well by her : él la trata bien> — *v aux* **1** (*used in interrogative sentences and negative statements*) <do you know her? : ¿la conoces?> <I don't like that : a mí no me gusta eso> **2** (*used for emphasis*) <I do hope you'll come : espero que vengas> **3** (*used as a substitute verb to avoid repetition*) <do you speak English? yes, I do : ¿habla inglés? sí>

docile [ˈdɑsəl] *adj* : dócil, sumiso

dock[1] [ˈdɑk] *vt* **1** CUT : cortar **2** : descontar dinero de (un sueldo) — *vi* ANCHOR, LAND : fondear, atracar

dock[2] *n* **1** PIER : atracadero *m* **2** WHARF : muelle *m* **3** : banquillo *m* de los acusados (en un tribunal)

doctor[1] [ˈdɑktər] *vt* **1** TREAT : tratar, curar **2** ALTER : adulterar, alterar, falsificar (un documento)

doctor[2] *n* **1** : doctor *m,* -tora *f* <Doctor of Philosophy : doctor en filosofía> **2** PHYSICIAN : médico *m,* -ca *f;* doctor *m,* -tora *f*

doctrine [ˈdɑktrɪn] *n* : doctrina *f*

document[1] [ˈdɑkjʊˌmɛnt] *vt* : documentar

document[2] [ˈdɑkjʊmənt] *n* : documento *m*

documentary[1] [ˌdɑkjʊˈmɛntəri] *adj* : documental

documentary[2] *n, pl* **-ries** : documental *m*

documentation [ˌdɑkjʊmənˈteɪʃən] *n* : documentación *f*

dodge[1] [ˈdɑdʒ] *v* **dodged; dodging** *vt* : esquivar, eludir, evadir (impuestos) — *vi* : echarse a un lado

dodge[2] *n* **1** RUSE : truco *m,* treta *f,* artimaña *f* **2** EVASION : regate *m,* evasión *f*

dodo [ˈdoːˌdoː] *n, pl* **-does** *or* **-dos** : dodo *m*

doe [ˈdoː] *n, pl* **does** *or* **doe** : gama *f,* cierva *f*

doer [ˈduːər] *n* : hacedor *m,* -dora *f*

does → **do**

doff [ˈdɑf, ˈdɔf] *vt* : quitarse <to doff one's hat : quitarse el sombrero>

dog[1] [ˈdɔg, ˈdɑg] *vt* **dogged; dogging** : seguir de cerca, perseguir, acosar <to dog someone's footsteps : seguir los pasos de alguien> <dogged by bad luck : perseguido por la mala suerte>

dog[2] *n* : perro *m,* -rra *f*

dogcatcher [ˈdɔgˌkætʃər] *n* : perrero *m,* -ra *f*

dog–eared [ˈdɔgˌɪrd] *adj* : con las esquinas dobladas

dogged [ˈdɔgəd] *adj* : tenaz, terco, obstinado

doggy [ˈdɔgi] *n, pl* **doggies** : perrito *m,* -ta *f*

doghouse [ˈdɔgˌhaʊs] *n* : casita *f* de perro

dogma [ˈdɔgmə] *n* : dogma *m*

dogmatic [dɔgˈmæt̬ɪk] *adj* : dogmático

dogmatism [ˈdɔgməˌtɪzəm] *n* : dogmatismo *m*

dogwood [ˈdɔgˌwʊd] *n* : cornejo *m*

doily [ˈdɔɪli] *n, pl* **-lies** : pañito *m*

doings [ˈduːɪŋz] *npl* : eventos *mpl,* actividades *fpl*

doldrums [ˈdoːldrəmz, ˈdɑl-] *npl* **1** : zona *f* de las calmas ecuatoriales **2 to be in the doldrums** : estar abatido (dícese de una persona), estar estancado (dícese de una empresa)

dole [ˈdoːl] *n* **1** ALMS : distribución *f* a los necesitados, limosna *f* **2** : subsidios *mpl* de desempleo

doleful [ˈdoːlfəl] *adj* : triste, lúgubre

dolefully [ˈdoːlfəli] *adv* : con pesar, de manera triste

dole out *vt* **doled out; doling out** : repartir

doll [ˈdɑl, ˈdɔl] *n* : muñeco *m,* -ca *f*

dollar [ˈdɑlər] *n* : dólar *m*

dolly ['dɑli] *n, pl* **-lies 1** → **doll 2** : plataforma *f* rodante

dolphin ['dɑlfən, 'dɔl-] *n* : delfín *m*

dolt ['do:lt] *n* : imbécil *mf;* tonto *m,* -ta *f*

domain [do'meɪn, də-] *n* **1** TERRITORY : dominio *m,* territorio *m* **2** FIELD : campo *m,* esfera *f,* ámbito *m* <the domain of art : el ámbito de las artes>

dome ['do:m] *n* : cúpula *f,* bóveda *f*

domestic[1] [də'mɛstɪk] *adj* **1** HOUSEHOLD : doméstico, casero **2** : nacional, interno <domestic policy : política interna> **3** TAME : domesticado

domestic[2] *n* : empleado *m* doméstico, empleada *f* doméstica

domestically [də'mɛstɪkli] *adv* : domésticamente

domesticate [də'mɛstɪ,keɪt] *vt* **-cated; -cating** : domesticar

domicile ['dɑmə,saɪl, 'do:-; 'dɑməsɪl] *n* : domicilio *m*

dominance ['dɑmənən*t*s] *n* : dominio *m,* dominación *f*

dominant ['dɑmənənt] *adj* : dominante

dominate ['dɑmə,neɪt] *v* **-nated; -nating** : dominar

domination [,dɑmə'neɪʃən] *n* : dominación *f*

domineer [,dɑmə'nɪr] *vt* : dominar sobre, avasallar, tiranizar

Dominican [də'mɪnɪkən] *n* : dominicano *m,* -na *f* — **Dominican** *adj*

dominion [də'mɪnjən] *n* **1** POWER : dominio *m* **2** DOMAIN, TERRITORY : dominio *m,* territorio *m*

domino ['dɑmə,no:] *n, pl* **-noes** *or* **-nos 1** : dominó *m* **2 dominoes** *npl* : dominó *m* (juego)

don ['dɑn] *vt* **donned; donning** : ponerse

donate ['do:,neɪt, do:'-] *vt* **-nated; -nating** : donar, hacer un donativo de

donation [do:'neɪʃən] *n* : donación *f,* donativo *m*

done[1] ['dʌn] → **do**

done[2] *adj* **1** FINISHED : terminado, acabado, concluido **2** COOKED : cocinado

donkey ['dɑŋki, 'dʌŋ-] *n, pl* **-keys** : burro *m,* asno *m*

donor ['do:nər] *n* : donante *mf;* donador *m,* -dora *f*

doodle[1] ['du:dəl] *v* **-dled; -dling** : garabatear

doodle[2] *n* : garabato *m*

doom[1] ['du:m] *vt* : condenar

doom[2] *n* **1** JUDGMENT : sentencia *f,* condena *f* **2** DEATH : muerte *f* **3** FATE : destino *m* **4** RUIN : perdición *f,* ruina *f*

door ['dor] *n* : puerta *f*

doorbell ['dor,bɛl] *n* : timbre *m*

doorknob ['dor,nɑb] *n* : pomo *m,* perilla *f*

doorman ['dormən] *n, pl* **-men** [-mən, -,mɛn] : portero *m*

doormat ['dor,mæt] *n* : felpudo *m*

doorstep ['dor,stɛp] *n* : umbral *m*

doorway ['dor,weɪ] *n* : entrada *f,* portal *m*

dope[1] ['do:p] *vt* **doped; doping** : drogar, narcotizar

dope[2] *n* **1** DRUG : droga *f,* estupefaciente *m,* narcótico *m* **2** IDIOT : idiota *mf;* tonto *m,* -ta *f* **3** INFORMATION : información *f*

dormant ['dɔrmənt] *adj* : inactivo, latente

dormer ['dɔrmər] *n* : buhardilla *f*

dormitory ['dɔrmə,tori] *n, pl* **-ries** : dormitorio *m,* residencia *f* de estudiantes

dormouse ['dɔr,maʊs] *n* : lirón *m*

dorsal ['dɔrsəl] *adj* : dorsal — **dorsally** *adv*

dory ['dori] *n, pl* **-ries** : bote *m* de fondo plano

dosage ['do:sɪdʒ] *n* : dosis *f*

dose[1] ['do:s] *vt* **dosed; dosing** : medicinar

dose[2] *n* : dosis *f*

dot[1] ['dɑt] *vt* **dotted; dotting 1** : poner el punto sobre (una letra) **2** SCATTER : esparcir, salpicar

dot[2] *n* : punto *m* <at six on the dot : a las seis en punto> <dots and dashes : puntos y rayas>

dote ['do:t] *vi* **doted; doting** : chochear

double[1] ['dʌbəl] *v* **-bled; -bling** *vt* **1** : doblar, duplicar (una cantidad), redoblar (esfuerzos) **2** FOLD : doblar, plegar **3 to double one's fist** : apretar el puño — *vi* **1** : doblarse, duplicarse **2 to double over** : retorcerse

double[2] *adj* : doble — **doubly** *adv*

double[3] *n* : doble *mf*

double bass *n* : contrabajo *m*

double–cross [,dʌbəl'krɔs] *vt* : traicionar

double–crosser [,dʌbəl'krɔsər] *n* : traidor *m,* -dora *f*

double–jointed [,dʌbəl'dʒɔintəd] *adj* : con articulaciones dobles

double–talk ['dʌbəl,tɔk] *n* : ambigüedades *fpl,* lenguaje *m* con doble sentido

doubt[1] ['daʊt] *vt* **1** QUESTION : dudar de, cuestionar **2** DISTRUST : desconfiar de **3** : dudar, creer poco probable <I doubt it very much : lo dudo mucho>

doubt[2] *n* **1** UNCERTAINTY : duda *f,* incertidumbre *f* **2** DISTRUST : desconfianza *f* **3** SKEPTICISM : duda *f,* escepticismo *m*

doubtful ['daʊtfəl] *adj* **1** QUESTIONABLE : dudoso **2** UNCERTAIN : dudoso, incierto

doubtfully ['daʊtfəli] *adv* : dudosamente, sin estar convencido

doubtless ['daʊtləs] *or* **doubtlessly** *adv* : sin duda

douche[1] ['du:ʃ] *vt* **douched; douching** : irrigar

douche[2] *n* : ducha *f,* irrigación *f*

dough ['do:] *n* : masa *f*

doughnut [ˈdoːˌnʌt] *n* : rosquilla *f*, dona *f Mex*
doughty [ˈdaʊṭi] *adj* **-tier; -est** : fuerte, valiente
dour [ˈdaʊər, ˈdʊr] *adj* **1** STERN : severo, adusto **2** SULLEN : hosco, taciturno — **dourly** *adv*
douse [ˈdaʊs, ˈdaʊz] *vt* **doused; dousing 1** DRENCH : empapar, mojar **2** EXTINGUISH : extinguir, apagar
dove[1] [ˈdoːv] → **dive**
dove[2] [ˈdʌv] *n* : paloma *f*
dovetail [ˈdʌvˌteɪl] *vi* : encajar, enlazar
dowdy [ˈdaʊdi] *adj* **dowdier; -est** : sin gracia, poco elegante
dowel [ˈdaʊəl] *n* : clavija *f*
down[1] [ˈdaʊn] *vt* **1** FELL : tumbar, derribar, abatir **2** DEFEAT : derrotar
down[2] *adv* **1** DOWNWARD : hacia abajo **2 to lie down** : acostarse, echarse **3 to put down (money)** : pagar un depósito (de dinero) **4 to sit down** : sentarse **5 to take down, to write down** : apuntar, anotar
down[3] *adj* **1** DESCENDING : de bajada <the down elevator : el ascensor de bajada> **2** REDUCED : reducido, rebajado <attendance is down : la concurrencia ha disminuido> **3** DOWNCAST : abatido, deprimido
down[4] *n* : plumón *m*
down[5] *prep* **1** : (hacia) abajo <down the mountain : montaña abajo> <I walked down the stairs : bajé por la escalera> **2** ALONG : por, a lo largo de <we ran down the beach : corrimos por la playa> **3** : a través de <down the years : a través de los años>
downcast [ˈdaʊnˌkæst] *adj* **1** SAD : triste, abatido **2 with downcast eyes** : con los ojos bajos, con los ojos mirando al suelo
downfall [ˈdaʊnˌfɔl] *n* : ruina *f*, perdición *f*
downgrade[1] [ˈdaʊnˌgreɪd] *vt* **-graded; -grading** : bajar de categoría
downgrade[2] *n* : bajada *f*
downhearted [ˈdaʊnˌhɑrṭəd] *adj* : desanimado, descorazonado
downhill [ˈdaʊnˈhɪl] *adv & adj* : cuesta abajo
down payment *n* : entrega *f* inicial
downpour [ˈdaʊnˌpor] *n* : aguacero *m*, chaparrón *m*
downright[1] [ˈdaʊnˌraɪt] *adv* THOROUGHLY : absolutamente, completamente
downright[2] *adj* : patente, manifiesto, absoluto <a downright refusal : un rechazo categórico>
downstairs[1] [ˈdaʊnˈstærz] *adv* : abajo
downstairs[2] [ˈdaʊnˌstærz] *adj* : del piso de abajo
downstairs[3] [ˈdaʊnˈstærz, -ˌstærz] *n* : planta *f* baja
downstream [ˈdaʊnˈstriːm] *adv* : río abajo
down-to-earth [ˌdaʊntuˈərth] *adj* : práctico, realista
downtown[1] [ˌdaʊnˈtaʊn] *adv* : hacia el centro, al centro, en el centro (de la ciudad)
downtown[2] *adj* : del centro (de la ciudad) <downtown Chicago : el centro de Chicago>
downtown[3] [ˌdaʊnˈtaʊn, ˈdaʊnˌtaʊn] *n* : centro *m* (de la ciudad)
downtrodden [ˈdaʊnˌtrɑdən] *adj* : oprimido
downward [ˈdaʊnwərd] *or* **downwards** [-wərdz] *adv & adj* : hacia abajo
downwind [ˈdaʊnˈwɪnd] *adv & adj* : en la dirección del viento
downy [ˈdaʊni] *adj* **downier; -est 1** : cubierto de plumón, plumoso **2** VELVETY : aterciopelado, velloso
dowry [ˈdaʊri] *n, pl* **-ries** : dote *f*
doze[1] [ˈdoːz] *vi* **dozed; dozing** : dormitar
doze[2] *n* : sueño *m* ligero, cabezada *f*
dozen [ˈdʌzən] *n, pl* **dozens** *or* **dozen** : docena *f*
drab [ˈdræb] *adj* **drabber; drabbest 1** BROWNISH : pardo **2** DULL, LACKLUSTER : monótono, gris, deslustrado
draft[1] [ˈdræft, ˈdraft] *vt* **1** CONSCRIPT : reclutar **2** COMPOSE, SKETCH : hacer el borrador de, redactar
draft[2] *adj* **1** : de barril <draft beer : cerveza de barril> **2** : de tiro <draft horses : caballos de tiro>
draft[3] *n* **1** HAULAGE : tiro *m* **2** DRINK, GULP : trago *m* **3** OUTLINE, SKETCH : bosquejo *m*, borrador *m*, versión *f* **4** : corriente *f* de aire, chiflón *m*, tiro *m* (de una chimenea) **5** CONSCRIPTION : conscripción *f* **6 bank draft** : giro *m* bancario, letra *f* de cambio
draftee [dræfˈtiː] *n* : recluta *mf*
draftsman [ˈdræftsmən] *n, pl* **-men** [-mən, -ˌmɛn] : dibujante *mf*
drafty [ˈdræfti] *adj* **draftier; -est** : con corrientes de aire
drag[1] [ˈdræg] *v* **dragged; dragging** *vt* **1** HAUL : arrastrar, jalar **2** DREDGE : dragar — *vi* **1** TRAIL : arrastrarse **2** LAG : rezagarse **3** : hacerse pesado, hacerse largo <the day dragged on : el día se hizo largo>
drag[2] *n* **1** RESISTANCE : resistencia *f* (aerodinámica) **2** HINDRANCE : traba *f*, estorbo *m* **3** BORE : pesadez *f*, plomo *m fam*
dragnet [ˈdrægˌnɛt] *n* **1** : red *f* barredera (en pesca) **2** : operativo *m* policial de captura
dragon [ˈdrægən] *n* : dragón *m*
dragonfly [ˈdrægənˌflaɪ] *n, pl* **-flies** : libélula *f*
drain[1] [ˈdreɪn] *vt* **1** EMPTY : vaciar, drenar **2** EXHAUST : agotar, consumir — *vi* **1** : escurrir, escurrirse <the dishes are draining : los platos están escurriéndose> **2** EMPTY : desaguar **3 to drain away** : irse agotando

drain[2] *n* **1** : desagüe *m* **2** SEWER : alcantarilla *f* **3** GRATING : sumidero *m,* resumidero *m,* rejilla *f* **4** EXHAUSTION : agotamiento *m,* disminución *f* (de energía, etc.) <to be a drain on : agotar, consumir> **5 to throw down the drain** : tirar por la ventana

drainage ['dreɪnɪdʒ] *n* : desagüe *m,* drenaje *m*

drainpipe ['dreɪn,paɪp] *n* : tubo *m* de desagüe, caño *m*

drake ['dreɪk] *n* : pato *m* (macho)

drama ['drɑmə, 'dræ-] *n* **1** THEATER : drama *m,* teatro *m* **2** PLAY : obra *f* de teatro, drama *m*

dramatic [drə'mæt̮ɪk] *adj* : dramático — **dramatically** [-t̮ɪkli] *adv*

dramatist ['dræmət̮ɪst, 'drɑ-] *n* : dramaturgo *m,* -ga *f*

dramatization [,dræmət̮ə'zeɪʃən, ,drɑ-] *n* : dramatización *f*

dramatize ['dræmə,taɪz, 'drɑ-] *vt* **-tized; -tizing** : dramatizar

drank → **drink**

drape[1] ['dreɪp] *vt* **draped; draping 1** COVER : cubrir (con tela) **2** HANG : drapear, disponer los pliegues de

drape[2] *n* **1** HANG : caída *f* **2 drapes** *npl* : cortinas *fpl*

drapery ['dreɪpəri] *n, pl* **-eries 1** CLOTH : pañería *f,* tela *f* para cortinas **2 draperies** *npl* : cortinas *fpl*

drastic ['dræstɪk] *adj* **1** HARSH, SEVERE : drástico, severo **2** EXTREME : radical, excepcional — **drastically** [-tɪkli] *adv*

draught ['dræft, 'draft] → **draft**[3]

draughty ['drafti] → **drafty**

draw[1] ['drɔ] *v* **drew** ['dru:]; **drawn** ['drɔn]; **drawing** *vt* **1** PULL : tirar de, jalar, correr (cortinas) **2** ATTRACT : atraer **3** PROVOKE : provocar, suscitar **4** INHALE : aspirar <to draw breath : respirar> **5** EXTRACT : sacar, extraer **6** TAKE : sacar <to draw a number : sacar un número> **7** COLLECT : cobrar, percibir (un sueldo, etc.) **8** BEND : tensar (un arco) **9** TIE : empatar (en deportes) **10** SKETCH : dibujar, trazar **11** FORMULATE : sacar, formular, llegar a <to draw a conclusion : llegar a una conclusión> **12 to draw out** : hacer hablar (sobre algo), hacer salir de sí mismo **13 to draw up** DRAFT : redactar — *vi* **1** SKETCH : dibujar **2** TUG : tirar, jalar **3 to draw near** : acercarse **4 to draw to a close** : terminar, finalizar **5 to draw up** STOP : parar

draw[2] *n* **1** DRAWING, RAFFLE : sorteo *m* **2** TIE : empate *m* **3** ATTRACTION : atracción *f* **4** PUFF : chupada *f* (de un cigarrillo, etc.)

drawback ['drɔ,bæk] *n* : desventaja *f,* inconveniente *m*

drawbridge ['drɔ,bridʒ] *n* : puente *m* levadizo

drawer ['drɔr, 'drɔər] *n* **1** ILLUSTRATOR : dibujante *mf* **2** : gaveta *f,* cajón *m* (en un mueble) **3 drawers** *npl* UNDERPANTS : calzones *mpl*

drawing ['drɔɪŋ] *n* **1** LOTTERY : sorteo *m,* lotería *f* **2** SKETCH : dibujo *m,* bosquejo *m*

drawl[1] ['drɔl] *vi* : hablar arrastrando las palabras

drawl[2] *n* : habla *f* lenta y con vocales prolongadas

dread[1] ['drɛd] *vt* : tenerle pavor a, temer

dread[2] *adj* : pavoroso, aterrado

dread[3] *n* : pavor *m,* temor *m*

dreadful ['drɛdfəl] *adj* **1** DREAD : pavoroso **2** TERRIBLE : espantoso, atroz, terrible — **dreadfully** *adv*

dream[1] ['dri:m] *v* **dreamed** ['drɛmpt, 'dri:md] *or* **dreamt** ['drɛmpt]; **dreaming** *vi* **1** : soñar <to dream about : soñar con> **2** FANTASIZE : fantasear — *vt* **1** : soñar **2** IMAGINE : imaginarse **3 to dream up** : inventar, idear

dream[2] *n* **1** : sueño *m,* ensueño *m* **2 bad dream** NIGHTMARE : pesadilla *f*

dreamer ['dri:mər] *n* : soñador *m,* -dora *f*

dreamlike ['dri:m,laɪk] *adj* : de ensueño

dreamy ['dri:mi] *adj* **dreamier; -est 1** DISTRACTED : soñador, distraído **2** DREAMLIKE : de ensueño **3** MARVELOUS : maravilloso

drearily ['drɪrəli] *adv* : sombríamente

dreary ['drɪri] *adj* **-rier; -est** : deprimente, lóbrego, sombrío

dredge[1] ['drɛdʒ] *vt* **dredged; dredging 1** DIG : dragar **2** COAT : espolvorear, enharinar

dredge[2] *n* : draga *f*

dredger ['drɛdʒər] *n* : draga *f*

dregs ['drɛgz] *npl* **1** LEES : posos *mpl,* heces *fpl* (de un líquido) **2** : heces *fpl,* escoria *f* <the dregs of society : la escoria de la sociedad>

drench ['drɛntʃ] *vt* : empapar, mojar, calar

dress[1] ['drɛs] *vt* **1** CLOTHE : vestir **2** DECORATE : decorar, adornar **3** : preparar (pollo o pescado), aliñar (ensalada) **4** : curar, vendar (una herida) **5** FERTILIZE : abonar (la tierra) — *vi* **1** : vestirse **2 to dress up** : ataviarse, engalanarse, ponerse de etiqueta

dress[2] *n* **1** APPAREL : indumentaria *f,* ropa *f* **2** : vestido *m,* traje *m* (de mujer)

dresser ['drɛsər] *n* : cómoda *f* con espejo

dressing ['drɛsɪŋ] *n* **1** : vestirse *m* **2** : aderezo *m,* aliño *m* (de ensalada), relleno *m* (de pollo) **3** BANDAGE : vendaje *m,* gasa *f*

dressmaker ['drɛs,meɪkər] *n* : modista *mf*

dressmaking ['drɛs,meɪkɪŋ] *n* : costura *f*

dressy ['drɛsi] *adj* **dressier; -est** : de mucho vestir, elegante

drew → **draw**

dribble[1] [ˈdrɪbəl] *vi* **-bled; -bling 1** DRIP : gotear **2** DROOL : babear **3** : driblar (en basquetbol)

dribble[2] *n* **1** TRICKLE : goteo *m,* hilo *m* **2** DROOL : baba *f* **3** : drible *m* (en basquetbol)

drier → **dry**[2], **dryer**

driest → **dry**[2]

drift[1] [ˈdrɪft] *vi* **1** : dejarse llevar por la corriente, ir a la deriva (dícese de un bote), ir sin rumbo (dícese de una persona) **2** ACCUMULATE : amontonarse, acumularse, apilarse

drift[2] *n* **1** DRIFTING : deriva *f* **2** HEAP, MASS : montón *m* (de arena, etc.), ventisquero *m* (de nieve) **3** MEANING : sentido *m*

drifter [ˈdrɪftər] *n* : vagabundo *m,* -da *f*

driftwood [ˈdrɪftˌwʊd] *n* : madera *f* flotante

drill[1] [ˈdrɪl] *vt* **1** BORE : perforar, taladrar **2** INSTRUCT : instruir por repetición — *vi* **1** TRAIN : entrenarse **2 to drill for oil** : perforar en busca de petróleo

drill[2] *n* **1** : taladro *m,* barrena *f* **2** EXERCISE, PRACTICE : ejercicio *m,* instrucción *f*

drily → **dryly**

drink[1] [ˈdrɪŋk] *v* **drank** [ˈdræŋk]; **drunk** [ˈdrʌŋk] *or* **drank; drinking** *vt* **1** IMBIBE : beber, tomar **2 to drink up** ABSORB : absorber — *vi* **1** : beber **2** : beber alcohol, tomar

drink[2] *n* **1** : bebida *f* **2** : bebida *f* alcohólica

drinkable [ˈdrɪŋkəbəl] *adj* : potable

drinker [ˈdrɪŋkər] *n* : bebedor *m,* -dora *f*

drip[1] [ˈdrɪp] *vi* **dripped; dripping** : gotear, chorrear

drip[2] *n* **1** DROP : gota *f* **2** DRIPPING : goteo *m*

drive[1] [ˈdraɪv] *v* **drove** [ˈdroːv]; **driven** [ˈdrɪvən]; **driving** *vt* **1** IMPEL : impeler, impulsar **2** OPERATE : guiar, conducir, manejar (un vehículo) **3** COMPEL : obligar, forzar **4** : clavar, hincar <to drive a stake : clavar una estaca> **5** *or* **to drive away** : ahuyentar, echar **6 to drive crazy** : volver loco — *vi* : manejar, conducir <do you know how to drive? : ¿sabes manejar?>

drive[2] *n* **1** RIDE : paseo *m* en coche **2** CAMPAIGN : campaña *f* <fund-raising drive : campaña para recaudar fondos> **3** DRIVEWAY : camino *m* de entrada, entrada *f* **4** TRANSMISSION : transmisión *f* <front-wheel drive : tracción delantera> **5** ENERGY : dinamismo *m,* energía *f* **6** INSTINCT, NEED : instinto *m,* necesidad *f* básica

drivel [ˈdrɪvəl] *n* : tontería *f,* estupidez *f*

driver [ˈdraɪvər] *n* : conductor *m,* -tora *f;* chofer *m*

driveway [ˈdraɪvˌweɪ] *n* : camino *m* de entrada, entrada *f* (para coches)

drizzle[1] [ˈdrɪzəl] *vi* **-zled; -zling** : lloviznar, garuar

drizzle[2] *n* : llovizna *f,* garúa *f*

droll [ˈdroːl] *adj* : cómico, gracioso, chistoso — **drolly** *adv*

dromedary [ˈdrɑməˌdɛri] *n, pl* **-daries** : dromedario *m*

drone[1] [ˈdroːn] *vi* **droned; droning 1** BUZZ : zumbar **2** MURMUR : hablar con monotonía, murmurar

drone[2] *n* **1** : zángano *m* (abeja) **2** FREELOADER : gorrón *m,* -rrona *f fam;* parásito *m,* -ta *f* **3** BUZZ, HUM : zumbido *m,* murmullo *m*

drool[1] [ˈdruːl] *vi* : babear

drool[2] *n* : baba *f*

droop[1] [ˈdruːp] *vi* **1** HANG : inclinarse (dícese de la cabeza), encorvarse (dícese de los escombros), marchitarse (dícese de las flores) **2** FLAG : decaer, flaquear <his spirits drooped : se desanimó>

droop[2] *n* : inclinación *f,* caída *f*

drop[1] [ˈdrɑp] *v* **dropped; dropping** *vt* **1** : dejar caer, soltar <she dropped the glass : se le cayó el vaso> <to drop a hint : dejar caer una indirecta> **2** SEND : mandar <drop me a line : mándame unas líneas> **3** ABANDON : abandonar, dejar <to drop the subject : cambiar de tema> **4** LOWER : bajar <he dropped his voice : bajó la voz> **5** OMIT : omitir **6 to drop off** : dejar — *vi* **1** DRIP : gotear **2** FALL : caer(se) **3** DECREASE, DESCEND : bajar, descender <the wind dropped : amainó el viento> **4 to drop back** *or* **to drop behind** : rezagarse, quedarse atrás **5 to drop by** *or* **to drop in** : pasar

drop[2] *n* **1** : gota *f* (de líquido) **2** DECLINE : caída *f,* bajada *f,* descenso *m* **3** INCLINE : caída *f,* pendiente *f* <a 20-foot drop : una caída de 20 pies> **4** SWEET : pastilla *f,* dulce *m* **5 drops** *npl* : gotas *fpl* (de medicina)

droplet [ˈdrɑplət] *n* : gotita *f*

dropper [ˈdrɑpər] *n* : gotero *m,* cuentagotas *m*

dross [ˈdrɑs, ˈdrɔs] *n* : escoria *f*

drought [ˈdraʊt] *n* : sequía *f*

drove[1] → **drive**

drove[2] [ˈdroːv] *n* : multitud *f,* gentío *m,* manada *f* (de ganado) <in droves : en manada>

drown [ˈdraʊn] *vt* **1** : ahogar **2** INUNDATE : anegar, inundar **3 to drown out** : ahogar — *vi* : ahogarse

drowse[1] [ˈdraʊz] *vi* **drowsed; drowsing** DOZE : dormitar

drowse[2] *n* : sueño *m* ligero, cabezada *f*

drowsiness [ˈdraʊzinəs] *n* : somnolencia *f,* adormecimiento *m*

drowsy [ˈdraʊzi] *adj* **drowsier; -est** : somnoliento, soñoliento

drub ['drʌb] *vt* **drubbed; drubbing 1** BEAT, THRASH : golpear, apalear **2** DEFEAT : derrotar por completo
drudge[1] ['drʌdʒ] *vi* **drudged; drudging** : trabajar como esclavo, trabajar duro
drudge[2] *n* : esclavo *m*, -va *f* del trabajo
drudgery ['drʌdʒəri] *n, pl* **-eries** : trabajo *m* pesado
drug[1] ['drʌg] *vt* **drugged; drugging** : drogar, narcotizar
drug[2] *n* **1** MEDICATION : droga *f*, medicina *f*, medicamento *m* **2** NARCOTIC : narcótico *m*, estupefaciente *m*, droga *f*
druggist ['drʌgɪst] *n* : farmacéutico *m*, -ca *f*
drugstore ['drʌg,stor] *n* : farmacia *f*, botica *f*, droguería *f*
drum[1] ['drʌm] *v* **drummed; drumming** *vt* : meter a fuerza <he drummed it into my head : me lo metió en la cabeza a fuerza> — *vi* : tocar el tambor
drum[2] *n* **1** : tambor *m* **2** : bidón *m* <oil drum : bidón de petróleo>
drummer ['drʌmər] *n* : baterista *mf*
drumstick ['drʌm,stɪk] *n* **1** : palillo *m* (de tambor), baqueta *f* **2** : muslo *m* de pollo
drunk[1] *pp* → **drink**
drunk[2] ['drʌŋk] *adj* : borracho, embriagado, ebrio
drunk[3] *n* : borracho *m*, -cha *f*
drunkard ['drʌŋkərd] *n* : borracho *m*, -cha *f*
drunken ['drʌŋkən] *adj* : borracho, ebrio <drunken driver : conductor ebrio> <drunken brawl : pleito de borrachos>
drunkenly ['drʌŋkənli] *adv* : como un borracho
drunkenness ['drʌŋkənnəs] *n* : borrachera *f*, embriaguez *f*, ebriedad *f*
dry[1] ['draɪ] *v* **dried; drying** *vt* : secar — *vi* : secarse
dry[2] *adj* **drier; driest 1** : seco **2** THIRSTY : sediento **3** : donde la venta de bebidas alcohólicas está prohibida <a dry county : un condado seco> **4** DULL : aburrido, árido **5** : seco (dícese del vino), brut (dícese de la champaña)
dry–clean ['draɪ,kli:n] *v* : limpiar en seco
dry cleaner *n* : tintorería *f* (servicio)
dry cleaning *n* : limpieza *f* en seco
dryer ['draɪər] *n* **1 hair dryer** : secador *m* **2 clothes dryer** : secadora *f*
dry goods *npl* : artículos *mpl* de confección
dry ice *n* : hielo *m* seco
dryly ['draɪli] *adv* : secamente
dryness ['draɪnəs] *n* : sequedad *f*, aridez *f*
dual ['du:əl, 'dju:-] *adj* : doble
dub ['dʌb] *vt* **dubbed; dubbing 1** CALL : apodar **2** : doblar (una película), mezclar (una grabación)
dubious ['du:biəs, 'dju:-] *adj* **1** UNCERTAIN : dudoso, indeciso **2** QUESTIONABLE : sospechoso, dudoso, discutible
dubiously ['du:biəsli, 'dju:-] *adv* **1** UNCERTAINLY : dudosamente, con desconfianza **2** SUSPICIOUSLY : de modo sospechoso, con recelo
duchess ['dʌtʃəs] *n* : duquesa *f*
duck[1] ['dʌk] *vt* **1** LOWER : agachar, bajar (la cabeza) **2** PLUNGE : zambullir **3** EVADE : eludir, evadir — *vi* **to duck down** : agacharse
duck[2] *n, pl* **duck** *or* **ducks** : pato *m*, -ta *f*
duckling ['dʌklɪŋ] *n* : patito *m*, -ta *f*
duct ['dʌkt] *n* : conducto *m*
ductile ['dʌktəl] *adj* : dúctil
dude ['du:d, 'dju:d] *n* **1** DANDY : dandi *m*, dandy *m* **2** GUY : tipo *m*
due[1] ['du:, 'dju:] *adv* : justo a, derecho hacia <due north : derecho hacia el norte>
due[2] *adj* **1** PAYABLE : pagadero, sin pagar **2** APPROPRIATE : debido, apropiado <after due consideration : con las debidas consideraciones> **3** EXPECTED : esperado <the train is due soon : esperamos el tren muy pronto, el tren debe llegar pronto> **4 due to** : debido a, por
due[3] *n* **1 to give someone his (her) due** : darle a alguien su merecido **2 dues** *npl* : cuota *f*
duel[1] ['du:əl, 'dju:-] *vi* : batirse en duelo
duel[2] *n* : duelo *m*
duet [du'ɛt, dju-] *n* : dúo *m*
due to *prep* : debido a
dug *pp* → **dig**
dugout ['dʌg,aʊt] *n* **1** CANOE : piragua *f* **2** SHELTER : refugio *m* subterráneo
duke ['du:k, 'dju:k] *n* : duque *m*
dull[1] ['dʌl] *vt* **1** DIM : opacar, quitar el brillo a, deslustrar **2** BLUNT : embotar (un filo), entorpecer (los sentidos), aliviar (el dolor), amortiguar (sonidos)
dull[2] *adj* **1** STUPID : torpe, lerdo, lento **2** BLUNT : desafilado, despuntado **3** LACKLUSTER : sin brillo, deslustrado **4** BORING : aburrido, soso, pesado — **dully** *adv*
dullness ['dʌlnəs] *n* **1** STUPIDITY : estupidez *f* **2** : embotamiento *m* (de los sentidos) **3** MONOTONY : monotonía *f*, insipidez *f* **4** : falta *f* de brillo **5** BLUNTNESS : falta *f* de filo, embotadura *f*
duly ['du:li, 'dju:-] *adv* PROPERLY : debidamente, a su debido tiempo
dumb ['dʌm] *adj* **1** MUTE : mudo **2** STUPID : estúpido, tonto, bobo — **dumbly** *adv*
dumbbell ['dʌm,bɛl] *n* **1** WEIGHT : pesa *f* **2** : estúpido *m*, -da *f*
dumbfound *or* **dumfound** [,dʌm'faʊnd] *vt* : dejar atónito, dejar sin habla
dummy ['dʌmi] *n, pl* **-mies 1** SHAM : imitación *f*, sustituto *m* **2** PUPPET

: muñeco *m* 3 MANNEQUIN : maniquí *m* 4 IDIOT : tonto *m,* -ta *f;* idiota *mf*

dump[1] [ˈdʌmp] *vt* : descargar, verter

dump[2] *n* **1** : vertedero *m,* tiradero *m Mex* **2 down in the dumps** : triste, deprimido

dumpling [ˈdʌmplɪŋ] *n* : bola *f* de masa hervida

dumpy [ˈdʌmpi] *adj* **dumpier; -est** : rechoncho, regordete

dun[1] [ˈdʌn] *vt* **dunned; dunning** : apremiar (a un deudor)

dun[2] *adj* : pardo (color)

dunce [ˈdʌnts] *n* : estúpido *m,* -da *f;* burro *m,* -rra *f fam*

dune [ˈduːn, ˈdjuːn] *n* : duna *f*

dung [ˈdʌŋ] *n* **1** FECES : excrementos *mpl* **2** MANURE : estiércol *m*

dungaree [ˌdʌŋgəˈriː] *n* **1** DENIM : tela *f* vaquera, mezclilla *f Chile, Mex* **2 dungarees** *npl* : pantalones *mpl* de trabajo hechos de tela vaquera

dungeon [ˈdʌndʒən] *n* : mazmorra *f,* calabozo *m*

dunk [ˈdʌŋk] *vt* : mojar, ensopar

duo [ˈduːoː, ˈdjuː-] *n, pl* **duos** : dúo *m,* par *m*

dupe[1] [ˈduːp, djuːp] *vt* **duped; duping** : engañar, embaucar

dupe[2] *n* : inocentón *m,* -tona *f;* simple *mf*

duplex[1] [ˈduːˌplɛks, ˈdjuː-] *adj* : doble

duplex[2] *n* : casa *f* de dos viviendas, dúplex *m*

duplicate[1] [ˈduːplɪˌkeɪt, ˈdjuː-] *vt* **-cated; -cating 1** COPY : duplicar, hacer copias de **2** REPEAT : repetir, reproducir

duplicate[2] [ˈduːplɪkət, ˈdjuː-] *adj* : duplicado <a duplicate invoice : una factura por duplicado>

duplicate[3] [ˈduːplɪkət, ˈdjuː-] *n* : duplicado *m,* copia *f*

duplication [ˌduːplɪˈkeɪʃən, ˌdjuː-] *n* **1** DUPLICATING : duplicación *f,* repetición *f* (de esfuerzos) **2** DUPLICATE : copia *f,* duplicado *m*

duplicity [dʊˈplɪsət̬i, ˌdjuː-] *n, pl* **-ties** : duplicidad *f*

durability [ˌdʊrəˈbɪlət̬i, ˌdjʊr-] *n* : durabilidad *f* (de un producto), permanencia *f*

durable [ˈdʊrəbəl, ˈdjʊr-] *adj* : duradero

duration [dʊˈreɪʃən, djʊ-] *n* : duración *f*

duress [dʊˈrɛs, djʊ-] *n* : coacción *f*

during [ˈdʊrɪŋ, ˈdjʊr-] *prep* : durante

dusk [ˈdʌsk] *n* : anochecer *m,* crepúsculo *m*

dusky [ˈdʌski] *adj* **duskier; -est** : oscuro (dícese de los colores)

dust[1] [ˈdʌst] *vt* **1** : quitar el polvo de **2** SPRINKLE : espolvorear

dust[2] *n* : polvo *m*

duster [ˈdʌstər] *n* **1** *or* **dust cloth** : trapo *m* de polvo **2** HOUSECOAT : guardapolvo *m* **3 feather duster** : plumero *m*

dustpan [ˈdʌstˌpæn] *n* : recogedor *m*

dusty [ˈdʌsti] *adj* **dustier; -est** : cubierto de polvo, polvoriento

Dutch[1] [ˈdʌtʃ] *adj* : holandés

Dutch[2] *n* **1** : holandés *m* (idioma) **2 the Dutch** *npl* : los holandeses

Dutch treat *n* : invitación *f* o pago *m* a escote

dutiful [ˈduːt̬ɪfəl, ˈdjuː-] *adj* : motivado por sus deberes, responsable

duty [ˈduːt̬i, ˈdjuː-] *n, pl* **-ties 1** OBLIGATION : deber *m,* obligación *f,* responsabilidad *f* **2** TAX : impuesto *m,* arancel *m*

dwarf[1] [ˈdwɔrf] *vt* **1** STUNT : arrestar el crecimiento de **2** : hacer parecer pequeño

dwarf[2] *n, pl* **dwarfs** [ˈdwɔrfs] *or* **dwarves** [ˈdwɔrvz] : enano *m,* -na *f*

dwell [ˈdwɛl] *vi* **dwelled** *or* **dwelt** [ˈdwɛlt]; **dwelling 1** RESIDE : residir, morar, vivir **2 to dwell on** : pensar demasiado en, insistir en

dweller [ˈdwɛlər] *n* : habitante *mf*

dwelling [ˈdwɛlɪŋ] *n* : morada *f,* vivienda *f,* residencia *f*

dwindle [ˈdwɪndəl] *vi* **-dled; -dling** : menguar, reducirse, disminuir

dye[1] [ˈdaɪ] *vt* **dyed; dyeing** : teñir

dye[2] *n* : tintura *f,* tinte *m*

dying → **die**

dyke → **dike**

dynamic [daɪˈnæmɪk] *adj* : dinámico

dynamite[1] [ˈdaɪnəˌmaɪt] *vt* **-mited; -miting** : dinamitar

dynamite[2] *n* : dinamita *f*

dynamo [ˈdaɪnəˌmoː] *n, pl* **-mos** : dínamo *m,* generador *m* de electricidad

dynasty [ˈdaɪnəsti, -ˌnæs-] *n, pl* **-ties** : dinastía *f*

dysentery [ˈdɪsənˌtɛri] *n, pl* **-teries** : disentería *f*

dystrophy [ˈdɪstrəfi] *n, pl* **-phies 1** : distrofia *f* **2** → **muscular dystrophy**

E

e [ˈiː] *n, pl* **e's** *or* **es** [ˈiːz] : quinta letra del alfabeto inglés

each[1] [ˈiːtʃ] *adv* : cada uno, por persona <they cost $10 each : costaron $10 cada uno>

each[2] *adj* : cada <each student : cada estudiante> <each and every one : todos sin excepción>

each[3] *pron* **1** : cada uno *m,* cada una *f* <each of us : cada uno de nosotros>

2 **each other :** el uno al otro, mutuamente <we are helping each other : nos ayudamos el uno al otro> <they love each other : se aman>

eager [ˈiːgər] *adj* **1** ENTHUSIASTIC **:** entusiasta, ávido, deseoso **2** ANXIOUS **:** ansioso, impaciente

eagerly [ˈiːgərli] *adv* **:** con entusiasmo, ansiosamente

eagerness [ˈiːgərnəs] *n* **:** entusiasmo *m,* deseo *m,* impaciencia *f*

eagle [ˈiːgəl] *n* **:** águila *f*

ear [ˈɪr] *n* **1 :** oído *m,* oreja *f* <inner ear : oído interno> <big ears : orejas grandes> **2 ear of corn :** mazorca *f,* choclo *m*

earache [ˈɪrˌeɪk] *n* **:** dolor *m* de oído

eardrum [ˈɪrˌdrʌm] *n* **:** tímpano *m*

earl [ˈərl] *n* **:** conde *m*

earlobe [ˈɪrˌloːb] *n* **:** lóbulo *m* de la oreja, perilla *f* de la oreja

early[1] [ˈərli] *adv* **earlier; -est :** temprano, pronto <he arrived early : llegó temprano> <as early as possible : lo más pronto posible, cuanto antes> <ten minutes early : diez minutos de adelanto>

early[2] *adj* **earlier; -est 1** (*referring to a beginning*) **:** primero <the early stages : las primeras etapas> <in early May : a principios de mayo> **2** (*referring to antiquity*) **:** primitivo, antiguo <early man : el hombre primitivo> <early painting : la pintura antigua> **3** (*referring to a designated time*) **:** temprano, antes de la hora, prematuro <he was early : llegó temprano> <early fruit : frutas tempraneras> <an early death : una muerte prematura>

earmark [ˈɪrˌmɑrk] *vt* **:** destinar <earmarked funds : fondos destinados>

earn [ˈərn] *vt* **1 :** ganar <to earn money : ganar dinero> **2** DESERVE **:** ganarse, merecer

earnest[1] [ˈərnəst] *adj* **:** serio, sincero

earnest[2] *n* **in ~ :** en serio, de verdad <we began in earnest : empezamos de verdad>

earnestly [ˈərnəstli] *adv* **1** SERIOUSLY **:** con seriedad, en serio **2** FERVENTLY **:** de todo corazón

earnestness [ˈərnəstnəs] *n* **:** seriedad *f,* sinceridad *f*

earnings [ˈərnɪŋz] *npl* **:** ingresos *mpl,* ganancias *fpl,* utilidades *fpl*

earphone [ˈɪrˌfoːn] *n* **:** audífono *m*

earring [ˈɪrˌrɪŋ] *n* **:** zarcillo *m,* arete *m,* aro *m Arg, Chile, Uru,* pendiente *m Spain*

earshot [ˈɪrˌʃɑt] *n* **:** alcance *m* del oído

earth [ˈərθ] *n* **1** LAND, SOIL **:** tierra *f,* suelo *m* **2 the Earth :** la Tierra

earthen [ˈərθən, -ðən] *adj* **:** de tierra, de barro

earthenware [ˈərθənˌwær, -ðən-] *n* **:** loza *f,* vajillas *fpl* de barro

earthly [ˈərθli] *adj* **:** terrenal, mundano

earthquake [ˈərθˌkweɪk] *n* **:** terremoto *m,* temblor *m*

earthworm [ˈərθˌwərm] *n* **:** lombriz *f* (de tierra)

earthy [ˈərθi] *adj* **earthier; -est 1 :** terroso <earthy colors : colores terrosos> **2** DOWN-TO- EARTH **:** realista, práctico, llano **3** COARSE, CRUDE **:** basto, grosero, tosco <earthy jokes : chistes groseros>

earwax [ˈɪrˌwæks] → **wax[2]**

earwig [ˈɪrˌwɪg] *n* **:** tijereta *f*

ease[1] [ˈiːz] *v* **eased; easing** *vt* **1** ALLEVIATE **:** aliviar, calmar, hacer disminuir **2** LOOSEN, RELAX **:** aflojar (una cuerda), relajar (restricciones), descargar (tensiones) **3** FACILITATE **:** facilitar — *vi* **:** calmarse, relajarse

ease[2] *n* **1** CALM, RELIEF **:** tranquilidad *f,* comodidad *f,* desahogo *m* **2** FACILITY **:** facilidad *f* **3 at ~ :** relajado, cómodo <to put someone at ease : tranquilizar a alguien>

easel [ˈiːzəl] *n* **:** caballete *m*

easily [ˈiːzəli] *adv* **1 :** fácilmente, con facilidad **2** UNQUESTIONABLY **:** con mucho, de lejos

easiness [ˈiːzinəs] *n* **:** facilidad *f,* soltura *f*

east[1] [ˈiːst] *adv* **:** al este

east[2] *adj* **:** este, del este, oriental <east winds : vientos del este>

east[3] *n* **1 :** este *m* **2 the East :** el Oriente

Easter [ˈiːstər] *n* **:** Pascua *f* (de Resurrección)

easterly [ˈiːstərli] *adv & adj* **:** del este

eastern [ˈiːstərn] *adj* **1 :** Oriental, del Este <Eastern Europe : Europa del Este> **2 :** oriental, este

Easterner [ˈiːstərnər] *n* **:** habitante *mf* del este

eastward [ˈiːstwərd] *adv & adj* **:** hacia el este

easy [ˈiːzi] *adj* **easier; -est 1 :** fácil **2** LENIENT **:** indulgente

easygoing [ˌiːziˈgoːɪŋ] *adj* **:** acomodaticio, tolerante, poco exigente

eat [ˈiːt] *v* **ate** [ˈeɪt]; **eaten** [ˈiːtən]; **eating** *vt* **1 :** comer **2** CONSUME **:** consumir, gastar, devorar <expenses ate up profits : los gastos devoraron las ganancias> **3** CORRODE **:** corroer — *vi* **1 :** comer **2 to eat away at** *or* **to eat into :** comerse **3 to eat out :** comer fuera

eatable[1] [ˈiːt̬əbəl] *adj* **:** comestible, comible *fam*

eatable[2] *n* **1 :** algo para comer **2 eatables** *npl* **:** comestibles *mpl,* alimentos *mpl*

eater [ˈiːt̬ər] *n* **:** comedor *m,* **-dora** *f*

eaves [ˈiːvz] *npl* **:** alero *m*

eavesdrop [ˈiːvzˌdrɑp] *vi* **-dropped; -dropping :** escuchar a escondidas

eavesdropper [ˈiːvzˌdrɑpər] *n* **:** persona *f* que escucha a escondidas

ebb[1] [ˈɛb] *vi* **1 :** bajar, menguar (dícese de la marea) **2** DECLINE **:** decaer, disminuir

ebb[2] *n* **1 :** reflujo *m* (de una marea) **2** DECLINE **:** decadencia *f,* declive *m,* disminución *f*

ebony[1] [ˈɛbəni] *adj* **1 :** de ébano **2** BLACK **:** de color ébano, negro

ebony[2] *n, pl* **-nies :** ébano *m*

ebullience [ɪˈbʊljənts, -ˈbʌl-] *n* **:** efervescencia *f,* vivacidad *f*

ebullient [ɪˈbʊljənt, -ˈbʌl-] *adj* **:** efervescente, vivaz

eccentric[1] [ɪkˈsɛntrɪk] *adj* **1 :** excéntrico <an eccentric wheel : una rueda excéntrica> **2** ODD, SINGULAR **:** excéntrico, extraño, raro — **eccentrically** [-trɪkli] *adv*

eccentric[2] *n* **:** ecéntrico *m,* -ca *f*

eccentricity [ˌɛkˌsɛnˈtrɪsəṭi] *n, pl* **-ties :** excentricidad *f*

ecclesiastic [ɪˌkliːziˈæstɪk] *n* **:** eclesiástico *m,* clérigo *m*

ecclesiastical [ɪˌkliːziˈæstɪkəl] *or* **ecclesiastic** *adj* **:** eclesiástico — **ecclesiastically** *adv*

echelon [ˈɛʃəˌlɑn] *n* **1 :** escalón *m* (de tropas o aviones) **2** LEVEL **:** nivel *m,* esfera *f,* estrato *m*

echo[1] [ˈɛˌkoː] *v* **echoed; echoing** *vi* **:** hacer eco, resonar — *vt* **:** repetir

echo[2] *n, pl* **echoes :** eco *m*

éclair [eɪˈklær, i-] *n* **:** pastel *m* relleno de crema

eclectic [ɛˈklɛktɪk, ɪ-] *adj* **:** ecléctico

eclipse[1] [ɪˈklɪps] *vt* **eclipsed; eclipsing :** eclipsar

eclipse[2] *n* **:** eclipse *m*

ecological *adj* [ˌiːkəˈlɑdʒɪkəl, ˌɛkə-] **:** ecológico — **ecologically** *adv*

ecologist [iˈkɑlədʒɪst, ɛ-] *n* **:** ecólogo *m,* -ga *f*

ecology [iˈkɑlədʒi, ɛ-] *n, pl* **-gies :** ecología *f*

economic [ˌiːkəˈnɑmɪk, ˌɛkə-] *adj* **:** económico

economical [ˌiːkəˈnɑmɪkəl, ˌɛkə-] *adj* **:** económico — **economically** *adv*

economics [ˌiːkəˈnɑmɪks, ˌɛkə-] *n* **:** economía *f*

economist [iˈkɑnəmɪst] *n* **:** economista *mf*

economize [iˈkɑnəˌmaɪz] *v* **-mized; -mizing :** economizar, ahorrar

economy [iˈkɑnəmi] *n, pl* **-mies 1 :** economía *f,* sistema *m* económico **2** THRIFT **:** economía *f,* ahorro *m*

ecosystem [ˈiːkoˌsɪstəm] *n* **:** ecosistema *m*

ecru [ˈɛˌkruː, ˈeɪ-] *n* **:** color *m* crudo

ecstasy [ˈɛkstəsi] *n, pl* **-sies :** éxtasis *m*

ecstatic [ɛkˈstæṭɪk, ɪk-] *adj* **:** extático

ecstatically [ɛkˈstæṭɪkli, ɪk-] *adv* **:** con éxtasis, con gran entusiasmo

Ecuadoran [ˌɛkwəˈdorən] *or* **Ecuadorean** *or* **Ecuadorian** [-ˈdoriən] *n* **:** ecuatoriano *m,* -na *f* — **Ecuadorean** *or* **Ecuadorian** *adj*

ecumenical [ˌɛkjʊˈmɛnɪkəl] *adj* **:** ecuménico

eczema [ɪgˈziːmə, ˈɛgzəmə, ˈɛksə-] *n* **:** eczema *m*

eddy[1] [ˈɛdi] *vi* **eddied; eddying :** arremolinarse, hacer remolinos

eddy[2] *n, pl* **-dies :** remolino *m*

edema [ɪˈdiːmə] *n* **:** edema *m*

Eden [ˈiːdən] *n* **:** Edén *m*

edge[1] [ˈɛdʒ] *v* **edged; edging** *vt* **1** BORDER **:** bordear, ribetear, orlar **2** SHARPEN **:** afilar, aguzar **3** *or* **to edge one's way :** avanzar poco a poco **4 to edge out :** derrotar por muy poco — *vi* ADVANCE **:** ir avanzando (poco a poco)

edge[2] *n* **1 :** filo *m* (de un cuchillo) **2** BORDER **:** borde *m,* orilla *f,* margen *m* **3** ADVANTAGE **:** ventaja *f*

edger [ˈɛdʒər] *n* **:** cortabordes *m*

edgewise [ˈɛdʒˌwaɪz] *adv* SIDEWAYS **:** de lado, de canto

edginess [ˈɛdʒinəs] *n* **:** tensión *f,* nerviosismo *m*

edgy [ˈɛdʒi] *adj* **edgier; -est :** tenso, nervioso

edible [ˈɛdəbəl] *adj* **:** comestible

edict [ˈiːˌdɪkt] *n* **:** edicto *m,* mandato *m,* orden *f*

edification [ˌɛdəfəˈkeɪʃən] *n* **:** edificación *f,* instrucción *f*

edifice [ˈɛdəfɪs] *n* **:** edificio *m*

edify [ˈɛdəˌfaɪ] *vt* **-fied; -fying :** edificar

edit [ˈɛdɪt] *vt* **1 :** editar, redactar, corregir **2** *or* **to edit out** DELETE **:** recortar, cortar

edition [ɪˈdɪʃən] *n* **:** edición *f*

editor [ˈɛdɪṭər] *n* **:** editor *m,* **-tora** *f;* redactor *m,* -tora *f*

editorial[1] [ˌɛdɪˈtoriəl] *adj* **1 :** de redacción **2 :** editorial <an editorial comment : un comentario editorial>

editorial[2] *n* **:** editorial *m*

editorship [ˈɛdəṭərˌʃɪp] *n* **:** dirección *f*

educable [ˈɛdʒəkəbəl] *adj* **:** educable

educate [ˈɛdʒəˌkeɪt] *vt* **-cated; -cating 1** TEACH **:** educar, enseñar **2** INSTRUCT **:** formar, educar, instruir **3** INFORM **:** informar, concientizar

education [ˌɛdʒəˈkeɪʃən] *n* **:** educación *f*

educational [ˌɛdʒəˈkeɪʃənəl] *adj* **1 :** docente, de enseñanza <an educational institution : una institución docente> **2** PEDAGOGICAL **:** pedagógico **3** INSTRUCTIONAL **:** educativo, instructivo

educator [ˈɛdʒəˌkeɪṭər] *n* **:** educador *m,* -dora *f*

eel [ˈiːl] *n* **:** anguila *f*

eerie [ˈɪri] *adj* **-rier; -est :** extraño, misterioso, fantasmagórico

eerily [ˈɪrəli] *adv* **:** de manera extraña y misteriosa

efface [ɪˈfeɪs, ɛ-] *vt* **-faced; -facing :** borrar

effect[1] [ɪˈfɛkt] *vt* **1** CARRY OUT **:** efectuar, llevar a cabo **2** ACHIEVE **:** lograr, realizar

effect[2] *n* **1** RESULT **:** efecto *m,* resultado *m,* consecuencia *f* <to no effect : sin resultado> **2** MEANING **:** sentido *m* <something to that effect : algo por el estilo> **3** INFLUENCE **:** efecto *m,* influen-

cia *f* **4 effects** *npl* BELONGINGS : efectos *mpl,* pertenencias *fpl* **5 to go into effect** : entrar en vigor **6 in ~** REALLY : en realidad, efectivamente
effective [ɪ'fɛktɪv] *adj* **1** EFFECTUAL : efectivo, eficaz **2** OPERATIVE : vigente — **effectively** *adv*
effectiveness [ɪ'fɛktɪvnəs] *n* : eficacia *f,* efectividad *f*
effectual [ɪ'fɛktʃʊəl] *adj* : eficaz, efectivo — **effectually** *adv*
effeminate [ə'fɛmənət] *adj* : afeminado
effervesce [ˌɛfər'vɛs] *vi* **-vesced; -vescing 1** : estar en efervescencia, burbujear (dícese de líquidos) **2** : estar eufórico, estar muy animado (dícese de las personas)
effervescence [ˌɛfər'vɛsənts] *n* **1** : efervescencia *f* **2** LIVELINESS : vivacidad *f*
effervescent [ˌɛfər'vɛsənt] *adj* **1** : efervescente **2** LIVELY, VIVACIOUS : vivaz, animado
effete [ɛ'fiːt, ɪ-] *adj* **1** WORN- OUT : desgastado, agotado **2** DECADENT : decadente **3** EFFEMINATE : afeminado
efficacious [ˌɛfə'keɪʃəs] *adj* : eficaz, efectivo
efficacy ['ɛfɪkəsi] *n, pl* **-cies** : eficacia *f*
efficiency [ɪ'fɪʃəntsi] *n, pl* **-cies** : eficiencia *f*
efficient [ɪ'fɪʃənt] *adj* : eficiente — **efficiently** *adv*
effigy ['ɛfədʒi] *n, pl* **-gies** : efigie *f*
effluent ['ɛˌfluːənt, ɛ'fluː-] *n* : efluente *m* — **effluent** *adj*
effort ['ɛfərt] *n* **1** EXERTION : esfuerzo *m* **2** ATTEMPT : tentativa *f,* intento *m* <it's not worth the effort : no vale la pena>
effortless ['ɛfərtləs] *adj* : fácil, sin esfuerzo
effortlessly ['ɛfərtləsli] *adv* : sin esfuerzo, fácilmente
effrontery [ɪ'frʌntəri] *n, pl* **-teries** : insolencia *f,* desfachatez *f,* descaro *m*
effusion [ɪ'fjuːʒən, ɛ-] *n* : efusión *f*
effusive [ɪ'fjuːsɪv, ɛ-] *adj* : efusivo — **effusively** *adv*
egg[1] ['ɛg] *vt* **to egg on** : incitar, azuzar, provocar
egg[2] *n* **1** : huevo *m* **2** OVUM : óvulo *m*
eggbeater ['ɛgˌbiːṭər] *n* : batidor *m* (de huevos)
eggnog ['ɛgˌnɑg] *n* : ponche *m* de huevo, rompope *m CA, Mex*
eggplant ['ɛgˌplænt] *n* : berenjena *f*
eggshell ['ɛgˌʃɛl] *n* : cascarón *m*
ego ['iːˌgoː] *n, pl* **egos 1** SELF-ESTEEM : amor *m* propio **2** SELF : ego *m,* yo *m*
egocentric [ˌiːgo'sɛntrɪk] *adj* : egocéntrico
egoism ['iːgoˌwɪzəm] *n* : egoísmo *m*
egoist ['iːgowɪst] *n* : egoísta *mf*
egoistic [ˌiːˌgo'wɪstɪk] *adj* : egoísta
egotism ['iːgəˌtɪzəm] *n* : egotismo *m*
egotist ['iːgətɪst] *n* : egotista *mf*
egotistic [ˌiːgə'tɪstɪk] *or* **egotistical** [-'tɪstɪkəl] *adj* : egotista — **egotistically** *adv*
egregious [ɪ'griːdʒəs] *adj* : atroz, flagrante, mayúsculo — **egregiously** *adv*
egress ['iːˌgrɛs] *n* : salida *f*
egret ['iːgrət, -ˌgrɛt] *n* : garceta *f*
eiderdown ['aɪdərˌdaʊn] *n* **1** : plumón *m* **2** COMFORTER : edredón *m*
eight[1] *adj* ['eɪt] : ocho
eight[2] *n* : ocho *m*
eight hundred[1] *adj* : ochocientos
eight hundred[2] *n* : ochocientos *m*
eighteen[1] [eɪt'tiːn] *adj* : dieciocho
eighteen[2] *n* : dieciocho *m*
eighteenth[1] [eɪt'tiːnθ] *adj* : decimoctavo
eighteenth[2] *n* **1** : decimoctavo *m,* -va *f* (en una serie) **2** : dieciochoavo *m,* dieciochoava parte *f*
eighth[1] ['eɪtθ] *adj* : octavo
eighth[2] *n* **1** : octavo *m,* -va *f* (en una serie) **2** : octavo *m,* octava parte *f*
eightieth[1] ['eɪṭiəθ] *adj* : octagésimo
eightieth[2] *n* **1** : octogésimo *m,* -ma *f* (en una serie) **2** : ochentavo *m,* ochentava parte *f*
eighty[1] ['eɪṭi] *adj* : ochenta
eighty[2] *n, pl* **eighties 1** : ochenta *m* **2 the eighties** : los ochenta *mpl*
either[1] ['iːðər, 'aɪ-] *adj* **1** : cualquiera (de los dos) <we can watch either movie : podemos ver cualquiera de las dos películas> **2** : ninguno de los dos <she wasn't in either room : no estaba en ninguna de las dos salas> **3** EACH : cada <on either side of the street : a cada lado de la calle>
either[2] *pron* **1** : cualquiera *mf* (de los dos) <either is fine : cualquiera de los dos está bien> **2** : ninguno *m,* -na *f* (de los dos) <I don't like either : no me gusta ninguno> **3** : algún *m,* alguna *f* <is either of you interested? : ¿está alguno de ustedes (dos) interesado?>
either[3] *conj* **1** : o, u <either David or Daniel could go : puede ir (o) David o Daniel> **2** : ni <we won't watch either this movie or the other : no veremos ni esta película ni la otra>
ejaculate [i'dʒækjəˌleɪt] *v* **-lated; -lating** *vt* **1** : eyacular **2** EXCLAIM : exclamar — *vi* : eyacular
ejaculation [iˌdʒækjə'leɪʃən] *n* **1** : eyaculación *f* (en fisiología) **2** EXCLAMATION : exclamación *f*
eject [i'dʒɛkt] *vt* : expulsar, expeler
ejection [i'dʒɛkʃən] *n* : expulsión *f*
eke ['iːk] *vt* **eked; eking** *or* **to eke out** : ganar a duras penas
elaborate[1] [i'læbəˌreɪt] *v* **-rated; -rating** *vt* : elaborar, idear, desarrollar — *vi* **to elaborate on** : ampliar, entrar en detalles
elaborate[2] [i'læbərət] *adj* **1** DETAILED : detallado, minucioso, elaborado **2** COMPLICATED : complicado, intrincado, elaborado — **elaborately** *adv*

elaboration [i,læbə'reɪʃən] *n* : elaboración *f*

elapse [i'læps] *vi* **elapsed; elapsing** : transcurrir, pasar

elastic[1] [i'læstɪk] *adj* : elástico

elastic[2] *n* **1** : elástico *m* **2** RUBBER BAND : goma *f*, gomita *f*, elástico *m*, liga *f*

elasticity [i,læs'tɪsəṭi, ,iː,læs-] *n, pl* **-ties** : elasticidad *f*

elate [i'leɪt] *vt* **elated; elating** : alborozar, regocijar

elation [i'leɪʃən] *n* : euforia *f*, júbilo *m*, alborozo *m*

elbow[1] ['ɛl,boː] *vt* : darle un codazo a

elbow[2] *n* : codo *m*

elder[1] ['ɛldər] *adj* : mayor

elder[2] *n* **1 to be someone's elder** : ser mayor que alguien **2** : anciano *m*, -na *f* (de un pueblo o una tribu) **3** : miembro *m* del consejo (en varias religiones)

elderberry ['ɛldər,bɛri] *n, pl* **-berries** : baya *f* de saúco (fruta), saúco *m* (árbol)

elderly ['ɛldərli] *adj* : mayor, de edad, anciano

eldest ['ɛldəst] *adj* : mayor, de más edad

elect[1] [i'lɛkt] *vt* : elegir

elect[2] *adj* : electo <the president-elect : el presidente electo>

elect[3] *npl* **the elect** : los elegidos *mpl*

election [i'lɛkʃən] *n* : elección *f*

elective[1] [i'lɛktɪv] *adj* **1** : electivo **2** OPTIONAL : facultativo, optativo

elective[2] *n* : asignatura *f* electiva

elector [i'lɛktər] *n* : elector *m*, -tora *f*

electoral [i'lɛktərəl] *adj* : electoral

electorate [i'lɛktərət] *n* : electorado *m*

electric [i'lɛktrɪk] *adj* **1** *or* **electrical** [-trɪkəl] : eléctrico **2** THRILLING : electrizante, emocionante

electrician [i,lɛk'trɪʃən] *n* : electricista *mf*

electricity [i,lɛk'trɪsəṭi] *n, pl* **-ties 1** : electricidad *f* **2** CURRENT : corriente *m* eléctrica

electrification [i,lɛktrəfə'keɪʃən] *n* : electrificación *f*

electrify [i'lɛktrə,faɪ] *vt* **-fied; -fying 1** : electrificar **2** THRILL : electrizar, emocionar

electrocardiogram [i,lɛktro'kɑrdiə,græm] *n* : electrocardiograma *m*

electrocardiograph [i,lɛktro'kɑrdiə,græf] *n* : electrocardiógrafo *m*

electrocute [i'lɛktrə,kjuːt] *vt* **-cuted; -cuting** : electrocutar

electrocution [i,lɛktrə'kjuːʃən] *n* : electrocución *f*

electrode [i'lɛk,troːd] *n* : electrodo *m*

electrolysis [i,lɛk'trɑləsɪs] *n* : electrólisis *f*

electrolyte [i'lɛktrə,laɪt] *n* : electrolito *m*

electromagnet [i,lɛktro'mægnət] *n* : electroimán *m*

electromagnetic [i,lɛktromæg'nɛṭɪk] *adj* : electromagnético — **electromagnetically** [-ṭɪkli] *adv*

electromagnetism [i,lɛktro'mægnə,tɪzəm] *n* : electromagnetismo *m*

electron [i'lɛk,trɑn] *n* : electrón *m*

electronic [i,lɛk'trɑnɪk] *adj* : electrónico — **electronically** [-nɪkli] *adv*

electronic mail *n* : correo *m* electrónico

electronics [i,lɛk'trɑnɪks] *n* : electrónica *f*

electroplate [i'lɛktrə,pleɪt] *vt* **-plated; plating** : galvanizar mediante electrólisis

elegance ['ɛlɪgənts] *n* : elegancia *f*

elegant ['ɛlɪgənt] *adj* : elegante — **elegantly** *adv*

elegy ['ɛlədʒi] *n, pl* **-gies** : elegía *f*

element ['ɛləmənt] *n* **1** COMPONENT : elemento *m*, factor *m* **2** : elemento *m* (en la química) **3** MILIEU : elemento *m*, medio *m* <to be in one's element : estar en su elemento> **4 elements** *npl* RUDIMENTS : elementos *mpl*, rudimentos *mpl*, bases *fpl* **5 the elements** WEATHER : los elementos *mpl*

elemental [,ɛlə'mɛntəl] *adj* **1** BASIC : elemental, primario **2** : elemental (dícese de los elementos químicos)

elementary [,ɛlə'mɛntri] *adj* **1** SIMPLE : elemental, simple, fundamental **2** : de enseñanza primaria

elementary school *n* : escuela *f* primaria

elephant ['ɛləfənt] *n* : elefante *m*, -ta *f*

elevate ['ɛlə,veɪt] *vt* **-vated; -vating 1** RAISE : elevar, levantar, alzar **2** EXALT, PROMOTE : elevar, exaltar, ascender **3** ELATE : alborozar, regocijar

elevation [,ɛlə'veɪʃən] *n* **1** : elevación *f* **2** ALTITUDE : altura *f*, altitud *f* **3** PROMOTION : ascenso *m*

elevator ['ɛlə,veɪṭər] *n* : ascensor *m*, elevador *m*

eleven[1] [ɪ'lɛvən] *adj* : once *m*

eleven[2] *n* : once *m*

eleventh[1] [ɪlɛvəntθ] *adj* : undécimo

eleventh[2] *n* **1** : undécimo *m*, -ma *f* (en una serie) **2** : onceavo *m*, onceava parte *f*

elf ['ɛlf] *n, pl* **elves** ['ɛlvz] : elfo *m*, geniecillo *m*, duende *m*

elfin ['ɛlfən] *adj* **1** : de elfo, menudo **2** ENCHANTING, MAGIC : mágico, encantador

elfish ['ɛlfɪʃ] *adj* **1** : de elfo **2** MISCHIEVOUS : travieso

elicit [ɪ'lɪsət] *vt* : provocar

eligibility [,ɛlədʒə'bɪləṭi] *n, pl* **-ties** : elegibilidad *f*

eligible ['ɛlədʒəbəl] *adj* **1** QUALIFIED : elegible **2** SUITABLE : idóneo

eliminate [ɪ'lɪmə,neɪt] *vt* **-nated; -nating** : eliminar

elimination [ɪ,lɪmə'neɪʃən] *n* : eliminación *f*

elite [eɪ'liːt, i-] *n* : elite *f*

elixir [i'lɪksər] *n* : elixir *m*
elk ['ɛlk] *n* : alce *m* (de Europa), uapití *m* (de América)
ellipse [ɪ'lɪps, ɛ-] *n* : elipse *f*
ellipsis [ɪ'lɪpsəs, ɛ-] *n, pl* **-lipses** [-ˌsiːz] **1** : elipsis *f* **2** : puntos *mpl* suspensivos (en la puntuación)
elliptical [ɪ'lɪptɪkəl, ɛ-] *or* **elliptic** [-tɪk] *adj* : elíptico
elm ['ɛlm] *n* : olmo *m*
elocution [ˌɛlə'kjuːʃən] *n* : elocución *f*
elongate [i'lɔŋˌgeɪt] *vt* **-gated; -gating** : alargar
elongation [ˌiːˌlɔŋ'geɪʃən] *n* : alargamiento *m*
elope [i'loːp] *vi* **eloped; eloping** : fugarse
elopement [i'loːpmənt] *n* : fuga *f*
eloquence ['ɛləkwənts] *n* : elocuencia *f*
eloquent ['ɛləkwənt] *adj* : elocuente — **eloquently** *adv*
El Salvadoran [ˌɛlˌsælvə'dorən] *n* : salvadoreño *m*, -ña *f* — **El Salvadoran** *adj*
else[1] ['ɛls] *adv* **1** DIFFERENTLY : de otro modo, de otra manera <how else? : ¿de qué otro modo?> **2** ELSEWHERE : de otro sitio, de otro lugar <where else? : ¿en qué otro sitio?> **3 or else** OTHERWISE : si no, de lo contrario
else[2] *adj* **1** OTHER : otro <anyone else : cualquier otro> <everyone else : todos los demás> <nobody else : ningún otro, nadie más> <somebody else : otra persona> **2** MORE : más <nothing else : nada más> <what else? : ¿qué más?>
elsewhere ['ɛlsˌhwɛr] *adv* : en otra parte, en otro sitio, en otro lugar
elucidate [i'luːsəˌdeɪt] *vt* **-dated; -dating** : dilucidar, elucidar, esclarecer
elucidation [iˌluːsə'deɪʃən] *n* : elucidación *f*, esclarecimiento *m*
elude [i'luːd] *vt* **eluded; eluding** : eludir, evadir
elusive [i'luːsɪv] *adj* **1** EVASIVE : evasivo, esquivo **2** SLIPPERY : huidizo, escurridizo **3** FLEETING, INTANGIBLE : impalpable, fugaz
elusively [i'luːsɪvli] *adv* : de manera esquiva
elves → **elf**
emaciate [i'meɪʃiˌeɪt] *vt* **-ated; -ating** : enflaquecer
emaciation [iˌmeɪsi'eɪʃən, -ʃi-] *n* : enflaquecimiento *m*, escualidez *f*, delgadez *f* extrema
E-mail ['iːˌmeɪl] → **electronic mail**
emanate ['ɛməˌneɪt] *v* **-nated; -nating** *vi* : emanar, provenir, proceder — *vt* : emanar
emanation [ˌɛmə'neɪʃən] *n* : emanación *f*
emancipate [i'mæntsəˌpeɪt] *vt* **-pated; -pating** : emancipar
emancipation [iˌmæntsə'peɪʃən] *n* : emancipación *f*
emasculate [i'mæskjəˌleɪt] *vt* **-lated; -lating 1** CASTRATE : castrar, emascular **2** WEAKEN : debilitar
embalm [ɪm'bɑm, ɛm-, -'bɑlm] *vt* : embalsamar
embankment [ɪm'bæŋkmənt, ɛm-] *n* : terraplén *m*, muro *m* de contención
embargo[1] [ɪm'bɑrgo, ɛm-] *vt* **-goed; -going** : imponer un embargo sobre
embargo[2] *n, pl* **-goes** : embargo *m*
embark [ɪm'bɑrk, ɛm-] *vt* : embarcar — *vi* **1** : embarcarse **2 to embark on** START : emprender, embarcarse en
embarkation [ˌɛmˌbɑr'keɪʃən] *n* : embarque *m*, embarco *m*
embarrass [ɪm'bærəs, ɛm-] *vt* : avergonzar, abochornar
embarrassing [ɪm'bærəsɪŋ, ɛm-] *adj* : embarazoso, violento
embarrassment [ɪm'bærəsmənt, ɛm-] *n* : vergüenza *f*, pena *f*
embassy ['ɛmbəsi] *n, pl* **-sies** : embajada *f*
embed [ɪm'bɛd, ɛm-] *vt* **-bedded; -bedding** : incrustar, empotrar, grabar (en la memoria)
embellish [ɪm'bɛlɪʃ, ɛm-] *vt* : adornar, embellecer
embellishment [ɪm'bɛlɪʃmənt, ɛm-] *n* : adorno *m*
ember ['ɛmbər] *n* : ascua *f*, brasa *f*
embezzle [ɪm'bɛzəl, ɛm-] *vt* **-zled; -zling** : desfalcar, malversar
embezzlement [ɪm'bɛzəlmənt, ɛm-] *n* : desfalco *m*, malversación *f*
embezzler [ɪm'bɛzələr, ɛm-] *n* : desfacador *m*, -dora *f*; malversador *m*, -dora *f*
embitter [ɪm'bɪtər, ɛm-] *vt* : amargar
emblem ['ɛmbləm] *n* : emblema *m*, símbolo *m*
emblematic [ˌɛmblə'mætɪk] *adj* : emblemático, simbólico
embodiment [ɪm'bɑdɪmənt, ɛm-] *n* : encarnación *f*, personificación *f*
embody [ɪm'bɑdi, ɛm-] *vt* **-bodied; -bodying** : encarnar, personificar
emboss [ɪm'bɑs, ɛm-, -'bɔs] *vt* : repujar, grabar en relieve
embrace[1] [ɪm'breɪs, ɛm-] *vt* **-braced; -bracing 1** HUG : abrazar **2** ADOPT, TAKE ON : adoptar, aceptar **3** INCLUDE : abarcar, incluir
embrace[2] *n* : abrazo *m*
embroider [ɪm'brɔɪdər, ɛm-] *vt* : bordar (una tela), adornar (una historia)
embroidery [ɪm'brɔɪdəri, ɛm-] *n, pl* **-deries** : bordado *m*
embroil [ɪm'brɔɪl, ɛm-] *vt* : embrollar, enredar
embryo ['ɛmbriˌoː] *n, pl* **embryos** : embrión *m*
embryonic [ˌɛmbri'ɑnɪk] *adj* : embrionario
emend [i'mɛnd] *vt* : enmendar, corregir

emendation [ˌiːˌmɛnˈdeɪʃən] *n* : enmienda *f*
emerald¹ [ˈɛmrəld, ˈɛmə-] *adj* : verde esmeralda
emerald² *n* : esmeralda *f*
emerge [iˈmərdʒ] *vi* **emerged; emerging** : emerger, salir, aparecer, surgir
emergence [iˈmərdʒənts] *n* : aparición *f,* surgimiento *m*
emergency [iˈmərdʒəntsi] *n, pl* **-cies** : emergencia *f*
emergent [iˈmərdʒənt] *adj* : emergente
emery [ˈɛməri] *n, pl* **-eries** : esmeril *m*
emetic¹ [iˈmɛt̬ɪk] *adj* : vomitivo, emético
emetic² *n* : vomitivo *m,* emético *m*
emigrant [ˈɛmɪgrənt] *n* : emigrante *mf*
emigrate [ˈɛməˌgreɪt] *vi* **-grated; -grating** : emigrar
emigration [ˌɛməˈgreɪʃən] *n* : emigración *f*
eminence [ˈɛmənənts] *n* **1** PROMINENCE : eminencia *f,* prestigio *m,* renombre *m* **2** DIGNITARY : eminencia *f;* dignatario *m,* -ria *f* <Your Eminence : Su Eminencia>
eminent [ˈɛmənənt] *adj* : eminente, ilustre
eminently [ˈɛmənəntli] *adv* : sumamente
emissary [ˈɛməˌsɛri] *n, pl* **-saries** : emisario *m,* **-ria** *f*
emission [iˈmɪʃən] *n* : emisión *f*
emit [iˈmɪt] *vt* **emitted; emitting** : emitir, despedir, producir
emote [iˈmoːt] *vi* **emoted; emoting** : exteriorizar las emociones
emotion [iˈmoːʃən] *n* : emoción *f,* sentimiento *m*
emotional [iˈmoːʃənəl] *adj* **1** : emocional, afectivo <an emotional reaction : una reacción emocional> **2** MOVING : emocionante, emotivo, conmovedor
emotionally [iˈmoːʃənəli] *adv* : emocionalmente
emperor [ˈɛmpərər] *n* : emperador *m*
emphasis [ˈɛmfəsɪs] *n, pl* **-phases** [-ˌsiːz] : énfasis *m,* hincapié *m*
emphasize [ˈɛmfəˌsaɪz] *vt* **-sized; -sizing** : enfatizar, destacar, subrayar, hacer hincapié en
emphatic [ɪmˈfætɪk, ɛm-] *adj* : enfático, enérgico, categórico — **emphatically** [-ɪkli] *adv*
empire [ˈɛmˌpaɪr] *n* : imperio *m*
empirical [ɪmˈpɪrɪkəl, ɛm-] *adj* : empírico — **empirically** [-ɪkli] *adv*
employ¹ [ɪmˈplɔɪ, ɛm-] *vt* **1** USE : usar, utilizar **2** HIRE : contratar, emplear **3** OCCUPY : ocupar, dedicar, emplear
employ² [ɪmˈplɔɪ, ɛm-; ˈɪmˌ-, ˈɛmˌ-] *n* **1** : puesto *m,* cargo *m,* ocupación *f* **2 to be in the employ of** : estar al servicio de, trabajar para
employee [ɪmˌplɔɪˈiː, ɛm-, -ˈplɔɪˌiː] *n* : empleado *m,* **-da** *f*
employer [ɪmˈplɔɪər, ɛm-] *n* : patrón *m,* -trona *f;* empleador *m,* -dora *f*
employment [ɪmˈplɔɪmənt, ɛm-] *n* : trabajo *m,* empleo *m*
empower [ɪmˈpaʊər, ɛm-] *vt* : facultar, autorizar, conferirle poder a
empowerment [ɪmˈpaʊərmənt, ɛm-] *n* : autorización *f*
empress [ˈɛmprəs] *n* : emperatriz *f*
emptiness [ˈɛmptinəs] *n* : vacío *m,* vacuidad *f*
empty¹ [ˈɛmpti] *v* **-tied; -tying** *vt* : vaciar — *vi* : desaguar (dícese de un río)
empty² *adj* **emptier; -est 1** : vacío **2** VACANT : desocupado, libre **3** MEANINGLESS : vacío, hueco, vano
empty–handed [ˌɛmptiˈhændəd] *adj* : con las manos vacías
empty–headed [ˌɛmptiˈhɛdəd] *adj* : cabeza hueca, tonto
emu [ˈiːˌmjuː] *n* : emú *m*
emulate [ˈɛmjəˌleɪt] *vt* **-lated; -lating** : emular
emulation [ˌɛmjəˈleɪʃən] *n* : emulación *f*
emulsifier [ɪˈmʌlsəˌfaɪər] *n* : emulsionante *m*
emulsify [ɪˈmʌlsəˌfaɪ] *vt* **-fied; -fying** : emulsionar
emulsion [ɪˈmʌlʃən] *n* : emulsión *f*
enable [ɪˈneɪbəl, ɛ-] *vt* **-abled; -abling 1** EMPOWER : habilitar, autorizar, facultar **2** PERMIT : hacer posible, posibilitar, permitar
enact [ɪˈnækt, ɛ-] *vt* **1** : promulgar (un ley o decreto) **2** : representar (un papel en el teatro)
enactment [ɪˈnæktmənt, ɛ-] *n* : promulgación *f*
enamel¹ [ɪˈnæməl] *vt* **-eled** *or* **-elled; -eling** *or* **-elling** : esmaltar
enamel² *n* : esmalte *m*
enamor [ɪˈnæmər] *vt* **1** : enamorar **2 to be enamored of** : estar enamorado de (una persona), estar entusiasmado con (algo)
encamp [ɪnˈkæmp, ɛn-] *vi* : acampar
encampment [ɪnˈkæmpmənt, ɛn-] *n* : campamento *m*
encase [ɪnˈkeɪs, ɛn-] *vt* **-cased; -casing** : encerrar, revestir
encephalitis [ɪnˌsɛfəˈlaɪtəs, ɛn-] *n, pl* **-litides** [-ˈlɪt̬əˌdiːz] : encefalitis *f*
enchant [ɪnˈtʃænt, ɛn-] *vt* **1** BEWITCH : hechizar, encantar, embrujar **2** CHARM, FASCINATE : cautivar, fascinar, encantar
enchanting [ɪnˈtʃæntɪŋ, ɛn-] *adj* : encantador
enchanter [ɪnˈtʃæntər, ɛn-] *n* SORCERER : mago *m,* encantador *m*
enchantment [ɪnˈtʃæntmənt, ɛn-] *n* **1** SPELL : encanto *m,* hechizo *m* **2** CHARM : encanto *m*
enchantress [ɪnˈtʃæntrəs, ɛn-] *n* **1** SORCERESS : maga *f,* hechicera *f* **2** CHARMER : mujer *f* cautivadora
encircle [ɪnˈsərkəl, ɛn-] *vt* **-cled; -cling** : rodear, ceñir, cercar
enclose [ɪnˈkloːz, ɛn-] *vt* **-closed; -closing 1** SURROUND : encerrar, cer-

car, rodear 2 INCLUDE : incluir, adjuntar, acompañar <please find enclosed : le enviamos adjunto>
enclosure [ɪn'klo:ʒər, ɛn-] *n* 1 ENCLOSING : encierro *m* 2 : cercado *m* (de terreno), recinto *m* <an enclosure for the press : un recinto para la prensa> 3 ADJUNCT : anexo *m* (con una carta), documento *m* adjunto
encompass [ɪn'kʌmpəs, ɛn-, -'kɑm-] *vt* 1 SURROUND : circundar, rodear 2 INCLUDE : abarcar, comprender
encore ['ɑn,kor] *n* : bis *m*, repetición *f*
encounter[1] [ɪn'kaʊntər, ɛn-] *vt* 1 MEET : encontrar, encontrarse con, toparse con, tropezar con 2 FIGHT : combatir, luchar contra
encounter[2] *n* : encuentro *m*
encourage [ɪn'kərɪdʒ, ɛn-] *vt* **-aged; -aging** 1 HEARTEN, INSPIRE : animar, alentar 2 FOSTER : fomentar, promover
encouragement [ɪn'kərɪdʒmənt, ɛn-] *n* : ánimo *m*, aliento *m*
encroach [ɪn'kro:tʃ, ɛn-] *vi* **to encroach on** : invadir, abusar (derechos), quitar (tiempo)
encroachment [ɪn'kro:tʃmənt, ɛn-] *n* : invasión *f*, usurpación *f*
encrust [ɪn'krʌst, ɛn-] *vt* 1 : recubrir con una costra 2 INLAY : incrustar <encrusted with gems : incrustado de gemas>
encumber [ɪn'kʌmbər, ɛn-] *vt* 1 BLOCK : obstruir, estorbar 2 BURDEN : cargar, gravar
encumbrance [ɪn'kʌmbrənts, ɛn-] *n* : estorbo *m*, carga *f*, gravamen *m*
encyclopedia [ɪn,saɪklə'pi:diə, ɛn-] *n* : enciclopedia *f*
encyclopedic [ɪn,saɪklə'pi:dɪk, ɛn-] *adj* : enciclopédico
end[1] ['ɛnd] *vt* 1 STOP : terminar, poner fin a 2 CONCLUDE : concluir, terminar — *vi* : terminar(se), acabar, concluir(se)
end[2] *n* 1 EXTREMITY : extremo *m*, final *m*, punta *f* 2 CONCLUSION : fin *m*, final *m* 3 AIM : fin *m*
endanger [ɪn'deɪndʒər, ɛn-] *vt* : poner en peligro
endear [ɪn'dɪr, ɛn-] *vt* **to endear oneself to** : ganarse la simpatía de, granjearse el cariño de
endearment [ɪn'dɪrmənt, ɛn-] *n* : expresión *f* de cariño
endeavor[1] [ɪn'dɛvər, ɛn-] *vt* : intentar, esforzarse por <he endeavored to improve his work : intentó por mejorar su trabajo>
endeavor[2] *n* : intento *m*, esfuerzo *m*
ending ['ɛndɪŋ] *n* 1 CONCLUSION : final *m*, desenlace *m* 2 SUFFIX : sufijo *m*, terminación *f*
endive ['ɛn,daɪv, ,ɑn'di:v] *n* : endibia *f*, endivia *f*
endless ['ɛndləs] *adj* 1 INTERMINABLE : interminable, inacabable, sin fin 2 INNUMERABLE : innumerable, incontable
endlessly ['ɛndləsli] *adv* : interminablemente, eternamente, sin parar
endocrine ['ɛndəkrən, -,kraɪn, -,kri:n] *adj* : endocrino
endorse [ɪn'dɔrs, ɛn-] *vt* **-dorsed; -dorsing** 1 SIGN : endosar, firmar 2 APPROVE : aprobar, sancionar
endorsement [ɪn'dɔrsmənt, ɛn-] *n* 1 SIGNATURE : endoso *m*, firma *f* 2 APPROVAL : aprobación *f*, aval *m*
endow [ɪn'daʊ, ɛn-] *vt* : dotar
endowment [ɪn'daʊmənt, ɛn-] *n* 1 FUNDING : dotación *f* 2 DONATION : donación *f*, legado *m* 3 ATTRIBUTE, GIFT : atributo *m*, dotes *fpl*
endurable [ɪn'dʊrəbəl, ɛn-, -'djʊr-] *adj* : tolerable, soportable
endurance [ɪn'dʊrənts, ɛn-, -'djʊr-] *n* : resistencia *f*, aguante *m*
endure [ɪn'dʊr, ɛn-, -'djʊr] *v* **-dured; -during** *vt* 1 BEAR : resistir, soportar, aguantar 2 TOLERATE : tolerar, soportar — *vi* LAST : durar, perdurar
enema ['ɛnəmə] *n* : enema *m*, lavativa *f*
enemy ['ɛnəmi] *n, pl* **-mies** : enemigo *m*, -ga *f*
energetic [,ɛnər'dʒɛtɪk] *adj* : enérgico, vigoroso — **energetically** [-tɪkli] *adv*
energize ['ɛnər,dʒaɪz] *vt* **-gized; -gizing** 1 ACTIVATE : activar 2 INVIGORATE : vigorizar
energy ['ɛnərdʒi] *n, pl* **-gies** 1 VITALITY : energía *f*, vitalidad *f* 2 EFFORT : esfuerzo *m*, energías *fpl* 3 POWER : energía *f* <atomic energy : energía atómica>
enervate ['ɛnər,veɪt] *vt* **-vated; -vating** : enervar, debilitar
enervation [,ɛnər'veɪʃən] *n* : enervación *f*, debilidad *f*
enfold [ɪn'fo:ld, ɛn-] *vt* : envolver
enforce [ɪn'fors, ɛn-] *vt* **-forced; -forcing** 1 : hacer respetar, hacer cumplir (una ley, etc.) 2 IMPOSE : imponer <to enforce obedience : imponer la obediencia>
enforcement [ɪn'forsmənt, ɛn-] *n* : imposición *f*
enfranchise [ɪn'fræn,tʃaɪz, ɛn-] *vt* **-chised; -chising** : conceder el voto a
enfranchisement [ɪn'fræn,tʃaɪzmənt, ɛn-] *n* : concesión *f* del voto
engage [ɪn'geɪdʒ, ɛn-] *v* **-gaged; -gaging** *vt* 1 ATTRACT : captar, atraer, llamar <to engage one's attention : captar la atención> 2 MESH : engranar <to engage the clutch : embragar> 3 COMMIT : comprometer <to get engaged : comprometerse> 4 HIRE : contratar 5 : entablar combate con (un enemigo) — *vi* 1 PARTICIPATE : participar 2 **to engage in combat** : entrar en combate

engagement [ɪn'geɪdʒmənt, ɛn-] *n* **1** APPOINTMENT : cita *f,* hora *f* **2** BETROTHAL : compromiso *m*
engaging [ɪn'geɪdʒɪŋ, ɛn-] *adj* : atractivo, encantador, interesante
engender [ɪn'dʒɛndər, ɛn-] *vt* **-dered; -dering** : engendrar
engine ['ɛndʒən] *n* **1** MOTOR : motor *m* **2** LOCOMOTIVE : locomotora *f,* máquina *f*
engineer[1] [ˌɛndʒə'nɪr] *vt* **1** : diseñar, construir (un sistema, un mecanismo, etc.) **2** CONTRIVE : maquinar, tramar, fraguar
engineer[2] *n* **1** : ingeniero *m,* -ra *f* **2** : maquinista *mf* (de locomotoras)
engineering [ˌɛndʒə'nɪrɪŋ] *n* : ingeniería *f*
English[1] ['ɪŋglɪʃ, 'ŋlɪʃ] *adj* : inglés
English[2] *n* **1** : inglés *m* (idioma) **2 the English** : los ingleses
Englishman ['ɪŋglɪʃmən, 'ɪŋlɪʃ-] *n, pl* **-men** [-mən, -ˌmɛn] : inglés *m*
Englishwoman ['ɪŋglɪʃˌwʊmən, 'ɪŋlɪʃ-] *n, pl* **-women** [-ˌwɪmən] : inglesa *f*
engrave [ɪn'greɪv, ɛn-] *vt* **-graved; -graving** : grabar
engraver [ɪn'greɪvər, ɛn-] *n* : grabador *m,* -dora *f*
engraving [ɪn'greɪvɪŋ, ɛn-] *n* : grabado *m*
engross [ɪn'groːs, ɛn-] *vt* : absorber
engrossed [ɪn'groːst, ɛn-] *adj* : absorto
engulf [ɪn'gʌlf, ɛn-] *vt* : envolver, sepultar
enhance [ɪn'hænts, ɛn-] *vt* **-hanced; -hancing** : realzar, aumentar, mejorar
enhancement [ɪn'hæntsmənt, ɛn-] *n* : mejora *f,* realce *m,* aumento *m*
enigma [ɪ'nɪgmə] *n* : enigma *m*
enigmatic [ˌɛnɪg'mæt̬ɪk, ˌiːnɪg-] *adj* : enigmático — **enigmatically** [-t̬ɪkli] *adv*
enjoin [ɪn'dʒɔɪn, ɛn-] *vt* **1** COMMAND : ordenar, imponer **2** FORBID : prohibir, vedar
enjoy [ɪn'dʒɔɪ, ɛn-] *vt* **1** : disfrutar, gozar de <did you enjoy the book? : ¿te gustó el libro?> <to enjoy good health : gozar de buena salud> **2 to enjoy oneself** : divertirse, pasarlo bien
enjoyable [ɪn'dʒɔɪəbəl, ɛn-] *adj* : agradable, placentero, divertido
enjoyment [ɪn'dʒɔɪmənt, ɛn-] *n* : placer *m,* goce *m,* disfrute *m,* deleite *m*
enlarge [ɪn'lɑrdʒ, ɛn-] *v* **-larged; -larging** *vt* : extender, agrandar, ampliar — *vi* **1** : ampliarse **2 to enlarge upon** : extenderse sobre, entrar en detalles sobre
enlargement [ɪn'lɑrdʒmənt, ɛn-] *n* : expansión *f,* ampliación *f* (dícese de fotografías)
enlarger [ɪn'lɑrdʒər, ɛn-] *n* : ampliadora *f*
enlighten [ɪn'laɪtən, ɛn-] *vt* : iluminar, aclarar
enlightenment [ɪn'laɪtənmənt, ɛn-] *n* **1** : ilustración *f* <the Enlightenment : la Ilustración> **2** CLARIFICATION : aclaración *f*
enlist [ɪn'lɪst, ɛn-] *vt* **1** ENROLL : alistar, reclutar **2** SECURE : conseguir <to enlist the support of : conseguir el apoyo de> — *vi* : alistarse
enlisted man [ɪn'lɪstəd, ɛn-] *n* : soldado *m* raso
enlistment [ɪn'lɪstmənt, ɛn-] *n* : alistamiento *m,* reclutamiento *m*
enliven [ɪn'laɪvən, ɛn-] *vt* : animar, alegrar, darle vida a
enmity ['ɛnmət̬i] *n, pl* **-ties** : enemistad *f,* animadversión *f*
ennoble [ɪ'noːbəl, ɛ-] *vt* **-bled; -bling** : ennoblecer
ennui [ˌɑn'wiː] *n* : hastío *m,* tedio *m,* fastidio *m,* aburrimiento *m*
enormity [ɪ'nɔrmət̬i] *n, pl* **-ties 1** ATROCITY : atrocidad *f,* barbaridad *f* **2** IMMENSITY : enormidad *f,* inmensidad *f*
enormous [ɪ'nɔrməs] *adj* : enorme, inmenso, tremendo — **enormously** *adv*
enough[1] [ɪ'nʌf] *adv* **1** : bastante, suficientemente **2 fair enough!** : ¡está bien!, ¡de acuerdo! **3 strangely enough** : por extraño que parezca **4 sure enough** : en efecto, sin duda alguna **5 well enough** : muy bien, bastante bien
enough[2] *adj* : bastante, suficiente <do we have enough chairs? : ¿tenemos suficientes sillas?>
enough[3] *pron* : (lo) suficiente, (lo) bastante <enough to eat : lo suficiente para comer> <it's not enough : no basta> <I've had enough! : ¡estoy harto!, ¡está bueno ya!>
enquire [ɪn'kwaɪr, ɛn-], **enquiry** ['ɪnˌkwaɪri, 'ɛn-, -kwəri; ɪn'kwaɪri, ɛn'-] → **inquire**, **inquiry**
enrage [ɪn'reɪdʒ, ɛn-] *vt* **-raged; -raging** : enfurecer, encolerizar
enraged [ɪn'reɪdʒd, ɛn-] *adj* : enfurecido, furioso
enrich [ɪn'rɪtʃ, ɛn-] *vt* : enriquecer
enrichment [ɪn'rɪtʃmənt, ɛn-] *n* : enriquecimiento *m*
enroll *or* **enrol** [ɪn'roːl, ɛn-] *v* **-rolled; -rolling** *vt* : matricular, inscribir — *vi* : matricularse, inscribirse
enrollment [ɪn'roːlmənt, ɛn-] *n* : matrícula *f,* inscripción *f*
en route [ɑ'ruːt, ɛn'raʊt] *adv* : de camino, por el camino
ensconce [ɪn'skɑnts, ɛn-] *vt* **-sconced; -sconcing** : acomodar, instalar, establecer cómodamente
ensemble [ɑn'sɑmbəl] *n* : conjunto *m*
enshrine [ɪn'ʃraɪn, ɛn-] *vt* **-shrined; -shrining** : conservar religiosamente, preservar
ensign ['ɛntsən, 'ɛnˌsaɪn] *n* **1** FLAG : enseña *f,* pabellón *m* **2** : alférez *mf* (de fragata)

enslave [ɪn'sleɪv, ɛn-] *vt* **-slaved; -slaving** : esclavizar
enslavement [ɪn'sleɪvmənt, ɛn-] *n* : esclavización *f*
ensnare [ɪn'snær, ɛn-] *vt* **-snared; -snaring** : atrapar
ensue [ɪn'suː, ɛn-] *vi* **-sued; -suing** : seguir, resultar
ensure [ɪn'ʃʊr, ɛn-] *vt* **-sured; -suring** : asegurar, garantizar
entail [ɪn'teɪl, ɛn-] *vt* : implicar, suponer, conllevar
entangle [ɪn'tæŋgəl, ɛn-] *vt* **-gled; -gling** : enredar
entanglement [ɪn'tæŋgəlmənt, ɛn-] *n* : enredo *m*
enter ['ɛntər] *vt* **1** : entrar en, entrar a **2** BEGIN : entrar en, comenzar, iniciar **3** RECORD : anotar, inscribir, dar entrada a **4** JOIN : entrar en, alistarse en, hacerse socio de — *vi* **1** : entrar **2 to enter into** : entrar en, firmar (un acuerdo), entablar (negociaciones, etc.)
enterprise ['ɛntər,praɪz] *n* **1** UNDERTAKING : empresa *f* **2** BUSINESS : empresa *f,* firma *f* **3** INITIATIVE : iniciativa *f,* empuje *m*
enterprising ['ɛntər,praɪzɪŋ] *adj* : emprendedor
entertain [,ɛntər'teɪn] *vt* **1** : recibir, agasajar <to entertain guests : tener invitados> **2** CONSIDER : considerar, contemplar **3** AMUSE : entretener, divertir
entertainer [,ɛntər'teɪnər] *n* : artista *mf*
entertainment [,ɛntər'teɪnmənt] *n* : entretenimiento *m,* diversión *f*
enthrall *or* **enthral** [ɪn'θrɔl, ɛn-] *vt* **-thralled; -thralling** : cautivar, embelesar
enthusiasm [ɪn'θuːzi,æzəm, ɛn-, -'θjuː-] *n* : entusiasmo *m*
enthusiast [ɪn'θuːzi,æst, ɛn-, -'θjuː-, -əst] *n* : entusiasta *mf;* aficionado *m,* -da *f*
enthusiastic [ɪn,θuːzi'æstɪk, ɛn-, -,θjuː-] *adj* : entusiasta, aficionado
enthusiastically [ɪn,θuːzi'æstɪkli, ɛn-, -,θjuː-] *adv* : con entusiasmo
entice [ɪn'taɪs, ɛn-] *vt* **-ticed; -ticing** : atraer, tentar
enticement [ɪn'taɪsmənt, ɛn-] *n* : tentación *f,* atracción *f,* señuelo *m*
entire [ɪn'taɪr, ɛn-] *adj* : entero, completo
entirely [ɪn'taɪrli, ɛn-] *adv* : completamente, totalmente
entirety [ɪn'taɪrti, ɛn-, -'taɪrəti] *n, pl* **-ties** : totalidad *f*
entitle [ɪn'taɪtəl, ɛn-] *vt* **-tled; -tling 1** NAME : titular, intitular **2** : dar derecho a <it entitles you to enter free : le da derecho a entrar gratis> **3 to be entitled to** : tener derecho a
entitlement [ɪn'taɪtəlmənt, ɛn-] *n* RIGHT : derecho *m*
entity ['ɛntəti] *n, pl* **-ties** : entidad *f,* ente *m*
entomologist [,ɛntə'mɑlədʒɪst] *n* : entomólogo *m,* -ga *f*
entomology [,ɛntə'mɑlədʒi] *n* : entomología *f*
entourage [,ɑntʊ'rɑʒ] *n* : séquito *m*
entrails ['ɛn,treɪlz, -trəlz] *npl* : entrañas *fpl,* vísceras *fpl*
entrance¹ [ɪn'træn*t*s, ɛn-] *vt* **-tranced; -trancing** : encantar, embelesar, fascinar
entrance² ['ɛntrən*t*s] *n* **1** ENTERING : entrada *f* <to make an entrance : entrar en escena> **2** ENTRY : entrada *f,* puerta *f* **3** ADMISSION : entrada *f,* ingreso *m* <entrance examination : examen de ingreso>
entrant ['ɛntrənt] *n* : candidato *m,* -ta *f* (en un examen); participante *mf* (en un concurso)
entrap [ɪn'træp, ɛn-] *vt* **-trapped; -trapping** : atrapar, entrampar, hacer caer en una trampa
entrapment [ɪn'træpmənt, ɛn-] *n* : captura *f*
entreat [ɪn'triːt, ɛn-] *vt* : suplicar, rogar
entreaty [ɪn'triːti, ɛn-] *n, pl* **-treaties** : ruego *m,* súplica *f*
entrée *or* **entree** ['ɑn,treɪ, ,ɑn'-] *n* : plato *m* principal
entrench [ɪn'trɛntʃ, ɛn-] *vt* **1** FORTIFY : atrincherar (una posición militar) **2** : consolidar, afianzar <firmly entrenched in his job : afianzado en su puesto>
entrepreneur [,ɑntrəprə'nər, -'njʊr] *n* : empresario *m,* -ria *f*
entrust [ɪn'trʌst, ɛn-] *vt* : confiar, encomendar
entry ['ɛntri] *n, pl* **-tries 1** ENTRANCE : entrada *f* **2** NOTATION : entrada *f,* anotación *f*
entwine [ɪn'twaɪn, ɛn-] *vt* **-twined; -twining** : entrelazar, entretejer, entrecruzar
enumerate [ɪ'nuːmə,reɪt, ɛ-, -'njuː-] *vt* **-ated; -ating 1** LIST : enumerar **2** COUNT : contar, enumerar
enumeration [ɪ,nuːmə'reɪʃən, ɛ-, -,njuː-] *n* : enumeración *f,* lista *f*
enunciate [i'nʌn*t*si,eɪt, ɛ-] *vt* **-ated; -ating 1** STATE : enunciar, decir **2** PRONOUNCE : articular, pronunciar
enunciation [i,nʌn*t*si'eɪʃən, ɛ-] *n* **1** STATEMENT : enunciación *f,* declaración *f* **2** ARTICULATION : articulación *f,* pronunciación *f,* dicción *f*
envelop [ɪn'vɛləp, ɛn-] *vt* : envolver, cubrir
envelope ['ɛnvə,loːp, 'ɑn-] *n* : sobre *m*
enviable ['ɛnviəbəl] *adj* : envidiable
envious ['ɛnviəs] *adj* : envidioso — **enviously** *adv*
environment [ɪn'vaɪrənmənt, ɛn-, -'vaɪərn-] *n* : medio *m* (ambiente), ambiente *m,* entorno *m*
environmental [ɪn,vaɪrən'mɛntəl, ɛn-, -,vaɪərn-] *adj* : ambiental

environmentalist [ɪn,vaɪrən'mɛn-təlɪst, ɛn-, -,vaɪərn-] *n* : ecologista *mf*
environs [ɪn'vaɪrənz, ɛn-, -'vaɪərnz] *npl* : alrededores *mpl*, entorno *m*, inmediaciones *fpl*
envisage [ɪn'vɪzɪdʒ, ɛn-] *vt* **-aged; -aging 1** IMAGINE : imaginarse, concebir **2** FORESEE : prever
envision [ɪn'vɪʒən, ɛn-] *vt* : imaginar
envoy ['ɛn,vɔɪ, 'ɑn-] *n* : enviado *m*, -da *f*
envy[1] ['ɛnvi] *vt* **-vied; -vying** : envidiar
envy[2] *n, pl* **envies** : envidia *f*
enzyme ['ɛn,zaɪm] *n* : enzima *f*
eon ['iːən, iː,ɑn] → **aeon**
epaulet [,ɛpə'lɛt] *n* : charretera *f*
ephemeral [ɪ'fɛmərəl, -'fiː-] *adj* : efímero, fugaz
epic[1] ['ɛpɪk] *adj* : épico
epic[2] *n* : poema *m* épico, epopeya *f*
epicure ['ɛpɪ,kjʊr] *n* : epicúreo *m*, -rea *f*; gastrónomo *m*, -ma *f*
epicurean [,ɛpɪkjʊ'riːən, -'kjʊriən] *adj* : epicúreo
epidemic[1] [,ɛpə'dɛmɪk] *adj* : epidémico
epidemic[2] *n* : epidemia *f*
epidermis [,ɛpə'dərməs] *n* : epidermis *f*
epigram ['ɛpə,græm] *n* : epigrama *m*
epilepsy ['ɛpə,lɛpsi] *n, pl* **-sies** : epilepsia *f*
epileptic[1] [,ɛpə'lɛptɪk] *adj* : epiléptico
epileptic[2] *n* : epiléptico *m*, -ca *f*
episcopal [ɪ'pɪskəpəl] *adj* : episcopal
episode ['ɛpə,soːd] *n* : episodio *m*
episodic [,ɛpə'sɑdɪk] *adj* : episódico
epistle [ɪ'pɪsəl] *n* : epístola *f*, carta *f*
epitaph ['ɛpə,tæf] *n* : epitafio *m*
epithet ['ɛpə,θɛt, -θət] *n* : epíteto *m*
epitome [ɪ'pɪt̬əmi] *n* **1** SUMMARY : epítome *m*, resumen *m* **2** EMBODIMENT : personificación *f*
epitomize [ɪ'pɪt̬ə,maɪz] *vt* **-mized; -mizing 1** SUMMARIZE : resumir **2** EMBODY : ser la personificación de, personificar
epoch ['ɛpək, 'ɛ,pɑk, 'iː,pɑk] *n* : época *f*, era *f*
equable ['ɛkwəbəl, 'iː-] *adj* **1** CALM, STEADY : ecuánime **2** UNIFORM : estable (dícese de la temperatura), constante (dícese del clima), uniforme
equably ['ɛkwəbli, 'iː-] *adv* : con ecuanimidad
equal[1] ['iːkwəl] *vt* **equaled** *or* **equalled; equaling** *or* **equalling 1** : ser igual a <two plus three equals five : dos más tres es igual a cinco> **2** MATCH : igualar
equal[2] *adj* **1** SAME : igual **2** ADEQUATE : adecuado, capaz
equal[3] *n* : igual *mf*
equality [ɪ'kwɑlət̬i] *n, pl* **-ties** : igualdad *f*
equalize ['iːkwə,laɪz] *vt* **-ized; -izing** : igualar, equiparar
equally ['iːkwəli] *adv* : igualmente, por igual
equanimity [,iːkwə'nɪmət̬i, ,ɛ-] *n, pl* **-ties** : ecuanimidad *f*
equate [ɪ'kweɪt] *vt* **equated; equating** : equiparar, identificar
equation [ɪ'kweɪʒən] *n* : ecuación *f*
equator [ɪ'kweɪt̬ər] *n* : ecuador *m*
equatorial [,iːkwə'toriəl, ,ɛ-] *adj* : ecuatorial
equestrian[1] [ɪ'kwɛstriən, ɛ-] *adj* : ecuestre
equestrian[2] *n* : jinete *mf*, caballista *mf*
equilateral [,iːkwə'læt̬ərəl, ,ɛ-] *adj* : equilátero
equilibrium [,iːkwə'lɪbriəm, ,ɛ-] *n, pl* **-riums** *or* **-ria** [-briə] : equilibrio *m*
equine ['iː,kwaɪn, 'ɛ-] *adj* : equino, hípico
equinox ['iːkwə,nɑks, 'ɛ-] *n* : equinoccio *m*
equip [ɪ'kwɪp] *vt* **equipped; equipping 1** FURNISH : equipar **2** PREPARE : preparar
equipment [ɪ'kwɪpmənt] *n* : equipo *m*
equitable ['ɛkwət̬əbəl] *adj* : equitativo, justo, imparcial
equity ['ɛkwət̬i] *n, pl* **-ties 1** FAIRNESS : equidad *f*, imparcialidad *f* **2** VALUE : valor *m* líquido
equivalence [ɪ'kwɪvələnts] *n* : equivalencia *f*
equivalent[1] [ɪ'kwɪvələnt] *adj* : equivalente
equivalent[2] *n* : equivalente *m*
equivocal [ɪ'kwɪvəkəl] *adj* **1** AMBIGUOUS : equívoco, ambiguo **2** QUESTIONABLE : incierto, dudoso, sospechoso
equivocate [ɪ'kwɪvə,keɪt] *vi* **-cated; -cating** : usar lenguaje equívoco, andarse con evasivas
equivocation [ɪ,kwɪvə'keɪʃən] *n* : evasiva *f*, subterfugio *m*
era ['ɪrə, 'ɛrə, 'iːrə] *n* : era *f*, época *f*
eradicate [ɪ'rædə,keɪt] *vt* **-cated; -cating** : erradicar
erase [ɪ'reɪs] *vt* **erased; erasing** : borrar
eraser [ɪ'reɪsər] *n* : goma *f* de borrar, borrador *m*
erasure [ɪ'reɪʃər] *n* : tachadura *f*
ere[1] ['ɛr] *conj* : antes de que
ere[2] *prep* **1** : antes de **2 ere long** : dentro de poco
erect[1] [ɪ'rɛkt] *vt* **1** CONSTRUCT : erigir, construir **2** RAISE : levantar **3** ESTABLISH : establecer
erect[2] *adj* : erguido, derecho, erecto
erection [ɪ'rɛkʃən] *n* **1** : erección *f* (en fisiología) **2** BUILDING : construcción *f*
ermine ['ərmən] *n* : armiño *m*
erode [ɪ'roːd] *vt* **eroded; eroding** : erosionar (el suelo), corroer (metales)
erosion [ɪ'roːʒən] *n* : erosión *f*, corrosión *f*
erotic [ɪ'rɑt̬ɪk] *adj* : erótico — **erotically** [-t̬ɪkli] *adv*

eroticism [ɪˈrɑt̬əˌsɪzəm] *n* : erotismo *m*

err [ˈɛr, ˈər] *vi* : cometer un error, equivocarse, errar

errand [ˈɛrənd] *n* : mandado *m,* encargo *m,* recado *m Spain* <an errand of mercy : una misión de caridad>

errant [ˈɛrənt] *adj* **1** WANDERING : errante **2** ASTRAY : descarriado

erratic [ɪˈræt̬ɪk] *adj* **1** INCONSISTENT : errático, irregular, inconsistente **2** ECCENTRIC : excéntrico, raro

erratically [ɪˈræt̬ɪkli] *adv* : erráticamente, de manera irregular

erroneous [ɪˈroːniəs, ɛ-] *adj* : erróneo — **erroneously** *adv*

error [ˈɛrər] *n* : error *m,* equivocación *f* <to be in error : estar equivocado>

ersatz [ˈɛrˌsɑts, ˈərˌsæts] *adj* : artificial, sustituto

erstwhile [ˈərstˌ*h*waɪl] *adj* : antiguo

erudite [ˈɛrəˌdaɪt, ˈɛrjʊ-] *adj* : erudito, letrado

erudition [ˌɛrəˈdɪʃən, ˌɛrjʊ-] *n* : erudición *f*

erupt [ɪˈrʌpt] *vi* **1** : hacer erupción (dícese de un volcán o un sarpullido) **2** : estallar (dícese de la cólera o la violencia)

eruption [ɪˈrʌpʃən] *n* : erupción *f,* estallido *m*

eruptive [ɪˈrʌptɪv] *adj* : eruptivo

escalate [ˈɛskəˌleɪt] *v* **-lated; -lating** *vt* : intensificar (un conflicto), aumentar (precios) — *vi* : intensificarse, aumentarse

escalation [ˌɛskəˈleɪʃən] *n* : intensificación *f,* escalada *f,* aumento *m,* subida *f*

escalator [ˈɛskəˌleɪt̬ər] *n* : escalera *f* mecánica

escapade [ˈɛskəˌpeɪd] *n* : aventura *f*

escape[1] [ɪˈskeɪp, ɛ-] *v* **-caped; -caping** *vt* : escaparse de, librarse de, evitar — *vi* : escaparse, fugarse, huir

escape[2] *n* **1** FLIGHT : fuga *f,* huida *f,* escapada *f* **2** LEAKAGE : escape *m,* fuga *f* **3** : escapatoria *f,* evasión *f* <to have no escape : no tener escapatoria> <escape from reality : evasión de la realidad>

escapee [ɪˌskeɪˈpiː, ˌɛ-] *n* : fugitivo *m,* -va *f*

escarole [ˈɛskəˌroːl] *n* : escarola *f*

escarpment [ɪsˈkɑrpmənt, ɛs-] *n* : escarpa *f,* escarpadura *f*

eschew [ɛˈʃuː, ɪsˈtʃuː] *vt* : evitar, rehuir, abstenerse de

escort[1] [ɪˈskɔrt, ɛ-] *vt* **1** : escoltar <to escort a ship : escoltar un barco> **2** ACCOMPANY : acompañar

escort[2] [ˈɛsˌkɔrt] *n* **1** : escolta *f* <armed escort : escolta armada> **2** COMPANION : acompañante *mf;* compañero *m,* -ra *f*

escrow [ˈɛsˌkroː] *n* **in escrow** : en depósito, en custodia de un tercero

esophagus [ɪˈsɑfəgəs, iː-] *n, pl* **-gi** [-ˌgaɪ, -ˌdʒaɪ] : esófago *m*

esoteric [ˌɛsəˈtɛrɪk] *adj* : esotérico, hermético

especially [ɪˈspɛʃəli] *adv* : especialmente, particularmente

espionage [ˈɛspiəˌnɑʒ, -ˌnɑdʒ] *n* : espionaje *m*

espouse [ɪˈspaʊz, ɛ-] *vt* **espoused; espousing** **1** MARRY : casarse con **2** ADOPT, ADVOCATE : apoyar, adherirse a, adoptar

espresso [ɛˈsprɛˌsoː] *n, pl* **-sos** : café *m* exprés

essay[1] [ɛˈseɪ, ˈɛˌseɪ] *vt* : intentar, tratar

essay[2] [ˈɛˌseɪ] *n* **1** COMPOSITION : ensayo *m,* trabajo *m* **2** ATTEMPT : intento *m*

essayist [ˈɛˌseɪɪst] *n* : ensayista *mf*

essence [ˈɛsən*t*s] *n* **1** CORE : esencia *f,* núcleo *m,* meollo *m* <in essence : esencialmente> **2** EXTRACT : esencia *f,* extracto *m* **3** PERFUME : esencia *f,* perfume *m*

essential[1] [ɪˈsɛntʃəl] *adj* : esencial, imprescindible, fundamental — **essentially** *adv*

essential[2] *n* : elemento *m* esencial, lo imprescindible

establish [ɪˈstæblɪʃ, ɛ-] *vt* **1** FOUND : establecer, fundar **2** SET UP : establecer, instaurar, instituir **3** PROVE : demostrar, probar

establishment [ɪˈstæblɪʃmənt, ɛ-] *n* **1** ESTABLISHING : establecimiento *m,* fundación *f,* instauración *f* **2** BUSINESS : negocio *m,* establecimiento *m* **3 the Establishment** : la clase dirigente

estate [ɪˈsteɪt, ɛ-] *n* **1** POSSESSIONS : bienes *mpl,* propiedad *f,* patrimonio *m* **2** PROPERTY : hacienda *f,* finca *f,* propiedad *f*

esteem[1] [ɪˈstiːm, ɛ-] *vt* : estimar, apreciar

esteem[2] *n* : estima *f,* aprecio *m*

ester [ˈɛstər] *n* : éster *m*

esthetic [ɛsˈθɛt̬ɪk] → **aesthetic**

estimable [ˈɛstəməbəl] *adj* : estimable

estimate[1] [ˈɛstəˌmeɪt] *vt* **-mated; -mating** : calcular, estimar

estimate[2] [ˈɛstəmət] *n* **1** : cálculo *m* aproximado <to make an estimate : hacer un cálculo> **2** ASSESSMENT : valoración *f,* estimación *f*

estimation [ˌɛstəˈmeɪʃən] *n* **1** JUDGMENT : juicio *m,* opinión *f* <in my estimation : en mi opinión, según mis cálculos> **2** ESTEEM : estima *f,* aprecio *m*

estimator [ˈɛstəˌmeɪt̬ər] *n* : tasador *m,* -dora *f*

Estonian [ɛˈstoːniən] *n* : estonio *m,* -nia *f* — **Estonian** *adj*

estrange [ɪˈstreɪndʒ, ɛ-] *vt* **-tranged; -tranging** : enajenar, apartar, alejar

estrangement [ɪˈstreɪndʒmənt, ɛ-] *n* : alejamiento *m,* distanciamiento *m*

estrogen [ˈɛstrədʒən] *n* : estrógeno *m*

estrus [ˈɛstrəs] *n* : celo *m*

estuary [ˈɛstʃʊˌwɛri] *n, pl* **-aries** : estuario *m,* -ria *f*

et cetera [ɛt'sɛt̬ərə, -'sɛtrə] : etcétera
etch ['ɛtʃ] *v* : grabar al aguafuerte
etching ['ɛtʃɪŋ] *n* : aguafuerte *m,* grabado *m* al aguafuerte
eternal [ɪ'tərnəl, iː-] *adj* **1** EVERLASTING : eterno **2** INTERMINABLE : constante, incesante
eternally [ɪ'tərnəli, iː-] *adv* : eternamente, para siempre
eternity [ɪ'tərnət̬i, iː-] *n, pl* **-ties** : eternidad *f*
ethane ['ɛ,θeɪn] *n* : etano *m*
ethanol ['ɛθə,nɔl, -,noːl] *n* : etanol *m*
ether ['iːθər] *n* : éter *m*
ethereal [ɪ'θɪriəl, iː-] *adj* **1** CELESTIAL : etéreo, celeste **2** DELICATE : delicado
ethical ['ɛθɪkəl] *adj* : ético — **ethically** *adv*
ethics ['ɛθɪks] *ns & pl* **1** : ética *f* **2** MORALITY : ética *f,* moral *f,* moralidad *f*
Ethiopian [,iːθi'oːpiən] *n* : etíope *mf* — **Ethiopian** *adj*
ethnic ['ɛθnɪk] *adj* : étnico
ethnologist [ɛθ'nɑlədʒɪst] *n* : etnólogo *m,* -ga *f*
ethnology [ɛθ'nɑlədʒi] *n* : etnología *f*
etiquette ['ɛt̬ɪkət, -,kɛt] *n* : etiqueta *f,* protocolo *m*
etymological [,ɛt̬əmə'lɑdʒɪkəl] *adj* : etimológico
etymology [,ɛt̬ə'mɑlədʒi] *n, pl* **-gies** : etimología *f*
eucalyptus [,juːkə'lɪptəs] *n, pl* **-ti** [-,taɪ] *or* **-tuses** [-təsəz] : eucalipto *m*
Eucharist ['juːkərɪst] *n* : Eucaristía *f*
eulogize ['juːlə,dʒaɪz] *vt* **-gized; -gizing** : elogiar, encomiar
eulogy ['juːlədʒi] *n, pl* **-gies** : elogio *m,* encomio *m,* panegírico *m*
eunuch ['juːnək] *n* : eunuco *m*
euphemism ['juːfə,mɪzəm] *n* : eufemismo *m*
euphemistic [,juːfə'mɪstɪk] *adj* : eufemístico
euphony ['juːfəni] *n, pl* **-nies** : eufonía *f*
euphoria [jʊ'foriə] *n* : euforia *f*
euphoric [jʊ'forɪk] *adj* : eufórico
euthanasia [,juːθə'neɪʒə, -ʒiə] *n* : eutanasia *f*
evacuate [ɪ'vækjʊ,eɪt] *v* **-ated; -ating** *vt* VACATE : evacuar, desalojar — *vi* WITHDRAW : retirarse
evacuation [ɪ,vækjʊ'eɪʃən] *n* : evacuación *f,* desalojo *m*
evade [ɪ'veɪd] *vt* **evaded; evading** : evadir, eludir, esquivar
evaluate [ɪ'væljʊ,eɪt] *vt* **-ated; -ating** : evaluar, valorar, tasar
evaluation [ɪ,væljʊ'eɪʃən] *n* : evaluación *f,* valoración *f,* tasación *f*
evangelical [,iː,væn'dʒɛlɪkəl, ,ɛvən-] *adj* : evangélico
evangelist [ɪ'vændʒəlɪst] *n* **1** : evangelista *m* **2** PREACHER : predicador *m,* -dora *f*
evaporate [ɪ'væpə,reɪt] *vi* **-rated; -rating 1** VAPORIZE : evaporarse **2** VANISH : evaporarse, desvanecerse, esfumarse
evaporation [ɪ,væpə'reɪʃən] *n* : evaporación *f*
evasion [ɪ'veɪʒən] *n* : evasión *f*
evasive [ɪ'veɪsɪv] *adj* : evasivo
evasiveness [ɪ'veɪsɪvnəs] *n* : carácter *m* evasivo
eve ['iːv] *n* **1** : víspera *f* <on the eve of the festivities : en vísperas de las festividades> **2** → **evening**
even[1] ['iːvən] *vt* **1** LEVEL : allanar, nivelar, emparejar **2** EQUALIZE : igualar, equilibrar — *vi* **to even out** : nivelarse, emparejarse
even[2] *adv* **1** : hasta, incluso <even a child can do it : hasta un niño puede hacerlo> <he looked content, even happy : se le veía satisfecho, incluso feliz> **2** (*in negative constructions*) : ni siquiera <he didn't even try : ni siquiera lo intentó> **3** (*in comparisons*) : aún, todavía <even better : aún mejor, todavía mejor> **4 even if** : aunque **5 even so** : aun así **6 even though** : aun cuando, a pesar de que
even[3] *adj* **1** SMOOTH : uniforme, liso, parejo **2** FLAT : plano, llano **3** EQUAL : igual, igualado <an even score : un marcador igualado> **4** REGULAR : regular, constante <an even pace : un ritmo constante> **5** EXACT : exacto, justo **6** : par <even number : número par> **7 to be even** : estar en paz, estar a mano **8 to get even** : desquitarse, vengarse
evening ['iːvnɪŋ] *n* : tarde *f,* noche *f* <in the evening : por la noche>
evenly ['iːvənli] *adv* **1** UNIFORMLY : de modo uniforme, de manera constante **2** FAIRLY : igualmente, equitativamente
evenness ['iːvənnəs] *n* : uniformidad *f,* igualdad *f,* regularidad *f*
event [ɪ'vɛnt] *n* **1** : acontecimiento *m,* suceso *m,* prueba *f* (en deportes) **2 in the event that** : en caso de que
eventful [ɪ'vɛntfəl] *adj* : lleno de incidentes, memorable
eventual [ɪ'vɛntʃʊəl] *adj* : final, consiguiente
eventuality [ɪ,vɛntʃʊ'ælət̬i] *n, pl* **-ties** : eventualidad *f*
eventually [ɪ'vɛntʃʊəli] *adv* : al fin, con el tiempo, algún día
ever ['ɛvər] *adv* **1** ALWAYS : siempre <as ever : como siempre> <ever since : desde entonces> **2** (*in questions*) : alguna vez, algún día <have you ever been to Mexico? : ¿has estado en México alguna vez?> **3** (*in negative constructions*) : nunca <doesn't he ever work? : ¿es que nunca trabaja?> <nobody ever helps me : nadie nunca me ayuda> **4** (*in comparisons*) : nunca <better than ever : mejor que nunca> **5** (*as intensifier*) <I'm ever so happy! : ¡estoy tan y tan feliz!> <he

looks ever so angry : parece estar muy enojado>
evergreen[1] ['ɛvər,gri:n] *adj* : de hoja perenne
evergreen[2] *n* : planta *f* de hoja perenne
everlasting [,ɛvər'læstɪŋ] *adj* : eterno, perpetuo, imperecedero
evermore [,ɛvər'mor] *adv* : eternamente
every ['ɛvri] *adj* **1** EACH : cada <every time : cada vez> <every other house : cada dos casas> **2** ALL : todo <every month : todos los meses> <every woman : toda mujer, todas las mujeres> **3** COMPLETE : pleno, entero <to have every confidence : tener plena confianza>
everybody ['ɛvri,bʌdi, -,bɑ-] *pron* : todos *mpl*, -das *fpl*; todo el mundo
everyday [,ɛvri'deɪ, 'ɛvri,-] *adj* : cotidiano, diario, corriente <everyday clothes : ropa de todos los días>
everyone ['ɛvri ,wʌn] → **everybody**
everything ['ɛvri,θɪŋ] *pron* : todo
everywhere ['ɛvri,*h*wɛr] *adv* : en todas partes, por todas partes, dondequiera <I looked everywhere : busqué en todas partes> <everywhere we go : dondequiera que vayamos>
evict [ɪ'vɪkt] *vt* : desalojar, desahuciar
eviction [ɪ'vɪkʃən] *n* : desalojo *m*, desahucio *m*
evidence ['ɛvədən*t*s] *n* **1** INDICATION : indicio *m*, señal *m* <to be in evidence : estar a la vista> **2** PROOF : evidencia *f*, prueba *f* **3** TESTIMONY : testimonio *m*, declaración *f* <to give evidence : declarar como testigo, prestar declaración>
evident ['ɛvidənt] *adj* : evidente, patente, manifiesto
evidently ['ɛvidəntli, ,ɛvi'dɛntli] *adv* **1** CLEARLY : claramente, obviamente **2** APPARENTLY : aparentemente, evidentemente, al parecer
evil[1] ['i:vəl, -vɪl] *adj* **eviler** *or* **eviller; evilest** *or* **evillest 1** WICKED : malvado, malo, maligno **2** HARMFUL : nocivo, dañino, pernicioso **3** UNPLEASANT : desagradable <an evil odor : un olor horrible>
evil[2] *n* **1** WICKEDNESS : mal *m*, maldad *f* **2** MISFORTUNE : desgracia *f*, mal *m*
evildoer [,i:vəl'du:ər, ,i:vɪl-] *n* : malvado *m*, -da *f*
evince [ɪ'vɪn*t*s] *vt* **evinced; evincing** : mostrar, manifestar, revelar
eviscerate [ɪ'vɪsə,reɪt] *vt* **-ated; -ating** : eviscerar, destripar (un pollo, etc.)
evocation [,i:vo'keɪʃən, ,ɛ-] *n* : evocación *f*
evocative [i'vɑkəţɪv] *adj* : evocador
evoke [i'vo:k] *vt* **evoked; evoking** : evocar, provocar
evolution [,ɛvə'lu:ʃən, ,i:-] *n* : evolución *f*, desarrollo *m*
evolutionary [,ɛvə'lu:ʃə,nɛri, ,i:-] *adj* : evolutivo
evolve [i'vɑlv] *vi* **evolved; evolving** : evolucionar, desarrollarse
ewe ['ju:] *n* : oveja *f*
exact[1] [ɪg'zækt, ɛ-] *vt* : exigir, imponer, arrancar
exact[2] *adj* : exacto, preciso — **exactly** *adv*
exacting [ɪ'zæktɪŋ, ɛg-] *adj* : exigente, riguroso
exactitude [ɪg'zæktə,tu:d, ɛg-, -,tju:d] *n* : exactitud *f*, precisión *f*
exaggerate [ɪg'zædʒə,reɪt, ɛg-] *v* **-ated; -ating** : exagerar
exaggerated [ɪg'zædʒə,reɪţəd, ɛg-] *adj* : exagerado — **exaggeratedly** *adv*
exaggeration [ɪg,zædʒə'reɪʃən, ɛg-] *n* : exageración *f*
exalt [ɪg'zɔlt, ɛg-] *vt* : exaltar, ensalzar, glorificar
exaltation [,ɛg,zɔl'teɪʃən, ,ɛk,sɔl-] *n* : exaltación *f*
exam [ɪg'zæm, ɛg-] → **examination**
examination [ɪg,zæmə'neɪʃən, ɛg-] *n* **1** TEST : examen *m* **2** INSPECTION : inspección *f*, revisión *f* **3** INVESTIGATION : examen *m*, estudio *m*
examine [ɪg'zæmən, ɛg-] *vt* **-ined; -ining 1** TEST : examinar **2** INSPECT : inspeccionar, revisar **3** STUDY : examinar
example [ɪg'zæmpəl, ɛg-] *n* : ejemplo *m* <for example : por ejemplo> <to set an example : dar ejemplo>
exasperate [ɪg'zæspə,reɪt, ɛg-] *vt* **-ated; -ating** : exasperar, sacar de quicio
exasperation [ɪg,zæspə'reɪʃən, ɛg-] *n* : exasperación *f*
excavate ['ɛkskə,veɪt] *vt* **-vated; -vating** : excavar
excavation [,ɛkskə'veɪʃən] *n* : excavación *f*
exceed [ɪk'si:d, ɛk-] *vt* **1** SURPASS : exceder, rebasar, sobrepasar **2** : exceder de, sobrepasar <not exceeding two months : que no exceda de dos meses>
exceedingly [ɪk'si:dɪŋli, ɛk-] *adv* : extremadamente, sumamente
excel [ɪk'sɛl, ɛk-] *v* **-celled; -celling** *vi* : sobresalir, descollar, lucirse — *vt* : superar
excellence ['ɛksələn*t*s] *n* : excelencia *f*
excellency ['ɛksələn*t*si] *n, pl* **-cies** : excelencia *f* <His Excellency : Su Excelencia>
excellent ['ɛksələnt] *adj* : excelente, sobresaliente — **excellently** *adv*
except[1] [ɪk'sɛpt] *vt* : exceptuar, excluir
except[2] *conj* : pero, si no fuera por
except[3] *prep* : excepto, menos, salvo <everyone except Carlos : todos menos Carlos>
exception [ɪk'sɛpʃən] *n* **1** : excepción *f* **2 to take exception to** : ofenderse por, objetar a
exceptional [ɪk'sɛpʃənəl] *adj* : excepcional, extraordinario — **exceptionally** *adv*

excerpt[1] [ɛk'sərpt, ɛg'zərpt, 'ɛk,-, 'ɛg,-] *vt* : escoger, seleccionar
excerpt[2] ['ɛk,sərpt, 'ɛg,zərpt] *n* : pasaje *m,* selección *f*
excess[1] ['ɛk,sɛs, ɪk'sɛs] *adj* **1** : excesivo, de sobra **2 excess baggage** : exceso *m* de equipaje
excess[2] [ɪk'sɛs, 'ɛk,sɛs] *n* **1** SUPERFLUITY : exceso *m,* superfluidad *f* <an excess of energy : un exceso de energía> **2** SURPLUS : excedente *m,* sobrante *m* <in excess of : superior a>
excessive [ɪk'sɛsɪv, ɛk-] *adj* : excesivo, exagerado, desmesurado — **excessively** *adv*
exchange[1] [ɪks'tʃeɪndʒ, ɛks-; 'ɛks-,tʃeɪndʒ] *vt* **-changed; -changing** : cambiar, intercambiar, canjear
exchange[2] *n* **1** : cambio *m,* intercambio *m,* canje *m* **2 stock exchange** : bolsa *f* (de valores)
exchangeable [ɪks'tʃeɪndʒəbəl, ɛks-] *adj* : canjeable
excise[1] [ɪk'saɪz, ɛk-] *vt* **-cised; -cising** : extirpar
excise[2] ['ɛk,saɪz] *n* **excise tax** : impuesto *m* interno, impuesto *m* sobre el consumo
excision [ɪk'sɪʒən, ɛk-] *n* : extirpación *f,* excisión *f*
excitability [ɪk,saɪtə'bɪləṭi, ɛk-] *n* : excitabilidad *f*
excitable [ɪk'saɪṭəbəl, ɛk-] *adj* : excitable
excitation [,ɛk,saɪ'teɪʃən] *n* : excitación *f*
excite [ɪk'saɪt, ɛk-] *vt* **-cited; -citing 1** AROUSE, STIMULATE : excitar, mover, estimular **2** ANIMATE : entusiasmar, animar **3** EVOKE, PROVOKE : provocar, despertar, suscitar <to excite curiousity : despertar la curiosidad>
excited [ɪk'saɪṭəd, ɛk-] *adj* **1** STIMULATED : excitado, estimulado **2** ENTHUSIASTIC : entusiasmado, emocionado
excitedly [ɪk'saɪṭədli, ɛk-] *adv* : con excitación, con entusiasmo
excitement [ɪk'saɪtmənt, ɛk-] *n* **1** ENTHUSIASM : entusiasmo *m,* emoción *f* **2** AGITATION : agitación *f,* alboroto *m,* conmoción *f* **3** AROUSAL : excitación *f*
exclaim [ɪks'kleɪm, ɛk-] *v* : exclamar
exclamation [,ɛksklə'meɪʃən] *n* : exclamación *f*
exclamation point *n* : signo *m* de admiración
exclamatory [ɪks'klæmə,tori, ɛks-] *adj* : exclamativo
exclude [ɪks'klu:d, ɛks-] *vt* **-cluded; -cluding 1** BAR : excluir, descartar, no admitir **2** EXPEL : expeler, expulsar
exclusion [ɪks'klu:ʒən, ɛks-] *n* : exclusión *f*
exclusive[1] [ɪks'klu:sɪv, ɛks-] *adj* **1** SOLE : exclusivo, único **2** SELECT : exclusivo, selecto
exclusive[2] *n* : exclusiva *f*
exclusively [ɪks'klu:sɪvli, ɛks-] *adv* : exclusivamente, únicamente
exclusiveness [ɪks'klu:sɪvnəs, ɛks-] *n* : exclusividad *f*
excommunicate [,ɛkskə'mju:nə,keɪt] *vt* **-cated; -cating** : excomulgar
excommunication [,ɛkskə,mju:nə-'keɪʃən] *n* : excomunión *f*
excrement ['ɛkskrəmənt] *n* : excremento *m*
excrete [ɪk'skri:t, ɛk-] *vt* **-creted; -creting** : excretar
excretion [ɪk'skri:ʃən, ɛk-] *n* : excreción *f*
excruciating [ɪk'skru:ʃi,eɪṭɪŋ, ɛk-] *adj* : insoportable, atroz, terrible — **excruciatingly** *adv*
exculpate ['ɛkskəl,peɪt] *vt* **-pated; -pating** : exculpar
excursion [ɪk'skərʒən, ɛk-] *n* **1** OUTING : excursión *f,* paseo *m* **2** DIGRESSION : digresión *f*
excuse[1] [ɪk'skju:z, ɛk-] *vt* **-cused; -cusing 1** PARDON : disculpar, perdonar <excuse me : con permiso, perdóneme, perdón> **2** EXEMPT : eximir, disculpar **3** JUSTIFY : excusar, justificar
excuse[2] [ɪk'skju:s, ɛk-] *n* **1** JUSTIFICATION : excusa *f,* justificación *f* **2** PRETEXT : pretexto *m* **3 to make one's excuses to someone** : pedirle disculpas a alguien
execute ['ɛksɪ,kju:t] *vt* **-cuted; -cuting 1** CARRY OUT : ejecutar, llevar a cabo, desempeñar **2** ENFORCE : ejecutar, cumplir (un testamento, etc.) **3** KILL : ejecutar, ajusticiar
execution [,ɛksɪ'kju:ʃən] *n* **1** PERFORMANCE : ejecución *f,* desempeño *m* **2** IMPLEMENTATION : cumplimiento *m* **3** : ejecución *f* (por un delito)
executioner [,ɛksɪ'kju:ʃənər] *n* : verdugo *m*
executive[1] [ɪg'zɛkjəṭɪv, ɛg-] *adj* : ejecutivo
executive[2] *n* : ejecutivo *m,* -va *f*
executor [ɪg'zɛkjəṭər, ɛg-] *n* : albacea *m,* testamentario *m*
executrix [ɪg'zɛkjə,trɪks, ɛg-] *n, pl* **executrices** [-,zɛkjə'traɪ,si:z] *or* **executrixes** [-'zɛkjə,trɪksəz] : albacea *f,* testamentaria *f*
exemplary [ɪg'zɛmpləri, ɛg-] *adj* : ejemplar
exemplify [ɪg'zɛmplə,faɪ, ɛg-] *vt* **-fied; -fying** : ejemplificar, ilustrar, demostrar
exempt[1] [ɪg'zɛmpt, ɛg-] *vt* : eximir, dispensar, exonerar
exempt[2] *adj* : exento, eximido
exemption [ɪg'zɛmpʃən, ɛg-] *n* : exención *f*
exercise[1] ['ɛksər,saɪz] *v* **-cised; -cising** *vt* **1** : ejercitar (el cuerpo) **2** USE : ejercer, hacer uso de — *vi* : hacer ejercicio
exercise[2] *n* **1** : ejercicio *m* **2 exercises** *npl* WORKOUT : ejercicios *mpl* físicos **3 exercises** *npl* CEREMONY : ceremonia *f*
exert [ɪg'zərt, ɛg-] *vt* **1** : ejercer, emplear **2 to exert oneself** : esforzarse

exertion [ɪg'zərʃən, ɛg-] *n* **1** USE : ejercicio *m* (de autoridad, etc.), uso *m* (de fuerza, etc.) **2** EFFORT : esfuerzo *m,* empeño *m*
exhalation [ˌɛksə'leɪʃən, ˌɛkshə-] *n* : exhalación *f,* espiración *f*
exhale [ɛks'heɪl] *v* **-haled; -haling** *vt* **1** : exhalar, espirar **2** EMIT : exhalar, despedir, emitir — *vi* : espirar
exhaust¹ [ɪg'zɔst, ɛg-] *vt* **1** DEPLETE : agotar **2** TIRE : cansar, fatigar, agotar **3** EMPTY : vaciar
exhaust² *n* **1 exhaust fumes** : gases *mpl* de escape **2 exhaust pipe** : tubo *m* de escape **3 exhaust system** : sistema *m* de escape
exhausted [ɪg'zɔstəd, ɛg-] *adj* : agotado, derrengado
exhausting [ɪg'zɔstɪŋ, ɛg-] *adj* : extenuante, agotador
exhaustion [ɪg'zɔstʃən, ɛg-] *n* : agotamiento *m*
exhaustive [ɪg'zɔstɪv, ɛg-] *adj* : exhaustivo
exhibit¹ [ɪg'zɪbət, ɛg-] *vt* **1** DISPLAY : exhibir, exponer **2** PRODUCE, SHOW : mostrar, presentar
exhibit² *n* **1** OBJECT : objeto *m* expuesto **2** EXHIBITION : exposición *f,* exhibición *f* **3** EVIDENCE : prueba *f* instrumental
exhibition [ˌɛksə'bɪʃən] *n* **1** : exposición *f,* exhibición *f* **2 to make an exhibition of oneself** : dar el espectáculo, hacer el ridículo
exhilarate [ɪg'zɪləˌreɪt, ɛg-] *vt* **-rated; -rating** : alegrar, levantar el ánimo de
exhilaration [ɪgˌzɪlə'reɪʃən, ɛg-] *n* : alegría *f,* regocijo *m,* júbilo *m*
exhort [ɪg'zɔrt, ɛg-] *vt* : exhortar
exhortation [ˌɛkˌsɔr'teɪʃən, -sər-; ˌɛgˌzɔr-] *n* : exhortación *f*
exhumation [ˌɛksju'meɪʃən, -hju-; ˌɛgzu-, -zju-] *n* : exhumación *f*
exhume [ɪg'zuːm, -'zjuːm; ɪks'juːm, -'hjuːm] *vt* **-humed; -huming** : exhumar, desenterrar
exigencies ['ɛksɪdʒən*t*siz, ɪg'zɪdʒənˌsiːz] *npl* : exigencias *fpl*
exile¹ ['ɛgˌzaɪl, 'ɛkˌsaɪl] *vt* **exiled; exiling** : exiliar, desterrar
exile² *n* **1** BANISHMENT : exilio *m,* destierro *m* **2** OUTCAST : exiliado *m,* **-da** *f;* desterrado *m,* **-da** *f*
exist [ɪg'zɪst, ɛg-] *vi* **1** BE : existir **2** LIVE : subsistir, vivir
existence [ɪg'zɪstən*t*s, ɛg-] *n* : existencia *f*
existent [ɪg'zɪstənt, ɛg-] *adj* : existente
exit¹ ['ɛgzət, 'ɛksət] *vi* : salir, hacer mutis (en el teatro) — *vt* : salir de
exit² *n* **1** DEPARTURE : salida *f,* partida *f* **2** EGRESS : salida *f* <emergency exit : salida de emergencia>
exodus ['ɛksədəs] *n* : éxodo *m*
exonerate [ɪg'zɑnəˌreɪt, ɛg-] *vt* **-ated; -ating** : exonerar, disculpar, absolver
exoneration [ɪgˌzɑnə'reɪʃən, ɛg-] *n* : exoneración *f*
exorbitant [ɪg'zɔrbətənt, ɛg-] *adj* : exorbitante, excesivo
exorcise ['ɛkˌsɔrˌsaɪz, -sər-] *vt* **-cised; -cising** : exorcizar
exorcism ['ɛksərˌsɪzəm] *n* : exorcismo *m*
exotic¹ [ɪg'zɑtɪk, ɛg-] *adj* : exótico — **exotically** [-ɪkli] *adv*
exotic² *n* : planta *f* exótica
expand [ɪk'spænd, ɛk-] *vt* **1** ENLARGE : expandir, dilatar, aumentar, ampliar **2** EXTEND : extender — *vi* **1** ENLARGE : ampliarse, extenderse **2** : expandirse, dilatarse (dícese de los metales, gases, etc.)
expanse [ɪk'spæn*t*s, ɛk-] *n* : extensión *f*
expansion [ɪk'spæntʃən, ɛk-] *n* **1** ENLARGEMENT : expansión *f,* ampliación *f* **2** EXPANSE : extensión *f*
expansive [ɪk'spæn*t*sɪv, ɛk-] *adj* **1** : expansivo **2** OUTGOING : expansivo, comunicativo **3** AMPLE : ancho, amplio — **expansively** *adv*
expansiveness [ɪk'spæn*t*sɪvnəs, ɛk-] *n* : expansibilidad *f*
expatriate¹ [ɛks'peɪtriˌeɪt] *vt* **-ated; -ating** : expatriar
expatriate² [ɛks'peɪtriət, -ˌeɪt] *adj* : expatriado
expatriate³ [ɛks'peɪtriət, -ˌeɪt] *n* : expatriado *m,* **-da** *f*
expect [ɪk'spɛkt, ɛk-] *vt* **1** SUPPOSE : suponer, imaginarse **2** ANTICIPATE : esperar **3** COUNT ON, REQUIRE : contar con, esperar — *vi* **to be expecting** : estar embarazada
expectancy [ɪk'spɛktən*t*si, ɛk-] *n, pl* **-cies** : expectativa *f,* esperanza *f*
expectant [ɪk'spɛktənt, ɛk-] *adj* **1** ANTICIPATING : expectante **2** EXPECTING : futuro <expectant mother : futura madre>
expectantly [ɪk'spɛktəntli, ɛk-] *adv* : con expectación
expectation [ˌɛkˌspɛk'teɪʃən] *n* **1** ANTICIPATION : expectación *f* **2** EXPECTANCY : expectativa *f*
expedient¹ [ɪk'spiːdiənt, ɛk-] *adj* : conveniente, oportuno
expedient² *n* : expediente *m,* recurso *m*
expedite ['ɛkspəˌdaɪt] *vt* **-dited; -diting 1** FACILITATE : facilitar, dar curso a **2** HASTEN : acelerar
expedition [ˌɛkspə'dɪʃən] *n* : expedición *f*
expeditious [ˌɛkspə'dɪʃəs] *adj* : pronto, rápido
expel [ɪk'spɛl, ɛk-] *vt* **-pelled; -pelling** : expulsar, expeler
expend [ɪk'spɛnd, ɛk-] *vt* **1** DISBURSE : gastar, desembolsar **2** CONSUME : consumir, agotar
expendable [ɪk'spɛndəbəl, ɛk-] *adj* : prescindible
expenditure [ɪk'spɛndɪtʃər, ɛk-, -ˌtʃʊr] *n* : gasto *m*
expense [ɪk'spɛn*t*s, ɛk-] *n* **1** COST : gasto *m* **2 expenses** *npl* : gastos *mpl,*

expensas *fpl* **3 at the expense of :** a expensas de
expensive [ɪk'spɛntsɪv, ɛk-] *adj* **:** costoso, caro — **expensively** *adv*
experience[1] [ɪk'spɪriənts, ɛk-] *vt* **-enced; -encing :** experimentar (sentimientos), tener (dificultades), sufrir (una pérdida)
experience[2] *n* **:** experiencia *f*
experiment[1] [ɪk'spɛrəmənt, ɛk-, -'spɪr-] *vi* **:** experimentar, hacer experimentos
experiment[2] *n* **:** experimento *m*
experimental [ɪk,spɛrə'mɛntəl, ɛk-, -,spɪr-] *adj* **:** experimental — **experimentally** *adv*
experimentation [ɪk,spɛrəmən'teɪʃən, ɛk-, -,spɪr-] *n* **:** experimentación *f*
expert[1] ['ɛk,spərt, ɪk'spərt] *adj* **:** experto, de experto, pericial (dícese de un testigo) — **expertly** *adv*
expert[2] ['ɛk,spərt] *n* **:** experto *m*, -ta *f*; perito *m*, -ta *f*; especialista *mf*
expertise [,ɛkspər'ti:z] *n* **:** pericia *f*, competencia *f*
expiate ['ɛkspi,eɪt] *vt* **-ated; -ating :** expiar
expiation [,ɛkspi'eɪʃən] *n* **:** expiación *f*
expiration [,ɛkspə'reɪʃən] *n* **1** EXHALATION **:** exhalación *f*, espiración *f* **2** DEATH **:** muerte *f* **3** TERMINATION **:** vencimiento *m*, caducidad *f*
expire [ɪk'spaɪr, ɛk-] *vi* **-pired; -piring 1** EXHALE **:** espirar **2** DIE **:** expirar, morir **3** TERMINATE **:** caducar, vencer
explain [ɪk'spleɪn, ɛk-] *vt* **:** explicar
explanation [,ɛksplə'neɪʃən] *n* **:** explicación *f*
explanatory [ɪk'splænə,tori, ɛk-] *adj* **:** explicativo, aclaratorio
expletive ['ɛkspləṭɪv] *n* **:** improperio *m*, palabrota *f fam*, grosería *f*
explicable [ɛk'splɪkəbəl, 'ɛksplɪ-] *adj* **:** explicable
explicit [ɪk'splɪsət, ɛk-] *adj* **:** explícito, claro, categórico, rotundo — **explicitly** *adv*
explicitness [ɪk'splɪsətnəs, ɛk-] *n* **:** claridad *f*, carácter *m* explícito
explode [ɪk'splo:d, ɛk-] *v* **-ploded; -ploding** *vt* **1** BURST **:** explosionar, hacer explotar **2** REFUTE **:** rebatir, refutar, desmentir — *vi* **1** BURST **:** explotar, estallar, reventar **2** SKYROCKET **:** dispararse
exploit[1] [ɪk'splɔɪt, ɛk-] *vt* **:** explotar, aprovecharse de
exploit[2] ['ɛk,splɔɪt] *n* **:** hazaña *f*, proeza *f*
exploitation [,ɛk,splɔɪ'teɪʃən] *n* **:** explotación *f*
exploration [,ɛksplə'reɪʃən] *n* **:** exploración *f*
exploratory [ɪk'splorə,tori, ɛk-] *adj* **:** exploratorio
explore [ɪk'splor, ɛk-] *vt* **-plored; -ploring :** explorar, investigar, examinar
explorer [ɪk'splorər, ɛk-] *n* **:** explorador *m*, -dora *f*
explosion [ɪk'splo:ʒən, ɛk-] *n* **:** explosión *f*, estallido *m*
explosive[1] [ɪk'splo:sɪv, ɛk-] *adj* **:** explosivo, fulminante — **explosively** *adv*
explosive[2] *n* **:** explosivo *m*
exponent [ɪk'spo:nənt, 'ɛk,spo:-] *n* **1 :** exponente *m* **2** ADVOCATE **:** defensor *m*, -sora *f*; partidario *m*, -ria *f*
exponential [,ɛkspə'nɛntʃəl] *adj* **:** exponencial — **exponentially** *adv*
export[1] [ɛk'sport, 'ɛk,sport] *vt* **:** exportar
export[2] ['ɛk,sport] *n* **1 :** artículo *m* de exportación **2** → **exportation**
exportation [,ɛk,spor'teɪʃən] *n* **:** exportación *f*
exporter [ɛk'sporṭər, 'ɛk,spor-] *n* **:** exportador *m*, -dora *f*
expose [ɪk'spo:z, ɛk-] *vt* **-posed; -posing 1 :** exponer (al peligro, a los elementos, a una enfermedad) **2 :** exponer (una película a la luz) **3** DISCLOSE **:** descubrir, revelar, poner en evidencia **4** UNMASK **:** desenmascarar
exposé *or* **expose** [,ɛkspo'zeɪ] *n* **:** exposición *f* (de hechos), relevación *f* (de un escándalo)
exposed [ɪk'spo:zd, ɛk-] *adj* **:** descubierto, sin protección
exposition [,ɛkspə'zɪʃən] *n* **:** exposición *f*
exposure [ɪk'spo:ʒər, ɛk-] *n* **1 :** exposición *f* **2** CONTACT **:** exposición *f*, experiencia *f*, contacto *m* **3** UNMASKING **:** desenmascaramiento *m* **4** ORIENTATION **:** orientación *f* <a room with a northern exposure : una sala orientada al norte>
expound [ɪk'spaʊnd, ɛk-] *vt* **:** exponer, explicar — *vi* **:** hacer comentarios detallados
express[1] [ɪk'sprɛs, ɛk-] *vt* **1** SAY **:** expresar, comunicar **2** SHOW **:** expresar, manifestar, externar *Mex* **3** SQUEEZE **:** exprimir <to express the juice from a lemon : exprimir el jugo de un limón>
express[2] *adv* **:** por correo exprés, por correo urgente
express[3] *adj* **1** EXPLICIT **:** expreso, manifiesto **2** SPECIFIC **:** específico <for that express purpose : con ese fin específico> **3** RAPID **:** expreso, rápido
express[4] *n* **1 :** correo *m* exprés, correo *m* urgente **2 :** expreso *m* (tren)
expression [ɪk'sprɛʃən, ɛk-] *n* **1** UTTERANCE **:** expresión *f* <freedom of expression : libertad de expresión> **2 :** expresión *f* (en la matemática) **3** PHRASE **:** frase *f*, expresión *f* **4** LOOK **:** expresión *f*, cara *f*, gesto *m* <with a sad expression : con un gesto de tristeza>
expressionless [ɪk'sprɛʃənləs, ɛk-] *adj* **:** inexpresivo

expressive [ɪk'sprɛsɪv, ɛk-] *adj* : expresivo

expressway [ɪk'sprɛs,weɪ, ɛk-] *n* : autopista *f*

expulsion [ɪk'spʌlʃən, ɛk-] *n* : expulsión *f*

expurgate ['ɛkspər,geɪt] *vt* **-gated; -gating** : expurgar

exquisite [ɛk'skwɪzət, 'ɛk,skwɪ-] *adj* **1** FINE : exquisito, delicado, primoroso **2** INTENSE : intenso, extremo

extant ['ɛkstənt, ɛk'stænt] *adj* : existente

extemporaneous [ɛk,stɛmpə'reɪniəs] *adj* : improvisado — **extemporaneously** *adv*

extend [ɪk'stɛnd, ɛk-] *vt* **1** STRETCH : extender, tender **2** PROLONG : prolongar, prorrogar **3** ENLARGE : agrandar, ampliar, aumentar **4** PROFFER : extender, dar, ofrecer — *vi* : extenderse

extended [ɪk'stɛndəd, ɛk-] *adj* LENGTHY : prolongado, largo

extension [ɪk'stɛntʃən, ɛk-] *n* **1** EXTENDING : extensión *f,* ampliación *f,* prórroga *f,* prolongación *f* **2** ANNEX : ampliación *f,* anexo *m* **3** : extensión *f* (de teléfono)

extensive [ɪk'stɛntsɪv, ɛk-] *adj* : extenso, vasto, amplio — **extensively** *adv*

extent [ɪk'stɛnt, ɛk-] *n* **1** SIZE : extensión *f,* magnitud *f* **2** DEGREE, SCOPE : alcance *m,* grado *m* <to a certain extent : hasta cierto punto>

extenuate [ɪk'stɛnjə,weɪt, ɛk-] *vt* **-ated; -ating** : atenuar, aminorar, mitigar <extenuating circumstances : circunstancias atenuantes>

extenuation [ɪk,stɛnjə'weɪʃən, ɛk-] *n* : atenuación *f,* aminoración *f*

exterior[1] [ɛk'stɪriər] *adj* : exterior

exterior[2] *n* : exterior *m*

exterminate [ɪk'stərmə,neɪt, ɛk-] *vt* **-nated; -nating** : exterminar

extermination [ɪk,stərmə'neɪʃən, ɛk-] *n* : exterminación *f,* exterminio *m*

exterminator [ɪk'stərmə,neɪṭər, ɛk-] *n* : exterminador *m,* -dora *f*

external [ɪk'stərnəl, ɛk-] *adj* : externo, exterior — **externally** *adv*

extinct [ɪk'stɪŋkt, ɛk-] *adj* : extinto

extinction [ɪk'stɪŋkʃən, ɛk-] *n* : extinción *f*

extinguish [ɪk'stɪŋgwɪʃ, ɛk-] *vt* : extinguir, apagar

extinguisher [ɪk'stɪŋgwɪʃər, ɛk-] *n* : extinguidor *m,* extintor *m*

extirpate ['ɛkstər,peɪt] *vt* **-pated; -pating** : extirpar, exterminar

extol [ɪk'sto:l, ɛk-] *vt* **-tolled; -tolling** : exaltar, ensalzar, alabar

extort [ɪk'stɔrt, ɛk-] *vt* : extorsionar

extortion [ɪk'stɔrʃən, ɛk-] *n* : extorsión *f*

extra[1] ['ɛkstrə] *adv* : extra, más, extremadamente, super <extra special : super especial>

extra[2] *adj* **1** ADDITIONAL : adicional, suplementario, de más **2** SUPERIOR : superior

extra[3] *n* : extra *m*

extract[1] [ɪk'strækt, ɛk-] *vt* : extraer, sacar

extract[2] ['ɛk,strækt] *n* **1** EXCERPT : pasaje *m,* selección *f,* trozo *m* **2** : extracto *m* <vanilla extract : extracto de vainilla>

extraction [ɪk'strækʃən, ɛk-] *n* : extracción *f*

extractor [ɪk'stræktər, ɛk-] *n* : extractor *m*

extracurricular [,ɛkstrəkə'rɪkjələr] *adj* : extracurricular

extradite ['ɛkstrə,daɪt] *vt* **-dited; -diting** : extraditar

extradition [,ɛkstrə'dɪʃən] *n* : extradición *f*

extramarital [,ɛkstrə'mærəṭəl] *adj* : extramatrimonial

extraneous [ɛk'streɪniəs] *adj* **1** OUTSIDE : extrínseco, externo **2** SUPERFLUOUS : superfluo, ajeno — **extraneously** *adv*

extraordinary [ɪk'strɔrdən,ɛri, ,ɛkstrə'ɔrd-] *adj* : extraordinario, excepcional — **extraordinarily** [ɪk,strɔrdən'ɛrəli, ,ɛkstrə,ɔrd-] *adv*

extrasensory [,ɛkstrə'sɛntsəri] *adj* : extrasensorial

extraterrestrial[1] [,ɛkstrətə'rɛstriəl] *adj* : extraterrestre

extraterrestrial[2] *n* : extraterrestre *mf*

extravagance [ɪk'strævɪgənts, ɛk-] *n* **1** EXCESS : exceso *m,* extravagancia *f* **2** WASTEFULNESS : derroche *m,* despilfarro *m* **3** LUXURY : lujo *m*

extravagant [ɪk'strævɪgənt, ɛk-] *adj* **1** EXCESSIVE : excesivo, extravagante **2** WASTEFUL : despilfarrador, derrochador, gastador **3** EXORBITANT : costoso, exorbitante

extravagantly [ɪk'strævɪgəntli, ɛk-] *adv* **1** LAVISHLY : a lo grande **2** EXCESSIVELY : exageradamente, desmesuradamente

extravaganza [ɪk,strævə'gænzə, ɛk-] *n* : gran espectáculo *m*

extreme[1] [ɪk'stri:m, ɛk-] *adj* **1** UTMOST : extremo, sumo <of extreme importance : de suma importancia> **2** INTENSE : intenso, extremado <extreme cold : frío extremado> **3** EXCESSIVE : excesivo, extremo <extreme views : opiniones extremas> <extreme measures : medidas excepcionales, medidas drásticas> **4** OUTERMOST : extremo <the extreme north : el norte extremo>

extreme[2] *n* **1** : extremo *m* **2 in the extreme** : en extremo, en sumo grado

extremely [ɪk'stri:mli, ɛk-] *adv* : sumamente, extremadamente, terriblemente

extremity [ɪk'strɛməṭi, ɛk-] *n, pl* **-ties** **1** EXTREME : extremo *m* **2 extremities** *npl* LIMBS : extremidades *fpl*

extricate [ˈɛkstrəˌkeɪt] *vt* **-cated; -cating** : librar, sacar
extrinsic [ɪkˈstrɪnzɪk, -ˈstrɪntsɪk] *adj* : extrínseco
extrovert [ˈɛkstrəˌvərt] *n* : extrovertido *m,* -da *f*
extroverted [ˈɛkstrəˌvərt̬əd] *adj* : extrovertido
extrude [ɪkˈstruːd, ɛk-] *vt* **-truded; -truding** : extrudir, expulsar
exuberance [ɪgˈzuːbərənts, ɛg-] *n* **1** JOYOUSNESS : euforia *f,* exaltación *f* **2** VIGOR : exuberancia *f,* vigor *m*
exuberant [ɪgˈzuːbərənt, ɛg-] *adj* **1** JOYOUS : eufórico **2** LUSH : exuberante — **exuberantly** *adv*
exude [ɪgˈzuːd, ɛg-] *vt* **-uded; -uding** **1** OOZE : rezumar, exudar **2** EMANATE : emanar, irradiar
exult [ɪgˈzʌlt, ɛg-] *vi* : exultar, regocijarse
exultant [ɪgˈzʌltənt, ɛg-] *adj* : exultante, jubiloso — **exultantly** *adv*
exultation [ˌɛksəlˈteɪʃən, ˌɛgzəl-] *n* : exultación *f,* júbilo *m,* alborozo *m*
eye¹ [ˈaɪ] *vt* **eyed; eyeing** *or* **eying** : mirar, observar
eye² *n* **1 :** ojo *m* **2** VISION : visión *f,* vista *f,* ojo *m* <a good eye for bargains : un buen ojo para las gangas> **3** GLANCE : mirada *f,* ojeada *f* **4** ATTENTION : atención *f* <to catch one's eye : llamar la atención> **5** POINT OF VIEW : punto *m* de vista <in the eyes of the law : según la ley> **6 :** ojo *m* (de una aguja, una papa, una tormenta)
eyeball [ˈaɪˌbɔl] *n* : globo *m* ocular
eyebrow [ˈaɪˌbraʊ] *n* : ceja *f*
eyedropper [ˈaɪˌdrɑpər] *n* : cuentagotas *f*
eyeglasses [ˈaɪˌglæsəz] *npl* : anteojos *mpl,* lentes *mpl,* espejuelos *mpl,* gafas *fpl*
eyelash [ˈaɪˌlæʃ] *n* : pestaña *f*
eyelet [ˈaɪlət] *n* : ojete *m*
eyelid [ˈaɪˌlɪd] *n* : párpado *m*
eye–opener [ˈaɪˌoːpənər] *n* : revelación *f,* sorpresa *f*
eye–opening [ˈaɪˌoːpənɪŋ] *adj* : revelador
eyepiece [ˈaɪˌpiːs] *n* : ocular *m*
eyesight [ˈaɪˌsaɪt] *n* : vista *f,* visión *f*
eyesore [ˈaɪˌsor] *n* : monstruosidad *f,* adefesio *m*
eyestrain [ˈaɪˌstreɪn] *n* : fatiga *f* visual, vista *f* cansada
eyetooth [ˈaɪˌtuːθ] *n* : colmillo *m*
eyewitness [ˈaɪˈwɪtnəs] *n* : testigo *mf* ocular, testigo *mf* presencial
eyrie [ˈaɪri] → **aerie**

F

f [ˈɛf] *n, pl* **f's** *or* **fs** [ˈɛfs] : sexta letra del alfabeto inglés
fable [ˈfeɪbəl] *n* : fábula *f*
fabled [ˈfeɪbəld] *adj* : legendario, fabuloso
fabric [ˈfæbrɪk] *n* **1** MATERIAL : tela *f,* tejido *m* **2** STRUCTURE : estructura *f* <the fabric of society : la estructura de la sociedad>
fabricate [ˈfæbrɪˌkeɪt] *vt* **-cated; -cating** **1** CONSTRUCT, MANUFACTURE : construir, fabricar **2** INVENT : inventar (excusas o mentiras)
fabrication [ˌfæbrɪˈkeɪʃən] *n* **1** LIE : mentira *f,* invención *f* **2** MANUFACTURE : fabricación *f*
fabulous [ˈfæbjələs] *adj* **1** LEGENDARY : fabuloso, legendario **2** INCREDIBLE : increíble, fabuloso <fabulous wealth : riqueza fabulosa> **3** WONDERFUL : magnífico, estupendo, fabuloso — **fabulously** *adv*
facade [fəˈsɑd] *n* : fachada *f*
face¹ [ˈfeɪs] *v* **faced; facing** *vt* **1** LINE : recubrir (una superficie), forrar (ropa) **2** CONFRONT : enfrentarse a, afrontar, hacer frente a <to face the music : afrontar las consecuencias> <to face the facts : aceptar la realidad> **3 :** estar de cara a, estar enfrente de <she's facing her brother : está de cara a su hermano> **4** OVERLOOK : dar a — *vi* : mirar (hacia), estar orientado (a)
face² *n* **1 :** cara *f,* rostro *m* <he told me to my face : me lo dijo a la cara> **2** EXPRESSION : cara *f,* expresión *f* <to pull a long face : poner mala cara> **3** GRIMACE : mueca *f* <to make faces : hacer muecas> **4** APPEARANCE : fisonomía *f,* aspecto *m* <the face of society : la fisonomía de la sociedad> **5** EFFRONTERY : desfachatez *f* **6** PRESTIGE : prestigio *m* <to lose face : desprestigiarse> **7** FRONT, SIDE : cara *f* (de una moneda), esfera *f* (de un reloj), fachada *f* (de un edificio), pared *f* (de una montaña) **8** SURFACE : superficie *f,* faz *f* (de la tierra), cara *f* (de la luna) **9 in the face of** DESPITE : en medio de, en visto de, ante
facedown [ˈfeɪsˌdaʊn] *adv* : boca abajo
faceless [ˈfeɪsləs] *adj* ANONYMOUS : anónimo
face–lift [ˈfeɪsˌlɪft] *n* **1 :** estiramiento *m* facial **2** RENOVATION : renovación *f,* remozamiento *m*
facet [ˈfæsət] *n* **1 :** faceta *f* (de una piedra) **2** ASPECT : faceta *f,* aspecto *m*
facetious [fəˈsiːʃəs] *adj* : gracioso, burlón, bromista
facetiously [fəˈsiːʃəsli] *adv* : en tono de burla
facetiousness [fəˈsiːʃəsnəs] *n* : jocosidad *f*
face–to–face *adv & adj* : cara a cara
faceup [ˈfeɪsˈʌp] *adv* : boca arriba

face value *n* : valor *m* nominal
facial[1] ['feɪʃəl] *adj* : de la cara, facial
facial[2] *n* : tratamiento *m* facial, limpieza *f* de cutis
facile ['fæsəl] *adj* SUPERFICIAL : superficial, simplista
facilitate [fə'sɪlə,teɪt] *vt* **-tated; -tating** : facilitar
facility [fə'sɪləṭi] *n, pl* **-ties 1** EASE : facilidad *f* **2** CENTER, COMPLEX : centro *m*, complejo *m* **3 facilities** *npl* AMENITIES : comodidades *fpl*, servicios *mpl*
facing ['feɪsɪŋ] *n* **1** LINING : entretela *f* (de una prenda) **2** : revestimiento *m* (de un edificio)
facsimile [fæk'sɪməli] *n* : facsímile *m*, facsímil *m*
fact ['fækt] *n* **1** : hecho *m* <as a matter of fact : de hecho> **2** INFORMATION : información *f*, datos *mpl* <facts and figures : datos y cifras> **3** REALITY : realidad *f* <in fact : en realidad>
faction ['fækʃən] *n* : facción *m*, bando *m*
factional ['fækʃənəl] *adj* : entre facciones
factious ['fækʃəs] *adj* : faccioso, contencioso
factitious [fæk'tɪʃəs] *adj* : artificial, facticio
factor ['fæktər] *n* : factor *m*
factory ['fæktəri] *n, pl* **-ries** : fábrica *f*
factual ['fæktʃʊəl] *adj* : basado en hechos, objetivo
factually ['fæktʃʊəli] *adv* : en cuanto a los hechos
faculty ['fækəlti] *n, pl* **-ties 1** : facultad *f* <the faculty of sight : las facultades visuales, el sentido de la vista> **2** APTITUDE : aptitud *f*, facilidad *f* **3** TEACHERS : cuerpo *m* docente
fad ['fæd] *n* : moda *f* pasajera, manía *f*
fade ['feɪd] *v* **faded; fading** *vi* **1** WITHER : debilitarse (dícese de las personas), marchitarse (dícese de las flores y las plantas) **2** DISCOLOR : desteñirse, decolorarse **3** DIM : apagarse (dícese de la luz), perderse (dícese de los sonidos), fundirse (dícese de las imágenes) **4** VANISH : desvanecerse, decaer — *vt* DISCOLOR : desteñir
fag ['fæg] *vt* **fagged; fagging** EXHAUST : cansar, fatigar
fagot *or* **faggot** ['fægət] *n* : haz *m* de leña
Fahrenheit ['færən,haɪt] *adj* : Fahrenheit
fail[1] ['feɪl] *vi* **1** WEAKEN : fallar, deteriorarse **2** STOP : fallar, detenerse <his heart failed : le falló el corazón> **3** : fracasar, fallar <her plan failed : su plan fracasó> <the crops failed : se perdió la cosecha> **4** : quebrar <a business about to fail : una empresa a punto de quebrar> **5 to fail in** : faltar a, no cumplir con <to fail in one's duties : faltar a sus deberes> — *vt* **1** FLUNK : reprobar (un examen) **2** : fallar <words fail me : las palabras me fallan, no encuentro palabras> **3** DISAPPOINT : fallar, decepcionar <don't fail me! : ¡no me falles!>
fail[2] *n* : fracaso *m*
failing ['feɪlɪŋ] *n* : defecto *m*
failure ['feɪljər] *n* **1** : fracaso *m*, malogro *m* <crop failure : pérdida de la cosecha> <heart failure : insuficiencia cardíaca> <engine failure : falla mecánica> **2** BANKRUPTCY : bancarrota *f*, quiebra *f* **3** : fracaso *m* (persona) <he was a failure as a manager : como gerente, fue un fracaso>
faint[1] ['feɪnt] *vi* : desmayarse
faint[2] *adj* **1** COWARDLY, TIMID : cobarde, tímido **2** DIZZY : mareado <faint with hunger : desfallecido de hambre> **3** SLIGHT : leve, ligero, vago <I haven't the faintest idea : no tengo la más mínima idea> **4** INDISTINCT : tenue, indistinto, apenas perceptible
faint[3] *n* : desmayo *m*
fainthearted ['feɪnt'hɑrṭəd] *adj* : cobarde, pusilánime
faintly ['feɪntli] *adv* : débilmente, ligeramente, levemente
faintness ['feɪntnəs] *n* **1** INDISTINCTNESS : lo débil, falta *f* de claridad **2** FAINTING : desmayo *m*, desfallecimiento *m*
fair[1] ['fær] *adj* **1** ATTRACTIVE, BEAUTIFUL : bello, hermoso, atractivo **2** (*relating to weather*) : bueno, despejado <fair weather : tiempo despejado> **3** JUST : justo, imparcial **4** ALLOWABLE : permisible **5** BLOND, LIGHT : rubio (dícese del pelo), blanco (dícese de la tez) **6** ADEQUATE : bastante, adecuado <fair to middling : mediano, regular> **7 fair game** : presa *f* fácil **8 to play fair** : jugar limpio
fair[2] *n* : feria *f*
fairground ['fær,graʊnd] *n* : parque *m* de diversiones
fairly ['færli] *adv* **1** IMPARTIALLY : imparcialmente, limpiamente, equitativamente **2** QUITE : bastante **3** MODERATELY : medianamente
fairness ['færnəs] *n* **1** IMPARTIALITY : imparcialidad *f*, justicia *f* **2** LIGHTNESS : blancura *f* (de la piel), lo rubio (del pelo)
fairy ['færi] *n, pl* **fairies 1** : hada *f* **2 fairy tale** : cuento *m* de hadas
fairyland ['færi,lænd] *n* **1** : país *m* de las hadas **2** : lugar *m* encantador
faith ['feɪθ] *n, pl* **faiths** ['feɪθs, 'feɪðz] **1** BELIEF : fe *f* **2** ALLEGIANCE : lealtad *f* **3** CONFIDENCE, TRUST : confianza *f*, fe *f* **4** RELIGION : religión *f*
faithful ['feɪθfəl] *adj* : fiel — **faithfully** *adv*
faithfulness ['feɪθfəlnəs] *n* : fidelidad *f*
faithless ['feɪθləs] *adj* **1** DISLOYAL : desleal **2** : infiel (en la religión) — **faithlessly** *adv*

faithlessness [ˈfeɪθləsnəs] *n* **:** deslealtad *f*
fake[1] [ˈfeɪk] *v* **faked; faking** *vt* **1** FALSIFY **:** falsificar, falsear **2** FEIGN **:** fingir — *vi* **1** PRETEND **:** fingir **2 :** hacer un engaño, hacer una finta (en deportes)
fake[2] *adj* **:** falso, fingido, postizo
fake[3] *n* **1** IMITATION **:** imitación *f,* falsificación *f* **2** IMPOSTOR **:** impostor *m,* -tora *f;* charlatán *m,* -tana *f;* farsante *mf* **3** FEINT **:** engaño *m,* finta *f* (en deportes)
faker [ˈfeɪkər] *n* **:** impostor *m,* -tora *f;* charlatán *m,* -tana *f;* farsante *mf*
fakir [fəˈkɪr, ˈfeɪkər] *n* **:** faquir *m*
falcon [ˈfælkən, ˈfɔl-] *n* **:** halcón *m*
falconry [ˈfælkənri, ˈfɔl-] *n* **:** cetrería *f*
fall[1] [ˈfɔl] *vi* **fell** [ˈfɛl]; **fallen** [fɔlən]; **falling 1 :** caer, caerse <to fall out of bed **:** caer de la cama> <to fall down **:** caerse> **2** HANG **:** caer **3** DESCEND **:** caer (dícese de la lluvia o de la noche), bajar (dícese de los precios), descender (dícese de la temperatura) **4 :** caer (a un enemigo), rendirse <the city fell **:** la ciudad se rindió> **5** OCCUR **:** caer <Christmas falls on a Friday **:** la Navidad cae en viernes> **6 to fall asleep :** dormirse, quedarse dormido **7 to fall from grace** SIN **:** perder la gracia **8 to fall sick :** caer enfermo, enfermarse **9 to fall through :** fracasar, caer en la nada **10 to fall to :** tocar a, corresponder a <the task fell to him **:** le tocó hacerlo>
fall[2] *n* **1** TUMBLE **:** caída *f* <to break one's fall **:** frenar uno su caída> <a fall of three feet **:** una caída de tres pies> **2** FALLING **:** derrumbe *m* (de rocas), aguacero *m* (de lluvia), nevada *f* (de nieve), bajada *f* (de precios), disminución *f* (de cantidades) **3** AUTUMN **:** otoño *m* **4** DOWNFALL **:** caída *f,* ruina *f* **5 falls** *npl* WATERFALL **:** cascada *f,* catarata *f*
fallacious [fəˈleɪʃəs] *adj* **:** erróneo, engañoso, falaz
fallacy [ˈfæləsi] *n, pl* **-cies :** falacia *f*
fall back *vi* **1** RETREAT **:** retirarse, replegarse **2 to fall back on :** recurrir a
fall guy *n* SCAPEGOAT **:** chivo *m* expiatorio
fallible [ˈfæləbəl] *adj* **:** falible
fallout [ˈfɔlˌaʊt] *n* **1 :** lluvia *f* radioactiva **2** CONSEQUENCES **:** secuelas *fpl,* consecuencias *fpl*
fallow[1] [ˈfælo] *vt* **:** barbechar
fallow[2] *adj* **to lie fallow :** estar en barbecho
fallow[3] *n* **:** barbecho *m*
false [ˈfɔls] *adj* **falser; falsest 1** UNTRUE **:** falso **2** ERRONEOUS **:** erróneo, equivocado **3** FAKE **:** falso, postizo **4** UNFAITHFUL **:** infiel **5** FRAUDULENT **:** fraudulento <under false pretenses **:** por fraude>
falsehood [ˈfɔlsˌhʊd] *n* **:** mentira *f,* falsedad *f*
falsely [ˈfɔlsli] *adv* **:** falsamente, con falsedad
falseness [ˈfɔlsnəs] *n* **:** falsedad *f*
falsetto [fɔlˈsɛt̬oː] *n, pl* **-tos :** falsete *m*
falsification [ˌfɔlsəfəˈkeɪʃən] *n* **:** falsificación *f,* falseamiento *m*
falsify [ˈfɔlsəˌfaɪ] *vt* **-fied; fying :** falsificar, falsear
falsity [ˈfɔlsət̬i] *n, pl* **-ties :** falsedad *f*
falter [ˈfɔltər] *vi* **-tered; -tering 1** TOTTER **:** tambalearse **2** STAMMER **:** titubear, tartamudear **3** WAVER **:** vacilar
faltering [ˈfɔltərɪŋ] *adj* **:** titubeante, vacilante
fame [ˈfeɪm] *n* **:** fama *f*
famed [ˈfeɪmd] *adj* **:** famoso, célebre, afamado
familial [fəˈmɪljəl, -liəl] *adj* **:** familiar
familiar[1] [fəˈmɪljər] *adj* **1** KNOWN **:** familiar, conocido <to be familiar with **:** estar familiarizado con> **2** INFORMAL **:** familiar, informal **3** INTIMATE **:** íntimo, de confianza **4** FORWARD **:** confianzudo, atrevido — **familiarly** *adv*
familiar[2] *n* **:** espíritu *m* guardián
familiarity [fəˌmɪliˈærət̬i, -ˌmɪlˈjær-] *n, pl* **-ties 1** KNOWLEDGE **:** conocimiento *m,* familiaridad *f* **2** INFORMALITY, INTIMACY **:** confianza *f,* familiaridad *f* **3** FORWARDNESS **:** exceso *m* de confianza, descaro *m*
familiarize [fəˈmɪljəˌraɪz] *vt* **-ized; -izing 1 :** familiarizar **2 to familiarize oneself :** familiarizarse
family [ˈfæmli, ˈfæmə-] *n, pl* **-lies :** familia *f*
family tree *n* **:** árbol *m* genealógico
famine [ˈfæmən] *n* **:** hambre *f,* hambruna *f*
famish [ˈfæmɪʃ] *vi* **to be famished :** estar famélico, estar hambriento, morir de hambre *fam*
famous [ˈfeɪməs] *adj* **:** famoso
famously [ˈfeɪməsli] *adv* **to get on famously :** llevarse de maravilla
fan[1] [ˈfæn] *vt* **fanned; fanning 1 :** abanicar (a una persona), avivar (un fuego) **2** STIMULATE **:** avivar, estimular
fan[2] *n* **1 :** ventilador *m,* abanico *m* **2** ADMIRER, ENTHUSIAST **:** aficionado *m,* -da *f;* entusiasta *mf;* admirador *m,* -dora *f*
fanatic[1] [fəˈnætɪk] *or* **fanatical** [-t̬ɪkəl] *adj* **:** fanático
fanatic[2] *n* **:** fanático *m,* -ca *f*
fanaticism [fəˈnæt̬əˌsɪzəm] *n* **:** fanatismo *m*
fanciful [ˈfæntsɪfəl] *adj* **1** CAPRICIOUS **:** caprichoso, fantástico, extravagante **2** IMAGINATIVE **:** imaginativo — **fancifully** *adv*
fancy[1] [ˈfæntsi] *vt* **-cied; -cying 1** IMAGINE **:** imaginarse, figurarse <fancy that! **:** ¡figúrate!, ¡imagínate!> **2** CRAVE **:** apetecer, tener ganas de
fancy[2] *adj* **-cier; -est 1** ELABORATE **:** elaborado **2** LUXURIOUS **:** lujoso, elegante — **fancily** [ˈfæntsəli] *adv*

fancy[3] *n, pl* **-cies 1** LIKING : gusto *m,* afición *f* **2** WHIM : antojo *m,* capricho *m* **3** IMAGINATION : fantasía *f,* imaginación *f*

fandango [fæn'dæŋgo] *n, pl* **-gos** : fandango *m*

fanfare ['fæn,fær] *n* : fanfarria *f*

fang ['fæŋ] *n* : colmillo *m* (de un animal), diente *m* (de una serpiente)

fanlight ['fæn,laɪt] *n* : tragaluz *m*

fantasia [fæn'teɪʒə, -ziə; ,fæntə'ziːə] *n* : fantasía *f*

fantasize ['fæntə,saɪz] *vi* **-sized; -sizing** : fantasear

fantastic [fæn'tæstɪk] *adj* **1** UNBELIEVABLE : fantástico, increíble, extraño **2** ENORMOUS : fabuloso, inmenso <fantastic sums : sumas fabulosas> **3** WONDERFUL : estupendo, fantástico, bárbaro *fam,* macanudo *fam* — **fantastically** [-tɪkli] *adv*

fantasy ['fæntəsi] *n, pl* **-sies** : fantasía *f*

far[1] ['fɑr] *adv* **farther** ['fɑrðər] *or* **further** ['fər-]; **farthest** *or* **furthest** [-ðəst] **1** : lejos <far from here : lejos de aquí> <to go far : llegar lejos> <as far as Chicago : hasta Chicago> <far away : a lo lejos> **2** MUCH : muy, mucho <far bigger : mucho más grande> <far superior : muy superior> <it's by far the best : es con mucho el mejor> **3** (*expressing degree or extent*) <the results are far off : salieron muy inexactos los resultados> <to go so far as : decir tanto como> <to go far enough : tener el alcance necesario> **4** (*expressing progress*) <the work is far advanced : el trabajo está muy avanzado> <to take (something) too far : llevar (algo) demasiado lejos> **5 far and wide** : por todas partes **6 far from it!** : ¡todo lo contrario! **7 so far** : hasta ahora, todavía

far[2] *adj* **farther** *or* **further; farthest** *or* **furthest 1** REMOTE : lejano, remoto <the Far East : el Lejano Oriente, el Extremo Oriente> <a far country : un país lejano> **2** LONG : largo <a far journey : un viaje largo> **3** EXTREME : extremo <the far right : la extrema derecha> <at the far end of the room : en el otro extremo de la sala>

faraway ['fɑrə,weɪ] *adj* : remoto, lejano

farce ['fɑrs] *n* : farsa *f*

farcical ['fɑrsɪkəl] *adj* : absurdo, ridículo

fare[1] ['fær] *vi* **fared; faring** : ir, salir <how did you fare? : ¿cómo te fue?>

fare[2] *n* **1** : pasaje *m,* billete *m,* boleto *m* <half fare : medio pasaje> **2** FOOD : comida *f*

farewell[1] [fær'wɛl] *adj* : de despedida

farewell[2] *n* : despedida *f*

far–fetched ['fɑr'fɛtʃt] *adj* : improbable, exagerado

farina [fə'riːnə] *n* : harina *f*

farm[1] ['fɑrm] *vt* **1** : cultivar, labrar **2** : criar (animales) — *vi* : ser agricultor

farm[2] *n* : granja *f,* hacienda *f,* finca *f,* estancia *f*

farmer ['fɑrmər] *n* : agricultor *m,* granjero *m*

farmhand ['fɑrm,hænd] *n* : peón *m*

farmhouse ['fɑrm,haʊs] *n* : granja *f,* vivienda *f* del granjero, casa *f* de hacienda

farming ['fɑrmɪŋ] *n* : labranza *f,* cultivo *m,* crianza *f* (de animales)

farmland ['fɑrm,lænd] *n* : tierras *fpl* de labranza

farmyard ['fɑrm,jɑrd] *n* : corral *m*

far–off ['fɑr,ɔf, -'ɔf] *adj* : remoto, distante, lejano

far–reaching ['fɑr'riːtʃɪŋ] *adj* : de gran alcance

farsighted ['fɑr,saɪţəd] *adj* **1** : hipermétrope **2** JUDICIOUS : con visión de futuro, previsor, precavido

farsightedness ['fɑr,saɪţədnəs] *n* **1** : hipermetropía *f* **2** PRUDENCE : previsión *f*

farther[1] ['fɑrðər] *adv* **1** AHEAD : más lejos (en el espacio), más adelante (en el tiempo) **2** MORE : más

farther[2] *adj* : más lejano, más remoto

farthermost ['fɑrðər,moːst] *adj* : (el) más lejano

farthest[1] ['fɑrðəst] *adv* **1** : lo más lejos <I jumped farthest : salté lo más lejos> **2** : lo más avanzado <he progressed farthest : progresó al punto más avanzado> **3** : más <the farthest developed plan : el plan más desarrollado>

farthest[2] *adj* : más lejano

fascicle ['fæsɪkəl] *n* : fascículo *m*

fascinate ['fæsən,eɪt] *vt* **-nated; -nating** : fascinar, cautivar

fascination [,fæsən'eɪʃən] *n* : fascinación *f*

fascism ['fæʃ,ɪzəm] *n* : fascismo *m*

fascist[1] ['fæʃɪst] *adj* : fascista

fascist[2] *n* : fascista *mf*

fashion[1] ['fæʃən] *vt* : formar, moldear

fashion[2] *n* **1** MANNER : manera *f,* modo *m* **2** CUSTOM : costumbre *f* **3** STYLE : moda *f*

fashionable ['fæʃənəbəl] *adj* : de moda, chic

fashionably ['fæʃənəbli] *adv* : a la moda

fast[1] ['fæst] *vi* : ayunar

fast[2] *adv* **1** SECURELY : firmemente, seguramente <to hold fast : agarrarse bien> **2** RAPIDLY : rápidamente, rápido, de prisa **3** SOUNDLY : profundamente <fast asleep : profundamente dormido>

fast[3] *adj* **1** SECURE : firme, seguro <to make fast : amarrar (un barco)> **2** FAITHFUL : leal <fast friends : amigos leales> **3** RAPID : rápido, veloz **4** : adelantado <10 minutes fast : 10 minutos adelantado> **5** DEEP : profundo <a fast sleep : un sueño pro-

fundo> **6** COLORFAST **:** inalterable, que no destiñe **7** DISSOLUTE **:** extravagante, disipado, disoluto

fast[4] *n* **:** ayuno *m*

fasten [ˈfæsən] *vt* **1** ATTACH **:** sujetar, atar **2** FIX **:** fijar <to fasten one's eyes on : fijar los ojos en> **3** SECURE **:** abrochar (ropa o cinturones), atar (cordones), cerrar (una maleta) — *vi* **:** abrocharse, cerrar

fastener [ˈfæsənər] *n* **:** cierre *m,* sujetador *m*

fastening [ˈfæsənɪŋ] *n* **:** cierre *m,* sujetador *m*

fastidious [fæsˈtɪdiəs] *adj* **:** quisquilloso, exigente — **fastidiously** *adv*

fat[1] [ˈfæt] *adj* **fatter; fattest 1** OBESE **:** gordo, obeso **2** THICK **:** grueso

fat[2] *n* **:** grasa *f*

fatal [ˈfeɪt̬əl] *adj* **1** DEADLY **:** mortal **2** ILL-FATED **:** malhadado, fatal **3** MOMENTOUS **:** fatídico

fatalism [ˈfeɪt̬əlˌɪzəm] *n* **:** fatalismo *m*

fatalist [ˈfeɪt̬əlɪst] *n* **:** fatalista *mf*

fatalistic [ˌfeɪt̬əlˈɪstɪk] *adj* **:** fatalista

fatality [feɪˈtæləti, fə-] *n, pl* **-ties :** víctima *f* mortal

fatally [ˈfeɪt̬əli] *adv* **:** mortalmente

fate [ˈfeɪt] *n* **1** DESTINY **:** destino *m* **2** END, LOT **:** final *m,* suerte *f*

fated [ˈfeɪt̬əd] *adj* **:** predestinado

fateful [ˈfeɪtfəl] *adj* **1** MOMENTOUS **:** fatídico, aciago **2** PROPHETIC **:** profético — **fatefully** *adv*

father[1] [ˈfɑðər] *vt* **:** engendrar

father[2] *n* **1 :** padre *m* <my father and my mother : mi padre y mi madre> <Father Smith : el padre Smith> **2 the Father** GOD **:** el Padre, Dios *m*

fatherhood [ˈfɑðərˌhʊd] *n* **:** paternidad *f*

father-in-law [ˈfɑðərɪnˌlɔ] *n, pl* **fathers-in-law :** suegro *m*

fatherland [ˈfɑðərˌlænd] *n* **:** patria *f*

fatherless [ˈfɑðərləs] *adj* **:** huérfano de padre, sin padre

fatherly [ˈfɑðərli] *adj* **:** paternal

fathom[1] [ˈfæðəm] *vt* UNDERSTAND **:** entender, comprender

fathom[2] *n* **:** braza *f*

fatigue[1] [fəˈtiːg] *vt* **-tigued; -tiguing :** fatigar, cansar

fatigue[2] *n* **:** fatiga *f*

fatness [ˈfætnəs] *n* **:** gordura *f* (de una persona o un animal), grosor *m* (de un objeto)

fatten [ˈfætən] *vt* **:** engordar, cebar

fatty [ˈfæti] *adj* **fattier; -est :** graso, grasoso, adiposo (dícese de los tejidos)

fatuous [ˈfætʃʊəs] *adj* **:** necio, fatuo — **fatuously** *adv*

faucet [ˈfɔsət] *n* **:** llave *f,* canilla *f Arg,Uru,* grifo *m*

fault[1] [ˈfɔlt] *vt* **:** encontrar defectos a

fault[2] *n* **1** SHORTCOMING **:** defecto *m,* falta *f* **2** DEFECT **:** falta *f,* defecto *m,* falla *f* **3** BLAME **:** culpa *f* **4** FRACTURE **:** falla *f* (geológica)

faultfinder [ˈfɔltˌfaɪndər] *n* **:** criticón *m,* -cona *f*

faultfinding [ˈfɔltˌfaɪndɪŋ] *n* **:** crítica *f*

faultless [ˈfɔltləs] *adj* **:** sin culpa, sin imperfecciones, impecable

faultlessly [ˈfɔltləsli] *adv* **:** impecablemente, perfectamente

faulty [ˈfɔlti] *adj* **faultier; -est :** defectuoso, imperfecto — **faultily** [ˈfɔltəli] *adv*

fauna [ˈfɔnə] *n* **:** fauna *f*

faux pas [ˌfoːˈpɑ] *n, pl* **faux pas** [*same or* -ˈpɑz] **:** metedura *f* de pata *fam*

favor[1] [ˈfeɪvər] *vt* **1** SUPPORT **:** estar a favor de, ser partidario de, apoyar **2** OBLIGE **:** hacerle un favor a **3** PREFER **:** preferir **4** RESEMBLE **:** parecerse a, salir a

favor[2] *n* **:** favor *m* <in favor of : a favor de> <an error in his favor : un error a su favor>

favorable [ˈfeɪvərəbəl] *adj* **:** favorable, propicio

favorably [ˈfeɪvərəbli] *adv* **:** favorablemente, bien

favorite[1] [ˈfeɪvərət] *adj* **:** favorito, preferido

favorite[2] *n* **:** favorito *m,* -ta *f;* preferido *m,* -da *f*

favoritism [ˈfeɪvərəˌtɪzəm] *n* **:** favoritismo *m*

fawn[1] [ˈfɔn] *vi* **:** adular, lisonjear

fawn[2] *n* **:** cervato *m*

fax [ˈfæks] *n* **:** facsímil *m,* facsímile *m*

faze [ˈfeɪz] *vt* **fazed; fazing :** desconcertar, perturbar

fear[1] [ˈfɪr] *vt* **:** temer, tener miedo de — *vi* **:** temer

fear[2] *n* **:** miedo *m,* temor *m* <for fear of : por temor a>

fearful [ˈfɪrfəl] *adj* **1** FRIGHTENING **:** espantoso, aterrador, horrible **2** FRIGHTENED **:** temeroso, miedoso

fearfully [ˈfɪrfəli] *adv* **1** EXTREMELY **:** extremadamente, terriblemente **2** TIMIDLY **:** con temor

fearless [ˈfɪrləs] *adj* **:** intrépido, impávido

fearlessly [ˈfɪrləsli] *adv* **:** sin temor

fearlessness [ˈfɪrləsnəs] *n* **:** intrepidez *f,* impavidez *f*

fearsome [ˈfɪrsəm] *adj* **:** aterrador

feasibility [ˌfiːzəˈbɪləti] *n* **:** viabilidad *f,* factibilidad *f*

feasible [ˈfiːzəbəl] *adj* **:** viable, factible, realizable

feast[1] [ˈfiːst] *vi* **:** banquetear — *vt* **1 :** agasajar, festejar **2 to feast one's eyes on :** regalarse la vista con

feast[2] *n* **1** BANQUET **:** banquete *m,* festín *m* **2** FESTIVAL **:** fiesta *f*

feat [ˈfiːt] *n* **:** proeza *f,* hazaña *f*

feather[1] [ˈfɛðər] *vt* **1 :** emplumar **2 to feather one's nest :** hacer su agosto

feather[2] *n* **1 :** pluma *f* **2 a feather in one's cap :** un triunfo personal

feathered [ˈfɛðərd] *adj* **:** con plumas

feathery [ˈfɛðəri] *adj* **1** DOWNY **:** plumoso **2** LIGHT **:** liviano

feature[1] ['fiːtʃər] *v* **-tured; -turing** *vt* **1** IMAGINE : imaginarse **2** PRESENT : presentar — *vi* : figurar

feature[2] *n* **1** CHARACTERISTIC : característica *f,* rasgo *m* **2** : largometraje *m* (en el cine), artículo *m* (en un periódico), documental *m* (en la televisión) **3 features** *npl* : rasgos *mpl,* facciones *fpl* <delicate features : facciones delicadas>

February ['fɛbjʊˌɛri, 'fɛbʊ-, 'fɛbrʊ-] *n* : febrero *m*

fecal ['fiːkəl] *adj* : fecal

feces ['fiːˌsiːz] *npl* : heces *fpl,* excrementos *mpl*

feckless ['fɛkləs] *adj* : irresponsable

fecund ['fɛkənd, 'fiː-] *adj* : fecundo

fecundity [fɪ'kʌndəṭi, fɛ-] *n* : fecundidad *f*

federal ['fɛdrəl, -dərəl] *adj* : federal

federalism ['fɛdrəˌlɪzəm, -dərə-] *n* : federalismo *m*

federalist[1] ['fɛdrəlɪst, -dərə-] *adj* : federalista

federalist[2] *n* : federalista *mf*

federate ['fɛdəˌreɪt] *vt* **-ated; -ating** : federar

federation [ˌfɛdə'reɪʃən] *n* : federación *f*

fedora [fɪ'dorə] *n* : sombrero *m* flexible de fieltro

fed up *adj* : harto

fee ['fiː] *n* **1** : honorarios *mpl* (a un médico, un abogado, etc.) **2 entrance fee** : entrada *f*

feeble ['fiːbəl] *adj* **-bler; -blest 1** WEAK : débil, endeble **2** INEFFECTIVE : flojo, pobre, poco convincente

feebleminded [ˌfiːbəl'maɪndəd] *adj* **1** : débil mental **2** FOOLISH, STUPID : imbécil, tonto

feebleness ['fiːbəlnəs] *n* : debilidad *f*

feebly ['fiːbli] *adv* : débilmente

feed[1] ['fiːd] *v* **fed** ['fɛd]; **feeding** *vt* **1** : dar de comer a, nutrir, alimentar (a una persona) **2** : alimentar (un fuego o una máquina), proveer (información), introducir (datos) — *vi* : comer, alimentarse

feed[2] *n* **1** NOURISHMENT : alimento *m* **2** FODDER : pienso *m*

feel[1] ['fiːl] *v* **felt** ['fɛlt]; **feeling** *vi* **1** : sentirse, encontrarse <I feel tired : me siento cansada> <he feels hungry : tiene hambre> <she feels like a fool : se siente como una idiota> <to feel like doing something : tener ganas de hacer algo> **2** SEEM : parecer <it feels like spring : parece primavera> **3** THINK : parecerse, opinar, pensar <how does he feel about that? : ¿qué opina él de eso?> — *vt* **1** TOUCH : tocar, palpar **2** SENSE : sentir <to feel the cold : sentir el frío> **3** CONSIDER : sentir, creer, considerar <to feel (it) necessary : creer necesario>

feel[2] *n* **1** SENSATION, TOUCH : sensación *f,* tacto *m* **2** ATMOSPHERE : ambiente *m,* atmósfera *f* **3 to have a feel for** : tener un talento especial para

feeler ['fiːlər] *n* : antena *f,* tentáculo *m*

feeling ['fiːlɪŋ] *n* **1** SENSATION : sensación *f,* sensibilidad *f* **2** EMOTION : sentimiento *m* **3** OPINION : opinión *f* **4 feelings** *npl* SENSIBILITIES : sentimientos *mpl* <to hurt someone's feelings : herir los sentimientos de alguien>

feet → **foot**

feign ['feɪn] *vt* : simular, aparentar, fingir

feint[1] ['feɪnt] *vi* : fintar, fintear

feint[2] *n* : finta *f*

felicitate [fɪ'lɪsəˌteɪt] *vt* **-tated; -tating** : felicitar, congratular

felicitation [fɪˌlɪsə'teɪʃən] *n* : felicitación *f*

felicitous [fɪ'lɪsəṭəs] *adj* : acertado, oportuno

feline[1] ['fiːˌlaɪn] *adj* : felino

feline[2] *n* : felino *m,* -na *f*

fell[1] ['fɛl] *vt* : talar (un árbol), derribar (a una persona)

fell[2] → **fall**

fellow ['fɛˌloː] *n* **1** COMPANION : compañero *m,* -ra *f;* camarada *mf* **2** ASSOCIATE : socio *m,* -cia *f* **3** MAN : tipo *m,* hombre *m*

fellowman [ˌfɛlo'mæn] *n, pl* **-men** : prójimo *m,* semejante *m*

fellowship ['fɛloˌʃɪp] *n* **1** COMPANIONSHIP : camaradería *f,* compañerismo *m* **2** ASSOCIATION : fraternidad *f* **3** GRANT : beca *f* (de investigación)

felon ['fɛlən] *n* : malhechor *m,* -chora *f;* criminal *mf*

felonious [fə'loːniəs] *adj* : criminal

felony ['fɛləni] *n, pl* **-nies** : delito *m* grave

felt[1] ['fɛlt] *n* : fieltro *m*

felt[2] → **feel**

female[1] ['fiːˌmeɪl] *adj* : femenino

female[2] *n* **1** : hembra *f* (de animal) **2** WOMAN : mujer *f*

feminine ['fɛmənən] *adj* : femenino

femininity [ˌfɛmə'nɪnəṭi] *n* : feminidad *f,* femineidad *f*

feminism ['fɛməˌnɪzəm] *n* : feminismo *m*

feminist[1] ['fɛmənɪst] *adj* : feminista

feminist[2] *n* : feminista *mf*

femoral ['fɛmərəl] *adj* : femoral

femur ['fiːmər] *n, pl* **femurs** *or* **femora** ['fɛmərə] : fémur *m*

fence[1] ['fɛnts] *v* **fenced; fencing** *vt* : vallar, cercar — *vi* : hacer esgrima

fence[2] *n* : cerca *f,* valla *f,* cerco *m*

fencer ['fɛntsər] *n* : esgrimista *mf;* esgrimidor *m,* -dora *f*

fencing ['fɛntsɪŋ] *n* **1** : esgrima *m* (deporte) **2** : materiales *mpl* para cercas **3** ENCLOSURE : cercado *m*

fend ['fɛnd] *vt* **to fend off** : rechazar (un enemigo), parar (un golpe), eludir (una pregunta) — *vi* **to fend for oneself** : arreglárselas sólo, valerse por sí mismo

fender [ˈfɛndər] *n* **:** guardabarros *mpl,* salpicadera *f Mex*

fennel [ˈfɛnəl] *n* **:** hinojo *m*

ferment[1] [fərˈmɛnt] *v* **:** fermentar

ferment[2] [ˈfərˌmɛnt] *n* **1 :** fermento *m* (en la química) **2** TURMOIL **:** agitación *f,* conmoción *f*

fermentation [ˌfərmənˈteɪʃən, -ˌmɛn-] *n* **:** fermentación *f*

fern [ˈfərn] *n* **:** helecho *m*

ferocious [fəˈroːʃəs] *adj* **:** feroz — **ferociously** *adv*

ferociousness [fəˈroːʃəsnəs] *n* **:** ferocidad *f*

ferocity [fəˈrɑsət̬i] *n* **:** ferocidad *f*

ferret[1] [ˈfɛrət] *vi* SNOOP **:** hurgar, husmear — *vt* **to ferret out :** descubrir

ferret[2] *n* **:** hurón *m*

ferric [ˈfɛrɪk] *or* **ferrous** [ˈfɛrəs] *adj* **:** férrico

Ferris wheel [ˈfɛrɪs] *n* **:** noria *f*

ferry[1] [ˈfɛri] *vt* **-ried; -rying :** llevar, transportar

ferry[2] *n, pl* **-ries :** transbordador *m,* ferry *m*

ferryboat [ˈfɛriˌboːt] *n* **:** transbordador *m,* ferry *m*

fertile [ˈfərt̬əl] *adj* **:** fértil, fecundo

fertility [fərˈtɪlət̬i] *n* **:** fertilidad *f*

fertilization [ˌfərt̬ələˈzeɪʃən] *n* **:** fertilización *f* (del suelo), fecundación (de un huevo)

fertilize [ˈfərt̬əlˌaɪz] *vt* **-ized; -izing 1 :** fecundar (un huevo) **2 :** fertilizar, abonar (el suelo)

fertilizer [ˈfərt̬əlˌaɪzər] *n* **:** fertilizante *m,* abono *m*

fervent [ˈfərvənt] *adj* **:** ferviente, fervoroso, ardiente — **fervently** *adv*

fervid [ˈfərvɪd] *adj* **:** ardiente, apasionado — **fervidly** *adv*

fervor [ˈfərvər] *n* **:** fervor *m,* ardor *m*

fester [ˈfɛstər] *vi* **:** enconarse, supurar

festival [ˈfɛstəvəl] *n* **:** fiesta *f,* festividad *f,* festival *m*

festive [ˈfɛstɪv] *adj* **:** festivo — **festively** *adv*

festivity [fɛsˈtɪvət̬i] *n, pl* **-ties :** festividad *f,* celebración *f*

festoon[1] [fɛsˈtuːn] *vt* **:** adornar, engalanar

festoon[2] *n* GARLAND **:** guirnalda *f*

fetal [ˈfiːt̬əl] *adj* **:** fetal

fetch [ˈfɛtʃ] *vt* **1** BRING **:** traer, recoger, ir a buscar **2** REALIZE **:** realizar, venderse por <the jewelry fetched $10,000 : las joyas se vendieron por $10,000>

fetching [ˈfɛtʃɪŋ] *adj* **:** atractivo, encantador

fête[1] [ˈfeɪt, ˈfɛt] *vt* **fêted; fêting :** festejar, agasajar

fête[2] *n* **:** fiesta *f*

fetid [ˈfɛt̬əd] *adj* **:** fétido

fetish [ˈfɛt̬ɪʃ] *n* **:** fetiche *m*

fetlock [ˈfɛtˌlɑk] *n* **:** espolón *m*

fetter [ˈfɛt̬ər] *vt* **:** encadenar, poner grillos a

fetters [ˈfɛt̬ərz] *npl* **:** grillos *mpl,* grilletes *mpl,* cadenas *fpl*

fettle [ˈfɛt̬əl] *n* **in fine fettle :** en buena forma, en plena forma

fetus [ˈfiːt̬əs] *n* **:** feto *m*

feud[1] [ˈfjuːd] *vi* **:** pelear, contender

feud[2] *n* **:** contienda *f,* enemistad *f* (heredada)

feudal [ˈfjuːdəl] *adj* **:** feudal

feudalism [ˈfjuːdəlˌɪzəm] *n* **:** feudalismo *m*

fever [ˈfiːvər] *n* **:** fiebre *f,* calentura *f*

feverish [ˈfiːvərɪʃ] *adj* **1 :** afiebrado, con fiebre, febril **2** FRANTIC **:** febril, frenético

few[1] [ˈfjuː] *adj* **:** pocos <with few exceptions : con pocas excepciones> <a few times : varias veces>

few[2] *pron* **1 :** pocos <few (of them) were ready : pocos estaban listos> **2 a few :** algunos, unos cuantos **3 few and far between :** contados

fewer [ˈfjuːər] *pron* **:** menos <the fewer the better : cuantos menos mejor>

fez [ˈfɛz] *n, pl* **fezzes :** fez *m*

fiancé [ˌfiːˌɑnˈseɪ, ˌfiːˈɑnˌseɪ] *n* **:** prometido *m,* novio *m*

fiancée [ˌfiːˌɑnˈseɪ, ˌfiːˈɑnˌseɪ] *n* **:** prometida *f,* novia *f*

fiasco [fiˈæsˌkoː] *n, pl* **-coes :** fiasco *m,* fracaso *m*

fiat [ˈfiːˌɑt, -ˌæt, -ət; ˈfaɪət, -ˌæt] *n* **:** decreto *m,* orden *m*

fib[1] [ˈfɪb] *vi* **fibbed; fibbing :** decir mentirillas

fib[2] *n* **:** mentirilla *f,* bola *f fam*

fibber [ˈfɪbər] *n* **:** mentirosillo *m,* -lla *f;* cuentista *mf fam*

fiber *or* **fibre** [ˈfaɪbər] *n* **:** fibra *f*

fiberboard [ˈfaɪbərˌbord] *n* **:** cartón *m* madera

fiberglass [ˈfaɪbərˌglæs] *n* **:** fibra *f* de vidrio

fibrillate [ˈfɪbrəˌleɪt, ˈfaɪ-] *vi* **-lated; -lating :** fibrilar

fibrillation [ˌfɪbrəˈleɪʃən, ˌfaɪ-] *n* **:** fibrilación *f*

fibrous [ˈfaɪbrəs] *adj* **:** fibroso

fibula [ˈfɪbjələ] *n, pl* **-lae** [-ˌliː, -ˌlaɪ] *or* **-las :** peroné *m*

fickle [ˈfɪkəl] *adj* **:** inconstante, voluble, veleidoso

fickleness [ˈfɪkəlnəs] *n* **:** volubilidad *f,* inconstancia *f,* veleidad *f*

fiction [ˈfɪkʃən] *n* **:** ficción *f*

fictional [ˈfɪkʃənəl] *adj* **:** ficticio

fictitious [fɪkˈtɪʃəs] *adj* **1** IMAGINARY **:** ficticio, imaginario **2** FALSE **:** falso, ficticio

fiddle[1] [ˈfɪdəl] *vi* **-dled; -dling 1 :** tocar el violín **2 to fiddle with :** juguetear con, toquetear

fiddle[2] *n* **:** violín *m*

fiddler [ˈfɪdlər, ˈfɪdələr] *n* **:** violinista *mf*

fiddlesticks [ˈfɪdəlˌstɪks] *interj* **:** ¡tonterías!

fidelity [fəˈdɛlət̬i, faɪ-] *n, pl* **-ties :** fidelidad *f*

fidget[1] [ˈfɪdʒət] *vi* **1 :** moverse, estarse inquieto **2 to fidget with :** juguetear con
fidget[2] *n* **1 :** persona *f* inquieta **2 fidgets** *npl* RESTLESSNESS **:** inquietud *f*
fidgety [ˈfɪdʒəti] *adj* **:** inquieto
fiduciary[1] [fəˈduːʃi,ɛri, -ˈdjuː-, -ʃəri] *adj* **:** fiduciario
fiduciary[2] *n, pl* **-ries :** fiduciario *m,* -ria *f*
field[1] [ˈfiːld] *vt* **:** interceptar y devolver (una pelota), presentar (un candidato), sortear (una pregunta)
field[2] *adj* **:** de campaña, de campo <field hospital : hospital de campaña> <field goal : gol de campo> <field trip : viaje de estudio>
field[3] *n* **1 :** campo *m* (de cosechas, de batalla, de magnetismo) **2 :** campo *m,* cancha *f* (en deportes) **3 :** campo *m* (de trabajo), esfera *f* (de actividades)
fielder [ˈfiːldər] *n* **:** jugador *m,* -dora *f* de campo; fildeador *m,* -dora *f*
field glasses *n* **:** binoculares *mpl*, gemelos *mpl*
fiend [ˈfiːnd] *n* **1** DEMON **:** demonio *m* **2** EVILDOER **:** persona *f* maligna; malvado *m,* -da *f* **3** FANATIC **:** fanático *m,* -ca *f*
fiendish [ˈfiːndɪʃ] *adj* **:** diabólico — **fiendishly** *adv*
fierce [ˈfɪrs] *adj* **fiercer; -est 1** FEROCIOUS **:** fiero, feroz **2** HEATED **:** acalorado **3** INTENSE **:** intenso, violento, fuerte — **fiercely** *adv*
fierceness [ˈfɪrsnəs] *n* **1** FEROCITY **:** ferocidad *f,* fiereza *f* **2** INTENSITY **:** intensidad *f,* violencia *f*
fieriness [ˈfaɪərinəs] *n* **:** pasión *f,* ardor *m*
fiery [ˈfaɪəri] *adj* **fierier; -est 1** BURNING **:** ardiente, llameante **2** GLOWING **:** encendido **3** PASSIONATE **:** acalorado, ardiente, fogoso
fiesta [fiˈɛstə] *n* **:** fiesta *f*
fife [ˈfaɪf] *n* **:** pífano *m*
fifteen[1] [fɪfˈtiːn] *adj* **:** quince
fifteen[2] *n* **:** quince *m*
fifteenth[1] [fɪfˈtiːnθ] *adj* **:** decimoquinto
fifteenth[2] *n* **1 :** decimoquinto *m,* -ta *f* (en una serie) **2 :** quinceavo *m,* quinceava parte *f*
fifth[1] [ˈfɪfθ] *adj* **:** quinto
fifth[2] *n* **1 :** quinto *m,* -ta *f* (en una serie) **2 :** quinto *m,* quinta parte *f* **3 :** quinta *f* (en la música)
fiftieth[1] [ˈfɪftiəθ] *adj* **:** quincuagésimo
fiftieth[2] *n* **1 :** quincuagésimo *m,* -ma *f* (en una serie) **2 :** cincuentavo *m,* cincuentava parte *f*
fifty[1] [ˈfɪfti] *adj* **:** cincuenta
fifty[2] *n, pl* **-ties :** cincuenta *m*
fifty–fifty[1] [,fɪftiˈfɪfti] *adv* **:** a medias, mitad y mitad
fifty–fifty[2] *adj* **to have a fifty–fifty chance :** tener un cincuenta por ciento de posibilidades
fig [ˈfɪg] *n* **:** higo *m*
fight[1] [ˈfaɪt] *v* **fought** [ˈfɔt]; **fighting** *vi* **:** luchar, combatir, pelear — *vt* **:** luchar contra, combatir contra
fight[2] *n* **1** COMBAT **:** lucha *f,* pelea *f,* combate *m* **2** MATCH **:** pelea *f,* combate *m* (en boxeo) **3** QUARREL **:** disputa *f,* pelea *f,* pleito *m*
fighter [ˈfaɪt̬ər] *n* **1** COMBATANT **:** luchador *m,* -dora *f;* combatiente *mf* **2** BOXER **:** boxeador *m,* -dora *f*
figment [ˈfɪgmənt] *n* **figment of the imagination :** producto *m* de la imaginación
figurative [ˈfɪgjərət̬ɪv, -gə-] *adj* **:** figurado, metafórico
figuratively [ˈfɪgjərət̬ɪvli, -gə-] *adv* **:** en sentido figurado, de manera metafórica
figure[1] [ˈfɪgjər, -gər] *v* **-ured; -uring** *vt* **1** CALCULATE **:** calcular **2** ESTIMATE **:** figurarse, calcular <he figured it was possible : se figuró que era posible> — *vi* **1** FEATURE, STAND OUT **:** figurar, destacar **2 that figures! :** ¡obvio!, ¡no me extraña nada!
figure[2] *n* **1** DIGIT **:** número *m,* cifra *f* **2** PRICE **:** precio *m,* cifra *f* **3** PERSONAGE **:** figura *f,* personaje *m* **4 :** figura *f,* tipo *m,* físico *m* <to have a good figure : tener buen tipo, tener un buen físico> **5** DESIGN, OUTLINE **:** figura *f* **6 figures** *npl* **:** aritmética *f*
figurehead [ˈfɪgjər,hɛd, -gər-] *n* **:** testaferro *m,* líder *mf* sin poder
figure of speech *n* **:** figura *f* retórica, figura *f* de hablar
figure out *vt* **1** UNDERSTAND **:** entender **2** RESOLVE **:** resolver (un problema, etc.)
figurine [,fɪgjəˈriːn] *n* **:** estatuilla *f*
Fijian [ˈfiːdʒiən, fɪˈjiːən] *n* **:** fijiano *m,* -na *f* — **Fijian** *adj*
filament [ˈfɪləmənt] *n* **:** filamento *m*
filbert [ˈfɪlbərt] *n* **:** avellana *f*
filch [ˈfɪltʃ] *vt* **:** hurtar, birlar *fam*
file[1] [ˈfaɪl] *v* **filed; filing** *vt* **1** CLASSIFY **:** clasificar **2 :** archivar (documentos) **3** SUBMIT **:** presentar <to file charges : presentar cargos> **4** SMOOTH **:** limar — *vi* **:** desfilar, entrar (o salir) en fila
file[2] *n* **1 :** lima *f* <nail file : lima de uñas> **2** DOCUMENTS **:** archivo *m* **3** LINE **:** fila *f*
filial [ˈfɪliəl, ˈfɪljəl] *adj* **:** filial
filibuster[1] [ˈfɪlə,bʌstər] *vi* **:** practicar el obstruccionismo
filibuster[2] *n* **:** obstruccionismo *m*
filibusterer [ˈfɪlə,bʌstərər] *n* **:** obstruccionista *mf*
filigree [ˈfɪlə,griː] *n* **:** filigrana *f*
Filipino [,fɪləˈpiːnoː] *n* **:** filipino *m,* -na *f* — **Filipino** *adj*
fill[1] [ˈfɪl] *vt* **1 :** llenar, ocupar <to fill a cup : llenar una taza> <to fill a room : ocupar una sala> **2** STUFF **:** rellenar **3** PLUG **:** tapar, rellenar, empastar (un diente) **4** SATISFY **:** cumplir con, satisfacer **5** *or* **to fill out :** llenar, re-

llenar <to fill out a form : rellenar un formulario>

fill[2] *n* **1** FILLING, STUFFING : relleno *m* **2 to eat one's fill :** comer lo suficiente **3 to have one's fill of :** estar harto de

filler [ˈfɪlər] *n* : relleno *m*

fillet[1] [ˈfɪlət, fɪˈleɪ, ˈfɪˌleɪ] *vt* : cortar en filetes

fillet[2] *n* : filete *m*

fill in *vt* INFORM : informar, poner al corriente — *vi* **to fill in for** : reemplazar a

filling [ˈfɪlɪŋ] *n* **1** : relleno *m* **2** : empaste *m* (de un diente)

filling station → **service station**

filly [ˈfɪli] *n, pl* **-lies** : potra *f,* potranca *f*

film[1] [ˈfɪlm] *vt* : filmar — *vi* : rodar

film[2] *n* **1** COATING : capa *f,* película *f* **2** : película *f* (fotográfica) **3** MOVIE : película *f,* filme *m*

filmy [ˈfɪlmi] *adj* **filmier; -est 1** GAUZY : diáfano, vaporoso **2** : cubierto de una película

filter[1] [ˈfɪltər] *vt* : filtrar

filter[2] *n* : filtro *m*

filth [ˈfɪlθ] *n* : mugre *f,* porquería *f,* roña *f*

filthiness [ˈfɪlθinəs] *n* : suciedad *f*

filthy [ˈfɪlθi] *adj* **filthier; -est 1** DIRTY : mugriento, sucio **2** OBSCENE : obsceno, indecente

filtration [fɪlˈtreɪʃən] *n* : filtración *f*

fin [ˈfɪn] *n* **1** : aleta *f* **2** : alerón *m* (de un automóvil o un avión)

finagle [fəˈneɪgəl] *vt* **-gled; -gling** : arreglárselas para conseguir

final[1] [ˈfaɪnəl] *adj* **1** DEFINITIVE : definitivo, final, inapelable **2** ULTIMATE : final **3** LAST : último, final

final[2] *n* **1** : final *f* (en deportes) **2 finals** *npl* : exámenes *mpl* finales

finale [fɪˈnæli, -ˈnɑ-] *n* : final *m* <grand finale : final triunfal>

finalist [ˈfaɪnəlɪst] *n* : finalista *mf*

finality [faɪˈnæləṭi, fə-] *n, pl* **-ties** : finalidad *f*

finalize [ˈfaɪnəlˌaɪz] *vt* **-ized; -izing** : finalizar

finally [ˈfaɪnəli] *adv* **1** LASTLY : por último, finalmente **2** EVENTUALLY : por fin, al final **3** DEFINITIVELY : definitivamente

finance[1] [fəˈnænts, ˈfaɪˌnænts] *vt* **-nanced; -nancing** : financiar

finance[2] *n* **1** : finanzas *fpl* **2 finances** *npl* RESOURCES : recursos *mpl* financieros

financial [fəˈnæntʃəl, faɪ-] *adj* : financiero, económico

financially [fəˈnæntʃəli, faɪ-] *adv* : económicamente

financier [ˌfɪnənˈsɪr, ˌfaɪˌnæn-] *n* : financiero *m,* -ra *f;* financista *mf*

finch [ˈfɪntʃ] *n* : pinzón *m*

find[1] [ˈfaɪnd] *vt* **found** [ˈfaʊnd]; **finding 1** LOCATE : encontrar, hallar <I can't find it : no lo encuentro> <to find one's way : encontrar el camino, orientarse> **2** DISCOVER, REALIZE : descubrir, darse cuenta de <he found it difficult : descubrió que era difícil> **3** DECLARE : declarar, hallar <they found him guilty : lo declararon culpable>

find[2] *n* : hallazgo *m*

finder [ˈfaɪndər] *n* : descubridor *m,* -dora *f*

finding [ˈfaɪndɪŋ] *n* **1** FIND : hallazgo *m* **2 findings** *npl* : conclusiones *fpl*

find out *vt* DISCOVER : descubrir, averiguar — *vi* LEARN : enterarse

fine[1] [ˈfaɪn] *vt* **fined; fining** : multar

fine[2] *adj* **finer; -est 1** PURE : puro (dícese del oro y de la plata) **2** THIN : fino, delgado **3** : fino <fine sand : arena fina> **4** SMALL : pequeño, minúsculo <fine print : letras minúsculas> **5** SUBTLE : sutil, delicado **6** EXCELLENT : excelente, magnífico, selecto **7** FAIR : bueno <it's a fine day : hace buen tiempo> **8** EXQUISITE : exquisito, delicado, fino **9 fine arts** : bellas artes *fpl*

fine[3] *n* : multa *f*

finely [ˈfaɪnli] *adv* **1** EXCELLENTLY : con arte **2** ELEGANTLY : elegantemente **3** PRECISELY : con precisión **4 to chop finely** : picar muy fino, picar en trozos pequeños

fineness [ˈfaɪnnəs] *n* **1** EXCELLENCE : excelencia *f* **2** ELEGANCE : elegancia *f,* refinamiento *m* **3** DELICACY : delicadeza *f,* lo fino **4** PRECISION : precisión *f* **5** SUBTLETY : sutileza *f* **6** PURITY : ley *f* (de oro y plata)

finery [ˈfaɪnəri] *n* : galas *fpl,* adornos *mpl*

finesse[1] [fəˈnɛs] *vt* **-nessed; -nessing** : ingeniar

finesse[2] *n* **1** REFINEMENT : refinamiento *m,* finura *f* **2** TACT : delicadeza *f,* tacto *m,* diplomacia *f* **3** CRAFTINESS : astucia *f*

finger[1] [ˈfɪŋgər] *vt* **1** HANDLE : tocar, toquetear **2** ACCUSE : acusar, delatar

finger[2] *n* : dedo *m*

fingerling [ˈfɪŋgərlɪŋ] *n* : pez *m* pequeño y joven

fingernail [ˈfɪŋgərˌneɪl] *n* : uña *f*

fingerprint[1] [ˈfɪŋgərˌprɪnt] *vt* : tomar las huellas digitales a

fingerprint[2] *n* : huella *f* digital

fingertip [ˈfɪŋgərˌtɪp] *n* : punta *f* del dedo, yema *f* del dedo

finicky [ˈfɪnɪki] *adj* : maniático, melindroso, mañoso

finish[1] [ˈfɪnɪʃ] *vt* **1** COMPLETE : acabar, terminar **2** : aplicar un acabado a (muebles, etc.)

finish[2] *n* **1** END : fin *m,* final *m* **2** REFINEMENT : refinamiento *m* **3** : acabado *m* <a glossy finish : un acabado brillante>

finite [ˈfaɪˌnaɪt] *adj* : finito

fink [ˈfɪŋk] *n* : mequetrefe *mf fam*

Finn [ˈfɪn] *n* : finlandés *m,* -desa *f*

Finnish[1] [ˈfɪnɪʃ] *adj* : finlandés

Finnish[2] *n* : finlandés *m* (idioma)

fiord [fiˈɔrd] → **fjord**

fir [ˈfər] *n* **:** abeto *m*

fire[1] [ˈfaɪr] *vt* **fired; firing 1** IGNITE, KINDLE **:** encender **2** ENLIVEN **:** animar, avivar **3** DISMISS **:** despedir **4** SHOOT **:** disparar **5** BAKE **:** cocer (cerámica)

fire[2] *n* **1 :** fuego *m* **2** BURNING **:** incendio *m* <fire alarm : alarma contra incendios> <to be on fire : estar en llamas> **3** ENTHUSIASM **:** ardor *m,* entusiasmo *m* **4** SHOOTING **:** disparos *mpl,* fuego *m*

firearm [ˈfaɪrˌɑrm] *n* **:** arma *f* de fuego

fireball [ˈfaɪrˌbɔl] *n* **1 :** bola *f* de fuego **2** METEOR **:** bólido *m*

firebreak [ˈfaɪrˌbreɪk] *n* **:** cortafuegos *m*

firebug [ˈfaɪrˌbʌg] *n* **:** pirómano *m,* -na *f;* incendiario *m,* -ria *f*

firecracker [ˈfaɪrˌkrækər] *n* **:** petardo *m*

fire escape *n* **:** escalera *f* de incendios

firefighter [ˈfaɪrˌfaɪt̬ər] *n* **:** bombero *m,* -ra *f*

firefly [ˈfaɪrˌflaɪ] *n, pl* **-flies :** luciérnaga *f*

fireman [ˈfaɪrmən] *n, pl* **-men** [-mən, -ˌmɛn] **1** FIREFIGHTER **:** bombero *m,* -ra *f* **2** STOKER **:** fogonero *m,* -ra *f*

fireplace [ˈfaɪrˌpleɪs] *n* **:** hogar *m,* chimenea *f*

fireproof[1] [ˈfaɪrˌpruːf] *vt* **:** hacer incombustible

fireproof[2] *adj* **:** incombustible, ignífugo

fireside[1] [ˈfaɪrˌsaɪd] *adj* **:** informal <fireside chat : charla informal>

fireside[2] *n* **1** HEARTH **:** chimenea *f,* hogar *m* **2** HOME **:** hogar *m,* casa *f*

firewood [ˈfaɪrˌwʊd] *n* **:** leña *f*

fireworks [ˈfaɪrˌwərks] *npl* **:** fuegos *mpl* artificiales, pirotecnia *f*

firm[1] [ˈfərm] *vi* **:** endurecer

firm[2] *adj* **1** VIGOROUS **:** fuerte, vigoroso **2** SOLID, UNYIELDING **:** firme, duro, sólido **3** UNCHANGING **:** firme, inalterable **4** RESOLUTE **:** firme, resuelto

firm[3] *n* **:** empresa *f,* firma *f,* compañía *f*

firmament [ˈfərməmənt] *n* **:** firmamento *m*

firmly [ˈfərmli] *adv* **:** firmemente

firmness [ˈfərmnəs] *n* **:** firmeza *f*

first[1] [ˈfərst] *adv* **1 :** primero <finish your homework first : primero termina tu tarea> <first and foremost : ante todo> <first of all : en primer lugar> **2 :** por primera vez <I saw it first in Boston : lo vi por primera vez en Boston>

first[2] *adj* **1 :** primero <the first time : la primera vez> <at first sight : a primera vista> <in the first place : en primer lugar> <the first ten applicants : los diez primeros candidatos> **2** FOREMOST **:** principal, primero <first tenor : tenor principal>

first[3] *n* **1 :** primero *m,* -ra *f* (en una serie) **2 :** primero *m,* primera parte *f* **3** *or* **first gear :** primera *f* **4 at ~ :** al principio

first aid *n* **:** primeros auxilios *mpl*

first–class[1] [ˈfərstˈklæs] *adv* **:** en primera <to travel first-class : viajar en primera>

first–class[2] *adj* **:** de primera

first class *n* **:** primera clase *f*

firsthand[1] [ˈfərstˈhænd] *adv* **:** directamente

firsthand[2] *adj* **:** de primera mano

first lieutenant *n* **:** teniente *mf;* teniente primero *m,* teniente primera *f*

firstly [ˈfərstli] *adv* **:** primeramente, principalmente, en primer lugar

first–rate[1] [ˈfərstˈreɪt] *adv* **:** muy bien

first–rate[2] *adj* **:** de primera, de primera clase

first sergeant *n* **:** sargento *mf*

firth [ˈfərθ] *n* **:** estuario *m*

fiscal [ˈfɪskəl] *adj* **:** fiscal — **fiscally** *adv*

fish[1] [ˈfɪʃ] *vi* **1 :** pescar **2 to fish for** SEEK **:** buscar, rebuscar <to fish for compliments : andar a la caza de cumplidos> — *vt* **:** pescar

fish[2] *n, pl* **fish** *or* **fishes :** pez *m* (vivo), pescado *m* (para comer)

fisherman [ˈfɪʃərmən] *n, pl* **-men** [-mən, -ˌmɛn] **:** pescador *m,* -dora *f*

fishery [ˈfɪʃəri] *n, pl* **-eries 1 → fishing 2 :** zona *f* pesquera, pesquería *f*

fishhook [ˈfɪʃˌhʊk] *n* **:** anzuelo *m*

fishing [ˈfɪʃɪŋ] *n* **:** pesca *f,* industria *f* pesquera

fishing pole *n* **:** caña *f* de pescar

fish market *n* **:** pescadería *f*

fishy [ˈfɪʃi] *adj* **fishier; -est 1 :** a pescado <a fishy taste : un sabor a pescado> **2** QUESTIONABLE **:** dudoso, sospechoso <there's something fishy going on : aquí hay gato encerrado>

fission [ˈfɪʃən, -ʒən] *n* **:** fisión *f*

fissure [ˈfɪʃər] *n* **:** fisura *f,* hendidura *f*

fist [ˈfɪst] *n* **:** puño *m*

fistful [ˈfɪstˌfʊl] *n* **:** puñado *m*

fisticuffs [ˈfɪstɪˌkʌfs] *npl* **:** lucha *f* a puñetazos

fit[1] [ˈfɪt] *v* **fitted; fitting** *vt* **1** MATCH **:** corresponder a, coincidir con <the punishment fits the crime : el castigo corresponde al crimen> **2 :** quedar <the dress doesn't fit me : el vestido no me queda> **3** GO **:** caber, encajar en <her key fits the lock : su llave encaja en la cerradura> **4** INSERT, INSTALL **:** poner, colocar **5** ADAPT **:** adecuar, ajustar, adaptar **6** *or* **to fit out** EQUIP **:** equipar — *vi* **1 :** quedar, entallar <these pants don't fit : estos pantalones no me quedan> **2** CONFORM **:** encajar, cuadrar **3 to fit in :** encajar, estar integrado

fit[2] *adj* **fitter; fittest 1** SUITABLE **:** adecuado, apropiado, conveniente **2** QUALIFIED **:** calificado, competente **3** HEALTHY **:** sano, en forma

fit[3] *n* **1** ATTACK **:** ataque *m,* acceso *m,* arranque *m* **2 to be a good fit :** quedar bien **3 to be a tight fit :** ser muy

entallado (de ropa), estar apretado (de espacios)
fitful ['fɪtfəl] *adj* **:** irregular, intermitente — **fitfully** *adv*
fitness ['fɪtnəs] *n* **1** HEALTH **:** salud *f,* buena forma *f* (física) **2** SUITABILITY **:** idoneidad *f*
fitting[1] ['fɪtɪŋ] *adj* **:** adecuado, apropiado
fitting[2] *n* **:** accesorio *m*
five[1] ['faɪv] *adj* **:** cinco
five[2] *n* **:** cinco *m*
five hundred[1] *adj* **:** quinientos
five hundred[2] *n* **:** quinientos *m*
fix[1] ['fɪks] *vt* **1** ATTACH, SECURE **:** sujetar, asegurar, fijar **2** ESTABLISH **:** fijar, concretar, establecer **3** REPAIR **:** arreglar, reparar **4** PREPARE **:** preparar <to fix dinner : preparar la cena> **5 :** arreglar, amañar <to fix a race : arreglar una carrera> **6** RIVET **:** fijar (los ojos, la mirada, etc.)
fix[2] *n* **1** PREDICAMENT **:** aprieto *m,* apuro *m* **2 :** posición *f* <to get a fix on : establecer la posición de>
fixate ['fɪk,seɪt] *vi* **-ated; -ating :** obsesionarse
fixation [fɪk'seɪʃən] *n* **:** fijación *f,* obsesión *f*
fixed ['fɪkst] *adj* **1** STATIONARY **:** estacionario, inmóvil **2** UNCHANGING **:** fijo, inalterable **3** INTENT **:** fijo <a fixed stare : una mirada fija> **4 to be comfortably fixed :** estar en posición acomodada
fixedly ['fɪksədli] *adv* **:** fijamente
fixedness ['fɪksədnəs, 'fikst-] *n* **:** rigidez *f*
fixture ['fɪkstʃər] *n* **1 :** parte *f* integrante, elemento *m* fijo **2 fixtures** *npl* **:** instalaciones *fpl* (de una casa)
fizz[1] ['fɪz] *vi* **:** burbujear
fizz[2] *n* **:** efervescencia *f,* burbujeo *m*
fizzle[1] ['fɪzəl] *vi* **-zled; -zling 1** FIZZ **:** burbujear **2** FAIL **:** fracasar
fizzle[2] *n* **:** fracaso *m,* fiasco *m*
fjord [fi'ɔrd] *n* **:** fiordo *m*
flab ['flæb] *n* **:** gordura *f*
flabbergast ['flæbər,gæst] *vt* **:** asombrar, pasmar, dejar atónito
flabby ['flæbi] *adj* **-bier; -est :** blando, fofo, aguado *CA, Col, Mex*
flaccid ['flæksəd, 'flæsəd] *adj* **:** fláccido
flag[1] ['flæg] *vi* **flagged; flagging 1 :** hacer señales con banderas **2** WEAKEN **:** flaquear, desfallecer
flag[2] *n* **:** bandera *f,* pabellón *m,* estandarte *m*
flagon ['flægən] *n* **:** jarra *f* grande
flagpole ['flæg,po:l] *n* **:** asta *f,* mástil *m*
flagrant ['fleɪgrənt] *adj* **:** flagrante — **flagrantly** *adv*
flagship ['flæg,ʃɪp] *n* **:** buque *m* insignia
flagstaff ['flæg,stæf] → **flagpole**
flagstone ['flæg,sto:n] *n* **:** losa *f,* piedra *f*
flail[1] ['fleɪl] *vt* **1 :** trillar (grano) **2 :** sacudir, agitar (los brazos)
flail[2] *n* **:** mayal *m*
flair ['flær] *n* **:** don *m,* facilidad *f*
flak ['flæk] *ns & pl* **flak 1 :** fuego *m* antiaéreo **2** CRITICISM **:** críticas *fpl*
flake[1] ['fleɪk] *vi* **flaked; flaking :** desmenuzarse, pelarse (dícese de la piel)
flake[2] *n* **:** copo *m* (de nieve), escama *f* (de la piel), astilla *f* (de madera)
flamboyance [flæm'bɔɪən*t*s] *n* **:** extravagancia *f,* rimbombancia *f*
flamboyant [flæm'bɔɪənt] *adj* **:** exuberante, extravagante, rimbombante
flame[1] ['fleɪm] *vi* **flamed; flaming 1** BLAZE **:** arder, llamear **2** GLOW **:** brillar, encenderse
flame[2] *n* BLAZE **:** llama *f* <to burst into flames : estallar en llamas> <to go up in flame : incendiarse>
flamethrower ['fleɪm,θro:ər] *n* **:** lanzallamas *m*
flamingo [flə'mɪŋgo] *n, pl* **-gos :** flamenco *m*
flammable ['flæməbəl] *adj* **:** inflamable, flamable
flange ['flændʒ] *n* **:** reborde *m,* pestaña *f*
flank[1] ['flæŋk] *vt* **1 :** flanquear (para defender o atacar) **2** BORDER, LINE **:** bordear
flank[2] *n* **:** ijada *f* (de un animal), costado *m* (de una persona), falda *f* (de una colina), flanco *m* (de un cuerpo de soldados)
flannel ['flænəl] *n* **:** franela *f*
flap[1] ['flæp] *v* **flapped; flapping** *vi* **1 :** aletear <the bird was flapping (its wings) : el pájaro aleteaba> **2** FLUTTER **:** ondear, agitarse — *vt* **:** batir, agitar
flap[2] *n* **1** FLAPPING **:** aleteo *m,* aletazo *m* (de alas) **2 :** soplada *f* (de un sobre), hoja *f* (de una mesa), faldón *m* (de una chaqueta)
flapjack ['flæp,dʒæk] → **pancake**
flare[1] ['flær] *vi* **flared; flaring 1** FLAME, SHINE **:** llamear, brillar **2 to flare up :** estallar, explotar (de cólera)
flare[2] *n* **1** FLASH **:** destello *m* **2** SIGNAL **:** (luz *f* de) bengala *f* **3 solar flare :** erupción *f* solar
flash[1] ['flæʃ] *vi* **1** SHINE, SPARKLE **:** destellar, brillar, relampaguear **2 :** pasar como un relámpago <an idea flashed through my mind : una idea me cruzó la mente como un relámpago> — *vt* **:** despedir, lanzar (una luz), transmitir (un mensaje)
flash[2] *adj* SUDDEN **:** repentino
flash[3] *n* **1 :** destello *m* (de luz), fogonazo *m* (de una explosión) **2 flash of lightning :** relámpago *m* **3 in a flash :** de repente, de un abrir y cerrar los ojos
flashiness ['flæʃinəs] *n* **:** ostentación *f*
flashlight ['flæʃ,laɪt] *n* **:** linterna *f*
flashy ['flæʃi] *adj* **flashier; -est :** llamativo, ostentoso
flask ['flæsk] *n* **:** frasco *m*

flat[1] [ˈflæt] *vt* **flatted; flatting 1** FLATTEN : aplanar, achatar **2** : bajar de tono (en música)
flat[2] *adv* **1** EXACTLY : exactamente <in ten minutes flat : en diez minutos exactos> **2** : desafinado, demasiado bajo (en la música)
flat[3] *adj* **flatter; flattest 1** EVEN, LEVEL : plano, llano **2** SMOOTH : liso **3** DEFINITE : categórico, rotundo, explícito <a flat refusal : una negativa categórica> **4** DULL : aburrido, soso, monótono (dícese la voz) **5** DEFLATED : desinflado, pinchado, ponchado *Mex* **6** : bemol (en música) <to sing flat : cantar desafinado>
flat[4] *n* **1** PLAIN : llano *m,* terreno *m* llano **2** : bemol *m* (en la música) **3** APARTMENT : apartamento *m,* departamento *m* **4** *or* **flat tire** : pinchazo *m,* ponchadura *f Mex*
flatbed [ˈflæt,bɛd] *n* : camión *m* de plataforma
flatcar [ˈflæt,kɑr] *n* : vagón *m* abierto
flatfish [ˈflæt,fɪʃ] *n* : platija *f*
flat–footed [ˈflæt,fʊt̬əd, ,flætˈ-] *adj* : de pies planos
flatly [ˈflætli] *adv* DEFINITELY : categóricamente, rotundamente
flatness [ˈflætnəs] *n* **1** EVENNESS : lo llano, lisura *f,* uniformidad *f* **2** DULLNESS : monotonía *f*
flat–out [ˈflætˈaʊt] *adj* **1** : frenético, a toda máquina <a flat-out effort : un esfuerzo frenético> **2** CATEGORICAL : descarado, rotundo, categórico
flatten [ˈflætən] *vt* : aplanar, achatar
flatter [ˈflæt̬ər] *vt* **1** OVERPRAISE : adular **2** COMPLIMENT : halagar **3** : favorecer <the photo flatters you : la foto te favorece>
flatterer [ˈflæt̬ərər] *n* : adulador *m,* -dora *f*
flattering [ˈflæt̬ərɪŋ] *adj* **1** COMPLIMENTARY : halagador **2** BECOMING : favorecedor
flattery [ˈflæt̬əri] *n, pl* **-ries** : halagos *mpl*
flatulence [ˈflætʃələnts] *n* : flatulencia *f,* ventosidad *f*
flatulent [ˈflætʃələnt] *adj* : flatulento
flatware [ˈflæt,wær] *n* : cubertería *f,* cubiertos *mpl*
flaunt[1] [ˈflɔnt] *vt* : alardear, hacer alarde de
flaunt[2] *n* : alarde *m,* ostentación *f*
flavor[1] [ˈfleɪvər] *vt* : dar sabor a, sazonar
flavor[2] *n* **1** : gusto *m,* sabor *m* **2** FLAVORING : sazón *f,* condimento *m*
flavorful [ˈfleɪvərfəl] *adj* : sabroso
flavoring [ˈfleɪvərɪŋ] *n* : condimento *m,* sazón *f*
flavorless [ˈfleɪvərləs] *adj* : sin sabor
flaw [ˈflɔ] *n* : falla *f,* defecto *m,* imperfección *f*
flawless [ˈflɔləs] *adj* : impecable, perfecto — **flawlessly** *adv*
flax [ˈflæks] *n* : lino *m*
flaxen [ˈflæksən] *adj* : rubio, blondo (dícese del pelo)
flay [ˈfleɪ] *vt* **1** SKIN : desollar, despellejar **2** VILIFY : criticar con dureza, vilipendiar
flea [ˈfliː] *n* : pulga *f*
fleck[1] [ˈflɛk] *vt* : salpicar
fleck[2] *n* : mota *f,* pinta *f*
fledgling [ˈflɛdʒlɪŋ] *n* : polluelo *m,* pollito *m*
flee [ˈfliː] *v* **fled** [ˈflɛd]; **fleeing** *vi* : huir, escapar(se) — *vt* : huir de
fleece[1] [ˈfliːs] *vt* **fleeced; fleecing 1** SHEAR : esquilar, trasquilar **2** SWINDLE : estafar, defraudar
fleece[2] *n* : lana *f,* vellón *m*
fleet[1] [ˈfliːt] *vi* : moverse con rapidez
fleet[2] *adj* SWIFT : rápido, veloz
fleet[3] *n* : flota *f*
fleet admiral *n* : almirante *mf*
fleeting [ˈfliːt̬ɪŋ] *adj* : fugaz, breve
flesh [ˈflɛʃ] *n* **1** : carne *f* (de seres humanos y animales) **2** : pulpa *f* (de frutas)
flesh out *vt* : desarrollar, darle cuerpo a
fleshy [ˈflɛʃi] *adj* **fleshier; -est** : gordo (dícese de las personas), carnoso (dícese de la fruta)
flew → **fly**
flex [ˈflɛks] *vt* : doblar, flexionar
flexibility [,flɛksəˈbɪlət̬i] *n, pl* **-ties** : flexibilidad *f,* elasticidad *f*
flexible [ˈflɛksəbəl] *adj* : flexible — **flexibly** [-bli] *adv*
flick[1] [ˈflɪk] *vt* : dar un capirotazo a (con el dedo) <to flick a switch : darle al interruptor> — *vi* **1** FLIT : revolotear **2 to flick through** : hojear (un libro)
flick[2] *n* : coletazo *m* (de una cola), capirotazo *m* (de un dedo)
flicker[1] [ˈflɪkər] *vi* **1** FLUTTER : revolotear, aletear **2** BLINK, TWINKLE : parpadear, titilar
flicker[2] *n* **1** : parpadeo *m,* titileo *m* **2** HINT, TRACE : indicio *m,* rastro *m* <a flicker of hope : un rayo de esperanza>
flier [ˈflaɪər] *n* **1** AVIATOR : aviador *m,* -dora *f* **2** CIRCULAR : folleto *m* publicitario, circular *f*
flight [ˈflaɪt] *n* **1** : vuelo *m* (de aves o aviones), trayectoria *f* (de proyectiles) **2** TRIP : vuelo *m* **3** FLOCK, SQUADRON : bandada *f* (de pájaros), escuadrilla *f* (de aviones) **4** ESCAPE : huida *f,* fuga *f* **5 flight of fancy** : ilusiones *fpl,* fantasía *f* **6 flight of stairs** : tramo *m*
flightless [ˈflaɪtləs] *adj* : no volador
flighty [ˈflaɪt̬i] *adj* **flightier; -est** : caprichoso, frívolo
flimsy [flɪmzi] *adj* **flimsier; -est 1** LIGHT, THIN : ligero, fino **2** WEAK : endeble, poco sólido **3** IMPLAUSIBLE : pobre, flojo, poco convincente <a flimsy excuse : una excusa floja>
flinch [ˈflɪntʃ] *vi* **1** WINCE : estremecerse **2** RECOIL : recular, retroceder

fling[1] [ˈflɪŋ] *vt* **flung** [ˈflʌŋ]; **flinging 1** THROW : lanzar, tirar, arrojar **2 to fling oneself** : lanzarse, tirarse, precipitarse

fling[2] *n* **1** THROW : lanzamiento *m* **2** ATTEMPT : intento *m* **3** AFFAIR : aventura *f* **4** BINGE : juerga *f*

flint [ˈflɪnt] *n* : pedernal *m*

flinty [ˈflɪnti] *adj* **flintier; -est 1** : de pedernal **2** STERN, UNYIELDING : severo, inflexible

flip[1] [ˈflɪp] *v* **flipped; flipping** *vt* **1** TOSS : tirar <to flip a coin : echar a cara o cruz> **2** OVERTURN : dar la vuelta a, voltear — *vi* **1** : moverse bruscamente **2 to flip through** : hojear (un libro)

flip[2] *adj* : insolente, descarado

flip[3] *n* **1** FLICK : capirotazo *m,* golpe *m* ligero **2** SOMERSAULT : voltereta *f*

flippancy [ˈflɪpən*t*si] *n, pl* **-cies** : ligereza *f,* falta *f* de seriedad

flippant [ˈflɪpənt] *adj* : ligero, frívolo, poco serio

flipper [ˈflɪpər] *n* : aleta *f*

flirt[1] [ˈflərt] *vi* **1** : coquetear, flirtear **2** TRIFLE : jugar <to flirt with death : jugar con la muerte>

flirt[2] *n* : coqueto *m,* -ta *f*

flirtation [ˌflərˈteɪʃən] *n* : devaneo *m,* coqueteo *m*

flirtatious [ˌflərˈteɪʃəs] *adj* : insinuante, coqueto

flit [ˈflɪt] *vi* **flitted; flitting 1** : revolotear **2 to flit about** : ir y venir rápidamente

float[1] [ˈfloːt] *vi* **1** : flotar **2** WANDER : vagar, errar — *vt* **1** : poner a flote, hacer flotar (un barco) **2** LAUNCH : hacer flotar (una empresa) **3** ISSUE : emitir (acciones en la bolsa)

float[2] *n* **1** : flotador *m,* corcho *m* (para pescar) **2** BUOY : boya *f* **3** : carroza *f* (en un desfile)

flock[1] [ˈflɑk] *vi* **1** : moverse en rebaño **2** CONGREGATE : congregarse, reunirse

flock[2] *n* : rebaño *m* (de ovejas), bandada *f* (de pájaros)

floe [ˈfloː] *n* : témpano *m* de hielo

flog [ˈflɑg] *vt* **flogged; flogging** : azotar, fustigar

flood[1] [ˈflʌd] *vt* : inundar, anegar

flood[2] *n* **1** INUNDATION : inundación *f* **2** TORRENT : avalancha *f,* diluvio *m,* torrente *m* <a flood of tears : un mar de lágrimas>

floodlight [ˈflʌdˌlaɪt] *n* : foco *m*

floodwater [ˈflʌdˌwɔ̌tər] *n* : crecida *f,* creciente *f*

floor[1] [ˈflor] *vt* **1** : solar, poner suelo a (una casa o una sala) **2** KNOCK DOWN : derribar, echar al suelo **3** NONPLUS : desconcertar, confundir, dejar perplejo

floor[2] *n* **1** : suelo *m,* piso *m* <dance floor : pista de baile> **2** STORY : piso *m,* planta *f* <ground floor : planta baja> <second floor : primer piso> **3** : mínimo *m* (de sueldos, precios, etc.)

floorboard [ˈflorˌbord] *n* : tabla *f* del suelo, suelo *m,* piso *m*

flop[1] [ˈflɑp] *vi* **flopped; flopping 1** FLAP : golpearse, agitarse **2** COLLAPSE : dejarse caer, desplomarse **3** FAIL : fracasar

flop[2] *n* **1** FAILURE : fracaso *m* **2 to take a flop** : caerse

floppy [ˈflɑpi] *adj* **-pier; -est 1** : blando, flexible **2 floppy disk** : diskette *m,* disquete *m*

flora [ˈflorə] *n* : flora *f*

floral [ˈflorəl] *adj* : floral, floreado

florid [ˈflorɪd] *adj* **1** FLOWERY : florido **2** REDDISH : rojizo

florist [ˈflorɪst] *n* : florista *mf*

floss[1] [ˈflɔs] *vi* : limpiarse los dientes con hilo dental

floss[2] *n* **1** : hilo *m* de seda (de brodar) **2** → **dental floss**

flotation [floˈteɪʃən] *n* : flotación *f*

flotilla [floˈtɪlə] *n* : flotilla *f*

flotsam [ˈflɑtsəm] *n* **1** : restos *mpl* flotantes (en el mar) **2 flotsam and jetsam** : desechos *mpl*, restos *mpl*

flounce[1] [ˈflaʊn*t*s] *vi* **flounced; flouncing** : moverse haciendo aspavientos <she flounced into the room : entró en la sala haciendo aspavientos>

flounce[2] *n* **1** RUFFLE : volante *m* **2** FLOURISH : aspaviento *m*

flounder[1] [ˈflaʊndər] *vi* **1** STRUGGLE : forcejear **2** STUMBLE : no saber qué hacer o decir, perder el hilo (en un discurso)

flounder[2] *n, pl* **flounder** *or* **flounders** : platija *f*

flour[1] [ˈflaʊər] *vt* : enharinar

flour[2] *n* : harina *f*

flourish[1] [ˈflərɪʃ] *vi* THRIVE : florecer, prosperar, crecer (dícese de las plantas) — *vt* BRANDISH : blandir

flourish[2] *n* : floritura *f,* floreo *m*

flourishing [ˈflərɪʃɪŋ] *adj* : floreciente, próspero

flout [ˈflaʊt] *vt* : desacatar, burlarse de

flow[1] [ˈfloː] *vi* **1** COURSE : fluir, manar, correr **2** CIRCULATE : circular, correr <traffic is flowing smoothly : el tránsito está circulando con fluidez>

flow[2] *n* **1** FLOWING : flujo *m,* circulación *f* **2** STREAM : corriente *f,* chorro *m*

flower[1] [ˈflaʊər] *vi* : florecer, florear

flower[2] *n* : flor *f*

flowered [ˈflaʊərd] *adj* : florido, floreado

floweriness [ˈflaʊərinəs] *n* : floritura *f*

flowering[1] [ˈflaʊərɪŋ] *adj* : floreciente

flowering[2] *n* : floración *f,* florecimiento *m*

flowerpot [ˈflaʊərˌpɑt] *n* : maceta *f,* tiesto *m,* macetero *m*

flowery [ˈflaʊəri] *adj* **1** : florido **2** FLOWERED : floreado, de flores

flowing [ˈfloːɪŋ] *adj* : fluido, corriente

flown → **fly**

flu [ˈfluː] *n* : gripe *f,* gripa *f Col, Mex*

fluctuate [ˈflʌktʃʊˌeɪt] *vi* **-ated; -ating** : fluctuar

fluctuation [ˌflʌktʃʊˈeɪʃən] *n* : fluctuación *f*

flue [ˈfluː] *n* : tiro *m,* salida *f* de humos

fluency [ˈfluːəntsi] *n* : fluidez *f,* soltura *f*

fluent [ˈfluːənt] *adj* : fluido

fluently [ˈfluːəntli] *adv* : con soltura, con fluidez

fluff[1] [ˈflʌf] *vt* **1** : mullir <to fluff up the pillows : mullir las almohadas> **2** BUNGLE : echar a perder, equivocarse

fluff[2] *n* **1** FUZZ : pelusa *f* **2** DOWN : plumón *m*

fluffy [ˈflʌfi] *adj* **fluffier; -est 1** DOWNY : lleno de pelusa, velloso **2** SPONGY : esponjoso

fluid[1] [ˈfluːɪd] *adj* : fluido

fluid[2] *n* : fluido *m,* líquido *m*

fluidity [fluˈɪdət̬i] *n* : fluidez *f*

fluid ounce *n* : onza *f* líquida (29.57 mililitros)

fluke [ˈfluːk] *n* : golpe *m* de suerte, chiripa *f,* casualidad *f*

flung → **fling**

flunk [ˈflʌŋk] *vt* FAIL : reprobar — *vi* : salir reprobando

fluorescence [ˌflʊrˈɛsənts, ˌflɔr-] *n* : fluorescencia *f*

fluorescent [ˌflʊrˈɛsənt, ˌflɔr-] *adj* : fluorescente

fluoridate [ˈflɔrəˌdeɪt, ˈflʊr-] *vt* **-dated; -dating** : fluorizar

fluoridation [ˌflɔrəˈdeɪʃən, ˌflʊr-] *n* : fluorización *f,* fluoración *f*

fluoride [ˈflɔrˌaɪd, ˈflʊr-] *n* : fluoruro *m*

fluorine [ˈflʊrˌiːn] *n* : flúor *m*

fluorocarbon [ˌflɔroˈkɑrbən, ˌflʊr-] *n* : fluorocarbono *m*

flurry [ˈflɘri] *n, pl* **-ries 1** GUST : ráfaga *f* **2** SNOWFALL : nevisca *f* **3** BUSTLE : frenesí *m,* bullicio *m* **4** BARRAGE : aluvión *m,* oleada *f* <a flurry of questions : un aluvión de preguntas>

flush[1] [ˈflʌʃ] *vt* **1** : limpiar con agua <to flush the toilet : jalar la cadena> **2** RAISE : hacer salir, levantar (en la caza) — *vi* BLUSH : ruborizarse, sonrojarse

flush[2] *adv* : al mismo nivel, a ras

flush[3] *adj* **1** *or* **flushed** [ˈflʌʃt] : colorado, rojo, encendido (dícese de la cara) **2** FILLED : lleno a rebosar **3** ABUNDANT : copioso, abundante **4** AFFLUENT : adinerado **5** ALIGNED, SMOOTH : alineado, liso **6 flush against** : pegado a, contra

flush[4] *n* **1** FLOW, JET : chorro *m,* flujo *m* rápido **2** SURGE : arrebato *m,* arranque *m* <a flush of anger : un arrebato de cólera> **3** BLUSH : rubor *m,* sonrojo *m* **4** GLOW : resplandor *m,* flor *f* <the flush of youth : la flor de la juventud> <in the flush of victory : en la euforia del triunfo>

fluster[1] [ˈflʌstər] *vt* : poner nervioso, aturdir

fluster[2] *n* : agitación *f,* confusión *f*

flute [ˈfluːt] *n* : flauta *f*

fluted [ˈfluːt̬əd] *adj* **1** GROOVED : estriado, acanalado **2** WAVY : ondulado

fluting [ˈfluːt̬ɪŋ] *n* : estrías *fpl*

flutist [ˈfluːt̬ɪst] *n* : flautista *mf*

flutter[1] [ˈflʌt̬ər] *vi* **1** : revolotear (dícese de un pájaro), ondear (dícese de una bandera), palpitar con fuerza (dícese del corazón) **2 to flutter about** : ir y venir, revoltear — *vt* : sacudir, batir

flutter[2] *n* **1** FLUTTERING : revoloteo *m,* aleteo *m* **2** COMMOTION, STIR : revuelo *m,* agitación *f*

flux [ˈflʌks] *n* **1** : flujo *m* (en física y medicina) **2** CHANGE : cambio *m* <to be in a state of flux : estar cambiando continuamente>

fly[1] [ˈflaɪ] *v* **flew** [ˈfluː]; **flown** [ˈfloːn]; **flying** *vi* **1** : volar (dícese de los pájaros, etc.) **2** TRAVEL : volar (dícese de los aviones), ir en avión (dícese de los pasajeros) **3** FLOAT : flotar, ondear **4** FLEE : huir, escapar **5** RUSH : correr, irse volando **6** PASS : pasar (volando) <how time flies! : ¡cómo pasa el tiempo!> **7 to fly open** : abrir de golpe — *vt* : pilotar (un avión), hacer volar (una cometa)

fly[2] *n, pl* **flies 1** : mosca *f* <to drop like flies : caer como moscas> **2** : bragueta *f* (de pantalones, etc.)

flyer → **flier**

flying saucer → **UFO**

flypaper [ˈflaɪˌpeɪpər] *n* : papel *m* matamoscas

flyspeck [ˈflaɪˌspɛk] *n* **1** : excremento *m* de mosca **2** SPECK : motita *f,* puntito *m*

flyswatter [ˈflaɪˌswɑt̬ər] *n* : matamoscas *m*

flywheel [ˈflaɪˌhwiːl] *n* : volante *m*

foal[1] [ˈfoːl] *vi* : parir

foal[2] *n* : potro *m,* -tra *f*

foam[1] [ˈfoːm] *vi* : hacer espuma

foam[2] *n* : espuma *f*

foamy [ˈfoːmi] *adj* **foamier; -est** : espumoso

focal [ˈfoːkəl] *adj* **1** : focal, central **2 focal point** : foco *m,* punto *m* de referencia

fo'c'sle [ˈfoːksəl] → **forecastle**

focus[1] [ˈfoːkəs] *v* **-cused** *or* **-cussed; -cusing** *or* **-cussing** *vt* **1** : enfocar (un instrumento) **2** CONCENTRATE : concentrar, centrar — *vi* : enfocar, fijar la vista

focus[2] *n, pl* **-ci** [ˈfoːˌsaɪ, -ˌkaɪ] **1** : foco *m* <to be in focus : estar enfocado> **2** FOCUSING : enfoque *m* **3** CENTER : centro *m,* foco *m*

fodder [ˈfɑdər] *n* : pienso *m,* forraje *m*

foe [ˈfoː] *n* : enemigo *m,* -ga *f*

fog[1] [ˈfɔg, ˈfɑg] *v* **fogged; fogging** *vt* : empañar — *vi* **to fog up** : empañarse

fog[2] *n* : niebla *f,* neblina *f*

foggy [ˈfɔgi, ˈfɑ-] *adj* **foggier; -est** : nebuloso, brumoso

foghorn [ˈfɔg,hɔrn, ˈfɑg-] *n* : sirena *f* de niebla

fogy [ˈfoːgi] *n, pl* **-gies** : carca *mf fam,* persona *f* chapada a la antigua

foible [ˈfɔɪbəl] *n* : flaqueza *f,* debilidad *f*

foil[1] [ˈfɔɪl] *vt* : frustrar, hacer fracasar

foil[2] *n* **1** : lámina *f* de metal, papel *m* de aluminio **2** CONTRAST : contraste *m,* complemento *m* **3** SWORD : florete *m* (en esgrima)

foist [ˈfɔɪst] *vt* : encajar, endilgar *fam,* colocar

fold[1] [ˈfoːld] *vt* **1** BEND : doblar, plegar **2** CLASP : cruzar (brazos), enlazar (manos), plegar (alas) **3** EMBRACE : estrechar, abrazar — *vi* **1** FAIL : fracasar **2 to fold up** : doblarse, plegarse

fold[2] *n* **1** SHEEPFOLD : redil *m* (para ovejas) **2** FLOCK : rebaño *m* <to return to the fold : volver al redil> **3** CREASE : pliegue *m,* doblez *m*

folder [ˈfoːldər] *n* **1** CIRCULAR : circular *f,* folleto *m* **2** BINDER : carpeta *f*

foliage [ˈfoːliɪdʒ, -lɪdʒ] *n* : follaje *m*

folio [ˈfoːli,oː] *n, pl* **-lios** : folio *m*

folk[1] [ˈfoːk] *adj* : popular, folklórico <folk customs : costumbres populares> <folk dance : danza folklórica>

folk[2] *n, pl* **folk** *or* **folks 1** PEOPLE : gente *f* **2 folks** *npl* : familia *f,* padres *mpl*

folklore [ˈfoːk,lor] *n* : folklore *m*

folklorist [ˈfoːk,lorɪst] *n* : folklorista *mf*

folksy [ˈfoːksi] *adj* **folksier; -est** : campechano

follicle [ˈfɑlɪkəl] *n* : folículo *m*

follow [ˈfɑlo] *vt* **1** : seguir <follow the guide : siga al guía> <she followed the road : siguió el camino, continuó por el camino> **2** PURSUE : perseguir, seguir **3** OBEY : seguir, cumplir, observar **4** UNDERSTAND : entender — *vi* **1** : seguir **2** UNDERSTAND : entender **3 it follows that...** : se deduce que...

follower [ˈfɑloər] *n* : seguidor *m,* -dora *f*

following[1] [ˈfɑloɪŋ] *adj* NEXT : siguiente

following[2] *n* FOLLOWERS : seguidores *mpl*

following[3] *prep* AFTER : después de

follow through *vi* **to follow through with** : continuar con, realizar

follow up *vt* : seguir (una sugerencia, etc.), investigar (una huella)

folly [ˈfɑli] *n, pl* **-lies** : locura *f,* desatino *m*

foment [foˈmɛnt] *vt* : fomentar

fond [ˈfɑnd] *adj* **1** LOVING : cariñoso, tierno **2** PARTIAL : aficionado **3** FERVENT : ferviente, fervoroso

fondle [ˈfɑndəl] *vt* **-dled; -dling** : acariciar

fondly [ˈfɑndli] *adv* : cariñosamente, afectuosamente

fondness [ˈfɑndnəs] *n* **1** LOVE : cariño *m* **2** LIKING : afición *f*

fondue [fɑnˈduː, -ˈdjuː] *n* : fondue *f*

font [ˈfɑnt] *n* **1** *or* **baptismal font** : pila *f* bautismal **2** FOUNTAIN : fuente *f*

food [ˈfuːd] *n* : comida *f,* alimento *m*

food chain *n* : cadena *f* alimenticia

foodstuffs [ˈfuːd,stʌfs] *npl* : comestibles *mpl*

fool[1] [ˈfuːl] *vi* **1** JOKE : bromear, hacer el tonto **2** TOY : jugar, juguetear <don't fool with the computer : no juegues con la computadora> **3 to fool around** : perder el tiempo <he fools around instead of working : pierde el tiempo en vez de trabajar> — *vt* DECEIVE : engañar, burlar

fool[2] *n* **1** IDIOT : idiota *mf;* tonto *m,* -ta *f;* bobo *m,* -ba *f* **2** JESTER : bufón *m,* -fona *f*

foolhardiness [ˈfuːl,hɑrdinəs] *n* : imprudencia *f*

foolhardy [ˈfuːl,hɑrdi] *adj* RASH : imprudente, temerario, precipitado

foolish [ˈfuːlɪʃ] *adj* **1** STUPID : insensato, estúpido **2** SILLY : idiota, tonto

foolishly [ˈfuːlɪʃli] *adv* : tontamente

foolishness [ˈfuːlɪʃnəs] *n* : insensatez *f,* estupidez *f,* tontería *f*

foolproof [ˈfuːl,pruːf] *adj* : infalible

foot [ˈfʊt] *n, pl* **feet** [ˈfiːt] : pie *m*

footage [ˈfʊtɪdʒ] *n* : medida *f* en pies, metraje *m* (en el cine)

football [ˈfʊt,bɔl] *n* : futbol *m* americano, fútbol *m* americano

footbridge [ˈfʊt,brɪdʒ] *n* : pasarela *f,* puente *m* peatonal

foothills [ˈfʊt,hɪlz] *npl* : estribaciones *fpl*

foothold [ˈfʊt,hoːld] *n* **1** : punto *m* de apoyo **2 to gain a foothold** : afianzarse en una posición

footing [ˈfʊtɪŋ] *n* **1** BALANCE : equilibrio *m* **2** FOOTHOLD : punto *m* de apoyo **3** BASIS : base *f* <on an equal footing : en igualdad>

footlights [ˈfʊt,laɪts] *npl* : candilejas *fpl*

footlocker [ˈfʊt,lɑkər] *n* : baúl *m* pequeño, cofre *m*

footloose [ˈfʊt,luːs] *adj* : libre y sin compromiso

footman [ˈfʊtmən] *n, pl* **-men** [-mən, -,mɛn] : lacayo *m*

footnote [ˈfʊt,noːt] *n* : nota *f* al pie de la página

footpath [ˈfʊt,pæθ] *n* : sendero *m,* senda *f,* vereda *f*

footprint [ˈfʊt,prɪnt] *n* : huella *f*

footrace [ˈfʊt,reɪs] *n* : carrera *f* pedestre

footrest [ˈfʊt,rɛst] *n* : apoyapiés *m,* reposapiés *m*

footstep [ˈfʊt,stɛp] *n* **1** STEP : paso *m* **2** FOOTPRINT : huella *f*

footstool [ˈfʊt,stuːl] *n* : taburete *m,* escabel *m*

footwear [ˈfʊt,wær] *n* : calzado *m*

footwork [ˈfʊt,wərk] *n* : juego *m* de piernas, juego *m* de pies

fop [ˈfɑp] *n* : petimetre *m,* dandi *m*

for[1] [ˈfɔr] *conj* : puesto que, porque

for[2] *prep* **1** (*indicating purpose*) : para, de <clothes for children : ropa para niños> <it's time for dinner : es la hora de comer> **2** BECAUSE OF : por <for fear of : por miedo de> **3** (*indicating a recipient*) : para, por <a gift for you : un regalo para ti> **4** (*indicating support*) : por <he fought for his country : luchó por su patria> **5** (*indicating a goal*) : por, para <a cure for cancer : una cura para el cáncer> <for your own good : por tu propio bien> **6** (*indicating correspondence or exchange*) : por, para <I bought it for $5 : lo compré por $5> <a lot of trouble for nothing : mucha molestia para nada> **7** AS FOR : para, con respecto a **8** (*indicating duration*) : durante, por <he's going for two years : se va por dos años> <I spoke for ten minutes : hablé (durante) diez minutos> <she has known it for three months : lo sabe desde hace tres meses>

forage[1] [ˈfɔrɪdʒ] *v* **-aged; -aging** *vi* : hurgar (en busca de alimento) — *vt* : buscar (provisiones)

forage[2] *n* : forraje *m*

foray [ˈfɔrˌeɪ] *n* : incursión *f*

forbear[1] [fɔrˈbær] *vi* **-bore** [-ˈbor]; **-borne** [-ˈborn]; **-bearing 1** ABSTAIN : abstenerse **2** : tener paciencia

forbear[2] → **forebear**

forbearance [fɔrˈbærənts] *n* **1** ABSTAINING : abstención *f* **2** PATIENCE : paciencia *f*

forbid [fərˈbɪd] *vt* **-bade** [-ˈbæd, -ˈbeɪd] *or* **-bad** [-ˈbæd]; **-bidden** [-ˈbɪdən]; **-bidding 1** PROHIBIT : prohibir **2** PREVENT : impedir

forbidding [fərˈbɪdɪŋ] *adj* **1** IMPOSING : imponente **2** DISAGREEABLE : desagradable, ingrato **3** GRIM : severo

force[1] [ˈfors] *vt* **forced; forcing 1** COMPEL : obligar, forzar **2** : forzar <to force open the window : forzar la ventana> <to force a lock : forzar una cerradura> **3** IMPOSE : imponer, obligar

force[2] *n* **1** : fuerza *f* **2 by force** : por la fuerza **3 in force** : en vigor, en vigencia

forced [ˈforst] *adj* : forzado, forzoso

forceful [ˈforsfəl] *adj* : fuerte, enérgico, contundente

forcefully [ˈforsfəli] *adv* : con energía, con fuerza

forcefulness [ˈforsfəlnəs] *n* : contundencia *f*, fuerza *f*

forceps [ˈfɔrsəps, -ˌsɛps] *ns & pl* : fórceps *m*

forcible [ˈforsəbəl] *adj* **1** FORCED : forzoso **2** CONVINCING : contundente, convincente — **forcibly** [-bli] *adv*

ford[1] [ˈford] *vt* : vadear

ford[2] *n* : vado *m*

fore[1] [ˈfor] *adv* **1** FORWARD : hacia adelante **2 fore and aft** : de popa a proa

fore[2] *adj* **1** FORWARD : delantero, de adelante **2** FORMER : anterior

fore[3] *n* **1** : frente *m*, delantera *f* **2 to come to the fore** : empezar a destacar, saltar a primera plana

fore–and–aft [ˈforənˈæft, -ənd-] *adj* : longitudinal

forearm [ˈforˌɑrm] *n* : antebrazo *m*

forebear [ˈforˌbær] *n* : antepasado *m*, -da *f*

foreboding [forˈboːdɪŋ] *n* : premonición *f*, presentimiento *m*

forecast[1] [ˈforˌkæst] *vt* **-cast; -casting** : pronosticar, predecir

forecast[2] *n* : predicción *f*, pronóstico *m*

forecastle [ˈfoːksəl] *n* : castillo *m* de proa

foreclose [forˈkloːz] *vt* **-closed; -closing** : ejecutar (una hipoteca)

forefather [ˈforˌfɑðər] *n* : antepasado *m*, ancestro *m*

forefinger [ˈforˌfɪŋgər] *n* : índice *m*, dedo *m* índice

forefoot [ˈforˌfʊt] *n* : pata *f* delantera

forefront [ˈforˌfrʌnt] *n* : frente *m*, vanguardia *f* <in the forefront : a la vanguardia>

forego [forˈgoː] *vt* **-went; -gone; -going 1** PRECEDE : preceder **2** → **forgo**

foregoing [forˈgoːɪŋ] *adj* : precedente, anterior

foregone [forˈgɔn] *adj* : previsto <a foregone conclusion : un resultado inevitable>

foreground [ˈforˌgraʊnd] *n* : primer plano *m*

forehand[1] [ˈforˌhænd] *adj* : directo, derecho

forehand[2] *n* : golpe *m* del derecho

forehead [ˈfɔrəd, ˈforˌhɛd] *n* : frente *f*

foreign [ˈfɔrən] *adj* **1** : extranjero, exterior <foreign countries : países extranjeros> <foreign trade : comercio exterior> **2** ALIEN : ajeno, extraño <foreign to their nature : ajeno a su carácter> <a foreign body : un cuerpo extraño>

foreigner [ˈfɔrənər] *n* : extranjero *m*, -ra *f*

foreknowledge [forˈnɑlɪdʒ] *n* : conocimiento *m* previo

foreleg [ˈforˌlɛg] *n* : pata *f* delantera

foreman [ˈformən] *n, pl* **-men** [-mən, -ˌmɛn] : capataz *mf* <foreman of the jury : presidente del jurado>

foremost[1] [ˈforˌmoːst] *adv* : en primer lugar

foremost[2] *adj* : más importante, principal, grande

forenoon [ˈforˌnuːn] *n* : mañana *m*

forensic [fəˈrɛntsɪk] *adj* **1** RHETORICAL : retórico, de argumentación **2** : forense <forensic medicine : medicina forense>

foreordain [ˌforɔr'deɪn] *vt* : predestinar, predeterminar
forequarter ['forˌkwɔrt̬ər] *n* : cuarto *m* delantero
forerunner ['forˌrʌnər] *n* : precursor *m*, -sora *f*
foresee [for'siː] *vt* **-saw; -seen; -seeing** : prever
foreseeable [for'siːəbəl] *adj* : previsible <in the foreseeable future : en el futuro inmediato>
foreshadow [for'ʃædoː] *vt* : anunciar, prefigurar
foresight ['forˌsaɪt] *n* : previsión *f*
foresighted ['forˌsaɪt̬əd] *adj* : previsto
forest ['fɔrəst] *n* : bosque *m* (en zonas templadas), selva *f* (en zonas tropicales)
forestall [for'stɔl] *vt* **1** PREVENT : prevenir, impedir **2** PREEMPT : adelantarse a
forested ['fɔrəstəd] *adj* : arbolado
forester ['fɔrəstər] *n* : silvicultor *m*, -tora *f*
forestland ['fɔrəstˌlænd] *n* : zona *f* boscosa
forest ranger → **ranger**
forestry ['fɔrəstri] *n* : silvicultura *f*, ingeniería *f* forestal
foreswear → **forswear**
foretaste[1] ['forˌteɪst] *vt* **-tasted; -tasting** : anticipar
foretaste[2] *n* : anticipo *m*
foretell [for'tɛl] *vt* **-told; -telling** : predecir, pronosticar, profetizar
forethought ['forˌθɔt] *n* : previsión *f*, reflexión *f* previa
forever [fɔr'ɛvər] *adv* **1** PERPETUALLY : para siempre, eternamente **2** CONTINUALLY : siempre, constantemente
forevermore [fɔrˌɛvər'mor] *adv* : por siempre jamás
forewarn [for'wɔrn] *vt* : prevenir, advertir
foreword ['forwərd] *n* : prólogo *m*
forfeit[1] ['fɔrfət] *vt* : perder el derecho a
forfeit[2] *n* **1** FINE, PENALTY : multa *f* **2** : prenda *f* (en un juego)
forge[1] ['fordʒ] *v* **forged; forging** *vt* **1** : forjar (metal o un plan) **2** COUNTERFEIT : falsificar — *vi* **to forge ahead** : avanzar, seguir adelante
forge[2] *n* : forja *f*
forger ['fordʒər] *n* : falsificador *m*, -dora *f*
forgery ['fordʒəri] *n, pl* **-eries** : falsificación *f*
forget [fər'gɛt] *v* **-got** [-'gɑt]; **-gotten** [-'gɑtən] *or* **-got; -getting** *vt* : olvidar — *vi* **to forget about** : olvidarse de, no acordarse de
forgetful [fər'gɛtfəl] *adj* : olvidadizo
forget-me-not [fər'gɛtmiˌnɑt] *n* : nomeolvides *mf*
forgettable [fər'gɛt̬əbəl] *adj* : poco memorable
forgivable [fər'gɪvəbəl] *adj* : perdonable
forgive [fər'gɪv] *vt* **-gave** [-'geɪv]; **-given** [-'gɪvən]; **-giving** : perdonar
forgiveness [fər'gɪvnəs] *n* : perdón *m*
forgiving [fər'gɪvɪŋ] *adj* : indulgente, comprensivo, clemente
forgo *or* **forego** [for'goː] *vt* **-went; -gone; -going** : privarse de, renunciar a
fork[1] ['fɔrk] *vi* : ramificarse, bifurcarse — *vt* **1** : levantar (con un tenedor, una horca, etc.) **2** **to fork over** : desembolsar
fork[2] *n* **1** : tenedor *m* (utensilio de cocina) **2** PITCHFORK : horca *f*, horquilla *f* **3** : bifurcación *f* (de un río o camino), horqueta *f* (de un árbol)
forked ['fɔrkt, 'fɔrkəd] *adj* : bífido, ahorquillado
forklift ['fɔrkˌlɪft] *n* : carretilla *f* elevadora
forlorn [fɔr'lɔrn] *adj* **1** DESOLATE : abandonado, desolado, desamparado **2** SAD : triste **3** DESPERATE : desesperado
forlornly [fɔr'lɔrnli] *adv* **1** SADLY : con tristeza **2** HALFHEARTEDLY : sin ánimo
form[1] ['fɔrm] *vt* **1** FASHION, MAKE : formar **2** DEVELOP : moldear, desarrollar **3** CONSTITUTE : constituir, formar **4** ACQUIRE : adquirir (un hábito), formar (una idea) — *vi* : tomar forma, formarse
form[2] *n* **1** SHAPE : forma *f*, figura *f* **2** MANNER : manera *f*, forma *f* **3** DOCUMENT : formulario *m* **4** : forma *f* <in good form : en buena forma> <true to form : en forma consecuente> **5** MOLD : molde *m* **6** KIND, VARIETY : clase *f*, tipo *m* **7** : forma *f* (en gramática) <plural forms : formas plurales>
formal[1] ['fɔrməl] *adj* **1** CEREMONIOUS : formal, de etiqueta, ceremonioso **2** OFFICIAL : formal, oficial, de forma
formal[2] *n* **1** BALL : baile *m* formal, baile *m* de etiqueta **2** *or* **formal dress** : traje *m* de etiqueta
formaldehyde [fɔr'mældəˌhaɪd] *n* : formaldehído *m*
formality [fɔr'mæləţi] *n, pl* **-ties** : formalidad *f*
formalize ['fɔrməˌlaɪz] *vt* **-ized; -izing** : formalizar
formally ['fɔrməli] *adv* : formalmente
format[1] ['fɔrˌmæt] *vt* **-matted; -matting** : formatear
format[2] *n* : formato *m*
formation [fɔr'meɪʃən] *n* **1** FORMING : formación *f* **2** SHAPE : forma *f* **3** **in formation** : en formación
formative ['fɔrməţɪv] *adj* : formativo
former ['fɔrmər] *adj* **1** PREVIOUS : antiguo, anterior <the former president : el antiguo presidente> **2** : primero (de dos)
formerly ['fɔrmərli] *adv* : anteriormente, antes
formidable ['fɔrmədəbəl, fɔr'mɪdə-] *adj* : formidable — **formidably** *adv*

formless [ˈfɔrmləs] *adj* : informe, amorfo
formula [ˈfɔrmjələ] *n, pl* **-las** *or* **-lae** [-ˌliː, -ˌlaɪ] **1** : fórmula *f* **2 baby formula** : preparado *m* para biberón
formulate [ˈfɔrmjəˌleɪt] *vt* **-lated; -lating** : formular, hacer
formulation [ˌfɔrmjəˈleɪʃən] *n* : formulación *f*
fornicate [ˈfɔrnəˌkeɪt] *vi* **-cated; -cating** : fornicar
fornication [ˌfɔrnəˈkeɪʃən] *n* : fornicación *f*
forsake [fərˈseɪk] *vt* **-sook** [-ˈsʊk]; **-saken** [-ˈseɪkən]; **-saking 1** ABANDON : abandonar, desamparar **2** RELINQUISH : renunciar a
forswear [fɔrˈswær] *v* **-swore; -sworn; -swearing** *vt* RENOUNCE : renunciar a — *vi* : perjurar
forsythia [fərˈsɪθiə] *n* : forsitia *f*
fort [ˈfort] *n* **1** STRONGHOLD : fuerte *m,* fortaleza *f,* fortín *m* **2** BASE : base *f* militar
forte [ˈfort, ˈforˌteɪ] *n* : fuerte *m*
forth [ˈforθ] *adv* **1** : adelante <from this day forth : de hoy en adelante> **2 and so forth** : etcétera
forthcoming [forθˈkʌmɪŋ, ˈforθˌ-] *adj* **1** COMING : próximo **2** DIRECT, OPEN : directo, franco, comunicativo
forthright [ˈforθˌraɪt] *adj* : directo, franco — **forthrightly** *adv*
forthrightness [ˈforθˌraɪtnəs] *n* : franqueza *f*
forthwith [forθˈwɪθ, -ˈwɪð] *adv* : inmediatamente, en el acto, enseguida
fortieth[1] [ˈfɔrtiəθ] *adj* : cuadragésimo
fortieth[2] *n* **1** : cuadragésimo *m,* -ma *f* (en una serie) **2** : cuarentavo *m,* cuarentava parte *f*
fortification [ˌfɔrtəfəˈkeɪʃən] *n* : fortificación *f*
fortify [ˈfɔrtəˌfaɪ] *vt* **-fied; -fying** : fortificar
fortitude [ˈfɔrtəˌtuːd, -ˌtjuːd] *n* : fortaleza *f,* valor *m*
fortnight [ˈfortˌnaɪt] *n* : quince días *mpl,* dos semanas *fpl*
fortnightly[1] [ˈfortˌnaɪtli] *adv* : cada quince días
fortnightly[2] *adj* : quincenal
fortress [ˈfɔrtrəs] *n* : fortaleza *f*
fortuitous [fɔrˈtuːətəs, -ˈtjuː-] *adj* : fortuito, accidental
fortunate [ˈfɔrtʃənət] *adj* : afortunado
fortunately [ˈfɔrtʃənətli] *adv* : afortunadamente, con suerte
fortune [ˈfɔrtʃən] *n* **1** : fortuna *f* <to seek one's fortune : buscar uno su fortuna> **2** LUCK : suerte *f,* fortuna *f* **3** DESTINY, FUTURE : destino *m,* buenaventura *f* **4** : dineral *m,* platal *m* <she spent a fortune : se gastó un dineral>
fortune-teller [ˈfɔrtʃənˌtɛlər] *n* : adivino *m,* -na *f*
fortune-telling [ˈfɔrtʃənˌtɛlɪŋ] *n* : adivinación *f*
forty[1] [ˈfɔrti] *adj* : cuarenta
forty[2] *n, pl* **forties** : cuarenta *m*
forum [ˈforəm] *n, pl* **-rums** : foro *m*
forward[1] [ˈfɔrwərd] *vt* **1** PROMOTE : promover, adelantar, fomentar **2** SEND : remitir, enviar
forward[2] *adv* **1** : adelante, hacia adelante <to go forward : irse adelante> **2 from this day forward** : de aquí en adelante
forward[3] *adj* **1** : hacia adelante, delantero **2** BRASH : atrevido, descarado
forward[4] *n* : delantero *m,* -ra *f* (en deportes)
forwarder [ˈfɔrwərdər] *n* : agencia *f* de transportes, agente *mf* expedidor
forwardness [ˈfɔrwərdnəs] *n* : atrevimiento *m,* descaro *m*
forwards [ˈfɔrwərdz] → **forward**[2]
fossil[1] [ˈfɑsəl] *adj* : fósil
fossil[2] *n* : fósil *m*
fossilize [ˈfɑsəˌlaɪz] *vt* **-ized; -izing** : fosilizar — *vi* : fosilizarse
foster[1] [ˈfɔstər] *vt* : promover, fomentar
foster[2] *adj* : adoptivo <foster child : niño adoptivo>
fought → **fight**
foul[1] [ˈfaʊl] *vi* : cometer faltas (en deportes) — *vt* **1** DIRTY, POLLUTE : contaminar, ensuciar **2** TANGLE : enredar
foul[2] *adv* **1** → **foully 2** : contra las reglas
foul[3] *adj* **1** REPULSIVE : asqueroso, repugnante **2** CLOGGED : atascado, obstruido **3** TANGLED : enredado **4** OBSCENE : obsceno **5** BAD : malo <foul weather : mal tiempo> **6** : antirreglamentario (en deportes)
foul[4] *n* : falta *f,* faul *m*
foully [ˈfaʊli] *adv* : asquerosamente
foulmouthed [ˈfaʊlˌmæʊːðd, -ˌmaʊθt] *adj* : malhablado
foulness [ˈfaʊlnəs] *n* **1** DIRTINESS : suciedad *f* **2** INCLEMENCY : inclemencia *f* **3** OBSCENITY : obscenidad *f,* grosería *f*
foul play *n* : actos *mpl* criminales
foul-up [ˈfaʊlˌʌp] *n* : lío *m,* confusión *f,* desastre *m*
foul up *vt* SPOIL : estropear, arruinar — *vi* BUNGLE : echar todo a perder
found[1] → **find**
found[2] [ˈfaʊnd] *vt* : fundar, establecer
foundation [faʊnˈdeɪʃən] *n* **1** FOUNDING : fundación *f* **2** BASIS : fundamento *m,* base *f* **3** INSTITUTION : fundación *f* **4** : cimientos *mpl* (de un edificio)
founder[1] [ˈfaʊndər] *vi* SINK : hundirse, irse a pique
founder[2] *n* : fundador *m,* -dora *f*
foundling [ˈfaʊndlɪŋ] *n* : expósito *m,* -ta *f*
foundry [ˈfaʊndri] *n, pl* **-dries** : fundición *f*
fount [ˈfaʊnt] *n* SOURCE : fuente *f,* origen *m*

fountain ['faʊntən] *n* **1** SPRING : fuente *f*, manantial *m* **2** SOURCE : fuente *f*, origen *m* **3** JET : chorro *m* (de agua), surtidor *m*
fountain pen *n* : pluma *f* fuente
four[1] ['for] *adj* : cuatro
four[2] *n* : cuatro *m*
fourfold ['for,fo:ld, -'fo:ld] *adj* : cuadruple
four hundred[1] *adj* : cuatrocientos
four hundred[2] *n* : cuatrocientos *m*
fourscore ['for'skor] *adj* EIGHTY : ochenta *m*
fourteen[1] [for'ti:n] *adj* : catorce
fourteen[2] *n* : catorce *m*
fourteenth[1] [for'ti:nθ] *adj* : decimocuarto
fourteenth[2] *n* **1** : decimocuarto *m*, -ta *f* (en una serie) **2** : catorceavo *m*, catorceava parte *f*
fourth[1] ['forθ] *adj* : cuarto
fourth[2] *n* **1** : cuarto *m*, -ta *f* (en una serie) **2** : cuarto *m*, cuarta parte *f*
fowl ['faʊl] *n, pl* **fowl** *or* **fowls 1** BIRD : ave *f* **2** CHICKEN : pollo *m*
fox[1] ['fɑks] *vt* **1** TRICK : engañar **2** BAFFLE : confundir
fox[2] *n, pl* **foxes** : zorro *m*, -ra *f*
foxglove ['fɑks,glʌv] *n* : dedalera *f*, digital *f*
foxhole ['fɑks,ho:l] *n* : hoyo *m* para atrincherarse, trinchera *f* individual
foxy ['fɑksi] *adj* **foxier; -est** SHREWD : astuto
foyer ['fɔɪər, 'fɔɪ,jeɪ] *n* : vestíbulo *m*
fracas ['freɪkəs, 'fræ-] *n, pl* **-cases** [-kəsəz] : altercado *m*, pelea *f*, reyerta *f*
fraction ['frækʃən] *n* **1** : fracción *f*, quebrado *m* **2** PORTION : porción *f*, parte *f*
fractional ['frækʃənəl] *adj* **1** : fraccionario **2** TINY : minúsculo, mínimo, insignificante
fractious ['frækʃəs] *adj* **1** UNRULY : rebelde **2** IRRITABLE : malhumorado, irritable
fracture[1] ['fræktʃər] *vt* **-tured; -turing** : fracturar
fracture[2] *n* **1** : fractura *f* (de un hueso) **2** CRACK : fisura *f*, grieta *f*, falla *f* (geológica)
fragile ['frædʒəl, -,dʒaɪl] *adj* : frágil
fragility [frə'dʒɪləṭi] *n, pl* **-ties** : fragilidad *f*
fragment[1] ['fræg,mɛnt] *vt* : fragmentar — *vi* : fragmentarse, hacerse añicos
fragment[2] ['frægmənt] *n* : fragmento *m*, trozo *m*, pedazo *m*
fragmentary ['frægmən,tɛri] *adj* : fragmentario, incompleto
fragmentation [,frægmən'teɪʃən, -,mɛn-] *n* : fragmentación *f*
fragrance ['freɪgrənts] *n* : fragancia *f*, aroma *m*
fragrant ['freɪgrənt] *adj* : fragante, aromático — **fragrantly** *adv*
frail ['freɪl] *adj* : débil, delicado
frailty ['freɪlti] *n, pl* **-ties** : debilidad *f*, flaqueza *f*
frame[1] ['freɪm] *vt* **framed; framing 1** FORMULATE : formular, elaborar **2** BORDER : enmarcar, encuadrar **3** INCRIMINATE : incriminar
frame[2] *n* **1** BODY : cuerpo *m* **2** : armazón *f* (de un edificio, un barco, o un avión), bastidor *m* (de un automóvil), cuadro *m* (de una bicicleta), marco *m* (de un cuadro, una ventana, una puerta, etc.) **3 frames** *npl* : armazón *mf*, montura *f* (para anteojos) **4 frame of mind** : estado *m* de ánimo
framework ['freɪm,wərk] *n* **1** SKELETON, STRUCTURE : armazón *f*, estructura *f* **2** BASIS : marco *m*
franc ['fræŋk] *n* : franco *m*
franchise ['fræn,tʃaɪz] *n* **1** LICENSE : licencia *f* exclusiva, concesión *f* (en comercio) **2** SUFFRAGE : sufragio *m*
franchisee [,fræn,tʃaɪ'zi:, -tʃə-] *n* : concesionario *m*, -ria *f*
frank[1] ['fræŋk] *vt* : franquear
frank[2] *adj* : franco, sincero, cándido — **frankly** *adv*
frank[3] *n* : franqueo *m* (de correo)
frankfurter ['fræŋkfərṭər, -,fər-] *or* **frankfurt** [-fərt] *n* : salchicha *f* (de Frankfurt, de Viena), perro *m* caliente
frankincense ['fræŋkən,sɛnts] *n* : incienso *m*
frankness ['fræŋknəs] *n* : franqueza *f*, sinceridad *f*, candidez *f*
frantic ['fræntɪk] *adj* : frenético, desesperado — **frantically** *adv*
fraternal [frə'tərnəl] *adj* : fraterno, fraternal
fraternity [frə'tərnəṭi] *n, pl* **-ties** : fraternidad *f*
fraternization [,fræṭərnə'zeɪʃən] *n* : fraternización *f*, confraternización *f*
fraternize ['fræṭər,naɪz] *vi* **-nized; -nizing** : fraternizar, confraternizar
fratricidal [,frætrə'saɪdəl] *adj* : fratricida
fratricide ['frætrə,saɪd] *n* : fratricidio *m*
fraud ['frɔd] *n* **1** DECEPTION, SWINDLE : fraude *m*, estafa *f*, engaño *m* **2** IMPOSTOR : impostor *m*, -tora *f*; farsante *mf*
fraudulent ['frɔdʒələnt] *adj* : fraudulento — **fraudulently** *adv*
fraught ['frɔt] *adj* **fraught with** : lleno de, cargado de
fray[1] ['freɪ] *vt* **1** WEAR : desgastar, deshilachar **2** IRRITATE : crispar, irritar (los nervios) — *vi* : desgastarse, deshilacharse
fray[2] *n* : pelea *f*, lucha *f*, refriega *f*
frazzle[1] ['fræzəl] *vt* **-zled; -zling 1** FRAY : desgastar, deshilachar **2** EXHAUST : agotar, fatigar
frazzle[2] *n* EXHAUSTION : agotamiento *m*
freak ['fri:k] *n* **1** ODDITY : ejemplar *m* anormal, fenómeno *m*, rareza *f* **2** ENTHUSIAST : entusiasta *mf*

freakish ['friːkɪʃ] *adj* : extraño, estrafalario, raro
freckle¹ ['frɛkəl] *vi* **-led; -ling** : cubrirse de pecas
freckle² *n* : peca *f*
free¹ ['friː] *vt* **freed; freeing 1** LIBERATE : libertar, liberar, poner en libertad **2** RELIEVE, RID : librar, eximir **3** RELEASE, UNTIE : desatar, soltar **4** UNCLOG : desatascar, destapar
free² *adv* **1** FREELY : libremente **2** GRATIS : gratuitamente, gratis
free³ *adj* **freer; freest 1** : libre <free as a bird : libre como un pájaro> **2** EXEMPT : libre <tax-free : libre de impuestos> **3** GRATIS : gratuito, gratis **4** VOLUNTARY : espontáneo, voluntario, libre **5** UNOCCUPIED : desocupado, libre **6** LOOSE : suelto
freebooter ['friːˌbuːt̬ər] *n* : pirata *mf*
freeborn ['friː'bɔrn] *adj* : nacido libre
freedom ['friːdəm] *n* : libertad *f*
free–for–all ['friːfərˌɔl] *n* : pelea *f,* batalla *f* campal
freelance¹ ['friːˌlæn*t*s] *vi* **-lanced; -lancing** : trabajar por cuenta propia
freelance² *adj* : por cuenta propia, independiente
freeload ['friːˌloːd] *vi* : gorronear *fam,* gorrear *fam*
freeloader ['friːˌloːdər] *n* : gorrón *m,* -rrona *f;* gorrero *m,* -ra *f;* vividor *m,* -dora *f*
freely ['friːli] *adv* **1** FREE : libremente **2** GRATIS : gratis, gratuitamente
freestanding ['friː'stændɪŋ] *adj* : de pie, no empotrado, independiente
freeway ['friːˌweɪ] *n* : autopista *f*
freewill ['friːˌwɪl] *adj* : de propia voluntad
free will *n* : libre albedrío *m,* propia voluntad *f*
freeze¹ ['friːz] *v* **froze** ['froːz]; **frozen** ['froːzən]; **freezing** *vi* **1** : congelarse, helarse <the water froze in the lake : el agua se congeló en el lago> <my blood froze : se me heló la sangre> <I'm freezing : me estoy helando> **2** STOP : quedarse inmóvil — *vt* : helar, congelar (líquidos), congelar (alimentos, precios, activos)
freeze² *n* **1** FROST : helada *f* **2** FREEZING : congelación *f,* congelamiento *m*
freeze–dried ['friːz'draɪd] *adj* : liofilizado
freeze–dry ['friːz'draɪ] *vt* **-dried; -drying** : liofilizar
freezer ['friːzər] *n* : congelador *m*
freezing ['friːzɪŋ] *adj* : helando <it's freezing! : ¡hace un frío espantoso!>
freezing point *n* : punto *m* de congelación
freight¹ ['freɪt] *vt* : enviar como carga
freight² *n* **1** SHIPPING, TRANSPORT : transporte *m,* porte *m,* flete *m* **2** GOODS : mercancías *fpl,* carga *f*
freighter ['freɪt̬ər] *n* : carguero *m,* buque *m* de carga
French¹ ['frɛn*t*ʃ] *adj* : francés
French² *n* **1** : francés *m* (idioma) **2 the French** *npl* : los franceses
Frenchman ['frɛn*t*ʃmən] *n, pl* **-men** [-mən, -ˌmɛn] : francés *m*
Frenchwoman ['frɛn*t*ʃˌwʊmən] *n, pl* **-women** [-ˌwɪmən] : francesa *f*
french fries ['frɛntʃˌfraɪz] *npl* : papas *fpl* fritas
frenetic [frɪ'nɛtɪk] *adj* : frenético — **frenetically** [-tɪkli] *adv*
frenzied ['frɛnzid] *adj* : frenético
frenzy ['frɛnzi] *n, pl* **-zies** : frenesí *m*
frequency ['friːkwən*t*si] *n, pl* **-cies** : frecuencia *f*
frequent¹ [fri'kwɛnt, 'friːkwənt] *vt* : frecuentar
frequent² ['friːkwənt] *adj* : frecuente — **frequently** *adv*
fresco ['frɛsˌkoː] *n, pl* **-coes** : fresco *m*
fresh ['frɛʃ] *adj* **1** : dulce <freshwater : agua dulce> **2** PURE : puro **3** : fresco <fresh fruits : frutas frescas> **4** CLEAN, NEW : limpio, nuevo <fresh clothes : ropa limpia> <fresh evidence : evidencia nueva> **5** REFRESHED : fresco, descansado **6** IMPEFTINENT : descarado, impertinente
freshen ['frɛʃən] *vt* : refrescar, arreglar — *vi* **to freshen up** : arreglarse, lavarse
freshet ['frɛʃət] *n* : arroyo *m* desbordado
freshly ['frɛʃli] *adv* : recientemente, recién
freshman ['frɛʃmən] *n, pl* **-men** [-mən, -ˌmɛn] : estudiante *mf* de primer año universitario
freshness ['frɛʃnəs] *n* : frescura *f*
freshwater ['frɛʃˌwɔt̬ər] *n* : agua *f* dulce
fret¹ ['frɛt] *vi* **fretted; fretting** : preocuparse, inquietarse
fret² *n* **1** VEXATION : irritación *f,* molestia *f* **2** WORRY : preocupación *f* **3** : traste *m* (de un instrumento musical)
fretful ['frɛtfəl] *adj* : fastidioso, quejoso, neurótico
fretfully ['frɛtfəli] *adv* : ansiosamente, fastidiosamente, inquieto
fretfulness ['frɛtfəlnəs] *n* : inquietud *f,* irritabilidad *f*
friable ['fraɪəbəl] *adj* : friable, pulverizable
friar ['fraɪər] *n* : fraile *m*
fricassee¹ ['frɪkəˌsiː, ˌfrɪkə'siː] *vt* **-seed; -seeing** : cocinar al fricasé
fricassee² *n* : fricasé *m*
friction ['frɪkʃən] *n* **1** RUBBING : fricción *f* **2** CONFLICT : fricción *f,* roce *m*
Friday ['fraɪˌdeɪ, -di] *n* : viernes *m*
fridge ['frɪdʒ] → **refrigerator**
friend ['frɛnd] *n* : amigo *m,* -ga *f*
friendless ['frɛndləs] *adj* : sin amigos
friendliness ['frɛndlinəs] *n* : simpatía *f,* amabilidad *f*
friendly ['frɛndli] *adj* **-lier; -est 1** : simpático, amable, de amigo <a friendly child : un niño simpático> <friendly advice : consejo de amigo>

2 : agradable, acogedor <a friendly atmosphere : un ambiente agradable> 3 GOOD-NATURED : amigable, amistoso <friendly competition : competencia amistosa>

friendship [frɛnd,ʃɪp] *n* : amistad *f*

frieze ['friːz] *n* : friso *m*

frigate ['frɪgət] *n* : fragata *f*

fright ['fraɪt] *n* : miedo *m,* susto *m*

frighten ['fraitən] *vt* : asustar, espantar

frightened ['fraitənd] *adj* : asustado, temeroso

frightening ['fraitənɪŋ] *adj* : espantoso, aterrador

frightful ['fraɪtfəl] *adj* **1** → **frightening** **2** TREMENDOUS : espantoso, tremendo

frightfully ['fraɪtfəli] *adv* : terriblemente, tremendamente

frigid ['frɪdʒɪd] *adj* : glacial, extremadamente frío

frigidity [frɪ'dʒɪdət̮i] *n* **1** COLDNESS : frialdad *f* **2** : frigidez *f* (sexual)

frill ['frɪl] *n* **1** RUFFLE : volante *m* **2** EMBELLISHMENT : floritura *f,* adorno *m*

frilly ['frɪli] *adj* **frillier; -est** **1** RUFFLY : con volantes **2** OVERDONE : recargado

fringe[1] ['frɪndʒ] *vt* **fringed; fringing** : orlar, bordear

fringe[2] *n* **1** BORDER : fleco *m,* orla *f* **2** EDGE : periferia *f,* margen *m* **3 fringe benefits** : incentivos *mpl*, extras *mpl*

frisk ['frɪsk] *vi* FROLIC : retozar, juguetear — *vt* SEARCH : cachear, registrar

friskiness ['frɪskinəs] *n* : vivacidad *f*

frisky ['frɪski] *adj* **friskier; -est** : retozón, juguetón

fritter[1] ['frɪt̮ər] *vt* : desperdiciar, malgastar <I frittered away the money : malgasté el dinero>

fritter[2] *n* : buñuelo *m*

frivolity [frɪ'vɑlət̮i] *n, pl* **-ties** : frivolidad *f*

frivolous ['frɪvələs] *adj* : frívolo, de poca importancia

frivolously ['frɪvələsli] *adv* : frívolamente, a la ligera

frizz[1] ['frɪz] *vi* : rizarse, encresparse, ponerse chino *Mex*

frizz[2] *n* : rizos *mpl* muy apretados

frizzy ['frɪzi] *adj* **frizzier; -est** : rizado, crespo, chino *Mex*

fro ['froː] *adv* **to and fro** : de aquí para allá, de un lado para otro

frock ['frɑk] *n* DRESS : vestido *m*

frog ['frɔg, 'frɑg] *n* **1** : rana *f* **2** FASTENER : alamar *m* 3 **to have a frog in one's throat** : tener carraspera

frogman ['frɔg,mæn, 'frɑg-, -mən] *n, pl* **-men** [-mən, -,mɛn] : hombre *m* rana, submarinista *mf*

frolic[1] ['frɑlɪk] *vi* **-icked; -icking** : retozar, juguetear

frolic[2] *n* FUN : diversión *f*

frolicsome ['frɑlɪksəm] *adj* : juguetón

from ['frʌm, 'frɑm] *prep* **1** (*indicating a starting point*) : desde, de, a partir de <from Cali to Bogota : de Cali a Bogotá> <where are you from? : ¿de dónde eres?> <from that time onward : desde entonces> <from tomorrow : a partir de mañana> **2** (*indicating a source or sender*) : de <a letter from my friend : una carta de mi amiga> <a quote from Shakespeare : una cita de Shakespeare> **3** (*indicating distance*) : de <10 feet from the entrance : a 10 pies de la entrada> **4** (*indicating a cause*) : de <red from crying : rojos de llorar> <he died from the cold : murió del frío> **5** OFF, OUT OF : de <she took it from the drawer : lo sacó del cajón> **6** (*with adverbs or adverbial phrases*) : de, desde <from above : desde arriba> <from among : de entre>

frond ['frɑnd] *n* : fronda *f,* hoja *f*

front[1] ['frʌnt] *vi* **1** FACE : dar, estar orientado <the house fronts north : la casa da al norte> **2** : servir de pantalla <he fronts for his boss : sirve de pantalla para su jefe>

front[2] *adj* : delantero, de adelante, primero <the front row : la primera fila>

front[3] *n* **1** : frente *m,* parte *f* de adelante, delantera *f* <the front of the class : el frente de la clase> <at the front of the train : en la parte delantera del tren> **2** AREA, ZONE : frente *m,* zona *f* <the Eastern front : el frente oriental> <on the educational front : en el frente de la enseñanza> **3** FACADE : fachada *f* (de un edificio o una persona> **4** : frente *m* (en meteorología)

frontage ['frʌntɪdʒ] *n* : fachada *f,* frente *m*

frontal ['frʌntəl] *adj* : frontal, de frente

frontier [,frʌn'tɪr] *n* : frontera *f*

frontiersman [,frʌn'tɪrzmən] *n, pl* **-men** [-mən, -,mɛn] : hombre *m* de la frontera

frontispiece ['frʌntəs,piːs] *n* : frontispicio *m*

frost[1] ['frɔst] *vt* **1** FREEZE : helar **2** ICE : escarchar (pasteles)

frost[2] *n* **1** : helada *f* (en meteorología) **2** : escarcha *f* <frost on the window : escarcha en la ventana>

frostbite ['frɔst,baɪt] *n* : congelación *f*

frostbitten ['frɔst,bɪtən] *adj* : congelado (dícese de una persona), quemado (dícese de una planta)

frosting ['frɔstɪŋ] *n* ICING : glaseado *m,* betún *m Mex*

frosty ['frɔsti] *adj* **frostier; -est** **1** CHILLY : helado, frío **2** COOL, UNFRIENDLY : frío, glacial

froth ['frɔθ] *n, pl* **froths** ['frɔθs, 'frɔðz] : espuma *f*

frothy ['frɔθi] *adj* **frothier; -est** : espumoso

frown[1] ['fraʊn] *vi* **1** : fruncir el ceño, fruncir el entrecejo **2 to frown at**

: mirar (algo) con ceño, mirar (a alguien) con ceño
frown[2] *n* : ceño *m* (fruncido)
frowsy *or* **frowzy** ['fraʊzi] *adj* **frowsier** *or* **frowzier; -est** : desaliñado, desaseado
froze → **freeze**
frozen → **freeze**
frugal ['fru:gəl] *adj* : frugal, ahorrativo, parco — **frugally** *adv*
frugality [fru'gæləti] *n* : frugalidad *f*
fruit[1] ['fru:t] *vi* : dar fruto
fruit[2] *n* **1** : fruta *f* (término genérico), fruto *m* (término particular) **2 fruits** *npl* REWARDS : frutos *mpl* <the fruits of his labor : los frutos de su trabajo>
fruitcake ['fru:t,keɪk] *n* : pastel *m* de frutas
fruitful ['fru:tfəl] *adj* : fructífero, provechoso
fruition [fru'ɪʃən] *n* **1** : cumplimiento *m,* realización *f* **2 to bring to fruition** : realizar
fruitless ['fru:tləs] *adj* : infructuoso, inútil — **fruitlessly** *adv*
fruity ['fru:ti] *adj* **fruitier; -est** : (con sabor) a fruta
frumpy ['frʌmpi] *adj* **frumpier; -est** : anticuado y sin atractivo
frustrate ['frʌs,treɪt] *vt* **-trated; -trating** : frustrar
frustrating ['frʌs,treɪtɪŋ] *adj* : frustrante — **frustratingly** *adv*
frustration [,frʌs'treɪʃən] *n* : frustración *f*
fry[1] ['fraɪ] *vt* **fried; frying** : freír
fry[2] *n, pl* **fries 1** : fritura *f,* plato *m* frito **2** : fiesta *f* en que se sirven frituras **3** *pl* **fry** : alevín *m* (pez)
fuddle ['fʌdəl] *vt* **-dled; -dling** : confundir, atontar
fuddy–duddy ['fʌdi,dʌdi] *n, pl* **-dies** : persona *f* chapada a la antigua, carca *mf*
fudge[1] ['fʌdʒ] *vt* **fudged; fudging 1** FALSIFY : amañar, falsificar **2** DODGE : esquivar
fudge[2] *n* : dulce *m* blando de chocolate y leche
fuel[1] ['fju:əl] *vt* **-eled** *or* **-elled; -eling** *or* **-elling 1** : abastecer de combustible **2** STIMULATE : estimular
fuel[2] *n* : combustible *m,* carburante *m* (para motores)
fugitive[1] ['fju:dʒətɪv] *adj* **1** RUNAWAY : fugitivo **2** FLEETING : efímero, pasajero, fugaz
fugitive[2] *n* : fugitivo *m,* -va *f*
fulcrum ['fʊlkrəm, 'fʌl-] *n, pl* **-crums** *or* **-cra** [-krə] : fulcro *m*
fulfill *or* **fulfil** [fʊl'fɪl] *vt* **-filled; -filling 1** PERFORM : cumplir con, realizar, llevar a cabo **2** SATISFY : satisfacer
fulfillment [fʊl'fɪlmənt] *n* **1** PERFORMANCE : cumplimiento *m,* ejecución *f* **2** SATISFACTION : satisfacción *f,* realización *f*
full[1] ['fʊl, 'fʌl] *adv* **1** VERY : muy <full well : muy bien, perfectamente> **2** ENTIRELY : completamente <she swung full around : giró completamente> **3** DIRECTLY : de lleno, directamente <he looked me full in the face : me miró directamente a la cara>
full[2] *adj* **1** FILLED : lleno **2** COMPLETE : completo, detallado **3** MAXIMUM : todo, pleno <at full speed : a toda velocidad> <in full bloom : en plena flor> **4** PLUMP : redondo, llenito *fam,* regordete *fam* <a full face : una cara redonda> <a full figure : un cuerpo llenito> **5** AMPLE : amplio <a full skirt : una falda amplia>
full[3] *n* **1 to pay in full** : pagar en su totalidad **2 to the full** : al máximo
full–fledged ['fʊl'flɛdʒd] *adj* : hecho y derecho
fullness ['fʊlnəs] *n* **1** ABUNDANCE : plenitud *f,* abundancia *f* **2** : amplitud *f* (de una falda)
fully ['fʊli] *adv* **1** COMPLETELY : completamente, totalmente **2** : al menos, por lo menos <fully half of them : al menos la mitad de ellos>
fulsome ['fʊlsəm] *adj* : excesivo, exagerado, efusivo
fumble[1] ['fʌmbəl] *v* **-bled; -bling** *vt* **1** : dejar caer, fumblear **2 to fumble one's way** : ir a tientas — *vi* **1** GROPE : hurgar, tantear **2 to fumble with** : manejar con torpeza
fumble[2] *n* : fumble *m* (en futbol americano)
fume[1] ['fju:m] *vi* **fumed; fuming 1** SMOKE : echar humo, humear **2** : enfadarse, enojarse
fume[2] *n* : gas *m,* humo *m,* vapor *m*
fumigate ['fju:mə,geɪt] *vt* **-gated; -gating** : fumigar
fumigation [,fju:mə'geɪʃən] *n* : fumigación *m*
fun[1] ['fʌn] *adj* : divertido, entretenido
fun[2] *n* **1** AMUSEMENT : diversión *f,* entretenimiento *m* **2** ENJOYMENT : disfrute *m* **3 to have fun** : divertirse **4 to make fun of** : reírse de, burlarse de
function[1] ['fʌŋkʃən] *vi* : funcionar, desempeñarse, servir
function[2] *n* **1** PURPOSE : función *f* **2** GATHERING : reunión *f* social, recepción *f* **3** CEREMONY : ceremonia *f,* acto *m*
functional ['fʌŋkʃənəl] *adj* : funcional — **functionally** *adv*
functionary ['fʌŋkʃə,nɛri] *n, pl* **-aries** : funcionario *m,* -ria *f*
fund[1] ['fʌnd] *vt* : financiar
fund[2] *n* **1** SUPPLY : reserva *f,* cúmulo *m* **2** : fondo *m* <investment fund : fondo de inversiones> **3 funds** *npl* RESOURCES : fondos *mpl*
fundamental[1] [,fʌndə'mɛntəl] *adj* **1** BASIC : fundamental, básico **2** PRINCIPAL : esencial, principal **3** INNATE : innato, intrínseco
fundamental[2] *n* : fundamento *m*

fundamentally [ˌfʌndəˈmɛntəli] *adv* : fundamentalmente, básicamente
funding [ˈfʌndɪŋ] *n* : financiación *f*
funeral[1] [ˈfjuːnərəl] *adj* **1** : funeral, funerario, fúnebre <funeral procession : cortejo fúnebre> **2 funeral home** : funeraria *f*
funeral[2] *n* : funeral *m,* funerales *mpl*
funereal [fjuːˈnɪriəl] *adj* : fúnebre
fungal [ˈfʌŋgəl] *adj* : de hongos, micótico
fungicidal [ˌfʌndʒəˈsaɪdəl, ˌfʌngə-] *adj* : fungicida
fungicide [ˈfʌndʒəˌsaɪd, ˈfʌŋgə-] *n* : fungicida *m*
fungous [ˈfʌŋgəs] *adj* : fungoso
fungus [ˈfʌŋgəs] *n, pl* **fungi** [ˈfʌnˌdʒaɪ, ˈfʌŋˌgaɪ] : hongo *m*
funk [ˈfʌŋk] *n* **1** FEAR : miedo *m* **2** DEPRESSION : depresión *f*
funky [ˈfʌŋki] *adj* **funkier; -est** ODD, QUAINT : raro, extraño, original
funnel[1] [ˈfʌnəl] *vt* **-neled; -neling** CHANNEL : canalizar, encauzar
funnel[2] *n* **1** : embudo *m* **2** SMOKESTACK : chimenea *f* (de un barco o vapor)
funnies [ˈfʌniz] *npl* : tiras *fpl* cómicas
funny [ˈfʌni] *adj* **funnier; -est 1** AMUSING : divertido, cómico **2** STRANGE : extraño, raro
fur[1] [ˈfər] *adj* : de piel
fur[2] *n* **1** : pelaje *m,* piel *f* **2** : prenda *f* de piel
furbish [ˈfərbɪʃ] *vt* : pulir, limpiar
furious [ˈfjʊriəs] *adj* **1** ANGRY : furioso **2** FRANTIC : violento, frenético, vertiginoso (dícese de la velocidad)
furiously [ˈfjʊriəsli] *adv* **1** ANGRILY : furiosamente **2** FRANTICALLY : frenéticamente
furlong [ˈfərˌlɔŋ] *n* : estadio *m* (201.2 m)
furlough[1] [ˈfərˌloː] *vt* : dar permiso a, dar licencia a
furlough[2] *n* LEAVE : permiso *m,* licencia *f*
furnace [ˈfərnəs] *n* : horno *m*
furnish [ˈfərnɪʃ] *vt* **1** SUPPLY : proveer, suministrar **2** : amueblar <furnished apartment : departamento amueblado>
furnishings [ˈfərnɪʃɪŋz] *npl* **1** ACCESSORIES : accesorios *mpl* **2** FURNITURE : muebles *mpl,* mobiliario *m*
furniture [ˈfərnɪtʃər] *n* : muebles *mpl,* mobiliario *m*
furor [ˈfjʊrˌɔr, -ər] *n* **1** RAGE : furia *f,* rabia *f* **2** UPROAR : escándalo *m,* jaleo *m,* alboroto *m*
furrier [ˈfəriər] *n* : peletero *m,* -ra *f*
furrow[1] [ˈfəroː] *vt* **1** : surcar **2 to furrow one's brow** : fruncir el ceño
furrow[2] *n* **1** GROOVE : surco *m* **2** WRINKLE : arruga *f,* surco *m*
furry [ˈfəri] *adj* **furrier; -est** : peludo (dícese de un animal), peluche (dícese de un objeto)
further[1] [ˈfərðər] *vt* : promover, fomentar
further[2] *adv* **1** FARTHER : más lejos, más adelante **2** MOREOVER : además **3** MORE : más <I'll consider it further in the morning : lo consideraré más en la mañana>
further[3] *adj* **1** FARTHER : más lejano **2** ADDITIONAL : adicional, más
furtherance [ˈfərðərənts] *n* : promoción *f,* fomento *m,* adelantamiento *m*
furthermore [ˈfərðərˌmor] *adv* : además
furthermost [ˈfərðərˌmoːst] *adj* : más lejano, más distante
furthest [ˈfərðəst] → **farthest**[1], **farthest**[2]
furtive [ˈfərt̬ɪv] *adj* : furtivo, sigiloso — **furtively** *adv*
furtiveness [ˈfərt̬ɪvnəs] *n* STEALTH : sigilo *m*
fury [ˈfjʊri] *n, pl* **-ries 1** RAGE : furia *f,* ira *f* **2** VIOLENCE : furia *f,* furor *m*
fuse[1] [ˈfjuːz] *or* **fuze** *vt* **fused** *or* **fuzed; fusing** *or* **fuzing** : equipar con un fusible
fuse[2] *v* **fused; fusing** *vt* **1** SMELT : fundir **2** MERGE : fusionar, fundir — *vi* : fundirse, fusionarse
fuse[3] *n* : fusible *m*
fuselage [ˈfjuːsəˌlɑʒ, -zə-] *n* : fuselage *m*
fusillade [ˈfjuːsəˌlɑd, -ˌleɪd, ˌfjuːsəˈ-, -zə-] *n* : descarga *f* de fusilería
fusion [ˈfjuːʒən] *n* : fusión *f*
fuss[1] [ˈfʌs] *vi* **1** WORRY : preocuparse **2 to fuss with** : juguetear con, toquetear **3 to fuss over** : mimar
fuss[2] *n* **1** COMMOTION : alboroto *m,* escándalo *m* **2** ATTENTION : atenciones *fpl* **3** COMPLAINT : quejas *fpl*
fussbudget [ˈfʌsˌbʌdʒət] *n* : quisquilloso *m,* -sa *f;* melindroso *m,* -sa *f*
fussiness [ˈfʌsinəs] *n* **1** IRRITABILITY : irritabilidad *f* **2** ORNATENESS : lo recargado **3** METICULOUSNESS : meticulosidad *f*
fussy [ˈfʌsi] *adj* **fussier; -est 1** IRRITABLE : irritable, nervioso **2** OVERELABORATE : recargado **3** METICULOUS : meticuloso **4** FASTIDIOUS : quisquilloso, exigente
futile [ˈfjuːt̬əl, ˈfjuːˌtaɪl] *adj* : inútil, vano
futility [fjuˈtɪlət̬i] *n, pl* **-ties** : inutilidad *f*
future[1] [ˈfjuːtʃər] *adj* : futuro
future[2] *n* : futuro *m*
futuristic [ˌfjuːtʃəˈrɪstɪk] *adj* : futurista
fuze → **fuse**[1]
fuzz [ˈfʌz] *n* : pelusa *f*
fuzziness [ˈfʌzinəs] *n* **1** DOWNINESS : vellosidad *f* **2** INDISTINCTNESS : falta *f* de claridad
fuzzy [ˈfʌzi] *adj* **fuzzier; -est 1** FLUFFY, FURRY : con pelusa, peludo **2** INDISTINCT : indistinto, borroso

G

g [ˈdʒiː] *n, pl* **g's** *or* **gs** [ˈdʒiːz] : séptima letra del alfabeto inglés
gab¹ [ˈgæb] *vi* **gabbed; gabbing** : charlar, cotorrear *fam,* parlotear *fam*
gab² *n* CHATTER : cotorreo *m fam,* parloteo *m fam*
gabardine [ˈgæbərˌdiːn] *n* : gabardina *f*
gabby [ˈgæbi] *adj* **gabbier; -est** : hablador, parlanchín
gable [ˈgeɪbəl] *n* : hastial *m,* aguilón *m*
Gabonese [ˌgæbəˈniːz, -ˈniːs] *n* : gabonés *m,* -nesa *f* — **Gabonese** *adj*
gad [ˈgæd] *vi* **gadded; gadding** WANDER : deambular, vagar, callejear
gadfly [ˈgædˌflaɪ] *n, pl* **-flies 1** : tábano *m* (insecto) **2** FAULTFINDER : criticón *m,* -cona *f fam*
gadget [ˈgædʒət] *n* : artilugio *m,* aparato *m*
gadgetry [ˈgædʒətri] *n* : artilugios *mpl,* aparatos *mpl*
gaff [ˈgæf] *n* **1** : garfio *m* **2** → **gaffe**
gaffe [ˈgæf] *n* : metedura *f* de pata *fam*
gag¹ [ˈgæg] *v* **gagged; gagging** *vt* : amordazar <to tie up and gag : atar y amordazar> — *vi* **1** CHOKE : atragantarse **2** RETCH : hacer arcadas
gag² *n* **1** : mordaza *f* (para la boca) **2** JOKE : chiste *m*
gage → **gauge**
gaggle [ˈgægəl] *n* : bandada *f,* manada *f* (de gansos)
gaiety [ˈgeɪəṭi] *n, pl* **-eties 1** MERRYMAKING : juerga *f* **2** MERRIMENT : alegría *f,* regocijo *m*
gaily [ˈgeɪli] *adv* : alegremente
gain¹ [ˈgeɪn] *vt* **1** ACQUIRE, OBTAIN : ganar, obtener, adquirir, conseguir <to gain knowledge : adquirir conocimientos> <to gain a victory : obtener una victoria> **2** REACH : alcanzar, llegar a **3** INCREASE : ganar, aumentar <to gain weight : aumentar de peso> **4** : adelantarse, ganar <the watch gains two minutes a day : el reloj se adelanta dos minutos por día> — *vi* **1** PROFIT : beneficiarse **2** INCREASE : aumentar
gain² *n* **1** PROFIT : beneficio *m,* ganancia *f,* lucro *m,* provecho *m* **2** INCREASE : aumento *m*
gainful [ˈgeɪnfəl] *adj* : lucrativo, beneficioso, provechoso <gainful employment : trabajo remunerado>
gait [ˈgeɪt] *n* : paso *m,* andar *m,* manera *f* de caminar
gal [ˈgæl] *n* : muchacha *f*
gala¹ [ˈgeɪlə, ˈgæ-, ˈgɑ-] *adj* : de gala
gala² *n* : gala *f,* fiesta *f*
galactic [gəˈlæktɪk] *adj* : galáctico
galaxy [ˈgæləksi] *n, pl* **-axies** : galaxia *f*
gale [ˈgeɪl] *n* **1** WIND : vendaval *f,* viento *m* fuerte **2 gales of laughter** : carcajadas *fpl*
gall¹ [ˈgɔl] *vt* **1** CHAFE : rozar **2** IRRITATE, VEX : irritar, molestar
gall² *n* **1** BILE : bilis *f,* hiel *f* **2** INSOLENCE : audacidad *f,* insolencia *f,* descaro *m* **3** SORE : rozadura *f* (de un caballo) **4** : agalla *f* (de una planta)
gallant [ˈgælənt] *adj* **1** BRAVE : valiente, gallardo **2** CHIVALROUS, POLITE : galante, cortés
gallantry [ˈgæləntri] *n, pl* **-ries** : galantería *f,* caballerosidad *f*
gallbladder [ˈgɔlˌblædər] *n* : vesícula *f* biliar
galleon [ˈgæljən] *n* : galeón *m*
gallery [ˈgæləri] *n, pl* **-leries 1** BALCONY : galería *f* (para espectadores) **2** CORRIDOR : pasillo *m,* galería *f,* corredor *m* **3** : galería *f* (para exposiciones)
galley [ˈgæli] *n, pl* **-leys** : galera *f*
gallium [ˈgæliəm] *n* : galio *m*
gallivant [ˈgæləˌvænt] *vi* : callejear
gallon [ˈgælən] *n* : galón *m*
gallop¹ [ˈgæləp] *vi* : galopar
gallop² *n* : galope *m*
gallows [ˈgæˌloːz] *n, pl* **-lows** *or* **-lowses** [-ˌloːzəz] : horca *f*
gallstone [ˈgɔlˌstoːn] *n* : cálculo *m* biliar
galore [gəˈlor] *adj* : en abundancia <bargains galore : muchísimas gangas>
galoshes [gəˈlɑʃəz] *n* : galochas *fpl,* chanclos *mpl*
galvanize [ˈgælvənˌaɪz] *vt* **-nized; -nizing 1** STIMULATE : estimular, excitar, impulsar **2** : galvanizar (metales)
Gambian [ˈgæmbiən] *n* : gambiano *m,* -na *f* — **Gambian** *adj*
gambit [ˈgæmbɪt] *n* **1** : gambito *m* (en ajedrez) **2** STRATAGEM : estratagema *f,* táctica *f*
gamble¹ [ˈgæmbəl] *v* **-bled; -bling** *vi* : jugar, arriesgarse — *vt* **1** BET, WAGER : apostar, jugarse **2** RISK : arriesgar
gamble² *n* **1** BET : apuesta *f* **2** RISK : riesga *f*
gambler [ˈgæmbələr] *n* : jugador *m,* -dora *f*
gambol [ˈgæmbəl] *vi* **-boled** *or* **-bolled; -boling** *or* **-bolling** FROLIC : retozar, juguetear
game¹ [ˈgeɪm] *adj* **1** READY : listo, dispuesto <we're game for anything : estamos listos para lo que sea> **2** LAME : cojo
game² *n* **1** AMUSEMENT : juego *m,* diversión *f* **2** CONTEST : juego *m,* partido *m,* concurso *m* **3** : caza *f* <big game : caza mayor>
gamecock [ˈgeɪmˌkɑk] *n* : gallo *m* de pelea
gamekeeper [ˈgeɪmˌkiːpər] *n* : guardabosque *mf*
gamely [ˈgeɪmli] *adv* : animosamente

gamma ray [ˈgæmə] *n* : rayo *m* gamma

gamut [ˈgæmət] *n* : gama *f,* espectro *m* <to run the gamut : pasar por toda la gama>

gamy *or* **gamey** [ˈgeɪmi] *adj* **gamier; -est** : con sabor de animal de caza, fuerte

gander [ˈgændər] *n* **1** : ganso *m* (animal) **2** GLANCE : mirada *f,* vistazo *m,* ojeada *f*

gang[1] [ˈgæŋ] *vi* **to gang up** : agruparse, unirse

gang[2] *n* : banda *f,* pandilla *f*

gangling [ˈgæŋglɪŋ] *adj* LANKY : larguirucho *fam*

ganglion [ˈgæŋgliən] *n, pl* **-glia** [-gliə] : ganglio *m*

gangplank [ˈgæŋˌplæŋk] *n* : pasarela *f*

gangrene [ˈgæŋˌgriːn, ˈgæn-; gæŋˈ-, gænˈ-] *n* : gangrena *f*

gangrenous [ˈgæŋgrənəs] *adj* : gangrenoso

gangster [ˈgæŋstər] *n* : gángster *mf*

gangway [ˈgæŋˌweɪ] *n* **1** : pasarela *f* **2 gangway!** : ¡abran paso!

gap [ˈgæp] *n* **1** BREACH, OPENING : espacio *m,* brecha *f,* abertura *f* **2** GORGE : desfiladero *m,* barranco *m* **3** : laguna *f* <a gap in my education : una laguna en mi educación> **4** INTERVAL : pausa *f,* intervalo *m* **5** DISPARITY : brecha *f,* disparidad *f*

gape[1] [ˈgeɪp] *vi* **gaped; gaping 1** OPEN : abrirse, estar abierto **2** STARE : mirar fijamente con la boca abierta, mirar boquiabierto

gape[2] *n* **1** OPENING : abertura *f,* brecha *f* **2** STARE : mirada *f* boquiabierta

garage[1] [gəˈrɑʒ, -ˈrɑdʒ] *vt* **-raged; -raging** : dejar en un garaje

garage[2] *n* : garaje *m,* cochera *f*

garb[1] [ˈgɑrb] *vt* : vestir, ataviar

garb[2] *n* : vestimenta *f,* atuendo *f*

garbage [ˈgɑrbɪdʒ] *n* : basura *f,* desechos *mpl*

garbageman [ˈgɑrbɪdʒmən] *n, pl* **-men** [-mən, -ˌmɛn] : basurero *m*

garble [ˈgɑrbəl] *vt* **-bled; -bling** : tergiversar, distorsionar

garbled [ˈgɑrbəld] *adj* : incoherente, incomprensible

garden[1] [ˈgɑrdən] *vi* : trabajar en el jardín

garden[2] *n* : jardín *m*

gardener [ˈgɑrdənər] *n* : jardinero *m,* -ra *f*

gardenia [gɑrˈdiːnjə] *n* : gardenia *f*

gargantuan [gɑrˈgæntʃuən] *adj* : gigantesco, colosal

gargle[1] [ˈgɑrgəl] *vi* **-gled; -gling** : hacer gárgaras, gargarizar

gargle[2] *n* : gárgara *f*

gargoyle [ˈgɑrˌgɔɪl] *n* : gárgola *f*

garish [ˈgærɪʃ] *adj* GAUDY : llamativo, chillón, charro — **garishly** *adv*

garland[1] [ˈgɑrlənd] *vt* : adornar con guirnaldas

garland[2] *n* : guirnalda *f*

garlic [ˈgɑrlɪk] *n* : ajo *m*

garment [ˈgɑrmənt] *n* : prenda *f*

garner [ˈgɑrnər] *vt* : recoger, cosechar

garnet [ˈgɑrnət] *n* : granate *m*

garnish[1] [ˈgɑrnɪʃ] *vt* : aderezar, guarnecer

garnish[2] *n* : aderezo *m,* guarnición *f*

garret [ˈgærət] *n* : buhardilla *f,* desván *m*

garrison[1] [ˈgærəsən] *vt* **1** QUARTER : acuartelar (tropas) **2** OCCUPY : guarnecer, ocupar (con tropas)

garrison[2] *n* **1** : guarnición *f* (ciudad) **2** FORT : fortaleza *f,* poste *m* militar

garrulous [ˈgærələs] *adj* : charlatán, parlanchín, garlero *Col fam*

garter [ˈgɑrtər] *n* : liga *f*

gas[1] [ˈgæs] *v* **gassed; gassing** *vt* : gasear — *vi* **to gas up** : llenar el tanque con gasolina

gas[2] *n, pl* **gases** [ˈgæsəz] **1** : gas *m* <tear gas : gas lacrimógeno> **2** GASOLINE : gasolina *f*

gaseous [ˈgæʃəs, ˈgæsiəs] *adj* : gaseoso

gash[1] [ˈgæʃ] *vt* : hacer un tajo en, cortar

gash[2] *n* : cuchillada *f,* tajo *m*

gasket [ˈgæskət] *n* : junta *f*

gas mask *n* : máscara *f* antigás

gasoline [ˈgæsəˌliːn, ˌgæsəˈ-] *n* : gasolina *f,* nafta *f*

gasp[1] [ˈgæsp] *vi* **1** : boquear <to gasp with surprise : gritar de asombro> **2** PANT : jadear, respirar con dificultad

gasp[2] *n* **1** : boqueada *f* <a gasp of surprise : un grito sofocado> **2** PANTING : jadeo *m*

gas station → **service station**

gastric [ˈgæstrɪk] *adj* : gástrico <gastric juice : jugo gástrico>

gastronomic [ˌgæstrəˈnɑmɪk] *adj* : gastronómico

gastronomy [gæsˈtrɑnəmi] *n* : gastronomía *f*

gate [ˈgeɪt] *n* : portón *m,* verja *f,* puerta *f*

gatekeeper [ˈgeɪtˌkiːpər] *n* : guarda *mf;* guardián *m,* -diana *f*

gateway [ˈgeɪtˌweɪ] *n* : puerta *f* (de acceso), entrada *f*

gather [ˈgæðər] *vt* **1** ASSEMBLE : juntar, recoger, reunir **2** HARVEST : recoger, cosechar **3** : fruncir (una tela) **4** INFER : deducir, suponer

gathering [ˈgæðərɪŋ] *n* : reunión *f*

gauche [ˈgoːʃ] *adj* : torpe, falto de tacto

gaudy [ˈgɔdi] *adj* **gaudier; -est** : chillón, llamativo

gauge[1] [ˈgeɪdʒ] *vt* **gauged; gauging 1** MEASURE : medir **2** ESTIMATE, JUDGE : estimar, evaluar, juzgar

gauge[2] *n* **1** : indicador *m* <pressure gauge : indicador de presión> **2** CALIBER : calibre *m* **3** INDICATION : indicio *m,* muestra *f*

gaunt ['gɔnt] *adj* : demacrado, enjuto, descarnado
gauntlet ['gɔntlət] *n* : guante *m* <to run the gauntlet of : exponerse a>
gauze ['gɔz] *n* : gasa *f*
gauzy ['gɔzi] *adj* **gauzier; -est** : diáfano, vaporoso
gave → **give**
gavel ['gævəl] *n* : martillo *m* (de un juez, un subastador, etc.)
gawk ['gɔk] *vi* GAPE : mirar boquiabierto
gawky ['gɔki] *adj* **gawkier; -est** : desmañado, torpe, desgarbado
gay ['geɪ] *adj* **1** MERRY : alegre **2** BRIGHT, COLORFUL : vistoso, vivo **3** HOMOSEXUAL : homosexual
gaze[1] ['geɪz] *vi* **gazed; gazing** : mirar (fijamente)
gaze[2] *n* : mirada *f* (fija)
gazelle [gə'zɛl] *n* : gacela *f*
gazette [gə'zɛt] *n* : gaceta *f*
gazetteer [ˌgæzə'tɪr] *n* : diccionario *m* geográfico
gear[1] ['gɪr] *vt* ADAPT, ORIENT : adaptar, ajustar, orientar <a book geared to children : un libro adaptado a los niños> — *vi* **to gear up** : prepararse
gear[2] *n* **1** CLOTHING : ropa *f* **2** BELONGINGS : efectos *mpl* personales **3** EQUIPMENT, TOOLS : equipo *m*, aparejo *m*, herramientas *fpl* <fishing gear : aparejo de pescar> <landing gear : tren de aterrizaje> **4** COGWHEEL : rueda *f* dentada **5** : marcha *f*, velocidad *f* (de un vehículo) <to put in gear : poner en marcha> <to change gear(s) : cambiar de velocidad>
gearshift ['gɪrˌʃɪft] *n* : palanca *f* de cambio, palanca *f* de velocidad
geese → **goose**
Geiger counter ['gaɪgərˌkaʊntər] *n* : contador *m* Geiger
gelatin ['dʒɛlətən] *n* : gelatina *f*
gem ['dʒɛm] *n* : joya *f*, gema *f*, alhaja *f*
Gemini ['dʒɛməˌnaɪ] *n* : Géminis *mf*
gemstone ['dʒɛmˌsto:n] *n* : piedra *f* (semipreciosa o preciosa), gema *f*
gender ['dʒɛndər] *n* **1** SEX : sexo *m* **2** : género *m* (en la gramática)
gene ['dʒi:n] *n* : gen *m*, gene *m*
genealogical [ˌdʒi:niə'lɑdʒɪkəl] *adj* : genealógico
genealogy [ˌdʒi:ni'ɑlədʒi, ˌdʒɛ-, -'æ-] *n, pl* **-gies** : genealogía *f*
genera → **genus**
general[1] ['dʒɛnrəl, 'dʒɛnə-] *adj* : general <in general : en general, por lo general>
general[2] *n* : general *mf*
generality [ˌdʒɛnə'rælət̬i] *n, pl* **-ties** : generalidad *f*
generalization [ˌdʒɛnrələ'zeɪʃən, ˌdʒɛnərə-] *n* : generalización *f*
generalize ['dʒɛnrəˌlaɪz, 'dʒɛnərə-] *v* **-ized; -izing** : generalizar
generally ['dʒɛnrəli, 'dʒɛnərə-] *adv* : generalmente, por lo general, en general
generate ['dʒɛnəˌreɪt] *vt* **-ated; -ating** : generar, producir
generation [ˌdʒɛnə'reɪʃən] *n* : generación *f*
generator ['dʒɛnəˌreɪt̬ər] *n* : generador *m*
generic [dʒə'nɛrɪk] *adj* : genérico
generosity [ˌdʒɛnə'rɑsət̬i] *n, pl* **-ties** : generosidad *f*
generous ['dʒɛnərəs] *adj* **1** OPENHANDED : generoso, dadivoso, desprendido **2** ABUNDANT, AMPLE : abundante, amplio, generoso — **generously** *adv*
genetic [dʒə'nɛt̬ɪk] *adj* : genético — **genetically** [-t̬ɪkli] *adv*
geneticist [dʒə'nɛt̬əsɪst] *n* : genetista *mf*
genetics [dʒə'nɛt̬ɪks] *n* : genética *f*
genial ['dʒi:niəl] *adj* GRACIOUS : simpático, cordial, afable — **genially** *adv*
geniality [ˌdʒi:ni'ælət̬i] *n* : simpatía *f*, afabilidad *f*
genie ['dʒi:ni] *n* : genio *m*
genital ['dʒɛnət̬əl] *adj* : genital
genitals ['dʒɛnət̬əlz] *npl* : genitales *mpl*
genius ['dʒi:njəs] *n* : genio *m*
genocide ['dʒɛnəˌsaɪd] *n* : genocidio *m*
genre ['ʒɑnrə, 'ʒɑr] *n* : género *m*
genteel [dʒɛn'ti:l] *adj* : cortés, fino, refinado
gentile[1] ['dʒɛnˌtaɪl] *adj* : gentil
gentile[2] *n* : gentil *mf*
gentility [dʒɛn'tɪlət̬i] *n, pl* **-ties** **1** : nobleza *f* (de nacimiento) **2** POLITENESS, REFINEMENT : cortesía *f*, refinamiento *m*
gentle ['dʒɛntəl] *adj* **-tler; -tlest** **1** NOBLE : bien nacido, noble **2** DOCILE : dócil, manso **3** KINDLY : bondadoso, amable **4** MILD : suave, apacible <a gentle breeze : una brisa suave> **5** SOFT : suave (dícese de un sonido), ligero (dícese del tacto) **6** MODERATE : moderado, gradual <a gentle slope : una cuesta gradual>
gentleman ['dʒɛntəlmən] *n, pl* **-men** [-mən, -ˌmɛn] : caballero *m*, señor *m*
gentlemanly ['dʒɛntəlmənli] *adj* : caballeroso
gentleness ['dʒɛntəlnəs] *n* : delicadeza *f*, suavidad *f*, ternura *f*
gentlewoman ['dʒɛntəlˌwʊmən] *n, pl* **-women** [-ˌwɪmən] : dama *f*, señora *f*
gently ['dʒɛntli] *adv* **1** CAREFULLY, SOFTLY : con cuidado, suavemente, ligeramente **2** KINDLY : amablemente, con delicadeza
gentry ['dʒɛntri] *n, pl* **-tries** : aristocracia *f*
genuflect ['dʒɛnjʊˌflɛkt] *vi* : doblar la rodilla, hacer una genuflexión
genuflection [ˌdʒɛnjʊ'flɛkʃən] *n* : genuflexión *f*

genuine [ˈdʒɛnjʊwən] *adj* **1** AUTHENTIC, REAL : genuino, verdadero, auténtico **2** SINCERE : sincero — **genuinely** *adv*
genus [ˈdʒiːnəs] *n, pl* **genera** [ˈdʒɛnərə] : género *m*
geographer [dʒiˈɑgrəfər] *n* : geógrafo *m,* -fa *f*
geographical [ˌdʒiːəˈgræfɪkəl] *or* **geographic** [-fɪk] *adj* : geográfico — **geographically** [-fɪkli] *adv*
geography [dʒiˈɑgrəfi] *n, pl* **-phies** : geografía *f*
geologic [ˌdʒiːəˈlɑdʒɪk] *or* **geological** [-dʒɪkəl] *adj* : geológico — **geologically** [-dʒɪkli] *adv*
geologist [dʒiˈɑlədʒɪst] *n* : geólogo *m,* -ga *f*
geology [dʒiˈɑlədʒi] *n* : geología *f*
geometric [ˌdʒiːəˈmɛtrɪk] *or* **geometrical** [-trɪkəl] *adj* : geométrico
geometry [dʒiˈɑmətri] *n, pl* **-tries** : geometría *f*
geranium [dʒəˈreɪniəm] *n* : geranio *m*
gerbil [ˈdʒərbəl] *n* : jerbo *m,* gerbo *m*
geriatric [ˌdʒɛriˈætrɪk] *adj* : geriátrico
geriatrics [ˌdʒɛriˈætrɪks] *n* : geriatría *f*
germ [ˈdʒərm] *n* **1** MICROORGANISM : microbio *m,* germen *m* **2** BEGINNING : germen *m,* principio *m* <the germ of a plan : el germen de un plan>
German [ˈdʒərmən] *n* **1** : alemán *m,* -mana *f* **2** : alemán *m* (idioma) — **German** *adj*
germane [dʒərˈmeɪn] *adj* : relevante, pertinente
germanium [dʒərˈmeɪniəm] *n* : germanio *m*
germ cell *n* : célula *f* germen
germicide [ˈdʒərməˌsaɪd] *n* : germicida *m*
germinate [ˈdʒərməˌneɪt] *v* **-nated; -nating** *vi* : germinar — *vt* : hacer germinar
germination [ˌdʒərməˈneɪʃən] *n* : germinación *f*
gerund [ˈdʒɛrənd] *n* : gerundio *m*
gestation [dʒɛˈsteɪʃən] *n* : gestación *f*
gesture¹ [ˈdʒɛstʃər] *vi* **-tured; -turing** : gesticular, hacer gestos
gesture² *n* **1** : gesto *m,* ademán *m* **2** SIGN, TOKEN : gesto *m,* señal *f* <a gesture of friendship : una señal de amistad>
get [ˈgɛt] *v* **got** [ˈgɑt]; **got** *or* **gotten** [ˈgɑtən]; **getting** *vt* **1** OBTAIN : conseguir, obtener, adquirir **2** RECEIVE : recibir <to get a letter : recibir una carta> **3** EARN : ganar <he gets $10 an hour : gana $10 por hora> **4** FETCH : traer <get me my book : tráigame el libro> **5** CATCH : tomar (un tren, etc.), agarrar (una pelota, una persona, etc.) **6** CONTRACT : contagiarse de, contraer <she got the measles : le dio el sarampión> **7** PREPARE : preparar (una comida) **8** PERSUADE : persuadir, mandar a hacer <I got him to agree : logré convencerlo> **9** (*to cause to be*) <to get one's hair cut : cortarse el pelo> **10** UNDERSTAND : entender <now I get it! : ¡ya entiendo!> **11 to have got** : tener <I've got a headache : tengo un dolor de cabeza> **12 to have got to** : tener que <you've got to come : tienes que venir> — *vi* **1** BECOME : ponerse, volverse, hacerse <to get angry : ponerse furioso, enojarse> **2** GO, MOVE : ir, avanzar <he didn't get far : no avanzó mucho> **3** ARRIVE : llegar <to get home : llegar a casa> **4 to get to be** : llegar a ser <she got to be the director : llegó a ser directora> **5 to get ahead** : adelantarse, progresar **6 to get along** : llevarse bien (con alguien), congeniar **7 to get by** MANAGE : arreglárselas **8 to get over** OVERCOME : superar, consolarse de **9 to get together** MEET : reunirse **10 to get up** : levantarse
getaway [ˈgɛtəˌweɪ] *n* ESCAPE : fuga *f,* huida *f,* escapada *f*
geyser [ˈgaɪzər] *n* : géiser *m*
Ghanaian [ˈgɑniən, ˈgæ-] *n* : ghanés *m,* -nesa *f* — **Ghanaian** *adj*
ghastly [ˈgæstli] *adj* **-lier; -est 1** HORRIBLE : horrible, espantoso **2** PALE : pálido, cadavérico
gherkin [ˈgərkən] *n* : pepinillo *m*
ghetto [ˈgɛtoː] *n, pl* **-tos** *or* **-toes** : gueto *m*
ghost [ˈgoːst] *n* **1** : fantasma *f,* espectro *m* **2 the Holy Ghost** : el Espíritu Santo
ghostly [ˈgoːstli] *adv* : fantasmal
ghoul [ˈguːl] *n* **1** : demonio *m* necrófago **2** : persona *f* de gustos macabros
GI [ˌdʒiːˈaɪ] *n, pl* **GI's** *or* **GIs** : soldado *m* estadounidense
giant¹ [ˈdʒaɪənt] *adj* : gigante, gigantesco, enorme
giant² *n* : gigante *m,* -ta *f*
gibberish [ˈdʒɪbərɪʃ] *n* : galimatías *m,* jerigonza *f*
gibbon [ˈgɪbən] *n* : gibón *m*
gibe¹ [ˈdʒaɪb] *vi* **gibed; gibing** : mofarse, burlarse
gibe² *n* : pulla *f,* burla *f,* mofa *f*
giblets [ˈdʒɪbləts] *npl* : menudos *mpl,* menudencias *fpl*
giddiness [ˈgɪdinəs] *n* **1** DIZZINESS : vértigo *m,* mareo *m* **2** SILLINESS : frivolidad *f,* estupidez *f*
giddy [ˈgɪdi] *adj* **-dier; -est 1** DIZZY : mareado, vertiginoso **2** FRIVOLOUS, SILLY : frívolo, tonto
gift [ˈgɪft] *n* **1** TALENT : don *m,* talento *m,* dotes *fpl* **2** PRESENT : regalo *m,* obsequio *m*
gifted [ˈgɪftəd] *adj* TALENTED : talentoso
gigantic [dʒaɪˈgæntɪk] *adj* : gigantesco, enorme, colosal
giggle¹ [ˈgɪgəl] *vi* **-gled; -gling** : reírse tontamente
giggle² *n* : risita *f,* risa *f* tonta
gild [ˈgɪld] *vt* **gilded** *or* **gilt** [ˈgɪlt]; **gilding** : dorar
gill [ˈgɪl] *n* : agalla *f,* branquia *f*

gilt[1] ['gɪlt] *adj* : dorado
gilt[2] *n* : dorado *m*
gimlet ['gɪmlət] *n* **1** : barrena *f* (herramiento) **2** : bebida *f* de vodka o ginebra y limón
gimmick ['gɪmɪk] *n* **1** GADGET : artilugio *m* **2** CATCH : engaño *m,* trampa *f* **3** SCHEME, TRICK : ardid *m,* truco *m*
gin[1] ['dʒɪn] *vt* **ginned; ginning** : desmotar (algodón)
gin[2] *n* **1** : desmotadora *f* (de algodón) **2** : ginebra *f* (bebida alcohólica)
ginger ['dʒɪndʒər] *n* : jengibre *m*
ginger ale *n* : ginger ale *m,* gaseosa *f* de jengibre
gingerbread ['dʒɪndʒər,brɛd] *n* : pan *m* de jengibre
gingerly ['dʒɪndʒərli] *adv* : con cuidado, cautelosamente
gingham ['gɪŋəm] *n* : guinga *f*
ginseng ['dʒɪn,sɪŋ, -,sɛŋ] *n* : ginseng *m*
giraffe [dʒə'ræf] *n* : jirafa *f*
gird ['gərd] *vt* **girded** *or* **girt** ['gərt]; **girding 1** BIND : ceñir, atar **2** ENCIRCLE : rodear **3 to gird oneself** : prepararse
girder ['gərdər] *n* : viga *f*
girdle[1] ['gərdəl] *vt* **-dled; -dling 1** GIRD : ceñir, atar **2** SURROUND : rodear, circundar
girdle[2] *n* : faja *f*
girl ['gərl] *n* **1** : niña *f,* muchacha *f,* chica *f* **2** SWEETHEART : novia *f* **3** DAUGHTER : hija *f*
girlfriend ['gərl,frɛnd] *n* : novia *f,* amiga *f*
girlhood ['gərl,hʊd] *n* : niñez *f,* juventud *f* (de una muchacha)
girlish ['gərlɪʃ] *adj* : de niña
girth ['gərθ] *n* **1** : circunferencia *f* (de un árbol, etc.), cintura *f* (de una persona) **2** CINCH : cincha *f* (para caballos, etc.)
gist ['dʒɪst] *n* : quid *m,* meollo *m*
give[1] ['gɪv] *v* **gave** ['geɪv]; **given** ['gɪvən]; **giving** *vt* **1** HAND, PRESENT : dar, regalar, obsequiar <give it to me : dámelo> <they gave him a gold watch : le regalaron un reloj de oro> **2** PAY : dar, pagar <I'll give you $10 for this one : te daré $10 por éste> **3** UTTER : dar, pronunciar <to give a shout : dar un grito> <to give a speech : pronunciar un discurso> <to give a verdict : dictar sentencia> **4** PROVIDE : dar <to give one's word : dar uno su palabra> <to give a party : dar una fiesta> **5** CAUSE : dar, causar, ocasionar <to give trouble : causar problemas> <to give someone to understand : darle a entender a alguien> **6** GRANT : dar, otorgar <to give permission : dar permiso> — *vi* **1** : hacer regalos **2** YIELD : ceder, romperse <it gave under the weight of the crowd : cedió bajo el peso de la muchedumbre> **3 to give in** *or* **to give up** SURRENDER : rendirse, entregarse **4 to give out** : agotarse, acabarse <the supplies gave out : las provisiones se agotaron>
give[2] *n* FLEXIBILITY : flexibilidad *f,* elasticidad *f*
giveaway ['gɪvə,weɪ] *n* **1** : revelación *f* involuntaria **2** GIFT : regalo *m,* obsequio *m*
given ['gɪvən] *adj* **1** INCLINED : dado, inclinado <he's given to quarreling : es muy dado a discutir> **2** SPECIFIC : dado, determinado <at a given time : en un momento dado>
given name *n* : nombre *m* de pila
give up *vt* : dejar, renunciar a, abandonar <to give up smoking : dejar de fumar>
gizzard ['gɪzərd] *n* : molleja *f*
glacial ['gleɪʃəl] *adj* : glacial — **glacially** *adv*
glacier ['gleɪʃər] *n* : glaciar *m*
glad ['glæd] *adj* **gladder; gladdest 1** PLEASED : alegre, contento <she was glad I came : se alegró de que haya venido> <glad to meet you! : ¡mucho gusto!> **2** HAPPY, PLEASING : feliz, agradable <glad tidings : buenas nuevas> **3** WILLING : dispuesto, gustoso <I'll be glad to do it : lo haré con mucho gusto>
gladden ['glædən] *vt* : alegrar
glade ['gleɪd] *n* : claro *m*
gladiator ['glædi,eɪt̬ər] *n* : gladiador *m*
gladiolus [,glædi'o:ləs] *n, pl* **-li** [-li, -,laɪ] : gladiolo *m,* gladíolo *m*
gladly ['glædli] *adv* : con mucho gusto
gladness ['glædnəs] *n* : alegría *f,* gozo *m*
glamor *or* **glamour** ['glæmər] *n* : atractivo *m,* hechizo *m,* encanto *m*
glamorous ['glæmərəs] *adj* : atractivo, encantador
glance[1] ['glænts] *vi* **glanced; glancing 1** RICOCHET : rebotar <it glanced off the wall : rebotó en la pared> **2 to glance at** : mirar, echar un vistazo a **3 to glance away** : apartar los ojos
glance[2] *n* : mirada *f,* vistazo *m,* ojeada *f*
gland ['glænd] *n* : glándula *f*
glandular ['glændʒʊlər] *adj* : glandular
glare[1] ['glær] *vi* **glared; glaring 1** SHINE : brillar, relumbrar **2** STARE : mirar con ira, lanzar una mirada feroz
glare[2] *n* **1** BRIGHTNESS : resplandor *m,* luz *f* deslumbrante **2** : mirada *f* feroz
glaring ['glærɪŋ] *adj* **1** BRIGHT : deslumbrante, brillante **2** FLAGRANT, OBVIOUS : flagrante, manifiesto <a glaring error : un error que salta a la vista>
glass ['glæs] *n* **1** : vidrio *m,* cristal *m* <stained glass : vidrio de color> **2** : vaso *m* <a glass of milk : un vaso de leche> **3 glasses** *npl* SPECTACLES : gafas *fpl,* anteojos *mpl,* lentes *mpl,* espejuelos *mpl*

glassblowing [ˈglæsˌbloːɪŋ] *n* : soplado *m* del vidrio

glassful [ˈglæsˌfʊl] *n* : vaso *m,* copa *f*

glassware [ˈglæsˌwær] *n* : cristalería *f*

glassy [ˈglæsi] *adj* **glassier; -est 1** VITREOUS : vítreo **2** : vidrioso <glassy eyes : ojos vidriosos>

glaze[1] [ˈgleɪz] *vt* **glazed; glazing 1** : ponerle vidrios a (una ventana, etc.) **2** : vidriar (cerámica) **3** : glasear (papel, verduras, etc.)

glaze[2] *n* : vidriado *m,* glaseado *m,* barniz *m*

glazier [ˈgleɪʒər] *n* : vidriero *m,* -ra *f*

gleam[1] [ˈgliːm] *vi* : brillar, destellar, relucir

gleam[2] *n* **1** LIGHT : luz *f* (oscura) **2** GLINT : destello *m* **3** GLIMMER : rayo *m,* vislumbre *f* <a gleam of hope : un rayo de esperanza>

glean [ˈgliːn] *vt* : recoger, espigar

glee [ˈgliː] *n* : alegría *f,* júbilo *m,* regocijo *m*

gleeful [ˈgliːfəl] *adj* : lleno de alegría

glen [ˈglɛn] *n* : cañada *f*

glib [ˈglɪb] *adj* **glibber; glibbest 1** : simplista <a glib reply : una respuesta simplista> **2** : con mucha labia (dícese de una persona)

glibly [ˈglɪbli] *adv* : con mucha labia

glide[1] [ˈglaɪd] *vi* **glided; gliding** : deslizarse (en una superficie), planear (en el aire)

glide[2] *n* : planeo *m*

glider [ˈglaɪdər] *n* **1** : planeador *m* (aeronave) **2** : mecedor *m* (tipo de columpio)

glimmer[1] [ˈglɪmər] *vi* : brillar con luz trémula

glimmer[2] *n* **1** : luz *f* trémula, luz *f* tenue **2** GLEAM : rayo *m,* vislumbre *f* <a glimmer of understanding : un rayo de entendimiento>

glimpse[1] [ˈglɪmps] *vt* **glimpsed; glimpsing** : vislumbrar, entrever

glimpse[2] *n* : mirada *f* breve <to catch a glimpse of : alcanzar a ver, vislumbrar>

glint[1] [ˈglɪnt] *vi* GLEAM, SPARKLE : destellar, fulgurar

glint[2] *n* **1** SPARKLE : destello *m,* centelleo *m* **2 to have a glint in one's eye** : chispearle los ojos a uno

glisten[1] [ˈglɪsən] *vi* : brillar, centellear

glisten[2] *n* : brillo *m,* centelleo *m*

glitter[1] [ˈglɪtər] *vi* **1** SPARKLE : destellar, relucir, brillar **2** FLASH : relampaguear <his eyes glittered in anger : le relampagueaban los ojos de ira>

glitter[2] *n* **1** BRIGHTNESS : brillo *m* **2** : purpurina *f* (para decoración)

gloat [ˈgloːt] *vi* **to gloat over** : regodearse en

glob [ˈglɑb] *n* : plasta *f,* masa *f,* grumo *m*

global [ˈgloːbəl] *adj* **1** SPHERICAL : esférico **2** WORLDWIDE : global, mundial — **globally** *adv*

globe [ˈgloːb] *n* **1** SPHERE : esfera *f,* globo *m* **2** EARTH : globo *m,* Tierra *f* **3** : globo *m* terráqueo (modelo de la Tierra)

globe–trotter [ˈgloːbˌtrɑt̬ər] *n* : trotamundos *mf*

globular [ˈglɑbjʊlər] *adj* : globular

globule [ˈglɑˌbjuːl] *n* : glóbulo *m*

gloom [ˈgluːm] *n* **1** DARKNESS : penumbra *f,* oscuridad *f* **2** MELANCHOLY : melancolía *f,* tristeza *f*

gloomily [ˈgluːməli] *adv* : tristemente

gloomy [ˈgluːmi] *adj* **gloomier; -est 1** DARK : oscuro, tenebroso <gloomy weather : tiempo gris> **2** MELANCHOLY : melancólico **3** PESSIMISTIC : pesimista **4** DEPRESSING : deprimente, lúgubre

glorification [ˌglorəfəˈkeɪʃən] *n* : glorificación *f*

glorify [ˈglorəˌfaɪ] *vt* **-fied; -fying** : glorificar

glorious [ˈgloriəs] *adj* **1** ILLUSTRIOUS : glorioso, ilustre **2** MAGNIFICENT : magnífico, espléndido, maravilloso — **gloriously** *adv*

glory[1] [ˈglori] *vi* **-ried; -rying** EXULT : exultar, regocijarse

glory[2] *n, pl* **-ries 1** RENOWN : gloria *f,* fama *f,* honor *m* **2** PRAISE : gloria *f* <glory to God : gloria a Dios> **3** MAGNIFICENCE : magnificencia *f,* esplendor *m,* gloria *f* **4 to be in one's glory** : estar uno en su gloria

gloss[1] [ˈglɔs, ˈglɑs] *vt* **1** EXPLAIN : glosar, explicar **2** POLISH : lustrar, pulir **3 to gloss over** : quitarle importancia a, minimizar

gloss[2] *n* **1** SHINE : lustre *m,* brillo *m* **2** EXPLANATION : glosa *f,* explicación *f* breve **3** → **glossary**

glossary [ˈglɔsəri, ˈglɑ-] *n, pl* **-ries** : glosario *m*

glossy [ˈglɔsi, ˈglɑ-] *adj* **glossier; -est** : brillante, lustroso, satinado (dícese del papel)

glove [ˈglʌv] *n* : guante *m*

glow[1] [ˈgloː] *vi* **1** SHINE : brillar, resplandecer **2** BRIM : rebosar <to glow with health : rebosar de salud>

glow[2] *n* **1** BRIGHTNESS : resplandor *m,* brillo *m,* luminosidad *f* **2** FEELING : sensación *f* (de bienestar), oleada *f* (de sentimiento) **3** INCANDESCENCE : incandescencia *f*

glower [ˈglaʊər] *vi* : fruncir el ceño

glowworm [ˈgloːˌwərm] *n* : luciérnaga *f*

glucose [ˈgluːˌkoːs] *n* : glucosa *f*

glue[1] [ˈgluː] *vt* **glued; gluing** *or* **glueing** : pegar, encolar

glue[2] *n* : pegamento *m,* cola *f*

gluey [ˈgluːi] *adj* **gluier; -est** : pegajoso

glum [ˈglʌm] *adj* **glummer; glummest 1** SULLEN : hosco, sombrío **2** DREARY, GLOOMY : sombrío, triste, melancólico

glut[1] [ˈglʌt] *vt* **glutted; glutting 1** SATIATE **:** saciar, hartar **2 :** inundar (el mercado)

glut[2] *n* **:** exceso *m,* superabundancia *f*

glutinous [ˈgluːtənəs] *adj* STICKY **:** pegajoso, glutinoso

glutton [ˈglʌtən] *n* **:** glotón *m,* -tona *f*

gluttonous [ˈglʌtənəs] *adj* **:** glotón

gluttony [ˈglʌtəni] *n, pl* **-tonies :** glotonería *f,* gula *f*

gnarled [ˈnɑrld] *adj* **1** KNOTTY **:** nudoso **2** TWISTED **:** retorcido

gnash [ˈnæʃ] *vt* **:** hacer rechinar (los dientes)

gnat [ˈnæt] *n* **:** jején *m*

gnaw [ˈnɔ] *vt* **:** roer

gnome [ˈnoːm] *n* **:** gnomo *m*

gnu [ˈnuː, ˈnjuː] *n, pl* **gnu** *or* **gnus :** ñu *m*

go[1] [ˈgoː] *v* **went** [ˈwɛnt]; **gone** [ˈgɔn, ˈgɑn]; **going; goes** [ˈgoːz] *vi* **1** PROCEED **:** ir <to go slow : ir despacio> <to go shopping : ir de compras> **2** LEAVE **:** irse, marcharse, salir <let's go! : ¡vámonos!> <the train went on time : el tren salió a tiempo> **3** DISAPPEAR **:** desaparecer, pasarse, irse <her fear is gone : se le ha pasado el miedo> <my pen is gone! : ¡mi pluma desapareció!> **4** EXTEND **:** ir, extenderse, llegar <this road goes to the river : este camino se extiende hasta el río> <to go from top to bottom : ir de arriba abajo> **5** FUNCTION **:** funcionar, marchar <the car won't go : el coche no funciona> <to get something going : poner algo en marcha> **6** SELL **:** venderse <it goes for $15 : se vende por $15> **7** PROGRESS **:** ir, andar, seguir <my exam went well : me fue bien en el examen> <how did the meeting go? : ¿qué tal la reunión?> **8** BECOME **:** volverse, quedarse <he's going crazy : está volviéndose loco> <the tire went flat : la llanta se desinfló> **9** FIT **:** caber <it will go through the door : cabe por la puerta> **10 anything goes! :** ¡todo vale! **11 to go :** faltar <only 10 days to go : faltan sólo 10 días> **12 to go back on :** faltar uno a (su promesa) **13 to go bad** SPOIL **:** estropearse, echarse a perder **14 to go for :** interesarse uno en, gustarle a uno (algo, alguien) <I don't go for that : eso no me interesa> **15 to go off** EXPLODE **:** estallar **16 to go with** MATCH **:** armonizar con, hacer juego con — *v aux* **to be going to :** ir a <I'm going to write a letter : voy a escribir una carta> <it's not going to last : no va a durar>

go[2] *n, pl* **goes 1** ATTEMPT **:** intento *m* <to have a go at : intentar, probar> **2** SUCCESS **:** éxito *m* **3** ENERGY **:** energía *f,* empuje *m* <to be on the go : no parar, no descansar>

goad[1] [ˈgoːd] *vt* **:** aguijonear (un animal), incitar (a una persona)

goad[2] *n* **:** aguijón *m*

goal [ˈgoːl] *n* **1 :** gol *m* (en deportes) <to score a goal : anotar un gol> **2** *or* **goalposts :** portería *f* **3** AIM, OBJECTIVE **:** meta *m,* objetivo *m*

goalie [ˈgoːli] → **goalkeeper**

goalkeeper [ˈgoːlˌkiːpər] *n* **:** portero *m,* -ra *f;* guardameta *mf;* arquero *m,* -ra *f*

goaltender [ˈgoːlˌtɛndər] → **goalkeeper**

goat [ˈgoːt] *n* **1 :** cabra *f* (hembra) **2 billy goat :** macho *m* cabrío, chivo *m*

goatee [goːˈtiː] *n* **:** barbita *f* de chivo, piocha *f Mex*

goatskin [ˈgoːtˌskɪn] *n* **:** piel *f* de cabra

gob [ˈgɑb] *n* **:** masa *f,* grumo *m*

gobble [ˈgɑbəl] *v* **-bled; -bling** *vt* **to gobble up :** tragar, engullir — *vi* **:** hacer ruidos de pavo

gobbledygook [ˈgɑbəldiˌgʊk, -ˌguːk] *n* GIBBERISH **:** jerigonza *f*

go–between [ˈgoːbɪˌtwiːn] *n* **:** intermediario *m,* -ria *f;* mediador *m,* -dora *f*

goblet [ˈgɑblət] *n* **:** copa *f*

goblin [ˈgɑblən] *n* **:** duende *m,* trasgo *m*

god [ˈgɑd, ˈgɔd] *n* **1 :** dios *m* **2 God :** Dios *m*

godchild [ˈgɑdˌtʃaɪld, ˈgɔd-] *n, pl* **-children :** ahijado *m,* -da *f*

goddess [ˈgɑdəs, ˈgɔ-] *n* **:** diosa *f*

godfather [ˈgɑdˌfɑðər, ˈgɔd-] *n* **:** padrino *m*

godless [ˈgɑdləs, ˈgɔd-] *adj* **:** ateo

godlike [ˈgɑdˌlaɪk, ˈgɔd-] *adj* **:** divino

godly [ˈgɑdli, ˈgɔd-] *adj* **-lier; -est 1** DIVINE **:** divino **2** DEVOUT, PIOUS **:** piadoso, devoto, beato

godmother [ˈgɑdˌmʌðər, ˈgɔd-] *n* **:** madrina *f*

godparents [ˈgɑdˌpærənts, ˈgɔd-] *npl* **:** padrinos *mpl*

godsend [ˈgɑdˌsɛnd, ˈgɔd-] *n* **:** bendición *f,* regalo *m* divino

goes → **go**

go–getter [ˈgoːˌgɛtər] *n* **:** persona *f* ambiciosa, buscavidas *mf fam*

goggle [ˈgɑgəl] *vi* **-gled; -gling :** mirar con ojos desorbitados

goggles [ˈgɑgəlz] *npl* **:** gafas *fpl* (protectoras), anteojos *mpl*

goings–on [ˌgoːɪŋzˈɑn, -ˈɔn] *npl* **:** sucesos *mpl,* ocurrencias *fpl*

goiter [ˈgɔɪtər] *n* **:** bocio *m*

gold [ˈgoːld] *n* **:** oro *m*

golden [ˈgoːldən] *adj* **1 :** (hecho) de oro **2 :** dorado, de color oro <golden hair : pelo rubio> **3** FLOURISHING, PROSPEROUS **:** dorado, próspero <golden years : años dorados> **4** FAVORABLE **:** favorable, excelente <a golden opportunity : una excelente oportunidad>

goldenrod [ˈgoːldənˌrɑd] *n* **:** vara *f* de oro

golden rule *n* **:** regla *f* de oro

goldfinch [ˈgoːldˌfɪntʃ] *n* **:** jilguero *m*

goldfish [ˈgoːld,fɪʃ] *n* : pez *m* de colores

goldsmith [ˈgoːld,smɪθ] *n* : orífice *mf,* orfebre *mf*

golf[1] [ˈgɑlf, ˈgɔlf] *vi* : jugar (al) golf

golf[2] *n* : golf *m*

golfer [ˈgɑlfər, ˈgɔl-] *n* : golfista *mf*

gondola [ˈgɑndələ, gɑnˈdoːlə] *n* : góndola *f*

gone [ˈgɔn] *adj* **1** DEAD : muerto **2** PAST : pasado, ido **3** LOST : perdido, desaparecido **4 to be far gone** : estar muy avanzado **5 to be gone on** : estar loco por

goner [ˈgɔnər] *n* **to be a goner** : estar en las últimas

gong [ˈgɔŋ, ˈgɑŋ] *n* : gong *m*

gonorrhea [,gɑnəˈriːə] *n* : gonorrea *f*

good[1] [ˈgʊd] *adv* **1** (*used as an intensifier*) : bien <a good strong rope : una cuerda bien fuerte> **2** WELL : bien

good[2] *adj* **better** [ˈbɛt̬ər]; **best** [ˈbɛst] **1** PLEASANT : bueno, agradable <good news : buenas noticias> <to have a good time : divertirse> **2** BENEFICIAL : bueno, beneficioso <good for a cold : beneficioso para los resfriados> <it's good for you : es bueno para uno> **3** FULL : completo, entero <a good hour : una hora entera> **4** CONSIDERABLE : bueno, bastante <a good many people : muchísima gente, un buen número de gente> **5** ATTRACTIVE, DESIRABLE : bueno, bien <a good salary : un buen sueldo> <to look good : quedar bien> **6** KIND, VIRTUOUS : bueno, amable <she's a good person : es buena gente> <that's good of you! : ¡qué amable!> <good deeds : buenas obras> **7** SKILLED : bueno, hábil <to be good at : tener facilidad para> **8** SOUND : bueno, sensato <good advice : buenos consejos> **9** (*in greetings*) : bueno <good morning : buenos días> <good afternoon (evening) : buenas tardes> <good night : buenas noches>

good[3] *n* **1** RIGHT : bien *m* <to do good : hacer el bien> **2** GOODNESS : bondad *f* **3** BENEFIT : bien *m,* provecho *m* <it's for your own good : es por tu propio bien> **4 goods** *npl* PROPERTY : efectos *mpl* personales, posesiones *fpl* **5 goods** *npl* WARES : mercancía *f,* mercadería *f,* artículos *mpl* **6 for ~** : para siempre

good–bye *or* **good–by** [gʊdˈbaɪ] *n* : adiós *m*

good–for–nothing [ˈgʊdfər,nʌθɪŋ] *n* : inútil *mf;* haragán *m,* -gana *f;* holgazán *m,* -zana *f*

Good Friday *n* : Viernes *m* Santo

good–hearted [ˈgʊdˈhɑrt̬əd] *adj* : bondadoso, benévolo, de buen corazón

good–looking [ˈgʊdˈlʊkɪŋ] *adj* : bello, bonito, guapo

goodly [ˈgʊdli] *adj* **-lier; -est** : considerable, importante <a goodly number : un número considerable>

good–natured [ˈgʊdˈneɪtʃərd] *adj* : amigable, amistoso, bonachón *fam*

goodness [ˈgʊdnəs] *n* **1** : bondad *f* **2 thank goodness!** : ¡gracias a Dios!, ¡menos mal!

good–tempered [ˈgʊdˈtɛmpərd] *adj* : de buen genio

goodwill [,gʊdˈwɪl] *n* **1** BENEVOLENCE : benevolencia *f,* buena voluntad *f* **2** : buen nombre *m* (de comercios), renombre *m* comercial

goody [ˈgʊdi] *n, pl* **goodies** : cosa *f* rica para comer, golosina *f*

gooey [ˈguːi] *adj* **gooier; gooiest** : pegajoso

goof[1] [ˈguːf] *vi* **1 to goof off** : holgazanear **2 to goof around** : hacer tonterías **3 to goof up** BLUNDER : cometer un error

goof[2] *n* **1** : bobo *m,* -ba *f;* tonto *m,* -ta *f* **2** BLUNDER : error *m,* planchazo *m fam*

goofy [ˈguːfi] *adj* **goofier; -est** SILLY : tonto, bobo

goose [ˈguːs] *n, pl* **geese** [ˈgiːs] : ganso *m,* -sa *f;* ánsar *m;* oca *f*

gooseberry [ˈguːs,bɛriː, ˈguːz-] *n, pl* **-berries** : grosella *f* espinosa

goose bumps *npl* : carne *f* de gallina

gooseflesh [ˈguːs,flɛʃ] → **goose bumps**

goose pimples → **goose bumps**

gopher [ˈgoːfər] *n* : taltuza *f*

gore[1] [ˈgor] *vt* **gored; goring** : cornear

gore[2] *n* BLOOD : sangre *f*

gorge[1] [ˈgɔrdʒ] *vt* **gorged; gorging 1** SATIATE : saciar, hartar **2 to gorge oneself** : hartarse, atiborrarse, atracarse *fam*

gorge[2] *n* RAVINE : desfiladero *m*

gorgeous [ˈgɔrdʒəs] *adj* : hermoso, espléndido, magnífico

gorilla [gəˈrɪlə] *n* : gorila *m*

gory [ˈgori] *adj* **gorier; -est** BLOODY : sangriento

gosling [ˈgɑzlɪŋ, ˈgɔz-] *n* : ansarino *m*

gospel [ˈgɑspəl] *n* **1** *or* **Gospel** : evangelio *m* <the four Gospels : los cuatro evangelios> **2 the gospel truth** : el evangelio, la pura verdad

gossamer [ˈgɑsəmər, ˈgɑzə-] *adj* : tenue, sutil <gossamer wings : alas tenues>

gossip[1] [ˈgɑsɪp] *vi* : chismear, contar chismes

gossip[2] *n* **1** : chismoso *m,* -sa *f* (persona) **2** RUMOR : chisme *m,* rumor *m*

gossipy [ˈgɑsɪpi] *adj* : chismoso

got → **get**

Gothic [ˈgɑθɪk] *adj* : gótico

gotten → **get**

gouge[1] [ˈgaʊdʒ] *vt* **gouged; gouging 1** : excavar, escoplear (con una gubia) **2** SWINDLE : estafar, extorsionar

gouge[2] *n* **1** CHISEL : gubia *f,* formón *m* **2** GROOVE : ranura *f,* hoyo *m* (hecho por un formón)

goulash [ˈguːˌlɑʃ, -ˌlæʃ] *n* : estofado *m,* guiso *m* al estilo húngaro

gourd [ˈgord, ˈgʊrd] *n* : calabaza *f*

gourmand [ˈgʊrˌmɑnd] *n* **1** GLUTTON : glotón *m,* -tona *f* **2** → **gourmet**

gourmet [ˈgʊrˌmeɪ, gʊrˈmeɪ] *n* : gourmet *mf;* gastrónomo *m,* -ma *f*

gout [ˈgaʊt] *n* : gota *f*

govern [ˈgʌvərn] *vt* **1** RULE : gobernar **2** CONTROL, DETERMINE : determinar, controlar, guiar **3** RESTRAIN : dominar (las emociones, etc.) — *vi* : gobernar

governess [ˈgʌvərnəs] *n* : institutriz *f*

government [ˈgʌvərmənt] *n* : gobierno *m*

governmental [ˌgʌvərˈmɛntəl] *adj* : gubernamental, gubernativo

governor [ˈgʌvənər, ˈgʌvərnər] *n* **1** : gobernador *m,* -dora *f* (de un estado, etc.) **2** : regulador *m* (de una máquina)

governorship [ˈgʌvənərˌʃɪp, ˈgʌvərnər-] *n* : cargo *m* de gobernador

gown [ˈgaʊn] *n* **1** : vestido *m* <evening gown : traje de fiesta> **2** : toga *f* (de magistrados, clérigos, etc.)

grab[1] [ˈgræb] *v* **grabbed; grabbing** *vt* SNATCH : agarrar, arrebatar — *vi* : agarrarse

grab[2] *n* **1 to make a grab for** : tratar de agarrar **2 up for grabs** : disponible, libre

grace[1] [ˈgreɪs] *vt* **graced; gracing 1** HONOR : honrar **2** ADORN : adornar, embellecer

grace[2] *n* **1** : gracia *f* <by the grace of God : por la gracia de Dios> **2** BLESSING : bendición *f* (de la mesa) **3** RESPITE : plazo *m,* gracia *f* <a five days' grace (period) : un plazo de cinco días> **4** GRACIOUSNESS : gentileza *f,* cortesía *f* **5** ELEGANCE : elegancia *f,* gracia *f* **6 to be in the good graces of** : estar en buenas relaciones con **7 with good grace** : de buena gana

graceful [ˈgreɪsfəl] *adj* : lleno de gracia, garboso, grácil

gracefully [ˈgreɪsfəli] *adv* : con gracia, con garbo

gracefulness [ˈgreɪsfəlnəs] *n* : gracilidad *f,* apostura *f,* gallardía *f*

graceless [ˈgreɪsləs] *adj* **1** DISCOURTEOUS : descortés **2** CLUMSY, INELEGANT : torpe, desgarbado, poco elegante

gracious [ˈgreɪʃəs] *adj* : cortés, gentil, cordial

graciously [ˈgreɪʃəsli] *adv* : gentilmente

graciousness [ˈgreɪʃəsnəs] *n* : gentileza *f*

gradation [greɪˈdeɪʃən, grə-] *n* : gradación *f*

grade[1] [ˈgreɪd] *vt* **graded; grading 1** SORT : clasificar **2** LEVEL : nivelar **3** : calificar (exámenes, alumnos)

grade[2] *n* **1** QUALITY : categoría *f,* calidad *f* **2** RANK : grado *m,* rango *m* (militar) **3** YEAR : grado *m,* curso *m,* año *m* <sixth grade : el sexto grado> **4** MARK : nota *f,* calificación *f* (en educación) **5** SLOPE : cuesta *f,* pendiente *f,* gradiente *f*

grade school → **elementary school**

gradual [ˈgrædʒʊəl] *adj* : gradual, paulatino

gradually [ˈgrædʒʊəli, ˈgrædʒəli] *adv* : gradualmente, poco a poco

graduate[1] [ˈgrædʒʊˌeɪt] *v* **-ated; -ating** *vi* : graduarse, licenciarse — *vt* : graduar <a graduated thermometer : un termómetro graduado>

graduate[2] [ˈgrædʒʊət] *adj* : de postgrado <graduate course : curso de postgrado>

graduate[3] *n* **1** : licenciado *m,* -da *f;* graduado *m,* -da *f* (de la universidad) **2** : bachiller *mf* (de la escuela secundaria)

graduate student *n* : postgraduado *m,* -da *f*

graduation [ˌgrædʒʊˈeɪʃən] *n* : graduación *f*

graffiti [grəˈfiːti, græ-] *npl* : pintadas *fpl,* graffiti *mpl*

graft[1] [ˈgræft] *vt* : injertar

graft[2] *n* **1** : injerto *m* <skin graft : injerto cutáneo> **2** CORRUPTION : soborno *m* (político), ganancia *f* ilegal

grain [ˈgreɪn] *n* **1** : grano *m* <a grain of corn : un grano de maíz> <like a grain of sand : como grano de arena> **2** CEREALS : cereales *mpl* **3** : veta *f,* vena *f,* grano *m* (de madera) **4** SPECK, TRACE : pizca *f,* ápice *m* <a grain of truth : una pizca de verdad> **5** : grano *m* (unidad de peso)

gram [ˈgræm] *n* : gramo *m*

grammar [ˈgræmər] *n* : gramática *f*

grammar school → **elementary school**

grammatical [grəˈmæt̬ɪkəl] *adj* : gramatical — **grammatically** [-kli] *adv*

granary [ˈgreɪnəri, ˈgræ-] *n, pl* **-ries** : granero *m*

grand [ˈgrænd] *adj* **1** FOREMOST : grande **2** IMPRESSIVE : impresionante, magnífico <a grand view : una vista magnífica> **3** LAVISH : grandioso, suntuoso, lujoso <to live in a grand manner : vivir a lo grande> **4** FABULOUS : fabuloso, magnífico <to have a grand time : pasarlo estupendamente, pasarlo en grande> **5 grand total** : total *m,* suma *f* total

grandchild [ˈgrændˌtʃaɪld] *n, pl* **-children** : nieto *m,* -ta *f*

granddaughter [ˈgrændˌdɔt̬ər] *n* : nieta *f*

grandeur [ˈgrændʒər] *n* : grandiosidad *f,* esplendor *m*

grandfather [ˈgrændˌfɑðər] *n* : abuelo *m*

grandiose [ˈgrændiˌoːs, ˌgrændiˈ-] *adj* **1** IMPOSING : imponente, grandioso **2** POMPOUS : pomposo, presuntuoso

grandmother ['grænd,mʌðər] *n* : abuela *f*

grandparents ['grænd,pærənts] *npl* : abuelos *mpl*

grandson ['grænd,sʌn] *n* : nieto *m*

grandstand ['grænd,stænd] *n* : tribuna *f*

granite ['grænɪt] *n* : granito *m*

grant[1] ['grænt] *vt* **1** ALLOW : conceder <to grant a request : conceder una petición> **2** BESTOW : conceder, dar, otorgar <to grant a favor : otorgar un favor> **3** ADMIT : reconocer, admitir <I'll grant that he's clever : reconozco que es listo> **4 to take for granted** : dar (algo) por sentado

grant[2] *n* **1** GRANTING : concesión *f*, otorgamiento *m* **2** SCHOLARSHIP : beca *f* **3** SUBSIDY : subvención *f*

granular ['grænjʊlər] *adj* : granular

granulated ['grænjʊ,leɪṭəd] *adj* : granulado

grape ['greɪp] *n* : uva *f*

grapefruit ['greɪp,fruːt] *n* : toronja *f*, pomelo *m*

grapevine ['greɪp,vaɪn] *n* **1** : vid *f*, parra *f* **2 through the grapevine** : por vías secretas <I heard it through the grapevine : me lo contaron>

graph ['græf] *n* : gráfica *f*, gráfico *m*

graphic ['græfɪk] *adj* **1** VIVID : vívido, gráfico **2 graphic arts** : artes gráficas

graphically ['græfɪkli] *adv* : gráficamente

graphite ['græ,faɪt] *n* : grafito *m*

grapnel ['græpnəl] *n* : rezón *m*

grapple ['græpəl] *vi* **-pled; -pling 1** GRIP : agarrar (con un garfio) **2** STRUGGLE : forcejear, luchar (con un problema, etc.)

grasp[1] ['græsp] *vt* **1** GRIP, SEIZE : agarrar, asir **2** COMPREHEND : entender, comprender — *vi* **to grasp at** : aprovechar

grasp[2] *n* **1** GRIP : agarre *m* **2** CONTROL : control *m*, garras *fpl* **3** REACH : alcance *m* <within your grasp : a su alcance> **4** UNDERSTANDING : comprensión *f*, entendimiento *m*

grass ['græs] *n* **1** : hierba *f* (planta) **2** PASTURE : pasto *m*, zacate *m CA*, *Mex* **3** LAWN : césped *m*, pasto *m*

grasshopper ['græs,hɑpər] *n* : saltamontes *m*

grassland ['græs,lænd] *n* : pradera *f*

grassy ['græsi] *adj* **grassier; -est** : cubierto de hierba

grate[1] ['greɪt] *v* **grated; -ing** *vt* **1** : rallar (en cocina) **2** SCRAPE : rascar **3 to grate one's teeth** : hacer rechinar los dientes — *vi* **1** RASP, SQUEAK : chirriar **2** IRRITATE : irritar <to grate on one's nerves : crisparle los nervios a uno>

grate[2] *n* **1** : parrilla *f* (para cocinar) **2** GRATING : reja *f*, rejilla *f*, verja *f* (en una ventana)

grateful ['greɪtfəl] *adj* : agradecido

gratefully ['greɪtfəli] *adv* : con agradecimiento

gratefulness ['greɪtfəlnəs] *n* : gratitud *f*, agradecimiento *m*

grater ['greɪṭər] *n* : rallador *m*

gratification [,græṭəfə'keɪʃən] *n* : gratificación *f*

gratify ['græṭə,faɪ] *vt* **-fied; -fying 1** PLEASE : complacer **2** SATISFY : satisfacer, gratificar

grating ['greɪṭɪŋ] *n* : reja *f*, rejilla *f*

gratis[1] ['græṭəs, 'greɪ-] *adv* : gratis, gratuitamente

gratis[2] *adj* : gratis, gratuito

gratitude ['græṭə,tuːd, -,tjuːd] *n* : gratitud *f*, agradecimiento *m*

gratuitous [grə'tuːəṭəs] *adj* : gratuito

gratuity [grə'tuːəṭi] *n, pl* **-ities** TIP : propina *f*

grave[1] ['greɪv] *adj* **graver; -est 1** IMPORTANT : grave, de mucha gravedad **2** SERIOUS, SOLEMN : grave, serio

grave[2] *n* : tumba *f*, sepultura *f*

gravel ['grævəl] *n* : grava *f*, gravilla *f*

gravelly ['grævəli] *adj* **1** : de grava **2** HARSH : áspero (dícese de la voz)

gravely ['greɪvli] *adv* : gravemente

gravestone ['greɪv,stoːn] *n* : lápida *f*

graveyard ['greɪv,jɑrd] *n* CEMETERY : cementerio *m*, panteón *m*, camposanto *m*

gravitate ['grævə,teɪt] *vi* **-tated; -tating** : gravitar

gravitation [,grævə'teɪʃən] *n* : gravitación *f*

gravitational [,grævə'teɪʃənəl] *adj* : gravitacional

gravity ['grævəṭi] *n, pl* **-ties 1** SERIOUSNESS : gravedad *f*, seriedad *f* **2** : gravedad *f* <the law of gravity : la ley de la gravedad>

gravy ['greɪvi] *n, pl* **-vies** : salsa *f* (preparada con el jugo de la carne asada)

gray[1] ['greɪ] *vt* : hacer gris — *vi* : encanecer, ponerse gris

gray[2] *adj* **1** : gris (dícese del color) **2** : cano, canoso <gray hair : pelo canoso> <to go gray : volverse cano> **3** DISMAL, GLOOMY : gris, triste

gray[3] *n* : gris *m*

grayish ['greɪɪʃ] *adj* : grisáceo

graze ['greɪz] *v* **grazed; grazing** *vi* : pastar, pacer — *vt* **1** : pastorear (ganado) **2** BRUSH : rozar **3** SCRATCH : raspar

grease[1] ['griːs, 'griːz] *vt* **greased; greasing** : engrasar, lubricar

grease[2] ['griːs] *n* : grasa *f*

greasy ['griːsi, -zi] *adj* **greasier; -est 1** : grasiento **2** OILY : graso, grasoso

great ['greɪt] *adj* **1** LARGE : grande <a great mountain : una montaña grande> <a great crowd : una gran muchedumbre> **2** INTENSE : intenso, fuerte, grande <great pain : gran dolor> **3** EMINENT : grande, eminente, distinguido <a great poet : un gran poeta> **4** EXCELLENT, TERRIFIC : excelente, estupendo, fabuloso <to have a

great time : pasarlo en grande> **5 a great while** : mucho tiempo

great-aunt [ˌgreɪtˈænt, -ˈant] *n* : tía *f* abuela

greater [ˈgreɪt̬ər] (*comparative of* **great**) : mayor

greatest [ˈgreɪt̬əst] (*superlative of* **great**) : el mayor, la mayor

great–grandchild [ˌgreɪtˈgrændˌtʃaɪld] *n, pl* **-children** [-ˌtʃɪldrən] : bisnieto *m*, -ta *f*

great–grandfather [ˌgreɪtˈgrændˌfɑðər] *n* : bisabuelo *m*

great–grandmother [ˌgreɪtˈgrændˌmʌðər] *n* : bisabuela *f*

greatly [ˈgreɪtli] *adv* **1** MUCH : mucho, sumamente <to be greatly improved : haber mejorado mucho> **2** VERY : muy <greatly superior : muy superior>

greatness [ˈgreɪtnəs] *n* : grandeza *f*

great–uncle [ˌgreɪtˈʌŋkəl] *n* : tío *m* abuelo

grebe [ˈgriːb] *n* : somorgujo *m*

greed [ˈgriːd] *n* **1** AVARICE : avaricia *f*, codicia *f* **2** GLUTTONY : glotonería *f*, gula *f*

greedily [ˈgriːdəli] *adv* : con avaricia, con gula

greediness [ˈgriːdinəs] → **greed**

greedy [ˈgriːdi] *adj* **greedier; -est 1** AVARICIOUS : codicioso, avaricioso **2** GLUTTONOUS : glotón

Greek [ˈgriːk] *n* **1** : griego *m*, -ga *f* **2** : griego *m* (idioma) — **Greek** *adj*

green¹ [ˈgriːn] *adj* **1** : verde (dícese del color) **2** UNRIPE : verde, inmaduro **3** INEXPERIENCED : verde, novato

green² *n* **1** : verde *m* **2 greens** *npl* VEGETABLES : verduras *fpl*

greenery [ˈgriːnəri] *n, pl* **-eries** : plantas *fpl* verdes, vegetación *f*

greenhorn [ˈgriːnˌhɔrn] *n* : novato *m*, -ta *f*

greenhouse [ˈgriːnˌhaʊs] *n* : invernadero *m*

greenhouse effect : efecto *m* invernadero

greenish [ˈgriːnɪʃ] *adj* : verdoso

Greenlander [ˈgriːnləndər, -ˌlæn-] *n* : groenlandés *m*, -desa *f*

greenness [ˈgriːnnəs] *n* **1** : verdor *m* **2** INEXPERIENCE : inexperiencia *f*

green thumb *n* **to have a green thumb** : tener buena mano para las plantas

greet [ˈgriːt] *vt* **1** : saludar <to greet a friend : saludar a un amigo> **2** : acoger, recibir <they greeted him with boos : lo recibieron con abucheos>

greeting [ˈgriːt̬ɪŋ] *n* **1** : saludo *m* **2 greetings** *npl* REGARDS : saludos *mpl*, recuerdos *mpl*

gregarious [grɪˈgæriəs] *adj* : gregario (dícese de los animales), sociable (dícese de las personas) — **gregariously** *adv*

gregariousness [grɪˈgæriəsnəs] *n* : sociabilidad *f*

gremlin [ˈgrɛmlən] *n* : duende *m*

grenade [grəˈneɪd] *n* : granada *f*

Grenadian [grəˈneɪdiən] *n* : granadino *m*, -na *f* — **Grenadian** *adj*

grew → **grow**

grey → **gray**

greyhound [ˈgreɪˌhaʊnd] *n* : galgo *m*

grid [ˈgrɪd] *n* **1** GRATING : rejilla *f* **2** NETWORK : red *f* (de electricidad, etc.) **3** : cuadriculado *m* (de un mapa)

griddle [ˈgrɪdəl] *n* : plancha *f*

griddle cake → **pancake**

gridiron [ˈgrɪdˌaɪərn] *n* **1** GRILL : parrilla *f* **2** : campo *m* de futbol americano

grief [ˈgriːf] *n* **1** SORROW : dolor *m*, pena *f* **2** ANNOYANCE, TROUBLE : problemas *mpl*, molestia *f*

grievance [ˈgriːvənts] *n* COMPLAINT : queja *f*

grieve [ˈgriːv] *v* **grieved; grieving** *vt* DISTRESS : afligir, entristecer, apenar — *vi* **1** : sufrir, afligirse **2 to grieve for** *or* **to grieve over** : llorar, lamentar

grievous [ˈgriːvəs] *adj* **1** OPPRESSIVE : gravoso, opresivo, severo **2** GRAVE, SERIOUS : grave, severo, doloroso

grievously [ˈgriːvəsli] *adv* : gravemente, de gravedad

grill¹ [ˈgrɪl] *vt* **1** : asar (a la parrilla) **2** INTERROGATE : interrogar

grill² *n* **1** : parrilla *f* (para cocinar) **2** : parrillada *f* (comida) **3** RESTAURANT : grill *m*

grille *or* **grill** [ˈgrɪl] *n* : reja *f*, enrejado *m*

grim [ˈgrɪm] *adj* **grimmer; grimmest 1** CRUEL : cruel, feroz **2** STERN : adusto, severo <a grim expression : un gesto severo> **3** GLOOMY : sombrío, deprimente **4** SINISTER : macabro, siniestro **5** UNYIELDING : inflexible, persistente <with grim determination : con una voluntad de hierro>

grimace¹ [ˈgrɪməs, grɪˈmeɪs] *vi* **-maced; -macing** : hacer muecas

grimace² *n* : mueca *f*

grime [ˈgraɪm] *n* : mugre *f*, suciedad *f*

grimly [ˈgrɪmli] *adv* **1** STERNLY : severamente **2** RESOLUTELY : inexorablemente

grimy [ˈgraɪmi] *adj* **grimier; -est** : mugriento, sucio

grin¹ [ˈgrɪn] *vi* **grinned; grinning** : sonreír abiertamente

grin² *n* : sonrisa *f* abierta

grind¹ [ˈgraɪnd] *v* **ground** [ˈgraʊnd]; **grinding** *vt* **1** CRUSH : moler, machacar, triturar **2** SHARPEN : afilar **3** POLISH : pulir, esmerilar (lentes, espejos) **4 to grind one's teeth** : rechinarle los dientes a uno **5 to grind down** OPPRESS : oprimir, agobiar — *vi* **1** : funcionar con dificultad, rechinar <to grind to a halt : pararse

poco a poco, llegar a un punto muerto> 2 STUDY : estudiar mucho

grind[2] *n* : trabajo *m* pesado <the daily grind : la rutina diaria>

grinder [ˈgraɪndər] *n* : molinillo *m* <coffee grinder : molinillo de café>

grindstone [ˈgraɪnd,stoːn] *n* : piedra *m* de afilar

grip[1] [ˈgrɪp] *vt* **gripped; gripping** 1 GRASP : agarrar, asir 2 HOLD, INTEREST : captar el interés de

grip[2] *n* 1 GRASP : agarre *m,* asidero *m* <to have a firm grip on something : agarrarse bien de algo> 2 CONTROL, HOLD : control *m,* dominio *m* <to lose one's grip on : perder el control de> <inflation tightened its grip on the economy : la inflación se afianzó en su dominio de la economía> 3 UNDERSTANDING : comprensión *f,* entendimiento *m* <to come to grips with : llegar a entender> 4 HANDLE : asidero *m,* empuñadura *f* (de un arma)

gripe[1] [ˈgraɪp] *v* **griped; griping** *vt* IRRITATE, VEX : irritar, fastidiar, molestar — *vi* COMPLAIN : quejarse, rezongar

gripe[2] *n* : queja *f*

grippe [ˈgrɪp] *n* : influenza *f,* gripe *f,* gripa *f Col, Mex*

grisly [ˈgrɪzli] *adj* **-lier; -est** : horripilante, horroroso, truculento

grist [ˈgrɪst] *n* : molienda *f* <it's all grist for the mill : todo ayuda, todo es provechoso>

gristle [ˈgrɪsəl] *n* : cartílago *m*

gristly [ˈgrɪsli] *adj* **-tlier; -est** : cartilaginoso

grit[1] [ˈgrɪt] *vt* **gritted; gritting** : hacer rechinar (los dientes, etc.)

grit[2] *n* 1 SAND : arena *f* 2 GRAVEL : grava *f* 3 COURAGE : valor *m,* coraje *m* 4 **grits** *npl* : sémola *f* de maíz

gritty [ˈgrɪţi] *adj* **-tier; -est** 1 : arenoso <a gritty surface : una superficie arenosa> 2 PLUCKY : valiente

grizzled [ˈgrɪzəld] *adj* : entrecano

grizzly bear [ˈgrɪzli] *n* : oso *m* pardo

groan[1] [ˈgroːn] *vi* 1 MOAN : gemir, quejarse 2 CREAK : crujir

groan[2] *n* 1 MOAN : gemido *m,* quejido *m* 2 CREAK : crujido *m*

grocer [ˈgroːsər] *n* : tendero *m,* -ra *f*

grocery [ˈgroːsəri, -ʃəri] *n, pl* **-ceries** 1 *or* **grocery store** : tienda *f* de comestibles, tienda *f* de abarrotes 2 **groceries** *npl* : comestibles *mpl,* abarrotes *mpl*

groggy [ˈgrɑgi] *adj* **-gier; -est** : atontado, grogui, tambaleante

groin [ˈgrɔɪn] *n* : ingle *f*

grommet [ˈgrɑmət, ˈgrʌ-] *n* : arandela *f*

groom[1] [ˈgruːm, ˈgrʊm] *vt* 1 : cepillar, almohazar (un animal) 2 : arreglar, cuidar <well-groomed : bien arreglado> 3 PREPARE : preparar

groom[2] *n* 1 : mozo *m,* -za *f* de cuadra 2 BRIDEGROOM : novio *m*

groove[1] [ˈgruːv] *vt* **grooved; grooving** : acanalar, hacer ranuras en, surcar

groove[2] *n* 1 FURROW, SLOT : ranura *f,* surco *m* 2 RUT : rutina *f*

grope [ˈgroːp] *v* **groped; groping** *vi* : andar a tientas, tantear <he groped for the switch : buscó el interruptor a tientas> — *vt* **to grope one's way** : avanzar a tientas

gross[1] [ˈgroːs] *vt* : tener entrada bruta de, recaudar en bruto

gross[2] *adj* 1 FLAGRANT : flagrante, grave <a gross error : un error flagrante> <a gross injustice : una injusticia grave> 2 FAT : muy gordo, obeso 3 : bruto <gross national product : producto nacional bruto> 4 COARSE, VULGAR : grosero, basto

gross[3] *n* 1 *pl* **gross** : gruesa *f* (12 docenas) 2 *or* **gross income** : ingresos *mpl* brutos

grossly [ˈgroːsli] *adv* 1 EXTREMELY : extremadamente <grossly unfair : totalmente injusto> 2 CRUDELY : groseramente

grotesque [groːˈtɛsk] *adj* : grotesco

grotesquely [groːˈtɛskli] *adv* : de forma grotesca

grotto [ˈgrɑţoː] *n, pl* **-toes** : gruta *f*

grouch[1] [ˈgraʊtʃ] *vi* : refunfuñar, rezongar

grouch[2] *n* 1 COMPLAINT : queja *f* 2 GRUMBLER : gruñón *m,* -ñona *f;* cascarrabias *mf fam*

grouchy [ˈgraʊtʃi] *adj* **grouchier; -est** : malhumorado, gruñón

ground[1] [ˈgraʊnd] *vt* 1 BASE : fundar, basar 2 INSTRUCT : enseñar los conocimientos básicos a <to be well grounded in : ser muy entendido en> 3 : conectar a tierra (un aparato eléctrico) 4 : varar, hacer encallar (un barco) 5 : restringir (un avión o un piloto) a la tierra

ground[2] *n* 1 EARTH, SOIL : suelo *m,* tierra *f* <to dig (in) the ground : cavar la tierra> <to fall to the ground : caerse al suelo> 2 LAND, TERRAIN : terreno *m* <hilly ground : terreno alto> <to lose ground : perder terreno> 3 BASIS, REASON : razón *f,* motivo *m* <grounds for complaint : motivos de queja> 4 BACKGROUND : fondo *m* 5 FIELD : campo *m,* plaza *f* <parade ground : plaza de armas> 6 : tierra *f* (para electricidad) 7 **grounds** *npl* PREMISES : recinto *m,* terreno *m* 8 **grounds** *npl* DREGS : posos *mpl* (de café)

ground[3] → **grind**

groundhog [ˈgraʊnd,hɔg] *n* : marmota *f* (de América)

groundless [ˈgraʊndləs] *adj* : infundado

groundwork [ˈgraʊnd,wərk] *n* 1 FOUNDATION : fundamento *m,* base *f* 2 PREPARATION : trabajo *m* preparatorio

group[1] [ˈgruːp] *vt* : agrupar

group[2] *n* : grupo *m,* agrupación *f,* conjunto *m,* compañía *f*

grouper ['gruːpər] *n* : mero *m*

grouse[1] ['graʊs] *vi* **groused; grousing** : quejarse, rezongar, refunfuñar

grouse[2] *n, pl* **grouse** *or* **grouses** : urogallo *m* (ave)

grout ['graʊt] *n* : lechada *f*

grove ['groːv] *n* : bosquecillo *m,* arboleda *f,* soto *m*

grovel ['grɑvəl, 'grʌ-] *vi* **-eled** *or* **-elled; -eling** *or* **-elling 1** CRAWL : arrastrarse **2** : humillarse, postrarse <to grovel before someone : postrarse ante alguien>

grow ['groː] *v* **grew** ['gruː]; **grown** ['groːn]; **growing** *vi* **1** : crecer <palm trees grow on the islands : las palmas crecen en las islas> <my hair grows very fast : mi pelo crece muy rápido> **2** DEVELOP, MATURE : desarrollarse, madurar **3** INCREASE : crecer, aumentar **4** BECOME : hacerse, volverse, ponerse <she was growing angry : se estaba poniendo furiosa> <to grow dark : oscurecerse> **5 to grow up** : hacerse mayor <grow up! : ¡no seas niño!> — *vt* **1** CULTIVATE, RAISE : cultivar **2** : dejar crecer <to grow one's hair : dejarse crecer el pelo>

grower ['groːər] *n* : cultivador *m,* -dora *f*

growl[1] ['graʊl] *vi* : gruñir (dícese de un animal), refunfuñar (dícese de una persona)

growl[2] *n* : gruñido *m*

grown–up[1] ['groːn,əp] *adj* : adulto, mayor

grown–up[2] *n* : adulto *m,* -ta *f;* persona *f* mayor

growth ['groːθ] *n* **1** : crecimiento *m* <to stunt one's growth : detener el crecimiento> **2** INCREASE : aumento *m,* crecimiento *m,* expansión *f* **3** DEVELOPMENT : desarrollo *m* <economic growth : desarrollo económico> <a five days' growth of beard : una barba de cinco días> **4** LUMP, TUMOR : bulto *m,* tumor *m*

grub[1] ['grʌb] *vi* **grubbed; grubbing 1** DIG : escarbar **2** RUMMAGE : hurgar, buscar **3** DRUDGE : trabajar duro

grub[2] *n* **1** : larva *f* <beetle grub : larva del escarabajo> **2** DRUDGE : esclavo *m,* -va *f* del trabajo **3** FOOD : comida *f*

grubby ['grʌbi] *adj* **grubbier; -est** : mugriento, sucio

grudge[1] ['grʌdʒ] *vt* **grudged; grudging** : resentir, envidiar

grudge[2] *n* : rencor *m,* resentimiento *m* <to hold a grudge : guardar rencor>

grueling *or* **gruelling** ['gruːlɪŋ, 'gruːə-] *adj* : extenuante, agotador, duro

gruesome ['gruːsəm] *adj* : horripilante, truculento, horroroso

gruff ['grʌf] *adj* **1** BRUSQUE : brusco <a gruff reply : una respuesta brusca> **2** HOARSE : ronco — **gruffly** *adv*

grumble[1] ['grʌmbəl] *vi* **-bled; -bling 1** COMPLAIN : refunfuñar, rezongar, quejarse **2** RUMBLE : hacer un ruido sordo, retumbar (dícese del trueno)

grumble[2] *n* **1** COMPLAINT : queja *f* **2** RUMBLE : ruido *m* sordo, estruendo *m*

grumbler ['grʌmbələr] *n* : gruñón *m,* -ñona *f*

grumpy ['grʌmpi] *adj* **grumpier; -est** : malhumorado, gruñón

grunt[1] ['grʌnt] *vi* : gruñir

grunt[2] *n* : gruñido *m*

guacamole [,gwɑkə'moːli] *n* : guacamole *m,* guacamol *m*

guarantee[1] [,gærən'tiː] *vt* **-teed; -teeing 1** PROMISE : asegurar, prometer **2** : poner bajo garantía, garantizar (un producto o servicio)

guarantee[2] *n* **1** PROMISE : garantía *f,* promesa *f* <lifetime guarantee : garantía de por vida> **2** → **guarantor**

guarantor [,gærən'tɔr] *n* : garante *mf;* fiador *m,* -dora *f*

guaranty [,gærən'tiː] → **guarantee**

guard[1] ['gɑrd] *vt* **1** DEFEND, PROTECT : defender, proteger **2** : guardar, vigilar, custodiar <to guard the frontier : vigilar la frontera> <she guarded my secret well : guardó bien mi secreto> — *vi* **to guard against** : protegerse contra, evitar

guard[2] *n* **1** WATCHMAN : guarda *mf* <security guard : guarda de seguridad> **2** VIGILANCE : guardia *f,* vigilancia *f* <to be on guard : estar en guardia> <to let one's guard down : bajar la guardia> **3** SAFEGUARD : salvaguardia *f,* dispositivo *m* de seguridad (en una máquina) **4** PRECAUTION : precaución *f,* protección *f*

guardhouse ['gɑrd,haʊs] *n* : cuartel *m* de la guardia

guardian ['gɑrdiən] *n* **1** PROTECTOR : guardián *m,* -diana *f;* custodio *m,* -dia *f* **2** : tutor *m,* -tora *f* (de un niño)

guardianship ['gɑrdiən,ʃɪp] *n* : custodia *f,* tutela *f*

Guatemalan [,gwɑtə'mɑlən] *n* : guatemalteco *m,* -ca *f* — **Guatemalan** *adj*

guava ['gwɑvə] *n* : guayaba *f*

gubernatorial [,guːbənə'toriːəl, ,gjuː-] *adj* : del gobernador

guerrilla *or* **guerilla** [gə'rɪlə] *n* : guerrillero *m,* -ra *f*

guess[1] ['gɛs] *vt* **1** CONJECTURE : adivinar, conjeturar <guess what happened! : ¡adivina lo que pasó!> **2** SUPPOSE : pensar, creer, suponer <I guess so : supongo que sí> **3** : adivinar correctamente, acertar <to guess the answer : acertar la respuesta> — *vi* : adivinar

guess[2] *n* : conjetura *f,* suposición *f*

guesswork ['gɛs,wərk] *n* : suposiciones *fpl,* conjeturas *fpl*

guest ['gɛst] *n* : huésped *mf;* invitado *m,* -da *f*

guffaw[1] [gə'fɔ] *vi* : reírse a carcajadas, carcajearse *fam*

guffaw[2] [gə'fɔ, 'gʌˌfɔ] *n* : carcajada *f,* risotada *f*
guidance ['gaɪdənts] *n* : orientación *f,* consejos *mpl*
guide[1] ['gaɪd] *vt* **guided; guiding 1** DIRECT, LEAD : guiar, dirigir, conducir **2** ADVISE, COUNSEL : aconsejar, orientar
guide[2] *n* : guía *f*
guidebook ['gaɪdˌbʊk] *n* : guía *f* (para viajeros)
guideline ['gaɪdˌlaɪn] *n* : pauta *f,* directriz *f*
guild ['gɪld] *n* : gremio *m,* sindicato *m,* asociación *f*
guile ['gaɪl] *n* : astucia *f,* engaño *m*
guileless ['gaɪlləs] *adj* : inocente, cándido, sin malicia
guillotine[1] ['gɪləˌtiːn, 'giːjəˌ-] *vt* **-tined; -tining** : guillotinar
guillotine[2] *n* : guillotina *f*
guilt ['gɪlt] *n* : culpa *f,* culpabilidad *f*
guilty ['gɪlti] *adj* **guiltier; -est** : culpable
guinea fowl ['gɪni] *n* : gallina *f* de Guinea
guinea pig *n* : conejillo *m* de Indias, cobaya *f*
guise ['gaɪz] *n* : apariencia *f,* aspecto *m,* forma *f*
guitar [gə'tɑr, gɪ-] *n* : guitarra *f*
gulch ['gʌltʃ] *n* : barranco *m,* quebrada *f*
gulf ['gʌlf] *n* **1** : golfo *m* <the Gulf of Mexico : el Golfo de México> **2** GAP : brecha *f* <the gulf between generations : la brecha entre las generaciones> **3** CHASM : abismo *m*
gull ['gʌl] *n* : gaviota *f*
gullet ['gʌlət] *n* : garganta *f*
gullible ['gʌlɪbəl] *adj* : crédulo
gully ['gʌli] *n, pl* **-lies** : barranco *m,* hondonada *f*
gulp[1] ['gʌlp] *vt* **1** : engullir, tragar <he gulped down the whiskey : engulló el whisky> **2** SUPPRESS : suprimir, reprimir, tragar <to gulp down a sob : reprimir un sollozo> — *vi* : tragar saliva, tener un nudo en la garganta
gulp[2] *n* : trago *m*
gum ['gʌm] *n* **1** CHEWING GUM : goma *f* de mascar, chicle *m* **2 gums** *npl* : encías *fpl*
gumbo ['gʌmˌboː] *n* : sopa *f* de quingombó
gumdrop ['gʌmˌdrɑp] *n* : pastilla *f* de goma
gummy ['gʌmi] *adj* **gummier; -est** : gomoso
gumption ['gʌmpʃən] *n* : iniciativa *f,* agallas *fpl fam*
gun[1] ['gʌn] *vt* **gunned; gunning 1** *or* **to gun down** : matar a tiros, asesinar **2** : acelerar (rápidamente) <to gun the engine : acelerar el motor>
gun[2] *n* **1** CANNON : cañón *m* **2** FIREARM : arma *f* de fuego **3** SPRAY GUN : pistola *f* **4 to jump the gun** : adelantarse, salir antes de tiempo
gunboat ['gʌnˌboːt] *n* : cañonero *m*
gunfight ['gʌnˌfaɪt] *n* : tiroteo *m,* balacera *f*
gunfire ['gʌnˌfaɪr] *n* : disparos *mpl*
gunman ['gʌnmən] *n, pl* **-men** [-mən, -ˌmɛn] : pistolero *m,* gatillero *m Mex*
gunner ['gʌnər] *n* : artillero *m,* -ra *f*
gunnysack ['gʌniˌsæk] *n* : saco *m* de yute
gunpowder ['gʌnˌpaʊdər] *n* : pólvora *f*
gunshot ['gʌnˌʃɑt] *n* : disparo *m,* tiro *m,* balazo *m*
gunwale ['gʌnəl] *n* : borda *f*
guppy ['gʌpi] *n, pl* **-pies** : lebistes *m*
gurgle[1] ['gərgəl] *vi* **-gled; -gling 1** : borbotar, gorgotear (dícese de un líquido) **2** : gorjear (dícese de un niño)
gurgle[2] *n* **1** : borboteo *m,* gorgoteo *m* (de un líquido) **2** : gorjeo *m* (de un niño)
gush ['gʌʃ] *vi* **1** SPOUT : surgir, salir a chorros, chorrear **2** : hablar con entusiasmo efusivo <she gushed with praise : se deshizo en elogios>
gust ['gʌst] *n* : ráfaga *f,* racha *f*
gusto ['gʌsˌtoː] *n, pl* **gustoes** : entusiasmo *m* <with gusto : con deleite, con ganas>
gusty ['gʌsti] *adj* **gustier; -est** : racheado
gut[1] ['gʌt] *vt* **gutted; gutting 1** EVISCERATE : destripar (un pollo, etc.), limpiar (un pescado) **2** : destruir el interior de (un edificio)
gut[2] *n* **1** INTESTINE : intestino *m* **2 guts** *npl* INNARDS : tripas *fpl fam,* entrañas *fpl* **3 guts** *npl* COURAGE : valentía *f,* agallas *fpl*
gutter ['gʌtər] *n* **1** : canal *mf,* canaleta *f* (de un techo) **2** : cuneta *f,* arroyo *m* (de una calle)
guttural ['gʌtərəl] *adj* : gutural
guy ['gaɪ] *n* **1** *or* **guyline** : cuerda *f* tensora, cable *m* **2** FELLOW : tipo *m,* hombre *m*
guzzle ['gʌzəl] *vt* **-zled; -zling** : chupar, tragarse
gym ['dʒɪm] → **gymnasium**
gymnasium [dʒɪm'neɪziəm, -ʒəm] *n, pl* **-siums** *or* **-sia** [-ziːə, -ʒə] : gimnasio *m*
gymnast ['dʒɪmnəst, -ˌnæst] *n* : gimnasta *mf*
gymnastic [dʒɪm'næstɪk] *adj* : gimnástico
gymnastics [dʒɪm'næstɪks] *ns & pl* : gimnasia *f*
gynecologist [ˌgaɪnə'kɑlədʒɪst, ˌdʒɪnə-] *n* : ginecólogo *m,* -ga *f*
gynecology [ˌgaɪnə'kɑlədʒi, ˌdʒɪnə-] *n* : ginecología *f*
gyp[1] ['dʒɪp] *vt* **gypped; gypping** : estafar, timar
gyp[2] *n* **1** SWINDLER : estafador *m,* -dora *f* **2** FRAUD, SWINDLE : estafa *f,* timo *m fam*
gypsum ['dʒɪpsəm] *n* : yeso *m*

Gypsy [ˈdʒɪpsi] *n, pl* **-sies** : gitano *m,* -na *f*

gyrate [ˈdʒaɪˌreɪt] *vi* **-rated; -rating** : girar, rotar

gyration [dʒaɪˈreɪʃən] *n* : giro *m,* rotación *f*

gyroscope [ˈdʒaɪrəˌskoːp] *n* : giroscopio *m,* giróscopo *m*

H

h [ˈeɪtʃ] *n, pl* **h's** *or* **hs** [ˈeɪtʃəz] : octava letra del alfabeto inglés

haberdashery [ˈhæbərˌdæʃəri] *n, pl* **-eries** : tienda *f* de ropa para caballeros

habit [ˈhæbɪt] *n* **1** CUSTOM : hábito *m,* costumbre *f* **2** : hábito *m* (de un monje o una religiosa) **3** ADDICTION : dependencia *f,* adicción *f*

habitable [ˈhæbɪt̬əbəl] *adj* : habitable

habitat [ˈhæbɪˌtæt] *n* : hábitat *m*

habitation [ˌhæbɪˈteɪʃən] *n* **1** OCCUPANCY : habitación *f* **2** RESIDENCE : residencia *f,* morada *f*

habit–forming [ˈhæbɪtˌfɔrmɪŋ] *adj* : que crea dependencia

habitual [həˈbɪtʃʊəl] *adj* **1** CUSTOMARY : habitual, acostumbrado **2** INVETERATE : incorregible, empedernido — **habitually** *adv*

habituate [həˈbɪtʃʊˌeɪt] *vt* **-ated; -ating** : habituar, acostumbrar

hack¹ [ˈhæk] *vt* : cortar, tajar <to hack one's way : abrirse paso> — *vi* **1** : hacer tajos **2** COUGH : toser

hack² *n* **1** CHOP : hachazo *m,* tajo *m* **2** HORSE : caballo *m* de alquiler **3** WRITER : escritor *m,* -tora *f* a sueldo; escritorzuelo *m,* -la *f* **4** COUGH : tos *f* seca

hackles [ˈhækəlz] *npl* **1** : pluma *f* erizada (de un ave), pelo *m* erizado (de un perro, etc.) **2 to get one's hackles up** : ponerse furioso

hackney [ˈhækni] *n, pl* **-neys** : caballo *m* de silla, caballo *m* de tiro

hackneyed [ˈhæknid] *adj* TRITE : trillado, gastado

hacksaw [ˈhækˌsɔ] *n* : sierra *f* para metales

had → **have**

haddock [ˈhædək] *ns & pl* : eglefino *m*

hadn't [ˈhædənt] (*contraction of* **had not**) → **have**

haft [ˈhæft] *n* : mango *m,* empuñadura *f*

hag [ˈhæg] *n* **1** WITCH : bruja *f,* hechicera *f* **2** CRONE : vieja *f* fea

haggard [ˈhægərd] *adj* : demacrado, macilento — **haggardly** *adv*

haggle [ˈhægəl] *vi* **-gled; -gling** : regatear

ha–ha [ˌhɑˈhɑ, ˈhɑˈhɑ] *interj* : ¡ja, ja!

hail¹ [ˈheɪl] *vt* **1** GREET : saludar **2** SUMMON : llamar <to hail a taxi : llamar un taxi> — *vi* : granizar (en meteorología)

hail² *n* **1** : granizo *m* **2** BARRAGE : aluvión *m,* lluvia *f*

hail³ *interj* : ¡salve!

hailstone [ˈheɪlˌstoːn] *n* : granizo *m,* piedra *f* de granizo

hailstorm [ˈheɪlˌstɔrm] *n* : granizada *f*

hair [ˈhær] *n* **1** : pelo *m,* cabello *m* <to get one's hair cut : cortarse el pelo> **2** : vello *m* (en las piernas, etc.)

hairbreadth [ˈhærˌbrɛdθ] *or* **hairsbreadth** [ˈhærz-] *n* **by a hairbreadth** : por un pelo

hairbrush [ˈhærˌbrʌʃ] *n* : cepillo *m* (del pelo)

haircut [ˈhærˌkʌt] *n* : corte *m* de pelo

hairdo [ˈhærˌduː] *n, pl* **-dos** : peinado *m*

hairdresser [ˈhærˌdrɛsər] *n* : peluquero *m,* -ra *f*

hairiness [ˈhærinəs] *n* : vellosidad *f*

hairless [ˈhærləs] *adj* : sin pelo, calvo, pelón

hairline [ˈhærˌlaɪn] *n* **1** : línea *f* delgada **2** : nacimiento *m* del pelo <to have a receding hairline : tener entradas>

hairpin [ˈhærˌpɪn] *n* : horquilla *f*

hair–raising [ˈhærˌreɪzɪŋ] *adj* : espeluznante

hairy [ˈhæri] *adj* **hairier; -est** : peludo, velludo

Haitian [ˈheɪʃən, ˈheɪt̬iən] *n* : haitiano *m,* -na *f* — **Haitian** *adj*

hake [ˈheɪk] *n* : merluza *f*

hale¹ [ˈheɪl] *vt* **haled; haling** : arrastrar, halar <to hale to court : arrastrar al tribunal>

hale² *adj* : saludable, robusto

half¹ [ˈhæf, ˈhaf] *adv* : medio, a medias <half cooked : medio cocido>

half² *adj* : medio, a medias <a half hour : una media hora> <a half truth : una verdad a medias>

half³ *n, pl* **halves** [ˈhævz, ˈhavz] **1** : mitad *f* <half of my friends : la mitad de mis amigos> <in half : por la mitad> **2** : tiempo *m* (en deportes)

half brother *n* : medio hermano *m,* hermanastro *m*

halfhearted [ˈhæfˈhɑrt̬əd] *adj* : sin ánimo, poco entusiasta

halfheartedly [ˈhæfˈhɑrt̬ədli] *adv* : con poco entusiasmo, sin ánimo

half–life [ˈhæfˌlaɪf] *n, pl* **half–lives** : media vida *f*

half sister *n* : media hermana *f,* hermanastra *f*

halfway¹ [ˈhæfˈweɪ] *adv* : a medio camino, a mitad de camino

halfway² *adj* : medio, intermedio <a halfway point : un punto intermedio>

half-wit [ˈhæfˌwɪt] *n* : tonto *m,* -ta *f;* imbécil *mf*

half-witted [ˈhæf,wɪt̬əd] *adj* : estúpido

halibut [ˈhælɪbət] *ns & pl* : halibut *m*

hall [ˈhɔl] *n* **1** BUILDING : residencia *f* estudiantil, facultad *f* (de una universidad) **2** VESTIBULE : entrada *f,* vestíbulo *m,* zaguán *m* **3** CORRIDOR : corredor *m,* pasillo *m* **4** AUDITORIUM : sala *f,* salón *m* <concert hall : sala de conciertos> **5 city hall** : ayuntamiento *m*

hallelujah [,hæləˈluːjə, ,hɑ-] *interj* : ¡aleluya!

hallmark [ˈhɔl,mɑrk] *n* : sello *m* (distintivo)

hallow [ˈhæ,loː] *vt* : santificar, consagrar

hallowed [ˈhæ,loːd, ˈhæ,loːəd, ˈhɑ,loːd] *adj* : sagrado

Halloween [,hæləˈwiːn, ,hɑ-] *n* : víspera *f* de Todos los Santos

hallucinate [hæˈluːsən,eɪt] *vi* **-nated; -nating** : alucinar

hallucination [hə,luːsənˈeɪʃən] *n* : alucinación *f*

hallucinatory [həˈluːsənə,tori] *adj* : alucinante

hallucinogen [həˈluːsənədʒən] *n* : alucinógeno *m*

hallucinogenic [hə,luːsənəˈdʒɛnɪk] *adj* : alucinógeno

hallway [ˈhɔl,weɪ] *n* **1** ENTRANCE : entrada *f* **2** CORRIDOR : corredor *m,* pasillo *m*

halo [ˈheɪ,loː] *n, pl* **-los** *or* **-loes** : aureola *f,* halo *m*

halt[1] [ˈhɔlt] *vi* : detenerse, pararse — *vt* **1** STOP : detener, parar (a una persona) **2** INTERRUPT : interrumpir (una actividad)

halt[2] *n* **1** : alto *m,* parada *f* **2 to come to a halt** : pararse, detenerse

halter [ˈhɔltər] *n* **1** : cabestro *m,* ronzal *m* (para un animal) **2** : blusa *f* sin espalda

halting [ˈhɔltɪŋ] *adj* HESITANT : vacilante, titubeante — **haltingly** *adv*

halve [ˈhæv, ˈhav] *vt* **halved; halving 1** DIVIDE : partir por la mitad **2** REDUCE : reducir a la mitad

halves → **half**

ham [ˈhæm] *n* **1** : jamón *m* **2** *or* **ham actor** : comicastro *m,* -tra *f* **3** *or* **ham radio operator** : radioaficionado *m,* -da *f* **4 hams** *npl* HAUNCHES : ancas *fpl*

hamburger [ˈhæm,bərgər] *or* **hamburg** [-,bərg] *n* **1** : carne *f* molida **2** : hamburguesa *f* (emparedado)

hamlet [ˈhæmlət] *n* VILLAGE : aldea *f,* poblado *m*

hammer[1] [ˈhæmər] *vt* **1** STRIKE : clavar, golpear **2** NAIL : clavar, martillar **3 to hammer out** NEGOTIATE : elaborar, negociar, llegar a — *vi* : martillar, golpear

hammer[2] *n* **1** : martillo *m* **2** : percusor *m,* percutor *m* (de un arma de fuego)

hammock [ˈhæmək] *n* : hamaca *f*

hamper[1] [ˈhæmpər] *vt* : obstaculizar, dificultar

hamper[2] *n* : cesto *m,* canasta *f*

hamster [ˈhæmpstər] *n* : hámster *m*

hamstring [ˈhæm,strɪŋ] *vt* **-strung** [-,strʌŋ]; **-stringing 1** : cortarle el tendón del corvejón a (un animal) **2** INCAPACITATE : incapacitar, inutilizar

hand[1] [ˈhænd] *vt* : pasar, dar, entregar

hand[2] *n* **1** : mano *f* <made by hand : hecho a mano> **2** POINTER : manecilla *f,* aguja *f* (de un reloj o instrumento) **3** SIDE : lado *m* <on the other hand : por otro lado> **4** HANDWRITING : letra *f,* escritura *f* **5** APPLAUSE : aplauso *m* **6** : mano *f,* cartas *fpl* (en juegos de naipes) **7** WORKER : obrero *m,* -ra *f;* trabajador *m,* -dora *f* **8 to ask for someone's hand (in marriage)** : pedir la mano de alguien **9 to lend a hand** : echar una mano

handbag [ˈhænd,bæg] *n* : cartera *f,* bolso *m,* bolsa *f Mex*

handball [ˈhænd,bɔl] *n* : frontón *m*

handbill [ˈhænd,bɪl] *n* : folleto *m,* volante *m*

handbook [ˈhænd,bʊk] *n* : manual *m*

handcuff [ˈhænd,kʌf] *vt* : esposar, ponerle esposas (a alguien)

handcuffs [ˈhænd,kʌfs] *npl* : esposas *fpl*

handful [ˈhænd,fʊl] *n* : puñado *m*

handgun [ˈhænd,gʌn] *n* : pistola *f,* revólver *m*

handicap[1] [ˈhændi,kæp] *vt* **-capped; -capping 1** : asignar un handicap a (en deportes) **2** HAMPER : obstaculizar, poner en desventaja

handicap[2] *n* **1** DISABILITY : minusvalía *f,* discapacidad *f* **2** DISADVANTAGE : desventaja *f,* handicap *m* (en deportes)

handicapped [ˈhændi,kæpt] *adj* DISABLED : minusválido, discapacitado

handicraft [ˈhændi,kræft] *n* : artesanía *f*

handily [ˈhændəli] *adv* EASILY : fácilmente, con facilidad

handiwork [ˈhændi,wərk] *n* **1** WORK : trabajo *m* **2** CRAFTS : artesanías *fpl*

handkerchief [ˈhæŋkərtʃəf, -,tʃiːf] *n, pl* **-chiefs** : pañuelo *m*

handle[1] [ˈhændəl] *v* **-dled; -dling** *vt* **1** TOUCH : tocar **2** MANAGE : tratar, manejar, despachar **3** SELL : comerciar con, vender — *vi* : responder, conducirse (dícese de un vehículo)

handle[2] *n* : asa *m,* asidero *m,* mango *m* (de un cuchillo, etc.), pomo *m* (de una puerta), tirador *m* (de un cajón)

handlebars [ˈhændəl,bɑrz] *npl* : manubrio *m,* manillar *m*

handler [ˈhændələr] *n* : cuidador *m,* -dora *f*

handmade [ˈhænd,meɪd] *adj* : hecho a mano

hand–me–downs [ˈhændmi,daʊnz] *npl* : ropa *f* usada

handout [ˈhændˌaʊt] *n* **1** AID : dádiva *f,* limosna *f* **2** LEAFLET : folleto *m*
handpick [ˈhændˈpɪk] *vt* : seleccionar con cuidado
handrail [ˈhændˌreɪl] *n* : pasamanos *m,* barandilla *f,* barandal *m*
handsaw [ˈhændˌsɔ] *n* : serrucho *m*
hands down *adv* **1** EASILY : con facilidad **2** UNQUESTIONABLY : con mucho, de lejos
handshake [ˈhændˌʃeɪk] *n* : apretón *m* de manos
handsome [ˈhæn*t*səm] *adj* **-somer; -est 1** ATTRACTIVE : apuesto, guapo, atractivo **2** GENEROUS : generoso **3** SIZABLE : considerable
handsomely [ˈhæn*t*səmli] *adv* **1** ELEGANTLY : elegantemente **2** GENEROUSLY : con generosidad
handspring [ˈhændˌsprɪŋ] *n* : voltereta *f*
handstand [ˈhændˌstænd] *n* **to do a handstand** : pararse de manos
hand–to–hand [ˈhæn*d*təˈhænd] *adj* : cuerpo a cuerpo
handwriting [ˈhændˌraɪt̬ɪŋ] *n* : letra *f,* escritura *f*
handwritten [ˈhændˌrɪtən] *adj* : escrito a mano
handy [ˈhændi] *adj* **handier; -est 1** NEARBY : a mano, cercano **2** USEFUL : útil, práctico **3** DEXTEROUS : hábil
hang[1] [ˈhæŋ] *v* **hung** [ˈhʌŋ]; **hanging** *vt* **1** SUSPEND : colgar, tender, suspender **2** (*past tense often* **hanged**) EXECUTE : colgar, ahorcar **3 to hang one's head** : bajar la cabeza — *vi* **1** FALL : caer (dícese de las telas y la ropa) **2** DANGLE : colgar **3** HOVER : flotar, sostenerse en el aire **4** : ser ahorcado **5** DROOP : inclinarse **6 to hang up** : colgar <he hung up on me : me colgó>
hang[2] *n* **1** DRAPE : caída *f* **2 to get the hang of something** : colgarle el truco a algo, lograr entender algo
hangar [ˈhæŋər, ˈhæŋgər] *n* : hangar *m*
hanger [ˈhæŋər] *n* : percha *f,* gancho *m* (para ropa)
hangman [ˈhæŋmən] *n, pl* **-men** [-mən, -ˌmɛn] : verdugo *m*
hangnail [ˈhæŋˌneɪl] *n* : padrastro *m*
hangout [ˈhæŋˌaʊt] *n* : lugar *m* popular, sitio *m* muy frecuentado
hangover [ˈhæŋˌoːvər] *n* : resaca *f*
hank [ˈhæŋk] *n* : madeja *f*
hanker [ˈhæŋkər] *vi* **to hanker for** : ansiar, anhelar, tener ganas de
hankering [ˈhæŋkərɪŋ] *n* : ansia *f,* anhelo *m*
hansom [ˈhæn*t*səm] *n* : coche *m* de caballos
Hanukkah [ˈxɑnəkə, ˈhɑ-] *n* : Januká, Hanukkah
haphazard [hæpˈhæzərd] *adj* : casual, fortuito, al azar — **haphazardly** *adv*
hapless [ˈhæpləs] *adj* UNFORTUNATE : desafortunado, desventurado — **haplessly**
happen [ˈhæpən] *vi* **1** OCCUR : pasar, ocurrir, suceder, tener lugar **2** BEFALL : pasar, acontecer <what happened to her? : ¿qué le ha pasado?> **3** CHANCE : resultar, ocurrir por casualidad <it happened that I wasn't home : resulta que estaba fuera de casa> <he happens to be right : da la casualidad de que tiene razón>
happening [ˈhæpənɪŋ] *n* : suceso *m,* acontecimiento *m*
happiness [ˈhæpinəs] *n* : felicidad *f,* dicha *f*
happy [ˈhæpi] *adj* **-pier; -est 1** JOYFUL : feliz, contento, alegre **2** FORTUNATE : afortunado, feliz — **happily** [-pəli] *adv*
happy–go–lucky [ˈhæpigoːˈlʌki] *adj* : despreocupado
harangue[1] [həˈræŋ] *vt* **-rangued; -ranguing** : arengar
harangue[2] *n* : arenga *f*
harass [həˈræs, ˈhærəs] *vt* **1** BESIEGE, HOUND : acosar, asediar, hostigar **2** ANNOY : molestar
harassment [həˈræsmənt, ˈhærəsmənt] *n* : acoso *m,* hostigamiento *m* <sexual harrassment : acoso sexual>
harbinger [ˈhɑrbɪndʒər] *n* **1** HERALD : heraldo *m,* precursor *m* **2** OMEN : presagio *m*
harbor[1] [ˈhɑrbər] *vt* **1** SHELTER : dar refugio a, albergar **2** CHERISH, KEEP : abrigar, guardar, albergar <to harbor doubts : guardar dudas>
harbor[2] *n* **1** REFUGE : refugio *m* **2** PORT : puerto *m*
hard[1] [ˈhɑrd] *adv* **1** FORCEFULLY : fuerte, con fuerza <the wind blew hard : el viento sopló fuerte> **2** STRENUOUSLY : duro, mucho <to work hard : trabajar duro> **3 to take something hard** : tomarse algo muy mal, estar muy afectado por algo
hard[2] *adj* **1** FIRM, SOLID : duro, firme, sólido **2** DIFFICULT : difícil, arduo **3** SEVERE : severo, duro <a hard winter : un invierno severo> **4** UNFEELING : insensible, duro **5** DILIGENT : diligente <to be a hard worker : ser muy trabajador> **6 hard liquor** : bebidas *fpl* fuertes **7 hard water** : agua *f* dura
harden [ˈhɑrdən] *vt* : endurecer
hardheaded [ˌhɑrdˈhɛdəd] *adj* **1** STUBBORN : testarudo, terco **2** REALISTIC : realista, práctico — **hardheadedly** *adv*
hard–hearted [ˌhɑrdˈhɑrt̬əd] *adj* : despiadado, insensible — **hard–heartedly** *adv*
hard–heartedness [ˌhɑrdˈhɑrt̬ədnəs] *n* : dureza *f* de corazón
hardly [ˈhɑrdli] *adv* **1** SCARCELY : apenas, casi <I hardly knew her : apenas la conocía> <hardly ever : casi nunca> **2** NOT : difícilmente,

poco, no <they can hardly blame me! : ¡difícilmente pueden echarme la culpa!> <it's hardly likely : es poco probable>

hardness [ˈhɑrdnəs] *n* **1** FIRMNESS : dureza *f* **2** DIFFICULTY : dificultad *f* **3** SEVERITY : severidad *f*

hardship [ˈhɑrd,ʃɪp] *n* : dificultad *f,* privación *f*

hardware [ˈhɑrd,wær] *n* **1** TOOLS : ferretería *f* **2** : hardware *m* (de una computadora)

hardwood [ˈhɑrd,wʊd] *n* : madera *f* dura, madera *f* noble

hardy [ˈhɑrdi] *adj* **-dier; -est** : fuerte, robusto, resistente (dícese de las plantas) — **hardily** [-dəli] *adv*

hare [ˈhær] *n, pl* **hare** *or* **hares** : liebre *f*

harebrained [ˈhær,breɪnd] *adj* : estúpido, absurdo, disparatado

harelip [ˈhær,lɪp] *n* : labio *m* leporino

harem [ˈhærəm] *n* : harén *m*

hark [ˈhɑrk] *vi* **1** (*used only in the imperative*) LISTEN : escuchar **2 hark back** RETURN : volver **3 hark back** RECALL : recordar

harlequin [ˈhɑrlɪkən, -kwən] *n* : arlequín *m*

harm¹ [ˈhɑrm] *vt* : hacerle daño a, perjudicar

harm² *n* : daño *m,* perjuicio *m*

harmful [ˈhɑrmfəl] *adj* : dañino, perjudicial — **harmfully** *adv*

harmless [ˈhɑrmləs] *adj* : inofensivo, inocuo — **harmlessly** *adv*

harmlessness [ˈhɑrmləsnəs] *n* : inocuidad *f*

harmonic [hɑrˈmɑnɪk] *adj* : armónico — **harmonically** [-nɪkli] *adv*

harmonica [hɑrˈmɑnɪkə] *n* : armónica *f*

harmonious [hɑrˈmoːniəs] *adj* : armonioso — **harmoniously** *adv*

harmonize [ˈhɑrmə,naɪz] *v* **-nized; -nizing** : armonizar

harmony [ˈhɑrməni] *n, pl* **-nies** : armonía *f*

harness¹ [ˈhɑrnəs] *vt* **1** : enjaezar (un animal) **2** UTILIZE : utilizar, aprovechar

harness² *n* : arreos *mpl*, guarniciones *fpl*, arnés *m*

harp¹ [ˈhɑrp] *vi* **to harp on** : insistir sobre, machacar sobre

harp² *n* : arpa *m*

harpist [ˈhɑrpɪst] *n* : arpista *mf*

harpoon¹ [hɑrˈpuːn] *vt* : arponear

harpoon² *n* : arpón *m*

harpsichord [ˈhɑrpsɪ,kɔrd] *n* : clavicémbalo *m*

harrow¹ [ˈhær,oː] *vt* **1** CULTIVATE : gradar, labrar (la tierra) **2** TORMENT : atormentar

harrow² *n* : grada *f,* rastra *f*

harry [ˈhæri] *vt* **-ried; -rying** HARASS : acosar, hostigar

harsh [ˈhɑrʃ] *adj* **1** ROUGH : áspero **2** SEVERE : duro, severo **3** : discordante (dícese de los sonidos) — **harshly** *adv*

harshness [ˈhɑrʃnəs] *n* **1** ROUGHNESS : aspereza *f* **2** SEVERITY : dureza *f,* severidad *f*

harvest¹ [ˈhɑrvəst] *v* : cosechar

harvest² *n* **1** HARVESTING : siega *f,* recolección *f* **2** CROP : cosecha *f*

harvester [ˈhɑrvəstər] *n* : segador *m,* -dora *f;* cosechadora *f* (máquina)

has → **have**

hash¹ [ˈhæʃ] *vt* **1** MINCE : picar **2 to hash over** DISCUSS : discutir, repasar

hash² *n* **1** : picadillo *m* (comida) **2** JUMBLE : revoltijo *m,* fárrago *m*

hasn't [ˈhæzənt] (*contraction of* **has not**) → **has**

hasp [ˈhæsp] *n* : picaporte *m,* pestillo *m*

hassle¹ [ˈhæsəl] *vt* **-sled; -sling** : fastidiar, molestar

hassle² *n* **1** ARGUMENT : discusión *f,* disputa *f,* bronca *f* **2** FIGHT : pelea *f,* riña *f* **3** BOTHER, TROUBLE : problemas *mpl,* lío *m*

hassock [ˈhæsək] *n* **1** CUSHION : almohadón *m,* cojín *m* **2** FOOTSTOOL : escabel *m*

haste [ˈheɪst] *n* **1** : prisa *f,* apuro *m* **2 to make haste** : darse prisa, apurarse

hasten [ˈheɪsən] *vt* : acelerar, precipitar — *vi* : apresurarse, apurarse

hasty [ˈheɪsti] *adj* **hastier; -est 1** HURRIED, QUICK : rápido, apresurado, apurado **2** RASH : precipitado — **hastily** [-təli] *adv*

hat [ˈhæt] *n* : sombrero *m*

hatch¹ [ˈhætʃ] *vt* **1** : incubar, empollar (huevos) **2** DEVISE : idear, tramar — *vi* : salir del cascarón

hatch² *n* : escotilla *f*

hatchery [ˈhætʃəri] *n, pl* **-ries** : criadero *m*

hatchet [ˈhætʃət] *n* : hacha *f*

hatchway [ˈhætʃ,weɪ] *n* : escotilla *f*

hate¹ [ˈheɪt] *vt* **hated; hating** : odiar, aborrecer, detestar

hate² *n* : odio *m*

hateful [ˈheɪtfəl] *adj* : odioso, aborrecible, detestable — **hatefully** *adv*

hatred [ˈheɪtrəd] *n* : odio *m*

hatter [ˈhætər] *n* : sombrerero *m,* -ra *f*

haughtiness [ˈhɔtinəs] *n* : altanería *f,* altivez *f*

haughty [ˈhɔti] *adj* **-tier; -est** : altanero, altivo — **haughtily** [-təli] *adv*

haul¹ [ˈhɔl] *vt* **1** DRAG, PULL : arrastrar, jalar **2** TRANSPORT : transportar

haul² *n* **1** PULL : tirón *m,* jalón *m* **2** CATCH : redada *f* **3** JOURNEY : viaje *m,* trayecto *m* <it's a long haul : es un trayecto largo>

haulage [ˈhɔlɪdʒ] *n* : transporte *m,* tiro *m*

hauler [ˈhɔlər] *n* : transportista *mf*

haunch [ˈhɔntʃ] *n* **1** HIP : cadera *f* **2 haunches** *npl* HINDQUARTERS : ancas *fpl*, cuartos *mpl* traseros

haunt[1] [ˈhɔnt] *vt* **1** : aparecer en (dícese de un fantasma) **2** FREQUENT : frecuentar, rondar **3** PREOCCUPY : perseguir, obsesionar

haunt[2] *n* : guarida *f* (de animales o ladrones), lugar *m* predilecto

haunting [ˈhɔntɪŋ] *adj* : obsesionante, evocador — **hauntingly** *adv*

have [ˈhæv, *in sense 3 as an auxiliary verb usu* ˈhæf] *v* **had** [ˈhæd]; **having; has** [ˈhæz, *in sense 3 as an auxiliary verb usu* ˈhæs] *vt* **1** POSSESS : tener <do you have change? : ¿tienes cambio?> **2** EXPERIENCE, UNDERGO : tener, experimentar, sufrir <I have a toothache : tengo un dolor de muelas> **3** INCLUDE : tener, incluir <April has 30 days : abril tiene 30 días> **4** CONSUME : comer, tomar **5** RECEIVE : tener, recibir <he had my permission : tenía mi permiso> **6** ALLOW : permitir, dejar <I won't have it! : ¡no lo permitiré!> **7** HOLD : hacer <to have a party : dar una fiesta> <to have a meeting : convocar una reunión> **8** HOLD : tener <he had me in his power : me tenía en su poder> **9** BEAR : tener (niños) **10** (*indicating causation*) <she had a dress made : mandó hacer un vestido> <to have one's hair cut : cortarse el pelo> — *v aux* **1** : haber <she has been very busy : ha estado muy ocupada> <I've lived here three years : hace tres años que vivo aquí> **2** (*used in tags*) <you've finished, haven't you? : ha terminado, ¿no?> **3 to have to** : deber, tener que <we have to leave : tenemos que salir>

haven [ˈheɪvən] *n* : refugio *m*

havoc [ˈhævək] *n* **1** DESTRUCTION : estragos *mpl*, destrucción *f* **2** CHAOS, DISORDER : desorden *m*, caos *m*

Hawaiian[1] [həˈwaɪən] *adj* : hawaiano

Hawaiian[2] *n* : hawaiano *m*, -na *f*

hawk[1] [ˈhɔk] *vt* : pregonar, vender (mercancías) en la calle

hawk[2] *n* : halcón *m*

hawker [ˈhɔkər] *n* : vendedor *m*, -dora *f* ambulante

hawthorn [ˈhɔˌθɔrn] *n* : espino *m*

hay [ˈheɪ] *n* : heno *m*

hay fever *n* : fiebre *f* del heno

hayloft [ˈheɪˌlɔft] *n* : pajar *m*

hayseed [ˈheɪˌsiːd] *n* : palurdo *m*, -da *f*

haystack [ˈheɪˌstæk] *n* : almiar *m*

haywire [ˈheɪˌwaɪr] *adj* : descompuesto, desbaratado <to go haywire : estropearse>

hazard[1] [ˈhæzərd] *vt* : arriesgar, aventurar

hazard[2] *n* **1** DANGER : peligro *m*, riesgo *m* **2** CHANCE : azar *m*

hazardous [ˈhæzərdəs] *adj* : arriesgado, peligroso

haze[1] [ˈheɪz] *vt* **hazed; hazing** : abrumar, acosar

haze[2] *n* : bruma *f*, neblina *f*

hazel [ˈheɪzəl] *n* **1** : avellano *m* (árbol) **2** : color *m* avellana

hazelnut [ˈheɪzəlˌnʌt] *n* : avellana *f*

haziness [ˈheɪzinəs] *n* **1** MISTINESS : nebulosidad *f* **2** VAGUENESS : vaguedad *f*

hazy [ˈheɪzi] *adj* **hazier; -est 1** MISTY : brumoso, neblinoso, nebuloso **2** VAGUE : vago, confuso

he [ˈhiː] *pron* : él

head[1] [ˈhɛd] *vt* **1** LEAD : encabezar **2** DIRECT : dirigir — *vi* : dirigirse

head[2] *adj* MAIN : principal <the head office : la oficina central, la sede>

head[3] *n* **1** : cabeza *f* <from head to foot : de pies a cabeza> **2** MIND : mente *f*, cabeza *f* **3** TIP, TOP : cabeza *f* (de un clavo, un martillo, etc.), cabecera *f* (de una mesa o un río), punta *f* (de una flecha), flor *m* (de un repollo, etc.), encabezamiento *m* (de una carta, etc.), espuma *f* (de cerveza) **4** DIRECTOR, LEADER : director *m*, -tora *f*; jefe *m*, -fa *f*; cabeza *f* (de una familia) **5** : cara *f* (de una moneda) <heads or tails : cara o cruz> **6** : cabeza *f* <500 head of cattle : 500 cabezas de ganado> <$10 a head : $10 por cabeza> **7 to come to a head** : llegar a un punto crítico

headache [ˈhɛdˌeɪk] *n* : dolor *m* de cabeza, jaqueca *f*

headband [ˈhɛdˌbænd] *n* : cinta *f* del pelo

headdress [ˈhɛdˌdrɛs] *n* : tocado *m*

headfirst [ˈhɛdˈfərst] *adv* : de cabeza

headgear [ˈhɛdˌgɪr] *n* : gorro *m*, casco *m*, sombrero *m*

heading [ˈhɛdɪŋ] *n* **1** DIRECTION : dirección *f* **2** TITLE : encabezamiento *m*, título *m* **3** : membrete *m* (de una carta)

headland [ˈhɛdlənd, -ˌlænd] *n* : cabo *m*

headlight [ˈhɛdˌlaɪt] *n* : faro *m*, foco *m*, farol *m Mex*

headline [ˈhɛdˌlaɪn] *n* : titular *m*

headlong[1] [ˈhɛdˈlɔŋ] *adv* **1** HEADFIRST : de cabeza **2** HASTILY : precipitadamente

headlong[2] [ˈhɛdˌlɔŋ] *adj* : precipitado

headmaster [ˈhɛdˌmæstər] *n* : director *m*

headmistress [ˈhɛdˌmɪstrəs, -ˈmɪs-] *n* : directora *f*

head–on [ˈhɛdˈɑn, -ˈɔn] *adv & adj* : de frente

headphones [ˈhɛdˌfoːnz] *npl* : audífonos *mpl*, cascos *mpl*

headquarters [ˈhɛdˌkwɔrt̬ərz] *ns & pl* **1** SEAT : oficina *f* central, sede *f* **2** : cuartel *m* general (de los militares)

headrest [ˈhɛdˌrɛst] *n* : apoyacabezas *m*

headship [ˈhɛdˌʃɪp] *n* : dirección *f*

head start *n* : ventaja *f*

headstone [ˈhɛdˌstoːn] *n* : lápida *f*

headstrong [ˈhɛdˈstrɔŋ] *adj* : testarudo, obstinado, empecinado

headwaiter [ˈhɛdˈweɪt̬ər] *n* : jefe *m,* -fa *f* de comedor

headwaters [ˈhɛd͵wɔ̌t̬ərz, -͵wɑ-] *npl* : cabecera *f*

headway [ˈhɛd͵weɪ] *n* : progreso *m* <to make headway against : avanzar contra>

heady [ˈhɛdi] *adj* **headier; -est 1** INTOXICATING : embriagador, excitante **2** SHREWD : astuto, sagaz

heal [ˈhiːl] *vt* : curar, sanar — *vi* **1** : sanar, curarse **2 to heal up** : cicatrizarse

healer [ˈhiːlər] *n* : curador *m,* -dora *f*

health [ˈhɛlθ] *n* : salud *f*

healthful [ˈhɛlθfəl] *adj* : saludable, salubre — **healthfully** *adv*

healthy [ˈhɛlθi] *adj* **healthier; -est** : sano, bien — **healthily** [-θəli] *adv*

heap[1] [ˈhiːp] *vt* **1** PILE : amontonar, apilar **2** SHOWER : colmar

heap[2] *n* : montón *m,* pila *f*

hear [ˈhɪr] *v* **heard** [ˈhərd]; **hearing** *vt* **1** : oír <do you hear me? : ¿me oyes?> **2** HEED : oír, prestar atención a **3** LEARN : oír, enterarse de — *vi* **1** : oír <to hear about : oír hablar de> **2 to hear from** : tener noticias de

hearing [ˈhɪrɪŋ] *n* **1** : oído *m* <hard of hearing : duro de oído> **2** : vista *f* (en un tribunal) **3** ATTENTION : consideración *f,* oportunidad *f* de expresarse **4** EARSHOT : alcance *m* del oído

hearing aid *n* : audífono *m*

hearken [ˈhɑrkən] *vt* : escuchar

hearsay [ˈhɪr͵seɪ] *n* : rumores *mpl*

hearse [ˈhərs] *n* : coche *m* fúnebre

heart [ˈhɑrt] *n* **1** : corazón *m* **2** CENTER, CORE : corazón *m,* centro *m* <the heart of the matter : el meollo del asunto> **3** FEELINGS : corazón *m,* sentimientos *mpl* <a broken heart : un corazón destrozado> <to have a good heart : tener buen corazón> <to take something to heart : tomarse algo a pecho> **4** COURAGE : valor *m,* corazón *m* <to take heart : animarse, cobrar ánimos> **5 hearts** *npl* : corazones *mpl* (en juegos de naipes) **6 by heart** : de memoria

heartache [ˈhɑrt̬͵eɪk] *n* : pena *f,* angustia *f*

heart attack *n* : infarto *m,* ataque *m* al corazón

heartbeat [ˈhɑrt͵biːt] *n* : latido *m* (del corazón)

heartbreak [ˈhɑrt͵breɪk] *n* : congoja *f,* angustia *f*

heartbreaking [ˈhɑrt͵breɪkɪŋ] *adj* : desgarrador, que parte el corazón

heartbroken [ˈhɑrt͵broːkən] *adj* : desconsolado, destrozado

heartburn [ˈhɑrt͵bərn] *n* : acidez *f* estomacal

hearten [ˈhɑrtən] *vt* : alentar, animar

hearth [ˈhɑrθ] *n* : hogar *m,* chimenea *f*

heartily [ˈhɑrt̬əli] *adv* **1** ENTHUSIASTICALLY : de buena gana, con entusiasmo **2** TOTALLY : totalmente, completamente

heartless [ˈhɑrtləs] *adj* : desalmado, despiadado, cruel

heartsick [ˈhɑrt͵sɪk] *adj* : abatido, desconsolado

heartstrings [ˈhɑrt͵strɪŋz] *npl* : fibras *fpl* del corazón

heartwarming [ˈhɑrt͵wɔrmɪŋ] *adj* : conmovedor, emocionante

hearty [ˈhɑrt̬i] *adj* **heartier; -est 1** CORDIAL, WARM : cordial, caluroso **2** STRONG : fuerte <to have a hearty appetite : ser de buen comer> **3** SUBSTANTIAL : abundante, sustancioso <a hearty breakfast : un desayuno abundante>

heat[1] [ˈhiːt] *vt* : calentar

heat[2] *n* **1** WARMTH : calor *m* **2** HEATING : calefacción *f* **3** EXCITEMENT : calor *m,* entusiasmo *m* <in the heat of the moment : en el calor del momento> **4** ESTRUS : celo *m*

heated [ˈhiːt̬əd] *adj* **1** WARMED : calentado **2** IMPASSIONED : acalorado, apasionado

heater [ˈhiːt̬ər] *n* : calentador *m,* estufa *f,* calefactor *m*

heath [ˈhiːθ] *n* **1** MOOR : brezal *m,* páramo *m* **2** HEATHER : brezo *m*

heathen[1] [ˈhiːðən] *adj* : pagano

heathen[2] *n, pl* **-thens** *or* **-then** : pagano *m,* -na *f;* infiel *mf*

heather [ˈhɛðər] *n* : brezo *m*

heave[1] [ˈhiːv] *v* **heaved** *or* **hove** [ˈhoːv]; **heaving** *vt* **1** LIFT, RAISE : levantar con esfuerzo **2** HURL : lanzar, tirar **3 to heave a sigh** : echar un suspiro, suspirar — *vi* **1** : subir y bajar, palpitar (dícese del pecho) **2 to heave up** RISE : levantarse

heave[2] *n* **1** EFFORT : gran esfuerzo *m* (para levantar algo) **2** THROW : lanzamiento *m*

heaven [ˈhɛvən] *n* **1** : cielo *m* <for heaven's sake : por Dios> **2 heavens** *npl* SKY : cielo *m* <the heavens opened up : empezó a llover a cántaros>

heavenly [ˈhɛvənli] *adj* **1** : celestial, celeste **2** DELIGHTFUL : divino, encantador

heavily [ˈhɛvəli] *adv* **1** : pesadamente, con mucho peso **2** LABORIOUSLY : trabajosamente, penosamente **3** : mucho

heaviness [ˈhɛvinəs] *n* : peso *m,* pesadez *f*

heavy [ˈhɛvi] *adj* **heavier; -est 1** WEIGHTY : pesado **2** DENSE, THICK : denso, espeso, grueso **3** BURDENSOME : oneroso, gravoso **4** PROFOUND : profundo **5** SLUGGISH : lento, tardo **6** STOUT : corpulento **7** SEVERE : severo, duro, fuerte

heavy–duty [ˈhɛviˈduːt̬i, -ˈdjuː-] *adj* : muy resistente, fuerte

heavyweight [ˈhɛvi͵weɪt] *n* : peso *m* pesado (en deportes)

Hebrew[1] [ˈhiːˌbruː] *adj* : hebreo
Hebrew[2] *n* **1** : hebreo *m*, -brea *f* **2** : hebreo *m* (idioma)
heckle [ˈhɛkəl] *vt* **-led; -ling** : interrumpir (a un orador)
hectic [ˈhɛktɪk] *adj* : agitado, ajetreado — **hectically** [-tɪkli] *adv*
he'd [ˈhiːd] (*contraction of* **he had** *or* **he would**) → **have, would**
hedge[1] [ˈhɛdʒ] *v* **hedged; hedging** *vt* **1** : cercar con un seto **2 to hedge one's bet** : cubrirse — *vi* **1** : dar rodeos, contestar con evasivas **2 to hedge against** : cubrirse contra, protegerse contra
hedge[2] *n* **1** : seto *m* vivo **2** SAFEGUARD : salvaguardia *f*, protección *f*
hedgehog [ˈhɛdʒˌhɔg, -hɑg] *n* : erizo *m*
heed[1] [ˈhiːd] *vt* : prestar atención a, hacer caso de
heed[2] *n* : atención *f*
heedless [ˈhiːdləs] *adj* : descuidado, despreocupado, inconsciente <to be heedless of : hacer caso omiso de> — **heedlessly** *adv*
heel[1] [ˈhiːl] *vi* : inclinarse
heel[2] *n* : talón *m* (del pie), tacón *m* (de calzado)
heft [ˈhɛft] *vt* : sopesar
hefty [ˈhɛfti] *adj* **heftier; -est** : robusto, fornido, pesado
heifer [ˈhɛfər] *n* : novilla *f*
height [ˈhaɪt] *n* **1** PEAK : cumbre *f*, cima *f*, punto *m* alto <at the height of her career : en la cumbre de su carrera> <the height of stupidity : el colmo de la estupidez> **2** TALLNESS : estatura *f* (de una persona), altura *f* (de un objeto) **3** ALTITUDE : altura *f*
heighten [ˈhaɪtən] *vt* **1** : hacer más alto **2** INTENSIFY : aumentar, intensificar — *vi* : aumentarse, intensificarse
heinous [ˈheɪnəs] *adj* : atroz, abominable, nefando
heir [ˈær] *n* : heredero *m*, -ra *f*
heiress [ˈærəs] *n* : heredera *f*
heirloom [ˈærˌluːm] *n* : reliquia *f* de familia
held → **hold**
helicopter [ˈhɛləˌkɑptər] *n* : helicóptero *m*
helium [ˈhiːliəm] *n* : helio *m*
hell [ˈhɛl] *n* : infierno *m*
he'll [ˈhiːl, ˈhɪl] (*contraction of* **he shall** *or* **he will**) → **shall, will**
hellish [ˈhɛlɪʃ] *adj* : horroroso, infernal
hello [həˈloː, hɛ-] *interj* : ¡hola!
helm [ˈhɛlm] *n* **1** : timón *m* **2 to take the helm** : tomar el mando
helmet [ˈhɛlmət] *n* : casco *m*
help[1] [ˈhɛlp] *vt* **1** AID, ASSIST : ayudar, auxiliar, socorrer, asistir **2** ALLEVIATE : aliviar **3** SERVE : servir <help yourself! : ¡sírvete!> **4** AVOID : evitar <it can't be helped : no lo podemos evitar, no hay más remedio> <I couldn't help smiling : no pude menos que sonreír>
help[2] *n* **1** ASSISTANCE : ayuda *f* <help! : ¡socorro!, ¡auxilio!> **2** STAFF : personal *m* (en una oficina), servicio *m* doméstico
helper [ˈhɛlpər] *n* : ayudante *mf*
helpful [ˈhɛlpfəl] *adj* **1** OBLIGING : servicial, amable, atento **2** USEFUL : útil, práctico — **helpfully** *adv*
helpfulness [ˈhɛlpfəlnəs] *n* **1** KINDNESS : bondad *f*, amabilidad *f* **2** USEFULNESS : utilidad *f*
helping [ˈhɛlpɪŋ] *n* : porción *f*
helpless [ˈhɛlpləs] *adj* **1** POWERLESS : incapaz, impotente **2** DEFENSELESS : indefenso
helplessly [ˈhɛlpləsli] *adv* : en vano, inútilmente
helplessness [ˈhɛlpləsnəs] *n* POWERLESSNESS : incapacidad *f*, impotencia *f*
helter-skelter [ˌhɛltərˈskɛltər] *adv* : atropelladamente, precipitadamente
hem[1] [ˈhɛm] *vt* **hemmed; hemming 1** : dobladillar **2 to hem in** : encerrar
hem[2] *n* : dobladillo *m*, bastilla *f*
hemisphere [ˈhɛməˌsfɪr] *n* : hemisferio *m*
hemispheric [ˌhɛməˈsfɪrɪk, -ˈsfɛr-] *or* **hemispherical** [-ɪkəl] *adj* : hemisférico
hemlock [ˈhɛmˌlɑk] *n* : cicuta *f*
hemoglobin [ˈhiːməˌgloːbən] *n* : hemoglobina *f*
hemophilia [ˌhiːməˈfɪliə] *n* : hemofilia *f*
hemorrhage[1] [ˈhɛmərɪdʒ] *vi* **-rhaged; -rhaging** : sufrir una hemorragia
hemorrhage[2] *n* : hemorragia *f*
hemorrhoids [ˈhɛməˌrɔɪdz, ˈhɛmˌrɔɪdz] *npl* : hemorroides *fpl*, almorranas *fpl*
hemp [ˈhɛmp] *n* : cáñamo *m*
hen [ˈhɛn] *n* : gallina *f*
hence [ˈhɛnts] *adv* **1** : de aquí, de ahí <10 years hence : de aquí a 10 años> <a dog bit me, hence my dislike of animals : un perro me mordió, de ahí mi aversión a los animales> **2** THEREFORE : por lo tanto, por consiguiente
henceforth [ˈhɛntsˌforθ, ˌhɛntsˈ-] *adv* : de ahora en adelante
henchman [ˈhɛntʃmən] *n, pl* **-men** [-mən, -ˌmɛn] : secuaz *mf*, esbirro *m*
henpeck [ˈhɛnˌpɛk] *vt* : dominar (al marido)
hepatitis [ˌhɛpəˈtaɪtəs] *n, pl* **-titides** [-ˈtɪtəˌdiːz] : hepatitis *f*
her[1] [ˈhər] *adj* : su, sus, de ella <her house : su casa, la casa de ella>
her[2] [ˈhər, ər] *pron* **1** (*used as direct object*) : la <I saw her yesterday : la vi ayer> **2** (*used as indirect object*) : le, se <he gave her the book : le dio el libro> <he sent it to her : se lo mandó> **3** (*used as object of a preposition*) : ella <we did it for her : lo hicimos por ella> <taller than her : más alto que ella>

herald[1] [ˈhɛrəld] *vt* ANNOUNCE **:** anunciar, proclamar

herald[2] *n* **1** MESSENGER **:** heraldo *m* **2** HARBINGER **:** precursor *m*

heraldic [hɛˈrældɪk, hə-] *adj* **:** heráldico

heraldry [ˈhɛrəldri] *n, pl* **-ries :** heráldica *f*

herb [ˈərb, ˈhərb] *n* **:** hierba *f*

herbal [ˈərbəl, ˈhər-] *adj* **:** herbario

herbicide [ˈərbəˌsaɪd, ˈhər-] *n* **:** herbicida *m*

herbivore [ˈərbəˌvor, ˈhər-] *n* **:** herbívoro *m*

herbivorous [ˌərˈbɪvərəs, ˌhər-] *adj* **:** herbívoro

herculean [ˌhərkjəˈliːən, ˌhərˈkjuːliən] *adj* **:** hercúleo, sobrehumano

herd[1] [ˈhərd] *vt* **:** reunir en manada, conducir en manada — *vi* **:** ir en manada (dícese de los animales), apiñarse (dícese de la gente)

herd[2] *n* **:** manada *f*

herder [ˈhərdər] → **herdsman**

herdsman [ˈhərdzmən] *n, pl* **-men** [-mən, -ˌmɛn] **:** vaquero *m* (de ganado), pastor *m* (de ovejas)

here [ˈhɪr] *adv* **1 :** aquí, acá <come here! : ¡ven acá!> <right here : aquí mismo> **2** NOW **:** en este momento, ahora, ya <here he comes : ya viene> <here it's three o'clock (already) : ahora son las tres> **3 :** en este punto <here we agree : estamos de acuerdo en este punto> **4 here you are! :** ¡toma!

hereabouts [ˈhɪrəˌbaʊts] *or* **hereabout** [-ˌbaʊt] *adv* **:** por aquí (cerca)

hereafter[1] [hɪrˈæftər] *adv* **1 :** de aquí en adelante, a continuación **2 :** en el futuro

hereafter[2] *n* **the hereafter :** el más allá

hereby [hɪrˈbaɪ] *adv* **:** por este medio

hereditary [həˈrɛdəˌtɛri] *adj* **:** hereditario

heredity [həˈrɛdət̬i] *n* **:** herencia *f*

herein [hɪrˈɪn] *adv* **:** aquí

hereof [hɪrˈʌv] *adv* **:** de aquí

hereon [hɪrˈɑn, -ˈɔn] *adv* **:** sobre esto

heresy [ˈhɛrəsi] *n, pl* **-sies :** herejía *f*

heretic [ˈhɛrəˌtɪk] *n* **:** hereje *mf*

heretical [həˈrɛt̬ɪkəl] *adj* **:** herético

hereto [hɪrˈtuː] *adv* **:** a esto

heretofore [ˈhɪrt̬əˌfor] *adv* HITHERTO **:** hasta ahora

hereunder [hɪrˈʌndər] *adv* **:** a continuación, abajo

hereupon [hɪrəˈpɑn, -ˈpɔn] *adv* **:** con esto, en ese momento

herewith [hɪrˈwɪθ] *adv* **:** adjunto

heritage [ˈhɛrət̬ɪdʒ] *n* **:** patrimonio *m* (nacional)

hermaphrodite [hərˈmæfrəˌdaɪt] *n* **:** hermafrodita *mf*

hermetic [hərˈmɛt̬ɪk] *adj* **:** hermético — **hermetically** [-t̬ɪkli] *adv*

hermit [ˈhərmət] *n* **:** ermitaño *m*, -ña *f*; eremita *mf*

hernia [ˈhərniə] *n, pl* **-nias** *or* **-niae** [-niˌiː, -niˌaɪ] **:** hernia *f*

hero [ˈhiːˌroː, ˈhɪrˌoː] *n, pl* **-roes 1 :** héroe *m* **2** PROTAGONIST **:** protagonista *mf*

heroic [hɪˈroːɪk] *adj* **:** heroico — **heroically** [-ɪkli] *adv*

heroics [hɪˈroːɪks] *npl* **:** actos *mpl* heroicos

heroin [ˈhɛroən] *n* **:** heroína *f*

heroine [ˈhɛroən] *n* **1 :** heroína *f* **2** PROTAGONIST **:** protagonista *f*

heroism [ˈhɛroˌɪzəm] *n* **:** heroísmo *m*

heron [ˈhɛrən] *n* **:** garza *f*

herpes [ˈhərˌpiːz] *n* **:** herpes *m*

herpetology [ˌhərpəˈtɑlədʒi] *n* **:** herpetología *f*

herring [ˈhɛrɪŋ] *n, pl* **-ring** *or* **-rings :** arenque *m*

hers [ˈhərz] *pron* **:** suyo, -ya; suyos, -yas; de ella <these shoes are hers : estos zapatos son suyos> <hers are bigger : los de ella son más grandes>

herself [hərˈsɛlf] *pron* **1** (*used reflexively*) **:** se <she dressed herself : se vistió> **2** (*used emphatically*) **:** ella misma <she fixed it herself : lo arregló ella misma, lo arregló por sí sola>

hertz [ˈhərts, ˈhɛrts] *ns & pl* **:** hercio *m*

he's [ˈhiːz] (*contraction of* **he is** *or* **he has**) → **be, have**

hesitancy [ˈhɛzət̬əntsi] *n, pl* **-cies :** vacilación *f*, titubeo *m*, indecisión *f*

hesitant [ˈhɛzət̬ənt] *adj* **:** titubeante, vacilante — **hesitantly** *adv*

hesitate [ˈhɛzəˌteɪt] *vi* **-tated; -tating :** vacilar, titubear

hesitation [ˌhɛzəˈteɪʃən] *n* **:** vacilación *f*, indecisión *f*, titubeo *m*

heterogeneous [ˌhɛt̬ərəˈdʒiːniəs, -njəs] *adj* **:** heterogéneo

heterosexual[1] [ˌhɛt̬əroˈsɛkʃʊəl] *adj* **:** heterosexual

heterosexual[2] *n* **:** heterosexual *mf*

heterosexuality [ˌhɛt̬əroˌsɛkʃʊˈælət̬i] *n* **:** heterosexualidad *f*

hew [ˈhjuː] *v* **hewed; hewed** *or* **hewn** [ˈhjuːn]; **hewing** *vt* **1** CUT **:** cortar, talar (árboles) **2** SHAPE **:** labrar, tallar — *vi* CONFORM **:** conformarse, ceñirse

hex[1] [ˈhɛks] *vt* **:** hacerle un maleficio (a alguien)

hex[2] *n* **:** maleficio *m*

hexagon [ˈhɛksəˌgɑn] *n* **:** hexágono *m*

hexagonal [hɛkˈsægənəl] *adj* **:** hexagonal

hey [ˈheɪ] *interj* **:** ¡eh!, ¡oye!

heyday [ˈheɪˌdeɪ] *n* **:** auge *m*, apogeo *m*

hi [ˈhaɪ] *interj* **:** ¡hola!

hiatus [haɪˈeɪt̬əs] *n* **1 :** hiato *m* **2** PAUSE **:** pausa *f*

hibernate [ˈhaɪbərˌneɪt] *vi* **-nated; -nating :** hibernar, invernar

hibernation [ˌhaɪbərˈneɪʃən] *n* **:** hibernación *f*

hiccup[1] [ˈhɪkəp] *vi* **-cuped; -cuping :** hipar, tener hipo

hiccup[2] *n* : hipo *m* <to have the hiccups : tener hipo>

hick [ˈhɪk] *n* BUMPKIN : palurdo *m*, -da *f*

hickory [ˈhɪkəri] *n, pl* **-ries** : nogal *m* americano

hidden [ˈhɪdən] *adj* : oculto

hide[1] [ˈhaɪd] *v* **hid** [ˈhɪd]; **hidden** [ˈhɪdən] *or* **hid; hiding** *vt* **1** CONCEAL : esconder **2** ocultar <to hide one's motives : ocultar uno sus motivos> **3** SCREEN : tapar, no dejar ver — *vi* : esconderse

hide[2] *n* : piel *f*, cuero *m* <to save one's hide : salvar el pellejo>

hide–and–seek [ˈhaɪdənd*ˈsiːk] *n* **to play hide–and–seek** : jugar a las escondidas

hidebound [ˈhaɪdˌbaʊnd] *adj* : rígido, conservador

hideous [ˈhɪdiəs] *adj* : horrible, horroroso, espantoso — **hideously** *adv*

hideout [ˈhaɪdˌaʊt] *n* : guarida *f*, escondrijo *m*

hierarchical [ˌhaɪəˈrɑrkɪkəl] *adj* : jerárquico

hierarchy [ˈhaɪəˌrɑrki] *n, pl* **-chies** : jerarquía *f*

hieroglyphic [ˌhaɪərəˈglɪfɪk] *n* : jeroglífico *m*

hi–fi [ˈhaɪˈfaɪ] *n* **1** → **high fidelity 2** : equipo *m* de alta fidelidad

high[1] [ˈhaɪ] *adv* : alto

high[2] *adj* **1** TALL : alto <a high wall : una pared alta> **2** ELEVATED : alto, elevado <high prices : precios elevados> <high blood pressure : presión alta> **3** GREAT, IMPORTANT : grande, importante, alto <a high number : un número grande> <high society : alta sociedad> <high hopes : grandes esperanzas> **4** : alto (en música) **5** INTOXICATED : borracho, drogado

high[3] *n* **1** : récord *m*, punto *m* máximo <to reach an all-time high : batir el récord> **2** : zona *f* de alta presión (en meteorología) **3** *or* **high gear** : directa *f* **4 on high** : en las alturas

highbrow [ˈhaɪˌbraʊ] *n* : intelectual *mf*

higher [ˈhaɪər] *adj* : superior

high fidelity *n* : alta fidelidad *f*

high–flown [ˈhaɪˈfloːn] *adj* : altisonante

high–handed [ˈhaɪˈhændəd] *adj* : arbitrario

highlands [ˈhaɪləndz] *npl* : tierras *fpl* altas, altiplano *m*

highlight[1] [ˈhaɪˌlaɪt] *vt* **1** EMPHASIZE : destacar, poner en relieve, subrayar **2** : ser el punto culminante de

highlight[2] *n* : punto *m* culminante

highly [ˈhaɪli] *adv* **1** VERY : muy, sumamente **2** FAVORABLY : muy bien <to speak highly of : hablar muy bien de> <to think highly of : tener en mucho a>

highness [ˈhaɪnəs] *n* **1** HEIGHT : altura *f* **2 Highness** : Alteza *f* <Your Royal Highness : Su Alteza Real>

high–rise [ˈhaɪˌraɪz] *adj* : alto, de muchas plantas

high school *n* : escuela *f* superior, escuela *f* secundaria

high seas *npl* : alta mar *f*

high–spirited [ˈhaɪˈspɪrəṭəd] *adj* : vivaz, muy animado, brioso

high–strung [ˌhaɪˈstrʌŋ] *adj* : nervioso, excitable

highway [ˈhaɪˌweɪ] *n* : carretera *f*

highwayman [ˈhaɪˌweɪmən] *n, pl* **-men** [- mən, -ˌmɛn] : salteador *m* (de caminos), bandido *m*

hijack[1] [ˈhaɪˌdʒæk] *vt* : secuestrar

hijack[2] *n* : secuestro *m*

hijacker [ˈhaɪˌdʒækər] *n* : secuestrador *m*, -dora *f*

hike[1] [ˈhaɪk] *v* **hiked; hiking** *vi* : hacer una caminata — *vt* RAISE : subir

hike[2] *n* **1** : caminata *f*, excursión *f* **2** INCREASE : subida *f* (de precios)

hiker [ˈhaɪkər] *n* : excursionista *mf*

hilarious [hɪˈlæriəs, haɪˈ-] *adj* : muy divertido, hilarante

hilarity [hɪˈlærəṭi, haɪ-] *n* : hilaridad *f*

hill [ˈhɪl] *n* **1** : colina *f*, cerro *m* **2** SLOPE : cuesta *f*, pendiente *f*

hillbilly [ˈhɪlˌbɪli] *n, pl* **-lies** : palurdo *m*, -da *f* (de las montañas)

hillock [ˈhɪlək] *n* : loma *f*, altozano *m*, otero *m*

hillside [ˈhɪlˌsaɪd] *n* : ladera *f*, cuesta *f*

hilltop [ˈhɪlˌtɑp] *n* : cima *f*, cumbre *f*

hilly [ˈhɪli] *adj* **hillier; -est** : montañoso, accidentado

hilt [ˈhɪlt] *n* : puño *m*, empuñadura *f*

him [ˈhɪm, əm] *pron* **1** (*used as direct object*) : lo <I found him : lo encontré> **2** (*used as indirect object*) : le, se <we gave him a present : le dimos un regalo> <I sent it to him : se lo mandé> **3** (*used as object of a preposition*) : él <she was thinking of him : pensaba en él> <younger than him : más joven que él>

himself [hɪmˈsɛlf] *pron* **1** (*used reflexively*) : se <he washed himself : se lavó> **2** (*used emphatically*) : él mismo <he did it himself : lo hizo él mismo, lo hizo por sí solo>

hind[1] [ˈhaɪnd] *adj* : trasero, posterior <hind legs : patas traseras>

hind[2] *n* : cierva *f*

hinder [ˈhɪndər] *vt* : dificultar, impedir, estorbar

hindquarters [ˈhaɪndˌkwɔrṭərz] *npl* : cuartos *mpl* traseros

hindrance [ˈhɪndrən*t*s] *n* : estorbo *m*, obstáculo *m*, impedimento *m*

hindsight [ˈhaɪndˌsaɪt] *n* : retrospectiva *f* <with the benefit of hindsight : en retrospectiva, con la perspectiva que da la experiencia>

Hindu[1] [ˈhɪnˌduː] *adj* : hindú

Hindu[2] *n* : hindú *mf*

Hinduism [ˈhɪnduːˌɪzəm] *n* : hinduismo *m*

hinge[1] ['hɪndʒ] *v* **hinged; hinging** *vt* : unir con bisagras — *vi* **to hinge on** : depender de

hinge[2] *n* : bisagra *f,* gozne *m*

hint[1] ['hɪnt] *vt* : insinuar, dar a entender — *vi* : soltar indirectas

hint[2] *n* **1** INSINUATION : insinuación *f,* indirecta *f* **2** TIP : consejo *m,* sugerencia *f* **3** TRACE : pizca *f,* indicio *m*

hinterland ['hɪntər,lænd, -lənd] *n* : interior *m* (de un país)

hip ['hɪp] *n* : cadera *f*

hippopotamus [,hɪpə'pɑtəməs] *n, pl* **-muses** *or* **-mi** [-,maɪ] : hipopótamo *m*

hippo ['hɪpo:] *n, pl* **hippos** → **hippopotamus**

hire[1] ['haɪr] *vt* **hired; hiring 1** EMPLOY : contratar, emplear **2** RENT : alquilar, arrendar

hire[2] *n* **1** RENT : alquiler *m* <for hire : se alquila> **2** WAGES : paga *f,* sueldo *m* **3** EMPLOYEE : empleado *m,* -da *f*

his[1] ['hɪz, ɪz] *adj* : su, sus, de él <his hat : su sombrero, el sombrero de él>

his[2] *pron* : suyo, -ya; suyos, suyas; de él <the decision is his : la decisión es suya> <it's his, not hers : es de él, no de ella>

Hispanic[1] [hɪ'spænɪk] *adj* : hispano, hispánico

Hispanic[2] *n* : hispano *m,* -na *f;* hispánico *m,* -ca *f*

hiss[1] ['hɪs] *vi* : sisear, silbar — *vt* : decir entre dientes

hiss[2] *n* : siseo *m,* silbido *m*

historian [hɪ'stɔriən] *n* : historiador *m,* -dora *f*

historic [hɪ'stɔrɪk] *or* **historical** [-ɪkəl] *adj* : histórico — **historically** [-ɪkli] *adv*

history ['hɪstəri] *n, pl* **-ries 1** : historia *f* **2** RECORD : historial *m*

histrionics [,hɪstri'ɑnɪks] *ns & pl* : histrionismo *m*

hit[1] ['hɪt] *v* **hit; hitting** *vt* **1** STRIKE : golpear, pegar, batear (una pelota) <he hit the dog : le pegó al perro> **2** : chocar contra, dar con, dar en (el blanco) <the car hit a tree : el coche chocó contra un árbol> **3** AFFECT : afectar <the news hit us hard : la noticia nos afectó mucho> **4** ENCOUNTER : tropezar con, toparse con <to hit a snag : tropezar con un obstáculo> **5** REACH : llegar a, alcanzar <the price hit $10 a pound : el precio alcanzó los $10 dólares por libra> <to hit town : llegar a la ciudad> <to hit the headlines : ser noticia> **6 to hit on** *or* **to hit upon** : dar con — *vi* : golpear

hit[2] *n* **1** BLOW : golpe *m* **2** : impacto *m* (de un arma) **3** SUCCESS : éxito *m*

hitch[1] ['hɪtʃ] *vt* **1** : mover con sacudidas **2** ATTACH : enganchar, atar, amarrar **3** → **hitchhike 4 to hitch up** : subirse (los pantalones, etc.)

hitch[2] *n* **1** JERK : tirón *m,* jalón *m* **2** OBSTACLE : obstáculo *m,* impedimento *m,* tropiezo *m*

hitchhike ['hɪtʃ,haɪk] *vi* **-hiked; -hiking** : hacer autostop, ir de aventón *Col, Mex fam*

hitchhiker ['hɪtʃ,haɪkər] *n* : autostopista *mf*

hither ['hɪðər] *adv* : acá, por aquí

hitherto ['hɪðər,tu:, ,hɪðər'-] *adv* : hasta ahora

hitter ['hɪt̬ər] *n* BATTER : bateador *m,* -dora *f*

HIV [,eɪtʃ,aɪ'vi:] *n* : VIH *m,* virus *m* del sida

hive ['haɪv] *n* **1** : colmena *f* **2** SWARM : enjambre *m* **3** : lugar *m* muy activo <a hive of activity : un hervidero de actividad>

hives ['haɪvz] *ns & pl* : urticaria *f*

hoard[1] ['hord] *vt* : acumular, atesorar

hoard[2] *n* : tesoro *m,* reserva *f,* provisión *f*

hoarfrost ['hor,frɔst] *n* : escarcha *f*

hoarse ['hors] *adj* **hoarser; -est** : ronco — **hoarsely** *adv*

hoarseness ['horsnəs] *n* : ronquera *f*

hoary ['hori] *adj* **hoarier; -est 1** : cano, canoso **2** OLD : vetusto, antiguo

hoax[1] ['ho:ks] *vt* : engañar, embaucar, bromar

hoax[2] *n* : engaño *m,* broma *f*

hobble[1] ['hɑbəl] *v* **-bled; -bling** *vi* LIMP : cojear, renguear — *vt* : manear (un animal)

hobble[2] *n* **1** LIMP : cojera *f,* rengo *m* **2** : maniota *f* (para un animal)

hobby ['hɑbi] *n, pl* **-bies** : pasatiempo *m,* afición *f*

hobgoblin ['hɑb,gɑblən] *n* : duende *m*

hobnail ['hɑb,neɪl] *n* : tachuela *f*

hobnob ['hɑb,nɑb] *vi* **-nobbed; -nobbing** : codearse

hobo ['ho:,bo:] *n, pl* **-boes** : vagabundo *m,* -da *f*

hock[1] ['hɑk] *vt* PAWN : empeñar

hock[2] *n* **in hock** : empeñado

hockey ['hɑki] *n* : hockey *m*

hod ['hɑd] *n* : capacho *m* (de albañil)

hodgepodge ['hɑdʒ,pɑdʒ] *n* : mezcolanza *f*

hoe[1] ['ho:] *vt* **hoed; hoeing** : azadonar

hoe[2] *n* : azada *f,* azadón *m*

hog[1] ['hɔg, 'hɑg] *vt* **hogged; hogging** : acaparar, monopolizar

hog[2] *n* **1** PIG : cerdo *m,* -da *f* **2** GLUTTON : glotón *m,* -tona *f*

hogshead ['hɔgz,hɛd, 'hɑgz-] *n* : tonel *m*

hoist[1] ['hɔɪst] *vt* : levantar, alzar, izar (una bandera, una vela)

hoist[2] *n* : grúa *f*

hold[1] ['ho:ld] *v* **held** ['hɛld]; **holding** *vt* **1** POSSESS : tener <to hold office : ocupar un puesto> **2** RESTRAIN : detener, controlar <to hold one's temper : controlar su mal genio> **3** CLASP, GRASP : agarrar, coger <to hold hands : agarrarse de la mano> **4** : sujetar, mantener fijo <hold this nail for me : sujétame este clavo> **5** CONTAIN : contener, dar cabida a **6** SUPPORT : aguantar, sostener **7** REGARD : considerar, tener <he held me responsible : me consideró responsable> **8** CONDUCT : celebrar (una reunión), realizar (un evento), mantener (una conversación) — *vi* **1** : aguantar, resistir <the rope will hold : la cuerda resistirá> **2** : ser válido, valer <my offer still holds : mi oferta todavía es válida> **3 to hold forth** : perorar, arengar **4 to hold to** : mantenerse firme en **5 to hold with** : estar de acuerdo con

hold[2] *n* **1** GRIP : agarre *m,* llave *f* (en deportes) **2** CONTROL : control *m,* dominio *m* <to get hold of oneself : controlarse> **3** DELAY : demora *f* <to put on hold : suspender temporalmente> **4** : bodega *f* (en un barco o un avión) **5 to get hold of** : conseguir, localizar

holder [ˈhoːldər] *n* : poseedor *m,* -dora *f;* titular *mf*

holdings [ˈhoːldɪŋz] *npl* : propiedades *fpl*

hold out *vi* **1** LAST : aguantar, durar **2** RESIST : resistir

holdup [ˈhoːldˌʌp] *n* **1** ROBBERY : atraco *m* **2** DELAY : retraso *m,* demora *f*

hold up *vt* **1** ROB : robarle (a alguien), atracar, asaltar **2** DELAY : retrasar

hole [ˈhoːl] *n* : agujero *m,* hoyo *m*

holiday [ˈhɑləˌdeɪ] *n* **1** : día *m* feriado, fiesta *f* **2** VACATION : vacaciones *fpl*

holiness [ˈhoːlinəs] *n* **1** : santidad *f* **2 His Holiness** : Su Santidad

holistic [hoːˈlɪstɪk] *adj* : holístico

holler[1] [ˈhɑlər] *vi* : gritar, chillar

holler[2] *n* : grito *m,* chillido *m*

hollow[1] [ˈhɑˌloː] *vt or* **to hollow out** : ahuecar

hollow[2] *adj* **-lower; -est 1** : hueco, hundido (dícese de las mejillas, etc.), cavernoso (dícese de un sonido) **2** EMPTY, FALSE : vacío, falso

hollow[3] *n* **1** CAVITY : hueco *m,* depresión *f,* cavidad *f* **2** VALLEY : hondonada *f,* valle *m*

hollowness [ˈhɑˌloːnəs] *n* **1** HOLLOW : hueco *m,* cavidad *f* **2** FALSENESS : falsedad *f* **3** EMPTINESS : vacuidad *f*

holly [ˈhɑli] *n, pl* **-lies** : acebo *m*

hollyhock [ˈhɑliˌhɑk] *n* : malvarrosa *f*

holocaust [ˈhɑləˌkɔst, ˈhoː-, ˈhɔ-] *n* : holocausto *m*

holster [ˈhoːlstər] *n* : pistolera *f*

holy [ˈhoːli] *adj* **-lier; -est** : santo, sagrado

Holy Ghost → **Holy Spirit**

Holy Spirit *n* **the Holy Spirit** : el Espíritu Santo

homage [ˈɑmɪdʒ, ˈhɑ-] *n* : homenaje *m*

home [ˈhoːm] *n* **1** : casa *f,* hogar *m,* domicilio *m* <to feel at home : sentirse en casa> **2** INSTITUTION : residencia *f,* asilo *m*

homecoming [ˈhoːmˌkʌmɪŋ] *n* : regreso *m* (a casa)

homegrown [ˈhoːmˈgroːn] *adj* **1** : de cosecha propia **2** LOCAL : local

homeland [ˈhoːmˌlænd] *n* : patria *f,* tierra *f* natal, terruño *m*

homeless [ˈhoːmləs] *adj* : sin hogar, sin techo

homely [ˈhoːmli] *adj* **-lier; -est 1** DOMESTIC : casero, hogareño **2** UGLY : feo, poco atractivo

homemade [ˈhoːmˈmeɪd] *adj* : casero, hecho en casa

homemaker [ˈhoːmˌmeɪkər] *n* : ama *f* de casa, persona *f* que se ocupa de la casa

home plate *n* : base *f* del bateador

home run *n* : jonrón *m*

homesick [ˈhoːmˌsɪk] *adj* : nostálgico <to be homesick : echar de menos a la familia>

homesickness [ˈhoːmˌsɪknəs] *n* : nostalgia *f,* morriña *f*

homespun [ˈhoːmˌspʌn] *adj* : simple, sencillo

homestead [ˈhoːmˌstɛd] *n* : estancia *f,* hacienda *f*

homeward[1] [ˈhoːmwərd] *or* **homewards** [-wərdz] *adv* : de vuelta a casa, hacia casa

homeward[2] *adj* : de vuelta, de regreso

homework [ˈhoːmˌwərk] *n* : tarea *f,* deberes *mpl Spain,* asignación *f PRi*

homey [ˈhoːmi] *adj* **homier; -est** : hogareño

homicidal [ˌhɑməˈsaɪdəl, ˌhoː-] *adj* : homicida

homicide [ˈhɑməˌsaɪd, ˈhoː-] *n* : homicidio *m*

hominy [ˈhɑməni] *n* : maíz *m* descascarillado

homogeneous [ˌhoːməˈdʒiːniəs, -njəs] *adj* : homogéneo — **homogeneously** *adv*

homogenize [hoːˈmɑdʒəˌnaɪz, hə-] *vt* **-nized; -nizing** : homogeneizar

homograph [ˈhɑməˌgræf, ˈhoː-] *n* : homógrafo *m*

homonym [ˈhɑməˌnɪm, ˈhoː-] *n* : homónimo *m*

homophone [ˈhɑməˌfoːn, ˈhoː-] *n* : homófono *m*

homosexual[1] [ˌhoːməˈsɛkʃʊəl] *adj* : homosexual

homosexual[2] *n* : homosexual *mf*

homosexuality [ˌhoːməˌsɛkʃʊˈæləṭi] *n* : homosexualidad *f*

Honduran [hɑnˈdʊrən, -ˈdjʊr-] *n* : hondureño *m,* -ña *f* — **Honduran** *adj*

hone [ˈhoːn] *vt* **honed; honing** : afilar

honest [ˈɑnəst] *adj* : honesto, honrado — **honestly** *adv*

honesty [ˈɑnəsti] *n, pl* **-ties** : honestidad *f,* honradez *f*

honey [ˈhʌni] *n, pl* **-eys** : miel *f*

honeybee [ˈhʌniˌbiː] *n* : abeja *f*

honeycomb [ˈhʌniˌkoːm] *n* : panal *m*

honeymoon[1] ['hʌni,muːn] *vi* : pasar la luna de miel
honeymoon[2] *n* : luna *f* de miel
honeysuckle ['hʌni,sʌkəl] *n* : madreselva *f*
honk[1] ['haŋk, 'hɔŋk] *vi* **1** : graznar (dícese del ganso) **2** : tocar la bocina (dícese de un vehículo), pitar
honk[2] *n* : graznido *m* (del ganso), bocinazo *m* (de un vehículo)
honor[1] ['ɑnər] *vt* **1** RESPECT : honrar **2** : cumplir con <to honor one's word : cumplir con su palabra> **3** : aceptar (un cheque, etc.)
honor[2] *n* **1** : honor *m* <in honor of : en honor de> **2 honors** *npl* AWARDS : honores *mpl*, condecoraciones *fpl* **3 Your Honor** : Su Señoría
honorable ['ɑnərəbəl] *adj* : honorable, honroso — **honorably** [-bli] *adv*
honorary ['ɑnə,rɛri] *adj* : honorario
hood ['hʊd] *n* **1** : capucha *f* **2** : capó *m*, bonete *m Car* (de un automóvil)
hooded ['hʊdəd] *adj* : encapuchado
hoodlum ['hʊdləm, 'huːd-] *n* THUG : maleante *mf*, matón *m*
hoodwink ['hʊd,wɪŋk] *vt* : engañar
hoof ['hʊf, 'huːf] *n, pl* **hooves** ['hʊvz, 'huːvz] *or* **hoofs** : pezuña *f*, casco *m*
hoofed ['hʊft, 'huːft] *adj* : ungulado
hook[1] ['hʊk] *vt* : enganchar — *vi* : abrocharse, engancharse
hook[2] *n* : gancho *m*, percha *f*
hookworm ['hʊk,wərm] *n* : anquilostoma *m*
hooligan ['huːlɪgən] *n* : gamberro *m*, -rra *f*
hoop ['huːp] *n* : aro *m*
hooray [hʊ'reɪ] → **hurrah**
hoot[1] ['huːt] *vi* **1** SHOUT : gritar <to hoot with laughter : morirse de risa, reírse a carcajadas> **2** : ulular (dícese de un búho), tocar la bocina (dícese de un vehículo), silbar (dícese de un tren o un barco)
hoot[2] *n* **1** : ululato *m* (de un búho), silbido *m* (de un tren), bocinazo *m* (de un vehículo) **2** GUFFAW : carcajada *f*, risotada *f* **3 I don't give a hoot** : me vale un comino, me importa un pito
hop[1] ['hɑp] *vi* **hopped; hopping** : brincar, saltar
hop[2] *n* **1** LEAP : salto *m*, brinco *m* **2** FLIGHT : vuelo *m* corto **3** : lúpulo *m* (planta)
hope[1] ['hoːp] *v* **hoped; hoping** *vi* : esperar — *vt* : esperar que <we hope she comes : esperamos que venga> <I hope not : espero que no>
hope[2] *n* : esperanza *f*
hopeful ['hoːpfəl] *adj* : esperanzado — **hopefully** *adv*
hopeless ['hoːpləs] *adj* **1** DESPAIRING : desesperado **2** IMPOSSIBLE : imposible <a hopeless case : un caso perdido>
hopelessly ['hoːpləsli] *adv* **1** : sin esperanzas, desesperadamente **2** COMPLETELY : totalmente, completamente **3** IMPOSSIBLY : imposiblemente
hopelessness ['hoːpləsnəs] *n* : desesperanza *f*
hopper ['hɑpər] *n* : tolva *f*
hopscotch ['hɑp,skɑtʃ] *n* : tejo *m*
horde ['hord] *n* : horda *f*, multitud *f*
horizon [hə'raɪzən] *n* : horizonte *m*
horizontal [,hɔrə'zɑntəl] *adj* : horizontal — **horizontally** *adv*
hormone ['hɔr,moːn] *n* : hormona *f* — **hormonal** [hɔr'moːnəl] *adj*
horn ['hɔrn] *n* **1** : cuerno *m* (de un toro, una vaca, etc.) **2** : cuerno *m*, trompa *f* (instrumento musical) **3** : bocina *f*, claxon *m* (de un vehículo)
horned ['hɔrnd, 'hɔrnəd] *adj* : cornudo, astado, con cuernos
hornet ['hɔrnət] *n* : avispón *m*
horn of plenty → **cornucopia**
horny ['hɔrni] *adj* **hornier; -est** CALLOUS : calloso
horoscope ['hɔrə,skoːp] *n* : horóscopo *m*
horrendous [hɔ'rɛndəs] *adj* : horrendo, horroroso, atroz
horrible ['hɔrəbəl] *adj* : horrible, espantoso, horroroso — **horribly** [-bli] *adv*
horrid ['hɔrɪd] *adj* : horroroso, horrible — **horridly** *adv*
horrify ['hɔrə,faɪ] *vt* **-fied; -fying** : horrorizar
horrifying ['hɔrə,faɪɪŋ] *adj* : horripilante, horroroso
horror ['hɔrər] *n* : horror *m*
hors d'oeuvre [ɔr'dərv] *n, pl* **hors d'oeuvres** [-'dərvz] : entremés *m*
horse ['hɔrs] *n* : caballo *m*
horseback ['hɔrs,bæk] *n* **on ~** : a caballo
horse chestnut *n* : castaña *f* de Indias
horsefly ['hɔrs,flaɪ] *n, pl* **-flies** : tábano *m*
horsehair ['hɔrs,hær] *n* : crin *f*
horseman ['hɔrsmən] *n, pl* **-men** [-mən, -,mɛn] : jinete *m*, caballista *m*
horsemanship ['hɔrsmən,ʃɪp] *n* : equitación *f*
horseplay ['hɔrs,pleɪ] *n* : payasadas *fpl*
horsepower ['hɔrs,paʊər] *n* : caballo *m* de fuerza
horseradish ['hɔrs,rædɪʃ] *n* : rábano *m* picante
horseshoe ['hɔrs,ʃuː] *n* : herradura *f*
horsewhip ['hɔrs,*h*wɪp] *vt* **-whipped; -whipping** : azotar, darle fuetazos (a alguien)
horsewoman ['hɔrs,wʊmən] *n, pl* **-women** [-,wɪmən] : amazona *f*, jinete *f*, caballista *f*
horsey *or* **horsy** ['hɔrsi] *adj* **horsier; -est** : relacionado a los caballos, caballar
horticultural [,hɔrt̬ə'kʌltʃərəl] *adj* : hortícola
horticulture ['hɔrt̬ə,kʌltʃər] *n* : horticultura *f*

hose[1] [ˈhoːz] *vt* **hosed; hosing :** regar o lavar con manguera
hose[2] *n* **1** *pl* **hose** SOCKS **:** calcetines *mpl,* medias *fpl* **2** *pl* **hose** STOCKINGS **:** medias *fpl* **3** *pl* **hoses :** manguera *f,* manga *f*
hosiery [ˈhoːʒəri, ˈhoːzə-] *n* **:** calcetería *f,* medias *fpl*
hospice [ˈhɑspəs] *n* **:** hospicio *m*
hospitable [hɑˈspɪtəbəl, ˈhɑs͵pɪ-] *adj* **:** hospitalario — **hospitably** [-bli] *adv*
hospital [ˈhɑs͵pɪtəl] *n* **:** hospital *m*
hospitality [͵hɑspəˈtæləti] *n, pl* **-ties :** hospitalidad *f*
hospitalization [͵hɑs͵pɪtələˈzeɪʃən] *n* **:** hospitalización *f*
hospitalize [ˈhɑs͵pɪtəl͵aɪz] *vt* **-ized; -izing :** hospitalizar
host[1] [ˈhoːst] *vt* **:** presentar (un programa de televisión, etc.)
host[2] *n* **1 :** anfitrión *m,* -triona *f* (en la casa, a un evento); presentador *m,* -dora *f* (de un programa de televisión, etc.) **2** *or* **host organism :** huésped *m* **3** TROOPS **:** huestes *fpl* **4** MULTITUDE **:** multitud *f* <for a host of reasons : por muchas razones> **5** EUCHARIST **:** hostia *f,* Eucaristía *f*
hostage [ˈhɑstɪdʒ] *n* **:** rehén *m*
hostel [ˈhɑstəl] *n* **:** albergue *m* juvenil
hostess [ˈhoːstɪs] *n* **:** anfitriona *f* (en la casa), presentadora *f* (de un programa)
hostile [ˈhɑstəl, -͵taɪl] *adj* **:** hostil — **hostilely** *adv*
hostility [hɑsˈtɪləti] *n, pl* **-ties :** hostilidad *f*
hot [ˈhɑt] *adj* **hotter; hottest 1 :** caliente, cálido, caluroso <hot water : agua caliente> <a hot climate : un clima cálido> <a hot day : un día caluroso> **2** ARDENT, FIERY **:** ardiente, acalorado <to have a hot temper : tener mal genio> **3** SPICY **:** picante **4** FRESH **:** reciente, nuevo <hot news : noticias de última hora> **5** EAGER **:** ávido **6** STOLEN **:** robado
hot air *n* **:** palabrería *f*
hotbed [ˈhɑt͵bɛd] *n* **1 :** semillero *m* (de plantas) **2 :** hervidero *m,* semillero *m* (de crimen, etc.)
hot dog *n* **:** perro *m* caliente
hotel [hoːˈtɛl] *n* **:** hotel *m*
hothead [ˈhɑt͵hɛd] *n* **:** exaltado *m,* -da *f*
hotheaded [ˈhɑtˈhɛdəd] *adj* **:** exaltado
hothouse [ˈhɑt͵haʊs] *n* **:** invernadero *m*
hot plate *n* **:** placa *f* (de cocina)
hot rod *n* **:** coche *m* con motor modificado
hot water *n* **to get into hot water :** meterse en un lío
hound[1] [ˈhaʊnd] *vt* **:** acosar, perseguir
hound[2] *n* **:** perro *m* (de caza)
hour [ˈaʊər] *n* **:** hora *f*
hourglass [ˈaʊər͵glæs] *n* **:** reloj *m* de arena
hourly [ˈaʊərli] *adv & adj* **:** cada hora, por hora
house[1] [ˈhaʊz] *vt* **housed; housing :** albergar, alojar, hospedar
house[2] [ˈhaʊs] *n, pl* **houses** [ˈhaʊzəz, -səz] **1** HOME **:** casa *f* **2 :** cámara *f* (del gobierno) **3** BUSINESS **:** casa *f,* empresa *f*
houseboat [ˈhaʊs͵boːt] *n* **:** casa *f* flotante
housebroken [ˈhaʊs͵broːkən] *adj* **:** enseñado
housefly [ˈhaʊs͵flaɪ] *n, pl* **-flies :** mosca *f* común
household[1] [ˈhaʊs͵hoːld] *adj* **1** DOMESTIC **:** doméstico, de la casa **2** FAMILIAR **:** conocido por todos
household[2] *n* **:** casa *f,* familia *f*
householder [ˈhaʊs͵hoːldər] *n* **:** dueño *m,* -ña *f* de casa
housekeeper [ˈhaʊs͵kiːpər] *n* **:** ama *f* de llaves
housekeeping [ˈhaʊs͵kiːpɪŋ] *n* **:** gobierno *m* de la casa, quehaceres *mpl* domésticos
housemaid [ˈhaʊs͵meɪd] *n* **:** criada *f,* mucama *f,* muchacha *f,* sirvienta *f*
housewarming [ˈhaʊs͵wɔrmɪŋ] *n* **:** fiesta *f* de estreno de una casa
housewife [ˈhaʊs͵waɪf] *n, pl* **-wives :** ama *f* de casa
housework [ˈhaʊs͵wərk] *n* **:** faenas *fpl* domésticas, quehaceres *mpl* domésticos
housing [ˈhaʊzɪŋ] *n* **1** HOUSES **:** vivienda *f* **2** COVERING **:** caja *f* protectora
hove → **heave**
hovel [ˈhʌvəl, ˈhɑ-] *n* **:** casucha *f,* tugurio *m*
hover [ˈhʌvər, ˈhɑ-] *vi* **1 :** cernerse, sostenerse en el aire **2 to hover about :** rondar
how [ˈhaʊ] *adv* **1 :** cómo <how are you? : ¿cómo estas?> <I don't know how to fix it : no se cómo arreglarlo> **2 :** qué <how beautiful! : ¡qué bonito!> **3 :** cuánto <how old are you? : ¿cuántos años tienes?> **4 how about...? :** ¿qué te parece...?
however[1] [haʊˈɛvər] *adv* **1 :** por mucho que, por más que <however hot it is : por mucho calor que haga> **2** NEVERTHELESS **:** sin embargo, no obstante
however[2] *conj* **:** comoquiera que, de cualquier manera que
howl[1] [ˈhaʊl] *vi* **:** aullar
howl[2] *n* **:** aullido *m,* alarido *m*
hub [ˈhʌb] *n* **1** CENTER **:** centro *m* **2 :** cubo *m* (de una rueda)
hubbub [ˈhʌ͵bʌb] *n* **:** algarabía *f,* alboroto *m,* jaleo *m*
hubcap [ˈhʌb͵kæp] *n* **:** tapacubos *m*
huckster [ˈhʌkstər] *n* **:** buhonero *m,* -ra *f;* vendedor *m,* -dora *f* ambulante
huddle[1] [ˈhʌdəl] *vi* **-dled; -dling 1 :** apiñarse, amontonarse **2 to huddle together :** acurrucarse

huddle[2] *n* **:** grupo *m* (cerrado) <to go into a huddle : conferenciar en secreto>

hue [ˈhjuː] *n* **:** color *m,* tono *m*

huff [ˈhʌf] *n* **:** enojo *m,* enfado *m* <to be in a huff : estar enojado>

huffy [ˈhʌfi] *adj* **huffier; -est :** enojado, enfadado

hug[1] [ˈhʌg] *vt* **hugged; hugging 1** EMBRACE **:** abrazar **2 :** ir pegado a <the road hugs the river : el camino está pegado al río>

hug[2] *n* **:** abrazo *m*

huge [ˈhjuːdʒ] *adj* **huger; hugest :** inmenso, enorme — **hugely** *adv*

hulk [ˈhʌlk] *n* **1 :** persona *f* fornida **2 :** casco *m* (barco), armatoste *m* (edificio, etc.)

hulking [ˈhʌlkɪŋ] *adj* **:** grandote *fam,* pesado

hull[1] [ˈhʌl] *vt* **:** pelar

hull[2] *n* **1** HUSK **:** cáscara *f* **2 :** casco *m* (de un barco, un avión, etc.)

hullabaloo [ˈhʌləbəˌluː] *n, pl* **-loos :** alboroto *m,* jaleo *m*

hum[1] [ˈhʌm] *v* **hummed; humming** *vi* **1** BUZZ **:** zumbar **2 :** estar muy activo, moverse <to hum with activity : bullir de actividad> — *vt* **:** tararear (una melodía)

hum[2] *n* **:** zumbido *m,* murmullo *m*

human[1] [ˈhjuːmən, ˈjuː-] *adj* **:** humano — **humanly** *adv*

human[2] *n* **:** ser *m* humano

humane [hjuːˈmeɪn, ˌjuː-] *adj* **:** humano, humanitario — **humanely** *adv*

humanism [ˈhjuːməˌnɪzəm, ˈjuː-] *n* **:** humanismo *m*

humanist [ˈhjuːmənɪst, ˈjuː-] *n* **:** humanista *mf*

humanitarian[1] [hjuːˌmænəˈtɛriən, juː-] *adj* **:** humanitario

humanitarian[2] *n* **:** humanitario *m,* -ria *f*

humanity [hjuːˈmænət̬i, juː-] *n, pl* **-ties :** humanidad *f*

humankind [ˈhjuːmənˈkaɪnd, ˈjuː-] *n* **:** género *m* humano

humble[1] [ˈhʌmbəl] *vt* **-bled; -bling 1 :** humillar **2 to humble oneself :** humillarse

humble[2] *adj* **-bler; -blest :** humilde, modesto — **humbly** [ˈhʌmbli] *adv*

humbug [ˈhʌmˌbʌg] *n* **1** FRAUD **:** charlatán *m,* -tana *f;* farsante *mf* **2** NONSENSE **:** patrañas *fpl,* tonterías *fpl*

humdrum [ˈhʌmˌdrʌm] *adj* **:** monótono, rutinario

humid [ˈhjuːməd, ˈjuː-] *adj* **:** húmedo

humidifier [hjuːˈmɪdəˌfaɪər, juː-] *n* **:** humidificador *m*

humidify [hjuːˈmɪdəˌfaɪ, juː-] *vt* **-fied; -fying :** humidificar

humidity [hjuːˈmɪdət̬i, juː-] *n, pl* **-ties :** humedad *f*

humiliate [hjuːˈmɪliˌeɪt, juː-] *vt* **-ated; -ating :** humillar

humiliating [hjuːˈmɪliˌeɪt̬ɪŋ, juː-] *adj* **:** humillante

humiliation [hjuːˌmɪliˈeɪʃən, juː-] *n* **:** humillación *f*

humility [hjuːˈmɪlət̬i, juː-] *n* **:** humildad *f*

hummingbird [ˈhʌmɪŋˌbərd] *n* **:** colibrí *m,* picaflor *m*

hummock [ˈhʌmək] *n* **:** montículo *m*

humor[1] [ˈhjuːmər, ˈjuː-] *vt* **:** seguir el humor a, complacer

humor[2] *n* **:** humor *m*

humorist [ˈhjuːmərɪst, ˈjuː-] *n* **:** humorista *mf*

humorless [ˈhjuːmərləs, ˈjuː-] *adj* **:** sin sentido del humor <a humorless smile : una sonrisa forzada>

humorous [ˈhjuːmərəs, ˈjuː-] *adj* **:** humorístico, cómico — **humorously** *adv*

hump [ˈhʌmp] *n* **:** joroba *f,* giba *f*

humpback [ˈhʌmpˌbæk] *n* **1** HUMP **:** joroba *f,* giba *f* **2** HUNCHBACK **:** jorobado *m,* -da *f;* giboso *m,* -sa *f*

humpbacked [ˈhʌmpˌbækt] *adj* **:** jorobado, giboso

humus [ˈhjuːməs, ˈjuː-] *n* **:** humus *m*

hunch[1] [ˈhʌntʃ] *vt* **:** encorvar — *vi or* **to hunch up :** encorvarse

hunch[2] *n* PREMONITION **:** presentimiento *m*

hunchback [ˈhʌntʃˌbæk] *n* **1** HUMP **:** joroba *f,* giba *f* **2** HUMPBACK **:** jorobado *m,* -da *f;* giboso *m,* -sa *f*

hunchbacked [ˈhʌntʃˌbækt] *adj* **:** jorobado, giboso

hundred[1] [ˈhʌndrəd] *adj* **:** cien, ciento

hundred[2] *n, pl* **-dreds** *or* **-dred :** ciento *m*

hundredth[1] [ˈhʌndrədθ] *adj* **:** centésimo

hundredth[2] *n* **1 :** centésimo *m,* -ma *f* (en una serie) **2 :** centésimo *m,* centésima parte *f*

hung → **hang**

Hungarian [hʌŋˈgæriən] *n* **1 :** húngaro *m,* -ra *f* **2 :** húngaro *m* (idioma) — **Hungarian** *adj*

hunger[1] [ˈhʌŋgər] *vi* **1 :** tener hambre **2 to hunger for :** ansiar, anhelar

hunger[2] *n* **:** hambre *m*

hungrily [ˈhʌŋgrəli] *adv* **:** ávidamente

hungry [ˈhʌŋgri] *adj* **-grier; -est 1 :** hambriento **2 to be hungry :** tener hambre

hunk [ˈhʌŋk] *n* **:** trozo *m,* pedazo *m*

hunt[1] [ˈhʌnt] *vt* **1** PURSUE **:** cazar **2 to hunt for :** buscar

hunt[2] *n* **1** PURSUIT **:** caza *f,* cacería *f* **2** SEARCH **:** búsqueda *f,* busca *f*

hunter [ˈhʌntər] *n* **:** cazador *m,* -dora *f*

hunting [ˈhʌntɪŋ] *n* **:** caza *f* <to go hunting : ir de caza>

hurdle[1] [ˈhərdəl] *vt* **-dled; -dling :** saltar, salvar (un obstáculo)

hurdle[2] *n* **:** valla *f* (en deportes), obstáculo *m*

hurl [ˈhərl] *vt* **:** arrojar, tirar, lanzar

hurrah [hʊˈrɑ, -ˈrɔ] *interj* **:** ¡hurra!

hurricane [ˈhərəˌkeɪn] *n* **:** huracán *m*

hurried [ˈhərid] *adj* **:** apresurado, precipitado
hurriedly [ˈhərədli] *adv* **:** apresuradamente, de prisa
hurry[1] [ˈhəri] *v* **-ried; -rying** *vi* **:** apurarse, darse prisa, apresurarse — *vt* **:** apurar, darle prisa (a alguien)
hurry[2] *n* **:** prisa *f,* apuro *f*
hurt[1] [ˈhərt] *v* **hurt; hurting** *vt* **1** INJURE **:** hacer daño a, herir, lastimar <to hurt oneself **:** hacerse daño> **2** DISTRESS, OFFEND **:** hacer sufrir, ofender, herir — *vi* **:** doler <my foot hurts **:** me duele el pie>
hurt[2] *n* **1** INJURY **:** herida *f* **2** DISTRESS, PAIN **:** dolor *m,* pena *f*
hurtful [ˈhərtfəl] *adj* **:** hiriente, doloroso
hurtle [ˈhərt̬əl] *vi* **-tled; -tling :** lanzarse, precipitarse
husband[1] [ˈhʌzbənd] *vt* **:** economizar, bien administrar
husband[2] *n* **:** esposo *m,* marido *m*
husbandry [ˈhʌzbəndri] *n* **1** MANAGEMENT, THRIFT **:** economía *f,* buena administración *f* **2** AGRICULTURE **:** agricultura *f* <animal husbandry **:** cría de animales>
hush[1] [ˈhʌʃ] *vt* **1** SILENCE **:** hacer callar, acallar **2** CALM **:** calmar, apaciguar
hush[2] *n* **:** silencio *m*
hush–hush [ˈhʌʃˌhʌʃ, ˌhʌʃˈhʌʃ] *adj* **:** muy secreto, confidencial
husk[1] [ˈhʌsk] *vt* **:** descascarar
husk[2] *n* **:** cáscara *f*
huskily [ˈhʌskəli] *adv* **:** con voz ronca
husky[1] [ˈhʌski] *adj* **-kier; -est 1** HOARSE **:** ronco **2** BURLY **:** fornido
husky[2] *n, pl* **-kies :** perro *m,* -rra *f* esquimal
hustle[1] [ˈhəsəl] *v* **-tled; -tling** *vt* **:** darle prisa (a alguien), apurar <they hustled me in **:** me hicieron entrar a empujones> — *vi* **:** apurarse, ajetrearse
hustle[2] *n* BUSTLE **:** ajetreo *m*
hut [ˈhʌt] *n* **:** cabaña *f,* choza *f,* barraca *f*
hutch [ˈhʌtʃ] *n* **1** CUPBOARD **:** alacena *f* **2 rabbit hutch :** conejera *f*
hyacinth [ˈhaɪəˌsɪnθ] *n* **:** jacinto *m*
hybrid[1] [ˈhaɪbrɪd] *adj* **:** híbrido
hybrid[2] *n* **:** híbrido *m*
hydrant [ˈhaɪdrənt] *n* **:** boca *f* de riego, hidrante *m CA, Col* <fire hydrant **:** boca de incendios>
hydraulic [haɪˈdrɔlɪk] *adj* **:** hidráulico — **hydraulically** *adv*
hydrocarbon [ˌhaɪdroˈkɑrbən] *n* **:** hidrocarburo *m*
hydrochloric acid [ˌhaɪdroˈklorɪk] *n* **:** ácido *m* clorohídrico
hydroelectric [ˌhaɪdroɪˈlɛktrɪk] *adj* **:** hidroeléctrico
hydrogen [ˈhaɪdrədʒən] *n* **:** hidrógeno *m*
hydrogen bomb *n* **:** bomba *f* de hidrógeno
hydrogen peroxide *n* **:** agua *f* oxigenada, peróxido *m* de hidrógeno
hydrophobia [ˌhaɪdrəˈfoːbiə] *n* **:** hidrofobia *f,* rabia *f*
hydroplane [ˈhaɪdrəˌpleɪn] *n* **:** hidroplano *m*
hyena [haɪˈiːnə] *n* **:** hiena *f*
hygiene [ˈhaɪˌdʒiːn] *n* **:** higiene *f*
hygienic [haɪˈdʒɛnɪk, -ˈdʒiː-; ˌhaɪdʒiˈɛnɪk] *adj* **:** higiénico — **hygienically** [-nɪkli] *adv*
hygienist [haɪˈdʒiːnɪst, -ˈdʒɛ-; ˈhaɪˌdʒiː-] *n* **:** higienista *mf*
hygrometer [haɪˈgrɑmət̬ər] *n* **:** higrómetro *m*
hymn [ˈhɪm] *n* **:** himno *m*
hymnal [ˈhɪmnəl] *n* **:** himnario *m*
hype [ˈhaɪp] *n* **:** bombo *m* publicitario
hyperactive [ˌhaɪpərˈæktɪv] *adj* **:** hiperactivo
hyperbole [haɪˈpərbəli] *n* **:** hipérbole *f*
hypercritical [ˌhaɪpərˈkrɪt̬əkəl] *adj* **:** hipercrítico
hypersensitivity [ˌhaɪpərˌsɛntsəˈtɪvət̬i] *n* **:** hipersensibilidad *f*
hypertension [ˈhaɪpərˌtɛntʃən] *n* **:** hipertensión *f*
hyphen [ˈhaɪfən] *n* **:** guión *m*
hyphenate [ˈhaɪfənˌeɪt] *vt* **-ated; -ating :** escribir con guión
hypnosis [hɪpˈnoːsɪs] *n, pl* **-noses** [-ˌsiːz] **:** hipnosis *f*
hypnotic [hɪpˈnɑt̬ɪk] *adj* **:** hipnótico, hipnotizador
hypnotism [ˈhɪpnəˌtɪzəm] *n* **:** hipnotismo *m*
hypnotize [ˈhɪpnəˌtaɪz] *vt* **-tized; -tizing :** hipnotizar
hypochondria [ˌhaɪpəˈkɑndriə] *n* **:** hipocondría *f*
hypochondriac [ˌhaɪpəˈkɑndriˌæk] *n* **:** hipocondríaco *m,* -ca *f*
hypocrisy [hɪpˈɑkrəsi] *n, pl* **-sies :** hipocresía *f*
hypocrite [ˈhɪpəˌkrɪt] *n* **:** hipócrita *mf*
hypocritical [ˌhɪpəˈkrɪt̬ɪkəl] *adj* **:** hipócrita
hypodermic[1] [ˌhaɪpəˈdərmɪk] *adj* **:** hipodérmico
hypodermic[2] *n* **:** aguja *f* hipodérmica
hypotenuse [haɪˈpɑtənˌuːs, -ˌuːz, -ˌjuːs, -ˌjuːz] *n* **:** hipotenusa *f*
hypothesis [haɪˈpɑθəsɪs] *n, pl* **-eses** [-ˌsiːz] **:** hipótesis *f*
hypothetical [ˌhaɪpəˈθɛt̬ɪkəl] *adj* **:** hipotético — **hypothetically** [-t̬ɪkli] *adv*
hysteria [hɪsˈtɛriə, -tɪr-] *n* **:** histeria *f,* histerismo *m*
hysterical [hɪsˈtɛrɪkəl] *adj* **:** histérico — **hysterically** [-ɪkli] *adv*
hysterics [hɪsˈtɛrɪks] *n* **:** histeria *f,* histerismo *m*

I

i [ˈaɪ] *n, pl* **i's** *or* **is** [ˈaɪz] : novena letra del alfabeto inglés
I [ˈaɪ] *pron* : yo
ibis [ˈaɪbəs] *n, pl* **ibis** *or* **ibises** : ibis *f*
ice[1] [ˈaɪs] *v* **iced; icing** *vt* **1** FREEZE : congelar, helar **2** CHILL : enfriar **3 to ice a cake** : escarchar un pastel — *vi* : helarse, congelarse
ice[2] *n* **1** : hielo *m* **2** SHERBET : sorbete *m,* nieve *f Cuba, Mex, PRi*
iceberg [ˈaɪs,bərg] *n* : iceberg *m*
icebox [ˈaɪs,bɑks] → **refrigerator**
icebreaker [ˈaɪs,breɪkər] *n* : rompehielos *m*
ice cap *n* : casquete *m* glaciar
ice–cold [ˈaɪsˈko:ld] *adj* : helado
ice cream *n* : helado *m,* mantecado *m PRi*
Icelander [ˈaɪs,lændər, -lən-] *n* : islandés *m,* -desa *f*
Icelandic[1] [aɪsˈlændɪk] *adj* : islandés
Icelandic[2] *n* : islandés *m* (idioma)
ice–skate [ˈaɪs,skeɪt] *vi* **-skated; -skating** : patinar
ice skater *n* : patinador *m,* -dora *f*
ichthyology [,ɪkθiˈɑləʤi] *n* : ictiología *f*
icicle [ˈaɪ,sɪkəl] *n* : carámbano *m*
icily [ˈaɪsəli] *adv* : fríamente, con frialdad <he stared at me icily : me fijó la mirada con mucha frialdad>
icing [ˈaɪsɪŋ] *n* : glaseado *m,* betún *m Mex*
icon [ˈaɪ,kɑn, -kən] *n* : icono *m*
iconoclasm [aɪˈkɑnə,klæzəm] *n* : iconoclasia *f*
iconoclast [aɪˈkɑnə,klæst] *n* : iconoclasta *mf*
icy [ˈaɪsi] *adj* **icier; -est 1** : cubierto de hielo <an icy road : una carretera cubierta de hielo> **2** FREEZING : helado, gélido, glacial **3** ALOOF : frío, distante
id [ˈɪd] *n* : id *m*
I'd [ˈaɪd] (*contraction of* **I should** *or* **I would**) → **should, would**
idea [aɪˈdi:ə] *n* : idea *f*
ideal[1] [aɪˈdi:əl] *adj* : ideal
ideal[2] *n* : ideal *m*
idealism [aɪˈdi:ə,lɪzəm] *n* : idealismo *m*
idealist [aɪˈdi:əlɪst] *n* : idealista *mf*
idealistic [aɪ,di:əˈlɪstɪk] *adj* : idealista
idealistically [aɪ,di:əˈlɪstɪkli] *adv* : con idealismo
idealization [aɪ,di:ələˈzeɪʃən] *n* : idealización *f*
idealize [aɪˈdi:ə,laɪz] *vt* **-ized; -izing** : idealizar
ideally [aɪˈdi:əli] *adv* : perfectamente
identical [aɪˈdɛntɪkəl] *adj* : idéntico — **identically** [-tɪkli] *adv*
identifiable [aɪ,dɛntəˈfaɪəbəl] *adj* : identificable
identification [aɪ,dɛntəfəˈkeɪʃən] *n* **1** : identificación *f* **2 identification card** : carnet *m,* cédula *f* de identidad, identificación *f*
identify [aɪˈdɛntə,faɪ] *v* **-fied; -fying** *vt* : identificar — *vi* **to identify with** : identificarse con
identity [aɪˈdɛntəti] *n, pl* **-ties** : identidad *f*
ideological [,aɪdiəˈlɑʤɪkəl, ,ɪ-] *adj* : ideológico — **ideologically** [-ʤɪkli] *adv*
ideology [,aɪdiˈɑləʤi, ,ɪ-] *n, pl* **-gies** : ideología *f*
idiocy [ˈɪdiəsi] *n, pl* **-cies 1** : idiotez *f* **2** NONSENSE : estupidez *f,* tontería *f*
idiom [ˈɪdiəm] *n* **1** LANGUAGE : lenguaje *m* **2** EXPRESSION : modismo *m,* expresión *f* idiomática
idiomatic [,ɪdiəˈmætɪk] *adj* : idiomático
idiosyncrasy [,ɪdioˈsɪŋkrəsi] *n, pl* **-sies** : idiosincrasia *f*
idiosyncratic [,ɪdiosɪnˈkrætɪk] *adj* : idiosincrásico — **idiosyncratically** [-tɪkli] *adv*
idiot [ˈɪdiət] *n* **1** : idiota *mf* (en medicina) **2** FOOL : idiota *mf;* tonto *m,* -ta *f;* imbécil *mf fam*
idiotic [,ɪdiˈɑtɪk] *adj* : estúpido, idiota
idiotically [,ɪdiˈɑtɪkli] *adv* : estúpidamente
idle[1] [ˈaɪdəl] *v* **idled; idling** *vi* **1** LOAF : holgazanear, flojear, haraganear **2** : andar al ralentí (dícese de un automóvil), marchar en vacío (dícese de una máquina) — *vt* : dejar sin trabajo
idle[2] *adj* **idler; idlest 1** VAIN : frívolo, vano, infundado <idle curiosity : pura curiosidad> **2** INACTIVE : inactivo, parado, desocupado **3** LAZY : holgazán, haragán, perezoso
idleness [ˈaɪdəlnəs] *n* **1** INACTIVITY : inactividad *f,* ociosidad *f* **2** LAZINESS : holgazanería *f,* flojera *f,* pereza *f*
idler [ˈaɪdələr] *n* : haragán *m,* -gana *f;* holgazán *m,* -zana *f*
idly [ˈaɪdəli] *adv* : ociosamente
idol [ˈaɪdəl] *n* : ídolo *m*
idolater *or* **idolator** [aɪˈdɑlətər] *n* : idólatra *mf*
idolatrous [aɪˈdɑlətrəs] *adj* : idólatra
idolatry [aɪˈdɑlətri] *n, pl* **-tries** : idolatría *f*
idolize [ˈaɪdəlaɪz] *vt* **-ized; -izing** : idolatrar
idyll [ˈaɪdəl] *n* : idilio *m*
idyllic [aɪˈdɪlɪk] *adj* : idílico
if [ˈɪf] *conj* **1** : si <I would do it if I could : lo haría si pudiera> <if so : si es así> <as if : como si> <if I were you : yo que tú> **2** WHETHER : si <I don't know if they're ready : no sé si están listos> **3** THOUGH : aunque, si bien <it's pretty, if somewhat old-fashioned : es lindo aunque algo anticuado>
igloo [ˈɪ,glu:] *n, pl* **-loos** : iglú *m*

ignite [ɪg'naɪt] *v* **-nited; -niting** *vt* : prenderle fuego a, encender — *vi* : prender, encenderse

ignition [ɪg'nɪʃən] *n* **1** IGNITING : ignición *f,* encendido *m* **2** *or* **ignition switch** : encendido *m,* arranque *m* <to turn on the ignition : arrancar el motor>

ignoble [ɪg'no:bəl] *adj* : innoble — **ignobly** *adv*

ignominious [ˌɪgnə'mɪniəs] *adj* : ignominioso, deshonroso — **ignominiously** *adv*

ignominy ['ɪgnəˌmɪni] *n, pl* **-nies** : ignominia *f*

ignoramus [ˌɪgnə'reɪməs] *n* : ignorante *mf;* bestia *mf;* bruto *m,* -ta *f*

ignorance ['ɪgnərənts] *n* : ignorancia *f*

ignorant ['ɪgnərənt] *adj* **1** : ignorante **2 to be ignorant of** : no ser consciente de, desconocer, ignorar

ignorantly ['ɪgnərəntli] *adv* : ignorantemente, con ignorancia

ignore [ɪg'nor] *vt* **-nored; -noring** : ignorar, hacer caso omiso de, no hacer caso de

iguana [ɪ'gwɑnə] *n* : iguana *f,* garrobo *f CA*

ilk ['ɪlk] *n* : tipo *m,* clase *f,* índole *f*

ill[1] ['ɪl] *adv* **worse** ['wərs]; **worst** ['wərst] : mal <to speak ill of : hablar mal de> <he can ill afford to fail : mal puede permitirse el lujo de fracasar>

ill[2] *adj* **worse; worst 1** SICK : enfermo **2** BAD : malo <ill luck : mala suerte>

ill[3] *n* **1** EVIL : mal *m* **2** MISFORTUNE : mal *m,* desgracia *f* **3** AILMENT : enfermedad *f*

I'll ['aɪl] (*contraction of* **I shall** *or* **I will**) → **shall, will**

illegal [ɪl'li:gəl] *adj* : ilegal — **illegally** *adv*

illegality [ɪli'gæləṭi] *n* : ilegalidad *f*

illegibility [ɪlˌlɛdʒə'bɪləṭi] *n, pl* **-ties** : ilegibilidad *f*

illegible [ɪl'lɛdʒəbəl] *adj* : ilegible — **illegibly** [-bli] *adv*

illegitimacy [ˌɪlɪ'dʒɪṭəməsi] *n* : ilegitimidad *f*

illegitimate [ˌɪlɪ'dʒɪṭəmət] *adj* **1** BASTARD : ilegítimo, bastardo **2** UNLAWFUL : ilegítimo, ilegal — **illegitimately** *adv*

ill–fated ['ɪl'feɪṭəd] *adj* : malhadado, infortunado, desventurado

illicit [ɪl'lɪsət] *adj* : ilícito — **illicitly** *adv*

illiteracy [ɪl'lɪṭərəsi] *n, pl* **-cies** : analfabetismo *m*

illiterate[1] [ɪl'lɪṭərət] *adj* : analfabeto

illiterate[2] *n* : analfabeto *m,* -ta *f*

ill–mannered [ˌɪl'manərd] *adj* : descortés, maleducado

ill–natured [ˌɪl'neɪtʃərd] *adj* : desagradable, de mal genio

ill–naturedly [ˌɪl'neɪtʃərdli] *adv* : desagradablemente

illness ['ɪlnəs] *n* : enfermedad *f*

illogical [ɪl'lɑdʒɪkəl] *adj* : ilógico — **illogically** [-kli] *adv*

ill–tempered [ˌɪl'tempərd] → **ill–natured**

ill–treat [ˌɪl'tri:t] *vt* : maltratar

ill–treatment [ˌɪl'tri:tmənt] *n* : maltrato *m*

illuminate [ɪ'lu:məˌneɪt] *vt* **-nated; -nating 1** : iluminar, alumbrar **2** ELUCIDATE : esclarecer, elucidar

illumination [ɪˌlu:mə'neɪʃən] *n* **1** LIGHTING : iluminación *f,* luz *f* **2** ELUCIDATION : esclarecimiento *m,* elucidación *f*

ill–use ['ɪl'ju:z] → **ill–treat**

illusion [ɪ'lu:ʒən] *n* : ilusión *f*

illusory [ɪ'lu:səri, -zəri] *adj* : engañoso, ilusorio

illustrate ['ɪləsˌtreɪt] *v* **-trated; -trating** : ilustrar

illustration [ˌɪlə'streɪʃən] *n* **1** PICTURE : ilustración *f* **2** EXAMPLE : ejemplo *m,* ilustración *f*

illustrative [ɪ'lʌstrəṭɪv, 'ɪləˌstreɪṭɪv] *adj* : ilustrativo — **illustratively** *adv*

illustrator ['ɪləˌstreɪṭər] *n* : ilustrador *m,* -dora *f;* dibujante *mf*

illustrious [ɪ'lʌstriəs] *adj* : ilustre, eminente, glorioso

illustriousness [ɪ'lʌstriəsnəs] *n* : eminencia *f,* prestigio *m*

ill will *n* : animosidad *f,* malquerencia *f,* mala voluntad *f*

I'm ['aɪm] (*contraction of* **I am**) → **be**

image[1] ['ɪmɪdʒ] *vt* **-aged; -aging** : imaginar, crear una imagen de

image[2] *n* : imagen *f*

imagery ['ɪmɪdʒri] *n, pl* **-eries 1** IMAGES : imágenes *fpl* **2** : imaginería *f* (en el arte)

imaginable [ɪ'mædʒənəbəl] *adj* : imaginable — **imaginably** [-bli] *adv*

imaginary [ɪ'mædʒəˌnɛri] *adj* : imaginario

imagination [ɪˌmædʒə'neɪʃən] *n* : imaginación *f*

imaginative [ɪ'mædʒənəṭɪv, -əˌneɪṭɪv] *adj* : imaginativo — **imaginatively** *adv*

imagine [ɪ'mædʒən] *vt* **-ined; -ining** : imaginar(se)

imbalance [ɪm'bælənts] *n* : desajuste *m,* desbalance *m,* desequilibrio *m*

imbecile[1] ['ɪmbəsəl, -ˌsɪl] *or* **imbecilic** [ˌɪmbə'sɪlɪk] *adj* : imbécil, estúpido

imbecile[2] *n* **1** : imbécil *mf* (en medicina) **2** FOOL : idiota *mf;* imbécil *mf fam;* estúpido *m,* -da *f*

imbecility [ˌɪmbə'sɪləṭi] *n, pl* **-ties** : imbecilidad *f*

imbibe [ɪm'baɪb] *v* **-bibed; -bibing** *vt* **1** DRINK : beber **2** ABSORB : absorber, embeber — *vi* : beber

imbue [ɪm'bju:] *vt* **-bued; -buing** : imbuir

imitate ['ɪməˌteɪt] *vt* **-tated; -tating** : imitar, remedar

imitation[1] [ˌɪməˈteɪʃən] *adj* **:** de imitación, artificial

imitation[2] *n* **:** imitación *f*

imitative [ˈɪməˌteɪt̬ɪv] *adj* **:** imitativo, imitador, poco original

imitator [ˈɪməˌteɪt̬ər] *n* **:** imitador *m*, -dora *f*

immaculate [ɪˈmækjələt] *adj* **1** PURE **:** inmaculado, puro **2** FLAWLESS **:** impecable, intachable — **immaculately** *adv*

immaterial [ˌɪməˈtɪriəl] *adj* **1** INCORPOREAL **:** incorpóreo **2** UNIMPORTANT **:** irrelevante, sin importancia

immature [ˌɪməˈtʃʊr, -ˈtjʊr, -ˈtʊr] *adj* **:** inmaduro, verde (dícese de la fruta)

immaturity [ˌɪməˈtʃʊrət̬i, -ˈtjʊr-, -ˈtʊr-] *n, pl* **-ties :** inmadurez *f*, falta *f* de madurez

immeasurable [ɪˈmɛʒərəbəl] *adj* **:** inconmensurable, incalculable — **immeasurably** [-bli] *adv*

immediate [ɪˈmiːdiət] *adj* **1** INSTANT **:** inmediato, instantáneo <immediate relief **:** alivio instantáneo> **2** DIRECT **:** inmediato, directo <the immediate cause of death **:** la causa directa de la muerte> **3** URGENT **:** urgente, apremiante **4** CLOSE **:** cercano, próximo, inmediato <her immediate family **:** sus familiares más cercanos> <in the immediate vicinity **:** en los alrededores, en las inmediaciones>

immediately [ɪˈmiːdiətli] *adv* **:** inmediatamente, enseguida

immemorial [ˌɪməˈmoriəl] *adj* **:** inmemorial

immense [ɪˈmɛnts] *adj* **:** inmenso, enorme — **immensely** *adv*

immensity [ɪˈmɛntsət̬i] *n, pl* **-ties :** inmensidad *f*

immerse [ɪˈmərs] *vt* **-mersed; -mersing 1** SUBMERGE **:** sumergir **2 to immerse oneself in :** enfrascarse en

immersion [ɪˈmərʒən] *n* **1 :** inmersión *f* (en un líquido) **2 :** enfrascamiento *m* (en una actividad)

immigrant [ˈɪmɪgrənt] *n* **:** inmigrante *mf*

immigrate [ˈɪməˌgreɪt] *vi* **-grated; -grating :** inmigrar

immigration [ˌɪməˈgreɪʃən] *n* **:** inmigración *f*

imminence [ˈɪmənənts] *n* **:** inminencia *f*

imminent [ˈɪmənənt] *adj* **:** inminente — **imminently** *adv*

immobile [ɪmˈoːbəl] *adj* **1** FIXED, IMMOVABLE **:** inmovible, fijo **2** MOTIONLESS **:** inmóvil

immobility [ˌɪmoˈbɪlət̬i] *n, pl* **-ties :** inmovilidad *f*

immobilize [ɪˈmoːbəˌlaɪz] *vt* **-lized; -lizing :** inmovilizar, paralizar

immoderate [ɪˈmɑdərət] *adj* **:** inmoderado, desmesurado, desmedido, excesivo — **immoderately** *adv*

immodest [ɪˈmɑdəst] *adj* **1** INDECENT **:** inmodesto, indecente, impúdico **2** CONCEITED **:** inmodesto, presuntuoso, engreído — **immodestly** *adv*

immodesty [ɪˈmɑdəsti] *n* **:** inmodestia *f*

immoral [ɪˈmɔrəl] *adj* **:** inmoral

immorality [ˌɪmɔˈrælət̬i, ˌɪmə-] *n, pl* **-ties :** inmoralidad *f*

immorally [ɪˈmɔrəli] *adv* **:** de manera inmoral

immortal[1] [ɪˈmɔrtəl] *adj* **:** inmortal

immortal[2] *n* **:** inmortal *mf*

immortality [ˌɪˌmɔrˈtælət̬i] *n* **:** inmortalidad *f*

immortalize [ɪˈmɔrtəlˌaɪz] *vt* **-ized; -izing :** inmortalizar

immovable [ɪˈmuːvəbəl] *adj* **1** FIXED **:** fijo, inmovible **2** UNYIELDING **:** inflexible

immune [ɪˈmjuːn] *adj* **1 :** inmune <immune to smallpox **:** inmune a la viruela> **2** EXEMPT **:** exento, inmune

immune system *n* **:** sistema *m* inmunológico

immunity [ɪˈmjuːnət̬i] *n, pl* **-ties 1 :** inmunidad *f* **2** EXEMPTION **:** exención *f*

immunization [ˌɪmjʊnəˈzeɪʃən] *n* **:** inmunización *f*

immunize [ˈɪmjʊˌnaɪz] *vt* **-nized; -nizing :** inmunizar

immunology [ˌɪmjʊˈnɑlədʒi] *n* **:** inmunología *f*

immutable [ɪˈmjuːt̬əbəl] *adj* **:** inmutable

imp [ˈɪmp] *n* RASCAL **:** diablillo *m*; pillo *m*, -lla *f*

impact[1] [ɪmˈpækt] *vt* **1** STRIKE **:** chocar con, impactar **2** AFFECT **:** afectar, impactar, impresionar — *vi* **1** STRIKE **:** hacer impacto, golpear **2 to impact on :** tener un impacto sobre

impact[2] [ˈɪmˌpækt] *n* **1** COLLISION **:** impacto *m*, choque *m*, colisión *f* **2** EFFECT **:** efecto *m*, impacto *m*, consecuencias *fpl*

impacted [ɪmˈpæktəd] *adj* **:** impactado, incrustado (dícese de los dientes)

impair [ɪmˈpær] *vt* **:** perjudicar, dañar, afectar

impairment [ɪmˈpærmənt] *n* **:** perjuicio *m*, daño *m*

impala [ɪmˈpɑlə, -ˈpæ-] *n, pl* **impalas** *or* **impala :** impala *m*

impale [ɪmˈpeɪl] *vt* **-paled; -paling :** empalar

impanel [ɪmˈpænəl] *vt* **-eled** *or* **-elled; eling** *or* **-elling :** elegir (un jurado)

impart [ɪmˈpɑrt] *vt* **1** CONVEY **:** impartir, dar, conferir **2** DISCLOSE **:** revelar, divulgar

impartial [ɪmˈpɑrʃəl] *adj* **:** imparcial — **impartially** *adv*

impartiality [ɪmˌpɑrʃiˈælət̬i] *n, pl* **-ties :** imparcialidad *f*

impassable [ɪmˈpæsəbəl] *adj* **:** infranqueable, intransitable — **impassably** [-bli] *adv*

impasse [ˈɪm,pæs] *n* **1** DEADLOCK : impasse *m,* punto *m* muerto **2** DEAD END : callejón *m* sin salida
impassioned [ɪmˈpæʃənd] *adj* : apasionado, vehemente
impassive [ɪmˈpæsɪv] *adj* : impasible, indiferente
impassively [ɪmˈpæsɪvli] *adv* : impasiblemente, sin emoción
impatience [ɪmˈpeɪʃənts] *n* : impaciencia *f*
impatient [ɪmˈpeɪʃənt] *adj* : impaciente — **impatiently** *adv*
impeach [ɪmˈpiːtʃ] *vt* : destituir (a un funcionario) de su cargo
impeachment [ɪmˈpiːtʃmənt] *n* **1** ACCUSATION : acusación *f* **2** DISMISSAL : destitución *f*
impeccable [ɪmˈpɛkəbəl] *adj* : impecable — **impeccably** [-bli] *adv*
impecunious [,ɪmpɪˈkjuːniəs] *adj* : falto de dinero
impede [ɪmˈpiːd] *vt* **-peded; -peding** : impedir, dificultar, obstaculizar
impediment [ɪmˈpɛdəmənt] *n* **1** HINDRANCE : impedimento *m,* obstáculo *m* **2 speech impediment** : defecto *m* del habla
impel [ɪmˈpɛl] *vt* **-pelled; -pelling** : impeler
impend [ɪmˈpɛnd] *vi* : ser inminente
impenetrable [ɪmˈpɛnətrəbəl] *adj* **1** : impenetrable <an impenetrable forest : una selva impenetrable> **2** INSCRUTABLE : incomprensible, inescrutable, impenetrable — **impenetrably** [-bli] *adv*
impenitent [ɪmˈpɛnətənt] *adj* : impenitente
imperative[1] [ɪmˈpɛrəṭɪv] *adj* **1** AUTHORITATIVE : imperativo, imperioso **2** NECESSARY : imprescindible — **imperatively** *adv*
imperative[2] *n* : imperativo *m*
imperceptible [,ɪmpərˈsɛptəbəl] *adj* : imperceptible — **imperceptibly** [-bli] *adv*
imperfect [ɪmˈpərfɪkt] *adj* : imperfecto, defectuoso — **imperfectly** *adv*
imperfection [ɪm,pərˈfɛkʃən] *n* : imperfección *f,* defecto *m*
imperial [ɪmˈpɪriəl] *adj* **1** : imperial **2** SOVEREIGN : soberano **3** IMPERIOUS : imperioso, señorial
imperialism [ɪmˈpɪriə,lɪzəm] *n* : imperialismo *m*
imperialist[1] [ɪmˈpɪriəlɪst] *adj* : imperialista
imperialist[2] *n* : imperialista *mf*
imperialistic [ɪm,pɪriːəˈlɪstɪk] *adj* : imperialista
imperil [ɪmˈpɛrəl] *vt* **-iled** *or* **-illed; -iling** *or* **-illing** : poner en peligro
imperious [ɪmˈpɪriəs] *adj* : imperioso — **imperiously** *adv*
imperishable [ɪmˈpɛrɪʃəbəl] *adj* : imperecedero
impermanent [ɪmˈpərmənənt] *adj* : pasajero, inestable, efímero — **impermanently** *adv*
impermeable [ɪmˈpərmiəbəl] *adj* : impermeable
impersonal [ɪmˈpərsənəl] *adj* : impersonal — **impersonally** *adv*
impersonate [ɪmˈpərsən,eɪt] *vt* **-ated; -ating** : hacerse pasar por, imitar
impersonation [ɪm,pərsənˈeɪʃən] *n* : imitación *f*
impersonator [ɪmˈpərsən,eɪṭər] *n* : imitador *m,* -dora *f*
impertinence [ɪmˈpərtənənts] *n* : impertinencia *f*
impertinent [ɪmˈpərtənənt] *adj* **1** IRRELEVANT : impertinente, irrelevante **2** INSOLENT : impertinente, insolente
impertinently [ɪmˈpərtənəntli] *adv* : con impertinencia, impertinentemente
imperturbable [,ɪmpərˈtərbəbəl] *adj* : imperturbable
impervious [ɪmˈpərviəs] *adj* **1** IMPENETRABLE : impermeable **2** INSENSITIVE : insensible <impervious to criticism : insensible a la crítica>
impetuosity [ɪm,pɛtʃʊˈɑsəṭi] *n, pl* **-ties** : impetuosidad *f*
impetuous [ɪmˈpɛtʃʊəs] *adj* : impetuoso, impulsivo
impetuously [ɪmˈpɛtʃʊəsli] *adv* : de manera impulsiva, impetuosamente
impetus [ˈɪmpəṭəs] *n* : ímpetu *m,* impulso *m*
impiety [ɪmˈpaɪəṭi] *n, pl* **-ties** : impiedad *f*
impinge [ɪmˈpɪndʒ] *vi* **-pinged; -pinging 1 to impinge on** AFFECT : afectar a, incidir en **2 to impinge on** VIOLATE : violar, vulnerar
impious [ˈɪmpiəs, ɪmˈpaɪəs] *adj* : impío, irreverente
impish [ˈɪmpɪʃ] *adj* MISCHIEVOUS : pícaro, travieso
impishly [ˈɪmpɪʃli] *adv* : con picardía
implacable [ɪmˈplækəbəl] *adj* : implacable — **implacably** [-bli] *adv*
implant[1] [ɪmˈplænt] *vt* **1** INCULCATE, INSTILL : inculcar, implantar **2** INSERT : implantar, insertar
implant[2] [ˈɪm,plænt] *n* : implante *m* (de pelo), injerto *m* (de piel)
implantation [,ɪm,plænˈteɪʃən] *n* : implantación *f*
implausibility [ɪm,plɔzəˈbɪləṭi] *n, pl* **-ties** : inverosimilitud *f*
implausible [ɪmˈplɔzəbəl] *adj* : inverosímil, poco convincente
implement[1] [ˈɪmplə,mɛnt] *vt* : poner en práctica, implementar
implement[2] [ˈɪmpləmənt] *n* : utensilio *m,* instrumento *m,* implemento *m*
implementation [,ɪmpləmənˈteɪʃən] *n* : implementación *f,* ejecución *f,* cumplimiento *m*
implicate [ˈɪmplə,keɪt] *vt* **-cated; -cating** : implicar, involucrar

implication [ˌɪmplə'keɪʃən] *n* **1** CONSEQUENCE : implicación *f,* consecuencia *f* **2** INFERENCE : insinuación *f,* inferencia *f*

implicit [ɪm'plɪsət] *adj* **1** IMPLIED : implícito, tácito **2** ABSOLUTE : absoluto, completo <implicit faith : fe ciega> — **implicitly** *adv*

implied [ɪm'plaɪd] *adj* : implícito, tácito

implode [ɪm'plo:d] *vi* **-ploded; -ploding** : implosionar

implore [ɪm'plor] *vt* **-plored; -ploring** : implorar, suplicar

imply [ɪm'plaɪ] *vt* **-plied; -plying 1** SUGGEST : insinuar, dar a entender **2** INVOLVE : implicar, suponer <rights imply obligations : los derechos implican unas obligaciones>

impolite [ˌɪmpə'laɪt] *adj* : descortés, maleducado

impoliteness [ˌɪmpə'laɪtnəs] *n* : descortesía *f,* falta *f* de educación

impolitic [ɪm'pɑləˌtɪk] *adj* : imprudente, poco político

imponderable[1] [ɪm'pɑndərəbəl] *adj* : imponderable

imponderable[2] *n* : imponderable *m*

import[1] [ɪm'port] *vt* **1** SIGNIFY : significar **2** : importar <to import foreign cars : importar autos extranjeros>

import[2] ['ɪmˌport] *n* **1** SIGNIFICANCE : importancia *f,* significación *f* **2** → **importation**

importance [ɪm'portənts] *n* : importancia *f*

important [ɪm'pɔrtənt] *adj* : importante

importantly [ɪm'pɔrtəntli] *adv* **1** : con importancia **2 more importantly** : lo que es más importante

importation [ˌɪmˌpɔr'teɪʃən] *n* : importación *f*

importer [ɪm'portər] *n* : importador *m,* -dora *f*

importunate [ɪm'pɔrtʃənət] *adj* : importuno, insistente

importune [ˌɪmpər'tu:n, -'tju:n; ɪm'pɔrtʃən] *vt* **-tuned; -tuning** : importunar, implorar

impose [ɪm'po:z] *v* **-posed; -posing** *vt* : imponer <to impose a tax : imponer un impuesto> — *vi* **to impose on** : abusar de, molestar <to impose on her kindness : abusar de su bondad>

imposing [ɪm'po:zɪŋ] *adj* : imponente, impresionante

imposition [ˌɪmpə'zɪʃən] *n* : imposición *f*

impossibility [ɪmˌpɑsə'bɪləti] *n, pl* **-ties** : imposibilidad *f*

impossible [ɪm'pɑsəbəl] *adj* **1** : imposible <an impossible task : una tarea imposible> <to make life impossible for : hacerle la vida imposible a> **2** UNACCEPTABLE : inaceptable

impossibly [ɪm'pɑsəbli] *adv* : imposiblemente, increíblemente

impostor *or* **imposter** [ɪm'pɑstər] *n* : impostor *m,* -tora *f*

imposture [ɪm'pɑstʃər] *n* : impostura *f*

impotence ['ɪmpətənts] *n* : impotencia *f*

impotency ['ɪmpətəntsi] → **impotence**

impotent ['ɪmpətənt] *adj* : impotente

impound [ɪm'paʊnd] *vt* : incautar, embargar, confiscar

impoverish [ɪm'pɑvərɪʃ] *vt* : empobrecer

impoverishment [ɪm'pɑvərɪʃmənt] *n* : empobrecimiento *m*

impracticable [ɪm'præktɪkəbəl] *adj* : impracticable

impractical [ɪm'præktɪkəl] *adj* : poco práctico

imprecise [ˌɪmprɪ'saɪs] *adj* : impreciso

imprecisely [ˌɪmprɪ'saɪsli] *adv* : con imprecisión

impreciseness [ˌɪmprɪ'saɪsnəs] → **imprecision**

imprecision [ˌɪmprɪ'sɪʒən] *n* : imprecisión *f,* falta de precisión *f*

impregnable [ɪm'prɛgnəbəl] *adj* : inexpugnable, impenetrable, inconquistable

impregnate [ɪm'prɛgˌneɪt] *vt* **-nated; -nating 1** FERTILIZE : fecundar **2** PERMEATE, SATURATE : impregnar, empapar, saturar

impresario [ˌɪmprə'sɑriˌo, -'sær-] *n, pl* **-rios** : empresario *m,* -ria *f*

impress [ɪm'prɛs] *vt* **1** IMPRINT : imprimir, estampar **2** : impresionar, causar impresión a <I was not impressed : no me hizo buena impresión> **3 to impress (something) on someone** : recalcarle (algo) a alguien — *vi* : impresionar, hacer una impresión

impression [ɪm'prɛʃən] *n* **1** IMPRINT : marca *f,* huella *f,* molde *m* (de los dientes) **2** EFFECT : impresión *f,* efecto *m,* impacto *m* **3** PRINTING : impresión *f* **4** NOTION : impresión *f,* noción *f*

impressionable [ɪm'prɛʃənəbəl] *adj* : impresionable

impressive [ɪm'prɛsɪv] *adj* : impresionante — **impressively** *adv*

impressiveness [ɪm'prɛsɪvnəs] *n* : calidad de ser impresionante

imprint[1] [ɪm'prɪnt, 'ɪmˌ-] *vt* : imprimir, estampar

imprint[2] ['ɪmˌprɪnt] *n* : marca *f,* huella *f*

imprison [ɪm'prɪzən] *vt* **1** JAIL : encarcelar, aprisionar **2** CONFINE : recluir, encerrar

imprisonment [ɪm'prɪzənmənt] *n* : encarcelamiento *m*

improbability [ɪmˌprɑbə'bɪləti] *n, pl* **-ties** : improbabilidad *f,* inverosimilitud *f*

improbable [ɪm'prɑbəbəl] *adj* : improbable, inverosímil

impromptu[1] [ɪmˈprɑmpˌtuː, -ˌtjuː] *adv* : sin preparación, espontáneamente
impromptu[2] *adj* : espontáneo, improvisado
impromptu[3] *n* : improvisación *f*
improper [ɪmˈprɑpər] *adj* **1** INCORRECT : incorrecto, impropio **2** INDECOROUS : indecoroso
improperly [ɪmˈprɑpərli] *adv* : incorrectamente, indebidamente
impropriety [ˌɪmprəˈpraɪəṭi] *n, pl* **-eties 1** INDECOROUSNESS : indecoro *m,* falta *f* de decoro **2** ERROR : impropiedad *f,* incorrección *f*
improve [ɪmˈpruːv] *v* **-proved; -proving** : mejorar
improvement [ɪmˈpruːvmənt] *n* : mejoramiento *m,* mejora *f*
improvidence [ɪmˈprɑvədən*t*s] *n* : imprevisión *f*
improvident [ɪmˈprɑvədənt] *adj* : sin previsión, imprevisor
improvisation [ɪmˌprɑvəˈzeɪʃən, ˌɪmprəvə-] *n* : improvisación *f*
improvise [ˈɪmprəˌvaɪz] *v* **-vised; -vising** : improvisar
imprudence [ɪmˈpruːdən*t*s] *n* : imprudencia *f,* indiscreción *f*
imprudent [ɪmˈpruːdənt] *adj* : imprudente, indiscreto
impudence [ˈɪmpjədən*t*s] *n* : insolencia *f,* descaro *m*
impudent [ˈɪmpjədənt] *adj* : insolente, descarado — **impudently** *adv*
impugn [ɪmˈpjuːn] *vt* : impugnar
impulse [ˈɪmˌpʌls] *n* **1** : impulso *m* **2 on impulse** : sin reflexionar
impulsive [ɪmˈpʌlsɪv] *adj* : impulsivo — **impulsively** *adv*
impulsiveness [ɪmˈpʌlsɪvnəs] *n* : impulsividad *f*
impunity [ɪmˈpjuːnəṭi] *n* **1** : impunidad *f* **2 with impunity** : impunemente
impure [ɪmˈpjʊr] *adj* **1** : impuro <impure thoughts : pensamientos impuros> **2** CONTAMINATED : con impurezas, impuro
impurity [ɪmˈpjʊrəṭi] *n, pl* **-ties** : impureza *f*
impute [ɪmˈpjuːt] *vt* **-puted; -puting** ATTRIBUTE : imputar, atribuir
in[1] [ˈɪn] *adv* **1** INSIDE : dentro, adentro <let's go in : vamos adentro> **2** HARVESTED : recogido <the crops are in : las cosechas ya están recogidas> **3 to be in** : estar <is Linda in? : ¿está Linda?> **4 to be in** : estar en poder <the Democrats are in : los demócratas están en el poder> **5 to be in for** : ser objeto de, estar a punto de <they're in for a treat : los van a agasajar> <he's in for a surprise : se va a llevar una sorpresa> **6 to be in on** : participar en, tomar parte en
in[2] *adj* **1** INSIDE : interior <the in part : la parte interior> **2** FASHIONABLE : de moda
in[3] *prep* **1** (*indicating location or position*) <in the lake : en el lago> <a pain in the leg : un dolor en la pierna> <in the sun : al sol> <in the rain : bajo la lluvia> <the best restaurant in Buenos Aires : el mejor restaurante de Buenos Aires> **2** INTO : en, a <he broke it in pieces : lo rompió en pedazos> <she went in the house : se metió a la casa> **3** DURING : por, durante <in the afternoon : por la tarde> **4** WITHIN : dentro de <I'll be back in a week : vuelvo dentro de una semana> **5** (*indicating manner*) : en, con, de <in Spanish : en español> <written in pencil : escrito con lápiz> <in this way : de esta manera> **6** (*indicating states or circumstances*) <to be in luck : tener suerte> <to be in love : estar enamorado> <to be in a hurry : tener prisa> **7** (*indicating purpose*) : en <in reply : en respuesta, como réplica>
inability [ˌɪnəˈbɪləṭi] *n, pl* **-ties** : incapacidad *f*
inaccessibility [ˌɪnɪkˌsɛsəˈbɪləṭi] *n, pl* **-ties** : inaccesibilidad *f*
inaccessible [ˌɪnɪkˈsɛsəbəl] *adj* : inaccesible
inaccuracy [ɪnˈækjərəsi] *n, pl* **-cies 1** : inexactitud *f* **2** MISTAKE : error *m*
inaccurate [ɪnˈækjərət] *n* : inexacto, erróneo, incorrecto
inaccurately [ɪnˈækjərətli] *adv* : incorrectamente, con inexactitud
inaction [ɪnˈækʃən] *n* : inactividad *f,* inacción *f*
inactive [ɪnˈæktɪv] *n* : inactivo
inactivity [ˌɪnˌækˈtɪvəṭi] *n, pl* **-ties** : inactividad *f,* ociosidad *f*
inadequacy [ɪnˈædɪkwəsi] *n, pl* **-cies 1** INSUFFICIENCY : insuficiencia *f* **2** INCOMPETENCE : ineptitud *f,* incompetencia *f*
inadequate [ɪnˈædɪkwət] *adj* **1** INSUFFICIENT : insuficiente, inadecuado **2** INCOMPETENT : inepto, incompetente
inadmissible [ˌɪnædˈmɪsəbəl] *adj* : inadmisible
inadvertent [ˌɪnədˈvərtənt] *adj* : inadvertido, involuntario — **inadvertently** *adv*
inadvisable [ˌɪnædˈvaɪzəbəl] *adj* : desaconsejable
inalienable [ɪnˈeɪljənəbəl, -ˈeɪliənə-] *adj* : inalienable
inane [ɪˈneɪn] *adj* **inaner; -est** : estúpido, idiota, necio
inanimate [ɪnˈænəmət] *adj* : inanimado, exánime
inanity [ɪˈnænəṭi] *n, pl* **-ties 1** STUPIDITY : estupidez *f* **2** NONSENSE : idiotez *f,* disparate *m*
inapplicable [ɪnˈæplɪkəbəl, ˌɪnəˈplɪkəbəl] *adj* IRRELEVANT : inaplicable, irrelevante
inappreciable [ˌɪnəˈpriːʃəbəl] *adj* : inapreciable, imperceptible
inappropriate [ˌɪnəˈproːpriət] *adj* : inapropiado, inadecuado, impropio

inappropriateness [ˌɪnəˈproːpriətnəs] *n* : lo inapropiado, impropiedad *f*

inapt [ɪnˈæpt] *adj* **1** UNSUITABLE : inadecuado, inapropiado **2** INEPT : inepto

inarticulate [ˌɪnɑrˈtɪkjələt] *adj* : inarticulado, incapaz de expresarse

inarticulately [ˌɪnɑrˈtɪkjələtli] *adv* : inarticuladamente

inasmuch as [ˌɪnæzˈmʌtʃæz] *conj* : ya que, dado que, puesto que

inattention [ˌɪnəˈtɛntʃən] *n* : falta *f* de atención, distracción *f*

inattentive [ˌɪnəˈtɛntɪv] *adj* : distraído, despistado

inattentively [ˌɪnəˈtɛntɪvli] *adv* : distraídamente, sin prestar atención

inaudible [ɪnˈɔdəbəl] *adj* : inaudible

inaudibly [ɪnˈɔdəbli] *adv* : de forma inaudible

inaugural[1] [ɪˈnɔgjərəl, -gərəl] *adj* : inaugural, de investidura

inaugural[2] *n* **1** *or* **inaugural address** : discurso *m* de investidura **2** INAUGURATION : investidura *f* (de una persona)

inaugurate [ɪˈnɔgjəˌreɪt, -gə-] *vt* **-rated; -rating 1** BEGIN : inaugurar **2** INDUCT : investir <to inaugurate the president : investir al presidente>

inauguration [ɪˌnɔgjəˈreɪʃən, -gə-] *n* **1** : inauguración *f* (de un edificio, un sistema, etc.) **2** : investidura *f* (de una persona)

inauspicious [ˌɪnɔˈspɪʃəs] *adj* : desfavorable, poco propicio

inborn [ˈɪnˌbɔrn] *adj* **1** CONGENITAL, INNATE : innato, congénito **2** HEREDITARY : hereditario

inbred [ˈɪnˌbrɛd] *adj* **1** : engendrado por endogamia **2** INNATE : innato

inbreed [ˈɪnˌbriːd] *vt* **-bred; -breeding** : engendrar por endogamia

inbreeding [ˈɪnˌbriːdɪŋ] *n* : endogamia *f*

incalculable [ɪnˈkælkjələbəl] *adj* : incalculable — **incalculably** [-bli] *adv*

incandescence [ˌɪnkənˈdɛsənts] *n* : incandescencia *f*

incandescent [ˌɪnkənˈdɛsənt] *adj* **1** : incandescente **2** BRILLIANT : brillante

incantation [ˌɪnˌkænˈteɪʃən] *n* : conjuro *m*, ensalmo *m*

incapable [ɪnˈkeɪpəbəl] *adj* : incapaz

incapacitate [ˌɪnkəˈpæsəˌteɪt] *vt* **-tated; -tating** : incapacitar

incapacity [ˌɪnkəˈpæsəti] *n, pl* **-ties** : incapacidad *f*

incarcerate [ɪnˈkɑrsəˌreɪt] *vt* **-ated; -ating** : encarcelar

incarceration [ɪnˌkɑrsəˈreɪʃən] *n* : encarcelamiento *m*, encarcelación *f*

incarnate[1] [ɪnˈkɑrˌneɪt] *vt* **-nated; -nating** : encarnar

incarnate[2] [ɪnˈkɑrnət, -ˌneɪt] *adj* : encarnado

incarnation [ˌɪnˌkɑrˈneɪʃən] *n* : encarnación *f*

incendiary[1] [ɪnˈsɛndiˌɛri] *adj* : incendiario

incendiary[2] *n, pl* **-aries** : incendiario *m*, -ria *f*; pirómano *m*, -na *f*

incense[1] [ɪnˈsɛnts] *vt* **-censed; -censing** : indignar, enfadar, enfurecer

incense[2] [ˈɪnˌsɛnts] *n* : incienso *m*

incentive [ɪnˈsɛntɪv] *n* : incentivo *m*, aliciente *m*, motivación *f*, acicate *m*

inception [ɪnˈsɛpʃən] *n* : comienzo *m*, principio *m*

incessant [ɪnˈsɛsənt] *adj* : incesante, continuo — **incessantly** *adv*

incest [ˈɪnˌsɛst] *n* : incesto *m*

incestuous [ɪnˈsɛstʃʊəs] *adj* : incestuoso

inch[1] [ˈɪntʃ] *v* : avanzar poco a poco

inch[2] *n* **1** : pulgada *f* **2 every inch** : absoluto, seguro <every inch a winner : un seguro ganador> **3 within an inch of** : a punto de

incidence [ˈɪntsədənts] *n* **1** FREQUENCY : frecuencia *f*, índice *m* <a high incidence of crime : un alto índice de crímenes> **2 angle of incidence** : ángulo *m* de incidencia

incident[1] [ˈɪntsədənt] *adj* : incidente

incident[2] *n* : incidente *m*, incidencia *f*, episodio *m* (en una obra de ficción)

incidental[1] [ˌɪntsəˈdɛntəl] *adj* **1** SECONDARY : incidental, secundario **2** ACCIDENTAL : casual, fortuito

incidental[2] *n* **1** : algo incidental **2 incidentals** *npl* : imprevistos *mpl*

incidentally [ˌɪntsəˈdɛntəli, -ˈdɛntli] *adv* **1** BY CHANCE : incidentalmente, casualmente **2** BY THE WAY : a propósito, por cierto

incinerate [ɪnˈsɪnəˌreɪt] *vt* **-ated; -ating** : incinerar

incinerator [ɪnˈsɪnəˌreɪt̬ər] *n* : incinerador *m*

incipient [ɪnˈsɪpiənt] *adj* : incipiente, naciente

incise [ɪnˈsaɪz] *vt* **-cised; -cising 1** ENGRAVE : grabar, cincelar, inscribir **2** : hacer una incisión en

incision [ɪnˈsɪʒən] *n* : incisión *f*

incisive [ɪnˈsaɪsɪv] *adj* : incisivo, penetrante

incisively [ɪnˈsaɪsɪvli] *adv* : con agudeza

incisor [ɪnˈsaɪzər] *n* : incisivo *m*

incite [ɪnˈsaɪt] *vt* **-cited; -citing** : incitar, instigar

incitement [ɪnˈsaɪtmənt] *n* : incitación *f*

inclemency [ɪnˈklɛməntsi] *n, pl* **-cies** : inclemencia *f*

inclement [ɪnˈklɛmənt] *adj* : inclemente, tormentuoso

inclination [ˌɪnkləˈneɪʃən] *n* **1** PROPENSITY : inclinación *f*, tendencia *f* **2** DESIRE : deseo *m*, ganas *fpl* **3** BOW : inclinación *f*

incline[1] [ɪnˈklaɪn] *v* **-clined; -clining** *vi* **1** SLOPE : inclinarse **2** TEND : inclinarse, tender <he is inclined to be late : tiende a llegar tarde> — *vt* **1** LOWER : inclinar, bajar <to incline one's head

: bajar la cabeza> 2 SLANT : inclinar 3 PREDISPOSE : predisponer

incline[2] [ˈɪnˌklaɪn] *n* : inclinación *f*, pendiente *f*

inclined [ɪnˈklaɪnd] *adj* 1 SLOPING : inclinado 2 PRONE : prono, dispuesto, dado

inclose, inclosure → **enclose, enclosure**

include [ɪnˈklu:d] *vt* **-cluded; -cluding** : incluir, comprender

inclusion [ɪnˈklu:ʒən] *n* : inclusión *f*

inclusive [ɪnˈklu:sɪv] *adj* : inclusivo

incognito [ˌɪnˌkɑgˈni:t̬o, ɪnˈkɑgnəˌto:] *adv & adj* : de incógnito

incoherence [ˌɪnkoˈhɪrənts, -ˈhɛr-] *n* : incoherencia *f*

incoherent [ˌɪnkoˈhɪrənt, -ˈhɛr-] *adj* : incoherente — **incoherently** *adv*

incombustible [ˌɪnkəmˈbʌstəbəl] *adj* : incombustible

income [ˈɪnˌkʌm] *n* : ingresos *mpl*, entradas *fpl*

income tax *n* : impuesto *m* sobre la renta

incoming [ˈɪnˌkʌmɪŋ] *adj* 1 ARRIVING : que se recibe (dícese del correo), que llega (dícese de las personas), ascendente (dícese de la marea) 2 NEW : nuevo, entrante <the incoming president : el nuevo presidente> <the incoming year : el año entrante>

incommunicado [ˌɪnkəˌmju:nəˈkɑdo] *adj* : incomunicado

incomparable [ɪnˈkɑmpərəbəl] *adj* : incomparable, sin igual

incompatible [ˌɪnkəmˈpæt̬əbəl] *adj* : incompatible

incompetence [ɪnˈkɑmpət̬ənts] *n* : incompetencia *f*, impericia *f*, ineptitud *f*

incompetent [ɪnˈkɑmpət̬ənt] *adj* : incompetente, inepto, incapaz

incomplete [ˌɪnkəmˈpli:t] *adj* : incompleto — **incompletely** *adv*

incomprehensible [ˌɪnˌkɑmpriˈhɛntsəbəl] *adj* : incomprensible

inconceivable [ˌɪnkənˈsi:vəbəl] *adj* 1 INCOMPREHENSIBLE : incomprensible 2 UNBELIEVABLE : inconcebible, increíble

inconceivably [ˌɪnkənˈsi:vəbli] *adv* : inconcebiblemente, increíblemente

inconclusive [ˌɪnkənˈklu:sɪv] *adj* : inconcluyente, no decisivo

incongruity [ˌɪnkənˈgru:əti, -ˌkɑn-] *n*, *pl* **-ties** : incongruencia *f*

incongruous [ɪnˈkɑŋgrʊəs] *adj* : incongruente, inapropiado, fuera de lugar

incongruously [ɪnˈkɑŋgrʊəsli] *adv* : de manera incongruente, inapropiadamente

inconsequential [ˌɪnˌkɑnsəˈkwɛntʃəl] *adj* : intrascendente, de poco importancia

inconsiderable [ˌɪnkənˈsɪdərəbəl] *adj* : insignificante

inconsiderate [ˌɪnkənˈsɪdərət] *adj* : desconsiderado, sin consideración — **inconsiderately** *adv*

inconsistency [ˌɪnkənˈsɪstəntsi] *n*, *pl* **-cies** : inconsecuencia *f*, inconsistencia *f*

inconsistent [ˌɪnkənˈsɪstənt] *adj* : inconsecuente, inconsistente

inconsolable [ˌɪnkənˈso:ləbəl] *adj* : inconsolable — **inconsolably** [-bli] *adv*

inconspicuous [ˌɪnkənˈspɪkjʊəs] *adj* : discreto, no conspicuo, que no llama la atención

inconspicuously [ˌɪnkənˈspɪkjʊəsli] *adv* : discretamente, sin llamar la atención

incontestable [ˌɪnkənˈtɛstəbəl] *adj* : incontestable, indiscutible — **incontestably** [-bli] *adv*

incontinence [ɪnˈkɑntənənts] *n* : incontinencia *f*

incontinent [ɪnˈkɑntənənt] *adj* : incontinente

inconvenience[1] [ˌɪnkənˈvi:njənts] **-nienced; -niencing** *vt* : importunar, incomodar, molestar

inconvenience[2] *n* : incomodidad *f*, molestia *f*

inconvenient [ˌɪnkənˈvi:njənt] *adj* : inconveniente, importuno, incómodo — **inconveniently** *adv*

incorporate [ɪnˈkɔrpəˌreɪt] *vt* **-rated; -rating** 1 INCLUDE : incorporar, incluir 2 : incorporar, constituir en sociedad (dícese de un negocio)

incorporation [ɪnˌkɔrpəˈreɪʃən] *n* : incorporación *f*

incorporeal [ˌɪnˌkɔrˈporiəl] *adj* : incorpóreo

incorrect [ˌɪnkəˈrɛkt] *adj* 1 INACCURATE : incorrecto 2 WRONG : equivocado, erróneo 3 IMPROPER : impropio — **incorrectly** *adv*

incorrigible [ɪnˈkɔrədʒəbəl] *adj* : incorregible

incorruptible [ˌɪnkəˈrʌptəbəl] *adj* : incorruptible

increase[1] [ɪnˈkri:s, ˈɪnˌkri:s] *v* **-creased; -creasing** *vi* GROW : aumentar, crecer, subir (dícese de los precios) — *vt* AUGMENT : aumentar, acrecentar

increase[2] [ˈɪnˌkri:s, ɪnˈkri:s] *n* : aumento *m*, incremento *m*, subida *f* (de precios)

increasing [ɪnˈkri:sɪŋ, ˈɪnˌkri:sɪŋ] *adj* : creciente

increasingly [ɪnˈkri:sɪŋli] *adv* : cada vez más

incredible [ɪnˈkrɛdəbəl] *adj* : increíble — **incredibly** [-bli] *adv*

incredulity [ˌɪnkrɪˈdu:lət̬i, -ˈdju:-] *n* : incredulidad *f*

incredulous [ɪnˈkrɛdʒələs] *adj* : incrédulo, escéptico

incredulously [ɪnˈkrɛdʒələsli] *adv* : con incredulidad

increment [ˈɪŋkrəmənt, ˈɪn-] *n* : incremento *m*, aumento *m*

incremental [ˌɪŋkrəˈmɛntəl, ˌɪn-] *adj* : de incremento

incriminate [ɪn'krɪmə,neɪt] *vt* **-nated; -nating** : incriminar
incrimination [ɪn,krɪmə'neɪʃən] *n* : incriminación *f*
incriminatory [ɪn'krɪmənə,tori] *adj* : incriminatorio
incubate ['ɪŋkjʊ,beɪt, 'ɪn-] *v* **-bated; -bating** *vt* : incubar, empollar — *vi* : incubar(se), empollar
incubation [,ɪŋkjʊ'beɪʃən, ,ɪn-] *n* : incubación *f*
incubator ['ɪŋkjʊ,beɪtər, 'ɪn-] *n* : incubadora *f*
inculcate [ɪn'kʌl,keɪt, 'ɪn,kʌl-] *vt* **-cated; -cating** : inculcar
incumbency [ɪn'kʌmbəntsi] *n, pl* **-cies** **1** OBLIGATION : incumbencia *f* **2** : mandato *m* (en la política)
incumbent[1] [ɪn'kʌmbənt] *adj* : obligatorio
incumbent[2] *n* : titular *mf*
incur [ɪn'kər] *vt* **incurred; incurring** : provocar (al enojo), incurrir en (gastos, obligaciones)
incurable [ɪn'kjʊrəbəl] *adj* : incurable, sin remedio
incursion [ɪn'kərʒən] *n* : incursión *f*
indebted [ɪn'dɛtəd] *adj* **1** : endeudado **2 to be indebted to** : estar en deuda con, estarle agracido a
indebtedness [ɪn'dɛtədnəs] *n* : endeudamiento *m*
indecency [ɪn'diːsəntsi] *n, pl* **-cies** : indecencia *f*
indecent [ɪn'diːsənt] *adj* : indecente — **indecently** *adv*
indecipherable [,ɪndɪ'saɪfərəbəl] *adj* : indescifrable
indecision [,ɪndɪ'sɪʒən] *n* : indecisión *f,* irresolución *f*
indecisive [,ɪndɪ'saɪsɪv] *adj* **1** INCONCLUSIVE : indeciso, que no es decisivo **2** IRRESOLUTE : indeciso, irresoluto, vacilante **3** INDEFINITE : indefinido — **indecisively** *adv*
indecorous [ɪn'dɛkərəs, ,ɪndɪ'korəs] *adj* : indecoroso — **indecorously** *adv*
indecorousness [ɪn'dɛkərəsnəs, ,ɪndɪ'korəs-] *n* : indecoro *m*
indeed [ɪn'diːd] *adv* **1** TRULY : verdaderamente, de veras **2** (*used as intensifier*) <thank you very much indeed : muchísimas gracias> **3** OF COURSE : claro, por supuesto
indefatigable [,ɪndɪ'fætɪgəbəl] *adj* : incansable, infatigable — **indefatigably** [-bli] *adv*
indefensible [,ɪndɪ'fɛntsəbəl] *adj* **1** VULNERABLE : indefendible, vulnerable **2** INEXCUSABLE : inexcusable
indefinable [,ɪndɪ'faɪnəbəl] *adj* : indefinible
indefinite [ɪn'dɛfənət] *adj* **1** : indefinido, indeterminado <indefinite pronouns : pronombres indefinidos> **2** VAGUE : vago, impreciso
indefinitely [ɪn'dɛfənətli] *adv* : indefinidamente, por un tiempo indefinido
indelible [ɪn'dɛləbəl] *adj* : indeleble, imborrable — **indelibly** [-bli] *adv*
indelicacy [ɪn'dɛləkəsi] *n* : falta *f* de delicadeza
indelicate [ɪn'dɛlɪkət] *adj* **1** IMPROPER : indelicado, indecoroso **2** TACTLESS : indiscreto, falto de tacto
indemnify [ɪn'dɛmnə,faɪ] *vt* **-fied; -fying** **1** INSURE : asegurar **2** COMPENSATE : indemnizar, compensar
indemnity [ɪn'dɛmnəti] *n, pl* **-ties** **1** INSURANCE : indemnidad *f* **2** COMPENSATION : indemnización *f*
indent [ɪn'dɛnt] *vt* : sangrar (un párrafo)
indentation [,ɪn,dɛn'teɪʃən] *n* **1** NOTCH : muesca *f,* mella *f* **2** INDENTING : sangría *f* (de un párrafo)
indenture[1] [ɪn'dɛntʃər] *vt* **-tured; -turing** : ligar por contrato
indenture[2] *n* : contrato de aprendizaje
independence [,ɪndə'pɛndənts] *n* : independencia *f*
Independence Day *n* : día *m* de la Independencia (4 de julio en los EE.UU.)
independent[1] [,ɪndə'pɛndənt] *adj* : independiente — **independently** *adv*
independent[2] *n* : independiente *mf*
indescribable [,ɪndɪ'skraɪbəbəl] *adj* : indescriptible, incalificable — **indescribably** [-bli] *adv*
indestructibility [,ɪndɪ,strʌktə'bɪləti] *n* : indestructibilidad *f*
indestructible [,ɪndɪ'strʌktəbəl] *adj* : indestructible
indeterminate [,ɪndɪ'tərmənət] *adj* **1** VAGUE : vago, impreciso, indeterminado **2** INDEFINITE : indeterminado, indefinido
index[1] ['ɪn,dɛks] *vt* **1** : ponerle un índice a (un libro o una revista) **2** : incluir en un índice <all proper names are indexed : todos los nombres propios están incluidos en el índice> **3** INDICATE : indicar, señalar **4** REGULATE : indexar, indiciar <to index prices : indiciar los precios>
index[2] *n, pl* **-dexes** *or* **-dices** ['ɪndə,siːz] **1** : índice *m* (de un libro, de precios) **2** INDICATION : indicio *m,* índice *m,* señal *f* <an index of her character : una señal de su carácter>
index finger *n* FOREFINGER : dedo *m* índice
Indian ['ɪndiən] *n* **1** : indio *m,* -dia *f* **2** → **American Indian** — **Indian** *adj*
indicate ['ɪndə,keɪt] *vt* **-cated; -cating** **1** POINT OUT : indicar, señalar **2** SHOW, SUGGEST : ser indicio de, ser señal de **3** EXPRESS : expresar, señalar **4** REGISTER : marcar, poner (una medida, etc.)
indication [,ɪndə'keɪʃən] *n* : indicio *m,* señal *f*
indicative [ɪn'dɪkətɪv] *adj* : indicativo

indicator ['ɪndə,keɪtər] *n* : indicador *m*
indict [ɪn'daɪt] *vt* : acusar, procesar (por un crímen)
indictment [ɪn'daɪtmənt] *n* : acusación *f*
indifference [ɪn'dɪfrənts, -'dɪfə-] *n* : indiferencia *f*
indifferent [ɪn'dɪfrənt, -'dɪfə-] *adj* **1** UNCONCERNED : indiferente **2** MEDIOCRE : mediocre
indifferently [ɪn'dɪfrəntli, -'dɪfə-] *adv* **1** : con indiferencia, indiferentemente **2** so-so : de modo regular, más o menos
indigence ['ɪndɪdʒənts] *n* : indigencia *f*
indigenous [ɪn'dɪdʒənəs] *adj* : indígena, nativo
indigent ['ɪndɪdʒənt] *adj* : indigente, pobre
indigestible [,ɪndaɪ'dʒɛstəbəl, -dɪ-] *adj* : difícil de digerir
indigestion [,ɪndaɪ'dʒɛstʃən, -dɪ-] *n* : indigestión *f*, empacho *m*
indignant [ɪn'dɪgnənt] *adj* : indignado
indignantly [ɪn'dɪgnəntli] *adv* : con indignación
indignation [,ɪndɪg'neɪʃən] *n* : indignación *f*
indignity [ɪn'dɪgnəti] *n, pl* **-ties** : indignidad *f*
indigo ['ɪndɪ,go:] *n, pl* **-gos** *or* **-goes** : añil *m*, índigo *m*
indirect [,ɪndə'rɛkt, -daɪ-] *adj* : indirecto — **indirectly** *adv*
indiscernible [,ɪndɪ'sərnəbəl, -'zər-] *adj* : imperceptible
indiscreet [,ɪndɪ'skri:t] *adj* : indiscreto, imprudente — **indiscreetly** *adv*
indiscretion [,ɪndɪ'skrɛʃən] *n* : indiscreción *f*, imprudencia *f*
indiscriminate [,ɪndɪ'skrɪmənət] *adj* : indiscriminado
indiscriminately [,ɪndɪ'skrɪmənətli] *adv* : sin discriminación, sin discernimiento
indispensable [,ɪndɪ'spɛntsəbəl] *adj* : indispensable, necesario, imprescindible — **indispensably** [-bli] *adv*
indisposed [,ɪndɪ'spo:zd] *adj* **1** ILL : indispuesto, enfermo **2** AVERSE, DISINCLINED : opuesto, reacio <to be indisposed toward working : no tener ganas de trabajar>
indisputable [,ɪndɪ'spju:təbəl, ɪn'dɪspjʊtə-] *adj* : indiscutible, incuestionable, incontestable — **indisputably** [-bli] *adv*
indistinct [,ɪndɪ'stɪŋkt] *adj* : indistinto — **indistinctly** *adv*
indistinctness [,ɪndɪ'stɪŋktnəs] *n* : falta *f* de claridad
individual[1] [,ɪndə'vɪdʒʊəl] *adj* **1** PERSONAL : individual, personal <individual traits : características personales> **2** SEPARATE : individual, separado **3** PARTICULAR : particular, propio
individual[2] *n* : individuo *m*
individualist [,ɪndə'vɪdʒʊəlɪst] *n* : individualista *mf*
individuality [,ɪndə,vɪdʒʊ'æləti] *n, pl* **-ties** : individualidad *f*
individually [,ɪndə'vɪdʒʊəli, -dʒəli] *adv* : individualmente
indivisible [,ɪndɪ'vɪzəbəl] *adj* : indivisible
indoctrinate [ɪn'dɑktrə,neɪt] *vt* **-nated; -nating 1** TEACH : enseñar, instruir **2** PROPAGANDIZE : adoctrinar
indoctrination [ɪn,dɑktrə'neɪʃən] *n* : adoctrinamiento *m*
indolence ['ɪndələnts] *n* : indolencia *f*
indolent ['ɪndələnt] *adj* : indolente
indomitable [ɪn'dɑmətəbəl] *adj* : invencible, indomable, indómito — **indomitably** [-bli] *adv*
Indonesian [,ɪndo'ni:ʒən, -ʃən] *n* : indonesio *m*, -sia *f* — **Indonesian** *adj*
indoor ['ɪn'dor] *adj* : interior (dícese de las plantas), para estar en casa (dícese de la ropa), cubierto (dícese de las piscinas, etc.), bajo techo (dícese de los deportes)
indoors ['ɪn'dorz] *adv* : adentro, dentro
indubitable [ɪn'du:bətəbəl, -'dju:-] *adj* : indudable, incuestionable, indiscutible
indubitably [ɪn'du:bətəbli, -'dju:-] *adv* : indudablemente
induce [ɪn'du:s, -'dju:s] *vt* **-duced; -ducing 1** PERSUADE : persuadir, inducir **2** CAUSE : inducir, provocar <to induce labor : provocar un parto>
inducement [ɪn'du:smənt, -'dju:s-] *n* **1** INCENTIVE : incentivo *m*, aliciente *m* **2** : inducción *f*, provocación *f* (de un parto)
induct [ɪn'dʌkt] *vt* **1** INSTALL : instalar, investir **2** ADMIT : admitir (como miembro) **3** CONSCRIPT : reclutar (al servicio militar)
inductee [,ɪn,dʌk'ti:] *n* : recluta *mf*, conscripto *m*, -ta *f*
induction [ɪn'dʌkʃən] *n* **1** INTRODUCTION : iniciación *f*, introducción *f* **2** : inducción *f* (en la lógica o la electricidad)
inductive [ɪn'dʌktɪv] *adj* : inductivo
indulge [ɪn'dʌldʒ] *v* **-dulged; -dulging** *vt* **1** GRATIFY : gratificar, satisfacer **2** SPOIL : consentir, mimar — *vi* **to indulge in** : permitirse
indulgence [ɪn'dʌldʒənts] *n* **1** SATISFYING : satisfacción *f*, gratificación *f* **2** HUMORING : complacencia *f*, indulgencia *f* **3** SPOILING : consentimiento *m* **4** : indulgencia *f* (en la religión)
indulgent [ɪŋ'dʌldʒənt] *adj* : indulgente, consentido — **indulgently** *adv*
industrial [ɪn'dʌstriəl] *adj* : industrial — **industrially** *adv*
industrialist [ɪn'dʌstriəlɪst] *n* : industrial *mf*

industrialization [ɪnˌdʌstriələˈzeɪʃən] *n* : industrialización *f*
industrialize [ɪnˈdʌstriəˌlaɪz] *vt* **-ized; -izing** : industrializar
industrious [ɪnˈdʌstriəs] *adj* : diligente, industrioso, trabajador
industriously [ɪnˈdʌstriəsli] *adv* : con diligencia, con aplicación
industriousness [ɪnˈdʌstriəsnəs] *n* : diligencia *f*, aplicación *f*
industry [ˈɪndəstri] *n, pl* **-tries 1** DILIGENCE : diligencia *f*, aplicación *f* **2** : industria *f* <the steel industry : la industria siderúrgica>
inebriated [ɪˈniːbriˌeɪt̬əd] *adj* : ebrio, embriagado
inebriation [ɪˌniːbriˈeɪʃən] *n* : ebriedad *f*, embriaguez *f*
ineffable [ɪnˈɛfəbəl] *adj* : inefable — **ineffably** [-bli] *adv*
ineffective [ˌɪnɪˈfɛktɪv] *adj* **1** INEFFECTUAL : ineficaz, inútil **2** INCAPABLE : incompetente, ineficiente, incapaz
ineffectively [ˌɪnɪˈfɛktɪvli] *adv* : ineficazmente, infructuosamente
ineffectual [ˌɪnɪˈfɛktʃʊəl] *adj* : inútil, ineficaz — **ineffectually** *adv*
inefficiency [ˌɪnɪˈfɪʃəntsi] *n, pl* **-cies** : ineficiencia *f*, ineficacia *f*
inefficient [ˌɪnɪˈfɪʃənt] *adj* **1** : ineficiente, ineficaz **2** INCAPABLE, INCOMPETENT : incompetente, incapaz — **inefficiently** *adv*
inelegance [ɪnˈɛləgənts] *n* : inelegancia *f*
inelegant [ɪnˈɛləgənt] *adj* : inelegante, poco elegante
ineligibility [ɪnˌɛlədʒəˈbɪlət̬i] *n* : inelegibilidad *f*
ineligible [ɪnˈɛlədʒəbəl] *adj* : inelegible
inept [ɪˈnɛpt] *adj* : inepto <inept at : incapaz para>
ineptitude [ɪˈnɛptəˌtuːd, -ˌtjuːd] *n* : ineptitud *f*, incompetencia *f*, incapacidad *f*
inequality [ˌɪnɪˈkwɑlət̬i] *n, pl* **-ties** : desigualdad *f*
inert [ɪˈnərt] *adj* **1** INACTIVE : inerte, inactivo **2** SLUGGISH : lento
inertia [ɪˈnərʃə] *n* : inercia *f*
inescapable [ˌɪnɪˈskeɪpəbəl] *adj* : inevitable, ineludible — **inescapably** [-bli] *adv*
inessential [ˌɪnɪˈsɛntʃəl] *adj* : que no es esencial, innecesario
inestimable [ɪnˈɛstəməbəl] *adj* : inestimable, inapreciable
inevitability [ɪnˌɛvət̬əˈbɪlət̬i] *n, pl* **-ties** : inevitabilidad *f*
inevitable [ɪnˈɛvət̬əbəl] *adj* : inevitable — **inevitably** [-bli] *adv*
inexact [ˌɪnɪgˈzækt] *adj* : inexacto
inexactly [ˌɪnɪgˈzæktli] *adv* : sin exactitud
inexcusable [ˌɪnɪkˈskjuːzəbəl] *adj* : inexcusable, imperdonable — **inexcusably** [-bli] *adv*
inexhaustible [ˌɪnɪgˈzɔstəbəl] *adj* **1** INDEFATIGABLE : infatigable, incansable **2** ENDLESS : inagotable — **inexhaustibly** [-bli] *adv*
inexorable [ɪnˈɛksərəbəl] *adj* : inexorable — **inexorably** [-bli] *adv*
inexpensive [ˌɪnɪkˈspɛntsɪv] *adj* : barato, económico
inexperience [ˌɪnɪkˈspɪriənts] *n* : inexperiencia *f*
inexperienced [ˌɪnɪkˈspɪriəntst] *adj* : inexperto, novato
inexplicable [ˌɪnɪkˈsplɪkəbəl] *adj* : inexplicable — **inexplicably** [-bli] *adv*
inexpressible [ˌɪnɪkˈsprɛsəbəl] *adj* : inexpresable, inefable
inextricable [ˌɪnɪkˈstrɪkəbəl, ɪˈnɛkˌstrɪ-] *adj* : inextricable — **inextricably** [-bli] *adv*
infallibility [ɪnˌfæləˈbɪlət̬i] *n* : infalibilidad *f*
infallible [ɪnˈfæləbəl] *adj* : infalible — **infallibly** [-bli] *adv*
infamous [ˈɪnfəməs] *adj* : infame — **infamously** *adv*
infamy [ˈɪnfəmi] *n, pl* **-mies** : infamia *f*
infancy [ˈɪnfəntsi] *n, pl* **-cies** : infancia *f*
infant [ˈɪnfənt] *n* : bebé *m;* niño *m*, -ña *f*
infantile [ˈɪnfənˌtaɪl, -təl, -ˌtiːl] *adj* : infantil, pueril
infantile paralysis → **poliomyelitis**
infantry [ˈɪnfəntri] *n, pl* **-tries** : infantería *f*
infatuated [ɪnˈfætʃʊˌeɪt̬əd] *adj* **to be infatuated with** : estar encaprichado con
infatuation [ɪnˌfætʃʊˈeɪʃən] *n* : encaprichamiento *m*, enamoramiento *m*
infect [ɪnˈfɛkt] *vt* : infectar, contagiar
infection [ɪnˈfɛkʃən] *n* : infección *f*, contagio *m*
infectious [ɪnˈfɛkʃəs] *adj* : infeccioso, contagioso
infer [ɪnˈfər] *vt* **inferred; inferring 1** DEDUCE : deducir, inferir **2** SURMISE : concluir, suponer, tener entendido **3** IMPLY : sugerir, insinuar
inference [ˈɪnfərənts] *n* : deducción *f*, inferencia *f*, conclusión *f*
inferior¹ [ɪnˈfɪriər] *adj* : inferior, malo
inferior² *n* : inferior *mf*
inferiority [ɪnˌfɪriˈɔrət̬i] *n, pl* **-ties** : inferioridad *f* <inferiority complex : complejo de inferioridad>
infernal [ɪnˈfərnəl] *adj* **1** : infernal <infernal fires : fuegos infernales> **2** DIABOLICAL : infernal, diabólico **3** DAMNABLE : maldito, condenado
inferno [ɪnˈfərˌnoː] *n, pl* **-nos** : infierno *m*
infertile [ɪnˈfərt̬əl, -ˌtaɪl] *adj* : estéril, infecundo
infertility [ˌɪnfərˈtɪlət̬i] *n* : esterilidad *f*, infecundidad *f*
infest [ɪnˈfɛst] *vt* : infestar, plagar
infidel [ˈɪnfədəl, -ˌdɛl] *n* : infiel *mf*

infidelity [ˌɪnfəˈdɛləṭi, -faɪ-] *n, pl* **-ties** **1** UNFAITHFULNESS : infidelidad *f* **2** DISLOYALTY : deslealtad *f*
infield [ˈɪnˌfiːld] *n* : cuadro *m,* diamante *m*
infiltrate [ɪnˈfɪlˌtreɪt, ˈɪnfɪl-] *v* **-trated; -trating** *vt* : infiltrar — *vi* : infiltrarse
infiltration [ˌɪnfɪlˈtreɪʃən] *n* : infiltración *f*
infinite [ˈɪnfənət] *adj* **1** LIMITLESS : infinito, sin límites **2** VAST : infinito, vasto, extenso
infinitely [ˈɪnfənətli] *adv* : infinitamente
infinitesimal [ˌɪnˌfɪnəˈtɛsəməl] *adj* : infinitésimo, infinitesimal — **infinitesimally** *adv*
infinitive [ɪnˈfɪnəṭɪv] *n* : infinitivo *m*
infinitude [ɪnˈfɪnəˌtuːd, -tjuːd] *n* : infinitud *f*
infinity [ɪnˈfɪnəṭi] *n, pl* **-ties** **1** : infinito *m* (en matemáticas, etc.) **2** : infinidad *f* <an infinity of stars : una infinidad de estrellas>
infirm [ɪnˈfərm] *adj* **1** FEEBLE : enfermizo, endeble **2** INSECURE : inseguro
infirmary [ɪnˈfərməri] *n, pl* **-ries** : enfermería *f,* hospital *m*
infirmity [ɪnˈfərməṭi] *n, pl* **-ties** **1** FRAILTY : debilidad *f,* endeblez *f* **2** AILMENT : enfermedad *f,* dolencia *f* <the infirmities of age : los achaques de la vejez>
inflame [ɪnˈfleɪm] *v* **-flamed; -flaming** *vt* **1** KINDLE : inflamar, encender **2** : inflamar (una herida) **3** STIR UP : encender, provocar, inflamar — *vi* : inflamarse
inflammable [ɪnˈflæməbəl] *adj* **1** FLAMMABLE : inflamable **2** IRASCIBLE : irascible, explosivo
inflammation [ˌɪnfləˈmeɪʃən] *n* : inflamación *f*
inflammatory [ɪnˈflæməˌtori] *adj* : inflamatorio, incendiario
inflatable [ɪnˈfleɪṭəbəl] *adj* : inflable
inflate [ɪnˈfleɪt] *vt* **-flated; -flating** : inflar, hinchar
inflation [ɪnˈfleɪʃən] *n* : inflación *f*
inflationary [ɪnˈfleɪʃəˌnɛri] *adj* : inflacionario, inflacionista
inflect [ɪnˈflɛkt] *vt* **1** CONJUGATE, DECLINE : conjugar, declinar **2** MODULATE : modular (la voz)
inflection [ɪnˈflɛkʃən] *n* : inflexión *f*
inflexibility [ɪnˌflɛksəˈbɪləṭi] *n, pl* **-ties** : inflexibilidad *f*
inflexible [ɪnˈflɛksɪbəl] *adj* : inflexible
inflict [ɪnˈflɪkt] *vt* **1** : infligir, causar, imponer **2 to inflict oneself on** : imponer uno su presencia (a alguien)
infliction [ɪnˈflɪkʃən] *n* : imposición *f*
influence[1] [ˈɪnˌfluːən*t*s, ɪnˈfluːən*t*s] *vt* **-enced; -encing** : influenciar, influir en
influence[2] *n* **1** : influencia *f,* influjo *m* <to exert influence over : ejercer influencia sobre> <the influence of gravity : el influjo de la gravidad> **2 under the influence** : bajo la influencia del alcohol, embriagado
influential [ˌɪnfluˈɛntʃəl] *adj* : influyente
influenza [ˌɪnfluˈɛnzə] *n* : gripe *f,* influenza *f,* gripa *f Col, Mex*
influx [ˈɪnˌflʌks] *n* : afluencia *f* (de gente), entrada *f* (de mercancías), llegada *f* (de ideas)
inform [ɪnˈfɔrm] *vt* : informar, notificar, avisar — *vi* **to inform on** : delatar, denunciar
informal [ɪnˈfɔrməl] *adj* **1** UNCEREMONIOUS : sin ceremonia, sin etiqueta **2** CASUAL : informal, familiar (dícese del lenguaje) **3** UNOFFICIAL : extraoficial
informality [ˌɪnfɔrˈmæləṭi, -fər-] *n, pl* **-ties** : informalidad *f,* familiaridad *f,* falta *f* de ceremonia
informally [ɪnˈfɔrməli] *adv* : sin ceremonias, de manera informal, informalmente
informant [ɪnˈfɔrmənt] *n* : informante *mf;* informador *m,* -dora *f*
information [ˌɪnfərˈmeɪʃən] *n* : información *f*
informative [ɪnˈfɔrməṭɪv] *adj* : informativo, instructivo
informer [ɪnˈfɔrmər] *n* : informante *mf;* informador *m,* -dora *f*
infraction [ɪnˈfrækʃən] *n* : infracción *f,* violación *f,* transgresión *f*
infrared [ˌɪnfrəˈrɛd] *adj* : infrarrojo
infrastructure [ˈɪnfrəˌstrʌktʃər] *n* : infraestructura *f*
infrequent [ɪnˈfriːkwənt] *adj* : infrequente, raro
infrequently [ɪnˈfriːkwəntli] *adv* : raramente, con poca frecuencia
infringe [ɪnˈfrɪndʒ] *v* **-fringed; -fringing** *vt* : infringir, violar — *vi* **to infringe on** : abusar de, violar
infringement [ɪnˈfrɪndʒmənt] *n* **1** VIOLATION : violación *f* (de la ley), incumplimiento *m* (de un contrato) **2** ENCROACHMENT : usurpación *f* (de derechos, etc.)
infuriate [ɪnˈfjʊriˌeɪt] *vt* **-ated; -ating** : enfurecer, poner furioso
infuriating [ɪnˈfjʊriˌeɪṭɪŋ] *adj* : indignante, exasperante
infuse [ɪnˈfjuːz] *vt* **-fused; -fusing** **1** INSTILL : infundir **2** STEEP : hacer una infusión de
infusion [ɪnˈfjuːʒən] *n* : infusión *f*
ingenious [ɪnˈdʒiːnjəs] *adj* : ingenioso — **ingeniously** *adv*
ingenue *or* **ingénue** [ˈɑndʒəˌnuː, ˈæn-; ˈæʒə-, ˈɑ-] *n* : ingenua *f*
ingenuity [ˌɪndʒəˈnuːəṭi, -ˈnjuː-] *n, pl* **-ities** : ingenio
ingenuous [ɪnˈdʒɛnjʊəs] *adj* **1** FRANK : cándido, franco **2** NAIVE : ingenuo — **ingenuously** *adv*
ingenuousness [ɪnˈdʒɛnjʊəsnəs] *n* **1** FRANKNESS : candidez *f,* candor *m* **2** NAÏVETÉ : ingenuidad *f*

ingest [ɪnˈdʒɛst] *vt* : ingerir
inglorious [ɪnˈgloriəs] *adj* : deshonroso, ignominioso
ingot [ˈɪŋgət] *n* : lingote *m*
ingrained [ɪnˈgreɪnd] *adj* : arraigado
ingrate [ˈɪn,greɪt] *n* : ingrato *m*, -ta *f*
ingratiate [ɪnˈgreɪʃi,eɪt] *vt* **-ated; -ating** : conseguir la benevolencia de <to ingratiate oneself with someone : congraciarse con alguien>
ingratiating [ɪnˈgreɪʃi,eɪt̬ɪŋ] *adj* : halagador, zalamero, obsequioso
ingratitude [ɪnˈgræt̬ə,tu:d, -,tju:d] *n* : ingratitud *f*
ingredient [ɪnˈgri:diənt] *n* : ingrediente *m*, componente *m*
ingrown [ˈɪn,gro:n] *adj* **1** : crecido hacia adentro **2 ingrown toenail** : uña *f* encarnada
inhabit [ɪnˈhæbət] *vt* : vivir en, habitar, ocupar
inhabitable [ɪnˈhæbət̬əbəl] *adj* : habitable
inhabitant [ɪnˈhæbət̬ənt] *n* : habitante *mf*
inhalant [ɪnˈheɪlənt] *n* : inhalante *m*
inhalation [,ɪnhəˈleɪʃən, ,ɪnə-] *n* : inhalación *f*
inhale [ɪnˈheɪl] *v* **-haled; -haling** *vt* : inhalar, aspirar — *vi* : inspirar
inhaler [ɪnˈheɪlər] *n* : inhalador *m*
inhere [ɪnˈhɪr] *vi* **-hered; -hering** : ser inherente
inherent [ɪnˈhɪrənt, -ˈhɛr-] *adj* : inherente, intrínseco — **inherently** *adv*
inherit [ɪnˈhɛrət] *vt* : heredar
inheritance [ɪnˈhɛrət̬əntsˌ] *n* : herencia *f*
inheritor [ɪnˈhɛrət̬ər] *n* : heredero *m*, -da *f*
inhibit [ɪnˈhɪbət] *vt* IMPEDE : inhibir, impedir
inhibition [,ɪnhəˈbɪʃən, ,ɪnə-] *n* : inhibición *f*, cohibición *f*
inhuman [ɪnˈhju:mən, -ˈju:-] *adj* : inhumano, cruel — **inhumanly** *adv*
inhumane [,ɪnhjuˈmeɪn, -ju-] *adj* INHUMAN : inhumano, cruel
inhumanity [,ɪnhjuˈmænəti, -ju-] *n, pl* **-ties** : inhumanidad *f*, crueldad *f*
inimical [ɪˈnɪmɪkəl] *adj* **1** UNFAVORABLE : adverso, desfavorable **2** HOSTILE : hostil — **inimically** *adv*
inimitable [ɪˈnɪmət̬əbəl] *adj* : inimitable
iniquitous [ɪˈnɪkwət̬əs] *adj* : inicuo, malvado
iniquity [ɪˈnɪkwət̬i] *n, pl* **-ties** : iniquidad *f*
initial[1] [ɪˈnɪʃəl] *vt* **-tialed** *or* **-tialled; -tialing** *or* **-tialling** : poner las iniciales a, firmar con las iniciales
initial[2] *adj* : inicial, primero — **initially** *adv*
initial[3] *n* : inicial *f*
initiate[1] [ɪˈnɪʃi,eɪt] *vt* **-ated; -ating 1** BEGIN : comenzar, iniciar **2** INDUCT : instruir **3** INTRODUCE : introducir, instruir
initiate[2] [ɪˈnɪʃiət] *n* : iniciado *m*, -da *f*
initiation [ɪ,nɪʃiˈeɪʃən] *n* : iniciación *f*
initiative [ɪˈnɪʃət̬ɪv] *n* : iniciativa *f*
initiatory [ɪˈnɪʃiə,tori] *adj* **1** INTRODUCTORY : introductorio **2** : de iniciación <initiatory rites : ritos de iniciación>
inject [ɪnˈdʒɛkt] *vt* : inyectar
injection [ɪnˈdʒɛkʃən] *n* : inyección *f*
injudicious [,ɪndʒʊˈdɪʃəs] *adj* : imprudente, indiscreto, poco juicioso
injunction [ɪnˈdʒʌŋkʃən] *n* **1** ORDER : orden *f*, mandato *m* **2** COURT ORDER : mandamiento *m* judicial
injure [ˈɪndʒər] *vt* **-jured; -juring 1** WOUND : herir, lesionar **2** HURT : lastimar, dañar, herir **3 to injure oneself** : hacerse daño
injurious [ɪnˈdʒʊriəs] *adj* : perjudicial <injurious to one's health : perjudicial a la salud>
injury [ˈɪndʒəri] *n, pl* **-ries 1** WRONG : mal *m*, injusticia *f* **2** DAMAGE, HARM : herida *f*, daño *m*, perjuicio *m*
injustice [ɪnˈdʒʌstəs] *n* : injusticia *f*
ink[1] [ˈɪŋk] *vt* : entintar
ink[2] *n* : tinta *f*
inkling [ˈɪŋklɪŋ] *n* : presentimiento *m*, indicio *m*, sospecho *m*
inkwell [ˈɪŋk,wɛl] *n* : tintero *m*
inky [ˈɪŋki] *adj* **1** : manchado de tinta **2** BLACK : negro, impenetrable <inky darkness : negra oscuridad>
inland[1] [ˈɪn,lænd, -lənd] *adv* : hacia el interior, tierra adentro
inland[2] *adj* : interior
inland[3] *n* : interior *m*
in–law [ˈɪn,lɔ] *n* **1** : pariente *m* político **2 in–laws** *npl* : suegros *mpl*
inlay[1] [ɪnˈleɪ, ˈɪn,leɪ] *vt* **-laid** [-ˈleɪd, -,leɪd]; **-laying** : incrustar, taracear
inlay[2] [ˈɪn,leɪ] *n* **1** : incrustación *f* **2** : empaste *m* (de un diente)
inlet [ˈɪn,lɛt, -lət] *n* : cala *f*, ensenada *f*
inmate [ˈɪn,meɪt] *n* : paciente *mf* (en un hospital); preso *m*, -sa *f* (en una prisión); interno *m*, -na *f* (en un asilo)
in memoriam [,ɪnməˈmoriəm] *prep* : en memoria de
inmost [ˈɪn,mo:st] → **innermost**
inn [ˈɪn] *n* **1** : posada *f*, hostería *f*, fonda *f* **2** TAVERN : taberna *f*
innards [ˈɪnərdz] *npl* : entrañas *fpl*, tripas *fpl fam*
innate [ɪˈneɪt] *adj* **1** INBORN : innato **2** INHERENT : inherente
inner [ˈɪnər] *adj* : interior, interno
innermost [ˈɪnər,mo:st] *adj* : más íntimo, más profundo
innersole [ˈɪnərˈso:l] → **insole**
inning [ˈɪnɪŋ] *n* : entrada *f*
innkeeper [ˈɪn,ki:pər] *n* : posadero *m*, -ra *f*
innocence [ˈɪnəsənts] *n* : inocencia *f*
innocent[1] [ˈɪnəsənt] *adj* : inocente — **innocently** *adv*
innocent[2] *n* : inocente *mf*

innocuous [ɪ'nɑkjəwəs] *adj* **1** HARMLESS : inocuo **2** INOFFENSIVE : inofensivo

innovate ['ɪnə,veɪt] *vi* **-vated; -vating** : innovar

innovation [,ɪnə'veɪʃən] *n* : innovación *f,* novedad *f*

innovative ['ɪnə,veɪt̬ɪv] *adj* : innovador

innovator ['ɪnə,veɪt̬ər] *n* : innovador *m,* -dora *f*

innuendo [,ɪnjʊ'ɛndo] *n, pl* **-dos** *or* **-does** : insinuación *f,* indirecta *f*

innumerable [ɪ'nuːmərəbəl, -'njuː-] *adj* : innumerable

inoculate [ɪ'nɑkjə,leɪt] *vt* **-lated; -lating** : inocular

inoculation [ɪ,nɑkjə'leɪʃən] *n* : inoculación *f*

inoffensive [,ɪnə'fɛntsɪv] *adj* : inofensivo

inoperable [ɪn'ɑpərəbəl] *adj* : inoperable

inoperative [ɪn'ɑpərət̬ɪv, -,reɪ-] *adj* : inoperante

inopportune [ɪn,ɑpər'tuːn, -'tjuːn] *adj* : inoportuno — **inopportunely** *adv*

inordinate [ɪn'ɔrdənət] *adj* : excesivo, inmoderado, desmesurado — **inordinately** *adv*

inorganic [,ɪn,ɔr'gænɪk] *adj* : inorgánico

inpatient ['ɪn,peɪʃənt] *n* : paciente *mf* hospitalizado

input[1] ['ɪn,pʊt] *vt* **inputted** *or* **input; inputting** : entrar (datos, información)

input[2] *n* **1** CONTRIBUTION : aportación *f,* contribución *f* **2** ENTRY : entrada *f* (de datos) **3** ADVICE, OPINION : consejos *mpl,* opinión *f*

inquest ['ɪn,kwɛst] *n* INQUIRY, INVESTIGATION : investigación *f,* averiguación *f,* pesquisa *f* (judicial)

inquire [ɪn'kwaɪr] *v* **-quired; -quiring** *vt* : preguntar, informarse de, inquirir <he inquired how to get in : preguntó como entrar> — *vi* **1** ASK : preguntar, informarse <to inquire about : informarse sobre> <to inquire after (someone) : preguntar por (alguien)> **2 to inquire into** INVESTIGATE : investigar, inquirir sobre

inquirer [ɪn'kwaɪrər] *n* : inquiridor *m,* -dora *f;* investigador *m,* -dora *f*

inquiringly [ɪn'kwaɪrɪŋli] *adv* : inquisitivamente

inquiry ['ɪn,kwaɪri, ɪn'kwaɪri; 'ɪnkwəri, 'ɪŋ-] *n, pl* **-ries 1** QUESTION : pregunta *f* <to make inquiries about : pedir información sobre> **2** INVESTIGATION : investigación *f,* inquisición *f,* pesquisa *f*

inquisition [,ɪnkwə'zɪʃən, ,ɪŋ-] *n* **1** : inquisición *f,* interrogatorio *m,* investigación *f* **2 the Inquisition** : la Inquisición *f*

inquisitive [ɪn'kwɪzət̬ɪv] *adj* : inquisidor, inquisitivo, curioso — **inquisitively** *adv*

inquisitiveness [ɪn'kwɪzət̬ɪvnəs] *n* : curiosidad *f*

inquisitor [ɪn'kwɪzət̬ər] *n* : inquisidor *m,* -dora *f;* interrogador *m,* -dora *f*

inroad ['ɪn,roːd] *n* **1** ENCROACHMENT, INVASION : invasión *f,* incursión *f* **2 to make inroads into** : ocupar parte de (un tiempo), agotar parte de (ahorros, recursos), invadir (un territorio)

insane [ɪn'seɪn] *adj* **1** MAD : loco, demente <to go insane : volverse loco> **2** ABSURD : absurdo, insensato <an insane scheme : un proyecto insensato>

insanely [ɪn'seɪnli] *adv* : como un loco <insanely suspicious : loco de recelo>

insanity [ɪn'sænət̬i] *n, pl* **-ties 1** MADNESS : locura *f* **2** FOLLY : locura *f,* insensatez *f*

insatiable [ɪn'seɪʃəbəl] *adj* : insaciable — **insatiably** [-bli] *adv*

inscribe [ɪn'skraɪb] *vt* **-scribed; -scribing 1** ENGRAVE : inscribir, grabar **2** ENROLL : inscribir **3** DEDICATE : dedicar (un libro)

inscription [ɪn'skrɪpʃən] *n* : inscripción *f* (en un monumento), dedicación *f* (en un libro), leyenda *f* (de una ilustración, etc.)

inscrutable [ɪn'skruːt̬əbəl] *adj* : inescrutable, misterioso — **inscrutably** [-bli] *adv*

inseam ['ɪn,siːm] *n* : entrepierna *f*

insect ['ɪn,sɛkt] *n* : insecto *m*

insecticidal [ɪn,sɛktə'saɪdəl] *adj* : insecticida

insecticide [ɪn'sɛktə,saɪd] *n* : insecticida *m*

insecure [,ɪnsɪ'kjʊr] *adj* : inseguro, poco seguro — **insecurely** *adv*

insecurely [,ɪnsɪ'kjʊrli] *adv* : inseguramente

insecurity [,ɪnsɪ'kjʊrət̬i] *n, pl* **-ties** : inseguridad *f*

inseminate [ɪn'sɛmə,neɪt] *vt* **-nated; -nating** : inseminar

insemination [ɪn,sɛmə'neɪʃən] *n* : inseminación *f*

insensibility [ɪn,sɛntsə'bɪlət̬i] *n, pl* **-ties** : insensibilidad *f*

insensible [ɪn'sɛntsəbəl] *adj* **1** UNCONSCIOUS : inconsciente, sin conocimiento **2** NUMB : insensible, entumecido **3** UNAWARE : inconsciente

insensitive [ɪn'sɛntsət̬ɪv] *adj* : insensible

insensitivity [ɪn,sɛntsə'tɪvət̬i] *n, pl* **-ties** : insensibilidad *f*

inseparable [ɪn'sɛpərəbəl] *adj* : inseparable

insert[1] [ɪn'sərt] *vt* **1** : insertar, introducir, poner, meter <insert your key in the lock : mete tu llave en la cerradura> **2** INTERPOLATE : interpolar, intercalar

insert[2] [ˈɪnˌsərt] *n* **:** inserción *f,* hoja *f* insertada (en una revista, etc.)
insertion [ɪnˈsərʃən] *n* **:** inserción *f*
inset [ˈɪnˌsɛt] *n* **:** página *f* intercalada (en un libro), entredós *m* (de encaje en la ropa)
inshore[1] [ˈɪnˈʃor] *adv* **:** hacia la costa
inshore[2] *adj* **:** cercano a la costa, costero <inshore fishing : pesca costera>
inside[1] [ɪnˈsaɪd, ˈɪnˌsaɪd] *adv* **:** adentro, dentro <to run inside : correr para adentro> <inside and out : por dentro y por fuera>
inside[2] *adj* **1 :** interior, de adentro, de dentro <the inside lane : el carril interior> **2 :** confidencial <inside information : información confidencial>
inside[3] *n* **1 :** interior *m,* parte *f* de adentro **2 insides** *npl* BELLY, GUTS **:** tripas *fpl fam* **3 inside out :** al revés
inside[4] *prep* **1** INTO **:** al interior de **2** WITHIN **:** dentro de **3** (*referring to time*) **:** en menos de <inside an hour : en menos de una hora>
inside of *prep* INSIDE **:** dentro de
insider [ɪnˈsaɪdər] *n* **:** persona *f* enterada
insidious [ɪnˈsɪdiəs] *adj* **:** insidioso — **insidiously** *adv*
insidiousness [ɪnˈsɪdiəsnəs] *n* **:** insidia *f*
insight [ˈɪnˌsaɪt] *n* **:** perspicacia *f,* penetración *f*
insightful [ɪnˈsaɪtfəl] *adj* **:** perspicaz
insignia [ɪnˈsɪgniə] *or* **insigne** [-ˌniː] *n, pl* **-nia** *or* **-nias :** insignia *f,* enseña *f*
insignificance [ˌɪnsɪgˈnɪfɪkən*t*s] *n* **:** insignificancia *f*
insignificant [ˌɪnsɪgˈnɪfɪkənt] *adj* **:** insignificante
insincere [ˌɪnsɪnˈsɪr] *adj* **:** insincero, poco sincero
insincerely [ˌɪnsɪnˈsɪrli] *adv* **:** con poca sinceridad
insincerity [ˌɪnsɪnˈsɛrət̬i, -ˈsɪr-] *n, pl* **-ties :** insinceridad *f*
insinuate [ɪnˈsɪnjʊˌeɪt] *vt* **-ated; -ating :** insinuar
insinuation [ɪnˌsɪnjʊˈeɪʃən] *n* **:** insinuación *f*
insipid [ɪnˈsɪpəd] *adj* **:** insípido
insist [ɪnˈsɪst] *v* **:** insistir
insistence [ɪnˈsɪstən*t*s] *n* **:** insistencia *f*
insistent [ɪnˈsɪstənt] *adj* **:** insistente — **insistently** *adv*
insofar as [ˌɪnsoˈfɑræz] *conj* **:** en la medida en que, en tanto que, en cuanto a
insole [ˈɪnˌsoːl] *n* **:** plantilla *f*
insolence [ˈɪn*t*sələn*t*s] *n* **:** insolencia *f*
insolent [ˈɪn*t*sələnt] *adj* **:** insolente
insolubility [ɪnˌsɑljʊˈbɪlət̬i] *n* **:** insolubilidad *f*
insoluble [ɪnˈsɑljʊbəl] *adj* **:** insoluble
insolvency [ɪnˈsɑlvən*t*si] *n, pl* **-cies :** insolvencia *f*
insolvent [ɪnˈsɑlvənt] *adj* **:** insolvente
insomnia [ɪnˈsɑmniə] *n* **:** insomnio *m*
insomuch as [ˌɪnsoˈmʌtʃæz] → **inasmuch as**
insomuch that *conj* so **:** así que, de manera que
inspect [ɪnˈspɛkt] *vt* **:** inspeccionar, examinar, revisar
inspection [ɪnˈspɛkʃən] *n* **:** inspección *f,* examen *m,* revisión *f,* revista *f* (de tropas)
inspector [ɪnˈspɛktər] *n* **:** inspector *m,* -tora *f*
inspiration [ˌɪn*t*spəˈreɪʃən] *n* **:** inspiración *f*
inspirational [ˌɪn*t*spəˈreɪʃənəl] *adj* **:** inspirador
inspire [ɪnˈspaɪr] *v* **-spired; -spiring** *vt* **1** INHALE **:** inhalar, aspirar **2** STIMULATE **:** estimular, animar, inspirar **3** INSTILL **:** inspirar, infundir — *vi* **:** inspirar
instability [ˌɪn*t*stəˈbɪlət̬i] *n, pl* **-ties :** inestabilidad *f*
install [ɪnˈstɔl] *vt* **-stalled; -stalling 1 :** instalar <to install the new president : instalar el presidente nuevo> <to install a fan : montar un abanico> **2 to install oneself :** instalarse
installation [ˌɪn*t*stəˈleɪʃən] *n* **:** instalación *f*
installment [ɪnˈstɔlmənt] *n* **1 :** plazo *m,* cuota *f* <to pay in four installments : pagar a cuatro plazos> **2 :** entrega *f* (de una publicación o telenovela) **3** INSTALLATION **:** instalación *f*
instance [ˈɪn*t*stən*t*s] *n* **1** INSTIGATION **:** instancia *f* **2** EXAMPLE **:** ejemplo *m* <for instance : por ejemplo> **3** OCCASION **:** instancia *f,* caso *m,* ocasión *f* <he prefers, in this instance, to remain anonymous : en este caso prefiere quedarse anónimo>
instant[1] [ˈɪn*t*stənt] *adj* **1** IMMEDIATE **:** inmediato, instantáneo <an instant reply : una respuesta inmediata> **2 :** instantáneo <instant coffee : café instantáneo>
instant[2] *n* **:** momento *m,* instante *m*
instantaneous [ˌɪn*t*stənˈteɪniəs] *adj* **:** instantáneo
instantaneously [ˌɪn*t*stənˈteɪniəsli] *adv* **:** instantáneamente, al instante
instantly [ˈɪn*t*stəntli] *adv* **:** al instante, instantáneamente
instead [ɪnˈstɛd] *adv* **1 :** en cambio, en lugar de eso, en su lugar <Dad was going, but Mom went instead : papá iba a ir, pero mamá fue en su lugar> **2** RATHER **:** al contrario
instead of *prep* **:** en vez de, en lugar de
instep [ˈɪnˌstɛp] *n* **:** empeine *m*
instigate [ˈɪn*t*stəˌgeɪt] *vt* **-gated; -gating** INCITE, PROVOKE **:** instigar, incitar, provocar, fomentar
instigation [ˌɪn*t*stəˈgeɪʃən] *n* **:** instancia *f,* incitación *f*
instigator [ˈɪn*t*stəˌgeɪtər] *n* **:** instigador *m,* -dora *f;* incitador *m,* -dora *f*

instill [ɪnˈstɪl] *vt* **-stilled; -stilling** : inculcar, infundir

instinct [ˈɪnˌstɪŋkt] *n* **1** TALENT : instinto *m,* don *m* <an instinct for the right word : un don para escoger la palabra apropiada> **2** : instinto *m* <maternal instincts : instintos maternales>

instinctive [ɪnˈstɪŋktɪv] *adj* : instintivo

instinctively [ɪnˈstɪŋktɪvli] *adv* : instintivamente, por instinto

instinctual [ɪnˈstɪŋktʃʊəl] *adj* : instintivo

institute[1] [ˈɪntstəˌtuːt, -ˌtjuːt] *vt* **-tuted; -tuting 1** ESTABLISH: establecer, instituir, fundar **2** INITIATE : iniciar, empezar, entablar

institute[2] *n* : instituto *m*

institution [ˌɪntstəˈtuːʃən, -ˈtjuː-] *n* **1** ESTABLISHING : institución *f,* establecimiento *m* **2** CUSTOM : institución *f,* tradición *f* <the institution of marriage : la institución del matrimonio> **3** ORGANIZATION : institución *f,* organismo *m* **4** ASYLUM : asilo *m*

institutional [ˌɪntstəˈtuːʃənəl, -ˈtjuː-] *adj* : institucional

institutionalize [ˌɪntstəˈtuːʃənəˌlaɪz, -ˈtjuː-] *vt* **-ized; -izing 1** : institucionalizar <institutionalized values : valores institucionalizados> **2** : internar <institutionalized orphans : huérfanos internados>

instruct [ɪnˈstrʌkt] *vt* **1** TEACH, TRAIN : instruir, adiestrar, enseñar **2** COMMAND : mandar, ordenar, dar instrucciones a

instruction [ɪnˈstrʌkʃən] *n* **1** TEACHING : instrucción *f,* enseñanza *f* **2** COMMAND : orden *f,* instrucción *f* **3 instructions** *npl* DIRECTIONS : instrucciones *fpl,* modo *m* de empleo

instructional [ɪnˈstrʌkʃənəl] *adj* : instructivo, educativo

instructive [ɪnˈstrʌktɪv] *adj* : instructivo

instructor [ɪnˈstrʌktər] *n* : instructor *m,* -tora *f*

instrument [ˈɪntstrəmənt] *n* : instrumento *m*

instrumental [ˌɪntstrəˈmɛntəl] *adj* : instrumental

instrumentalist [ˌɪntstrəˈmɛntəlɪst] *n* : instrumentista *mf*

insubordinate [ˌɪnsəˈbɔrdənət] *adj* : insubordinado

insubordination [ˌɪnsəˌbɔrdənˈeɪʃən] *n* : insubordinación *f*

insubstantial [ˌɪnsəbˈstæntʃəl] *adj* : insustancial, poco nutritivo (dícese de una comida), poco sólido (dícese de una estructura o un argumento)

insufferable [ɪnˈsʌfərəbəl] *adj* UNBEARABLE : insufrible, intolerable, inaguantable, insoportable — **insufferably** [-bli] *adv*

insufficiency [ˌɪnsəˈfɪʃəntsi] *n, pl* **-cies** : insuficiencia *f*

insufficient [ˌɪnsəˈfɪʃənt] *adj* : insuficiente — **insufficiently** *adv*

insular [ˈɪntsʊlər, -sjʊ-] *adj* **1** : isleño (dícese de la gente), insular (dícese del clima) <insular residents : residentes de la isla> **2** NARROW-MINDED : de miras estrechas

insularity [ˌɪntsʊˈlærət̬i, -sjʊ-] *n* : insularidad *f*

insulate [ˈɪntsəˌleɪt] *vt* **-lated; -lating** : aislar

insulation [ˌɪntsəˈleɪʃən] *n* : aislamiento *m*

insulator [ˈɪntsəˌleɪt̬ər] *n* : aislante *m,* aislador *m*

insulin [ˈɪntsələn] *n* : insulina *f*

insult[1] [ɪnˈsʌlt] *vt* : insultar, ofender, injuriar

insult[2] [ˈɪnˌsʌlt] *n* : insulto *m,* injuria *f,* agravio *m*

insulting [ɪnˈsʌltɪŋ] *adj* : ofensivo, injurioso, insultante

insultingly [ɪnˈsʌltɪŋli] *adv* : ofensivamente, de manera insultante

insuperable [ɪnˈsuːpərəbəl] *adj* : insuperable — **insuperably** [-bli] *adv*

insurable [ɪnˈʃʊrəbəl] *adj* : asegurable

insurance [ɪnˈʃʊrənts, ˈɪnˌʃʊr-] *n* : seguro *m* <life insurance : seguro de vida> <insurance company : compañía de seguros>

insure [ɪnˈʃʊr] *vt* **-sured; -suring 1** UNDERWRITE : asegurar **2** ENSURE : asegurar, garantizar

insured [ɪnˈʃʊrd] *n* : asegurado *m,* -da *f*

insurer [ɪnˈʃʊrər] *n* : asegurador *m,* -dora *f*

insurgent[1] [ɪnˈsərdʒənt] *adj* : insurgente

insurgent[2] *n* : insurgente *mf*

insurmountable [ˌɪnsərˈmaʊntəbəl] *adj* : insuperable, insalvable — **insurmountably** [-bli] *adv*

insurrection [ˌɪnsəˈrɛkʃən] *n* : insurrección *f,* levantamiento *m,* alzamiento *m*

intact [ɪnˈtækt] *adj* : intacto

intake [ˈɪnˌteɪk] *n* **1** OPENING : entrada *f,* toma *f* <fuel intake : toma de combustible> **2** : entrada *f* (de agua o aire), consumo *m* (de sustancias nutritivas) **3 intake of breath** : inhalación *f*

intangible [ɪnˈtændʒəbəl] *adj* : intangible, impalpable — **intangibly** [-bli] *adv*

integer [ˈɪntɪdʒər] *n* : entero *m*

integral [ˈɪntɪgrəl] *adj* : integral, esencial

integrate [ˈɪntəˌgreɪt] *v* **-grated; -grating** *vt* **1** UNITE : integrar, unir **2** DESEGREGATE : eliminar la segregación de — *vi* : integrarse

integration [ˌɪntəˈgreɪʃən] *n* : integración *f*

integrity [ɪnˈtɛgrət̬i] *n* : integridad *f*

intellect [ˈɪntəlˌɛkt] *n* : intelecto *m,* inteligencia *f,* capacidad *f* intelectual

intellectual[1] [ˌɪntəˈlɛktʃʊəl] *adj* : intelectual — **intellectually** *adv*

intellectual[2] *n* : intelectual *mf*

intellectualism [ˌɪntəˈlɛktʃʊəˌlɪzəm] *n* : intelectualismo *m*

intelligence [ɪnˈtɛlədʒən*t*s] *n* **1** : inteligencia *f* **2** INFORMATION, NEWS : inteligencia *f,* información *f,* noticias *fpl*

intelligent [ɪnˈtɛlədʒənt] *adj* : inteligente — **intelligently** *adv*

intelligibility [ɪnˌtɛlədʒəˈbɪləṭi] *n* : inteligibilidad *f*

intelligible [ɪnˈtɛlədʒəbəl] *adj* : inteligible, comprensible — **intelligibly** [-bli] *adv*

intemperance [ɪnˈtɛmpərən*t*s] *n* : inmoderación *f,* intemperancia *f*

intemperate [ɪnˈtɛmpərət] *adj* : excesivo, inmoderado, desmedido

intend [ɪnˈtɛnd] *vt* **1** MEAN : querer decir <that's not what I intended : eso no es lo que quería decir> **2** PLAN : tener planeado, proyectar, proponerse <I intend to finish by Thursday : me propongo acabar para el jueves>

intended [ɪnˈtɛndəd] *adj* **1** PLANNED : previsto, proyectado **2** INTENTIONAL : intencional, deliberado

intense [ɪnˈtɛn*t*s] *adj* **1** EXTREME : intenso, extremo <intense pain : dolor intenso> **2** : profundo, intenso <to my intense relief : para mi alivio profundo> <intense enthusiasm : entusiasmo ardiente>

intensely [ɪnˈtɛn*t*sli] *adv* : sumamente, profundamente, intensamente

intensification [ɪnˌtɛn*t*səfəˈkeɪʃən] *n* : intensificación *f*

intensify [ɪnˈtɛn*t*səˌfaɪ] *v* **-fied; -fying** *vt* **1** STRENGTHEN : intensificar, redoblar <to intensify one's efforts : redoblar uno sus esfuerzos> **2** SHARPEN : intensificar, agudizar (dolor, ansiedad) — *vi* : intensificarse, hacerse más intenso

intensity [ɪnˈtɛn*t*səṭi] *n, pl* **-ties** : intensidad *f*

intensive [ɪnˈtɛn*t*sɪv] *adj* : intensivo — **intensively** *adv*

intent[1] [ɪnˈtɛnt] *adj* **1** FIXED : concentrado, fijo <an intent stare : una mirada fija> **2 intent on** *or* **intent upon** : resuelto a, atento a

intent[2] *n* **1** PURPOSE : intención *f,* propósito *m* **2 for all intents and purposes** : a todos los efectos, prácticamente

intention [ɪnˈtɛntʃən] *n* : intención *f,* propósito *m*

intentional [ɪnˈtɛntʃənəl] *adj* : intencional, deliberado

intentionally [ɪnˈtɛntʃənəli] *adv* : a propósito, adrede

intently [ɪnˈtɛntli] *adv* : atentamente, fijamente

inter [ɪnˈtər] *vt* **-terred; -terring** : enterrar, inhumar

interact [ˌɪntərˈækt] *vi* : interactuar, actuar recíprocamente, relacionarse

interaction [ˌɪntərˈækʃən] *n* : interacción *f,* interrelación *f*

interactive [ˌɪntərˈæktɪv] *adj* : interactivo

interbreed [ˌɪntərˈbriːd] *v* **-bred** [-ˈbrɛd]; **-breeding** *vt* : cruzar — *vi* : cruzarse

intercalate [ɪnˈtərkəˌleɪt] *vt* **-lated; -lating** : intercalar

intercede [ˌɪntərˈsiːd] *vi* **-ceded; -ceding** : interceder

intercept [ˌɪntərˈsɛpt] *vt* : interceptar

interception [ˌɪntərˈsɛpʃən] *n* : intercepción *f*

intercession [ˌɪntərˈsɛʃən] *n* : intercesión *f*

interchange[1] [ˌɪntərˈtʃeɪndʒ] *vt* **-changed; -changing** : intercambiar

interchange[2] [ˈɪntərˌtʃeɪndʒ] *n* **1** EXCHANGE : intercambio *m,* cambio *m* **2** JUNCTION : empalme *m,* enlace *m* de carreteras

interchangeable [ˌɪntərˈtʃeɪndʒəəl] *adj* : intercambiable

intercity [ˈɪntərˈsɪṭi] *adj* : interurbano

intercollegiate [ˌɪntərkəˈliːdʒət, -dʒiət] *adj* : interuniversitario

intercontinental [ˌɪntərˌkantənˈɛntəl] *adj* : intercontinental

intercourse [ˈɪntərˌkors] *n* **1** RELATIONS : relaciones *fpl,* trato *m* **2** COPULATION : acto *m* sexual, relaciones *fpl* sexuales, coito *m*

interdenominational [ˌɪntərdɪˌnaməˈneɪʃənəl] *adj* : interconfesional

interdepartmental [ˌɪntərdɪˌpartˈmɛntəl, -ˌdiː-] *adj* : interdepartamental

interdependence [ˌɪntərdɪˈpɛndən*t*s] *n* : interdependencia *f*

interdependent [ˌɪntərdɪˈpɛndənt] *adj* : interdependiente

interdict [ˌɪntərˈdɪkt] *vt* **1** PROHIBIT : prohibir **2** : cortar (las líneas de comunicación o provisión del enemigo)

interest[1] [ˈɪntrəst, -təˌrɛst] *vt* : interesar

interest[2] *n* **1** SHARE, STAKE : interés *m,* participación *f* **2** BENEFIT : provecho *m,* beneficio *m,* interés *m* <in the public interest : en el interés público> **3** CHARGE : interés *m,* cargo *m* <compound interest : interés compuesto> **4** CURIOSITY : interés *m,* curiosidad *f* **5** COLOR : color *m,* interés *m* <places of local interest : lugares de color local> **6** HOBBY : afición *f*

interesting [ˈɪntrəstɪŋ, -təˌrɛstɪŋ] *adj* : interesante — **interestingly** *adv*

interface [ˈɪntərˌfeɪs] *n* **1** : punto *m* de contacto <oil-water interface : punto de contacto entre el agua y el aceite> **2** : interfase *f,* interfaz *f* (de una computadora)

interfere [ˌɪntərˈfɪr] *vi* **-fered; -fering** **1** INTERPOSE : interponerse, hacer interferencia <to interfere with a play : obstruir una jugada> **2** MEDDLE : entrometerse, interferir, intervenir **3 to interfere with** DISRUPT : afectar (una actividad), interferir (la radiotransmisión) **4 to interfere with** TOUCH : tocar <someone interfered with my papers : alguien tocó mis papeles>

interference [ˌɪntərˈfɪrənts] *n* : interferencia *f,* intromisión *f*

intergalactic [ˌɪntərgəˈlæktɪk] *adj* : intergaláctico

intergovernmental [ˌɪntərˌgʌvərˈmɛntəl, -vərn-] *adj* : intergubernamental

interim[1] [ˈɪntərəm] *adj* : interino, provisional

interim[2] *n* 1 : interín *m,* intervalo *m* **2 in the interim :** en el interín, mientras tanto

interior[1] [ɪnˈtɪriər] *adj* : interior

interior[2] *n* : interior *m*

interject [ˌɪntərˈdʒɛkt] *vt* : interponer, agregar

interjection [ˌɪntərˈdʒɛkʃən] *n* **1** : interjección *f* (en lingüística) **2** EXCLAMATION : exclamación *f* **3** INTERPOSITION, INTERRUPTION : interposición *f,* interrupción *f*

interlace [ˌɪntərˈleɪs] *vt* **-laced; -lacing 1** INTERWEAVE : entrelazar **2** INTERSPERSE : intercalar

interlock [ˌɪntərˈlɑk] *vt* **1** UNITE : trabar, unir **2** ENGAGE, MESH : engranar — *vi* : entrelazarse, trabarse

interloper [ˌɪntərˈloːpər] *n* **1** INTRUDER : intruso *m,* -sa *f* **2** MEDDLER : entrometido *m,* -da *f*

interlude [ˈɪntərˌluːd] *n* **1** INTERVAL : intervalo *m,* intermedio *m* (en el teatro) **2** : interludio *m* (en música)

intermarriage [ˌɪntərˈmærɪdʒ] *n* **1** : matrimonio *m* mixto (entre miembros de distintas razas o religiones) **2** : matrimonio *m* entre miembros del mismo grupo

intermarry [ˌɪntərˈmæri] *vi* **-married; -marrying 1 :** casarse (con miembros de otros grupos) **2 :** casarse entre sí (con miembros del mismo grupo)

intermediary[1] [ˌɪntərˈmiːdiˌɛri] *adj* : intermediario

intermediary[2] *n, pl* **-aries** : intermediario *m,* -ria *f*

intermediate[1] [ˌɪntərˈmiːdiət] *adj* : intermedio

intermediate[2] *n* GO-BETWEEN : intermediario *m,* -ria *f;* mediador *m,* -dora *f*

interment [ɪnˈtərmənt] *n* : entierro *m*

interminable [ɪnˈtərmənəbəl] *adj* : interminable, constante — **interminably** [-bli] *adv*

intermingle [ˌɪntərˈmɪŋgəl] *vt* **-mingled; -mingling :** entremezclar, mezclar — *vi* : entremezclarse

intermission [ˌɪntərˈmɪʃən] *n* : intermisión *f,* intervalo *m,* intermedio *m*

intermittent [ˌɪntərˈmɪtənt] *adj* : intermitente — **intermittently** *adv*

intermix [ˌɪntərˈmɪks] *vt* : entremezclar

intern[1] [ˈɪnˌtərn, ɪnˈtərn] *vt* : confinar (durante la guerra) — *vi* : servir de interno, hacer las prácticas

intern[2] [ˈɪnˌtərn] *n* : interno *m,* -na *f*

internal [ɪnˈtərnəl] *adj* : interno, interior <internal bleeding : hemorragia interna> <internal affairs : asuntos interiores, asuntos domésticos> — **internally** *adv*

international [ˌɪntərˈnæʃənəl] *adj* : internacional — **internationally** *adv*

internationalize [ˌɪntərˈnæʃənəˌlaɪz] *vt* **-ized; -izing :** internacionalizar

internee [ˌɪnˌtərˈniː] *n* : interno *m,* -na *f*

internist [ˈɪnˌtərnɪst] *n* : internista *mf*

interpersonal [ˌɪntərˈpərsənəl] *adj* : interpersonal

interplay [ˈɪntərˌpleɪ] *n* : interacción *f,* juego *m*

interpolate [ɪnˈtərpəˌleɪt] *vt* **-lated; -lating :** interpolar

interpose [ˌɪntərˈpoːz] *v* **-posed; -posing** *vt* : interponer, interrumpir con — *vi* : interponerse

interposition [ˌɪntərpəˈzɪʃən] *n* : interposición *f*

interpret [ɪnˈtərprət] *vt* : interpretar

interpretation [ɪnˌtərprəˈteɪʃən] *n* : interpretación *f*

interpretative [ɪnˈtərprəˌteɪṭɪv] *adj* : interpretativo

interpreter [ɪnˈtərprəṭər] *n* : intérprete *mf*

interpretive [ɪnˈtərprəṭɪv] *adj* : interpretativo

interracial [ˌɪntərˈreɪʃəl] *adj* : interracial

interrelate [ˌɪntərɪˈleɪt] *vi* **-related; -relating :** interelacionar

interrelationship [ˌɪntərɪˈleɪʃənˌʃɪp] *n* : interrelación *f*

interrogate [ɪnˈtɛrəˌgeɪt] *vt* **-gated; -gating :** interrogar, someter a un interrogatorio

interrogation [ɪnˌtɛrəˈgeɪʃən] *n* : interrogación *f*

interrogative[1] [ˌɪntəˈrɑgəṭɪv] *adj* : interrogativo

interrogative[2] *n* : interrogativo *m*

interrogator [ɪnˈtɛrəˌgeɪṭər] *n* : interrogador *m,* -dora *f*

interrogatory [ˌɪntəˈrɑgəˌtɔri] → **interrogative**[1]

interrupt [ˌɪntəˈrʌpt] *v* : interrumpir

interruption [ˌɪntəˈrʌpʃən] *n* : interrupción *f*

intersect [ˌɪntərˈsɛkt] *vt* : cruzar, cortar — *vi* : cruzarse (dícese de los caminos), intersectarse (dícese de las líneas o figuras), cortarse

intersection [ˌɪntərˈsɛkʃən] *n* : intersección *f,* cruce *m*

intersperse [ˌɪntərˈspərs] *vt* **-spersed; -spersing :** intercalar, entremezclar

interstate [ˌɪntər'steɪt] *adj* : interestatal

interstellar [ˌɪntər'stɛlər] *adj* : interestelar

interstice [ɪn'tərstəs] *n, pl* **-stices** [-stəˌsiːz, -stəsəz] : intersticio *m*

intertwine [ˌɪntər'twaɪn] *vi* **-twined; -twining** : entrelazarse

interval ['ɪntərvəl] *n* : intervalo *m*

intervene [ˌɪntər'viːn] *vi* **-vened; -vening 1** ELAPSE : transcurrir, pasar <the intervening years : los años intermediarios> **2** INTERCEDE : intervenir, interceder, mediar

intervention [ˌɪntər'vɛntʃən] *n* : intervención *f*

interview[1] ['ɪntərˌvjuː] *vt* : entrevistar — *vi* : hacer entrevistas

interview[2] *n* : entrevista *f*

interviewer ['ɪntərˌvjuːər] *n* : entrevistador *m*, -dora *f*

interweave [ˌɪntər'wiːv] *v* **-wove** [-'woːv]; **-woven** [-'woːvən]; **-weaving** *vt* : entretejer, entrelazar — *vi* INTERTWINE : entrelazarse, entretejerse

interwoven [ˌɪntər'woːvən] *adj* : entretejido

intestate [ɪn'tɛsˌteɪt, -tət] *adj* : intestado

intestinal [ɪn'tɛstənəl] *adj* : intestinal

intestine [ɪn'tɛstən] *n* **1** : intestino *m* **2 small intestine** : intestino *m* delgado **3 large intestine** : intestino *m* grueso

intimacy ['ɪntəməsi] *n, pl* **-cies 1** CLOSENESS : intimidad *f* **2** FAMILIARITY : familiaridad *f*

intimate[1] ['ɪntəˌmeɪt] *vt* **-mated; -mating** : insinuar, dar a entender

intimate[2] ['ɪntəmət] *adj* **1** CLOSE : íntimo, de confianza <intimate friends : amigos íntimos> **2** PRIVATE : íntimo, privado <intimate clubs : clubes íntimos> **3** INNERMOST, SECRET : íntimo, secreto <intimate fantasies : fantasías secretas>

intimate[3] *n* : amigo *m* íntimo, amiga *f* íntima

intimidate [ɪn'tɪməˌdeɪt] *vt* **-dated; -dating** : intimidar

intimidation [ɪnˌtɪmə'deɪʃən] *n* : intimidación *f*

into ['ɪnˌtuː] *prep* **1** (*indicating motion*) : en, a, contra, dentro de <she got into bed : se metió en la cama> <to get into a plane : subir a un avión> <he crashed into the wall : chocó contra la pared> <looking into the sun : mirando al sol> **2** (*indicating state or condition*) : a, en <to burst into tears : echarse a llorar> <the water turned into ice : el agua se convirtió en hielo> <to translate into English : traducir al inglés> **3** (*indicating time*) <far into the night : hasta bien entrada la noche> <he's well into his eighties : tiene los ochenta bien cumplidos> **4** (*in mathematics*) <3 into 12 is 4 : 12 dividido por 3 es 4>

intolerable [ɪn'tɑlərəbəl] *adj* : intolerable — **intolerably** [-bli] *adv*

intolerance [ɪn'tɑlərən*t*s] *n* : intolerancia *f*

intolerant [ɪn'tɑlərənt] *adj* : intolerante

intonation [ˌɪnto'neɪʃən] *n* : intonación *f*

intone [ɪn'toːn] *vt* **-toned; -toning** : entonar

intoxicant [ɪn'tɑksɪkənt] *n* : bebida *f* alcohólica

intoxicate [ɪn'tɑksəˌkeɪt] *vt* **-cated; -cating** : emborrachar, embriagar

intoxicated [ɪn'tɑksəˌkeɪt̬əd] *adj* : borracho, embriagado

intoxicating [ɪn'tɑksəˌkeɪt̬ɪŋ] *adj* : embriagador

intoxication [ɪnˌtɑksə'keɪʃən] *n* : embriaguez *f*

intractable [ɪn'træktəbəl] *adj* : obstinado, intratable

intramural [ˌɪntrə'mjʊrəl] *adj* : interno, dentro de la universidad

intransigence [ɪn'træn*t*sədʒən*t*s, -'trænzə-] *n* : intransigencia *f*

intransigent [ɪn'træn*t*sədʒənt, -'trænzə-] *adj* : intransigente

intravenous [ˌɪntrə'viːnəs] *adj* : intravenoso — **intravenously** *adv*

intrepid [ɪn'trɛpəd] *adj* : intrépido

intricacy ['ɪntrɪkəsi] *n, pl* **-cies** : complejidad *f*, lo intrincado

intricate ['ɪntrɪkət] *adj* : intrincado, complicado — **intricately** *adv*

intrigue[1] [ɪn'triːg] *v* **-trigued; -triguing** : intrigar

intrigue[2] ['ɪnˌtriːg, ɪn'triːg] *n* : intriga *f*

intriguing [ɪn'triːgɪŋli] *adj* : intrigante, fascinante

intrinsic [ɪn'trɪnzɪk, -'trɪn*t*sɪk] *adj* : intrínseco, esencial — **intrinsically** [-zɪkli, -sɪ-] *adv*

introduce [ˌɪntrə'duːs, -'djuːs] *vt* **-duced; -ducing 1** : presentar <let me introduce my father : permítame presentar a mi padre> **2** : introducir (algo nuevo), lanzar (un producto), presentar (una ley), proponer (una idea o un tema)

introduction [ˌɪntrə'dʌkʃən] *n* : introducción *f*, presentación *f*

introductory [ˌɪntrə'dʌktəri] *adj* : introductorio, preliminar, de introducción

introspection [ˌɪntrə'spɛkʃən] *n* : introspección *f*

introspective [ˌɪntrə'spɛktɪv] *adj* : introspectivo — **introspectively** *adv*

introvert ['ɪntrəˌvərt] *n* : introvertido *m*, -da *f*

introverted ['ɪntrəˌvərt̬əd] *adj* : introvertido

intrude [ɪn'truːd] *v* **-truded; -truding** *vi* **1** INTERFERE : inmiscuirse, entrometerse **2** DISTURB, INTERRUPT : molestar, estorbar, interrumpir — *vt* : introducir por fuerza

intruder [ɪn'truːdər] *n* : intruso *m,* -sa *f*
intrusion [ɪn'truːʒən] *n* : intrusión *f*
intrusive [ɪn'truːsɪv] *adj* : intruso
intuit [ɪn'tuːɪt, -'tjuː-] *vt* : intuir
intuition [ˌɪntʊ'ɪʃən, -tjʊ-] *n* : intuición *f*
intuitive [ɪn'tuːət̬ɪv, -'tjuː-] *adj* : intuitivo — **intuitively** *adv*
inundate ['ɪnənˌdeɪt] *vt* **-dated; -dating** : inundar
inundation [ˌɪnən'deɪʃən] *n* : inundación *f*
inure [ɪ'nʊr, -'njʊr] *vt* **-ured; -uring** : acostumbrar, habituar
invade [ɪn'veɪd] *vt* **-vaded; -vading** : invadir
invader [ɪn'veɪdər] *n* : invasor *m,* -sora *f*
invalid[1] [ɪn'væləd] *adj* : inválido, nulo
invalid[2] ['ɪnvələd] *adj* : inválido, discapacitado
invalid[3] ['ɪnvələd] *n* : inválido *m,* -da *f*
invalidate [ɪn'væləˌdeɪt] *vt* **-dated; -dating** : invalidar
invalidity [ˌɪnvə'lɪdət̬i] *n, pl* **-ties** : invalidez *f,* falta de validez *f*
invaluable [ɪn'væljəbəl, -'væljʊə-] *adj* : invalorable, inestimable, inapreciable
invariable [ɪn'væriəbəl] *adj* : invariable, constante — **invariably** [-bli] *adv*
invasion [ɪn'veɪʒən] *n* : invasión *f*
invasive [ɪn'veɪsɪv] *adj* : invasivo
invective [ɪn'vɛktɪv] *n* : invectiva *f,* improperio *m,* vituperio *m*
inveigh [ɪn'veɪ] *vi* **to inveigh against** : arremeter contra, lanzar invectivas contra
inveigle [ɪn'veɪgəl, -'viː-] *vt* **-gled; -gling** : engatusar, embaucar, persuadir con engaños
invent [ɪn'vɛnt] *vt* : inventar
invention [ɪn'vɛntʃən] *n* : invención *f,* invento *m*
inventive [ɪn'vɛntɪv] *adj* : inventivo
inventiveness [ɪn'vɛntɪvnəs] *n* : ingenio *m,* inventiva *f*
inventor [ɪn'vɛntər] *n* : inventor *m,* -tora *f*
inventory[1] ['ɪnvənˌtɔri] *vt* **-ried; -rying** : inventariar
inventory[2] *n, pl* **-ries 1** LIST : inventario *m* **2** STOCK : existencias *fpl*
inverse[1] [ɪn'vərs, 'ɪnˌvərs] *adj* : inverso — **inversely** *adv*
inverse[2] *n* : inverso *m*
inversion [ɪn'vɛrʒən] *n* : inversión *f*
invert [ɪn'vərt] *vt* : invertir
invertebrate[1] [ɪn'vərt̬əbrət, -ˌbreɪt] *adj* : invertebrado
invertebrate[2] *n* : invertebrado *m*
invest [ɪn'vɛst] *vt* **1** AUTHORIZE : investir, autorizar **2** CONFER : conferir **3** : invertir, dedicar <he invested his savings in stocks : invirtió sus ahorros en acciones> <to invest one's time : dedicar uno su tiempo>
investigate [ɪn'vɛstəˌgeɪt] *v* **-gated; -gating** : investigar
investigation [ɪnˌvɛstə'geɪʃən] *n* : investigación *f,* estudio *m*
investigative [ɪn'vɛstəˌgeɪt̬ɪv] *adj* : investigador
investigator [ɪn'vɛstəˌgeɪt̬ər] *n* : investigador *m,* -dora *f*
investiture [ɪn'vɛstəˌtʃʊr, -tʃər] *n* : investidura *f*
investment [ɪn'vɛstmənt] *n* : inversión *f*
investor [ɪn'vɛstər] *n* : inversor *m,* -sora *f;* inversionista *mf*
inveterate [ɪn'vɛt̬ərət] *adj* **1** DEEP-SEATED : inveterado, enraizado **2** HABITUAL : empedernido, incorregible
invidious [ɪn'vɪdiəs] *adj* **1** OBNOXIOUS : repugnante, odioso **2** UNJUST : injusto — **invidiously** *adv*
invigorate [ɪn'vɪgəˌreɪt] *vt* **-rated; -rating** : vigorizar, animar
invigorating [ɪn'vɪgəˌreɪt̬ɪŋ] *adj* : vigorizante, estimulante
invigoration [ɪnˌvɪgə'reɪʃən] *n* : animación *f*
invincibility [ɪnˌvɪntsə'bɪlət̬i] *n* : invencibilidad *f*
invincible [ɪn'vɪntsəbəl] *adj* : invencible — **invincibly** [-bli] *adv*
inviolable [ɪn'vaɪələbəl] *adj* : inviolable
inviolate [ɪn'vaɪələt] *adj* : inviolado, puro
invisibility [ɪnˌvɪzə'bɪlət̬i] *n* : invisibilidad *f*
invisible [ɪn'vɪzəbəl] *adj* : invisible — **invisibly** [-bli] *adv*
invitation [ˌɪnvə'teɪʃən] *n* : invitación *f*
invite [ɪn'vaɪt] *vt* **-vited; -viting 1** ATTRACT : atraer, tentar <a book that invites interest : un libro que atrae el interés> **2** PROVOKE : provocar, buscar <to invite trouble : buscarse problemas> **3** ASK : invitar <we invited them for dinner : los invitamos a cenar> **4** SOLICIT : solicitar, buscar (preguntas, comentarios, etc.)
inviting [ɪn'vaɪt̬ɪŋ] *adj* : atractivo, atrayente
invocation [ˌɪnvə'keɪʃən] *n* : invocación *f*
invoice[1] ['ɪnˌvɔɪs] *vt* **-voiced; -voicing** : facturar
invoice[2] *n* : factura *f*
invoke [ɪn'voːk] *vt* **-voked; -voking 1** : invocar, apelar a <she invoked our aid : apeló a nuestra ayuda> **2** CITE : invocar, citar <to invoke a precedent : invocar un precedente> **3** CONJURE UP : hacer aparecer, invocar
involuntary [ɪn'vɑlənˌtɛri] *adj* : involuntario — **involuntarily** [ɪnˌvɑlən'tɛrəli] *adv*

involve [ɪn'vɑlv] *vt* **-volved; -volving** 1 ENGAGE : ocupar <workers involved in construction : trabajadores ocupados con la construcción> 2 IMPLICATE : involucrar, enredar, implicar <to be involved in a crime : estar involucrado en un crimen> 3 CONCERN : concernir, afectar 4 CONNECT : conectar, relacionar 5 ENTAIL, INCLUDE : suponer, incluir, consistir en <what does the job involve? : ¿en qué consiste el trabajo?> 6 **to be involved with someone** : tener una relación (amorosa) con alguien

involved [ɪn'vɑlvd] *adj* 1 COMPLEX, INTRICATE : complicado, complejo, enrevesado 2 CONCERNED : interesado, afectado

involvement [ɪn'vɑlvmənt] *n* 1 PARTICIPATION : participación *f,* complicidad *f* 2 RELATIONSHIP : relación *f*

invulnerable [ɪn'vʌlnərəbəl] *adj* : invulnerable

inward[1] ['ɪnwərd] *or* **inwards** [-wərdz] *adv* : hacia adentro, hacia el interior

inward[2] *adj* INSIDE : interior, interno

inwardly ['ɪnwərdli] *adv* 1 MENTALLY, SPIRITUALLY : por dentro 2 INTERNALLY : internamente, interiormente 3 PRIVATELY : para sus adentros, para sí

iodide ['aɪəˌdaɪd] *n* : yoduro *m*

iodine ['aɪəˌdaɪn, -dən] *n* : yodo *m,* tintura *f* de yodo

iodize ['aɪəˌdaɪz] *vt* **-dized; -dizing** : yodar

ion ['aɪən, 'aɪˌɑn] *n* : ion *m*

ionic [aɪ'ɑnɪk] *adj* : iónico

ionize ['aɪəˌnaɪz] *v* **ionized; ionizing** : ionizar

ionosphere [aɪ'ɑnəˌsfɪr] *n* : ionosfera *f*

iota [aɪ'oːt̬ə] *n* : pizca *f,* ápice *m*

IOU [ˌaɪˌo'juː] *n* : pagaré *m,* vale *m*

Iranian [ɪ'reɪniən, -'ræ-, -'rɑ-; aɪ'-] *n* : iraní *mf* — **Iranian** *adj*

Iraqi [ɪ'rakiː] *n* : iraquí *mf* — **Iraqi** *adj*

irascibility [ɪˌræsə'bɪlət̬i] *n* : irascibilidad *f*

irascible [ɪ'ræsəbəl] *adj* : irascible

irate [aɪ'reɪt] *adj* : furioso, airado, iracundo — **irately** *adv*

ire ['aɪr] *n* : ira *f,* cólera *f*

iridescence [ˌɪrə'dɛsənts] *n* : iridiscencia *f*

iridescent [ˌɪrə'dɛsənt] *adj* : iridiscente

iris ['aɪrəs] *n, pl* **irises** *or* **irides** ['aɪrəˌdiːz, 'ɪr-] 1 : iris *m* (del ojo) 2 : lirio *m* (planta)

Irish[1] ['aɪrɪʃ] *adj* : irlandés

Irish[2] 1 : irlandés *m* (idioma) 2 **the Irish** *npl* : los irlandeses

Irishman ['aɪrɪʃmən] *n* : irlandés *m*

Irishwoman ['aɪrɪʃˌwʊmən] *n* : irlandesa *f*

irk ['ərk] *vt* : fastidiar, irritar, preocupar

irksome ['ərksəm] *adj* : irritante, fastidioso — **irksomely** *adv*

iron[1] ['aɪərn] *v* : planchar

iron[2] *n* 1 : hierro *m,* fierro *m* <a will of iron : una voluntad de hierro, una voluntad férrea> 2 : plancha *f* (para planchar la ropa)

ironclad ['aɪərn'klæd] *adj* 1 : acorazado, blindado 2 STRICT : riguroso, estricto

ironic [aɪ'rɑnɪk] *or* **ironical** [-nɪkəl] *adj* : irónico — **ironically** [-kli] *adv*

ironing ['aɪərnɪŋ] *n* 1 PRESSING : planchada *f* 2 : ropa *f* para planchar

ironing board *n* : tabla *f* (de planchar)

ironwork ['aɪərnˌwərk] *n* 1 : obra *f* de hierro 2 **ironworks** *npl* : fundición *f*

ironworker ['aɪərnˌwərkər] *n* : fundidor *m,* -dora *f*

irony ['aɪrəni] *n, pl* **-nies** : ironía *f*

irradiate [ɪ'reɪdiˌeɪt] *vt* **-ated; -ating** : irradiar, radiar

irradiation [ɪˌreɪdi'eɪʃən] *n* : irradiación *f,* radiación *f*

irrational [ɪ'ræʃənəl] *adj* : irracional — **irrationally** *adv*

irrationality [ɪˌræʃə'nælət̬i] *n, pl* **-ties** : irracionalidad *f*

irreconcilable [ɪˌrɛkən'saɪləbəl] *adj* : irreconciliable

irrecoverable [ˌɪrɪ'kʌvərəbəl] *adj* : irrecuperable — **irrecoverably** [-bli] *adv*

irredeemable [ˌɪrɪ'diːməbəl] *adj* 1 : irredimible (dícese de un bono) 2 HOPELESS : irremediable, irreparable

irreducible [ˌɪrɪ'duːsəbəl, -'djuː-] *adj* : irreducible — **irreducibly** [-bli] *adv*

irrefutable [ˌɪrɪ'fjuːt̬əbəl, ɪr'rɛfjə-] *adj* : irrefutable

irregular[1] [ɪ'rɛgjələr] *adj* : irregular — **irregularly** *adv*

irregular[2] *n* 1 : soldado *m* irregular 2 **irregulars** *npl* : artículos *mpl* defectuosos

irregularity [ɪˌrɛgjə'lærət̬i] *n, pl* **-ties** : irregularidad *f*

irrelevance [ɪ'rɛləvənts] *n* : irrelevancia *f*

irrelevant [ɪ'rɛləvənt] *adj* : irrelevante

irreligious [ˌɪrɪ'lɪdʒəs] *adj* : irreligioso

irreparable [ɪ'rɛpərəbəl] *adj* : irreparable

irreplaceable [ˌɪrɪ'pleɪsəbəl] *adj* : irreemplazable, insustituible

irrepressible [ˌɪrɪ'prɛsəbəl] *adj* : incontenible, incontrolable

irreproachable [ɪrɪ'proːtʃəbəl] *adj* : irreprochable, intachable

irresistible [ˌɪrɪ'zɪstəbəl] *adj* : irresistible — **irresistibly** [-bli] *adv*

irresolute [ɪ'rɛzəˌluːt] *adj* : irresoluto, indeciso

irresolutely [ɪ'rɛzəˌluːtli, -ˌrɛzə'luːt-] *adv* : de manera indecisa

irresolution [ɪˌrɛzə'luːʃən] *n* : irresolución *f*

irrespective of [ˌɪrɪˈspɛktɪvəv] *prep* : sin tomar en consideración, sin tener en cuenta

irresponsibility [ˌɪrɪˌspɑntsəˈbɪləṭi] *n, pl* **-ties** : irresponsabilidad *f,* falta *f* de responsabilidad

irresponsible [ˌɪrɪˈspɑntsəbəl] *adj* : irresponsable — **irresponsibly** [-bli] *adv*

irretrievable [ˌɪrɪˈtriːvəbəl] *adj* IRRECOVERABLE : irrecuperable

irreverence [ɪˈrɛvərənts] *n* : irreverencia *f,* falta *f* de respeto

irreverent [ɪˈrɛvərənt] *adj* : irreverente, irrespetuoso

irreversible [ˌɪrɪˈvərsəbəl] *adj* : irreversible

irrevocable [ɪˈrɛvəkəbəl] *adj* : irrevocable — **irrevocably** [-bli] *adv*

irrigate [ˈɪrəˌgeɪt] *vt* **-gated; -gating** : irrigar, regar

irrigation [ˌɪrəˈgeɪʃən] *n* : irrigación *f,* riego *m*

irritability [ˌɪrəṭəˈbɪləṭi] *n, pl* **-ties** : irritabilidad *f*

irritable [ˈɪrəṭəbəl] *adj* : irritable, colérico

irritably [ˈɪrəṭəbli] *adv* : con irritación

irritant¹ [ˈɪrəṭənt] *adj* : irritante

irritant² *n* : agente *m* irritante

irritate [ˈɪrəˌteɪt] *vt* **-tated; -tating 1** ANNOY : irritar, molestar **2** : irritar (en medicina)

irritating [ˈɪrəˌteɪṭɪŋ] *adj* : irritante

irritatingly [ˈɪrəˌteɪṭɪŋli] *adv* : de modo irritante, fastidiosamente

irritation [ˌɪrəˈteɪʃən] *n* : irritación *f*

is → **be**

Islam [ɪsˈlɑm, ɪz-, -ˈlæm; ˈɪsˌlɑm, ˈɪz-, -ˌlæm] *n* : el Islam

Islamic [ɪsˈlɑmɪk, ɪz-, -ˈlæ-] *adj* : islámico

island [ˈaɪlənd] *n* : isla *f*

islander [ˈaɪləndər] *n* : isleño *m,* -ña *f*

isle [ˈaɪl] *n* : isla *f,* islote *m*

islet [ˈaɪlət] *n* : islote *m*

isolate [ˈaɪsəˌleɪt] *vt* **-lated; -lating** : aislar

isolated [ˈaɪsəˌleɪṭəd] *adj* : aislado, solo

isolation [ˌaɪsəˈleɪʃən] *n* : aislamiento *m*

isometric [ˌaɪsəˈmɛtrɪk] *adj* : isométrico

isometrics [ˌaɪsəˈmɛtrɪks] *ns & pl* : isometría *f*

isosceles [aɪˈsɑsəˌliːz] *adj* : isósceles

isotope [ˈaɪsəˌtoːp] *n* : isótopo *m*

Israeli [ɪzˈreɪli] *n* : israelí *mf* — **Israeli** *adj*

issue¹ [ˈɪˌʃuː] *v* **-sued; -suing** *vi* **1** EMERGE : emerger, salir, fluir **2** DESCEND : descender (dícese de los padres o antepasados específicos) **3** EMANATE, RESULT : emanar, surgir, resultar — *vt* **1** EMIT : emitir **2** DISTRIBUTE : emitir, distribuir <to issue a new stamp : emitir un sello nuevo> **3** PUBLISH : publicar

issue² *n* **1** EMERGENCE, FLOW : emergencia *f,* flujo *m* **2** PROGENY : descendencia *f,* progenie *f* **3** OUTCOME, RESULT : desenlace *m,* resultado *m,* consecuencia *f* **4** MATTER, QUESTION : asunto *m,* cuestión *f* **5** PUBLICATION : publicación *f,* distribución *f,* emisión *f* **6** : número *m* (de un periódico o una revista)

isthmus [ˈɪsməs] *n* : istmo *m*

it [ˈɪt] *pron* **1** (*as subject; generally omitted*) : él, ella, ello <it's a big building : es un edificio grande> <who was it? : ¿quién era?> **2** (*as indirect object*) : le <I'll give it some water : voy a darle agua> **3** (*as direct object*) : lo, la <give it to me : dámelo> **4** (*as object of a preposition; generally omitted*) : él, ella, ello <behind it : detrás, detrás de él> **5** (*in impersonal constructions*) <it's raining : está lloviendo> <it's 8 o'clock : son las ocho> **6** (*as the implied subject or object of a verb*) <it is necessary to study : es necesario estudiar> <to give it all one's got : dar lo mejor de sí>

Italian [ɪˈtæliən, aɪ-] *n* **1** : italiano *m,* -na *f* **2** : italiano *m* (idioma) — **Italian** *adj*

italic¹ [ɪˈtælɪk, aɪ-] *adj* : en cursiva, en bastardilla

italic² *n* : cursiva *f,* bastardilla *f*

italicize [ɪˈtæləˌsaɪz, aɪ-] *vt* **-cized; -cizing** : poner en cursiva

itch¹ [ˈɪtʃ] *vi* **1** : picar <her arm itched : le pica el brazo> **2** : morirse <they were itching to go outside : se morían por salir> — *vt* : dar picazón, hacer picar

itch² *n* **1** ITCHING : picazón *f,* picor *m,* comezón *f* **2** RASH : sarpullido *m,* erupción *f* **3** DESIRE : ansia *f,* deseo *m*

itchy [ˈɪtʃi] *adj* **itchier; -est** : que pica, que da comezón

it'd [ˈɪṭəd] (*contraction of* **it had** *or* **it would**) → **have, would**

item [ˈaɪṭəm] *n* **1** OBJECT : artículo *m,* pieza *f* <item of clothing : prenda de vestir> **2** : punto *m* (en una agenda), número *m* (en el teatro), ítem *m* (en un documento) **3 news item** : noticia *f*

itemize [ˈaɪṭəˌmaɪz] *vt* **-ized; -izing** : detallar, enumerar, listar

itinerant [aɪˈtɪnərənt] *adj* : itinerante, ambulante

itinerary [aɪˈtɪnəˌrɛri] *n, pl* **-aries** : itinerario *m*

it'll [ˈɪṭəl] (*contraction of* **it shall** *or* **it will**) → **shall, will**

its [ˈɪts] *adj* : su, sus <its kennel : su perrera> <a city and its inhabitants : una ciudad y sus habitantes>

it's [ˈɪts] (*contraction of* **it is** *or* **it has**) → **be, have**

itself [ɪtˈsɛlf] *pron* **1** (*used reflexively*) : se <the cat gave itself a bath : el gato se bañó> **2** (*used for emphasis*) : (él) mismo, (ella) misma, sí (mismo), solo <he is courtesy itself : es la misma cortesía> <in and of itself : por sí

mismo> <it opened by itself : se abrió solo>

I've [ˈaɪv] (*contraction of* **I have**) → **have**

ivory [ˈaɪvəri] *n, pl* **-ries 1 :** marfil *m* **2 :** color *m* de marfil

ivy [ˈaɪvi] *n, pl* **ivies 1 :** hiedra *f,* yedra *f* **2** → **poison ivy**

J

j [ˈdʒeɪ] *n, pl* **j's** *or* **js** [ˈdʒeɪz] **:** décima letra del alfabeto inglés

jab[1] [ˈdʒæb] *v* **jabbed; jabbing** *vt* **1** PUNCTURE **:** clavar, pinchar **2** POKE **:** dar, golpear (con la punta de algo) <he jabbed me in the ribs : me dio un codazo en las costillas> — *vi* **to jab at :** dar, golpear

jab[2] *n* **1** PRICK **:** pinchazo *m* **2** POKE **:** golpe *m* abrupto

jabber[1] [ˈdʒæbər] *v* **:** farfullar

jabber[2] *n* **:** galimatías *m,* farfulla *f*

jack[1] [ˈdʒæk] *vt* **to jack up 1 :** levantar (con un gato) **2** INCREASE **:** subir, aumentar

jack[2] *n* **1 :** gato *m,* cric *m* <hydraulic jack : gato hidráulico> **2** FLAG **:** pabellón *m* **3** SOCKET **:** enchufe *m* hembra **4 :** jota *f,* valet *m* <jack of hearts : jota de corazones> **5 jacks** *npl* **:** cantillos *mpl*

jackal [ˈdʒækəl] *n* **:** chacal *m*

jackass [ˈdʒækˌæs] *n* **:** asno *m,* burro *m*

jacket [ˈdʒækət] *n* **1 :** chaqueta *f* **2** COVER **:** sobrecubierta *f* (de un libro), carátula *f* (de un disco)

jackhammer [ˈdʒækˌhæmər] *n* **:** martillo *m* neumático

jack–in–the–box [ˈdʒækɪnðəˌbɑks] *n* **:** caja *f* de sorpresa

jackknife[1] [ˈdʒækˌnaɪf] *vi* **-knifed; -knifing :** doblarse como una navaja, plegarse

jackknife[2] *n* **:** navaja *f*

jack–of–all–trades *n* **:** persona *f* que sabe un poco de todo, persona *f* de muchos oficios

jack–o'–lantern [ˈdʒækəˌlæntərn] *n* **:** linterna *f* hecha de una calabaza

jackpot [ˈdʒækˌpɑt] *n* **1 :** primer premio *m,* gordo *m* **2 to hit the jackpot :** sacarse la lotería, sacarse el gordo

jackrabbit [ˈdʒækˌræbət] *n* **:** liebre *f* grande de Norteamérica

jade [ˈdʒeɪd] *n* **:** jade *m*

jaded [ˈdʒeɪdəd] *adj* **1** TIRED **:** agotado **2** BORED **:** hastiado

jagged [ˈdʒægəd] *adj* **:** dentado, mellado

jaguar [ˈdʒægˌwɑr, ˈdʒægjʊˌwɑr] *n* **:** jaguar *m*

jai alai [ˈhaɪˌlaɪ] *n* **:** jai alai *m,* pelota *f* vasca

jail[1] [ˈdʒeɪl] *vt* **:** encarcelar

jail[2] *n* **:** cárcel *f*

jailbreak [ˈdʒeɪlˌbreɪk] *n* **:** fuga *f,* huida *f* (de la cárcel)

jailer *or* **jailor** [ˈdʒeɪlər] *n* **:** carcelero *m,* -ra *f*

jalapeño [ˌhɑləˈpeɪnjo, ˌhæ-, -ˈpiːno] *n* **:** jalapeño *m*

jalopy [dʒəˈlɑpi] *n, pl* **-lopies :** cacharro *m fam,* carro *m* destartalado

jalousie [ˈdʒæləsi] *n* **:** celosía *f*

jam[1] [ˈdʒæm] *v* **jammed; jamming** *vt* **1** CRAM **:** apiñar, embutir **2** BLOCK **:** atascar, atorar **3 to jam on the brakes :** frenar en seco — *vi* STICK **:** atascarse, atrancarse

jam[2] *n* **1** *or* **traffic jam :** atasco *m,* embotellamiento *m* (de tráfico) **2** PREDICAMENT **:** lío *m,* aprieto *m,* apuro *m* **3 :** mermelada *f* <strawberry jam : mermelada de fresa>

jamb [ˈdʒæm] *n* **:** jamba *f*

jamboree [ˌdʒæmbəˈriː] *n* **:** fiesta *f* grande

jangle[1] [ˈdʒæŋgəl] *v* **-gled; -gling** *vi* **:** hacer un ruido metálico — *vt* **1 :** hacer sonar **2 to jangle one's nerves :** irritar, crispar

jangle[2] *n* **:** ruido *m* metálico

janitor [ˈdʒænət̬ər] *n* **:** portero *m,* -ra *f;* conserje *mf*

January [ˈdʒænjʊˌɛri] *n* **:** enero *m*

Japanese [ˌdʒæpəˈniːz, -ˈniːs] *n* **1 :** japonés *m,* -nesa *f* **2 :** japonés *m* (idioma) — **Japanese** *adj*

jar[1] [ˈdʒɑr] *v* **jarred; jarring** *vi* **1** GRATE **:** chirriar **2** CLASH **:** desentonar **3** SHAKE **:** sacudirse **4 to jar on :** crispar, enervar — *vt* JOLT **:** sacudir

jar[2] *n* **1** GRATING **:** chirrido *m* **2** JOLT **:** vibración *f,* sacudida *f* **3 :** tarro *m,* bote *m,* pote *m* <a jar of honey : un tarro de miel>

jargon [ˈdʒɑrgən] *n* **:** jerga *f*

jasmine [ˈdʒæzmən] *n* **:** jazmín *m*

jasper [ˈdʒæspər] *n* **:** jaspe *m*

jaundice [ˈdʒɔndɪs] *n* **:** ictericia *f*

jaundiced [ˈdʒɔndɪst] *adj* **1 :** ictérico **2** EMBITTERED, RESENTFUL **:** amargado, resentido, negativo <with a jaundiced eye : con una actitud de cinismo>

jaunt [ˈdʒɔnt] *n* **:** excursión *f,* paseo *m*

jauntily [ˈdʒɔntəli] *adv* **:** animadamente

jauntiness [ˈdʒɔntinəs] *n* **:** animación *f,* vivacidad *f*

jaunty [ˈdʒɔnti] *adj* **-tier; -est 1** SPRIGHTLY **:** animado, alegre **2** RAKISH **:** desenvuelto, desenfadado

javelin [ˈdʒævələn] *n* **:** jabalina *f*

jaw[1] [ˈdʒɔ] *vi* GAB **:** cotorrear *fam,* parlotear *fam*

jaw[2] *n* **1 :** mandíbula *f,* quijada *f* **2 :** mordaza *f* (de una herramienta) **3 the jaws of death :** las garras *f* de la muerte

jawbone [ˈdʒɔˌboːn] *n* **:** mandíbula *f*
jay [ˈdʒeɪ] *n* **:** arrendajo *m,* chara *f Mex,* azulejo *m Mex*
jaybird [ˈdʒeɪˌbərd] → **jay**
jaywalk [ˈdʒeɪˌwɔk] *vi* **:** cruzar la calle sin prudencia
jaywalker [ˈdʒeɪˌwɔkər] *n* **:** peatón *m* imprudente
jazz[1] [ˈdʒæz] *vt* **to jazz up :** animar, alegrar
jazz[2] *n* **:** jazz *m*
jazzy [ˈdʒæzi] *adj* **jazzier; -est 1 :** con ritmo de jazz **2** FLASHY, SHOWY **:** llamativo, ostentoso
jealous [ˈdʒɛləs] *adj* **:** celoso, envidioso — **jealously** *adv*
jealousy [ˈdʒɛləsi] *n* **:** celos *mpl,* envidia *f*
jeans [ˈdʒiːnz] *npl* **:** jeans *mpl,* vaqueros *mpl*
jeep [ˈdʒiːp] *n* **:** jeep *m*
jeer[1] [ˈdʒɪr] *vi* **1** BOO **:** abuchear **2** SCOFF **:** mofarse, burlarse — *vt* RIDICULE **:** mofarse de, burlarse de
jeer[2] *n* **1 :** abucheo *m* **2** TAUNT **:** mofa *f,* burla *f*
Jehovah [dʒɪˈhoːvə] *n* **:** Jehová *m*
jell [ˈdʒɛl] *vi* **1** SET **:** gelificarse, cuajar **2** FORM **:** cuajar, formarse (una idea, etc.)
jelly[1] [ˈdʒɛli] *v* **jellied; jellying** *vi* **1** JELL **:** gelificarse, cuajar **2 :** hacer jalea — *vt* **:** gelificar
jelly[2] *n, pl* **-lies 1 :** jalea *f* **2** GELATIN **:** gelatina *f*
jellyfish [ˈdʒɛliˌfɪʃ] *n* **:** medusa *f*
jeopardize [ˈdʒɛpərˌdaɪz] *vt* **-dized; -dizing :** arriesgar, poner en peligro
jeopardy [ˈdʒɛpərdi] *n* **:** peligro *m,* riesgo *m*
jerk[1] [ˈdʒərk] *vt* **1** JOLT **:** sacudir **2** TUG, YANK **:** darle un tirón a — *vi* JOLT **:** dar sacudidas <the train jerked along : el tren iba moviéndose a sacudidas>
jerk[2] *n* **1** TUG **:** tirón *m,* jalón *m* **2** JOLT **:** sacudida *f* brusca **3** FOOL **:** estúpido *m,* -da *f;* idiota *mf*
jerkin [ˈdʒərkən] *n* **:** chaqueta *f* sin mangas, chaleco *m*
jerky [ˈdʒərki] *adj* **jerkier; -est 1 :** espasmódico (dícese de los movimientos) **2** CHOPPY **:** inconexo (dícese de la prosa) — **jerkily** [-kəli] *adv*
jerry-built [ˈdʒɛriˌbɪlt] *adj* **:** mal construido, chapucero
jersey [ˈdʒərzi] *n, pl* **-seys :** jersey *m*
jest[1] [ˈdʒɛst] *vi* **:** bromear
jest[2] *n* **:** broma *f,* chiste *m*
jester [ˈdʒɛstər] *n* **:** bufón *m,* -fona *f*
Jesus [ˈdʒiːzəs, -zəz] *n* **:** Jesús *m*
jet[1] [ˈdʒɛt] *v* **jetted; jetting** *vt* SPOUT **:** arrojar a chorros — *vi* **1** GUSH **:** salir a chorros, chorrear **2** FLY **:** viajar en avión, volar
jet[2] *n* **1** STREAM **:** chorro *m* **2** *or* **jet airplane :** avión *m* a reacción, reactor *m* **3 :** azabache *m* (mineral) **4 jet engine :** reactor *m,* motor *m* a reacción **5 jet lag :** desajuste *m* de horario (debido a un vuelo largo)
jet-propelled *adj* **:** a reacción
jetsam [ˈdʒɛtsəm] *n* **flotsam and jetsam :** restos *mpl,* desechos *mpl*
jettison [ˈdʒɛtəsən] *vt* **1 :** echar al mar **2** DISCARD **:** desechar, deshacerse de
jetty [ˈdʒɛti] *n, pl* **-ties 1** PIER, WHARF **:** desembarcadero *m,* muelle *m* **2** BREAKWATER **:** malecón *m,* rompeolas *m*
Jew [ˈdʒuː] *n* **:** judío *m,* -día *f*
jewel [ˈdʒuːəl] *n* **1 :** joya *f,* alhaja *f* **2** GEM **:** piedra *f* preciosa, gema *f* **3 :** rubí *m* (de un reloj) **4** TREASURE **:** joya *f,* tesoro *m*
jeweler *or* **jeweller** [ˈdʒuːələr] *n* **:** joyero *m,* -ra *f*
jewelry [ˈdʒuːəlri] *n* **:** joyas *fpl,* alhajas *fpl*
Jewish [ˈdʒuːɪʃ] *adj* **:** judío
jib [ˈdʒɪb] *n* **:** foque *m* (de un barco)
jibe [ˈdʒaɪb] *vi* **jibed; jibing** AGREE **:** concordar
jiffy [ˈdʒɪfi] *n, pl* **-fies :** santiamén *m,* segundo *m,* momento *m*
jig[1] [ˈdʒɪg] *vi* **jigged; jigging :** bailar la giga
jig[2] *n* **1 :** giga *f* **2 the jig is up :** se acabó la fiesta
jigger [ˈdʒɪgər] *n* **:** medida de 1 a 2 onzas (para licores)
jiggle[1] [ˈdʒɪgəl] *v* **-gled; -gling** *vt* **:** agitar o sacudir ligeramente — *vi* **:** agitarse, vibrar
jiggle[2] *n* **:** sacudida *f,* vibración *f*
jigsaw [ˈdʒɪgˌsɔ] *n* **1 :** sierra *f* de vaivén **2 jigsaw puzzle :** rompecabezas *m*
jilt [ˈdʒɪlt] *vt* **:** dejar plantado, dar calabazas a
jimmy[1] [ˈdʒɪmi] *vt* **-mied; -mying :** forzar con una palanqueta
jimmy[2] *n, pl* **-mies :** palanqueta *f*
jingle[1] [ˈdʒɪŋgəl] *v* **-gled; -gling** *vi* **:** tintinear — *vt* **:** hacer sonar
jingle[2] *n* **1** TINKLE **:** tintineo *m,* retintín *m* **2 :** canción *f* rimada
jingoism [ˈdʒɪŋgoˌɪzəm] *n* **:** jingoísmo *m,* patriotería *f*
jingoistic [ˌdʒɪŋgoˈɪstɪk] *or* **jingoist** [ˈdʒɪŋgoɪst] *adj* **:** jingoísta, patriotero
jinx[1] [ˈdʒɪŋks] *vt* **:** traer mala suerte a, salar *CoRi, Mex*
jinx[2] *n* **1 :** cenizo *m,* -za *f* **2 to put a jinx on :** echarle el mal de ojo a
jitters [ˈdʒɪtərz] *npl* **:** nervios *mpl* <he got the jitters : se puso nervioso>
jittery [ˈdʒɪtəri] *adj* **:** nervioso
job [ˈdʒɑb] *n* **1 :** trabajo *m* <he did odd jobs for her : le hizo algunos trabajos> **2** CHORE, TASK **:** tarea *f,* quehacer *m* **3** EMPLOYMENT **:** trabajo *m,* empleo *m,* puesto *m*
jobber [ˈdʒɑbər] *n* MIDDLEMAN **:** intermediario *m,* -ria *f*
jockey[1] [ˈdʒɑki] *v* **-eyed; -eying** *vt* **1** MANIPULATE **:** manipular **2** MANEUVER

: maniobrar — *vi* **to jockey for position :** maniobrar para conseguir algo
jockey[2] *n, pl* **-eys :** jockey *mf*
jocose [dʒoˈkoːs] *adj* **:** jocoso
jocular [ˈdʒɑkjʊlər] *adj* **:** jocoso — **jocularly** *adv*
jocularity [ˌdʒɑkjʊˈlærət̬i] *n* **:** jocosidad *f*
jodhpurs [ˈdʒɑdpərz] *npl* **:** pantalones *mpl* de montar
jog[1] [ˈdʒɑg] *v* **jogged; jogging** *vt* **1** NUDGE **:** dar, empujar, codear **2 to jog one's memory :** refrescar la memoria — *vi* **1** RUN **:** correr despacio, trotar, hacer footing (como ejercicio) **2** TRUDGE **:** andar a trote corto
jog[2] *n* **1** PUSH, SHAKE **:** empujoncito *m,* sacudida *f* leve **2** TROT **:** trote *m* corto, footing *m* (en deportes) **3** TWIST **:** recodo *m,* vuelta *f,* curva *f*
jogger [ˈdʒɑgər] *n* **:** persona *f* que hace footing
join [ˈdʒɔɪn] *vt* **1** CONNECT, LINK **:** unir, juntar <to join in marriage : unir en matrimonio> **2** ADJOIN **:** lindar con, colindar con **3** MEET **:** reunirse con, encontrarse con <we joined them for lunch : nos reunimos con ellos para almorzar> **4 :** hacerse socio de (una organización), afiliarse a (un partido), entrar en (una empresa) — *vi* **1** UNITE **:** unirse **2** MERGE **:** empalmar (dícese de las carreteras), confluir (dícese de los ríos) **3 to join up :** hacerse socio, enrolarse
joiner [ˈdʒɔɪnər] *n* **1** CARPENTER **:** carpintero *m,* -ra *f* **2 :** persona *f* que se une a varios grupos
joint[1] [ˈdʒɔɪnt] *adj* **:** conjunto, colectivo, mutuo <a joint effort : un esfuerzo conjunto> — **jointly** *adv*
joint[2] *n* **1 :** articulación *f,* coyuntura *f* <out of joint : dislocado> **2** ROAST **:** asado *m* **3** JUNCTURE **:** juntura *f,* unión *f* **4** DIVE **:** antro *m,* tasca *f*
joist [ˈdʒɔɪst] *n* **:** viga *f*
joke[1] [ˈdʒoːk] *vi* **joked; joking :** bromear
joke[2] *n* **1** STORY **:** chiste *m* **2** PRANK **:** broma *f*
joker [ˈdʒoːkər] *n* **1** PRANKSTER **:** bromista *mf* **2 :** comodín *m* (en los naipes)
jokingly [ˈdʒoːkɪŋli] *adv* **:** en broma
jollity [ˈdʒɑlət̬i] *n, pl* **-ties** MERRIMENT **:** alegría *f,* regocijo *m*
jolly [ˈdʒɑli] *adj* **-lier; -est :** alegre, jovial
jolt[1] [ˈdʒoːlt] *vi* JERK **:** dar tumbos, dar sacudidas — *vt* **:** sacudir
jolt[2] *n* **1** JERK **:** sacudida *f* brusca **2** SHOCK **:** golpe *m* (emocional)
jonquil [ˈdʒɑnkwɪl] *n* **:** junquillo *m*
Jordanian [dʒɔrˈdeɪniən] *n* **:** jordano *m,* -na *f* — **Jordanian** *adj*
josh [ˈdʒɑʃ] *vt* TEASE **:** tomarle el pelo (a alguien) — *vi* JOKE **:** bromear
jostle [ˈdʒɑsəl] *v* **-tled; -tling** *vi* **1** SHOVE **:** empujar, dar empellones **2** CONTEND **:** competir — *vt* **1** SHOVE **:** empujar **2 to jostle one's way :** abrirse paso a empellones
jot[1] [ˈdʒɑt] *vt* **jotted; jotting :** anotar, apuntar <jot it down : apúntalo>
jot[2] *n* BIT **:** ápice *m,* jota *f,* pizca *f*
jounce[1] [ˈdʒæʊnts] *v* **jounced; jouncing** *vt* JOLT **:** sacudir — *vi* **:** dar tumbos, dar sacudidas
jounce[2] *n* JOLT **:** sacudida *f,* tumbo *m*
journal [ˈdʒərnəl] *n* **1** DIARY **:** diario *m* **2** PERIODICAL **:** revista *f,* publicación *f* periódica **3** NEWSPAPER **:** periódico *m,* diario *m*
journalism [ˈdʒərnəlˌɪzəm] *n* **:** periodismo *m*
journalist [ˈdʒərnəlɪst] *n* **:** periodista *mf*
journalistic [ˌdʒərnəlˈɪstɪk] *adj* **:** periodístico
journey[1] [ˈdʒərni] *vi* **-neyed; -neying :** viajar
journey[2] *n, pl* **-neys :** viaje *m*
journeyman [ˈdʒərnimən] *n, pl* **-men** [-mən, -ˌmɛn] **:** oficial *m*
joust[1] [ˈdʒæʊst] *vi* **:** justar
joust[2] *n* **:** justa *f*
jovial [ˈdʒoːviəl] *adj* **:** jovial — **jovially** *adv*
joviality [ˌdʒoːviˈælət̬i] *n* **:** jovialidad *f*
jowl [ˈdʒæʊl] *n* **1** JAW **:** mandíbula *f* **2** CHEEK **:** mejilla *f,* cachete *m*
joy [ˈdʒɔɪ] *n* **1** HAPPINESS **:** gozo *m,* alegría *f,* felicidad *f* **2** DELIGHT **:** placer *m,* deleite *m* <the child is a real joy : el niño es un verdadero placer>
joyful [ˈdʒɔɪfəl] *adj* **:** gozoso, alegre, feliz — **joyfully** *adv*
joyless [ˈdʒɔɪləs] *adj* **:** sin alegría, triste
joyous [ˈdʒɔɪəs] *adj* **:** alegre, feliz, eufórico — **joyously** *adv*
joyousness [ˈdʒɔɪəsnəs] *n* **:** alegría *f,* felicidad *f,* euforia *f*
joyride [ˈdʒɔɪˌraɪd] *n* **:** paseo *m* temerario e irresponsable (en coche)
jubilant [ˈdʒuːbələnt] *adj* **:** jubiloso, alborozado — **jubilantly** *adv*
jubilation [ˌdʒuːbəˈleɪʃən] *n* **:** júbilo *m*
jubilee [ˈdʒuːbəˌliː] *n* **1 :** quincuagésimo aniversario *m* **2** CELEBRATION **:** celebración *f,* festejos *mpl*
Judaic [dʒʊˈdeɪɪk] *adj* **:** judaico
Judaism [ˈdʒuːdəˌɪzəm, ˈdʒuːdi-, ˈdʒuːˌdeɪ-] *n* **:** judaísmo *m*
judge[1] [ˈdʒʌdʒ] *vt* **judged; judging 1** ASSESS **:** evaluar, juzgar **2** DEEM **:** juzgar, considerar **3** TRY **:** juzgar (ante el tribuno) **4 judging by :** a juzgar por
judge[2] *n* **1 :** juez *mf,* jueza *f* **2 to be a good judge of :** saber juzgar a, entender mucho de
judgment *or* **judgement** [ˈdʒʌdʒmənt] *n* **1** RULING **:** fallo *m,* sentencia *f* **2** OPINION **:** opinión *f* **3** DISCERNMENT **:** juicio *m,* discernimiento *m*
judgmental [ˌdʒʌdʒˈmɛnt̬əl] *adj* **:** crítico — **judgmentally** *adv*

judicature [ˈdʒuːdɪkəˌtʃʊr] *n* : judicatura *f*

judicial [dʒʊˈdɪʃəl] *adj* : judicial — **judicially** *adv*

judiciary[1] [dʒʊˈdɪʃiˌɛri, -ˈdɪʃəri] *adj* : judicial

judiciary[2] *n* **1** JUDICATURE : judicatura *f* **2** : poder *m* judicial

judicious [dʒʊˈdɪʃəs] *adj* SOUND, WISE : juicioso, sensato — **judiciously** *adv*

judo [ˈdʒuːˌdoː] *n* : judo *m*

jug [ˈdʒʌg] *n* **1** : jarra *f,* jarro *m,* cántaro *m* **2** JAIL : cárcel *f,* chirona *f fam*

juggernaut [ˈdʒʌgərˌnɔt] *n* : gigante *m,* fuerza *f* irresistible <a political juggernaut : un gigante político>

juggle [ˈdʒʌgəl] *v* **-gled; -gling** *vt* **1** : hacer juegos malabares con **2** MANIPULATE : manipular, jugar con — *vi* : hacer juegos malabares

juggler [ˈdʒʌgələr] *n* : malabarista *mf*

jugular [ˈdʒʌgjʊlər] *adj* : yugular <jugular vein : vena yugular>

juice [ˈdʒuːs] *n* **1** : jugo *m* (de carne, de frutas) *m,* zumo *m* (de frutas) **2** ELECTRICITY : electricidad *f,* luz *f*

juicer [ˈdʒuːsər] *n* : exprimidor *m*

juiciness [ˈdʒuːsinəs] *n* : jugosidad *f*

juicy [ˈdʒuːsi] *adj* **juicier; -est 1** SUCCULENT : jugoso, suculento **2** PROFITABLE : jugoso, lucrativo **3** RACY : picante

jukebox [ˈdʒuːkˌbɑks] *n* : rocola *f,* máquina *f* de discos

julep [ˈdʒuːləp] *n* : bebida *f* hecha con whisky americano y menta

July [dʒʊˈlaɪ] *n* : julio *m*

jumble[1] [ˈdʒʌmbəl] *vt* **-bled; -bling** : mezclar, revolver

jumble[2] *n* : revoltijo *m,* fárrago *m,* embrollo *m*

jumbo[1] [ˈdʒʌmˌboː] *adj* : gigante, enorme, de tamaño extra grande

jumbo[2] *n, pl* **-bos** : coloso *m,* cosa *f* de tamaño extra grande

jump[1] [ˈdʒʌmp] *vi* **1** LEAP : saltar, brincar **2** START : levantarse de un salto, sobresaltarse **3** MOVE, SHIFT : moverse, pasar <to jump from job to job : pasar de un empleo a otro> **4** INCREASE, RISE : dar un salto, aumentarse de golpe, subir bruscamente **5** BUSTLE : animarse, ajetrearse **6 to jump to conclusions** : sacar conclusiones precipitadas — *vt* **1** : saltar <to jump a fence : saltar una valla> **2** SKIP : saltarse **3** ATTACK : atacar, asaltar **4 to jump the gun** : precipitarse

jump[2] *n* **1** LEAP : salto *m* **2** START : sobresalto *m,* respingo *m* **3** INCREASE : subida *f* brusca, aumento *m* **4** ADVANTAGE : ventaja *f* <we got the jump on them : les llevamos la ventaja>

jumper [ˈdʒʌmpər] *n* **1** : saltador *m,* -dora *f* (en deportes) **2** : jumper *m,* vestido *m* sin mangas

jumpy [ˈdʒʌmpi] *adj* **jumpier; -est** : asustadizo, nervioso

junction [ˈdʒʌŋkʃən] *n* **1** JOINING : unión *f* **2** : cruce *m* (de calles), empalme *m* (de un ferrocarril), confluencia *f* (de ríos)

juncture [ˈdʒʌŋktʃər] *n* **1** UNION : juntura *f,* unión *f* **2** MOMENT, POINT : coyuntura *f* <at this juncture : en esta coyuntura, en este momento>

June [ˈdʒuːn] *n* : junio *m*

jungle [ˈdʒʌŋgəl] *n* : jungla *f,* selva *f*

junior[1] [ˈdʒuːnjər] *adj* **1** YOUNGER : más joven <John Smith, Junior : John Smith, hijo> **2** SUBORDINATE : subordinado, subalterno

junior[2] *n* **1** : persona *f* de menor edad <she's my junior : es menor que yo> **2** SUBORDINATE : subalterno *m,* -na *f;* subordinado *m,* -da *f* **3** : estudiante *mf* de penúltimo año

juniper [ˈdʒuːnəpər] *n* : enebro *m*

junk[1] [ˈdʒʌŋk] *vt* : echar a la basura

junk[2] *n* **1** RUBBISH : desechos *mpl,* desperdicios *mpl* **2** STUFF : trastos *mpl fam,* cachivaches *mpl fam* **3 piece of junk** : cacharro *m,* porquería *f*

junket [ˈdʒʌŋkət] *n* : viaje *m* (pagado con dinero público)

junta [ˈhʊntə, ˈdʒʌn-, ˈhʌn-] *n* : junta *f* militar

Jupiter [ˈdʒuːpətər] *n* : Júpiter *m*

jurisdiction [ˌdʒʊrəsˈdɪkʃən] *n* : jurisdicción *f*

jurisprudence [ˌdʒʊrəsˈpruːdənts] *n* : jurisprudencia *f*

jurist [ˈdʒʊrɪst] *n* : jurista *mf;* magistrado *m,* -da *f*

juror [ˈdʒʊrər] *n* : jurado *m,* -da *f*

jury [ˈdʒʊri] *n, pl* **-ries** : jurado *m*

just[1] [ˈdʒʌst] *adv* **1** EXACTLY : justo, precisamente, exactamente **2** POSSIBLY : posiblemente <it just might work : tal vez resulte> **3** BARELY : justo, apenas <just in time : justo a tiempo> **4** ONLY : sólo, solamente, nada más <just us : sólo nosotros> **5** QUITE : muy, simplemente <it's just horrible! : ¡qué horrible!> **6 to have just (done something)** : acabar de (hacer algo) <he just called : acaba de llamar>

just[2] *adj* : justo — **justly** *adv*

justice [ˈdʒʌstɪs] *n* **1** : justicia *f* **2** JUDGE : juez *mf,* jueza *f*

justification [ˌdʒʌstəfəˈkeɪʃən] *n* : justificación *f*

justify [ˈdʒʌstəˌfaɪ] *vt* **-fied; -fying** : justificar — **justifiable** [ˌdʒʌstəˈfaɪəbəl] *adj*

jut [ˈdʒʌt] *vi* **jutted; jutting** : sobresalir

jute [ˈdʒuːt] *n* : yute *m*

juvenile[1] [ˈdʒuːvəˌnaɪl, -vənəl] *adj* **1** : juvenil <juvenile delinquent : delincuente juvenil> <juvenile court : tribunal de menores> **2** CHILDISH : infantil

juvenile[2] *n* : menor *mf*

juxtapose [ˈdʒʌkstəˌpoːz] *vt* **-posed; -posing** : yuxtaponer

juxtaposition [ˌdʒʌkstəpəˈzɪʃən] *n* : yuxtaposición *f*

K

k [ˈkeɪ] *n, pl* **k's** *or* **ks** [ˈkeɪz] : undécima letra del alfabeto inglés
kaiser [ˈkaɪzər] *n* : káiser *m*
kale [ˈkeɪl] *n* : col *f* rizada
kaleidoscope [kəˈlaɪdəˌskoːp] *n* : calidoscopio *m*
kangaroo [ˌkæŋgəˈruː] *n, pl* **-roos** : canguro *m*
kaolin [ˈkeɪələn] *n* : caolín *m*
karat [ˈkærət] *n* : quilate *m*
karate [kəˈrɑt̬i] *n* : karate *m*
katydid [ˈkeɪt̬iˌdɪd] *n* : saltamontes *m*
kayak [ˈkaɪˌæk] *n* : kayac *m,* kayak *m*
keel[1] [ˈkiːl] *vi* **to keel over** : volcar (dícese de un barco), desplomarse (dícese de una persona)
keel[2] *n* : quilla *f*
keen [ˈkiːn] *adj* **1** SHARP : afilado, filoso <a keen blade : una hoja afilada> **2** PENETRATING : cortante, penetrante <a keen wind : un viento cortante> **3** ENTHUSIASTIC : entusiasta **4** ACUTE : agudo, fino <keen hearing : oído fino> <keen intelligence : inteligencia aguda>
keenly [ˈkiːnli] *adv* **1** ENTHUSIASTICALLY : con entusiasmo **2** INTENSELY : vivamente, profundamente <keenly aware of : muy consciente de>
keenness [ˈkiːnnəs] *n* **1** SHARPNESS : lo afilado, lo filoso **2** ENTHUSIASM : entusiasmo *m* **3** ACUTENESS : agudeza *f*
keep[1] [ˈkiːp] *v* **kept** [ˈkɛpt]; **keeping** *vt* **1** : cumplir (la palabra a uno), acudir a (una cita) **2** OBSERVE : observar (una fiesta) **3** GUARD : guardar, cuidar **4** CONTINUE : mantener <to keep silence : mantener silencio> **5** SUPPORT : mantener (una familia) **6** RAISE : criar (animales) **7** : llevar, escribir (un diario, etc.) **8** RETAIN : guardar, conservar, quedarse con **9** STORE : guardar **10** DETAIN : hacer quedar, detener **11** PRESERVE : guardar <to keep a secret : guardar un secreto> — *vi* **1** : conservarse (dícese de los alimentos) **2** CONTINUE : seguir, no dejar <he keeps on pestering us : no deja de molestarnos> **3 to keep from** : abstenerse de <I couldn't keep from laughing : no podía contener la risa>
keep[2] *n* **1** TOWER : torreón *m* (de un castillo), torre *f* del homenaje **2** SUSTENANCE : manutención *f,* sustento *m* **3 for keeps** : para siempre
keeper [ˈkiːpər] *n* **1** : guarda *mf* (en un zoológico); conservador *m,* -dora *f* (en un museo) **2** GAMEKEEPER : guardabosque *mf*
keeping [ˈkiːpɪŋ] *n* **1** CONFORMITY : conformidad *f,* acuerdo *m* <in keeping with : de acuerdo con> **2** CARE : cuidado *m* <in the keeping of : al cuidado de>
keepsake [ˈkiːpˌseɪk] *n* : recuerdo *m*
keep up *vt* CONTINUE, MAINTAIN : mantener, seguir con — *vi* **1** : mantenerse al corriente <he kept up with the news : se mantenía al tanto de las noticias> **2** CONTINUE : continuar **3 to keep up with someone** : mantener contacto con alguien
keg [ˈkɛg] *n* : barril *m*
kelp [ˈkɛlp] *n* : alga *f* marina
ken [ˈkɛn] *n* **1** SIGHT : vista *f,* alcance *m* de la vista **2** UNDERSTANDING : comprensión *f,* alcance *m* del conocimiento <it's beyond his ken : no lo puede entender>
kennel [ˈkɛnəl] *n* : caseta *f* para perros, perrera *f*
Kenyan [ˈkɛnjən, ˈkiːn-] *n* : keniano *m,* -na *f* — **Kenyan** *adj*
kept → **keep**
kerchief [ˈkərtʃəf, -ˌtʃiːf] *n* : pañuelo *m*
kernel [ˈkərnəl] *n* **1** : almendra *f* (de semillas y nueces) **2** : grano *m* (de cereales) **3** CORE : meollo *m* <a kernel of truth : un fondo de verdad>
kerosene *or* **kerosine** [ˈkɛrəˌsiːn, ˌkɛrəˈ-] *n* : queroseno *m,* kerosén *m,* kerosene *m*
ketchup [ˈkɛtʃəp, ˈkæ-] *n* : salsa *f* catsup
kettle [ˈkɛtəl] *n* **1** : hervidor *m,* pava *f Arg, Bol, Chile* **2** → **teakettle**
kettledrum [ˈkɛtəlˌdrʌm] *n* : timbal *m*
key[1] [ˈkiː] *vt* **1** ATTUNE : adaptar, adecuar **2 to key up** : poner nervioso, inquietar
key[2] *adj* : clave, fundamental
key[3] *n* **1** : llave *f* **2** SOLUTION : clave *f,* soluciones *fpl* **3** : tecla *f* (de un piano o una máquina) **4** : tono *m,* tonalidad *f* (en la música) **5** ISLET, REEF : cayo *m,* islote *m*
keyboard [ˈkiːˌbord] *n* : teclado *m*
keyhole [ˈkiːˌhoːl] *n* : bocallave *f,* ojo *m* (de una cerradura)
keynote[1] [ˈkiːˌnoːt] *vt* **-noted; -noting** **1** : establecer la tónica de (en música) **2** : pronunciar el discurso principal de
keynote[2] *n* **1** : tónica *f* (en música) **2** : idea *f* fundamental
keystone [ˈkiːˌstoːn] *n* : clave *f,* dovela *f*
khaki [ˈkæki, ˈkɑ-] *n* : caqui *m*
khan [ˈkɑn, ˈkæn] *n* : kan *m*
kibbutz [kəˈbʊts, -ˈbuːts] *n, pl* **-butzim** [-ˌbʊtˈsiːm, -ˌbuːt-] : kibutz *m*
kibitz [ˈkɪbɪts] *vi* : dar consejos molestos
kibitzer [ˈkɪbɪtsər, kɪˈbɪt-] *n* : persona *f* que da consejos molestos
kick[1] [ˈkɪk] *vi* **1** : dar patadas (dícese de una persona), cocear (dícese de un animal) **2** PROTEST : patalear, protestar **3** RECOIL : dar un culatazo (dícese de

un arma de fuego) — *vt* : patear, darle una patada (a alguien)

kick[2] *n* **1** : patada *f,* puntapié *m,* coz *f* (de un animal) **2** RECOIL : culatazo *m* (de un arma de fuego) **3** : fuerza *f* <a drink with a kick : una bebida fuerte>

kicker ['kɪkər] *n* : pateador *m,* -dora *f* (en deportes)

kickoff ['kɪk,ɔf] *n* : saque *m* (inicial)

kick off *vi* **1** : hacer el saque inicial (en deportes) **2** BEGIN : empezar — *vt* : empezar

kid[1] ['kɪd] *v* **kidded; kidding** *vt* **1** FOOL : engañar **2** TEASE : tomarle el pelo (a alguien) — *vi* JOKE : bromear <I'm only kidding : lo digo en broma>

kid[2] *n* **1** : chivo *m,* -va *f;* cabrito *m,* -ta *f* **2** CHILD : chico *m,* -ca *f;* niño *m,* -ña *f*

kidder ['kɪdər] *n* : bromista *mf*

kiddingly ['kɪdɪŋli] *adv* : en broma

kidnap ['kɪd,næp] *vt* **-napped** *or* **-naped** [-,næpt]; **-napping** *or* **-naping** [-,næpɪŋ] : secuestrar, raptar

kidnapper *or* **kidnaper** ['kɪd,næpər] *n* : secuestrador *m,* -dora *f;* raptor *m,* -tora *f*

kidney ['kɪdni] *n, pl* **-neys** : riñón *m*

kidney bean *n* : frijol *m*

kill[1] ['kɪl] *vt* **1** : matar **2** END : acabar con, poner fin a **3 to kill time** : matar el tiempo

kill[2] *n* **1** KILLING : matanza *f* **2** PREY : presa *f*

killer ['kɪlər] *n* : asesino *m,* -na *f*

kiln ['kɪl, 'kɪln] *n* : horno *m*

kilo ['kiː,loː] *n, pl* **-los** : kilo *m*

kilocycle ['kɪlə,saɪkəl] *n* : kilociclo *m*

kilogram ['kɪlə,græm, 'kiː-] *n* : kilogramo *m*

kilohertz ['kɪlə,hərts] *n* : kilohertzio *m*

kilometer [kɪ'lɑmət̬ər, 'kɪlə,miː-] *n* : kilómetro *m*

kilowatt ['kɪlə,wɑt] *n* : kilovatio *m*

kilt ['kɪlt] *n* : falda *f* escocesa

kilter ['kɪltər] *n* **1** ORDER : buen estado *m* **2 out of kilter** : descompuesto, estropeado

kimono [kə'moːno, -nə] *n, pl* **-nos** : kimono *m,* quimono *m*

kin ['kɪn] *n* : familiares *mpl*, parientes *mpl*

kind[1] ['kaɪnd] *adj* : amable, bondadoso, benévolo

kind[2] *n* **1** ESSENCE : esencia *f* <a difference in degree, not in kind : una diferencia cuantitativa y no cualitativa> **2** CATEGORY : especie *f,* género *m* **3** TYPE : clase *f,* tipo *m,* índole *f*

kindergarten ['kɪndər,gɑrtən, -dən] *n* : kinder *m,* kindergarten *m,* jardín *m* de infantes, jardín *m* de niños *Mex*

kindhearted [,kaɪnd'hɑrt̬əd] *adj* : bondadoso, de buen corazón

kindle ['kɪndəl] *v* **-dled; -dling** *vt* **1** IGNITE : encender **2** AROUSE : despertar, suscitar — *vi* : encenderse

kindliness ['kaɪndlinəs] *n* : bondad *f*

kindling ['kɪndlɪŋ, 'kɪndlən] *n* : astillas *fpl*, leña *f*

kindly[1] ['kaɪndli] *adv* **1** AMIABLY : amablemente, bondadosamente **2** COURTEOUSLY : cortésmente, con cortesía <we kindly ask you not smoke : les rogamos que no fumen> **3** PLEASE : por favor **4 to take kindly to** : aceptar de buena gana

kindly[2] *adj* **-lier; -est** : bondadoso, amable

kindness ['kaɪndnəs] *n* : bondad *f*

kind of *adv* SOMEWHAT : un tanto, algo

kindred[1] ['kɪndrəd] *adj* SIMILAR : similar, afín <kindred spirits : almas gemelas>

kindred[2] *n* **1** FAMILY : familia *f,* parentela *f* **2** → **kin**

kinfolk ['kɪn,foːk] *or* **kinfolks** [-,foːks] *npl* → **kin**

king ['kɪŋ] *n* : rey *m*

kingdom ['kɪŋdəm] *n* : reino *m*

kingfisher ['kɪŋ,fɪʃər] *n* : martín *m* pescador

kingly ['kɪŋli] *adj* **-lier; -est** : regio, real

king–size ['kɪŋ,saɪz] *or* **king–sized** [-,saɪzd] *adj* : de tamaño muy grande, extra largo (dícese de cigarillos)

kink ['kɪŋk] *n* **1** : rizo *m* (en el pelo), vuelta *f* (en una cuerda) **2** CRAMP : calambre *m* <to have a kink in the neck : tener tortícolis>

kinky ['kɪŋki] *adj* **-kier; -est** : rizado (dícese del pelo), enroscado (dícese de una cuerda)

kinship ['kɪn,ʃɪp] *n* : parentesco *m*

kinsman ['kɪnzmən] *n, pl* **-men** [-mən, -,mɛn] : familiar *m,* pariente *m*

kinswoman ['kɪnz,wʊmən] *n, pl* **-women** [-,wɪmən] : familiar *f,* pariente *f*

kipper ['kɪpər] *n* : arenque *m* ahumado

kiss[1] ['kɪs] *vt* : besar — *vi* : besarse

kiss[2] *n* : beso *m*

kit ['kɪt] *n* **1** SET : juego *m,* kit *m* **2** CASE : estuche *m,* caja *f* **3 first–aid kit** : botiquín *m* **4 tool kit** : caja *f* de herramientas **5 travel kit** : neceser *m*

kitchen ['kɪtʃən] *n* : cocina *f*

kite ['kaɪt] *n* **1** : milano *m* (ave) **2** : cometa *f,* papalote *m Mex* <to fly a kite : hacer volar una cometa>

kith ['kɪθ] *n* : amigos *mpl* <kith and kin : amigos y parientes>

kitten ['kɪtən] *n* : gatito *m,* -ta *f*

kitty ['kɪt̬i] *n, pl* **-ties 1** FUND, POOL : bote *m,* fondo *m* común **2** CAT : gato *m,* gatito *m*

kitty–corner ['kɪt̬i,kɔrnər] *or* **kitty–cornered** [-nərd] → **catercorner**

kiwi ['kiː,wiː] *n* : kiwi *m*

kleptomania [,klɛptə'meɪniə] *n* : cleptomanía *f*

kleptomaniac [,klɛptə'meɪni,æk] *n* : cleptómano *m,* -na *f*

knack ['næk] *n* : maña *f,* facilidad *f*

knapsack ['næp,sæk] *n* : mochila *f,* morral *m*

knave [ˈneɪv] *n* : bellaco *m,* pícaro *m*
knead [ˈniːd] *vt* **1** : amasar, sobar **2** MASSAGE : masajear
knee [ˈniː] *n* : rodilla *f*
kneecap [ˈniːˌkæp] *n* : rótula *f*
kneel [ˈniːl] *vi* **knelt** [ˈnɛlt] *or* **kneeled** [ˈniːld]; **kneeling** : arrodillarse, ponerse de rodillas
knell [ˈnɛl] *n* : doble *m,* toque *m* <death knell : toque de difuntos>
knew → **know**
knickers [ˈnɪkərz] *npl* : pantalones *mpl* bombachos de media pierna
knickknack [ˈnɪkˌnæk] *n* : chuchería *f,* baratija *f*
knife[1] [ˈnaɪf] *vt* **knifed** [ˈnaɪft]; **knifing** : acuchillar, apuñalar
knife[2] *n, pl* **knives** [ˈnaɪvz] : cuchillo *m*
knight[1] [ˈnaɪt] *vt* : conceder el título de *Sir* a
knight[2] *n* **1** : caballero *m* <knight errant : caballero andante> **2** : caballo *m* (en ajedrez) **3** : uno que tiene el título de *Sir*
knighthood [ˈnaɪtˌhʊd] *n* **1** : caballería *f* **2** : título *m* de *Sir*
knightly [ˈnaɪtli] *adj* : caballeresco
knit[1] [ˈnɪt] *v* **knit** *or* **knitted** [ˈnɪt̬əd]; **knitting** *vt* **1** UNITE : unir, enlazar **2** : tejer <to knit a sweater : tejer un suéter> **3 to knit one's brows** : fruncir el ceño — *vi* **1** : tejer **2** : soldarse (dícese de los huesos)
knit[2] *n* : prenda *f* tejida
knitter [ˈnɪt̬ər] *n* : tejedor *m,* -dora *f*
knob [ˈnɑb] *n* **1** LUMP : bulto *m,* protuberancia *f* **2** HANDLE : perilla *f,* tirador *m,* botón *m*
knobbed [ˈnɑbd] *adj* **1** KNOTTY : nudoso **2** : que tiene perilla o botón
knobby [ˈnɑbi] *adj* **knobbier; -est 1** KNOTTY : nudoso **2 knobby knees** : rodillas *fpl* huesudas
knock[1] [ˈnɑk] *vt* **1** HIT, RAP : golpear, golpetear **2** : hacer chocar <they knocked heads : se dieron en la cabeza> **3** CRITICIZE : criticar — *vi* **1** RAP : dar un golpe, llamar (a la puerta) **2** COLLIDE : darse, chocar
knock[2] *n* : golpe *m,* llamada *f* (a la puerta), golpeteo *m* (de un motor)
knock down *vt* : derribar, echar al suelo
knocker [ˈnɑkər] *n* : aldaba *f,* llamador *m*
knock–kneed [ˈnɑkˈniːd] *adj* : patizambo
knock out *vt* : dejar sin sentido, poner fuera de combate (en el boxeo)
knoll [ˈnoːl] *n* : loma *f,* otero *m,* montículo *m*
knot[1] [ˈnɑt] *v* **knotted; knotting** *vt* : anudar — *vi* : anudarse
knot[2] *n* **1** : nudo *m* (en cordel o madera), nódulo *m* (en los músculos) **2** CLUSTER : grupo *m* **3** : nudo *m* (unidad de velocidad)
knotty [ˈnɑt̬i] *adj* **-tier; -est 1** GNARLED : nudoso **2** COMPLEX : espinoso, enredado, complejo
know [ˈnoː] *v* **knew** [ˈnuː, ˈnjuː]; **known** [ˈnoːn]; **knowing** *vt* **1** : saber <he knows the answer : sabe la respuesta> **2** : conocer (a una persona, un lugar) <do you know Julia? : ¿conoces a Julia?> **3** RECOGNIZE : reconocer **4** DISCERN, DISTINGUISH : distinguir, discernir **5 to know how to** : saber <I don't know how to dance : no sé bailar> — *vi* : saber
knowable [ˈnoːəbəl] *adj* : conocible
knowing [ˈnoːɪŋ] *adj* **1** KNOWLEDGEABLE : informado <a knowing look : una mirada de complicidad> **2** ASTUTE : astuto **3** DELIBERATE : deliberado, intencional
knowingly [ˈnoːɪŋli] *adv* **1** : con complicidad <she smiled knowingly : sonrió con una mirada de complicidad> **2** DELIBERATELY : a sabiendas, adrede, a propósito
know–it–all [ˈnoːɪt̬ˌɔl] *n* : sabelotodo *mf fam*
knowledge [ˈnɑlɪdʒ] *n* **1** AWARENESS : conocimiento *m* **2** LEARNING : conocimientos *mpl,* saber *m*
knowledgeable [ˈnɑlɪdʒəbəl] *adj* : informado, entendido, enterado
known [ˈnoːn] *adj* : conocido, familiar
knuckle [ˈnʌkəl] *n* : nudillo *m*
koala [koˈwɑlə] *n* : koala *m*
kohlrabi [ˌkoːlˈrɑbi, -ˈræ-] *n, pl* **-bies** : colinabo *m*
Koran [kəˈrɑn, -ˈræn] *n* **the Koran** : el Corán
Korean [kəˈriːən] *n* : coreano *m,* -na *f* — **Korean** *adj*
kosher [ˈkoːʃər] *adj* : aprobado por la ley judía
kowtow [ˌkaʊˈtaʊ, ˈkaʊˌtaʊ] *vi* **to kowtow to** : humillarse ante, doblegarse ante
krypton [ˈkrɪpˌtɑn] *n* : criptón *m*
kudos [ˈkjuːˌdɑs, ˈkuː-, -ˌdoːz] *n* : fama *f,* renombre *m*
kumquat [ˈkʌmˌkwɑt] *n* : naranjita *f* china
Kuwaiti [kʊˈweɪt̬i] *n* : kuwaití *mf* — **Kuwaiti** *adj*

L

l [ˈɛl] *n, pl* **l's** *or* **ls** [ˈɛlz] : duodécima letra del alfabeto inglés
lab [ˈlæb] → **laboratory**
label[1] [ˈleɪbəl] *vt* **-beled** *or* **-belled; -beling** *or* **-belling 1** : etiquetar, poner etiqueta a **2** BRAND, CATEGORIZE

: calificar, tildar, tachar <they labeled him as a fraud : lo calificaron de farsante>
label[2] *n* **1** : etiqueta *f,* rótulo *m* **2** DESCRIPTION : calificación *f,* descripción *f* **3** BRAND : marca *f*
labial [ˈleɪbiəl] *adj* : labial
labor[1] [ˈleɪbər] *vi* **1** WORK : trabajar **2** STRUGGLE : avanzar penosamente (dícese de una persona), funcionar con dificultad (dícese de un motor) **3 to labor under a delusion** : hacerse ilusiones, tener una falsa impresión — *vt* BELABOR : insistir en, extenderse sobre
labor[2] *n* **1** EFFORT, WORK : trabajo *m,* esfuerzos *mpl* **2** : parto *m* <to be in labor : estar de parto> **3** TASK : tarea *f,* labor *m* **4** WORKERS : mano *f* de obra
laboratory [ˈlæbrəˌtori, ləˈbɔrə-] *n, pl* **-ries** : laboratorio *m*
Labor Day *n* : Día *m* del Trabajo
laborer [ˈleɪbərər] *n* : peón *m;* trabajador *m,* -dora *f*
laborious [ləˈboriəs] *adj* : laborioso, difícil
laboriously [ləˈboriəsli] *adv* : laboriosamente, trabajosamente
labor union → **union**
labyrinth [ˈlæbəˌrɪnθ] *n* : laberinto *m*
lace[1] [ˈleɪs] *vt* **laced; lacing 1** TIE : acordonar, atar los cordones de **2** : adornar de encaje <I laced the dress in white : adorné el vestido de encaje blanco> **3** SPIKE : echar licor a
lace[2] *n* **1** : encaje *m* **2** SHOELACE : cordón *m* (de zapatos), agujeta *f Mex*
lacerate [ˈlæsəˌreɪt] *vt* **-ated; -ating** : lacerar
laceration [ˌlæsəˈreɪʃən] *n* : laceración *f*
lack[1] [ˈlæk] *vt* : carecer de, no tener <she lacks patience : carece de paciencia> — *vi* : faltar <they lack for nothing : no les falta nada>
lack[2] *n* : falta *f,* carencia *f*
lackadaisical [ˌlækəˈdeɪzɪkəl] *adj* : apático, indiferente, lánguido — **lackadaisically** [-kli] *adv*
lackey [ˈlæki] *n, pl* **-eys 1** FOOTMAN : lacayo *m* **2** TOADY : adulador *m,* -dora *f*
lackluster [ˈlækˌlʌstər] *adj* **1** DULL : sin brillo, apagado, deslustrado **2** MEDIOCRE : deslucido, mediocre
laconic [ləˈkɑnɪk] *adj* : lacónico — **laconically** [-nɪkli] *adv*
lacquer[1] [ˈlækər] *vt* : laquear, pintar con laca
lacquer[2] *n* : laca *f*
lacrosse [ləˈkrɔs] *n* : lacrosse *f*
lactic acid [ˈlæktɪk] *n* : ácido *m* láctico
lacuna [ləˈkuːnə, -ˈkjuː-] *n, pl* **-nae** [-ˌniː, -ˌnaɪ] *or* **-nas** : laguna *f*
lacy [ˈleɪsi] *adj* **lacier; -est** : de encaje, como de encaje
lad [ˈlæd] *n* : muchacho *m,* niño *m*
ladder [ˈlædər] *n* : escalera *f*
laden [ˈleɪdən] *adj* : cargado
ladle[1] [ˈleɪdəl] *vt* **-dled; -dling** : servir con cucharón
ladle[2] *n* : cucharón *m,* cazo *m*
lady [ˈleɪdi] *n, pl* **-dies 1** : señora *f,* dama *f* **2** WOMAN : mujer *f*
ladybird [ˈleɪdiˌbərd] → **ladybug**
ladybug [ˈleɪdiˌbʌg] *n* : mariquita *f*
lag[1] [ˈlæg] *vi* **lagged; lagging** : quedarse atrás, retrasarse, rezagarse
lag[2] *n* **1** DELAY : retraso *m,* demora *f* **2** INTERVAL : lapso *m,* intervalo *m*
lager [ˈlɑgər] *n* : cerveza *f* rubia
laggard[1] [ˈlægərd] *adj* : retardado, retrasado
laggard[2] *n* : rezagado *m,* -da *f*
lagoon [ləˈguːn] *n* : laguna *f*
laid *pp* → **lay**
lain *pp* → **lie**
lair [ˈlær] *n* : guarida *f,* madriguera *f*
laissez–faire [ˌlɛˌseɪˈfær, ˌleɪˌzeɪ-] *n* : liberalismo *m* económico
laity [ˈleɪəṭi] *n* **the laity** : los laicos, el laicado
lake [ˈleɪk] *n* : lago *m*
lama [ˈlɑmə] *n* : lama *m*
lamb [ˈlæm] *n* **1** : cordero *m,* borrego *m* (animal) **2** : carne *f* de cordero
lambaste [læmˈbeɪst] *or* **lambast** [-ˈbæst] *vt* **-basted; -basting 1** BEAT, THRASH : golpear, azotar, darle una paliza (a alguien) **2** CENSURE : arremeter contre, censurar
lame[1] [ˈleɪm] *vt* **lamed; laming** : lisiar, hacer cojo
lame[2] *adj* **lamer; lamest 1** : cojo, renco, rengo **2** WEAK : pobre, débil, poco convincente <a lame excuse : una excusa débil>
lamé [lɑˈmeɪ, læ-] *n* : lamé *m*
lame duck *n* : persona *f* sin poder <a lame-duck President : un presidente saliente>
lamely [ˈleɪmli] *adv* : sin convicción
lameness [ˈleɪmnəs] *n* **1** : cojera *f,* renquera *f* **2** : falta *f* de convicción, debilidad *f,* pobreza *f* <the lameness of her response : la pobreza de su respuesta>
lament[1] [ləˈmɛnt] *vt* **1** MOURN : llorar, llorar por **2** DEPLORE : lamentar, deplorar — *vi* : llorar
lament[2] *n* : lamento *m*
lamentable [ˈlæməntəbəl, ləˈmɛntə-] *adj* : lamentable, deplorable — **lamentably** [-bli] *adv*
lamentation [ˌlæmənˈteɪʃən] *n* : lamentación *f,* lamento *m*
laminate[1] [ˈlæməˌneɪt] *vt* **-nated; -nating** : laminar
laminate[2] [ˈlæmənət] *n* : laminado *m*
laminated [ˈlæməˌneɪṭəd] *adj* : laminado
lamp [ˈlæmp] *n* : lámpara *f*
lampoon[1] [læmˈpuːn] *vt* : satirizar
lampoon[2] *n* : sátira *f*
lamprey [ˈlæmpri] *n, pl* **-preys** : lamprea *f*
lance[1] [ˈlænts] *vt* **lanced; lancing** : abrir con lanceta, sajar

lance² *n* **:** lanza *f*
lance corporal *n* **:** cabo *m* interino, soldado *m* de primera clase
lancet [ˈlæntsət] *n* **:** lanceta *f*
land¹ [ˈlænd] *vt* **1 :** desembarcar (pasajeros de un barco), hacer aterrizar (un avión) **2** CATCH **:** pescar, sacar (un pez) del agua **3** GAIN, SECURE **:** conseguir, ganar <to land a job : conseguir empleo> **4** DELIVER **:** dar, asestar <he landed a punch : asestó un puñetazo> — *vi* **1 :** aterrizar, tomar tierra, atracar <the plane just landed : el avión acaba de aterrizar> <the ship landed an hour ago : el barco atracó hace una hora>**2** ALIGHT **:** posarse, aterrizar <to land on one's feet : caer de pie>
land² *n* **1** GROUND **:** tierra *f* <dry land : tierra firme> **2** TERRAIN **:** terreno *m* **3** NATION **:** país *m,* nación *f* **4** DOMAIN **:** mundo *m,* dominio *m* <the land of dreams : el mundo de los sueños>
landfill [ˈlændˌfɪl] *n* **:** vertadero *m* (de basuras)
landing [ˈlændɪŋ] *n* **1 :** aterrizaje *m* (de aviones), desembarco *m* (de barcos) **2 :** descansillo *m* (de una escalera)
landing field *n* **:** campo *m* de aterrizaje
landing strip → **airstrip**
landlady [ˈlændˌleɪdi] *n, pl* **-dies :** casera *f,* dueña *f,* arrendadora *f*
landless [ˈlændləs] *adj* **:** sin tierra
landlocked [ˈlændˌlɑkt] *adj* **:** sin salida al mar
landlord [ˈlændˌlɔrd] *n* **:** dueño *m,* casero *m,* arrendador *m*
landlubber [ˈlændˌlʌbər] *n* **:** marinero *m* de agua dulce
landmark [ˈlændˌmɑrk] *n* **1 :** señal *f* (geográfica), punto *m* de referencia **2** MILESTONE **:** hito *m* <a landmark in our history : un hito en nuestra historia> **3** MONUMENT **:** monumento *m* histórico
landowner [ˈlændˌoːnər] *n* **:** hacendado *m,* -da *f;* terrateniente *mf*
landscape¹ [ˈlændˌskeɪp] *vt* **-scaped; -scaping :** ajardinar
landscape² *n* **:** paisaje *m*
landslide [ˈlændˌslaɪd] *n* **1 :** desprendimiento *m* de tierras, derrumbe *m* **2 landslide victory :** victoria *f* arrolladora
landward [ˈlændwərd] *adv* **:** en dirección de la tierra, hacia tierra
lane [ˈleɪn] *n* **1** PATH, WAY **:** camino *m,* sendero *m* **2 :** carril *m* (de una carretera)
language [ˈlæŋgwɪdʒ] *n* **1 :** idioma *m,* lengua *f* <the English language : el idioma inglés> **2 :** lenguaje *m* <body language : lenguaje corporal>
languid [ˈlæŋgwɪd] *adj* **:** lánguido — **languidly** *adv*
languish [ˈlæŋgwɪʃ] *vi* **1** WEAKEN **:** languidecer, debilitarse **2** PINE **:** consumirse, suspirar (por) <to languish for love : suspirar por el amor> <he languished in prison : estuvo pudriéndose en la cárcel>
languor [ˈlæŋgər] *n* **:** languidez *f*
languorous [ˈlæŋgərəs] *adj* **:** lánguido — **languorously** *adv*
lank [ˈlæŋk] *adj* **1** THIN **:** delgado, larguirucho *fam* **2** LIMP **:** lacio
lanky [ˈlæŋki] *adj* **lankier; -est :** delgado, larguirucho *fam*
lanolin [ˈlænəlɪn] *n* **:** lanolina *f*
lantern [ˈlæntərn] *n* **:** linterna *f,* farol *m*
Laotian [leɪˈoːʃən, ˈlaʊʃən] *n* **:** laosiano *m,* -na *f* — **Laotian** *adj*
lap¹ [ˈlæp] *v* **lapped; lapping** *vt* **1** FOLD **:** plegar, doblar **2** WRAP **:** envolver **3 :** lamer, besar <waves were lapping the shore : las olas lamían la orilla> **4 to lap up :** beber a lengüetadas (como un gato) — *vi* OVERLAP **:** traslaparse
lap² *n* **1 :** falda *f,* regazo *m* (del cuerpo) **2** OVERLAP **:** traslapo *m* **3 :** vuelta *f* (en deportes) **4** STAGE **:** etapa *f* (de un viaje)
lapdog [ˈlæpˌdɔg] *n* **:** perro *m* faldero
lapel [ləˈpɛl] *n* **:** solapa *f*
Lapp [ˈlæp] *n* **:** lapón *m,* -pona *f* — **Lapp** *adj*
lapse¹ [ˈlæps] *vi* **lapsed; lapsing 1** FALL, SLIP **:** caer <to lapse into bad habits : caer en malos hábitos> <to lapse into unconsciousness : perder el conocimiento> <to lapse into silence : quedarse callado> **2** FADE **:** decaer, desvanecerse <her dedication lapsed : su dedicación se desvaneció> **3** CEASE **:** cancelarse, perderse **4** ELAPSE **:** transcurrir, pasar **5** EXPIRE **:** caducar
lapse² *n* **1** SLIP **:** lapsus *m,* deliz *m,* falla *f* <a lapse of memory : una falla de memoria> **2** INTERVAL **:** lapso *m,* intervalo *m,* período *m* **3** EXPIRATION **:** caducidad *f*
laptop [ˈlæpˌtɑp] *adj* **:** portátil, laptop
larboard [ˈlɑrbərd] *n* **:** babor *m*
larcenous [ˈlɑrsənəs] *adj* **:** de robo
larceny [ˈlɑrsəni] *n, pl* **-nies :** robo *m,* hurto *m*
larch [ˈlɑrtʃ] *n* **:** alerce *f*
lard [ˈlɑrd] *n* **:** manteca *f* de cerdo
larder [ˈlɑrdər] *n* **:** despensa *f,* alacena *f*
large [ˈlɑrdʒ] *adj* **larger; largest 1** BIG **:** grande **2** COMPREHENSIVE **:** amplio, extenso **3 by and large :** por lo general
largely [ˈlɑrdʒli] *adv* **:** en gran parte, en su mayoría
largeness [ˈlɑrdʒnəs] *n* **:** lo grande
largesse *or* **largess** [lɑrˈʒɛs, -ˈdʒɛs] *n* **:** generosidad *f,* largueza *f*
lariat [ˈlæriət] *n* **:** lazo *m*
lark [ˈlɑrk] *n* **1** FUN **:** diversión *f* <what a lark! : ¡qué divertido!> **2 :** alondra *f* (pájaro)
larva [ˈlɑrvə] *n, pl* **-vae** [-ˌviː, -ˌvaɪ] **:** larva *f* — **larval** [-vəl] *adj*
laryngitis [ˌlærənˈdʒaɪtəs] *n* **:** laringitis *f*

larynx [ˈlærɪŋks] *n, pl* **-rynges** [ləˈrɪn,dʒiːz] *or* **-ynxes** [ˈlærɪŋksəz] : laringe *f*

lasagna [ləˈzɑnjə] *n* : lasaña *f*

lascivious [ləˈsɪviəs] *adj* : lascivo

lasciviousness [ləˈsɪviəsnəs] *n* : lascivia *f,* lujuria *f*

laser [ˈleɪzər] *n* : láser *m*

lash[1] [ˈlæʃ] *vt* **1** WHIP : azotar **2** BIND : atar, amarrar

lash[2] *n* **1** WHIP : látigo *m* **2** STROKE : latigazo *m* **3** EYELASH : pestaña *f*

lass [ˈlæs] *or* **lassie** [ˈlæsi] *n* : muchacha *f,* chica *f*

lassitude [ˈlæsə,tuːd, -,tjuːd] *n* : lasitud *f*

lasso[1] [ˈlæ,soː, læˈsuː] *vt* : lazar

lasso[2] *n, pl* **-sos** *or* **-soes** : lazo *m,* reata *f Mex*

last[1] [ˈlæst] *vi* **1** CONTINUE : durar <how long will it last? : ¿cuánto durará?> **2** ENDURE : aguantar, durar **3** SURVIVE : durar, sobrevivir **4** SUFFICE : durar, bastar — *vt* **1** : durar <it will last a lifetime : durará toda la vida> **2** **to last out** : aguantar

last[2] *adv* **1** : en último lugar, al último <we came in last : llegamos en último lugar> **2** : por última vez, la última vez <I saw him last in Bogota : lo vi por última vez en Bogotá> **3** FINALLY : por último, en conclusión

last[3] *adj* **1** FINAL : último, final **2** PREVIOUS : pasado <last year : el año pasado>

last[4] *n* **1** : el último, la última, lo último <at last : por fin, al fin, finalmente> **2** : horma *f* (de zapatero)

lasting [ˈlæstɪŋ] *adj* : perdurable, duradero, estable

lastly [ˈlæstli] *adv* : por último, finalmente

latch[1] [ˈlætʃ] *vt* : cerrar con picaporte

latch[2] *n* : picaporte *m,* pestillo *m,* pasador *m*

late[1] [ˈleɪt] *adv* **later; latest** **1** : tarde <to arrive late : llegar tarde> <to sleep late : dormir hasta tarde> **2** : a última hora, a finales <late in the month : a finales del mes> **3** RECENTLY : recién, últimamente <as late as last year : todavía en el año pasado>

late[2] *adj* **later; latest** **1** TARDY : tardío, de retraso <to be late : llegar tarde> **2** : avanzado <because of the late hour : a causa de la hora avanzada> **3** DECEASED : difunto, fallecido **4** RECENT : reciente, último <our late quarrel : nuestra última pelea>

latecomer [ˈleɪt,kʌmər] *n* : rezagado *m,* -da *f*

lately [ˈleɪtli] *adv* : recientemente, últimamente

lateness [ˈleɪtnəs] *n* **1** DELAY : retraso *m,* atraso *m,* tardanza *f* **2** : lo avanzado (de la hora)

latent [ˈleɪtənt] *adj* : latente — **latently** *adv*

lateral [ˈlæt̬ərəl] *adj* : lateral — **laterally** *adv*

latex [ˈleɪ,tɛks] *n, pl* **-tices** [ˈleɪt̬ə,siːz, ˈlæt̬ə-] *or* **-texes** : látex *m*

lath [ˈlæθ, ˈlæð] *n, pl* **laths** *or* **lath** : listón *m*

lathe [ˈleɪð] *n* : torno *m*

lather[1] [ˈlæðər] *vt* : enjabonar — *vi* : espumar, hacer espuma

lather[2] *n* **1** : espuma *f* (de jabón) **2** : sudor *m* (de caballo) **3** **to get into a lather** : ponerse histérico

Latin[1] *adj* : latino

Latin[2] *n* **1** : latín *m* (idioma) **2** → **Latin American**

Latin–American [ˈlætənəˈmɛrikən] *adj* : latinoamericano

Latin American *n* : latinoamericano *m,* -na *f*

latitude [ˈlæt̬ə,tuːd, -,tjuːd] *n* : latitud *f*

latrine [ləˈtriːn] *n* : letrina *f*

latter[1] [ˈlæt̬ər] *adj* **1** SECOND : segundo **2** LAST : último

latter[2] *pron* **the latter** : éste, ésta, éstos *pl,* éstas *pl*

lattice [ˈlæt̬əs] *n* : enrejado *m,* celosía *f*

Latvian [ˈlætviən] *n* : letón *m,* -tona *f* — **Latvian** *adj*

laud[1] [ˈlɔd] *vt* : alabar, loar

laud[2] *n* : alabanza *f,* loa *f*

laudable [ˈlɔdəbəl] *adj* : loable — **laudably** [-bli] *adv*

laugh[1] [ˈlæf] *vi* : reír, reírse

laugh[2] *n* **1** LAUGHTER : risa *f* **2** JOKE : chiste *m,* broma *f* <he did it for a laugh : lo hizo en broma, lo hizo para divertirse>

laughable [ˈlæfəbəl] *adj* : risible, de risa

laughingstock [ˈlæfɪŋ,stɑk] *n* : hazmerreír *m*

laughter [ˈlæftər] *n* : risa *f,* risas *fpl*

launch[1] [ˈlɔntʃ] *vt* **1** HURL : lanzar **2** : botar (un barco) **3** START : iniciar, empezar

launch[2] *n* **1** : lancha *f* (bote) **2** LAUNCHING : lanzamiento *m*

launder [ˈlɔndər] *vt* **1** : lavar y planchar (ropa) **2** : blanquear, lavar (dinero)

launderer [ˈlɔndərər] *n* : lavandero *m,* -ra *f*

laundress [ˈlɔndrəs] *n* : lavandera *f*

laundry [ˈlɔndri] *n, pl* **laundries** **1** : ropa *f* sucia, ropa *f* para lavar <to do the laundry : lavar la ropa> **2** : lavandería *f* (servicio de lavar)

laureate [ˈlɔriət] *n* : laureado *m,* -da *f* <poet laureate : poeta laureado>

laurel [ˈlɔrəl] *n* **1** : laurel *m* (planta) **2** **laurels** *npl* : laureles *mpl* <to rest on one's laurels : dormirse uno en sus laureles>

lava [ˈlɑvə, ˈlæ-] *n* : lava *f*

lavatory [ˈlævə,tori] *n, pl* **-ries** : baño *m,* cuarto *m* de baño

lavender ['lævəndər] *n* : lavanda *f,* espliego *m*
lavish[1] ['lævɪʃ] *vt* : prodigar (a), colmar (de)
lavish[2] *adj* **1** EXTRAVAGANT : pródigo, generoso, derrochador **2** ABUNDANT : abundante **3** LUXURIOUS : lujoso, espléndido
lavishly ['lævɪʃli] *adv* : con generosidad, espléndidamente <to live lavishly : vivir a lo grande>
lavishness ['lævɪʃnəs] *n* : generosidad *f,* esplendidez *f*
law ['lɔ] *n* **1** : ley *f* <to break the law : violar la ley> **2** : derecho *m* <criminal law : derecho criminal> **3** : abogacía *f* <to practice law : ejercer la abogacía>
law–abiding ['lɔə,baɪdɪŋ] *adj* : observante de la ley
lawbreaker ['lɔ,breɪkər] *n* : infractor *m,* -tora *f* de la ley
lawful ['lɔfəl] *adj* : legal, legítimo, lícito — **lawfully** *adv*
lawgiver ['lɔ,gɪvər] *n* : legislador *m,* -dora *f*
lawless ['lɔləs] *adj* : anárquico, ingobernable — **lawlessly** *adv*
lawlessness ['lɔləsnəs] *n* : anarquía *f,* desorden *m*
lawmaker ['lɔ,meɪkər] *n* : legislador *m,* -dora *f*
lawman ['lɔmən] *n, pl* **-men** [-mən, -,mɛn] : agente *m* del orden
lawn ['lɔn] *n* : césped *m,* pasto *m*
lawn mower *n* : cortadora *f* de césped
lawsuit ['lɔ,su:t] *n* : pleito *m,* litigio *m,* demanda *f*
lawyer ['lɔɪər, 'lɔjər] *n* : abogado *m,* -da *f*
lax ['læks] *adj* : laxo, relajado — **laxly** *adv*
laxative ['læksət̬ɪv] *n* : laxante *m*
laxity ['læksət̬i] *n* : relajación *f,* descuido *m,* falta *f* de rigor
lay[1] ['leɪ] *vt* **laid** ['leɪd]; **laying 1** PLACE, PUT : poner, colocar <she laid it on the table : lo puso en la mesa> <to lay eggs : poner huevos> **2** : hacer <to lay a bet : hacer una apuesta> **3** IMPOSE : imponer <to lay a tax : imponer un impuesto> <to lay the blame on : echarle la culpa a> **4 to lay out** PRESENT : presentar, exponer <he laid out his plan : presentó su proyecto> **5 to lay out** DESIGN : diseñar (el trazado de)
lay[2] *pp* → **lie**
lay[3] *adj* SECULAR : laico, lego
lay[4] *n* **1** : disposición *f,* configuración *f* <the lay of the land : la configuración del terreno> **2** BALLAD : romance *m,* balada *f*
layer ['leɪər] *n* **1** : capa *f* (de pintura, etc.), estrato *m* (de roca) **2** : gallina *f* ponedora
layman ['leɪmən] *n, pl* **-men** [-mən, -,mɛn] : laico *m,* lego *m*
layoff ['leɪ,ɔf] *n* : despido *m*
lay off *vt* : despedir
layout ['leɪ,aʊt] *n* : disposición *f,* distribución *f* (de una casa, etc.), trazado *m* (de una ciudad)
lay up *vt* **1** STORE : guardar, almacenar **2 to be laid up** : estar enfermo, tener que guardar cama
laywoman ['leɪ,wʊmən] *n, pl* **-women** [-,wɪmən] : laica *f,* lega *f*
laziness ['leɪzinəs] *n* : pereza *f,* flojera *f*
lazy ['leɪzi] *adj* **-zier; -est** : perezoso, holgazán — **lazily** ['leɪzəli] *adv*
leach ['li:tʃ] *vt* : filtrar
lead[1] ['li:d] *vt* **led** ['lɛd]; **leading 1** GUIDE : conducir, llevar, guiar **2** DIRECT : dirigir **3** HEAD : encabezar, ir al frente de **4 to lead to** : resultar en, llevar a <it only leads to trouble : sólo resulta en problemas>
lead[2] *n* : delantera *f,* primer lugar *m* <to take the lead : tomar la delantera>
lead[3] ['lɛd] *n* **1** : plomo *m* (metal) **2** : mina *f* (de lápiz) **3 lead poisoning** : saturnismo *m*
leaden ['lɛdən] *adj* **1** : plomizo <a leaden sky : un ciel plomizo> **2** HEAVY : pesado
leader ['li:dər] *n* : jefe *m,* -fa *f;* líder *mf;* dirigente *mf;* gobernante *mf*
leadership ['li:dər,ʃɪp] *n* : mando *m,* dirección *f*
leaf[1] ['li:f] *vi* **1** : echar hojas (dícese de un árbol) **2 to leaf through** : hojear (un libro)
leaf[2] *n, pl* **leaves** ['li:vz] **1** : hoja *f* (de plantas o libros) **2 to turn over a new leaf** : hacer borrón y cuenta nueva
leafless ['li:fləs] *adj* : sin hojas, pelado
leaflet ['li:flət] *n* : folleto *m*
leafy ['li:fi] *adj* **leafier; -est** : frondoso
league[1] ['li:g] *v* **leagued; leaguing** *vt* : aliar, unir — *vi* : aliarse, unirse
league[2] *n* **1** : legua *f* (medida de distancia) **2** ASSOCIATION : alianza *f,* sociedad *f,* liga *f*
leak[1] ['li:k] *vt* **1** : perder, dejar escapar (un líquido o un gas) **2** : filtrar (información) — *vi* **1** : gotear, escaparse, fugarse (dícese de un líquido o un gas) **2** : hacer agua (dícese de un bote) **3** : filtrarse, divulgarse (dícese de información)
leak[2] *n* **1** HOLE : agujero *m* (en recipientes), gotera *f* (en un tejado) **2** ESCAPE : fuga *f,* escape *m* **3** : filtración *f* (de información)
leakage ['li:kɪdʒ] *n* : escape *m,* fuga *f*
leaky ['li:ki] *adj* **leakier; -est** : agujereado (dícese de un recipiente), que hace agua (dícese de un bote), con goteras (dícese de un tejado)
lean[1] ['li:n] *vi* **1** BEND : inclinarse, ladearse **2** RECLINE : reclinarse **3** RELY : apoyarse (en), depender (de) **4** INCLINE, TEND : inclinarse, tender — *vt* : apoyar

lean[2] *adj* 1 THIN : delgado, flaco 2 : sin grasa, magro (dícese de la carne)

leanness [ˈliːnnəs] *n* : delgadez *f*

lean–to [ˈliːnˌtuː] *n* : cobertizo *m*

leap[1] [ˈliːp] *vi* **leapt** *or* **leaped** [ˈliːpt, ˈlɛpt]; **leaping** : saltar, brincar

leap[2] *n* : salto *m,* brinco *m*

leap year *n* : año *m* bisiesto

learn [ˈlərn] *vt* **1** : aprender <to learn to sing : aprender a cantar> **2** MEMORIZE : aprender de memoria **3** DISCOVER : saber, enterarse de — *vi* **1** : aprender <to learn from experience : aprender por experiencia> **2** FIND OUT : enterarse, saber

learned [ˈlərnəd] *adj* : erudito

learner [ˈlərnər] *n* : principiante *mf,* estudiante *mf*

learning [ˈlərnɪŋ] *n* : erudición *f,* saber *m*

lease[1] [ˈliːs] *vt* **leased; leasing** : arrendar

lease[2] *n* : contrato *m* de arrendamiento

leash[1] [ˈliːʃ] *vt* : atraillar (un animal)

leash[2] *n* : traílla *f*

least[1] [ˈliːst] *adv* : menos <when least expected : cuando menos se espera>

least[2] *adj* (*superlative of* **little**) : menor, más mínimo

least[3] *n* **1** : lo menos <at least : por lo menos> **2 to say the least** : por no decir más

leather [ˈlɛðər] *n* : cuero *m*

leathery [ˈlɛðəri] *adj* : curtido (dícese de la piel), correoso (dícese de la carne)

leave[1] [ˈliːv] *v* **left** [ˈlɛft]; **leaving** *vt* **1** BEQUEATH : dejar, legar **2** DEPART : dejar, salir(se) de **3** ABANDON : abandonar, dejar **4** FORGET : dejar, olvidarse de <I left the books at the library : dejé los libros en la biblioteca> **5 to be left** : quedar <it's all I have left : es todo lo que me queda> **6 to be left over** : sobrar **7 to leave out** : omitir, excluir — *vi* : irse, salir, partir, marcharse <she left yesterday morning : se fue ayer por la mañana>

leave[2] *n* **1** PERMISSION : permiso *m* <by your leave : con su permiso> **2** *or* **leave of absence** : permiso *m,* licencia *f* <maternity leave : licencia por maternidad> **3 to take one's leave** : despedirse

leaven [ˈlɛvən] *n* : levadura *f*

leaves → **leaf**[2]

leaving [ˈliːvɪŋ] *n* **1** : salida *f,* partida *f* **2 leavings** *npl* : restos *mpl,* sobras *fpl*

Lebanese [ˌlɛbəˈniːz, -ˈniːs] *n* : libanés *m,* -nesa *f* — **Lebanese** *adj*

lecherous [ˈlɛtʃərəs] *adj* : lascivo, libidinoso — **lecherously** *adv*

lechery [ˈlɛtʃəri] *n* : lascivia *f,* lujuria *f*

lecture[1] [ˈlɛktʃər] *v* **-tured; -turing** *vi* : dar clase, dictar clase, dar una conferencia — *vt* SCOLD : sermonear, echar una reprimenda a, regañar

lecture[2] *n* **1** : conferencia *f* **2** REPRIMAND : reprimenda *f*

led *pp* → **lead**[1]

ledge [ˈlɛdʒ] *n* : repisa *f* (de una pared), antepecho *m* (de una ventana), saliente *m* (de una montaña)

ledger [ˈlɛdʒər] *n* : libro *m* mayor, libro *m* de contabilidad

lee[1] [ˈliː] *adj* : de sotavento

lee[2] *n* : sotavento *m*

leech [ˈliːtʃ] *n* : sanguijuela *f*

leek [ˈliːk] *n* : puerro *m*

leer[1] [ˈlɪr] *vi* : mirar con lascivia

leer[2] *n* : mirada *f* lasciva

leery [ˈlɪri] *adj* : receloso

lees [ˈliːz] *npl* : posos *mpl,* heces *fpl*

leeward[1] [ˈliːwərd, ˈluːərd] *adj* : de sotavento

leeward[2] *n* : sotavento *m*

leeway [ˈliːˌweɪ] *n* : libertad *f,* margen *m*

left[1] [ˈlɛft] *adv* : hacia la izquierda

left[2] *pp* → **leave**

left[3] *adj* : izquierdo

left[4] *n* : izquierda *f* <on the left : a la izquierda>

left–hand [ˈlɛftˈhand] *adj* **1** : de la izquierda **2** → **left–handed**

left–handed [ˈlɛftˈhandəd] *adj* **1** : zurdo (dícese de una persona) **2** : con doble sentido <a left-handed compliment : un cumplido a medias>

leftovers [ˈlɛftˌoːvərz] *npl* : restos *mpl,* sobras *fpl*

left wing *n* **the left wing** : la izquierda

left–winger [ˈlɛftˈwɪŋər] *n* : izquierdista *mf*

leg [ˈlɛg] *n* **1** : pierna *f* (de una persona, de carne, de ropa), pata *f* (de un animal, de muebles) **2** STAGE : etapa *f* (de un viaje), vuelta *f* (de una carrera)

legacy [ˈlɛgəsi] *n, pl* **-cies** : legado *m,* herencia *f*

legal [ˈliːgəl] *adj* **1** : legal, jurídico <legal advisor : asesor jurídico> <the legal profession : la abogacía> **2** LAWFUL : legítimo, legal

legalistic [ˌliːgəˈlɪstɪk] *adj* : legalista

legality [lɪˈgæləṭi] *n, pl* **-ties** : legalidad *f*

legalize [ˈliːgəˌlaɪz] *vt* **-ized; -izing** : legalizar

legally [ˈliːgəli] *adv* : legalmente

legate [ˈlɛgət] *n* : legado *m*

legation [lɪˈgeɪʃən] *n* : legación *f*

legend [ˈlɛdʒənd] *n* **1** STORY : leyenda *f* **2** INSCRIPTION : leyenda *f,* inscripción *f* **3** : signos *mpl* convencionales (en un mapa)

legendary [ˈlɛdʒənˌdɛri] *adj* : lengendario

legerdemain [ˌlɛdʒərdəˈmeɪn] → **sleight of hand**

leggings [ˈlɛgɪŋz, ˈlɛgənz] *npl* : mallas *fpl*

legibility [ˌlɛdʒəˈbɪləṭi] *n* : legibilidad *f*

legible [ˈlɛdʒəbəl] *adj* : legible

legibly [ˈlɛdʒəbli] *adv* **:** de manera legible
legion [ˈliːdʒən] *n* **:** legión *f*
legionnaire [ˌliːdʒəˈnær] *n* **:** legionario *m,* -ria *f*
legislate [ˈlɛdʒəsˌleɪt] *vi* **-lated; -lating :** legislar
legislation [ˌlɛdʒəsˈleɪʃən] *n* **:** legislación *f*
legislative [ˈlɛdʒəsˌleɪt̬ɪv] *adj* **:** legislativo, legislador
legislator [ˈlɛdʒəsˌleɪt̬ər] *n* **:** legislador *m,* -dora *f*
legislature [ˈlɛdʒəsˌleɪtʃər] *n* **:** asamblea *f* legislativa
legitimacy [lɪˈdʒɪt̬əməsi] *n* **:** legitimidad *f*
legitimate [lɪˈdʒɪt̬əmət] *adj* **1** VALID **:** legítimo, válido, justificado **2** LAWFUL **:** legítimo, legal
legitimately [lɪˈdʒɪt̬əmətli] *adv* **:** legítimamente
legitimize [lɪˈdʒɪt̬əˌmaɪz] *vt* **-mized; -mizing :** legitimar, hacer legítimo
legume [ˈlɛˌgjuːm, lɪˈgjuːm] *n* **:** legumbre *f*
leisure [ˈliːʒər, ˈlɛ-] *n* **1 :** ocio *m,* tiempo *m* libre <a life of leisure : una vida de ocio>**2 to take one’s leisure :** reposar **3 at your leisure :** cuando te venga bien, cuando tengas tiempo
leisurely [ˈliːʒərli, ˈlɛ-] *adj & adv* **:** lento, sin prisas
lemming [ˈlɛmɪŋ] *n* **:** lemming *m*
lemon [ˈlɛmən] *n* **:** limón *m*
lemonade [ˌlɛməˈneɪd] *n* **:** limonada *f*
lemony [ˈlɛməni] *adj* **:** a limón
lend [ˈlɛnd] *vt* **lent** [ˈlɛnt]; **lending 1 :** prestar <to lend money : prestar dinero> **2** GIVE **:** dar <it lends force to his criticism : da fuerza a su crítica> **3 to lend oneself to :** prestarse a
length [ˈlɛŋkθ] *n* **1 :** longitud *f,* largo *m* <10 feet in length : 10 pies de largo> **2** DURATION **:** duración *f* **3 :** trozo *m* (de madera), corte *m* (de tela) **4 to go to any lengths :** hacer todo lo posible **5 at ~ :** extensamente <to speak at length : hablar largo y tendido>
lengthen [ˈlɛŋkθən] *vt* **1 :** alargar <can they lengthen the dress? : ¿se puede alargar el vestido?> **2** EXTEND, PROLONG **:** prolongar, extender — *vi* **:** alargarse, crecer <the days are lengthening : los días están creciendo>
lengthways [ˈlɛŋkθˌweɪz] → **lengthwise**
lengthwise [ˈlɛŋkθˌwaɪz] *adv* **:** a lo largo, longitudinalmente
lengthy [ˈlɛŋkθi] *adj* **lengthier; -est 1** OVERLONG **:** largo y pesado **2** EXTENDED **:** prolongado, largo
leniency [ˈliːniəntsi] *n, pl* **-cies :** lenidad *f,* indulgencia *f*
lenient [ˈliːniənt] *adj* **:** indulgente, poco severo
leniently [ˈliːniəntli] *adv* **:** con lenidad, con indulgencia
lens [ˈlɛnz] *n* **1 :** cristalino *m* (del ojo) **2 :** lente *mf* (de un instrumento o una cámara) **3** → **contact lens**
lent → **lend**
Lent [ˈlɛnt] *n* **:** Cuaresma *f*
lentil [ˈlɛntəl] *n* **:** lenteja *f*
Leo [ˈliːoː] *n* **:** Leo *mf*
leopard [ˈlɛpərd] *n* **:** leopardo *m*
leotard [ˈliːəˌtɑrd] *n* **:** leotardo *m,* malla *f*
leper [ˈlɛpər] *n* **:** leproso *m,* -sa *f*
leprechaun [ˈlɛprəˌkɑn] *n* **:** duende *m* (irlandés)
leprosy [ˈlɛprəsi] *n* **:** lepra *f* — **leprous** [ˈlɛprəs] *adj*
lesbian[1] [ˈlɛzbiən] *adj* **:** lesbiano
lesbian[2] *n* **:** lesbiana *f*
lesbianism [ˈlɛzbiəˌnɪzəm] *n* **:** lesbianismo *m*
lesion [ˈliːʒən] *n* **:** lesión *f*
less[1] [ˈlɛs] *adv* (*comparative of* **little[1]**) **:** menos <the less you know, the better : cuanto menos sepas, mejor> <less and less : cada vez menos>
less[2] *adj* (*comparative of* **little[2]**) **:** menos <less than three : menos de tres> <less money : menos dinero> <nothing less than perfection : nada menos que la perfección>
less[3] *pron* **:** menos <I’m earning less : estoy ganando menos>
less[4] *prep* **:** menos <one month less two days : un mes menos dos días>
lessee [lɛˈsiː] *n* **:** arrendatario *m,* -ria *f*
lessen [ˈlɛsən] *vt* **:** disminuir, reducir — *vi* **:** disminuir, reducirse
lesser [ˈlɛsər] *adj* **:** menor <to a lesser degree : en menor grado>
lesson [ˈlɛsən] *n* **1** CLASS **:** clase *f,* curso *m* **2 :** lección *f* <the lessons of history : las lecciones de la historia>
lessor [ˈlɛˌsɔr, lɛˈsɔr] *n* **:** arrendador *m,* -dora *f*
lest [ˈlɛst] *conj* **:** para (que) no <lest we forget : para que no olvidemos>
let [ˈlɛt] *vt* **let; letting 1** ALLOW **:** dejar, permitir <let me see it : déjame verlo> **2** MAKE **:** hacer <let me know : házmelo saber, avísame> <let them wait : que esperen, haz que esperen> **3** RENT **:** alquilar **4** (*used in the first person plural imperative*) <let’s go! : ¡vamos!, ¡vámonos!> <let us pray : oremos> **5 to let down** DISAPPOINT **:** fallar **6 to let off** FORGIVE **:** perdonar **7 to let out** REVEAL **:** revelar **8 to let up** ABATE **:** amainar, disminuir <the pace never lets up : el ritmo nunca disminuye>
letdown *n* **:** chasco *m,* decepción *f*
lethal [ˈliːθəl] *adj* **:** letal — **lethally** *adv*
lethargic [lɪˈθɑrdʒɪk] *adj* **:** letárgico
lethargy [ˈlɛθərdʒi] *n* **:** letargo *m*
let on *vi* **1** ADMIT **:** reconocer <don’t let on! : ¡no digas nada!> **2** PRETEND **:** fingir
let’s [ˈlɛts] (*contraction of* **let us**) → **let**

letter[1] [ˈlɛt̬ər] *vt* : marcar con letras, inscribir letras en
letter[2] *n* **1** : letra *f* (del alfabeto) **2** : carta *f* <a letter to my mother : una carta a mi madre> **3 letters** *npl* ARTS : letras *fpl* **4 to the letter** : al pie de la letra
lettering [ˈlɛt̬ərɪŋ] *n* : letra *f*
lettuce [ˈlɛt̬əs] *n* : lechuga *f*
leukemia [luːˈkiːmiə] *n* : leucemia *f*
levee [ˈlɛvi] *n* : dique *m*
level[1] [ˈlɛvəl] *vt* **-eled** *or* **-elled; -eling** *or* **-elling 1** FLATTEN : nivelar, aplanar **2** AIM : apuntar (una pistola), dirigir (una acusación) **3** RAZE : rasar, arrasar
level[2] *adj* **1** EVEN : llano, plano, parejo **2** CALM : tranquilo <to keep a level head : no perder la cabeza>
level[3] *n* : nivel *m*
leveler [ˈlɛvələr] *n* : nivelador *m*, -dora *f*
levelheaded [ˈlɛvəlˈhɛdəd] *adj* : sensato, equilibrado
levelly [ˈlɛvəli] *adv* CALMLY : con ecuanimidad *f*, con calma
levelness [ˈlɛvəlnəs] *n* : uniformidad *f*
lever [ˈlɛvər, ˈliː-] *n* : palanca *f*
leverage [ˈlɛvərɪdʒ, ˈliː-] *n* **1** : apalancamiento *m* (en física) **2** INFLUENCE : influencia *f*, palanca *f fam*
leviathan [lɪˈvaɪəθən] *n* : leviatán *m*, gigante *m*
levity [ˈlɛvət̬i] *n* : ligereza *f*, frivolidad *f*
levy[1] [ˈlɛvi] *vt* **levied; levying 1** IMPOSE : imponer, exigir, gravar (un impuesto) **2** COLLECT : recaudar (un impuesto)
levy[2] *n, pl* **levies** : impuesto *m*, gravamen *m*
lewd [ˈluːd] *adj* : lascivo — **lewdly** *adv*
lewdness [ˈluːdnəs] *n* : lascivia *f*
lexicographer [ˌlɛksəˈkɑgrəfər] *n* : lexicógrafo *m*, -fa *f*
lexicographical [ˌlɛksəkoˈgræfɪkəl] *or* **lexicographic** [-ˈgræfɪk] *adj* : lexicográfico
lexicography [ˌlɛksəˈkɑgrəfi] *n* : lexicografía *f*
lexicon [ˈlɛksɪˌkɑn] *n, pl* **-ica** [-kə] *or* **-icons** : léxico *m*, lexicón *m*
liability [ˌlaɪəˈbɪlət̬i] *n, pl* **-ties 1** RESPONSIBILITY : responsabilidad *f* **2** SUSCEPTIBILITY : propensión *f* **3** DRAWBACK : desventaja *f* **4 liabilities** *npl* DEBTS : deudas *fpl*, pasivo *m*
liable [ˈlaɪəbəl] *adj* **1** RESPONSIBLE : responsable **2** SUSCEPTIBLE : propenso **3** PROBABLE : probable <it's liable to happen : es probable que suceda>
liaison [ˈliːəˌzɑn, liˈeɪ-] *n* **1** CONNECTION : enlace *m*, relación *f* **2** AFFAIR : amorío *m*, aventura *f*
liar [ˈlaɪər] *n* : mentiroso *m*, -sa *f*; embustero *m*, -ra *f*
libel[1] [ˈlaɪbəl] *vt* **-beled** *or* **-belled; -beling** *or* **-belling** : difamar, calumniar
libel[2] *n* : difamación *f*, calumnia *f*
libeler [ˈlaɪbələr] *n* : difamador *m*, -dora *f*; calumniador *m*, -dora *f*; libelista *mf*
libelous *or* **libellous** [ˈlaɪbələs] *adj* : difamatorio, calumnioso, injurioso
liberal[1] [ˈlɪbrəl, ˈlɪbərəl] *adj* **1** TOLERANT : liberal, tolerante **2** GENEROUS : generoso **3** ABUNDANT : abundante **4 liberal arts** : humanidades *fpl*, artes *fpl* liberales
liberal[2] *n* : liberal *mf*
liberalism [ˈlɪbrəˌlɪzəm, ˈlɪbərə-] *n* : liberalismo *m*
liberality [ˌlɪbəˈrælət̬i] *n, pl* **-ties** : liberalidad *f*, generosidad *f*
liberalize [ˈlɪbrəˌlaɪz, ˈlɪbərə-] *vt* **-ized; -izing** : liberalizar
liberally [ˈlɪbrəli, ˈlɪbərə-] *adv* **1** GENEROUSLY : generosamente **2** ABUNDANTLY : abundantemente **3** FREELY : libremente
liberate [ˈlɪbəˌreɪt] *vt* **-ated; -ating** : liberar, libertar
liberation [ˌlɪbəˈreɪʃən] *n* : liberación *f*
liberator [ˈlɪbəˌreɪt̬ər] *n* : libertador *m*, -dora *f*
Liberian [laɪˈbɪriən] *n* : liberiano *m*, -na *f* — **Liberian** *adj*
libertine [ˈlɪbərˌtiːn] *n* : libertino *m*, -na *f*
liberty [ˈlɪbərt̬i] *n, pl* **-ties 1** : libertad *f* **2 to take the liberty of** : tomarse la libertad de **3 to take liberties with** : tomarse confianzas con, tomarse libertades con
libido [ləˈbiːdoː, -ˈbaɪ-] *n, pl* **-dos** : libido *f* — **libidinous** [ləˈbɪdənəs] *adj*
Libra [ˈliːbrə] *n* : Libra *mf*
librarian [laɪˈbrɛriən] *n* : bibliotecario *m*, -ria *f*
library [ˈlaɪˌbrɛri] *n, pl* **-braries** : biblioteca *f*
librettist [lɪˈbrɛt̬ɪst] *n* : libretista *mf*
libretto [lɪˈbrɛt̬o] *n, pl* **-tos** *or* **-ti** [-tiː] : libreto *m*
Libyan [ˈlɪbiən] *n* : libio *m*, -bia *f* — **Libyan** *adj*
lice → **louse**
license[1] [ˈlaɪsənts] *vt* **licensed; licensing** : licenciar, autorizar, dar permiso a
license[2] *or* **licence** *n* **1** PERMISSION : licencia *f*, permiso *m* **2** PERMIT : licencia *f*, carnet *m Spain* <driver's license : licencia de conducir> **3** FREEDOM : libertad *f* **4** LICENTIOUSNESS : libertinaje *m*
licentious [laɪˈsɛntʃəs] *adj* : licencioso, disoluto — **licentiously** *adv*
licentiousness [laɪˈsɛntʃəsnəs] *n* : libertinaje *m*
lichen [ˈlaɪkən] *n* : liquen *m*
licit [ˈlɪsət] *adj* : lícito
lick[1] [ˈlɪk] *vt* **1** : lamer **2** BEAT : darle una paliza (a alguien)

lick[2] *n* **:** lamida *f,* lengüetada *f* <a lick of paint : una mano de pintura> **2** BIT **:** pizca *f,* ápice *m* **3 a lick and a promise :** una lavada a la carrera

licorice [ˈlɪkərɪʃ, -rəs] *n* **:** regaliz *m,* dulce *m* de regaliz

lid [ˈlɪd] *n* **1** COVER **:** tapa *f* **2** EYELID **:** párpado *m*

lie[1] [ˈlaɪ] *vi* **lay** [ˈleɪ]; **lain** [ˈleɪn]; **lying** [ˈlaɪɪŋ] **1 :** acostarse, echarse <I lay down : me acosté> **2 :** estar, estar situado, encontrarse <the book lay on the table : el libro estaba en la mesa> <the city lies to the south : la ciudad se encuentra al sur> **3** CONSIST **:** consistir **4 to lie in :** residir en <the power lies in the people : el poder reside en el pueblo>

lie[2] *vi* **lied; lying** [ˈlaɪɪŋ] **:** mentir

lie[3] *n* **1** UNTRUTH **:** mentira *f* <to tell lies : decir mentiras> **2** POSITION **:** posición *f*

liege [ˈliːdʒ] *n* **:** señor *m* feudal

lien [ˈliːn, ˈliːən] *n* **:** derecho *m* de retención

lieutenant [luːˈtɛnənt] *n* **:** teniente *mf*

lieutenant colonel *n* **:** teniente *mf* coronel

lieutenant commander *n* **:** capitán *m,* -tana *f* de corbeta

lieutenant general *n* **:** teniente *mf* general

life [ˈlaɪf] *n, pl* **lives** [ˈlaɪvz] **1 :** vida *f* <plant life : la vida vegetal> **2** EXISTENCE **:** vida *f,* existencia *f* **3** BIOGRAPHY **:** biografía *f,* vida *f* **4** DURATION **:** duración *f,* vida *f* **5** LIVELINESS **:** vivacidad *f,* animación *f*

lifeblood [ˈlaɪf,blʌd] *n* **:** parte *f* vital, sustento *m*

lifeboat [ˈlaɪf,boːt] *n* **:** bote *m* salvavidas

lifeguard [ˈlaɪf,gɑrd] *n* **:** socorrista *mf,* salvavidas *mf*

lifeless [ˈlaɪfləs] *adj* **:** sin vida, muerto

lifelike [ˈlaɪf,laɪk] *adj* **:** que parece vivo, natural, verosímil

lifelong [ˈlaɪfˈlɔŋ] *adj* **:** de toda la vida <a lifelong friend : un amigo de toda la vida>

life preserver *n* **:** salvavidas *m*

lifesaver [ˈlaɪf,seɪvər] *n* **1 :** salvación *f* **2** → **lifeguard**

lifesaving [ˈlaɪf,seɪvɪŋ] *n* **:** socorrismo *m*

lifestyle [ˈlaɪf,staɪl] *n* **:** estilo *m* de vida

lifetime [ˈlaɪf,taɪm] *n* **:** vida *f,* curso *m* de la vida

lift[1] [ˈlɪft] *vt* **1** RAISE **:** levantar, alzar, subir **2** END **:** levantar <to lift a ban : levantar una prohibición> — *vi* **1** RISE **:** levantarse, alzarse **2** CLEAR UP **:** despejar <the fog lifted : se disipó la niebla>

lift[2] *n* **1** LIFTING **:** levantamiento *m,* alzamiento *m* **2** BOOST **:** impulso *m,* estímulo *m* **3 to give someone a lift :** llevar en coche a alguien

liftoff [ˈlɪft,ɔf] *n* **:** despegue *m*

ligament [ˈlɪgəmənt] *n* **:** ligamento *m*

ligature [ˈlɪgə,tʃʊr, -tʃər] *n* **:** ligadura *f*

light[1] [ˈlaɪt] *v* **lit** [ˈlɪt] *or* **lighted; lighting** *vt* **1** ILLUMINATE **:** iluminar, alumbrar **2** IGNITE **:** encender, prenderle fuego a — *vi* **:** encenderse, prender

light[2] *vi* **lighted** *or* **lit** [ˈlɪt]; **lighting 1** LAND, SETTLE **:** posarse **2** DISMOUNT **:** bajarse, apearse

light[3] [ˈlaɪt] *adv* **1** LIGHTLY **:** suavemente, ligeramente **2 to travel light :** viajar con poco equipaje

light[4] *adj* **1** LIGHTWEIGHT **:** ligero, liviano, poco pesado **2** EASY **:** fácil, ligero, liviano <light reading : lectura fácil> <light work : trabajo liviano> **3** GENTLE, MILD **:** fino, suave, leve <a light breeze : una brisa suave> <a light rain : una lluvia fina> **4** FRIVOLOUS **:** de poca importancia, superficial **5** BRIGHT **:** bien iluminado, claro **6** PALE **:** claro (dícese de los colores), rubio (dícese del pelo)

light[5] *n* **1** ILLUMINATION **:** luz *f* **2** DAYLIGHT **:** luz *f* del día **3** DAWN **:** amanecer *m,* madrugada *f* **4** LAMP **:** lámpara *f* <to turn on off the light : apagar la luz> **5** ASPECT **:** aspecto *m* <in a new light : con otros ojos> <in the light of : en vista de, a la luz de> **6** MATCH **:** fósforo *m,* cerillo *m* **7 to bring to light :** sacar a (la) luz

lightbulb [ˈlaɪt,bʌlb] *n* **:** bombilla *f,* foco *m,* bombillo *m CA, Col, Ven*

lighten [ˈlaɪtən] *vt* **1** ILLUMINATE **:** iluminar, dar más luz a **2 :** aclararse (el pelo) **3 :** aligerar (una carga, etc.) **4** RELIEVE **:** aliviar **5** GLADDEN **:** alegrar <it lightened his heart : alegró su corazón>

lighter [ˈlaɪtər] *n* **:** encendedor *m*

lighthearted [ˈlaɪtˈhɑrt̬əd] *adj* **:** alegre, despreocupado, desenfadado — **lightheartedly** *adv*

lightheartedness [ˈlaɪtˈhɑrt̬ədnəs] *n* **:** desenfado *m,* alegría *f*

lighthouse [ˈlaɪt,haʊs] *n* **:** faro *m*

lighting [ˈlaɪtɪŋ] *n* **:** iluminación *f*

lightly [ˈlaɪtli] *adv* **1** GENTLY **:** suavemente **2** SLIGHTLY **:** ligeramente **3** FRIVOLOUSLY **:** a la ligera **4 to let off lightly :** tratar con indulgencia

lightness [ˈlaɪtnəs] *n* **1** BRIGHTNESS **:** luminosidad *f,* claridad *f* **2** GENTLENESS **:** ligereza *f,* suavidad *f,* delicadeza *f* **3 :** ligereza *f,* liviandad *f* (de peso)

lightning [ˈlaɪtnɪŋ] *n* **:** relámpago *m,* rayo *m*

lightning bug → **firefly**

lightproof [ˈlaɪt,pruːf] *adj* **:** impenetrable por la luz, opaco

lightweight [ˈlaɪtˈweɪt] *adj* **:** ligero, liviano, de poco peso

light–year [ˈlaɪt,jɪr] *n* **:** año *m* luz

lignite [ˈlɪg,naɪt] *n* **:** lignito *m*

likable *or* **likeable** [ˈlaɪkəbəl] *adj* **:** simpático, agradable

like[1] [ˈlaɪk] *v* **liked; liking** *vt* **1 :** agradar, gustarle (algo a uno) <he likes rice : le gusta el arroz> <she doesn't like flowers : a ella no le gustan las flores> <I like you : me caes bien> **2** WANT **:** querer, desear <I'd like a hamburger : quiero una hamburguesa> <he would like more help : le gustaría tener más ayuda> — *vi* **:** querer <do as you like : haz lo que quieras>

like[2] *adj* **:** parecido, semejante, similar

like[3] *n* **1** PREFERENCE **:** preferencia *f,* gusto *m* **2 the like :** cosa *f* parecida, cosas *fpl* por el estilo <I've never seen the like : nunca he visto cosa parecida>

like[4] *conj* **1** AS IF **:** como si <they looked at me like I was crazy : se me quedaron mirando como si estuviera loca> **2** AS **:** como, igual que <she doesn't love you like I do : ella no te quiere como yo>

like[5] *prep* **1 :** como, parecido a <she acts like my mother : se comporta como mi madre> <he looks like me : se parece a mí> **2 :** propio de, típico de <that's just like her : eso es muy típico de ella> **3 :** como <animals like cows : animales como vacas> **4 like this, like that :** así <do it like that : hazlo así>

likelihood [ˈlaɪkliˌhʊd] *n* **:** probabilidad *f* <in all likelihood : con toda probabilidad>

likely[1] [ˈlaɪkli] *adv* **:** probablemente <most likely he's sick : lo más probable es que esté enfermo> <they're likely to come : es probable que vengan>

likely[2] *adj* **-lier; -est 1** PROBABLE **:** probable <to be likely to : ser muy probable que> **2** SUITABLE **:** apropiado, adecuado **3** BELIEVABLE **:** verosímil, creíble **4** PROMISING **:** prometedor

liken [ˈlaɪkən] *vt* **:** comparar

likeness [ˈlaɪknəs] *n* **1** SIMILARITY **:** semejanza *f,* parecido *m* **2** PORTRAIT **:** retrato *m*

likewise [ˈlaɪkˌwaɪz] *adv* **1** SIMILARLY **:** de la misma manera, asimismo **2** ALSO **:** también, además, asimismo

liking [ˈlaɪkɪŋ] *n* **1** FONDNESS **:** afición *f* (por una cosa), simpatía *f* (por una persona) **2** TASTE **:** gusto *m* <is it to your liking? : ¿te gusta?>

lilac [ˈlaɪlək, -ˌlæk, -ˌlɑk] *n* **:** lila *f*

lilt [ˈlɪlt] *n* **:** cadencia *f,* ritmo *m* alegre

lily [ˈlɪli] *n, pl* **lilies 1 :** lirio *m,* azucena *f* **2 lily of the valley :** lirio *m* de los valles, muguete *m*

lima bean [ˈlaɪmə] *n* **:** frijol *m* de media luna

limb [ˈlɪm] *n* **1** APPENDAGE **:** miembro *m,* extremidad *f* **2** BRANCH **:** rama *f*

limber[1] [ˈlɪmbər] *vi or* **to limber up :** calentarse, prepararse

limber[2] *adj* **:** ágil (dícese de las personas), flexible (dícese de los objetos)

limbo [ˈlɪmˌboː] *n, pl* **-bos 1 :** limbo *m* (en la religión) **2** OBLIVION **:** olvido *m* <the project is in limbo : el proyecto ha caído en el olvido>

lime [ˈlaɪm] *n* **1 :** cal *f* (óxido) **2 :** lima *f* (fruta), limón *m* verde *Mex*

limelight [ˈlaɪmˌlaɪt] *n* **to be in the limelight :** ser el centro de atención, estar en el candelero

limerick [ˈlɪmərɪk] *n* **:** poema *m* jocoso de cinco versos

limestone [ˈlaɪmˌstoːn] *n* **:** piedra *f* caliza, caliza *f*

limit[1] [ˈlɪmət] *vt* **:** limitar, restringir

limit[2] *n* **1** MAXIMUM **:** límite *m,* máximo *m* <speed limit : límite de velocidad> **2 limits** *npl* **:** límites *mpl,* confines *mpl* <city limits : límites de la ciudad> **3 that's the limit! :** ¡eso es el colmo!

limitation [ˌlɪməˈteɪʃən] *n* **:** limitación *f,* restricción *f*

limited [ˈlɪmət̬əd] *adj* **:** limitado, restringido

limitless [ˈlɪmətləs] *adj* **:** ilimitado, sin límites

limousine [ˈlɪməˌziːn, ˌlɪməˈ-] *n* **:** limusina *f*

limp[1] [ˈlɪmp] *vi* **:** cojear

limp[2] *adj* **1** FLACCID **:** fláccido **2** LANK **:** lacio (dícese del pelo) **3** WEAK **:** débil <to feel limp : sentirse desfallecer, sentirse sin fuerzas>

limp[3] *n* **:** cojera *f*

limpid [ˈlɪmpəd] *adj* **:** límpido, claro

limply [ˈlɪmpli] *adv* **:** sin fuerzas

limpness [ˈlɪmpnəs] *n* **:** flaccidez *f,* debilidad *f*

linden [ˈlɪndən] *n* **:** tilo *m*

line[1] [ˈlaɪn] *v* **lined; lining** *vt* **1 :** forrar, cubrir <to line a dress : forrar un vestido> <to line the walls : cubrir las paredes> **2** MARK **:** rayar, trazar líneas en **3** BORDER **:** bordear **4** ALIGN **:** alinear — *vi* **to line up :** ponerse in fila, hacer cola

line[2] *n* **1** CORD, ROPE **:** cuerda *f* **2** WIRE **:** cable *m* <power line : cable eléctrico> **3 :** línea *f* (de teléfono) **4** ROW **:** fila *f,* hilera *f* **5** NOTE **:** nota *f,* líneas *fpl* <drop me a line : mándame unas líneas> **6** COURSE **:** línea *f* <line of inquiry : línea de investigación> **7** AGREEMENT **:** conformidad *f* <to be in line with : ser conforme a> <to fall into line : estar de acuerdo> **8** OCCUPATION **:** ocupación *f,* rama *f,* especialidad *f* **9** LIMIT **:** línea *f,* límite *m* <dividing line : línea divisoria> <to draw the line : fijar límites> **10** SERVICE **:** línea *f* <bus line : línea de autobuses> **11** MARK **:** línea *f,* arruga *f* (de la cara)

lineage [ˈlɪniɪdʒ] *n* **:** linaje *m,* abolengo *m*

lineal [ˈlɪniəl] *adj* **:** en línea directa

lineaments [ˈlɪniəmənts] *npl* **:** facciones *fpl* (de la cara), rasgos *mpl*

linear [ˈlɪniər] *adj* **:** lineal

linen [ˈlɪnən] *n* : lino *m*

liner [ˈlaɪnər] *n* **1** LINING : forro *m* **2** SHIP : buque *m,* transatlántico *m*

lineup [ˈlaɪn,əp] *n* **1** : fila *f* de sospechosos **2** : formación *f* (en deportes) **3** ALIGNMENT : alineación *f*

linger [ˈlɪŋgər] *vi* **1** TARRY : quedarse, entretenerse, rezagarse **2** PERSIST : persistir, sobrevivir

lingerie [,lɑndʒəˈreɪ, ,læʒəˈriː] *n* : ropa *f* íntima femenina, lencería *f*

lingo [ˈlɪŋgo] *n, pl* **-goes 1** LANGUAGE : idioma *m* **2** JARGON : jerga *f*

linguist [ˈlɪŋgwɪst] *n* : lingüista *mf*

linguistic [lɪŋˈgwɪstɪk] *adj* : lingüístico

linguistics [lɪŋˈgwɪstɪks] *n* : lingüística *f*

liniment [ˈlɪnəmənt] *n* : linimento *m*

lining [ˈlaɪnɪŋ] *n* : forro *m*

link[1] [ˈlɪŋk] *vt* : unir, enlazar, conectar — *vi* **to link up** : unirse, conectar

link[2] *n* **1** : eslabón *m* (de una cadena) **2** BOND : conexión *f,* lazo *m,* vínculo *m*

linkage [ˈlɪŋkɪdʒ] *n* : conexión *f,* unión *f,* enlace *m*

linoleum [ləˈnoːliəm] *n* : linóleo *m*

linseed oil [ˈlɪn,siːd] *n* : aceite *m* de linaza

lint [ˈlɪnt] *n* : pelusa *f*

lintel [ˈlɪntəl] *n* : dintel *m*

lion [ˈlaɪən] *n* : león *m*

lioness [ˈlaɪənɪs] *n* : leona *f*

lionize [ˈlaɪə,naɪz] *vt* **-ized; -izing** : tratar a una persona como muy importante

lip [ˈlɪp] *n* **1** : labio *m* **2** EDGE, RIM : pico *m* (de una jarra), borde *m* (de una taza)

lipreading [ˈlɪp,riːdɪŋ] *n* : lectura *f* de los labios

lipstick [ˈlɪp,stɪk] *n* : lápiz *m* de labios, barra *f* de labios

liquefy [ˈlɪkwə,faɪ] *v* **-fied; -fying** *vt* : licuar — *vi* : licuarse

liqueur [lɪˈkʊr, -ˈkər, -ˈkjʊr] *n* : licor *m*

liquid[1] [ˈlɪkwəd] *adj* : líquido

liquid[2] *n* : líquido *m*

liquidate [ˈlɪkwə,deɪt] *vt* **-dated; -dating** : liquidar

liquidation [,lɪkwəˈdeɪʃən] *n* : liquidación *f*

liquidity [lɪkˈwɪdət̬i] *n* : liquidez *f*

liquor [ˈlɪkər] *n* : alcohol *m,* bebidas *fpl* alcohólicas, licor *m*

lisp[1] [ˈlɪsp] *vi* : cecear

lisp[2] *n* : ceceo *m*

lissome [ˈlɪsəm] *adj* **1** FLEXIBLE : flexible **2** LITHE : ágil y grácil

list[1] [ˈlɪst] *vt* **1** ENUMERATE : hacer una lista de, enumerar **2** INCLUDE : poner en una lista, incluir — *vi* : escorar (dícese de un barco)

list[2] *n* **1** ENUMERATION : lista *f* **2** SLANT : escora *f,* inclinación *f*

listen [ˈlɪsən] *vi* **1** : escuchar, oír **2 to listen to** HEED : prestar atención a, hacer caso de, escuchar **3 to listen to reason** : atender a razones

listener [ˈlɪsənər] *n* : oyente *mf,* persona *f* que sabe escuchar

listless [ˈlɪstləs] *adj* : lánguido, apático — **listlessly** *adv*

listlessness [ˈlɪstləsnəs] *n* : apatía *f,* languidez *f,* desgana *f*

lit [ˈlɪt] *pp* → **light**

litany [ˈlɪtəni] *n, pl* **-nies** : letanía *f*

liter [ˈliːt̬ər] *n* : litro *m*

literacy [ˈlɪt̬ərəsi] *n* : alfabetismo *m*

literal [ˈlɪt̬ərəl] *adj* : literal — **literally** *adv*

literary [ˈlɪt̬ə,rɛri] *adj* : literario

literate [ˈlɪt̬ərət] *adj* : alfabetizado

literature [ˈlɪt̬ərə,tʃʊr, -tʃər] *n* : literatura *f*

lithe [ˈlaɪð, ˈlaɪθ] *adj* : ágil y grácil

lithesome [ˈlaɪðsəm, ˈlaɪθ-] → **lissome**

lithograph [ˈlɪθə,græf] *n* : litografía *f*

lithographer [lɪˈθɑgrəfər, ˈlɪθə,græfər] *n* : litógrafo *m,* -fa *f*

lithography [lɪˈθɑgrəfi] *n* : litografía *f*

litigant [ˈlɪtɪgənt] *n* : litigante *mf*

litigate [ˈlɪt̬ə,geɪt] *vi* **-gated; -gating** : litigar

litigation [,lɪt̬əˈgeɪʃən] *n* : litigio *m*

litmus paper [ˈlɪtməs] *n* : papel *m* de tornasol

litter[1] [ˈlɪt̬ər] *vt* : tirar basura en, ensuciar — *vi* : tirar basura

litter[2] *n* **1** : camada *f,* cría *f* <a litter of kittens : una cría de gatitos> **2** STRETCHER : camilla *f* **3** RUBBISH : basura *f* **4** : arena *f* higiénica (para gatos)

little[1] [ˈlɪt̬əl] *adv* **less** [ˈlɛs]; **least** [ˈliːst] **1** : poco <she sings very little : canta muy poco> **2 little did I know that...** : no tenía la menor idea de que ... **3 as little as possible** : lo menos posible

little[2] *adj* **littler** *or* **less** [ˈlɛs] *or* **lesser** [ˈlɛsər]; **littlest** *or* **least** [ˈliːst] **1** SMALL : pequeño **2** : poco <they speak little Spanish : hablan poco español> <little by little : poco a poco> **3** TRIVIAL : sin importancia, trivial

little[3] *n* **1** : poco *m* <little has changed : poco ha cambiado> **2 a little** : un poco, algo <it's a little surprising : es algo sorprendente>

Little Dipper → **dipper**

liturgical [ləˈtərdʒɪkəl] *adj* : litúrgico — **liturgically** [-kli] *adv*

liturgy [ˈlɪt̬ərdʒi] *n, pl* **-gies** : liturgia *f*

livable [ˈlɪvəbəl] *adj* : habitable

live[1] [ˈlɪv] *vi* **lived; living 1** EXIST : vivir <as long as I live : mientras viva> <to live from day to day : vivir al día> **2** : llevar una vida, vivir <he lived simply : llevó una vida sencilla> **3** SUBSIST : mantenerse, vivir **4** RESIDE : vivir, residir

live[2] [ˈlaɪv] *adj* **1** LIVING : vivo **2** BURNING : encendido <a live coal : una brasa> **3** : con corriente <live wires

: cables con corriente> **4** : cargado, sin estallar <a live bomb : una bomba sin estallar> **5** CURRENT : de actualidad <a live issue : un asunto de actualidad> **6** : en vivo, en directo <a live interview : una entrevista en vivo>
livelihood [ˈlaɪvli,hʊd] *n* : sustento *m*, vida *f*, medio *m* de vida
liveliness [ˈlaɪvlinəs] *n* : animación *f*, vivacidad *f*
livelong [ˈlɪvˈlɔŋ] *adj* : entero, completo
lively [ˈlaɪvli] *adj* **-lier; -est** : animado, vivaz, vivo, enérgico
liven [ˈlaɪvən] *vt* : animar — *vi* : animarse
liver [ˈlɪvər] *n* : hígado *m*
livery [ˈlɪvəri] *n, pl* **-eries** : librea *f*
lives → **life**
livestock [ˈlaɪv,stɑk] *n* : ganado *m*
live wire *n* : persona *f* vivaz y muy activa
livid [ˈlɪvəd] *adj* **1** BLACK-AND-BLUE : amoratado **2** PALE : lívido **3** ENRAGED : furioso
living[1] [ˈlɪvɪŋ] *adj* : vivo
living[2] *n* **to make a living** : ganarse la vida
living room *n* : living *m*, sala *f* de estar
lizard [ˈlɪzərd] *n* : lagarto *m*
llama [ˈlɑmə, ˈjɑ-] *n* : llama *f*
load[1] [ˈlo:d] *vt* : cargar, embarcar
load[2] *n* **1** CARGO : carga *f* **2** WEIGHT : peso *m* **3** BURDEN : carga *f*, peso *m* **4 loads** *npl* : montón *m*, pila *f*, cantidad *f* <loads of work : un montón de trabajo>
loaf[1] [ˈlo:f] *vi* : holgazanear, flojear, haraganear
loaf[2] *n, pl* **loaves** [ˈlo:vz] **1** : pan *m*, pan *m* de molde, barra *f* de pan **2 meat loaf** : pan *m* de carne
loafer [ˈlo:fər] *n* : holgazán *m*, -zana *f*; haragán *m*, -gana *f*; vago *m*, -ga *f*
loam [ˈlo:m] *n* : marga *f*, suelo *m*
loan[1] [ˈlo:n] *vt* : prestar
loan[2] *n* : préstamo *m*, empréstito *m* (del banco)
loath [ˈlo:θ, ˈlo:ð] *adj* : poco dispuesto <I am loath to say it : me resisto a decirlo>
loathe [ˈlo:ð] *vt* **loathed; loathing** : odiar, aborrecer
loathing [ˈlo:ðɪŋ] *n* : aversión *f*, odio *m*, aborrecimiento *m*
loathsome [ˈlo:θsəm, ˈlo:ð-] *adj* : odioso, repugnante
lob[1] [ˈlɑb] *vt* **lobbed; lobbing** : hacerle un globo (a otro jugador)
lob[2] *n* : globo *m* (en deportes)
lobby[1] [ˈlɑbi] *v* **-bied; -bying** *vt* : presionar, ejercer presión sobre — *vi* **to lobby for** : presionar para (lograr algo)
lobby[2] *n, pl* **-bies 1** FOYER : vestíbulo *m* **2** LOBBYISTS : grupo *m* de presión, lobby *m*
lobbyist [ˈlɑbiɪst] *n* : miembro *m* de un lobby
lobe [ˈlo:b] *n* : lóbulo *m*
lobed [ˈlo:bd] *adj* : lobulado
lobotomy [ləˈbɑt̬əmi, lo-] *n, pl* **-mies** : lobotomía *f*
lobster [ˈlɑbstər] *n* : langosta *f*
local[1] [ˈlo:kəl] *adj* : local
local[2] *n* **1** : anestesia *f* local **2 the locals** : los vecinos del lugar, los habitantes
locale [loˈkæl] *n* : lugar *m*, escenario *m*
locality [loˈkæləṭi] *n, pl* **-ties** : localidad *f*
localize [ˈlo:kə,laɪz] *vt* **-ized; -izing** : localizar
locally [ˈlo:kəli] *adv* : en la localidad, en la zona
locate [ˈlo:,keɪt, loˈkeɪt] *v* **-cated; -cating** *vt* **1** POSITION : situar, ubicar **2** FIND : localizar, ubicar — *vi* SETTLE : establecerse
location [loˈkeɪʃən] *n* **1** POSITION : posición *f*, emplazamiento *m*, ubicación *f* **2** PLACE : lugar *m*, sitio *m*
lock[1] [ˈlɑk] *vt* **1** FASTEN : cerrar **2** CONFINE : encerrar <they locked me in the room : me encerraron en la sala> **3** IMMOBILIZE : bloquear (una rueda) — *vi* **1** : cerrarse (dícese de una puerta) **2** : trabarse, bloquearse (dícese de una rueda)
lock[2] *n* **1** : mechón *m* (de pelo) **2** FASTENER : cerradura *f*, cerrojo *m*, chapa *f* **3** : esclusa *f* (de un canal)
locker [ˈlɑkər] *n* : armario *m*, cajón *m* con llave, lócker *m*
locket [ˈlɑkət] *n* : medallón *m*, guardapelo *m*, relicario *m*
lockjaw [ˈlɑk,jɔ] *n* : tétano *m*
lockout [ˈlɑk,aʊt] *n* : cierre *m* patronal, lockout *m*
locksmith [ˈlɑk,smɪθ] *n* : cerrajero *m*, -ra *f*
lockup [ˈlɑk,ʌp] *n* JAIL : cárcel *f*
locomotion [,lo:kəˈmo:ʃən] *n* : locomoción *f*
locomotive[1] [,lo:kəˈmo:ṭɪv] *adj* : locomotor
locomotive[2] *n* : locomotora *f*
locust [ˈlo:kəst] *n* **1** : langosta *f*, chapulín *m CA, Mex* **2** CICADA : cigarra *f*, chicharra *f* **3** : acacia *f* blanca (árbol)
locution [loˈkju:ʃən] *n* : locución *f*
lode [ˈlo:d] *n* : veta *f*, vena *f*, filón *m*
lodestar [ˈlo:d,stɑr] *n* : estrella *f* polar
lodestone [ˈlo:d,sto:n] *n* : piedra *f* imán
lodge[1] [ˈlɑdʒ] *v* **lodged; lodging** *vt* **1** HOUSE : hospedar, alojar **2** FILE : presentar <to lodge a complaint : presentar una demanda> — *vi* **1** : posarse, meterse <the bullet lodged in the door : la bala se incrustó en la puerta> **2** STAY : hospedarse, alojarse
lodge[2] *n* **1** : pabellón *m*, casa *f* de campo <hunting lodge : refugio de caza> **2** : madriguera *f* (de un castor) **3** : logia *f* <Masonic lodge : logia masónica>

lodger [ˈlɑdʒər] *n* : inquilino *m,* -na *f;* huésped *m,* -peda *f*

lodging [ˈlɑdʒɪŋ] *n* **1** : alojamiento *m* **2 lodgings** *npl* ROOMS : habitaciones *fpl*

loft [ˈlɔft] *n* **1** ATTIC : desván *m,* ático *m,* buhardilla *f* **2** : loft *m* (en un depósito comercial) **3** HAYLOFT : pajar *m* **4** : galería *f* <choir loft : galería del coro>

loftily [ˈlɔftəli] *adv* : altaneramente, con altivez

loftiness [ˈlɔftinəs] *n* **1** NOBILITY : nobleza *f* **2** ARROGANCE : altanería *f,* arrogancia *f* **3** HEIGHT : altura *f,* elevación *f*

lofty [ˈlɔfti] *adj* **loftier; -est 1** NOBLE : noble, elevado **2** HAUGHTY : altivo, arrogante, altanero **3** HIGH : majestuoso, elevado

log[1] [ˈlɔg, ˈlɑg] *vi* **logged; logging 1** : talar (árboles) **2** RECORD : registrar, anotar **3 to log on** : entrar (al sistema) **4 to log off** : salir (del sistema)

log[2] *n* **1** : tronco *m,* leño *m* **2** RECORD : diario *m*

logarithm [ˈlɔgəˌrɪðəm, ˈlɑ-] *n* : logaritmo *m*

logger [ˈlɔgər, ˈlɑ-] *n* : leñador *m,* -dora *f*

loggerhead [ˈlɔgərˌhɛd, ˈlɑ-] *n* **1** : tortuga *f* boba **2 to be at loggerheads** : estar en pugna, estar en desacuerdo

logic [ˈlɑdʒɪk] *n* : lógica *f* — **logical** [ˈlɑdʒɪkəl] *adj* — **logically** [-kli] *adv*

logistic [ləˈdʒɪstɪk, lo-] *adj* : logístico

logistics [ləˈdʒɪstɪks, lo-] *ns & pl* : logística *f*

logo [ˈloːˌgoː] *n, pl* **logos** [-ˌgoːz] : logotipo *m*

loin [ˈlɔɪn] *n* **1** : lomo *m* <pork loin : lomo de cerdo> **2 loins** *npl* : lomos *mpl* <to gird one's loins : prepararse para la lucha>

loiter [ˈlɔɪt̬ər] *vi* : vagar, perder el tiempo

loll [ˈlɑl] *vi* **1** SLOUCH : repantigarse **2** IDLE : holgazanear, hacer el vago

lollipop *or* **lollypop** [ˈlɑliˌpɑp] *n* : dulce *m* en palito, chupete *m Chile, Peru,* paleta *f CA, Mex*

lone [ˈloːn] *adj* **1** SOLITARY : solitario **2** ONLY : único

loneliness [ˈloːnlinəs] *n* : soledad *f*

lonely [ˈloːnli] *adj* **-lier; -est 1** SOLITARY : solitario, aislado **2** LONESOME : solo <to feel lonely : sentirse muy solo>

loner [ˈloːnər] *n* : solitario *m,* -ria *f;* recluso *m,* -sa *f*

lonesome [ˈloːnsəm] *adj* : solo, solitario

long[1] [ˈlɔŋ] *vi* **1 to long for** : añorar, desear, anhelar **2 to long to** : anhelar, estar deseando <they longed to see her : estaban deseando verla, tenían muchas ganas de verla>

long[2] *adv* **1** : mucho, mucho tiempo <it didn't take long : no llevó mucho tiempo> <will it last long? : ¿va a durar mucho?> **2 all day long** : todo el día **3 as long as** *or* **so long as** : mientras, con tal que **4 long before** : mucho antes **5 so long!** : ¡hasta luego!, ¡adiós!

long[3] *adj* **longer** [ˈlɔngər]; **longest** [ˈlɔŋgəst] **1** (*indicating length*) : largo <the dress is too long : el vestido es demasiado largo> <a long way from : bastante lejos de> <in the long run : a la larga> **2** (*indicating time*) : largo, prolongado <a long illness : una enfermedad prolongada> <a long walk : un paseo largo> <at long last : por fin> **3 to be long on** : estar cargado de

long[4] *n* **1 before long** : dentro de poco **2 the long and the short** : lo esencial, lo fundamental

longevity [lɑnˈdʒɛvət̬i] *n* : longevidad *f*

longhand [ˈlɔŋˌhænd] *n* : escritura *f* a mano, escritura *f* cursiva

longhorn [ˈlɔŋˌhɔrn] *n* : longhorn *mf*

longing [lɔŋɪŋ] *n* : vivo deseo *m,* ansia *f,* anhelo *m*

longingly [lɔŋɪŋlli] *adv* : ansiosamente, con ansia

longitude [ˈlɑndʒəˌtuːd, -ˌtjuːd] *n* : longitud *f*

longitudinal [ˌlɑndʒəˈtuːdənəl, -ˈtjuː-] *adj* : longitudinal — **longitudinally** *adv*

longshoreman [ˈlɔŋˈʃormən] *n, pl* **-men** [-mən, -ˌmɛn] : estibador *m,* -dora *f*

long–suffering [ˈlɔŋˈsʌfərɪŋ] *adj* : paciente, sufrido

look[1] [ˈlʊk] *vi* **1** GLANCE : mirar <to look out the window : mirar por la ventana> **2** INVESTIGATE : buscar, mirar <look in the closet : busca en el closet> <look before you leap : mira lo que haces> **3** SEEM : parecer <he looks happy : parece estar contento> <I look like my mother : me parezco a mi madre> **4 to look after** : cuidar, cuidar de **5 to look for** EXPECT : esperar **6 to look for** SEEK : buscar — *vt* : mirar

look[2] *n* **1** GLANCE : mirada *f* **2** EXPRESSION : cara *f* <a look of disapproval : una cara de desaprobación> **3** ASPECT : aspecto *m,* apariencia *f,* aire *m*

lookout [ˈlʊkˌaʊt] *n* **1** : centinela *mf,* vigía *mf* **2 to be on the lookout for** : estar al acecho de, andar a la caza de

loom[1] [ˈluːm] *vi* **1** : aparecer, surgir <the city loomed up in the distance : la ciudad surgió en la distancia> **2** IMPEND : amenazar, ser inminente **3 to loom large** : cobrar mucha importancia

loom[2] *n* : telar *m*

loon [ˈluːn] *n* : somorgujo *m,* somormujo *m*

loony *or* **looney** [ˈluːni] *adj* **-nier; -est** : loco, chiflado *fam*

loop[1] [ˈluːp] *vt* **1** : hacer lazadas con **2 to loop around** : pasar alrededor de — *vi* **1** : rizar el rizo (dícese de un avión) **2** : serpentear (dícese de una carretera)

loop[2] *n* **1** : lazada *f* (en hilo o cuerda) **2** BEND : curva *f* **3** CIRCUIT : circuito *m* cerrado **4** : rizo *m* (en la aviación) <to loop the loop : rizar el rizo>

loophole [ˈluːpˌhoːl] *n* : escapatoria *f*, pretexto *m*

loose[1] [ˈluːs] *vt* **loosed; loosing 1** RELEASE : poner en libertad, soltar **2** UNTIE : deshacer, desatar **3** DISCHARGE, UNLEASH : descargar, desatar

loose[2] → **loosely**

loose[3] *adj* **looser; -est 1** INSECURE : flojo, suelto, poco seguro <a loose tooth : un diente flojo> **2** ROOMY : suelto, holgado <loose clothing : ropa holgada> **3** OPEN : suelto, abierto <loose soil : suelo suelto> <a loose weave : una tejida abierta> **4** FREE : suelto <to break loose : soltarse> **5** SLACK : flojo, flexible **6** APPROXIMATE : libre, aproximado <a loose translation : una traducción aproximada>

loosely [ˈluːsli] *adv* **1** : sin apretar **2** ROUGHLY : aproximadamente, más o menos

loosen [ˈluːsən] *vt* : aflojar

loose–leaf [ˈluːsˈliːf] *adj* : de hojas sueltas

looseness [ˈluːsnəs] *n* **1** : aflojamiento *m*, holgura *f* (de ropa) **2** IMPRECISION : imprecisión *f*

loot[1] [ˈluːt] *vt* : saquear, robar

loot[2] *n* : botín *m*

looter [ˈluːt̬ər] *n* : saqueador *m*, -dora *f*

lop [ˈlɑp] *vt* **lopped; lopping** : cortar, podar

lope[1] [ˈloːp] *vi* **loped; loping** : correr a paso largo

lope[2] *n* : paso *m* largo

lopsided [ˈlɑpˌsaɪdəd] *adj* **1** CROOKED : torcido, chueco, ladeado **2** ASYMETRICAL : asimétrico

loquacious [loˈkweɪʃəs] *adj* : locuaz

lord [ˈlɔrd] *n* **1** : señor *m*, noble *m* **2** : lord *m* (en la Gran Bretaña) **3 the Lord** : el Señor **4 good Lord!** : ¡Dios mío!

lordly [ˈlɔrdli] *adj* **-lier; -est** HAUGHTY : arrogante, altanero

lordship [ˈlɔrdˌʃɪp] *n* : señoría *f*

Lord's Supper *n* : Eucaristía *f*

lore [ˈlor] *n* : saber *m* popular, tradición *f*

lose [ˈluːz] *v* **lost** [ˈlɔst]; **losing** [ˈluːzɪŋ] *vt* **1** : perder <I lost my umbrella : perdí mi paraguas> <to lose blood : perder sangre> <to lose one's voice : quedarse afónico> <to have nothing to lose : no tener nada que perder> <to lose no time : no perder tiempo> <to lose weight : perder peso, adelgazar> <to lose one's temper : perder los estribos, enojarse, enfadarse> <to lose sight of : perder de vista> **2** : costar, hacer perder <the errors lost him his job : los errores le costaron su empleo> **3** : atrasar <my watch loses 5 minutes a day : mi reloj atrasa 5 minutos por día> **4 to lose oneself** : perderse, ensimismarse — *vi* **1** : perder <we lost to the other team : perdimos contra el otro equipo> **2** : atrasarse <the clock loses time : el reloj se atrasa>

loser [ˈluːzər] *n* : perdedor *m*, -dora *f*

loss [ˈlɔs] *n* **1** LOSING : pérdida *f* <loss of memory : pérdida de memoria> <to sell at a loss : vender con pérdida> <to be at a loss to : no saber como> **2** DEFEAT : derrota *f*, juego *m* perdido **3 losses** *npl* DEATHS : muertos *mpl*

lost [ˈlɔst] *adj* **1** : perdido <a lost cause : una causa perdida> <lost in thought : absorto> **2 to get lost** : perderse **3 to make up for lost time** : recuperar el tiempo perdido

lot [ˈlɑt] *n* **1** DRAWING : sorteo *m* <by lot : por sorteo> **2** SHARE : parte *f*, porción *f* **3** FATE : suerte *f* **4** LAND, PLOT : terreno *m*, solar *m*, lote *m*, parcela *f* **5 a lot of** *or* **lots of** : mucho, un montón de, bastante <lots of books : un montón de libros, muchos libros> <a lot of people : mucha gente>

loth [ˈloːθ, ˈloːð] → **loath**

lotion [ˈloːʃən] *n* : loción *f*

lottery [ˈlɑt̬əri] *n*, *pl* **-teries** : lotería *f*

lotus [ˈloːt̬əs] *n* : loto *m*

loud[1] [ˈlaʊd] *adv* : alto, fuerte <out loud : en voz alta>

loud[2] *adj* **1** : alto, fuerte <a loud voice : una voz alta> **2** NOISY : ruidoso <a loud party : una fiesta ruidosa> **3** FLASHY : llamativo, chillón

loudly [ˈlaʊdli] *adv* : alto, fuerte, en voz alta

loudness [ˈlaʊdnəs] *n* : volumen *m*, fuerza *f* (del ruido)

loudspeaker [ˈlaʊdˌspiːkər] *n* : altavoz *m*, altoparlante *m*

lounge[1] [ˈlaʊndʒ] *vi* **lounged; lounging** : holgazanear, gandulear

lounge[2] *n* : salón *m*, sala *f* de estar

louse [ˈlaʊs] *n*, *pl* **lice** [ˈlaɪs] : piojo *m*

lousy [ˈlaʊzi] *adj* **lousier; -est 1** : piojoso, lleno de piojos **2** BAD : pésimo, muy malo

lout [ˈlaʊt] *n* : bruto *m*, patán *m*

louver *or* **louvre** [ˈluːvər] *n* : persiana *f*, listón *m* de persiana

lovable [ˈlʌvəbəl] *adj* : adorable, amoroso, encantador

love[1] [ˈlʌv] *v* **loved; loving** *vt* **1** : querer, amar <I love you : te quiero> **2** ENJOY : encantarle a alguien, ser (muy) aficionado a, gustarle mucho a uno (algo) <she loves flowers : le encantan las flores> <he loves golf : es muy aficionado al golf> <I'd love

to go with you : me gustaría mucho acompañarte> — *vi* : querer, amar

love[2] *n* **1** : amor *m,* cariño *m* <to be in love with : estar enamorado de> <to fall in love with : enamorarse de> **2** ENTHUSIASM, INTEREST : amor *m,* afición *m,* gusto *m* <love of music : afición a la música> **3** BELOVED : amor *m;* amado *m,* -da *f;* enamorado *m,* -da *f*

loveless [ˈlʌvləs] *adj* : sin amor

loveliness [ˈlʌvlinəs] *n* : belleza *f,* hermosura *f*

lovelorn [ˈlʌvˌlɔrn] *adj* : herido de amor, perdidamente enamorado

lovely [ˈlʌvli] *adj* **-lier; -est** : hermoso, bello, lindo, precioso

lover [ˈlʌvər] *n* : amante *mf* (de personas); aficionado *m,* -da *f* (a alguna actividad)

loving [ˈlʌvɪŋ] *adj* : amoroso, cariñoso

lovingly [ˈlʌvɪŋli] *adv* : cariñosamente

low[1] [ˈloː] *vi* : mugir

low[2] *adv* : bajo, profundo <to aim low : apuntar bajo> <to lie low : mantenerse escondido> <to turn the lights down low : bajar las luces>

low[3] *adj* **lower** [ˈloːər]; **-est 1** : bajo <a low building : un edificio bajo> <a low bow : una profunda reverencia> **2** SOFT : bajo, suave <in a low voice : en voz baja> **3** SHALLOW : bajo, poco profundo **4** HUMBLE : humilde, modesto **5** DEPRESSED : deprimido, bajo de moral **6** INFERIOR : bajo, inferior **7** UNFAVORABLE : mal <to have a low opinion of him : tener un mal concepto de él> **8 to be low on** : tener poco de, estar escaso de

low[4] *n* **1** : punto *m* bajo <to reach an all-time low : estar más bajo que nunca> **2** *or* **low gear** : primera velocidad *f* **3** : mugido *m* (de una vaca)

lowbrow [ˈloːˌbraʊ] *n* : persona *f* inculta

lower[1] [ˈloːər] *vt* **1** DROP : bajar <to lower one's voice : bajar la voz> **2** : arriar, bajar <to lower the flag : arriar la bandera> **3** REDUCE : reducir, bajar **4 to lower oneself** : rebajarse

lower[2] [ˈloːər] *adj* : inferior, más bajo, de abajo

lowland [ˈloːlənd, -ˌlænd] *n* : tierras *fpl* bajas

lowly [ˈloːli] *adj* **-lier; -est** : humilde, modesto

loyal [ˈlɔɪəl] *adj* : leal, fiel — **loyally** *adv*

loyalist [ˈlɔɪəlɪst] *n* : partidario *m,* -ria *f* del régimen

loyalty [ˈlɔɪəlti] *n, pl* **-ties** : lealtad *f,* fidelidad *f*

lozenge [ˈlɑzəndʒ] *n* : pastilla *f*

LSD [ˌɛlˌɛsˈdiː] *n* : LSD *m*

lubricant [ˈluːbrɪkənt] *n* : lubricante *m*

lubricate [ˈluːbrɪˌkeɪt] *vt* **-cated; -cating** : lubricar — **lubrication** [ˌluːbrɪˈkeɪʃən] *n*

lucid [ˈluːsəd] *adj* : lúcido, claro — **lucidly** *adv*

lucidity [luːˈsɪdəṭi] *n* : lucidez *f*

luck [ˈlʌk] *n* **1** : suerte *f* **2 to have bad luck** : tener mala suerte **3 good luck!** : ¡(buena) suerte!

luckily [ˈlʌkəli] *adv* : afortunadamente, por suerte

luckless [ˈlʌkləs] *adj* : desafortunado

lucky [ˈlʌki] *adj* **luckier; -est 1** : afortunado, que tiene suerte <a lucky woman : una mujer afortunada **2** FORTUITOUS : fortuito, de suerte **3** OPPORTUNE : oportuno **4** : de (la) suerte <lucky number : número de la suerte>

lucrative [ˈluːkrəṭɪv] *adj* : lucrativo, provechoso — **lucratively** *adv*

ludicrous [ˈluːdəkrəs] *adj* : ridículo, absurdo — **ludicrously** *adv*

ludicrousness [ˈluːdəkrəsnəs] *n* : ridiculez *f,* absurdo *m*

lug [ˈlʌg] *vt* **lugged; lugging** : arrastrar, transportar con dificultad

luggage [ˈlʌgɪdʒ] *n* : equipaje *m*

lugubrious [lʊˈguːbriəs] *adj* : lúgubre — **lugubriously** *adv*

lukewarm [ˈluːkˈwɔrm] *adj* **1** TEPID : tibio **2** HALFHEARTED : poco entusiasta

lull[1] [ˈlʌl] *vt* **1** CALM, SOOTHE : calmar, sosegar **2 to lull to sleep** : arrullar, adormecer

lull[2] *n* : calma *f,* pausa *f*

lullaby [ˈlʌləˌbaɪ] *n, pl* **-bies** : canción *f* de cuna, arrullo *m,* nana *f*

lumbago [ˌlʌmˈbeɪgo] *n* : lumbago *m*

lumber[1] [ˈlʌmbər] *vt* : aserrar (madera) — *vi* : moverse pesadamente

lumber[2] *n* : madera *f*

lumberjack [ˈlʌmbərˌdʒæk] *n* : leñador *m,* -dora *f*

lumberyard [ˈlʌmbərˌjɑrd] *n* : almacén *m* de maderas

luminary [ˈluːməˌnɛri] *n, pl* **-naries** : lumbrera *f,* luminaria *f*

luminescence [ˌluːməˈnɛsənts] *n* : luminiscencia *f* — **luminescent** [-ˈnɛsənt] *adj*

luminosity [ˌluːməˈnɑsəṭi] *n, pl* **-ties** : luminosidad *f*

luminous [ˈluːmənəs] *adj* : luminoso — **luminously** *adv*

lump[1] [ˈlʌmp] *vt or* **to lump together** : juntar, agrupar, amontonar — *vi* CLUMP : agruparse, aglutinarse

lump[2] *n* **1** GLOB : grumo *m* **2** PIECE : pedazo *m,* trozo *m,* terrón *m* <a lump of coal : un trozo de carbón> <a lump of sugar : un terrón de azúcar> **3** SWELLING : bulto *m,* hinchazón *f,* protuberancia *f* **4 to have a lump in one's throat** : tener un nudo en la garganta

lumpy [ˈlʌmpi] *adj* **lumpier; -est 1** : lleno de grumos (dícese de una salsa) **2** UNEVEN : desigual, disparejo

lunacy [ˈluːnəsi] *n, pl* **-cies** : locura *f*

lunar [ˈluːnər] *adj* : lunar

lunatic[1] [ˈluːnəˌtɪk] *adj* : lunático, loco

lunatic[2] *n* : loco *m,* -ca *f*
lunch[1] [ˈlʌntʃ] *vi* : almorzar, comer
lunch[2] *n* : almuerzo *m,* comida *f,* lonche *m*
luncheon [ˈlʌntʃən] *n* **1** : comida *f,* almuerzo *m* **2 luncheon meat** : fiambres *fpl*
lung [ˈlʌŋ] *n* : pulmón *m*
lunge[1] [ˈlʌndʒ] *vi* **lunged; lunging 1** THRUST : atacar (en la esgrima) **2 to lunge forward** : arremeter, lanzarse
lunge[2] *n* **1** : arremetida *f,* embestida *f* **2** : estocada *f* (en la esgrima)
lurch[1] [ˈlərtʃ] *vi* **1** PITCH : cabecear, dar bandazos, dar sacudidas **2** STAGGER : tambalearse
lurch[2] *n* **1** : sacudida *f,* bandazo *m* (de un vehículo) **2** : tambaleo *m* (de una persona)
lure[1] [ˈlʊr] *vt* **lured; luring** : atraer
lure[2] *n* **1** ATTRACTION : atractivo *m* **2** ENTICEMENT : señuelo *m,* aliciente *m* **3** BAIT : cebo *m* artificial (en la pesca)
lurid [ˈlʊrəd] *adj* **1** GRUESOME : espeluznante, horripilante **2** SENSATIONAL : sensacionalista, chocante **3** GAUDY : chillón
lurk [ˈlərk] *vi* : estar al acecho
luscious [ˈlʌʃəs] *adj* **1** DELICIOUS : delicioso, exquisito **2** SEDUCTIVE : seductor, cautivador
lush [ˈlʌʃ] *adj* **1** LUXURIANT : exuberante, lozano **2** LUXURIOUS : suntuoso, lujoso
lust[1] [ˈlʌst] *vi* **to lust after** : desear (a una persona), codiciar (riquezas, etc.)
lust[2] *n* **1** LASCIVIOUSNESS : lujuria *f,* lascivia *f* **2** CRAVING : deseo *m,* ansia *f,* anhelo *m*
luster *or* **lustre** [ˈlʌstər] *n* **1** GLOSS, SHEEN : lustre *m,* brillo *m* **2** SPLENDOR : lustre *m,* esplendor *m*
lusterless [ˈlʌstərləs] *adj* : deslustrado, sin brillo
lustful [ˈlʌstfəl] *adj* : lujurioso, lascivo, lleno de deseo
lustrous [ˈlʌstrəs] *adj* : brillante, brilloso, lustroso
lusty [ˈlʌsti] *adj* **lustier; -est** : fuerte, robusto, vigoroso — **lustily** [ˈlʌstəli] *adv*
lute [ˈluːt] *n* : laúd *m*
luxuriant [ˌlʌgˈʒʊriənt, ˌlʌkˈʃʊr-] *adj* **1** : exuberante, lozano (dícese de las plantas) **2** : abundante y hermoso (dícese del pelo) — **luxuriantly** *adv*
luxuriate [ˌlʌgˈʒʊriˌeɪt, ˌlʌkˈʃʊr-] *vi* **-ated; -ating 1** : disfrutar **2 to luxuriate in** : deleitarse con
luxurious [ˌlʌgˈʒʊriəs, ˌlʌkˈʃʊr-] *adj* : lujoso, suntuoso — **luxuriously** *adv*
luxury [ˈlʌkʃəri, ˈlʌgʒə-] *n, pl* **-ries** : lujo *m*
lye [ˈlaɪ] *n* : lejía *f*
lying → **lie**[1], **lie**[2]
lymph [ˈlɪmpf] *n* : linfa *f*
lymphatic [lɪmˈfætɪk] *adj* : linfático
lynch [ˈlɪntʃ] *vt* : linchar
lynx [ˈlɪŋks] *n, pl* **lynx** *or* **lynxes** : lince *m*
lyre [ˈlaɪr] *n* : lira *f*
lyric[1] [ˈlɪrɪk] *adj* : lírico
lyric[2] *n* **1** : poema *m* lírico **2 lyrics** *npl* : letra *f* (de una canción)
lyrical [ˈlɪrɪkəl] *adj* : lírico, elocuente

M

m [ˈɛm] *n, pl* **m's** *or* **ms** [ˈɛmz] : decimotercera letra del alfabeto inglés
ma'am [ˈmæm] → **madam**
macabre [məˈkɑb, -ˈkɑbər, -ˈkɑbrə] *adj* : macabro
macadam [məˈkædəm] *n* : macadán *m*
macaroni [ˌmækəˈroːni] *n* : macarrones *mpl*
macaroon [ˌmækəˈruːn] *n* : macarrón *m,* mostachón *m*
macaw [məˈkɔ] *n* : guacamayo *m*
mace [ˈmeɪs] *n* **1** : maza *f* (arma o símbolo) **2** : macis *f* (especia)
machete [məˈʃɛti] *n* : machete *m*
machination [ˌmækəˈneɪʃən, ˌmæʃə-] *n* : maquinación *f,* intriga *f*
machine[1] [məˈʃiːn] *vt* **-chined; -chining** : trabajar a máquina
machine[2] *n* **1** : máquina *f* <machine shop : taller de máquinas> <machine language : lenguaje de la máquina> **2** : aparato *m,* maquinaria *f* (en política)
machine gun *n* : ametralladora *f*
machinery [məˈʃiːnəri] *n, pl* **-eries 1** : maquinaria *f* **2** WORKS : mecanismo *m*
machinist [məˈʃiːnɪst] *n* : maquinista *mf*
mackerel [ˈmækərəl] *n, pl* **-el** *or* **-els** : caballa *f*
mackinaw [ˈmækəˌnɔ] *n* : chaqueta *f* escocesa de lana
mad [ˈmæd] *adj* **madder; maddest 1** INSANE : loco, demente **2** RABID : rabioso **3** FOOLISH : tonto, insensato **4** ANGRY : enojado, furioso **5** CRAZY : loco <I'm mad about you : estoy loco por ti>
Madagascan [ˌmædəˈgæskən] *n* : malgache *mf* — **Madagascan** *adj*
madam [ˈmædəm] *n, pl* **mesdames** [meɪˈdɑm, -ˈdæm] : señora *f*
madcap[1] [ˈmædˌkæp] *adj* ZANY : alocado, disparatado
madcap[2] *n* : alocado *m,* -da *f*
madden [ˈmædən] *vt* : enloquecer, enfurecer
maddeningly [ˈmædənɪŋli] *adv* : irritantemente <maddeningly vague : tan vago que te exaspera>

made → **make**[1]
madhouse ['mæd,haʊs] *n* : manicomio *m* <the office was a madhouse : la oficina parecía una casa de locos>
madly ['mædli] *adv* : como un loco, locamente
madman ['mæd,mæn, -mən] *n, pl* **-men** [-mən, -,mɛn] : loco *m,* demente *m*
madness ['mædnəs] *n* : locura *f,* demencia *f*
madwoman ['mæd,wʊmən] *n, pl* **-women** [-,wɪmən] : loca *f,* demente *f*
maelstrom ['meɪlstrəm] *n* : remolino *m,* vorágine *f*
maestro ['maɪ,stroː] *n, pl* **-stros** *or* **-stri** [-,striː] : maestro *m*
Mafia ['mɑfiə] *n* : Mafia *f*
magazine ['mægə,ziːn] *n* **1** STOREHOUSE : almacén *m,* polvorín *m* (de explosivos) **2** PERIODICAL : revista *f* **3** : cargador *m* (de un arma de fuego)
magenta [mə'dʒɛntə] *n* : magenta *f,* color *m* magenta
maggot ['mægət] *n* : gusano *m*
magic[1] ['mædʒɪk] *or* **magical** ['mædʒɪkəl] *adj* : mágico
magic[2] *n* : magia *f*
magically ['mædʒɪkli] *adv* : mágicamente <they magically appeared : aparecieron como por arte de magia>
magician [mə'dʒɪʃən] *n* **1** SORCERER : mago *m,* -ga *f* **2** CONJURER : prestidigitador *m,* -dora *f;* mago *m,* -ga *f*
magistrate ['mædʒə,streɪt] *n* : magistrado *m,* -da *f*
magma ['mægmə] *n* : magma *m*
magnanimity [,mægnə'nɪməti] *n, pl* **-ties** : magnanimidad *f*
magnanimous [mæg'nænəməs] *adj* : magnánimo, generoso — **magnanimously** *adv*
magnate ['mæg,neɪt, -nət] *n* : magnate *mf*
magnesium [mæg'niːziəm, -ʒəm] *n* : magnesio *m*
magnet ['mægnət] *n* : imán *m*
magnetic [mæg'nɛtɪk] *adj* : magnético — **magnetically** [-tɪkli] *adv*
magnetic field *n* : campo *m* magnético
magnetism ['mægnə,tɪzəm] *n* : magnetismo *m*
magnetize ['mægnə,taɪz] *vt* **-tized; -tizing 1** : magnetizar, imantar **2** ATTRACT : magnetizar, atraer
magnification [,mægnəfə'keɪʃən] *n* : aumento *m,* ampliación *f*
magnificence [mæg'nɪfəsənts] *n* : magnificencia *f*
magnificent [mæg'nɪfəsənt] *adj* : magnífico — **magnificently** *adv*
magnify ['mægnə,faɪ] *vt* **-fied; -fying 1** ENLARGE : ampliar **2** EXAGGERATE : magnificar, exagerar
magnifying glass *n* : lupa *f*
magnitude ['mægnə,tuːd, -,tjuːd] *n* **1** GREATNESS : magnitud *f,* grandeza *f* **2** QUANTITY : cantidad *f* **3** IMPORTANCE : magnitud *f,* envergadura *f*
magnolia [mæg'noːljə] *n* : magnolia *f* (flor), magnolio *m* (árbol)
magpie ['mæg,paɪ] *n* : urraca *f*
mahogany [mə'hɑgəni] *n, pl* **-nies** : caoba *f*
maid ['meɪd] *n* **1** MAIDEN : doncella *f* **2** *or* **maidservant** ['meɪd,sərvənt] : sirvienta *f,* muchacha *f,* mucama *f,* criada *f*
maiden[1] ['meɪdən] *adj* **1** UNMARRIED : soltera **2** FIRST : primero <maiden voyage : primera travesía>
maiden[2] *n* : doncella *f*
maidenhood ['meɪdən,hʊd] *n* : doncellez *f*
maiden name *n* : nombre *m* de soltera
mail[1] ['meɪl] *vt* : enviar por correo, echar al correo
mail[2] *n* **1** : correo *m* <airmail : correo aéreo> **2** : malla *f* <coat of mail : cota de malla>
mailbox ['meɪl,bɑks] *n* : buzón *m*
mailman ['meɪl,mæn, -mən] *n, pl* **-men** [-mən, -,mɛn] : cartero *m*
maim ['meɪm] *vt* : mutilar, desfigurar, lisiar
main[1] ['meɪn] *adj* : principal, central <the main office : la oficina central>
main[2] *n* **1** HIGH SEAS : alta mar *f* **2** : tubería *f* principal (de agua o gas), cable *m* principal (de un circuito) **3 with might and main** : con todas sus fuerzas
mainframe ['meɪn,freɪm] *n* : mainframe *m,* computadora *f* central
mainland ['meɪn,lænd, -lənd] *n* : continente *m*
mainly ['meɪnli] *adv* **1** PRINCIPALLY : principalmente, en primer lugar **2** MOSTLY : principalmente, en la mayor parte
mainstay ['meɪn,steɪ] *n* : pilar *m,* sostén *m* principal
mainstream[1] ['meɪn,striːm] *adj* : dominante, corriente, convencional
mainstream[2] *n* : corriente *f* principal
maintain [meɪn'teɪn] *vt* **1** SERVICE : dar mantenimiento a (una máquina) **2** PRESERVE : mantener, conservar <to maintain silence : guardar silencio> **3** SUPPORT : mantener, sostener **4** ASSERT : mantener, sostener, afirmar
maintenance ['meɪntənənts] *n* : mantenimiento *m*
maize ['meɪz] *n* : maíz *m*
majestic [mə'dʒɛstɪk] *adj* : majestuoso — **majestically** [-tɪkli] *adv*
majesty ['mædʒəsti] *n, pl* **-ties 1** : majestad *f* <Your Majesty : su Majestad> **2** SPLENDOR : majestuosidad *f,* esplendor *m*
major[1] ['meɪdʒər] *vi* **-jored; -joring** : especializarse

major[2] *adj* **1** GREATER : mayor **2** NOTEWORTHY : mayor, notable **3** SERIOUS : grave **4** : mayor (en la música)
major[3] *n* **1** : mayor *mf,* comandante *mf* (en las fuerzas armadas) **2** : especialidad *f* (universitaria)
Majorcan [mɑˈdʒɔrkən, mə-, -ˈjɔr-] *n* : mallorquín *m,* -quina *f* — **Majorcan** *adj*
major general *n* : general *mf* de división
majority [məˈdʒɔrət̬i] *n, pl* **-ties 1** ADULTHOOD : mayoría *f* de edad **2** : mayoría *f,* mayor parte *f* <the vast majority : la inmensa mayoría>
make[1] [ˈmeɪk] *v* **made** [ˈmeɪd]; **making** *vt* **1** CREATE : hacer <to make noise : hacer ruido> **2** FASHION, MANUFACTURE : hacer, fabricar <she made a dress : hizo un vestido> **3** DEVISE, FORM : desarrollar, elaborar, formar **4** CONSTITUTE : hacer, constituir <made of stone : hecho de piedra> **5** PREPARE : hacer, preparar **6** RENDER : hacer, poner <it makes him nervous : lo pone nervioso> <to make someone happy : hacer feliz a alguien> <it made me sad : me dio pena> **7** PERFORM : hacer <to make a gesture : hacer un gesto> **8** COMPEL : hacer, forzar, obligar **9** EARN : ganar <to make a living : ganarse la vida> — *vi* **1** HEAD : ir, dirigirse <we made for home : nos fuimos a casa> **2 to make do** : arreglárselas **3 to make good** REPAY : pagar **4 to make good** SUCCEED : tener éxito
make[2] *n* BRAND : marca *f*
make–believe[1] [ˌmeɪkbəˈliːv] *adj* : imaginario
make–believe[2] *n* : fantasía *f,* invención *f* <a world of make-believe : un mundo de ensueño>
make out *vt* **1** WRITE : hacer (un cheque) **2** DISCERN : distinguir, divisar **3** UNDERSTAND : comprender, entender — *vi* : arreglárselas <how did you make out? : ¿qué tal te fue?>
maker [ˈmeɪkər] *n* : fabricante *mf*
makeshift [ˈmeɪkˌʃɪft] *adj* : provisional, improvisado
makeup [ˈmeɪkˌʌp] *n* **1** COMPOSITION : composición *f* **2** CHARACTER : carácter *m,* temperamento *m* **3** COSMETICS : maquillaje *m*
make up *vt* **1** INVENT : inventar **2** : recuperar <she made up the time : recuperó las horas perdidas> — *vi* RECONCILE : hacer las paces, reconciliarse
maladjusted [ˌmæləˈdʒʌstəd] *adj* : inadaptado
malady [ˈmælədi] *n, pl* **-dies** : dolencia *f,* enfermedad *f,* mal *m*
malaise [məˈleɪz, mæ-] *n* : malestar *m*
malapropism [ˈmæləˌprɑˌpɪzəm] *n* : uso *m* incorrecto y cómico de una palabra
malaria [məˈlɛriə] *n* : malaria *f,* paludismo *m*
malarkey [məˈlɑrki] *n* : tonterías *fpl,* estupideces *fpl*
Malawian [məˈlɑwiən] *n* : malauiano *m,* -na *f* — **Malawian** *adj*
Malay [məˈleɪ, ˈmeɪˌleɪ] *n* **1** *or* **Malayan** [məˈleɪən, meɪ-; ˈmeɪˌleɪən] : malayo *m,* -ya *f* **2** : malayo *m* (idioma) — **Malay** *or* **Malayan** *adj*
male[1] [ˈmeɪl] *adj* **1** : macho **2** MASCULINE : masculino
male[2] *n* : macho *m* (de animales o plantas), varón *m* (de personas)
malefactor [ˈmæləˌfæktər] *n* : malhechor *m,* -chora *f*
maleness [ˈmeɪlnəs] *n* : masculinidad *f*
malevolence [məˈlɛvələnts] *n* : malevolencia *f*
malevolent [məˈlɛvələnt] *adj* : malévolo
malformation [ˌmælfɔrˈmeɪʃən] *n* : malformación *f*
malformed [mælˈfɔrmd] *adj* : mal formado, deforme
malfunction[1] [mælˈfʌŋkʃən] *vi* : funcionar mal
malfunction[2] *n* : mal funcionamiento *m*
malice [ˈmælɪs] *n* **1** : malicia *f,* malevolencia *f* **2 with malice aforethought** : con premeditación
malicious [məˈlɪʃəs] *adj* : malicioso, malévolo — **maliciously** *adv*
malign[1] [məˈlaɪn] *vt* : calumniar, difamar
malign[2] *adj* : maligno
malignancy [məˈlɪgnəntsi] *n, pl* **-cies** : malignidad *f*
malignant [məˈlɪgnənt] *adj* : maligno
malinger [məˈlɪŋgər] *vi* : fingirse enfermo
malingerer [məˈlɪŋgərər] *n* : uno que se finge enfermo
mall [ˈmɔl] *n* **1** PROMENADE : alameda *f,* paseo *m* (arbolado) **2** : centro *m* comercial <shopping mall : galería comercial>
mallard [ˈmælərd] *n, pl* **-lard** *or* **-lards** : pato *m* real, ánade *mf* real
malleable [ˈmæliəbəl] *adj* : maleable
mallet [ˈmælət] *n* : mazo *m*
malnourished [mælˈnərɪʃt] *adj* : desnutrido, malnutrido
malnutrition [ˌmælnʊˈtrɪʃən, -njʊ-] *n* : desnutrición *f,* malnutrición *f*
malodorous [mælˈoːdərəs] *adj* : maloliente
malpractice [ˌmælˈpræktəs] *n* : mala práctica *f,* negligencia *f*
malt [ˈmɔlt] *n* : malta *f*
maltreat [mælˈtriːt] *vt* : maltratar
mama *or* **mamma** [ˈmɑmə] *n* : mamá *f*
mammal [ˈmæməl] *n* : mamífero *m*
mammalian [məˈmeɪliən, mæ-] *adj* : mamífero
mammary [ˈmæməri] *adj* **1** : mamario **2 mammary gland** : glándula mamaria

mammogram ['mæmə,græm] *n* : mamografía *f*
mammoth[1] ['mæməθ] *adj* : colosal, gigantesco
mammoth[2] *n* : mamut *m*
man[1] ['mæn] *vt* **manned; manning** : tripular (un barco o avión), encargarse de (un servicio)
man[2] *n, pl* **men** ['mɛn] **1** PERSON : hombre *m,* persona *f* **2** MALE : hombre *m* **3** MANKIND : humanidad *f*
manacles ['mænɪkəlz] *npl* HANDCUFFS : esposas *fpl*
manage ['mænɪdʒ] *v* **-aged; -aging** *vt* **1** HANDLE : controlar, manejar **2** DIRECT : administrar, dirigir **3** CONTRIVE : lograr, ingeniárselas para — *vi* COPE : arreglárselas
manageable ['mænɪdʒəbəl] *adj* : manejable
management ['mænɪdʒmənt] *n* **1** DIRECTION : administración *f,* gestión *f,* dirección *f* **2** HANDLING : manejo *m* **3** MANAGERS : dirección *f,* gerencia *f*
manager ['mænɪdʒər] *n* : director *m,* -tora *f;* gerente *mf;* administrador *m,* -dora *f*
managerial [,mænə'dʒɪriəl] *adj* : directivo, gerencial
mandarin ['mændərən] *n* **1** : mandarín *m* **2** *or* **mandarin orange** : mandarina *f*
mandate ['mæn,deɪt] *n* : mandato *m*
mandatory ['mændə,tori] *adj* : obligatorio
mandible ['mændəbəl] *n* : mandíbula *f*
mandolin [,mændə'lɪn, 'mændələn] *n* : mandolina *f*
mane ['meɪn] *n* : crin *f* (de un caballo), melena *f* (de un león o una persona)
maneuver[1] [mə'nu:vər, -'nju:-] *vt* **1** PLACE, POSITION : maniobrar, posicionar, colocar **2** MANIPULATE : manipular, maniobrar — *vi* : maniobrar
maneuver[2] *n* : maniobra *f*
manfully ['mænfəli] *adj* : valientemente
manganese ['mæŋgə,ni:z, -,ni:s] *n* : manganeso *m*
mange ['meɪndʒ] *n* : sarna *f*
manger ['meɪndʒər] *n* : pesebre *m*
mangle ['mæŋgəl] *vt* **-gled; -gling 1** CRUSH, DESTROY : aplastar, despedazar, destrozar **2** MUTILATE : mutilar <to mangle a text : mutilar un texto>
mango ['mæŋ,go:] *n, pl* **-goes** : mango *m*
mangrove ['mæn,gro:v, 'mæŋ-] *n* : mangle *m*
mangy ['meɪndʒi] *adj* **mangier; -est 1** : sarnoso **2** SHABBY : gastoso
manhandle ['mæn,hændəl] *vi* **-dled; -dling** : maltratar, tratar con poco cuidado
manhole ['mæn,ho:l] *n* : boca *f* de alcantarilla
manhood ['mæn,hʊd] *n* **1** : madurez *f* (de un hombre) **2** COURAGE, MANLINESS : hombría *f,* valor *m* **3** MEN : hombres *mpl*
manhunt ['mæn,hʌnt] *n* : búsqueda *f* (de un criminal)
mania ['meɪniə, -njə] *n* : manía *f*
maniac ['meɪni,æk] *n* : maníaco *m,* -ca *f;* maniático *m,* -ca *f*
maniacal [mə'naɪəkəl] *adj* : maníaco, maniaco
manicure[1] ['mænə,kjʊr] *vt* **-cured; -curing 1** : hacer la manicura a **2** TRIM : recortar
manicure[2] *n* : manicura *f*
manicurist ['mænə,kjʊrɪst] *n* : manicuro *m,* -ra *f*
manifest[1] ['mænə,fɛst] *vt* : manifestar
manifest[2] *adj* : manifiesto, patente — **manifestly** *adv*
manifestation [,mænəfə'steɪʃən] *n* : manifestación *f*
manifesto [,mænə'fɛs,to:] *n, pl* **-tos** *or* **-toes** : manifiesto *m*
manifold[1] ['mænə,fo:ld] *adj* : diverso, variado
manifold[2] *n* : colector *m* (de escape)
manipulate [mə'nɪpjə,leɪt] *vt* **-lated; -lating** : manipular
manipulation [mə,nɪpjə'leɪʃən] *n* : manipulación *f*
manipulative [mə'nɪpjə,leɪt̬ɪv, -lət̬ɪv] *adj* : manipulador
mankind ['mæn'kaɪnd, ,kaɪnd] *n* : género *m* humano, humanidad *f*
manliness ['mænlinəs] *n* : hombría *f,* masculinidad *f*
manly ['mænli] *adj* **-lier; -est** : varonil, viril
man–made ['mæn'meɪd] *adj* : artificial <man-made fabrics : telas sintéticas>
manna ['mænə] *n* : maná *m*
mannequin ['mænɪkən] *n* **1** DUMMY : maniquí *m* **2** MODEL : modelo *mf*
manner ['mænər] *n* **1** KIND, SORT : tipo *m,* clase *f* **2** WAY : manera *f,* modo *m* **3** STYLE : estilo *m* (artístico) **4 manners** *npl* CUSTOMS : costumbres *fpl* <Victorian manners : costumbres victorianas> **5 manners** *npl* ETIQUETTE : modales *mpl,* educación *f,* etiqueta *f* <good manners : buenos modales>
mannered ['mænərd] *adj* **1** AFFECTED, ARTIFICIAL : amanerado, afectado **2 well–mannered** : educado, cortés **3** → **ill–mannered**
mannerism ['mænə,rɪzəm] *n* : peculiaridad *f,* gesto *m* particular
mannerly ['mænərli] *adj* : cortés, bien educado
mannish ['mænɪʃ] *adj* : masculino, hombruno
man–of–war [,mænə'wɔr, -əv'wɔr] *n, pl* **men–of–war** [,mɛn-] WARSHIP : buque *m* de guerra
manor ['mænər] *n* **1** : casa *f* solariega, casa *f* señorial **2** ESTATE : señorío *m*

manpower [ˈmæn,paʊər] *n* : personal *m,* mano *f* de obra
mansion [ˈmæntʃən] *n* : mansión *f*
manslaughter [ˈmæn,slɔt̬ər] *n* : homicidio *m* sin premeditación
mantel [ˈmæntəl] *n* : repisa *f* de chimenea
mantelpiece [ˈmæntəl,piːs] → **mantel**
mantis [ˈmæntəs] *n, pl* **-tises** *or* **-tes** [ˈmæn,tiːz] : mantis *f* religiosa
mantle [ˈmæntəl] *n* : manto *m*
manual[1] [ˈmænjʊəl] *adj* : manual — **manually** *adv*
manual[2] *n* : manual *m*
manufacture[1] [,mænjəˈfæktʃər] *vt* **-tured; -turing** : fabricar, manufacturar, confeccionar (ropa), elaborar (comestibles)
manufacture[2] *n* : manufactura *f,* fabricación *f,* confección *f* (de ropa), elaboración *f* (de comestibles)
manufacturer [,mænjəˈfæktʃərər] *n* : fabricante *m;* manufacturero *m,* -ra *f*
manure [məˈnʊr, -ˈnjʊr] *n* : estiércol *m*
manuscript [ˈmænjə,skrɪpt] *n* : manuscrito *m*
many[1] [ˈmɛni] *adj* **more** [ˈmor]; **most** [ˈmoːst] : muchos
many[2] *pron* : muchos *pl,* -chas *pl*
map[1] [ˈmæp] *vt* **mapped; mapping 1** : trazar el mapa de **2** PLAN : planear, proyectar <to map out a program : planear un programa>
map[2] *n* : mapa *m*
maple [ˈmeɪpəl] *n* : arce *m*
mar [ˈmɑr] *vt* **marred; marring 1** SPOIL : estropear, echar a perder **2** DEFACE : desfigurar
maraschino [,mærəˈskiːnoː, -ˈʃiː-] *n, pl* **-nos** : cereza *f* al marrasquino
marathon [ˈmærə,θɑn] *n* **1** RACE : maratón *m* **2** CONTEST : competencia *f* de resistencia
maraud [məˈrɔd] *vi* : merodear
marauder [məˈrɔdər] *n* : merodeador *m,* -dora *f*
marble [ˈmɑrbəl] *n* **1** : mármol *m* **2** : canica *f* <to play marbles : jugar a las canicas>
march[1] [ˈmɑrtʃ] *vi* **1** : marchar, desfilar <they marched past the grandstand : desfilaron ante la tribuna> **2** : caminar con resolución <she marched right up to him : se le acercó sin vacilación>
march[2] *n* **1** MARCHING : marcha *f* **2** PASSAGE : paso *m* (del tiempo) **3** PROGRESS : avance *m,* progreso *m* **4** : marcha *f* (en música)
March [ˈmɑrtʃ] *n* : marzo *m*
marchioness [ˈmɑrʃənɪs] *n* : marquesa *f*
Mardi Gras [ˈmɑrdi,grɑ] *n* : martes *m* de Carnaval
mare [ˈmær] *n* : yegua *f*
margarine [ˈmɑrdʒərən] *n* : margarina *f*
margin [ˈmɑrdʒən] *n* : margen *m*
marginal [ˈmɑrdʒənəl] *adj* **1** : marginal **2** MINIMAL : mínimo — **marginally** *adv*
marigold [ˈmærə,goːld] *n* : maravilla *f,* caléndula *f*
marijuana [,mærəˈhwɑnə] *n* : marihuana *f*
marina [məˈriːnə] *n* : puerto *m* deportivo
marinate [ˈmærə,neɪt] *vt* **-nated; -nating** : marinar
marine[1] [məˈriːn] *adj* **1** : marino <marine life : vida marina> **2** NAUTICAL : náutico, marítimo **3** : de la infantería de marina
marine[2] *n* : soldado *m* de marina
mariner [ˈmærɪnər] *n* : marinero *m,* marino *m*
marionette [,mæriəˈnɛt] *n* : marioneta *f,* títere *m*
marital [ˈmærət̬əl] *adj* **1** : matrimonial **2 marital status** : estado *m* civil
maritime [ˈmærə,taɪm] *adj* : marítimo
marjoram [ˈmɑrdʒərəm] *n* : mejorana *f*
mark[1] [ˈmɑrk] *vt* **1** : marcar **2** CHARACTERIZE : caracterizar **3** SIGNAL : señalar **4** NOTICE : prestar atención a, hacer caso de **5 to mark off** : demarcar, delimitar
mark[2] *n* **1** TARGET : blanco *m* **2** : marca *f,* señal *f* <put a mark where you left off : pon una señal donde terminaste> **3** INDICATION : señal *f,* indicio *m* **4** GRADE : nota *f* **5** IMPRINT : huella *f,* marca *f* **6** BLEMISH : marca *f,* imperfección *f*
marked [ˈmɑrkt] *adj* : marcado, notable — **markedly** [ˈmɑrkədli] *adv*
marker [ˈmɑrkər] *n* : marcador *m*
market[1] [ˈmɑrkət] *vt* : poner en venta, comercializar
market[2] *n* **1** MARKETPLACE : mercado *m* <the open market : el mercado libre> **2** DEMAND : demanda *f,* mercado *m* **3** STORE : tienda *f* **4** → **stock market**
marketable [ˈmɑrkət̬əbəl] *adj* : vendible
marketplace [ˈmɑrkət,pleɪs] *n* : mercado *m*
marksman [ˈmɑrksmən] *n, pl* **-men** [-mən, -,mɛn] : tirador *m*
marksmanship [ˈmɑrksmən,ʃɪp] *n* : puntería *f*
marlin [ˈmɑrlɪn] *n* : marlín *m*
marmalade [ˈmɑrmə,leɪd] *n* : mermelada *f*
marmoset [ˈmɑrmə,sɛt] *n* : tití *m*
marmot [ˈmɑrmət] *n* : marmota *f*
maroon[1] [məˈruːn] *vt* : abandonar, aislar
maroon[2] *n* : rojo *m* oscuro, granate *m*
marquee [mɑrˈkiː] *n* : marquesina *f*
marquess [ˈmɑrkwɪs] *or* **marquis** [ˈmɑrkwɪs, mɑrˈkiː] *n, pl* **-quesses** *or* **-quises** [-ˈkiːz, -ˈkiːzəz] *or* **-quis** [-ˈkiː, -ˈkiːz] : marqués *m*
marquise [mɑrˈkiːz] → **marchioness**

marriage ['mærɪdʒ] *n* **1** : matrimonio *m* **2** WEDDING : casamiento *m,* boda *f*

marriageable ['mærɪdʒəbəl] *adj* **of marriageable age** : de edad de casarse

married ['mærid] *adj* **1** : casado **2 to get married** : casarse

marrow ['mæroː] *n* : médula *f,* tuétano *m*

marry ['mæri] *vt* **-ried; -rying 1** : casar <the priest married them : el cura los casó> **2** : casarse con <she married John : se casó con John>

Mars ['mɑrz] *n* : Marte *m*

marsh ['mɑrʃ] *n* **1** : pantano *m* **2 salt marsh** : marisma *f*

marshal[1] ['mɑrʃəl] *vt* **-shaled** *or* **-shalled; -shaling** *or* **-shalling 1** : poner en orden, reunir **2** USHER : conducir

marshal[2] *n* **1** : maestro *m* de ceremonias **2** : mariscal *m* (en el ejército); jefe *m,* -fa *f* (de la policía, de los bomberos, etc.)

marshmallow ['mɑrʃˌmɛloː, -ˌmæloː] *n* : malvavisco *m*

marshy ['mɑrʃi] *adj* **marshier; -est** : pantanoso

marsupial [mɑr'suːpiəl] *n* : marsupial *m*

mart ['mɑrt] *n* MARKET : mercado *m*

marten ['mɑrtən] *n, pl* **-ten** *or* **-tens** : marta *f*

martial ['mɑrʃəl] *adj* : marcial

martin ['mɑrtən] *n* **1** SWALLOW : golondrina *f* **2** SWIFT : vencejo *m*

martyr[1] ['mɑrtər] *vt* : martirizar

martyr[2] *n* : mártir *mf*

martyrdom ['mɑrtərdəm] *n* : martirio *m*

marvel[1] ['mɑrvəl] *vi* **-veled** *or* **-velled; -veling** *or* **-velling** : maravillarse

marvel[2] *n* : maravilla *f*

marvelous ['mɑrvələs] *or* **marvellous** *adj* : maravilloso — **marvelously** *adv*

Marxism ['mɑrkˌsɪzəm] *n* : marxismo *m*

Marxist[1] ['mɑrksɪst] *adj* : marxista

Marxist[2] *n* : marxista *mf*

mascara [mæs'kærə] *n* : rímel *m,* rimel *m*

mascot ['mæsˌkɑt, -kət] *n* : mascota *f*

masculine ['mæskjələn] *adj* : masculino

masculinity [ˌmæskjə'lɪnəti] *n* : masculinidad *f*

mash[1] ['mæʃ] *vt* **1** : hacer puré de (papas, etc.) **2** CRUSH : aplastar, majar

mash[2] *n* **1** FEED : afrecho *m* **2** : malta *f* (para hacer bebidas alcohólicas) **3** PASTE, PULP : papilla *f,* pasta *f*

mask[1] ['mæsk] *vt* **1** CONCEAL, DISGUISE : enmascarar, ocultar **2** COVER : cubrir, tapar

mask[2] *n* : máscara *f,* careta *f,* mascarilla *f* (de un cirujano o dentista)

masochism ['mæsəˌkɪzəm, 'mæzə-] *n* : masoquismo *m*

masochist ['mæsəˌkɪst, 'mæzə-] *n* : masoquista *mf*

masochistic [ˌmæsə'kɪstɪk, ˌmæzə-] *adj* : masoquista

mason ['meɪsən] *n* **1** BRICKLAYER : albañil *mf* **2** *or* **stonemason** ['stoːnˌ-] : mampostero *m,* cantero *m*

masonry ['meɪsənri] *n, pl* **-ries 1** BRICKLAYING : albañería *f* **2** *or* **stonemasonry** ['stoːnˌ-] : mampostería *f*

masquerade[1] [ˌmæskə'reɪd] *vi* **-aded; -ading 1** : disfrazarse (de), hacerse pasar (por) **2** : asistir a una mascarada

masquerade[2] *n* **1** : mascarada *f,* baile *m* de disfraces **2** FACADE : farsa *f,* fachada *f*

mass[1] ['mæs] *vi* : concentrarse, juntarse en masa — *vt* : concentrar

mass[2] *n* **1** : masa *f* <atomic mass : masa atómica> **2** BULK : mole *f,* volumen *m* **3** MULTITUDE : cantidad *f,* montón *m* (de cosas), multitud *f* (de gente) **4 the masses** : las masas, el pueblo, el populacho

Mass ['mæs] *n* : misa *f*

massacre[1] ['mæsɪkər] *vt* **-cred; -cring** : masacrar

massacre[2] *n* : masacre *f*

massage[1] [mə'sɑʒ, -'sɑdʒ] *vt* **-saged; -saging** : masajear

massage[2] *n* : masaje *m*

masseur [mæ'sər] *n* : masajista *m*

masseuse [mæ'søz, -'suːz] *n* : masajista *f*

massive ['mæsɪv] *adj* **1** BULKY : voluminoso, macizo **2** HUGE : masivo, enorme — **massively** *adv*

mast ['mæst] *n* : mástil *m,* palo *m*

master[1] ['mæstər] *vt* **1** SUBDUE : dominar **2** : llegar a dominar <she mastered French : llegó a dominar el francés>

master[2] *n* **1** TEACHER : maestro *m,* profesor *m* **2** EXPERT : experto *m,* -ta *f;* maestro *m,* -tra *f* **3** : amo *m* (de animales o esclavos), señor *m* (de la casa) **4 master's degree** : maestría *f*

masterful ['mæstərfəl] *adj* **1** IMPERIOUS : autoritario, imperioso, dominante **2** SKILLFUL : magistral — **masterfully** *adv*

masterly ['mæstərli] *adj* : magistral

masterpiece ['mæstərˌpiːs] *n* : obra *f* maestra

masterwork ['mæstərˌwərk] → **masterpiece**

mastery ['mæstəri] *n* **1** DOMINION : dominio *m,* autoridad *f* **2** SUPERIORITY : superioridad *f* **3** EXPERTISE : maestría *f*

masticate ['mæstəˌkeɪt] *v* **-cated; -cating** : masticar

mastiff ['mæstɪf] *n* : mastín *m*

mastodon ['mæstəˌdɑn] *n* : mastodonte *m*

masturbate ['mæstərˌbeɪt] *v* **-bated; bating** *vi* : masturbarse — *vt* : masturbar

masturbation [ˌmæstər'beɪʃən] *n* : masturbación *f*

mat¹ [ˈmæt] *v* **matted; matting** *vt* TANGLE : enmarañar — *vi* : enmarañarse

mat² *n* **1** : estera *f* **2** TANGLE : maraña *f* **3** PAD : colchoneta *f* (de gimnasia) **4** *or* **matt** *or* **matte** [ˈmæt] FRAME : marco *m* (de cartón)

mat³ → **matte**

matador [ˈmæṭəˌdɔr] *n* : matador *m*

match¹ [ˈmætʃ] *vt* **1** PIT : enfrentar, oponer **2** EQUAL, FIT : igualar, corresponder a, coincidir con **3** : combinar con, hacer juego con <her shoes match her dress : sus zapatos hacen juego con su vestido> — *vi* **1** CORRESPOND : concordar, coincidir **2** : hacer juego <with a tie to match : con una corbata que hace juego>

match² *n* **1** EQUAL : igual *mf* <he's no match for her : no puede competir con ella> **2** FIGHT, GAME : partido *m*, combate *m* (en boxeo) **3** MARRIAGE : matrimonio *m*, casamiento *m* **4** : fósforo *m*, cerilla *f*, cerillo *m* (*in various countries*) <he lit a match : encendió un fósforo> **5 to be a good match** : hacer buena pareja (dícese de las personas), hacer juego (dícese de la ropa)

matchless [ˈmætʃləs] *adj* : sin igual, sin par

matchmaker [ˈmætʃˌmeɪkər] *n* : casamentero *m*, -ra *f*

mate¹ [ˈmeɪt] *v* **mated; mating** *vi* **1** FIT : encajar **2** PAIR : emparejarse **3** (*relating to animals*) : aparearse, copular — *vt* : aparear, acoplar (animales)

mate² *n* **1** COMPANION : compañero *m*, -ra *f*; camarada *mf* **2** : macho *m*, hembra *f* (de animales) **3** : oficial *mf* (de un barco) <first mate : primer oficial> **4** : compañero *m*, -ra *f*; pareja *f* (de un zapato, etc.)

material¹ [məˈtɪriəl] *adj* **1** PHYSICAL : material, físico <the material world : el mundo material> <material needs : necesidades materiales> **2** IMPORTANT : importante, esencial **3 material evidence** : prueba *f* sustancial

material² *n* **1** : material *m* **2** CLOTH : tejido *m*, tela *f*

materialism [məˈtɪriəˌlɪzəm] *n* : materialismo *m*

materialist [məˈtɪriəlɪst] *n* : materialista *mf*

materialistic [məˌtɪriəˈlɪstɪk] *adj* : materialista

materialize [məˈtɪriəˌlaɪz] *v* **-ized; -izing** *vt* : materializar, hacer aparecer — *vi* : materializarse, aparecer

maternal [məˈtərnəl] *adj* MOTHERLY : maternal — **maternally** *adv*

maternity¹ [məˈtərnəṭi] *adj* : de maternidad <maternity clothes : ropa de futura mamá> <maternity leave : licencia por maternidad>

maternity² *n, pl* **-ties** : maternidad *f*

math [ˈmæθ] → **mathematics**

mathematical [ˌmæθəˈmæṭɪkəl] *adj* : matemático — **mathematically** *adv*

mathematician [ˌmæθəməˈtɪʃən] *n* : matemático *m*, -ca *f*

mathematics [ˌmæθəˈmæṭɪks] *ns & pl* : matemáticas *fpl*, matemática *f*

matinee *or* **matinée** [ˌmætənˈeɪ] *n* : matiné *f*

matriarch [ˈmeɪtriˌɑrk] *n* : matriarca *f*

matriarchy [ˈmeɪtriˌɑrki] *n, pl* **-chies** : matriarcado *m*

matriculate [məˈtrɪkjəˌleɪt] *v* **-lated; -lating** *vt* : matricular — *vi* : matricularse

matriculation [məˌtrɪkjəˈleɪʃən] *n* : matrícula *f*, matriculación *f*

matrimony [ˈmætrəˌmoːni] *n* : matrimonio *m* — **matrimonial** [ˌmætrəˈmoːniəl] *adj*

matrix [ˈmeɪtrɪks] *n, pl* **-trices** [ˈmeɪtrəˌsiːz, ˈmæ-] *or* **-trixes** [ˈmeɪtrɪksəz] : matriz *f*

matron [ˈmeɪtrən] *n* : matrona *f*

matronly [ˈmeɪtrənli] *adj* : de matrona, matronal

matte [ˈmæt] *adj* : mate, de acabado mate

matter¹ [ˈmæṭər] *vi* : importar <it doesn't matter : no importa>

matter² *n* **1** QUESTION : asunto *m*, cuestión *f* <a matter of taste : una cuestión de gusto> **2** SUBSTANCE : materia *f*, sustancia *f* **3 matters** *npl* CIRCUMSTANCES : situación *f*, cosas *fpl* <to make matters worse : para colmo de males> **4 to be the matter** : pasar <what's the matter? : ¿qué pasa?> **5 as a matter of fact** : en efecto, en realidad **6 for that matter** : de hecho **7 no matter how much** : por mucho que

matter–of–fact [ˈmæṭərəvˈfækt] *adj* : práctico, realista

mattress [ˈmætrəs] *n* : colchón *m*

mature¹ [məˈtʊr, -ˈtjʊr, -ˈtʃʊr] *vi* **-tured; -turing 1** : madurar **2** : vencer <when does the loan mature? : ¿cuándo vence el préstamo?>

mature² *adj* **-turer; -est 1** : maduro **2** DUE : vencido

maturity [məˈtʊrəṭi, -ˈtjʊr-, -ˈtʃʊr-] *n* : madurez *f*

maudlin [ˈmɔdlɪn] *adj* : sensiblero

maul¹ [ˈmɔl] *vt* **1** BEAT : golpear, pegar **2** MANGLE : mutilar **3** MANHANDLE : maltratar

maul² *n* MALLET : mazo *m*

Mauritanian [ˌmɔrəˈteɪniən] *n* : mauritano *m*, -na *f* — **Mauritanian** *adj*

mausoleum [ˌmɔsəˈliːəm, ˌmɔzə-] *n, pl* **-leums** *or* **-lea** [-ˈliːə] : mausoleo *m*

mauve [ˈmoːv, ˈmɔv] *n* : malva *m*

maven *or* **mavin** [ˈmeɪvən] *n* EXPERT : experto *m*, -ta *f*

maverick [ˈmævrɪk, ˈmævə-] *n* **1** : ternero *m* sin marcar **2** NONCONFORMIST : inconformista *mf*, disidente *mf*

mawkish [ˈmɔkɪʃ] *adj* : sensiblero

maxim [ˈmæksəm] *n* : máxima *f*

maximize [ˈmæksəˌmaɪz] *vt* **-mized; -mizing** : maximizar, llevar al máximo
maximum[1] [ˈmæksəməm] *adj* : máximo
maximum[2] *n, pl* **-ma** [ˈmæksəmə] *or* **-mums** : máximo *m*
may [ˈmeɪ] *v aux, past* **might** [ˈmaɪt]; *present s & pl* **may 1** (*expressing permission*) : poder <you may go : puedes ir> **2** (*expressing possibility or probability*) : poder <you may be right : puede que tengas razón> <it may happen occasionally : puede pasar de vez en cuando> **3** (*expressing desires, intentions, or contingencies*) <may the best man win : que gane el mejor> <I laugh that I may not weep : me río para no llorar> <come what may : pase lo que pase>
May [ˈmeɪ] *n* : mayo *m*
maybe [ˈmeɪbi] *adv* PERHAPS : quizás, tal vez
mayfly [ˈmeɪˌflaɪ] *n, pl* **-flies** : efímera *f*
mayhem [ˈmeɪˌhɛm, ˈmeɪəm] *n* **1** MUTILATION : mutilación *f* **2** DEVASTATION : estragos *mpl*
mayonnaise [ˈmeɪəˌneɪz] *n* : mayonesa *f*
mayor [ˈmeɪər, ˈmɛr] *n* : alcalde *m*, -desa *f*
mayoral [ˈmeɪərəl, ˈmɛrəl] *adj* : de alcalde
maze [ˈmeɪz] *n* : laberinto *m*
me [ˈmiː] *pron* **1** : me <she called me : me llamó> <give it to me : dámelo> **2** (*after a preposition*) : mí <for me : para mí> <with me : conmigo> **3** (*after conjunctions and verbs*) : yo <it's me : soy yo> <as big as me : tan grande como yo> **4** (*emphatic use*) : yo <me, too! : ¡yo también!> <who, me? : ¿quién, yo?>
meadow [ˈmɛdoː] *n* : prado *m*, pradera *f*
meadowland [ˈmɛdoˌlænd] *n* : pradera *f*
meadowlark [ˈmɛdoˌlɑrk] *n* : pájaro *m* cantor con el pecho amarillo
meager *or* **meagre** [ˈmiːgər] *adj* **1** THIN : magro, flaco **2** POOR, SCANTY : exiguo, escaso, pobre
meagerly [ˈmiːgərli] *adv* : pobremente
meagerness [ˈmiːgərnəs] *n* : escasez *f*, pobreza *f*
meal [ˈmiːl] *n* **1** : comida *f* <a hearty meal : una comida sustanciosa> **2** : harina *f* (de maíz, etc.)
mealtime [ˈmiːlˌtaɪm] *n* : hora *f* de comer
mean[1] [ˈmiːn] *vt* **meant** [ˈmɛnt]; **meaning 1** INTEND : querer, pensar, tener la intención de <I didn't mean to do it : lo hice sin querer> <what do you mean to do? : ¿qué piensas hacer?> **2** SIGNIFY : querer decir, significar <what does that mean? : ¿qué quiere decir eso?> **3** : importar <health means everything : lo que más importa es la salud>
mean[2] *adj* **1** HUMBLE : humilde **2** NEGLIGIBLE : despreciable <it's no mean feat : no es poca cosa> **3** STINGY : mezquino, tacaño **4** CRUEL : malo, cruel <to be mean to someone : tratar mal a alguien> **5** AVERAGE, MEDIAN : medio
mean[3] *n* **1** MIDPOINT : término *m* medio **2** AVERAGE : promedio *m*, media *f* aritmética **3 means** *npl* WAY : medio *m*, manera *f*, vía *f* **4 means** *npl* RESOURCES : medios *mpl*, recursos *mpl* **5 by all means** : por supuesto, cómo no **6 by means of** : por medio de **7 by no means** : de ninguna manera, de ningún modo
meander [miˈændər] *vi* **-dered; -dering 1** WIND : serpentear **2** WANDER : vagar, andar sin rumbo fijo
meaning [ˈmiːnɪŋ] *n* **1** : significado *m*, sentido *m* <double meaning : doble sentido> **2** INTENT : intención *f*, propósito *m*
meaningful [ˈmiːnɪŋfəl] *adj* : significativo — **meaningfully** *adv*
meaningless [ˈmiːnɪŋləs] *adj* : sin sentido
meanness [ˈmiːnnəs] *n* **1** CRUELTY : crueldad *f*, mezquindad *f* **2** STINGINESS : tacañería *f*
meantime[1] [ˈmiːnˌtaɪm] *adv* → **meanwhile[1]**
meantime[2] *n* **1** : interín *m* **2 in the meantime** : entretanto, mientras tanto
meanwhile[1] [ˈmiːnˌ*h*waɪl] *adv* : entretanto, mientras tanto
meanwhile[2] *n* → **meantime[2]**
measles [ˈmiːzəlz] *ns & pl* : sarampión *m*
measly [ˈmiːzli] *adj* **-slier; -est** : miserable, mezquino
measurable [ˈmɛʒərəbəl, ˈmeɪ-] *adj* : mensurable — **measurably** [-bli] *adv*
measure[1] [ˈmɛʒər, ˈmeɪ-] *v* **-sured; -suring** : medir <he measured the table : midió la mesa> <it measures 15 feet tall : mide 15 pies de altura>
measure[2] *n* **1** AMOUNT : medida *f*, cantidad *f* <in large measure : en gran medida> <a full measure : una cantidad exacta> <a measure of proficiency : una cierta competencia> <for good measure : de ñapa, por añadidura> **2** DIMENSIONS, SIZE : medida *f*, tamaño *m* **3** RULER : regla *f* <tape measure : cinta métrica> **4** MEASUREMENT : medida *f* <cubic measure : medida de capacidad> **5** MEASURING : medición *f* **6 measures** *npl* : medidas *fpl* <security measures : medidas de seguridad>
measureless [ˈmɛʒərləs, ˈmeɪ-] *adj* : inmensurable
measurement [ˈmɛʒərmənt, ˈmeɪ-] *n* **1** MEASURING : medición *f* **2** DIMENSION : medida *f*

measure up *vi* **to measure up to :** estar a la altura de

meat [ˈmiːt] *n* **1** FOOD : comida *f* **2** : carne *f* <meat and fish : carne y pescado> **3** SUBSTANCE : sustancia *f,* esencia *f* <the meat of the story : la sustancia del cuento>

meatball [ˈmiːtˌbɔl] *n* : albóndiga *f*

meaty [ˈmiːt̬i] *adj* **meatier; -est** : con mucha carne, carnoso

mechanic [mɪˈkænɪk] *n* : mecánico *m,* -ca *f*

mechanical [mɪˈkænɪkəl] *adj* : mecánico — **mechanically** *adv*

mechanics [mɪˈkænɪks] *ns & pl* **1** : mecánica *f* <fluid mechanics : la mecánica de fluidos> **2** MECHANISMS : mecanismos *mpl,* aspectos *mpl* prácticos

mechanism [ˈmɛkəˌnɪzəm] *n* : mecanismo *m*

mechanization [ˌmɛkənəˈzeɪʃən] *n* : mecanización *f*

mechanize [ˈmɛkəˌnaɪz] *vt* **-nized; -nizing** : mecanizar

medal [ˈmɛdəl] *n* : medalla *f,* condecoración *f*

medalist [ˈmɛdəlɪst] *or* **medallist** *n* : medallista *mf*

medallion [məˈdæljən] *n* : medallón *m*

meddle [ˈmɛdəl] *vi* **-dled; -dling** : meterse, entrometerse

meddler [ˈmɛdələr] *n* : entrometido *m,* -da *f*

meddlesome [ˈmɛdəlsəm] *adj* : entrometido

media [ˈmiːdiə] *npl* : medios *mpl* de comunicación

median[1] [ˈmiːdiən] *adj* : medio

median[2] *n* : valor *m* medio

mediate [ˈmiːdiˌeɪt] *vi* **-ated; -ating** : mediar

mediation [ˌmiːdiˈeɪʃən] *n* : mediación *f*

mediator [ˈmiːdiˌeɪt̬ər] *n* : mediador *m,* -dora *f*

medical [ˈmɛdɪkəl] *adj* : médico

medicate [ˈmɛdəˌkeɪt] *vt* **-cated; -cating** : medicar <medicated powder : polvos medicinales>

medication [ˌmɛdəˈkeɪʃən] *n* **1** TREATMENT : tratamiento *m,* medicación *f* **2** MEDICINE : medicamento *m* <to be on medication : estar medicado>

medicinal [məˈdɪsənəl] *adj* : medicinal

medicine [ˈmɛdəsən] *n* **1** MEDICATION : medicina *f,* medicamento *m* **2** : medicina *f* <he's studying medicine : estudia medicina>

medicine man *n* : hechicero *m*

medieval *or* **mediaeval** [mɪˈdiːvəl, ˌmiː-, ˌmɛ-, -diˈiːvəl] *adj* : medieval

mediocre [ˌmiːdiˈoːkər] *adj* : mediocre

mediocrity [ˌmiːdiˈɑkrət̬i] *n, pl* **-ties** : mediocridad *f*

meditate [ˈmɛdəˌteɪt] *vi* **-tated; -tating** : meditar

meditation [ˌmɛdəˈteɪʃən] *n* : meditación *f*

meditative [ˈmɛdəˌteɪt̬ɪv] *adj* : meditabundo

medium[1] [ˈmiːdiəm] *adj* : mediano <of medium height : de estatura mediana, de estatura regular>

medium[2] *n, pl* **-diums** *or* **-dia** [ˈmiːdiə] **1** MEAN : punto *m* medio, término *m* medio <happy medium : justo medio> **2** MEANS : medio *m* **3** SUBSTANCE : medio *m,* sustancia *f* <a viscous medium : un medio viscoso> **4** : medio *m* de comunicación **5** : medio *m* (artístico)

medley [ˈmɛdli] *n, pl* **-leys** : popurrí *m* (de canciones)

meek [ˈmiːk] *adj* **1** LONG-SUFFERING : paciente, sufrido **2** SUBMISSIVE : sumiso, dócil, manso

meekly [ˈmiːkli] *adv* : dócilmente

meekness [ˈmiːknəs] *n* : mansedumbre *f,* docilidad *f*

meet[1] [ˈmiːt] *v* **met** [ˈmɛt]; **meeting** *vt* **1** ENCOUNTER : encontrarse con **2** JOIN : unirse con **3** CONFRONT : enfrentarse a **4** SATISFY : satisfacer, cumplir con <to meet costs : pagar los gastos> **5** : conocer <I met his sister : conocí a su hermana> — *vi* ASSEMBLE : reunirse, congregarse

meet[2] *n* : encuentro *m*

meeting [ˈmiːt̬ɪŋ] *n* **1** : reunión *f* <to open the meeting : abrir la sesión> **2** ENCOUNTER : encuentro *m* **3** : entrevista *f* (formal)

meetinghouse [ˈmiːt̬ɪŋˌhaʊs] *n* : iglesia *f* (de ciertas confesiones protestantes)

megabyte [ˈmɛgəˌbaɪt] *n* : megabyte *m*

megahertz [ˈmɛgəˌhərts, -ˌhɛrts] *n* : megahercio *m*

megaphone [ˈmɛgəˌfoːn] *n* : megáfono *m*

melancholy[1] [ˈmɛlənˌkɑli] *adj* : melancólico, triste, sombrío

melancholy[2] *n, pl* **-cholies** : melancolía *f*

melanoma [ˌmɛləˈnoːmə] *n, pl* **-mas** : melanoma *m*

melee [ˈmeɪˌleɪ, meɪˈleɪ] *n* BRAWL : reyerta *f,* riña *f,* pelea *f*

meliorate [ˈmiːljəˌreɪt, ˈmiːliə-] → **ameliorate**

mellow[1] [ˈmɛloː] *vt* : suavizar, endulzar — *vi* : suavizarse, endulzarse

mellow[2] *adj* **1** RIPE : maduro **2** MILD : apacible <a mellow character : un carácter apacible> <mellow wines : vinos añejos> **3** : suave, dulce <mellow colors : colores suaves> <mellow tones : tonos dulces>

mellowness [ˈmɛlonəs] *n* : suavidad *f,* dulzura *f*

melodic [məˈlɑdɪk] *adj* : melódico — **melodically** [-dɪkli] *adv*

melodious [məˈloːdiəs] *adj* : melodioso — **melodiously** *adv*

melodiousness [mə'loːdiəsnəs] *n* : calidad *f* de melódico

melodrama ['mɛlə͵drɑmə, -͵dræ-] *n* : melodrama *m*

melodramatic [͵mɛlədrə'mæt̬ɪk] *adj* : melodramático — **melodramatically** [-t̬ɪkli] *adv*

melody ['mɛlədi] *n, pl* **-dies** : melodía *f,* tonada *f*

melon ['mɛlən] *n* : melón *m*

melt ['mɛlt] *vt* **1** : derretir, disolver **2** SOFTEN : ablandar <it melted his heart : ablandó su corazón> — *vi* **1** : derretirse, disolverse **2** SOFTEN : ablandarse **3** DISAPPEAR : desvanecerse, esfumarse <the clouds melted away : las nubes se desvanecieron>

melting point *n* : punto *m* de fusión

member ['mɛmbər] *n* **1** LIMB : miembro *m* **2** : miembro *m* (de un grupo); socio *m,* -cia *f* (de un club) **3** PART : miembro *m,* parte *f*

membership ['mɛmbər͵ʃɪp] *n* **1** : membresía *f* <application for membership : solicitud de entrada> **2** MEMBERS : membresía *f,* miembros *mpl,* socios *mpl*

membrane ['mɛm͵breɪn] *n* : membrana *f* — **membranous** ['mɛmbrənəs] *adj*

memento [mɪ'mɛn͵toː] *n, pl* **-tos** *or* **-toes** : recuerdo *m*

memo ['mɛmoː] *n, pl* **memos** : memorándum *m*

memoirs ['mɛm͵wɑrz] *npl* : memorias *fpl,* autobiografía *f*

memorabilia [͵mɛmərə'biliə, -'bɪljə] *npl* **1** : objetos *mpl* de interés histórico **2** MEMENTOS : recuerdos *mpl*

memorable ['mɛmərəbəl] *adj* : memorable, notable — **memorably** [-bli] *adv*

memorandum [͵mɛmə'rændəm] *n, pl* **-dums** *or* **-da** [-də] : memorándum *m*

memorial[1] [mə'moriəl] *adj* : conmemorativo

memorial[2] *n* : monumento *m* conmemorativo

Memorial Day *n* : el último lunes de mayo (observado en Estados Unidos como día feriado para conmemorar a los caídos en guerra)

memorialize [mə'moriə͵laɪz] *vt* **-ized; -izing** COMMEMORATE : conmemorar

memorization [͵mɛmərə'zeɪʃən] *n* : memorización *f*

memorize ['mɛmə͵raɪz] *vt* **-rized; -rizing** : memorizar, aprender de memoria

memory ['mɛmri, 'mɛmə-] *n, pl* **-ries** **1** : memoria *f* <he has a good memory : tiene buena memoria> **2** RECOLLECTION : recuerdo *m* **3** COMMEMORATION : memoria *f,* conmemoración *f*

men → **man**[2]

menace[1] ['mɛnəs] *vt* **-aced; -acing** **1** THREATEN : amenazar **2** ENDANGER : poner en peligro

menace[2] *n* : amenaza *f*

menacing ['mɛnəsɪŋli] *adj* : amenazador, amenazante

menagerie [mə'nædʒəri, -'næʒəri] *n* : colección *f* de animales salvajes

mend[1] ['mɛnd] *vt* **1** CORRECT : enmendar, corregir <to mend one's ways : enmendarse> **2** REPAIR : remendar, arreglar, reparar — *vi* HEAL : curarse

mend[2] *n* : remiendo *m*

mendicant ['mɛndɪkənt] *n* BEGGAR : mendigo *m,* -ga *f*

menhaden [mɛn'heɪdən, mən-] *ns & pl* : pez *m* de la misma familia que los arenques

menial[1] ['miːniəl] *adj* : servil, bajo

menial[2] *n* : sirviente *m,* -ta *f*

meningitis [͵mɛnən'dʒaɪt̬əs] *n, pl* **-gitides** [-'dʒɪt̬ə͵diːz] : meningitis *f*

menopause ['mɛnə͵pɔz] *n* : menopausia *f*

menorah [mə'norə] *n* : candelabro *m* (usado en los oficios religiosos judíos)

menstrual ['mɛn*t*strʊəl] *adj* : menstrual

menstruate ['mɛn*t*strʊ͵eɪt] *vi* **-ated; -ating** : menstruar

menstruation [͵mɛn*t*strʊ'eɪʃən] *n* : menstruación *f*

mental ['mɛntəl] *adj* : mental <mental hospital : hospital psiquiátrico> — **mentally** *adv*

mentality [mɛn'tæləti] *n, pl* **-ties** : mentalidad *f*

menthol ['mɛn͵θɔl, -͵θoːl] *n* : mentol *m*

mentholated [͵mɛn*t*θə͵leɪt̬əd] *adj* : mentolado

mention[1] ['mɛntʃən] *vt* : mencionar, mentar, referirse a <don't mention it! : ¡de nada!, ¡no hay de qué!>

mention[2] *n* : mención *f*

mentor ['mɛn͵tɔr, 'mɛntər] *n* : mentor *m*

menu ['mɛn͵juː] *n* **1** : menú *m,* carta *f* (en un restaurante) **2** : menú *m* (de computadoras)

meow[1] [miː'aʊ] *vi* : maullar

meow[2] *n* : maullido *m,* miau *m*

mercantile ['mərkən͵tiːl, -͵taɪl] *adj* : mercantil

mercenary[1] ['mərsən͵ɛri] *adj* : mercenario

mercenary[2] *n, pl* **-naries** : mercenario *m,* -ria *f*

merchandise ['mərtʃən͵daɪz, -͵daɪs] *n* : mercancía *f,* mercadería *f*

merchandiser ['mərtʃən͵daɪzər] *n* : comerciante *mf;* vendedor *m,* -dora *f*

merchant ['mərtʃənt] *n* : comerciante *mf*

merchant marine *n* : marina *f* mercante

merciful ['mərsɪfəl] *adj* : misericordioso, clemente

mercifully ['mərsɪfli] *adv* **1** : con misericordia, con compasión **2** FORTUNATELY : afortunadamente

merciless [ˈmərsɪləs] *adj* : despiadado — **mercilessly** *adv*
mercurial [ˌmərˈkjʊriəl] *adj* TEMPERAMENTAL : temperamental, volátil
mercury [ˈmərkjəri] *n, pl* **-ries** : mercurio *m*
Mercury *n* : Mercurio *m*
mercy [ˈmərsi] *n, pl* **-cies 1** CLEMENCY : misericordia *f,* clemencia *f* **2** BLESSING : bendición *f*
mere [ˈmɪr] *adj, superlative* **merest** : mero, simple
merely [ˈmɪrli] *adv* : solamente, simplemente
merge [ˈmərdʒ] *v* **merged; merging** *vi* : unirse, fusionarse (dícese de las compañías), confluir (dícese de los ríos, las calles, etc.) — *vt* : unir, fusionar, combinar
merger [ˈmərdʒər] *n* : unión *f,* fusión *f*
meridian [məˈrɪdiən] *n* : meridiano *m*
meringue [məˈræŋ] *n* : merengue *m*
merino [məˈriːno] *n, pl* **-nos 1** : merino *m,* -na *f* **2** *or* **merino wool** : lana *f* merino
merit¹ [ˈmɛrət] *vt* : merecer, ser digno de
merit² *n* : mérito *m,* valor *m*
meritorious [ˌmɛrəˈtoriəs] *adj* : meritorio
mermaid [ˈmərˌmeɪd] *n* : sirena *f*
merriment [ˈmɛrɪmənt] *n* : alegría *f,* júbilo *m,* regocijo *m*
merry [ˈmɛri] *adj* **-rier; -est** : alegre — **merrily** [ˈmɛrəli] *adv*
merry–go–round [ˈmɛrigoˌraʊnd] *n* : carrusel *m,* tiovivo *m*
merrymaker [ˈmɛriˌmeɪkər] *n* : juerguista *mf*
merrymaking [ˈmɛriˌmeɪkɪŋ] *n* : juerga *f*
mesa [ˈmeɪsə] *n* : mesa *f*
mesdames → **madam, Mrs.**
mesh¹ [ˈmɛʃ] *vi* **1** ENGAGE : engranar (dícese de las piezas mecánicas) **2** TANGLE : enredarse **3** COORDINATE : coordinarse, combinar
mesh² *n* **1** : malla *f* <wire mesh : malla metálica> **2** NETWORK : red *f* **3** MESHING : engranaje *m* <in mesh : engranado>
mesmerize [ˈmɛzməˌraɪz] *vt* **-ized; -izing 1** HYPNOTIZE : hipnotizar **2** FASCINATE : cautivar, embelesar, fascinar
mess¹ [ˈmɛs] *vt* **1** SOIL : ensuciar **2 to mess up** DISARRANGE : desordenar, desarreglar **3 to mess up** BUNGLE : echar a perder — *vi* **1** PUTTER : entretenerse **2** INTERFERE : meterse, entrometerse <don't mess with me : no te metas conmigo>
mess² *n* **1** : rancho *m* (para soldados, etc.) **2** DISORDER : desorden *m* <your room is a mess : tienes el cuarto hecho un desastre> **3** CONFUSION, TURMOIL : confusión *f,* embrollo *m,* lío *m fam*
message [ˈmɛsɪdʒ] *n* : mensaje *m,* recado *m*
messenger [ˈmɛsəndʒər] *n* : mensajero *m,* -ra *f*
Messiah [məˈsaɪə] *n* : Mesías *m*
Messrs. → **Mr.**
messy [ˈmɛsi] *adj* **messier; -est** UNTIDY : desordenado, sucio
met → **meet**
metabolic [ˌmɛt̬əˈbɑlɪk] *adj* : metabólico
metabolism [məˈtæbəˌlɪzəm] *n* : metabolismo *m*
metabolize [məˈtæbəˌlaɪz] *vt* **-lized; -lizing** : metabolizar
metal [ˈmɛt̬əl] *n* : metal *m*
metallic [məˈtælɪk] *adj* : metálico
metallurgical [ˌmɛt̬əlˈərdʒɪkəl] *adj* : metalúrgico
metallurgy [ˈmɛt̬əlˌərdʒi] *n* : metalurgia *f*
metalwork [ˈmɛt̬əlˌwərk] *n* : objeto *m* de metal
metalworking [ˈmɛt̬əlˌwərkɪŋ] *n* : metalistería *f*
metamorphosis [ˌmɛt̬əˈmɔrfəsɪs] *n, pl* **-phoses** [-ˌsiːz] : metamorfosis *f*
metaphor [ˈmɛt̬əˌfɔr, -fər] *n* : metáfora *f*
metaphoric [ˌmɛt̬əˈfɔrɪk] *or* **metaphorical** [-ɪkəl] *adj* : metafórico
metaphysical [ˌmɛt̬əˈfɪzəkəl] *adj* : metafísico
metaphysics [ˌmɛt̬əˈfɪzɪks] *n* : metafísica *f*
mete [ˈmiːt] *vt* **meted; meting** ALLOT : repartir, distribuir <to mete out punishment : imponer castigos>
meteor [ˈmiːt̬iər, -t̬iːˌɔr] *n* : meteoro *m*
meteoric [ˌmiːt̬iˈɔrɪk] *adj* : meteórico
meteorite [ˈmiːt̬iəˌraɪt] *n* : meteorito *m*
meteorologic [ˌmiːt̬iˌɔrəˈlɑdʒɪk] *or* **meteorological** [-ˈlɑdʒɪkəl] *adj* : meteorológico
meteorologist [ˌmiːt̬iəˈrɑlədʒɪst] *n* : meteorólogo *m,* -ga *f*
meteorology [ˌmiːt̬iəˈrɑlədʒi] *n* : meteorología *f*
meter [ˈmiːt̬ər] *n* **1** : metro *m* <it measures 2 meters : mide 2 metros> **2** : contador *m,* medidor *m* (de electricidad, etc.) <parking meter : parquímetro> **3** : metro *m* (en literatura o música)
methane [ˈmɛˌθeɪn] *n* : metano *m*
method [ˈmɛθəd] *n* : método *m*
methodical [məˈθɑdɪkəl] *adj* : metódico — **methodically** *adv*
meticulous [məˈtɪkjələs] *adj* : meticuloso — **meticulously** *adv*
meticulousness [məˈtɪkjələsnəs] *n* : meticulosidad *f*
metric [ˈmɛtrɪk] *or* **metrical** [-trɪkəl] *adj* : métrico
metric system *n* : sistema *m* métrico
metronome [ˈmɛtrəˌnoːm] *n* : metrónomo *m*
metropolis [məˈtrɑpələs] *n* : metrópoli *f,* metrópolis *f*
metropolitan [ˌmɛtrəˈpɑlətən] *adj* : metropolitano

mettle ['mɛtəl] *n* : temple *m,* valor *m* <on one's mettle : dispuesto a mostrar su valía>
Mexican ['mɛksɪkən] *n* : mexicano *m,* -na *f* — **Mexican** *adj*
mezzanine ['mɛzə,ni:n, ,mɛzə'ni:n] *n* **1** : entrepiso *m,* entresuelo *m* **2** : primer piso *m* (de un teatro)
miasma [maɪ'æzmə] *n* : miasma *m*
mica ['maɪkə] *n* : mica *f*
mice → **mouse**
micro ['maɪkro] *adj* : muy pequeño, microscópico
microbe ['maɪ,kro:b] *n* : microbio *m*
microbiology [,maɪkrobaɪ'ɑlədʒi] *n* : microbiología *f*
microcomputer ['maɪkrokəm,pju:tər] *n* : microcomputadora *f*
microcosm ['maɪkro,kɑzəm] *n* : microcosmo *m*
microfilm ['maɪkro,fɪlm] *n* : microfilm *m*
micrometer [maɪ'krɑmətər] *n* : micrómetro *m*
micron ['maɪ,krɑn] *n* : micrón *m*
microorganism [,maɪkro'ɔrgə,nɪzəm] *n* : microorganismo *m,* microbio *m*
microphone ['maɪkrə,fo:n] *n* : micrófono *m*
microprocessor ['maɪkro,prɑ,sɛsər] *n* : microprocesador *m*
microscope ['maɪkrə,sko:p] *n* : microscopio *m*
microscopic [,maɪkrə'skɑpɪk] *adj* : microscópico
microscopy [maɪ'krɑskəpi] *n* : microscopía *f*
microwave ['maɪkrə,weɪv] *n* **1** : microonda *f* **2** *or* **microwave oven** : microondas *m*
mid ['mɪd] *adj* : medio <mid morning : a media mañana> <in mid-August : a mediados de agosto> <in mid ocean : en alta mar>
midair ['mɪd'ær] *n* **in ~** : en el aire <to catch in midair : agarrar al vuelo>
midday ['mɪd'deɪ] *n* NOON : mediodía *m*
middle[1] ['mɪdəl] *adj* **1** CENTRAL : medio, del medio, de en medio **2** INTERMEDIATE : intermedio, mediano <middle age : la mediana edad>
middle[2] *n* **1** CENTER : medio *m,* centro *m* <fold it down the middle : dóblalo por la mitad> **2 in the middle of** : en medio de (un espacio), a mitad de (una actividad) <in the middle of the month : a mediados del mes>
Middle Ages *npl* : Edad *f* Media
middle class *n* : clase *f* media
middleman ['mɪdəl,mæn] *n, pl* **-men** [-mən, -,mɛn] : intermediario *m,* -ria *f*
middling ['mɪdlɪŋ, -lən] *adj* **1** MEDIUM, MIDDLE : mediano **2** MEDIOCRE : mediocre, regular
midge ['mɪdʒ] *n* : mosca *f* pequeña
midget ['mɪdʒət] *n* **1** : enano *m,* -na *f* (persona) **2** : cosa *f* diminuta
midland ['mɪdlənd, -,lænd] *n* : región *f* central (de un país)
midnight ['mɪd,naɪt] *n* : medianoche *f*
midpoint ['mɪd,pɔɪnt] *n* : punto *m* medio, término *m* medio
midriff ['mɪd,rɪf] *n* : diafragma *m*
midshipman ['mɪd,ʃɪpmən, ,mɪd'ʃɪp-] *n, pl* **-men** [-mən, -,mɛn] : guardiamarina *m*
midst[1] ['mɪdst] *n* : medio *m* <in our midst : entre nosotros> <in the midst of : en medio de>
midst[2] *prep* : entre
midstream ['mɪd'stri:m, -,stri:m] *n* : medio *m* de la corriente <in the midstream of his career : en medio de su carrera>
midsummer ['mɪd'sʌmər, -,sʌ-] *n* : pleno verano *m*
midtown ['mɪd,taʊn] *n* : centro *m* (de una ciudad)
midway ['mɪd,weɪ] *adv* HALFWAY : a mitad de camino
midweek ['mɪd,wi:k] *n* : medio *m* de la semana <in midweek : a media semana>
midwife ['mɪd,waɪf] *n, pl* **-wives** [-,waɪvz] : partera *f,* comadrona *f*
midwinter ['mɪd'wɪntər, -,wɪn-] *n* : pleno invierno *m*
midyear ['mɪd,jɪr] *n* : medio *m* del año <at midyear : a mediados del año>
mien ['mi:n] *n* : aspecto *m,* porte *m,* semblante *m*
miff ['mɪf] *vt* : ofender
might[1] ['maɪt] (*used to express permission or possibility or as a polite alternative to* **may**) → **may** <it might be true : podría ser verdad> <might I speak with Sarah? : ¿se puede hablar con Sarah?>
might[2] *n* : fuerza *f,* poder *m*
mightily ['maɪtəli] *adv* : con mucha fuerza, poderosamente
mighty[1] ['maɪti] *adv* VERY : muy <mighty good : muy bueno, buenísimo>
mighty[2] *adj* **mightier; -est 1** POWERFUL : poderoso, potente **2** GREAT : grande, imponente
migraine ['maɪ,greɪn] *n* : jaqueca *f,* migraña *f*
migrant ['maɪgrənt] *n* : trabajador *m,* -dora *f* ambulante
migrate ['maɪ,greɪt] *vi* **-grated; -grating** : emigrar
migration [maɪ'greɪʃən] *n* : migración *f*
migratory ['maɪgrə,tori] *adj* : migratorio
mild ['maɪld] *adj* **1** GENTLE : apacible, suave <a mild disposition : un temperamento suave> **2** LIGHT : leve, ligero <a mild punishment : un castigo leve, un castigo poco severo> **3** TEMPERATE : templado (dícese del clima) — **mildly** *adv*

mildew[1] ['mɪl͵du:, -͵dju:] *vi* : enmohecerse
mildew[2] *n* : moho *m*
mildness ['maɪldnəs] *n* : apacibilidad *f,* suavidad *f*
mile ['maɪl] *n* : milla *f*
mileage ['maɪlɪdʒ] *n* **1** ALLOWANCE : viáticos *mpl* (pagados por milla recorrida) **2** : distancia *f* recorrida (en millas), kilometraje *m*
milestone ['maɪl͵sto:n] *n* LANDMARK : hito *m,* jalón *m* <a milestone in his life : un hito en su vida>
milieu [mi:l'ju:, -'jø] *n, pl* **-lieus** *or* **-lieux** [-'ju:z, -'jø] SURROUNDINGS : entorno *m,* medio *m,* ambiente *m*
militant[1] ['mɪlətənt] *adj* : militante, combativo
militant[2] *n* : militante *mf*
militarism ['mɪlət̬ə͵rɪzəm] *n* : militarismo *m*
militaristic [͵mɪlət̬ə'rɪstɪk] *adj* : militarista
military[1] ['mɪlə͵tɛri] *adj* : militar
military[2] *n* **the military** : las fuerzas armadas
militia [mə'lɪʃə] *n* : milicia *f*
milk[1] ['mɪlk] *vt* **1** : ordeñar (una vaca, etc.) **2** EXPLOIT : explotar
milk[2] *n* : leche *f*
milkman ['mɪlk͵mæn, -mən] *n, pl* **-men** [-mən, -͵mɛn] : lechero *m*
milk shake *n* : batido *m,* licuado *m*
milkweed ['mɪlk͵wi:d] *n* : algodoncillo *m*
milky ['mɪlki] *adj* **milkier; -est** : lechoso
Milky Way *n* : Vía *f* Láctea
mill[1] ['mɪl] *vt* : moler (granos), fresar (metales), acordonar (monedas) — *vi* **to mill about** : arremolinarse
mill[2] *n* **1** : molino *m* (para moler granos) **2** FACTORY : fábrica *f* <textile mill : fábrica textil> **3** GRINDER : molinillo *m*
millennium [mə'lɛniəm] *n, pl* **-nia** [-niə] *or* **-niums** : milenio *m*
miller ['mɪlər] *n* : molinero *m,* -ra *f*
millet ['mɪlət] *n* : mijo *m*
milligram ['mɪlə͵græm] *n* : miligramo *m*
milliliter ['mɪlə͵li:t̬ər] *n* : mililitro *m*
millimeter ['mɪlə͵mi:t̬ər] *n* : milímetro *m*
milliner ['mɪlənər] *n* : sombrerero *m,* -ra *f* (de señoras)
millinery ['mɪlə͵nɛri] *n* : sombreros *mpl* de señora
million[1] ['mɪljən] *adj* **a million** : un millón de
million[2] *n, pl* **millions** *or* **million** : millón *m*
millionaire [͵mɪljə'nær, 'mɪljə͵nær] *n* : millonario *m,* -ria *f*
millionth[1] ['mɪljənθ] *adj* : millonésimo
millionth[2] *n* : millonésimo *m*
millipede ['mɪlə͵pi:d] *n* : milpiés *m*
millstone ['mɪl͵sto:n] *n* : rueda *f* de molino, muela *f*
mime[1] ['maɪm] *v* **mimed; miming** *vt* MIMIC : imitar, remedar — *vi* PANTOMIME : hacer la mímica
mime[2] *n* **1** : mimo *mf* **2** PANTOMIME : pantomima *f*
mimeograph ['mɪmiə͵græf] *n* : mimeógrafo *m*
mimic[1] ['mɪmɪk] *vt* **-icked; -icking** : imitar, remedar
mimic[2] *n* : imitador *m,* -dora *f*
mimicry ['mɪmɪkri] *n, pl* **-ries** : mímica *f,* imitación *f*
minaret [͵mɪnə'rɛt] *n* : alminar *m,* minarete *m*
mince ['mɪnts] *v* **minced; mincing** *vt* **1** CHOP : picar, moler (carne) **2 not to mince one's words** : no tener uno pelos en la lengua — *vi* : caminar de manera afectada
mincemeat ['mɪnts͵mi:t] *n* : mezcla *f* de fruta picada, sebo, y especias
mind[1] ['maɪnd] *vt* **1** TEND : cuidar, atender <mind the children : cuida a los niños> **2** OBEY : obedecer **3** : preocuparse por, sentirse molestado por <I don't mind his jokes : sus bromas no me molestan> **4** : tener cuidado con <mind the ladder! : ¡cuidado con la escalera!> — *vi* **1** OBEY : obedecer **2** CARE : importarle a uno <I don't mind : no me importa, me es igual>
mind[2] *n* **1** MEMORY : memoria *f,* recuerdo *m* <keep it in mind : téngalo en cuenta> **2** : mente *f* <the mind and the body : la mente y el cuerpo> **3** INTENTION : intención *f,* propósito *m* <to have a mind to do something : tener intención de hacer algo> **4** : razón *f* <he's out of his mind : está loco> **5** OPINION : opinión *f* <to change one's mind : cambiar de opinión> **6** INTELLECT : capacidad *f* intelectual
minded ['maɪndəd] *adj* **1** (*used in combination*) <narrow-minded : de mentalidad cerrada> <health-minded : preocupado por la salud> **2** INCLINED : inclinado
mindful ['maɪndfəl] *adj* AWARE : consciente — **mindfully** *adv*
mindless ['maɪndləs] *adj* **1** SENSELESS : estúpido, sin sentido <mindless violence : violencia sin sentido> **2** HEEDLESS : inconsciente
mindlessly ['maɪndləsli] *adv* **1** SENSELESSLY : sin sentido **2** HEEDLESSLY : inconscientemente
mine[1] ['maɪn] *vt* **mined; mining 1** : extraer (oro, etc.) **2** : minar (con artefactos explosivos)
mine[2] *n* : mina *f* <gold mine : mina de oro>
mine[3] *pron* : mío, mía <that one's mine : ése es el mío> <some friends of mine : unos amigos míos>
minefield ['maɪn͵fi:ld] *n* : campo *m* de minas
miner ['maɪnər] *n* : minero *m,* -ra *f*

mineral [ˈmɪnərəl] *n* : mineral *m* — **mineral** *adj*

mineralogy [ˌmɪnəˈrɑlədʒi, -ˈræ-] *n* : mineralogía *f*

mingle [ˈmɪŋgəl] *v* **-gled; -gling** *vt* MIX : mezclar — *vi* **1** MIX : mezclarse **2** CIRCULATE : circular

miniature[1] [ˈmɪniəˌtʃʊr, ˈmɪnɪˌtʃʊr, -tʃər] *adj* : en miniatura, diminuto

miniature[2] *n* : miniatura *f*

minibus [ˈmɪniˌbʌs] *n* : microbús *m*, pesera *f Mex*

minicomputer [ˈmɪnikəmˌpjuːt̬ər] *n* : minicomputadora *f*

minimal [ˈmɪnəməl] *adj* : mínimo

minimally [ˈmɪnəməli] *adv* : en grado mínimo

minimize [ˈmɪnəˌmaɪz] *vt* **-mized; -mizing** : minimizar

minimum[1] [ˈmɪnəməm] *adj* : mínimo

minimum[2] *n, pl* **-ma** [ˈmɪnəmə] *or* **-mums** : mínimo *m*

miniskirt [ˈmɪniˌskərt] *n* : minifalda *f*

minister[1] [ˈmɪnəstər] *vi* **to minister to** : cuidar (de), atender a

minister[2] *n* **1** : pastor *m*, -tora *f* (de una iglesia) **2** : ministro *m*, -tra *f* (en política)

ministerial [ˌmɪnəˈstɪriəl] *adj* : ministerial

ministry [ˈmɪnəstri] *n, pl* **-tries 1** : ministerio *m* (en política) **2** : sacerdocio *m* (en el catolicismo), clerecía *f* (en el protestantismo)

minivan [ˈmɪniˌvæn] *n* : minivan *f*

mink [ˈmɪŋk] *n, pl* **mink** *or* **minks** : visón *m*

minnow [ˈmɪnoː] *n, pl* **-nows** : pececillo *m* de agua dulce

minor[1] [ˈmaɪnər] *adj* : menor

minor[2] *n* **1** : menor *mf* (de edad) **2** : asignatura *f* secundaria (de estudios)

minority [məˈnɔrət̬i, maɪ-] *n, pl* **-ties** : minoría *f*

minstrel [ˈmɪnᵗstrəl] *n* : juglar *m*, trovador *m* (en el medioevo)

mint[1] [ˈmɪnt] *vt* : acuñar

mint[2] *adj* : sin usar <in mint condition : como nuevo>

mint[3] *n* **1** : menta *f* <mint tea : té de menta> **2** : pastilla *f* de menta **3** : casa *f* de la moneda <the U.S. Mint : la casa de la moneda de los EE.UU.> **4** FORTUNE : dineral *m*, fortuna *f*

minuet [ˌmɪnjʊˈɛt] *n* : minué *m*

minus[1] [ˈmaɪnəs] *n* **1** : cantidad *f* negativa **2 minus sign** : signo *m* de menos

minus[2] *prep* **1** : menos <four minus two : cuatro menos dos> **2** WITHOUT : sin <minus his hat : sin su sombrero>

minuscule *or* **miniscule** [ˈmɪnəsˌkjuːl, mɪˈnʌs-] *adj* : minúsculo

minute[1] [maɪˈnuːt, mɪ-, -ˈnjuːt] *adj* **-nuter; -est 1** TINY : diminuto, minúsculo **2** DETAILED : minucioso

minute[2] [ˈmɪnət] *n* **1** : minuto *m* <ten minutes late : diez minutos de retraso> **2** MOMENT : momento *m* **3 minutes** *npl* : actas *fpl* (de una reunión)

minutely [maɪˈnuːtli, mɪ-, -ˈnjuːt-] *adv* : minuciosamente

miracle [ˈmɪrɪkəl] *n* : milagro *m*

miraculous [məˈrækjələs] *adj* : milagroso — **miraculously** *adv*

mirage [mɪˈrɑʒ, *chiefly Brit* ˈmɪrˌɑʒ] *n* : espejismo *m*

mire[1] [ˈmaɪr] *vi* **mired; miring** : atascarse

mire[2] *n* : lodo *m*, barro *m*, fango *m*

mirror[1] [ˈmɪrər] *vt* : reflejar

mirror[2] *n* : espejo *m*

mirth [ˈmərθ] *n* : alegría *f*, regocijo *m*

mirthful [ˈmərθfəl] *adj* : alegre, regocijado

misanthrope [ˈmɪsənˌθroːp] *n* : misántropo *m*, -pa *f*

misanthropic [ˌmɪsənˈθrɑpɪk] *adj* : misantrópico

misanthropy [mɪˈsænθrəpi] *n* : misantropía *f*

misapprehend [ˌmɪsˌæprəˈhɛnd] *vt* : entender mal

misapprehension [ˌmɪsˌæprəˈhɛntʃən] *n* : malentendido *m*

misappropriate [ˌmɪsəˈproːpriˌeɪt] *vt* **-ated; -ating** : malversar

misbegotten [ˌmɪsbiˈgɑtən] *adj* **1** ILLEGITIMATE : ilegítimo **2** : mal concebido <misbegotten laws : leyes mal concebidas>

misbehave [ˌmɪsbiˈheɪv] *vi* **-haved; -having** : portarse mal

misbehavior [ˌmɪsbiˈheɪvjər] *n* : mala conducta *f*

miscalculate [mɪsˈkælkjəˌleɪt] *v* **-lated; -lating** : calcular mal

miscalculation [mɪsˌkælkjəˈleɪʃən] *n* : error *m* de cálculo, mal cálculo *m*

miscarriage [ˌmɪsˈkærɪdʒ, ˈmɪsˌkærɪdʒ] *n* **1** : aborto *m* **2** FAILURE : fracaso *m*, malogro *m* <a miscarriage of justice : una injusticia, un error judicial>

miscarry [ˌmɪsˈkæri, ˈmɪsˌkæri] *vi* **-ried; -rying 1** ABORT : abortar **2** FAIL : malograrse, fracasar

miscellaneous [ˌmɪsəˈleɪniəs] *adj* : misceláneo

miscellany [ˈmɪsəˌleɪni] *n, pl* **-nies** : miscelánea *f*

mischance [mɪsˈtʃænᵗs] *n* : desgracia *f*, infortunio *m*, mala suerte *f*

mischief [ˈmɪstʃəf] *n* : diabluras *fpl*, travesuras *fpl*

mischievous [ˈmɪstʃəvəs] *adj* : travieso, pícaro

mischievously [ˈmɪstʃəvəsli] *adv* : de manera traviesa

misconception [ˌmɪskənˈsɛpʃən] *n* : concepto *m* erróneo, idea *f* falsa

misconduct [mɪsˈkɑndəkt] *n* : mala conducta *f*

misconstrue [ˌmɪskənˈstruː] *vt* **-strued; -struing** : malinterpretar

misdeed [mɪsˈdiːd] *n* : fechoría *f*

misdemeanor [ˌmɪsdɪˈmiːnər] *n* : delito *m* menor
miser [ˈmaɪzər] *n* : avaro *m,* -ra *f;* tacaño *m,* -ña *f*
miserable [ˈmɪzərəbəl] *adj* **1** UNHAPPY : triste, desdichado **2** WRETCHED : miserable, desgraciado <a miserable hut : una choza miserable> **3** UNPLEASANT : desagradable, malo <miserable weather : tiempo malísimo> **4** CONTEMPTIBLE : despreciable, mísero <for a miserable $10 : por unos míseros diez dólares>
miserably [ˈmɪzərəbli] *adv* **1** SADLY : tristemente **2** WRETCHEDLY : miserablemente, lamentablemente **3** UNFORTUNATELY : desgraciadamente
miserly [ˈmaɪzərli] *adj* : avaro, tacaño
misery [ˈmɪzəri] *n, pl* **-eries** : miseria *f,* sufrimiento *m*
misfire [mɪsˈfaɪr] *vi* **-fired; -firing** : fallar
misfit [ˈmɪsˌfɪt] *n* : inadaptado *m,* -da *f*
misfortune [mɪsˈfɔrtʃən] *n* : desgracia *f,* desventura *f,* infortunio *m*
misgiving [mɪsˈgɪvɪŋ] *n* : duda *f,* recelo *m*
misguided [mɪsˈgaɪdəd] *adj* : desacertado, equivocado, mal informado
mishap [ˈmɪsˌhæp] *n* : contratiempo *m,* percance *m,* accidente *m*
misinform [ˌmɪsɪnˈfɔrm] *vt* : informar mal
misinterpret [ˌmɪsɪnˈtərprət] *vt* : malinterpretar
misinterpretation [ˌmɪsɪnˌtərprəˈteɪʃən] *n* : mala interpretación *f,* malentendido *m*
misjudge [mɪsˈdʒʌdʒ] *vt* **-judged; -judging** : juzgar mal
mislay [mɪsˈleɪ] *vt* **-laid** [-leɪd]; **-laying** : extraviar, perder
mislead [mɪsˈliːd] *vt* **-led** [-ˈlɛd]; **-leading** : engañar
misleading [mɪsˈliːdɪŋ] *adj* : engañoso
mismanage [mɪsˈmænɪdʒ] *vt* **-aged; -aging** : administrar mal
mismanagement [mɪsˈmænɪdʒmənt] *n* : mala administración *f*
misnomer [mɪsˈnoːmər] *n* : nombre *m* inapropiado
misogynist [mɪˈsɑdʒənɪst] *n* : misógino *m*
misplace [mɪsˈpleɪs] *vt* **-placed; -placing** : extraviar, perder
misprint [ˈmɪsˌprɪnt, mɪsˈ-] *n* : errata *f,* error *m* de imprenta
mispronounce [ˌmɪsprəˈnaʊnts] *vt* **-nounced; -nouncing** : pronunciar mal
mispronunciation [ˌmɪsprəˌnʌntsiˈeɪʃən] *n* : pronunciación *f* incorrecta
misquote [mɪsˈkwoːt] *vt* **-quoted; -quoting** : citar incorrectamente
misread [mɪsˈriːd] *vt* **-read; -reading 1** : leer mal <she misread the sentence : leyó mal la frase> **2** MISUNDERSTAND : malinterpretar <they misread his intention : malinterpretaron su intención>
misrepresent [ˌmɪsˌrɛprɪˈzɛnt] *vt* : distorsionar, falsear, tergiversar
misrule[1] [mɪsˈruːl] *vt* **-ruled; -ruling** : gobernar mal
misrule[2] *n* : mal gobierno *m*
miss[1] [ˈmɪs] *vt* **1** : errar, faltar <to miss the target : no dar en el blanco> **2** : no encontrar, perder <they missed each other : no se encontraron> <I missed the plane : perdí el avión> **3** : echar de menos, extrañar <we miss him a lot : lo echamos mucho de menos> **4** OVERLOOK : pasar por alto, perder (una oportunidad, etc.) **5** AVOID : evitar <they just missed hitting the tree : por muy poco chocan contra el árbol> **6** OMIT : saltarse <he missed breakfast : se saltó el desayuno>
miss[2] *n* **1** : fallo *m* (de un tiro, etc.) **2** FAILURE : fracaso *m* **3** : señorita *f* <Miss Jones : la señorita Jones> <excuse me, miss : perdone, señorita>
missal [ˈmɪsəl] *n* : misal *m*
misshapen [mɪˈʃeɪpən] *adj* : deforme
missile [ˈmɪsəl] *n* **1** : misil *m* <guided missile : misil guiado> **2** PROJECTILE : proyectil *m*
missing [ˈmɪsɪŋ] *adj* **1** ABSENT : ausente <who's missing? : ¿quién falta?> **2** LOST : perdido, desaparecido <missing persons : los desaparecidos>
mission [ˈmɪʃən] *n* **1** : misión *f* (mandada por una iglesia) **2** DELEGATION : misión *f,* delegación *f,* embajada *f* **3** TASK : misión *f*
missionary[1] [ˈmɪʃəˌnɛri] *adj* : misionero
missionary[2] *n, pl* **-aries** : misionero *m,* -ra *f*
missive [ˈmɪsɪv] *n* : misiva *f*
misspell [mɪsˈspɛl] *vt* : escribir mal
misspelling [mɪsˈspɛlɪŋ] *n* : falta *f* de ortografía
misstep [ˈmɪsˌstɛp] *n* : traspié *m,* tropezón *m*
mist [ˈmɪst] *n* **1** HAZE : neblina *f,* niebla *f* **2** SPRAY : rocío *m*
mistake[1] [mɪˈsteɪk] *vt* **-took** [-ˈstʊk]; **-taken** [-ˈsteɪkən]; **-taking 1** MISINTERPRET : malinterpretar **2** CONFUSE : confundir <he mistook her for Clara : la confundió con Clara>
mistake[2] *n* **1** MISUNDERSTANDING : malentendido *m,* confusión *f* **2** ERROR : error *m* <I made a mistake : me equivoqué, cometí un error>
mistaken [mɪˈsteɪkən] *adj* WRONG : equivocado — **mistakenly** *adv*
mister [ˈmɪstər] *n* : señor *m* <watch out, mister : cuidado, señor>
mistiness [ˈmɪstinəs] *n* : nebulosidad *f*
mistletoe [ˈmɪsəlˌtoː] *n* : muérdago *m*
mistreat [mɪsˈtriːt] *vt* : maltratar
mistreatment [mɪsˈtriːtmənt] *n* : maltrato *m,* abuso *m*

mistress [ˈmɪstrəs] *n* **1** : dueña *f,* señora *f* (de una casa) **2** LOVER : amante *f*
mistrust[1] [mɪsˈtrʌst] *vt* : desconfiar de
mistrust[2] *n* : desconfianza *f*
mistrustful [mɪsˈtrʌstfəl] *adj* : desconfiado
misty [ˈmɪsti] *adj* **mistier; -est 1** : neblinoso, nebuloso **2** TEARFUL : lloroso
misunderstand [ˌmɪsˌʌndərˈstænd] *vt* **-stood** [-ˈstʊd]; **-standing 1** : entender mal **2** MISINTERPRET : malinterpretar <don't misunderstand me : no me malinterpretes>
misunderstanding [ˌmɪsˌʌndərˈstændɪŋ] *n* **1** MISINTERPRETATION : malentendido *m* **2** DISAGREEMENT, QUARREL : disputa *f,* discusión *f*
misuse[1] [mɪsˈjuːz] *vt* **-used; -using 1** : emplear mal **2** ABUSE, MISTREAT : abusar de, maltratar
misuse[2] [mɪsˈjuːs] *n* **1** : mal empleo *m,* mal uso *m* **2** WASTE : derroche *m,* despilfarro *m* **3** ABUSE : abuso *m*
mite [ˈmaɪt] *n* **1** : ácaro *m* **2** BIT : poco *m* <a mite tired : un poquito cansado>
miter *or* **mitre** [ˈmaɪt̬ər] *n* **1** : mitra *f* (de un obispo) **2** *or* **miter joint** : inglete *m*
mitigate [ˈmɪt̬əˌgeɪt] *vt* **-gated; -gating** : mitigar, aliviar
mitigation [ˌmɪt̬əˈgeɪʃən] *n* : mitigación *f,* alivio *m*
mitosis [maɪˈtoːsɪs] *n, pl* **-toses** [-ˌsiːz] : mitosis *f*
mitt [ˈmɪt] *n* : manopla *f,* guante *m* (de béisbol)
mitten [ˈmɪtən] *n* : manopla *f,* mitón *m*
mix[1] [ˈmɪks] *vt* **1** COMBINE : mezclar **2** STIR : remover, revolver **3 to mix up** CONFUSE : confundir — *vi* : mezclarse
mix[2] *n* : mezcla *f*
mixer [ˈmɪksər] *n* **1** : batidora *f* (de la cocina) **2 cement mixer** : hormigonera *f*
mixture [ˈmɪkstʃər] *n* : mezcla *f*
mix–up [ˈmɪksˌʌp] *n* CONFUSION : confusión *f,* lío *m fam*
mnemonic [nɪˈmɑnɪk] *adj* : mnemónico
moan[1] [ˈmoːn] *vi* : gemir
moan[2] *n* : gemido *m*
moat [ˈmoːt] *n* : foso *m*
mob[1] [ˈmɑb] *vt* **mobbed; mobbing 1** ATTACK : atacar en masa **2** HOUND : acosar, rodear
mob[2] *n* **1** THRONG : multitud *f,* turba *f,* muchedumbre *f* **2** GANG : pandilla *f*
mobile[1] [ˈmoːbəl, -ˌbiːl, -ˌbaɪl] *adj* : móvil <mobile home : caravana, casa rodante>
mobile[2] [ˈmoˌbiːl] *n* : móvil *m*
mobility [moˈbɪlət̬i] *n* : movilidad *f*
mobilize [ˈmoːbəˌlaɪz] *vt* **-lized; -lizing** : movilizar
moccasin [ˈmɑkəsən] *n* **1** : mocasín *m* **2** *or* **water moccasin** : serpiente *f* venenosa de Norteamérica
mocha [ˈmoːkə] *n* **1** : mezcla *f* de café y chocolate **2** : color *m* chocolate
mock[1] [ˈmɑk, ˈmɔk] *vt* **1** RIDICULE : burlarse de, mofarse de **2** MIMIC : imitar, remedar (de manera burlona)
mock[2] *adj* **1** SIMULATED : simulado **2** PHONY : falso
mockery [ˈmɑkəri, ˈmɔ-] *n, pl* **-eries 1** JEER, TAUNT : burla *f,* mofa *f* <to make a mockery of : burlarse de> **2** FAKE : imitación *f* (burlona)
mockingbird [ˈmɑkɪŋˌbərd, ˈmɔ-] *n* : sinsonte *m*
mode [ˈmoːd] *n* **1** FORM : modo *m,* forma *f* **2** MANNER : modo *m,* manera *f,* estilo *m* **3** FASHION : moda *f*
model[1] [ˈmɑdəl] *v* **-eled** *or* **-elled; -eling** *or* **-elling** *vt* SHAPE : modelar — *vi* : trabajar de modelo
model[2] *adj* **1** EXEMPLARY : modelo, ejemplar <a model student : un estudiante modelo> **2** MINIATURE : en miniatura
model[3] *n* **1** PATTERN : modelo *m* **2** MINIATURE : modelo *m,* miniatura *f* **3** EXAMPLE : modelo *m,* ejemplo *m* **4** MANNEQUIN : modelo *mf* **5** DESIGN : modelo *m* <the '97 model : el modelo '97>
modem [ˈmoːdəm, -ˌdɛm] *n* : módem *m*
moderate[1] [ˈmɑdəˌreɪt] *v* **-ated; -ating** *vt* : moderar, temperar — *vi* **1** CALM : moderarse, calmarse **2** : fungir como moderador (en un debate, etc.)
moderate[2] [ˈmɑdərət] *adj* : moderado
moderate[3] [ˈmɑdərət] *n* : moderado *m,* -da *f*
moderately [ˈmɑdərətli] *adv* **1** : con moderación **2** FAIRLY : medianamente
moderation [ˌmɑdəˈreɪʃən] *n* : moderación *f*
moderator [ˈmɑdəˌreɪt̬ər] *n* : moderador *m,* -dora *f*
modern [ˈmɑdərn] *adj* : moderno
modernity [məˈdərnət̬i] *n* : modernidad *f*
modernization [ˌmɑdərnəˈzeɪʃən] *n* : modernización *f*
modernize [ˈmɑdərˌnaɪz] *v* **-ized; -izing** *vt* : modernizar — *vi* : modernizarse
modest [ˈmɑdəst] *adj* **1** HUMBLE : modesto **2** DEMURE : recatado, pudoroso **3** MODERATE : modesto, moderado — **modestly** *adv*
modesty [ˈmɑdəsti] *n* : modestia *f*
modicum [ˈmɑdɪkəm] *n* : mínimo *m,* pizca *f*
modification [ˌmɑdəfəˈkeɪʃən] *n* : modificación *f*
modifier [ˈmɑdəˌfaɪər] *n* : modificante *m,* modificador *m*
modify [ˈmɑdəˌfaɪ] *vt* **-fied; -fying** : modificar, calificar (en gramática)
modish [ˈmoːdɪʃ] *adj* STYLISH : a la moda, de moda
modular [ˈmɑdʒələr] *adj* : modular
modulate [ˈmɑdʒəˌleɪt] *vt* **-lated; -lating** : modular

modulation [ˌmɑdʒəˈleɪʃən] *n* : modulación *f*
module [ˈmɑˌdʒuːl] *n* : módulo *m*
mogul [ˈmoːgəl] *n* : magnate *mf;* potentado *m,* -da *f*
mohair [ˈmoːˌhær] *n* : mohair *m*
moist [ˈmɔɪst] *adj* : húmedo
moisten [ˈmɔɪsən] *vt* : humedecer
moistness [ˈmɔɪstnəs] *n* : humedad *f*
moisture [ˈmɔɪstʃər] *n* : humedad *f*
moisturize [ˈmɔɪstʃəˌraɪz] *vt* **-ized; -izing** : humedecer (el aire), humectar (la piel)
moisturizer [ˈmɔɪtʃəˌraɪzər] *n* : crema *f* hidratante, crema *f* humectante
molar [ˈmoːlər] *n* : muela *f,* molar *m*
molasses [məˈlæsəz] *n* : melaza *f*
mold[1] [ˈmoːld] *vt* : moldear, formar (carácter, etc.) — *vi* : enmohecerse <the bread will mold : el pan se enmohecerá>
mold[2] *n* **1** *or* **leaf mold** : mantillo *m* **2** FORM : molde *m* <to break the mold : romper el molde> **3** FUNGUS : moho *m*
molder [ˈmoːldər] *vi* CRUMBLE : desmoronarse
molding [ˈmoːldɪŋ] *n* : moldura *f* (en arquitectura)
moldy [ˈmoːldi] *adj* **moldier; -est** : mohoso
mole [ˈmoːl] *n* **1** : lunar *m* (en la piel) **2** : topo *m* (animal)
molecule [ˈmɑlɪˌkjuːl] *n* : molécula *f* — **molecular** [məˈlɛkjələr] *adj*
molehill [ˈmoːlˌhɪl] *n* : topera *f*
molest [məˈlɛst] *vt* **1** ANNOY, DISTURB : molestar **2** : abusar (sexualmente)
mollify [ˈmɑləˌfaɪ] *vt* **-fied; -fying** : apaciguar, aplacar
mollusk *or* **mollusc** [ˈmɑləsk] *n* : molusco *m*
mollycoddle [ˈmɑliˌkɑdəl] *vt* **-dled; -dling** PAMPER : consentir, mimar
molt [ˈmoːlt] *vi* : mudar, hacer la muda
molten [ˈmoːltən] *adj* : fundido
mom [ˈmɑm, ˈmʌm] *n* : mamá *f*
moment [ˈmoːmənt] *n* **1** INSTANT : momento *m* <one moment, please : un momento, por favor> **2** TIME : momento *m* <at the moment : de momento, actualmente> <from that moment : desde entonces> **3** IMPORTANCE : importancia *f* <of great moment : de gran importancia>
momentarily [ˌmoːmənˈtɛrəli] *adv* **1** : momentáneamente **2** SOON : dentro de poco, pronto
momentary [ˈmoːmənˌtɛri] *adj* : momentáneo
momentous [moˈmɛntəs] *adj* : de suma importancia, fatídico
momentum [moˈmɛntəm] *n, pl* **-ta** [-tə] *or* **-tums 1** : momento *m* (en física) **2** IMPETUS : ímpetu *m,* impulso *m*
monarch [ˈmɑˌnɑrk, -nərk] *n* : monarca *mf*
monarchism [ˈmɑˌnɑrˌkɪzəm, -nər-] *n* : monarquismo *m*
monarchist [ˈmɑˌnɑrkɪst, -nər-] *n* : monárquico *m,* -ca *f*
monarchy [ˈmɑˌnɑrki, -nər-] *n, pl* **-chies** : monarquía *f*
monastery [ˈmɑnəˌstɛri] *n, pl* **-teries** : monasterio *m*
monastic [məˈnæstɪk] *adj* : monástico — **monastically** [-tɪkli] *adv*
Monday [ˈmʌnˌdeɪ, -di] *n* : lunes *m*
monetary [ˈmɑnəˌtɛri, ˈmʌnə-] *adj* : monetario
money [ˈmʌni] *n, pl* **-eys** *or* **-ies** [ˈmʌniz] : dinero *m,* plata *f*
moneyed [ˈmʌnid] *adj* : adinerado
moneylender [ˈmʌniˌlɛndər] *n* : prestamista *mf*
money order *n* : giro *m* postal
Mongolian [mɑnˈgoːliən, mɑŋ-] *n* : mongol *m,* -gola *f* — **Mongolian** *adj*
mongoose [ˈmɑnˌguːs, ˈmɑŋ-] *n, pl* **-gooses** : mangosta *f*
mongrel [ˈmɑŋgrəl, ˈmʌŋ-] *n* **1** : perro *m* mestizo, perro *m* corriente *Mex* **2** HYBRID : híbrido *m*
monitor[1] [ˈmɑnət̬ər] *vt* : controlar, monitorear
monitor[2] *n* **1** : ayudante *mf* (en una escuela) **2** : monitor *m* (de una computadora, etc.)
monk [ˈmʌŋk] *n* : monje *m*
monkey[1] [ˈmʌŋki] *vi* **-keyed; -keying 1 to monkey around** : hacer payasadas, payasear **2 to monkey with** : juguetear con
monkey[2] *n, pl* **-keys** : mono *m,* -na *f*
monkeyshines [ˈmʌŋkiˌʃaɪnz] *npl* PRANKS : picardías *fpl,* travesuras *fpl*
monkey wrench *n* : llave *f* inglesa
monkshood [ˈmʌŋksˌhʊd] *n* : acónito *m*
monocle [ˈmɑnɪkəl] *n* : monóculo *m*
monogamous [məˈnɑgəməs] *adj* : monógamo
monogamy [məˈnɑgəmi] *n* : monogamia *f*
monogram[1] [ˈmɑnəˌgræm] *vt* **-grammed; -gramming** : marcar con monograma <monogrammed towels : toallas con monograma>
monogram[2] *n* : monograma *m*
monograph [ˈmɑnəˌgræf] *n* : monografía *f*
monolingual [ˌmɑnəˈlɪŋgwəl] *adj* : monolingüe
monolith [ˈmɑnəˌlɪθ] *n* : monolito *m*
monolithic [ˌmɑnəˈlɪθɪk] *adj* : monolítico
monologue [ˈmɑnəˌlɔg] *n* : monólogo *m*
monoplane [ˈmɑnəˌpleɪn] *n* : monoplano *m*
monopolize [məˈnɑpəˌlaɪz] *vt* **-lized; -lizing** : monopolizar
monopoly [məˈnɑpəli] *n, pl* **-lies** : monopolio *m*
monosyllabic [ˌmɑnosəˈlæbɪk] *adj* : monosilábico

monosyllable ['mɑno,sɪləbəl] *n* : monosílabo *m*
monotheism ['mɑnoθiː,ɪzəm] *n* : monoteísmo *m*
monotheistic [,mɑnoθiː'ɪstɪk] *adj* : monoteísta
monotone ['mɑnə,toːn] *n* : voz *f* monótona
monotonous [mə'nɑtənəs] *adj* : monótono — **monotonously** *adv*
monotony [mə'nɑtəni] *n* : monotonía *f,* uniformidad *f*
monoxide [mə'nɑk,saɪd] *n* : monóxido *m*
monsoon [mɑn'suːn] *n* : monzón *m*
monster ['mɑn*t*stər] *n* : monstruo *m*
monstrosity [mɑn'strɑsəṭi] *n, pl* **-ties** : monstruosidad *f*
monstrous ['mɑn*t*strəs] *adj* : monstruoso — **monstrously** *adv*
montage [mɑn'tɑʒ] *n* : montaje *m*
month ['mʌnθ] *n* : mes *m*
monthly[1] ['mʌnθli] *adv* : mensualmente
monthly[2] *adj* : mensual
monthly[3] *n, pl* **-lies** : publicación *f* mensual
monument ['mɑnjəmənt] *n* : monumento *m*
monumental [,mɑnjə'mɛntəl] *adj* : monumental — **monumentally** *adv*
moo[1] ['muː] *vi* : mugir
moo[2] *n* : mugido *m*
mood ['muːd] *n* : humor *m* <to be in a good mood : estar de buen humor> <to be in the mood for : tener ganas de> <to be in no mood for : no estar para>
moodiness ['muːdinəs] *n* **1** SADNESS : melancolía *f,* tristeza *f* **2** : cambios *mpl* de humor, carácter *m* temperamental
moody ['muːdi] *adj* **moodier; -est 1** GLOOMY : melancólico, deprimido **2** TEMPERAMENTAL : temperamental, de humor variable
moon ['muːn] *n* : luna *f*
moonbeam ['muːn,biːm] *n* : rayo *m* de luna
moonlight[1] ['muːn,laɪt] *vi* : estar pluriempleado
moonlight[2] *n* : claro *m* de luna, luz *f* de la luna
moonlit ['muːn,lɪt] *adj* : iluminado por la luna <a moonlit night : una noche de luna>
moonshine ['muːn,ʃaɪn] *n* **1** MOONLIGHT : luz *f* de la luna **2** NONSENSE : disparates *mpl,* tonterías *fpl* **3** : whiskey *m* destilado ilegalmente
moor[1] ['mʊr, 'mɔr] *vt* : amarrar
moor[2] *n* : brezal *m,* páramo *m*
mooring ['mʊrɪŋ, 'mɔr-] *n* DOCK : atracadero *m*
moose ['muːs] *ns & pl* : alce *m* (norteamericano)
moot ['muːt] *adj* DEBATABLE : discutible
mop[1] ['mɑp] *vt* **mopped; mopping** : trapear
mop[2] *n* : trapeador *m*
mope ['moːp] *vi* **moped; moping** : andar deprimido, quedar abatido
moped ['moː,pɛd] *n* : ciclomotor *m*
moral[1] ['mɔrəl] *adj* : moral <moral judgment : juicio moral> <moral support : apoyo moral> — **morally** *adv*
moral[2] *n* **1** : moraleja *f* (de un cuento, etc.) **2 morals** *npl* : moral *f,* moralidad *f*
morale [mə'ræl] *n* : moral *f*
morality [mə'ræləṭi] *n, pl* **-ties** : moralidad *f*
morass [mə'ræs] *n* **1** SWAMP : ciénaga *f,* pantano *m* **2** CONFUSION, MESS : lío *m fam,* embrollo *m*
moratorium [,mɔrə'toriəm] *n, pl* **-riums** *or* **-ria** [-iə] : moratoria *f*
moray ['mɔr,eɪ, mə'reɪ] *n* : morena *f*
morbid ['mɔrbɪd] *adj* **1** : mórbido, morboso (en medicina) **2** GRUESOME : morboso, horripilante
morbidity [mɔr'bɪdəṭi] *n* : morbosidad *f*
more[1] ['mor] *adv* : más <what more can I say? : ¿qué más puedo decir?> <more important : más importante> <once more : una vez más>
more[2] *adj* : más <nothing more than that : nada más que eso> <more work : más trabajo>
more[3] *n* : más *m* <the more you eat, the more you want : cuanto más comes, tanto más quieres>
more[4] *pron* : más <more were found : se encontraron más>
moreover [mor'oːvər] *adv* : además
mores ['mɔr,eɪz, -iːz] *npl* CUSTOMS : costumbres *fpl,* tradiciones *fpl*
morgue ['mɔrg] *n* : morgue *f*
moribund ['mɔrə,bʌnd] *adj* : moribundo
morn ['mɔrn] → **morning**
morning ['mɔrnɪŋ] *n* : mañana *f* <good morning! : ¡buenos días!>
Moroccan [mə'rɑkən] *n* : marroquí *mf* — **Moroccan** *adj*
moron ['mor,ɑn] *n* **1** : retrasado *m,* -da *f* mental **2** DUNCE : estúpido *m,* -da *f;* tonto *m,* -ta *f*
morose [mə'roːs] *adj* : hosco, sombrío — **morosely** *adv*
moroseness [mə'roːsnəs] *n* : malhumor *m*
morphine ['mɔr,fiːn] *n* : morfina *f*
morrow ['mɑroː] *n* : día *m* siguiente
Morse code ['mɔrs] *n* : código *m* morse
morsel ['mɔrsəl] *n* **1** BITE : bocado *m* **2** FRAGMENT : pedazo *m*
mortal[1] ['mɔrṭəl] *adj* : mortal <mortal blow : golpe mortal> <mortal fear : miedo mortal> — **mortally** *adv*
mortal[2] *n* : mortal *mf*
mortality [mɔr'tæləṭi] *n* : mortalidad *f*
mortar ['mɔrṭər] *n* **1** : mortero *m,* molcajete *m Mex* <mortar and pestle

: mortero y maja> **2** : mortero *m* <mortar shell : granada de mortero> **3** CEMENT : mortero *m,* argamasa *f*
mortgage[1] ['mɔrgɪdʒ] *vt* **-gaged; -gaging** : hipotecar
mortgage[2] *n* : hipoteca *f*
mortification [ˌmɔrṭəfə'keɪʃən] *n* **1** : mortificación *f* **2** HUMILIATION : humillación *f,* vergüenza *f*
mortify ['mɔrṭəˌfaɪ] *vt* **-fied; -fying 1** : mortificar (en religión) **2** HUMILIATE : humillar, avergonzar
mortuary ['mɔrtʃəˌwɛri] *n, pl* **-aries** FUNERAL HOME : funeraria *f*
mosaic [mo'zeɪɪk] *n* : mosaico *m*
Moslem ['mɑzləm] → **Muslim**
mosque ['mɑsk] *n* : mezquita *f*
mosquito [mə'ski:ṭo] *n, pl* **-toes** : mosquito *m,* zancudo *m*
moss ['mɔs] *n* : musgo *m*
mossy ['mɔsi] *adj* **-ier; -est** : musgoso
most[1] ['mo:st] *adv* : más <the most interesting book : el libro más interesante>
most[2] *adj* **1** : la mayoría de, la mayor parte de <most people : la mayoría de la gente> **2** GREATEST : más (dícese de los números), mayor (dícese de las cantidades) <the most ability : la mayor capacidad>
most[3] *n* : más *m,* máximo *m* <the most I can do : lo más que puedo hacer> <three weeks at the most : tres semanas como máximo>
most[4] *pron* : la mayoría, la mayor parte <most will go : la mayoría irá>
mostly ['mo:stli] *adv* MAINLY : en su mayor parte, principalmente
mote ['mo:t] *n* SPECK : mota *f*
motel [mo'tɛl] *n* : motel *m*
moth ['mɔθ] *n* : palomilla *f,* polilla *f*
mother[1] ['mʌðər] *vt* **1** BEAR : dar a luz a **2** PROTECT : cuidar de, proteger
mother[2] *n* : madre *f*
motherhood ['mʌðərˌhʊd] *n* : maternidad *f*
mother–in–law ['mʌðərɪnˌlɔ] *n, pl* **mothers–in–law** : suegra *f*
motherland ['mʌðərˌlænd] *n* : patria *f*
motherly ['mʌðərli] *adj* : maternal
mother–of–pearl [ˌmʌðərəv'pərl] *n* : nácar *m,* madreperla *f*
motif [mo'ti:f] *n* : motivo *m*
motion[1] ['mo:ʃən] *vt* : hacerle señas (a alguien) <she motioned us to come in : nos hizo señas para que entráramos>
motion[2] *n* **1** MOVEMENT : movimiento *m* <to set in motion : poner en marcha> **2** PROPOSAL : moción *f* <to second a motion : apoyar una moción>
motionless ['mo:ʃənləs] *adj* : inmóvil, quieto
motion picture *n* MOVIE : película *f*
motivate ['mo:ṭəˌveɪt] *vt* **-vated; -vating** : motivar, mover, inducir
motivation [ˌmo:ṭə'veɪʃən] *n* : motivación *f*
motive[1] ['mo:ṭɪv] *adj* : motor <motive power : fuerza motriz>
motive[2] *n* : motivo *m,* móvil *m*
motley ['mɑtli] *adj* : abigarrado, variopinto
motor[1] ['mo:ṭər] *vi* : viajar en coche
motor[2] *n* : motor *m*
motorbike ['mo:ṭərˌbaɪk] *n* : motocicleta *f* (pequeña), moto *f*
motorboat ['mo:ṭərˌbo:t] *n* : bote *m* a motor, lancha *f* motora
motorcar ['mo:ṭərˌkɑr] *n* : automóvil *m*
motorcycle ['mo:ṭərˌsaɪkəl] *n* : motocicleta *f*
motorcyclist ['mo:ṭərˌsaɪkəlɪst] *n* : motociclista *mf*
motorist ['mo:ṭərɪst] *n* : automovilista *mf,* motorista *mf*
mottle ['mɑṭəl] *vt* **-tled; -tling** : manchar, motear <mottled skin : piel manchada> <a mottled surface : una superficie moteada>
motto ['mɑṭo:] *n, pl* **-toes** : lema *m*
mould ['mo:ld] → **mold**
mound ['maʊnd] *n* **1** PILE : montón *m* **2** KNOLL : montículo *m* **3 burial mound** : túmulo *m*
mount[1] ['maʊnt] *vt* **1** : montar a (un caballo), montar en (una bicicleta), subir a **2** : montar (artillería, etc.) — *vi* INCREASE : aumentar
mount[2] *n* **1** SUPPORT : soporte *m* **2** HORSE : caballería *f,* montura *f* **3** MOUNTAIN : monte *m,* montaña *f*
mountain ['maʊntən] *n* : montaña *f*
mountaineer [ˌmaʊntən'ɪr] *n* : alpinista *mf;* montañero *m,* -ra *f*
mountainous ['maʊntənəs] *adj* : montañoso
mountaintop ['maʊntənˌtɑp] *n* : cima *f,* cumbre *f*
mourn ['morn] *vt* : llorar (por), lamentar <to mourn the death of : llorar la muerte de> — *vi* : llorar, estar de luto
mourner ['mornər] *n* : doliente *mf*
mournful ['mornfəl] *adj* **1** SORROWFUL : lloroso, plañidero, triste **2** GLOOMY : deprimente, entristecedor — **mournfully** *adv*
mourning ['mornɪŋ] *n* : duelo *m,* luto *m*
mouse ['maʊs] *n, pl* **mice** ['maɪs] **1** : ratón *m,* -tona *f* **2** : ratón *m* (de una computadora)
mousetrap ['maʊsˌtræp] *n* : ratonera *f*
moustache ['mʌˌstæʃ, mə'stæʃ] → **mustache**
mouth[1] ['maʊð] *vt* **1** : decir con poca sinceridad, repetir sin comprensión **2** : articular en silencio <she mouthed the words : formó las palabras con los labios>
mouth[2] ['maʊθ] *n* : boca *f* (de una persona o un animal), entrada *f* (de un túnel), desembocadura *f* (de un río)
mouthful ['maʊθˌfʊl] *n* : bocado *m* (de comida), bocanada *f* (de líquido o humo)

mouthpiece [ˈmaʊθˌpiːs] *n* **:** boquilla *f* (de un instrumento musical)
movable [ˈmuːvəbəl] *or* **moveable** *adj* **:** movible, móvil
move[1] [ˈmuːv] *v* **moved; moving** *vi* **1** GO **:** ir **2** RELOCATE **:** mudarse, trasladarse **3** STIR **:** moverse <¡no te muevas! : don't move!> **4** ACT **:** actuar — *vt* **1 :** mover <move it over there : ponlo allí> <he kept moving his feet : no dejaba de mover los pies> **2** INDUCE, PERSUADE **:** inducir, persuadir, mover **3** TOUCH **:** conmover <it moved him to tears : lo hizo llorar> **4** PROPOSE **:** proponer
move[2] *n* **1** MOVEMENT **:** movimiento *m* **2** RELOCATION **:** mudanza *f* (de casa), traslado *m* **3** STEP **:** paso *m* <a good move : un paso acertado>
movement [ˈmuːvmənt] *n* **:** movimiento *m*
mover [ˈmuːvər] *n* **:** persona *f* que hace mudanzas
movie [ˈmuːvi] *n* **1 :** película *f* **2 movies** *npl* **:** cine *m*
moving [ˈmuːvɪŋ] *adj* **1 :** en movimiento <a moving target : un blanco móvil> **2** TOUCHING **:** conmovedor, emocionante
mow[1] [ˈmoː] *vt* **mowed; mowed** *or* **mown** [ˈmoːn]; **mowing :** cortar (la hierba)
mow[2] [ˈmaʊ] *n* **:** pajar *m*
mower [ˈmoːər] → **lawn mower**
Mr. [ˈmɪstər] *n, pl* **Messrs.** [ˈmɛsərz] **:** señor *m*
Mrs. [ˈmɪsəz, -səs, *esp South* ˈmɪzəz, -zəs] *n, pl* **Mesdames** [meɪ-ˈdɑm, -ˈdæm] **:** señora *f*
Ms. [ˈmɪz] *n* **:** señora *f,* señorita *f*
much[1] [ˈmʌtʃ] *adv* **more** [ˈmor]; **most** [ˈmoːst] **:** mucho <I'm much happier : estoy mucho más contenta> <she talks as much as I do : habla tanto como yo>
much[2] *adj* **more; most :** mucho <it has much validity : tiene mucha validez> <too much time : demasiado tiempo>
much[3] *pron* **:** mucho, -cha <I don't need much : no necesito mucho>
mucilage [ˈmjuːsəlɪdʒ] *n* **:** mucílago *m*
muck [ˈmʌk] *n* **1** MANURE **:** estiércol *m* **2** DIRT, FILTH **:** mugre *f,* suciedad *f* **3** MIRE, MUD **:** barro *m,* fango *m,* lodo *m*
mucous [ˈmjuːkəs] *adj* **:** mucoso <mucous membrane : membrana mucosa>
mucus [ˈmjuːkəs] *n* **:** mucosidad *f*
mud [ˈmʌd] *n* **:** barro *m,* fango *m,* lodo *m*
muddle[1] [ˈmʌdəl] *v* **-dled; -dling** *vt* **1** CONFUSE **:** confundir **2** BUNGLE **:** echar a perder, malograr — *vi* **:** andar confundido <to muddle through : arreglárselas>
muddle[2] *n* **:** confusión *f,* embrollo *m,* lío *m*
muddleheaded [ˌmʌdəlˈhɛdəd, ˈmʌdəlˌ-] *adj* CONFUSED **:** confuso, despistado
muddy[1] [ˈmʌdi] *vt* **-died; -dying :** llenar de barro
muddy[2] *adj* **-dier; -est :** barroso, fangoso, lodoso, enlodado <you're all muddy : estás cubierto de barro>
muff[1] [ˈmʌf] *vt* BUNGLE **:** echar a perder, fallar (un tiro, etc.)
muff[2] *n* **:** manguito *m*
muffin [ˈmʌfən] *n* **:** magdalena *f,* mantecada *f Mex*
muffle [ˈmʌfəl] *vt* **-fled; -fling 1** ENVELOP **:** cubrir, tapar **2** DEADEN **:** amortiguar (un sonido)
muffler [ˈmʌflər] *n* **1** SCARF **:** bufanda *f* **2 :** silenciador *m,* mofle *m CA, Mex* (de un automóvil)
mug[1] [ˈmʌg] *v* **mugged; mugging** *vi* **:** posar (con afectación), hacer muecas <mugging for the camera : haciendo muecas para la cámara> — *vt* ASSAULT **:** asaltar, atracar
mug[2] *n* CUP **:** tazón *m*
mugger [ˈmʌgər] *n* **:** atracador *m,* -dora *f*
mugginess [ˈmʌginəs] *n* **:** bochorno *m*
muggy [ˈmʌgi] *adj* **-gier; -est :** bochornoso
mulatto [mʊˈlɑto, -ˈlæ-] *n, pl* **-toes** *or* **-tos :** mulato *m,* -ta *f*
mulberry [ˈmʌlˌbɛri] *n, pl* **-ries :** morera *f* (árbol), mora *f* (fruta)
mulch[1] [ˈmʌltʃ] *vt* **:** cubrir con pajote
mulch[2] *n* **:** pajote *m*
mule [ˈmjuːl] *n* **1 :** mula *f* **2 :** obstinado *m,* -da *f;* terco *m,* -ca *f*
mulish [ˈmjuːlɪʃ] *adj* **:** obstinado, terco
mull [ˈmʌl] *vt* **to mull over :** reflexionar sobre
mullet [ˈmʌlət] *n, pl* **-let** *or* **-lets :** mújol *m,* múgil *m*
multicolored [ˌmʌltiˈkʌlərd, ˌmʌltaɪ-] *adj* **:** multicolor, abigarrado
multifaceted [ˌmʌltiˈfæsət̬əd, ˌmʌltaɪ-] *adj* **:** multifacético
multifamily [ˌmʌltiˈfæmli, ˌmʌltaɪ-] *adj* **:** multifamiliar
multifarious [ˌmʌltəˈfæriəs] *adj* DIVERSE **:** diverso, variado
multilateral [ˌmʌltiˈlæt̬ərəl, ˌmʌltaɪ-] *adj* **:** multilateral
multimedia [ˌmʌltiˈmiːdiə, ˌmʌltaɪ-] *adj* **:** multimedia
multimillionaire [ˌmʌltiˌmɪljəˈnær, ˌmʌltaɪ-, -ˈmɪljəˌnær] *adj* **:** multimillonario
multinational [ˌmʌltiˈnæʃənəl, ˌmʌltaɪ-] *adj* **:** multinacional
multiple[1] [ˈmʌltəpəl] *adj* **:** múltiple
multiple[2] *n* **:** múltiplo *m*
multiple sclerosis [skləˈroːsɪs] *n* **:** esclerosis *f* múltiple
multiplication [ˌmʌltəpləˈkeɪʃən] *n* **:** multiplicación *f*
multiplicity [ˌmʌltəˈplɪsət̬i] *n, pl* **-ties :** multiplicidad *f*
multiplier [ˈmʌltəˌplaɪər] *n* **:** multiplicador *m* (en matemáticas)

multiply ['mʌltəˌplaɪ] *v* **-plied; -plying** *vt* : multiplicar — *vi* : multiplicarse
multipurpose [ˌmʌlti'pərpəs, ˌmʌltaɪ-] *adj* : multiuso
multitude ['mʌltəˌtu:d, -ˌtju:d] *n* **1** CROWD : multitud *f*, muchedumbre *f* **2** HOST : multitud *f*, gran cantidad *f* <a multitude of ideas : numerosas ideas>
multivitamin [ˌmʌlti'vaɪṭəmən, ˌmʌltaɪ-] *adj* : multivitamínico
mum¹ ['mʌm] *adj* SILENT : callado
mum² *n* → **chrysanthemum**
mumble¹ ['mʌmbəl] *v* **-bled; -bling** *vt* : mascullar, musitar — *vi* : mascullar, hablar entre dientes, murmurar
mumble² *n* **to speak in a mumble** : hablar entre dientes
mummy ['mʌmi] *n, pl* **-mies** : momia *f*
mumps ['mʌmps] *ns & pl* : paperas *fpl*
munch ['mʌntʃ] *v* : mascar, masticar
mundane [ˌmʌn'deɪn, 'mʌnˌ-] *adj* **1** EARTHLY, WORLDLY : mundano, terrenal **2** COMMONPLACE : rutinario, ordinario
municipal [mjʊ'nɪsəpəl] *adj* : municipal
municipality [mjʊˌnɪsə'pæləṭi] *n, pl* **-ties** : municipio *m*
munitions [mjʊ'nɪʃənz] *npl* : municiones *fpl*
mural¹ ['mjʊrəl] *adj* : mural
mural² ['mjʊrəlɪst] *n* : mural *m*
murder¹ ['mərdər] *vt* : asesinar, matar — *vi* : matar
murder² *n* : asesinato *m*, homicidio *m*
murderer ['mərdərər] *n* : asesino *m*, -na *f*; homicida *mf*
murderess ['mərdərɪs, -dəˌrɛs, -dərəs] *n* : asesina *f*, homicida *f*
murderous ['mərdərəs] *adj* : asesino, homicida
murk ['mərk] *n* DARKNESS : oscuridad *f*, tinieblas *fpl*
murkiness ['mərkinəs] *n* : oscuridad *f*, tenebrosidad *f*
murky ['mərki] *adj* **-kier; -est** : oscuro, tenebroso
murmur¹ ['mərmər] *vi* **1** DRONE : murmurar **2** GRUMBLE : refunfuñar, regañar, rezongar — *vt* MUMBLE : murmurar
murmur² *n* **1** COMPLAINT : queja *f* **2** DRONE : murmullo *m*, rumor *m*
muscle¹ ['mʌsəl] *vi* **-cled; -cling** : meterse <to muscle in on : meterse por la fuerza en, entrometerse en>
muscle² *n* **1** : músculo *m* **2** STRENGTH : fuerza *f*
muscular ['mʌskjələr] *adj* **1** : muscular <muscular tissue : tejido muscular> **2** BRAWNY : musculoso
muscular dystrophy *n* : distrofia *f* muscular
musculature ['mʌskjələˌtʃʊr, -tʃər] *n* : musculatura *f*
muse¹ ['mju:z] *vi* **mused; musing** PONER, REFLECT : cavilar, meditar, reflexionar
muse² *n* : musa *f*
museum [mjʊ'zi:əm] *n* : museo *m*
mush ['mʌʃ] *n* **1** : gachas *fpl* (de maíz) **2** SENTIMENTALITY : sensiblería *f*
mushroom¹ ['mʌʃˌru:m, -ˌrʊm] *vi* GROW, MULTIPLY : crecer rápidamente, multiplicarse
mushroom² *n* : hongo *m*, champiñón *m*, seta *f*
mushy ['mʌʃi] *adj* **mushier; -est** **1** SOFT : blando **2** MAWKISH : sensiblero
music ['mju:zɪk] *n* : música *f*
musical¹ ['mju:zɪkəl] *adj* : musical, de música — **musically** *adv*
musical² *n* : comedia *f* musical
music box *n* : cajita *f* de música
musician [mjʊ'zɪʃən] *n* : músico *m*, -ca *f*
musk ['mʌsk] *n* : almizcle *m*
musket ['mʌskət] *n* : mosquete *m*
musketeer [ˌmʌskə'tɪr] *n* : mosquetero *m*
muskrat ['mʌskˌræt] *n, pl* **-rat** *or* **-rats** : rata *f* almizclera
Muslim¹ ['mʌzləm, 'mʊs-, 'mʊz-] *adj* : musulmán
Muslim² *n* : musulmán *m*, -mana *f*
muslin ['mʌzlən] *n* : muselina *f*
muss¹ ['mʌs] *vt* : desordenar, despeinar (el pelo)
muss² *n* : desorden *m*
mussel ['mʌsəl] *n* : mejillón *m*
must¹ ['mʌst] *v aux* **1** (*expressing obligation or necessity*) : deber, tener que <you must stop : debes parar> <we must obey : tenemos que obedecer> **2** (*expressing probability*) : deber (de), haber de <you must be tired : debes de estar cansado> <it must be late : ha de ser tarde>
must² *n* : necesidad *f* <exercise is a must : el ejercicio es imprescindible>
mustache ['mʌˌstæʃ, mʌ'stæʃ] *n* : bigote *m*, bigotes *mpl*
mustang ['mʌˌstæŋ] *n* : mustang *m*
mustard ['mʌstərd] *n* : mostaza *f*
muster¹ ['mʌstər] *vt* **1** ASSEMBLE : reunir **2 to muster up** : armarse de, cobrar (valor, fuerzas, etc.)
muster² *n* **1** INSPECTION : revista *f* (de tropas) <it didn't pass muster : no resistió un examen minucioso> **2** COLLECTION : colección *f*
mustiness ['mʌstinəs] *n* : lo mohoso
musty ['mʌsti] *adj* **mustier; -est** : mohoso, que huele a moho, que huele a encerrado
mutant¹ ['mju:tənt] *adj* : mutante
mutant² *n* : mutante *m*
mutate ['mju:ˌteɪt] *vi* **-tated; -tating** **1** : mutar (genéticamente) **2** CHANGE : transformarse
mutation [mju:'teɪʃən] *n* : mutación *f* (genética)

mute[1] ['mjuːt] *vt* **muted; muting** MUFFLE : amortiguar, ponerle sordina a (un instrumento musical)
mute[2] *adj* **muter; mutest** : mudo — **mutely** *adv*
mute[3] *n* **1** : mudo *m*, -da *f* (persona) **2** : sordina *f* (para un instrumento musical)
mutilate ['mjuːt̬ə,leɪt] *vt* **-lated; -lating** : mutilar
mutilation [,mjuːt̬ə'leɪʃən] *n* : mutilación *f*
mutineer [,mjuːtən'ɪr] *n* : amotinado *m*, -da *f*
mutinous ['mjuːtənəs] *adj* : amotinado
mutiny[1] ['mjuːtəni] *vi* **-nied; -nying** : amotinarse
mutiny[2] *n, pl* **-nies** : amotinamiento *m*, motín *m*
mutt ['mʌt] *n* MONGREL : perro *m* mestizo, perro *m* corriente *Mex*
mutter ['mʌt̬ər] *vi* **1** MUMBLE : mascullar, hablar entre dientes, murmurar **2** GRUMBLE : refunfuñar, regañar, rezongar
mutton ['mʌtən] *n* : carne *f* de carnero
mutual ['mjuːtʃʊəl] *adj* **1** : mutuo <mutual respect : respeto mutuo> **2** COMMON : común <a mutual friend : un amigo común>
mutually ['mjuːtʃʊəli, -tʃəli] *adv* **1** : mutuamente <mutually beneficial : mutuamente beneficioso> **2** JOINTLY : conjuntamente
muzzle[1] ['mʌzəl] *vt* **-zled; -zling** : ponerle un bozal a (un animal), amordazar
muzzle[2] *n* **1** SNOUT : hocico *m* **2** : bozal *m* (para un perro, etc.) **3** : boca *f* (de un arma de fuego)
my[1] ['maɪ] *adj* : mi <my parents : mis padres>
my[2] *interj* : ¡caramba!, ¡Dios mío!
myopia [maɪ'oːpiə] *n* : miopía *f*
myopic [maɪ'oːpɪk, -'ɑ-] *adj* : miope
myriad[1] ['mɪriəd] *adj* INNUMERABLE : innumerable
myriad[2] *n* : miríada *f*
myrrh ['mər] *n* : mirra *f*
myrtle ['mərt̬əl] *n* : mirto *m*, arrayán *m*
myself [maɪ'sɛlf] *pron* **1** (*used reflexively*) : me <I washed myself : me lavé> **2** (*used for emphasis*) : yo mismo, yo misma <I did it myself : lo hice yo mismo>
mysterious [mɪ'stɪriəs] *adj* : misterioso — **mysteriously** *adv*
mysteriousness [mɪ'stɪriəsnəs] *n* : lo misterioso
mystery ['mɪstəri] *n, pl* **-teries** : misterio *m*
mystic[1] ['mɪstɪk] *adj* : místico
mystic[2] *n* : místico *m*, -ca *f*
mystical ['mɪstɪkəl] *adj* : místico — **mystically** *adv*
mysticism ['mɪstə,sɪzəm] *n* : misticismo *m*
mystify ['mɪstə,faɪ] *vt* **-fied; -fying** : dejar perplejo, confundir
mystique [mɪ'stiːk] *n* : aura *f* de misterio
myth ['mɪθ] *n* : mito *m*
mythical ['mɪθɪkəl] *adj* : mítico
mythological [,mɪθə'lɑdʒɪkəl] *adj* : mitológico
mythology [mɪ'θɑlədʒi] *n, pl* **-gies** : mitología *f*

N

n ['ɛn] *n, pl* **n's** *or* **ns** ['ɛnz] : decimocuarta letra del alfabeto inglés
nab ['næb] *vt* **nabbed; nabbing** : prender, pillar *fam*, pescar *fam*
nadir ['neɪdər, 'neɪ,dɪr] *n* : nadir *m*, punto *m* más bajo
nag[1] ['næg] *v* **nagged; nagging** *vi* **1** COMPLAIN : quejarse, rezongar **2 to nag at** HASSLE : molestar, darle (la) lata (a alguien) — *vt* **1** PESTER : molestar, fastidiar **2** SCOLD : regañar, estarle encima a *fam*
nag[2] *n* **1** GRUMBLER : gruñón *m*, -ñona *f* **2** HORSE : jamelgo *m*
naiad ['neɪəd, 'naɪ-, -,æd] *n, pl* **-iads** *or* **-iades** [-ə,diːz] : náyade *f*
nail[1] ['neɪl] *vt* : clavar, sujetar con clavos
nail[2] *n* **1** FINGERNAIL : uña *f* <nail file : lima (de uñas)> <nail polish : laca de uñas> **2** : clavo *m* <to hit the nail on the head : dar en el clavo>
naive *or* **naïve** [nɑ'iːv] *adj* **-iver; -est** **1** INGENUOUS : ingenuo, cándido **2** GULLIBLE : crédulo
naively [nɑ'iːvli] *adv* : ingenuamente
naïveté [,nɑ,iːvə'teɪ, nɑ'iːvə,-] *n* : ingenuidad *f*
naked ['neɪkəd] *adj* **1** UNCLOTHED : desnudo **2** UNCOVERED : desenvainado (dícese de una espada), pelado (dícese de los árboles), expuesto al aire (dícese de una llama) **3** OBVIOUS, PLAIN : manifiesto, puro, desnudo <the naked truth : la pura verdad> **4 to the naked eye** : a simple vista
nakedly ['neɪkədli] *adv* : manifiestamente
nakedness ['neɪkədnəs] *n* : desnudez *f*
name[1] ['neɪm] *vt* **named; naming** **1** CALL : llamar, bautizar, ponerle nombre a **2** MENTION : mentar, mencionar, dar el nombre de <they have named a suspect : han dado el nombre de un

sospechoso> 3 APPOINT : nombrar 4 **to name a price** : fijar un precio

name[2] *adj* 1 KNOWN : de nombre <name brand : marca conocida> 2 PROMINENT : de renombre, de prestigio

name[3] *n* 1 : nombre *m* <what is your name : ¿cómo se llama?> 2 SURNAME : apellido *m* 3 EPITHET : epíteto *m* <to call somebody names : llamar a alguien de todo> 4 REPUTATION : fama *f*, reputación *f* <to make a name for oneself : darse a conocer, hacerse famoso>

nameless ['neɪmləs] *adj* 1 ANONYMOUS : anónimo 2 INDESCRIBABLE : indecible, indescriptible

namelessly ['neɪmləsli] *adv* : anónimamente

namely ['neɪmli] *adv* : a saber

namesake ['neɪm,seɪk] *n* : tocayo *m*, -ya *f*; homónimo *m*, -ma *f*

Namibian [nə'mɪbiən] *n* : namibio *m*, -bia *f* — **Namibian** *adj*

nap[1] ['næp] *vi* **napped; napping** 1 : dormir, dormir la siesta 2 **to be caught napping** : estar desprevenido

nap[2] *n* 1 SLEEP : siesta *f* <to take a nap : echarse una siesta> 2 FUZZ, PILE : pelo *m*, pelusa *f* (de telas)

nape ['neɪp, 'næp] *n* : nuca *f*, cerviz *f*, cogote *m*

naphtha ['næfθə] *n* : nafta *f*

napkin ['næpkən] *n* : servilleta *f*

narcissism ['nɑrsə,sɪzəm] *n* : narcisismo *m*

narcissist ['nɑrsəsɪst] *n* : narcisista *mf*

narcissistic [,nɑrsə'sɪstɪk] *adj* : narcisista

narcissus [nɑr'sɪsəs] *n, pl* **-cissus** *or* **-cissuses** *or* **-cissi** [-'sɪ,saɪ, -,siː] : narciso *m*

narcotic[1] [nɑr'kɑtɪk] *adj* : narcótico

narcotic[2] *n* : narcótico *m*, estupefaciente *m*

narrate ['nær,eɪt] *vt* **-rated; -rating** : narrar, relatar

narration [næ'reɪʃən] *n* : narración *f*

narrative[1] ['nærət̬ɪv] *adj* : narrativo

narrative[2] *n* : narración *f*, narrativa *f*, relato *m*

narrator ['nær,eɪt̬ər] *n* : narrador *m*, -dora *f*

narrow[1] ['nær,oː] *vi* : estrecharse, angostarse <the river narrowed : el río se estrechó> — *vt* 1 : estrechar, angostar 2 LIMIT : restringir, limitar <to narrow the search : limitar la búsqueda>

narrow[2] *adj* 1 : estrecho, angosto 2 LIMITED : estricto, limitado <in the narrowest sense of the word : en el sentido más estricto de la palabra> 3 **to have a narrow escape** : escapar por un pelo

narrowly ['næroli] *adv* 1 BARELY : por poco 2 CLOSELY : de cerca

narrow-minded [,næro'maɪndəd] *adj* : de miras estrechas

narrowness ['næronəs] *n* : estrechez *f*

narrows ['næroːz] *npl* STRAIT : estrecho *m*

narwhal ['nɑr,*h*wɑl, 'nɑrwəl] *n* : narval *m*

nasal ['neɪzəl] *adj* : nasal, gangoso <a nasal voice : una voz gangosa>

nasally ['neɪzəli] *adv* 1 : por la nariz 2 : con voz gangosa

nastily ['næstəli] *adv* : con maldad, cruelmente

nastiness ['næstinəs] *n* : porquería *f*

nasturtium [nə'stərʃəm, næ-] *n* : capuchina *f*

nasty ['næsti] *adj* **-tier; -est** 1 FILTHY : sucio, mugriento 2 OBSCENE : obsceno 3 MEAN, SPITEFUL : malo, malicioso 4 UNPLEASANT : desagradable, feo 5 REPUGNANT : asqueroso, repugnante <a nasty smell : un olor asqueroso>

natal ['neɪt̬əl] *adj* : natal

nation ['neɪʃən] *n* : nación *f*

national[1] ['næʃənəl] *adj* : nacional

national[2] *n* : ciudadano *m*, -na *f*; nacional *mf*

nationalism ['næʃənə,lɪzəm] *n* : nacionalismo *m*

nationalist[1] ['næʃənəlɪst] *adj* : nacionalista

nationalist[2] *n* : nacionalista *mf*

nationalistic [,næʃənə'lɪstɪk] *adj* : nacionalista

nationality [,næʃə'nælət̬i] *n, pl* **-ties** : nacionalidad *f*

nationalization [,næʃənələ'zeɪʃən] *n* : nacionalización *f*

nationalize ['næʃənə,laɪz] *vt* **-ized; -izing** : nacionalizar

nationally ['næʃənəli] *adv* : a escala nacional, a nivel nacional

nationwide ['neɪʃən'waɪd] *adj* : en toda la nación, por todo el país

native[1] ['neɪt̬ɪv] *adj* 1 INNATE : innato 2 : natal <her native city : su ciudad natal> 3 INDIGENOUS : indígeno, autóctono

native[2] *n* 1 ABORIGINE : nativo *m*, -va *f*; indígena *mf* 2 : natural *m* <he's a native of Mexico : es natural de México>

Native American → **American Indian**

nativity [nə'tɪvət̬i, neɪ-] *n, pl* **-ties** 1 BIRTH : navidad *f* 2 **the Nativity** : la Natividad, la Navidad

natty ['næt̬i] *adj* **-tier; -est** : elegante, garboso

natural[1] ['nætʃərəl] *adj* 1 : natural, de la naturaleza <natural woodlands : bosques naturales> <natural childbirth : parto natural> 2 INNATE : innato, natural 3 UNAFFECTED : natural, sin afectación 4 LIFELIKE : natural, vivo

natural[2] *n* **to be a natural** : tener un talento innato (para algo)

natural gas *n* : gas *m* natural

natural history *n* : historia *f* natural

naturalist [ˈnætʃərəlɪst] *n* : naturalista *mf*

naturalization [ˌnætʃərələˈzeɪʃən] *n* : naturalización *f*

naturalize [ˈnætʃərəˌlaɪz] *vt* **-ized; -izing** : naturalizar

naturally [ˈnætʃərəli] *adv* **1** INHERENTLY : naturalmente, intrínsecamente **2** UNAFFECTEDLY : de manera natural **3** OF COURSE : por supuesto, naturalmente

naturalness [ˈnætʃərəlnəs] *n* : naturalidad *f*

natural science *n* : ciencias *fpl* naturales

nature [ˈneɪtʃər] *n* **1** : naturaleza *f* <the laws of nature : las leyes de la naturaleza> **2** KIND, SORT : índole *f,* clase *f* <things of this nature : cosas de esta índole> **3** DISPOSITION : carácter *m,* natural *m,* naturaleza *f* <it is his nature to be friendly : es de natural simpático> <human nature : la naturaleza humana>

naught [ˈnɔt] *n* **1** : nada *f* <to come to naught : reducirse a nada, fracasar> **2** ZERO : cero *m*

naughtily [ˈnɔt̬əli] *adv* : traviesamente, con malicia

naughtiness [ˈnɔt̬inəs] *n* : mala conducta *f,* travesuras *fpl*, malicia *f*

naughty [ˈnɔt̬i] *adj* **-tier; -est 1** MISCHIEVOUS : travieso, pícaro **2** RISQUÉ : picante, subido de tono

nausea [ˈnɔziə, ˈnɔʃə] *n* **1** SICKNESS : náuseas *fpl* **2** DISGUST : asco *m*

nauseate [ˈnɔziˌeɪt, -ʒi-, -si-, -ʃi-] *vt* **-ated; -ating 1** SICKEN : darle náuseas (a alguien) **2** DISGUST : asquear, darle asco (a alguien)

nauseating *adj* : nauseabundo, repugnante

nauseatingly [ˈnɔziˌeɪt̬ɪŋli, -ʒi-, -si-, -ʃi-] *adv* : hasta el punto de dar asco <nauseatingly sweet : tan dulce que da asco>

nauseous [ˈnɔʃəs, -ziəs] *adj* **1** SICK : mareado, con náuseas **2** SICKENING : nauseabundo

nautical [ˈnɔt̬ɪkəl] *adj* : náutico

nautilus [ˈnɔt̬ələs] *n, pl* **-luses** *or* **-li** [-ˌlaɪ, -ˌliː] : nautilo *m*

naval [ˈneɪvəl] *adj* : naval

nave [ˈneɪv] *n* : nave *f*

navel [ˈneɪvəl] *n* : ombligo *m*

navigability [ˌnævɪgəˈbɪlət̬i] *n* : navegabilidad *f*

navigable [ˈnævɪgəbəl] *adj* : navegable

navigate [ˈnævəˌgeɪt] *v* **-gated; -gating** *vi* : navegar — *vt* **1** STEER : gobernar (un barco), pilotar (un avión) **2** : navegar por (un río, etc.)

navigation [ˌnævəˈgeɪʃən] *n* : navegación *f*

navigator [ˈnævəˌgeɪt̬ər] *n* : navegante *mf*

navy [ˈneɪvi] *n, pl* **-vies 1** FLEET : flota *f* **2** : marina *f* de guerra, armada *f* <the United States Navy : la armada de los Estados Unidos> **3** *or* **navy blue** : azul *m* marino

nay[1] [ˈneɪ] *adv* : no

nay[2] *n* : no *m,* voto *m* en contra

Nazi [ˈnɑtsi, ˈnæt-] *n* : nazi *mf*

Nazism [ˈnɑtˌsɪzəm, ˈnæt-] *or* **Naziism** [ˈnɑtsiˌɪzəm, ˈnæt-] *n* : nazismo *m*

Neanderthal man [niˈændərˌθɔl, -ˌtɔl] *n* : hombre *m* de Neanderthal

near[1] [ˈnɪr] *vt* **1** : acercarse a <the ship is nearing port : el barco se está acercando al puerto> **2** : estar a punto de <she is nearing graduation : está a punto de graduarse>

near[2] *adv* **1** CLOSE : cerca <my family lives quite near : mi familia vive muy cerca> **2** NEARLY : casi <I came near to finishing : casi terminé>

near[3] *adj* **1** CLOSE : cercano, próximo **2** SIMILAR : parecido, semejante

near[4] *prep* : cerca de

nearby[1] [nɪrˈbaɪ, ˈnɪrˌbaɪ] *adv* : cerca

nearby[2] *adj* : cercano

nearly [ˈnɪrli] *adv* **1** ALMOST : casi <nearly asleep : casi dormido> **2 not nearly** : ni con mucho, ni mucho menos <it was not nearly so bad as I had expected : no fue ni con mucho tan malo como esperaba>

nearness [ˈnɪrnəs] *n* : proximidad *f*

nearsighted [ˈnɪrˌsaɪt̬əd] *adj* : miope, corto de vista

nearsightedly [ˈnɪrˌsaɪt̬ədli] *adv* : con miopía

nearsightedness [ˈnɪrˌsaɪt̬ədnəs] *n* : miopía *f*

neat [ˈniːt] *adj* **1** CLEAN, ORDERLY : ordenado, pulcro, limpio **2** UNDILUTED : solo, sin diluir **3** SIMPLE, TASTEFUL : sencillo y de buen gusto **4** CLEVER : hábil, ingenioso <a neat trick : un truco ingenioso>

neatly [ˈniːtli] *adv* **1** TIDILY : ordenadamente **2** CLEVERLY : ingeniosamente

neatness [ˈniːtnəs] *n* : pulcritud *f,* limpieza *f,* orden *m*

nebula [ˈnɛbjʊlə] *n, pl* **-lae** [-ˌliː, -ˌlaɪ] : nebulosa *f*

nebulous [ˈnɛbjʊləs] *adj* : nebuloso, vago

necessarily [ˌnɛsəˈsɛrəli] *adv* : necesariamente, forzosamente

necessary[1] [ˈnɛsəˌsɛri] *adj* **1** INEVITABLE : inevitable **2** COMPULSORY : necesario, obligatorio **3** ESSENTIAL : imprescindible, preciso, necesario

necessary[2] *n, pl* **-saries** : lo esencial, lo necesario

necessitate [nɪˈsɛsəˌteɪt] *vt* **-tated; -tating** : necesitar, requerir

necessity [nɪˈsɛsət̬i] *n, pl* **-ties 1** NEED : necesidad *f* **2** REQUIREMENT : requisito *m* indispensable **3** POVERTY : indigencia *f,* necesidad *f* **4** INEVITABILITY : inevitabilitad *f*

neck[1] [ˈnɛk] *vi* : besuquearse

neck[2] *n* **1 :** cuello *m* (de una persona), pescuezo *m* (de un animal) **2** COLLAR **:** cuello *m* **3 :** cuello *m* (de una botella), mástil *m* (de una guitarra)
neckerchief [ˈnɛkərtʃəf, -ˌtʃiːf] *n, pl* **-chiefs** [-tʃəfs, -ˌtʃiːfs] **:** pañuelo *m* (para el cuello), mascada *f Mex*
necklace [ˈnɛkləs] *n* **:** collar *m*
neckline [ˈnɛkˌlaɪn] *n* **:** escote *m*
necktie [ˈnɛkˌtaɪ] *n* **:** corbata *f*
nectar [ˈnɛktər] *n* **:** néctar *m*
nectarine [ˌnɛktəˈriːn] *n* **:** nectarina *f*
née *or* **nee** [ˈneɪ] *adj* **:** de soltera <Mrs. Smith, née Whitman **:** la señora Smith, de soltera Whitman>
need[1] [ˈniːd] *vt* **1 :** necesitar <I need your help **:** necesito su ayuda> <I need money **:** me falta dinero> **2** REQUIRE **:** requerir, exigir <that job needs patience **:** ese trabajo exige paciencia> **3 to need to :** tener que <he needs to study **:** tiene que estudiar> <they need to be scolded **:** hay que reprenderlos> — *v aux* **1** MUST **:** tener que, deber <need you shout? **:** ¿tienes que gritar?> **2 to be needed :** hacer falta <you needn't worry **:** no hace falta que te preocupes, no hay por qué preocuparse>
need[2] *n* **1** NECESSITY **:** necesidad *f* <in case of need **:** en caso de necesidad> **2** LACK **:** falta *f* <the need for better training **:** la falta de mejor capacitación> <to be in need **:** necesitar> **3** POVERTY **:** necesidad *f,* indigencia *f* **4 needs** *npl* **:** requisitos *mpl,* carencias *fpl*
needful [ˈniːdfəl] *adj* **:** necesario
needle[1] [ˈniːdəl] *vt* **-dled; -dling :** pinchar
needle[2] *n* **1 :** aguja *f* <to thread a needle **:** enhebrar una aguja> <knitting needle **:** aguja de tejer> **2** POINTER **:** aguja *f,* indicador *m*
needlepoint [ˈniːdəlˌpɔɪnt] *n* **1** LACE **:** encaje *m* de mano **2** EMBROIDERY **:** bordado *m* en cañamazo
needless [ˈniːdləs] *adj* **:** innecesario
needlessly [ˈniːdləsli] *adv* **:** sin ninguna necesidad, innecesariamente
needlework [ˈniːdəlˌwərk] *n* **:** bordado *m*
needn't [ˈniːdənt] (*contraction of* **need not**) → **need**
needy[1] [ˈniːdi] **needier; -est** *adj* **:** necesitado
needy[2] *n* **the needy :** los necesitados *mpl*
nefarious [nɪˈfæriəs] *adj* **:** nefario, nefando, infame
negate [nɪˈgeɪt] *vt* **-gated; -gating 1** DENY **:** negar **2** NULLIFY **:** invalidar, anular
negation [nɪˈgeɪʃən] *n* **:** negación *f*
negative[1] [ˈnɛgət̬ɪv] *adj* **:** negativo
negative[2] *n* **1 :** negación *f* (en lingüística) **2 :** negativa *f* <to answer in the negative **:** contestar con una negativa> **3 :** término *m* negativo (en matemáticas) **4 :** negativo *m,* imagen *f* en negativo (en fotografía)
negatively [ˈnɛgət̬ɪvli] *adv* **:** negativamente
neglect[1] [nɪˈglɛkt] *vt* **1 :** desatender, descuidar <to neglect one's health **:** descuidar la salud> **2 :** no cumplir con, faltar a <to neglect one's obligations **:** faltar uno a sus obligaciones> <he neglected to tell me **:** omitió decírmelo>
neglect[2] *n* **1 :** negligencia *f,* descuido *m,* incumplimiento *m* <through neglect **:** por negligencia> <neglect of duty **:** incumplimiento del deber> **2 in a state of neglect :** abandonado, descuidado
neglectful [nɪˈglɛktfəl] *adj* **:** descuidado *m*
negligee [ˌnɛgləˈʒeɪ] *n* **:** negligé *m*
negligence [ˈnɛglɪdʒən*t*s] *n* **:** descuido *m,* negligencia *f*
negligent [ˈnɛglɪdʒənt] *adj* **:** negligente, descuidado — **negligently** *adv*
negligible [ˈnɛglɪdʒəbəl] *adj* **:** insignificante, despreciable
negotiable [nɪˈgoːʃəbəl, -ʃiə-] *adj* **:** negociable
negotiate [nɪˈgoːʃiˌeɪt] *v* **-ated; -ating** *vi* **:** negociar — *vt* **1 :** negociar, gestionar <to negotiate a treaty **:** negociar un trato> **2 :** salvar, franquear <they negotiated the obstacles **:** salvaron los obstáculos> <to negotiate a turn **:** tomar una curva>
negotiation [nɪˌgoːʃiˈeɪʃən, -siˈeɪ-] *n* **:** negociación *f*
negotiator [nɪˈgoːʃiˌeɪtər, -siˌeɪ-] *n* **:** negociador *m,* -dora *f*
Negro [ˈniːˌgroː] *n, pl* **-groes :** negro *m,* -gra *f*
neigh[1] [ˈneɪ] *vi* **:** relinchar
neigh[2] *n* **:** relincho *m*
neighbor[1] [ˈneɪbər] *vt* **:** ser vecino de, estar junto a <her house neighbors mine **:** su casa está junto a la mía> — *vi* **:** estar cercano, lindar, colindar <her land neighbors on mine **:** sus tierras lindan con las mías>
neighbor[2] *n* **1 :** vecino *m,* -na *f* **2 love thy neighbor :** ama a tu prójimo
neighborhood [ˈneɪbərˌhʊd] *n* **1 :** barrio *m,* vecindad *f,* vecindario *m* **2 in the neighborhood of :** alrededor de, cerca de
neighborly [ˈneɪbərli] *adv* **:** amable, de buena vecindad
neither[1] [ˈniːðər, ˈnaɪ-] *adj* **:** ninguno (de los dos)
neither[2] *conj* **1 :** ni <neither asleep nor awake **:** ni dormido ni despierto> **2** NOR **:** ni (tampoco) <I'm not asleep — neither am I **:** no estoy dormido — ni yo tampoco>
neither[3] *pron* **:** ninguno
nemesis [ˈnɛməsɪs] *n, pl* **-eses** [-ˌsiːz] **1** RIVAL **:** rival *mf* **2** RETRIBUTION **:** justo castigo *m*

neologism [niˈɑlə,dʒɪzəm] *n* **:** neologismo *m*
neon[1] [ˈni:,ɑn] *adj* **:** de neón <neon sign : letrero de neón>
neon[2] *n* **:** neón *m*
Nepali [nəˈpɔli, -ˈpɑ-, -ˈpæ-] *n* **:** nepalés *m*, -lesa *f* — **Nepali** *adj*
neophyte [ˈni:ə,faɪt] *n* **:** neófito *m*, -ta *f*
nephew [ˈnɛ,fju:, *chiefly British* ˈnɛ,vju:] *n* **:** sobrino *m*
nepotism [ˈnɛpə,tɪzəm] *n* **:** nepotismo *m*
Neptune [ˈnɛp,tu:n, -,tju:n] *n* **:** Neptuno *m*
nerd [ˈnərd] *n* **:** ganso *m*, -sa *f*
nerve [ˈnərv] *n* **1 :** nervio *m* **2** COURAGE **:** coraje *m*, valor *m*, fuerza *f* de la voluntad <to lose one's nerve : perder el valor> **3** AUDACITY, GALL **:** atrevimiento *m*, descaro *m* <of all the nerve! : ¡qué descaro!> **4 nerves** *npl* **:** nervios *mpl* <a fit of nerves : un ataque de nervios>
nervous [ˈnərvəs] *adj* **1 :** nervioso <the nervous system : el sistema nervioso> **2** EXCITABLE **:** nervioso, excitable <to get nervous : excitarse, ponerse nervioso> **3** FEARFUL **:** miedoso, temeroso
nervously [ˈnərvəsli] *adv* **:** nerviosamente
nervousness [ˈnərvəsnəs] *n* **:** nerviosismo *m*, nerviosidad *f*, ansiedad *f*
nervy [ˈnərvi] *adj* **nervier; -est 1** COURAGEOUS **:** valiente **2** IMPUDENT **:** atrevido, descarado, fresco *fam* **3** NERVOUS **:** nervioso
nest[1] [ˈnɛst] *vi* **:** anidar
nest[2] *n* **1 :** nido *m* (de un ave), avispero *m* (de una avispa), madriguera *f* (de un animal) **2** REFUGE **:** nido *m*, refugio *m* **3** SET **:** juego *m* <a nest of tables : un juego de mesitas>
nestle [ˈnɛsəl] *vi* **-tled; -tling :** acurrucarse, arrimarse cómodamente
net[1] [ˈnɛt] *vt* **netted; netting 1** CATCH **:** pescar, atrapar con una red **2** CLEAR **:** ganar neto <they netted $5000 : ganaron $5000 netos> **3** YIELD **:** producir neto
net[2] *adj* **:** neto <net weight : peso neto> <net gain : ganancia neta>
net[3] *n* **:** red *f*, malla *f*
nether [ˈnɛðər] *adj* **1 :** inferior, más bajo **2 the nether regions :** el infierno
nettle[1] [ˈnɛtəl] *vt* **-tled; -tling :** irritar, provocar, molestar
nettle[2] *n* **:** ortiga *f*
network [ˈnɛt,wərk] *n* **1** SYSTEM **:** red *f* **2** CHAIN **:** cadena *f* <a network of supermarkets : una cadena de supermercados>
neural [ˈnʊrəl, ˈnjʊr-] *adj* **:** neural
neuralgia [nʊˈrældʒə, njʊ-] *n* **:** neuralgia *f*
neuritis [nʊˈraɪtəs, njʊ-] *n, pl* **-ritides** [-ˈrɪtə,di:z] *or* **-ritises :** neuritis *f*
neurological [,nʊrəˈlɑdʒɪkəl, ,njʊr-] *or* **neurologic** [,nʊrəˈlɑdʒɪk, ,njʊr-] *adj* **:** neurológico
neurologist [nʊˈrɑlədʒɪst, njʊ-] *n* **:** neurólogo *m*, -ga *f*
neurology [nʊˈrɑlədʒi, njʊ-] *n* **:** neurología *f*
neurosis [nʊˈro:sɪs, njʊ-] *n, pl* **-roses** [-,si:z] **:** neurosis *f*
neurotic[1] [nʊˈrɑtɪk, njʊ-] *adj* **:** neurótico
neurotic[2] *n* **:** neurótico *m*, -ca *f*
neuter[1] [ˈnu:tər, ˈnju:-] *vt* **:** castrar
neuter[2] *adj* **:** neutro
neutral[1] [ˈnu:trəl, ˈnju:-] *adj* **1** IMPARTIAL **:** neutral, imparcial <to remain neutral : permanecer neutral> **2 :** neutro <a neutral color : un color neutro> **3 :** neutro (en la química o la electricidad)
neutral[2] *n* **:** punto *m* muerto (de un automóvil)
neutrality [nu:ˈtræləti:, nju:-] *n* **:** neutralidad *f*
neutralization [,nu:trələˈzeɪʃən, ,nju:-] *n* **:** neutralización *f*
neutralize [ˈnu:trə,laɪz, ˈnju:-] *vt* **-ized; -izing :** neutralizar
neutron [ˈnu:,trɑn, ˈnju:-] *n* **:** neutrón *m*
never [ˈnɛvər] *adv* **1 :** nunca, jamás <he never studies : nunca estudia> **2 never again :** nunca más, nunca jamás **3 never mind :** no importa
nevermore [,nɛvərˈmor] *adv* **:** nunca más
nevertheless [,nɛvərðəˈlɛs] *adv* **:** sin embargo, no obstante
new [ˈnu:, ˈnju:] *adj* **1 :** nuevo <a new dress : un vestido nuevo> **2** RECENT **:** nuevo, reciente <what's new? : ¿qué hay de nuevo?> <a new arrival : un recién llegado> **3** DIFFERENT **:** nuevo, distinto <this problem is new : este problema es distinto> <new ideas : ideas nuevas> **4 like new :** como nuevo
newborn [ˈnu:,bɔrn, ˈnju:-] *adj* **:** recién nacido
newcomer [ˈnu:,kʌmər, ˈnju:-] *n* **:** recién llegado *m*, recién llegada *f*
newfangled [ˈnu:ˈfæŋgəld, ˈnju:-] *adj* **:** novedoso
newfound [ˈnu:ˈfaʊnd, ˈnju:-] *adj* **:** recién descubierto
newly [ˈnu:li, ˈnju:-] *adv* **:** recién, recientemente
newlywed [ˈnu:li,wɛd, ˈnju:-] *n* **:** recién casado *m*, -da *f*
new moon *n* **:** luna *f* nueva
newness [ˈnu:nəs, ˈnju:-] *n* **:** novedad *f*
news [ˈnu:z, ˈnju:z] *n* **:** noticias *fpl*
newscast [ˈnu:z,kæst, ˈnju:z-] *n* **:** noticiero *m*, informativo *m*
newscaster [ˈnu:z,kæstər, ˈnju:z-] *n* **:** presentador *m*, -dora *f*; locutor *m*, -tora *f*

newsletter ['nuːzˌlɛtər, 'njuːz-] *n* : boletín *m* informativo

newsman ['nuːzmən, 'njuːz-, -ˌmæn] *n, pl* **-men** [-mən, -ˌmɛn] : periodista *m,* reportero *m*

newspaper ['nuːzˌpeɪpər, 'njuːz-] *n* : periódico *m,* diario *m*

newspaperman ['nuːzˌpeɪpərˌmæn, 'njuːz-] *n, pl* **-men** [-mən, -ˌmɛn] **1** REPORTER : periodista *m,* reportero *m* **2** : dueño *m* de un periódico

newsprint ['nuːzˌprɪnt, 'njuːz-] *n* : papel *m* de prensa

newsstand ['nuːzˌstænd, 'njuːz-] *n* : quiosco *m,* puesto *m* de periódicos

newswoman ['nuːzˌwʊmən, 'njuːz-] *n, pl* **-women** [-ˌwɪmən] : periodista *f,* reportera *f*

newsworthy ['nuːzˌwərði, 'njuːz-] *adj* : de interés periodístico

newsy ['nuːziː, 'njuː-] *adj* **newsier; -est** : lleno de noticias

newt ['nuːt, 'njuːt] *n* : tritón *m*

New Year *n* : Año *m* Nuevo

New Year's Day *n* : día *m* del Año Nuevo

New Yorker [nuː'jɔrkər, njuː-] *n* : neoyorquino *m,* -na *f*

New Zealander [nuː'ziːləndər, njuː-] *n* : neozelandés *m,* -desa *f*

next[1] ['nɛkst] *adv* **1** AFTERWARD : después, luego <what will you do next? : ¿qué harás después?> **2** NOW : después, ahora, entonces <next I will sing a song : ahora voy a cantar una canción> **3** : la próxima vez <when next we meet : la próxima vez que nos encontremos>

next[2] *adj* **1** ADJACENT : contiguo, de al lado **2** COMING : que viene, próximo <next Friday : el viernes que viene> **3** FOLLOWING : siguiente <the next year : el año siguiente>

next–door ['nɛkst'dor] *adj* : de al lado

next to[1] *adv* ALMOST : casi, prácticamente <next to impossible : casi imposible>

next to[2] *prep* : junto a, al lado de

nib ['nɪb] *n* : plumilla *f*

nibble[1] ['nɪbəl] *v* **-bled; -bling** *vt* : pellizcar, mordisquear, picar — *vi* : picar

nibble[2] *n* : mordisco *m*

Nicaraguan [ˌnɪkə'rɑgwən] *n* : nicaragüense *mf* — **Nicaraguan** *adj*

nice ['naɪs] *adj* **nicer; nicest 1** REFINED : pulido, refinado **2** SUBTLE : fino, sutil **3** PLEASING : agradable, bueno, lindo <nice weather : buen tiempo> **4** RESPECTABLE : bueno, decente **5 nice and** : bien, muy <nice and hot : bien caliente> <nice and slow : despacito>

nicely ['naɪsli] *adv* **1** KINDLY : amablemente **2** POLITELY : con buenos modales **3** ATTRACTIVELY : de buen gusto

niceness ['naɪsnəs] *n* : simpatía *f,* amabilidad *f*

nicety ['naɪsəti] *n, pl* **-ties 1** DETAIL, SUBTLETY : sutileza *f,* detalle *m* **2 niceties** *npl* : lujos *mpl,* detalles *mpl*

niche ['nɪtʃ] *n* **1** RECESS : nicho *m,* hornacina *f* **2** : nicho *m,* hueco *m* <to make a niche for oneself : hacerse un hueco, encontrarse una buena posición>

nick[1] ['nɪk] *vt* : cortar, hacer una muesca en

nick[2] *n* **1** CUT : corte *m,* muesca *f* **2 in the nick of time** : en el momento crítico, justo a tiempo

nickel ['nɪkəl] *n* **1** : níquel *m* **2** : moneda *f* de cinco centavos

nickname[1] ['nɪkˌneɪm] *vt* **-named; -naming** : apodar

nickname[2] *n* : apodo *m,* mote *m,* sobrenombre *m*

nicotine ['nɪkəˌtiːn] *n* : nicotina *f*

niece ['niːs] *n* : sobrina *f*

Nigerian [naɪ'dʒɪriən] *n* : nigeriano *m,* -na *f* — **Nigerian** *adj*

niggardly ['nɪgərdli] *adj* : mezquino, tacaño

niggling ['nɪgəlɪŋ] *adj* **1** PETTY : insignificante **2** PERSISTENT : constante, persistente <a niggling doubt : una duda constante>

nigh[1] ['naɪ] *adv* **1** NEARLY : casi **2 to draw nigh** : acercarse, avecinarse

nigh[2] *adj* : cercano, próximo

night[1] ['naɪt] *adj* : nocturno, de la noche <the night sky : el cielo nocturno> <night shift : turno de la noche>

night[2] *n* **1** EVENING : noche *f* <at night : de noche> <last night : anoche> <tomorrow night : mañana por la noche> **2** DARKNESS : noche *f,* oscuridad *f* <night fell : cayó la noche>

nightclothes ['naɪtˌkloːðz, -ˌkloːz] *npl* : ropa *f* de dormir

nightclub ['naɪtˌklʌb] *n* : cabaret *m,* club *m* nocturno

night crawler ['naɪtˌkrɔlər] *n* EARTHWORM : lombriz *f* (de tierra)

nightfall ['naɪtˌfɔl] *n* : anochecer *m*

nightgown ['naɪtˌgaʊn] *n* : camisón *m* (de noche)

nightingale ['naɪtənˌgeɪl, 'naɪtɪŋ-] *n* : ruiseñor *m*

nightly[1] ['naɪtli] *adv* : cada noche, todas las noches

nightly[2] *adj* : de todas las noches

nightmare ['naɪtˌmær] *n* : pesadilla *f*

nightmarish ['naɪtˌmærɪʃ] *adj* : de pesadilla

night owl *n* : noctámbulo *m,* -la *f*

nightshade ['naɪtˌʃeɪd] *n* : hierba *f* mora

nightshirt ['naɪtˌʃərt] *n* : camisa *f* de dormir

nightstick ['naɪtˌstɪk] *n* : porra *f*

nighttime ['naɪtˌtaɪm] *n* : noche *f*

nil ['nɪl] *n* : nada *f,* cero *m*

nimble ['nɪmbəl] *adj* **-bler; -blest 1** AGILE : ágil **2** CLEVER : hábil, ingenioso

nimbleness ['nɪmbəlnəs] *n* : agilidad *f*

nimbly [ˈnɪmbli] *adv* : con agilidad, ágilmente

nincompoop [ˈnɪnkəm,puːp, ˈnɪŋ-] *n* FOOL : tonto *m*, -ta *f;* bobo *m*, -ba *f*

nine[1] [ˈnaɪn] *adj* **1** : nueve **2 nine times out of ten** : casi siempre

nine[2] *n* : nueve *m*

nine hundred[1] *adj* : novecientos

nine hundred[2] *n* : novecientos *m*

ninepins [ˈnaɪn,pɪnz] *n* : bolos *mpl*

nineteen[1] [naɪnˈtiːn] *adj* : diecinueve

nineteen[2] *n* : diecinueve *m*

nineteenth[1] [naɪnˈtiːnθ] *adj* : decimonoveno, decimonono <the nineteenth century : el siglo diecinueve>

nineteenth[2] *n* : decimonoveno *m*, -na *f;* decimonono *m*, -na *f* (en una serie) **2** : diecinueveavo *m*, diecinueveava parte *f*

ninetieth[1] [ˈnaɪntiəθ] *adj* : nonagésimo

ninetieth[2] *n* **1** : nonagésimo *m*, -ma *f* (en una serie) **2** : noventavo *m*, noventava parte *f*

ninety[1] [ˈnaɪnti] *adj* : noventa

ninety[2] *n, pl* **-ties** : noventa *m*

ninth[1] [ˈnaɪnθ] *adj* : noveno

ninth[2] *n* **1** : noveno *m*, -na *f* (en una serie) **2** : noveno *m*, novena parte *f*

ninny [ˈnɪni] *n, pl* **ninnies** FOOL : tonto *m*, -ta *f;* bobo *m*, -ba *f*

nip[1] [ˈnɪp] *vt* **nipped; nipping 1** PINCH : pellizcar **2** BITE : morder, mordisquear **3 to nip in the bud** : cortar de raíz

nip[2] *n* **1** TANG : sabor *m* fuerte **2** PINCH : pellizco *m* **3** NIBBLE : mordisco *m* **4** SWALLOW : trago *m*, traguito *m* **5 there's a nip in the air** : hace fresco

nipple [ˈnɪpəl] *n* : pezón *m* (de una mujer), tetilla *f* (de un hombre)

nippy [ˈnɪpi] *adj* **-pier; -est 1** SHARP : fuerte, picante **2** CHILLY : frío <it's nippy today : hoy hace frío>

nit [ˈnɪt] *n* : liendre *f*

nitrate [ˈnaɪ,treɪt] *n* : nitrato *m*

nitric acid [ˈnaɪtrɪk] *n* : ácido *m* nítrico

nitrite [ˈnaɪ,traɪt] *n* : nitrito *m*

nitrogen [ˈnaɪtrədʒən] *n* : nitrógen *m*

nitroglycerin *or* **nitroglycerine** [,naɪtroˈglɪsərən] *n* : nitroglicerina *f*

nitwit [ˈnɪt,wɪt] *n* : zonzo *m*, -za *f;* bobo *m*, -ba *f*

no[1] [ˈnoː] *adv* : no <are you leaving?—no : ¿te vas?—no> <no less than : no menos de> <to say no : decir que no> <like it or no : quieras o no quieras>

no[2] *adj* **1** : ninguno <it's no trouble : no es ningún problema> <she has no money : no tiene dinero> **2** (*indicating a small amount*) <we'll be there in no time : llegamos dentro de poco, no tardamos nada> **3** (*expressing a negation*) <he's no liar : no es mentiroso>

no[3] *n, pl* **noes** *or* **nos** [ˈnoːz] **1** DENIAL : no *m* <I won't take no for an answer : no aceptaré un no por respuesta> **2** : vota *f* en contra <the noes have it : se ha rechazado la moción>

nobility [noˈbɪləti] *n* : nobleza *f*

noble[1] [ˈnoːbəl] *adj* **-bler; -blest 1** ILLUSTRIOUS : noble, glorioso **2** ARISTOCRATIC : noble **3** STATELY : majestuoso, magnífico **4** LOFTY : noble, elevado <noble sentiments : sentimientos elevados>

noble[2] *n* : noble *mf*, aristócrata *mf*

nobleman [ˈnoːbəlmən] *n, pl* **-men** [-mən, -,mɛn] : noble *m*, aristócrata *m*

nobleness [ˈnoːbəlnəs] *n* : nobleza *f*

noblewoman [ˈnoːbəl,wʊmən] *n, pl* **-women** [-,wɪmən] : noble *f*, aristócrata *f*

nobly [ˈnoːbli] *adv* : noblemente

nobody[1] [ˈnoːbədi, -,bɑdi] *n, pl* **-bodies** : don nadie *m* <he's a mere nobody : es un don nadie>

nobody[2] *pron* : nadie

nocturnal [nɑkˈtərnəl] *adj* : nocturno

nocturne [ˈnɑk,tərn] *n* : nocturno *m*

nod[1] [ˈnɑd] *v* **nodded; nodding** *vi* **1** : saludar con la cabeza, asentir con la cabeza **2 to nod off** : dormirse, quedarse dormido — *vt* : inclinar (la cabeza) <to nod one's head in agreement : asentir con la cabeza>

nod[2] *n* : saludo *m* con la cabeza, señal *m* con la cabeza, señal *m* de asentimiento

node [ˈnoːd] *n* : nudo *m* (de una planta)

nodule [ˈnɑ,dʒuːl] *n* : nódulo *m*

noel [noˈɛl] *n* **1** CAROL : villancico *m* de Navidad **2 Noel** CHRISTMAS : Navidad *f*

noes → **no**[3]

noise[1] [ˈnɔɪz] *vt* **noised; noising** : rumorear, publicar

noise[2] *n* : ruido *m*

noiseless [ˈnɔɪzləs] *adj* : silencioso, sin ruido

noiselessly [ˈnɔɪzləsli] *adv* : silenciosamente

noisemaker [ˈnɔɪz,meɪkər] *n* : matraca *f*

noisiness [ˈnɔɪzinəs] *n* : ruido *m*

noisome [ˈnɔɪsəm] *adj* : maloliente, fétido

noisy [ˈnɔɪzi] *adj* **noisier; -est** : ruidoso — **noisily** [ˈnɔɪzəli] *adv*

nomad[1] [ˈnoː,mæd] → **nomadic**

nomad[2] *n* : nómada *mf*

nomadic [noˈmædɪk] *adj* : nómada

nomenclature [ˈnoːmən,kleɪtʃər] *n* : nomenclatura *f*

nominal [ˈnɑmənəl] *adj* **1** : nominal <the nominal head of his party : el jefe nominal de su partido> **2** TRIFLING : insignificante

nominally [ˈnɑmənəli] *adv* : sólo de nombre, nominalmente

nominate [ˈnɑmə,neɪt] *vt* **-nated; -nating 1** PROPOSE : proponer (como candidato), nominar **2** APPOINT : nombrar

nomination [ˌnɑmə'neɪʃən] *n* **1** PROPOSAL : propuesta *f,* postulación *f* **2** APPOINTMENT : nombramiento *m*
nominative¹ ['nɑmənət̬ɪv] *adj* : nominativo
nominative² *n or* **nominative case** : nominativo *m*
nominee [ˌnɑmə'niː] *n* : candidato *m,* -ta *f*
nonaddictive [ˌnɑnə'dɪktɪv] *adj* : que no crea dependencia
nonalcoholic [ˌnɑnˌælkə'hɔlɪk] *adj* : sin alcohol, no alcohólico
nonaligned [ˌnɑnə'laɪnd] *adj* : no alineado
nonbeliever [ˌnɑnbə'liːvər] *n* : no creyente *mf*
nonbreakable [ˌnɑn'breɪkəbəl] *adj* : irrompible
nonce ['nɑn*t*s] *n* **for the nonce** : por el momento
nonchalance [ˌnɑnʃə'lɑn*t*s] *n* : indiferencia *f,* despreocupación *f*
nonchalant [ˌnɑnʃə'lɑnt] *adj* : indiferente, despreocupado, impasible
nonchalantly [ˌnɑnʃə'lɑntli] *adv* : con aire despreocupado, con indiferencia
noncombatant [ˌnɑnkəm'bætənt, -'kɑmbə-] *adj* : no combatiente *mf*
noncommissioned officer [ˌnɑnkə'mɪʃənd] *n* : suboficial *mf*
noncommittal [ˌnɑnkə'mɪt̬əl] *adj* : evasivo, que no se compromete
nonconductor [ˌnɑnkən'dʌktər] *n* : aislante *m*
nonconformist [ˌnɑnkən'fɔrmɪst] *n* : inconformista *mf,* inconforme *mf*
nonconformity [ˌnɑnkən'fɔrmət̬i] *n* : inconformidad *f,* no conformidad *f*
noncontagious [ˌnɑnkən'teɪdʒəs] *adj* : no contagioso
nondenominational [ˌnɑndɪˌnɑmə'neɪʃənəl] *adj* : no sectario
nondescript [ˌnɑndɪ'skrɪpt] *adj* : anodino, soso
nondiscriminatory [ˌnɑndɪ'skrɪmənəˌtori] *adj* : no discriminatorio
nondrinker [ˌnɑn'drɪŋkər] *n* : abstemio *m,* -mia *f*
none¹ ['nʌn] *adv* : de ninguna manera, de ningún modo, nada <he was none too happy : no se sintió nada contento> <I'm none the worse for it : no estoy peor por ello> <none too soon : a buena hora>
none² *pron* : ninguno, ninguna
nonentity [ˌnɑn'ɛntət̬i] *n, pl* **-ties** : persona *f* insignificante, nulidad *f*
nonessential [ˌnɑnɪ'sɛntʃəl] *adj* : secundario, no esencial
nonessentials [ˌnɑnɪ'sɛntʃəlz] *npl* : cosas *fpl* secundarias, cosas *fpl* accesorias
nonetheless [ˌnʌnðə'lɛs] *adv* : sin embargo, no obstante
nonexistence [ˌnɑnɪg'zɪstən*t*s] *n* : inexistencia *f*
nonexistent [ˌnɑnɪg'zɪstənt] *adj* : inexistente

nonfat [ˌnɑn'fæt] *adj* : sin grasa
nonfattening [ˌnɑn'fætənɪŋ] *adj* : que no engorda
nonfiction [ˌnɑn'fɪkʃən] *n* : no ficción *f*
nonflammable [ˌnɑn'flæməbəl] *adj* : no inflamable
nonintervention [ˌnɑnˌɪntər'vɛntʃən] *n* : no intervención *f*
nonmalignant [ˌnɑnmə'lɪgnənt] *adj* : no maligno, benigno
nonnegotiable [ˌnɑnnɪ'goːʃəbəl, -ʃiə-] *adj* : no negociable
nonpareil¹ [ˌnɑnpə'rɛl] *adj* : sin parangón, sin par
nonpareil² *n* : persona *f* sin igual, cosa *f* sin par
nonpartisan [ˌnɑn'pɑrt̬əzən, -sən] *adj* : imparcial
nonpaying [ˌnɑn'peɪɪŋ] *adj* : que no paga
nonpayment [ˌnɑn'peɪmənt] *n* : impago *m,* falta *f* de pago
nonperson [ˌnɑn'pərsən] *n* : persona *f* sin derechos
nonplus [ˌnɑn'plʌs] *vt* **-plussed; -plussing** : confundir, desconcertar, dejar perplejo
nonprescription [ˌnɑnprɪ'skrɪpʃən] *adj* : disponible sin receta del médico
nonproductive [ˌnɑnprə'dʌktɪv] *adj* : improductivo
nonprofit [ˌnɑn'prɑfət] *adj* : sin fines lucrativos
nonproliferation [ˌnɑnprəˌlɪfə'reɪʃən] *adj* : no proliferación
nonresident [ˌnɑn'rɛzədənt, -ˌdɛnt] *n* : no residente *mf*
nonscheduled [ˌnɑn'skɛˌdʒuːld] *adj* : no programado, no regular
nonsectarian [ˌnɑnˌsɛk'tæriən] *adj* : no sectario
nonsense ['nɑnˌsɛn*t*s, 'nɑn*t*sən*t*s] *n* : tonterías *fpl,* disparates *mpl*
nonsensical [nɑn'sɛn*t*sɪkəl] *adj* ABSURD : absurdo, disparatado — **nonsensically** [-kli] *adv*
nonsmoker [ˌnɑn'smoːkər] *n* : no fumador *m,* -dora *f;* persona *f* que no fuma
nonstandard [ˌnɑn'stændərd] *adj* : no regular, no estándar
nonstick [ˌnɑn'stɪk] *adj* : antiadherente
nonstop¹ [ˌnɑn'stɑp] *adv* : sin parar <he talked nonstop : habló sin parar>
nonstop² *adj* : directo, sin escalas <nonstop flight : vuelo directo>
nonsupport [ˌnɑnsə'pɔrt] *n* : falta *f* de manutención
nontaxable [ˌnɑn'tæksəbəl] *adj* : exento de impuestos
nontoxic [ˌnɑn'tɑksɪk] *adj* : no tóxico
nonviolence [ˌnɑn'vaɪlən*t*s, -'vaɪə-] *n* : no violencia *f*
nonviolent [ˌnɑn'vaɪlənt, -'vaɪə-] *adj* : pacífico, no violento
noodle ['nuːdəl] *n* : fideo *m,* tallarín *m*

nook [ˈnʊk] *n* **:** rincón *m,* recoveco *m,* escondrijo *m* <in every nook and cranny : en todos los rincones>

noon [ˈnuːn] *n* **:** mediodía *m*

noonday [ˈnuːnˌdeɪ] *n* **:** mediodía *m* <the noonday sun : el sol de mediodía>

no one *pron* NOBODY **:** nadie

noontime [ˈnuːnˌtaɪm] *n* **:** mediodía *m*

noose [ˈnuːs] *n* **1** LASSO **:** lazo *m* **2 hangman's noose:** dogal *m,* soga *f*

nor [ˈnɔr] *conj* **:** ni <neither good nor bad : ni bueno ni malo> <nor I! : ¡ni yo tampoco!>

Nordic [ˈnɔrdɪk] *adj* **:** nórdico

norm [ˈnɔrm] *n* **1** STANDARD **:** norma *f,* modelo *m* **2** CUSTOM, RULE **:** regla *f* general, lo normal

normal [ˈnɔrməl] *adj* **:** normal — **normally** *adv*

normalcy [ˈnɔrməlsi] *n* **:** normalidad *f*

normality [nɔrˈmæləṯi] *n* **:** normalidad *f*

normalize [ˈnɔrməˌlaɪz] *vt* **:** normalizar

Norse [ˈnɔrs] *adj* **:** nórdico

north[1] [ˈnɔrθ] *adv* **:** al norte

north[2] *adj* **:** norte, del norte <the north coast : la costa del norte>

north[3] *n* **1 :** norte *m* **2 the North :** el Norte *m*

northbound [ˈnɔrθˌbaʊnd] *adv* **:** con rumbo al norte

North American *n* **:** norteamericano *m,* -na *f* — **North American** *adj*

northeast[1] [nɔrθˈiːst] *adv* **:** hacia el nordeste

northeast[2] *adj* **:** nordeste, del nordeste

northeast[3] *n* **:** nordeste *m,* noreste *m*

northeasterly[1] [nɔrθˈiːstərli] *adv* **:** hacia el nordeste

northeasterly[2] *adj* **:** nordeste, del nordeste

northeastern [nɔrθˈiːstərn] *adj* **:** nordeste, del nordeste

northerly[1] [ˈnɔrðərli] *adv* **:** hacia el norte

northerly[2] *adj* **:** del norte <a northerly wind : un viento del norte>

northern [ˈnɔrðərn] *adj* **:** norte, norteño, septentrional

Northerner [ˈnɔrðərnər] *n* **:** norteño *m,* -ña *f*

northern lights → aurora borealis

North Pole : Polo *m* Norte

North Star *n* **:** estrella *f* polar

northward [ˈnɔrθwərd] *adv & adj* **:** hacia el norte

northwest[1] [nɔrθˈwɛst] *adv* **:** hacia el noroeste

northwest[2] *adj* **:** del noroeste

northwest[3] *n* **:** noroeste *m*

northwesterly[1] [nɔrθˈwɛstərli] *adv* **:** hacia el noroeste

northwesterly[2] *adj* **:** del noroeste

northwestern [nɔrθˈwɛstərn] *adj* **:** noroeste, del noroeste

Norwegian [nɔrˈwiːdʒən] *n* **1 :** noruego *m,* -ga *f* **2 :** noruego *m* (idioma) — **Norwegian** *adj*

nose[1] [ˈnoːz] *v* **nosed; nosing** *vt* **1** SMELL **:** olfatear **2 :** empujar con el hocico <the dog nosed open the bag : el perro abrió el saco con el hocico> **3** EDGE, MOVE **:** mover poco a poco — *vi* **1** PRY **:** entrometerse, meter las narices **2** EDGE **:** avanzar poco a poco

nose[2] *n* **1 :** nariz *f* (de una persona), hocico *m* (de un animal) <to blow one's nose : sonarse las narices> **2** SMELL **:** olfato *m,* sentido *m* del olfato **3** FRONT **:** parte *f* delantera, nariz *f* (de un avión), proa *f* (de un barco) **4 to follow one's nose :** dejarse guiar por el instinto

nosebleed [ˈnoːzˌbliːd] *n* **:** hemorragia *f* nasal

nosedive [ˈnoːzˌdaɪv] *n* **1 :** descenso *m* en picada (de un avión) **2 :** caída *f* súbita (de precios, etc.)

nose–dive [ˈnoːzˌdaɪv] *vi* **:** descender en picada, caer en picada

nostalgia [nɑˈstældʒə, nə-] *n* **:** nostalgia *f*

nostalgic [nɑˈstældʒɪk, nə-] *adj* **:** nostálgico

nostril [ˈnɑstrəl] *n* **:** ventana *f* de la nariz

nostrum [ˈnɑstrəm] *n* **:** panacea *f*

nosy *or* **nosey** [ˈnoːzi] *adj* **nosier; -est :** entrometido

not [ˈnɑt] *adv* **1** (*used to form a negative*) **:** no <she is not tired : no está cansada> <not to say something would be wrong : no decir nada sería injusto> **2** (*used to replace a negative clause*) **:** no <are we going or not? : ¿vamos a ir o no?> <of course not! : ¡claro que no!>

notable[1] [ˈnoːṯəbəl] *adj* **1** NOTEWORTHY **:** notable, de notar **2** DISTINGUISHED, PROMINENT **:** distinguido, destacado

notable[2] *n* **:** persona *f* importante, personaje *m*

notably [ˈnoːṯəbli] *adv* **:** notablemente, particularmente

notarize [ˈnoːṯəˌraɪz] *vt* **-rized; -rizing :** autenticar, autorizar

notary public [ˈnoːṯəri] *n, pl* **-ries public** *or* **-ry publics :** notario *m,* -ria *f;* escribano *m,* -na *f*

notation [noˈteɪʃən] *n* **1** NOTE **:** anotación *f,* nota *f* **2 :** notación *f* <musical notation : notación musical>

notch[1] [ˈnɑtʃ] *vt* **:** hacer una muesca en, cortar

notch[2] *n* **:** muesca *f,* corte *m*

note[1] [ˈnoːt] *vt* **noted; noting 1** NOTICE **:** notar, observar, tomar nota de **2** RECORD **:** anotar, apuntar

note[2] *n* **1 :** nota *f* (musical) **2** COMMENT **:** nota *f,* comentario *m* **3** LETTER **:** nota *f,* cartita *f* **4** PROMINENCE **:** prestigio *m* <a musician of note : un músico destacado> **5** ATTENTION **:** atención *f* <to take note of : prestar atención a>

notebook [ˈnoːt,bʊk] *n* : libreta *f,* cuaderno *m*
noted [ˈnoːṭəd] *adj* EMINENT : renombrado, eminente, celebrado
noteworthy [ˈnoːt,wərði] *adj* : notable, de notar, de interés
nothing[1] [ˈnʌθɪŋ] *adv* **1** : de ninguna manera <nothing daunted, we carried on : sin amilanarnos, seguimos adelante> **2 nothing like** : no...en nada <he's nothing like his brother : no se parece en nada a su hermano>
nothing[2] *n* **1** NOTHINGNESS : nada *f* **2** ZERO : cero *m* **3** : persona *f* de poca importancia, cero *m* **4** TRIFLE : nimiedad *f*
nothing[3] *pron* : nada <there's nothing better : no hay nada mejor> <nothing else : nada más> <nothing but : solamente> <they mean nothing to me : ellos me son indiferentes>
nothingness [ˈnʌθɪŋnəs] *n* **1** VOID : vacío *m,* nada *f* **2** NONEXISTENCE : inexistencia *f* **3** TRIFLE : nimiedad *f*
notice[1] [ˈnoːṭɪs] *vt* **-ticed; -ticing** : notar, observar, advertir, darse cuenta de
notice[2] *n* **1** NOTIFICATION : aviso *m,* notificación *f* **2** ATTENTION : atención *f* <to take notice of : prestar atención a>
noticeable [ˈnoːṭɪsəbəl] *adj* : evidente, perceptible — **noticeably** [-bli] *adv*
notification [,noːṭəfəˈkeɪʃən] *n* : notificación *f,* aviso *m*
notify [ˈnoːṭə,faɪ] *vt* **-fied; -fying** : notificar, avisar
notion [ˈnoːʃən] *n* **1** IDEA : idea *f,* noción *f* **2** WHIM : capricho *m,* antojo *m* **3 notions** *npl* : artículos *mpl* de mercería
notoriety [,noːṭəˈraɪəṭi] *n* : mala fama *f,* notoriedad *f*
notorious [noˈtoːriəs] *adj* : de mala fama, célebre, bien conocido
notwithstanding[1] [,nɑtwɪθˈstændɪŋ, -wɪð-] *adv* NEVERTHELESS : no obstante, sin embargo
notwithstanding[2] *conj* : a pesar de que
notwithstanding[3] *prep* : a pesar de, no obstante
nougat [ˈnuːgət] *n* : turrón *m*
nought [ˈnɔt, ˈnɑt] → **naught**
noun [ˈnaʊn] *n* : nombre *m,* sustantivo *m*
nourish [ˈnərɪʃ] *vt* **1** FEED : alimentar, nutrir, sustentar **2** FOSTER : fomentar, alentar
nourishing [ˈnərɪʃɪŋ] *adj* : alimenticio, nutritivo
nourishment [ˈnərɪʃmənt] *n* : nutrición *f,* alimento *m,* sustento *m*
novel[1] [ˈnɑvəl] *adj* : original, novedoso
novel[2] *n* : novela *f*
novelist [ˈnɑvəlɪst] *n* : novelista *mf*
novelty [ˈnɑvəlṭi] *n, pl* **-ties 1** : novedad *f* **2 novelties** *npl* TRINKETS : baratijas *fpl,* chucherías *fpl*
November [noˈvɛmbər] *n* : noviembre *m*
novice [ˈnɑvɪs] *n* : novato *m,* -ta *f;* principiante *mf;* novicio *m,* -cia *f*
now[1] [ˈnaʊ] *adv* **1** PRESENTLY : ahora, ya, actualmente <from now on : de ahora en adelante> <long before now : ya hace tiempo> <now and then : de vez en cuando> **2** IMMEDIATELY : ahora (mismo), inmediatamente <do it right now! : ¡hazlo ahora mismo!> **3** THEN : ya, entonces <now they were ready : ya estaban listos> **4** (*used to introduce a statement, a question, a command, or a transition*) <now hear this! : ¡presten atención!> <now what do you think of that? : ¿qué piensas de eso?>
now[2] *n* (*indicating the present time*) <until now : hasta ahora> <by now : ya> <ten years from now : dentro de 10 años>
now[3] *conj* **now that** : ahora que, ya que
nowadays [ˈnaʊə,deɪz] *adv* : hoy en día, actualmente, en la actualidad
nowhere[1] [ˈnoː,*h*wɛr] *adv* **1** : en ninguna parte, a ningún lado <nowhere to be found : en ninguna parte, por ningún lado> <you're going nowhere : no estás yendo a ningún lado, no estás yendo a ninguna parte> **2 nowhere near** : ni con mucho, nada cerca <it's nowhere near here : no está nada cerca de aquí>
nowhere[2] *n* **1** : ninguna parte *f* **2 out of nowhere** : de la nada
noxious [ˈnɑkʃəs] *adj* : nocivo, dañino, tóxico
nozzle [ˈnɑzəl] *n* : boca *f*
nuance [ˈnuː,ɑn*t*s, ˈnjuː-] *n* : matiz *m*
nub [ˈnʌb] *n* **1** KNOB, LUMP : protuberancia *f,* nudo *m* **2** GIST : quid *m,* meollo *m*
nuclear [ˈnuːkliər, ˈnjuː-] *adj* : nuclear
nucleus [ˈnuːkliəs, ˈnjuː-] *n, pl* **-clei** [-kli,aɪ] : núcleo *m*
nude[1] [ˈnuːd, ˈnjuːd] *adj* **nuder; nudest** : desnudo
nude[2] *n* : desnudo *m*
nudge[1] [ˈnʌdʒ] *vt* **nudged; nudging** : darle con el codo (a alguien)
nudge[2] *n* : toque *m* que se da con el codo
nudism [ˈnuː,dɪzəm, ˈnjuː-] *n* : nudismo *m*
nudist [ˈnuːdɪst, ˈnjuː-] *n* : nudista *mf*
nudity [ˈnuːdəṭi, ˈnjuː-] *n* : desnudez *f*
nugget [ˈnʌgət] *n* : pepita *f*
nuisance [ˈnuːsən*t*s, ˈnjuː-] *n* **1** BOTHER : fastidio *m,* molestia *f,* lata *f* **2** PEST : peste *f;* pesado *m,* -da *f fam*
null [ˈnʌl] *adj* : nulo <null and void : nulo y sin efecto>
nullify [ˈnʌlə,faɪ] *vt* **-fied; -fying** : invalidar, anular
numb[1] [ˈnʌm] *vt* : entumecer, adormecer

numb[2] *adj* **:** entumecido, dormido <numb with fear **:** paralizado de miedo>

number[1] [ˈnʌmbər] *vt* **1** COUNT, INCLUDE **:** contar, incluir **2 :** numerar <number the pages **:** numera las páginas> **3** TOTAL **:** ascender a, sumar

number[2] *n* **1 :** número *m* <in round numbers **:** en números redondos> <telephone number **:** número de teléfono> **2 a number of :** varios, unos pocos, unos cuantos

numberless [ˈnʌmbərləs] *adj* **:** innumerable, sin número

numbness [ˈnʌmnəs] *n* **:** entumecimiento *m*

numeral [ˈnuːmərəl, ˈnjuː-] *n* **:** número *m* <Roman numeral **:** número romano>

numerator [ˈnuːməˌreɪt̬ər, ˈnjuː-] *n* **:** numerador *m*

numeric [nʊˈmɛrɪk, njʊ-] *adj* **:** numérico

numerical [nʊˈmɛrɪkəl, njʊ-] *adj* **:** numérico — **numerically** [-kli] *adv*

numerous [ˈnuːmərəs, ˈnjuː-] *adj* **:** numeroso

numismatics [ˌnuːməzˈmæt̬ɪks, ˌnjuː-] *n* **:** numismática *f*

numskull [ˈnʌmˌskʌl] *n* **:** tonto *m*, -ta *f;* mentecato *m*, -ta *f;* zoquete *m fam*

nun [ˈnʌn] *n* **:** monja *f*

nuptial [ˈnʌpʃəl] *adj* **:** nupcial

nuptials [ˈnʌpʃəlz] *npl* WEDDING **:** nupcias *fpl*, boda *f*

nurse[1] [ˈnərs] *vt* **nursed; nursing 1** SUCKLE **:** amamantar **2 :** cuidar (de), atender <to nurse the sick **:** cuidar a los enfermos> <to nurse a cold **:** curarse de un resfriado>

nurse[2] *n* **1 :** enfermero *m*, -ra *f* **2 → nursemaid**

nursemaid [ˈnərsˌmeɪd] *n* **:** niñera *f*

nursery [ˈnərsəri] *n, pl* **-eries 1** *or* **day nursery :** guardería *f* **2 :** vivero *m* (de plantas)

nursing home *n* **:** hogar *m* de ancianos, clínica *f* de reposo

nurture[1] [ˈnərtʃər] *vt* **-tured; -turing 1** FEED, NOURISH **:** nutrir, alimentar **2** EDUCATE **:** criar, educar **3** FOSTER **:** alimentar, fomentar

nurture[2] *n* **1** UPBRINGING **:** crianza *f*, educación *f* **2** FOOD **:** alimento *m*

nut [ˈnʌt] *n* **1 :** nuez *f* **2 :** tuerca *f* <nuts and bolts **:** tuercas y tornillos> **3** LUNATIC **:** loco *m*, -ca *f;* chiflado *m*, -da *f fam* **4** ENTHUSIAST **:** fanático *m*, -ca *f;* entusiasta *mf*

nutcracker [ˈnʌtˌkrækər] *n* **:** cascanueces *m*

nuthatch [ˈnʌtˌhætʃ] *n* **:** trepador *m*

nutmeg [ˈnʌtˌmɛg] *n* **:** nuez *f* moscada

nutrient [ˈnuːtriənt, ˈnjuː-] *n* **:** nutriente *m*, alimento *m* nutritivo

nutriment [ˈnuːtrəmənt, ˈnjuː-] *n* **:** nutrimento *m*

nutrition [nʊˈtrɪʃən, njʊ-] *n* **:** nutrición *f*

nutritional [nʊˈtrɪʃənəl, njʊ-] *adj* **:** alimenticio

nutritious [nʊˈtrɪʃəs, njʊ-] *adj* **:** nutritivo, alimenticio

nuts [ˈnʌts] *adj* **1** FANATICAL **:** fanático **2** CRAZY **:** loco, chiflado *fam*

nutshell [ˈnʌtˌʃɛl] *n* **1 :** cáscara *f* de nuez **2 in a nutshell :** en pocas palabras

nutty [ˈnʌt̬i] *adj* **-tier; -tiest :** loco, chiflado *fam*

nuzzle [ˈnʌzəl] *v* **-zled; -zling** *vi* NESTLE **:** acurrucarse, arrimarse — *vt* **:** acariciar con el hocico

nylon [ˈnaɪˌlɑn] *n* **1 :** nilón *m* **2 nylons** *npl* **:** medias *fpl* de nilón

nymph [ˈnɪmpf] *n* **:** ninfa *f*

O

o [ˈoː] *n, pl* **o's** *or* **os** [ˈoːz] **1 :** decimoquinta letra del alfabeto inglés **2** ZERO **:** cero *m*

O [ˈoː] **→ oh**

oaf [ˈoːf] *n* **:** zoquete *m;* bruto *m*, -ta *f*

oafish [ˈoːfɪʃ] *adj* **:** torpe, lerdo

oak [ˈoːk] *n, pl* **oaks** *or* **oak :** roble *m*

oaken [ˈoːkən] *adj* **:** de roble

oar [ˈor] *n* **:** remo *m*

oarlock [ˈorˌlɑk] *n* **:** tolete *m*, escálamo *m*

oasis [oˈeɪsɪs] *n, pl* **oases** [-ˌsiːz] **:** oasis *m*

oat [ˈoːt] *n* **:** avena *f*

oath [ˈoːθ] *n, pl* **oaths** [ˈoːðz, ˈoːθs] **1 :** juramento *m* <to take an oath **:** prestar juramento> **2** SWEARWORD **:** mala palabra *f*, palabrota *f*

oatmeal [ˈoːtˌmiːl] *n* **:** avena *f* <instant oatmeal **:** avena instantánea>

obdurate [ˈɑbdʊrət, -djʊ-] *adj* **:** inflexible, firme, obstinado

obedience [oˈbiːdiənts] *n* **:** obediencia *f*

obedient [oˈbiːdiənt] *adj* **:** obediente — **obediently** *adv*

obelisk [ˈɑbəˌlɪsk] *n* **:** obelisco *m*

obese [oˈbiːs] *adj* **:** obeso

obesity [oˈbiːsəti] *n* **:** obesidad *f*

obey [oˈbeɪ] *v* **obeyed; obeying :** obedecer <to obey the law **:** cumplir la ley>

obfuscate [ˈɑbfəˌskeɪt] *vt* **-cated; -cating :** ofuscar, confundir

obituary [əˈbɪtʃʊˌɛri] *n, pl* **-aries :** obituario *m*, necrología *f*

object[1] [əbˈdʒɛkt] *vt* **:** objetar — *vi* **:** oponerse, poner reparos, hacer objeciones

object[2] [ˈɑbdʒɪkt] *n* **1 :** objeto *m* **2** OBJECTIVE, PURPOSE **:** objetivo *m*, propósito *m* **3 :** complemento *m* (en gramática)

objection [əbˈdʒɛkʃən] *n* **:** objeción *f*

objectionable [əbˈdʒɛkʃənəbəl] *adj* **:** ofensivo, indeseable — **objectionably** [-bli] *adv*

objective[1] [əbˈdʒɛktɪv] *adj* **1** IMPARTIAL **:** objetivo, imparcial **2 :** de complemento, directo (en gramática)

objective[2] *n* **1 :** objetivo *m* **2** *or* **objective case :** acusativo *m*

objectively [əbˈdʒɛktɪvli] *adv* **:** objetivamente

objectivity [ˌɑbˌdʒɛkˈtɪvət̬i] *n, pl* **-ties :** objetividad *f*

obligate [ˈɑbləˌgeɪt] *vt* **-gated; -gating :** obligar

obligation [ˌɑbləˈgeɪʃən] *n* **:** obligación *f*

obligatory [əˈblɪgəˌtori] *adj* **:** obligatorio

oblige [əˈblaɪdʒ] *vt* **obliged; obliging 1** COMPEL **:** obligar **2 :** hacerle un favor (a alguien), complacer <to oblige a friend : hacerle un favor a un amigo> **3 to be much obliged :** estar muy agradecido

obliging [əˈblaɪdʒɪŋ] *adj* **:** servicial, complaciente — **obligingly** *adv*

oblique [oˈbliːk] *adj* **1** SLANTING **:** oblicuo **2** INDIRECT **:** indirecto — **obliquely** *adv*

obliterate [əˈblɪt̬əˌreɪt] *vt* **-ated; -ating 1** ERASE **:** obliterar, borrar **2** DESTROY **:** destruir, eliminar

obliteration [əˌblɪt̬əˈreɪʃən] *n* **:** obliteración *f*

oblivion [əˈblɪviən] *n* **:** olvido *m*

oblivious [əˈblɪviəs] *adj* **:** inconsciente — **obliviously** *adv*

oblong[1] [ˈɑˌblɔŋ] *adj* **:** oblongo

oblong[2] *n* **:** figura *f* oblonga, rectángulo *m*

obnoxious [ɑbˈnɑkʃəs, əb-] *adj* **:** repugnante, odioso — **obnoxiously** *adv*

oboe [ˈoːˌboː] *n* **:** oboe *m*

oboist [ˈoˌboɪst] *n* **:** oboe *mf*

obscene [ɑbˈsiːn, əb-] *adj* **:** obsceno, indecente — **obscenely** *adv*

obscenity [ɑbˈsɛnət̬i, əb-] *n, pl* **-ties :** obscenidad *f*

obscure[1] [ɑbˈskjʊr, əb-] *vt* **-scured; -scuring 1** CLOUD, DIM **:** oscurecer, nublar **2** HIDE **:** ocultar

obscure[2] *adj* **1** DIM **:** oscuro **2** REMOTE, SECLUDED **:** recóndito **3** VAGUE **:** oscuro, confuso, vago **4** UNKNOWN **:** desconocido <an obscure poet : un poeta desconocido> — **obscurely** *adv*

obscurity [ɑbˈskjʊrət̬i, əb-] *n, pl* **-ties :** oscuridad *f*

obsequious [əbˈsiːkwiəs] *adj* **:** servil, excesivamente atento

observable [əbˈzərvəbəl] *adj* **:** observable, perceptible

observance [əbˈzərvənts] *n* **1** FULFILLMENT **:** observancia *f*, cumplimiento *m* **2** PRACTICE **:** práctica *f*

observant [əbˈzərvənt] *adj* **:** observador

observation [ˌɑbsərˈveɪʃən, -zər-] *n* **:** observación *f*

observatory [əbˈzərvəˌtori] *n, pl* **-ries :** observatorio *m*

observe [əbˈzərv] *v* **-served; -serving** *vt* **1** OBEY **:** observar, obedecer **2** CELEBRATE **:** celebrar, guardar (una práctica religiosa) **3** WATCH **:** observar, mirar **4** REMARK **:** observar, comentar — *vi* LOOK **:** mirar

obsess [əbˈsɛs] *vt* **:** obsesionar

obsession [ɑbˈsɛʃən, əb-] *n* **:** obsesión *f*

obsessive [ɑbˈsɛsɪv, əb-] *adj* **:** obsesivo — **obsessively** *adv*

obsolescence [ˌɑbsəˈlɛsənts] *n* **:** obsolescencia *f*

obsolescent [ˌɑbsəˈlɛsənt] *adj* **:** obsolescente <to become obsolescent : caer en desuso>

obsolete [ˌɑbsəˈliːt, ˈɑbsəˌ-] *adj* **:** obsoleto, anticuado

obstacle [ˈɑbstɪkəl] *n* **:** obstáculo *m*, impedimento *m*

obstetric [əbˈstɛtrɪk] *or* **obstetrical** [-trɪkəl] *adj* **:** obstétrico

obstetrician [ˌɑbstəˈtrɪʃən] *n* **:** obstetra *mf;* tocólogo *m*, -ga *f*

obstetrics [əbˈstɛtrɪks] *ns & pl* **:** obstetricia *f*, tocología *f*

obstinacy [ˈɑbstənəsi] *n, pl* **-cies :** obstinación *f*, terquedad *f*

obstinate [ˈɑbstənət] *adj* **:** obstinado, terco — **obstinately** *adv*

obstreperous [əbˈstrɛpərəs] *adj* **1** CLAMOROUS **:** ruidoso, clamoroso **2** UNRULY **:** rebelde, indisciplinado

obstruct [əbˈstrʌkt] *vt* **:** obstruir, bloquear

obstruction [əbˈstrʌkʃən] *n* **:** obstrucción *f*, bloqueo *m*

obstructive [əbˈstrəktɪv] *adj* **:** obstructor

obtain [əbˈteɪn] *vt* **:** obtener, conseguir — *vi* PREVAIL **:** imperar, prevalecer

obtainable [əbˈteɪnəbəl] *adj* **:** obtenible, asequible

obtrude [əbˈtruːd] *v* **-truded; -truding** *vt* **1** EXTRUDE **:** expulsar **2** IMPOSE **:** imponer — *vi* INTRUDE **:** inmiscuirse, entrometerse

obtrusive [əbˈtruːsɪv] *adj* **1** IMPERTINENT, MEDDLESOME **:** impertinente, entrometido **2** PROTRUDING **:** prominente

obtuse [ɑbˈtuːs, əb-, -ˈtjuːs] *adj* **:** obtuso, torpe

obtuse angle *n* **:** ángulo obtuso

obviate [ˈɑbviˌeɪt] *vt* **-ated; -ating :** obviar, evitar

obvious [ˈɑbviəs] *adj* **:** obvio, evidente, manifiesto

obviously [ˈɑbviəsli] *adv* **1** CLEARLY **:** obviamente, evidentemente **2** OF COURSE **:** claro, por supuesto

occasion[1] [əˈkeɪʒən] *vt* **:** ocasionar, causar

occasion[2] *n* **1** OPPORTUNITY : oportunidad *f,* ocasión *f* **2** CAUSE : motivo *m,* razón *f* **3** INSTANCE : ocasión *f* **4** EVENT : ocasión *f,* acontecimiento *m* **5 on ~** : de vez en cuando, ocasionalmente

occasional [əˈkeɪʒənəl] *adj* : ocasional

occasionally [əˈkeɪʒənəli] *adv* : de vez en cuando, ocasionalmente

occidental [ˌɑksəˈdɛntəl] *adj* : oeste, del oeste, occidental

occult[1] [əˈkʌlt, ˈɑˌkʌlt] *adj* **1** HIDDEN, SECRET : oculto, secreto **2** ARCANE : arcano, esotérico

occult[2] *n* **the occult** : las ciencias ocultas

occupancy [ˈɑkjəpən*t*si] *n, pl* **-cies** : ocupación *f,* habitación *f*

occupant [ˈɑkjəpənt] *n* : ocupante *mf*

occupation [ˌɑkjəˈpeɪʃən] *n* : ocupación *f,* profesión *f,* oficio *m*

occupational [ˌɑkjəˈpeɪʃənəl] *adj* : ocupacional

occupy [ˈɑkjəˌpaɪ] *vt* **-pied; -pying** : ocupar

occur [əˈkər] *vi* **occurred; occurring** **1** EXIST : encontrarse, existir **2** HAPPEN : ocurrir, acontecer, suceder, tener lugar **3** : ocurrirse <it occurred to him that. . . : se le ocurrió que. . .>

occurrence [əˈkərən*t*s] *n* : acontecimiento *m,* suceso *m,* ocurrencia *f*

ocean [ˈoːʃən] *n* : océano *m*

oceanic [ˌoːʃiˈænɪk] *adj* : oceánico

oceanography [ˌoːʃəˈnɑgrəfi] *n* : oceanografía *f*

ocelot [ˈɑsəˌlɑt, ˈoː-] *n* : ocelote *m*

ocher *or* **ochre** [ˈoːkər] *n* : ocre *m*

o'clock [əˈklɑk] *adv* (*used in telling time*) <it's ten o'clock : son las diez> <at six o'clock : a las seis>

octagon [ˈɑktəˌgɑn] *n* : octágono *m*

octagonal [ɑkˈtægənəl] *adj* : octagonal

octave [ˈɑktɪv] *n* : octava *f*

October [ɑkˈtoːbər] *n* : octubre *m*

octopus [ˈɑktəˌpʊs, -pəs] *n, pl* **-puses** *or* **-pi** [-ˌpaɪ] : pulpo *m*

ocular [ˈɑkjələr] *adj* : ocular

oculist [ˈɑkjəlɪst] *n* **1** OPHTHALMOLOGIST : oftalmólogo *m,* -ga *f;* oculista *mf* **2** OPTOMETRIST : optometrista *mf*

odd [ˈɑd] *adj* **1** : sin pareja, suelto <an odd sock : un calcetín sin pareja> **2** UNEVEN : impar <odd numbers : números impares> **3** : y pico, y tantos <forty odd years ago : hace cuarenta y pico años> **4** : alguno, uno que otro <odd jobs : algunos trabajos> **5** STRANGE : extraño, raro

oddball [ˈɑdˌbɔl] *n* : excéntrico *m,* -ca *f;* persona *f* rara

oddity [ˈɑdət̬i] *n, pl* **-ties** : rareza *f,* cosa *f* rara

oddly [ˈɑdli] *adv* : de manera extraña

oddness [ˈɑdnəs] *n* : rareza *f,* excentricidad *f*

odds [ˈɑdz] *npl* **1** CHANCES : probabilidades *fpl* **2** : puntos *mpl* de ventaja (de una apuesta) **3 to be at odds** : estar en desacuerdo

odds and ends *npl* : costillas *fpl,* cosas *fpl* sueltas, cachivaches *mpl*

ode [ˈoːd] *n* : oda *f*

odious [ˈoːdiəs] *adj* : odioso — **odiously** *adv*

odor [ˈoːdər] *n* : olor *m*

odorless [ˈoːdərləs] *adj* : inodoro, sin olor

odorous [ˈoːdərəs] *adj* : oloroso

odyssey [ˈɑdəsi] *n, pl* **-seys** : odisea *f*

o'er [ˈor] → **over**

of [ˈʌv, ˈɑv] *prep* **1** FROM : de <a man of the city : un hombre de la ciudad> **2** (*indicating character or background*) : de <a woman of great ability : una mujer de gran capacidad> **3** (*indicating cause*) : de <he died of the flu : murió de la gripe> **4** BY : de <the works of Shakespeare : las obras de Shakespeare> **5** (*indicating contents, material or quantity*) : de <a house of wood : una casa de madera> <a glass of water : un vaso de agua> **6** (*indicating belonging or connection*) : de <the front of the house : el frente de la casa> **7** ABOUT : sobre, de <tales of the West : los cuentos del Oeste> **8** (*indicating a particular example*) : de <the city of Caracas : la ciudad de Caracas> **9** FOR : por, a <love of country : amor por la patria> **10** (*indicating time or date*) <five minutes of ten : las diez menos cinco> <the eighth of April : el ocho de abril>

off[1] [ˈɔf] *adv* **1** (*indicating change of position or state*) <to march off : marcharse> <he dozed off : se puso a dormir> **2** (*indicating distance in space or time*) <some miles off : a varias millas> <the holiday is three weeks off : faltan tres semanas para la fiesta> **3** (*indicating removal*) <the knob came off : se le cayó el pomo> **4** (*indicating termination*) <shut the television off : apaga la televisión> **5** (*indicating suspension of work*) <to take a day off : tomarse un día de descanso> **6 off and on** : de vez en cuando

off[2] *adj* **1** FARTHER : más remoto, distante <the off side of the building : el lado distante del edificio> **2** STARTED : empezado <to be off on a spree : irse de juerga> **3** OUT : apagado <the light is off : la luz está apagada> **4** CANCELED : cancelado, suspendido **5** INCORRECT : erróneo, incorrecto **6** REMOTE : remoto, lejano <an off chance : una posibilidad remota> **7** FREE : libre <I'm off today : hoy estoy libre> **8 to be well off** : vivir con desahogo, tener bastante dinero

off[3] *prep* **1** (*indicating physical separation*) : de <she took it off the table : lo tomó de la mesa> <a shop off the main street : una tienda al lado de la calle principal> **2** : a la costa de, a expensas de <he lives off his sister : vive a expensas de su hermana> **3** (*indicating the suspension of an activity*) <to be off duty : estar libre> <he's off liquor : ha dejado el alcohol> **4** BELOW : por debajo de <he's off his game : está por debajo de su juego normal>

offal [ˈɔfəl] *n* **1** RUBBISH, WASTE : desechos *mpl*, desperdicios *mpl* **2** VISCERA : vísceras *fpl*, asaduras *fpl*

offend [əˈfɛnd] *vt* **1** VIOLATE : violar, atentar contra **2** HURT : ofender <to be easily offended : ser muy susceptible>

offender [əˈfɛndər] *n* : delincuente *mf;* infractor *m*, -tora *f*

offense *or* **offence** [əˈfɛnts, ˈɔˌfɛnts] *n* **1** INSULT : ofensa *f*, injuria *f*, agravio *m* <to take offense : ofenderse> **2** ASSAULT : ataque *m* **3** : ofensiva *f* (en deportes) **4** CRIME, INFRACTION : infracción *f*, delito *m*

offensive[1] [əˈfɛntsɪv, ˈɔˌfɛnt-] *adj* : ofensivo — **offensively** *adv*

offensive[2] *n* : ofensiva *f*

offer[1] [ˈɔfər] *vt* **1** : ofrecer <they offered him the job : le ofrecieron el puesto> **2** PROPOSE : proponer, sugerir **3** SHOW : ofrecer, mostrar <to offer resistance : ofrecer resistencia>

offer[2] *n* : oferta *f*, ofrecimiento *m*, propuesta *f*

offering [ˈɔfərɪŋ] *n* : ofrenda *f*

offhand[1] [ˈɔfˈhænd] *adv* : sin preparación, sin pensarlo

offhand[2] *adj* **1** IMPROMPTU : improvisado **2** ABRUPT : brusco

office [ˈɔfəs] *n* **1** : cargo *m* <to run for office : presentarse como candidato> **2** : oficina *f*, despacho *m*, gabinete *m* (en la casa) <office hours : horas de oficina>

officeholder [ˈɔfəsˌhoːldər] *n* : titular *mf*

officer [ˈɔfəsər] *n* **1** *or* **police officer** : policía *mf*, agente *mf* de policía **2** OFFICIAL : oficial *mf;* funcionario *m*, -ria *f;* director *m*, -tora *f* (en una empresa) **3** COMMISSIONED OFFICER : oficial *mf*

official[1] [əˈfɪʃəl] *adj* : oficial — **officially** *adv*

official[2] *n* : funcionario *m*, -ria *f;* oficial *mf*

officiate [əˈfɪʃiˌeɪt] *v* **-ated; -ating** *vi* **1** : arbitrar (en deportes) **2 to officiate at** : oficiar, celebrar — *vt* : arbitrar

officious [əˈfɪʃəs] *adj* : oficioso

offing [ˈɔfɪŋ] *n* **in the offing** : en perspectiva

offset [ˈɔfˌsɛt] *vt* **-set; -setting** : compensar

offshoot [ˈɔfˌʃuːt] *n* **1** OUTGROWTH : producto *m*, resultado *m* **2** BRANCH, SHOOT : retoño *m*, rama *f*, vástago *m* (de una planta)

offshore[1] [ˈɔfˈʃor] *adv* : a una distancia de la costa

offshore[2] *adj* **1** : de (la) tierra <an offshore wind : un viento que sopla de tierra> **2** : (de) costa afuera, cercano a la costa <an offshore island : una isla costera>

offspring [ˈɔfˌsprɪŋ] *ns & pl* **1** YOUNG : crías *fpl* (de los animales) **2** PROGENY : prole *f*, progenie *f*

off-the-road [ˈɔfðəˈroːd] *adj* : extraoficial

often [ˈɔfən, ˈɔftən] *adv* : muchas veces, a menudo, seguido

oftentimes [ˈɔfənˌtaɪmz, ˈɔftən-] *or* **ofttimes** [ˈɔftˌtaɪms] → **often**

ogle [ˈoːgəl] *vt* **ogled; ogling** : comerse con los ojos, quedarse mirando a

ogre [ˈoːgər] *n* : ogro *m*

oh [ˈoː] *interj* : ¡oh!, ¡ah!, ¡ay! <oh, of course : ah, por supuesto> <oh no! : ¡ay no!> <oh really? : ¿de veras?>

ohm [ˈoːm] *n* : ohm *m*, ohmio *m*

oil[1] [ˈɔɪl] *vt* : lubricar, engrasar, aceitar

oil[2] *n* **1** : aceite *m* **2** PETROLEUM : petróleo *m* **3** *or* **oil painting** : óleo *m*, pintura *f* al óleo **4** *or* **oil paint(s)** : óleo *m*

oilcloth [ˈɔɪlˌklɔθ] *n* : hule *m*

oiliness [ˈɔɪlinəs] *n* : lo aceitoso

oilskin [ˈɔɪlˌskɪn] *n* **1** : hule *m* **2 oilskins** *npl* : impermeable *m*

oily [ˈɔɪli] *adj* **oilier; -est** : aceitoso, grasiento, grasoso <oily fingers : dedos grasientos>

ointment [ˈɔɪntmənt] *n* : ungüento *m*, pomada *f*

OK[1] [ˌoːˈkeɪ] *vt* **OK'd** *or* **okayed** [ˌoːˈkeɪd]; **OK'ing** *or* **okaying** APPROVE, AUTHORIZE : dar el visto bueno a, autorizar, aprobar

OK[2] *or* **okay** [ˌoːˈkeɪ] *adv* **1** WELL : bien **2** YES : sí, por supuesto

OK[3] *adj* : bien <he's OK : está bien> <it's OK with me : estoy de acuerdo>

OK[4] *n* : autorización *f*, visto *m* bueno

okra [ˈoːkrə, *South also* -kri] *n* : quingombó *m*

old[1] [ˈoːld] *adj* **1** ANCIENT : antiguo <old civilizations : civilizaciones antiguas> **2** FAMILIAR : viejo <old friends : viejos amigos> <the same old story : el mismo cuento> **3** (*indicating a certain age*) <he's ten years old : tiene diez años (de edad)> **4** AGED : viejo, anciano <an old woman : una anciana> **5** FORMER : antiguo <her old neighborhood : su antiguo barrio> **6** WORN-OUT : viejo, gastado

old[2] *n* **1 the old** : los viejos, los ancianos **2 in the days of old** : antaño, en los tiempos antiguos

olden [ˈoːldən] *adj* : de antaño, de antigüedad

old-fashioned [ˈoːldˈfæʃənd] *adj* : anticuado, pasado de moda

old maid *n* **1** SPINSTER : soltera *f* **2** FUSSBUDGET : maniático *m*, -ca *f;* melindroso *m*, -sa *f*

old-time [ˈoːldˈtaɪm] *adj* : antiguo

old–timer [ˈoːldˈtaɪmər] *n* **1** VETERAN : veterano *m,* -na *f* **2** *or* **oldster** : anciano *m,* -na *f*

old–world [ˈoːldˈwərld] *adj* : pintoresco (de antaño)

oleander [ˈoːliˌændər] *n* : adelfa *f*

oleomargarine [ˌoːlioˈmɑrdʒərən] → **margarine**

olfactory [ɑlˈfæktəri,ol-] *adj* : olfativo

oligarchy [ˈɑləˌgɑrki, ˈoːlə-] *n, pl* **-chies** : oligarquía *f*

olive [ˈɑlɪv, -ləv] *n* **1** : aceituna *f,* oliva *f* (fruta) **2** : olivo *m* (árbol) **3** *or* **olive green** : color *m* aceituna, verde *m* oliva

Olympic Games [oˈlɪmpɪk] *npl* : Juegos *mpl* Olímpicos

Omani [oˈmɑni, -ˈmæ-] *n* : omaní *mf* — **Omani** *adj*

ombudsman [ˈɑmˌbʊdzmən, ɑmˈbʊdz-] *n, pl* **-men** [-mən, -ˌmɛn] : ombudsman *m*

omelet *or* **omelette** [ˈɑmlət, ˈɑmə-] *n* : omelette *mf,* tortilla *f* de huevo

omen [ˈoːmən] *n* : presagio *m,* augurio *m,* agüero *m*

ominous [ˈɑmənəs] *adj* : ominoso, agorero, de mal agüero

ominously [ˈɑmənəsli] *adv* : de manera amenazadora

omission [oˈmɪʃən] *n* : omisión *f*

omit [oˈmɪt] *vt* **omitted; omitting 1** LEAVE OUT : omitir, excluir **2** NEGLECT : omitir <they omitted to tell us : omitieron decírnoslo>

omnipotence [ɑmˈnɪpət̬ənts] *n* : omnipotencia *f* — **omnipotent** [ɑmˈnɪpət̬ənt] *adj*

omnipresent [ˌɑmnɪˈprɛzənt] *adj* : omnipresente

omniscient [ɑmˈnɪʃənt] *adj* : omnisciente

omnivorous [ɑmˈnɪvərəs] *adj* **1** : omnívoro **2** AVID : ávido, voraz

on[1] [ˈɑn, ˈɔn] *adv* **1** (*indicating contact with a surface*) <put the top on : pon la tapa> <he has a hat on : lleva un sombrero puesto> **2** (*indicating forward movement*) <from that moment on : a partir de ese momento> <farther on : más adelante> **3** (*indicating operation or an operating position*) <turn the light on : prende la luz>

on[2] *adj* **1** (*being in operation*) <the radio is on : el radio está prendido> **2** (*taking place*) <the game is on : el juego ha comenzado> **3 to be on to** : estar enterado de

on[3] *prep* **1** (*indicating position*) : en, sobre, encima de <on the table : en (sobre, encima de) la mesa> <shadows on the wall : sombras en la pared> <on horseback : a caballo> **2** AT, TO : a <on the right : a la derecha> **3** ABOARD, IN : en, a <on the plane : en el avión> <he got on the train : subió al tren> **4** (*indicating time*) <she worked on Saturdays : trabajaba los sábados> <every hour on the hour : a la hora en punto> **5** (*indicating means or agency*) : por <he cut himself on a tin can : se cortó con una lata> <to talk on the telephone : hablar por teléfono> **6** (*indicating a state or process*) : en <on fire : en llamas> <on the increase : en aumento> **7** (*indicating connection or membership*) : en <on a committee : en una comisión> **8** (*indicating an activity*) <on vacation : de vacaciones> <on a diet : a dieta> **9** ABOUT, CONCERNING : sobre <a book on insects : un libro sobre insectos> <reflect on that : reflexiona sobre eso>

once[1] [ˈwʌnts] *adv* **1** : una vez <once a month : una vez al mes> <once and for all : de una vez por todas> **2** EVER : alguna vez **3** FORMERLY : antes, anteriormente

once[2] *adj* FORMER : antiguo

once[3] *n* **1** : una vez **2 at ~** SIMULTANEOUSLY : al mismo tiempo, simultáneamente **3 at ~** IMMEDIATELY : inmediatamente, en seguida

once[4] *conj* : una vez que, tan pronto como

once–over [ˌwʌntsˈoːvər, ˈwʌntsˌ-] *n* **to give someone the once–over** : echarle un vistazo a alguien

oncoming [ˈɑnˌkʌmɪŋ, ˈɔn-] *adj* : que viene

one[1] [ˈwʌn] *adj* **1** (*being a single unit*) : un, una <he only wants one apple : sólo quiere una manzana> **2** (*being a particular one*) : un, una <he arrived early one morning : llegó temprano una mañana> **3** (*being the same*) : mismo, misma <they're all members of one team : todos son miembros del mismo equipo> <one and the same thing : la misma cosa> **4** SOME : alguno, alguna; un, una <I'll see you again one day : algún día te veré otra vez> <at one time or another : en una u otra ocasión>

one[2] *n* **1** : uno *m* (número) **2** (*indicating the first of a set or series*) <from day one : desde el primer momento> **3** (*indicating a single person or thing*) <the one (girl) on the right : la de la derecha> <he has the one but needs the other : tiene uno pero necesita el otro>

one[3] *pron* **1** : uno, una <one of his friends : una de sus amigas> <one never knows : uno nunca sabe, nunca se sabe> <to cut one's finger : cortarse el dedo> **2 one and all** : todos, todo el mundo **3 one another** : el uno al otro, se <they loved one another : se amaban> **4 that one** : aquél, aquella **5 which one?** : ¿cuál?

onerous [ˈɑnərəs, ˈoːnə-] *adj* : oneroso, gravoso

oneself [ˌwʌnˈsɛlf] *pron* **1** (*used reflexively or for emphasis*) : se, sí mismo, uno mismo <to control oneself : controlarse> <to talk to oneself

: hablarse a sí mismo> <to do it oneself : hacérselo uno mismo> **2 by ~** : solo

one–sided [ˈwʌnˈsaɪdəd] *adj* **1** : de un solo lado **2** LOPSIDED : asimétrico **3** BIASED : parcial, tendencioso **4** UNILATERAL : unilateral

onetime [ˈwʌnˈtaɪm] *adj* FORMER : antiguo

one–way [ˈwʌnˈweɪ] *adj* **1** : de sentido único, de una sola dirección <a one-way street : una calle de sentido único> **2** : de ida, sencillo <a one-way ticket : un boleto de ida>

ongoing [ˈɑnˌgoːɪŋ] *adj* **1** CONTINUING : en curso, corriente **2** DEVELOPING : en desarrollo

onion [ˈʌnjən] *n* : cebolla *f*

only[1] [ˈoːnli] *adv* **1** MERELY : sólo, solamente, nomás <for only two dollars : por tan sólo dos dólares> <only once : sólo una vez, no más de una vez> <I only did it to help : lo hice por ayudar nomás> **2** SOLELY : únicamente, sólo, solamente <only he knows it : solamente él lo sabe> **3** (*indicating a result*) <it will only cause him problems : no hará más que crearle problemas> **4 if only** : ojalá, por lo menos <if only it were true! : ¡ojalá sea cierto!> <if he could only dance : si por lo menos pudiera bailar>

only[2] *adj* : único <an only child : un hijo único> <the only chance : la única oportunidad>

only[3] *conj* BUT : pero <I would go, only I'm sick : iría, pero estoy enfermo>

onset [ˈɑnˌsɛt] *n* : comienzo *m,* llegada *f*

onslaught [ˈɑnˌslɔt, ˈɔn-] *n* : arremetida *f,* embestida *f,* embate *m*

onto [ˈɑnˌtuː, ˈɔn-] *prep* : sobre

onus [ˈoːnəs] *n* : responsabilidad *f,* carga *f*

onward[1] [ˈɑnwərd, ˈɔn-] *or* **onwards** *adv* FORWARD : adelante, hacia adelante

onward[2] *adj* : hacia adelante

onyx [ˈɑnɪks] *n* : ónix *m*

ooze[1] [ˈuːz] *v* **oozed; oozing** *vi* : rezumar — *vt* **1** : rezumar **2** EXUDE : irradiar, rebosar <to ooze confidence : irradiar confianza>

ooze[2] *n* SLIME : cieno *m,* limo *m*

opal [ˈoːpəl] *n* : ópalo *m*

opaque [oˈpeɪk] *adj* **1** : opaco **2** UNCLEAR : poco claro

open[1] [ˈoːpən] *vt* **1** : abrir <open the door : abre la puerta> **2** UNCOVER : destapar **3** UNFOLD : desplegar, abrir **4** CLEAR : abrir (un camino, etc.) **5** INAUGURATE : abrir (una tienda), inaugurar (una exposición, etc.) **6** INITIATE : initiar, entablar, abrir <to open the meeting : abrir la sesión> <to open a discussion : entablar un debate> — *vi* **1** : abrirse **2** BEGIN : empezar, comenzar

open[2] *adj* **1** : abierto <an open window : una ventana abierta> **2** FRANK : abierto, franco, directo **3** UNCOVERED : descubierto, abierto **4** EXTENDED : extendido, abierto <with open arms : con los brazos abiertos> **5** UNRESTRICTED : libre, abierto **6** UNDECIDED : pendiente, por decidir, sin resolver <an open question : una cuestión pendiente> **7** AVAILABLE : vacante, libre <the job is open : el puesto está vacante>

open[3] *n* **in the open 1** OUTDOORS : al aire libre **2** KNOWN : conocido, sacado a la luz

open-air [ˈoːpənˈær] *adj* OUTDOOR : al aire libre

open-and-shut [ˈoːpənəndˈʃʌt] *adj* : claro, evidente <an open-and-shut case : un caso muy claro>

opener [ˈoːpənər] *n* : destapador *m,* abrelatas *m,* abridor *m*

openhanded [ˌoːpənˈhændəd] *adj* : generoso, liberal

openhearted [ˌoːpənˈhɑrt̬əd] *adj* **1** FRANK : franco, sincero **2** : generoso, de gran corazón

opening [ˈoːpənɪŋ] *n* **1** BEGINNING : comienzo *m,* principio *m,* apertura *f* **2** APERTURE : abertura *f,* brecha *f,* claro *m* (en el bosque) **3** OPPORTUNITY : oportunidad *f*

openly [ˈoːpənli] *adv* **1** FRANKLY : abiertamente, francamente **2** PUBLICLY : públicamente, declaradamente

openness [ˈoːpənnəs] *n* : franqueza *f*

opera [ˈɑprə, ˈɑpərə] *n* **1** : ópera *f* **2** → **opus**

opera glasses *npl* : gemelos *mpl* de teatro

operate [ˈɑpəˌreɪt] *v* **-ated; -ating** *vi* **1** ACT, FUNCTION : operar, funcionar, actuar **2 to operate on (someone)** : operar a (alguien) — *vt* **1** WORK : operar, manejar, hacer funcionar (una máquina) **2** MANAGE : manejar, administrar (un negocio)

operatic [ˌɑpəˈræt̬ɪk] *adj* : operístico

operation [ˌɑpəˈreɪʃən] *n* **1** FUNCTIONING : funcionamiento *m* **2** USE : uso *m,* manejo *m* (de máquinas) **3** SURGERY : operación *f,* intervención *f* quirúrgica

operational [ˌɑpəˈreɪʃənəl] *adj* : operacional, de operación

operative [ˈɑpərət̬ɪv, -ˌreɪ-] *adj* **1** OPERATING : vigente, en vigor **2** WORKING : operativo **3** SURGICAL : quirúrgico

operator [ˈɑpəˌreɪt̬ər] *n* : operador *m,* -dora *f*

operetta [ˌɑpəˈrɛt̬ə] *n* : opereta *f*

ophthalmologist [ˌɑfˌθælˈmɑlədʒɪst, -θəˈmɑ-] *n* : oftalmólogo *m,* -ga *f*

ophthalmology [ˌɑfˌθælˈmɑlədʒi, -θəˈmɑ-] *n* : oftalmología *f*

opiate [ˈoːpiət, -piˌeɪt] *n* : opiato *m*

opinion [əˈpɪnjən] *n* : opinión *f*

opinionated [əˈpɪnjəˌneɪt̬əd] *adj* : testarudo, dogmático

opium [ˈoːpiəm] *n* : opio *m*

opossum [əˈpɑsəm] *n* : zarigüeya *f,* oposum *m*

opponent [əˈpoːnənt] *n* : oponente *mf;* opositor *m,* -tora *f;* contrincante *mf* (en deportes)

opportune [ˌɑpərˈtuːn, -ˈtjuːn] *adj* : oportuno — **opportunely** *adv*

opportunist [ˌɑpərˈtuːnɪst, -ˈtjuː-] *n* : oportunista *mf*

opportunity [ˌɑpərˈtuːnət̬i, -ˈtjuː-] *n, pl* **-ties** : oportunidad *f,* ocasión *f,* chance *m,* posibilidades *fpl*

oppose [əˈpoːz] *vt* **-posed; -posing 1** : ir en contra de, oponerse a <good opposes evil : el bien se opone al mal> **2** COMBAT : luchar contra, combatir, resistir

opposite[1] [ˈɑpəzət] *adv* : enfrente

opposite[2] *adj* **1** FACING : de enfrente <the opposite side : el lado de enfrente> **2** CONTRARY : opuesto, contrario <in opposite directions : en direcciones contrarias> <the opposite sex : el sexo opuesto, el otro sexo>

opposite[3] *n* : lo contrario, lo opuesto

opposite[4] *prep* : enfrente de, frente a

opposition [ˌɑpəˈzɪʃən] *n* **1** : oposición *f,* resistencia *f* **2 in opposition to** AGAINST : en contra de

oppress [əˈprɛs] *vt* **1** PERSECUTE : oprimir, perseguir **2** BURDEN : oprimir, agobiar

oppression [əˈprɛʃən] *n* : opresión *f*

oppressive [əˈprɛsɪv] *adj* **1** HARSH : opresivo, severo **2** STIFLING : agobiante, sofocante <oppressive heat : calor sofocante>

oppressor [əˈprɛsər] *n* : opresor *m,* -sora *f*

opprobrium [əˈproːbriəm] *n* : oprobio *m*

opt [ˈɑpt] *vi* : optar

optic [ˈɑptɪk] *or* **optical** [-tɪkəl] *adj* : óptico

optician [ɑpˈtɪʃən] *n* : óptico *m,* -ca *f*

optics [ˈɑptɪks] *npl* : óptica *f*

optimal [ˈɑptəməl] *adj* : óptimo

optimism [ˈɑptəˌmɪzəm] *n* : optimismo *m*

optimist [ˈɑptəmɪst] *n* : optimista *mf*

optimistic [ˌɑptəˈmɪstɪk] *adj* : optimista

optimistically [ˌɑptəˈmɪstɪkli] *adv* : con optimismo, positivamente

optimum[1] [ˈɑptəməm] *adj* → **optimal**

optimum[2] *n, pl* **-ma** [ˈɑptəmə] : lo óptimo, lo ideal

option [ˈɑpʃən] *n* : opción *f* <she has no option : no tiene más remedio>

optional [ˈɑpʃənəl] *adj* : facultativo, optativo

optometrist [ɑpˈtɑmətrɪst] *n* : optometrista *mf*

optometry [ɑpˈtɑmətri] *n* : optometría *f*

opulence [ˈɑpjələnts] *n* : opulencia *f*

opulent [ˈɑpjələnt] *adj* : opulento

opus [ˈoːpəs] *n, pl* **opera** [ˈoːpərə, ˈɑpə-] : opus *m,* obra *f* (de música)

or [ˈɔr] *conj* **1** (*indicating an alternative*) : o (u *before words beginning with* o *or* ho) <coffee or tea : café o té> <one day or another : un día u otro> **2** (*following a negative*) : ni <he didn't have his keys or his wallet : no llevaba ni sus llaves ni su billetera>

oracle [ˈɔrəkəl] *n* : oráculo *m*

oral [ˈorəl] *adj* : oral — **orally** *adv*

orange [ˈɔrɪndʒ] *n* **1** : naranja *f,* china *f PRi* (fruto) **2** : naranja *m* (color), color *m* de china *PRi*

orangeade [ˌɔrɪndʒˈeɪd] *n* : naranjada *f*

orangutan [əˈræŋəˌtæŋ, -ˈræŋgə-, -ˌtæn] *n* : orangután *m*

oration [əˈreɪʃən] *n* : oración *f,* discurso *m*

orator [ˈɔrət̬ər] *n* : orador *m,* -dora *f*

oratorio [ˌɔrəˈtoriˌoː] *n, pl* **-rios** : oratorio *m*

oratory [ˈɔrəˌtori] *n, pl* **-ries** : oratoria *f*

orb [ˈɔrb] *n* : orbe *m*

orbit[1] [ˈɔrbət] *vt* **1** CIRCLE : girar alrededor de **2** : poner en órbita (un satélite, etc.) — *vi* : orbitar

orbit[2] *n* : órbita *f*

orbital [ˈɔrbət̬əl] *adj* : orbital

orchard [ˈɔrtʃərd] *n* : huerto *m*

orchestra [ˈɔrkəstrə] *n* : orquesta *f*

orchestral [ɔrˈkɛstrəl] *adj* : orquestal

orchestrate [ˈɔrkəˌstreɪt] *vt* **-trated; -trating 1** : orquestar, instrumentar (en música) **2** ORGANIZE : arreglar, organizar

orchestration [ˌɔrkəˈstreɪʃən] *n* : orquestación *f*

orchid [ˈɔrkɪd] *n* : orquídea *f*

ordain [ɔrˈdeɪn] *vt* **1** : ordenar (en religión) **2** DECREE : decretar, ordenar

ordeal [ɔrˈdiːl, ˈɔrˌdiːl] *n* : prueba *f* dura, experiencia *f* terrible

order[1] [ˈɔrdər] *vt* **1** ORGANIZE : arreglar, ordenar, poner en orden **2** COMMAND : ordenar, mandar **3** REQUEST : pedir, encargar <to order a meal : pedir algo de comer> — *vi* : hacer un pedido

order[2] *n* **1** : orden *f* <a religious order : una orden religiosa> **2** COMMAND : orden *f,* mandato *m* <to give an order : dar una orden> **3** REQUEST : orden *f,* pedido *m* <purchase order : orden de compra> **4** ARRANGEMENT : orden *m* <in chronological order : por orden cronológico> **5** DISCIPLINE : orden *m* <law and order : el orden público> **6 in order to** : para **7 out of order** : descompuesto, averiado **8 orders** *npl or* **holy orders** : órdenes *fpl* sagradas

orderliness [ˈɔrdərlinəs] *n* : orden *m*

orderly[1] [ˈɔrdərli] *adj* **1** METHODICAL : ordenado, metódico **2** PEACEFUL : pacífico, disciplinado

orderly[2] *n, pl* **-lies 1** : ordenanza *m* (en el ejército) **2** : camillero *m* (en un hospital)

ordinal ['ɔrdənəl] *n or* **ordinal number :** ordinal *m,* número *m* ordinal
ordinance ['ɔrdənənts] *n* **:** ordenanza *f,* reglamento *m*
ordinarily [ˌɔrdən'ɛrəli] *adv* **:** ordinariamente, por lo general
ordinary ['ɔrdənˌɛri] *adj* **1** NORMAL, USUAL **:** normal, usual **2** AVERAGE **:** común y corriente, normal **3** MEDIOCRE **:** mediocre, ordinario
ordination [ˌɔrdən'eɪʃən] *n* **:** ordenación *f*
ordnance ['ɔrdnənts] *n* **:** artillería *f*
ore ['or] *n* **:** mineral *m* (metalífero), mena *f*
oregano [ə'rɛgəˌnoː] *n* **:** orégano *m*
organ ['ɔrgən] *n* **1 :** órgano *m* (instrumento) **2 :** órgano *m* (del cuerpo) **3** PERIODICAL **:** publicación *f* periódica, órgano *m*
organic [ɔr'gænɪk] *adj* **:** orgánico — **organically** *adv*
organism ['ɔrgəˌnɪzəm] *n* **:** organismo *m*
organist ['ɔrgənɪst] *n* **:** organista *mf*
organization [ˌɔrgənə'zeɪʃən] *n* **1** ORGANIZING **:** organización *f* **2** BODY **:** organización *f,* organismo *m*
organizational [ˌɔrgənə'zeɪʃənəl] *adj* **:** organizativo
organize ['ɔrgəˌnaɪz] *vt* **-nized; -nizing :** organizar, arreglar, poner en orden
organizer ['ɔrgəˌnaɪzər] *n* **:** organizador *m,* -dora *f*
orgasm ['ɔrˌgæzəm] *n* **:** orgasmo *m*
orgy ['ɔrdʒi] *n, pl* **-gies :** orgía *f*
orient ['oriˌɛnt] *vt* **:** orientar
Orient *n* **the Orient :** el Oriente
oriental [ˌori'ɛntəl] *adj* **:** del Oriente, oriental
Oriental *n* **:** oriental *mf*
orientation [ˌoriən'teɪʃən] *n* **:** orientación *f*
orifice ['ɔrəfəs] *n* **:** orificio *m*
origin ['ɔrədʒən] *n* **1** ANCESTRY **:** origen *m,* ascendencia *f* **2** SOURCE **:** origen *m,* raíz *f,* fuente *f*
original[1] [ə'rɪdʒənəl] *adj* **:** original
original[2] *n* **:** original *m*
originality [əˌrɪdʒə'nælət̬i] *n* **:** originalidad *f*
originally [ə'rɪdʒənəli] *adv* **1** AT FIRST **:** al principio, originariamente **2** CREATIVELY **:** originalmente, con originalidad
originate [ə'rɪdʒəˌneɪt] *v* **-nated; -nating** *vt* **:** originar, iniciar, crear — *vi* **1** BEGIN **:** originarse, empezar **2** COME **:** provenir, proceder, derivarse
originator [ə'rɪdʒəˌneɪt̬ər] *n* **:** creador *m,* -dora *f;* inventor *m,* -tora *f*
oriole ['oriˌoːl, -iəl] *n* **:** oropéndola *f*
ornament[1] ['ɔrnəmənt] *vt* **:** adornar, decorar, ornamentar
ornament[2] *n* **:** ornamento *m,* adorno *m,* decoración *f*
ornamental [ˌɔrnə'mɛntəl] *adj* **:** ornamental, de adorno, decorativo
ornamentation [ˌɔrnəmən'teɪʃən, -mɛn-] *n* **:** ornamentación *f*
ornate [ɔr'neɪt] *adj* **:** elaborado, recargado
ornery ['ɔrnəri, 'ɑrnəri] *adj* **ornerier; -est :** de mal genio, malhumorado
ornithologist [ˌɔrnə'θɑlədʒɪst] *n* **:** ornitólogo *m,* -ga *f*
ornithology [ˌɔrnə'θɑlədʒi] *n, pl* **-gies :** ornitología *f*
orphan[1] ['ɔrfən] *vt* **:** dejar huérfano
orphan[2] *n* **:** huérfano *m,* -na *f*
orphanage ['ɔrfənɪdʒ] *n* **:** orfelinato *m,* orfanato *m*
orthodontics [ˌɔrθə'dɑntɪks] *n* **:** ortodoncia *f*
orthodontist [ˌɔrθə'dɑntɪst] *n* **:** ortodoncista *mf*
orthodox ['ɔrθəˌdɑks] *adj* **:** ortodoxo
orthodoxy ['ɔrθəˌdɑksi] *n, pl* **-doxies :** ortodoxia *f*
orthographic [ˌɔrθə'græfɪk] *adj* **:** ortográfico
orthography [ɔr'θɑgrəfi] *n, pl* **-phies** SPELLING **:** ortografía *f*
orthopedic [ˌɔrθə'piːdɪk] *adj* **:** ortopédico
orthopedics [ˌɔrθə'piːdɪks] *ns & pl* **:** ortopedia *f*
orthopedist [ˌɔrθə'piːdɪst] *n* **:** ortopedista *mf*
oscillate ['ɑsəˌleɪt] *vi* **-lated; -lating :** oscilar
oscillation [ˌɑsə'leɪʃən] *n* **:** oscilación *f*
osmosis [ɑz'moːsɪs, ɑs-] *n* **:** ósmosis *f,* osmosis *f*
ostensible [ɑ'stɛntsəbəl] *adj* APPARENT **:** aparente, ostensible — **ostensibly** [-bli] *adv*
ostentation [ˌɑstən'teɪʃən] *n* **:** ostentación *f,* boato *m*
ostentatious [ˌɑstən'teɪʃəs] *adj* **:** ostentoso — **ostentatiously** *adv*
osteopath ['ɑstiəˌpæθ] *n* **:** osteópata *f*
osteopathy [ˌɑsti'ɑpəθi] *n* **:** osteopatía *f*
osteoporosis [ˌɑstiopə'roːsɪs] *n, pl* **-roses** [-ˌsiːz] **:** osteoporosis *f*
ostracism ['ɑstrəˌsɪzəm] *n* **:** ostracismo *m*
ostracize ['ɑstrəˌsaɪz] *vt* **-cized; -cizing :** condenar al ostracismo, marginar, aislar
ostrich ['ɑstrɪtʃ, 'ɔs-] *n* **:** avestruz *m*
other[1] ['ʌðər] *adv* **other than :** aparte de, fuera de
other[2] *adj* **:** otro <the other boys : los otros muchachos> <smarter than other people : más inteligente que los demás> <on the other hand : por otra parte, por otro lado> <every other day : cada dos días>
other[3] *pron* **:** otro, otra <one in front of the other : uno tras otro> <myself and three others : yo y tres otros, yo y tres más> <somewhere or other : en alguna parte>

otherwise[1] [ˈʌðər,waɪz] *adv* **1** DIFFERENTLY : de otro modo, de manera distinta <he could not act otherwise : no pudo actuar de manera distinta> **2** : eso aparte, por lo demás <I'm dizzy, but otherwise I'm fine : estoy mareado pero, por lo demás, estoy bien> **3** OR ELSE : de lo contario, si no <do what I tell you, otherwise you'll be sorry : haz lo que te digo, de lo contario, te arrepentirás>

otherwise[2] *adj* : diferente, distinto <the facts are otherwise : la realidad es diferente>

otter [ˈɑtər] *n* : nutria *f*

ought [ˈɔt] *v aux* : deber <you ought to take care of yourself : deberías cuidarte>

oughtn't [ˈɔtənt] (*contraction of* **ought not**) → **ought**

ounce [ˈaʊnts] *n* : onza *f*

our [ˈɑr, ˈaʊr] *adj* : nuestro

ours [ˈaʊrz, ˈɑrz] *pron* : nuestro, nuestra <a cousin of ours : un primo nuestro>

ourselves [ɑrˈsɛlvz, aʊr-] *pron* **1** (*used reflexively*) : nos, nosotros <we amused ourselves : nos divertimos> <we were always thinking of ourselves : siempre pensábamos en nosotros> **2** (*used for emphasis*) : nosotros mismos, nosotras mismas <we did it ourselves : lo hicimos nosotros mismos>

oust [ˈaʊst] *vt* : desbancar, expulsar

ouster [ˈaʊstər] *n* : expulsión *f* (de un país, etc.), destitución *f* (de un puesto)

out[1] [ˈaʊt] *vi* : revelarse, hacerse conocido

out[2] *adv* **1** (*indicating direction or movement*) : para afuera <she opened the door and looked out : abrió la puerta y miró para afuera> **2** (*indicating a location away from home or work*) : fuera, afuera <to eat out : comer afuera> **3** (*indicating loss of control or possession*) <they let the secret out : sacaron el secreto a la luz> **4** (*indicating completion or discontinuance*) <his money ran out : se le acabó el dinero> <to turn out the light : apagar la luz> **5** OUTSIDE : fuera, afuera <out in the garden : afuera en el jardín> **6** ALOUD : en voz alta, en alto <to cry out : gritar>

out[3] *adj* **1** EXTERNAL : externo, exterior **2** OUTLYING : alejado, distante <the out islands : las islas distantes> **3** ABSENT : ausente **4** UNFASHIONABLE : fuera de moda **5** EXTINGUISHED : apagado

out[4] *prep* **1** (*used to indicate an outward movement*) : por <I looked out the window : miré por la ventana> <she ran out the door : corrió por la puerta> **2** → **out of**

out-and-out [ˈaʊtənˈaʊt] *adj* UTTER : redomado, absoluto

outboard motor [ˈaʊt,bord] *n* : motor *m* fuera de borde

outbound [ˈaʊt,baʊnd] *adj* : que sale, de salida

outbreak [ˈaʊt,breɪk] *n* : brote *m* (de una enfermedad), comienzo *m* (de guerra), ola *f* (de violencia), erupción *f* (de granos)

outbuilding [ˈaʊt,bɪldɪŋ] *n* : edificio *m* anexo

outburst [ˈaʊt,bərst] *n* : arranque *m*, arrebato *m*

outcast [ˈaʊt,kæst] *n* : marginado *m*, -da *f;* paria *mf*

outcome [ˈaʊt,kʌm] *n* : resultado *m*, desenlace *m*, consecuencia *f*

outcrop [ˈaʊt,krɑp] *n* : afloramiento *m*

outcry [ˈaʊt,kraɪ] *n, pl* **-cries** : clamor *m*, protesta *f*

outdated [,aʊtˈdeɪtəd] *adj* : anticuado, fuera de moda

outdistance [,aʊtˈdɪstənts] *vt* **-tanced; -tancing** : aventajar, dejar atrás

outdo [,aʊtˈdu:] *vt* **-did** [-ˈdɪd]; **-done** [-ˈdʌn]; **-doing**; **-does** [-ˈdʌz] : superar

outdoor [ˈaʊtˈdor] *adj* : al aire libre <outdoor sports : deportes al aire libre> <outdoor clothing : ropa de calle>

outdoors[1] [ˈaʊtˈdorz] *adv* : afuera, al aire libre

outdoors[2] *n* : aire *m* libre

outer [ˈaʊtər] *adj* **1** : exterior, externo **2 outer space** : espacio *m* exterior

outermost [ˈaʊtər,mo:st] *adj* : más remoto, más exterior, extremo

outfield [ˈaʊt,fi:ld] *n* **the outfield** : los jardines

outfielder [ˈaʊt,fi:ldər] *n* : jardinero *m*, -ra *f*

outfit[1] [ˈaʊt,fɪt] *vt* **-fitted; -fitting** EQUIP : equipar

outfit[2] *n* **1** EQUIPMENT : equipo *m* **2** COSTUME, ENSEMBLE : traje *m*, conjunto *m* **3** GROUP : conjunto *m*

outgo [ˈaʊt,go:] *n, pl* **outgoes** : gasto *m*

outgoing [ˈaʊt,go:ɪŋ] *adj* **1** OUTBOUND : que sale **2** DEPARTING : saliente <an outgoing president : un presidente saliente> **3** EXTROVERTED : extrovertido, expansivo

outgrow [,aʊtˈgro:] *vt* **-grew** [-ˈgru:]; **-grown** [-ˈgro:n]; **-growing 1** : crecer más que <that tree outgrew all the others : ese árbol creció más que todos los otros> **2 to outgrow one's clothes** : quedarle pequeña la ropa a uno

outgrowth [ˈaʊt,gro:θ] *n* **1** OFFSHOOT : brote *m*, vástago *m* (de una planta) **2** CONSEQUENCE : consecuencia *f*, producto *m*, resultado *m*

outing [ˈaʊtɪŋ] *n* : excursión *f*

outlandish [aʊtˈlændɪʃ] *adj* : descabellado, muy extraño

outlast [,aʊtˈlæst] *vt* : durar más que

outlaw[1] [ˈaʊt,lɔ] *vt* : hacerse ilegal, declarar fuera de la ley, prohibir

outlaw[2] *n* : bandido *m,* -da *f;* bandolero *m,* -ra *f;* forajido *m,* -da *f*

outlay [ˈaʊt,leɪ] *n* : gasto *m,* desembolso *m*

outlet [ˈaʊt,lɛt, -lət] *n* **1** EXIT : salida *f,* escape *m* <electrical outlet : toma de corriente> **2** RELIEF : desahogo *m* **3** MARKET : mercado *m,* salida *f*

outline[1] [ˈaʊt,laɪn] *vt* **-lined; -lining 1** SKETCH : diseñar, esbozar, bosquejar **2** DEFINE, EXPLAIN : perfilar, delinear, explicar <she outlined our responsibilities : delineó nuestras responsabilidades>

outline[2] *n* **1** PROFILE : perfil *m,* silueta *f,* contorno *m* **2** SKETCH : bosquejo *m,* boceto *m* **3** SUMMARY : esquema *m,* resumen *m,* sinopsis *m* <an outline of world history : un esquema de la historia mundial>

outlive [,aʊtˈlɪv] *vt* **-lived; -living** : sobrevivir a

outlook [ˈaʊt,lʊk] *n* **1** VIEW : vista *f,* panorama *f* **2** POINT OF VIEW : punto *m* de vista **3** PROSPECTS : perspectivas *fpl*

outlying [ˈaʊt,laɪɪŋ] *adj* : alejado, distante, remoto <the outlying areas : las afueras>

outmoded [,aʊtˈmoːdəd] *adj* : pasado de moda, anticuado

outnumber [,aʊtˈnʌmbər] *vt* : superar en número a, ser más numeroso de

out of *prep* **1** (*indicating direction or movement from within*) : de, por <we ran out of the house : salimos corriendo de la casa> <to look out of the window : mirar por la ventana> **2** (*being beyond the limits of*) <out of control : fuera de control> <to be out of sight : desaparecer de vista> **3** OF : de <one out of four : uno de cada cuatro> **4** (*indicating absence or loss*) : sin <out of money : sin dinero> <we're out of matches : nos hemos quedado sin fósforos> **5** BECAUSE OF : por <out of curiosity : por curiosidad> **6** FROM : de <made out of plastic : hecho de plástico>

out–of–date [,aʊtəvˈdeɪt] *adj* : anticuado, obsoleto, pasado de moda

out-of-door [,aʊtəvˈdor] *or* **out-of-doors** [-ˈdorz] *adj* → **outdoor**

out-of-doors *n* → **outdoors**

outpatient [ˈaʊt,peɪʃənt] *n* : paciente *m* externo, paciente *f* externa

outpost [ˈaʊt,poːst] *n* : puesto *m* avanzado

output[1] [ˈaʊt,pʊt] *vt* **-putted** *or* **-put; -putting** : producir

output[2] *n* : producción *f* (de una fábrica), rendimiento *m* (de una máquina), productividad *f* (de una persona)

outrage[1] [ˈaʊt,reɪdʒ] *vt* **-raged; -raging 1** INSULT : ultrajar, injuriar **2** INFURIATE : indignar, enfurecer

outrage[2] *n* **1** ATROCITY : atropello *m,* atrocidad *f,* atentado *m* **2** SCANDAL : escándalo *m* **3** ANGER : ira *f,* furia *f*

outrageous [,aʊtˈreɪdʒəs] *adj* **1** SCANDALOUS : escandaloso, ofensivo, atroz **2** UNCONVENTIONAL : poco convencional, extravagante **3** EXORBITANT : exorbitante, excesivo (dícese de los precios, etc.)

outright[1] [,aʊtˈraɪt] *adv* **1** COMPLETELY : por completo, totalmente <to sell outright : vender por completo> <he refused it outright : lo rechazó rotundamente> **2** DIRECTLY : directamente, sin reserva **3** INSTANTLY : al instante, en el acto

outright[2] [ˈaʊt,raɪt] *adj* **1** COMPLETE : completo, absoluto, categórico <an outright lie : una mentira absoluta> **2** : sin reservas <an outright gift : un regalo sin reservas>

outset [ˈaʊt,sɛt] *n* : comienzo *m,* principio *m*

outshine [,aʊtˈʃaɪn] *vt* **-shone** [-ˈʃoːn, -ˈʃɒn] *or* **-shined; -shining** : eclipsar

outside[1] [,aʊtˈsaɪd, ˈaʊt,-] *adv* : fuera, afuera

outside[2] *adj* **1** : exterior, externo <the outside edge : el borde exterior> <outside influences : influencias externas> **2** REMOTE : remoto <an outside chance : una posibilidad remota>

outside[3] *n* **1** EXTERIOR : parte *f* de afuera, exterior *m* **2** MOST : máximo *m* <three weeks at the outside : tres semanas como máximo> **3 from the outside** : desde afuera, desde fuera

outside[4] *prep* : fuera de, afuera de <outside my window : fuera de mi ventana> <outside regular hours : fuera del horario normal> <outside the law : afuera de la ley>

outside of *prep* **1** → **outside**[4] **2** → **besides**[2]

outsider [,aʊtˈsaɪdər] *n* : forastero *m,* -ra *f*

outskirts [ˈaʊt,skərts] *npl* : afueras *fpl,* alrededores *mpl*

outsmart [,aʊtˈsmɑrt] → **outwit**

outspoken [,aʊtˈspoːkən] *adj* : franco, directo

outstanding [,aʊtˈstændɪŋ] *adj* **1** UNPAID : pendiente **2** NOTABLE : destacado, notable, excepcional, sobresaliente

outstandingly [,aʊtˈstændɪŋli] *adv* : excepcionalmente

outstrip [,aʊtˈstrɪp] *vt* **-stripped** *or* **-stript** [-ˈstrɪpt]; **-stripping 1** : aventajar, dejar atrás <he outstripped the other runners : aventajó a los otros corredores> **2** SURPASS : aventajar, sobrepasar

outward[1] [ˈaʊtwərd] *or* **outwards** [-wərdz] *adv* : hacia afuera, hacia el exterior

outward[2] *adj* **1** : hacia afuera <an outward flow : un flujo hacia afuera> **2** : externo, external <outward beauty : belleza externa>

outwardly ['aʊtwərdli] *adv* **1** EXTERNALLY : externalmente **2** APPARENTLY : aparentemente <outwardly friendly : aparentemente simpático>
outwit [ˌaʊt'wɪt] *vt* **-witted; -witting** : ser más listo que
ova → **ovum**
oval[1] ['oːvəl] *adj* : ovalado, oval
oval[2] *n* : óvalo *m*
ovary ['oːvəri] *n, pl* **-ries** : ovario *m*
ovation [o'veɪʃən] *n* : ovación *f*
oven ['ʌvən] *n* : horno *m*
over[1] ['oːvər] *adv* **1** (*indicating movement across*) <he flew over to London : voló a Londres> <come on over! : ¡ven acá!> **2** (*indicating an additional amount*) <the show ran 10 minutes over : el espectáculo terminó 10 minutos de tarde> **3** ABOVE, OVERHEAD : por encima **4** AGAIN : otra vez, de nuevo <over and over : una y otra vez> <to start over : volver a empezar> **5 all over** EVERYWHERE : por todas partes **6 to fall over** : caerse **7 to turn over** : poner boca abajo, voltear
over[2] *adj* **1** HIGHER, UPPER : superior **2** REMAINING : sobrante, que sobra **3** ENDED : terminado, acabado <the work is over : el trabajo está terminado>
over[3] *prep* **1** ABOVE : encima de, arriba de, sobre <over the fireplace : encima de la chimenea> <the hawk flew over the hills : el halcón voló sobre los cerros> **2** : más de <over $50 : más de $50> **3** ALONG : por, sobre <to glide over the ice : deslizarse sobre el hielo> **4** (*indicating motion through a place or thing*) <they showed me over the house : me mostraron la casa> **5** ACROSS : por encima de, sobre <he jumped over the ditch : saltó por encima de la zanja> **6** UPON : sobre <a cape over my shoulders : una capa sobre los hombros> **7** ON : por <to speak over the telephone : hablar por teléfono> **8** DURING : en, durante <over the past 25 years : durante los últimos 25 años> **9** BECAUSE OF : por <they fought over the money : se pelearon por el dinero>
overabundance [ˌoːvərə'bʌndəntk] *n* : superabundancia *f*
overabundant [ˌoːvərə'bʌndənt] *adj* : superabundante
overactive [ˌoːvər'æktɪv] *adj* : hiperactivo
overall [ˌoːvər'ɔl] *adj* : total, global, de conjunto
overalls ['oːvərˌɔlz] *npl* : overol *m*
overawe [ˌoːvər'ɔ] *vt* **-awed; -awing** : intimidar, impresionar
overbearing [ˌoːvər'bærɪŋ] *adj* : dominante, imperioso, prepotente
overboard ['oːvərˌbord] *adv* : por la borda, al agua
overburden [ˌoːvər'bərdən] *vt* : sobrecargar, agobiar
overcast ['oːvərˌkæst] *adj* CLOUDY : nublado
overcharge [ˌoːvər'tʃɑrdʒ] *vt* **-charged; -charging** : cobrarle de más (a alguien)
overcoat ['oːvərˌkoːt] *n* : abrigo *m*
overcome [ˌoːvər'kʌm] *v* **-came** [-'keɪm]; **-come; -coming** *vt* **1** CONQUER : vencer, derrotar, superar **2** OVERWHELM : abrumar, agobiar — *vi* : vencer
overconfidence [ˌoːvər'kɑnfədənts] *n* : exceso *m* de confianza
overconfident [ˌoːvər'kɑnfədənt] *adj* : demasiado confiado
overcook [ˌoːvər'kʊk] *vt* : recocer, cocer demasiado
overcrowded [ˌoːvər'kraʊdəd] *adj* **1** PACKED : abarrotado, atestado de gente **2** OVERPOPULATED : superpoblado
overdo [ˌoːvər'duː] *vt* **-did** [-'dɪd]; **-done** [-'dʌn]; **-doing; -does** [-'dʌz] **1** : hacer demasiado **2** EXAGGERATE : exagerar **3** OVERCOOK : recocer
overdose ['oːvərˌdoːs] *n* : sobredosis *f*
overdraft ['oːvərˌdræft] *n* : sobregiro *m*, descubierto *m*
overdraw [ˌoːvər'drɔ] *vt* **-drew** [-'druː]; **-drawn** [-'drɔn]; **-drawing 1** : sobregirar <my account is overdrawn : tengo la cuenta en descubierto> **2** EXAGGERATE : exagerar
overdue [ˌoːvər'duː] *adj* **1** UNPAID : vencido y sin pagar **2** TARDY : de retraso, tardío
overeat [ˌoːvər'iːt] *vi* **-ate** [-'eɪt]; **-eaten** [-'iːtən]; **-eating** : comer demasiado
overelaborate [ˌoːvərɪ'læbərət] *adj* : recargado
overestimate [ˌoːvər'ɛstəˌmeɪt] *vt* **-mated; -mating** : sobreestimar
overexcited [ˌoːvərɪk'saɪt̬əd] *adj* : sobreexcitado
overexpose [ˌoːvərɪk'spoːz] *vt* **-posed; -posing** : sobreexponer
overfeed [ˌoːvər'fiːd] *vt* **-fed** [-'fɛd]; **-feeding** : sobrealimentar
overflow[1] [ˌoːvər'floː] *vt* **1** : desbordar **2** INUNDATE : inundar — *vi* : desbordarse, rebosar
overflow[2] ['oːvərˌfloː] *n* **1** : derrame *m*, desbordamiento *m* (de un río) **2** SURPLUS : exceso *m*, excedente *m*
overfly [ˌoːvər'flaɪ] *vt* **-flew** [-'fluː]; **-flown** [-'floːn]; **-flying** : sobrevolar
overgrown [ˌoːvər'groːn] *adj* **1** : cubierto <overgrown with weeds : cubierto de malas hierbas> **2** : demasiado grande
overhand[1] ['oːvərˌhænd] *adv* : por encima de la cabeza
overhand[2] *adj* : por lo alto (tirada)
overhang[1] [ˌoːvər'hæŋ] *v* **-hung** [-'hʌŋ]; **-hanging** *vt* **1** : sobresalir por encima de **2** THREATEN : amenazar — *vi* : sobresalir
overhang[2] ['oːvərˌhæŋ] *n* : saliente *mf*

overhaul [ˌoːvərˈhɔl] *vt* **1** : revisar <to overhaul an engine : revisar un motor> **2** OVERTAKE : adelantar
overhead[1] [ˌoːvərˈhɛd] *adv* : por encima, arriba, por lo alto
overhead[2] [ˈoːvərˌhɛd] *adj* : de arriba
overhead[3] [ˈoːvərˌhɛd] *n* : gastos *mpl* generales
overhear [ˌoːvərˈhɪr] *vt* **-heard; -hearing** : oír por casualidad
overheat [ˌoːvərˈhiːt] *vt* : recalentar, sobrecalentar, calentar demasiado
overjoyed [ˌoːvərˈdʒɔɪd] *adj* : rebosante de alegría
overkill [ˈoːvərˌkɪl] *n* : exceso *m,* excedente *m*
overland[1] [ˈoːvərˌlænd, -lənd] *adv* : por tierra
overland[2] *adj* : terrestre, por tierra
overlap[1] [ˌoːvərˈlæp] *v* **-lapped; -lapping** *vt* : traslapar — *vi* : traslaparse, solaparse
overlap[2] [ˈoːvərˌlæp] *n* : traslapo *m*
overlay[1] [ˌoːvərˈleɪ] *vt* **-laid** [-ˈleɪd]; **-laying** : recubrir, revestir
overlay[2] [ˈoːvərˌleɪ] *n* : revestimiento *m*
overload [ˌoːvərˈloːd] *vt* : sobrecargar
overlong [ˌoːvərˈlɔŋ] *adj* : excesivamente largo, largo y pesado
overlook [ˌoːvərˈlʊk] *vt* **1** INSPECT : inspeccionar, revisar **2** : tener vista a, dar a <a house overlooking the valley : una casa que tiene vista al valle> **3** MISS : pasar por alto **4** EXCUSE : dejar pasar, disculpar
overly [ˈoːvərli] *adv* : demasiado
overnight[1] [ˌoːvərˈnaɪt] *adv* **1** : por la noche, durante la noche **2** : de la noche a la mañana <we can't do it overnight : no podemos hacerlo de la noche a la mañana>
overnight[2] [ˈoːvərˈnaɪt] *adj* **1** : de noche <an overnight stay : una estancia de una noche> <an overnight bag : una bolsa de viaje> **2** SUDDEN : repentino
overpass [ˈoːvərˌpæs] *n* : paso *m* elevado, paso *m* a desnivel *Mex*
overpopulated [ˌoːvərˈpɑpjəˌleɪt̬əd] *adj* : sobrepoblado
overpower [ˌoːvərˈpaʊər] *vt* **1** CONQUER, SUBDUE : vencer, superar **2** OVERWHELM : abrumar, agobiar <overpowered by the heat : sofocado por el calor>
overpraise [ˌoːvərˈpreɪz] *vt* **-praised; -praising** : adular
overrate [ˌoːvərˈreɪt] *vt* **-rated; -rating** : sobrevalorar, sobrevaluar
override [ˌoːvərˈraɪd] *vt* **-rode** [-ˈroːd]; **-ridden** [-ˈrɪdən]; **-riding 1** : predominar sobre, contar más que <hunger overrode our manners : el hambre predominó sobre los modales> **2** ANNUL : anular, invalidar <to override a veto : anular un veto>
overrule [ˌoːvərˈruːl] *vt* **-ruled; -ruling** : anular (una decisión), desautorizar (una persona), denegar (un pedido)
overrun [ˌoːvərˈrʌn] *v* **-ran** [-ˈræn]; **-running** *vt* **1** INVADE : invadir **2** INFEST : infestar, plagar **3** EXCEED : exceder, rebasar — *vi* : rebasar el tiempo previsto
overseas[1] [ˌoːvərˈsiːz] *adv* : en el extranjero <to travel overseas : viajar al extranjero>
overseas[2] [ˈoːvərˌsiːz] *adj* : extranjero, exterior
oversee [ˌoːvərˈsiː] *vt* **-saw** [-ˈsɔ]; **-seen** [-ˈsiːn]; **-seeing** SUPERVISE : supervisar
overseer [ˈoːvərˌsiːər] *n* : supervisor *m,* -sora *f;* capataz *mf*
overshadow [ˌoːvərˈʃæˌdoː] *vt* **1** DARKEN : oscurecer, ensombrecer **2** ECLIPSE, OUTSHINE : eclipsar
overshoe [ˈoːvərˌʃuː] *n* : chanclo *m*
overshoot [ˌoːvərˈʃuːt] *vt* **-shot** [-ˈʃɑt]; **-shooting** : pasarse de <to overshoot the mark : pasarse de la raya>
oversight [ˈoːvərˌsaɪt] *n* : descuido *m,* inadvertencia *f*
oversleep [ˌoːvərˈsliːp] *vi* **-slept** [-ˈslɛpt]; **-sleeping** : no despertarse a tiempo, quedarse dormido
overspread [ˌoːvərˈsprɛd] *vt* **-spread; -spreading** : extenderse sobre
overstaffed [ˌoːvərˈstæft] *adj* : con exceso de personal
overstate [ˌoːvərˈsteɪt] *vt* **-stated; -stating** EXAGGERATE : exagerar
overstatement [ˌoːvərˈsteɪtmənt] *n* : exageración *f*
overstep [ˌoːvərˈstɛp] *vt* **-stepped; -stepping** EXCEED : sobrepasar, traspasar, exceder
overt [oˈvərt, ˈoːˌvərt] *adj* : evidente, manifiesto, patente
overtake [ˌoːvərˈteɪk] *vt* **-took** [-ˈtʊk]; **-taken** [-ˈteɪkən]; **-taking** : pasar, adelantar, rebasar *Mex*
overthrow[1] [ˌoːvərˈθroː] *vt* **-threw** [-ˈθruː]; **-thrown** [-ˈθroːn]; **-throwing 1** OVERTURN : dar la vuelta a, volcar **2** DEFEAT, TOPPLE : derrocar, derribar, deponer
overthrow[2] [ˈoːvərˌθroː] *n* : derrocamiento *m,* caída *f*
overtime [ˈoːvərˌtaɪm] *n* **1** : horas *fpl* extras (de trabajo) **2** : prórroga *f* (en deportes)
overtly [oˈvərtli, ˈoːˌvərt-] *adv* OPENLY : abiertamente
overtone [ˈoːvərˌtoːn] *n* **1** : armónico *m* (en música) **2** HINT, SUGGESTION : tinte *m,* insinuación *f*
overture [ˈoːvərˌtʃʊr, -tʃər] *n* **1** PROPOSAL : propuesta *f* **2** : obertura *f* (en música)
overturn [ˌoːvərˈtərn] *vt* **1** UPSET : dar la vuelta a, volcar **2** NULLIFY : anular, invalidar — *vi* TURN OVER : volcar, dar un vuelco

overuse [ˌoːvərˈjuːz] *vt* **-used; -using** : abusar de

overview [ˈoːvərˌvjuː] *n* : resumen *m,* visión *f* general

overweening [ˌoːvərˈwiːnɪŋ] *adj* **1** ARROGANT : arrogante, soberbio **2** IMMODERATE : desmesurado

overweight [ˌoːvərˈweɪt] *adj* : demasiado gordo, demasiado pesado

overwhelm [ˌoːvərˈ*h*wɛlm] *vt* **1** CRUSH, DEFEAT : aplastar, arrollar **2** SUBMERGE : inundar, sumergir **3** OVERPOWER : abrumar, agobiar <overwhelmed by remorse : abrumado de remordimiento>

overwhelming [ˌoːvərˈ*h*wɛlmɪŋ] *adj* **1** CRUSHING : abrumador, apabullante **2** SWEEPING : arrollador, aplastante <an overwhelming majority : una mayoría aplastante>

overwork [ˌoːvərˈwərk] *vt* **1** : hacer trabajar demasiado **2** OVERUSE : abusar de — *vi* : trabajar demasiado

overwrought [ˌoːvərˈrɔt] *adj* : alterado, sobreexcitado

ovoid [ˈoːˌvɔɪd] *or* **ovoidal** [oˈvɔɪdəl] *adj* : ovoide

ovulate [ˈɑvjəˌleɪt, ˈoː-] *vi* **-lated; -lating** : ovular

ovulation [ˌɑvjəˈleɪʃən, ˌoː-] *n* : ovulación *f*

ovum [ˈoːvəm] *n, pl* **ova** [-və] : óvulo *m*

owe [ˈoː] *vt* **owed; owing** : deber <you owe me $10 : me debes $10> <he owes his wealth to his father : le debe su riqueza a su padre>

owing to *prep* : debido a

owl [ˈaʊl] *n* : búho *m,* lechuza *f,* tecolote *m Mex*

own[1] *v* [ˈoːn] *vt* **1** POSSESS : poseer, tener, ser dueño de **2** ADMIT : reconocer, admitir — *vi* **to own up** : reconocer (algo), admitir (algo)

own[2] *adj* : propio, personal, particular <his own car : su propio coche>

own[3] *pron* **my** (**your, his/her, our, their**) **own** : el mío, la mía; el tuyo, la tuya; el suyo, la suya; el nuestro, la nuestra <to each his own : cada uno a lo suyo> <money of my own : mi propio dinero> <to be on one's own : estar solo>

owner [ˈoːnər] *n* : dueño *m,* -ña *f;* propietario *m,* -ria *f*

ownership [ˈoːnərˌʃɪp] *n* : propiedad *f*

ox [ˈɑks] *n, pl* **oxen** [ˈɑksən] : buey *m*

oxidation [ˌɑksəˈdeɪʃən] *n* : oxidación *f*

oxide [ˈɑkˌsaɪd] *n* : óxido *m*

oxidize [ˈɑksəˌdaɪz] *vt* **-dized; -dizing** : oxidar

oxygen [ˈɑksɪdʒən] *n* : oxígeno *m*

oyster [ˈɔɪstər] *n* : ostra *f,* ostión *m Mex*

ozone [ˈoːˌzoːn] *n* : ozono *m*

P

p [ˈpiː] *n, pl* **p's** *or* **ps** [ˈpiːz] : decimosexta letra del alfabeto inglés

pace[1] [ˈpeɪs] *v* **paced; pacing** *vi* : caminar, ir y venir — *vt* **1** : caminar por <she paced the floor : caminaba de un lado a otro del cuarto> **2 to pace a runner** : marcarle el ritmo a un corredor

pace[2] *n* **1** STEP : paso *m* **2** RATE : paso *m,* ritmo *m* <to set the pace : marcar el paso, marcar la pauta>

pacemaker [ˈpeɪsˌmeɪkər] *n* : marcapasos *m*

pacific [pəˈsɪfɪk] *adj* : pacífico

pacifier [ˈpæsəˌfaɪər] *n* : chupete *m,* chupón *m,* mamila *f Mex*

pacifism [ˈpæsəˌfɪzəm] *n* : pacifismo *m*

pacifist [ˈpæsəfɪst] *n* : pacifista *mf*

pacify [ˈpæsəˌfaɪ] *vt* **-fied; -fying** **1** SOOTHE : apaciguar, pacificar **2** : pacificar (un país, una región, etc.)

pack[1] [ˈpæk] *vt* **1** PACKAGE : empaquetar, embalar, envasar **2** : empacar, meter (en una maleta) <to pack one's bag : hacer la maleta> **3** FILL : llenar, abarrotar <a packed theater : un teatro abarrotado> **4 to pack off** SEND : mandar — *vi* : empacar, hacer las maletas

pack[2] *n* **1** BUNDLE : bulto *m,* fardo *m* **2** BACKPACK : mochila *f* **3** PACKAGE : paquete *m,* cajetilla *f* (de cigarillos, etc.) **4** : manada *f* (de lobos, etc.), jauría *f* (de perros) <a pack of thieves : una pandilla de ladrones>

package[1] [ˈpækɪdʒ] *vt* **-aged; -aging** : empaquetar, embalar

package[2] *n* : paquete *m,* bulto *m*

packer [ˈpækər] *n* : empacador *m,* -dora *f*

packet [ˈpækət] *n* : paquete *m*

pact [ˈpækt] *n* : pacto *m,* acuerdo *m*

pad[1] [ˈpæd] *vt* **padded; padding** **1** FILL, STUFF : rellenar, acolchar (una silla, una pared) **2** : meter paja en, rellenar <to pad a speech : rellenar un discurso>

pad[2] *n* **1** CUSHION : almohadilla *f* <a shoulder pad : una hombrera> **2** TABLET : bloc *m* (de papel) **3** *or* **lily pad** : hoja *f* grande (de un nenúfar) **4 ink pad** : tampón *m* **5 launching pad** : plataforma *f* (de lanzamiento)

padding [ˈpædɪŋ] *n* **1** FILLING : relleno *m* **2** : paja *f* (en un discurso, etc.)

paddle[1] [ˈpædəl] *v* **-dled; -dling** *vt* **1** : hacer avanzar (una canoa) con canalete **2** HIT : azotar, darle nalgadas a (con una pala o paleta) — *vi* **1** : remar (en una canoa) **2** SPLASH : chapotear, mojarse los pies

paddle² *n* **1 :** canalete *m,* zagual *m* (de una canoa, etc.) **2 :** pala *f,* paleta *f* (en deportes)
paddock ['pædək] *n* **1** PASTURE **:** potrero *m* **2 :** paddock *m,* cercado *m* (en un hipódromo)
paddy ['pædi] *n, pl* **-dies :** arrozal *m*
padlock¹ ['pæd,lɑk] *vt* **:** cerrar con candado
padlock² *n* **:** candado *m*
pagan¹ ['peɪgən] *adj* **:** pagano
pagan² *n* **:** pagano *m,* -na *f*
paganism ['peɪgən,ɪzəm] *n* **:** paganismo *m*
page¹ ['peɪdʒ] *vt* **paged; paging :** llamar por altavoz
page² *n* **1** BELLHOP **:** botones *m* **2 :** página *f* (de un libro, etc.)
pageant ['pædʒənt] *n* **1** SPECTACLE **:** espectáculo *m* **2** PROCESSION **:** desfile *m*
pageantry ['pædʒəntri] *n* **:** pompa *f,* fausto *m*
pagoda [pə'go:də] *n* **:** pagoda *f*
paid → **pay**
pail ['peɪl] *n* **:** balde *m,* cubo *m,* cubeta *f Mex*
pailful ['peɪl,fʊl] *n* **:** balde *m,* cubo *m,* cubeta *f Mex*
pain¹ ['peɪn] *vt* **:** doler
pain² *n* **1** PENALTY **:** pena *f* <under pain of death : so pena de muerte> **2** SUFFERING **:** dolor *m,* malestar *m,* pena *f* (mental) **3 pains** *npl* EFFORT **:** esmero *m,* esfuerzo *m* <to take pains : esmerarse>
painful ['peɪnfəl] *adj* **:** doloroso — **painfully** *adv*
painkiller ['peɪn,kɪlər] *n* **:** analgésico *m*
painless ['peɪnləs] *adj* **:** indoloro, sin dolor
painlessly ['peɪnləsli] *adv* **:** sin dolor
painstaking ['peɪn,steɪkɪŋ] *adj* **:** esmerado, cuidadoso, meticuloso — **painstakingly** *adv*
paint¹ ['peɪnt] *v* **:** pintar
paint² *n* **:** pintura *f*
paintbrush ['peɪnt,brʌʃ] *n* **:** pincel *m* (de un artista), brocha *f* (para pintar casas, etc.)
painter ['peɪntər] *n* **:** pintor *m,* -tora *f*
painting ['peɪntɪŋ] *n* **:** pintura *f*
pair¹ ['pær] *vt* **:** emparejar, poner en parejas — *vi* **:** emparejarse
pair² *n* **:** par *m* (de objetos), pareja *f* (de personas o animales) <a pair of scissors : unas tijeras>
pajamas [pə'dʒɑməz, -'dʒæ-] *npl* **:** pijama *m,* piyama *mf*
Pakistani [,pækɪ'stæni, ,pɑkɪ'stɑni] *n* **:** paquistaní *mf* — **Pakistani** *adj*
pal ['pæl] *n* **:** amigo *m,* -ga *f;* compinche *mf fam;* chamo *m,* -ma *f Ven fam;* cuate *m,* -ta *f Mex*
palace ['pæləs] *n* **:** palacio *m*
palatable ['pælətəbəl] *adj* **:** sabroso
palate ['pælət] *n* **1 :** paladar *m* (de la boca) **2** TASTE **:** paladar *m,* gusto *m*
palatial [pə'leɪʃəl] *adj* **:** suntuoso, espléndido
palaver [pə'lævər, -'lɑ-] *n* **:** palabrería *f*
pale¹ ['peɪl] *v* **paled; paling** *vi* **:** palidecer — *vt* **:** hacer pálido
pale² *adj* **paler; palest 1 :** pálido <to turn pale : palidecer, ponerse pálido> **2 :** claro (dícese de los colores)
paleness ['peɪlnəs] *n* **:** palidez *f*
Palestinian [,pælə'stɪniən] *n* **:** palestino *m,* -na *f* — **Palestinian** *adj*
palette ['pælət] *n* **:** paleta *f* (para mezclar pigmentos)
palisade [,pælə'seɪd] *n* **1** FENCE **:** empalizada *f,* estacada *f* **2** CLIFFS **:** acantilado *m*
pall¹ ['pɔl] *vi* **:** perder su sabor, dejar de gustar
pall² *n* **1 :** paño *m* mortuario (sobre un ataúd) **2** COVER **:** cortina *f* (de humo, etc.) **3 to cast a pall over :** ensombrecer
pallbearer ['pɔl,bɛrər] *n* **:** portador *m,* -dora *f* del féretro
pallet ['pælət] *n* **1** BED **:** camastro *m* **2** PLATFORM **:** plataforma *f* de carga
palliative ['pæli,eɪṭɪv, 'pæljəṭɪv] *adj* **:** paliativo
pallid ['pæləd] *adj* **:** pálido
pallor ['pælər] *n* **:** palidez *f*
palm¹ ['pɑm, 'pɑlm] *vt* **1** CONCEAL **:** escamotear (un naipe, etc.) **2 to palm off :** encajar, endilgar *fam* <he palmed it off on me : me lo endilgó>
palm² *n* **1** *or* **palm tree :** palmera *f* **2 :** palma *f* (de la mano)
Palm Sunday *n* **:** Domingo *m* de Ramos
palomino [,pælə'mi:,no:] *n, pl* **-nos :** caballo *m* de color dorado
palpable ['pælpəbəl] *adj* **:** palpable — **palpably** [-bli] *adv*
palpitate ['pælpə,teɪt] *vi* **-tated; -tating :** palpitar
palpitation [,pælpə'teɪʃən] *n* **:** palpitación *f*
palsy ['pɔlzi] *n, pl* **-sies 1 :** parálisis *f* **2** → **cerebral palsy**
paltry ['pɔltri] *adj* **-trier; -est :** mísero, mezquino, insignificante <a paltry excuse : una mala excusa>
pampas ['pæmpəz, 'pɑmpəs] *npl* **:** pampa *f*
pamper ['pæmpər] *vt* **:** mimar, consentir, chiquear *Mex*
pamphlet ['pæmpflət] *n* **:** panfleto *m,* folleto *m*
pan¹ ['pæn] *vt* **panned; panning** CRITICIZE **:** poner por los suelos — *vi* **to pan for gold :** cribar el oro con batea, lavar oro
pan² *n* **1 :** cacerola *f,* cazuela *f* **2 frying pan :** sartén *mf,* freidera *f Mex*
panacea [,pænə'si:ə] *n* **:** panacea *f*
Panamanian [,pænə'meɪniən] *n* **:** panameño *m,* -ña *f* — **Panamanian** *adj*
pancake ['pæn,keɪk] *n* **:** panqueque *m*

pancreas [ˈpæŋkriəs, ˈpæn-] *n* : páncreas *m*

panda [ˈpændə] *n* : panda *mf*

pandemonium [ˌpændəˈmoːniəm] *n* : pandemonio *m,* pandemónium *m*

pander [ˈpændər] *vi* **to pander to** : satisfacer, complacer (a alguien) <to pander to popular taste : satisfacer el gusto popular>

pane [ˈpeɪn] *n* : cristal *m,* vidrio *m*

panel[1] [ˈpænəl] *vt* **-eled** *or* **-elled; -eling** *or* **-elling** : adornar con paneles

panel[2] *n* **1** : lista *f* de nombres (de un jurado, etc.) **2** GROUP : panel *m,* grupo *m* <discussion panel : panel de discusión> **3** : panel *m* (de una pared, etc.) **4 instrument panel** : tablero *m* de instrumentos

paneling [ˈpænəlɪŋ] *n* : paneles *mpl*

pang [ˈpæŋ] *n* : puntada *f,* punzada *f*

panic[1] [ˈpænɪk] *v* **-icked; -icking** *vt* : llenar de pánico — *vi* : ser presa de pánico

panic[2] *n* : pánico *m*

panicky [ˈpænɪki] *adj* : presa de pánico

panorama [ˌpænəˈræmə, -ˈrɑ-] *n* : panorama *m*

panoramic [ˌpænəˈræmɪk, -ˈrɑ-] *adj* : panorámico

pansy [ˈpænzi] *n, pl* **-sies** : pensamiento *m*

pant[1] [ˈpænt] *vi* : jadear, resoplar

pant[2] *n* : jadeo *m,* resoplo *m*

pantaloons [ˌpæntəˈluːnz] → **pants**

panther [ˈpænθər] *n* : pantera *f*

panties [ˈpæntiz] *npl* : calzones *mpl,* pantaletas *fpl*

pantomime[1] [ˈpæntəˌmaɪm] *v* **-mimed; -miming** *vt* : representar mediante la pantomima — *vi* : hacer la mímica

pantomime[2] *n* : pantomima *f*

pantry [ˈpæntri] *n, pl* **-tries** : despensa *f*

pants [ˈpænts] *npl* **1** TROUSERS : pantalón *m,* pantalones *mpl* **2** → **panties**

pap [ˈpæp] *n* : papilla *f* (para bebés, etc.)

papal [ˈpeɪpəl] *adj* : papal

papaya [pəˈpaɪə] *n* : papaya *f* (fruta)

paper[1] [ˈpeɪpər] *vt* WALLPAPER : empapelar

paper[2] *adj* : de papel

paper[3] *n* **1** : papel *m* <a piece of paper : un papel> **2** DOCUMENT : papel *m,* documento *m* **3** NEWSPAPER : periódico *m,* diario *m*

paperback [ˈpeɪpərˌbæk] *n* : libro *m* en rústica

paper clip *n* : clip *m,* sujetapapeles *m*

paperweight [ˈpeɪpərˌweɪt] *n* : pisapapeles *m*

papery [ˈpeɪpəri] *adj* : parecido al papel

papier–mâché [ˌpeɪpərməˈʃeɪ, ˌpæˌpjeɪmæˈʃeɪ] *n* : papel *m* maché

papoose [pæˈpuːs, pə-] *n* : niño *m,* -ña *f* de los indios norteamericanos

paprika [pəˈpriːkə, pæ-] *n* : pimentón *m,* paprika *f*

papyrus [pəˈpaɪrəs] *n, pl* **-ruses** *or* **-ri** [-ri, -ˌraɪ] : papiro *m*

par [ˈpɑr] *n* **1** VALUE : valor *m* (nominal), par *f* <below par : debajo de la par> **2** EQUALITY : igualdad *f* <to be on a par with : estar al mismo nivel que> **3** : par *m* (en golf)

parable [ˈpærəbəl] *n* : parábola *f*

parachute[1] [ˈpærəˌʃuːt] *vi* **-chuted; -chuting** : lanzarse en paracaídas

parachute[2] *n* : paracaídas *m*

parachutist [ˈpærəˌʃuːt̬ɪst] *n* : paracaidista *mf*

parade[1] [pəˈreɪd] *vi* **-raded; -rading 1** MARCH : desfilar **2** SHOW OFF : pavonearse, lucirse

parade[2] *n* **1** PROCESSION : desfile *m* **2** DISPLAY : alarde *m*

paradigm [ˈpærəˌdaɪm] *n* : paradigma *m*

paradise [ˈpærəˌdaɪs, -ˌdaɪz] *n* : paraíso *m*

paradox [ˈpærəˌdɑks] *n* : paradoja *f*

paradoxical [ˌpærəˈdɑksɪkəl] *adj* : paradójico — **paradoxically** *adv*

paraffin [ˈpærəfən] *n* : parafina *f*

paragraph[1] [ˈpærəˌgræf] *vt* : dividir en párrafos

paragraph[2] *n* : párrafo *m,* acápite *m*

Paraguayan [ˌpærəˈgwaɪən, -ˈgweɪ-] *n* : paraguayo *m,* -ya *f* — **Paraguayan** *adj*

parakeet [ˈpærəˌkiːt] *n* : periquito *m*

parallel[1] [ˈpærəˌlɛl, -ləl] *vt* **1** MATCH, RESEMBLE : ser paralelo a, ser análogo a, corresponder con **2** : extenderse en línea paralela con <the road parallels the river : el camino se extiende a lo largo del río>

parallel[2] *adj* : paralelo

parallel[3] *n* **1** : línea *f* paralela, superficie *f* paralela **2** : paralelo *m* (en geografía) **3** SIMILARITY : paralelismo *m,* semejanza *f*

parallelogram [ˌpærəˈlɛləˌgræm] *n* : paralelogramo *m*

paralysis [pəˈræləsɪs] *n, pl* **-yses** [-ˌsiːz] : parálisis *f*

paralyze [ˈpærəˌlaɪz] *vt* **-lyzed; -lyzing** : paralizar

parameter [pəˈræmət̬ər] *n* : parámetro *m*

paramount [ˈpærəˌmaʊnt] *adj* : supremo <of paramount importance : de suma importancia>

paranoia [ˌpærəˈnɔɪə] *n* : paranoia *f*

paranoid [ˈpærəˌnɔɪd] *adj* : paranoico

parapet [ˈpærəpət, -ˌpɛt] *n* : parapeto *m*

paraphernalia [ˌpærəfəˈneɪljə, -fər-] *ns & pl* : parafernalia *f*

paraphrase[1] [ˈpærəˌfreɪz] *vt* **-phrased; -phrasing** : parafrasear

paraphrase[2] *n* : paráfrasis *f*

paraplegic[1] [ˌpærəˈpliːdʒɪk] *adj* : parapléjico

paraplegic[2] *n* : parapléjico *m,* -ca *f*

parasite ['pærə,saɪt] *n* : parásito *m*
parasitic [,pærə'sɪt̬ɪk] *adj* : parasitario
parasol ['pærə,sɔl] *n* : sombrilla *f,* quitasol *m,* parasol *m*
paratrooper ['pærə,tru:pər] *n* : paracaidista *mf* (militar)
parboil ['pɑr,bɔɪl] *vt* : sancochar, cocer a medias
parcel[1] ['pɑrsəl] *vt* **-celed** *or* **-celled; -celing** *or* **-celling** *or* **to parcel out** : repartir, parcelar (tierras)
parcel[2] *n* **1** LOT : parcela *f,* lote *m* **2** PACKAGE : paquete *m,* bulto *m*
parch ['pɑrtʃ] *vt* : resecar
parchment ['pɑrtʃmənt] *n* : pergamino *m*
pardon[1] ['pɑrdən] *vt* **1** FORGIVE : perdonar, disculpar <pardon me! : ¡perdone!, ¡disculpe la molestia!> **2** REPRIEVE : indultar (a un delincuente)
pardon[2] *n* **1** FORGIVENESS : perdón *m* **2** REPRIEVE : indulto *m*
pardonable ['pɑrdənəbəl] *adj* : perdonable, disculpable
pare ['pær] *vt* **pared; paring 1** PEEL : pelar **2** TRIM : recortar **3** REDUCE : reducir <he pared it (down) to 50 pages : lo redujo a 50 páginas>
parent ['pærənt] *n* **1** : madre *f,* padre *m* **2 parents** *npl* : padres *mpl*
parentage ['pærəntɪdʒ] *n* : linaje *m,* abolengo *m,* origen *m*
parental [pə'rɛntəl] *adj* : de los padres
parenthesis [pə'rɛnθəsɪs] *n, pl* **-theses** [-,si:z] : paréntesis *m*
parenthetic [,pærən'θɛt̬ɪk] *or* **parenthetical** [-tɪkəl] *adj* : parentético — **parenthetically** [-t̬ɪkli] *adv*
parenthood ['pærənt,hʊd] *n* : paternidad *f*
parfait [pɑr'feɪ] *n* : postre *m* elaborado con frutas y helado
pariah [pə'raɪə] *n* : paria *mf*
parish ['pærɪʃ] *n* : parroquia *f*
parishioner [pə'rɪʃənər] *n* : feligrés *m,* -gresa *f*
parity ['pærət̬i] *n, pl* **-ties** : paridad *f*
park[1] ['pɑrk] *vt* : estacionar, parquear, aparcar *Spain* — *vi* : estacionarse, parquearse, aparcar *Spain*
park[2] *n* : parque *m*
parka ['pɑrkə] *n* : parka *f*
parkway ['pɑrk,weɪ] *n* : carretera *f* ajardinada, bulevar *m*
parley[1] ['pɑrli] *vi* : parlamentar, negociar
parley[2] *n, pl* **-leys** : negociación *f,* parlamento *m*
parliament ['pɑrləmənt, 'pɑrljə-] *n* : parlamento *m*
parliamentary [,pɑrlə'mɛntəri, ,pɑrljə-] *adj* : parlamentario
parlor ['pɑrlər] *n* **1** : sala *f,* salón *m* (en una casa) **2** : salón *m* <beauty parlor : salón de belleza> **3 funeral parlor** : funeraria *f*
parochial [pə'ro:kiəl] *adj* **1** : parroquial **2** PROVINCIAL : pueblerino, de miras estrechas
parody[1] ['pærədi] *vt* **-died; -dying** : parodiar
parody[2] *n, pl* **-dies** : parodia *f*
parole [pə'ro:l] *n* : libertad *f* condicional
paroxysm ['pærək,sɪzəm, pə'rɑk-] *n* : paroxismo *m*
parquet ['pɑr,keɪ, pɑr'keɪ] *n* : parquet *m,* parqué *m*
parrakeet → **parakeet**
parrot ['pærət] *n* : loro *m,* papagayo *m*
parry[1] ['pæri] *v* **-ried; -rying** *vi* : parar un golpe — *vt* EVADE : esquivar (una pregunta, etc.)
parry[2] *n, pl* **-ries** : parada *f*
parsimonious [,pɑrsə'mo:niəs] *adj* : tacaño, mezquino
parsley ['pɑrsli] *n* : perejil *m*
parsnip ['pɑrsnɪp] *n* : chirivía *f*
parson ['pɑrsən] *n* : pastor *m,* -tora *f;* clérigo *m*
parsonage ['pɑrsənɪdʒ] *n* : rectoría *f,* casa *f* del párroco
part[1] ['pɑrt] *vi* **1** SEPARATE : separarse, despedirse <we should part as friends : debemos separarnos amistosamente> **2** OPEN : abrirse <the curtains parted : las cortinas se abrieron> **3 to part with** : dehacerse de — *vt* **1** SEPARATE : separar **2 to part one's hair** : hacerse la raya, peinarse con raya
part[2] *n* **1** SECTION, SEGMENT : parte *f,* sección *f* **2** PIECE : pieza *f* (de una máquina, etc.) **3** ROLE : papel *m* **4** : raya *f* (del pelo)
partake [pɑr'teɪk, pər-] *vi* **-took** [-'tʊk]; **-taken** [-'teɪkən]; **-taking 1 to partake of** CONSUME : comer, beber, tomar **2 to partake in** : participar en (una actividad, etc.)
partial ['pɑrʃəl] *adj* **1** BIASED : parcial, tendencioso **2** INCOMPLETE : parcial, incompleto **3 to be partial to** : ser aficionado a
partiality [,pɑrʃi'ælət̬i] *n, pl* **-ties** : parcialidad *f*
partially ['pɑrʃəli] *adv* : parcialmente
participant [pər'tɪsəpənt, pɑr-] *n* : participante *mf*
participate [pər'tɪsə,peɪt, pɑr-] *vi* **-pated; -pating** : participar
participation [pər,tɪsə'peɪʃən, pɑr-] *n* : participación *f*
participle ['pɑrt̬ə,sɪpəl] *n* : participio *m*
particle ['pɑrt̬ɪkəl] *n* : partícula *f*
particular[1] [pɑr'tɪkjələr] *adj* **1** SPECIFIC : particular, en particular <this particular person : esta persona en particular> **2** SPECIAL : particular, especial <with particular emphasis : con un énfasis especial> **3** FUSSY : exigente, maniático <to be very particular : ser muy especial> <I'm not particular : me da igual>
particular[2] *n* **1** DETAIL : detalle *m,* sentido *m* **2 in particular** : en particular, en especial

particularly [pɑr'tɪkjələrli] *adv* **1** ESPECIALLY : particularmente, especialmente **2** SPECIFICALLY : específicamente, en especial

partisan ['pɑrtəzən, -sən] *n* **1** ADHERENT : partidario *m,* -ria *f* **2** GUERRILLA : partisano *m,* -na *f;* guerrillero *m,* -ra *f*

partition¹ [pər'tɪʃən, pɑr-] *vt* : dividir <to partition off (a room) : dividir con un tabique>

partition² *n* **1** DISTRIBUTION : partición *f,* división *f,* reparto *m* **2** DIVIDER : tabique *m,* mampara *f,* biombo *m*

partly ['pɑrtli] *adv* : en parte, parcialmente

partner ['pɑrtnər] *n* **1** COMPANION : compañero *m,* -ra *f* **2** : pareja *f* (en un juego, etc.) <dancing partner : pareja de baile> **3** SPOUSE : cónyuge *mf* **4** *or* **business partner** : socio *m,* -cia *f;* asociado *m,* -da *f*

partnership ['pɑrtnər,ʃɪp] *n* **1** ASSOCIATION : asociación *f,* compañerismo *m* **2** : sociedad *f* (de negociantes) <to form a partnership : asociarse>

part of speech : categoría *f* gramatical

partridge ['pɑrtrɪdʒ] *n, pl* **-tridge** *or* **-tridges** : perdiz *f*

party ['pɑrti] *n, pl* **-ties** **1** : partido *m* (político) **2** PARTICIPANT : parte *f,* participante *mf* **3** GROUP : grupo *m* (de personas) **4** GATHERING : fiesta *f* <to throw a party : dar una fiesta>

parvenu ['pɑrvə,nu:, -,nju:] *n* : advenedizo *m,* -za *f*

pass¹ ['pæs] *vi* **1** : pasar, cruzarse <a car passed by : pasó un coche> <we passed in the hallway : nos cruzamos en el pasillo> **2** CEASE : pasarse <the pain passed : se pasó el dolor> **3** ELAPSE : pasar, transcurrir **4** PROCEED : pasar <let me pass : déjame pasar> **5** HAPPEN : pasar, ocurrir **6** : pasar, aprobar (en un examen) **7** RULE : fallar <the jury passed on the case : el jurado falló en el caso> **8** *or* **to pass down** : pasar <the throne passed to his son : el trono pasó a su hijo> **9 to let pass** OVERLOOK : pasar por alto **10 to pass as** : pasar por **11 to pass away** *or* **to pass on** DIE : fallecer, morir — *vt* **1** : pasar por <they passed the house : pasaron por la casa> **2** OVERTAKE : pasar, adelantar **3** SPEND : pasar (tiempo) **4** HAND : pasar <pass me the salt : pásame la sal> **5** : aprobar (un examen, una ley)

pass² *n* **1** CROSSING, GAP : paso *m,* desfiladero *m,* puerto *m* <mountain pass : puerto de montaña> **2** PERMIT : pase *m,* permiso *m* **3** : pase *m* (en deportes) **4** SITUATION : situación *f* (difícil) <things have come to a pretty pass! : ¡hasta dónde hemos llegado!>

passable ['pæsəbəl] *adj* **1** ADEQUATE : adecuado, pasable **2** : transitable (dícese de un camino, etc.)

passably ['pæsəbli] *adv* : pasablemente

passage ['pæsɪdʒ] *n* **1** PASSING : paso *m* <the passage of time : el paso del tiempo> **2** PASSAGEWAY : pasillo *m* (dentro de un edificio), pasaje *m* (entre edificios) **3** VOYAGE : travesía *f* (por el mar), viaje *m* <to grant safe passage : dar un salvoconducto> **4** SECTION : pasaje *m* (en música o literatura)

passageway ['pæsɪdʒ,weɪ] *n* : pasillo *m,* pasadizo *m,* corredor *m*

passbook ['pæs,bʊk] *n* BANKBOOK : libreta *f* de ahorros

passé [pæ'seɪ] *adj* : pasado de moda

passenger ['pæsəndʒər] *n* : pasajero *m,* -ra *f*

passerby [,pæsər'baɪ, 'pæsər,-] *n, pl* **passersby** : transeúnte *mf*

passing ['pæsɪŋ] *n* DEATH : fallecimiento *m*

passion ['pæʃən] *n* : pasión *f,* ardor *m*

passionate ['pæʃənət] *adj* **1** IRASCIBLE : irascible, iracundo **2** ARDENT : apasionado, ardiente, ferviente, fogoso

passionately ['pæʃənətli] *adv* : apasionadamente, fervientemente, con pasión

passive¹ ['pæsɪv] *adj* : pasivo — **passively** *adv*

passive² *n* : voz *f* pasiva (en gramática)

Passover ['pæs,o:vər] *n* : Pascua *f* (en el judaísmo)

passport ['pæs,port] *n* : pasaporte *m*

password ['pæs,wərd] *n* : contraseña *f*

past¹ ['pæst] *adv* : por delante <he drove past : pasamos en coche>

past² *adj* **1** AGO : hace <10 years past : hace 10 años> **2** LAST : último <the past few months : los últimos meses> **3** BYGONE : pasado <in past times : en tiempos pasados> **4** : pasado (en gramática)

past³ *n* : pasado *m*

past⁴ *prep* **1** BY : por, por delante de <he ran past the house : pasó por la casa corriendo> **2** BEYOND : más allá de <just past the corner : un poco más allá de la esquina> <we went past the exit : pasamos la salida> **3** AFTER : despúes de <past noon : después del mediodía> <half past two : las dos y media>

pasta ['pɑstə, 'pæs-] *n* : pasta *f*

paste¹ ['peɪst] *vt* **pasted; pasting** : pegar (con engrudo)

paste² *n* **1** : pasta *f* <tomato paste : pasta de tomate> **2** : engrudo *m* (para pegar)

pasteboard ['peɪst,bord] *n* : cartón *m,* cartulina *f*

pastel [pæ'stɛl] *n* : pastel *m* — **pastel** *adj*

pasteurization [,pæstʃərə'zeɪʃən, ,pæstjə-] *n* : pasteurización *f*

pasteurize ['pæstʃə,raɪz, 'pæstjə-] *vt* **-ized; -izing** : pasteurizar

pastime ['pæs,taɪm] *n* : pasatiempo *m*

pastor ['pæstər] *n* : pastor *m,* -tora *f*

pastoral [ˈpæstərəl] *adj* **:** pastoral
past participle *n* **:** participio *m* pasado
pastry [ˈpeɪstri] *n, pl* **-ries 1** DOUGH **:** pasta *f,* masa *f* **2 pastries** *npl* **:** pasteles *mpl*
pasture¹ [ˈpæstʃər] *v* **-tured; -turing** *vi* GRAZE **:** pacer, pastar — *vt* **:** apacentar, pastar
pasture² *n* **:** pastizal *m,* potrero *m,* pasto *m*
pasty [ˈpeɪsti] *adj* **pastier; -est 1 :** pastoso (en consistencia) **2** PALLID **:** pálido
pat¹ [ˈpæt] *vt* **patted; patting :** dar palmaditas a, tocar
pat² *adv* **:** de memoria <to have down pat : saberse de memoria>
pat³ *adj* **1** APT **:** apto, apropiado **2** GLIB **:** fácil **3** UNYIELDING **:** firme <to stand pat : mantenerse firme>
pat⁴ *n* **1** TAP **:** golpecito *m,* palmadita *f* <a pat on the back : una palmadita en la espalda> **2** CARESS **:** caricia *f* **3 :** porción *f* <a pat of butter : una porción de mantequilla>
patch¹ [ˈpætʃ] *vt* **1** MEND, REPAIR **:** remender, parchar, ponerle un parche a **2 to patch together** IMPROVISE **:** confeccionar, improvisar **3 to patch up :** arreglar <they patched things up : hicieron las paces>
patch² *n* **1 :** parche *m,* remiendo *m* (para la ropa) <eye patch : parche para el ojo> **2** PIECE **:** mancha *f,* trozo *m* <a patch of sky : un trozo de cielo> **3** PLOT **:** parcela *f,* terreno *m* <cabbage patch : parcela de repollos>
patchwork [ˈpætʃˌwərk] *n* **:** labor *f* de retazos
patchy [ˈpætʃi] *adj* **patchier; -est 1** IRREGULAR **:** irregular, desigual **2** INCOMPLETE **:** parcial, incompleto
patent¹ [ˈpætənt] *vt* **:** patentar
patent² *adj* [ˈpætənt, ˈpeɪt-] **1** OBVIOUS **:** patente, evidente **2** [ˈpæt-] PATENTED **:** patentado
patent³ [ˈpætənt] *n* **:** patente *f*
patently [ˈpætəntli] *adv* **:** patentemente, evidentemente
paternal [pəˈtərnəl] *adj* **1** FATHERLY **:** paternal **2 :** paterno <paternal grandfather : abuelo paterno>
paternity [pəˈtərnət̬i] *n* **:** paternidad *f*
path [ˈpæθ, ˈpaθ] *n* **1** TRACK, TRAIL **:** camino *m,* sendero *m,* senda *f* **2** COURSE, ROUTE **:** recorrido *m,* trayecto *m,* trayectoria *f*
pathetic [pəˈθɛt̬ɪk] *adj* **:** patético — **pathetically** [-t̬ɪkli] *adv*
pathological [ˌpæθəˈlɑdʒɪkəl] *adj* **:** patológico
pathologist [pəˈθɑlədʒɪst] *n* **:** patólogo *m,* -ga *f*
pathology [pəˈθɑlədʒi] *n, pl* **-gies :** patología *f*
pathos [ˈpeɪˌθɑs, ˈpæ-, -ˌθɔs] *n* **:** patetismo *m*
pathway [ˈpæθˌweɪ] *n* **:** camino *m,* sendero *m,* senda *f,* vereda *f*
patience [ˈpeɪʃənts] *n* **:** paciencia *f*
patient¹ [ˈpeɪʃənt] *adj* **:** paciente — **patiently** *adv*
patient² *n* **:** paciente *mf*
patio [ˈpæt̬iˌoː] *n, pl* **-tios :** patio *m*
patriarch [ˈpeɪtriˌɑrk] *n* **:** patriarca *m*
patrimony [ˈpætrəˌmoːni] *n, pl* **-nies :** patrimonio *m*
patriot [ˈpeɪtriət] *n* **:** patriota *mf*
patriotic [ˌpeɪtriˈɑt̬ɪk] *adj* **:** patriótico — **patriotically** *adv*
patriotism [ˈpeɪtriəˌtɪzəm] *n* **:** patriotismo *m*
patrol¹ [pəˈtroːl] *v* **-trolled; -trolling :** patrullar
patrol² *n* **:** patrulla *f*
patrolman [pəˈtroːlmən] *n, pl* **-men** [-mən, -ˌmɛn] **:** policía *mf,* guardia *mf*
patron [ˈpeɪtrən] *n* **1** SPONSOR **:** patrocinador *m,* -dora *f* **2** CUSTOMER **:** cliente *m,* -ta *f* **3** *or* **patron saint :** patrono *m,* -na *f*
patronage [ˈpeɪtrənɪdʒ, ˈpæ-] *n* **1** SPONSORSHIP **:** patrocinio *m* **2** CLIENTELE **:** clientela *f* **3 :** influencia *f* (política)
patronize [ˈpeɪtrəˌnaɪz, ˈpæ-] *vt* **-ized; -izing 1** SPONSOR **:** patrocinar **2 :** ser cliente de (un negocio) **3 :** tratar con condescendencia
patter¹ [ˈpæt̬ər] *vi* **1** TAP **:** golpetear, tamborilear (dícese de la lluvia) **2 to patter about :** corretear (con pasos ligeros)
patter² *n* **1** TAPPING **:** golpeteo *m,* tamborileo *m* (de la lluvia), correteo *m* (de pies) **2** CHATTER **:** palabrería *f,* parloteo *m fam*
pattern¹ [ˈpæt̬ərn] *vt* **1** BASE **:** basar (en un modelo) **2 to pattern after :** hacer imitación de
pattern² *n* **1** MODEL **:** modelo *m,* patrón *m* (de costura) **2** DESIGN **:** diseño *m,* dibujo *m,* estampado *m* (de tela) **3** NORM, STANDARD **:** pauta *f,* norma *f,* patrón *m*
patty [ˈpæt̬i] *n, pl* **-ties :** porción *f* de carne picada (u otro alimento) en forma de ruedita <a hamburger patty : una hamburguesa>
paucity [ˈpɔsət̬i] *n* **:** escasez *f*
paunch [ˈpɔntʃ] *n* **:** panza *f,* barriga *f*
pauper [ˈpɔpər] *n* **:** pobre *mf,* indigente *mf*
pause¹ [ˈpɔz] *vi* **paused; pausing :** hacer una pausa, pararse (brevemente)
pause² *n* **:** pausa *f*
pave [ˈpeɪv] *vt* **paved; paving :** pavimentar <to pave with stones : empedrar>
pavement [ˈpeɪvmənt] *n* **:** pavimento *m,* empedrado *m*
pavilion [pəˈvɪljən] *n* **:** pabellón *m*
paving [ˈpeɪvɪŋ] → **pavement**
paw¹ [ˈpɔ] *vt* **:** tocar, manosear, sobar
paw² *n* **:** pata *f,* garra *f,* zarpa *f*
pawn¹ [ˈpɔn] *vt* **:** empeñar, prendar

pawn[2] *n* **1** PLEDGE, SECURITY : prenda *f* **2** PAWNING : empeño *m* **3** : peón *m* (en ajedrez)

pawnbroker ['pɔn,bro:kər] *n* : prestamista *mf*

pawnshop ['pɔn,ʃɑp] *n* : casa *f* de empeños, monte *m* de piedad

pay[1] ['peɪ] *v* **paid** ['peɪd]; **paying** *vt* **1** : pagar (una cuenta, a un empleado, etc.) **2 to pay attention** : poner atención, prestar atención, hacer caso **3 to pay back** : pagar, devolver <she paid them back : les devolvió el dinero> <I'll pay you back for what you did! : ¡me las pagarás!> **4 to pay off** SETTLE : saldar, cancelar (una deuda, etc.) **5 to pay one's respects** : presentar uno sus respetos **6 to pay a visit** : hacer una visita — *vi* : valer la pena <crime doesn't pay : no hay crimen sin castigo>

pay[2] *n* : paga *f*

payable ['peɪəbəl] *adj* DUE : pagadero

paycheck ['peɪ,tʃɛk] *n* : sueldo *m*, cheque *m* del sueldo

payee [peɪ'i:] *n* : beneficiario *m*, -ria *f* (de un cheque, etc.)

payment ['peɪmənt] *n* **1** : pago *m* **2** INSTALLMENT : plazo *m*, cuota *f* **3** REWARD : recompensa *f*

payroll ['peɪ,ro:l] *n* : nómina *f*

PC [,pi:'si:] *n, pl* **PCs** *or* **PC's** : PC *mf*, computadora *f* personal

pea ['pi:] *n* : chícharo *m*, guisante *m*, arveja *f*

peace ['pi:s] *n* **1** : paz *f* <peace treaty : tratado de paz> <peace and tranquillity : paz y tranquilidad> **2** ORDER : orden *m* (público)

peaceable ['pi:səbəl] *adj* : pacífico — **peaceably** [-bli] *adv*

peaceful ['pi:sfəl] *adj* **1** PEACEABLE : pacífico **2** CALM, QUIET : tranquilo, sosegado — **peacefully** *adv*

peacemaker ['pi:s,meɪkər] *n* : conciliador *m*, -dora *f*; mediador *m*, -dora *f*

peach ['pi:tʃ] *n* : durazno *m*, melocotón *m*

peacock ['pi:,kɑk] *n* : pavo *m* real

peak[1] ['pi:k] *vi* : alcanzar su nivel máximo

peak[2] *adj* : máximo

peak[3] *n* **1** POINT : punta *f* **2** CREST, SUMMIT : cima *f*, cumbre *f* **3** APEX : cúspide *f*, apogeo *m*, nivel *m* máximo

peaked ['pi:kəd] *adj* SICKLY : pálido

peal[1] ['pi:l] *vi* : repicar

peal[2] *n* : repique *m*, tañido *m* (de campanada) <peals of laughter : carcajadas>

peanut ['pi:,nʌt] *n* : maní *m*, cacahuate *m Mex*, cacahuete *m Spain*

pear ['pær] *n* : pera *f*

pearl ['pərl] *n* : perla *f*

pearly ['pərli] *adj* **pearlier; -est** : nacarado

peasant ['pɛzənt] *n* : campesino *m*, -na *f*

peat ['pi:t] *n* : turba *f*

pebble ['pɛbəl] *n* : piedrita *f*, piedrecita *f*, guijarro *m*

pecan [pɪ'kɑn, -'kæn, 'pi:,kæn] *n* : pacana *f*, nuez *f Mex*

peccadillo [,pɛkə'dɪlo] *n, pl* **-loes** *or* **-los** : pecadillo *m*

peccary ['pɛkəri] *n, pl* **-ries** : pécari *m*, pecarí *m*

peck[1] ['pɛk] *vt* : picar, picotear

peck[2] *n* **1** : medida *f* de áridos equivalente a 8.810 litros **2** : picotazo *m* (de un pájaro) <a peck on the cheek : un besito en la mejilla>

pectoral ['pɛktərəl] *adj* : pectoral

peculiar [pɪ'kju:ljər] *adj* **1** DISTINCTIVE : propio, peculiar, característico <peculiar to this area : propio de esta zona> **2** STRANGE : extraño, raro — **peculiarly** *adv*

peculiarity [pɪ,kju:l'jærəṭi, -,kju:li'ær-] *n, pl* **-ties 1** DISTINCTIVENESS : peculiaridad *f* **2** ODDITY, QUIRK : rareza *f*, idiosincrasia *f*, excentricidad *f*

pecuniary [pɪ'kju:ni,ɛri] *adj* : pecuniario

pedagogical [,pɛdə'gɑdʒɪkəl, -'go:-] *adj* : pedagógico

pedagogy ['pɛdə,go:dʒi, -,gɑ-] *n* : pedagogía *f*

pedal[1] ['pɛdəl] *v* **-aled** *or* **-alled; -aling** *or* **-alling** *vi* : pedalear — *vt* : darle a los pedales de

pedal[2] *n* : pedal *m*

pedant ['pɛdənt] *n* : pedante *mf*

pedantic [pɪ'dæntɪk] *adj* : pedante

pedantry ['pɛdəntri] *n, pl* **-ries** : pedantería *f*

peddle ['pɛdəl] *vt* **-dled; -dling** : vender (en las calles)

peddler ['pɛdlər] *n* : vendedor *m*, -dora *f* ambulante; mercachifle *m*

pedestal ['pɛdəstəl] *n* : pedestal *m*

pedestrian[1] [pə'dɛstriən] *adj* **1** COMMONPLACE : pedestre, ordinario **2** : de peatón <pedestrian crossing : paso de peatones>

pedestrian[2] *n* : peatón *m*, -tona *f*

pediatric [,pi:di'ætrɪk] *adj* : pediátrico

pediatrician [,pi:diə'trɪʃən] *n* : pediatra *mf*

pediatrics [,pi:di'ætrɪks] *ns & pl* : pediatría *f*

pedigree ['pɛdə,gri:] *n* **1** FAMILY TREE : árbol *m* genealógico **2** LINEAGE : pedigrí *m* (de un animal), linaje *m* (de una persona)

peek[1] ['pi:k] *vi* **1** PEEP : espiar, mirar furtivamente **2** GLANCE : echar un vistazo

peek[2] *n* **1** : miradita *f* (furtiva) **2** GLANCE : vistazo *m*, ojeada *f*

peel[1] ['pi:l] *vt* **1** : pelar (fruta, etc.) **2** *or* **to peel away** : quitar — *vi* : pelarse (dícese de la piel), desconcharse (dícese de la pintura)

peel[2] *n* : cáscara *f*

peep¹ [ˈpiːp] *vi* **1** PEEK : espiar, mirar furtivamente **2** CHEEP : piar **3 to peep out** SHOW : asomarse
peep² *n* **1** CHEEP : pío *m* (de un pajarito) **2** GLANCE : vistazo *m,* ojeada *f*
peer¹ [ˈpɪr] *vi* : mirar detenidamente, mirar con atención
peer² *n* **1** EQUAL : par *m,* igual *mf* **2** NOBLE : noble *mf*
peerage [ˈpɪrɪdʒ] *n* : nobleza *f*
peerless [ˈpɪrləs] *adj* : sin par, incomparable
peeve¹ [ˈpiːv] *vt* **peeved; peeving** : fastidiar, irritar, molestar
peeve² *n* : queja *f*
peevish [ˈpiːvɪʃ] *adj* : quejoso, fastidioso — **peevishly** *adv*
peevishness [ˈpiːvɪʃnəs] *n* : irritabilidad *f*
peg¹ [ˈpɛg] *vt* **pegged; pegging 1** PLUG : tapar (con una clavija) **2** FASTEN, FIX : sujetar (con estaquillas) **3 to peg out** MARK : marcar (con estaquillas)
peg² *n* : estaquilla *f* (para clavar), clavija *f* (para tapar)
pejorative [pɪˈdʒɔrət̬ɪv] *adj* : peyorativo — **pejoratively** *adv*
pelican [ˈpɛlɪkən] *n* : pelícano *m*
pellagra [pəˈlægrə, -ˈleɪ-] *n* : pelagra *f*
pellet [ˈpɛlət] *n* **1** BALL : bolita *f* <food pellet : bolita de comida> **2** SHOT : perdigón *m*
pell–mell [ˈpɛlˈmɛl] *adv* : desordenadamente, atropelladamente
pelt¹ [ˈpɛlt] *vt* **1** THROW : lanzar, tirar (algo a alguien) **2 to pelt with stones** : apedrear — *vi* BEAT : golpear con fuerza <the rain was pelting down : llovía a cántaros>
pelt² *n* : piel *f,* pellejo *m*
pelvic [ˈpɛlvɪk] *adj* : pélvico
pelvis [ˈpɛlvɪs] *n, pl* **-vises** *or* **-ves** [ˈpɛlˌviːz] : pelvis *f*
pen¹ [ˈpɛn] *vt* **penned; penning 1** *or* **pen in** : encerrar (animales) **2** WRITE : escribir
pen² *n* **1** CORRAL : corral *m,* redil *m* (para ovejas) **2** : pluma *f* <fountain pen : pluma fuente> <ballpoint pen : bolígrafo>
penal [ˈpiːnəl] *adj* : penal
penalize [ˈpiːnəlˌaɪz, ˈpɛn-] *vt* **-ized; -izing** : penalizar, sancionar, penar
penalty [ˈpɛnəlti] *n, pl* **-ties 1** PUNISHMENT : pena *f,* castigo *m* **2** DISADVANTAGE : desventaja *f,* castigo *m,* penalty *m* (en deportes) **3** FINE : multa *f*
penance [ˈpɛnənts] *n* : penitencia *f*
pence → **penny**
penchant [ˈpɛntʃənt] *n* : inclinación *f,* afición *f*
pencil¹ [ˈpɛntsəl] *vt* **-ciled** *or* **-cilled; -ciling** *or* **-cilling** : escribir con lápiz, dibujar con lápiz
pencil² *n* : lápiz *m*
pendant [ˈpɛndənt] *n* : colgante *m*
pending¹ [ˈpɛndɪŋ] *adj* : pendiente
pending² *prep* **1** DURING : durante **2** AWAITING : en espera de
pendulum [ˈpɛndʒələm, -djʊləm] *n* : péndulo *m*
penetrate [ˈpɛnəˌtreɪt] *vt* **-trated; -trating** : penetrar
penetrating [ˈpɛnəˌtreɪt̬ɪŋ] *adj* : penetrante, cortante
penetration [ˌpɛnəˈtreɪʃən] *n* : penetración *f*
penguin [ˈpɛŋgwɪn, ˈpɛn-] *n* : pingüino *m*
penicillin [ˌpɛnəˈsɪlən] *n* : penicilina *f*
peninsula [pəˈnɪntsələ, -ˈnɪntʃʊlə] *n* : península *f*
penis [ˈpiːnəs] *n, pl* **-nes** [-ˌniːz] *or* **-nises** : pene *m*
penitence [ˈpɛnət̬ənts] *n* : arrepentimiento *m,* penitencia *f*
penitent¹ [ˈpɛnət̬ənt] *adj* : arrepentido, penitente
penitent² *n* : penitente *mf*
penitentiary [ˌpɛnəˈtɛntʃəri] *n, pl* **-ries** : penitenciaría *f,* prisión *m,* presidio *m*
penmanship [ˈpɛnmənˌʃɪp] *n* : escritura *f,* caligrafía *f*
pen name *n* : seudónimo *m*
pennant [ˈpɛnənt] *n* : gallardete *m* (de un barco), banderín *m*
penniless [ˈpɛniləs] *adj* : sin un centavo
penny [ˈpɛni] *n, pl* **-nies** *or* **pence** [ˈpɛnts] **1** : penique *m* (del Reino Unido) **2** *pl* **-nies** CENT : centavo *m* (de los Estados Unidos)
pension¹ [ˈpɛntʃən] *vt or* **to pension off** : jubilar
pension² *n* : pensión *m,* jubilación *f*
pensive [ˈpɛntsɪv] *adj* : pensativo, meditabundo — **pensively** *adv*
pent [ˈpɛnt] *adj* : encerrado <pent-up feelings : emociones reprimidas>
pentagon [ˈpɛntəˌgɑn] *n* : pentágono *m*
pentagonal [pɛnˈtægənəl] *adj* : pentagonal
penthouse [ˈpɛntˌhaʊs] *n* : ático *m,* penthouse *m*
penury [ˈpɛnjəri] *n* : penuria *f,* miseria *f*
peon [ˈpiːˌɑn, -ən] *n, pl* **-ons** *or* **-ones** [peɪˈoːniːz] : peón *m*
peony [ˈpiːəni] *n, pl* **-nies** : peonía *f*
people¹ [ˈpiːpəl] *vt* **-pled; -pling** : poblar
people² *ns & pl* **1 people** *npl* : gente *f,* personas *fpl* <people like him : él le cae bien a la gente> <many people : mucha gente, muchas personas> **2** *pl* **peoples** : pueblo *m* <the Cuban people : el pueblo cubano>
pep¹ [ˈpɛp] *vt* **pepped; pepping** *or* **to pep up** : animar
pep² *n* : energía *f,* vigor *m*
pepper¹ [ˈpɛpər] *vt* **1** : añadir pimienta a **2** RIDDLE : acribillar (a balazos) **3** SPRINKLE : salpicar <peppered with quotations : salpicado de citas>

pepper[2] *n* **1 :** pimienta *f* (condimento) **2 :** pimiento *m,* pimentón *m* (fruta) **3** → **chili**

peppermint [ˈpɛpərˌmɪnt] *n* **:** menta *f*

peppery [ˈpɛpəri] *adj* **:** picante

peppy [ˈpɛpi] *adj* **peppier; -est :** lleno de energía, vivaz

peptic [ˈpɛptɪk] *adj* **peptic ulcer :** úlcera *f* estomacal

per [ˈpər] *prep* **1 :** por <miles per hour : millas por hora> **2** ACCORDING TO **:** según <per his specifications : según sus especificaciones>

per annum [pərˈænəm] *adv* **:** al año, por año

percale [ˌpərˈkeɪl, ˈpər-ˌ; ˌpərˈkæl] *n* **:** percal *m*

per capita [pərˈkæpɪt̬ə] *adv & adj* **:** per cápita

perceive [pərˈsiːv] *vt* **-ceived; -ceiving 1** REALIZE **:** percatarse de, concientizarse de, darse cuenta de **2** NOTE **:** percibir, notar

percent[1] [pərˈsɛnt] *adv* **:** por ciento

percent[2] *n, pl* **-cent** *or* **-cents 1 :** por ciento <10 percent of the population : el 10 por ciento de la población> **2** → **percentage**

percentage [pərˈsɛntɪdʒ] *n* **:** porcentaje *m*

perceptible [pərˈsɛptəbəl] *adj* **:** perceptible — **perceptibly** [-bli] *adv*

perception [pərˈsɛpʃən] *n* **1 :** percepción *f* <color perception : la percepción de los colores> **2** INSIGHT **:** perspicacia *f* **3** IDEA **:** idea *f,* imagen *f*

perceptive [pərˈsɛptɪv] *adj* **:** perspicaz

perceptively [pərˈsɛptɪvli] *adv* **:** con perspicacia

perch[1] [ˈpərtʃ] *vi* **1** ROOST **:** posarse **2** SIT **:** sentarse (en un sitio elevado) — *vt* PLACE **:** posar, colocar

perch[2] *n* **1** ROOST **:** percha *f* (para los pájaros) **2** *pl* **perch** *or* **perches :** perca *f* (pez)

percolate [ˈpərkəˌleɪt] *vi* **-lated; -lating :** colarse, filtrarse <percolated coffee : café filtrado>

percolator [ˈpərkəˌleɪt̬ər] *n* **:** cafetera *f* de filtro

percussion [pərˈkʌʃən] *n* **1** STRIKING **:** percusión *f* **2** *or* **percussion instruments :** instrumentos *mpl* de percusión

peremptory [pəˈrɛmptəri] *adj* **:** perentorio

perennial[1] [pəˈrɛniəl] *adj* **1 :** perenne, vivaz <perennial flowers : flores perennes> **2** RECURRENT **:** perenne, continuo <a perennial problem : un problema eterno>

perennial[2] *n* **:** planta *f* perenne, planta *f* vivaz

perfect[1] [pərˈfɛkt] *vt* **:** perfeccionar

perfect[2] [ˈpərfɪkt] *adj* **:** perfecto — **perfectly** *adv*

perfection [pərˈfɛkʃən] *n* **:** perfección *f*

perfectionist [pərˈfɛkʃənɪst] *n* **:** perfeccionista *mf*

perfidious [pərˈfɪdiəs] *adj* **:** pérfido

perforate [ˈpərfəˌreɪt] *vt* **-rated; -rating :** perforar

perforation [ˌpərfəˈreɪʃən] *n* **:** perforación *f*

perform [pərˈfɔrm] *vt* **1** CARRY OUT **:** realizar, hacer, desempeñar **2** PRESENT **:** representar, dar (una obra teatral, etc.) — *vi* **:** actuar (en una obra teatral), cantar (en una ópera, etc.), tocar (en un concierto, etc.), bailar (en un ballet, etc.)

performance [pərˈfɔrmənts] *n* **1** EXECUTION **:** ejecución *f,* realización *f,* desempeño *m,* rendimiento *m* **2** INTERPRETATION **:** interpretación *f* <his performance of Hamlet : su interpretación de Hamlet> **3** PRESENTATION **:** representación *f* (de una obra teatral), función *f*

performer [pərˈfɔrmər] *n* **:** artista *mf;* actor *m,* -triz *f;* intérprete *mf* (de música)

perfume[1] [pərˈfjuːm, ˈpərˌ-] *vt* **-fumed; -fuming :** perfumar

perfume[2] [ˈpərˌfjuːm, pərˈ-] *n* **:** perfume *m*

perfunctory [pərˈfʌŋktəri] *adj* **:** mecánico, superficial, somero

perhaps [pərˈhæps] *adv* **:** tal vez, quizá, quizás

peril [ˈpɛrəl] *n* **:** peligro *m*

perilous [ˈpɛrələs] *adj* **:** peligroso — **perilously** *adv*

perimeter [pəˈrɪmət̬ər] *n* **:** perímetro *m*

period [ˈpɪriəd] *n* **1 :** punto *m* (en puntuación) **2 :** período *m* <a two-hour period : un período de dos horas> **3** STAGE **:** época *f* (histórica), fase *f,* etapa *f*

periodic [ˌpɪriˈɑdɪk] *or* **periodical** [-dɪkəl] *adj* **:** periódico — **periodically** [-dɪkli] *adv*

periodical [ˌpɪriˈɑdɪkəl] *n* **:** publicación *f* periódica, revista *f*

peripheral [pəˈrɪfərəl] *adj* **:** periférico

periphery [pəˈrɪfəri] *n, pl* **-eries :** periferia *f*

periscope [ˈpɛrəˌskoːp] *n* **:** periscopio *m*

perish [ˈpɛrɪʃ] *vi* DIE **:** perecer, morirse

perishable[1] [ˈpɛrɪʃəbəl] *adj* **:** perecedero

perishable[2] *n* **:** producto *m* perecedero

perjure [ˈpərdʒər] *vt* **-jured; -juring** (*used in law*) **to perjure oneself :** perjurar, perjurarse

perjury [ˈpərdʒəri] *n* **:** perjurio *m*

perk[1] [ˈpərk] *vt* **1 :** levantar (las orejas, etc.) **2** *or* **to perk up** FRESHEN **:** arreglar — *vi* **to perk up :** animarse, reanimarse

perk[2] *n* **:** extra *m*

perky [ˈpərki] *adj* **perkier; -est :** animado, alegre, lleno de vida

permanence [ˈpərmənənts] *n* **:** permanencia *f*

permanent[1] [ˈpərmənənt] *adj* : permanente — **permanently** *adv*
permanent[2] *n* : permanente *f*
permeable [ˈpərmiəbəl] *adj* : permeable
permeate [ˈpərmi,eɪt] *v* **-ated; -ating** *vt* **1** PENETRATE : penetrar, impregnar **2** PERVADE : penetrar, difundirse por — *vi* : penetrar
permissible [pərˈmɪsəbəl] *adj* : permisible, lícito
permission [pərˈmɪʃən] *n* : permiso *m*
permissive [pərˈmɪsɪv] *adj* : permisivo
permit[1] [pərˈmɪt] *vt* **-mitted; -mitting** : permitir, dejar <weather permitting : si el tiempo lo permite>
permit[2] [ˈpər,mɪt, pərˈ-] *n* : permiso *m,* licencia *f*
pernicious [pərˈnɪʃəs] *adj* : pernicioso
peroxide [pəˈrɑk,saɪd] *n* **1** : peróxido *m* **2** → **hydrogen peroxide**
perpendicular[1] [,pərpənˈdɪkjələr] *adj* **1** VERTICAL : vertical **2** : perpendicular <perpendicular lines : líneas perpendiculares> — **perpendicularly** *adv*
perpendicular[2] *n* : perpendicular *f*
perpetrate [ˈpərpə,treɪt] *vt* **-trated; -trating** : perpetrar, cometer (un delito)
perpetrator [ˈpərpə,treɪtər] *n* : autor *m,* -tora *f* (de un delito)
perpetual [pərˈpɛtʃʊəl] *adj* **1** EVERLASTING : perpetuo, eterno **2** CONTINUAL : perpetuo, continuo, constante
perpetually [pərˈpɛtʃʊəli, -tʃəli] *adv* : para siempre, eternamente
perpetuate [pərˈpɛtʃʊ,eɪt] *vt* **-ated; -ating** : perpetuar
perpetuity [,pərpəˈtuːəti, -ˈtjuː-] *n, pl* **-ties** : perpetuidad *f*
perplex [pərˈplɛks] *vt* : dejar perplejo, confundir
perplexed [pərˈplɛkst] *adj* : perplejo
perplexity [pərˈplɛksəti] *n, pl* **-ties** : perplejidad *f,* confusión *f*
persecute [ˈpərsɪ,kjuːt] *vt* **-cuted; -cuting** : perseguir
persecution [,pərsɪˈkjuːʃən] *n* : persecución *f*
perseverance [,pərsəˈvɪrənts] *n* : perseverancia *f*
persevere [,pərsəˈvɪr] *vi* **-vered; -vering** : perseverar
Persian [ˈpərʒən] *n* **1** : persa *mf* **2** : persa *m* (idioma) — **Persian** *adj*
persist [pərˈsɪst] *vi* : persistir
persistence [pərˈsɪstənts] *n* **1** CONTINUATION : persistencia *f* **2** TENACITY : perseverancia *f,* tenacidad *f*
persistent [pərˈsɪstənt] *adj* : persistente — **persistently** *adv*
person [ˈpərsən] *n* **1** HUMAN, INDIVIDUAL : persona *f,* individuo *m,* ser *m* humano **2** : persona *f* (en gramática) **3 in person** : en persona
personable [ˈpərsənəbəl] *adj* : agradable
personage [ˈpərsənɪdʒ] *n* : personaje *m*
personal [ˈpərsənəl] *adj* **1** OWN, PRIVATE : personal, particular, privado <for personal reasons : por razones personales> **2** : en persona <to make a personal appearance : presentarse en persona, hacerse acto de presencia> **3** : íntimo, personal <personal hygiene : higiene personal> **4** INDISCREET, PRYING : indiscreto, personal
personality [,pərsənˈæləti] *n, pl* **-ties** **1** DISPOSITION : personalidad *f,* temperamento *m* **2** CELEBRITY : personalidad *f,* personaje *m,* celebridad *f*
personalize [ˈpərsənə,laɪz] *vt* **-ized; -izing** : personalizar
personally [ˈpərsənəli] *adv* **1** : personalmente, en persona <I'll do it personally : lo haré personalmente> **2** : como persona <personally she's very amiable : como persona es muy amable> **3** : personalmente <personally, I don't believe it : yo, personalmente, no me lo creo>
personification [pər,sɑnəfəˈkeɪʃən] *n* : personificación *f*
personify [pərˈsɑnə,faɪ] *vt* **-fied; -fying** : personificar
personnel [,pərsənˈɛl] *n* : personal *m*
perspective [pərˈspɛktɪv] *n* : perspectiva *f*
perspicacious [,pərspəˈkeɪʃəs] *adj* : perspicaz
perspiration [,pərspəˈreɪʃən] *n* : transpiración *f,* sudor *m*
perspire [pərˈspaɪr] *vi* **-spired; -spiring** : transpirar, sudar
persuade [pərˈsweɪd] *vt* **-suaded; -suading** : persuadir, convencer
persuasion [pərˈsweɪʒən] *n* : persuasión *f*
persuasive [pərˈsweɪsɪv, -zɪv] *adj* : persuasivo — **persuasively** *adv*
persuasiveness [pərˈsweɪsɪvnəs, -zɪv-] *n* : persuasión *f*
pert [ˈpərt] *adj* **1** SAUCY : descarado, impertinente **2** JAUNTY : alegre, animado <a pert little hat : un sombrero coqueto>
pertain [pərˈteɪn] *vi* **1** BELONG : pertenecer (a) **2** RELATE : estar relacionado (con)
pertinence [ˈpərtənənts] *n* : pertinencia *f*
pertinent [ˈpərtənənt] *adj* : pertinente
perturb [pərˈtərb] *vt* : perturbar
perusal [pəˈruːzəl] *n* : lectura *f* cuidadosa
peruse [pəˈruːz] *vt* **-rused; -rusing** **1** READ : leer con cuidado **2** SCAN : recorrer con la vista <he perused the newspaper : echó un vistazo al periódico>
Peruvian [pəˈruːviən] *n* : peruano *m,* -na *f* — **Peruvian** *adj*
pervade [pərˈveɪd] *vt* **-vaded; -vading** : penetrar, difundirse por
pervasive [pərˈveɪsɪv, -zɪv] *adj* : penetrante

perverse [pər'vərs] *adj* **1** CORRUPT : perverso, corrompido **2** STUBBORN : obstinado, porfiado, terco (sin razón) — **perversely** *adv*
perversion [pər'vərʒən] *n* : perversión *f*
perversity [pər'vərsəṭi] *n, pl* **-ties 1** CORRUPTION : corrupción *f* **2** STUBBORNNESS : obstinación *f,* terquedad *f*
pervert[1] [pər'vərt] *vt* **1** DISTORT : pervertir, distorsionar **2** CORRUPT : pervertir, corromper
pervert[2] ['pər,vərt] *n* : pervertido *m,* -da *f*
peso ['peɪ,so:] *n, pl* **-sos** : peso *m*
pessimism ['pɛsə,mɪzəm] *n* : pesimismo *m*
pessimist ['pɛsəmɪst] *n* : pesimista *mf*
pessimistic [,pɛsə'mɪstɪk] *adj* : pesimista
pest ['pɛst] *n* **1** NUISANCE : peste *f;* latoso *m,* -sa *f fam* <to be a pest : dar (la) lata> **2** : insecto *m* nocivo, animal *m* nocivo <the squirrels were pests : las ardillas eran una plaga>
pester ['pɛstər] *vt* **-tered; -tering** : molestar, fastidiar
pesticide ['pɛstə,saɪd] *n* : pesticida *m*
pestilence ['pɛstələn*t*s] *n* : pestilencia *f,* peste *f*
pestle ['pɛsəl, 'pɛstəl] *n* : mano *f* de mortero, mazo *m,* maja *f*
pet[1] ['pɛt] *vt* **petted; petting** : acariciar
pet[2] *n* **1** : animal *m* doméstico **2** FAVORITE : favorito *m,* -ta *f*
petal ['pɛṭəl] *n* : pétalo *m*
petite [pə'ti:t] *adj* : pequeña, menuda, chiquita
petition[1] [pə'tɪʃən] *vt* : peticionar
petition[2] *n* : petición *f*
petitioner [pə'tɪʃənər] *n* : peticionario *m,* -ria *f*
petrify ['pɛtrə,faɪ] *vt* **-fied; -fying** : petrificar
petroleum [pə'tro:liəm] *n* : petróleo *m*
petticoat ['pɛṭi,ko:t] *n* : enagua *f,* fondo *m Mex*
pettiness ['pɛṭinəs] *n* **1** INSIGNIFICANCE : insignificancia *f* **2** MEANNESS : mezquindad *f*
petty ['pɛṭi] *adj* **-tier; -est 1** MINOR : menor <petty cash : dinero para gastos menores> **2** INSIGNIFICANT : insignificante, trivial, nimio **3** MEAN : mezquino
petty officer *n* : suboficial *mf*
petulance ['pɛtʃələn*t*s] *n* : irritabilidad *f,* mal genio *m*
petulant ['pɛtʃələnt] *adj* : irritable, de mal genio
petunia [pɪ'tu:njə, -'tju:-] *n* : petunia *f*
pew ['pju:] *n* : banco *m* (de iglesia)
pewter ['pju:ṭər] *n* : peltre *m*
pH [,pi:'eɪtʃ] *n* : pH *m*
phallic ['fælɪk] *adj* : fálico
phallus ['fæləs] *n, pl* **-li** ['fæ,laɪ] *or* **-luses** : falo *m*
phantasy ['fæntəsi] → **fantasy**
phantom ['fæntəm] *n* : fantasma *m*
pharaoh ['fɛr,o:, 'feɪ,ro:] *n* : faraón *m*
pharmaceutical [,fɑrmə'su:ṭɪkəl] *adj* : farmacéutico
pharmacist ['fɑrməsɪst] *n* : farmacéutico *m,* -ca *f*
pharmacology [,fɑrmə'kɑlədʒi] *n* : farmacología *f*
pharmacy ['fɑrməsi] *n, pl* **-cies** : farmacia *f*
pharynx ['færɪŋks] *n, pl* **pharynges** [fə'rɪn,dʒi:z] : faringe *f*
phase[1] ['feɪz] *vt* **phased; phasing 1** SYNCHRONIZE : sincronizar, poner en fase **2** STAGGER : escalonar **3 to phase in** : introducir progresivamente **4 to phase out** : retirar progresivamente, dejar de producir
phase[2] *n* **1** : fase *f* (de la luna, etc.) **2** STAGE : fase *f,* etapa *f*
pheasant ['fɛzənt] *n, pl* **-ant** *or* **-ants** : faisán *m*
phenomenal [fɪ'nɑmənəl] *adj* : extraordinario, excepcional
phenomenon [fɪ'nɑmə,nɑn, -nən] *n, pl* **-na** [-nə] *or* **-nons 1** : fenómeno *m* **2** *pl* **-nons** PRODIGY : fenómeno *m,* prodigio *m*
philanthropic [,fɪlən'θrɑpɪk] *adj* : filantrópico
philanthropist [fə'læn*t*θrəpɪst] *n* : filántropo *m,* -pa *f*
philanthropy [fə'læn*t*θrəpi] *n, pl* **-pies** : filantropía *f*
philately [fə'læṭəli] *n* : filatelia *f*
philodendron [,fɪlə'dɛndrən] *n, pl* **-drons** *or* **-dra** [-drə] : arácea *f*
philosopher [fə'lɑsəfər] *n* : filósofo *m,* -fa *f*
philosophic [,fɪlə'sɑfɪk] *or* **philosophical** [-fɪkəl] *adj* : filosófico — **philosophically** [-kli] *adv*
philosophize [fə'lɑsə,faɪz] *vi* **-phized; -phizing** : filosofar
philosophy [fə'lɑsəfi] *n, pl* **-phies** : filosofía *f*
phlebitis [flɪ'baɪṭəs] *n* : flebitis *f*
phlegm ['flɛm] *n* : flema *f*
phlox ['flɑks] *n, pl* **phlox** *or* **phloxes** : polemonio *m*
phobia ['fo:biə] *n* : fobia *f*
phoenix ['fi:nɪks] *n* : fénix *m*
phone[1] ['fo:n] *v* → **telephone**[1]
phone[2] *n* → **telephone**[2]
phoneme ['fo:,ni:m] *n* : fonema *m*
phonetic [fə'nɛṭɪk] *adj* : fonético
phonetics [fə'nɛṭɪks] *n* : fonética *f*
phonics ['fɑnɪks] *n* : método *m* fonético de aprender a leer
phonograph ['fo:nə,græf] *n* : fonógrafo *m,* tocadiscos *m*
phony[1] *or* **phoney** ['fo:ni] *adj* **-nier; -est** : falso
phony[2] *or* **phoney** *n, pl* **-nies** : farsante *mf;* charlatán *m,* -tana *f*
phosphate ['fɑs,feɪt] *n* : fosfato *m*
phosphorescence [,fɑsfə'rɛsən*t*s] *n* : fosforescencia *f*

phosphorescent [ˌfɑsfəˈrɛsənt] *adj* : fosforescente — **phosphorescently** *adv*

phosphorus [ˈfɑsfərəs] *n* : fósforo *m*

photo [ˈfoːtoː] *n, pl* **-tos** : foto *f*

photocopier [ˈfoːt̬oˌkɑpiər] *n* : fotocopiadora *f*

photocopy[1] [ˈfoːt̬oˌkɑpi] *vt* **-copied; -copying** : fotocopiar

photocopy[2] *n, pl* **-copies** : fotocopia *f*

photoelectric [ˌfoːt̬oɪˈlɛktrɪk] *adj* : fotoeléctrico

photogenic [ˌfoːt̬əˈdʒɛnɪk] *adj* : fotogénico

photograph[1] [ˈfoːt̬əˌgræf] *vt* : fotografiar

photograph[2] *n* : fotografía *f,* foto *f* <to take a photograph of : tomarle una fotografía a, tomar una fotografía de>

photographer [fəˈtɑgrəfər] *n* : fotógrafo *m,* -fa *f*

photographic [ˌfoːt̬əˈgræfɪk] *adj* : fotográfico — **photographically** [-fɪkli] *adv*

photography [fəˈtɑgrəfi] *n* : fotografía *f*

photosynthesis [ˌfoːt̬oˈsɪnθəsɪs] *n* : fotosíntesis *f*

photosynthetic [ˌfoːtosɪnˈθɛtɪk] *adj* : fotosintético, de fotosíntesis

phrase[1] [ˈfreɪz] *vt* **phrased; phrasing** : expresar

phrase[2] *n* : frase *f,* locución *f* <to coin a phrase : para decirlo así>

phylum [ˈfaɪləm] *n, pl* **-la** [-lə] : phylum *m*

physical[1] [ˈfɪzɪkəl] *adj* **1** : físico <physical laws : leyes físicas> **2** MATERIAL : material, físico **3** BODILY : físico, corpóreo — **physically** [-kli] *adv*

physical[2] *n* CHECKUP : chequeo *m,* reconocimiento *m* médico

physician [fəˈzɪʃən] *n* : médico *m,* -ca *f*

physicist [ˈfɪzəsɪst] *n* : físico *m,* -ca *f*

physics [ˈfɪzɪks] *ns & pl* : física *f*

physiognomy [ˌfɪziˈɑgnəmi] *n, pl* **-mies** : fisonomía *f*

physiological [ˈfɪziəˈlɑdʒɪkəl] *or* **physiologic** [-dʒɪk] *adj* : fisiológico

physiologist [ˌfɪziˈɑlədʒɪst] *n* : fisiólogo *m,* -ga *f*

physiology [ˌfɪziˈɑlədʒi] *n* : fisiología *f*

physique [fəˈziːk] *n* : físico *m*

pi [ˈpaɪ] *n, pl* **pis** [ˈpaɪz] : pi *f*

pianist [piˈænɪst, ˈpiːənɪst] *n* : pianista *mf*

piano [piˈænoː] *n, pl* **-anos** : piano *m*

piazza [piˈæzə, -ˈɑtsə] *n, pl* **-zas** *or* **-ze** [-ˈɑtˌseɪ] : plaza *f*

picayune [ˌpɪkiˈjuːn] *adj* : trivial, nimio, insignificante

piccolo [ˈpɪkəˌloː] *n, pl* **-los** : flautín *m*

pick[1] [ˈpɪk] *vt* **1** : picar, labrar (con un pico) <he picked the hard soil : picó la tierra dura> **2** : quitar, sacar (poco a poco) <to pick meat off the bones : quitar pedazos de carne de los huesos> **3** : recoger, arrancar (frutas, flores, etc.) **4** SELECT : escoger, elegir **5** PROVOKE : provocar <to pick a quarrel : buscar pleito, buscar pelea> **6 to pick a lock** : forzar una cerradura **7 to pick someone's pocket** : robarle algo del bolsillo de alguien <someone picked my pocket! : ¡me robaron la cartera del bolsillo!> — *vi* **1** NIBBLE : picar, picotear **2 to pick and choose** : ser exigente **3 to pick at** : tocar, rascarse (una herida, etc.) **4 to pick on** TEASE : mofarse de, atormentar

pick[2] *n* **1** CHOICE : selección *f* **2** BEST : lo mejor <the pick of the crop : la crema y nata> **3** → **pickax**

pickax [ˈpɪkˌæks] *n* : pico *m,* zapapico *m,* piqueta *f*

pickerel [ˈpɪkərəl] *n, pl* **-el** *or* **-els** : lucio *m* pequeño

picket[1] [ˈpɪkət] *v* : piquetear

picket[2] *n* **1** STAKE : estaca *f* **2** STRIKER : huelguista *mf,* integrante *mf* de un piquete

pickle[1] [ˈpɪkəl] *vt* **-led; -ling** : encurtir, escabechar

pickle[2] *n* **1** BRINE : escabeche *m* **2** GHERKIN : pepinillo *m* (encurtido) **3** JAM, TROUBLE : lío *m,* apuro *m*

pickpocket [ˈpɪkˌpɑkət] *n* : carterista *mf*

pickup [ˈpɪkˌəp] *n* **1** IMPROVEMENT : mejora *f* **2** *or* **pickup truck** : camioneta *f*

pick up *vt* **1** LIFT : levantar **2** TIDY : arreglar, ordenar — *vi* IMPROVE : mejorar

picnic[1] [ˈpɪkˌnɪk] *vi* **-nicked; -nicking** : ir de picnic

picnic[2] *n* : picnic *m*

pictorial [pɪkˈtoriəl] *adj* : pictórico

picture[1] [ˈpɪktʃər] *vt* **-tured; -turing 1** DEPICT : representar **2** IMAGINE : imaginarse <can you picture it? : ¿te lo puedes imaginar?>

picture[2] *n* **1** : cuadro *m* (pintado o dibujado), ilustración *f,* fotografía *f* **2** DESCRIPTION : descripción *f* **3** IMAGE : imagen *f* <he's the picture of his father : es la viva imagen de su padre> **4** MOVIE : película *f*

picturesque [ˌpɪktʃəˈrɛsk] *adj* : pintoresco

pie [ˈpaɪ] *n* : pastel *m* (con fruta o carne), empanada *f* (con carne)

piebald [ˈpaɪˌbɔld] *adj* : picazo, pío

piece[1] [ˈpiːs] *vt* **pieced; piecing 1** PATCH : parchar, arreglar **2 to piece together** : construir pieza por pieza

piece[2] *n* **1** FRAGMENT : trozo *m,* pedazo *m* **2** COMPONENT : pieza *f* <a three-piece suit : un traje de tres piezas> **3** UNIT : pieza *f* <a piece of fruit : una (pieza de) fruta> **4** WORK : obra *f,* pieza *f* (de música, etc.) **5** (*in board games*) : ficha *f,* pieza *f,* figura *f* (en ajedrez)

piecemeal[1] [ˈpiːsˌmiːl] *adv* **:** poco a poco, por partes
piecemeal[2] *adj* **:** hecho poco a poco, poco sistemático
pied [ˈpaɪd] *adj* **:** pío
pier [ˈpɪr] *n* **1 :** pila *f* (de un puente) **2** WHARF **:** muelle *m,* atracadero *m,* embarcadero *m* **3** PILLAR **:** pilar *m*
pierce [ˈpɪrs] *vt* **pierced; piercing 1** PENETRATE **:** atravesar, traspasar, penetrar (en) <the bullet pierced his leg : la bala le atravesó la pierna> <to pierce one's heart : traspasarle el corazón a uno> **2** PERFORATE **:** perforar, agujerear (las orejas, etc.) **3 to pierce the silence :** desgarrar el silencio
piety [ˈpaɪəṭi] *n, pl* **-eties :** piedad *f*
pig [ˈpɪg] *n* **1** HOG, SWINE **:** cerdo *m,* -da *f;* puerco *m,* -ca *f* **2** SLOB **:** persona *f* desaliñada; cerdo *m,* -da *f* **3** GLUTTON **:** glotón *m,* -tona *f* **4** *or* **pig iron :** lingote *m* de hierro
pigeon [ˈpɪdʒən] *n* **:** paloma *f*
pigeonhole [ˈpɪdʒənˌhoːl] *n* **:** casilla *f*
pigeon–toed [ˈpɪdʒənˌtoːd] *adj* **:** patituerto
piggish [ˈpɪgɪʃ] *adj* **1** GREEDY **:** glotón **2** DIRTY **:** cochino, sucio
piggyback [ˈpɪgiˌbæk] *adv & adj* **:** a cuestas
pigheaded [ˈpɪgˌhɛdəd] *adj* **:** terco, obstinado
piglet [ˈpɪglət] *n* **:** cochinillo *m;* lechón *m,* -chona *f*
pigment [ˈpɪgmənt] *n* **:** pigmento *m*
pigmentation [ˌpɪgmənˈteɪʃən] *n* **:** pigmentación *f*
pigmy → **pygmy**
pigpen [ˈpɪgˌpɛn] *n* **:** chiquero *m,* pocilga *f*
pigsty [ˈpɪgˌstaɪ] → **pigpen**
pigtail [ˈpɪgˌteɪl] *n* **:** coleta *f,* trenza *f*
pike [ˈpaɪk] *n, pl* **pike** *or* **pikes 1 :** lucio *m* (pez) **2** LANCE **:** pica *f* **3** → **turnpike**
pile[1] [ˈpaɪl] *v* **piled; piling** *vt* **:** amontonar, apilar — *vi* **to pile up :** amontonarse, acumularse
pile[2] *n* **1** STAKE **:** pilote *m* **2** HEAP **:** montón *m,* pila *f* **3** NAP **:** pelo *m* (de telas)
piles [ˈpaɪlz] *npl* HEMORRHOIDS **:** hemorroides *fpl,* almorranas *fpl*
pilfer [ˈpɪlfər] *vt* **:** robar (cosas pequeñas), ratear
pilgrim [ˈpɪlgrəm] *n* **:** peregrino *m,* -na *f*
pilgrimage [ˈpɪlgrəmɪdʒ] *n* **:** peregrinación *f*
pill [ˈpɪl] *n* **:** pastilla *f,* píldora *f*
pillage[1] [ˈpɪlɪdʒ] *vt* **-laged; -laging :** saquear
pillage[2] *n* **:** saqueo *m*
pillar [ˈpɪlər] *n* **:** pilar *m,* columna *f*
pillory [ˈpɪləri] *n, pl* **-ries :** picota *f*
pillow [ˈpɪˌloː] *n* **:** almohada *f*
pillowcase [ˈpɪˌloːˌkeɪs] *n* **:** funda *f*
pilot[1] [ˈpaɪlət] *vt* **:** pilotar, pilotear
pilot[2] *n* **:** piloto *mf*
pilot light *n* **:** piloto *m*
pimento [pəˈmɛnˌtoː] → **pimiento**
pimiento [pəˈmɛnˌtoː, -ˈmjɛn-] *n, pl* **-tos :** pimiento *m* morrón
pimp [ˈpɪmp] *n* **:** proxeneta *m*
pimple [ˈpɪmpəl] *n* **:** grano *m*
pimply [ˈpɪmpəli] *adj* **-plier; -est :** cubierto de granos
pin[1] [ˈpɪn] *vt* **pinned; pinning 1** FASTEN **:** prender, sujetar (con alfileres) **2** HOLD, IMMOBILIZE **:** inmovilizar, sujetar **3 to pin one's hopes on :** poner sus esperanzas en
pin[2] *n* **1 :** alfiler *m* <safety pin : alfiler de gancho> <a bobby pin : una horquilla> **2** BROOCH **:** alfiler *m,* broche *m,* prendedor *m* **3** *or* **bowling pin :** bolo *m*
pinafore [ˈpɪnəˌfor] *n* **:** delantal *m*
pincer [ˈpɪntsər] *n* **1** CLAW **:** pinza *f* (de una langosta, etc.) **2 pincers** *npl* **:** pinzas *fpl,* tenazas *fpl,* tenaza *f*
pinch[1] [ˈpɪntʃ] *vt* **1 :** pellizcar <she pinched my cheek : me pellizcó el cachete> **2** STEAL **:** robar — *vi* **:** apretar <my shoes pinch : me aprietan los zapatos>
pinch[2] *n* **1** EMERGENCY **:** emergencia *f* <in a pinch : en caso necesario> **2** PAIN **:** dolor *m,* tormento *m* **3** SQUEEZE **:** pellizco *m* (con los dedos) **4** BIT **:** pizca *f,* pellizco *m* <a pinch of cinnamon : una pizca de canela>
pinch hitter *n* **1** SUBSTITUTE **:** sustituto *m,* -ta *f* **2 :** bateador *m* emergente (en beisbol)
pincushion [ˈpɪnˌkʊʃən] *n* **:** acerico *m,* alfiletero *m*
pine[1] [ˈpaɪn] *vi* **pined; pining 1 to pine away :** languidecer, consumirse **2 to pine for :** añorar, suspirar por
pine[2] *n* **1 :** pino *m* (árbol) **2 :** madera *f* de pino
pineapple [ˈpaɪnˌæpəl] *n* **:** piña *f,* ananá *m,* ananás *m*
pinion[1] [ˈpɪnjən] *vt* **:** sujetar los brazos de, inmovilizar
pinion[2] *n* **:** piñón *m*
pink[1] [ˈpɪŋk] *adj* **:** rosa, rosado
pink[2] *n* **1 :** clavelito *m* (flor) **2 :** rosa *m,* rosado *m* (color) **3 to be in the pink :** estar en plena forma, rebosar de salud
pinkeye [ˈpɪŋkˌaɪ] *n* **:** conjuntivitis *f* aguda
pinkish [ˈpɪŋkɪʃ] *adj* **:** rosáceo
pinnacle [ˈpɪnɪkəl] *n* **1 :** pináculo *m* (de un edificio) **2** PEAK **:** cima *f,* cumbre *f* (de una montaña) **3** ACME **:** pináculo *m,* cúspide *f,* apogeo *m*
pinpoint [ˈpɪnˌpɔɪnt] *vt* **:** precisar, localizar con precisión
pint [ˈpaɪnt] *n* **:** pinta *f*
pinto [ˈpɪnˌtoː] *n, pl* **pintos :** caballo *m* pinto
pinworm [ˈpɪnˌwərm] *n* **:** oxiuro *m*
pioneer[1] [ˌpaɪəˈnɪr] *vt* **:** promover, iniciar, introducir
pioneer[2] *n* **:** pionero *m,* -ra *f*

pious [ˈpaɪəs] *adj* **1** DEVOUT : piadoso, devoto **2** SANCTIMONIOUS : beato
piously [ˈpaɪəsli] *adv* **1** DEVOUTLY : piadosamente **2** SANCTIMONIOUSLY : santurronamente
pipe[1] [ˈpaɪp] *v* **piped; piping** *vi* : hablar en voz chillona — *vt* **1** PLAY : tocar (el caramillo o la flauta) **2** : conducir por tuberías <to pipe water : transportar el agua por tubería>
pipe[2] *n* **1** : caramillo *m* (instrumento musical) **2** BAGPIPE : gaita *f* **3** : tubo *m*, caño *m* <gas pipes : tubería de gas> **4** : pipa *f* (para fumar)
pipeline [ˈpaɪpˌlaɪn] *n* **1** : conducto *m*, oleoducto *m* (para petróleo), gasoducto *m* (para gas) **2** CONDUIT : vía *f* (de información, etc.)
piper [ˈpaɪpər] *n* : músico *m*, -ca *f* que toca el caramillo o la gaita
piping [ˈpaɪpɪŋ] *n* **1** : música *f* del caramillo o de la gaita **2** TRIM : cordoncillo *m*, ribete *m* con cordón
piquant [ˈpiːkənt, ˈpɪkwənt] *adj* **1** SPICY : picante **2** INTRIGUING : intrigante, estimulante
pique[1] [ˈpiːk] *vt* **piqued; piquing 1** IRRITATE : picar, irritar **2** AROUSE : despertar (la curiosidad, etc.)
pique[2] *n* : pique *m*, resentimiento *m*
piracy [ˈpaɪrəsi] *n, pl* **-cies** : piratería *f*
piranha [pəˈrɑnə, -ˈrɑnjə, -ˈrænjə] *n* : piraña *f*
pirate [ˈpaɪrət] *n* : pirata *mf*
pirouette [ˌpɪrəˈwɛt] *n* : pirueta *f*
pis → **pi**
Pisces [ˈpaɪˌsiːz, ˈpɪ-; ˈpɪsˌkeɪs] *n* : Piscis *mf*
pistachio [pəˈstæʃiˌoː, -ˈstɑ-] *n, pl* **-chios** : pistacho *m*
pistil [ˈpɪstəl] *n* : pistilo *m*
pistol [ˈpɪstəl] *n* : pistola *f*
piston [ˈpɪstən] *n* : pistón *m*, émbolo *m*
pit[1] [ˈpɪt] *v* **pitted; pitting** *vt* **1** : marcar de hoyos, picar (una superficie) **2** : deshuesar (una fruta) **3 to pit against** : enfrentar a, oponer a — *vi* : quedar marcado
pit[2] *n* **1** HOLE : fosa *f*, hoyo *m* <a bottomless pit : un pozo sin fondo> **2** MINE : mina *f* **3** : foso *m* <orchestra pit : foso orquestal> **4** POCKMARK : marca *f* (en la cara), cicatriz *f* de viruela **5** STONE : hueso *m*, pepa *f* (de una fruta) **6 pit of the stomach** : boca *f* del estómago
pitch[1] [ˈpɪtʃ] *vt* **1** SET UP : montar, armar (una tienda) **2** THROW : lanzar, arrojar **3** ADJUST, SET : dar el tono de (un discurso, un instrumento musical) — *vi* **1** *or* **pitch forward** FALL : caerse **2** LURCH : cabecear (dícese de un barco o un avión), dar bandazos
pitch[2] *n* **1** LURCHING : cabezada *f*, cabeceo *m* (de un barco o un avión) **2** SLOPE : (grado de) inclinación *f*, pendiente *f* **3** : tono *m* (en música) <perfect pitch : oído absoluto> **4** THROW : lanzamiento *m* **5** DEGREE : grado *m*, nivel *m*, punto *m* <the excitement reached a high pitch : la excitación llegó a un punto culminante> **6** *or* **sales pitch** : presentación *f* (de un vendedor) **7** TAR : pez *f*, brea *f*
pitcher [ˈpɪtʃər] *n* **1** JUG : jarra *f*, jarro *m*, cántaro *m*, pichel *m* **2** : lanzador *m*, -dora *f* (en béisbol, etc.)
pitchfork [ˈpɪtʃˌfɔrk] *n* : horquilla *f*, horca *f*
piteous [ˈpɪt̬iəs] *adj* : lastimoso, lastimero — **piteously** *adv*
pitfall [ˈpɪtˌfɔl] *n* : peligro *m* (poco obvio), dificultad *f*
pith [ˈpɪθ] *n* **1** : médula *f* (de una planta) **2** CORE : meollo *m*, entraña *f*
pithy [ˈpɪθi] *adj* **pithier; -est** : conciso y sustancioso <pithy comments : comentarios sucintos>
pitiable [ˈpɪt̬iəbəl] → **pitiful**
pitiful [ˈpɪt̬ɪfəl] *adj* **1** LAMENTABLE : lastimero, lastimoso, lamentable **2** CONTEMPTIBLE : despreciable, lamentable — **pitifully** [-fli] *adv*
pitiless [ˈpɪt̬ɪləs] *adj* : despiadado — **pitilessly** *adv*
pittance [ˈpɪtənts] *n* : miseria *f*
pituitary [pəˈtuːəˌtɛri, -ˈtjuː-] *adj* : pituitario
pity[1] [ˈpɪt̬i] *vt* **pitied; pitying** : compadecer, compadecerse de
pity[2] *n, pl* **pities 1** COMPASSION : compasión *f*, piedad *f* **2** SHAME : lástima *f*, pena *f* <what a pity! : ¡qué lástima!>
pivot[1] [ˈpɪvət] *vi* **1** : girar sobre un eje **2 to pivot on** : girar sobre, depender de
pivot[2] *n* : pivote *m*
pivotal [ˈpɪvət̬əl] *adj* : fundamental, central
pixie *or* **pixy** [ˈpɪksi] *n, pl* **pixies** : elfo *m*, hada *f*
pizza [ˈpiːtsə] *n* : pizza *f*
pizzazz *or* **pizazz** [pəˈzæz] *n* **1** GLAMOR : encanto *m* **2** VITALITY : animación *f*, vitalidad *f*
placard [ˈplækərd, -ˌkɑrd] *n* POSTER : cartel *m*, póster *m*, afiche *m*
placate [ˈpleɪˌkeɪt, ˈplæ-] *vt* **-cated; -cating** : aplacar, apaciguar
place[1] [ˈpleɪs] *vt* **placed; placing 1** PUT, SET : poner, colocar **2** SITUATE : situar, ubicar, emplazar <to be well placed : estar bien situado> <to place in a job : colocar en un trabajo> **3** IDENTIFY, RECALL : identificar, ubicar, recordar <I can't place him : no lo ubico> **4 to place an order** : hacer un pedido
place[2] *n* **1** SPACE : sitio *m*, lugar *m* <there's no place to sit : no hay sitio para sentarse> **2** LOCATION, SPOT : lugar *m*, sitio *m*, parte *f* <place of work : lugar de trabajo> <our summer place : nuestra casa de verano> <all over the place : por todas partes> **3** RANK : lugar *m*, puesto *m* <he took first place : ganó el primer lugar> **4**

POSITION : lugar *m* <everything in its place : todo en su debido lugar> <to feel out of place : sentirse fuera de lugar> **5** SEAT : asiento *m,* cubierto *m* (a la mesa) **6** JOB : puesto *m* **7** ROLE : papel *m,* lugar *m* <to change places : cambiarse los papeles> **8 to take place :** tener lugar **9 to take the place of :** sustituir a

placebo [plə'siː,boː] *n, pl* **-bos :** placebo *m*

placement ['pleɪsmənt] *n* **:** colocación *f*

placenta [plə'sɛntə] *n, pl* **-tas** *or* **-tae** [-ti, -,taɪ] **:** placenta *f*

placid ['plæsəd] *adj* **:** plácido, tranquilo **— placidly** *adv*

plagiarism ['pleɪdʒə,rɪzəm] *n* **:** plagio *m*

plagiarist ['pleɪdʒərɪst] *n* **:** plagiario *m,* -ria *f*

plagiarize ['pleɪdʒə,raɪz] *vt* **-rized; -rizing :** plagiar

plague[1] ['pleɪg] *vt* **plagued; plaguing 1** AFFLICT **:** plagar, afligir **2** HARASS **:** acosar, atormentar

plague[2] *n* **1 :** plaga *f* (de insectos, etc.) **2 :** peste *f* (en medicina)

plaid[1] ['plæd] *adj* **:** escocés, de cuadros <a plaid skirt : una falda escocesa>

plaid[2] *n* TARTAN **:** tela *f* escocesa, tartán *m*

plain[1] ['pleɪn] *adj* **1** SIMPLE, UNADORNED **:** liso, sencillo, sin adornos **2** CLEAR **:** claro <in plain language : en palabras claras> **3** FRANK **:** franco, puro <the plain truth : la pura verdad> **4** HOMELY **:** ordinario, poco atractivo **5 in plain sight :** a la vista de todos

plain[2] *n* **:** llanura *f,* llano *m,* planicie *f*

plainly ['pleɪnli] *adv* **1** CLEARLY **:** claramente **2** FRANKLY **:** francamente, con franqueza **3** SIMPLY **:** sencillamente

plaintiff ['pleɪntɪf] *n* **:** demandante *mf*

plaintive ['pleɪntɪv] *adj* MOURNFUL **:** lastimero, plañidero

plait[1] ['pleɪt, 'plæt] *vt* **1** PLEAT **:** plisar **2** BRAID **:** trenzar

plait[2] *n* **1** PLEAT **:** pliegue *m* **2** BRAID **:** trenza *f*

plan[1] ['plæn] *v* **planned; planning** *vt* **1 :** planear, proyectar, planificar <to plan a trip : planear un viaje> <to plan a city : planificar una ciudad> **2** INTEND **:** tener planeado, proyectar **—** *vi* **:** hacer planes

plan[2] *n* **1** DIAGRAM **:** plano *m,* esquema *m* **2** SCHEME **:** plan *m,* proyecto *m,* programa *m* <to draw up a plan : elaborar un proyecto>

plane[1] ['pleɪn] *vt* **planed; planing :** cepillar (madera)

plane[2] *adj* **:** plano

plane[3] *n* **1 :** plano *m* (en matemáticas, etc.) **2** LEVEL **:** nivel *m* **3 :** cepillo *m* (de carpintero) **4 → airplane**

planet ['plænət] *n* **:** planeta *f*

planetarium [,plænə'tɛriəm] *n, pl* **-iums** *or* **-ia** [-iə] **:** planetario *m*

planetary ['plænə,tɛri] *adj* **:** planetario

plank ['plæŋk] *n* **1** BOARD **:** tablón *m,* tabla *f* **2 :** artículo *m,* punto *m* (de una plataforma política)

plankton ['plæŋktən] *n* **:** plancton *m*

plant[1] ['plænt] *vt* **1 :** plantar (flores, árboles), sembrar (semillas) **2** PLACE **:** plantar, colocar <to plant an idea : inculcar una idea>

plant[2] *n* **1 :** planta *f* <leafy plants : plantas frondosas> **2** FACTORY **:** planta *f,* fábrica *f* <hydroelectric plant : planta hidroeléctrica> **3** MACHINERY **:** maquinaria *f,* equipo *m*

plantain ['plæntən] *n* **1 :** llantén *m* (mala hierba) **2 :** plátano *m,* plátano *m* macho *Mex* (fruta)

plantation [plæn'teɪʃən] *n* **:** plantación *f,* hacienda *f* <a coffee plantation : un cafetal>

planter ['plæntər] *n* **1 :** hacendado *m,* -da *f* (de una hacienda) **2** FLOWERPOT **:** tiesto *m,* maceta *f*

plaque ['plæk] *n* **1** TABLET **:** placa *f* **2 :** placa *f* (dental)

plasma ['plæzmə] *n* **:** plasma *m*

plaster[1] ['plæstər] *vt* **1 :** enyesar, revocar (con yeso) **2** COVER **:** cubrir, llenar <a wall plastered with notices : una pared cubierta de avisos>

plaster[2] *n* **1 :** yeso *m,* revoque *m* (para paredes, etc.) **2 :** escayola *f,* yeso *m* (en medicina) **3 plaster of Paris** ['pærɪs] **:** yeso *m* mate

plaster cast *n* **:** vaciado *m* de yeso

plasterer ['plæstərər] *n* **:** revocador *m,* -dora *f*

plastic[1] ['plæstɪk] *adj* **1 :** de plástico **2** PLIABLE **:** plástico, flexible **3 plastic surgery :** cirugía *f* plástica

plastic[2] *n* **:** plástico *m*

plate[1] ['pleɪt] *vt* **plated; plating :** chapar (en metal)

plate[2] *n* **1** PLAQUE, SHEET **:** placa *f* <a steel plate : una placa de acero> **2** UTENSILS **:** vajilla *f* (de metal) <silver plate : vajilla de plata> **3** DISH **:** plato *m* **4** DENTURES **:** dentadura *f* postiza **5** ILLUSTRATION **:** lámina *f* (en un libro) **6 license plate :** matrícula *f,* placa *f* de matrícula

plateau [plæ'toː] *n, pl* **-teaus** *or* **-teaux** [-'toːz] **:** meseta *f*

platform ['plæt,fɔrm] *n* **1** STAGE **:** plataforma *f,* estrado *m,* tribuna *f* **2 :** andén *m* (de una estación de ferrocarril) **3 political platform :** plataforma *f* política, programa *m* electoral

plating ['pleɪtɪŋ] *n* **1 :** enchapado *m* **2 silver plating :** plateado *m*

platinum ['plætənəm] *n* **:** platino *m*

platitude ['plætə,tuːd, -,tjuːd] *n* **:** lugar *m* común, perogrullada *f*

platoon [plə'tuːn] *n* **:** sección *f* (en el ejército)

platter ['plætər] *n* **:** fuente *f*

platypus [ˈplætɪpəs, -ˌpʊs] *n, pl* **platypuses** *or* **platypi** [-ˌpaɪ, -ˌpiː] **:** ornitorrinco *m*

plausibility [ˌplɔzəˈbɪləṭi] *n, pl* **-ties :** credibilidad *f,* verosimilitud *f*

plausible [ˈplɔzəbəl] *adj* **:** creíble, convincente, verosímil — **plausibly** [-bli] *adv*

play[1] [ˈpleɪ] *vi* **1 :** jugar <to play with a doll : jugar con una muñeca> <to play with an idea : darle vueltas a una idea> **2** FIDDLE, TOY **:** jugar, juguetear <don't play with your food : no juegues con la comida> **3 :** tocar <to play in a band : tocar en un grupo> **4 :** actuar (en una obra de teatro) — *vt* **1 :** jugar (un deporte, etc.), jugar a (un juego), jugar contra (un contrincante) **2 :** tocar (música o un instrumento) **3** PERFORM **:** interpretar, hacer el papel de (un carácter), representar (una obra de teatro) <she plays the lead : hace el papel principal>

play[2] *n* **1** GAME, RECREATION **:** juego *m* <children at play : niños jugando> <a play on words : un juego de palabras> **2** ACTION **:** juego *m* <the ball is in play : la pelota está en juego> <to bring into play : poner en juego> **3** DRAMA **:** obra *f* de teatro, pieza *f* (de teatro) **4** MOVEMENT **:** juego *m* (de la luz, una brisa, etc.) **5** SLACK **:** juego *m* <there's not enough play in the wheel : la rueda no da lo suficiente>

playacting [ˈpleɪˌæktɪŋ] *n* **:** actuación *f,* teatro *m*

player [ˈpleɪər] *n* **1 :** jugador *m,* -dora *f* (en un juego) **2** ACTOR **:** actor *m,* actriz *f* **3** MUSICIAN **:** músico *m,* -ca *f*

playful [ˈpleɪfəl] *adj* **1** FROLICSOME **:** juguetón **2** JOCULAR **:** jocoso — **playfully** *adv*

playfulness [ˈpleɪfəlnəs] *n* **:** lo juguetón, jocosidad *f,* alegría *f*

playground [ˈpleɪˌgraʊnd] *n* **:** patio *m* de recreo, jardín *m* para jugar

playhouse [ˈpleɪˌhaʊs] *n* **1** THEATER **:** teatro *m* **2 :** casita *f* de juguete

playing card *n* **:** naipe *m,* carta *f*

playmate [ˈpleɪˌmeɪt] *n* **:** compañero *m,* -ra *f* de juego

play–off [ˈpleɪˌɔf] *n* **:** desempate *m*

playpen [ˈpleɪˌpɛn] *n* **:** corral *m* (para niños)

plaything [ˈpleɪˌθɪŋ] *n* **:** juguete *m*

playwright [ˈpleɪˌraɪt] *n* **:** dramaturgo *m,* -ga *f*

plaza [ˈplæzə, ˈplɑ-] *n* **1** SQUARE **:** plaza *f* **2 shopping plaza** MALL **:** centro *m* comercial

plea [ˈpliː] *n* **1 :** acto *m* de declararse <he entered a plea of guilty : se declaró culpable> **2** APPEAL **:** ruego *m,* súplica *f*

plead [ˈpliːd] *v* **pleaded** *or* **pled** [ˈplɛd]; **pleading** *vi* **1 :** declararse (culpable o inocente) **2 to plead for :** suplicar, implorar — *vt* **1 :** alegar, pretextar <he pleaded illness : pretextó la enfermedad> **2 to plead a case :** defender un caso

pleasant [ˈplɛzənt] *adj* **:** agradable, grato, bueno — **pleasantly** *adv*

pleasantness [ˈplɛzəntnəs] *n* **:** lo agradable, amenidad *f*

pleasantries [ˈplɛzəntriz] *npl* **:** cumplidos *mpl,* cortesías *fpl* <to exchange pleasantries : intercambiar cumplidos>

please[1] [ˈpliːz] *v* **pleased; pleasing** *vt* **1** GRATIFY **:** complacer <please yourself! : ¡cómo quieras!> **2** SATISFY **:** contentar, satisfacer — *vi* **1** SATISFY **:** complacer, agradar <anxious to please : deseoso de complacer> **2** LIKE **:** querer <do as you please : haz lo que quieras, haz lo que te parezca>

please[2] *adv* **:** por favor

pleased [ˈpliːzd] *adj* **:** contento, satisfecho, alegre

pleasing [ˈpliːzɪŋ] *adj* **:** agradable — **pleasingly** *adv*

pleasurable [ˈplɛʒərəbəl] *adj* PLEASANT **:** agradable

pleasure [ˈplɛʒər] *n* **1** WISH **:** deseo *m,* voluntad *f* <at your pleasure : cuando guste> **2** ENJOYMENT **:** placer *m,* disfrute *m,* goce *m* <with pleasure : con mucho gusto> **3 :** placer *m,* gusto *m* <it's a pleasure to be here : me da gusto estar aquí> <the pleasures of reading : los placeres de leer>

pleat[1] [ˈpliːt] *vt* **:** plisar

pleat[2] *n* **:** pliegue *m*

plebeian [plɪˈbiən] *adj* **:** ordinario, plebeyo

pledge[1] [ˈplɛdʒ] *vt* **pledged; pledging 1** PAWN **:** empeñar, prendar **2** PROMISE **:** prometer, jurar

pledge[2] *n* **1** SECURITY **:** garantía *f,* prenda *f* **2** PROMISE **:** promesa *f*

plenteous [ˈplɛntiəs] *adj* **:** copioso, abundante

plentiful [ˈplɛntɪfəl] *adj* **:** abundante — **plentifully** [-fli] *adv*

plenty [ˈplɛnti] *n* **:** abundancia *f* <plenty of time : tiempo de sobra> <plenty of visitors : muchos visitantes>

plethora [ˈplɛθərə] *n* **:** plétora *f*

pleurisy [ˈplʊrəsi] *n* **:** pleuresía *f*

pliable [ˈplaɪəbəl] *adj* **:** flexible, maleable

pliant [ˈplaɪənt] → **pliable**

pliers [ˈplaɪərz] *npl* **:** alicates *mpl,* pinzas *fpl*

plight [ˈplaɪt] *n* **:** situación *f* difícil, apuro *m*

plod [ˈplɑd] *vi* **plodded; plodding 1** TRUDGE **:** caminar pesadamente y lentamente **2** DRUDGE **:** trabajar laboriosamente

plot[1] [ˈplɑt] *v* **plotted; plotting** *vt* **1** DEVISE **:** tramar **2 to plot out :** trazar, determinar (una posición, etc.) — *vi* CONSPIRE **:** conspirar

plot[2] *n* **1** LOT **:** terreno *m,* parcela *f,* lote *m* **2** STORY **:** argumento *m* (en el teatro), trama *f* (en un libro, etc.) **3** CONSPIRACY, INTRIGUE : complot *m,* intriga *f*

plotter [ˈplɑt̬ər] *n* : conspirador *m,* -dora *f;* intrigante *mf*

plow[1] *or* **plough** [ˈplaʊ] *vt* **1** : arar (la tierra) **2 to plow the seas** : surcar los mares

plow[2] *or* **plough** *n* **1** : arado *m* **2** → **snowplow**

plowshare [ˈplaʊˌʃɛr] *n* : reja *f* del arado

ploy [ˈplɔɪ] *n* : estratagema *f,* maniobra *f*

pluck[1] [ˈplʌk] *vt* **1** PICK : arrancar **2** : desplumar (un pollo, etc.) — *vi* **to pluck at** : tirar de

pluck[2] *n* **1** TUG : tirón *m* **2** COURAGE, SPIRIT : valor *m,* ánimo *m*

plucky [ˈplʌki] *adj* **pluckier; -est** : valiente, animoso

plug[1] [ˈplʌg] *vt* **plugged; plugging 1** BLOCK : tapar **2** PROMOTE : hacerle publicidad a, promocionar **3 to plug in** : enchufar

plug[2] *n* **1** STOPPER : tapón *m* **2** : enchufe *m* (eléctrico) **3** ADVERTISEMENT : publicidad *f,* propaganda *f*

plum [ˈplʌm] *n* **1** : ciruela *f* (fruta) **2** : color *m* ciruela **3** PRIZE : premio *m,* algo muy atractivo

plumage [ˈpluːmɪdʒ] *n* : plumaje *m*

plumb[1] [ˈplʌm] *vt* **1** : aplomar <to plumb a wall : aplomar una pared> **2** SOUND : sondear, sondar

plumb[2] *adv* **1** VERTICALLY : a plomo, verticalmente **2** EXACTLY : justo, exactamente **3** COMPLETELY : completamente, absolutamente <plumb crazy : loco de remate>

plumb[3] *adj* : a plomo

plumb[4] *n or* **plumb line** : plomada *f*

plumber [ˈplʌmər] *n* : plomero *m,* -ra *f;* fontanero *m,* -ra *f*

plumbing [ˈplʌmɪŋ] *n* **1** : plomería *f,* fontanería *f* (trabajo del plomero) **2** PIPES : cañería *f,* tubería *f*

plume [ˈpluːm] *n* **1** FEATHER : pluma *f* **2** TUFT : penacho *m* (en un sombrero, etc.)

plumed [ˈpluːmd] *adj* : con plumas <white-plumed birds : aves de plumaje blanco>

plummet [ˈplʌmət] *vi* : caer en picada, desplomarse

plump[1] [ˈplʌmp] *vi or* **to plump down** : dejarse caer (pesadamente)

plump[2] *adv* **1** STRAIGHT : a plomo **2** DIRECTLY : directamente, sin rodeos <he ran plump into the door : dio de cara con la puerta>

plump[3] *adj* : llenito *fam,* regordete *fam,* rechoncho *fam*

plumpness [ˈplʌmpnəs] *n* : gordura *f*

plunder[1] [ˈplʌndər] *vi* : saquear, robar

plunder[2] *n* : botín *m*

plunderer [ˈplʌndərər] *n* : saqueador *m,* -dora *f*

plunge[1] [ˈplʌndʒ] *v* **plunged; plunging** *vt* **1** IMMERSE : sumergir **2** THRUST : hundir, clavar — *vi* **1** DIVE : zambullirse (en el agua) **2** : meterse precipitadamente o violentamente <they plunged into war : se enfrascaron en una guerra> <he plunged into depression : cayó en la depresión> **3** DESCEND : descender en picada <the road plunges dizzily : la calle desciende vertiginosamente>

plunge[2] *n* **1** DIVE : zambullida *f* **2** DROP : descenso *m* abrupto <the plunge in prices : el desplome de los precios>

plural[1] [ˈplʊrəl] *adj* : plural

plural[2] *n* : plural *m*

plurality [plʊˈrælət̬i] *n, pl* **-ties** : pluralidad *f*

pluralize [ˈplʊrəˌlaɪz] *vt* **-ized; -izing** : pluralizar

plus[1] [ˈplʌs] *adj* **1** POSITIVE : positivo <a plus factor : un factor positivo> **2** (*indicating a quantity in addition*) <a grade of C plus : una calificación entre C y B> <a salary of $30,000 plus : un sueldo de más de $30,000>

plus[2] *n* **1** *or* **plus sign** : más *m,* signo *m* de más **2** ADVANTAGE : ventaja *f*

plus[3] *prep* : más (en matemáticas)

plus[4] *conj* AND : y

plush[1] [ˈplʌʃ] *adj* **1** : afelpado **2** LUXURIOUS : lujoso

plush[2] *n* : felpa *f,* peluche *m*

plushy [ˈplʌʃi] *adj* **plushier; -est** : lujoso

Pluto [ˈpluːt̬oː] *n* : Plutón *m*

plutocracy [pluːˈtɑkrəsi] *n, pl* **-cies** : plutocracia *f*

plutonium [pluːˈtoːniəm] *n* : plutonio *m*

ply[1] [ˈplaɪ] *v* **plied; plying** *vt* **1** USE, WIELD : manejar <to ply an ax : manejar un hacha> **2** PRACTICE : ejercer <to ply a trade : ejercer un oficio> **3 to ply with questions** : acosar con preguntas

ply[2] *n, pl* **plies 1** LAYER : chapa *f* (de madera), capa *f* (de papel) **2** STRAND : cabo *m* (de hilo, etc.)

plywood [ˈplaɪˌwʊd] *n* : contrachapado *m*

pneumatic [nʊˈmæt̬ɪk, njʊ-] *adj* : neumático

pneumonia [nʊˈmoːnjə, njʊ-] *n* : pulmonía *f,* neumonía *f*

poach [ˈpoːtʃ] *vt* **1** : cocer a fuego lento <to poach an egg : escalfar un huevo> **2 to poach game** : cazar ilegalmente — *vi* : cazar ilegalmente

poacher [ˈpoːtʃər] *n* : cazador *m* furtivo, cazadora *f* furtiva

pock [ˈpɑk] *n* **1** PUSTULE : pústula *f* **2** → **pockmark**

pocket[1] [ˈpɑkət] *vt* **1** : meterse en el bolsillo <he pocketed the pen : se metió la pluma en el bolsillo> **2** STEAL : embolsarse

pocket[2] *n* **1** : bolsillo *m,* bolsa *f Mex* <a coat pocket : el bolsillo de un abrigo>

<air pockets : bolsas de aire> **2** CENTER : foco *m,* centro *m* <a pocket of resistance : un foco de resistencia>
pocketbook [ˈpɑkət,bʊk] *n* **1** PURSE : cartera *f,* bolso *m,* bolsa *f Mex* **2** MEANS : recursos *mpl*
pocketknife [ˈpɑkət,naɪf] *n, pl* **-knives** : navaja *f*
pocket-size [ˈpɑkətˈsaɪz] *adj* : de bolsillo
pockmark [ˈpɑk,mɑrk] *n* : cicatriz *f* de viruela, viruela *f*
pod [ˈpɑd] *n* : vaina *f* <pea pod : vaina de guisantes>
podiatrist [pəˈdaɪətrɪst, po-] *n* : podólogo *m,* -ga *f*
podiatry [pəˈdaɪətri, po-] *n* : podología *f,* podiatría *f*
podium [ˈpoːdiəm] *n, pl* **-diums** *or* **-dia** [-diə] : podio *m,* estrado *m,* tarima *f*
poem [ˈpoːəm] *n* : poema *m,* poesía *f*
poet [ˈpoːət] *n* : poeta *mf*
poetic [poˈɛtɪk] *or* **poetical** [-tɪkəl] *adj* : poético
poetry [ˈpoːətri] *n* : poesía *f*
pogrom [ˈpoːgrəm, pəˈgrɑm, ˈpɑgrəm] *n* : pogrom *m*
poignancy [ˈpɔɪnjəntsi] *n, pl* **-cies** : lo conmovedor
poignant [ˈpɔɪnjənt] *adj* **1** PAINFUL : penoso, doloroso <poignant grief : profundo dolor> **2** TOUCHING : conmovedor, emocionante
poinsettia [pɔɪnˈsɛtiə, -ˈsɛtə] *n* : flor *f* de Nochebuena
point[1] [ˈpɔɪnt] *vt* **1** SHARPEN : afilar (la punta de) **2** INDICATE : señalar, indicar <to point the way : señalar el camino> **3** AIM : apuntar **4** **to point out** : señalar, indicar — *vi* **1** **to point at** : señalar (con el dedo) **2** **to point to** INDICATE : señalar, indicar
point[2] *n* **1** ITEM : punto *m* <the main points : los puntos principales> **2** QUALITY : cualidad *f* <her good points : sus buenas cualidades> <it's not his strong point : no es su (punto) fuerte> **3** (*indicating a chief idea or meaning*) <it's beside the point : no viene al caso> <to get to the point : ir al grano> <to stick to the point : no salirse del tema> **4** PURPOSE : fin *m,* propósito *m* <there's no point to it : no vale la pena, no sirve para nada> **5** PLACE : punto *m,* lugar *m* <points of interest : puntos interesantes> **6** : punto *m* (en una escala) <boiling point : punto de ebullición> **7** MOMENT : momento *m,* coyuntura *f* <at this point : en este momento> **8** TIP : punta *f* **9** HEADLAND : punta *f,* cabo *m* **10** PERIOD : punto *m* (marca de puntuación) **11** UNIT : punto *m* <he scored 15 points : ganó 15 puntos> <shares fell 10 points : las acciones bajaron 10 enteros> **12** **compass points** : puntos *mpl* cardinales **13** **decimal point** : punto *m* decimal, coma *f*
point–blank[1] [ˈpɔɪntˈblæŋk] *adv* **1** : a quemarropa <to shoot point-blank : disparar a quemarropa> **2** BLUNTLY, DIRECTLY : a bocajarro, sin rodeos, francamente
point–blank[2] *adj* **1** : a quemarropa <point-blank shots : disparos a quemarropa> **2** BLUNT, DIRECT : directo, franco
pointedly [ˈpɔɪntədli] *adv* : intencionadamente, directamente
pointer [ˈpɔɪntər] *n* **1** STICK : puntero *m* (para maestros, etc.) **2** INDICATOR, NEEDLE : indicador *m,* aguja *f* **3** : perro *m* de muestra **4** HINT, TIP : consejo *m*
pointless [ˈpɔɪntləs] *adj* : inútil, ocioso, vano <it's pointless to continue : no tiene sentido continuar>
point of view *n* : perspectiva *f,* punto *m* de vista
poise[1] [ˈpɔɪz] *vt* **poised; poising** BALANCE : equilibrar, balancear
poise[2] *n* : aplomo *m,* compostura *f*
poison[1] [ˈpɔɪzən] *vt* **1** : envenenar, intoxicar **2** CORRUPT : corromper
poison[2] *n* : veneno *m*
poison ivy *n* : hiedra *f* venenosa
poisonous [ˈpɔɪzənəs] *adj* : venenoso, tóxico, ponzoñoso
poke[1] [ˈpoːk] *v* **poked; poking** *vt* **1** JAB : golpear (con la punta de algo), dar <he poked me with his finger : me dio con el dedo> **2** THRUST : introducir, asomar <I poked my head out the window : asomé la cabeza por la ventana> — *vi* **1** **to poke around** RUMMAGE : hurgar **2** **to poke along** DAWDLE : demorarse, entretenerse
poke[2] *n* : golpe *m* abrupto (con la punta de algo)
poker [ˈpoːkər] *n* **1** : atizador *m* (para el fuego) **2** : póker *m,* poker *m* (juego de naipes)
polar [ˈpoːlər] *adj* : polar
polar bear *n* : oso *m* blanco
Polaris [poˈlærɪs, -ˈlɑr-] → **North Star**
polarize [ˈpoːlə,raɪz] *vt* **-ized; -izing** : polarizar
pole [ˈpoːl] *n* **1** : palo *m,* poste *m,* vara *f* <telephone pole : poste de teléfonos> **2** : polo *m* <the South Pole : el Polo Sur> **3** : polo *m* (eléctrico o magnético)
Pole [ˈpoːl] *n* : polaco *m,* -ca *f*
polecat [ˈpoːl,kæt] *n, pl* **polecats** *or* **polecat** **1** : turón *m* (de Europa) **2** SKUNK : mofeta *f,* zorrillo *m*
polemical [pəˈlɛmɪkəl] *adj* : polémico
polemics [pəˈlɛmɪks] *ns & pl* : polémica *f*
polestar [ˈpoːl,stɑr] → **North Star**
police[1] [pəˈliːs] *vt* **-liced; -licing** : mantener el orden en <to police the streets : patrullar las calles>
police[2] *ns & pl* **1** : policía *f* (organización) **2** POLICE OFFICERS : policías *mfpl*
policeman [pəˈliːsmən] *n, pl* **-men** [-mən, -,mɛn] : policía *m*

police officer *n* : policía *mf,* agente *mf* de policía
policewoman [pəˈliːsˌwʊmən] *n, pl* **-women** [-ˌwɪmən] : policía *f,* mujer *f* policía
policy [ˈpɑləsi] *n, pl* **-cies** **1** : política *f* <foreign policy : política exterior> **2** *or* **insurance policy** : póliza *f* de seguros, seguro *m*
polio[1] [ˈpoːliˌoː] *adj* : de polio <polio vaccine : vacuna contra la polio>
polio[2] *n* → **poliomyelitis**
poliomyelitis [ˌpoːliˌoːˌmaɪəˈlaɪṭəs] *n* : poliomielitis *f,* polio *f*
polish[1] [ˈpɑlɪʃ] *vt* **1** : pulir, lustrar, sacar brillo a <to polish one's nails : pintarse las uñas> **2** REFINE : pulir, perfeccionar
polish[2] *n* **1** LUSTER : brillo *m,* lustre *m* **2** REFINEMENT : refinamiento *m* **3** : betún *m* (para zapatos), cera *f* (para suelos y muebles), esmalte *m* (para las uñas)
Polish[1] [ˈpoːlɪʃ] *adj* : polaco
Polish[2] *n* : polaco *m* (idioma)
polite [pəˈlaɪt] *adj* **-liter; -est** : cortés, correcto, educado
politely [pəˈlaɪtli] *adv* : cortésmente, correctamente, con buenos modales
politeness [pəˈlaɪtnəs] *n* : cortesía *f*
politic [ˈpɑləˌtɪk] *adj* : diplomático, prudente
political [pəˈlɪṭɪkəl] *adj* : político — **politically** [-ṭɪkli] *adv*
politician [ˌpɑləˈtɪʃən] *n* : político *m,* -ca *f*
politics [ˈpɑləˌtɪks] *ns & pl* : política *f*
polka [ˈpoːlkə, ˈpoːkə] *n* : polka *f*
polka dot [ˈpoːkəˌdɑt] *n* : lunar *m* (en un diseño)
poll[1] [ˈpoːl] *vt* **1** : obtener (votos) <she polled over 1000 votes : obtuvo más de 1000 votos> **2** CANVASS : encuestar, sondear — *vi* : obtener votos
poll[2] *n* **1** SURVEY : encuesta *f,* sondeo *m* **2 polls** *npl* : urnas *fpl* <to go to the polls : acudir a las urnas, ir a votar>
pollen [ˈpɑlən] *n* : polen *m*
pollinate [ˈpɑləˌneɪt] *vt* **-nated; -nating** : polinizar
pollination [ˌpɑləˈneɪʃən] *n* : polinización *f*
pollster [ˈpoːlstər] *n* : encuestador *m,* -dora *f*
pollutant [pəˈluːtənt] *n* : contaminante *m*
pollute [pəˈluːt] *vt* **-luted; -luting** : contaminar
pollution [pəˈluːʃən] *n* : contaminación *f*
pollywog *or* **polliwog** [ˈpɑliˌwɔg] *n* TADPOLE : renacuajo *m*
polo [ˈpoːˌloː] *n* : polo *m*
poltergeist [ˈpoːltərˌgaɪst] *n* : poltergeist *m,* fantasma *m* travieso
polyester [ˈpɑliˌɛstər, ˌpɑliˈ-] *n* : poliéster *m*
polygamous [pəˈlɪgəməs] *adj* : polígamo
polygamy [pəˈlɪgəmi] *n* : poligamia *f*
polygon [ˈpɑliˌgɑn] *n* : polígono *m*
polymer [ˈpɑləmər] *n* : polímero *m*
polyunsaturated [ˌpɑliˌʌnˈsætʃəˌreɪṭəd] *adj* : poliinsaturado
pomegranate [ˈpɑməˌgrænət, ˈpɑmˌgrænət] *n* : granada *f* (fruta)
pommel[1] [ˈpʌməl] *vt* → **pummel**
pommel[2] [ˈpʌməl, ˈpɑ-] *n* **1** : pomo *m* (de una espada) **2** : perilla *f* (de una silla de montar)
pomp [ˈpɑmp] *n* **1** SPLENDOR : pompa *f,* esplendor *m* **2** OSTENTATION : boato *m,* ostentación *f*
pom-pom [ˈpɑmˌpɑm] *n* : borla *f,* pompón *m*
pomposity [pɑmˈpɑsəṭi] *n, pl* **-ties** : pomposidad *f*
pompous [ˈpɑmpəs] *adj* : pomposo — **pompously** *adv*
poncho [ˈpɑnˌtʃoː] *n, pl* **-chos** : poncho *m*
pond [ˈpɑnd] *n* : charca *f* (natural), estanque *m* (artificial)
ponder [ˈpɑndər] *vt* : reflexionar, considerar — *vi* **to ponder over** : reflexionar sobre, sopesar
ponderous [ˈpɑndərəs] *adj* : pesado
pontiff [ˈpɑntɪf] *n* POPE : pontífice *m*
pontificate [pɑnˈtɪfəˌkeɪt] *vi* **-cated; -cating** : pontificar
pontoon [pɑnˈtuːn] *n* : pontón *m*
pony [ˈpoːni] *n, pl* **-nies** : poni *m,* poney *m,* jaca *f*
ponytail [ˈpoːniˌteɪl] *n* : cola *f* de caballo, coleta *f*
poodle [ˈpuːdəl] *n* : caniche *m*
pool[1] [ˈpuːl] *vt* : mancomunar, hacer un fondo común de
pool[2] *n* **1** : charca *f* <a swimming pool : una piscina> **2** PUDDLE : charco *m* **3** RESERVE, SUPPLY : fondo *m* común (de recursos), reserva *f* **4** : billar *m* (juego)
poor [ˈpʊr, ˈpor] *adj* **1** : pobre <poor people : los pobres> **2** SCANTY : pobre, escaso <poor attendance : baja asistencia> **3** UNFORTUNATE : pobre <poor thing! : ¡pobrecito!> **4** BAD : malo <to be in poor health : estar mal de salud>
poorly [ˈpʊrli, ˈpor-] *adv* : mal
pop[1] [ˈpɑp] *v* **popped; popping** *vi* **1** BURST : reventarse, estallar **2** : ir, venir, o aparecer abruptamente <he popped into the house : se metió en la casa> <a menu pops up : aparece un menú> **3 to pop out** PROTRUDE : salirse, saltarse <my eyes popped out of my head : se me saltaban los ojos> — *vt* **1** BURST : reventar **2** : hacer o meter abruptamente <he popped it into his mouth : se lo metió en la boca>
pop[2] *adj* : popular <pop music : música popular>
pop[3] *n* **1** : estallido *m* pequeño (de un globo, etc.) **2** SODA : refresco *m,* gaseosa *f*

popcorn ['pɑp,kɔrn] *n* : palomitas *fpl* (de maíz)
pope ['po:p] *n* : papa *m* <Pope John : el Papa Juan>
poplar ['pɑplər] *n* : álamo *m*
poplin ['pɑplɪn] *n* : popelín *m*, popelina *f*
poppy ['pɑpi] *n, pl* **-pies** : amapola *f*
populace ['pɑpjələs] *n* **1** MASSES : pueblo *m* **2** POPULATION : población *f*
popular ['pɑpjələr] *adj* **1** : popular <the popular vote : el voto popular> **2** COMMON : generalizado, común <popular beliefs : creencias generalizadas> **3** : popular, de gran popularidad <a popular singer : un cantante popular>
popularity [,pɑpjə'lærət̬i] *n* : popularidad *f*
popularize ['pɑpjələ,raɪz] *vt* **-ized; -izing** : popularizar
popularly ['pɑpjələrli] *adv* : popularmente, vulgarmente
populate ['pɑpjə,leɪt] *vt* **-lated; -lating** : poblar
population [,pɑpjə'leɪʃən] *n* : población *f*
populous ['pɑpjələs] *adj* : populoso
porcelain ['porsələn] *n* : porcelana *f*
porch ['portʃ] *n* : porche *m*
porcupine ['pɔrkjə,paɪn] *n* : puerco *m* espín
pore[1] ['por] *vi* **pored; poring 1** GAZE : mirar (con atención) **2 to pore over** : leer detenidamente, estudiar
pore[2] *n* : poro *m*
pork ['pork] *n* : carne *f* de cerdo, carne *f* de puerco
pornographic [,pɔrnə'græfɪk] *adj* : pornográfico
pornography [pɔr'nɑgrəfi] *n* : pornografía *f*
porous ['porəs] *adj* : poroso
porpoise ['pɔrpəs] *n* **1** : marsopa *f* **2** DOLPHIN : delfín *m*
porridge ['pɔrɪdʒ] *n* : sopa *f* espesa de harina, gachas *fpl*
port[1] ['port] *adj* : de babor <on the port side : a babor>
port[2] *n* **1** HARBOR : puerto *m* **2** ORIFICE : orificio *m* (de una válvula, etc.) **3** : puerto *m* (de una computadora) **4** PORTHOLE : portilla *f* **5** *or* **port side** : babor *m* (de un barco) **6** : oporto *m* (vino)
portable ['portəbəl] *adj* : portátil
portal ['portəl] *n* : portal *m*
portend [pɔr'tɛnd] *vt* : presagiar, augurar
portent ['pɔr,tɛnt] *n* : presagio *m*, augurio *m*
portentous [pɔr'tɛntəs] *adj* : profético, que presagia
porter ['portər] *n* : maletero *m*, mozo *m* (de estación)
portfolio [port'fo:li,o] *n, pl* **-lios 1** FOLDER : cartera *f* (para llevar papeles), carpeta *f* **2** : cartera *f* (diplomática) **3 investment portfolio** : cartera de inversiones
porthole ['port,ho:l] *n* : portilla *f* (de un barco), ventanilla *f* (de un avión)
portico ['port̬ɪ,ko] *n, pl* **-coes** *or* **-cos** : pórtico *m*
portion[1] ['porʃən] *vt* DISTRIBUTE : repartir
portion[2] *n* PART, SHARE : porción *f*, parte *f*
portly ['portli] *adj* **-lier; -est** : corpulento
portrait ['portrət, -,treɪt] *n* : retrato *m*
portray [por'treɪ] *vt* **1** DEPICT : representar, retratar **2** DESCRIBE : describir **3** PLAY : interpretar (un personaje)
portrayal [por'treɪəl] *n* **1** REPRESENTATION : representación *f* **2** PORTRAIT : retrato *m*
Portuguese [,portʃə'gi:z, -'gi:s] *n* **1** : portugués *m*, -guesa *f* (persona) **2** : portugués *m* (idioma) — **Portuguese** *adj*
pose[1] ['po:z] *v* **posed; posing** *vt* PRESENT : plantear (una pregunta, etc.), representar (una amenaza) — *vi* **1** : posar (para una foto, etc.) **2 to pose as** : hacerse pasar por
pose[2] *n* **1** : pose *f* <to strike a pose : asumir una pose> **2** PRETENSE : pose *f*, afectación *f*
posh ['pɑʃ] *adj* : elegante, de lujo
position[1] [pə'zɪʃən] *vt* : colocar, situar, ubicar
position[2] *n* **1** APPROACH, STANCE : posición *f*, postura *f*, planteamiento *m* **2** LOCATION : posición *f*, ubicación *f* **3** STATUS : posición *f* (en una jerarquía) **4** JOB : puesto *m*
positive ['pɑzət̬ɪv] *adj* **1** DEFINITE : incuestionable, inequívoco <positive evidence : pruebas irrefutables> **2** CONFIDENT : seguro **3** : positivo (en gramática, matemáticas, y física) **4** AFFIRMATIVE : positivo, afirmativo <a positive response : una respuesta positiva>
positively ['pɑzət̬ɪvli] *adv* **1** FAVORABLY : favorablemente **2** OPTIMISTICALLY : positivamente **3** DEFINITELY : definitivamente, en forma concluyente **4** (*used for emphasis*) : realmente, verdaderamente <it's positively awful! : ¡es verdaderamente malo!>
possess [pə'zɛs] *vt* **1** HAVE, OWN : poseer, tener **2** SEIZE : apoderarse de <he was possessed by fear : el miedo se apoderó de él>
possession [pə'zɛʃən] *n* **1** POSSESSING : posesión *f* **2** : posesión *f* (por un demonio, etc.) **3 possessions** *npl* PROPERTY : bienes *mpl*, propiedad *f*
possessive[1] [pə'zɛsɪv] *adj* **1** : posesivo (en gramática) **2** JEALOUS : posesivo, celoso
possessive[2] *n or* **possessive case** : posesivo *m*

possessor [pəˈzɛsər] *n* **:** poseedor *m,* -dora *f*
possibility [ˌpɑsəˈbɪləṭi] *n, pl* **-ties :** posibilidad *f*
possible [ˈpɑsəbəl] *adj* **:** posible
possibly [ˈpɑsəbli] *adv* **1** CONCEIVABLY **:** posiblemente <it can't possibly be true! : ¡no puede ser!> **2** PERHAPS **:** quizás, posiblemente
possum [ˈpɑsəm] → **opossum**
post[1] [ˈpoːst] *vt* **1** MAIL **:** echar al correo, mandar por correo **2** ANNOUNCE **:** anunciar <they've posted the grades : han anunciado las notas> **3** AFFIX **:** fijar, poner (noticias, etc.) **4** STATION **:** apostar **5 to keep** (**someone**) **posted :** tener al corriente (a alguien)
post[2] *n* **1** POLE **:** poste *m,* palo *m* **2** STATION **:** puesto *m* **3** CAMP **:** puesto *m* (militar) **4** JOB, POSITION **:** puesto *m,* empleo *m,* cargo *m*
postage [ˈpoːstɪdʒ] *n* **:** franqueo *m*
postal [ˈpoːstəl] *adj* **:** postal
postcard [ˈpoːstˌkɑrd] *n* **:** postal *f,* tarjeta *f* postal
poster [ˈpoːstər] *n* **:** póster *m,* cartel *m,* afiche *m*
posterior[1] [pɑˈstɪriər, po-] *adj* **:** posterior
posterior[2] *n* BUTTOCKS **:** trasero *m,* nalgas *fpl,* asentaderas *fpl*
posterity [pɑˈstɛrəṭi] *n* **:** posteridad *f*
postgraduate[1] [ˌpoːstˈgrædʒʊət] *adj* **:** de postgrado
postgraduate[2] *n* **:** postgraduado *m,* -da *f*
posthaste [ˈpoːstˈheɪst] *adv* **:** a toda prisa
posthumous [ˈpɑstʃəməs] *adj* **:** póstumo — **posthumously** *adv*
postman [ˈpoːstmən, -ˌmæn] → **mailman**
postmark[1] [ˈpoːstˌmɑrk] *vt* **:** matasellar
postmark[2] *n* **:** matasellos *m*
postmaster [ˈpoːstˌmæstər] *n* **:** administrador *m,* -dora *f* de correos
postmortem [ˌpoːstˈmɔrṭəm] *n* **:** autopsia *f*
postnatal [ˌpoːstˈneɪṭəl] *adj* **:** postnatal <postnatal depression : depresión posparto>
post office *n* **:** correo *m,* oficina *f* de correos
postoperative [ˌpoːstˈɑpərəṭɪv, -ˌreɪ-] *adj* **:** posoperatorio
postpaid [ˌpoːstˈpeɪd] *adv* **:** con franqueo pagado
postpone [ˌpoːstˈpoːn] *vt* **-poned; -poning :** postergar, aplazar, posponer
postponement [ˌpoːstˈpoːnmənt] *n* **:** postergación *f,* aplazamiento *m*
postscript [ˈpoːstˌskrɪpt] *n* **:** postdata *f,* posdata *f*
postulate [ˈpɑstʃəˌleɪt] *vt* **-lated; -lating :** postular
posture[1] [ˈpɑstʃər] *vi* **-tured; -turing :** posar, asumir una pose
posture[2] *n* **:** postura *f*
postwar [ˌpoːstˈwɔr] *adj* **:** de (la) posguerra
posy [ˈpoːzi] *n, pl* **-sies 1** FLOWER **:** flor *f* **2** BOUQUET **:** ramo *m,* ramillete *m*
pot[1] [ˈpɑt] *vt* **potted; potting :** plantar (en una maceta)
pot[2] *n* **1 :** olla *f* (de cocina) **2 pots and pans :** cacharros *mpl*
potable [ˈpoːṭəbəl] *adj* **:** potable
potash [ˈpɑtˌæʃ] *n* **:** potasa *f*
potassium [pəˈtæsiəm] *n* **:** potasio *m*
potato [pəˈteɪṭo] *n, pl* **-toes :** papa *f,* patata *f Spain*
potato chips *npl* **:** papas *fpl* fritas (de bolsa)
potbellied [ˈpɑtˌbɛlid] *adj* **:** panzón, barrigón *fam*
potbelly [ˈpɑtˌbɛli] *n* **:** panza *f,* barriga *f*
potency [ˈpoːtənᵗsi] *n, pl* **-cies 1** POWER **:** fuerza *f,* potencia *f* **2** EFFECTIVENESS **:** eficacia *f*
potent [ˈpoːtənt] *adj* **1** POWERFUL **:** potente, poderoso **2** EFFECTIVE **:** eficaz <a potent medicine : una medicina bien fuerte>
potential[1] [pəˈtɛntʃəl] *adj* **:** potencial, posible
potential[2] *n* **1 :** potencial *m* <growth potential : potencial de crecimiento> <a child with potential : un niño que promete> **2 :** potencial *m* (eléctrico) — **potentially** *adv*
potful [ˈpɑtˌfʊl] *n* **:** contenido *m* de una olla <a potful of water : una olla de agua>
pothole [ˈpɑtˌhoːl] *n* **:** bache *m*
potion [ˈpoːʃən] *n* **:** brebaje *m,* poción *f*
potluck [ˈpɑtˌlʌk] *n* **to take potluck :** tomar lo que haya
potpourri [ˌpoːpʊˈriː] *n* **:** popurrí *m*
potshot [ˈpɑtˌʃɑt] *n* **1 :** tiro *m* al azar <to take potshots at : disparar al azar a> **2** CRITICISM **:** crítica *f* (hecha al azar)
potter [ˈpɑṭər] *n* **:** alfarero *m,* -ra *f*
pottery [ˈpɑṭəri] *n, pl* **-teries :** cerámica *f*
pouch [ˈpaʊtʃ] *n* **1** BAG **:** bolsa *f* pequeña **2 :** bolsa *f* (de un animal)
poultice [ˈpoːltəs] *n* **:** emplasto *m,* cataplasma *f*
poultry [ˈpoːltri] *n* **:** aves *fpl* de corral
pounce [ˈpaʊnᵗs] *vi* **pounced; pouncing :** abalanzarse
pound[1] [ˈpaʊnd] *vt* **1** CRUSH **:** machacar, machucar, majar **2** BEAT **:** golpear, machacar <she pounded the lessons into them : les machacaba las lecciones> <he pounded home his point : les hizo entender su razonamiento> — *vi* **1** BEAT **:** palpitar (dícese del corazón) **2** RESOUND **:** retumbar, resonar **3 :** andar con paso pesado <we pounded through the mud : caminamos pesadamente por el barro>

pound[2] *n* **1 :** libra *f* (unidad de peso) **2 :** libra *f* (unidad monetaria) **3 dog pound :** perrera *f*

pour [ˈpor] *vt* **1 :** echar, verter, servir (bebidas) <pour it into a pot : viértalo en una olla> **2 :** proveer con abundancia <they poured money into it : le invirtieron mucho dinero> **3 to pour out :** dar salida a <he poured out his feelings to her : se desahogó con ella> — *vi* **1** FLOW **:** manar, fluir, salir <blood was pouring from the wound : la sangre le salía de la herida> **2 it's pouring (outside) :** está lloviendo a cántaros

pout[1] [ˈpaʊt] *vi* **:** hacer pucheros

pout[2] *n* **:** puchero *m*

poverty [ˈpɑvərti] *n* **:** pobreza *f,* indigencia *f*

powder[1] [ˈpaʊdər] *vt* **1 :** empolvar <to powder one's face : empolvarse la cara> **2** PULVERIZE **:** pulverizar

powder[2] *n* **:** polvo *m,* polvos *mpl*

powdery [ˈpaʊdəri] *adj* **:** polvoriento, como polvo

power[1] [ˈpaʊər] *vt* **:** impulsar, propulsar

power[2] *n* **1** AUTHORITY **:** poder *m,* autoridad *f* <executive powers : poderes ejecutivos> **2** ABILITY **:** capacidad *f,* poder *m* **3 :** potencia *f* (política) <foreign powers : potencias extranjeras> **4** STRENGTH **:** fuerza *f* **5 :** potencia *f* (en física y matemáticas)

powerful [ˈpaʊərfəl] *adj* **:** poderoso, potente — **powerfully** *adv*

powerhouse [ˈpaʊərˌhaʊs] *n* **:** persona *f* dinámica

powerless [ˈpaʊərləs] *adj* **:** impotente

power plant *n* **:** central *f* eléctrica

powwow [ˈpaʊˌwaʊ] *n* **:** conferencia *f*

pox [ˈpɑks] *n, pl* **pox** *or* **poxes 1** CHICKEN POX **:** varicela *f* **2** SYPHILIS **:** sífilis *f*

practicable [ˈpræktɪkəbəl] *adj* **:** practicable, viable, factible

practical [ˈpræktɪkəl] *adj* **:** práctico

practicality [ˌpræktɪˈkæləti] *n, pl* **-ties :** factibilidad *f,* viabilidad *f*

practical joke *n* **:** broma *f* (pesada)

practically [ˈpræktɪkli] *adv* **1 :** de manera práctica **2** ALMOST **:** casi, prácticamente

practice[1] *or* **practise** [ˈpræktəs] *vt* **-ticed** *or* **-tised; -ticing** *or* **-tising 1 :** practicar <he practiced his German on us : practicó el alemán con nosotros> <to practice politeness : practicar la cortesía> **2 :** ejercer <to practice medicine : ejercer la medicina>

practice[2] *n* **1** USE **:** práctica *f* <to put into practice : poner en práctica> **2** CUSTOM **:** costumbre *f* <it's a common practice here : por aquí se acostumbra hacerlo> **3** TRAINING **:** práctica *f* **4 :** ejercicio *m* (de una profesión)

practitioner [prækˈtɪʃənər] *n* **1 :** profesional *mf* **2 general practitioner :** médico *m,* -ca *f*

pragmatic [prægˈmæṭɪk] *adj* **:** pragmático — **pragmatically** *adv*

pragmatism [ˈprægməˌtɪzəm] *n* **:** pragmatismo

prairie [ˈprɛri] *n* **:** pradera *f,* llanura *f*

praise[1] [ˈpreɪz] *vt* **praised; praising :** elogiar, alabar <to praise God : alabar a Dios>

praise[2] *n* **:** elogio *m,* alabanza *f*

praiseworthy [ˈpreɪzˌwərði] *adj* **:** digno de alabanza, loable

prance[1] [ˈprænts] *vi* **pranced; prancing 1 :** hacer cabriolas, cabriolar <a prancing horse : un caballo haciendo cabriolas> **2** SWAGGER **:** pavonearse

prance[2] *n* **:** cabriola *f*

prank [ˈpræŋk] *n* **:** broma *f,* travesura *f*

prankster [ˈpræŋkstər] *n* **:** bromista *mf*

prattle[1] [ˈprætəl] *vt* **-tled; -tling :** parlotear *fam,* cotorrear *fam,* balbucear (como un niño)

prattle[2] *n* **:** parloteo *m fam,* cotorreo *m fam,* cháchara *f fam*

prawn [ˈprɔn] *n* **:** langostino *m,* camarón *m,* gamba *f*

pray [ˈpreɪ] *vt* ENTREAT **:** rogar, suplicar — *vi* **:** rezar

prayer [ˈprɛr] *n* **1 :** plegaria *f,* oración *f* <to say one's prayers : orar, rezar> <the Lord's Prayer : el Padrenuestro> **2** PRAYING **:** rezo *m,* oración *f* <to kneel in prayer : arrodillarse para rezar>

praying mantis → **mantis**

preach [ˈpriːtʃ] *vi* **:** predicar — *vt* ADVOCATE **:** abogar por <to preach cooperation : promover la cooperación>

preacher [ˈpriːtʃər] *n* **1 :** predicador *m,* -dora *f* **2** MINISTER **:** pastor *m,* -tora *f*

preamble [ˈpriːˌæmbəl] *n* **:** preámbulo *m*

prearrange [ˌpriːəˈreɪndʒ] *vt* **-ranged; -ranging :** arreglar de antemano

precarious [priˈkæriəs] *adj* **:** precario — **precariously** *adv*

precariousness [priˈkæriəsnəs] *n* **:** precariedad *f*

precaution [priˈkɔʃən] *n* **:** precaución *f*

precautionary [priˈkɔʃəˌnɛri] *adj* **:** preventivo, cautelar, precautorio

precede [priˈsiːd] *v* **-ceded; -ceding :** preceder a

precedence [ˈprɛsədənts, prɪˈsiːdənts] *n* **:** precedencia *f*

precedent [ˈprɛsədənt] *n* **:** precedente *m*

precept [ˈpriːˌsɛpt] *n* **:** precepto *m*

precinct [ˈpriːˌsɪŋkt] *n* **1** DISTRICT **:** distrito *m* (policial, electoral, etc.) **2 precincts** *npl* PREMISES **:** recinto *m,* predio *m,* límites *mpl* (de una ciudad)

precious [ˈprɛʃəs] *adj* **1 :** precioso <precious gems : piedras preciosas> **2** DEAR **:** querido **3** AFFECTED **:** afectado

precipice [ˈprɛsəpəs] *n* **:** precipicio *m*

precipitate [priˈsɪpəˌteɪt] *v* **-tated; -tating** *vt* **1** HASTEN, PROVOKE **:** precipitar, provocar **2** HURL **:** arrojar **3**

: precipitar (en química) — *vi* : precipitarse (en química), condensarse (en meteorología)

precipitation [priˌsɪpəˈteɪʃən] *n* **1** HASTE : precipitación *f*, prisa *f* **2** : precipitaciones *fpl* (en meteorología)

precipitous [priˈsɪpəṭəs] *adj* **1** HASTY, RASH : precipitado **2** STEEP : escarpado, empinado <a precipitous drop : una caída vertiginosa>

précis [preɪˈsiː] *n, pl* **précis** [-ˈsiːz] : resumen *m*

precise [priˈsaɪs] *adj* **1** DEFINITE : preciso, explícito **2** EXACT : exacto, preciso <precise calculations : cálculos precisos> — **precisely** *adv*

preciseness [priˈsaɪsnəs] *n* : precisión *f*, exactitud *f*

precision [priˈsɪʒən] *n* : precisión *f*

preclude [priˈkluːd] *vt* **-cluded; -cluding** : evitar, impedir, excluir (una posibilidad, etc.)

precocious [priˈkoːʃəs] *adj* : precoz — **precociously** *adv*

precocity [priˈkɑsəṭi] *n* : precocidad *f*

preconceive [ˌpriːkənˈsiːv] *vt* **-ceived; -ceiving** : preconcebir

preconception [ˌpriːkənˈsɛpʃən] *n* : idea *f* preconcebida

precondition [ˌpriːkənˈdɪʃən] *n* : precondición *f*, condición *f* previa

precook [ˌpriːˈkʊk] *vt* : precocinar

precursor [priˈkərsər] *n* : precursor *m*, -sora *f*

predator [ˈprɛdəṭər] *n* : depredador *m*, -dora *f*

predatory [ˈprɛdəˌtori] *adj* : depredador

predecessor [ˈprɛdəˌsɛsər, ˈpriː-] *n* : antecesor *m*, -sora *f*; predecesor *m*, -sora *f*

predestination [priˌdɛstəˈneɪʃən] *n* : predestinación *f*

predestine [priˈdɛstən] *vt* **-tined; -tining** : predestinar

predetermine [ˌpriːdɪˈtərmən] *vt* **-mined; -mining** : predeterminar

predicament [priˈdɪkəmənt] *n* : apuro *m*, aprieto *m*

predicate¹ [ˈprɛdəˌkeɪt] *vt* **-cated; -cating 1** AFFIRM : afirmar, aseverar **2 to be predicated on** : estar basado en

predicate² [ˈprɛdɪkət] *n* : predicado *m*

predict [priˈdɪkt] *vt* : pronosticar, predecir

predictable [priˈdɪktəbəl] *adj* : previsible — **predictably** [-bli] *adv*

prediction [priˈdɪkʃən] *n* : pronóstico *m*, predicción *f*

predilection [ˌprɛdəlˈɛkʃən, ˌpriː-] *n* : predilección *f*

predispose [ˌpriːdɪˈspoːz] *vt* **-posed; -posing** : predisponer

predominance [priˈdɑmənənts] *n* : predominio *m*

predominant [priˈdɑmənənt] *adj* : predominante — **predominantly** *adv*

predominate [priˈdɑməˌneɪt] *vi* **-nated; -nating 1** : predominar (en cantidad) **2** PREVAIL : prevalecer

preeminence [priˈɛmənənts] *n* : preeminencia *f*

preeminent [priˈɛmənənt] *adj* : preeminente

preeminently [priˈɛmənəntli] *adv* : especialmente

preempt [priˈɛmpt] *vt* **1** APPROPRIATE : apoderarse de, apropriarse de **2** : reemplazar (un programa de televisión, etc.) **3** FORESTALL : adelantarse a (un ataque, etc.)

preen [ˈpriːn] *vt* : arreglarse (el pelo, las plumas, etc.)

prefabricated [ˌpriːˈfæbrəˌkeɪṭəd] *adj* : prefabricado

preface [ˈprɛfəs] *n* : prefacio *m*, prólogo *m*

prefatory [ˈprɛfəˌtori] *adj* : preliminar

prefer [priˈfər] *vt* **-ferred; -ferring 1** : preferir <I prefer coffee : prefiero café> **2 to prefer charges against** : presentar cargos contra

preferable [ˈprɛfərəbəl] *adj* : preferible

preferably [ˈprɛfərəbli] *adv* : preferentemente, de preferencia

preference [ˈprɛfrənts, ˈprɛfər-] *n* : preferencia *f*, gusto *m*

preferential [ˌprɛfəˈrɛntʃəl] *adj* : preferencial, preferente

prefigure [priˈfɪgjər] *vt* **-ured; -uring** FORESHADOW : prefigurar, anunciar

prefix [ˈpriːˌfɪks] *n* : prefijo *m*

pregnancy [ˈprɛgnəntsi] *n, pl* **-cies** : embarazo *m*, preñez *f*

pregnant [ˈprɛgnənt] *adj* **1** : embarazada (dícese de una mujer), preñada (dícese de un animal) **2** MEANINGFUL : significativo

preheat [ˌpriːˈhiːt] *vt* : precalentar

prehensile [priˈhɛntsəl, -ˈhɛnˌsaɪl] *adj* : prensil

prehistoric [ˌpriːhɪsˈtɔrɪk] *or* **prehistorical** [-ɪkəl] *adj* : prehistórico

prejudge [ˌpriːˈdʒʌdʒ] *vt* **-judged; -judging** : prejuzgar

prejudice¹ [ˈprɛdʒədəs] *vt* **-diced; -dicing 1** DAMAGE : perjudicar **2** BIAS : predisponer, influir en

prejudice² *n* **1** DAMAGE : perjuicio *m* (en derecho) **2** BIAS : prejuicio *m*

prelate [ˈprɛlət] *n* : prelado *m*

preliminary¹ [priˈlɪməˌnɛri] *adj* : preliminar

preliminary² *n, pl* **-naries 1** : preámbulo *m*, preludio *m* **2 preliminaries** *npl* : preliminares *mpl*

prelude [ˈprɛˌluːd, ˈprɛlˌjuːd; ˈpreɪˌluːd, ˈpriː-] *n* : preludio *m*

premarital [ˌpriːˈmærəṭəl] *adj* : prematrimonial

premature [ˌpriːməˈtʊr, -ˈtjʊr, -ˈtʃʊr] *adj* : prematuro — **prematurely** *adv*

premeditate [priˈmɛdəˌteɪt] *vt* **-tated; -tating** : premeditar

premeditation [pri,mɛdə'teɪʃən] *n* : premeditación *f*
premenstrual [pri'mɛn*t*strʊəl] *adj* : premenstrual
premier[1] [pri'mɪr, -'mjɪr; 'pri:miər] *adj* : principal
premier[2] *n* PRIME MINISTER : primer ministro *m,* primera ministra *f*
premiere[1] [prɪ'mjɛr, -'mɪr] *vt* **-miered; -miering** : estrenar
premiere[2] *n* : estreno *m*
premise ['prɛmɪs] *n* **1** : premisa *f* <the premise of his arguments : la premisa de sus argumentos> **2 premises** *npl* : recinto *m,* local *m*
premium ['pri:miəm] *n* **1** BONUS : prima *f* **2** SURCHARGE : recargo *m* <to sell at a premium : vender (algo) muy caro> **3 insurance premium** : prima *f* (de seguros) **4 to set a premium on** : darle un gran valor (a algo)
premonition [,pri:mə'nɪʃən, ,prɛmə-] *n* : presentimiento *m,* premonición *f*
prenatal [,pri:'neɪt̬əl] *adj* : prenatal
preoccupation [pri,ɑkjə'peɪʃən] *n* : preocupación *f*
preoccupied [pri'ɑkjə,paɪd] *adj* : abstraído, ensimismado, preocupado
preoccupy [pri'ɑkjə,paɪ] *vt* **-pied; -pying** : preocupar
preparation [,prɛpə'reɪʃən] *n* **1** PREPARING : preparación *f* **2** MIXTURE : preparado *m* <a preparation for burns : un preparado para quemaduras> **3 preparations** *npl* ARRANGEMENTS : preparativos *mpl*
preparatory [pri'pærə,tori] *adj* : preparatorio
prepare [pri'pær] *v* **-pared; -paring** *vt* : preparar — *vi* : prepararse
prepay [,pri:'peɪ] *vt* **-paid; -paying** : pagar por adelantado
preponderance [pri'pɑndərən*t*s] *n* : preponderancia *f*
preponderant [pri'pɑndərənt] *adj* : preponderante — **preponderantly** *adv*
preposition [,prɛpə'zɪʃən] *n* : preposición *f*
prepositional [,prɛpə'zɪʃənəl] *adj* : preposicional
prepossessing [,pri:pə'zɛsɪŋ] *adj* : atractivo, agradable
preposterous [pri'pɑstərəs] *adj* : absurdo, ridículo
prerequisite[1] [pri'rɛkwəzət] *adj* : necesario, esencial
prerequisite[2] *n* : condición *f* necesario, requisito *m* previo
prerogative [pri'rɑgət̬ɪv] *n* : prerrogativa *f*
presage ['prɛsɪdʒ, pri'seɪdʒ] *vt* **-saged; -saging** : presagiar
preschool ['pri:,sku:l] *adj* : preescolar <preschool students : estudiantes de preescolar>
prescribe [pri'skraɪb] *vt* **-scribed; -scribing 1** ORDAIN : prescribir, ordenar **2** : recetar (medicinas, etc.)
prescription [pri'skrɪpʃən] *n* : receta *f*
presence ['prɛzən*t*s] *n* : presencia *f*
present[1] [pri'zɛnt] *vt* **1** INTRODUCE : presentar <to present oneself : presentarse> **2** : presentar (una obra de teatro, etc.) **3** GIVE : entregar (un regalo, etc.), regalar, obsequiar **4** SHOW : presentar, ofrecer <it presents a lovely view : ofrece una vista muy linda>
present[2] ['prɛzənt] *adj* **1** : actual <present conditions : condiciones actuales> **2** : presente <all the students were present : todos los estudiantes estaban presentes>
present[3] ['prɛzənt] *n* **1** GIFT : regalo *m,* obsequio *m* **2** : presente *m* <at present : en este momento> **3** *or* **present tense** : presente *m*
presentation [,pri:,zɛn'teɪʃən, ,prɛzən-] *n* : presentación *f* <presentation ceremony : ceremonia de entrega>
presentiment [pri'zɛntəmənt] *n* : presentimiento *m,* premonición *f*
presently ['prɛzəntli] *adv* **1** SOON : pronto, dentro de poco **2** NOW : actualmente, ahora
present participle *n* : participio *m* presente, participio *m* activo
preservation [,prɛzər'veɪʃən] *n* : conservación *f,* preservación *f*
preservative [pri'zərvət̬ɪv] *n* : conservante *m*
preserve[1] [pri'zərv] *vt* **-served; -serving 1** PROTECT : proteger, preservar **2** : conservar (los alimentos, etc.) **3** MAINTAIN : conservar, mantener
preserve[2] *n* **1** *or* **preserves** *npl* : conserva *f* <peach preserves : duraznos en conserva> **2** : coto *m* <game preserve : coto de caza>
preside [pri'zaɪd] *vi* **-sided; -siding 1 to preside over** : presidir <he presided over the meeting : presidió la reunión> **2 to preside over** : supervisar <she presides over the department : dirige el departamento>
presidency ['prɛzədən*t*si] *n, pl* **-cies** : presidencia *f*
president ['prɛzədənt] *n* : presidente *m,* -ta *f*
presidential [,prɛzə'dɛntʃəl] *adj* : presidencial
press[1] ['prɛs] *vt* **1** PUSH : apretar **2** SQUEEZE : apretar, prensar (frutas, flores, etc.) **3** IRON : planchar (ropa) **4** URGE : instar, apremiar <he pressed me to come : insistió en que viniera> — *vi* **1** PUSH : apretar <press hard : aprieta con fuerza> **2** CROWD : apiñarse **3** : abrirse paso <I pressed through the crowd : me abrí paso entre el gentío> **4** URGE : presionar
press[2] *n* **1** CROWD : multitud *f* **2** : imprenta *f,* prensa *f* <to go to press : entrar en prensa> **3** URGENCY : urgencia *f,* prisa *f* **4** PRINTER, PUBLISHER : imprenta *f,* editorial *f* **5 the press** : la

prensa <freedom of the press : libertad de prensa>

pressing [ˈprɛsɪŋ] *adj* URGENT : urgente

pressure[1] [ˈprɛʃər] *vt* **-sured; -suring** : presionar, apremiar

pressure[2] *n* **1** : presión *f* <to be under pressure : estar bajo presión> **2** → **blood pressure**

pressurize [ˈprɛʃəˌraɪz] *vt* **-ized; -izing** : presurizar

prestige [prɛˈstiːʒ, -ˈstiːdʒ] *n* : prestigio *m*

prestigious [prɛˈstɪdʒəs] *adj* : prestigioso

presto [ˈprɛsˌtoː] *adv* : de pronto

presumably [priˈzuːməbli] *adv* : es de suponer, supuestamente <presumably, he's guilty : supone que es culpable>

presume [priˈzuːm] *vt* **-sumed; -suming 1** ASSUME, SUPPOSE : suponer, asumir, presumir **2 to presume to** : atreverse a, osar

presumption [priˈzʌmpʃən] *n* **1** AUDACITY : atrevimiento *m,* osadía *f* **2** ASSUMPTION : presunción *f,* suposición *f*

presumptuous [priˈzʌmptʃʊəs] *adj* : descarado, atrevido

presuppose [ˌpriːsəˈpoːz] *vt* **-posed; -posing** : presuponer

pretend [priˈtɛnd] *vt* **1** CLAIM : pretender **2** FEIGN : fingir, simular — *vi* : fingir

pretense *or* **pretence** [ˈpriːˌtɛnts, priˈtɛnts] *n* **1** CLAIM : afirmación *f* (falsa), pretensión *f* **2** FEIGNING : fingimiento *m,* simulación *f* <to make a pretense of doing something : fingir hacer algo> <a pretense of order : una apariencia de orden> **3** PRETEXT : pretexto *m* <under false pretenses : con pretextos falsos, de manera fraudulenta>

pretension [priˈtɛntʃən] *n* **1** CLAIM : pretensión *f,* afirmación *f* **2** ASPIRATION : aspiración *f,* ambición *f* **3** PRETENTIOUSNESS : pretensiones *fpl*, presunción *f*

pretentious [priˈtɛntʃəs] *adj* : pretencioso

pretentiousness [priˈtɛntʃəsnəs] *n* : presunción *f,* pretenciones *fpl*

pretext [ˈpriːˌtɛkst] *n* : pretexto *m,* excusa *f*

prettily [ˈprɪtəli] *adv* : atractivamente

prettiness [ˈprɪt̬inəs] *n* : lindeza *f*

pretty[1] [ˈprɪt̬i] *adv* : bastante, bien <it's pretty obvious : está bien claro> <it's pretty much the same : es más o menos igual>

pretty[2] *adj* **-tier; -est** : bonito, lindo, guapo <a pretty girl : una muchacha guapa> <what a pretty dress! : ¡qué vestido más lindo!>

pretzel [ˈprɛtsəl] *n* : galleta *f* salada (en forma de nudo)

prevail [priˈveɪl] *vi* **1** TRIUMPH : prevalecer **2** PREDOMINATE : predominar **3 to prevail upon** : persuadir, convencer <I prevailed upon her to sing : la convencí para que cantara>

prevalence [ˈprɛvələnts] *n* : preponderancia *f,* predominio *m*

prevalent [ˈprɛvələnt] *adj* **1** COMMON : común y corriente, general **2** WIDESPREAD : extendido

prevaricate [priˈværəˌkeɪt] *vi* **-cated; -cating** LIE : mentir

prevarication [priˌværəˈkeɪʃən] *n* : mentira *f*

prevent [priˈvɛnt] *vt* **1** AVOID : prevenir, evitar <steps to prevent war : medidas para evitar la guerra> **2** HINDER : impedir

preventable [priˈvɛntəbəl] *adj* : evitable

preventative [priˈvɛntət̬ɪv] → **preventive**

prevention [priˈvɛntʃən] *n* : prevención *f*

preventive [priˈvɛntɪv] *adj* : preventivo

preview [ˈpriːˌvju] *n* : preestreno *m*

previous [ˈpriːviəs] *adj* : previo, anterior <previous knowledge : conocimientos previos> <the previous day : el día anterior> <in the previous year : en el año pasado>

previously [ˈpriːviəsli] *adv* : antes

prewar [ˌpriːˈwɔr] *adj* : de antes de la guerra

prey [ˈpreɪ] *n, pl* **preys** : presa *f*

prey on *vt* **1** : cazar, alimentarse de <it preys on fish : se alimenta de peces> **2 to prey on one's mind** : hacer presa en alguien, atormentar a alguien

price[1] [ˈpraɪs] *vt* **priced; pricing** : poner un precio a

price[2] *n* : precio *m* <peace at any price : la paz a toda costa>

priceless [ˈpraɪsləs] *adj* : inestimable, inapreciable

prick[1] [ˈprɪk] *vt* **1** : pinchar **2 to prick up one's ears** : levantar las orejas — *vi* : pinchar

prick[2] *n* **1** STAB : pinchazo *m* <a prick of conscience : un remordimiento> **2** → **pricker**

pricker [ˈprɪkər] *n* THORN : espina *f*

prickle[1] [ˈprɪkəl] *vi* **-led; -ling** : sentir un cosquilleo, tener un hormigueo

prickle[2] *n* **1** : espina *f* (de una planta) **2** TINGLE : cosquilleo *m,* hormigueo *m*

prickly [ˈprɪkəli] *adj* **1** THORNY : espinoso **2** : que pica <a prickly sensation : un hormigueo>

prickly pear *n* : tuna *f*

pride[1] [ˈpraɪd] *vt* **prided; priding** : estar orgulloso de <to pride oneself on : preciarse de, enorgullecerse de>

pride[2] *n* : orgullo *m*

priest [ˈpriːst] *n* : sacerdote *m,* cura *m*

priestess [ˈpriːstɪs] *n* : sacerdotisa *f*

priesthood [ˈpriːstˌhʊd] *n* : sacerdocio *m*

priestly [ˈpriːstli] *adj* : sacerdotal

prig [ˈprɪg] *n* : mojigato *m,* -ta *f;* gazmoño *m,* -ña *f*

prim ['prɪm] *adj* **primmer; primmest 1** PRISSY : remilgado **2** PRUDISH : mojigato, gazmoño

primarily [praɪ'mɛrəli] *adv* : principalmente, fundamentalmente

primary[1] ['praɪ,mɛri, 'praɪməri] *adj* **1** FIRST : primario **2** PRINCIPAL : principal **3** BASIC : fundamental

primary[2] *n, pl* **-ries** : elección *f* primaria

primary color *n* : color *m* primario

primary school → **elementary school**

primate *n* **1** ['praɪ,meɪt, -mət] : primado *m* (obispo) **2** [-,meɪt] : primate *m* (animal)

prime[1] ['praɪm] *vt* **primed; priming 1** : cebar <to prime a pump : cebar una bomba> **2** PREPARE : preparar (una superficie para pintar) **3** COACH : preparar (a un testigo, etc.)

prime[2] *adj* **1** CHIEF, MAIN : principal, primero **2** EXCELLENT : de primera (categoría), excelente

prime[3] *n* **the prime of one's life** : la flor de la vida

prime minister *n* : primer ministro *m*, primera ministra *f*

primer[1] ['prɪmər] *n* **1** READER : cartilla *f* **2** MANUAL : manual *m*

primer[2] ['praɪmər] *n* **1** : cebo *m* (para explosivos) **2** : base *f* (de pintura)

primeval [praɪ'mi:vəl] *adj* : primitivo, primigenio

primitive ['prɪmət̬ɪv] *adj* : primitivo

primly ['prɪmli] *adv* : mojigatamente

primness ['prɪmnəs] *n* : mojigatería *f*, gazmoñería *f*

primordial [praɪ'mɔrdiəl] *adj* : primordial, fundamental

primp ['prɪmp] *vi* : arreglarse, acicalarse

primrose ['prɪm,ro:z] *n* : primavera *f*, prímula *f*

prince ['prɪnts] *n* : príncipe *m*

princely ['prɪntsli] *adj* : principesco

princess ['prɪntsəs, 'prɪn,sɛs] *n* : princesa *f*

principal[1] ['prɪntsəpəl] *adj* : principal — **principally** *adv*

principal[2] *n* **1** PROTAGONIST : protagonista *mf* **2** : director *m*, -tora *f* (de una escuela) **3** CAPITAL : principal *m*, capital *m* (en finanzas)

principality [,prɪntsə'pæləṭi] *n, pl* **-ties** : principado *m*

principle ['prɪntsəpəl] *n* : principio *m*

print[1] ['prɪnt] *vt* : imprimir (libros, etc.) — *vi* : escribir con letra de molde

print[2] *n* **1** IMPRESSION : marca *f*, huella *f*, impresión *f* **2** : texto *m* impreso <to be out of print : estar agotado> **3** LETTERING : letra *f* **4** ENGRAVING : grabado *m* **5** : copia *f* (en fotografía) **6** : estampado *m* (de tela)

printer ['prɪntər] *n* **1** : impresor *m*, -sora *f* (persona) **2** : impresora *f* (máquina)

printing ['prɪntɪŋ] *n* **1** : impresión *f* (acto) <the third printing : la tercera tirada> **2** : imprenta *f* (profesión) **3** LETTERING : letras *fpl* de molde

printing press *n* : prensa *f*

print out *vt* : imprimir (de una computadora)

printout ['prɪnt,aʊt] *n* : copia *f* impresa (de una computadora)

prior ['praɪər] *adj* **1** : previo **2 prior to** : antes de

priority [praɪ'ɔrəṭi] *n, pl* **-ties** : prioridad *f*

priory ['praɪəri] *n, pl* **-ries** : priorato *m*

prism ['prɪzəm] *n* : prisma *m*

prison ['prɪzən] *n* : prisión *f*, cárcel *f*

prisoner ['prɪzənər] *n* : preso *m*, -sa *f*; recluso *m*, -sa *f* <prisoner of war : prisionero de guerra>

prissy ['prɪsi] *adj* **-sier; -est** : remilgado, melindroso

pristine ['prɪs,ti:n, prɪs'-] *adj* : puro, pristino

privacy ['praɪvəsi] *n, pl* **-cies** : privacidad *f*

private[1] ['praɪvət] *adj* **1** PERSONAL : privado, particular <private property : propiedad privada> **2** INDEPENDENT : privado, independiente <private studies : estudios privados> **3** SECRET : secreto **4** SECLUDED : aislado, privado — **privately** *adv*

private[2] *n* : soldado *m* raso

privateer [,praɪvə'tɪr] *n* : corsario *m*

privation [praɪ'veɪʃən] *n* : privación *f*

privilege ['prɪvlɪdʒ, 'prɪvə-] *n* : privilegio *m*

privileged ['prɪvlɪdʒd, 'prɪvə-] *adj* : privilegiado

privy[1] ['prɪvi] *adj* **to be privy to** : estar enterado de

privy[2] *n, pl* **privies** : excusado *m*, retrete *m* (exterior)

prize[1] ['praɪz] *vt* **prized; prizing** : valorar, apreciar

prize[2] *adj* **1** : premiado <a prize stallion : un semental premiado> **2** OUTSTANDING : de primera, excepcional

prize[3] *n* **1** AWARD : premio *m* <third prize : el tercer premio> **2** : joya *f*, tesoro *m* <he's a real prize : es un tesoro>

prizefighter ['praɪz,faɪt̬ər] *n* : boxeador *m*, -dora *f* profesional

prizewinning ['praɪz,wɪnɪŋ] *adj* : premiado

pro[1] ['pro:] *adv* : a favor

pro[2] *adj* → **professional[1]**

pro[3] *n* **1** : pro *m* <the pros and cons : los pros y los contras> **2** → **professional[2]**

probability [,prɑbə'bɪləṭi] *n, pl* **-ties** : probabilidad *f*

probable ['prɑbəbəl] *adj* : probable — **probably** [-bli] *adv*

probate[1] ['pro:,beɪt] *vt* **-bated; -bating** : autenticar (un testamento)

probate[2] *n* : autenticación *f* (de un testamento)

probation [pro'beɪʃən] *n* **1 :** período *m* de prueba (para un empleado, etc.) **2 :** libertad *f* condicional (para un preso)

probationary [pro'beɪʃəˌnɛri] *adj* **:** de prueba

probe[1] ['pro:b] *vt* **probed; probing 1 :** sondar (en medicina y tecnología) **2** INVESTIGATE **:** investigar, sondear

probe[2] *n* **1 :** sonda *f* (en medicina, etc.) <space probe : sonda espacial> **2** INVESTIGATION **:** investigación *f,* sondeo *m*

probity ['pro:bəti] *n* **:** probidad *f*

problem[1] ['prɑbləm] *adj* **:** difícil

problem[2] *n* **:** problema *m*

problematic [ˌprɑblə'mætɪk] *or* **problematical** [-tɪkəl] *adj* **:** problemático

proboscis [prə'bɑsɪs] *n, pl* **-cises** *also* **-cides** [-səˌdi:z] **:** probóscide *f*

procedural [prə'si:dʒərəl] *adj* **:** de procedimiento

procedure [prə'si:dʒər] *n* **:** procedimiento *m* <administrative procedures : trámites administrativos>

proceed [pro'si:d] *vi* **1 :** proceder <to proceed to do something : proceder a hacer algo> **2** CONTINUE **:** continuar, proseguir, seguir <he proceeded to the next phase : pasó a la segunda fase> **3** ADVANCE **:** avanzar <as the conference proceeded : mientras seguía avanzando la conferencia> <the road proceeds south : la calle sigue hacia el sur>

proceeding [pro'si:dɪŋ] *n* **1** PROCEDURE **:** procedimiento *m* **2 proceedings** *npl* EVENTS **:** acontecimientos *mpl* **3 proceedings** *npl* MINUTES **:** actas *fpl* (de una reunión, etc.)

proceeds ['pro:ˌsi:dz] *npl* **:** ganancias *fpl*

process[1] ['prɑˌsɛs, 'pro:-] *vt* **:** procesar, tratar

process[2] *n, pl* **-cesses** ['prɑˌsɛsəz, 'pro:-, -səsəz, -səˌsi:z] **1 :** proceso *m* <the process of elimination : el proceso de eliminación> **2** METHOD **:** proceso *m,* método *m* <manufacturing processes : procesos industriales> **3 :** acción *f* judicial <due process of law : el debido proceso (de la ley)> **4** SUMMONS **:** citación *f* **5** PROJECTION **:** protuberancia *f* (anatómica) **6 in the process of :** en vías de <in the process of repair : en reparaciones>

procession [prə'sɛʃən] *n* **:** procesión *f,* desfile *m* <a funeral procession : un cortejo fúnebre>

processional [prə'sɛʃənəl] *n* **:** himno *m* para una procesión

processor ['prɑˌsɛsər, 'pro:-, -səsər] *n* **1 :** procesador *m* (de una computadora) **2 food processor :** procesador *m* de alimentos

proclaim [pro'kleɪm] *vt* **:** proclamar

proclamation [ˌprɑklə'meɪʃən] *n* **:** proclamación *f*

proclivity [pro'klɪvəti] *n, pl* **-ties :** proclividad *f*

procrastinate [prə'kræstəˌneɪt] *vi* **-nated; -nating :** demorar, aplazar las responsabilidades

procrastination [prəˌkræstə'neɪʃən] *n* **:** aplazamiento *m,* demora *f,* dilación *f*

procreate ['pro:kriˌeɪt] *vi* **-ated; -ating :** procrear

procreation [ˌpro:kri'eɪʃən] *n* **:** procreación *f*

proctor[1] ['prɑktər] *vt* **:** supervisar (un examen)

proctor[2] *n* **:** supervisor *m,* -sora *f* (de un examen)

procure [prə'kjʊr] *vt* **-cured; -curing 1** OBTAIN **:** procurar, obtener **2** BRING ABOUT **:** provocar, lograr, conseguir

procurement [prə'kjʊrmənt] *n* **:** obtención *f*

prod[1] ['prɑd] *vt* **prodded; prodding 1** JAB, POKE **:** pinchar, golpear (con la punta de algo) **2** GOAD **:** incitar, estimular

prod[2] *n* **1** JAB, POKE **:** golpe *m* (con la punta de algo), pinchazo *m* **2** STIMULUS **:** estímulo *m* **3 cattle prod :** picana *f,* aguijón *m*

prodigal[1] ['prɑdɪgəl] *adj* SPENDTHRIFT **:** pródigo, despilfarrador, derrochador

prodigal[2] *n* **:** pródigo *m,* -ga *f;* derrochador *m,* -dora *f*

prodigious [prə'dɪdʒəs] *adj* **1** MARVELOUS **:** prodigioso, maravilloso **2** HUGE **:** enorme, vasto <prodigious sums : muchísimo dinero> **— prodigiously** *adv*

prodigy ['prɑdədʒi] *n, pl* **-gies :** prodigio *m* <child prodigy : niño prodigio>

produce[1] [prə'du:s, -'dju:s] *vt* **-duced; -ducing 1** EXHIBIT **:** presentar, mostrar **2** YIELD **:** producir **3** CAUSE **:** producir, causar **4** CREATE **:** producir <to produce a poem : escribir un poema> **5 :** poner en escena (una obra de teatro), producir (una película)

produce[2] ['prɑˌdu:s, 'pro:-, -ˌdju:s] *n* **:** productos *mpl* agrícolas

producer [prə'du:sər, -'dju:-] *n* **:** productor *m,* -tora *f*

product ['prɑˌdʌkt] *n* **:** producto *m*

production [prə'dʌkʃən] *n* **:** producción *f*

productive [prə'dʌktɪv] *adj* **:** productivo

productivity [ˌpro:ˌdʌk'tɪvəti, ˌprɑ-] *n* **:** productividad *f*

profane[1] [pro'feɪn] *vt* **-faned; -faning :** profanar

profane[2] *adj* **1** SECULAR **:** profano **2** IRREVERENT **:** irreverente, impío

profanity [pro'fænəti] *n, pl* **-ties 1** IRREVERENCE **:** irreverencia *f,* impiedad *f* **2 :** blasfemias *fpl,* obscenidades *fpl* <don't use profanity : no digas blasfemias>

profess [prə'fɛs] *vt* **1** DECLARE **:** declarar, manifestar **2** CLAIM **:** pretender **3 :** profesar (una religión, etc.)

professedly [prəˈfɛsədli] *adv* **1** OPENLY : declaradamente **2** ALLEGEDLY : supuestamente

profession [prəˈfɛʃən] *n* : profesión *f*

professional[1] [prəˈfɛʃənəl] *adj* : profesional — **professionally** *adv*

professional[2] *n* : profesional *mf*

professionalism [prəˈfɛʃənəˌlizəm] *n* : profesionalismo *m*

professor [prəˈfɛsər] *n* : profesor *m* (universitario), profesora *f* (universitaria); catedrático *m*, -ca *f*

proffer [ˈprɑfər] *vt* **-fered; -fering** : ofrecer, dar

proficiency [prəˈfɪʃəntsi] *n* : competencia *f*, capacidad *f*

proficient [prəˈfɪʃənt] *adj* : competente, experto — **proficiently** *adv*

profile [ˈproːˌfaɪl] *n* : perfil *m* <a portrait in profile : un retrato de perfil> <to keep a low profile : no llamar la atención, hacerse pasar desapercibido>

profit[1] [ˈprɑfət] *vi* : sacar provecho (de), beneficiarse (de)

profit[2] *n* **1** ADVANTAGE : provecho *m*, partido *m*, beneficio *m* **2** GAIN : beneficio *m*, utilidad *f*, ganancia *f* <to make a profit : sacar beneficios>

profitable [ˈprɑfət̬əbəl] *adj* : rentable, lucrativo — **profitably** [-bli] *adv*

profitless [ˈprɑfətləs] *adj* : infructuoso, inútil

profligate [ˈprɑflɪgət, -ˌgeɪt] *adj* **1** DISSOLUTE : disoluto, licencioso **2** SPENDTHRIFT : despilfarrador, derrochador, pródigo

profound [prəˈfaʊnd] *adj* : profundo

profoundly [prəˈfaʊndli] *adv* : profundamente, en profundidad

profundity [prəˈfʌndət̬i] *n, pl* **-ties** : profundidad *f*

profuse [prəˈfjuːs] *adj* **1** COPIOUS : profuso, copioso **2** LAVISH : pródigo — **profusely** *adv*

profusion [prəˈfjuːʒən] *n* : abundancia *f*, profusión *f*

progeny [ˈprɑdʒəni] *n, pl* **-nies** : progenie *f*

progesterone [proˈdʒɛstəˌroːn] *n* : progesterona *f*

prognosis [prɑgˈnoːsɪs] *n, pl* **-noses** [-ˌsiːz] : pronóstico *m* (médico)

program[1] [ˈproːˌgræm, -grəm] *vt* **-grammed** *or* **-gramed; -gramming** *or* **-graming** : programar

program[2] *n* : programa *m*

programmer [ˈproːˌgræmər] *n* : programador *m*, -dora *f*

programming [ˈproːˌgræmɪŋ] *n* : programación *f*

progress[1] [prəˈgrɛs] *vi* **1** PROCEED : progresar, adelantar **2** IMPROVE : mejorar

progress[2] [ˈprɑgrəs, -ˌgrɛs] *n* **1** ADVANCE : progreso *m*, adelanto *m*, avance *m* <to make progress : hacer progresos> **2** BETTERMENT : mejora *f*, mejoramiento *m*

progression [prəˈgrɛʃən] *n* **1** ADVANCE : avance *m* **2** SEQUENCE : desarrollo *m* (de eventos)

progressive [prəˈgrɛsɪv] *adj* **1** : progresista <a progressive society : una sociedad progresista> **2** : progresivo <a progressive disease : una enfermedad progresiva> **3** *or* **Progressive** : progresista (en política) **4** : progresivo (en gramática)

progressively [prəˈgrɛsɪvli] *adv* : progresivamente, poco a poco

prohibit [proˈhɪbət] *vt* : prohibir

prohibition [ˌproːəˈbɪʃən, ˌproːhə-] *n* : prohibición *f*

prohibitive [proˈhɪbət̬ɪv] *adj* : prohibitivo

project[1] [prəˈdʒɛkt] *vt* **1** PLAN : proyectar, planear **2** : proyectar (imágenes, misiles, etc.) — *vi* PROTRUDE : sobresalir, salir

project[2] [ˈprɑˌdʒɛkt, -dʒɪkt] *n* : proyecto *m*, trabajo *m* (de un estudiante) <research project : proyecto de investigación>

projectile [prəˈdʒɛktəl, -ˌtaɪl] *n* : proyectil *m*

projection [prəˈdʒɛkʃən] *n* **1** PLAN : plan *m*, proyección *f* **2** : proyección *f* (de imágenes, misiles, etc.) **3** PROTRUSION : saliente *m*

projector [prəˈdʒɛktər] *n* : proyector *m*

proletarian[1] [ˌproːləˈtɛriən] *adj* : proletario

proletarian[2] *n* : proletario *m*, -ria *f*

proletariat [ˌproːləˈtɛriət] *n* : proletariado *m*

proliferate [prəˈlɪfəˌreɪt] *vi* **-ated; -ating** : proliferar

proliferation [prəˌlɪfəˈreɪʃən] *n* : proliferación *f*

prolific [prəˈlɪfɪk] *adj* : prolífico

prologue [ˈproːˌlɔg] *n* : prólogo *m*

prolong [prəˈlɔŋ] *vt* : prolongar

prolongation [ˌproːˌlɔŋˈgeɪʃən] *n* : prolongación *f*

prom [ˈprɑm] *n* : baile *m* formal (de un colegio)

promenade[1] [ˌprɑməˈneɪd, -ˈnɑd] *vi* **-naded; -nading** : pasear, pasearse, dar un paseo

promenade[2] *n* : paseo *m*

prominence [ˈprɑmənənts] *n* **1** PROJECTION : prominencia *f* **2** EMINENCE : eminencia *f*, prestigio *m*

prominent [ˈprɑmənənt] *adj* **1** OUTSTANDING : prominente, destacado **2** PROJECTING : prominente, saliente

prominently [ˈprɑmənəntli] *adv* : destacadamente, prominentemente

promiscuity [ˌprɑmɪsˈkjuːət̬i] *n, pl* **-ties** : promiscuidad *f*

promiscuous [prəˈmɪskjʊəs] *adj* : promiscuo — **promiscuously** *adv*

promise[1] [ˈprɑməs] *v* **-ised; -ising** : prometer

promise[2] *n* **1 :** promesa *f* <he kept his promise : cumplió su promesa> **2 to show promise :** prometer

promising ['prɑməsɪŋ] *adj* **:** prometedor

promissory ['prɑmə,sori] *adj* **:** que promete <a promissory note : un pagaré>

promontory ['prɑmən,tori] *n, pl* **-ries** **:** promontorio *m*

promote [prə'mo:t] *vt* **-moted; -moting 1 :** ascender (a un alumno o un empleado) **2** ADVERTISE **:** promocionar, hacerle publicidad a **3** FURTHER **:** promover, fomentar

promoter [prə'mo:t̬ər] *n* **:** promotor *m,* -tora *f;* empresario *m,* -ria *f* (en deportes)

promotion [prə'mo:ʃən] *n* **1 :** ascenso *m* (de un alumno o un empleado) **2** FURTHERING **:** promoción *f,* fomento *m* **3** ADVERTISING **:** publicidad *f,* propaganda *f*

promotional [prə'mo:ʃənəl] *adj* **:** promocional

prompt[1] ['prɑmpt] *vt* **1** INDUCE **:** provocar (una cosa), inducir (a una persona) <curiosity prompted me to ask you : la curiosidad me indujo a preguntarle> **2 :** apuntar (a un actor, etc.)

prompt[2] *adj* **:** pronto, rápido <prompt payment : pago puntual>

prompter ['prɑmptər] *n* **:** apuntador *m,* -dora *f* (en teatro)

promptly ['prɑmptli] *adv* **:** inmediatamente, rápidamente

promptness ['prɑmptnəs] *n* **:** prontitud *f,* rapidez *f*

prone ['pro:n] *adj* **1** LIABLE **:** propenso, proclive <accident-prone : propenso a los accidentes> **2 :** boca abajo, decúbito prono <in a prone position : en decúbito prono>

prong ['prɔŋ] *n* **:** punta *f,* diente *m*

pronoun ['pro:,naʊn] *n* **:** pronombre *m*

pronounce [prə'naʊnts] *vt* **-nounced; -nouncing 1 :** pronunciar <how do you pronounce your name? : ¿cómo se pronuncia su nombre?> **2** DECLARE **:** declarar **3 to pronounce sentence :** dictar sentencia, pronunciar un fallo

pronounced [prə'naʊntst] *adj* MARKED **:** pronunciado, marcado

pronouncement [prə'naʊntsmənt] *n* **:** declaración *f*

pronunciation [prə,nʌntsi'eɪʃən] *n* **:** pronunciación *f*

proof[1] ['pru:f] *adj* **:** a prueba <proof against tampering : a prueba de manipulación>

proof[2] *n* **:** prueba *f*

proofread ['pru:f,ri:d] *v* **-read; -reading** *vt* **:** corregir — *vi* **:** corregir pruebas

proofreader ['pru:f,ri:dər] *n* **:** corrector *m,* -tora *f* (de pruebas)

prop[1] ['prɑp] *vt* **propped; propping 1 to prop against :** apoyar contra **2 to prop up** SUPPORT **:** apoyar, apuntalar, sostener **3 to prop up** SUSTAIN **:** alentar (a alguien), darle ánimo (a alguien)

prop[2] *n* **1** SUPPORT **:** puntal *m,* apoyo *m,* soporte *m* **2 :** accesorio *m* (en teatro)

propaganda [,prɑpə'gændə, ,pro:-] *n* **:** propaganda *f*

propagandize [,prɑpə'gæn,daɪz, ,pro:-] *v* **-dized; -dizing** *vt* **:** someter a propaganda — *vi* **:** hacer propaganda

propagate ['prɑpə,geɪt] *v* **-gated; -gating** *vi* **:** propagarse — *vt* **:** propagar

propagation [,prɑpə'geɪʃən] *n* **:** propagación *f*

propane ['pro:,peɪn] *n* **:** propano *m*

propel [prə'pɛl] *vt* **-pelled; -pelling** **:** impulsar, propulsar, impeler

propellant *or* **propellent** [prə'pɛlənt] *n* **:** propulsor *m*

propeller [prə'pɛlər] *n* **:** hélice *f*

propensity [prə'pɛntsət̬i] *n, pl* **-ties** **:** propensión *f,* tendencia *f,* inclinación *f*

proper ['prɑpər] *adj* **1** RIGHT, SUITABLE **:** apropiado, adecuado **2 :** propio, mismo <the city proper : la propia ciudad> **3** CORRECT **:** correcto **4** GENTEEL **:** fino, refinado, cortés **5** OWN, SPECIAL **:** propio <proper name : nombre propio> — **properly** *adv*

property ['prɑpərt̬i] *n, pl* **-ties 1** CHARACTERISTIC **:** característica *f,* propiedad *f* **2** POSSESSIONS **:** propiedad *f* **3** BUILDING **:** inmueble *m* **4** LAND, LOT **:** terreno *m,* lote *m,* parcela *f* **5** PROP **:** accesorio *m* (en teatro)

prophecy ['prɑfəsi] *n, pl* **-cies** **:** profecía *f,* vaticinio *m*

prophesy ['prɑfə,saɪ] *v* **-sied; -sying** *vt* **1** FORETELL **:** profetizar (como profeta) **2** PREDICT **:** profetizar, predecir, vaticinar — *vi* **:** hacer profecías

prophet ['prɑfət] *n* **:** profeta *m,* profetisa *f*

prophetic [prə'fɛt̬ɪk] *or* **prophetical** [-t̬ɪkəl] *adj* **:** profético — **prophetically** [-t̬ɪkli] *adv*

propitiate [pro'pɪʃi,eɪt] *vt* **-ated; -ating** **:** propiciar

propitious [prə'pɪʃəs] *adj* **:** propicio

proponent [prə'po:nənt] *n* **:** defensor *m,* -sora *f;* partidario *m,* -ria *f*

proportion[1] [prə'porʃən] *vt* **:** proporcionar <well-proportioned : de buenas proporciones>

proportion[2] *n* **1** RATIO **:** proporción *f* **2** SYMMETRY **:** proporción *f,* simetría *f* <out of proportion : desproporcionado> **3** SHARE **:** parte *f* **4 proportions** *npl* SIZE **:** dimensiones *fpl*

proportional [prə'porʃənəl] *adj* **:** proporcional — **proportionally** *adv*

proportionate [prə'porʃənət] *adj* **:** proporcional — **proportionately** *adv*

proposal [prə'po:zəl] *n* **1** PROPOSITION **:** propuesta *f,* proposición *f* <marriage

proposal : propuesta de matrimonio> 2 PLAN : proyecto *m,* propuesta *f*

propose [prə'po:z] *v* **-posed; -posing** *vi* : proponer matrimonio — *vt* 1 INTEND : pensar, proponerse 2 SUGGEST : proponer

proposition [ˌprɑpə'zɪʃən] *n* 1 PROPOSAL : proposición *f,* propuesta *f* 2 STATEMENT : proposición *f*

propound [prə'paʊnd] *vt* : proponer, exponer

proprietary [prə'praɪəˌtɛri] *adj* : propietario, patentado

proprietor [prə'praɪət̬ər] *n* : propietario *m,* -ria *f*

propriety [prə'praɪət̬i] *n, pl* **-eties** 1 DECORUM : decencia *f,* decoro *m* 2 **proprieties** *npl* CONVENTIONS : convenciones *fpl,* cánones *mpl* sociales

propulsion [prə'pʌlʃən] *n* : propulsión *f*

prosaic [pro'zeɪɪk] *adj* : prosaico

proscribe [pro'skraɪb] *vt* **-scribed; -scribing** : proscribir

prose ['pro:z] *n* : prosa *f*

prosecute ['prɑsɪˌkju:t] *vt* **-cuted; -cuting** 1 CARRY OUT : llevar a cabo 2 : procesar, enjuiciar <prosecuted for fraud : procesado por fraude>

prosecution [ˌprɑsɪ'kju:ʃən] *n* 1 : procesamiento *m* <the prosecution of forgers : el procesamiento de falsificadores> 2 PROSECUTORS : acusación *f* <witness for the prosecution : testigo de cargo>

prosecutor ['prɑsɪˌkju:t̬ər] *n* : acusador *m,* -dora *f;* fiscal *mf*

prospect[1] ['prɑˌspɛkt] *vi* : prospectar (el terreno) <to prospect for gold : buscar oro>

prospect[2] *n* 1 VISTA : vista *f,* panorama *m* 2 POSSIBILITY : posibilidad *f* 3 OUTLOOK : perspectiva *f* 4 : posible cliente *m,* -ta *f* <a salesman looking for prospects : un vendedor buscando nuevos clientes>

prospective [prə'spɛktɪv, 'prɑˌspɛk-] *adj* 1 EXPECTANT : futuro <prospective mother : futura madre> 2 POTENTIAL : potencial, posible <prospective employee : posible empleado>

prospector ['prɑˌspɛktər, prɑ'spɛk-] *n* : prospector *m,* -tora *f;* explorador *m,* -dora *f*

prospectus [prə'spɛktəs] *n* : prospecto *m*

prosper ['prɑspər] *vi* : prosperar

prosperity [prɑ'spɛrət̬i] *n* : prosperidad *f*

prosperous ['prɑspərəs] *adj* : próspero

prostate ['prɑˌsteɪt] *n* : próstata *f*

prosthesis [prɑs'θi:sɪs, 'prɑsθə-] *n, pl* **-theses** [-ˌsi:z] : prótesis *f*

prostitute[1] ['prɑstəˌtu:t, -ˌtju:t] *vt* **-tuted; -tuting** 1 : prostituir 2 **to prostitute oneself** : prostituirse

prostitute[2] *n* : prostituto *m,* -ta *f*

prostitution [ˌprɑstə'tu:ʃən, -'tju:-] *n* : prostitución *f*

prostrate[1] ['prɑˌstreɪt] *vt* **-trated; -trating** 1 : postrar 2 **to prostrate oneself** : postrarse

prostrate[2] *adj* : postrado

prostration [prɑ'streɪʃən] *n* : postración *f*

protagonist [pro'tægənɪst] *n* : protagonista *mf*

protect [prə'tɛkt] *vt* : proteger

protection [prə'tɛkʃən] *n* : protección *f*

protective [prə'tɛktɪv] *adj* : protector

protector [prə'tɛktər] *n* 1 : protector *m,* -tora *f* (persona) 2 GUARD : protector *m* (aparato)

protectorate [prə'tɛktərət] *n* : protectorado *m*

protégé ['pro:təˌʒeɪ] *n* : protegido *m,* -da *f*

protein ['pro:ˌti:n] *n* : proteína *f*

protest[1] [pro'tɛst] *vt* 1 ASSERT : afirmar, declarar 2 : protestar <they protested the decision : protestaron (por) la decisión> — *vi* **to protest against** : protestar contra

protest[2] ['pro:ˌtɛst] *n* 1 DEMONSTRATION : manifestación *f* (de protesta) <a public protest : una manifestación pública> 2 COMPLAINT : queja *f,* protesta *f*

Protestant ['prɑt̬əstənt] *n* : protestante *mf*

Protestantism ['prɑt̬əstənˌtɪzəm] *n* : protestantismo *m*

protocol ['pro:t̬əˌkɔl] *n* : protocolo *m*

proton ['proˌtɑn] *n* : protón *m*

protoplasm ['pro:t̬əˌplæzəm] *n* : protoplasma *m*

prototype ['pro:t̬əˌtaɪp] *n* : prototipo *m*

protozoan [ˌpro:t̬ə'zo:ən] *n* : protozoario *m,* protozoo *m*

protract [pro'trækt] *vt* : prolongar

protractor [pro'træktər] *n* : transportador *m* (instrumento)

protrude [pro'tru:d] *vi* **-truded; -truding** : salir, sobresalir

protrusion [pro'tru:ʒən] *n* : protuberancia *f,* saliente *m*

protuberance [pro'tu:bərənts, -'tju:-] *n* : protuberancia *f*

proud ['praʊd] *adj* 1 HAUGHTY : altanero, orgulloso, arrogante 2 : orgulloso <she was proud of her work : estaba orgullosa de su trabajo> <too proud to beg : demasiado orgulloso para rogar> 3 GLORIOUS : glorioso — **proudly** *adv*

prove ['pru:v] *v* **proved; proved** *or* **proven** ['pru:vən]; **proving** *vt* 1 TEST : probar 2 DEMONSTRATE : probar, demostrar — *vi* : resultar <it proved effective : resultó efectivo>

Provençal [ˌpro:vɑn'sɑl, ˌprɑvən-] *n* 1 : provenzal *mf* 2 : provenzal *m* (idioma) — **Provençal** *adj*

proverb [ˈprɑˌvərb] *n* **:** proverbio *m,* refrán *m*

proverbial [prəˈvərbiəl] *adj* **:** proverbial

provide [prəˈvaɪd] *v* **-vided; -viding** *vt* **1** STIPULATE **:** estipular **2 to provide with :** proveer de, proporcionar — *vi* **1 :** proveer <the Lord will provide : el Señor proveerá> **2 to provide for** SUPPORT **:** mantener **3 to provide for** ANTICIPATE **:** hacer previsiones para, prever

provided [prəˈvaɪdəd] *or* **provided that** *conj* **:** con tal (de) que, siempre que

providence [ˈprɑvədənts] *n* **1** PRUDENCE **:** previsión *f,* prudencia *f* **2** *or* **Providence :** providencia *f* <divine providence : la Divina Providencia> **3 Providence** GOD **:** Providencia *f*

provident [ˈprɑvədənt] *adj* **1** PRUDENT **:** previsor, prudente **2** FRUGAL **:** frugal, ahorrativo

providential [ˌprɑvəˈdɛntʃəl] *adj* **:** providencial

providing that → **provided**

province [ˈprɑvɪnts] *n* **1 :** provincia *f* (de un país) <to live in the provinces : vivir en las provincias> **2** FIELD, SPHERE **:** campo *m,* competencia *f* <it's not in my province : no es de mi competencia>

provincial [prəˈvɪntʃəl] *adj* **1 :** provincial <provincial government : gobierno provincial> **2 :** provinciano, pueblerino <a provincial mentality : una mentalidad provinciana>

provision[1] [prəˈvɪʒən] *vt* **:** aprovisionar, abastecer

provision[2] *n* **1** PROVIDING **:** provisión *f,* suministro *m* **2** STIPULATION **:** condición *f,* salvedad *f,* estipulación *f* **3 provisions** *npl* **:** despensa *f,* víveres *mpl,* provisiones *fpl*

provisional [prəˈvɪʒənəl] *adj* **:** provisional, provisorio — **provisionally** *adv*

proviso [prəˈvaɪˌzoː] *n, pl* **-sos** *or* **-soes :** condición *f,* salvedad *f,* estipulación *f*

provocation [ˌprɑvəˈkeɪʃən] *n* **:** provocación *f*

provocative [prəˈvɑkət̬ɪv] *adj* **:** provocador, provocativo <a provocative article : un artículo que hace pensar>

provoke [prəˈvoːk] *vt* **-voked; -voking :** provocar

prow [ˈpraʊ] *n* **:** proa *f*

prowess [ˈpraʊəs] *n* **1** VALOR **:** valor *m,* valentía *f* **2** SKILL **:** habilidad *f,* destreza *f*

prowl [ˈpraʊl] *vi* **:** merodear, rondar — *vt* **:** rondar por

prowler [ˈpraʊlər] *n* **:** merodeador *m,* -dora *f*

proximity [prɑkˈsɪmət̬i] *n* **:** proximidad *f*

proxy [ˈprɑksi] *n, pl* **proxies 1 :** poder *m* (de actuar en nombre de alguien) <by proxy : por poder> **2** AGENT **:** apoderado *m,* -da *f;* representante *mf*

prude [ˈpruːd] *n* **:** mojigato *m,* -ta *f;* gazmoño *m,* -ña *f*

prudence [ˈpruːdənts] *n* **1** SHREWDNESS **:** prudencia *f,* sagacidad *f* **2** CAUTION **:** prudencia *f,* cautela *f* **3** THRIFTINESS **:** frugalidad *f*

prudent [ˈpruːdənt] *adj* **1** SHREWD **:** prudente, sagaz **2** CAUTIOUS, FARSIGHTED **:** prudente, previsor, precavido **3** THRIFTY **:** frugal, ahorrativo — **prudently** *adv*

prudery [ˈpruːdəri] *n, pl* **-eries :** mojigatería *f,* gazmoñería *f*

prudish [ˈpruːdɪʃ] *adj* **:** mojigato, gazmoño

prune[1] [ˈpruːn] *vt* **pruned; pruning :** podar (arbustos, etc.), acortar (un texto), recortar (gastos, etc.)

prune[2] *n* **:** ciruela *f* pasa

prurient [ˈprʊriənt] *adj* **:** lascivo

pry [ˈpraɪ] *v* **pried; prying** *vi* **:** curiosear, huronear <to pry into other people's business : meterse uno en lo que no le importa> — *vt or* **to pry open :** abrir (con una palanca), apalancar

psalm [ˈsɑm, ˈsɑlm] *n* **:** salmo *m*

pseudonym [ˈsuːdəˌnɪm] *n* **:** seudónimo *m*

psoriasis [səˈraɪəsɪs] *n* **:** soriasis *f,* psoriasis *f*

psyche [ˈsaɪki] *n* **:** psique *f,* psiquis *f*

psychiatric [ˌsaɪkiˈætrɪk] *adj* **:** psiquiátrico, siquiátrico

psychiatrist [səˈkaɪətrɪst, saɪ-] *n* **:** psiquiatra *mf,* siquiatra *mf*

psychiatry [səˈkaɪətri, saɪ-] *n* **:** psiquiatría *f,* siquiatría *f*

psychic[1] [ˈsaɪkɪk] *adj* **1 :** psíquico, síquico (en psicología) **2** CLAIRVOYANT **:** clarividente

psychic[2] *n* **:** vidente *mf,* clarividente *mf*

psychoanalysis [ˌsaɪkoəˈnæləsɪs] *n, pl* **-yses :** psicoanálisis *m,* sicoanálisis *m*

psychoanalyst [ˌsaɪkoˈænəlɪst] *n* **:** psicoanalista *mf,* sicoanalista *mf*

psychoanalytic [ˌsaɪkoˌænəlˈɪt̬ɪk] *adj* **:** psicoanalítico, sicoanalítico

psychoanalyze [ˌsaɪkoˈænəlˌaɪz] *vt* **-lyzed; -lyzing :** psicoanalizar, sicoanalizar

psychological [ˌsaɪkəˈlɑdʒɪkəl] *adj* **:** psicológico, sicológico — **psychologically** *adv*

psychologist [saɪˈkɑlədʒɪst] *n* **:** psicólogo *m,* -ga *f;* sicólogo *m,* -ga *f*

psychology [saɪˈkɑlədʒi] *n, pl* **-gies :** psicología *f,* sicología *f*

psychopath [ˈsaɪkəˌpæθ] *n* **:** psicópata *mf,* sicópata *mf*

psychopathic [ˌsaɪkəˈpæθɪk] *adj* **:** psicopático, sicopático

psychosis [saɪˈkoːsɪs] *n, pl* **-choses** [-ˈkoːˌsiːz] **:** psicosis *f,* sicosis *f*

psychosomatic [ˌsaɪkəsəˈmæt̬ɪk] *adj* **:** psicosomático, sicosomático

psychotherapist [ˌsaɪkoˈθɛrəpɪst] *n* **:** psicoterapeuta *mf,* sicoterapeuta *mf*

psychotherapy [ˌsaɪko'θɛrəpi] *n, pl* **-pies** : psicoterapia *f,* sicoterapia *f*

psychotic[1] [saɪ'kɑt̬ɪk] *adj* : psicótico, sicótico

psychotic[2] *n* : psicótico *m,* -ca *f;* sicótico *m,* -ca *f*

puberty ['pjuːbərt̬i] *n* : pubertad *f*

pubic ['pjuːbɪk] *adj* : pubiano, púbico

public[1] ['pʌblɪk] *adj* : público — **publicly** *adv*

public[2] *n* : público *m*

publication [ˌpʌblə'keɪʃən] *n* : publicación *f*

publicist ['pʌbləsɪst] *n* : publicista *mf*

publicity [pə'blɪsət̬i] *n* : publicidad *f*

publicize ['pʌbləˌsaɪz] *vt* **-cized; -cizing** : publicitar

public school *n* : escuela *f* pública

publish ['pʌblɪʃ] *vt* : publicar

publisher ['pʌblɪʃər] *n* : casa *f* editorial (compañía); editor *m,* -tora *f* (persona)

pucker[1] ['pʌkər] *vt* : fruncir, arrugar — *vi* : arrugarse

pucker[2] *n* : arruga *f,* frunce *m,* fruncido *m*

pudding ['pʊdɪŋ] *n* : budín *m,* pudín *m*

puddle ['pʌdəl] *n* : charco *m*

pudgy ['pʌdʒi] *adj* **pudgier; -est** : regordete *fam,* rechoncho *fam,* gordinflón *fam*

puerile ['pjʊrəl] *adj* : pueril

Puerto Rican[1] [ˌpwɛrt̬ə'riːkən, ˌport̬ə-] *adj* : puertorriqueño

Puerto Rican[2] *n* : puertorriqueño *m,* -ña *f*

puff[1] ['pʌf] *vi* **1** BLOW : soplar **2** PANT : resoplar, jadear **3 to puff up** SWELL : hincharse — *vt* **1** BLOW : soplar <to puff smoke : echar humo> **2** INFLATE : inflar, hinchar <to puff out one's cheeks : inflar las mejillas>

puff[2] *n* **1** GUST : soplo *m,* ráfaga *f,* bocanada *f* (de humo) **2** DRAW : chupada *f* (a un cigarrillo) **3** SWELLING : hinchazón *f* **4 cream puff** : pastelito *m* de crema **5 powder puff** : borla *f*

puffy ['pʌfi] *adj* **puffier; -est 1** SWOLLEN : hinchado, inflado **2** SPONGY : esponjoso, suave

pug ['pʌg] *n* **1** : doguillo *m* (perro) **2** *or* **pug nose** : nariz *f* achatada

pugnacious [ˌpʌg'neɪʃəs] *adj* : pugnaz, agresivo

puke ['pjuːk] *vi* **puked; puking** : vomitar, devolver

pull[1] ['pʊl, 'pʌl] *vt* **1** DRAW, TUG : tirar de, jalar **2** EXTRACT : sacar, extraer <to pull teeth : sacar muelas> <to pull a gun on : amenazar a (alguien) con pistola> **3** TEAR : desgarrarse (un músculo, etc.) **4 to pull down** : bajar, echar abajo, derribar (un edificio) **5 to pull in** ATTRACT : atraer (una muchedumbre, etc.) <to pull in votes : conseguir votos> **6 to pull off** REMOVE : sacar, quitar **7 to pull oneself together** : calmarse, tranquilizarse **8 to pull up** RAISE : levantar, subir — *vi* **1** DRAW, TUG : tirar, jalar **2** (*indicating movement in a specific direction*) <they pulled in front of us : se nos metieron delante> <to pull to a stop : pararse> **3 to pull through** RECOVER : recobrarse, reponerse **4 to pull together** COOPERATE : trabajar juntos, cooperar

pull[2] *n* **1** TUG : tirón *m,* jalón *m* <he gave it a pull : le dio un tirón> **2** ATTRACTION : atracción *f,* fuerza *f* <the pull of gravity : la fuerza de la gravedad> **3** INFLUENCE : influencia *f* **4** HANDLE : tirador *m* (de un cajón, etc.) **5 bell pull** : cuerda *f*

pullet ['pʊlət] *n* : polla *f,* gallina *f* (joven)

pulley ['pʊli] *n, pl* **-leys** : polea *f*

pullover ['pʊlˌoːvər] *n* : suéter *m*

pulmonary ['pʊlməˌnɛri, 'pʌl-] *adj* : pulmonar

pulp ['pʌlp] *n* **1** : pulpa *f* (de una fruta, etc.) **2** MASH : papilla *f,* pasta *f* <wood pulp : pasta de papel, pulpa de papel> <to beat to a pulp : hacer papilla (a alguien)> **3** : pulpa *f* (de los dientes)

pulpit ['pʊlˌpɪt] *n* : púlpito *m*

pulsate ['pʌlˌseɪt] *vi* **-sated; -sating 1** BEAT : latir, palpitar **2** VIBRATE : vibrar

pulsation [ˌpʌl'seɪʃən] *n* : pulsación *f*

pulse ['pʌls] *n* : pulso *m*

pulverize ['pʌlvəˌraɪz] *vt* **-ized; -izing** : pulverizar

puma ['puːmə, 'pjuː-] *n* : puma *m;* león *m,* leona *f* (in various countries)

pumice ['pʌməs] *n* : piedra *f* pómez

pummel ['pʌməl] *vt* **-meled; -meling** : aporrear, apalear

pump[1] ['pʌmp] *vt* **1** : bombear <to pump water : bombear agua> <to pump (up) a tire : inflar una llanta> **2** : mover (una manivela, un pedal, etc.) de arriba abajo <to pump someone's hand : darle un fuerte apretón de manos (a alguien)> **3 to pump out** : sacar, vaciar (con una bomba)

pump[2] *n* **1** : bomba *f* <water pump : bomba de agua> **2** SHOE : zapato *m* de tacón

pumpernickel ['pʌmpərˌnɪkəl] *n* : pan *m* negro de centeno

pumpkin ['pʌmpkɪn, 'pʌŋkən] *n* : calabaza *f,* zapallo *m Arg, Chile, Peru, Uru*

pun[1] ['pʌn] *vi* **punned; punning** : hacer juegos de palabras

pun[2] *n* : juego *m* de palabras, albur *m Mex*

punch[1] ['pʌntʃ] *vt* **1** HIT : darle un puñetazo (a alguien), golpear <she punched him in the nose : le dio un puñetazo en la nariz> **2** PERFORATE : perforar (papel, etc.), picar (un boleto)

punch[2] *n* **1** : perforadora *f* <paper punch : perforadora de papel> **2** BLOW : golpe *m,* puñetazo *m* **3** : ponche *m* <fruit punch : ponche de frutas>

punctilious [pəŋk'tɪliəs] *adj* **:** puntilloso
punctual ['pʌŋktʃʊəl] *adj* **:** puntual
punctuality [ˌpʌŋktʃʊ'æləṯi] *n* **:** puntualidad *f*
punctually ['pʌŋktʃʊəli] *adv* **:** puntualmente, a tiempo
punctuate ['pʌŋktʃʊˌeɪt] *vt* **-ated; -ating :** puntuar
punctuation [ˌpʌŋktʃʊ'eɪʃən] *n* **:** puntuación *f*
puncture[1] ['pʌŋktʃər] *vt* **-tured; -turing :** pinchar, punzar, perforar, ponchar *Mex*
puncture[2] *n* **:** pinchazo *m,* ponchadura *f Mex*
pundit ['pʌndɪt] *n* **:** experto *m,* -ta *f*
pungency ['pʌndʒən*t*si] *n* **:** acritud *f,* acrimonia *f*
pungent ['pʌndʒənt] *adj* **:** acre
punish ['pʌnɪʃ] *vt* **:** castigar
punishable ['pʌnɪʃəbəl] *adj* **:** punible
punishment ['pʌnɪʃmənt] *n* **:** castigo *m*
punitive ['pju:nəṯɪv] *adj* **:** punitivo
punt[1] ['pʌnt] *vt* **:** impulsar (un barco) con una pértiga — *vi* **:** despejar (en deportes)
punt[2] *n* **1 :** batea *f* (barco) **2 :** patada *f* de despeje (en deportes)
puny ['pju:ni] *adj* **-nier; -est :** enclenque, endeble
pup ['pʌp] *n* **:** cachorro *m,* -rra *f* (de un perro); cría *f* (de otros animales)
pupa ['pju:pə] *n, pl* **-pae** [-pi, -ˌpaɪ] *or* **-pas :** crisálida *f,* pupa *f*
pupil ['pju:pəl] *n* **1 :** alumno *m,* -na *f* (de colegio) **2 :** pupila *f* (del ojo)
puppet ['pʌpət] *n* **:** títere *m,* marioneta *f*
puppy ['pʌpi] *n, pl* **-pies :** cachorro *m,* -rra *f*
purchase[1] ['pərtʃəs] *vt* **-chased; -chasing :** comprar
purchase[2] *n* **1** PURCHASING **:** compra *f,* adquisición *f* **2 :** compra *f* <last-minute purchases : compras de última hora> **3** GRIP **:** agarre *m,* asidero *m* <she got a firm purchase on the wheel : se agarró bien del volante>
purchase order *n* **:** orden *f* de compra
pure ['pjʊr] *adj* **purer; purest :** puro
puree[1] [pjʊ'reɪ, -'ri:] *vt* **-reed; -reeing :** hacer un puré con
puree[2] *n* **:** puré *m*
purely ['pjʊrli] *adv* **1** WHOLLY **:** puramente, completamente <purely by chance : por pura casualidad> **2** SIMPLY **:** sencillamente, meramente
purgative ['pərgəṯɪv] *n* **:** purgante *m*
purgatory ['pərgəˌtori] *n, pl* **-ries :** purgatorio *m*
purge[1] ['pərdʒ] *vt* **purged; purging :** purgar
purge[2] *n* **:** purga *f*
purification [ˌpjʊrəfə'keɪʃən] *n* **:** purificación *f*
purify ['pjʊrəˌfaɪ] *vt* **-fied; -fying :** purificar
puritan ['pjʊrətən] *n* **:** puritano *m,* -na *f*
puritanical [ˌpju:rə'tænɪkəl] *adj* **:** puritano
purity ['pjʊrəṯi] *n* **:** pureza *f*
purl[1] ['pərl] *v* **:** tejer al revés, tejer del revés
purl[2] *n* **:** punto *m* del revés
purloin [pər'lɔɪn, 'pərˌlɔɪn] *vt* **:** hurtar, robar
purple ['pərpəl] *n* **:** morado *m,* color *m* púrpura
purport [pər'port] *vt* **:** pretender <to purport to be : pretender ser>
purpose ['pərpəs] *n* **1** INTENTION **:** propósito *m,* intención *f* <on purpose : a propósito, adrede> **2** FUNCTION **:** función *f* **3** RESOLUTION **:** resolución *f,* determinación *f*
purposeful ['pərpəsfəl] *adj* **:** determinado, decidido, resuelto
purposefully ['pərpəsfəli] *adv* **:** decididamente, resueltamente
purposely ['pərpəsli] *adv* **:** intencionadamente, a propósito, adrede
purr[1] ['pər] *vi* **:** ronronear
purr[2] *n* **:** ronroneo *m*
purse[1] ['pərs] *vt* **pursed; pursing :** fruncir <to purse one's lips : fruncir la boca>
purse[2] *n* **1** HANDBAG **:** cartera *f,* bolso *m,* bolsa *f Mex* <a change purse : un monedero> **2** FUNDS **:** fondos *mpl* **3** PRIZE **:** premio *m*
pursue [pər'su:] *vt* **-sued; -suing 1** CHASE **:** perseguir **2** SEEK **:** buscar, tratar de encontrar <to pursue pleasure : buscar el placer> **3** FOLLOW **:** seguir <the road pursues a northerly course : el camino sigue hacia el norte> **4 :** dedicarse a <to pursue a hobby : dedicarse a un pasatiempo>
pursuer [pər'su:ər] *n* **:** perseguidor *m,* -dora *f*
pursuit [pər'su:t] *n* **1** CHASE **:** persecución *f* **2** SEARCH **:** búsqueda *f,* busca *f* **3** ACTIVITY **:** actividad *f,* pasatiempo *m*
purveyor [pər'veɪər] *n* **:** proveedor *m,* -dora *f*
pus ['pʌs] *n* **:** pus *m*
push[1] ['pʊʃ] *vt* **1** SHOVE **:** empujar **2** PRESS **:** aprietar, pulsar <push that button : aprieta ese botón> **3** PRESSURE, URGE **:** presionar **4 to push around** BULLY **:** intimidar, mangonear — *vi* **1** SHOVE **:** empujar **2** INSIST **:** insistir, presionar **3 to push off** LEAVE **:** marcharse, irse, largarse *fam* **4 to push on** PROCEED **:** seguir
push[2] *n* **1** SHOVE **:** empujón *m* **2** DRIVE **:** empuje *m,* energía *f,* dinamismo *m* **3** EFFORT **:** esfuerzo *m*
push-button ['pʊʃ'bʌṯən] *adj* **:** de botones
pushcart ['pʊʃˌkɑrt] *n* **:** carretilla *f* de mano
pushy ['pʊʃi] *adj* **pushier; -est :** mandón, prepotente

pussy [ˈpʊsi] *n, pl* **pussies** : gatito *m,* -ta *f;* minino *m,* -na *f*

pussy willow *n* : sauce *m* blanco

pustule [ˈpʌsˌtʃuːl] *n* : pústula *f*

put [ˈpʊt] *v* **put; putting** *vt* **1** PLACE : poner, colocar <put it on the table : ponlo en la mesa> **2** INSERT : meter **3** (*indicating causation of a state or feeling*) : poner <it put her in a good mood : la puso de buen humor> <to put into effect : poner en práctica> **4** IMPOSE : imponer <they put a tax on it : lo gravaron con un impuesto> **5** SUBJECT : someter, poner <to put to the test : poner a prueba> <to put to death : ejecutar> **6** EXPRESS : expresar, decir <he put it simply : lo dijo sencillamente> **7** APPLY : aplicar <to put one's mind to something : proponerse hacer algo> 8 SET : poner <I put him to work : lo puse a trabajar> **9** ATTACH : dar <to put a high value on : dar gran valor a> **10** PRESENT : presentar, exponer <to put a question to someone : hacer una pregunta a alguien> — *vi* **1 to put to sea** : hacerse a la mar **2 to put up with** : aguantar, soportar

put away *vt* **1** KEEP : guardar **2** *or* **to put aside** : dejar a un lado

put by *vt* SAVE : ahorrar

put down *vt* **1** SUPPRESS : aplastar, suprimir **2** ATTRIBUTE : atribuir <she put it down to luck : lo atribuyó a la suerte>

put in *vi* : presentarse <I've put in for the position : me presenté para el puesto> — *vt* DEVOTE : dedicar (unas horas, etc.)

put off *vt* DEFER : aplazar, posponer

put on *vt* **1** ASSUME : afectar, adoptar **2** PRODUCE : presentar (una obra de teatro, etc.) **3** WEAR : ponerse

put out *vt* INCONVENIENCE : importunar, incomodar

putrefy [ˈpjuːtrəˌfaɪ] *v* **-fied; -fying** *vt* : pudrir — *vi* : pudrirse

putrid [ˈpjuːtrɪd] *adj* : putrefacto, pútrido

putter [ˈpʌt̬ər] *vi or* **to putter around** : entretenerse

putty¹ [ˈpʌt̬i] *vt* **-tied; -tying** : poner masilla en

putty² *n, pl* **-ties** : masilla *f*

put up *vt* **1** LODGE : alojar **2** CONTRIBUTE : contribuir, pagar

puzzle¹ [ˈpʌzəl] *vt* **-zled; -zling 1** CONFUSE : confundir, dejar perplejo **2 to puzzle out** : dar vueltas a, tratar de resolver

puzzle² *n* **1** : rompecabezas *m* <a crossword puzzle : un crucigrama> **2** MYSTERY : misterio *m,* enigma *m*

puzzlement [ˈpʌzəlmənt] *n* : desconcierto *m,* perplejidad *f*

pygmy¹ [ˈpɪgmi] *adj* : enano, pigmeo

pygmy² *n, pl* **-mies 1** DWARF : enano *m,* -na *f* **2 Pygmy** : pigmeo *m,* -mea *f*

pylon [ˈpaɪˌlɑn, -lən] *n* **1** : torre *f* de conducta eléctrica **2** : pilón *m* (de un puente)

pyramid [ˈpɪrəˌmɪd] *n* : pirámide *f*

pyre [ˈpaɪr] *n* : pira *f*

pyromania [ˌpaɪroˈmeɪniə] *n* : piromanía *f*

pyromaniac [ˌpaɪroˈmeɪniˌæk] *n* : pirómano *m,* -na *f*

pyrotechnics [ˌpaɪrəˈtɛknɪks] *npl* **1** FIREWORKS : fuegos *mpl* artificiales **2** DISPLAY, SHOW : espectáculo *m,* muestra *f* de virtuosismo <computer pyrotechnics : efectos especiales hechos por computadora>

python [ˈpaɪˌθɑn, -θən] *n* : pitón *f,* serpiente *f* pitón

Q

q [ˈkjuː] *n, pl* **q's** *or* **qs** [ˈkjuːz] : decimoséptima letra del alfabeto inglés

quack¹ [ˈkwæk] *vi* : graznar

quack² *n* **1** : graznido *m* (de pato) **2** CHARLATAN : curandero *m,* -ra *f;* matasanos *m fam*

quadrangle [ˈkwɑˌdræŋgəl] *n* **1** COURTYARD : patio *m* interior **2** → **quadrilateral**

quadrant [ˈkwɑdrənt] *n* : cuadrante *m*

quadrilateral [ˌkwɑdrəˈlæt̬ərəl] *n* : cuadrilátero *m*

quadruped [ˈkwɑdrəˌpɛd] *n* : cuadrúpedo *m*

quadruple [kwɑˈdruːpəl, -ˈdrʌ-; ˈkwɑdrə-] *v* **-pled; -pling** *vt* : cuadruplicar — *vi* : cuadruplicarse

quadruplet [kwɑˈdruːplət, -ˈdrʌ-; ˈkwɑdrə-] *-n* : cuatrillizo *m,* -za *f*

quagmire [ˈkwægˌmaɪr, ˈkwɑg-] *n* : cenagal *m,* lodazal *m*

quail¹ [ˈkweɪl] *vi* : encogerse, acobardarse

quail² *n, pl* **quail** *or* **quails** : codorniz *f*

quaint [ˈkweɪnt] *adj* **1** ODD : extraño, curioso **2** PICTURESQUE : pintoresco — **quaintly** *adv*

quaintness [ˈkweɪntnəs] *n* : rareza *f,* lo curioso

quake¹ [ˈkweɪk] *vi* **quaked; quaking** : temblar

quake² *n* : temblor *m,* terremoto *m*

qualification [ˌkwɑləfəˈkeɪʃən] *n* **1** LIMITATION, RESERVATION : reserva *f,* limitación *f* <without qualification : sin reservas> **2** REQUIREMENT : requisito *m* **3 qualifications** *npl* ABILITY : aptitud *f,* capacidad *f*

qualified [ˈkwɑləˌfaɪd] *adj* : competente, capacitado

qualify [ˈkwɑləˌfaɪ] *v* **-fied; -fying** *vt* **1** : matizar <to qualify a statement

: matizar una declaración> **2** MODIFY : calificar (en gramática) **3** : habilitar <the certificate qualified her to teach : el certificado la habilitó para enseñar> — *vi* **1** : obtener el título, recibirse <to qualify as an engineer : recibirse de ingeniero> **2** : clasificarse (en deportes)

quality ['kwɑləṭi] *n, pl* **-ties 1** NATURE : carácter *m* **2** ATTRIBUTE : cualidad *f* **3** GRADE : calidad *f* <of good quality : de buena calidad>

qualm ['kwɑm, 'kwɑlm, 'kwɔm] *n* **1** MISGIVING : duda *f*, aprensión *f* **2** RESERVATION, SCRUPLE : escrúpulo *m*, reparo *m*

quandary ['kwɑndri] *n, pl* **-ries** : dilema *m*

quantity ['kwɑntəṭi] *n, pl* **-ties** : cantidad *f*

quantum theory ['kwɑntəm] *n* : teoría *f* cuántica

quarantine[1] ['kwɔrən,ti:n] *vt* **-tined; -tining** : poner en cuarentena

quarantine[2] *n* : cuarentena *f*

quarrel[1] ['kwɔrəl] *vi* **-reled** *or* **-relled; -reling** *or* **-relling** : pelearse, reñir, discutir

quarrel[2] *n* : pelea *f*, riña *f*, disputa *f*

quarrelsome ['kwɔrəlsəm] *adj* : pendenciero, discutidor

quarry[1] ['kwɔri] *vt* **quarried; quarrying 1** EXTRACT : extraer, sacar <to quarry marble : extraer mármol> **2** EXCAVATE : excavar <to quarry a hill : excavar un cerro>

quarry[2] *n, pl* **quarries 1** PREY : presa *f* **2** *or* **stone quarry** : cantera *f*

quart ['kwɔrt] *n* : cuarto *m* de galón

quarter[1] ['kwɔrṭər] *vt* **1** : dividir en cuatro partes **2** LODGE : alojar, acuartelar (tropas)

quarter[2] *n* **1** : cuarto *m*, cuarta parte *f* <a foot and a quarter : un pie y cuarto> <a quarter after three : las tres y cuarto> **2** : moneda *f* de 25 centavos, cuarto *m* de dólar **3** DISTRICT : barrio *m* <business quarter : barrio comercial> **4** PLACE : parte *f* <from all quarters : de todas partes> <at close quarters : de muy cerca> **5** MERCY : clemencia *f*, cuartel *m* <to give no quarter : no dar cuartel> **6 quarters** *npl* LODGING : alojamiento *m*, cuartel *m* (militar)

quarterly[1] ['kwɔrṭərli] *adv* : cada tres meses, trimestralmente

quarterly[2] *adj* : trimestral

quarterly[3] *n, pl* **-lies** : publicación *f* trimestral

quartermaster ['kwɔrṭər,mæstər] *n* : intendente *mf*

quartet [kwɔr'tɛt] *n* : cuarteto *m*

quartz ['kwɔrts] *n* : cuarzo *m*

quash ['kwɑʃ, 'kwɔʃ] *vt* **1** ANNUL : anular **2** QUELL : sofocar, aplastar

quaver[1] ['kweɪvər] *vi* **1** SHAKE : temblar <her voice was quavering : su voz temblaba> **2** TRILL : trinar

quaver[2] *n* : temblor *m* (de la voz)

quay ['ki:, 'keɪ, 'kweɪ] *n* : muelle *m*

queasiness ['kwi:zinəs] *n* : mareo *m*, náusea *f*

queasy ['kwi:zi] *adj* **-sier; -est** : mareado

queen ['kwi:n] *n* : reina *f*

queenly ['kwi:nli] *adj* **-lier; -est** : de reina, regio

queer ['kwɪr] *adj* : extraño, raro, curioso — **queerly** *adv*

quell ['kwɛl] *vt* : aplastar, sofocar

quench ['kwɛntʃ] *vt* **1** EXTINGUISH : apagar, sofocar **2** SATISFY : saciar, satisfacer (la sed)

querulous ['kwɛrələs, 'kwɛrjələs, 'kwɪr-] *adj* : quejumbroso, quejoso — **querulously** *adv*

query[1] ['kwɪri, 'kwɛr-] *vt* **-ried; -rying 1** ASK : preguntar, interrogar <we queried the professor : preguntamos al profesor> **2** QUESTION : cuestionar, poner en duda <to query a matter : cuestionar un asunto>

query[2] *n, pl* **-ries 1** QUESTION : pregunta *f* **2** DOUBT : duda *f*

quest[1] ['kwɛst] *v* : buscar

quest[2] *n* : búsqueda *f*

question[1] ['kwɛstʃən] *vt* **1** ASK : preguntar **2** DOUBT : poner en duda, cuestionar **3** INTERROGATE : interrogar — *vi* INQUIRE : inquirir, preguntar

question[2] *n* **1** QUERY : pregunta *f* **2** ISSUE : asunto *m*, problema *f*, cuestión *f* **3** POSSIBILITY : posibilidad *f* <it's out of the question : es indiscutible> **4** DOUBT : duda *f* <to call into question : poner en duda>

questionable ['kwɛstʃənəbəl] *adj* : dudoso, discutible, cuestionable <questionable results : resultados discutibles> <questionable motives : motivos sospechosos>

questioner ['kwɛstʃənər] *n* : interrogador *m*, -dora *f*

question mark *n* : signo *m* de interrogación

questionnaire [,kwɛstʃə'nær] *n* : cuestionario *m*

queue[1] ['kju:] *vi* **queued; queuing** *or* **queueing** : hacer cola

queue[2] *n* **1** PIGTAIL : coleta *f*, trenza *f* **2** LINE : cola *f*, fila *f*

quibble[1] ['kwɪbəl] *vi* **-bled; -bling** : quejarse por nimiedades, andar con sutilezas

quibble[2] *n* : objeción *f* de poca monta, queja *f* insignificante

quick[1] ['kwɪk] *adv* : rápidamente

quick[2] *adj* **1** RAPID : rápido **2** ALERT, CLEVER : listo, vivo, agudo **3 a quick temper** : un genio vivo

quick[3] *n* **1** FLESH : carne *f* viva **2 to cut someone to the quick** : herir a alguien en lo más vivo

quicken ['kwɪkən] *vt* **1** REVIVE : resucitar **2** AROUSE : estimular, despertar **3** HASTEN : acelerar <she quickened her pace : aceleró el paso>

quickly [ˈkwɪkli] *adv* : rápidamente, rápido, de prisa

quickness [ˈkwɪknəs] *n* : rapidez *f*

quicksand [ˈkwɪkˌsænd] *n* : arena *f* movediza

quicksilver [ˈkwɪkˌsɪlvər] *n* : mercurio *m,* azogue *m*

quick–tempered [ˈkwɪkˈtɛmpərd] *adj* : irascible, de genio vivo

quick–witted [ˈkwɪkˈwɪt̬əd] *adj* : agudo

quiet[1] *v* [ˈkwaɪət] *vt* **1** SILENCE : hacer callar, acallar **2** CALM : calmar, tranquilizar — *vi* **to quiet down** : calmarse, tranquilizarse

quiet[2] *adv* : silenciosamente <a quiet-running engine : un motor silencioso>

quiet[3] *adj* **1** CALM : tranquilo, calmoso **2** MILD : sosegado, suave <a quiet disposition : un temperamento sosegado> **3** SILENT : silencioso **4** UNOBTRUSIVE : discreto **5** SECLUDED : aislado <a quiet nook : un rincón aislado> — **quietly** *adv*

quiet[4] *n* **1** CALM : calma *f,* tranquilidad *f* **2** SILENCE : silencio *m*

quietness [ˈkwaɪətnəs] *n* : suavidad *f,* tranquilidad *f,* quietud *f*

quietude [ˈkwaɪəˌtuːd, -ˌtjuːd] *n* : quietud *f,* reposo *m*

quill [ˈkwɪl] *n* **1** SPINE : púa *f* (de un puerco espín) **2** : pluma *f* (para escribir)

quilt[1] [ˈkwɪlt] *vt* : acolchar

quilt[2] *n* : colcha *f,* edredón *m*

quince [ˈkwɪnts] *n* : membrillo *m*

quinine [ˈkwaɪˌnaɪn] *n* : quinina *f*

quintessence [kwɪnˈtɛsənts] *n* : quintaesencia *f*

quintet [kwɪnˈtɛt] *n* : quinteto *m*

quintuple [kwɪnˈtuːpəl, -ˈtjuː-, -ˈtʌ-; ˈkwɪntə-] *adj* : quíntuplo

quintuplet [kwɪnˈtʌplət, -ˈtuː-, -ˈtjuː-; ˈkwɪntə-] *n* : quintillizo *m,* -za *f*

quip[1] [ˈkwɪp] *vi* **quipped; quipping** : bromear

quip[2] *n* : ocurrencia *f,* salida *f*

quirk [ˈkwərk] *n* : peculiaridad *f,* rareza *f* <a quirk of fate : un capricho del destino>

quirky [ˈkwərki] *adj* **-kier; -est** : peculiar, raro

quit [ˈkwɪt] *v* **quit; quitting** *vt* : dejar, abandonar <to quit smoking : dejar de fumar> — *vi* **1** STOP : parar **2** RESIGN : dimitir, renunciar

quite [ˈkwaɪt] *adv* **1** COMPLETELY : completamente, totalmente **2** RATHER : bastante <quite near : bastante cerca>

quits [ˈkwɪts] *adj* **to call it quits** : quedar en paz

quitter [ˈkwɪt̬ər] *n* : derrotista *mf*

quiver[1] [ˈkwɪvər] *vi* : temblar, estremecerse, vibrar

quiver[2] *n* **1** : carcaj *m,* aljaba *f* (para flechas) **2** TREMBLING : temblor *m,* estremecimiento *m*

quixotic [kwɪkˈsɑt̬ɪk] *adj* : quijotesco

quiz[1] [ˈkwɪz] *vt* **quizzed; quizzing** : interrogar, hacer una prueba a (en el colegio)

quiz[2] *n, pl* **quizzes** : examen *m* corto, prueba *f*

quizzical [ˈkwɪzɪkəl] *adj* **1** TEASING : burlón **2** CURIOUS : curioso, interrogativo

quorum [ˈkworəm] *n* : quórum *m*

quota [ˈkwoːt̬ə] *n* : cuota *f,* cupo *m*

quotable [ˈkwoːt̬əbəl] *adj* : citable

quotation [kwoˈteɪʃən] *n* **1** CITATION : cita *f* **2** ESTIMATE : presupuesto *m,* estimación *f* **3** PRICE : cotización *f*

quotation marks *npl* : comillas *fpl*

quote[1] [ˈkwoːt] *vt* **quoted; quoting 1** CITE : citar **2** VALUE : cotizar (en finanzas)

quote[2] *n* **1** → **quotation 2 quotes** *npl* → **quotation marks**

quotient [ˈkwoːʃənt] *n* : cociente *m*

R

r [ˈɑr] *n, pl* **r's** *or* **rs** [ˈɑrz] : decimoctava letra del alfabeto inglés

rabbi [ˈræˌbaɪ] *n* : rabino *m,* -na *f*

rabbit [ˈræbət] *n, pl* **-bit** *or* **-bits** : conejo *m,* -ja *f*

rabble [ˈræbəl] *n* **1** MASSES : populacho *m* **2** RIFFRAFF : chusma *f,* gentuza *f*

rabid [ˈræbɪd] *adj* **1** : rabioso, afectado con la rabia **2** FURIOUS : furioso **3** FANATIC : fanático

rabies [ˈreɪbiːz] *ns & pl* : rabia *f*

raccoon [ræˈkuːn] *n, pl* **-coon** *or* **-coons** : mapache *m*

race[1] [ˈreɪs] *vi* **raced; racing 1** : correr, competir (en una carrera) **2** RUSH : ir a toda prisa, ir corriendo

race[2] *n* **1** CURRENT : corriente *f* (de agua) **2** : carrera *f* <dog race : carrera de perros> <the presidential race : la carrera presidential> **3** : raza *f* <the black race : la raza negra> <the human race : el género humano>

racecourse [ˈreɪsˌkors] *n* : pista *f* (de carreras)

racehorse [ˈreɪsˌhors] *n* : caballo *m* de carreras

racer [ˈreɪsər] *n* : corredor *m,* -dora *f*

racetrack [ˈreɪsˌtræk] *n* : pista *f* (de carreras)

racial [ˈreɪʃəl] *adj* : racial — **racially** *adv*

racism [ˈreɪˌsɪzəm] *n* : racismo *m*

racist [ˈreɪsɪst] *n* : racista *mf*

rack¹ ['ræk] *vt* **1** : atormentar <racked with pain : atormentado por el dolor> **2 to rack one's brains** : devanarse los sesos
rack² *n* **1** SHELF, STAND : estante *m* <a luggage rack : un portaequipajes> <a coatrack : un perchero, una percha> **2** : potro *m* (instrumento de la tortura)
racket ['rækət] *n* **1** : raqueta *f* (en deportes) **2** DIN : estruendo *m,* bulla *f,* jaleo *m fam* **3** SWINDLE : estafa *f,* timo *m fam*
racketeer [ˌrækə'tɪr] *n* : estafador *m,* -dora *f*
raconteur [ˌræˌkɑn'tər] *n* : anecdotista *mf*
racy ['reɪsi] *adj* **racier; -est** : subido de tono, picante
radar ['reɪˌdɑr] *n* : radar *m*
radial ['reɪdiəl] *adj* : radial
radiance ['reɪdiən*t*s] *n* : resplandor *m*
radiant ['reɪdiənt] *adj* : radiante — **radiantly** *adv*
radiate ['reɪdiˌeɪt] *v* **-ated; -ating** *vt* : irradiar, emitir <to radiate heat : irradiar el calor> <to radiate happiness : rebosar de alegría> — *vi* **1** : irradiar **2** SPREAD : salir, extenderse <to radiate (out) from the center : salir del centro>
radiation [ˌreɪdi'eɪʃən] *n* : radiación *f*
radiator ['reɪdiˌeɪtər] *n* : radiador *m*
radical¹ ['rædɪkəl] *adj* : radical — **radically** [-kli] *adv*
radical² *n* : radical *mf*
radii → **radius**
radio¹ ['reɪdiˌoː] *v* : llamar por radio, transmitir por radio
radio² *n, pl* **-dios** : radio *m* (aparato), radio *f* (emisora, radiodifusión)
radioactive ['reɪdio'æktɪv] *adj* : radiactivo, radioactivo
radioactivity [ˌreɪdioˌæk'tɪvəti] *n, pl* **-ties** : radiactividad *f,* radioactividad *f*
radiologist [ˌreɪdi'ɑləʤɪst] *n* : radiólogo *m,* -ga *f*
radiology [ˌreɪdi'ɑləʤi] *n* : radiología *f*
radish ['rædɪʃ] *n* : rábano *m*
radium ['reɪdiəm] *n* : radio *m*
radius ['reɪdiəs] *n, pl* **radii** [-diˌaɪ] : radio *m*
radon ['reɪˌdɑn] *n* : radón *m*
raffle¹ ['ræfəl] *vt* **-fled; -fling** : rifar, sortear
raffle² *n* : rifa *f,* sorteo *m*
raft ['ræft] *n* **1** : balsa *f* <rubber rafts : balsas de goma> **2** LOT, SLEW : montón *m* <a raft of documents : un montón de documentos>
rafter ['ræftər] *n* : par *m,* viga *f*
rag ['ræg] *n* **1** CLOTH : trapo *m* **2 rags** *npl* TATTERS : harapos *mpl*, andrapos *mpl*
ragamuffin ['rægəˌmʌfən] *n* : pilluelo *m,* -la *f*
rage¹ ['reɪʤ] *vi* **raged; raging 1** : estar furioso, rabiar <to fly into a rage : enfurecerse> **2** : bramar, hacer estragos <the wind was raging : el viento bramaba> <flu raged through the school : la gripe hizo estragos por el colegio>
rage² *n* **1** ANGER : furia *f,* ira *f,* cólera *f* **2** FAD : moda *f,* furor *m*
ragged ['rægəd] *adj* **1** UNEVEN : irregular, desigual **2** TORN : hecho jirones **3** TATTERED : andrajoso, harapiento
ragout [ræ'guː] *n* : ragú *m,* estofado *m*
ragtime ['rægˌtaɪm] *n* : ragtime *m*
ragweed ['rægˌwiːd] *n* : ambrosía *f*
raid¹ ['reɪd] *vt* **1** : invadir, hacer una incursión en <raided by enemy troops : invadido por tropas enemigas> **2** : asaltar, atracar <the gang raided the warehouse : la pandilla asaltó el almacén> **3** : allanar, hacer una redada en <police raided the house : la policía allanó la vivienda>
raid² *n* **1** : invasión *f* (militar) **2** : asalto *m* (por delincuentes) **3** : redada *f,* allanamiento *m* (por la policía)
raider ['reɪdər] *n* **1** ATTACKER : asaltante *mf;* invasor *m,* -sora *f* **2 corporate raider** : tiburón *m*
rail¹ ['reɪl] *vi* **1 to rail against** REVILE : denostar contra **2 to rail at** SCOLD : regañar, reprender
rail² *n* **1** BAR : barra *f,* barrera *f* **2** HANDRAIL : pasamanos *m,* barandilla *f* **3** TRACK : riel *m* (para ferrocarriles) **4** RAILROAD : ferrocarril *m*
railing ['reɪlɪŋ] *n* **1** : baranda *f* (de un balcón, etc.) **2** RAILS : verja *f*
raillery ['reɪləri] *n, pl* **-leries** : bromas *fpl*
railroad ['reɪlˌroːd] *n* : ferrocarril *m*
railway ['reɪlˌweɪ] → **railroad**
raiment ['reɪmənt] *n* : vestiduras *fpl*
rain¹ ['reɪn] *vi* **1** : llover <it's raining : está lloviendo> **2 to rain down** SHOWER : llover <insults rained down on him : le llovieron los insultos>
rain² *n* : lluvia *f*
rainbow ['reɪnˌboː] *n* : arco *m* iris
raincoat ['reɪnˌkoːt] *n* : impermeable *m*
raindrop ['reɪnˌdrɑp] *n* : gota *f* de lluvia
rainfall ['reɪnˌfɔl] *n* : lluvia *f,* precipitación *f*
rainstorm ['reɪnˌstɔrm] *n* : temporal *m* (de lluvia)
rainwater ['reɪnˌwɔtər] *n* : agua *f* de lluvia
rainy ['reɪni] *adj* **rainier; -est** : lluvioso
raise¹ ['reɪz] *vt* **raised; raising 1** LIFT : levantar, subir, alzar <to raise one's spirits : levantarle el ánimo a alguien> **2** ERECT : levantar, erigir **3** COLLECT : recaudar <to raise money : recaudar dinero> **4** REAR : criar <to raise one's children : criar uno a sus niños> **5** GROW : cultivar **6** INCREASE : aumentar, subir **7** PROMOTE : ascender **8** PROVOKE : provocar <it raised

a laugh : provocó una risa> **9** BRING UP : sacar (temas, objeciones, etc.)

raise[2] *n* : aumento *m*

raisin [ˈreɪzən] *n* : pasa *f*

raja *or* **rajah** [ˈrɑʤə, -ˌʤɑ, -ˌʒɑ] *n* : rajá *m*

rake[1] [ˈreɪk] *v* **raked; raking** *vt* **1** : rastrillar <to rake leaves : rastrillar las hojas> **2** SWEEP : barrer <raked with gunfire : barrido con metralla> — *vi* **to rake through** : revolver, hurgar en

rake[2] *n* **1** : rastrillo *m* **2** LIBERTINE : libertino *m,* -na *f;* calavera *m*

rakish [ˈreɪkɪʃ] *adj* **1** JAUNTY : desenvuelto, desenfadado **2** DISSOLUTE : libertino, disoluto

rally[1] [ˈræli] *v* **-lied; -lying** *vi* **1** MEET, UNITE : reunirse, congregarse **2** RECOVER : recuperarse — *vt* **1** ASSEMBLE : reunir (tropas, etc.) **2** RECOVER : recobrar (la fuerza, el ánimo, etc.)

rally[2] *n, pl* **-lies** : reunión *f,* mitin *m,* manifestación *f*

ram[1] [ˈræm] *v* **rammed; ramming** *vt* **1** DRIVE : hincar, clavar <he rammed it into the ground : lo hincó en la tierra> **2** SMASH : estrellar, embestir — *vi* COLLIDE : chocar (contra), estrellarse

ram[2] *n* **1** : carnero *m* (animal) **2 battering ram** : ariete *m*

RAM [ˈræm] *n* : RAM *f*

ramble[1] [ˈræmbəl] *vi* **-bled; -bling 1** WANDER : pasear, deambular **2 to ramble on** : divagar, perder el hilo **3** SPREAD : trepar (dícese de una planta)

ramble[2] *n* : paseo *m,* excursión *f*

rambler [ˈræmblər] *n* **1** WALKER : excursionista *mf* **2** ROSE : rosa *f* trepadora

rambunctious [ræmˈbʌŋkʃəs] *adj* UNRULY : alborotado

ramification [ˌræməfəˈkeɪʃən] *n* : ramificación *f*

ramify [ˈræməˌfaɪ] *vi* **-fied; -fying** : ramificarse

ramp [ˈræmp] *n* : rampa *f*

rampage[1] [ˈræmˌpeɪʤ, ræmˈpeɪʤ] *vi* **-paged; -paging** : andar arrasando todo, correr destrozando

rampage[2] [ˈræmˌpeɪʤ] *n* : alboroto *m,* frenesí *m* (de violencia)

rampant [ˈræmpənt] *adj* : desenfrenado

rampart [ˈræmˌpɑrt] *n* : terraplén *m,* muralla *f*

ramrod [ˈræmˌrɑd] *n* : baqueta *f*

ramshackle [ˈræmˌʃækəl] *adj* : destartalado

ran → **run**

ranch [ˈræntʃ] *n* **1** : hacienda *f,* rancho *m,* finca *f* ganadera **2** FARM : granja *f* <fruit ranch : granja de frutas>

rancher [ˈræntʃər] *n* : estanciero *m,* -ra *f;* ranchero *m,* -ra *f*

rancid [ˈræntsɪd] *adj* : rancio

rancor [ˈræŋkər] *n* : rencor *m*

random [ˈrændəm] *adj* **1** : fortuito, aleatorio **2 at ~** : al azar — **randomly** *adv*

rang → **ring**

range[1] [ˈreɪnʤ] *v* **ranged; ranging** *vt* ARRANGE : alinear, ordenar, arreglar — *vi* **1** ROAM : deambular <to range through the town : deambular por el pueblo> **2** EXTEND : extenderse <the results range widely : los resultados se extienden mucho> **3** VARY : variar <discounts range from 20% to 40% : los descuentos varían entre 20% y 40%>

range[2] *n* **1** ROW : fila *f,* hilera *f* <a mountain range : una cordillera> **2** GRASSLAND : pradera *f,* pampa *f* **3** STOVE : cocina *f* **4** VARIETY : variedad *f,* gama *f* **5** SPHERE : ámbito *m,* esfera *f,* campo *m* **6** REACH : registro *m* (de la voz), alcance *m* (de un arma de fuego) **7 shooting range** : campo *m* de tiro

ranger [ˈreɪnʤər] *n or* **forest ranger** : guardabosque *mf*

rangy [ˈreɪnʤi] *adj* **rangier; -est** : alto y delgado

rank[1] [ˈræŋk] *vt* **1** RANGE : alinear, ordenar, poner en fila **2** CLASSIFY : clasificar — *vi* **1 to rank above** : ser superior a **2 to rank among** : encontrarse entre, figurar entre

rank[2] *adj* **1** LUXURIANT : lozano, exuberante (dícese de una planta) **2** SMELLY : fétido, maloliente **3** OUTRIGHT : completo, absoluto <a rank injustice : una injusticia manifiesta>

rank[3] *n* **1** LINE, ROW : fila *f* <to close ranks : cerrar filas> **2** GRADE, POSITION : grado *m,* rango *m* (militar) <to pull rank : abusar de su autoridad> **3** CLASS : categoría *f,* clase *f* **4 ranks** *npl* : soldados *mpl* rasos

rank and file *n* **1** RANKS : soldados *mpl* rasos **2** : bases *fpl* (de un partido, etc.)

rankle [ˈræŋkəl] *v* **-kled; -kling** *vi* : doler — *vt* : irritar, herir

ransack [ˈrænˌsæk] *vt* : revolver, desvalijar, registrar de arriba abajo

ransom[1] [ˈræntsəm] *vt* : rescatar, pagar un rescate por

ransom[2] *n* : rescate *m*

rant [ˈrænt] *vi or* **to rant and rave** : despotricar, desvariar

rap[1] [ˈræp] *v* **rapped; rapping** *vt* **1** KNOCK : golpetear, dar un golpe en **2** CRITICIZE : criticar — *vi* **1** CHAT : charlar, cotorrear *fam* **2** KNOCK : dar un golpe

rap[2] *n* **1** BLOW, KNOCK : golpe *m,* golpecito *m* **2** CHAT : charla *f* **3** *or* **rap music** : rap *m* **4 to take the rap** : pagar el pato *fam*

rapacious [rəˈpeɪʃəs] *adj* **1** GREEDY : avaricioso, codicioso **2** PREDATORY : rapaz, de rapiña **3** RAVENOUS : voraz

rape[1] [ˈreɪp] *vt* **raped; raping** : violar

rape[2] *n* **1** : colza *f* (planta) **2** : violación *f* (de una persona)

rapid [ˈræpɪd] *adj* : rápido — **rapidly** *adv*
rapidity [rəˈpɪdət̬i] *n* : rapidez *f*
rapids [ˈræpɪdz] *npl* : rápidos *mpl*
rapier [ˈreɪpiər] *n* : estoque *m*
rapist [ˈreɪpɪst] *n* : violador *m,* -dora *f*
rapport [ræˈpor] *n* : relación *f* armoniosa, entendimiento *m*
rapt [ˈræpt] *adj* : absorto, embelesado
rapture [ˈræptʃər] *n* : éxtasis *m*
rapturous [ˈræptʃərəs] *adj* : extasiado, embelesado
rare [ˈrær] *adj* **rarer; rarest 1** RAREFIED : enrarecido **2** FINE : excelente, excepcional <a rare talent : un talento excepcional> **3** UNCOMMON : raro, poco común **4** : poco cocido (dícese de la carne)
rarefy [ˈrærəˌfaɪ] *vt* **-fied; -fying** : rarificar, enrarecer
rarely [ˈrærli] *adv* SELDOM : pocas veces, rara vez
raring [ˈrærən, -ɪŋ] *adj* : lleno de entusiasmo, con muchas ganas
rarity [ˈrærət̬i] *n, pl* **-ties** : rareza *f*
rascal [ˈræskəl] *n* : pillo *m,* -lla *f;* pícaro *m,* -ra *f*
rash¹ [ˈræʃ] *adj* : imprudente, precipitado — **rashly** *adv*
rash² *n* : sarpullido *m,* erupción *f*
rashness [ˈræʃnəs] *n* : precipitación *f,* impetuosidad *f*
rasp¹ [ˈræsp] *vt* **1** SCRAPE : raspar, escofinar **2 to rasp out** : decir en voz áspera
rasp² *n* : escofina *f*
raspberry [ˈræzˌbɛri] *n, pl* **-ries** : frambuesa *f*
rat [ˈræt] *n* : rata *f*
ratchet [ˈrætʃət] *n* : trinquete *m*
rate¹ [ˈreɪt] *vt* **rated; rating 1** CONSIDER, REGARD : considerar, estimar **2** DESERVE : merecer
rate² *n* **1** PACE, SPEED : velocidad *f,* ritmo *m* <at this rate : a este paso> **2** : índice *m,* tasa *f* <birth rate : índice de natalidad> <interest rate : tasa de interés> **3** CHARGE, PRICE : precio *m,* tarifa *f*
rather [ˈræðər, ˈrʌ-, ˈrɑ-] *adv* **1** (*indicating preference*) <she would rather stay in the house : preferiría quedarse en casa> <I'd rather not : mejor que no> **2** (*indicating preciseness*) <my father, or rather my stepfather : mi padre, o mejor dicho mi padrastro> **3** INSTEAD : sino que, más que, al contrario <I'm not pleased; rather I'm disappointed : no estoy satisfecho, sino desilusionado> **4** SOMEWHAT : algo, un tanto <rather strange : un poco extraño> **5** QUITE : bastante <rather difficult : bastante difícil>
ratification [ˌræt̬əfəˈkeɪʃən] *n* : ratificación *f*
ratify [ˈræt̬əˌfaɪ] *vt* **-fied; -fying** : ratificar
rating [ˈreɪt̬ɪŋ] *n* **1** STANDING : clasificación *f,* posición *f* **2 ratings** *npl* : índice *m* de audiencia
ratio [ˈreɪʃio] *n, pl* **-tios** : proporción *f,* relación *f*
ration¹ [ˈræʃən, ˈreɪʃən] *vt* : racionar
ration² *n* **1** : ración *f* **2 rations** *npl* PROVISIONS : víveres *mpl*
rational [ˈræʃənəl] *adj* : racional, razonable, lógico — **rationally** *adv*
rationale [ˌræʃəˈnæl] *n* **1** EXPLANATION : explicación *f* **2** BASIS : base *f,* razones *fpl*
rationalization [ˌræʃənələˈzeɪʃən] *n* : racionalización *f*
rationalize [ˈræʃənəˌlaɪz] *vt* **-ized; -izing** : racionalizar
rattle¹ [ˈræt̬əl] *v* **-tled; -tling** *vi* **1** CLATTER : traquetear, hacer ruido **2 to rattle on** CHATTER : parlotear *fam* — *vt* **1** : hacer sonar, agitar <the wind rattled the door : el viento sacudió la puerta> **2** DISCONCERT, WORRY : desconcertar, poner nervioso **3 to rattle off** : despachar, recitar, decir de corrido
rattle² *n* **1** CLATTER : traqueteo *m,* ruido *m* **2** *or* **baby's rattle** : sonajero *m* **3** : cascabel *m* (de una culebra)
rattler [ˈræt̬ələr] → **rattlesnake**
rattlesnake [ˈræt̬əlˌsneɪk] *n* : serpiente *f* de cascabel
ratty [ˈræt̬i] *adj* **rattier; -est** : raído, andrajoso
raucous [ˈrɔkəs] *adj* **1** HOARSE : ronco **2** BOISTEROUS : escandaloso, bullicioso — **raucously** *adv*
ravage¹ [ˈrævɪdʒ] *vt* **-aged; -aging** : devastar, arrasar, hacer estragos
ravage² *n* : destrozo *m,* destrucción *f* <the ravages of war : los estragos de la guerra>
rave [ˈreɪv] *vi* **raved; raving 1** : delirar, desvariar <to rave like a maniac : desvariar como un loco> **2 to rave about** : hablar con entusiasmo sobre, entusiasmarse por
ravel [ˈrævəl] *v* **-eled** *or* **-elled; -eling** *or* **-elling** *vt* UNRAVEL : desenredar, desenmarañar — *vi* FRAY : deshilacharse
raven [ˈreɪvən] *n* : cuervo *m*
ravenous [ˈrævənəs] *adj* : hambriento, voraz — **ravenously** *adv*
ravine [rəˈviːn] *n* : barranco *m,* quebrada *f*
ravish [ˈrævɪʃ] *vt* **1** PLUNDER : saquear **2** ENCHANT : embelesar, cautivar, encantar
raw [ˈrɔ] *adj* **rawer; rawest 1** UNCOOKED : crudo **2** UNTREATED : sin tratar, sin refinar, puro <raw data : datos en bruto> <raw materials : materias primas> **3** INEXPERIENCED : novato, inexperto **4** OPEN : abierto, en carne viva <a raw sore : una llaga abierta> **5** : frío y húmedo <a raw day : un día crudo> **6** UNFAIR : injusto <a raw deal : un trato injusto, una injusticia>

rawhide [ˈrɔ,haɪd] *n* : cuero *m* sin curtir

ray [ˈreɪ] *n* **1** : rayo *m* (de la luz, etc.) <a ray of hope : un resquicio de esperanza> **2** : raya *f* (pez)

rayon [ˈreɪ,ɑn] *n* : rayón *m*

raze [ˈreɪz] *vt* **razed; razing** : arrasar, demoler

razor [ˈreɪzər] *n* **1 straight razor** : navaja *f* (de afeitar) **2 safety razor** : maquinilla *f* de afeitar, rastrillo *m Mex*

reach¹ [ˈriːtʃ] *vt* **1** EXTEND : extender, alargar <to reach out one's hand : extender la mano> **2** : alcanzar <I couldn't reach the apple : no pude alcanzar la manzana> **3** : llegar a, llegar hasta <the shadow reached the wall : la sombra llegó hasta la pared> **4** CONTACT : contactar, ponerse en contacto con — *vi* **1** *or* **to reach out** : extender la mano **2** STRETCH : extenderse **3 to reach for** : tratar de agarrar

reach² *n* : alcance *m,* extensión *f*

react [riˈækt] *vi* : reaccionar

reaction [riˈækʃən] *n* : reacción *f*

reactionary¹ [riˈækʃə,nɛri] *adj* : reaccionario

reactionary² *n, pl* **-ries** : reaccionario *m,* -ria *f*

reactor [riˈæktər] *n* : reactor *m* <nuclear reactor : reactor nuclear>

read¹ [ˈriːd] *v* **read** [ˈrɛd]; **reading** *vt* **1** : leer <to read a story : leer un cuento> **2** INTERPRET : interpretar <it can be read two ways : se puede interpretar de dos maneras> **3** : decir, poner <the sign read ‘‘No smoking’’ : el letrero decía ‘‘No Fumar’’> **4** : marcar <the thermometer reads 70° : el termómetro marca 70°> — *vi* **1** : leer <he can read : sabe leer> **2** SAY : decir <the list reads as follows : la lista dice lo siguiente>

read² *n* **to be a good read** : ser una lectura amena

readable [ˈriːdəbəl] *adj* : legible — **readably** [-bli] *adv*

reader [ˈriːdər] *n* : lector *m,* -tora *f*

readily [ˈrɛdəli] *adv* **1** WILLINGLY : de buena gana, con gusto **2** EASILY : fácilmente, con facilidad

readiness [ˈrɛdinəs] *n* **1** WILLINGNESS : buena disposición *f* **2 to be in readiness** : estar preparado

reading [ˈriːdɪŋ] *n* : lectura *f*

readjust [,riːəˈdʒʌst] *vt* : reajustar — *vi* : volverse a adaptar

readjustment [,riːəˈdʒʌstmənt] *n* : reajuste *m*

ready¹ [ˈrɛdi] *vt* **readied; readying** : preparar

ready² *adj* **readier; -est 1** PREPARED : listo, preparado **2** WILLING : dispuesto **3** : a punto de <ready to cry : a punto de llorar> **4** AVAILABLE : disponible <ready cash : efectivo> **5** QUICK : vivo, agudo <a ready wit : un ingenio agudo>

ready–made [ˈrɛdiˈmeɪd] *adj* : preparado, confeccionado

reaffirm [,riːəˈfərm] *vt* : reafirmar

real¹ [ˈriːl] *adv* VERY : muy <we had a real good time : lo pasamos muy bien>

real² *adj* **1** : inmobilario <real property : bien inmueble, bien raíz> **2** GENUINE : auténtico, genuino **3** ACTUAL, TRUE : real, verdadero <a real friend : un verdadero amigo> **4 for real** SERIOUSLY : de veras, de verdad

real estate *n* : propiedad *f* inmobiliaria, bienes *mpl* raíces

realign [,riːəˈlaɪn] *vt* : realinear

realignment [,riːəˈlaɪnmənt] *n* : realineamiento *m*

realism [ˈriːə,lɪzəm] *n* : realismo *m*

realist [ˈriːəlɪst] *n* : realista *mf*

realistic [,riːəˈlɪstɪk] *adj* : realista

realistically [,riːəˈlɪstɪkli] *adv* : de manera realista

reality [riˈæləṭi] *n, pl* **-ties** : realidad *f*

realization [,riːələˈzeɪʃən] *n* : realización *f*

realize [ˈriːə,laɪz] *vt* **-ized; -izing 1** ACCOMPLISH : realizar, llevar a cabo **2** GAIN : obtener, realizar, sacar <to realize a profit : realizar beneficios> **3** UNDERSTAND : darse cuenta de, saber

really [ˈrɪli, ˈriː-] *adv* **1** ACTUALLY : de verdad, en realidad **2** TRULY : verdaderamente, realmente **3** FRANKLY : francamente, en serio

realm [ˈrɛlm] *n* **1** KINGDOM : reino *m* **2** SPHERE : esfera *f,* campo *m*

ream¹ [ˈriːm] *vt* : escariar

ream² *n* **1** : resma *f* (de papel) **2 reams** *npl* LOADS : montones *mpl*

reap [ˈriːp] *v* : cosechar

reaper [ˈriːpər] *n* **1** : cosechador *m,* -dora *f* (persona) **2** : cosechadora *f* (máquina)

reappear [,riːəˈpɪr] *vi* : reaparecer

reappearance [,riːəˈpɪrənts] *n* : reaparición *f*

rear¹ [ˈrɪr] *vt* **1** LIFT, RAISE : levantar **2** BREED, BRING UP : criar — *vi or* **to rear up** : encabritarse

rear² *adj* : trasero, posterior, de atrás

rear³ *n* **1** BACK : parte *f* de atrás <to bring up the rear : cerrar la marcha> **2** *or* **rear end** : trasero *m*

rear admiral *n* : contraalmirante *mf*

rearrange [,riːəˈreɪndʒ] *vt* **-ranged; -ranging** : colocar de otra manera, volver a arreglar, reorganizar

reason¹ [ˈriːzən] *vt* THINK : pensar — *vi* : razonar <I can't reason with her : no puedo razonar con ella>

reason² *n* **1** CAUSE, GROUND : razón *f,* motivo *m* <the reason for his trip : el motivo de su viaje> <for this reason : por esta razón, por lo cual> <the reason why : la razón por la cual, el porqué> **2** SENSE : razón *f* <to lose

one's reason : perder los sesos> <to listen to reason : avenirse a razones>
reasonable [ˈriːzənəbəl] *adj* **1** SENSIBLE : razonable **2** INEXPENSIVE : barato, económico
reasonably [ˈriːzənəbli] *adv* **1** SENSIBLY : razonablemente **2** FAIRLY : bastante
reasoning [ˈriːzənɪŋ] *n* : razonamiento *m,* raciocinio *m,* argumentos *mpl*
reassess [ˌriːəˈsɛs] *vt* : revaluar, reconsiderar
reassurance [ˌriːəˈʃʊrənts] *n* : consuelo *m,* palabras *fpl* alentadoras
reassure [ˌriːəˈʃʊr] *vt* **-sured; -suring** : tranquilizar
reawaken [ˌriːəˈweɪkən] *vt* : volver a despertar, reavivar
rebate [ˈriːˌbeɪt] *n* : reembolso *m,* devolución *f*
rebel[1] [rɪˈbɛl] *vi* **-belled; -belling** : rebelarse, sublevarse
rebel[2] [ˈrɛbəl] *adj* : rebelde
rebel[3] [ˈrɛbəl] *n* : rebelde *mf*
rebellion [rɪˈbɛljən] *n* : rebelión *f*
rebellious [rɪˈbɛljəs] *adj* : rebelde
rebelliousness [rɪˈbɛljəsnəs] *n* : rebeldía *f*
rebirth [ˌriːˈbərθ] *n* : renacimiento *m*
rebound[1] [ˈriːˌbaʊnd, ˌriːˈbaʊnd] *vi* : rebotar
rebound[2] [ˈriːˌbaʊnd] *n* : rebote *m*
rebuff[1] [riˈbʌf] *vt* : desairar, rechazar
rebuff[2] *n* : desaire *m,* rechazo *m*
rebuild [ˌriːˈbɪld] *vt* **-built** [-ˈbɪlt]; **-building** : reconstruir
rebuke[1] [riˈbjuːk] *vt* **-buked; -buking** : reprender, regañar
rebuke[2] *n* : reprimenda *f,* reproche *m*
rebut [riˈbʌt] *vt* **-butted; -butting** : rebatir, refutar
rebuttal [riˈbʌtəl] *n* : refutación *f*
recalcitrant [riˈkælsətrənt] *adj* : recalcitrante
recall[1] [riˈkɔl] *vt* **1** : llamar, retirar <recalled to active duty : llamado al servicio activo> **2** REMEMBER : recordar, acordarse de **3** REVOKE : revocar
recall[2] [riˈkɔl, ˈriːˌkɔl] *n* **1** : retirada *f* (de personas o mercancías) **2** MEMORY : memoria *f* <to have total recall : poder recordar todo>
recant [riˈkænt] *vt* : retractarse de — *vi* : retractarse, renegar
recapitulate [ˌriːkəˈpɪtʃəˌleɪt] *v* **-lated; -lating** : resumir, recapitular
recapture [ˌriːˈkæptʃər] *vt* **-tured; -turing 1** REGAIN : volver a tomar, reconquistar **2** RELIVE : revivir (la juventud, etc.)
recede [riˈsiːd] *vi* **-ceded; -ceding 1** WITHDRAW : retirarse, retroceder **2** FADE : desvanecerse, alejarse **3** SLANT : inclinarse **4 to have a receding hairline** : tener entradas
receipt [riˈsiːt] *n* **1** : recibo *m* **2 receipts** *npl* : ingresos *mpl,* entradas *fpl*
receivable [riˈsiːvəbəl] *adj* **accounts receivable** : cuentas por cobrar
receive [riˈsiːv] *vt* **-ceived; -ceiving 1** GET : recibir <to receive a letter : recibir una carta> <to receive a blow : recibir un golpe> **2** WELCOME : acoger, recibir <to receive guests : tener invitados> **3** : recibir, captar (señales de radio)
receiver [riˈsiːvər] *n* **1** : receptor *m,* -tora *f* (en futbol americano) **2** : receptor *m* (de radio o televisión) **3 telephone receiver** : auricular *m*
recent [ˈriːsənt] *adj* : reciente — **recently** *adv*
receptacle [riˈsɛptɪkəl] *n* : receptáculo *m,* recipiente *m*
reception [riˈsɛpʃən] *n* : recepción *f*
receptionist [riˈsɛpʃənɪst] *n* : recepcionista *mf*
receptive [riˈsɛptɪv] *adj* : receptivo
receptivity [ˌriːˌsɛpˈtɪvət̬i] *n* : receptividad *f*
recess[1] [ˈriːˌsɛs, rɪˈsɛs] *vt* **1** : poner en un hueco <recessed lighting : iluminación empotrada> **2** ADJOURN : suspender, levantar
recess[2] *n* **1** ALCOVE : hueco *m,* nicho *m* **2** BREAK : receso *m,* descanso *m,* recreo *m* (en el colegio)
recession [riˈsɛʃən] *n* : recesión *f,* depresión *f* económica
recessive [riˈsɛsɪv] *adj* : recesivo
recharge [ˌriːˈtʃɑrdʒ] *vt* **-charged; -charging** : recargar
rechargeable [ˌriːˈtʃɑrdʒəbəl] *adj* : recargable
recipe [ˈrɛsəˌpiː] *n* : receta *f*
recipient [riˈsɪpiənt] *n* : recipiente *mf*
reciprocal [riˈsɪprəkəl] *adj* : recíproco
reciprocate [riˈsɪprəˌkeɪt] *vi* **-cated; -cating** : reciprocar
reciprocity [ˌrɛsəˈprɑsət̬i] *n, pl* **-ties** : reciprocidad *f*
recital [riˈsaɪt̬əl] *n* **1** PERFORMANCE : recital *m* **2** ENUMERATION : relato *m,* enumeración *f*
recitation [ˌrɛsəˈteɪʃən] *n* : recitación *f*
recite [riˈsaɪt] *vt* **-cited; -citing 1** : recitar (un poema, etc.) **2** RECOUNT : narrar, relatar, enumerar
reckless [ˈrɛkləs] *adj* : imprudente, temerario — **recklessly** *adv*
recklessness [ˈrɛkləsnəs] *n* : imprudencia *f,* temeridad *f*
reckon [ˈrɛkən] *vt* **1** CALCULATE : calcular, contar **2** CONSIDER : considerar
reckoning [ˈrɛkənɪŋ] *n* **1** CALCULATION : cálculo *m* **2** SETTLEMENT : ajuste *m* de cuentas <day of reckoning : día del juicio final>
reclaim [riˈkleɪm] *vt* **1** : ganar, sanear <to reclaim marshy land : sanear las tierras pantanosas> **2** RECOVER : recobrar, reciclar <to reclaim old tires : reciclar llantas desechadas> **3** REGAIN : reclamar, recuperar <to reclaim one's rights : reclamar uno sus derechos>

recline [ri'klaɪn] *vi* **-clined; -clining 1** LEAN : reclinarse **2** REPOSE : recostarse

recluse ['rɛ,kluːs, ri'kluːs] *n* : solitario *m*, -ria *f*

recognition [,rɛkɪg'nɪʃən] *n* : reconocimiento *m*

recognizable ['rɛkəg,naɪzəbəl] *adj* : reconocible

recognize ['rɛkɪg,naɪz] *vt* **-nized; -nizing** : reconocer

recoil[1] [ri'kɔɪl] *vi* : retroceder, dar un culatazo

recoil[2] ['riː,kɔɪl, ri'-] *n* : retroceso *m*, culatazo *m*

recollect [,rɛkə'lɛkt] *v* : recordar

recollection [,rɛkə'lɛkʃən] *n* : recuerdo *m*

recommend [,rɛkə'mɛnd] *vt* **1** : recomendar <she recommended the medicine : recomendó la medicina> **2** ADVISE, COUNSEL : aconsejar, recomendar

recommendation [,rɛkəmən'deɪʃən] *n* : recomendación *f*

recompense[1] ['rɛkəm,pɛnts] *vt* **-pensed; -pensing** : indemnizar, recompensar

recompense[2] *n* : indemnización *f*, compensación *f*

reconcile ['rɛkən,saɪl] *v* **-ciled; -ciling** *vt* **1** : reconciliar (personas), conciliar (ideas, etc.) **2 to reconcile oneself to** : resignarse a — *vi* MAKE UP : reconciliarse, hacer las paces

reconciliation [,rɛkən,sɪli'eɪʃən] *n* : reconciliación *f* (con personas), conciliación *f* (con ideas, etc.)

recondite ['rɛkən,daɪt, ri'kɑn-] *adj* : recóndito, abstruso

recondition [,riːkən'dɪʃən] *vt* : reacondicionar

reconnaissance [ri'kɑnəzənts, -sənts] *n* : reconocimiento *m*

reconnoiter *or* **reconnoitre** [,riːkə'nɔɪtər, ,rɛkə-] *v* **-tered** *or* **-tred; -tering** *or* **-tring** *vt* : reconocer — *vi* : hacer un reconocimiento

reconsider [,riːkən'sɪdər] *vt* : reconsiderar, repensar

reconsideration [,riːkən,sɪdə'reɪʃən] *n* : reconsideración *f*

reconstruct [,riːkən'strʌkt] *vt* : reconstruir

record[1] [ri'kɔrd] *vt* **1** WRITE DOWN : anotar, apuntar **2** REGISTER : registrar, hacer constar **3** INDICATE : marcar (una temperatura, etc.) **4** TAPE : grabar

record[2] ['rɛkərd] *n* **1** DOCUMENT : registro *m*, documento *m* oficial **2** HISTORY : historial *m* <a good academic record : un buen historial académico> <criminal record : antecedentes penales> **3** : récord *m* <the world record : el récord mundial> **4** : disco *m* (de música, etc.) <to make a record : grabar un disco>

recorder [ri'kɔrdər] *n* **1** : flauta *f* dulce (instrumento de viento) **2 tape recorder** : grabadora *f*

recount[1] [ri'kaʊnt] *vt* **1** NARRATE : narrar, relatar **2** : volver a contar (votos, etc.)

recount[2] ['riː,kaʊnt, ,ri'-] *n* : recuento *m*

recoup [ri'kuːp] *vt* : recuperar, recobrar

recourse ['riː,kors, ri'-] *n* : recurso *m* <to have recourse to : recurrir a>

recover [ri'kʌvər] *vt* REGAIN : recobrar — *vi* RECUPERATE : recuperarse

recovery [ri'kʌvəri] *n, pl* **-eries** : recuperación *f*

re–create [,riːkri'eɪt] *vt* **-ated; -ating** : recrear

recreation [,rɛkri'eɪʃən] *n* : recreo *m*, esparcimiento *m*, diversión *f*

recreational [,rɛkri'eɪʃənəl] *adj* : recreativo, de recreo

recrimination [ri,krɪmə'neɪʃən] *n* : recriminación *f*

recruit[1] [ri'kruːt] *vt* : reclutar

recruit[2] *n* : recluta *mf*

recruitment [ri'kruːtmənt] *n* : reclutamiento *m*, alistamiento *m*

rectal ['rɛktəl] *adj* : rectal

rectangle ['rɛk,tæŋgəl] *n* : rectángulo *m*

rectangular [rɛk'tæŋgjələr] *adj* : rectangular

rectify ['rɛktə,faɪ] *vt* **-fied; -fying** : rectificar

rectitude ['rɛktə,tuːd, -,tjuːd] *n* : rectitud *f*

rector ['rɛktər] *n* : rector *m*, -tora *f*

rectory ['rɛktəri] *n, pl* **-ries** : rectoría *f*

rectum ['rɛktəm] *n, pl* **-tums** *or* **-ta** [-tə] : recto *m*

recuperate [ri'kuːpə,reɪt, -'kjuː-] *v* **-ated; -ating** *vt* : recuperar — *vi* : recuperarse, restablecerse

recuperation [ri,kuːpə'reɪʃən, -,kjuː-] *n* : recuperación *f*

recur [ri'kər] *vi* **-curred; -curring** : volver a ocurrir, volver a producirse, repetirse

recurrence [ri'kərənts] *n* : repetición *f*, reaparición *f*

recurrent [ri'kərənt] *adj* : recurrente, que se repite

recycle [ri'saɪkəl] *vt* **-cled; -cling** : reciclar

red[1] ['rɛd] *adj* **1** : rojo, colorado <to be red in the face : ponerse colorado> <to have red hair : ser pelirrojo> **2** COMMUNIST : rojo, comunista

red[2] *n* **1** : rojo *m*, colorado *m* **2 Red** COMMUNIST : comunista *mf*

red blood cell *n* : glóbulo *m* rojo

red–blooded ['rɛd'blʌdəd] *adj* : vigoroso

redcap ['rɛd,kæp] → **porter**

redden ['rɛdən] *vt* : enrojecer — *vi* BLUSH : enrojecerse, ruborizarse

reddish ['rɛdɪʃ] *adj* : rojizo

redecorate [,riː'dɛkə,reɪt] *vt* **-rated; -rating** : renovar, pintar de nuevo

redeem [ri'di:m] *vt* **1** RESCUE, SAVE : rescatar, salvar **2** : desempeñar <she redeemed it from the pawnshop : lo desempeñó de la casa de empeños> **3** : redimir (en religión) **4** : canjear, vender <to redeem coupons : canjear cupones>
redeemer [ri'di:mər] *n* : redentor *m*, -tora *f*
redemption [ri'dɛmpʃən] *n* : redención *f*
redesign [ˌri:di'zaɪn] *vt* : rediseñar
red–handed ['rɛd'hændəd] *adj* : con las manos en la masa
redhead ['rɛdˌhɛd] *n* : pelirrojo *m*, -ja *f*
red–hot ['rɛd'hɑt] *adj* **1** : candente **2** ARDENT : ardiente, fervoroso
rediscover [ˌri:di'skʌvər] *vt* : redescubrir
redistribute [ˌri:di'strɪˌbju:t] *vt* **-uted; -uting** : redistribuir
red–letter ['rɛd'lɛt̬ər] *adj* **red–letter day** : día *m* memorable
redness ['rɛdnəs] *n* : rojez *f*
redo [ˌri:'du:] *vt* **-did** [-dɪd]; **-done** [-'dʌn]; **-doing 1** : hacer de nuevo **2** → **redecorate**
redolence ['rɛdələnts] *n* : fragancia *f*
redolent ['rɛdələnt] *adj* **1** FRAGRANT : fragante, oloroso **2** SUGGESTIVE : evocador
redouble [ri'dʌbəl] *vt* **-bled; -bling** : redoblar, intensificar (esfuerzos, etc.)
redoubtable [rɛ'daʊt̬əbəl] *adj* : temible
redress [ri'drɛs] *vt* : reparar, remediar, enmendar
red snapper *n* : pargo *m*, huachinango *m Mex*
red tape *n* : papeleo *m*
reduce [ri'du:s, -'dju:s] *v* **-duced; -ducing** *vt* **1** LESSEN : reducir, disminuir, rebajar (precios) **2** DEMOTE : bajar de categoría, degradar **3 to be reduced to** : verse rebajado a, verse forzado a **4 to reduce someone to tears** : hacer llorar a alguien — *vi* SLIM : adelgazar
reduction [ri'dʌkʃən] *n* : reducción *f*, rebaja *f*
redundant [ri'dʌndənt] *adj* : superfluo, redundante
redwood ['rɛdˌwʊd] *n* : secoya *f*
reed ['ri:d] *n* **1** : caña *f*, carrizo *m*, junco *m* **2** : lengüeta *f* (para instrumentos de viento)
reef ['ri:f] *n* : arrecife *m*, escollo *m*
reek[1] ['ri:k] *vi* : apestar
reek[2] *n* : hedor *m*
reel ['ri:l] *vt* **1 to reel in** : enrollar, sacar (un pez) del agua **2 to reel off** : recitar de un tirón — *vi* **1** SPIN, WHIRL : girar, dar vueltas **2** STAGGER : tambalearse
reel[2] *n* **1** : carrete *m* (de pescar etc.), rollo *m* (de fotos) **2** : baile *m* escocés **3** STAGGER : tambaleo *m*
reelect [ˌri:ɪ'lɛkt] *vt* : reelegir
reenact [ˌri:ɪ'nækt] *vt* : representar de nuevo, reconstruir
reenter [ˌri:'ɛntər] *vt* : volver a entrar
reestablish [ˌri:ɪ'stæblɪʃ] *vt* : restablecer
reevaluate [ˌri:ɪ'væljʊˌeɪt] *vt* **-ated; -ating** : revaluar
reevaluation [ˌri:ɪˌvæljʊ'eɪʃən] *n* : revaluación *f*
reexamine [ˌri:ɪg'zæmən, -ɛg-] *vt* **-ined; -ining** : volver a examinar, reexaminar
refer [ri'fər] *v* **-ferred; -ferring** *vt* DIRECT, SEND : remitir, enviar <to refer a patient to a specialist : enviar a un paciente a un especialista> — *vi* **to refer to** MENTION : referirse a, aludir a
referee[1] [ˌrɛfə'ri:] *v* **-eed; -eeing** : arbitrar
referee[2] *n* : árbitro *m*, -tra *f*; réferi *mf*
reference ['rɛfrənts, 'rɛfə-] *n* **1** ALLUSION : referencia *f*, alusión *f* <to make reference to : hacer referencia a> **2** CONSULTATION : consulta *f* <for future reference : para futuras consultas> **3** *or* **reference book** : libro *m* de consulta **4** TESTIMONIAL : informe *m*, referencia *f*, recomendación *f*
referendum [ˌrɛfə'rɛndəm] *n, pl* **-da** [-də] *or* **-dums** : referéndum *m*
refill[1] [ˌri:'fɪl] *vt* : rellenar
refill[2] ['ri:ˌfɪl] *n* : recambio *m*
refinance [ˌri:'faɪˌnænts] *vt* **-nanced; -nancing** : refinanciar
refine [ri'faɪn] *vt* **-fined; -fining 1** : refinar (azúcar, petróleo, etc.) **2** PERFECT : perfeccionar, pulir
refined [ri'faɪnd] *adj* **1** : refinado (dícese del azúcar, etc.) **2** CULTURED : culto, educado, refinado
refinement [ri'faɪnmənt] *n* : refinamiento *m*, fineza *f*, finura *f*
refinery [ri'faɪnəri] *n, pl* **-eries** : refinería *f*
reflect [ri'flɛkt] *vt* **1** : reflejar <to reflect light : reflejar la luz> <happiness is reflected in her face : la felicidad se refleja en su cara> **2 to reflect that** : pensar que, considerar que — *vi* **1 to reflect on** : reflexionar sobre **2 to reflect badly on** : desacreditar, perjudicar
reflection [ri'flɛkʃən] *n* **1** : reflexión *f*, reflejo *m* (de la luz, de imágenes, etc.) **2** THOUGHT : reflexión *f*, meditación *f*
reflective [ri'flɛktɪv] *adj* **1** THOUGHTFUL : reflexivo, pensativo **2** : reflectante (en física)
reflector [ri'flɛktər] *n* : reflector *m*
reflex ['ri:ˌflɛks] *n* : reflejo *m*
reflexive [ri'flɛksɪv] *adj* : reflexivo <a reflexive verb : un verbo reflexivo>
reform[1] [ri'fɔrm] *vt* : reformar — *vi* : reformarse
reform[2] *n* : reforma *f*
reformation [ˌrɛfər'meɪʃən] *n* : reforma *f* <the Reformation : la Reforma>

reformatory [ri'fɔrmə,tori] *n, pl* **-ries** : reformatorio *m*

reformer [ri'fɔrmər] *n* : reformador *m*, -dora *f*

refract [ri'frækt] *vt* : refractar — *vi* : refractarse

refraction [ri'frækʃən] *n* : refracción *f*

refractory [ri'fræktəri] *adj* OBSTINATE : refractario, obstinado

refrain[1] [ri'freɪn] *vi* **to refrain from** : abstenerse de

refrain[2] *n* : estribillo *m* (en música)

refresh [ri'frɛʃ] *vt* : refrescar <to refresh one's memory : refrescarle la memoria a uno>

refreshment [ri'frɛʃmənt] *n* **1** : refresco *m* **2 refreshments** *npl* : refrigerio *m*

refrigerate [ri'frɪdʒə,reɪt] *vt* **-ated; -ating** : refrigerar

refrigeration [ri,frɪdʒə'reɪʃən] *n* : refrigeración *f*

refrigerator [ri'frɪdʒə,reɪt̬ər] *n* : refrigerador *mf*, nevera *f*

refuel [ri:'fju:əl] *v* **-eled** *or* **-elled; -eling** *or* **-elling** *vi* : repostar — *vt* : llenar de combustible

refuge ['rɛ,fju:dʒ] *n* : refugio *m*

refugee [,rɛfjʊ'dʒi:] *n* : refugiado *m*, -da *f*

refund[1] [ri'fʌnd, 'ri:,fʌnd] *vt* : reembolsar, devolver

refund[2] ['ri:,fʌnd] *n* : reembolso *m*, devolución *f*

refundable [ri'fʌndəbəl] *adj* : reembolsable

refurbish [ri'fərbɪʃ] *vt* : renovar, restaurar

refusal [ri'fju:zəl] *n* : negativa *f*, rechazo *m*, denegación *f* (de una petición)

refuse[1] [ri'fju:z] *vt* **-fused; -fusing 1** REJECT : rechazar, rehusar **2** DENY : negar, rehusar, denegar <to refuse permission : negar el permiso> **3 to refuse to** : negarse a

refuse[2] ['rɛ,fju:s, -,fju:z] *n* : basura *f*, desechos *mpl*, desperdicios *m*

refutation [,rɛfjʊ'teɪʃən] *n* : refutación *f*

refute [ri'fju:t] *vt* **-futed; -futing 1** DENY : desmentir, negar **2** DISPROVE : refutar, rebatir

regain [ri:'geɪn] *vt* **1** RECOVER : recuperar, recobrar **2** REACH : alcanzar <to regain the shore : llegar a la tierra>

regal ['ri:gəl] *adj* : real, regio

regale [ri'geɪl] *vt* **-galed; -galing 1** ENTERTAIN : agasajar, entretener **2** AMUSE, DELIGHT : deleitar, divertir

regalia [ri'geɪljə] *npl* : ropaje *m*, vestiduras *fpl*, adornos *mpl*

regard[1] [ri'gɑrd] *vt* **1** OBSERVE : observar, mirar **2** HEED : tener en cuenta, hacer caso de **3** CONSIDER : considerar **4** RESPECT : respetar <highly regarded : muy estimado> **5 as regards** : en cuanto a, en lo que se refiere a

regard[2] *n* **1** CONSIDERATION : consideración *f* **2** ESTEEM : respeto *m*, estima *f* **3** PARTICULAR : aspecto *m*, sentido *m* <in this regard : en este sentido> **4 regards** *npl* : saludos *mpl*, recuerdos *mpl* **5 with regard to** : con relación a, con respecto a

regarding [ri'gɑrdɪŋ] *prep* : con respecto a, en cuanto a

regardless [ri'gɑrdləs] *adv* : a pesar de todo

regardless of *prep* : a pesar de, sin tener en cuenta <regardless of our mistakes : a pesar de nuestros errores> <regardless of age : sin tener en cuenta la edad>

regenerate [ri'dʒɛnə,reɪt] *v* **-ated; -ating** *vt* : regenerar — *vi* : regenerarse

regeneration [ri,dʒɛnə'reɪʃən] *n* : regeneración *f*

regent ['ri:dʒənt] *n* **1** RULER : regente *mf* **2** : miembro *m* de la junta directiva (de una universidad, etc.)

regime [reɪ'ʒi:m, rɪ-] *n* : régimen *m*

regimen ['rɛdʒəmən] *n* : régimen *m*

regiment[1] ['rɛdʒə,mɛnt] *vt* : reglamentar

regiment[2] ['rɛdʒəmənt] *n* : regimiento *m*

region ['ri:dʒən] *n* **1** : región *f* **2 in the region of** : alrededor de

regional ['ri:dʒənəl] *adj* : regional — **regionally** *adv*

register[1] ['rɛdʒəstər] *vt* **1** RECORD : registrar, inscribir **2** INDICATE : marcar (temperatura, medidas, etc.) **3** REVEAL : manifestar, acusar <to register surprise : acusar sorpresa> **4** : certificar (correo) — *vi* ENROLL : inscribirse, matricularse

register[2] *n* : registro *m*

registrar ['rɛdʒə,strɑr] *n* : registrador *m*, -dora *f* oficial

registration [,rɛdʒə'streɪʃən] *n* **1** REGISTERING : inscripción *f*, matriculación *f*, registro *m* **2** *or* **registration number** : matrícula *f*, número *m* de matrícula

registry ['rɛdʒəstri] *n, pl* **-tries** : registro *m*

regress [ri'grɛs] *vi* : retroceder

regression [ri'grɛʃən] *n* : retroceso *m*, regresión *f*

regressive [ri'grɛsɪv] *adj* : regresivo

regret[1] [ri'grɛt] *vt* **-gretted; -gretting** : arrepentirse de, lamentar <he regrets nothing : no se arrepiente de nada> <I regret to tell you : lamento decirle>

regret[2] *n* **1** REMORSE : arrepentimiento *m*, remordimientos *mpl* **2** SADNESS : pesar *m*, dolor *m* **3 regrets** *npl* : excusas *fpl* <to send one's regrets : excusarse>

regretful [ri'grɛtfəl] *adj* : arrepentido, pesaroso

regretfully [ri'grɛtfəli] *adv* : con pesar

regrettable [ri'grɛt̬əbəl] *adj* : lamentable — **regrettably** [-bli] *adv*

regular[1] [ˈrɛgjələr] *adj* **1** NORMAL : regular, normal, usual **2** STEADY : uniforme, regular <a regular pace : un paso regular> **3** CUSTOMARY, HABITUAL : habitual, de costumbre

regular[2] *n* : cliente *mf* habitual

regularity [ˌrɛgjəˈlærət̬i] *n, pl* **-ties** : regularidad *f*

regularly [ˈrɛgjələrli] *adv* : regularmente, con regularidad

regulate [ˈrɛgjəˌleɪt] *vt* **-lated; -lating** : regular

regulation [ˌrɛgjəˈleɪʃən] *n* **1** REGULATING : regulación *f* **2** RULE : regla *f*, reglamento *m*, norma *f* <safety regulations : reglas de seguridad>

regurgitate [riˈgərdʒəˌteɪt] *v* **-tated; -tating** : regurgitar, vomitar

rehabilitate [ˌriːhəˈbɪləˌteɪt, ˌriːə-] *vt* **-tated; -tating** : rehabilitar

rehabilitation [ˌriːhəˌbɪləˈteɪʃən, ˌriːə-] *n* : rehabilitación *f*

rehearsal [riˈhərsəl] *n* : ensayo *m*

rehearse [riˈhərs] *v* **-hearsed; -hearsing** : ensayar

reheat [ˌriːˈhiːt] *vt* : recalentar

reign[1] [ˈreɪn] *vi* **1** RULE : reinar **2** PREVAIL : reinar, predominar

reign[2] *n* : reinado *m*

reimburse [ˌriːəmˈbərs] *vt* **-bursed; -bursing** : reembolsar

reimbursement [ˌriːəmˈbərsmənt] *n* : reembolso *m*

rein[1] [ˈreɪn] *vt* : refrenar (un caballo)

rein[2] *n* **1** : rienda *f* <to give free rein to : dar rienda suelta a> **2** CHECK : control *m* <to keep a tight rein on : llevar un estricto control de>

reincarnation [ˌriːɪnˌkɑrˈneɪʃən] *n* : reencarnación *f*

reindeer [ˈreɪnˌdɪr] *n* : reno *m*

reinforce [ˌriːənˈfors] *vt* **-forced; -forcing** : reforzar

reinforcement [ˌriːənˈforsmənt] *n* : refuerzo *m*

reinstate [ˌriːənˈsteɪt] *vt* **-stated; -stating 1** : reintegrar, restituir (una persona) **2** RESTORE : restablecer (un servicio, etc.)

reinstatement [ˌriːənˈsteɪtmənt] *n* : reintegración *f*, restitución *f*, restablecimiento *m*

reiterate [riˈɪt̬əˌreɪt] *vt* **-ated; -ating** : reiterar, repetir

reiteration [riˌɪt̬əˈreɪʃən] *n* : reiteración *f*, repetición *f*

reject[1] [riˈdʒɛkt] *vt* : rechazar

reject[2] [ˈriːˌdʒɛkt] *n* : desecho *m* (cosa), persona *f* rechazada

rejection [riˈdʒɛkʃən] *n* : rechazo *m*

rejoice [riˈdʒɔɪs] *vi* **-joiced; -joicing** : alegrarse, regocijarse

rejoin *vt* [ˌriːˈdʒɔɪn] **1** : reincorporarse a, reintegrarse a <he rejoined the firm : se reincorporó a la firma> **2** [riˈ-] REPLY, RETORT : replicar

rejoinder [riˈdʒɔɪndər] *n* : réplica *f*

rejuvenate [riˈdʒuːvəˌneɪt] *vt* **-nated; -nating** : rejuvenecer

rejuvenation [riˌdʒuːvəˈneɪʃən] *n* : rejuvenecimiento *m*

rekindle [ˌriːˈkɪndəl] *vt* **-dled; -dling** : reavivar

relapse[1] [riˈlæps] *vi* **-lapsed; -lapsing** : recaer, volver a caer

relapse[2] [ˈriːˌlæps, riˈlæps] *n* : recaída *f*

relate [riˈleɪt] *v* **-lated; -lating** *vt* **1** TELL : relatar, contar **2** ASSOCIATE : relacionar, asociar <to relate crime to poverty : relacionar la delincuencia a la pobreza> — *vi* **1** CONNECT : conectar, estar relacionado (con) **2** INTERACT : relacionarse (con), llevarse bien (con) **3 to relate to** UNDERSTAND : identificarse con, simpatizar con

related [riˈleɪt̬əd] *adj* : emparentado <to be related to : ser pariente de>

relation [riˈleɪʃən] *n* **1** NARRATION : relato *m*, narración *f* **2** RELATIVE : pariente *mf*, familiar *mf* **3** RELATIONSHIP : relación *f* <in relation to : en relación con, con relación a> **4 relations** *npl* : relaciones *fpl* <public relations : relaciones públicas>

relationship [riˈleɪʃənˌʃɪp] *n* **1** CONNECTION : relación *f* **2** KINSHIP : parentesco *m*

relative[1] [ˈrɛlət̬ɪv] *adj* : relativo — **relatively** *adv*

relative[2] *n* : pariente *mf*, familiar *mf*

relativity [ˌrɛləˈtɪvət̬i] *n, pl* **-ties** : relatividad *f*

relax [riˈlæks] *vt* : relajar, aflojar — *vi* : relajarse

relaxation [ˌriːˌlækˈseɪʃən] *n* **1** RELAXING : relajación *f*, aflojamiento *m* **2** DIVERSION : esparcimiento *m*, distracción *f*

relay[1] [ˈriːˌleɪ, riˈleɪ] *vt* **-layed; -laying** : transmitir

relay[2] [ˈriːˌleɪ] *n* **1** : relevo *m* **2** *or* **relay race** : carrera de relevos

release[1] [riˈliːs] *vt* **-leased; -leasing 1** FREE : liberar, poner en libertad **2** LOOSEN : soltar, aflojar <to release the brake : soltar el freno> **3** RELINQUISH : renunciar a, ceder **4** ISSUE : publicar (un libro), estrenar (una película), sacar (un disco)

release[2] *n* **1** LIBERATION : liberación *f*, puesta *f* en libertad **2** RELINQUISHMENT : cesión *f* (de propiedad, etc.) **3** ISSUE : estreno *m* (de una película), puesta *f* en venta (de un disco), publicación *f* (de un libro) **4** ESCAPE : escape *m*, fuga *f* (de un gas)

relegate [ˈrɛləˌgeɪt] *vt* **-gated; -gating** : relegar

relent [riˈlɛnt] *vi* : ablandarse, ceder

relentless [riˈlɛntləs] *adj* : implacable, sin tregua

relentlessly [riˈlɛntləsli] *adv* : implacablemente

relevance [ˈrɛləvənts] *n* : pertinencia *f*, relación *f*

relevant [ˈrɛləvənt] *adj* : pertinente — **relevantly** *adv*

reliability [ri,laɪə'bɪləti] *n, pl* **-ties 1** : fiabilidad *f,* seguridad *f* (de una cosa) **2** : formalidad *f,* seriedad *f* (de una persona)

reliable [ri'laɪəbəl] *adj* : confiable, fiable, fidedigno, seguro

reliably [ri'laɪəbli] *adv* : sin fallar <to be reliably informed : saber (algo) de fuentes fidedignas>

reliance [ri'laɪən*t*s] *n* **1** DEPENDENCE : dependencia *f* **2** CONFIDENCE : confianza *f*

reliant [ri'laɪənt] *adj* : confiable, dependente

relic ['rɛlɪk] *n* **1** : reliquia *f* **2** VESTIGE : vestigio *m*

relief [ri'liːf] *n* **1** : alivio *m,* desahogo *m* <relief from pain : alivio del dolor> **2** AID, WELFARE : ayuda *f* (benéfica), asistencia *f* social **3** : relieve *m* (en la escultura) <relief map : mapa en relieve> **4** REPLACEMENT : relevo *m*

relieve [ri'liːv] *vt* **-lieved; -lieving 1** ALLEVIATE : aliviar, mitigar <to feel relieved : sentirse aliviado> **2** FREE : liberar, eximir <to relieve someone of responsibility for : eximir a alguien de la responsabilidad de> **3** REPLACE : relevar (a un centinela, etc.) **4** BREAK : romper <to relieve the monotony : romper la monotonía>

religion [ri'lɪdʒən] *n* : religión *f*

religious [ri'lɪdʒəs] *adj* : religioso — **religiously** *adv*

relinquish [ri'lɪŋkwɪʃ, -'lɪn-] *vt* **1** GIVE UP : renunciar a, abandonar **2** RELEASE : soltar

relish[1] ['rɛlɪʃ] *vt* : saborear (comida), disfrutar con (una idea, una perspectiva, etc.)

relish[2] *n* **1** ENJOYMENT : gusto *m,* deleite *m* **2** : salsa *f* (condimento)

relive [,riː'lɪv] *vt* **-lived; -living** : revivir

relocate [,riː'loː,keɪt, ,riːlo'keɪt] *v* **-cated; -cating** *vt* : reubicar, trasladar — *vi* : trasladarse

relocation [,riːlo'keɪʃən] *n* : reubicación *f,* traslado *m*

reluctance [ri'lʌktən*t*s] *n* : renuencia *f,* reticencia *f,* desgana *f*

reluctant [ri'lʌktənt] *adj* : renuente, reacio, reticente

reluctantly [ri'lʌktəntli] *adv* : a regañadientes

rely [ri'laɪ] *vi* **-lied; -lying 1** DEPEND : depender (de), contar (con) **2** TRUST : confiar (en)

remain [ri'meɪn] *vi* **1** : quedar <very little remains : queda muy poco> <the remaining 10 minutes : los 10 minutos que quedan> **2** STAY : quedarse, permanecer **3** CONTINUE : continuar, seguir <to remain the same : continuar siendo igual> **4 to remain to** : quedar por <to remain to be done : quedar por hacer> <it remains to be seen : está por ver>

remainder [ri'meɪndər] *n* : resto *m,* remanente *m*

remains [ri'meɪnz] *npl* : restos *mpl* <mortal remains : restos mortales>

remark[1] [ri'mɑrk] *vt* **1** NOTICE : observar **2** SAY : comentar, observar — *vi* **to remark on** : hacer observaciones sobre

remark[2] *n* : comentario *m,* observación *f*

remarkable [ri'mɑrkəbəl] *adj* : extraordinario, notable — **remarkably** [-bli] *adv*

rematch ['riː,mætʃ] *n* : revancha *f*

remedial [ri'miːdiəl] *adj* : correctivo <remedial classes : clases para alumnos atrasados>

remedy[1] ['rɛmədi] *vt* **-died; -dying** : remediar

remedy[2] *n, pl* **-dies** : remedio *m,* medicamento *m*

remember [ri'mɛmbər] *vt* **1** RECOLLECT : acordarse de, recordar **2** : no olvidar <remember my words : no olvides mis palabras> <to remember to : acordarse de> **3** : dar saludos, dar recuerdos <remember me to her : dale saludos de mi parte> **4** COMMEMORATE : recordar, conmemorar

remembrance [ri'mɛmbrən*t*s] *n* **1** RECOLLECTION : recuerdo *m* <in remembrance of : en conmemoración de> **2** MEMENTO : recuerdo *m*

remind [ri'maɪnd] *vt* : recordar <remind me to do it : recuérdame que lo haga> <she reminds me of Clara : me recuerda de Clara>

reminder [ri'maɪndər] *n* : recuerdo *m*

reminisce [,rɛmə'nɪs] *vi* **-nisced; -niscing** : rememorar los viejos tiempos

reminiscence [,rɛmə'nɪsən*t*s] *n* : recuerdo *m,* reminiscencia *f*

reminiscent [,rɛmə'nɪsənt] *adj* **1** NOSTALGIC : reminiscente, nostálgico **2** SUGGESTIVE : evocador, que recuerda — **reminiscently** *adv*

remiss [ri'mɪs] *adj* : negligente, descuidado, remiso

remission [ri'mɪʃən] *n* : remisión *f*

remit [ri'mɪt] *vt* **-mitted; -mitting 1** PARDON : perdonar **2** SEND : remitir, enviar (dinero)

remittance [ri'mɪtən*t*s] *n* : remesa *f*

remnant ['rɛmnənt] *n* : restos *mpl,* vestigio *m*

remodel [ri'mɑdəl] *vt* **-eled** *or* **-elled; -eling** *or* **-elling** : remodelar, reformar

remonstrate [ri'mɑn,streɪt] *vi* **-strated; -strating** : protestar <to remonstrate with someone : quejarse a alguien>

remorse [ri'mɔrs] *n* : remordimiento *m*

remorseful [ri'mɔrsfəl] *adj* : arrepentido, lleno de remordimiento

remorseless [ri'mɔrsləs] *adj* **1** PITILESS : despiadado **2** RELENTLESS : implacable

remote [ri'mo:t] *adj* **-moter; -est 1** FAR-OFF : lejano, remoto <remote countries : países remotos> <in the remote past : en el pasado lejano> **2** SECLUDED : recóndito **3** : a distancia, remoto <remote control : control remoto> **4** SLIGHT : remoto **5** ALOOF : distante
remotely [ri'mo:tli] *adv* **1** SLIGHTLY : remotamente **2** DISTANTLY : en un lugar remoto, muy lejos
remoteness [ri'mo:tnəs] *n* : lejanía *f*
removable [ri'mu:vəbəl] *adj* : movible, separable
removal [ri'mu:vəl] *n* : separación *f,* extracción *f,* supresión *f* (en algo escrito), eliminación *f* (de problemas, etc.)
remove [ri'mu:v] *vt* **-moved; -moving 1** : quitar, quitarse <remove the lid : quite la tapa> <to remove one's hat : quitarse el sombrero> **2** EXTRACT : sacar, extraer <to remove the contents of : sacar el contenido de> **3** ELIMINATE : eliminar, disipar
remunerate [ri'mju:nə,reɪt] *vt* **-ated; -ating** : remunerar
remuneration [ri,mju:nə'reɪʃən] *n* : remuneración *f*
remunerative [ri'mju:nərət̬ɪv, -,reɪ-] *adj* : remunerativo
renaissance [,rɛnə'sɑnts, -'zɑnts; 'rɛnə,-] *n* : renacimiento *m* <the Renaissance : el Renacimiento>
renal ['ri:nəl] *adj* : renal
rename [,ri:'neɪm] *vt* **-named; -naming** : ponerle un nombre nuevo a
rend ['rɛnd] *vt* **rent** ['rɛnt]; **rending** : desgarrar
render ['rɛndər] *vt* **1** : derretir <to render lard : derretir la manteca> **2** GIVE : prestar, dar <to render aid : prestar ayuda> **3** MAKE : hacer, volver, dejar <it rendered him helpless : lo dejó incapacitado> **4** TRANSLATE : traducir, verter <to render into English : traducir al inglés>
rendezvous ['rɑndɪ,vu:, -deɪ-] *ns & pl* : encuentro *m,* cita *f*
rendition [rɛn'dɪʃən] *n* : interpretación *f*
renegade ['rɛnɪ,geɪd] *n* : renegado *m,* -da *f*
renege [ri'nɪg, -'nɛg] *vi* **-neged; -neging** : no cumplir con (una promesa, etc.)
renew [ri'nu:, -'nju:] *vt* **1** REVIVE : renovar, reavivar <to renew the sentiments of youth : renovar los sentimientos de la juventud> **2** RESUME : reanudar **3** EXTEND : renovar <to renew a subscription : renovar una suscripción>
renewable [ri'nu:əbəl, -'nju:-] *adj* : renovable
renewal [ri'nu:əl, -'nju:-] *n* : renovación *f*
renounce [ri'naʊnts] *vt* **-nounced; -nouncing** : renunciar a
renovate ['rɛnə,veɪt] *vt* **-vated; -vating** : restaurar, renovar
renovation [,rɛnə'veɪʃən] *n* : restauración *f,* renovación *f*
renown [ri'naʊn] *n* : renombre *m,* fama *f,* celebridad *f*
renowned [ri'naʊnd] *adj* : renombrado, célebre, famoso
rent¹ ['rɛnt] *vt* : rentar, alquilar
rent² *n* **1** : renta *f,* alquiler *m* <for rent : se alquila> **2** RIP : rasgadura *f*
rental¹ ['rɛntəl] *adj* RENT : de alquiler
rental² *n* : alquiler *m*
renter ['rɛntər] *n* : arrendatario *m,* -ria *f*
renunciation [ri,nʌntsi'eɪʃən] *n* : renuncia *f*
reopen [,ri:'o:pən] *vt* : volver a abrir
reorganization [,ri:,ɔrgənə'zeɪʃən] *n* : reorganización *f*
reorganize [,ri:'ɔrgən,aɪz] *vt* **-nized; -nizing** : reorganizar
repair¹ [ri'pær] *vt* : reparar, arreglar, refaccionar
repair² *n* **1** : reparación *f,* arreglo *m* **2** CONDITION : estado *m* <in bad repair : en mal estado>
reparation [,rɛpə'reɪʃən] *n* **1** AMENDS : reparación *f* **2 reparations** *npl* COMPENSATION : indemnización *f*
repartee [,rɛpər'ti:, -,pɑr-, -'teɪ] *n* : intercambio *m* de réplicas ingeniosas
repast [ri'pæst, 'ri:,pæst] *n* : comida *f*
repatriate [ri'peɪtri,eɪt] *vt* **-ated; -ating** : repatriar
repay [ri'peɪ] *vt* **-paid; -paying** : pagar, devolver, reembolsar
repeal¹ [ri'pi:l] *vt* : abrogar, revocar
repeal² *n* : abrogación *f,* revocación *f*
repeat¹ [ri'pi:t] *vt* : repetir
repeat² *n* : repetición *f*
repeatedly [ri'pi:t̬ədli] *adv* : repetidamente, repetidas veces
repel [ri'pɛl] *vt* **-pelled; -pelling 1** REPULSE : repeler (un enemigo, etc.) **2** RESIST : repeler **3** REJECT : rechazar, repeler **4** DISGUST : repugnar, darle asco (a alguien)
repellent *or* **repellant** [ri'pɛlənt] *n* : repelente *m*
repent [ri'pɛnt] *vi* : arrepentirse
repentance [ri'pɛntənts] *n* : arrepentimiento *m*
repentant [ri'pɛntənt] *adj* : arrepentido
repercussion [,ri:pər'kʌʃən, ,rɛpər-] *n* : repercusión *f*
repertoire ['rɛpər,twɑr] *n* : repertorio *m*
repertory ['rɛpər,tori] *n, pl* **-ries** : repertorio *m*
repetition [,rɛpə'tɪʃən] *n* : repetición *f*
repetitious [,rɛpə'tɪʃəs] *adj* : repetitivo, reiterativo — **repetitiously** *adv*

repetitive [ri'pɛt̬ət̬ɪv] *adj* : repetitivo, reiterativo

replace [ri'pleɪs] *vt* **-placed; -placing 1** : volver a poner <replace it in the drawer : vuelve a ponerlo en el cajón> **2** SUBSTITUTE : reemplazar, sustituir **3** : reponer <to replace the worn carpet : reponer la alfombra raída>

replaceable [ri'pleɪsəbəl] *adj* : reemplazable

replacement [ri'pleɪsmənt] *n* **1** SUBSTITUTION : reemplazo *m,* sustitución *f* **2** SUBSTITUTE : sustituto *m,* -ta *f;* suplente *mf* (persona) **3 replacement part :** repuesto *m,* pieza *f* de recambio

replenish [ri'plɛnɪʃ] *vt* : rellenar, llenar de nuevo

replenishment [ri'plɛnɪʃmənt] *n* : reabastecimiento *m*

replete [ri'pli:t] *adj* : repleto, lleno

replica ['rɛplɪkə] *n* : réplica *f,* reproducción *f*

reply¹ [ri'plaɪ] *vi* **-plied; -plying :** contestar, responder

reply² *n, pl* **-plies** : respuesta *f,* contestación *f*

report¹ [ri'port] *vt* **1** ANNOUNCE : relatar, anunciar **2 :** dar parte de, informar de, reportar <he reported an accident : dio parte de un accidente> <to report a crime : denunciar un delito> **3 :** informar acerca de (en un periódico, la televisión, etc.) — *vi* **1** : hacer un informe, informar **2 to report for duty :** presentarse, reportarse

report² *n* **1** RUMOR : rumor *m* **2** REPUTATION : reputación *f* <people of evil report : personas de mala fama> **3** ACCOUNT : informe *m,* reportaje *m* (en un periódico, etc.) **4** BANG : estallido *m* (de un arma de fuego)

report card *n* : boletín *m* de calificaciones, boletín *m* de notas

reportedly [ri'portədli] *adv* : según se dice, según se informa

reporter [ri'portər] *n* : periodista *mf;* reportero *m,* -ra *f*

repose¹ [ri'po:z] *vi* **-posed; -posing** : reposar, descansar

repose² *n* **1** : reposo *m,* descanso *m* **2** CALM : calma *f,* tranquilidad *f*

repository [ri'pɑzə,tori] *n, pl* **-ries** : depósito *m*

repossess [,ri:pə'zɛs] *vt* : recuperar, recobrar la posesión de

reprehensible [,rɛpri'hɛntsəbəl] *adj* : reprensible — **reprehensibly** *adv*

represent [,rɛprɪ'zɛnt] *vt* **1** SYMBOLIZE : representar <the flag represents our country : la bandera representa a nuestro país> **2** : representar, ser un representante de <an attorney who represents his client : un abogado que representa su cliente> **3** PORTRAY : presentar <he represents himself as a friend : se presenta como amigo>

representation [,rɛprɪ,zɛn'teɪʃən, -zən-] *n* : representación *f*

representative¹ [,rɛprɪ'zɛntət̬ɪv] *adj* : representativo

representative² *n* **1** : representante *mf* **2** : diputado *m,* -da *f* (en la política)

repress [ri'prɛs] *vt* : reprimir

repression [ri'prɛʃən] *n* : represión *f*

repressive [ri'prɛsɪv] *adj* : represivo

reprieve¹ [ri'pri:v] *vt* **-prieved; -prieving** : indultar

reprieve² *n* : indulto *m*

reprimand¹ ['rɛprə,mænd] *vt* : reprender

reprimand² *n* : reprimenda *f*

reprint¹ [ri'prɪnt] *vt* : reimprimir

reprint² ['ri:,prɪnt, ri'prɪnt] *n* : reedición *f*

reprisal [ri'praɪzəl] *n* : represalia *f*

reproach¹ [ri'pro:tʃ] *vt* : reprochar

reproach² *n* **1** DISGRACE : deshonra *f* **2** REBUKE : reproche *m,* recriminación *f*

reproachful [ri'pro:tʃfəl] *adj* : de reproche

reproduce [,ri:prə'du:s, -'dju:s] *v* **-duced; -ducing** *vt* : reproducir — *vi* BREED : reproducirse

reproduction [,ri:prə'dʌkʃən] *n* : reproducción *f*

reproductive [,ri:prə'dʌktɪv] *adj* : reproductor

reproof [ri'pru:f] *n* : reprobación *f,* reprimenda *f,* reproche *m*

reprove [ri'pru:v] *vt* **-proved; -proving** : reprender, censurar

reptile ['rɛp,taɪl] *n* : reptil *m*

republic [ri'pʌblɪk] *n* : república *f*

republican¹ [ri'pʌblɪkən] *adj* : republicano

republican² *n* : republicano *m,* -na *f*

repudiate [ri'pju:di,eɪt] *vt* **-ated; -ating 1** REJECT : rechazar **2** DISOWN : repudiar, renegar de

repudiation [ri,pju:di'eɪʃən] *n* : rechazo *m,* repudio *m*

repugnance [ri'pʌgnənts] *n* : repugnancia *f*

repugnant [ri'pʌgnənt] *adj* : repugnante, asqueroso

repulse¹ [ri'pʌls] *vt* **-pulsed; -pulsing 1** REPEL : repeler **2** REBUFF : desairar, rechazar

repulse² *n* : rechazo *m*

repulsive [ri'pʌlsɪv] *adj* : repulsivo, repugnante, asqueroso — **repulsively** *adv*

reputable ['rɛpjət̬əbəl] *adj* : acreditado, de buena reputación

reputation [,rɛpjə'teɪʃən] *n* : reputación *f,* fama *f*

repute [ri'pju:t] *n* : reputación *f,* fama *f*

reputed [ri'pju:təd] *adj* : reputado, supuesto <she's reputed to be the best : tiene fama de ser la mejor>

reputedly [ri'pju:tədli] *adv* : supuestamente, según se dice

request¹ [ri'kwɛst] *vt* : pedir, solicitar, rogar <to request assistance : solicitar asistencia, pedir ayuda> <I requested him to do it : le pedí que lo hiciera>

request[2] *n* **:** petición *f,* solicitud *f,* pedido *m*

requiem [ˈrɛkwiəm, ˈreɪ-] *n* **:** réquiem *m*

require [riˈkwaɪr] *vt* **-quired; -quiring 1** CALL FOR, DEMAND **:** requerir, exigir <if required **:** si se requiere> <to require that something be done **:** exigir que algo se haga> **2** NEED **:** necesitar, requerir

requirement [riˈkwaɪrmənt] *n* **1** NECESSITY **:** necesidad *f* **2** DEMAND **:** requisito *m,* demanda *f*

requisite[1] [ˈrɛkwəzɪt] *adj* **:** esencial, necesario

requisite[2] *n* **:** requisito *m,* necesidad *f*

requisition[1] [ˌrɛkwəˈzɪʃən] *vt* **:** requisar

requisition[2] *n* **:** requisición *f,* requisa *f*

reread [ˌriːˈriːd] *vt* **-read; -reading :** releer

reroute [ˌriːˈruːt, -ˈraʊt] *vt* **-routed; -routing :** desviar

resale [ˈriːˌseɪl, ˌriːˈseɪl] *n* **:** reventa *f* <resale price **:** precio de venta>

rescind [riˈsɪnd] *vt* **1** CANCEL **:** rescindir, cancelar **2** REPEAL **:** abrogar, revocar

rescue[1] [ˈrɛsˌkjuː] *vt* **-cued; -cuing :** rescatar, salvar

rescue[2] *n* **:** rescate *m*

rescuer [ˈrɛskjuər] *n* **:** salvador *m,* -dora *f*

research[1] [riˈsərtʃ, ˈriːˌsərtʃ] *v* **:** investigar

research[2] *n* **:** investigación *f*

researcher [riˈsərtʃər, ˈriːˌ-] *n* **:** investigador *m,* -dora *f*

resemblance [riˈzɛmblən*t*s] *n* **:** semejanza *f,* parecido *m*

resemble [riˈzɛmbəl] *vt* **-sembled; -sembling :** parecerse a, asemejarse a

resent [riˈzɛnt] *vt* **:** resentirse de, ofenderse por

resentful [riˈzɛntfəl] *adj* **:** resentido, rencoroso **— resentfully** *adv*

resentment [riˈzɛntmənt] *n* **:** resentimiento *m*

reservation [ˌrɛzərˈveɪʃən] *n* **1 :** reservación *f,* reserva *f* <to make a reservation **:** hacer una reservación> **2** DOUBT, MISGIVING **:** reserva *f,* duda *f* <without reservations **:** sin reservas> **3 :** reserva *f* (de indios americanos)

reserve[1] [riˈzərv] *vt* **-served; -serving :** reservar

reserve[2] *n* **1** STOCK **:** reserva *f* <to keep in reserve **:** guardar en reserva> **2** RESTRAINT **:** reserva *f,* moderación *f* **3 reserves** *npl* **:** reservas *fpl* (militares)

reserved [riˈzərvd] *adj* **:** reservado

reservoir [ˈrɛzərˌvwɑr, -ˌvwɔr, -ˌvɔr] *n* **:** embalse *m*

reset [ˌriːˈsɛt] *vt* **-set; -setting :** reajustar, poner en hora (un reloj), reinicializar (una computadora)

reside [riˈzaɪd] *vi* **-sided; -siding 1** DWELL **:** residir **2** LIE **:** radicar, residir <the power resides in the presidency **:** el poder radica en la presidencia>

residence [ˈrɛzədən*t*s] *n* **:** residencia *f*

resident[1] [ˈrɛzədənt] *adj* **:** residente

resident[2] *n* **:** residente *mf*

residential [ˌrɛzəˈdɛntʃəl] *adj* **:** residencial

residual [riˈzɪdʒʊəl] *adj* **:** residual

residue [ˈrɛzəˌduː, -ˌdjuː] *n* **:** residuo *m,* resto *m*

resign [riˈzaɪn] *vt* **1** QUIT **:** dimitir, renunciar **2 to resign oneself :** aguantarse, resignarse

resignation [ˌrɛzɪgˈneɪʃən] *n* **:** resignación *f*

resignedly [riˈzaɪnədli] *adv* **:** con resignación

resilience [riˈzɪljən*t*s] *n* **1 :** capacidad *f* de recuperación, adaptabilidad *f* **2** ELASTICITY **:** elasticidad *f*

resiliency [riˈzɪljən*t*si] → **resilience**

resilient [riˈzɪljənt] *adj* **1** STRONG **:** resistente, fuerte **2** ELASTIC **:** elástico

resin [ˈrɛzən] *n* **:** resina *f*

resist [riˈzɪst] *vt* **1** WITHSTAND **:** resistir <to resist heat **:** resistir el calor> **2** OPPOSE **:** oponerse a

resistance [riˈzɪstən*t*s] *n* **:** resistencia *f*

resistant [riˈzɪstənt] *adj* **:** resistente

resolute [ˈrɛzəˌluːt] *adj* **:** firme, resuelto, decidido

resolutely [ˈrɛzəˌluːtli, ˌrɛzəˈ-] *adv* **:** resueltamente, firmemente

resolution [ˌrɛzəˈluːʃən] *n* **1** SOLUTION **:** solución *f* **2** RESOLVE **:** resolución *f,* determinación *f* **3** DECISION **:** propósito *m,* decisión *f* <New Year's resolutions **:** propósitos para el Año Nuevo> **4** MOTION, PROPOSAL **:** moción *f,* resolución *f* (legislativa)

resolve[1] [riˈzɑlv] *vt* **-solved; -solving 1** SOLVE **:** resolver, solucionar **2** DECIDE **:** resolver <she resolved to get more sleep **:** resolvió dormir más>

resolve[2] *n* **:** resolución *f,* determinación *f*

resonance [ˈrɛzənən*t*s] *n* **:** resonancia *f*

resonant [ˈrɛzənənt] *adj* **:** resonante, retumbante

resort[1] [riˈzɔrt] *vi* **to resort to :** recurrir <to resort to force **:** recurrir a la fuerza>

resort[2] *n* **1** RECOURSE **:** recurso *m* <as a last resort **:** como último recurso> **2** HANGOUT **:** lugar *m* popular, lugar *m* muy frecuentado **3 :** lugar *m* de vacaciones <tourist resort **:** centro turístico>

resound [riˈzaʊnd] *vi* **:** retumbar, resonar

resounding [riˈzaʊndɪŋ] *adj* **1** RESONANT **:** retumbante, resonante **2** ABSOLUTE, CATEGORICAL **:** rotundo, tremendo <a resounding success **:** un éxito rotundo>

resource [ˈriːˌsors, riˈsors] *n* **1** RESOURCEFULNESS **:** ingenio *m,* recursos *mpl* **2 resources** *npl* **:** recursos *mpl*

<natural resources : recursos naturales> **3 resources** *npl* MEANS : recursos *mpl,* medios *mpl,* fondos *mpl*

resourceful [ri'sorsfəl, -'zors-] *adj* : ingenioso

resourcefulness [ri'sorsfəlnəs, -'zors-] *n* : ingenio *m,* recursos *mpl,* inventiva *f*

respect[1] [ri'spɛkt] *vt* : respetar, estimar

respect[2] *n* **1** REFERENCE : relación *f,* respeto *m* <with respect to : en lo que respecta a> **2** ESTEEM : respeto *m,* estima *f* **3** DETAIL, PARTICULAR : detalle *m,* sentido *m,* respeto *m* <in some respects : en algunos sentidos> **4 respects** *npl* : respetos *mpl* <to pay one's respects : presentar uno sus respetos>

respectability [ri,spɛktə'bɪləṱi] *n* : respetabilidad *f*

respectable [ri'spɛktəbəl] *adj* **1** PROPER : respetable, decente **2** CONSIDERABLE : considerable, respetable <a respectable amount : una cantidad respetable> — **respectably** [-bli] *adv*

respectful [ri'spɛktfəl] *adj* : respetuoso — **respectfully** *adv*

respectfulness [ri'spɛktfəlnəs] *n* : respetuosidad *f*

respective [ri'spɛktɪv] *adj* : respectivo <their respective homes : sus casas respectivas> — **respectively** *adv*

respiration [,rɛspə'reɪʃən] *n* : respiración *f*

respirator ['rɛspə,reɪṱər] *n* : respirador *m*

respiratory ['rɛspərə,tori, rɪ'spaɪrə-] *adj* : respiratorio

respite ['rɛspɪt, rɪ'spaɪt] *n* : respiro *m,* tregua *f*

resplendent [ri'splɛndənt] *adj* : resplandeciente — **resplendently** *adv*

respond [ri'spɑnd] *vi* **1** ANSWER : contestar, responder **2** REACT : responder, reaccionar <to respond to treatment : responder al tratamiento>

response [ri'spɑnts] *n* : respuesta *f*

responsibility [ri,spɑntsə'bɪləṱi] *n, pl* **-ties** : responsabilidad *f*

responsible [ri'spɑntsəbəl] *adj* : responsable — **responsibly** [-bli] *adv*

responsive [ri'spɑntsɪv] *adj* **1** ANSWERING : que responde **2** SENSITIVE : sensible, receptivo

responsiveness [ri'spɑntsɪvnəs] *n* : receptividad *f,* sensibilidad *f*

rest[1] ['rɛst] *vi* **1** REPOSE : reposar, descansar **2** RELAX : quedarse tranquilo **3** STOP : pararse, detenerse **4** DEPEND : basarse (en), descansar (sobre), depender (de) <the decision rests with her : la decisión pesa sobre ella> **5 to rest on** : apoyarse en, descansar sobre <to rest on one's arm : apoyarse en el brazo> — *vt* **1** RELAX : descansar **2** SUPPORT : apoyar **3 to rest one's eyes on** : fijar la mirada en

rest[2] *n* **1** RELAXATION, REPOSE : reposo *m,* descanso *m* **2** SUPPORT : soporte *m,* apoyo *m* **3** : silencio *m* (en música) **4** REMAINDER : resto *m* **5 to come to rest** : pararse

restatement [,riː'steɪtmənt] *n* : repetición *f*

restaurant ['rɛstə,rɑnt, -rənt] *n* : restaurante *m*

restful ['rɛstfəl] *adj* **1** RELAXING : relajante **2** PEACEFUL : tranquilo, sosegado

restitution [,rɛstə'tuːʃən, -'tjuː-] *n* : restitución *f*

restive ['rɛstɪv] *adj* : inquieto, nervioso

restless ['rɛstləs] *adj* **1** FIDGETY : inquieto, agitado **2** IMPATIENT : impaciente **3** SLEEPLESS : desvelado <a restless night : una noche en blanco>

restlessly ['rɛstləsli] *adv* : nerviosamente

restlessness ['rɛstləsnəs] *n* : inquietud *f,* agitación *f*

restoration [,rɛstə'reɪʃən] *n* : restauración *f,* restablecimiento *m*

restore [ri'stor] *vt* **-stored; -storing 1** RETURN : volver **2** REESTABLISH : restablecer **3** REPAIR : restaurar

restrain [ri'streɪn] *vt* **1** : refrenar, contener **2 to restrain oneself** : contenerse

restrained [ri'streɪnd] *adj* : comedido, templado, contenido

restraint [ri'streɪnt] *n* **1** RESTRICTION : restricción *f,* limitación *f,* control *m* **2** CONFINEMENT : encierro *m* **3** RESERVE : reserva *f,* control *m* de sí mismo

restrict [ri'strɪkt] *vt* : restringir, limitar, constreñir

restricted [ri'strɪktəd] *adj* **1** LIMITED : limitado, restringido **2** CLASSIFIED : secreto, confidencial

restriction [ri'strɪkʃən] *n* : restricción *f*

restrictive [ri'strɪktɪv] *adj* : restrictivo — **restrictively** *adv*

restructure [ri'strʌktʃər] *vt* **-tured; -turing** : reestructurar

result[1] [ri'zʌlt] *vi* : resultar <to result in : resultar en, tener por resultado>

result[2] *n* : resultado *m,* consecuencia *f* <as a result of : como consecuencia de>

resultant [ri'zʌltənt] *adj* : resultante

resume [ri'zuːm] *v* **-sumed; -suming** *vt* : reanudar — *vi* : reanudarse

résumé *or* **resume** *or* **resumé** ['rɛzə,meɪ, ,rɛzə'-] *n* **1** SUMMARY : resumen *m* **2** CURRICULUM VITAE : currículum *m,* currículo *m*

resumption [ri'zʌmpʃən] *n* : reanudación *f*

resurface [,riː'sərfəs] *v* **-faced; -facing** *vt* : pavimentar (una carretera) de nuevo — *vi* : volver a salir en la superficie

resurgence [ri'sərdʒənts] *n* : resurgimiento *m*

resurrect [ˌrɛzəˈrɛkt] *vt* : resucitar, desempolvar

resurrection [ˌrɛzəˈrɛkʃən] *n* : resurrección *f*

resuscitate [riˈsʌsəˌteɪt] *vt* **-tated; -tating** : resucitar, revivir

retail[1] [ˈriːˌteɪl] *vt* : vender al por menor, vender al detalle

retail[2] *adv* : al por menor, al detalle

retail[3] *adj* : detallista, minorista

retail[4] *n* : venta *f* al detalle, venta *f* al por menor

retailer [ˈriːˌteɪlər] *n* : detallista *mf,* minorista *mf*

retain [riˈteɪn] *vt* : retener, conservar, guardar

retainer [riˈteɪnər] *n* **1** SERVANT : criado *m,* -da *f* **2** ADVANCE : anticipo *m*

retaliate [riˈtæliˌeɪt] *vi* **-ated; -ating** : responder, contraatacar, tomar represalias

retaliation [riˌtæliˈeɪʃən] *n* : represalia *f,* retaliación *f*

retard [riˈtɑrd] *vt* : retardar, retrasar

retarded [riˈtɑrdəd] *adj* : retrasado

retch [ˈrɛtʃ] *vi* : hacer arcadas

retention [riˈtɛntʃən] *n* : retención *f*

retentive [riˈtɛntɪv] *adj* : retentivo

reticence [ˈrɛtəsən*t*s] *n* : reticencia *f*

reticent [ˈrɛtəsənt] *adj* : reticente

retina [ˈrɛtənə] *n, pl* **-nas** *or* **-nae** [-əni, -ənˌaɪ] : retina *f*

retinue [ˈrɛtənˌuː, -ˌjuː] *n* : séquito *m,* comitiva *f,* cortejo *m*

retire [riˈtaɪr] *vi* **-tired; -tiring 1** RETREAT, WITHDRAW : retirarse, retraerse **2** : retirarse, jubilarse (de su trabajo) **3** : acostarse, irse a dormir

retiree [riˌtaɪˈriː] *n* : jubilado *m,* -da *f*

retirement [riˈtaɪrmənt] *n* : jubilación *f*

retiring [riˈtaɪrɪŋ] *adj* SHY : retraído

retort[1] [riˈtɔrt] *vt* : replicar

retort[2] *n* : réplica *f*

retrace [ˌriːˈtreɪs] *vt* **-traced; -tracing** : volver sobre, desandar <to retrace one's steps : volver uno sobre sus pasos>

retract [riˈtrækt] *vt* **1** TAKE BACK, WITHDRAW : retirar, retractarse de **2** : retraer (las garras) — *vi* : retractarse

retractable [riˈtræktəbəl] *adj* : retractable

retrain [ˌriːˈtreɪn] *vt* : reciclar, reconvertir

retreat[1] [riˈtriːt] *vi* : retirarse

retreat[2] *n* **1** WITHDRAWAL : retirada *f,* repliegue *m,* retiro *m* <to beat a retreat : batirse en retirada> **2** REFUGE : retiro *m,* refugio *m*

retrench [riˈtrɛntʃ] *vt* : reducir (gastos) — *vi* : economizar

retribution [ˌrɛtrəˈbjuːʃən] *n* PUNISHMENT : castigo *m,* pena *f* merecida

retrieval [riˈtriːvəl] *n* : recuperación *f* <beyond retrieval : irrecuperable> <data retrieval : recuperación de datos>

retrieve [riˈtriːv] *vt* **-trieved; -trieving 1** : cobrar <to retrieve game : cobrar la caza> **2** RECOVER : recuperar

retriever [riˈtriːvər] *n* : perro *m* cobrador

retroactive [ˌrɛtroˈæktɪv] *adj* : retroactivo — **retroactively** *adv*

retrograde [ˈrɛtrəˌgreɪd] *adj* : retrógrado

retrospect [ˈrɛtrəˌspɛkt] *n* **in retrospect** : mirando hacia atrás, retrospectivamente

retrospective [ˌrɛtrəˈspɛktɪv] *adj* : retrospectivo

return[1] [riˈtərn] *vi* **1** : volver, regresar <to return home : regresar a casa> **2** REAPPEAR : reaparecer, resurgir **3** ANSWER : responder — *vt* **1** REPLACE, RESTORE : devolver, volver (a poner), restituir <to return something to its place : volver a poner algo en su lugar> **2** YIELD : producir, redituar, rendir **3** REPAY : pagar, devolver <to return a compliment : devolver un cumplido>

return[2] *adj* : de vuelta

return[3] *n* **1** RETURNING : regreso *m,* vuelta *f,* retorno *m* **2** *or* **tax return** : declaración *f* de impuestos **3** YIELD : rédito *m,* rendimiento *m,* ganancia *f* **4 returns** *npl* DATA, RESULTS : resultados *mpl,* datos *mpl*

reunion [riˈjuːnjən] *n* : reunión *f,* reencuentro *m*

reunite [ˌriːjʊˈnaɪt] *v* **-nited; -niting** *vt* : (volver a) reunir — *vi* : (volver a) reunirse

reusable [riˈjuːzəbəl] *adj* : reutilizable

reuse [riˈjuːz] *vt* **-used; -using** : reutilizar, usar de nuevo

revamp [ˌriˈvæmp] *vt* : renovar

reveal [riˈviːl] *vt* **1** DIVULGE : revelar, divulgar <to reveal a secret : revelar un secreto> **2** SHOW : manifestar, mostrar, dejar ver

reveille [ˈrɛvəli] *n* : toque *m* de diana

revel[1] [ˈrɛvəl] *vi* **-eled** *or* **-elled; -eling** *or* **-elling 1** CAROUSE : ir de juerga **2 to revel in** : deleitarse en

revel[2] *n* : juerga *f,* parranda *f fam*

revelation [ˌrɛvəˈleɪʃən] *n* : revelación *f*

reveler *or* **reveller** [ˈrɛvələr] *n* : juerguista *mf*

revelry [ˈrɛvəlri] *n, pl* **–ries** : juerga *f,* parranda *f fam,* jarana *f fam*

revenge[1] [riˈvɛndʒ] *vt* **-venged; -venging** : vengar <to revenge oneself on : vengarse de>

revenge[2] *n* : venganza *f*

revenue [ˈrɛvəˌnuː, -ˌnjuː] *n* : ingresos *mpl,* rentas *fpl*

reverberate [riˈvərbəˌreɪt] *vi* **-ated; -ating** : reverberar

reverberation [riˌvərbəˈreɪʃən] *n* : reverberación *f*

revere [riˈvɪr] *vt* **-vered; -vering** : reverenciar, venerar

reverence ['rɛvərənts] *n* : reverencia *f,* veneración *f*
reverend ['rɛvərənd] *adj* : reverendo <the Reverend John Chapin : el reverendo John Chapin>
reverent ['rɛvərənt] *adj* : reverente — **reverently** *adv*
reverie ['rɛvəri] *n, pl* **-eries** : ensueño *m*
reversal ['rɛvərsəl] *n* **1** INVERSION : inversión *f* (del orden normal) **2** CHANGE : cambio *m* total **3** SETBACK : revés *m,* contratiempo *m*
reverse[1] [ri'vərs] *v* **-versed; -versing** *vt* **1** INVERT : invertir **2** CHANGE : cambiar totalmente **3** ANNUL : anular, revocar — *vi* : dar marcha atrás
reverse[2] *adj* **1** : inverso <in reverse order : en orden inverso> <the reverse side : el reverso> **2** OPPOSITE : contrario, opuesto
reverse[3] *n* **1** OPPOSITE : lo contrario, lo opuesto **2** SETBACK : revés *m,* contratiempo *m* **3** BACK : reverso *m,* dorso *m,* revés *m* **4** *or* **reverse gear** : marcha *f* atrás, reversa *f Col, Mex*
reversible [ri'vərsəbəl] *adj* : reversible
reversion [ri'vərʒən] *n* : reversión *f,* vuelta *f*
revert [ri'vərt] *vi* : revertir
review[1] [ri'vjuː] *vt* **1** REEXAMINE : volver a examinar, repasar (una lección) **2** CRITICIZE : reseñar, hacer una crítica de **3** EXAMINE : examinar, analizar <to review one's life : examinar su vida> **4 to review the troops** : pasar revista a las tropas
review[2] *n* **1** INSPECTION : revista *f* (de tropas) **2** ANALYSIS, OVERVIEW : resumen *m,* análisis *m* <a review of current affairs : un análisis de las actualidades> **3** CRITICISM : reseña *f,* crítica *f* (de un libro, etc.) **4** : repaso *m* (para un examen) **5** REVUE : revista *f* (musical)
reviewer [ri'vjuːər] *n* : crítico *m,* -ca *f*
revile [ri'vaɪl] *vt* **-viled; -viling** : injuriar, denostar
revise [ri'vaɪz] *vt* **-vised; -vising** : revisar, corregir, refundir <to revise a dictionary : corregir un diccionario>
revision [ri'vɪʒən] *n* : revisión *f*
revival [ri'vaɪvəl] *n* **1** : renacimiento *m* (de ideas, etc.), restablecimiento *m* (de costumbres, etc.), reactivación *f* (de la economía) **2** : reanimación *f,* resucitación *f* (en medicina) **3** *or* **revival meeting** : asamblea *f* evangelista
revive [ri'vaɪv] *v* **-vived; -viving** *vt* **1** REAWAKEN : reavivar, reanimar, reactivar (la economía), resucitar (a un paciente) **2** REESTABLISH : restablecer — *vi* **1** : renacer, reanimarse, reactivarse **2** COME TO : recobrar el sentido, volver en sí
revoke [ri'voːk] *vt* **-voked; -voking** : revocar
revolt[1] [ri'voːlt] *vi* **1** REBEL : rebelarse, sublevarse **2 to revolt at** : sentir repugnancia por — *vt* DISGUST : darle asco (a alguien), repugnar
revolt[2] *n* REBELLION : rebelión *f,* revuelta *f,* sublevación *f*
revolting [ri'voːltɪŋ] *adj* : asqueroso, repugnante
revolution [ˌrɛvə'luːʃən] *n* : revolución *f*
revolutionary[1] [ˌrɛvə'luːʃənˌɛri] *adj* : revolucionario
revolutionary[2] *n, pl* **-aries** : revolucionario *m,* -ria *f*
revolutionize [ˌrɛvə'luːʃənˌaɪz] *vt* **-ized; -izing** : cambiar radicalmente, revolucionar
revolve [ri'vɑlv] *v* **-volved; -volving** *vt* ROTATE : hacer girar — *vi* **1** ROTATE : girar <to revolve around : girar alrededor de> **2 to revolve in one's mind** : darle vueltas en la cabeza a alguien
revolver [ri'vɑlvər] *n* : revólver *m*
revue [ri'vjuː] *n* : revista *f* (musical)
revulsion [ri'vʌlʃən] *n* : repugnancia *f*
reward[1] [ri'wɔrd] *vt* : recompensar, premiar
reward[2] *n* : recompensa *f*
rewrite [ˌriː'raɪt] *vt* **-wrote; -written; -writing** : escribir de nuevo, volver a escribir
rhapsody ['ræpsədi] *n, pl* **-dies 1** : elogio *m* excesivo <to go into rhapsodies over : extasiarse por> **2** : rapsodia *f* (en música)
rhetoric ['rɛṭərɪk] *n* : retórica *f*
rhetorical [rɪ'tɔrɪkəl] *adj* : retórico
rheumatic [rʊ'mæṭɪk] *adj* : reumático
rheumatism ['ruːməˌtɪzəm, 'rʊ-] *n* : reumatismo *m*
rhinestone ['raɪnˌstoːn] *n* : diamante *m* de imitación
rhino ['raɪˌnoː] *n, pl* **rhino** *or* **rhinos** → **rhinoceros**
rhinoceros [raɪ'nɑsərəs] *n, pl* **-eroses** *or* **-eros** *or* **-eri** [-ˌraɪ] : rinoceronte *m*
rhododendron [ˌroːdə'dɛndrən] *n* : rododendro *m*
rhombus ['rɑmbəs] *n, pl* **-buses** *or* **-bi** [-ˌbaɪ, -bi] : rombo *m*
rhubarb ['ruːˌbɑrb] *n* : ruibarbo *m*
rhyme[1] ['raɪm] *vi* **rhymed; rhyming** : rimar
rhyme[2] *n* **1** : rima *f* **2** VERSE : verso *m* (en rima)
rhythm ['rɪðəm] *n* : ritmo *m*
rhythmic ['rɪðmɪk] *or* **rhythmical** [-mɪkəl] *adj* : rítmico — **rhythmically** [-mɪkli] *adv*
rib[1] ['rɪb] *vt* **ribbed; ribbing 1** : hacer en canalé <a ribbed sweater : un suéter en canalé> **2** TEASE : tomarle el pelo (a alguien)
rib[2] *n* **1** : costilla *f* (de una persona o un animal) **2** : nervio *m* (de una bóveda o una hoja), varilla *f* (de un

paraguas), canalé *m* (de una prenda tejida)

ribald [ˈrɪbəld] *adj* **:** escabroso, procaz

ribbon [ˈrɪbən] *n* **1 :** cinta *f* **2 to tear to ribbons :** hacer jirones

rice [ˈraɪs] *n* **:** arroz *m*

rich [ˈrɪtʃ] *adj* **1** WEALTHY **:** rico **2** SUMPTUOUS **:** suntuoso, lujoso **3 :** pesado <rich foods : comida pesada> **4** ABUNDANT **:** abundante **5 :** vivo, intenso <rich colors : colores vivos> **6** FERTILE **:** fértil, rico

riches [ˈrɪtʃəz] *npl* **:** riquezas *fpl*

richly [ˈrɪtʃli] *adv* **1** SUMPTUOUSLY **:** suntuosamente, ricamente **2** ABUNDANTLY **:** abundantemente **3 richly deserved :** bien merecido

richness [ˈrɪtʃnəs] *n* **:** riqueza *f*

rickets [ˈrɪkəts] *n* **:** raquitismo *m*

rickety [ˈrɪkət̬i] *adj* **:** desvencijado, destartalado

ricksha *or* **rickshaw** [ˈrɪkˌʃɔ] *n* **:** cochecillo *m* tirado por un hombre

ricochet[1] [ˈrɪkəˌʃeɪ] *vi* **-cheted** [-ˌʃeɪd] *or* **-chetted** [-ˌʃɛt̬əd]; **-cheting** [-ˌʃeɪɪŋ] *or* **-chetting** [-ˌʃɛt̬ɪŋ] **:** rebotar

ricochet[2] *n* **:** rebote *m*

rid [ˈrɪd] *vt* **rid; ridding 1** FREE **:** librar <to rid the city of thieves : librar la ciudad de ladrones> **2 to rid oneself of :** desembarazarse de

riddance [ˈrɪdənts] *n* **:** libramiento *m* <good riddance! : ¡adiós y buen viaje!, ¡vete con viento fresco!>

riddle[1] [ˈrɪdəl] *vt* **-dled; -dling :** acribillar <riddled with bullets : acribillado a balazos> <riddled with errors : lleno de errores>

riddle[2] *n* **:** acertijo *m,* adivinanza *f*

ride[1] [ˈraɪd] *v* **rode** [ˈroːd]; **ridden** [ˈrɪdən]; **riding** *vt* **1 :** montar, ir, andar <to ride a horse : montar a caballo> <to ride a bicycle : montar en bicicleta, andar en bicicleta> <to ride the bus : ir en autobús> **2** TRAVERSE **:** recorrer <he rode 5 miles : recorrió 5 millas> **3** TEASE **:** burlarse de, ridiculizar **4** CARRY **:** llevar **5** WEATHER **:** capear <they rode out the storm : capearon el temporal> **6 to ride the waves :** surcar los mares — *vi* **1 :** montar a caballo, cabalgar **2** TRAVEL **:** ir, viajar (en coche, en bicicleta, etc.) **3** RUN **:** andar, marchar <the car rides well : el coche anda bien> **4 to ride at anchor :** estar fondeado **5 to let things ride :** dejar pasar las cosas

ride[2] *n* **1 :** paseo *m,* vuelta *f* (en coche, en bicicleta, a caballo) <to go for a ride : dar una vuelta> <to give someone a ride : llevar en coche a alguien> **2 :** aparato *m* (en un parque de diversiones)

rider [ˈraɪdər] *n* **1 :** jinete *mf* <the rider fell off his horse : el jinete se cayó de su caballo> **2** CYCLIST **:** ciclista *mf* **3** MOTORCYCLIST **:** motociclista *mf* **4** CLAUSE **:** cláusula *f* añadida

ridge [ˈrɪdʒ] *n* **1** CHAIN **:** cadena *f* (de montañas o cerros) **2 :** caballete *m* (de un techo), cresta *f* (de una ola o una montaña), cordoncillo *m* (de telas)

ridicule[1] [ˈrɪdəˌkjuːl] *vt* **-culed; -culing :** burlarse de, mofarse de, ridiculizar

ridicule[2] *n* **:** burlas *fpl*

ridiculous [rəˈdɪkjələs] *adj* **:** ridículo, absurdo

ridiculously [rəˈdɪkjələsli] *adv* **:** de forma ridícula

rife [ˈraɪf] *adj* **:** abundante, común <to be rife with : estar plagado de>

riffraff [ˈrɪfˌræf] *n* **:** chusma *f,* gentuza *f*

rifle[1] [ˈraɪfəl] *v* **-fled; -fling** *vt* RANSACK **:** desvalijar, saquear — *vi* **: to rifle through :** revolver

rifle[2] *n* **:** rifle *m,* fusil *m*

rift [ˈrɪft] *n* **1** FISSURE **:** grieta *f,* fisura *f* **2** BREAK **:** ruptura *f* (entre personas), división *f* (dentro de un grupo)

rig[1] [ˈrɪg] *vt* **rigged; rigging 1 :** aparejar (un barco) **2** EQUIP **:** equipar **3** FIX **:** amañar (una elección, etc.) **4 to rig up** CONSTRUCT **:** construir, erigir **5 to rig oneself out as :** vestirse de

rig[2] *n* **1 :** aparejo *m* (de un barco) **2** *or* **oil rig :** torre *f* de perforación, plataforma *f* petrolífera

rigging [ˈrɪgɪŋ, -gən] *n* **:** jarcia *f,* aparejo *m*

right[1] [ˈraɪt] *vt* **1** FIX, RESTORE **:** reparar <to right the economy : reparar la economía> **2** STRAIGHTEN **:** enderezar

right[2] *adv* **1 :** bien <to live right : vivir bien> **2** PRECISELY **:** precisamente, justo <right in the middle : justo en medio> **3** DIRECTLY, STRAIGHT **:** derecho, directamente <he went right home : fue derecho a casa> **4** IMMEDIATELY **:** inmediatamente <right after lunch : inmediatamente después del almuerzo> **5** COMPLETELY **:** completamente <he felt right at home : se sintió completamente cómodo> **6 :** a la derecha <to look left and right : mirar a la izquierda y a la derecha>

right[3] *adj* **1** UPRIGHT **:** bueno, honrado <right conduct : conducta honrada> **2** CORRECT **:** correcto <the right answer : la respuesta correcta> **3** APPROPRIATE **:** apropiado, adecuado, debido <the right man for the job : el hombre perfecto para el trabajo> **4** STRAIGHT **:** recto <a right line : una línea recta> **5 :** derecho <the right hand : la mano derecha> **6** SOUND **:** bien <he's not in his right mind : no está bien de la cabeza>

right[4] *n* **1** GOOD **:** bien *m* <to do right : hacer el bien> **2 :** derecha *f* <on the right : a la derecha> **3** *or* **right hand :** mano *f* derecha **4** ENTITLEMENT **:** derecho *m* <the right to vote : el derecho a votar> <women's rights : los derechos de la mujer> **5 the Right :** la derecha (en la política)

right angle *n* **:** ángulo *m* recto
right–angled [ˈraɪtˈæŋgəld] *or* **right–angle** [-gəl] *adj* **1 :** en ángulo recto **2 right–angled triangle :** triángulo *m* rectángulo
righteous [ˈraɪtʃəs] *adj* **:** recto, honrado — **righteously** *adv*
righteousness [ˈraɪtʃəsnəs] *n* **:** rectitud *f,* honradez *f*
rightful [ˈraɪtfəl] *adj* **1** JUST **:** justo **2** LAWFUL **:** legítimo — **rightfully** *adv*
right–hand [ˈraɪtˈhænd] *adj* **1 :** situado a la derecha **2** RIGHT-HANDED **:** para la mano derecha, con la mano derecha **3 right–hand man :** brazo *m* derecho
right–handed [ˈraɪtˈhændəd] *adj* **1 :** diestro <a right-handed pitcher : un lanzador diestro> **2 :** para la mano derecha, con la mano derecha **3** CLOCKWISE **:** en la dirección de las manecillas del reloj
rightly [ˈraɪtli] *adv* **1** JUSTLY **:** justamente, con razón **2** PROPERLY **:** debidamente, apropiadamente **3** CORRECTLY **:** correctamente
right–of–way [ˈraɪt̬əˈweɪ, -əv-] *n, pl* **rights–of–way 1 :** preferencia (del tráfico) **2** ACCESS **:** derecho *m* de paso
rightward [ˈraɪtwərd] *adj* **:** a la derecha, hacia la derecha
right–wing [ˈraɪtˈwɪŋ] *adj* **:** derechista
right wing *n* **the right wing :** la derecha
right–winger [ˈraɪtˈwɪŋər] *n* **:** derechista *mf*
rigid [ˈrɪdʒɪd] *adj* **:** rígido — **rigidly** *adv*
rigidity [rɪˈdʒɪdət̬i] *n, pl* **-ties :** rigidez *f*
rigmarole [ˈrɪgməˌroːl, ˈrɪgə-] *n* **1** NONSENSE **:** galimatías *m,* disparates *mpl* **2** PROCEDURES **:** trámites *mpl*
rigor [ˈrɪgər] *n* **:** rigor *m*
rigor mortis [ˌrɪgərˈmɔrt̬əs] *n* **:** rigidez *f* cadavérica
rigorous [ˈrɪgərəs] *adj* **:** rigoroso — **rigorously** *adv*
rile [ˈraɪl] *vt* **riled; riling :** irritar
rill [ˈrɪl] *n* **:** riachuelo *m*
rim [ˈrɪm] *n* **1** EDGE **:** borde *m* **2 :** llanta *f,* rin *m Col, Mex* (de una rueda) **3** FRAME **:** montura *f* (de anteojos)
rime [ˈraɪm] *n* **:** escarcha *f*
rind [ˈraɪnd] *n* **:** corteza *f*
ring[1] [ˈrɪŋ] *v* **rang** [ˈræŋ]; **rung** [ˈrʌŋ]; **ringing** *vi* **1 :** sonar <the doorbell rang : el timbre sonó> <to ring for : llamar> **2** RESOUND **:** resonar **3** SEEM **:** parecer <to ring true : parecer cierto> — *vt* **1 :** tocar, hacer sonar (un timbre, una alarma, etc.) **2** SURROUND **:** cercar, rodear
ring[2] *n* **1 :** anillo *m,* sortija *f* <wedding ring : anillo de matrimonio> **2** BAND **:** aro *m,* anillo *m* <piston ring : aro de émbolo> **3** CIRCLE **:** círculo *m* **4** ARENA **:** arena *f,* ruedo *m* <a boxing ring : un cuadrilátero, un ring> **5** GANG **:** banda *f* (de ladrones, etc.) **6** SOUND **:** timbre *m,* sonido *m* **7** CALL **:** llamada *f* (por teléfono)
ringer [ˈrɪŋər] *n* **to be a dead ringer for :** ser un vivo retrato de
ringleader [ˈrɪŋˌliːdər] *n* **:** cabecilla *mf*
ringlet [ˈrɪŋlət] *n* **:** sortija *f,* rizo *m*
ringworm [ˈrɪŋˌwərm] *n* **:** tiña *f*
rink [ˈrɪŋk] *n* **:** pista *f* <skating rink : pista de patinaje>
rinse[1] [ˈrɪnts] *vt* **rinsed; rinsing :** enjuagar <to rinse out one's mouth : enjuagarse la boca>
rinse[2] *n* **:** enjuague *m*
riot[1] [ˈraɪət] *vi* **:** amotinarse
riot[2] *n* **:** motín *m,* tumulto *m,* alboroto *m*
rioter [ˈraɪət̬ər] *n* **:** alborotador *m,* -dora *f*
riotous [ˈraɪət̬əs] *adj* **1** UNRULY, WILD **:** desenfrenado, alborotado **2** ABUNDANT **:** abundante
rip[1] [ˈrɪp] *v* **ripped; ripping** *vt* **:** rasgar, arrancar, desgarrar — *vi* **:** rasgarse, desgarrarse
rip[2] *n* **:** rasgón *m,* desgarrón *m*
ripe [ˈraɪp] *adj* **riper; ripest 1** MATURE **:** maduro <ripe fruit : fruta madura> **2** READY **:** listo, preparado
ripen [ˈraɪpən] *v* **:** madurar
ripeness [ˈraɪpnəs] *n* **:** madurez *f*
rip–off [ˈrɪpˌɔf] *n* **1** THEFT **:** robo *m* **2** SWINDLE **:** estafa *f,* timo *m fam*
ripple[1] [ˈrɪpəl] *v* **-pled; -pling** *vi* **:** rizarse, ondear, ondular — *vt* **:** rizar
ripple[2] *n* **:** onda *f,* ondulación *f*
rise[1] [ˈraɪz] *vi* **rose** [ˈroːz]; **risen** [ˈrɪzən]; **rising 1** GET UP **:** levantarse <to rise to one's feet : ponerse de pie> **2 :** elevarse, alzarse <the mountains rose to the west : las montañas se elevaron al oeste> **3 :** salir (dícese del sol y de la luna) **4 :** subir (dícese de las aguas, del humo, etc.) <the river rose : las aguas subieron de nivel> **5** INCREASE **:** aumentar, subir **6** ORIGINATE **:** nacer, proceder **7 to rise in rank :** ascender **8 to rise up** REBEL **:** sublevarse, rebelarse
rise[2] *n* **1** ASCENT **:** ascensión *f,* subida *f* **2** ORIGIN **:** origen *m* **3** ELEVATION **:** elevación *f* **4** INCREASE **:** subida *f,* aumento *m,* alzamiento *m* **5** SLOPE **:** pendiente *f,* cuesta *f*
riser [ˈraɪzər] *n* **1 :** contrahuella *f* (de una escalera) **2 early riser :** madrugador *m,* -dora *f* **3 late riser :** dormilón *m,* -lona *f*
risk[1] [ˈrɪsk] *vt* **:** arriesgar
risk[2] *n* **:** riesgo *m,* peligro *m* <at risk : en peligro> <at your own risk : por su cuenta y riesgo>
risky [ˈrɪski] *adj* **riskier; -est :** arriesgado, peligroso, riesgoso
risqué [rɪˈskeɪ] *adj* **:** escabroso, picante, subido de tono
rite [ˈraɪt] *n* **:** rito *m*

ritual[1] [ˈrɪtʃʊəl] *adj* : ritual — **ritually** *adv*

ritual[2] *n* : ritual *m*

rival[1] [ˈraɪvəl] *vt* **-valed** *or* **-valled; -valing** *or* **-valling** : rivalizar con, competir con

rival[2] *adj* : competidor, rival

rival[3] *n* : rival *mf;* competidor *m,* -dora *f*

rivalry [ˈraɪvəlri] *n, pl* **-ries** : rivalidad *f,* competencia *f*

river [ˈrɪvər] *n* : río *m*

riverbank [ˈrɪvərˌbæŋk] *n* : ribera *f,* orilla *f*

riverbed [ˈrɪvərˌbɛd] *n* : cauce *m,* lecho *m*

riverside [ˈrɪvərˌsaɪd] *n* : ribera *f,* orilla *f*

rivet[1] [ˈrɪvət] *vt* **1** : remachar **2** FIX : fijar (los ojos, etc.) **3** FASCINATE : fascinar, cautivar

rivet[2] *n* : remache *m*

rivulet [ˈrɪvjələt] *n* : arroyo *m,* riachuelo *m* <rivulets of sweat : gotas de sudor>

roach [ˈroːtʃ] → **cockroach**

road [ˈroːd] *n* **1** : carretera *f,* calle *f,* camino *m* **2** PATH : camino *m,* sendero *m,* vía *f* <on the road to a solution : en vías de una solución>

roadblock [ˈroːdˌblɑk] *n* : control *m*

roadrunner [ˈroːdˌrʌnər] *n* : correcaminos *m*

roadside [ˈroːdˌsaɪd] *n* : borde *m* de la carretera

roadway [ˈroːdˌweɪ] *n* : carretera *f,* calzada *f*

roam [ˈroːm] *vi* : vagar, deambular, errar — *vt* : vagar por

roan[1] [ˈroːn] *adj* : ruano

roan[2] *n* : caballo *m* ruano

roar[1] [ˈror] *vi* : rugir, bramar <to roar with laughter : reírse a carcajadas> — *vt* : decir a gritos

roar[2] *n* **1** : rugido *m,* bramido *m* (de un animal) **2** DIN : clamor *m* (de gente), fragor *m* (del trueno), estruendo *m* (del tráfico, etc.)

roast[1] [ˈroːst] *vt* : asar (carne, papas), tostar (café, nueces) — *vi* : asarse

roast[2] *adj* **1** : asado <roast chicken : pollo asado> **2 roast beef** : rosbif *m*

roast[3] *n* : asado *m*

rob [ˈrɑb] *v* **robbed; robbing** *vt* **1** STEAL : robar **2** DEPRIVE : privar, quitar — *vi* : robar

robber [ˈrɑbər] *n* : ladrón *m,* -drona *f*

robbery [ˈrɑbəri] *n, pl* **-beries** : robo *m*

robe[1] [ˈroːb] *vt* **robed; robing** : vestirse

robe[2] *n* **1** : toga *f* (de magistrados, etc.), sotana *f* (de eclesiásticos) <robe of office : traje de ceremonias> **2** BATHROBE : bata *f*

robin [ˈrɑbən] *n* : petirrojo *m*

robot [ˈroːˌbɑt, -bət] *n* : robot *m*

robust [roˈbʌst, ˈroːˌbʌst] *adj* : robusto, fuerte — **robustly** *adv*

rock[1] [ˈrɑk] *vt* **1** : acunar (a un niño), mecer (una cuna) **2** SHAKE : sacudir — *vi* SWAY : mecerse, balancearse

rock[2] *adj* : de rock

rock[3] *n* **1** ROCKING : balanceo *m* **2** *or* **rock music** : rock *m,* música *f* rock **3** : roca *f* (substancia) **4** STONE : piedra *f*

rock and roll *n* : rock and roll *m*

rocker [ˈrɑkər] *n* **1** : balancín *m* **2** *or* **rocking chair** : mecedora *f,* balancín *m* **3 to be off one's rocker** : estar chiflado, estar loco

rocket[1] [ˈrɑkət] *vi* : dispararse, subir rápidamente

rocket[2] *n* : cohete *m*

rocking horse *n* : caballito *m* (de balancín)

rock salt *n* : sal *f* gema

rocky [ˈrɑki] *adj* **rockier; -est 1** : rocoso, pedregoso **2** UNSTEADY : inestable

rod [ˈrɑd] *n* **1** BAR : barra *f,* varilla *f,* vara *f* (de madera) <a fishing rod : una caña (de pescar)> **2** : medida *f* de longitud equivalente a 5.03 metros (5 yardas)

rode → **ride**[1]

rodent [ˈroːdənt] *n* : roedor *m*

rodeo [ˈroːdiˌoː, roˈdeɪˌoː] *n, pl* **-deos** : rodeo *m*

roe [ˈroː] *n* : hueva *f*

roe deer *n* : corzo *m*

rogue [ˈroːg] *n* SCOUNDREL : pícaro *m,* -ra *f;* pillo *m,* -lla *f*

roguish [ˈroːgɪʃ] *adj* : pícaro, travieso

role [ˈroːl] *n* : papel *m,* función *f,* rol *m*

roll[1] [ˈroːl] *vt* **1** : hacer rodar <to roll the ball : hacer rodar la pelota> <to roll one's eyes : poner los ojos en blanco> **2** : liar (un cigarillo) **3** *or* **to roll up** : enrollar <to roll (oneself) up into a ball : hacerse una bola> **4** FLATTEN : estirar (masa), laminar (metales), pasar el rodillo por (el césped) **5 to roll up one's sleeves** : arremangarse — *vi* **1** : rodar <the ball kept on rolling : la pelota siguió rodando> **2** SWAY : balancearse <the ship rolled in the waves : el barco se balanceó en las olas> **3** REVERBERATE, SOUND : tronar (dícese del trueno), redoblar (dícese de un tambor) **4 to roll along** PROCEED : ponerse en marcha **5 to roll around** : revolcarse **6 to roll by** : pasar **7 to roll over** : dar una vuelta

roll[2] *n* **1** LIST : lista *f* <to call the roll : pasar lista> <to have on the roll : tener inscrito> **2** *or* **bread roll** : panecito *m,* bolillo *m Mex* **3** : rollo *m* (de papel, de tela, etc.) <a roll of film : un carrete> <a roll of bills : un fajo> **4** : redoble *m* (de tambores), retumbo *m* (del trueno, etc.) **5** ROLLING, SWAYING : balanceo *m*

roller [ˈroːlər] *n* **1** : rodillo *m* **2** CURLER : rulo *m*

roller coaster [ˈroːlərˌkoːstər] *n* : montaña *f* rusa

roller–skate [ˈroːlər͵skeɪt] *vi* **-skated; -skating** : patinar (sobre ruedas)
roller skate *n* : patín *m* (de ruedas)
rollicking [ˈrɑlɪkɪŋ] *adj* : animado, alegre
rolling pin *n* : rodillo *m*
Roman[1] [ˈroːmən] *adj* : romano
Roman[2] *n* : romano *m,* -na *f*
Roman Catholic *n* : católico *m,* -ca *f* — **Roman Catholic** *adj*
Roman Catholicism *n* : catolicismo *m*
romance[1] [roˈmænts, ˈroː͵mænts] *vi* **-manced; -mancing** FANTASIZE : fantasear
romance[2] *n* **1** : romance *m,* novela *f* de caballerías **2** : novela *f* de amor, novela *f* romántica **3** AFFAIR : romance *m,* amorío *m*
Romanian [rʊˈmeɪniən, ro-] *n* **1** : rumano *m,* -na *f* **2** : rumano *m* (idioma) — **Romanian** *adj*
Roman numeral *n* : número *m* romano
romantic [roˈmæntɪk] *adj* : romántico — **romantically** [-tɪkli] *adv*
romp[1] [ˈrɑmp] *vi* FROLIC : retozar, jugetear
romp[2] *n* : retozo *m*
roof[1] [ˈruːf, ˈrʊf] *vt* : techar
roof[2] *n, pl* **roofs** [ˈruːfs, ˈrʊfs; ˈruːvz, ˈrʊvz] **1** : techo *m,* tejado *m,* techado *m* **2** **roof of the mouth** : paladar *m*
roofing [ˈruːfɪŋ, ˈrʊfɪŋ] *n* : techumbre *f*
rooftop [ˈruːf͵tɑp, ˈrʊf-] *n* ROOF : tejado *m*
rook[1] [ˈrʊk] *vt* CHEAT : defraudar, estafar, timar
rook[2] *n* **1** : grajo *m* (ave) **2** : torre *f* (en ajedrez)
rookie [ˈrʊki] *n* : novato *m,* -ta *f*
room[1] [ˈruːm, ˈrʊm] *vi* LODGE : alojarse, hospedarse
room[2] *n* **1** SPACE : espacio *m,* sitio *m,* lugar *m* <to make room for : hacer lugar para> **2** : cuarto *m,* habitación *f* (en una casa), sala *f* (para reuniones, etc.) **3** BEDROOM : dormitorio *m,* habitación *f,* pieza *f* **4** (*indicating possibility or opportunity*) <room for improvement : posibilidad de mejorar> <there's no room for error : no hay lugar para errores>
roomer [ˈruːmər, ˈrʊmər] *n* : inquilino *m,* -na *f*
rooming house *n* : pensión *f*
roommate [ˈruːm͵meɪt, ˈrʊm-] *n* : compañero *m,* -ra *f* de cuarto
roomy [ˈruːmi, ˈrʊmi] *adj* **roomier; -est** **1** SPACIOUS : espacioso, amplio **2** LOOSE : suelto, holgado <a roomy blouse : una blusa holgada>
roost[1] [ˈruːst] *vi* : posarse, dormir (en una percha)
roost[2] *n* : percha *f*
rooster [ˈruːstər, ˈrʊs-] *n* : gallo *m*
root[1] [ˈruːt, ˈrʊt] *vi* **1** : arraigar <the plant rooted easily : la planta arraigó con facilidad> <deeply rooted traditions : tradiciones profundamente arraigadas> **2** : hozar (dícese de los cerdos) <to root around in : hurgar en> **3** **to root for** : apoyar a, alentar — *vt* **to root out** *or* **to root up** : desarraigar (plantas), extirpar (problemas, etc.)
root[2] *n* **1** : raíz *f* (de una planta) **2** ORIGIN : origen *m,* raíz *f* **3** CORE : centro *m,* núcleo *m* <to get to the root of the matter : ir al centro del asunto>
rootless [ˈruːtləs, ˈrʊt-] *adj* : desarraigado
rope[1] [ˈroːp] *vt* **roped; roping** **1** TIE : amarrar, atar **2** LASSO : lazar **3** **to rope off** : acordonar
rope[2] *n* : soga *f,* cuerda *f*
rosary [ˈroːzəri] *n, pl* **-ries** : rosario *m*
rose[1] → **rise**[1]
rose[2] [ˈroːz] *adj* : rosa, color de rosa
rose[3] *n* **1** : rosal *m* (planta), rosa *f* (flor) **2** : rosa *m* (color)
rosebush [ˈroːz͵bʊʃ] *n* : rosal *m*
rosemary [ˈroːz͵mɛri] *n, pl* **-maries** : romero *m*
rosette [roˈzɛt] *n* : escarapela *f* (hecho de cintas), roseta *f* (en arquitectura)
Rosh Hashanah [͵rɑʃhɑˈʃɑnə, ͵roːʃ-] *n* : el Año Nuevo judío
rosin [ˈrɑzən] *n* : colofonia *f*
roster [ˈrɑstər] *n* : lista *f*
rostrum [ˈrɑstrəm] *n, pl* **-trums** *or* **-tra** [-trə] : tribuna *f,* estrado *m*
rosy [ˈroːzi] *adj* **rosier; -est** **1** : sonrosado, de color rosa **2** PROMISING : prometedor, halagüeno
rot[1] [ˈrɑt] *v* **rotted; rotting** *vi* : pudrirse, descomponerse — *vt* : pudrir, descomponer
rot[2] *n* : putrefacción *f,* descomposición *f,* podredumbre *f*
rotary[1] [ˈroːt̬əri] *adj* : rotativo, rotatorio
rotary[2] *n, pl* **-ries** **1** : máquina *f* rotativa **2** TRAFFIC CIRCLE : rotonda *f,* glorieta *f*
rotate [ˈroː͵teɪt] *v* **-tated; -tating** *vi* REVOLVE : girar, rotar — *vt* **1** TURN : hacer girar, darle vueltas a **2** ALTERNATE : alternar
rotation [roˈteɪʃən] *n* : rotación *f*
rote [ˈroːt] *n* **to learn by rote** : aprender de memoria
rotor [ˈroːt̬ər] *n* : rotor *m*
rotten [ˈrɑt̬ən] *adj* **1** PUTRID : podrido, putrefacto **2** CORRUPT : corrompido **3** BAD : malo <a rotten day : un día malísimo>
rottenness [ˈrɑtənnəs] *n* : podredumbre *f*
rotund [roˈtʌnd] *adj* **1** ROUNDED : redondeado **2** PLUMP : regordete *fam,* llenito *fam*
rouge [ˈruːʒ, ˈruːdʒ] *n* : colorete *m*
rough[1] [ˈrʌf] *vt* **1** ROUGHEN : poner áspero **2** **to rough out** SKETCH : esbozar, bosquejar **3** **to rough up** BEAT : darle una paliza (a alguien) **4** **to rough it** : vivir sin comodidades

rough[2] *adj* **1** COARSE **:** áspero, basto **2** UNEVEN **:** desigual, escabroso, accidentado (dícese del terreno) **3 :** agitado (dícese del mar), tempestuoso (dícese del tiempo), violento (dícese del viento) **4** VIOLENT **:** violento, brutal <a rough neighborhood : un barrio peligroso> **5** DIFFICULT **:** duro, difícil **6** CRUDE **:** rudo, tosco, burdo <a rough cottage : una casita tosca> <a rough draft : un borrador> <a rough sketch : un bosquejo> **7** APPROXIMATE **:** aproximado <a rough idea : una idea aproximada>

rough[3] *n* **1 the rough :** el rough (en golf) **2 in the rough :** en borrador

roughage [ˈrʌfɪdʒ] *n* **:** fibra *f*

roughen [ˈrʌfən] *vt* **:** poner áspero — *vi* **:** ponerse áspero

roughly [ˈrʌfli] *adv* **1 :** bruscamente <to treat roughly : maltratar> **2** CRUDELY **:** burdamente **3** APPROXIMATELY **:** aproximadamente, más o menos

roughneck [ˈrʌfˌnɛk] *n* **:** matón *m*

roughness [ˈrʌfnəs] *n* **:** rudeza *f,* aspereza *f*

roulette [ruːˈlɛt] *n* **:** ruleta *f*

round[1] [ˈraʊnd] *vt* **1 :** redondear <she rounded the edges : redondeó los bordes> **2** TURN **:** doblar <to round the corner : dar la vuelta a la esquina> **3 to round off :** redondear (un número) **4 to round off** *or* **to round out** COMPLETE **:** rematar, terminar **5 to round up** GATHER **:** reunir

round[2] *adv* → **around**[1]

round[3] *adj* **1 :** redondo <a round table : una mesa redonda> <in round numbers : en números redondos> <round shoulders : espaldas cargadas> **2 round trip :** viaje *m* de ida y vuelta

round[4] *n* **1** CIRCLE **:** círculo *m* **2** SERIES **:** serie *f,* sucesión *f* <a round of talks : una ronda de negociaciones> <the daily round : la rutina cotidiana> **3 :** asalto *m* (en boxeo), recorrido *m* (en golf), vuelta *f* (en varios juegos) **4 :** salva *f* (de aplausos) **5 round of drinks :** ronda *f* **6 round of ammunition :** disparo *m,* cartucho *m* **7 rounds** *npl* **:** recorridos *mpl* (de un cartero), rondas *fpl* (de un vigilante), visitas *fpl* (de un médico) <to make the rounds : hacer visitas>

round[5] *prep* → **around**[2]

roundabout [ˈraʊndəˌbaʊt] *adj* **:** indirecto <to speak in a roundabout way : hablar con rodeos>

roundly [ˈraʊndli] *adv* **1** THOROUGHLY **:** completamente **2** BLUNTLY **:** francamente, rotundamente **3** VIGOROUSLY **:** con vigor

roundness [ˈraʊndnəs] *n* **:** redondez *f*

roundup [ˈraʊndˌʌp] *n* **1 :** rodeo *m* (de animales), redada *f* (de delincuentes, etc.) **2** SUMMARY **:** resumen *m*

round up *vt* **1 :** rodear (ganado), reunir (personas) **2** SUMMARIZE **:** hacer un resumen de

roundworm [ˈraʊndˌwərm] *n* **:** lombriz *f* intestinal

rouse [ˈraʊz] *vt* **roused; rousing 1** AWAKE **:** despertar **2** EXCITE **:** excitar <it roused him to fury : lo enfureció>

rout[1] [ˈraʊt] *vt* **1** DEFEAT **:** derrotar, aplastar **2 to rout out :** hacer salir

rout[2] *n* **1** DISPERSAL **:** desbandada *f,* dispersión *f* **2** DEFEAT **:** derrota *f* aplastante

route[1] [ˈruːt, ˈraʊt] *vt* **routed; routing :** dirigir, enviar, encaminar

route[2] *n* **:** camino *m,* ruta *f,* recorrido *m*

routine[1] [ruːˈtiːn] *adj* **:** rutinario — **routinely** *adv*

routine[2] *n* **:** rutina *f*

rove [ˈroːv] *v* **roved; roving** *vi* **:** vagar, errar — *vt* **:** errar por

rover [ˈroːvər] *n* **:** vagabundo *m,* -da *f*

row[1] [ˈroː] *vt* **1 :** avanzar a remo <to row a boat : remar> **2 :** llevar a remo <he rowed me to shore : me llevó hasta la orilla> — *vi* **:** remar

row[2] [ˈraʊ] *n* **1 :** paseo *m* en barca <to go for a row : salir a remar> **2** LINE, RANK **:** fila *f,* hilera *f* **3** SERIES **:** serie *f* <three days in a row : tres días seguidos> **4** RACKET **:** estruendo *m,* bulla *f* **5** QUARREL **:** pelea *f,* riña *f*

rowboat [ˈroːˌboːt] *n* **:** bote *m* de remos

rowdiness [ˈraʊdinəs] *n* **:** bulla *f*

rowdy[1] [ˈraʊdi] *adj* **-dier; -est :** escandaloso, alborotador

rowdy[2] *n, pl* **-dies :** alborotador *m,* -dora *f*

royal[1] [ˈrɔɪəl] *adj* **:** real — **royally** *adv*

royal[2] *n* **:** persona de linaje real, miembro de la familia real

royalty [ˈrɔɪəlti] *n, pl* **-ties 1 :** realeza *f* (posición) **2 :** miembros *mpl* de la familia real **3 royalties** *npl* **:** derechos *mpl* de autor

rub[1] [ˈrʌb] *v* **rubbed; rubbing** *vt* **1 :** frotar, restregar <to rub one's hands together : frotarse las manos> **2** MASSAGE **:** friccionar, masajear **3** CHAFE **:** rozar **4** POLISH **:** frotar, pulir **5** SCRUB **:** fregar **6 to rub elbows with :** codarse con **7 to rub someone the wrong way :** sacar de quicio a alguien, caerle mal a alguien — *vi* **to rub against :** rozar

rub[2] *n* **1** RUBBING **:** frotamiento *m,* fricción *f* **2** DIFFICULTY **:** problema *m*

rubber [ˈrʌbər] *n* **1 :** goma *f,* caucho *m,* hule *m Mex* **2 rubbers** *npl* OVERSHOES **:** chanclos *mpl*

rubber band *n* **:** goma *f* (elástica), gomita *f*

rubber–stamp [ˈrʌbərˈstæmp] *vt* **1** APPROVE **:** aprobar, autorizar **2** STAMP **:** sellar

rubber stamp *n* **:** sello *m* (de goma)

rubbery [ˈrʌbəri] *adj* **:** gomoso

rubbish [ˈrʌbɪʃ] *n* **:** basura *f,* desechos *mpl,* desperdicios *mpl*
rubble [ˈrʌbəl] *n* **:** escombros *mpl,* ripio *m*
ruble [ˈruːbəl] *n* **:** rublo *m*
ruby [ˈruːbi] *n, pl* **-bies 1 :** rubí *m* (gema) **2 :** color *m* de rubí
rudder [ˈrʌdər] *n* **:** timón *m*
ruddy [ˈrʌdi] *adj* **-dier; -est :** rubicundo (dícese de la cara, etc.), rojizo (dícese del cielo)
rude [ˈruːd] *adj* **ruder; rudest 1** CRUDE **:** tosco, rústico **2** IMPOLITE **:** grosero, descortés, maleducado **3** ABRUPT **:** brusco <a rude awakening : una sorpresa desagradable>
rudely [ˈruːdli] *adv* **:** groseramente
rudeness [ˈruːdnəs] *n* **1** IMPOLITENESS **:** grosería *f,* descortesía *f,* falta *f* de educación **2** ROUGHNESS **:** tosquedad *f* **3** SUDDENNESS **:** brusquedad *f*
rudiment [ˈruːdəmənt] *n* **:** rudimento *m,* noción *f* básica <the rudiments of Spanish : los rudimentos del español>
rudimentary [ˌruːdəˈmɛntəri] *adj* **:** rudimentario, básico
rue [ˈruː] *vt* **rued; ruing :** lamentar, arrepentirse de
rueful [ˈruːfəl] *adj* **1** PITIFUL **:** lastimoso **2** REGRETFUL **:** arrepentido, pesaroso
ruffian [ˈrʌfiən] *n* **:** matón *m*
ruffle[1] [ˈrʌfəl] *vt* **-fled; -fling 1** AGITATE **:** agitar, rizar (agua) **2** RUMPLE **:** arrugar (ropa), despeinar (pelo) **3** ERECT **:** erizar (plumas) **4** VEX **:** alterar, irritar, perturbar **5 :** fruncir volantes en (tela)
ruffle[2] *n* FLOUNCE **:** volante *m*
ruffly [ˈrʌfəli] *adj* **:** con volantes
rug [ˈrʌg] *n* **:** alfombra *f,* tapete *m*
rugged [ˈrʌgəd] *adj* **1** ROUGH, UNEVEN **:** accidentado, escabroso <rugged mountains : montañas accidentadas> **2** HARSH **:** duro, severo **3** ROBUST, STURDY **:** robusto, fuerte
ruin[1] [ˈruːən] *vt* **1** DESTROY **:** destruir, arruinar **2** BANKRUPT **:** arruinar, hacer quebrar
ruin[2] *n* **1 :** ruina *f* <to fall into ruin : caer en ruinas> **2 :** ruina *f,* perdición *f* <to be the ruin of : ser la perdición de> **3 ruins** *npl* **:** ruinas *fpl,* restos *mpl* <the ruins of the ancient temple : las ruinas del templo antiguo>
ruinous [ˈruːənəs] *adj* **:** ruinoso
rule[1] [ˈruːl] *v* **ruled; ruling** *vt* **1** CONTROL, GOVERN **:** gobernar (un país), controlar (las emociones) **2** DECIDE **:** decidir, fallar <the judge ruled that... : el juez falló que...> **3** DRAW **:** trazar con una regla — *vi* **1** GOVERN **:** gobernar, reinar **2** PREVAIL **:** prevalecer, imperar **3 to rule against :** fallar en contra de
rule[2] *n* **1** REGULATION **:** regla *f,* norma *f* **2** CUSTOM, HABIT **:** regla *f* general <as a rule : por lo general> **3** GOVERNMENT **:** gobierno *m,* dominio *m* **4** RULER **:** regla *f* (para medir)
ruler [ˈruːlər] *n* **1** LEADER, SOVEREIGN **:** gobernante *mf;* soberano *m,* -na *f* **2 :** regla *f* (para medir)
ruling [ˈruːlɪŋ] *n* **:** resolución *f,* fallo *m*
rum [ˈrʌm] *n* **:** ron *m*
Rumanian [rʊˈmeɪniən] → **Romanian**
rumble[1] [ˈrʌmbəl] *vi* **-bled; -bling :** retumbar, hacer ruidos (dícese del estómago)
rumble[2] *n* **:** estruendo *m,* ruido *m* sordo, retumbo *m*
ruminant[1] [ˈruːmənənt] *adj* **:** rumiante
ruminant[2] *n* **:** rumiante *m*
ruminate [ˈruːməˌneɪt] *vi* **-nated; -nating 1 :** rumiar (en zoología) **2** REFLECT **:** reflexionar, rumiar
rummage [ˈrʌmɪdʒ] *v* **-maged; -maging** *vi* **:** hurgar — *vt* RANSACK **:** revolver <they rummaged the attic : revolvieron el ático>
rummy [ˈrʌmi] *n* **:** rummy *m* (juego de naipes)
rumor[1] [ˈruːmər] *vt* **:** rumorear <it is rumored that. . . : se rumorea que. . . , se dice que. . .>
rumor[2] *n* **:** rumor *m*
rump [ˈrʌmp] *n* **1 :** ancas *fpl,* grupa *f* (de un animal) **2 :** cadera *f* <rump steak : filete de cadera>
rumple [ˈrʌmpəl] *vt* **-pled; -pling :** arrugar (ropa, etc.), despeinar (pelo)
rumpus [ˈrʌmpəs] *n* **:** lío *m,* jaleo *m fam*
run[1] [ˈrʌn] *v* **ran** [ˈræn]; **run; running** *vi* **1 :** correr <she ran to catch the bus : corrió para alcanzar el autobús> <run and fetch the doctor : corre a buscar al médico> **2 :** circular, correr <the train runs between Detroit and Chicago : el tren circula entre Detroit y Chicago> <to run on time : ser puntual> **3** FUNCTION **:** funcionar, ir <the engine runs on gasoline : el motor funciona con gasolina> <to run smoothly : ir bien> **4** FLOW **:** correr, ir **5** LAST **:** durar <the movie runs for two hours : la película dura dos horas> <the contract runs for three years : el contrato es válido por tres años> **6 :** desteñir, despintar (dícese de los colores) **7** EXTEND **:** correr, extenderse **8 to run for office :** postularse, presentarse — *vt* **1 :** correr <to run 10 miles : correr 10 millas> <to run errands : hacer los mandados> <to run out of town : hacer salir del pueblo> **2** PASS **:** pasar **3** DRIVE **:** llevar en coche **4** OPERATE **:** hacer funcionar (un motor, etc.) **5 :** echar <to run water : echar agua> **6** MANAGE **:** dirigir, llevar (un negocio, etc.) **7** EXTEND **:** tender (un cable, etc.) **8 to run a risk :** correr un riesgo
run[2] *n* **1 :** carrera *f* <at a run : a la carrera, corriendo> <to go for a run : ir a correr> **2** TRIP **:** vuelta *f,* paseo *m* (en coche), viaje *m* (en avión) **3** SERIES **:** serie *f* <a run of disappointments : una serie de desilusiones> <in

the long run : a la larga> <in the short run : a corto plazo> 4 DEMAND : gran demanda *f* <a run on the banks : una corrida bancaria> **5** (*used for theatrical productions and films*) <to have a long run : mantenerse mucho tiempo en la cartelera> **6** TYPE : tipo *m* <the average run of students : el tipo más común de estudiante> **7** : carrera *f* (en béisbol) **8** : carrera *f* (en una media) **9 to have the run of** : tener libre acceso de (una casa, etc.) **10 ski run** : pista *f* (de esquí)
runaway[1] [ˈrʌnəˌweɪ] *adj* **1** FUGITIVE : fugitivo **2** UNCONTROLLABLE : incontrolable, fuera de control <runaway inflation : inflación desenfrenada> <a runaway success : un éxito aplastante>
runaway[2] *n* : fugitivo *m*, -va *f*
rundown [ˈrʌnˌdaʊn] *n* SUMMARY : resumen *m*
run–down [ˈrʌnˈdaʊn] *adj* **1** DILAPIDATED : ruinoso, destartalado **2** SICKLY, TIRED : cansado, débil
rung[1] → **ring**[1]
rung[2] [ˈrʌŋ] *n* : peldaño *m*, escalón *m*
run–in [ˈrʌnˌɪn] *n* : disputa *f*, altercado *m*
runner [ˈrʌnər] *n* **1** RACER : corredor *m*, -dora *f* **2** MESSENGER : mensajero *m*, -ra *f* **3** TRACK : riel *m* (de un cajón, etc.) **4** : patín *m* (de un trineo), cuchilla *f* (de un patín) **5** : estolón *m* (planta)
runner–up [ˌrʌnərˈʌp] *n, pl* **runners–up** : subcampeón *m*, -peona *f*
running [ˈrʌnɪŋ] *adj* **1** FLOWING : corriente <running water : agua corriente> **2** CONTINUOUS : continuo <a running battle : una lucha continua> **3** CONSECUTIVE : seguido <six days running : por seis días seguidos>
run over *vt* : atropellar — *vi* OVERFLOW : rebosar
runt [ˈrʌnt] *n* : animal *m* pequeño <the runt of the litter : el más pequeño de la camada>
runway [ˈrʌnˌweɪ] *n* : pista *f* de aterrizaje
rupee [ruːˈpiː, ˈruːˌ-] *n* : rupia *f*
rupture[1] [ˈrʌptʃər] *v* **-tured; -turing** *vt* **1** BREAK, BURST : romper, reventar **2** : causar una hernia en — *vi* : reventarse
rupture[2] *n* **1** BREAK : ruptura *f* **2** HERNIA : hernia *f*
rural [ˈrʊrəl] *adj* : rural, campestre
ruse [ˈruːs, ˈruːz] *n* : treta *f*, ardid *m*, estratagema *f*
rush[1] [ˈrʌʃ] *vi* : correr, ir de prisa <to rush around : correr de un lado a otro> <to rush off : irse corriendo> — *vt* **1** HURRY : apresurar, apurar **2** ATTACK : abalanzarse sobre, asaltar
rush[2] *adj* : urgente
rush[3] *n* **1** HASTE : prisa *f*, apuro *m* **2** SURGE : ráfaga *f* (de aire), torrente *m* (de aguas), avalancha *f* (de gente) **3** DEMAND : demanda *f* <a rush on sugar : una gran demanda para el azúcar> **4** : carga *f* (en futbol americano) **5** : junco *m* (planta)
russet [ˈrʌsət] *n* : color *m* rojizo
Russian [ˈrʌʃən] *n* **1** : ruso *m*, -sa *f* **2** : ruso *m* (idioma) — **Russian** *adj*
rust[1] [ˈrʌst] *vi* : oxidarse — *vt* : oxidar
rust[2] *n* **1** : herrumbre *f*, orín *m*, óxido *m* (en los metales) **2** : roya *f* (en las plantas)
rustic[1] [ˈrʌstɪk] *adj* : rústico, campestre — **rustically** [-tɪkli] *adv*
rustic[2] *n* : rústico *m*, -ca *f*; campesino *m*, -na *f*
rustle[1] [ˈrʌsəl] *v* **-tled; -tling** *vt* **1** : hacer susurrar, hacer crujir <to rustle a newspaper : hacer crujir un periódico> **2** STEAL : robar (ganado) — *vi* : susurrar, crujir
rustle[2] *n* : murmullo *m*, susurro *m*, crujido *m*
rustler [ˈrʌsələr] *n* : ladrón *m*, -drona *f* de ganado
rusty [ˈrʌsti] *adj* **rustier; -est** : oxidado, herrumbroso
rut [ˈrʌt] *n* **1** GROOVE, TRACK : rodada *f*, surco *m* **2 to be in a rut** : ser esclavo de la rutina
ruthless [ˈruːθləs] *adj* : despiadado, cruel — **ruthlessly** *adv*
ruthlessness [ˈruːθləsnəs] *n* : crueldad *f*, falta *f* de piedad
Rwandan [rʊˈɑndən] *n* : ruandés *m*, -desa *f* — **Rwandan** *adj*
rye [ˈraɪ] *n* **1** : centeno *m* **2** *or* **rye whiskey** : whisky *m* de centeno

S

s [ˈɛs] *n, pl* **s's** *or* **ss** [ˈɛsəz] : decimonovena letra del alfabeto inglés
Sabbath [ˈsæbəθ] *n* **1** : sábado *m* (en el judaísmo) **2** : domingo *m* (en el cristianismo)
saber [ˈseɪbər] *n* : sable *m*
sable [ˈseɪbəl] *n* **1** BLACK : negro *m* **2** : marta *f* cebellina (animal)
sabotage[1] [ˈsæbəˌtɑʒ] *vt* **-taged; -taging** : sabotear
sabotage[2] *n* : sabotaje *m*
sac [ˈsæk] *n* : saco *m* (anatómico)
saccharin [ˈsækərən] *n* : sacarina *f*
saccharine *adj* [ˈsækərən, -ˌriːn, -ˌraɪn] : meloso, empalagoso
sachet [sæˈʃeɪ] *n* : bolsita *f* (perfumada)
sack[1] [ˈsæk] *vt* **1** FIRE : echar (del trabajo), despedir **2** PLUNDER : saquear
sack[2] *n* BAG : saco *m*
sacrament [ˈsækrəmənt] *n* : sacramento *m*

sacramental [ˌsækrəˈmɛntəl] *adj* : sacramental
sacred [ˈseɪkrəd] *adj* **1** RELIGIOUS : sagrado, sacro <sacred texts : textos sagrados> **2** HOLY : sagrado **3 sacred to** : consagrado a
sacrifice[1] [ˈsækrəˌfaɪs] *vt* **-ficed; -ficing 1** : sacrificar **2 to sacrifice oneself** : sacrificarse
sacrifice[2] *n* : sacrificio *m*
sacrilege [ˈsækrəlɪdʒ] *n* : sacrilegio *m*
sacrilegious [ˌsækrəˈlɪdʒəs, -ˈliː-] *adj* : sacrílego
sacrosanct [ˈsækroˌsæŋkt] *adj* : sacrosanto
sad [ˈsæd] *adj* **sadder; saddest** : triste — **sadly** *adv*
sadden [ˈsædən] *vt* : entristecer
saddle[1] [ˈsædəl] *vt* **-dled; -dling** : ensillar
saddle[2] *n* : silla *f* (de montar)
sadism [ˈseɪˌdɪzəm, ˈsæ-] *n* : sadismo *m*
sadist [ˈseɪdɪst, ˈsæ-] *n* : sádico *m*, -ca *f*
sadistic [səˈdɪstɪk] *adj* : sádico — **sadistically** [-tɪkli] *adv*
sadness [ˈsædnəs] *n* : tristeza *f*
safari [səˈfɑri, -ˈfær-] *n* : safari *m*
safe[1] [ˈseɪf] *adj* **safer; safest 1** UNHARMED : ileso <safe and sound : sano y salvo> **2** SECURE : seguro **3 to be on the safe side** : para mayor seguridad **4 to play it safe** : ir a la segura
safe[2] *n* : caja *f* fuerte
safeguard[1] [ˈseɪfˌgɑrd] *vt* : salvaguardar, proteger
safeguard[2] *n* : salvaguarda *f*, protección *f*
safekeeping [ˈseɪfˈkiːpɪŋ] *n* : custodia *f*, protección *f* <to put into safekeeping : poner en buen recaudo>
safely [ˈseɪfli] *adv* **1** UNHARMED : sin incidentes, sin novedades <they landed safely : aterrizaron sin novedades> **2** SECURELY : con toda seguridad, sin peligro
safety [ˈseɪfti] *n, pl* **-ties** : seguridad *f*
safety belt *n* : cinturón *m* de seguridad
safety pin *n* : alfiler *m* de gancho, alfiler *m* de seguridad, imperdible *m Spain*
saffron [ˈsæfrən] *n* : azafrán *m*
sag[1] [ˈsæg] *vi* **sagged; sagging 1** DROOP, SINK : combarse, hundirse, inclinarse **2** : colgar, caer <his jowls sagged : le colgaban las mejillas> **3** FLAG : flaquear, decaer <his spirits sagged : se le flaqueó el ánimo>
sag[2] *n* : combadura *f*
saga [ˈsɑgə, ˈsæ-] *n* : saga *f*
sagacious [səˈgeɪʃəs] *adj* : sagaz
sage[1] [ˈseɪdʒ] *adj* **sager; -est** : sabio — **sagely** *adv*
sage[2] *n* **1** : sabio *m*, -bia *f* **2** : salvia *f* (planta)
sagebrush [ˈseɪdʒˌbrʌʃ] *n* : artemisa *f*
Sagittarius [ˌsædʒəˈtɛriəs] *n* : Sagitario *mf*
said → **say**
sail[1] [ˈseɪl] *vi* **1** : navegar (en un barco) **2** : ir fácilmente <we sailed right in : entramos sin ningún problema> — *vt* **1** : gobernar (un barco) **2 to sail the seas** : cruzar los mares
sail[2] *n* **1** : vela *f* (de un barco) **2** : viaje *m* en velero <to go for a sail : salir a navegar>
sailboat [ˈseɪlˌboːt] *n* : velero *m*, barco *m* de vela
sailfish [ˈseɪlˌfɪʃ] *n* : pez *m* vela
sailor [ˈseɪlər] *n* : marinero *m*
saint [ˈseɪnt, *before a name* ˌseɪnt *or* sənt] *n* : santo *m*, -ta *f* <Saint Francis : San Francisco> <Saint Rose : Santa Rosa>
saintliness [ˈseɪntlinəs] *n* : santidad *f*
saintly [ˈseɪntli] *adj* **saintlier; -est** : santo
sake [ˈseɪk] *n* **1** BENEFIT : bien *m* <for the children's sake : por el bien de los niños> **2** (*indicating an end or a purpose*) <art for art's sake : el arte por el arte> <let's say, for argument's sake, that he's wrong : pongamos que está equivocado> **3 for goodness' sake!** : ¡por (el amor de) Dios!
salable *or* **saleable** [ˈseɪləbəl] *adj* : vendible
salacious [səˈleɪʃəs] *adj* : salaz — **salaciously** *adv*
salad [ˈsæləd] *n* : ensalada *f*
salamander [ˈsæləˌmændər] *n* : salamandra *f*
salami [səˈlɑmi] *n* : salami *m*
salary [ˈsæləri] *n, pl* **-ries** : sueldo *m*
sale [ˈseɪl] *n* **1** SELLING : venta *f* **2** : liquidación *f*, rebajas *fpl* <on sale : de rebaja> **3 sales** *npl* : ventas *fpl* <to work in sales : trabajar en ventas>
salesman [ˈseɪlzmən] *n, pl* **-men** [-mən, -ˌmɛn] **1** : vendedor *m*, dependiente *m* (en una tienda) **2 traveling salesman** : viajante *m*, representante *m*
salesperson [ˈseɪlzˌpərsən] *n* : vendedor *m*, -dora *f*; dependiente *m*, -ta *f* (en una tienda)
saleswoman [ˈseɪlzˌwʊmən] *n, pl* **-women** [-ˌwɪmən] **1** : vendedora *f*, dependienta *f* (en una tienda) **2 traveling saleswoman** : viajante *f*, representante *f*
salient [ˈseɪljənt] *adj* : saliente, sobresaliente
saline [ˈseɪˌliːn, -ˌlaɪn] *adj* : salino
saliva [səˈlaɪvə] *n* : saliva *f*
salivary [ˈsæləˌvɛri] *adj* : salival <salivary gland : glándula salival>
salivate [ˈsæləˌveɪt] *vi* **-vated; -vating** : salivar
sallow [ˈsæloː] *adj* : amarillento, cetrino
sally[1] [ˈsæli] *vi* **-lied; -lying** SET OUT : salir, hacer una salida
sally[2] *n, pl* **-lies 1** : salida *f* (militar), misión *f* **2** QUIP : salida *f*, ocurrencia *f*

salmon ['sæmən] *ns & pl* **1** : salmón *m* (pez) **2** : color *m* salmón

salon [sə'lɑn, 'sæ,lɑn, sæ'lɔ̃] *n* : salón *m* <beauty salon : salón de belleza>

saloon [sə'lu:n] *n* **1** HALL : salón *m* (en un barco) **2** BARROOM : bar *m*

salsa ['sɔlsə, 'sɑl-] *n* : salsa *f* mexicana, salsa *f* picante

salt[1] ['sɔlt] *vt* : salar, echarle sal a

salt[2] *adj* : salado

salt[3] *n* : sal *f*

saltwater ['sɔlt,wɔtər, -,wɑ-] *adj* : de agua salada

salty ['sɔlti] *adj* **saltier; -est** : salado

salubrious [sə'lu:briəs] *adj* : salubre

salutary ['sæljə,tɛri] *adj* : saludable, salubre

salutation [,sæljə'teɪʃən] *n* : saludo *m*, salutación *f*

salute[1] [sə'lu:t] *v* **-luted; -luting** *vt* **1** : saludar (con gestos o ceremonias) **2** ACCLAIM : reconocer, aclamar — *vi* : hacer un saludo

salute[2] *n* **1** : saludo *m* (gesto), salva *f* (de cañonazos) **2** TRIBUTE : reconocimiento *m*, homenaje *m*

salvage[1] ['sælvɪdʒ] *vt* **-vaged; -vaging** : salvar, rescatar

salvage[2] *n* **1** SALVAGING : salvamento *m*, rescate *m* **2** : objetos *mpl* salvados

salvation [sæl'veɪʃən] *n* : salvación *f*

salve[1] ['sæv, 'sav] *vt* **salved; salving** : calmar, apaciguar <to salve one's conscience : aliviarse la conciencia>

salve[2] *n* : ungüento *m*

salvo ['sæl,vo:] *n, pl* **-vos** *or* **-voes** : salva *f*

same[1] ['seɪm] *adj* : mismo, igual <the results are the same : los resultados son iguales> <he said the same thing as you : dijo lo mismo que tú>

same[2] *pron* : mismo <it's all the same to me : me da lo mismo> <the same to you! : ¡igualmente!>

sameness ['seɪmnəs] *n* **1** SIMILARITY : identidad *f*, semejanza *f* **2** MONOTONY : monotonía *f*

sample[1] ['sæmpəl] *vt* **-pled; -pling** : probar

sample[2] *n* : muestra *f*, prueba *f*

sampler ['sæmplər] *n* : dechado *m* (en bordado)

sanatorium [,sænə'toriəm] *n, pl* **-riums** *or* **-ria** [-iə] : sanatorio *m*

sanctify ['sæŋktə,faɪ] *vt* **-fied; -fying** : santificar

sanctimonious [,sæŋktə'mo:niəs] *adj* : beato, santurrón

sanction[1] ['sæŋkʃən] *vt* : sancionar, aprobar

sanction[2] *n* **1** AUTHORIZATION : sanción *f*, autorización *f* **2 sanctions** *npl* : sanciones *fpl* <to impose sanctions on : imponer sanciones a>

sanctity ['sæŋktəti] *n, pl* **-ties** : santidad *f*

sanctuary ['sæŋktʃʊ,ɛri] *n, pl* **-aries 1** : presbiterio *m* (en una iglesia) **2** REFUGE : refugio *m*, asilo *m*

sand[1] ['sænd] *vt* : lijar (madera)

sand[2] *n* : arena *f*

sandal ['sændəl] *n* : sandalia *f*

sandbank ['sænd,bæŋk] *n* : banco *m* de arena

sandpaper *n* : papel *m* de lija

sandpiper ['sænd,paɪpər] *n* : andarríos *m*

sandstone ['sænd,sto:n] *n* : arenisca *f*

sandstorm ['sænd,stɔrm] *n* : tormenta *f* de arena

sandwich[1] ['sænd,wɪtʃ] *vt* : intercalar, encajonar, meter (entre dos cosas)

sandwich[2] *n* : sandwich *m*, emparedado *m*, bocadillo *m Spain*

sandy ['sændi] *adj* **sandier; -est** : arenoso

sane ['seɪn] *adj* **saner; sanest 1** : cuerdo **2** SENSIBLE : sensato, razonable

sang → **sing**

sanguine ['sæŋgwən] *adj* **1** RUDDY : sanguíneo, rubicundo **2** HOPEFUL : optimista

sanitarium [,sænə'tɛriəm] *n, pl* **-iums** *or* **-ia** [-iə] → **sanatorium**

sanitary ['sænətɛri] *adj* **1** : sanitario <sanitary measures : medidas sanitarias> **2** HYGIENIC : higiénico **3 sanitary napkin** : compresa *f*, paño *m* higiénico

sanitation [,sænə'teɪʃən] *n* : sanidad *f*

sanity ['sænəti] *n* : cordura *f*, razón *f* <to lose one's sanity : perder el juicio>

sank → **sink**

Santa Claus ['sæntə,klɔz] *n* : Papá Noel, San Nicolás

sap[1] ['sæp] *vt* **sapped; sapping 1** UNDERMINE : socavar **2** WEAKEN : minar, debilitar

sap[2] *n* **1** : savia *f* (de una planta) **2** SUCKER : inocentón *m*, -tona *f*

sapling ['sæplɪŋ] *n* : árbol *m* joven

sapphire ['sæ,faɪr] *n* : zafiro *m*

sarcasm ['sɑr,kæzəm] *n* : sarcasmo *m*

sarcastic [sɑr'kæstɪk] *adj* : sarcástico — **sarcastically** [-tɪkli] *adv*

sarcophagus [sɑr'kɑfəgəs] *n, pl* **-gi** [-,gaɪ, -,dʒaɪ] : sarcófago *m*

sardine [sɑr'di:n] *n* : sardina *f*

sardonic [sɑr'dɑnɪk] *adj* : sardónico — **sardonically** [-nɪkli] *adv*

sarsaparilla [,sæspə'rɪlə, ,sɑrs-] *n* : zarzaparrilla *f*

sash ['sæʃ] *n* **1** : faja *f* (de un vestido), fajín *m* (de un uniforme) **2** *pl* **sash** : marco *m* (de una ventana)

sassafras ['sæsə,fræs] *n* : sasafrás *m*

sassy ['sæsi] *adj* **sassier; -est** → **saucy**

sat → **sit**

Satan ['seɪtən] *n* : Satanás *m*, Satán *m*

satanic [sə'tænɪk, seɪ-] *adj* : satánico — **satanically** [-nɪkli] *adv*

satchel ['sætʃəl] *n* : cartera *f*, saco *m*

sate ['seɪt] *vt* **sated; sating** : saciar

satellite [ˈsætə͵laɪt] *n* **:** satélite *m* <spy satellite : satélite espía>
satiate [ˈseɪʃi͵eɪt] *vt* **-ated; -ating :** saciar, hartar
satin [ˈsætən] *n* **:** raso *m,* satín *m,* satén *m*
satire [ˈsæ͵taɪr] *n* **:** sátira *f*
satiric [səˈtɪrɪk] *or* **satirical** [-ɪkəl] *adj* **:** satírico
satirize [ˈsætə͵raɪz] *vt* **-rized; -rizing :** satirizar
satisfaction [͵sætəsˈfækʃən] *n* **:** satisfacción *f*
satisfactory [͵sætəsˈfæktəri] *adj* **:** satisfactorio, bueno — **satisfactorily** [-rəli] *adv*
satisfy [ˈsætəs͵faɪ] *v* **-fied; -fying** *vt* **1** PLEASE **:** satisfacer, contentar **2** CONVINCE **:** convencer **3** FULFILL **:** satisfacer, cumplir con, llenar **4** SETTLE **:** pagar, saldar (una cuenta) — *vi* SUFFICE **:** bastar
saturate [ˈsætʃə͵reɪt] *vt* **-rated; -rating 1** SOAK **:** empapar **2** FILL **:** saturar
saturation [͵sætʃəˈreɪʃən] *n* **:** saturación *f*
Saturday [ˈsætər͵deɪ, -di] *n* **:** sábado *m*
Saturn [ˈsætərn] *n* **:** Saturno *m*
satyr [ˈseɪtər, ˈsæ-] *n* **:** sátiro *m*
sauce [ˈsɔs] *n* **:** salsa *f*
saucepan [ˈsɔs͵pæn] *n* **:** cacerola *f,* cazo *m,* cazuela *f*
saucer [ˈsɔsər] *n* **:** platillo *m*
sauciness [ˈsɔsinəs] *n* **:** descaro *m,* frescura *f*
saucy [ˈsɔsi] *adj* **saucier; -est** IMPUDENT **:** descarado, fresco *fam* — **saucily** *adv*
sauna [ˈsɔnə, ˈsaʊnə] *n* **:** sauna *mf*
saunter [ˈsɔntər, ˈsɑn-] *vi* **:** pasear, parsearse
sausage [ˈsɔsɪdʒ] *n* **:** salchicha *f,* embutido *m*
sauté [sɔˈteɪ, soː-] *vt* **-téed** *or* **-téd; -téing :** saltear, sofreír
savage[1] [ˈsævɪdʒ] *adj* **:** salvaje, feroz — **savagely** *adv*
savage[2] *n* **:** salvaje *mf*
savagery [ˈsævɪdʒri, -dʒəri] *n, pl* **-ries 1** FEROCITY **:** ferocidad *f* **2** WILDNESS **:** salvajismo *m*
save[1] [ˈseɪv] *vt* **saved; saving 1** RESCUE **:** salvar, rescatar **2** PRESERVE **:** preservar, conservar **3** KEEP **:** guardar, ahorrar (dinero), almacenar (alimentos)
save[2] *prep* EXCEPT **:** salvo, excepto, menos
savior [ˈseɪvjər] *n* **1 :** salvador *m,* -dora *f* **2 the Savior :** el Salvador *m*
savor[1] [ˈseɪvər] *vt* **:** saborear
savor[2] *n* **:** sabor *m*
savory [ˈseɪvəri] *adj* **:** sabroso
saw[1] → **see**
saw[2] [ˈsɔ] *vt* **sawed; sawed** *or* **sawn** [ˈsɔn]; **sawing :** serrar, cortar (con sierra)
saw[3] *n* **:** sierra *f*
sawdust [ˈsɔ͵dʌst] *n* **:** aserrín *m,* serrín *m*
sawhorse [ˈsɔ͵hɔrs] *n* **:** caballete *m,* burro *m* (en carpintería)
sawmill [ˈsɔ͵mɪl] *n* **:** aserradero *m*
saxophone [ˈsæksə͵foːn] *n* **:** saxofón *m*
say[1] [ˈseɪ] *v* **said** [ˈsɛd]; **saying; says** [ˈsɛz] *vt* **1** EXPRESS, UTTER **:** decir, expresar <to say no : decir que no> <that goes without saying : ni que decir tiene> <no sooner said than done : dicho y hecho> <to say again : repetir> <to say one's prayers : rezar> **2** INDICATE **:** marcar, poner <my watch says three o'clock : mi reloj marca las tres> <what does the sign say? : ¿qué pone el letrero?> **3** ALLEGE **:** decir <it's said that she's pretty : se dice que es bonita> — *vi* **:** decir
say[2] *n, pl* **says** [ˈseɪz] **:** voz *f,* opinión *f* <to have no say : no tener ni voz ni voto> <to have one's say : dar uno su opinión>
saying [ˈseɪɪŋ] *n* **:** dicho *m,* refrán *m*
scab [ˈskæb] *n* **1 :** costra *f,* postilla *f* (en una herida) **2** STRIKEBREAKER **:** rompehuelgas *mf,* esquirol *mf*
scabbard [ˈskæbərd] *n* **:** vaina *f* (de una espada), funda *f* (de un puñal, etc.)
scabby [ˈskæbi] *adj* **scabbier; -est :** lleno de costras
scaffold [ˈskæfəld, -͵foːld] *n* **1** *or* **scaffolding :** andamio *m* (para obreros, etc.) **2 :** patíbulo *m,* cadalso *m* (para ejecuciones)
scald [ˈskɔld] *vt* **1** BURN **:** escaldar **2** HEAT **:** calentar (hasta el punto de ebullición)
scale[1] [ˈskeɪl] *v* **scaled; scaling** *vt* **1 :** escamar (un pescado) **2** CLIMB **:** escalar (un muro, etc.) **3 to scale down :** reducir — *vi* WEIGH **:** pesar <he scaled in at 200 pounds : pesó 200 libras>
scale[2] *n* **1** *or* **scales :** balanza *f,* báscula *f* (para pesar) **2 :** escama *f* (de un pez, etc.) **3** EXTENT **:** escala *f,* proporción *f* <wage scale : escala salarial> **4 :** escala *f* (en música, en cartografía, etc.) <to draw to scale : dibujar a escala>
scallion [ˈskæljən] *n* **:** cebollino *m,* cebolleta *f*
scallop [ˈskɑləp, ˈskæ-] *n* **1 :** vieira *f* (molusco) **2 :** festón *m* (decoración)
scalp[1] [ˈskælp] *vt* **:** arrancar la cabellera a
scalp[2] *n* **:** cuero *m* cabelludo
scalpel [ˈskælpəl] *n* **:** bisturí *m,* escalpelo *m*
scaly [ˈskeɪli] *adj* **scalier; -est :** escamoso
scam [ˈskæm] *n* **:** estafa *f,* timo *m fam,* chanchullo *m fam*
scamp [ˈskæmp] *n* **:** bribón *m,* -bona *f;* granuja *mf;* travieso *m,* -sa *f*
scamper [ˈskæmpər] *vi* **:** corretear

scan[1] ['skæn] *vt* **scanned; scanning 1** : escandir (versos) **2** SCRUTINIZE : escudriñar, escrutar <to scan the horizon : escudriñar el horizonte> **3** PERUSE : echarle un vistazo a (un periódico, etc.) **4** EXPLORE : explorar (con radar), hacer un escáner de (en ecografía) **5** : escanear (una imagen)

scan[2] *n* **1** : ecografía *f,* examen *m* ultrasónico (en medicina) **2** : imagen *f* escaneada (en una computadora)

scandal ['skændəl] *n* **1** DISGRACE, OUTRAGE : escándalo *m* **2** GOSSIP : habladurías *fpl,* chismes *mpl*

scandalize ['skændəlˌaɪz] *vt* **-ized; -izing** : escandalizar

scandalous ['skændələs] *adj* : de escándalo

Scandinavian[1] [ˌskændə'neɪviən] *adj* : escandinavo

Scandinavian[2] *n* : escandinavo *m,* -va *f*

scanner ['skænər] *n* : escáner *m,* scanner *m*

scant ['skænt] *adj* : escaso

scanty ['skænti] *adj* **scantier; -est** : exiguo, escaso <a scanty meal : una comida insuficiente> — **scantily** [-təli] *adv*

scapegoat ['skeɪpˌgoːt] *n* : chivo *m* expiatorio, cabeza *f* de turco

scapula ['skæpjələ] *n, pl* **-lae** [-ˌliː, -ˌlaɪ] *or* **-las** → **shoulder blade**

scar[1] ['skɑr] *v* **scarred; scarring** *vt* : dejar una cicatriz en — *vi* : cicatrizar

scar[2] *n* : cicatriz *f,* marca *f*

scarab ['skærəb] *n* : escarabajo *m*

scarce ['skɛrs] *adj* **scarcer; -est** : escaso

scarcely ['skɛrsli] *adv* **1** BARELY : apenas **2** : ni mucho menos, ni nada que se le parezca <he's scarcely an expert : ciertamente no es experto>

scarcity ['skɛrsət̬i] *n, pl* **-ties** : escasez *f*

scare[1] ['skɛr] *vt* **scared; scaring** : asustar, espantar

scare[2] *n* **1** FRIGHT : susto *m,* sobresalto *m* **2** ALARM : pánico *m*

scarecrow ['skɛrˌkroː] *n* : espantapájaros *m,* espantajo *m*

scarf ['skɑrf] *n, pl* **scarves** ['skɑrvz] *or* **scarfs 1** MUFFLER : bufanda *f* **2** KERCHIEF : pañuelo *m*

scarlet ['skɑrlət] *n* : escarlata *f* — **scarlet** *adj*

scarlet fever *n* : escarlatina *f*

scary ['skɛri] *adj* **scarier; -est** : espantoso, pavoroso

scathing ['skeɪðɪŋ] *adj* : mordaz, cáustico

scatter ['skæt̬ər] *vt* : esparcir, desparramar — *vi* DISPERSE : dispersarse

scavenge ['skævəndʒ] *v* **-venged; -venging** *vt* : rescatar (de la basura), pepenar *CA, Mex* — *vi* : rebuscar, hurgar en la basura <to scavenge for food : andar buscando comida>

scavenger ['skævəndʒər] *n* **1** : persona *f* que rebusca en las basuras; pepenador *m,* -dora *f CA, Mex* **2** : carroñero *m,* -ra *f* (animal)

scenario [sə'næriˌoː, -'nɑr-] *n, pl* **-ios 1** PLOT : argumento *m* (en teatro), guión *m* (en cine) **2** SITUATION : situación *f* hipotética <in the worst-case scenario : en el peor de los casos>

scene ['siːn] *n* **1** : escena *f* (en una obra de teatro) **2** SCENERY : decorado *m* (en el teatro) **3** VIEW : escena *f* **4** LOCALE : escenario *m* **5** COMMOTION, FUSS : escándalo *m,* escena *f* <to make a scene : armar un escándalo>

scenery ['siːnəri] *n, pl* **-eries 1** : decorado *m* (en el teatro) **2** LANDSCAPE : paisaje *m*

scenic ['siːnɪk] *adj* : pintoresco

scent[1] ['sɛnt] *vt* **1** SMELL : oler, olfatear **2** PERFUME : perfumar **3** SENSE : sentir, percibir

scent[2] *n* **1** ODOR : olor *m,* aroma *m* **2** : olfato *m* <a dog with a keen scent : un perro con un buen olfato> **3** PERFUME : perfume *m*

scented ['sɛntəd] *adj* : perfumado

scepter ['sɛptər] *n* : cetro *m*

sceptic ['skɛptɪk] → **skeptic**

schedule[1] ['skɛˌdʒuːl, -dʒəl, *esp Brit* 'ʃɛdˌjuːl] *vt* **-uled; -uling** : planear, programar

schedule[2] *n* **1** PLAN : programa *m,* plan *m* <on schedule : según lo previsto> <behind schedule : atrasado, con retraso> **2** TIMETABLE : horario *m*

scheme[1] ['skiːm] *vi* **schemed; scheming** : intrigar, conspirar

scheme[2] *n* **1** PLAN : plan *m,* proyecto *m* **2** PLOT, TRICK : intriga *f,* ardid *m* **3** FRAMEWORK : esquema *f* <a color scheme : una combinación de colores>

schemer ['skiːmər] *n* : intrigante *mf*

schism ['sɪzəm, 'skɪ-] *n* : cisma *m*

schizophrenia [ˌskɪtsə'friːniə, ˌskɪzə-, -'frɛ-] *n* : esquizofrenia *f*

schizophrenic [ˌskɪtsə'frɛnɪk, ˌskɪzə-] *n* : esquizofrénico *m,* -ca *f* — **schizophrenic** *adj*

scholar ['skɑlər] *n* **1** STUDENT : escolar *mf;* alumno *m,* -na *f* **2** EXPERT : especialista *mf*

scholarly ['skɑlərli] *adj* : erudito

scholarship ['skɑlərˌʃɪp] *n* **1** LEARNING : erudición *f* **2** GRANT : beca *f*

scholastic [skə'læstɪk] *adj* : académico

school[1] ['skuːl] *vt* : instruir, enseñar

school[2] *n* **1** : escuela *f,* colegio *m* (institución) **2** : estudiantes *mfpl* y profesores *mpl* (de una escuela) **3** : escuela *f* (en pintura, etc.) <the Flemish school : la escuela flamenca> **4 school of fish** : banco *m,* cardumen *m*

schoolboy ['skuːlˌbɔɪ] *n* : escolar *m,* colegial *m*

schoolgirl ['skuːlˌgərl] *n* : escolar *f,* colegiala *f*

schoolhouse [ˈskuːlˌhaʊs] *n* : escuela *f*

schoolmate [ˈskuːlˌmeɪt] *n* : compañero *m*, -ra *f* de escuela

schoolroom [ˈskuːlˌruːm, -ˌrʊm] → **classroom**

schoolteacher [ˈskuːlˌtiːtʃər] *n* : maestro *m*, -tra *f*; profesor *m*, -sora *f*

schooner [ˈskuːnər] *n* : goleta *f*

science [ˈsaɪənts] *n* : ciencia *f*

scientific [ˌsaɪənˈtɪfɪk] *adj* : científico — **scientifically** [-fɪkli] *adv*

scientist [ˈsaɪəntɪst] *n* : científico *m*, -ca *f*

scintillating [ˈsɪntəˌleɪt̬ɪŋ] *adj* : chispeante, brillante

scissors [ˈsɪzərz] *npl* : tijeras *fpl*

scoff [ˈskɑf] *vi* **to scoff at** : burlarse de, mofarse de

scold [ˈskoːld] *vt* : regañar, reprender, reñir

scoop[1] [ˈskuːp] *vt* **1** : sacar (con pala o cucharón) **2 to scoop out** HOLLOW : vaciar, ahuecar

scoop[2] *n* : pala *f* (para harina, etc.), cucharón *m* (para helado, etc.)

scoot [ˈskuːt] *vi* : ir rápidamente <she scooted around the corner : volvió la esquina a toda prisa>

scooter [ˈskuːt̬ər] *n* : patineta *f*, monopatín *m*, patinete *m*

scope [ˈskoːp] *n* **1** RANGE : alcance *m*, ámbito *m*, extensión *f* **2** OPPORTUNITY : posibilidades *fpl*, libertad *f*

scorch [ˈskɔrtʃ] *vt* : chamuscar, quemar

score[1] [ˈskor] *v* **scored; scoring** *vt* **1** RECORD : anotar **2** MARK, SCRATCH : marcar, rayar **3** : marcar, meter (en deportes) **4** GAIN : ganar, apuntarse **5** GRADE : calificar (exámenes, etc.) **6** : instrumentar, orquestar (música) — *vi* **1** : marcar (en deportes) **2** : obtener una puntuación (en un examen)

score[2] *n, pl* **scores 1** *or pl* **score** TWENTY : veintena *f* **2** LINE, SCRATCH : línea *f*, marca *f* **3** : resultado *m* (en deportes) <what's the score? : ¿cómo va el marcador?> **4** GRADE, POINTS : calificación *f* (en un examen), puntuación *f* (en un concurso) **5** ACCOUNT : cuenta *f* <to settle a score : ajustar una cuenta> <on that score : a ese respecto> **6** : partitura *f* (musical)

scorn[1] [ˈskɔrn] *vt* : despreciar, menospreciar, desdeñar

scorn[2] *n* : desprecio *m*, menosprecio *m*, desdén *m*

scornful [ˈskɔrnfəl] *adj* : desdeñoso, despreciativo — **scornfully** *adv*

Scorpio [ˈskɔrpiˌoː] *n* : Escorpio *mf*, Escorpión *mf*

scorpion [ˈskɔrpiən] *n* : alacrán *m*, escorpión *m*

Scot [ˈskɑt] *n* : escocés *m*, -cesa *f*

Scotch[1] [ˈskɑtʃ] *adj* → **Scottish[1]**

Scotch[2] *npl* **the Scotch** : los escoceses

scot–free [ˈskɑtˈfriː] *adj* **to get off scot–free** : salir impune, quedar sin castigo

Scots [ˈskɑts] *n* : escocés *m* (idioma)

Scottish[1] [ˈskɑt̬ɪʃ] *adj* : escocés

Scottish[2] *n* → **Scots**

scoundrel [ˈskaʊndrəl] *n* : sinvergüenza *mf*; bellaco *m*, -ca *f*

scour [ˈskaʊər] *vt* **1** EXAMINE, SEARCH : registrar (un área), revisar (documentos, etc.) **2** SCRUB : fregar, restregar

scourge[1] [ˈskərdʒ] *vt* **scourged; scourging** : azotar

scourge[2] *n* : azote *m*

scout[1] [ˈskaʊt] *vi* **1** RECONNOITER : reconocer **2 to scout around for** : explorar en busca de

scout[2] *n* **1** : explorador *m*, -dora *f* **2** *or* **talent scout** : cazatalentos *mf*

scow [ˈskaʊ] *n* : barcaza *f*, gabarra *f*

scowl[1] [ˈskaʊl] *vi* : fruncir el ceño

scowl[2] *n* : ceño *m* fruncido

scram [ˈskræm] *vi* **scrammed; scramming** : largarse

scramble[1] [ˈskræmbəl] *v* **-bled; -bling** *vi* **1** : trepar, gatear (con torpeza) <he scrambled over the fence : se trepó a la cerca con dificultad> **2** STRUGGLE : pelearse (por) <they scrambled for seats : se pelearon por los asientos> — *vt* **1** JUMBLE : mezclar **2 to scramble eggs** : hacer huevos revueltos

scramble[2] *n* : rebatiña *f*, pelea *f*

scrap[1] [ˈskræp] *v* **scrapped; scrapping** *vt* DISCARD : desechar — *vi* FIGHT : pelearse

scrap[2] *n* **1** FRAGMENT : pedazo *m*, trozo *m* **2** FIGHT : pelea *f* **3** *or* **scrap metal** : chatarra *f* **4 scraps** *npl* LEFTOVERS : restos *mpl*, sobras *fpl*

scrapbook [ˈskræpˌbʊk] *n* : álbum *m* de recortes

scrape[1] [ˈskreɪp] *v* **scraped; scraping** *vt* **1** GRAZE, SCRATCH : rozar, rascar <to scrape one's knee : rasparse la rodilla> **2** CLEAN : raspar <to scrape carrots : raspar zanahorias> **3 to scrape off** : raspar (pintura, etc.) **4 to scrape up** *or* **to scrape together** : juntar, reunir poco a poco — *vi* **1** RUB : rozar **2 to scrape by** : arreglárselas, ir tirando

scrape[2] *n* **1** SCRAPING : raspadura *f* **2** SCRATCH : rasguño *m* **3** PREDICAMENT : apuro *m*, aprieto *m*

scratch[1] [ˈskrætʃ] *vt* **1** : arañar, rasguñar <to scratch an itch : rascarse> **2** MARK : rayar, marcar **3 to scratch out** : tachar

scratch[2] *n* **1** : rasguño *m*, arañazo *m* (en la piel), rayón *m* (en un mueble, etc.) **2** : sonido *m* rasposo <I heard a scratch at the door : oí como que raspaban a la puerta>

scratchy [ˈskrætʃi] *adj* **scratchier; -est** : áspero, que pica <a scratchy sweater : un suéter que pica>

scrawl[1] [ˈskrɔl] *v* : garabatear

scrawl[2] *n* : garabato *m*

scrawny ['skrɔni] *adj* **scrawnier; -est** : flaco, escuálido

scream1 ['skri:m] *vi* : chillar, gritar

scream2 *n* : chillido *m,* grito *m*

screech1 ['skri:tʃ] *vi* : chillar (dícese de las personas o de los animales), chirriar (dícese de los frenos, etc.)

screech2 *n* 1 : chillido *m,* grito *m* (de una persona o un animal) **2** : chirrido *m* (de frenos, etc.)

screen1 ['skri:n] *vt* **1** SHIELD : proteger **2** CONCEAL : tapar, ocultar **3** EXAMINE : someter a una revisión, hacerle un chequeo (a un paciente) **4** SIEVE : cribar

screen2 *n* **1** PARTITION : biombo *m,* pantalla *f* **2** SIEVE : criba *f* **3** : pantalla *f* (de un televisor, una computadora, etc.) **4** MOVIES : cine *m* **5** *or* **window screen** : ventana *f* de tela metálica

screw1 ['skru:] *vt* : atornillar — *vi* **to screw in** : atornillarse

screw2 *n* **1** : tornillo *m* (para fijar algo) **2** TWIST : vuelta *f* **3** PROPELLER : hélice *f*

screwdriver ['skru:ˌdraɪvər] *n* : destornillador *m,* desarmador *m Mex*

scribble1 ['skrɪbəl] *v* **-bled; -bling** : garabatear

scribble2 *n* : garabato *m*

scribe ['skraɪb] *n* : escriba *m*

scrimp ['skrɪmp] *vi* **1 to scrimp on** : escatimar **2 to scrimp and save** : hacer economías

script ['skrɪpt] *n* **1** HANDWRITING : letra *f,* escritura *f* **2** : guión *m* (de una película, etc.)

scriptural ['skrɪptʃərəl] *adj* : bíblico

scripture ['skrɪptʃər] *n* **1** : escritos *mpl* sagrados (de una religión) **2 the Scriptures** *npl* : las Sagradas Escrituras

scroll ['skro:l] *n* **1** : rollo *m* (de pergamino, etc.) **2** : voluta *f* (adorno en arquitectura)

scrotum ['skro:təm] *n, pl* **scrota** [-tə] *or* **scrotums** : escroto *m*

scrounge ['skraʊndʒ] *v* **scrounged; scrounging** *vt* **1** BUM : gorrear *fam,* sablear *fam* (dinero) **2 to scrounge around for** : buscar, andar a la busca de — *vi* **to scrounge off someone** : vivir a costa de alguien

scrub1 ['skrʌb] *vt* **scrubbed; scrubbing** : restregar, fregar

scrub2 *n* **1** THICKET, UNDERBRUSH : maleza *f,* matorral *m,* matorrales *mpl* **2** SCRUBBING : fregado *m,* restregadura *f*

scrubby ['skrʌbi] *adj* **-bier; -est 1** STUNTED : achaparrado **2** : cubierto de maleza

scruff ['skrʌf] *n* **by the scruff of the neck** : por el cogote, por el pescuezo

scrumptious ['skrʌmpʃəs] *adj* : delicioso, muy rico

scruple ['skru:pəl] *n* : escrúpulo *m*

scrupulous ['skru:pjələs] *adj* : escrupuloso — **scrupulously** *adv*

scrutinize ['skru:tənˌaɪz] *vt* **-nized; -nizing** : escrutar, escudriñar

scrutiny ['skru:təni] *n, pl* **-nies** : escrutinio *m,* inspección *f*

scuff ['skʌf] *vt* : rayar, raspar <to scuff one's feet : arrastrar los pies>

scuffle1 ['skʌfəl] *vi* **-fled; -fling 1** TUSSLE : pelearse **2** SHUFFLE : caminar arrastrando los pies

scuffle2 *n* **1** TUSSLE : refriega *f,* pelea *f* **2** SHUFFLE : arrastre *m* de los pies

scull1 ['skʌl] *vi* : remar (con espadilla)

scull2 *n* OAR : espadilla *f*

sculpt ['skʌlpt] *v* : esculpir

sculptor ['skʌlptər] *n* : escultor *m,* -tora *f*

sculpture1 ['skʌlptʃər] *vt* **-tured; -turing** : esculpir

sculpture2 *n* : escultura *f*

scum ['skʌm] *n* **1** FROTH : espuma *f,* nata *f* **2** : verdín *m* (encima de un líquido)

scurrilous ['skərələs] *adj* : difamatorio, calumnioso, injurioso

scurry ['skəri] *vi* **-ried; -rying** : corretear

scurvy ['skərvi] *n* : escorbuto *m*

scuttle1 ['skʌtəl] *v* **-tled; -tling** *vt* : hundir (un barco) — *vi* SCAMPER : corretear

scuttle2 *n* : cubo *m* (para carbón)

scythe ['saɪð] *n* : guadaña *f*

sea1 ['si:] *adj* : del mar

sea2 *n* **1** : mar *mf* <the Black Sea : el Mar Negro> <on the high seas : en alta mar> <heavy seas : mar gruesa, mar agitada> **2** MASS : mar *m,* multitud *f* <a sea of faces : un mar de rostros>

seabird ['si:ˌbərd] *n* : ave *f* marina

seacoast ['si:ˌko:st] *n* : costa *f,* litoral *m*

seafarer ['si:ˌfærər] *n* : marinero *m*

seafaring1 ['si:ˌfærɪŋ] *adj* : marinero

seafaring2 *n* : navegación *f*

seafood ['si:ˌfu:d] *n* : mariscos *mpl*

seagull ['si:ˌgʌl] *n* : gaviota *f*

sea horse ['si:ˌhɔrs] *n* : hipocampo *m,* caballito *m* de mar

seal1 ['si:l] *vt* **1** CLOSE : sellar, cerrar <to seal a letter : cerrar una carta> <to seal an agreement : sellar un acuerdo> **2 to seal up** : tapar, rellenar (una grieta, etc.)

seal2 *n* **1** : foca *f* (animal) **2** : sello *m* <seal of approval : sello de aprobación> **3** CLOSURE : cierre *m,* precinto *m*

sea level *n* : nivel *m* del mar

sea lion *n* : león *m* marino

sealskin ['si:lˌskɪn] *n* : piel *f* de foca

seam1 ['si:m] *vt* **1** STITCH : unir con costuras **2** MARK : marcar

seam2 *n* **1** STITCHING : costura *f* **2** LODE, VEIN : veta *f,* filón *m*

seaman ['si:mən] *n, pl* **-men** [-mən, -ˌmɛn] **1** SAILOR : marinero *m* **2** : marino *m* (en la armada)

seamless ['si:mləs] *adj* **1** : sin costuras, de una pieza **2** : perfecto <a seamless transition : una transición fluida>

seamstress [ˈsiːmpstrəs] *n* : costurera *f*

seamy [ˈsiːmi] *adj* **seamier; -est** : sórdido

séance [ˈseɪˌɑnts] *n* : sesión *f* de espiritismo

seaplane [ˈsiːˌpleɪn] *n* : hidroavión *m*

seaport [ˈsiːˌport] *n* : puerto *m* marítimo

sear [ˈsɪr] *vt* **1** PARCH, WITHER : secar, resecar **2** SCORCH : chamuscar, quemar

search[1] [ˈsərtʃ] *vt* : registrar (un edificio, un área), cachear (a una persona), buscar en — *vi* **to search for** : buscar

search[2] *n* : búsqueda *f*, registro *m* (de un edificio, etc.), cacheo *m* (de una persona)

searchlight [ˈsərtʃˌlaɪt] *n* : reflector *m*

seashell [ˈsiːˌʃɛl] *n* : concha *f* (marina)

seashore [ˈsiːˌʃor] *n* : orilla *f* del mar

seasick [ˈsiːˌsɪk] *adj* : mareado <to get seasick : marearse>

seasickness [ˈsiːˌsɪknəs] *n* : mareo *m*

seaside → **seacoast**

season[1] [ˈsiːzən] *vt* **1** FLAVOR, SPICE : sazonar, condimentar **2** CURE : curar, secar <seasoned wood : madera seca> <a seasoned veteran : un veterano avezado>

season[2] *n* **1** : estación *f* (del año) **2** : temporada *f* (en deportes, etc.) <baseball season : temporada de beisbol>

seasonable [ˈsiːzənəbəl] *adj* **1** : propio de la estación (dícese del tiempo, de las temperaturas, etc.) **2** TIMELY : oportuno

seasonal [ˈsiːzənəl] *adj* : estacional — **seasonally** *adv*

seasoning [ˈsiːzənɪŋ] *n* : condimento *m*, sazón *f*

seat[1] [ˈsiːt] *vt* **1** SIT : sentar <please be seated : siéntense, por favor> **2** HOLD : tener cabida para <the stadium seats 40,000 : el estadio tiene 40,000 asientos>

seat[2] *n* **1** : asiento *m*, plaza *f* (en un vehículo) <take a seat : tome asiento> **2** BOTTOM : fondillos *mpl* (de la ropa), trasero *m* (del cuerpo) **3** : sede *f* (de un gobierno, etc.)

seat belt *n* : cinturón *m* de seguridad

sea urchin *n* : erizo *m* de mar

seawall [ˈsiːˌwɑl] *n* : rompeolas *m*, dique *m* marítimo

seawater [ˈsiːˌwɔt̬ər, -ˌwɑ-] *n* : agua *f* de mar

seaweed [ˈsiːˌwiːd] *n* : alga *f* marina

seaworthy [ˈsiːˌwərðí] *adj* : en condiciones de navegar

secede [sɪˈsiːd] *vi* **-ceded; -ceding** : separarse (de una nación, etc.)

seclude [sɪˈkluːd] *vt* **-cluded; -cluding** : aislar

seclusion [sɪˈkluːʒən] *n* : aislamiento *m*

second[1] [ˈsɛkənd] *vt* : secundar, apoyar (una moción)

second[2] *or* **secondly** [ˈsɛkəndli] *adv* : en segundo lugar

second[3] *adj* : segundo

second[4] *n* **1** : segundo *m*, -da *f* (en una serie) **2** : segundo *m*, segunda parte *f* **3** : segundo *m*, ayudante *m* (en deportes) **4** MOMENT : segundo *m*, momento *m*

secondary [ˈsɛkənˌdɛri] *adj* : secundario

secondhand [ˈsɛkəndˈhænd] *adj* : de segunda mano

second lieutenant *n* : alférez *mf*, subteniente *mf*

second–rate [ˈsɛkəndˈreɪt] *adj* : mediocre, de segunda categoría

secrecy [ˈsiːkrəsi] *n, pl* **-cies** : secreto *m*

secret[1] [ˈsiːkrət] *adj* : secreto — **secretly** *adv*

secret[2] *n* : secreto *m*

secretarial [ˌsɛkrəˈtɛriəl] *adj* : de secretario, de oficina

secretariat [ˌsɛkrəˈtɛriət] *n* : secretaría *f*, secretariado *m*

secretary [ˈsɛkrəˌtɛri] *n, pl* **-taries 1** : secretario *m*, -ria *f* (en una oficina, etc.) **2** : ministro *m*, -tra *f*; secretario *m*, -ria *f* <Secretary of State : Secretario de Estado>

secrete [sɪˈkriːt] *vt* **-creted; -creting 1** : secretar, segregar (en fisiología) **2** HIDE : ocultar

secretion [sɪˈkriːʃən] *n* : secreción *f*

secretive [ˈsiːkrət̬ɪv, sɪˈkriːt̬ɪv] *adj* : reservado, callado, secreto

sect [ˈsɛkt] *n* : secta *f*

sectarian [sɛkˈtɛriən] *adj* : sectario

section [ˈsɛkʃən] *n* : sección *f*, parte *f* (de un mueble, etc.), sector *m* (de la población), barrio *m* (de una ciudad)

sectional [ˈsɛkʃənəl] *adj* **1** : en sección, en corte <a sectional diagram : un gráfico en corte> **2** FACTIONAL : de grupo, entre facciones **3** : modular <sectional furniture : muebles modulares>

sector [ˈsɛktər] *n* : sector *m*

secular [ˈsɛkjələr] *adj* **1** : secular, laico <secular life : la vida secular> **2** : seglar (dícese de los sacerdotes, etc.)

secure[1] [sɪˈkjʊr] *vt* **-cured; -curing 1** FASTEN : asegurar (una puerta, etc.), sujetar **2** GET : conseguir

secure[2] *adj* **-curer; -est** : seguro — **securely** *adv*

security [sɪˈkjʊrət̬i] *n, pl* **-ties 1** SAFETY : seguridad *f* **2** GUARANTEE : garantía *f* **3 securities** *npl* : valores *mpl*

sedan [sɪˈdæn] *n* **1** *or* **sedan chair** : silla *f* de manos **2** : sedán *m* (automóvil)

sedate[1] [sɪˈdeɪt] *vt* **-dated; -dating** : sedar

sedate[2] *adj* : sosegado — **sedately** *adv*

sedation [sɪˈdeɪʃən] *n* : sedación *f*

sedative[1] [ˈsɛdət̬ɪv] *adj* : sedante

sedative[2] *n* : sedante *m*, calmante *m*

sedentary [ˈsɛdən,tɛri] *adj* : sedentario
sedge [ˈsɛdʒ] *n* : juncia *f*
sediment [ˈsɛdəmənt] *n* : sedimento *m* (geológico), poso *m* (en un líquido)
sedimentary [,sɛdəˈmɛntəri] *adj* : sedimentario
sedition [sɪˈdɪʃən] *n* : sedición *f*
seditious [sɪˈdɪʃəs] *adj* : sedicioso
seduce [sɪˈdu:s, -ˈdju:s] *vt* **-duced; -ducing** : seducir
seduction [sɪˈdʌkʃən] *n* : seducción *f*
seductive [sɪˈdʌktɪv] *adj* : seductor, seductivo
see[1] [ˈsi:] *v* **saw** [ˈsɔ]; **seen** [ˈsi:n]; **seeing** *vt* **1** : ver <I saw a dog : vi un perro> <see you later! : ¡hasta luego!> **2** EXPERIENCE : ver, conocer **3** UNDERSTAND : ver, entender **4** ENSURE : asegurarse <see that it's correct : asegúrese de que sea correcto> **5** ACCOMPANY : acompañar **6 to see off** : despedir, despedirse de — *vi* **1** : ver <seeing is believing : ver para creer> **2** UNDERSTAND : entender, ver <now I see! : ¡ya entiendo!> **3** CONSIDER : ver <let's see : vamos a ver> **4 to see to** : ocuparse de
see[2] *n* : sede *f* <the Holy See : la Santa Sede>
seed[1] [ˈsi:d] *vt* **1** SOW : sembrar **2** : despepitar, quitarle las semillas a
seed[2] *n, pl* **seed** *or* **seeds** **1** : semilla *f,* pepita *f* (de una fruta) **2** SOURCE : germen *m,* semilla *f*
seedless [ˈsi:dləs] *adj* : sin semillas
seedling [ˈsi:dlɪŋ] *n* : plantón *m*
seedpod [ˈsi:d,pɑd] → **pod**
seedy [ˈsi:di] *adj* **seedier; -est** **1** : lleno de semillas **2** SHABBY : raído (dícese de la ropa) **3** RUN-DOWN : ruinoso (dícese de los edificios, etc.), sórdido
seek [ˈsi:k] *v* **sought** [ˈsɔt]; **seeking** *vt* **1** : buscar <to seek an answer : buscar una solución> **2** REQUEST : solicitar, pedir **3 to seek to** : tratar de, intentar de — *vi* SEARCH : buscar
seem [ˈsi:m] *vi* : parecer
seeming [ˈsi:mɪŋ] *adj* : aparente, ostensible
seemingly [ˈsi:mɪŋli] *adv* : aparentemente, según parece
seemly [ˈsi:mli] *adj* **seemlier; -est** : apropiado, decoroso
seep [ˈsi:p] *vi* : filtrarse
seer [ˈsi:ər] *n* : vidente *mf,* clarividente *mf*
seesaw[1] [ˈsi:,sɔ] *vi* **1** : jugar en un subibaja **2** VACILLATE : vacilar, oscilar
seesaw[2] *n* : balancín *m,* subibaja *m*
seethe [ˈsi:ð] *vi* **seethed; seething** **1** : bullir, hervir **2 to seethe with anger** : rabiar, estar furioso
segment [ˈsɛgmənt] *n* : segmento *m*
segmented [ˈsɛg,mɛntəd, sɛgˈmɛn-] *adj* : segmentado
segregate [ˈsɛgrɪ,geɪt] *vt* **-gated; -gating** : segregar
segregation [,sɛgrɪˈgeɪʃən] *n* : segregación *f*
seismic [ˈsaɪzmɪk, ˈsaɪs-] *adj* : sísmico
seize [ˈsi:z] *v* **seized; seizing** *vt* **1** CAPTURE : capturar, tomar, apoderarse de **2** ARREST : detener **3** CLUTCH, GRAB : agarrar, coger, aprovechar (una oportunidad) **4 to be seized with** : estar sobrecogido por — *vi or* **to seize up** : agarrotarse
seizure [ˈsi:ʒər] *n* **1** CAPTURE : toma *f,* captura *f* **2** ARREST : detención *f* **3** : ataque *m* <an epileptic seizure : un ataque epiléptico>
seldom [ˈsɛldəm] *adv* : pocas veces, rara vez, casi nunca
select[1] [səˈlɛkt] *vt* : escoger, elegir, seleccionar (a un candidato, etc.)
select[2] *adj* : selecto
selection [səˈlɛkʃən] *n* : selección *f,* elección *f*
selective [səˈlɛktɪv] *adj* : selectivo
selenium [səˈli:niəm] *n* : selenio *m*
self [ˈsɛlf] *n, pl* **selves** [ˈsɛlvz] **1** : ser *m,* persona *f* <the self : el yo> <with his whole self : con todo su ser> <her own self : su propia persona> **2** SIDE : lado (de la personalidad) <his better self : su lado bueno>
self–addressed [,sɛlfəˈdrɛst] *adj* : con la dirección del remitente <include a self-addressed envelope : incluya un sobre con su nombre y dirección>
self–appointed [,sɛlfəˈpɔɪntəd] *adj* : autoproclamado, autonombrado
self–assurance [,sɛlfəˈʃʊrən*t*s] *n* : seguridad *f* en sí mismo
self–assured [,sɛlfəˈʃʊrd] *adj* : seguro de sí mismo
self–centered [,sɛlfˈsɛntərd] *adj* : egocéntrico
self–confidence [,sɛlfˈkɑnfədən*t*s] *n* : confianza *f* en sí mismo
self–confident [,sɛlfˈkɑnfədənt] *adj* : seguro de sí mismo
self–conscious [,sɛlfˈkɑntʃəs] *adj* : cohibido, tímido
self–consciously [,sɛlfˈkɑntʃəsli] *adv* : de manera cohibida
self–consciousness [,sɛlfˈkɑntʃəsnəs] *n* : vergüenza *f,* timidez *f*
self–contained [,sɛlfkənˈteɪnd] *adj* **1** INDEPENDENT : independiente **2** RESERVED : reservado
self–control [,sɛlfkənˈtro:l] *n* : autocontrol *m,* control *m* de sí mismo
self–defense [,sɛlfdɪˈfɛn*t*s] *n* : defensa *f* propia, defensa *f* personal <to act in self-defense : actuar en defensa propia> <self-defense class : clase de defensa personal>
self–denial [,sɛlfdɪˈnaɪəl] *n* : abnegación *f*
self–destructive [,sɛlfdɪˈstrʌktɪv] *adj* : autodestructivo
self–determination [,sɛlfdɪ,tərməˈneɪʃən] *n* : autodeterminación *f*
self–discipline [,sɛlfˈdɪsəplən] *n* : autodisciplina *f*

self–employed [ˌsɛlfɪm'plɔɪd] *adj* : que trabaja por cuenta propia, autónomo

self–esteem [ˌsɛlfɪ'stiːm] *n* : autoestima *f,* amor *m* propio

self–evident [ˌsɛlf'ɛvədənt] *adj* : evidente, manifiesto

self–explanatory [ˌsɛlfɪk'splænəˌtori] *adj* : fácil de entender, evidente

self–expression [ˌsɛlfɪk'sprɛʃən] *n* : expresión *f* personal

self–government [ˌsɛlf'gʌvərmənt, -vərn-] *n* : autogobierno *m*

self–help [ˌsɛlf'hɛlp] *n* : autoayuda *f*

self–important [ˌsɛlfɪm'pɔrtənt] *adj* **1** VAIN : vanidoso, presumido **2** ARROGANT : arrogante

self–indulgent [ˌsɛlfɪn'dʌldʒənt] *adj* : que se permite excesos

self–inflicted [ˌsɛlfɪn'flɪktəd] *adj* : autoinfligido

self–interest [ˌsɛlf'ɪntrəst, -təˌrɛst] *n* : interés *m* personal

selfish ['sɛlfɪʃ] *adj* : egoísta

selfishly ['sɛlfɪʃli] *adv* : de manera egoísta

selfishness ['sɛlfɪʃnəs] *n* : egoísmo *m*

selfless ['sɛlfləs] *adj* UNSELFISH : desinteresado

self–made [ˌsɛlf'meɪd] *adj* : próspero gracias a sus propios esfuerzos

self–pity [ˌsɛlf'pɪt̬i] *n, pl* **-ties** : autocompasión *f*

self–portrait [ˌsɛlf'pɔrtrət] *n* : autorretrato *m*

self–propelled [ˌsɛlfpro'pɛld] *adj* : autopropulsado

self–reliance [ˌsɛlfri'laɪənts] *n* : independencia *f,* autosuficiencia *f*

self–respect [ˌsɛlfri'spɛkt] *n* : autoestima *f,* amor *m* propio

self–restraint [ˌsɛlfri'streɪnt] *n* : autocontrol *m,* moderación *f*

self–righteous [ˌsɛlf'raɪtʃəs] *adj* : santurrón, moralista

self–sacrifice [ˌsɛlf'sækrəˌfaɪs] *n* : abnegación *f*

selfsame ['sɛlfˌseɪm] *adj* : mismo

self–service [ˌsɛlf'sərvɪs] *adj* **1** : de autoservicio **2 self-service restaurant** : autoservicio *m*

self–sufficiency [ˌsɛlfsə'fɪʃəntsi] *n* : autosuficiencia *f*

self–sufficient [ˌsɛlfsə'fɪʃənt] *adj* : autosuficiente

self–taught [ˌsɛlf'tɔt] *adj* : autodidacto

sell ['sɛl] *v* **sold** ['soːld]; **selling** *vt* : vender — *vi* : venderse

seller ['sɛlər] *n* : vendedor *m,* -dora *f*

selves → **self**

semantics [sɪ'mæntɪks] *ns & pl* : semántica *f*

semaphore ['sɛməˌfor] *n* : semáforo *m*

semblance ['sɛmbləntṡ] *n* : apariencia *f*

semen ['siːmən] *n* : semen *m*

semester [sə'mɛstər] *n* : semestre *m*

semicolon ['sɛmiˌkoːlən, 'sɛˌmaɪ-] *n* : punto y coma *m*

semiconductor ['sɛmikənˌdʌktər, 'sɛˌmaɪ-] *n* : semiconductor *m*

semifinal ['sɛmiˌfaɪnəl, 'sɛˌmaɪ-] *n* : semifinal *f*

seminar ['sɛməˌnɑr] *n* : seminario *m*

seminary ['sɛməˌnɛri] *n, pl* **-naries** : seminario *m*

senate ['sɛnət] *n* : senado *m*

senator ['sɛnət̬ər] *n* : senador *m,* -dora *f*

send ['sɛnd] *vt* **sent** ['sɛnt]; **sending 1** : mandar, enviar <to send a letter : mandar una carta> <to send word : avisar, mandar decir> **2** PROPEL : mandar, lanzar <he sent it into left field : lo mandó al jardín izquierdo> <to send up dust : alzar polvo> **3 to send into a rage** : poner furioso

sender ['sɛndər] *n* : remitente *mf* (de una carta, etc.)

Senegalese [ˌsɛnəgə'liːz, -'liːs] *n* : senegalés *m,* -lesa *f* — **Senegalese** *adj*

senile ['siːˌnaɪl] *adj* : senil

senility [sɪ'nɪlət̬i] *n* : senilidad *f*

senior¹ ['siːnjər] *adj* **1** ELDER : mayor <John Doe, Senior : John Doe, padre> **2** : superior (en rango), más antiguo (en años de servicio) <a senior official : un alto oficial>

senior² *n* **1** : superior *m* (en rango) **2 to be someone's senior** : ser mayor que alguien <she's two years my senior : me lleva dos años>

seniority [ˌsiː'njɔrət̬i] *n* : antigüedad *f* (en años de servicio)

sensation [sɛn'seɪʃən] *n* : sensación *f*

sensational [sɛn'seɪʃənəl] *adj* : que causa sensación <sensational stories : historias sensacionalistas>

sense¹ ['sɛnts] *vt* **sensed; sensing** : sentir <he sensed danger : se dio cuenta del peligro>

sense² *n* **1** MEANING : sentido *m,* significado *m* **2** : sentido *m* <the sense of smell : el sentido del olfato> **3 to make sense** : tener sentido

senseless ['sɛntsləs] *adj* **1** MEANINGLESS : sin sentido, sin razón **2** UNCONSCIOUS : inconsciente

senselessly ['sɛntsləsli] *adv* : sin sentido

sensibility [ˌsɛntsə'bɪlət̬i] *n, pl* **-ties** : sensibilidad *f*

sensible ['sɛntsəbəl] *adj* **1** PERCEPTIBLE : sensible, perceptible **2** AWARE : consciente **3** REASONABLE : sensato <a sensible man : un hombre sensato> <sensible shoes : zapatos prácticos> — **sensibly** [-bli] *adv*

sensibleness ['sɛntsəbəlnəs] *n* : sensatez *f,* solidez *f*

sensitive ['sɛntsət̬ɪv] *adj* **1** : sensible, delicado <sensitive skin : piel sensible> **2** IMPRESSIONABLE : sensible, impresionable **3** TOUCHY : susceptible

sensitiveness ['sɛntsət̬ɪvnəs] → **sensitivity**
sensitivity [ˌsɛntsə'tɪvət̬i] *n, pl* **-ties** : sensibilidad *f*
sensor ['sɛnˌsɔr, 'sɛntsər] *n* : sensor *m*
sensory ['sɛntsəri] *adj* : sensorial
sensual ['sɛntʃʊəl] *adj* : sensual — **sensually** *adv*
sensuous ['sɛntʃʊəs] *adj* : sensual
sent → **send**
sentence[1] ['sɛntənts, -ənz] *vt* **-tenced; -tencing** : sentenciar
sentence[2] *n* **1** JUDGMENT : sentencia *f* **2** : oración *f,* frase *f* (en gramática)
sentiment ['sɛntəmənt] *n* **1** BELIEF : opinión *f* **2** FEELING : sentimiento *m* **3** → **sentimentality**
sentimental [ˌsɛntə'mɛntəl] *adj* : sentimental
sentimentality [ˌsɛntəˌmɛn'tæləṭi] *n, pl* **-ties** : sentimentalismo *m,* sensiblería *f*
sentinel ['sɛntənəl] *n* : centinela *mf,* guardia *mf*
sentry ['sɛntri] *n, pl* **-tries** : centinela *mf*
sepal ['si:pəl, 'sɛ-] *n* : sépalo *m*
separable ['sɛpərəbəl] *adj* : separable
separate[1] ['sɛpəˌreɪt] *v* **-rated; -rating** *vt* **1** DETACH, SEVER : separar **2** DISTINGUISH : diferenciar, distinguir — *vi* PART : separarse
separate[2] ['sɛprət, 'sɛpə-] *adj* **1** INDIVIDUAL : separado, aparte <a separate state : un estado separado> <in a separate envelope : en un sobre aparte> **2** DISTINCT : distinto
separately ['sɛprətli, 'sɛpə-] *adv* : por separado, separadamente, aparte
separation [ˌsɛpə'reɪʃən] *n* : separación *f*
sepia ['si:piə] *n* : color *m* sepia
September [sɛp'tɛmbər] *n* : septiembre *m,* setiembre *m*
sepulchre ['sɛpəlkər] *n* : sepulcro *m*
sequel ['si:kwəl] *n* **1** CONSEQUENCE : secuela *f,* consecuencia *f* **2** : continuación *f* (de una película, etc.)
sequence ['si:kwənts] *n* **1** SERIES : serie *f,* sucesión *f,* secuencia *f* (matemática o musical) **2** ORDER : orden *m*
sequester [sɪ'kwɛstər] *vt* : aislar
sequin ['si:kwən] *n* : lentejuela *f*
sequoia [sɪ'kwɔɪə] *n* : secoya *f,* secuoya *f*
sera → **serum**
Serb ['sərb] *or* **Serbian** ['sərbiən] *n* : serbio *m,* -bia *f* — **Serb** *or* **Serbian** *adj*
Serbo–Croatian [ˌsərbokro'eɪʃən] *n* : serbocroata *m* (idioma) — **Serbo–Croatian** *adj*
serenade[1] [ˌsɛrə'neɪd] *vt* **-naded; -nading** : darle una serenata (a alguien)
serenade[2] *n* : serenata *f*
serene [sə'ri:n] *adj* : sereno — **serenely** *adv*
serenity [sə'rɛnəṭi] *n* : serenidad *f*
serf ['sərf] *n* : siervo *m,* -va *f*
serge ['sərdʒ] *n* : sarga *f*
sergeant ['sɑrdʒənt] *n* : sargento *mf*
serial[1] ['sɪriəl] *adj* : seriado
serial[2] *n* : serie *f,* serial *m* (de radio o televisión), publicación *f* por entregas
serially ['sɪriəli] *adv* : en serie
series ['sɪrˌi:z] *n, pl* **series** : serie *f,* sucesión *f*
serious ['sɪriəs] *adj* **1** SOBER : serio **2** DEDICATED, EARNEST : serio, dedicado <to be serious about something : tomar algo en serio> **3** GRAVE : serio, grave <serious problems : problemas graves>
seriously ['sɪriəsli] *adv* **1** EARNESTLY : seriamente, con seriedad, en serio **2** SEVERELY : gravemente
seriousness ['sɪriəsnəs] *n* : seriedad *f,* gravedad *f*
sermon ['sərmən] *n* : sermón *m*
serpent ['sərpənt] *n* : serpiente *f*
serrated [sə'reɪṭəd, 'sɛrˌeɪṭəd] *adj* : dentado, serrado
serum ['sɪrəm] *n, pl* **serums** *or* **sera** ['sɪrə] : suero *m*
servant ['sərvənt] *n* : criado *m,* -da *f;* sirviente *m,* -ta *f*
serve ['sərv] *v* **served; serving** *vi* **1** : servir <to serve in the navy : servir en la armada> <to serve on a jury : ser miembro de un jurado> **2** DO, FUNCTION : servir <to serve as : servir de, servir como> **3** : sacar (en deportes) — *vt* **1** : servir <to serve God : servir a Dios> **2** HELP : servir <it serves no purpose : no sirve para nada> **3** : servir (comida o bebida) <dinner is served : la cena está servida> **4** SUPPLY : abastecer **5** CARRY OUT : cumplir, hacer <to serve time : servir una pena> **6 to serve a summons** : entregar una citación
server ['sərvər] *n* **1** : camarero *m,* -ra *f;* mesero *m,* -ra *f* (en un restaurante) **2** *or* **serving dish** : fuente *f* (para servir comida)
service[1] ['sərvəs] *vt* **-viced; -vicing 1** MAINTAIN : darle mantenimiento a (una máquina), revisar **2** REPAIR : arreglar, reparar
service[2] *n* **1** HELP, USE : servicio *m* <to do someone a service : hacerle un servicio a alguien> <at your service : a sus órdenes> <to be out of service : no funcionar> **2** CEREMONY : oficio *m* (religioso) **3** DEPARTMENT, SYSTEM : servicio *m* <social services : servicios sociales> <train service : servicio de trenes> **4** SET : juego *m,* servicio *m* <tea service : juego de té> **5** MAINTENANCE : mantenimiento *m,* revisión *f,* servicio *m* **6** : saque *m* (en deportes) **7 armed services** : fuerzas *fpl* armadas
serviceable ['sərvəsəbəl] *adj* **1** USEFUL : útil **2** DURABLE : duradero
serviceman ['sərvəsˌmæn, -mən] *n, pl* **-men** [-mən, -ˌmɛn] : militar *m*

service station *n* : estación *f* de servicio
servicewoman [ˈsərvəsˌwʊmən] *n, pl* **-women** [-ˌwɪmən] : militar *f*
servile [ˈsərvəl, -ˌvaɪl] *adj* : servil
serving [ˈsərvɪŋ] *n* HELPING : porción *f,* ración *f*
servitude [ˈsərvəˌtuːd, -ˌtjuːd] *n* : servidumbre *f*
sesame [ˈsɛsəmi] *n* : ajonjolí *m,* sésamo *m*
session [ˈsɛʃən] *n* : sesión *f*
set[1] [ˈsɛt] *v* **set; setting** *vt* **1** SEAT : sentar **2** *or* **to set down** PLACE : poner, colocar **3** ARRANGE : fijar, establecer <to set the date : poner la fecha> <he set the agenda : estableció la agenda> **4** ADJUST : poner (un reloj, etc.) **5** (*indicating the causing of a certain condition*) <to set fire to : prenderle fuego a> <she set it free : lo soltó> **6** MAKE, START : poner, hacer <I set them working : los puse a trabajar> — *vi* **1** SOLIDIFY : fraguar (dícese del cemento, etc.), cuajar (dícese de la gelatina, etc.) **2** : ponerse (dícese del sol o de la luna)
set[2] *adj* **1** ESTABLISHED, FIXED : fijo, establecido **2** RIGID : inflexible <to be set in one's ways : tener costumbres muy arraigadas> **3** READY : listo, preparado
set[3] *n* **1** COLLECTION : juego *m* <a set of dishes : un juego de platos, una vajilla> <a tool set : una caja de herramientas> **2** *or* **stage set** : decorado *m* (en el teatro), plató *m* (en el cine) **3** APPARATUS : aparato *m* <a television set : un televisor> **4** : conjunto *m* (en matemáticas)
setback [ˈsɛtˌbæk] *n* : revés *m,* contratiempo *m*
set in *vi* BEGIN : comenzar, empezar
set off *vt* **1** PROVOKE : provocar **2** EXPLODE : hacer estallar (una bomba, etc.) — *vi or* **to set forth** : salir
set out *vi* : salir (de viaje) — *vt* INTEND : proponerse
settee [sɛˈtiː] *n* : sofá *m*
setter [ˈsɛt̬ər] *n* : setter *mf* <Irish setter : setter irlandés>
setting [ˈsɛt̬ɪŋ] *n* **1** : posición *f,* ajuste *m* (de un control) **2** : engaste *m,* montura *f* (de una gema) **3** SCENE : escenario *m* (de una novela, etc.) **4** SURROUNDINGS : ambiente *m,* entorno *m,* marco *m*
settle [ˈsɛt̬əl] *v* **settled; settling** *vi* **1** ALIGHT, LAND : posarse (dícese de las aves), depositarse (dícese del polvo) **2** SINK : asentarse (dícese de los edificios) <he settled into the chair : se arrellanó en la silla> **3** : instalarse (en una casa), establecerse (en una ciudad o región) **4 to settle down** : calmarse, tranquilizarse <settle down! : ¡tranquilízate!, ¡cálmate!> **5 to settle down** : sentar cabeza, hacerse sensato <to marry and settle down : casarse y sentar cabeza> — *vt* **1** ARRANGE, DECIDE : fijar, decidir, acordar (planes, etc.) **2** RESOLVE : resolver, solucionar <to settle an argument : resolver una discusión> **3** PAY : pagar <to settle an account : saldar una cuenta> **4** CALM : calmar (los nervios), asentar (el estómago) **5** COLONIZE : colonizar **6 to settle oneself** : acomodarse, hacerse cómodo
settlement [ˈsɛt̬əlmənt] *n* **1** PAYMENT : pago *m,* liquidación *f* **2** COLONY : asentamiento *m* **3** RESOLUTION : acuerdo *m*
settler [ˈsɛt̬ələr] *n* : poblador *m,* -dora *f;* colono *m,* -na *f*
set up *vt* **1** ASSEMBLE : montar, armar **2** ERECT : levantar, erigir **3** ESTABLISH : establecer, fundar, montar (un negocio) **4** CAUSE : armar <they set up a clamor : armaron un alboroto>
seven[1] [ˈsɛvən] *adj* : siete
seven[2] *n* : siete *m*
seven hundred[1] *adj* : setecientos
seven hundred[2] *n* : setecientos *m*
seventeen[1] [ˌsɛvənˈtiːn] *adj* : diecisiete
seventeen[2] *n* : diecisiete *m*
seventeenth[1] [ˌsɛvənˈtiːnθ] *adj* : decimoséptimo
seventeenth[2] *n* **1** : decimoséptimo *m,* -ma *f* (en una serie) **2** : diecisieteavo *m,* diecisieteava parte *f*
seventh[1] [ˈsɛvənθ] *adj* : séptimo
seventh[2] *n* **1** : séptimo *m,* -ma *f* (en una serie) **2** : séptimo *m,* séptima parte *f*
seventieth[1] [ˈsɛvəntiəθ] *adj* : septuagésimo
seventieth[2] *n* **1** : septuagésimo *m,* -ma *f* (en una serie) **2** : setentavo *m,* setentava parte *f,* septuagésima parte *f*
seventy[1] [ˈsɛvənti] *adj* : setenta
seventy[2] *n, pl* **-ties** : setenta *m*
sever [ˈsɛvər] *vt* **-ered; -ering** : cortar, romper
several[1] [ˈsɛvrəl, ˈsɛvə-] *adj* **1** DISTINCT : distinto **2** SOME : varios <several weeks : varias semanas>
several[2] *pron* : varios, varias
severance [ˈsɛvrənts, sɛvə-] *n* **1** : ruptura *f* (de relaciones, etc.) **2 severance pay** : indemnización *f* (por despido)
severe [səˈvɪr] *adj* **severer; -est 1** STRICT : severo **2** AUSTERE : sobrio, austero **3** SERIOUS : grave <a severe wound : una herida grave> <severe aches : dolores fuertes> **4** DIFFICULT : duro, difícil — **severely** *adv*
severity [səˈvɛrət̬i] *n* **1** HARSHNESS : severidad *f* **2** AUSTERITY : sobriedad *f,* austeridad *f* **3** SERIOUSNESS : gravedad *f* (de una herida, etc.)
sew [ˈsoː] *v* **sewed; sewn** [ˈsoːn] *or* **sewed; sewing** : coser
sewage [ˈsuːɪdʒ] *n* : aguas *fpl* negras, aguas *fpl* residuales
sewer[1] [ˈsoːər] *n* : uno que cose
sewer[2] [ˈsuːər] *n* : alcantarilla *f,* cloaca *f*

sewing ['soːɪŋ] *n* : costura *f*

sex ['sɛks] *n* **1** : sexo *m* <the opposite sex : el sexo opuesto> **2** COPULATION : relaciones *fpl* sexuales

sexism ['sɛk,sɪzəm] *n* : sexismo *m*

sexist[1] ['sɛksɪst] *adj* : sexista

sexist[2] *n* : sexista *mf*

sextant ['sɛkstənt] *n* : sextante *m*

sextet [sɛk'stɛt] *n* : sexteto *m*

sexton ['sɛkstən] *n* : sacristán *m*

sexual ['sɛkʃʊəl] *adj* : sexual — **sexually** *adv*

sexuality [,sɛkʃʊ'æləṭi] *n* : sexualidad *f*

sexy ['sɛksi] *adj* **sexier; -est** : sexy

shabbily ['ʃæbəli] *adv* **1** : pobremente <shabbily dressed : pobremente vestido> **2** UNFAIRLY : mal, injustamente

shabbiness ['ʃæbinəs] *n* **1** : lo gastado (de ropa, etc.) **2** : lo mal vestido (de personas) **3** UNFAIRNESS : injusticia *f*

shabby ['ʃæbi] *adj* **shabbier; -est 1** : gastado (dícese de la ropa, etc.) **2** : mal vestido (dícese de las personas) **3** UNFAIR : malo, injusto <shabby treatment : mal trato>

shack ['ʃæk] *n* : choza *f,* rancho *m*

shackle[1] ['ʃækəl] *vt* **-led; -ling** : ponerle grilletes (a alguien)

shackle[2] *n* : grillete *m*

shad ['ʃæd] *n* : sábalo *m*

shade[1] ['ʃeɪd] *v* **shaded; shading** *vt* **1** SHELTER : proteger (del sol o de la luz) **2** *or* **to shade in** : matizar los colores de — *vi* : convertirse gradualmente <his irritation shaded into rage : su irritación iba convirtiéndose en furia>

shade[2] *n* **1** : sombra *f* <to give shade : dar sombra> **2** : tono *m* (de un color) **3** NUANCE : matiz *m* **4** : pantalla *f* (de una lámpara), persiana *f* (de una ventana)

shadow[1] ['ʃædoː] *vt* **1** DARKEN : ensombrecer **2** TRAIL : seguir de cerca, seguirle la pista (a alguien)

shadow[2] *n* **1** : sombra *f* **2** DARKNESS : oscuridad *f* **3** TRACE : sombra *f,* atisbo *m,* indicio *m* <without a shadow of a doubt : sin sombra de duda, sin lugar a dudas> **4 to cast a shadow over** : ensombrecer

shadowy ['ʃædowi] *adj* **1** INDISTINCT : vago, indistinto **2** DARK : oscuro

shady ['ʃeɪdi] *adj* **shadier; -est 1** : sombreado (dícese de un lugar), que da sombra (dícese de un árbol) **2** DISREPUTABLE : sospechoso (dícese de una persona), turbio (dícese de un negocio, etc.)

shaft ['ʃæft] *n* **1** : asta *f* (de una lanza), astil *m* (de una flecha), mango *m* (de una herramienta) **2** *or* **mine shaft** : pozo *m*

shaggy ['ʃægi] *adj* **shaggier; -est 1** HAIRY : peludo <a shaggy dog : un perro peludo> **2** UNKEMPT : enmarañado, despeinado (dícese del pelo, de las barbas, etc.)

shake[1] ['ʃeɪk] *v* **shook** ['ʃʊk]; **shaken** ['ʃeɪkən]; **shaking** *vt* **1** : sacudir, agitar, hacer temblar <he shook his head : negó con la cabeza> **2** WEAKEN : debilitar, hacer flaquear <it shook her faith : debilitó su confianza> **3** UPSET : afectar, alterar **4 to shake hands with someone** : darle la mano a alguien, estrecharle la mano a alguien — *vi* : temblar, sacudirse

shake[2] *n* : sacudida *f,* apretón *m* (de manos)

shaker ['ʃeɪkər] *n* **1 salt shaker** : salero *m* **2 pepper shaker** : pimentero *m* **3 cocktail shaker** : coctelera *f*

shake–up ['ʃeɪk,ʌp] *n* : reorganización *f*

shakily ['ʃeɪkəli] *adv* : temblorosamente

shaky ['ʃeɪki] *adj* **shakier; -est 1** SHAKING : tembloroso **2** UNSTABLE : poco firme, inestable **3** PRECARIOUS : precario, incierto **4** QUESTIONABLE : dudoso, cuestionable <shaky arguments : argumentos discutibles>

shale ['ʃeɪl] *n* : esquisto *m*

shall ['ʃæl] *v aux, past* **should** ['ʃʊd]; *present s & pl* **shall 1** (*used to express a command*) <you shall do as I say : harás lo que te digo> **2** (*used to express futurity*) <we shall see : ya veremos> <when shall we expect you? : ¿cuándo te podemos esperar?> **3** (*used to express determination*) <you shall have the money : tendrás el dinero> **4** (*used to express a condition*) <if he should die : si muriera> <if they should call, tell me : si llaman, dímelo> **5** (*used to express obligation*) <he should have said it : debería haberlo dicho> **6** (*used to express probability*) <they should arrive soon : deben (de) llegar pronto> <why should he lie? : ¿porqué ha de mentir?>

shallow ['ʃæloː] *adj* **1** : poco profundo (dícese del agua, etc.) **2** SUPERFICIAL : superficial

shallows ['ʃæloːz] *npl* : bajío *m,* bajos *mpl*

sham[1] ['ʃæm] *v* **shammed; shamming** : fingir

sham[2] *adj* : falso, fingido

sham[3] *n* **1** FAKE, PRETENSE : farsa *f,* simulación *f,* imitación *f* **2** FAKER : impostor *m,* -tora *f;* farsante *mf*

shamble ['ʃæmbəl] *vi* **-bled; -bling** : caminar arrastrando los pies

shambles ['ʃæmbəlz] *ns & pl* : caos *m,* desorden *m,* confusión *f*

shame[1] ['ʃeɪm] *vt* **shamed; shaming 1** : avergonzar <he was shamed by their words : sus palabras le dieron vergüenza> **2** DISGRACE : deshonrar

shame[2] *n* **1** : vergüenza *f* <to have no shame : no tener vergüenza> **2** DISGRACE : vergüenza *f,* deshonra *f* **3** PITY : lástima *f,* pena *f* <what a shame! : ¡qué pena!>

shamefaced [ˈʃeɪm,feɪst] *adj* : avergonzado
shameful [ˈʃeɪmfəl] *adj* : vergonzoso — **shamefully** *adv*
shameless [ˈʃeɪmləs] *adj* : descarado, desvergonzado — **shamelessly** *adv*
shampoo[1] [ʃæmˈpuː] *vt* : lavar (el pelo)
shampoo[2] *n, pl* **-poos** : champú *m*
shamrock [ˈʃæm,rɑk] *n* : trébol *m*
shank [ˈʃæŋk] *n* : parte *f* baja de la pierna
shan't [ˈʃænt] (*contraction of* **shall not**) → **shall**
shanty [ˈʃænti] *n, pl* **-ties** : choza *f*, rancho *m*
shape[1] [ˈʃeɪp] *v* **shaped; shaping** *vt* **1** : dar forma a, modelar (arcilla, etc.), tallar (madera, piedra), formar (carácter) <to be shaped like : tener forma de> **2** DETERMINE : decidir, determinar — *vi or* **to shape up** : tomar forma
shape[2] *n* **1** : forma *f*, figura *f* <in the shape of a circle : en forma de círculo> **2** CONDITION : estado *m*, condiciones *fpl*, forma *f* (física) <to get in shape : ponerse en forma>
shapeless [ˈʃeɪpləs] *adj* : informe
shapely [ˈʃeɪpli] *adj* **shapelier; -est** : curvilíneo, bien proporcionado
shard [ˈʃɑrd] *n* : fragmento *m*, casco *m* (de cerámica, etc.)
share[1] [ˈʃɛr] *v* **shared; sharing** *vt* **1** APPORTION : dividir, repartir **2** : compartir <they share a room : comparten una habitación> — *vi* : compartir
share[2] *n* **1** PORTION : parte *f*, porción *f* <one's fair share : lo que le corresponde a uno> **2** : acción *f* (en una compañía) <to hold shares : tener acciones>
sharecropper [ˈʃɛr,krɑpər] *n* : aparcero *m*, -ra *f*
shareholder [ˈʃɛr,hoːldər] *n* : accionista *mf*
shark [ˈʃɑrk] *n* : tiburón *m*
sharp[1] [ˈʃɑrp] *adv* : en punto <at two o'clock sharp : a las dos en punto>
sharp[2] *adj* **1** : afilado, filoso <a sharp knife : un cuchillo afilado> **2** PENETRATING : cortante, fuerte **3** CLEVER : agudo, listo, perspicaz **4** ACUTE : agudo <sharp eyesight : vista aguda> **5** HARSH, SEVERE : duro, severo, agudo <a sharp rebuke : una reprimenda mordaz> **6** STRONG : fuerte <sharp cheese : queso fuerte> **7** ABRUPT : brusco, repentino **8** DISTINCT : nítido, definido <a sharp image : una imagen bien definida> **9** ANGULAR : anguloso (dícese de la cara) **10** : sostenido (en música)
sharp[3] *n* : sostenido *m* (en música)
sharpen [ˈʃɑrpən] *vt* : afilar, aguzar <to sharpen a pencil : sacarle punta a un lápiz> <to sharpen one's wits : aguzar el ingenio>
sharpener [ˈʃɑrpənər] *n* : afilador *m* (para cuchillos, etc.), sacapuntas *m* (para lápices)
sharply [ˈʃɑrpli] *adv* **1** ABRUPTLY : bruscamente **2** DISTINCTLY : claramente, marcadamente
sharpness [ˈʃɑrpnəs] *n* **1** : lo afilado (de un cuchillo, etc.) **2** ACUTENESS : agudeza *f* (de los sentidos o de la mente) **3** INTENSITY : intensidad *f*, agudeza *f* (de dolores, etc.) **4** HARSHNESS : dureza *f*, severidad *f* **5** ABRUPTNESS : brusquedad *f* **6** CLARITY : nitidez *f*
sharpshooter [ˈʃɑrp,ʃuːtər] *n* : tirador *m*, -dora *f* de primera
shatter [ˈʃætər] *vt* **1** : hacer añicos <to shatter the silence : romper el silencio> **2 to be shattered by** : quedar destrozado por — *vi* : hacerse añicos, romperse en pedazos
shave[1] [ˈʃeɪv] *v* **shaved; shaved** *or* **shaven** [ˈʃeɪvən]; **shaving** *vt* **1** : afeitar, rasurar <she shaved her legs : se rasuró las piernas> <they shaved (off) his beard : le afeitaron la barba> **2** SLICE : cortar (en pedazos finos) — *vi* : afeitarse, rasurarse
shave[2] *n* : afeitada *f*, rasurada *f*
shaver [ˈʃeɪvər] *n* : afeitadora *f*, máquina *f* de afeitar, rasuradora *f*
shawl [ˈʃɔl] *n* : chal *m*, mantón *m*, rebozo *m*
she [ˈʃiː] *pron* : ella
sheaf [ˈʃiːf] *n, pl* **sheaves** [ˈʃiːvz] : gavilla *f* (de cereales), haz *m* (de flechas), fajo *m* (de papeles)
shear [ˈʃɪr] *vt* **sheared; sheared** *or* **shorn** [ˈʃorn]; **shearing 1** : esquilar, trasquilar <to shear sheep : trasquilar ovejas> **2** CUT : cortar (el pelo, etc.)
shears [ˈʃɪrz] *npl* : tijeras *fpl* (grandes)
sheath [ˈʃiːθ] *n, pl* **sheaths** [ˈʃiːðz, ˈʃiːθs] : funda *f*, vaina *f*
sheathe [ˈʃiːð] *vt* **sheathed; sheathing** : envainar, enfundar
shed[1] [ˈʃɛd] *vt* **shed; shedding 1** : derramar (sangre o lágrimas) **2** EMIT : emitir (luz) <to shed light on : aclarar> **3** DISCARD : mudar (la piel, etc.) <to shed one's clothes : quitarse uno la ropa>
shed[2] *n* : cobertizo *m*
she'd [ˈʃiːd] (*contraction of* **she had** *or* **she would**) → **have, would**
sheen [ˈʃiːn] *n* : brillo *m*, lustre *m*
sheep [ˈʃiːp] *ns & pl* : oveja *f*
sheepfold [ˈʃiːp,foːld] *n* : redil *m*
sheepish [ˈʃiːpɪʃ] *adj* : avergonzado
sheepskin [ˈʃiːp,skɪn] *n* : piel *f* de oveja, piel *f* de borrego
sheer[1] [ˈʃɪr] *adv* **1** COMPLETELY : completamente, totalmente **2** VERTICALLY : verticalmente
sheer[2] *adj* **1** TRANSPARENT : vaporoso, transparente **2** ABSOLUTE, UTTER : puro <by sheer luck : por pura suerte> **3** STEEP : escarpado, vertical
sheet [ˈʃiːt] *n* **1** *or* **bedsheet** [ˈbɛd,ʃiːt] : sábana *f* **2** : hoja *f* (de papel) **3**

: capa *f* (de hielo, etc.) **4 :** lámina *f,* placa *f* (de vidrio, metal, etc.), plancha *f* (de metal, madera, etc.) <baking sheet : placa de horno>

sheikh *or* **sheik** [ˈʃiːk, ˈʃeɪk] *n* **:** jeque *m*

shelf [ˈʃɛlf] *n, pl* **shelves** [ˈʃɛlvz] **1 :** estante *m,* anaquel *m* (en una pared) **2 :** banco *m,* arrecife *m* (en geología) <continental shelf : plataforma continental>

shell¹ [ˈʃɛl] *vt* **1 :** desvainar (chícharos), pelar (nueces, etc.) **2** BOMBARD **:** bombardear

shell² *n* **1** SEASHELL **:** concha *f* **2 :** cáscara *f* (de huevos, nueces, etc.), vaina *f* (de chícharos, etc.), caparazón *m* (de crustáceos, tortugas, etc.) **3 :** cartucho *m,* casquillo *m* <a .45 caliber shell : un cartucho calibre .45> **4** *or* **racing shell :** bote *m* (para hacer regatas de remos)

she'll [ˈʃiːl, ˈʃɪl] (*contraction of* **she shall** *or* **she will**) → **shall, will**

shellac¹ [ʃəˈlæk] *vt* **-lacked; -lacking 1 :** laquear (madera, etc.) **2** DEFEAT **:** darle una paliza (a alguien), derrotar

shellac² *n* **:** laca *f*

shellfish [ˈʃɛlˌfɪʃ] *n* **:** marisco *m*

shelter¹ [ˈʃɛltər] *vt* **1** PROTECT **:** proteger, abrigar **2** HARBOR **:** dar refugio a, albergar

shelter² *n* **:** refugio *m,* abrigo *m* <to take shelter : refugiarse>

shelve [ˈʃɛlv] *vt* **shelved; shelving 1 :** poner en estantes **2** DEFER **:** dar carpetazo a

shenanigans [ʃəˈnænɪgənz] *npl* **1** TRICKERY **:** artimañas *fpl* **2** MISCHIEF **:** travesuras *fpl*

shepherd¹ [ˈʃɛpərd] *vt* **1 :** cuidar (ovejas, etc.) **2** GUIDE **:** conducir, guiar

shepherd² *n* **:** pastor *m*

shepherdess [ˈʃɛpərdəs] *n* **:** pastora *f*

sherbet [ˈʃərbət] *or* **sherbert** [-bərt] *n* **:** sorbete *m,* nieve *f Cuba, Mex, PRi*

sheriff [ˈʃɛrɪf] *n* **:** sheriff *mf*

sherry [ˈʃɛri] *n, pl* **-ries :** jerez *m*

she's [ˈʃiːz] (*contraction of* **she is** *or* **she has**) → **be, have**

shield¹ [ˈʃiːld] *vt* **1** PROTECT **:** proteger **2** CONCEAL **:** ocultar <to shield one's eyes : taparse los ojos>

shield² *n* **1 :** escudo *m* (armadura) **2** PROTECTION **:** protección *f,* blindaje *m* (de un cable)

shier, shiest → **shy**

shift¹ [ˈʃɪft] *vt* **1** CHANGE **:** cambiar <to shift gears : cambiar de velocidad> **2** MOVE **:** mover **3** TRANSFER **:** transferir <to shift the blame : echarle la culpa (a otro)> **—** *vi* **1** CHANGE **:** cambiar **2** MOVE **:** moverse **3 to shift for oneself :** arreglárselas solo

shift² *n* **1** CHANGE, TRANSFER **:** cambio *m* <a shift in priorities : un cambio de prioridades> **2 :** turno *m* <night shift : turno de noche> **3** DRESS **:** vestido *m* (suelto) **4** → **gearshift**

shiftless [ˈʃɪftləs] *adj* **:** perezoso, vago, holgazán

shifty [ˈʃɪfti] *adj* **shiftier; -est :** taimado, artero <a shifty look : una mirada huidiza>

shilling [ˈʃɪlɪŋ] *n* **:** chelín *m*

shimmer [ˈʃɪmər] *vi* GLIMMER **:** brillar con luz trémula

shin¹ [ˈʃɪn] *vi* **shinned; shinning :** trepar, subir <she shinned up the pole : subió al poste>

shin² *n* **:** espinilla *f,* canilla *f*

shine¹ [ˈʃaɪn] *v* **shone** [ˈʃoːn, *esp Brit and Canadian* ˈʃɒn] *or* **shined; shining** *vi* **1 :** brillar, relucir <the stars were shining : las estrellas brillaban> **2** EXCEL **:** brillar, lucirse **—** *vt* **1 :** alumbrar <he shined the flashlight at it : lo alumbró con la linterna> **2** POLISH **:** sacarle brillo a, lustrar

shine² *n* **:** brillo *m,* lustre *m*

shingle¹ [ˈʃɪŋgəl] *vt* **-gled; -gling :** techar

shingle² *n* **:** tablilla *f* (para techar)

shingles [ˈʃɪŋgəlz] *npl* **:** herpes *m*

shinny [ˈʃɪni] *vi* **-nied; -nying** → **shin¹**

shiny [ˈʃaɪni] *adj* **shinier; -est :** brillante

ship¹ [ˈʃɪp] *vt* **shipped; shipping 1** LOAD **:** embarcar (en un barco) **2** SEND **:** transportar (en barco), enviar <to ship by air : enviar por avión>

ship² *n* **1 :** barco *m,* buque *m* **2** → **spaceship**

shipboard [ˈʃɪpˌbord] *n* **on ~ :** a bordo

shipbuilder [ˈʃɪpˌbɪldər] *n* **:** constructor *m,* -tora *f* naval

shipment [ˈʃɪpmənt] *n* **1** SHIPPING **:** transporte *m,* embarque *m* **2 :** envío *m,* remesa *f* <a shipment of medicine : un envío de medicina>

shipping [ˈʃɪpɪŋ] *n* **1** SHIPS **:** barcos *mpl,* embarcaciones *fpl* **2** TRANSPORTATION **:** transporte *m* (de mercancías)

shipshape [ˈʃɪpˈʃeɪp] *adj* **:** ordenado

shipwreck¹ [ˈʃɪpˌrɛk] *vt* **to be shipwrecked :** naufragar

shipwreck² *n* **:** naufragio *m*

shipyard [ˈʃɪpˌjɑrd] *n* **:** astillero *m*

shirk [ˈʃərk] *vt* **:** eludir, rehuir <to shirk one's responsibilities : esquivar uno sus responsabilidades>

shirt [ˈʃərt] *n* **:** camisa *f*

shiver¹ [ˈʃɪvər] *vi* **1 :** tiritar (de frío) **2** TREMBLE **:** estremecerse, temblar

shiver² *n* **:** escalofrío *m,* estremecimiento *m*

shoal [ˈʃoːl] *n* **:** banco *m,* bajío *m*

shock¹ [ˈʃɑk] *vt* **1** UPSET **:** conmover, conmocionar **2** STARTLE **:** asustar, sobresaltar **3** SCANDALIZE **:** escandalizar **4 :** darle una descarga eléctrica a

shock² *n* **1** COLLISION, JOLT **:** choque *m,* sacudida *f* **2** UPSET **:** conmoción *f,* golpe *m* emocional **3 :** shock *m* (en medicina) **4** *or* **electric shock :** descarga *f* eléctrica **5** SHEAVES **:** gavillas *fpl* **6 shock of hair :** mata *f* de pelo

shock absorber *n* : amortiguador *m*

shoddy [ˈʃɑdi] *adj* **shoddier; -est** : de mala calidad <a shoddy piece of work : un trabajo chapucero>

shoe[1] [ˈʃuː] *vt* **shod** [ˈʃɑd]; **shoeing** : herrar (un caballo)

shoe[2] *n* **1** : zapato *m* <the shoe industry : la industria del calzado> **2** HORSESHOE : herradura *f* **3 brake shoe** : zapata *f*

shoelace [ˈʃuːˌleɪs] *n* : cordón *m* (de zapatos)

shoemaker [ˈʃuːˌmeɪkər] *n* : zapatero *m*, -ra *f*

shone → **shine**

shook → **shake**

shoot[1] [ˈʃuːt] *v* **shot** [ˈʃɑt]; **shooting** *vt* **1** : disparar, tirar <to shoot a bullet : tirar una bala> **2** : pegarle un tiro a, darle un balazo a <he shot her : le pegó un tiro> <they shot and killed him : lo mataron a balazos> **3** THROW : lanzar (una pelota, etc.), echar (una mirada) **4** PHOTOGRAPH : fotografiar **5** FILM : filmar — *vi* **1** : disparar (con un arma de fuego) **2** DART : ir rápidamente <it shot past : pasó como una bala>

shoot[2] *n* : brote *m*, retoño *m*, vástago *m*

shooting star *n* : estrella *f* fugaz

shop[1] [ˈʃɑp] *vi* **shopped; shopping** : hacer compras <to go shopping : ir de compras>

shop[2] *n* **1** WORKSHOP : taller *m* **2** STORE : tienda *f*

shopkeeper [ˈʃɑpˌkiːpər] *n* : tendero *m*, -ra *f*

shoplift [ˈʃɑpˌlɪft] *vi* : hurtar mercancía (de una tienda) — *vt* : hurtar (de una tienda)

shoplifter [ˈʃɑpˌlɪftər] *n* : ladrón *m*, -drona *f* (que roba en una tienda)

shopper [ˈʃɑpər] *n* : comprador *m*, -dora *f*

shore[1] [ˈʃor] *vt* **shored; shoring** : apuntalar <they shored up the wall : apuntalaron la pared>

shore[2] *n* **1** : orilla *f* (del mar, etc.) **2** PROP : puntal *m*

shoreline [ˈʃorˌlaɪn] *n* : orilla *f*

shorn → **shear**

short[1] [ˈʃɔrt] *adv* **1** ABRUPTLY : repentinamente, súbitamente <the car stopped short : el carro se paró en seco> **2 to fall short** : no alcanzar, quedarse corto

short[2] *adj* **1** : corto (de medida), bajo (de estatura) **2** BRIEF : corto <short and sweet : corto y bueno> <a short time ago : hace poco> **3** CURT : brusco, cortante, seco **4** : corto (de tiempo, de dinero) <I'm one dollar short : me falta un dólar>

short[3] *n* **1 shorts** *npl* : shorts *mpl*, pantalones *mpl* cortos **2** → **short circuit**

shortage [ˈʃɔrtɪdʒ] *n* : falta *f*, escasez *f*, carencia *f*

shortcake [ˈʃɔrtˌkeɪk] *n* : tarta *f* de fruta

shortchange [ˈʃɔrtˈtʃeɪndʒ] *vt* **-changed; -changing** : darle mal el cambio (a alguien)

short circuit *n* : cortocircuito *m*, corto *m* (eléctrico)

shortcoming [ˈʃɔrtˌkʌmɪŋ] *n* : defecto *m*

shortcut [ˈʃɔrtˌkʌt] *n* **1** : atajo *m* <to take a shortcut : cortar camino> **2** : alternativa *f* fácil, método *m* rápido

shorten [ˈʃɔrtən] *vt* : acortar — *vi* : acortarse

shorthand [ˈʃɔrtˌhænd] *n* : taquigrafía *f*

short–lived [ˈʃɔrtˈlɪvd, -ˈlaɪvd] *adj* : efímero

shortly [ˈʃɔrtli] *adv* **1** BRIEFLY : brevemente <to put it shortly : para decirlo en pocas palabras> **2** SOON : dentro de poco

shortness [ˈʃɔrtnəs] *n* **1** : lo corto <shortness of stature : estatura baja> **2** BREVITY : brevedad *f* **3** CURTNESS : brusquedad *f* **4** SHORTAGE : falta *f*, escasez *f*, carencia *f*

shortsighted [ˈʃɔrtˌsaɪt̬əd] → **nearsighted**

shot [ˈʃɑt] *n* **1** : disparo *m*, tiro *m* <to fire a shot : disparar> **2** PELLETS : perdigones *mpl* **3** : tiro *m* (en deportes) **4** ATTEMPT : intento *m*, tentativa *f* <to have a shot at : hacer un intento por> **5** RANGE : alcance *m* <a long shot : una posibilidad remota> **6** PHOTOGRAPH : foto *f* **7** INJECTION : inyección *f* **8** : trago *m* (de licor)

shotgun [ˈʃɑtˌɡʌn] *n* : escopeta *f*

should → **shall**

shoulder[1] [ˈʃoːldər] *vt* **1** JOSTLE : empujar (con el hombro) **2** : ponerse al hombro (una mochila, etc.) **3** : cargar con (la responsabilidad, etc.)

shoulder[2] *n* **1** : hombro *m* <to shrug one's shoulders : encogerse los hombros> **2** : arcén *m* (de una carretera)

shoulder blade *n* : omóplato *m*, omoplato *m*, escápula *f*

shouldn't [ˈʃʊdənt] (*contraction of* **should not**) → **should**

shout[1] [ˈʃaʊt] *v* : gritar, vocear

shout[2] *n* : grito *m*

shove[1] [ˈʃʌv] *v* **shoved; shoving** : empujar bruscamente

shove[2] *n* : empujón *m*, empellón *m*

shovel[1] [ˈʃʌvəl] *vt* **-veled** *or* **-velled; -veling** *or* **-velling 1** : mover con (una) pala <they shoveled the dirt out : sacaron la tierra con palas> **2** DIG : cavar (con una pala)

shovel[2] *n* : pala *f*

show[1] [ˈʃoː] *v* **showed; shown** [ˈʃoːn] *or* **showed; showing** *vt* **1** DISPLAY : mostrar, enseñar **2** REVEAL : demostrar, manifestar, revelar <he showed himself to be a coward : se reveló como cobarde> **3** TEACH : enseñar **4** PROVE : demostrar, probar **5** CON-

DUCT, DIRECT : llevar, acompañar <to show someone the way : indicarle el camino a alguien> **6** : proyectar (una película), dar (un programa de televisión) — *vi* **1** : notarse, verse <the stain doesn't show : la mancha no se ve> **2** APPEAR : aparecer, dejarse ver
show² *n* **1** : demostración *f* <a show of force : una demostración de fuerza> **2** EXHIBITION : exposición *f,* exhibición *f* <flower show : exposición de flores> <to be on show : estar expuesto> **3** : espectáculo *m* (teatral), programa *m* (de televisión, etc.) <to go to a show : ir al teatro>
showcase [ˈʃoːˌkeɪs] *n* : vitrina *f*
showdown [ˈʃoːˌdaʊn] *n* : confrontación *f* (decisiva)
shower¹ [ˈʃaʊər] *vt* **1** SPRAY : regar, mojar **2** HEAP : colmar <they showered him with gifts : lo colmaron de regalos, le llovieron los regalos> — *vi* **1** BATHE : ducharse, darse una ducha **2** RAIN : llover
shower² *n* **1** : chaparrón *m,* chubasco *m* <a chance of showers : una posibilidad de chaparrones> **2** : ducha *f* <to take a shower : ducharse> **3** PARTY : fiesta *f* <a bridal shower : una despedida de soltera>
show off *vt* : hacer alarde de, ostentar — *vi* : lucirse
show up *vi* APPEAR : aparecer — *vt* EXPOSE : revelar
showy [ˈʃoːi] *adj* **showier; -est** : llamativo, ostentoso — **showily** *adv*
shrank → **shrink**
shrapnel [ˈʃræpnəl] *ns & pl* : metralla *f*
shred¹ [ˈʃrɛd] *vt* **shredded; shredding** : hacer trizas, desmenuzar (con las manos), triturar (con una máquina) <to shred vegetables : cortar verduras en tiras>
shred² *n* **1** STRIP : tira *f,* jirón *m* (de tela) **2** BIT : pizca *f* <not a shred of evidence : ni la mínima prueba>
shrew [ˈʃruː] *n* **1** : musaraña *f* (animal) **2** : mujer *f* regañona, arpía *f*
shrewd [ˈʃruːd] *adj* : astuto, inteligente, sagaz — **shrewdly** *adv*
shrewdness [ˈʃruːdnəs] *n* : astucia *f*
shriek¹ [ˈʃriːk] *vi* : chillar, gritar
shriek² *n* : chillido *m,* alarido *m,* grito *m*
shrill [ˈʃrɪl] *adj* : agudo, estridente
shrilly [ˈʃrɪli] *adv* : agudamente
shrimp [ˈʃrɪmp] *n* : camarón *m,* langostino *m*
shrine [ˈʃraɪn] *n* **1** TOMB : sepulcro *m* (de un santo) **2** SANCTUARY : lugar *m* sagrado, santuario *m*
shrink [ˈʃrɪŋk] *vi* **shrank** [ˈʃræŋk]; **shrunk** [ˈʃrʌŋk] *or* **shrunken** [ˈʃrʌŋkən]; **shrinking 1** RECOIL : retroceder <he shrank back : se echó para atrás> **2** : encogerse (dícese de la ropa)
shrinkage [ˈʃrɪŋkɪdʒ] *n* : encogimiento *m* (de ropa, etc.), contracción *f,* reducción *f*
shrivel [ˈʃrɪvəl] *vi* **-veled** *or* **-velled; -veling** *or* **-velling** : arrugarse, marchitarse
shroud¹ [ˈʃraʊd] *vt* : envolver
shroud² *n* **1** : sudario *m,* mortaja *f* **2** VEIL : velo *m* <wrapped in a shroud of mystery : envuelto en un aura de misterio>
shrub [ˈʃrʌb] *n* : arbusto *m,* mata *f*
shrubbery [ˈʃrʌbəri] *n, pl* **-beries** : arbustos *mpl,* matas *fpl*
shrug [ˈʃrʌg] *vi* **shrugged; shrugging** : encogerse de hombros
shrunk → **shrink**
shuck¹ [ˈʃʌk] *vt* : pelar (mazorcas, etc.), abrir (almejas, etc.)
shuck² *n* **1** HUSK : cascarilla *f,* cáscara *f* (de una nuez, etc.), hojas *fpl* (de una mazorca) **2** SHELL : concha *f* (de una almeja, etc.)
shudder¹ [ˈʃʌdər] *vi* : estremecerse
shudder² *n* : estremecimiento *m,* escalofrío *m*
shuffle¹ [ˈʃʌfəl] *v* **-fled; -fling** *vt* MIX : mezclar, revolver, barajar (naipes) — *vi* : caminar arrastrando los pies
shuffle² *n* **1** : acto *m* de revolver <each player gets a shuffle : a cada jugador le toca barajar> **2** JUMBLE : revoltijo *m* **3** : arrastramiento *m* de los pies
shun [ˈʃʌn] *vt* **shunned; shunning** : evitar, esquivar, eludir
shunt [ˈʃʌnt] *vt* : desviar, cambiar de vía (un tren)
shut [ˈʃʌt] *v* **shut; shutting** *vt* **1** CLOSE : cerrar <shut the lid : tápalo> **2 to shut out** EXCLUDE : excluir, dejar fuera a (personas), no dejar que entre (luz, ruido, etc.) **3 to shut up** CONFINE : encerrar — *vi* : cerrarse <the factory shut down : la fábrica cerró sus puertas>
shut–in [ˈʃʌtˌɪn] *n* : inválido *m,* -da *f* (que no puede salir de casa)
shutter [ˈʃʌtər] *n* **1** : contraventana *f,* postigo *m* (de una ventana o puerta) **2** : obturador *m* (de una cámara)
shuttle¹ [ˈʃʌtəl] *v* **-tled; -tling** *vt* : transportar <she shuttled him back and forth : lo llevaba de acá para allá> — *vi* : ir y venir
shuttle² *n* **1** : lanzadera *f* (para tejer) **2** : vehículo *m* que hace recorridos cortos **3** → **space shuttle**
shuttlecock [ˈʃʌtəlˌkɑk] *n* : volante *m*
shut up *vi* : callarse <shut up! : ¡cállate (la boca)!>
shy¹ [ˈʃaɪ] *vi* **shied; shying** : retroceder, asustarse
shy² *adj* **shier** *or* **shyer** [ˈʃaɪər]; **shiest** *or* **shyest** [ˈʃaɪəst] **1** TIMID : tímido **2** WARY : cauteloso <he's not shy about asking : no vacila en preguntar> **3** SHORT : corto (de dinero, etc.) <I'm two dollars shy : me faltan dos dólares>

shyly [ˈʃaɪli] *adv* **:** tímidamente

shyness [ˈʃaɪnəs] *n* **:** timidez *f*

sibling [ˈsɪblɪŋ] *n* **:** hermano *m,* hermana *f*

Sicilian [səˈsɪljən] *n* **:** siciliano *m,* -na *f* — **Sicilian** *adj*

sick [ˈsɪk] *adj* **1 :** enfermo **2** NAUSEOUS **:** mareado, con náuseas <to get sick : vomitar> **3 :** para uso de enfermos <sick day : día de permiso (por enfermedad)>

sickbed [ˈsɪk,bɛd] *n* **:** lecho *m* de enfermo

sicken [ˈsɪkən] *vt* **1 :** poner enfermo **2** REVOLT **:** darle asco (a alguien) — *vi* **:** enfermar(se), caer enfermo

sickening [ˈsɪkənɪŋ] *adj* **:** asqueroso, repugnante, nauseabundo

sickle [ˈsɪkəl] *n* **:** hoz *f*

sickly [ˈsɪkli] *adj* **sicklier; -est 1 :** enfermizo **2 → sickening**

sickness [ˈsɪknəs] *n* **1 :** enfermedad *f* **2** NAUSEA **:** náuseas *fpl*

side [ˈsaɪd] *n* **1 :** lado *m,* costado *m* (de una persona), ijada *f* (de un animal) **2 :** lado *m,* cara *f* (de una moneda, etc.) **3 :** lado *m,* parte *f* <he's on my side : está de mi parte> <to take sides : tomar partido>

sideboard [ˈsaɪd,bord] *n* **:** aparador *m*

sideburns [ˈsaɪd,bərnz] *npl* **:** patillas *fpl*

sided [ˈsaɪdəd] *adj* **:** que tiene lados <one-sided : de un lado>

side effect *n* **:** efecto *m* secundario

sideline [ˈsaɪd,laɪn] *n* **1 :** línea *f* de banda (en deportes) **2 :** actividad *f* suplementaria (en negocios) **3 to be on the sidelines :** estar al margen

sidelong [ˈsaɪd,lɔŋ] *adj* **:** de reojo, de soslayo

sideshow [ˈsaɪd,ʃoː] *n* **:** espectáculo *m* secundario, atracción *f* secundaria

sidestep [ˈsaɪd,stɛp] *v* **-stepped; -stepping** *vi* **:** dar un paso hacia un lado — *vt* AVOID **:** esquivar, eludir

sidetrack [ˈsaɪd,træk] *vt* **:** desviar (una conversación, etc.), distraer (a una persona)

sidewalk [ˈsaɪd,wɔk] *n* **:** acera *f,* vereda *f,* andén *m CA, Col,* banqueta *f Mex*

sideways[1] [ˈsaɪd,weɪz] *adv* **1 :** hacia un lado <it leaned sideways : se inclinaba hacia un lado> **2 :** de lado, de costado <lie sideways : acuéstese de costado>

sideways[2] *adj* **:** hacia un lado <a sideways glance : una mirada de reojo>

siding [ˈsaɪdɪŋ] *n* **1 :** apartadero *m* (para trenes) **2 :** revestimiento *m* exterior (de un edificio)

sidle [ˈsaɪdəl] *vi* **-dled; -dling :** moverse furtivamente

siege [ˈsiːdʒ, ˈsiːʒ] *n* **:** sitio *m* <to be under siege : estar sitiado>

siesta [siːˈɛstə] *n* **:** siesta *f*

sieve [ˈsɪv] *n* **:** tamiz *m,* cedazo *m,* criba *f* (en minerología)

sift [ˈsɪft] *vt* **1 :** tamizar, cerner <sift the flour : tamice la harina> **2** *or* **sift through :** examinar cuidadosamente, pasar por el tamiz

sifter [ˈsɪftər] *n* **:** tamiz *m,* cedazo *m*

sigh[1] [ˈsaɪ] *vi* **:** suspirar

sigh[2] *n* **:** suspiro *m*

sight[1] [ˈsaɪt] *vt* **:** ver (a una persona), divisar (la tierra, un barco)

sight[2] *n* **1 :** vista *f* (facultad) <out of sight : fuera de vista> **2 :** algo visto <it's a familiar sight : se ve con frecuencia> <she's a sight for sore eyes : da gusto verla> **3 :** lugar *m* de interés (para turistas, etc.) **4 :** mira *f* (de un rifle, etc.) **5** GLIMPSE **:** mirada *f* breve <I caught sight of her : la divisé, alcancé a verla>

sightless [ˈsaɪtləs] *adj* **:** invidente, ciego

sightseer [ˈsaɪt,siːər] *n* **:** turista *mf*

sign[1] [ˈsaɪn] *vt* **1 :** firmar <to sign a check : firmar un cheque> **2** *or* **to sign on** HIRE **:** contratar (a un empleado), fichar (a un jugador) — *vi* **1 :** hacer una seña <she signed for him to stop : le hizo una seña para que se parara> **2 :** comunicarse por señas

sign[2] *n* **1** SYMBOL **:** símbolo *m,* signo *m* <minus sign : signo de menos> **2** GESTURE **:** seña *f,* señal *f,* gesto *m* **3 :** letrero *m,* cartel *m* <neon sign : letrero de neón> **4** TRACE **:** señal *f,* indicio *m*

signal[1] [ˈsɪgnəl] *vt* **-naled** *or* **-nalled; -naling** *or* **-nalling 1 :** hacerle señas (a alguien) <she signaled me to leave : me hizo señas para que saliera> **2** INDICATE **:** señalar, indicar — *vi* **:** hacer señas, comunicar por señas

signal[2] *adj* NOTABLE **:** señalado, notable

signal[3] *n* **:** señal *f*

signature [ˈsɪgnə,tʃʊr] *n* **:** firma *f*

signet [ˈsɪgnət] *n* **:** sello *m*

significance [sɪgˈnɪfɪkən*t*s] *n* **1** MEANING **:** significado *m* **2** IMPORTANCE **:** importancia *f*

significant [sɪgˈnɪfɪkənt] *adj* **1** IMPORTANT **:** importante **2** MEANINGFUL **:** significativo — **significantly** *adv*

signify [ˈsɪgnə,faɪ] *vt* **-fied; -fying 1 :** indicar <he signified his desire for more : haciendo señas indicó que quería más> **2** MEAN **:** significar

sign language *n* **:** lenguaje *m* por señas

signpost [ˈsaɪn,poːst] *n* **:** poste *m* indicador

silence[1] [ˈsaɪlən*t*s] *vt* **-lenced; -lencing :** silenciar, acallar

silence[2] *n* **:** silencio *m*

silent [ˈsaɪlənt] *adj* **1 :** callado <to remain silent : quedarse callado, guardar silencio> **2** QUIET, STILL **:** silencioso **3** MUTE **:** mudo <a silent letter : una letra muda>

silently [ˈsaɪləntli] *adv* **:** silenciosamente, calladamente

silhouette[1] [,sɪləˈwɛt] *vt* **-etted; -etting :** destacar la silueta de <it was

silhouetted against the sky : se perfilaba contra el cielo>
silhouette[2] *n* : silueta *f*
silica ['sɪlɪkə] *n* : sílice *f*
silicon ['sɪlɪkən, -ˌkɑn] *n* : silicio *m*
silk ['sɪlk] *n* : seda *f*
silken ['sɪlkən] *adj* **1** : de seda <a silken veil : un velo de seda> **2** SILKY : sedoso <silken hair : cabellos sedosos>
silkworm ['sɪlkˌwərm] *n* : gusano *m* de seda
silky ['sɪlki] *adj* **silkier; -est** : sedoso
sill ['sɪl] *n* : alféizar *m* (de una ventana), umbral *m* (de una puerta)
silliness ['sɪlinəs] *n* : tontería *f*, estupidez *f*
silly ['sɪli] *adj* **sillier; -est** : tonto, estúpido, ridículo
silo ['saɪˌloː] *n, pl* **silos** : silo *m*
silt ['sɪlt] *n* : cieno *m*
silver[1] ['sɪlvər] *adj* **1** : de plata <a silver spoon : una cuchara de plata> **2** → **silvery**
silver[2] *n* **1** : plata *f* **2** COINS : monedas *fpl* **3** → **silverware** **4** : color *m* plata
silverware ['sɪlvərˌwær] *n* **1** : artículos *mpl* de plata, platería *f* **2** FLATWARE : cubertería *f*
silvery ['sɪlvəri] *adj* : plateado
similar ['sɪmələr] *adj* : similar, parecido, semejante
similarity [ˌsɪmə'lærəṭi] *n, pl* **-ties** : semejanza *f*, parecido *m*
similarly ['sɪmələrli] *adv* : de manera similar
simile ['sɪməˌliː] *n* : símil *m*
simmer ['sɪmər] *v* : hervir a fuego lento
simper[1] ['sɪmpər] *vi* : sonreír como un tonto
simper[2] *n* : sonrisa *f* tonta
simple ['sɪmpəl] *adj* **simpler; -plest** **1** INNOCENT : inocente **2** PLAIN : sencillo, simple **3** EASY : simple, sencillo, fácil **4** STRAIGHTFORWARD : puro, simple <the simple truth : la pura verdad> **5** NAIVE : ingenuo, simple
simpleton ['sɪmpəltən] *n* : bobo *m*, -ba *f*; tonto *m*, -ta *f*
simplicity [sɪm'plɪsəṭi] *n* : simplicidad *f*, sencillez *f*
simplification [ˌsɪmpləfə'keɪʃən] *n* : simplificación *f*
simplify ['sɪmpləˌfaɪ] *vt* **-fied; -fying** : simplificar
simply ['sɪmpli] *adv* **1** PLAINLY : sencillamente **2** SOLELY : simplemente, sólo **3** REALLY : absolutamente
simulate ['sɪmjəˌleɪt] *vt* **-lated; -lating** : simular
simultaneous [ˌsaɪməl'teɪniəs] *adj* : simultáneo — **simultaneously** *adv*
sin[1] ['sɪn] *vi* **sinned; sinning** : pecar
sin[2] *n* : pecado *m*
since[1] ['sɪnts] *adv* **1** : desde entonces <they've been friends ever since : desde entonces han sido amigos> <she's since become mayor : más tarde se hizo alcalde> **2** AGO : hace <he's long since dead : murió hace mucho>
since[2] *conj* **1** : desde que <since he was born : desde que nació> **2** INASMUCH AS : ya que, puesto que, dado que
since[3] *prep* : desde
sincere [sɪn'sɪr] *adj* **-cerer; -est** : sincero — **sincerely** *adv*
sincerity [sɪn'sɛrəṭi] *n* : sinceridad *f*
sinew ['sɪnˌjuː, 'sɪˌnuː] *n* **1** TENDON : tendón *m*, nervio *m* (en la carne) **2** POWER : fuerza *f*
sinewy ['sɪnjʊi, 'sɪnʊi] *adj* **1** STRINGY : fibroso **2** STRONG, WIRY : fuerte, nervudo
sinful ['sɪnfəl] *adj* : pecador (dícese de las personas), pecaminoso
sing ['sɪŋ] *v* **sang** ['sæŋ] *or* **sung** ['sʌŋ]; **sung; singing** : cantar
singe ['sɪnʤ] *vt* **singed; singeing** : chamuscar, quemar
singer ['sɪŋər] *n* : cantante *mf*
single[1] ['sɪŋgəl] *vt* **-gled; -gling** *or* **to single out** **1** SELECT : escoger **2** DISTINGUISH : señalar
single[2] *adj* **1** UNMARRIED : soltero **2** SOLE : solo <a single survivor : un solo sobreviviente> <every single one : cada uno, todos>
single[3] *n* **1** : soltero *m*, -ra *f* <for married couples and singles : para los matrimonios y los solteros> **2** *or* **single room** : habitación *f* individual **3** DOLLAR : billete *m* de un dólar
single–handed ['sɪŋgəl'hændəd] *adj* : sin ayuda, solo
singly ['sɪŋgli] *adv* : individualmente, uno por uno
singular[1] ['sɪŋgjələr] *adj* **1** : singular (en gramática) **2** OUTSTANDING : singular, sobresaliente **3** STRANGE : singular, extraño
singular[2] *n* : singular *m*
singularly ['sɪŋgjələrli] *adv* : singularmente
sinister ['sɪnəstər] *adj* : siniestro
sink[1] ['sɪŋk] *v* **sank** ['sæŋk] *or* **sunk** ['sʌŋk]; **sunk; sinking** *vi* **1** : hundirse (dícese de un barco) **2** DROP, FALL : descender, caer <to sink into a chair : dejarse caer en una silla> <her heart sank : se le cayó el alma a los pies> **3** DECREASE : bajar — *vt* **1** : hundir (un barco, etc.) **2** EXCAVATE : excavar (un pozo para minar), perforar (un pozo de agua) **3** PLUNGE, STICK : clavar, hincar **4** INVEST : invertir (fondos)
sink[2] *n* **1 kitchen sink** : fregadero *m*, lavaplatos *m Chile, Col, Mex* **2 bathroom sink** : lavabo *m*, lavamanos *m*
sinner ['sɪnər] *n* : pecador *m*, -dora *f*
sinuous ['sɪnjʊəs] *adj* : sinuoso — **sinuously** *adv*
sinus ['saɪnəs] *n* : seno *m*
sip[1] ['sɪp] *v* **sipped; sipping** *vt* : sorber — *vi* : beber a sorbos
sip[2] *n* : sorbo *m*
siphon[1] ['saɪfən] *vt* : sacar con sifón

siphon² *n* : sifón *m*
sir ['sər] *n* **1** (*in titles*) : sir *m* **2** (*as a form of address*) : señor *m* <Dear Sir : Muy señor mío> <yes sir! : ¡sí, señor!>
sire¹ ['saɪr] *vt* **sired; siring** : engendrar, ser el padre de
sire² *n* : padre *m*
siren ['saɪrən] *n* : sirena *f*
sirloin ['sər,lɔɪn] *n* : solomillo *m*
sirup → **syrup**
sisal ['saɪsəl, -zəl] *n* : sisal *m*
sissy ['sɪsi] *n, pl* **-sies** : mariquita *f fam*
sister ['sɪstər] *n* : hermana *f*
sisterhood ['sɪstər,hʊd] *n* **1** : condición *f* de ser hermana **2** : sociedad *f* de mujeres
sister–in–law ['sɪstərɪn,lɔ] *n, pl* **sisters–in–law** : cuñada *f*
sisterly ['sɪstərli] *adj* : de hermana
sit ['sɪt] *v* **sat** ['sæt]; **sitting** *vi* **1** : sentarse, estar sentado <he sat down : se sentó> **2** ROOST : posarse **3** : sesionar <the legislature is sitting : la legislatura está en sesión> **4** POSE : posar (para un retrato) **5** LIE, REST : estar (ubicado) <the house sits on a hill : la casa está en una colina> — *vt* SEAT : sentar, colocar <I sat him on the sofa : lo senté en el sofá>
site ['saɪt] *n* 1 PLACE : sitio *m,* lugar *m* **2** LOCATION : emplazamiento *m,* ubicación *f*
sitting room → **living room**
sitter ['sɪt̬ər] → **baby–sitter**
situated ['sɪtʃʊ,eɪt̬əd] *adj* LOCATED : ubicado, situado
situation [,sɪtʃʊ'eɪʃən] *n* **1** LOCATION : situación *f,* ubicación *f,* emplazamiento *m* **2** CIRCUMSTANCES : situación *f* **3** JOB : empleo *m*
six¹ ['sɪks] *adj* : seis
six² *n* : seis *m*
six–gun ['sɪks,gʌn] *n* : revólver *m* (con seis cámaras)
six hundred¹ *adj* : seiscientos
six hundred² *n* : seiscientos *m*
six–shooter ['sɪks,ʃuːt̬ər] → **six–gun**
sixteen¹ [sɪks'tiːn] *adj* : dieciséis
sixteen² *n* : dieciséis *m*
sixteenth¹ [sɪks'tiːnθ] *adj* : decimosexto
sixteenth² *n* **1** : decimosexto *m,* -ta *f* (en una serie) **2** : dieciseisavo *m,* dieciseisava parte *f*
sixth¹ ['sɪksθ, 'sɪkst] *adj* : sexto
sixth² *n* **1** : sexto *m,* -ta *f* (en una serie) **2** : sexto *m,* sexta parte *f*
sixtieth¹ ['sɪkstiəθ] *adj* : sexagésimo
sixtieth² *n* **1** : sexagésimo *m,* -ma *f* (en una serie) **2** : sesentavo *m,* sesentava parte *f*
sixty¹ ['sɪksti] *adj* : sesenta
sixty² *n, pl* **-ties** : sesenta *m*
sizable *or* **sizeable** ['saɪzəbəl] *adj* : considerable
size¹ ['saɪz] *vt* **sized; sizing 1** : clasificar según el tamaño **2 to size up** : evaluar, apreciar
size² *n* **1** DIMENSIONS : tamaño *m,* talla *f* (de ropa), número *m* (de zapatos) **2** MAGNITUDE : magnitud *f*
sizzle ['sɪzəl] *vi* **-zled; -zling** : chisporrotear
skate¹ ['skeɪt] *vi* **skated; skating** : patinar
skate² *n* **1** : patín *m* <roller skate : patín de ruedas> **2** : raya *f* (pez)
skateboard ['skeɪt,bord] *n* : monopatín *m*
skater ['skeɪt̬ər] *n* : patinador *m,* -dora *f*
skein ['skeɪn] *n* : madeja *f*
skeletal ['skɛlət̬əl] *adj* **1** : óseo (en anatomía) **2** EMACIATED : esquelético
skeleton ['skɛlətən] *n* **1** : esqueleto *m* (anatómico) **2** FRAMEWORK : armazón *mf*
skeptic ['skɛptɪk] *n* : escéptico *m,* -ca *f*
skeptical ['skɛptɪkəl] *adj* : escéptico
skepticism ['skɛptə,sɪzəm] *n* : escepticismo *m*
sketch¹ ['skɛtʃ] *vt* : bosquejar — *vi* : hacer bosquejos
sketch² *n* **1** DRAWING, OUTLINE : esbozo *m,* bosquejo *m* **2** ESSAY : ensayo *m*
sketchy ['skɛtʃi] *adj* **sketchier; -est** : incompleto, poco detallado
skewer¹ ['skjuːər] *vt* : ensartar (carne, etc.)
skewer² *n* : brocheta *f,* broqueta *f*
ski¹ ['skiː] *vi* **skied; skiing** : esquiar
ski² *n, pl* **skis** : esquí *m*
skid¹ ['skɪd] *vi* **skidded; skidding** : derrapar, patinar
skid² *n* : derrape *m,* patinazo *m*
skier ['skiːər] *n* : esquiador *m,* -dora *f*
skiff ['skɪf] *n* : esquife *m*
skill ['skɪl] *n* **1** DEXTERITY : habilidad *f,* destreza *f* **2** CAPABILITY : capacidad *f,* arte *m,* técnica *f* <organizational skills : la capacidad para organizar>
skilled ['skɪld] *adj* : hábil, experto
skillet ['skɪlət] *n* : sartén *mf*
skillful ['skɪlfəl] *adj* : hábil, diestro
skillfully ['skɪlfəli] *adv* : con habilidad, con destreza
skim¹ ['skɪm] *vt* **skimmed; skimming 1** *or* **to skim off** : espumar, descremar (leche) **2** : echarle un vistazo a (un libro, etc.), pasar rozando (un superficie)
skim² *adj* : descremado <skim milk : leche descremada>
skimp ['skɪmp] *vi* **to skimp on** : escatimar
skimpy ['skɪmpi] *adj* **skimpier; -est** : exiguo, escaso, raquítico
skin¹ ['skɪn] *vt* **skinned; skinning** : despellejar, desollar
skin² *n* **1** : piel *f,* cutis *m* (de la cara) <dark skin : piel morena> **2** RIND : piel *f*
skin diving *n* : buceo *m,* submarinismo *m*
skinflint ['skɪn,flɪnt] *n* : tacaño *m,* -ña *f*

skinned [ˈskɪnd] *adj* **:** de piel <tough-skinned : de piel dura>

skinny [ˈskɪni] *adj* **skinnier; -est :** flaco

skip[1] [ˈskɪp] *v* **skipped; skipping** *vi* **:** ir dando brincos — *vt* **:** saltarse

skip[2] *n* **:** brinco *m,* salto *m*

skipper [ˈskɪpər] *n* **:** capitán *m,* -tana *f*

skirmish[1] [ˈskərmɪʃ] *vi* **:** escaramuzar

skirmish[2] *n* **:** escaramuza *f,* refriega *f*

skirt[1] [ˈskərt] *vt* **1** BORDER **:** bordear **2** EVADE **:** evadir, esquivar

skirt[2] *n* **:** falda *f,* pollera *f*

skit [ˈskɪt] *n* **:** sketch *m* (teatral)

skittish [ˈskɪṭɪʃ] *adj* **:** asustadizo, nervioso

skulk [ˈskʌlk] *vi* **:** merodear

skull [ˈskʌl] *n* **1 :** cráneo *m,* calavera *f* **2 skull and crossbones :** calavera *f* (bandera pirata)

skunk [ˈskʌŋk] *n* **:** zorrillo *m,* mofeta *f*

sky [ˈskaɪ] *n, pl* **skies :** cielo *m*

skylark [ˈskaɪˌlɑrk] *n* **:** alondra *f*

skylight [ˈskaɪˌlaɪt] *n* **:** claraboya *f,* tragaluz *m*

skyline [ˈskaɪˌlaɪn] *n* **:** horizonte *m*

skyrocket [ˈskaɪˌrɑkət] *vi* **:** dispararse

skyscraper [ˈskaɪˌskreɪpər] *n* **:** rascacielos *m*

slab [ˈslæb] *n* **:** losa *f* (de piedra), tabla *f* (de madera), pedazo *m* grueso (de pan, etc.)

slack[1] [ˈslæk] *adj* **1** CARELESS **:** descuidado, negligente **2** LOOSE **:** flojo **3** SLOW **:** de poco movimiento

slack[2] *n* **1 :** parte *f* floja <to take up the slack : tensar (una cuerda, etc.)> **2 slacks** *npl* **:** pantalones *mpl*

slacken [ˈslækən] *vt* **:** aflojar — *vi* **:** aflojarse

slag [ˈslæg] *n* **:** escoria *f*

slain → **slay**

slake [ˈsleɪk] *vt* **slaked; slaking :** saciar (la sed), satisfacer (la curiosidad)

slam[1] [ˈslæm] *v* **slammed; slamming** *vt* **1 :** cerrar de golpe <he slammed the door : dio un portazo> **2 :** tirar o dejar caer de golpe <he slammed down the book : dejó caer el libro de un golpe> — *vi* **1 :** cerrarse de golpe **2 to slam into :** chocar contra

slam[2] *n* **:** golpe *m,* portazo *m* (de una puerta)

slander[1] [ˈslændər] *vt* **:** calumniar, difamar

slander[2] *n* **:** calumnia *f,* difamación *f*

slanderous [ˈslændərəs] *adj* **:** difamatorio, calumnioso

slang [ˈslæŋ] *n* **:** argot *m,* jerga *f*

slant[1] [ˈslænt] *vi* **:** inclinarse, ladearse — *vt* **1** SLOPE **:** inclinar **2** ANGLE **:** sesgar, orientar, dirigir <a story slanted towards youth : un artículo dirigido a los jóvenes>

slant[2] *n* **1** INCLINE **:** inclinación *f* **2** PERSPECTIVE **:** perspectiva *f,* enfoque *m*

slap[1] [ˈslæp] *vt* **slapped; slapping :** bofetear, cachetear, dar una palmada (en la espalda, etc.)

slap[2] *n* **:** bofetada *f,* cachetada *f,* palmada *f*

slash[1] [ˈslæʃ] *vt* **1** GASH **:** cortar, hacer un tajo en **2** REDUCE **:** reducir, rebajar (precios)

slash[2] *n* **:** tajo *m,* corte *m*

slat [ˈslæt] *n* **:** tablilla *f,* listón *m*

slate [ˈsleɪt] *n* **1 :** pizarra *f* <a slate roof : un techo de pizarra> **2 :** lista *f* de candidatos (políticos)

slaughter[1] [ˈslɔṭər] *vt* **1** BUTCHER **:** matar (animales) **2** MASSACRE **:** masacrar (personas)

slaughter[2] *n* **1 :** matanza *f* (de animales) **2** MASSACRE **:** masacre *f,* carnicería *f*

slaughterhouse [ˈslɔṭərˌhaʊs] *n* **:** matadero *m*

Slav [ˈslɑv, ˈslæv] *n* **:** eslavo *m,* -va *f*

slave[1] [ˈsleɪv] *vi* **slaved; slaving :** trabajar como un burro

slave[2] *n* **:** esclavo *m,* -va *f*

slaver [ˈslævər, ˈsleɪ-] *vi* **:** babear

slavery [ˈsleɪvəri] *n* **:** esclavitud *f*

Slavic [ˈslɑvɪk, ˈslæ-] *adj* **:** eslavo

slavish [ˈsleɪvɪʃ] *adj* **1** SERVILE **:** servil **2** IMITATIVE **:** poco original

slay [ˈsleɪ] *vt* **slew** [ˈsluː]; **slain** [ˈsleɪn]; **slaying :** asesinar, matar

slayer [ˈsleɪər] *n* **:** asesino *m,* -na *f*

sleazy [ˈsliːzi] *adj* **sleazier; -est 1** SHODDY **:** chapucero, de mala calidad **2** DILAPIDATED **:** ruinoso **3** DISREPUTABLE **:** de mala fama

sled[1] [ˈslɛd] *v* **sledded; sledding** *vi* **:** ir en trineo — *vt* **:** transportar en trineo

sled[2] *n* **:** trineo *m*

sledge [ˈslɛdʒ] *n* **1 :** trineo *m* (grande) **2** → **sledgehammer**

sledgehammer [ˈslɛdʒˌhæmər] *n* **:** almádena *f,* combo *m Chile, Peru*

sleek[1] [ˈsliːk] *vt* SLICK **:** alisar

sleek[2] *adj* **:** liso y brillante

sleep[1] [ˈsliːp] *vi* **slept** [ˈslɛpt]; **sleeping :** dormir

sleep[2] *n* **1 :** sueño *m* **2 to go to sleep :** dormirse

sleeper [ˈsliːpər] *n* **1 :** durmiente *mf* <to be a light sleeper : tener el sueño ligero> **2** *or* **sleeping car :** coche *m* cama, coche *m* dormitorio

sleepily [ˈsliːpəli] *adv* **:** de manera somnolienta

sleepiness [ˈsliːpinəs] *n* **:** somnolencia *f*

sleepless [ˈsliːpləs] *adj* **:** sin dormir, desvelado <to have a sleepless night : pasar la noche en blanco>

sleepwalker [ˈsliːpˌwɔkər] *n* **:** sonámbulo *m,* -la *f*

sleepy [ˈsliːpi] *adj* **sleepier; -est 1** DROWSY **:** somnoliento, soñoliento <to be sleepy : tener sueño> **2** LETHARGIC **:** aletargado, letárgico

sleet[1] [ˈsliːt] *vi* **to be sleeting :** caer aguanieve

sleet[2] *n* **:** aguanieve *f*
sleeve [ˈsliːv] *n* **:** manga *f* (de una camisa, etc.)
sleeveless [ˈsliːvləs] *adj* **:** sin mangas
sleigh[1] [ˈsleɪ] *vi* **:** ir en trineo
sleigh[2] *n* **:** trineo *m* (tirado por caballos)
sleight of hand [ˌslaɪt̬əvˈhænd] **:** prestidigitación *f,* juegos *mpl* de manos
slender [ˈslɛndər] *adj* **1** SLIM **:** esbelto, delgado **2** SCANTY **:** exiguo, escaso <a slender hope : una esperanza lejana>
sleuth [ˈsluːθ] *n* **:** detective *mf;* sabueso *m,* -sa *f*
slew → **slay**
slice[1] [ˈslaɪs] *vt* **sliced; slicing :** cortar
slice[2] *n* **:** rebanada *f,* tajada *f,* lonja *f* (de carne, etc.), rodaja *f* (de una verdura, fruta, etc.), trozo *m* (de pastel, etc.)
slick[1] [ˈslɪk] *vt* **:** alisar
slick[2] *adj* **1** SLIPPERY **:** resbaladizo, resbaloso **2** CRAFTY **:** astuto, taimado
slicker [ˈslɪkər] *n* **:** impermeable *m*
slide[1] [ˈslaɪd] *v* **slid** [ˈslɪd]; **sliding** [ˈslaɪdɪŋ] *vi* **1** SLIP **:** resbalar **2** GLIDE **:** deslizarse **3** DECLINE **:** bajar <to let things slide : dejar pasar las cosas> — *vt* **:** correr, deslizar
slide[2] *n* **1** SLIDING **:** deslizamiento *m* **2** SLIP **:** resbalón *m* **3 :** tobogán *m* (para niños) **4 :** TRANSPARENCY **:** diapositiva *f* (fotográfica) **5** DECLINE **:** descenso *m*
slier, sliest → **sly**
slight[1] [ˈslaɪt] *vt* **:** desairar, despreciar
slight[2] *adj* **1** SLENDER **:** esbelto, delgado **2** FLIMSY **:** endeble **3** TRIFLING **:** leve, insignificante <a slight pain : un leve dolor> **4** SMALL **:** pequeño, ligero <not in the slightest : en absoluto>
slight[3] *n* SNUB **:** desaire *m*
slightly [ˈslaɪtli] *adv* **:** ligeramente, un poco
slim[1] [ˈslɪm] *v* **slimmed; slimming :** adelgazar
slim[2] *adj* **slimmer; slimmest 1** SLENDER **:** esbelto, delgado **2** SCANTY **:** exiguo, escaso
slime [ˈslaɪm] *n* **1 :** baba *f* (secretado por un animal) **2** MUD, SILT **:** fango *m,* cieno *m*
slimy [ˈslaɪmi] *adj* **slimier; -est :** viscoso
sling[1] [ˈslɪŋ] *vt* **slung** [ˈslʌŋ]; **slinging 1** THROW **:** lanzar, tirar **2** HANG **:** colgar
sling[2] *n* **1 :** honda *f* (arma) **2 :** cabestrillo *m* <my arm is in a sling : llevo el brazo en cabestrillo>
slingshot [ˈslɪŋˌʃɑt] *n* **:** tiragomas *m,* resortera *f Mex*
slink [ˈslɪŋk] *vi* **slunk** [ˈslʌŋk]; **slinking :** caminar furtivamente
slip[1] [ˈslɪp] *v* **slipped; slipping** *vi* **1** STEAL **:** ir sigilosamente <to slip away : escabullirse> <to slip out the door : escaparse por la puerta> **2** SLIDE **:** resbalarse, deslizarse **3** LAPSE **:** caer <to slip into error : equivocarse> **4 to let slip :** dejar escapar **5 to slip into** PUT ON **:** ponerse — *vt* **1** PUT **:** meter, poner **2** PASS **:** pasar <she slipped me a note : me pasó una nota> **3 to slip one's mind :** olvidársele a uno
slip[2] *n* **1** PIER **:** atracadero *m* **2** MISHAP **:** percance *m,* contratiempo *m* **3** MISTAKE **:** error *m,* desliz *m* <a slip of the tongue : un lapsus> **4** PETTICOAT **:** enagua *f* **5 :** injerto *m,* esqueje *m* (de una planta) **6 slip of paper :** papelito *m*
slipper [ˈslɪpər] *n* **:** zapatilla *f,* pantufla *f*
slipperiness [ˈslɪpərinəs] *n* **1 :** lo resbaloso, lo resbaladizo **2** TRICKINESS **:** astucia *f*
slippery [ˈslɪpəri] *adj* **slipperier; -est 1 :** resbaloso, resbaladizo <a slippery road : un camino resbaloso> **2** TRICKY **:** artero, astuto, taimado **3** ELUSIVE **:** huidizo, escurridizo
slipshod [ˈslɪpˌʃɑd] *adj* **:** descuidado, chapucero
slip up *vi* **:** equivocarse
slit[1] [ˈslɪt] *vt* **slit; slitting :** cortar, abrir por lo largo
slit[2] *n* **1** OPENING **:** abertura *f,* rendija *f* **2** CUT **:** corte *m,* raja *f,* tajo *m*
slither [ˈslɪðər] *vi* **:** deslizarse
sliver [ˈslɪvər] *n* **:** astilla *f*
slob [ˈslɑb] *n* **:** persona *f* desaliñada <what a slob! : ¡qué cerdo!>
slobber[1] [ˈslɑbər] *vi* **:** babear
slobber[2] *n* **:** baba *f*
slogan [ˈsloːgən] *n* **:** lema *m,* eslogan *m*
sloop [ˈsluːp] *n* **:** balandra *f*
slop[1] [ˈslɑp] *v* **slopped; slopping** *vt* **:** derramar — *vi* **:** derramarse
slop[2] *n* **:** bazofia *f*
slope[1] [ˈsloːp] *vi* **sloped; sloping :** inclinarse <the road slopes upward : el camino sube (en pendiente)>
slope[2] *n* **:** inclinación *f,* pendiente *f,* declive *m*
sloppy [ˈslɑpi] *adj* **sloppier; -est 1** MUDDY, SLUSHY **:** lodoso, fangoso **2** UNTIDY **:** descuidado (en el trabajo, etc.), desaliñado (de aspecto)
slot [ˈslɑt] *n* **:** ranura *f*
sloth [ˈslɔθ, ˈsloːθ] *n* **1** LAZINESS **:** pereza *f* **2 :** perezoso *m* (animal)
slouch[1] [ˈslaʊtʃ] *vi* **:** andar con los hombros caídos, repantigarse (en un sillón)
slouch[2] *n* **1** SLUMPING **:** mala postura *f* **2** BUNGLER, IDLER **:** haragán *m,* -gana *f;* inepto *m,* -ta *f* <to be no slouch : no quedarse atrás>
slough[1] [ˈslʌf] *vt* **:** mudar de (piel)
slough[2] [ˈsluː, ˈslaʊ] *n* SWAMP **:** ciénaga *f*
Slovak [ˈsloːˌvɑk, -ˌvæk] *or* **Slovakian** [sloːˈvɑkiən, -ˈvæ-] *n* **:** eslovaco *m,* -ca *f* — **Slovak** *or* **Slovakian** *adj*
Slovene [ˈsloːˌviːn] *or* **Slovenian** [sloːˈviːniən] *n* **:** esloveno *m,* -na *f* — **Slovene** *or* **Slovenian** *adj*

slovenly ['slɑvənli, 'slʌv-] *adj* **:** descuidado (en el trabajo, etc.), desaliñado (de aspecto)
slow[1] [slo:] *vt* **:** retrasar, reducir la marcha de — *vi* **:** ir más despacio
slow[2] *adv* **:** despacio, lentamente
slow[3] *adj* **1 :** lento <a slow process : un proceso lento> **2 :** atrasado <my watch is slow : mi reloj está atrasado, mi reloj se atrasa> **3** SLUGGISH **:** lento, poco activo **4** STUPID **:** lento, torpe, corto de alcances
slowly [slo:li] *adv* **:** lentamente, despacio
slowness [slo:nəs] *n* **:** lentitud *f,* torpeza *f*
sludge ['slʌdʒ] *n* **:** aguas *fpl* negras, aguas *fpl* residuales
slug[1] ['slʌg] *vt* **slugged; slugging :** pegarle un porrazo (a alguien)
slug[2] *n* **1 :** babosa *f* (molusco) **2** BULLET **:** bala *f* **3** TOKEN **:** ficha *f* **4** BLOW **:** porrazo *m,* puñetazo *m*
sluggish ['slʌgɪʃ] *adj* **:** aletargado, lento
sluice[1] ['slu:s] *vt* **sluiced; sluicing :** lavar en agua corriente
sluice[2] *n* **:** canal *m*
slum ['slʌm] *n* **:** barriada *f,* barrio *m* bajo
slumber[1] ['slʌmbər] *vi* **:** dormir
slumber[2] *n* **:** sueño *m*
slump[1] ['slʌmp] *vi* **1** DECLINE, DROP **:** disminuir, bajar **2** SLOUCH **:** encorvarse, dejarse caer (en una silla, etc.)
slump[2] *n* **:** bajón *m,* declive *m* (económico)
slung → **sling**
slunk → **slink**
slur[1] ['slər] *vt* **slurred; slurring :** ligar (notas musicales), tragarse (las palabras)
slur[2] *n* **1 :** ligado *m* (en música), mala pronunciación *f* (de las palabras) **2** ASPERSION **:** calumnia *f,* difamación *f*
slurp[1] ['slərp] *vi* **:** beber o comer haciendo ruido — *vt* **:** sorber ruidosamente
slurp[2] *n* **:** sorbo *m* (ruidoso)
slush ['slʌʃ] *n* **:** nieve *f* medio derretida
slut ['slʌt] *n* PROSTITUTE **:** ramera *f,* fulana *f*
sly ['slaɪ] *adj* **slier** ['slaɪər]; **sliest** ['slaɪəst] **1** CUNNING **:** astuto, taimado **2** UNDERHANDED **:** soplado — **slyly** *adv*
slyness ['slaɪnəs] *n* **:** astucia *f*
smack[1] ['smæk] *vi* **to smack of :** oler a, saber a — *vt* **1** KISS **:** besar, plantarle un beso (a alguien) **2** SLAP **:** pegarle una bofetada (a alguien) **3 to smack one's lips :** relamerse
smack[2] *adv* **:** justo, exactamente <smack in the face : en plena cara>
smack[3] *n* **1** TASTE, TRACE **:** sabor *m,* indicio *m* **2 :** chasquido *m* (de los labios) **3** SLAP **:** bofetada *f* **4** KISS **:** beso *m*
small ['smɔl] *adj* **1 :** pequeño, chico <a small house : una casa pequeña> <small change : monedas de poco valor> **2** TRIVIAL **:** pequeño, insignificante
smallness ['smɔlnəs] *n* **:** pequeñez *f*
smallpox ['smɔl,pɑks] *n* **:** viruela *f*
smart[1] ['smɑrt] *vi* **1** STING **:** escocer, picar, arder **2** HURT **:** dolerse, resentirse <to smart under a rejection : dolerse ante un rechazo>
smart[2] *adj* **1** BRIGHT **:** listo, vivo, inteligente **2** STYLISH **:** elegante — **smartly** *adv*
smart[3] *n* **:** escozor *m,* dolor *m*
smartness ['smɑrtnəs] *n* **1** INTELLIGENCE **:** inteligencia *f* **2** ELEGANCE **:** elegancia *f*
smash[1] ['smæʃ] *vt* **1** BREAK **:** romper, quebrar, hacer pedazos **2** WRECK **:** destrozar, arruinar **3** CRASH **:** estrellar, chocar — *vi* **1** SHATTER **:** hacerse pedazos, hacerse añicos **2** COLLIDE, CRASH **:** estrellarse, chocar
smash[2] *n* **1** BLOW **:** golpe *m* **2** COLLISION **:** choque *m* **3** BANG, CRASH **:** estrépito *m*
smattering ['smætərɪŋ] *n* **1 :** nociones *fpl* <she has a smattering of programming : tiene nociones de programación> **2 :** un poco, unos cuantos <a smattering of spectators : unos cuantos espectadores>
smear[1] ['smɪr] *vt* **1** DAUB **:** embadurnar, untar (mantequilla, etc.) **2** SMUDGE **:** emborronar **3** SLANDER **:** calumniar, difamar
smear[2] *n* **1** SMUDGE **:** mancha *f* **2** SLANDER **:** calumnia *f*
smell[1] ['smɛl] *v* **smelled** *or* **smelt** ['smɛlt]; **smelling** *vt* **:** oler, olfatear <to smell danger : olfatear el peligro> — *vi* **:** oler <to smell good : oler bien>
smell[2] *n* **1 :** olfato *m,* sentido *m* del olfato **2** ODOR **:** olor *m*
smelly ['smɛli] *adj* **smellier; -est :** maloliente
smelt[1] ['smɛlt] *vt* **:** fundir
smelt[2] *n, pl* **smelts** *or* **smelt :** eperlano *m* (pez)
smile[1] ['smaɪl] *vi* **smiled; smiling :** sonreír
smile[2] *n* **:** sonrisa *f*
smirk[1] ['smərk] *vi* **:** sonreír con suficiencia
smirk[2] *n* **:** sonrisa *f* satisfecha
smite ['smaɪt] *vt* **smote** ['smo:t]; **smitten** ['smɪtən] *or* **smote; smiting 1** STRIKE **:** golpear **2** AFFLICT **:** afligir
smith ['smɪθ] *n* **:** herrero *m,* -ra *f*
smithy ['smɪθi] *n, pl* **smithies :** herrería *f*
smock ['smɑk] *n* **:** bata *f,* blusón *m*
smog ['smɑg, 'smɔg] *n* **:** smog *m*
smoke[1] ['smo:k] *v* **smoked; smoking** *vi* **1 :** echar humo, humear <a smoking chimney : una chimenea que echa humo> **2 :** fumar <I don't smoke : no fumo> — *vt* **:** ahumar (carne, etc.)
smoke[2] *n* **:** humo *m*

smoke detector [dɪˈtɛktər] *n* : detector *m* de humo
smoker [ˈsmoːkər] *n* : fumador *m,* -dora *f*
smokestack [ˈsmoːkˌstæk] *n* : chimenea *f*
smoky [ˈsmoːki] *adj* **smokier; -est 1** SMOKING : humeante **2** : a humo <a smoky flavor : un sabor a humo> **3** : lleno de humo <a smoky room : un cuarto lleno de humo>
smolder [ˈsmoːldər] *vi* **1** : arder sin llama **2** : arder (en el corazón) <his anger smoldered : su rabia ardía>
smooth[1] [ˈsmuːð] *vt* : alisar
smooth[2] *adj* **1** : liso (dícese de una superficie) <smooth skin : piel lisa> **2** : suave (dícese de un movimiento) <a smooth landing : un aterrizaje suave> **3** : sin grumos <a smooth sauce : una salsa sin grumos> **4** : fluido <smooth writing : escritura fluida>
smoothly [ˈsmuːðli] *adv* **1** GENTLY, SOFTLY : suavemente **2** EASILY : con facilidad, sin problemas
smoothness [ˈsmuːðnəs] *n* : suavidad *f*
smother [ˈsmʌðər] *vt* **1** SUFFOCATE : ahogar, sofocar **2** COVER : cubrir **3** SUPPRESS : contener — *vi* : asfixiarse
smudge[1] [ˈsmʌdʒ] *v* **smudged; smudging** *vt* : emborronar — *vi* : correrse
smudge[2] *n* : mancha *f,* borrón *m*
smug [ˈsmʌg] *adj* **smugger; smuggest** : suficiente, pagado de sí mismo
smuggle [ˈsmʌgəl] *vt* **-gled; -gling** : contrabandear, pasar de contrabando
smuggler [ˈsmʌgələr] *n* : contrabandista *mf*
smugly [ˈsmʌgli] *adv* : con suficiencia
smut [ˈsmʌt] *n* **1** SOOT : tizne *m,* hollín *m* **2** FUNGUS : tizón *m* **3** OBSCENITY : obscenidad *f,* inmundicia *f*
smutty [ˈsmʌti] *adj* **smuttier; -est 1** SOOTY : tiznado **2** OBSCENE : obsceno, indecente
snack [ˈsnæk] *n* : refrigerio *m,* bocado *m,* tentempié *m fam* <an afternoon snack : una merienda>
snag[1] [ˈsnæg] *v* **snagged; snagging** *vt* : enganchar — *vi* : engancharse
snag[2] *n* : problema *m,* inconveniente *m*
snail [ˈsneɪl] *n* : caracol *m*
snake [ˈsneɪk] *n* : culebra *f,* serpiente *f*
snakebite [ˈsneɪkˌbaɪt] *n* : mordedura *f* de serpiente
snap[1] [ˈsnæp] *v* **snapped; snapping** *vi* **1** : intentar morder (dícese de un perro, etc.), picar (dícese de un pez) **2** : hablar con severidad <he snapped at me! : ¡me gritó!> **3** BREAK : romperse, quebrarse (haciendo un chasquido) — *vt* **1** BREAK : partir (en dos), quebrar **2** : hacer (algo) de un golpe <to snap open : abrir de golpe> **3** RETORT : decir bruscamente **4** CLICK : chasquear <to snap one's fingers : chasquear los dedos>
snap[2] *n* **1** CLICK, CRACK : chasquido *m* **2** FASTENER : broche *m* **3** CINCH : cosa *f* fácil <it's a snap : es facilísimo>
snapdragon [ˈsnæpˌdrægən] *n* : dragón *m* (flor)
snapper [ˈsnæpər] → **red snapper**
snappy [ˈsnæpi] *adj* **snappier; -est 1** FAST : rápido <make it snappy! : ¡date prisa!> **2** LIVELY : vivaz **3** CHILLY : frío **4** STYLISH : elegante
snapshot [ˈsnæpˌʃɑt] *n* : instantánea *f*
snare[1] [ˈsnær] *vt* **snared; snaring** : atrapar
snare[2] *n* : trampa *f,* red *f*
snare drum *n* : tambor *m* con bordón
snarl[1] [ˈsnɑrl] *vi* **1** TANGLE : enmarañar, enredar **2** GROWL : gruñir
snarl[2] *n* **1** TANGLE : enredo *m,* maraña *f* **2** GROWL : gruñido *m*
snatch[1] [ˈsnætʃ] *vt* : arrebatar
snatch[2] *n* : fragmento *m*
sneak[1] [ˈsniːk] *vi* : ir a hurtadillas — *vt* : hacer furtivamente <to sneak a look : mirar con disimulo> <he sneaked a smoke : fumó un cigarrillo a escondidas>
sneak[2] *n* : soplón *m,* -plona *f*
sneakers [ˈsniːkərz] *npl* : tenis *mpl,* zapatillas *fpl*
sneaky [ˈsniːki] *adj* **sneakier; -est** : solapado
sneer[1] [ˈsnɪr] *vi* : sonreír con desprecio
sneer[2] *n* : sonrisa *f* de desprecio
sneeze[1] [ˈsniːz] *vi* **sneezed; sneezing** : estornudar
sneeze[2] *n* : estornudo *m*
snicker[1] [ˈsnɪkər] *vi* : reírse disimuladamente
snicker[2] *n* : risita *f*
snide [ˈsnaɪd] *adj* : sarcástico
sniff[1] [ˈsnɪf] *vi* **1** SMELL : oler, husmear (dícese de los animales) **2 to sniff at** : despreciar, desdeñar — *vt* **1** SMELL : oler **2 to sniff out** : olerse, husmear
sniff[2] *n* **1** SNIFFING : aspiración *f* por la nariz **2** SMELL : olor *m*
sniffle [ˈsnɪfəl] *vi* **-fled; -fling** : respirar con la nariz congestionada
sniffles [ˈsnɪfəlz] *npl* : resfriado *m*
snip[1] [ˈsnɪp] *vt* **snipped; snipping** : cortar (con tijeras)
snip[2] *n* : tijeretada *f,* recorte *m*
snipe[1] [ˈsnaɪp] *vi* **sniped; sniping** : disparar
snipe[2] *n, pl* **snipes** *or* **snipe** : agachadiza *f*
sniper [ˈsnaɪpər] *n* : francotirador *m,* -dora *f*
snivel [ˈsnɪvəl] *vi* **-veled** *or* **-velled; -veling** *or* **-velling 1** → **snuffle 2** WHINE : lloriquear
snob [ˈsnɑb] *n* : esnob *mf,* snob *mf*
snobbery [ˈsnɑbəri] *n, pl* **-beries** : esnobismo *m*
snobbish [ˈsnɑbɪʃ] *adj* : esnob, snob
snobbishness [ˈsnɑbɪʃnəs] *n* : esnobismo *m*
snoop[1] [ˈsnuːp] *vi* : husmear, curiosear
snoop[2] *n* : fisgón *m,* -gona *f*

snooze[1] [ˈsnuːz] *vi* **snoozed; snoozing** : dormitar
snooze[2] *n* : siestecita *f,* siestita *f*
snore[1] [ˈsnor] *vi* **snored; snoring** : roncar
snore[2] *n* : ronquido *m*
snort[1] [ˈsnɔrt] *vi* : bufar, resoplar
snort[2] *n* : bufido *m,* resoplo *m*
snout [ˈsnaʊt] *n* : hocico *m,* morro *m*
snow[1] [ˈsnoː] *vi* **1** : nevar <I'm snowed in : estoy aislado por la nieve> **2 to be snowed under** : estar inundado
snow[2] *n* : nieve *f*
snowball [ˈsnoːˌbɔl] *n* : bola *f* de nieve
snowdrift [ˈsnoːˌdrɪft] *n* : ventisquero *m*
snowfall [ˈsnoːˌfɔl] *n* : nevada *f*
snowplow [ˈsnoːˌplaʊ] *n* : quitanieves *m*
snowshoe [ˈsnoːˌʃuː] *n* : raqueta *f* (para nieve)
snowstorm [ˈsnoːˌstɔrm] *n* : tormenta *f* de nieve, ventisca *f*
snowy [ˈsnoːi] *adj* **snowier; -est** : nevoso <a snowy road : un camino nevado>
snub[1] [ˈsnʌb] *vi* **snubbed; snubbing** : desairar
snub[2] *n* : desaire *m*
snub–nosed [ˈsnʌbˌnoːzd] *adj* : de nariz respingada
snuff[1] [ˈsnʌf] *vt* **1** : apagar (una vela) **2** : sorber (algo) por la nariz
snuff[2] *n* : rapé *m*
snuffle [ˈsnʌfəl] *vi* **-fled; -fling** : respirar con la nariz congestionada
snug [ˈsnʌg] *adj* **snugger; snuggest 1** COMFORTABLE : cómodo **2** TIGHT : ajustado, ceñido <snug pants : pantalones ajustados>
snuggle [ˈsnʌgəl] *vi* **-gled; -gling** : acurrucarse <to snuggle up to someone : arrimársele a alguien>
snugly [ˈsnʌgli] *adv* **1** COMFORTABLY : cómodamente **2** : de manera ajustada <the shirt fits snugly : la camisa queda ajustada>
so[1] [ˈsoː] *adv* **1** (*referring to something indicated or suggested*) <do you think so? : ¿tú crees?> <so it would seem : eso parece> <I told her so : se lo dije> <he's ready, or so he says : según dice, está listo> <it so happened that. . . : resultó que. . .> <do it like so : hazlo así> <so be it : así sea> **2** ALSO : también <so do I : yo también> **3** THUS : así, de esta manera **4** : tan <he'd never been so happy : nunca había estado tan contento> **5** CONSEQUENTLY : por lo tanto
so[2] *conj* **1** THEREFORE : así que **2** *or* **so that** : para que, así que, de manera que **3 so what?** : ¿y qué?
soak[1] [ˈsoːk] *vi* : estar en remojo — *vt* **1** : poner en remojo **2 to soak up** ABSORB : absorber
soak[2] *n* : remojo *m*
soap[1] [ˈsoːp] *vt* : enjabonar
soap[2] *n* : jabón *m*
soapsuds [ˈsoːpˌsʌdz] → **suds**
soapy [ˈsoːpi] **soapier; -est** *adj* : jabonoso <a soapy taste : un gusto a jabón> <a soapy texture : una textura de jabón>
soar [ˈsor] *vi* **1** FLY : volar **2** RISE : remontar el vuelo (dícese de las aves) <her hopes soared : su esperanza renació> <prices are soaring : los precios están subiendo vertiginosamente>
sob[1] [ˈsɑb] *vi* **sobbed; sobbing** : sollozar
sob[2] *n* : sollozo *m*
sober [ˈsoːbər] *adj* **1** : sobrio <he's not sober enough to drive : está demasiado borracho para manejar> **2** SERIOUS : serio
soberly [ˈsoːbərli] *adv* **1** : sobriamente **2** SERIOUSLY : seriamente
sobriety [səˈbraɪəti, so-] *n* **1** : sobriedad *f* <sobriety test : prueba de alcoholemia> **2** SERIOUSNESS : seriedad *f*
so–called [ˈsoːˈkɔld] *adj* : supuesto, presunto <the so-called experts : los expertos, así llamados>
soccer [ˈsɑkər] *n* : futbol *m,* fútbol *m*
sociable [ˈsoːʃəbəl] *adj* : sociable
social[1] [ˈsoːʃəl] *adj* : social — **socially** *adv*
social[2] *n* : reunión *f* social
socialism [ˈsoːʃəˌlɪzəm] *n* : socialismo *m*
socialist[1] [ˈsoːʃəlɪst] *adj* : socialista
socialist[2] *n* : socialista *mf*
socialize [ˈsoːʃəˌlaɪz] *v* **-ized; -izing** *vt* **1** NATIONALIZE : nacionalizar **2** : socializar (en psicología) — *vi* : alternar, circular <to socialize with friends : alternar con amigos>
social work *n* : asistencia *f* social
society [səˈsaɪəti] *n, pl* **-eties 1** COMPANIONSHIP : compañía *f* **2** : sociedad *f* <a democratic society : una sociedad democrática> <high society : alta sociedad> **3** ASSOCIATION : sociedad *f,* asociación *f*
sociology [ˌsoːsiˈɑləʤi] *n* : sociología *f*
sociological [ˌsoːsiəˈlɑʤɪkəl] *adj* : sociológico
sociologist [ˌsoːsiˈɑləʤɪst] *n* : sociólogo *m,* -ga *f*
sock[1] [ˈsɑk] *vt* : pegar, golpear, darle un puñetazo a
sock[2] *n* **1** *pl* **socks** *or* **sox** [ˈsɑks] : calcetín *m,* media *f* <shoes and socks : zapatos y calcetines> **2** *pl* **socks** [ˈsɑks] PUNCH : puñetazo *m*
socket [ˈsɑkət] *n* **1** *or* **electric socket** : enchufe *m,* toma *f* de corriente **2** : glena *f* (de una articulación) <shoulder socket : glena del hombro> **3 eye socket** : órbita *f,* cuenca *f*
sod[1] [ˈsɑd] *vt* **sodded; sodding** : cubrir de césped
sod[2] *n* TURF : césped *m,* tepe *m*

soda [ˈsoːdə] *n* **1** *or* **soda water :** soda *f* **2** *or* **soda pop :** gaseosa *f,* refresco *m* **3** *or* **ice–cream soda :** refresco *m* con helado
sodden [ˈsɑdən] *adj* SOGGY : empapado
sodium [ˈsoːdiəm] *n* : sodio *m*
sodium bicarbonate *n* : bicarbonato *m* de soda
sodium chloride → salt
sofa [ˈsoːfə] *n* : sofá *m*
soft [ˈsɔft] *adj* **1 :** blando <a soft pillow : una almohada blanda> **2** SMOOTH : suave (dícese de las texturas, de los sonidos, etc.) **3** NONALCOHOLIC : no alcohólico <a soft drink : un refresco>
softball [ˈsɔftˌbɔl] *n* : softbol *m*
soften [ˈsɔfən] *vt* : ablandar (algo sólido), suavizar (la piel, un golpe, etc.), amortiguar (un impacto) — *vi* : ablandarse, suavizarse
softly [ˈsɔftli] *adv* : suavemente <she spoke softly : habló en voz baja>
softness [ˈsɔftnəs] *n* **1 :** blandura *f,* lo blando (de una almohada, de la mantequilla, etc.) **2** SMOOTHNESS : suavidad *f*
software [ˈsɔftˌwær] *n* : software *m*
soggy [ˈsɑgi] *adj* **soggier; -est** : empapado
soil[1] [ˈsɔɪl] *vt* : ensuciar — *vi* : ensuciarse
soil[2] *n* **1** DIRTINESS : suciedad *f* **2** DIRT, EARTH : suelo *m,* tierra *f* **3** COUNTRY : patria *f* <her native soil : su tierra natal>
sojourn[1] [ˈsoːˌdʒərn, soːˈdʒərn] *vi* : pasar una temporada
sojourn[2] *n* : estadía *f,* estancia *f,* permanencia *f*
solace [ˈsɑləs] *n* : consuelo *m*
solar [ˈsoːlər] *adj* : solar <the solar system : el sistema solar>
sold → sell
solder[1] [ˈsɑdər, ˈsɔ-] *vt* : soldar
solder[2] *n* : soldadura *f*
soldier[1] [ˈsoːldʒər] *vi* : servir como soldado
soldier[2] *n* : soldado *mf*
sole[1] [ˈsoːl] *adj* : único
sole[2] *n* **1 :** suela *f* (de un zapato) **2 :** lenguado *m* (pez)
solely [ˈsoːli] *adv* : únicamente, sólo
solemn [ˈsɑləm] *adj* : solemne, serio — **solemnly** *adv*
solemnity [səˈlɛmnət̬i] *n, pl* **-ties** : solemnidad *f*
solicit [səˈlɪsət] *vt* : solicitar
solicitous [səˈlɪsət̬əs] *adj* : solícito
solicitude [səˈlɪsəˌtuːd, -ˌtjuːd] *n* : solicitud *f*
solid[1] [ˈsɑləd] *adj* **1 :** macizo <a solid rubber ball : una bola maciza de caucho> **2** CUBIC : tridimensional **3** COMPACT : compacto, denso **4** STURDY : sólido **5** CONTINUOUS : seguido, continuo <two solid hours : dos horas seguidas> <a solid line : una línea continua> **6** UNANIMOUS : unánime **7** DEPENDABLE : serio, fiable **8** PURE : macizo, puro <solid gold : oro macizo>
solid[2] *n* : sólido *m*
solidarity [ˌsɑləˈdærət̬i] *n* : solidaridad *f*
solidify [səˈlɪdəˌfaɪ] *v* **-fied; -fying** *vt* : solidificar — *vi* : solidificarse
solidity [səˈlɪdət̬i] *n, pl* **-ties** : solidez *f*
solidly [ˈsɑlədli] *adv* **1 :** sólidamente **2** UNANIMOUSLY : unánimemente
soliloquy [səˈlɪləkwi] *n, pl* **-quies** : soliloquio *m*
solitaire [ˈsɑləˌtɛr] *n* : solitario *m*
solitary [ˈsɑləˌtɛri] *adj* **1** ALONE : solitario **2** SECLUDED : apartado, retirado **3** SINGLE : solo
solitude [ˈsɑləˌtuːd, -ˌtjuːd] *n* : soledad *f*
solo[1] [ˈsoːˌloː] *vi* : volar en solitario (dícese de un piloto)
solo[2] *adv & adj* : en solitario, a solas
solo[3] *n, pl* **solos** : solo *m*
soloist [ˈsoːloɪst] *n* : solista *mf*
solstice [ˈsɑlstɪs] *n* : solsticio *m*
soluble [ˈsɑljəbəl] *adj* : soluble
solution [səˈluːʃən] *n* : solución *f*
solve [ˈsɑlv] *vt* **solved; solving** : resolver, solucionar
solvency [ˈsɑlvən*t*si] *n* : solvencia *f*
solvent [ˈsɑlvənt] *n* : solvente *m*
Somali [soˈmɑli, sə-] *n* : somalí *mf* — **Somali** *adj*
somber [ˈsɑmbər] *adj* **1** DARK : sombrío, oscuro <somber colors : colores oscuros> **2** GRAVE : sombrío, serio **3** MELANCHOLY : sombrío, lúgubre
sombrero [səmˈbrɛrˌoː] *n, pl* **-ros** : sombrero *m* (mexicano)
some[1] [ˈsʌm] *adj* **1 :** un, algún <some lady stopped me : una mujer me detuvo> <some distant galaxy : alguna galaxia lejana> **2 :** algo de, un poco de <he drank some water : tomó (un poco de) agua> **3 :** unos <do you want some apples? : ¿quieres unas manzanas?> <some years ago : hace varios años>
some[2] *pron* **1 :** algunos <some went, others stayed : algunos se fueron, otros se quedaron> **2 :** un poco, algo <there's some left : queda un poco> <I have gum; do you want some? : tengo chicle, ¿quieres?>
somebody [ˈsʌmbədi, -ˌbɑdi] *pron* : alguien
someday [ˈsʌmˌdeɪ] *adv* : algún día
somehow [ˈsʌmˌhaʊ] *adv* **1 :** de alguna manera, de algún modo <I'll do it somehow : lo haré de alguna manera> **2 :** por alguna rázon <somehow I don't trust her : por alguna razón no me fío de ella>
someone [ˈsʌmˌwʌn] *pron* : alguien
somersault[1] [ˈsʌmərˌsɔlt] *vi* : dar volteretas, dar un salto mortal
somersault[2] *n* : voltereta *f,* salto *m* mortal

something [ˈsʌmθɪŋ] *pron* : algo <I want something else : quiero otra cosa> <she's writing a novel or something : está escribiendo una novela o no sé qué>

sometime [ˈsʌmˌtaɪm] *adv* : algún día, en algún momento <sometime next month : durante el mes que viene>

sometimes [ˈsʌmˌtaɪmz] *adv* : a veces, algunas veces, de vez en cuando

somewhat [ˈsʌmˌhwʌt, -ˌhwɑt] *adv* : algo, un tanto

somewhere [ˈsʌmˌ*h*wɛr] *adv* **1** : en alguna parte, a algún lugar **2 somewhere else** : en otro sitio

son [ˈsʌn] *n* : hijo *m*

sonar [ˈsoːˌnɑr] *n* : sonar *m*

sonata [səˈnɑṭə] *n* : sonata *f*

song [ˈsɔŋ] *n* : canción *f,* canto *m* (de un pájaro)

songbird [ˈsɔŋˌbərd] *n* : pájaro *m* cantor

sonic [ˈsɑnɪk] *adj* **1** : sónico **2 sonic boom** : estampido *m* sónico

son–in–law [ˈsʌnɪnˌlɔ] *n, pl* **sons–in–law** : yerno *m,* hijo *m* político

sonnet [ˈsɑnət] *n* : soneto *m*

sonorous [ˈsɑnərəs, səˈnorəs] *adj* : sonoro

soon [ˈsuːn] *adv* **1** : pronto, dentro de poco <he'll arrive soon : llegará pronto> **2** QUICKLY : pronto <as soon as possible : lo más pronto posible> <the sooner the better : cuanto antes mejor>

soot [ˈsʊt, ˈsuːt, ˈsʌt] *n* : hollín *m,* tizne *m*

soothe [ˈsuːð] *vt* **soothed; soothing 1** CALM : calmar, tranquilizar **2** RELIEVE : aliviar

soothsayer [ˈsuːθˌseɪər] *n* : adivino *m,* -na *f*

sooty [ˈsʊṭi, ˈsuː-, ˈsʌ-] *adj* **sootier; -est** : cubierto de hollín, tiznado

sop[1] [ˈsɑp] *vt* **sopped; sopping 1** DIP : mojar **2** SOAK : empapar **3 to sop up** : rebañar, absorber

sop[2] *n* **1** CONCESSION : concesión *f* **2** BRIBE : soborno *m*

sophisticated [səˈfɪstəˌkeɪṭəd] *adj* **1** COMPLEX : complejo **2** WORLDLY-WISE : sofisticado

sophistication [səˌfɪstəˈkeɪʃən] *n* **1** COMPLEXITY : complejidad *f* **2** URBANITY : sofisticación *f*

sophomore [ˈsɑfˌmor, ˈsɑfəˌmor] *n* : estudiante *mf* de segundo año

soporific [ˌsɑpəˈrɪfɪk, ˌsoː-] *adj* : soporífero

soprano [səˈpræˌnoː] *n, pl* **-nos** : soprano *mf*

sorcerer [ˈsɔrsərər] *n* : hechicero *m,* brujo *m,* mago *m*

sorceress [ˈsɔrsərəs] *n* : hechicera *f,* bruja *f,* maga *f*

sorcery [ˈsɔrsəri] *n* : hechicería *f,* brujería *f*

sordid [ˈsɔrdɪd] *adj* : sórdido

sore[1] [ˈsor] *adj* **sorer; sorest 1** PAINFUL : dolorido, doloroso <I have a sore throat : me duele la garganta> **2** ACUTE, SEVERE : extremo, grande <in sore straits : en grandes apuros> **3** ANGRY : enojado, enfadado

sore[2] *n* : llaga *f*

sorely [ˈsorli] *adv* : muchísimo <it was sorely needed : se necesitaba urgentemente> <she was sorely missed : la echaban mucho de menos>

soreness [ˈsornəs] *n* : dolor *m*

sorghum [ˈsɔrgəm] *n* : sorgo *m*

sorority [səˈrɔrəṭi] *n, pl* **-ties** : hermandad *f* (de estudiantes femeninas)

sorrel [ˈsɔrəl] *n* **1** : alazán *m* (color o animal) **2** : acedera *f* (hierba)

sorrow [ˈsɑrˌoː] *n* : pesar *m,* dolor *m,* pena *f*

sorrowful [ˈsɑrofəl] *adj* : triste, afligido, apenado

sorrowfully [ˈsɑrofəli] *adv* : con tristeza

sorry [ˈsɑri] *adj* **sorrier; -est 1** PITIFUL : lastimero, lastimoso **2 to be sorry** : sentir, lamentar <I'm sorry : lo siento> **3 to feel sorry for** : compadecer <I feel sorry for him : me da pena>

sort[1] [ˈsɔrt] *vt* : clasificar

sort[2] *n* **1** KIND : tipo *m,* clase *f* <a sort of writer : una especie de escritor> **2** NATURE : índole *f* **3 out of sorts** : de mal humor

sortie [ˈsɔrṭi, sɔrˈtiː] *n* : salida *f*

SOS [ˌɛsˌoːˈɛs] *n* : SOS *m*

so–so [ˈsoːˈsoː] *adj & adv* : así así, de modo regular

soufflé [suːˈfleɪ] *n* : suflé *m*

sought → **seek**

soul [ˈsoːl] *n* **1** SPIRIT : alma *f* **2** ESSENCE : esencia *f* **3** PERSON : persona *f,* alma *f*

soulful [ˈsoːlfəl] *adj* : conmovedor, lleno de emoción

sound[1] [ˈsaʊnd] *vt* **1** : sondar (en navegación) **2** *or* **to sound out** PROBE : sondear **3** : hacer sonar, tocar (una trompeta, etc.) — *vi* **1** : sonar <the alarm sounded : la alarma sonó> **2** SEEM : parecer

sound[2] *adj* **1** HEALTHY : sano <safe and sound : sano y salvo> <of sound mind and body : en pleno uso de sus facultades> **2** FIRM, SOLID : sólido **3** SENSIBLE : lógico, sensato **4** DEEP : profundo <a sound sleep : un sueño profundo>

sound[3] *n* **1** : sonido *m* <the speed of sound : la velocidad del sonido> **2** NOISE : sonido *m,* ruido *m* <I heard a sound : oí un sonido> **3** CHANNEL : brazo *m* de mar, canal *m* (ancho)

soundless [ˈsaʊndləs] *adj* : sordo

soundlessly [ˈsaʊndləsli] *adv* : silenciosamente

soundly [ˈsaʊndli] *adv* **1** SOLIDLY : sólidamente **2** SENSIBLY : lógicamente, sensatamente **3** DEEPLY : profunda-

mente <sleeping soundly : durmiendo profundamente>
soundness [ˈsaʊndnəs] *n* **1** SOLIDITY : solidez *f* **2** SENSIBLENESS : sensatez *f,* solidez *f*
soundproof [ˈsaʊnd,pruːf] *adj* : insonorizado
sound wave *n* : onda *f* sonora
soup [ˈsuːp] *n* : sopa *f*
sour¹ [ˈsaʊər] *vi* : agriarse, cortarse (dícese de la leche) — *vt* : agriar, cortar (leche)
sour² *adj* **1** ACID : agrio, ácido (dícese de la fruta, etc.), cortado (dícese de la leche) **2** DISAGREEABLE : desagradable, agrio
source [ˈsors] *n* : fuente *f,* origen *m,* nacimiento *m* (de un río)
sourness [ˈsaʊərnəs] *n* : acidez *f*
south¹ [ˈsaʊθ] *adv* : al sur, hacia el sur <the window looks south : la ventana mira al sur> <she continued south : continuó hacia el sur>
south² *adj* : sur, del sur <the south entrance : la entrada sur> <South America : Sudamérica, América del Sur>
south³ *n* : sur *m*
South African *n* : sudafricano *m,* -na *f* — **South African** *adj*
South American¹ *adj* : sudamericano, suramericano
South American² *n* : sudamericano *m,* -na *f;* suramericano *m,* -na *f*
southbound [ˈsaʊθ,baʊnd] *adj* : con rumbo al sur
southeast¹ [saʊˈθiːst] *adj* : sureste, sudeste, del sureste
southeast² *n* : sureste *m,* sudeste *m*
southeasterly [saʊˈθiːstərli] *adv & adj* **1** : del sureste (dícese del viento) **2** : hacia el sureste
southeastern [saʊˈθiːstərn] → **southeast¹**
southerly [ˈsʌðərli] *adv & adj* : del sur
southern [ˈsʌðərn] *adj* : sur, sureño, meridional, austral <a southern city : una ciudad del sur del país, una ciudad meridional> <the southern side : el lado sur>
Southerner [ˈsʌðərnər] *n* : sureño *m,* -ña *f*
South Pole : Polo *m* Sur
southward [ˈsaʊθwərd] *or* **southwards** [-wərdz] *adv & adj* : hacia el sur
southwest¹ [saʊθˈwɛst, *as a nautical term often* saʊˈwɛst] *adj* : suroeste, sudoeste, del suroeste
southwest² *n* : suroeste *m,* sudoeste *m*
southwesterly [saʊθˈwɛstərli] *adv & adj* **1** : del suroeste (dícese del viento) **2** : hacia el suroeste
southwestern [saʊθˈwɛstərn] → **southwest¹**
souvenir [,suːvəˈnɪr, ˈsuːvə,-] *n* : recuerdo *m,* souvenir *m*
sovereign¹ [ˈsɑvərən] *adj* : soberano
sovereign² *n* **1** : soberano *m,* -na *f* (monarca) **2** : soberano *m* (moneda)
sovereignty [ˈsɑvərənti] *n, pl* **-ties** : soberanía *f*
Soviet [ˈsoːvi,ɛt, ˈsɑ-, -viət] *adj* : soviético
sow¹ [ˈsoː] *vt* **sowed; sown** [ˈsoːn] *or* **sowed; sowing 1** PLANT : sembrar **2** SCATTER : esparcir
sow² [ˈsaʊ] *n* : cerda *f*
sox → **sock**
soybean [ˈsɔɪ,biːn] *n* : soya *f,* soja *f*
spa [ˈspɑ] *n* : balneario *m*
space¹ [ˈspeɪs] *vt* **spaced; spacing** : espaciar
space² *n* **1** PERIOD : espacio *m,* lapso *m,* período *m* **2** ROOM : espacio *m,* sitio *m,* lugar *m* <is there space for me? : ¿hay sitio para mí?> **3** : espacio *m* <blank space : espacio en blanco> **4** : espacio *m* (en física) **5** PLACE : plaza *f,* sitio *m* <to reserve space : reservar plazas> <parking space : sitio para estacionarse>
spacecraft [ˈspeɪs,kræft] *n* : nave *f* espacial
spaceflight [ˈspeɪs,flaɪt] *n* : vuelo *m* espacial
spaceman [ˈspeɪsmən, -,mæn] *n, pl* **-men** [-mən, -,mɛn] : astronauta *m,* cosmonauta *m*
spaceship [ˈspeɪs,ʃɪp] *n* : nave *f* espacial
space shuttle *n* : transbordador *m* espacial
space suit *n* : traje *m* espacial
spacious [ˈspeɪʃəs] *adj* : espacioso, amplio
spade¹ [ˈspeɪd] *v* **spaded; spading** *vt* : palear — *vi* : usar una pala
spade² *n* **1** SHOVEL : pala *f* **2** : pica *f* (naipe)
spaghetti [spəˈgɛti] *n* : espagueti *m,* espaguetis *mpl,* spaghetti *mpl*
span¹ [ˈspæn] *vt* **spanned; spanning** : abarcar (un período de tiempo), extenderse sobre (un espacio)
span² *n* **1** : lapso *m,* espacio *m* (de tiempo) <life span : duración de la vida> **2** : luz *f* (entre dos soportes)
spangle [ˈspæŋgəl] *n* : lentejuela *f*
Spaniard [ˈspænjərd] *n* : español *m,* -ñola *f*
spaniel [ˈspænjəl] *n* : spaniel *m*
Spanish¹ [ˈspænɪʃ] *adj* : español
Spanish² *n* **1** : español *m* (idioma) **2 the Spanish** *npl* : los españoles
spank [ˈspæŋk] *vt* : darle nalgadas (a alguien)
spar¹ [ˈspɑr] *vi* **sparred; sparring** : entrenarse (en boxeo)
spar² *n* : palo *m,* verga *f* (de un barco)
spare¹ [ˈspær] *vt* **spared; sparing 1** : perdonar <to spare someone's life : perdonarle la vida a alguien> **2** SAVE : ahorrar, evitar <I'll spare you the trouble : le evitaré la molestia> **3** : prescindir de <I can't spare her : no puedo prescindir de ella> <can you

spare a dollar? : ¿me das un dólar?> **4** STINT : escatimar <they spared no expense : no repararon en gastos> **5 to spare** : de sobra

spare[2] *adj* **1** : de repuesto, de recambio <spare tire : llanta de repuesto> **2** EXCESS : de más, de sobra <spare time : tiempo libre> **3** LEAN : delgado

spare[3] *n or* **spare part** : repuesto *m,* recambio *m*

sparing [ˈspærɪŋ] *adj* : parco, económico — **sparingly** *adv*

spark[1] [ˈspɑrk] *vi* : chispear, echar chispas — *vt* PROVOKE : despertar, provocar <to spark interest : despertar interés>

spark[2] *n* **1** : chispa *f* <to throw off sparks : echar chispas> **2** GLIMMER, TRACE : destello *m,* pizca *f*

sparkle[1] [ˈspɑrkəl] *vi* **-kled; -kling 1** FLASH, SHINE : destellar, centellear, brillar **2** : estar muy animado (dícese de una conversación, etc.)

sparkle[2] *n* : destello *m,* centelleo *m*

sparkler [ˈspɑrklər] *n* : luz *f* de bengala

spark plug *n* : bujía *f*

sparrow [ˈspæroː] *n* : gorrión *m*

sparse [ˈspɑrs] *adj* **sparser; -est** : escaso — **sparsely** *adv*

spasm [ˈspæzəm] *n* **1** : espasmo *m* (muscular) **2** BURST, FIT : arrebato *m*

spasmodic [spæzˈmɑdɪk] *adj* **1** : espasmódico **2** SPORADIC : irregular, esporádico — **spasmodically** [-dɪkli] *adv*

spastic [ˈspæstɪk] *adj* : espástico

spat[1] → **spit**[1]

spat[2] [ˈspæt] *n* : discusión *f,* disputa *f,* pelea *f*

spatial [ˈspeɪʃəl] *adj* : espacial

spatter[1] [ˈspæt̬ər] *v* : salpicar

spatter[2] *n* : salpicadura *f*

spatula [ˈspætʃələ] *n* : espátula *f,* paleta *f* (para servir)

spawn[1] [ˈspɔn] *vi* : desovar, frezar — *vt* GENERATE : generar, producir

spawn[2] *n* : hueva *f,* freza *f*

spay [ˈspeɪ] *vt* : esterilizar (una perra, etc.)

speak [ˈspiːk] *v* **spoke** [ˈspoːk]; **spoken** [ˈspoːkən]; **speaking** *vi* **1** TALK : hablar <to speak to someone : hablar con alguien> <who's speaking? : ¿de parte de quien?> <so to speak : por así decirlo> **2 to speak out** : hablar claramente **3 to speak out against** : denunciar **4 to speak up** : hablar en voz alta **5 to speak up for** : defender — *vt* **1** SAY : decir <she spoke her mind : habló con franqueza> **2** : hablar (un idioma)

speaker [ˈspiːkər] *n* **1** : hablante *mf* <a native speaker : un hablante nativo> **2** : orador *m,* -dora *f* <the keynote speaker : el orador principal> **3** LOUDSPEAKER : altavoz *m,* altoparlante *m*

spear[1] [ˈspɪr] *vt* : atravesar con una lanza

spear[2] *n* : lanza *f*

spearhead[1] [ˈspɪrˌhɛd] *vt* : encabezar

spearhead[2] *n* : punta *f* de lanza

spearmint [ˈspɪrmɪnt] *n* : menta *f* verde

special [ˈspɛʃəl] *adj* : especial <nothing special : nada en especial, nada en particular> — **specially** *adv*

specialist [ˈspɛʃəlɪst] *n* : especialista *mf*

specialization [ˌspɛʃələˈzeɪʃən] *n* : especialización *f*

specialize [ˈspɛʃəˌlaɪz] *vi* **-ized; -izing** : especializarse

specialty [ˈspɛʃəlt̬i] *n, pl* **-ties** : especialidad *f*

species [ˈspiːˌʃiːz, -ˌsiːz] *ns & pl* : especie *f*

specific [spɪˈsɪfɪk] *adj* : específico, determinado — **specifically** [-fɪkli] *adv*

specification [ˌspɛsəfəˈkeɪʃən] *n* : especificación *f*

specify [ˈspɛsəˌfaɪ] *vt* **-fied; -fying** : especificar

specimen [ˈspɛsəmən] *n* **1** SAMPLE : espécimen *m,* muestra *f* **2** EXAMPLE : espécimen *m,* ejemplar *m*

speck [ˈspɛk] *n* **1** SPOT : manchita *f* **2** BIT, TRACE : mota *f,* pizca *f,* ápice *m*

speckled [ˈspɛkəld] *adj* : moteado

spectacle [ˈspɛktɪkəl] *n* **1** : espectáculo *m* **2 spectacles** *npl* GLASSES : lentes *fpl,* gafas *fpl,* anteojos *mpl,* espejuelos *mpl*

spectacular [spɛkˈtækjələr] *adj* : espectacular

spectator [ˈspɛkˌteɪt̬ər] *n* : espectador *m,* -dora *f*

specter *or* **spectre** [ˈspɛktər] *n* : espectro *m,* fantasma *m*

spectrum [ˈspɛktrəm] *n, pl* **spectra** [-trə] *or* **spectrums 1** : espectro *m* (de colores, etc.) **2** RANGE : gama *f,* abanico *m*

speculate [ˈspɛkjəˌleɪt] *vi* **-lated; -lating 1** : especular (en finanza) **2** WONDER : preguntarse, hacer conjeturas

speculation [ˌspɛkjəˈleɪʃən] *n* : especulación *f*

speculative [ˈspɛkjəˌleɪt̬ɪv] *adj* : especulativo

speculator [ˈspɛkjəˌleɪt̬ər] *n* : especulador *m,* -dora *f*

speech [ˈspiːtʃ] *n* **1** : habla *f,* modo *m* de hablar, expresión *f* **2** ADDRESS : discurso *m*

speechless [ˈspiːtʃləs] *adj* : enmudecido, estupefacto

speed[1] [ˈspiːd] *v* **sped** [ˈspɛd] *or* **speeded; speeding** *vi* **1** : ir a toda velocidad, correr a toda prisa <he sped off : se fue a toda velocidad> **2** : conducir a exceso de velocidad <a ticket for speeding : una multa por exceso de velocidad> — *vt* **to speed up** : acelerar

speed[2] *n* **1** SWIFTNESS : rapidez *f* **2** VELOCITY : velocidad *f*

speedboat ['spi:d,bo:t] *n* : lancha *f* motora
speed bump *n* : badén *m*
speed limit *n* : velocidad *f* máxima, límite *m* de velocidad
speedometer [spɪ'dɑmət̬ər] *n* : velocímetro *m*
speedup ['spi:d,ʌp] *n* : aceleracion *f*
speedy ['spi:di] *adj* **speedier, -est** : rápido — **speedily** [-dəli] *adv*
spell[1] ['spɛl] *vt* **1** : escribir, deletrear (verbalmente) <how do you spell it? : ¿cómo se escribe?, ¿cómo se deletrea?> **2** MEAN : significar <that could spell trouble : eso puede significar problemas> **3** RELIEVE : relevar
spell[2] *n* **1** TURN : turno *m* **2** PERIOD, TIME : período *m* (de tiempo) **3** ENCHANTMENT : encanto *m,* hechizo *m,* maleficio *m*
spellbound ['spɛl,baʊnd] *adj* : embelesado
speller ['spɛlər] *n* : persona *f* que escribe <she's a good speller : tiene buena ortografía>
spelling ['spɛlɪŋ] *n* : ortografía *f*
spend ['spɛnd] *vt* **spent** ['spɛnt]; **spending 1** : gastar (dinero, etc.) **2** PASS : pasar (el tiempo) <to spend time on : dedicar tiempo a>
spendthrift ['spɛnd,θrɪft] *n* : derrochador *m,* -dora *f;* despilfarrador *m,* -dora *f*
sperm ['spərm] *n, pl* **sperm** *or* **sperms** : esperma *mf*
spew ['spju:] *vi* : salir a chorros — *vt* : vomitar, arrojar (lava, etc.)
sphere ['sfɪr] *n* : esfera *f*
spherical ['sfɪrɪkəl, 'sfɛr-] *adj* : esférico
spice[1] ['spaɪs] *vt* **spiced; spicing 1** SEASON : condimentar, sazonar **2** *or* **to spice up** : salpimentar, hacer más interesante
spice[2] *n* **1** : especia *f* **2** FLAVOR, INTEREST : sabor *m* <the spice of life : la sal de la vida>
spick–and–span ['spɪkənd'spæn] *adj* : limpio y ordenado
spicy ['spaɪsi] *adj* **spicier; -est 1** SPICED : condimentado, sazonado **2** HOT : picante **3** RACY : picante
spider ['spaɪdər] *n* : araña *f*
spigot ['spɪgət, -kət] *n* : llave *f,* grifo *m,* canilla *Arg, Uru*
spike[1] ['spaɪk] *vt* **spiked; spiking 1** FASTEN : clavar (con clavos grandes) **2** PIERCE : atravesar **3** : añadir alcohol a <he spiked her drink with rum : le puso ron a la bebida>
spike[2] *n* : clavo *m* grande
spill[1] ['spɪl] *vt* **1** SHED : derramar, verter <to spill blood : derrame sangre> **2** DIVULGE : revelar, divulgar — *vi* : derramarse
spill[2] *n* **1** SPILLING : derrame *m,* vertido *m* <oil spill : derrame de petróleo> **2** FALL : caída *f*
spin[1] ['spɪn] *v* **spun** ['spʌn]; **spinning** *vi* **1** : hilar **2** TURN : girar **3** REEL : dar vueltas <my head is spinning : la cabeza me está dando vueltas> — *vt* **1** : hilar (hilo, etc.) **2** : tejer <to spin a web : tejer una telaraña> **3** TWIRL : hacer girar
spin[2] *n* : vuelta *f,* giro *m* <to go for a spin : dar una vuelta (en coche)>
spinach ['spɪnɪtʃ] *n* : espinacas *fpl,* espinaca *f*
spinal column ['spaɪnəl] *n* BACKBONE : columna *f* vertebral
spinal cord *n* : médula *f* espinal
spindle ['spɪndəl] *n* **1** : huso *m* (para hilar) **2** : eje *m* (de un mecanismo)
spindly ['spɪndli] *adj* : larguirucho *fam,* largo y débil (dícese de una planta)
spine ['spaɪn] *n* **1** BACKBONE : columna *f* vertebral, espina *f* dorsal **2** QUILL : púa *f* (de un animal) **3** THORN : espina *f* **4** : lomo *m* (de un libro)
spineless ['spaɪnləs] *adj* **1** : sin púas, sin espinas **2** INVERTEBRATE : invertebrado **3** WEAK : débil (de carácter)
spinet ['spɪnət] *n* : espineta *f*
spinster ['spɪn*t*stər] *n* : soltera *f*
spiny ['spaɪni] *adj* **spinier; -est** : con púas (dícese de los animales), espinoso (dícese de las plantas)
spiral[1] ['spaɪrəl] *vi* **-raled** *or* **-ralled; -raling** *or* **-ralling** : ir en espiral
spiral[2] *adj* : espiral, en espiral <a spiral staircase : una escalera de caracol>
spiral[3] *n* : espiral *f*
spire ['spaɪr] *n* : aguja *f*
spirit[1] ['spɪrət] *vt* **to spirit away** : hacer desaparecer
spirit[2] *n* **1** : espíritu *m* <body and spirit : cuerpo y espíritu> **2** GHOST : espíritu *m,* fantasma *m* **3** MOOD : espíritu *m,* humor *m* <in the spirit of friendship : en el espíritu de amistad> <to be in good spirits : estar de buen humor> **4** ENTHUSIASM, VIVACITY : espíritu *m,* ánimo *m,* brío *m* **5 spirits** *npl* : licores *mpl*
spirited ['spɪrət̬əd] *adj* : animado, energético
spiritless ['spɪrətləs] *adj* : desanimado
spiritual[1] ['spɪrɪtʃʊəl, -tʃəl] *adj* : espiritual — **spiritually** *adv*
spiritual[2] *n* : espiritual *m* (canción)
spiritualism ['spɪrɪtʃʊə,lɪzəm, -tʃə-] *n* : espiritismo *m*
spirituality [,spɪrɪtʃʊ'ælət̬i] *n, pl* **-ties** : espiritualidad *f*
spit[1] ['spɪt] *v* **spit** *or* **spat** ['spæt]; **spitting** : escupir
spit[2] *n* **1** SALIVA : saliva *f* **2** ROTISSERIE : asador *m* **3** POINT : lengua *f* (de tierra)
spite[1] ['spaɪt] *vt* **spited; spiting** : fastidiar, molestar
spite[2] *n* **1** : despecho *m,* rencor *m* **2 in spite of** : a pesar de (que), pese a (que)

spiteful ['spaɪtfəl] *adj* : malicioso, rencoroso
spitting image *n* **to be the spitting image of** : ser el vivo retrato de
spittle ['spɪtəl] *n* : saliva *f*
splash[1] ['splæʃ] *vt* : salpicar — *vi* **1** : salpicar **2 to splash around** : chapotear
splash[2] *n* **1** SPLASHING : salpicadura *f* **2** SQUIRT : chorrito *m* **3** SPOT : mancha *f*
splatter ['splætər] → **spatter**
splay ['spleɪ] *vt* : extender (hacia afuera) <to splay one's fingers : abrir los dedos> — *vi* : extenderse (hacia afuera)
spleen ['spli:n] *n* **1** : bazo *m* (órgano) **2** ANGER, SPITE : ira *f*, rencor *m*
splendid ['splɛndəd] *adj* : espléndido — **splendidly** *adv*
splendor ['splɛndər] *n* : esplendor *m*
splice[1] ['splaɪs] *vt* **spliced; splicing** : empalmar, unir
splice[2] *n* : empalme *m*, unión *f*
splint ['splɪnt] *n* : tablilla *f*
splinter[1] ['splɪntər] *vt* : astillar — *vi* : astillarse
splinter[2] *n* : astilla *f*
split[1] ['splɪt] *v* **split; splitting** *vt* **1** CLEAVE : partir, hender <to split wood : partir madera> **2** BURST : romper, rajar <to split open : abrir> **3** DIVIDE, SHARE : dividir, repartir — *vi* **1** : partirse (dícese de la madera, etc.) **2** BURST, CRACK : romperse, rajarse **3** *or* **to split up** : dividirse
split[2] *n* **1** CRACK : rajadura *f* **2** TEAR : rotura *f* **3** DIVISION : división *f*, escisión *f*
splurge[1] ['splərdʒ] *v* **splurged; splurging** *vt* : derrochar — *vi* : derrochar dinero
splurge[2] *n* : derroche *m*
spoil[1] ['spɔɪl] *v* **spoiled** *or* **spoilt** ['spɔɪlt]; **spoiling** *vt* **1** PILLAGE : saquear **2** RUIN : estropear, arruinar **3** PAMPER : consentir, mimar — *vi* : estropearse, echarse a perder
spoil[2] *n* PLUNDER : botín *m*
spoke[1] → **speak**
spoke[2] ['spo:k] *n* : rayo *m* (de una rueda)
spoken → **speak**
spokesman ['spo:ksmən] *n, pl* **-men** [-mən, -ˌmɛn] : portavoz *mf;* vocero *m*, -ra *f*
spokeswoman ['spo:ksˌwʊmən] *n, pl* **-women** [-ˌwɪmən] : portavoz *f*, vocera *f*
sponge[1] ['spʌndʒ] *vt* **sponged; sponging** : limpiar con una esponja
sponge[2] *n* : esponja *f*
spongy ['spʌndʒi] *adj* **spongier; -est** : esponjoso
sponsor[1] ['spɑntsər] *vt* : patrocinar, auspiciar, apadrinar (a una persona)
sponsor[2] *n* : patrocinador *m*, -dora *f;* padrino *m*, madrina *f*
sponsorship ['spɑntsərˌʃɪp] *n* : patrocinio *m*, apadrinamiento *m*
spontaneity [ˌspɑntə'ni:əti, -'neɪ-] *n* : espontaneidad *f*
spontaneous [spɑn'teɪniəs] *adj* : espontáneo — **spontaneously** *adv*
spoof ['spu:f] *n* : burla *f*, parodia *f*
spook[1] ['spu:k] *vt* : asustar
spook[2] *n* : fantasma *m*, espíritu *m*, espectro *m*
spooky ['spu:ki] *adj* **spookier; -est** : que da miedo, espeluzante
spool ['spu:l] *n* : carrete *m*
spoon[1] ['spu:n] *vt* : comer, servir, o echar con cuchara
spoon[2] *n* : cuchara *f*
spoonful ['spu:nˌfʊl] *n* : cucharada *f* <by the spoonful : a cucharadas>
spoor ['spʊr, 'spor] *n* : rastro *m*, pista *f*
sporadic [spə'rædɪk] *adj* : esporádico — **sporadically** [-dɪkli] *adv*
spore ['spor] *n* : espora *f*
sport[1] ['sport] *vi* FROLIC : retozar, juguetear — *vt* SHOW OFF : lucir, ostentar
sport[2] *n* **1** : deporte *m* <outdoor sports : deportes al aire libre> **2** JEST : broma *f* **3 to be a good sport** : tener espíritu deportivo
sportsman ['sportsmən] *n, pl* **-men** [-mən, -ˌmɛn] : deportista *m*
sportsmanship ['sportsmənˌʃɪp] *n* : espíritu *m* deportivo, deportividad *f Spain*
sportswoman ['sportsˌwʊmən] *n, pl* **-women** [-ˌwɪmən] : deportista *f*
sporty ['sporti] *adj* **sportier; -est** : deportivo
spot[1] ['spɑt] *v* **spotted; spotting** *vt* **1** STAIN : manchar **2** RECOGNIZE, SEE : ver, reconocer <to spot an error : descubrir un error> — *vi* : mancharse
spot[2] *adj* : hecho al azar <a spot check : un vistazo, un control aleatorio>
spot[3] *n* **1** STAIN : mancha *f* **2** DOT : punto *m* **3** PIMPLE : grano *m* <to break out in spots : salirle granos a alguien> **4** PREDICAMENT : apuro *m*, aprieto *m*, lío *m* <in a tight spot : en apuros> **5** PLACE : lugar *m*, sitio *m* <to be on the spot : estar en el lugar>
spotless ['spɑtləs] *adj* : impecable, inmaculado — **spotlessly** *adv*
spotlight[1] ['spɑtˌlaɪt] *vt* **-lighted** *or* **-lit** [-ˌlɪt]; **-lighting 1** LIGHT : iluminar (con un reflector) **2** HIGHLIGHT : destacar, poner en relieve
spotlight[2] *n* **1** : reflector *m*, foco *m* **2 to be in the spotlight** : ser el centro de atención
spotty ['spɑti] *adj* **spottier; -est** : irregular, desigual
spouse ['spaʊs] *n* : cónyuge *mf*
spout[1] ['spaʊt] *vt* **1** : lanzar chorros de **2** DECLAIM : declamar — *vi* : salir a chorros
spout[2] *n* **1** : pico *m* (de una jarra, etc.) **2** STREAM : chorro *m*
sprain[1] ['spreɪn] *vt* : sufrir un esguince en

sprain[2] *n* : esguince *m,* torcedura *f*
sprawl[1] ['sprɔl] *vi* **1** LIE : tumbarse, echarse, despatarrarse **2** EXTEND : extenderse
sprawl[2] *n* **1** : postura *f* despatarrada **2** SPREAD : extensión *f,* expansión *f*
spray[1] ['spreɪ] *vt* : rociar (una superficie), pulverizar (un líquido)
spray[2] *n* **1** BOUQUET : ramillete *m* **2** MIST : rocío *m* **3** ATOMIZER : atomizador *m,* pulverizador *m*
spray gun *n* : pistola *f*
spread[1] ['sprɛd] *v* **spread; spreading** *vt* **1** *or* **to spread out** : desplegar, extender **2** SCATTER, STREW : esparcir **3** SMEAR : untar (mantequilla, etc.) **4** DISSEMINATE : difundir, sembrar, propagar — *vi* **1** : difundirse, correr, propagarse **2** EXTEND : extenderse
spread[2] *n* **1** EXTENSION : extensión *f,* difusión *f* (de noticias, etc.), propagación *f* (de enfermedades, etc.) **2** : colcha *f* (para una cama), mantel *m* (para una mesa) **3** PASTE : pasta *f* <cheese spread : pasta de queso>
spreadsheet ['sprɛd,ʃiːt] *n* : hoja *f* de cálculo
spree ['spri] *n* **1** : acción *f* desenfrenada <to go on a shopping spree : comprar como loco> **2** BINGE : parranda *f,* juerga *f* <on a spree : de parranda, de juerga>
sprig ['sprɪg] *n* : ramita *f,* ramito *m*
sprightly ['spraɪtli] *adj* **sprightlier; -est** : vivo, animado <with a sprightly step : con paso ligero>
spring[1] ['sprɪŋ] *v* **sprang** ['spræŋ] *or* **sprung** ['sprʌŋ]; **sprung; springing** *vi* **1** LEAP : saltar **2** : mover rápidamente <the lid sprang shut : la tapa se cerró de un golpe> <he sprang to his feet : se paró de un salto> **3 to spring up** : brotar (dícese de las plantas), surgir **4 to spring from** : surgir de — *vt* **1** RELEASE : soltar (de repente) <to spring the news on someone : sorprender a alguien con las noticias> <to spring a trap : hacer saltar una trampa> **2** ACTIVATE : accionar (un mecanismo) **3 to spring a leak** : hacer agua
spring[2] *n* **1** SOURCE : fuente *f,* origen *m* **2** : manantial *m,* fuente *f* <hot spring : fuente termal> **3** : primavera *f* <spring and summer : la primavera y el verano> **4** : resorte *m,* muelle *m* (de metal, etc.) **5** LEAP : salto *m,* brinco *m* **6** RESILIENCE : elasticidad *f*
springboard ['sprɪŋ,bord] *n* : trampolín *m*
springtime ['sprɪŋ,taɪm] *n* : primavera *f*
springy ['sprɪŋi] *adj* **springier; -est 1** RESILIENT : elástico **2** LIVELY : enérgico
sprinkle[1] ['sprɪŋkəl] *vt* **-kled; -kling** : rociar (con agua), espolvorear (con azúcar, etc.), salpicar
sprinkle[2] *n* : llovizna *f*
sprinkler ['sprɪŋkələr] *n* : rociador *m,* aspersor *m*
sprint[1] ['sprɪnt] *vi* : echar la carrera, esprintar (en deportes)
sprint[2] *n* : esprint *m* (en deportes)
sprite ['spraɪt] *n* : hada *f,* elfo *m*
sprocket ['sprɑkət] *n* : diente *m* (de una rueda dentada)
sprout[1] ['spraʊt] *vi* : brotar
sprout[2] *n* : brote *m,* retoño *m,* vástago *m*
spruce[1] ['spruːs] *v* **spruced; sprucing** *vt* : arreglar — *vi or* **to spruce up** : arreglarse, acicalarse
spruce[2] *adj* **sprucer; sprucest** : pulcro, arreglado
spruce[3] *n* : picea *f* (árbol)
spry ['spraɪ] *adj* **sprier** *or* **spryer** ['spraɪər]; **spriest** *or* **spryest** ['spraɪəst] : ágil, activo
spun → **spin**
spunk ['spʌŋk] *n* : valor *m,* coraje *m,* agallas *fpl fam*
spunky ['spʌŋki] *adj* **spunkier; -est** : animoso, corajudo
spur[1] ['spər] *vt* **spurred; spurring** *or* **to spur on** : espolear (un caballo), motivar (a una persona, etc.)
spur[2] *n* **1** : espuela *f,* acicate *m* **2** STIMULUS : acicate *m* **3** : espolón *m* (de aves gallináceas)
spurious ['spjʊriəs] *adj* : espurio
spurn ['spərn] *vt* : desdeñar, rechazar
spurt[1] ['spərt] *vt* SQUIRT : lanzar un chorro de — *vi* SPOUT : salir a chorros
spurt[2] *n* **1** : actividad *f* repentina <a spurt of energy : una explosión de energía> <to do in spurts : hacer por rachas> **2** JET : chorro *m* (de agua, etc.)
sputter[1] ['spʌt̬ər] *vi* **1** JABBER : farfullar **2** : chisporrotear (dícese de la grasa, etc.), petardear (dícese de un motor)
sputter[2] *n* **1** JABBER : farfulla *f* **2** : chisporroteo *m* (de grasa, etc.), petardeo *m* (de un motor)
spy[1] ['spaɪ] *v* **spied; spying** *vt* SEE : ver, divisar — *vi* : espiar <to spy on someone : espiar a alguien>
spy[2] *n* : espía *mf*
squab ['skwɑb] *n, pl* **squabs** *or* **squab** : pichón *m*
squabble[1] ['skwɑbəl] *vi* **-bled; -bling** : reñir, pelearse, discutir
squabble[2] *n* : riña *f,* pelea *f,* discusión *f*
squad ['skwɑd] *n* : pelotón *m* (militar), brigada *f* (de policías), cuadrilla *f* (de obreros, etc.)
squadron ['skwɑdrən] *n* : escuadrón *m* (de militares), escuadrilla *f* (de aviones), escuadra *f* (de naves)
squalid ['skwɑlɪd] *adj* : miserable
squall ['skwɔl] *n* **1** : aguacero *m* tormentoso, chubasco *m* tormentoso **2** **snow squall** : tormenta *f* de nieve
squalor ['skwɑlər] *n* : miseria *f*
squander ['skwɑndər] *vt* : derrochar (dinero, etc.), desaprovechar (una

oportunidad, etc.), desperdiciar (talentos, energías, etc.)

square[1] ['skwær] *vt* **squared; squaring 1 :** cuadrar **2 :** elevar al cuadrado (en matemáticas) **3** CONFORM **:** conciliar (con), ajustar (con) **4** SETTLE **:** saldar (una cuenta) <I squared it with him : lo arreglé con él>

square[2] *adj* **squarer; -est 1 :** cuadrado <a square house : una casa cuadrada> **2** RIGHT-ANGLED **:** a escuadra, en ángulo recto **3 :** cuadrado (en matemáticas) <a square mile : una milla cuadrada> **4** HONEST **:** justo <a square deal : un buen acuerdo> <fair and square : en buena lid>

square[3] *n* **1 :** escuadra *f* (instrumento) **2 :** cuadrado *m,* cuadro *m* <to fold into squares : plegar en cuadrados> **3 :** plaza *f* (de una ciudad) **4 :** cuadrado *m* (en matemáticas)

squarely ['skwærli] *adv* **1** EXACTLY **:** exactamente, directamente, justo **2** HONESTLY **:** honradamente, justamente

square root *n* **:** raíz *f* cuadrada

squash[1] ['skwɑʃ, 'skwɔʃ] *vt* **1** CRUSH **:** aplastar **2** SUPPRESS **:** acallar (protestas), sofocar (una rebelión)

squash[2] *n* **1** *pl* **squashes** *or* **squash :** calabaza *f* (vegetal) **2** *or* **squash racquets :** squash *m* (deporte)

squat[1] ['skwɑt] *vi* **squatted; squatting 1** CROUCH **:** agacharse, ponerse en cuclillas **2 :** ocupar un lugar sin derecho

squat[2] *adj* **squatter; squattest :** bajo y ancho, rechoncho *fam* (dícese de una persona)

squat[3] *n* **1 :** posición *f* en cuclillas **2 :** ocupación *f* ilegal (de un lugar)

squaw ['skwɔ] *n* **:** india *f* (norteamericana)

squawk[1] ['skwɔk] *vi* **:** graznar (dícese de las aves), chillar

squawk[2] *n* **:** graznido *m* (de un ave), chillido *m*

squeak[1] ['skwiːk] *vi* **:** chillar (dícese de un animal), chirriar (dícese de un objeto)

squeak[2] *n* **:** chillido *m,* chirrido *m*

squeaky ['skwiːki] *adj* **squeakier; -est :** chirriante <a squeaky voice : una voz chillona>

squeal[1] ['skwiːl] *vi* **1 :** chillar (dícese de las personas o los animales), chirriar (dícese de los frenos, etc.) **2** PROTEST **:** quejarse

squeal[2] *n* **1 :** chillido *m* (de una persona o un animal) **2** SCREECH **:** chirrido *m* (de frenos, etc.)

squeamish ['skwiːmɪʃ] *adj* **:** impresionable, sensible <he's squeamish about cockroaches : las cucarachas le dan asco>

squeeze[1] ['skwiːz] *vt* **squeezed; squeezing 1** PRESS **:** apretar, exprimir (naranjas, etc.) **2** EXTRACT **:** extraer (jugo, etc.)

squeeze[2] *n* **:** apretón *m*

squelch ['skwɛltʃ] *vt* **:** aplastar (una rebelión, etc.)

squid ['skwɪd] *n, pl* **squid** *or* **squids :** calamar *m*

squint[1] ['skwɪnt] *vi* **:** mirar con los ojos entornados

squint[2] *adj or* **squint-eyed** ['skwɪnt,aɪd] **:** bizco

squint[3] *n* **:** ojos *mpl* bizcos, bizquera *f*

squire ['skwaɪr] *n* **:** hacendado *m,* -da *f;* terrateniente *mf*

squirm ['skwərm] *vi* **:** retorcerse

squirrel ['skwərəl] *n* **:** ardilla *f*

squirt[1] ['skwərt] *vt* **:** lanzar un chorro de — *vi* SPURT **:** salir a chorros

squirt[2] *n* **:** chorrito *m*

stab[1] [stæb] *vt* **stabbed; stabbing 1** KNIFE **:** acuchillar, apuñalar **2** STICK **:** clavar (con una aguja, etc.), golpear (con el dedo, etc.)

stab[2] *n* **1 :** puñalada *f,* cuchillada *f* **2** JAB **:** pinchazo *m* (con una aguja, etc.), golpe *m* (con un dedo, etc.) **3 to take a stab at :** intentar

stability [stə'bɪləti] *n, pl* **-ties :** estabilidad *f*

stabilize ['steɪbə,laɪz] *v* **-lized; -lizing** *vt* **:** estabilizar — *vi* **:** estabilizarse

stable[1] ['steɪbəl] *vt* **-bled; -bling :** poner (ganado) en un establo, poner (caballos) en una caballeriza

stable[2] *adj* **-bler; -blest 1** FIXED, STEADY **:** fijo, sólido, estable **2** LASTING **:** estable, perdurable <a stable government : un gobierno estable> **3 :** estacionario (en medicina), equilibrado (en psicología)

stable[3] *n* **:** establo *m* (para ganado), caballeriza *f* o cuadra *f* (para caballos)

staccato [stə'kɑtoː] *adj* **:** staccato

stack[1] ['stæk] *vt* **1** PILE **:** amontonar, apilar **2** COVER **:** cubrir, llenar <he stacked the table with books : cubrió la mesa de libros>

stack[2] *n* **1** PILE **:** montón *m,* pila *f* **2** SMOKESTACK **:** chimenea *f*

stadium ['steɪdiəm] *n, pl* **-dia** [-diə] *or* **-diums :** estadio *m*

staff[1] ['stæf] *vt* **:** proveer de personal

staff[2] *n, pl* **staffs** ['stæfs, stævz] *or* **staves** ['stævz, 'steɪvz] **1 :** bastón *m* (de mando), báculo *m* (de obispo) **2** *pl* **staffs** PERSONNEL **:** personal *m* **3** *pl* **staffs :** pentagrama *m* (en música)

stag[1] ['stæg] *adv* **:** solo, sin pareja <to go stag : ir solo>

stag[2] *adj* **:** sólo para hombres

stag[3] *n, pl* **stags** *or* **stag :** ciervo *m,* venado *m*

stage[1] ['steɪdʒ] *vt* **staged; staging :** poner en escena (una obra de teatro)

stage[2] *n* **1** PLATFORM **:** estrado *m,* tablado *m,* escenario *m* (de un teatro) **2** PHASE, STEP **:** fase *f,* etapa *f* <stage of development : fase de desarrollo> <in stages : por etapas> **3 the stage :** el teatro *m*

stagecoach ['steɪdʒ,koːtʃ] *n* **:** diligencia *f*

stagger[1] [ˈstægər] *vi* TOTTER : tambalearse — *vt* **1** ALTERNATE : alternar, escalonar (turnos de trabajo) **2** : hacer tambalear <to be staggered by : quedarse estupefacto por>

stagger[2] *n* : tambaleo *m*

staggering [ˈstægərɪŋli] *adj* : asombroso

stagnant [ˈstægnənt] *adj* : estancado

stagnate [ˈstæg,neɪt] *vi* **-nated; -nating** : estancarse

staid [ˈsteɪd] *adj* : serio, sobrio

stain[1] [ˈsteɪn] *vt* **1** DISCOLOR : manchar **2** DYE : teñir (madera, etc.) **3** SULLY : manchar, empañar

stain[2] *n* **1** SPOT : mancha *f* **2** DYE : tinte *m*, tintura *f* **3** BLEMISH : mancha *f*, mácula *f*

stainless [ˈsteɪnləs] *adj* : sin mancha <stainless steel : acero inoxidable>

stair [ˈstær] *n* **1** STEP : escalón *m*, peldaño *m* **2 stairs** *npl* : escalera *f*, escaleras *fpl*

staircase [ˈstær,keɪs] *n* : escalera *f*, escaleras *fpl*

stairway [ˈstær,weɪ] *n* : escalera *f*, escaleras *fpl*

stake[1] [ˈsteɪk] *vt* **staked; staking 1** : estacar, marcar con estacas (una propiedad) **2** BET : jugarse, apostar **3 to stake a claim to** : reclamar, reivindicar

stake[2] *n* **1** POST : estaca *f* **2** BET : apuesta *f* <to be at stake : estar en juego> **3** INTEREST, SHARE : interés *m*, participación *f*

stalactite [stəˈlæk,taɪt] *n* : estalactita *f*

stalagmite [stəˈlæg,maɪt] *n* : estalagmita *f*

stale [ˈsteɪl] *adj* **staler; stalest** : viejo <stale bread : pan duro> <stale news : viejas noticias>

stalemate [ˈsteɪl,meɪt] *n* : punto *m* muerto, impasse *m*

stalk[1] [ˈstɔk] *vt* : acechar — *vi* : caminar rígidamente (por orgullo, ira, etc.)

stalk[2] *n* : tallo *m* (de una planta)

stall[1] [ˈstɔl] *vt* **1** : parar (un motor) **2** DELAY : entretener (a una persona), demorar — *vi* **1** : pararse (dícese de un motor) **2** DELAY : demorar, andar con rodeos

stall[2] *n* **1** : compartimiento *m* (de un establo) **2** : puesto *m* (en un mercado, etc.)

stallion [ˈstæljən] *n* : caballo *m* semental

stalwart [ˈstɔlwərt] *adj* **1** STRONG : fuerte <a stalwart supporter : un firme partidario> **2** BRAVE : valiente, valeroso

stamen [ˈsteɪmən] *n* : estambre *m*

stamina [ˈstæmənə] *n* : resistencia *f*

stammer[1] [ˈstæmər] *vi* : tartamudear, titubear

stammer[2] *n* : tartamudeo *m*, titubeo *m*

stamp[1] [ˈstæmp] *vt* **1** : pisotear (con los pies) <to stamp one's feet : patear, dar una patada> **2** IMPRESS, IMPRINT : sellar (una factura, etc.), acuñar (monedas) **3** : franquear, ponerle estampillas a (correo)

stamp[2] *n* **1** : sello *m* (para documentos, etc.) **2** DIE : cuño *m* (para monedas) **3** *or* **postage stamp** : sello *m*, estampilla *f*, timbre *m CA, Mex*

stampede[1] [stæmˈpi:d] *vi* **-peded; -peding** : salir en estampida

stampede[2] *n* : estampida *f*

stance [ˈstænts] *n* : postura *f*

stanch [ˈstɔntʃ, ˈstɑntʃ] *vt* : detener, estancar (un líquido)

stand[1] [ˈstænd] *v* **stood** [ˈstʊd]; **standing** *vi* **1** : estar de pie, estar parado <I was standing on the corner : estaba parada en la esquina> **2** *or* **to stand up** : levantarse, pararse, ponerse de pie **3** *(indicating a specified position or location)* <they stand third in the country : ocupan el tercer lugar en el país> <the machines are standing idle : las máquinas están paradas> **4** *(referring to an opinion)* <how does he stand on the matter ? : ¿cuál es su postura respecto al asunto?> **5** BE : estar <the house stands on a hill : la casa está en una colina> **6** CONTINUE : seguir <the order still stands : el mandato sigue vigente> — *vt* **1** PLACE, SET : poner, colocar <he stood them in a row : los colocó en hilera> **2** TOLERATE : aguantar, soportar <he can't stand her : no la puede tragar> **3 to stand firm** : mantenerse firme **4 to stand guard** : hacer la guardia

stand[2] *n* **1** RESISTANCE : resistencia *f* <to make a stand against : resistir a> **2** BOOTH, STALL : stand *m*, puesto *m*, kiosko *m* (para vender periódicos, etc.) **3** BASE : pie *m*, base *f* **4** : grupo *m* (de árboles, etc.) **5** POSITION : posición *f*, postura *f* **6 stands** *npl* GRANDSTAND : tribuna *f*

standard[1] [ˈstændərd] *adj* **1** ESTABLISHED : estándar, oficial <standard measures : medidas oficiales> <standard English : el inglés estándar> **2** NORMAL : normal, estándar, común **3** CLASSIC : estándar, clásico <a standard work : una obra clásica>

standard[2] *n* **1** BANNER : estandarte *m* **2** CRITERION : criterio *m* **3** RULE : estándar *m*, norma *f*, regla *f* **4** LEVEL : nivel *m* <standard of living : nivel de vida> **5** SUPPORT : poste *m*, soporte *m*

standardize [ˈstændər,daɪz] *vt* **-ized; -izing** : estandarizar

standard time *n* : hora *f* oficial

stand by *vt* : atenerse a, cumplir con (una promesa, etc.) — *vi* **1** : mantenerse aparte <to stand by and do nothing : mirar sin hacer nada> **2** : estar preparado, estar listo (para un anuncio, un ataque, etc.)

stand for *vt* **1** REPRESENT : significar **2** PERMIT, TOLERATE : permitir, tolerar

standing [ˈstændɪŋ] *n* **1** POSITION, RANK : posición *f* **2** DURATION : duración *f*

stand out *vi* **1 :** destacar(se) <she stands out from the rest : se destaca entre los otros> **2 to stand out against** RESIST **:** oponerse a
standpoint [ˈstænd,pɔint] *n* **:** punto *m* de vista
standstill [ˈstænd,stɪl] *n* **1** STOP **:** detención *f,* paro *m* <to come to a standstill : pararse> **2** DEADLOCK **:** punto *m* muerto, impasse *m*
stand up *vt* **:** dejar plantado <he stood me up again : otra vez me dejó plantado> — *vi* **1** ENDURE **:** durar, resistir **2 to stand up for :** defender **3 to stand up to :** hacerle frente (a alguien)
stank → **stink**
stanza [ˈstænzə] *n* **:** estrofa *f*
staple[1] [ˈsteɪpəl] *vt* **-pled; -pling :** engrapar, grapar
staple[2] *adj* **:** principal, básico <a staple food : un alimento básico>
staple[3] *n* **1 :** producto *m* principal **2 :** grapa *f* (para engrapar papeles)
stapler [ˈsteɪplər] *n* **:** engrapadora *f,* grapadora *f*
star[1] [ˈstɑr] *v* **starred; starring** *vt* **1 :** marcar con una estrella o un asterisco **2** FEATURE **:** ser protagonizado por — *vi* **:** tener el papel principal <to star in : protagonizar>
star[2] *n* **:** estrella *f*
starboard [ˈstɑrbərd] *n* **:** estribor *m*
starch[1] [ˈstɑrtʃ] *vt* **:** almidonar
starch[2] *n* **:** almidón *m,* fécula *f* (comida)
starchy [ˈstɑrtʃi] *adj* **starchier; -est :** lleno de almidón <a starchy diet : una dieta feculenta>
stardom [ˈstɑrdəm] *n* **:** estrellato *m*
stare[1] [ˈstær] *vi* **stared; staring :** mirar fijamente
stare[2] *n* **:** mirada *f* fija
starfish [ˈstɑr,fɪʃ] *n* **:** estrella *f* de mar
stark[1] [ˈstɑrk] *adv* **:** completamente <stark raving mad : loco de remate> <stark naked : completamente desnudo>
stark[2] *adj* **1** ABSOLUTE **:** absoluto **2** BARREN, DESOLATE **:** desolado, desierto **3** BARE **:** desnudo **4** HARSH **:** severo, duro
starlight [ˈstɑr,laɪt] *n* **:** luz *f* de las estrellas
starling [ˈstɑrlɪŋ] *n* **:** estornino *m*
starry [ˈstɑri] *adj* **starrier; -est :** estrellado
start[1] [ˈstɑrt] *vi* **1** JUMP **:** levantarse de un salto, sobresaltarse, dar un respingo **2** BEGIN **:** empezar, comenzar **3** SET OUT **:** salir (de viaje, etc.) **4 :** arrancar (dícese de un motor) — *vt* **1** BEGIN **:** empezar, comenzar, iniciar **2** CAUSE **:** provocar, causar **3** ESTABLISH **:** fundar, montar, establecer <to start a business : montar un negocio> **4 :** arrancar, poner en marcha, encender <to start the car : arrancar el motor>
start[2] *n* **1** JUMP **:** sobresalto *m,* respingo *m* **2** BEGINNING **:** principio *m,* comienzo *m* <to get an early start : salir temprano>
starter [ˈstɑrt̬ər] *n* **1** ENTRANT **:** participante *mf* (en deportes) **2** APPETIZER **:** entremés *m,* aperitivo *m* **3 :** motor *m* de arranque (de un vehículo)
startle [ˈstɑrt̬əl] *vt* **-tled; -tling :** asustar, sobresaltar
starvation [stɑrˈveɪʃən] *n* **:** inanición *f,* hambre *f*
starve [ˈstɑrv] *v* **starved; starving** *vi* **:** morirse de hambre — *vt* **:** privar de comida
stash [ˈstæʃ] *vt* **:** esconder, guardar (en un lugar secreto)
state[1] [ˈsteɪt] *vt* **stated; stating 1** REPORT **:** puntualizar, exponer (los hechos, etc.) <state your name : diga su nombre> **2** ESTABLISH, FIX **:** establecer, fijar
state[2] *n* **1** CONDITION **:** estado *m,* condición *f* <a liquid state : un estado líquido> <state of mind : estado de ánimo> <in a bad state : en malas condiciones> **2** NATION **:** estado *m,* nación *f* **3 :** estado *m* (dentro de un país) <the States : los Estados Unidos>
stateliness [ˈsteɪtlinəs] *n* **:** majestuosidad *f*
stately [ˈsteɪtli] *adj* **statelier; -est :** majestuoso
statement [ˈsteɪtmənt] *n* **1** DECLARATION **:** declaración *f,* afirmación *f* **2** *or* **bank statement :** estado *m* de cuenta
stateroom [ˈsteɪt,ruːm, -,rʊm] *n* **:** camarote *m*
statesman [ˈsteɪtsmən] *n, pl* **-men** [-mən, -,mɛn] **:** estadista *mf*
static[1] [ˈstæt̬ɪk] *adj* **:** estático
static[2] *n* **:** estática *f,* interferencia *f*
station[1] [ˈsteɪʃən] *vt* **:** apostar, estacionar
station[2] *n* **1 :** estación *f* (de trenes, etc.) **2** RANK, STANDING **:** condición *f* (social) **3 :** canal *m* (de televisión), estación *f* o emisora *f* (de radio) **4 police station :** comisaría *f* **5 fire station :** estación *f* de bomberos, cuartel *m* de bomberos
stationary [ˈsteɪʃə,nɛri] *adj* **1** IMMOBILE **:** estacionario, inmovible **2** UNCHANGING **:** inmutable, inalterable
stationery [ˈsteɪʃə,nɛri] *n* **:** papel *m* y sobres *mpl* (para correspondencia)
station wagon *n* **:** camioneta *f* guayín, camioneta *f* ranchera
statistic [stəˈtɪstɪk] *n* **:** estadística *f* <according to statistics : según las estadísticas>
statistical [stəˈtɪstɪkəl] *adj* **:** estadístico
statue [ˈstæ,tʃuː] *n* **:** estatua *f*
statuesque [,stætʃʊˈɛsk] *adj* **:** escultural
statuette [,stætʃʊˈɛt] *n* **:** estatuilla *f*
stature [ˈstætʃər] *n* **1** HEIGHT **:** estatura *f,* talla *f* **2** PRESTIGE **:** talla *f,* prestigio *m*

status [ˈsteɪtəs, ˈstæ-] *n* : condición *f,* situación *f,* estatus *m* (social) <marital status : estado civil>

statute [ˈstæˌtʃuːt] *n* : ley *f,* estatuto *m*

staunch [ˈstɔntʃ] *adj* : acérrimo, incondicional, leal <a staunch supporter : un partidario incondicional> — **staunchly** *adv*

stave[1] [ˈsteɪv] *vt* **staved** *or* **stove** [ˈstoːv]; **staving 1 to stave in** : romper **2 to stave off** : evitar (un ataque), prevenir (un problema)

stave[2] *n* : duela *f* (de un barril)

staves → **staff**

stay[1] [ˈsteɪ] *vi* **1** REMAIN : quedarse, permanecer <to stay in : quedarse en casa> <he stayed in the city : permaneció en la ciudad> **2** CONTINUE : seguir, quedarse <it stayed cloudy : siguió nublado> <to stay awake : mantenerse despierto> **3** LODGE : hospedarse, alojarse (en un hotel, etc.) — *vt* **1** HALT : detener, suspender (una ejecución, etc.) **2 to stay the course** : aguantar hasta el final

stay[2] *n* **1** SOJOURN : estadía *f,* estancia *f,* permanencia *f* **2** SUSPENSION : suspensión *f* (de una sentencia) **3** SUPPORT : soporte *m*

stead [ˈstɛd] *n* **1** : lugar *m* <she went in his stead : fue en su lugar> **2 to stand (someone) in good stead** : ser muy útil a, servir de mucho a

steadfast [ˈstɛdˌfæst] *adj* : firme, resuelto <a steadfast friend : un fiel amigo> <a steadfast refusal : una negativa categórica>

steadily [ˈstɛdəli] *adv* **1** CONSTANTLY : continuamente, sin parar **2** FIRMLY : con firmeza **3** FIXEDLY : fijamente

steady[1] [ˈstɛdi] *v* **steadied; steadying** *vt* : sujetar <she steadied herself : recobró el equilibrio> — *vi* : estabilizarse

steady[2] *adj* **steadier; -est 1** FIRM, SURE : seguro, firme <to have a steady hand : tener buen pulso> **2** FIXED, REGULAR : fijo <a steady income : ingresos fijos> **3** CALM : tranquilo, ecuánime <she has steady nerves : es imperturbable> **4** DEPENDABLE : responsable, fiable **5** CONSTANT : constante

steak [ˈsteɪk] *n* : bistec *m,* filete *m,* churrasco *m,* bife *m Arg, Chile, Uru*

steal [ˈstiːl] *v* **stole** [ˈstoːl]; **stolen** [ˈstoːlən]; **stealing** *vt* : robar, hurtar — *vi* **1** : robar, hurtar **2** : ir sigilosamente <to steal away : escabullirse>

stealth [ˈstɛlθ] *n* : sigilo *m*

stealthily [ˈstɛlθəli] *adv* : furtivamente

stealthy [ˈstɛlθi] *adj* **stealthier; -est** : furtivo, sigiloso

steam[1] [ˈstiːm] *vi* : echar vapor <to steam away : moverse echando vapor> — *vt* **1** : cocer al vapor (en cocina) **2 to steam open** : abrir con vapor

steam[2] *n* **1** : vapor *m* **2 to let off steam** : desahogarse

steamboat [ˈstiːmˌboːt] → **steamship**

steam engine *n* : motor *m* de vapor

steamroller [ˈstiːmˌroːlər] *n* : apisonadora *f*

steamship [ˈstiːmˌʃɪp] *n* : vapor *m,* barco *m* de vapor

steamy [ˈstiːmi] *adj* **steamier; -est 1** : lleno de vapor **2** EROTIC : erótico <a steamy romance : un tórrido romance>

steed [ˈstiːd] *n* : corcel *m*

steel[1] [ˈstiːl] *vt* **to steel oneself** : armarse de valor

steel[2] *adj* : de acero

steel[3] *n* : acero *m*

steely [ˈstiːli] *adj* **steelier; -est** : como acero <a steely gaze : una mirada fría> <steely determination : determinación férrea>

steep[1] [ˈstiːp] *vt* : remojar, dejar (té, etc.) en infusión

steep[2] *adj* **1** : empinado, escarpado <a steep cliff : un precipicio escarpado> **2** CONSIDERABLE : considerable, marcado **3** EXCESSIVE : excesivo <steep prices : precios muy altos>

steeple [ˈstiːpəl] *n* : aguja *f,* campanario *m*

steeplechase [ˈstiːpəlˌtʃeɪs] *n* : carrera *f* de obstáculos

steeply [ˈstiːpli] *adv* : abruptamente

steer[1] [ˈstɪr] *vt* **1** : conducir (un coche), gobernar (un barco) **2** GUIDE : dirigir, guiar

steer[2] *n* : buey *m*

steering wheel *n* : volante *m*

stein [ˈstaɪn] *n* : jarra *f* (para cerveza)

stellar [ˈstɛlər] *adj* : estelar

stem[1] [ˈstɛm] *v* **stemmed; stemming** *vt* : detener, contener, parar <to stem the tide : detener el curso> — *vi* **to stem from** : provenir de, ser el resultado de

stem[2] *n* : tallo *m* (de una planta)

stench [ˈstɛntʃ] *n* : hedor *m,* mal olor *m*

stencil[1] [ˈstɛntsəl] *vt* **-ciled** *or* **-cilled; -ciling** *or* **-cilling** : marcar utilizando una plantilla

stencil[2] *n* : plantilla *f* (para marcar)

stenographer [stəˈnɑgrəfər] *n* : taquígrafo *m,* -fa *f*

stenographic [ˌstɛnəˈgræfɪk] *adj* : taquigráfico

stenography [stəˈnɑgrəfi] *n* : taquigrafía *f*

step[1] [ˈstɛp] *vi* **stepped; stepping 1** : dar un paso <step this way, please : pase por aquí, por favor> <he stepped outside : salió> **2 to step on** : pisar

step[2] *n* **1** : paso *m* <step by step : paso por paso> **2** STAIR : escalón *m,* peldaño *m* **3** RUNG : escalón *m,* travesaño *m* **4** MEASURE, MOVE : medida *f,* paso *m* <to take steps : tomar medidas> **5** STRIDE : paso *m* <with a quick step : con paso rápido>

stepbrother ['stɛp,brʌðər] *n* **:** hermanastro *m*
stepdaughter ['stɛp,dɔt̬ər] *n* **:** hijastra *f*
stepfather ['stɛp,fɑðər, -,fa-] *n* **:** padrastro *m*
stepladder ['stɛp,lædər] *n* **:** escalera *f* de tijera
stepmother ['stɛp,mʌðər] *n* **:** madrastra *f*
steppe ['stɛp] *n* **:** estepa *f*
stepping–stone ['stɛpɪŋ,sto:n] *n* **:** pasadera *f* (en un río, etc.), trampolín *m* (al éxito)
stepsister ['stɛp,sɪstər] *n* **:** hermanastra *f*
stepson ['stɛp,sʌn] *n* **:** hijastro *m*
step up *vt* INCREASE **:** aumentar
stereo[1] ['stɛri,o:, 'stɪr-] *adj* **:** estéreo
stereo[2] *n, pl* **stereos :** estéreo *m*
stereophonic [,stɛrio'fɑnɪk, ,stɪr-] *adj* **:** estereofónico
stereotype[1] ['stɛrio,taɪp, 'stɪr-] *vt* **-typed; -typing :** estereotipar
stereotype[2] *n* **:** estereotipo *m*
sterile ['stɛrəl] *adj* **:** estéril
sterility [stə'rɪlət̬i] *n* **:** esterilidad *f*
sterilization [,stɛrələ'zeɪʃən] *n* **:** esterilización *f*
sterilize ['stɛrə,laɪz] *vt* **-ized; -izing :** esterilizar
sterling ['stərlɪŋ] *adj* **1 :** de ley <sterling silver **:** plata de ley> **2** EXCELLENT **:** excelente
stern[1] ['stərn] *adj* **:** severo, adusto — **sternly** *adv*
stern[2] *n* **:** popa *f*
sternness ['stərnnəs] *n* **:** severidad *f*
sternum ['stərnəm] *n, pl* **sternums** *or* **sterna** [-nə] **:** esternón *m*
stethoscope ['stɛθə,sko:p] *n* **:** estetoscopio *m*
stevedore ['sti:və,dor] *n* **:** estibador *m*, -dora *f*
stew[1] ['stu:, 'stju:] *vt* **:** estofar, guisar — *vi* **1 :** cocer (dícese de la carne, etc.) **2** FRET **:** preocuparse
stew[2] *n* **1 :** estofado *m*, guiso *m* **2 to be in a stew :** estar agitado
steward ['stu:ərd, 'stju:-] *n* **1** MANAGER **:** administrador *m* **2 :** auxiliar *m* de vuelo (en un avión), camarero *m* (en un barco)
stewardess ['stu:ərdəs, 'stju:-] *n* **1** MANAGER **:** administradora *f* **2 :** camarera *f* (en un barco) **3 :** auxiliar *f* de vuelo, azafata *f*, aeromoza *f* (en un avión)
stick[1] ['stɪk] *v* **stuck** ['stʌk]; **sticking** *vt* **1** STAB **:** clavar **2** ATTACH **:** pegar **3** PUT **:** poner **4 to stick out :** sacar (la lengua, etc.), extender (la mano) — *vi* **1** ADHERE **:** pegarse, adherirse **2** JAM **:** atascarse **3 to stick around :** quedarse **4 to stick out** PROJECT **:** sobresalir (de una superficie), asomar (por detrás o debajo de algo) **5 to stick to :** no abandonar <stick to your guns **:** manténgase firme> **6 to stick up :** estar parado (dícese del pelo, etc.), sobresalir (de una superficie) **7 to stick with :** serle fiel a (una persona), seguir con (una cosa) <I'll stick with what I know **:** prefiero lo conocido>
stick[2] *n* **1** BRANCH, TWIG **:** ramita *f* **2 :** palo *m*, vara *f* <a walking stick **:** un bastón>
sticker ['stɪkər] *n* **:** etiqueta *f* adhesiva
stickler ['stɪklər] *n* **:** persona *f* exigente <to be a stickler for **:** insistir mucho en>
sticky ['stɪki] *adj* **stickier; -est 1** ADHESIVE **:** pegajoso, adhesivo **2** MUGGY **:** bochornoso **3** DIFFICULT **:** difícil
stiff ['stɪf] *adj* **1** RIGID **:** rígido, tieso <a stiff dough **:** una masa firme> **2 :** agarrotado, entumecido <stiff muscles **:** músculos entumecidos> **3** STILTED **:** acartonado, poco natural **4** STRONG **:** fuerte (dícese del viento, etc.) **5** DIFFICULT, SEVERE **:** severo, difícil, duro
stiffen ['stɪfən] *vt* **1** STRENGTHEN **:** fortalecer, reforzar (tela, etc.) **2 :** hacer más duro (un castigo, etc.) — *vi* **1** HARDEN **:** endurecerse **2 :** entumecerse (dícese de los músculos)
stiffly ['stɪfli] *adv* **1** RIGIDLY **:** rígidamente **2** COLDLY **:** con frialdad
stiffness ['stɪfnəs] *n* **1** RIGIDITY **:** rigidez *f* **2** COLDNESS **:** frialdad *f* **3** SEVERITY **:** severidad *f*
stifle ['staɪfəl] *vt* **-fled; -fling** SMOTHER, SUPPRESS **:** sofocar, reprimir, contener <to stifle a yawn **:** reprimir un bostezo>
stigma ['stɪgmə] *n, pl* **stigmata** [stɪg'mɑt̬ə, 'stɪgmət̬ə] *or* **stigmas :** estigma *m*
stigmatize ['stɪgmə,taɪz] *vt* **-tized; -tizing :** estigmatizar
stile ['staɪl] *n* **:** escalones *mpl* para cruzar un cerco
stiletto [stə'lɛ,t̬o:] *n, pl* **-tos** *or* **-toes :** estilete *m*
still[1] ['stɪl] *vt* CALM **:** pacificar, apaciguar — *vi* **:** pacificarse, apaciguarse
still[2] *adv* **1** QUIETLY **:** quieto <sit still! **:** ¡quédate quieto!> **2 :** de todos modos, aún, todavía <she still lives there **:** aún vive allí> <it's still the same **:** sigue siendo lo mismo> **3** IN ANY CASE **:** de todos modos, aún así <he still has doubts **:** aún así le quedan dudas> <I still prefer that you stay **:** de todos modos prefiero que te quedes>
still[3] *adj* **1** MOTIONLESS **:** quieto, inmóvil **2** SILENT **:** callado
still[4] *n* **1** SILENCE **:** quietud *f*, calma *f* **2 :** alambique *m* (para destilar alcohol)
stillborn ['stɪl,bɔrn] *adj* **:** nacido muerto
stillness ['stɪlnəs] *n* **:** calma *f*, silencio *m*
stilt ['stɪlt] *n* **:** zanco *m*
stilted ['stɪltəd] *adj* **:** afectado, poco natural

stimulant [ˈstɪmjələnt] *n* **:** estimulante *m* — **stimulant** *adj*
stimulate [ˈstɪmjəˌleɪt] *vt* **-lated; -lating :** estimular
stimulation [ˌstɪmjəˈleɪʃən] *n* **1** STIMULATING **:** estimulación *f* **2** STIMULUS **:** estímulo *m*
stimulus [ˈstɪmjələs] *n, pl* **-li** [-ˌlaɪ] **1 :** estímulo *m* **2** INCENTIVE **:** acicate *m*
sting[1] [ˈstɪŋ] *v* **stung** [ˈstʌŋ]; **stinging** *vt* **1 :** picar <a bee stung him : le picó una abeja> **2** HURT **:** hacer escocer (físicamente), herir (emocionalmente) — *vi* **1 :** picar (dícese de las abejas, etc.) **2** SMART **:** escocer, arder
sting[2] *n* **:** picadura *f* (herida), escozor *m* (sensación)
stinger [ˈstɪŋər] *n* **:** aguijón *m* (de una abeja, etc.)
stinginess [ˈstɪndʒinəs] *n* **:** tacañería *f*
stingy [ˈstɪndʒi] *adj* **stingier; -est 1** MISERLY **:** tacaño, avaro **2** PALTRY **:** mezquino, mísero
stink[1] [ˈstɪŋk] *vi* **stank** [ˈstæŋk] *or* **stunk** [ˈstʌŋk]; **stunk; stinking :** apestar, oler mal
stink[2] *n* **:** hedor *m,* mal olor *m,* peste *f*
stint[1] [ˈstɪnt] *vt* **:** escatimar <to stint oneself of : privarse de> — *vi* **to stint on :** escatimar
stint[2] *n* **:** período *m*
stipend [ˈstaɪˌpɛnd, -pənd] *n* **:** estipendio *m*
stipulate [ˈstɪpjəˌleɪt] *vt* **-lated; -lating :** estipular
stipulation [ˌstɪpjəˈleɪʃən] *n* **:** estipulación *f*
stir[1] [ˈstər] *v* **stirred; stirring** *vt* **1** AGITATE **:** mover, agitar **2** MIX **:** revolver, remover **3** INCITE **:** incitar, impulsar, motivar **4** *or* **to stir up** AROUSE **:** despertar (memorias, etc.), provocar (ira, etc.) — *vi* **:** moverse, agitarse
stir[2] *n* **1** MOTION **:** movimiento *m* **2** COMMOTION **:** revuelo *m*
stirrup [ˈstərəp, ˈstɪr-] *n* **:** estribo *m*
stitch[1] [ˈstɪtʃ] *vt* **:** coser, bordar (para decorar) — *vi* **:** coser
stitch[2] *n* **1 :** puntada *f* **2** TWINGE **:** punzada *f,* puntada *f*
stock[1] [ˈstɑk] *vt* **:** surtir, abastecer, vender — *vi* **to stock up :** abastecerse
stock[2] *n* **1** SUPPLY **:** reserva *f,* existencias *fpl* (en comercio) <to be out of stock : estar agotadas las existencias> **2** SECURITIES **:** acciones *fpl,* valores *mpl* **3** LIVESTOCK **:** ganado *m* **4** ANCESTRY **:** linaje *m,* estirpe *f* **5** BROTH **:** caldo *m* **6 to take stock :** evaluar
stockade [stɑˈkeɪd] *n* **:** estacada *f*
stockbroker [ˈstɑkˌbroːkər] *n* **:** corredor *m,* -dora *f* de bolsa
stockholder [ˈstɑkˌhoːldər] *n* **:** accionista *mf*
stocking [ˈstɑkɪŋ] *n* **:** media *f* <a pair of stockings : unas medias>
stock market *n* **:** bolsa *f*
stockpile[1] [ˈstɑkˌpaɪl] *vt* **-piled; -piling :** acumular, almacenar
stockpile[2] *n* **:** reservas *fpl*
stocky [ˈstɑki] *adj* **stockier; -est :** robusto, fornido
stockyard [ˈstɑkˌjɑrd] *n* **:** corral *m*
stodgy [ˈstɑdʒi] *adj* **stodgier; -est 1** DULL **:** aburrido, pesado **2** OLD-FASHIONED **:** anticuado
stoic[1] [ˈstoːɪk] *or* **stoical** [-ɪkəl] *adj* **:** estoico — **stoically** [-ɪkli] *adv*
stoic[2] *n* **:** estoico *m,* -ca *f*
stoicism [ˈstoːəˌsɪzəm] *n* **:** estoicismo *m*
stoke [ˈstoːk] *vt* **stoked; stoking :** atizar (un fuego), echarle carbón a (un horno)
stole[1] → **steal**
stole[2] [ˈstoːl] *n* **:** estola *f*
stolen → **steal**
stolid [ˈstɑlɪd] *adj* **:** impasible, imperturbable — **stolidly** *adv*
stomach[1] [ˈstʌmɪk] *vt* **:** aguantar, soportar
stomach[2] *n* **1 :** estómago *m* **2** BELLY **:** vientre *m,* barriga *f,* panza *f* **3** DESIRE **:** ganas *fpl* <he had no stomach for a fight : no quería pelea>
stomachache [ˈstʌmɪkˌeɪk] *n* **:** dolor *m* de estómago
stomp [ˈstɑmp, ˈstɔmp] *vt* **:** pisotear — *vi* **:** pisar fuerte
stone[1] [ˈstoːn] *vt* **stoned; stoning :** apedrear, lapidar
stone[2] *n* **1 :** piedra *f* **2** PIT **:** hueso *m,* pepa *f* (de una fruta)
Stone Age *n* **:** Edad *f* de Piedra
stony [ˈstoːni] *adj* **stonier; -est 1** ROCKY **:** pedregoso **2** UNFEELING **:** insensible, frío <a stony stare : una mirada glacial>
stood → **stand**
stool [ˈstuːl] *n* **1** SEAT **:** taburete *m,* banco *m* **2** FOOTSTOOL **:** escabel *m* **3** FECES **:** deposición *f* de heces
stoop[1] [ˈstuːp] *vi* **1** CROUCH **:** agacharse **2 to stoop to :** rebajarse a
stoop[2] *n* **1 :** espaldas *fpl* encorvadas <to have a stoop : ser encorvado> **2 :** entrada *f* (de una casa)
stop[1] [ˈstɑp] *v* **stopped; stopping** *vt* **1** PLUG **:** tapar **2** PREVENT **:** impedir, evitar <she stopped me from leaving : me impidió que saliera> **3** HALT **:** parar, detener **4** CEASE **:** dejar de <he stopped talking : dejó de hablar> — *vi* **1** HALT **:** detenerse, parar **2** CEASE **:** cesar, terminar <the rain won't stop : no deja de llover> **3** STAY **:** quedarse <she stopped with friends : se quedó en casa de unos amigos> **4 to stop by :** visitar
stop[2] *n* **1** STOPPER **:** tapón *m* **2** HALT **:** parada *f,* alto *m* <to come to a stop : pararse, detenerse> <to put a stop to : poner fin a> **3 :** parada *f* <bus stop : parada de autobús>
stopgap [ˈstɑpˌgæp] *n* **:** arreglo *m* provisorio
stoplight [ˈstɑpˌlaɪt] *n* **:** semáforo *m*

stoppage [ˈstɑpɪdʒ] *n* **:** acto *m* de parar <a work stoppage : un paro>
stopper [ˈstɑpər] *n* **:** tapón *m*
storage [ˈstorɪdʒ] *n* **:** almacenamiento *m,* almacenaje *m*
storage battery *n* **:** acumulador *m*
store[1] [ˈstor] *vt* **stored; storing :** guardar, almacenar
store[2] *n* **1** RESERVE, SUPPLY **:** reserva *f* **2** SHOP **:** tienda *f* <grocery store : tienda de comestibles>
storehouse [ˈstorˌhaʊs] *n* **:** almacén *m,* depósito *m*
storekeeper [ˈstorˌkiːpər] *n* **:** tendero *m,* -ra *f*
storeroom [ˈstorˌruːm, -ˌrʊm] *n* **:** almacén *m,* depósito *m*
stork [ˈstɔrk] *n* **:** cigüeña *f*
storm[1] [ˈstɔrm] *vi* **1 :** llover o nevar tormentosamente **2** RAGE **:** ponerse furioso, vociferar **3 to storm out :** salir echando pestes — *vt* ATTACK **:** asaltar
storm[2] *n* **1 :** tormenta *f,* tempestad *f* **2** UPROAR **:** alboroto *m,* revuelo *m,* escándalo *m* <a storm of abuse : un torrente de abusos>
stormy [ˈstɔrmi] *adj* **stormier; -est :** tormentoso
story [ˈstori] *n, pl* **stories 1** NARRATIVE **:** cuento *m,* relato *m* **2** ACCOUNT **:** historia *f,* relato *m* **3 :** piso *m,* planta *f* (de un edificio) <first story : planta baja>
stout [ˈstaʊt] *adj* **1** FIRM, RESOLUTE **:** firme, resuelto **2** STURDY **:** fuerte, robusto, sólido **3** FAT **:** corpulento, gordo
stove[1] [ˈstoːv] *n* **:** cocina *f* (para cocinar), estufa *f* (para calentar)
stove[2] → **stave**[1]
stow [ˈstoː] *vt* **1** STORE **:** poner, meter, guardar **2** LOAD **:** cargar — *vi* **to stow away :** viajar de polizón
stowaway [ˈstoːəˌweɪ] *n* **:** polizón *m*
straddle [ˈstrædəl] *vt* **-dled; -dling :** sentarse a horcajadas sobre
straggle [ˈstrægəl] *vi* **-gled; -gling :** rezagarse, quedarse atrás
straggler [ˈstrægələr] *n* **:** rezagado *m,* -da *f*
straight[1] [ˈstreɪt] *adv* **1 :** derecho, directamente <go straight, then turn right : sigue derecho, luego gira a la derecha> **2** HONESTLY **:** honestamente <to go straight : enmendarse> **3** CLEARLY **:** con claridad **4** FRANKLY **:** francamente, con franqueza
straight[2] *adj* **1 :** recto (dícese de las líneas, etc.), derecho (dícese de algo vertical), lacio (dícese del pelo) **2** HONEST, JUST **:** honesto, justo **3** NEAT, ORDERLY **:** arreglado, ordenado
straighten [ˈstreɪtən] *vt* **1 :** enderezar, poner derecho **2 to straighten up :** arreglar, ordenar <he straightened up the house : arregló la casa>
straightforward [streɪtˈfɔrwərd] *adj* **1** FRANK **:** franco, sincero **2** CLEAR, PRECISE **:** puro, simple, claro
straightway [ˈstreɪtˈweɪ, -ˌweɪ] *adv* **:** inmediatamente
strain[1] [ˈstreɪn] *vt* **1** EXERT **:** forzar (la vista, la voz) <to strain oneself : hacer un gran esfuerzo> **2** FILTER **:** colar, filtrar **3** INJURE **:** lastimarse, hacerse daño en <to strain a muscle : sufrir un esguince>
strain[2] *n* **1** LINEAGE **:** linaje *m,* abolengo *m* **2** STREAK, TRACE **:** veta *f* **3** VARIETY **:** tipo *m,* variedad *f* **4** STRESS **:** tensión *f,* presión *f* **5** SPRAIN **:** esguince *m,* torcedura *f* (del tobillo, etc.) **6 strains** *npl* TUNE **:** melodía *f,* acordes *mpl,* compases *fpl*
strainer [ˈstreɪnər] *n* **:** colador *m*
strait [ˈstreɪt] *n* **1 :** estrecho *m* **2 straits** *npl* DISTRESS **:** aprietos *mpl,* apuros *mpl* <in dire straits : en serios aprietos>
straitened [ˈstreɪtənd] *adj* **in straitened circumstances :** en apuros económicos
strand[1] [ˈstrænd] *vt* **1 :** varar **2 to be left stranded :** quedar(se) varado, quedar colgado <they left me stranded : me dejaron abandonado>
strand[2] *n* **1 :** hebra *f* (de hilo, etc.) <a strand of hair : un pelo> **2** BEACH **:** playa *f*
strange [ˈstreɪndʒ] *adj* **stranger; -est 1** QUEER, UNUSUAL **:** extraño, raro **2** UNFAMILIAR **:** desconocido, nuevo
strangely [ˈstreɪndʒli] *adv* ODDLY **:** de manera extraña <to behave strangely : portarse de una manera rara> <strangely, he didn't call : curiosamente, no llamó>
strangeness [ˈstreɪndʒnəs] *n* **1** ODDNESS **:** rareza *f* **2** UNFAMILIARITY **:** lo desconocido
stranger [ˈstreɪndʒər] *n* **:** desconocido *m,* -da *f;* extraño *m,* -ña *f*
strangle [ˈstræŋgəl] *vt* **-gled; -gling :** estrangular
strangler [ˈstræŋglər] *n* **:** estrangulador *m,* -dora *f*
strap[1] [ˈstræp] *vt* **strapped; strapping 1** FASTEN **:** sujetar con una correa **2** FLOG **:** azotar (con una correa)
strap[2] *n* **1 :** correa *f* **2 shoulder strap :** tirante *m*
strapless [ˈstræpləs] *n* **:** sin tirantes
strapping [ˈstræpɪŋ] *adj* **:** robusto, fornido
stratagem [ˈstrætədʒəm, -ˌdʒɛm] *n* **:** estratagema *f,* artimaña *f*
strategic [strəˈtiːdʒɪk] *adj* **:** estratégico
strategy [ˈstrætədʒi] *n, pl* **-gies :** estrategia *f*
stratified [ˈstrætəˌfaɪd] *adj* **:** estratificado
stratosphere [ˈstrætəˌsfɪr] *n* **:** estratosfera *f*
stratum [ˈstreɪtəm, ˈstræ-] *n, pl* **strata** [-tə] **:** estrato *m,* capa *f*
straw *n* **1 :** paja *f* <the last straw : el colmo> **2** *or* **drinking straw :** pajita *f,* popote *m Mex*

strawberry ['strɔ,bɛri] *n, pl* **-ries** : fresa *f*

stray[1] ['streɪ] *vi* **1** WANDER : alejarse, extraviarse <the cattle strayed away : el ganado se descarrió> **2** DIGRESS : desviarse, divagar

stray[2] *adj* : perdido, callejero (dícese de un perro o un gato), descarriado (dícese del ganado)

stray[3] *n* : animal *m* perdido, animal *m* callejero

streak[1] ['stri:k] *vt* : hacer rayas en <blue streaked with grey : azul veteado con gris> — *vi* : ir como una flecha

streak[2] *n* **1** : raya *f,* veta *f* (en mármol, queso, etc.), mechón *m* (en el pelo) **2** : rayo *m* (de luz) **3** TRACE : veta *f* **4** : racha *f* <a streak of luck : una racha de suerte>

stream[1] ['stri:m] *vi* : correr, salir a chorros <tears streamed from his eyes : las lágrimas brotaban de sus ojos> — *vt* : derramar, dejar correr <to stream blood : derramar sangre>

stream[2] *n* **1** BROOK : arroyo *m,* riachuelo *m* **2** RIVER : río *m* **3** FLOW : corriente *f,* chorro *m*

streamer ['stri:mər] *n* **1** PENNANT : banderín *m* **2** RIBBON : serpentina *f* (de papel), cinta *f* (de tela)

streamlined ['stri:m,laɪnd] *adj* **1** : aerodinámico (dícese de los automóviles, etc.) **2** EFFICIENT : eficiente, racionalizado

street ['stri:t] *n* : calle *f*

streetcar ['stri:t,kɑr] *n* : tranvía *m*

strength ['strɛŋkθ] *n* **1** POWER : fuerza *f* **2** SOLIDITY, TOUGHNESS : solidez *f,* resistencia *f,* dureza *f* **3** INTENSITY : intensidad *f* (de emociones, etc.), lo fuerte (de un sabor, etc.) **4** : punto *m* fuerte <strengths and weaknesses : virtudes y defectos> **5** NUMBER : número *m,* complemento *m* <in full strength : en gran número>

strengthen ['strɛŋkθən] *vt* **1** : fortalecer (los músculos, el espíritu, etc.) **2** REINFORCE : reforzar **3** INTENSIFY : intensificar, redoblar (esfuerzos, etc.) — *vi* **1** : fortalecerse, hacerse más fuerte **2** INTENSIFY : intensificarse

strenuous ['strɛnjʊəs] *adj* **1** VIGOROUS : vigoroso, enérgico **2** ARDUOUS : duro, riguroso

strenuously ['strɛnjʊəsli] *adv* : vigorosamente, duro

stress[1] ['strɛs] *vt* **1** : someter a tensión (física) **2** EMPHASIZE : enfatizar, recalcar **3 to stress out** : estresar

stress[2] *n* **1** : tensión *f* (en un material) **2** EMPHASIS : énfasis *m,* acento *m* (en lingüística) **3** TENSION : tensión *f* (nerviosa), estrés *m*

stressful ['strɛsfəl] *adj* : estresante

stretch[1] ['strɛtʃ] *vt* **1** EXTEND : estirar, extender, desplegar (alas) **2 to stretch the truth** : forzar la verdad, exagerar — *vi* : estirarse

stretch[2] *n* **1** STRETCHING : extensión *f,* estiramiento *m* (de músculos) **2** ELASTICITY : elasticidad *f* **3** EXPANSE : tramo *m,* trecho *m* <the home stretch : la recta final> **4** PERIOD : período *m* (de tiempo)

stretcher ['strɛtʃər] *n* : camilla *f*

strew ['stru:] *vt* **strewed; strewed** *or* **strewn** ['stru:n]; **strewing 1** SCATTER : esparcir (semillas, etc.), desparramar (papeles, etc.) **2 to strew with** : cubrir de

stricken ['strɪkən] *adj* **stricken with** : aquejado de (una enfermedad), afligido por (tristeza, etc.)

strict ['strɪkt] *adj* : estricto — **strictly** *adv*

strictness ['strɪktnəs] *n* : severidad *f,* lo estricto

stricture ['strɪktʃər] *n* : crítica *f,* censura *f*

stride[1] ['straɪd] *vi* **strode** ['stro:d]; **stridden** ['strɪdən]; **striding** : ir dando trancos, ir dando zancadas

stride[2] *n* : tranco *m,* zancada *f*

strident ['straɪdənt] *adj* : estridente

strife ['straɪf] *n* : conflictos *mpl,* disensión *f*

strike[1] ['straɪk] *v* **struck** ['strʌk]; **struck; striking** *vt* **1** HIT : golpear (a una persona) <to strike a blow : pegar un golpe> **2** DELETE : suprimir, tachar **3** COIN, MINT : acuñar (monedas) **4** : dar (la hora) **5** AFFLICT : sobrevenir <he was stricken with a fever : le sobrevino una fiebre> **6** IMPRESS : impresionar, parecer <her voice struck me : su voz me impresionó> <it struck him as funny : le pareció chistoso> **7** : encender (un fósforo) **8** FIND : descubrir (oro, petróleo) **9** ADOPT : adoptar (una pose, etc.) — *vi* **1** HIT : golpear <to strike against : chocar contra> **2** ATTACK : atacar **3** : declararse en huelga

strike[2] *n* **1** BLOW : golpe *m* **2** : huelga *f,* paro *m* <to be on strike : estar en huelga> **3** ATTACK : ataque *m*

strikebreaker ['straɪk,breɪkər] *n* : rompehuelgas *mf,* esquirol *mf*

strike out *vi* **1** HEAD : salir (para) **2** : ser ponchado (en béisbol) <the batter struck out : poncharon al bateador>

striker ['straɪkər] *n* : huelgista *mf*

strike up *vt* START : entablar, empezar

striking ['straɪkɪŋ] *adj* : notable, sorprendente, llamativo <a striking beauty : una belleza imponente> — **strikingly** *adv*

string[1] ['strɪŋ] *vt* **strung** ['strʌŋ]; **stringing 1** THREAD : ensartar <to string beads : ensartar cuentas> **2** HANG : colgar (con un cordel)

string[2] *n* **1** : cordel *m,* cuerda *f* **2** SERIES : serie *f,* sarta *f* (de insultos, etc.) **3 strings** *npl* : cuerdas *fpl* (en música)

string bean *n* : judía *f,* ejote *m Mex*

stringent ['strɪndʒənt] *adj* : estricto, severo

stringy [ˈstrɪŋi] *adj* **stringier; -est** : fibroso

strip[1] [ˈstrɪp] *v* **stripped; stripping** *vt* : quitar (ropa, pintura, etc.), desnudar, despojar — *vi* UNDRESS : desnudarse

strip[2] *n* : tira *f* <a strip of land : una faja>

stripe[1] [ˈstraɪp] *vt* **striped** [ˈstraɪpt]; **striping** : marcar con rayas o listas

stripe[2] *n* **1** : raya *f,* lista *f* **2** BAND : franja *f*

striped [ˈstraɪpt, ˈstraɪpəd] *adj* : a rayas, de rayas, rayado, listado

strive [ˈstraɪv] *vi* **strove** [ˈstroːv]; **striven** [ˈstrɪvən] *or* **strived; striving 1 to strive for :** luchar por lograr **2 to strive to :** esforzarse por

strode → **stride**

stroke[1] [ˈstroːk] *vt* **stroked; stroking** : acariciar

stroke[2] *n* : golpe *m* <a stroke of luck : un golpe de suerte>

stroll[1] [ˈstroːl] *vi* : pasear, pasearse, dar un paseo

stroll[2] *n* : paseo *m*

stroller [ˈstroːlər] *n* : cochecito *m* (para niños)

strong [ˈstrɔŋ] *adj* **1** : fuerte **2** HEALTHY : sano **3** ZEALOUS : ferviente

stronghold [ˈstrɔŋˌhoːld] *n* : fortaleza *f,* fuerte *m,* bastión *m* <a cultural stronghold : un baluarte de la cultura>

strongly [ˈstrɔŋli] *adv* **1** POWERFULLY : fuerte, con fuerza **2** STURDILY : fuertemente, sólidamente **3** INTENSELY : intensamente, profundamente **4** WHOLEHEARTEDLY : totalmente

struck → **strike**[1]

structural [ˈstrʌktʃərəl] *adj* : estructural

structure[1] [ˈstrʌktʃər] *vt* **-tured; -turing** : estructurar

structure[2] *n* **1** BUILDING : construcción *f* **2** ARRANGEMENT, FRAMEWORK : estructura *f*

struggle[1] [ˈstrʌgəl] *vi* **-gled; -gling 1** CONTEND : forcejear (físicamente), luchar, contender **2** : hacer con dificultad <she struggled forward : avanzó con dificultad>

struggle[2] *n* : lucha *f,* pelea *f* (física)

strum [ˈstrʌm] *vt* **strummed; strumming** : rasguear

strung → **string**[1]

strut[1] [ˈstrʌt] *vi* **strutted; strutting** : pavonearse

strut[2] *n* **1** : pavoneo *m* <he walked with a strut : se pavoneaba> **2** : puntal *m* (en construcción, etc.)

strychnine [ˈstrɪkˌnaɪn, -nən, -ˌniːn] *n* : estricnina *f*

stub[1] [ˈstʌb] *vt* **stubbed; stubbing 1 to stub one's toe :** darse en el dedo (del pie) **2 to stub out :** apagarse

stub[2] *n* : colilla *f* (de un cigarrillo), cabo *m* (de un lápiz, etc.), talón *m* (de un cheque)

stubble [ˈstʌbəl] *n* **1** : rastrojo *m* (de plantas) **2** BEARD : barba *f*

stubborn [ˈstʌbərn] *adj* **1** OBSTINATE : terco, obstinado, empecinado **2** PERSISTENT : pertinaz, persistente — **stubbornly** *adv*

stubbornness [ˈstʌbərnnəs] *n* **1** OBSTINACY : terquedad *f,* obstinación *f* **2** PERSISTENCE : persistencia *f*

stubby [ˈstʌbi] *adj* **stubbier; -est** : corto y grueso <stubby fingers : dedos regordetes>

stucco [ˈstʌkoː] *n, pl* **stuccos** *or* **stuccoes** : estuco *m*

stuck → **stick**[1]

stuck–up [ˈstʌkˈʌp] *adj* : engreído, creído *fam*

stud[1] [ˈstʌd] *vt* **studded; studding :** tachonar, salpicar

stud[2] *n* **1** *or* **stud horse** : semental *m* **2** : montante *m* (en construcción) **3** HOBNAIL : tachuela *f,* tachón *m*

student [ˈstuːdənt, ˈstjuː-] *n* : estudiante *mf;* alumno *m,* -na *f* (de un colegio)

studied [ˈstʌdid] *adj* : intencionado, premeditado

studio [ˈstuːdiˌoː, ˈstjuː-] *n, pl* **studios** : estudio *m*

studious [ˈstuːdiəs, ˈstjuː-] *adj* : estudioso — **studiously** *adv*

study[1] [ˈstʌdi] *v* **studied; studying 1** : estudiar **2** EXAMINE : examinar, estudiar

study[2] *n, pl* **studies 1** STUDYING : estudio *m* **2** OFFICE : estudio *m,* gabinete *m* (en una casa) **3** RESEARCH : investigación *f,* estudio *m*

stuff[1] [ˈstʌf] *vt* : rellenar, llenar, atiborrar

stuff[2] *n* **1** POSSESSIONS : cosas *fpl* **2** ESSENCE : esencia *f* **3** SUBSTANCE : cosa *f,* cosas *fpl* <some sticky stuff : una cosa pegajosa> <she knows her stuff : es experta>

stuffing [ˈstʌfɪŋ] *n* : relleno *m*

stuffy [ˈstʌfi] *adj* **stuffier; -est 1** CLOSE : viciado, cargado <a stuffy room : una sala mal ventilada> <stuffy weather : tiempo bochornoso> **2** : tapado (dícese de la nariz) **3** STODGY : pesado, aburrido

stumble[1] [ˈstʌmbəl] *vi* **-bled; -bling 1** TRIP : tropezar, dar un traspié **2** FLOUNDER : quedarse sin saber qué hacer o decir **3 to stumble across** *or* **to stumble upon :** dar con, tropezar con

stumble[2] *n* : tropezón *m,* traspié *m*

stump[1] [ˈstʌmp] *vt* : dejar perplejo <to be stumped : no tener respuesta>

stump[2] *n* **1** : muñón *m* (de un brazo o una pierna) **2** *or* **tree stump** : cepa *f,* tocón *m* **3** STUB : cabo *m*

stun [ˈstʌn] *vt* **stunned; stunning 1** : aturdir (con un golpe) **2** ASTONISH, SHOCK : dejar estupefacto, dejar atónito, aturdir

stung → **sting**[1]

stunk → **stink**[1]

stunning ['stʌnɪŋ] *adj* **1** ASTONISHING : asombroso, pasmoso, increíble **2** STRIKING : imponente, impresionante (dícese de la belleza)
stunt[1] ['stʌnt] *vt* : atrofiar
stunt[2] *n* : proeza *f* (acrobática)
stupefy ['stu:pə,faɪ, 'stju:-] *vt* **-fied; -fying 1** : aturdir, atontar (con drogas, etc.) **2** AMAZE : dejar estupefacto, dejar atónito
stupendous [stʊ'pɛndəs, stjʊ-] *adj* **1** MARVELOUS : estupendo, maravilloso **2** TREMENDOUS : tremendo — **stupendously** *adv*
stupid ['stu:pəd, 'stju:-] *adj* **1** IDIOTIC, SILLY : tonto, bobo, estúpido **2** DULL, OBTUSE : lento, torpe, lerdo
stupidity [stʊ'pɪdəṭi, stjʊ-] *n* : tontería *f*, estupidez *f*
stupidly ['stu:pədli, 'stju:-] *adv* **1** IDIOTICALLY : estúpidamente, tontamente **2** DENSELY : torpemente
stupor ['stu:pər, 'stju:-] *n* : estupor *m*
sturdily ['stərdəli] *adv* : sólidamente
sturdiness ['stərdinəs] *n* : solidez *f* (de muebles, etc.), robustez *f* (de una persona)
sturdy ['stərdi] *adj* **sturdier; -est** : fuerte, robusto, sólido
sturgeon ['stərdʒən] *n* : esturión *m*
stutter[1] ['stʌṭər] *vi* : tartamudear
stutter[2] *n* STAMMER : tartamudeo *m*
sty ['staɪ] *n* **1** *pl* **sties** PIGPEN : chiquero *m*, polcilga *f* **2** *pl* **sties** *or* **styes** : orzuelo *m* (en el ojo)
style[1] ['staɪl] *vt* **styled; styling 1** NAME : llamar **2** : peinar (pelo), diseñar (vestidos, etc.) <carefully styled prose : prosa escrita con gran esmero>
style[2] *n* **1** : estilo *m* <that's just his style : él es así> <to live in style : vivir a lo grande> **2** FASHION : moda *f*
stylish ['staɪlɪʃ] *adj* : de moda, elegante, chic
stylishly ['staɪlɪʃli] *adv* : con estilo
stylishness ['staɪlɪʃnəs] *n* : estilo *m*
stylize ['staɪ,laɪz, 'staɪə-] *vt* : estilizar
stylus ['staɪləs] *n, pl* **styli** ['staɪ,laɪ] **1** PEN : estilo *m* **2** NEEDLE : aguja *f* (de un tocadiscos)
stymie ['staɪmi] *vt* **-mied; -mieing** : obstaculizar
suave ['swɑv] *adj* : fino, urbano
sub[1] ['sʌb] *vi* **subbed; subbing** → **substitute**[1]
sub[2] *n* **1** → **substitute**[2] **2** → **submarine**
subcommittee ['sʌbkə,mɪṭi] *n* : subcomité *m*
subconscious[1] [səb'kɑntʃəs] *adj* : subconsciente — **subconsciously** *adv*
subconscious[2] *n* : subconsciente *m*
subcontract [,sʌb'kɑn,trækt] *vt* : subcontratar
subdivide [,sʌbdə'vaɪd, 'sʌbdə,vaɪd] *vt* **-vided; -viding** : subdividir
subdivision ['sʌbdə,vɪʒən] *n* : subdivisión *f*
subdue [səb'du:, -'dju:] *vt* **-dued; -duing 1** OVERCOME : sojuzgar (a un enemigo), vencer, superar **2** CONTROL : dominar **3** SOFTEN : suavizar, atenuar (luz, etc.), moderar (lenguaje)
subhead ['sʌb,hɛd] *or* **subheading** [-,hɛdɪŋ] *n* : subtítulo *m*
subject[1] [səb'dʒɛkt] *vt* **1** CONTROL, DOMINATE : controlar, dominar **2** : someter <they subjected him to pressure : lo sometieron a presiones>
subject[2] ['sʌbdʒɪkt] *adj* **1** : subyugado, sometido <a subject nation : una nación subyugada> **2** PRONE : sujeto, propenso <subject to colds : sujeto a resfriarse> **3 subject to** : sujeto a <subject to congressional approval : sujeto a la aprobación del congreso>
subject[3] ['sʌbdʒɪkt] *n* **1** : súbdito *m*, -ta *f* (de un gobierno) **2** TOPIC : tema *m* **3** : sujeto *m* (en gramática)
subjection [səb'dʒɛkʃən] *n* : sometimiento *m*
subjective [səb'dʒɛktɪv] *adj* : subjetivo — **subjectively** *adv*
subjectivity [,sʌb,dʒɛk'tɪvəṭi] *n* : subjetividad *f*
subjugate ['sʌbdʒɪ,geɪt] *vt* **-gated; -gating** : subyugar, someter, sojuzgar
subjunctive [səb'dʒʌŋktɪv] *n* : subjuntivo *m* — **subjunctive** *adj*
sublet ['sʌb,lɛt] *vt* **-let; -letting** : subarrendar
sublime [sə'blaɪm] *adj* : sublime
sublimely [sə'blaɪmli] *adv* **1** : de manera sublime **2** UTTERLY : absolutamente, completamente
submarine[1] ['sʌbmə,ri:n, ,sʌbmə'-] *adj* : submarino
submarine[2] *n* : submarino *m*
submerge [səb'mərdʒ] *v* **-merged; -merging** *vt* : sumergir — *vi* : sumergirse
submission [səb'mɪʃən] *n* **1** YIELDING : sumisión *f* **2** PRESENTATION : presentación *f*
submissive [səb'mɪsɪv] *adj* : sumiso, dócil
submit [səb'mɪt] *v* **-mitted; -mitting** *vi* YIELD : rendirse <to submit to : someterse a> — *vt* PRESENT : presentar
subnormal [,sʌb'nɔrməl] *adj* : por debajo de lo normal
subordinate[1] [sə'bɔrdən,eɪt] *vt* **-nated; -nating** : subordinar
subordinate[2] [sə'bɔrdənət] *adj* : subordinado <a subordinate clause : una oración subordinada>
subordinate[3] *n* : subordinado *m*, -da *f*; subalterno *m*, -na *f*
subordination [sə,bɔrdən'eɪʃən] *n* : subordinación *f*
subpoena[1] [sə'pi:nə] *vt* **-naed; -naing** : citar
subpoena[2] *n* : citación *f*, citatorio *m*
subscribe [səb'skraɪb] *vi* **-scribed; -scribing 1** : suscribirse (a una revista, etc.) **2 to subscribe to** : sus-

cribir (una opinión, etc.), estar de acuerdo con

subscriber [səbˈskraɪbər] *n* : suscriptor *m,* -tora *f* (de una revista, etc.); abonado *m,* -da *f* (de un servicio)

subscription [səbˈskrɪpʃən] *n* : suscripción *f*

subsequent [ˈsʌbsɪkwənt, -səˌkwɛnt] *adj* : subsiguiente <subsequent to : posterior a>

subsequently [ˈsʌbˌkwɛntli, -kwənt-] *adv* : posteriormente

subservient [səbˈsərviənt] *adj* : servil

subside [səbˈsaɪd] *vi* **-sided; -siding 1** SINK : hundirse, descender **2** ABATE : calmarse (dícese de las emociones), amainar (dícese del viento, etc.)

subsidiary[1] [səbˈsɪdiˌɛri] *adj* : secundario

subsidiary[2] *n, pl* **-ries** : filial *f,* subsidiaria *f*

subsidize [ˈsʌbsəˌdaɪz] *vt* **-dized; -dizing** : subvencionar, subsidiar

subsidy [ˈsʌbsədi] *n, pl* **-dies** : subvención *f,* subsidio *m*

subsist [səbˈsɪst] *vi* : subsistir, mantenerse, vivir

subsistence [səbˈsɪstən*t*s] *n* : subsistencia *f*

substance [ˈsʌbstən*t*s] *n* **1** ESSENCE : sustancia *f,* esencia *f* **2** : sustancia *f* <a toxic substance : una sustancia tóxica> **3** WEALTH : riqueza *f* <a woman of substance : una mujer acaudalada>

substandard [ˌsʌbˈstændərd] *adj* : inferior, deficiente

substantial [səbˈstæntʃəl] *adj* **1** ABUNDANT : sustancioso <a substantial meal : una comida sustanciosa> **2** CONSIDERABLE : considerable, apreciable **3** SOLID, STURDY : sólido

substantially [səbˈstæntʃəli] *adv* : considerablemente

substantiate [səbˈstæntʃiˌeɪt] *vt* **-ated; -ating** : confirmar, probar, justificar

substitute[1] [ˈsʌbstəˌtuːt, -ˌtjuːt] *v* **-tuted; -tuting** *vt* : sustituir — *vi* **to substitute for** : sustituir

substitute[2] *n* **1** : sustituto *m,* -ta *f;* suplente *mf* (persona) **2** : sucedáneo *m* <sugar substitute : sucedáneo de azúcar>

substitute teacher *n* : profesor *m,* -sora *f* suplente

substitution [ˌsʌbstəˈtuːʃən, -ˈtjuː-] *n* : sustitución *f*

subterfuge [ˈsʌbtərˌfjuːdʒ] *n* : subterfugio *m*

subterranean [ˌsʌbtəˈreɪniən] *adj* : subterráneo

subtitle [ˈsʌbˌtaɪtəl] *n* : subtítulo *m*

subtle [ˈsʌtəl] *adj* **-tler; -tlest 1** DELICATE, ELUSIVE : sutil, delicado **2** CLEVER : sutil, ingenioso

subtlety [ˈsʌtəlti] *n, pl* **-ties** : sutileza *f*

subtly [ˈsʌtəli] *adv* : sutilmente

subtotal [ˈsʌbˌtoːtəl] *n* : subtotal *m*

subtract [səbˈtrækt] *vt* : restar, sustraer

subtraction [səbˈtrækʃən] *n* : resta *f,* sustracción *f*

suburb [ˈsʌˌbərb] *n* : municipio *m* periférico, suburbio *m*

suburban [səˈbərbən] *adj* : de las afueras (de una ciudad), suburbano

subversion [səbˈvərʒən] *n* : subversión *f*

subversive [səbˈvərsɪv] *adj* : subversivo

subway [ˈsʌbˌweɪ] *n* : metro *m,* subterráneo *m Arg, Uru*

succeed [səkˈsiːd] *vt* FOLLOW : suceder a — *vi* : tener éxito (dícese de las personas), dar resultado (dícese de los planes, etc.) <she succeeded in finishing : logró terminar>

success [səkˈsɛs] *n* : éxito *m*

successful [səkˈsɛsfəl] *adj* : exitoso, logrado — **successfully** *adv*

succession [səkˈsɛʃən] *n* : sucesión *f* <in succesion : sucesivamente>

successive [səkˈsɛsɪv] *adj* : sucesivo, consecutivo — **successively** *adv*

successor [səkˈsɛsər] *n* : sucesor *m,* -sora *f*

succinct [səkˈsɪŋkt, səˈsɪŋkt] *adj* : sucinto — **succinctly** *adv*

succor[1] [ˈsʌkər] *vt* : socorrer

succor[2] *n* : socorro *m*

succotash [ˈsʌkəˌtæʃ] *n* : guiso *m* de maíz y frijoles

succulent[1] [ˈsʌkjələnt] *adj* : suculento, jugoso

succulent[2] *n* : suculenta *f* (planta)

succumb [səˈkʌm] *vi* : sucumbir

such[1] [ˈsʌtʃ] *adv* **1** SO : tan <such tall buildings : edificios tan grandes> **2** VERY : muy <he's not in such good shape : anda un poco mal> **3 such that** : de tal manera que

such[2] *adj* : tal <there's no such thing : no existe tal cosa> <in such cases : en tales casos> <animals such as cows and sheep : animales como vacas y ovejas>

such[3] *pron* **1** : tal <such was the result : tal fue el resultado> <he's a child, and acts as such : es un niño, y se porta como tal> **2** : algo o alguien semejante <books, papers and such : libros, papeles y cosas por el estilo>

suck [ˈsʌk] *vi* **1** : chupar (por la boca), aspirar (dícese de las máquinas) **2** SUCKLE : mamar — *vt* : sorber (bebidas), chupar (dulces, etc.)

sucker [ˈsʌkər] *n* **1** : ventosa *f* (de un insecto, etc.) **2** : chupón *m* (de una planta) **3** → **lollipop 4** FOOL : tonto *m,* -ta *f;* idiota *mf*

suckle [ˈsʌkəl] *v* **-led; -ling** *vt* : amamantar — *vi* : mamar

suckling [ˈsʌklɪŋ] *n* : lactante *mf*

sucrose [ˈsuːˌkroːs, -ˌkroːz] *n* : sacarosa *f*

suction [ˈsʌkʃən] *n* : succión *f*

Sudanese [ˌsuːdənˈiːz, -ˈiːs] *n* : sudanés *m,* -nesa *f* — **Sudanese** *adj*

sudden [ˈsʌdən] *adj* **1** : repentino, súbito <all of a sudden : de pronto, de repente> **2** UNEXPECTED : inesperado, improvisto **3** ABRUPT, HASTY : precipitado, brusco

suddenly [ˈsʌdənli] *adv* **1** : de repente, de pronto **2** ABRUPTLY : bruscamente

suddenness [ˈsʌdənnəs] *n* **1** : lo repentino **2** ABRUPTNESS : brusquedad *f* **3** HASTINESS : lo precipitado

suds [ˈsʌdz] *npl* : espuma *f* (de jabón)

sue [ˈsuː] *v* **sued; suing** *vt* : demandar — *vi* **to sue for** : demandar por (daños, etc.)

suede [ˈsweɪd] *n* : ante *m,* gamuza *f*

suet [ˈsuːət] *n* : sebo *m*

suffer [ˈsʌfər] *vi* : sufrir — *vt* **1** : sufrir, padecer (dolores, etc.) **2** PERMIT : permitir, dejar

sufferer [ˈsʌfərər] *n* : persona que padece (una enfermedad, etc.)

suffering [ˈsʌfərɪŋ] *n* : sufrimiento *m*

suffice [səˈfaɪs] *vi* **-ficed; -ficing** : ser suficiente, bastar

sufficient [səˈfɪʃənt] *adj* : suficiente

sufficiently [səˈfɪʃəntli] *adv* : (lo) suficientemente, bastante

suffix [ˈsʌˌfɪks] *n* : sufijo *m*

suffocate [ˈsʌfəˌkeɪt] *v* **-cated; -cating** *vt* : asfixiar, ahogar — *vi* : asfixiarse, ahogarse

suffocation [ˌsʌfəˈkeɪʃən] *n* : asfixia *f,* ahogo *m*

suffrage [ˈsʌfrɪdʒ] *n* : sufragio *m,* derecho *m* al voto

suffuse [səˈfjuːz] *vt* **-fused; -fusing** : impregnar (de olores, etc.), bañar (de luz), teñir (de colores), llenar (de emociones)

sugar[1] [ˈʃʊgər] *vt* : azucarar

sugar[2] *n* : azúcar *mf*

sugarcane [ˈʃʊgərˌkeɪn] *n* : caña *f* de azúcar

sugary [ˈʃʊgəri] *adj* **1** : azucarado <sugary desserts : postres azucarados> **2** SACCHARINE : empalagoso

suggest [səgˈdʒɛst, sə-] *vt* **1** PROPOSE : sugerir **2** IMPLY : indicar, dar a entender

suggestible [səgˈdʒɛstəbəl, sə-] *adj* : influenciable

suggestion [səgˈdʒɛstʃən, sə-] *n* **1** PROPOSAL : sugerencia *f* **2** INDICATION : indicio *m* **3** INSINUATION : insinuación *f*

suggestive [səgˈdʒɛstɪv, sə-] *adj* : insinuante — **suggestively** *adv*

suicidal [ˌsuːəˈsaɪdəl] *adj* : suicida

suicide [ˈsuːəˌsaɪd] *n* **1** : suicidio *m* (acto) **2** : suicida *mf* (persona)

suit[1] [ˈsuːt] *vt* **1** ADAPT : adaptar **2** BEFIT : convenir a, ser apropiado a **3** BECOME : favorecer, quedarle bien (a alguien) <the dress suits you : el vestido te queda bien> **4** PLEASE : agradecer, satisfacer, convenirle bien (a alguien) <does Friday suit you? : ¿le conviene el viernes?> <suit yourself! : ¡como quieras!>

suit[2] *n* **1** LAWSUIT : pleito *m,* litigio *m* **2** : traje *m* (ropa) **3** : palo *m* (de naipes)

suitability [ˌsuːt̬əˈbɪlət̬i] *n* : idoneidad *f,* lo apropiado

suitable [ˈsuːt̬əbəl] *adj* : apropiado, idóneo — **suitably** [-bli] *adv*

suitcase [ˈsuːtˌkeɪs] *n* : maleta *f,* valija *f,* petaca *f Mex*

suite [ˈswiːt, *for 2 also* ˈsuːt] *n* **1** : suite *f* (de habitaciones) **2** SET : juego *m* (de muebles)

suitor [ˈsuːt̬ər] *n* : pretendiente *m*

sulfur [ˈsʌlfər] *n* : azufre *m*

sulfuric acid [ˌsʌlˈfjʊrɪk] *adj* : ácido *m* sulfúrico

sulfurous [ˌsʌlˈfjʊrəs, ˈsʌlfərəs, ˈsʌlfjə-] *adj* : sulfuroso

sulk[1] [ˈsʌlk] *vi* : estar de mal humor, enfurruñarse *fam*

sulk[2] *n* : mal humor *m*

sulky [ˈsʌlki] *adj* **sulkier; -est** : malhumorado, taimado *Chile*

sullen [ˈsʌlən] *adj* **1** MOROSE : hosco, taciturno **2** DREARY : sombrío, deprimente

sullenly [ˈsʌlənli] *adv* **1** MOROSELY : hoscamente **2** GLOOMILY : sombríamente

sully [ˈsʌli] *vt* **sullied; sullying** : manchar, empañar

sultan [ˈsʌltən] *n* : sultán *m*

sultry [ˈsʌltri] *adj* **sultrier; -est 1** : bochornoso <sultry weather : tiempo sofocante, tiempo bochornoso> **2** SENSUAL : sensual, seductor

sum[1] [ˈsʌm] *vt* **summed; summing 1** : sumar (números) **2** → **sum up**

sum[2] *n* **1** AMOUNT : suma *f,* cantidad *f* **2** TOTAL : suma *f,* total *f* **3** : suma *f,* adición *f* (en matemáticas)

sumac [ˈʃuːˌmæk, ˈsuː-] *n* : zumaque *m*

summarize [ˈsʌməˌraɪz] *v* **-rized; -rizing** : resumir, compendiar

summary[1] [ˈsʌməri] *adj* **1** CONCISE : breve, conciso **2** IMMEDIATE : inmediato <a summary dismissal : un despido inmediato>

summary[2] *n, pl* **-ries** : resumen *m,* compendio *m*

summer [ˈsʌmər] *n* : verano *m*

summery [ˈsʌməri] *adj* : veraniego

summit [ˈsʌmət] *n* **1** : cumbre *f,* cima *f* (de una montaña) **2** *or* **summit conference** : cumbre *f*

summon [ˈsʌmən] *vt* **1** CALL : convocar (una reunión, etc.), llamar (a una persona) **2** : citar (en derecho) **3 to summon up** : armarse de (valor, etc.) <to summon up one's strength : reunir fuerzas>

summons [ˈsʌmənz] *n, pl* **summonses 1** SUBPOENA : citación *f,* citatorio *m Mex* **2** CALL : llamada *f,* llamamiento *m*

sumptuous [ˈsʌmptʃʊəs] *adj* : suntuoso

sum up *vt* **1** SUMMARIZE : resumir **2** EVALUATE : evaluar — *vi* : recapitular

sun[1] ['sʌn] *vt* **sunned; sunning 1** : poner al sol **2 to sun oneself** : asolearse, tomar el sol

sun[2] *n* **1** : sol *m* **2** SUNSHINE : luz *f* del sol

sunbeam ['sʌn,bi:m] *n* : rayo *m* de sol

sunblock ['sʌn,blɑk] *n* : filtro *m* solar

sunburn[1] ['sʌn,bərn] *vi* **-burned** [-,bərnd] *or* **-burnt** [-,bərnt]; **-burning** : quemarse por el sol

sunburn[2] ['sʌn,bərn] *n* : quemadura *f* de sol

sundae ['sʌndi] *n* : sundae *m*

Sunday ['sʌn,deɪ, -di] *n* : domingo *m*

sundial ['sʌn,daɪl] *n* : reloj *m* de sol

sundown ['sʌn,daʊn] → **sunset**

sundries ['sʌndriz] *npl* : artículos *mpl* diversos

sundry ['sʌndri] *adj* : varios, diversos

sunflower ['sʌn,flaʊər] *n* : girasol *m,* mirasol *m*

sung → **sing**

sunglasses ['sʌn,glæsəz] *npl* : gafas *fpl* de sol, lentes *mpl* de sol

sunk → **sink**[1]

sunken ['sʌŋkən] *adj* : hundido

sunlight ['sʌn,laɪt] *n* : sol *m,* luz *f* del sol

sunny ['sʌni] *adj* **sunnier; -est** : soleado

sunrise ['sʌn,raɪz] *n* : salida *f* del sol

sunset ['sʌn,sɛt] *n* : puesta *f* del sol

sunshine ['sʌn,ʃaɪn] *n* : sol *m,* luz *f* del sol

sunspot ['sʌn,spɑt] *n* : mancha *f* solar

sunstroke ['sʌn,stro:k] *n* : insolación *f*

suntan ['sʌn,tæn] *n* : bronceado *m*

sup ['sʌp] *vi* **supped; supping** : cenar

super ['su:pər] *adj* : súper <super! : ¡fantástico!>

superabundance [,su:pərə'bʌndənts] *n* : superabundancia *f*

superb [sʊ'pərb] *adj* : magnífico, espléndido — **superbly** *adv*

supercilious [,su:pər'sɪliəs] *adj* : altivo, altanero, desdeñoso

supercomputer ['su:pərkəm,pju:tər] *n* : supercomputadora *f*

superficial [,su:pər'fɪʃəl] *adj* : superficial — **superficially** *adv*

superfluous [sʊ'pərflʊəs] *adj* : superfluo

superhighway ['su:pər,haɪ,weɪ, ,su:pər'-] *n* : autopista *f*

superhuman [,su:pər'*h*ju:mən] *adj* **1** SUPERNATURAL : sobrenatural **2** HERCULEAN : sobrehumano

superimpose [,su:pərɪm'po:z] *vt* **-posed; -posing** : superponer, sobreponer

superintend [,su:pərɪn'tɛnd] *vt* : supervisar

superintendent [,su:pərɪn'tɛndənt] *n* : portero *m,* -ra *f* (de un edificio); director *m,* -tora *f* (de una escuela, etc.); superintendente *mf* (de policía)

superior[1] [sʊ'pɪriər] *adj* **1** BETTER : superior **2** HAUGHTY : altivo, altanero

superior[2] *n* : superior *m*

superiority [sʊ,pɪri'ɔrəti] *n, pl* **-ties** : superioridad *f*

superlative[1] [sʊ'pərlətɪv] *adj* **1** : superlativo (en gramática) **2** SUPREME : supremo **3** EXCELLENT : excelente, excepcional

superlative[2] *n* : superlativo *m*

supermarket ['su:pər,mɑrkət] *n* : supermercado *m*

supernatural [,su:pər'nætʃərəl] *adj* : sobrenatural

supernaturally [,su:pər'nætʃərəli] *adv* : de manera sobrenatural

superpower ['su:pər,paʊər] *n* : superpotencia *f*

supersede [,su:pər'si:d] *vt* **-seded; -seding** : suplantar, reemplazar, sustituir

supersonic [,su:pər'sɑnɪk] *adj* : supersónico

superstition [,su:pər'stɪʃən] *n* : superstición *f*

superstitious [,su:pər'stɪʃəs] *adj* : supersticioso

superstructure ['su:pər,strʌktʃər] *n* : superestructura *f*

supervise ['su:pər,vaɪz] *vt* **-vised; -vising** : supervisar, dirigir

supervision [,su:pər'vɪʒən] *n* : supervisión *f,* dirección *f*

supervisor ['su:pər,vaɪzər] *n* : supervisor *m,* -sora *f*

supervisory [,su:pər'vaɪzəri] *adj* : de supervisor

supine [sʊ'paɪn] *adj* **1** : en decúbito supino, en decúbito dorsal **2** ABJECT, INDIFFERENT : indiferente, apático

supper ['sʌpər] *n* : cena *f,* comida *f*

supplant [sə'plænt] *vt* : suplantar

supple ['sʌpəl] *adj* **-pler; -plest** : flexible

supplement[1] ['sʌplə,mɛnt] *vt* : complementar, completar

supplement[2] ['sʌpləmənt] *n* **1** : complemento *m* <dietary supplement : complemento alimenticio> **2** : suplemento *m* (de un libro o periódico)

supplementary [,sʌplə'mɛntəri] *adj* : suplementario

supplicate ['sʌplə,keɪt] *v* **-cated; -cating** *vi* : rezar — *vt* : suplicar

supplier [sə'plaɪər] *n* : proveedor *m,* -dora *f;* abastecedor *m,* -dora *f*

supply[1] [sə'plaɪ] *vt* **-plied; -plying** : suministrar, proveer de, proporcionar

supply[2] *n, pl* **-plies 1** PROVISION : provisión *f,* suministro *m* <supply and demand : la oferta y la demanda> **2** STOCK : reserva *f,* existencias *fpl* (de un negocio) **3 supplies** *npl* PROVISIONS : provisiones *fpl,* víveres *mpl,* despensa *f*

support[1] [sə'port] *vt* **1** BACK : apoyar, respaldar **2** MAINTAIN : mantener, sostener, sustentar **3** PROP UP **:** sostener, apoyar, apuntalar, soportar

support² *n* **1 :** apoyo *m* (moral), ayuda *f* (económica) **2** PROP **:** soporte *m,* apoyo *m*

supporter [sə'portər] *n* **:** partidario *m,* -ria *f*

suppose [sə'po:z] *vt* **-posed; -posing 1** ASSUME **:** suponer, imaginarse **2** BELIEVE **:** suponer, creer **3 to be supposed to :** tener que, deber

supposition [ˌsʌpə'zɪʃən] *n* **:** suposición *f*

suppository [sə'pɑzəˌtori] *n, pl* **-ries :** supositorio *m*

suppress [sə'prɛs] *vt* **1** SUBDUE **:** sofocar, suprimir, reprimir (una rebelión, etc.) **2 :** suprimir, ocultar (información) **3** REPRESS **:** reprimir, contener <to suppress a yawn **:** reprimir un bostezo>

suppression [sə'prɛʃən] *n* **1** SUBDUING **:** represión *f* **2 :** supresión *f* (de información) **3** REPRESSION **:** represión *f,* inhibición *f*

supremacy [sʊ'prɛməsi] *n, pl* **-cies :** supremacía *f*

supreme [sʊ'pri:m] *adj* **:** supremo

Supreme Being *n* **:** Ser *m* Supremo

supremely [sʊ'pri:mli] *adv* **:** totalmente, sumamente

surcharge ['sərˌtʃɑrdʒ] *n* **:** recargo *m*

sure¹ ['ʃʊr] *adv* **1** ALL RIGHT **:** por supuesto, claro **2** *(used as an intensifier)* <it sure is hot! **:** ¡hace tanto calor!> <she sure is pretty! **:** ¡qué linda es!>

sure² *adj* **surer; -est :** seguro <to be sure about something **:** estar seguro de algo> <a sure sign **:** una clara señal> <for sure **:** seguro, con seguridad>

surely ['ʃʊrli] *adv* **1** CERTAINLY **:** seguramente **2** (*used as an intensifier*) <you surely don't mean that! **:** ¡no me digas que estás hablando en serio!>

sureness ['ʃʊrnəs] *n* **:** certeza *f,* seguridad *f*

surety ['ʃʊrəti] *n, pl* **-ties :** fianza *f,* garantía *f*

surf ['sərf] *n* **1** WAVES **:** oleaje *m* **2** FOAM **:** espuma *f*

surface¹ ['sərfəs] *v* **-faced; -facing** *vi* **:** salir a la superficie — *vt* **:** revestir (una carretera)

surface² *n* **1 :** superficie *f* **2 on the surface :** en apariencia

surfboard ['sərfˌbord] *n* **:** tabla *f* de surf, tabla *f* de surfing

surfeit ['sərfət] *n* **:** exceso *m*

surfing ['sərfɪŋ] *n* **:** surf *m,* surfing *m*

surge¹ ['sərdʒ] *vi* **surged; surging 1 :** hincharse (dícese del mar), levantarse (dícese de las olas) **2** SWARM **:** salir en tropel (dícese de la gente, etc.)

surge² *n* **1 :** oleaje *m* (del mar), oleada *f* (de gente) **2** FLUSH **:** arranque *m,* arrebato *m* (de ira, etc.) **3** INCREASE **:** aumento *m* (súbito)

surgeon ['sərdʒən] *n* **:** cirujano *m,* -na *f*

surgery ['sərdʒəri] *n, pl* **-geries :** cirugía *f*

surgical ['sərdʒɪkəl] *adj* **:** quirúrgico — **surgically** [-kli] *adv*

surly ['sərli] *adj* **surlier; -est :** hosco, arisco

surmise¹ [sər'maɪz] *vt* **-mised; -mising :** conjeturar, suponer, concluir

surmise² *n* **:** conjetura *f*

surmount [sər'maʊnt] *vt* **1** OVERCOME **:** superar, vencer, salvar **2** CLIMB **:** escalar **3** CAP, TOP **:** coronar

surname ['sərˌneɪm] *n* **:** apellido *m*

surpass [sər'pæs] *vt* **:** superar, exceder, rebasar, sobrepasar

surplus ['sərˌplʌs] *n* **:** excedente *m,* sobrante *m,* superávit *m* (de dinero)

surprise¹ [sə'praɪz, sər-] *vt* **-prised; -prising :** sorprender

surprise² *n* **:** sorpresa *f* <to take by surprise **:** sorprender>

surprising [sə'praɪzɪŋ, sər-] *adj* **:** sorprendente — **surprisingly** *adv*

surrender¹ [sə'rɛndər] *vt* **1 :** entregar, rendir **2 to surrender oneself :** entregarse — *vi* **:** rendirse

surrender² *n* **:** rendición *m* (de una ciudad, etc.), entrega *f* (de posesiones)

surreptitious [ˌsərəp'tɪʃəs] *adj* **:** subrepticio — **surreptitiously** *adv*

surrogate ['sərəgət, -ˌgeɪt] *n* **:** sustituto *m*

surround [sə'raʊnd] *vt* **:** rodear

surroundings [sə'raʊndɪŋz] *npl* **:** ambiente *m,* entorno *m*

surveillance [sər'veɪlənts, -'veɪljənts, -'veɪənts] *n* **:** vigilancia *f*

survey¹ [sər'veɪ] *vt* **-veyed; -veying 1 :** medir (un terreno) **2** EXAMINE **:** inspeccionar, examinar, revisar **3** POLL **:** hacer una encuesta de, sondear

survey² ['sərˌveɪ] *n, pl* **-veys 1** INSPECTION **:** inspección *f,* revisión *f* **2 :** medición *f* (de un terreno) **3** POLL **:** encuesta *f,* sondeo *m*

surveyor [sər'veɪər] *n* **:** agrimensor *m,* -sora *f*

survival [sər'vaɪvəl] *n* **:** supervivencia *f,* sobrevivencia *f*

survive [sər'vaɪv] *v* **-vived; -viving** *vi* **:** sobrevivir — *vt* OUTLIVE **:** sobrevivir a

survivor [sər'vaɪvər] *n* **:** superviviente *mf,* sobreviviente *mf*

susceptibility [səˌsɛptə'bɪləti] *n, pl* **-ties :** vulnerabilidad *f,* propensión *f* (a enfermedades, etc.)

susceptible [sə'sɛptəbəl] *adj* **1** VULNERABLE **:** vulnerable, sensible <susceptible to flattery **:** sensible a halagos> **2** PRONE **:** propenso <susceptible to colds **:** propenso a resfriarse>

suspect¹ [sə'spɛkt] *vt* **1** DISTRUST **:** dudar de **2 :** sospechar (algo), sospechar de (una persona) **3** IMAGINE, THINK **:** imaginarse, creer

suspect[2] [ˈsʌs͵pɛkt, səˈspɛkt] *adj* : sospechoso, dudoso, cuestionable

suspect[3] [ˈsʌs͵pɛkt] *n* : sospechoso *m*, -sa *f*

suspend [səˈspɛnd] *vt* : suspender

suspenders [səˈspɛndərz] *npl* : tirantes *mpl*

suspense [səˈspɛn*t*s] *n* : incertidumbre *f*, suspenso *m* (en una película, etc.)

suspenseful [səˈspɛn*t*sfəl] *adj* : de suspenso

suspension [səˈspɛntʃən] *n* : suspensión *f*

suspicion [səˈspɪʃən] *n* **1** : sospecha *f* **2** TRACE : pizca *f*, atisbo *m*

suspicious [səˈspɪʃəs] *adj* **1** QUESTIONABLE : sospechoso, dudoso **2** DISTRUSTFUL : suspicaz, desconfiado

suspiciously [səˈspɪʃəsli] *adv* : de modo sospechoso, con recelo

sustain [səˈsteɪn] *vt* **1** NOURISH : sustentar **2** PROLONG : sostener **3** SUFFER : sufrir **4** SUPPORT, UPHOLD : apoyar, respaldar, sostentar

sustenance [ˈsʌstənən*t*s] *n* **1** NOURISHMENT : sustento *m* **2** SUPPORT : sostén *m*

svelte [ˈsfɛlt] *adj* : esbelto

swab[1] [ˈswɑb] *vt* **swabbed; swabbing** **1** CLEAN : lavar, limpiar **2** : aplicar a (con hisopo)

swab[2] *n or* **cotton swab** : hisopo *m* (para aplicar medicinas, etc.)

swaddle [ˈswɑdəl] *vt* **-dled; -dling** [ˈswɑdəlɪŋ] : envolver (en pañales)

swagger[1] [ˈswægər] *vi* : pavonearse

swagger[2] *n* : pavoneo *m*

swallow[1] [ˈswɑloː] *vt* **1** : tragar (comida, etc.) **2** ENGULF : tragarse, envolver **3** REPRESS : tragarse (insultos, etc.) — *vi* : tragar

swallow[2] *n* **1** : golondrina *f* (pájaro) **2** GULP : trago *m*

swam → **swim**[1]

swamp[1] [ˈswɑmp] *vt* : inundar

swamp[2] *n* : pantano *m*, ciénaga *f*

swampy [ˈswɑmpi] *adj* **swampier; -est** : pantanoso, cenagoso

swan [ˈswɑn] *n* : cisne *f*

swap[1] [ˈswɑp] *vt* **swapped; swapping** : cambiar, intercambiar <to swap places : cambiarse de sitio>

swap[2] *n* : cambio *m*, intercambio *m*

swarm[1] [ˈswɔrm] *vi* : enjambrar

swarm[2] *n* : enjambre *m*

swarthy [ˈswɔrði, -θi] *adj* **swarthier; -est** : moreno

swashbuckling [ˈswɑʃ͵bʌklɪŋ] *adj* : de aventurero

swat[1] [ˈswɑt] *vt* **swatted; swatting** : aplastar (un insecto), darle una palmada (a alguien)

swat[2] *n* : palmada *f* (con la mano), golpe *m* (con un objeto)

swatch [ˈswɑtʃ] *n* : muestra *f*

swath [ˈswɑθ, ˈswɔθ] *or* **swathe** [ˈswɑð, ˈswɔð, ˈsweɪð] *n* : franja *f* (de grano segado)

swathe [ˈswɑð, ˈswɔð, ˈsweɪð] *vt* **swathed; swathing** : envolver

swatter [ˈswɑtər] → **flyswatter**

sway[1] [ˈsweɪ] *vi* : balancearse, mecerse — *vt* INFLUENCE : influir en, convencer

sway[2] *n* **1** SWINGING : balanceo *m* **2** INFLUENCE : influjo *m*

swear [ˈswær] *v* **swore** [ˈswor]; **sworn** [ˈsworn]; **swearing** *vi* **1** VOW : jurar **2** CURSE : decir palabrotas — *vt* : jurar

swearword [ˈswær͵wərd] *n* : mala palabra *f*, palabrota *f*

sweat[1] [ˈswɛt] *vi* **sweat** *or* **sweated; sweating** **1** PERSPIRE : sudar, transpirar **2** OOZE : rezumar **3 to sweat over** : sudar la gota gorda por

sweat[2] *n* : sudor *m*, transpiración *f*

sweater [ˈswɛtər] *n* : suéter *m*

sweatshirt [ˈswɛt͵ʃərt] *n* : sudadera *f*

sweaty [ˈswɛti] *adj* **sweatier; -est** : sudoroso, sudado, transpirado

Swede [ˈswiːd] *n* : sueco *m*, -ca *f*

Swedish[1] [ˈswiːdɪʃ] *adj* : sueco

Swedish[2] *n* **1** : sueco *m* (idioma) **2 the Swedish** *npl* : los suecos

sweep[1] [ˈswiːp] *v* **swept** [ˈswɛpt]; **sweeping** *vt* **1** : barrer (el suelo, etc.), limpiar (suciedad, etc.) <he swept the books aside : apartó los libros de un manotazo> **2** *or* **to sweep through** : extenderse por (dícese del fuego, etc.), azotar (dícese de una tormenta) — *vi* **1** : barrer, limpiar **2** : extenderse (en una curva), describir una curva <the sun swept across the sky : el sol describía una curva en el cielo>

sweep[2] *n* **1** : barrido *m*, barrida *f* (con una escoba) **2** : movimiento *m* circular **3** SCOPE : alcance *m*

sweeper [ˈswiːpər] *n* : barrendero *m*, -ra *f*

sweeping [ˈswiːpɪŋ] *adj* **1** WIDE : amplio (dícese de un movimiento) **2** EXTENSIVE : extenso, radical **3** INDISCRIMINATE : indiscriminado, demasiado general **4** OVERWHELMING : arrollador, aplastante

sweepstakes [ˈswiːp͵steɪks] *ns & pl* **1** : carrera *f* (en que el ganador se lleva el premio entero) **2** LOTTERY : lotería *f*

sweet[1] [ˈswiːt] *adj* **1** : dulce <sweet desserts : postres dulces> **2** FRESH : fresco **3** : sin sal (dícese de la mantequilla, etc.) **4** PLEASANT : dulce, agradable **5** DEAR : querido

sweet[2] *n* : dulce *m*

sweeten [ˈswiːtən] *vt* : endulzar

sweetener [ˈswiːtənər] *n* : endulzante *m*

sweetheart [ˈswiːt͵hɑrt] *n* : novio *m*, -via *f* <thanks, sweetheart : gracias, cariño>

sweetly [ˈswiːtli] *adv* : dulcemente

sweetness [ˈswiːtnəs] *n* : dulzura *f*

sweet potato *n* : batata *f*, boniato *m*

swell[1] [ˈswɛl] *vi* **swelled; swelled** *or* **swollen** [ˈswoːlən, ˈswʌl-]; **swelling** **1** *or* **to swell up** : hincharse <her

ankle swelled : se le hinchó el tobillo> 2 *or* **to swell out** : inflarse, hincharse (dícese de las velas, etc.) 3 INCREASE : aumentar, crecer

swell[2] *n* **1** : oleaje *m* (del mar) **2** → **swelling**

swelling [ˈswɛlɪŋ] *n* : hinchazón *f*

swelter [ˈswɛltər] *vi* : sofocarse de calor

swept → **sweep**[1]

swerve[1] [ˈswərv] *vi* **swerved; swerving** : virar bruscamente

swerve[2] *n* : viraje *m* brusco

swift[1] [ˈswɪft] *adj* **1** FAST : rápido, veloz **2** SUDDEN : repentino, súbito — **swiftly** *adv*

swift[2] *n* : vencejo *m* (pájaro)

swiftness [ˈswɪftnəs] *n* : rapidez *f,* velocidad *f*

swig[1] [ˈswɪg] *vi* **swigged; swigging** : tomar a tragos, beber a tragos

swig[2] *n* : trago *m*

swill[1] [ˈswɪl] *vt* : chupar, beber a tragos grandes

swill[2] *n* **1** SLOP : bazofia *f* **2** GARBAGE : basura *f*

swim[1] [ˈswɪm] *vi* **swam** [ˈswæm]; **swum** [ˈswʌm]; **swimming 1** : nadar **2** FLOAT : flotar **3** REEL : dar vueltas <his head was swimming : la cabeza le daba vueltas>

swim[2] *n* : baño *m,* chapuzón *m* <to go for a swim : ir a nadar>

swimmer [ˈswɪmər] *n* : nadador *m,* -dora *f*

swindle[1] [ˈswɪndəl] *vt* **-dled; -dling** : estafar, timar

swindle[2] *n* : estafa *f,* timo *m fam*

swindler [ˈswɪndələr] *n* : estafador *m,* -dora *f;* timador *m,* -dora *f*

swine [ˈswaɪn] *ns & pl* : cerdo *m,* -da *f*

swing[1] [ˈswɪŋ] *v* **swung** [ˈswʌŋ]; **swinging** *vt* **1** : describir una curva con <he swung the ax at the tree : le dio al arbol con el hacha> **2** : balancear (los brazos, etc.), hacer oscilar **3** SUSPEND : colgar — *vi* **1** SWAY : balancearse (dícese de los brazos, etc.), oscilar (dícese de un objeto), columpiarse, mecerse (en un columpio) **2** SWIVEL : girar (en un pivote) <the door swung shut : la puerta se cerró> **3** CHANGE : virar, cambiar (dícese de las opiniones, etc.)

swing[2] *n* **1** SWINGING : vaivén *m,* balanceo *m* **2** CHANGE, SHIFT : viraje *m,* movimiento *m* **3** : columpio *m* (para niños) **4 to take a swing at someone** : intentar pegarle a alguien

swipe[1] [ˈswaɪp] *vt* **swiped; swiping 1** STRIKE : dar, pegar (con un movimiento amplio) **2** WIPE : limpiar **3** STEAL : birlar *fam,* robar

swipe[2] *n* BLOW : golpe *m*

swirl[1] [ˈswərl] *vi* : arremolinarse

swirl[2] *n* **1** EDDY : remolino *m* **2** SPIRAL : espiral *f*

swish[1] [ˈswɪʃ] *vt* : mover (produciendo un sonido) <she swished her skirt : movía la falda> — *vi* : moverse (produciendo un sonido) <the cars swished by : se oían pasar los coches>

swish[2] *n* : silbido *m* (de un látigo, etc.), susurro *m* (de agua), crujido *m* (de ropa, etc.)

Swiss [ˈswɪs] *n* : suizo *m,* -za *f* — **Swiss** *adj*

swiss chard *n* : acelga *f*

switch[1] [ˈswɪtʃ] *vt* **1** LASH, WHIP : azotar **2** CHANGE : cambiar de **3** EXCHANGE : intercambiar **4 to switch on** : encender, prender **5 to switch off** : apagar — *vi* **1** : moverse de un lado al otro **2** CHANGE : cambiar **3** SWAP : intercambiarse

switch[2] *n* **1** WHIP : vara *f* **2** CHANGE, SHIFT : cambio *m* **3** : interruptor *m,* llave *f* (de la luz, etc.)

switchboard [ˈswɪtʃˌbord] *n* : conmutador *m,* centralita *f*

swivel[1] [ˈswɪvəl] *vi* **-veled** *or* **-velled; -veling** *or* **-velling** : girar (sobre un pivote)

swivel[2] *n* : base *f* giratoria

swollen → **swell**[1]

swoon[1] [ˈswuːn] *vi* : desvanecerse, desmayarse

swoon[2] *n* : desvanecimiento *m,* desmayo *m*

swoop[1] [ˈswuːp] *vi* : abatirse (dícese de las aves), descender en picada (dícese de un avión)

swoop[2] *n* : descenso *m* en picada

sword [ˈsɔrd] *n* : espada *f*

swordfish [ˈsɔrdˌfɪʃ] *n* : pez *m* espada

swore, sworn → **swear**

swum → **swim**[1]

swung → **swing**[1]

sycamore [ˈsɪkəˌmor] *n* : sicomoro *m*

sycophant [ˈsɪkəfənt, -ˌfænt] *n* : adulador *m,* -dora *f*

syllabic [səˈlæbɪk] *adj* : silábico

syllable [ˈsɪləbəl] *n* : sílaba *f*

syllabus [ˈsɪləbəs] *n, pl* **-bi** [-ˌbaɪ] *or* **-buses** : programa *m* (de estudios)

symbol [ˈsɪmbəl] *n* : símbolo *m*

symbolic [sɪmˈbɑlɪk] *adj* : simbólico — **symbolically** [-kli] *adv*

symbolism [ˈsɪmbəˌlɪzəm] *n* : simbolismo *m*

symbolize [ˈsɪmbəˌlaɪz] *vt* **-ized; -izing** : simbolizar

symmetrical [səˈmɛtrɪəl] *or* **symmetric** [-trɪk] *adj* : simétrico — **symmetrically** [-trɪkli] *adv*

symmetry [ˈsɪmətri] *n, pl* **-tries** : simetría *f*

sympathetic [ˌsɪmpəˈθɛtɪk] *adj* **1** PLEASING : agradable **2** RECEPTIVE : receptivo, favorable **3** COMPASSIONATE, UNDERSTANDING : comprensivo, compasivo

sympathetically [ˌsɪmpəˈθɛtɪkli] *adv* : con compasión, con comprensión

sympathize ['sɪmpə,θaɪz] *vi* **-thized; -thizing :** compadecer <I sympathize with you : te compadezco>
sympathy ['sɪmpəθi] *n, pl* **-thies 1** COMPASSION **:** compasión *f* **2** UNDERSTANDING **:** comprensión *f* **3** AGREEMENT **:** solidaridad *f* <in sympathy with : de acuerdo con> **4** CONDOLENCES **:** pésame *m,* condolencias *fpl*
symphonic [sɪm'fɑnɪk] *adj* **:** sinfónico
symphony ['sɪmpfəni] *n, pl* **-nies :** sinfonía *f*
symposium [sɪm'po:ziəm] *n, pl* **-sia** [-ziə] *or* **-siums :** simposio *m*
symptom ['sɪmptəm] *n* **:** síntoma *m*
symptomatic [,sɪmptə'mæṭɪk] *adj* **:** sintomático
synagogue ['sɪnə,gɑg, -,gɔg] *n* **:** sinagoga *f*
synchronize ['sɪŋkrə,naɪz, 'sɪn-] *v* **-nized; -nizing** *vi* **:** estar sincronizado — *vt* **:** sincronizar
syncopate ['sɪŋkə,peɪt, 'sɪn-] *vt* **-pated; -pating :** sincopar
syncopation [,sɪŋkə'peɪʃən, ,sɪn-] *n* **:** síncopa *f*
syndicate¹ ['sɪndə,keɪt] *vi* **-cated; -cating :** formar una asociación
syndicate² ['sɪndɪkət] *n* **:** asociación *f,* agrupación *f*
syndrome ['sɪn,dro:m] *n* **:** síndrome *m*
synonym ['sɪnə,nɪm] *n* **:** sinónimo *m*
synonymous [sə'nɑnəməs] *adj* **:** sinónimo
synopsis [sə'nɑpsɪs] *n, pl* **-opses** [-,si:z] **:** sinopsis *f*
syntax ['sɪn,tæks] *n* **:** sintaxis *f*
synthesis ['sɪnθəsɪs] *n, pl* **-theses** [-,si:z] **:** síntesis *f*
synthesize ['sɪnθə,saɪz] *vt* **-sized; -sizing :** sintetizar
synthetic¹ [sɪn'θɛṭɪk] *adj* **:** sintético, artificial — **synthetically** [-ṭɪkli] *adv*
synthetic² *n* **:** producto *m* sintético
syphilis ['sɪfələs] *n* **:** sífilis *f*
Syrian ['sɪriən] *n* **:** sirio *m,* -ria *f* — **Syrian** *adj*
syringe [sə'rɪndʒ, 'sɪrɪndʒ] *n* **:** jeringa *f,* jeringuilla *f*
syrup ['sərəp, 'sɪrəp] *n* **:** jarabe *m,* almíbar *m* (de azúcar y agua)
system ['sɪstəm] *n* **1** METHOD **:** sistema *m,* método *m* **2** APPARATUS **:** sistema *m,* instalación *f,* aparato *m* <electrical system : instalación eléctrica> <digestive system : aparato digestivo> **3** BODY **:** organismo *m,* cuerpo *m* <diseases that affect the whole system : enfermedades que afectan el organismo entero> **4** NETWORK **:** red *f*
systematic [,sɪstə'mæṭɪk] *adj* **:** sistemático — **systematically** [-ṭɪkli] *adv*
systematize ['sɪstəmə,taɪz] *vt* **-tized; -tizing :** sistematizar
systemic [sɪs'tɛmɪk] *adj* **:** sistémico

T

t ['ti:] *n, pl* **t's** *or* **ts** ['ti:z] **:** vigésima letra del alfabeto inglés
tab ['tæb] *n* **1** FLAP, TAG **:** lengüeta *f* (de un sobre, una caja, etc.), etiqueta *f* (de ropa) **2** → **tabulator 3** BILL, CHECK **:** cuenta *f* **4 to keep tabs on :** tener bajo vigilancia
tabby ['tæbi] *n, pl* **-bies 1** *or* **tabby cat :** gato *m* atigrado **2 :** gata *f*
tabernacle ['tæbər,nækəl] *n* **:** tabernáculo *m*
table ['teɪbəl] *n* **1 :** mesa *f* <a table for two : una mesa para dos> **2** LIST **:** tabla *f* <multiplication table : tabla de multiplicar> **3 table of contents :** índice *m* de materias
tableau [tæ'blo:, 'tæ,-] *n, pl* **-leaux** [-'blo:z, -,blo:z] **:** retablo *m,* cuadro *m* vivo (en teatro)
tablecloth ['teɪbəl,klɔθ] *n* **:** mantel *m*
tablespoon ['teɪbəl,spu:n] *n* **1 :** cuchara *f* (de mesa) **2** → **tablespoonful**
tablespoonful ['teɪbəl,spu:n,fʊl] *n* **:** cucharada *f*
tablet ['tæblət] *n* **1** PLAQUE **:** placa *f* **2** PAD **:** bloc *m* (de papel) **3** PILL **:** tableta *f,* pastilla *f,* píldora *f* <an aspirin tablet : una tableta de aspirina>
table tennis *n* **:** tenis *m* de mesa
tableware ['teɪbəl,wær] *n* **:** vajillas *fpl,* cubiertos *mpl* (de mesa)
tabloid ['tæ,blɔɪd] *n* **:** tabloide *m*
taboo¹ [tə'bu:, tæ-] *adj* **:** tabú
taboo² *n* **:** tabú *m*
tabular ['tæbjələr] *adj* **:** tabular
tabulate ['tæbjə,leɪt] *vt* **-lated; -lating :** tabular
tabulator ['tæbjə,leɪṭər] *n* **:** tabulador *m*
tacit ['tæsɪt] *adj* **:** tácito, implícito — **tacitly** *adv*
taciturn ['tæsɪ,tərn] *adj* **:** taciturno
tack¹ ['tæk] *vt* **1 :** sujetar con tachuelas **2 to tack on** ADD **:** añadir, agregar
tack² *n* **1 :** tachuela *f* **2** COURSE **:** rumbo *m* <to change tack : cambiar de rumbo>
tackle¹ ['tækəl] *vt* **-led; -ling 1 :** taclear (en futbol americano) **2** CONFRONT **:** abordar, enfrentar, emprender (un problema, un trabajo, etc.)
tackle² *n* **1** EQUIPMENT, GEAR **:** equipo *m,* aparejo *m* **2 :** aparejo *m* (de un buque) **3 :** tacleada *f* (en futbol americano)
tacky ['tæki] *adj* **tackier; -est 1** STICKY **:** pegajoso **2** CHEAP, GAUDY **:** de mal gusto, naco *Mex*
tact ['tækt] *n* **:** tacto *m,* delicadeza *f,* discreción *f*

tactful [ˈtæktfəl] *adj* **:** discreto, diplomático, de mucho tacto

tactfully [ˈtæktfəli] *adv* **:** discretamente, con mucho tacto

tactic [ˈtæktɪk] *n* **:** táctica *f*

tactical [ˈtæktɪkəl] *adj* **:** táctico, estratégico

tactics [ˈtæktɪks] *ns & pl* **:** táctica *f,* estrategia *f*

tactile [ˈtæktəl, -ˌtaɪl] *adj* **:** táctil

tactless [ˈtæktləs] *adj* **:** indiscreto, poco delicado

tactlessly [ˈtæktləsli] *adv* **:** rudamente, sin tacto

tadpole [ˈtædˌpoːl] *n* **:** renacuajo *m*

taffeta [ˈtæfətə] *n* **:** tafetán *m,* tafeta *f Arg, Mex, Uru*

taffy [ˈtæfi] *n, pl* **-fies :** caramelo *m* de melaza, chicloso *m Mex*

tag[1] [ˈtæg] *v* **tagged; tagging** *vt* **1** LABEL **:** etiquetar **2** TAIL **:** seguir de cerca **3** TOUCH **:** tocar (en varios juegos) — *vi* **to tag along :** pegarse, acompañar

tag[2] *n* **1** LABEL **:** etiqueta *f* **2** SAYING **:** dicho *m,* refrán *m*

tail[1] [ˈteɪl] *vt* FOLLOW **:** seguir de cerca, pegarse

tail[2] *n* **1 :** cola *f,* rabo *m* (de un animal) **2 :** cola *f,* parte *f* posterior <a comet's tail : la cola de un cometa> **3 tails** *npl* **:** cruz *f* (de una moneda) <heads or tails : cara o cruz>

tailed [ˈteɪld] *adj* **:** que tiene cola

tailgate[1] [ˈteɪlˌgeɪt] *vi* **-gated; -gating :** seguir a un vehículo demasiado de cerca

tailgate[2] *n* **:** puerta *f* trasera (de un vehículo)

taillight [ˈteɪlˌlaɪt] *n* **:** luz *f* trasera (de un vehículo), calavera *f Mex*

tailor[1] [ˈteɪlər] *vt* **1 :** confeccionar o alterar (ropa) **2** ADAPT **:** adaptar, ajustar

tailor[2] *n* **:** sastre *m,* -tra *f*

tailpipe [ˈteɪlˌpaɪp] *n* **:** tubo *m* de escape

tailspin [ˈteɪlˌspɪn] *n* **:** barrena *f*

taint[1] [ˈteɪnt] *vt* **:** contaminar, corromper

taint[2] *n* **:** corrupción *f,* impureza *f*

take[1] [ˈteɪk] *v* **took** [ˈtʊk]; **taken** [ˈteɪkən]; **taking** *vt* **1** CAPTURE **:** capturar, apresar **2** GRASP **:** tomar, agarrar <to take the bull by the horns : tomar al toro por los cuernos> **3** CATCH **:** tomar, agarrar <taken by surprise : tomado por sorpresa> **4** CAPTIVATE **:** encantar, fascinar **5** INGEST **:** tomar, ingerir <take two pills : tome dos píldoras> **6** REMOVE **:** sacar, extraer <take an orange : saca una naranja> **7 :** tomar, coger (un tren, un autobús, etc.) **8** NEED, REQUIRE **:** tomar, requirir <these things take time : estas cosas toman tiempo> **9** BRING, CARRY **:** llevar, sacar, cargar <take them with you : llévalos contigo> <take the trash out : saca la basura> **10** BEAR, ENDURE **:** soportar, aguantar (dolores, etc.) **11** ACCEPT **:** aceptar (un cheque, etc.), seguir (consejos), asumir (la responsabilidad) **12** SUPPOSE **:** suponer <I take it that... : supongo que...> **13** (*indicating an action or an undertaking*) <to take a walk : dar un paseo> <to take a class : tomar una clase> **14 to take place** HAPPEN **:** tener lugar, suceder, ocurrir — *vi* **:** agarrar (dícese de un tinte), prender (dícese de una vacuna)

take[2] *n* **1** PROCEEDS **:** recaudación *f,* ingresos *mpl,* ganancias *fpl* **2 :** toma *f* (de un rodaje o una grabación)

take back *vt* **:** retirar (palabras, etc.)

take in *vt* **1 :** tomarle a, achicar (un vestido, etc.) **2** INCLUDE **:** incluir, abarcar **3** ATTEND **:** ir a <to take in a movie : ir al cine> **4** GRASP, UNDERSTAND **:** captar, entender **5** DECEIVE **:** engañar

takeoff [ˈteɪkˌɔf] *n* **1** PARODY **:** parodia *f* **2 :** despegue *m* (de un avión o cohete)

take off *vt* REMOVE **:** quitar <take off your hat : quítate el sombrero> — *vi* **1 :** despegar (dícese de un avión o un cohete) **2** LEAVE **:** irse, partir

take on *vt* **1** TACKLE **:** abordar, emprender (problemas, etc.) **2** ACCEPT **:** aceptar, encargarse de, asumir (una responsabilidad) **3** CONTRACT **:** contratar (trabajadores) **4** ASSUME **:** adoptar, asumir, adquirir <the neighborhood took on a dingy look : el barrio asumió una apariencia deprimente>

takeover [ˈteɪkˌoːvər] *n* **:** toma *f* (de poder o de control), adquisición *f* (de una empresa por otra)

take over *vt* **:** tomar el poder de, tomar las riendas de — *vi* **:** asumir el mando

taker [ˈteɪkər] *n* **:** persona *f* interesada <available to all takers : disponible a cuantos estén interesados>

take up *vt* **1** LIFT **:** levantar **2** SHORTEN **:** acortar (una falda, etc.) **3** BEGIN **:** empezar, dedicarse a (un pasatiempo, etc.) **4** OCCUPY **:** ocupar, llevar (tiempo, espacio) **5** PURSUE **:** volver a (una cuestión, un asunto) **6** CONTINUE **:** seguir con

talc [ˈtælk] *n* **:** talco *m*

talcum powder [ˈtælkəm] *n* **:** talco *m,* polvos *mpl* de talco

tale [ˈteɪl] *n* **1** ANECDOTE, STORY **:** cuento *m,* relato *m,* anécdota *f* **2** FALSEHOOD **:** cuento *m,* mentira *f*

talent [ˈtælənt] *n* **:** talento *m,* don *m*

talented [ˈtæləntəd] *adj* **:** talentoso

talisman [ˈtælɪsmən, -lɪz-] *n, pl* **-mans :** talismán *m*

talk[1] [ˈtɔk] *vi* **1 :** hablar <he talks for hours : se pasa horas hablando> **2** CHAT **:** charlar, platicar — *vt* **1** SPEAK **:** hablar <to talk French : hablar francés> <to talk business : hablar de negocios> **2** PERSUADE **:** influenciar, convencer <she talked me out of it : me convenció que no lo hiciera> **3**

to talk over DISCUSS : hablar de, discutir

talk[2] *n* **1** CONVERSATION : charla *f,* plática *f,* conversación *f* **2** GOSSIP, RUMOR : chisme *m,* rumores *mpl*

talkative [ˈtɔkətɪv] *adj* : locuaz, parlanchín, charlatán

talker [ˈtɔkər] *n* : conversador *m,* -dora *f;* hablador *m,* -dora *f*

tall [ˈtɔl] *adj* : alto <how tall is he? : ¿cuánto mide?>

tallness [ˈtɔlnəs] *n* HEIGHT : estatura *f* (de una persona), altura *f* (de un objeto)

tallow [ˈtæloː] *n* : sebo *m*

tally[1] [ˈtæli] *v* **-lied; -lying** *vt* RECKON : contar, hacer una cuenta de — *vi* MATCH : concordar, corresponder, cuadrar

tally[2] *n, pl* **-lies** : cuenta *f* <to keep a tally : llevar la cuenta>

talon [ˈtælən] *n* : garra *f* (de un ave de rapiña)

tambourine [ˌtæmbəˈriːn] *n* : pandero *m,* pandereta *f*

tame[1] [ˈteɪm] *vt* **tamed; taming** : domar, amansar, domesticar

tame[2] *adj* **tamer; -est 1** DOMESTICATED : domesticado, manso **2** DOCILE : manso, dócil **3** DULL : aburrido, soso

tamely [ˈteɪmli] *adv* : mansamente, dócilmente

tamer [ˈteɪmər] *n* : domador *m,* -dora *f*

tamp [ˈtæmp] *vt* : apisonar

tamper [ˈtæmpər] *vi* **to tamper with** : adulterar (una sustancia), forzar (un sello, una cerradura), falsear (documentos), manipular (una máquina)

tampon [ˈtæmˌpɑn] *n* : tampón *m*

tan[1] [ˈtæn] *v* **tanned; tanning** *vt* **1** : curtir (pieles) **2** : broncear — *vi* : broncearse

tan[2] *n* **1** SUNTAN : bronceado *m* <to get a tan : broncearse> **2** : color *m* canela, color *m* café con leche

tandem[1] [ˈtændəm] *adv or* **in tandem** : en tándem

tandem[2] *n* : tándem *m* (bicicleta)

tang [ˈtæŋ] *n* : sabor *m* fuerte

tangent [ˈtændʒənt] *n* : tangente *f* <to go off on a tangent : irse por la tangente>

tangerine [ˈtændʒəˌriːn, ˌtændʒəˈ-] *n* : mandarina *f*

tangible [ˈtændʒəbəl] *adj* : tangible, palpable — **tangibly** [-bli] *adv*

tangle[1] [ˈtæŋgəl] *v* **-gled; -gling** *vt* : enredar, enmarañar — *vi* : enredarse

tangle[2] *n* : enredo *m,* maraña *f*

tango[1] [ˈtæŋˌgoː] *vi* : bailar el tango

tango[2] *n, pl* **-gos** : tango *m*

tangy [ˈtæŋi] *adj* **tangier; -est** : que tiene un sabor fuerte

tank [ˈtæŋk] *n* : tanque *m,* depósito *m* <fuel tank : depósito de combustibles>

tankard [ˈtæŋkərd] *n* : jarra *f*

tanker [ˈtæŋkər] *n* : buque *m* cisterna, camión *m* cisterna, avión *m* cisterna <an oil tanker : un petrolero>

tanner [ˈtænər] *n* : curtidor *m,* -dora *f*

tannery [ˈtænəri] *n, pl* **-neries** : curtiduría *f,* tenería *f*

tannin [ˈtænən] *n* : tanino *m*

tantalize [ˈtæntəˌlaɪz] *vt* **-lized; -lizing** : tentar, atormentar (con algo inasequible)

tantalizing [ˈtæntəˌlaɪzɪŋ] *adj* : tentador, seductor

tantamount [ˈtæntəˌmaʊnt] *adj* : equivalente

tantrum [ˈtæntrəm] *n* : rabieta *f,* berrinche *m* <to throw a tantrum : hacer un berrinche>

tap[1] [ˈtæp] *vt* **tapped; tapping 1** : ponerle una espita a, sacar líquido de (un barril, un tanque, etc.) **2** : intervenir (una línea telefónica) **3** PAT, TOUCH : tocar, golpear ligeramente <he tapped me on the shoulder : me tocó en el hombro>

tap[2] *n* **1** FAUCET : llave *f,* grifo *m* <beer on tap : cerveza de barril> **2** : extracción *f* (de líquido) <a spinal tap : una punción lumbar> **3** PAT, TOUCH : golpecito *m,* toque *m*

tape[1] [ˈteɪp] *vt* **taped; taping 1** : sujetar o mendar con cinta adhesiva **2** RECORD : grabar

tape[2] *n* **1** : cinta *f* (adhesiva, magnética, etc.) **2** → **tape measure**

tape measure *n* : cinta *f* métrica

taper[1] [ˈteɪpər] *vi* **1** : estrecharse gradualmente <its tail tapers towards the tip : su cola va estrechándose hacia la punta> **2** *or* **to taper off** : disminuir gradualmente

taper[2] *n* **1** CANDLE : vela *f* larga y delgada **2** TAPERING : estrechamiento *m* gradual

tapestry [ˈtæpəstri] *n, pl* **-tries** : tapiz *m*

tapeworm [ˈteɪpˌwərm] *n* : solitaria *f,* tenia *f*

tapioca [ˌtæpiˈoːkə] *n* : tapioca *f*

tar[1] [ˈtɑr] *vt* **tarred; tarring** : alquitranar

tar[2] *n* : alquitrán *m,* brea *f,* chapopote *m Mex*

tarantula [təˈræntʃələ, -ˈræntələ] *n* : tarántula *f*

tardiness [ˈtɑrdinəs] *n* : tardanza *f,* retraso *m*

tardy [ˈtɑrdi] *adj* **-dier; -est** LATE : tardío, de retraso

target[1] [ˈtɑrgət] *vt* : fijar como objetivo, dirigir, destinar

target[2] *n* **1** : blanco *m* <target practice : tiro al blanco> **2** GOAL, OBJECTIVE : meta *f,* objetivo *m*

tariff [ˈtærɪf] *n* DUTY : tarifa *f,* arancel *m*

tarnish[1] [ˈtɑrnɪʃ] *vt* **1** DULL : deslustrar **2** SULLY : empañar, manchar (una reputación, etc.) — *vi* : deslustrarse

tarnish[2] *n* : deslustre *m*

tarpaulin [tɑrˈpɔlən, ˈtɑrpə-] *n* **:** lona *f* (impermeable)

tarry[1] [ˈtæri] *vi* **-ried; -rying :** demorarse, entretenerse

tarry[2] [ˈtɑri] *adj* **1 :** parecido al alquitrán **2 :** cubierto de alquitrán

tart[1] [ˈtɑrt] *adj* **1** SOUR **:** ácido, agrio **2** CAUSTIC **:** mordaz, acrimonioso — **tartly** *adv*

tart[2] *n* **:** tartaleta *f*

tartan [ˈtɑrtən] *n* **:** tartán *m*

tartar [ˈtɑrtər] *n* **1 :** tártaro *m* <tartar sauce : salsa tártara> **2 :** sarro *m* (dental)

tartness [ˈtɑrtnəs] *n* **1** SOURNESS **:** acidez *f* **2** ACRIMONY, SHARPNESS **:** mordacidad *f*, acrimonia *f*, acritud *f*

task [ˈtæsk] *n* **:** tarea *f*, trabajo *m*

taskmaster [ˈtæskˌmæstər] *n* **to be a hard taskmaster :** ser exigente, ser muy estricto

tassel [ˈtæsəl] *n* **:** borla *f*

taste[1] [ˈteɪst] *v* **tasted; tasting** *vt* **:** probar (alimentos), degustar, catar (vinos) <taste this soup : prueba esta sopa> — *vi* **:** saber <this tastes good : esto sabe bueno>

taste[2] *n* **1** SAMPLE **:** prueba *f*, bocado *m* (de comida), trago *m* (de bebidas) **2** FLAVOR **:** gusto *m*, sabor *m* **3 :** gusto *m* <she has good taste : tiene buen gusto> <in bad taste : de mal gusto>

taste bud *n* **:** papila *f* gustativa

tasteful [ˈteɪstfəl] *adj* **:** de buen gusto

tastefully [ˈteɪstfəli] *adv* **:** con buen gusto

tasteless [ˈteɪstləs] *adj* **1** FLAVORLESS **:** sin sabor, soso, insípido **2 :** de mal gusto <a tasteless joke : un chiste de mal gusto>

taster [ˈteɪstər] *n* **:** degustador *m*, -dora *f*; catador *m*, -dora *f* (de vinos)

tastiness [ˈteɪstinəs] *n* **:** lo sabroso

tasty [ˈteɪsti] *adj* **tastier; -est :** sabroso, gustoso

tatter [ˈtætər] *n* **1** SHRED **:** tira *f*, jirón *m* (de tela) **2 tatters** *npl* **:** andrajos *mpl*, harapos *mpl* <to be in tatters : estar por los suelos>

tattered [ˈtætərd] *adj* **:** andrajoso, en jirones

tattle [ˈtætəl] *vi* **-tled; -tling 1** CHATTER **:** parlotear *fam*, cotorrear *fam* **2 to tattle on someone :** acusar a alguien

tattletale [ˈtætəlˌteɪl] *n* **:** soplón *m*, -plona *f fam*

tattoo[1] [tæˈtuː] *vt* **:** tatuar

tattoo[2] *n* **:** tatuaje *m* <to get a tattoo : tatuarse>

taught → **teach**

taunt[1] [ˈtɔnt] *vt* MOCK **:** mofarse de, burlarse de

taunt[2] *n* **:** mofa *f*, burla *f*

Taurus [ˈtɔrəs] *n* **:** Tauro *mf*

taut [ˈtɔt] *adj* **:** tirante, tenso — **tautly** *adv*

tautness [ˈtɔtnəs] *n* **:** tirantez *f*, tensión *f*

tavern [ˈtævərn] *n* **:** taberna *f*

tawdry [ˈtɔdri] *adj* **-drier; -est :** chabacano, vulgar

tawny [ˈtɔni] *adj* **-nier; -est :** leonado

tax[1] [ˈtæks] *vt* **1 :** gravar, cobrar un impuesto sobre **2** CHARGE **:** acusar <they taxed him with neglect : fue acusado de incumplimiento> **3 to tax someone's strength :** ponerle a prueba las fuerzas (a alguien)

tax[2] *n* **1 :** impuesto *m*, tributo *m* **2** BURDEN **:** carga *f*

taxable [ˈtæksəbəl] *adj* **:** sujeto a un impuesto

taxation [tækˈseɪʃən] *n* **:** impuestos *mpl*

tax–exempt [ˈtæksɪgˈzɛmpt, -ɛg-] *adj* **:** libre de impuestos

taxi[1] [ˈtæksi] *vi* **taxied; taxiing** *or* **taxying; taxis** *or* **taxies 1 :** ir en taxi **2 :** rodar sobre la pista de aterrizaje (dícese de un avión)

taxi[2] *n, pl* **taxis :** taxi *m*, libre *m Mex*

taxicab [ˈtæksiˌkæb] → **taxi**[2]

taxidermist [ˈtæksəˌdərmɪst] *n* **:** taxidermista *mf*

taxidermy [ˈtæksəˌdərmi] *n* **:** taxidermia *f*

taxpayer [ˈtæksˌpeɪər] *n* **:** contribuyente *mf*, causante *mf Mex*

TB [ˌtiːˈbiː] → **tuberculosis**

tea [ˈtiː] *n* **1 :** té *m* (planta y bebida) **2 :** merienda *f*, té *m* (comida)

teach [ˈtiːtʃ] *v* **taught** [ˈtɔt]; **teaching** *vt* **:** enseñar, dar clases de <she teaches math : da clases de matemáticas> <she taught me everything I know : me enseñó todo lo que sé> — *vi* **:** enseñar, dar clases

teacher [ˈtiːtʃər] *n* **:** maestro *m*, -tra *f* (de enseñanza primaria); profesor *m*, -sora *f* (de enseñanza secundaria)

teaching [ˈtiːtʃɪŋ] *n* **:** enseñanza *f*

teacup [ˈtiːˌkʌp] *n* **:** taza *f* para té

teak [ˈtiːk] *n* **:** teca *f*

teakettle [ˈtiːˌkɛtəl] *n* **:** tetera *f*

teal [ˈtiːl] *n, pl* **teal** *or* **teals :** cerceta *f* (pato)

team[1] [ˈtiːm] *vi or* **to team up 1 :** formar un equipo (en deportes) **2** COLLABORATE **:** asociarse, juntarse, unirse

team[2] *adj* **:** de equipo

team[3] *n* **1 :** tiro *m* (de caballos), yunta *f* (de bueyes o mulas) **2 :** equipo *m* (en deportes, etc.)

teammate [ˈtiːmˌmeɪt] *n* **:** compañero *m*, -ra *f* de equipo

teamster [ˈtiːmstər] *n* **:** camionero *m*, -ra *f*

teamwork [ˈtiːmˌwərk] *n* **:** trabajo *m* en equipo, cooperación *f*

teapot [ˈtiːˌpɑt] *n* **:** tetera *f*

tear[1] [ˈtær] *v* **tore** [ˈtor]; **torn** [ˈtorn]; **tearing** *vt* **1** RIP **:** desgarrar, romper, rasgar (tela) <to tear to pieces : hacer pedazos> **2** *or* **to tear apart** DIVIDE **:** dividir **3** REMOVE **:** arrancar <torn from his family : arrancado de su familia> **4 to tear down :** derribar — *vi* **1** RIP **:** desgarrarse, romperse **2** RUSH

: ir a gran velocidad <she went tearing down the street : se fue como rayo por la calle>
tear[2] *n* : desgarradura *f,* rotura *f,* desgarro *m* (muscular)
tear[3] ['tɪr] *n* : lágrima *f*
teardrop ['tɪrˌdrɑp] → **tear**[3]
tearful ['tɪrfəl] *adj* : lloroso, triste — **tearfully** *adv*
tease[1] ['tiːz] *vt* **teased; teasing 1** MOCK : burlarse de, mofarse de **2** ANNOY : irritar, fastidiar
tease[2] *n* **1** TEASING : burla *f,* mofa *f* **2** : bromista *mf;* guasón *m,* -sona *f*
teaspoon ['tiːˌspuːn] *n* **1** : cucharita *f* **2** → **teaspoonful**
teaspoonful ['tiːˌspuːnˌfʊl] *n, pl* **-spoonfuls** [-ˌfʊlz] *or* **-spoonsful** [-ˌspuːnzˌfʊl] : cucharadita *f*
teat ['tiːt] *n* : tetilla *f*
technical ['tɛknɪkəl] *adj* : técnico — **technically** [-kli] *adv*
technicality [ˌtɛknə'kæləṯi] *n, pl* **-ties** : detalle *m* técnico
technician [tɛk'nɪʃən] *n* : técnico *m,* -ca *f*
technique [tɛk'niːk] *n* : técnica *f*
technological [ˌtɛknə'lɑdʒɪkəl] *adj* : tecnológico
technology [tɛk'nɑlədʒi] *n, pl* **-gies** : tecnología *f*
teddy bear ['tɛdi] *n* : oso *m* de peluche
tedious ['tiːdiəs] *adj* : aburrido, pesado, monótono — **tediously** *adv*
tediousness ['tiːdiəsnəs] *n* : lo aburrido, lo pesado
tedium ['tiːdiəm] *n* : tedio *m,* pesadez *f*
tee ['tiː] *n* : tee *mf*
teem ['tiːm] *vi* **to teem with** : estar repleto de, estar lleno de
teenage ['tiːnˌeɪdʒ] *or* **teenaged** [-eɪdʒd] *adj* : adolescente, de adolescencia
teenager ['tiːnˌeɪdʒər] *n* : adolescente *mf*
teens ['tiːnz] *npl* : adolescencia *f*
teepee → **tepee**
teeter[1] ['tiːṯər] *vi* : balancearse, tambalearse
teeter[2] *n or* **teeter–totter** ['tiːṯərˌtɑṯər] → **seesaw**
teeth → **tooth**
teethe ['tiːð] *vi* **teethed; teething** : formársele a uno los dientes <the baby's teething : le están saliendo los dientes al niño>
telecast[1] ['tɛləˌkæst] *vt* **-cast; -casting** : televisar, transmitir por televisión
telecast[2] *n* : transmisión *f* por televisión
telecommunication ['tɛləkəˌmjuːnə'keɪʃən] *n* : telecomunicación *f*
telegram ['tɛləˌgræm] *n* : telegrama *m*
telegraph[1] ['tɛləˌgræf] *v* : telegrafiar
telegraph[2] *n* : telégrafo *m*
telepathic [ˌtɛlə'pæθɪk] *adj* : telepático — **telepathically** [-θɪkli] *adv*
telepathy [tə'lɛpəθi] *n* : telepatía *f*
telephone[1] ['tɛləˌfoːn] *v* **-phoned; -phoning** *vt* : llamar por teléfono a, telefonear — *vi* : telefonear
telephone[2] *n* : teléfono *m*
telescope[1] ['tɛləˌskoːp] *vi* **-scoped; -scoping** : plegarse (como un telescopio)
telescope[2] *n* : telescopio *m*
telescopic [ˌtɛlə'skɑpɪk] *adj* : telescópico
televise ['tɛləˌvaɪz] *vt* **-vised; -vising** : televisar
television ['tɛləˌvɪʒən] *n* : televisión *f*
tell ['tɛl] *v* **told** ['toːld]; **telling** *vt* **1** COUNT : contar, enumerar <all told : en total> **2** INSTRUCT : decir <he told me how to fix it : me dijo cómo arreglarlo> <they told her to wait : le dijeron que esperara> **3** RELATE : contar, relatar, narrar <to tell a story : contar una historia> **4** DIVULGE, REVEAL : revelar, divulgar <he told me everything about her : me contó todo acerca de ella> **5** DISCERN : discernir, notar <I can't tell the difference : no noto la diferencia> — *vi* **1** SAY : decir <I won't tell : no voy a decírselo a nadie> **2** KNOW : saber <you never can tell : nunca se sabe> **3** SHOW . notarse, hacerse sentir <the strain is beginning to tell : la tensión se empieza a notar>
teller ['tɛlər] *n* **1** NARRATOR : narrador *m,* -dora *f* **2** *or* **bank teller** : cajero *m,* -ra *f*
temerity [tə'mɛrəṯi] *n, pl* **-ties** : temeridad *f*
temp ['tɛmp] *n* : empleado *m,* -da *f* temporal
temper[1] ['tɛmpər] *vt* **1** MODERATE : moderar, temperar **2** ANNEAL : templar (acero, etc.)
temper[2] *n* **1** DISPOSITION : carácter *m,* genio *m* **2** HARDNESS : temple *m,* dureza *f* (de un metal) **3** COMPOSURE : calma *f,* serenidad *f* <to lose one's temper : perder los estribos> **4** RAGE : furia *f* <to fly into a temper : ponerse furioso>
temperament ['tɛmpərmənt, -prə-, -pərə-] *n* : temperamento *m*
temperamental [ˌtɛmpər'mɛntəl, -prə-, -pərə-] *adj* : temperamental
temperance ['tɛmprənts] *n* : templanza *f,* temperancia *f*
temperate ['tɛmpərət] *adj* : templado (dícese del clima, etc.), moderado
temperature ['tɛmpərˌtʃʊr, -prə-, -pərə-, -tʃər] *n* **1** : temperatura *f* **2** FEVER : calentura *f,* fiebre *f*
tempest ['tɛmpəst] *n* : tempestad *f*
tempestuous [tɛm'pɛstʃʊəs] *adj* : tempestuoso
temple ['tɛmpəl] *n* **1** : templo *m* (en religión) **2** : sien *f* (en anatomía)
tempo ['tɛmˌpoː] *n, pl* **-pi** [-ˌpiː] *or* **-pos** : ritmo *m,* tempo *m* (en música)
temporal ['tɛmpərəl] *adj* : temporal
temporarily [ˌtɛmpə'rɛrəli] *adv* : temporalmente, provisionalmente

temporary ['tɛmpəˌrɛri] *adj* : temporal, provisional, provisorio
tempt ['tɛmpt] *vt* : tentar
temptation [tɛmp'teɪʃən] *n* : tentación *f*
tempter ['tɛmptər] *n* : tentador *m*
temptress ['tɛmptrəs] *n* : tentadora *f*
ten[1] ['tɛn] *adj* : diez
ten[2] *n* **1** : diez *m* (número) **2** : decena *f* <tens of thousands : decenas de millares>
tenable ['tɛnəbəl] *adj* : sostenible, defendible
tenacious [tə'neɪʃəs] *adj* : tenaz
tenacity [tə'næsət̬i] *n* : tenacidad *f*
tenancy ['tɛnən*t*si] *n, pl* **-cies** : tenencia *f,* inquilinato *m* (de un inmueble)
tenant ['tɛnənt] *n* : inquilino *m,* -na *f;* arrendatario *m,* -ria *f*
tend ['tɛnd] *vt* : atender, cuidar (de), ocuparse de — *vi* : tender <it tends to benefit the consumer : tiende a beneficiar al consumidor>
tendency ['tɛndən*t*si] *n, pl* **-cies** : tendencia *f,* proclividad *f,* inclinación *f*
tender[1] ['tɛndər] *vt* : entregar, presentar <I tendered my resignation : presenté mi renuncia>
tender[2] *adj* **1** : tierno, blando <tender steak : bistec tierno> **2** AFFECTIONATE, LOVING : tierno, cariñoso, afectuoso **3** DELICATE : tierno, sensible, delicado
tender[3] *n* **1** OFFER : propuesta *f,* oferta *f* (en negocios) **2 legal tender** : moneda *f* de curso legal
tenderize ['tɛndəˌraɪz] *vt* **-ized; -izing** : ablandar (carnes)
tenderloin ['tɛndɛrˌlɔɪn] *n* : lomo *f* (de res o de puerco)
tenderly ['tɛndərli] *adv* : tiernamente, con ternura
tenderness ['tɛndərnəs] *n* : ternura *f*
tendon ['tɛndən] *n* : tendón *m*
tendril ['tɛndrɪl] *n* : zarcillo *m*
tenement ['tɛnəmənt] *n* : casa *f* de vecindad
tenet ['tɛnət] *n* : principio *m*
tennis ['tɛnəs] *n* : tenis *m*
tenor ['tɛnər] *n* **1** PURPORT : tenor *m,* significado *m* **2** : tenor *m* (en música)
tenpins ['tɛnˌpɪnz] *npl* : bolos *mpl,* boliche *m*
tense[1] ['tɛn*t*s] *v* **tensed; tensing** *vt* : tensar — *vi* : tensarse, ponerse tenso
tense[2] *adj* **tenser; tensest 1** TAUT : tenso, tirante **2** NERVOUS : tenso, nervioso
tense[3] *n* : tiempo *m* (de un verbo)
tensely ['tɛn*t*sli] *adv* : tensamente
tenseness ['tɛn*t*snəs] → **tension**
tension ['tɛntʃən] *n* **1** TAUTNESS : tensión *f,* tirantez *f* **2** STRESS : tensión *f,* nerviosismo *m,* estrés *m*
tent ['tɛnt] *n* : tienda *f* de campaña
tentacle ['tɛntɪkəl] *n* : tentáculo *m*
tentative ['tɛntət̬ɪv] *adj* **1** HESITANT : indeciso, vacilante **2** PROVISIONAL : sujeto a cambios, provisional
tentatively ['tɛntət̬ɪvli] *adv* : provisionalmente
tenth[1] ['tɛnθ] *adj* : décimo
tenth[2] *n* **1** : décimo *m,* -ma *f* (en una serie) **2** : décimo *m,* décima parte *f*
tenuous ['tɛnjʊəs] *adj* : tenue, débil <tenuous reasons : razones poco convincentes>
tenuously ['tɛnjʊəsli] *adv* : tenuemente, ligeramente
tenure ['tɛnjər] *n* : tenencia *f* (de un cargo o una propiedad), titularidad *f* (de un puesto académico)
tepee ['tiːˌpiː] *n* : tipi *m*
tepid ['tɛpid] *adj* : tibio
term[1] ['tərm] *vt* : calificar de, llamar, nombrar
term[2] *n* **1** PERIOD : término *m,* plazo *m,* período *m* **2** : término *m* (en matemáticas) **3** WORD : término *m,* vocablo *m* <legal terms : términos legales> **4 terms** *npl* CONDITIONS : términos *mpl,* condiciones *fpl* **5 terms** *npl* RELATIONS : relaciones *fpl* <to be on good terms with : tener buenas relaciones con> **6 in terms of** : con respecto a, en cuanto a
terminal[1] ['tərmənəl] *adj* : terminal
terminal[2] *n* **1** : terminal *m,* polo *m* (en electricidad) **2** : terminal *m* (de una computadora) **3** STATION : terminal *f,* estación *f* (de transporte público)
terminate ['tərməˌneɪt] *v* **-nated; -nating** *vi* : terminar(se), concluirse — *vt* : terminar, poner fin a
termination [ˌtərmə'neɪʃən] *n* : cese *m,* terminación *f*
terminology [ˌtərmə'nɑlədʒi] *n, pl* **-gies** : terminología *f*
terminus ['tərmənəs] *n, pl* **-ni** [-ˌnaɪ] *or* **-nuses 1** END : término *m,* fin *m* **2** : terminal *f* (de transporte público)
termite ['tərˌmaɪt] *n* : termita *f*
tern ['tərn] *n* : golondrina *f* de mar
terrace[1] ['tɛrəs] *vt* **-raced; -racing** : formar en terrazas, disponer en bancales
terrace[2] *n* **1** PATIO : terraza *f,* patio *m* **2** : terraplén *m,* terraza *f,* bancal *m* (en agricultura)
terra–cotta [ˌtɛrə'kɑt̬ə] *n* : terracota *f*
terrain [tə'reɪn] *n* : terreno *m*
terrapin ['tɛrəpɪn] *n* : galápago *m* norteamericano
terrarium [tə'ræriəm] *n, pl* **-ia** [-iə] *or* **-iums** : terrario *m*
terrestrial [tə'rɛstriəl] *adj* : terrestre
terrible ['tɛrəbəl] *adj* : atroz, horrible, terrible
terribly ['tɛrəbli] *adv* **1** BADLY : muy mal **2** EXTREMELY : terriblemente, extremadamente
terrier ['tɛriər] *n* : terrier *mf*
terrific [tə'rɪfɪk] *adj* **1** FRIGHTFUL : aterrador **2** EXTRAORDINARY : extraordinario, excepcional **3** EXCELLENT : excelente, estupendo
terrify ['tɛrəˌfaɪ] *vt* **-fied; -fying** : aterrorizar, aterrar, espantar

terrifying [ˈtɛrəˌfaɪɪŋ] *adj* : espantoso, aterrador
territory [ˈtɛrəˌtori] *n, pl* **-ries** : territorio *m* — **territorial** [ˌtɛrəˈtoriəl] *adj*
terror [ˈtɛrər] *n* : terror *m*
terrorism [ˈtɛrərˌɪzəm] *n* : terrorismo *m*
terrorist[1] [ˈtɛrərɪst] *adj* : terrorista
terrorist[2] *n* : terrorista *mf*
terrorize [ˈtɛrərˌaɪz] *vt* **-ized; -izing** : aterrorizar
terry [ˈtɛri] *n, pl* **-ries** *or* **terry cloth** : (tela de) toalla *f*
terse [ˈtərs] *adj* **terser; tersest** : lacónico, conciso, seco — **tersely** *adv*
tertiary [ˈtərʃiˌɛri] *adj* : terciario
test[1] [ˈtɛst] *vt* : examinar, evaluar — *vi* : hacer pruebas
test[2] *n* : prueba *f,* examen *m,* test *m* <to put to the test : poner a prueba>
testament [ˈtɛstəmənt] *n* **1** WILL : testamento *m* **2** : Testamento *m* (en la Biblia) <the Old Testament : el Antiguo Testamento>
testicle [ˈtɛstɪkəl] *n* : testículo *m*
testify [ˈtɛstəˌfaɪ] *v* **-fied; -fying** *vi* : testificar, atestar, testimoniar — *vt* : testificar
testimonial [ˌtɛstəˈmoːniəl] *n* **1** REFERENCE : recomendación *f* **2** TRIBUTE : homenaje *m,* tributo *m*
testimony [ˈtɛstəˌmoːni] *n, pl* **-nies** : testimonio *m,* declaración *f*
test tube *n* : probeta *f,* tubo *m* de ensayo
testy [ˈtɛsti] *adj* **-tier; -est** : irritable
tetanus [ˈtɛtənəs] *n* : tétano *m,* tétanos *m*
tête–à–tête [ˌtɛtəˈtɛt, ˌteɪtəˈteɪt] *n* : conversación *f* en privado
tether[1] [ˈtɛðər] *vt* : atar (con una cuerda), amarrar
tether[2] *n* : atadura *f,* cadena *f,* correa *f*
text [ˈtɛkst] *n* **1** : texto *m* **2** TOPIC : tema *m* **3** → **textbook**
textbook [ˈtɛkstˌbʊk] *n* : libro *m* de texto
textile [ˈtɛkˌstaɪl, ˈtɛkstəl] *n* : textil *m,* tela *f* <the textile industry : la industria textil>
textual [ˈtɛkstʃuəl] *adj* : textual
texture [ˈtɛkstʃər] *n* : textura *f*
than[1] [ˈðæn] *conj* : que, de <it's worth more than that : vale más que eso> <more than you think : más de lo que piensas>
than[2] *prep* : que, de <you're better than he is : eres mejor que él> <more than once : más de una vez>
thank [ˈθæŋk] *vt* : agradecer, darle (las) gracias (a alguien) <thank you! : ¡gracias!> <I thanked her for the present : le di las gracias por el regalo> <I thank you for your help : le agradezco su ayuda>
thankful [ˈθæŋkfəl] *adj* : agradecido
thankfully [ˈθæŋkfəli] *adv* **1** GRATEFULLY : con agradecimiento **2** FORTUNATELY : afortunadamente, por suerte <thankfully, it's over : se acabó, gracias a Dios>
thankfulness [ˈθæŋkfəlnəs] *n* : agradecimiento *m,* gratitud *f*
thankless [ˈθæŋkləs] *adj* : ingrato <a thankless task : un trabajo ingrato>
thanks [ˈθæŋks] *npl* **1** : agradecimiento *m* **2** **thanks!** : ¡gracias!
Thanksgiving [θæŋksˈgɪvɪŋ, ˈθæŋksˌ-] *n* : el día de Acción de Gracias (fiesta estadounidense)
that[1] [ˈðæt] *adv* (*in negative constructions*) : tan <it's not that expensive : no es tan caro> <not that much : no tanto>
that[2] *adj, pl* **those** : ese, esa, aquel, aquella <do you see those children? : ¿ves a aquellos niños?>
that[3] *conj & pron* : que <he said that he was afraid : dijo que tenía miedo> <the book that he wrote : el libro que escribió>
that[4] *pron, pl* **those** [ˈðoːz] **1** : ése, ésa, eso <that's my father : ése es mi padre> <those are the ones he likes : ésos son los que le gustan> <what's that? : ¿qué es eso?> **2** (*referring to more distant objects or time*) : aquél, aquélla, aquello <those are maples and these are elms : aquéllos son arces y éstos son olmos> <that came to an end : aquello se acabó>
thatch[1] [ˈθætʃ] *vt* : cubrir o techar con paja
thatch[2] *n* : paja *f* (usada para techos)
thaw[1] [ˈθɔ] *vt* : descongelar — *vi* : derretirse (dícese de la nieve), descongelarse (dícese de los alimentos)
thaw[2] *n* : deshielo *m*
the[1] [ðə, *before vowel sounds usu* ðiː] *adv* **1** (*used to indicate comparison*) <the sooner the better : cuanto más pronto, mejor> <she likes this one the best : éste es el que más le gusta> **2** (*used as a conjunction*) : cuanto <the more I learn, the less I understand : cuanto más aprendo, menos entiendo>
the[2] *art* : el, la, los, las <the gloves : los guantes> <the suitcase : la maleta> <forty cookies to the box : cuarenta galletas por caja>
theater *or* **theatre** [ˈθiːətər] *n* **1** : teatro *m* (edificio) **2** DRAMA : teatro *m,* drama *m*
theatrical [θiˈætrɪkəl] *adj* : teatral, dramático
thee [ˈðiː] *pron* : te, ti
theft [ˈθɛft] *n* : robo *m,* hurto *m*
their [ˈðɛr] *adj* : su <their friends : sus amigos>
theirs [ˈðɛrz] *pron* : (el) suyo, (la) suya, (los) suyos, (las) suyas <they came for theirs : vinieron por el suyo> <theirs is bigger : la suya es más grande, la de ellos es más grande> <a brother of theirs : un hermano suyo, un hermano de ellos>

them [ˈðɛm] *pron* **1** (*as a direct object*) : los (*Spain sometimes* les), las <I know them : los conozco> **2** (*as indirect object*) : les, se <I sent them a letter : les mandé una carta> <give it to them : dáselo (a ellos)> **3** (*as object of a preposition*) : ellos, ellas <go with them : ve con ellos> **4** (*for emphasis*) : ellos, ellas <I wasn't expecting them : no los esperaba a ellos>

theme [ˈθiːm] *n* **1** SUBJECT, TOPIC : tema *m* **2** COMPOSITION : composición *f,* trabajo *m* (escrito) **3** : tema *m* (en música)

themselves [ðəmˈsɛlvz, ðɛm-] *pron* **1** (*as a reflexive*) : se, sí <they enjoyed themselves : se divirtieron> <they divided it among themselves : lo repartieron entre sí, se lo repartieron> **2** (*for emphasis*) : ellos mismos, ellas mismas <they built it themselves : ellas mismas lo construyeron>

then[1] [ˈðɛn] *adv* **1** : entonces, en ese tiempo <I was sixteen then : tenía entonces dieciséis años> <since then : desde entonces> **2** NEXT : después, luego <we'll go to Toronto, then to Winnipeg : iremos a Toronto, y luego a Winnipeg> **3** BESIDES : además, aparte <then there's the tax : y aparte está el impuesto> **4** : entonces, en ese caso <if you like music, then you should attend : si te gusta la música, entonces deberías asistir>

then[2] *adj* : entonces <the then governor of Georgia : el entonces gobernador de Georgia>

thence [ˈðɛnts, ˈθɛnts] *adv* : de ahí, de ahí en adelante

theologian [ˌθiːəˈloːdʒən] *n* : teólogo *m,* -ga *f*

theological [ˌθiːəˈlɑdʒɪkəl] *adj* : teológico

theology [θiˈɑlədʒi] *n, pl* **-gies** : teología *f*

theorem [ˈθiːərəm, ˈθɪrəm] *n* : teorema *m*

theoretical [ˌθiːəˈrɛt̬ɪkəl] *adj* : teórico — **theoretically** *adv*

theorize [ˈθiːəˌraɪz] *vi* **-rized; -rizing** : teorizar

theory [ˈθiːəri, ˈθɪri] *n, pl* **-ries** : teoría *f*

therapeutic [ˌθɛrəˈpjuːt̬ɪk] *adj* : terapéutico — **therapeutically** *adv*

therapist [ˈθɛrəpɪst] *n* : terapeuta *mf*

therapy [ˈθɛrəpi] *n, pl* **-pies** : terapia *f*

there[1] [ˈðær] *adv* **1** : ahí, allí, allá <stand over there : párate ahí> <over there : por allí, por allá> <who's there? : ¿quién es?> **2** : ahí, en esto, en eso <there is where we disagree : en eso es donde no estamos de acuerdo>

there[2] *pron* **1** (*introducing a sentence or clause*) <there comes a time to decide : llega un momento en que tiene uno que decidir> **2 there is, there are :** hay <there are many children here : aquí hay muchos niños> <there's a good hotel downtown : hay un buen hotel en el centro>

thereabouts [ðærəˈbaʊts, ˈðærəˌ-] *or* **thereabout** [-ˈbaʊt, -ˌbaʊt] *adv* **or thereabouts :** por ahí, más o menos <at five o'clock or thereabouts : por ahí de las cinco>

thereafter [ðærˈæftər] *adv* : después <shortly thereafter : poco después>

thereby [ðærˈbaɪ, ˈðærˌbaɪ] *adv* : de tal modo, de ese manera, así

therefore [ˈðærˌfor] *adv* : por lo tanto, por consiguiente

therein [ðærˈɪn] *adv* **1** : allí adentro, ahí adentro <the contents therein : lo que allí se contiene> **2** : allí, en ese aspecto <therein lies the problem : allí está el problema>

thereof [ðærˈʌv, -ˈɑv] *adv* : de eso, de esto

thereupon [ˈðærəˌpɑn, -ˌpɔn; ˌðærəˈpɑn, -ˈpɔn] *adv* : acto seguido, inmediatamente (después)

therewith [ðærˈwɪð, -ˈwɪθ] *adv* : con eso, con ello

thermal [ˈθərməl] *adj* **1** : térmico (en física) **2** HOT : termal

thermodynamics [ˌθərmodaɪˈnæmɪks] *ns & pl* : termodinámica *f*

thermometer [θərˈmɑmət̬ər] *n* : termómetro *m*

thermos [ˈθərməs] *n* : termo *m*

thermostat [ˈθərməˌstæt] *n* : termostato *m*

thesaurus [θɪˈsɔrəs] *n, pl* **-sauri** [-ˈsɔrˌaɪ] *or* **-sauruses** [-ˈsɔrəsəz] : diccionario *m* de sinónimos

these → **this**

thesis [ˈθiːsɪs] *n, pl* **theses** [ˈθiːˌsiːz] : tesis *f*

they [ˈðeɪ] *pron* : ellos, ellas <they are here : están aquí> <they don't know : ellos no saben>

they'd [ˈðeɪd] (*contraction of* **they had** *or* **they would**) → **have, would**

they'll [ˈðeɪl, ˈðɛl] (*contraction of* **they shall** *or* **they will**) → **shall, will**

they're [ˈðɛr] (*contraction of* **they are**) → **be**

they've [ˈðeɪv] (*contraction of* **they have**) → **have**

thiamine [ˈθaɪəmɪn, -ˌmiːn] *n* : tiamina *f*

thick[1] [ˈθɪk] *adj* **1** : grueso <a thick plank : una tabla gruesa> **2** : espeso, denso <thick syrup : jarabe espeso> — **thickly** *adv*

thick[2] *n* **1 in the thick of :** en medio de <in the thick of the battle : en lo más reñido de la batalla> **2 through thick and thin :** a las duras y a las maduras

thicken [ˈθɪkən] *vt* : espesar (un líquido) — *vi* : espesarse

thickener [ˈθɪkənər] *n* : espesante *m*

thicket [ˈθɪkət] *n* : matorral *m,* maleza *f,* espesura *f*

thickness [ˈθɪknəs] *n* : grosor *m,* grueso *m,* espesor *m*
thickset [ˈθɪkˈsɛt] *adj* STOCKY : robusto, fornido
thick–skinned [ˈθɪkˈskɪnd] *adj* : poco sensible, que no se ofende fácilmente
thief [ˈθiːf] *n, pl* **thieves** [ˈθiːvz] : ladrón *m,* -drona *f*
thieve [ˈθiːv] *v* **thieved; thieving** : hurtar, robar
thievery [ˈθiːvəri] *n* : hurto *m,* robo *m,* latrocinio *m*
thigh [ˈθaɪ] *n* : muslo *m*
thighbone [ˈθaɪˌboːn] *n* : fémur *m*
thimble [ˈθɪmbəl] *n* : dedal *m*
thin[1] [ˈθɪn] *v* **thinned; thinning** *vt* : hacer menos denso, diluir, aguar (un líquido), enrarecer (un gas) — *vi* : diluirse, aguarse (dícese de un líquido), enrarecerse (dícese de un gas)
thin[2] *adj* **thinner; -est 1** LEAN, SLIM : delgado, esbelto, flaco **2** SPARSE : ralo, escaso <a thin beard : una barba rala> **3** WATERY : claro, aguado, diluido **4** FINE : delgado, fino <thin slices : rebanadas finas>
thing [ˈθɪŋ] *n* **1** AFFAIR, MATTER : cosa *f,* asunto *m* <don't talk about those things : no hables de esas cosas> <how are things? : ¿cómo van las cosas?> **2** ACT, EVENT : cosa *f,* suceso *m,* evento *m* <the flood was a terrible thing : la inundación fue una cosa terrible> **3** OBJECT : cosa *f,* objeto *m* <don't forget your things : no olvides tus cosas>
think [ˈθɪŋk] *v* **thought** [ˈθɔt]; **thinking** *vt* **1** : pensar <I thought to return early : pensaba regresar temprano> **2** BELIEVE : pensar, creer, opinar **3** PONDER : pensar, reflexionar **4** CONCEIVE : ocurrirse, concebir <we've thought up a plan : se nos ha ocurrido un plan> — *vi* **1** REASON : pensar, razonar **2** CONSIDER : pensar, considerar <think of your family first : primero piensa en tu familia>
thinker [ˈθɪŋkər] *n* : pensador *m,* -dora *f*
thinly [ˈθɪnli] *adv* **1** LIGHTLY : ligeramente **2** SPARSELY : escasamente <thinly populated : poco populado> **3** BARELY : apenas
thinness [ˈθɪnnəs] *n* : delgadez *f*
thin–skinned [ˈθɪnˈskɪnd] *adj* : susceptible, muy sensible
third[1] [ˈθərd] *or* **thirdly** [-li] *adv* : en tercer lugar <she came in third : llegó en tercer lugar>
third[2] *adj* : tercero <the third day : el tercer día>
third[3] *n* **1** : tercero *m,* -ra *f* (en una serie) **2** : tercero *m,* tercera parte *f*
third world *n* **the Third World** : el Tercer Mundo *m*
thirst[1] [ˈθərst] *vi* **1** : tener sed **2 to thirst for** DESIRE : tener sed de, estar sediento de
thirst[2] *n* : sed *f*
thirsty [ˈθərsti] *adj* **thirstier; -est** : sediento, que tiene sed <I'm thirsty : tengo sed>
thirteen[1] [ˌθərˈtiːn] *adj* : trece
thirteen[2] *n* : trece *m*
thirteenth[1] [ˌθərˈtiːnθ] *adj* : décimo tercero
thirteenth[2] *n* **1** : decimotercero *m,* -ra *f* (en una serie) **2** : treceavo *m,* treceava parte *f*
thirtieth[1] [ˈθərtiəθ] *adj* : trigésimo
thirtieth[2] *n* **1** : trigésimo *m,* -ma *f* (en una serie) **2** : treintavo *m,* treintava parte *f*
thirty[1] [ˈθərti] *adj* : treinta
thirty[2] *n, pl* **thirties** : treinta *m*
this[1] [ˈðɪs] *adv* : así, a tal punto <this big : así de grande>
this[2] *adj, pl* **these** [ˈðiːz] : este <these things : estas cosas> <read this book : lee este libro>
this[3] *pron, pl* **these** : esto <what's this? : ¿qué es esto?> <this wasn't here yesterday : esto no estaba aquí ayer>
thistle [ˈθɪsəl] *n* : cardo *m*
thong [ˈθɔŋ] *n* **1** STRAP : correa *f,* tira *f* **2** *or* **thong sandal** : chancla *f,* chancleta *f*
thorax [ˈθorˌæks] *n, pl* **-raxes** *or* **-races** [ˈθorəˌsiːz] : tórax *m*
thorn [ˈθɔrn] *n* : espina *f*
thorny [ˈθɔrni] *adj* **thornier; -est** : espinoso
thorough [ˈθəroː] *adj* **1** CONSCIENTIOUS : concienzudo, meticuloso **2** COMPLETE : absoluto, completo — **thoroughly** *adv*
thoroughbred [ˈθəroˌbrɛd] *adj* : de pura sangre (dícese de un caballo)
Thoroughbred *n or* **Thoroughbred horse** : pura sangre *mf*
thoroughfare [ˈθəroˌfær] *n* : vía *f* pública, carretera *f*
thoroughness [ˈθəronəs] *n* : esmero *m,* meticulosidad *f*
those → **that**
thou [ˈðaʊ] *pron* : tú
though[1] [ˈðoː] *adv* **1** HOWEVER, NEVERTHELESS : sin embargo, no obstante **2 as ~** : como si <as though nothing had happened : como si nada hubiera pasado>
though[2] *conj* : aunque, a pesar de <though it was raining, we went out : salimos a pesar de la lluvia>
thought[1] → **think**
thought[2] [ˈθɔt] *n* **1** THINKING : pensamiento *m,* ideas *fpl* <Western thought : el pensamiento occidental> **2** COGITATION : pensamiento *m,* reflexión *f,* raciocinio *m* **3** IDEA : idea *f,* ocurrencia *f* <it was just a thought : fue sólo una idea>
thoughtful [ˈθɔtfəl] *adj* **1** PENSIVE : pensativo, meditabundo **2** CONSIDERATE : considerado, atento, cortés — **thoughtfully** *adv*
thoughtfulness [ˈθɔtfəlnəs] *n* : consideración *f,* atención *f,* cortesía *f*

thoughtless ['θɔtləs] *adj* **1** CARELESS : descuidado, negligente **2** INCONSIDERATE : desconsiderado — **thoughtlessly** *adv*
thousand[1] ['θaʊzənd] *adj* : mil
thousand[2] *n, pl* **-sands** *or* **-sand** : mil *m*
thousandth[1] ['θaʊzəntθ] *adj* : milésimo
thousandth[2] *n* **1** : milésimo *m,* -ma *f* (en una serie) **2** : milésimo *m,* milésima parte *f*
thrash ['θræʃ] *vt* **1** → **thresh 2** BEAT : golpear, azotar, darle una paliza (a alguien) **3** FLAIL : sacudir, agitar bruscamente
thread[1] ['θrɛd] *vt* **1** : enhilar, enhebrar (una aguja) **2** STRING : ensartar (cuentas en un hilo) **3 to thread one's way** : abrirse paso
thread[2] *n* **1** : hilo *m,* hebra *f* <needle and thread : aguja e hilo> <the thread of an argument : el hilo de un debate> **2** : rosca *f,* filete *m* (de un tornillo)
threadbare ['θrɛd'bær] *adj* **1** SHABBY, WORN : raído, gastado **2** TRITE : trillado, tópico, manido
threat ['θrɛt] *n* : amenaza *f*
threaten ['θrɛtən] *v* : amenazar
threatening ['θrɛtənɪŋ] *adj* : amenazador — **threateningly** *adv*
three[1] ['θri:] *adj* : tres
three[2] *n* : tres *m*
threefold ['θri:ˌfo:ld] *adj* TRIPLE : triple
three hundred[1] *adj* : trescientos
three hundred[2] *n* : trescientos *m*
threescore ['θri:'skor] *adj* SIXTY : sesenta
thresh ['θrɛʃ] *vt* : trillar (grano)
thresher ['θrɛʃər] *n* : trilladora *f*
threshold ['θrɛʃˌho:ld, -ˌo:ld] *n* : umbral *m*
threw → **throw**[1]
thrice ['θraɪs] *adv* : tres veces
thrift ['θrɪft] *n* : economía *f,* frugalidad *f*
thriftless ['θrɪftləs] *adj* : despilfarrador, manirroto
thrifty ['θrɪfti] *adj* **thriftier; -est** : económico, frugal — **thriftily** ['θrɪftəli] *adv*
thrill[1] ['θrɪl] *vt* : emocionar — *vi* **to thrill to** : dejarse conmover por, estremecerse con
thrill[2] *n* : emoción *f*
thriller ['θrɪlər] *n* **1** : evento *m* emocionante **2** : obra *f* de suspenso
thrilling ['θrɪlɪŋ] *adj* : emocionante, excitante
thrive ['θraɪv] *vi* **throve** ['θro:v] *or* **thrived; thriven** ['θrɪvən] **1** FLOURISH : florecer, crecer abundantemente **2** PROSPER : prosperar
throat ['θro:t] *n* : garganta *f*
throaty ['θro:ṭi] *adj* **throatier; -est** : ronco (dícese de la voz)
throb[1] ['θrɑb] *vi* **throbbed; throbbing** : palpitar, latir (dícese del corazón), vibrar (dícese de un motor, etc.)
throb[2] *n* : palpitación *f,* latido *m,* vibración *f*
throe ['θro:] *n* **1** PAIN, SPASM : espasmo *m,* dolor *m* <the throes of childbirth : los dolores de parto> **2 throes** *npl* : lucha *f* larga y ardua <in the throes of : en el medio de>
throne ['θro:n] *n* : trono *m*
throng[1] ['θrɔŋ] *vt* CROWD : atestar, atiborrar, llenar — *vi* : aglomerarse, amontonarse
throng[2] *n* : muchedumbre *f,* gentío *m,* multitud *f*
throttle[1] ['θrɑtəl] *vt* **-tled; -tling 1** STRANGLE : estrangular, ahogar **2 to throttle down** : desacelerar (un motor)
throttle[2] *n* **1** : válvula *f* reguladora **2 at full throttle** : a toda máquina
through[1] ['θru:] *adv* **1** : a través, de un lado a otro <let them through : déjenlos pasar> **2** : de principio a fin <she read the book through : leyó el libro de principio a fin> **3** COMPLETELY : completamente <soaked through : completamente empapado>
through[2] *adj* **1** DIRECT : directo <a through train : un tren directo> **2** FINISHED : terminado, acabado <we're through : hemos terminado>
through[3] *prep* **1** : a través de, por <through the door : por la puerta> <a road through the woods : un camino que atraviesa el bosque> **2** BETWEEN : entre <a path through the trees : un sendero entre los árboles> **3** BECAUSE OF : a causa de, como consecuencia de **4** (*in expressions of time*) <through the night : durante la noche> <to go through an experience : pasar por una experiencia> **5** : a, hasta <from Monday through Friday : de lunes a viernes>
throughout[1] [θru:'aʊt] *adv* **1** EVERYWHERE : por todas partes **2** THROUGH : desde el principio hasta el fin de (algo)
throughout[2] *prep* **1** : en todas partes de, a través de <throughout the United States : en todo Estados Unidos> **2** : de principio a fin de, durante <throughout the winter : durante todo el invierno>
throve → **thrive**
throw[1] ['θro:] *vt* **threw** ['θru:]; **thrown** ['θro:n]; **throwing 1** TOSS : tirar, lanzar, echar, arrojar, aventar *Col, Mex* <to throw a ball : tirar una pelota> **2** UNSEAT : desmontar (a un jinete) **3** CAST : proyectar <it threw a long shadow : proyectó una sombra larga> **4 to throw a party** : dar una fiesta **5 to throw into confusion** : desconcertar **6 to throw out** DISCARD : botar, tirar (en la basura)

throw[2] *n* TOSS **:** tiro *m,* tirada *f,* lanzamiento *m,* lance *m* (de dados)

thrower [ˈθroːər] *n* **:** lanzador *m,* -dora *f*

throw up *v* VOMIT **:** vomitar, devolver

thrush [ˈθrʌʃ] *n* **:** tordo *m,* zorzal *m*

thrust[1] [ˈθrʌst] *vt* **thrust; thrusting 1** SHOVE **:** empujar bruscamente **2** PLUNGE, STAB **:** apuñalar, clavar <he thrust a dagger into her heart : la apuñaló en el corazón> **3 to thrust one's way :** abrirse paso **4 to thrust upon :** imponer a

thrust[2] *n* **1** PUSH, SHOVE **:** empujón *m,* empellón *m* **2** LUNGE **:** estocada *f* (en esgrima) **3** IMPETUS **:** ímpetu *m,* impulso *m,* propulsión *f* (de un motor)

thud[1] [ˈθʌd] *vi* **thudded; thudding :** producir un ruido sordo

thud[2] *n* **:** ruido *m* sordo (que produce un objeto al caer)

thug [ˈθʌg] *n* **:** matón *m*

thumb[1] [ˈθʌm] *vt* **:** hojear (con el pulgar)

thumb[2] *n* **:** pulgar *m,* dedo *m* pulgar

thumbnail [ˈθʌm,neɪl] *n* **:** uña *f* del pulgar

thumbtack [ˈθʌm,tæk] *n* **:** tachuela *f,* chinche *f*

thump[1] [ˈθʌmp] *vt* POUND **:** golpear, aporrear — *vi* **:** latir con vehemencia (dícese del corazón)

thump[2] *n* THUD **:** ruido *m* sordo

thunder[1] [ˈθʌndər] *vi* **1 :** tronar <it rained and thundered all night : llovió y tronó durante la noche> **2** BOOM **:** retumbar, bramar, resonar — *vt* ROAR, SHOUT **:** decir a gritos, vociferar

thunder[2] *n* **:** truenos *mpl*

thunderbolt [ˈθʌndər,boːlt] *n* **:** rayo *m*

thunderclap [ˈθʌndər,klæp] *n* **:** trueno *m*

thunderous [ˈθʌndərəs] *adj* **:** atronador, ensordecedor, estruendoso

thundershower [ˈθʌndər,ʃaʊər] *n* **:** lluvia *f* con truenos y relámpagos

thunderstorm [ˈθʌndər,stɔrm] *n* **:** tormenta *f* con truenos y relámpagos

thunderstruck [ˈθʌndər,strʌk] *adj* **:** atónito

Thursday [ˈθərz,deɪ, -di] *n* **:** jueves *m*

thus [ˈðʌs] *adv* **1 :** así, de esta manera **2** SO **:** hasta (cierto punto) <the weather's been nice thus far : hasta ahora ha hecho buen tiempo> **3** HENCE **:** por consiguiente, por lo tanto

thwart [ˈθwɔrt] *vt* **:** frustrar

thy [ˈðaɪ] *adj* **:** tu

thyme [ˈtaɪm, ˈθaɪm] *n* **:** tomillo *m*

thyroid [ˈθaɪ,rɔɪd] *n or* **thyroid gland :** tiroides *mf,* glándula *f* tiroidea

thyself [ðaɪˈsɛlf] *pron* **:** ti, ti mismo

tiara [tiˈærə, -ˈɑr-] *n* **:** diadema *f*

tibia [ˈtɪbiə] *n, pl* **-iae** [-bi,iː] **:** tibia *f*

tic [ˈtɪk] *n* **:** tic *m*

tick[1] [ˈtɪk] *vi* **1 :** hacer tictac **2** OPERATE, RUN **:** operar, andar (dícese de un mecanismo) <what makes him tick? : ¿qué es lo que lo mueve?> — *vt or* **to tick off** CHECK **:** marcar

tick[2] *n* **1 :** tictac *m* (de un reloj) **2** CHECK **:** marca *f* **3 :** garrapata *f* (insecto)

ticket[1] [ˈtɪkət] *vt* LABEL **:** etiquetar

ticket[2] *n* **1 :** boleto *m,* entrada *f* (de un espectáculo), pasaje *m* (de avión, tren, etc.) **2** SLATE **:** lista *f* de candidatos

tickle[1] [ˈtɪkəl] *v* **-led; -ling** *vt* **1** AMUSE **:** divertir, hacerle gracia (a alguien) **2 :** hacerle cosquillas (a alguien) <don't tickle me! : ¡no me hagas cosquillas!> — *vi* **:** picar

tickle[2] *n* **:** cosquilla *f*

ticklish [ˈtɪkəlɪʃ] *adj* **1 :** cosquilloso (dícese de una persona) **2** DELICATE, TRICKY **:** delicado, peliagudo

tidal [ˈtaɪdəl] *adj* **:** de marea, relativo a la marea

tidal wave *n* **:** maremoto *m*

tidbit [ˈtɪd,bɪt] *n* **1** BITE, SNACK **:** bocado *m,* golosina *f* **2 :** dato *m* o noticia *f* interesante <useful tidbits of information : informaciones útiles>

tide[1] [ˈtaɪd] *vt* **tided; tiding** *or* **to tide over :** proveer lo necesario para aguantar una dificultad <this money will tide you over until you find work : este dinero te mantendrá hasta que encuentres empleo>

tide[2] *n* **1 :** marea *f* **2** CURRENT **:** corriente *f* (de eventos, opiniones, etc.)

tidily [ˈtaɪdəli] *adv* **:** ordenadamente

tidiness [ˈtaɪdinəs] *n* **:** aseo *m,* limpieza *f,* orden *m*

tidings [ˈtaɪdɪŋz] *npl* **:** nuevas *fpl*

tidy[1] [ˈtaɪdi] *vt* **-died; -dying :** asear, limpiar, poner en orden

tidy[2] *adj* **-dier; -est 1** CLEAN, NEAT **:** limpio, aseado, en orden **2** SUBSTANTIAL **:** grande, considerable <a tidy sum : una suma considerable>

tie[1] [ˈtaɪ] *v* **tied; tying** *or* **tieing** *vt* **1 :** atar, amarrar <to tie a knot : atar un nudo> <to tie one's shoelaces : atarse los cordones> **2** BIND, UNITE **:** ligar, atar **3 :** empatar <they tied the score : empataron el marcador> — *vi* **:** empatar <the two teams were tied : los dos equipos empataron>

tie[2] *n* **1 :** ligadura *f,* cuerda *f,* cordón *m* (para atar algo) **2** BOND, LINK **:** atadura *f,* ligadura *f,* vínculo *m,* lazo *m* <family ties : lazos familiares> **3** *or* **railroad tie :** traviesa *f* **4** DRAW **:** empate *m* (en deportes) **5** NECKTIE **:** corbata *f*

tier [ˈtɪr] *n* **:** hilera *f,* escalón *m*

tiff [ˈtɪf] *n* **:** disgusto *m,* disputa *f*

tiger [ˈtaɪgər] *n* **:** tigre *m*

tight[1] [ˈtaɪt] *adv* TIGHTLY **:** bien, fuerte <shut it tight : ciérralo bien>

tight[2] *adj* **1 :** bien cerrado, hermético <a tight seal : un cierre hermético> **2** STRICT **:** estricto, severo **3** TAUT **:** tirante, tenso **4** SNUG **:** apretado, ajustado, ceñido <a tight dress : un vestido ceñido> **5** DIFFICULT **:** difícil <to be in a tight spot : estar en un aprieto> **6** STINGY **:** apretado, avaro, agarrado *fam* 7 CLOSE : reñido <a tight game : un juego reñido> 8 SCARCE : escaso <money is tight : escasea el dinero>

tighten [ˈtaɪtən] *vt* : tensar (una cuerda, etc.), apretar (un nudo, un tornillo, etc.), apretarse (el cinturón), reforzar (las reglas)

tightly [ˈtaɪtli] *adv* : bien, fuerte

tightness [ˈtaɪtnəs] *n* : lo apretado, lo tenso, tensión *f*

tightrope [ˈtaɪtˌroːp] *n* : cuerda *f* floja

tights [ˈtaɪts] *npl* : leotardo *m,* malla *f*

tightwad [ˈtaɪtˌwɑd] *n* : avaro *m,* -ra *f;* tacaño *m,* -ña *f*

tigress [ˈtaɪgrəs] *n* : tigresa *f*

tile[1] [ˈtaɪl] *vt* **tiled; tiling :** embaldosar (un piso), revestir de azulejos (una pared), tejar (un techo)

tile[2] *n* **1** *or* **floor tile :** losa *f,* baldosa *f,* mosaico *m Mex* (de un piso) **2 :** azulejo *m* (de una pared) **3 :** teja *f* (de un techo)

till[1] [ˈtɪl] *vt* : cultivar, labrar

till[2] *n* : caja *f,* caja *f* registradora

till[3] *prep & conj* → **until**

tiller [ˈtɪlər] *n* **1 :** cultivador *m,* -dora *f* (de la tierra) **2 :** caña *f* del timón (de un barco)

tilt[1] [ˈtɪlt] *vt* : ladear, inclinar — *vi* : ladearse, inclinarse

tilt[2] *n* **1** SLANT : inclinación *f* **2 at full tilt :** a toda velocidad

timber [ˈtɪmbər] *n* **1 :** madera *f* (para construcción) **2** BEAM : viga *f*

timberland [ˈtɪmbərˌlænd] *n* : bosque *m* maderero

timbre [ˈtæmbər, ˈtɪm-] *n* : timbre *m*

time[1] [ˈtaɪm] *vt* **timed; timing 1** SCHEDULE : fijar la hora de, calcular el momento oportuno para **2** CLOCK : cronometrar, medir el tiempo de (una competencia, etc.)

time[2] *n* **1 :** tiempo *m* <the passing of time : el paso del tiempo> <she doesn't have time : no tiene tiempo> **2** MOMENT : tiempo *m,* momento *m* <this is not the time to bring it up : no es el momento de sacar el tema> **3** : vez *f* <she called you three times : te llamó tres veces> <three times greater : tres veces mayor> **4** AGE : tiempo *m,* era *f* <in your grandparents' time : en el tiempo de tus abuelos> **5** TEMPO : tiempo *m,* ritmo *m* (en música) **6** : hora *f* <what time is it? : ¿qué hora es?> <at the usual time : a la hora acostumbrada> <to keep time : ir a la hora> <to lose time : atrasar> **7** EXPERIENCE : rato *m,* experiencia *f* <we had a nice time together : pasamos juntos un rato agradable> <to have a rough time : pasarlo mal> <have a good time! : ¡que se diviertan!> **8 at times** SOMETIMES : a veces **9 for the time being :** por el momento, de momento **10 from time to time** OCCASIONALLY : de vez en cuando **11 in time** PUNCTUALLY : a tiempo **12 in time** EVENTUALLY : con el tiempo **13 time after time :** una y otra vez

timekeeper [ˈtaɪmˌkiːpər] *n* : cronometrador *m,* -dora *f*

timeless [ˈtaɪmləs] *adj* : eterno

timely [ˈtaɪmli] *adj* **-lier; -est :** oportuno

timepiece [ˈtaɪmˌpiːs] *n* : reloj *m*

timer [ˈtaɪmər] *n* : temporizador *m,* cronómetro *m*

times [ˈtaɪmz] *prep* : por <3 times 4 is 12 : 3 por 4 son 12>

timetable [ˈtaɪmˌteɪbəl] *n* : horario *m*

timid [ˈtɪmɪd] *adj* : tímido — **timidly** *adv*

timidity [təˈmɪdəti] *n* : timidez *f*

timorous [ˈtɪmərəs] *adj* : timorato, miedoso

timpani [ˈtɪmpəni] *npl* : timbales *mpl*

tin [ˈtɪn] *n* **1 :** estaño *m,* hojalata *f* (metal) **2** CAN : lata *f,* bote *m,* envase *m*

tincture [ˈtɪŋktʃər] *n* : tintura *f*

tinder [ˈtɪndər] *n* : yesca *f*

tine [ˈtaɪn] *n* : diente *m* (de un tenedor, etc.)

tinfoil [ˈtɪnˌfɔɪl] *n* : papel *m* (de) aluminio

tinge[1] [ˈtɪndʒ] *vt* **tinged; tingeing** *or* **tinging** [ˈtɪndʒɪŋ] TINT : matizar, teñir ligeramente

tinge[2] *n* **1** TINT : matiz *m,* tinte *m* sutil **2** TOUCH : dejo *m,* sensación *f* ligera

tingle[1] [ˈtɪŋgəl] *vi* **-gled; -gling :** sentir (un) hormigueo, sentir (un) cosquilleo

tingle[2] *n* : hormigueo *m,* cosquilleo *m*

tinker [ˈtɪŋkər] *vi* **to tinker with :** arreglar con pequeños ajustes, toquetear (con intento de arreglar)

tinkle[1] [ˈtɪŋkəl] *vi* **-kled; -kling :** tintinear

tinkle[2] *n* : tintineo *m*

tinsel [ˈtɪn*t*səl] *n* : oropel *m*

tint[1] [ˈtɪnt] *vt* : teñir, colorar

tint[2] *n* : tinte *m*

tiny [ˈtaɪni] *adj* **-nier; -est :** diminuto, minúsculo

tip[1] [ˈtɪp] *v* **tipped; tipping** *vt* **1** *or* **to tip over :** volcar, voltear, hacer caer **2** TILT : ladear, inclinar <to tip one's hat : saludar con el sombrero> **3** TAP : tocar, golpear ligeramente **4 :** darle una propina (a un mesero, etc.) <I tipped him $5 : le di $5 de propina> **5** : adornar o cubrir la punta de <wings tipped in red : alas que tienen las puntas rojas> **6 to tip off :** dar información a — *vi* TILT : ladearse, inclinarse

tip[2] *n* **1** END, POINT : punta *f,* extremo *m* <on the tip of one's tongue : en la punta de la lengua> **2** GRATUITY : propina *f* **3** ADVICE, INFORMATION : consejo *m,* información *f* (confidencial)

tip–off [ˈtɪpˌɔf] *n* **1** SIGN : indicación *f,* señal *f* **2** TIP : información *f* (confidencial)

tipple ['tɪpəl] *vi* **-pled; -pling** : tomarse unas copas

tipsy ['tɪpsi] *adj* **-sier; -est** : achispado

tiptoe[1] ['tɪp,toː] *vi* **-toed; -toeing** : caminar de puntillas

tiptoe[2] *adv* : de puntillas

tiptoe[3] *n* : punta *f* del pie

tip–top[1] ['tɪp'tɑp, -,tɑp] *adj* EXCELLENT : excelente

tip–top[2] *n* SUMMIT : cumbre *f,* cima *f*

tirade ['taɪ,reɪd] *n* : diatriba *f*

tire[1] ['taɪr] *v* **tired; tiring** *vt* : cansar, agotar, fatigar — *vi* : cansarse

tire[2] *n* : llanta *f,* neumático *m,* goma *f*

tired ['taɪrd] *adj* : cansado, agotado, fatigado <to get tired : cansarse>

tireless ['taɪrləs] *adj* : incansable, infatigable — **tirelessly** *adv*

tiresome ['taɪrsəm] *adj* : fastidioso, pesado, tedioso — **tiresomely** *adv*

tissue ['tɪ,ʃuː] *n* **1** : pañuelo *m* de papel **2** : tejido *m* <lung tissue : tejido pulmonar>

titanic [taɪ'tænɪk, tə-] *adj* GIGANTIC : titánico, gigantesco

titanium [taɪ'teɪniəm, tə-] *n* : titanio *m*

titillate ['tɪtəl,eɪt] *vt* **-lated; -lating** : excitar, estimular placenteramente

title[1] ['taɪtəl] *vt* **-tled; -tling** : titular, intitular

title[2] *n* : título *m*

titter[1] ['tɪtər] *vi* GIGGLE : reírse tontamente

titter[2] *n* : risita *f,* risa *f* tonta

tizzy ['tɪzi] *n, pl* **tizzies** : estado *m* agitado o nervioso <I'm all in a tizzy : estoy todo alterado>

TNT [,tiː,ɛn'tiː] *n* : TNT *m*

to[1] ['tuː] *adv* **1** : a un estado consciente <to come to : volver en sí> **2 to and fro** : de aquí para allá, de un lado para otro

to[2] *prep* **1** (*indicating a place*) : a <to go to the doctor : ir al médico> <I'm going to John's : voy a la casa de John> **2** TOWARD : a, hacia <two miles to the south : dos millas hacia el sur> **3** ON : en, sobre <apply salve to the wound : póngale ungüento a la herida> **4** UP TO : hasta, a <to a degree : hasta cierto grado> <from head to toe : de pies a cabeza> **5** (*in expressions of time*) <it's quarter to seven : son las siete menos cuarto> **6** UNTIL : a, hasta <from May to December : de mayo a diciembre> **7** (*indicating belonging or possession*) : de, a <the key to the lock : la llave del candado> **8** (*indicating response*) : a <dancing to the rhythm : bailando al compás> **9** (*indicating comparison or proportion*) : a <it's similar to mine : es parecido al mío> <they won 4 to 2 : ganaron 4 a 2> **10** (*indicating agreement or conformity*) : a, de acuerdo con <made to order : hecho a la orden> <to my knowledge : a mi saber> **11** (*indicating inclusion*) : en cada, por <twenty to the box : veinte por caja> **12** (*used to form the infinitive*) <to understand : entender> <to go away : irse>

toad ['toːd] *n* : sapo *m*

toadstool ['toːd,stuːl] *n* : hongo *m* (no comestible)

toady ['toːdi] *n, pl* **toadies** : adulador *m,* -dora *f*

toast[1] ['toːst] *vt* **1** : tostar (pan) **2** : brindar por <to toast the victors : brindar por los vencedores> **3** WARM : calentar <to toast oneself : calentarse>

toast[2] *n* **1** : pan *m* tostado, tostadas *fpl* **2** : brindis *m* <to propose a toast : proponer un brindis>

toaster ['toːstər] *n* : tostador *m*

tobacco [tə'bækoː] *n, pl* **-cos** : tabaco *m*

toboggan[1] [tə'bɑgən] *vi* : deslizarse en tobogán

toboggan[2] *n* : tobogán *m*

today[1] [tə'deɪ] *adv* **1** : hoy <she arrives today : hoy llega> **2** NOWADAYS : hoy en día

today[2] *n* : hoy *m* <today is a holiday : hoy es día de fiesta>

toddle ['tɑdəl] *vi* **-dled; -dling** : hacer pininos, hacer pinitos

toddler ['tɑdələr] *n* : niño *m* pequeño, niña *f* pequeña (que comienza a caminar)

to–do [tə'duː] *n, pl* **to–dos** [-'duːz] FUSS : lío *m,* alboroto *m*

toe ['toː] *n* : dedo *m* del pie

toenail ['toː,neɪl] *n* : uña *f* del pie

toffee *or* **toffy** ['tɔfi, 'tɑ-] *n, pl* **toffees** *or* **toffies** : caramelo *m* elaborado con azúcar y mantequilla

toga ['toːgə] *n* : toga *f*

together [tə'gɛðər] *adv* **1** : juntamente, juntos (el uno con el otro) <Susan and Sarah work together : Susan y Sarah trabajan juntas> **2 ~ with** : junto con

togetherness [tə'gɛðərnəs] *n* : unión *f,* compañerismo *m*

togs ['tɑgz, 'tɔgz] *npl* : ropa *f*

toil[1] ['tɔɪl] *vi* : trabajar arduamente

toil[2] *n* : trabajo *m* arduo

toilet ['tɔɪlət] *n* **1** : arreglo *m* personal **2** BATHROOM : (cuarto de) baño *m,* servicios *mpl* (públicos), sanitario *m Col, Mex, Ven* **3** : inodoro *m* <to flush the toilet : jalar la cadena>

toilet paper *n* : papel *m* higiénico

toiletries ['tɔɪlətriz] *npl* : artículos *mpl* de tocador

token ['toːkən] *n* **1** PROOF, SIGN : prueba *f,* muestra *f,* señal *m* **2** SYMBOL : símbolo *m* **3** SOUVENIR : recuerdo *m* **4** : ficha *f* (para transporte público, etc.)

told → **tell**

tolerable ['tɑlərəbəl] *adj* : tolerable — **tolerably** [-bli] *adv*

tolerance ['tɑlərənts] *n* : tolerancia *f*

tolerant ['tɑlərənt] *adj* : tolerante — **tolerantly** *adv*

tolerate ['tɑlə͵reɪt] *vt* **-ated; -ating 1** ACCEPT : tolerar, aceptar **2** BEAR, ENDURE : tolerar, aguantar, soportar
toleration [͵tɑlə'reɪʃən] *n* : tolerancia *f*
toll[1] ['toːl] *vt* : tañer, sonar (una campana) — *vi* : sonar, doblar (dícese de las campanas)
toll[2] *n* **1** : peaje *m* (de una carretera, un puente, etc.) **2** CASUALTIES : pérdida *f,* número *m* de víctimas **3** TOLLING : tañido *m* (de campanas)
tollbooth ['toːl͵buːθ] *n* : caseta *f* de peaje
tollgate ['toːl͵geɪt] *n* : barrera *f* de peaje
tomahawk ['tɑmə͵hɔk] *n* : hacha *f* de guerra (de los indígenas norteamericanos)
tomato [tə'meɪt̬o, -'mɑ-] *n, pl* **-toes** : tomate *m*
tomb ['tuːm] *n* : sepulcro *m,* tumba *f*
tomboy ['tɑm͵bɔɪ] *n* : marimacho *mf;* niña *f* que se porta como muchacho
tombstone ['tuːm͵stoːn] *n* : lápida *f*
tomcat ['tɑm͵kæt] *n* : gato *m* (macho)
tome ['toːm] *n* : tomo *m*
tomorrow[1] [tə'mɑro] *adv* : mañana
tomorrow[2] *n* : mañana *m*
tom–tom ['tɑm͵tɑm] *n* : tam-tam *m*
ton ['tən] *n* : tonelada *f*
tone[1] ['toːn] *vt* **toned; toning 1** *or* **to tone down** : atenuar, suavizar, moderar **2** *or* **to tone up** STRENGTHEN : tonificar, vigorizar
tone[2] *n* : tono *m* <in a friendly tone : en tono amistoso> <a greyish tone : un tono grisáceo>
tongs ['tɑŋz, 'tɔŋz] *npl* : tenazas *fpl*
tongue ['tʌŋ] *n* **1** : lengua *f* **2** LANGUAGE : lengua *f,* idioma *m*
tongue–tied ['tʌŋ͵taɪd] *adj* **to get tongue–tied** : trabársele la lengua a uno
tonic[1] ['tɑnɪk] *adj* : tónico
tonic[2] *n* **1** : tónico *m* **2** *or* **tonic water** : tónica *f*
tonight[1] [tə'naɪt] *adv* : esta noche
tonight[2] *n* : esta noche *f*
tonsil ['tɑntsəl] *n* : amígdala *f,* angina *f Mex*
tonsillitis [͵tɑntsə'laɪt̬əs] *n* : amigdalitis *f,* anginas *fpl Mex*
too ['tuː] *adv* **1** ALSO : también **2** EXCESSIVELY : demasiado <it's too hot in here : aquí hace demasiado calor>
took → **take**[1]
tool[1] ['tuːl] *vt* **1** : fabricar, confeccionar (con herramientas) **2** EQUIP : instalar maquinaria en (una fábrica)
tool[2] *n* : herramienta *f*
toolbox ['tuːl͵bɑks] *n* : caja *f* de herramientas
toot[1] ['tuːt] *vt* : sonar (un claxon o un pito)
toot[2] *n* : pitido *m,* bocinazo *m* (de un claxon)
tooth ['tuːθ] *n, pl* **teeth** ['tiːθ] : diente *m*
toothache ['tuːθ͵eɪk] *n* : dolor *m* de muelas
toothbrush ['tuːθ͵brʌʃ] *n* : cepillo *m* de dientes
toothless ['tuːθləs] *adj* : desdentado
toothpaste ['tuːθ͵peɪst] *n* : pasta *f* de dientes, crema *f* dental, dentífrico *m*
toothpick ['tuːθ͵pɪk] *n* : palillo *m* (de dientes), mondadientes *m*
top[1] ['tɑp] *vt* **topped; topping 1** COVER : cubrir, coronar **2** SURPASS : sobrepasar, superar **3** CLEAR : pasar por encima de
top[2] *adj* : superior <the top shelf : la repisa superior> <one of the top lawyers : uno de los mejores abogados>
top[3] *n* **1** : parte *f* superior, cumbre *f,* cima *f* (de un monte, etc.) <to climb to the top : subir a la cumbre> **2** COVER : tapa *f,* cubierta *f* **3** : trompo *m* (juguete) **4 on top of** : encima de
topaz ['toː͵pæz] *n* : topacio *m*
topcoat ['tɑp͵koːt] *n* : sobretodo *m,* abrigo *m*
topic ['tɑpɪk] *n* : tema *f,* tópico *m*
topical ['tɑpɪkəl] *adj* : de interés actual
topmost ['tɑp͵moːst] *adj* : más alto
top–notch ['tɑp'nɑtʃ] *adj* : de lo mejor, de primera categoría
topographic [͵tɑpə'græfɪk,] *or* **topographical** [-fɪkəl] *adj* : topográfico
topography [tə'pɑgrəfi] *n, pl* **-phies** : topografía *f*
topple ['tɑpəl] *v* **-pled; -pling** *vi* : caerse, venirse abajo — *vt* : volcar, derrocar (un gobierno, etc.)
topsoil ['tɑp͵sɔɪl] *n* : capa *f* superior del suelo
topsy–turvy [͵tɑpsi'tərvi] *adv & adj* : patas arriba, al revés
torch ['tɔrtʃ] *n* : antorcha *f*
tore → **tear**[1]
torment[1] [tɔr'mɛnt, 'tɔr͵-] *vt* : atormentar, torturar, martirizar
torment[2] ['tɔr͵mɛnt] *n* : tormento *m,* suplicio *m,* martirio *m*
tormentor [tɔr'mɛntər] *n* : atormentador *m,* -dora *f*
torn → **tear**[1]
tornado [tɔr'neɪdo] *n, pl* **-does** *or* **-dos** : tornado *m*
torpedo[1] [tɔr'piːdo] *vt* : torpedear
torpedo[2] *n, pl* **-does** : torpedo *m*
torpid ['tɔrpɪd] *adj* **1** SLUGGISH : aletargado **2** APATHETIC : apático
torpor ['tɔrpər] *n* : letargo *m,* apatía *f*
torrent ['tɔrənt] *n* : torrente *m*
torrential [tɔ'rɛntʃəl, tə-] *adj* : torrencial
torrid ['tɔrɪd] *adj* : tórrido
torso ['tɔr͵soː] *n, pl* **-sos** *or* **-si** [-͵siː] : torso *m*
tortilla [tɔr'tiːjə] *n* : tortilla *f*
tortoise ['tɔrt̬əs] *n* : tortuga *f* (terrestre)
tortoiseshell ['tɔrt̬əs͵ʃɛl] *n* : carey *m,* concha *f*
tortuous ['tɔrtʃʊəs] *adj* : tortuoso

torture[1] [ˈtɔrtʃər] *vt* **-tured; -turing** : torturar, atormentar

torture[2] *n* : tortura *f,* tormento *m* <it was sheer torture! : ¡fue un verdadero suplicio!>

torturer [ˈtɔrtʃərər] *n* : torturador *m,* -dora *f*

toss[1] [ˈtɔs, ˈtɑs] *vt* **1** AGITATE, SHAKE : sacudir, agitar, mezclar (una ensalada) **2** THROW : tirar, echar, lanzar — *vi* : sacudirse, moverse agitadamente <to toss and turn : dar vueltas>

toss[2] *n* THROW : lanzamiento *m,* tiro *m,* tirada *f,* lance *m* (de dados, etc.)

toss–up [ˈtɔsˌʌp] *n* : posibilidad *f* igual <it's a toss-up : quizá sí, quizá no>

tot [ˈtɑt] *n* : pequeño *m,* -ña *f*

total[1] [ˈtoːtəl] *vt* **-taled** *or* **-talled; -taling** *or* **-talling 1** *or* **to total up** ADD : sumar, totalizar **2** AMOUNT TO : ascender a, llegar a

total[2] *adj* : total, completo, absoluto — **totally** *adv*

total[3] *n* : total *m*

totalitarian [toːˌtæləˈtɛriən] *adj* : totalitario

totalitarianism [toːˌtæləˈtɛriəˌnɪzəm] *n* : totalitarismo *m*

totality [toːˈtæləṭi] *n, pl* **-ties** : totalidad *f*

tote [ˈtoːt] *vt* **toted; toting** : cargar, llevar

totem [ˈtoːtəm] *n* : tótem *m*

totter [ˈtɑtər] *vi* : tambalearse

touch[1] [ˈtʌtʃ] *vt* **1** FEEL, HANDLE : tocar, tentar **2** AFFECT, MOVE : conmover, afectar, tocar <his gesture touched our hearts : su gesto nos tocó el corazón> — *vi* : tocarse

touch[2] *n* **1** : tacto *m* (sentido) **2** DETAIL : toque *m,* detalle *m* <a touch of color : un toque de color> **3** BIT : pizca *f,* gota *f,* poco *m* **4** ABILITY : habilidad *f* <to lose one's touch : perder la habilidad> **5** CONTACT : contacto *m,* comunicación *f* <to keep in touch : mantenerse en contacto>

touchdown [ˈtʌtʃˌdaʊn] *n* : touchdown *m* (en futbol americano)

touch up *vt* : retocar

touchy [ˈtʌtʃi] *adj* **touchier; -est 1** : sensible, susceptible (dícese de una persona) **2** : delicado <a touchy subject : un tema delicado>

tough[1] [ˈtʌf] *adj* **1** STRONG : fuerte, resistente (dícese de materiales) **2** LEATHERY : correoso <a tough steak : un bistec duro> **3** HARDY : fuerte, robusto (dícese de una persona) **4** STRICT : severo, exigente **5** DIFFICULT : difícil **6** STUBBORN : terco, obstinado

tough[2] *n* : matón *m,* persona *f* ruda y brusca

toughen [ˈtʌfən] *vt* : fortalecer, endurecer — *vi* : endurecerse, hacerse más fuerte

toughness [ˈtʌfnəs] *n* : dureza *f*

toupee [tuːˈpeɪ] *n* : peluquín *m,* bisoñé *m*

tour[1] [ˈtʊr] *vi* : tomar una excursión, viajar — *vt* : recorrer, hacer una gira por

tour[2] *n* **1** : gira *f,* tour *m,* excursión *f* **2 tour of duty** : período *m* de servicio

tourist [ˈtʊrɪst, ˈtər-] *n* : turista *mf*

tournament [ˈtərnəmənt, ˈtʊr-] *n* : torneo *m*

tourniquet [ˈtərnɪkət, ˈtʊr-] *n* : torniquete *m*

tousle [ˈtaʊzəl] *vt* **-sled; -sling** : desarreglar, despeinar (el cabello)

tout [ˈtaʊt] *vt* : promocionar, elogiar (con exageración)

tow[1] [ˈtoː] *vt* : remolcar

tow[2] *n* : remolque *m*

toward [ˈtord, təˈwɔrd] *or* **towards** [ˈtordz, təˈwɔrdz] *prep* **1** (*indicating direction*) : hacia, rumbo a <heading toward town : dirigiéndose rumbo al pueblo> <efforts towards peace : esfuerzos hacia la paz> **2** (*indicating time*) : alrededor de <toward midnight : alrededor de la medianoche> **3** REGARDING : hacia, con respecto a <his attitude toward life : su actitud hacia la vida> **4** FOR : para, como pago parcial de (una compra o deuda)

towel [ˈtaʊəl] *n* : toalla *f*

tower[1] [ˈtaʊər] *vi* **to tower over** : descollar sobre, elevarse sobre, dominar

tower[2] *n* : torre *f*

towering [ˈtaʊərɪŋ] *adj* : altísimo, imponente

town [ˈtaʊn] *n* : pueblo *m,* ciudad *f* (pequeña)

township [ˈtaʊnˌʃɪp] *n* : municipio *m*

tow truck [ˈtoːˌtrʌk] *n* : grúa *f*

toxic [ˈtɑksɪk] *adj* : tóxico

toxicity [tɑkˈsɪsəṭi] *n, pl* **-ties** : toxicidad *f*

toxin [ˈtɑksɪn] *n* : toxina *f*

toy[1] [ˈtɔɪ] *vi* : juguetear, jugar

toy[2] *adj* : de juguete <a toy rifle : un rifle de juguete>

toy[3] *n* : juguete *m*

trace[1] [ˈtreɪs] *vt* **traced; tracing 1** : calcar (un dibujo, etc.) **2** OUTLINE : delinear, trazar (planes, etc.) **3** TRACK : describir (un curso, una historia) **4** FIND : localizar, ubicar

trace[2] *n* **1** SIGN, TRACK : huella *f,* rastro *m,* indicio *m,* vestigio *m* <he disappeared without a trace : desapareció sin dejar rastro> **2** BIT, HINT : pizca *f,* ápice *m,* dejo *m*

trachea [ˈtreɪkiə] *n, pl* **-cheae** [-kiˌiː] : tráquea *f*

tracing paper *n* : papel *m* de calcar

track[1] [ˈtræk] *vt* **1** TRAIL : seguir la pista de, rastrear **2** : dejar huellas de <he tracked mud all over : dejó huellas de lodo por todas partes>

track[2] *n* **1** : rastro *m,* huella *f* (de animales), pista *f* (de personas) **2** PATH : pista *f,* sendero *m,* camino *m* **3** *or* **railroad track** : vía *f* (férrea) **4** → **racetrack 5** : oruga *f* (de un tanque,

etc.) **6** : pista *f* (deporte) **7 to keep track of** : llevar la cuenta de
track–and–field ['trækənd'fi:ld] *adj* : de pista y campo
tract ['trækt] *n* **1** AREA : terreno *m,* extensión *f,* área *f* **2** : tracto *m* <digestive tract : tracto digestivo> **3** PAMPHLET : panfleto *m,* folleto *m*
traction ['trækʃən] *n* : tracción *f*
tractor ['træktər] *n* **1** : tractor *m* (vehículo agrícola) **2** TRUCK : camión *m* (con remolque)
trade¹ ['treɪd] *v* **traded; trading** *vi* : comerciar, negociar — *vt* EXCHANGE : intercambiar, canjear
trade² *n* **1** OCCUPATION : oficio *m,* profesión *f,* ocupación *f* <a carpenter by trade : carpintero de oficio> **2** COMMERCE : comercio *m,* industria *f* <free trade : libre comercio> <the book trade : la industria del libro> **3** EXCHANGE : intercambio *m,* canje *m*
trade–in ['treɪd,ɪn] *n* : artículo *m* que se canjea por otro
trademark ['treɪd,mɑrk] *n* **1** : marca *f* registrada **2** CHARACTERISTIC : sello *m* característico (de un grupo, una persona, etc.)
trader ['treɪdər] *n* : negociante *mf,* tratante *mf,* comerciante *mf*
tradesman ['treɪdzmən] *n, pl* **-men** [-mən, -,mɛn] **1** CRAFTSMAN : artesano *m,* -na *f* **2** SHOPKEEPER : tendero *m,* -ra *f;* comerciante *mf*
trade wind *n* : viento *m* alisio
tradition [trə'dɪʃən] *n* : tradición *f*
traditional [trə'dɪʃənəl] *adj* : tradicional — **traditionally** *adv*
traffic¹ ['træfɪk] *vi* **trafficked; trafficking** : traficar (en)
traffic² *n* **1** COMMERCE : tráfico *m,* comercio *m* <the drug traffic : el narcotráfico> **2** : tráfico *m,* tránsito *m,* circulación *f* (de vehículos, etc.)
traffic circle *n* : rotonda *f,* glorieta *f*
trafficker ['træfɪkər] *n* : traficante *mf*
traffic light *n* : semáforo *m,* luz *f* (de tránsito)
tragedy ['trædʒədi] *n, pl* **-dies** : tragedia *f*
tragic ['trædʒɪk] *adj* : trágico — **tragically** *adv*
trail¹ ['treɪl] *vi* **1** DRAG : arrastrarse **2** LAG : quedarse atrás, retrasarse **3 to trail away** *or* **to trail off** : disminuir, menguar, desvanecerse — *vt* **1** DRAG : arrastrar **2** PURSUE : perseguir, seguir la pista de
trail² *n* **1** TRACK : rastro *m,* huella *f,* pista *f* <a trail of blood : un rastro de sangre> **2** : cola *f,* estela *f* (de un meteoro) **3** PATH : sendero *m,* camino *m,* vereda *f*
trailer ['treɪlər] *n* **1** : remolque *m,* tráiler *m* (de un camión) **2** : caravana *f* (vivienda ambulante)
train¹ ['treɪn] *vt* **1** : entrenar (atletas), capacitar (empleados), adiestrar, amaestrar (animales) **2** POINT : apuntar (un arma, etc.) — *vi* : entrenar(se) (físicamente), prepararse (profesionalmente) <she's training at the gym : se está entrenando en el gimnasio>
train² *n* **1** : cola *f* (de un vestido) **2** RETINUE : cortejo *m,* séquito *m* **3** SERIES : serie *f* (de eventos) **4** : tren *m* <passenger train : tren de pasajeros>
trainee [treɪ'ni:] *n* : aprendiz *m,* -diza *f*
trainer ['treɪnər] *n* : entrenador *m,* -dora *f*
traipse ['treɪps] *vi* **traipsed; traipsing** : andar de un lado para otro, vagar
trait ['treɪt] *n* : rasgo *m,* característica *f*
traitor ['treɪtər] *n* : traidor *m,* -dora *f*
traitorous ['treɪtərəs] *adj* : traidor
trajectory [trə'dʒɛktəri] *n, pl* **-ries** : trayectoria *f*
tramp¹ ['træmp] *vi* : caminar (a paso pesado) — *vt* : deambular por, vagar por <to tramp the streets : vagar por las calles>
tramp² *n* **1** VAGRANT : vagabundo *m,* -da *f* **2** HIKE : caminata *f*
trample ['træmpəl] *vt* **-pled; -pling** : pisotear, hollar
trampoline [,træmpə'li:n, 'træmpə,-] *n* : trampolín *m,* cama *f* elástica
trance ['trænts] *n* : trance *m*
tranquil ['træŋkwəl] *adj* : calmo, tranquilo, sereno — **tranquilly** *adv*
tranquilize ['træŋkwə,laɪz] *vt* **-ized; -izing** : tranquilizar
tranquilizer ['træŋkwə,laɪzər] *n* : tranquilizante *m*
tranquillity *or* **tranquility** [træŋ'kwɪləṭi] *n* : sosiego *m,* tranquilidad *f*
transact [træn'zækt] *vt* : negociar, gestionar, hacer (negocios)
transaction [træn'zækʃən] *n* **1** : transacción *f,* negocio *m,* operación *f* **2 transactions** *npl* RECORDS : actas *fpl*
transatlantic [,træntsət'læntɪk, ,trænz-] *adj* : transatlántico
transcend [træn'sɛnd] *vt* : trascender, sobrepasar
transcribe [træn'skraɪb] *vt* **-scribed; -scribing** : transcribir
transcript ['træn,skrɪpt] *n* : copia *f* oficial
transcription [træn'skrɪpʃən] *n* : transcripción *f*
transfer¹ [trænts'fər, 'trænts,fər] *v* **-ferred; -ferring** *vt* **1** : trasladar (a una persona), transferir (fondos) **2** : transferir, traspasar, ceder (propiedad) **3** PRINT : imprimir (un diseño) — *vi* **1** MOVE : trasladarse, cambiarse **2** CHANGE : transbordar, cambiar (de un transporte a otro) <she transferred at E Street : hizo un transborde a la calle E>
transfer² ['trænts,fər] *n* **1** TRANSFERRING : transferencia *f* (de fondos, de

propiedad, etc.), traslado *m* (de una persona) **2** DECAL **:** calcomanía *f* **3** **:** boleto *m* (para cambiar de un avión, etc., a otro)

transferable [træn*t*s'fərəbəl] *adj* **:** transferible

transference [træn*t*s'fərən*t*s] *n* **:** transferencia *f*

transfigure [træn*t*s'fɪgjər] *vt* **-ured; -uring :** transfigurar, transformar

transfix [træn*t*s'fɪks] *vt* **1** PIERCE **:** traspasar, atravesar **2** IMMOBILIZE **:** paralizar

transform [træn*t*s'fɔrm] *vt* **:** transformar

transformation [ˌtræn*t*sfər'meɪʃən] *n* **:** transformación *f*

transformer [træn*t*s'fɔrmər] *n* **:** transformador *m*

transfusion [træn*t*s'fjuːʒən] *n* **:** transfusión *f*

transgress [træn*t*s'grɛs, trænz-] *vt* **:** transgredir, infringir

transgression [træn*t*s'grɛʃən, trænz-] *n* **:** transgresión *f*

transient¹ ['træntʃənt, 'trænsiənt] *adj* **:** pasajero, transitorio — **transiently** *adv*

transient² *n* **:** transeúnte *mf*

transistor [træn'zɪstər, -'sɪs-] *n* **:** transistor *m*

transit ['træn*t*sɪt, 'trænzɪt] *n* **1** PASSAGE **:** pasaje *m,* tránsito *m* <in transit : en tránsito> **2** TRANSPORTATION **:** transporte *m* (público) **3 :** teodolito *m* (instrumento topográfico)

transition [træn'sɪʃən, -'zɪʃ-] *n* **:** transición *f*

transitional [træn'sɪʃənəl, -'zɪʃ-] *adj* **:** de transición

transitive ['træn*t*sət̬ɪv, 'trænzə-] *adj* **:** transitivo

transitory ['træn*t*səˌtori, 'trænzə-] *adj* **:** transitorio

translate [træn*t*s'leɪt, trænz-; 'træn*t*sˌ-, 'trænsˌ-] *vt* **-lated; -lating :** traducir

translation [træn*t*s'leɪʃən, trænz-] *n* **:** traducción *f*

translator [træn*t*s'leɪt̬ər, trænz-; 'træn*t*sˌ-, 'trænsˌ-] *n* **:** traductor *m,* -tora *f*

translucent [træn*t*s'luːsənt, trænz-] *adj* **:** translúcido

transmission [træn*t*s'mɪʃən, trænz-] *n* **:** transmisión *f*

transmit [træn*t*s'mɪt, trænz-] *vt* **-mitted; -mitting :** transmitir

transmitter [træn*t*s'mɪt̬ər, trænz-; 'træn*t*sˌ-, 'trænsˌ-] *n* **:** transmisor *m,* emisor *m*

transom ['træn*t*səm] *n* **:** montante *m* (de una puerta), travesaño *m* (de una ventana)

transparency [træn*t*s'pærən*t*si] *n, pl* **-cies :** transparencia *f*

transparent [træn*t*s'pærənt] *adj* **1** **:** transparente, traslúcido <a transparent fabric : una tela transparente> **2** OBVIOUS **:** transparente, obvio, claro — **transparently** *adv*

transpiration [ˌtræn*t*spə'reɪʃən] *n* **:** transpiración *f*

transpire [træn*t*s'paɪr] *vi* **-spired; -spiring 1 :** transpirar (en biología y botanía) **2** TURN OUT **:** resultar **3** HAPPEN **:** suceder, ocurrir, tener lugar

transplant¹ [træn*t*s'plænt] *vt* **:** trasplantar

transplant² ['træn*t*sˌplænt] *n* **:** trasplante *m*

transport¹ [træn*t*s'port, 'træn*t*sˌ-] *vt* **1** CARRY **:** transportar, acarrear **2** ENRAPTURE **:** transportar, extasiar

transport² ['træn*t*sˌport] *n* **1** TRANSPORTATION **:** transporte *m,* transportación *f* **2** RAPTURE **:** éxtasis *m* **3** *or* **transport ship :** buque *m* de transporte (de personal militar)

transportation [ˌtræn*t*spər'teɪʃən] *n* **:** transporte *m,* transportación *f*

transpose [træn*t*s'poːz] *vt* **-posed; -posing :** trasponer, trasladar, transportar (una composición musical)

transverse [træn*t*s'vərs, trænz-] *adj* **:** transversal, transverso, oblicuo — **transversely** *adv*

trap¹ ['træp] *vt* **trapped; trapping :** atrapar, apresar (en una trampa)

trap² *n* **:** trampa *f* <to set a trap : tender una trampa>

trapdoor ['træp'dor] *n* **:** trampilla *f,* escotillón *m*

trapeze [træ'piːz] *n* **:** trapecio *m*

trapezoid ['træpəˌzɔɪd] *n* **:** trapezoide *m,* trapecio *m*

trapper ['træpər] *n* **:** trampero *m,* -ra *f;* cazador *m,* -dora *f* (que usa trampas)

trappings ['træpɪŋz] *npl* **1 :** arreos *mpl,* jaeces *mpl* (de un caballo) **2** ADORNMENTS **:** adornos *mpl,* pompa *f*

trash ['træʃ] *n* **:** basura *f*

trauma ['trɔmə, 'traʊ-] *n* **:** trauma *m*

traumatic [trə'mæt̬ɪk, trɔ-, traʊ-] *adj* **:** traumático

travel¹ ['trævəl] *vi* **-eled** *or* **-elled; -eling** *or* **-elling 1** JOURNEY **:** viajar **2** GO, MOVE **:** desplazarse, moverse, ir <the waves travel at uniform speed : las ondas se desplazan a una velocidad uniforme>

travel² *n* **:** viajes *mpl*

traveler *or* **traveller** ['trævələr] *n* **:** viajero *m,* -ra *f*

traverse [trə'vərs, træ'vərs, 'trævərs] *vt* **-versed; -versing** CROSS **:** atravesar, extenderse a través de, cruzar

travesty ['trævəsti] *n, pl* **-ties :** parodia *f*

trawl¹ ['trɔl] *vi* **:** pescar con red de arrastre, rastrear

trawl² *n or* **trawl net :** red *f* de arrastre

trawler ['trɔlər] *n* **:** barco *m* de pesca (utilizado para rastrear)

tray ['treɪ] *n* **:** bandeja *f,* charola *f Bol, Mex, Peru*

treacherous ['trɛtʃərəs] *adj* **1** TRAITOROUS : traicionero, traidor **2** DANGEROUS : peligroso
treacherously ['trɛtʃərəsli] *adv* : a traición
treachery ['trɛtʃəri] *n, pl* **-eries** : traición *f*
tread[1] ['trɛd] *v* **trod** ['trɑd]; **trodden** ['trɑdən] *or* **trod; treading** *vt* TRAMPLE : pisotear, hollar — *vi* **1** WALK : caminar, andar **2 to tread on** : pisar
tread[2] *n* **1** STEP : paso *m,* andar *m* **2** : banda *f* de rodadura (de un neumático, etc.) **3** : escalón *m* (de una escalera)
treadle ['trɛdəl] *n* : pedal *m* (de una máquina)
treadmill ['trɛd,mɪl] *n* **1** : rueda *f* de andar **2** ROUTINE : rutina *f*
treason ['triːzən] *n* : traición *f* (a la patria, etc.)
treasure[1] ['trɛʒər, 'treɪ-] *vt* **-sured; -suring** : apreciar, valorar
treasure[2] *n* : tesoro *m*
treasurer ['trɛʒərər, 'treɪ-] *n* : tesorero *m,* -ra *f*
treasury ['trɛʒəri, 'treɪ-] *n, pl* **-suries** : tesorería *f,* tesoro *m*
treat[1] ['triːt] *vt* **1** DEAL WITH : tratar (un asunto) <the article treats of poverty : el artículo trata de la pobreza> **2** HANDLE : tratar (a una persona), manejar (un objeto) <to treat something as a joke : tomar(se) algo a broma> **3** INVITE : invitar, convidar <he treated me to a meal : me invitó a comer> **4** : tratar, atender (en medicina) **5** PROCESS : tratar <to treat sewage : tratar las aguas negras>
treat[2] *n* : gusto *m,* placer *m* <it was a treat to see you : fue un placer verte> <it's my treat : yo invito>
treatise ['triːtɪs] *n* : tratado *m,* estudio *m*
treatment ['triːtmənt] *n* : trato *m,* tratamiento *m* (médico)
treaty ['triːti] *n, pl* **-ties** : tratado *m,* convenio *m*
treble[1] ['trɛbəl] *vt* **-bled; -bling** : triplicar
treble[2] *adj* **1** → **triple 2** : de tiple, soprano (en música) **3 treble clef** : clave *f* de sol
treble[3] *n* : tiple *m,* parte *f* soprana
tree ['triː] *n* : árbol *m*
treeless ['triːləs] *adj* : carente de árboles
trek[1] ['trɛk] *vi* **trekked; trekking** : hacer un viaje largo y difícil
trek[2] *n* : viaje *m* largo y difícil
trellis ['trɛlɪs] *n* : enrejado *m,* espaldera *f,* celosía *f*
tremble ['trɛmbəl] *vi* **-bled; -bling** : temblar
tremendous [trɪ'mɛndəs] *adj* : tremendo — **tremendously** *adv*
tremor ['trɛmər] *n* : temblor *m*
tremulous ['trɛmjələs] *adj* : trémulo, tembloroso
trench ['trɛntʃ] *n* **1** DITCH : zanja *f* **2** : trinchera *f* (militar)
trenchant ['trɛntʃənt] *adj* : cortante, mordaz
trend[1] ['trɛnd] *vi* : tender, inclinarse
trend[2] *n* **1** TENDENCY : tendencia *f* **2** FASHION : moda *f*
trendy ['trɛndi] *adj* **trendier; -est** : de moda
trepidation [,trɛpə'deɪʃən] *n* : inquietud *f,* ansiedad *f*
trespass[1] ['trɛspəs, -,pæs] *vi* **1** SIN : pecar, transgredir **2** : entrar ilegalmente (en propiedad ajena)
trespass[2] *n* **1** SIN : pecado *m,* transgresión *f* <forgive us our trespasses : perdónanos nuestras deudas> **2** : entrada *f* ilegal (en propiedad ajena)
tress ['trɛs] *n* : mechón *m*
trestle ['trɛsəl] *n* **1** : caballete *m* (armazón) **2** *or* **trestle bridge** : puente *m* de caballete
triad ['traɪ,æd] *n* : tríada *f*
trial[1] ['traɪəl] *adj* : de prueba <trial period : período de prueba>
trial[2] *n* **1** : juicio *m,* proceso *m* <to stand trial : ser sometido a juicio> **2** AFFLICTION : aflicción *f,* tribulación *f* **3** TEST : prueba *f,* ensayo *m*
triangle ['traɪ,æŋgəl] *n* : triángulo *m*
triangular [traɪ'æŋgjələr] *adj* : triangular
tribal ['traɪbəl] *adj* : tribal
tribe ['traɪb] *n* : tribu *f*
tribesman ['traɪbzmən] *n, pl* **-men** [-mən, -,mɛn] : miembro *m* de una tribu
tribulation [,trɪbjə'leɪʃən] *n* : tribulación *f*
tribunal [traɪ'bjuːnəl, trɪ-] *n* : tribunal *m,* corte *f*
tributary ['trɪbjə,tɛri] *n, pl* **-taries** : afluente *m*
tribute ['trɪb,juːt] *n* : tributo *m*
trick[1] ['trɪk] *vt* : engañar, embaucar
trick[2] *n* **1** RUSE : trampa *f,* treta *f,* artimaña *f* **2** PRANK : broma *f* <we played a trick on her : le gastamos una broma> **3** : truco *m* <magic tricks : trucos de magia> <the trick is to wait five minutes : el truco está en esperar cinco minutos> **4** MANNERISM : peculiaridad *f,* manía *f* **5** : baza *f* (en juegos de naipes)
trickery ['trɪkəri] *n* : engaños *mpl,* trampas *fpl*
trickle[1] ['trɪkəl] *vi* **-led; -ling** : gotear, chorrear
trickle[2] *n* : goteo *m,* hilo *m*
trickster ['trɪkstər] *n* : estafador *m,* -dora *f;* embaucador *m,* -dora *f*
tricky ['trɪki] *adj* **trickier; -est 1** SLY : astuto, taimado **2** DIFFICULT : delicado, peliagudo, difícil
tricycle ['traɪsəkəl, -,sɪkəl] *n* : triciclo *m*
trident ['traɪdənt] *n* : tridente *m*
triennial [traɪ'ɛniəl] *adj* : trienal
trifle[1] ['traɪfəl] *vi* **-fled; -fling** : jugar, juguetear

trifle[2] *n* : nimiedad *f,* insignificancia *f*
trifling ['traɪflɪŋ] *adj* : trivial, insignificante
trigger[1] ['trɪgər] *vt* : causar, provocar
trigger[2] *n* : gatillo *m*
trigonometry [ˌtrɪgə'nɑmətri] *n* : trigonometría *f*
trill[1] ['trɪl] *vi* QUAVER : trinar, gorjear — *vt* : vibrar <to trill the *r* : vibrar la *r*>
trill[2] *n* **1** QUAVER : trino *m,* gorjeo *m* **2** : vibración *f* (en fonología)
trillion ['trɪljən] *n* : billón *m*
trilogy ['trɪlədʒi] *n, pl* **-gies** : trilogía *f*
trim[1] ['trɪm] *vt* **trimmed; trimming 1** DECORATE : adornar, decorar **2** CUT : recortar **3** REDUCE : recortar, reducir <to trim the excess : recortar el exceso>
trim[2] *adj* **trimmer; trimmest 1** SLIM : esbelto **2** NEAT : limpio y arreglado, bien cuidado
trim[3] *n* **1** CONDITION : condición *f,* estado *m* <to keep in trim : mantenerse en buena forma> **2** CUT : recorte *m* **3** TRIMMING : adornos *mpl*
trimming ['trɪmɪŋ] *n* : adornos *mpl,* accesorios *mpl*
Trinity ['trɪnət̬i] *n* : Trinidad *f*
trinket ['trɪŋkət] *n* : chuchería *f,* baratija *f*
trio ['triːˌoː] *n, pl* **trios** : trío *m*
trip[1] ['trɪp] *v* **tripped; tripping** *vi* **1** : caminar (a paso ligero) **2** STUMBLE : tropezar **3 to trip up** ERR : equivocarse, cometer un error — *vt* **1** : hacerle una zancadilla (a alguien) <you tripped me on purpose! : ¡me hiciste la zancadilla a propósito!> **2** ACTIVATE : activar (un mecanismo) **3 to trip up** : hacer equivocar (a alguien)
trip[2] *n* **1** JOURNEY : viaje *m* <to take a trip : hacer un viaje> **2** STUMBLE : tropiezo *m,* traspié *m*
tripartite [traɪ'pɑrˌtaɪt] *adj* : tripartito
tripe ['traɪp] *n* **1** : mondongo *m,* callos *mpl,* pancita *f Mex* **2** TRASH : porquería *f*
triple[1] ['trɪpəl] *vt* **-pled; -pling** : triplicar
triple[2] *adj* : triple
triple[3] *n* : triple *m*
triplet ['trɪplət] *n* **1** : terceto *m* (en poesía, música, etc.) **2** : trillizo *m,* -za *f* (persona)
triplicate ['trɪplɪkət] *n* : triplicado *m*
tripod ['traɪˌpɑd] *n* : trípode *m*
trite ['traɪt] *adj* **triter; tritest** : trillado, tópico, manido
triumph[1] ['traɪəmpf] *vi* : triunfar
triumph[2] *n* : triunfo *m*
triumphal [traɪ'ʌmpfəl] *adj* : triunfal
triumphant [traɪ'ʌmpfənt] *adj* : triunfante, triunfal — **triumphantly** *adv*
trivia ['trɪviə] *ns & pl* : trivialidades *fpl,* nimiedades *fpl*
trivial ['trɪviəl] *adj* : trivial, intrascendente, insignificante
triviality [ˌtrɪvi'æləţi] *n, pl* **-ties** : trivialidad *f*
trod, trodden → **tread**[1]
troll ['troːl] *n* : duende *m* o gigante *m* de cuentos folklóricos
trolley ['trɑli] *n, pl* **-leys** : tranvía *m*
trombone [trɑm'boːn] *n* : trombón *m*
trombonist [trɑm'boːnɪst] *n* : trombón *m*
troop[1] ['truːp] *vi* : desfilar, ir en tropel
troop[2] *n* **1** : escuadrón *m* (de caballería) **2** GROUP : grupo *m,* banda *f* (de personas) **3 troops** *npl* SOLDIERS : tropas *fpl,* soldados *mpl*
trooper ['truːpər] *n* **1** : soldado *m* (de caballería) **2** : policía *m* montado **3** : policía *m* (estatal)
trophy ['troːfi] *n, pl* **-phies** : trofeo *m*
tropic[1] ['trɑpɪk] *or* **tropical** [-pɪkəl] *adj* : tropical
tropic[2] *n* **1** : trópico *m* <tropic of Cancer : trópico de Cáncer> **2 the tropics** : el trópico
trot[1] ['trɑt] *vi* **trotted; trotting** : trotar
trot[2] *n* : trote *m*
trouble[1] ['trʌbəl] *v* **-bled; -bling** *vt* **1** DISTURB, WORRY : molestar, perturbar, inquietar **2** AFFLICT : afligir, afectar — *vi* : molestarse, hacer un esfuerzo <they didn't trouble to come : no se molestaron en venir>
trouble[2] *n* **1** PROBLEMS : problemas *mpl,* dificultades *fpl* <to be in trouble : estar en un aprieto> <heart trouble : problemas de corazón> **2** EFFORT : molestia *f,* esfuerzo *m* <to take the trouble : tomarse la molestia> <it's not worth the trouble : no vale la pena>
troublemaker ['trʌbəlˌmeɪkər] *n* : agitador *m,* -dora *f;* alborotador *m,* -dora *f*
troublesome ['trʌbəlsəm] *adj* : problemático, dificultoso — **troublesomely** *adv*
trough ['trɔf] *n, pl* **troughs** ['trɔfs, 'trɔvz] **1** : comedero *m,* bebedero *m* (de animales) **2** CHANNEL, HOLLOW : depresión *f* (en el suelo), seno *m* (de olas)
trounce ['traʊnts] *vt* **trounced; trouncing 1** THRASH : apalear, darle una paliza (a alguien) **2** DEFEAT : derrotar contundentemente
troupe ['truːp] *n* : troupe *f*
trousers ['traʊzərz] *npl* : pantalón *m,* pantalones *mpl*
trout ['traʊt] *n, pl* **trout** : trucha *f*
trowel ['traʊəl] *n* **1** : llana *f,* paleta *f* (de albañil) **2** : desplantador *m* (de jardinero)
truant ['truːənt] *n* : alumno *m,* -na *f* que falta a clase sin permiso
truce ['truːs] *n* : tregua *f,* armisticio *m*
truck[1] ['trʌk] *vt* : transportar en camión
truck[2] *n* **1** : camión *m* (vehículo automóvil), carro *m* (manual) **2** DEAL-

INGS : tratos *mpl* <to have no truck with : no tener nada que ver con>
trucker ['trʌkər] *n* : camionero *m,* -ra *f*
truculent ['trʌkjələnt] *adj* : agresivo, beligerante
trudge ['trʌdʒ] *vi* **trudged; trudging** : caminar a paso pesado
true[1] ['tru:] *vt* **trued; trueing** : aplomar (algo vertical), nivelar (algo horizontal), centrar (una rueda)
true[2] *adv* **1** TRUTHFULLY : lealmente, sinceramente **2** ACCURATELY : exactamente, certeramente
true[3] *adj* **truer; truest 1** LOYAL : fiel, leal **2** : cierto, verdadero, verídico <it's true : es cierto, es la verdad> <a true story : una historia verídica> **3** GENUINE : auténtico, genuino — **truly** *adv*
true–blue ['tru:'blu:] *adj* LOYAL : leal, fiel
truffle ['trʌfəl] *n* : trufa *f*
truism ['tru:ˌɪzəm] *n* : perogrullada *f,* verdad *f* obvia
trump[1] ['trʌmp] *vt* : matar (en juegos de naipes)
trump[2] *n* : triunfo *m* (en juegos de naipes)
trumped–up ['trʌmpt'ʌp] *adj* : inventado, fabricado <trumped-up charges : falsas acusaciones>
trumpet[1] ['trʌmpət] *vi* **1** : sonar una trompeta **2** : berrear, bramar (dícese de un animal) — *vt* : proclamar a los cuatro vientos
trumpet[2] *n* : trompeta *f*
trumpeter ['trʌmpət̬ər] *n* : trompetista *mf*
truncate ['trʌŋˌkeɪt, 'trʌn-] *vt* **-cated; -cating** : truncar
trundle ['trʌndəl] *v* **-dled; -dling** *vi* : rodar lentamente — *vt* : hacer rodar, empujar lentamente
trunk ['trʌŋk] *n* **1** : tronco *m* (de un árbol o del cuerpo) **2** : trompa *f* (de un elefante) **3** CHEST : baúl *m* **4** : maletero *m,* cajuela *f Mex* (de un auto) **5 trunks** *npl* : traje *m* de baño (de caballero)
truss[1] ['trʌs] *vt* : atar (con fuerza)
truss[2] *n* **1** FRAMEWORK : armazón *m* (de una estructura) **2** : braguero *m* (en medicina)
trust[1] ['trʌst] *vi* : confiar, esperar <to trust in God : confiar en Dios> — *vt* **1** ENTRUST : confiar, encomendar **2** : confiar en, tenerle confianza a <I trust you : te tengo confianza>
trust[2] *n* **1** CONFIDENCE : confianza *f* **2** HOPE : esperanza *f,* fe *f* **3** CREDIT : crédito *m* <to sell on trust : fiar> **4** : fideicomiso *m* <to hold in trust : guardar en fideicomiso> **5** : trust *m* (consorcio empresarial) **6** CUSTODY : responsabilidad *f,* custodia *f*
trustee [ˌtrʌs'ti:] *n* : fideicomisario *m,* -ria *f;* fiduciario *m,* -ria *f*
trustful ['trʌstfəl] *adj* : confiado — **trustfully** *adv*
trustworthiness ['trəstˌwərðinəs] *n* : integridad *f,* honradez *f*
trustworthy ['trəstˌwərði] *adj* : digno de confianza, confiable
trusty ['trəsti] *adj* **trustier; -est** : fiel, confiable
truth ['tru:θ] *n, pl* **truths** ['tru:ðz, 'tru:θs] : verdad *f*
truthful ['tru:θfəl] *adj* : sincero, veraz — **truthfully** *adv*
truthfulness ['tru:θfəlnəs] *n* : sinceridad *f,* veracidad *f*
try[1] ['traɪ] *v* **tried; trying** *vt* **1** : enjuiciar, juzgar, procesar <he was tried for murder : fue procesado por homicidio> **2** : probar <did you try the salad? : ¿probaste la ensalada?> **3** TEST : tentar, poner a prueba <to try one's patience : tentarle la paciencia a uno> **4** ATTEMPT : tratar (de), intentar **5** *or* **to try on** : probarse (ropa) — *vi* : tratar, intentar
try[2] *n, pl* **tries** : intento *m,* tentativa *f*
tryout ['traɪˌaʊt] *n* : prueba *f*
tsar ['zɑr, 'tsɑr, 'sɑr] → **czar**
T–shirt ['ti:ˌʃərt] *n* : camiseta *f*
tub ['tʌb] *n* **1** CASK : cuba *f,* barril *m,* tonel *m* **2** CONTAINER : envase *m* (de plástico, etc.) <a tub of margarine : un envase de margarina> **3** BATHTUB : tina *f* (de baño), bañera *f*
tuba ['tu:bə, 'tju:-] *n* : tuba *f*
tube ['tu:b, 'tju:b] *n* **1** PIPE : tubo *m* **2** : tubo *m* (de dentífrico, etc.) **3** *or* **inner tube** : cámara *f* **4** : tubo *m* (de un aparato electrónico) **5** : trompa *f* (en anatomía)
tubeless ['tu:bləs, 'tju:b-] *adj* : sin cámara (dícese de una llanta)
tuber ['tu:bər, 'tju:-] *n* : tubérculo *m*
tubercular [tʊ'bərkjələr, tjʊ-] → **tuberculous**
tuberculosis [tʊˌbərkjə'lo:sɪs, tjʊ-] *n, pl* **-loses** [-ˌsi:z] : tuberculosis *f*
tuberculous [tʊ'bərkjələs, tjʊ-] *adj* : tuberculoso
tuberous ['tu:bərəs, 'tju:-] *adj* : tuberoso
tubing ['tu:bɪŋ, 'tju:-] *n* : tubería *f*
tubular ['tu:bjələr, 'tju:-] *adj* : tubular
tuck[1] ['tʌk] *vt* **1** PLACE, PUT : meter, colocar <tuck in your shirt : métete la camisa> **2** : guardar, esconder <to tuck away one's money : guardar uno bien su dinero> **3** COVER : arropar (a un niño en la cama)
tuck[2] *n* : pliegue *m,* alforza *f*
Tuesday ['tu:zˌdeɪ, 'tju:z-, -di] *n* : martes *m*
tuft ['tʌft] *n* : penacho *m* (de plumas), copete *m* (de pelo)
tug[1] ['tʌg] *v* **tugged; tugging** *vi* : tirar, jalar, dar un tirón — *vt* : jalar, arrastrar, remolcar (con un barco)
tug[2] *n* **1** : tirón *m,* jalón *m* **2** → **tugboat**
tugboat ['tʌgˌbo:t] *n* : remolcador *m*
tug–of–war [ˌtʌgə'wɔr] *n, pl* **tugs–of–war** : tira y afloja *m*
tulip ['tu:lɪp, 'tju:-] *n* : tulipán *m*

tumble[1] ['tʌmbəl] *v* **-bled; -bling** *vi* **1** : dar volteretas (en acrobacia) **2** FALL : caerse, venirse abajo — *vt* **1** TOPPLE : volcar **2** TOSS : hacer girar

tumble[2] *n* : voltereta *f,* caída *f*

tumbler ['tʌmblər] *n* **1** ACROBAT : acróbata *mf,* saltimbanqui *mf* **2** GLASS : vaso *m* (de mesa) **3** : clavija *f* (de una cerradura)

tummy ['tʌmi] *n, pl* **-mies** BELLY : panza *f,* vientre *m*

tumor ['tu:mər 'tju:-] *n* : tumor *m*

tumult ['tu:ˌmʌlt 'tju:-] *n* : tumulto *m,* alboroto *m*

tumultuous [tʊ'mʌltʃʊəs, tju:-] *adj* : tumultuoso

tuna ['tu:nə 'tju:-] *n, pl* **-na** *or* **-nas** : atún *m*

tundra ['tʌndrə] *n* : tundra *f*

tune[1] ['tu:n, 'tju:n] *v* **tuned; tuning** *vt* **1** ADJUST : ajustar, hacer más preciso, afinar (un motor) **2** : afinar (un instrumento musical) **3** : sintonizar (un radio o televisor) — *vi* **to tune in** : sintonizar (con una emisora)

tune[2] *n* **1** MELODY : tonada *f,* canción *f,* melodía *f* **2 in tune** : afinado (dícese de un instrumento o de la voz), sintonizado, en sintonía

tuneful ['tu:nfəl, 'tju:n-] *adj* : armonioso, melódico

tuner ['tu:nər, 'tju:-] *n* : afinador *m,* -dora *f* (de instrumentos); sintonizador *m* (de un radio o un televisior)

tungsten ['tʌŋkstən] *n* : tungsteno *m*

tunic ['tu:nɪk, 'tju:-] *n* : túnica *f*

tuning fork *n* : diapasón *m*

Tunisian [tu:'ni:ʒən, tju:'nɪziən] *n* : tunecino *m,* -na *f* — **Tunisian** *adj*

tunnel[1] ['tʌnəl] *vi* **-neled** *or* **-nelled; -neling** *or* **-nelling** : hacer un túnel

tunnel[2] *n* : túnel *m*

turban ['tərbən] *n* : turbante *m*

turbid ['tərbɪd] *adj* : turbio

turbine ['tərbən, -ˌbaɪn] *n* : turbina *f*

turboprop ['tərbo:ˌprɑp] *n* : turbopropulsor *m* (motor), avión *m* turbopropulsado

turbulence ['tərbjələnts] *n* : turbulencia *f*

turbulent ['tərbjələnt] *adj* : turbulento — **turbulently** *adv*

tureen [tə'ri:n, tjʊ-] *n* : sopera *f*

turf ['tərf] *n* SOD : tepe *m*

turgid ['tərdʒɪd] *adj* **1** SWOLLEN : turgente **2** : ampuloso, hinchado <turgid style : estilo ampuloso>

turkey ['tərki] *n, pl* **-keys** : pavo *m*

turmoil ['tərˌmɔɪl] *n* : agitación *f,* desorden *m,* confusión *f*

turn[1] ['tərn] *vt* **1** : girar, voltear, volver <to turn one's head : voltear la cabeza> <she turned her chair toward the fire : giró su asiento hacia la hoguera> **2** ROTATE : darle vuelta a, hacer girar <turn the handle : dale vuelta a la manivela> **3** SPRAIN, WRENCH : dislocar, torcer **4** UPSET : revolver (el estómago) **5** TRANSFORM : convertir <to turn water into wine : convertir el agua en vino> **6** SHAPE : tornear (en carpintería) — *vi* **1** ROTATE : girar, dar vueltas **2** : girar, doblar, dar una vuelta <turn left : doble a la izquierda> <to turn around : dar la media vuelta> **3** BECOME : hacerse, volverse, ponerse **4** SOUR : agriarse, cortarse (dícese de la leche) **5 to turn to** : recurrir a <they have no one to turn to : no tienen quien les ayude>

turn[2] *n* **1** : vuelta *f,* giro *m* <a sudden turn : una vuelta repentina> **2** CHANGE : cambio *m* **3** CURVE : curva *f* (en un camino) **4** : turno *m* <they're awaiting their turn : están esperando su turno> <whose turn is it? : ¿a quién le toca?>

turncoat ['tərnˌko:t] *n* : traidor *m,* -dora *f*

turn down *vt* **1** REFUSE : rehusar, rechazar <they turned down our invitation : rehusaron nuestra invitación> **2** LOWER : bajar (el volumen)

turn in *vt* : entregar <to turn in one's work : entregar uno su trabajo> <they turned in the suspect : entregaron al sospechoso> — *vi* : acostarse, irse a la cama

turnip ['tərnəp] *n* : nabo *m*

turn off *vt* : apagar (la luz, la radio, etc.)

turn on *vt* : prender (la luz, etc.), encender (un motor, etc.)

turnout ['tərnˌaʊt] *n* : concurrencia *f*

turn out *vt* **1** EVICT, EXPEL : expulsar, echar, desalojar **2** PRODUCE : producir **3** → **turn off** — *vi* **1** : concurrir, presentarse <many turned out to vote : muchos concurrieron a votar> **2** PROVE, RESULT : resultar

turnover ['tərnˌo:vər] *n* **1** : tarta *f* (rellena de fruta) **2** : volumen *m* (de ventas) **3** : rotación *f* (de personal) <a high turnover : un alto nivel de rotación>

turn over *vt* **1** TRANSFER : entregar, transferir (un cargo o una responsabilidad) **2** : voltear, darle la vuelta a <turn the cassette over : voltea el cassette>

turnpike ['tərnˌpaɪk] *n* : carretera *f* de peaje

turnstile ['tərnˌstaɪl] *n* : torniquete *m* (de acceso)

turntable ['tərnˌteɪbəl] *n* : tornamesa *mf*

turn up *vi* **1** APPEAR : aparecer, presentarse **2** HAPPEN : ocurrir, suceder (inesperadamente) — *vt* : subir (el volumen)

turpentine ['tərpənˌtaɪn] *n* : aguarrás *m,* trementina *f*

turquoise ['tərˌkɔɪz, -ˌkwɔɪz] *n* : turquesa *f*

turret ['tərət] *n* **1** TOWER : torre *f* pequeña **2** : torreta *f* (de un tanque, un avión, etc.)

turtle ['tərt̬əl] *n* : tortuga *f* (marina)

turtledove ['tərtəl,dʌv] *n* **:** tórtola *f*
turtleneck ['tərtəl,nɛk] *n* **:** cuello *m* de tortuga, cuello *m* alto
tusk ['tʌsk] *n* **:** colmillo *m*
tussle[1] ['tʌsəl] *vi* **-sled; -sling** SCUFFLE **:** pelearse, reñir
tussle[2] *n* **:** riña *f,* pelea *f*
tutor[1] ['tu:tər, 'tju:-] *vt* **:** darle clases particulares (a alguien)
tutor[2] *n* **:** tutor *m,* -tora *f;* maestro *m,* -tra *f* (particular)
tuxedo [,tək'si:,do:] *n, pl* **-dos** *or* **-does :** esmoquin *m,* smoking *m*
TV [,ti:'vi:, 'ti:,vi:] → **television**
twain ['tweɪn] *n* **:** dos *m*
twang[1] ['twæŋ] *vt* **:** pulsar la cuerda de (una guitarra) — *vi* **:** hablar en tono nasal
twang[2] *n* **1 :** tañido *m* (de una cuerda de guitarra) **2 :** tono *m* nasal (de voz)
tweak[1] ['twi:k] *vt* **:** pellizcar
tweak[2] *n* **:** pellizco *m*
tweed ['twi:d] *n* **:** tweed *m*
tweet[1] ['twi:t] *vi* **:** piar
tweet[2] *n* **:** gorjeo *m,* pío *m*
tweezers ['twi:zərz] *npl* **:** pinzas *fpl*
twelfth[1] ['twɛlfθ] *adj* **:** duodécimo
twelfth[2] *n* **1 :** duodécimo *m,* -ma *f* (en una serie) **2 :** doceavo *m,* doceava parte *f*
twelve[1] ['twɛlv] *adj* **:** doce
twelve[2] *n* **:** doce *m*
twentieth[1] ['twʌntiəθ, 'twɛn-] *adj* **:** vigésimo
twentieth[2] *n* **1 :** vigésimo *m,* -ma *f* (en una serie) **2 :** veinteavo *m,* veinteava parte *f*
twenty[1] ['twʌnti, 'twɛn-] *adj* **:** veinte
twenty[2] *n, pl* **-ties :** veinte *m*
twice ['twaɪs] *adv* **:** dos veces <twice a day : dos veces al día> <it costs twice as much : cuesta el doble>
twig ['twɪg] *n* **:** ramita *f*
twilight ['twaɪ,laɪt] *n* **:** crepúsculo *m*
twill ['twɪl] *n* **:** sarga *f,* tela *f* cruzada
twin[1] ['twɪn] *adj* **:** gemelo, mellizo
twin[2] *n* **:** gemelo *m,* -la *f;* mellizo *m,* -za *f*
twine[1] ['twaɪn] *v* **twined; twining** *vt* **:** entrelazar, entrecruzar — *vi* **:** enroscarse (alrededor de algo)
twine[2] *n* **:** cordel *m,* cuerda *f,* mecate *m CA, Mex, Ven*
twinge[1] ['twɪndʒ] *vi* **twinged; twinging** *or* **twingeing :** sentir punzadas
twinge[2] *n* **:** punzada *f,* dolor *m* agudo
twinkle[1] ['twɪŋkəl] *vi* **-kled; -kling 1 :** centellear, titilar (dícese de las estrellas o de la luz) **2 :** chispear, brillar (dícese de los ojos)
twinkle[2] *n* **:** centelleo *m* (de las estrellas), brillo *m* (de los ojos)
twirl[1] ['twərl] *vt* **:** girar, darle vueltas a — *vi* **:** girar, dar vueltas (rápidamente)
twirl[2] *n* **:** giro *m,* vuelta *f*
twist[1] ['twɪst] *vt* **:** torcer, retorcer <he twisted my arm : me torció el brazo> — *vi* **:** retorcerse, enroscarse, serpentear (dícese de un río, un camino, etc.)
twist[2] *n* **1** BEND **:** vuelta *f,* recodo *m* (en el camino, el río, etc.) **2** TURN **:** giro *m* <give it a twist : hazlo girar> **3** SPIRAL **:** espiral *f* <a twist of lemon : una rodajita de limón> **4 :** giro *m* inesperado (de eventos, etc.)
twister ['twɪstər] **1** → **tornado 2** → **waterspout**
twitch[1] ['twɪtʃ] *vi* **:** moverse nerviosamente, contraerse espasmódicamente (dícese de un músculo)
twitch[2] *n* **:** espasmo *m,* sacudida *f* <a nervous twitch : un tic nervioso>
twitter[1] ['twɪtər] *vi* CHIRP **:** gorjear, cantar (dícese de los pájaros)
twitter[2] *n* **:** gorjeo *m*
two[1] ['tu:] *adj* **:** dos
two[2] *n, pl* **twos :** dos *m*
twofold[1] ['tu:'fo:ld] *adv* **:** al doble
twofold[2] ['tu:,fo:ld] *adj* **:** doble
two hundred[1] *adj* **:** doscientos
two hundred[2] *n* **:** doscientos *m*
twosome ['tu:səm] *n* COUPLE **:** pareja *f*
tycoon [taɪ'ku:n] *n* **:** magnate *mf*
tying → **tie[1]**
type[1] ['taɪp] *v* **typed; typing** *vt* **1** TYPEWRITE **:** escribir a máquina, pasar (un texto) a máquina **2** CATEGORIZE **:** categorizar, identificar — *vi* **:** escribir a máquina
type[2] *n* **1** KIND **:** tipo *m,* clase *f,* categoría *f* **2** *or* **printing type :** tipo *m*
typewrite ['taɪp,raɪt] *v* **-wrote; -written :** escribir a máquina
typewriter ['taɪp,raɪtər] *n* **:** máquina *f* de escribir
typhoid[1] ['taɪ,fɔɪd, taɪ'-] *adj* **:** relativo al tifus o a la tifoidea
typhoid[2] *n or* **typhoid fever :** tifoidea *f*
typhoon [taɪ'fu:n] *n* **:** tifón *m*
typhus ['taɪfəs] *n* **:** tifus *m,* tifo *m*
typical ['tɪpɪkəl] *adj* **:** típico, característico — **typically** *adv*
typify ['tɪpə,faɪ] *vt* **-fied; -fying :** ser típico o representativo de (un grupo, una clase, etc.)
typist ['taɪpɪst] *n* **:** mecanógrafo *m,* -fa *f*
typographic [,taɪpə'græfɪk] *or* **typographical** [-fɪkəl] *adj* **:** tipográfico — **typographically** [-fɪkli] *adv*
typography [taɪ'pɑgrəfi] *n* **:** tipografía *f*
tyrannical [tə'rænɪkəl, taɪ-] *adj* **:** tiránico — **tyrannically** [-nɪkli] *adv*
tyrannize ['tɪrə,naɪz] *vt* **-nized; -nizing :** tiranizar
tyranny ['tɪrəni] *n, pl* **-nies :** tiranía *f*
tyrant ['taɪrənt] *n* **:** tirano *m,* -na *f*
tzar ['zɑr, 'tsɑr, 'sɑr] → **czar**

U

u [ˈjuː] *n, pl* **u's** *or* **us** [ˈjuːz] **:** vigésima primera letra del alfabeto inglés
ubiquitous [juːˈbɪkwət̬əs] *adj* **:** ubicuo, omnipresente
udder [ˈʌdər] *n* **:** ubre *f*
UFO [ˌjuːˌɛfˈoː, ˈjuːˌfoː] *n, pl* **UFO's** *or* **UFOs** (*unidentified flying object*) **:** ovni *m,* OVNI *m*
Ugandan [juːˈgændən, -ˈgɑn-; uːˈgɑn-] *n* **:** ugandés *m,* -desa *f* — **Ugandan** *adj*
ugliness [ˈʌglinəs] *n* **:** fealdad *f*
ugly [ˈʌgli] *adj* **uglier; -est 1** UNATTRACTIVE **:** feo **2** DISAGREEABLE **:** desagradable, feo <ugly weather **:** tiempo feo> <to have an ugly temper **:** tener mal genio>
Ukrainian [juːˈkreɪniən, -ˈkraɪ-] *n* **:** ucraniano *m,* -na *f* — **Ukrainian** *adj*
ukulele [ˌjuːkəˈleɪli] *n* **:** ukelele *m*
ulcer [ˈʌlsər] *n* **:** úlcera *f* (interna), llaga *f* (externa)
ulcerate [ˈʌlsəˌreɪt] *vi* **-ated; -ating :** ulcerarse
ulceration [ˌʌlsəˈreɪʃən] *n* **1 :** ulceración *f* **2** ULCER **:** úlcera *f,* llaga *f*
ulcerous [ˈʌlsərəs] *adj* **:** ulceroso
ulna [ˈʌlnə] *n* **:** cúbito *m*
ulterior [ˌʌlˈtɪriər] *adj* **:** oculto <ulterior motive **:** motivo oculto, segunda intención>
ultimate [ˈʌltəmət] *adj* **1** FINAL **:** último, final **2** SUPREME **:** supremo, máximo **3** FUNDAMENTAL **:** fundamental, esencial
ultimately [ˈʌltəmətli] *adv* **1** FINALLY **:** por último, finalmente **2** EVENTUALLY **:** a la larga, con el tiempo
ultimatum [ˌʌltəˈmeɪt̬əm, -ˈmɑ-] *n, pl* **-tums** *or* **-ta** [-t̬ə] **:** ultimátum *m*
ultraviolet [ˌʌltrəˈvaɪələt] *adj* **:** ultravioleta
umbilical cord [ˌʌmˈbɪlɪkəl] *adj* **:** cordón umbilical
umbrage [ˈʌmbrɪʤ] *n* **to take umbrage at :** ofenderse por
umbrella [ˌʌmˈbrɛlə] *n* **1 :** paraguas *m* **2 beach umbrella :** sombrilla *f*
umpire¹ [ˈʌmˌpaɪr] *v* **-pired; -piring :** arbitrar
umpire² *n* **:** árbitro *m,* -tra *f*
umpteenth [ˌʌmpˈtiːnθ] *adj* **:** enésimo
unable [ˌʌnˈeɪbəl] *adj* **:** incapaz <to be unable to **:** no poder>
unabridged [ˌʌnəˈbrɪʤd] *adj* **:** íntegro
unacceptable [ˌʌnɪkˈsɛptəbəl] *adj* **:** inaceptable
unaccompanied [ˌʌnəˈkʌmpənid] *adj* **:** solo, sin acompañamiento (en música)
unaccountable [ˌʌnəˈkaʊntəbəl] *adj* **:** inexplicable, incomprensible — **unaccountably** [-bli] *adv*
unaccustomed [ˌʌnəˈkʌstəmd] *adj* **1** UNUSUAL **:** desacostumbrado, inusual **2** UNUSED **:** inhabituado <unaccustomed to noise **:** inhabituado al ruido>
unacquainted [ˌʌnəˈkweɪnt̬əd] *adj* **to be unacquainted with :** desconocer, ignorar
unadorned [ˌʌnəˈdɔrnd] *adj* **:** sin adornos, puro y simple
unadulterated [ˌʌnəˈdʌltəˌreɪt̬əd] *adj* **1** PURE **:** puro <unadulterated food **:** comida pura> **2** ABSOLUTE **:** completo, absoluto
unaffected [ˌʌnəˈfɛktəd] *adj* **1 :** no afectado, indiferente **2** NATURAL **:** sin afectación, natural
unaffectedly [ˌʌnəˈfɛktədli] *adv* **:** de manera natural
unafraid [ˌʌnəˈfreɪd] *adj* **:** sin miedo
unaided [ˌʌnˈeɪdəd] *adj* **:** sin ayuda, solo
unambiguous [ˌʌnæmˈbɪgjʊəs] *adj* **:** inequívoco
unanimity [ˌjuːnəˈnɪmət̬i] *n* **:** unanimidad *f*
unanimous [jʊˈnænəməs] *adj* **:** unánime — **unanimously** *adv*
unannounced [ˌʌnəˈnaʊnst] *adj* **:** sin dar aviso
unanswered [ˌʌnˈæntsərd] *adj* **:** sin contestar
unappealing [ˌʌnəˈpiːlɪŋ] *adj* **:** desagradable
unappetizing [ˌʌnˈæpəˌtaɪzɪŋ] *adj* **:** poco apetitoso, poco apetecible
unarmed [ˌʌnˈɑrmd] *adj* **:** sin armas, desarmado
unassisted [ˌʌnəˈsɪstəd] *adj* **:** sin ayuda
unassuming [ˌʌnəˈsuːmɪŋ] *adj* **:** modesto, sin pretensiones
unattached [ˌʌnəˈtætʃt] *adj* **1** LOOSE **:** suelto **2** INDEPENDENT **:** independiente **3 :** solo (ni casado ni prometido)
unattractive [ˌʌnəˈtræktɪv] *adj* **:** poco atractivo
unauthorized [ˌʌnˈɔθəˌraɪzd] *adj* **:** sin autorización, no autorizado
unavailable [ˌʌnəˈveɪləbəl] *adj* **:** no disponible
unavoidable [ˌʌnəˈvɔɪdəbəl] *adj* **:** inevitable, ineludible
unaware¹ [ˌʌnəˈwær] *adv* → **unawares**
unaware² *adj* **:** inconsciente
unawares [ˌʌnəˈwærz] *adv* **1 :** por sorpresa <to catch someone unawares **:** agarrar a alguien desprevenido> **2** UNINTENTIONALLY **:** inconscientemente, inadvertidamente
unbalanced [ˌʌnˈbæləntst] *adj* **:** desequilibrado
unbearable [ˌʌnˈbærəbəl] *adj* **:** insoportable, inaguantable — **unbearably** [-bli] *adv*
unbecoming [ˌʌnbɪˈkʌmɪŋ] *adj* **1** UNSEEMLY **:** impropio, indecoroso **2** UNFLATTERING **:** poco favorecedor

unbelievable [ˌʌnbəˈliːvəbəl] *adj* : increíble — **unbelievably** [-bli] *adv*
unbend [ˌʌnˈbɛnd] *vi* **-bent** [-ˈbɛnt]; **-bending** RELAX : relajarse
unbending [ˌʌnˈbɛndɪŋ] *adj* : inflexible
unbiased [ˌʌnˈbaɪəst] *adj* : imparcial, objetivo
unbind [ˌʌnˈbaɪnd] *vt* **-bound** [-ˈbaʊnd]; **-binding 1** UNFASTEN, UNTIE : desatar, desamarrar **2** RELEASE : liberar
unbolt [ˌʌnˈboːlt] *vt* : abrir el cerrojo de, descorrer el pestillo de
unborn [ˌʌnˈbɔrn] *adj* : aún no nacido, que va a nacer
unbosom [ˌʌnˈbʊzəm, -ˈbuː-] *vt* : revelar, divulgar
unbreakable [ˌʌnˈbreɪkəbəl] *adj* : irrompible
unbridled [ˌʌnˈbraɪdəld] *adj* : desenfrenado
unbroken [ˌʌnˈbroːkən] *adj* **1** INTACT : intacto, sano **2** CONTINUOUS : continuo, ininterrumpido
unbuckle [ˌʌnˈbʌkəl] *vt* **-led; -ling** : desabrochar
unburden [ˌʌnˈbərdən] *vt* **1** UNLOAD : descargar **2 to unburden oneself** : desahogarse
unbutton [ˌʌnˈbʌtən] *vt* : desabrochar, desabotonar
uncalled–for [ˌʌnˈkɔldˌfɔr] *adj* : inapropiado, innecesario
uncanny [ənˈkæni] *adj* **-nier; -est 1** STRANGE : extraño **2** EXTRAORDINARY : raro, extraordinario — **uncannily** [-ˈkænəli] *adv*
unceasing [ˌʌnˈsiːsɪŋ] *adj* : incesante, continuo — **unceasingly** *adv*
unceremonious [ˌʌnˌsɛrəˈmoːniəs] *adj* **1** INFORMAL : sin ceremonia, sin pompa **2** ABRUPT : abrupto, brusco — **unceremoniously** *adv*
uncertain [ˌʌnˈsərtən] *adj* **1** INDEFINITE : indeterminado **2** UNSURE : incierto, dudoso **3** CHANGEABLE : inestable, variable <uncertain weather : tiempo inestable> **4** HESITANT : indeciso **5** VAGUE : poco claro
uncertainly [ˌʌnˈsərtənli] *adv* : dudosamente, con desconfianza
uncertainty [ˌʌnˈərtənti] *n, pl* **-ties** : duda *f*, incertidumbre *f*
unchangeable [ˌʌnˈtʃeɪndʒəbəl] *adj* : inalterable, inmutable
unchanged [ˌʌnˈtʃeɪndʒd] *adj* : sin cambiar
unchanging [ˌʌnˈtʃeɪdʒɪŋ] *adj* : inalterable, inmutable, firme
uncharacteristic [ˌʌnˌkærɪktəˈrɪstɪk] *adj* : inusual, desacostumbrado
uncharged [ˌʌnˈtʃɑrdʒd] *adj* : sin carga (eléctrica)
uncivilized [ˌʌnˈsɪvəˌlaɪzd] *adj* **1** BARBAROUS : incivilizado, bárbaro **2** WILD : salvaje
uncle [ˈʌŋkəl] *n* : tío *m*
unclean [ˌʌnˈkliːn] *adj* **1** IMPURE : impuro **2** DIRTY : sucio
unclear [ˌʌnˈklɪr] *adj* : confuso, borroso, poco claro
Uncle Sam [ˈsæm] *n* : el Tío Sam
unclog [ˌʌnˈklɑg] *vt* **-clogged; -clogging** : desatascar, destapar
unclothed [ˌʌnˈkloːðd] *adj* : desnudo
uncomfortable [ˌʌnˈkʌmpfərtəbəl] *adj* **1** : incómodo (dícese de una silla, etc.) **2** UNEASY : inquieto, incómodo
uncommitted [ˌʌnkəˈmɪtəd] *adj* : sin compromisos
uncommon [ˌʌnˈkɑmən] *adj* **1** UNUSUAL : raro, poco común **2** REMARKABLE : excepcional, extraordinario
uncommonly [ˌʌnˈkɑmənli] *adv* : extraordinariamente
uncompromising [ˌʌnˈkɑmprəˌmaɪzɪŋ] *adj* : inflexible, intransigente
unconcerned [ˌʌnkənˈsərnd] *adj* : indiferente — **unconcernedly** [-ˈsərnədli] *adv*
unconditional [ˌʌnkənˈdɪʃənəl] *adj* : incondicional — **unconditionally** *adv*
unconscious[1] [ˌʌnˈkɑntʃəs] *adj* : inconsciente — **unconsciously** *adv*
unconscious[2] *n* : inconsciente *m*
unconsciousness [ˌʌnˈkɑntʃəsnəs] *n* : inconsciencia *f*
unconstitutional [ˌʌnˌkɑntstəˈtuːʃənəl, -ˈtjuː-] *adj* : inconstitucional
uncontrollable [ˌʌnkənˈtroːləbəl] *adj* : incontrolable, incontenible — **uncontrollably** [-bli] *adv*
uncontrolled [ˌʌnkənˈtroːld] *adj* : incontrolado
unconventional [ˌʌnkənˈvɛntʃənəl] *adj* : poco convencional
unconvincing [ˌʌnkənˈvɪntsɪŋ] *adj* : poco convincente
uncouth [ˌʌnˈkuːθ] *adj* CRUDE, ROUGH : grosero, rudo
uncover [ˌʌnˈkʌvər] *vt* **1** : destapar (un objeto), dejar al descubierto **2** EXPOSE, REVEAL : descubrir, revelar, exponer
uncultivated [ˌʌnˈkʌltəˌveɪtəd] *adj* : inculto
uncurl [ˌʌnˈkərl] *vt* UNROLL : desenrollar — *vi* : desenrollarse, desrizarse (dícese del pelo)
uncut [ˌʌnˈkʌt] *adj* **1** : sin cortar <uncut grass : hierba sin cortar> **2** : sin tallar, en bruto <an uncut diamond : un diamante en bruto> **3** UNABRIDGED : completo, íntegro
undaunted [ˌʌnˈdɔntəd] *adj* : impávido
undecided [ˌʌndiˈsaɪdəd] *adj* **1** IRRESOLUTE : indeciso, irresoluto **2** UNRESOLVED : pendiente, no resuelto
undefeated [ˌʌndiˈfiːtəd] *adj* : invicto
undeniable [ˌʌndiˈnaɪəbəl] *adj* : innegable — **undeniably** [-bli] *adv*
under[1] [ˈʌndər] *adv* **1** LESS : menos <$10 or under : $10 o menos> **2** UNDERWATER : debajo del agua **3** : bajo los efectos de la anestesia

under[2] *adj* **1** LOWER : (más) bajo, inferior **2** SUBORDINATE : inferior **3** : insuficiente <an under dose of medicine : una dosis insuficiente de medicina>

under[3] *prep* **1** BELOW, BENEATH : debajo de, abajo de <under the table : abajo de la mesa> <we walked under the arch : pasamos por debajo del arco> <under the sun : bajo el sol> **2** : menos de <in under 20 minutes : en menos de 20 minutos> **3** (*indicating rank or authority*) : bajo <under the command of : bajo las órdenes de> **4** SUBJECT TO : bajo <under suspicion : bajo sospecha> <under the circumstances : dadas las circunstancias> **5** ACCORDING TO : según, de acuerdo con, conforme a <under the present laws : según las leyes actuales>

underage [ˌʌndərˈeɪdʒ] *adj* : menor de edad

underbrush [ˈʌndərˌbrəʃ] *n* : maleza *f*

underclothes [ˈʌndərˌkloːz, -ˌkloːðz] → **underwear**

underclothing [ˈʌndərˌkloːðɪŋ] → **underwear**

undercover [ˌʌndərˈkʌvər] *adj* : secreto, clandestino

undercurrent [ˈʌndərˌkərənt] *n* **1** : corriente *f* submarina **2** UNDERTONE : corriente *f* oculta, trasfondo *m*

undercut [ˌʌndərˈkʌt] *vt* **-cut; -cutting** : vender más barato que

underdeveloped [ˌʌndərdɪˈvɛləpt] *adj* : subdesarrollado, atrasado

underdog [ˈʌndərˌdɔg] *n* : persona *f* que tiene menos posibilidades

underdone [ˌʌndərˈdʌn] *adj* RARE : poco cocido

underestimate [ˌʌndərˈɛstəˌmeɪt] *vt* **-mated; -mating** : subestimar, menospreciar

underexposed [ˌʌndərɪkˈspoːzd] *adj* : subexpuesto (en fotografía)

underfoot [ˌʌndərˈfʊt] *adv* **1** : bajo los pies <to trample underfoot : pisotear> **2 to be underfoot** : estorbar <they're always underfoot : están siempre estorbando>

undergarment [ˈʌndərˌgɑrmənt] *n* : prenda *f* íntima

undergo [ˌʌndərˈgoː] *vt* **-went** [-ˈwɛnt;]; **-gone** [-ˈgɔn]; **-going** : sufrir, experimentar <to undergo an operation : someterse a una intervención quirúrgica>

undergraduate [ˌʌndərˈgrædʒʊət] *n* : estudiante *m* universitario, estudiante *f* universitaria

underground[1] [ˌʌndərˈgraʊnd] *adv* **1** : bajo tierra **2** SECRETLY : clandestinamente, en secreto <to go underground : pasar a la clandestinidad>

underground[2] [ˈʌndərˌgraʊnd] *adj* **1** SUBTERRANEAN : subterráneo **2** SECRET : secreto, clandestino

underground[3] [ˈʌndərˌgraʊnd] *n* : movimiento *m* o grupo *m* clandestino

undergrowth [ˈʌndərˈgroːθ] *n* : maleza *f*, broza *f*

underhand[1] [ˈʌndərˌhænd] *adv* **1** SECRETLY : de manera clandestina **2** *or* **underhanded** : sin levantar el brazo por encima del hombro (en deportes)

underhand[2] *adj* **1** SLY : solapado **2** : por debajo del hombro (en deportes)

underhanded [ˌʌndərˈhændəd] *adj* **1** SLY : solapado **2** SHADY : turbio, poco limpio

underline [ˈʌndərˌlaɪn] *vt* **-lined; -lining 1** : subrayar **2** EMPHASIZE : subrayar, acentuar, hacer hincapié en

underlying [ˌʌndərˈlaɪɪŋ] *adj* **1** : subyacente <the underlying rock : la roca subyacente> **2** FUNDAMENTAL : fundamental, esencial

undermine [ˌʌndərˈmaɪn] *vt* **-mined; -mining 1** : socavar (una estructura, etc.) **2** SAP, WEAKEN : minar, debilitar

underneath[1] [ˌʌndərˈniːθ] *adv* : debajo, abajo <the part underneath : la parte de abajo>

underneath[2] *prep* : debajo de, abajo de

undernourished [ˌʌndərˈnərɪʃt] *adj* : desnutrido

underpants [ˈʌndərˌpænts] *npl* : calzoncillos *mpl*, calzones *mpl*

underpass [ˈʌndərˌpæs] *n* : paso *m* a desnivel

underprivileged [ˌʌndərˈprɪvlɪdʒd] *adj* : desfavorecido

underrate [ˌʌndərˈreɪt] *vt* **-rated; -rating** : subestimar, menospreciar

underscore [ˈʌndərˌskor] *vt* **-scored; -scoring** → **underline**

undersea[1] [ˌʌndərˈsiː] *or* **underseas** [-ˈsiːz] *adv* : bajo la superficie del mar

undersea[2] *adj* : submarino

undersecretary [ˌʌndərˈsɛkrəˌtɛri] *n, pl* **-ries** : subsecretario *m*, -ria *f*

undersell [ˌʌndərˈsɛl] *vt* **-sold; -selling** : vender más barato que

undershirt [ˈʌndərˌʃərt] *n* : camiseta *f*

undershorts [ˈʌndərˌʃɔrts] *npl* : calzoncillos *mpl*

underside [ˈʌndərˌsaɪd, ˌʌndərˈsaɪd] *n* : parte *f* de abajo

undersized [ˌʌndərˈsaɪzd] *adj* : más pequeño de lo normal

understand [ˌʌndərˈstænd] *v* **-stood** [-ˈstʊd;]; **-standing** *vt* **1** COMPREHEND : comprender, entender <I don't understand it : no lo entiendo> <that's understood : eso se comprende> <to make oneself understood : hacerse entender> **2** BELIEVE : entender <to give someone to understand : dar a alguien a entender> **3** INFER : tener entendido <I understand that she's leaving : tengo entendido que se va> — *vi* : comprender, entender

understandable [ˌʌndərˈstændəbəl] *adj* : comprensible

understanding[1] [ˌʌndərˈstændɪŋ] *adj* : comprensivo, compasivo

understanding[2] *n* **1** GRASP : comprensión *f,* entendimiento *m* **2** SYMPATHY : comprensión *f* (mutua) **3** INTERPRETATION : interpretación *f* <it's my understanding that... : tengo la impresión de que..., tengo entendido que...> **4** AGREEMENT : acuerdo *m,* arreglo *m*

understate [ˌʌndərˈsteɪt] *vt* **-stated; -stating** : minimizar, subestimar

understatement [ˌʌndərˈsteɪtmənt] *n* : atenuación *f* <that's an understatement : decir sólo eso es quedarse corto>

understudy [ˈʌndərˌstʌdi] *n, pl* **-dies** : sobresaliente *mf,* suplente *mf* (en el teatro)

undertake [ˌʌndərˈteɪk] *vt* **-took** [-ˈtʊk]; **-taken** [-ˈteɪkən]; **-taking 1** : emprender (una tarea), asumir (una responsabilidad) **2** PROMISE : comprometerse (a hacer algo)

undertaker [ˈʌndərˌteɪkər] *n* : director *m,* -tora *f* de funeraria

undertaking [ˈʌndərˌteɪkɪŋ, ˌʌndərˈ-] *n* **1** ENTERPRISE, TASK : empresa *f,* tarea *f* **2** PLEDGE : promesa *f,* garantía *f*

undertone [ˈʌndərˌtoːn] *n* **1** : voz *f* baja <to speak in an undertone : hablar en voz baja> **2** HINT, UNDERCURRENT : trasfondo *m,* matiz *m*

undertow [ˈʌndərˌtoː] *n* : resaca *f*

undervalue [ˌʌndərˈvælˌjuː] *vt* **-ued; -uing** : menospreciar, subestimar

underwater[1] [ˌʌndərˈwɔt̬ər, -ˈwɑ-] *adv* : debajo (del agua)

underwater[2] *adj* : submarino

under way [ˌʌndərˈweɪ] *adv* : en marcha, en camino <to get under way : ponerse en marcha>

underwear [ˈʌndərˌwær] *n* : ropa *f* interior, ropa *f* íntima

underworld [ˈʌndərˌwərld] *n* **1** HELL : infierno *m* **2 the underworld** CRIMINALS : la hampa, los bajos fondos

underwrite [ˈʌndərˌraɪt, ˌʌndərˈ-] *vt* **-wrote** [-ˌroːt, -ˈroːt]; **-written** [-ˌrɪtən, -ˈrɪtən]; **-writing 1** INSURE : asegurar **2** FINANCE : financiar **3** BACK, ENDORSE : suscribir, respaldar

underwriter [ˈʌndərˌraɪt̬ər, ˌʌndərˈ-] *n* INSURER : asegurador *m,* -dora *f*

undeserving [ˌʌndiˈzərvɪŋ] *adj* : indigno

undesirable[1] [ˌʌndiˈzaɪrəbəl] *adj* : indeseable

undesirable[2] *n* : indeseable *mf*

undeveloped [ˌʌndiˈvɛləpt] *adj* : sin desarrollar, sin revelar (dícese de una película)

undies [ˈʌndiːz] → **underwear**

undignified [ˌʌnˈdɪgnəfaɪd] *adj* : indecoroso

undiluted [ˌʌndaɪˈluːt̬əd, -də-] *adj* : sin diluir, concentrado

undiscovered [ˌʌndɪˈskʌvərd] *adj* : no descubierto

undisputed [ˌʌndɪˈspjuːt̬əd] *adj* : indiscutible

undisturbed [ˌʌndɪˈstərbd] *adj* : tranquilo (dícese de una persona), sin tocar (dícese de un objeto)

undivided [ˌʌndɪˈvaɪdəd] *adj* : íntegro, completo

undo [ˌʌnˈduː] *vt* **-did** [-ˈdɪd]; **-done** [-ˈdʌn]; **-doing 1** UNFASTEN : desabrochar, desatar, abrir **2** ANNUL : anular **3** REVERSE : deshacer, reparar (daños, etc.) **4** RUIN : arruinar, destruir

undoing [ˌʌnˈduːɪŋ] *n* : ruina *f,* perdición *f*

undoubted [ˌʌnˈdaʊt̬əd] *adj* : cierto, indudable — **undoubtedly** *adv*

undress [ˌʌnˈdrɛs] *vt* : desvestir, desabrigar, desnudar — *vi* : desvestirse, desnudarse

undrinkable [ˌʌnˈdrɪŋkəbəl] *adj* : no potable

undue [ˌʌnˈduː, -ˈdjuː] *adj* : excesivo, indebido — **unduly** *adv*

undulate [ˈʌndʒəˌleɪt] *vi* **-lated; -lating** : ondular

undulation [ˌʌndʒəˈleɪʃən] *n* : ondulación *f*

undying [ˌʌnˈdaɪɪŋ] *adj* : perpetuo, imperecedero

unearth [ˌʌnˈərθ] *vt* **1** EXHUME : desenterrar, exhumar **2** DISCOVER : descubrir

unearthly [ˌʌnˈərθli] *adj* **-lier; -est** : sobrenatural, de otro mundo

uneasily [ˌʌnˈiːzəli] *adv* : inquietamente, con inquietud

uneasiness [ˌʌnˈiːzinəs] *n* : inquietud *f*

uneasy [ˌʌnˈiːzi] *adj* **-easier; -est 1** AWKWARD : incómodo **2** WORRIED : preocupado, inquieto **3** RESTLESS : inquieto, agitado

uneducated [ˌʌnˈɛdʒəˌkeɪt̬əd] *adj* : inculto, sin educación

unemployed [ˌʌnɪmˈplɔɪd] *adj* : desempleado

unemployment [ˌʌnɪmˈplɔɪmənt] *n* : desempleo *m*

unending [ˌʌnˈɛndɪŋ] *adj* : sin fin, interminable

unendurable [ˌʌnɪnˈdʊrəbəl, -ɛn-, -ˈdjʊr-] *adj* : insoportable, intolerable

unequal [ˌʌnˈiːkwəl] *adj* **1** : desigual **2** INADEQUATE : incapaz, incompetente <to be unequal to a task : no estar a la altura de una tarea>

unequaled *or* **unequalled** [ˌʌnˈiːkwəld] *adj* : sin igual

unequivocal [ˌʌnɪˈkwɪvəkəl] *adj* : inequívoco, claro — **unequivocally** *adv*

unerring [ˌʌnˈɛrɪŋ, -ˈər-] *adj* : infalible

unethical [ˌʌnˈɛθɪkəl] *adj* : poco ético

uneven [ˌʌnˈiːvən] *adj* **1** ODD : impar (dícese de un número) **2** : desigual, desnivelado (dícese de una superficie) <uneven terrain : terreno accidentado> **3** IRREGULAR : irregular, poco uniforme **4** UNEQUAL : desigual

unevenly [ˌʌnˈiːvənli] *adv* : desigualmente, irregularmente
uneventful [ˌʌnɪˈvɛntfəl] *adj* : sin incidentes, tranquilo
unexpected [ˌʌnɪkˈspɛktəd] *adj* : imprevisto, inesperado — **unexpectedly** *adv*
unfailing [ˌʌnˈfeɪlɪŋ] *adj* **1** CONSTANT : constante **2** INEXHAUSTIBLE : inagotable **3** SURE : a toda prueba, indefectible
unfair [ˌʌnˈfær] *adj* : injusto — **unfairly** *adv*
unfairness [ˌʌnˈfærnəs] *n* : injusticia *f*
unfaithful [ˌʌnˈfeɪθfəl] *adj* : desleal, infiel — **unfaithfully** *adv*
unfaithfulness [ˌʌnˈfeɪθfəlnəs] *n* : infidelidad *f,* deslealtad *f*
unfamiliar [ˌʌnfəˈmɪljər] *adj* **1** STRANGE : desconocido, extraño <an unfamiliar place : un lugar nuevo> **2** **to be unfamiliar with** : no estar familiarizado con, desconocer
unfamiliarity [ˌʌnfəˌmɪliˈærət̬i] *n* : falta *f* de familiaridad
unfashionable [ˌʌnˈfæʃənəbəl] *adj* : fuera de moda
unfasten [ˌʌnˈfæsən] *vt* : desabrochar, desatar (una cuerda, etc.), abrir (una puerta)
unfavorable [ˌʌnˈfeɪvərəbəl] *adj* : desfavorable, mal — **unfavorably** [-bli] *adv*
unfeeling [ˌʌnˈfiːlɪŋ] *adj* : insensible — **unfeelingly** *adv*
unfinished [ˌʌnˈfɪnɪʃd] *adj* : inacabado, incompleto
unfit [ˌʌnˈfɪt] *adj* **1** UNSUITABLE : inadecuado, impropio **2** UNSUITED : no apto, incapaz **3** : incapacitado (físicamente) <to be unfit : no estar en forma>
unflappable [ˌʌnˈflæpəbəl] *adj* : imperturbable
unflattering [ˌʌnˈflæt̬ərɪŋ] *adj* : poco favorecedor
unfold [ˌʌnˈfoːld] *vt* **1** EXPAND : desplegar, desdoblar, extender <to unfold a map : desplegar un mapa> **2** DISCLOSE, REVEAL : revelar, exponer (un plan, etc.) — *vi* **1** DEVELOP : desarrollarse, desenvolverse <the story unfolded : el cuento se desarrollaba> **2** EXPAND : extenderse, desplegarse
unforeseeable [ˌʌnforˈsiːəbəl] *adj* : imprevisible
unforeseen [ˌʌnforˈsiːn] *adj* : imprevisto
unforgettable [ˌʌnfərˈgɛt̬əbəl] *adj* : inolvidable, memorable — **unforgettably** [-bli] *adv*
unforgivable [ˌʌnfərˈgɪvəbəl] *adj* : imperdonable
unfortunate[1] [ˌʌnˈfɔrtʃənət] *adj* **1** UNLUCKY : desgraciado, infortunado, desafortunado <how unfortunate! : ¡qué mala suerte!> **2** INAPPROPRIATE : inoportuno <an unfortunate comment : un comentario poco feliz>
unfortunate[2] *n* : desgraciado *m,* -da *f*
unfortunately [ˌʌnˈfɔrtʃənətli] *adv* : desafortunadamente
unfounded [ˌʌnˈfaʊndəd] *adj* : infundado
unfreeze [ˌʌnˈfriːz] *v* **-froze** [-ˈfroːz]; **-frozen** [-ˈfroːzən]; **-freezing** *vt* : descongelar — *vi* : descongelarse
unfriendliness [ˌʌnˈfrɛndlinəs] *n* : hostilidad *f,* antipatía *f*
unfriendly [ˌʌnˈfrɛndli] *adj* **-lier; -est** : poco amistoso, hostil
unfurl [ˌʌnˈfərl] *vt* : desplegar, desdoblar — *vi* : desplegarse
unfurnished [ˌʌnˈfərnɪʃt] *adj* : desamueblado
ungainly [ˌʌnˈgeɪnli] *adj* : desgarbado
ungodly [ˌʌnˈgɔdli, -ˈgɑd-] *adj* **1** IMPIOUS : impío **2** OUTRAGEOUS : atroz, terrible <at an ungodly hour : a una hora intempestiva>
ungrateful [ˌʌnˈgreɪtfəl] *adj* : desagradecido, ingrato — **ungratefully** *adv*
ungratefulness [ˌʌnˈgreɪtfəlnəs] *n* : ingratitud *f*
unhappily [ˌʌnˈhæpəli] *adv* **1** SADLY : tristemente **2** UNFORTUNATELY : desafortunadamente, lamentablemente
unhappiness [ˌʌnˈhæpinəs] *n* : infelicidad *f,* tristeza *f,* desdicha *f*
unhappy [ˌʌnˈhæpi] *adj* **-pier; -est** **1** UNFORTUNATE : desafortunado, desventurado **2** MISERABLE, SAD : infeliz, triste, desdichado **3** INOPPORTUNE : inoportuno, poco feliz
unharmed [ˌʌnˈhɑrmd] *adj* : salvo, ileso
unhealthy [ˌʌnˈhɛlθi] *adj* **-thier; -est** **1** UNWHOLESOME : insalubre, malsano, nocivo a la salud <an unhealthy climate : un clima insalubre> **2** SICKLY : de mala salud, enfermizo
unheard–of [ˌʌnˈhərdəv] *adj* : sin precedente, inaudito, insólito
unhinge [ˌʌnˈhɪndʒ] *vt* **-hinged; -hinging** **1** : desquiciar (una puerta, etc.) **2** DISRUPT, UNSETTLE : trastornar, perturbar
unholy [ˌʌnˈhoːli] *adj* **-lier; -est** **1** : profano, impío **2** UNGODLY : atroz, terrible
unhook [ˌʌnˈhʊk] *vt* **1** : desenganchar, descolgar (de algo) **2** UNDO : desabrochar
unhurt [ˌʌnˈhərt] *adj* : ileso
unicorn [ˈjuːnəˌkɔrn] *n* : unicornio *m*
unidentified [ˌʌnaɪˈdɛntəˌfaɪd] *adj* : no identificado <unidentified flying object : objeto volador no identificado>
unification [ˌjuːnəfəˈkeɪʃən] *n* : unificación *f*
uniform[1] [ˈjuːnəˌfɔrm] *adj* : uniforme, homogéneo, constante
uniform[2] *n* : uniforme *m*
uniformity [ˌjuːnəˈfɔrmət̬i] *n, pl* **-ties** : uniformidad *f*

unify [ˈjuːnəˌfaɪ] *vt* **-fied; -fying** : unificar, unir
unilateral [ˌjuːnəˈlætərəl] *adj* : unilateral — **unilaterally** *adv*
unimaginable [ˌʌnɪˈmædʒənəbəl] *adj* : inimaginable, inconcebible
unimportant [ˌʌnɪmˈpɔrtənt] *adj* : intrascendente, insignificante, sin importancia
uninhabited [ˌʌnɪnˈhæbət̬əd] *adj* : deshabitado, desierto, despoblado
uninhibited [ˌʌnɪnˈhɪbət̬əd] *adj* : desenfadado, desinhibido, sin reservas
uninjured [ˌʌnˈindʒərd] *adj* : ileso
unintelligent [ˌʌnɪnˈtɛlədʒənt] *adj* : poco inteligente
unintelligible [ˌʌnɪnˈtɛlədʒəbəl] *adj* : ininteligible, incomprensible
unintentional [ˌʌnɪnˈtɛntʃənəl] *adj* : no deliberado, involuntario
unintentionally [ˌʌnɪnˈtɛntʃənəli] *adv* : involuntariamente, sin querer
uninterested [ˌʌnˈɪntəˌrɛstəd, -trəstəd] *adj* : indiferente
uninteresting [ˌʌnˈɪntəˌrɛstɪŋ, -trəstɪŋ] *adj* : poco interesante, sin interés
uninterrupted [ˌʌnˌɪntəˈrʌptəd] *adj* : ininterrumpido, continuo
union [ˈjuːnjən] *n* **1** : unión *f* **2** *or* **labor union** : sindicato *m*, gremio *m*
unionize [ˈjuːnjəˌnaɪz] *v* **-ized; -izing** *vt* : sindicalizar, sindicar — *vi* : sindicalizarse
unique [jʊˈniːk] *adj* **1** SOLE : único, solo **2** UNUSUAL : extraordinario
uniquely [jʊˈniːkli] *adv* **1** EXCLUSIVELY : exclusivamente **2** EXCEPTIONALLY : excepcionalmente
unison [ˈjuːnəsən, -zən] *n* **1** : unísono *m* (en música) **2** CONCORD : acuerdo *m*, armonía *f*, concordia *f* **3 in ~** SIMULTANEOUSLY : simultáneamente, al unísono
unit [ˈjuːnɪt] *n* **1** : unidad *f* **2** : módulo *m* (de un mobiliario)
unite [jʊˈnaɪt] *v* **united; uniting** *vt* : unir, juntar, combinar — *vi* : unirse, juntarse
unity [ˈjuːnət̬i] *n*, *pl* **-ties 1** UNION : unidad *f*, unión *f* **2** HARMONY : armonía *f*, acuerdo *m*
universal [ˌjuːnəˈvərsəl] *adj* **1** GENERAL : general, universal <a universal rule : una regla universal> **2** WORLDWIDE : universal, mundial — **universally** *adv*
universe [ˈjuːnəˌvərs] *n* : universo *m*
university [ˌjuːnəˈvərsət̬i] *n*, *pl* **-ties** : universidad *f*
unjust [ˌʌnˈdʒʌst] *adj* : injusto — **unjustly** *adv*
unjustifiable [ˌʌnˌdʒʌstəˈfaɪəbəl] *adj* : injustificable
unjustified [ˌʌnˈdʒʌstəˌfaɪd] *adj* : injustificado
unkempt [ˌʌnˈkɛmpt] *adj* : descuidado, desaliñado, despeinado (dícese del pelo)
unkind [ˌʌnˈkaɪnd] *adj* : poco amable, cruel — **unkindly** *adv*
unkindness [ˌʌnˈkaɪndnəs] *n* : crueldad *f*, falta *f* de amabilidad
unknowing [ˌʌnˈnoːɪŋ] *adj* : inconsciente, ignorante — **unknowingly** *adv*
unknown [ˌʌnˈnoːn] *adj* : desconocido
unlawful [ˌʌnˈlɔfəl] *adj* : ilícito, ilegal — **unlawfully** *adv*
unleash [ˌʌnˈliːʃ] *vt* : soltar, desatar
unless [ənˈlɛs] *conj* : a menos que, salvo que, a no ser que
unlike[1] [ˌʌnˈlaɪk] *adj* **1** DIFFERENT : diferente, distinto **2** UNEQUAL : desigual
unlike[2] *prep* **1** : diferente de, distinto de <unlike the others : distinto a los demás> **2** : a diferencia de <unlike her sister, she is shy : a diferencia de su hermana, es tímida>
unlikelihood [ˌʌnˈlaɪkliˌhʊd] *n* : improbabilidad *f*
unlikely [ˌʌnˈlaɪkli] *adj* **-lier; -est 1** IMPROBABLE : improbable, poco probable **2** UNPROMISING : poco prometedor
unlimited [ˌʌnˈlɪmət̬əd] *adj* : ilimitado
unload [ˌʌnˈloːd] *vt* **1** REMOVE : descargar, desembarcar (mercancías o pasajeros) **2** : descargar (un avión, un camión, etc.) **3** DUMP : deshacerse de — *vi* : descargar (dícese de un avión, un camión, etc.)
unlock [ˌʌnˈlɑk] *vt* **1** : abrir (con llave) **2** DISCLOSE, REVEAL : revelar
unluckily [ˌʌnˈlʌkəli] *adv* : desgraciadamente
unlucky [ˌʌnˈlʌki] *adj* **-luckier; -est 1** : de mala suerte, desgraciado, desafortunado <an unlucky year : un año de mala suerte> **2** INAUSPICIOUS : desfavorable, poco propicio **3** REGRETTABLE : lamentable
unmanageable [ˌʌnˈmænɪdʒəbəl] *adj* : difícil de controlar, poco manejable, ingobernable
unmarried [ˌʌnˈmærid] *adj* : soltero
unmask [ˌʌnˈmæsk] *vt* EXPOSE : desenmascarar
unmerciful [ˌʌnˈmərsɪfəl] *adj* MERCILESS : despiadado — **unmercifully** *adv*
unmistakable [ˌʌnmɪˈsteɪkəbəl] *adj* : evidente, inconfundible, obvio — **unmistakably** [-bli] *adv*
unmoved [ˌʌnˈmuːvd] *adj* : impasible <to be unmoved by : permanecer impasible ante>
unnatural [ˌʌnˈnætʃərəl] *adj* **1** ABNORMAL, UNUSUAL : anormal, poco natural, poco normal **2** AFFECTED : afectado, forzado <an unnatural smile : una sonrisa forzada> **3** PERVERSE : perverso, antinatural
unnecessary [ˌʌnˈnɛsəˌsɛri] *adj* : innecesario — **unnecessarily** [-ˌnɛsəˈsɛrəli] *adv*

unnerve [ˌʌnˈnərv] *vt* **-nerved; -nerving** : turbar, desconcertar, poner nervioso

unnoticed [ˌʌnˈnoːtəst] *adj* : inadvertido <to go unnoticed : pasar inadvertido>

unobstructed [ˌʌnəbˈstrʌktəd] *adj* : libre, despejado

unobtainable [ˌʌnəbˈteɪnəbəl] *adj* : inasequible

unobtrusive [ˌʌnəbˈstruːsɪv] *adj* : discreto

unoccupied [ˌʌnˈɑkjəˌpaɪd] *adj* **1** IDLE : desempleado, desocupado **2** EMPTY : desocupado, libre, deshabitado

unofficial [ˌʌnəˈfɪʃəl] *adj* : extraoficial, oficioso, no oficial

unorganized [ˌʌnˈɔrgəˌnaɪzd] *adj* : desorganizado

unorthodox [ˌʌnˈɔrθəˌdɑks] *adj* : poco ortodoxo, poco convencional

unpack [ˌʌnˈpæk] *vt* : desempacar — *vi* : desempacar, deshacer las maletas

unpaid [ˌʌnˈpeɪd] *adj* : no remunerado, no retribuido <an unpaid bill : una cuenta pendiente>

unparalleled [ˌʌnˈpærəˌlɛld] *adj* : sin igual

unpatriotic [ˌʌnˌpeɪtriˈɑt̬ɪk] *adj* : antipatriótico

unpleasant [ˌʌnˈplɛzənt] *adj* : desagradable — **unpleasantly** *adv*

unplug [ˌʌnˈplʌg] *vt* **-plugged; -plugging 1** UNCLOG : destapar, desatascar **2** DISCONNECT : desconectar, desenchufar

unpopular [ˌʌnˈpɑpjələr] *adj* : impopular, poco popular

unpopularity [ˌʌnˌpɑpjəˈlærət̬i] *n* : impopularidad *f*

unprecedented [ˌʌnˈprɛsəˌdɛntəd] *adj* : sin precedentes, inaudito, nuevo

unpredictable [ˌʌnpriˈdɪktəbəl] *adj* : impredecible

unprejudiced [ˌʌnˈprɛdʒədəst] *adj* : imparcial, objetivo

unprepared [ˌʌnpriˈpærd] *adj* : no preparado <an unprepared speech : un discurso improvisado>

unpretentious [ˌʌnpriˈtɛntʃəs] *adj* : modesto, sin pretensiones

unprincipled [ˌʌnˈprɪntsəpəld] *adj* : sin principios, carente de escrúpulos

unproductive [ˌʌnprəˈdʌktɪv] *adj* : improductivo

unprofitable [ˌʌnˈprɑfət̬əbəl] *adj* : no rentable, poco provechoso

unpromising [ˌʌnˈprɑməsɪŋ] *adj* : poco prometedor

unprotected [ˌʌnprəˈtɛktəd] *adj* : sin protección, desprotegido

unprovoked [ˌʌnprəˈvoːkt] *adj* : no provocado

unpunished [ˌʌnˈpʌnɪʃt] *adj* : impune <to go unpunished : escapar sin castigo>

unqualified [ˌʌnˈkwɑləˌfaɪd] *adj* **1** : no calificado, sin título **2** COMPLETE : completo, absoluto <an unqualified denial : una negación incondicional>

unquestionable [ˌʌnˈkwɛstʃənəbəl] *adj* : incuestionable, indudable, indiscutible — **unquestionably** [-bli] *adv*

unquestioning [ˌʌnˈkwɛstʃənɪŋ] *adj* : incondicional, absoluto, ciego

unravel [ˌʌnˈrævəl] *v* **-eled** *or* **-elled; -eling** *or* **-elling** *vt* **1** DISENTANGLE : desenmarañar, desenredar **2** SOLVE : aclarar, desenmarañar, desentrañar — *vi* : deshacerse

unreal [ˌʌnˈriːl] *adj* : irreal

unrealistic [ˌʌnˌriːəˈlɪstɪk] *adj* : poco realista

unreasonable [ˌʌnˈriːzənəbəl] *adj* **1** IRRATIONAL : poco razonable, irrazonable, irracional **2** EXCESSIVE : excesivo <unreasonable prices : precios excesivos>

unreasonably [ˌʌnˈriːzənəbli] *adv* **1** IRRATIONALLY : irracionalmente, de manera irrazonable **2** EXCESSIVELY : excesivamente

unrefined [ˌʌnriˈfaɪnd] *adj* **1** : no refinado, sin refinar (dícese del azúcar, de la harina, etc.) **2** : poco refinado, inculto (dícese de una persona)

unrelated [ˌʌnriˈleɪt̬əd] *adj* : no relacionado, inconexo

unrelenting [ˌʌnriˈlɛntɪŋ] *adj* **1** STERN : severo, inexorable **2** CONSTANT, RELENTLESS : constante, implacable

unreliable [ˌʌnriˈlaɪəbəl] *adj* : que no es de fiar, de poca confianza, inestable (dícese del tiempo)

unrepentant [ˌʌnriˈpɛntənt] *adj* : impenitente

unresolved [ˌʌnriˈzɑlvd] *adj* : pendiente, no resuelto

unrest [ˌʌnˈrɛst] *n* : inquietud *f,* malestar *m* <political unrest : disturbios políticos>

unrestrained [ˌʌnriˈstreɪnd] *adj* : desenfrenado, incontrolado

unrestricted [ˌʌnriˈstrɪktəd] *adj* : sin restricción <unrestricted access : libre acceso>

unrewarding [ˌʌnriˈwɔrdɪŋ] *adj* THANKLESS : ingrato

unripe [ˌʌnˈraɪp] *adj* : inmaduro, verde

unrivaled *or* **unrivalled** [ˌʌnˈraɪvəld] *adj* : incomparable

unroll [ˌʌnˈroːl] *vt* : desenrollar — *vi* : desenrollarse

unruffled [ˌʌnˈrʌfəld] *adj* **1** SERENE : sereno, tranquilo **2** SMOOTH : tranquilo, liso <unruffled waters : aguas tranquilas>

unruliness [ˌʌnˈruːlinəs] *n* : indisciplina *f*

unruly [ˌʌnˈruːli] *adj* : indisciplinado, díscolo, rebelde

unsafe [ˌʌnˈseɪf] *adj* : inseguro

unsaid [ˌʌnˈsɛd] *adj* : sin decir <to leave unsaid : quedar por decir>

unsanitary [ˌʌnˈsænəˌtɛri] *adj* : antihigiénico

unsatisfactory [ˌʌnˌsæt̬əsˈfæktəri] *adj* : insatisfactorio
unsatisfied [ˌʌnˈsæt̬əsˌfaɪd] *adj* : insatisfecho
unscathed [ˌʌnˈskeɪðd] *adj* UNHARMED : ileso
unscheduled [ˌʌnˈskɛˌdʒuːld] *adj* : no programado, imprevisto
unscientific [ˌʌnˌsaɪənˈtɪfɪk] *adj* : poco científico
unscrupulous [ˌʌnˈskruːpjələs] *adj* : inescrupuloso, sin escrúpulos — **unscrupulously** *adv*
unseal [ˌʌnˈsiːl] *vt* : abrir, quitarle el sello a
unseasonable [ˌʌnˈsiːzənəbəl] *adj* **1** : extemporáneo <unseasonable rain : lluvia extemporánea> **2** UNTIMELY : extemporáneo, inoportuno
unseemly [ˌʌnˈsiːmli] *adj* **-lier; -est 1** INDECOROUS : indecoroso **2** INAPPROPRIATE : impropio, inapropiado
unseen [ˌʌnˈsiːn] *adj* **1** UNNOTICED : inadvertido **2** INVISIBLE : oculto, invisible
unselfish [ˌʌnˈsɛlfɪʃ] *adj* : generoso, desinteresado — **unselfishly** *adv*
unselfishness [ˌʌnˈsɛlfɪʃnəs] *n* : generosidad *f,* desinterés *m*
unsettle [ˌʌnˈsɛt̬əl] *vt* **-tled; -tling** DISTURB : trastornar, alterar, perturbar
unsettled [ˌʌnˈsɛt̬əld] *adj* **1** CHANGEABLE : inestable, variable <unsettled weather : tiempo inestable> **2** DISTURBED : agitado, inquieto <unsettled waters : aguas agitadas> **3** UNDECIDED : pendiente (dícese de un asunto), indeciso (dícese de una persona) **4** UNPAID : sin saldar, pendiente **5** UNINHABITED : despoblado, no colonizado
unshaped [ˌʌnˈʃeɪpt] *adj* : sin forma, informe
unsightly [ˌʌnˈsaɪtli] *adj* UGLY : feo, de aspecto malo
unskilled [ˌʌnˈskɪld] *adj* : no calificado
unskillful [ˌʌnˈskɪlfəl] *adj* : inexperto, poco hábil
unsnap [ˌʌnˈsnæp] *vt* **-snapped; -snapping** : desabrochar
unsociable *adj* : poco sociable
unsolved [ˌʌnˈsɔlvd] *adj* : no resuelto, sin resolver
unsophisticated [ˌʌnsəˈfɪstəˌkeɪt̬əd] *adj* **1** NAIVE, UNWORLDLY : ingenuo, de poco mundo **2** SIMPLE : simple, poco sofisticado, rudimentario
unsound [ˌʌnˈsaʊnd] *adj* **1** UNHEALTHY : enfermizo, de mala salud **2** : poco sólido, defectuoso (dícese de una estructura, etc.) **3** INVALID : inválido, erróneo **4 of unsound mind** : mentalmente incapacitado
unspeakable [ˌʌnˈspiːkəbəl] *adj* **1** INDESCRIBABLE : indecible, inexpresable, incalificable **2** HEINOUS : atroz, nefando, abominable — **unspeakably** [-bli] *adv*
unspecified [ˌʌnˈspɛsəˌfaɪd] *adj* : indeterminado, sin especificar
unspoiled [ˌʌnˈspɔɪld] *adj* **1** : conservado, sin estropear (dícese de un lugar) **2** : que no está mimado (dícese de un niño)
unstable [ˌʌnˈsteɪbəl] *adj* **1** CHANGEABLE : variable, inestable, cambiable <an unstable pulse : un pulso irregular> **2** UNSTEADY : inestable, poco sólido (dícese de una estructura)
unsteadily [ˌʌnˈstɛdəli] *adv* : de modo inestable
unsteadiness [ˌʌnˈstɛdinəs] *n* : inestabilidad *f,* inseguridad *f*
unsteady [ˌʌnˈstɛdi] *adj* **1** UNSTABLE : inestable, variable **2** SHAKY : tembloroso
unstoppable [ˌʌnˈstɑpəbəl] *adj* : irrefrenable, incontenible
unsubstantiated [ˌʌnsəbˈstæntʃiˌeɪt̬əd] *adj* : no corroborado, no demostrado
unsuccessful [ˌʌnsəkˈsɛsfəl] *adj* : fracasado, infructuoso
unsuitable [ˌʌnˈsuːt̬əbəl] *adj* : inadecuado, impropio, inapropiado <an unsuitable time : una hora inconveniente>
unsuited [ˌʌnˈsuːt̬əd] *adj* : inadecuado, inepto
unsung [ˌʌnˈsʌŋ] *adj* : olvidado
unsure [ˌʌnˈʃʊr] *adj* : incierto, dudoso
unsurpassed [ˌʌnsərˈpæst] *adj* : sin par, sin igual
unsuspecting [ˌʌnsəˈspɛktɪŋ] *adj* : desprevenido, desapercibido, confiado
unsympathetic [ˌʌnˌsɪmpəˈθɛt̬ɪk] *adj* : poco comprensivo, indiferente
untangle [ˌʌnˈteɪŋgəl] *vt* **-gled; -gling** : desenmarañar, desenredar
unthinkable [ˌʌnˈθɪŋkəbəl] *adj* : inconcebible, impensable
unthinking [ˌʌnˈθɪŋkɪŋ] *adj* : irreflexivo, inconsciente — **unthinkingly** *adv*
untidy [ˌʌnˈtaɪdi] *adj* **1** SLOVENLY : desaliñado **2** DISORDERLY : desordenado, desarreglado
untie [ˌʌnˈtaɪ] *vt* **-tied; -tying** *or* **-tieing** : desatar, deshacer
until[1] [ˌʌnˈtɪl] *prep* : hasta <until now : hasta ahora>
until[2] *conj* : hasta que <until they left : hasta que salieron> <don't answer until you're sure : no contestes hasta que (no) estés seguro>
untimely [ˌʌnˈtaɪmli] *adj* **1** PREMATURE : prematuro <an untimely death : una muerte prematura> **2** INOPPORTUNE : inoportuno, intempestivo
untold [ˌʌnˈtoːld] *adj* **1** : nunca dicho <the untold secret : el secreto sin contar> **2** INCALCULABLE : incalculable, indecible
untouched [ˌʌnˈtʌtʃt] *adj* **1** INTACT : intacto, sin tocar, sin probar (dícese de la comida) **2** UNAFFECTED : insensible, indiferente

untoward [ˌʌnˈtɔrd, -ˈtoːərd, -tə-ˈwɔrd] *adj* **1** : indecoroso, impropio (dícese del comportamiento) **2** ADVERSE, UNFORTUNATE : desafortunado, adverso <untoward effects : efectos perjudiciales> **3** UNSEEMLY : indecoroso

untrained [ˌʌnˈtreɪnd] *adj* : inexperto, no capacitado

untreated [ˌʌnˈtriːt̬əd] *adj* : no tratado (dícese de una enfermedad, etc.), sin tratar (dícese de un material)

untroubled [ˌʌnˈtrʌbəld] *adj* : tranquilo <to be untroubled by : no estar afectado por>

untrue [ˌʌnˈtruː] *adj* **1** UNFAITHFUL : infiel **2** FALSE : falso

untrustworthy [ˌʌnˈtrʌstˌwərði] *adj* : de poca confianza (dícese de una persona), no fidedigno (dícese de la información)

untruth [ˌʌnˈtruːθ, ˈʌnˌ-] *n* : mentira *f,* falsedad *f*

untruthful [ˌʌnˈtruːθfəl] *adj* : mentiroso, falso

unusable [ˌʌnˈjuːzəbəl] *adj* : inútil, inservible

unused [ˌʌnˈjuːzd, *in sense 1 usually* -ˈjuːst] *adj* **1** UNACCUSTOMED : inhabituado **2** NEW : nuevo **3** IDLE : no utilizado (dícese de la tierra) **4** REMAINING : restante <the unused portion : la porción restante>

unusual [ˌʌnˈjuːʒʊəl] *adj* : inusual, poco común, raro

unusually [ˌʌnˈjuːʒʊəli, -ˈjuːʒəli] *adv* : excepcionalmente, extraordinariamente, fuera de lo común

unwanted [ˌʌnˈwɑntəd] *adj* : superfluo, de sobre

unwarranted [ˌʌnˈwɔrəntəd] *adj* : injustificado

unwary [ˌʌnˈwæri] *adj* : incauto

unwavering [ˌʌnˈweɪvərɪŋ] *adj* : firme, inquebrantable <an unwavering gaze : una mirada fija>

unwelcome [ˌʌnˈwɛlkəm] *adj* : importuno, molesto

unwell [ˌʌnˈwɛl] *adj* : enfermo, mal

unwholesome [ˌʌnˈhoːlsəm] *adj* **1** UNHEALTHY : malsano, insalubre **2** PERNICIOUS : pernicioso **3** LOATHSOME : repugnante, muy desagradable

unwieldy [ˌʌnˈwiːldi] *adj* CUMBERSOME : difícil de manejar, torpe y pesado

unwilling [ˌʌnˈwɪlɪŋ] *adj* : poco dispuesto <to be unwilling to : no estar dispuesto a>

unwillingly [ˌʌnˈwɪlɪŋli] *adv* : a regañadientes, de mala gana

unwind [ˌʌnˈwaɪnd] *v* **-wound** [-ˈwaʊnd]; **-winding** *vt* **1** UNROLL : desenrollar **2** RELAX : relajar — *vi* : desenrollarse

unwise [ˌʌnˈwaɪz] *adj* : imprudente, desacertado, poco aconsejable

unwisely [ˌʌnˈwaɪzli] *adv* : imprudentemente

unwitting [ˌʌnˈwɪt̬ɪŋ] *adj* **1** UNAWARE : inconsciente **2** INADVERTENT : involuntario, inadvertido <an unwitting mistake : un error inadvertido> — **unwittingly** *adv*

unworthiness [ˌʌnˈwərðinəs] *n* : falta *f* de valía

unworthy [ˌʌnˈwərði] *adj* **1** UNDESERVING : indigno <to be unworthy of : no ser digno de> **2** UNMERITED : inmerecido

unwrap [ˌʌnˈræp] *vt* **-wrapped; -wrapping** : desenvolver, deshacer

unwritten [ˌʌnˈrɪtən] *adj* : no escrito

unyielding [ˌʌnˈjiːldɪŋ] *adj* : firme, inflexible, rígido

unzip [ˌʌnˈzɪp] *vt* **-zipped; -zipping** : abrir el cierre de

up[1] [ˈʌp] *v* **upped** [ˈʌpt]; **upping; ups** *vt* INCREASE : aumentar, subir <they upped the prices : aumentaron los precios> — *vi* **to up and** : agarrar y *fam* <she up and left : agarró y se fue>

up[2] *adv* **1** ABOVE : arriba, en lo alto <up in the mountains : arriba en las montañas> **2** UPWARDS : hacia arriba <push it up : empújalo hacia arriba> <the sun came up : el sol salió> <prices went up : los precios subieron> **3** (*indicating an upright position or waking state*) <to sit up : ponerse derecho> <they got up late : se levantaron tarde> <I stayed up all night : pasé toda la noche sin dormir> **4** (*indicating volume or intensity*) <to speak up : hablar más fuerte> **5** (*indicating a northerly direction*) <the climate up north : el clima del norte> <I'm going up to Canada : voy para Canadá> **6** (*indicating the appearance or existence of something*) <the book turned up : el libro apareció> **7** (*indicating consideration*) <she brought the matter up : mencionó el asunto> **8** COMPLETELY : completamente <eat it up : cómetelo todo> **9** : en pedazos <he tore it up : lo rompió en pedazos> **10** (*indicating a stopping*) <the car pulled up to the curb : el carro paró al borde de la acera> **11** (*indicating an even score*) <the game was 10 up : empataron a 10>

up[3] *adj* **1** (*risen above the horizon*) <the sun is up : ha salido el sol> **2** (*being above a normal or former level*) <prices are up : los precios han aumentado> <the river is up : las aguas están altas> **3** : despierto, levantado <up all night : despierto toda la noche> **4** BUILT : construido <the house is up : la casa está construida> **5** OPEN : abierto <the windows are up : las ventanas están abiertas> **6** (*moving or going upward*) <the up staircase : la escalera para subir> **7** ABREAST : enterado, al día, al corriente <to be up on the news : estar al corriente de las noticias> **8** PREPARED : preparado <we were up for the test

: estuvimos preparados para el examen> 9 FINISHED : terminado, acabado <time is up : se ha terminado el tiempo permitido> **10 to be up** : pasar <what's up? : ¿qué pasa?>

up[4] *prep* **1** (*to, toward, or at a higher point of*) <he went up the stairs : subió la escalera> **2** (*to or toward the source of*) <to go up the river : ir río arriba> **3** ALONG : a lo largo, por <up the coast : a lo largo de la costa> <just up the way : un poco más adelante> <up and down the city : por toda la ciudad>

upbraid [ˌʌpˈbreɪd] *vt* : reprender, regañar

upbringing [ˈʌpˌbrɪŋɪŋ] *n* : crianza *f,* educación *f*

upcoming [ˌʌpˈkʌmɪŋ] *adj* : próximo

update[1] [ˌʌpˈdeɪt] *vt* **-dated; -dating** : poner al día, poner al corriente, actualizar

update[2] [ˈʌpˌdeɪt] *n* : actualización *f,* puesta *f* al día

upend [ˌʌpˈɛnd] *vt* **1** : poner vertical **2** OVERTURN : volcar

upgrade[1] [ˈʌpˌgreɪd, ˌʌpˈ-] *vt* **-graded; -grading** : elevar la categoría de (un puesto, etc.), implementar mejoras a (una facilidad, etc.)

upgrade[2] [ˈʌpˌgreɪd] *n* **1** SLOPE : cuesta *f,* pendiente *f* **2** RISE : aumento *m* de categoría (de un puesto), ascenso *m* (de un empleado)

upheaval [ˌʌpˈhiːvəl] *n* **1** : levantamiento *m* (en geología) **2** DISTURBANCE, UPSET : trastorno *m,* agitación *f,* conmoción *f*

uphill[1] [ˌʌpˈhɪl] *adv* : cuesta arriba

uphill[2] [ˈʌpˌhɪl] *adj* **1** ASCENDING : en subida **2** DIFFICULT : difícil, arduo

uphold [ˌʌpˈhoːld] *vt* **-held; -holding** **1** SUPPORT : sostener, apoyar, mantener **2** RAISE : levantar **3** CONFIRM : confirmar (una decisión judicial)

upholster [ˌʌpˈhoːlstər] *vt* : tapizar

upholsterer [ˌʌpˈhoːlstərər] *n* : tapicero *m,* -ra *f*

upholstery [ˌʌpˈhoːlstəri] *n, pl* **-steries** : tapicería *f*

upkeep [ˈʌpˌkiːp] *n* : mantenimiento *m*

upland [ˈʌplənd, -ˌlænd] *n* : altiplanicie *f,* altiplano *m*

uplift[1] [ˌʌpˈlɪft] *vt* **1** RAISE : elevar, levantar **2** ELEVATE : elevar, animar (el espíritu, la mente, etc.)

uplift[2] [ˈʌpˌlɪft] *n* : elevación *f*

upon [əˈpɔn, əˈpɑn] *prep* : en, sobre <upon the desk : sobre el escritorio> <upon leaving : al salir> <questions upon questions : pregunta tras pregunta>

upper[1] [ˈʌpər] *adj* **1** HIGHER : superior <the upper classes : las clases altas> **2** : alto (en geografía) <the upper Mississippi : el alto Mississippi>

upper[2] *n* : parte *f* superior (del calzado, etc.)

uppercase [ˌʌpərˈkeɪs] *adj* : mayúsculo

upper hand *n* : ventaja *f,* dominio *m*

uppermost [ˈʌpərˌmoːst] *adj* : más alto <it was uppermost in his mind : era lo que más le preocupaba>

upright[1] [ˈʌpˌraɪt] *adj* **1** VERTICAL : vertical **2** ERECT : erguido, derecho <to sit upright : sentarse derecho>**3** JUST : recto, honesto, justo

upright[2] *n* : montante *m,* poste *m,* soporte *m*

uprising [ˈʌpˌraɪzɪŋ] *n* : insurrección *f,* revuelta *f,* alzamiento *m*

uproar [ˈʌpˌror] *n* COMMOTION : alboroto *m,* jaleo *m,* escándalo *m*

uproarious [ˌʌpˈroriəs] *adj* **1** CLAMOROUS : estrepitoso, clamoroso **2** HILARIOUS : muy divertido, hilarante — **uproariously** *adv*

uproot [ˌʌpˈruːt, -ˈrʊt] *vt* : desarraigar

upset[1] [ˌʌpˈsɛt] *vt* **-set; -setting** **1** OVERTURN : volcar **2** SPILL : derramar **3** DISTURB : perturbar, disgustar, inquietar, alterar **4** SICKEN : sentar mal a <it upsets my stomach : me sienta mal al estómago> **5** DISRUPT : trastornar, desbaratar (planes, etc.) **6** DEFEAT : derrotar (en deportes)

upset[2] *adj* **1** DISPLEASED, DISTRESSED : disgustado, alterado **2 to have an upset stomach** : estar mal del estómago, estar descompuesto (de estómago)

upset[3] [ˈʌpˌsɛt] *n* **1** OVERTURNING : vuelco *m* **2** DISRUPTION : trastorno *m* (de planes, etc.) **3** DEFEAT : derrota *f* (en deportes)

upshot [ˈʌpˌʃɑt] *n* : resultado *m* final

upside–down [ˌʌpˌsaɪdˈdaʊn] *adj* : al revés

upside down [ˌʌpˌsaɪdˈdaʊn] *adv* **1** : al revés **2** : en confusión, en desorden

upstairs[1] [ˌʌpˈstærz] *adv* : arriba, en el piso superior

upstairs[2] [ˈʌpˌstærz, ˌʌpˈ-] *adj* : de arriba

upstairs[3] [ˈʌpˌstærz, ˌʌpˈ-] *ns & pl* : piso *m* de arriba, planta *f* de arriba

upstanding [ˌʌpˈstændɪŋ, ˈʌpˌ-] *adj* HONEST, UPRIGHT : honesto, íntegro, recto

upstart [ˈʌpˌstɑrt] *n* : advenedizo *m,* -za *f*

upswing [ˈʌpˌswɪŋ] *n* : alza *f,* mejora *f* notable <to be on the upswing : estar mejorándose>

uptight [ˌʌpˈtaɪt] *adj* : tenso, nervioso

up to *prep* **1** : hasta <up to a year : hasta un año> <in mud up to my ankles : en barro hasta los tobillos> **2 to be up to** : estar a la altura de <I'm not up to going : no estoy en condiciones de ir> **3 to be up to** : depender de <it's up to the director : depende del director>

up–to–date [ˌʌptəˈdeɪt] *adj* **1** CURRENT : corriente, al día <to keep up-to-date

: mantenerse al corriente> **2** MODERN : moderno

uptown [ˈʌpˈtaʊn] *adv* : hacia la parte alta de la ciudad, hacia el distrito residencial

upturn [ˈʌpˌtərn] *n* : mejora *f,* auge *m* (económico)

upward[1] [ˈʌpwərd] *or* **upwards** [-wərdz] *adv* : hacia arriba

upward[2] *adj* : ascendente, hacia arriba

upwind [ˌʌpˈwɪnd] *adv & adj* : contra el viento

uranium [jʊˈreɪniəm] *n* : uranio *m*

Uranus [jʊˈreɪnəs, ˈjʊrənəs] *n* : Urano *m*

urban [ˈərbən] *adj* : urbano

urbane [ˌərˈbeɪn] *adj* : urbano, cortés

urchin [ˈərtʃən] *n* **1** SCAMP : granuja *mf;* pillo *m,* -lla *f* **2 sea urchin** : erizo *m* de mar

urethra [jʊˈriːθrə] *n, pl* **-thras** *or* **-thrae** [-ˌθriː] : uretra *f*

urge[1] [ˈərdʒ] *vt* **urged; urging 1** PRESS : instar, apremiar, insistir <we urged him to come : insistimos en que viniera> **2** ADVOCATE : recomendar, abogar por **3 to urge on** : animar, alentar

urge[2] *n* : impulso *m,* ganas *fpl,* compulsión *f*

urgency [ˈərdʒən*t*si] *n, pl* **-cies** : urgencia *f*

urgent [ˈərdʒənt] *adj* **1** PRESSING : urgente, apremiante **2** INSISTENT : insistente **3 to be urgent** : urgir

urgently [ˈərdʒəntli] *adv* : urgentemente

urinal [ˈjʊrənəl, *esp Brit* jʊˈraɪnəl] *n* : orinal *m* (recipiente), urinario *m* (lugar)

urinary [ˈjʊrəˌnɛri] *adj* : urinario

urinate [ˈjʊrəˌneɪt] *vi* **-nated; -nating** : orinar

urination [ˌjʊrəˈneɪʃən] *n* : orinación *f*

urine [ˈjʊrən] *n* : orina *f*

urn [ˈərn] *n* **1** VASE : urna *f* **2** : recipiente *m* (para servir café, etc.)

Uruguayan [ˌʊrəˈgwaɪən, ˌjʊr-, -ˈgweɪ-] *n* : uruguayo *m,* -ya *f* — **Uruguayan** *adj*

us [ˈʌs] *pron* **1** (*as direct object*) : nos <they were visiting us : nos visitaban> **2** (*as indirect object*) : nos <he gave us a present : nos dio un regalo> **3** (*as object of preposition*) : nosotros, nosotras <stay with us : quédese con nosotros> <both of us : nosotros dos> **4** (*for emphasis*) : nosotros <it's us! : ¡somos nosotros!>

usable [ˈjuːzəbəl] *adj* : utilizable

usage [ˈjuːsɪdʒ, -zɪdʒ] *n* **1** HABIT : costumbre *f,* hábito *m* **2** USE : uso *m*

use[1] [ˈjuːz] *v* **used** [ˈjuːzd, *in phrase "used to" usually* ˈjuːstuː]; **using** *vt* **1** EMPLOY : emplear, usar **2** CONSUME : consumir, tomar (drogas, etc.) **3** UTILIZE : usar, utilizar <to use tact : usar tacto> <he used his friends to get ahead : usó a sus amigos para mejorar su posición> **4** TREAT : tratar <they used the horse cruelly : maltrataron al caballo> **5 to use up** : agotar, consumir, gastar — *vi* (*used in the past with* **to** *to indicate a former fact or state*) : soler, acostumbrar <winters used to be colder : los inviernos solían ser más fríos, los inviernos eran más fríos> <she used to dance : acostumbraba bailar>

use[2] [ˈjuːs] *n* **1** APPLICATION, EMPLOYMENT : uso *m,* empleo *m,* utilización *f* <out of use : en desuso> <ready for use : listo para usar> <to be in use : usarse, estar funcionando> <to make use of : servirse de, aprovechar> **2** USEFULNESS : utilidad *f* <to be of no use : no servir (para nada)> <it's no use! : ¡es inútil!> **3 to have the use of** : poder usar, tener acceso a **4 to have no use for** : no necesitar <she has no use for poetry : a ella no le gusta la poesía>

used [ˈjuːzd] *adj* **1** SECONDHAND : usado, de segunda mano <used cars : coches usados> **2 used to** ACCUSTOMED : acostumbrado <used to the heat : acostumbrado al calor>

useful [ˈjuːsfəl] *adj* : útil, práctico — **usefully** *adv*

usefulness [ˈjuːsfəlnəs] *n* : utilidad *f*

useless [ˈjuːsləs] *adj* : inútil — **uselessly** *adv*

uselessness [ˈjuːsləsnəs] *n* : inutilidad *f*

user [ˈjuːzər] *n* : usuario *m,* -ria *f*

usher[1] [ˈʌʃər] *vt* **1** ESCORT : acompañar, conducir **2 to usher in** : hacer pasar (a alguien) <to usher in a new era : anunciar una nueva época>

usher[2] *n* : acomodador *m,* -dora *f*

usherette [ˌʌʃəˈrɛt] *n* : acomodadora *f*

usual [ˈjuːʒʊəl] *adj* **1** NORMAL : usual, normal **2** CUSTOMARY : acostumbrado, habitual, de costumbre **3** ORDINARY : ordinario, típico

usually [ˈjuːʒʊəli, ˈjuːʒəli] *adv* : usualmente, normalmente

usurp [jʊˈsərp, -ˈzərp] *vt* : usurpar

usurper [jʊˈsərpər, -ˈzər-] *n* : usurpador *m,* -dora *f*

utensil [jʊˈtɛn*t*səl] *n* **1** : utensilio *m* (de cocina) **2** IMPLEMENT : implemento *m,* útil *m* (de labranza, etc.)

uterus [ˈjuːtərəs] *n, pl* **uteri** [-ˌraɪ] : útero *m,* matriz *f*

utilitarian [juːˌtɪləˈtɛriən] *adj* : utilitario

utility [juːˈtɪləṭi] *n, pl* **-ties 1** USEFULNESS : utilidad *f* **2 public utility** : empresa *f* de servicio público

utilization [ˌjuːṭələˈzeɪʃən] *n* : utilización *f*

utilize [ˈjuːṭəlˌaɪz] *vt* **-lized; -lizing** : utilizar, hacer uso de

utmost[1] [ˈʌtˌmoːst] *adj* **1** FARTHEST : extremo, más lejano **2** GREATEST : sumo, mayor <of the utmost importance : de suma importancia>

utmost[2] *n* : lo más posible <to the utmost : al máximo>

utopia [jʊˈtoːpiə] *n* : utopía *f*

utopian [jʊˈtoːpiən] *adj* : utópico

utter[1] [ˈʌtər] *vt* : decir, articular, pronunciar (palabras)

utter[2] *adj* : absoluto — **utterly** *adv*

utterance [ˈʌtərənts] *n* : declaración *f*, articulación *f*

V

v [ˈviː] *n, pl* **v's** *or* **vs** [ˈviːz] : vigésima segunda letra del alfabeto inglés

vacancy [ˈveɪkəntsi] *n, pl* **-cies 1** EMPTINESS : vacío *m*, vacuidad *f* **2** : vacante *f*, puesto *m* vacante <to fill a vacancy : ocupar un puesto> **3** : habitación *f* libre (en un hotel) <no vacancies : completo>

vacant [ˈveɪkənt] *adj* **1** EMPTY : libre, desocupado (dícese de los edificios, etc.) **2** : vacante (dícese de los puestos) **3** BLANK : vacío, ausente <a vacant stare : una mirada ausente>

vacate [ˈveɪˌkeɪt] *vt* **-cated; -cating** : desalojar, desocupar

vacation[1] [veɪˈkeɪʃən, və-] *vi* : pasar las vacaciones, vacacionar *Mex*

vacation[2] *n* : vacaciones *fpl* <to be on vacation : estar de vacaciones>

vacationer [veɪˈkeɪʃənər, və-] *n* : turista *mf*, veraneante *mf*, vacacionista *mf CA, Mex*

vaccinate [ˈvæksəˌneɪt] *vt* **-nated; -nating** : vacunar

vaccination [ˌvæksəˈneɪʃən] *n* : vacunación *f*

vaccine [vækˈsiːn, ˈvækˌ-] *n* : vacuna *f*

vacillate [ˈvæsəˌleɪt] *vi* **-lated; -lating 1** HESITATE : vacilar **2** SWAY : oscilar

vacillation [ˌvæsəˈleɪʃən] *n* : indecisión *f*, vacilación *f*

vacuous [ˈvækjʊəs] *adj* **1** EMPTY : vacío **2** INANE : vacuo, necio, estúpido

vacuum[1] [ˈvæˌkjuːm, -kjəm] *vt* : limpiar con aspiradora, pasar la aspiradora por

vacuum[2] *n, pl* **vacuums** *or* **vacua** [ˈvækjʊə] : vacío *m*

vacuum cleaner *n* : aspiradora *f*

vagabond[1] [ˈvægəˌbɑnd] *adj* : vagabundo

vagabond[2] *n* : vagabundo *m*, -da *f*

vagary [ˈveɪgəri, vəˈgɛri] *n, pl* **-ries** : capricho *m*

vagina [vəˈdʒaɪnə] *n, pl* **-nae** [-ˌniː, -ˌnaɪ] *or* **-nas** : vagina *f*

vagrancy [ˈveɪgrəntsi] *n* : vagancia *f*

vagrant[1] [ˈveɪgrənt] *adj* : vagabundo

vagrant[2] *n* : vagabundo *m*, -da *f*

vague [ˈveɪg] *adj* **vaguer; -est 1** IMPRECISE : vago, impreciso <a vague feeling : una sensación indefinida> <I haven't the vaguest idea : no tengo la más remota idea> **2** UNCLEAR : borroso, poco claro <a vague outline : un perfil indistinto> **3** ABSENTMINDED : distraído

vaguely [ˈveɪgli] *adv* : vagamente, de manera imprecisa

vagueness [ˈveɪgnəs] *n* : vaguedad *f*, imprecisión *f*

vain [ˈveɪn] *adj* **1** WORTHLESS : vano **2** FUTILE : vano, inútil <in vain : en vano> **3** CONCEITED : vanidoso, presumido

vainly [ˈveɪnli] *adv* : en vano, vanamente, inútilmente

valance [ˈvælənts, ˈveɪ-] *n* **1** FLOUNCE : volante *m* (de una cama, etc.) **2** : galería *f* de cortina (sobre una ventana)

vale [ˈveɪl] *n* : valle *m*

valedictorian [ˌvæləˌdɪkˈtoriən] *n* : estudiante *mf* que pronuncia el discurso de despedida en ceremonia de graduación

valedictory [ˌvæləˈdɪktəri] *adj* : de despedida

valentine [ˈvælənˌtaɪn] *n* : tarjeta *f* que se manda el Día de los Enamorados (el 14 de febrero)

Valentine's Day *n* : Día *m* de los Enamorados

valet [ˈvæˌleɪ, væˈleɪ, ˈvælət] *n* : ayuda *m* de cámara

valiant [ˈvæljənt] *adj* : valiente, valeroso

valiantly [ˈvæljəntli] *adv* : con valor, valientemente

valid [ˈvæləd] *adj* : válido

validate [ˈvæləˌdeɪt] *vt* **-dated; -dating** : validar, dar validez a

validity [vəˈlɪdəṭi, væ-] *n* : validez *f*

valise [vəˈliːs] *n* : maleta *f* (de mano)

valley [ˈvæli] *n, pl* **-leys** : valle *m*

valor [ˈvælər] *n* : valor *m*, valentía *f*

valorous [ˈvælərəs] *adj* : valeroso, valiente

valuable[1] [ˈvæljʊəbəl, ˈvæljəbəl] *adj* **1** EXPENSIVE : valioso, de valor **2** WORTHWHILE : valioso, apreciable

valuable[2] *n* : objeto *m* de valor

valuation [ˌvæljʊˈeɪʃən] *n* **1** APPRAISAL : valoración *f*, tasación *f* **2** VALUE : valuación *f*

value[1] [ˈvælˌjuː] *vt* **-ued; -uing 1** APPRAISE : valorar, avaluar, tasar **2** APPRECIATE : valorar, apreciar

value[2] *n* **1** : valor *m* <of little value : de poco valor> <to be a good value : estar bien de precio, tener buen precio> <at face value : en su sentido literal>

2 values *npl* : valores *mpl* (morales), principios *mpl*
valueless ['væljuːləs] *adj* : sin valor
valve ['vælv] *n* : válvula *f*
vampire ['væm,paɪr] *n* **1** : vampiro *m* **2** *or* **vampire bat** : vampiro *m*
van[1] ['væn] → **vanguard**
van[2] *n* : furgoneta *f*, camioneta *f*
vanadium [və'neɪdiəm] *n* : vanadio *m*
vandal ['vændəl] *n* : vándalo *m*
vandalism ['vændəl,ɪzəm] *n* : vandalismo *m*
vandalize ['vændəl,aɪz] *vt* : destrozar, destruir, estropear
vane ['veɪn] *n* *or* **weather vane** : veleta *f*
vanguard ['væn,gɑrd] *n* : vanguardia *f*
vanilla [və'nɪlə, -'nɛ-] *n* : vainilla *f*
vanish ['vænɪʃ] *vi* : desaparecer, disiparse, desvanecerse
vanity ['vænət̬i] *n, pl* **-ties 1** : vanidad *f* **2** *or* **vanity table** : tocador *m*
vanquish ['væŋkwɪʃ, 'væn-] *vt* : vencer, conquistar
vantage point ['væntɪdʒ] *n* : posición *f* ventajosa
vapid ['væpəd, 'veɪ-] *adj* : insípido, insulso
vapor ['veɪpər] *n* : vapor *m*
vaporize ['veɪpə,raɪz] *v* **-rized; -rizing** *vt* : vaporizar — *vi* : vaporizarse, evaporarse
vaporizer ['veɪpə,raɪzər] *n* : vaporizador *m*
variability [,vɛriə'bɪlət̬i] *n, pl* **-ties** : variabilidad *f*
variable[1] ['vɛriəbəl] *adj* : variable <variable cloudiness : nubosidad variable>
variable[2] *n* : variable *f*, factor *m*
variance ['vɛriənts] *n* **1** DISCREPANCY : varianza *f*, discrepancia *f* **2** DISAGREEMENT : desacuerdo *m* <at variance with : en desacuerdo con>
variant[1] ['vɛriənt] *adj* : variante, divergente
variant[2] *n* : variante *f*
variation [,vɛri'eɪʃən] *n* : variación *f*, diferencias *fpl*
varicose ['værə,koːs] *adj* : varicoso
varicose veins *npl* : varices *fpl*, várices *fpl*
varied ['vɛrid] *adj* : variado, dispar, diferente
variegated ['vɛriə,geɪt̬əd] *adj* : abigarrado, multicolor
variety [və'raɪət̬i] *n, pl* **-ties 1** DIVERSITY : diversidad *f*, variedad *f* **2** ASSORTMENT : surtido *m* <for a variety of reasons : por diversas razones> **3** SORT : clase *f* **4** BREED : variedad *f* (de plantas)
various ['vɛriəs] *adj* : varios, diversos
varnish[1] ['vɑrnɪʃ] *vt* : barnizar
varnish[2] *n* : barniz *f*
varsity ['vɑrsət̬i] *n, pl* **-ties** : equipo *m* universitario
vary ['vɛri] *v* **varied; varying** *vt* : variar, diversificar — *vi* **1** CHANGE : variar, cambiar **2** DEVIATE : desviarse
vascular ['væskjələr] *adj* : vascular
vase ['veɪs, 'veɪz, 'vɑz] *n* : jarrón *m*, florero *m*
vassal ['væsəl] *n* : vasallo *m*, -lla *f*
vast ['væst] *adj* : inmenso, enorme, vasto
vastly ['væstli] *adv* : enormemente
vastness ['væstnəs] *n* : vastedad *f*, inmensidad *f*
vat ['væt] *n* : cuba *f*, tina *f*
vaudeville ['vɔdvəl, -,vɪl; 'vɔdə,vɪl] *n* : vodevil *m*
vault[1] ['vɔlt] *vi* LEAP : saltar
vault[2] *n* **1** JUMP : salto *m* <pole vault : salto de pértiga, salto con garrocha> **2** DOME : bóveda *f* **3** : bodega *f* (para vino), bóveda *f* de seguridad (de un banco) **4** CRYPT : cripta *f*
vaulted ['vɔltəd] *adj* : abovedado
vaunted ['vɔntəd] *adj* : cacareado, alardeado <a much vaunted wine : un vino muy alardeado>
VCR [,viː,siː'ɑr] *n* : video *m*, videocasetera *f*
veal ['viːl] *n* : ternera *f*, carne *f* de ternera
veer ['vɪr] *vi* : virar (dícese de un barco), girar (dícese de un coche), torcer (dícese de un camino)
vegetable[1] ['vɛdʒtəbəl, 'vɛdʒət̬ə-] *adj* : vegetal
vegetable[2] *n* **1** : vegetal *m* <the vegetable kingdom : el reino vegetal> **2** : verdura *f*, hortaliza *f* (para comer)
vegetarian [,vɛdʒə'tɛriən] *n* : vegetariano *mf*
vegetarianism [,vɛdʒə'tɛriə,nɪzəm] *n* : vegetarianismo *m*
vegetate ['vɛdʒə,teɪt] *vi* **-tated; -tating** : vegetar
vegetation [,vɛdʒə'teɪʃən] *n* : vegetación *f*
vehemence ['viːəmənts] *n* : intensidad *f*, vehemencia *f*
vehement ['viːəmənt] *adj* : intenso, vehemente
vehemently ['viːəməntli] *adv* : vehementemente, con vehemencia
vehicle ['viːəkəl, 'viː,hɪkəl] *n* **1** *or* **motor vehicle** : vehículo *m* **2** MEDIUM : vehículo *m*, medio *m*
vehicular [vi'hɪkjələr, və-] *adj* : vehicular <vehicular homicide : muerte por atropello>
veil[1] ['veɪl] *vt* **1** CONCEAL : velar, disimular **2** : cubrir con un velo <to veil one's face : cubrirse con un velo>
veil[2] *n* : velo *m* <bridal veil : velo de novia>
vein ['veɪn] *n* **1** : vena *f* (en anatomía, botánica, etc.) **2** LODE : veta *f*, vena *f*, filón *m* **3** STYLE : vena *f* <in a humorous vein : en vena humorística>
veined ['veɪnd] *adj* : veteado (dícese del queso, de los minerales, etc.)

velocity [vəˈlɑsət̬i] *n, pl* **-ties** : velocidad *f*
velour [vəˈlʊr] *or* **velours** [-ˈlʊrz] *n* : velour *m*
velvet[1] [ˈvɛlvət] *adj* **1** : de terciopelo **2** → **velvety**
velvet[2] *n* : terciopelo *m*
velvety [ˈvɛlvət̬i] *adj* : aterciopelado
venal [ˈviːnəl] *adj* : venal, sobornable
vend [ˈvɛnd] *vt* : vender
vendetta [vɛnˈdɛt̬ə] *n* : vendetta *f*
vendor [ˈvɛndər] *n* : vendedor *m*, -dora *f*; puestero *m*, -ra *f*
veneer[1] [vəˈnɪr] *vt* : enchapar, chapar
veneer[2] *n* **1** : enchapado *m*, chapa *f* **2** APPEARANCE : apariencia *f*, barniz *m* <a veneer of culture : un barniz de cultura>
venerable [ˈvɛnərəbəl] *adj* : venerable
venerate [ˈvɛnəˌreɪt] *vt* **-ated; -ating** : venerar
veneration [ˌvɛnəˈreɪʃən] *n* : veneración *f*
venereal disease [vəˈnɪriəl] *n* : enfermedad *f* venérea
venetian blind [vəˈniːʃən] *n* : persiana *f* veneciana
Venezuelan [ˌvɛnəˈzweɪlən, -zʊˈeɪ-] *n* : venezolano *m*, -na *f* — **Venezuelan** *adj*
vengeance [ˈvɛndʒənts] *n* : venganza *f* <to take vengeance on : vengarse de>
vengeful [ˈvɛndʒfəl] *adj* : vengativo
venial [ˈviːniəl] *adj* : venial <a venial sin : un pecado venial>
venison [ˈvɛnəsən, -zən] *n* : venado *m*, carne *f* de venado
venom [ˈvɛnəm] *n* **1** : veneno *m* **2** MALICE : veneno *m*, malevolencia *f*
venomous [ˈvɛnəməs] *adj* : venenoso
vent[1] [ˈvɛnt] *vt* : desahogar, dar salida a <to vent one's feelings : desahogarse>
vent[2] *n* **1** OPENING : abertura *f* (de escape), orificio *m* **2** *or* **air vent** : respiradero *m*, rejilla *f* de ventilación **3** OUTLET : desahogo *m* <to give vent to one's anger : desahogar la ira>
ventilate [ˈvɛntəlˌeɪt] *vt* **-lated; -lating** : ventilar
ventilation [ˌvɛntəlˈeɪʃən] *n* : ventilación *f*
ventilator [ˈvɛntəlˌeɪt̬ər] *n* : ventilador *m*
ventricle [ˈvɛntrɪkəl] *n* : ventrículo *m*
ventriloquism [vɛnˈtrɪləˌkwɪzəm] *n* : ventriloquia *f*
ventriloquist [vɛnˈtrɪləˌkwɪst] *n* : ventrílocuo *m*, -cua *f*
venture[1] [ˈvɛntʃər] *v* **-tured; -turing** *vt* **1** RISK : arriesgar **2** OFFER : aventurar <to venture an opinion : aventurar una opinión> — *vi* : arriesgarse, atreverse, aventurarse
venture[2] *n* **1** UNDERTAKING : empresa *f* **2** GAMBLE, RISK : aventura *f*, riesgo *m*
venturesome [ˈvɛntʃərsəm] *adj* **1** ADVENTUROUS : audaz, atrevido **2** RISKY : arriesgado
venue [ˈvɛnˌjuː] *n* **1** PLACE : lugar *m* **2** : jurisdicción *f* (en derecho)
Venus [ˈviːnəs] *n* : Venus *m*
veracity [vəˈræsət̬i] *n, pl* **-ties** : veracidad *f*
veranda *or* **verandah** [vəˈrændə] *n* : terraza *f*, veranda *f*
verb [ˈvərb] *n* : verbo *m*
verbal [ˈvərbəl] *adj* : verbal
verbalize [ˈvərbəˌlaɪz] *vt* **-ized; -izing** : expresar con palabras, verbalizar
verbally [ˈvərbəli] *adv* : verbalmente, de palabra
verbatim[1] [vərˈbeɪt̬əm] *adv* : palabra por palabra, textualmente
verbatim[2] *adj* : literal, textual
verbose [vərˈboːs] *adj* : verboso, prolijo
verdant [ˈvərdənt] *adj* : verde, verdeante
verdict [ˈvərdɪkt] *n* **1** : veredicto *m* (de un jurado) **2** JUDGMENT, OPINION : juicio *m*, opinión *f*
verge[1] [ˈvərdʒ] *vi* **verged; verging** : estar al borde, rayar <it verges on madness : raya en la locura>
verge[2] *n* **1** EDGE : borde *m* **2 to be on the verge of** : estar a pique de, estar al borde de, estar a punto de
verification [ˌvɛrəfəˈkeɪʃən] *n* : verificación *f*
verify [ˈvɛrəˌfaɪ] *vt* **-fied; -fying** : verificar, comprobar, confirmar
veritable [ˈvɛrət̬əbəl] *adj* : verdadero — **veritably** *adv*
vermicelli [ˌvərməˈtʃɛli, -ˈsɛli] *n* : fideos *mpl* finos
vermin [ˈvərmən] *ns & pl* : alimañas *fpl*, bichos *mpl*, sabandijas *fpl*
vermouth [vərˈmuːth] *n* : vermut *m*
vernacular[1] [vərˈnækjələr] *adj* : vernáculo
vernacular[2] *n* : lengua *f* vernácula
versatile [ˈvərsət̬əl] *adj* : versátil
versatility [ˌvərsəˈtɪlət̬i] *n* : versatilidad *f*
verse [ˈvərs] *n* **1** LINE, STANZA : verso *m*, estrofa *f* **2** POETRY : poesía *f* **3** : versículo *m* (en la Biblia)
versed [ˈvərst] *adj* : versado <to be well versed in : ser muy versado en>
version [ˈvərʒən] *n* : versión *f*
versus [ˈvərsəs] *prep* : versus
vertebra [ˈvərt̬əbrə] *n, pl* **-brae** [-ˌbreɪ, -ˌbriː] *or* **-bras** : vértebra *f*
vertebrate[1] [ˈvərt̬əbrət, -ˌbreɪt] *adj* : vertebrado
vertebrate[2] *n* : vertebrado *m*
vertex [ˈvərˌtɛks] *n, pl* **vertices** [ˈvərt̬əˌsiːz] **1** : vértice *m* (en matemáticas y anatomía) **2** SUMMIT, TOP : ápice *m*, cumbre *f*, cima *f*
vertical[1] [ˈvərt̬ɪkəl] *adj* : vertical — **verticalmente** *adv*
vertical[2] *n* : vertical *f*
vertigo [ˈvərt̬ɪˌgoː] *n, pl* **-goes** *or* **-gos** : vértigo *m*
verve [ˈvərv] *n* : brío *m*

very[1] ['vɛri] *adv* **1** EXTREMELY **:** muy, sumamente <very few : muy pocos> <I am very sorry : lo siento mucho> **2** (*used for emphasis*) <at the very least : por lo menos, como mínimo> <the same dress : el mismo vestido>

very[2] *adj* **verier; -est 1** EXACT, PRECISE **:** mismo, exacto <at that very moment : en ese mismo momento> <it's the very thing : es justo lo que hacía falta> **2** BARE, MERE **:** solo, mero <the very thought of it : sólo pensarlo> **3** EXTREME **:** extremo, de todo <at the very top : arriba de todo>

vespers ['vɛspərz] *npl* **:** vísperas *fpl*

vessel ['vɛsəl] *n* **1** CONTAINER **:** vasija *f,* recipiente *m* **2** BOAT, CRAFT **:** nave *f,* barco *m,* buque *m* **3 :** vaso *m* <blood vessel : vaso sanguíneo>

vest[1] ['vɛst] *vt* **1** CONFER **:** conferir <to vest authority in : conferirle la autoridad a> **2** CLOTHE **:** vestir

vest[2] *n* **1 :** chaleco *m* **2** UNDERSHIRT **:** camiseta *f*

vestibule ['vɛstə,bju:l] *n* **:** vestíbulo *m*

vestige ['vɛstɪdʒ] *n* **:** vestigio *m,* rastro *m*

vestment ['vɛstmənt] *n* **:** vestidura *f*

vestry ['vɛstri] *n, pl* **-tries :** sacristía *f*

vet ['vɛt] *n* **1** → **veterinarian 2** → **veteran**[2]

veteran[1] ['vɛtərən, 'vɛtrən] *adj* **:** veterano

veteran[2] *n* **:** veterano *m,* -na *f*

Veterans Day *n* **:** día *m* del Armisticio (celebrado el 11 de noviembre en los Estados Unidos)

veterinarian [,vɛtərə'nɛriən, ,vɛtə'nɛr-] *n* **:** veterinario *m,* -ria *f*

veterinary ['vɛtərə,nɛri] *adj* **:** veterinario

veto[1] ['vi:to] *vt* **1** FORBID **:** prohibir **2 :** vetar <to veto a bill : vetar un proyecto de ley>

veto[2] *n, pl* **-toes 1 :** veto *m* <the power of veto : el derecho de veto> **2** BAN **:** veto *m,* prohibición *f*

vex ['vɛks] *vt* **:** contrariar, molestar, irritar

vexation [vɛk'seɪʃən] *n* **:** contrariedad *f,* irritación *f*

via ['vaɪə, 'vi:ə] *prep* **:** por, vía

viability [,vaɪə'bɪləti] *n* **:** viabilidad *f*

viable ['vaɪəbəl] *adj* **:** viable

viaduct ['vaɪə,dʌkt] *n* **:** viaducto *m*

vial ['vaɪəl] *n* **:** frasco *m*

vibrant ['vaɪbrənt] *adj* **1** LIVELY **:** vibrante, animado, dinámico **2** BRIGHT **:** fuerte, vivo (dícese de los colores)

vibrate ['vaɪ,breɪt] *vi* **-brated; -brating 1** OSCILLATE **:** vibrar, oscilar **2** THRILL **:** bullir <to vibrate with excitement : bullir de emoción>

vibration [vaɪ'breɪʃən] *n* **:** vibración *f*

vicar ['vɪkər] *n* **:** vicario *m,* -ria *f*

vicarious [vaɪ'kæri:əs, vɪ-] *adj* **:** indirecto **— vicariously** *adv*

vice ['vaɪs] *n* **:** vicio *m*

vice admiral *n* **:** vicealmirante *mf*

vice president *n* **:** vicepresidente *m,* -ta *f*

viceroy ['vaɪs,rɔɪ] *n* **:** virrey *m,* -rreina *f*

vice versa [,vaɪsɪ'vərsə, ,vaɪs'vər-] *adv* **:** viceversa

vicinity [və'sɪnəti] *n, pl* **-ties 1** NEIGHBORHOOD **:** vecindad *f,* inmediaciones *fpl* **2** NEARNESS **:** proximidad *f*

vicious ['vɪʃəs] *adj* **1** DEPRAVED **:** depravado, malo **2** SAVAGE **:** malo, fiero, salvaje <a vicious dog : un perro feroz> **3** MALICIOUS **:** malicioso

viciously ['vɪʃəsli] *adv* **:** con saña, brutalmente

viciousness ['vɪʃəsnəs] *n* **:** brutalidad *f,* ferocidad *f* (de un animal), malevolencia *f* (de un comentario, etc.)

vicissitudes [və'sɪsə,tu:dz, vaɪ-, -,tju:dz] *npl* **:** vicisitudes *fpl*

victim ['vɪktəm] *n* **:** víctima *f*

victimize ['vɪktə,maɪz] *vt* **-mized; -mizing :** tomar como víctima, perseguir, victimizar *Arg, Mex*

victor ['vɪktər] *n* **:** vencedor *m,* -dora *f*

Victorian [vɪk'to:riən] *adj* **:** victoriano

victorious [vɪk'to:riəs] *adj* **:** victorioso **— victoriously** *adv*

victory ['vɪktəri] *n, pl* **-ries :** victoria *f,* triunfo *m*

victuals ['vɪtəlz] *npl* **:** víveres *mpl,* provisiones *fpl*

video[1] ['vɪdi,o:] *adj* **:** de video <video recording : grabación de video>

video[2] *n* **1 :** video *m* (medio o grabación) **2** → **videotape**[2]

videocassette [,vɪdiokə'sɛt] *n* **:** videocasete *m,* videocassette *m*

videocassette recorder → **VCR**

videotape[1] ['vɪdio,teɪp] *vt* **-taped; -taping :** grabar en video, videograbar

videotape[2] *n* **:** videocinta *f*

vie ['vaɪ] *vi* **vied; vying** ['vaɪɪŋ] **:** competir, rivalizar

Vietnamese [vi,ɛtnə'mi:z, -'mi:s] *n* **:** vietnamita *mf* **— Vietnamese** *adj*

view[1] ['vju:] *vt* **1** OBSERVE **:** mirar, ver, observar **2** CONSIDER **:** considerar, contemplar

view[2] *n* **1** SIGHT **:** vista *f* <to come into view : aparecer> **2** ATTITUDE, OPINION **:** opinión *f,* parecer *m,* actitud *f* <in my view : en mi opinión> **3** SCENE **:** vista *f,* panorama *f* **4** INTENTION **:** idea *f,* vista *f* <with a view to : con vistas a, con la idea de> **5 in view of :** dado que, en vista de (que)

viewer ['vju:ər] *n or* **television viewer :** telespectador *m,* -dora *f;* televidente *mf*

viewpoint ['vju:,pɔɪnt] *n* **:** punto *m* de vista

vigil ['vɪdʒəl] *n* **1 :** vigilia *f,* vela *f* **2 to keep vigil :** velar

vigilance ['vɪdʒələnts] *n* **:** vigilancia *f*

vigilant ['vɪdʒələnt] *adj* **:** vigilante

vigilante [ˌvɪdʒəˈlænˌtiː] *n* : integrante *mf* de un comité de vigilancia (que actúa como policía)
vigilantly [ˈvɪdʒələntli] *adv* : con vigilancia
vigor [ˈvɪgər] *n* : vigor *m,* energía *f,* fuerza *f*
vigorous [ˈvɪgərəs] *adj* : vigoroso, enérgico — **vigorously** *adv*
Viking [ˈvaɪkɪŋ] *n* : vikingo *m,* -ga *f*
vile [ˈvaɪl] *adj* **viler; vilest 1** WICKED : vil, infame **2** REVOLTING : asqueroso, repugnante **3** TERRIBLE : horrible, atroz <vile weather : tiempo horrible> <to be in a vile mood : estar de un humor de perros>
vilify [ˈvɪləˌfaɪ] *vt* **-fied; -fying** : vilipendiar, denigrar, difamar
villa [ˈvɪlə] *n* : casa *f* de campo, quinta *f*
village [ˈvɪlɪdʒ] *n* : pueblo *m* (grande), aldea *f* (pequeña)
villager [ˈvɪlɪdʒər] *n* : vecino *m,* -na *f* (de un pueblo); aldeano *m,* -na *f* (de una aldea)
villain [ˈvɪlən] *n* : villano *m,* -na *f;* malo *m,* -la *f* (en ficción, películas, etc.)
villainess [ˈvɪlənɪs, -nəs] *n* : villana *f*
villainous [ˈvɪlənəs] *adj* : infame, malvado
villainy [ˈvɪləni] *n, pl* **-lainies** : vileza *f,* maldad *f*
vim [ˈvɪm] *n* : brío *m,* vigor *m,* energía *f*
vindicate [ˈvɪndəˌkeɪt] *vt* **-cated; -cating 1** EXONERATE : vindicar, disculpar **2** JUSTIFY : justificar
vindication [ˌvɪndəˈkeɪʃən] *n* : vindicación *f,* justificación *f*
vindictive [vɪnˈdɪktɪv] *adj* : vengativo
vine [ˈvaɪn] *n* **1** GRAPEVINE : vid *f,* parra *f* **2** : planta *f* trepadora, enredadera *f*
vinegar [ˈvɪnɪgər] *n* : vinagre *m*
vinegary [ˈvɪnɪgəri] *adj* : avinagrado
vineyard [ˈvɪnjərd] *n* : viña *f,* viñedo *m*
vintage[1] [ˈvɪntɪdʒ] *adj* **1** : añejo (dícese de un vino) **2** CLASSIC : clásico, de época
vintage[2] *n* **1** : cosecha *f* <the 1947 vintage : la cosecha de 1947> **2** ERA : época *f,* era *f* <slang of recent vintage : argot de la época reciente>
vinyl [ˈvaɪnəl] *n* : vinilo
viola [viːˈoːlə] *n* : viola *f*
violate [ˈvaɪəˌleɪt] *vt* **-lated; -lating 1** BREAK : infringir, violar, quebrantar <to violate the rules : violar las reglas> **2** RAPE : violar **3** DESECRATE : profanar
violation [ˌvaɪəˈleɪʃən] *n* **1** : violación *f,* infracción *f* (de una ley) **2** DESECRATION : profanación *f*
violence [ˈvaɪlənts, ˈvaɪə-] *n* : violencia *f*
violent [ˈvaɪlənt, ˈvaɪə-] *adj* : violento
violently [ˈvaɪləntli, ˈvaɪə-] *adv* : violentamente, con violencia
violet [ˈvaɪlət, ˈvaɪə-] *n* : violeta *f*
violin [ˌvaɪəˈlɪn] *n* : violín *m*
violinist [ˌvaɪəˈlɪnɪst] *n* : violinista *mf*
violoncello [ˌvaɪələnˈtʃɛloː, ˌviː-] → **cello**
VIP [ˌviːˌaɪˈpiː] *n, pl* **VIPs** [-ˈpiːz] : VIP *mf,* persona *f* de categoría
viper [ˈvaɪpər] *n* : víbora *f*
viral [ˈvaɪrəl] *adj* : viral, vírico <viral pneumonia : pulmonía viral>
virgin[1] [ˈvərdʒən] *adj* **1** CHASTE : virginal <the virgin birth : el alumbramiento virginal> **2** : virgen, intacto <a virgin forest : una selva virgen> <virgin wool : lana virgen>
virgin[2] *n* : virgen *mf*
virginity [vərˈdʒɪnət̬i] *n* : virginidad *f*
Virgo [ˈvərˌgoː, ˈvɪr-] *n* : Virgo *mf*
virile [ˈvɪrəl, -ˌaɪl] *adj* : viril, varonil
virility [vəˈrɪlət̬i] *n* : virilidad *f*
virtual [ˈvərtʃʊəl] *adj* : virtual <a virtual dictator : un virtual dictador> <virtual reality : realidad virtual>
virtually [ˈvərtʃʊəli, ˈvərtʃəli] *adv* : en realidad, de hecho, casi
virtue [ˈvərˌtʃuː] *n* **1** : virtud *f* **2 by virtue of** : en virtud de, debido a
virtuosity [ˌvərtʃʊˈɑsət̬i] *n, pl* **-ties** : virtuosismo *m*
virtuoso [ˌvərtʃʊˈoːsoː, -zoː] *n, pl* **-sos** *or* **-si** [-ˌsiː, -ˌziː] : virtuoso *m,* -sa *f*
virtuous [ˈvərtʃʊəs] *adj* : virtuoso, bueno — **virtuously** *adv*
virulence [ˈvɪrələnts, ˈvɪrjə-] *n* : virulencia *f*
virulent [ˈvɪrələnt, ˈvɪrjə-] *adj* : virulento
virus [ˈvaɪrəs] *n* : virus *m*
visa [ˈviːzə, -sə] *n* : visa *f*
vis-à-vis [ˌviːzəˈviː, -sə-] *prep* : con relación a, con respecto a
viscera [ˈvɪsərə] *npl* : vísceras *fpl*
visceral [ˈvɪsərəl] *adj* : visceral
viscosity [vɪsˈkɑsət̬i] *n, pl* **-ties** : viscosidad *f*
viscount [ˈvaɪˌkæʊnt] *n* : vizconde *m*
viscountess [ˈvaɪˌkæʊntɪs] *n* : vizcondesa *f*
viscous [ˈvɪskəs] *adj* : viscoso
vise [ˈvaɪs] *n* : torno *m* de banco, tornillo *m* de banco
visibility [ˌvɪzəˈbɪlət̬i] *n, pl* **-ties** : visibilidad *f*
visible [ˈvɪzəbəl] *adj* **1** : visible <the visible stars : las estrellas visibles> **2** OBVIOUS : evidente, patente
visibly [ˈvɪzəbli] *adv* : visiblemente
vision [ˈvɪʒən] *n* **1** EYESIGHT : vista *f,* visión *f* **2** APPARITION : visión *f,* aparición *f* **3** FORESIGHT : visión *f* (del futuro), previsión *f* **4** IMAGE : imagen *f* <she had visions of a disaster : se imaginaba un desastre>
visionary[1] [ˈvɪʒəˌnɛri] *adj* **1** FARSIGHTED : visionario, con visión de futuro **2** UTOPIAN : utópico, poco realista
visionary[2] *n, pl* **-ries** : visionario *m,* -ria *f*

visit[1] [ˈvɪzət] *vt* **1** : visitar, ir a ver **2** AFFLICT : azotar, afligir <visited by troubles : afligido con problemas> — *vi* : hacer (una) visita
visit[2] *n* : visita *f*
visitor [ˈvɪzət̬ər] *n* : visitante *mf* (a una ciudad, etc.), visita *f* (a una casa)
visor [ˈvaɪzər] *n* : visera *f*
vista [ˈvɪstə] *n* : vista *f*
visual [ˈvɪʒʊəl] *adj* : visual <the visual arts : las artes visuales> — **visually** *adv*
visualize [ˈvɪʒʊəˌlaɪz] *vt* **-ized; -izing** : visualizar, imaginarse, hacerse una idea de
vital [ˈvaɪt̬əl] *adj* **1** : vital <vital organs : órganos vitales> **2** CRUCIAL : esencial, crucial, decisivo <of vital importance : de suma importancia> **3** LIVELY : enérgico, lleno de vida, vital
vitality [vaɪˈtæləţi] *n, pl* **-ties** : vitalidad *f*, energía *f*
vitally [ˈvaɪt̬əli] *adv* : sumamente
vital statistics *npl* : estadísticas *fpl* demográficas
vitamin [ˈvaɪt̬əmən] *n* : vitamina *f* <vitamin deficiency : carencia vitamínica>
vitreous [ˈvɪtriəs] *adj* : vítreo
vitriolic [ˌvɪtriˈɑlɪk] *adj* : mordaz, virulento
vituperation [vaɪˌtuːpəˈreɪʃən, -ˌtjuː-] *n* : vituperio *m*
vivacious [vəˈveɪʃəs, vaɪ-] *adj* : vivaz, animado, lleno de vida
vivaciously [vəˈveɪʃəsli, vaɪ-] *adv* : con vivacidad, animadamente
vivacity [vəˈvæsəţi, vaɪ-] *n* : vivacidad *f*
vivid [ˈvɪvəd] *adj* **1** LIVELY : lleno de vitalidad **2** BRILLIANT : vivo, intenso <vivid colors : colores vivos> **3** INTENSE, SHARP : vívido, gráfico <a vivid dream : un sueño vívido>
vividly [ˈvɪvədli] *adv* **1** BRIGHTLY : con colores vivos **2** SHARPLY : vívidamente
vividness [ˈvɪvədnəs] *n* **1** BRIGHTNESS : intensidad *f*, viveza *f* **2** SHARPNESS : lo gráfico, nitidez *f*
vivisection [ˌvɪvəˈsɛkʃən, ˈvɪvəˌ-] *n* : vivisección *f*
vixen [ˈvɪksən] *n* : zorra *f*, raposa *f*
vocabulary [voːˈkæbjəˌlɛri] *n, pl* **-laries 1** : vocabulario *m* **2** LEXICON : léxico *m*
vocal [ˈvoːkəl] *adj* **1** : vocal **2** LOUD, OUTSPOKEN : ruidoso, muy franco
vocal cords *npl* : cuerdas *fpl* vocales
vocalist [ˈvoːkəlɪst] *n* : cantante *mf*, vocalista *mf*
vocalize [ˈvoːkəlˌaɪz] *vt* **-ized; -izing** : vocalizar
vocation [voˈkeɪʃən] *n* : vocación *f* <to have a vocation for : tener vocación de>
vocational [voˈkeɪʃənəl] *adj* : profesional <vocational guidance : orientación profesional>
vociferous [voˈsɪfərəs] *adj* : ruidoso, vociferante
vodka [ˈvɑdkə] *n* : vodka *m*
vogue [ˈvoːg] *n* : moda *f*, boga *f* <to be in vogue : estar de moda, estar en boga>
voice[1] [ˈvɔɪs] *vt* **voiced; voicing** : expresar
voice[2] *n* **1** : voz *f* <in a low voice : en voz baja> <to lose one's voice : quedarse sin voz> <the voice of the people : la voz del pueblo> **2 to make one's voice heard** : hacerse oír
voice box → **larynx**
voiced [ˈvɔɪst] *adj* : sonoro
void[1] [ˈvɔɪd] *vt* : anular, invalidar <to void a contract : anular un contrato>
void[2] *adj* **1** EMPTY : vacío, desprovisto <void of content : desprovisto de contenido> **2** INVALID : inválido, nulo
void[3] *n* : vacío *m*
volatile [ˈvɑləţəl] *adj* : volátil, inestable
volatility [ˌvɑləˈtɪləţi] *n* : volatilidad *f*, inestabilidad *f*
volcanic [vɑlˈkænɪk] *adj* : volcánico
volcano [vɑlˈkeɪˌnoː] *n, pl* **-noes** *or* **-nos** : volcán *m*
vole [ˈvoːl] *n* : campañol *m*
volition [voˈlɪʃən] *n* : volición *f*, voluntad *f* <of one's own volition : por voluntad propia>
volley [ˈvɑli] *n, pl* **-leys 1** : descarga *f* (de tiros) **2** : torrente *m*, lluvia *f* (de insultos, etc.) **3** : salva *f* (de aplausos) **4** : volea *f* (en deportes)
volleyball [ˈvɑliˌbɔl] *n* : voleibol *m*
volt [ˈvoːlt] *n* : voltio *m*
voltage [ˈvoːltɪdʒ] *n* : voltaje *m*
volubility [ˌvɑljəˈbɪləţi] *n* : locuacidad *f*
voluble [ˈvɑljəbəl] *adj* : locuaz
volume [ˈvɑljəm, -ˌjuːm] *n* **1** BOOK : volumen *m*, tomo *m* **2** SPACE : capacidad *f*, volumen *m* (en física) **3** AMOUNT : cantidad *f*, volumen *m* **4** LOUDNESS : volumen *m*
voluminous [vəˈluːmənəs] *adj* : voluminoso
voluntary [ˈvɑlənˌtɛri] *adj* : voluntario — **voluntarily** [ˌvɑlənˈtɛrəli] *adv*
volunteer[1] [ˌvɑlənˈtɪr] *vt* : ofrecer, dar <to volunteer one's assistance : ofrecer la ayuda> — *vi* : ofrecerse, alistarse como voluntario
volunteer[2] *n* : voluntario *m*, -ria *f*
voluptuous [vəˈlʌptʃʊəs] *adj* : voluptuoso
vomit[1] [ˈvɑmət] *v* : vomitar
vomit[2] *n* : vómito *m*
voodoo [ˈvuːˌduː] *n, pl* **voodoos** : vudú *m*
voracious [vɔˈreɪʃəs, və-] *adj* : voraz
voraciously [vɔˈreɪʃəsli, və-] *adv* : vorazmente, con voracidad
vortex [ˈvɔrˌtɛks] *n, pl* **vortices** [ˈvɔrtəˌsiːz] : vórtice *m*

vote[1] ['voːt] *vi* **voted; voting** : votar <to vote Democratic : votar por los demócratas>
vote[2] *n* **1** : voto *m* **2** SUFFRAGE : sufragio *m,* derecho *m* al voto
voter ['voːtər] *n* : votante *mf*
voting ['voːtɪŋ] *n* : votación *f*
vouch ['væʊtʃ] *vi* **to vouch for** : garantizar (algo), responder de (algo), responder por (alguien)
voucher ['væʊtʃər] *n* **1** RECEIPT : comprobante *m* **2** : vale *m* <travel voucher : vale de viajar>
vow[1] [væʊ] *vt* : jurar, prometer, hacer voto de
vow[2] *n* : promesa *f,* voto *m* (en la religión) <a vow of poverty : un voto de pobreza>
vowel ['væʊəl] *n* : vocal *m*
voyage[1] ['vɔɪɪdʒ] *vi* **-aged; -aging** : viajar
voyage[2] *n* : viaje *m*
voyager ['vɔɪɪdʒər] *n* : viajero *m,* -ra *f*
vulcanize ['vʌlkəˌnaɪz] *vt* **-nized; -nizing** : vulcanizar
vulgar ['vʌlgər] *adj* **1** COMMON, PLEBIAN : ordinario, populachero, del vulgo **2** COARSE, CRUDE : grosero, de mal gusto, majadero *Mex* **3** INDECENT : indecente, colorado (dícese de un chiste, etc.)
vulgarity [ˌvʌl'gærəti] *n, pl* **-ties** : grosería *f,* vulgaridad *f*
vulgarly ['vʌlgərli] *adv* : vulgarmente, groseramente
vulnerability [ˌvʌlnərə'bɪləti] *n, pl* **-ties** : vulnerabilidad *f*
vulnerable ['vʌlnərəbəl] *adj* : vulnerable
vulture ['vʌltʃər] *n* : buitre *m,* zopilote *m CA, Mex*
vying → **vie**

W

w ['dʌbəlˌjuː] *n, pl* **w's** *or* **ws** [-ˌjuːz] : vigésima tercera letra del alfabeto inglés
wad[1] ['wɑd] *vt* **wadded; wadding 1** : hacer un taco con, formar en una masa **2** STUFF : rellenar
wad[2] *n* : taco *m* (de papel), bola *f* (de algodón, etc.), fajo *m* (de billetes)
waddle[1] ['wɑdəl] *vi* **-dled; -dling** : andar como un pato
waddle[2] *n* : andar *m* de pato
wade ['weɪd] *v* **waded; wading** *vi* **1** : caminar por el agua **2 to wade through** : leer (algo) con dificultad — *vt or* **to wade across** : vadear
wading bird *n* : zancuda *f,* ave *f* zancuda
wafer ['weɪfər] *n* : barquillo *m,* galleta *f* de barquillo
waffle ['wɑfəl] *n* **1** : wafle *m* **2 waffle iron** : waflera *f*
waft ['wɑft, 'wæft] *vt* : llevar por el aire — *vi* : flotar
wag[1] ['wæg] *v* **wagged; wagging** *vt* : menear — *vi* : menearse, moverse
wag[2] *n* **1** : meneo *m* (de la cola) **2** JOKER, WIT : bromista *mf*
wage[1] ['weɪdʒ] *vt* **waged; waging** : hacer, librar <to wage war : hacer la guerra>
wage[2] *n or* **wages** *npl* : sueldo *m,* salario *m* <minimum wage : salario mínimo>
wager[1] ['weɪdʒər] *v* : apostar
wager[2] *n* : apuesta *f*
waggish ['wægɪʃ] *adj* : burlón, bromista (dícese de una persona), chistoso (dícese de un comentario)
waggle ['wægəl] *vt* **-gled; -gling** : menear, mover (de un lado a otro)
wagon ['wægən] *n* **1** : carro *m* (tirado por caballos) **2** CART : carrito *m* **3** → **station wagon**
waif ['weɪf] *n* : niño *m* abandonado, animal *m* sin hogar
wail[1] ['weɪl] *vi* : gemir, lamentarse
wail[2] *n* : gemido *m,* lamento *m*
wainscot ['weɪnskət, -ˌskɑt, -ˌskoːt] *or* **wainscoting** [-skətɪŋ, -ˌskɑ-, -ˌskoː-] *n* : boiserie *f,* revestimiento *m* de paneles de madera
waist ['weɪst] *n* : cintura *f* (del cuerpo humano), talle *m* (de ropa)
waistline ['weɪstˌlaɪn] → **waist**
wait[1] ['weɪt] *vi* : esperar <to wait for something : esperar algo> <wait and see! : ¡espera y verás!> <I can't wait : me muero de ganas> — *vt* **1** AWAIT : esperar **2** DELAY : retrasar <don't wait lunch : no retrase el almuerzo> **3** SERVE : servir, atender <to wait tables : servir (a la mesa)>
wait[2] *n* **1** : espera *f* **2 to lie in wait** : estar al acecho
waiter ['weɪtər] *n* : mesero *m,* camarero *m,* mozo *m Arg, Chile, Col, Peru*
waiting room *n* : sala *f* de espera
waitress ['weɪtrəs] *n* : mesera *f,* camarera *f,* moza *f Arg, Chile, Col, Peru*
waive ['weɪv] *vt* **waived; waiving** : renunciar a <to waive one's rights : renunciar a sus derechos> <to waive the rules : no aplicar las reglas>
waiver ['weɪvər] *n* : renuncia *f*
wake[1] ['weɪk] *v* **woke** ['woːk]; **woken** ['woːkən] *or* **waked; waking** *vi or* **to wake up** : despertar(se) <he woke at noon : se despertó al mediodía> <wake up! : ¡despiértate!> — *vt* : despertar
wake[2] *n* **1** VIGIL : velatorio *m,* velorio *m* (de un difunto) **2** TRAIL : estela *f* (de un barco, un huracán, etc.) **3** AFTERMATH : consecuencias *fpl* <in the wake of : tras, como consecuencia de>

wakeful [ˈweɪkfəl] *adj* **1** SLEEPLESS **:** desvelado **2** VIGILANT **:** alerta, vigilante

waken [ˈweɪkən] → **awake**

walk[1] [ˈwɔk] *vi* **1 :** caminar, andar, pasear <you're walking too fast : estás caminando demasiado rápido> <to walk around the city : pasearse por la ciudad> **2 :** ir andando, ir a pie <we had to walk home : tuvimos que ir a casa a pie> **3 :** darle base por bolas (a un bateador) — *vt* **1 :** recorrer, caminar <she walked two miles : caminó dos millas> **2** ACCOMPANY **:** acompañar **3 :** sacar a pasear (a un perro)

walk[2] *n* **1 :** paseo *m,* caminata *f* <to go for a walk : ir a caminar, dar un paseo> **2** PATH **:** camino *m* **3** GAIT **:** andar *m* **4 :** marcha *f* (en beisbol) **5 walk of life :** esfera *f,* condición *f*

walker [ˈwɔkər] *n* **1 :** paseante *mf;* andador *m,* -dora *f* **2** HIKER **:** excursionista *mf* **3** *or* **baby walker :** andador *m*

walking stick *n* **:** bastón *m*

walkout [ˈwɔkˌaʊt] *n* STRIKE **:** huelga *f*

walk out *vi* **1** STRIKE **:** declararse en huelga **2** LEAVE **:** salir, irse **3 to walk out on :** abandonar, dejar

wall[1] [ˈwɔl] *vt* **1 to wall in :** cercar con una pared o un muro, tapiar, amurallar **2 to wall off :** separar con una pared o un muro **3 to wall up :** tapiar, condenar (una ventana, etc.)

wall[2] *n* **1 :** muro *m* (exterior) <the walls of the city : las murallas de la ciudad> **2 :** pared *f* (interior) **3** BARRIER **:** barrera *f* <a wall of mountains : una barrera de montañas> **4 :** pared *f* (en anatomía)

wallaby [ˈwɑləbi] *n, pl* **-bies :** ualabí *m*

walled [ˈwɔld] *adj* **:** amurallado

wallet [ˈwɑlət] *n* **:** billetera *f,* cartera *f*

wallflower [ˈwɔlˌflaʊər] *n* **1 :** alhelí *m* (flor) **2 to be a wallflower :** comer pavo

wallop[1] [ˈwɑləp] *vt* **1** TROUNCE **:** darle una paliza (a alguien) **2** SOCK **:** pegar fuerte

wallop[2] *n* **:** golpe *m* fuerte, golpazo *m*

wallow[1] [ˈwɑˌloː] *vi* **1 :** revolcarse <to wallow in the mud : revolcarse en el lodo> **2** DELIGHT **:** deleitarse <to wallow in luxury : nadar en lujos>

wallow[2] *n* **:** revolcadero *m* (para animales)

wallpaper[1] [ˈwɔlˌpeɪpər] *vt* **:** empapelar

wallpaper[2] *n* **:** papel *m* pintado

walnut [ˈwɔlˌnʌt] *n* **1 :** nuez *f* (fruta) **2 :** nogal *m* (árbol y madera)

walrus [ˈwɔlrəs, ˈwɑl-] *n, pl* **-rus** *or* **-ruses :** morsa *f*

waltz[1] [ˈwɔlts] *vi* **1 :** valsar, bailar el vals **2** BREEZE **:** pasar con ligereza <to waltz in : entrar tan campante>

waltz[2] *n* **:** vals *m*

wan [ˈwɑn] *adj* **wanner; -est 1** PALLID **:** pálido **2** DIM **:** tenue <wan light : luz tenue> **3** LANGUID **:** lánguido <a wan smile : una sonrisa lánguida> — **wanly** *adv*

wand [ˈwɑnd] *n* **:** varita *f* (mágica)

wander [ˈwɑndər] *vi* **1** RAMBLE **:** deambular, vagar, vagabundear **2** STRAY **:** alejarse, desviarse, divagar <she let her mind wander : dejó vagar la imaginación> — *vt* **:** recorrer <to wander the streets : vagar por las calles>

wanderer [ˈwɑndərər] *n* **:** vagabundo *m,* -da *f;* viajero *m,* -ra *f*

wanderlust [ˈwɑndərˌlʌst] *n* **:** pasión *f* por viajar

wane[1] [ˈweɪn] *vi* **waned; waning 1 :** menguar (dícese de la luna) **2** DECLINE **:** disminuir, decaer, menguar

wane[2] *n* **on the wane :** decayendo, en decadencia

wangle [ˈwæŋgəl] *vt* **-gled; -gling** FINAGLE **:** arreglárselas para conseguir

want[1] [ˈwɑnt, ˈwɔnt] *vt* **1** LACK **:** faltar **2** REQUIRE **:** requerir, necesitar **3** DESIRE **:** querer, desear

want[2] *n* **1** LACK **:** falta *f* **2** DESTITUTION **:** indigencia *f,* miseria *f* **3** DESIRE, NEED **:** deseo *m,* necesidad *f*

wanting [ˈwɑntɪŋ, ˈwɔn-] *adj* **1** ABSENT **:** ausente **2** DEFICIENT **:** deficiente <he's wanting in common sense : le falta sentido común>

wanton [ˈwɑntən, ˈwɔn-] *adj* **1** LEWD, LUSTFUL **:** lascivo, lujurioso, licencioso **2** INHUMANE, MERCILESS **:** despiadado <wanton cruelty : crueldad despiadada>

wapiti [ˈwɑpəti] *n, pl* **-ti** *or* **-tis :** uapití *m*

war[1] [ˈwɔr] *vi* **warred; warring :** combatir, batallar, hacer la guerra

war[2] *n* **:** guerra *f* <to go to war : entrar en guerra>

warble[1] [ˈwɔrbəl] *vi* **-bled; -bling :** gorjear, trinar

warble[2] *n* **:** trino *m,* gorjeo *m*

warbler [ˈwɔrblər] *n* **:** pájaro *m* gorjeador, curruca *f*

ward[1] [ˈwɔrd] *vt* **to ward off :** desviar, protegerse contra

ward[2] *n* **1 :** sala *f* (de un hospital, etc.) <maternity ward : sala de maternidad> **2 :** distrito *m* electoral o administrativo (de una ciudad) **3 :** pupilo *m,* -la *f* (de un tutor, etc.)

warden [ˈwɔrdən] *n* **1** KEEPER **:** guarda *mf;* guardián *m,* -diana *f* <game warden : guardabosque> **2** *or* **prison warden :** alcaide *m*

wardrobe [ˈwɔrdˌroːb] *n* **1** CLOSET **:** armario *m* **2** CLOTHES **:** vestuario *m,* guardarropa *f*

ware [ˈwær] *n* **1** POTTERY **:** cerámica *f* **2 wares** *npl* GOODS **:** mercancía *f,* mercadería *f*

warehouse [ˈwærˌhaʊs] *n* **:** depósito *m,* almacén *m,* bodega *f Chile, Col, Mex*

warfare ['wɔr,fær] *n* **1** WAR : guerra *f* **2** STRUGGLE : lucha *f* <the warfare against drugs : la lucha contra las drogas>

warhead ['wɔr,hɛd] *n* : ojiva *f,* cabeza *f* (de un misil)

warily ['wærəli] *adv* : cautelosamente, con cautela

wariness ['wærinəs] *n* : cautela *f*

warlike ['wær,laɪk] *adj* : belicoso, guerrero

warm[1] ['wɔrm] *vt* **1** HEAT : calentar, recalentar **2 to warm one's heart** : reconfortar a uno, alegrar el corazón **3 to warm up** : calentar (los músculos, un automóvil, etc.) — *vi* **1** : calentarse **2 to warm to** : tomarle simpatía (a alguien), entusiasmarse con (algo)

warm[2] *adj* **1** LUKEWARM : tibio, templado **2** : caliente, cálido, caluroso <a warm wind : un viento cálido> <a warm day : un día caluroso, un día de calor> <warm hands : manos calientes> **3** : caliente, que abriga <warm clothes : ropa de abrigo> <I feel warm : tengo calor> **4** CARING, CORDIAL : cariñoso, cordial **5** : cálido (dícese de colores) **6** FRESH : fresco, reciente <a warm trail : un rastro reciente> **7** (*used for riddles*) : caliente

warm–blooded ['wɔrm'blʌdəd] *adj* : de sangre caliente

warmhearted ['wɔrm'hɑrt̬əd] *adj* : cariñoso

warmly ['wɔrmli] *adv* **1** AFFECTIONATELY : calurosamente, afectuosamente **2 to dress warmly** : abrigarse

warmonger ['wɔr,mɑŋgər, -,mʌŋ-] *n* : belicista *mf*

warmth ['wɔrmpθ] *n* **1** : calor *m* **2** AFFECTION : cariño *m,* afecto *m* **3** ENTHUSIASM : ardor *m,* entusiasmo *m*

warm–up ['wɔrm,ʌp] *n* : calentamiento *m*

warn ['wɔrn] *vt* **1** CAUTION : advertir, alertar **2** INFORM : avisar, informar

warning ['wɔrnɪŋ] *n* **1** ADVICE : advertencia *f,* aviso *m* **2** ALERT : alerta *f,* alarma *f*

warp[1] ['wɔrp] *vt* **1** : alabear, combar **2** PERVERT : pervertir, deformar — *vi* : pandearse, alabearse, combarse

warp[2] *n* **1** : urdimbre *f* <the warp and the weft : la urdimbre y la trama> **2** : alabeo *m* (en la madera, etc.)

warrant[1] ['wɔrənt] *vt* **1** ASSURE : asegurar, garantizar **2** GUARANTEE : garantizar **3** JUSTIFY, MERIT : justificar, merecer

warrant[2] *n* **1** AUTHORIZATION : autorización *f,* permiso *m* <an arrest warrant : una orden de detención> **2** JUSTIFICATION : justificación *f*

warranty ['wɔrənti, ,wɔrən'ti:] *n, pl* **-ties** : garantía *f*

warren ['wɔrən] *n* : madriguera *f* (de conejos)

warrior ['wɔriər] *n* : guerrero *m,* -ra *f*

warship ['wɔr,ʃɪp] *n* : buque *m* de guerra

wart ['wɔrt] *n* : verruga *f*

wartime ['wɔr,taɪm] *n* : tiempo *m* de guerra

wary ['wæri] *adj* **warier; -est** : cauteloso, receloso <to be wary of : desconfiar de>

was → **be**

wash[1] ['wɔʃ, 'wɑʃ] *vt* **1** CLEAN : lavar(se), limpiar, fregar <to wash the dishes : lavar los platos> <to wash one's hands : lavarse las manos> **2** DRENCH : mojar **3** LAP : bañar <waves were washing the shore : las olas bañaban la orilla> **4** CARRY, DRAG : arrastrar **5 to wash away** : llevarse (un puente, etc.) — *vi* **1** : lavarse (dícese de una persona o la ropa) <the dress washes well : el vestido se lava bien> **2 to wash against** *or* **to wash over** : bañar

wash[2] *n* **1** : lavado *m* <to give something a wash : lavar algo> **2** LAUNDRY : artículos *mpl* para lavar, ropa *f* sucia **3** : estela *f* (de un barco)

washable ['wɔʃəbəl, 'wɑ-] *adj* : lavable

washboard ['wɔʃ,bord, 'wɑʃ-] *n* : tabla *f* de lavar

washbowl ['wɔʃ,bo:l, 'wɑʃ-] *n* : lavabo *m,* lavamanos *m*

washcloth ['wɔʃ,klɔθ, 'wɑʃ-] *n* : toallita *f* (para lavarse)

washed–out ['wɔʃt'aʊt, 'wɑʃt-] *adj* **1** : desvaído (dícese de colores) **2** EXHAUSTED : agotado, desanimado

washed–up ['wɔʃt'ʌp, 'wɑʃt-] *adj* : acabado (dícese de una persona), fracasado (dícese de un negocio, etc.)

washer ['wɔʃər, 'wɑ-] *n* **1** → **washing machine 2** : arandela *f* (de una llave, etc.)

washing ['wɔʃɪŋ, 'wɑ-] *n* WASH : ropa *f* para lavar

washing machine *n* : máquina *f* de lavar, lavadora *f*

washout ['wɔʃ,aʊt, 'wɑʃ-] *n* **1** : erosión *f* (de la tierra) **2** FAILURE : fracaso *m* <she's a washout : es un desastre>

washroom ['wɔʃ,ru:m, 'wɑʃ-, -,rʊm] *n* : servicios *mpl* (públicos), baño *m,* sanitario *m Col, Mex, Ven*

wasn't ['wʌzənt] (*contraction of* **was not**) → **be**

wasp ['wɑsp] *n* : avispa *f*

waspish ['wɑspɪʃ] *adj* **1** IRRITABLE : irritable, irascible **2** CAUSTIC : cáustico, mordaz

waste[1] ['weɪst] *v* **wasted; wasting** *vt* **1** DEVASTATE : arrasar, arruinar, devastar **2** SQUANDER : desperdiciar, despilfarrar, malgastar <to waste time : perder tiempo> — *vi or* **to waste away** : consumirse, chuparse

waste[2] *adj* **1** BARREN : yermo, baldío **2** DISCARDED : de desecho **3** EXCESS : sobrante

waste[3] *n* **1** → **wasteland** **2** MISUSE : derroche *m,* desperdicio *m,* despilfarro *m* <a waste of time : una pérdida de tiempo> **3** RUBBISH : basura *f,* desechos *mpl,* desperdicios *mpl* **4** EXCREMENT : excremento *m*

wastebasket [ˈweɪstˌbæskət] *n* : cesto *m* (de basura), papelera *f,* zafacón *m Car*

wasteful [ˈweɪstfəl] *adj* : despilfarrador, derrochador, pródigo

wastefulness [ˈweɪstfəlnəs] *n* : derroche *m,* despilfarro *m*

wasteland [ˈweɪstˌlænd, -lənd] *n* : baldío *m,* yermo *m,* desierto *m*

watch[1] [ˈwɑtʃ] *vi* **1** *or* **to keep watch** : velar **2** OBSERVE : mirar, ver, observar **3 to watch for** AWAIT : esperar, quedar a la espera de **4 to watch out** : tener cuidado <watch out! : ¡ten cuidado!, ¡ojo!> — *vt* **1** OBSERVE : mirar, observar **2** *or* **to watch over** : vigilar, cuidar **3** : tener cuidado de <watch what you do : ten cuidado con lo que haces>

watch[2] *n* **1** : guardia *f* <to be on watch : estar de guardia> **2** SURVEILLANCE : vigilancia *f* **3** LOOKOUT : guardia *mf,* centinela *f,* vigía *mf* **4** TIMEPIECE : reloj *m*

watchdog [ˈwɑtʃˌdɔg] *n* : perro *m* guardián

watcher [ˈwɑtʃər] *n* : observador *m,* -dora *f*

watchful [ˈwɑtʃfəl] *adj* : alerta, vigilante, atento

watchfulness [ˈwɑtʃfəlnəs] *n* : vigilancia *f*

watchman [ˈwɑtʃmən] *n, pl* **-men** [-mən, -ˌmɛn] : vigilante *m,* guarda *m*

watchword [ˈwɑtʃˌwərd] *n* **1** PASSWORD : contraseña *f* **2** SLOGAN : lema *m,* eslogan *m*

water[1] [ˈwɔt̬ər, ˈwɑ-] *vt* **1** : regar (el jardín, etc.) **2 to water down** DILUTE : diluir, aguar — *vi* : lagrimar (dícese de los ojos), hacérsele agua la boca a uno <my mouth is watering : se me hace agua la boca>

water[2] *n* : agua *f*

water buffalo *n* : búfalo *m* de agua

watercolor [ˈwɔt̬ərˌkʌlər, ˈwɑ-] *n* : acuarela *f*

watercourse [ˈwɔt̬ərˌkors, ˈwɑ-] *n* : curso *m* de agua

watercress [ˈwɔt̬ərˌkrɛs, ˈwɑ-] *n* : berro *m*

waterfall [ˈwɔt̬ərˌfɔl, ˈwɑ-] *n* : cascada *f,* salto *m* de agua, catarata *f*

waterfowl [ˈwɔt̬ərˌfaʊl, ˈwɑ-] *n* : ave *f* acuática

waterfront [ˈwɔt̬ərˌfrʌnt, ˈwɑ-] *n* **1** : tierra *f* que bordea un río, un lago, o un mar **2** WHARF : muelle *m*

water lily *n* : nenúfar *m*

waterlogged [ˈwɔt̬ərˌlɔgd, ˈwɑt̬ərˌlɑgd] *adj* : lleno de agua, empapado, inundado (dícese del suelo)

watermark [ˈwɔt̬ərˌmɑrk, ˈwɑ-] *n* **1** : marca *f* del nivel de agua **2** : filigrana *f* (en el papel)

watermelon [ˈwɔt̬ərˌmɛlən, ˈwɑ-] *n* : sandía *f*

water moccasin → **moccasin**

waterpower [ˈwɔt̬ərˌpaʊər, ˈwɑ-] *n* : energía *f* hidráulica

waterproof[1] [ˈwɔt̬ərˌpruːf, ˈwɑ-] *vt* : hacer impermeable, impermeabilizar

waterproof[2] *adj* : impermeable, a prueba de agua

watershed [ˈwɔt̬ərˌʃɛd, ˈwɑ-] *n* **1** : línea *f* divisoria de aguas **2** BASIN : cuenca *f* (de un río)

waterskiing [ˈwɔt̬ərˌskiːɪŋ, ˈwɑ-] *n* : esquí *m* acuático

waterspout [ˈwɔt̬ərˌspaʊt, ˈwɑ-] *n* WHIRLWIND : tromba *f* marina

watertight [ˈwɔt̬ərˌtaɪt, ˈwɑ-] *adj* **1** : hermético **2** IRREFUTABLE : irrebatible, irrefutable <a watertight contract : un contrato sin lagunas>

waterway [ˈwɔt̬ərˌweɪ, ˈwɑ-] *n* : vía *f* navegable

waterworks [ˈwɔt̬ərˌwərks, ˈwɑ-] *npl* : central *f* de abastecimiento de agua

watery [ˈwɔt̬əri, ˈwɑ-] *adj* **1** : acuoso, como agua **2** : aguado, diluido <watery soup : sopa aguada> **3** : lloroso <watery eyes : ojos llorosos> **4** WASHED-OUT : desvaído (dícese de colores)

watt [ˈwɑt] *n* : vatio *m*

wattage [ˈwɑt̬ɪdʒ] *n* : vataje *m*

wattle [ˈwɑt̬əl] *n* : carúncula *f* (de un ave, etc.)

wave[1] [ˈweɪv] *v* **waved; waving** *vi* **1** : saludar con la mano, hacer señas con la mano <she waved at him : lo saludó con la mano> **2** FLUTTER, SHAKE : ondear, agitarse **3** UNDULATE : ondular — *vt* **1** SHAKE : agitar **2** BRANDISH : blandir **3** CURL : ondular, marcar (el pelo) **4** SIGNAL : hacerle señas a (con la mano) <he waved farewell : se despidió con la mano>

wave[2] *n* **1** : ola *f* (de agua) **2** CURL : onda *f* (en el pelo) **3** : onda *f* (en física) **4** SURGE : oleada *f* <a wave of enthusiasm : una oleada de entusiasmo> **5** GESTURE : señal *f* con la mano, saludo *m* con la mano

wavelength [ˈweɪvˌlɛŋkθ] *n* : longitud *f* de onda

waver [ˈweɪvər] *vi* **1** VACILLATE : vacilar, fluctuar **2** FLICKER : parpadear, titilar, oscilar **3** FALTER : flaquear, tambalearse

wavy [ˈweɪvi] *adj* **wavier; -est** : ondulado

wax[1] [ˈwæks] *vi* **1** : crecer (dícese de la luna) **2** BECOME : volverse, ponerse <to wax indignant : indignarse> — *vt* : encerar

wax[2] *n* **1** BEESWAX : cera *f* de abejas **2** : cera *f* <floor wax : cera para el piso>

3 *or* **earwax** [ˈɪrˌwæks] **:** cerilla *f,* cerumen *m*

waxen [ˈwæksən] *adj* **:** de cera

waxy [ˈwæksi] *adj* **waxier; -est** **:** ceroso

way [ˈweɪ] *n* **1** PATH, ROAD **:** camino *m,* vía *f* **2** ROUTE **:** camino *m,* ruta *f* <to go the wrong way : equivocarse de camino> <I'm on my way : estoy de camino> **3 :** línea *f* de conducta, camino *m* <he chose the easy way : optó por el camino fácil> **4** MANNER, MEANS **:** manera *f,* modo *m,* forma *f* <in the same way : del mismo modo, igualmente> <there are no two ways about it : no cabe la menor duda> **5** (*indicating a wish*) <have it your way : como tú quieras> <to get one's own way : salirse uno con la suya> **6** STATE **:** estado *m* <things are in a bad way : las cosas marchan mal> **7** RESPECT **:** aspecto *m,* sentido *m* **8** CUSTOM **:** costumbre *f* <to mend one's ways : dejar las malas costumbres> **9** PASSAGE **:** camino *m* <to get in the way : meterse en el camino> **10** DISTANCE **:** distancia *f* <to come a long way : hacer grandes progresos> **11** DIRECTION **:** dirección *f* <come this way : venga por aquí> <which way did he go? : ¿por dónde fue?> **12 by the way :** a propósito, por cierto **13 by way of** VIA **:** vía, pasando por **14 out of the way** REMOTE **:** remoto, recóndito **15** → **under way**

wayfarer [ˈweɪˌfærər] *n* **:** caminante *mf*

waylay [ˈweɪˌleɪ] *vt* **-laid** [-ˌleɪd]; **-laying** ACCOST **:** abordar

wayside [ˈweɪˌsaɪd] *n* **:** borde *m* del camino

wayward [ˈweɪwərd] *adj* **1** UNRULY **:** díscolo, rebelde **2** UNTOWARD **:** adverso

we [ˈwiː] *pron* **:** nosotros, nosotras

weak [ˈwiːk] *adj* **1** FEEBLE **:** débil, endeble **2 :** flojo, pobre <a weak excuse : una excusa poco convincente> **3** DILUTED **:** aguado, diluido <weak tea : té poco cargado> **4** FAINT **:** tenue (dícese de los colores, las luces, los sonidos, etc.)

weaken [ˈwiːkən] *vt* **:** debilitar — *vi* **:** debilitarse, flaquear

weakling [ˈwiːklɪŋ] *n* **:** alfeñique *m fam;* debilucho *m,* -cha *f*

weakly[1] [ˈwiːkli] *adv* **:** débilmente

weakly[2] *adj* **weaklier; -est :** débil, enclenque

weakness [ˈwiːknəs] *n* **1** FEEBLENESS **:** debilidad *f* **2** FAULT, FLAW **:** flaqueza *f,* punto *m* débil

wealth [ˈwɛlθ] *n* **1** RICHES **:** riqueza *f* **2** PROFUSION **:** abundancia *f,* profusión *f*

wealthy [ˈwɛlθi] *adj* **wealthier; -est** **:** rico, acaudalado, adinerado

wean [ˈwiːn] *vt* **1 :** destetar (a los niños o las crías) **2 to wean someone away from :** quitarle a alguien la costumbre de

weapon [ˈwɛpən] *n* **:** arma *f*

weaponless [ˈwɛpənləs] *adj* **:** desarmado

wear[1] [ˈwær] *v* **wore** [ˈwor]; **worn** [ˈworn]; **wearing** *vt* **1 :** llevar (ropa, un reloj, etc.), calzar (zapatos) <to wear a happy smile : sonreír alegremente> **2** *or* **to wear away :** desgastar, erosionar (rocas, etc.) **3 to wear out :** gastar <he wore out his shoes : gastó sus zapatos> **4 to wear out** EXHAUST **:** agotar, fatigar <to wear oneself out : agotarse> — *vi* **1** LAST **:** durar **2 to wear off** DIMINISH **:** disminuir **3 to wear out :** gastarse

wear[2] *n* **1** USE **:** uso *m* <for everyday wear : para todos los días> **2** CLOTHING **:** ropa *f* <children's wear : ropa de niños> **3** DETERIORATION **:** desgaste *m* <to be the worse for wear : estar deteriorado>

wearable [ˈwærəbəl] *adj* **:** que puede ponerse (dícese de una prenda)

wear and tear *n* **:** desgaste *m*

weariness [ˈwɪrinəs] *n* **:** fatiga *f,* cansancio *m*

wearisome [ˈwɪrisəm] *adj* **:** aburrido, pesado, cansado

weary[1] [ˈwɪri] *v* **-ried; -rying** *vt* **1** TIRE **:** cansar, fatigar **2** BORE **:** hastiar, aburrir — *vi* **:** cansarse

weary[2] *adj* **-rier; -est 1** TIRED **:** cansado **2** FED UP **:** harto **3** BORED **:** aburrido

weasel [ˈwiːzəl] *n* **:** comadreja *f*

weather[1] [ˈwɛðər] *vt* **1** WEAR **:** erosionar, desgastar **2** ENDURE **:** aguantar, sobrellevar, capear <to weather the storm : capear el temporal>

weather[2] *n* **:** tiempo *m*

weather–beaten [ˈwɛðərˌbiːtən] *adj* **:** curtido

weatherman [ˈwɛðərˌmæn] *n, pl* **-men** [-mən, -ˌmɛn] METEOROLOGIST **:** meteorólogo *m,* -ga *f*

weatherproof [ˈwɛðərˌpruːf] *adj* **:** que resiste a la intemperie, impermeable

weather vane → **vane**

weave[1] [ˈwiːv] *v* **wove** [ˈwoːv] *or* **weaved; woven** [ˈwoːvən] *or* **weaved; weaving** *vt* **1 :** tejer (tela) **2** INTERLACE **:** entretejer, entrelazar **3 to weave one's way through :** abrirse camino por — *vi* **1 :** tejer **2** WIND **:** serpentear, zigzaguear

weave[2] *n* **:** tejido *m,* trama *f*

weaver [ˈwiːvər] *n* **:** tejedor *m,* -dora *f*

web[1] [ˈwɛb] *vt* **webbed; webbing :** cubrir o proveer con una red

web[2] *n* **1** COBWEB, SPIDERWEB **:** telaraña *f,* tela *f* de araña **2** ENTANGLEMENT, SNARE **:** red *f,* enredo *m* <a web of intrigue : una red de intriga> **3 :** membrana *f* interdigital (de aves) **4** NETWORK **:** red *f* <a web of highways : una red de carreteras>

webbed ['wɛbd] *adj* : palmeado <webbed feet : patas palmeadas>

wed ['wɛd] *vt* **wedded; wedding 1** MARRY : casarse con **2** UNITE : ligar, unir

we'd ['wi:d] (*contraction of* **we had, we should,** *or* **we would**) → **have, should, would**

wedding ['wɛdɪŋ] *n* : boda *f,* casamiento *m*

wedge[1] ['wɛdʒ] *vt* **wedged; wedging 1** : apretar (con una cuña) <to wedge open : mantener abierto con una cuña> **2** CRAM : meter, embutir

wedge[2] *n* **1** : cuña *f* **2** PIECE : porción *f,* trozo *m*

wedlock ['wɛd,lɑk] → **marriage**

Wednesday ['wɛnz,deɪ, -di] *n* : miércoles *m*

wee ['wi:] *adj* : pequeño, minúsculo <in the wee hours : a las altas horas>

weed[1] ['wi:d] *vt* **1** : desherbar, desyerbar **2 to weed out** : eliminar, quitar

weed[2] *n* : mala hierba *f*

weedy ['wi:di] *adj* **weedier; -est 1** : cubierto de malas hierbas **2** LANKY, SKINNY : flaco, larguirucho *fam*

week ['wi:k] *n* : semana *f*

weekday ['wi:k,deɪ] *n* : día *m* laborable

weekend ['wi:k,ɛnd] *n* : fin *m* de semana

weekly[1] ['wi:kli] *adv* : semanalmente

weekly[2] *adj* : semanal

weekly[3] *n, pl* **-lies** : semanario *m*

weep ['wi:p] *v* **wept** ['wɛpt]; **weeping** : llorar

weeping willow *n* : sauce *m* llorón

weepy ['wi:pi] *adj* **weepier; -est** : lloroso, triste

weevil ['wi:vəl] *n* : gorgojo *m*

weft ['wɛft] *n* : trama *f*

weigh ['weɪ] *vt* **1** : pesar **2** CONSIDER : considerar, sopesar **3 to weigh anchor** : levar anclas **4 to weigh down** : sobrecargar (con una carga), abrumar (con preocupaciones, etc.) — *vi* **1** : pesar <it weighs 10 pounds : pesa 10 libras> **2** COUNT : tener importancia, contar **3 to weigh on one's mind** : preocuparle a uno

weight[1] ['weɪt] *vt* **1** : poner peso en, sujetar con un peso **2** BURDEN : cargar, oprimir

weight[2] *n* **1** HEAVINESS : peso *m* <to lose weight : bajar de peso, adelgazar> **2** : peso *m* <weights and measures : pesos y medidas> **3** : pesa *f* <to lift weights : levantar pesas> **4** BURDEN : peso *m,* carga *f* <to take a weight off one's mind : quitarle un peso de encima a uno> **5** IMPORTANCE : peso *m* **6** INFLUENCE : influencia *f,* autoridad *f* <to throw one's weight around : hacer sentir su influencia>

weighty ['weɪţi] *adj* **weightier; -est 1** HEAVY : pesado **2** IMPORTANT : importante, de peso

weird ['wɪrd] *adj* **1** MYSTERIOUS : misterioso **2** STRANGE : extraño, raro — **weirdly** *adv*

welcome[1] ['wɛlkəm] *vt* **-comed; -coming** : darle la bienvenida a, recibir

welcome[2] *adj* : bienvenido <to make someone welcome : acoger bien a alguien> <you're welcome! : ¡de nada!, ¡no hay de qué!>

welcome[3] *n* : bienvenida *f,* recibimiento *m,* acojida *f*

weld[1] ['wɛld] *v* : soldar

weld[2] *n* : soldadura *f*

welder ['wɛldər] *n* : soldador *m,* -dora *f*

welfare ['wɛl,fær] *n* **1** WELL-BEING : bienestar *m* **2** : asistencia *f* social

well[1] ['wɛl] *vi or* **to well up** : brotar, manar

well[2] *adv* **better** ['bɛţər]; **best** ['bɛst] **1** RIGHTLY : bien, correctamente **2** SATISFACTORILY : bien <to turn out well : resultar bien, salir bien> **3** COMPLETELY : completamente <well-hidden : completamente escondido> **4** INTIMATELY : bien <I knew him well : lo conocía bien> **5** CONSIDERABLY, FAR : muy, bastante <well ahead : muy adelante> <well before the deadline : bastante antes de la fecha> **6 as well** ALSO : también **7** → **as well as**

well[3] *adj* **1** SATISFACTORY : bien <all is well : todo está bien> **2** DESIRABLE : conveniente <it would be well if you left : sería conveniente que te fueras> **3** HEALTHY : bien, sano

well[4] *n* **1** : pozo *m* (de agua, petróleo, gas, etc.), aljibe *m* (de agua) **2** SOURCE : fuente *f* <a well of information : una fuente de información> **3** *or* **stairwell** : caja *f,* hueco *m* (de la escalera)

well[5] *interj* **1** (*used to introduce a remark*) : bueno **2** (*used to express surprise*) : ¡vaya!

we'll ['wi:l, wɪl] (*contraction of* **we shall** *or* **we will**) → **shall, will**

well–balanced ['wɛl'bælənst] *adj* : equilibrado

well–being ['wɛl'bi:ɪŋ] *n* : bienestar *m*

well–bred ['wɛl'brɛd] *adj* : fino, bien educado

well–done ['wɛl'dʌn] *adj* **1** : bien hecho <well-done! : ¡bravo!> **2** : bien cocido

well–known ['wɛl'no:n] *adj* : famoso, bien conocido

well–meaning ['wɛl'mi:nɪŋ] *adj* : bienintencionado, que tiene buenas intenciones

well–nigh ['wɛl'naɪ] *adv* : casi <well-nigh impossible : casi imposible>

well–off ['wɛl'ɔf] → **well–to–do**

well–rounded ['wɛl'raʊndəd] *adj* : completo, equilibrado

well–to–do [,wɛltə'du:] *adj* : próspero, adinerado, rico

welt [ˈwɛlt] *n* **1 :** vira *f* (de un zapato) **2** WHEAL **:** verdugón *m*

welter [ˈwɛltər] *n* **:** fárrago *m,* revoltijo *m* <a welter of data : un fárrago de datos>

wend [ˈwɛnd] *vi* **to wend one's way :** ponerse en camino, encaminar sus pasos

went → **go**

wept → **weep**

were → **be**

we're [ˈwɪr, ˈwər, ˈwiːər] (*contraction of* **we are**) → **be**

werewolf [ˈwɪrˌwʊlf, ˈwɛr-, ˈwər-, -ˌwʌlf] *n, pl* **-wolves** [-ˌwʊlvz, -ˌwʌlvz] **:** hombre *m* lobo

west[1] [ˈwɛst] *adv* **:** al oeste

west[2] *adj* **:** oeste, del oeste, occidental <west winds : vientos del oeste>

west[3] *n* **1 :** oeste *m* **2 the West :** el Oeste, el Occidente

westerly [ˈwɛstərli] *adv & adj* **:** del oeste

western [ˈwɛstərn] *adj* **1 :** Occidental, del Oeste **2 :** occidental, oeste

Westerner [ˈwɛstərnər] *n* **:** habitante *mf* del oeste

West Indian *n* **:** antillano *m,* -na *f* — **West Indian** *adj*

westward [ˈwɛstwərd] *adv & adj* **:** hacia el oeste

wet[1] [ˈwɛt] *vt* **wet** *or* **wetted; wetting :** mojar, humedecer

wet[2] *adj* **wetter; wettest 1 :** mojado, húmedo <wet clothes : ropa mojada> **2** RAINY **:** lluvioso **3 wet paint :** pintura *f* fresca

wet[3] *n* **1** MOISTURE **:** humedad *f* **2** RAIN **:** lluvia *f*

we've [ˈwiːv] (*contraction of* **we have**) → **have**

whack[1] [ˈhwæk] *vt* **:** golpear (fuertemente), aporrear

whack[2] *n* **1 :** golpe *m* fuerte, porrazo *m* **2** ATTEMPT **:** intento *m,* tentativa *f*

whale[1] [ˈhweɪl] *vi* **whaled; whaling :** cazar ballenas

whale[2] *n, pl* **whales** *or* **whale :** ballena *f*

whaleboat [ˈhweɪlˌboːt] *n* **:** ballenero *m*

whalebone [ˈhweɪlˌboːn] *n* **:** barba *f* de ballena

whaler [ˈhweɪlər] *n* **1 :** ballenero *m,* -ra *f* **2** → **whaleboat**

wharf [ˈhwɔrf] *n, pl* **wharves** [ˈhwɔrvz] **:** muelle *m,* embarcadero *m*

what[1] [ˈhwɑt, ˈhwʌt] *adv* **1** HOW **:** cómo, cúanto <what he suffered! : ¡cómo sufría!> **2 what with :** entre <what with one thing and another : entre una cosa y otra>

what[2] *adj* **1** (*used in questions*) **:** qué <what more do you want? : ¿qué más quieres?> <what color is it? : ¿de qué color es?> **2** (*used in exclamations*) **:** qué <what an idea! : ¡qué idea!> **3** ANY, WHATEVER **:** cualquier <give what help you can : da cualquier contribución que puedas>

what[3] *pron* **1** (*used in direct questions*) **:** qué <what happened? : ¿qué pasó?> <what does it cost? : ¿cuánto cuesta?> **2** (*used in indirect statements*) **:** lo que, que <I don't know what to do : no sé que hacer> <do what I tell you : haz lo que te digo> **3 what for** WHY **:** porqué **4 what if :** y si <what if he knows? : ¿y si lo sabe?>

whatever[1] [hwɑtˈɛvər, ˌhwʌt-] *adj* **1** ANY **:** cualquier, cualquier...que <whatever way you prefer : de cualquier manera que prefiera, como prefiera> **2** (*in negative constructions*) <there's no chance whatever : no hay ninguna posibilidad> <nothing whatever : nada en absoluto>

whatever[2] *pron* **1** ANYTHING **:** (todo) lo que <I'll do whatever I want : haré lo que quiera> **2** (*no matter what*) <whatever it may be : sea lo que sea> **3** WHAT **:** qué <whatever do you mean? : ¿qué quieres decir?>

whatsoever[1] [ˌhwɑtsoˈɛvər, ˌhwʌt-] *adj* → **whatever**[1]

whatsoever[2] *pron* → **whatever**[2]

wheal [ˈhwiːl] *n* **:** verdugón *m*

wheat [ˈhwiːt] *n* **:** trigo *m*

wheaten [ˈhwiːtən] *adj* **:** de trigo

wheedle [ˈhwiːdəl] *vt* **-dled; -dling** CAJOLE **:** engatusar <to wheedle something out of someone : sonsacarle algo a alguien>

wheel[1] [ˈhwiːl] *vt* **:** empujar (una bicicleta, etc.), mover (algo sobre ruedas) — *vi* **1** ROTATE **:** girar, rotar **2 to wheel around** TURN **:** darse la vuelta

wheel[2] *n* **1 :** rueda *f* **2** *or* **steering wheel :** volante *m* (de automóviles, etc.), timón *m* (de barcos o aviones) **3 wheels** *npl* **:** maquinaria *f,* fuerza *f* impulsora <the wheels of government : la maquinaria del gobierno>

wheelbarrow [ˈhwiːlˌbærˌoː] *n* **:** carretilla *f*

wheelchair [ˈhwiːlˌtʃær] *n* **:** silla *f* de ruedas

wheeze[1] [ˈhwiːz] *vi* **wheezed; wheezing :** resollar, respirar con dificultad

wheeze[2] *n* **:** resuello *m*

whelk [ˈhwɛlk] *n* **:** buccino *m*

whelp[1] [ˈhwɛlp] *vi* **:** parir

whelp[2] *n* **:** cachorro *m,* -rra *f*

when[1] [ˈhwɛn] *adv* **:** cuándo <when will you return? : ¿cuándo volverás?> <he asked me when I would be home : me preguntó cuándo estaría en casa>

when[2] *conj* **1** (*referring to a particular time*) **:** cuando, en que <when you are ready : cuando estés listo> <the days when I clean the house : los días en que limpio la casa> **2** IF **:** cuando, si <how can I go when I have no money? : ¿cómo voy a ir si no tengo dinero?> **3** ALTHOUGH **:** cuando <you said it was big when actually it's

small : dijiste que era grande cuando en realidad es pequeño>

when[3] *pron* : cuándo <since when are you the boss? : ¿desde cuándo eres el jefe?>

whence [ˈ*h*wɛnts] *adv* : de donde

whenever[1] [*h*wɛnˈɛvər] *adv* **1** : cuando sea <tomorrow or whenever : mañana o cuando sea> **2** (*in questions*) : cuándo

whenever[2] *conj* **1** : siempre que, cada vez que <whenever I go, I'm disappointed : siempre que voy, quedo desilusionado> **2** WHEN : cuando <whenever you like : cuando quieras>

where[1] [ˈ*h*wɛr] *adv* : dónde, adónde <where is he? : ¿dónde está?> <where did they go? : ¿adónde fueron?>

where[2] *conj* : donde, adonde <she knows where the house is : sabe donde está la casa> <she goes where she likes : va adonde quiera>

where[3] *pron* : donde <Chicago is where I live : Chicago es donde vivo>

whereabouts[1] [ˈ*h*wɛrəˌbaʊts] *adv* : dónde, por dónde <whereabouts is the house? : ¿dónde está la casa?>

whereabouts[2] *ns & pl* : paradero *m*

whereas [*h*wɛrˈæz] *conj* **1** : considerando que (usado en documentos legales) **2** : mientras que <I like the white one whereas she prefers the black : me gusta el blanco mientras que ella prefiere el negro>

whereby [*h*wɛrˈbaɪ] *adv* : por lo cual

wherefore [ˈ*h*wɛrˌfor] *adv* : por qué

wherein [*h*wɛrˈɪn] *adv* : en el cual, en el que

whereof [*h*wɛrˈʌv, -ɑv] *conj* : de lo cual

whereupon [ˈ*h*wɛrəˌpɑn, -ˌpɔn] *conj* : con lo cual, después de lo cual

wherever[1] [*h*wɛrˈɛvər] *adv* **1** WHERE : dónde, adónde **2** : en cualquier parte <or wherever : o donde sea>

wherever[2] *conj* : dondequiera que, donde sea <wherever you go : dondequiera que vayas>

wherewithal [ˈ*h*wɛrwɪˌðɔl, -ˌθɔl] *n* : medios *mpl*, recursos *mpl*

whet [ˈ*h*wɛt] *vt* **whetted; whetting 1** SHARPEN : afilar **2** STIMULATE : estimular <to whet the appetite : estimular el apetito>

whether [ˈ*h*wɛðər] *conj* **1** : si <I don't know whether it is finished : no sé si está acabado> <we doubt whether he'll show up : dudamos que aparezca> **2** (*used in comparisons*) <whether I like it or not : tanto si quiero como si no> <whether he comes or he doesn't : venga o no>

whetstone [ˈ*h*wɛtˌstoːn] *n* : piedra *f* de afilar

whey [ˈ*h*weɪ] *n* : suero *m* (de la leche)

which[1] [ˈ*h*wɪtʃ] *adj* : qué, cuál <which tie do you prefer? : ¿cuál corbata prefieres?> <which ones? : ¿cuáles?> <tell me which house is yours : dime qué casa es la tuya>

which[2] *pron* **1** : cuál <which is the right answer? : ¿cuál es la respuesta correcta?> **2** : que, el (la) cual <the cup which broke : la taza que se quebró> <the house, which is made of brick : la casa, la cual es de ladrillo>

whichever[1] [*h*wɪtʃˈɛvər] *adj* : el (la) que, cualquiera que <whichever book you like : cualquier libro que te guste>

whichever[2] *pron* : el (la) que, cualquiera que <take whichever you want : toma el que quieras> <whichever I choose : cualquiera que elija>

whiff[1] [ˈ*h*wɪf] *v* PUFF : soplar

whiff[2] *n* **1** PUFF : soplo *m*, ráfaga *f* **2** SNIFF : olor *m* **3** HINT : dejo *m*, pizca *f*

while[1] [ˈ*h*waɪl] *vt* **whiled; whiling** : pasar <to while away the time : matar el tiempo>

while[2] *n* **1** TIME : rato *m*, tiempo *m* <after a while : después de un rato> <in a while : dentro de poco> **2 to be worth one's while** : valer la pena

while[3] *conj* **1** : mientras <whistle while you work : silba mientras trabajas> **2** WHEREAS : mientras que **3** ALTHOUGH : aunque <while it's very good, it's not perfect : aunque es muy bueno, no es perfecto>

whim [ˈ*h*wɪm] *n* : capricho *m*, antojo *m*

whimper[1] [ˈ*h*wɪmpər] *vi* : lloriquear, gimotear

whimper[2] *n* : quejido *m*

whimsical [ˈ*h*wɪmzɪkəl] *adj* **1** CAPRICIOUS : caprichoso, fantasioso **2** ERRATIC : errático — **whimsically** *adv*

whine[1] [ˈ*h*waɪn] *vi* **whined; whining 1** : lloriquear, gimotear, gemir **2** COMPLAIN : quejarse

whine[2] *n* : quejido *m*, gemido *m*

whinny[1] [ˈ*h*wɪni] *vi* **-nied; -nying** : relinchar

whinny[2] *n, pl* **-nies** : relincho *m*

whip[1] [ˈ*h*wɪp] *v* **whipped; whipping** *vt* **1** SNATCH : sacar (rápidamente), arrebatar <she whipped the cloth off the table : arrebató el mantel de la mesa> **2** LASH : azotar **3** DEFEAT : vencer, derrotar **4** INCITE : incitar, despertar <to whip up enthusiasm : despertar el entusiasmo> **5** BEAT : batir (huevos, crema, etc.) — *vi* FLAP : agitarse

whip[2] *n* **1** : látigo *m*, azote *m*, fusta *f* (de jinete) **2** : miembro *m* de un cuerpo legislativo encargado de disciplina

whiplash [ˈ*h*wɪpˌlæʃ] *n or* **whiplash injury** : traumatismo *m* cervical

whippet [ˈ*h*wɪpət] *n* : galgo *m* pequeño, galgo *m* inglés

whippoorwill [ˈ*h*wɪpərˌwɪl] *n* : chotacabras *mf*

whir[1] [ˈ*h*wər] *vi* **whirred; whirring** : zumbar

whir[2] *n* : zumbido *m*

whirl[1] ['*h*wərl] *vi* **1** SPIN : dar vueltas, girar <my head is whirling : la cabeza me está dando vueltas> **2 to whirl about** : arremolinarse, moverse rápidamente
whirl[2] *n* **1** SPIN : giro *m,* vuelta *f,* remolino *m* (dícese del polvo, etc.) **2** BUSTLE : bullicio *m,* torbellino *m* (de actividad, etc.) **3 to give it a whirl** : intentar hacer, probar
whirlpool ['*h*wərl,pu:l] *n* : vorágine *f,* remolino *m*
whirlwind ['*h*wərl,wɪnd] *n* : remolino *m,* torbellino *m,* tromba *f*
whisk[1] ['*h*wɪsk] *vt* **1** : llevar <she whisked the children off to bed : llevó a los niños a la cama> **2** : batir <to whisk eggs : batir huevos> **3 to whisk away** *or* **to whisk off** : sacudir
whisk[2] *n* **1** WHISKING : sacudida *f* (movimiento) **2** : batidor *m* (para batir huevos, etc.)
whisk broom *n* : escobilla *f*
whisker ['*h*wɪskər] *n* **1** : pelo *m* (de la barba o el bigote) **2 whiskers** *npl* : bigotes *mpl* (de animales)
whiskey *or* **whisky** ['*h*wɪski] *n, pl* **-keys** *or* **-kies** : whisky *m*
whisper[1] ['*h*wɪspər] *vi* : cuchichear, susurrar — *vt* : decir en voz baja, susurrar
whisper[2] *n* **1** WHISPERING : susurro *m,* cuchicheo *m* **2** RUMOR : rumor *m* **3** TRACE : dejo *m,* pizca *f*
whistle[1] ['*h*wɪsəl] *v* **-tled; -tling** *vi* : silbar, chiflar, pitar (dícese de un tren, etc.) — *vt* : silbar <to whistle a tune : silbar una melodía>
whistle[2] *n* **1** WHISTLING : chiflido *m,* silbido *m* **2** : silbato *m,* pito *m* (instrumento)
whit ['*h*wɪt] *n* BIT : ápice *m,* pizca *f*
white[1] ['*h*waɪt] *adj* **whiter; -est** : blanco
white[2] *n* **1** : blanco *m* (color) **2** : clara *f* (de huevos) **3** *or* **white person** : blanco *m,* -ca *f*
white blood cell *n* : glóbulo *m* blanco
whitecaps ['*h*waɪt,kæps] *npl* : cabrillas *fpl*
white–collar ['*h*waɪt'kɑlər] *adj* **1** : de oficina **2 white–collar worker** : oficinista *mf*
whitefish ['*h*waɪt,fɪʃ] *n* : pescado *m* blanco
whiten ['*h*waɪtən] *vt* : blanquear — *vi* : ponerse blanco
whiteness ['*h*waɪtnəs] *n* : blancura *f*
white–tailed deer ['*h*waɪt'teɪld] *n* : ciervo *f* de Virginia
whitewash[1] ['*h*waɪt,wɔʃ] *vt* **1** : enjalbegar, blanquear <to whitewash a fence : enjalbegar una valla> **2** CONCEAL : encubrir (un escándalo, etc.)
whitewash[2] *n* **1** : jalbegue *m,* lechada *f* **2** COVER-UP : encubrimiento *m*
whither ['*h*wɪðər] *adv* : adónde
whiting ['*h*waɪṭɪŋ] *n* : merluza *f,* pescadilla *f* (pez)
whitish ['*h*waɪṭɪʃ] *adj* : blancuzco
whittle ['*h*wɪṭəl] *vt* **-tled; -tling 1** : tallar (madera) **2 to whittle down** : reducir, recortar <to whittle down expenses : reducir los gastos>
whiz[1] *or* **whizz** ['*h*wɪz] *vi* **whizzed; whizzing 1** BUZZ : zumbar **2 to whiz by** : pasar muy rápido, pasar volando
whiz[2] *or* **whizz** *n, pl* **whizzes 1** BUZZ : zumbido *m* **2 to be a whiz** : ser un prodigio, ser muy hábil
who ['hu:] *pron* **1** (*used in direct and indirect questions*) : quién <who is that? : ¿quién es ése?> <who did it? : ¿quién lo hizo?> <we know who they are : sabemos quiénes son> **2** (*used in relative clauses*) : que, quien <the lady who lives there : la señora que vive allí> <for those who wait : para los que esperan, para quienes esperan>
whodunit [hu:'dʌnɪt] *n* : novela *f* policíaca
whoever [hu:'ɛvər] *pron* **1** : quienquiera que, quien <whoever did it : quienquiera que lo hizo> <give it to whoever you want : dalo a quien quieras> **2** (*used in questions*) : quién <whoever could that be? : ¿quién podría ser?>
whole[1] ['ho:l] *adj* **1** UNHURT : ileso **2** INTACT : intacto, sano **3** ENTIRE : entero, íntegro <the whole island : toda la isla> <whole milk : leche entera> **4 a whole lot** : muchísimo
whole[2] *n* **1** : todo *m* **2 as a whole** : en conjunto **3 on the whole** : en general
wholehearted ['ho:l'hɑrṭəd] *adj* : sin reservas, incondicional
whole number *n* : entero *m*
wholesale[1] ['ho:l,seɪl] *v* **-saled; -saling** *vt* : vender al por mayor — *vi* : venderse al por mayor
wholesale[2] *adv* : al por mayor
wholesale[3] *adj* **1** : al por mayor <wholesale grocer : tendero al por mayor> **2** TOTAL : total, absoluto <wholesale slaughter : matanza sistemática>
wholesale[4] *n* : mayoreo *m*
wholesaler ['ho:l,seɪlər] *n* : mayorista *mf*
wholesome ['ho:lsəm] *adj* **1** : sano <wholesome advice : consejo sano> **2** HEALTHY : sano, saludable
whole wheat *adj* : de trigo integral
wholly ['ho:li] *adv* **1** COMPLETELY : completamente **2** SOLELY : exclusivamente, únicamente
whom ['hu:m] *pron* **1** (*used in direct questions*) : a quién <whom did you choose? : ¿a quién elegiste?> **2** (*used in indirect questions*) : de quién, con quién, en quién <I don't know whom to consult : no sé con quién consultar> **3** (*used in relative clauses*) : que, a quien <the lawyer whom I recommended to you : el abogado que te recomendé>

whomever [huːmˈɛvər] *pron* **:** a quienquiera que, a quien

whoop[1] [ˈ*h*wuːp, ˈ*h*wʊp] *vi* **:** gritar, chillar

whoop[2] *n* **:** grito *m*

whooping cough *n* **:** tos *f* ferina

whopper [ˈ*h*wɑpər] *n* **1 :** cosa *f* enorme **2** LIE **:** mentira *f* colosal

whopping [ˈ*h*wɑpɪŋ] *adj* **:** enorme

whore [ˈhor] *n* **:** puta *f,* ramera *f*

whorl [ˈ*h*wɔrl, ˈ*h*wərl] *n* **:** espiral *f,* espira *f* (de una concha), línea *f* (de una huella digital)

whose[1] [ˈhuːz] *adj* **1** (*used in questions*) **:** de quién <whose truck is that? **:** ¿de quién es ese camión?> **2** (*used in relative clauses*) **:** cuyo <the person whose work is finished **:** la persona cuyo trabajo está terminado>

whose[2] *pron* **:** de quién <tell me whose it was **:** dime de quién era>

why[1] [ˈ*h*waɪ] *adv* **:** por qué <why did you do it? **:** ¿por qué lo hizo?>

why[2] *n, pl* **whys** REASON **:** porqué *m,* razón *f*

why[3] *conj* **:** por qué <I know why he left **:** yo sé por qué salió> <there's no reason why it should exist **:** no hay razón para que exista>

why[4] *interj* (*used to express surprise*) **:** ¡vaya!, ¡mira!

wick [ˈwɪk] *n* **:** mecha *f*

wicked [ˈwɪkəd] *adj* **1** EVIL **:** malo, malvado **2** MISCHIEVOUS **:** travieso, pícaro <a wicked grin **:** una sonrisa traviesa> **3** TERRIBLE **:** terrible, horrible <a wicked storm **:** una tormenta horrible>

wickedly [ˈwɪkədli] *adv* **:** con maldad

wickedness [ˈwɪkədnəs] *n* **:** maldad *f*

wicker[1] [ˈwɪkər] *adj* **:** de mimbre

wicker[2] *n* **1 :** mimbre *m* **2** → **wickerwork**

wickerwork [ˈwɪkər,wərk] *n* **:** artículos *mpl* de mimbre

wicket [ˈwɪkət] *n* **1** WINDOW **:** ventanilla *f* **2** *or* **wicket gate :** postigo *m* **3 :** aro *m* (en croquet), palos *mpl* (en críquet)

wide[1] [ˈwaɪd] *adv* **wider; widest 1** WIDELY **:** por todas partes <to travel far and wide **:** viajar por todas partes> **2** COMPLETELY **:** completamente, totalmente <wide open **:** abierto de par en par> **3 wide apart :** muy separados

wide[2] *adj* **wider; widest 1** VAST **:** vasto, extensivo <a wide area **:** una área extensiva> **2 :** ancho <three meters wide **:** tres metros de ancho> **3** BROAD **:** ancho, amplio **4** *or* **wide–open :** muy abierto **5 wide of the mark :** desviado, lejos del blanco

wide–awake [ˈwaɪdəˈweɪk] *adj* **:** (completamente) despierto

wide–eyed [ˈwaɪdˈaɪd] *adj* **1 :** con los ojos muy abiertos **2** NAIVE **:** inocente, ingenuo

widely [ˈwaɪdli] *adv* **:** extensivamente, por todas partes

widen [ˈwaɪdən] *vt* **:** ampliar, ensanchar — *vi* **:** ampliarse, ensancharse

widespread [ˈwaɪdˈsprɛd] *adj* **:** extendido, extenso, difuso

widow[1] [ˈwɪ,doː] *vt* **:** dejar viuda <to be widowed **:** enviudar>

widow[2] *n* **:** viuda *f*

widower [ˈwɪdowər] *n* **:** viudo *m*

width [ˈwɪdθ] *n* **:** ancho *m,* anchura *f*

wield [ˈwiːld] *vt* **1** USE **:** usar, manejar <to wield a broom **:** usar una escoba> **2** EXERCISE **:** ejercer <to wield influence **:** influir>

wiener [ˈwiːnər] → **frankfurter**

wife [ˈwaɪf] *n, pl* **wives** [ˈwaɪvz] **:** esposa *f,* mujer *f*

wifely [ˈwaɪfli] *adj* **:** de esposa, conyugal

wig [ˈwɪg] *n* **:** peluca *f*

wiggle[1] [ˈwɪgəl] *v* **-gled; -gling** *vt* **:** menear, contonear <to wiggle one's hips **:** contonearse> — *vi* **:** menearse

wiggle[2] *n* **:** meneo *m,* contoneo *m*

wiggly [ˈwɪgəli] *adj* **-glier; -est 1 :** que se menea **2** WAVY **:** ondulado

wigwag [ˈwɪg,wæg] *vi* **-wagged; -wagging :** comunicar por señales

wigwam [ˈwɪg,wɑm] *n* **:** wigwam *m*

wild[1] [ˈwaɪld] *adv* **1** → **wildly 2 to run wild :** descontrolarse

wild[2] *adj* **1 :** salvaje, silvestre, cimarrón <wild horses **:** caballos salvajes> <wild rice **:** arroz silvestre> **2** DESOLATE **:** yermo, agreste **3** UNRULY **:** desenfrenado **4** CRAZY **:** loco, fantástico <wild ideas **:** ideas locas> **5** BARBAROUS **:** salvaje, bárbaro **6** ERRATIC **:** errático <a wild throw **:** un tiro errático>

wild[3] *n* → **wilderness**

wildcat [ˈwaɪld,kæt] *n* **1 :** gato *m* montés **2** BOBCAT **:** lince *m* rojo

wilderness [ˈwɪldərnəs] *n* **:** yermo *m,* desierto *m*

wildfire [ˈwaɪld,faɪr] *n* **1 :** fuego *m* descontrolado **2 to spread like wildfire :** propagarse como un reguero de pólvora

wildflower [ˈwaɪld,flaʊər] *n* **:** flor *f* silvestre

wildfowl [ˈwaɪld,faʊl] *n* **:** ave *f* de caza

wildlife [ˈwaɪld,laɪf] *n* **:** fauna *f*

wildly [ˈwaɪldli] *adv* **1** FRANTICALLY **:** frenéticamente, como un loco **2** EXTREMELY **:** extremadamente <wildly happy **:** loco de felicidad>

wile[1] [ˈwaɪl] *vt* **wiled; wiling** LURE **:** atraer

wile[2] *n* **:** ardid *m,* artimaña *f*

will[1] [ˈwɪl] *v past* **would** [ˈwʊd]; *pres sing & pl* **will** *vi* WISH **:** querer <do what you will **:** haz lo que quieras> — *v aux* **1** (*expressing willingness*) <no one would take the job **:** nadie aceptaría el trabajo> <I won't do it **:** no lo haré> **2** (*expressing habitual action*) <he will get angry over nothing **:** se pone furioso por cualquier cosa> **3** (*forming the future tense*)

<tomorrow we will go shopping : mañana iremos de compras> **4** (*expressing capacity*) <the couch will hold three people : en el sofá cabrán tres personas> **5** (*expressing determination*) <I will go despite them : iré a pesar de ellos> **6** (*expressing probability*) <that will be the mailman : eso ha de ser el cartero> **7** (*expressing inevitability*) <accidents will happen : los accidentes ocurrirán> **8** (*expressing a command*) <you will do as I say : harás lo que digo>

will[2] *vt* **1** ORDAIN : disponer, decretar <if God wills it : si Dios lo dispone, si Dios quiere> **2** : lograr a fuerza de voluntad <they were willing him to succeed : estaban deseando que tuviera éxito> **3** BEQUEATH : legar

will[3] *n* **1** DESIRE : deseo *m,* voluntad *f* **2** VOLITION : voluntad *f* <free will : libre albedrío> **3** WILLPOWER : voluntad *f,* fuerza *f* de voluntad <a will of iron : una voluntad férrea> **4** : testamento *m* <to make a will : hacer testamento>

willful *or* **wilful** [ˈwɪlfəl] *adj* **1** OBSTINATE : obstinado, terco **2** INTENTIONAL : intencionado, deliberado — **willfully** *adv*

willing [ˈwɪlɪŋ] *adj* **1** INCLINED, READY : listo, dispuesto **2** OBLIGING : servicial, complaciente

willingly [ˈwɪlɪŋli] *adv* : con gusto

willingness [ˈwɪlɪŋnəs] *n* : buena voluntad *f*

willow [ˈwɪˌloː] *n* : sauce *m*

willowy [ˈwɪlowi] *adj* : esbelto

willpower [ˈwɪlˌpaʊər] *n* : voluntad *f,* fuerza *f* de voluntad

wilt [ˈwɪlt] *vi* **1** : marchitarse (dícese de las flores) **2** LANGUISH : debilitarse, languidecer

wily [ˈwaɪli] *adj* **wilier; -est** : artero, astuto

win[1] [ˈwɪn] *v* **won** [ˈwʌn]; **winning** *vi* : ganar — *vt* **1** : ganar, conseguir **2 to win over** : ganarse a **3 to win someone's heart** : conquistar a alguien

win[2] *n* : triunfo *m,* victoria *f*

wince[1] [ˈwɪnts] *vi* **winced; wincing** : estremecerse, hacer una mueca de dolor

wince[2] *n* : mueca *f* de dolor

winch [ˈwɪntʃ] *n* : torno *m*

wind[1] [ˈwɪnd] *vt* : dejar sin aliento <to be winded : quedarse sin aliento>

wind[2] [ˈwaɪnd] *v* **wound** [ˈwaʊnd]; **winding** *vi* MEANDER : serpentear — *vt* **1** COIL, ROLL : envolver, enrollar **2** TURN : hacer girar <to wind a clock : darle cuerda a un reloj>

wind[3] [ˈwɪnd] *n* **1** : viento *m* <against the wind : contra el viento> **2** BREATH : aliento *m* **3** FLATULENCE : flatulencia *f,* ventosidad *f* **4 to get wind of** : enterarse de

wind[4] [ˈwaɪnd] *n* **1** TURN : vuelta *f* **2** BEND : recodo *m,* curva *f*

windbreak [ˈwɪndˌbreɪk] *n* : barrera *f* contra el viento, abrigadero *m*

windfall [ˈwɪndˌfɔl] *n* **1** : fruta *f* caída **2** : beneficio *m* imprevisto

wind instrument *n* : instrumento *m* de viento

windlass [ˈwɪndləs] *n* : cabrestante *m*

windmill [ˈwɪndˌmɪl] *n* : molino *m* de viento

window [ˈwɪnˌdoː] *n* **1** : ventana *f* (de un edificio o una computadora), ventanilla *f* (de un vehículo o avión), vitrina *f* (de una tienda) **2** → **windowpane**

windowpane [ˈwɪnˌdoːˌpeɪn] *n* : vidrio *m*

window–shop [ˈwɪndoˌʃɑp] *vi* **-shopped; -shopping** : mirar las vitrinas

windpipe [ˈwɪndˌpaɪp] *n* : tráquea *f*

windshield [ˈwɪndˌʃiːld] *n* **1** : parabrisas *m* **2 windshield wiper** : limpiaparabrisas *m*

windup [ˈwaɪndˌʌp] *n* : conclusión *f*

wind up *vt* END : terminar, concluir — *vi* : terminar, acabar

windward[1] [ˈwɪndwərd] *adj* : de barlovento

windward[2] *n* : barlovento *m*

windy [ˈwɪndi] *adj* **windier; -est 1** : ventoso <it's windy : hace viento> **2** VERBOSE : verboso, prolijo

wine[1] [ˈwaɪn] *v* **wined; wining** *vi* : beber vino — *vt* **to wine and dine** : agasajar

wine[2] *n* : vino *m*

wing[1] [ˈwɪŋ] *vi* FLY : volar

wing[2] *n* **1** : ala *f* (de un ave, un avión, o un edificio) **2** FACTION : ala *f* <the right wing of the party : el ala derecha del partido> **3 wings** *npl* : bastidores *mpl* (de un teatro) **4 on the wing** : al vuelo, volando **5 under one's wing** : bajo el cargo de uno

winged [ˈwɪŋd, ˈwɪŋəd] *adj* : alado

wink[1] [ˈwɪŋk] *vi* **1** : guiñar el ojo **2** BLINK : pestañear, parpadear **3** FLICKER : parpadear, titilar

wink[2] *n* **1** : guiño *m* (del ojo) **2** NAP : siesta *f* <not to sleep a wink : no pegar el ojo>

winner [ˈwɪnər] *n* : ganador *m,* -dora *f*

winning [ˈwɪnɪŋ] *adj* **1** VICTORIOUS : ganador **2** CHARMING : encantador

winnings [ˈwɪnɪŋz] *npl* : ganancias *fpl*

winnow [ˈwɪˌnoː] *vt* : aventar (el grano, etc.)

winsome [ˈwɪnsəm] *adj* CHARMING : encantador

winter[1] [ˈwɪntər] *adj* : invernal, de invierno

winter[2] *n* : invierno *m*

wintergreen [ˈwɪntərˌgriːn] *n* : gaulteria *f*

wintertime [ˈwɪntərˌtaɪm] *n* : invierno *m*

wintry [ˈwɪntri] *adj* **wintrier; -est 1** WINTER : invernal, de invierno **2** COLD

: frío <she gave us a wintry greeting : nos saludó fríamente>

wipe[1] [ˈwaɪp] *vt* **wiped; wiping 1** : limpiar, pasarle un trapo a <to wipe one's feet : limpiarse los pies> **2 to wipe away** : enjugar (lágrimas), borrar (una memoria) **3 to wipe out** ANNIHILATE : aniquilar, destruir

wipe[2] *n* : pasada *f* (con un trapo, etc.)

wire[1] [ˈwaɪr] *vt* **-wired; wiring 1** : instalar el cableado en (una casa, etc.) **2** BIND : atar con alambre **3** TELEGRAPH : telegrafiar, mandarle un telegrama (a alguien)

wire[2] *n* **1** : alambre *m* <barbed wire : alambre de púas> **2** : cable *m* (eléctrico o telefónico) **3** CABLEGRAM, TELEGRAM : telegrama *m,* cable *m*

wireless [ˈwaɪrləs] *adj* : inalámbrico

wiretapping [ˈwaɪrˌtæpɪŋ] *n* : intervención *f* electrónica

wiring [ˈwaɪrɪŋ] *n* : cableado *m*

wiry [ˈwaɪri] *adj* **wirier; -est 1** : hirsuto, tieso (dícese del pelo) **2** : esbelto y musculoso (dícese del cuerpo)

wisdom [ˈwɪzdəm] *n* **1** KNOWLEDGE : sabiduría *f* **2** JUDGMENT, SENSE : sensatez *f*

wisdom tooth *n* : muela *f* de juicio

wise[1] [ˈwaɪz] *adj* **wiser; wisest 1** LEARNED : sabio **2** SENSIBLE : sabio, sensato, prudente **3** KNOWLEDGEABLE : entendido, enterado <they're wise to his tricks : conocen muy bien sus mañas>

wise[2] *n* : manera *f,* modo *m* <in no wise : de ninguna manera>

wisecrack [ˈwaɪzˌkræk] *n* : broma *f,* chiste *m*

wisely [ˈwaɪzli] *adv* : sabiamente, sensatamente

wish[1] [ˈwɪʃ] *vt* **1** WANT : desear, querer **2 to wish (something) for** : desear <they wished me well : me desearon lo mejor> — *vi* **1** : pedir (como deseo) **2** : querer <as you wish : como quieras>

wish[2] *n* **1** : deseo *m* <to grant a wish : conceder un deseo> **2 wishes** *npl* : saludos *mpl,* recuerdos *mpl* <to send best wishes : mandar muchos recuerdos>

wishbone [ˈwɪʃˌboːn] *n* : espoleta *f*

wishful [ˈwɪʃfəl] *adj* **1** HOPEFUL : deseoso, lleno de esperanza **2 wishful thinking** : ilusiones *fpl*

wishy–washy [ˈwɪʃiˌwɔʃi, -ˌwɑʃi] *adj* : insípido, soso

wisp [ˈwɪsp] *n* **1** BUNCH : manojo *m* (de paja) **2** STRAND : mechón *m* (de pelo) **3** : voluta *f* (de humo)

wispy [ˈwɪspi] *adj* **wispier; -est** : tenue, ralo (dícese del pelo)

wisteria [wɪsˈtɪriə] *n* : glicinia *f*

wistful [ˈwɪstfəl] *adj* : añorante, anhelante, melancólico — **wistfully** *adv*

wistfulness [ˈwɪstfəlnəs] *n* : añoranza *f,* melancolía *f*

wit [ˈwɪt] *n* **1** INTELLIGENCE : inteligencia *f* **2** CLEVERNESS : ingenio *m,* gracia *f,* agudeza *f* **3** HUMOR : humorismo *m* **4** JOKER : chistoso *m,* -sa *f* **5 wits** *npl* : razón *f,* buen juicio *m* <scared out of one's wits : muerto de miedo> <to be at one's wits' end : estar desesperado>

witch [ˈwɪtʃ] *n* : bruja *f*

witchcraft [ˈwɪtʃˌkræft] *n* : brujería *f,* hechicería *f*

witch doctor *n* : hechicero *m,* -ra *f*

witchery [ˈwɪtʃəri] *n, pl* **-eries 1** → **witchcraft 2** CHARM : encanto *m*

witch–hunt [ˈwɪtʃˌhʌnt] *n* : caza *f* de brujas

with [ˈwɪð, ˈwɪθ] *prep* **1** : con <I'm going with you : voy contigo> <coffee with milk : café con leche> **2** AGAINST : con <to argue with someone : discutir con alguien> **3** (*used in descriptions*) : con, de <the girl with red hair : la muchacha de pelo rojo> **4** (*indicating manner, means, or cause*) : con <to cut with a knife : cortar con un cuchillo> <fix it with tape : arréglalo con cinta> <with luck : con suerte> **5** DESPITE : a pesar de, aún con <with all his work, the business failed : a pesar de su trabajo, el negocio fracasó> **6** REGARDING : con respecto a, con <the trouble with your plan : el problema con su plan> **7** ACCORDING TO : según <it varies with the season : varía según la estación> **8** (*indicating support or understanding*) : con <I'm with you all the way : estoy contigo hasta el fin>

withdraw [wɪðˈdrɔ, wɪθ-] *v* **-drew** [-ˈdruː]; **-drawn** [-ˈdrɔn]; **-drawing** *vt* **1** REMOVE : retirar, apartar, sacar (dinero) **2** RETRACT : retractarse de — *vi* : retirarse, recluirse (de la sociedad)

withdrawal [wɪðˈdrɔəl, wɪθ-] *n* **1** : retirada *f,* retiro *m* (de fondos, etc.), retraimiento *m* (social) **2** RETRACTION : retractación *f* **3 withdrawal symptoms** : síndrome *m* de abstinencia

withdrawn [wɪðˈdrɔn, wɪθ-] *adj* : retraído, reservado, introvertido

wither [ˈwɪðər] *vt* : marchitar, agostar — *vi* **1** WILT : marchitarse **2** WEAKEN : decaer, debilitarse

withhold [wɪθˈhoːld, wɪð-] *vt* **-held** [-ˈhɛld]; **-holding** : retener (fondos), aplazar (una decisión), negar (permiso, etc.)

within[1] [wɪðˈɪn, wɪθ-] *adv* : dentro

within[2] *prep* **1** : dentro de <within the limits : dentro de los límites> **2** (*in expressions of distance*) : a menos de <within 10 miles of the ocean : a menos de 10 millas del mar> **3** (*in expressions of time*) : dentro de <within an hour : dentro de una hora> <within a month of her birthday : a poco menos de un mes de su cumpleaños>

without[1] [wɪð'aʊt, wɪθ-] *adv* **1** OUTSIDE : fuera **2 to do without** : pasar sin algo
without[2] *prep* **1** OUTSIDE : fuera de **2** : sin <without fear : sin temor> <he left without his briefcase : se fue sin su portafolios>
withstand [wɪθ'stænd, wɪð-] *vt* **-stood** [-'stʊd]; **-standing 1** BEAR : aguantar, soportar **2** RESIST : resistir, resistirse a
witless ['wɪtləs] *adj* : estúpido, tonto
witness[1] ['wɪtnəs] *vt* **1** SEE : presenciar, ver, ser testigo de **2** : atestiguar (una firma, etc.) — *vi* TESTIFY : atestiguar, testimoniar
witness[2] *n* **1** TESTIMONY : testimonio *m* <to bear witness : atestiguar, testimoniar> **2** : testigo *mf* <witness for the prosecution : testigo de cargo>
witticism ['wɪṭə,sɪzəm] *n* : agudeza *f,* ocurrencia *f*
witty ['wɪṭi] *adj* **-tier; -est** : ingenioso, ocurrente, gracioso
wives → **wife**
wizard ['wɪzərd] *n* **1** SORCERER : mago *m,* brujo *m,* hechicero *m* **2** : genio *m* <a math wizard : un genio en matemáticas>
wizened ['wɪzənd, 'wiː-] *adj* : arrugado, marchito
wobble[1] ['wɑbəl] *vi* **-bled; -bling** : bambolearse, tambalearse, temblar (dícese de la voz)
wobble[2] *n* : tambaleo *m,* bamboleo *m*
wobbly ['wɑbəli] *adj* : bamboleante, tambaleante, inestable
woe ['woː] *n* **1** GRIEF, MISFORTUNE : desgracia *f,* infortunio *m,* aflicción *f* **2 woes** *npl* TROUBLES : penas *fpl,* males *mpl*
woeful ['woːfəl] *adj* **1** SORROWFUL : afligido, apenado, triste **2** UNFORTUNATE : desgraciado, infortunado **3** DEPLORABLE : lamentable
woke, woken → **wake**[1]
wolf[1] ['wʊlf] *vt or* **to wolf down** : engullir
wolf[2] *n, pl* **wolves** ['wʊlvz] : lobo *m,* -ba *f*
wolfram ['wʊlfrəm] → **tungsten**
wolverine [,wʊlvə'riːn] *n* : glotón *m* (animal)
woman ['wʊmən] *n, pl* **women** ['wɪmən] : mujer *f*
womanhood ['wʊmən,hʊd] *n* **1** : condición *f* de mujer **2** WOMEN : mujeres *fpl*
womanly ['wʊmənli] *adj* : femenino
womb ['wuːm] *n* : útero *m,* matriz *f*
won → **win**
wonder[1] ['wʌndər] *vi* **1** SPECULATE : preguntarse, pensar <to wonder about : preguntarse por> **2** MARVEL : asombrarse, maravillarse — *vt* : preguntarse <I wonder if they're coming : me pregunto si vendrán>
wonder[2] *n* **1** MARVEL : maravilla *f,* milagro *m* <to work wonders : hacer maravillas> **2** AMAZEMENT : asombro *m*
wonderful ['wʌndərfəl] *adj* : maravilloso, estupendo
wonderfully ['wʌndərfəli] *adv* : maravillosamente, de maravilla
wonderland ['wʌndər,lænd, -lənd] *n* : país *m* de las maravillas
wonderment ['wʌndərmənt] *n* : asombro *m*
wondrous ['wʌndrəs] → **wonderful**
wont[1] ['wɔnt, 'woːnt, 'wɑnt] *adj* : acostumbrado, habituado
wont[2] *n* : hábito *m,* costumbre *f*
won't ['woːnt] (*contraction of* **will not**) → **will**[1]
woo ['wuː] *vt* **1** COURT : cortejar **2** : buscar el apoyo de (clientes, votantes, etc.)
wood[1] ['wʊd] *adj* : de madera
wood[2] *n* **1** *or* **woods** *npl* FOREST : bosque *m* **2** : madera *f* (materia) **3** FIREWOOD : leña *f*
woodchuck ['wʊd,tʃʌk] *n* : marmota *f* de América
woodcut ['wʊd,kʌt] *n* **1** : plancha *f* de madera (para imprimir imágenes) **2** : grabado *m* en madera
woodcutter ['wʊd,kʌṭər] *n* : leñador *m,* -dora *f*
wooded ['wʊdəd] *adj* : arbolado, boscoso
wooden ['wʊdən] *adj* **1** : de madera <a wooden cross : una cruz de madera> **2** STIFF : rígido, inexpresivo (dícese del estilo, de la cara, etc.)
woodland ['wʊdlənd, -,lænd] *n* : bosque *m*
woodpecker ['wʊd,pɛkər] *n* : pájaro *m* carpintero
woodshed ['wʊd,ʃɛd] *n* : leñera *f*
woodsman ['wʊdzmən] → **woodcutter**
woodwind ['wʊd,wɪnd] *n* : instrumento *m* de viento de madera
woodworking ['wʊd,wərkɪŋ] *n* : carpintería *f*
woody ['wʊdi] *adj* **woodier; -est 1** → **wooded 2** : leñoso <woody plants : plantas leñosas> **3** : leñoso (dícese de la textura), a madera (dícese del aroma, etc.)
woof ['wʊf] → **weft**
wool ['wʊl] *n* : lana *f*
woolen[1] *or* **woollen** ['wʊlən] *adj* : de lana
woolen[2] *or* **woollen** *n* **1** : lana *f* (tela) **2 woolens** *npl* : prendas *fpl* de lana
woolly ['wʊli] *adj* **-lier; -est 1** : lanudo **2** CONFUSED : confuso, vago
woozy ['wuːzi] *adj* **-zier; -est** : mareado
word[1] ['wərd] *vt* : expresar, formular, redactar
word[2] *n* **1** : palabra *f,* vocablo *m,* voz *f* <word for word : palabra por palabra> <in one's own words : en sus

propias palabras> <words fail me : me quedo sin habla> **2** REMARK : palabra *f* <by word of mouth : de palabra> <to have a word with : hablar (dos palabras) con> **3** COMMAND : orden *f* <to give the word : dar la orden> <just say the word : no tienes que decirlo> **4** MESSAGE, NEWS : noticias *fpl* <is there any word from her? : ¿hay noticias de ella?> <to send word : mandar un recado> **5** PROMISE : palabra *f* <to keep one's word : cumplir uno su palabra> **6 words** *npl* QUARREL : palabra *f,* riña *f* <to have words with : tener unas palabras con, reñir con> **7 words** *npl* TEXT : letra *f* (de una canción, etc.)

wordiness ['wərdinəs] *n* : verbosidad *f*

wording ['wərdɪŋ] *n* : redacción *f,* lenguaje *m* (de un documento)

word processing *n* : procesamiento *m* de textos

word processor *n* : procesador *m* de textos

wordy ['wərdi] *adj* **wordier; -est** : verboso, prolijo

wore → **wear[1]**

work[1] ['wərk] *v* **worked** ['wərkt] *or* **wrought** ['rɔt]; **working** *vt* **1** OPERATE : trabajar, operar <to work a machine : operar una máquina> **2** : lograr, conseguir (algo) con esfuerzo <to work one's way up : lograr subir por sus propios esfuerzos> **3** EFFECT : efectuar, llevar a cabo, obrar (milagros) **4** MAKE, SHAPE : elaborar, fabricar, formar <a beautifully wrought vase : un florero bellamente elaborado> **5 to work up** : estimular, excitar <don't get worked up : no te agites> — *vi* **1** LABOR : trabajar <to work full-time : trabajar a tiempo completo> **2** FUNCTION : funcionar, servir

work[2] *adj* : laboral

work[3] *n* **1** LABOR : trabajo *m,* labor *f* **2** EMPLOYMENT : trabajo *m,* empleo *m* **3** TASK : tarea *f,* faena *f* **4** DEED : obra *f,* labor *f* <works of charity : obras de caridad> **5** : obra *f* (de arte o literatura) **6** → **workmanship 7 works** *npl* FACTORY : fábrica *f* **8 works** *npl* MECHANISM : mecanismo *m*

workable ['wərkəbəl] *adj* **1** : explotable (dícese de una mina, etc.) **2** FEASIBLE : factible, realizable

workaday ['wərkə,deɪ] *adj* : ordinario, banal

workbench ['wərk,bɛntʃ] *n* : mesa *f* de trabajo

workday ['wərk,deɪ] *n* **1** : jornada *f* laboral **2** WEEKDAY : día *m* hábil, día *m* laborable

worker ['wərkər] *n* : trabajador *m,* -dora *f;* obrero *m,* -ra *f*

working ['wərkɪŋ] *adj* **1** : que trabaja <working mothers : madres que trabajan> <the working class : la clase obrera> **2** : de trabajo <working hours : horas de trabajo> **3** FUNCTIONING : que funciona, operativo **4** SUFFICIENT : suficiente <a working majority : una mayoría suficiente> <working knowledge : conocimientos básicos>

workingman ['wərkɪŋ,mæn] *n, pl* **-men** [-mən, -,mɛn] : obrero *m*

workman ['wərkmən] *n, pl* **-men** [-mən, -,mɛn] **1** → **workingman 2** ARTISAN : artesano *m*

workmanlike ['wərkmən,laɪk] *adj* : bien hecho, competente

workmanship ['wərkmən,ʃɪp] *n* **1** WORK : ejecución *f,* trabajo *m* **2** CRAFTSMANSHIP : artesanía *f,* destreza *f*

workout ['wərk,aʊt] *n* : ejercicios *mpl* físicos, entrenamiento *m*

work out *vt* **1** DEVELOP, PLAN : idear, planear, desarrollar **2** RESOLVE : solucionar, resolver <to work out the answer : calcular la solución> — *vi* **1** TURN OUT : resultar **2** SUCCEED : lograr, dar resultado, salir bien **3** EXERCISE : hacer ejercicio

workroom ['wərk,ruːm, -,rʊm] *n* : taller *m*

workshop ['wərk,ʃɑp] *n* : taller *m* <ceramics workshop : taller de cerámica>

world[1] ['wərld] *adj* : mundial, del mundo <world championship : campeonato mundial>

world[2] *n* : mundo *m* <around the world : alrededor del mundo> <a world of possibilities : un mundo de posibilidades> <to think the world of someone : tener a alguien en alta estima> <to be worlds apart : no tener nada que ver (uno con otro)>

worldly ['wərldli] *adj* **1** : mundano <wordly goods : bienes materiales> **2** SOPHISTICATED : sofisticado, de mundo

worldwide[1] ['wərld'waɪd] *adv* : mundialmente, en todo el mundo

worldwide[2] *adj* : global, mundial

worm[1] ['wərm] *vi* **1** CRAWL : arrastrarse, deslizarse (como gusano) <to worm one's way into someone's confidence : ganarse la confianza de alguien> **2 to worm something out of someone** : sonsacarle algo a alguien — *vt* : desparasitar (un animal)

worm[2] *n* **1** : gusano *m,* lombriz *f* **2 worms** *npl* : lombrices *fpl* (parásitos)

wormy ['wərmi] *adj* **wormier; -est** : infestado de gusanos

worn → **wear[1]**

worn–out ['worn'aʊt] *adj* **1** USED : gastado, desgastado **2** TIRED : agotado

worried ['wərid] *adj* : inquieto, preocupado

worrier ['wəriər] *n* : persona *f* que se preocupa mucho

worrisome ['wərisəm] *adj* **1** DISTURBING : preocupante, inquietante **2** : que se preocupa mucho (dícese de una persona)

worry[1] ['wəri] *v* **-ried; -rying** *vt* : preocupar, inquietar — *vi* : preocuparse, inquietarse, angustiarse

worry[2] *n, pl* **-ries :** preocupación *f,* inquietud *f,* angustia *f*

worse[1] [ˈwərs] *adv* (*comparative of* **bad** *or of* **ill**) **:** peor <to feel worse : sentirse peor>

worse[2] *adj* (*comparative of* **bad** *or of* **ill**) **:** peor <from bad to worse : de mal en peor> <to get worse : empeorar>

worse[3] *n* **:** estado *m* peor <to take a turn for the worse : ponerse peor> <so much the worse : tanto peor>

worsen [ˈwərsən] *vt* **:** empeorar — *vi* **:** empeorar(se)

worship[1] [ˈwərʃəp] *v* **-shiped** *or* **-shipped; -shiping** *or* **-shipping** *vt* **:** adorar, venerar <to worship God : adorar a Dios> — *vi* **:** practicar una religión

worship[2] *n* **:** adoración *f,* culto *m*

worshiper *or* **worshipper** [ˈwərʃəpər] *n* **:** devoto *m,* -ta *f;* adorador *m,* -dora *f*

worst[1] [ˈwərst] *vt* DEFEAT **:** derrotar

worst[2] *adv* (*superlative of* **ill** *or of* **bad** *or* **badly**) **:** peor <the worst dressed of all : el peor vestido de todos>

worst[3] *adj* (*superlative of* **bad** *or of* **ill**) **:** peor <the worst movie : la peor película>

worst[4] *n* **the worst :** lo peor, el (la) peor <the worst is over : ya ha pasado lo peor>

worsted [ˈwʊstəd, ˈwərstəd] *n* **:** estambre *m*

worth[1] [ˈwərθ] *n* **1 :** valor *m* (monetario) <ten dollars' worth of gas : diez dólares de gasolina> **2** MERIT **:** valor *m,* mérito *m,* valía *f* <an employee of great worth : un empleado de gran valía>

worth[2] *prep* **to be worth :** valer <her holdings are worth a fortune : sus propiedades valen una fortuna> <it's not worth it : no vale la pena>

worthiness [ˈwərðinəs] *n* **:** mérito *m*

worthless [ˈwərθləs] *adj* **1 :** sin valor <worthless trinkets : chucherías sin valor> **2** USELESS **:** inútil

worthwhile [wərθˈ*h*waɪl] *adj* **:** que vale la pena

worthy [ˈwərðil] *adj* **-thier; -est 1 :** digno <worthy of promotion : digno de un ascenso> **2** COMMENDABLE **:** meritorio, encomiable

would [ˈwʊd] *past of* **will 1** (*expressing preference*) <I would rather go alone than with her : preferiría ir sola que con ella> **2** (*expressing intent*) <those who would ban certain books : aquellos que prohibirían ciertos libros> **3** (*expressing habitual action*) <he would often take his kids to the park : solía llevar a sus hijos al parque> **4** (*expressing contingency*) <I would go if I had the money : iría yo si tuviera el dinero> **5** (*expressing probability*) <she would have won if she hadn't tripped : habría ganado si no hubiera tropezado> **6** (*expressing a request*) <would you kindly help me with this? : ¿tendría la bondad de ayudarme con esto?>

would–be [ˈwʊdˈbiː] *adj* **:** potencial <a would-be celebrity : un aspirante a celebridad>

wouldn't [ˈwʊdˈənt] (*contraction of* **would not**) → **would**

wound[1] [ˈwuːnd] *vt* **:** herir

wound[2] *n* **:** herida *f*

wound[3] [ˈwaʊnd] → **wind**[2]

wove, woven → **weave**[1]

wrangle[1] [ˈræŋgəl] *vi* **-gled; -gling :** discutir, reñir <to wrangle over : discutir por>

wrangle[2] *n* **:** riña *f,* disputa *f*

wrap[1] [ˈræp] *v* **wrapped; wrapping** *vt* **1** COVER **:** envolver, cubrir <to wrap a package : envolver un paquete> <wrapped in mystery : envuelto en misterio> **2** ENCIRCLE **:** rodear, ceñir <to wrap one's arms around someone : estrechar a alguien> **3 to wrap up** FINISH **:** darle fin a (algo) — *vi* **1** COIL **:** envolverse, enroscarse **2 to wrap up** DRESS **:** abrigarse <wrap up warmly : abrígate bien>

wrap[2] *n* **1** WRAPPER **:** envoltura *f* **2 :** prenda *f* que envuelve (como un chal, una bata, etc.)

wrapper [ˈræpər] *n* **:** envoltura *f,* envoltorio *m*

wrapping [ˈræpɪŋ] *n* **:** envoltura *f,* envoltorio *m*

wrath [ˈræθ] *n* **:** ira *f,* cólera *f*

wrathful [ˈræθfəl] *adj* **:** iracundo

wreak [ˈriːk] *vt* **:** infligir, causar <to wreak havoc : crear caos, causar estragos>

wreath [ˈriːθ] *n, pl* **wreaths** [ˈriːðz, ˈriːθs] **:** corona *f* (de flores, etc.)

wreathe [ˈriːð] *vt* **wreathed; wreathing 1** ADORN **:** coronar (de flores, etc.) **2** ENVELOP **:** envolver <wreathed in mist : envuelto en niebla>

wreck[1] [ˈrɛk] *vt* **:** destruir, arruinar, estrellar (un automóvil), naufragar (un barco)

wreck[2] *n* **1** WRECKAGE **:** restos *mpl* (de un buque naufragado, un avión siniestrado, etc.) **2** RUIN **:** ruina *f,* desastre *m* <this place is a wreck! : ¡este lugar está hecho un desastre!> <to be a nervous wreck : tener los nervios destrozados>

wreckage [ˈrɛkɪdʒ] *n* **:** restos *mpl* (de un buque naufragado, un avión siniestrado, etc.), ruinas *fpl* (de un edificio)

wrecker [ˈrɛkər] *n* **1** TOW TRUCK **:** grúa *f* **2 :** desguazador *m* (de autos, barcos, etc.), demoledor *m* (de edificios)

wren [ˈrɛn] *n* **:** chochín *m*

wrench[1] [ˈrɛntʃ] *vt* **1** PULL **:** arrancar (de un tirón) **2** SPRAIN, TWIST **:** torcerse (un tobillo, un músculo, etc.)

wrench[2] *n* **1** TUG **:** tirón *m,* jalón *m* **2** SPRAIN **:** torcedura *f* **3** *or* **monkey wrench :** llave *f* inglesa

wrest ['rɛst] *vt* **:** arrancar

wrestle[1] ['rɛsəl] *v* **-tled; -tling** *vi* **1 :** luchar, practicar la lucha (en deportes) **2** STRUGGLE **:** luchar <to wrestle with a dilemma : lidiar con un dilema> — *vt* **:** luchar contra

wrestle[2] *n* STRUGGLE **:** lucha *f*

wrestler ['rɛsələr] *n* **:** luchador *m,* -dora *f*

wrestling ['rɛsəlɪŋ] *n* **:** lucha *f*

wretch ['rɛtʃ] *n* **:** infeliz *mf;* desgraciado *m,* -da *f*

wretched ['rɛtʃəd] *adj* **1** MISERABLE, UNHAPPY **:** desdichado, afligido <I feel wretched : me siento muy mal> **2** UNFORTUNATE **:** miserable, desgraciado, lastimoso <wretched weather : tiempo espantoso> **3** INFERIOR **:** inferior, malo

wretchedly ['rɛtʃədli] *adv* **:** miserablemente, lamentablemente

wriggle ['rɪgəl] *vi* **-gled; -gling :** retorcerse, menearse

wring ['rɪŋ] *vt* **wrung** ['rʌŋ]; **wringing 1** *or* **to wring out :** escurrir, exprimir (el lavado) **2** EXTRACT **:** arrancar, sacar (por la fuerza) **3** TWIST **:** torcer, retorcer **4 to wring someone's heart :** partirle el corazón a alguien

wringer ['rɪŋər] *n* **:** escurridor *m*

wrinkle[1] ['rɪŋkəl] *v* **-kled; -kling** *vt* **:** arrugar — *vi* **:** arrugarse

wrinkle[2] *n* **:** arruga *f*

wrinkly ['rɪŋkəli] *adj* **wrinklier; -est :** arrugado

wrist ['rɪst] *n* **1 :** muñeca *f* (en anatomía) **2** *or* **wristband** ['rɪst,bænd] CUFF **:** puño *m*

writ ['rɪt] *n* **:** orden *f* (judicial)

write ['raɪt] *v* **wrote** ['ro:t]; **written** ['rɪtən]; **writing :** escribir

write down *vt* **:** apuntar, anotar

write off *vt* CANCEL **:** cancelar

writer ['raɪtər] *n* **:** escritor *m,* -tora *f*

writhe ['raɪð] *vi* **writhed; writhing :** retorcerse

writing ['raɪtɪŋ] *n* **:** escritura *f*

wrong[1] ['rɔŋ] *vt* **wronged; wronging :** ofender, ser injusto con

wrong[2] *adv* **:** mal, incorrectamente

wrong[3] *adj* **wronger** ['rɔŋər]; **wrongest** ['rɔŋəst] **1** EVIL, SINFUL **:** malo, injusto, inmoral **2** IMPROPER, UNSUITABLE **:** inadecuado, inapropiado, malo **3** INCORRECT **:** incorrecto, erróneo, malo <a wrong answer : una mala respuesta> **4 to be wrong :** equivocarse, estar equivocado

wrong[4] *n* **1** INJUSTICE **:** injusticia *f,* mal *m* **2** OFFENSE **:** ofensa *f,* agravio *m* (en derecho) **3 to be in the wrong :** haber hecho mal, estar equivocado

wrongdoer ['rɔŋ,du:ər] *n* **:** malhechor *m,* -chora *f*

wrongdoing ['rɔŋ,du:ɪŋ] *n* **:** fechoría *f,* maldad *f*

wrongful ['rɔŋfəl] *adj* **1** UNJUST **:** injusto **2** UNLAWFUL **:** ilegal

wrongly ['rɔŋli] *adv* **1 :** injustamente **2** INCORRECTLY **:** erróneamente, incorrectamente

wrote → **write**

wrought ['rɔt] *adj* **1** SHAPED **:** formado, forjado <wrought iron : hierro forjado> **2** *or* **wrought up :** agitado, excitado

wrung → **wring**

wry ['raɪ] *adj* **wrier** ['raɪər]; **wriest** ['raɪəst] **1** TWISTED **:** torcido <a wry neck : un cuello torcido> **2 :** irónico, sardónico (dícese del humor)

X

x[1] *n, pl* **x's** *or* **xs** ['ɛksəz] **1 :** vigésima cuarta letra del alfabeto inglés **2 :** incógnita *f* (en matemáticas)

x[2] ['ɛks] *vt* **x–ed** ['ɛkst]; **x–ing** *or* **x'ing** ['ɛksiŋ] DELETE **:** tachar

xenon ['zi:,nɑn, 'zɛ-] *n* **:** xenón *m*

xenophobia [,zɛnə'fo:biə, ,zi:-] *n* **:** xenofobia *f*

Xmas ['krɪsməs] *n* **:** Navidad *f*

x–ray ['ɛks,reɪ] *vt* **:** radiografiar

X ray ['ɛks,reɪ] *n* **1 :** rayo *m* X **2** *or* **X–ray photograph :** radiografía *f*

xylophone ['zaɪlə,fo:n] *n* **:** xilófono *m*

Y

y ['waɪ] *n, pl* **y's** *or* **ys** ['waɪz] **:** vigésima quinta letra del alfabeto inglés

yacht[1] ['jɑt] *vi* **:** navegar (a vela), ir en yate <to go yachting : irse a navegar>

yacht[2] *n* **:** yate *m*

yak ['jæk] *n* **:** yac *m*

yam ['jæm] *n* **1 :** ñame *m* **2** SWEET POTATO **:** batata *f,* boniato *m*

yank[1] ['jæŋk] *vt* **:** tirar de, jalar, darle un tirón a

yank[2] *n* **:** tirón *m*

Yankee ['jæŋki] *n* **:** yanqui *mf*

yap[1] ['jæp] *vi* **yapped; yapping 1** BARK, YELP **:** ladrar, gañir **2** CHATTER **:** cotorrear *fam,* parlotear *fam*

yap[2] *n* **:** ladrido *m,* gañido *m*

yard ['jɑrd] *n* **1** : yarda *f* (medida) **2** SPAR : verga *f* (de un barco) **3** COURTYARD : patio *m* **4** : jardín *m* (de una casa) **5** : depósito *m* (de mercancías, etc.)
yardage ['jɑrdɪdʒ] *n* : medida *f* en yardas
yardarm ['jɑrd,ɑrm] *n* : penol *m*
yardstick ['jɑrd,stɪk] *n* **1** : vara *f* **2** CRITERION : criterio *m,* norma *f*
yarn ['jɑrn] *n* **1** : hilado *m* **2** TALE : historia *f,* cuento *m* <to spin a yarn : inventar una historia>
yawl ['jɔl] *n* : yola *f*
yawn¹ ['jɔn] *vi* **1** : bostezar **2** OPEN : abrirse
yawn² *n* : bostezo *m*
ye ['ji:] *pron* : vosotros, vosotras
yea¹ ['jeɪ] *adv* YES : sí
yea² *n* : voto *m* a favor
year ['jɪr] *n* **1** : año *m* <last year : el año pasado> <he's ten years old : tiene diez años> **2** : curso *m,* año *m* (escolar) **3 years** *npl* AGES : siglos *mpl,* años *mpl* <I haven't seen them in years : hace siglos que no los veo>
yearbook ['jɪr,bʊk] *n* : anuario *m*
yearling ['jɪrlɪŋ, 'jərlən] *n* : animal *m* menor de dos año
yearly¹ ['jɪrli] *adv* : cada año, anualmente
yearly² *adj* : anual
yearn ['jərn] *vi* : anhelar, ansiar
yearning ['jərnɪŋ] *n* : anhelo *m*
yeast ['ji:st] *n* : levadura *f*
yell¹ ['jɛl] *vi* : gritar, chillar — *vt* : gritar
yell² *n* : grito *m,* alarido *m* <to let out a yell : dar un grito>
yellow¹ ['jɛlo] *vi* : ponerse amarillo, volverse amarillo
yellow² *adj* **1** : amarillo **2** COWARDLY : cobarde
yellow³ *n* : amarillo *m*
yellow fever *n* : fiebre *f* amarilla
yellowish ['jɛloɪʃ] *adj* : amarillento
yellow jacket *n* : avispa *f* (con rayas amarillas)
yelp¹ ['jɛlp] *vi* : dar un gañido (dícese de un animal), dar un grito (dícese de una persona)
yelp² *n* : gañido *m* (de un animal), grito *m* (de una persona)
yen ['jɛn] *n* **1** DESIRE : deseo *m,* ganas *fpl* **2** : yen *m* (moneda japonesa)
yeoman ['jo:mən] *n, pl* **-men** [-mən, -mɛn] : suboficial *mf* de marina
yes¹ ['jɛs] *adv* : sí <to say yes : decir que sí>
yes² *n* : sí *m*
yesterday¹ ['jɛstər,deɪ, -di] *adv* : ayer
yesterday² *n* **1** : ayer *m* **2 the day before yesterday** : anteayer
yet¹ ['jɛt] *adv* **1** BESIDES, EVEN : aún <yet more problems : más problemas aún> <yet again : otra vez> **2** SO FAR : aún, todavía <not yet : todavía no> <as yet : hasta ahora, todavía> **3** : ya <has he come yet? : ¿ya ha venido?> **4** EVENTUALLY : todavía, algún día **5** NEVERTHELESS : sin embargo
yet² *conj* : pero
yew ['ju:] *n* : tejo *m*
yield¹ ['ji:ld] *vt* **1** SURRENDER : ceder <to yield the right of way : ceder el paso> **2** PRODUCE : producir, dar, rendir (en finanzas) — *vi* **1** GIVE : ceder <to yield under pressure : ceder por la presión> **2** GIVE IN, SURRENDER : ceder, rendirse, entregarse
yield² *n* : rendimiento *m,* rédito *m* (en finanzas)
yodel¹ ['jo:dəl] *vi* **-deled** *or* **-delled; -deling** *or* **-delling** : cantar al estilo tirolés
yodel² *n* : canción *f* al estilo tirolés
yoga ['jo:gə] *n* : yoga *m*
yogurt ['jo:gərt] *n* : yogur *m,* yogurt *m*
yoke¹ ['jo:k] *vt* **yoked; yoking** : uncir (animales)
yoke² *n* **1** : yugo *m* (para uncir animales) <the yoke of oppression : el yugo de la opresión> **2** TEAM : yunta *f* (de bueyes) **3** : canesú *m* (de ropa)
yokel ['jo:kəl] *n* : palurdo *m,* -da *f*
yolk ['jo:k] *n* : yema *f* (de un huevo)
Yom Kippur [,jo:mkɪ'pʊr, ,jɑm-, -'kɪpər] *n* : el Día *m* del Perdón, Yom Kippur
yon ['jɑn] → **yonder**
yonder¹ ['jɑndər] *adv* : allá <over yonder : allá lejos>
yonder² *adj* : aquel <yonder hill : aquella colina>
yore ['jo:r] *n* **in days of yore** : antaño
you ['ju:] *pron* **1** (*used as subject — familiar*) : tú; vos (*in some Latin American countries*); ustedes *pl;* vosotros, vosotras *pl Spain* **2** (*used as subject — formal*) : usted, ustedes *pl* **3** (*used as indirect object — familiar*) : te, les *pl* (se *before lo, la, los, las*), os *pl Spain* <he told it to you : te lo contó> <I gave them to (all of, both of) you : se los di> **4** (*used as indirect object — formal*) : lo (*Spain sometimes* le), la; los (*Spain sometimes* les), las *pl* **5** (*used after a preposition — familiar*) : ti; vos (*in some Latin American countries*); ustedes *pl;* vosotros, vosotras *pl Spain* **6** (*used after a preposition — formal*) : usted, ustedes *pl* **7** (*used as an impersonal subject*) <you never know : nunca se sabe> <you have to be aware : hay que ser consciente> <you mustn't do that : eso no se hace> **8 with you** (*familiar*) : contigo; con ustedes *pl;* con vosotros, con vosotras *pl Spain* **9 with you** (*formal*) : con usted, con ustedes *pl*
you'd ['ju:d, 'jʊd] (*contraction of* **you had** *or* **you would**) → **have, would**
you'll ['ju:l, 'jʊl] (*contraction of* **you shall** *or* **you will**) → **shall, will**
young¹ ['jʌŋ] *adj* **younger** ['jʌŋgər]; **youngest** [-gəst] **1** : joven, pequeño, menor <young people : los jóvenes>

<my younger brother : mi hermano menor> <she is the youngest : es la más pequeña> **2** FRESH, NEW : tierno (dícese de las verduras), joven (dícese del vino) **3** YOUTHFUL : joven, juvenil

young[2] *npl* : jóvenes *mfpl* (de los humanos), crías *fpl* (de los animales)

youngster [ˈjʌŋkstər] *n* **1** YOUTH : joven *mf* **2** CHILD : chico *m*, -ca *f;* niño *m*, -ña *f*

your [ˈjʊr, ˈjoːr, jər] *adj* **1** (*familiar singular*) : tu <your cat : tu gato> <your books : tus libros> <wash your hands : lávate las manos> **2** (*familiar plural*) su, vuestro *Spain* <your car : su coche, el coche de ustedes> **3** (*formal*) : su <your houses : sus casas> **4** (*impersonal*) : el, la, los, las <on your left : a la izquierda>

you're [ˈjʊr, ˈjoːr, ˈjər, ˈjuːər] (*contraction of* **you are**) → **be**

yours [ˈjʊrz, ˈjoːrz] *pron* **1** (*belonging to one person — familiar*) : (el) tuyo, (la) tuya, (los) tuyos, (las) tuyas <those are mine; yours are there : ésas son mías; las tuyas están allí> <is this one yours? : ¿éste es tuyo?> **2** (*belonging to more than one person — familiar*) : (el) suyo, (la) suya, (los) suyos, (las) suyas; (el) vuestro, (la) vuestra, (los) vuestros, (las) vuestras *Spain* <our house and yours : nuestra casa y la suya> **3** (*formal*) : (el) suyo, (la) suya, (los) suyos, (las) suyas

yourself [jərˈsɛlf] *pron, pl* **yourselves** [-ˈsɛlvz] **1** (*used reflexively — familiar*) : te, se *pl*, os *pl Spain* <wash yourself : lávate> <you dressed yourselves : se vistieron, os vestisteis> **2** (*used reflexively — formal*) : se <did you hurt yourself? : ¿se hizo daño?> <you've gotten yourselves dirty : se ensuciaron> **3** (*used for emphasis*) : tú mismo, tú misma; usted mismo, usted misma; ustedes mismos, ustedes mismas *pl;* vosotros mismos, vosotras mismas *pl Spain* <you did it yourselves? : ¿lo hicieron ustedes mismos?, ¿lo hicieron por sí solos?>

youth [ˈjuːθ] *n, pl* **youths** [ˈjuːðz, ˈjuːθs] **1** : juventud *f* <in her youth : en su juventud> **2** BOY : joven *m* **3** : jóvenes *mfpl*, juventud *f* <the youth of our city : los jóvenes de nuestra ciudad>

youthful [ˈjuːθfəl] *adj* **1** : de juventud **2** YOUNG : joven **3** JUVENILE : juvenil

youthfulness [ˈjuːθfəlnəs] *n* : juventud *f*

you've [ˈjuːv] (*contraction of* **you have**) → **have**

yowl[1] [ˈjæʊl] *vi* : aullar

yowl[2] *n* : aullido *m*

yo–yo [ˈjoːˌjoː] *n, pl* **-yos** : yoyo *m*, yoyó *m*

yucca [ˈjʌkə] *n* : yuca *f*

Yugoslavian [ˌjuːgoˈslɑviən] *n* : yugoslavo *m*, -va *f* — **Yugoslavian** *adj*

yule [ˈjuːl] *n* CHRISTMAS : Navidad *f*

yuletide [ˈjuːlˌtaɪd] *n* : Navidades *fpl*

Z

z [ˈziː] *n, pl* **z's** *or* **zs** : vigésima sexta letra del alfabeto inglés

Zambian [ˈzæmbiən] *n* : zambiano *m*, -na *f* — **Zambian** *adj*

zany[1] [ˈzeɪni] *adj* **-nier; -est** : alocado, disparatado

zany[2] *n, pl* **-nies** : bufón *m*, -fona *f*

zeal [ˈziːl] *n* : fervor *m*, celo *m*, entusiasmo *m*

zealot [ˈzɛlət] *n* : fanático *m*, -ca *f*

zealous [ˈzɛləs] *adj* : celoso — **zealously** *adv*

zebra [ˈziːbrə] *n* : cebra *f*

zenith [ˈziːnəθ] *n* **1** : cenit *m* (en astronomía) **2** PEAK : apogeo *m*, cenit *m* <at the zenith of his career : en el apogeo de su carrera>

zephyr [ˈzɛfər] *n* : céfiro *m*

zeppelin [ˈzɛplən, -pəlɪn] *n* : zepelín *m*

zero[1] [ˈziːro, ˈzɪro] *vi* **to zero in on** : apuntar hacia, centrarse en (un problema, etc.)

zero[2] *adj* : cero, nulo <zero degrees : cero grados> <zero opportunities : oportunidades nulas>

zero[3] *n, pl* **-ros** : cero *m* <below zero : bajo cero>

zest [ˈzɛst] *n* **1** GUSTO : entusiasmo *m*, brío *m* **2** FLAVOR : sabor *m*, sazón *f*

zestful [ˈzɛstfəl] *adj* : brioso

zigzag[1] [ˈzɪgˌzæg] *vi* **-zagged; -zagging** : zigzaguear

zigzag[2] *adv & adj* : en zigzag

zigzag[3] *n* : zigzag *m*

Zimbabwean [zɪmˈbɑbwiən, -bweɪ-] *n* : zimbabuense *mf* — **Zimbabwean** *adj*

zinc [ˈzɪŋk] *n* : cinc *m*, zinc *m*

zing [ˈzɪŋ] *n* **1** HISS, HUM : zumbido *m*, silbido *m* **2** ENERGY : brío *m*

zinnia [ˈzɪniə, ˈziː-, -njə] *n* : zinnia *f*

Zionism [ˈzaɪəˌnɪzəm] *n* : sionismo *m*

Zionist [ˈzaɪənɪst] *n* : sionista *mf*

zip[1] [ˈzɪp] *v* **zipped; zipping** *vt or* **to zip up** : cerrar el cierre de — *vi* **1** SPEED : pasarse volando <the day zipped by : el día se pasó volando> **2** HISS, HUM : silbar, zumbar

zip[2] *n* **1** ZING : zumbido *m*, silbido *m* **2** ENERGY : brío *m*

zip code *n* : código *m* postal

zipper [ˈzɪpər] *n* : cierre *m*, cremallera *f*, zíper *m CA, Mex*

zippy [ˈzɪpi] *adj* **-pier; -est** : brioso

zircon [ˈzər,kɑn] *n* : circón *m,* zircón *m*

zirconium [,zərˈko:niəm] *n* : circonio *m*

zither [ˈzɪðər, -θər] *n* : cítara *f*

zodiac [ˈzo:di,æk] *n* : zodíaco *m*

zombie [ˈzɑmbi] *n* : zombi *mf,* zombie *mf*

zone[1] [ˈzo:n] *vt* **zoned; zoning 1** : dividir en zonas **2** DESIGNATE : declarar <to zone for business : declarar como zona comercial>

zone[2] *n* : zona *f*

zoo [ˈzu:] *n, pl* **zoos** : zoológico *m,* zoo *m*

zoological [,zo:əˈlɑdʒɪkəl, ,zu:ə-] *adj* : zoológico

zoologist [zoˈɑlədʒɪst, zu:-] *n* : zoólogo *m,* -ga *f*

zoology [zoˈɑlədʒi, zu:-] *n* : zoología *f*

zoom[1] [ˈzu:m] *vi* **1** : zumbar, ir volando <to zoom past : pasar volando> **2** CLIMB : elevarse <the plane zoomed up : el avión se elevó>

zoom[2] *n* **1** : zumbido *m* <the zoom of an engine : el zumbido de un motor> **2** : subida *f* vertical (de un avión, etc.) **3** *or* **zoom lens** : zoom *m*

zucchini [zʊˈki:ni] *n, pl* **-ni** *or* **-nis** : calabacín *m,* calabacita *f Mex*

zygote [ˈzaɪ,go:t] *n* : zigoto *m,* cigoto *m*

Common Spanish Abbreviations Abreviaturas comunes en español

SPANISH ABBREVIATION AND EXPANSION		ENGLISH EQUIVALENT	
abr.	abril	**Apr.**	April
A.C., a.C.	antes de Cristo	**BC**	before Christ
a. de J.C.	antes de Jesucristo	**BC**	before Christ
admon., admón.	administración	—	administration
a/f	a favor	—	in favor
ago.	agosto	**Aug.**	August
Apdo.	apartado (de correos)	—	P.O. box
aprox.	aproximadamente	**approx.**	approximately
Aptdo.	apartado (de correos)	—	P.O. box
Arq.	arquitecto	**arch.**	architect
A.T.	Antiguo Testamento	**O. T.**	Old Testament
atte.	atentamente	—	sincerely
atto., atta.	atento, atenta	—	kind, courteous
av., avda.	avenida	**ave.**	avenue
a/v.	a vista	—	on receipt
BID	Banco Interamericano de Desarrollo	**IDB**	Interamerican Development Bank
B⁰	banco	—	bank
BM	Banco Mundial		World Bank
c/, C/	calle	**st.**	street
C	centígrado, Celsius	**C**	centigrade, Celsius
C.	compañía	**Co.**	company
CA	corriente alterna	**AC**	alternating current
cap.	capítulo	**ch., chap.**	chapter
c/c	cuenta corriente	—	current account, checking account
c.c.	centímetros cúbicos	**cu. cm**	cubic centimeters
CC	corriente continua	**DC**	direct current
c/d	con descuento	—	with discount
Cd.	ciudad	—	city
CE	Comunidad Europea	**EC**	European Community
CEE	Comunidad Económica Europea	**EEC**	European Economic Community
cf.	confróntese	**cf.**	compare
cg.	centígramo	**cg**	centigram
CGT	Confederación General de Trabajadores *or* del Trabajo	—	confederation of workers, workers' union
CI	coeficiente intelectual *or* de inteligencia	**IQ**	intelligence quotient
Cía.	compañía	**Co.**	company
cm.	centímetro	**cm**	centimeter

SPANISH ABBREVIATION AND EXPANSION		ENGLISH EQUIVALENT	
Cnel.	coronel	**Col.**	colonel
col.	columna	**col.**	column
Col. *Mex*	Colonia	—	—
Com.	comandante	**Cmdr.**	commander
comp.	compárese	**comp.**	compare
Cor.	coronel	**Col.**	colonel
C.P.	código postal	—	zip code
CSF, c.s.f.	coste, seguro y flete	**c.i.f.**	cost, insurance, and freight
cta.	cuenta	**ac., acct.**	account
cte.	corriente	**cur.**	current
c/u	cada uno, cada una	**ea.**	each
CV	caballo de vapor	**hp**	horsepower
D.	Don	—	—
Da., D.ª	Doña	—	—
d.C.	después de Cristo	**AD**	anno Domini (in the year of our Lord)
dcha.	derecha	—	right
d. de J.C.	después de Jesucristo	**AD**	anno Domini (in the year of our Lord)
dep.	departamento	**dept.**	department
DF, D.F.	Distrito Federal	—	Federal District
dic.	diciembre	**Dec.**	December
dir.	director, directora	**dir.**	director
dir.	dirección	—	address
Dña.	Doña	—	—
do.	domingo	**Sun.**	Sunday
dpto.	departamento	**dept.**	department
Dr.	doctor	**Dr.**	doctor
Dra.	doctora	**Dr.**	doctor
dto.	descuento	—	discount
E, E.	Este, este	**E**	East, east
Ed.	editorial	—	publishing house
Ed., ed.	edición	**ed.**	edition
edif.	edificio	**bldg.**	building
edo.	estado	**st.**	state
EEUU, EE.UU.	Estados Unidos	**US, U.S.**	United States
ej.	por ejemplo	**e.g.**	for example
E.M.	esclerosis multiple	**MS**	multiple sclerosis
ene.	enero	**Jan.**	January
etc.	etcétera	**etc.**	et cetera
ext.	extensión	**ext.**	extension
F	Fahrenheit	**F**	Fahrenheit
f.a.b.	franco a bordo	**f.o.b.**	free on board
FC	ferrocarril	**RR**	railroad
feb.	febrero	**Feb.**	February
FF AA, FF.AA.	Fuerzas Armadas	—	armed forces
FMI	Fondo Monetario Internacional	**IMF**	International Monetary Fund
g.	gramo	**g., gm, gr.**	gram
G.P.	giro postal	**M.O.**	money order
gr.	gramo	**g., gm, gr.**	gram